The Oxford Handbook of Nonsuicidal Self-Injury

OXFORD LIBRARY OF PSYCHOLOGY
AREA EDITORS:

Clinical Psychology
David H. Barlow

Cognitive Neuroscience
Kevin N. Ochsner and Stephen M. Kosslyn

Cognitive Psychology
Daniel Reisberg

Counseling Psychology
Elizabeth M. Altmaier and Jo-Ida C. Hansen

Developmental Psychology
Philip David Zelazo

Health Psychology
Howard S. Friedman

History of Psychology
David B. Baker

Methods and Measurement
Todd D. Little

Neuropsychology
Kenneth M. Adams

Organizational Psychology
Steve W. J. Kozlowski

Personality and Social Psychology
Kay Deaux and Mark Snyder

OXFORD LIBRARY OF PSYCHOLOGY

The Oxford Handbook of Nonsuicidal Self-Injury

Edited by

Elizabeth E. Lloyd-Richardson,
Imke Baetens,
and
Janis L. Whitlock

OXFORD
UNIVERSITY PRESS

Oxford University Press is a department of the University of Oxford. It furthers
the University's objective of excellence in research, scholarship, and education
by publishing worldwide. Oxford is a registered trade mark of Oxford University
Press in the UK and certain other countries.

Published in the United States of America by Oxford University Press
198 Madison Avenue, New York, NY 10016, United States of America.

© Oxford University Press 2024

All rights reserved. No part of this publication may be reproduced, stored in
a retrieval system, or transmitted, in any form or by any means, without the
prior permission in writing of Oxford University Press, or as expressly permitted
by law, by license, or under terms agreed with the appropriate reproduction
rights organization. Inquiries concerning reproduction outside the scope of the
above should be sent to the Rights Department, Oxford University Press, at the
address above.

You must not circulate this work in any other form
and you must impose this same condition on any acquirer.

Library of Congress Cataloging-in-Publication Data
Names: Lloyd-Richardson, Elizabeth E., editor. | Baetens, Imke, editor. |
Whitlock, Janis L., editor.
Title: The Oxford handbook of nonsuicidal self-injury / [edited by]
Elizabeth E. Lloyd-Richardson, Imke Baetens, Janis L. Whitlock.
Description: 1 edition. | New York, NY : Oxford University Press, [2024] |
Includes bibliographical references and index. |
Identifiers: LCCN 2023051631 (print) | LCCN 2023051632 (ebook) |
ISBN 9780197611272 (hardback) | ISBN 9780197611302 |
ISBN 9780197611296 (epub)
Subjects: LCSH: Self-injurious behavior.
Classification: LCC RC569.5.S48 O94 2024 (print) | LCC RC569.5.S48 (ebook) |
DDC 616.85/82—dc23/eng/20240117
LC record available at https://lccn.loc.gov/2023051631
LC ebook record available at https://lccn.loc.gov/2023051632

DOI: 10.1093/oxfordhb/9780197611272.001.0001

Printed by Sheridan Books, Inc., United States of America

CONTENTS

Acknowledgments xi
List of Contributors xiii

1. Introduction 1
    Elizabeth E. Lloyd-Richardson, Imke Baetens, and *Janis L. Whitlock*
2. NSSI in the DSM-5 7
    Greg Lengel, Brooke A. Ammerman, and *Jason Washburn*
3. A Comparison of the Theoretical Models of NSSI 24
    Kirsty Hird, Penelope Hasking, and *Mark Boyes*
4. Direct and Indirect Self-Injury 41
    Lotte Rubæk and *Bo Møhl*
5. Theoretical Models Linking NSSI to Suicide 72
    Sarah E. Victor, Kirsten Christensen, and *Terry H. Trieu*
6. The Functions of Nonsuicidal Self-Injury 89
    Peter James Taylor, Katie Dhingra, Kelly-Marie Peel-Wainwright, and *Kathryn Jane Gardner*
7. The Epidemiology of Nonsuicidal Self-Injury and Self-Harm in Nonclinical Samples: Population-Level Trends 107
    Louise Staring, Glenn Kiekens, and *Olivia J. Kirtley*
8. Overview and Epidemiology of NSSI in Clinical Samples 127
    Jennifer J. Muehlenkamp and *Victoria Tillotson*
9. NSSI and Self-Harm Behavior and the COVID-19 Pandemic 149
    Amy Brausch and *Rebekah Clapham*
10. Cross-Cultural Representations of NSSI 167
    Marc Stewart Wilson
11. Stairway to Heaven: NSSI as an Addiction 187
    Hilario Blasco-Fontecilla
12. A Roadmap Overview of the Research Domain Criteria: A Shift from Diagnostic to Transdiagnostic Processes 204
    Tim Bastiaens and *Laurence Claes*

13. Negative Affect and Nonsuicidal Self-Injury   226
    Benjamin A. Swerdlow, Jennifer G. Pearlstein, Devon B. Sandel, and *Sheri L. Johnson*
14. The Brain and Body's Threat System Functioning in Those with NSSI   251
    Katherine A. Carosella, Andrea Wiglesworth, Zeynep Başgöze, Kathryn R. Cullen, and *Bonnie Klimes-Dougan*
15. Positive Valence Systems and Nonsuicidal Self-Injury   278
    Laurence Claes, Koen Luyckx, and *Glenn Kiekens*
16. Cognitive Systems in NSSI and Co-Occurring Conditions   309
    Morgan E. Browning and *Jennifer J. Muehlenkamp*
17. Social Processes in Nonsuicidal Self-Injury   328
    Maria Zetterqvist and *Johan Bjureberg*
18. Autonomic Nervous System Function in Nonsuicidal Self-Injury—A Research Domain Criteria Perspective on the Arousal/Regulatory Systems   349
    Christine Sigrist, Michael Kaess, and *Julian Koenig*
19. Bridging Brain and Behavior: Using Biology to Inform NSSI Interventions   377
    Mindy Westlund Schreiner, Summer B. Frandsen, Nicolette C. Molina, and *Alina K. Dillahunt*
20. Lived Experience Perspectives on Self-Injury: Current Evidence and Practical Applications   393
    Penelope Hasking, Therese E. Kenny, and *Stephen P. Lewis*
21. Beyond "Stopping": Reconceptualizing NSSI Recovery in Favor of Healing and Growth   412
    Janis L. Whitlock, Elizabeth E. Lloyd-Richardson, and *Josie Woolsen*
22. The Dynamics and Perception of Pain During Self-Injury   440
    Edward A. Selby and *Christopher Hughes*
23. The Role of Self and Blood in Ritual and Nonritual Self-Injury   468
    Annette Hornbacher, William Sax, Janina Naoum, and *Christian Schmahl*
24. The Significance of Location of Self-Injury   481
    Kathryn Jane Gardner, Caroline Clements, Harriet Bickley, Gillian Rayner, and *Peter James Taylor*
25. NSSI in Elementary School   500
    Lisa Van Hove, Imke Baetens, Amanda Simundic, Elana Bloom, and *Nancy Heath*
26. NSSI in Adolescence and Emerging Adulthood   514
    Glenn Kiekens, Penelope Hasking, and *Laurence Claes*
27. Understanding and Working with Adults with NSSI   540
    Margaret Andover, Hae-Joon Kim, Vincent Corcoran, Michelle Hiner, Ana Rabasco, and *Joshua DeSon*

28. Understanding and Treating Atypical, Severe Nonsuicidal Self-Injury 555
    Barent W. Walsh, Leonard Doerfler, and *Lisa Van Hove*
29. NSSI in Older Adults 572
    Lisa Van Hove, Imke Baetens, Chloe A. Hamza, Eva Dierckx, An Haekens, Lila Fieremans, and *Steven Vanderstichelen*
30. What Do NCI Data Tell Us About People Who Need Support for Self-Injurious Behavior 593
    Valerie J. Bradley, Dorothy Hiersteiner, David A. Rotholz, and *Henan Li*
31. Self-Injury in Prison Populations 616
    Natalie Winicov
32. NSSI Among Military Service Members and Veterans 638
    Molly Gromatsky, Adam J. Mann, Nathan A. Kimbrel, and *Kirsten H. Dillon*
33. NSSI Among Sexual and Gender Diverse Youth 659
    Lucas Zullo, Megan L. Rogers, and *Lindsay A. Taliaferro*
34. Understanding the Link Between Direct and Indirect Self-Injurious Behavior 680
    Bo Møhl and *Lotte Rubæk*
35. An Integrated Cognitive-Emotional Perspective of NSSI 702
    Kate Tonta, Danyelle Greene, Penelope Hasking, and *Mark Boyes*
36. Intrapersonal Risk and Protective Factors for NSSI 719
    Saskia Jorgensen, Erica A. Hart, Emily Burns, and *Kathryn R. Fox*
37. Early Childhood Trauma and Nonsuicidal Self-Injury 737
    Gianluca Serafini, Nicolò Cipriani, Laura Costanza De Angelis, and *Mario Amore*
38. The Parent-Child Dyad and Other Family Factors Associated with Youth Nonsuicidal Self-Injury 753
    Kiera M. James and *Brandon E. Gibb*
39. Media Representations of Nonsuicidal Self-Injury 771
    Nicholas J. Westers
40. Understanding Online Self-Injury Activity: Implications for Research, Practice, and Outreach 787
    Tyler R. Pritchard and *Stephen P. Lewis*
41. Understanding the Social Context of NSSI: Interpersonal Stress in Romantic and Peer Relationships and Peer Socialization of NSSI 806
    Olivia H. Pollak, Matthew G. Clayton, Benjamin W. Nelson, and *Mitchell J. Prinstein*
42. Social Contagion of Nonsuicidal Self-Injury 830
    Stephanie Jarvi Steele, Nigel Jaffe, and *Grace Murray*

43. Assessing NSSI in Clinical and Community Settings   847
    Charlotte Cliffe, Rosemary Sedgwick, Sophie Epstein, Catherine Polling,
    and *Dennis Ougrin*
44. Risk Assessment, Intervention, and Guidance for First Responders and
    Medical Settings   873
    Nicholas J. Westers and *Brittany Tinsley*
45. Novel Assessment Methods for Differentiating Those at Risk for Suicidal and
    Nonsuicidal Self-Injurious Behaviors   894
    Taylor A. Burke, Brooke A. Ammerman, and *Richard T. Liu*
46. Fine-Grained Assessment of Nonsuicidal Self-Injury   912
    Nicole K. Legg, Andrew C. Switzer, and *Brianna J. Turner*
47. Guidelines, Policies, and Recommendations for Responding to NSSI in Schools
    and Universities   930
    *Imke Baetens, Elizabeth E. Lloyd-Richardson, Elana Bloom, Chloe A. Hamza,
    Penelope Hasking, Stephen P. Lewis, Dariya Bezugla, Esther Meers,* and
    Lisa Van Hove
48. Promising Approaches in Prevention and Intervention in Secondary
    School Settings   952
    *Julia Petrovic, Laurianne Bastien, Jessica Mettler, Elana Bloom,
    Chloe A. Hamza,* and *Nancy Heath*
49. Promising Approaches to Prevention and Intervention in Higher Education   971
    Alexandra L. Morena, Akshay V. Trisal, and *Elizabeth E. Lloyd-Richardson*
50. Digital Interventions for Nonsuicidal Self-Injury   998
    Kaylee P. Kruzan and *Janis L. Whitlock*
51. Machine Learning for Detection, Prediction, and Treatment of Nonsuicidal
    Self-Injury: Challenges and Future Directions   1024
    Shirley B. Wang, Walter Dempsey, Rowan A. Hunt, and *Matthew K. Nock*
52. Managing NSSI Across Different Treatment Contexts   1039
    Franziska Rockstroh and *Michael Kaess*
53. Medical and Pharmaceutical Interventions in NSSI   1061
    Paul L. Plener
54. Online Approaches to NSSI Treatment   1076
    Jill M. Hooley and *Kathryn R. Fox*
55. Application of the Unified Protocol for Treatment of Nonsuicidal Self-Injury   1091
    Kate H. Bentley and *Adam C. Jaroszewski*
56. Cognitive-Behavioral and Dialectical Behavior Therapy for
    Nonsuicidal Self-Injury   1112
    Alexander L. Chapman, Philippa Hood, and *Cassandra J. Turner*
57. Family Therapy for NSSI   1127
    Imke Baetens, Lisa Van Hove, and *Tinne Buelens*

58. Mentalizing and Psychodynamic Approaches to Nonsuicidal Self-Injury 1146
    Anna Motz, Anthony Bateman, Peter Fonagy, and *Patrick Luyten*
59. Experiential Therapies and Nonsuicidal Self-Injury 1169
    Victoria E. Kress, Julia Whisenhunt, Nicole A. Stargell, and
    Christine A. McAllister
60. Collaborative Strengths-Based Family Therapy with Nonsuicidal Self-Injuring Adolescents and Their Families 1191
    Matthew D. Selekman
61. Conclusion and Future Directions 1237
    Elizabeth E. Lloyd-Richardson, Imke Baetens, and *Janis L. Whitlock*

Index 1247

ACKNOWLEDGMENTS

We are immensely grateful to all the authors who believed in the mission of this book from the start and have willingly contributed their insightful and groundbreaking ideas. Their remarkable contributions have enriched the content and added immense value to its pages, and our collective knowledge of nonsuicidal self-injury is stronger as a result. We are deeply appreciative of the guidance provided by the Oxford University Press team and our two wonderful editors in particular, Sarah Harrington and Mary Funchion, who helped early on in shaping the book and continued to support the work as it evolved. It certainly takes a village, and this book would not have been possible without all of our collective efforts!

Notes from Elizabeth:
I am filled with admiration and respect for my two wonderful co-editors and friends, Janis and Imke. You are each filled with determination, compassion, and curiosity, and I have truly enjoyed our time working on this project. None of us knew how long this effort was going to take (or how many Zoom hours!) but it has been an excellent adventure, and I hope we continue to find ways to connect, collaborate, and celebrate with each other!

I am grateful for my students over the years and want to particularly thank Akshay Trisal for his careful and thoughtful reviews of chapter content and Morgan Browning for her willingness to add NSSI to her vast clinical research knowledge. I hope you find joy and satisfaction in your professional careers ahead!

Thanks to my husband, Tom, for offering much support at home, and to my sweet and sassy children, Max, Summer, and Daicey. The three of you were so young when I wrote my first book about NSSI, and now that you are teenagers, I appreciate even more the immense joy and richness you bring to my life every single day. Thank you for helping me to keep a balanced perspective on life and a healthy appreciation for the value of play!

Notes from Imke:
I would like to express my heartfelt gratitude to the co-editors of this book. Their guidance, expertise, and unwavering commitment have made this journey truly magnificent. I extend my sincerest appreciation to my exceptional team whose dedication and support

have been instrumental in bringing this project to fruition. Their hard work and unwavering commitment have made a significant difference.

A special acknowledgment goes to Dariya Bezugla for her invaluable assistance in setting up the tracking systems. Her meticulous attention to detail has ensured the smooth functioning of our processes.

I would also like to express my gratitude to Lisa Van Hove, Shokoufeh Vatandoost, and Joyce Van Den Meersschaut for their invaluable help in the copyediting work. Their keen eye for detail and expertise have greatly enhanced the quality of the book.

I am deeply indebted to Lisa for her outstanding contribution in keeping all the processes on track and providing invaluable backend support. Her efficiency and organizational skills have been vital throughout this endeavor.

I cannot express enough gratitude to my family for their unwavering support and love throughout this entire journey. Their encouragement and understanding have been the driving force behind my work.

A special mention goes to Bram for being my rock and for his unwavering love and support. His presence has been a constant source of strength and inspiration.

Last but certainly not least to my sons, Teo and Bas, you are my greatest blessings, and I am forever grateful for your love and presence in my life. Thank you for being my guiding light and for making every day an extraordinary adventure.

Notes from Janis:
I would like to acknowledge my wonderful co-editors, colleagues, and friends, Elizabeth Lloyd Richardson and Imke Baetens. This project was a labor of love that required steady persistence and good humor, and our meetings were good for both the book and for my soul. Having the opportunity to serve as the Francqui International Professor at VUB for the spring semester of 2022, thanks to Imke, the Department of Psychology at VUB, and the Francqui Foundation created vital space for collaboration and was pivotal in getting this volume across the finish line. I'd also like to thank Josie Woolsen for the administrative and moral support along the way as well as the many graduate students from Imke and Elizabeth's labs who worked diligently to help us process the many, many chapters contained in this book. My son and daughter, Aliya and Aidan, contributed just by being a source of love and light in my life. Finally, I'd like to thank all of the authors who contributed to this volume. Many friends and esteemed colleagues devoted valuable time, energy, and attention to creating what I know will be an important contribution to the field.

CONTRIBUTORS

Brooke A. Ammerman
    Assistant Professor, Department of Psychology, University of Notre Dame

Mario Amore
    Visiting Professor, Universitia di Genova

Margaret Andover
    Professor, Department of Psychology, Fordham University

Imke Baetens
    Associate Professor, Department of Psychology, Vrije Universiteit Brussel

Zeynep Başgöze
    Neuroimaging Research Scientist/ Psychiatry and Behavioral Sciences, University of Minnesota

Tim Bastiaens
    Clinical Psychologist, Centre for Psychological Assessment (head), UPC KU Leuven

Laurianne Bastien
    PhD Candidate in Educational and Counselling Psychology, McGill University

Anthony Bateman
    Visiting Professor, Department of Clinical, Educational and Health Psychology, University College London

Kate H. Bentley
    Assistant Professor of Psychology, Department of Psychiatry, Massachusetts General Hospital/ Harvard Medical School

Dariya Bezugla
    The Faculty of Psychology and Educational Sciences, VUB

Harriet Bickley
    Research Associate and Data Manager, University of Manchester

Johan Bjureberg
    Associate Professor of Clinical Psychology, Department of Clinical Neuroscience, Karolinska Institutet

Hilario Blasco-Fontecilla
    Associate Professor Autonoma University of Madrid and Head of the Traslational Research Mental Health Group at the IDIPHIPSA, Autonoma University of Madrid

Elana Bloom
    Director Campus Wellness and Support Services, Concordia University

Mark Boyes
    Associate Professor, Curtin University

Valerie J. Bradley
    President Emerita, Human Services Research Institute

Amy Brausch
    Professor of Psychological Sciences, Western Kentucky University

Morgan E. Browning
    Graduate Student, Department of Psychology, University of Massachusetts Dartmouth

Tinne Buelens
    Assistant Professor of Clinical Psychology, Faculty of Social and Behavioural Sciences, University of Amsterdam

Taylor A. Burke
: Assistant Professor, Department of Psychiatry, Harvard Medical School

Emily Burns
: University of Denver Graduate School of Professional Psychology

Katherine A. Carosella
: Graduate Student, Department of Psychology, University of Minnesota

Alexander L. Chapman
: Professor and Director of Clinical Training, Department of Psychology, Simon Fraser University

Kirsten Christensen
: Graduate Student, Texas Tech University

Nicolò Cipriani
: Psychiatrist, ASL AL

Laurence Claes
: Professor of Clinical Psychology, Faculty of Psychology and Educational Sciences, KU Leuven

Rebekah Clapham
: Clinical-Community Psychology PhD graduate student, Psychology Department, University of Illinois Urbana-Champaign

Matthew G. Clayton
: Doctoral Candidate in Clinical Psychology, Department of Psychology and Neuroscience, University of North Carolina at Chapel Hill

Caroline Clements
: Research Fellow, School of Health Sciences, University of Manchester

Charlotte Cliffe
: Psychiatrist (general adult higher specialty trainee) and Academic Clinical Fellow, Surrey and Borders NHS Trust and King's College London

Vincent Corcoran
: Assistant Professor, Psychology Department, Russell Sage College

Kathryn R. Cullen
: Professor, Psychiatry and Behavioral Sciences, University of Minnesota Medical School

Laura Costanza De Angelis
: PhD student, Istituto Giannina Gaslini

Walter Dempsey
: Assistant Professor of Biostatistics and Assistant Research Professor, d3lab, Institute of Social Research, University of Michigan

Joshua DeSon
: Senior Teaching Fellow, Psychology, Fordham University

Katie Dhingra
: Reader/Associate Professor in Psychology in Psychology, Criminology Department, Leeds Beckett University

Eva Dierckx
: Professor of Clinical Psychology. Department of Psychology, Vrije Universiteit Brussel

Alina K. Dillahunt
: PhD Student in the Mend2Lab, School of Medicine, University of Utah

Kirsten H. Dillon
: Psychologist, Research and Development, Durham VA Health Care System

Leonard Doerfler
: Professor of Psychology, Assumption University

Sophie Epstein
: Clinical Research Training Fellow, Department of Psychological Medicine, Institute of Psychiatry, Psychology and Neuroscience, King's College London

Lila Fieremans
: Former student, Vrije Universiteit Brussels

Peter Fonagy
: Professor of Contemporary Psychoanalysis and Developmental Science and Director of Division, Division of Psychology and Language Sciences, University College London (UCL)

Kathryn R. Fox
: Assistant Professor, Department of Psychology, University of Denver

Summer B. Frandsen
: Senior Research Assistant, Center for Brain Circuit Therapeutics, Neurology Department, Brigham and Women's Hospital

Kathryn Jane Gardner
: Senior Lecturer in Psychology, School of Psychology and Humanities, University of Central Lancashire

Brandon E. Gibb
: Professor, Department of Psychology, Binghamton University (SUNY)

Danyelle Greene
: Postdoctoral Research Fellow, The University of Queensland

Molly Gromatsky
: Postdoctoral Research Fellow, James J. Peters VA Medical Center

An Haekens
: Medical Director, Alexian Brothers Hospital

Chloe A. Hamza
: Associate Professor, Ontario Institute for Studies in Education (OISE), University of Toronto

Erica A. Hart
: MA Psychology, Mile High Behavioral Healthcare

Penelope Hasking
: Professor of Psychology, Curtin University

Nancy Heath
: Professor, Department of Educational and Counselling Psychology, McGill University

Dorothy Hiersteiner
: Co-Director of National Core Indicators, Human Services Research Institute

Michelle Hiner
: Graduate Student, Department of Psychology, Fordham University

Kirsty Hird
: PhD Candidate, Curtin University Philippa Hood, graduate student, Simon Fraser University

Jill M. Hooley
: John Lindsley Professor of Psychology, Department of Psychology, Harvard University

Annette Hornbacher
: Professor of Anthropology, Heidelberg University

Christopher Hughes
: Assistant Professor (Research), Department of Psychiatry and Human Behavior, Warren Alpert Medical School of Brown University

Rowan A. Hunt
: Graduate Student, Department of Psychological and Brain Sciences, University of Louisville

Nigel Jaffe
: Undergraduate Student, Psychology Department, Williams College

Kiera M. James
: Postdoctoral Scholar, Department of Psychology, University of Pittsburgh

Adam C. Jaroszewski
: Psychologist, Department of Psychiatry, Massachusetts General Hospital

Sheri L. Johnson
: Distinguished Professor of Psychology, University of California Berkeley

Saskia Jorgensen
: George Washington University Department of Psychology

Michael Kaess
: Chair and Clinical Director, University Hospital of Child and Adolescent Psychiatry and Psychotherapy, University of Bern

Therese E. Kenny
: PhD Candidate, Clinical Child and Adolescent Psychology, University of Guelph

Glenn Kiekens
: Postdoctoral Researcher, KU Leuven

Hae-Joon Kim
: PhD Student, Clinical Psychology, Fordham University

Nathan A. Kimbrel
: Associate Professor in Psychiatry and Behavioral Sciences, Behavioral Medicine & Neurosciences Division, Duke University School of Medicine

Olivia J. Kirtley
: Assistant Professor, KU Leuven

Bonnie Klimes-Dougan
: Teaching Professor of Psychology, University of Minnesota

Julian Koenig
: Professor of Biological Child and Adolescent Psychiatry, Department of Child and Adolescent Psychiatry, Psychosomatics and Psychotherapy, University of Cologne

Victoria E. Kress
: Distinguished Professor, Youngstown State University

Kaylee P. Kruzan
: Research Assistant Professor, Department of Preventive Medicine, Northwestern University

Nicole K. Legg
: Doctoral Candidate in Clinical Psychology, University of Victoria

Greg Lengel
: Associate Professor, Department of Psychology & Neuroscience, Drake University

Stephen P. Lewis
: Professor, Department of Psychology, University of Guelph

Henan Li
: Research Associate, Human Services Research Institute

Richard T. Liu
: Associate Professor, Massachusetts General Hospital and Harvard Medical School

Elizabeth E. Lloyd-Richardson
: Professor of Psychology, University of Massachusetts Dartmouth

Koen Luyckx
: Associate Professor of Psychology and Educational Sciences, KU Leuven

Patrick Luyten
: Professor of Clinical Psychology, Faculty of Psychology and Educational Sciences, University of Leuven

Adam J. Mann
: Graduate Student, University of Toledo

Christine A. McAllister
: Part-Time Faculty, Department of Counseling, School Psychology, and Educational Leadership, Youngstown State University

Esther Meers
  Former student, Vrije Universiteit Brussels
Jessica Mettler
  Educational and Counselling Psychology, McGill University
Bo Møhl
  Professor Emeritus in Clinical Psychology, Department of Communication and Psychology, Aalborg University
Nicolette C. Molina
  PhD Student, Department of Psychology, University of Oregon
Alexandra L. Morena
  Doctoral Student in Applied Psychology and Prevention Science, Psychology Department, University of Massachusetts Lowell
Anna Motz
  Consultant Clinical and Forensic Psychologist
Jennifer J. Muehlenkamp
  Professor, Department of Psychology, University of Wisconsin Eau Claire
Grace Murray
  Doctoral Student, Department of Psychological and Brain Sciences, Boston University
Janina Naoum
  Senior Physician Obstetrics, Klinik St. Elisabeth GmbH
Benjamin W. Nelson
  Postdoctoral Scholar, Department of Psychology and Neuroscience, The University of North Carolina
Matthew K. Nock
  Edgar Pierce Professor and Chair, Department of Psychology, Harvard University
Dennis Ougrin
  Professor of Child and Adolescent Psychiatry, Queen Mary University of London
Jennifer G. Pearlstein
  Postdoctoral Fellow, Department of Rehabilitatoi Medicine, University of Washington
Kelly-Marie Peel-Wainwright
  Greater Manchester Mental Health NHS Foundation Trust
Julia Petrovic
  PhD Candidate, Department of Educational and Counselling Psychology, McGill University
Paul L. Plener
  Head of the Department of Child and Adolescent Psychiatry, Medical University Vienna
Olivia H. Pollak
  Doctoral Student, Department of Psychology and Neuroscience, University of North Carolina at Chapel Hill
Catherine Polling
  Clinical Lecturer in General Psychiatry, Department of Psychological Medicine, Institute of Psychiatry, Psychology and Neuroscience, King's College London
Mitchell J. Prinstein
  John Van Seters Distinguished Professor, The University of North Carolina at Chapel Hill
Tyler R. Pritchard
  Visiting Professor, Department of Psychology, Grenfell Campus, Memorial University
Ana Rabasco
  Postdoctoral Fellow, Department of Psychiatry and Human Behavior, Brown University
Gillian Rayner
  Reader in Counselling & Psychotherapy, School of Health, University of Central Lancashire (UCLan)

Franziska Rockstroh
Research Assistant, University Hospital of Child and Adolescent Psychiatry and Psychotherapy, University of Bern

Megan L. Rogers
Assistant Professor, Department of Psychology, Texas State University

David A. Rotholz
Executive Director, Center for Disability Resources, Clinical Professor, University of South Carolina School of Medicine

Lotte Rubæk
Leader of Team of Self-Injury, Child and Adolescent Mental Health Services, The Capital Region of Denmark

Devon B. Sandel
Doctoral Candidate, Department of Psychology, University of California, Berkeley

William Sax
Professor and Head of Department, South Asia Institute

Christian Schmahl
Medical Director, Department of Psychosomatic Medicine, Central Institute of Mental Health

Mindy Westlund Schreiner
Assistant Professor of Psychiatry, University of Utah

Rosemary Sedgwick
Consultant Child and Adolescent Psychiatrist, South London and Maudsley NHS Foundation Trust

Edward A. Selby
Associate Professor, Department of Psychology, Rutgers, The State University of New Jersey

Matthew D. Selekman
Director, Partners for Collaborative Solutions

Gianluca Serafini
Professor of Psychiatry, Department of Neuroscience, University of Genoa

Christine Sigrist
Research Coordinator and Postdoc, Department of Child and Adolescent Psychiatry, Psychosomatics, and Psychotherapy, University Hospital Cologne and University of Cologne

Amanda Simundic
PhD Candidate, Department of Educational and Counselling Psychology, McGill University

Nicole A. Stargell
Associate Professor, Department of Counseling, The University of North Carolina at Pembroke

Louise Staring
PhD Researcher, Psychology Department, Vrije Universiteit Brussel

Stephanie Jarvi Steele
Assistant Professor of Psychology, Smith College

Benjamin A. Swerdlow
Assistant Professor, Department of Psychology, Lake Forest College

Andrew C. Switzer
Graduate Student, University of Victoria

Lindsay A. Taliaferro
Associate Professor of Medicine, Department of Population Health Sciences, University of Central Florida

Peter James Taylor
Senior Clinic Lecturer, Division of Psychology and Mental Health, School of Health Sciences, University of Manchester, Manchester Academic Health Sciences Centre, University of Manchester

Victoria Tillotson
Student, University of Wisconsin

Brittany Tinsley
   Freelance Writer
Kate Tonta
   Lecturer, School of Population Health, Curtin University
Terry H. Trieu
   Graduate Student, Department of Psychological Sciences, Texas Tech University
Akshay V. Trisal
   Graduate Student, University of Massachusetts Dartmouth
Brianna J. Turner
   Associate Professor, Department of Psychology, University of Victoria
Cassandra J. Turner
   Graduate Student, Clinical Psychology, Simon Fraser University
Steven Vanderstichelen
   Scientific Coordinator, Compassionate Communities Centre of Expertise (COCO), Vrije Universiteit Brussel
Lisa Van Hove
   Doctoral Candidate, Brussels University Consultation Center (BRUCC), Faculty of Psychology and Educational Sciences, Vrije Universiteit Brussel
Sarah E. Victor
   Assistant Professor, Department of Psychological Sciences, Texas Tech University
Barent W. Walsh
   Senior Consultant Open Sky Community Services, Open Sky Community Services
Shirley B. Wang
   PhD Candidate, Harvard University
Jason Washburn
   Professor and Chief, Division of Psychology, Department of Psychiatry & Behavioral Sciences, Northwestern University
Nicholas J. Westers
   Clinical Psychologist, Department of Psychiatry, Children's Health Systems of Texas
Julia Whisenhunt
   Professor, Department of Counseling, Higher Education, and Speech-Language Pathology, University of West Georgia
Janis L. Whitlock
   Emerita Research Scientist, Cornell University
Andrea Wiglesworth
   Graduate Student, Department of Psychology, University of Minnesota Twin Cities
Marc Stewart Wilson
   Professor of Psychology, School of Psychology, Te Herenga Waka Victoria University of Wellington
Natalie Winicov
   Social Worker, Columbia University School of Social Work
Josie Woolsen
   Teaching Support, Cornell College of Human Ecology, Cornell University
Maria Zetterqvist
   Associate Professor, Clinical Psychology (with focus on child and adolescent psychiatric activities), Department of Child and Adolescent Psychiatry and Department of Clinical and Biomedical Sciences, Linköping University
Lucas Zullo
   Clinical Psychologist, Department of Psychiatry and Biobehavioral Sciences, University of California Los Angeles

CHAPTER 1

Introduction

Elizabeth E. Lloyd-Richardson, Imke Baetens, *and* Janis L. Whitlock

> **Abstract**
>
> This chapter introduces the notion of nonsuicidal self-injury (NSSI). NSSI encompasses a wide variety of behaviors including but not limited to carving or cutting of the skin and subdermal tissue, scratching, and burning. NSSI became an indelible part of the mental health landscape in populations of all types. Moreover, NSSI occurs across cultures, geography, and population which eventually became a leading signal for suicide risk. The chapter looks into Bronfenbrenner's ecological systems theory and a transdiagnostic perspective at the levels of conceptualization, therapeutic assessment, intervention, and treatment as per the Research Domain Criteria. It considers case vignettes and summaries of implications for research, clinical practice, and intervention.
>
> **Key Words:** nonsuicidal self-injury, behaviors, mental health, suicide risk, ecological systems theory, conceptualization, Research Doman Criteria, case vignettes

Why This Volume and Why Now?

Defined as self-inflicted destruction of the body for purposes not socially sanctioned and without suicidal intent (International Society for the Study of Self-injury, 2022), nonsuicidal self-injury (NSSI) encompasses a wide variety of behaviors including but not limited to carving or cutting of the skin and subdermal tissue, scratching, burning, ripping or pulling skin or hair, bruising, and breaking bones. Once regarded as a disorder primarily associated with significant cognitive or emotional impairment, it was largely assumed to be present as a comorbid condition in individuals with existing clinical or otherwise acute conditions. The only two recognized epidemiological studies prior to the late 1980s (Clendenin & Murphy, 1971; Weissman, 1975) were based on emergency room populations. It was not until the first part of the 21st century that reports of NSSI were noted in a growing number of populations, such as youth in school settings, which led to significant empirical interest in mapping its epidemiological contours.

In the course of less than two decades, NSSI has gone from what appeared to be a rather rare condition, particularly in community populations, to one that has become an indelible part of the mental health landscape in populations of all types. While a large and internationally diverse body of research confirms that adolescents and young adults are those most likely to have lived NSSI experience (Gandhi et al., 2018), two decades of epidemiological investigation suggests that NSSI is present across both the globe and the life course (Cipriano et al., 2015; Xiao et al., 2022; also see Staring et al., this volume, and Muehlenkamp & Tillotson, this volume, for NSSI prevalence rates in nonclinical and clinical samples). NSSI has been documented in children as young as age 5 (see Van Hove et al., this volume) as well as in older adults (see Van Hove et al., this volume). Moreover, it occurs across culture, geography, and population (see Wilson, this volume). Not only has it become a leading signal for suicide risk, especially when present in youth (e.g., see Staring et al., this volume), it has moved from being one of a number of indicators for borderline personality disorder to being considered a unique classified condition according to the fifth edition of *Diagnostic and Statistical Manual of Mental Disorders* (DSM-5; American Psychiatric Association 2013; see Lengel et al., this volume).

Perhaps the most striking marker of its significance is that the current volume required nearly 60 chapters to review what has been learned in just two decades of focused research on NSSI. Indeed, having the opportunity to assemble the most current and cutting-edge science, authored by many of the most distinguished and prolific NSSI scholars in the world, left us in awe of what has been accomplished in a rather short period of time. This book offers insight and hope for greater understanding of the complexities of NSSI and shines a light on the research occurring worldwide that will allow us to collectively effect change in our understanding of NSSI and best support those who self-injure, their loved ones, and their care providers.

This volume is intended to provide a robust review of topics germane to the field of NSSI across a wide array of both established and newer topic areas. Designed to capture and explore both the current "state of the science" as well as new directions for the field, it reflects a rich diversity of science, approach, and novel areas for development authored by both well-known scholars and emerging NSSI researchers likely to make significant contributions to the field. Each chapter offers critical review of literature and ample discussion of key discoveries, perspectives, and future directions of clinical and research efforts.

Two primary ideas guide formulation of this handbook. First, while critical to consider individual factors at the heart of self-injurious thoughts and behaviors, we aim to place these within broader, nested ecological contexts of family, peers, schools, social media, and cultural and historical events, a framework consistent with Bronfenbrenner's ecological systems theory (Bronfenbrenner, 1979). Second, we aim to consider NSSI from a transdiagnostic perspective at the levels of conceptualization, therapeutic assessment, intervention, and treatment that is informed by the Research Domain Criteria (RDoC; Insel et al., 2010) framework. While these transdiagnostic approaches were developed more than a decade ago, many researchers and clinicians remain unfamiliar with how these might fit within their own theoretical frame of reference. RDoC aims to better understand basic dimensions of functioning underlying the full range of human behavior from normal to abnormal. Section three of this book aims to thoroughly present the transdiagnostic perspective and core RDoC processes as applied to NSSI.

Beyond highlighting research advancements in a wide variety of areas, this handbook is intended to provide a platform for diversity of voice and perspective. By integrating international perspectives and scholars, we hope to broaden the collective knowledge network and to provide a wide-angle portrait of NSSI in diverse global contexts. Of similar importance is including lived experience perspectives. Recognizing that we are likely to be most effective at understanding NSSI and advancing authentic healing and well-being when theory, empirical research, and lived experience perspectives are considered and aligned, we place high value in this volume on amplifying each of these vantage points. In keeping with this, we encouraged authors to incorporate both quantitative research findings as well as illustrative or formative qualitative work (qualitative research findings, case vignettes, etc.), as well as consideration of strengths- and growth-based frameworks and approaches. Toward this end, nearly every chapter includes case vignettes and summaries of implications for research, clinical practice, and intervention, where indicated.

Volume Organization

In order to facilitate easy access to desired content, we have divided the volume into nine parts. Part I aims to offer historical context on the evolution of how NSSI is conceptualized and perceived, as well as to review up-to-date information on NSSI classification in DSM-5 (American Psychiatric Association, 2013). Theoretical frameworks that ground our current understanding of NSSI are discussed, including comparing and contrasting what is currently known of traditionally defined NSSI with suicidal behaviors and other forms of indirect and direct self-harm, and discussion of NSSI functions. Readers will note that there are occasional references to terms other than NSSI (e.g., direct and indirect self-harm). We chose not to fully regulate the terminology that authors use in their chapters and defer to how our collaborators on this project have chosen to frame their various chapters. Nevertheless, this illustrates the challenges the field continues to experience with regard to consensus on terminology.

Part II is dedicated to a broad review of NSSI epidemiology. Starting off with separate chapters focused on reviewing population-level trends for community and clinical samples, this section includes information on key demographic trends, age of onset and offset, features and forms of NSSI, and description of relevant typologies. While work on this volume began prior to the COVID-19 pandemic, it is hard not to reflect on the influences this worldwide pandemic has had on global mental health challenges, access to care, socioeconomic inequities, and the need for scalable solutions. Thus, we include here chapters on NSSI trends during the COVID-19 pandemic and NSSI in cross-cultural contexts. The final chapter considers the question of whether NSSI is consistent enough with standard addiction models to be regarded as an addiction, at least in some individuals.

From here we move on to Part III where we take a deep dive into the burgeoning literature related to transdiagnostic processes and its application to NSSI. Using the RDoC framework, which consists of domains of functioning that reflect current knowledge surrounding major systems of cognition, emotion, motivation, and social behavior (Insel et al., 2010), chapters review how each of these systems helps us to understand and productively address NSSI. Leaning on contributions by several experienced teams of clinical scholars, this full-bodied section includes chapters that review NSSI behavior within a RDoC framework. With regard to the negative valence system domain, Swerdlow et al., this volume, describes research on NSSI and negative affectivity, and Carosella et al., this volume dives into the sustained threat construct. Claes et al., this volume, empirically review different theoretical models on NSSI and positive valence systems, and the role of the positive valence systems in between NSSI and other adverse emotion regulating behaviors, like substance use and eating disorder behavior. Browning and Muehlenkamp, this volume, summarize what is currently known about cognitive processes that activate NSSI (e.g., rumination and attentional bias) and those that maintain and increase it, namely, rule-governed behavior and expectancies. RDoC systems for social processes and their relationship with NSSI behaviors are described by Zetterqvist and Bjureberg, this volume, and explain the effects of social exclusion and negative social bias. To date, there is a lacuna in studies on NSSI within the arousal and regulatory systems domain and the sensorimotor domain, these are not described in this handbook. All chapters in Part III start with a review of literature relevant to the RDoC domains, where different units of analyses are described, and conclude with implications for clinicians for transdiagnostic interventions and avenues for future research. Part III concludes with a chapter aimed at elucidating application of transdiagnostic biological processes to NSSI interventions. Although RDoC is nascent in application to NSSI, the chapters in this section offer thoughtful and promising considerations for scholars and clinicians alike.

Part IV is dedicated to exploring NSSI from the phenomenological angle, focusing primarily on lived experience perceptions and experiences. It starts with a review of the way that lived experience is and is not currently integrated into research, practice, and policy, and what opportunities and challenges exist for remedying current gaps. Subsequent chapters explore the meaning and role of blood in ritual and nonritual NSSI, as well as the significance of wound location. These chapters are complemented by exploration of the dynamics of pain and pain perception—a fundamental component of NSSI behavior and its regulatory processes. Finally, this section includes a review of how NSSI recovery is currently conceptualized and measured, and how shifting the lens from recovery to healing and growth may be more reflective and supportive of the lived experience.

In Part V, we consider NSSI epidemiology and significance within a wide variety of special populations. Four of the chapters in this section are devoted to NSSI across various segments of the lifespan—childhood, adolescence and emerging adulthood, adults, and older adults. Additional chapters focus on self-injurious behavior among those with intellectual and developmental disabilities, within prison populations, military veterans, and sexual and gender diverse youth. While NSSI is present at concerning levels across all these populations, their unique features have important and differing implications for research, clinical, and community-based intervention approaches.

Part VI is focused on the array of risk and protective factors that have empirically or theoretically surfaced as key forces in either increasing or decreasing NSSI risk. Many of these reflect the complexity of the phenomenon itself by examining the interplay of various contributing factors. Chapters are dedicated to understanding the links between direct and indirect forms of self-harm and the way that cognitive and emotional processes interact to increase NSSI risk. These chapters extend the depth and breadth of basic understanding and include important implications for intervention and treatment. Chapters focused on contextual contributors, such as early childhood trauma and abuse, address long recognized but poorly understood dynamics at play in both enhancing NSSI risk and protection. Family- and peer-related processes are the subject of two chapters dedicated to untangling the myriad factors and processes that both enhance risk and mitigate harm. Closely linked to these areas is the subject of social contagion, where authors review what we do and do not know about the tendency of NSSI to spread in groups, particularly among young people. Of particular salience in the current era of social media are two chapters that thoughtfully consider the ways in which media representations contribute to and reflect NSSI behavior, particularly in youth, and another that reviews what we know about the relationship of online activity vis-à-vis self-injurious activity. Taken as a whole, this section both advances basic insight into core NSSI processes and contains a diverse array of very useful implications.

Part VII is devoted to assessment. The first chapter reviews assessment-linked considerations and tools in two distinct settings: community and clinical. The remaining chapters review assessment approaches for risk assessment in first responder groups and others in medical settings, differentiating risk for suicidal and nonsuicidal behaviors, and use of "fine-grained" assessment tools/methodologies, such as ecological momentary assessment, virtual reality, and various apps.

Building on all the previous sections, the final two sections are devoted to intervention and treatment. Part VIII contains chapters devoted to promising intervention and prevention approaches within secondary schools, at universities, and via online venues. It includes recommendations for the development of context-specific protocols, such as an example of a protocol for guiding universities on NSSI issues. This section closes with a review of the present and future of applying machine learning techniques to detection, predicting, and treating NSSI.

The final section of the book, Part IX, is dedicated to the review and discussion of treatment approaches across a variety of contexts. There are chapters dedicated to medical and pharmacological interventions, online interventions, mentalizing and psychodynamic approaches, and experiential therapies. One chapter lays out the unified protocol for transdiagnostic treatment of emotional disorders, and NSSI in particular. Mentalizing and psychoanalytic approaches, as well as experiential therapies, are chapters included in this section that offer excellent description and illustration of their implementation and processes. As the still favored treatment approaches for NSSI, there are detailed chapters on cognitive behavioral therapy (CBT) and dialectical behavior therapy (DBT), and two chapters devoted to examining the evidence for family therapy in treating NSSI, as well as a chapter highlighting the value and importance of using collaborative and strength-based approaches, particularly with youth and families in challenging situations. This chapter also includes an appendix containing a number of hands-on questions and exercises that can be used in treatment settings.

In sum, it is our hope that readers of this volume will encounter a rich array of resources to guide us forward in understanding the most contemporary thinking, research, and clinical applications related to NSSI etiology, epidemiology, phenomenology, risk and protective factors, and intervention and treatment. Through the astute and extremely knowledgeable work of nearly 100 NSSI expert chapter authors from a dozen countries worldwide, we hope this volume educates, intrigues, and inspires readers as it has inspired us!

References

American Psychiatric Association. (2013). *Diagnostic and Statistical Manual of Mental Disorders* (5th ed.).

Bronfenbrenner, U. (1979). Contexts of child rearing: Problems and prospects. *American Psychologist, 34*(10), 844.

Cipriano, A., Cella, S., & Cotrufo, P. (2017). Nonsuicidal self-injury: A systematic review. *Frontiers in Psychology, 8*, Article 1946. https://doi.org/10.3389/fpsyg.2017.01946

Clendenin, W. W., & Murphy, G. E. (1971). Wrist cutting: New epidemiological findings. *Archives of General Psychiatry, 25*(5), 465–469.

Insel, T., Cuthbert, B., Garvey, M., Heinssen, R., Pine, D. S., Quinn, K., Sanislow, C., & Wang, P. (2010). Research domain criteria (RDoC): Toward a new classification framework for research on mental disorders. *The American Journal of Psychiatry, 167*(7), 748–751.

International Society for the Study of Self-Injury. (2022, November). What is self-injury? Retrieved from https://itriples.org/about-self-injury/what-is-self-injury

Gandhi, A., Luyckx, K., Baetens, I., Kiekens, G., Sleuwaegen, E., Berens, A., Shubhada Maitra, & Claes, L. (2018). Age of onset of non-suicidal self-injury in Dutch-speaking adolescents and emerging adults: An event history analysis of pooled data. *Comprehensive Psychiatry, 80*, 170–178.

Xiao, Q., Song, X., Huang, L., Hou, D., & Huang, X. (2022). Global prevalence and characteristics of non-suicidal self-injury between 2010 and 2021 among a non-clinical sample of adolescents: A meta-analysis. *Frontiers in Psychiatry, 13*, Article 912441. https://doi.org/10.3389/fpsyt.2022.912441

Weissman, M. M. (1975). Wrist cutting: Relationship between clinical observations and epidemiological findings. *Archives of General Psychiatry, 32*(9), 1166–1171.

CHAPTER 2

NSSI in the DSM-5

Greg Lengel, Brooke A. Ammerman, *and* Jason Washburn

> **Abstract**
>
> Since the proposal for an NSSI disorder (NSSI-D) in DSM-5, there has been an expanding literature exploring the reliability, validity, and utility of NSSI-D and its proposed criteria. This chapter aims to identify NSSI features that may advance the construct from a behavior subordinated within other mental disorders to an independent diagnosis, and examines historical conceptualizations of NSSI as a clinical behavior and discrete syndrome, the initial proposal to include NSSI-D in DSM-5 and recent and future directions for NSSI-D. The chapter also identifies NSSI features that differentiate the construct from related diagnoses and behaviors (e.g., borderline personality disorder), explores challenges with the current NSSI-D criteria and its categorization in the diagnostic manual, and summarizes arguments for and against NSSI-D.
>
> **Key Words:** non-suicidal self-injury, mental disorders, NSSI disorder, generalizability, research, assessment, intervention, syndrome, DSM-5

Introduction

Nonsuicidal self-injury (NSSI), or the purposeful, self-inflicted damage of body tissue without suicidal intent (International Society for the Study of Self-Injury, 2023), is recognized as a relatively common pathological behavior. Lifetime prevalence rates for NSSI are estimated at 17.9% for adolescents and 13.4% for young adults (Swannell et al., 2014). These lifetime rates of NSSI behavior, however, obscure substantial variation in the severity of NSSI. For example, while Klonsky (2011) found a lifetime prevalence of NSSI of 5.9% among adults in a national sample in the United States, only 2.7% of adults engaged in NSSI five or more times in their life. Latent class analyses of community and clinical samples routinely find a substantial proportion (51%–78%) of individuals who engage in only mild or moderate NSSI (e.g., Case et al., 2020; Klonsky & Olino, 2008; Shahwan et al., 2020). This variation in NSSI severity complicates our understanding of if—and when—NSSI should be considered a separate condition for the purposes of research or clinical practice.

The goal of this chapter is to identify NSSI features that may elevate it from a discrete behavior subordinated within other mental disorders to a separate disorder in and of itself.

The consideration of NSSI as an independent syndrome is a natural extension of decades of literature that have articulated the importance of NSSI in mental health, particularly with regard to the risk for suicide. By examining historical attempts to conceptualize NSSI as a syndrome, as well as current attempts to refine the diagnosis of NSSI disorder (NSSI-D), this chapter builds upon prior reviews of NSSI as a disorder (e.g., Brausch, 2019; Hooley et al., 2020; Selby et al., 2015; Zetterqvist, 2015).

From Aberrant Behavior to Clinical Diagnosis: A Brief History Early Identification of NSSI as a Behavior and "Condition"

Recognition and discussion of behavior that is now considered NSSI has existed since at least the 19th century (Richards, 1877; see Angelotta, 2015, for a detailed history of NSSI). Menninger (1933, 1938) has been credited as being the first to describe this behavior as a unique clinical entity (Shaffer & Jacobson, 2009), which he described as "self-mutilation," and a behavior that functions as a "partial suicide" in an effort to thwart suicidal impulses. Throughout history, however, NSSI has been inconsistently conceptualized and labeled. For example, early discussions of NSSI often conflated NSSI with suicide attempts (Hooley et al., 2020). In time, researchers and clinicians began to explicitly distinguish between deliberate self-injurious behaviors without suicide intent from suicidal self-injury (e.g., Butler & Malone, 2013; Favazza, 1987; Kessel, 1965; Ross & McKay, 1979). Conceptualization has been complicated by an array of different labels for what is now commonly referred to as NSSI, including *deliberate self-harm*, *self-mutilation*, *parasuicide*, *self-injury*, *self-destructive behavior*, *self-defeating behavior*, *self-assault*, and *self-directed aggression*. Collectively, the cacophony of terms applied to NSSI has led to "semantic obfuscation" (Prinstein, 2008, p. 2), which has hindered generalizability across the literature and impeded advancement in research, assessment, and intervention, as well as communication across disciplines. Moreover, disagreement remains among professionals as to specific behaviors that should be considered NSSI, as well as how NSSI is defined and conceptualized (Lengel et al., 2022). These concerns gave rise to discussions of NSSI as a syndrome in an effort to both clarify NSSI behavior as well as what constitutes clinically relevant NSSI.

Early Conceptualizations and Discussions of NSSI as a Syndrome

As the self-injury literature advanced, conceptualizations and proposals of NSSI as a stand-alone diagnostic construct began to emerge. Early examples include Graff and Mallin's (1967) "syndrome of the wrist cutter," Pao's (1969) "syndrome of delicate self-cutting," and Rosenthal et al.'s (1972) description of a "wrist cutting syndrome." These early syndrome proposals were ultimately unsuccessful in their influence due to a shortage of supporting research as well as their conflation with suicidal self-injury (Muehlenkamp, 2005).

Building on these early syndrome conceptualizations, several researchers proposed clinical self-harm syndromes separate from suicide and other psychopathology. For example, Pattison and Kahan (1983) and Kahan and Pattison (1984) proposed a distinct "deliberate self-harm syndrome" as a potential diagnosis according to the *Diagnostic and Statistical Manual of Mental Disorders* (DSM), which included "low-lethality deliberate physical self-harm" (Kahan & Pattison, 1984, p. 27), omitting injury with apparent suicidal intent (e.g., gunshot), overdose, and indirect self-harm (e.g., compulsive eating), as well as harm resulting from a neurodevelopmental disorder. Additionally, Favazza and Rosenthal (1990) suggested a distinct "repetitive self-mutilation" disorder, which was conceptualized as an impulse control disorder and associated with a preoccupation with self-harm, increased tension prior to the act, and tension reduction following the act. Favazza (1992) also argued that the supporting literature for this condition was more robust than all other impulse control disorders not elsewhere specified, apart from pathological gambling. Further, he noted that other impulsive behaviors (e.g., binge eating and shoplifting) included with the borderline personality disorder (BPD) criteria are recognized as independent diagnostic constructs when engaged in repetitively, thus making the case for a similar treatment of NSSI (Favazza, 1992). Leading up to the fifth edition of the DSM (DSM-5; American Psychiatric Association, 2013), Muehlenkamp (2005) proposed an adoption of a "deliberate self-injury syndrome" as an independent clinical construct, basing proposed criteria, in part, on the aforementioned conditions. A significant step toward the adoption of an NSSI-D occurred following Shaffer and Jacobson's (2009) proposal to the DSM-5 Childhood Disorder and Mood Disorder Work Groups to recognize and adopt NSSI-D into the DSM. This proposal and the suggested criteria represented the first significant and "official" effort to provide a strong rationale for why NSSI merits recognition as a psychological disorder, independent from BPD.

Early Attempts to Conceptualize a Clinical Form or Threshold of NSSI

One primary challenge in delineating NSSI as a diagnosis is setting clear clinical boundaries. To this end, researchers have attempted to establish thresholds distinguishing clinically significant and subthreshold/superficial NSSI. One early-recognized distinction is recurrence. Individuals who recurrently self-injure report higher impulsiveness (Evans et al., 1996) as well as depressive symptoms, anger, lower self-esteem, and problem-solving skills (Hawton et al., 1999). Early attempts were also made to identify an appropriate frequency threshold. There is some evidence for, and suggestion that, five or more acts of NSSI in one's lifetime is indicative of a syndrome (e.g., Favazza & Rosenthal, 1990; Graff & Mallin, 1967; Manca et al., 2014; Muehlenkamp, 2005); however, the empirical support for this threshold of five has been equivocal. As discussed in greater depth later in the chapter, more recent research suggests a higher threshold, such as 10 or more lifetime incidences, may be more appropriate at discriminating between clinically significant and subthreshold NSSI (e.g., Muehlenkamp & Brausch, 2016).

Differentiating NSSI from Other Diagnoses and Behaviors

An additional challenge in establishing NSSI as a clinical diagnosis is differentiating it from existing diagnoses. The conflation of NSSI with existing disorders, such as Borderline Personality Disorder, serves as a primary impetus for identifying NSSI as a separate disorder; however, differentiating NSSI from this and other disorders remains a significant challenge for the inclusion of a standalone NSSI-D in the DSM. The next section explores relationships between NSSI and other adjacent DSM diagnoses and behaviors.

Borderline Personality Disorder

Historically, NSSI has been closely associated with BPD. Notably, this association is not without justification—NSSI frequently occurs amongst individuals with BPD (American Psychiatric Association, 2013), and until DSM-5, NSSI's only representation in the DSM was as the fifth criterion for BPD. Despite the fact that many individuals with BPD engage in NSSI, it is important to recognize that there is overwhelming evidence that NSSI is not unique to BPD. NSSI occurs in other personality disorders; other psychological disorders such as depression, anxiety, eating, and substance use disorders; and possibly in the absence of psychopathology (Bentley et al., 2015; Glenn & Klonsky, 2013; Kerr et al., 2010; Klonsky, 2011; Wilkinson, 2013).

Moreover, the association between BPD and NSSI may be exaggerated. Glenn and Klonsky (2013) found that the overlap between NSSI-D and BPD in an adolescent sample was no different from BPD and other psychopathology (i.e., previously referred to as Axis I disorders). They further found that NSSI-D had unique relationships with clinical impairment when controlling for BPD. Similarly, Gratz et al. (2015) found unique associations between NSSI-D and psychopathology, NSSI severity, and emotion dysregulation even when controlling for BPD. Additionally, in another sample of adolescents, In-Albon et al. (2013) found that 80% of participants who met criteria for NSSI-D did not meet BPD criteria. Moreover, studies comparing self-injuring individuals with and without BPD have found differences in NSSI functions and methods, as well as diagnostic comorbidities and emotion dysregulation (Bracken-Minor & McDevitt-Murphy, 2014; Turner et al., 2015). Collectively, empirical evidence suggests while many individuals with BPD engage in NSSI, NSSI is distinct from BPD.

Suicide

Like BPD, the relationship between NSSI and suicide is nuanced, as there is significant overlap and distinction between these constructs. History of NSSI is theorized to increase one's capability for suicide (Joiner, 2005), and is one of the strongest predictors of suicidal thoughts and behaviors (Ribeiro et al., 2016). Despite the contribution of NSSI to suicide risk, research has identified several differences between NSSI and suicidal self-injury. For example, Muehlenkamp (2005) reported that an estimated ~59%–72% of individuals do not have suicidal ideation while engaging in NSSI, and ~15%–45% of individuals with an

NSSI history deny history of suicide attempts. Further, many individuals engage in NSSI to help cope with, thwart, and avoid acting on suicidal ideations (Klonsky, 2007). NSSI also differs from suicide in its prevalence, the methods utilized, and the lack of desire to end one's life (Klonsky et al., 2014). Collectively, the extant research suggests that NSSI is distinct from suicidal self-injury, and conflating NSSI and suicidal self-injury can lead to negative clinical outcomes, misdiagnosis, and inappropriate treatment (e.g., unnecessary hospitalization; Glenn & Klonsky, 2013).

Excoriation, Trichotillomania, and Self-Harm in Developmental Disabilities
Several definitions of NSSI, along with the NSSI-D diagnostic criteria proposed in the DSM-5, exclude excoriation (skin picking), trichotillomania (hair pulling), and repetitive/stereotypic self-harming behaviors associated with neurodevelopmental disorders. While these behaviors can lead to direct harm and tissue damage and have some overlap with NSSI (Jurska et al., 2019), there are some important differences. NSSI is a deliberate and purposeful behavior that serves a variety of intra- and interpersonal functions (Klonsky, 2007). In contrast, skin picking and hair pulling are conceptualized as obsessive and compulsive related behaviors that occur with lower awareness than NSSI and may be more likely to serve the functions of reducing boredom and addressing skin imperfections (Mathew et al., 2020).

Compared to NSSI, stereotypic self-harm that occurs in neurodevelopmental disorders (e.g., head banging and biting) is often restrictive, rhythmic, and repetitive (Maddox et al., 2017) and typically occurs at a significantly higher frequency, leads to minor harm, and rarely involves tools (Nock & Favazza, 2009). These behaviors are also distinguished from traditional NSSI in that they are associated with severe intellectual disability, deficits in receptive and expressive communication, and lower adaptive functioning (Maddox et al., 2017). That said, it is important to note that NSSI can occur within these populations. For example, Maddox et al. (2017) compared a sample of adults with and without autism spectrum disorder (ASD) and found that 50% of the adults with ASD reported at least one NSSI episode, suggesting a significantly elevated risk for NSSI within this population. Additional research is needed to better understand NSSI in ASD and other populations with neurodevelopmental disorders (for more information, see Bradley et al., this volume).

First Attempt at Inclusion in the DSM-5
As noted above, the initial DSM-5 NSSI-D proposal (Shaffer & Jacobson, 2009) was a significant step forward for NSSI becoming an independent diagnosis, stimulating a significant amount of discussion and debate within the field. While there was a promising degree of support among NSSI clinicians and researchers regarding the proposal, significant challenges arose during the DSM-5 field trials. In short, the NSSI-D field trials were unsuccessful in demonstrating acceptable interrater reliability (Regier et al., 2013). It

was hard to imagine, however, how the field trials for NSSI-D could have been successful given the associated limitations. For example, the evaluation of NSSI-D was restricted to only child and adolescent sites and multiple sites failed to obtain adequate sample sizes (Brausch, 2019); one site recruited zero participants while the other two sites recruited only seven participants each (Clarke et al., 2013). As a result of these unsuccessful trials, the NSSI-D proposal was assigned to Section III Conditions for Further Study.

Current Status of NSSI-D

Since the publication of Shaffer and Jacobson's (2009) proposal and the release of the DSM-5, there has been an active literature that has explored the reliability, validity, and utility of the proposed criteria for NSSI-D (e.g., Ammerman et al., 2017; Ammerman et al., 2021; Brausch et al., 2016; In-Albon et al., 2013; Lengel & Mullins-Sweatt, 2013; Muehlenkamp & Brausch, 2016; Victor et al., 2017; Washburn et al., 2015). Collectively, this research will be instrumental in informing and improving proposals for future diagnostic manuals. In addition, at the time of this writing, a workgroup comprised of clinicians and researchers, and sponsored by the International Society for the Study of Self-Injury, is in the process of conducting empirical research and developing a data-driven proposal to the American Psychiatric Association for revised DSM NSSI-D criteria. Accordingly, one can expect interest in, and progress toward, an official NSSI-D to continue.

Challenges with the Current NSSI-D Criteria and Categorization

Researchers in the field of NSSI have responded robustly to the call for better empirical support and delineation of an NSSI-D diagnosis. Although the field has progressed in its understanding of how best to articulate and define NSSI-D, several challenges and considerations have emerged concerning to the proposed NSSI-D diagnostic criteria. Even fundamental questions, such as the appropriate categorization of NSSI-D in the DSM, remain a point of disagreement within the field. The next section explores current challenges with how to define NSSI-D criteria and where to categorize NSSI diagnostically.

Determining the Threshold for Criterion A

Currently, the NSSI-D criteria are listed in Section III (i.e., Conditions for Further Study) of the DSM-5 (American Psychiatric Association, 2013) and include six primary criteria: criteria A–F. Of these criteria, criterion A—which includes a definition of behaviors considered to be NSSI, as well as a time frame and frequency threshold for the behavior—may be the most studied, and also the most contested and controversial. The first aspect of criterion A that raises concern is what general categories of behaviors should be considered NSSI. A body of research has investigated potential differences between traditionally accepted NSSI behaviors (e.g., self-cutting) and indirect forms of self-inflicted self-harm (e.g., substance use, risky sex, and reckless behavior). While these two categories of behaviors can serve similar functions (Jonsson et al., 2019) and have comparable relations to clinical outcomes (St. Germain & Hooley, 2012), they often have different intentions (Walsh, 2012) (for more information on indirect self-harm, see Rubæk & Møhl, this volume). Further, while NSSI results in immediate tissue damage, indirect self-harm may result in little or no immediate tissue damage, only accumulating damage—or risk for it—over time (Green et al., 2017). Given these differences, there is general support in the literature that NSSI should be considered a distinct clinical phenomenon, separate from indirect forms of self-harm (Hooley et al., 2014; St. Germain & Hooley, 2012).

Despite general agreement that NSSI needs to represent a direct (i.e., on the surface of the body) self-inflicted injury, as highlighted in the NSSI-D criteria, other aspects of the current behavioral definition of NSSI remain debatable. For example, experts in the field report acceptable agreement with the notion that NSSI should be injurious, causing either tissue damage *or* pain (Lengel et al., 2022). In contrast to the current DSM-5 definition, which identifies the essential feature of NSSI to be the repeated self-infliction of "shallow, yet painful injuries to the surface of his or her body" (American Psychiatric Association, 2013, p. 804), experts also report acceptable agreement that NSSI does *not* need to be a painful injury. Further, there is good agreement among experts that NSSI does not need to necessarily result in a wound (i.e., break tissues or cause bruising or bleeding; Lengel et al., 2022). Considering this research, in combination with the definition of NSSI as proposed in the DSM-5, there are potential discrepancies in determining whether or not a given behavior, such as scratching without breaking the skin or cutting through the skin without feeling pain, would meet threshold for NSSI (Lengel et al., 2022). Although the field has begun to coalesce around the general features of behaviors that qualify as NSSI, the behavioral definition of NSSI would benefit from increased clarity and specificity, as well as agreement on a core and extended set of specific NSSI behaviors.

The time frame to meet criterion A in the proposed DSM-5 criteria uses a given number of *days* of NSSI in the past year. This time frame is in contrast to many NSSI assessment tools, which evaluate the frequency of specific NSSI acts or episodes, not the number of days. The use of days instead of specific acts or episodes can be beneficial, as it helps to reduce individual variation in definitions of NSSI acts or episodes. For example, if an individual engages in two NSSI acts 10 minutes apart, should this be considered one or two NSSI acts? If the latter, this may artificially inflate an individual's behavioral frequency, allowing them to meet criterion A with only two days of NSSI behavior based on two to three acts per day. Relying on reports of days during which NSSI occurs, versus the number of acts regardless of days, also has the benefit of reducing the potential of retrospective recall bias, allowing for a more accurate understanding of an individual's NSSI course and enhancing clinical utility of the disorder. Although there are many advantages to using days instead of acts or episodes in criterion A, days may fail to capture true behavioral severity (Selby et al., 2015). For example, an individual who engages in an isolated act of NSSI over five days would meet criterion A, whereas an individual who engages in NSSI a hundred times across four days would not meet the criterion. Although some measures examine both number of days and average number of acts or episodes per day (e.g., Washburn et al., 2015), given the lack of validated measures that utilize NSSI days, and the limited prior empirical research following this classification (e.g., Andover, 2014, Buelens et al., 2020), there is a need for further work to more directly examine the impact of conceptualizing NSSI severity based on days as opposed to behavioral acts or episodes.

One of the most widely studied aspects of criterion A is the outlined frequency threshold. The proposed criteria of five or more days in the past year was established based on the reasoning that more than one episode should be required for a NSSI disorder diagnosis, and beyond that, the threshold should be relatively conservative (Shaffer & Jacobson, 2009). Since this criterion was first presented, numerous researchers have highlighted the need for a higher threshold in criterion A to more meaningfully demarcate individuals with clinically significant NSSI. Such propositions have been based on the high percentage of individuals engaging in NSSI who meet the criterion as currently proposed (i.e., Andover, 2014; Buelens et al., 2020; Washburn et al., 2015), as well as distributions of NSSI frequency. Across several studies, researchers have variously concluded that the frequency of NSSI behavior should increase anywhere from six or more acts of NSSI to 30 or more days of NSSI in the past year (Ammerman et al., 2017; Ammerman et al., 2019; Ammerman et al., 2021; Muehlenkamp & Brausch, 2016; Muehlenkamp et al., 2017). Similarly, several studies have suggested that a time frame shorter than the 12-month time frame outlined in the current criterion A may be more clinically meaningful. The majority of experts in the field of NSSI agree that a three-month time frame would be most useful (Ammerman et al., 2021), with other empirical work suggesting that demarcating past-month behavior may enhance the ability of the diagnostic criterion to serve as a clinical indicator (Ammerman et al., 2019; Graham et al., 2003). Despite research highlighting the need to modify criterion A to include a shorter time frame of assessment and likely a higher threshold for behavioral frequency, the exact parameters of those revisions have yet to reach a consensus in the field.

Articulating—and Differentiating—Criteria B and C
Whereas additional work is needed to reach consensus for criterion A, research regarding criteria B and C has been relatively uniform. These two criteria require the endorsement of one of three NSSI functions (i.e., negative affect regulation, interpersonal problem-solving, and induction of positive emotion) and the engagement of NSSI following one of three proximal precipitants (i.e., interpersonal difficulties or negative thoughts/feelings, NSSI urges, preoccupation with NSSI), respectively (American Psychiatric Association, 2013). Research examining these criteria highlight their limited utility in differentiating clinically significantly NSSI (e.g., Victor et al., 2017; Zetterqvist et al., 2013). For example, across research studies, 87%–99% of individuals with a lifetime NSSI history met criterion B (Brausch et al., 2016; Buelens et al., 2020) and 82%–99% met criterion C (Andover, 2014; Buelens et al., 2020). Some research has highlighted that individuals who

meet the currently proposed criterion A endorse a greater number of NSSI functions more broadly (Brausch et al., 2016), suggesting a revision of the criterion B that assesses number, rather than presence, of functions may increase the clinical utility of the criterion. Despite this, experts have generally agreed that criteria B and C may be removed from the NSSI disorder diagnostic criteria, without reducing the diagnostic utility.

Criteria D, E, and F

The remaining NSSI-D proposed criteria require that the NSSI behavior not be socially sanctioned (criterion D), causes clinically significant distress or impairment (criterion E), and does not occur exclusively in the context of other, specified psychological conditions (i.e., psychotic episodes and substance intoxication; criterion F; American Psychiatric Association, 2013). The determination of NSSI not being a socially sanctioned behavior has been long discussed (i.e., Favazza, 1987; St. Germain & Hooley, 2012; Jonsson et al., 2019). The need to prevent the inappropriate application of an NSSI label to bona fide cultural and religious practices that may involve self-injurious behavior is clear. Indeed, early examinations of NSSI were careful to differentiate *culturally sanctioned body modifications* that include accepted rituals and practices within specific cultures and religions from *pathological self-injury* (Favazza, 1987). For example, some Aboriginal and Torres Strait Islander peoples may engage in cutting of the skin as part of traditional initiation or mourning ceremonies (Farrelly & Francis, 2009). Although it is critical to avoid pathologizing socially sanctioned behaviors that involve self-injury, it is also possible that socially sanctioned behaviors may be used as a form of NSSI. For example, while tattooing is specifically identified in criterion D as exclusionary of NSSI-D, case examples in which tattooing is used as a form of NSSI have been identified in the literature (Mann et al., 2020). Further, among patients in treatment for NSSI, 11.9% reported engaging in tattooing specifically for the purposes of causing pain or harm (Washburn et al., 2015). Similar to scrupulosity, in which obsessive and compulsive symptoms can resemble extreme adherence to religious practices, extreme forms of behaviors that are socially sanctioned within a particular culture or religion serve the function of NSSI for some individuals (Mann et al., 2020) (cross-cultural representations of NSSI are discussed further in Wilson, this volume).

Criterion E relies on the presence of distress or impairment due to one's NSSI, the measurement of which has yet to be solidified in the literature. There are two validated assessment tools that aim to assess distress and impairment (i.e., Impact of Nonsuicidal Self-Injury Scale; Nonsuicidal Self-Injury Disorder Scale; Burke et al., 2017; Victor et al., 2017), with the former offering a more comprehensive assessment of distress and impairment and latter mapping more directly on the proposed NSSI-D criteria. Despite the existence of such measures, their use has been limited, with the majority of existing research utilizing study specific, single items. This lack of standardization is unfortunate as research has highlighted that criterion E may be meaningful in its ability to distinguish those who engage in clinically significant NSSI behavior (Buelens et al., 2020). Understanding distress and impairment may be particularly important for NSSI, given that some people report limited concern regarding their NSSI behavior (Ammerman et al., 2020; Klonsky & Muehlenkamp, 2007). Moreover, some patients view NSSI as a lifestyle choice that does not harm others and facilitates interpersonal connections (Adler & Adler, 2007; Whitlock et al., 2006). It will be important for future research to consider how, in these cases and elsewise, distress and impairment should be conceptualized in NSSI-D.

Categorizing and Specifying NSSI-D

Beyond the proposed criteria, several other diagnostic aspects of NSSI disorder have received attention in the literature, albeit limited. As NSSI-D is currently included in the section designed for conditions for future study, it is unclear how it will be categorized in DSM-5. One study examined this question, finding overwhelming support among experts in the field for NSSI-D to be housed in the diagnostic category of disruptive, impulse-control, and conduct disorder (Ammerman et al., 2021). Despite this consensus, more research is necessary to understand the ramifications of the classification of NSSI-D in this category. For example, while NSSI precipitants (e.g., negative affect) may be similar to disorders catalogued under this classification, it may also lead to a biased or incomplete conceptualization of NSSI and its functions, as well as potentially perpetuate the stigmatization of NSSI.

The use of diagnostic specifiers, including remission status, must also be considered if NSSI-D is to move out of Section III. NSSI researchers and clinicians endorse the utility of diagnostic specifiers, such as the presence of NSSI urges and suicidality (Ammerman et al., 2021). NSSI-D may also benefit from a severity specifier based on key NSSI features, such as frequency and number of methods, which may provide valuable information necessary for identifying treatment targets (Ammerman et al., 2021). Importantly, the inclusion of remission specifiers must recognize the complexity and nonlinearity associated with the recovery process of NSSI and consider factors beyond just cessation of NSSI (Lewis & Hasking, 2021) (see Whitlock et al., this volume, for more information on NSSI recovery).

Should NSSI Be a Diagnosis?

While there is growing support and evidence for a stand-alone NSSI syndrome, the proposal for the inclusion of NSSI-D is not without criticism. Many have critiqued and challenged the validity, necessity, and utility of an NSSI-D, which has fostered spirited debate among clinicians and researchers. The next section presents some of the major arguments in support of, and against, NSSI-D.

Pro-NSSI-D Arguments

Muehlenkamp (2005) initially suggested that NSSI warrants consideration as a unique diagnostic category because it has a "prominent symptom pattern and a relatively clear presentation of biological and associated features (e.g., age of onset, precipitants, course)" (p. 327). Additionally, Shaffer and Jacobson (2009) argued that NSSI-D meets the criteria in the DSM for a disorder because it is "common, impairing, and distinctive, both with respect to clinical presentation and antecedent and future characteristics" (p. 10). Accordingly, there is theoretical justification for NSSI-D.

Further, despite being associated with numerous psychological disorders, as well as occurring in the absence of other psychopathology, NSSI is currently only represented in DSM-5 as a criterion of BPD. The relegation of NSSI to a BPD criterion erroneously suggests that NSSI is not relevant outside the context of BPD (Glenn & Klonsky, 2013). An NSSI-D could, in theory, reduce misdiagnosis of BPD in those with NSSI, but lacking other prominent BPD symptoms, as well as reduce referrals for inappropriate treatment (Shaffer & Jacobson, 2009). NSSI is also often falsely conflated with, and misinterpreted as, suicidal behavior, which can contribute to inaccurate epidemiological data and overly restrictive care, resulting in inappropriate, and potentially harmful, hospitalization and misallocation of resources (Glenn & Klonsky, 2013; Shaffer & Jacobson, 2009). Although unique from suicidal self-injury, identifying a clinical level of NSSI as a substantial contributor to suicidal lethality could facilitate risk assessment (Cunningham et al., 2021).

NSSI-D could have significant clinical utility. Having a clearly defined definition and criteria set for NSSI could help mitigate the "semantic obfuscation" of labeling and definitional problems that have negatively impacted the generalizability and interpretability of the NSSI literature for decades, as well as lead to clear and consistent communication between researchers, clinicians, patients, and the public. NSSI-D could also lead to the development of improved assessment measures and targeted clinical interventions, as well as aid treatment planning. NSSI-D may also help reduce stigma associated with NSSI behavior, validating and empowering those who engage in NSSI to seek treatment, particularly for those individuals whose symptom profiles do not neatly fit into another diagnostic category (Lewis et al, 2017).

Inclusion of NSSI-D into diagnostic nomenclature could also accelerate and advance NSSI research. As found in the eating disorder field, simply designating NSSI as a clinical disorder may promote research focused on the behavior (Striegel-Moore & Franko, 2008). Further, NSSI-D would standardize an operational definition for NSSI and clearly delineate the criteria needed for clinically relevant NSSI. As it currently stands, researchers frequently utilize various assessment classifications (i.e., days, frequency, and methods), as well as differing behavioral time frames (i.e., past month, past year, and lifetime), thwarting attempts to compare findings across studies and to generalize findings to different contexts. A consistent framework for measuring NSSI would also allow for the inclusion of NSSI-D in epidemiological studies, enhancing knowledge of the prevalence across age ranges and special populations, as well as potentially increasing funding opportunities for understanding and treating NSSI (Glenn & Klonsky, 2013; Selby et al., 2015). Finally, the classification of NSSI as a diagnostic category would increase opportunities for learning from individuals with lived experience. For example, it would allow researchers to explore how the inclusion of NSSI disorder as clinical diagnostic impacts both the public and self-stigma associated with the behavior, as well as the downstream effects on prevention efforts and intervention availability.

Anti-NSSI-D Arguments

While there is substantial support and strong justification for NSSI-D, critics of NSSI-D have offered several arguments against adoption of NSSI as a stand-alone syndrome. Despite a growing research base for NSSI-D, Kapur et al. (2013) noted that there are relatively few studies that utilized adult samples or samples outside of North America, as well as a lack of longitudinal studies. Although research on NSSI-D has increased exponentially in recent years, including with diverse ages and populations (e.g., Buelens et al., 2020; Cunningham et al., 2021; Kiekens et al., 2018; Tschan et al., 2019; Zetterqvist et al., 2020), the field could benefit from more longitudinal studies of NSSI-D.

Further, it has been argued that an NSSI diagnostic classification is simply unnecessary, or worse, invalid. Some may contend that NSSI-D contributes to an unwarranted, ever-expanding, proliferation of diagnoses in the DSM (Frances, 2013). A related argument is that NSSI does not reach the level of a distinct disorder. Ghinea et al. (2020) suggested that NSSI may only be a precursor or indicator behavior of a psychological disorder, as opposed to an independent cause of a disorder. Similarly, it has been asserted that the significant comorbidity NSSI shares with several other psychological disorders (e.g., BPD and eating disorders) suggests that NSSI is a distinct *symptom* of psychopathology, as opposed to an independent diagnosis (Muehlenkamp, 2005). Indeed, rather than including NSSI as a separate disorder, NSSI could be included in DSM-5 as a specifier across other diagnoses. Additionally, Kapur et al. (2013) critiqued NSSI-D by describing a "false dichotomy" between NSSI and suicidal self-injury, arguing that NSSI is part of a dimensional continuum of suicidal behavior. The lack of a clear cutoff point or definition for clinically relevant NSSI as well as potential ambiguity with the suicidal intent of self-injurious behavior support the use of a more inclusive construct, like self-harm, to refer to either NSSI or suicidal self-injury (Kapur et al., 2013). Building on concerns with criterion D, Gilman (2013) argued that the line between societally acceptable and unacceptable NSSI is constantly in flux (e.g., body modification is accepted and skin cutting is not), and therefore defining NSSI as a psychological disorder is inappropriate.

Finally, while an NSSI-D can have a positive impact on individuals, one must consider potential negative side effects of labeling, as a diagnostic label has the potential of being stigmatizing and may lead to inappropriate stereotypes and prejudices. For example, in addition to finding support for an NSSI-D from individuals with lived experience, Lewis et al. (2017) also found that several respondents expressed concern about stigmatization. Similarly, Crowe (2014) expressed concern about NSSI-D, citing that the majority of NSSI occurs among adolescents and young adults, which may resolve spontaneously

(Moran et al., 2012), and questioned whether it is appropriate for "young people to be labeled as abnormal during a turbulent period in their development" (p. 857) (for more on the specifics of NSSI in adolescence, see Kiekens et al., this volume).

Conclusion and Future Directions

The consideration of NSSI for inclusion in DSM-5 represents a major milestone for the field. Although arguments for and against identifying NSSI as a disorder both have merit, the fact that the field is having this discussion indicates the maturity of research and clinical practice related to NSSI. Yet, NSSI remains a relatively new construct and there is much still to be learned. Indeed, research on NSSI only began to get traction in the literature in the early 2000s. Regardless of whether NSSI becomes an officially recognized clinical disorder, it remains critical for both research and clinical practice to develop standards for understanding what constitutes NSSI, what features should be considered when determining the severity of NSSI, and thresholds for identifying different levels of severity.

References

Adler, P. A., & Adler, P. (2007). The demedicalization of self-injury: From psychopathology to sociological deviance. *Journal of Contemporary Ethnography*, *36*, 537–570. https://doi.org/10.1177%2F0891241607301968

American Psychiatric Association. (2013). *Diagnostic and statistical manual of mental disorders* (5th ed.). https://doi.org/10.1176/appi.books.9780890425596

Ammerman, B. A., Jacobucci, R., Kleiman, E. M., Muehlenkamp, J. J., & McCloskey, M. S. (2017). Development and validation of empirically derived frequency criteria for NSSI disorder using exploratory data mining. *Psychological Assessment*, *29*, 221–231. https://doi.org/doi/10.1037/pas0000334

Ammerman, B. A., Jacobucci, R., & McCloskey, M. S. (2019). Reconsidering important outcomes of the nonsuicidal self-injury disorder diagnostic criterion A. *Journal of Clinical Psychology*, *75*, 1084–1097. https://doi.org/10.1002/jclp.22754

Ammerman, B. A., Lengel, G. J., & Washburn, J. J. (2021). Consideration of clinician and researcher opinions on the parameters of nonsuicidal self-injury disorder diagnostic criteria. *Psychiatry Research*, *296*, 113642. https://doi.org/10.1016/j.psychres.2020.113642

Ammerman, B. A., Wilcox, K. T., O'Loughlin, C. M., & McCloskey, M. S. (2020). Characterizing the choice to disclose nonsuicidal self-injury. *Journal of Clinical Psychology*, *77*, 683–700. https://doi.org/10.1002/jclp.23045

Andover, M. S. (2014). Non-suicidal self-injury disorder in a community sample of adults. *Psychiatry Research*, *219*, 305–310. https://doi.org/10.1016/j.psychres.2014.06.001

Angelotta, C. (2015). Defining and refining self-harm: A historical perspective on nonsuicidal self-injury. *The Journal of Nervous and Mental Disease*, *203*, 75–80. https://doi.org/10.1097/nmd.0000000000000243

Bentley, K. H., Cassiello-Robbins, C. F., Vittorio, L., Sauer-Zavala, S., & Barlow, D. H. (2015). The association between nonsuicidal self-injury and the emotional disorders: A meta-analytic review. *Clinical Psychology Review*, *37*, 72–88. https://doi.org/10.1016/j.cpr.2015.02.006

Bracken-Minor, K. L., & McDevitt-Murphy, M. E. (2014). Differences in features of non-suicidal self-injury according to borderline personality disorder screening status. *Archives of Suicide Research*, *18*, 88–103. https://doi.org/10.1080/13811118.2013.809040

Brausch, A. M. (2019). Diagnostic classification of NSSI. In J. J. Washburn (Ed.), *Nonsuicidal self-injury: Advances in research and practice* (pp. 71–87). Routledge. https://doi.org/10.4324/9781315164182

Brausch, A. M., Muehlenkamp, J. J., & Washburn, J. J. (2016). Nonsuicidal self-injury disorder: Does Criterion B add diagnostic utility? *Psychiatry Research*, *244*, 179–184. https://doi.org/10.1016/j.psychres.2016.07.025

Buelens, T., Luyckx, K., Kiekens, G., Gandhi, A., Muehlenkamp, J. J., & Claes, L. (2020). Investigating the DSM-5 criteria for non-suicidal self-injury disorder in a community sample of adolescents. *Journal of Affective Disorders*, *260*, 314–322. https://doi.org/10.1016/j.jad.2019.09.009

Burke, T. A., Ammerman, B. A., Hamilton, J. L., & Alloy, L. B. (2017). Impact of non-suicidal self-injury scale: Initial psychometric validation. *Cognitive Therapy and Research*, *41*, 130–142. https://doi.org/10.1007/s10608-016-9806-9

Butler, A. M., & Malone, K. (2013). Attempted suicide v. non-suicidal self-injury: Behaviour, syndrome or diagnosis? *The British Journal of Psychiatry*, *202*, 324–325. https://doi.org/10.1192/bjp.bp.112.113506

Case, J. A. C., Burke, T. A., Siegel, D. M., Piccirillo, M. L., Alloy, L. B., & Olino, T. M. (2020). Functions of non-suicidal self-injury in late adolescence: A latent class analysis. *Archives of Suicide Research*, *24*(Supp.2). https://doi.org/10.1080/13811118.2019.1586607

Clarke, D. E., Narrow, W. E., Regier, D. A., Kuramoto, S. J., Kupfer, D. J., Kuhl, E. A., Greiner, L., & Kraemer, H. C. (2013). DSM–5 field trials in the United States and Canada, Part I: Study design, sampling strategy, implementation, and analytic approaches. *American Journal of Psychiatry*, *170*, 43–58. https://doi.org/10.1176/appi.ajp.2012.12070998

Crowe, M. (2014). From expression to symptom to disorder: The psychiatric evolution of self- harm in the DSM. *Journal of Psychiatric and Mental Health Nursing*, *21*, 857–858. https://doi.org/10.1111/jpm.12183

Cunningham, K. C., Aunon, F. M., Patel, T. A., Mann, A. J., DeBeer, B. B., Meyer, E. C., Morissette, S. B., Silvia, P. J., Gratz, K. L., Calhoun, P. S., Beckham, J. C., & Kimbrel, N. A. (2021). Nonsuicidal self-injury disorder, borderline personality disorder, and lifetime history of suicide attempts among male and female veterans with mental health disorders. *Journal of Affective Disorders*, *287*, 276–281. https://doi.org/10.1016/j.jad.2021.03.033

Evans, J., Platts, H., & Liebenau, A. (1996). Impulsiveness and deliberate self-harm: A comparison of "first-timers" and "repeaters." *Acta Psychiatrica Scandinavica*, *93*, 378–380. https://doi.org/10.1111/j.1600-0447.1996.tb10663.x

Farrelly, T., & Francis, K. (2009). Definitions of suicide and self-harm behavior in an Australian Aboriginal Community. *Suicide and Life-Threatening Behavior*, *39*, 182–189. https://doi.org/10.1521/suli.2009.39.2.182

Favazza, A. R. (1987). *Bodies under siege: Self-mutilation and body modification in culture and psychiatry*. Johns Hopkins University Press.

Favazza, A. R. (1992). Repetitive self-mutilation. *Psychiatric Annals*, *22*, 60–63. https://doi.org/10.3928/0048-5713-19920201-06

Favazza, A. R. & Rosenthal, R. J. (1990). Varieties of pathological self-mutilation. *Behavioural Neurology*, *3*, 77–85. https://doi.org/10.3233/ben-1990-3202

Frances, A. (2013). The new crisis of confidence in psychiatric diagnosis. *Annals of Internal Medicine*, *159*, 221–222. https://doi.org/10.7326/0003-4819-159-3-201308060-00655

Ghinea, D., Edinger, A., Parzer, P., Koenig, J., Resch, F., & Kaess, M. (2020). Non-suicidal self-injury disorder as a stand-alone diagnosis in a consecutive help-seeking sample of adolescents. *Journal of Affective Disorders*, *274*, 1122–1125. https://doi.org/10.1016/j.jad.2020.06.009

Gilman, S. L. (2013). From psychiatric symptom to diagnostic category: Self-harm from the Victorians to DSM-5. *History of Psychiatry*, *24*, 148–165. https://doi.org/10.1177%2F0957154X13478082

Glenn, C. R. & Klonsky, E. D. (2013). Nonsuicidal self-injury disorder: An empirical investigation in adolescent psychiatric patients. *Journal of Clinical Child & Adolescent Psychology*, *42*, 496–507. https://doi.org/10.1080/15374416.2013.794699

Graff, H., & Mallin, R. (1967). The syndrome of the wrist cutter. *The American Journal of Psychiatry*, *124*, 36–42. https://doi.org/10.1176/ajp.124.1.36

Graham, C. A., Catania, J. A., Brand, R., Duong, T., & Canchola, J. A. (2003). Recalling sexual behavior: A methodological analysis of memory recall bias via interview using the diary as the gold standard. *Journal of Sex Research*, *40*, 325–332. https://doi.org/10.1080/00224490209552198

Gratz, K. L., Dixon-Gordon, K. L., Chapman, A. L., & Tull, M. T. (2015). Diagnosis and characterization of DSM-5 nonsuicidal self-injury disorder using the clinician-administered nonsuicidal self-injury disorder index. *Assessment*, *22*, 527–539. https://doi.org/10.1177/1073191114565878

Green, J. D., Hatgis, C., Kearns, J. C., Nock, M. K., & Marx, B. P. (2017). The direct and indirect self-harm inventory (DISH): A new measure for assessing high-risk and self-harm behaviors among military veterans. *Psychology of Men and Masculinity*, *18*, 208–214. http://dx.doi.org/10.1037/men0000116

Hawton, K., Kingsbury, S., Steinhardt, K., James, A., & Fagg, J. (1999). Repetition of deliberate self-harm by adolescents: The role of psychological factors. *Journal of Adolescence, 22*, 369–378. https://doi.org/10.1006/jado.1999.0228

Hooley, J. M., Fox, K. R., & Boccagno, C. (2020). Nonsuicidal self-injury: Diagnostic challenges and current perspectives. *Neuropsychiatric Disease and Treatment, 16*, 101–112. https://doi.org/10.2147/ndt.s198806

Hooley, J. M., St. Germain, S. A., & Nock, M. K. (2014). Should we expand the conceptualization of self-injurious behavior? Rationale, review, and recommendations. The Oxford handbook of suicide and self-injury (pp. 47–60). Oxford University Press. https://doi.org/10.1093/oxfordhb/9780195388565.013.0006

In-Albon, T., Ruf, C., & Schmid, M. (2013). Proposed diagnostic criteria for the DSM-5 of nonsuicidal self-injury in female adolescents: Diagnostic and clinical correlates. *Psychiatry Journal, 2013*, 1–12. https://doi.org/10.1155/2013/159208

International Society for the Study of Self-Injury. (2023, July 25). *What is self-injury?* Retrieved from: https://www.itriples.org/what-is-nssi

Joiner, T. (2005). *Why people die by suicide.* Harvard University Press.

Jonsson, L. S., Svedin, C. G., Priebe, G., Fredlund, C., Wadsby, M., & Zetterqvist, M. (2019). Similarities and differences in the functions of nonsuicidal self-injury (NSSI) and sex as self-injury (SASI). *Suicide and Life-Threatening Behavior, 49*, 120–136. https://doi.org/10.1111/sltb.12417

Jurska, J., Corcoran, V., Andover, M. (2019). Nonsuicidal self-injury and compulsive disorders. In J. Washburn (Ed.), *Nonsuicidal self-injury: Advances in research and practice* (pp. 88–108). Routledge. https://doi.org/10.4324/9781315164182

Kahan, J., & Pattison, E. M. (1984). Proposal for a distinctive diagnosis: The deliberate self-harm syndrome (DSH). *Suicide & Life-Threatening Behavior, 14*, 17–35. https://doi.org/10.1111/j.1943-278x.1984.tb00334.x

Kapur, N., Cooper, J., O'Connor, R. C., & Hawton, K. (2013). Non-suicidal self-injury v. attempted suicide: New diagnosis or false dichotomy? *British Journal of Psychiatry, 202*, 326–328. https://doi.org/10.1192/bjp.bp.112.116111

Kerr, P. L., Muehlenkamp, J. J., & Turner, J. M. (2010). Nonsuicidal self-injury: A review of current research for family medicine and primary care physicians. *Journal of the American Board of Family Medicine, 23*, 240–259. https://doi.org/10.3122/jabfm.2010.02.090110

Kessel, N. (1965). Repeated acts of self-poisoning and self-injury. *Journal of the Royal Society of Medicine, 50*, 651–654.

Kiekens, G., Hasking, P., Claes, L., Mortier, P., Auerbach, R. P., Boyes, M., Cuijpers, P., Demyttenaere, K., Green, J. G., Kessler, R. C., Nock, M. K., & Bruffaerts, R. (2018). The DSM-5 nonsuicidal self-injury disorder among incoming college students: Prevalence and associations with 12-month mental disorders and suicidal thoughts and behaviors. *Depression and Anxiety, 35*, 629–637. https://doi.org/10.1002/da.22754

Klonsky, E. D. (2007). The functions of deliberate self-injury: A review of the evidence. *Clinical Psychology Review, 27*, 226–239. https://doi.org/10.1016/j.cpr.2006.08.002

Klonsky, E. D. (2011). Non-suicidal self-injury in United States adults: Prevalence, sociodemographics, topography and functions. *Psychological Medicine, 41*, 1981–1986. https://doi.org/10.1017/s0033291710002497

Klonsky, E. D., & Muehlenkamp, J. J. (2007). Self-injury: A research review for the practitioner. *Journal of Clinical Psychology, 63*, 1045–1056. https://doi.org/10.1002/jclp.20412

Klonsky, E. D., & Olino, T. M. (2008). Identifying clinically distinct subgroups of self-injurers among young adults: A latent class analysis. *Journal of Consulting and Clinical Psychology, 76*, 22–27. https://doi.org/10.1037/0022-006x.76.1.22

Klonsky, E. D., Victor, S. E., & Saffer, B. Y. (2014). Nonsuicidal self-injury: What we know, and what we need to know. *Canadian Journal of Psychiatry, 59*, 565–568. https://dx.doi.org/10.1177%2F070674371405901101

Lengel, G. J., Ammerman, B. A., & Washburn, J. J. (2022). Clarifying the definition of nonsuicidal self-injury: Clinician and researcher perspectives. *Crisis: The Journal of Crisis Intervention and Suicide Prevention, 43*, 119–126. https://doi.org/10.1027/0227-5910/a000764

Lengel, G. J., & Mullins-Sweatt, S. N. (2013). Nonsuicidal self-injury disorder: Clinician and expert ratings. *Psychiatry Research, 210*, 940–944. https://doi.org/10.1016/j.psychres.2013.08.047

Lewis, S. P., Bryant, L. A., Schaefer, B. M., & Grunberg, P. H. (2017). In their own words: Perspectives on nonsuicidal self-injury disorder among those with lived experience. *Journal of Nervous and Mental Disease, 205*, 771–779. https://doi.org/10.1097/nmd.0000000000000733

Lewis, S. P., & Hasking, P. A. (2021). Self-injury recovery: A person-centered framework. *Journal of Clinical Psychology, 77*, 884–895. https://doi.org/10.1002/jclp.23094

Maddox, B. B., Trubanova, A., & White, S. W. (2017). Untended wounds: Non-suicidal self-injury in adults with autism spectrum disorder. *Autism, 21*, 412–422. https://doi.org/10.1177/1362361316644731

Manca, M., Presaghi, F., & Cerutti, R. (2014). Clinical specificity of acute versus chronic self-injury: Measurement and evaluation of repetitive non-suicidal self-injury. *Psychiatry Research, 215*, 111–119. https://doi.org/10.1016/j.psychres.2013.10.010

Mann, A. J. D., van Voorhees, E. E., Patel, T. A., Wilson, S. M., Gratz, K. L., Calhoun, P. S., Beckham, J. C., & Kimbrel, N. A. (2020). Nail-biting, scab-picking, and tattooing as nonsuicidal self-injury (NSSI): A deviant case series analysis of the proposed NSSI disorder diagnostic criteria. *Journal of Clinical Psychology, 76*, 2296–2313. https://doi.org/10.1002/jclp.23008

Mathew, A. S., Davine, T. P., Snorrason, I., Houghton, D. C., Woods, D. W., & Lee, H. (2020). Body-focused repetitive behaviors and non-suicidal self-injury: A comparison of clinical characteristics and symptom features. *Journal of Psychiatric Research, 124*, 115–122. https://doi.org/10.1016/j.jpsychires.2020.02.020

Menninger K. A. (1933) Psychoanalytic aspects of suicide. *International Journal of Psychoanalysis, 14*, 376–390.

Menninger, K. A. (1938). *Man against himself*. Harcourt and Brace.

Moran, P., Coffey, C., Romaniuk, H., Olsson, C., Borschmann, R., Carlin, J.B., & Patton, G.C., (2012). The natural history of self-harm from adolescence to young adulthood: A population-based cohort study. *Lancet, 379*, 236–243. https://doi.org/10.1016/s0140-6736(11)61141-0

Muehlenkamp, J. J. (2005). Self-injurious behavior as a separate clinical syndrome. *American Journal of Orthopsychiatry, 75*, 324–333. https://doi.org/10.1037/0002-9432.75.2.324

Muehlenkamp, J. J., & Brausch, A. M. (2016). Reconsidering criterion A for the diagnosis of non-suicidal self-injury disorder. *Journal of Psychopathology and Behavioral Assessment, 38*(4), 547–558. https://psycnet.apa.org/doi/10.1007/s10862-016-9543-0

Muehlenkamp, J. J., Brausch, A. M., & Washburn, J. J. (2017). How much is enough? Examining frequency criteria for NSSI disorder in adolescent inpatients. *Journal of Consulting and Clinical Psychology, 85*, 611–619. https://doi.org/10.1037/ccp0000209

Nock, M. K., & Favazza, A. (2009). Nonsuicidal self-injury: Definition and classification. In M. K. Nock (Ed.), U*nderstanding nonsuicidal self- injury: Origins, assessment, and treatment*. (pp. 9–18). American Psychological Association. https://doi.org/10.1037/11875-001

Pao, P. N. (1969). The syndrome of delicate self-cutting. *British Journal of Medical Psychology, 42*, 195–206. https://doi.org/10.1111/j.2044-8341.1969.tb02071.x

Pattison, E. M., & Kahan, J. (1983). The deliberate self-harm syndrome. *American Journal of Psychiatry, 140*, 867–872. https://doi.org/10.1176/ajp.140.7.867

Prinstein, M. J. (2008). Introduction to the special section on suicide and nonsuicidal self-injury: A review of unique challenges and important directions for self-injury science. *Journal of Consulting and Clinical Psychology, 76*, 1–8. https://doi.org/10.1037/0022-006x.76.1.1

Regier, D. A., Narrow, W. E., Clarke, D. E., Kraemer, H. C., Kuramoto, S. J., Kuhl, E. A., & Kupfer, D. J. (2013). DSM–5 field trials in the United States and Canada, Part II: Test–retest reliability of selected categorical diagnoses. *American Journal of Psychiatry, 170*, 59–70. https://doi.org/10.1176/appi.ajp.2012.12070999

Ribeiro, J. D., Franklin, J. C., Fox, K. R., Bentley, K. H., Kleiman, E. M., Chang, B. P., & Nock, M. K. (2016). Self-injurious thoughts and behaviors as risk factors for future suicide ideation, attempts, and death: A meta-analysis of longitudinal studies. *Psychological Medicine, 46*, 225–236. https://doi.org/10.1017/s0033291715001804

Richards, V. (1877). Self-mutilation by a boy. *Indian Medical Gazette, 12*(1), 13.

Rosenthal, R. J., Rinzler, C., Wallsh, R., & Klausner, E. (1972). Wrist-cutting syndrome: The meaning of a gesture. *The American Journal of Psychiatry, 128*, 1363–1368. https://doi.org/10.1176/ajp.128.11.1363

Ross, R. R., & McKay, H. B. (1979). *Self-mutilation*. Lexington Books.

Selby, E. A., Kranzler, A., Fehling, K. B., & Panza, E. (2015). Nonsuicidal self-injury disorder: The path to diagnostic validity and final obstacles. *Clinical Psychology Review, 38*, 79–91. https://doi.org/10.1016/j.cpr.2015.03.003

Shaffer, D., & Jacobson, C. (2009). *Proposal to the DSM-V childhood disorder and mood disorder work groups to include non-suicidal self-injury (NSSI) as a DSM-V disorder*. American Psychiatric Association.

Shahwan, S., Lau, J. H., Abdin, E., Zhang, Y., Sambasivam, R., Teh, W. L., Gupta, B., Ong, S. H., Chong, S. A., & Subramaniam, M. (2020). A typology of nonsuicidal self-injury in a clinical sample: A latent class analysis. *Clinical Psychology and Psychotherapy, 27*, 791–803. https://doi.org/10.1002/cpp.2463

St. Germain, A. S., & Hooley, J. M. (2012). Direct and indirect forms of non-suicidal self-injury: Evidence for a distinction. *Psychiatry Research, 197*, 78–84. https://doi.org/10.1016/j.psychres.2011.12.050

Striegel-Moore, R. H., & Franko, D. L. (2008). Should binge eating disorder be included in the DSM-V? A critical review of the state of the evidence. *Annual Review of Clinical Psychology, 4*, 305–324. https://doi.org/10.1146/annurev.clinpsy.4.022007.141149

Swannell, S. V., Graham, E. M., Page, A., Hasking, P., & St. John, N. J. (2014). Prevalence of nonsuicidal self-injury in nonclinical samples: Systematic review, meta-analysis and meta-regression. *Suicide and Life Threatening Behavior, 44*, 273–303. https://doi.org/10.1111/sltb.12070

Tschan, T., Lüdtke, J., Schmid, M., & In-Albon, T. (2019). Sibling relationships of female adolescents with nonsuicidal self-injury disorder in comparison to a clinical and a nonclinical control group. *Child and Adolescent Psychiatry and Mental Health, 13*, Article 15. https://doi.org/10.1186/s13034-019-0275-2

Turner, B. J., Dixon-Gordon, K. L., Austin, S. B., Rodriguez, M. A., Rosenthal, M. Z., & Chapman, A. L. (2015). Non-suicidal self-injury with and without borderline personality disorder: Differences in self-injury and diagnostic comorbidity. *Psychiatry Research, 230*, 28–35. https://doi.org/10.1016/j.psychres.2015.07.058

Victor, S. E., Davis, T., & Klonsky, E. D. (2017). Descriptive characteristics and initial psychometric properties of the non-suicidal self-injury disorder scale. *Archives of Suicide Research, 21*, 265–278. https://doi.org/10.1080/13811118.2016.1193078

Walsh, B. W. (2012). *Treating self-injury: A practical guide*. Guilford Press.

Washburn, J. J., Potthoff, L. M., Juzwin, K. R., & Styer, D. M. (2015). Assessing DSM-5 nonsuicidal self-injury disorder in a clinical sample. *Psychological Assessment, 27*, 31–41. https://doi.org/10.1037/pas0000021

Whitlock, J. L., Powers, J. L., & Eckenrode, J. (2006). The virtual cutting edge: The internet and adolescent self-injury. *Developmental Psychology, 42*, 407–417. https://doi.org/10.1037/0012-1649.42.3.407

Wilkinson, P. (2013). Non-suicidal self-injury. *European Child and Adolescent Psychiatry, 22* (Supp. 1), 75–79. https://doi.org/10.1007/s00787-012-0365-7

Zetterqvist, M. (2015). The DSM-5 diagnosis of nonsuicidal self-injury disorder: A review of the empirical literature. *Child and Adolescent Psychiatry and Mental Health, 9*, Article 31. https://doi.org/10.1186/s13034-015-0062-7

Zetterqvist, M., Lundh, L. G., Dahlström, Ö., & Svedin, C. G. (2013). Prevalence and function of non-suicidal self-injury (NSSI) in a community sample of adolescents, using suggested DSM-5 criteria for a potential NSSI disorder. *Journal of Abnormal Child Psychology, 41*, 759–773. https://doi.org/10.1007/s10802-013-9712-5

Zetterqvist, M., Perini, I., Mayo, L. M., & Gustafsson, P. A. (2020). Nonsuicidal self-injury disorder in adolescents: Clinical utility of the diagnosis using the Clinical Assessment of Nonsuicidal Self-Injury Disorder Index. *Frontiers in Psychiatry, 11*, Article 8. https://doi.org/10.3389/fpsyt.2020.00008

CHAPTER 3

A Comparison of the Theoretical Models of NSSI

Kirsty Hird, Penelope Hasking, *and* Mark Boyes

Abstract

This chapter examines the leading models of non-suicidal self-injury (NSSI) and synthesizes what is known from relevant research. These include the four-function model, the experiential avoidance model, the emotional cascade model, the integrated model, the cognitive-emotional model, and the barriers and benefits model. While each model differs in the suggested processes by which the behavior is developed and maintained, there are commonalities between the theories. Each theorist agrees that self-injury serves an affect regulation function, a finding that has been central to most of the NSSI literature to date. They also share the concept of behavioral reinforcement, in which the outcomes of self-injury reinforce the behavior as an effective strategy for achieving a desired function. Ultimately, the balance of barriers and benefits that a person experiences will determine whether or not they might self-injure.

Key Words: non-suicidal self-injury, four-function model, experiential avoidance model, emotional cascade model, integrated model, cognitive-emotional model, barriers and benefits model, affect regulation, behavioral reinforcement

In recent years, nonsuicidal self-injury (NSSI) has garnered attention from researchers and health professionals alike. Generally speaking, people aim to avoid painful experiences as often as possible. To intentionally inflict injury on oneself goes against the human instinct of self-preservation, and the absence of suicidal intent in the behavior eliminates the desire to die as a potential explanation. Despite this, self-injury is a prevalent behavior with significant health outcomes. Such behavior is reported most often among adolescents (17.2%), but it is also seen among young adults (13.4%) and adults (5.5%; Swannell et al., 2014). Some groups are also at greater risk of self-injury than others, including university students (20.2%; Swannell et al., 2014) and the LGBTQIA + community (30–47%; Liu et al., 2019). Given the prevalence of the behavior, as well as its perplexing nature, researchers are paying considerable attention to understanding factors that contribute to the onset, maintenance, and cessation of NSSI.

There are several theories of self-injury that aim to explain the behavior. These theories cover a range of functions, risk factors, and underlying cognitions thought to contribute to the behavior. Although each model differs in the suggested processes by which the behavior is developed and maintained, there are commonalities between theories. Each theorist agrees that self-injury serves an affect regulation function, a finding that has been central to most of the NSSI literature to date (McKenzie & Gross, 2014). They also share the concept of behavioral reinforcement, in which the outcomes of self-injury reinforce the behavior as an effective strategy for achieving a desired function. The aim of this chapter is to present a narrative review of the leading models of NSSI and synthesize what is known from relevant research.

The Four-Function Model of NSSI

Nock and Prinstein (2004) took a functional approach to NSSI in which self-injury is understood based on the motives that precede the behavior and the outcomes that reinforce it. Functional approaches have been effective in understanding other behaviors too, as well as many psychological disorders (Hayes et al., 1996). A functional approach has also been used in developing an intervention targeting NSSI (Andover et al., 2015). The four-function model proposes that NSSI can serve four functions across two dimensions: automatic versus social motives and positive versus negative reinforcement. Automatic negative reinforcement occurs when a person self-injures in order to avoid, reduce, or distract from an unwanted emotional state. Automatic positive reinforcement occurs when a person self-injures in order to induce a desired affective state, such as the desire to feel something when feeling empty or numb, or in order to punish oneself. Social negative reinforcement occurs when a person self-injures in order to avoid an unpleasant situation or task. Social positive reinforcement occurs when a person self-injures in order to gain something from others, such as care or attention (Nock & Prinstein, 2004).

Nock and Prinstein (2004) tested their model using confirmatory factor analysis and found that self-reported functions of NSSI from a group of adolescents mapped onto each of the four reinforcement styles. They found that automatic functions (24%–43%) were more widely endorsed than social functions (6%–24%), with the most widely endorsed function being automatic-negative reinforcement (52.9%). This is congruent with more recent findings that emotion regulation is the most commonly reported function of NSSI (Taylor et al., 2018).

The four-function model is strengthened by the finding that the four functions are correlated with contextual features of self-injury as well as theoretically related clinical constructs (Nock & Prinstein, 2005). Specifically, those who endorsed an automatic negative reinforcement function were more likely to report higher feelings of hopelessness and past suicide attempts, which likely reflects the emotion regulation function of NSSI. Those who endorsed an automatic positive reinforcement function were more likely to report symptoms of major depressive disorder and posttraumatic stress disorder—both of which are associated with feelings of emptiness and detachment—which may reflect the tendency to engage in self-injury in order to "feel something." Additionally, those who endorsed a social positive function also reported being aware of a greater number of self-injury occurrences carried out by friends, which might suggest that self-injury contributed to a sense of peer group affiliation for these participants. Subsequent research has demonstrated further support for the four-function model (Bentley et al., 2014). However, there is much research focusing only on differentiating automatic and social motives without considering whether reinforcement is positive or negative. Klonsky et al. (2015) have suggested that such a two-factor model may offer a more parsimonious representation of NSSI functions.

The four-function model differs from many other models as it doesn't focus purely on the affect regulation hypothesis—it is one of the few models in this chapter that also considers social determinants and consequences of self-injury. However, the theory is somewhat limited in its ability to explain self-injurious behavior. Although this functional approach allows for an understanding of why a person would self-injure and how reinforcement serves to maintain the behavior, it does not attempt to understand relevant risk factors or cognitive processes that may lead a person to self-injure rather than engage in other behaviors that serve a similar function.

Experiential Avoidance Model

The experiential avoidance model of deliberate self-harm (Chapman et al., 2006) classifies NSSI as an avoidance behavior, in which a person self-injures as a way to avoid, escape, or distract from an unwanted emotion or the external factors that promote unwanted emotions. Chapman et al. suggested that self-injury functions to regulate emotion and is maintained by negative reinforcement. In creating the experiential avoidance model, the authors aimed to provide a framework for understanding self-injury across general populations, as opposed to clinical populations, which had dominated NSSI research prior to this model's conception.

The process outlined in the experiential avoidance model begins with a stimulus, which elicits an unwanted emotional response. Among individuals with avoidance tendencies, this emotional response may trigger the urge to self-injure in order to escape the discomfort or distress they are experiencing. The emotional relief provided by self-injury then negatively reinforces the behavior, which over time becomes a conditioned escape response. Research into the experiential avoidance model has been substantially supportive of the link between avoidance and self-injury (see Brereton & McGlinchey, 2020, for a review). People who have a history of self-injury generally report higher levels of both expressive suppression and thought suppression, both of which are elements of experiential avoidance (Anderson et al., 2018; Anderson & Crowther, 2012; Howe-Martin et al., 2012).

Chapman et al. (2006) also outlined a number of emotion regulation deficits that may contribute to an individual's propensity for avoidant behaviors such as NSSI, and these too have found support in subsequent research. One such factor is heightened emotional reactivity, in that individuals who experience particularly intense emotions may self-injure to avoid becoming overwhelmed. Research has found that people who self-injure tend to report greater emotion reactivity (C. R. Glenn et al., 2011; Nock et al., 2008); however, it has been suggested that the association between the two does not hold up when tested outside cross-sectional methodology (Hooley & Franklin, 2018). Similarly, a person who has lower distress tolerance, regardless of their actual levels of arousal, may be more likely to self-injure as a form of avoidance rather than attempting to tolerate the emotional experience. The association between low distress tolerance and NSSI has found significant support in relevant literature, with associations between the two found across cross-sectional (Anestis et al., 2013; Slabbert et al., 2022), experimental (Nock & Mendes, 2008), and longitudinal studies (Lin et al., 2018).

Another suggested factor contributing to avoidance tendencies is access to appropriate emotion regulation strategies. If a person does not have skillful strategies in place for responding to difficult emotions, they may be more likely to self-injure as an avoidance strategy (Nielsen et al., 2016). Alternatively, a person may have the necessary skills to regulate their emotions but fail to implement them under intense arousal due to a breakdown of cognitive processes, instead using avoidance strategies such as NSSI. This supposition is supported by significant research demonstrating a relationship between emotion regulation difficulties and NSSI (Wolff et al., 2019).

The experiential avoidance model offers a straightforward approach to understanding self-injurious behavior that is supported by subsequent literature. This model is harmonious with the four-function model presented by Nock and Prinstein (2004), in that avoidance of an unwanted emotional state or social situation through engagement in NSSI could be categorized as negative reinforcement (either automatic or social). However, the process outlined in the experiential avoidance model is somewhat simplistic in that it does not offer an understanding of why a person might self-injure, as opposed to using other avoidance strategies such as substance use or disordered eating.

Emotional Cascade Model

The emotional cascade model (Selby & Joiner, 2009) was developed to understand a range of risky health behaviors, including NSSI, specifically in the context of borderline personality disorder (BPD). However, the model has often been applied to understanding self-injury in the absence of BPD, or indeed of any mental health diagnosis.

At the core of this model is rumination, in which an individual repetitively thinks about negative thoughts, feelings, or experiences. An individual may engage in rumination with the hope that it will help them to better understand their emotions or to solve a social or emotional problem (Papageorgiou & Wells, 2001). In reality, rumination is likely to achieve the opposite outcome, as research shows that it increases negative affect rather than reducing it (Kirkegaard Thomsen, 2006). In the emotional cascade model, rumination heightens the intensity of negative affect, causing further rumination on the initial experience, which in turn further increases negative affect. This cycle of heightening rumination and emotional response is known as an "emotional cascade." Among individuals who are prone to such a response, any negative stimuli—no matter how small—has the potential to spiral into an intense emotional experience causing severe distress. A person experiencing this emotional cascade may engage in NSSI to create a distraction that disrupts the cycle, allowing them to return to a more neutral affective state and, in turn, reinforcing the behavior as an escape strategy. Due to the intensity of the emotional experience and ruminative cycle, it is thought that other methods of distraction (e.g., going for a walk or taking a cold shower) are not enough to short-circuit the cascade. Self-injury, on the other hand, results in more salient stimuli to focus on, such as the sight of blood or wounds. These more severe stimuli are thought to be distracting enough to break the cycle of rumination.

Research has found rumination to be positively associated with negative affect (see Kirkegaard Thomsen, 2006, for a review). Moberly and Watkins (2008) also found that the relationship between negative affect and rumination is bidirectional, such that rumination predicts negative affect and negative affect predicts rumination, in line with the suppositions of the emotional cascade model. Further, several studies have confirmed an association between rumination, negative affect, and NSSI using a variety of research methods. Longitudinal and experience-sampling methods have found that rumination is predictive of future NSSI (Buelens et al., 2019; Nicolai et al., 2016; Selby et al., 2013). Nicolai et al. (2016) also found that rumination strengthened the relationship between negative affect and NSSI. Arbuthnott et al. (2015) found that experimentally induced rumination preceded increases in negative affect among participants who had a history of self-injury. Taken together, these findings support the predictions of the emotional cascade model.

The emotional cascade model also accounts for risk factors that may render a person susceptible to an emotional cascade. One such factor is low distress tolerance which, as previously discussed, has demonstrated associations with NSSI. Selby and Joiner (2009) suggested that a person with low distress tolerance will have more difficulty withstanding an emotional cascade, rendering them more likely to self-injure as an escape strategy. Another risk factor considered in the emotional cascade model is thought suppression, in which a person takes deliberate action to avoid negative cognitions. As previously discussed, thought suppression is an aspect of avoidance which has been empirically linked to NSSI. That both distress tolerance and thought suppression are shared constructs between the emotional cascade model and the experiential avoidance model is unsurprising; the two models are conceptually similar in that they both categorize NSSI as a strategy for escaping or avoiding an emotional experience the individual perceives as unmanageable. In this, the emotional cascade model can also be considered to represent a negative reinforcement function of NSSI.

Integrated Model

Building upon his previously described four-function model of NSSI, Nock (2010) outlined a new model of self-injury which attempts to explain the processes by which a person comes to self-injure in order to achieve a desired outcome, instead of engaging in other behaviors that may serve a similar function. The integrated model outlines a number of early genetic and environmental factors that promote the development of intra- and interpersonal difficulties, which in turn increase the risk that a person will engage in dysregulated behaviors (such as self-injury) in response to stressful stimuli. Nock (2010) explained that early life stressors, such as childhood maltreatment or a hostile familial environment, can contribute to cognitive and emotional problems (i.e., high negative thoughts and emotions, and poor distress tolerance) as well as social difficulties (i.e., poor communication skills and poor social problem-solving).

This model also suggests that these intra- and interpersonal vulnerability factors for engaging in NSSI correlate with the functions of NSSI outlined in Nock and Prinstein's four-function model. For example, a person possessing negative thoughts and emotions and/or poor distress tolerance may be at greater risk of engaging in NSSI as a vehicle for affect regulation. Here we can see parallels between the integrated model and the previously discussed experiential avoidance and emotional cascade models, which also link distress tolerance and negative cognitions and emotions with NSSI for the purpose of regulating difficult emotions. Alternatively, a person possessing poor communication and/or social problem-solving skills may be at greater risk of engaging in NSSI in order to modulate a social situation.

Finally, the integrated model outlines a number of processes by which a person possessing these general risk factors might come to self-injure in order to achieve a desired outcome. One such process is the social learning hypothesis, in which a person who is exposed to self-injury, through parents, friends, or the media, may in turn be influenced to engage in the behavior themselves. There is evidence to suggest that people with a history of self-injury are more likely to also know a friend or peer who self-injures (Hasking & Rose, 2016; Heath et al., 2009; Victor & Klonsky, 2018), and longitudinal work shows that knowing somebody who self-injures can predict future NSSI engagement (Hasking et al., 2013; You et al., 2013). Dawkins et al. (2019a) found that people who knew of self-injury by a parent were three times more likely to have engaged in the behavior themselves, and this relationship was mediated by the belief that self-injury would assist the individual with regulating their emotions.

People may self-injure simply because they find it to be a fast and effective way to regulate their emotional experience, particularly if they do not have access to other, more appropriate coping strategies. This is backed up by significant evidence in favor of the affect regulation function of self-injury (McKenzie & Gross, 2014). Similarly, the pain analgesia hypothesis presents an argument as to how self-injury serves to regulate affect. It is suggested that following self-injury, endorphins are released into the body which can dull the experience of pain and increase positive affect to give a sense of euphoria. This is consistent with findings that some people do not experience pain during self-injury (Selby et al., 2019). Another suggested process for the emotion regulatory function of NSSI is the self-punishment hypothesis, in which a person engages in NSSI to satisfy self-punishment desires. Self-punishment is a commonly endorsed function of self-injury; meta-analytic work has found that 51% of people with a history of self-injurious behavior endorse self-punishment motives (Taylor et al., 2018). This is reinforced by the high levels of self-directed negative thoughts and emotions (e.g., self-criticism) reported by people who self-injure (Forrester et al., 2017; Muehlenkamp & Brausch, 2012; Smith et al., 2015).

The Cognitive-Emotional Model

While prior research has focused on the risk factors related to NSSI, such as emotional reactivity, emotion regulation difficulties, and negative cognitions, the cognitive-emotional model of NSSI (Hasking et al., 2017) seeks to explain why a person possessing these risk factors would self-injure rather than engage in other emotion regulation strategies. This theory borrows elements of social cognitive theory (outcome expectancies and self-efficacy) to explain the underlying cognitions that drive a person to self-injure. Outcome expectancies are the consequences a person anticipates will occur if they were to engage in a behavior (Bandura, 1989). In relation to NSSI, a person may be more likely to engage in this behavior if they expect it will yield a desirable outcome (e.g., reduction of negative affect) as opposed to an undesirable outcome (e.g., negative reactions from loved ones). Self-efficacy refers to a person's perceived ability to engage in a behavior (Bandura, 1997), and in the case of NSSI it can also refer to a person's perceived ability to resist self-injury (Hasking & Rose, 2016). Hasking et al. (2017) posited that a person who expects that engaging in NSSI will yield a desirable outcome and has low self-efficacy to resist NSSI will be at greater risk of engaging in NSSI compared to others.

Research so far has supported the cognitive-emotional model. Hasking and Boyes (2018) found five key anticipated outcomes relating to NSSI. "Affect regulation" expectancies relate to anticipated relief from unwanted emotions after engaging in NSSI. "Negative social outcomes" expectancies reflect anticipated negative reactions from friends and peers in response to NSSI. "Communication" expectancies reflect the belief that NSSI will facilitate communication with others (i.e., to influence behavior or elicit care). "Pain" expectancies relate to the anticipation that NSSI will be painful. Finally, "Negative self beliefs" expectancies reflect the anticipation that NSSI will result in negative feelings toward oneself, such as feelings of failure or self-hatred.

Hasking and Boyes (2018) also found that outcome expectancies could differentiate between individuals with and without a history of self-injury, and similar results have been found in research testing the predictions of the cognitive-emotional model. Specifically, individuals with a history of self-injury generally hold stronger affect regulation expectancies than those without (Dawkins et al., 2019a, 2019b; Dawkins et al., 2021; Hasking & Boyes, 2018). This is consistent with findings that emotion regulation is the most commonly reported function of self-injury (Taylor et al., 2018) and likely also reflects the fact that self-injury has been found to be effective at regulating emotion (McKenzie & Gross, 2014). Conversely, those with a history of self-injury are less likely to anticipate pain from the behavior (Dawkins et al., 2019a, 2019b; Hasking & Boyes, 2018), consistent with findings that some people do not experience pain during self-injury (Selby et al., 2019). Individuals who have never self-injured are more likely to endorse communication expectancies (Dawkins et al., 2019a, 2019b; Hasking & Boyes, 2018), which is likely a reflection of the stigma surrounding self-injury in which many people see the behavior as attention-seeking or manipulative in design (Gratz, 2003). Similarly, those who have never self-injured are more likely to expect the behavior to result in negative self-beliefs (Hasking & Boyes, 2018; Hasking & Rose, 2016), which may be a further stigmatization of individuals who self-injure.

The literature has also been supportive of the role of self-efficacy to resist NSSI as a protective factor against the behavior itself, with diminished self-efficacy to resist NSSI being associated with more recent self-injury (Dawkins et al., 2019b; Dawkins, Hasking, Boyes, Greene, et al., 2019; Hasking & Rose, 2016). It has been consistently noted in NSSI literature that people are more likely to engage in NSSI if they have difficulties with emotion regulation—however, recent research has found that this relationship is even stronger among people who have low self-efficacy to resist NSSI (Hird et al., 2022). Using ecological momentary assessment, Kiekens et al. (2020) also found that low self-efficacy to resist NSSI could predict future self-injury. It has also been found that greater self-efficacy to resist NSSI can be protective against the behavior among individuals who expect NSSI to yield a desirable outcome. For instance, a person who expects NSSI to assist with affect regulation is less likely to do so if their self-efficacy to resist the behavior is high (Dawkins et al., 2019b). Inversely, low self-efficacy to resist NSSI can be a risk factor for self-injury even when an individual expects an undesirable outcome from the behavior. For instance, a person who expects NSSI to result in negative social outcomes may still self-injure when their self-efficacy to resist NSSI is low (Dawkins et al., 2019b).

The cognitive-emotional model is novel in that it seeks to explain why a person would self-injure rather than engage in other emotion regulatory behaviors. This is demonstrated by research that shows that outcome expectancies and self-efficacy can differentiate people who self-injure from those who engage in risky drinking. Specifically, individuals who expected NSSI to yield a positive outcome and had less belief in their ability to resist self-injury, coupled with negative outcome expectancies related to alcohol consumption and high self-efficacy to resist drinking, were more likely to self-injure than drink as a means of emotion regulation (Hasking, 2017). The cognitive-emotional model also considers both affective and social functions of self-injury, through affect regulation and communication expectancies, respectively.

The Barriers and Benefits Model

Moving away from emotion regulation models, the barriers and benefits model (Hooley & Franklin, 2018) suggests that there are many factors that may motivate a person to self-injure, and a number of factors that may deter a person from self-injuring. The benefits of NSSI are universal and may be accessed by anybody; however, many people will never engage in self-injury due to the barriers they encounter. The balance of barriers and benefits that a person experiences will determine whether or not they might self-injure.

Benefits

Congruent with previous NSSI models, as well as substantial supporting research, people who self-injure may experience a reduction of negative affect and/or an increase in positive affect (McKenzie & Gross, 2014). These affective outcomes are arguably the most salient benefit of self-injury, given that emotion regulation is the most commonly reported function of NSSI (Taylor et al., 2018). The authors of the barriers and benefits model suggested that emotional benefits have little to do with why a person would first engage in self-injury, but, once they have done so and recognize these benefits, they will be more likely to continue the behavior in the future. This is in line with the automatic reinforcement processes outlined in the four-function model. Among people who hold negative self-schemas, NSSI can serve a self-punishment function that can reduce feelings of guilt and shame (as also suggested in the integrated model by Nock, 2010). Hooley and Franklin (2018) argued that self-punishment is a cognitive benefit that should be considered separately to purely affective benefits. Supporting evidence shows that people who self-injure specifically for self-punishment show a decrease in guilt and shame on top of the general affective improvements reported by those who self-injure for other reasons (Hamza & Willoughby, 2018).

A less common benefit of NSSI is peer group affiliation, in which a person self-injures in order to enhance or maintain status within a group of people who also engage in the behavior. Though there is a small body of work supporting this theory (Giletta et al., 2013; Prinstein et al., 2010), meta-analytic work has found interpersonal influence to be among the least commonly endorsed functions of NSSI (Taylor et al., 2018). It has also been suggested that NSSI can serve to communicate distress or strength, and Taylor et al. (2018) found this to be the most commonly endorsed interpersonal function of self-injury. However, as previously discussed, research testing the cognitive-emotional model found that people with a history of self-injury were less likely to expect the behavior to facilitate communication. This may suggest that some people are motivated to self-injure by the desire to communicate distress or strength but do not find it to be particularly effective.

Barriers

One suggested barrier to engaging in NSSI is a lack of awareness about the behavior. Those who have not been exposed to NSSI are less likely to engage in the behavior as they have not considered it an option or been made aware of the benefits. The social-learning hypothesis by Nock (2010) suggested that a person who is exposed to self-injury through peers, family, or the media is more likely to engage in the behavior themselves. As previously discussed in relation to the integrated model, there is significant research to support this theory. As such, the idea that a lack of awareness about NSSI is a barrier to the behavior is a logical deduction from this line of inquiry.

People with positive representations of self may also be less likely to self-injure, as the behavior is associated with higher levels of negative self-beliefs. There is a growing body of evidence revealing a relationship between self-criticism and NSSI (Burke et al., 2021; Fox et al., 2019; Fox et al., 2018). People with negative views of the self may be more likely to engage in NSSI instead of other behaviors due to its self-directed nature, as they are less likely to care about harming the body and may even see this as desirable, as demonstrated by the self-punishment function sometimes endorsed by individuals who self-injure. In fact, positive representations of the self as a protective barrier against NSSI can be seen as inverse to self-punishment desires as a benefit of the behavior.

Humans have an evolutionary instinct to avoid pain, and so the prospect of physical pain can also act as a barrier to NSSI. Engagement in self-injury requires the individual to overcome this barrier. In support of this notion, studies have found that many who self-injure have a higher pain tolerance/endurance (J. J. Glenn et al., 2014), or report experiencing little to no pain during self-injury (Selby et al., 2019). The previously discussed pain analgesia hypothesis may also provide an explanation as to how people who self-injure overcome the barrier of physical pain. Alternatively, the pain offset hypothesis suggests that the relief from physical pain also provides relief from emotional pain, and self-injury is an easy way for a person to induce and then terminate physical pain in order to simultaneously offset emotion pain (Franklin et al., 2013). Finally, it is possible that the induction of pain may be an intentional outcome of self-injury in order to distract from difficult thoughts and emotions, as suggested by the experiential avoidance and emotional cascade models.

People who self-injure also tend to be less averse to related stimuli such as blood and wounds, which would deter many people from engaging in the behavior. The authors suggest that this barrier may be overcome by exposure to stimuli over time, making them less averse. Due to the pain analgesia effect, these stimuli may, over time, become associated with relief from pain rather than pain itself (Fox et al., 2018). It is also suggested that the motivation to self-injure may simply be greater than the aversion to stimuli in many cases.

Social norms are suggested as a fifth barrier to NSSI. Self-injury is not a socially sanctioned behavior, and those who self-injure often experience a great deal of stigma (Burke et al., 2019), which may deter some people from engaging in the behavior. This barrier can be overcome by engaging in self-injury privately, which is the case for most people (Klonsky et al., 2014), as well as by concealing scars (Staniland et al., 2020). It can also be overcome by aligning oneself with a peer group that endorses the behavior, as suggested by the peer group affiliation benefit. Thirdly, if a person is engaging in NSSI to communicate distress or strength, it is likely to reduce the potential of social norms to act as a barrier, as the very act of violating social norms is being used to serve a communicative function.

The barriers and benefits model subsumes many of the other theories of NSSI. It is partially harmonious with the integrated model, as many of the barriers and benefits map onto the NSSI-specific processes outlined by Nock (2010), such as affect regulation, self-punishment, and peer group affiliation. The barriers and benefits model is also conceptually similar to the cognitive-emotional model (outcome expectancies, specifically), as both models suggest that a person's NSSI-specific thoughts or cognitions can ultimately govern whether or not they will self-injure in order to achieve a desired outcome.

What We Already Know

Through amalgamation of the literature, we can infer that emotion regulation is intrinsically linked to NSSI. All the models outlined in this chapter focus, at least in part, on the internal, emotional experience in understanding why a person might self-injure. In addition, some models outline a number of social factors and functions that may explain self-injurious behavior. However, it may be that these interpersonal functions are ultimately driven by the desire to modulate one's emotions (e.g., avoiding a social situation likely to invoke unwanted emotions, or influencing others to provide care in order to reduce negative affect) (for more on the connections between social processes and NSSI, see Zetterqvist & Bjureberg, this volume). Various aspects of emotion regulation can be seen across multiple theories. The idea that emotional reactivity is associated with NSSI is common to the experiential avoidance model, the emotional cascade theory, the integrated model, and the cognitive-emotional model, and it is refuted only by the barriers and benefits model. Avoidance of emotions is also a common theme throughout the literature; central to the experiential avoidance model, it is also a theme in the emotional cascade model and the four-function model. Many models also outline the importance of emotion regulation ability in the onset and maintenance of the behavior. The experiential avoidance model suggests that a person is more likely to engage in self-injury if they do not have access to alternative regulation strategies, and the emotional cascade model suggests that poor regulation strategies, such as rumination or thought suppression, are also risk factors for the behavior.

Among the reviewed models are also a number of shared constructs not specific to emotion regulation. Common to every theory in this chapter is the idea that self-injury is maintained by reinforcement, in which NSSI becomes a learned behavior for the purpose of escaping or avoiding a negative state or inducing a desired state. This is the basis of the four-function model of Nock and Prinstein (2004), and the many functions of NSSI reflected throughout the literature can be categorized in accordance with these four reinforcement styles (see Taylor et al., this volume, for functions of NSSI). Throughout the body of literature, a number of prominent risk factors for self-injury have also emerged, such as poor distress tolerance, negative views of the self, reduced aversion to pain or self-injury stimuli, and a reduced belief in one's ability to resist NSSI.

Future Directions for NSSI Research

There is a wealth of research on various constructs associated with NSSI, and each of the models reviewed in this chapter has a substantial body of research supporting it. However, a significant majority of this research is cross-sectional in nature. The use of alternative research methods could greatly improve our understanding of self-injurious behavior. This is particularly true for the more recent theories of NSSI for which support is still emerging.

Longitudinal methods show promise for investigating the developmental trajectories of NSSI (Plener et al., 2015). Further longitudinal research may be utilized in order to test the predictions of models that seek to explain the onset of self-injury. For example, a longitudinal investigation of the integrated model could help to confirm the association between early risk factors, intra- and interpersonal difficulties, and the functions of NSSI. Alternatively, similar methods could be used to examine the specific factors related to NSSI cessation. For example, does the long-term reduction of self-criticism see an equivalent reduction in self-injury, as suggested by the barriers and benefits model? Some self-injury research has been conducted using ecological momentary assessment (EMA; see Rodríguez-Blanco et al., 2018, for a review). However, EMA research testing the specific predictions of leading NSSI models is limited. This method could be further utilized in order to shed light onto the factors that predict NSSI in real time. For example, investigation of how NSSI-specific outcome expectancies and self-efficacy differ before and after NSSI engagement could be used to test the predictions of the cognitive-emotional model. Understanding how risk factors for NSSI develop and fluctuate over time may be instrumental in creating interventions targeting the onset, maintenance, and cessation of the behavior.

Implications for Clinical Practice

Most of the current treatments and interventions targeting NSSI focus on improving emotion regulation ability, such as cognitive behavioral therapy and dialectical behavior therapy (DBT) (Harvey et al., 2019; Hawton et al., 2016). This is unsurprising given the dominant focus on affect regulation throughout the NSSI literature. However, more recent theories of NSSI have departed from conceptualizations grounded purely in emotion to integrate other social and cognitive considerations into their understanding of NSSI. In so doing, these theories have created space for new self-injury interventions to be proposed. For example, preliminary research has found support for the inclusion of an intervention targeting self-criticism in DBT. Based on the supposition of the barriers and benefits model that self-criticism is a risk factor for NSSI, Ramsey et al. (2021) found that including a self-criticism intervention in a course of DBT for adolescents reduced the number of NSSI occurrences recorded at posttreatment, when compared to treatment as usual. In addition, a novel intervention in the form of a mobile app also found early support (Franklin et al., 2016). In line with the barriers and benefits model, this intervention aimed to decrease self-criticism and increase aversion to NSSI stimuli, such as blood or wounds, with the aim of reducing self-injurious thoughts and behaviors. While these results are preliminary, they demonstrate the potential of focusing on NSSI-specific cognitions in the treatment of self-injury.

Alternatively, it has previously been suggested that NSSI-specific outcome expectancies could be targets for intervention programs (Dawkins et al., 2019b; Hasking, 2017; Hasking & Rose, 2016), similar to existing expectancy challenges targeting risky drinking (Labbe & Maisto, 2011). For example, informing individuals of the negative outcomes associated with NSSI, such as feelings of shame (Mahtani et al., 2019), self-stigmatization (Piccirillo et al., 2020), and long-term decreases in emotion regulation ability (Robinson et al., 2019) could serve to counter the belief that self-injury is an effective emotion regulation strategy by highlighting the ways in which the behavior can contribute to negative affect over time. Challenging outcome expectancies in this way may assist those who currently self-injure to resist the behavior in the future or prevent at-risk individuals from engaging in the behavior in the first instance.

In discussing the treatment of NSSI in clinical practice, it is important to consider how we conceptualize "recovery" from self-injury (for more information on recovery, see Whitlock et al., this volume). Whereas most understanding of NSSI recovery focuses on cessation of the behavior, Lewis and Hasking (2021) put forward a person-centered framework for understanding NSSI recovery which highlights individual differences in the recovery process. Specifically, this framework asserts that NSSI recovery is not a linear process, and that the process will ultimately differ from person to person depending on what they consider recovery to be. Future research aiming to create a new intervention for NSSI should apply this framework in order to promote realistic and achievable goals for individualized treatment.

Conclusion

In summary, research shows that self-injury is a complex behavior that can take many forms and functions, and it can be developed and maintained through a variety of processes. There are a few common assumptions shared by leading theorists in the field of NSSI research. Self-injury serves an affect regulation function and is also often used in order to modulate a social situation. When engaging in self-injury elicits a desired outcome, the behavior is reinforced as an effective strategy. In addition to these fundamental constructs, each theorist offers unique processes and risk factors to supplement our understanding of NSSI. Further research is required to delineate the developmental trajectories of self-injury, as well as to advance our efforts to target the behavior through treatment and intervention.

References

Anderson, N. L., & Crowther, J. H. (2012). Using the experiential avoidance model of non-suicidal self-injury: Understanding who stops and who continues. *Archives of Suicide Research, 16*(2), 124–134. https://doi.org/10.1080/13811118.2012.667329

Anderson, N. L., Smith, K. E., Mason, T. B., & Crowther, J. H. (2018). Testing an integrative model of affect regulation and avoidance in non-suicidal self-injury and disordered eating. *Archives of Suicide Research, 22*(2), 295–310. https://doi.org/10.1080/13811118.2017.1340854

Andover, M. S., Schatten, H. T., Morris, B. W., & Miller, I. W. (2015). Development of an intervention for nonsuicidal self-injury in young adults: An open pilot trial. *Cognitive and Behavioral Practice, 22*(4), 491–503. https://doi.org/10.1016/j.cbpra.2014.05.003

Anestis, M. D., Knorr, A. C., Tull, M. T., Lavender, J. M., & Gratz, K. L. (2013). The importance of high distress tolerance in the relationship between nonsuicidal self-injury and suicide potential. *Suicide and Life-Threatening Behavior, 43*(6), 663–675. https://doi.org/10.1111/sltb.12048

Arbuthnott, A. E., Lewis, S. P., & Bailey, H. N. (2015). Rumination and emotions in nonsuicidal self-injury and eating disorder behaviors: A preliminary test of the emotional cascade model. *Journal of Clinical Psychology, 71*(1), 62–71. https://doi.org/10.1002/jclp.22115

Bandura, A. (1989). Human agency in social cognitive theory. *American Psychologist, 44*(9), 1175–1184. https://doi.org/10.1037/0003-066X.44.9.1175

Bandura, A. (1997). *Self-efficacy: The exercise of control.* W. H. Freeman.

Bentley, K. H., Nock, M. K., & Barlow, D. H. (2014). The four-function model of nonsuicidal self-injury: Key directions for future research. *Clinical Psychological Science, 2*(5), 638–656. https://doi.org/10.1177/2167702613514563

Brereton, A., & McGlinchey, E. (2020). Self-harm, emotion regulation, and experiential avoidance: A systematic review. *Archives of Suicide Research, 24*(1), 1–24. https://doi.org/10.1080/13811118.2018.1563575

Buelens, T., Luyckx, K., Gandhi, A., Kiekens, G., & Claes, L. (2019). Non-suicidal self-injury in adolescence: Longitudinal associations with psychological distress and rumination. *Journal of Abnormal Child Psychology, 47*(9), 1569–1581. https://doi.org/10.1007/s10802-019-00531-8

Burke, T. A., Fox, K., Kautz, M. M., Rodriguez-Seijas, C., Bettis, A. H., & Alloy, L. B. (2021). Self-critical and self-punishment cognitions differentiate those with and without a history of nonsuicidal self-injury: An ecological momentary assessment study. *Behavior Therapy, 52*(3), 686–697. https://doi.org/10.1016/j.beth.2020.08.006

Burke, T. A., Piccirillo, M. L., Moore-Berg, S. L., Alloy, L. B., & Heimberg, R. G. (2019). The stigmatization of nonsuicidal self-injury. *Journal of Clinical Psychology, 75*(3), 481–498. https://doi.org/10.1002/jclp.22713

Chapman, A. L., Gratz, K. L., & Brown, M. Z. (2006). Solving the puzzle of deliberate self-harm: The experiential avoidance model. *Behaviour Research and Therapy, 44*(3), 371–394. https://doi.org/10.1016/j.brat.2005.03.005

Dawkins, J. C., Hasking, P. A., & Boyes, M. E. (2019a). Knowledge of parental nonsuicidal self-injury in young people who self-injure: The mediating role of outcome expectancies. *Journal of Family Studies, 27*(4), 479–490. https://doi.org/10.1080/13229400.2019.1633385

Dawkins, J. C., Hasking, P. A., & Boyes, M. E. (2019b). Thoughts and beliefs about nonsuicidal self-injury: An application of social cognitive theory. *Journal of American College Health, 69*(4), 428–434. https://doi.org/10.1080/07448481.2019.1679817

Dawkins, J. C., Hasking, P. A., Boyes, M. E., Greene, D., & Passchier, C. (2019). Applying a cognitive-emotional model to nonsuicidal self-injury. *Stress Health, 35*(1), 39–48. https://doi.org/10.1002/smi.2837

Dawkins, J., Hasking, P., Luck, C., & Boyes, M. (2021). Implicit assessment of self-injury related outcome expectancies: A comparison of three behavioural tasks. *Psychological Reports, 124*, 2524–2548. https://doi.org/10.1177/0033294120961512

Forrester, R. L., Slater, H., Jomar, K., Mitzman, S., & Taylor, P. J. (2017). Self-esteem and non-suicidal self-injury in adulthood: A systematic review. *Journal of Affective Disorders, 221*, 172–183. https://doi.org/10.1016/j.jad.2017.06.027

Fox, K. R., O'Sullivan, I. M., Wang, S. B., & Hooley, J. M. (2019). Self-criticism impacts emotional responses to pain. *Behavior Therapy, 50*(2), 410–420. https://doi.org/https://doi.org/10.1016/j.beth.2018.07.008

Fox, K. R., Ribeiro, J. D., Kleiman, E. M., Hooley, J. M., Nock, M. K., & Franklin, J. C. (2018). Affect toward the self and self-injury stimuli as potential risk factors for nonsuicidal self-injury. *Psychiatry Research, 260*, 279–285. https://doi.org/https://doi.org/10.1016/j.psychres.2017.11.083

Franklin, J. C., Fox, K. R., Franklin, C. R., Kleiman, E. M., Ribeiro, J. D., Jaroszewski, A. C., Hooley, J. M., & Nock, M. K. (2016). A brief mobile app reduces nonsuicidal and suicidal self-injury: Evidence from three randomized controlled trials. *Journal of Consulting and Clinical Psychology, 84*(6), 544–557. https://doi.org/10.1037/ccp0000093

Franklin, J. C., Puzia, M. E., Lee, K. M., Lee, G. E., Hanna, E. K., Spring, V. L., & Prinstein, M. J. (2013). The nature of pain offset relief in nonsuicidal self-injury. *Clinical Psychological Science, 1*(2), 110–119. https://doi.org/10.1177/2167702612474440

Giletta, M., Burk, W. J., Scholte, R. H. J., Engels, R. C. M. E., & Prinstein, M. J. (2013). Direct and indirect peer socialization of adolescent nonsuicidal self-injury. *Journal of Research on Adolescence, 23*(3), 450–463. https://doi.org/10.1111/jora.12036

Glenn, C. R., Blumenthal, T. D., Klonsky, E. D., & Hajcak, G. (2011). Emotional reactivity in nonsuicidal self-injury: Divergence between self-report and startle measures. *International Journal of Psychophysiology 80*(2), 166–170. https://doi.org/10.1016/j.ijpsycho.2011.02.016

Glenn, J. J., Michel, B. D., Franklin, J. C., Hooley, J. M., & Nock, M. K. (2014). Pain analgesia among adolescent self-injurers. *Psychiatry Research, 220*(3), 921–926. https://doi.org/10.1016/j.psychres.2014.08.016

Gratz, K. L. (2003). Risk factors for and functions of deliberate self-harm: An empirical and conceptual review. *Clinical Psychology: Science and Practice, 10*(2), 192–205. https://doi.org/10.1093/clipsy.bpg022

Hamza, C. A., & Willoughby, T. (2018). A lab-based study exploring the associations among nonsuicidal self-injury, pain, and emotion among university students. *Psychiatry Research, 269*, 462–468. https://doi.org/10.1016/j.psychres.2018.08.096

Harvey, L. J., Hunt, C., & White, F. A. (2019). Dialectical behaviour therapy for emotion regulation difficulties: A systematic review. *Behaviour Change, 36*(3), 143–164. https://doi.org/10.1017/bec.2019.9

Hasking, P. (2017). Differentiating non-suicidal self-injury and risky drinking: A role for outcome expectancies and self-efficacy beliefs. *Prevention Science, 18*(6), 694–703. https://doi.org/10.1007/s11121-017-0755-7

Hasking, P., Andrews, T., & Martin, G. (2013). The role of exposure to self-injury among peers in predicting later self-injury. *Journal of Youth and Adolescence, 42*(10), 1543–1556. https://doi.org/10.1007/s10964-013-9931-7

Hasking, P., & Boyes, M. (2018). The non-suicidal self-injury expectancy questionnaire: Factor structure and initial validation. *Clinical Psychologist, 22*(2), 251–261. https://doi.org/10.1111/cp.12127

Hasking, P., & Rose, A. (2016). A preliminary application of social cognitive theory to nonsuicidal self-injury. *Journal of Youth and Adolescence, 45*(8), 1560–1574. https://doi.org/10.1007/s10964-016-0449-7

Hasking, P., Whitlock, J., Voon, D., & Rose, A. (2017). A cognitive-emotional model of NSSI: Using emotion regulation and cognitive processes to explain why people self-injure. *Cognition and Emotion, 31*(8), 1543–1556. https://doi.org/10.1080/02699931.2016.1241219

Hawton, K., Witt, K. G., Salisbury, T. L. T., Arensman, E., Gunnell, D., Hazell, P., Townsend, E., & Van Heeringen, K. (2016). Psychosocial interventions following self-harm in adults: A systematic review and meta-analysis. *The Lancet Psychiatry, 3*(8), 740–750. https://doi.org/10.1016/s2215-0366(16)30070-0

Hayes, S. C., Wilson, K. G., Gifford, E. V., Follette, V. M., & Strosahl, K. (1996). Experiential avoidance and behavioral disorders: A functional dimensional approach to diagnosis and treatment. *Journal of Consulting and Clinical Psychology, 64*(6), 1152–1168. https://doi.org/10.1037/0022-006X.64.6.1152

Heath, N. L., Ross, S., Toste, J. R., Charlebois, A., & Nedecheva, T. (2009). Retrospective analysis of social factors and nonsuicidal self-injury among young adults. *Canadian Journal of Behavioural Science, 41*(3), 180–186. https://doi.org/10.1037/a0015732

Hird, K., Hasking, P., & Boyes, M. (2022). Relationships between outcome expectancies and non-suicidal self-injury: Moderating roles of emotion regulation difficulties and self-efficacy to resist self-injury. *Archives of Suicide Research, 26*(4), 1688–1701. https://doi.org/10.1080/13811118.2021.1983492

Hooley, J. M., & Franklin, J. C. (2018). Why do people hurt themselves? A new conceptual model of non-suicidal self-injury. *Clinical Psychological Science, 6*(3), 428–451. https://doi.org/10.1177/2167702617745641

Howe-Martin, L. S., Murrell, A. R., & Guarnaccia, C. A. (2012). Repetitive nonsuicidal self-injury as experiential avoidance among a community sample of adolescents. *Journal of Clinical Psychology, 68*(7), 809–829. https://doi.org/10.1002/jclp.21868

Kiekens, G., Hasking, P., Nock, M. K., Boyes, M., Kirtley, O., Bruffaerts, R., Myin-Germeys, I., & Claes, L. (2020). Fluctuations in affective states and self-efficacy to resist non-suicidal self-injury as real-time predictors of non-suicidal self-injurious thoughts and behaviors. *Frontiers in Psychiatry*, Article 11. https://doi.org/10.3389/fpsyt.2020.00214

Kirkegaard Thomsen, D. (2006). The association between rumination and negative affect: A review. *Cognition & Emotion*, *20*(8), 1216–1235. https://doi.org/10.1080/02699930500473533

Klonsky, E. D., Glenn, C. R., Styer, D. M., Olino, T. M., & Washburn, J. J. (2015). The functions of nonsuicidal self-injury: Converging evidence for a two-factor structure. *Child and Adolescent Psychiatry and Mental Health*, *9*, Article 44. https://doi.org/10.1186/s13034-015-0073-4

Klonsky, E. D., Victor, S. E., & Saffer, B. Y. (2014). Nonsuicidal self-injury: What we know, and what we need to know. *The Canadian Journal of Psychiatry*, *59*(11), 565–568. https://doi.org/10.1177/070674371405901101

Labbe, A. K., & Maisto, S. A. (2011). Alcohol expectancy challenges for college students: A narrative review. *Clinical Psychology Review*, *31*(4), 673–683. https://doi.org/10.1016/j.cpr.2011.02.007

Lewis, S. P., & Hasking, P. A. (2021). Self-injury recovery: A person-centered framework. *Journal of Clinical Psychology*, *77*(4), 884–895. https://doi.org/10.1002/jclp.23094

Lin, M.-P., You, J., Wu, Y. W., & Jiang, Y. (2018). Depression mediates the relationship between distress tolerance and nonsuicidal self-injury among adolescents: One-year follow-up. *Suicide and Life-Threatening Behavior*, *48*(5), 589–600. https://doi.org/10.1111/sltb.12382

Liu, R. T., Sheehan, A. E., Walsh, R. F. L., Sanzari, C. M., Cheek, S. M., & Hernandez, E. M. (2019). Prevalence and correlates of non-suicidal self-injury among lesbian, gay, bisexual, and transgender individuals: A systematic review and meta-analysis. *Clinical Psychology Review*, *74*, Article 101783. https://doi.org/10.1016/j.cpr.2019.101783

Mahtani, S., Hasking, P., & Melvin, G. A. (2019). Shame and non-suicidal self-injury: Conceptualization and preliminary test of a novel developmental model among emerging adults. *Journal of Youth and Adolescence*, *48*(4), 753–770. https://doi.org/10.1007/s10964-018-0944-0

McKenzie, K. C., & Gross, J. J. (2014). Nonsuicidal self-injury: An emotion regulation perspective. *Psychopathology*, *47*(4), 207–219. https://doi.org/10.1159/000358097

Moberly, N. J., & Watkins, E. R. (2008). Ruminative self-focus and negative affect: An experience sampling study. *Journal of Abnormal Psychology*, *117*(2), 314–323. https://doi.org/10.1037/0021-843X.117.2.314

Muehlenkamp, J. J., & Brausch, A. M. (2012). Body image as a mediator of non-suicidal self-injury in adolescents. *Journal of Adolescence*, *35*(1), 1–9. https://doi.org/10.1016/j.adolescence.2011.06.010

Nicolai, K. A., Wielgus, M. D., & Mezulis, A. (2016). Identifying risk for self-harm: Rumination and negative affectivity in the prospective prediction of nonsuicidal self-injury. *Suicide and Life-Threatening Behavior*, *46*(2), 223–233. https://doi.org/10.1111/sltb.12186

Nielsen, E., Sayal, K., & Townsend, E. (2016). Exploring the relationship between experiential avoidance, coping functions and the recency and frequency of self-harm. *PLoS One*, *11*(7), Article: e0159854. https://doi.org/10.1371/journal.pone.0159854

Nock, M. K. (2010). Self-injury. *Annual Review of Clinical Psychology*, *6*(1), 339–363. https://doi.org/10.1146/annurev.clinpsy.121208.131258

Nock, M. K., & Mendes, W. B. (2008). Physiological arousal, distress tolerance, and social problem-solving deficits among adolescent self-injurers. *Journal of Consulting and Clinical Psychology*, *76*(1), 28–38. https://doi.org/10.1037/0022-006X.76.1.28

Nock, M. K., & Prinstein, M. J. (2004). A functional approach to the assessment of self-mutilative behavior. *Journal of Consulting and Clinical Psychology*, *72*(5), 885–890. https://doi.org/10.1037/0022-006X.72.5.885

Nock, M. K., & Prinstein, M. J. (2005). Contextual features and behavioral functions of self-mutilation among adolescents. *Journal of Abnormal Psychology*, *114*(1), 140–146. https://doi.org/10.1037/0021-843X.114.1.140

Nock, M. K., Wedig, M. M., Holmberg, E. B., & Hooley, J. M. (2008). The emotion reactivity scale: Development, evaluation, and relation to self-injurious thoughts and behaviors. *Behavior Therapy*, *39*(2), 107–116. https://doi.org/10.1016/j.beth.2007.05.005

Papageorgiou, C., & Wells, A. (2001). Positive beliefs about depressive rumination: Development and preliminary validation of a self-report scale. *Behavior Therapy*, *32*(1), 13–26. https://doi.org/10.1016/s0005-7894(01)80041-1

Piccirillo, M. L., Burke, T. A., Moore-Berg, S. L., Alloy, L. B., & Heimberg, R. G. (2020). Self-stigma toward nonsuicidal self-injury: An examination of implicit and explicit attitudes. *Suicide and Life-Threatening Behavior*, *50*(5), 1007–1024. https://doi.org/10.1111/sltb.12640

Plener, P. L., Schumacher, T. S., Munz, L. M., & Groschwitz, R. C. (2015). The longitudinal course of nonsuicidal self-injury and deliberate self-harm: A systematic review of the literature. *Borderline Personality Disorder and Emotion Dysregulation, 2*(1), Article 2. https://doi.org/10.1186/s40479-014-0024-3

Prinstein, M. J., Heilbron, N., Guerry, J. D., Franklin, J. C., Rancourt, D., Simon, V., & Spirito, A. (2010). Peer influence and nonsuicidal self injury: Longitudinal results in community and clinically-referred adolescent samples. *Journal of Abnormal Child Psychology, 38*(5), 669–682. https://doi.org/10.1007/s10802-010-9423-0

Ramsey, W. A., Berlin, K. S., Del Conte, G., Lightsey, O. R., Schimmel-Bristow, A., Marks, L. R., & Strohmer, D. C. (2021). Targeting self-criticism in the treatment of nonsuicidal self-injury in dialectical behavior therapy for adolescents: A randomized clinical trial. *Child and Adolescent Mental Health, 26*(4), 320–330. https://doi.org/10.1111/camh.12452

Robinson, K., Garisch, J. A., Kingi, T., Brocklesby, M., O'Connell, A., Langlands, R. L., Russell, L., & Wilson, M. S. (2019). Reciprocal risk: The longitudinal relationship between emotion regulation and non-suicidal self-injury in adolescents. *Journal of Abnormal Child Psychology, 47*(2), 325–332. https://doi.org/10.1007/s10802-018-0450-6

Rodríguez-Blanco, L., Carballo, J. J., & Baca-García, E. (2018). Use of ecological momentary assessment (ema) in non-suicidal self-injury (NSSI): A systematic review. *Psychiatry Research, 263*, 212–219. https://doi.org/10.1016/j.psychres.2018.02.051

Selby, E. A., Franklin, J., Carson-Wong, A., & Rizvi, S. L. (2013). Emotional cascades and self-injury: Investigating instability of rumination and negative emotion. *Journal of Clinical Psychology, 69*(12), 1213–1227. https://doi.org/10.1002/jclp.21966

Selby, E. A., & Joiner, T. E. (2009). Cascades of emotion: The emergence of borderline personality disorder from emotional and behavioral dysregulation. *Review of General Psychology, 13*(3), 219–229. https://doi.org/10.1037/a0015687

Selby, E. A., Kranzler, A., Lindqvist, J., Fehling, K. B., Brillante, J., Yuan, F., Gao, X., & Miller, A. L. (2019). The dynamics of pain during nonsuicidal self-injury. *Clinical Psychological Science, 7*(2), 302–320. https://doi.org/10.1177/2167702618807147

Slabbert, A., Hasking, P., Notebaert, L., & Boyes, M. (2022). The role of distress tolerance in the relationship between affect and NSSI. *Archives of Suicide Research, 26*(2), 761–775. https://doi.org/10.1080/13811118.2020.1833797

Smith, N. B., Steele, A. M., Weitzman, M. L., Trueba, A. F., & Meuret, A. E. (2015). Investigating the role of self-disgust in nonsuicidal self-injury. *Archives of Suicide Research, 19*(1), 60–74. https://doi.org/10.1080/13811118.2013.850135

Staniland, L., Hasking, P., Boyes, M., & Lewis, S. (2020). Stigma and nonsuicidal self-injury: Application of a conceptual framework. *Stigma and Health, 6*(3), 312–323. https://doi.org/10.1037/sah0000257

Swannell, S. V., Martin, G. E., Page, A., Hasking, P., & St John, N. J. (2014). Prevalence of nonsuicidal self-injury in nonclinical samples: Systematic review, meta-analysis and meta-regression. *Suicide and Life-Threatening Behavior, 44*(3), 273–303. https://doi.org/10.1111/sltb.12070

Taylor, P. J., Jomar, K., Dhingra, K., Forrester, R., Shahmalak, U., & Dickson, J. M. (2018). A meta-analysis of the prevalence of different functions of non-suicidal self-injury. *Journal of Affective Disorders, 227*, 759–769. https://doi.org/10.1016/j.jad.2017.11.073

Victor, S. E., & Klonsky, E. D. (2018). Understanding the social context of adolescent nonsuicidal self-injury. *Journal of Clinical Psychology, 74*(12), 2107–2116. https://doi.org/10.1002/jclp.22657

Wolff, J. C., Thompson, E., Thomas, S. A., Nesi, J., Bettis, A. H., Ransford, B., Scopelliti, K., Frazier, E. A., & Liu, R. T. (2019). Emotion dysregulation and non-suicidal self-injury: A systematic review and meta-analysis. *European Psychiatry, 59*, 25–36. https://doi.org/10.1016/j.eurpsy.2019.03.004

You, J., Lin, M. P., Fu, K., & Leung, F. (2013). The best friend and friendship group influence on adolescent nonsuicidal self-injury. *Journal of Abnormal Child Psychology, 41*(6), 993–1004. https://doi.org/10.1007/s10802-013-9734-z

CHAPTER 4

Direct and Indirect Self-Injury

Lotte Rubæk *and* Bo Møhl

Abstract

This chapter provides an overview of different forms of self-injurious behavior (SIB). A general distinction is made between direct and indirect SIB. Direct SIB is a deliberate intentional harmful behavior such as cutting or burning oneself while indirect SIB, such as overeating or substance abuse, is in itself not immediately harmful but increases the risk of harm occurring subsequently. Indirect SIB consists of various behaviors, and it does not make sense to describe indirect SIB as a uniform phenomenon. The authors propose a categorization of indirect non-suicidal SIB and review examples of behaviors that belong in each of the three categories proposed: (1) indirect self-injury (active or passive), (2) self-injury by proxy, and (3) risk-taking behavior. Persons who use direct and/or indirect SIB do so because they achieve a positive effect (benefit) here and now (e.g., in the form of emotion regulation) although it can have negative consequences in the short and/or long term. A positive correlation between direct and indirect SIB is found, but this varies for different types of indirect SIB. Barriers to different forms of SIB also vary and are more often lower in indirect SIBs that border on normal cultural behaviors (e.g., tobacco or alcohol use), than in more serious forms such as eating disorders. Further research is needed on the relationship between the different forms of direct and indirect SIBs to gain a better understanding of development trajectories and mediators to be able to make preventative and therapeutic efforts.

Key Words: direct self-injurious behaviour, indirect self-injurious behaviour, self-injury by proxy, eating disorders, substance use, compulsive exercise, sex as self-injury (SASI), risk taking behavior

Introduction

Most people occasionally do things that are not entirely healthy, such as drinking, having a cigarette after dinner, or working long hours, with the stress and sleep deprivation that this involves. People harm, neglect, or endanger themselves in countless ways. According to Favazza (1989a, 1989b), "normal" and accepted self-injurious behavior (SIB) exists in all cultures. Turp (2002) has labeled these behaviors "CASHAS," an acronym that stands for "*c*ulturally *a*ccepted *s*elf-*h*arming *a*cts/*a*ctivities," which vary from culture to culture. Many of these SIB methods escape attention because they are so commonplace, while other direct forms of SIB are more visible and eye-catching.

When adolescents and young adults cut, burn, bite, hit, or scratch themselves to the point of drawing blood, there is no doubt that their behavior constitutes self-injury. This type of behavior is cause for great concern and media attention in the Western world, in part because it is on the rise (McManus et al., 2019; Wester et al., 2018) and in part because it is a clear sign of poor emotional health and well-being. But what about the young woman who in a "drive for thinness" and healthy living limits herself to such restrictive eating that she becomes severely underweight and develops physical symptoms? Or the young man who numbs his inner pain and anxiety with recurring episodes of binge eating and consequently develops severe overweight and a metabolic syndrome? What about individuals who regularly engage in high-risk behavior, like balancing on bridges, standing on the edge of tall buildings, or train-surfing?

The point is that SIB has many different forms and levels of severity, and just as the behavior itself exists on a continuum, ranging from normal behavior that is potentially harmful in the long run to pathological behavior that results in life-threatening damage, the conscious awareness of the behavior also varies. Sometimes self-injury is deliberate and direct with the intention of achieving an immediate effect, and sometimes it is indirect and results in damage over time. Sometimes, the behavior only leads to the *risk* of injury. The fact that self-injury is such a heterogeneous constellation of phenomena gives rise to a dilemma between, on the one hand, establishing a definition of self-injury that includes the full range and diversity of SIB and, on the other hand, is specific in its categorization and delimitation of SIB, like the proposed diagnostic criteria for nonsuicidal self-injury disorder (NSSI-D; see Lengel et al., this volume) in the DSM-5.

In a study of how clinicians and researchers define direct nonsuicidal self-injury (NSSI), Lengel et al. (2021) confirm that there is a lack of clarity about what should be categorized as NSSI, which is defined, in part, by being self-inflicted, intentional, direct, and with immediate physical effect. The chapter discusses a number of issues that influence whether an injury is categorized as direct or indirect (e.g., what time frame is considered "immediate"). Approximately three quarters of respondents argued that damage should occur within "minutes" or sooner, while others considered damage that occurs within hours or even days as being immediate. Another example relevant for our discussion of self-injury by proxy is whether intentionally causing or provoking another person (or animal) to inflict injury should be categorized as NSSI. Respondents were nearly equally divided on this latter issue.

Definitions

Direct SIB

Lengel et al. (2021) point out that despite several points of consensus, there are differences between the three most frequently applied definitions of NSSI (American Psychiatric

Association, 2013; International Society for the Study of Self-injury, 2018; Nock, 2009), and that the instruments used in the assessment of NSSI include different behaviors as part of NSSI. For example, the Self-Harm Inventory (SHI) (Sansone et al., 1998) includes *reckless driving on purpose*, *lost a job on purpose*, and *substance abuse* as forms of NSSI, although these behaviors are commonly regarded as examples of indirect SIB.

Despite these differences, the three definitions agree that NSSI must be self-inflicted and intentional/deliberate, and they all exclude culturally sanctioned behaviors (e.g., tattooing and ear piercing) and suicidal intent. The requirement that the injury has to be direct and *intentional*, that is, with the deliberate intention of self-injury, excludes accidental injuries as well as the wide range of indirect SIBs which the person will often but not necessarily know to be potentially harmful, and where the harmful effect is rarely what drives the behavior but rather an unintended side effect.

The distinction between suicidal and nonsuicidal intention is maintained in the United States, Canada, and other parts of the world that use one of the above-mentioned definitions of NSSI (e.g., the one from the International Society for the Study of Self-Injury, 2018), while the UK uses *deliberate self-harm* or *self-harm* to describe all SIBs, regardless of intent (Kapur et al., 2013). The most common forms of NSSI are cutting, scoring, burning, hitting, biting, pinching, or scratching oneself in various parts of the body to the point of drawing blood (Slesinger et al., 2019; Victor et al., 2018). In figure 4.1, we propose an overview of different forms of SIB and how to distinguish direct NSSI from indirect NSSI and other forms of self-harm.

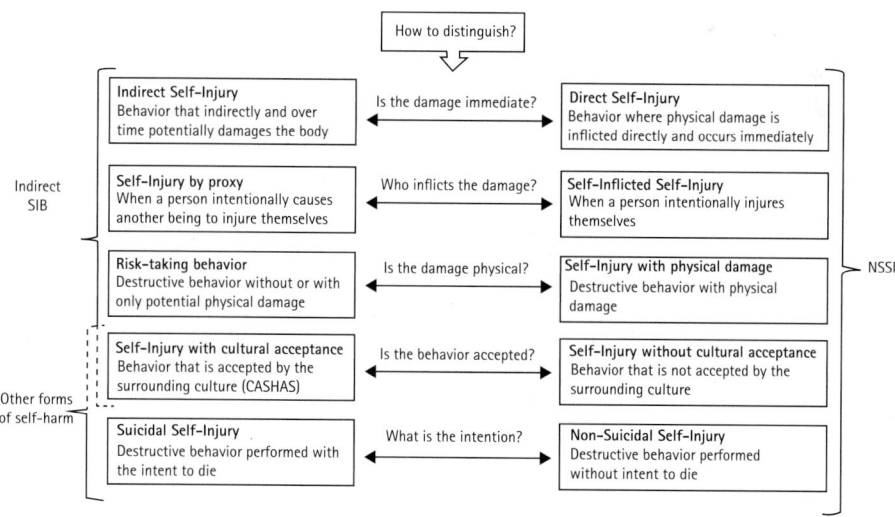

Figure 4.1 Overview of Self-Injurious Behavior and how to Distinguish Direct NSSI From Indirect NSSI and Other Forms of Self-Harm

Indirect SIB

Indirect NSSI is defined by Hooley and St. Germain (2014b) as a "purposeful behavior that is a source of concern for clinicians or family members, occurs in repetitive patterns (i.e., not sporadic or context dependent), and which, in indirect ways, has the potential to compromise physical integrity and be harmful to one's body" (Hooley & St. Germain, 2014b, p. 48). Hooley and St. Germain add that *"Indirect SIB must (a) be repeated or persistent, (b) be clinically significant (ideally indicated by established diagnostic criteria or previously validated cutoffs on clinical assessments), (c) represent a source of serious concern to either the person or others, and (d) have the potential to lead to marked and lasting physical damage over time"* (Hooley & St. Germain, 2014b, pp. 48–49).

Criterion (a) points out that the behavior has to be repeated and persistent. This rules out behavior that occurs sporadically (such as occasionally skipping a meal) or context-dependent (such as drinking too much alcohol at a party). Thus, the behavior has to be persistent over time and will often serve as the person's preferred coping strategy for dealing with difficult situations or troubling emotional states.

Criterion (b) specifies that the behavior must be clinically significant and possibly, but not necessarily, defined as pathological through a diagnostic code or cut-off score that distinguishes normal from abnormal behavior (e.g., in the case of eating disorders or an addiction syndrome) or otherwise have a certain clinical significance.

Criterion (c) underscores that the behavior should be a cause of concern to the person themself or to others. That is, if the person is unconcerned by, for example, their anorexic behavior or drinking due to lack of insight into their own disease, it is sufficient that the behavior gives others cause for concern.

Finally, criterion (d) establishes that the behavior must have the potential to lead to significant or enduring physical damage over time. This excludes behavior such as digital self-harm (e.g., "auto-trolling"), compulsive gambling, and impulse shopping, which may lead to stress or discomfort for the person but does not have the potential to cause *physical* damage.

While physical damage due to NSSI is primary (immediate) and leads to the desired, secondary, effect (e.g., affect regulation, self-punishment, or influencing others), the opposite is the case for indirect self-injury: here, the desired effect is primary, while the damage is typically secondary (occurring subsequently or over time) (see fig. 4.2). In anorexia, for example, the person is primarily driven by a desire to be thin and to achieve control through restrictive eating, while the physical damage is often an unintended, secondary effect (however, cf. Fox et al., 2018). Likewise, in substance abuse, the person is primarily driven by the urge for intoxication or a kick, while the physical damage occurs secondarily.

Categorization of Indirect SIB

With the above definition in mind, we propose the typology of indirect nonsuicidal SIB below and mention examples of behaviors that belong in each of the three categories

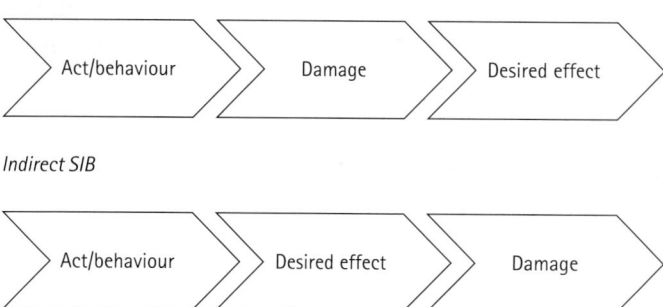

Figure 4.2 Illustration of the Temporality of Damage and Desired Effect in Direct and Indirect SIB

proposed: (1) indirect self-injury (active or passive), (2) self-injury by proxy, and (3) risk-taking behavior.

1. **Indirect SIB** is characterized by physical damage occurring indirectly due to an active act or more passive omission by the person. The damage typically accumulates over time, and often, the individual's active or passive indirect self-injury episodes are not harmful in themselves. With indirect self-injury, such as heavy drinking or smoking, the actual harm stemming from the behavior is unclear, and in many cases, the harmful effects are a matter of chance. Some people can consume large quantities of alcohol over several years without suffering major long-term effects. Although the habit increases their risk of liver damage, with luck, they may avoid this outcome. This is an important difference compared to direct SIB, where the damage is predictable and occurs as an immediate result of the behavior.

   The consequences of indirect self-injury are usually internal and follow from unhealthy and harmful behavior or the omission of healthy or life-sustaining behavior with harmful consequences for the body (Hooley & St. Germain, 2014b; Nock, 2010). Indirect SIB can thus be further categorized into:

1a. ***Active indirect SIB***, characterized by indirect damage as the result of active behavior. Examples of active indirect self-injury include eating disorders, such as bulimia, binge eating disorder, and (some aspects of) anorexia, which are all characterized by active behaviors such as overeating, vomiting, compulsive exercise, or the ingestion of laxatives. Similarly, drug and alcohol abuse are examples of active indirect self-injury, in which the person repeatedly uses substances that are toxic and harmful to the body (see table 4.1). Although the behavior is active, it is not always deliberate or intentional. At some point, for example, many people with eating disorders find that they lose control, so that the eating disorder takes over. The same applies to drug and alcohol abuse.

1b. *Passive indirect SIB* describes indirect damage that may be caused by the omission of health-promoting or life-sustaining behaviors. Turp (2002) describes this as "compromised self-care." Examples of passive indirect self-injury include those aspects of anorexia that involve fasting and maintaining a restrictive eating pattern or failing to adhere to a medically prescribed course of treatment, such as not taking prescription medicine (e.g., insulin for diabetes) (see table 4.1).

2. Self-injury by proxy refers to a situation where the person enlists the cooperation of another person to inflict the injuries (Møhl, 2019). *Merriam-Webster Dictionary* describes *proxy* as "power or authority that is given to allow a person to act for someone else." The indirect aspect of the behavior is contained in the fact that there is an intermediary, namely, the involvement of another person (or animal), between the intention of self-harm and the actual bodily damage (see fig. 4.3).

Thus, in self-injury by proxy, the person actively provokes or encourages someone else to inflict the injury on them. This may be done either deliberately or subconsciously and results in physical and often also mental damage. Some researchers have suggested that self-injury by proxy should be considered a form of indirect self-injury, given that it is the proxy causing the injury, rather than the individual doing so directly (Green et al., 2017). Others suggest that indirect self-injury is a distinct construct that differs in important ways from self-injury by proxy, in that it refers to behaviors that are not immediately or deliberately damaging to body tissue (Mann et al., 2022; St. Germain & Hooley, 2012). In our opinion, it makes sense to understand self-injury by proxy as a subcategory of indirect SIB given the nondirect infliction of damage, although self-injury by proxy results in damage that is more intentional, physical, and immediate than other forms of indirect SIB.

Unique to self-injury by proxy is the added component of an "other" as the inflictor of the injury (Møhl, 2019). The "other" can obfuscate the self-injurious intentions of the behavior and increase its perceived social acceptability (Mann et al., 2022). Also, by "enlisting" others to inflict the injury, the person (a) has an opportunity to engage with others, (b) is able to absolve themself of responsibility for the SIB which allows for an

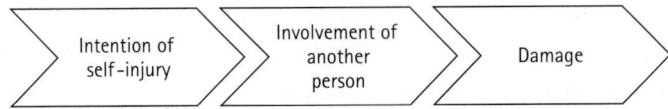

Figure 4.3 Self-Injury by Proxy

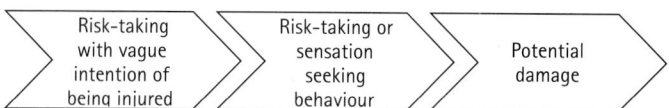

Figure 4.4 Risk-Taking Behavior

external attribution of the injury and the possibility to take the role of victim ("others are doing this to me"), (c) is able to legitimize and act out their anger, which may in itself provide relief, and (d) generates intense drama, which not only results in self-injury by proxy but also in the kind of intense engagements with others that many patients with borderline personality disorder (BPD) are longing for due to a feeling of inner emptiness.

Scholars have described self-injury by proxy as a clinically meaningful construct and suggested a subcategorization of behaviors that could be included in the construct. These include initiating injury via (a) tattooing or body piercing, (b) an animal, (c) sexual activity with a partner, (d) instigating a physical fight, (e) sports, and (f) engaging in elective or cosmetic medical procedures (Mann et al., 2022).

3. **Risk-taking behavior** is behavior that involves a significant risk of bodily harm. The intention behind the behavior and the potential damage are more diffuse and vaguer than in direct self-injury. Risk-taking behavior thus has the *potential* to cause harm, but as in other forms of indirect self-injury, whether the person actually does experience damage is a matter of chance (see fig. 4.4).

Examples of risk-taking behavior include reckless driving, unprotected sex, balancing on bridge railings, standing on the edge of tall buildings, train surfing, walking on the roadway or train tracks, and various self-asphyxial practices (see table 4.1).

Relationship between Direct and Indirect SIB
Until a few years ago, direct and indirect self-injury were largely unrelated research areas, and thus the correlations between the two different forms of self-injury went undescribed. However, in a number of recent studies (e.g., Boccagno & Hooley, 2023; Brausch & Muehlenkamp, 2014; Cipriano et al., 2020; D'Agostino et al., 2020; Greene et al., 2020; Hooley & St. Germain, 2014a; Pak et al., 2021; St. Germain & Hooley, 2012), the focus has shifted, and clinical and theoretical insight into similarities and differences has grown. Several studies have documented a positive correlation between direct and indirect SIB, which means that persons who engage in direct self-injury have a higher likelihood of also engaging in indirect self-injury, and vice versa. Thus, indirect SIBs such as eating disorders (Ahn et al., 2021; Cucchi et al., 2016; Warne et al., 2021), alcohol abuse (Bresin & Mekawi, 2022), cannabis use (Escelsior et al., 2021), substance misuse (Klassen et al.,

Table 4.1 Examples of Behaviors Included in and Excluded from the Categories of Indirect SIB

Category	Included behavior	Excluded behavior
Indirect self-injury—*active*	– Alcohol abuse – Drug abuse – Bulimia – Compulsive overeating – Compulsive/excessive exercise – Overdosing on medicine (nonlethal)	– Occasional drinking binges – Occasional drug use – Occasional overeating – Excessive exercise that does not lead to physical damage – Frequent use of pain medicine due to pain
Indirect self-injury—*passive*	– Starving/fasting – Failure to take prescription medicine	– Occasional restrictive eating or dieting – Forgetting to take or not being able to afford prescription medicine
Self-injury by proxy	– Entering violent relationships or instigating physical fights with the intention to cause immediate and direct physical injury to oneself – Initiating sexual activity with a partner for the purpose of causing direct injury to oneself – Arranging to be subjected to the use of force with the intention of experiencing injury or pain – Getting a tattoo or piercing for the explicit purpose of injuring oneself physically – Intentionally provoking an animal to scratch, bite, or otherwise cause direct physical injury to oneself – Participating in sports for the explicit purpose of causing immediate and direct physical injury to oneself – Engaging in cosmetic or elective medical procedures for the explicit purpose of causing physical injury to oneself	– Entering and then ending a violent relationship – Having multiple sex partners or engaging in S/M for pleasure – Being subjected to the use of force without intention of self-injury – Having many piercings or tattoos for aesthetic reasons – Getting scratches after playing with an animal – Getting an accidental sports injury – Engaging in cosmetic medical procedures for aesthetic reasons
Risk-taking behaviour	– Reckless driving – Unprotected sex – Train surfing – Walking on the roadway or train tracks at the risk of being run over – Stepping close to the edge of a tall building – Balancing on the railing of a bridge – Climbing high at the risk of falling – Practising self-asphyxiation	– Walking on the roadway in a rural area with limited traffic – Speeding slightly in an area with light traffic – Other behaviours that do not involve a *high* risk of damage, for example to ski down mountain slopes

Note: With inspiration from Hooley and St. Germain (2014b) and Mann et al. (2022).

2018; Monto et al., 2018; Richardson et al., 2020), sexual risk-taking behaviors (Brown et al., 2005; Zetterqvist et al., 2018), cigarette smoking (Korhonen et al., 2018), general reckless and risk-taking behaviors (Duggan & Heath, 2014), and self-asphyxial risk-taking behavior (Brausch et al., 2011) occur more frequently in adolescents and young adults with a history of NSSI. Similarly, various forms of impulse control disorders, such as problematic shopping (Greenberg et al., 2021), problematic gaming (Farhat et al., 2020), digital self-harm (Patchin & Hinduja, 2017), which are not associated with physical damage but are associated with negative long-term consequences for the person, are more common among adolescents and young adults with a history of NSSI than among those without experience with NSSI.

Indirect SIB covers a wide spectrum of behaviors that cannot be addressed as one. Some of the common features of the different forms of indirect and direct SIB are that they all represent attempts at using the body or physical actions to control state of mind and social situations, are associated with other forms of mental disorders and cause, or have the potential to cause physical damage (Boccagno & Hooley, 2023; Brausch & Muehlenkamp, 2014; Nock, 2010). Based on the frequent comorbidity or co-occurrence of direct and indirect SIB, Hooley and St. Germain (2014a) raised the question of how direct and indirect SIB might be related. They pointed to three possible relationships: One possibility is to regard direct and indirect SIB as alternate forms of SIB with the choice of method depending on personal preference, needs, and convenience. Another possibility is to regard direct and indirect SIB as related behaviors that represent different points on a severity continuum, with direct SIB being a more extreme and severe form of SIB. Finally, there is the possibility that direct SIB is not simply a more severe variant of SIB but a separate variant with its own distinct psychological characteristics (Hooley & St. Germain, 2014a, pp. 52–53). In their conclusion, the authors lean toward direct and indirect SIB as separate behaviors with distinct characteristics. In a more recent study, Fox et al. (2018) point out that rather than considering direct and indirect SIB as entirely unique and nonoverlapping categories, it may be more accurate to consider self-harming intentions as lying on a continuum.

Correlations between NSSI and Active and Passive Indirect SIB

NSSI and Eating Disorders

Although eating disorders and eating-disordered behavior (such as starving oneself, overeating episodes, or compensatory purging) are excluded from the definition of NSSI, and despite the obvious differences between NSSI and eating disorders, the two behaviors have been found to be strongly correlated (Claes & Muehlenkamp, 2014b; Kiekens & Claes, 2020). On this basis, it has been suggested that the correlation between eating disorders and NSSI is one of the 10 most important future research topics in the study of eating disorders (van Furth et al., 2016). In phenomenological terms, NSSI and eating disorders are comparable in several regards (Svirko & Hawton, 2007). In addition to both involving damage to the body, they also typically occur during early adolescence and youth (Volpe et al., 2016), just as they are both more prevalent in girls and women than in boys and men (Galmiche et al., 2019). In addition, scholars have argued that the two behaviors have a similar underlying pathogenesis (Ahn et al., 2021; Muehlenkamp et al., 2019; Svirko & Hawton, 2007) and shared underlying neurobiological and psychological mechanisms, such as noradrenergic dysfunction, impulsivity, obsessive-compulsive features, affect dysregulation, dissociation, self-criticism, and an urge for control (Ahn et al., 2021; Oquendo & Mann, 2000; Svirko & Hawton, 2007).

Often, NSSI and eating disorders display the same psychiatric comorbidities, for example depression, personality disorder, and anxiety (Hawton et al., 2013), as well as the same psychosocial risk factors, such as childhood trauma (Muehlenkamp et al., 2010; Wonderlich et al., 2007) or an invalidating childhood environment (Gonçalves et al., 2021; Svirko & Hawton, 2007).

Several scholars have also focused on the fact that both NSSI and an eating disorder, such as anorexia, leave clear marks on the body and thus may be seen as a signal to others of poor emotional health and well-being (Lader, 2006; Møhl, 2019). In this sense, the body or the skin becomes the "canvas" for displaying the inner pain. This urge to give inner suffering an outward manifestation may have several explanations, including alexithymia (the inability to identify and express or describe one's feelings) (Raffagnato et al., 2020), poor mentalizing capacity (Bateman & Fonagy, 2006), negative or distorted body image (Muehlenkamp, 2012), a desire to regain control over one's own body (Svirko & Hawton, 2007), an urge to mark the boundary between self and others (Lader, 2006) or a rejection of/rebellion against a social culture of perfection (Møhl, 2019).

NSSI among Persons with an Eating Disorder

A literature review from Svirko and Hawton (2007) found that 24.4%–55.2% of eating-disordered patients also have direct SIB. According to the authors, this strong correlation can be explained by factors such as impulsivity, obsessive-compulsive features, affect dysregulation, dissociation, a self-critical cognitive style, and an urge for control. Among outpatients with an eating disorder, 32% had experience with NSSI (Solano et al., 2005), while among inpatients with an eating disorder, 44% had experience with NSSI (Claes et al., 2001).

Looking at specific eating disorders, a meta-analysis shows that 21.8% of anorexia nervosa (AN) patients and 32.7% of bulimia nervosa (BN) patients had experience with NSSI (Cucchi et al., 2016). Among patients with binge eating disorder (BED), researchers have found a lifetime prevalence of direct SIB of 20.4% (Islam et al., 2015). There is consensus that NSSI is more common among persons with bulimia (26%–55.2%) and anorexia of the "binge-purge" subtype (27.8%–68.1%) than among patients with the restrictive subtype of anorexia (13.6%–42.1%) (Claes et al.,

2001, 2003; Claes & Muehlenkamp, 2014; Davico et al., 2019; Svirko & Hawton, 2007). Dzombak et al. (2020) found that among young inpatients with overeating episodes and purging, more than half reported having engaged in NSSI during the month leading up to their treatment start, compared to 17% among patients with a restrictive eating pattern. A similar pattern was found among adult inpatients with an eating disorder (Pérez et al., 2018).

Many young people have disordered eating behavior without necessarily meeting diagnostic criteria of an eating disorder (Croll et al., 2002; Swanson et al., 2011), and they also have high co-occurrence of self-harm. In a UK population-based cohort study (N = 3,384 females and 2,326 males), Warne et al. (2021) found that 29.9% of females and 23.7% of males at age 16 with disordered eating also reported self-harm in the last year. At age 24, 16.1% of females and 11.1% of males with disordered eating had also self-harmed.

Eating Disorders among Persons with NSSI

From the opposite perspective, studies of persons with NSSI have similarly found a high prevalence of eating-disordered behavior (Shingleton et al., 2013; Turner et al., 2016; Washburn et al., 2015; Wright et al., 2009). Studies suggest that between 25% and 61% of persons with NSSI also have disordered eating (Claes & Muehlenkamp, 2014a; Gollust et al., 2008; Heath et al., 2008; Muehlenkamp et al., 2012; Svirko & Hawton, 2007). In the above-mentioned population-based cohort study Warne et al. (2021) found that, 63.7% of females and 32.7% of males at age 16 who self-harmed also reported disordered eating and at age 24, 60.9% of females who had self-harmed (vs. 34.3% who had not) and 41.9% of males who had self-harmed (vs. 18.0% who had not) reported disordered eating. In a sample of persons with NSSI recruited from online self-injury forums, Yiu et al. (2015) found that almost four in five had engaged in at least one type of eating-disordered behavior over the previous week, and that 66.1% had compensatory weight control behavior at least once a week, while 57.6% fasted, and another 57.6% had weekly overeating episodes.

Characteristics of Persons with Coexisting SIB and Eating-Disordered Behavior

A study of 1,355 adult eating-disordered psychiatric outpatients found that patients with NSSI had an earlier onset of the eating disorder as well as higher likelihood of having a history of alcohol abuse, depression, hospitalization, and suicide attempts than patients without NSSI (Ahn et al., 2021). Similarly, a higher frequency of NSSI, greater variation in NSSI methods and a history of medical treatment of NSSI have been found to correlate with more severe eating disorders (Turner et al., 2015; Whitlock et al., 2006; Yiu et al., 2015).

Meta-analyses find that both NSSI and eating disorders increase the risk of future suicide attempts (Franklin et al., 2017; Smith et al., 2019), and theorists suggest that persons with multiple forms of SIB have a higher risk of suicide compared to the ones who only have one SIB (Arnold et al., 2022; Joiner, 2005).

However, although the above-mentioned findings provide important information about how the coexistence of NSSI and eating disorders may affect the severity of both, they do not shed light on the temporal relationship between the behaviors.

The Temporal Relationship between SIB and Eating-Disordered Behavior

In a cohort study, Wilkinson et al. (2018) found that repeated NSSI at the age of 14 years predicted an eating disorder at the age of 17 years. Other studies yield similar findings (Peterson & Fischer, 2012; Riley et al., 2016; Turner et al., 2015). On the other hand, several studies have documented the occurrence of an eating disorder as predictive of future NSSI. Riley et al. (2016) found that college students who had engaged in purging behavior over the previous month were at increased risk of debuting with NSSI during their first year in college. This is consistent with other studies as well (Kiekens et al., 2019; Micali et al., 2017).

The following case illustrates a possible example of the temporal relationship between eating disorders and NSSI:

> *A 17-year-old high school (upper secondary) student is hospitalized in a special ward for eating disorders due to anorexia. Her body mass index (BMI) at the time of admission was only 14.3, so she is in critical condition but also scared of gaining weight. During her hospital stay, she develops direct self-injury in the form of cutting. She uses cutting especially when it is time for her to go on the scale "in order to escape the anxiety" and also when she has gained weight, in accordance with her treatment plan. She uses cutting as self-punishment and a way to regain control, because "I have been gorging on food and I'm growing fat and disgusting." In addition to diet and restrictive exercise, the main focus in her psychotherapeutic sessions was on her self-hatred, feelings of shame, and vulnerable affect regulation.*

Compulsive Exercise and NSSI

Persons with an eating disorder (especially AN) often have an abnormally high level of physical activity with the purpose of losing weight. This has been found in 31%–48% of patients with AN (Rizk et al., 2020) and is associated with poor treatment outcome and increased risk of relapse and chronicity (Strober et al., 1997; Taranis & Meyer, 2011). However, studies show that compulsive exercise in itself can be regarded as indirect SIB, which is associated with long-term physical damage and psychosocial problems. Compulsive exercise is often driven by body dissatisfaction, as women typically exercise to lose weight (Holland & Tiggemann, 2017), while men do it to increase their muscle mass and modify their body shape (Dawson & Hammer, 2020); both sexes also use compulsive exercise as a means of affect regulation. There is no formal definition (Mond & Gorrell, 2021), but compulsive exercise means that the individual feels compelled to exercise excessively in order to avoid the distress associated with "missing a workout," the exercise is time-consuming, it continues despite injuries, it impairs social functioning, the exercise routines are intense and vigorous (Dittmer et al., 2018), and there is a marked obsessive quality to the exercise (Bratland-Sanda et al., 2019). Compulsive exercise has also been described as "exercise addiction," a term that underscores the addictive aspects of excessive exercise (Trott et al., 2021).

Ganson et al. (2021) studied some of the harmful effects of compulsive exercise in college students (N = 8,251). In the study, 11% of men and 17% of women reported engaging in compulsive exercise over the past four weeks. Both male and female respondents who reported compulsive exercise over the past four weeks are more likely to report illicit drug use (e.g., stimulants) and to be assessed as having mental health symptoms, including a positive depression screen, a positive anxiety screen, a positive eating disorder screen, self-reported suicidal ideation during the past 12 months, and self-reported NSSI during the past 12 months. The authors argued that compulsive exercise used for the purpose of weight loss or changing body shape may be considered a form of SIB with emotion regulation functions, like NSSI (see Taylor et al., this volume). Participation in organized sports is found to help adolescents refrain from self-harm (Latina et al., 2022), and other studies have found that sport and exercise are one of the most helpful ways of resisting SIB (Plener et al., 2013; Wallenstein & Nock, 2007). The next section turns to more classic addiction conditions, such as drug and alcohol abuse, and their connection with NSSI.

NSSI and Substance Use

Several researchers have described that in some individuals, SIB can be regarded as an addictive behavior comparable to substance abuse, including craving, loss of control, development of tolerance, withdrawal symptoms, and relapse (Blasco-Fontecilla et al., 2016; Buser & Buser, 2013; Nixon et al., 2002; Rubæk & Møhl, 2016). Some 89.7% of young psychiatric patients with SIB have tried in vain to resist the urge to self-injure (Klonsky & Glenn, 2008). In a study of craving and addiction in connection with NSSI and drug use Victor et al. (2012) found, however, that the level of craving associated with NSSI is generally lower than in drug abuse, and that craving mainly occurs when the self-injuring person is under the influence of negative emotions.

In addition to SIB in itself leading to psychological and physiological addiction, numerous studies of both clinical and nonclinical samples have found that adolescents with a history of substance use are much more likely to have also engaged in NSSI (e.g., Klassen et al., 2018; St. Germain & Hooley, 2013). Substance use refers to the use of drugs or alcohol, including cigarettes, illegal drugs, and prescription drugs. Since this category includes a very heterogeneous group of substances with different effect profiles, health risks, and prevalence, it does not make sense to treat them as one. Besides, adolescents with SIB often use and/or are addicted to several different substances. In a study of NSSI among schoolchildren in grades 6 to 8 (roughly 12–14 years) (N = 508), Hill et al. (2008) found that significantly more (46.7%) participants with a history of NSSI had used drugs compared to those who had no such history (4.4%). Of the NSSI group, 73.3% had smoked cigarettes over the past year, compared to 28% of study participants without NSSI. In a sample of 541 clinically referred adolescents, Klassen et al. (2018) found that 29.1% of adolescents who engaged in SIB also engaged in substance use, and among adolescents who reported substance use, 52.0% also reported engagement in direct SIB. Female sex, higher age, high levels of depressive symptoms, and neighborhood violence were associated with increased likelihood of engagement in SIB. A study of university students (ages 19–28 years) found that substance use was less likely when the perceived risk was high (Hanauer et al., 2021). In a clinical sample of psychiatric inpatient adolescents, Nock et al. (2006) found that 59.6% of young people who had engaged in NSSI during the past 12 months met the criteria for a substance use disorder. The majority of them (38.6%) were dependent on nicotine, but many had alcohol abuse (18%) or dependency (16.8%); marijuana abuse (12.6%) or dependency (29.5%) or met the criteria for other substance abuse (3.4%) or dependency (5.6%).

Tobacco

Young people's substance use often begins with tobacco, alcohol, or cannabis (Klassen et al., 2018). At most ages over 16 years, women exceeded men in rates of smoking initiation (59.8% vs. 50.3%, $p < 0.001$), and early onset comes with a heightened risk of various somatic and mental adverse health outcomes. For both sexes, smoking increases the risk of major depressive and generalized anxiety disorder (Thompson et al., 2015). A prospective study from adolescence to young adulthood found that adolescents who initiated regular tobacco use before the age of 14 years had a significantly increased risk of SIB, such as cutting or burning, at age 22 (adjusted odds ratio = 4.57, 95% CI [1.93–10.8], $p = 0.001$) compared to those who had not initiated tobacco use. Girls who initiated regular tobacco use before the age of 14 years had a particularly heightened risk of SIB by age 22 (Korhonen et al., 2018).

Cannabis

Men are more likely to use and become dependent on cannabis than women, but the gender gap is narrowing (Hemsing & Greaves, 2020). Several studies have documented the link between cannabis use and SIB. In a systematic review, Escelsior et al. (2021) found that cannabis use was associated with an increased prevalence of SIB and may act as a causative factor in a duration-dependent manner. Cannabis use was associated with a significantly increased likelihood of displaying (OR = 1.57) or developing SIB (OR = 2.57) compared with nonusers. The presence of severe psychiatric disorders, such as major depression or posttraumatic stress disorder (PTSD), seems to increase the risk of SIB following cannabis use (Kimbrel et al., 2018); however, the risk is generally significantly greater for any psychiatric population, regardless of the specific disorder (Carabellese et al., 2013). Even in the absence of a psychiatric diagnosis, specific psychopathological traits may predispose cannabis users for SIB (e.g., Hodgson et al., 2020; Taliaferro et al., 2019). These factors are reciprocally associated, and the direction of causality remains partially unclear (Escelsior et al., 2021). Hodgson et al. (2020) found that the risk of SIB is greater with continued use of cannabis (OR = 3.89) than with initial use (OR = 2.38). They also found a link between the polygenic risk for cannabis use and SIB. Similarly, a duration-related increase of odds for SIB was found by Few et al. (2016), with OR = 2.15 for early onset and OR = 2.84 for lifetime cannabis use. The increased odds of SIB were found particularly among monozygotic twin pairs discordant for early cannabis use. The latter suggests the role of shared genes.

Alcohol

In the United States, more males than females drink, and male drinkers tend to drink more often and more heavily than females, consuming nearly three times as much alcohol per year (19 liters for males, 6.7 liters for females). However, the gender gap is narrowing among adolescents and emerging adults, primarily because alcohol use among males has declined more than alcohol use among females (White, 2020). In a review of 57 samples (N = 141,669) in their mid-20s (M = 26.91, SD = 11.29), Bresin and Mekawi (2022) found a significant positive correlation between alcohol use and NSSI. Across all studies, they found that SIB was associated with a heightened risk of alcohol use (OR = 1.78; 95% CI [1.53–2.07]). The risk of SIB was lower in connection with alcohol use (OR = 1.63; 95% CI [1.41–1.89]) than with alcohol use disorder (OR = 2.82; 95% CI [1.80–4.48]), which suggests a dose-response connection. Alcohol and SIB both serve similar emotion regulation functions, including the reduction of negative affect (Greene et al., 2020; Nock & Prinstein, 2004) and the increase of positive affect (Selby et al., 2014). Besides, alcohol may intensify negative emotions and increase pain tolerance, the latter being an important barrier to engaging in SIB (Hooley & Franklin, 2018); in particular, the combination of cutting and substance use disorder has been found to increase the risk of suicidal behavior (Baer et al., 2020).

Overall, studies of SIB and substance use provide robust documentation of a high correlation between substance abuse and NSSI (Andrews et al., 2012; Few et al., 2016; Klassen et al., 2018; Moller et al., 2013). However, there seem to be gender differences, as shown in a study of U.S. high school students which found that drug and alcohol use increased the odds of NSSI among females but not among male adolescents (Monto et al., 2018).

There has been limited research into the impact of various substances on the pattern of SIB. In a study of 309 adults (average age 29.28 years; SD = 9.19) recruited through MTURK (Amazon Mechanical Turk), Richardson et al. (2020) found that opiates, barbiturates, and sedatives all had a small but statistically significant influence on the frequency of NSSI, and that marijuana, antianxiety medication, and PCP (Phencyclidine) had a small but statistically significant relationship with the severity of NSSI.

Correlations between NSSI and Self-Injury by Proxy

NSSI and self-injury by proxy (provoking others to inflict physical harm to yourself) can take on a variety of forms, for example, getting a tattoo or piercing with the intention of injury, sex as self-injury, or deliberately seeking to get into fights or provoking people or animals in order to incur an injury (Mann et al., 2022; Møhl, 2019). Some psychiatric inpatients may provoke the use of force with the primary purpose of achieving physical damage or pain. About half of the clinicians and researchers who have knowledge and clinical experience with NSSI define injury inflicted by other people or animals as direct self-injury (Lengel et al., 2021). However, in our assessment, self-injury by proxy differs from direct self-injury, and although it is a significant phenomenon in clinical practice, it is often overlooked, perhaps because it borders on normal behavior and seems more legitimate, and perhaps because we have not previously had a specific term for it.

NSSI and Sex as Self-Injury

Sex as self-injury (SASI) is defined as "a sexual behavior in relation to another person in order to self-injure" (Fredlund et al., 2017, p. 3). Using sex as affect regulation will be familiar to most people, but when this involves seeking out potentially dangerous situations that are known to involve the risk of rough treatment, abuse, or being pressured into unwanted sex with one or more partners, this behavior is associated with SIB (Jonsson et al., 2015; Houck et al., 2008). Risk-taking sexual behavior also includes, for example, selling sex, poor condom use, and other ways of disregarding one's own safety in connection with sex.

In a representative national sample of 5,750 students in the third year of Swedish upper secondary school, Fredlund et al. (2017) found that 100 (3.2%) of the girls, 20 (0.8%) of the boys, and 5 (9.4%) of those who stated that the male/female classification did not fit them reported SASI on at least one occasion (median five times). Over the previous 12 months, 58.5% had engaged in SASI one to five times and 16.3% more than five times, and 25.2% had not engaged in SASI during the previous year. NSSI was found among 65.6% of the SASI group compared to 16.6% of the non-SASI group. Pain associated with SASI activity was experienced by 70.7% of the females and 55.6% of the males. Seventy-five percent of persons in the SASI group had been exposed to sexual abuse. In a study, Zetterqvist et al. (2018) compared the SASI group with an NSSI group and found that significantly more adolescents (48.8%) reported having been exposed to penetrating sex against their will compared to adolescents who reported NSSI only (11.9%). The relationship between SASI and penetrating sexual abuse was further confirmed by higher levels of trauma symptoms, such as dissociation, posttraumatic stress, and sexual concerns. Significantly more adolescents (7.1%) from the SASI group had sold sex, compared to 1% in the NSSI group. Drug use was more common in the SASI group (45.2%) versus 29.6% in the NSSI group, but there was no difference in alcohol consumption. However, adolescents who had engaged in both SASI and NSSI stood out as the most troubled group, which potentially explains their need for more forms of SIB to cope with distress.

SASI may be regarded as a form of reenactment of sexual abuse (revictimization), in which a person, driven by intense self-hatred, seeks contact with others who confirm their self-perception (theory of self-verification) (Swann, 1997) or act with anger toward them; this is consistent with the finding of self-punishment as one of the reasons for SASI behavior (Jonsson et al., 2019). Furthermore, SASI may be seen as an attempt at turning the passive childhood role into an active one, as the person replaces feelings of helplessness with an illusory sense of control (van der Kolk, 1989).

Jonsson et al. (2019) debated whether SASI should be categorized as direct or indirect SIB and concluded that SASI might include both direct and indirect SIB with and without tissue damage. This suggests that SASI might best be seen as a behavioral continuum ranging from indirect to direct SIB. However, we choose to highlight the relational perspective, as the person makes someone else inflict the damage, and thus categorize SASI as SIB by proxy.

However, sex may also serve as a protective factor against SIB. Monto et al. (2018) found that youth who reported sexual activity during the past three months were only 83% as likely to report NSSI compared with responders who reported no sexual activity. This negative association between sexual activity and NSSI was statistically significant for girls but not for boys.

NSSI and Staying in Abusive Relationships

According to Capaldi et al. (2012), the rate of physical violence toward an intimate partner during the prior year for couples in the United States ranges from 17% to 39%. Most victims of partner violence are women and most eventually leave the abusive partner, but not everyone. Some stay in the violent relationship for a long time despite the risk to their safety, perhaps because they fear the consequences of breaking up (Estrellado & Loh, 2019; Karakurt et al., 2021). There seem to be cultural variations among women both in the tolerance of intimate partner violence (IPV) and in help-seeking behaviors. For example, Monterrosa (2021) found that there were differences in the ways that Black and White women seek help for IPV, and Li et al. (2020) found that Chinese college students had a higher level of tolerance for IPV than their U.S. counterparts. The correlates with the finding that Chinese students have a stronger belief in male dominance than their American counterparts, which may imply that women in China are more likely to perceive IPV as expectable and acceptable (Pugh et al., 2018).

Women living in abusive relationships have higher rates of depression, anxiety, PTSD, and SIB (Chen, 2022; Karakurt et al., 2021; Sansone & Sansone, 2007) in addition to a higher occurrence of gynecological and other somatic conditions than in the general female population (Karakurt et al., 2017). The question is what makes victims choose to stay in abusive relationships. One explanation may be financial and social dependence on the partner, especially since the survivor may have become isolated from family and friends, as well as concern for any children in the relationship; however, as a result of the severe psychological consequences of the constant degradation of self-esteem and self-worth, the survivor will often lack sufficient strength and confidence to leave (Jacobson & Gottman, 1998). Other scholars suggest that dehumanization by the partner will subsequently cause the survivor to dehumanize themself and adopt the view that they are not worthy of having a partner who treats them better (Bastian, 2019), or that the survivor stays in the relationship out of fear of abandonment due to insecure attachment. Insecure attachment to a caregiver during childhood or to an intimate partner has also been associated with direct SIB (Gratz et al., 2002; Levesque et al., 2010).

NSSI and Using Staff in Psychiatric Institutions for Self-Injury by Proxy

Restraint and seclusion of psychiatric patients may be necessary measures to prevent patients from harming themselves or others. Some patients have found that the staff acted with unnecessary force as a form of punishment, with harmful physical and psychological effects, when the patient was placed in restraints because they were upset or acting out (Lindgren et al., 2018). Some have compared this experience with rape or physical abuse (Singh et al., 1999). To the best of our knowledge, there are no systematic studies of how often patients deliberately provoke or precipitate restraint, which some patients describe as corresponding to SIB (Møhl, 2019).

The vignette is about a young woman with BPD who has been cutting, burning, and tearing herself to blood several times a week since she was 13 years old. She is fully aware of why she is provoking the staff of the psychiatric ward to place her in restraints:

> *An 18-year-old woman who is hospitalized in a psychiatric youth ward due to severe SIB says that she sometimes deliberately breaks a glass or throws a book against the window because she knows that the staff is going to respond by immediately placing her in restraints. Being held down or restrained with straps gives her the same experience of sensing her body and the subsequent relief that direct SIB can provide.*

Correlations between NSSI and Risk-Taking Behavior

Risk-taking behavior can be defined as a behavior that can potentially result in negative consequences for physical and mental health in the future (Buelow, 2020). Several of the abovementioned behaviors, for example, reckless driving or daredevil behavior such as balancing on the railing of bridges, walking to the edge of tall buildings, hanging on to the back of trains, walking on the roadway, on train tracks, or various self-asphyxial practices are different expressions of risk-taking behavior which is associated with increased risk of damage to the body (Schonberg et al., 2011). The person may be motivated by an unconscious desire to harm themselves or by sensation seeking, which may be linked to a magical notion of being invulnerable/invincible or an indifference to getting hurt. The short-term effect can be emotion regulation or getting a kick that overshadows concerns about the long-term risk (Zetterqvist, 2017). Risk-taking behavior has been identified as a marker for early identification of vulnerability to develop psychiatric disorders in adolescence (King et al., 2001) and is associated with a range of psychological problems (Carli et al., 2014; Ghinea et al., 2019).

Youth is a time of greater risk-taking than other periods in life (Cohen et al., 2016). According to Shulman et al. (2016), risk-taking peaks during adolescence because activation of an early-maturing socioemotional incentive-processing system amplifies adolescents' affinity for exciting, pleasurable, and novel activities at a time when the as-yet immature cognitive control system is not strong enough to consistently restrain potentially hazardous impulses. Thus, the disparate developmental trajectories of the cognitive control system and the socioemotional system make youth such a vulnerable period in terms of daredevil behavior, such as reckless driving, train-surfing, balancing on bridges and near the edge of tall buildings, or trying trends or online challenges (such as "the choking game," which involves deliberately cutting off oxygen to the brain without having an intention to die).

Several studies have examined the correlation between direct self-injury and risk-taking behavior (e.g., Knorr et al., 2013; Laye-Gindhu & Schonert-Reichl, 2005). In a study of impulsivity and self-injury, Glenn and Klonsky (2010) found that self-injurious students were more sensation seeking, were more likely to make rash decisions under the influence of negative emotions, and had difficulty planning before acting. Brausch et al. (2011) studied self-asphyxial risk-taking behavior ("the choking game") which is a dangerous behavior among children and young people that involves cutting off oxygen to one's brain to the point of fainting and then experiencing a "high" as one comes round (Linkletter et al., 2010; Ullrich et al., 2008). In a sample of 4,693 high school students, the researchers found that during the past 12 months, 21% had engaged in direct SIB, 16.5% had experience with self-asphyxial behavior, and 6.5% had experience with both. The group who had both SIB and experience with self-asphyxial behavior also engaged in other forms of risk-taking behavior. This group also seems to be at increased risk of developing BPD (Ghinea et al., 2019).

To investigate whether sensation seeking may alter the balance between the benefits and barriers of engaging in NSSI (Hooley & Franklin, 2018), Kentopp et al. (2021) studied NSSI and risk-taking behavior in a sample of 200 young psychiatric inpatients. They found that increased sensation seeking was associated with greater likelihood of ever engaging in NSSI and a greater number of different methods of SIB tried. Sensation seeking is thus associated with an elevated risk of direct SIB and with a wider range of methods, which may be regarded as a sign of more severe NSSI.

After reviewing the suggested categories of indirect self-injury and their relation to direct self-injury, we will now turn to the topic of challenges and recommendations for clinical practice and future research.

Discussion of Challenges

It is a challenge that SIB includes a very wide range of diverse behaviors. Direct SIB is fairly well defined, although it does remain a subject of discussion, and some definitions still include suicidal behavior. Indirect self-injury, on the other hand, covers a wide spectrum, ranging from culturally accepted forms, such as tobacco, alcohol, and cannabis use, to severe psychopathology. Anorexia nervosa is the psychiatric illness with the highest mortality rate (Westmoreland et al., 2016). In reflection of this diversity, the balance between benefits and barriers (Hooley & Franklin, 2018) in different forms of SIB will vary, and systematic research and descriptions are needed (see Møhl & Rubæk, this volume).

Although a new transdiagnostic understanding of SIB is emerging, our knowledge is limited by the fact that much of the research into different forms of self-injury has been conducted with an isolated focus on the respective forms without consideration of interactions, for example, between direct and indirect SIB. It is a challenge to integrate the existing knowledge about specific forms of SIB in an effort to develop a general transdiagnostic understanding of the psychology of self-injury.

Recommendations for Clinical Practice

In clinical practice, it is a challenge to develop effective prevention and feasible short-term treatment models that take into account the fact that SIB constitutes a wide range of behaviors. The transdiagnostic understanding, which incorporates the common underlying factors in and functions of different forms of SIB, should be a high priority (see also Møhl & Rubæk, this volume). Another challenge is the inclusion of modern technology, such as online solutions and smartphone apps, which are an increasingly integral part of everyday life for the young generation of "digital natives" who are far more familiar with these media than the generations before them. Future treatments of SIB will need to incorporate modern technology to make it possible to offer more flexible treatment. Since many forms of SIB are associated with a high level of shame, in-home treatment options may be beneficial because they avoid the risk of stigmatization implied in a face-to-face encounter with a therapist (Berger et al., 2005). Pilot studies of online treatment of adolescents and young adults using emotion regulation individual therapy for adolescents (ERITA) are showing promising results (Bjureberg et al., 2018; Bjureberg et al., 2023) and suggest that online solutions are effective and feasible. Larger RCTs are ongoing (Morthorst et al., 2022).

However, it is necessary to develop models and test the transdiagnostic treatment approach in clinical trials before it can be recommended.

Recommendations for Future Research

Most of the research on direct and indirect SIB has focused on NSSI, eating disorders, and substance use, and there is a need for additional insight into the relationship between other, and maybe newer, indirect forms of SIB. For example, a study from 2022 shows that eating disorder psychopathology was significantly higher among individuals who reported that they also performed digital self-harm compared with age-matched controls (Lydecker et al., 2022). There is also a need for more knowledge about what causes a person to choose one form of SIB over another.

Over the past 20 years, research into SIB has developed in leaps and bounds, and today, this is one of the best researched fields within psychology and other behavioral sciences. To prevent this development from stagnating, we see an important research task in developing well-defined, nonstigmatizing and uniform concepts, and debating and clarifying disagreements about concepts and definitions (Lengel et al., 2021). This effort should involve researchers, clinicians, and people with lived experience with SIB (Victor et al., 2021) working together to create and consolidate the language necessary for conducting and exchanging research.

Conclusion

In this chapter we have described a positive correlation between direct and indirect SIB, which means that persons who engage in direct self-injury have a higher likelihood of also engaging in indirect self-injury, and vice versa. In particular, indirect SIB consists of a series of diverse behaviors, some of which border on normal cultural behaviors (e.g., tobacco, alcohol, or cannabis use), and it does not make sense to describe indirect SIB as a uniform and well-defined phenomenon.

In this chapter, we have proposed a categorization of indirect SIB. In addition to distinguishing between passive and active indirect SIB, we have described self-injury by proxy as a form of indirect SIB. Self-injury by proxy is characterized by provoking another person (or an animal) to inflict physical injury to oneself. Finally, we have categorized risk-taking behavior as a form of indirect self-injury, because it only potentially causes bodily injury.

The fact that self-injury is such a heterogeneous constellation of phenomena gives rise to a dilemma between, on the one hand, establishing a definition of self-injury that includes the full range and diversity of SIB and, on the other hand, is specific in its categorization and delimitation of SIB, like the proposed diagnostic criteria NSSI-D (see Lengel et al., this volume) in DSM-5 (American Psychiatric Assoiciation, 2013).

Despite ambiguity and overlaps in the definitions of different types of self-injury which makes it difficult to maintain absolute categories, we would advocate continuing to distinguish between direct SIB, which causes immediate physical damage (e.g., burning or cutting), although we cannot define a precise time limit for "immediate" (cf. Lengel et al., 2021), and indirect SIB, which increases the risk of physical damage but in which such damage is inherently a matter of chance.

Key points

1. Both direct and indirect SIB consists of a series of diverse behaviors, some of which border on normal cultural behaviors (e.g., tobacco, alcohol, or cannabis use). Due to its heterogeneous nature it does not make sense to describe indirect SIB as a uniform and well-defined phenomenon. We propose a categorization of indirect nonsuicidal SIB as follows (a) indirect self-injury (active or passive), (b) self-injury by proxy, and (c) risk-taking behavior.
2. There is a positive correlation between direct and indirect SIB, which means that persons who engage in direct self-injury have a higher likelihood of also engaging in indirect self-injury, and vice versa.
3. Even though there is great diversity within both direct and indirect self-harm and despite the fact that it can be difficult to distinguish categorically between direct and indirect self-harm, it is constructive and relevant to maintain a distinction between the two forms of SIB.

References

Ahn, J., Lee, J. H., & Jung, Y. C. (2021). Identifying predictors of non-suicidal self-injuries in individuals with eating disorders. *Yonsei Medical Journal, 62*(2), 159–163. https://doi.org/10.3349/ymj.2021.62.2.159

American Psychiatric Association. (2013). *Diagnostic and statistical manual of mental disorders*. 5th ed. https://doi.org/10.1176/appi.books.9780890425596

Andrews, T., Martin, G., & Hasking, P. (2012). Differential and common correlates of non-suicidal self-injury and alcohol use among community-based adolescents. *Advances in Mental Health, 11*(1), 55–66. https://doi.org/10.5172/jamh.2012.11.1.55

Arnold, S., Wiese, A., Zaid, S., Correll, C. U., & Jaite, C. (2022). Lifetime prevalence and clinical correlates of nonsuicidal self-injury in youth inpatients with eating disorders: A retrospective chart review. *Child and Adolescent Psychiatry and Mental Health, 16*(1), 1–20. https://doi.org/10.1186/s13034-022-00446-1

Baer, M. M., Tull, M. T., Forbes, C. N., Richmond, J. R., & Gratz, K. L. (2020). Methods matter: Non-suicidal self-injury in the form of cutting is uniquely associated with suicide attempt severity in patients with substance use disorders. *Suicide and Life-Threatening Behavior, 50*(2), 397–407. https://doi.org/10.1111/sltb.12596

Bastian, B. (2019). A dehumanization perspective on dependence in low-satisfaction (abusive) relationships. *Journal of Social and Personal Relationships, 36*(5), 1421–1440. https://doi.org/10.1177/0265407519835978

Bateman, A., & Fonagy, P. (2006). Mentalizing and borderline personality disorder. In J. G. Allen & P. Fonagy (Eds.), *Handbook of mentalization-based treatment*. John Wiley and Sons (pp. 183–200). https://doi.org/10.1093/med/9780198570905.003.003

Berger, M., Wagner, T. H., & Baker, L. C. (2005). Internet use and stigmatized illness. *Social Science & Medicine, 61*(8), 1821–1827. https://doi.org/10.1016/j.socscimed.2005.03.025

Bjureberg, J., Ojala, O., Hesser, H., Häbel, H., Sahlin, H., Gratz, K. L., Tull, M. T., Claesdotter-Knutsson, E., Hedman-Lagerlöf, E., Ljótsson, B., & Hellner, C. (2023). *Internet-delivered emotion regulation therapy for adolescents with nonsuicidal self-injury disorder: A randomized clinical trial* [Manuscript submitted for publication].

Bjureberg, J., Sahlin, H., Hedman-Lagerlöf, E., Gratz, K. L., Tull, M. T., Jokinen, J., Hellner, C., & Ljótsson, B. (2018). Extending research on emotion regulation individual therapy for adolescents (ERITA) with non-suicidal self-injury disorder: Open pilot trial and mediation analysis of a novel online version. *BMC Psychiatry, 18*(1), 1–13. https://doi.org/10.1186/s12888-018-1885-6

Blasco-Fontecilla, H., Fernández-Fernández, R., Colino, L., Fajardo, L., Perteguer-Barrio, R., & De Leon, J. (2016). The addictive model of self-harming (non-suicidal and suicidal) behavior. *Frontiers In Psychiatry, 7*, Article 8. https://doi.org/10.3389/fpsyt.2016.00008

Boccagno, C., & Hooley, J. M. (2023). Emotion regulation strategy choices following aversive self-awareness in people who engage in non-suicidal self-injury or indirect self-injury. *Journal of Emotion and Psychopathology, 1*(1), 8–22. https://doi.org/10.31234/osf.io/7m69

Bratland-Sanda, S., Mathisen, T. F., Sundgot-Borgen, J., & Rosenvinge, J. H. (2019). Defining compulsive exercise in eating disorders: Acknowledging the exercise paradox and exercise obsessions. *Journal of Eating Disorders, 7*(1), 13. https://doi.org/10.1186/s40337-019-0238-2

Brausch, A. M., Decker, K. M., & Hadley, A. G. (2011). Risk of suicidal ideation in adolescents with both self-asphyxial risk-taking behavior and non-suicidal self-injury. *Suicide and Life-Threatening Behavior, 41*(4), 424–434. https://doi.org/10.1111/j.1943-278X.2011.00042.x

Brausch A. M., & Muehlenkamp, J. J. (2014). Experience of the body. In L. Claes & J. J. Muehlenkamp (Eds.), *Non-suicidal self-injury in eating disorders* (pp. 3–18). Springer. https://doi.org/10.1007/978-3-642-40107-7_14

Bresin, K., & Mekawi, Y. (2022). Different ways to drown out the pain: A meta-analysis of the association between non-suicidal self-injury and alcohol use. *Archives of Suicide Research, 26*(2), 348–369. https://doi.org/10.1080/13811118.2020.1802378

Brown, L. K., Houck, C. D., Hadley, W. S., & Lescano, C. M. (2005). Self-cutting and sexual risk among adolescents in intensive psychiatric treatment. *Psychiatric Services, 56*(2), 216–218. https://doi.org/10.1176/appi.ps.56.2.216

Buelow, M. T. (2020). *Risky decision making in psychological disorders*. Elsevier.

Buser, T. J., & Buser, J. K. (2013). Conceptualizing non-suicidal self-injury as a process addiction: Review of research and implications for counselor training and practice. *Journal of Addictions & Offender Counseling, 34*(1), 16–29. https://doi.org/10.1002/j.2161-1874.2013.00011.x

Capaldi, D. M., Knoble, N. B., Shortt, J. W., & Kim, H. K. (2012). A systematic review of risk factors for intimate partner violence. *Partner Abuse, 3*(2), 231–280. https://doi.org/10.1891/1946-6560.3.2.231

Carabellese, F., Candelli, C., Martinelli, D., La Tegola, D., & Catanesi, R. (2013). Cannabis use and violent behaviour: A psychiatric patients cohort study in Southern Italy. *Rivista di psichiatria, 48*(1), 43–50. https://doi.org/10.1708/1228.13614

Carli, V., Hoven, C. W., Wasserman, C., Chiesa, F., Guffanti, G., Sarchiapone, M., Apter, A., Balazs, J., Brunner,R., Corcoran, P., Cosman, D.,Haring, C., Iosue,M., Kaess, M., Kahn, J. P.,Keeley, H., Postuvan, V., Saiz, P., Varnik, A., & Wasserman, D. (2014). A newly identified group of adolescents at "invisible" risk for psychopathology and suicidal behavior: Findings from the SEYLE study. *World Psychiatry, 13*(1), 78–86. https://doi.org/10.1002/wps.20088

Chen, Y. (2022). Intimate partner violence as a risk factor for self-harm behaviors: A meta-analysis. *Advances in Social Science, Education and Humanities Research, 638*, 882–887. https://doi.org/10.2991/assehr.k.220110.167

Cipriano, A., Claes, L., Gandhi, A., Cella, S., & Cotrufo, P. (2020). Does anger expression mediate the relationship between parental rejection and direct and indirect forms of non-suicidal self-injury?. *Journal of Child and Family Studies, 29*(12), 3575–3585. https://doi.org/10.1007/s10826-020-01844-9

Claes, L., & Muehlenkamp J. J. (2014a). *Non-suicidal self-injury in eating disorders: Advancements in etiology and treatment*. Springer-Verlag. https://doi.org/10.1007/978-3-642-40107-7

Claes, L., & Muehlenkamp J. J. (2014b). Non-suicidal self-injury and eating disorders: Dimensions of self-harm. In L. Claes & J. J. Muehlenkamp (Eds.), *Non-suicidal self-injury in eating disorders*. Springer. https://doi.org/10.1007/978-3-642-40107-7_1

Claes, L., Vandereycken, W., & Vertommen, H. (2001). Self-injurious behaviors in eating-disordered patients. *Eating Behaviors, 2*(3), 263–272. https://doi.org/10.1016/S1471-0153(01)00033-2

Claes, L., Vandereycken, W., & Vertommen, H. (2003). Eating-disordered patients with and without self-injurious behaviours: A comparison of psychopathological features. *European Eating Disorders Review: The Professional Journal of the Eating Disorders Association, 11*(5), 379–396.

Cohen, A. O., Breiner, K., Steinberg, L., Bonnie, R. J., Scott, E. S., Taylor-Thompson, K., Rudolph, M. D., Chein, J., Richeson, J. A, Heller, A. S., Silverman, M. R., Dellarco, D. V., Fair, D. A., Galvan, A., & Casey, B. J. (2016). When is an adolescent an adult? Assessing cognitive control in emotional and nonemotional contexts. *Psychological Science, 27*(4), 549–562. https://doi.org/10.1177/0956797615627625

Croll, J., Neumark-Sztainer, D., Story, M., & Ireland, M. (2002). Prevalence and risk and protective factors related to disordered eating behaviors among adolescents: Relationship to gender and ethnicity. *Journal of Adolescent Health, 31*(2), 166–175. https://doi.org/10.1016/S1054-139X(02)00368-3

Cucchi, A., Ryan, D., Konstantakopoulos, G., Stroumpa, S., Kaçar, A. Ş., Renshaw, S., Landau, S., & Kravariti, E. (2016). Lifetime prevalence of non-suicidal self-injury in patients with eating disorders: A systematic review and meta-analysis. *Psychological Medicine, 46*(7), 1345–1358. https://doi.org/10.1017/S0033291716000027

D'Agostino, A., Boni, M., Aportone, A., Pepi, R., & Monti, M. R. (2020). Direct and indirect self-injury: Is it really all the same?. *Mediterranean Journal of Clinical Psychology, 8*(2), 1–18. https://doi.org/10.6092/2282-1619/mjcp-2434

Davico, C., Amianto, F., Gaiotti, F., Lasorsa, C., Peloso, A., Bosia, C., Vesco, S., Arletti, L., Reale, L. & Vitiello, B. (2019). Clinical and personality characteristics of adolescents with anorexia nervosa with or without non-suicidal self-injurious behavior. *Comprehensive Psychiatry, 94*, Article 152115. https://doi.org/10.1016/j.comppsych.2019.152115

Dawson, N., & Hammer, J. H. (2020). No pain, no gains: Conformity to masculine norms, body dissatisfaction, and exercise dependence. *Psychology of Men & Masculinities, 21*(3), Article 430. https://doi.org/10.1037/men0000243

Dittmer, N., Jacobi, C., & Voderholzer, U. (2018). Compulsive exercise in eating disorders: Proposal for a definition and a clinical assessment. *Journal of Eating Disorders, 6*(1), 1–9. https://doi.org/10.1186/s40337-018-0219-x

Duggan, J. M., & Heath, N. L. (2014). Co-occurring health-risk behaviors of non-suicidal self-injury and eating disorders. In L. Claes & J. J. Muehlenkamp (Eds.), *Non-suicidal self-injury in eating disorders*. Springer-Verlag. https://doi.org/10.1007/978-3-642-40107-7_13

Dzombak, J. W., Haynos, A. F., Rienecke, R. D., & Van Huysse, J. L. (2020). Brief report: Differences in non-suicidal self-injury according to binge eating and purging status in an adolescent sample seeking eating disorder treatment. *Eating Behaviors, 37*, Article 101389. https://doi.org/10.1016/j.eatbeh.2020.101389

Escelsior, A., Murri, M. B., Corsini, G. P., Serafini, G., Aguglia, A., Zampogna, D., Cattedra, S., Nebbia, J., Trabucco, A., Prestia, D., Olcese, M., Barletta, E., da Silva, B. P., & Amore, M. (2021). Cannabinoid use and self-injurious behaviours: A systematic review and meta-analysis. *Journal of Affective Disorders, 278*, 85–98. https://doi.org/10.1016/j.jad.2020.09.020

Estrellado, A. F., & Loh, J. (2019). To stay in or leave an abusive relationship: Losses and gains experienced by battered Filipino women. *Journal of Interpersonal Violence, 34*(9), 1843–1863. https://doi.org/10.1177/0886260516657912

Farhat, L. C., Roberto, A. J., Wampler, J., Steinberg, M. A., Krishnan-Sarin, S., Hoff, R. A., & Potenza, M. N. (2020). Self-injurious behavior and gambling-related attitudes, perceptions and behaviors in adolescents. *Journal of Psychiatric Research, 124*, 77–84. https://doi.org/10.1016/j.jpsychires.2020.02.016

Favazza, A. (1989a). Normal and deviant self-mutilation: An essay review. *Transcultural Psychiatric Research Review, 26*(2), 113–127. https://doi.org/10.1177/136346158902600020

Favazza, A. (1989b). Why patients mutilate themselves. *Hospital and Community Psychiatry, 40*(2), 137–145. https://doi.org/10.1176/ps.40.2.137

Few, L. R., Grant, J. D., Nelson, E. C., Trull, T. J., Grucza, R. A., Bucholz, K. K., Verweij, K. J. H., Martin, N. G., Statham, D. J., Madden, P. A. F., Heath, A. C., Lynskey, M. T., & Agrawal, A. (2016). Cannabis involvement and non-suicidal self-injury: A discordant twin approach. *Journal of Studies on Alcohol and Drugs, 77*(6), 873–880. https://doi.org/10.15288/jsad.2016.77.873

Fox, K. R., Ribeiro, J. D., Kleiman, E. M., Hooley, J. M., Nock, M. K., & Franklin, J. C. (2018). Affect toward the self and self-injury stimuli as potential risk factors for non-suicidal self-injury. *Psychiatry Research, 260*, Article 279285. https://doi.org/10.1016/j.psychres.2017.11.083

Franklin, J. C., Ribeiro, J. D., Fox, K. R., Bentley, K. H., Kleiman, E. M., Huang, X., Musacchio, K.M., Jaroszewski, A. C., Chang, B. P., & Nock, M. K. (2017). Risk factors for suicidal thoughts and behaviors: A meta-analysis of 50 years of research. *Psychological Bulletin, 143*(2), Article 187. https://doi.org/10.1037/bul0000084

Fredlund, C., Svedin, C. G., Priebe, G., Jonsson, L., & Wadsby, M. (2017). Self-reported frequency of sex as self-injury (SASI) in a national study of Swedish adolescents and association to sociodemographic factors, sexual behaviors, abuse and mental health. *Child and Adolescent Psychiatry and Mental Health, 11*(1), 1–11. https://doi.org/10.1186/s13034-017-0146-7

Galmiche, M., Déchelotte, P., Lambert, G., & Tavolacci, M. P. (2019). Prevalence of eating disorders over the 2000-2018 period: A systematic literature review. *The American Journal of Clinical Nutrition*, *109*(5), 1402–1413. https://doi.org/10.1093/ajcn/nqy342

Ganson, K. T., Mitchison, D., Rodgers, R. F., Cunningham, M. L., Murray, S. B., & Nagata, J. M. (2021). Compulsive exercise among college students: 5-year time trends in prevalence and demographic, substance use, and mental health correlates. *Eating and Weight Disorders-Studies on Anorexia, Bulimia and Obesity*, *27*(2), 717–728. https://doi.org/10.1007/s40519-021-01210-8

Ghinea, D., Koenig, J., Parzer, P., Brunner, R., Carli, V., Hoven, C. W., Sarchiapone, M., Wasserman, D., Resch, F., & Kaess, M. (2019). Longitudinal development of risk-taking and self-injurious behavior in association with late adolescent borderline personality disorder symptoms. *Psychiatry Research*, *273*, 127–133. https://doi.org/10.1016/j.psychres.2019.01.010

Glenn, C. R., & Klonsky, E. D. (2010). A multimethod analysis of impulsivity in non-suicidal self-injury. *Personality Disorders: Theory, Research, and Treatment*, *1*(1), 67. https://doi.org/10.1037/a0017427

Gollust, S. E., Eisenberg, D., & Golberstein, E. (2008). Prevalence and correlates of self-injury among university students. *Journal of American College Health*, *56*(5), 491–498. https://doi.org/10.3200/JACH.56.5.491-498

Gonçalves, S., Vieira, A. I., Rodrigues, T., Machado, P. P., Brandão, I., Timóteo, S., Nunes, P., & Machado, B. (2021). Adult attachment in eating disorders mediates the association between perceived invalidating childhood environments and eating psychopathology. *Current Psychology*, *40*(11), 5478–5488. https://doi.org/10.1007/s12144-019-00524-2

Gratz, K. L., Conrad, S. D., & Roemer, L. (2002). Risk factors for deliberate self-harm among college students. *American Journal of Orthopsychiatry*, *72*(1), 128–140. https://doi.org/10.1037/0002-9432.72.1.128

Green, J. D., Hatgis, C., Kearns, J. C., Nock, M. K., & Marx, B. P. (2017). The Direct and Indirect Self-Harm Inventory (DISH): A new measure for assessing high-risk and self-harm behaviors among military veterans. *Psychology of Men & Masculinity*, *18*(3), 208. https://doi.org/10.1037/men0000116

Greenberg, N. R., Zhai, Z. W., Hoff, R. A., Krishnan-Sarin, S., & Potenza, M. N. (2021). Problematic shopping and self-injurious behaviors in adolescents. *Journal of Behavioral Addictions*, *9*(4), 1068–1078. https://doi.org/10.1556/2006.2020.00093

Greene, D., Boyes, M., & Hasking, P. (2020). The associations between alexithymia and both non-suicidal self-injury and risky drinking: A systematic review and meta-analysis. *Journal of Affective Disorders*, *260*, 140–166. https://doi.org/10.1016/j.jad.2019.08.088

Hanauer, M., Walker, M. R., Machledt, K., Ragatz, M., & Macy, J. T. (2021). Association between perceived risk of harm and self-reported binge drinking, cigarette smoking, and marijuana smoking in young adults. *Journal of American College Health*, *69*(4), 345–352. https://doi.org/10.1080/07448481.2019.1676757

Hawton, K., Saunders, K., Topiwala, A., & Haw, C. (2013). Psychiatric disorders in patients presenting to hospital following self-harm: A systematic review. *Journal of Affective Disorders*, *151*(3), 821–830. https://doi.org/10.1016/j.jad.2013.08.020

Heath, N. L., Toste, J. R., Nedechava, T., & Charlebois, A. (2008). An examination of non-suicidal self-injury among college students. *Journal of Mental Health Counseling*, *30*(2), 137–156. https://doi.org/10.17744/mehc.30.2.8p879p3443514678

Hemsing, N., & Greaves, L. (2020). Gender norms, roles and relations and cannabis-use patterns: A scoping review. *International Journal of Environmental Research and Public Health*, *17*(3), Article 947. https://doi.org/10.3390/ijerph17030947

Hill, E. M., Jenkins, J., & Farmer, L. (2008). Family unpredictability, future discounting, and risk taking. *The Journal of Socio-Economics*, *37*(4), 1381–1396. https://doi.org/10.1016/j.socec.2006.12.081

Hodgson, K., Coleman, J. R., Hagenaars, S. P., Purves, K. L., Glanville, K., Choi, S. W., O'Reilly, P., Breen, G., & Lewis, C. M. (2020). Cannabis use, depression and self-harm: Phenotypic and genetic relationships. *Addiction*, *115*(3), 482–492. https://doi.org/10.1111/add.14845

Holland, G., & Tiggemann, M. (2017). "Strong beats skinny every time": Disordered eating and compulsive exercise in women who post fitspiration on Instagram. *International Journal of Eating Disorders*, *50*(1), 76–79. https://doi.org/10.1002/eat.22559

Hooley, J. M., & Franklin, J. C. (2018). Why do people hurt themselves? A new conceptual model of non-suicidal self-injury. *Clinical Psychological Science*, *6*(3), 428–451. https://doi.org/10.1177/2167702617745641

Hooley, J. M., & St. Germain, S. A. (2014a). Non-suicidal self-injury, pain, and self-criticism: Does changing self-worth change pain endurance in people who engage in self-injury?. *Clinical Psychological Science*, *2*(3), 297–305. https://doi.org/10.1177/2167702613509372

Hooley, J. M., & St. Germain, S. A. (2014b). Should we expand the conceptualization of self-injurious behavior? Rationale, review, and recommendations. In M. K. Nock (Ed.), *The Oxford handbook of suicide and self-injury* (pp. 47–61). Oxford University Press. https://doi.org/10.1093/oxfordhb/9780195388565.013.0006

Houck, C. D., Hadley, W., Lescano, C. M., Pugatch, D., Brown, L. K., & Project SHIELD Study Group. (2008). Suicide attempt and sexual risk behavior: Relationship among adolescents. *Archives of Suicide Research*, *12*(1), 39–49. https://doi.org/10.1080/13811110701800715

International Society for the Study of Self-INJURY. (2018, May). *What is self-injury?* https://itriples.org/about-self-injury/what-is-selfinjury

Islam, M. A., Steiger, H., Jimenez-Murcia, S., Israel, M., Granero, R., Agüera, Z., Castro, R., Sànchez, I., Riesco, N., Menchón, J.M., & Fernández-Aranda, F. (2015). Non-suicidal self-injury in different eating disorder types: Relevance of personality traits and gender. *European Eating Disorders Review*, *23*(6), 553–560. https://doi.org/10.1002/erv.2374

Jacobson, N. S., & Gottman, J. M. (1998). *When men batter women: New insights into ending abusive relationships*. Simon and Schuster.

Joiner, T. E. (2005). *Why people die by suicide*. Harvard University Press.

Jonsson, L. S., Svedin, C. G., & Hydén, M. (2015). Young women selling sex online-narratives on regulating feelings. *Adolescent Health, Medicine and Therapeutics*, *6*, Article 17. https://doi.org/10.2147/AHMT.S77324

Jonsson, L. S., Svedin, C. G., Priebe, G., Fredlund, C., Wadsby, M., & Zetterqvist, M. (2019). Similarities and differences in the functions of non-suicidal self-injury (NSSI) and sex as self-injury (SASI). *Suicide and Life-Threatening Behavior*, *49*(1), 120–136. https://doi.org/10.1111/sltb.12417

Kapur, N., Cooper, J., O'connor, R. C., & Hawton, K. (2013). Non-suicidal self-injury v. Attempted suicide: New diagnosis or false dichotomy? *The British Journal of Psychiatry*, *202*(5), 326–328. https://doi.org/10.1192/bjp.bp.112.116111

Karakurt, G., Ayluçtarhan, Z., Ergüner-Tekinalp, B., & Köse, Ö. (2021). Regaining courage to leave abusive relationships: Theoretical framework. *The American Journal of Family Therapy*, *50*(1), 1–15. https://doi.org/10.1080/01926187.2021.1877208

Karakurt, G., Patel, V., Whiting, K., & Koyutürk, M. (2017). Mining electronic health records data: Domestic violence and adverse health effects. *Journal of Family Violence*, *32*(1), 79–87. https://doi.org/10.1007/s10896-016-9872-5

Kentopp, S. D., Conner, B. T., Fetterling, T. J., Delgadillo, A. A., & Rebecca, R. A. (2021). Sensation seeking and non-suicidal self-injurious behavior among adolescent psychiatric patients. *Clinical Child Psychology and Psychiatry*, *26*(2), 430–442. https://doi.org/10.1177/1359104521994627

Kiekens, G., & Claes, L. (2020). Non-suicidal self-injury and eating disordered behaviors: An update on what we do and do not know. *Current Psychiatry Reports*, *22*(12), 1–11. https://doi.org/10.1007/s11920-020-01191-y

Kiekens, G., Hasking, P., Claes, L., Boyes, M., Mortier, P., Auerbach, R. P., Cuijpers, P., Demyttenaere, K., Green, J. G., Kessler, R. C., Myin-Germeys, I. M., Nock, K., & Bruffaerts, R. (2019). Predicting the incidence of non-suicidal self-injury in college students. *European Psychiatry*, *59*, 44–51. https://doi.org/10.1016/j.eurpsy.2019.04.002

Kimbrel, N. A., Meyer, E. C., De Beer, B. B., Gulliver, S. B., & Morissette, S. B. (2018). The impact of cannabis use disorder on suicidal and non-suicidal self-injury in Iraq/Afghanistan-era veterans with and without mental health disorders. *Suicide and Life-Threatening Behavior*, *48*(2), 140–148. https://doi.org/10.1111/sltb.12345

King, R. A., Schwab-Stone, M., Flisher, A. J., Greenwald, S., Kramer, R. A., Goodman, S. H., Lahey, B. B., Shaffer, D., & Gould, M. S. (2001). Psychosocial and risk behavior correlates of youth suicide attempts and suicidal ideation. *Journal of the American Academy of Child & Adolescent Psychiatry*, *40*(7), 837–846. https://doi.org/10.1097/00004583-200107000-00019

Klassen, J. A., Hamza, C. A., & Stewart, S. L. (2018). An examination of correlates for adolescent engagement in non-suicidal self-injury, suicidal self-injury, and substance use. *Journal of Research on Adolescence*, *28*(2), 342–353. https://doi.org/10.1111/jora.12333

Klonsky, E. D., & Glenn, C. R. (2008). Resisting urges to self-injure. *Behavioural and Cognitive Psychotherapy*, *36*(2), 211–220. https://doi.org/10.1017/S1352465808004128

Knorr, A. C., Jenkins, A. L., & Conner, B. T. (2013). The role of sensation seeking in non-suicidal self-injury. *Cognitive Therapy and Research*, *37*(6), 1276–1284. https://doi.org/10.1007/s10608-013-9554-z

Korhonen, T., Sihvola, E., Latvala, A., Dick, D. M., Pulkkinen, L., Nurnberger, J., Rose, R. J., & Kaprio, J. (2018). Early-onset tobacco use and suicide-related behavior—A prospective study from adolescence to young adulthood, *Addictive Behaviors*, *79*, 32–38. https://doi.org/10.1016/j.addbeh.2017.12.008

Lader, W. (2006). A look at the increase in body focused behaviors. *Paradigm*, *11*, 14–18.

Latina, D., Jaf, D., Alberti, R., & Tilton-Weaver, L. (2022). Can participation in organized sports help adolescents refrain from self-harm? An analysis of underlying mechanisms. *Psychology of Sport and Exercise*, *59*, Article 102133. https://doi.org/10.1016/j.psychsport.2022.102133

Laye-Gindhu, A., & Schonert-Reichl, K. (2005). Non-suicidal self-harm among community adolescents: Understanding the "whats" and "whys" of self-harm. *Journal of Youth and Adolescence*, *34*(5), 447–457. https://doi.org/10.1007/s10964-005-7262-z

Lengel, G. J., Ammerman, B. A., & Washburn, J. J. (2021). Clarifying the definition of non-suicidal self-injury: Clinician and researcher perspectives. *Crisis: The Journal of Crisis Intervention and Suicide Prevention*, *43*(2), 119. https://doi.org/10.1027/0227-5910/a000764

Levesque, C., Lafontaine, M. F., Bureau, J. F., Cloutier, P., & Dandurand, C. (2010). The influence of romantic attachment and intimate partner violence on non-suicidal self-injury in young adults. *Journal of Youth and Adolescence*, *39*(5), 474–483. https://doi.org/10.1007/s10964-009-9471-3

Li, L., Sun, I. Y., & Button, D. M. (2020). Tolerance for intimate partner violence: A comparative study of Chinese and American college students. *Journal of Interpersonal Violence*, *35*(21–22), 4533–4557. https://doi.org/10.1177/0886260517716941

Lindgren, B. M., Svedin, C. G., & Werkö, S. (2018). A systematic literature review of experiences of professional care and support among people who self-harm. *Archives of Suicide Research*, *22*(2), 173–192. https://doi.org/10.1080/13811118.2017.1319309

Linkletter, M., Gordon, K., & Dooley, J. (2010). The choking game and YouTube: A dangerous combination. *Clinical Pediatrics*, *49*(3), 274–279. https://doi.org/10.1177/0009922809339203

Lydecker, J. A., Grilo, C. M., Hamilton, A., & Barnes, R. D. (2022). Digital self-harm is associated with disordered eating behaviors in adults. *Eating and Weight Disorders—Studies on Anorexia, Bulimia and Obesity*, *27*(6), 2129–2136. https://doi.org/10.1007/s40519-021-01355-6

Mann, A. J. D., Tull, M. T., & Gratz, K. L. (2022). Hiding in the open: Consideration of nonsuicidal self-injury by proxy as a clinically meaningful construct. *Suicide and Life-Threatening Behavior*, *52*(5), 1024–1036. https://doi.org/10.1111/sltb.12899

McManus, S., Gunnell, D., Cooper, C., Bebbington, P. E., Howard, L. M., Brugha, T. Jenkins, R., Hassiotis, A., Weich, S., & Appleby, L. (2019). Prevalence of non-suicidal self-harm and service contact in England, 2000-14: Repeated cross-sectional surveys of the general population. *The Lancet Psychiatry*, *6*(7), 573–581. https://doi.org/10.1016/S2215-0366(19)30188-9

Micali, N., Horton, N. J., Crosby, R. D., Swanson, S. A., Sonneville, K. R., Solmi, F., Calzo, J.P., Eddy, K.T., & Field, A. E. (2017). Eating disorder behaviours amongst adolescents: In classification, persistence and prospective associations with adverse outcomes using latent class models. *European Child & Adolescent Psychiatry*, *26*(2), 231–240. https://doi.org/10.1007/s00787-016-0877-7

Møhl, B. (2019). *Assessment and treatment of non-suicidal self-injury: A clinical perspective*. Routledge. https://doi.org/10.4324/9780429296352

Moller, C. I., Tait, R. J., & Byrne, D. G. (2013). Deliberate self-harm, substance use, and negative affect in nonclinical samples: A systematic review. *Substance Abuse*, *34*(2), 188–207. https://doi.org/10.1080/08897077.2012.693462

Mond, J., & Gorrell, S. (2021). "Excessive exercise" in eating disorders research: Problems of definition and perspective. Eating and Weight Disorders—Studies *on Anorexia, Bulimia and Obesity*, *26*(4), 1017–1020. https://doi.org/10.1007/s40519-020-01075-3

Monterrosa, A. E. (2021). How race and gender stereotypes influence help-seeking for intimate partner violence. *Journal of Interpersonal Violence*, *36*(17–18), NP9153–NP9174. https://doi.org/10.1177/0886260519853403

Monto, M. A., McRee, N., & Deryck, F. S. (2018). Non-suicidal self-injury among a representative sample of US adolescents, 2015. *American Journal of Public Health*, *108*(8), 1042–1048. https://doi.org/10.2105/AJPH.2018.304470

Morthorst, B., Harboe Olsen, M., Jakobsen, J. C., Lindschou, J., Gluud, C., Heinrichsen, M., Møhl, B., Rubæk, L., Bjureberg, B., Ojala, O., Hellner, C., & Pagsberg, A. K. (2022). *Internet-based intervention*

(ERITA) as add-on to treatment as usual for non-suicidal self-injury in adolescent outpatients: The TEENS randomized feasibility trial. *JCPP Advances, 2*(4), e12115.

Muehlenkamp, J. J. (2012). Body regard in non-suicidal self-injury: Theoretical explanations and treatment directions. *Journal of Cognitive Psychotherapy, 26*(4), 331–347. https://doi.org/10.1891/0889-8391.26.4.331

Muehlenkamp, J. J., Kerr, P. L., Bradley, A. R., & Larsen, M. A. (2010). Abuse subtypes evidence and non-suicidal self-injury. Preliminary evidence of complex emotion regulation patterns. *Journal of Nervous and Mental Disease, 198*(4), 258–263. https://doi.org/10.1097/NMD.0b013e3181d612ab

Muehlenkamp, J. J., Peat, C. M., Claes, L., & Smits, D. (2012). Self-injury and disordered eating: Expressing emotion dysregulation through the body. *Suicide and Life-Threatening Behavior, 42*(4), 416–425. https://doi.org/10.1111/j.1943-278X.2012.00100.x

Muehlenkamp, J. J., Suzuki, T., Brausch, A. M., & Peyerl, N. (2019). Behavioral functions underlying NSSI and eating disorder behaviors. *Journal of Clinical Psychology, 75*(7), 1219–1232. https://doi.org/10.1002/jclp.22745

Nixon, M. K., Cloutier, P. F., & Aggarwal, S. (2002). Affect regulation and addictive aspects of repetitive self-injury in hospitalized adolescents. *Journal of the American Academy of Child & Adolescent Psychiatry, 41*(11), 1333–1341. https://doi.org/10.1097/00004583-200211000-00015

Nock, M. K. (2009). Why do people hurt themselves? New insights into the nature and functions of self-injury. *Current Directions in Psychological Science, 18*(2), 78–83. https://doi.org/10.1111/j.1467-8721.2009.01613.x

Nock, M. K. (2010). Self-injury. *Annual Review of Clinical Psychology, 6*(1), 339–363. https://doi.org/10.1146/annurev.clinpsy.121208.131258

Nock, M. K., Joiner, T. E., Gordon, K. H., Lloyd-Richardson, E., & Prinstein, M. J. (2006). Non-suicidal self-injury among adolescents: Diagnostic correlates and relation to suicide attempts. *Psychiatry Research, 144*(1), 65–72. https://doi.org/10.1016/j.psychres.2006.05.010

Nock, M. K., & Prinstein, M. (2004). A functional approach to the assessment of self-mutilative behavior. *Journal of Consulting and Clinical Psychology, 72*(5), 885–890. https://doi.org/10.1037/0022-006X.72.5.885

Oquendo, M. A., & Mann, J. J. (2000). The biology of impulsivity and suicidality. *Psychiatric Clinics of North America, 23*(1), 11–25. https://doi.org/10.1016/S0193-953X(05)70140-4

Pak, K. N., Nelson, J., Adams, L. M., & Fischer, S. (2021). Mixture modeling of non-suicidal self-injury and binge eating: Behaviors and motives. *Behavior Therapy, 52*(5), 1265–1276. https://doi.org/10.1016/j.beth.2021.02.005

Patchin, J. W., & Hinduja, S. (2017). Digital self-harm among adolescents. *Journal of Adolescent Health, 61*(6), 761–766. https://doi.org/10.1016/j.jadohealth.2017.06.012

Pérez, S., Marco, J. H., & Cañabate, M. (2018). Non-suicidal self-injury in patients with eating disorders: Prevalence, forms, functions, and body image correlates. *Comprehensive Psychiatry, 84*, 32–38. https://doi.org/10.1016/j.comppsych.2018.04.003

Peterson, C. M., & Fischer, S. (2012). A prospective study of the influence of the UPPS model of impulsivity on the co-occurrence of bulimic symptoms and non-suicidal self-injury. *Eating Behaviors, 13*(4), 335–341. https://doi.org/10.1016/j.eatbeh.2012.05.007

Plener, P. L., Fischer, C. J., In-Albon, T., Rollett, B., Nixon, M. K., Groschwitz, R. C., & Schmid, M. (2013). Adolescent non-suicidal self-injury (NSSI) in German-speaking countries: Comparing prevalence rates from three community samples. *Social Psychiatry and Psychiatric Epidemiology, 48*(9), 1439–1445. https://doi.org/10.1007/s00127-012-0645-z

Pugh, B., Li, L., & Sun, I. Y. (2018). Perceptions of why women stay in physically abusive relationships: A comparative study of Chinese and U.S. college students. *Journal of Interpersonal Violence, 36*(7–8), 3778–3813. https://doi.org/10.1177/0886260518778264

Raffagnato, A., Angelico, C., Valentini, P., Miscioscia, M., & Gatta, M. (2020). Using the body when there are no words for feelings: Alexithymia and somatization in self-harming adolescents. *Frontiers in Psychiatry, 11*, Article 262. https://doi.org/10.3389/fpsyt.2020.00262

Richardson, E., DePue, M. K., Therriault, D. J., Alli, S., & Liu, R. (2020). The influence of substance use on engagement in non-suicidal self-injury (NSI) in adults. *Substance Use & Misuse, 55*(1), 89–94. https://doi.org/10.1080/10826084.2019.1656254

Riley, E. N., Davis, H. A., Combs, J. L., Jordan, C. E., & Smith, G. T. (2016). Non-suicidal self-injury as a risk factor for purging onset: Negatively reinforced behaviours that reduce emotional distress. *European Eating Disorders Review, 24*(1), 78–82. https://doi.org/10.1002/erv.2407

Rizk, M., Mattar, L., Kern, L., Berthoz, S., Duclos, J., Viltart, O., & Godart, N. (2020). Physical activity in eating disorders: A systematic review. *Nutrients*, *12*(1), Article 183. https://doi.org/10.3390/nu12010183

Rubæk, L., & Møhl, B. (2016). Ikke-suicidal selvskade-et afhængighedssyndrom? (Non-suicidal self-harm - a dependency syndrome?). *Psyke & Logos*, *37*(2), 205–219.

Sansone, R. A., & Sansone, L. A. (2007). Childhood trauma, borderline personality, and eating disorders: A developmental cascade. *Eating Disorders*, *15*(4), 333–346. https://doi.org/10.1080/10640260701454345

Sansone, R. A., Wiederman, M. W., & Sansone, L. A. (1998). The self-harm inventory (SHI): Development of a scale for identifying self-destructive behaviors and borderline personality disorder. *Journal of Clinical Psychology*, *54*(7), 973–983. https://doi.org/10.1002/(SICI)1097-4679(199811)54:7<973::AID-JCLP11>3.0.CO;2-H

Schonberg, T., Fox, C. R., & Poldrack, R. A. (2011). Mind the gap: Bridging economic and naturalistic risk-taking with cognitive neuroscience. *Trends in Cognitive Sciences*, *15*(1), 11–19. https://doi.org/10.1016/j.tics.2010.10.002

Selby, E. A., Nock, M. K., & Kranzler, A. (2014). How does self-injury feel? Examining automatic positive reinforcement in adolescent self-injurers with experience sampling. *Psychiatry Research*, *215*(2), 417–423. https://doi.org/10.1016/j.psychres.2013.12.005

Shingleton, R. M., Eddy, K. T., Keshaviah, A., Franko, D. L., Swanson, S. A., Yu, J. S., Krishna, M., Nock, M.K., & Herzog, D. B. (2013). Binge/purge thoughts in non-suicidal self-injurious adolescents: An ecological momentary analysis. *International Journal of Eating Disorders*, *46*(7), 684–689. https://doi.org/10.1002/eat.22142

Shulman, E. P., Smith, A. R., Silva, K., Icenogle, G., Duell, N., Chein, J., & Steinberg, L. (2016). The dual systems model: Review, reappraisal, and reaffirmation. *Developmental Cognitive Neuroscience*, *17*, 103–117. https://doi.org/10.1016/j.dcn.2015.12.010

Singh, N. N., Singh, S. D., Davis, C. M., Latham, L. L., & Ayers, J. G. (1999). Reconsidering the use of seclusion and restraints in inpatient child and adult psychiatry. *Journal of Child and Family Studies*, *8*(3), 243–253. https://doi.org/10.1023/A:1022039711096

Slesinger, N. C., Hayes, N. A., & Washburn, J. J. (2019). In J. J. Washburn (Ed.), *Non-suicidal self-injury. Advances in research and practice*. Routledge. https://doi.org/10.4324/9781315164182-1

Smith, A. R., Velkoff, E. A., Ribeiro, J. D., & Franklin, J. (2019). Are eating disorders and related symptoms risk factors for suicidal thoughts and behaviors? A meta-analysis. *Suicide and Life-Threatening Behavior*, *49*(1), 221–239. https://doi.org/10.1111/sltb.12427

Solano, R., Fernández-Aranda, F., Aitken, A., López, C., & Vallejo, J. (2005). Self-injurious behaviour in people with eating disorders. *European Eating Disorders Review: The Professional Journal of the Eating Disorders Association*, *13*(1), 3–10. https://doi.org/10.1002/erv.618

St. Germain, S. A., & Hooley, J. M. (2012). Direct and indirect forms of non-suicidal self-injury: Evidence for a distinction. *Psychiatry Research*, *197*(1–2), 78–84. https://doi.org/10.1016/j.psychres.2011.12.050

St. Germain, S. A., & Hooley, J. M. (2013). Aberrant pain perception in direct and indirect non-suicidal self-injury: An empirical test of Joiner's interpersonal theory. *Comprehensive Psychiatry*, *54*(6), 694–701. https://doi.org/10.1016/j.comppsych.2012.12.029

Strober, M., Freeman, R., & Morrell, W. (1997). The long-term course of severe anorexia nervosa in adolescents: Survival analysis of recovery, relapse, and outcome predictors over 10-15 years in a prospective study. *International Journal of Eating Disorders*, *22*(4), 339–360. https://doi.org/10.1002/(SICI)1098-108X(199712)22:4<339::AID-EAT1>3.0.CO;2-N

Svirko, E., & Hawton, K. (2007). Self-injurious behavior and eating disorders: The extent and nature of the association. *Suicide and Life-Threatening Behavior*, *37*(4), 409–421. https://doi.org/10.1521/suli.2007.37.4.409

Swann, W. B. (1997). The trouble with change. Self-verification and allegiance to the self. *Psychological Science*, *8*(3), 177–180. https://doi.org/10.1111/j.1467-9280.1997.tb00407.x

Swanson, S. A., Crow, S. J., Le Grange, D., Swendsen, J., & Merikangas, K. R. (2011). Prevalence and correlates of eating disorders in adolescents: Results from the national comorbidity survey replication adolescent supplement. *Archives of General Psychiatry*, *68*(7), 714–723. https://doi.org/10.1001/archgenpsychiatry.2011.22

Taliaferro, L. A., McMorris, B. J., Rider, G. N., & Eisenberg, M. E. (2019). Risk and protective factors for self-harm in a population-based sample of transgender youth. *Archives of Suicide Research*, *23*(2), 203–221. https://doi.org/10.1080/13811118.2018.1430639

Taranis, L., & Meyer, C. (2011). Associations between specific components of compulsive exercise and eating-disordered cognitions and behaviors among young women. *International Journal of Eating Disorders*, *44*(5), 452–458. https://doi.org/10.1002/eat.20838

Thompson, A. B., Tebes, J. K., & McKee, S. A. (2015). Gender differences in age of smoking initiation and its association with health. *Addiction Research & Theory*, *23*(5), 413–420. https://doi.org/10.3109/16066 359.2015.1022159

Trott, M., Jackson, S. E., Firth, J., Jacob, L., Grabovac, I., Mistry, A., Stubbs, B., & Smith, L. (2021). A comparative meta-analysis of the prevalence of exercise addiction in adults with and without indicated eating disorders. *Eating and Weight Disorders—Studies on Anorexia, Bulimia and Obesity*, *26*(1), 37–46. https://doi.org/10.1007/s40519-019-00842-1

Turner, B. J., Yiu, A., Claes, L., Muehlenkamp, J. J., & Chapman, A. L. (2016). Occurrence and co-occurrence of non-suicidal self-injury and disordered eating in a daily diary study: Which behavior, when?. *Psychiatry Research*, *246*, 39–47. https://doi.org/10.1016/j.psychres.2016.09.012

Turner, B. J., Yiu, A., Layden, B. K., Claes, L., Zaitsoff, S., & Chapman, A. L. (2015). Temporal associations between disordered eating and non-suicidal self-injury: Examining symptom overlap over 1 year. *Behavior Therapy*, *46*(1), 125–138. https://doi.org/10.1016/j.beth.2014.09.002

Turp, M. (2002). The many faces of self-harm. *Psychodynamic Practice*, *8*(2), 197–217. https://doi.org/10.1080/13533330210154655

Ullrich, N. J., Bergin, A. M., & Goodkin, H. P. (2008). "The choking game": Self-induced hypoxia presenting as recurrent seizurelike events. *Epilepsy & Behavior*, *12*(3), 486–488. https://doi.org/10.1016/j.yebeh.2007.12.008

van der Kolk, B. A. (1989). The compulsion to repeat the trauma re-enactment, revictimization, and masochism. *Psychiatric Clinics of North America*, *12*(2), 389–411. https://doi.org/10.1016/S0193-953X(18)30439-8

van Furth, E. F., van der Meer, A., & Cowan, K. (2016). Top 10 research priorities for eating disorders. *The Lancet Psychiatry*, *3*(8), 706–707. https://doi.org/10.1016/S2215-0366(16)30147-X

Victor, S. E., Glenn, C. R., & Klonsky, E. D. (2012). Is non-suicidal self-injury an "addiction"? A comparison of craving in substance use and non-suicidal self-injury. *Psychiatry Research*, *197*(1-2), 73–77. https://doi.org/10.1016/j.psychres.2011.12.011

Victor, S. E., Lewis, S. P., & Muehlenkamp, J. J. (2021). Psychologists with lived experience of non-suicidal self-injury: Priorities, obstacles, and recommendations for inclusion. *Psychological Services*, *19*(1), 21. https://doi.org/10.1037/ser0000510

Victor, S. E., Muehlenkamp, J. J., Hayes, N. A., Lengel, G. J., Styer, D. M., & Washburn, J. J. (2018). Characterizing gender differences in non-suicidal self-injury: Evidence from a large clinical sample of adolescents and adults. *Comprehensive Psychiatry*, *82*, 53–60. https://doi.org/10.1016/j.comppsych.2018.01.009

Volpe, U., Tortorella, A., Manchia, M., Monteleone, A. M., Albert, U., & Monteleone, P. (2016). Eating disorders: What age at onset? *Psychiatry Research*, *238*, 225–227. https://doi.org/10.1016/j.psychres.2016.02.048

Wallenstein, M. B., & Nock, M. K. (2007). Physical exercise as a treatment for non-suicidal self-injury: Evidence from a single-case study. *American Journal of Psychiatry*, *164*(2), 350–351. https://doi.org/10.1176/ajp.2007.164.2.350a

Warne, N., Heron, J., Mars, B., Moran, P., Stewart, A., Munafò, M., Biddle, L., Skinner, A., Gunell, D., & Bould, H. (2021). Comorbidity of self-harm and disordered eating in young people: Evidence from a UK population-based cohort. *Journal of Affective Disorders*, *282*, 386–390. https://doi.org/10.1016/j.jad.2020.12.053

Washburn, J. J., Potthoff, L. M., Juzwin, K. R., & Styer, D. M. (2015). Assessing DSM-5 non-suicidal self-injury disorder in a clinical sample. *Psychological Assessment*, *27*(1), 31–41. https://doi.org/10.1037/pas0000021

Wester, K., Trepal, H., & King, K. (2018). Nonsuicidal self-injury: Increased prevalence in engagement. *Suicide and Life-Threatening Behavior*, *48*(6), 690–698. https://doi.org/10.1111/sltb.12389

Westmoreland, P., Krantz, M. J., & Mehler, P. S. (2016). Medical complications of anorexia nervosa and bulimia. *The American Journal of Medicine*, *129*(1), 30–37. https://doi.org/10.1016/j.amjmed.2015.06.031

White, A. M. (2020). Gender differences in the epidemiology of alcohol use and related harms in the United States. *Alcohol Research: Current Reviews*, *40*(2), Article 01. https://doi.org/10.35946/arcr.v40.2.01

Whitlock, J., Eckenrode, J., & Silverman, D. (2006). Self-injurious behaviors in a college population. *Pediatrics*, *117*(6), 1939–1948. https://doi.org/10.1542/peds.2005-2543

Wilkinson, P. O., Qiu, T., Neufeld, S., Jones, P. B., & Goodyer, I. M. (2018). Sporadic and recurrent non-suicidal self-injury before age 14 and incident onset of psychiatric disorders by 17 years: Prospective cohort study. *The British Journal of Psychiatry*, *212*(4), 222–226. https://doi.org/10.1192/bjp.2017.45

Wonderlich, S. A., Rosenfeldt, S., Crosby, R. D., Mitchell, J. E., Engel, S. G., Smyth, J., & Miltenberger, R. (2007). The effects of childhood trauma on daily mood lability and comorbid psychopathology in bulimia nervosa. *Journal of Traumatic Stress*, *20*(1), 77–87. https://doi.org/10.1002/jts.20184

Wright, F., Bewick, B. M., Barkham, M., House, A. O., & Hill, A. J. (2009). Co-occurrence of self-reported disordered eating and self-harm in UK university students. *British Journal of Clinical Psychology*, *48*(4), 397–410. https://doi.org/10.1348/014466509X410343

Yiu, A., Turner, B. J., Layden, B. K., Chapman, A. L., & Zaitsoff, S. L. (2015). Prevalence and correlates of eating disorder symptoms in a community sample with non-suicidal self-injury. *Journal of Psychopathology and Behavioral Assessment*, *37*(3), 504–511. https://doi.org/10.1007/s10862-014-9470-x

Zetterqvist, M. (2017). Nonsuicidal self-injury in adolescents: Characterization of the disorder and the issue of distress and impairment. *Suicide and Life-Threatening Behavior*, *47*(3), 321–335. https://doi.org/10.1111/sltb.12283

Zetterqvist, M., Svedin, C. G., Fredlund, C., Priebe, G., Wadsby, M., & Jonsson, L. S. (2018). Self-reported nonsuicidal self-injury (NSSI) and sex as self-injury (SASI): Relationship to abuse, risk behaviors, trauma symptoms, self-esteem and attachment. *Psychiatry Research*, *265*, 309–316. https://doi.org/10.1016/j.psychres.2018.05.013

CHAPTER 5

Theoretical Models Linking NSSI to Suicide

Sarah E. Victor, Kirsten Christensen, *and* Terry H. Trieu

Abstract

Nonsuicidal self-injury (NSSI) is associated with suicidal ideation (SI) and capability for suicidal behavior. This chapter describes theoretical models of suicide in relation to NSSI, with implications for research and clinical practice. First, theories emphasize cognitive influences on suicide associated with NSSI, such as rumination, impaired problem-solving, and negative attributional style. These factors may exacerbate hopelessness, increasing risk for both NSSI and SI. Second, interpersonal difficulties are core to several suicide theories. NSSI is associated with loneliness, poor social support, and victimization; moreover, NSSI may prompt negative reactions from others, exacerbating interpersonal risk factors for SI. Finally, suicide theories often highlight the role of negative views of self in desire for suicide. NSSI is strongly associated with self-criticism, occurs as a means of self-punishment, and is frequently followed by guilt and shame, which may exacerbate negative self-views contributing to SI. NSSI is also associated with suicide capability. This may be due to differences in pain sensitivity or tolerance, fearlessness about death, exposure to painful and provocative events, or impulsivity, each of which has exhibited associations with NSSI. Further, NSSI involves repeated exposure to injury and pain, which may explain why chronic and severe NSSI elevates risk of suicide attempts. Taken together, research highlights the importance of assessing NSSI and suicide risk and protective factors in clinical practice, while leaving open unanswered questions about potentially causal relationships between these related, but distinct, experiences. Longitudinal work is needed to understand how NSSI most appropriately fits within existing theoretical models of suicide.

Key Words: psychache, NSSI, hopelessness, suicidal ideation, suicidal behavior, self-criticism, interpersonal problems, suicide capability, ideation-to-action

Introduction

Nonsuicidal self-injury (NSSI) is, by its very definition, not suicidal in nature (International Society for the Study of Self-Injury, 2018). However, a large body of literature demonstrates that NSSI is a prospective risk factor for suicidal thoughts and behaviors (Ribeiro et al., 2016). Research suggests that increased engagement in NSSI, such as higher frequency and number of methods used, is associated with elevated risk of suicidal behavior (Victor & Klonsky, 2014). Thus, understanding the basis on which NSSI serves to increase risk for suicide is a critical element of NSSI-focused research.

Consistent with theoretical models of NSSI differentiating risk for NSSI urges and NSSI behaviors (see Hird et al., this volume), modern theories of suicide are typically characterized by ideation-to-action approaches (Klonsky et al., 2018). These models emphasize the unique predictors of suicidal thoughts, relative to suicidal behaviors, and consider specific risk factors that contribute to the transition from thoughts to behaviors over time. Prior work has found NSSI to predict suicidal desire over time (Brausch & Woods, 2019), which may be due to its association with negative emotional experiences (Selby et al., 2013) or other life stressors (Steinhoff et al., 2020). NSSI also appears to increase capability for suicidal behavior (Willoughby et al., 2015), which may be due to habituation to pain, injury, and self-directed violence (May & Victor, 2018).

This chapter describes a number of theoretical models of suicide as they relate to NSSI. Further, the chapter briefly describes the empirical literature providing evidentiary support for NSSI as a risk factor for suicidal thoughts and/or behaviors within each model. Finally, the chapter identifies ways in which this work can be expanded upon in later research, as well as how this work can be utilized in clinical practice.

Theoretical Models of Suicidal Ideation

Suicidal ideation has been conceptualized as developing in response to numerous intrapersonal and interpersonal processes, which can be broadly characterized as falling within three domains: cognitive processes, interpersonal difficulties, and negative views of self.

Cognitive Biases and Hopelessness

Shneidman (1993) proposed that unbearable psychological pain, which he termed "psychache," was a necessary condition for suicide. In this model, he defined 10 commonalities of suicide: purpose of seeking a solution, goal of ending consciousness, stimulus of psychological pain, stressor of unmet psychological needs, emotions of helplessness and hopelessness, state of ambivalence about life versus death, state of mental constriction, act of escape, communication of intention, and pattern of lifelong styles of coping. Thus, suicidal behavior is seen as a problem-solving action that occurs when someone experiences intolerable psychache as a result of unmet psychological needs and insufficient means of coping.

Beck et al. (1990) also saw hopelessness as central to suicidal thinking, but they conceptualized the phenomenon as a maladaptive schema consisting of thoughts about oneself, others, and the world that forms from biases in attention, information processing, and memory, which lead to mental constriction and impairment in recalling hope or reasons for living. Impulsivity and aggression, problem-solving deficits, overly general memory style, maladaptive cognitive style, and certain personality traits form a disposition that can be vulnerable to suicidal thinking if it interacts with stressors, cognitive processes that are part of psychopathology, or cognitive processes that are part of suicidal behavior.

From studies of problem-solving among people who have been suicidal, Schotte and Clum (1987) theorized that cognitive rigidity leads to an inability to identify alternative solutions to problems or a tendency to fixate on negative possible consequences for imagined solutions, which can result in hopelessness in the face of high stress. However, what is unclear is if these deficits are state dependent such that they occur only in stressful circumstances or if they represent a trait.

The three-step theory (Klonsky & May, 2015) posited that the combination of pain and hopelessness is necessary to the development of suicidal ideation. If an individual is in considerable emotional, mental, or physical pain but has hope of their situation improving, then they are not likely to seriously consider suicide. Similarly, if an individual does not have hope of their situation improving but is not in a level of pain that they consider unbearable, they are not likely to become suicidal.

Research has demonstrated that NSSI is associated with decreased hope (Jiang et al., 2018) and optimism (Tanner et al., 2014), particularly in the context of psychological symptoms or distress. Further, a recent meta-analysis demonstrated that hopelessness is one of the strongest risk factors for later NSSI (Fox et al., 2015). Rumination (the tendency to focus on the causes, consequences, and meanings of one's negative emotions; Nolen-Hoeksema, 1991) and negative attributional style (the tendency to interpret negative events as being caused by factors that are stable, internal to oneself, and globally relevant; Abramson et al., 1989) have shown prospective associations with NSSI (Barrocas et al., 2015; Selby et al., 2013), highlighting the relevance of biased cognitive processes in contributing to both NSSI and suicide. In addition, impaired problem-solving has been associated with NSSI in ethnically diverse college students (Lucas et al., 2019), and problem-solving deficits have been shown to moderate the association between NSSI and suicidal behavior (Walker et al., 2017). Taken together, negative cognitive biases and difficulties solving life problems may exacerbate hopelessness, which then increases the risk for both NSSI and suicidal ideation.

Although hopelessness may be a risk factor for both NSSI and suicidal thoughts, NSSI itself can be used as a temporary strategy to cope with suicidal thoughts and avoid suicidal behavior. In a large sample of university students, only 4.5% of participants with a history of NSSI reported using NSSI to avoid attempting suicide; however, participants with a history of suicidal thoughts, plans, or attempts were more likely to report NSSI as serving an antisuicide function (Paul et al., 2015). In a study of female adolescents in inpatient psychiatric treatment with NSSI disorder, 32% reported NSSI serving as a coping strategy to avoid attempting suicide (Kraus et al., 2020). Thus, NSSI may serve as a short-term coping mechanism for suicidal thoughts, simultaneously increasing later risk for suicidal behavior (Taylor et al., 2018).

Interpersonal Processes and Challenges
The interpersonal theory of suicide by Joiner (2005) linked two interpersonal constructs—perceived burdensomeness and thwarted belongingness—as key to the development of suicidal ideation (Van Orden et al., 2010). When an individual feels that they are a

burden on the people around them (i.e., perceived burdensomeness) or feels that they do not belong or have connection to any social group (i.e., thwarted belongingness), then they are more likely to believe that others would be better off without them alive. These perceptions can come about due to actual or perceived interpersonal challenges. In particular, thwarted belongingness is associated with conditions such as living alone or having low social support (Van Orden et al., 2012). Higher levels of perceived burdensomeness and thwarted belongingness are associated with a history of NSSI (Chu et al., 2016), and higher levels of thwarted belongingness are also associated with a greater frequency of NSSI (Assavedo & Anestis, 2015). Perceived burdensomeness and thwarted belongingness may account for associations between NSSI and suicidal thoughts (Chu et al., 2016).

In the second step of the three-step theory by Klonsky and May (2015), connectedness is what separates moderate from severe suicidal ideation. Connectedness in this context refers to a sense of connection to not only other people but also work, hobbies, or another source of meaning. An individual experiencing a wish to die who does not feel connected is more likely to have suicidal thoughts with some intent to carry them out. While connectedness here can be likened to the concepts of perceived burdensomeness and thwarted belongingness, according to Joiner (2005), connectedness in the three-step theory refers to a broader sense of fulfillment or attachment to some aspect of living. Regardless, challenges in interpersonal functioning can result in lack of connectedness.

NSSI is associated with a variety of interpersonal challenges. Loneliness has been linked cross-sectionally (Gandhi et al., 2018; Giletta et al., 2012) to a history of NSSI and prospectively (Wang et al., 2020) to initiation of NSSI among adolescents. Other interpersonal experiences, including parental harsh punishment, low parental monitoring, and more negative perceptions of peers, are also associated with greater likelihood of initiating NSSI among adolescent girls (Victor, Hipwell, et al., 2019). Individuals with a history of NSSI perceive less interpersonal support compared to individuals who have never engaged in NSSI (Trepal et al., 2015), and are more likely to report experiencing peer victimization (Giletta et al., 2012; van Geel et al., 2015). Additionally, lower perceived social support from family members and fewer individuals to seek advice from are associated with repetitive NSSI, compared to individuals with a single experience of NSSI or no history of NSSI (Muehlenkamp et al., 2013). Individuals with recent, repeated NSSI have less contact with family and friends, perceive less support from friends, and are less likely to seek support to cope (Turner et al., 2017). However, individuals with recent NSSI may not differ from those without a history of NSSI on perceived support in romantic relationships, and they actually report more contact with romantic partners than do individuals with no history of NSSI (Turner et al., 2017). In intensive longitudinal research, NSSI urges and behaviors have been linked to interpersonal conflict (Turner et al., 2016) and being rejected or criticized (Victor, Scott, et al., 2019) over the course of hours or days.

In addition to the likelihood that NSSI is influenced by interpersonal processes, NSSI itself may be used as an interpersonal communication strategy, thus contributing to changes in individuals' interpersonal experiences. A 2018 meta-analysis found that interpersonal functions (reasons) were reported by 44% of individuals who engaged in NSSI (Taylor et al., 2018). The most commonly reported interpersonal function was to communicate levels of distress (42%), followed by using NSSI for interpersonal influence (28%) and to punish others (18%; Taylor et al., 2018). Use of NSSI for interpersonal reasons may contribute to negative reactions from others, which could then indirectly influence suicide risk through changes in depressive symptoms (Park & Ammerman, 2020). In fact, studies examining perceived reactions to NSSI disclosure have found that reactions from others are often perceived as negative and unhelpful, which may discourage future disclosure and help-seeking (Muehlenkamp et al., 2013; Park et al., 2021).

Negative Views of the Self
Baumeister (1990) observed that the most common motive for suicidal behavior is the desire to escape either from oneself or from an unbearable situation. Suicidal thinking consists of six steps: perceiving a discrepancy between expectations and reality, interpreting that discrepancy as due to personal failure, comparing oneself to one's excessively high standards, experiencing negative emotions as a result of seeing oneself as falling short, engaging in cognitive deconstruction such that one focuses on concrete sensations and immediate goals, and being less behaviorally inhibited such that harming oneself is easier. Similar to the model by Shneidman (1993), Baumeister saw suicide as coming from the desire to end unbearable mental pain through the loss of consciousness.

The arrested flight model by Williams (1997), however, saw suicidal thinking as resulting from perceived entrapment, which comes from feelings of defeat following humiliation or rejection, which interacts with problem-solving deficits that prevent identifying alternative solutions. When a suicidal individual believes that their attempts to problem-solve are unsuccessful, they experience hopelessness and helplessness about their ability to escape their current situation in the future. Thus, both models expand upon literature emphasizing the role of hopelessness and impaired problem-solving to also include negative views of oneself in relation to expectations, demands, and goals.

Per the perceived burdensomeness construct proposed by Joiner (2005), people can have such a negative view of themselves that they believe they are a burden on others or that their loved ones would be better off without them, which occurs when there is an unmet need for social competence. Circumstances such as impaired functioning, poor family relations, or unemployment (Van Orden et al., 2012) can result in the perception that one is a burden; however, this belief can also occur regardless of one's material circumstances.

The integrated motivational-volitional model (O'Connor & Kirtley, 2018) incorporates elements of prior theoretical models of suicide in its conceptualization of how suicidal ideation and intention develop. When an individual experiences defeat or humiliation, threat-to-self moderators (e.g., cognitive biases and hopelessness) can lead them to feel trapped. Defeat and humiliation are often associated with acute or chronic stressors that the individual feels they have not or are unable to resolve successfully, and these stressors interact with background factors and the environment of the individual's life. Motivational moderators, such as lack of connectedness, perceived burdensomeness, or thwarted belongingness, can then lead that individual to seriously consider suicide.

NSSI is associated with self-criticism cross-sectionally (Burke et al., 2020; Gilbert et al., 2010; Itzhaky et al., 2016; Zelkowitz & Cole, 2019) and longitudinally (Perkins et al., 2020). Self-criticism has also been shown to mediate the relationship between childhood emotional abuse (Glassman et al., 2007) and perceived parental expressed emotion (Ammerman & Brown, 2018) and engagement in NSSI. Improving feelings of self-worth has been shown to reduce pain endurance among individuals with a history of NSSI in a laboratory setting (Hooley & St. Germain, 2014). However, one study found that NSSI predicted self-criticism a year later, but self-criticism did not predict later NSSI (Daly & Willoughby, 2019). Thus, it is unclear whether self-criticism is a risk factor for both NSSI and suicide or whether NSSI itself increases self-criticism, thereby increasing suicide risk. Self-disgust also appears to differentiate individuals with and without a history of NSSI (Hamza et al., 2021; Smith et al., 2015), as well as individuals with recent NSSI compared to individuals with past NSSI (Smith et al., 2015), but has been less well studied in relation to suicide.

Self-esteem is lower in individuals with a history of NSSI compared to those without in both clinical and nonclinical populations (Forrester et al., 2017). Specifically, lower coping self-efficacy is associated with increased frequency of NSSI among individuals with a history of NSSI (Midkiff et al., 2018) and differentiates individuals with past-year NSSI from individuals with more distal histories of NSSI (Heath et al., 2016). Emotion regulation self-efficacy has shown associations with NSSI frequency in community and clinical samples (Gratz et al., 2020) and lower emotion regulation self-efficacy is also associated with recent NSSI (Spitzen et al., 2022). Emotion regulation self-efficacy may also mediate the relationship between NSSI frequency and suicide attempts (Gratz et al., 2020). Taken together, these results suggest that negative views of oneself *specific to one's ability to cope with negative emotions* may serve as a unique risk factor for both NSSI and suicide.

The association between NSSI and negative self-views is further supported by research on NSSI functions (see Taylor et al., this volume). In fact, more than half (51%) of people who engage in NSSI report doing so as a means of self-punishment (Taylor et al., 2018), and higher self-punishment cognitions differentiate individuals with a history of NSSI from individuals with no history of NSSI (Burke et al., 2020). Using NSSI to cope with self-hatred is also associated with suicide attempts (Paul et al., 2015).

Theoretical Models of Suicide Capability

Suicide capability has been conceptualized as driven by individual differences in personality, habituation to injury and pain, and practical capability, such as access to lethal means.

Personality and Individual Differences

The interpersonal theory of suicide (Joiner, 2005) argues that a lethal or near-lethal suicide attempt occurs only when there is acquired capability for suicide, in addition to suicidal desire. Acquired capability for suicide consists of fearlessness about death and increased pain tolerance. Suicide attempts are difficult to enact, due to both the human instinct to survive and the physical pain associated with killing oneself. Being able to transition from suicidal desire to suicide attempt thus takes a certain fearlessness about death. This reduced fear of mortality includes stoicism about the fact of one's death, lack of fear about death itself or the pain of dying, and lack of anxiety about the concept of death or talking about death (Ribeiro et al., 2014). While fearlessness about death is associated with making a suicide attempt, increased pain tolerance is associated with the medical lethality of an attempt (Van Orden et al., 2010).

The three-step theory (Klonsky & May, 2015) broadens the concept of capability for suicide to encompass three categories: acquired, dispositional, and practical. While acquired capability is the same construct proposed by Joiner (2005), dispositional capability refers to genetic or temperamental traits that remain unchanged by life circumstances, such as harm avoidance, pain sensitivity, and personality traits (Anestis et al., 2018). Dispositional factors may act directly on suicide risk, such that an individual with high pain sensitivity would be less likely to attempt suicide due to aversion to physical pain, or they may act indirectly, such that an individual with high sensation-seeking may have higher capability by virtue of higher likelihood of exposure to painful and provocative events (May & Victor, 2018). However, there is relatively little work investigating the role of dispositional capability for suicide.

The integrated motivational-volitional model (O'Connor & Kirtley, 2018) incorporates previously theorized capability factors as volitional moderators that facilitate the transition from suicidal ideation to suicidal behavior. These moderators include access to lethal means, suicide planning, exposure to suicidal behavior, impulsivity, pain sensitivity, fearlessness about death, mental imagery or rehearsal, and past suicidal behavior. While the operational definition of impulsivity has little consensus (May & Klonsky, 2016), the model conceptualizes impulsivity as acting on "the spur of the moment" without considerable forethought or planning of the suicide attempt.

Impulsivity is associated with NSSI cross-sectionally and prospectively (Fox et al., 2015; Hamza et al., 2015). However, the association between impulsivity and NSSI is most consistent for self-report measures of negative urgency and less reliable for other measures of impulsivity, including lab-based measures (Hamza et al., 2015). Some evidence suggests that different types of impulsivity may relate to different aspects of NSSI; one study found that negative urgency predicted the onset of NSSI during the first year of college, while lack of perseverance predicted maintenance of NSSI (Riley et al., 2015). The literature on fearlessness about death in relation to NSSI is similarly mixed. For example, fearlessness about death differentiated between adolescents with and without

NSSI in one study (Krantz et al., 2021) but was not associated with NSSI frequency in undergraduate students in another study (Brackman et al., 2016).

Exposure and Habituation to Injury and Pain

According to the interpersonal theory of suicide (Joiner, 2005), acquired capability for suicide develops through repeated exposure to painful and provocative events. Through habituation and opponent processes, painful and provocative events result in lessened fear of the pain associated with a suicide attempt and amplification of the opponent process (e.g., exhilaration) involved in dangerous or risky activities. Painful and provocative events are defined as events that are either physically painful or frightening, and they can include such proximal events as imagining one's suicide death or engaging in preparation or rehearsal for an eventual suicide attempt, as well as distal events like childhood maltreatment, combat exposure, risky behaviors, or NSSI itself. These experiences decrease fears about death (see above) as well as potentially increasing pain tolerance and acceptability.

The integrated motivational-volitional model (O'Connor & Kirtley, 2018) lists exposure to suicide as a social volitional moderator. Suicidal behaviors by loved ones may become a model for how to enact a suicide attempt or for problem-solving seemingly hopeless situations. Additionally, exposure to suicide may result in cognitive accessibility of suicide as an option. Social learning is a particular issue with regard to media portrayals of suicide in a positive or glamorized light, making suicide appear to be an attractive option for individuals who are vulnerable.

Painful and provocative events have shown mixed associations with suicide attempts and NSSI. Relationships between childhood abuse/neglect, NSSI, and suicide attempts are relatively well established in the literature (Glassman et al., 2007; McMahon et al., 2018). However, other painful and provocative events have also shown mixed associations with suicide attempts (Bond et al., 2021; Stanley et al., 2020). For example, one study found that while injuries requiring medical attention and using intravenous drugs were associated with a suicide attempt history, behaviors like skydiving and jumping from high places were not associated with suicide attempts, and shooting a gun was actually associated with a lower likelihood of having attempted suicide (Bond et al., 2021). While certain painful or provocative experiences may increase risk for suicide or NSSI, these experiences may need to be considered individually rather than as a group of similar risk factors, and may differ in the extent to which they influence pain tolerance, one theorized component of suicide capability.

With respect to NSSI itself, indicators of greater severity or exposure to NSSI have shown robust associations with suicidal behaviors. Greater NSSI frequency, greater number of NSSI methods, and earlier age of onset of NSSI are linked to increased risk for suicide attempts (Andover & Gibb, 2010; Kiekens et al., 2018; Matney et al., 2018; Muehlenkamp et al., 2019; Paul et al., 2015; Victor & Klonsky, 2014). More medically severe NSSI methods may also be associated with risk for suicide attempts (Stewart et al.,

2017). Pain tolerance may be higher among individuals who engage in NSSI, although associations between NSSI and specific aspects of pain tolerance (e.g., pain persistence and pain threshold) have been mixed (Law et al., 2017; St. Germain & Hooley, 2013; Tuna & Gençöz, 2021; van der Venne et al., 2021).

Evidence suggests that both NSSI and suicide may involve social contagion (see Jarvi et al., this volume), including imitation or clustering of behaviors, which may be associated with increased suicide capability. A 2015 meta-analysis found that exposure to peer NSSI significantly predicted later NSSI, with a weighted odds ratio of 2.13 (Fox et al., 2015). Among adolescents in an inpatient psychiatric unit, exposure to specific NSSI methods was associated with greater likelihood of use of that method (Zhu et al., 2016). Research on suicide contagion has focused largely on media reporting of suicide deaths. A meta-analysis of media reporting and suicide deaths found that suicides increased by 13% after media reports of a celebrity death by suicide, but no increase following non-celebrity suicide deaths (Niederkrotenthaler et al., 2020). A 2020 meta-analysis found that exposure to suicide attempts or suicide death was associated with greater odds of suicidal behavior, but the pattern of finding was not consistent across suicide-related outcomes (suicidal thoughts, suicide attempt, or suicide death; Hill et al., 2020). Research on suicide clusters has proposed possible risk factors and mechanisms (e.g., contagion, imitation, and learning) for suicide in these contexts, but studies have been limited by methodological problems and there is limited evidence for proposed mechanisms (Haw et al., 2013). Unfortunately, studies of NSSI clustering or contagion are even more sparse. Thus, further work is needed to understand how social learning may relate to suicide capability in the context of NSSI.

Practical Capability and Access to Lethal Means
Practical capability in the three-step theory (Klonsky & May, 2015) and integrated motivational-volitional model (O'Connor & Kirtley, 2018) refers to concrete factors that facilitate a suicide attempt, which can include knowledge of and ready access to lethal means. Individuals who, through research, their occupation, exposure, or other circumstance, are aware of how to use a specific method are more likely to engage in a suicide attempt. For instance, veterinary professionals are at elevated risk of suicide, which may be due to exposure to, and familiarity with, medications used for veterinary euthanasia (Tomasi et al., 2019). Practical capability may also occur through availability, such as in the case of firearms; handgun ownership is associated with predicted suicidal behavior, which in turn is predictive of actual suicidal behavior (Houtsma & Anestis, 2017).

The most commonly reported NSSI methods are cutting and scratching (Brausch et al., 2016; Klonsky, 2011; Plener et al., 2009; Saraff & Pepper, 2014). In contrast, the most common suicide attempt method is overdose (Andover & Gibb, 2010; Brausch et al., 2016), and the most common method of death by suicide in the United States is a firearm (Drapeau & McIntosh, 2020). Even among individuals with a history of both NSSI and suicide attempt, individuals may use different methods for NSSI and suicide attempts (Brausch et al., 2016). Thus, knowledge of NSSI or the availability of NSSI methods is unlikely to serve as a significant contributor to suicide attempts, although further research is needed in this domain.

Challenges, Recommendations, and Future Directions
Ample research shows that NSSI is an important risk factor for suicidal thoughts and behaviors. Prior work has been limited, however, by a reliance on cross-sectional approaches, which can tell us how constructs are related but not the underlying mechanisms contributing to those relationships. For example, NSSI has been associated with a number of known risk factors for suicidal ideation, such as rumination (Selby et al., 2013), hopelessness (Jiang et al., 2018), limited interpersonal connections or supports (Trepal et al., 2015), and negative views of oneself (Burke et al., 2020). Longitudinal research has implicated many of these experiences in predicting later NSSI, suggesting that they also serve as indicators of risk for NSSI onset and maintenance. Thus, the association between NSSI and suicidal ideation may be attributable, at least in part, to shared etiological factors that increase risk for both experiences over time.

However, it is also possible that NSSI itself exacerbates or contributes to these experiences in meaningful ways, such that NSSI contributes to risk of suicidal thoughts through (mediated by) other experiences. For instance, NSSI prospectively predicts increases in self-criticism (Daly & Willoughby, 2019), which may be driven by the shame and guilt one feels about engaging in NSSI, or by negative reactions to NSSI disclosures from others (Park & Ammerman, 2020). Thus, NSSI not only may serve as a marker of other risk factors, but also may itself confer suicide risk due to the negative intrapersonal and interpersonal consequences of NSSI.

With respect to the association between NSSI and suicidal behavior, results are far from clear. Trait-like risk factors for suicidal behavior include impulsivity and fearlessness about death, both of which have shown inconsistent relationships to NSSI. NSSI may be most strongly associated with negative urgency, the tendency to behave impulsively when experiencing negative emotions (Hamza et al., 2015), which has also been shown to relate to suicide (Anestis & Joiner, 2011); however, whether NSSI itself changes the experience of negative urgency in a way that would contribute to suicide risk is unclear. There is some longitudinal evidence that more frequent NSSI precedes increased capability for suicide, as indexed by fearlessness about death and decreased self-reported pain sensitivity (Willoughby et al., 2015), but the mechanisms underlying this relationship remain unexamined. Similarly, little research has directly examined how NSSI experiences may influence access to, and awareness of, lethal means for suicide in ways that could potentially change risk for suicidal behavior and/or death.

The most plausible and well-supported relationship between NSSI and suicidal capability is through habituation to pain and self-directed violence. Robust evidence shows that increased NSSI engagement, such as a higher frequency of NSSI or more versatile use of different NSSI methods, increases risk for suicidal behavior (Matney et al., 2018; Victor & Klonsky, 2014); there is also evidence that NSSI is associated with increased pain tolerance and endurance (Koenig et al., 2016), with the most pronounced effects specific to willingness to tolerate painful stimuli rather than the perception of pain intensity (Law et al., 2017; St. Germain & Hooley, 2013). Thus, NSSI may function to change one's comfort with, and willingness to experience, pain and injury, which could then decrease evolutionary and sociocultural barriers to engaging in suicidal behavior.

Relevance to Clinical Practice

NSSI is now well established as an indicator of risk for suicide. Thus, it is essential to assess for NSSI when working with clients experiencing suicidal thoughts or behaviors *as well as* to assess for suicide risk when working with clients who engage in NSSI. NSSI may indicate the presence of other, shared risk factors for suicidal thoughts (hopelessness, cognitive biases, social difficulties, negative self-views), and may also exacerbate these problems through intrapersonal (e.g., feelings of shame and guilt; see Fox, this volume) and interpersonal (e.g., negative reactions from others; see Zetterqvist & Bjureberg, this volume) mechanisms. NSSI may also be indicative of underlying risk processes relevant to the transition from suicidal thoughts to behaviors, such as elevated impulsivity, increased pain tolerance, and exposure to NSSI and suicidal behaviors in others. Of greatest import, NSSI appears to be associated with increased habituation to pain and self-inflicted injury, which may decrease barriers to engaging in suicidal behavior among those at risk. Thus, understanding the severity and extent of NSSI (e.g., frequency, recency, number and types of methods used, and functions) is critical to explicate and address suicide risk among people with a history of NSSI. Further, when assessing and responding to experiences that serve as shared risk factors for both NSSI and suicide, it is valuable for clinicians to ask clients to what extent they view these difficulties as contributing to their experiences of NSSI, suicidal thoughts or behaviors, or both, to identify the most appropriate intervention targets.

Because of the association between NSSI and suicide, some argue that stopping NSSI must be a primary treatment target when working with clients at risk. However, it is critical to note that some individuals use NSSI as a coping strategy to avoid suicide (Kraus et al., 2020), and no research has been conducted to suggest that stopping NSSI is itself an effective suicide prevention strategy. As a result, requiring or obligating a client to cease NSSI may be counterproductive in the short-term prevention of suicide.

Much of the research examining associations between NSSI and suicidal thoughts and behaviors has used cross-sectional approaches that consider these experiences over the course of one's life. As a result, we know comparatively little about how suicide risk changes over time after someone stops engaging in NSSI. For instance, does suicide risk decrease immediately following NSSI cessation, or does risk decline slowly over time?

Does the presence of continued urges for NSSI, even without NSSI behaviors, serve as an indicator of suicide risk? Or, is any lifetime history of NSSI a marker of elevated risk regardless of the time since a person last self-injured, in the same way that adverse childhood experiences confer risk for negative psychosocial outcomes throughout the lifespan? Because these remain open questions in the literature, it is critical to engage in regular suicide risk assessment and crisis planning for clients with any history of NSSI, regardless of whether the person is engaging in NSSI at the time of treatment.

Conclusion

Taken together, these results highlight the lack of clarity with respect to how NSSI fits into extant theoretical models of suicide. In particular, longitudinal research is needed to understand whether and how NSSI serves as a *marker* of other indicators of risk, an *independent risk factor* for suicidal behavior, or both. Crucially, work is needed not only to understand how NSSI as an overarching category relates to suicide but how specific components of the experience of NSSI (urges, behaviors, recency, functions) contribute to, or protect against, suicidal thoughts and behaviors, and how changes in these phenomena increase or decrease suicide risk over time.

References

Abramson, L. Y., Metalsky, G. I., & Alloy, L. B. (1989). Hopelessness depression: A theory- based subtype of depression. *Psychological Review, 96*(2), 358–372. https://doi.org/gxf

Ammerman, B. A., & Brown, S. (2018). The mediating role of self-criticism in the relationship between parental expressed emotion and NSSI. *Current Psychology, 37*(1), 325–333. https://doi.org/10.1007/s12144-016-9516-1

Andover, M. S., & Gibb, B. E. (2010). Non-suicidal self-injury, attempted suicide, and suicidal intent among psychiatric inpatients. *Psychiatry Research, 178*(1), 101–105. https://doi.org/10.1016/j.psychres.2010.03.019

Anestis, J. C., Anestis, M. D., & Preston, O. C. (2018). Psychopathic personality traits as a form of dispositional capability for suicide. *Psychiatry Research, 262*, 193–202. https://doi.org/10.1016/j.psychres.2018.02.003

Anestis, M. D., & Joiner, T. E. (2011). Examining the role of emotion in suicidality: Negative urgency as an amplifier of the relationship between components of the interpersonal-psychological theory of suicidal behavior and lifetime number of suicide attempts. *Journal of Affective Disorders, 129*(1–3), 261–269. https://doi.org/10/b7cxtb

Assavedo, B. L., & Anestis, M. D. (2015). The relationship between non-suicidal self-injury and both perceived burdensomeness and thwarted belongingness. *Journal of Psychopathology and Behavioral Assessment, 38*, 251–257. https://doi.org/10/gdcgnq

Barrocas, A. L., Giletta, M., Hankin, B. L., Prinstein, M. J., & Abela, J. R. Z. (2015). Nonsuicidal self-injury in adolescence: Longitudinal course, trajectories, and intrapersonal predictors. *Journal of Abnormal Child Psychology, 43*, 369–380. https://doi.org/10/f63bpr

Baumeister, R. F. (1990). Suicide as escape from self. *Psychological Bulletin, 97*(1), 90–113. https://doi.org/10/bpntdx

Beck, A. T., Brown, G., Berchick, R. J., Stewart, B. L., & Steer, R. A. (1990). Relationship between hopelessness and ultimate suicide: A replication with psychiatric outpatients. *The American Journal of Psychiatry, 147*(2), 190–195. https://doi.org/gd3vf2

Bond, A. E., Bandel, S. L., Daruwala, S. E., & Anestis, M. D. (2021). Painful and provocative events: Determining which events are associated with increased odds of attempting suicide. *Suicide and Life-Threatening Behavior, 51*(5), 961–968. https://doi.org/10.1111/sltb.12781

Brackman, E. H., Morris, B. W., & Andover, M. S. (2016). Predicting risk for suicide: A preliminary examination of non-suicidal self-injury and the acquired capability construct in a college sample. *Archives of Suicide Research, 20*(4), 663–676. https://doi.org/10/gdcgrb

Brausch, A. M., Williams, A. G., & Cox, E. M. (2016). Examining intent to die and methods for nonsuicidal self-injury and suicide attempts. *Suicide and Life-Threatening Behavior, 46*(6), 737–744. https://doi.org/10/f9dqgf

Brausch, A. M., & Woods, S. E. (2019). Emotion regulation deficits and nonsuicidal self-injury prospectively predict suicide ideation in adolescents. *Suicide and Life-Threatening Behavior, 49*(3), 868–880. https://doi.org/10/gdpfgc

Burke, T. A., Fox, K., Kautz, M. M., Rodriguez-Seijas, C., Bettis, A. H., & Alloy, L. B. (2020). Self-critical and self-punishment cognitions differentiate those with and without a history of nonsuicidal self-injury: An ecological momentary assessment study. *Behavior Therapy, 52*(3), 686–697. https://doi.org/10/ghrpw8

Chu, C., Rogers, M. L., & Joiner, T. E. (2016). Cross-sectional and temporal association between non-suicidal self-injury and suicidal ideation in young adults: The explanatory roles of thwarted belongingness and perceived burdensomeness. *Psychiatry Research, 246*, 573–580. https://doi.org/10/gdcgmm

Daly, O., & Willoughby, T. (2019). A longitudinal study investigating bidirectionality among nonsuicidal self-injury, self-criticism, and parental criticism. *Psychiatry Research, 271*, 678–683. https://doi.org/10/gfzfhz

Drapeau, C. W., & McIntosh, J. L. (2020). *U.S.A. suicide: 2018 Official final data.* American Association of Suicidology. https://suicidology.org/wp-content/uploads/2020/02/2018datapgsv2_Final.pdf

Forrester, R. L., Slater, H., Jomar, K., Mitzman, S., & Taylor, P. J. (2017). Self-esteem and non-suicidal self-injury in adulthood: A systematic review. *Journal of Affective Disorders, 221*, 172–183. https://doi.org/10.1016/j.jad.2017.06.027

Fox, K. R., Franklin, J. C., Ribeiro, J. D., Kleiman, E. M., Bentley, K. H., & Nock, M. K. (2015). Meta-analysis of risk factors for nonsuicidal self-injury. *Clinical Psychology Review, 42*, 156–167. https://doi.org/10.1016/j.cpr.2015.09.002

Gandhi, A., Luyckx, K., Goossens, L., Maitra, S., & Claes, L. (2018). Association between non-suicidal self-injury, parents and peers related loneliness, and attitude towards aloneness in Flemish adolescents: An empirical note. *Psychologica Belgica, 58*(1), 3–12. https://doi.org/10.5334/pb.385

Gilbert, P., McEwan, K., Irons, C., Bhundia, R., Christie, R., Broomhead, C., & Rockliff, H. (2010). Self-harm in a mixed clinical population: The roles of self-criticism, shame, and social rank. *British Journal of Clinical Psychology, 49*(4), 563–576. https://doi.org/10.1348/014466509X479771

Giletta, M., Scholte, R. H. J., Engels, R. C. M. E., Ciairano, S., & Prinstein, M. J. (2012). Adolescent non-suicidal self-injury: A cross-national study of community samples from Italy, the Netherlands and the United States. *Psychiatry Research, 197*(1–2), 66–72. https://doi.org/10.1016/j.psychres.2012.02.009

Glassman, L. H., Weierich, M. R., Hooley, J. M., Deliberto, T. L., & Nock, M. K. (2007). Child maltreatment, non-suicidal self-injury, and the mediating role of self-criticism. *Behaviour Research and Therapy, 45*(10), 2483–2490. https://doi.org/10/ch8k2j

Gratz, K. L., Spitzen, T. L., & Tull, M. T. (2020). Expanding our understanding of the relationship between nonsuicidal self-injury and suicide attempts: The roles of emotion regulation self-efficacy and the acquired capability for suicide. *Journal of Clinical Psychology, 76*(9), 1653–1667. https://doi.org/10/ggtq2f

Hamza, C. A., Goldstein, A. L., Heath, N. L., & Ewing, L. (2021). Stressful experiences in university predict non-suicidal self-injury through emotional reactivity. *Frontiers in Psychology, 12*, Article 610670. https://doi.org/10.3389/fpsyg.2021.610670

Hamza, C. A., Willoughby, T., & Heffer, T. (2015). Impulsivity and nonsuicidal self-injury: A review and meta-analysis. *Clinical Psychology Review, 38*, 13–24. https://doi.org/10/f7fmvw

Haw, C., Hawton, K., Niedzwiedz, C., & Platt, S. (2013). Suicide clusters: A review of risk factors and mechanisms. *Suicide and Life-Threatening Behavior, 43*(1), 97–108. https://doi.org/10.1111/j.1943-278X.2012.00130.x

Heath, N. L., Joly, M., & Carsley, D. (2016). Coping self-efficacy and mindfulness in non-suicidal self-injury. *Mindfulness, 7*(5), 1132–1141. https://doi.org/10/f83dk2

Hill, N. T. M., Robinson, J., Pirkis, J., Andriessen, K., Krysinska, K., Payne, A., Boland, A., Clarke, A., Milner, A., Witt, K., Krohn, S., & Lampit, A. (2020). Association of suicidal behavior with exposure to suicide and suicide attempt: A systematic review and multilevel meta-analysis. *PLOS Medicine, 17*(3), Article 1003074. https://doi.org/ggtq2c

Hooley, J. M., & St. Germain, S. A. (2014). Nonsuicidal self-injury, pain, and self-criticism: Does changing self-worth change pain endurance in people who engage in self-injury? *Clinical Psychological Science, 2*(3), 297–305. https://doi.org/10/gdcg5j

Houtsma, C., & Anestis, M. D. (2017). Practical capability: The impact of handgun ownership among suicide attempt survivors. *Psychiatry Research, 258*, 88–92. https://doi.org/10.1016/j.psychres.2017.09.064

International Society for the Study of Self-Injury. (2018). *What is nonsuicidal self-injury?* ISSS. https://itriples.org/category/about-self-injury/

Itzhaky, L., Shahar, G., Stein, D., & Fennig, S. (2016). In eating-disordered inpatient adolescents, self-criticism predicts nonsuicidal self-injury. *Suicide and Life-Threatening Behavior, 46*(4), 385–397. https://doi.org/10/f88kc8

Jiang, Y., Ren, Y., Liang, Q., & You, J. (2018). The moderating role of trait hope in the association between adolescent depressive symptoms and nonsuicidal self-injury. *Personality and Individual Differences, 135*, 137–142. https://doi.org/10/gfj6c3

Joiner, T. (2005). *Why people die by suicide.* Harvard University Press.

Kiekens, G., Hasking, P., Boyes, M., Claes, L., Mortier, P., Auerbach, R. P., Cuijpers, P., Demyttenaere, K., Green, J. G., Kessler, R. C., Myin-Germeys, I., Nock, M. K., & Bruffaerts, R. (2018). The associations between non-suicidal self-injury and first onset suicidal thoughts and behaviors. *Journal of Affective Disorders, 239*, 171–179. https://doi.org/10.1016/j.jad.2018.06.033

Klonsky, E. D. (2011). Non-suicidal self-injury in United States adults: Prevalence, sociodemographics, topography and functions. *Psychological Medicine, 41*(9), 1981–1986. https://doi.org/10.1017/S0033291710002497

Klonsky, E. D., & May, A. M. (2015). The three-step theory (3ST): A new theory of suicide rooted in the ideation-to-action framework. *International Journal of Cognitive Therapy, 8*(2), 114–129. https://doi.org/f7j7c6

Klonsky, E. D., Saffer, B. Y., & Bryan, C. J. (2018). Ideation-to-action theories of suicide: A conceptual and empirical update. *Current Opinion in Psychology, 22*, 38–43. https://doi.org/10/gd3vjd

Koenig, J., Thayer, J. F., & Kaess, M. (2016). A meta-analysis on pain sensitivity in self-injury. *Psychological Medicine, 46*(8), 1597–1612. https://doi.org/10/f8mhkh

Krantz, S. M., Yang, X., King, J., Kennard, B. D., Emslie, G. J., & Stewart, S. M. (2021). Validation of Fearlessness about Death Scale in adolescents. *Psychological Assessment.* https://doi.org/10.1037/pas0001035

Kraus, L., Schmid, M., & In-Albon, T. (2020). Anti-suicide function of nonsuicidal self-injury in female inpatient adolescents. *Frontiers in Psychiatry, 11*, Article 490. https://doi.org/gp3v

Law, K. C., Khazem, L. R., Jin, H. M., & Anestis, M. D. (2017). Non-suicidal self-injury and frequency of suicide attempts: The role of pain persistence. *Journal of Affective Disorders, 209*, 254–261. https://doi.org/10.1016/j.jad.2016.11.028

Lucas, A. G., Chang, E. C., Li, M., Chang, O. D., & Hirsch, J. K. (2019). Perfectionism and social problem solving as predictors of nonsuicidal self-injury in ethnoracially diverse college students: Findings controlling for concomitant suicide risk. *Social Work, 64*(2), 165–174. https://doi.org/10/gf246w

Matney, J., Westers, N. J., Horton, S. E., King, J. D., Eaddy, M., Emslie, G. J., Kennard, B. D., & Stewart, S. M. (2018). Frequency and methods of nonsuicidal self-injury in relation to acquired capability for suicide among adolescents. *Archives of Suicide Research, 22*(1), 91–105. https://doi.org/10/gdcgjg

May, A. M., & Klonsky, E. D. (2016). "Impulsive" suicide attempts: What do we really mean? *Personality Disorders: Theory, Research, and Treatment, 7*(3), 293–302. https://doi.org/10.1037/per0000160

May, A. M., & Victor, S. E. (2018). From ideation to action: Recent advances in understanding suicide capability. *Current Opinion in Psychology, 22*, 1–6. https://doi.org/10/gdcgjm

McMahon, K., Hoertel, N., Olfson, M., Wall, M., Wang, S., & Blanco, C. (2018). Childhood maltreatment and impulsivity as predictors of interpersonal violence, self-injury and suicide attempts: A national study. *Psychiatry Research, 269*, 386–393. https://doi.org/10/gfpg33

Midkiff, M. F., Lindsey, C. R., & Meadows, E. A. (2018). The role of coping self-efficacy in emotion regulation and frequency of NSSI in young adult college students. *Cogent Psychology, 5*(1), Article 1520437. https://doi.org/10.1080/23311908.2018.1520437

Muehlenkamp, J., Brausch, A., Quigley, K., & Whitlock, J. (2013). Interpersonal features and functions of nonsuicidal self-injury. *Suicide and Life-Threatening Behavior, 43*(1), 67–80. https://doi.org/10/f4kkxr

Muehlenkamp, J. J., Xhunga, N., & Brausch, A. M. (2019). Self-injury age of onset: A risk factor for NSSI severity and suicidal behavior. *Archives of Suicide Research, 23*(4), 551–563. https://doi.org/10/gdshq2

Niederkrotenthaler, T., Braun, M., Pirkis, J., Till, B., Stack, S., Sinyor, M., Tran, U. S., Voracek, M., Cheng, Q., Arendt, F., Scherr, S., Yip, P. S. F., & Spittal, M. J. (2020). Association between suicide reporting in the media and suicide: Systematic review and meta-analysis. *Britisch Medical Journal*, 2020, Article m575. https://doi.org/10.1136/bmj.m575

Nolen-Hoeksema, S. (1991). Responses to depression and their effects on the duration of depressive episodes. *Journal of Abnormal Psychology*, *100*(4), 569–582. https://doi.org/cpds2q

O'Connor, R. C., & Kirtley, O. J. (2018). The integrated motivational-volitional model of suicidal behaviour. *Philosophical Transactions of the Royal Society B*, *373*(1754), Article 20170268. https://doi.org/10.1098/rstb.2017.0268

Park, Y., & Ammerman, B. A. (2020). How should we respond to non-suicidal self-injury disclosures?: An examination of perceived reactions to disclosure, depression, and suicide risk. *Psychiatry Research*, *293*, Article 113430. https://doi.org/10/ghrksj

Park, Y., Mahdy, J. C., & Ammerman, B. A. (2021). How others respond to non-suicidal self-injury disclosure: A systematic review. *Journal of Community & Applied Social Psychology*, *31*(1), 107–119. https://doi.org/10.1002/casp.2478

Paul, E., Tsypes, A., Eidlitz, L., Ernhout, C., & Whitlock, J. (2015). Frequency and functions of non-suicidal self-injury: Associations with suicidal thoughts and behaviors. *Psychiatry Research*, *225*(3), 276–282. https://doi.org/10/f63xnj

Perkins, N. M., Ortiz, S. N., & Smith, A. R. (2020). Self-criticism longitudinally predicts nonsuicidal self-injury in eating disorders. *Eating Disorders*, *28*(2), 157–170. https://doi.org/10/ggf2nd

Plener, P. L., Libal, G., Keller, F., Fegert, J. M., & Muehlenkamp, J. J. (2009). An international comparison of adolescent non-suicidal self-injury (NSSI) and suicide attempts: Germany and the USA. *Psychological Medicine*, *39*(9), 1549–1558. https://doi.org/10.1017/S0033291708005114

Ribeiro, J. D., Franklin, J. C., Fox, K. R., Bentley, K. H., Kleiman, E. M., Chang, B. P., & Nock, M. K. (2016). Self-injurious thoughts and behaviors as risk factors for future suicide ideation, attempts, and death: A meta-analysis of longitudinal studies. *Psychological Medicine*, *46*(2), 225–236. https://doi.org/10/f84cbj

Ribeiro, J. D., Witte, T. K., Van Orden, K. A., Selby, E. A., Gordon, K. H., Bender, T. W., & Joiner, T. E. (2014). Fearlessness about death: The psychometric properties and construct validity of the revision to the Acquired Capability for Suicide Scale. *Psychological Assessment*, *26*(1), 115–126. https://doi.org/10.1037/a0034858

Riley, E. N., Combs, J. L., Jordan, C. E., & Smith, G. T. (2015). Negative urgency and lack of perseverance: Identification of differential pathways of onset and maintenance risk in the longitudinal prediction of non-suicidal self-injury. *Behavior Therapy*, *46*(4), 439–448. https://doi.org/10/f7mgrb

Saraff, P. D., & Pepper, C. M. (2014). Functions, lifetime frequency, and variety of methods of non-suicidal self-injury among college students. *Psychiatry Research*, *219*(2), 298–304. https://doi.org/10.1016/j.psychres.2014.05.044

Schotte, D. E., & Clum, G. A. (1987). Problem-solving skills in suicidal psychiatric patients. *Journal of Consulting and Clinical Psychology*, *55*(1), 49–54. https://doi.org/10.1037/0022-006X.55.1.49

Selby, E. A., Franklin, J., Carson-Wong, A., & Rizvi, S. L. (2013). Emotional cascades and self-injury: Investigating instability of rumination and negative emotion. *Journal of Clinical Psychology*, *69*(12), 1213–1227. https://doi.org/10/f5ftg3

Shneidman, E. S. (1993). Suicide as psychache. *The Journal of Nervous and Mental Disease*, *181*(3), 145–147. https://doi.org/10/c3k3rn

Smith, N. B., Steele, A. M., Weitzman, M. L., Trueba, A. F., & Meuret, A. E. (2015). Investigating the role of self-disgust in nonsuicidal self-injury. *Archives of Suicide Research*, *19*(1), 60–74. https://doi.org/10/gdcg3v

Spitzen, T. L., Tull, M. T., & Gratz, K. L. (2022). The roles of emotion regulation self-efficacy and emotional avoidance in self-injurious thoughts and behaviors. *Archives of Suicide Research*, *26*(2), 595–613. https://doi.org/10.1080/13811118.2020.1818654

St. Germain, S. A., & Hooley, J. M. (2013). Aberrant pain perception in direct and indirect non-suicidal self-injury: An empirical test of Joiner's interpersonal theory. *Comprehensive Psychiatry*, *54*(6), 694–701. https://doi.org/f45tzx

Stanley, I. H., Hom, M. A., Gallyer, A. J., Gray, J. S., & Joiner, T. E. (2020). Suicidal behaviors among American Indian/Alaska Native firefighters: Evidence for the role of painful and provocative events. *Transcultural Psychiatry*, *57*(2), 275–287. https://doi.org/10.1177/1363461519847812

Steinhoff, A., Bechtiger, L., Ribeaud, D., Eisner, M., & Shanahan, L. (2020). Stressful life events in different social contexts are associated with self-injury from early adolescence to early adulthood. *Frontiers in Psychiatry, 11*, Article 487200. https://doi.org/10/ghrkr3

Stewart, J. G., Esposito, E. C., Glenn, C. R., Gilman, S. E., Pridgen, B., Gold, J., & Auerbach, R. P. (2017). Adolescent self-injurers: Comparing non-ideators, suicide ideators, and suicide attempters. *Journal of Psychiatric Research, 84*, 105–112. https://doi.org/10.1016/j.jpsychires.2016.09.031

Tanner, A. K., Hasking, P., & Martin, G. (2014). Effects of rumination and optimism on the relationship between psychological distress and non-suicidal self-injury. *Prevention Science, 15*, 860–868. https://doi.org/10/f6ps9j

Taylor, P. J., Jomar, K., Dhingra, K., Forrester, R., Shahmalak, U., & Dickson, J. M. (2018). A meta-analysis of the prevalence of different functions of non-suicidal self-injury. *Journal of Affective Disorders, 227*, 759–769. https://doi.org/10/gc2skk

Tomasi, S. E., Fechter-Leggett, E. D., Edwards, N. T, Reddish, A. D., Crosby, A. E., & Nett, R. J. (2019). Suicide among veterinarians in the United States from 1979 through 2015. *Journal of the American Veterinary Medical Association, 254*(1), 104–112. https://doi.org/10.2460/javma.254.1.104

Trepal, H. C., Wester, K. L., & Merchant, E. (2015). A cross-sectional matched sample study of nonsuicidal self-injury among young adults: Support for interpersonal and intrapersonal factors, with implications for coping strategies. *Child and Adolescent Psychiatry and Mental Health, 9*, 36. https://doi.org/10/f8b68c

Tuna, E., & Gençöz, T. (2021). Pain perception, distress tolerance and self-compassion in Turkish young adults with and without a history of non-suicidal self-injury. *Current Psychology, 40*, 4143–4155. https://doi.org/10.1007/s12144-020-00634-2

Turner, B. J., Cobb, R. J., Gratz, K. L., & Chapman, A. L. (2016). The role of interpersonal conflict and perceived social support in nonsuicidal self-injury in daily life. *Journal of Abnormal Psychology, 125*(4), 588–598. https://doi.org/10/f8kfd5

Turner, B. J., Wakefield, M. A., Gratz, K. L., & Chapman, A. L. (2017). Characterizing interpersonal difficulties among young adults who engage in nonsuicidal self-injury using a daily diary. *Behavior Therapy, 48*(3), 366–379. https://doi.org/10/f96hbw

van der Venne, P., Balint, A., Drews, E., Parzer, P., Resch, F., Koenig, J., & Kaess, M. (2021). Pain sensitivity and plasma beta-endorphin in adolescent non-suicidal self-injury. *Journal of Affective Disorders, 278*, 199–208. https://doi.org/gp3w

van Geel, M., Goemans, A., & Vedder, P. (2015). A meta-analysis on the relation between peer victimization and adolescent non-suicidal self-injury. *Psychiatry Research, 230*(2), 364–368. https://doi.org/10/f74jpp

Van Orden, K. A., Cukrowicz, K. C., Witte, T. K., & Joiner, T. E. (2012). Thwarted belongingness and perceived burdensomeness: Construct validity and psychometric properties of the Interpersonal Needs Questionnaire. *Psychological Assessment, 24*(1), 197–215. https://doi.org/10/ft6h58

Van Orden, K. A., Witte, T. K., Cukrowicz, K. C., Braithwaite, S. R., Selby, E. A., & Joiner, T. E. (2010). The interpersonal theory of suicide. *Psychological Review, 117*, 575–600. https://doi.org/10/b44zs2

Victor, S. E., Hipwell, A. E., Stepp, S. D., & Scott, L. N. (2019). Parent and peer relationships as longitudinal predictors of adolescent non-suicidal self-injury onset. *Child and Adolescent Psychiatry and Mental Health, 13*, 1. https://doi.org/10/gfst9t

Victor, S. E., & Klonsky, E. D. (2014). Correlates of suicide attempts among self-injurers: A meta-analysis. *Clinical Psychology Review, 34*(4), 282–297. https://doi.org/f56b82

Victor, S. E., Scott, L. N., Stepp, S. D., & Goldstein, T. R. (2019). I want you to want me: Interpersonal stress and affective experiences as within-person predictors of nonsuicidal self-injury and suicide urges in daily life. Suicide and Life-Threatening *Behavior, 49*(4), 1157–1177. https://doi.org/10/gd3z4q

Walker, K. L., Hirsch, J. K., Chang, E. C., & Jeglic, E. L. (2017). Non-suicidal self-injury and suicidal behavior in a diverse sample: The moderating role of social problem-solving ability. *International Journal of Mental Health and Addiction, 15*, 471–484. https://doi.org/10/gdcg7v

Wang, H., Wang, Q., Liu, X., Gao, Y., & Chen, Z. (2020). Prospective interpersonal and intrapersonal predictors of initiation and cessation of non-suicidal self-injury among Chinese adolescents. *International Journal of Environmental Research and Public Health, 17*(24), 9454. https://doi.org/10/ghs86h

Williams, J. M. G. (1997). *Cry of pain: Understanding suicide and self-harm.* Penguin Books.

Willoughby, T., Heffer, T., & Hamza, C. A. (2015). The link between nonsuicidal self-injury and acquired capability for suicide: A longitudinal study. *Journal of Abnormal Psychology, 124*(4), 1110–1115. https://doi.org/10/f72h8c

Zelkowitz, R. L., & Cole, D. A. (2019). Self-criticism as a transdiagnostic process in nonsuicidal self-injury and disordered eating: Systematic review and meta-analysis. *Suicide and Life-Threatening Behavior, 49*(1), 310–327. https://doi.org/10/gc3gqb

Zhu, L., Westers, N. J., Horton, S. E., King, J. D., Diederich, A., Stewart, S. M., & Kennard, B. D. (2016). Frequency of exposure to and engagement in nonsuicidal self-injury among inpatient adolescents. *Archives of Suicide Research, 20*(4), 580–590. https://doi.org/10.1080/13811118.2016.1162240

CHAPTER 6

The Functions of Nonsuicidal Self-Injury

Peter James Taylor, Katie Dhingra, Kelly-Marie Peel-Wainwright, *and* Kathryn Jane Gardner

Abstract

This chapter explores the extant research concerning the functions of nonsuicidal self-injury (NSSI), highlighting the key implications of this work for future research, clinical practice, and prevention. It uses the term "function" to refer to either the self-reported reasons for engaging in NSSI behaviors, or the expected or actual consequences of the behaviors. Many of the functions of NSSI are considered intrapersonal (sometimes called autonomic), focusing on changing or affecting a person's internal states in some way. These include self-injury as a form of affect regulation, helping the person to cope with or reduce emotional distress. In addition to intrapersonal functions, many reported functions of NSSI are interpersonal in nature, involving other people. These include NSSI providing a means to express or communicate the level of distress one is experiencing, or as a way of seeking help from others. It has also been noted that NSSI may act as a means of hurting others. The chapter then outlines implications for future research and clinical practice based on what is known so far about the functions of NSSI.

Key Words: nonsuicidal self-injury, NSSI behaviors, affect regulation, emotional distress, functions of NSSI

Introduction

There is a long history of research and clinical work attempting to understand why some people engage in nonsuicidal self-injury (NSSI). A significant observation that emerges from this work is that NSSI is a *functional* behavior rather than a symptom of mental disorder (Klonsky, 2011; Nock, 2009; Nock & Cha, 2009). That is, self-injury appears to occur with the purpose (whether held consciously or unconsciously) of achieving some goal or end state; it serves a function for the person. This is of course not to say that NSSI always feels like a choice. For example, some people experience their NSSI as akin to an addiction over which they have limited control (Buser & Buser, 2013; although see Victor et al., 2012). However, even in these cases NSSI appears to meet some need(s) in the individual's life. An understanding of NSSI as inherently functional has had a major influence on our understanding of what potentially causes people to engage in NSSI, and in guiding clinical practice and the interventions developed to help those who self-injure.

In this chapter, we aim to provide an overview of the extant research concerning the functions of NSSI and to highlight the major implications of this work for future research, clinical practice, and prevention. In this chapter, *function* is used to refer to either the self-reported reasons for engaging in NSSI behaviors or the expected or actual consequences of the behaviors. We begin by summarizing research concerning the prevalence and structure of different functions of NSSI. We then consider the conceptual insights that are offered by the research into NSSI functions. Finally, we outline implications for future research and clinical practice (including prevention and intervention) based on what we know so far about the functions of these behaviors.

Variety of NSSI Functions

A large body of research has focused on asking individuals who self-injure about the reasons for or functions of this behavior (see reviews by Edmondson et al., 2016; Klonsky, 2007; Suyemoto, 1998). This research has highlighted a wide variety of different functions. Many of these functions are considered intrapersonal (sometimes called autonomic), focusing on changing or affecting a person's internal states in some way. These include self-injury as a form of affect regulation, helping the person to cope with or reduce emotional distress. NSSI is experienced by some as an emotional "release" of pent-up feelings (Stänicke et al., 2018). Some individuals describe NSSI as a means of escaping specific aversive states of awareness, such as a feeling of emotional numbness or periods of dissociation (e.g., allowing the person to feel "something"; Klonsky & Glenn, 2009; Rallis et al., 2020). Relatedly, NSSI may also be a means of generating a positive or desired state, such as producing a rush or period of brief euphoria. Self-punishment (i.e., engaging in NSSI as a way to punish oneself for perceived wrongdoings or personal flaws) is often presented as a distinct function to affect regulation but may still relate to the regulation of internal experiences, perhaps as a means of quelling feelings of shame, guilt, or self-criticism (Hooley & Franklin, 2017; Sheehy et al., 2019). Although NSSI is an established risk factor for subsequent suicidal behavior (Hamza et al., 2012; Ribeiro et al., 2016), some people self-injure explicitly as a way to cope with and resist suicidal feelings (Kraus et al., 2020). It is speculated that NSSI may provide a way of responding to suicidal urges and feelings, without engaging in suicidal behavior, but through various mechanisms, including an increasing acquired capability to harm oneself, the risk of suicidal behavior also grows over time (Hamza et al., 2012; see Victor et al., this volume).

In addition to intrapersonal functions, many reported functions of NSSI are interpersonal in nature, involving other people (Edmondson et al., 2016; Klonsky, 2007; Stänicke et al., 2018; Suyemoto, 1998). These include NSSI providing a means to express or communicate the level of distress one is experiencing, or as a way of seeking help from others. NSSI may also become a form of peer bonding or affiliation (Klonsky & Glenn, 2009; Stänicke et al., 2018). It has been suggested that NSSI may have other communicatory functions, such as to indicate toughness or to keep others (e.g., bullies or abusers) away

(Nock, 2008). Such functions may relate to certain settings such as prisons, in particular (Dixon-Gordon et al., 2012; Gambetta, 2009; see Winicov, this volume). This may reflect the limited avenues available to people in prison to impact their surroundings. The use of self-injury to affirm boundaries between self and other, or as a result of anger toward others being redirected toward the self, have also been reported (Yakeley & Burbridge-James, 2018). Finally, it has been noted that NSSI may act as a means of hurting others. For example, in Huey et al. (2015), in their qualitative study of homeless women who self-injure, one participant described the use of self-injury as a way to hurt her mother who had been physically abusive to her.

The functions described here, while capturing those most common in the research, do not cover every possible reason. It should also be noted that NSSI may serve multiple co-occurring functions for a particular individual (Cipriano et al., 2017), and that different acts of self-injury may have had a different function for the same person. For instance, in a study of adults sampled using random-digit dialing, two thirds of those engaging in NSSI reported two or more functions for their NSSI behaviors (Klonsky, 2011).

Neuropsychology of NSSI Functions

Neuropsychological investigations into why people may self-injure have indicated differences in brain regions associated with emotion and reward processing (Pambianchi & Whitlock, 2019; Poon et al., 2019). Such evidence is consistent with the use of NSSI as a way to regulate emotions (although some researchers have questioned the idea that self-injury arises primarily from problems with emotion regulation; Hooley & Franklin, 2017). There is also evidence of differential neural responses to social rejection and when asked to reflect on how others perceive them, among people who self-injure (Pambianchi & Whitlock, 2019). Such findings are consistent with the idea that self-injury may serve to regulate responses to experiences of social exclusion or negative self-image. A putative biological mechanism through which self-injury may regulate affect (reduction of negative affect and possible increase in positive affect) is the release of endogenous opioids. However, the evidence supporting this hypothesis is limited (Bresin & Gordon, 2013; Kirtley et al., 2015).

Structure of NSSI Functions

Various studies have investigated the underlying structure of NSSI functions, using factor-analytic methods. A consistent finding is that intrapersonal and interpersonal functions do not appear to load onto the same factors in these studies but instead typically load onto distinct factors. Studies have largely focused on data from two self-report measures, the Inventory of Statements about Self-Injury (ISAS; Klonsky & Glenn, 2009), or the Functional Assessment of Self-Mutilation (FASM; Lloyd et al., 1997), and findings differ depending on the scale used. Studies using the ISAS have supported a two-factor structure with separate intra and interpersonal factors (Klonsky & Glenn, 2009; Klonsky et al., 2015; Kortge et al., 2013). Studies using the FASM have led to much less consistent results. Early studies supported a four-factor structure, where intra and interpersonal functions could also be distinguished in terms of whether they reflected positive reinforcement (i.e., NSSI in order to create a desired, rewarding state) or negative reinforcement (i.e., NSSI to escape from a negative state; Lloyd-Richardson et al., 2007; Nock & Prinstein, 2004). However, subsequent studies have failed to replicate this structure and have identified two-factor, three-factor, or alternate four-factor solutions as the preferred models (Dahlström et al., 2015; Kaess et al., 2013; Leong et al., 2014; Zetterqvist et al., 2013). A robust study in a large sample of Swedish adolescents, using both exploratory and confirmatory approaches and replicating models across independent samples, suggested an alternate four-factor solution, with three interpersonal factors (social influence, peer identification, avoiding demands) and a single intrapersonal factor (Dahlström et al., 2015). Other studies have similarly supported the idea of a distinct peer identification and social influence factors (Kaess et al., 2013). The reason for the varied results with the FASM is unclear, but differences in population and analytic approach are likely important here.

Prevalence of NSSI Functions

It is clear that a wide range of different potential NSSI functions exist. This heterogeneity represents a challenge to trying to understand NSSI within a particular model or theory, or to intervene with a specific therapeutic approach. However, research highlights that certain functions are more prevalent than others. Though studies have varied in the reported prevalence of the different reported functions of NSSI, a common theme is that those functions related to affect regulation appear most commonly cited. For example, in a large sample of Swedish adolescents (n = 836 providing relevant data) the most commonly endorsed functions were "to stop bad feelings" (47%), "to relieve feeling numb or empty" (46%) and "to punish yourself" (41%). These same three functions were the most endorsed in a sample of adolescents at a psychiatric inpatient unit (endorsed by 52%, 30%, and 31% of participants, respectively; Nock & Prinstein, 2004). Data from an Australian household survey similarly found that among those reporting NSSI (n = 133) the most common function was to manage emotions (41–58%; Martin et al., 2010).

Attempts to generate pooled estimates for the prevalence of different functions are complex, since the measures and labels used to describe functions vary across studies, and different functions are not mutually exclusive. In Taylor et al. (2018), an attempt was made to overcome these challenges by applying a prespecified framework to categorize data into different types of function using broader (e.g., interpersonal) and more specific categories (e.g., communication of distress). Where a study reported data on different functions that related to the same category (e.g., a study reports prevalence data for several different functions that all describe a form of affect regulation), the most prevalent was used. These decision rules allowed pooled estimates to be generated. Across the 50 studies included in the meta-analysis, intrapersonal functions were most commonly reported, in particular those related to affect regulation (71%, 95% CI: 63–78), or more specifically the escape from a negative or unwanted state (70%, 95% CI: 62–78). Inducing a positive state (50%, 95% CI: 42–57) and self-punishment (51%, 95% CI: 41–62) were less common but still endorsed by around half of participants. Interpersonal functions, including communication of distress (42%, 95% CI: 30–55) and interpersonal influence (i.e., attempts to affect the behavior of others; 28%, 95% CI: 23–33), were less common, although still not rare. A limitation of this meta-analysis is that the method used to organize the data means that the prevalence estimates provided for broader function categories, such as "interpersonal" or "intrapersonal," are likely underestimates, whereas estimates for more specific functions (e.g., "affect regulation" and "communication of distress") are likely to be better.

Within the meta-analysis by Taylor et al. (2018), it was found that factors such as the choice of assessment tool and the population studied affected the prevalence estimates obtained. Prevalence estimates tended to be lower in university student samples (compared with nonstudent samples). Prevalence estimates also tended to be higher when the ISAS was used, and lower when the FASM was used, though this was potentially attributable to the response options used for these measures (the FASM has a "rarely" option, which for the purposes of the meta-analysis was counted as nonendorsement of that function). When results were restricted to a specific measurement tool (either the ISAS or FASM), the relative ordering of different functions in terms of their prevalence still remained largely consistent, with emotion regulation as the most prevalent, and functions related to influencing or punishing others being among the least endorsed of those investigated.

There is some evidence that the functions underlying NSSI may change over time. Muehlenkamp et al. (2013), using the Nonsuicidal Self-Injury Assessment Tool (NSSI-AT; Whitlock et al., 2014), found that interpersonal functions were more commonly reported as a motivation for the first incident of NSSI but became less prevalently endorsed for subsequent NSSI (28% vs. 20%). Gardner et al. (2021) further found that among adolescents who self-injured, 8% reported only interpersonal functions, but for adults who self-injured, interpersonal functions always occurred alongside intrapersonal functions (36% of adults endorsed intra- and interpersonal functions, while the remainder only reported intrapersonal functions). Thus, interpersonal functions may sometimes relate to self-harm initiation but only reinforce repeated NSSI in the presence of intrapersonal functions. Similarly, it has been argued that affect-regulation based functions for NSSI may become more important in maintaining this behavior over time (Halpin & Duffy, 2020; Hooley & Franklin, 2017).

Despite evidence that the prevalence of different functions may vary depending on population, method of assessment, and even within-individuals over time, the predominance of affect regulation-related functions remains a consistent finding. This observation is mirrored in the emergence of theoretical models (Chapman et al., 2006; Hasking et al., 2017) and treatment approaches (e.g., Emotion Regulation Group Therapy; Turner et al., 2014) that emphasize difficulties in this area. It has been argued, however, that methodological issues may have contributed to predominance of affect regulation functions. Edmondson et al. (2016) highlight how the assessment tools used, may restrict participants to a number of prespecified functions and consequently introduce bias. They also note that even where participants are providing more open-ended accounts of the reasons for their self-injury, the interpretation and categorization of these data may again introduce bias, favoring certain models and understandings of NSSI. Edmondson et al. (2016) suggest there may be underexplored functions of NSSI, including the use of self-injury as a way to seek gratification, or as a way to protect the self from others (e.g., creating a barrier to unwanted attention by making oneself appear unattractive), or as a way of defining or validating the self. These other functions have received less attention within theoretical models and clinical approaches to NSSI (though psychodynamic approaches do highlight the use of self-injury as a process of self-definition; Yakeley & Burbridge-James, 2018) but nonetheless play an important part in the experience of NSSI for some individuals.

NSSI is a highly stigmatized behavior, and the idea that NSSI is "attention-seeking" is a recognized pejorative stereotype. Research suggests that NSSI does have an important interpersonal dimension for many people, though this is rarely just about eliciting attention from others, and typically reflects some deeper interpersonal need (e.g., to have one's distress recognized, to be supported, and to maintain a sense of self). This stigma may impact on individuals' willingness to disclose interpersonal reasons for NSSI, however, and could mean such reasons are underreported.

Contextualizing the Functions of NSSI

While NSSI functions are typically grouped into the intra- and interpersonal, and the factor-analytic evidence supports this distinction, it is worth noting that no function is purely interpersonal or purely intrapersonal. While regulating emotional distress is a common example of an intrapersonal function, these feelings do not occur in a void, and social stresses and adversity can be a major factor driving the emotional distress that individuals are trying to cope with through their self-injury (Cawley et al., 2019; Turner et al., 2016; Victor et al., 2018). Thus, although the reduction of negative emotional states may be the proximal function of NSSI, the wider interpersonal context remains relevant in understanding the occurrence and persistence of these emotional states.

The social context may help us to understand why a person may come to self-injury as a way to regulate their feelings, as opposed to other methods of affect regulation. Seeking support from others is a common way to cope with distress (Taylor, 2011), but where the immediate social environment is highly invalidating or disregarding of one's feelings, a person may be left to struggle with such emotions alone and be more likely to engage in self-injury as a way to respond (Peel-Wainwright et al., 2021). This may be especially likely where a person has not had the opportunity to develop alternative, more adaptive, ways to regulate such feelings, perhaps as a result of having grown up in a suboptimal social environment. As another example, an individual may engage in self-injury as a response to feelings of anger about others in their lives (Huey et al., 2015; Mangnall, 2006). They may fear expressing these feelings directly due to how it could impact on their relationships or hurt others, and so self-injury may become a private way to respond to these emotions. Therefore, instances of self-injury with what appears to be an intrapersonal functional may still have a fundamentally relational dimension. A systematic review and metasynthesis focusing on interpersonal processes underlying NSSI indicated that many individuals had the experience of being trapped in an aversive and disempowered social environment, where avenues for support could be limited. In this context, NSSI became a means of regaining control and taking the ability to manage difficult feelings into one's own hands (Peel-Wainwright et al., 2021). Consequently, when considering the functions of NSSI, especially at an individual level, it is important that this is grounded in a consideration of the wider social context within which self-injury occurs.

Inferred and Implicit Functions

The research described so far has largely relied on individuals' self-reports of the functions of their self-injury. Self-report measures operate at conscious controlled level of processing and while these produce valuable data, they are prone to bias such as inaccurate retrospective recall of events and responding in a manner deemed favorable by others (i.e., social desirability). The perceived social stigma around NSSI (e.g., Burke et al., 2019) may encourage socially desirable responding and this may be especially likely when responding to questions about NSSI functions that might attract more criticism and judgement from others (e.g., self-injuring to elicit care/support). One way to circumvent the potential bias inherent in explicit measures of NSSI functions is to use implicit measures to assess people's automatic, unconscious thoughts. With this aim, a number of studies have used variants of the performance-based Implicit Association Test (IAT; Greenwald et al., 2003) and found stronger associations between NSSI and the self in those who do rather than do not self-injure (C. R. Glenn et al., 2016; J. J. Glenn et al., 2017). This implicit identification with NSSI is indicated by, for example, a faster reaction time when "cutting" and "me" are paired rather than when "cutting" and "not me" are paired. Some of the work that has used the IAT to assess the functions of NSSI has adapted the measure and found stronger implicit associations between NSSI and emotional relief among those who do rather than do not self-injure (Gratz et al., 2016; Gratz et al., 2018). There are also studies that have used the IAT to test mechanisms that might underpin NSSI functions. For example, Nagy et al. (2021) found that experimentally induced self-criticism (which might underpin functions such as self-punishment) strengthened implicit identification with NSSI (Nagy et al., 2021), though this effect was present in both individuals who do and who do not self-injure. Caution is needed in interpreting these studies, given concerns about the reliability and validity of IAT (Schimmack, 2021). Further work into the idea of implicit NSSI functions, including the validity of this concept and the interaction between explicit and implicit functions, is warranted.

Characteristics of NSSI Associated with Function

Understanding the functions served by NSSI is important for several reasons. Endorsement of a greater number of functions served, or function accumulation, is associated with increased risk of psychopathology, as well as suicide ideation and behaviors (Nock & Prinstein, 2005; Paul et al., 2015; Victor & Klonsky, 2014). NSSI functions also vary in their association with specific types of psychopathology. Intrapersonal functions are associated more strongly with depression, borderline personality disorder (BPD) symptomology, nonsuicidal self-injury disorder (NSSID) criteria, and suicidal ideation than interpersonal functions (Glenn & Klonsky, 2013; Gratz et al., 2015; Klonsky & Glenn, 2009; Nock & Prinstein, 2005; Victor et al., 2015). Further, intrapersonal negative reinforcement functions (e.g., to reduce negative feelings) have been shown to relate to hopelessness and prior suicide attempts, while intrapersonal positive reinforcement functions (e.g., to feel something) have been shown to be associated with posttraumatic stress disorder (PTSD) and major depressive disorder (MDD) (Nock & Prinstein, 2005). Individuals with high scores on both intra- and interpersonal NSSI functions report higher depression and anxiety than other people who self-injure (Klonsky & Olino, 2008). Higher endorsement of both intra- and interpersonal NSSI functions was also positively associated with suicidal ideation (though not attempts) in one study (Klonsky & Glenn, 2009) though in another those with high intra- but low interpersonal scores have the highest prevalence of suicidal ideation and suicide attempts compared to other people who engage in NSSI (Klonsky & Olino, 2008). Notably when investigating gender differences in a large U.S. student sample, females were more likely to endorse affect regulation related functions, or using NSSI as a form of self-control, compared to men (Whitlock et al., 2011). The study did not consider nonbinary or other gender groups, however.

The individual functions comprising the intra- and interpersonal superordinate functions importantly also appear to differ in their strength of association with suicidal ideation and attempt history. For example, Paul et al. (2015) found that all but three ("to get a rush/surge of energy," "to deal with frustration," and as "self-punishment") of the 17 functions assessed (using the NSSI-AT; Whitlock et al., 2014) were significantly associated with suicidal behavior, with functions related to avoiding attempting suicide, coping with self-hatred, and feeling generation (i.e., antidissociation) showing the strongest associations. NSSI for interpersonal communication and antidissociation (i.e., feeling generation) were the only functions significantly related to suicidal ideation. A number of studies have found that, perhaps unsurprisingly, endorsement of antisuicide functions (i.e., using self-injury to prevent oneself acting on suicidal feelings) is associated with current suicidal ideation and planning (Burke et al., 2018; Robinson et al., 2021; Victor et al., 2015). Together, these findings suggest that individuals who use NSSI to avoid suicide, to cope with self-hatred, or to terminate dissociative states may be at a higher risk for making a suicide attempt than those who do not.

Several studies have found an association between NSSI functions and trajectories of behavioral engagement. For example, in a three-year longitudinal study, using the NSSI-AT (Whitlock et al., 2014), Kiekens et al. (2017) examined the prospective association between NSSI functions and continuation of NSSI among college students and found that certain functions, specifically, those associated with intrapersonal positive reinforcement (i.e., "get a rush or surge of energy"), predicted the persistence of NSSI behaviors beyond adolescence. Similarly, Yen et al. (2016) found that use of NSSI for intrapersonal positive reinforcement predicted persistence of NSSI behaviors among adolescent psychiatric inpatients during the six months following hospitalization. Conversely, intrapersonal negative reinforcement and interpersonal reinforcement functions (interpersonal positive and negative reinforcement) did not predict NSSI behaviors after hospitalization. These findings suggest that use of NSSI to regulate emotions, specifically, to generate emotion, predicts continuation of NSSI over time, perhaps because NSSI is effective in enhancing positive emotion and, therefore, reinforces continued engagement (Paul et al., 2015; Pollak et al., 2020; Selby et al., 2014). Indeed, research suggests that individuals rate intrapersonal functions as significantly more effective than interpersonal functions (Brausch & Muehlenkamp, 2018). These findings suggest that identifying individuals' reasons for NSSI engagement may help to distinguish those at higher risk (and those at lower risk) of NSSI persistence. In contrast, in a clinically severe sample of adolescents, duration of NSSI engagement did not vary by function, after controlling for relevant demographic and clinical characteristics (Victor et al., 2016). Knowledge and understanding of NSSI functions can also help clarify the types of difficulties that people engaging in NSSI may experience. For example, research suggests that individuals using NSSI for intrapersonal functions have greater difficulties with emotional reactivity and regulation, as well as self-criticism; while individuals using NSSI for interpersonal functions have greater difficulty in their relationships with others (Hilt et al., 2008; Nock, 2008; Turner et al., 2016).

Clinical Assessment of the Functions of NSSI

Understanding the functions behind NSSI appears essential in identifying the underlying factors and processes that maintain this behavior, and thus in guiding treatment decisions. It therefore is important to consider functions of NSSI as part of clinical assessments, and to factor this information into clinical formulations of individual's difficulties (Klonsky & Lewis, 2014). Understanding the functions of NSSI can be essential to tailoring treatment interventions for people engaging in NSSI (Klonsky & Muehlenkamp, 2007; Walsh, 2007; Washburn et al., 2012).

Myriad validated assessment tools of NSSI exist that cover the functions of the behavior. Widely used measures include the ISAS (Klonsky & Glenn, 2009), FASM (Lloyd et al., 1997), NSSI-AT (Whitlock et al., 2014), and the Suicide Attempt Self-Injury

Interview (SASII; Linehan et al., 2006). While all these tools tend to cover the same general categories of NSSI functions, as noted, the choice of measure may have an impact on the reported prevalence of different functions. While these tools are helpful in better understanding the characteristics of an individual's NSSI, it should be noted that the reliance on predetermined categories runs the risk of missing important nuance in an individual's particular experience of NSSI (Edmondson et al., 2016). Consequently, we recommend that such NSSI assessment tools are used as part of a wider clinical interview where practicable to do so. Many tools have been explicitly developed based on discussions with people who self-injure, with items mapping the functions and language used (e.g., Whitlock et al., 2014). Nonetheless, given the presentation of a list of predetermined categories may still bias or influence how a person describes their self-injury, it may often be preferable that such assessments begin with more open-ended questioning about the function of NSSI, before specific assessment tools are introduced. Given the evidence that the importance of different functions may change over time for individuals who self-injure (Muehlenkamp et al., 2013), there may also be a value in asking about both functions related to the onset of NSSI as well as current functions. Repeated measurement of NSSI functions may also be important given these may change over time. Finally, it is important to note that just because an episode of NSSI influences the behavior of others (e.g., elicits a caregiving response), this does not mean that such a consequence influenced the person's decision to engage in NSSI.

Implications for Intervention

Having a thorough understanding of the functions that underlie someone's self-injury may be important as this may inform the effectiveness of particular interventions used. For example, if a client engages in self-injury primarily in response to feels of shame and self-criticism, as a form of self-punishment, then therapeutic approaches that target these psychological processes of shame and self-criticism, such as compassion-focused approaches (e.g., van Vliet & Kalnins, 2011), may be helpful. For others, where self-injury is a way to regulate unexpressed feelings of anger toward family members, systemic interventions may be of value, alongside work on developing alternative emotion-regulation techniques.

In making clinical judgments about treatment based on NSSI functions we advocate a contextualized approach to thinking about the function of NSSI, whereby the function that self-injury serves is positioned and understood within the wider psychological and social context of a person's life and history. For example, negative self-concept and self-criticism are elevated among those who self-injure (Forrester et al., 2017; Hooley & Franklin, 2017; Taylor et al., 2020). For such individuals, even though the function of self-injury may be about regulating negative emotions, adopting alternative strategies for regulating emotions that are perceived as being kind to oneself (e.g., soothing or relaxation techniques) may be difficult as they are dystonic with this underlying psychological context of self-criticism. One reason NSSI may come to be adopted by such individuals is that it provides an ego-syntonic (in that it is self-attacking in nature) means of regulating negative emotions (Hooley & Franklin, 2017). While the function of NSSI is an important piece of clinical information, it is arguably just one piece of the jigsaw and unlikely to be helpful if used as a guide for treatment in the absence of a broader understanding of someone's life and experiences (Lewis et al., 2017).

Self-Injury and the Therapeutic Relationship

Given its functional nature, NSSI can play an important role in someone's life. People can form strong positive beliefs about their NSSI and their reliance on this behavior (Sandel et al., 2020), and for some it may seem that NSSI is the thing that has kept them alive through incredibly difficult times. These positive beliefs about NSSI may exist alongside negative beliefs about the adverse consequences self-injury has had for them (Sandel et al., 2020). Consequently, some individuals are understandably ambivalent about cessation of their self-injury. This ambivalence about stopping self-injury has been shown in qualitative studies (Hambleton et al., 2020; Shaw, 2006). Interventions for NSSI often have the cessation of the behavior as a primary goal (Lewis & Hasking, 2021; Warner & Spandler, 2012). There are various driving factors for this focus, but this may include the framing in some psychotherapeutic circles of NSSI as a therapy-interfering behavior that needs to stop for other therapeutic work to occur (Prada et al., 2018), and also due to concerns about risk to self that are associated with NSSI (such concerns can create an individual pressure to stop a client self-injuring but can also result in an organizational pressure as well). This focus on cessation or reduction of NSSI has the potential to clash with clients' own ambivalence or concerns about ending their self-injury. This tension has the potential to create ruptures in the therapeutic relationship and lead to a mismatch in therapeutic goals, which may disrupt therapeutic work going forward. Shared goals are an important foundation for effective therapy (Blake et al., 2019). Hence, when working with NSSI, careful negotiation of what the goals of therapy should be, holding in mind the function NSSI serves for the person, will likely be important. Mental health staff have described how an awareness of the role self-injury plays in a client's life can help them to see the client as a whole person, leading to better therapeutic work (O'Connor & Glover, 2017). Likewise, an investigation by the UK mental health charity the Samaritans (2020) suggested that people who self-injure want interventions to take a holistic approach and think about the underlying drivers and not just the behavior itself. Indeed, individuals engaging in NSSI discuss a range of concerns (e.g., disclosure, scarring, and alternative viable coping strategies) that extend well beyond NSSI cessation (Lewis & Hasking, 2021).

Implications for Prevention

The growing understanding of the functions that NSSI serves has several implications for prevention efforts in a variety of different settings. Programs designed to prevent the initial onset of self-injury in settings like schools and colleges, for example, could base aspects of the program around the common functions of NSSI. This could include basic psychoeducation and skills training with the aim of improving young people's ability to identify, label, communicate, and regulate difficult feelings. This may help undermine the emergence of NSSI as a means of communicating or coping with difficult emotional states. So far there have been few investigations of prevention programs for NSSI. Klingman and Hochdorf (1993) trialed a school-based prevention program for self-destructive behaviors (not NSSI specifically) that focused on developing distress coping skills. While well received by participants, there was no evidence that it led to a reduction in self-destructive behavior. The Happyles program (Baetens et al., 2020) was designed for school-based prevention of NSSI, which included general psychoeducation and exercises relating to emotional well-being and regulation, alongside more focused content on NSSI (including psychoeducation about the functions of NSSI). Although there were some positive results, such as improvements over time in emotional awareness, there was no evidence relating to the prevention of NSSI (Baetens et al., 2020). Further research is clearly needed investigating the potential benefit of prevention programs for NSSI. Consideration of the common functions of NSSI may help in development of such programs. Notably, in both examples above, there is content on emotional regulation and coping. However, given the preliminary evidence that interpersonal NSSI functions may have a greater role in the initial onset of NSSI (compared to ongoing maintenance), consideration of preventative activities linked to these functions of NSSI may also be important (Muehlenkamp et al., 2013).

Implications for Research

The functions of NSSI have been the focus of a large amount of research to date, but there remain important areas where research has been scarce that could be a helpful focus for future studies. First, to date only a few studies have attempted to investigate the temporal characteristics of different functions, including how the importance of different functions changes over time, and in turn how such changes may relate to NSSI behavior. Understanding these temporal changes may help inform our understanding of how the processes that maintain NSSI change over time. Further research using intensive longitudinal methods would be well suited to investigating this area. Second, research investigating the link between the function NSSI serves and the broader social or environmental context, is needed. Currently, qualitative research highlights how the functions of self-injury are closely tied to the broader social context and psychological needs of the individual (Peel-Wainwright et al., 2021). Experience sampling methodologies (also referred to as ecological momentary assessment) are well suited to exploring psychological phenomena situated within the day-to-day context of a person's life, and so might provide a means of further examining how the functions of NSSI varies across different social contexts (Selby et al., 2014). Third, we suggest above that therapeutic approaches may vary in efficacy depending on the extent to which they match the underlying function of self-injury. This could be investigated through mechanistic clinical trials and individual-patient data meta-analysis, taking a "what works for who" approach to evaluating treatments. Fourth, the interpersonal functions of NSSI have received less research attention, but appear important, and may have more of a role at certain points in the development of NSSI. Further research focused on interpersonal NSSI functions, including when and what contexts they may play a greater role in driving NSSI, is therefore warranted.

Conclusions

Consideration of the functions that NSSI serves, has been essential to the development of our understanding of these behaviors, guiding the development of theory and intervention. Research has identified a wide range of different NSSI functions and has established that some functions, such as those associated with emotion regulation, are more prevalent than others. Research has also indicated that important differences in the severity and experience of NSSI may exist between people who engage in NSSI for different reasons. It is also becoming clear that the functions of NSSI are not completely fixed, but potentially change over time, and are likely to be closely tied to the wider social and psychological context of someone's life. With these considerations in mind, we recommend the adoption of a contextualized approach to thinking about NSSI functions, treating them not as a stable individual property but instead as something that emerges from the interplay between a person's broader psychosocial needs and constraints and their self-injury. The function of NSSI may act as a helpful guide in considering which preventative activities or interventions will be helpful and can help inform clinical formulation of clients' difficulties. However, we argue that within clinical decision making about individual clients it is beneficial to treat the function of NSSI as one (albeit important) jigsaw piece within the broader picture of that individual.

References

Baetens, I., Decruy, C., Vatandoost, S., Vanderhaegen, B., & Kiekens, G. (2020). School-based prevention targeting non-suicidal self-injury: A pilot study. *Frontiers in Psychiatry, 11*, 437. https://doi.org/10.3389/fpsyt.2020.00437

Blake, A., Larkin, A., & Taylor, P. J. (2019). The relationship with the therapist. In P. J. Taylor, O. Gianfrancesco, & N. Fisher (Eds.), *Personal experiences of psychological therapy for psychosis and related experiences* (pp. 166–184). Routledge.

Brausch, A. M., & Muehlenkamp, J. J. (2018). Perceived effectiveness of NSSI in achieving functions on severity and suicide risk. *Psychiatry Research, 265*, 144–150. https://doi.org/10.1016/j.psychres.2018.04.038

Bresin, K., & Gordon, K. H. (2013). Endogenous opioids and nonsuicidal self-injury: A mechanism of affect regulation. *Neuroscience & Biobehavioral Reviews, 37*(3), 374–383. https://doi.org/10.1016/j.neubiorev.2013.01.020

Burke, T. A., Jacobucci, R., Ammerman, B. A., Piccirillo, M., McCloskey, M. S., Heimberg, R. G., & Alloy, L. B. (2018). Identifying the relative importance of non-suicidal self-injury features in classifying suicidal ideation, plans, and behavior using exploratory data mining. *Psychiatry Research, 262*, 175–183. https://doi.org/10.1016/j.psychres.2018.01.045

Burke, T. A., Piccirillo, M. L., Moore-Berg, S. L., Alloy, L. B., & Heimberg, R. G. (2019). The stigmatization of nonsuicidal self-injury. *Journal of Clinical Psychology, 75*(3), 481–498. https://doi.org/10.1002/jclp.22713

Buser, T. J., & Buser, J. K. (2013). Conceptualizing nonsuicidal self-injury as a process addiction: Review of research and implications for counselor training and practice. *Journal of Addictions & Offender Counseling, 34*(1), 16–29. https://doi.org/https://doi.org/10.1002/j.2161-1874.2013.00011.x

Cawley, R., Pontin, E. E., Touhey, J., Sheehy, K., & Taylor, P. J. (2019). What is the relationship between rejection and self-harm or suicidality in adulthood? *Journal of Affective Disorders, 242*, 123–134. https://doi.org/https://doi.org/10.1016/j.jad.2018.08.082

Chapman, A. L., Gratz, K. L., & Brown, M. Z. (2006). Solving the puzzle of deliberate self-harm: The experiential avoidance model. *Behaviour Research and Therapy, 44*, 371–394. https://doi.org/10.1016/j.brat.2005.03.005

Cipriano, A., Cella, S., & Cotrufo, P. (2017). Nonsuicidal self-injury: A systematic review. *Frontiers in Psychology, 8*, Article 1946. https://doi.org/10.3389/fpsyg.2017.01946

Dahlström, Ö., Zetterqvist, M., Lundh, L.-G., & Svedin, C. G. (2015). Functions of nonsuicidal self-injury: Exploratory and confirmatory factor analyses in a large community sample of adolescents. *Psychological Assessment, 27*(1), 302–313. https://doi.org/10.1037/pas0000034

Dixon-Gordon, K. L., Harrison, N., & Roesch, R. (2012). Non-suicidal self-injury within offender populations: A systematic review. *International Journal of Forensic Mental Health, 11*, 33–50. https://doi.org/10.1080/14999013.2012.667513

Edmondson, A. J., Brennan, C. A., & House, A. O. (2016). Non-suicidal reasons for self-harm: A systematic review of self-reported accounts. *Journal of Affective Disorders, 191*, 109–117. https://doi.org/http://dx.doi.org/10.1016/j.jad.2015.11.043

Forrester, R. L., Slater, H., Jomar, K., Mitzman, S., & Taylor, P. J. (2017). Self-esteem and non-suicidal self-injury in adulthood: A systematic review. *Journal of Affective Disorders, 221*, 172–183. https://doi.org/10.1016/j.jad.2017.06.027

Gambetta, D. (2009). *Codes of the underworld: How criminals communicate.* Princeton University Press.

Gardner, K. J., Paul, E., Selby, E., A., Klonsky, E. D., & Mars, B. (2021). Intrapersonal and interpersonal functions as pathways to future self-harm repetition and suicide attempts. *Frontiers in Psychology, 12*, 688472. https://doi.org/10.3389/fpsyg.2021.688472

Glenn, C. R., Kleiman, E. M., Cha, C. B., Nock, M. K., & Prinstein, M. J. (2016). Implicit cognition about self-injury predicts actual self-injurious behavior: Results from a longitudinal study of adolescents. *Journal of Child Psychology and Psychiatry, and Allied Disciplines, 57*(7), 805–813. https://doi.org/10.1111/jcpp.12500

Glenn, C. R., & Klonsky, E. D. (2013). Nonsuicidal self-injury disorder: An empirical investigation in adolescent psychiatric patients. *Journal of Clinical Child & Adolescent Psychology, 42*(4), 496–507. https://doi.org/10.1080/15374416.2013.794699

Glenn, J. J., Werntz, A. J., Slama, S. J. K., Steinman, S. A., Teachman, B. A., & Nock, M. K. (2017). Suicide and self-injury-related implicit cognition: A large-scale examination and replication. *Journal of Abnormal Psychology, 126*(2), 199–211. https://doi.org/10.1037/abn0000230

Gratz, K. L., Chapman, A. L., Dixon-Gordon, K. L., & Tull, M. T. (2016). Exploring the association of deliberate self-harm with emotional relief using a novel Implicit Association Test. *Personality Disorders, 7*(1), 91–102. https://doi.org/10.1037/per0000138

Gratz, K. L., Dixon-Gordon, K. L., Chapman, A. L., & Tull, M. T. (2015). Diagnosis and characterization of DSM-5 nonsuicidal self-injury disorder using the clinician-administered nonsuicidal self-injury disorder index. *Assessment, 22*(5), 527–539. https://doi.org/10.1177/1073191114565878

Gratz, K. L., Tull, M. T., Dixon-Gordon, K. L., Turner, B. J., & Chapman, A. L. (2018). Is the association of deliberate self-harm with emotional relief stable or dependent on emotional context? *Journal of Behavioural Therapy & Experimental Psychiatry, 60*, 61–68. https://doi.org/10.1016/j.jbtep.2018.03.003

Greenwald, A. G., Nosek, B. A., & Banaji, M. R. (2003). Understanding and using the Implicit Association Test: I. An improved scoring algorithm. *Journal of Personality and Social Psychology, 85*(2), 197–216. https://doi.org/10.1037/0022-3514.85.2.197

Halpin, S. A., & Duffy, N. M. (2020). Predictors of non-suicidal self-injury cessation in adults who self-injured during adolescence. *Journal of Affective Disorders Reports, 1*, 100017. https://doi.org/https://doi.org/10.1016/j.jadr.2020.100017

Hambleton, A. L., Hanstock, T. L., Halpin, S., & Dempsey, C. (2020). Initiation, meaning and cessation of self-harm: Australian adults' retrospective reflections and advice to adolescents who currently self-harm. *Counselling Psychology Quarterly, 35*(2), 260–283.

Hamza, C. A., Stewart, S. L., & Willoughby, T. (2012). Examining the link between nonsuicidal self-injury and suicidal behavior: A review of the literature and an integrated model. *Clinical Psychology Review*, *32*(6), 482–495. https://doi.org/http://dx.doi.org/10.1016/j.cpr.2012.05.003

Hasking, P., Whitlock, J., Voon, D., & Rose, A. (2017). A cognitive-emotional model of NSSI: Using emotion regulation and cognitive processes to explain why people self-injure. *Cognition and Emotion*, *31*(8), 1543–1556. https://doi.org/10.1080/02699931.2016.1241219

Hilt, L. M., Nock, M. K., Lloyd-Richardson, E. E., & Prinstein, M. J. (2008). Longitudinal study of nonsuicidal self-injury among young adolescents: Rates, correlates, and preliminary test of an interpersonal model. *The Journal of Early Adolescence*, *28*(3), 455–469. https://doi.org/10.1177/0272431608316604

Hooley, J. M., & Franklin, J. C. (2017). Why do people hurt themselves? A new conceptual model of non-suicidal self-injury. *Clinical Psychological Science*, *6*(3), 428–451. https://doi.org/10.1177/2167702617745641

Huey, L., Hryniewicz, D., & Fthenos, G. (2015). "I had a lot of anger and that's what kind of led me to cutting myself": Employing a social stress framework to explain why some homeless women self-injure. *Health Sociology Review*, *23*, 148–158. https://doi.org/10.1080/14461242.2014.11081969

Kaess, M., Parzer, P., Mattern, M., Plener, P. L., Bifulco, A., Resch, F., & Brunner, R. (2013). Adverse childhood experiences and their impact on frequency, severity, and the individual function of nonsuicidal self-injury in youth. *Psychiatry Research*, *206*(2–3), 265–272.

Kiekens, G., Hasking, P., Bruffaerts, R., Claes, L., Baetens, I., Boyes, M., Mortier, P., Demyttenaere, K., & Whitlock, J. (2017). What predicts ongoing nonsuicidal self-injury?: A comparison between persistent and ceased self-injury in emerging adults. *Journal of Nervous and Mental Disease*, *205*(10), 762–770. https://doi.org/10.1097/NMD.0000000000000726

Kirtley, O. J., O'Carroll, R. E., & O'Connor, R. C. (2015). The role of endogenous opioids in non-suicidal self-injurious behavior: Methodological challenges. *Neuroscience & Biobehavioral Reviews*, *48*, 186–189. https://doi.org/https://doi.org/10.1016/j.neubiorev.2014.11.007

Klingman, A., & Hochdorf, Z. (1993). Coping with distress and self-harm: The impact of a primary prevention program among adolescents. *Journal of Adolescence*, *16*(2), 121–140. https://doi.org/10.1006/jado.1993.1012

Klonsky, E. D. (2007). The functions of deliberate self-injury: A review of the evidence [Review article]. *Clinical Psychology Review*, *27*, 226–239. https://doi.org/10.1016/j.cpr.2006.08.002

Klonsky, E. D. (2011). Non-suicidal self-injury in United States adults: Prevalence, sociodemographics, topography and functions. *Psychological Medicine*, *41*(09), 1981–1986. https://doi.org/doi:10.1017/S0033291710002497

Klonsky, E. D., & Glenn, C. R. (2009). Assessing the functions of non-suicidal self-injury: Psychometric properties of the inventory of statements about self-injury (ISAS). *Journal of Psychopathology & Behavioral Assessment*, *31*(3), 215–219. https://doi.org/10.1007/s10862-008-9107-z

Klonsky, E. D., Glenn, C. R., Styer, D. M., Olino, T. M., & Washburn, J. J. (2015). The functions of nonsuicidal self-injury: Converging evidence for a two-factor structure. *Child and Adolescent Psychiatry and Mental Health*, *9*, 44–53. https://doi.org/10.1186/s13034-015-0073-4

Klonsky, E. D., & Lewis, S. P. (2014). Assessment of nonsuicidal self-injury. In M. K. Nock (Ed.), *The Oxford handbook of suicide and self-injury* (pp. 337–354). Oxford University Press.

Klonsky, E. D., & Muehlenkamp, J. J. (2007). Self-injury: A research review for the practitioner. *Journal of Clinical Psychology*, *63*(11), 1045–1056. https://doi.org/10.1002/jclp.20412

Klonsky, E. D., & Olino, T. M. (2008). Identifying clinically distinct subgroups of self-injurers among young adults: A latent class analysis. *Journal of Consulting & Clinical Psychology*, *76*(1), 22–27. https://doi.org/10.1037/0022-006x.76.1.22

Kortge, R., Meade, T., & Tennant, A. (2013). Interpersonal and intrapersonal functions of deliberate self-harm (DSH): A psychometric examination of the inventory of statements about self-injury (ISAS) scale. *Behaviour Change*, *30*(1), 24–35. https://doi.org/10.1017/bec.2013.3

Kraus, L., Schmid, M., & In-Albon, T. (2020). Anti-suicide function of nonsuicidal self-injury in female inpatient adolescents [original research]. *Frontiers in Psychiatry*, *11*, 490. https://doi.org/10.3389/fpsyt.2020.00490

Leong, C. H., Wu, A. M., & Poon, M. M.-y. (2014). Measurement of perceived functions of non-suicidal self-injury for Chinese adolescents. *Archives of Suicide Research*, *18*(2), 193–212.

Lewis, S. P., Bryant, L. A., Schaefer, B. M., & Grunberg, P. H. (2017). In their own words: Perspectives on nonsuicidal self-injury disorder among those with lived experience. *Journal of Nervous and Mental Disease*, *205*(10), 771–779. https://doi.org/10.1097/NMD.0000000000000733

Lewis, S. P., & Hasking, P. A. (2021). Self-injury recovery: A person-centered framework. *Journal of Clinical Psychology*, *77*(4), 884–895. https://doi.org/https://doi.org/10.1002/jclp.23094

Linehan, M. M., Comtois, K. A., Brown, M. Z., Heard, H. L., & Wagner, A. (2006). Suicide Attempt Self-Injury Interview (SASII): Development, reliability, and validity of a scale to assess suicide attempts and intentional self-injury. *Psychological Assessment*, *18*(3), 303–312. https://doi.org/10.1037/1040-3590.18.3.303

Lloyd, E., Kelley, M. L., & Hope, T. (1997). *Self-mutilation in a community sample of adolescents: Descriptive characteristics and provisional prevalence rates* [Paper presentation]. Annual Meeting of the Society for Behavioral Medicine, New Orleans, LA.

Lloyd-Richardson, E. E., Perrine, N., Dierker, L., & Kelley, M. L. (2007). Characteristics and functions of non-suicidal self-injury in a community sample of adolescents. *Psychological Medicine*, *37*(8), 1183–1192. https://doi.org/10.1017/S003329170700027X

Mangnall, J. (2006). *Needing To act: Exploring deliberate self-harm in incarcerated women*. University of North Dakota Press. https://search.proquest.com/openview/d26bdbf54791ece7723ba00a1706a8f7/1?pq-origsite=gscholar&cbl=18750&diss=y

Martin, G., Swannell, S., Hazell, P., Harrison, J., & Taylor, A. (2010). Self-injury in Australia: A community survey. *Medical Journal of Australia*, *193*(9), 506–510.

Muehlenkamp, J., Brausch, A., Quigley, K., & Whitlock, J. (2013). Interpersonal features and functions of nonsuicidal self-injury. *Suicide & Life-Threatening Behavior*, *43*(1), 67–80. https://doi.org/10.1111/j.1943-278X.2012.00128.x

Nagy, L. M., Shanahan, M. L., & Baer, R. A. (2021). An experimental investigation of the effects of self-criticism and self-compassion on implicit associations with non-suicidal self-injury. *Behaviour Research and Therapy*, *139*, 103819. https://doi.org/https://doi.org/10.1016/j.brat.2021.103819

Nock, M. K. (2008). Actions speak louder than words: An elaborated theoretical model of the social functions of self-injury and other harmful behaviors. *Applied and Preventive Psychology*, *12*(4), 159–168. https://doi.org/https://doi.org/10.1016/j.appsy.2008.05.002

Nock, M. K. (2009). Why do people hurt themselves? New insights into the nature and functions of self-injury. *Current Directions in Psychological Science*, *18*(2), 78–83. https://doi.org/10.1111/j.1467-8721.2009.01613.x

Nock, M. K., & Cha, C. B. (2009). Psychological models of nonsuicidal self-injury. In M. K. Nock (Ed.), Understanding nonsuicidal self-injury: Origins, assessment, and treatment (pp. 65–77). American Psychological Association. https://doi.org/10.1037/11875-004

Nock, M. K., & Prinstein, M. J. (2004). A functional approach to the assessment of self-mutilative behaviour. *Journal of Consulting and Clinical Psychology*, *72*(5), 885–890. https://doi.org/10.1037/0022-006x.72.5.885

Nock, M. K., & Prinstein, M. J. (2005). Contextual features and behavioral functions of self-mutilation among adolescents. *Journal of Abnormal Psychology*, *114*(1), 140–146. https://doi.org/10.1037/0021-843x.114.1.140

O'Connor, S., & Glover, L. (2017). Hospital staff experiences of their relationships with adults who self-harm: A meta-synthesis. *Psychology and Psychotherapy: Theory, Research and Practice*, *90*(3), 480–501. https://doi.org/10.1111/papt.12113

Pambianchi, H., & Whitlock, J. (2019). Understanding the neurobiology of non-suicidal self-injury. In *Brief series, Cornell research program on self-injury and recovery*. Cornell University. http://www.selfinjury.bctr.cornell.edu/perch/resources/the-neurobiology-of-nssi.pdf

Paul, E., Tsypes, A., Eidlitz, L., Ernhout, C., & Whitlock, J. (2015). Frequency and functions of non-suicidal self-injury: Associations with suicidal thoughts and behaviors. *Psychiatry research*, *225*(3), 276–282. https://doi.org/10.1016/j.psychres.2014.12.026

Peel-Wainwright, K., Hartley, S., Rocca, E., Boland, A., Langer, S., & Taylor, P. J. (2021). The interpersonal processes of non-suicidal self-injury: A systematic review and meta-synthesis. *Psychology and Psychotherapy: Theory, Research and Practice*, *94*(4), 1059–1082. https://doi.org/10.1111/papt.12352

Pollak, O. H., D'Angelo, E. J., & Cha, C. B. (2020). Does function predict persistence? Nonsuicidal self-injury among adolescents during and after hospitalisation. *Psychiatry Research*, *286*, Article 112839. https://doi.org/10.1016/j.psychres.2020.112839

Poon, J. A., Thompson, J. C., Forbes, E. E., & Chaplin, T. M. (2019). Adolescents' reward-related neural activation: Links to thoughts of nonsuicidal self-injury. *Suicide & Life-Threatening Behavior*, *49*, 76–89. https://doi.org/10.1111/sltb.12418

Prada, P., Perroud, N., Rüfenacht, E., & Nicastro, R. (2018). Strategies to deal with suicide and non-suicidal self-injury in borderline personality disorder, the case of DBTT. *Frontiers in Psychology*, *9*, 2595. https://doi.org/10.3389/fpsyg.2018.02595

Rallis, B. A., Deming, C. A., Glenn, J. J., & Nock, M. K. (2020). What is the role of dissociation and emptiness in the occurrence of nonsuicidal self-injury? *Journal of Cognitive Psychotherapy*, *26*(4), 287–298. https://doi.org/10.1891/0889-8391.26.4.287

Ribeiro, J. D., Franklin, J. C., Fox, K. R., Bentley, K. H., Kleiman, E. M., Chang, B. P., & Nock, M. K. (2016). Self-injurious thoughts and behaviors as risk factors for future suicide ideation, attempts, and death: A meta-analysis of longitudinal studies. *Psychological Medicine*, *46*(2), 225–236. https://doi.org/10.1017/S0033291715001804

Robinson, K., Garisch, J. A., & Wilson, M. S. (2021). Nonsuicidal self-injury thoughts and behavioural characteristics: Associations with suicidal thoughts and behaviours among community adolescents. *Journal of Affective Disorders*, *282*, 1247–1254. https://doi.org/10.1016/j.jad.2020.12.201

Samaritans. (2020). *Pushed from pillar to post: Improving the availability and quality of support after self-harm in England*. https://media.samaritans.org/documents/Samaritans_-_Pushed_from_pillar_to_post_web.pdf

Sandel, D. B., Jomar, K., Johnson, S. L., Dickson, J. M., Dandy, S., Forrester, R., & Taylor, P. J. (2020). Beliefs about one's non-suicidal self-injury: The experiences of self-injury questionnaire (ESIQ). *Archives of Suicide Research*, *25*(3), 458–474. https://doi.org/10.1080/13811118.2020.1712285

Schimmack, U. (2021). Invalid claims about the validity of implicit association tests by prisoners of the implicit social-cognition paradigm. *Perspectives on Psychological Science*, *16*(2), 435–442. https://doi.org/10.1177/1745691621991860

Selby, E. A., Nock, M. K., & Kranzler, A. (2014). How does self-injury feel? Examining automatic positive reinforcement in adolescent self-injurers with experience sampling. *Psychiatry Research*, *215*(2), 417–423. https://doi.org/10.1016/j.psychres.2013.12.005

Shaw, S. (2006). Certainty, revision, and ambivalence: A qualitative Investigation into women's journeys to stop self-injuring. *Women & Therapy*, *29*(1–2), 153–177. https://doi.org/10.1300/J015v29n01_08

Sheehy, K., Noureen, A., Khaliq, A., Dhingra, K., Husain, N., Pontin, E. E., Cawley, R., & Taylor, P. J. (2019). An examination of the relationship between shame, guilt and self-harm: A systematic review and meta-analysis. *Clinical Psychology Review*, *73*, 101779. https://doi.org/https://doi.org/10.1016/j.cpr.2019.101779

Stänicke, L. I., Haavind, H., & Gullestad, S. E. (2018). How do young people understand their own self-harm? A meta-synthesis of adolescents' subjective experience of self-harm. *Adolescent Research Review*, *3*(2), 173–191. https://doi.org/10.1007/s40894-018-0080-9

Suyemoto, K. L. (1998). The functions of self-mutilation. *Clinical Psychology Review*, *18*(5), 531–554. https://doi.org/10.1016/S0272-7358(97)00105-0

Taylor, P. J., Jomar, K., Dhingra, K., Forrester, R., Shahmalak, U., & Dickson, J. M. (2018). A meta-analysis of the prevalence of different functions of non-suicidal self-injury. *Journal of Affective Disorders*, *227*, 759–769. https://doi.org/10.1016/j.jad.2017.11.073

Taylor, P. J., Usher, S., Jomar, K., & Forrester, R. (2020). Investigating self-concept in self-harm: A repertory grid study. *Psychology and Psychotherapy: Theory, Research and Practice*. https://doi.org/https://doi.org/10.1111/papt.12269

Taylor, S. E. (2011). Social support: A review. In H. S. Friedman (Ed.), *The Oxford handbook of health psychology* (pp. 189–214). Oxford University Press. https://doi.org/10.1093/oxfordhb/9780195342819.013.0009

Turner, B. J., Austin, S. B., & Chapman, A. L. (2014). Treating nonsuicidal self-injury: A systematic review of psychological and pharmacological interventions. *Canadian Journal of Psychiatry*, *59*(11), 576–585. https://doi.org/10.1177/070674371405901103

Turner, B. J., Cobb, R. J., Gratz, K. L., & Chapman, A. L. (2016). The role of interpersonal conflict and perceived social support in nonsuicidal self-injury in daily life. *Journal of Abnormal Psychology*, *125*(4), 588–598. https://doi.org/10.1037/abn0000141

van Vliet, K. J., & Kalnins, G. R. C. (2011). A compassion-focused approach to nonsuicidal self-injury. *Journal of Mental Health Counseling*, *33*(4), 295–311. https://doi.org/10.17744/mehc.33.4.j7540338q223t417

Victor, S. E., Glenn, C. R., & Klonsky, E. D. (2012). Is non-suicidal self-injury an "addiction"? A comparison of craving in substance use and non-suicidal self-injury. *Psychiatry Research, 197*(1–2), 73–77. https://doi.org/10.1016/j.psychres.2011.12.011

Victor, S. E., & Klonsky, E. D. (2014). Correlates of suicide attempts among self-injurers: A meta-analysis. *Clinical Psychology Review, 34*(4), 282–297. https://doi.org/10.1016/j.cpr.2014.03.005

Victor, S. E., Scott, L. N., Stepp, S. D., & Goldstein, T. R. (2018). I want you to want me: Interpersonal stress and affective experiences as within-person predictors of nonsuicidal self-injury and suicide urges in daily life. *Suicide and Life-Threatening Behavior, 49*(4),1157–1177. https://doi.org/10.1111/sltb.12513

Victor, S. E., Styer, D., & Washburn, J. J. (2015). Characteristics of nonsuicidal self-injury associated with suicidal ideation: Evidence from a clinical sample of youth. *Child and Adolescent Psychiatry and Mental Health, 9*(20), Article PMC4495693. https://doi.org/10.1186/s13034-015-0053-8

Victor, S. E., Styer, D., & Washburn, J. J. (2016). Functions of nonsuicidal self-injury (NSSI): Cross-sectional associations with NSSI duration and longitudinal changes over time and following treatment. *Psychiatry Research, 241,* 83–90. https://doi.org/10.1016/j.psychres.2016.04.083

Walsh, B. (2007). Clinical assessment of self-injury: A practical guide. *Journal of Clinical Psychology, 63*(11), 1057–1068. https://doi.org/10.1002/jclp.20413

Warner, S., & Spandler, H. (2012). New strategies for practice-based evidence: A focus on self-harm. *Qualitative Research in Psychology, 9*(1), 13–26. https://doi.org/10.1080/14780887.2012.630631

Washburn, J. J., Richardt, S. L., Styer, D. M., Gebhardt, M., Juzwin, K. R., Yourek, A., & Aldridge, D. (2012). Psychotherapeutic approaches to non-suicidal self-injury in adolescents. *Child and Adolescent Psychiatry and Mental Health, 6*(1), 14–14. https://doi.org/10.1186/1753-2000-6-14

Whitlock, J., Exner-Cortens, D., & Purington, A. (2014). Assessment of nonsuicidal self-injury: Development and initial validation of the n on-suicidal self-injury-assessment tool (NSSI-AT). *Psychological Assessment, 26,* 935–946. https://doi.org/10.1037/a0036611

Whitlock, J., Muehlkamp, J., Purington, A., Eckenrode, J., Barreira, P., Baral Abrams, G., Marchell, T., Kress, V., Girard, K., Chin, C., & Knox, K. (2011). Nonsuicidal self-injury in a college population: General trends and sex differences. *Journal of American College Health, 59,* 691–698. https://doi.org/10.1080/07448481.2010.529626

Yakeley, J., & Burbridge-James, W. (2018). Psychodynamic approaches to suicide and self-harm. *BJPsych Advances, 24,* 37–45. https://doi.org/10.1192/bja.2017.6

Yen, S., Kuehn, K., Melvin, C., Weinstock, L. M., Andover, M. S., Selby, E. A., Solomon, J. B., & Spirito, A. (2016). Predicting persistence of nonsuicidal self-injury in suicidal adolescents. *Suicide & Life-Threatening Behavior, 46*(1), 13–22. https://doi.org/10.1111/sltb.12167

Zetterqvist, M., Lundh, L. G., Dahlström, O., & Svedin, C. G. (2013). Prevalence and function of nonsuicidal self-injury (NSSI) in a community sample of adolescents, using suggested DSM-5 criteria for a potential NSSI disorder. *Journal of Abnormal Child Psychology, 41*(5), 759–773. https://doi.org/10.1007/s10802-013-9712-5

CHAPTER 7

The Epidemiology of Nonsuicidal Self-Injury and Self-Harm in Nonclinical Samples: Population-Level Trends

Louise Staring, Glenn Kiekens, *and* Olivia J. Kirtley

> **Abstract**
>
> This chapter evaluates current and emerging knowledge about the epidemiology of nonsuicidal self-injury (NSSI) and self-harm in nonclinical populations. It begins by discussing epidemiological patterns of NSSI and self-harm, including global prevalence rates across different age groups, the onset, and course, as well as cohort effects. The chapter then summarizes research on sociodemographic correlates and risk factors, including sex, ethnicity and race, and socioeconomic status. It also looks at the correlates of NSSI and self-harm in low- and middle-income countries. Moreover, the chapter assesses whether rates of NSSI and self-harm have increased more recently due to the COVID-19 pandemic. Finally, it considers challenges, recommendations, and future directions to advance research on the epidemiology of NSSI and self-harm.
>
> **Key Words:** nonsuicidal self-injury, self-harm, epidemiological patterns, prevalence, risk factors, COVID-19 pandemic

Introduction

This chapter will provide a timely overview of current and emerging knowledge about the epidemiology of non-suicidal self-injury (NSSI) and self-harm in nonclinical populations. NSSI and self-harm are two different conceptualizations of self-injury that are frequently used in research and practice. The term "NSSI" is predominantly used in the American research literature, which refers to the deliberate, self-inflicted damaging of one's body tissue without the intention to die, and for purposes not socially or culturally sanctioned (International Society for the Study of Self-Injury, 2022). NSSI can take many forms but usually involves cutting, hitting, burning, or scratching oneself (International Society for the Study of Self-Injury, 2022; Nock & Favazza, 2009). The fifth edition of the *Diagnostic and Statistical Manual for Mental Disorders* (DSM-5) included NSSI disorder as a "condition for further study" (American Psychiatric Association, 2013). Diagnosis of NSSI disorder requires NSSI on at least five days in the past year, significant distress due to NSSI, and several other criteria to be met (e.g., a psychological precipitant, intense urges, and expectation of a favorable outcome following NSSI; American Psychiatric Association,

2013). In contrast, the term "self-harm" is mainly used in British research literature and refers to self-injurious behaviors irrespective of suicidal intent, such as cutting, but also includes self-poisoning (Hawton & Harriss, 2008; National Institute for Health and Care Excellence, 2011).

To provide a comprehensive overview of the epidemiology of self-injury, we draw upon research on both NSSI and self-harm and refer to the terms used in the relevant literature. First, we will discuss epidemiological patterns of NSSI and self-harm, including global prevalence rates (i.e., lifetime, 12-month, and current estimates) across different age groups, the onset, and course (i.e., age of onset, persistence rates, and thoughts-behavior transitions) as well as cohort effects. Second, we will summarize research on sociodemographic correlates and risk factors, including sex, ethnicity and race, and socioeconomic status. Here, we will also discuss the correlates of NSSI and self-harm in low- and middle-income countries. Third, we will discuss whether rates of NSSI and self-harm have increased more recently due to the COVID-19 pandemic (see Brausch & Clapham, this volume). Finally, we will consider challenges, recommendations, and future directions to advance research on the epidemiology of NSSI and self-harm. In doing so, we propose a research agenda for epidemiological studies and discuss the implications for clinical practice and community settings (e.g., schools and colleges).

Prevalence

A variety of epidemiological outcomes indicate a higher prevalence of NSSI and self-harm during adolescence (12–18 years: Jaworska & MacQueen, 2015) and emerging adulthood (18–29 years: Arnett, 2000, 2015)—both sensitive developmental periods for the onset of mental health problems (World Health Organization, 2020).

Lifetime Prevalence

Lifetime prevalence refers to the proportion of individuals who report NSSI or self-harm at least once in their life. NSSI prevalence is highest among adolescents (22.6%, Gillies et al., 2018; 17.2%, Swannell et al., 2014) and emerging adults (13.4%, Swannell et al., 2014) compared to in children (7.6%, Luby et al., 2019) and adults (~5%; Klonsky, 2011; Swannell et al., 2014). In addition, some evidence suggests that rates are higher in college students (~20%) compared to non-college-attending peers (~12%; Swannell et al., 2014).

Lifetime prevalence of self-harm is also highest among adolescents (11.4%, Gillies et al., 2018; 16.1%, Muehlenkamp et al., 2012) and emerging adults (16.2%, O'Connor et al., 2018) compared to in children (1.3%; Meltzer et al., 2001) and adults (3–7%, McManus et al., 2020; Soomro & Kakhi, 2015).

Twelve-Month Prevalence

Twelve-month prevalence refers to the proportion of individuals who report NSSI or self-harm during the past year. To the best of our knowledge, no study has investigated the 12-month prevalence of NSSI among children. Among adolescents, the 12-month prevalence of NSSI is estimated as 18.6% (Gillies et al., 2018), compared to 3–8% in emerging adults (Benjet et al., 2017; Kiekens et al., 2016, 2023), and 0.9% in adults (Klonsky, 2011).

NSSI disorder appears to be less common, with 12-month prevalence estimates ranging from 1.5% to 7.6% in adolescents (Benjet et al., 2017; Brown & Plener, 2017; Buelens et al., 2020; Plener et al., 2016), 0.8% to 2.3% in emerging adults (Kiekens et al., 2018b, 2023), and 0.3% to 3% in adults (Andover, 2014; Plener et al., 2016).

For self-harm, the 12-month prevalence is estimated to be 8% among children and adolescents (Zubrick et al., 2016), but studies including only adolescents indicate a higher rate (13%, Gillies et al., 2018). In emerging adults, 12-month prevalence is estimated to be in the 4–10% range (Lin et al., 2021; O'Connor et al., 2018). To the best of our knowledge, no studies have investigated the 12-month prevalence of self-harm in adults.

Developmental Course

In what follows, we discuss epidemiological literature on the age of onset and incidence and persistence rates of NSSI and self-harm as well as evidence for potential increases over time.

Age of Onset

The onset of NSSI and self-harm peaks during adolescence and emerging adulthood (see Kiekens et al., this volume). NSSI often first occurs between the ages of 14 and 16, with a second (smaller) peak in the onset of NSSI between 17 and 24 years of age (Gandhi et al., 2018; Kiekens et al., 2019). Similarly, self-harm behaviors mostly have their onset between the ages of 12 and 16 years (Gillies et al., 2018; Morey et al., 2017; Stallard et al., 2013) and 20 and 24 years (Griffin et al., 2018). Earlier onset of self-injury is associated with a higher risk of (more frequent) engagement in NSSI (Ammerman et al., 2018; Muehlenkamp et al., 2019) later in life and of making a future suicide attempt (Kiekens et al., 2018a; Ribeiro et al., 2017).

Incidence Rates

Incidence refers to the proportion of individuals without a lifetime history of NSSI or self-harm who report an onset of NSSI or self-harm within a specified period. The one-year incidence of NSSI is 3.8% (Andrews et al., 2014) in adolescents and ranges from 2% to 4% in emerging adults (Hamza & Willoughby, 2014; Riley et al., 2015). Specifically, in the study of Kiekens et al. (2019), the incidence of NSSI in college students was 10.3% in the first year of college, and at 6% in the second year.

For self-harm, one-year incidence rates of 3.6% (Larsson & Sund, 2008) to 15% (Stallard et al., 2013) have been observed in adolescents. To the best of our knowledge, there are no large-scale studies assessing incidence rates of NSSI and self-harm among adults.

Persistence Rates

Persistence refers to the proportion of individuals with a lifetime history of NSSI or self-harm who report ongoing engagement within a specified period. Although studies that estimate persistence rates are scarce, 12-month NSSI persistence rates are in the 20–39% range among adolescents (X. Liu et al., 2021; Steinhoff et al., 2021). Among first-year college students, 12-month persistence was recently estimated at 44% (Kiekens et al., 2023).

Figures for self-harm persistence generally come from hospital presentation data, and meta-analytic evidence suggests a 12-month persistence rate of 16.3% for individuals ages 10 years and older (Carroll et al., 2014). More recently, large-scale prospective research reported a 12-month persistence rate of 12% among individuals ages 16 years and over (Steeg et al., 2016). Further research has suggested a 12-month persistence rate of 19.2% among children, adolescents, and young adults ages 10–29 years (Bennardi et al., 2016).

Increases over Time

Emerging evidence suggests that the prevalence of NSSI (e.g., Duffy et al., 2019) and self-harm (e.g., Gillies et al., 2018) has increased over time. In a meta-analysis by Lang and Yao (2018), the lifetime prevalence of NSSI increased from 18.8% in 2008 to 28.5% in 2018 among Chinese middle school students. Likewise, the lifetime prevalence of self-harm appears to have increased significantly over time among adolescents (between 1990 and 2015 in Gillies et al., 2018; from 11% to 14% between 2005 and 2015 in Patalay & Gage, 2019) and adults (from 2.4% in 2000 to 6.4% in 2014 in McManus et al., 2019). The incidence of self-harm also appears to have increased over time (between 2003 and 2018; incidence rate ratio = 2.25 in Cybulski et al., 2021).

An important caveat is that, in some studies, apparent increases may be due to a nonresponse bias (Mortier et al., 2018). For example, in a study by Wester et al. (2018), which reported an increased lifetime and current prevalence of NSSI over time, response rates also decreased across the three assessment points (from 19.3% in 2008 to 11.9% in 2011, and 14.7% in 2015). A similar trend was also observed in the study of Duffy et al. (2019) (from 43% between 2007 and 2009 to 25% between 2010 and 2013). Prospective cohort studies are needed with sufficiently high retention rates to confirm the possibility of an increase in the prevalence of NSSI.

Thoughts-Behavior Transitions

The past decades have seen a shift toward "ideation-to-action" theoretical models of suicidal behavior, which distinguish between factors associated with thoughts (ideation) about suicide and those associated with suicidal behavior (Klonsky et al., 2018). While such ideation-to-action approaches have thus far primarily been applied in the context of suicidal ideation and behavior, researchers have argued that self-injurious thoughts and behaviors should also be differentiated from each other (Kiekens et al., 2019; Klonsky et al., 2021; Klonsky & May, 2015). However, to date, few epidemiological studies have considered this differentiation. In what follows, we discuss what is known about the prevalence of NSSI and self-harm thoughts, the transition from thoughts to NSSI and self-harm behavior, and the transition from NSSI and self-harm to suicidal behavior (see Victor et al., this volume).

Thoughts of NSSI and self-harm occur more frequently than behaviors. This is reflected in a higher lifetime prevalence of NSSI thoughts versus behaviors in college students (24.9% vs. 22.9%, Kiekens et al., 2018b) and self-harm thoughts versus behaviors in school pupils (12.2% vs. 11.4%, O'Connor et al., 2012), college students (22.6% vs. 19.6%, Sivertsen et al., 2019), and adults (12.3% vs. 11.6%, O'Connor et al., 2018). A recent study found that only 2% of college students reported experiencing NSSI thoughts in the absence of subsequent NSSI behavior, suggesting that most young people who think about NSSI also act upon their thoughts—within an average transition window of two months (Kiekens et al., 2018a). Furthermore, among adolescents with a history of self-harm thoughts—but no self-harm behavior—researchers observed that 17.3% developed self-harm behavior six months later (Stallard et al., 2013). Finally, studies using ecological momentary assessment or experience sampling methods have also shown that it typically takes people who engage in self-injury between 1 and 30 minutes to transition from thoughts to behavior in daily life (Fitzpatrick et al., 2020; Nock et al., 2009). Hence, these findings underscore the relevance of differentiating thoughts and behavior in future work on prevention of self-injurious thoughts and behaviors.

Engaging in NSSI (Kiekens et al., 2018a; Ribeiro et al., 2017; Whitlock et al., 2013) and self-harm (Owens et al., 2002; Zahl & Hawton, 2004) increases individuals' risk of making a suicide attempt. In adolescents and young adults, the population attributable risk of self-injurious thoughts and behaviors for future suicide attempt was estimated at 26% (Castellví et al., 2017). In college students with a history of NSSI and suicide ideation, plan, and attempt, NSSI behavior precedes the emergence of suicidal thoughts and behaviors 55.8% to 80.1% of the time, with on average ten months, 1.6 years, and 3.2 years between NSSI and the transition to suicide ideation, a suicide plan, and a first suicide attempt, respectively (Kiekens et al., 2018a). The risk of death by suicide following a self-harm episode is higher in men (3.2%) than in women (0.8%) and is further elevated in the case of multiple self-harm episodes (5.7% of men and 2.7% of women) among all ages (Zahl & Hawton, 2004).

Sociodemographic Correlates and Risk Factors

A number of sociodemographic factors have been associated with the presence of NSSI and self-harm in the community, which will be reviewed here: sex, sexuality and gender identity, ethnicity and race, and socio economic status. We end this section by considering geographical region and review what is known about the epidemiology of NSSI and self-harm in low- and middle-income countries.

Sex

Research often suggests that NSSI occurs slightly more often in females than in males. For example, in a meta-analysis, Bresin and Schoenleber (2015) observed that females (33.8%) are 1.5 times more likely than males (26.4%) to report engaging in NSSI. Of note, men and women use different NSSI methods. For example, while females are more likely to report cutting and scratching, biting, hair pulling, and interfering with wound healing, men are more likely to report burning, hitting, and head-banging than females (Bresin & Schoenleber, 2015).

Evidence regarding sex-related differences in self-harm in the community is mixed—some studies suggest that females more frequently report a history of self-harm (e.g. Gillies et al., 2018), while others do not (e.g., Geulayov et al., 2018).

Sexuality and Gender Identity

Individuals identifying as Lesbian, Gay, Bisexual, Transgender, Queer or Questioning, or as having another sexual identity (LGBTQ+) report higher rates of NSSI thoughts and behaviors (Marshall et al., 2016) and self-harm behaviors (Williams et al., 2021) compared to individuals identifying as heterosexual and cisgender (see Taliaferro et al., this volume). In their meta-analytic review, Batejan et al. (2015) found that individuals from a sexual minority group (i.e., lesbian, gay, bisexual, and questioning)—especially adolescents—more often reported a history of NSSI (40.6%) compared to those identifying as heterosexuals (24%). Specifically, individuals identifying as transgender and bisexual reported the highest lifetime prevalence of NSSI (46.65% and 41.47%, respectively) compared to individuals identifying as heterosexual and/or cisgender (14.57%; R. T. Liu et al., 2019).

Similarly, compared to those identifying as heterosexual, individuals identifying as LGBT have an elevated lifetime (47% vs. 23%) and 12-month (45% vs. 18%) prevalence of self-harm (Quarshie et al., 2020). Furthermore, adolescents identifying as a sexual minority (i.e., lesbian, gay, bisexual, pansexual, asexual, queer, and unknown/unwilling to answer) are twice as likely to self-harm as their heterosexual peers (O'Reilly et al., 2021).

Ethnicity and Race

NSSI (Rojas-Velasquez et al., 2021) and self-harm (Al-Sharifi et al., 2015) are present across all ethnic and racial groups. While some studies indicate slight differences in the prevalence of NSSI (e.g., Monto et al., 2018) and self-harm (e.g., Gratz et al., 2012) according to race and ethnicity, no conclusions can be drawn from the sparse research currently available.

Socioeconomic Status

People from different socioeconomic groups are exposed to different levels of stress, which is associated with various negative psychological outcomes (Aneshensel & Avison, 2015). However, it remains unclear whether a low socioeconomic status (SES) is associated with a higher or lower prevalence of NSSI. Evidence is mixed and differs according to the conceptualization of SES. For instance, low SES—defined by low income and unemployment—has been correlated with a history of NSSI and/or a suicide attempt (Coppersmith et al., 2017). SES (also conceptualized as low income and unemployment) has also been shown to moderate the relationship between stressful life events and NSSI, where encountering stressful life events is associated with NSSI in those from a low but not from a high SES background (Wang et al., 2020). Conversely, high educational performance—linked with a high SES (Sharma, 2017)—has been associated with a higher NSSI prevalence among adolescents (Baetens et al., 2011).

Similarly, low SES is associated with a higher prevalence of self-harm thoughts (Kokkevi et al., 2012) and behaviors (Gratz et al., 2012) in adolescents. Notably, researchers observed that the risk of self-harm increased the longer a child experiences socioeconomic deprivation (i.e., low parental income; Mok et al., 2018) or the more SES decreases over time (i.e., a lower parental income, uptake of social welfare benefits, and changing to a one-parent household; Jablonska et al., 2008). Additionally, poor school performance—linked with a low SES (Sharma, 2017)—has been associated with an increased risk for self-harm in adolescents (Brunner et al., 2007; Zhang et al., 2016).

Low- and Middle-Income Countries

Although NSSI and self-harm have mostly been examined in Western societies, lifetime and 12-month prevalence rates of NSSI (11.5–33.8%, Thippaiah et al., 2020) and self-harm (15.5–31.3%, Aggarwal et al., 2017) in low- and middle-income countries (LMICs) seem based on the currently available evidence similar to those in high-income countries (HICs).

However, Knipe et al. (2019) posit that *repeated* self-harm might be lower in LMICs than in HICs, as they found a lower risk for repeated self-harm in the 12 months following a hospital presentation for self-harm in Sri Lanka (3.1%) compared to HICs (16.3%, Carroll et al., 2014). A higher prevalence of self-poisoning can potentially explain this lower risk of repeated self-harm in LMICs (Aggarwal et al., 2017; Knipe et al., 2019)—which is more fatal than other methods of self-harm and, therefore, less often repeated (Carroll et al., 2014; Knipe et al., 2019; Vijayakumar & Armstrong, 2019). However, these findings should be interpreted tentatively, as cross-national epidemiological studies that compare rates across countries using a similar methodology are lacking (Vijayakumar & Armstrong, 2019).

Methods

The most commonly reported method of NSSI is cutting (94.7%), followed by burning (78.9%), self-battery (73.7%), scratching (58.9%), biting (50.5%), wound interference

(48.4%), and head-banging (46.3%; Cipriano et al., 2017; Swannell et al., 2014). Within the self-harm literature, the most commonly reported methods are intentional drug overdoses (68.3%), self-cutting (23.8%), attempted hanging (6.6%), and attempted drowning (3.0%) (Cully et al., 2019).

A few studies have investigated risk associations of specific methods among people who engage in NSSI and self-harm. For instance, individuals who report cutting are at higher risk of repeated self-harm (Bennardi et al., 2016; Cully et al., 2019) and a subsequent suicide attempt (Hawton et al., 2012; Kiekens et al., 2018a). Conversely, self-poisoning has been associated with less repeated self-harm, because the fatality rate of this method is higher than other methods of self-harm (Carroll et al., 2014; Knipe et al., 2019; Vijayakumar & Armstrong, 2019).

Functions

Individuals engage in NSSI and self-harm behaviors for various reasons (Edmondson et al., 2016; see Taylor et al., this volume). According to the Four-Function Model (FFM), negative and positive reinforcement processes maintain NSSI on interpersonal and intrapersonal levels (Bentley et al., 2014; Nock & Prinstein, 2004). When individuals engage in NSSI to fulfill intrapersonal functions, it could be used to relieve or distract from negative or unwanted thoughts and feelings (automatic negative reinforcement) or as a form of stimulation or emotion generation (automatic positive reinforcement; Bentley et al., 2014). Interpersonal reasons for engaging in NSSI include escaping uncomfortable social situations (social negative reinforcement) or seeking help from others (social positive reinforcement; Bentley et al., 2014). Studies have consistently shown that most people report engaging in NSSI to relieve or distract from negative or unwanted thoughts and feelings (Bentley et al., 2014; Taylor et al., 2018). For instance, in a recent meta-analysis, intrapersonal functions were endorsed by 74% of individuals (especially emotion regulation), while an interpersonal function of NSSI was reported by approximately half of those with a history of NSSI (44%). Interestingly, one recent study demonstrated that the functions of NSSI can change within one person over time and can vary depending on the social context (Coppersmith et al., 2021).

The main reported reasons for engaging in self-harm are also emotion regulation (Edmondson et al., 2016), including escaping from a terrible state of mind (Gillies et al., 2018; Rasmussen et al., 2016) and self-punishment (Edmondson et al., 2016; Gillies et al., 2018). Less commonly reported functions of self-harm include dissociation and sensation-seeking (Edmondson et al., 2016).

COVID-19

Questions have been raised about the potential effects of the recent COVID-19 pandemic on suicidal thoughts and behaviors—including NSSI (Hasking et al., 2021; Plener, 2021) and self-harm (Kapur et al., 2021)—especially among young people. Research on the impact of the COVID-19 pandemic on mental health outcomes is quickly evolving. However, it remains challenging to draw definitive conclusions, as epidemiological studies comparing NSSI and self-harm rates before and after the lockdown are scarce.

Nonetheless, several studies suggest the prevalence of NSSI (e.g., Tang et al., 2021; Zetterqvist et al., 2021) and self-harm (e.g., Iob et al., 2020; Paul & Fancourt, 2021) may have increased as a result of the COVID-19 pandemic, while others did not find significant differences (Hamza et al., 2021). In the study of Tang et al. (2021) 12-month NSSI prevalence increased during the first lockdown in March 2020 (40.9%) compared to before COVID-19 (8–24%, Tang et al., 2021). Similarly, NSSI lifetime rates increased from the spring of 2020 (24.4%) to the spring of 2021 (30.6%) among adolescents (Zetterqvist et al., 2021). In addition, among different age groups, slight increases in self-harm have also been observed. For example, one study comparing past week rates of self-harm across the first six weeks of the lockdown found an increase from 0.7% to 1.4% (O'Connor et al., 2021).

Several studies also show how service utilization for self-harm has changed during the first wave of the COVID-19 pandemic (March to August 2020), with decreasing self-harm presentations to general practitioners (GPs), hospital emergency departments, and psychiatric units (DelPozo-Banos et al., 2021; Henry et al., 2021; John et al., 2020). At GP practices, the incidence of self-harm decreased by 37.6% between April 1 and May 1, 2020 (Carr et al., 2021). The weekly number of self-harm presentations in hospital emergency departments was also 30.6% lower than in the pre-lockdown period (January 6 to March 22, 2020 in Hawton et al., 2021). This decrease in self-harm presentations was also found during the second pandemic wave (August 2020 to March 2021 in Delpozo-Banos et al., 2021).

Notably, during the first wave, those who self-harmed were more likely to consult their GP rather than present to an emergency department or a psychiatric unit, possibly due to fears about contracting the virus or increasing pressure on strained hospital services (DelPozo-Banos et al., 2021). Additionally, the use of more lethal self-harm methods were observed, especially during the first wave. However, during the second wave, the number of hospitalizations following a presentation to an emergency department for self-harm decreased. These findings suggest that there were more stringent criteria for hospital admission (linked with the COVID-19 restrictions) and that people might not have received the care they needed (DelPozo-Banos et al., 2021).

Challenges and Recommendations

While the literature on the epidemiology of NSSI and self-harm continues to expand, several critical challenges should be addressed in future research. In the following section, we discuss some challenges, along with recommendations for future research.

The first and most significant challenge includes the lack of common terminology, making it difficult to compare findings across studies (Muehlenkamp et al., 2012).

Various terms are used to conceptualize self-injurious thoughts and behaviors, among which "NSSI" and "self-harm" are most frequently used in research and practice. NSSI emphasizes the importance of studying and treating self-injury as distinct from suicidal thoughts and behaviors (Angelotta, 2015; Butler & Malone, 2013). Conversely, the term "self-harm" is broader, and does not distinguish self-injury based on its intent but aims to reflect that motivations for engaging in self-harm behavior may differ within individuals from episode to episode, or even within a single episode (Kapur et al., 2013). Although standardized, validated assessment methods exist to measure NSSI (e.g., Self-Injurious Thoughts and Behaviors Interview-Revised [SITBI-R]; Hooley et al., 2020) and self-harm (Inventory of Statements About Self-Injury [ISAS]: Klonsky & Glenn, 2009), little attention has been devoted to the conceptual overlap and distinctions between NSSI and self-harm. See Hooley et al. (2020) for a thoughtful discussion of this issue. In part, this may be due to heterogeneity in self-harm assessment methods—an issue already highlighted some time ago in a review by Borschmann et al. (2012)—and whether they do in fact capture self-harm, as per the NICE (2011) guidelines definition. Therefore, it is essential to open up discussion and research on the conceptualization of and assessment methods for NSSI and self-harm (Silverman & De Leo, 2016). This would facilitate the creation of national and international guidelines on how to collect self-injury data that are cross-culturally and internationally applicable.

The second challenge encompasses the need for a broader geographical focus. Most of the existing research on NSSI and self-harm has been conducted in WEIRD (Western, Educated, Industrialized, Rich, and Democratic) samples (i.e., Henrich, 2020), making it difficult to compare and explain findings across different cultures and countries. The research leading up to the development of NSSI disorder, for instance, mainly relies upon studies conducted in the United States and Canada. This raises questions about the cultural validity of this potential diagnosis (Muehlenkamp et al., 2012). Similarly, few studies have investigated self-harm in low- and middle-income countries (Knipe et al., 2019; Vijayakumar & Armstrong, 2019). Therefore, large, high-quality, cross-national studies are needed to provide better insights into the cross-cultural differences in the epidemiology of NSSI and self-harm (for more information, also see Wilson, this volume).

The third challenge encompasses the lack of differentiation between epidemiological outcomes (e.g., prevalence, onset, persistence, and remission). Having a detailed understanding of the epidemiology and course of NSSI and self-harm is a prerequisite for risk screening, targeted prevention, and intervention planning. However, even though governments should establish national surveillance systems for all forms of suicidal behaviors (World Health Organization, 2014)—which can provide us with these data—such national registries are not systematically implemented (Silverman & De Leo, 2016). Instead, we should draw upon examples such as the long-running, multicenter study of self-harm, which records self-harm presentations to emergency departments in general hospitals in Oxford, Manchester, and Leeds (Hawton et al., 2007), or the National

Self-harm Registry in Ireland: a population-level system for monitoring hospital-treated self-harm (Griffin et al., 2017). While regional and national registry systems provide myriad opportunities for advancing our understanding of NSSI and self-harm epidemiology, a key limitation of these systems—which generally rely upon hospital presentations—is that most people do not present to healthcare services for self-injurious thoughts and behaviors (Geulayov et al., 2018; McMahon et al., 2014).

Consequently, registry-based estimates of NSSI and self-harm are likely to be an underestimate, as they do not account for community-occurring NSSI and self-harm. Furthermore, the phenomenology of those presenting to healthcare services for NSSI or self-harm may differ from those who stay unnoticed in the community. Therefore, we need to optimize the assessment of NSSI and self-harm also in nonclinical populations. For instance, asking about NSSI or self-harm thoughts and behaviors should become standard in mental health assessments. International school- or university-based screening, for example, the Child and Adolescent Self-Harm in Europe Study (CASE) (Madge et al., 2008) or the World Mental Health International College Student Initiative (Cuijpers et al., 2019), could also significantly increase our knowledge about non-hospital-presenting NSSI and self-harm thoughts and behaviors. Furthermore, large-scale epidemiological population surveys should include NSSI and self-harm measures (e.g., McManus et al., 2020). Given that NSSI and self-harm are major public health issues—and are important antecedents of suicide—a radical public health approach to gathering data may be to implement questions on NSSI and self-harm in national censuses.

The fourth challenge encompasses the lack of differentiation between thoughts and behaviors in research on NSSI and self-harm. Consistent with ideation-to-action frameworks, including the Interpersonal Psychological Theory (Joiner, 2005; Van Orden et al., 2010), the Three Step Theory (Klonsky & May, 2015), and the Integrated Motivational-Volitional model (O'Connor & Kirtley, 2018), such differentiation is becoming increasingly common practice in self-harm and suicide research (e.g., Kokkevi et al., 2012; O'Connor et al., 2018; Stallard et al., 2013). Making this distinction is essential as the factors leading to the development of thoughts about NSSI and self-harm are not necessarily the same as the factors that cause an individual to act upon their thoughts and engage in NSSI or self-harm behavior. For instance, those who have self-harmed report more negative life stress than those who have thought about self-harm without engaging in the behavior (O'Connor et al., 2012). Some studies have also started to differentiate NSSI thoughts from behaviors (e.g., Kiekens et al., 2018a; Kranzler et al., 2018; Martin et al., 2011), but more work on this topic is needed. For example, one recent study indicated that fluctuations in affect predict thoughts of NSSI, while a low sense of self-efficacy to resist NSSI predicted NSSI behavior (Kiekens et al., 2020). Hence, to determine what predicts the emergence of thoughts and the transition from these self-injurious thoughts to behavior, we should measure NSSI and self-harm thoughts and behaviors separately in future studies.

The fifth and final challenge is our lack of understanding about the factors involved in the emergence and development of NSSI and self-harm thoughts and behaviors in the short and long term. If we are to understand the long-term course of NSSI and self-harm, prospective longitudinal cohort studies are needed, which span from childhood up to adulthood (e.g., Kirtley et al., 2021; Zubrick et al., 2016). However, we should also expand our focus to short-term changes in NSSI and self-harm thoughts and behaviors in daily life, as clinicians face the challenge of gauging an individual's risk in the next hours and days (Glenn & Nock, 2014). Real-time assessments—using experience sampling methodology (ESM; Myin-Germeys et al., 2018)—within longitudinal cohort studies (i.e., measurement burst designs) can advance knowledge of individual-level momentary predictors of NSSI and self-harm and illuminate how such short-term patterns relate to long-term developmental change and outcomes (see Kiekens et al., 2021). Research employing ESM would allow us to better understand the differences between those who do and do not experience NSSI and self-harm thoughts and/or behaviors (i.e., the between-person perspective), as well as what makes an individual think about NSSI or self-harm, or act upon such thoughts (i.e., the within-person perspective)—not only throughout developmental periods, but also in the short term, across hours and days. Taking an epidemiological perspective in this type of research can provide a rich and detailed understanding of who is at risk when and why, enabling the development of more tailored public health and clinical interventions to prevent NSSI and self-harm.

References

Aggarwal, S., Patton, G., Reavley, N., Sreenivasan, S. A., & Berk, M. (2017). Youth self-harm in low- and middle-income countries: Systematic review of the risk and protective factors. *International Journal of Social Psychiatry*, *63*(4), 359–375. https://doi.org/10.1177/0020764017700175

Al-Sharifi, A., Krynicki, C. R., & Upthegrove, R. (2015). Self-harm and ethnicity: A systematic review. *International Journal of Social Psychiatry*, *61*(6), 600–612. https://doi.org/10.1177/0020764015573085

American Psychiatric Association. (2013). *Diagnostic and statistical manual of mental disorders*. https://doi.org/10.1176/appi.books.9780890425596

Ammerman, B. A., Jacobucci, R., Kleiman, E. M., Uyeji, L. L., & McCloskey, M. S. (2018). The relationship between nonsuicidal self-injury age of onset and severity of self-harm. *Suicide and Life-Threatening Behavior*, *48*(1), 31–37. https://doi.org/10.1111/sltb.12330

Andover, M. S. (2014). Non-suicidal self-injury disorder in a community sample of adults. *Psychiatry Research*, *219*(2), 305–310. https://doi.org/10.1016/j.psychres.2014.06.001

Andrews, T., Martin, G., Hasking, P., & Page, A. (2014). Predictors of onset for non-suicidal delf-injury within a school-based sample of adolescents. *Prevention Science*, *15*(6), 850–859. https://doi.org/10.1007/s11121-013-0412-8

Aneshensel, C. S., & Avison, W. R. (2015). The stress process: An appreciation of Leonard I. Pearlin. *Society and Mental Health*, *5*(2), 67–85. https://doi.org/10.1177/2156869315585388

Angelotta, C. (2015). Defining and refining self-harm: A historical perspective on nonsuicidal self-injury. *Journal of Nervous & Mental Disease*, *203*(2), 75–80. https://doi.org/10.1097/NMD.0000000000000243

Arnett, J. J. (2000). Emerging adulthood: A theory of development from the late teens through the twenties. *American Psychologist*, *55*(5), 469–480. https://doi.org/10.1037/0003-066X.55.5.469

Arnett, J. J. (2015). *The Oxford handbook of emerging adulthood*. Oxford: Oxford University Press.

Baetens, I., Claes, L., Muehlenkamp, J., Grietens, H., & Onghena, P. (2011). Non-suicidal and suicidal self-injurious behavior among Flemish adolescents: A web-survey. *Archives of Suicide Research*, *15*(1), 56–67. https://doi.org/10.1080/13811118.2011.540467

Batejan, K. L., Jarvi, S. M., & Swenson, L. P. (2015). Sexual orientation and non-suicidal self-injury: A meta-analytic review. *Archives of Suicide Research*, *19*(2), 131–150. https://doi.org/10.1080/13811118.2014.957450

Benjet, C., González-Herrera, I., Castro-Silva, E., Méndez, E., Borges, G., Casanova, L., & Medina-Mora, M. E. (2017). Non-suicidal self-injury in Mexican young adults: Prevalence, associations with suicidal behavior and psychiatric disorders, and DSM-5 proposed diagnostic criteria. *Journal of Affective Disorders*, *215*, 1–8. https://doi.org/10.1016/j.jad.2017.03.025

Bennardi, M., McMahon, E., Corcoran, P., Griffin, E., & Arensman, E. (2016). Risk of repeated self-harm and associated factors in children, adolescents and young adults. *BMC Psychiatry*, *16*(1), 1–12. https://doi.org/10.1186/s12888-016-1120-2

Bentley, K. H., Nock, M. K., & Barlow, D. H. (2014). The four-function model of nonsuicidal self-injury: Key directions for future research. *Clinical Psychological Science*, *2*(5), 638–656. https://doi.org/10.1177/2167702613514563

Borschmann, R., Hogg, J., Phillips, R., & Moran, P. (2012). Measuring self-harm in adults: A systematic review. *European Psychiatry*, *27*(3), 176–180. https://doi.org/10.1016/j.eurpsy.2011.04.005

Bresin, K., & Schoenleber, M. (2015). Gender differences in the prevalence of nonsuicidal self-injury: A meta-analysis. *Clinical Psychology Review*, *38*, 55–64. https://doi.org/10.1016/j.cpr.2015.02.009

Brown, R. C., & Plener, P. L. (2017). Non-suicidal self-injury in adolescence. *Current Psychiatry Reports*, *19*(3), 1–8. https://doi.org/10.1007/s11920-017-0767-9

Brunner, R., Parzer, P., Haffner, J., Steen, R., Roos, J., Klett, M., & Resch, F. (2007). Prevalence and psychological correlates of occasional and repetitive deliberate self-harm in adolescents. *Archives of Pediatrics and Adolescent Medicine*, *161*(7), 641–649. https://doi.org/10.1001/archpedi.161.7.641

Buelens, T., Luyckx, K., Kiekens, G., Gandhi, A., Muehlenkamp, J. J., & Claes, L. (2020). Investigating the DSM-5 criteria for non-suicidal self-injury disorder in a community sample of adolescents. *Journal of Affective Disorders*, *260*, 314–322. https://doi.org/10.1016/j.jad.2019.09.009

Butler, A. M., & Malone, K. (2013). Attempted suicide v. non-suicidal self-injury: Behaviour syndrome or diagnosis? *British Journal of Psychiatry*, *202*(5), 324–325. https://doi.org/10.1192/bjp.bp.112.113506

Carr, M. J., Steeg, S., Webb, R. T., Kapur, N., Chew-Graham, C. A., Abel, K. M., Hope, H., Pierce, M., & Ashcroft, D. M. (2021). Effects of the COVID-19 pandemic on primary care-recorded mental illness and self-harm episodes in the UK: A population-based cohort study. *The Lancet Public Health*, *6*(2), e124–e135. https://doi.org/10.1016/S2468-2667(20)30288-7

Carroll, R., Metcalfe, C., & Gunnell, D. (2014). Hospital presenting self-harm and risk of fatal and non-fatal repetition: Systematic review and meta-analysis. *PLoS One*, *9*(2), Article e8994. https://doi.org/10.1371/journal.pone.0089944

Castellví, P., Lucas-Romero, E., Miranda-Mendizábal, A., Parés-Badell, O., Almenara, J., Alonso, I., Blasco, M. J., Cebrià, A., Gabilondo, A., Gili, M., Lagares, C., Piqueras, J. A., Roca, M., Rodríguez-Marín, J., Rodríguez-Jimenez, T., Soto-Sanz, V., & Alonso, J. (2017). Longitudinal association between self-injurious thoughts and behaviors and suicidal behavior in adolescents and young adults: A systematic review with meta-analysis. *Journal of Affective Disorders*, *215*, 37–48. https://doi.org/10.1016/j.jad.2017.03.035

Cipriano, A., Cella, S., & Cotrufo, P. (2017). Nonsuicidal self-injury: A systematic review. *Frontiers in Psychology*, *8*, 1–14. https://doi.org/10.3389/fpsyg.2017.01946

Coppersmith, D. D. L., Bentley, K. H., Kleiman, E. M., & Nock, M. K. (2021). Variability in the functions of nonsuicidal self-injury: Evidence from three real-time monitoring studies. *Behavior Therapy*, *52*(6), 1516–1528. https://doi.org/10.1016/j.beth.2021.05.003

Coppersmith, D. D. L., Nada-Raja, S., & Beautrais, A. (2017). Non-suicidal self-injury and suicide attempts in a New Zealand birth cohort. *Journal of Affective Disorders*, *221*, 89–96. https://doi.org/10.3389/fpsyg.2017.01946

Cuijpers, P., Auerbach, R. P., Benjet, C., Bruffaerts, R., Ebert, D., Karyotaki, E., & Kessler, R. C. (2019). The World Health Organization World Mental Health International College Student initiative: An overview. *International Journal of Methods in Psychiatric Research*, *28*(2), Article e1761. https://doi.org/10.1002/mpr.1761

Cully, G., Corcoran, P., Leahy, D., Griffin, E., Dillon, C., Cassidy, E., & Shiely, F. (2019). Method of self-harm and risk of self-harm repetition: Findings from a national self-harm registry. *Journal of Affective Disorders, 246*, 843–850. https://doi.org/10.1016/j.jad.2018.10.372

Cybulski, L., Ashcroft, D. M., Carr, M. J., Garg, S., Chew-Graham, C. A., Kapur, N., & Webb, R. T. (2021). Temporal trends in annual incidence rates for psychiatric disorders and self-harm among children and adolescents in the UK, 2003–2018. *BMC Psychiatry, 21*(1), 229. https://doi.org/10.1186/s12888-021-03235-w

DelPozo-Banos, M., Lee, S. C., Friedmann, Y., Akbari, A., Torabi, F., Lloyd, K., Lyons, R. A., & John, A. (2021). Healthcare presentations with self-harm and the association with COVID-19: an e-cohort whole-population-based study using individual-level linked routine electronic health records in Wales, UK, 2016 – March 2021. *medRxiv*. https://doi.org/10.1101/2021.08.13.21261861

Duffy, M. E., Twenge, J. M., & Joiner, T. E. (2019). Trends in mood and anxiety symptoms and suicide-related outcomes among U.S. undergraduates, 2007–2018: Evidence from two national surveys. *Journal of Adolescent Health, 65*(5), 590–598. https://doi.org/10.1016/j.jadohealth.2019.04.033

Edmondson, A. J., Brennan, C. A., & House, A. O. (2016). Non-suicidal reasons for self-harm: A systematic review of self-reported accounts. *Journal of Affective Disorders, 191*, 109–117. https://doi.org/10.1016/j.jad.2015.11.043

Fitzpatrick, S., Kranzler, A., Fehling, K., Lindqvist, J., & Selby, E. (2020). Investigating the role of the intensity and duration of self-injury thoughts in self-injury with ecological momentary assessment. *Psychiatry Research, 284*, 112761. https://doi.org/10.1016/j.psychres.2020.112761

Gandhi, A., Luyckx, K., Baetens, I., Kiekens, G., Sleuwaegen, E., Berens, A., Maitra, S., & Claes, L. (2018). Age of onset of non-suicidal self-injury in Dutch-speaking adolescents and emerging adults: An event history analysis of pooled data. *Comprehensive Psychiatry, 80*, 170–178. https://doi.org/10.1016/j.comppsych.2017.10.007

Geulayov, G., Casey, D., McDonald, K. C., Foster, P., Pritchard, K., Wells, C., Clements, C., Kapur, N., Ness, J., Waters, K., & Hawton, K. (2018). Incidence of suicide, hospital-presenting non-fatal self-harm, and community-occurring non-fatal self-harm in adolescents in England (the iceberg model of self-harm): A retrospective study. *The Lancet Psychiatry, 5*(2), 167–174. https://doi.org/10.1016/S2215-0366(17)30478-9

Gillies, D., Christou, M. A., Dixon, A. C., Featherson, O. J., Rapti, I., Garcia-Anguita, A., Villasis-Keever, M., Reebye, P., Christou, E., Al Kabir, N., & Christou, P. A. (2018). Prevalence and characteristics of self-harm in adolescents: Meta-analysis of community-based studies. *Journal of the American Academy of Child & Adolescent Psychiatry, (57)*10, 733–741. https://doi.org/10.1016/j.jaac.2018.06.018

Glenn, C. R., & Nock, M. K. (2014). Improving the short-term prediction of suicidal behavior. *American Journal of Preventive Medicine 47*(3), S176–S180. https://doi.org/10.1016/j.amepre.2014.06.004

Gratz, K. L., Latzman, R. D., Young, J., Heiden, L. J., Damon, J., Hight, J., & Tull., M. T. (2012). Deliberate self-harm among underserved adolescents: The moderating roles of gender, race, and school-level and association with borderline personality features. *Personality Disorders: Theory, Research, and Treatment, 3*(1), 39–54. https://doi.org/10.1037/a0022107

Griffin, E., Dillon, C. B., Arensman, E., Corcoran, P., Williamson, E., & Perry, I. J. (2017). *National Self-Harm Registry Ireland Annual Report 2016*. National Suicide Research Foundation.

Griffin, E., McMahon, E., McNicholas, F., Corcoran, P., Perry, I. J., & Arensman, E. (2018). Increasing rates of self-harm among children, adolescents and young adults: A 10-year national registry study 2007–2016. *Social Psychiatry and Psychiatric Epidemiology, 53*(7), 663–671. https://doi.org/10.1007/s00127-018-1522-1

Hamza, C. A., Ewing, L., Heath, N. L., & Goldstein, A. L. (2021). When social isolation is nothing new: A longitudinal study on psychological distress during COVID-19 among university students with and without preexisting mental health concerns. *Canadian Psychology/Psychologie canadienne, 62*(1), 20–30. https://doi.org/10.1037/cap0000255

Hamza, C. A., & Willoughby, T. (2014). A longitudinal person-centered examination of nonsuicidal self-injury among university students. *Journal of Youth and Adolescence, 43*(4), 671–685. https://doi.org/10.1007/s10964-013-9991-8

Hasking, P., Lewis, S. P., Bloom, E., Brausch, A., Kaess, M., & Robinson, K. (2021). Impact of the COVID-19 pandemic on students at elevated risk of self-injury: The importance of virtual and online resources. *School Psychology International, 42*(1), 57–78. https://doi.org/10.1177/0143034320974414

Hawton, K., Bergen, H., Casey, D., Simkin, S., Palmer, B., Cooper, J., Kapur, N., Horrocks, J., House, A., Lilley, R., Noble, R., & Owens, D. (2007). Self-harm in England: A tale of three cities. *Social Psychiatry and Psychiatric Epidemiology*, *42*(7), 513–521. https://doi.org/10.1007/s00127-007-0199-7

Hawton, K., Bergen, H., Kapur, N., Cooper, J., Steeg, S., Ness, J., & Waters, K. (2012). Repetition of self-harm and suicide following self-harm in children and adolescents: Findings from the multicentre study of self-harm in England. *Journal of Child Psychology and Psychiatry*, *53*(12), 1212–1219. https://doi.org/10.1111/j.1469-7610.2012.02559.x

Hawton, K., Casey, D., Bale, E., Brand, F., Ness, J., Waters, K., Kelly, S., & Geulayov, G. (2021). Self-harm during the early period of the COVID-19 pandemic in England: Comparative trend analysis of hospital presentations. *Journal of Affective Disorders*, *282*, 991–995. https://doi.org/10.1016/j.jad.2021.01.015

Hawton, K., & Harriss, L. (2008). How often does deliberate self-harm occur relative to each suicide? A study of variations by gender and age. *Suicide and Life-Threatening Behavior*, *38*(6), 650–660. https://doi.org/10.1521/suli.2008.38.6.650

Henrich, J. (2020). *The weirdest people in the world: How the West became psychologically peculiar and particularly prosperous*. Farrar, Straus and Giroux.

Henry, N., Parthiban, S., & Farroha, A. (2021). The effect of COVID-19 lockdown on the incidence of deliberate self-harm injuries presenting to the emergency room. *The International Journal of Psychiatry in Medicine*, *56*(4), 266–277. https://doi.org/10.1177/0091217420982100

Hooley, J. M., Fox, K. R., & Boccagno, C. (2020). Nonsuicidal self-injury: Diagnostic challenges and current perspectives. *Neuropsychiatric disease and treatment*, *16*, 101–112. https://doi.org/10.2147/NDT.S198806

International Society for the Study of Self-Injury. (2022). *What is self-injury?* ISSS. https://www.itriples.org/what-is-nssi

Iob, E., Steptoe, A., & Fancourt, D. (2020). Abuse, self-harm and suicidal ideation in the UK during the COVID-19 pandemic. *The British Journal of Psychiatry*, *217*(4), 543–546. https://doi.org/10.1192/bjp.2020.130

Jablonska, B., Lindberg, L., Lindblad, F., & Hjern, A. (2008). Ethnicity, socio-economic status and self-harm in Swedish youth: A national cohort study. *Psychological Medicine*, *39*(1), 87–94. https://doi.org/10.1017/S0033291708003176

Jaworska, N., & MacQueen, G. (2015). Adolescence as a unique developmental period. *Journal of Psychiatry and Neuroscience*, *40*(5), 291–293. https://doi.org/10.1503/jpn.150268

John, A., Eyles, E., Webb, R. T., Okolie, C., Schmidt, L., Arensman, E., Hawton, K., O'Connor, R., Kapur, N., Moran, P., O'Neill, S., McGuinness, L. A., Olorisade, B. K., Dekel, D., Macleod-Hall, C., Cheng, H., Higgins, J. P. T., & Gunnell, D. (2020). The impact of the COVID-19 pandemic on self-harm and suicidal behavior: update of living systematic review. *F1000 Research*, *9*, 1097. https://doi.org/10.12688/f1000research.25522.1

Joiner, T. (2005). *Why people die by suicide*. Harvard University Press.

Kapur, N., Clements, C., Appleby, L., Hawton, K., Steeg, S., Waters, K., & Webb, R. (2021). Effects of the COVID-19 pandemic on self-harm. *The Lancet Psychiatry*, *8*(2), Article e4. https://doi.org/10.1016/S2215-0366(20)30528-9

Kapur, N., Cooper, J., O'Connor, R. C., & Hawton, K. (2013). Non-suicidal self-injury v. attempted suicide: New diagnosis or false dichotomy? *British Journal of Psychiatry*, *202*(5), 326–328. https://doi.org/10.1192/bjp.bp.112.116111

Kiekens, G., Claes, L., Demyttenaere, K., Auerbach, R. P., Green, J. G., Kessler, R. C., Mortier, P., Nock, M. K., & Bruffaerts, R. (2016). Lifetime and 12-month non-suicidal self-injury and academic performance in college freshmen. *Suicide and Life-Threatening Behavior*, *46*(5), 563–576. https://doi.org/10.1111/sltb.12237

Kiekens, G., Hasking, P., Boyes, M., Claes, L., Mortier, P., Auerbach, R. P., Cuijpers, P., Demyttenaere, K., Green, J. G., Kessler, R. C., Myin-Germeys, I., Nock, M. K., & Bruffaerts, R. (2018a). The associations between non-suicidal self-injury and first onset suicidal thoughts and behaviors. *Journal of Affective Disorders*, *239*, 171–179. https://doi.org/10.1016/j.jad.2018.06.033

Kiekens, G., Hasking, P., Bruffaerts, R., Alonso, J., Auerbach, R. P., Bantjes, J., Benjet, C., Boyes, M., Chiu, W. T., Claes, L., Cuijpers, P., Ebert, D. D., Mak, A., Mortier, P., O'Neill, S., Sampson, N. A., Stein, D. J., Vilagut, G., Nock, M. K., & Kessler, R. C. (2023). Nonsuicidal self-injury among first-year college students and its association with mental disorders: Results from the World Mental Health International

College Student (WMHICS) initiative. *Psychological Medicine*, *53*, 875–886. https://doi.org/10.1017/S0033291721002245

Kiekens, G., Hasking, P., Claes, L., Boyes, M., Mortier, P., Auerbach, R. P., Cuijpers, P., Demyttenaere, K., Green, J. G., Kessler, R. C., Myin-Germeys, I., Nock, M. K., & Bruffaerts, R. (2019). Predicting the incidence of non-suicidal self-injury in college students. *European Psychiatry*, *59*, 44–51. https://doi.org/10.1016/j.eurpsy.2019.04.002

Kiekens, G., Hasking, P., Claes, L., Mortier, P., Auerbach, R. P., Boyes, M., Cuijpers, P., Demyttenaere, K., Green, J. G., Kessler, R. C., Nock, M. K., & Bruffaerts, R. (2018b). The DSM-5 nonsuicidal self-injury disorder among incoming college students: Prevalence and associations with 12-month mental disorders and suicidal thoughts and behaviors. *Depression and Anxiety*, *35*(7), 629–637. https://doi.org/10.1002/da.22754

Kiekens, G., Hasking, P., Nock, M. K., Boyes, M., Kirtley, O., Bruffaerts, R., Myin-Germeys, I., & Claes, L. (2020). Fluctuations in affective states and self-efficacy to resist non-suicidal self-injury as real-time predictors of non-suicidal self-injurious thoughts and behaviors. *Frontiers in Psychiatry*, *11*, 1–13. https://doi.org/10.3389/fpsyt.2020.00214

Kiekens, G., Robinson, K., Tatnell, R., & Kirtley, O. J. (2021). Opening the black box of daily life in non-suicidal self-injury research: with great opportunity comes great responsibility. *JMIR mental health*, *8*(11), e30915. https://doi.org/10.2196/30915

Kirtley, O. J., Achterhof, R., Hagemann, N., Hermans, K. S. F. M., Hiekkaranta, A. P., Lecei, A., Boets, B., Henquet, C., Kasanova, Z., Schneider, M., van Winkel, R., Reininghaus, U., Viechtbauer, W., & Myin-Germeys, I. (2021). Initial cohort characteristics and protocol for SIGMA: An accelerated longitudinal study of environmental factors, inter- and intrapersonal processes, and mental health in adolescence. *PsyArXiv*. https://doi.org/10.31234/osf.io/jp2fk

Klonsky, E. D. (2011). Non-suicidal self-injury in United States adults: Prevalence, sociodemographics, topography and functions. *Psychological Medicine*, *41*(9), 1981–1986. https://doi.org/10.1017/S0033291710002497

Klonsky, E. D., Dixon-Luinenberg, T., & May, A. M. (2021). The critical distinction between suicidal ideation and suicide attempts. *World Psychiatry*, *20*(3), 439–441. https://doi.org/10.1002/wps.20909

Klonsky, E. D., & Glenn, C. R. (2009). Assessing the functions of non-suicidal self-injury: Psychometric properties of the inventory of statements about self-injury (ISAS). *Journal of Psychopathology and Behavioral Assessment*, *31*(3), 215–219. https://doi.org/10.1007/s10862-008-9107-z

Klonsky, E. D., & May, A. M. (2015). The Three-Step Theory (3ST): A new theory of suicide rooted in the "Ideation-to-Action" framework. *International Journal of Cognitive Therapy*, *8*(2), 114–129. https://doi.org/10.1521/ijct.2015.8.2.114

Klonsky, E. D., Saffer, B. Y., & Bryan, C. J. (2018). Ideation-to-action theories of suicide: A conceptual and empirical update. *Current Opinion in Psychology*, *22*, 38. https://doi.org/10.1016/j.copsyc.2017.07.020

Knipe, D., Metcalfe, C., Hawton, K., Pearson, M., Dawson, A., Jayamanne, S., Konradsen, F., Eddleston, M., & Gunnell, D. (2019). Risk of suicide and repeat self-harm after hospital attendance for non-fatal self-harm in Sri Lanka: A cohort study. *The Lancet Psychiatry*, *6*(8), 659–666. https://doi.org/10.1016/S2215-0366(19)30214-7

Kokkevi, A., Rotsika, V., Arapaki, A., & Richardson, C. (2012). Adolescents' self-reported suicide attempts, self-harm thoughts and their correlates across 17 European countries. *Journal of Child Psychology and Psychiatry and Allied Disciplines*, *53*(4), 381–389. https://doi.org/10.1111/j.1469-7610.2011.02457.x

Kranzler, A., Fehling, K. B., Lindqvist, J., Brillante, J., Yuan, F., Gao, X., Miller, A. L., & Selby, E. A. (2018). An ecological investigation of the emotional context surrounding nonsuicidal self-injurious thoughts and behaviors in adolescents and young adults. *Suicide and Life-Threatening Behavior*, *48*(2), 149–159. https://doi.org/10.1111/sltb.12373

Lang, J., & Yao, Y. (2018). Prevalence of nonsuicidal self-injury in Chinese middle school and high school students. *Medicine*, *97*(42), e12916. https://doi.org/10.1097/MD.0000000000012916

Larsson, B., & Sund, A. M. (2008). Prevalence, course, incidence, and 1-year prediction of deliberate self-harm and suicide attempts in early Norwegian school adolescents. *Suicide and Life-Threatening Behavior*, *38*(2), 152–165. https://doi.org/10.1521/suli.2008.38.2.152

Lin, H. C., Li, M., Stevens, C., Pinder-Amaker, S., Chen, J. A., & Liu, C. H. (2021). Self-harm and suicidality in US college students: Associations with emotional exhaustion versus multiple psychiatric symptoms. *Journal of Affective Disorders*, *280*(Pt A), 345–353. https://doi.org/10.1016/j.jad.2020.11.014

Liu, R. T., Sheehan, A. E., Walsh, R. F. L., Sanzari, C. M., Cheek, S. M., & Hernandez, A. M. (2019). *Clinical Psychology Review, 74*(3), 101789. https://doi.org/10.1016/j.cpr.2019.101783

Liu, X., Liu, Z. Z., & Jia, C. X. (2021). Repeat self-harm among Chinese adolescents: 1-year incidence and psychosocial predictors. *Social Psychiatry and Psychiatric Epidemiology*, 0123456789. https://doi.org/10.1007/s00127-021-02085-x

Luby, J. L., Whalen, D., Tillman, R., & Barch, D. M. (2019). Clinical and psychosocial characteristics of young children with suicidal ideation, behaviors, and non-suicidal self-injurious behaviors. *Journal of the American Academy of Child & Adolescent Psychiatry, (58)*1, 117–127. https://doi.org/10.1016/j.jaac.2018.06.031

Madge, N., Hewitt, A., Hawton, K., de Wilde, E. J., Corcoran, P., Fekete, S., van Heeringen, K., De Leo, D., & Ystgaard, M. (2008). Deliberate self-harm within an international community sample of young people: Comparative findings from the Child & Adolescent Self-harm in Europe (CASE) Study. *Journal of Child Psychology and Psychiatry and Allied Disciplines, 49*(6), 667–677. https://doi.org/10.1111/j.1469-7610.2008.01879.x

Marshall, E., Claes, L., Bouman, W. P., Witcomb, G. L., & Arcelus, J. (2016). Non-suicidal self-injury and suicidality in trans people: A systematic review of the literature. *International Review of Psychiatry, 28*(1), 58–69. https://doi.org/10.3109/09540261.2015.1073143

Martin, J., Bureau, J., Cloutier, P., & Lafontaine, M. (2011). A comparison of invalidating family environment characteristics between university students engaging in self-injurious thoughts & actions and non-self-injuring university students. *Journal of Youth and Adolescence, 40*(11), 1477–1488. https://doi.org/10.1007/s10964-011-9643-9

McMahon, A. M., Keeley, H., Cannon, M., Arensman, E., Perry, I. J., Clarke, M., Chambers, D., & Corcoran, P. (2014). The iceberg of suicide and self-harm in Irish adolescents: A population-based study. *Social Psychiatry and Psychiatric Epidemiology, 49*(12), 1929–1935. https://doi.org/10.1007/s00127-014-0907-z

McManus, S., Bebbington, P. E., Jenkins, R., Morgan, Z., Brown, L., Collinson, D., & Brugha, T. (2020). Data resource profile: Adult Psychiatric Morbidity Survey (APMS). *International Journal of Epidemiology, 49*(2), 361–362e. https://doi.org/10.1093/ije/dyz224

McManus, S., Gunnell, D., Cooper, C., Bebbington, P. E., Howard, L. M., Brugha, T., Jenkins, R., Hassiotis, A., Weich, S., & Appleby, L. (2019). Prevalence of non-suicidal self-harm and service contact in England, 2000–14: Repeated cross-sectional surveys of the general population. *The Lancet Psychiatry, 6*(7), 573–581. https://doi.org/10.1016/S2215-0366(19)30188-9

Meltzer, H., Harrington, R., Goodman, R., & Jenkins, R. (2001). *Children and adolescents who try to harm, hurt of kill themselves*. Crown.

Mok, P. L. H., Antonsen, S., Pedersen, C. B., Carr, M. J., Kapur, N., Nazroo, J., & Webb, R. T. (2018). Family income inequalities and trajectories through childhood and self-harm and violence in young adults: A population-based, nested case-control study. *The Lancet Public Health, 3*(10), e498–e507. https://doi.org/10.1016/S2468-2667(18)30164-6

Monto, M. A., McRee, N., & Deryck, F. S. (2018). Nonsuicidal self-Injury among a representative sample of US adolescents, 2015. *American Journal of Public Health, 108*(8), 1042–1048. https://doi.org/10.2105/AJPH.2018.304470

Morey, Y., Mellon, D., Dailami, N., Verne, J., & Tapp, A. (2017). Adolescent self-harm in the community: An update on prevalence using a self-report survey of adolescents aged 13–18 in England. *Journal of Public Health (United Kingdom), 39*(1), 58–64. https://doi.org/10.1093/pubmed/fdw010

Mortier, P., Cuijpers, P., Kiekens, G., Auerbach, R. P., Demyttenaere, K., Green, J. G., Kessler, K. C., Nock, M. K., & Bruffaerts, R. (2018). The prevalence of suicidal thoughts and behaviours among college students: A meta-analysis. *Psychological medicine, 48*(4), 554–565. https://doi.org/10.1017/S0033291717002215

Muehlenkamp, J. J., Claes, L., Havertape, L., & Plener, P. L. (2012). International prevalence of adolescent non-suicidal self-injury and deliberate self-harm. *Child and Adolescent Psychiatry and Mental Health, 6*(1), Article 10. https://doi.org/10.1186/1753-2000-6-10

Muehlenkamp, J. J., Xhunga, N., & Brausch, A. M. (2019). Self-injury age of O-onset: A risk factor for NSSI severity and suicidal behavior. *Archives of Suicide Research, 23*(4), 551–563. https://doi.org/10.1080/13811118.2018.1486252

Myin-Germeys, I., Kasanova, Z., Vaessen, T., Vachon, H., Kirtley, O., Viechtbauer, W., & Reininghaus, U. (2018). Experience sampling methodology in mental health research: New insights and technical developments. *World Psychiatry, 17*, 123–132. https://doi.org/10.1002/wps.20513F

National Institute for Health and Care Excellence. (2011). *Self-harm (NICE Guideline)*. https://www.nice.org.uk/guidance

Nock, M. K., & Favazza, A. R. (2009). Nonsuicidal self-injury: Definition and classification. In M. K. Nock (Ed.), *Understanding nonsuicidal self-injury: Origins, assessment, and treatment* (pp. 9–18). American Psychological Association. https://doi.org/10.1037/11875-001

Nock, M. K., & Prinstein, M. J. (2004). A functional approach to the assessment of self-mutilative behavior. *Journal of Consulting and Clinical Psychology, 72*(5), 885–890. https://doi.org/10.1037/0022-006X.72.5.885

Nock, M. K., Prinstein, M. J., & Sterba, S. K. (2009). Revealing the form and function of self-injurious thoughts and behaviors: A real-time ecological assessment study among adolescents and young adults. *Journal of Abnormal Psychology, 118*(4), 816–827. https://doi.org/10.1037/a0016948

O'Connor, R. C., & Kirtley, O. J. (2018). The integrated motivational-volitional model of suicidal behaviour. *Philosophical transactions of the Royal Society of London. Series B, Biological sciences, 373*(1754), 20170268. https://doi.org/10.1098/rstb.2017.0268

O'Connor, R. C., Rasmussen, S., & Hawton, K. (2012). Distinguishing adolescents who think about self-harm from those who engage in self-harm. *British Journal of Psychiatry, 200*(4), 330–335. https://doi.org/10.1192/bjp.bp.111.097808

O'Connor, R. C., Wetherall, K., Cleare, S., Eschle, S., Drummond, J., Ferguson, E., O'Connor, D. B., & O'Carroll, R. E. (2018). Suicide attempts and non-suicidal self-harm: National prevalence study of young adults. *BJPsych Open, 4*(3), 142–148. https://doi.org/10.1192/bjo.2018.14

O'Connor, R. C., Wetherall, K., Cleare, S., McClelland, H., Melson, A. J., Niedzwiedz, C. L., O'Carroll, R. E., O'Connor, D. B., Platt, S., Scowcroft, E., Watson, B., Zortea, T., Ferguson, E., & Robb, K. A. (2021). Mental health and well-being during the COVID-19 pandemic: Longitudinal analyses of adults in the UK COVID-19 Mental Health & Wellbeing study. *The British Journal of Psychiatry, 218*(6), 326–333. https://doi.org/10.1192/bjp.2020.212

O'Reilly, L. M., Petterson, E., Donahue, K., Quinn, P. D., Klonsky, E. D., Lundström, S., Larsson, H., Lichtenstein, P., & D'Onofrio, B. M. (2021). Sexual orientation and adolescent suicide attempt and self-harm: A co-twin control study. *Journal of Child Psychology and Psychiatry, 62*(7), 834–841. https://doi.org/10.1111/jcpp.13325

Owens, D., Horrocks, J., & House, A. (2002). Fatal and non-fatal repetition of self-harm. Systematic review. *British Journal of Psychiatry, 181*(3), 193–199. https://doi.org/10.1192/bjp.181.3.193

Patalay, P., & Gage, S. H. (2019). Changes in millennial adolescent mental health and health-related behaviours over 10 years: A population cohort comparison study. *International Journal of Epidemiology, 48*(5), 1650–1664. https://doi.org/10.1093/ije/dyz006

Paul, E., & Fancourt, D. (2021). Factors influencing self-harm thoughts and self-harm behaviours over the first 45 weeks of the COVID-19 pandemic in the UK: A longitudinal analysis of 48,446 adults. *Medrixv*. https://doi.org/10.1101/2021.02.19.21252050

Plener, P. (2021). COVID-19 and nonsuicidal self-injury: The pandemic's influence on an adolescent epidemic. *American Journal of Public Health, 111*(2), 195–196. https://doi.org/10.2105/AJPH.2020.306037

Plener, P. L., Allroggen, M., Kapusta, N. D., Brähler, E., Fegert, J. M., & Groschwitz, R. C. (2016). The prevalence of Nonsuicidal Self-Injury (NSSI) in a representative sample of the German population. *BMC Psychiatry, 16*(1), 1–7. https://doi.org/10.1186/s12888-016-1060-x

Quarshie, E. N., Waterman, M. G., & House, A. O. (2020). Prevalence of self-harm among lesbian, gay, bisexual, and transgender adolescents: A comparison of personal and social adversity with a heterosexual sample in Ghana. *BMC Research Notes, 13*(1), 1–6. https://doi.org/10.1186/s13104-020-05111-4

Rasmussen, S., Hawton, K., Philpott-Morgan, S., & O'Connor, R. C. (2016). Why Do Adolescents Self-Harm? *Crisis, 37*(3), 176–183. https://doi.org/10.1027/0227-5910/a000369

Ribeiro, J. D., Franklin, J. C., Fox, K. R., Bentley, K. H., Kleiman, E. M., Chang, B. P., & Nock, M. K. (2017). Risk factors for suicidal thoughts and behaviors: A meta-analysis of 50 years of research. *Psychological Medicine, 46*(2), 225–236. https://doi.org/10.1037/bul0000084

Riley, E. N., Combs, J. L., Jordan, C. E., & Smith, G. T. (2015). Negative urgency and lack of perseverance: Identification of differential pathways of onset and maintenance risk in the longitudinal prediction of non-suicidal self-injury. *Behavior Therapy, 46*(4), 439–448. https://doi.org/10.1016/j.beth.2015.03.002

Rojas-Velasquez, D. A., Pluhar, A. I., Burns, P. A., & Burton, E. T. (2021). Nonsuicidal self-injury among African American and Hispanic Adolescents and young adults: A systematic review. *Prevention Science, 22*(3), 367–377. https://doi.org/10.1007/s11121-020-01147-x

Sharma, R. (2017). Revised Kuppuswamy's socio-economic status scale: Explained and updated. *Indian Pediatrics, 54*(10), 867–870. https://doi.org/10.1007/s13312-017-1151-x

Silverman, M. M., & De Leo, D. (2016). Why there is a need for an international nomenclature and classification system for suicide. *Crisis, 37*(2), 83–87. https://doi.org/10.1027/0227-5910/a000419

Sivertsen, B., Hysing, M., Knapstad, M., Harvey, A. G., Reneflot, A., Lønning, K. J., & O'Connor, R. C. (2019). Suicide attempts and non-suicidal self-harm among university students: Prevalence study. *BJPsych Open, 5*(2), Article e26. https://doi.org/10.1192/bjo.2019.4

Soomro, G. M., & Kakhi, S. (2015). Deliberate self-harm (and attempted suicide). *BMJ Clinical Evidence, 2015*, 1012.

Stallard, P., Spears, M., Montgomery, A. A., Phillips, R., & Sayal, K. (2013). Self-harm in young adolescents (12–16 years): Onset and short-term continuation in a community sample. *BMC Psychiatry, 13*(1), 328. https://doi.org/10.1186/1471-244X-13-328

Steeg, S., Haigh, M., Webb, R. T., Kapur, N., Awenat, Y., Gooding, P., Pratt, D., & Cooper, J. (2016). The exacerbating influence of hopelessness on other known risk factors for repeat self-harm and suicide. *Journal of Affective Disorders, 190*, 522–528. https://doi.org/10.1016/j.jad.2015.09.050

Steinhoff, A., Ribeaud, D., Kupferschmid, S., Raible-Destan, N., Quednow, B. B., Hepp, U., Eisner, M., & Shanahan, L. (2021). Self-injury from early adolescence to early adulthood: Age-related course, recurrence, and services use in males and females from the community. *European Child & Adolescent Psychiatry, 30*(6), 937–951. https://doi.org/10.1007/s00787-020-01573-w

Swannell, S. V., Martin, G. E., Page, A., Hasking, P., & St John, N. J. (2014). Prevalence of nonsuicidal self-injury in nonclinical samples: Systematic review, meta-analysis and meta-regression. *Suicide and Life-Threatening Behavior, 44*(3), 273–303. https://doi.org/10.1111/sltb.12070

Tang, W., Lin, M., You, W., Wu, J. Y., & Chen, K. (2021). Prevalence and psychosocial risk factors of nonsuicidal self-injury among adolescents during the COVID-19 outbreak. *Current Psychology*, 1–10. https://doi.org/10.1007/s12144-021-01931-0

Taylor, P. J., Jomar, K., Dhingra, K., Forrester, R., Shahmalak, U., & Dickson, J. M. (2018). A meta-analysis of the prevalence of different functions of non-suicidal self-injury. *Journal of Affective Disorders, 227*, 759–769. https://doi.org/10.1016/j.jad.2017.11.073

Thippaiah, S. M., Nanjappa, M. S., Gude, J. G., Voyiaziakis, E., Patwa, S., Birur, B., & Pandurangi, A. (2020). Non-suicidal self-injury in developing countries: A review. *International Journal of Social Psychiatry, 67*(5), 472–482. https://doi.org/10.1177/0020764020943627

Van Orden, K. A., Witte, T. K., Cukrowicz, K. C., Braithwaite, S., Selby, E. A., & Joiner, T. E. (2010). The interpersonal theory of suicide. *Psychological Review, 117*(2), 575–600. https://doi.org/10.1037/a0018697

Vijayakumar, L., & Armstrong, G. (2019). Surveillance for self-harm: An urgent need in low-income and middle-income countries. *The Lancet Psychiatry, 6*(8), 633–634. https://doi.org/10.1016/S2215-0366(19)30207-X

Wang, H., Wang, Q., Liu, X., Gao, Y., & Chen, Z. (2020). Prospective interpersonal and intrapersonal predictors of initiation and cessation of non-suicidal self-injury among Chinese adolescents. *International Journal of Environmental Research and Public Health, 17*(24), Article 9454. https://doi.org/10.3390/ijerph17249454

Wester, K., Trepal, H., & King, K. (2018). Nonsuicidal self-injury: Increased prevalence in engagement. *Suicide and Life-Threatening Behavior, 48*(6), 690–698. https://doi.org/10.1111/sltb.12389

Whitlock, J., Muehlenkamp, J., Eckenrode, J., Purington, A., Baral Abrams, G., Barreira, P., & Kress, V. (2013). Nonsuicidal self-injury as a gateway to suicide in young adults. *Journal of Adolescent Health, 52*(4), 486–492. https://doi.org/10.1016/j.jadohealth.2012.09.010

Williams, A. J., Jones, C., Arcelus, J., Townsend, E., Lazaridou, A., & Michail, M. (2021). A systematic review and meta-analysis of victimisation and mental health prevalence among LGBTQ+ young people with experiences of self-harm and suicide. *PLoS One, 16*(1), e0245268. https://doi.org/10.1371/journal.pone.0245268

World Health Organization. (2014). *Preventing suicide: A global imperative.*

World Health Organization. (2020). *Adolescent mental health.* https://www.who.int/news-room/fact-sheets/detail/adolescent-mental-health#:~:text=Mental%20health%20conditions%20account%20for,illness%20and%20disability%20among%20adolescents

Zahl, D., & Hawton, K. (2004). Repetition of deliberate self-harm and subsequent suicide risk: Long-term follow-up study of 11 583 patients. *British Journal of Psychiatry, 185*(1), 70–75. https://doi.org/10.1192/bjp.185.1.70

Zetterqvist, M., Jonsson, L. S., Landberg, A., & Svedin, C. G. (2021). A potential increase in adolescent nonsuicidal self-injury during COVID-19: A comparison of data from three different time points during 2011–2021. *Psychiatry Research, 305*, Article 114208. https://doi.org/10.1016/j.psychres.2021.114208

Zhang, J., Song, J., & Wang, J. (2016). Adolescent self-harm and risk factors. *Asia-Pacific Psychiatry, 8*(4), 287–295. https://doi.org/10.1111/appy.12243

Zubrick, S. R., Hafekost, J., Johnson, S. E., Lawrence, D., Saw, S., Sawyer, M., Ainley, J., & Buckingham, W. J. (2016). Self-harm: Prevalence estimates from the second Australian Child and Adolescent Survey of Mental Health and Wellbeing. *Australian and New Zealand Journal of Psychiatry, 50*(9), 911–921. https://doi.org/10.1177/0004867415617837

CHAPTER 8

Overview and Epidemiology of NSSI in Clinical Samples

Jennifer J. Muehlenkamp *and* Victoria Tillotson

Abstract

This chapter provides a comprehensive overview of the prevalence and characteristics of nonsuicidal self-injury (NSSI) within clinical samples. To provide some depth to understanding the clinical epidemiology of NSSI, it presents the risk and protective factors that appear most salient to clinically significant manifestations of NSSI. The prevalent occurrence of NSSI across a wide variety of diagnostic categories supports the conclusion that NSSI is a transdiagnostic behavior. Thus, treatments targeting transdiagnostic features will likely be most effective in reducing both NSSI as well as any co-occurring psychopathology. The chapter then discusses NSSI typologies or subgroups with implications for treatment. Interventions may need to consider the general profile of NSSI that best represents each person's presentation, adapting treatment approaches to the self-injury in alignment with the profile patterns. Ultimately, the chapter calls for future research that can meaningfully advance the understanding of NSSI within clinical populations.

Key Words: nonsuicidal self-injury, risk factors, protective factors, transdiagnostic behavior, NSSI treatment, psychopathology, diagnostic categories, clinical epidemiology

Introduction

NSSI is a behavior found within clinical samples as well as the general population. A large portion of the research on NSSI comes from general population samples which is perplexing given the focus on NSSI as a potential disorder (American Psychiatric Association, 2022). To consider NSSI as a diagnostic entity, its prevalence and distinction from other disorders within clinical samples is necessary. Currently, the research suggests that NSSI is more likely to be a transdiagnostic behavior than a unique disorder (Ghinea et al., 2020; Hooley et al., 2020) because it co-occurs across a wide variety of existing mental disorders and shares many of the same risk factors. Yet, our understanding of NSSI is incomplete given the sparse number of studies examining this behavior within clinical populations. The current chapter aims to advance the field by providing a comprehensive overview of the prevalence and characteristics of NSSI within clinical samples. To provide some depth to understanding the clinical epidemiology of NSSI, risk and protective factors that appear most salient to clinically significant manifestations of NSSI will be presented. A discussion of NSSI typologies or subgroups with implications for treatment is provided along with a call to action for future research that can meaningfully advance our understanding of NSSI within clinical populations.

Prevalence in Clinical Samples

There is significant variation in prevalence estimates of NSSI within clinical samples, ranging from 13% to as much as 80% (Daukantaitė et al., 2020; Hauber et al., 2019). This substantial variation in rates is likely the result of having few epidemiological studies that specifically examine prevalence rates and trends strictly within clinical samples. Consequently, prevalence rate estimates are highly dependent on sample sizes and characteristics. Detailed descriptions of the prevalence of NSSI in clinical samples across different age groups is also limited, but the data suggest NSSI is most prevalent during adolescence (Bresin & Schoenleber, 2015). Some data suggest that around 8% of adults in general outpatient clinical samples report recent (past 14 days) engagement in NSSI (Ose et al., 2021), which is lower than typically reported rates of approximately 60% among adolescent clinical samples (e.g., Hauber et al., 2019). Additional studies posit prevalence rates for adolescent clinical samples, ranging from 13% to 23.3% (R. T. Liu et al., 2014) up to 70% (Nock et al., 2006; Prinstein et al., 2010). Although recent studies on prevalence in clinical samples are lacking, research regarding the proportion of samples meeting proposed NSSI disorder criteria (American Psychiatric Association, 2022) suggest that among clinical samples, more than 60% meet criteria (Muehlenkamp et al., 2017; Zetterqvist et al., 2020) whereas 1–8% of community samples meet criteria (Andover, 2014; Buelens et al., 2020; Kiekens et al., 2018). There is some research to suggest that NSSI is present in elderly clinical samples; however, studies are sparse. In the one study identified, Morgan et al. (2018) reported that 58% of females and 42% of males between the ages of 65 and 85+ reported recent self-harm. The challenge with these rates is that the authors did not distinguish between nonsuicidal and suicidal self-injury, so these results need to be considered cautiously.

Despite the lack of epidemiological data and consensus on the overall prevalence of NSSI within clinical samples and across age groups, several studies concur that NSSI rates are likely substantially higher in clinical samples relative to community samples. A consistent body of literature with clinical samples indicates that females are more likely to engage in NSSI than males (OR [odds ratio] = 1.50 to 1.80; Bresin & Schoenleber, 2015; Fox et al., 2015). Additionally, within their clinical sample of adolescent inpatients, Hauber et al. (2019) reported that 70.4% females compared to 48.0% of males endorsed NSSI, which is consistent with gender differences reported in other clinical samples studying NSSI correlates (Victor et al., 2018). This disproportion may be partially explained by the increased help-seeking observed in females compared to males. Although new data are emerging from community samples to suggest that transgender and gender nonbinary individuals have some of the highest rates of NSSI relative to cisgender persons (Taliaferro et al., 2019; Staples et al., 2018; see Taliaferro et al., this volume), these gender-inclusive data are rarely reported in clinical samples. One exception is a recent study of adolescent inpatients conducted by Bettis et al. (2020), who found that gender minority youth reported higher rates of NSSI (77.5%) than cisgender youth (46.24%), but past-year frequency of NSSI did not differ between gender minority and cisgender youth; however, their sample was small. Similarly, Leon et al. (2021) reported high rates of NSSI (36.8%) within a small sample of rural gender minority youth seeking outpatient care and found a transmasculine spectrum gender identity was predictive of recent NSSI.

The data, however, are less clear about race/ethnicity due to a lack of studies examining cultural variations in NSSI within clinical samples. In the one study that examined NSSI prevalence by race/ethnicity within a treatment-seeking sample of young adults, Polanco-Roman et al. (2014) reported similar rates of NSSI among White, Latino, Asian, Black, and "other-ethnicity" groups. This finding contrasts with research in nonclinical samples, where NSSI has been identified as being more common for Whites (Rojas-Velasquez et al., 2021; Sornberger et al., 2012), although others report comparable rates across race/ethnicity (Cipriano et al., 2017). In a review of NSSI studies within non-Western cultures, Gholamrezaei et al. (2017) reported some differences in NSSI features, functions, and risk correlates by race/ethnicity but suggested that these variations were mediated by socioeconomic status and gender. Given the discrepancies and lack of research on racial/ethnic/cultural influences on NSSI, further research is required especially within clinical populations.

Co-Occurring Clinical Diagnoses

NSSI can be conceptualized as a transdiagnostic behavior because it co-occurs alongside many psychiatric disorders but does appear to be more prevalent in some conditions than others. A meta-analysis of the relationship between emotional disorders and NSSI by Bentley et al. (2015) found that individuals with a diagnosed mood disorder were significantly more likely to have engaged in NSSI (OR = 2.09) relative to those without a mood disorder. While individuals with any diagnosed emotional disorder were at an increased likelihood of engaging in NSSI (OR = 1.75 and 1.86, respectively), those with bipolar disorder (OR = 1.05) or social anxiety disorder (OR = 1.44) did not show an increased likelihood of NSSI. Most notably, individuals with diagnosed panic disorder or posttraumatic stress disorder (PTSD) had the highest likelihood of co-occurring NSSI (OR = 2.67 and 2.06, respectively) among all the diagnoses reported, although a PTSD diagnosis was not found to be a significant prospective risk factor for NSSI in Fox et al.'s meta-analysis of risk factors (Fox et al., 2015). This overall pattern of association between emotional disorders and NSSI has been observed across a variety of clinical samples (e.g., Ose et al., 2021; Victor et al., 2018).

Eating disorders also tend to have a high prevalence of co-occurring NSSI (25.4% to 55.2%; Claes et al., 2018), with the rates being highest within eating disorders of the binge-eating/purging subtype than in the restrictive subtype (Cucchi et al., 2016; Kiekens & Claes, 2020). Recent data suggest the lifetime prevalence of NSSI among patients with a diagnosis of bulimia nervosa is approximately 32.7%, anorexia nervosa approximately 21.8%, and binge-eating disorder approximately 20% (Kiekens & Claes, 2020). It is estimated that around 43% of individuals in clinical samples with eating disorders engaged in NSSI within the past year (Claes et al., 2010), and eating disorder pathology was found to have a significant weighted OR of 1.81 for NSSI in the meta-analysis conducted by Fox et al. (2015).

Additionally, there are some data to suggest that NSSI may be meaningfully prevalent in behavioral disorders such as attention deficit/hyperactivity disorder (ADHD) and other externalizing disorders (Fox et al., 2015; Meszaros et al., 2017). In their study of adolescents with an ADHD diagnosis, Balázs et al. (2018) estimated the prevalence to be as high as 67.3%. By contrast, Fox et al. (2015) reported an OR of 1.11 for ADHD, suggesting a nonsignificant association with NSSI, but general externalizing symptoms were significantly associated with NSSI (OR = 1.68). The data remain inconclusive due to the lack of studies. Szewczuk-Boguslawska et al. (2018) reported 50% of their female adolescent sample with conduct disorder engaged in NSSI, which is comparable to other studies documenting NSSI rates ranging from 15% to 62% among those with conduct disorder (see Meszaros et al., 2017; Nock et al., 2006). A couple of studies examining NSSI within samples meeting criteria for intermittent explosive disorder reported that approximately 7% to 12% also endorse NSSI (Jenkins et al., 2015; McCloskey et al., 2008). Although studies are scarce, some early research with clinical samples of adolescents suggest NSSI co-occurs in around 40% of those diagnosed with oppositional defiant disorder (Esposito-Smythers et al., 2010; Nock et al., 2006). Overall, existing studies indicate NSSI co-occurs at substantial rates with behavioral disorders, but the limited number of studies exploring this prevalence and relationship highlights an area for further study.

Borderline personality disorder (BPD) is currently the only disorder in the fifth edition of *Diagnostic and Statistical Manual of Mental Disorders-Text Revised* (DSM-5TR) with presentation of self-injurious behavior as a diagnostic criterion (American Psychiatric Association, 2022). Because of this, there are a significant portion of individuals with BPD who also report NSSI resulting in a high co-occurrence. In samples of adults with BPD, NSSI prevalence rates have been estimated to fall between 50% to 90% (Reichl & Kaess, 2021), similar to rates reported among adolescents with BPD features (e.g., 75% to 95%; Andrewes et al., 2019; Reichl & Kaess, 2021). In their meta-analysis of risk factors, Fox et al. (2015) reported that cluster B symptoms (including BPD) were associated with a 5.9-fold increased likelihood of reporting NSSI behavior, highlighting the strong co-occurrence of NSSI and BPD. However, sharing NSSI behavior as part of its symptom set inflates the comorbidity, and most studies have not accounted for this. Furthermore, few studies have examined the presence of NSSI across other personality disorders making our understanding of the relationship between NSSI and personality pathology incomplete and largely biased toward cluster B and BPD disorders.

It is also important to briefly mention the co-occurrence of NSSI and suicidal thoughts and behaviors given the clinical importance of suicide. Studies frequently report a high rate of co-occurrence between NSSI and suicide in clinical settings. Some research estimates that in clinical samples of adolescents, up to 70% report both NSSI and suicide attempts whereas rates of co-occurrence tend to be less than 50% within nonclinical populations (Horváth et al., 2020). Additionally, a history of NSSI is associated with a significantly increased likelihood of a subsequent suicide attempt (OR = 4.27, Ribeiro et al., 2015). Although it is important to note that many individuals who engage in NSSI do not attempt suicide, the strong correlation between these behaviors means that clinicians need to attend to possible suicide risk when working with individuals who engage in NSSI. See Victor et al., this volume for a more detailed discussion of the relationship between NSSI and suicide.

Collectively, our review of the existing literature demonstrates that NSSI co-occurs with a multitude of psychiatric disorders, suggesting that it a transdiagnostic behavior and may represent a marker of severity. Although most of the research on NSSI within clinical samples focuses upon emotional disorders, there is some evidence to suggest a high prevalence within behavioral disorders as well. Surprisingly, there was a notable lack of research exploring NSSI among clinical samples within psychotic disorders. Two recent studies, however, indicate that psychotic experiences, such as auditory and visual hallucinations or delusions, are significantly associated with NSSI engagement (Lee et al., 2021; Hielscher et al., 2021). In their two-year prospective cohort study of 1.100 adolescents, Hielscher et al. (2021) found that persistent psychotic experiences had a stronger correlation with NSSI and predicted subsequent NSSI more so than transient or remitting psychotic experiences. Persistent auditory hallucinatory experiences held much stronger odd ratios for later NSSI than did the other psychotic experiences, suggesting auditory hallucinations may be an understudied risk factor for NSSI. Recently, Ose et al. (2021) reported on rates of NSSI within a large clinical sample of adults from Norway and within their sample, they identified that approximately 7% of those with NSSI had a diagnosis of schizophrenia. Still, the prevalence of psychotic disorders among those who engage in NSSI remains largely unknown, so researchers are encouraged to consider exploring NSSI within these clinical populations as well.

Despite evidence of a high co-occurrence of NSSI across disorders, the proportion of studies examining NSSI within clinical samples is small in comparison to the prominence of those within community samples. As such, researchers are strongly encouraged to utilize clinical samples alongside community samples so that the complete spectrum of NSSI prevalence and features can be understood and guide decision-making about clinically significant thresholds.

Risk Factors

A myriad of risk factors have been identified for NSSI. Some of these risk factors warrant special focus because they represent transdiagnostic vulnerabilities that can be a focus for treatment interventions of NSSI that also reduce concomitant diagnostic symptoms. Personality features such as neuroticism have shown particularly strong relationships to NSSI, often differentiating those who self-injure from those who do not (Perlman et al., 2018). Studies have shown that trait neuroticism, which also underlies many anxiety and mood disorders (Merino et al., 2016) that co-occur with NSSI, is positively associated with both episodic and repetitive engagement in NSSI (Grigoryan & Jurick, 2020; You et al., 2016). Neuroticism has been purported to increase risk for self-injury due to its contributing role in precursors to NSSI acts, such as emotional dysregulation (Hughes et al., 2020). Emotion dysregulation has been consistently identified as a significant risk factor for NSSI (Hasking et al., 2017; Wolff et al., 2019). Negative emotions are the most endorsed reason for motivating acts of NSSI (Taylor et al., 2019), and ecological momentary assessment studies show that negative affect precedes acts of NSSI, which are then followed by positive emotions which subsequently reinforce NSSI engagement (e.g., Andrewes et al., 2017; Houben et al., 2017; Kranzler et al., 2018). The contribution and intersecting influence of neuroticism and emotion regulation on NSSI may partially be explained by shared limbic system malfunction. Studies indicate that neuroticism may result in poor emotion regulation due to a failure of the inhibitory neurocircuitry within the amygdala–ventromedial prefrontal cortex, resulting in difficulties controlling and downregulating emotions (Silverman et al., 2019). Similar limbic system deficits among self-injurers have been observed (Auerbach et al., 2020) and others find increases in ß-endorphin levels post-NSSI acts that correspond with self-reported emotion regulation benefits of NSSI (Stoerkel et al., 2019), providing evidence of biological mechanisms for neuroticism and emotion regulation as risk factors for NSSI (see Swerdlow et al., this volume and Carosella et al., this volume for more detailed discussion). Consequently, targeting personality features such as neuroticism and subsequent emotion dysregulation as part of a transdiagnostic approach (e.g., Sauer-Zavala et al., 2020) may lead to a reduction of NSSI.

Impulsivity has also been identified as a notable risk factor for several comorbidities of NSSI and may partially explain the elevated rates of NSSI within eating disorders, BPD, and impulse control disorders such as ADHD. Studies have shown that individuals engaging in NSSI self-report higher levels of impulsivity than those who do not (Lockwood et al., 2017; Hamza et al., 2015). When considered multidimensionally, behavioral impulsivity (i.e., difficulty preventing initiation of, or stopping, a behavior) appears to have the strongest association with NSSI (Lockwood et al., 2017; R. T. Liu et al., 2017). However, mixed results have been observed with task-based measures of behavioral impulsivity with some failing to support the relationship (e.g., Hamza et al., 2015; Lutz et al., 2021) and others finding higher behavioral impulsivity among those with NSSI (Kim et al., 2020).

The inconsistent findings may be due to the varying severity of NSSI within the samples given that studies using community samples tend to find weak or no effects while those drawing from clinical samples do find effects. This suggests that for clinically relevant NSSI, behavioral impulsivity is likely an important risk factor to consider.

Similarly, negative urgency, which can be considered a mood-based impulsivity where an individual feels they must act immediately to relieve distress, is strongly and consistently associated with NSSI across community and clinical samples (Hamza et al., 2015; Lockwood et al., 2017). In their sample of outpatients with eating disorders, Vieira et al. (2017) reported that negative urgency was significantly predictive of current NSSI and interacted with parental invalidation, weakening the effect of parental invalidation on NSSI engagement when impulsivity was high. Although not a clinical sample, Cassels et al. (2020) provide evidence that impulsivity uniquely predicted future NSSI engagement after controlling for the effects of other risk factors suggesting impulsivity is a risk factor. Hamza and Willoughby (2019) reported similar results from a three-year longitudinal study of young adults but also found that frequent engagement in NSSI predicted subsequent increases in impulsivity suggesting a reciprocal influence that perpetuates self-injury acts. It is speculated that negative urgency interacts with emotion dysregulation to exacerbate NSSI urges which, for those with high behavioral impulsivity, are difficult to resist, resulting in acts of self-injury when distressed or emotionally overwhelmed. Thus, impulsivity has strong clinical relevance for understanding and treating NSSI. Increasing self-regulation and decreasing emotionally reactive behaviors may help to reduce or decrease NSSI occurrence.

Along with impulsivity, several other cognitive aspects have been associated with increased risk of NSSI, including self-criticism, low self-esteem, maladaptive perfectionism, and a negative cognitive attribution style (Forrester et al., 2017; Hooley & Franklin, 2018; Zelkowitz & Cole, 2019). Most of these features fall under the umbrella construct of negative self-perceptions (see Swerdlow et al., this volume). In their benefits and barriers model of NSSI, Hooley and Franklin (2018) suggest that negative self-perceptions, and self-criticism in particular, are essential to eroding protective barriers to engaging in NSSI. Meta-analytic findings from cross-sectional studies suggest a moderate to large effect of self-criticism on NSSI (Zelkowitz & Cole, 2019). Prospective studies with treatment-seeking adults report that baseline self-report and behavioral measures of self-criticism predicted future NSSI acts (Fox et al., 2018; Perkins et al., 2020), and ecological momentary assessment studies find that self-criticism predicts increases in concurrent and future NSSI urges and behaviors sometimes through an effect on self-punishment motivations (Burke et al., 2021; Lear et al., 2019). Perfectionism (Chester et al., 2015; Claes et al., 2012) and low self-esteem (Forrester et al., 2017) are observed correlates for NSSI, and are likely to influence, precede, or interact with self-criticism to create a context where NSSI is more likely to occur. The relationship between self-criticism and NSSI may also be partially explained by a negative cognitive attribution style, which refers to the tendency to think that negative life events are caused by internal, global, and stable factors (Rubenstein et al., 2016). This attribution style may increase the tendency to overfocus on negative stimuli (Wolff et al., 2013, 2014), leading to greater amounts of self-criticism, which then feed into aversive emotional states preceding a self-injurious act. Emerging research indicates that negative self-perceptions and factors that contribute to or exacerbate negative self-perceptions are prime targets for clinical intervention to reduce NSSI behaviors.

In addition to the individual risk factors noted, there are some environmental risk factors with salience to clinical intervention and risk for NSSI. Those who engage in NSSI report experiencing a slightly higher rate of negative life events than those who do not (R. T. Liu et al., 2014), and these negative events may be what motivates help-seeking. The most identified negative life event linked to NSSI is the experience of childhood trauma, particularly within adolescent clinical samples (Baiden et al., 2017; Serafini et al., 2017; see Serafini et al., this volume). In a meta-analysis of more than 70 studies, R. T. Liu et al. (2018) found that childhood maltreatment in general has a strong association with NSSI (OR = 3.42). When broken down across maltreatment types, childhood emotional abuse (OR = 3.03) held the strongest association followed by sexual abuse (OR = 2.65) and physical abuse (OR = 2.32) or neglect (OR = 2.22). Other prospective studies have also demonstrated significant predictive relationships between recent experiences of trauma and NSSI behavior (e.g., Tatnell et al., 2017). Severity of trauma experiences has also differentiated among subgroups of individuals with NSSI, with more severe trauma being present among those also reporting more severe self-injury (Shahwan et al., 2020). The robust connection between childhood trauma and NSSI is partially explained by trauma's influence on the development of psychiatric disorders such as PTSD, BPD, and mood disorders, all of which have a high comorbidity with NSSI (Bentley et al., 2015; Reichl & Kaess, 2021). Furthermore, childhood trauma is linked to a disruption in normal neurobiological development, particularly within the frontal cortex, amygdala, limbic (emotional) and hypothalamic-pituitary-adrenal axis (stress response) systems. Dysfunction within these regions has been implicated in difficulties with self—and emotion—regulation as well as impulsivity (Assogna et al., 2020); all of which are significant risk factors for NSSI. Thus, trauma experiences, especially in childhood, appear to confer significant risk for NSSI behavior directly and indirectly through its influence on other risk processes. Screening for trauma and treating existing sequelae of traumatic experiences for those interested in doing so may be beneficial for decreasing both NSSI and co-occurring symptomatology.

Finally, there is emerging but mixed evidence regarding the influence of peer engagement in NSSI as a risk factor (Fox et al., 2015; Jarvi et al., 2013). It has been proposed that peer influence could result in NSSI through a "contagion effect" that has been observed in some inpatient settings as well as among community samples (Hauber et al., 2019; see Jarvi Steele et al., this volume). In one of the few longitudinal studies available,

Schwartz-Mette and Lawrence (2019) found that friends' NSSI frequency at baseline predicted one's own NSSI frequency at both three and six months later after controlling for other risk factors. This provides evidence of peer NSSI behavior influencing risk for NSSI. Additionally, poor peer relationships and peer victimization have been shown to be significant predictors of NSSI in adolescents (Grigoryan & Jurick, 2020; Valencia-Agudo et al., 2018) and peer bonding is endorsed as a motivation for NSSI for some individuals (Case et al., 2019). Whereas the current literature has examined peer influence more extensively in nonclinical populations, the evidence suggests the effects are likely to generalize to clinical samples as well.

Protective Factors for Clinical Consideration

Few studies have examined protective factors for NSSI and of those that do, they draw from community samples of adolescents and young adults. Despite this limitation, it is relevant to briefly review protective factors as they can provide unique avenues for clinical intervention and prevention. To be protective, a variable must modify or alter the strength of risk conferred for a behavior or be associated with a decreased likelihood the behavior occurs. To date, there appear to be two consistently identified protective factors for NSSI: positive self-perceptions and adaptive or positive family connection. In addition, coping self-efficacy and sharing values or norms against self-harm may also serve a protective role, but the data are limited at this time.

In their theoretical model, Hooley and Franklin (2018) described potential barriers to NSSI, or processes that prevent a person from engaging in the behavior. As discussed previously, self-perceptions are viewed as a key feature to understanding self-injury engagement, with positive self-perceptions providing a powerful protective effect. Hooley and Franklin (2018) argued that positive self-associations, which include self-worth and self-compassion, support a desire to protect oneself making it extremely difficult to physically harm the body. A few studies support this notion, finding that self-compassion (Kaniuka et al., 2020; Valencia-Agudo et al., 2018; Xavier et al., 2016), positive body regard (e.g., Muehlenkamp et al., 2013), and self-esteem (e.g., Lan et al., 2019) moderate the effects of selected risk factors, essentially buffering and reducing the strength of the relationship between the risk factors and NSSI. Furthermore, in studies of individuals with lived experience (Lewis & Hasking, 2020; Sutherland et al., 2014), self-acceptance was identified as an essential component to recovery from NSSI.

A few studies have also demonstrated that brief self-affirming exercises were associated with short-term reduced NSSI urge/actions (Franklin et al., 2017) and decreased pain tolerance—a proxy for NSSI risk (Gregory et al., 2017; Hooley & St. Germain, 2013). Physiological studies suggest that self-compassion may serve a protective role because it deactivates the stress-response system by lowering cortisol levels and increases heart-rate variability which activates self-soothing/regulation systems (e.g., Arch et al., 2014; Luo et al., 2018; Rockliff et al., 2008) supporting a neurobiological mechanism for the protective effects. These preliminary findings provide evidence that positive self-perceptions are likely protective against NSSI, and they represent common targets for treatment across a variety of the disorders that commonly co-occur with NSSI (e.g., mood disorders and eating disorders). Addressing self-perceptions as part of treatment is highly encouraged and integrating self-compassion exercises into prevention programs would likely produce strong, positive results.

Having an adaptive and supportive family connection is also emerging as a potentially robust protective factor for NSSI, although results are mixed (Valencia-Agudo et al., 2018). Although most studies have identified that poor family relationships are linked to increased NSSI (e.g., DeVille et al., 2020), others show that positive family connections and cohesion are associated with decreased NSSI behaviors and NSSI recovery (Jiang et al., 2017; Kelada et al., 2016). Within a large sample of adolescents Victor et al. (2019) found that positive parenting significantly reduced the odds of NSSI onset one year later. These results indicate that when family relationships are perceived as supportive, engagement in NSSI is lower, suggesting a potential protective influence. Other studies have also identified that having a positive connection with family or a trusted adult is associated with decreased likelihood of NSSI (e.g., Taliaferro et al., 2019, 2020), often above and beyond the effect of positive peer relationships (Jiang et al., 2017; Taliaferro & Muehlenkamp, 2017). Including family members or trusted adults in treatment and utilizing family therapy alongside individual therapy for NSSI is strongly recommended by experts and may produce better or faster positive outcomes (Bean et al., 2021; Glenn et al., 2014).

Finally, there are early studies to suggest that social norms rejecting NSSI are an important barrier for preventing NSSI (Hooley & Franklin, 2018). Although there are few data examining peer or self-norms regarding NSSI, studies have shown that having friends who engage in NSSI is positively associated with one's own NSSI both cross-sectionally (Jarvi et al., 2013; Syed et al., 2020) and prospectively (Schwartz-Mette & Lawrence, 2019). Thus, challenging the acceptability or perceived normalcy of NSSI behaviors as part of therapy, possibly using a treatment like acceptance and commitment therapy (ACT; Hayes et al., 2011) may also help to reduce the likelihood a person turns to, or continues to engage in, self-injury. Many treatments recommended for NSSI focus on strengthening coping skills, and some recent research has found that coping self-efficacy, or the belief in one's ability to cope through distress and resist NSSI, was prospectively associated with decreased NSSI acts (Kiekens & Claes, 2020). Other studies have found coping self-efficacy to moderate the effect of emotional reactivity on NSSI, decreasing the likelihood and frequency of NSSI (Hasking et al., 2018; S. Liu et al., 2020). While these findings need to be replicated, they provide preliminary evidence that building an individual's confidence in their ability to cope through emotional distress and resist NSSI may serve to protect against NSSI behaviors and aid recovery. This can be accomplished as part of treatment but also through skill- and resilience-building prevention programs offered in schools or within the community.

Clinical Profiles and Treatment Considerations

NSSI is characterized by extensive heterogeneity in its features, characteristics, and demographic elements including co-occurring psychopathology. Due to this heterogeneity, several researchers have attempted to identify subgroups of individuals with a history of NSSI to better understand the behavior and provide insight into clinically meaningful profiles using latent class analysis procedures. Across studies, a consistent pattern identifying three to four distinct and reliable groups characterized by increasing severity have been observed within samples of adolescents (Reinhardt et al., 2021; Somer et al., 2015; Xin et al., 2016), young adults (e.g., Case et al., 2019; Dhingra et al., 2016; Peterson et al., 2019), and adults (Vaughn et al., 2015) as well as across countries and cultures (Singhal et al., 2021; Somer et al., 2015; Xin et al., 2016). In studies where four groups are identified, the primary difference is a split within the "moderate" group, with one of the moderate groups endorsing a greater variety and stronger salience of motivations for the NSSI (e.g., Case et al., 2019; Klonsky & Olino, 2008) or being more populated by individuals identifying as male (e.g., Singhal et al., 2021; Whitlock, et al., 2008). Although almost all these studies have been conducted within community samples, a recent study with a clinical outpatient sample of individuals ages 14 to 35 years in Singapore found very similar results; a three-class solution that mirrored the characteristics found in community samples (Shahwan et al., 2020). Replication is essential, but the data appear to converge around clear subgroups of NSSI that represent a continuum of severity and likely warrant different clinical interventions.

Within all studies, there is an experimental subgroup characterized by infrequent (e.g., one to four acts), superficial/minor NSSI injuries, with few reported motivations for the behavior and low levels of co-occurring psychopathology. Of note, Hamza and Willoughby (2013) found their experimental subgroup did not differ from no-NSSI controls on any of the psychosocial risk factors or clinical symptoms assessed, including suicidal thoughts and behaviors, although others have reported some differences (Whitlock et al., 2008). Thus, it is possible individuals who fall into the experimental subgroup may not require formal treatment and instead would benefit from monitoring of risk and prevention efforts that bolster coping skills, emotional awareness, and general resilience building. The low-moderate subgroup represents those who have slightly greater frequency (e.g., 4–10 acts), use a couple of methods with superficial wounds, and have low endorsement of motivations outside emotion regulation (e.g., Case et al., 2019; Peterson et al., 2019). By contrast, the high-moderate group tend to report greater frequency (e.g., 8–20 acts), to use three to four methods, to have slight scarring, and to endorse multiple motivations with *inter*personal and self-punishment motivations having strong salience (e.g., Case et al., 2019; Shahwan et al., 2020). These moderate NSSI groups tend to be similar with regard to co-occurring psychopathology symptoms, suicidal thoughts/behaviors, and risk factors, although higher than the experimental subgroup. As such, treatment strategies may want to focus on emotional awareness and regulation and learning additional coping strategies. For those in the high-moderate group, including brief cognitive-behavioral or solution-focused approaches that build self-compassion and strengthen interpersonal and problem-solving skills may be particularly useful (e.g., Andover et al., 2017; Kaess et al., 2019; Rees et al., 2015).

The empirically derived "severe" subgroup is mostly likely to represent a clinically significant presentation and is characterized by high NSSI frequencies (e.g., >20 acts), more diverse and severe methods (>4 methods, cutting/burning as primary), some significant scarring and/or injuries requiring medical attention, and high endorsement of multiple motivations with *intra*personal reasons being dominant. This group is heavily populated by females and has the highest levels of psychopathology, risk factors including past trauma, impairment/life interference, and suicidal thoughts and behaviors. Multifaceted treatment interventions that target the drivers of the individual's NSSI motivational and maintaining factors, alongside co-occurring psychopathology, are recommended, which is why transdiagnostic approaches (Barlow et al., 2011) may be the most useful. Other promising treatments include those that address underlying risk factors such as emotion dysregulation, impulsivity, negative self-perceptions, and problem-solving/coping (see Bentley et al., 2015; Klonsky et al., 2011). While there is not a clearly established treatment specifically for NSSI at this time, encouraging results have been observed for dialectical behavior therapy (DBT; see Kothgassner et al., 2021), emotion regulation group therapy (ERGT; Gratz et al., 2019), emotion regulation individual therapy for adolescents (ERITA; Bjureberg et al., 2018), and treatment for self-injurious behaviors (T-SIB; Andover et al., 2017). Similarly, Bentley (2017) describes a successful application of the unified protocol to treating NSSI, showing promise of that approach as well. Incorporating any of these approaches and skill sets into treatment with clients who are self-injuring would likely enhance positive outcomes.

Challenges and Implications for Research and Treatment

The most significant challenge to understanding NSSI within clinical populations and settings is the very limited number of studies that have included clinical samples as the focus of study. Of the studies that do exist, many samples have been small and often centralized around a specific disorder such as BPD or eating disorders. As such, much of the data pertaining to co-occurring disorders presented in this chapter had to be extracted from sample descriptions within studies testing hypotheses unrelated to co-occurrence. Consequently, the field lacks a depth of understanding of NSSI within clinical populations. Additionally, it was widely assumed across studies that major depressive disorder (MDD) is very prevalent in NSSI. Yet, very few studies intentionally examined or diagnostically evaluated the presence of MDD or other mood disorders, instead, assessing symptoms rather than diagnoses. To really understand the transdiagnostic representation of NSSI or potential existence of a unique NSSI disorder, we need studies that intentionally assess for disorders within the sample in addition to more general symptomology.

Larger-scale, or epidemiological, studies within clinical populations are needed to have a solidly accurate understanding of co-occurring psychopathology, as well as to fully comprehend the features and continuum of NSSI severity. Few to no studies have compared clinical samples with and without NSSI, so it remains unknown whether the risk factors identified are unique, or more salient, to the emergence of NSSI or if they instead represent global, generalized risk factors that increase vulnerability for a range of difficulties one of which may be NSSI. Short- and long-term prospective studies with clinical samples across age groups are essential to identifying actual risk factors, documenting that the factor is a precursor to, and predictive of, future NSSI behavior. As noted above, there are very few studies of protective factors, and within that scant literature, we were unable to locate any that drew from a clinical sample. Our ability to prevent NSSI and effectively intervene is severely limited without an understanding of specific protective factors as these are areas to strengthen and build upon within interventions.

There are also notable Eurocentric and gender-based biases within the existing data pertaining to clinical populations (for more information also see Wilson, this volume). Females are significantly overrepresented within the clinical samples and there are some data to suggest males may have different clinical presentations of NSSI that might require different treatment approaches (e.g., Victor et al., 2018). The few emerging studies of NSSI within transgender populations also point to some unique variations in risk, protection, and severity of NSSI that may warrant a tailored approach (Angoff et al., 2021; R. T. Liu et al., 2019), but additional research is needed. Similarly, there is a lack of global or multicultural data in the current literature, particularly for clinical samples. While Aggarwal et al. (2017) found that NSSI prevalence, features, and risk factors appear similar across low- and middle-income countries, there were several conflicting results indicating further examination of culture, and intersectionality is needed to best understand the clinical presentation of NSSI around the world. Understanding NSSI across cultures within clinical samples can help identify "universal" and culturally specific features of the behavior which can help to inform considerations of whether NSSI is a unique disorder, as well as to identify appropriate therapeutic approaches.

To help the field achieve a more representative and thorough understanding of NSSI, a focus on examining NSSI within clinical samples is urgently needed. Much of the field's knowledge about NSSI comes from adolescent community and college-student samples. Although diverse features of NSSI have been described across these samples, they tend to represent less severe manifestations of NSSI when compared to clinical samples. Consequently, current understanding of NSSI has been restricted and can lead to misjudgments or misunderstandings of the true severity and clinical implications of the behavior (e.g., Muehlenkamp et al., 2017). Advancing the field requires prospective studies in clinical samples that examine both risk and protective factors, assess for co-occurrence across a variety of disorders, and considers intersectionality of identities and culture. It is imperative that researchers begin to tackle these more complex elements so that we have a thoroughly comprehensive understanding of NSSI and the continuum of its manifestation across populations and severity.

Conclusion

The prevalence of NSSI across a wide variety of diagnostic categories supports the conclusion that NSSI is a transdiagnostic behavior. This comorbidity also highlights the importance for clinicians to routinely assess for NSSI regardless of the client's diagnostic label. Many of the risk factors and underlying difficulties for NSSI are shared by the commonly co-occurring disorders (e.g., Muehlenkamp et al., 2019), further supporting the transdiagnostic nature of this behavior. Thus, treatments targeting these transdiagnostic features will likely be most effective in reducing both NSSI as well as any co-occurring psychopathology (e.g., Bentley et al., 2015). Interventions may also need to consider the general profile of NSSI that best represents each person's presentation, adapting treatment approaches to the self-injury in alignment with the profile patterns. There is great need to advance treatment for NSSI and identify what treatments, or treatment targets and strategies, work best for the different NSSI profiles and presentations. Furthermore, considering sociocultural factors influencing risk, protection, and recovery processes are essential but remain largely unknown. There is opportunity for clinicians and researchers to improve interventions for NSSI through a cultural lens.

However, research on NSSI within clinical samples lags behind knowledge of other disorders. To overcome this limitation, we recommend that researchers studying NSSI within any population integrate valid diagnostic tools such as diagnostic interviews or self-report symptom scales with established clinical thresholds to aid evaluation of NSSI among those meeting criteria for different disorders. Furthermore, researchers with access to clinical samples or medical records could include chart review studies to understand prevalence and examine how demographic or other health-related factors associate with NSSI. Researchers studying other related clinical domains could consider including assessments of NSSI behaviors and features as a supplement to their work. Such an approach can open opportunities for collaboration to understand NSSI from new and transdiagnostic frameworks, along with expanding NSSI data from clinical samples. Finally, given the robust findings of different subgroups within those who report NSSI, our knowledge of the behavior would be enhanced if researchers began to examine similarities and differences across the severity continuum or between subgroups (also see Møhl & Rubæk, this volume).

Additional exploration of NSSI within clinical samples will also aid treatment and prevention. As noted, most treatments for NSSI have been extrapolated from those that effectively treat co-occurring disorders (e.g., BPD). The current review suggests that clinicians may also want to consider approaches that address self-perceptions, enhance self-regulation, strengthen connections with family, and consider developmental phenomena given that the behavior occurs across the lifespan. Integrating culturally specific elements into treatment is also needed, but research needs to first discover the unique factors contributing to clinically severe NSSI across diverse populations. Furthermore, additional exploration of the clinical presentation and treatment approaches for addressing NSSI among those with externalizing or psychotic disorders is greatly needed as different interventions may prove more effective based on co-occurring difficulties. Clinicians are encouraged to share case reports of treatment efforts to guide understanding of NSSI within clinical populations and inspire intervention development. Documenting factors that seem to reduce or protect against NSSI engagement within clinical populations would make substantial contributions to the field and are important elements for clinicians to attend to, and enhance, within their treatments. Given the transdiagnostic nature of NSSI, treatments that target the shared symptomology and risk or protective factors are most likely to be effective in ameliorating NSSI while also affecting change in accompanying psychopathology. However, studies examining the effectiveness of transdiagnostic treatments (e.g., unified protocol) and/or those outside emotion regulation interventions (e.g., ACT) are greatly needed to know if they do indeed help to stop NSSI behavior.

Although there is substantial research characterizing NSSI, our understanding of this behavior and the most effective ways to treat it within clinical populations is severely limited. The field will not have sufficient knowledge of NSSI as a transdiagnostic behavior or independent disorder, or know the best way to prevent or treat it, until research on NSSI within clinical samples is expanded.

References

Aggarwal, S., Patton, G., Reavley, N., Sreenivasan, S. A., & Berk, M. (2017). Youth self-harm in low- and middle-income countries: Systematic review of the risk and protective factors. *International Journal of Social Psychiatry*, *63*(4), 359–375. https://doi.org/10.1177/0020764017700175

American Psychiatric Association. (2022). *Diagnostic and statistical manual of mental disorders* (Text Revised). https://doi.org/10.1176/appi.books.9780890425596

Andover, M. S. (2014). Non-suicidal self-injury disorder in a community sample of adults. *Psychiatry Research*, *219*(2), 305–310. https://doi.org/10.1016/j.psychres.2014.06.001

Andover, M. S., Schatten, H. T., Morris, B. W., Holman, C. S., & Miller, I. W. (2017). An intervention for nonsuicidal self-injury in young adults: A pilot randomized controlled trial. *Journal of Consulting and Clinical Psychology*, *85*(6), 620–631. https://doi.org/10.1037/ccp0000206

Andrewes, H. E., Hulbert, C., Cotton, S. M., Betts, J., & Chanen, A. M. (2019). Relationships between the frequency and severity of non-suicidal self-injury and suicide attempts in youth with borderline personality disorder. *Early Intervention in Psychiatry*, *13*(2), 194–201. https://doi.org/10.1111/eip.12461

Andrewes, H. E., Hulbert, C., Cotton, S. M., Betts, J., & Chanen, A. M. (2017). An ecological momentary assessment investigation of complex and conflicting emotions in youth with borderline personality disorder. *Psychiatry Research*, *252*, 102–110. https://doi.org/10.1016/j.psychres.2017.01.100

Angoff, H. D., McGraw, J. S., & Docherty, M. (2021). Intersecting identities and nonsuicidal self-injury among youth. *Identity*, *21*(2), 98–114. https://doi.org/proxy.uwec.edu/10.1080/15283488.2020.1863216

Arch, J. J., Warren Brown, K., Dean, D. J., Landy, L. N., Brown, K. D., & Laudenslager, M. L. (2014). Self-compassion training modulates alpha-amylase, heart rate variability, and subjective responses to social evaluative threat in women. *Psychoneuroendocrinology*, *42*, 49–58. https://doi.org/10.1016/j.psyneuen.2013.12.018

Assogna, F., Piras, F., & Spalletta, G. (2020). Neurobiological basis of childhood trauma and the risk for neurological deficits later in life. *Childhood Trauma in Mental Disorders*, 385–410. https://doi.org/10.1007/978-3-030-49414-8_18

Auerbach, R. P., Pagliaccio, D., Allison, G. O., Alqueza, K. L., & Alonso, M. F. (2020). Neural correlates associated with suicide and non-suicidal self-injury in youth. *Biological Psychiatry, 89*(2), 119–133. https://doi.org/10.1016/j.biopsych.2020.06.002

Baiden, P., Stewart, S. L., & Fallon, B. (2017). The role of adverse childhood experiences as determinants of non-suicidal self-injury among children and adolescents referred to community and inpatient mental health settings. *Child Abuse and Neglect, 69*, 163–176. https://doi.org/10.1016/j.chiabu.2017.04.011

Balázs, J., Gyori, D., Horváth, L. O., Meszáros, G., Szentiványi, D. (2018). Attention-deficit hyperactivity disorder and nonsuicidal self-injury in a clinical sample of adolescents: The role of comorbidities and gender. *BMC Psychiatry, 18*(34). https://doi.org/10.1186/s12888-018-1620-3

Barlow, D. H., Farchione, T. J., Bullis, J. R., Gallagher, M. W., Murray-Latin, H., Sauer-Zavala, S., Bentley, K. H., Thompson-Hollands, J., Conklin, L. R., Boswell, J. F., Ametaj, A., Carl, J. R., Boettcher, H. T., & Cassiello-Robbins, C. (2011). The unified protocol for transdiagnostic treatment of emotional disorders compared with diagnosis-specific protocols for anxiety disorders: A randomized clinical trial. *JAMA Psychiatry, 9*, 875–884. https://doi.org/10.1001/jamapsychiatry.2017.2164

Bean, R. A., Keenan, B. H., & Fox, C. (2021). Treatment of adolescent non-suicidal self-injury: A review of family factors and family therapy. *The American Journal of Family Therapy*, 1–16. https://doi.org/10.1080/01926187.2021.1909513

Bentley, K. H. (2017). Applying the unified protocol transdiagnostic treatment to nonsuicidal self-injury and co-occurring emotional disorders: A case illustration. *Journal of Clinical Psychology, 73*(5), 547–558. https://doi.org/10.1002/jclp.22452

Bentley, K. H., Cassiellao-Robbins, C. F., Vittorio, L., Sauer-Zavaala, S., & Barlow, D. H. (2015). The association between nonsuicidal self-injury and the emotional disorders: A meta-analytic review. *Clinical Psychology Review, 37*, 72–88. https://doi.org/10.1016/j.cpr.2015.02.006

Bettis, A. H., Thompson, E. C., Burke, T. A., Nesi, J., Kudinova, A. Y., Hunt, J. I., Liu, R. T., & Wolff, J. C. (2020). Prevalence and clinical indices of risk for sexual and gender minority youth in an adolescent inpatient sample. *Journal of psychiatric research, 130*, 327–332. https://doi.org/10.1016/j.jpsychires.2020.08.022

Bjureberg, J., Sahlin, H., Hedman-Lagerlöf, E., Gratz, K. L., Tull, M. T., Jokinen, J., Hellner, C., & Ljótsson, B. (2018). Extending research on emotion regulation individual therapy for adolescents (ERITA) with nonsuicidal self-injury disorder: Open pilot trial and mediation analysis of a novel online version. *BMC Psychiatry, 18*(1). https://doi.org/10.1186/s12888-018-1885-6

Bresin, K., & Schoenleber, M. (2015). Gender differences in the prevalence of nonsuicidal self-injury: A meta-analysis. *Clinical Psychology Review, 38*, 55–64. https://doi.org/10.1016/j.cpr.2015.02.009

Buelens, T., Luyckx, K., Kiekens, G., Gandhi, A., Muehlenkamp, J. J., & Claes, L. (2020). Investigating the DSM-5 criteria for non-suicidal self-injury disorder in a community sample of adolescents. *Journal of affective disorders, 260*, 314–322. https://doi.org/10.1016/j.jad.2019.09.009

Burke, T. A., Fox, K., Kautz, M., Siegel, D. M., Kleiman, E., & Alloy, L. B. (2021). Real-time monitoring of the associations between self-critical and self-punishment cognitions and nonsuicidal self-injury. *Behaviour Research and Therapy, 137*. https://doi.org/10.1016/j.brat.2020.103775

Case, J. A. C., Burke, T. A., Siegel, D. M., Piccirillo, M. L., Alloy, L. B., & Olino, T. M. (2019). Functions of non-suicidal self-injury in late adolescence: A latent class analysis. *Archives of Suicide Research, 24*, S165–S186. https://doi-org/10.1080/13811118.2019.1586607

Cassels, M., Neufeld, S., Van Harmelen, A. L., Goodyer, I., & Wilkinson, P. (2020). Prospective pathways from impulsivity to non-suicidal self-injury among youth. *Archives of Suicide Research*, 1–14. https://doi.org/10.1080/13811118.2020.1811180

Chester, D. S., Merwin, L. M., & DeWall, N. (2015). Maladaptive perfectionism's link to aggression and self-harm: Emotion regulation as a mechanism. *Aggressive Behavior, 41*(5), 443–454. https://doi.org/10.1002/ab.21578

Cipriano, A., Cella, S., & Cotrufo, P. (2017). Nonsuicidal self-injury: A systematic review. *Frontiers in Psychology, 8*(1946). https://doi.org/10.3389/fpsyg.2017.01946

Claes, L., Klonsky, D. E., Muehlenkamp, J., Kuppens, P., & Vandereycken, W. (2010). The affect-regulation function of nonsuicidal self-injury in eating-disordered patients: Which affect states are regulated? *Comprehensive Psychiatry, 51*(4), 386–392. https://doi.org/10.1016/j.comppsych.2009.09.001

Claes, L., Soenens, L., Vansteenkiste, M., & Vandereycken, W. (2012). The scars of the inner critic: Perfectionism and nonsuicidal self-injury in eating disorders. *European Eating Disorders Review,20*, 196–202. https://doi.org/10.1002/erv.1158

Claes, L., Turner, B., Dierckx, E., Luyckx, K., Verschueren, M., & Schoevaerts, K. (2018). Different clinical presentations in eating disorder patients with non-suicidal self-injury based on the co-occurrence of borderline personality disorder. *Psychologica Belgica*, *58*(1), 243–255. https://doi.org/10.5334/pb.420

Cucchi, A., Ryan, D., Konstantakopoulos, G., Stroumpa, S., Kaçar, A., Renshaw, S., Landau, S., & Kravariti, E. (2016). Lifetime prevalence of non-suicidal self-injury in patients with eating disorders: A systematic review and meta-analysis. *Psychological Medicine*, *46*(7), 1345–1358. https://doi.org/10.1017/S0033291716000027

Daukantaitė, D., Lantto, R., Liljedahl, S. I., Helleman, M., & Westling, S. (2020). One-year consistency in lifetime frequency estimates and functions of non-suicidal self-injury in a clinical sample. *Frontiers in Psychiatry*, *11*(538). https://doi.org/10.3389/fpsyt.2020.00538

DeVille, D. C., Whalen, D., Breslin, F. J., Breslin, F. J., Morris, A. S., Khalsa, S. S., Paulus, M. P., & Barch, D. M. (2020). Prevalence and family-related factors associated with suicidaldeation, suicide attempts, and self-injury in children aged 9 to 10 years. *JAMA Netw Open*, *3*(2). https://doi.org/10.1001/jamanetworkopen.2019.20956

Dhingra, K., Boduszek, D., & Klonsky, E. D. (2016). Empirically derived subgroups of self-injurious thoughts and behavior: Application of latent class analysis. *Suicide and Life-Threatening Behavior*, *46*(4), 486–499. https://doi.org/10.1111/sltb.12232

Esposito-Smythers, C., Goldstein, T., Birmaher, B., Goldstein, B., Hunt, J., Ryan, N., Axelson, D., Strober, M., Gill, M. K., Hanley, A., & Keller, M. (2010). Clinical and psychosocial correlates of non-suicidal self-injury within a sample of children and adolescents with bipolar disorder. *Journal of Affective Disorders*, *125*(1–3), 89–97. https://doi.org/10.1016/j.jad.2009.12.029

Forrester, R. L., Slater, H., Jomar, K., Mitzman, S., & Taylor, P. J. (2017). Self-esteem and non-suicidal self-injury in adulthood: A systematic review. *Journal of Affective Disorders*, *221*, 172–183. https://doi.org/10.1016/j.jad.2017.06.027

Fox, K. R., Franklin, J. C., Ribeiro, J. D., Kleiman, E. M., Bentley, K. H., & Nock, M. K. (2015). Meta-analysis of risk factors for nonsuicidal self-injury. *Clinical Psychology Review*, *42*, 156–167. https://doi.org/10.1016/j.cpr.2015.09.002

Fox, K. R., Ribeiro, J. D., Kleiman, E. M., Hooley, J. M., Nock, M. K., & Franklin, J. C. (2018). Affect toward the self and self-injury stimuli as potential risk factors for nonsuicidal self-injury. *Psychiatry Research*, *260*, 279–285. https://doi.org/10.1016/j.psychres.2017.11.083

Franklin, J. C., Ribeiro, J. D., Fox, K. R., Bentley, K. H., Kleiman, E. M., Huang, X., Musacchio, K. M., Jaroszewski, A. C., Chang, B. P., & Nock, M. K. (2017). Risk factors for suicidal thoughts and behaviors: A meta-analysis of 50 years of research. *Psychological Bulletin*, *143*(2), 187–232. https://doi.org/10.1037/bul0000084

Ghinea, D., Edinger, A., Parzer, P., Koenig, J., Resch, F., & Kaess, M. (2020). Non-suicidal self-injury disorder as a stand-alone diagnosis in a consecutive help-seeking sample of adolescents. *Journal of affective disorders*, *274*, 1122–1125. https://doi.org/10.1016/j.jad.2020.06.009

Gholamrezaei, M., De Stefano, J., & Heath, N. L. (2017). Nonsuicidal self-injury across cultures and ethnic and racial minorities: A review. *International journal of psychology*, *52*(4), 316–326. https://doi.org/10.1002/ijop.12230

Glenn, J. J., Michel, B. D., Franklin, J. C., Hooley, J. M., & Nock, M. K. (2014). Pain analgesia among adolescent self-injurers. *Psychiatry Research*, *220*(3), 921–926. https://doi.org/10.1016/j.psychres.2014.08.016

Gratz, K. L., Bjureberg, J., Sahlin, H., & Tull, M. T. (2019). Emotion regulation group therapy for nonsuicidal self-injury. In J. J. Washburn (Ed.), Nonsuicidal Self-Injury: Advances in Research and Practice (pp. 148–163). Routledge. https://doi.org/10.4324/9781315164182-9

Gregory, W. E., Glazer, J. V. & Berenson, K. R. Self-compassion, self-injury, and pain. (2017). *Cognitive Therapy and Research*, *41*, 777–786. https://doi.org/10.1007/s10608-017-9846-9

Grigoryan, K., & Jurick, T. (2020). Psychosocial predictors of non-suicidal self-injury (NSSI) in adolescents: Literature review. *Mental Health and Family Medicine*, *16*, 905–912.

Hamza, C. A., & Willoughby, T. (2013). Nonsuicidal self-injury and suicidal behavior: A latent class analysis among young adults. *PLoS One*, *8*(3). https://doi.org/10.1371/journal.pone.0059955

Hamza, C. A., & Willoughby, T. (2019). Impulsivity and nonsuicidal self-injury: A longitudinal examination among emerging adults. *Journal of Adolescence*, *75*, 37–46. https://doi.org/10.1016/j.adolescence.2019.07.003

Hamza, C. A., Willoughby, T., & Heffer, T. (2015). Impulsivity and nonsuicidal self-injury: A review and meta-analysis. *Clinical Psychology Review, 38*, 13–24. https://doi.org/10.1016/j.cpr.2015.02.010

Hasking, P., Boyes, M., & Greves, S. (2018). Self-efficacy and emotionally dysregulated behavior: An exploratory test of the role of emotion regulatory and behavior-specific beliefs. *Psychiatry Research, 270*, 335–340. https://doi.org/10.1016/j.psychres.2018.09.045

Hasking, P., Whitlock, J., Voon, D., & Rose, A. (2017). A cognitive-emotional model of NSSI: Using emotion regulation and cognitive processes to explain why people self-injure. *Cognition and Emotion, 31*(8), 1543–1556. https://doi.org/10.1080/02699931.2016.1241219

Hauber, K., Boon, A., & Vermeiren, R. (2019). Non-suicidal self-injury in clinical practice. *Frontiers in Psychology, 10*(502). https://doi.org/10.3389/fpsyg.2019.00502

Hayes, S. C., Strosahl, K. D., & Wilson, K. G. (2011). *Acceptance and commitment therapy: The process and practice of mindful change* (2nd ed.). Guilford Press.

Hielscher, E., DeVylder, J., Hasking, P., Connell, M., Martin, G., & Scott, J. G. (2021). Can't get you out of my head: Persistence and remission of psychotic experiences in adolescents and its association with self-injury and suicide attempts. *Schizophrenia Research, 229*, 63–72. https://doi.org/10.1016/j.schres.2020.11.019

Hooley, J. M., & Franklin, J. C. (2018). Why do people hurt themselves? A new conceptual model of nonsuicidal self-injury. *Clinical Psychological Science, 6*(3), 428–451. https://doi.org/10.1177/2167702617745641

Hooley, J. M., & St. Germain, S. A. (2013). Nonsuicidal self-injury, pain, and self-criticism. *Clinical Psychological Science, 2*(3), 297–305. https://doi.org/10.1177/2167702613509372

Hooley, J. M., Fox, K. R., & Boccagno, C. (2020). Nonsuicidal self-injury: Diagnostic challenges and current perspectives. *Neuropsychiatric Disease and Treatment, 16*, 101–112. https://doi.org/10.2147/NDT.S198806

Horváth, L. O., Győri, D., Komáromy, D., Mészáros, G., Szentiványi, D., & Balázs, J. (2020). Nonsuicidal self-injury and suicide: The role of life events in clinical and non-clinical populations of adolescents. *Frontiers in Psychiatry, 11*(307). https://doi.org/10.3389/fpsyt.2020.00370

Houben, M., Claes, L., Vansteelandt, K., Berens, A., Sleuwaegen, E., & Kuppens, P. (2017). The emotion regulation function of nonsuicidal self-injury: A momentary assessment study in inpatients with borderline personality disorder features. *Journal of Abnormal Psychology, 126*(1), 89–95. https://doi.org/10.1037/abn0000229

Hughes, D. J., Kratsiotis, I. K., Niven, K., & Holman, D. (2020). Personality traits and emotion regulation: A targeted review and recommendations. *Emotion, 20*(1), 63–67. https://doi.org/10.1037/emo0000644

Jarvi, S., Jackson, B., Swenson, L., & Crawford, H. (2013). The impact of social contagion on non-suicidal self-injury: A review of the literature. *Archives of Suicide Research, 17*(1), 1–19. https://doi.org/10.1080/13811118.2013.748404

Jenkins, A. L., McCloskey, M. S., Kulper, D., Berman, M. E., & Coccaro, E. F. (2015). Self-harm behavior among individuals with intermittent explosive disorder and personality disorders. *Journal of Psychiatric Research, 60*, 125–131. https://doi.org/10.1016/j.jpsychires.2014.08.013

Jiang, Y., You, J., Zheng, X., & Lin, M.-P. (2017). The qualities of attachment with significant others and self-compassion protect adolescents from non suicidal self-injury. *School Psychology Quarterly, 32*(2), 143–155. https://doi.org/10.1037/spq0000187

Kaess, M., Edinger, A., Fischer-Waldschmidt, G., Parzer, P., Brunner, R., & Resch, F. (2019). Effectiveness of a brief psychotherapeutic intervention compared with treatment as usual for adolescent nonsuicidal self-injury: A single-centre, randomised controlled trial. *European Child & Adolescent Psychiatry*, 1–11. https://doi.org/10.1007/s00787-019-01399-1

Kaniuka, A. R., Kelliher-Rabon, J., Chang, E. C., Sirois, F. M., & Hirsch, J. K. (2020). Symptoms of anxiety and depression and suicidal behavior in college students: Conditional indirect effects of non-suicidal self-injury and self-compassion. *Journal of College Student Psychotherapy, 34*(4), 316–338. https://doi.org/10.1080/07448481.2019.1705838

Kelada, L., Hasking, P., & Melvin, G. (2016). Adolescent NSSI and recovery. *Youth & Society, 50*(8), 1056–1077. https://doi.org/10.1177/0044118x16653153

Kiekens, G., & Claes, L. (2020). Non-suicidal self-injury and eating disordered behaviors: An update on what we do and do not know. *Current Psychiatry Reports, 22*(68). https://doi.org/10.1007/s11920-020-01191-y

Kiekens, G., Hasking, P., Claes, L., Mortier, P., Auerbach, R. P., Boyes, M., Cuijpers, P., Demyttenaere, K., Green, J. G., Kessler, R. C., Nock, M. K., & Bruffaerts, R. (2018). The DSM-5 nonsuicidal self-injury disorder among incoming college students: Prevalence and associations with 12-month mental disorders and suicidal thoughts and behaviors. *Depression and Anxiety, 35*(7), 629–637. https://doi.org/10.1002/da.22754

Kim, J. S., Kang, E. S., Bahk, Y. C., Jang, S., Hong, K. S., & Baek, J. H. (2020). Exploratory analysis of behavioral impulsivity, pro-inflammatory cytokines, and resting-state frontal EEG activity associated with non-suicidal self-injury in patients with mood disorder. *Frontiers in psychiatry, 11*, 124. https://doi.org/10.3389/fpsyt.2020.00124

Klonsky, E. D., Muehlenkamp, J. J., Lewis, S., & Walsh, B. W. (2011). *Nonsuicidal self-injury*. Hogrefe.

Klonsky, E. D., & Olino, T. M. (2008). Identifying clinically distinct subgroups of self-injurers among young adults: A latent class analysis. *Journal of Consulting and Clinical Psychology, 76*(1), 22. https://doi.org/10.1037/0022-006X.76.1.22

Kothgassner, O. D., Goreis, A., Robinson, K., Huscsava, M. M., Schmahl, C., & Plener, P. L. (2021). Efficacy of dialectical behavior therapy for adolescent self-harm and suicidal ideation: A systematic review and meta-analysis. *Psychological Medicine, 51*(7), 1–11. https://doi.org/10.1017/s0033291721001355

Kranzler, A., Fehling, K. B., Lindqvist, J., Brillante, J., Yuan, F., Gao, X., Miller, A. L., & Selby, E. A. (2018). An ecological investigation of the emotional context surrounding nonsuicidal self-injurious thoughts and behaviors in adolescents and young adults. *Suicide and Life-Threatening Behavior, 48*(2), 149–159. https://doi.org/10.1111/sltb.12373

Lan, T., Jia, X., Lin, D., & Lin, X. (2019). Stressful life events, depression, and non-suicidal self-injury among Chinese left-behind children: Moderating effects of self-esteem. *Frontiers in Psychiatry, 10*(244). https://doi.org/10.3389/fpsyt.2019.00244

Lear, M. K., Wilkowski, B. M., & Pepper, C. M. (2019). A daily diary investigation of the defective self-model among college students with recent self-injury. *Behavior Therapy, 50*(5), 1002–1012. https://doi.org/10.1016/j.beth.2019.03.005

Lee, J. Y., Kim, H., Kim, S. Y., Kim, J. M., Shin, I. S., & Kim, S. W. (2021). Non-suicidal self-injury is associated with psychotic like experiences, depression, and bullying in Korean adolescents. *Early Intervention in Psychiatry*. https://doi.org/10.1111/eip.13115

Leon, K., O'Bryan, J., Wolf-Gould, C., Turell, S. C., & Gadomski, A. (2021). Prevalence and risk factors for nonsuicidal self-injury in transgender and gender-expansive youth at a rural gender wellness clinic. *Transgender Health, 6*(1), 43–50. https://doi.org/10.1089/trgh.2020.0031

Lewis, S., & Hasking, P. (2020). Rethinking self-injury recovery: A commentary and conceptual reframing. *BJPsych Bulletin, 44*(2), 44–46. https://doi.org/10.1192/bjb.2019.51

Liu, R. T., Frazier, E. A., Cataldo, A.M., Simon, V. A., Spirito, A., & Prinstein, M. J. (2014). Negative life events and non-suicidal self-injury in an adolescent inpatient sample. *Archives of Suicide Research, 18*(3), 251–258. https://doi.org/10.1080/13811118.2013.824835

Liu, R. T., Scopelliti, K. M., Pittman, S. K., & Zamora, A. S. (2018). Childhood maltreatment and non-suicidal self-injury: A systematic review and meta-analysis. *The Lancet Psychiatry, 5*(1), 51–64. https://doi.org/10.1016/S2215-0366(17)30469-8

Liu, R. T., Sheehan, A. E., Walsh, R. F. L., Sanzari, C. M., Cheek, S. M., & Hernandez, E. M. (2019). Prevalence and correlates of non-suicidal self-injury among lesbian, gay, bisexual, and transgender individuals: A systematic review and meta-analysis. *Clinical Psychology Review, 74*, https://doi.org/10.1016/j.cpr.2019.101783

Liu, R. T., Trout, Z. M., Hernandez, E. M., Cheek, S. M., & Gerlus, N. (2017). A behavioral and cognitive neuroscience perspective on impulsivity, suicide, and non-suicidal self-injury: Meta-analysis and recommendations for future research. *Neuroscience & Biobehavioral Reviews, 83*, 440–450. https://doi.org/10.1016/j.neubiorev.2017.09.019

Liu, S., You, J., Ying, J., Li, X., & Shi, Q. (2020). Emotion reactivity, nonsuicidal self-injury, and regulatory emotional self-efficacy: A moderated mediation model of suicide ideation. *Journal of Affective Disorders, 266*, 82–89. https://doi.org/10.1016/j.jad.2020.01.083

Lockwood, J., Daley, D., Townsend, E., & Sayal, K. (2017). Impulsivity and self-harm in adolescence: A systematic review. *European Child & Adolescent Psychiatry, 26*(4), 387–402. https://doi.org/10.1007/s00787-016-0915-5

Luo, X., Qiao, L., & Che, X. (2018). Self-compassion modulates heart rate variability and negative affect to experimentally induced stress. *Mindfulness, 9*(5), 1522–1528. https://doi.org/10.1007/s12671-018-0900-9

Lutz, N. M., Chamberlain, S. R., Goodyer, I. M., Bhardwaj, A., Sahakian, B. J., Jones, P. B., & Wilkinson, P. O. (2021). Behavioral measures of impulsivity and compulsivity in adolescents with nonsuicidal self-injury. *CNS Spectrums*, 1–9. https://doi.org/10.1017/S1092852921000274

McCloskey, M. S., Ben-Zeev, D., Lee, R., & Coccaro, E. F. (2008). Prevalence of suicidal and self-injurious behavior among subjects with intermittent explosive disorder. *Psychiatry Research, 158*(2), 248–250. https://doi.org/10.1016/j.psychres.2007.09.011

Merino, H., Senra, C., & Ferreiro, F. (2016). Are worry and rumination specific pathways linking neuroticism and symptoms of anxiety and depression in patients with generalized anxiety disorder, major depressive disorder, and mixed anxiety-depressive disorder? *PLoS One, 11*(5) https://doi.org/10.1371/journal.pone.0156169

Meszaros, G., Horvath, L. O., & Balazs, J. (2017). Self-injury and externalizing pathology: A systematic literature review. *BMC Psychiatry, 17*. https://doi.org/10.1186/s12888-017-1326-y

Morgan, C., Webb, R. T., Carr, M. J., Kontopantelis, E., Chew-Graham, C. A., Kapur, N., & Ashcroft, D. M. (2018). Self-harm in a primary care cohort of older people: Incidence, clinical management, and risk of suicide and other causes of death. *The Lancet Psychiatry, 5*(11), 905–912. https://doi.org/10.1016/S2215-0366(18)30348-1

Muehlenkamp, J. J., Bagge, C. L., Tull, M. T., & Gratz, K. L. (2013). Body regard as a moderator of the relation between emotion dysregulation and nonsuicidal self-injury. *Suicide and Life-Threatening Behavior, 43*(5), 479–493. https://doi.org/10.1111/sltb.12032

Muehlenkamp, J. J., Brausch, A. M., & Washburn, J. J. (2017). How much is enough? Examining frequency criteria for NSSI disorder in adolescent inpatients. *Journal of Consulting and Clinical Psychology, 85*(6), 611–619. https://doi.org/10.1037/ccp0000209

Muehlenkamp, J. J., Suzuki, T., Brausch, A. M., & Peyerl, N. (2019). Behavioral functions underlying NSSI and eating disorder behaviors. *Journal of Clinical Psychology, 75*(7), 1219–1232. https://doi.org/10.1002/jclp.22745

Nock, M. K., Joiner Jr, T. E., Gordon, K. H., Lloyd-Richardson, E., & Prinstein, M. J. (2006). Non-suicidal self-injury among adolescents: Diagnostic correlates and relation to suicide attempts. *Psychiatry Research, 144*(1), 65–72. https://doi.org/10.1016/j.psychres.2006.05.010

Ose, S. O., Tveit, T., & Mehlum, L. (2021). Non-suicidal self-injury (NSSI) in adult psychiatric outpatients—A nationwide study. *Journal of Psychiatric Research, 133*, 1–9. https://doi.org/10.1016/j.jpsychires.2020.11.031

Perkins, N. M., Ortiz, S. N., & Smith, A. R. (2020). Self-criticism longitudinally predicts nonsuicidal self-injury in eating disorders. *Eating Disorders, 28*(2), 157–170. https://doi.org/10.1080/10640266.2019.1695450

Perlman, G., Gromatsky, M., Salis, K. L., Klein, D. N., & Kotov, R. (2018). Personality correlates of self-injury in adolescent girls: Disentangling the effects of lifetime psychopathology. *Journal of Abnormal Child Psychology, 46*(8), 1677–1685. https://doi.org/10.1007/s10802-018-0403-0

Peterson, A. L., Chen, J. I., Karver, M. S., & Labouliere, C. D. (2019). Frustration with feeling: Latent classes of non-suicidal self-injury and emotion regulation difficulties. *Psychiaatry Research, 275*, 61–70. https://doi.org/10.1016/j.psychres.2019.03.014

Polanco-Roman, L., Tsypes, A., Soffer, A., & Miranda, R. (2014). Ethnic differences in prevalence and correlates of self-harm behaviors in a treatment-seeking sample of emerging adults. *Psychiatry Research, 220*(3), 927–934. https://doi.org/10.1016/j.psychres.2014.09.017

Prinstein, M. J., Helibron, N., Guerry, J. D., Franklin, J. C., Rancourt, D., Simon, V., & Spirito, A. (2010). Peer influence and nonsuicidal self injury: Longitudinal results in community and clinically-referred adolescent samples. *Journal of Abnormal Child Psychology, 38*(5), 669–682. https://doi.org/10.1007/s10802-010-9423-0

Rees, C. S., Hasking, P., Breen, L. J., Lipp, O. V., & Mamotte, C. (2015). Group mindfulness based cognitive therapy vs group support for self-injury among young people: Study protocol for a randomised controlled trial. *BMC Psychiatry, 15*(1). https://doi.org/10.1186/s12888-015-0527-5

Reichl, C., & Kaess, M. (2021). Self-harm in the context of borderline personality disorder. *Current Opinion in Psychology, 37*, 139–144. https://doi.org/10.1016/j.copsyc.2020.12.007

Reinhardt, M., Horváth, Z., Drubina, B., Kökönyei, G., & Rice, K. G. (2021). Latent class analysis of nonsuicidal self-injury among justice-involved juveniles: Association with motivational and emotional aspects of self-harm behavior. *Criminal Justice and Behavior, 48*(7), 902–922. https://doi.org/10.1177/0093854821998411

Ribeiro, J. D., Franklin, J. C., Fox, K. R., Bentley, K. H., Kleiman, E. M., Chang, B. P., & Nock, M. K. (2015). Self-injurious thoughts and behaviors as risk factors for future suicide ideation, attempts, and death: A meta-analysis of longitudinal studies. *Psychological Medicine, 46*(2), 225–236. https://doi.org/10.1017/S0033291715001804

Rockliff, H., Gilbert, P., McEwan, K., Lightman, S., & Glover, D. (2008) A pilot exploration of heart rate variability and salivary cortisol responses to compassion-focused imagery. *Clinical Neuropsychiatry: Journal of Treatment Evaluation*, *5*(3), 132–139.

Rojas-Velasquez, D. A., Pluhar, E. I., Burns, P. A., & Burton, E. T. (2021). Nonsuicidal self-injury among African American and Hispanic adolescents and young adults: A systematic review. *Prevention Science*, *22*, 367–377. https://doi.org/10.1007/s11121-020-01147-x

Rubenstein, L. M., Freed, R. D., Shapero, B. G., Fauber, R. L., & Alloy, L. B. (2016). Cognitive attributions in depression: Bridging the gap between research and clinical practice. *Journal of Psychotherapy Integration*, *26*(2), 103–115. https://doi.org/10.1037/int0000030

Sauer-Zavala, S., Fournier, J. C., Steele, S. J., Woods, B. K., Wang, M., Farchione, T. J., & Barlow, D. H. (2020). Does the unified protocol really change neuroticism? Results from a randomized trial. *Psychological Medicine*, *51*(14), 2378–2387. https://doi.org/10.1017/S0033291720000975

Schwartz-Mette, R. A., & Lawrence, H. R. (2019). Peer socialization of non-suicidal self-injury in adolescents' close friendships. *Journal of Abnormal Child Psychology*, *47*(11), 1851–1862. https://doi.org/10.1007/s10802-019-00569-8

Serafini, G., Canepa, G., Adavastro, G., Nebbia, J., Belvederi Murri, M., Erbuto, D., Pocai, B., Fiorillo, A., Pompili, M., Flouri, E., & Amore, M. (2017). The relationship between childhood maltreatment and non-suicidal self-injury: A systematic review. *Frontiers in Psychiatry*, *8*(149). https://doi.org/10.3389/fpsyt.2017.00149

Shahwan, S., Lau, J. H., Abdin, E., Zhang, Y., Sambasivam, R., Teh, W. L., Gupta, B., Ong, S. H., Chong, S. A., & Subramaniam, M. (2020). A typology of nonsuicidal self-injury in a clinical sample: A latent class analysis. *Clinical Psychology and Psychotherapy*, *27*(6), 791–803. https://doi.org/10.1002/cpp.2463

Silverman, M. H., Wilson, S., Ramsay, I. S., Hunt, R. H., Thomas, K. M., Krueger, R. F., & Iacono, W. G. (2019). Trait neuroticism and emotion neurocircuitry: fMRI evidence for a failure in emotion regulation. *Development and Psychopathology*, *31*(3), 1085–1099. https://doi.org/10.1017%2FS0954579419000610

Singhal, N., Bhola, P., Reddi, V. S. K., Bhaskarapillai, B., & Joseph, S. (2021). Non-suicidal self-injury (NSSI) among emerging adults: Sub-group profiles and their clinical relevance. *Psychiatry Research*, *300*. https://doi.org/10.1016/j.psychres.2021.113877

Somer, O., Bildik, T., Kabukçu-Başay, B., Güngör, D., Başay, Ö., & Farmer, R. F. (2015). Prevalence of non-suicidal self-injury and distinct groups of self-injurers in a community sample of adolescents. *Social Psychiatry and Psychiatric Epidemiology*, *50*(7), 1163–1171. https://doi.org/10.1007/s00127-015-1060-z

Sornberger, M. J., Heath, N. L., Toste, J. R., & McLouth, R. (2012). Nonsuicidal self-injury and gender: Patterns of prevalence, methods, and locations among adolescents. *Suicide and Life-Threatening Behavior*, *42*(3), 266–278. https://doi.org/10.1111/j.1943-278X.2012.0088.x

Staples, J. M., Neilson, E. C., Bryan, A. E., & George, W. H. (2018). The role of distal minority stress and internalized transnegativity in suicidal ideation and nonsuicidal self-injury among transgender adults. *The Journal of Sex Research*, *55*(4–5), 591–603. https://doi.org/10.1080/00224499.2017.1393651

Stoerkel, L., Karabatsiakis, A., Hepp, J., Schmahl, C., & Niedtfeld, I. (2019). 150. Ecological momentary assessment of psychological and biological antecedents and consequences of non-suicidal self-injury. *Biological Psychiatry*, *85*(10). https://doi.org/10.1016/j.biopsych.2019.03.164

Sutherland, O., Dawczyk, A., De Leon, K., Cripps, J., & Lewis, S. P. (2014). Self-compassion in online accounts of nonsuicidal self-injury: An interpretive phenomenological analysis. *Counseling Psychology Quarterly*, *27*, 409–433, https://doi.org/10.1080/09515070.2014.948809

Syed, S., Kingsbury, M., Bennett, K., Manion, I., & Colman, I. (2020). Adolescents' knowledge of a peer's non-suicidal self-injury and own non-suicidal self-injury and suicidality. *Acta Psychiatrica Scandinavica*. https://doi.org/10.1111/acps.13229

Szewczuk-Bogusławska, M., Kaczmarek-Fojtar, M., Moustafa, A. A., Frydecka, D., Oleszkowicz, A., Bak, O., & Misiak, B. (2018). Assessment of the frequency criterion for the diagnosis of non-suicidal self-injury disorder in female adolescents with conduct disorder. *Psychiatry Research*, *267*, 333–339. https://doi.org/10.1016/j.psychres.2018.05.054

Taliaferro, L. A., Jang, S. T., Westers, N. J., Muehlenkamp, J. J., Whitlock, J. L., & McMorris, B. J. (2020). Associations between connections to parents and friends and non-suicidal self-injury among adolescents. *Clinical Child Psychology and Psychiatry*, *25*(2), 359–371. https://doi.org/10.1177%2F1359104519868493

Taliaferro, L. A., McMorris, B. J., Rider, G. N., & Eisenberg, M. E. (2019). Risk and protective factors for self-harm in a population-based sample of transgender youth. *Archives of Suicide Research*, *23*(2), 203–221. https://doi.org/10.1080/13811118.2018.1430639

Taliaferro, L. A., & Muehlenkamp, J. J. (2017). Nonsuicidal self-injury and suicidality among sexual minority youth: Risk factors and protective connectedness factors. *Academic Pediatrics*, *17*(7), 715–722. https://doi.org/10.1016/j.acap.2016.11.002

Tatnell, R., Hasking, P., Newman, L., Taffe, J., & Martin, G. (2017). Attachment, emotion regulation, childhood abuse and assault: Examining predictors of NSSI among adolescents. *Archives of Suicide Research*, *21*(4), 610–620. https://doi.org/10.1080/13811118.2016.1246267

Taylor, P. J., Jomar, K., Dhingra, K, Forrester, R., Shahmalak, U., & Dickson, J. M. (2019). A meta-analysis of the prevalence of different functions of non-suicidal self-injury. *Journal of Affective Disord*ers 227, 759–769.https://doi.org/10.1016/j.jad.2017.11.073

Valencia-Agudo, F., Burcher, G. C., Ezpeleta, L., & Kramer, T. (2018). Nonsuicidal self-injury in community adolescents: A systematic review of prospective predictors, mediators and moderators. *Journal of Adolescence*, *65*, 25–38. https://doi.org/10.1016/j.adolescence.2018.02.012

Vaughn, M. G., Salas-Wright, C. P., Underwood, S., & Gochez-Kerr, T. (2015). Subtypes of non-suicidal self-injury based on childhood adversity. *Psychiatric Quarterly*, *86*(1), 137–151. https://doi.org/10.1007/s11126-014-9313-7

Victor, S. E., Muehlenkamp, J. J., Hayes, N. A., Lengel, G. J., Styer, D. M., & Washburn, J. J. (2018). Characterizing gender differences in nonsuicidal self-injury: Evidence form a large clinical sample of adolescents and adults. *Comprehensive Psychiatry*, *82*, 53–60. https://doi.org/proxy.uwec.edu/10.1016/j.comppsych.2018.01.009

Victor, S. E., Scott, L. N., Stepp, S. D., & Goldstein, T. R. (2019). I want you to want me: Interpersonal stress and affective experiences as within-person predictors of nonsuicidal self-injury and suicide urges in daily life. *Suicide and Life-Threatening Behavior*, *49*(4), 1157–1177. https://doi.org/10.1111/sltb.12513

Vieira, A. I., Machado, B. C., Machado, P. P. P., Brandão, I., Roma-Torres, A., & Gonçalves, S. (2017). Putative risk factors for non-suicidal self-injury in eating disorders. *European Eating Disorder Review*, *25*(6), 544–550. https://doi.org/10.1002/erv.2545

Whitlock, J., Muehlenkamp, J., & Eckenrode, J. (2008). Variation in nonsuicidal self-injury: Identification and features of latent classes in a college population of emerging adults. *Journal of Clinical Child & Adolescent Psychology*, *37*(4), 725–735. https://doi.org/.10.1080/15374410802359734

Wolff, J. C., Frazier, E. A., Esposito-Smythers, C., Becker, S. J., Burke, T. A., Cataldo, A., & Spirito, A. (2014). Negative cognitive style and perceived social support mediate the relationship between aggression and NSSI in hospitalized adolescents. *Journal of Adolescence*, *37*(4), 483–491. https://doi.org/10.1016/j.adolescence.2014.03.016

Wolff, J., Frazier, E. A., Esposito-Smythers, C., Burke, T., Sloan, E., & Spirito, A. (2013). Cognitive and social factors associated with NSSI and suicide attempts in psychiatrically hospitalized adolescents. *Journal of Abnormal Child Psychology*, *41*(6). 1005–1013. https://doi.org/10.1007/s10802-013-9743-y

Wolff, J. C., Thompson, E., Thomas, S. A., Nesi, J., Bettis, A. H., Ransford, B., Scopelliti, K., Fraizer, E. A., & Liu, R. T. (2019). Emotion dysregulation and non-suicidal self-injury: A systematic review and meta-analysis. *European Psychiatry*, *59*, 25–36. https://doi.org/10.1016/j.eurpsy.2019.03.004

Xavier, A., Pinto-Gouveia, J., & Cunha, M. (2016). The protective role of self-compassion on risk factors for non-suicidal self-injury in adolescence. *School Mental Health*, *8*(4), 476–485. https://doi.org/10.1007/s12310-016-9197-9

Xin, X., Ming, Q., Zhang, J., Wang, Y., Liu, M., & Yao, S. (2016). Four distinct subgroups of self-injurious behavior among Chinese adolescents: Findings from a latent class analysis. *PLOS ONE*, *11*(7). https://doi.org/10.1371/journal.pone.0158609

You, J., Lin, M. P., Xu, S., & Hu, W. H. (2016). Big Five personality traits in the occurrence and repetition of nonsuicidal self-injury among adolescents: The mediating effects of depressive symptoms. *Personality and Individual Differences*, *101*, 227–231. https://doi.org/10.1016/j.paid.2016.05.057

Zelkowitz, R. L., & Cole, D. A. (2019). Self-criticism as a transdiagnostic process in nonsuicidal self-injury and disordered eating: Systematic review and meta-analysis. *Suicide and Life-Threatening Behavior*, *49*(1), 310–327. https://doi.org/10.1111/sltb.12436

Zetterqvist, M., Perini, I., Mayo, L. M., & Gustafsson, P. A. (2020). Nonsuicidal self-injury disorder in adolescents: Clinical utility of the diagnosis using the clinical assessment of nonsuicidal self-injury disorder index. *Frontiers in Psychiatry*, *11*. https://doi.org/10.3389%2Ffpsyt.2020.00008

CHAPTER 9

NSSI and Self-Harm Behavior and the COVID-19 Pandemic

Amy Brausch *and* Rebekah Clapham

Abstract

This chapter reviews the effects of previous pandemics on mental health and self-harm, as well as the current research available about the effects of COVID-19 on nonsuicidal self-injury and suicide risk. Initial evidence on the effects of COVID-19 on deliberate self-harm behavior suggests that in general, individuals are experiencing a significant amount of collective stress and trauma, regardless of their views about or access to masks or vaccines. Some researchers have suggested that factors such as social distancing, less access to social supports, barriers to mental health treatments, fear of and experience with physical illness, and increased feelings of responsibility and guilt may be reducing general resilience of the population and increasing deliberate self-harm risk. However, it is also possible that the COVID-19 pandemic has created situations that serve as protective factors against deliberate self-harm. With opportunities to work from home, the closures of schools, and increased interaction with family members, individuals may be experiencing less work-related stress, more distance from negative or harmful peers, and an increased sense of family connection. The chapter then considers identity-related factors in the context of COVID-19 and self-harm. In addition to adolescents and the LGBTQ community potentially being disproportionally influenced by COVID-19, there have been reports of deliberate self-harm behaviors increasing among other minoritized individuals as well.

Key Words: self-harm, COVID-19 pandemic, nonsuicidal self-injury, suicide risk, collective stress, collective trauma, self-harm risk, adolescents, minoritized individuals

Rates of deliberate self-harm (broadly defined as the combination of suicidal and nonsuicidal self-injury; Hawton et al., 2003) have been leading health concerns across the world even before the COVID-19 pandemic (World Health Organization, 2020). However, the current pandemic has introduced circumstances that could increase risk factors, or create new risk factors for engagement in deliberate self-harm, such as financial insecurity, social isolation, and increased levels of stress. Consequently, rates of deliberate self-harm during the COVID-19 pandemic have become an important area of focus for mental health researchers. However, the majority of research on this topic is extremely limited and still developing, and the research that does exist tends to be cross-sectional, making definitive conclusions premature at this time. This chapter reviews the effects of previous pandemics on mental health and self-harm, as well as the current research available about the effects of COVID-19 on nonsuicidal self-injury and suicide risk.

Increases in self-harm are associated with times of stress (Miller et al., 2019), uncertainty (Hawton et al., 2012), isolation (Endo et al., 2017), anxiety (Hughes et al., 2019), and interpersonal problems (Victor et al., 2019), all of which are relevant to COVID-19. Additionally, research on past pandemics and epidemics have found exacerbated effects on suicidality; the 1918 flu longitudinally increased suicide rates in the United States (Johnson & Mueller, 2002; Wasserman, 1992). The 1918 flu pandemic (sometimes referred to as the Spanish flu pandemic) is similar to the COVID-19 pandemic in that worldwide infections and mortality rates were high, both experienced multiple waves, and both seemed to affect individuals across many age groups. The 1918 flu is documented to have occurred across four waves from 1918 to 1920, and as of this writing, the COVID-19 pandemic began in late 2019 and has endured multiple waves depending on country and continent, with many locations finding themselves in the midst of new waves with new variants (Eghigian, 2020). Research conducted following the 1918 pandemic found increases in psychiatric hospitalizations, reports of sleep disturbance, feeling distracted, and difficulties coping at home and work among flu survivors, as well as increased associations with suicide (Eghigian, 2020). Similarly, the 2003 outbreak of SARS was associated with peak suicide rates in older adults in Hong Kong (Chan et al., 2006), as well as higher rates of posttraumatic stress disorder (PTSD) and depression (Mak et al., 2009), and higher rates of anger, anxiety, suicide ideation, and depressive symptoms among patients with SARS across all ages. Additionally, there was an increase of suicide attempts related to Ebola exposure (Zortea et al., 2021).

Many countries experienced ebbs and flows in COVID-19 transmission, resulting in ever-changing health and safety protocols and requirements—vaccine requirements, mask mandates, social distancing, online versus in-person schooling, and so on. Research has documented that these fluctuations in COVID-19 severity and associated safety measures prolonged feelings of uncertainty and anxiety and led many individuals to feel they were in a constant state of evaluating risk and making related decisions for themselves and loved ones. We review the existing research on the effects of the COVID-19 pandemic, which have been mixed thus far in terms of showing associations with increased or decreased rates of self-harm. Longitudinal research in the years and decades to follow will provide even more insight into the long-term effects of the current pandemic.

Evidence of Increasing Deliberate Self-Harm Behaviors During COVID-19

John et al. (2020) conducted a systematic review of studies examining deliberate self-harm and suicidal thoughts during the pandemic. Although there have been mixed findings, John et al. (2020) ultimately concluded that at this time there was not enough evidence to claim deliberate self-harm rates rose. However, they reviewed several studies that found significant increases. For example, Lee (2020) found that higher levels of deliberate self-harm thoughts were reported in people with anxiety relating to COVID-19 in the United States. Similarly, increases in deliberate self-harm thoughts were reported in individuals with worry related to the pandemic, mediated by insomnia (Killgore et al., 2020), in students (Kaparounaki et al., 2020) and in people recovering from COVID-19 (Hao et al., 2020). Additionally, Killgore et al. (2020) found that loneliness was also associated with increased suicidal and self-harm thoughts, and Wu et al. (2020) reported increased levels of self-harm thoughts among pregnant women in China after the start of the pandemic compared to pregnant women in China before the pandemic.

Furthermore, reports from hospitals and treatment centers have suggested a significant increase in the number of people seeking medical attention or support for deliberate self-harm since the pandemic onset. A study in an Irish hospital that took place from March to May of 2020 reported an increased number of visits to the emergency room from people seeking help for self-harm behaviors, with the peak of visits occurring in mid-May (McIntyre et al., 2021). The researchers also noted an increase in the lethality of self-harm behaviors, with the number of people needing medical attention for their injuries almost tripling. When the 2020 reports were compared to the reports for the previous four years, McIntyre et al. (2021) found a significant increase in the lethality of attempts after accounting for age and gender. In a hospital in the UK, 25% of penetrating injuries (defined as the physical trauma that occurs when an object pierces the skin) were found to be the direct result of self-harm, such as cutting, as compared to 11% of penetrating injuries in 2019, and 2% in 2018 (Olding et al., 2021). A study of UK adults analyzed from April 2020 to February 2021 found that both financial concern and COVID-19 infection were associated with increased self-harm thoughts and behaviors (Paul & Fancourt, 2021). On a global scale, a study that examined data from 10 countries compared reports of emergency services from March–April 2019 to March–April 2020 and observed a substantial growth in the number of children presenting for help with self-harm (Ougrin et al., 2022). In India, researchers examined 72 suicide cases to determine their relation to COVID-19 and found that the most common reasons for suicide were fear of COVID-19 infection, financial crisis, loneliness, work-related stress, and distance from family (Dsouza et al., 2020). Taken together, these alarming reports suggested a growing increase of deliberate self-harm across nationalities, age groups, and gender in relation to the effects of the COVID-19 pandemic.

Beyond the reports from clinical settings, research conducted online with the general public also revealed concerning increases in deliberate self-harm. In a 2020 online survey of more than 4,909 individuals in the United States, researchers found that among adolescents, loneliness and more exposure to media reporting on COVID-19 were associated with increased suicidal thoughts and behaviors as compared to data taken prior to COVID-19 (Murata et al., 2020). Loneliness was also linked to an increase in nonsuicidal self-injury (NSSI) and suicide ideation during COVID-19 in a sample of adults

(Hammond, 2020). Similarly, COVID-19 related experiences, such as distress, social distancing, and fear of physical harm, were associated with past-month suicide ideation and attempts. Approximately 45% of adults, who reported experiencing past-month suicide ideation specifically linked their suicidal thoughts to COVID-19, and 9.2% of sampled adults disclosed they intentionally exposed themselves to the virus with the intent to die (Ammerman et al., 2021).

A few studies have suggested that certain groups may be more at risk for deliberate self-harm during COVID-19 than others, such as healthcare workers, those with preexisting mental health issues, and people of certain economic status or family background. For example, a survey among Canadian adults showed that thoughts of self-harm increased post-COVID and those most at risk were people who were 25 years of age, indigenous, unemployed, single, and/or living with family and with increased anxiety (Sapara et al., 2021). Hospital staff who reported having family members infected with COVID-19, or felt a high likelihood of contracting it themselves, reported more thoughts of self-harm (Xu et al., 2021). Additionally, healthcare workers with perceived high stress and low support, as well as anxiety and depression, were at increased risk for suicide ideation.

People with preexisting mental health conditions, such as anxiety and depression, are more at risk for deliberate self-harm and suicidal thoughts generally (Klonsky et al., 2003). It is possible that the pandemic may have put these individuals even further at risk. Researchers have suggested that uncertainties caused by COVID-19, in combination with public health responses (such as lockdown), heightened depression, anxiety, loneliness, stress, and substance abuse among people across the globe (Courtet et al., 2020; Khan, 2020; Tull et al., 2020). As a result, individuals with heightened mental health problems may be at especially high risk for deliberate self-harm behaviors. One study of the Central Denmark Region seems to support this theory; researchers screened more than 11,000 clinical notes recorded from February to March 2020 in an adult psychiatric center and found that one of the most common manifestations of psychopathology related to COVID-19 was deliberate self-harm (Rohde et al., 2020). This suggestion is also supported by prior research on previous pandemics and epidemics; researchers found that the 2003 SARS outbreak was associated with increased rates of anxiety, depression, and stress, as well as peak suicide rates (Chan et al., 2006; Lee et al., 2007; Mak et al., 2009). It is possible that a similar trend will exist with COVID-19, however, there is not yet enough existing research to support this conclusion.

In contrast to these suggestions, Hamza et al. (2020) found that since the start of the pandemic, students without preexisting mental health concerns were more likely to report declining mental health and more NSSI behaviors when compared to students who had preexisting mental health conditions. This may be because students with preexisting mental health conditions that are largely tied to, or influenced by, the environment, such as anxiety or depression related to school stress, bullying, or ostracism, may feel more comfortable and supported outside the school environment. However, students who do not deal with those issues at school may suddenly be facing new challenges, such as loneliness and disconnection while in lockdown at home. Students already experiencing mental health concerns prior to the pandemic may have already been connected to therapists or other resources and were able to continue to access those resources during the pandemic. Students with the onset of mental health concerns during the pandemic may have struggled to reach out and connect to therapists or resources, especially during times of lockdown and/or quarantine.

In general, it is critical to consider why deliberate self-harm rates may have increased during the pandemic in order to provide effective, immediate, and preventative support. Some researchers have suggested that factors such as social distancing, less access to social supports, barriers to mental health treatments, fear of and experience with physical illness, and increased feelings of responsibility and guilt may be reducing general resilience of the population and increasing deliberate self-harm risk (Reger et al., 2020). Other researchers also argue that screen time and social media played a role, with extensive social media usage among adults being linked to increased anxiety and depression during COVID-19 lockdowns (Gao et al., 2020). It may be that with increased social media use, individuals are absorbing more upsetting or negative news more frequently, or "doomscrolling," which in turn, may lower resilience and increase risk of self-harm. It could also be that more time on social media may increase feelings of loneliness and disconnection. Furthermore, if individuals are already struggling with NSSI behaviors or thoughts of suicide, social media may increase these urges by exposing them to pro-self-harming websites, or triggering images or news of deliberate self-harm (Lewis & Seko, 2016; also see Westers, this volume and Pritchard & Lewis, this volume, for online NSSI).

It is also critical to consider the surrounding cultural climate that could have contributed to the stress surrounding the pandemic. For example, in more collectivist cultures that emphasize the needs of the larger community over the needs of the individual, a person who contracted COVID-19 may have experienced a greater sense of burdensomeness and guilt than a person from an individualistic culture, particularly if that person may have exposed others, relied on others for support or help, and/or was unable to provide for their family during their illness. For instance, in case report studies in India, these feelings of burdensomeness on family and society were linked to at least two suicide deaths (Sahoo et al., 2020). In addition, the social climate of a culture may play a significant role. In the United States, the COVID-19 pandemic coincided with the resurgence of divided social justice movements, and in combination with the closure of schools, isolation, loss of businesses, and unemployment, the social unrest may have contributed to general feelings of hopelessness and despair that an increasing number of adults have reported feeling since the start of the pandemic (Vahratian et al., 2021).

However, with the current lack of research and longitudinal data on deliberate self-harm during COVID-19, it is only possible to speculate about causes, relationships, and outcomes. Furthermore, there has been contradicting evidence, some of which suggests that deliberate self-harm rates have *decreased* during the pandemic; thus, it is imperative to examine how COVID-19 may also have created circumstances that serve as potential protective factors.

Evidence of Decreasing Deliberate Self-Harm Behaviors During COVID-19

In opposition to theories that argue that increased stress, isolation, financial strain, and loneliness brought on by the pandemic may increase self-harm and suicidal thoughts, it is also possible that the COVID-19 pandemic created situations that served as protective factors against deliberate self-harm. It may be that with opportunities to work from home, the closures of schools, and increased interaction with family members, individuals may have experienced less work-related stress, more distance from negative or harmful peers, and an increased sense of family connection.

Research from previous pandemics shows a general trend of increases in self-harm and suicide rates, but research conducted during the COVID-19 pandemic thus far indicates that self-harm may decrease in certain situations. This may be in part because the context of the current pandemic is significantly different than previous pandemics. The current availability of technology and the internet has made it easier for people to engage in school and work from home and also to establish and maintain strong connections with others. Health systems across the globe have improved; communication, updates, and news are more accessible; and a vaccine was created in record time (Cohen, 2020). These advancements may provide people with feelings of hope, resiliency, control, and a greater sense of safety, which, in turn, may serve as a buffer for self-harm thoughts and behaviors.

However, it is important to recognize that these protective factors may only apply to certain groups of people, such as people who have higher-paying or more flexible jobs, feel safe at home, have affordable and stable health care, and have access to internet and technological equipment. Thus, the factors that may be protective for some may ultimately serve as increased risk factors for other groups of people; we will discuss particularly at-risk groups in the later section "Identity-Related Factors in Relation to COVID-19 and Deliberate Self-Harm."

NSSI and suicide have been shown to decrease in the presence of family support (Kelada et al., 2018; Shamsian, 2001) and the absence of bullying (Esposito et al., 2019; Holt et al., 2015). Additionally, deliberate self-harm has been tied to work stress (Milner et al., 2018) and feelings of isolation and loneliness (Joiner, 2005). With the pandemic generally increasing time spent with family, removing the presence of peers, and forcing people to adapt to new ways of working, it is possible that these changes served as protective factors and, thus, help explain why some of the existing cross-sectional data found both a lack of increase in deliberate self-harm as well as a decrease.

It is important to note that data are difficult to collect on this topic, and the pandemic and related research are still developing. John et al. (2020) concluded their living systematic review by stating that there was no clear and definitive evidence of increases in self-harm, suicidal behavior, or suicidal thoughts associated with the COVID-19 pandemic. Across the 28 studies reviewed by John et al. (2020), none were able to directly link harmful effects of lockdown or physical distancing to increases in suicidal thoughts or behavior, or self-harm. One study that did examine the prevalence of suicidal behavior and suicidal thoughts in people across different areas of the United States with varying lockdown procedures, still found no differences between groups (Bryan et al., 2020), suggesting that lockdown did not have an effect on deliberate self-harm engagement.

Additionally, although Ammerman et al. (2021) concluded that COVID-19-related experiences, such as distress, social distancing, and fear of physical harm, were ultimately associated with past-month suicide ideation and attempts, they also noted a decrease in suicidal thoughts associated with social distancing during the early stages of lockdown. This finding indicates that a changing relationship between suicidality and social distancing and may be informative of how lockdown could have served as both a protective and risk factor for self-harm. Perhaps in the beginning of lockdown, aspects such as time off from work, more time with family, and less time with colleagues and peers was beneficial, yet as time went on, these protective factors transformed into risk factors as stress and hopelessness increased; work became stagnant; or feelings of hope, independence, and resilience dissipated.

There have also been reports from hospital and treatment centers that show no significant increases in people seeking medical treatment or support for NSSI behaviors; some hospitals and treatment centers have even found decreasing numbers. For example, data collected during the first 12 weeks of lockdown restrictions from two medical centers in England showed that there was a significant decrease in the number of people reporting to hospitals for self-harm compared to the weeks prior to lockdown in 2020 and in 2019 (Hawton et al., 2021). This decrease was consistent across all age groups, although, it was significantly greater in females than males, and there was a larger decrease in self-injury behaviors compared to suicide attempts through self-poisoning. It is also not known if the decrease was due to actual decreases in self-harm requiring medical treatment or if it was due to fears of possible COVID-19 exposure at hospitals. Furthermore, these data were collected during the beginning of lockdown; thus, it may be that the situations created by lockdown were only protective in the beginning. It is necessary to examine how these trends continued across waves of COVID-19 and associated health and safety mandates. Further, as the study consists of a comparison between the beginning of lockdown to the pre-COVID rates of 2019 and 2020, it is impossible to know if COVID-related factors are responsible for the decrease.

Similarly, a suicide surveillance system in Queensland, Australia, found no increases in suicide rates from February to August 2020 when compared to the time period pre-COVID (Leske et al., 2020). The register also found no change in the motives for suicides including unemployment, financial problems, or relationship issues. Additionally, a study of 1,500 general practices in the UK found that recorded incidence of self-harm was 38% lower in April 2020 than it had been compared to the previous years (Carr et al., 2021). A similar study among young people ages 0–17 in England, found that the total number of presentations to the emergency room in April 2020 decreased by 56.6% when compared to the same month of the previous year (Ougrin, 2020). A smaller, but significant reduction was also seen when comparing March 2020 emergency room presentations to the emergency room presentations in March 2019. Further, the total number of psychiatric inpatient admissions was recorded to be the lowest number since records began (Ougrin, 2020).

Another study in the UK also saw a drop in reports of self-harm and suicide ideation, with referrals and presentations to nearly all mental and physical health services declining at lockdown, consequently decreasing the supply of treatment services (Chen et al., 2020). Again, this evidence supports the idea that lockdown may have been somewhat protective against deliberate self-harm in the beginning; however, there is no evidence that this continued throughout the rest of the year. Even if these numbers are decreasing, it is unclear why; it could be that there is a protective element to being in lockdown, or it could be that people are less likely to seek or receive help for self-harm or suicide, which could be because they may no longer have support systems, such as health insurance, supportive peers or friends, or access to educational resources.

However, it is also possible that fewer people have been engaging in deliberate self-harm behaviors since the pandemic began; this possibility has prompted researchers to speculate about the potential benefits of lockdown, social distancing, and working from home. Hasking et al. (2021) highlighted more family bonding, less social and academic pressure, and more independence as potential protective factors. It may also be that lockdown leads to an increasing availability of online support resources, such as Tele-health and potentially allowing people struggling to access help more easily and earlier on.

The UK study that observed significant decreases in emergency room presentations in young people (Ougrin, 2020) is particularly interesting considering youth are one demographic most significantly impacted by the pandemic. Specifically, with the closure of schools, youth lost peer interaction, friendships, extracurricular activities, milestone celebrations like graduation ceremonies and formal dances, and in-person learning opportunities. One would assume that with these significant losses, rates of deliberate self-harm would increase, yet, Ougrin (2020) reported the opposite. It may be that with school closures, there was less pressure to perform (e.g., the cancellation of school exams and the waived entrance exam requirement for university); more opportunity to connect and bond with parents or siblings; and less exposure to bullies, drug and alcohol abuse, and risky behavior (Ougrin, 2020).

Thus, if future longitudinal work demonstrates that there were significantly fewer youth engaging in deliberate self-harm during the pandemic, and it can verify that rates declined due to these protective factors, it may be beneficial to consider how to introduce these elements of protection into active school environments. In this respect, the pandemic may have exposed specific ways to make the school system healthier, such as by minimizing the importance of exams, adapting more flexibility to assignments and schedules, and working to create supportive peer relationships. These suggestions may also extend beyond youth and hold true across age groups and surroundings. Thus, it may be beneficial to think about how, going forward, society can implement positive changes seen in the pandemic, such as reduced work load and more family time, and encourage aspects of healthy living. However, much more research is needed on the topic, including specific research examining what aspects of lockdown were protective (if any), before we can begin to enact changes.

Identity-Related Factors in Relation to COVID-19 and Deliberate Self-Harm

Despite potential protective factors created by COVID-19-related circumstances, there are still groups of people who were disproportionally and negatively affected by the pandemic. People of certain identities and demographic backgrounds are more at risk for deliberate self-harm (e.g., LGBTQ individuals; see Taliaferro, Rogers, & Zullo, this volume), and these risk factors may be made worse by the pandemic. Similarly, there are people of certain identities who were not necessarily at higher risk for deliberate self-harm before the pandemic; however, the existence of the pandemic has created situations that have put them at heightened risk (e.g., essential workers). Consequently, it is essential to consider these identity-related factors in the context of COVID-19 and self-harm in order to provide immediate and effective support.

Adolescents are a particular group of individuals who by nature of their age and stage in life have been significantly impacted by the pandemic and may be more or less at risk for deliberate self-harm as a result. While the current research on adolescent deliberate self-harm during the pandemic is lacking, there have been reports of increases in depression and anxiety symptoms among adolescents since the pandemic began (O'Sullivan et al., 2021). As depression and anxiety symptoms are tied to deliberate self-harm (Hawton et al., 2003), and adolescents are already at increased risk for NSSI and suicide (Hawton et al., 2012), it is likely that future research will show that deliberate self-harm increased among certain groups of adolescents during the pandemic.

Considering the closure of schools, adolescents adjusted to a new way of handling schoolwork, friendships, free time, and planning for their future. With school being mostly online for many students around the world for various amounts of time, there was less of an adjustment period, specifically for new students (e.g., freshmen in college or high school). As feeling unprepared to transition to school and online learning has been tied to anxiety among adolescents (Abdous, 2019), this lack of preparedness or transition period may increase the risk for self-harm. Additionally, the online format of schooling results in less time for individuals to make new friends or rely on the support of existing friendships. As social support is associated with significantly decreased NSSI engagement (Muehlenkamp et al., 2013) and suicide (Kaminski et al., 2010), removing this aspect of support may have led to increases in deliberate self-harm (see Zetterqvist & Bjureberg, this volume, for social processes in NSSI). Similarly, online schooling could have fostered more feelings of loneliness and social isolation, both of which have been tied to deliberate self-harm (Endo et al., 2017; Rönkä et al., 2013).

The pandemic may have increased feelings of anxiety directly, through concerns about the safety of one's own health or the health of one's family members. There is also a lingering increased level of uncertainty because of the pandemic, especially for students, as qualifying exams were cancelled, the job market fluctuates, and university acceptance rates decrease, all of which may increase feelings of hopelessness, anxiety, and suicide ideation. For example, a teen suicide in the UK was tied to the announcement that qualifying exams would be cancelled and the score from mock exams would be used to determine university admission (Murphy-Bates, 2020). The dynamics of stress and anxiety get more complicated when considering family relationships. In households where both youth and parents were working or doing virtual learning from home, there was likely more general family interaction, which may serve as an increased risk factor for some youth. Specifically, youth who already had tumultuous or strained relationships with their family members may have felt increasingly trapped, anxious, or overwhelmed without external outlets such as school. Many youth experienced cancelled extracurricular activities and sports which may have resulted in spending more time alone, feeling stagnant, exercising less, and using technology more frequently. All these may consequently impair sleep and generally increase feelings of loneliness and despair. Excessive social media use specifically has been tied to increased anxiety and depression during COVID-19 lockdowns (Gao et al., 2020). Furthermore, when removed from school, students lost access to mental health resources such as counselors and teachers, as well as the ability to reach out for help and support. Teachers who may have been able to identify at-risk students through their behavior or demeanor in the classroom attempted to monitor and identify at-risk students via Zoom, which was a far more difficult task.

However, it is also possible that school closings served as a protective factor for certain youth, particularly those who do not "fit in" at school or feel comfortable in their school environments. Students who are bullied at school or have social anxiety may feel safer at home (Ingul & Nordahl, 2013; Williams et al., 2018). Additionally, students who feel pressured to perform well academically may find some of this pressure is reduced when they are not surrounded by high-achieving peers. As a result, there may be decreases in deliberate self-harm if youth feel safer and less anxious in their homes. This may be particularly true for individuals who hold a stigmatized identity, such as members of the LGBTQ community. People who are being targeted for their sexual orientation or gender identity, whether that be at school or in a workplace environment, may feel safer and more secure working from home. However, the reverse may also be true. Depending on one's home environment, people may not be "out" to their family members and thus feel suppressed and alone at home. Others may be "out" to their families but feel unaccepted and unsafe at home (Fish et al., 2020). Additionally, people who identify as LGBTQ are already two to five times more likely to engage in NSSI than their heterosexual or cisgender peers (Batejan et al., 2015), and having a supportive peer-based queer community can serve as a protective factor (Higa et al., 2014). Similarly, schools commonly provide access to and resources for mental health services for LGBTQ people (Dunbar et al., 2017). Therefore, school closures may be removing access to supportive peers and resources and consequently increasing the risk of self-harm thoughts or behaviors.

In addition to adolescents and LGBTQ indivdiuals potentially being disproportionally influenced by COVID-19, there have been reports of deliberate self-harm behaviors increasing among other minoritized individuals. A UK study examining patterns of self-harm thoughts and behaviors during the first month of the pandemic found that reports of self-harm and thoughts of suicide were higher among Black, Asian minority ethnic groups (BAME) and socioeconomically disadvantaged people (Iob et al., 2020). In the United States, minoritized racial and ethnic individuals were disproportionally affected by the pandemic as these groups were at heightened risk for getting sick, having more severe illness, and dying from COVID-19 compared to White people (Stokes et al., 2020). These individuals were also more profoundly and unequally affected by the economic, social, and secondary health consequences of COVID-19, such as business closures and social distancing (Stokes et al., 2020). The increased risk of losing loved ones and financial safety to COVID-19, as well as experiencing unequal access to health care for COVID-19 prevention and treatment, may be increasing depression, hopelessness, anxiety, and self-harm behaviors among these populations (Polanco-Roman et al., 2014). Additionally, self-harm rates may be on the rise among Asian individuals as discrimination against Asian people has been growing since the start of the pandemic (Haynes, 2021). Again, the research on these relationships is currently limited; however, it is likely that future research will show increases in deliberate self-harm among minoritized individuals.

Another group at heightened risk for deliberate self-harm are those with pre-existing psychological conditions that have potentially been made worse by COVID-19. Eating disorders among teens dramatically increased during the pandemic (Damour, 2021), as well as symptoms of anxiety, depression, and substance use disorders among the general public (Fowers & Wan, 2020; Murata et al., 2020). Furthermore, some researchers noted increases in OCD symptoms since the pandemic began (Jelinek et al., 2021). Preliminary studies in China noted significant increases in psychological distress (i.e., PTSD, depression, and anxiety) as a result of the pandemic (Wang et al., 2020; Zhang et al., 2020), and a survey out of the UK found that 83% of participants up to age 25 said the pandemic made their existing psychological conditions worse (Thomas, 2020). Many mental health conditions are known to be associated with increased for suicide and NSSI (Kiekens et al., 2018; Van Orden et al., 2020), and stress is known to increase symptom severity for those who are already suffering (Bangasser & Valentino, 2014). The stress brought on by the pandemic, in combination with the reduction in available psychiatric resources (Van Dorn et al., 2020), suggests that a ripple effect may be seen in the coming years. Stress may exacerbate prevalence and severity of psychological conditions, which may lead to more individuals using maladaptive coping mechanisms such as deliberate self-harm. In addition, it is possible that the prolonged stress caused by COVID-19 will impact neurological, immunological, and health functioning, particularly among older adults, which, in turn, will increase the risk of suicide (Sheffler et al., 2021).

Other at-risk groups worth discussing are those without technology access, those with limited child or care-giving support at home, those who have lost jobs or businesses, and essential workers. In the United States, a national survey showed that the percentage of respondents who reported seriously considering suicide was significantly higher among people ages 18–24 years (25.5%), minority/racial ethnic groups (15.2–18.6%), self-reported caregivers for adults (30.7%), and essential workers (21.7%) (Czeisler et al., 2020). Additionally, older adults may also be at increased risk—during the pandemic, older adults have continually been sent the message that their health needs are not worthy of resources or treatment and that their existence is a burden on society (Cohn-Schwartz & Ayalon, 2020; Frakt, 2020); these feelings of burdensomeness may lead to suicide or self-harm (Joiner, 2005).

Conclusions

Initial evidence on the effects of COVID-19 on deliberate self-harm behavior suggests that in general, individuals are experiencing a significant amount of collective stress and trauma, regardless of their views about or access to masks or vaccines.

Clinical Implications

People everywhere have experienced job loss, school and work disruption, major changes to daily routines, and the inability to plan too far into the future. Researchers and clinicians should be aware of the trauma of this pandemic and respond with increasingly tailored support as we learn more about its psychological consequences. We don't yet know the long-term effects of prolonged stress and uncertainty of this magnitude, but we can focus our efforts on effective coping, keeping people connected, increasing access to social support, and ensuring access to medical and mental health treatment. Humans are resilient, and drawing on existing knowledge for working through adversity, as well as new ways to cope with the specific challenges of COVID-19, will ideally result in the majority of us moving beyond coping and surviving to fully functioning and thriving.

Future Research Directions

We are still dealing with the effects of a major global pandemic and the long-term effects of COVID-19 on NSSI and self-harm behavior are yet to be determined. Initial evidence suggests that hardships endured from the pandemic will likely increase risk for self-harm in certain groups, and that aspects of the pandemic may serve to be protective for self-harm among other groups. Future research should continue to investigate the harmful and protective aspects of the pandemic, as well as examine how the pandemic differentially affects people of varying identities, occupations, and circumstances. Further, it is critical to assess the accessibility and effectiveness of clinical response during the pandemic in order to create more efficacious support networks for COVID-19-related psychological distress, including support specifically tailored to deliberate self-harm. Finally, as we continue to move further from the start of the pandemic, longitudinal research will identify the long-term effects of COVID-19 on individuals' mental health, as well as explore the psychological consequences of living through a constantly evolving, multiyear pandemic.

References

Abdous, M. H. (2019). Influence of satisfaction and preparedness on online students' feelings of anxiety. *The Internet and Higher Education*, *41*, 34–44. https://doi.org/10.1016/j.iheduc.2019.01.001

Ammerman, B. A., Burke, T. A., Jacobucci, R., & McClure, K. (2021). Preliminary investigation of the association between COVID-19 and suicidal thoughts and behaviors in the US. *Journal of Psychiatric Research*, *134*, 32–38. https://doi.org/10.1016/j.jpsychires.2020.12.037

Bangasser, D. A., & Valentino, R. J. (2014). Sex differences in stress-related psychiatric disorders: Neurobiological perspectives. *Frontiers in Neuroendocrinology*, *35*(3), 303–319. https://doi.org/10.1016/j.yfrne.2014.03.008

Batejan, K. L., Jarvi, S. M., & Swenson, L. P. (2015). Sexual orientation and non-suicidal self-injury: A meta-analytic review. *Archives of Suicide Research*, *19*(2), 131–150. https://doi.org/10.1080/13811118.2014.957450

Bryan, C. J., Bryan, A. O., & Baker, J. C. (2020). Associations among state-level physical distancing measures and suicidal thoughts and behaviors among US adults during the early COVID-19 pandemic. *Suicide and Life-Threatening Behavior*, *50*(6), 1223–1229. https://doi.org/10.1111/sltb.12653

Carr, M. J., Steeg, S., Webb, R. T., Kapur, N., Chew-Graham, C. A., Abel, K. M., Hope, H., Pierce, M., & Ashcroft, D. M. (2021). Effects of the COVID-19 pandemic on primary care-recorded mental illness and self-harm episodes in the UK: A population-based cohort study. *The Lancet Public Health*, *6*(2), 124–135. https://doi.org/10.1016/s2468-2667(20)30288-7

Chan, S. M. S., Chiu, F. K. H., Lam, C. W. L., Leung, P. Y. V., & Conwell, Y. (2006). Elderly suicide and the 2003 SARS epidemic in Hong Kong. *International Journal of Geriatric Psychiatry: A Journal of the Psychiatry of Late Life and Allied Sciences*, *21*(2), 113–118. https://doi.org/10.1002/gps.1432

Chen, S., Jones, P. B., Underwood, B. R., Moore, A., Bullmore, E. T., Banerjee, S., Osimo, E. F., Deakin, J. B., Hatfield, C. F., Thompson, F. J., Artingstall, J. D., Slann, M. P., Lewis, J. R., & Cardinal, R. N. (2020). The early impact of COVID-19 on mental health and community physical health services and their patients' mortality in Cambridgeshire and Peterborough, UK. *Journal of Psychiatric Research*, *131*, 244–254. https://doi.org/10.2139/ssrn.3648247

Cohen, S. (2020, December 30). The fastest vaccine in history. *UCLA Health*. Retrieved fromhttps://www.scribbr.com/apa-examples/website/.

Cohn-Schwartz, E., & Ayalon, L. (2020). Societal views of older adults as vulnerable and a burden to society during the COVID-19 outbreak: Results from an Israeli nationally representative sample. *The Journals of Gerontology: Series*,*150*, e313–e317. https://doi.org/10.1093/geronb/gbaa150

Courtet, P., Olié, E., Debien, C., & Vaiva, G. (2020). Keep socially (but not physically) connected and carry on: Preventing suicide in the age of COVID-19. *The Journal of Clinical Psychiatry*, *81*(3), 20com13370. https://doi.org/10.4088/jcp.20com13370

Czeisler M.É., Lane R.I., Petrosky E., Wiley, J. F., Christensen, A., Njai, R., Weaver, M. D., Robbins, R., Facer-Childs, E. R., Barger, L. K., Czeisler, C. A., Howard, M. E., & Rajaratnam, S. M. (2020) Mental health, substance use, and suicidal ideation during the COVID-19 pandemic—United States, June 24–30, 2020. *Morbidity and Mortality Weekly Report*, *69*, 1049–1057. https://doi.org/10.15585/mmwr.mm6932a1

Damour, L. (2021, April 28). Eating disorders in teens have "Exploded" in the pandemic. *The New York Times.* https://www.nytimes.com/2021/04/28/well/family/teens-eating-disorders.html?smid=url-share

Dsouza, D. D., Quadros, S., Hyderabadwala, Z. J., & Mamun, M. A. (2020). Aggregated COVID-19 suicide incidences in India: Fear of COVID-19 infection is the prominent causative factor. *Psychiatry Research, 290,* Article 113145. https://doi.org/10.1016/j.psychres.2020.113145

Dunbar, M. S., Sontag-Padilla, L., Ramchand, R., Seelam, R., & Stein, B. D. (2017). Mental health service utilization among lesbian, gay, bisexual, and questioning or queer college students. *Journal of Adolescent Health, 61*(3), 294–301. https://doi.org/10.1016/j.jadohealth.2017.03.008

Endo, K., Ando, S., Shimodera, S., Yamasaki, S., Usami, S., Okazaki, Y., Sasaki, T., Richards, M., Hatch, S., & Nishida, A. (2017). Preference for solitude, social isolation, suicidal ideation, and self-harm in adolescents. *Journal of Adolescent Health, 61*(2), 187–191. https://doi.org/10.1016/j.jadohealth.2017.02.018

Eghigian, G. (2020). The spanish flu pandemic and mental health: A historical perspective. *Psychiatric Times, 37*(5), 26.

Esposito, C., Bacchini, D., & Affuso, G. (2019). Adolescent non-suicidal self-injury and its relationships with school bullying and peer rejection. *Psychiatry Research, 274,* 1–6. https://doi.org/10.1016/j.psychres.2019.02.018

Fish, J. N., McInroy, L. B., Paceley, M. S., Williams, N. D., Henderson, S., Levine, D. S., & Edsall, R. N. (2020). "I'm kinda stuck at home with unsupportive parents right now": LGBTQ youths' experiences with COVID-19 and the importance of online support. *Journal of Adolescent Health, 67*(3), 450–452. https://doi.org/10.1016/j.jadohealth.2020.06.002

Fowers, A., & Wan, W. (2020, May 26). A third of Americans now show signs of clinical anxiety or depression, Census Bureau finds amid coronavirus pandemic. *Washington Post.* https://www.washingtonpost.com/health/2020/05/26/americans-with-depression-anxiety-pandemic/.

Frakt, A. (2020, March 29). Who should be saved first? Experts offer ethical guidance. *New York Times.* https://www.globalchildrenssurgery.org/wp-content/uploads/2020/03/25-Who-Should-Be-Saved-First_-Experts-Offer-Ethical-Guidance-The-New-York-Times.pdf.

Gao, J., Zheng, P., Jia, Y., Chen, H., Mao, Y., Chen, S., Wang, Y., Fu, H., & Dai, J. (2020). Mental health problems and social media exposure during COVID-19 outbreak. *PLoS One, 15*(4), e0231924. https://doi.org/10.2139/ssrn.3541120

Hammond, L. E. (2020). *The costs of COVID-19: Loneliness, coping, and psychological distress in the United States population* [Doctoral dissertation, Seattle Pacific University]. ProQuest Dissertations & Theses Global. https://digitalcommons.spu.edu/cgi/viewcontent.cgi?article=1055&context=cpy_etd

Hamza, C. A., Ewing, L., Heath, N. L., & Goldstein, A. L. (2020). When social isolation is nothing new: A longitudinal study psychological distress during COVID-19 among university students with and without preexisting mental health concerns. *Canadian Psychology, 62*(1), 20–30. https://doi.org/10.1037/cap0000255

Hao, F., Tan, W., Jiang, L., Zhang, L., Zhao, X., Zou, Y., Hu, Y., Luo, X., Jiang, X., McIntyre, R. S., Tran, B., Sun, J., Zhang, Z., Ho, R., Ho, C., & Tam, W. (2020). Do psychiatric patients experience more psychiatric symptoms during COVID-19 pandemic and lockdown? A case-control study with service and research implications for immunopsychiatry. *Brain, Behavior, and Immunity, 87,* 100–106. https://doi.org/10.1016/j.bbi.2020.04.069

Hasking, P., Lewis, S. P., Bloom, E., Brausch, A., Kaess, M., & Robinson, K. (2021). Impact of the COVID-19 pandemic on students at elevated risk of self-injury: The importance of virtual and online resources. *School Psychology International, 42*(1), 57–78. https://doi.org/10.1177/0143034320974414

Hawton, K., Casey, D., Bale, E., Brand, F., Ness, J., Waters, K., Kelly, S., & Geulayov, G. (2021). Self-harm during the early period of the COVID-19 pandemic in England: Comparative trend analysis of hospital presentations. *Journal of Affective Disorders, 282,* 991–995. https://doi.org/10.1016/j.jad.2021.01.015

Hawton, K., Hall, S., Simkin, S., Bale, L., Bond, A., Codd, S., & Stewart, A. (2003). Deliberate self-harm in adolescents: A study of characteristics and trends in Oxford, 1990–2000. *Journal of Child Psychology and Psychiatry, 44*(8), 1191–1198. https://doi.org/10.1111/1469-7610.00200

Hawton, K., Saunders, K. E., & O'Connor, R. C. (2012). Self-harm and suicide in adolescents. *The Lancet, 379*(9834), 2373–2382. https://doi.org/10.1016/s0140-6736(12)60322-5

Haynes, S. (2021, March 22). "This isn't just a problem for North America." The Atlanta shooting highlights the painful reality of rising anti-Asian violence around the world. *Time.* https://time.com/5947862/anti-asian-attacks-rising-worldwide.

Higa, D., Hoppe, M. J., Lindhorst, T., Mincer, S., Beadnell, B., Morrison, D. M., Wells, E. A., Todd, A., & Mountz, S. (2014). Negative and positive factors associated with the well-being of lesbian, gay, bisexual, transgender, queer, and questioning (LGBTQ) youth. *Youth & Society*, *46*(5), 663–687. https://doi.org/10.1177/0044118x12449630

Holt, M. K., Vivolo-Kantor, A. M., Polanin, J. R., Holland, K. M., DeGue, S., Matjasko, J. L., Wolfe, M., & Reid, G. (2015). Bullying and suicidal ideation and behaviors: A meta-analysis. *Pediatrics*, *135*(2), e496–e509. https://doi.org/10.1542/peds.2014-1864

Hughes, C. D., King, A. M., Kranzler, A., Fehling, K., Miller, A., Lindqvist, J., & Selby, E. A. (2019). Anxious and overwhelming affects and repetitive negative thinking as ecological predictors of self-injurious thoughts and behaviors. *Cognitive Therapy and Research*, *43*(1), 88–101. https://doi.org/10.1007/s10608-019-09996-9

Ingul, J. M., & Nordahl, H. M. (2013). Anxiety as a risk factor for school absenteeism: What differentiates anxious school attenders from non-attenders?. *Annals of General Psychiatry*, *12*(1), 1–9. https://doi.org/10.1186/1744-859x-12-25

Iob, E., Steptoe, A., & Fancourt, D. (2020). Abuse, self-harm and suicidal ideation in the UK during the COVID-19 pandemic. *The British Journal of Psychiatry*, *217*(4), 543–546. https://doi.org/10.1192/bjp.2020.130

Jelinek, L., Moritz, S., Miegel, F., & Voderholzer, U. (2021). Obsessive-compulsive disorder during COVID-19: Turning a problem into an opportunity? *Journal of Anxiety Disorders*, *77*, Article 102329. https://doi.org/10.1016/j.janxdis.2020.102329

John, A., Okolie, C., Eyles, E., Webb, R. T., Schmidt, L., McGuiness, L. A., Olorisade, B. K., Arensman, E., Hawton, K., Kapur, N., Moran, P., O'Connor, R. C., O'Neill, S., Higgins, J. P., & Gunnell, D. (2020). The impact of the COVID-19 pandemic on self-harm and suicidal behaviour: A living systematic review. *F1000Research*, *9*, Article 1097. https://doi.org/10.12688/f1000research.25522.1

Johnson, N.P.A.S. and Mueller, J. (2002), Updating the accounts: Global mortality of the 1918-1920 'Spanish' influenza pandemic. *Bulletin of the History of Medicine*, *76*(1), 105–115. https://doi.org/10.1353/bhm.2002.0022

Joiner, T. E. (2005). *Why people die by suicide*. Harvard University Press.

Kaminski, J. W., Puddy, R. W., Hall, D. M., Cashman, S. Y., Crosby, A. E., & Ortega, L. A. (2010). The relative influence of different domains of social connectedness on self-directed violence in adolescence. *Journal of Youth and Adolescence*, *39*(5), 460–473. https://doi.org/10.1007/s10964-009-9472-2

Kaparounaki, C. K., Patsali, M. E., Mousa, D. P. V., Papadopoulou, E. V., Papadopoulou, K. K., & Fountoulakis, K. N. (2020). University students' mental health amidst the COVID-19 quarantine in Greece. *Psychiatry Research*, *290*, Article 113111. https://doi.org/10.1016/j.psychres.2020.113111

Kelada, L., Hasking, P., & Melvin, G. (2018). Adolescent NSSI and recovery: The role of family functioning and emotion regulation. *Youth & Society*, *50*(8), 1056–1077. https://doi.org/10.1177/0044118x16653153

Khan, A. R., Ratele, K., & Arendse, N. (2020). Men, suicide, and Covid-19: Critical masculinity analyses and interventions. *Postdigital Science and Education*, *2*(3), 651–656. https://doi.org/10.1007/s42438-020-00152-1

Kiekens, G., Hasking, P., Claes, L., Mortier, P., Auerbach, R. P., Boyes, M., Cuijpers, P., Demyttenaere, K., Green, J. G., Kessler, R. C., Nock, M. K., & Bruffaerts, R. (2018). The DSM-5 nonsuicidal self-injury disorder among incoming college students: Prevalence and associations with 12-month mental disorders and suicidal thoughts and behaviors. *Depression and Anxiety*, *35*(7), 629–637. https://doi.org/10.1002/da.22754

Killgore, W. D., Cloonan, S. A., Taylor, E. C., Fernandez, F., Grandner, M. A., & Dailey, N. S. (2020). Suicidal ideation during the COVID-19 pandemic: The role of insomnia. *Psychiatry Research*, *290*, Article 113134. https://doi.org/10.1016/j.psychres.2020.113134

Klonsky, E. D., Oltmanns, T. F., & Turkheimer, E. (2003). Deliberate self-harm in a nonclinical population: Prevalence and psychological correlates. *American Journal of Psychiatry*, *160*(8), 1501–1508. https://doi.org/10.1176/appi.ajp.160.8.1501

Lee, A. M., Wong, J. G., McAlonan, G. M., Cheung, V., Cheung, C., Sham, P. C., Chu, C. M., Wong, P. C., Tsang, K. W., & Chua, S. E. (2007). Stress and psychological distress among SARS survivors 1 year after the outbreak. *The Canadian Journal of Psychiatry*, *52*(4), 233–240. https://doi.org/10.1177/070674370705200405

Lee, S. A. (2020). Coronavirus Anxiety Scale: A brief mental health screener for COVID-19 related anxiety. *Death Studies, 44*(7), 393–401. https://doi.org/10.1080/07481187.2020.1748481

Leske S., Kõlves K., Crompton D., Arensman E., & de Leo, D. (2020). Real-time suicide mortality data from police reports in Queensland, Australia, during the COVID-19 pandemic: An interrupted time-series analysis. *Lancet Psychiatry, 8*(1), 58–63. https://doi.org/10.1016/s2215-0366(20)30435-1

Lewis, S. P., & Seko, Y. (2016). A double-edged sword: A review of benefits and risks of online nonsuicidal self-injury activities. *Journal of Clinical Psychology, 72*(3), 249–262. https://doi.org/10.1002/jclp.22242

Mak, I. W. C., Chu, C. M., Pan, P. C., Yiu, M. G. C., & Chan, V. L. (2009). Long-term psychiatric morbidities among SARS survivors. *General Hospital Psychiatry, 31*(4), 318–326. https://doi.org/10.1016/j.genhosppsych.2009.03.001

McIntyre, A., Tong, K., McMahon, E., & Doherty, A. (2021). COVID-19 and its effect on emergency presentations to a tertiary hospital with self-harm in Ireland. *Irish Journal of Psychological Medicine, 38*(2), 116–122. https://doi.org/10.1017/ipm.2020.116

Miller, A. B., Eisenlohr-Moul, T., Glenn, C. R., Turner, B. J., Chapman, A. L., Nock, M. K., & Prinstein, M. J. (2019). Does higher-than-usual stress predict nonsuicidal self-injury? Evidence from two prospective studies in adolescent and emerging adult females. *Journal of Child Psychology and Psychiatry, 60*(10), 1076–1084. https://doi.org/10.1111/jcpp.13072

Milner, A., Witt, K., LaMontagne, A. D., & Niedhammer, I. (2018). Psychosocial job stressors and suicidality: Ameta-analysis and systematic review. *Occupational and Environmental Medicine, 75*(4), 245–253. https://doi.org/10.1136/oemed-2017-104531

Muehlenkamp, J., Brausch, A., Quigley, K., & Whitlock, J. (2013). Interpersonal features and functions of nonsuicidal self-injury. *Suicide and Life-Threatening Behavior, 43*(1), 67–80. https://doi.org/10.1111/j.1943-278x.2012.00128.x

Murata, S., Rezeppa, T., Thoma, B., Marengo, L., Krancevich, K., Chiyka, E., Hayes, B., Goodfriend, E., Deal, M., Zhong, Y., Brummit, B., Coury, T., Riston, S., Brent, D. A., & Melhem, N. M. (2020). The psychiatric sequelae of the COVID-19 pandemic in adolescents, adults, and health care workers. *Depression and Anxiety, 38*(2), 233–246. https://doi.org/10.1002/da.23120

Murphy-Bates, S. (2020, March 30). Body is found in woodland by police hunting boy, 17, who vanished having despaired when his A level exams were called off amid coronavirus. *Daily Mail.* https://www.dailymail.co.uk/news/article-8169427/Body-woodland-police-hunting-boy-17-vanished-amid-coronavirus-panic.html.

Olding, J., Zisman, S., Olding, C., & Fan, K. (2021). Penetrating trauma during a global pandemic: Changing patterns in interpersonal violence, self-harm and domestic violence in the Covid-19 outbreak. *The Surgeon, 19*(1), 9–13. https://doi.org/10.1016/j.surge.2020.07.004

O'Sullivan, K., Clark, S., McGrane, A., Rock, N., Burke, L., Boyle, N., Joksimovic, N., & Marshall, K. (2021). A qualitative study of child and adolescent mental health during the COVID-19 pandemic in Ireland. *International Journal of Environmental Research and Public Health, 18*(3), 1062. https://doi.org/10.3390/ijerph18031062

Ougrin, D. (2020). Debate: Emergency mental health presentations of young people during the COVID-19 lockdown. *Child and Adolescent Mental Health, 25*(3), 171. https://doi.org/10.1111/camh.12411

Ougrin, D., Wong, B. H. C., Vaezinejad, M., PleBarrett, E., Hussain, H., Lloyd, A., Tolmac, J., Rao, M., Chakrabarti, S., Carucci, S., Moghraby, O. S., Elvins, R., Rozali, F., Skouta, E., McNicholas, F., Kuruppuaracchi, N., Nagy, P., Davico, C., Mirza, H., . . . Landau, S. (2022). Pandemic-related emergency psychiatric presentations for self-harm of children and adolescents in 10 countries (PREP-kids): A retrospective international cohort study. *European Child & Adolescent Psychiatry, 31*(7), 1–13. https://doi.org/10.1007/s00787-021-01741-6

Paul, E., & Fancourt, D. (2021). Factors influencing self-harm thoughts and self-harm behaviours over the first 45 weeks of the COVID-19 pandemic in the UK: A longitudinal analysis of 48,446 adults. *medRxiv.* https://doi.org/10.1101/2021.02.19.21252050

Polanco-Roman, L., Tsypes, A., Soffer, A., & Miranda, R. (2014). Ethnic differences in prevalence and correlates of self-harm behaviors in a treatment-seeking sample of emerging adults. *Psychiatry Research, 220*(3), 927–934. https://doi.org/10.1016/j.psychres.2014.09.017

Reger, M. A., Stanley, I. H., & Joiner, T. E. (2020). Suicide mortality and coronavirus disease 2019—A perfect storm? *JAMA Psychiatry, 77*(11), 1093–1094. https://doi.org/10.1001/jamapsychiatry.2020.1060

Rohde C., Jefsen O.H., Nørremark B., Danielsen A.A., Østergaard S.D. (2020). Psychiatric symptoms related to the COVID-19 pandemic. *Acta Neuropsychiatrica Scandinavica*, *32*(5), 274–276. https://doi.org/10.1017/neu.2020.24

Rönkä, A. R., Taanila, A., Koiranen, M., Sunnari, V., & Rautio, A. (2013). Associations of deliberate self-harm with loneliness, self-rated health and life satisfaction in adolescence: Northern Finland Birth Cohort 1986 Study. *International Journal of Circumpolar Health*, *72*(1), 21085. https://doi.org/10.3402/ijch.v72i0.21085

Sahoo, S., Bharadwaj, S., Parveen, S., Singh, A. P., Tandup, C., Mehra, A., Chakrabarti, S., Grover, S., & Tandup, C. (2020). Self-harm and COVID-19 Pandemic: An emerging concern–A report of 2 cases from India. *Asian Journal of Psychiatry*, *51*, Article 102104. https://doi.org/10.1016/j.ajp.2020.102104

Sapara, A., Shalaby, R., Osiogo, F., Hrabok, M., Gusnowski, A., Vuong, W., Surood, S., Urichuk, L., Greenshaw, A. J., & Agyapong, V. I. (2021). COVID-19 pandemic: Demographic and clinical correlates of passive death wish and thoughts of self-harm among Canadians. *Journal of Mental Health*, 30(2), 170–178. https://doi.org/10.1080/09638237.2021.1875417

Shamsian, N. (2001). Family support decreases suicide risk. *BMJ*, *322*(4) 485–493.

Sheffler, J. L., Joiner, T. E., & Sachs-Ericsson, N. J. (2021). The interpersonal and psychological impacts of COVID-19 on risk for late-life suicide. *The Gerontologist*, *61*(1), 23–29. https://doi.org/10.1093/geront/gnaa123

Stokes E.K., Zambrano L.D., Anderson K.N., & Fullerton, K. E. (2020). Coronavirus Disease 2019 Case Surveillance—United States, January 22–May 30, 2020. *Morbidity and Mortality Weekly Report*, *69*, 759–765. http://dx.doi.org/10.15585/mmwr.mm6924e2

Thomas, E. (2020, September). Coronavirus: Impact on young people with mental health needs. *YoungMinds*. https://youngminds.org.uk/about-us/reports/coronavirus-impact-on-young-people-with-mental-health-needs/#covid-19-autumn-2020-survey.

Tull, M. T., Edmonds, K. A., Scamaldo, K. M., Richmond, J. R., Rose, J. P., & Gratz, K. L. (2020). Psychological outcomes associated with stay-at-home orders and the perceived impact of COVID-19 on daily life. *Psychiatry Research*, *289*, Article 113098. https://doi.org/10.1016/j.psychres.2020.113098

Van Orden, K. A., Bower, E., Lutz, J., Silva, C., Gallegos, A. M., Podgorski, C. A., Santos, E. J., & Conwell, Y. (2020). Strategies to promote social connections among older adults during "social distancing" restrictions. *The American Journal of Geriatric Psychiatry*, *29*(8), 816–827. https://doi.org/10.1016/j.jagp.2020.05.004.

Vahratian, A., Blumberg, S. J., Terlizzi, E. P., Schiller, J. S. (2021). Symptoms of anxiety or depressive disorder and use of mental health care among adults during the COVID-19 Pandemic—United States, August 2020–February 2021. *Morbidity and Mortality Weekly Report*, 70, 490–494. https://doi.org/10.15585/mmwr.mm7013e2

Van Dorn, A., Cooney, R. E., & Sabin, M. L. (2020). COVID-19 exacerbating inequalities in the US. *Lancet*, *395*(10232), Article 1243.

Victor, S. E., Hipwell, A. E., Stepp, S. D., & Scott, L. N. (2019). Parent and peer relationships as longitudinal predictors of adolescent non-suicidal self-injury onset. *Child and Adolescent Psychiatry and Mental Health*, *13*(1), 1–13. https://doi.org/10.1186/s13034-018-0261-0

Wang, C., Pan, R., Wan, X., Tan, Y., Xu, L., McIntyre, R. S., Choo, F. N., Tran, B., Ho, R., Sharma, V. K., & Ho, C. (2020). A longitudinal study on the mental health of general population during the COVID-19 epidemic in China. *Brain, Behavior, and Immunity*, *87*, 40–48. https://doi.org/10.1016/j.bbi.2020.04.028

Wasserman, I. M. (1992). The impact of epidemic, war, prohibition and media on suicide: United States, 1910–1920. *Suicide and Life-Threatening Behavior*, *22*(2), 240–254.

Williams, S., Schneider, M., Wornell, C., & Langhinrichsen-Rohling, J. (2018). Student's perceptions of school safety: It is not just about being bullied. *The Journal of School Nursing*, *34*(4), 319–330. https://doi.org/10.1177/1059840518761792

World Health Organization. (2020). Suicide prevention. *International statistical classification of diseases and related health problems* (10th rev., ICD-10).

Wu, Y., Zhang, C., Liu, H., Duan, C., Li, C., Fan, J., Li, H., Chen, L., Xu, H., Li, X., Guo, Y., Wang, Y., Li, X., Li, J., Zhang, T., You, Y., Li, H., Yang, S., Tao, X., . . . Huang, H. F. (2020). Perinatal depressive and anxiety symptoms of pregnant women along with COVID-19 outbreak in China. *American Journal of Obstetrics and Gynecology*, *223*(2), 240–249. https://doi.org/10.1016/j.ajog.2020.05.009

Xu, X., Wang, W., Chen, J., Ai, M., Shi, L., Wang, L., Hong, S., Zhang, Q., Hu, H., Li, X., Cao, J., Lv, Z., Du, L., Li, J., Yang, H., He, X., Chen, X., Chen, R., Luo, Q., . . . Kuang, L. (2021). Suicidal and self-harm ideation among Chinese hospital staff during the COVID-19 pandemic: Prevalence and correlates. *Psychiatry Research*, *296*, Article 113654. https://doi.org/10.1016/j.psychres.2020.113654

Zhang, J., Lu, H., Zeng, H., Zhang, S., Du, Q., Jiang, T., & Du, B. (2020). The differential psychological distress of populations affected by the COVID-19 pandemic. *Brain, Behavior, and Immunity*, *87*, Article 49. https://doi.org/10.1016/j.bbi.2020.04.031

Zortea, T. C., Brenna, C. T., Joyce, M., McClelland, H., Tippett, M., Tran, M. M., Arensman, E., Corcoran, P., Hatcher, S., Heise, M. J., Links, P., O'Connor, R. C., Edgar, N. E., Cha, Y., Guaiana, G., Williamson, E., Sinyor, M., & Platt, S. (2021). The impact of infectious disease-related public health emergencies on suicide, suicidal behavior, and suicidal thoughts. *Crisis*, *42*(6), 474–487. https://doi.org/10.1027/0227-5910/a000753

CHAPTER 10
Cross-Cultural Representations of NSSI

Marc Stewart Wilson

Abstract

Much of what we know about nonsuicidal self-injury is based on research and practice from cultures that can be described as Western and English-speaking, but there is increasing appreciation of the need to step outside these traditional boundaries. This chapter summarizes research comparing nonsuicidal self-injury characteristics and correlates across four "families" of research: explicit comparisons across nations, considering minority groups within nations, conducted on non-Western/English-speaking nations, and among indigenous minorities. This research highlights variation that may be attributable to culture but that may not have been fully informed by what "culture" means. Therefore, the author explores how cultural and cross-cultural research can contribute to our understanding, with particular attention to the notion of "cultural scripts" in the context of mental health in general, and nonsuicidal self-injury in particular. Finally, the author considers nonsuicidal self-injury in cultural contexts that aren't defined, as has traditionally been done, by national or ethnic distinctions.

Key Words: nonsuicidal self-injury, NSSI, NSSI prevalence, NSSI functions, culture, cultural script

Cross-Cultural Representations of Nonsuicidal Self-Injury

From a cultural psychiatry perspective, *behavior* is considered to be determined by the interplay among a person's environment, life experiences, and biological endowment. *Culture* is the matrix within which these psychological, social, and biological forces operate and become meaningful to human beings (Favazza, 2009, p. 19).

It would be cliché to characterize the relatively new field of research on nonsuicidal self-injury (NSSI) as "in its infancy," though perhaps gangly adolescence would be reasonable. As a result of this relative youth, the last two decades have seen blooming research that investigates how many people hurt themselves, who hurts themselves, and what predicts their doing so. We have several useful frameworks for explaining why people hurt themselves (e.g., Chapman et al., 2006; Hasking et al., 2017; Nock, 2010), growing evidence of the correlates that may actually be causal (e.g., Fox et al., 2015; Robinson et al., 2019), and several fruitful avenues for intervention (e.g., Kothgassner et al., 2021). And now, finally and belatedly, we have turned to ask how culture fits into this equation. Or perhaps how self-injury fits into "culture"—the matrix within which Favazza (2009) tells us self-injury occurs.

Given the nature of this volume, I shall avoid restating in great detail what I mean by NSSI, beyond briefly noting that it is defined as "the deliberate, self-inflicted damage of body tissue without suicidal intent and for purposes not socially or culturally sanctioned" (International Society for the Study of Self-Injury, 2018; see Lengel et al., this volume). The same cannot be said for the term "culture," however, though we likely have at least an intuitive understanding of what this common term means. Having made the argument that we need such a definition, we will now create suspense by first reviewing what we think we know about NSSI culturally and cross-culturally, before returning to this important question.

In the context of this volume, NSSI is a behavior and, like other behaviors, can mean different things to different people. The definition provided above explicitly excludes "culturally sanctioned" deliberate behaviors that cause tissue damage in the absence of suicidal intent—what kinds of self-injury does this mean?

Favazza (2009, 2011) argues that culturally sanctioned destruction of tissue has a widespread and long history, and almost universally serves the function of remediating external (e.g., crop failure or disease) or internal (e.g., moral or religious transgressions or violation of expectations around social order) threats to individuals, their communities, or both. The forms of tissue destruction associated with this remediation varies in nature and extent. Favazza (2011) goes on to discuss more contemporary self-injurious rituals that include behaviors that may feel almost ubiquitous—such as tattooing and piercing—and speculates that at least some of these socially tolerated behaviors parallel traditional coming-of-age or initiation rituals. What if a young person's attempts to mature are subjectively or objectively unsuccessful? Favazza (2009) suggests that self-injury may provide avoidance of the loneliness or other negative emotions that go along with this "failure," or even to facilitate or signal maturation. Our assumption is that, by definition, NSSI is not socially sanctioned, but Favazza (2009) observes that this may not be the case—given, for example, the increase in NSSI-related websites and chat rooms, as well as schoolyard discussions.

Why is "culture" important? Intuitively we know this to be true, but how *exactly* is culture important. Broadly, we know that culture is important for mental health and ill health. The fifth edition of *Diagnostic and Statistical Manual of Mental Disorders* (DSM-5; American Psychiatric Association, 2013) expands on its predecessor's treatment of culture to include discussion of incorporating consideration of culture into assessment and formulation, as well as including a glossary of *cultural concepts of distress*—"ways that cultural groups experience, understand and communicate suffering" (p. 787). Examples of culturally bound syndromes might include semen loss anxiety in India or ghost sickness (recurring nightmares, fear, confusion, etc., believed to be the product of witchcraft) among

Native American populations. While these syndromes may possess characteristics that lend to "Western" diagnoses, DSM-5 advocates for locating "symptoms" in the context of the client's culture.

Appreciation of culture is, therefore, important not only for informing appropriate assessment, avoiding misdiagnosis, and facilitating effective treatment but also potentially assisting in rapport between therapist and client in the first place. The DSM-5 "Cultural Formulation Interview" emphasizes cultural definition of the presenting issue, cultural understandings of causes and supports, and cultural factors associated with coping, including past and present help-seeking.

However, over the past 10 years, the majority of published psychological research (60%) has been based on samples that are overwhelmingly North American, and half as much again draws from other Western, developed nations. The rest of the world (or almost 90% of the world's population) is characterized by the remainder—approximately 10% of published papers (Thalmayer et al., 2021). Like the majority of all published psychological research, much research on the ways that people conceive of and manifest NSSI, not to mention the "causes" of self-injurious thoughts and behaviors, typically focuses on people within nations (or cultures), and predominantly Western nations. Between them, NSSI reviews authored by Muehlenkamp et al. (2012), Swannell et al. (2014), Gholamrezaei et al. (2015), and Lim et al. (2019) identified 161 samples, available between 1993 and 2018, in which NSSI was assessed. More than half of all samples (52%) came from North America (85% of these were from the United States). A further 24% came from Europe (a third of which came from the United Kingdom) and 9% from Australia and New Zealand. Eleven percent of samples were drawn from Asia and fewer than 1% of samples were drawn from South America. Four further samples were drawn from Turkey (2%, on the border of Asia and Europe). Just over two thirds (69%) of samples represented English-speaking countries; only three samples represent participants in developing nations.

Having established that NSSI research parallels psychological research more generally in its relatively narrow sampling focus, I first review what this small but growing literature tells us about NSSI based on explicit comparison of samples collected in different nations, between groups within nations, within non-Western nations, and minority indigenous people within nations. Finally, I shall return to the question of "culture" and reflect on what this means for our understanding of NSSI based on these various studies.

NSSI across Nations

Meta-analytic studies of NSSI prevalence have shown significant heterogeneity in estimates attributed to a variety of moderators, including methods of assessing NSSI (e.g., Muehlenkamp et al., 2012), geographical location, and development status (e.g., Lim et al., 2019). Where studies directly compare or contrast groups in different settings they typically do so at the level of nations—for example, do people in Germany engage in

NSSI in different ways or at different frequency compared to those in the United States (Plener et al., 2009), or the United States and Greece (Kokaliari et al., 2017b), or Belgium compared to India (Gandhi et al., 2021)?

These studies, though limited in scope by the small numbers of samples solicited, are important. Given the variation in NSSI prevalence (that we know at least partly reflects how NSSI is assessed: Muehlenkamp et al., 2012), these studies allow direct comparisons of similar samples, using similar assessment tools but in different contexts. Equivalence of measures and samples allows us to make inferences about the "true" differences in cross-national NSSI prevalence, forms, functions, and contributory factors.

Plener et al. (2009) report no differences in NSSI prevalence or characteristics across their German and American samples (excepting that cutting was more common in the U.S. sample). Gandhi et al. (2021) found that, while past-year prevalence in Belgian and Indian samples was essentially the same, Indian participants were more likely to report head-banging, but less likely to report self-scratching or cutting. Additionally, Belgians reported an earlier peak in NSSI engagement (ages 14–16 vs. 16–18) and endorsed more intrapersonal (but similar interpersonal) NSSI functions (Gandhi et al., 2021). Meanwhile Kokaliari et al. (2017b) reported higher NSSI prevalence in their U.S. college subsample (27% vs. 17%), while their Greek subsample reported higher rates of self-biting, carving, and injuring themselves with glass objects.

In one of the only cross-national studies to include an African sample, Boduszek et al. (2021) surveyed thousands of Ugandan and Jamaican young people about their NSSI, suicidal ideation, and suicidal attempts. They report similar lifetime NSSI among Ugandan girls (23.2%) and boys (25.5%), but higher lifetime NSS among Jamaican girls (32.6%) than boys (21.0%).

NSSI among Minority Groups within Nations

Studies comparing NSSI prevalence and presentation among minorities in ethnically diverse samples are relatively more common than are cross-national comparison studies described above. They also more commonly come from North America. For example, Rojas-Velasquez et al. (2021) reviewed NSSI characteristics among African American and Hispanic adolescents, based on 15 studies with mixed-ethnicity samples including enough of each group (>10%). Again, prevalence rates were highly variable (between 7.3% and 46.5%). For instance, Chesin et al. (2013) found that White *and* Asian participants reported significantly more NSSI than Hispanics and African Americans, in a sample of more than 700 predominantly non-White university students (see also Brausch & Gutierrez, 2010). However, Walker et al. (2017) reported no differences in self-injury by ethnicity in a diverse North American sample. Meanwhile, Gratz et al. (2012) reported that African American boys reported more engagement than their peers in all forms of NSSI, though White girls reported statistically similar levels of cutting.

Rojas-Velasquez et al. (2021) conclude that the majority of studies reported higher rates among non-Hispanic White youth compared to minority youth, but that NSSI may be elevated among African American male youth specifically. Whereas experiences of discrimination and prejudice were *not* associated with NSSI among minority participants, minority youth NSSI appear to reflect (in part) acculturation and immigration stress, peer victimization, and stress associated with familial drug use, particularly among Hispanic youth. Social support and connection to others and community, on the other hand, were protective for African American and Hispanic young people (Brausch & Gutierrez, 2010; Wester & Trepal, 2015), as was cultural identity among Mexican men (Croyle, 2007) and church attendance for African American women (Davis et al., 2017).

While Sami and Hallaq (2018) reported similar NSSI prevalence among Palestinian youth (18.4%) living in Israel compared to Western and majority group samples (Muehlenkamp et al., 2012), they did find that young Palestinian males reported the highest frequency of NSSI (see also Madjar et al., 2021). Consistent with this, Verroken et al. (2018) found that refugee youth in Belgium reported similar rates, forms, and functions of NSSI compared to nonrefugee youth but went on to argue that NSSI among such a vulnerable group should perhaps be taken particularly seriously.

NSSI in Non-Western Nations

As already noted, the majority of NSSI research has been conducted in Western and English-speaking countries. Gholamrezaei et al. (2015) first reviewed research on NSSI across non-Western cultures and non-White ethnicities, published up until 2015, identifying 35 samples that satisfied their criteria. Of these, 17 focused specifically on non-Western cultures, 6 on ethnic/racial minorities, while a further 12 present analysis by ethnicity/race as a demographic variable. Twelve of 17 non-Western samples were drawn from Chinese or Japanese territories, three from Turkey, and one each drawn from India and Indonesia. In these non-Western samples, prevalence rates vary between 2.2% (Turkish adults) and 38% (Indonesian university students), broadly consistent with meta-analytic mean prevalence (Muehlenkamp et al., 2012; note that a small number of the samples are common to both reviews). The consistently inconsistent gender differences typically found in Western samples were also manifest, with approximately half of studies finding no difference (e.g., Zoroglu et al., 2003), some relating that women reported more NSSI (e.g., Cheung et al., 2013; Law & Shek, 2013) and others still finding the reverse (e.g., Tang et al., 2011; Tang et al., 2018) or that gender differences depended on NSSI forms (e.g., Izutsu et al., 2006). More recently, Lim et al. (2019) reported that meta-analytic lifetime prevalence of NSSI was greater in low-/middle-income and non-Western (33.7% and 32.6%) than high-income and Western (19.4% and 20.0%, respectively) countries, though past-year prevalence was essentially the same (19.1% vs. 19.7%).

Though Ghaedi Heidari et al. (2020) provide a narrative review of 18 studies investigating self-injury in Iran, it is not clear how many of these studies focus specifically on

NSSI. Gholamrezaei et al. (2016) reported comparatively low rates of NSSI (12.3%) in their own Iranian sample, with no evidence of gender differences. However, aspects of emotion dysregulation predicted NSSI among women, but not men.

There is an important caveat on my previous claim about the lack of non-Western NSSI research—this may not reflect research on NSSI published in non-English-language journals. Lang and Yao (2018) identified 26 articles based on Chinese samples of middle school students (combined N = 160,348), only 7 of which were reported in English-language journals. At the same time, the results of this larger set of Chinese studies parallels those published in English-language journals—the meta-analytic prevalence of NSSI across these samples was 22.4%, with females reporting slightly higher consolidated meta-analytic estimates (21.9%) of lifetime NSSI than males (20.6%).

Additionally and importantly, just as studies in the West utilize a variety of NSSI assessments the same is true of NSSI research in other contexts, but there is also limited evidence of cross-cultural validity of measures adapted for use in non-English contexts (see Chávez-Flores et al., 2019; Faura-Garcia et al., 2020).

NSSI in Indigenous Peoples
Even less is known about self-injury among "indigenous" peoples than about most other minorities within nations. One reason is that indigenous people are often minorities in their own lands, and even large-scale studies may include only small numbers of indigenous/first-nations participants, or may include indigenous participants but not report NSSI information by culture/ethnicity (e.g., Klonsky et al., 2013; Sornberger et al., 2012).

Gholamrezaei et al. (2015) note that two large studies with ethnically diverse samples that *have* reported NSSI rates for indigenous participants (Native Americans: Kuentzel et al., 2012; Yates et al., 2008) both indicate higher rates of self-injury than for participants of (most) other groups. However, only 24 and 10 participants (respectively) identified as Native American in these studies. 71% (five) of the seven Native American participants in Bryan and Bryan's (2014) research with college-enrolled military reported lifetime NSSI—by far the strongest predictor of NSSI among the background variables collected. One analysis of case files drawn from the White Mountain Apache Surveillance System (Cwik et al., 2011) extrapolated from presentations for self-injury to conclude a lifetime NSSI presentation to health services of around 1% among all ages, and 3% among those ages 15 to 19. However, actual rates *will* be higher given that the vast majority of NSSI is typically conducted in private (Klonsky et al., 2014), with few people presenting for medical treatment (Lloyd-Richardson et al., 2007).

In a notable large-scale exception, Monto et al. (2018) report NSSI rates from the nationally representative Centers for Disease Control and Prevention's (CDC) Youth Risk Behavior Surveillance System sample of 64,671 adolescents. Participants were asked "during the past 12 months, how many times did you do something to purposely hurt yourself without wanting to die, such as cutting or burning yourself on purpose?" NSSI rates were highest among Native Americans and Alaska Natives (20.79%), compared to Hispanic youth (19.9%), Whites (17.71%), and African Americans (12.1%). Similarly, slightly elevated NSSI rates among Sami, compared to non-Sami, Norwegians were not statistically different (Eckhoff et al., 2019; Kiærbech et al., 2021).

In the southern hemisphere, Black and Kisely (2018) identified six studies published between 1990 and 2015 investigating "NSSI" among Aboriginal Australians and Torres Strait Islanders, and one with New Zealand Māori. Where reported, prevalence in the Australian and Torres Strait samples ranged from 0.9% to 22.5%, while the single New Zealand study identified 4% of Māori hospital presentations were for "serious non-fatal injury." One of the larger studies in this group (Martin et al., 2010) reported no differences in past-four-week NSSI prevalence in a relatively small subsample (183 of 9,480 community adolescents) of indigenous Australians. However, it was not clear that all studies assessed NSSI and, further, Black and Kisely (2018) conclude, "Findings are limited due to a small pool of literature" (p. 3).

Garisch and Wilson (2015) found no significant differences in Deliberate Self-Harm Inventory scores by ethnicity in a sample of 1,126 16–18-year-olds (including 99 Māori/indigenous New Zealanders, 43 Pasifika, and 127 "Asian" youth). In one of the largest studies of its kind, Kingi (2018) analyzed survey responses from a subset of 322 Māori participants (of more than 2,000 adolescent participants; Robinson et al., 2021), 27% of which indicated NSSI (and a further 8% thoughts of NSSI). Importantly, Māori youth NSSI did not statistically differ from the majority New Zealand European youth (see also Fitzgerald & Curtis, 2017).

At the same time, numerous qualitative studies suggest that indigenous people may understand NSSI in ways that are broader than the definitions commonly adopted and measured by researchers. A significant minority of Cwik et al. (2011) Apache medical presentees had described other self-destructive behaviors in "terms similar to NSSI" (p. 867), most notably alcohol and drug use (see also Barlow et al., 2012). Consistent with this, Tingey et al. (2012) reported that in focus groups with 55 White Mountain Apache adolescents, Apache youth almost consistently agreed that substance use often functioned as self-injury, in order to serve two broad families of functions: "to avoid problems" or "to reduce negative feelings," versus "to be cool" or "to feel part of a group."" (p. 409). In other words, for intra- and interpersonal reasons. Farrelly and Francis (2009) also describe a broader conceptualization of NSSI among aboriginal Australians, including substance use and cutting off one's hair (to "harm" one's appearance). Critically, it is not clear how we should approach such "traditional" self-injury (e.g., self-inflicted "sorry cuts" and head-striking associated with mourning, particularly among women; Farrelly & Francis, 2009)—it may be culturally sanctioned or merely tolerated. That is, tolerated but not sanctioned behaviors fall within conventional definitions of NSSI. Additionally, Dash et al. (2017) reported that Pasifika mental health professionals extended the notion of self-injury beyond the physical—including "harm" to the mental or spiritual self (see also

Kingi, 2018; Kingi et al., 2017). Both Kingi et al. (2017) and Dash et al. (2017) suggest that tattoos (not usually considered self-injury in spite of the relatively permanent change to one's tissue) that do not authentically represent Māori or Pasifika culture can function to harm one's own spirit or even that of one's extended family (Dash et al., 2017; Wilson et al., 2016).

Forms and Functions of NSSI

As well as variation in the prevalence of NSSI, these cultural NSSI studies also indicate variation in the forms of NSSI "routinely" engaged in by different samples. For example, Kokaliari et al. (2017a) reported that among Jordanians, NSSI included avulsion of fingernails, jumping from a height, and masturbation. In Turkey, hitting oneself and specifically around the head were more common than cutting (Zoroglu et al., 2003), while ethnic Indians may also report more head-banging but less self-scratching or cutting (Gandhi et al., 2021). Lang and Yao (2018) reported that across 18 Chinese samples, young women tend to report cutting more than young men, but the reverse is true for self-battery.

It is something of a truism that affect regulation is the primary function of NSSI. Two recent meta-analytic reviews of the relationship between NSSI and emotion regulation (Wolff et al., 2019) and dysregulation (You et al., 2018) indicate that both are consistently and moderately associated with NSSI but did not include culture (or nation) as a potential moderator. At the same time, emotional experience is clearly important in the context of culture. For example, Rojas-Velasquez et al. (2021) found that emotional dysregulation emerged as a common risk factor for NSSI across the ethnic minority samples they reviewed. Taylor et al. (2018) reported a meta-analysis of 53 samples in which functions of NSSI were assessed. More than half (28) were North American, and 15 more came from Europe and Australia. Across samples, 66% to 81% of individuals reported NSSI as a means to regulate one's internal states, while 33% to 56% endorsed some interpersonal function. Once again, the lack of cultural diversity did not allow for tests of moderation by culture. However, this may not be the case for at least some other cultures, or perhaps not to the same extent.

Individual studies in non-Western cultures hint at considerable heterogeneity. You et al. (2013) identified three clusters of NSSI functions in a large sample of Chinese youth: affect regulation, social influence, and social avoidance. Consistent with the majority of published research (Wolff et al., 2019), affect regulation was the most commonly endorsed function, followed by social avoidance and social influence (see Taylor et al., this volume). Similarly, Zhang et al. (2019) reported emotion regulation (88% of adolescent participants) as the most common function of NSSI, followed by emotional release (82%), social influence (57%), and sensation-seeking (28%). However, Leong et al. (2014) found that functions associated with social-positive reinforcement were most strongly endorsed among a young adolescent Chinese sample (mean age 11.51 years). Meanwhile, "moderate" or "severe" self-injury by Indian young adults was more strongly associated with affect regulation than for "minor" self-injury, which was more likely to reflect regulation of the social environment (Kharsati & Bhola, 2014). Longitudinally, You et al. (2012) found that while negative emotion and relationship problems were both concurrently associated with NSSI for Chinese adolescents, only relationship problems *prospectively* predicted NSSI. Further, NSSI prospectively predicted negative affect but not future relationship problems. Finally, participants in Williams et al. (2018) interviews with a small sample of South Korean young adults reported engaging in NSSI to manage emotions in response to family and athletic/academic pressures (see also Wong & Chung, 2021).

What Is Culture?

To this point, I have resisted asking this question. Even Gholamrezaei et al. (2015) do not address this question, though they, and others, ostensibly review the relationship between NSSI and "culture." As Ryder et al. (2011) note, "The word 'culture' has long been used in psychology to stand for ethnicity or nationality, and invoked as a black box explanation: groups differ because of 'culture,' but the specific ways in which this happens remain unclear" (p. 961).

Rohner (1984) argued that culture can be thought of as the understanding of experiences of the world that are shared between individuals in a particular social system. Markus and Hamedani (2019) go on to define "culture" as a "label for any significant social category associated with shared ideas (e.g., values, beliefs, meanings assumptions) and practices (e.g., ways of doing, making, and being) that organize people's experiences and behaviours" (pp. 11–12). Much of the research described above, comparing NSSI characteristics and associated factors in people from different nations, or characterizing NSSI and associated factors in people in non-Western nations, may therefore not automatically qualify as cultural or cross-cultural research on NSSI. For example, Japan is ethnically much more homogeneous than China, and New Zealand is more electorally diverse than much-larger Australia.

If DSM-5 didn't tell us that culture is important for mental health, research increasingly suggests that it is important for other aspects of well-being. In the context of physical health, we know that emotion and affect may demonstrate culturally differentiable effects. For example, daily negative affect is a better predictor of poor physical health among Americans than Japanese (e.g., Kitayama & Park, 2017). Similarly, greater biological health risk is predicted by lower big-five emotional stability scores among Americans, but by higher emotional stability among Japanese (Kitayama et al., 2018). A similar pattern is found for anger expression (Kitayama & Park, 2017). There is also evidence of similar disjunctions in other cultures (see Shattuck, 2019).

Emotional experience and interpretation and understanding of emotional experience have been identified as consistently important in understanding NSSI. Emotional dysregulation is a cross-sectional (Wolff et al., 2019) and prospective (e.g., Robinson et al., 2019) predictor of NSSI and plays a key role in our theoretical frameworks (Chapman et al., 2006; Hasking et al., 2017; Nock, 2010). Alexithymia, a dimensional construct commonly assessed using the Toronto Alexithymia Scale (TAS-20; Taylor et al., 1985) reflecting difficulties in identifying feelings (DIF), difficulties in describing feelings (DDF), and a preference for pragmatic matters of everyday life over internal emotional life (externally oriented thinking, or EOT), has been identified as a risk factor in this research (see Greene et al., 2020; Norman et al., 2020). Our theories of NSSI lead us to expect that difficulties in identifying and describing emotions, and devaluation of emotional life, should be a problem. Indeed, DIF and DDF consistently predict lifetime and recent NSSI (Greene et al., 2020), but the effect size for EOT as a positive predictor of NSSI was notably smaller (e.g., $g = .10$) than the overall scale effect size (e.g., $g = .57$; Norman et al., 2020).

Again, this Alexithymia-NSSI literature is both small and dominated by Western samples (23 of 25 samples: Norman et al., 2020). Additionally, the reliability of the EOT subscale is notably lower, and lower still for non-English-language versions (Ryder et al., 2018). This suggests that whatever EOT is supposed to measure may make sense in different ways in different settings. Further, not only do Chinese patients appear to report more somatic symptoms of psychiatric conditions relative to Europeans (e.g., Haroz et al., 2017), but also appear to score higher on Alexithymia than Americans, and this appears to be driven entirely by the EOT subscale of the Toronto Alexithymia Scale (Ryder et al., 2008). While somatic symptoms of depression are common in all nations, there is considerable variation in their frequency of presentation (e.g., Simon et al., 1999).

One explanation for this phenomenon is that different cultural settings value the expression of emotions differently. Ryder et al. (2018) argue that this variation may reflect different kinds of pathologies relating to healthy expression (or suppression) of emotions, or it may instead reflect the adherence to contextually appropriate norms (or "cultural scripts")—it just makes more cultural sense in some settings to focus on somatic symptoms. We'll return to this notion of cultural scripts shortly.

One potentially fruitful direction is to investigate how NSSI engagement, nature, and function are associated with or influenced by cultural variables. Although there are many lenses through which people sharing a culture may understand and enact the world, a relatively finite set of dimensions of culture has been identified. Perhaps the most influential characterization of cultural multidimensionality is that of Hofstede (1984) who argued that national cultures vary in terms of individualism versus collectivism, power distance versus closeness, uncertainty avoidance versus acceptance, and masculinity versus femininity. Two further dimensions (long-term vs. short-term orientation and indulgence vs. restraint) were subsequently added (Hofstede et al., 2010).

As well as national-level variation in how cultural citizens vary on these dimensions, there is, unsurprisingly, individual-level variation. The most heavily studied of these dimensions is individualism versus collectivism. For individualists, maintaining a positive sense of one's individual self is key, expressing one's emotions is important for life satisfaction, and relationships are important primarily for attainment of one's personal goals and well-being. Meanwhile, for collectivists, not only is ingroup membership central to the self-concept but harmonious group relationships are likely enhanced by restraint in emotional expression, and satisfaction of the obligations that go with those memberships are a source of well-being (Oyserman et al., 2002). The United States is a highly individualistic culture, while China is highly collectivist. Japan is less collectivistic than China but still notably more so than the United States.

A stronger collectivist orientation may predict greater stigmatization of mental distress (Papadopoulos et al., 2013). Greater endorsement of individualism versus collectivism also appears to differentially predict more negative affect in response to achievement-related or social stressors (respectively: Tafarodi & Smith, 2001). Finally, these cultural orientations also have implications regarding who seeks help, who from, and how to offer appropriate support regarding NSSI—collectivists may be uncomfortable explicitly seeking support for NSSI from close others or mental health services. In turn, it may be particularly valuable to consider electronic NSSI interventions for both collectivist and indigenous people (cultures that, incidentally, are typically considered collectivist). In some, but not all, places indigenous and other minority groups may be geographically spread, living in rural and remote areas, and may be particularly likely to benefit from e-mental health interventions (e.g., Toombs et al., 2020).

The notion of cultural scripts is a useful one for considering what the research reviewed above suggests about NSSI. For example, Kokaliari et al. (2017a) identified marked differences in beliefs about the role of different cultural influences on NSSI between social work students in Greece, Cyprus, Jordan, and the United States. U.S. participants were less likely to endorse family and societal pressures as the main contributors to NSSI and, along with Greek and Cypriot participants, identified mental illness and deprivation as potential causes. U.S. participants also saw NSSI treatment as a responsibility of the individual. Jordanian social work students thought that NSSI reflected absence or weakening of religious faith and, therefore, saw a role for faith leaders in intervention, while participants from the other three countries disagreed. We see multiple "scripts" informing understanding and behavior—not only does the contextually "appropriate" *form* that NSSI takes potentially vary, but the causes and appropriate remediation may also follow what makes cultural sense in these different contexts in ways that may be informed by appreciating the distinction between, for example, individualistic and collectivistic cultures. It makes sense, for example, that the endorsement of interpersonal NSSI functions may be more common for members of collectivist cultures. Cultural scripts have the potential to help us understand the variations in prevalence, forms, and functions that characterize NSSI research both across as well as within cultures.

Other Cultures?

Smith et al. (2013) note that the notion that culture reflects a system of shared understandings can apply at various levels of increasing specificity—for example, within racial groups, within faith-based groups that may themselves be part of racial groups, within families nested within faith-based groups that are part of racial groups, and so on (see also Markus & Hamedani, 2019). Culture, then, can differentiate groups that are *not* racially or nationally defined. A cultural lens may, therefore, potentially be useful for considering understanding of NSSI and its treatment among groups that aren't necessarily nationally or ethnicity based. Such intersections might include, for example, gender, sexuality, religion, or subculture, among others.

GENDER

As noted above, and elsewhere, there is a great deal of inconsistency across studies as to whether there is a gender difference in NSSI (Bresin & Schoenleber, 2015 also see Taliaferro et al., this volume). However, where gender differences are identified, it is not unreasonable to suggest that this may reflect a different kind of cultural script—in which women (particularly young women) engage in self-injury more or in particular ways (e.g., cutting) in part because that is the stereotype or expectation. Just as it may make more sense for Chinese patients to express their distress in terms of somatic symptoms (e.g., Haroz et al., 2017), maybe young women perceive it as culturally understandable to manage or express emotional challenges through NSSI?

SEXUALITY

Self-injury is around three times more common among minority sexuality youth (Batejan et al., 2015) than among their straight peers (see Taliaferro et al., this volume). Among other things identified in a systematic narrative review of qualitative NSSI research, Peel-Wainwright et al. (2021) noted that minority sexuality individuals commonly express that they do not see themselves as "counting" or mattering in the eyes of others—NSSI represents a way to both deal with this apparent lack of care as well as manage or communicate difficulties and feelings. It may be less threatening to engage in NSSI than to engage with close others directly about sexuality. Similarly, Morris and Galupo (2019) argue that their finding that people who identify as agender report NSSI for interpersonal reasons more than other genderqueer individuals is consistent with Joiner's (2015; Joiner, 2005; Van Orden et al., 2010) interpersonal theory of suicide—rejection of societal gender-binary expectations contributes to a sense of rejection by society. Additionally, some transgender participants reported using NSSI to alter their bodies in order to improve their self-image (Morris & Galupo, 2019; Liu et al., 2019).

RELIGION

Religion appears to be protective. Haney (2020) reported a small but significant meta-analytic correlation of -0.10 between holding a faith and NSSI engagement. Though there was significant heterogeneity, this result was *not* moderated by age, gender, or location (American vs. international). However, relatively few studies have assessed religiosity and, therefore, we cannot yet make claims about risky or protective intersectionality. Unfortunately, relatively few studies of NSSI have large and diverse enough samples to compare denominational differences. Kuentzel et al. (2012) found that self-reported religiosity predicted less NSSI engagement, with Muslim and Baptist participants four to five times less likely to engage in NSSI than the irreligious. Further, faith can be both a risk *and* protective factor for NSSI among intersectional groups—Longo et al. (2013) found that minority sexuality youth who adhered to liberal Christian doctrine were less likely to self-injure than conservative Christian minority sexuality youth. Additionally, while Kiærbech et al. (2021) found no significant differences in NSSI across indigenous and non-indigenous Norwegians, they report that religiosity predicted less NSSI, and particularly among those observing Laestadianism—a Swedish Lutheran revival movement that was also more common among indigenous Sami Norwegians.

YOUTH SUBCULTURES

NSSI has often been seen to be associated with membership of several nonconforming subcultural groups, particularly emo and goth identities, and particularly among youth. There have been relatively few studies looking specifically at NSSI among youth subcultures, but Hughes et al. (2018) identified 10 quantitative studies assessing NSSI, self-harm, or suicidal thoughts and behaviors, concluding that members of alternative subcultures present elevated risk for all three. In one of the only NSSI-specific studies, Young et al. (2014) found that German youths holding an "Alternative" (emo, goth, or punk) identity were two and a half times more likely to report NSSI, and reported greater frequency of both NSSI and suicidal thoughts and attempts. A "jock" identity was more weakly but significantly protective. Additionally, alternative youth more commonly endorsed communicative and social functions of their self-injury (Young et al., 2014).

Implications and Future Directions

This growing body of research, alongside DSM-5 recommendations to attend to culture and, potentially importantly, the notion of cultural scripts, suggests several implications and applications in clinical practice. First, when assessing NSSI it would be important to consider cultural scripts regarding the underlying drivers of the behavior/background factors that are considered important. For example, "scripts" around expression of emotion (e.g., whether expressed emotion centers on the goals of the individual or the collective), help-seeking (e.g., whether help-seeking for emotional distress is considered shameful/discredit to family or community), and/or understanding and experiences of the body (e.g., the finding that different cultural or religious groups may be less likely to engage in NSSI may reflect scripts related to the body as sacred/taboo and therefore imperatives to treat it as such).

Second, when asking questions about NSSI, practitioners (and researchers) may need to be broader in our definition of this behavior when working with minority groups, or indigenous groups in particular. Superficially, behaviors that involve isolating oneself from one's culture (or religion) functioning as self-punishment or self-harm may appear inconsistent with definitions of NSSI privileging tissue damage but are also based on Western understandings that privilege separation of body, mind, and spirit in ways that other cultures may not.

Third, in treatment, awareness and interrogation of cultural scripts may heighten the client's experience of emotional validation and also strengthen the capacity to reach a shared formulation and treatment pathway. Additionally, if NSSI is a high-frequency behavior in a certain cultural group (e.g., "Alternative cultures") this is important to acknowledge. This may suggest that cultural scripts place NSSI as an acceptable means of expressing distress and engaging in help-seeking. If alternative youth are more likely to use NSSI as a form of communication, then it will be important to assess what *other* "scripts" may be available to communicate distress, or manage social stressors.

In terms of future research, there is tremendous opportunity to both expand what we know about self-injury and also to reflect on what we mean by it, as we work to expand the representation of non-Western, minority, and indigenous groups in our research. It is an interesting thought experiment to wonder what self-injury research and practice might look like had we first explored these behaviors through a cultural lens? On the one hand, grasping this challenge means expanding our samples, and the groups and places from which we recruit from, as well as collaborating with researchers in hard-to-reach places. Most importantly it may mean reflecting on our own understandings and operationalizations of self-injury, and psychology more broadly.

Concluding Summary

A consistent theme in this chapter has been "too few studies/samples to be sure." However, we can be confident that the same kinds of inconsistencies seen across (and within) Western, English-speaking cultures are found in samples reflecting greater diversity. Gholamrezaei et al. (2015) counseled that:

> Accepting a Western construction of NSSI means that researchers sometimes inadvertently ignore the norms and values of populations that are substantially different from the dominant Western culture. It is important to situate NSSI within the contexts of race, ethnicity and culture if we are to make better sense of what is occurring at a deeper level. (p. 323).

I have suggested that we might usefully think of NSSI as informed by this idea of a cultural script (Ryder et al., 2018)—that the form and characteristics thatNSSI can, and who engages in NSSI, may not immutably tie to a particular cause or preferred form but rather reflect contextually sensible shared understandings of distress, how distress is communicated, and also how to seek support. In short, they reflect culture.

References

American Psychiatric Association. (2013). *Diagnostic and statistical manual of mental disorders* (5th ed.).

Barlow, A., Tingey, L., Cwik, M., Goklish, N., Larzelere-Hinton, F., Lee, A., Suttle, R., Mullany, B., & Walkup, J. T. (2012). Understanding the relationship between substance use and self-injury in American Indian youth. *The American Journal of Drug and Alcohol Abuse, 38*(5), 403–408. https://doi.org/10.3109/00952990.2012.696757

Batejan, K. L., Jarvi, S. M., & Swenson, L. P. (2015). Sexual orientation and non-suicidal self-injury: A meta-analytic review. *Archives of Suicide Research, 19*(2), 131–150. https://doi.org/10.1080/13811118.2014.957450

Black, E. B., & Kisely, S. (2018). A systematic review: Non-suicidal self-injury in Australia and New Zealand's indigenous populations. *Australian Psychologist, 53*(1), 3–12. https://doi.org/10.1111/ap.12274

Boduszek, D., Debowska, A., Ochen, E. A., Fray, C., Nanfuka, E. K., Powell-Booth, K., Turyomurugyendo, F., Nelson, K., Harvey, R., Willmott, D., & Mason, S. J. (2021). Prevalence and correlates of non-suicidal self-injury, suicidal ideation, and suicide attempt among children and adolescents: Findings from Uganda and Jamaica. *Journal of Affective Disorders, 283*, 172–178. https://doi.org/10.1016/j.jad.2021.01.063

Brausch, A. M., & Gutierrez, P. M. (2010). Differences in non-suicidal self-injury and suicide attempts in adolescents. *Journal of Youth and Adolescence, 39*, 233–242. https://doi.org/10.1007/s10964-009-9482-0

Bresin, K., & Schoenleber, M. (2015). Gender differences in the prevalence of nonsuicidal self-injury: A meta-analysis. *Clinical Psychology Review, 38*, 55–64. https://doi.org/10.1016/j.cpr.2015.02.009

Bryan, C., & Bryan, A. (2014). Nonsuicidal self-injury among a sample of united states military personnel and veterans enrolled in college classes. *Journal of Clinical Psychology, 70*(9), 874–885. https://doi.org/10.1002/jclp.22075

Chapman, A. L., Gratz, K. L., & Brown, M. Z. (2006). Solving the puzzle of deliberate self-harm: The experiential avoidance model. *Behaviour Research and Therapy, 44*(3), 371–394. https://doi.org/10.1016/j.brat.2005.03.005

Chávez-Flores, Y. V., Hidalgo-Rasmussen, C. A., & Yanez-Peñúñuri, L. Y. (2019). Assessment tools of non-suicidal self-injury in adolescents 1990–2016: A systematic review. *Ciencia & Saude Coletiva, 24*, 2871–2882. https://doi.org/10.1590/1413-81232018248.18502017

Chesin, M. S., Moster, A. N., & Jeglic, E. L. (2013). Non-suicidal self-injury among ethnically and racially diverse emerging adults: Do factors unique to the minority experience matter? *Current Psychology, 32*(4), 318–328. https://doi.org/10.1007/s12144-013-9185-2

Cheung, Y. T. D., Wong, P. W. C., Lee, A. M., Lam, T. H., Fan, Y. S. S., & Yip, P. S. F. (2013). Non-suicidal self-injury and suicidal behavior: Prevalence, co-occurrence, and correlates of suicide among adolescents in Hong Kong. *Social Psychiatry and Psychiatric Epidemiology, 48*(7), 1133–1144. https://doi.org/10.1007/s00127-012-0640-4

Croyle, K. L. (2007). Self-harm experiences among Hispanic and non-Hispanic White young adults. *Hispanic Journal of Behavioral Sciences, 29*, 242–253. https://doi.org/10.1177/0739986307299452

Cwik, M. F., Barlow, A., Tingey, L., Larzelere-Hinton, F., Goklish, N., & Walkup, J. T. (2011). Nonsuicidal self-injury in an American Indian reservation community: Results from the White Mountain Apache surveillance system, 2007–2008. *Journal of the American Academy of Child & Adolescent Psychiatry, 50*(9), 860–869. https://doi.org/10.1016/j.jaac.2011.06.007

Dash, S., Taylor, T., Ofanoa, M., & Taufa, N. (2017). Conceptualisations of deliberate self-harm as it occurs within the context of Pacific populations living in New Zealand. *New Zealand Journal of Psychology, 46*(3), 115–125.

Davis, L. T., Weiss, N. H., Tull, M. T., & Gratz, K. L. (2017). The relation of protective factors to deliberate self-harm among African-American adults: Moderating roles of gender and sexual orientation identity. *Journal of Mental Health, 26*, 351–358. https://doi.org/10.1080/09638237.2017.1340610

Eckhoff, C., Sørvold, M. T., & Kvernmo, S. (2019). Adolescent self-harm and suicidal behavior and young adult outcomes in indigenous and non-indigenous people. *European Child & Adolescent Psychiatry, 29*, 917–927. https://doi.org/10.1007/s00787-019-01406-5

Farrelly, T., & Francis, K. (2009). Definitions of suicide and self-harm behavior in an Australian Aboriginal community. *Suicide and Life-Threatening Behavior, 39*(2), 182–189. https://doi.org/10.1521/suli.2009.39.2.182

Faura-Garcia, J., Orue, I., & Calvete, E. (2020). Clinical assessment of non-suicidal self-injury: A systematic review of instruments. *Clinical Psychology & Psychotherapy, 28*(4), 739–765. https://doi.org/10.1002/cpp.2537

Favazza, A. R. (2009). A cultural understanding of nonsuicidal self-injury. In M.K. Nock (Ed.), *Understanding nonsuicidal self-injury: Origins, assessment, and treatment.* American Psychological Association.

Favazza, A. R. (2011). *Bodies under siege: Self-mutilation, nonsuicidal self-injury, and body modification in culture and psychiatry.* JHU Press.

Fitzgerald, J., & Curtis, C. (2017). Non-suicidal self-injury in a New Zealand student population: Demographic and self-harm characteristics. *New Zealand Journal of Psychology, 46*(3), 156–163.

Fox, K. R., Franklin, J. C., Ribeiro, J. D., Kleiman, E. M., Bentley, K. H., & Nock, M. K. (2015). Meta-analysis of risk factors for nonsuicidal self-injury. *Clinical Psychology Review, 42*, 156–167. https://doi.org/10.1016/j.cpr.2015.09.002

Gandhi, A., Luyckx, K., Adhikari, A., Parmar, D., Desousa, A., Shah, N.,Maitra, S., & Claes, L. (2021). Non-suicidal self-injury and its association with identity formation in India and Belgium: A cross-cultural case-control study. *Transcultural Psychiatry, 58*(1), 52–62. https://doi.org/10.1177/1363461520933759

Garisch, J. A., & Wilson, M. S. (2015). Prevalence, correlates, and prospective predictors of non-suicidal self-injury among New Zealand adolescents: Cross-sectional and longitudinal survey data. *Child and Adolescent Psychiatry and Mental Health, 9*(1), 1–11. https://doi.org/10.1186/s13034-015-0055-6

Ghaedi Heidari, F., Bahrami, M., Kheirabadi, G., & Maghsoudi, J. (2020). Factors associated with non-suicidal self-injury (NSSI) in Iran: A narrative systematic review. *International Journal of Pediatrics, 8*(1), 10785–10799.

Gholamrezaei, M., De Stefano, J., & Heath, N. L. (2015). Nonsuicidal self-injury across cultures and ethnic and racial minorities: A review. *International Journal of Psychology, 52*(4), 316–326. https://doi.org/10.1002/ijop.12230

Gholamrezaei, M., Heath, N., & Panaghi, L. (2016). Non-suicidal self-injury in a sample of university students in Tehran, Iran: Prevalence, characteristics and risk factors. *International Journal of Culture and Mental Health, 10*(2), 136–149. https://doi.org/10.1080/17542863.2016.1265999

Gratz, K. L., Latzman, R. D., Young, J., Heiden, L. J., Damon, J., Hight, T., & Tull, M. T. (2012). Deliberate self-harm among underserved adolescents: The moderating roles of gender, race, and school-level and association with borderline personality features. *Personality Disorders: Theory, Research, and Treatment, 3*(1), 39–54. https://doi.org/10.1037/a0022107

Greene, D., Boyes, M., & Hasking, P. (2020). The associations between alexithymia and both non-suicidal self-injury and risky drinking: A systematic review and meta-analysis. *Journal of Affective Disorders, 260*, 140–166. https://doi.org/10.1016/j.jad.2019.08.088

Haney, A. M. (2020). Nonsuicidal self-injury and religiosity: A meta-analytic investigation. *American Journal of Orthopsychiatry, 90*(1), 78–89. https://doi.org/10.1037/ort0000395

Haroz, E. E., Ritchey, M., Bass, J. K., Kohrt, B. A., Augustinavicius, J., Michalopoulos, L., Burkey, M., & Bolton, P. (2017). How is depression experienced around the world? A systematic review of qualitative literature. *Social Science & Medicine, 183*, 151–162. https://doi.org/10.1016/j.socscimed.2016.12.030

Hasking, P., Whitlock, J., Voon, D., & Rose, A. (2017). A cognitive-emotional model of NSSI: Using emotion regulation and cognitive processes to explain why people self-injure. *Cognition and Emotion, 31*(8), 1543–1556. https://doi.org/10.1080/02699931.2016.1241219

Hofstede, G. (1984). *Culture's consequences: International differences in work-related values* (Vol. 5). SAGE.

Hofstede, G., Hofstede, G. J., & Minkov, M. (2010). *Cultures and organizations: Software of the mind* (3rd ed.). McGraw Hill.

Hughes, M. A., Knowles, S. F., Dhingra, K., Nicholson, H. L., & Taylor, P. J. (2018). This corrosion: A systematic review of the association between alternative subcultures and the risk of self-harm and suicide. *British Journal of Clinical Psychology, 57*(4), 491–513. https://doi.org/10.1111/bjc.12179

International Society for the Study of Self-Injury. (2018, May). What is self-injury? Retrieved from https://itriples.org/about-self-injury/what-is-self-injury

Izutsu, T., Shimotsu, S., Matsumoto, T., Okada, T., Kikuchi, A., Kojimoto, M., & Yoshikawa, K. (2006). Deliberate self-harm and childhood hyperactivity in junior high school students. *European Child & Adolescent Psychiatry, 15*(3), 172–176. https://doi.org/10.1007/s00787-005-0520-5

Joiner, T. E. (2005). *Why people die by suicide.* Harvard University Press.

Kharsati, N., & Bhola, P. (2014). Patterns of non-suicidal self-injurious behaviours among college students in India. *International Journal of Social Psychiatry, 61*(1), 39–49. https://doi.org/10.1177/0020764014535755

Kiærbech, H., Silviken, A., Lorem, G. F., Kristiansen, R. E., & Spein, A. R. (2021). Religion and Health In Arctic Norway—The association of religious and spiritual factors with non-suicidal self-injury in the Sami and non-Sami adult population—The SAMINOR 2 Questionnaire Survey. *Mental Health, Religion & Culture, 24*(7), 670–686. https://doi.org/10.1080/13674676.2021.1924125

Kingi, T., Russell, L., & Ashby, W. (2017). Mā te mātau, ka ora: The use of traditional Indigenous knowledge to support contemporary rangatahi Māori who self-injure. *New Zealand Journal of Psychology, 46*(3), 137–145.

Kingi, T. E. T. A. M. (2018). *Ko ngā pūtake o te mātānawe ki tā te rangatahi: An exploration of self-injury in rangatahi Māori* [Unpublished doctoral dissertation]. Victoria University of Wellington.

Kitayama, S., Park, J., Miyamoto, Y., Date, H., Boylan, J. M., Markus, H. R., Karasawa, M., Kawakami, N., Coe, C. L., Love, G. D., & Ryff, C. D. (2018). Behavioral adjustment moderates the link between neuroticism and biological health risk: A US–Japan comparison study. *Personality and Social Psychology Bulletin, 44*(6), 809–822. https://doi.org/10.1177/0146167217748603

Kitayama, S., & Park, J. (2017). Emotion and biological health: The socio-cultural moderation. *Current Opinion in Psychology, 17*, 99–105. https://doi.org/10.1016/j.copsyc.2017.06.016

Klonsky, E. D., May, A. M., & Glenn, C. R. (2013). The relationship between nonsuicidal self-injury and attempted suicide: Converging evidence from four samples. *Journal of Abnormal Psychology, 122*(1), 231–237. https://doi.org/10.1037/a0030278

Klonsky, E. D., Victor, S. E., & Saffer, B. Y. (2014). Nonsuicidal self-injury: What we know, and what we need to know. *Canadian Journal of Psychiatry, 59*(11), 565–568. https://doi.org/10.1177/070674371405901101

Kokaliari, E. D., Roy, A. W., & Koutra, K. (2017a). A cross-sectional study comparing predictors of non-suicidal self-injury among college students in the United States and Greece. *International Journal of Culture and Mental Health, 10*(1), 50–61. https://doi.org/10.1080/17542863.2016.1259339

Kokaliari, E. D., Roy, A. W., Panagiotopoulos, C., & Al-Makhamreh, S. (2017b). An exploratory comparative study of perspectives on non-suicidal self-injurious behaviors among social work students in the United States, Greece, Cyprus, and Jordan: Implications for social work practice and education. *International Social Work, 60*(4), 1015–1027. https://doi.org/10.1177/0020872815594225

Kothgassner, O. D., Goreis, A., Robinson, K., Huscsava, M. M., Schmahl, C., & Plener, P. L. (2021). Efficacy of dialectical behavior therapy for adolescent self-harm and suicidal ideation: A systematic review and meta-analysis. *Psychological Medicine, 51*, 1057–1067. https://doi.org/10.1017/s0033291721001355

Kuentzel, J. G., Arble, E., Boutros, N., Chugani, D., & Barnett, D. (2012). Nonsuicidal self-injury in an ethnically diverse college sample. *American Journal of Orthopsychiatry, 82*(3), 291–297. https://doi.org/10.1111/j.1939-0025.2012.01167.x

Lang, J., & Yao, Y. (2018). Prevalence of nonsuicidal self-injury in Chinese middle school and high school students: A meta-analysis. *Medicine, 97*(42), Article 12916. https://doi.org/10.1097/md.0000000000012916

Law, B. M. F., & Shek, D. T. L. (2013). Self-harm and suicide attempts among young Chinese adolescents in Hong Kong: Prevalence, correlates, and changes. *Journal of Pediatric and Adolescent Gynecology, 26*(3), S26–S32. https://doi.org/10.1016/j.jpag.2013.03.012

Leong, C. H., Wu, A. M., & Poon, M. M. Y. (2014). Measurement of perceived functions of non-suicidal self-injury for Chinese adolescents. *Archives of Suicide Research, 18*(2), 193–212. https://doi.org/10.1080/13811118.2013.824828

Lim, K. S., Wong, C. H., McIntyre, R. S., Wang, J., Zhang, Z., Tran, B. X., Ho, C. S., & Ho, R. C. (2019). Global lifetime and 12-month prevalence of suicidal behavior, deliberate self-harm and non-suicidal self-injury in children and adolescents between 1989 and 2018: A meta-analysis. *International Journal of Environmental Research and Public Health, 16*(22), 4581. https://doi.org/10.3390/ijerph16224581

Liu, R. T., Sheehan, A. E., Walsh, R. F., Sanzari, C. M., Cheek, S. M., & Hernandez, E. M. (2019). Prevalence and correlates of non-suicidal self-injury among lesbian, gay, bisexual, and transgender individuals: A systematic review and meta-analysis. *Clinical Psychology Review, 74*, 101783. https://doi.org/10.1016/j.cpr.2019.101783

Lloyd-Richardson, E. E., Perrine, N., Dierker, L., & Kelley, M. L. (2007). Characteristics and functions of non-suicidal self-injury in a community sample of adolescents. *Psychological Medicine, 37*(8), 1183–1192. https://doi.org/10.1017/s003329170700027x

Longo, J., Walls, N. E., & Wisneski, H. (2013). Religion and religiosity: Protective or harmful factors for sexual minority youth?. *Mental Health, Religion & Culture*, *16*(3), 273–290. https://doi.org/10.1080/13674676.2012.659240

Madjar, N., Daka, D., Zalsman, G., & Shoval, G. (2021). Depression symptoms as a mediator between social support, non-suicidal self-injury, and suicidal ideation among Arab adolescents in Israel. *School Psychology International*, *42*, 358–378. https://doi.org/10.1177/0143034321998741

Markus, H. R., & Hamedani, M. G. (2019). People are culturally shaped shapers: The psychological science of culture and culture change. In D. Cohen & S. Kitayama (Eds.), *Handbook of Cultural Psychology* (pp. 11–52). Guilford Press.

Martin, G., Swannell, S. V., Hazell, P. L., Harrison, J. E., & Taylor, A. W. (2010). Self-injury in Australia: A community survey. *Medical Journal of Australia*, *193*(9), 506–510. https://doi.org/10.5694/j.1326-5377.2010.tb04033.x

Monto, M. A., McRee, N., & Deryck, F. S. (2018). Nonsuicidal self-injury among a representative sample of US adolescents, 2015. *American Journal of Public Health*, *108*(8), 1042–1048. https://doi.org/10.2105/ajph.2018.304470

Morris, E. R., & Galupo, M. P. (2019). "Attempting to dull the dysphoria": Nonsuicidal self-injury among transgender individuals. *Psychology of Sexual Orientation and Gender Diversity*, *6*(3), 296–307. https://doi.org/10.1037/sgd0000327

Muehlenkamp, J. J., Claes, L., Havertape, L., & Plener, P. L. (2012). International prevalence of adolescent non-suicidal self-injury and deliberate self-harm. *Child and Adolescent Psychiatry and Mental Health*, *6*(1), 1–9. https://doi.org/10.1186/1753-2000-6-10

Nock, M. K. (2010). Self-injury. *Annual Review of Clinical Psychology*, *6*, 339–363.

Norman, H., Oskis, A., Marzano, L., & Coulson, M. (2020). The relationship between self-harm and alexithymia: A systematic review and meta-analysis. *Scandinavian Journal of Psychology*, *61*(6), 855–876. https://doi.org/10.1111/sjop.12668

Oyserman, D., Coon, H. M., & Kemmelmeier, M. (2002). Rethinking individualism and collectivism: Evaluation of theoretical assumptions and meta-analyses. *Psychological Bulletin*, *128*, 3–72. https://doi.org/10.1037/0033-2909.128.1.3

Papadopoulos, C., Foster, J., & Caldwell, K. (2013). "Individualism-collectivism" as an explanatory device for mental illness stigma. *Community Mental Health Journal*, *49*(3), 270–280. https://doi.org/10.1007/s10597-012-9534-x

Peel-Wainwright, K. M., Hartley, S., Boland, A., Rocca, E., Langer, S., & Taylor, P. J. (2021). The interpersonal processes of non-suicidal self-injury: A systematic review and meta-synthesis. *Psychology and Psychotherapy: Theory, Research and Practice*, *94*(4), 1059–1082. https://doi.org/10.1111/papt.12352

Plener, P. L., Libal, G., Keller, F., Fegert, J. M., & Muehlenkamp, J. J. (2009). An international comparison of adolescent non-suicidal self-injury (NSSI) and suicide attempts: Germany and the USA. *Psychological Medicine*, *39*(9), 1549–1558. https://doi.org/10.1017/s0033291708005114

Robinson, K., Garisch, J. A., Kingi, T., Brocklesby, M., O'Connell, A., Langlands, R. L., Russell, L., & Wilson, M. S. (2019). Reciprocal risk: The longitudinal relationship between emotion regulation and non-suicidal self-injury in adolescents. *Journal of Abnormal Child Psychology*, *47*(2), 325–332. https://doi.org/10.1007/s10802-018-0450-6

Robinson, K., Garisch, J. A., & Wilson, M. S. (2021). Nonsuicidal self-injury thoughts and behavioural characteristics: Associations with suicidal thoughts and behaviours among community adolescents. *Journal of Affective Disorders*, *282*, 1247–1254. https://doi.org/10.1016/j.jad.2020.12.201

Rohner, R. P. (1984). Toward a conception of culture for cross-cultural psychology. *Journal of Cross-Cultural Psychology*, *15*(2), 111–138.

Rojas-Velasquez, D. A., Pluhar, E. I., Burns, P. A., & Burton, E. T. (2021). Nonsuicidal self-injury among African American and Hispanic adolescents and young adults: A systematic review. *Prevention Science*, *22*(3), 367–377. https://doi.org/10.1007/s11121-020-01147-x

Ryder, A. G., Yang, J., Zhu, X., Yao, S., Yi, J., Heine, S. J., & Bagby, R. M. (2008). The cultural shaping of depression: Somatic symptoms in China, psychological symptoms in North America? *Journal of Abnormal Psychology*, *117*(2), 300–313. https://doi.org/10.1037/0021-843x.117.2.300

Ryder, A. G., Ban, L. M., & Chentsova-Dutton, Y. E. (2011). Towards a cultural–clinical psychology. *Social and Personality Psychology Compass*, *5*(12), 960–975. https://doi.org/10.1111/j.1751-9004.2011.00404.x

Ryder, A. G., Sunohara, M., Dere, J., & Chentsova-Dutton, Y. E. (2018). The cultural shaping of alexithymia. In O. Luminet, R. M. Bagby, & G. J. Taylor (Eds.), *Alexithymia: Advances in research, theory, and clinical practice* (pp. 33–48). Cambridge University Press.

Sami, H., & Hallaq, E. (2018). Nonsuicidal self-injury among adolescents and young adults with prolonged exposure to violence: The effect of post-traumatic stress symptoms. *Psychiatry Research, 270*, 510–516. https://doi.org/10.1016/j.psychres.2018.10.028

Shattuck, E.C. (2019). A biocultural approach to psychiatric illnesses. *Psychopharmacology, 236*(10), 2923–2936. https://doi.org/10.1007/s00213-019-5178-7

Simon, G. E., VonKorff, M., Piccinelli, M., Fullerton, C., & Ormel, J. (1999). An international study of the relation between somatic symptoms and depression. *New England Journal of Medicine, 341*(18), 1329–1335. https://doi.org/10.1056/nejm199910283411801

Smith, P. B., Fischer, R., Vignoles, V. L., & Bond, M. H. (2013). *Understanding social psychology across cultures: Engaging with others in a changing world.* SAGE.

Sornberger, M. J., Heath, N. L., Toste, J. R., & McLouth, R. (2012). Nonsuicidal self-injury and gender: Patterns of prevalence, methods, and locations among adolescents. *Suicide and Life-Threatening Behavior, 42*(3), 266–278. https://doi.org/10.1111/j.1943-278x.2012.0088.x

Swannell, S. V., Martin, G. E., Page, A., Hasking, P., & St John, N. J. (2014). Prevalence of nonsuicidal self-injury in nonclinical samples: Systematic review, meta-analysis and meta-regression. *Suicide and Life-Threatening Behavior, 44*(3), 273–303. https://doi.org/10.1111/sltb.12070

Tafarodi, R. W., & Smith, A. J. (2001). Individualism–collectivism and depressive sensitivity to life events: The case of Malaysian sojourners. *International Journal of Intercultural Relations, 25*(1), 73–88. https://doi.org/10.1016/s0147-1767(00)00043-2

Tang, J., Li, G., Chen, B., Huang, Z., Zhang, Y., Chang, H.,Wu, C., Ma, X., Wang, J., & Yu, Y. (2018). Prevalence of and risk factors for non-suicidal self-injury in rural China: Results from a nationwide survey in China. *Journal of Affective Disorders, 226*, 188–195. 195. https://doi.org/10.1016/j.jad.2017.09.051

Tang, J., Yu, Y., Wu, Y., Du, Y., Ma, Y., Zhu, H., & Liu, Z. (2011). Association between non-suicidal self-injuries and suicide attempts in Chinese adolescents and college students: A cross-section study. *PLoS One, 6*(4), Article e17977. https://doi.org/10.1371/journal.pone.0017977

Taylor, G. J., Ryan, D., and Bagby, R.M. (1985). Toward the development of a new self-report alexithymia scale. *Psychotherapy and Psychosomatics, 44*, 191–199.

Taylor, P. J., Jomar, K., Dhingra, K., Forrester, R., Shahmalak, U., & Dickson, J. M. (2018). A meta-analysis of the prevalence of different functions of non-suicidal self-injury. *Journal of Affective Disorders, 227*, 759–769. https://doi.org/10.1016/j.jad.2017.11.073

Thalmayer, A. G., Toscanelli, C., & Arnett, J. J. (2021). The neglected 95% revisited: Is American psychology becoming less American? *American Psychologist, 76*, 116–129. https://doi.org/10.1037/amp0000622

Tingey, L., Cwik, M., Goklish, N., Alchesay, M., Lee, A., Strom, R., Walkup, J., & Barlow, A. (2012). Exploring binge drinking and drug use among American Indians: Data from adolescent focus groups. *The American Journal of Drug and Alcohol Abuse, 38*(5), 409–415. https://doi.org/10.3109/00952990.2012.705204

Toombs, E., Kowatch, K. R., Dalicandro, L., McConkey, S., Hopkins, C., & Mushquash, C. J. (2020). A systematic review of electronic mental health interventions for Indigenous youth: Results and recommendations. *Journal of Telemedicine and Telecare, 27*(9), 539–552. https://doi.org/10.1177/1357633x19899231

Van Orden, K. A., Witte, T. K., Cukrowicz, K. C., Braithwaite, S. R., Selby, E. A., & Joiner Jr, T. E. (2010). The interpersonal theory of suicide. *Psychological Review, 117*(2), 575–600. https://doi.org/10.1037/a0018697

Verroken, S., Schotte, C., Derluyn, I., & Baetens, I. (2018). Starting from scratch: Prevalence, methods, and functions of non-suicidal self-injury among refugee minors in Belgium. *Child and Adolescent Psychiatry and Mental Health, 12*(1), 1–12. https://doi.org/10.1186/s13034-018-0260-1

Walker, K.L., Hirsch, J.K., Chang, E.C. et al. (2017). Non-suicidal self-injury and suicidal behavior in a diverse sample: The moderating role of social problem-solving ability. *International Journal of Mental Health and Addiction, 15*, 471–484. https://doi.org/10.1007/s11469-017-9755-x

Wester, K. L., & Trepal, H. C. (2015). Nonsuicidal self-injury: Exploring the connection among race, ethnic identity, and ethnic belonging. *Journal of College Student Development, 56*, 127–139. https://doi.org/10.1353/csd.2015.0013

Williams, K. A., Lee, E. J., Shahour, G., & Kanan, S. (2018). Perspectives of non-suicidal self-injury behaviors in ten South Korean young adults. *Journal of Cultural Diversity, 25*(3), 101–109.

Wilson, M. S., Robinson, K., Brocklesby, M., Kingi, T., Garisch, J. A., Langlands, R., Russell, L., O'Connell, A., & Fraser, G. (2016, June). *Results of a longitudinal study of the development, maintenance and cessation of self-injury among a large sample of community adolescents.* 11th Annual Conference of the International Society for the Study of Self-injury, Wisconsin.

Wolff, J. C., Thompson, E., Thomas, S. A., Nesi, J., Bettis, A. H., Ransford, B., Scopelliti, K., Frazier, E. A., & Liu, R. T. (2019). Emotion dysregulation and non-suicidal self-injury: A systematic review and meta-analysis. *European Psychiatry, 59*, 25–36. https://doi.org/10.1016/j.eurpsy.2019.03.004

Wong, S. L., & Chung, M. C. (2021). The subjective experience of non-suicidal self-injury among female Chinese university students. *Nordic Journal of Psychiatry, 76*(1), 18–28. https://doi.org/10.1080/08039488.2021.1929461

Yates, T. M., Tracy, A. J., & Luthar, S. S. (2008). Nonsuicidal self-injury among "privileged" youths: Longitudinal and cross-sectional approaches to developmental process. *Journal of Consulting and Clinical Psychology, 76*(1), 52–62. https://doi.org/10.1037/0022-006x.76.1.52

You, J., Leung, F., & Fu, K. (2012). Exploring the reciprocal relations between nonsuicidal self-injury, negative emotions and relationship problems in Chinese adolescents: A longitudinal cross-lag study. *Journal of Abnormal Child Psychology, 40*(5), 829–836. https://doi.org/10.1007/s10802-011-9597-0

You, J., Lin, M. P., & Leung, F. (2013). Functions of nonsuicidal self-injury among Chinese community adolescents. *Journal of Adolescence, 36*(4), 737–745. https://doi.org/10.1016/j.adolescence.2013.05.007

You, J., Ren, Y., Zhang, X., Wu, Z., Xu, S., & Lin, M. P. (2018). Emotional dysregulation and nonsuicidal self-injury: A meta-analytic review. *Neuropsychiatry, 8*, 733–748. https://doi.org/10.4172/neuropsychiatry.1000399

Young, R., Sproeber, N., Groschwitz, R. C., Preiss, M., & Plener, P. L. (2014). Why alternative teenagers self-harm: Exploring the link between non-suicidal self-injury, attempted suicide and adolescent identity. *BMC Psychiatry, 14*(1), 1–14. https://doi.org/10.1186/1471-244x-14-137

Zhang, F., Cloutier, P. F., Yang, H., Liu, W., Cheng, W., & Xiao, Z. (2019). Non-suicidal self-injury in Shanghai inner bound middle school students. *General Psychiatry, 32*(4), e100083. https://doi.org/10.1136/gpsych-2019-100083

Zoroglu, S. S., Tuzun, U., Sar, V., Tutkun, H., Savaçs, H. A., Ozturk, M., & Kora, M. E. (2003). Suicide attempt and self-mutilation among Turkish high school students in relation with abuse, neglect and dissociation. *Psychiatry and Clinical Neurosciences, 57*(1), 119–126. https://doi.org/10.1046/j.1440-1819.2003.01088.x

CHAPTER 11

Stairway to Heaven: NSSI as an Addiction

Hilario Blasco-Fontecilla

> **Abstract**
>
> This chapter describes a model for nonsuicidal self-injury (NSSI) as an addictive behavior, and its implications. The framing of self-injury as an "addiction" is controversial. Some authors argue that the repetition of NSSI is better explained by emotional processes rather than by addictive mechanisms. These authors stress the works that argued that whereas both positive and negative reinforcement sustain substance use, NSSI is only perpetuated thanks to negative reinforcement. However, some authors do not fully agree with the assumption that self-harm is not inherently pleasurable for some patients. Many describe it as such, and indeed, self-harm serves homeostatic functions as well as sensation-seeking functions. In any case, emotional dysregulation appears to characterize those patients who display NSSI with addictive characteristics. The chapter then considers the pathophysiology of NSSI before looking at the increasing number of solid empirical studies demonstrating the addictive properties of NSSI. A clear consequence of considering repetitive NSSI as an addiction is that treatments traditionally used in drug addictions may also be implemented in this field. A recent systematic review focused on the treatment of NSSI concluded that both brief psychotherapies and pharmacological interventions can be effective for treating NSSI.
>
> **Key Words:** nonsuicidal self-injury, addiction, self-harm, emotional dysregulation, addictive behavior, psychotherapies, pharmacological interventions, NSSI treatment

Introduction

Nonsuicidal self-injury (NSSI) is "the deliberate destruction of one's own body tissue in the absence of suicidal intent" (Franklin et al., 2012). NSSI is frequent, with a prevalence ranging from 6% to 20% in adolescents and young adults worldwide (Beauchaine et al., 2019; Csorba et al., 2009; Muehlenkamp et al., 2012; see Staring, Kiekens, & Kirtley, this volume, for an overview of NSSI epidemiology). NSSI is more common in females between 16 and 19 years of age, but there are no relevant gender differences at either younger or older ages (Wilkinson et al., 2022). NSSI characteristically begins between 12 and 17 years (Martin et al., 2013). However, some female adolescents initiate NSSI before age 10 (Beauchaine et al., 2019). In addition, although it is a controversial topic, there is a growing literature on understanding NSSI as addictive behavior (Nixon et al., 2002).

NSSI has usually been associated with four functions: internal self-regulation, external self-regulation, social influence, and sensation seeking (Martin et al., 2013; see Taylor et al., this volume). In a confirmatory factor analysis of the Ottawa Self-Injury Inventory (OSI) using a sample of 316 young university students ages between 17 and 25 (84.8% female) who had a history of lifetime NSSI, the authors reported that NSSI severity was associated with internal and external self-regulation, whereas NSSI addictive features were related to (a) more frequent lifetime NSSI, (b) recent (past six months) NSSI; and (c) greater distress regarding NSSI urges (Guérin-Marion et al., 2018).

Relationship to Addiction

Behavioral addictions such as gambling, shopping, video games, suntanning, work, exercise, or even sex (Cassin & von Ranson, 2007; Favazza, 1989; Goodman, 1992; Kourosh et al., 2010; Reynaud et al., 2010; Sanchez-Carbonell et al., 2008; Tantam & Whittaker, 1992; Tao et al., 2010) are frequent, and share common neurobiological underpinnings with substance addictions (i.e., tolerance, withdrawal, and relapse) (Grant et al., 2006). Recent literature suggests that NSSI could also be understood as an addiction in some individuals (Blasco-Fontecilla, 2012; Blasco-Fontecilla et al., 2014; Blasco-Fontecilla et al., 2015; Nixon et al., 2002; Victor et al., 2012).

This is relevant because it could represent a Copernican turning point in the therapeutic approach. Thus, individuals "addicted" to NSSI may benefit from treatments traditionally used for other addictions instead of focusing on the symptom itself. The objective of this chapter is to describe a model for NSSI as an addictive behavior and its implications.

The Framing of Self-injury as an "Addiction"

The framing of self-injury as an "addiction" is controversial (Victor et al., 2012; Whitlock et al., 2006). Regarding the proxy concept of suicidal behavior (SB), Ken Tullis (1998) proposed a theory of suicide addiction. In order to test this compelling hypothesis, we proposed that some suicide attempters (major repeaters, individuals with ≥ 5 lifetime suicide attempts) were the patients addicted to SB (Blasco-Fontecilla, 2012). Later on, we empirically tested our hypothesis in a series of different studies (Blasco-Fontecilla et al., 2020; Blasco-Fontecilla et al., 2014).

Tullis (1998) suggested that individuals addicted to SB would be characterized by the presence of (a) childhood trauma, (b) mood disorders, and (c) multiple addictions. He based his theory on a sample of 50 patients from his own private practice. The clinical profile of these patients can be summarized as follows: (a) all patients had a history of physical, emotional, and/or sexual abuse in childhood or early adolescence; (b) all patients had an affective disorder; and (c) most patients had both drug and behavioral addictions. Within the behavioral addictions, sex addiction stood out in both genders. He also reported that these patients exhibited all seven addiction criteria. Furthermore, he paralleled sex and suicide addiction in the sense that both addictions include elements of three basic addictions: arousal, satiation, and fantasy addictions. Finally, he suggested that people addicted to suicide may display elevated blood biomarkers such as endogenous opioids, adrenaline, phenylethylamine, and oxytocin, while recognizing that the exact neurochemistry of suicide addiction remained a mystery, placing early childhood trauma at the very core of suicide addiction. Whether or not this framing of suicidal addiction can be used for NSSI is a matter of debate.

The factors pointed out by Tullis, basically the history of maltreatment in childhood and early adolescence, and the presence of affective and particularly addictive psychopathology, borderline personality disorder (BPD), and a poor self-regulation refer precisely to risk factors for NSSI yet described (Glenn & Klonsky, 2013; Gromatsky et al., 2017).

Up to 80% of individuals with a history of NSSI report a history of childhood trauma (Gratz et al., 2002) (see Serafini et al., this volume). Using data of 9,526 adult twins from two cohorts of the Australian Twin Registry, the authors concluded that there are common genetic contributions to NSSI and high-risk traumatic experiences, but also that past trauma exposure may confer some direct risk for NSSI among females (Richmond-Rakerd et al., 2019). Furthermore, in a study including 957 undergraduate students, perceived parent-child relational trauma was linked with NSSI, whereas perceived paternal maltreatment was related with NSSI's addictive features (Martin et al., 2016).

But not just trauma. Both parenting styles and parental psychopathology are also associated with NSSI (see James & Gibb, this volume, for a review of parent-child dynamics in NSSI). For instance, parental substance use disorder, attention deficit/hyperactivity disorder (ADHD) symptoms, self-criticism, and lower conscientiousness and agreeableness were related to offspring's NSSI (Gromatsky et al., 2017). Negative parenting styles (mother and father's rejection, low level of mother and father's emotional warmth, and high level of mother's overprotection) is also associated with NSSI, repeated NSSI, and severe NSSI (Y. Liu, Xiaio, et al., 2020).

Regarding psychopathology, sporadic NSSI (one episode per year), but particularly recurrent NSSI (two or more NSSI episodes per year), is a potent marker for increased risk of mental illness between the ages of 14 and 17 (Wilkinson et al., 2018). Thus, repetitive NSSI has traditionally been linked with BPD. Not surprisingly, in a study of BPD patients, the authors found that having no meaning in life predicted the frequency and severity of NSSI (Marco et al., 2015). However, NSSI usually precedes the development and diagnosis of BPD. The authors of a recent study comparing 69 11–13-year-old adolescents with a history of NSSI with 61 matched controls who were reassessed between 18 and 20 years old reported that the risk factors for NSSI continuation over time were greater BPD symptomatology and psychosocial impairment. Both were mediated by emotion dysregulation (Biskin et al., 2021). In another study, repetitive NSSI was associated with disadvantageous decision-making and increased behavioral compulsivity, but not with behavioral impulsivity (Lutz et al., 2021).

NSSI has also been associated with major depressive disorder (MDD) (Glenn & Klonsky, 2013), ADHD (Balázs et al., 2018), or even autism (Moseley et al., 2019). But NSSI is particularly comorbid with addictions and, particularly, internet addiction (IA) (Y. Liu, Xiaio, et al., 2020; Steinbüchel et al., 2018; Tang et al., 2020). Thus, in a sample of 555 Turkish students, NSSI was correlated with having "toxic" friends, and addictions such as high internet usage, smoking, and substance use (Çimen et al., 2017). Furthermore, a recent study suggests that the relationship between IA and NSSI is mediated by psychopathology (Mészáros et al., 2020). Finally, in a case-control study comparing 220 women with eating disorders (ED) with 121 healthy controls (HC), women presenting food addiction (FA) showed a high prevalence of lifetime NSSI in both groups. Moreover, FA and difficulties in emotion regulation predicted the presence of lifetime NSSI. Accordingly, these authors concluded that ED, FA, and NSSI appear to share a common etiology partly explained by emotion regulation deficits (Carlson et al., 2018).

In this context, some authors argue that the repetition of NSSI is better explained by emotional processes rather than by addictive mechanisms (Victor et al., 2012). These authors stress the works by Nixon et al. who argued that, whereas both positive and negative reinforcement sustain substance use, NSSI is only perpetuated thanks to negative reinforcement (Nixon et al., 2002). Victor et al. (2012) studied craving in a sample of 58 adolescents and stated that NSSI was not positively reinforcing. They thought that a behavior that was not inherently pleasurable was unlikely "to be craved and/or be utilized in contexts other than aversive affect." In contrast, we have reported that major repetition of SB is associated with both negative and positive reinforcement, in a similar way to substance dependence. Furthermore, some authors do not fully agree with the assumption that self-harm is not inherently pleasurable for some patients, as many patients do describe it as pleasurable. Indeed, as we will see below, self-harm serves not only homeostatic functions but also sensation-seeking functions (Martin et al., 2013).

Addictive Model of Self-harm (Including NSSI and SSI)

Indeed, we proposed a common addictive model of self-harming (nonsuicidal and suicidal) behavior (Blasco-Fontecilla et al., 2016). We think that the addiction to self-harm (either NSSI or SB) can be explained either by psychological or neurobiological mechanisms (see below). For instance, Faye (1995) suggested the emotional state preceding NSSI is similar to the withdrawal symptoms of drug addicts. She also stressed that self-injurers and drug users share similar histories of childhood abuse. Furthermore, individuals displaying NSSI often have strong urges to self-injure (Washburn et al., 2010). As such, the author of this chapter argues that NSSI can better be explained as a process characterized by addictive features such as compulsion, increasing tolerance, and loss of control (Blasco-Fontecilla et al., 2016; Buser & Buser, 2013).

In a study using thematic analysis to explore why individuals might use addiction references to describe their NSSI behaviors, the authors examined 71 posts from a popular NSSI social media. They found that four topics emerged: difficulty in stopping, authentication, warning others, and communication (Pritchard et al., 2021). Indeed, adolescents and young adults who present with NSSI frequently make references to the addictive component of these behaviors. Thus, NSSI can be used as a signaling strategy within the "bargaining model" of depression, and used as a way of imposing costs on the group in the event of a conflict (Hagen, 2003). This is relevant because adolescents and young adults who engage in NSSI often participate in social media regarding their self-injury (Pritchard et al., 2021). As a matter of fact, most NSSI websites depict NSSI as an effective coping mechanism (91.55%), and addictive (Lewis & Baker, 2011).

Finally, NSSI may be considered a compulsive, addictive behavior, rather than an impulsive one, and engaged in in order to reduce suicidal risk (Miller et al., 2021). Thus, the NSSI could be considered a dam of containment, as the last barrier that protects some adolescents from crossing the barrier into suicidal behaviors.

Emotional Dysregulation

In any case, emotional dysregulation appears to characterize those patients who will display NSSI with addictive characteristics (Guérin-Marion et al., 2021; Guérin-Marion et al., 2018; Nixon et al., 2002). Here, I would like to stress that in one of our recent studies, emotional maltreatment and neglect were, by far, the most relevant maltreatments for major repeaters (Blasco-Fontecilla et al., 2020). Thus, it is possible that emotional dysregulation displayed by NSSI patients may simply be reflecting the emotional abuse and neglect they suffered in childhood.

Addictive Mechanisms

The pathophysiology of NSSI is controversial (Bunderla & Kumperščak, 2015). The addiction to NSSI can be explained by either psychological or neurobiological mechanisms.

Psychological Mechanisms

As stated before, NSSI serves different functions, but mainly to deal with psychological pain and to regulate emotions (homeostasis) (Franklin et al., 2012; Stanley et al., 2001). Some authors have tried to explain why self-harm, which is painful and should be aversive, instead becomes reinforcing in some people (Osuch et al., 2014). Many NSSI individuals have lower pain sensitivity, and subsequently no aversion to pain, thus reporting little or no pain at all (Glenn et al., 2014). A recent systematic review confirmed that people with a history of NSSI have a higher pain threshold and tolerance (Kirtley et al., 2016). Recent neuroimaging studies also demonstrated abnormal pain-and/or reward-processing neurocircuits in people with NSSI patients (Osuch et al., 2014). This altered pain perception has been related to "emotional dysregulation, self-criticism, neuroticism and painful and provocative experiences" (Bunderla & Kumperščak, 2015).

Some authors have suggested that self-injury is craved due to negative reinforcement (reduction of aversive emotions such as psychological pain) rather than by positive reinforcement (Victor et al., 2012). In other words, negative reinforcement perpetuates NSSI, thus contributing to NSSI addiction. This negative reinforcement is frequently described as a cathartic feeling of calm after a previous unpleasant, overwhelming feeling (i.e., psychological or emotional pain). This catharsis can be explained by the emotional venting of an unbearable emotional or physical state (Jallade et al., 2005; van Praag & Plutchik, 1985), but also by the mobilization of interpersonal support (i.e., medical attention and caring family) (Jallade et al., 2005; Walker et al., 2001).

Another theory that may explain the addictive nature of NSSI is the pain offset relief mechanism (Franklin et al., 2013). The pain offset relief might be one of the primary mechanisms of emotional regulation in NSSI. Given the overlap between physical and emotional pain, and considering that physical pain is more easily controlled than emotional pain, many patients may use physical pain to control emotional pain. Indeed, pain offset simultaneously diminishes negative affect and stimulates positive affect and thus may explain "why people engage in both normal and abnormal behaviors associated with relief" (Franklin et al., 2013, p. 521).

Thus, NSSI can be used as a way of self-regulating negative emotions in the short term (Esposito et al., 2003). The question is whether or not, in the long term, NSSI maintains this cathartic effect or, on the contrary, increases negative affectivity and becomes another stressor (see, e.g., Linehan, 1993). Indeed, NSSI predicted concurrent and later SB in a study with more than 1,000 U.S. college students (Whitlock et al., 2013). The authors also reported that the transition between NSSI and SB was buffered by presence of meaning in life and reporting parents as confidants. They concluded that NSSI might serve as a "gateway" for concurrent or later SB and more serious SB, thus stressing the need for early NSSI intervention. Other authors have reported that NSSI is associated with increased odds of subsequent SB controlling for mental disorders (Kiekens et al., 2018).

When self-injury no longer serves as a means for the subject to self-regulate, suicide attempts may replace self-mutilation to regulate negative emotions, at least in multiple-suicide attempters (Esposito et al., 2003; see Victor et al., this volume, for review of the relationship between NSSI and suicide). In keeping with this, we found that, compared to non-major repeaters ($n = 71$), major repeaters ($n = 11$, 13%) more frequently endorsed automatic positive reinforcement ("To feel something, because you felt numb or empty") to explain their repetitive SB. Automatic positive reinforcement (relieving emptiness) was the factor most closely related to the category of major repeaters, even more relevant than BPD diagnosis (Blasco-Fontecilla et al., 2014). In other words, in contrast with the findings suggesting that NSSI is perpetuated mainly through negative reinforcement (Victor et al., 2012), our study suggested that major repetition of suicide attempts was perpetuated primarily through positive reinforcement. Thus, it is possible that, some major repeaters initially use NSSI as a way of emotional regulation or communication, and when repetitive NSSI is no longer useful, they take the step to suicide attempts. In keeping with this suggestion, Kiekens et al. (2018) reported that several NSSI characteristics (e.g., earlier-onset NSSI and automatic positive reinforcement) were associated with increased risk of transitioning to SB.

In addition to automatic positive reinforcement, another mechanism that may help to understand the development of an addiction to NSSI is the "sensitizing" hypothesis. In 1996, Beck suggested that, as self-harming episodes become more easily triggered by stressful life events, they become more persistent and severe. In other words, repetitive self-harm can become more autonomous and easily precipitated (Beck, 1996). Beck's "sensitizing" hypothesis of SB has gained some empirical support (Bradvik & Berglund, 2011; Joiner & Rudd, 2000). Furthermore, even after prolonged "free" periods, there is the risk of relapse, often precipitated by similar life events, in a similar way to that of drug addiction (Hyman, 2005).

Neurobiological Mechanisms

The search for the biological mechanisms underlying the addiction to NSSI is relevant because it allows the search for pharmacological treatments that hinder its development (see Plener, this volume, for a review of current work in this area). As previously mentioned, one of the main functions of the NSSI is to gain control over emotions that are painful. That is, to control psychological suffering. Since physical and mental pain share the same brain circuits, it is logical to think that the opioid system will be involved in the regulation of psychological pain. If humans are vulnerable to addiction to exogenous opioids such as morphine or heroin, why should we not be vulnerable to addiction to endogenous opioids?

Pain perception is regulated by the pain-relieving endogenous opioid system (Akil et al., 1984). If we accept that NSSI can become an addiction in some individuals, it is reasonable to think that individuals addicted to NSSI will have a compromised functioning of the brain's motivational systems, including (a) the endogenous opioid system, (b) the mesocortical dopamine reward system (Grigson, 2002; Volkow & Wise, 2005; Wise & Koob, 2014), and (c) the hypothalamic-pituitary-adrenal axis (HPA Axis) (stress) (Lovallo, 2006; Wise & Koob, 2014). These three systems interact in the forebrain and are closely related (Lovallo, 2006; Traskman-Bendz et al., 1992; Volkow & Wise, 2005). This is not surprising, given that adrenocorticotropic hormone (ACTH) and β-endorphin (BE) are derived from the pro-opiomelanocortin (POMC) (Dent et al., 1986; Oquendo et al., 2014). Furthermore, there is substantial literature on this issue. For instance, chronic stress in mice produces opioid dependence (Christie & Chesher, 1982), and repetitive mutilation behaviors increase met-enkephalins (Coid et al., 1983).

Regarding the role of the endogenous opioid system, some authors have reported that people engaging in NSSI have lower resting levels of BE (opioid deficiency theories) (Bresin & Gordon, 2013; Stanley et al., 2010), but evidence contradicting this hypothesis is also reported (see Victor et al., 2012, for a review). Regardless of the reasons for the NSSI, it is likely that NSSI results in releases of BE (Bresin & Gordon, 2013), which can produce euphoric and analgesic effects (Sandman et al., 2008). This opioid release may ultimately produce an addiction to NSSI in vulnerable people (Blasco-Fontecilla, 2012).

Within the opioid system, endogenous BE is the best-studied candidate biomarker. BE is a μ-and δ-receptor agonist, which modulates pain perception through central and peripheral nervous BE release alike (Benarroch, 2012). In a recent study comparing 94 female patients with NSSI and 35 healthy controls, the authors reported lower fasting BE levels in patients compared to the healthy controls. These authors did not find a relationship either between BE levels and pain sensitivity or between the number of NSSI in the past 12 months and BE levels (van der Venne et al., 2021). Unfortunately, there is virtually no literature addressing the relationship between BE levels and repetitive NSSI. In the closely related concept of major repeaters, we found that the level of fasting serum BE increased with a higher number of criteria met for the addiction to SB (Blasco-Fontecilla et al., 2020).

Regarding the HPA axis, both acute and chronic stress are associated with substance use disorders (Volkow & Wise, 2005). The corticotropin-releasing factor (CRF) is involved in vulnerability to drug withdrawal (Kreek & Koob, 1998) and relapse (Sarnyai et al., 2001), and gene polymorphisms of the CRF receptor have been related to exacerbated stress responses and/or the vulnerability to develop drug addiction (Logrip et al., 2011). In a study exploring the intersection between childhood trauma, HPA axis, and NSSI, the authors reported that adolescents engaging in NSSI had significantly higher cortisol awakening responses compared to HCs. Interestingly, in the presence of childhood adversities, HCs showed flattened diurnal cortisol slopes, while NSSI adolescents exhibited significantly steeper ones (Reichl et al., 2016). Furthermore, patients engaging in repetitive NSSI, which could point to NSSI addiction, are more likely to display lower levels of blood ACTH (Sandman et al., 2008) and cortisol (Klimes-Dougan et al., 2019).

Regarding the potential role of dopamine in the development of an NSSI addiction, there is virtually no research, with the remarkable exception of the study by Barbara Stanley and colleagues comparing 14 suicide attempters with a history of repetitive NSSI with 15 suicide attempters without a history of NSSI (Stanley et al., 2010). They reported that there were no statistically significant differences in the cerebrospinal fluid (CSF) dopamine metabolite, and homovanillic acid (HVA) between both groups. Most research on the dopaminergic system are basic studies based on Lesch-Nyhan, a genetic disease characterized by dopamine deficiency and aggression and self-injurious behavior, among others (Breese et al., 1990).

Finally, preliminary studies have addressed the role of the endocannabinoid system on SB, but little research has explored the association between cannabis use and lifetime NSSI (Few et al., 2016). Few et al. (2016) examined the odds of NSSI associated with early cannabis use (< 17 years of age) in the Australian Twin Registry (N = 9,583). They found an increased risk for NSSI in monozygotic (MZ) twin pairs who had early cannabis use (OR = 3.20, 95% CI [1.17, 8.73]), suggesting that person-specific factors contributing to the relationship between early cannabis use and NSSI exist. Interestingly, the co-occurrence of alcohol and cannabis use increased 30 times the odds of engaging in NSSI in a sample 71 adolescents hospitalized for suicide risk (Sellers et al., 2021). Regarding the association between the endocannabinoid system and repetitive NSSI, a study comparing patients with eating disorders with repetitive NSSI with HCs found that the first group had lower levels of CB1 receptor mRNA in peripheral blood samples (Schroeder et al., 2012).

Evidence for NSSI as an Addictive Behavior

Even if most evidence comes from either case reports or anecdotal evidence, there is an increasing number of solid empirical studies demonstrating the addictive properties of NSSI (Martin et al., 2013). In a study of 42 adolescents endorsing NSSI, the authors tested if adolescents displaying repetitive NSSI were addicted to NSSI (Nixon et al., 2002). They reported that 97.6% and 80.1% of adolescents endorsed three and five criteria, respectively, of a self-report measure of NSSI addiction adapted from the criteria for substance dependence according to the fourth edition of *Diagnostic and Statistical Manual of Mental Disorders* (DSM-IV; American Psychiatric Association, 1994). In a study following a similar strategy, we explored if major repeaters (individuals with ≥ 5 lifetime suicide attempts) were addicted to SB using seven criteria, modified from the DSM-IV criteria for substance dependence: (a) tolerance, (b) withdrawal, (c) loss of control, (d) problems in quitting/cutting down, (e) much time spent using, (e) substantial reduction in activities, and (f) adverse physiological/physical consequences (Blasco-Fontecilla et al., 2014). In total, 83% of major repeaters met criteria for an addiction to SB, which is pretty similar to the 81% of adolescents displaying an addiction to NSSI (Nixon et al., 2002). Furthermore, our study suggested that the addiction to SB was not mediated by the diagnosis of BPD (Blasco-Fontecilla et al., 2014). More recently, we brought some support to the addictive hypothesis of SB by reporting that addicts to SB (patients with ≥ 6 of a modified DSM-IV criteria for substance dependence) displayed higher serum β-endorphin concentrations than nonaddicts to SB (Blasco-Fontecilla et al., 2020). Furthermore, we were fairly capable of correctly classifying suicide attempters addicted to SB just by using blood β-endorphin levels and the S-PLE values, a brief six-item scale (ROC analysis evaluating offered an area under the curve (AUC) of .782.

In another study, the development of NSSI addiction was related to more frequent NSSI, feelings of relief following NSSI behavior, and harming themselves after thinking about it (Martin et al., 2013). In other words, patients who engaged frequently in NSSI after thinking about doing so and then feeling some relief were the patients who developed addictive characteristics, which is clinically coherent. As we have explained elsewhere, it is possible for some patients to transition from NSSI to SB when NSSI is no longer giving them enough relief.

Implications of NSSI Addiction

The addictive model of self-harming may have an important impact on the way we treat repetitive NSSI. A recent systematic review focused on the treatment of NSSI concluded that both brief psychotherapies and pharmacological interventions can be effective for treating NSSI (Turner et al., 2014). Regarding psychotherapies, they appear to be efficient if they are structured, focused on collaborative therapeutic relationships and motivation for change, and directly addressing NSSI behaviors. Drugs targeting the dopaminergic (i.e., atypical antipsychotics), serotonergic (i.e., selective serotonin reuptake inhibitors, or SSRIs), and opioid systems (i.e., naltrexone) also demonstrated some benefits, in keeping with the neurobiological systems altered in NSSI.

A clear consequence of considering repetitive NSSI as an addiction is that treatments traditionally used in drug addictions may also be implemented in this field. Regarding psychotherapies, aberrant and maladaptive emotional memories can lead to addictions (J. Liu, Lu, & Mueller, 2020). Thus, one strategy has been to focus on extinction, a type of inhibitory learning that suppresses a previously conditioned response. Enhancing the consolidation of extinction learning is one strategy that may be used to reduce motivating either drug-seeking or drug-taking behavior (Torregrossa & Taylor, 2013), and it may also be useful in behavioral addictions. Furthermore, a recent systematic review on the effectiveness of specific psychotherapeutic interventions (SPI) devoted to the reduction of NSSI, the authors concluded that six SPI were found to significantly reduce NSSI in adolescents: intensive contextual treatment (ICT), developmental group psychotherapy (DGP), therapeutic assessment (TA), emotional regulation individual therapy for adolescents (ERITA), particularly, treatment for self-injurious behaviors (T-SIB), and cutting down program (CDP) (Calvo et al., 2022). However, brief dialectical behavior therapy (DBT) may also be particularly useful, as DBT has proven to be an effective psychotherapy to diminish the frequency of NSSI (Krantz et al., 2018; McMain et al., 2017). Another strategy that can pay off is to focus on comorbidities, particularly, the relationship between IA and NSSI. A recent study concluded that offline social support was negatively associated with both IA and NSSI, whereas online social support was positively associated with both IA and NSSI (S. Liu et al., 2021). In other words, real, meaningful relationships appear to be helpful, whereas the role of social media relationships appear negative for NSSI.

As for medications, the most evident targets to halt the development of an NSSI addiction are the HPA axis, and opioid systems (Kreek & Koob, 1998). In 1989, some advocated for clinical trials using opiate antagonists to treat NSSI (Konicki & Schulz, 1989). Recently, some authors suggested that both naltrexone and buprenorphine have displayed promising results (Serafini et al., 2018; Turner et al., 2014). CRF receptor antagonists, particularly CRF1 antagonists (i.e., antalarmin) have shown promising results for treating addictions (Logrip et al., 2011), but evidence is lacking regarding its use in NSSI. As for the dopaminergic system, most studies are either many animal models for self-injurious behavior (Visser et al., 2000) or the yet commented on human model focused on the Lesch-Nyhan diseases. Interestingly, calcium blockers (i.e., nifedipine) suppress self-injurious behavior in animal models (Blake et al., 2007), which is probably due to the coupling between L-type calcium channels and striatal dopamine receptors.

But probably the most interesting development of the last few years is the use of N-acetylcysteine (NAC). There have been some suggestions about the potential use of drugs acting on the glutamatergic pathway (i.e., gabapentin, lamotrigine, topiramate, acamprosate, D-cycloserine, modafinil, memantine, and NAC) for treating drug and behavioral addictions (Olive et al., 2012). A recent open-label, single-arm study design, tested the use of high doses of NAC in 35 female adolescents and young adults with NSSI (Cullen et al., 2018). NAC use was related to a significant decrease in NSSI frequency, depression scores, but not impulsivity scores, thus providing preliminary evidence about NAC as a potential treatment option for patients with NSSI.

Conclusion

NSSI is not easily changed. Around 50% of individuals engaging in NSSI will have very frequent, repetitive NSSI (Madjar et al., 2017). Whether or not this repetitive pattern of NSSI is an addiction is still open to debate. But this may be just a semantic debate, and both proposals—that repetitive NSSI behaviors are better explained either under an addictive umbrella or simply as a way to regulate emotions—are correct and complementary. In any case, some data that point toward NSSI addiction are engaging with repetitive NSSI, having increased stress associated with NSSI urges and/or feelings of relief following NSSI behavior, or displaying emotional dysregulation. Some other factors associated with NSSI addictive characteristics are lower levels of blood ACTH *and* CB1 receptor of the data that may point toward the use of CRF and/or opiate antagonists to treat NSSI. All these data point to potential therapeutic avenues at both the psychotherapeutic and pharmacological levels.

In any case, even if NSSI can be found in individuals with no apparent psychopathology, who may see NSSI either as a normal way to deal with emotional discomfort or just for sensation seeking, this is not the case for most individuals who engage in NSSI. For most patients, NSSI is the last barrier before crossing into SB. Thus, the relevance of NSSI should not be trivialized. Likewise, the gaps in knowledge about potential biomarkers of potential NSSI addiction or the efficacy of psychotherapeutic or pharmacological approaches is overwhelming.

Conflicts of Interest

In the last three years, Dr. Blasco-Fontecilla has received lecture fees from AB-Biotics, Janssen, and Shire. He is member of the board of directors at Korian. He is currently participating in the ESKETINSUI2002 clinical trial.

References

Akil, H., Watson, S. J., Young, E., Lewis, M. E., Khachaturian, H., & Walker, J. M. (1984). Endogenous opioids: Biology and function. *Annual Review of Neuroscience*, 7, 223–255. https://doi.org/10.1146/annurev.ne.07.030184.001255

American Psychiatric Association. (1994). *Diagnostic and statistical manual of mental disorders* (4th ed.; DSM-IV).

Balázs, J., Győri, D., Horváth, L. O., Mészáros, G., & Szentiványi, D. (2018). Attention-deficit hyperactivity disorder and nonsuicidal self-injury in a clinical sample of adolescents: The role of comorbidities and gender. *BMC Psychiatry*, 18(1), 34. https://doi.org/10.1186/s12888-018-1620-3

Beauchaine, T. P., Hinshaw, S. P., & Bridge, J. A. (2019). Nonsuicidal self-injury and suicidal behaviors in girls: The case for targeted prevention in preadolescence. *Clinical Psychological Science*, 7(4), 643–667. https://doi.org/10.1177/2167702618818474

Beck, A. T. (1996). Beyond belief: A theory of modes, personality, and psychopathology. In P. M. Salkovskis (Ed.), *Frontiers of cognitive therapy* (pp. 1–25). Guilford Press.

Benarroch, E. E. (2012). Endogenous opioid systems: Current concepts and clinical correlations. *Neurology*, 79(8), 807–814. https://doi.org/10.1212/WNL.0b013e3182662098

Biskin, R. S., Paris, J., Zelkowitz, P., Mills, D., Laporte, L., & Heath, N. (2021). Nonsuicidal self-injury in early adolescence as a predictor of borderline personality disorder in early adulthood. *Journal of Personality Disorders*, 35(5), 764–775. https://doi.org/10.1521/pedi.2021.35.5.764

Blake, B. L., Muehlmann, A. M., Egami, K., Breese, G. R., Devine, D. P., & Jinnah, H. A. (2007). Nifedipine suppresses self-injurious behaviors in animals. *Developmental Neuroscience*, 29(3), 241–250. https://doi.org/10.1159/000096414

Blasco-Fontecilla, H. (2012). The addictive hypothesis of suicidal behavior. *Medical Hypotheses*, 78(2), 350. https://doi.org/10.1016/j.mehy.2011.11.005

Blasco-Fontecilla, H., Artieda-Urrutia, P., Berenguer-Elias, N., Garcia-Vega, J.M., Fernández-Rodriguez, M., Rodriguez-Lomas, C., González-Villalobos, I., Iruela-Cuadrado, L., & de Leon, J. (2014). Are major repeater patients addicted to suicidal behavior? *Adicciones*, 26(4), 321–333. https://doi.org/10.20882/adicciones.38

Blasco-Fontecilla, H., Baca-García, E., Courtet, P., García Nieto, R., & de Leon, J. (2015). Horror vacui: Emptiness might distinguish between major suicide repeaters and nonmajor suicide repeaters: A pilot study. *Psychotherapy and Psychosomatics*, 84(2), 117–119. https://doi.org/10.1159/000369937

Blasco-Fontecilla, H., Fernandez-Fernandez, R., Colino, L., Fajardo, L., Perteguer-Barrio, R., & de Leon, J. (2016). The addictive model of self-harming (non-suicidal and suicidal) behavior. *Frontiers in Psychiatry*, 7, Article 8. https://doi.org/10.3389/fpsyt.2016.00008

Blasco-Fontecilla, H., Herranz-Herrer, J., Ponte-Lopez, T., Gil-Benito, E., Donoso-Navarro, E., Hernandez-Alvarez, E., Gil-Ligero, M., Horrillo, I., Meana, J. J., Royuela, A., Rosado-Garcia, S., & Sánchez-López, A. J. (2020). Serum β-endorphin levels are associated with addiction to suicidal behavior: A pilot study. *European Neuropsychopharmacology*, 40, 38–51. https://doi.org/10.1016/j.euroneuro.2020.07.010

Blasco-Fontecilla, H., Jaussent, I., Olie, E., Beziat, S., Guillaume, S., Artieda-Urrutia, P., Baca-Garcia, E., de Leon, J., & Courtet, P. (2014). A cross-sectional study of major repeaters: A distinct phenotype of suicidal behavior. *The Primary Care Companion for CNS Disorders*, 16(4). https://doi.org/10.4088/PCC.14m01633

Bradvik, L., & Berglund, M. (2011). Repetition of suicide attempts across episodes of severe depression. Behavioural sensitisation found in suicide group but not in controls. *BMC Psychiatry*, 11, Article 5. https://doi.org/10.1186/1471-244X-11-5

Breese, G. R., Criswell, H. E., & Mueller, R. A. (1990). Evidence that lack of brain dopamine during development can increase the susceptibility for aggression and self-injurious behavior by influencing D1-dopamine receptor function. *Progress in Neuro-psychopharmacology and Biological Psychiatry*, 14(1), S65–80. https://doi.org/10.1016/0278-5846(90)90089-y

Bresin, K., & Gordon, K. H. (2013). Endogenous opioids and nonsuicidal self-injury: A mechanism of affect regulation. *Neuroscience & Biobehavioral Reviews*, 37(3), 374–383. https://doi.org/10.1016/j.neubiorev.2013.01.020

Bunderla, T., & Kumperščak, H. G. (2015). Altered pain perception in self-injurious behavior and the association of psychological elements with pain perception measures: A systematic review. *Psychiatria Danubina*, 27(4), 346–354.

Buser, T. J., & Buser, J. K. (2013). Conceptualizing nonsuicidal self-injury as a process addiction: Review of research and implications for counselor training and practice. *Journal of Addictions & Offender Counseling*, *34*(1), 16–29. https://doi.org/10.1002/j.2161-1874.2013.00011.x

Calvo, N., García-González, S., Perez-Galbarro, C., Regales-Peco, C., Lugo-Marin, J., Ramos-Quiroga, J. A., & Ferrer, M. (2022). Psychotherapeutic interventions specifically developed for NSSI in adolescence: A systematic review. *European Neuropsychopharmacology*, *58*, 86–98. https://doi.org/10.1016/j.euroneuro.2022.02.009

Carlson, L., Steward, T., Agüera, Z., Mestre-Bach, G., Magaña, P., Granero, R., Jimenéz-Murcia, S., Claes, L., Gearhandt, A. N., Menchón, J. M., & Fernández-Aranda, F. (2018). Associations of food addiction and nonsuicidal self-injury among women with an eating disorder: A common strategy for regulating emotions? *European Eating Disorders Review*, *26*(6), 629–637. https://doi.org/10.1002/erv.2646

Cassin, S. E., & von Ranson, K. M. (2007). Is binge eating experienced as an addiction? *Appetite*, *49*(3), 687–690. https://doi.org/10.1016/j.appet.2007.06.012

Christie, M. J., & Chesher, G. B. (1982). Physical dependence on physiologically released endogenous opiates. *Life Sciences*, *30*(14), 1173–1177. https://doi.org/10.1016/0024-3205(82)90659-2

Çimen İ, D., Coşkun, A., & Etiler, N. (2017). Non-suicidal self-injury behaviors` features and relationship with adolescents` daily life activities and mental status. *Turkish Journal of Pediatrics*, *59*(2), 113–121. https://doi.org/10.24953/turkjped.2017.02.002

Coid, J., Allolio, B., & Rees, L. H. (1983). Raised plasma metenkephalin in patients who habitually mutilate themselves. *Lancet*, *2*(8349), 545–546. https://doi.org/10.1016/S0140-6736(83)90572-X

Csorba, J., Dinya, E., Plener, P., Nagy, E., & Páli, E. (2009). Clinical diagnoses, characteristics of risk behaviour, differences between suicidal and non-suicidal subgroups of Hungarian adolescent outpatients practising self-injury. *European Child and Adolescent Psychiatry*, *18*(5), 309–320. https://doi.org/10.1007/s00787-008-0733-5

Cullen, K. R., Klimes-Dougan, B., Westlund Schreiner, M., Carstedt, P., Marka, N., Nelson, K., Miller, M. J., Reigstad, K., Westervelt, A., Gunlicks-Stoessel, M., & Eberly, L. E. (2018). N-acetylcysteine for non-suicidal self-injurious behavior in adolescents: An open-label pilot study. *Journal of Child & Adolescent Psychopharmacology*, *28*(2), 136–144. https://doi.org/10.1089/cap.2017.0032

Dent, R. R., Ghadirian, A. M., Kusalic, M., & Young, S. N. (1986). Diurnal rhythms of plasma cortisol, beta-endorphin and prolactin, and cerebrospinal fluid amine metabolite levels before suicide. Case report. *Neuropsychobiology*, *16*(2–3), 64–67. https://doi.org/10.1159/000118299

Esposito, C., Spirito, A., Boergers, J., & Donaldson, D. (2003). Affective, behavioral, and cognitive functioning in adolescents with multiple suicide attempts. *Suicide and Life-Threatening Behavior*, *33*(4), 389–399. https://doi.org/10.1521/suli.33.4.389.25231

Favazza, A. R. (1989). Suicide gestures and self-mutilation. *American Journal of Psychiatry*, *146*(3), 408–409. https://doi.org/10.1176/ajp.146.3.408c

Faye, P. (1995). Addictive characteristics of the behavior of self-mutilation. *Journal of Psychosocial Nursing and Mental Health Services*, *33*(6), 36–39. https://doi.org/10.3928/0279-3695-19950601-08

Few, L. R., Grant, J. D., Nelson, E. C., Trull, T. J., Grucza, R. A., Bucholz, K. K., Verweij, K. J. H., Martin, N. G., Statham, D. J., Madden, P. A. F., Heath, A. C., Lynskey, M. T., & Agrawal, A. (2016). Cannabis involvement and nonsuicidal self-injury: A discordant twin approach. *Journal of Studies on Alcohol and Drugs*, *77*(6), 873–880. https://doi.org/10.15288/jsad.2016.77.873

Franklin, J. C., Aaron, R. V., Arthur, M. S., Shorkey, S. P., & Prinstein, M. J. (2012). Nonsuicidal self-injury and diminished pain perception: The role of emotion dysregulation. *Comprehensive Psychiatry*, *53*(6), 691–700. https://doi.org/10.1016/j.comppsych.2011.11.008

Franklin, J. C., Lee, K. M., Hanna, E. K., & Prinstein, M. J. (2013). Feeling worse to feel better: Pain-offset relief simultaneously stimulates positive affect and reduces negative affect. *Psychological Sciences*, *24*(4), 521–529. https://doi.org/10.1177/0956797612458805

Glenn, C. R., & Klonsky, E. D. (2013). Nonsuicidal self-injury disorder: An empirical investigation in adolescent psychiatric patients. *Journal of Clinical Child & Adolescent Psychology*, *42*(4), 496–507. https://doi.org/10.1080/15374416.2013.794699

Glenn, J. J., Michel, B. D., Franklin, J. C., Hooley, J. M., & Nock, M. K. (2014). Pain analgesia among adolescent self-injurers. *Psychiatry Research*, *220*(3), 921–926. https://doi.org/10.1016/j.psychres.2014.08.016

Goodman, A. (1992). Sexual addiction: Designation and treatment. *Journal of Sex and Marital Therapy*, *18*(4), 303–314. https://doi.org/10.1080/00926239208412855

Grant, J. E., Brewer, J. A., & Potenza, M. N. (2006). The neurobiology of substance and behavioral addictions. *CNS Spectrums*, *11*(12), 924–930. https://doi.org/10.1017/s109285290001511x

Gratz, K. L., Conrad, S. D., & Roemer, L. (2002). Risk factors for deliberate self-harm among college students. *American Journal of Orthopsychiatry*, *72*(1), 128–140. https://doi.org/10.1037//0002-9432.72.1.128

Grigson, P. S. (2002). Like drugs for chocolate: Separate rewards modulated by common mechanisms? *Physiology & Behavior*, *76*(3), 389–395. https://doi.org/10.1016/S0031-9384(02)00758-8

Gromatsky, M. A., Waszczuk, M. A., Perlman, G., Salis, K. L., Klein, D. N., & Kotov, R. (2017). The role of parental psychopathology and personality in adolescent non-suicidal self-injury. *Journal of Psychiatric Research*, *85*, 15–23. https://doi.org/10.1016/j.jpsychires.2016.10.013

Guérin-Marion, C., Bureau, J. F., Lafontaine, M. F., Gaudreau, P., & Martin, J. (2021). Profiles of emotion dysregulation among university students who self-injure: Associations with parent-child relationships and non-suicidal self-injury characteristics. *Journal of Youth and Adolescence*, *50*(4), 767–787. https://doi.org/10.1007/s10964-020-01378-9

Guérin-Marion, C., Martin, J., Deneault, A. A., Lafontaine, M. F., & Bureau, J. F. (2018). The functions and addictive features of non-suicidal self-injury: A confirmatory factor analysis of the Ottawa self-injury inventory in a university sample. *Psychiatry Research*, *264*, 316–321. https://doi.org/10.1016/j.psychres.2018.04.019

Hagen, E. H. (2003). The bargaining model of depression. In P. Hammerstein (Ed.), *Genetic and cultural evolution of cooperation* (pp. 95–123). MIT Press in cooperation with Dahlem University Press.

Hyman, S. E. (2005). Addiction: A disease of learning and memory. *American Journal of Psychiatry*, *162*(8), 1414–1422. https://doi.org/10.1176/appi.ajp.162.8.1414

Jallade, C., Sarfati, Y., & Hardy-Bayle, M. C. (2005). Clinical evolution after self-induced or accidental traumatism: A controlled study of the extent and the specificity of suicidal catharsis. *Journal of Affective Disorders*, *85*(3), 283–292. https://doi.org/10.1016/j.jad.2004.11.002

Joiner, T. E., Jr., & Rudd, M. D. (2000). Intensity and duration of suicidal crises vary as a function of previous suicide attempts and negative life events. *Journal of Consulting and Clinical Psychology*, *68*(5), 909–916. https://doi.org/10.1037/0022-006X.68.5.909

Kiekens, G., Hasking, P., Boyes, M., Claes, L., Mortier, P., Auerbach, R. P., Cuijpers, P., Demyttenaere, K., Green, J. G., Kessler, R. C., Myin-Germeys, I., Nock, M. K., & Bruffaerts, R. (2018). The associations between non-suicidal self-injury and first onset suicidal thoughts and behaviors. *Journal of Affective Disorders*, *239*, 171–179. https://doi.org/10.1016/j.jad.2018.06.033

Kirtley, O. J., O'Carroll, R. E., & O'Connor, R. C. (2016). Pain and self-harm: A systematic review. *Journal of Affective Disorders*, *203*, 347–363. https://doi.org/10.1016/j.jad.2016.05.068

Klimes-Dougan, B., Begnel, E., Almy, B., Thai, M., Schreiner, M. W., & Cullen, K. R. (2019). Hypothalamic-pituitary-adrenal axis dysregulation in depressed adolescents with non-suicidal self-injury. *Psychoneuroendocrinology*, *102*, 216–224. https://doi.org/10.1016/j.psyneuen.2018.11.004

Konicki, P. E., & Schulz, S. C. (1989). Rationale for clinical trials of opiate antagonists in treating patients with personality disorders and self-injurious behavior. *Psychopharmacological Bulletin*, *25*(4), 556–563.

Kourosh, A. S., Harrington, C. R., & Adinoff, B. (2010). Tanning as a behavioral addiction. *American Journal of Drug and Alcohol Abuse*, *36*(5), 284–290. https://doi.org/10.3109/00952990.2010.491883

Krantz, L. H., McMain, S., & Kuo, J. R. (2018). The unique contribution of acceptance without judgment in predicting nonsuicidal self-injury after 20-weeks of dialectical behaviour therapy group skills training. *Behaviour Research and Therapy*, *104*, 44–50. https://doi.org/10.1016/j.brat.2018.02.006

Kreek, M. J., & Koob, G. F. (1998). Drug dependence: Stress and dysregulation of brain reward pathways. *Drug and Alcohol Dependence*, *51*(1–2), 23–47. https://doi.org/10.1016/S0376-8716(98)00064-7

Lewis, S. P., & Baker, T. G. (2011). The possible risks of self-injury web sites: A content analysis. *Archives of Suicide Research*, *15*(4), 390–396. https://doi.org/10.1080/13811118.2011.616154

Linehan, M. M. (1993). *Cognitive behavioral treatment of borderline personality disorder*. Guilford Press.

Liu, J., Lu, L., & Mueller, D. (2020). Editorial: Overcome fear and addiction by manipulating reconsolidation and extinction of emotional memories. *Frontiers in Behavioral Neuroscience*, *14*, Article 613612. https://doi.org/10.3389/fnbeh.2020.613612

Liu, S., Lin, M. P., Lee, Y. T., Wu, J. Y., Hu, W. H., & You, J. (2021). Internet addiction and nonsuicidal self-injury in adolescence: Associations with offline and online social support. *Journal of Clinical Psychology*, *78*(5), 971–982. https://doi.org/10.1002/jclp.23264

Liu, Y., Xiao, Y., Ran, H., He, X., Jiang, L., Wang, T., Yang, R., Xu, X., Yang, G., & Lu, J. (2020). Association between parenting and non-suicidal self-injury among adolescents in Yunnan, China: A cross-sectional survey. *PeerJ*, *8*, Article e10493. https://doi.org/10.7717/peerj.10493

Logrip, M. L., Koob, G. F., & Zorrilla, E. P. (2011). Role of corticotropin-releasing factor in drug addiction: Potential for pharmacological intervention. *CNS Drugs*, *25*(4), 271–287. https://doi.org/10.2165/11587790-000000000-00000

Lovallo, W. R. (2006). Cortisol secretion patterns in addiction and addiction risk. *International Journal of Psychophysiology*, *59*(3), 195–202. https://doi.org/10.1016/j.ijpsycho.2005.10.007

Lutz, N. M., Chamberlain, S. R., Goodyer, I. M., Bhardwaj, A., Sahakian, B. J., Jones, P. B., & Wilkinson, P. O. (2021). Behavioral measures of impulsivity and compulsivity in adolescents with nonsuicidal self-injury. *CNS Spectrum*, 1–9. https://doi.org/10.1017/s1092852921000274

Madjar, N., Zalsman, G., Ben Mordechai, T. R., & Shoval, G. (2017). Repetitive vs. occasional non-suicidal self-injury and school-related factors among Israeli high school students. *Psychiatry Research*, *257*, 358–360. https://doi.org/10.1016/j.psychres.2017.07.073

Marco, J. H., Garcia-Alandete, J., Pérez, S., Guillen, V., Jorquera, M., Espallargas, P., & Botella, C. (2015). Meaning in life and non-suicidal self-injury: A follow-up study with participants with borderline personality disorder. *Psychiatry Research*, *230*(2), 561–566. https://doi.org/10.1016/j.psychres.2015.10.004

Martin, J., Bureau, J. F., Yurkowski, K., Fournier, T. R., Lafontaine, M. F., & Cloutier, P. (2016). Family-based risk factors for non-suicidal self-injury: Considering influences of maltreatment, adverse family-life experiences, and parent-child relational risk. *Journal of Adolescence*, *49*, 170–180. https://doi.org/10.1016/j.adolescence.2016.03.015

Martin, J., Cloutier, P. F., Levesque, C., Bureau, J. F., Lafontaine, M. F., & Nixon, M. K. (2013). Psychometric properties of the functions and addictive features scales of the Ottawa Self-Injury Inventory: A preliminary investigation using a university sample. *Psychological Assessment*, *25*(3), 1013–1018. https://doi.org/10.1037/a0032575

McMain, S. F., Guimond, T., Barnhart, R., Habinski, L., & Streiner, D. L. (2017). A randomized trial of brief dialectical behaviour therapy skills training in suicidal patients suffering from borderline disorder. *Acta Psychiatrica Scandinavica*, *135*(2), 138–148. https://doi.org/10.1111/acps.12664

Miller, M., Redley, M., & Wilkinson, P. O. (2021). A qualitative study of understanding reasons for self-harm in adolescent girls. *International Journal of Environmental Research and Public Health*, *18*(7). https://doi.org/10.3390/ijerph18073361

Moseley, R. L., Gregory, N. J., Smith, P., Allison, C., & Baron-Cohen, S. (2019). A "choice," an "addiction," a way "out of the lost": Exploring self-injury in autistic people without intellectual disability. *Molecular Autism*, *10*, Article 18. https://doi.org/10.1186/s13229-019-0267-3

Muehlenkamp, J. J., Claes, L., Havertape, L., & Plener, P. L. (2012). International prevalence of adolescent non-suicidal self-injury and deliberate self-harm. *Child and Adolescent Psychiatry and Mental Health*, *6*, Article 10. https://doi.org/10.1186/1753-2000-6-10

Mészáros, G., Győri, D., Horváth, L. O., Szentiványi, D., & Balázs, J. (2020). Nonsuicidal self-injury: Its associations with pathological internet use and psychopathology among adolescents. *Frontiers in Psychiatry*, *11*, Article 814. https://doi.org/10.3389/fpsyt.2020.00814

Nixon, M. K., Cloutier, P. F., & Aggarwal, S. (2002). Affect regulation and addictive aspects of repetitive self-injury in hospitalized adolescents. *Journal of the American Academy of Child and Adolescent Psychiatry*, *41*(11), 1333–1341. https://doi.org/10.1097/00004583-200211000-00015

Olive, M. F., Cleva, R. M., Kalivas, P. W., & Malcolm, R. J. (2012). Glutamatergic medications for the treatment of drug and behavioral addictions. *Pharmacology Biochemistry and Behavior*, *100*(4), 801–810. https://doi.org/10.1016/j.pbb.2011.04.015

Oquendo, M. A., Sullivan, G. M., Sudol, K., Baca-Garcia, E., Stanley, B. H., Sublette, M. E., & Mann, J. J. (2014). Toward a biosignature for suicide. *American Journal of Psychiatry*. https://doi.org/10.1176/appi.ajp.2014.14020194

Osuch, E., Ford, K., Wrath, A., Bartha, R., & Neufeld, R. (2014). Functional MRI of pain application in youth who engaged in repetitive non-suicidal self-injury vs. psychiatric controls. *Psychiatry Research*, *223*(2), 104–112. https://doi.org/10.1016/j.pscychresns.2014.05.003

Pritchard, T. R., Fedchenko, C. A., & Lewis, S. P. (2021). Self-injury is my drug: The functions of describing nonsuicidal self-injury as an addiction. *Journal of Nervous Mental Disease*, *209*(9), 628–635. https://doi.org/10.1097/nmd.0000000000001359

Reichl, C., Heyer, A., Brunner, R., Parzer, P., Völker, J. M., Resch, F., & Kaess, M. (2016). Hypothalamic-pituitary-adrenal axis, childhood adversity and adolescent nonsuicidal self-injury. *Psychoneuroendocrinology, 74*, 203–211. https://doi.org/10.1016/j.psyneuen.2016.09.011

Reynaud, M., Karila, L., Blecha, L., & Benyamina, A. (2010). Is love passion an addictive disorder? *American Journal of Drug and Alcohol Abuse, 36*(5), 261–267. https://doi.org/10.3109/00952990.2010.495183

Richmond-Rakerd, L. S., Trull, T. J., Gizer, I. R., McLaughlin, K., Scheiderer, E. M., Nelson, E. C., Agrawal, A., Lynskey, M. T., Madden, P. A. F., Heath, A. C., Statham, D. J., & Martin, N. G. (2019). Common genetic contributions to high-risk trauma exposure and self-injurious thoughts and behaviors. *Psychological Medicine, 49*(3), 421–430. https://doi.org/10.1017/s0033291718001034

Sanchez-Carbonell, X., Beranuy, M., Castellana, M., Chamarro, A., & Oberst, U. (2008). Internet and cell phone addiction: Passing fad or disorder? *Adicciones, 20*(2), 149–159.

Sandman, C. A., Touchette, P. E., Marion, S. D., & Chicz-DeMet, A. (2008). The role of proopiomelanocortin (POMC) in sequentially dependent self-injurious behavior. *Developmental Psychobiology, 50*(7), 680–689. https://doi.org/10.1002/dev.20323

Sarnyai, Z., Shaham, Y., & Heinrichs, S. C. (2001). The role of corticotropin-releasing factor in drug addiction. *Pharmacological Review, 53*(2), 209–243.

Schroeder, M., Eberlein, C., de Zwaan, M., Kornhuber, J., Bleich, S., & Frieling, H. (2012). Lower levels of cannabinoid 1 receptor mRNA in female eating disorder patients: Association with wrist cutting as impulsive self-injurious behavior. *Psychoneuroendocrinology, 37*(12), 2032–2036. https://doi.org/10.1016/j.psyneuen.2012.03.025

Sellers, C. M., Díaz-Valdés, A., Oliver, M. M., Simon, K. M., & O'Brien, K. H. M. (2021). The relationship between alcohol and cannabis use with nonsuicidal self-injury among adolescent inpatients: Examining the 90 days prior to psychiatric hospitalization. *Addictive Behaviors, 114*, 106759. https://doi.org/10.1016/j.addbeh.2020.106759

Serafini, G., Adavastro, G., Canepa, G., De Berardis, D., Valchera, A., Pompili, M., Nasrallah, H., & Amore, M. (2018). The efficacy of buprenorphine in major depression, treatment-resistant depression and suicidal behavior: A systematic review. *International Journal of Molecular Sciences, 19*(8). https://doi.org/10.3390/ijms19082410

Stanley, B., Gameroff, M. J., Michalsen, V., & Mann, J. J. (2001). Are suicide attempters who self-mutilate a unique population? *American Journal of Psychiatry, 158*(3), 427–432. https://doi.org/10.1176/appi.ajp.158.3.427

Stanley, B., Sher, L., Wilson, S., Ekman, R., Huang, Y. Y., & Mann, J. J. (2010). Non-suicidal self-injurious behavior, endogenous opioids and monoamine neurotransmitters. *Journal of Affective Disorders, 124*(1–2), 134–140. https://doi.org/10.1016/j.jad.2009.10.028

Steinbüchel, T. A., Herpertz, S., Külpmann, I., Kehyayan, A., Dieris-Hirche, J., & Te Wildt, B. T. (2018). Internet addiction, suicidality and non-suicidal self-harming behavior-A systematic review. *Psychotherapie, Psychosomatik, Medizinische Psychologie, 68*(11), 451–461. https://doi.org/10.1055/s-0043-120448

Tang, J., Ma, Y., Lewis, S. P., Chen, R., Clifford, A., Ammerman, B. A., Gazimbi, M. M., Byrne, A., Wu, Y., Lu, X., Chang, H., Kang, C., Tiemeier, H., & Yu, Y. (2020). Association of internet addiction with non-suicidal self-injury among adolescents in China. *JAMA Network Open, 3*(6), Article e206863. https://doi.org/10.1001/jamanetworkopen.2020.6863

Tantam, D., & Whittaker, J. (1992). Personality disorder and self-wounding. *British Journal of Psychiatry, 161*, 451–464. https://doi.org/10.1192/bjp.161.4.451

Tao, R., Huang, X., Wang, J., Zhang, H., Zhang, Y., & Li, M. (2010). Proposed diagnostic criteria for internet addiction. *Addiction, 105*(3), 556–564. https://doi.org/10.1111/j.1360-0443.2009.02828.x

Torregrossa, M. M., & Taylor, J. R. (2013). Learning to forget: Manipulating extinction and reconsolidation processes to treat addiction. *Psychopharmacology, 226*(4), 659–672. https://doi.org/10.1007/s00213-012-2750-9

Traskman-Bendz, L., Ekman, R., Regnell, G., & Ohman, R. (1992). HPA-related CSF neuropeptides in suicide attempters. *European Neuropsychopharmacology, 2*(2), 99–106. https://doi.org/10.1016/0924-977x(92)90018-4

Tullis, K. (1998). A theory of suicide addiction. *Sexual addiction & Compulsivity, 5*, 311–324. https://doi.org/10.1080/10720169808402339

Turner, B. J., Austin, S. B., & Chapman, A. L. (2014). Treating nonsuicidal self-injury: A systematic review of psychological and pharmacological interventions. *Canadian Journal of Psychiatry, 59*(11), 576–585. https://doi.org/10.1177/070674371405901103

van der Venne, P., Balint, A., Drews, E., Parzer, P., Resch, F., Koenig, J., & Kaess, M. (2021). Pain sensitivity and plasma beta-endorphin in adolescent non-suicidal self-injury. *Journal of Affective Disorders, 278*, 199–208. https://doi.org/10.1016/j.jad.2020.09.036

van Praag, H., & Plutchik, R. (1985). An empirical study on the "cathartic effect" of attempted suicide. *Psychiatry Research, 16*(2), 123–130. https://doi.org/0165-1781(85)90005-8

Victor, S. E., Glenn, C. R., & Klonsky, E. D. (2012). Is non-suicidal self-injury an "addiction"? A comparison of craving in substance use and non-suicidal self-injury. *Psychiatry Research, 197*(1–2), 73–77. https://doi.org/10.1016/j.psychres.2011.12.011

Visser, J. E., Bar, P. R., & Jinnah, H. A. (2000). Lesch-Nyhan disease and the basal ganglia. *Brain Research Reviews, 32*(2–3), 449–475. https://doi.org/10.1016/S0165-0173(99)00094-6

Volkow, N. D., & Wise, R. A. (2005). How can drug addiction help us understand obesity? *Nature Neuroscience, 8*(5), 555–560. https://doi.org/10.1038/nn1452

Walker, R. L., Joiner, T. E., Jr., & Rudd, M. D. (2001). The course of post-crisis suicidal symptoms: How and for whom is suicide "cathartic"? *Suicide and Life-Threatening Behavior, 31*(2), 144–152.

Washburn, J. J., Juzwin, K. R., Styer, D. M., & Aldridge, D. (2010). Measuring the urge to self-injure: Preliminary data from a clinical sample. *Psychiatry Research, 178*(3), 540–544. https://doi.org/10.1016/j.psychres.2010.05.018

Whitlock, J., Muehlenkamp, J., Eckenrode, J., Purington, A., Baral Abrams, G., Barreira, P., & Kress, V. (2013). Nonsuicidal self-injury as a gateway to suicide in young adults. *Journal of Adolescent Health, 52*(4), 486–492. https://doi.org/10.1016/j.jadohealth.2012.09.010

Whitlock, J. L., Powers, J. L., & Eckenrode, J. (2006). The virtual cutting edge: The internet and adolescent self-injury. *Developmental Psychology, 42*(3), 407–417. https://doi.org/10.1037/0012-1649.42.3.407

Wilkinson, P. O., Qiu, T., Jesmont, C., Neufeld, S. A. S., Kaur, S. P., Jones, P. B., & Goodyer, I. M. (2022). Age and gender effects on non-suicidal self-injury, and their interplay with psychological distress. *Journal of Affective Disorders, 306*, 240–245. https://doi.org/10.1016/j.jad.2022.03.021

Wilkinson, P. O., Qiu, T., Neufeld, S., Jones, P. B., & Goodyer, I. M. (2018). Sporadic and recurrent non-suicidal self-injury before age 14 and incident onset of psychiatric disorders by 17 years: Prospective cohort study. *British Journal of Psychiatry, 212*(4), 222–226. https://doi.org/10.1192/bjp.2017.45

Wise, R. A., & Koob, G. F. (2014). The development and maintenance of drug addiction. *Neuropsychopharmacology, 39*(2), 254–262. https://doi.org/10.1038/npp.2013.261

CHAPTER 12

A Roadmap Overview of the Research Domain Criteria: A Shift from Diagnostic to Transdiagnostic Processes

Tim Bastiaens *and* Laurence Claes

Abstract

In this chapter, the authors familiarize the reader with the Research Domain Criteria (RDoC) and the paradigm shift it represents towards a new conceptualization of psychopathology. The authors first provide an overview of the problems currently encountered in the present classification systems of mental disorders, advocated by either the fifth edition of the *Diagnostic and Statistical Manual of Mental Disorders* (DSM-5) or the International Classification of Diseases, 11th edition (ICD-11). The authors discuss the RDoC matrix as the transdiagnostic framework from which a future, neurobiologically grounded, diagnostic system might arise. The authors introduce the reader to the rows of the matrix, representing of the RDoC domains and underlying constructs. They then discuss the seven columns of the matrix, representing the different levels of analysis at which each domain/construct can be investigated. Afterward, the authors first address RDoC's general implications using a clinical case example and subsequently focus on the promising intersection between RDoC and nonsuicidal self-injury (NSSI). The authors finish by discussing three of RDoC's current limitations, which can subsequently be addressed to advance future research. Notwithstanding its exciting prospects, acknowledging RDoC's current limitations can help avoid future obstacles not unlike the current hampering publication requirement of DSM/ICD categorical delineation of research groups the RDoC approach sets out to overcome.

Key Words: Research Domain Criteria, psychopathology, mental disorders, transdiagnostic framework, nonsuicidal self injury, International Classification of Diseases, Diagnostic and Statistical Manual

Introduction

In 2008, the National Institute of Mental Health (NIMH) started their Research Domain Criteria (RDoC; Insel et al., 2010) project, intending to create, for research purposes, new ways to classify mental disorders. Important to note is that the RDoC project in itself does not claim to offer a new, ready-to-use diagnostic system at its current point of development. Rather, it wants to offer a framework that surpasses the present classification systems of mental disorders, advocated by either the fifth edition of the *Diagnostic* and *Statistical Manual of Mental Disorders* (DSM-5; American Psychiatric Association, 2013) or the *International Classification of Diseases*, 11th edition (ICD-11; World Health Organization, 2019). The RDoC framework builds upon advances in neurobiological and behavioral research, and as such, contrary to the former, offers the capacity for causation (Cuthbert, 2014).

The Problems with the DSM–ICD Assumptions

Both the DSM and ICD classification systems are constructed to generate a common language on mental disorders, grounded in observational symptoms and intentionally void of theoretical explanatory models (Insel, 2014). By means of this common language, mental disorders are defined as distinct entities composed of standardized diagnostic criteria. Subsequent scientific research investigates correlations, etiology, and treatment of mental disorders defined by these classification systems. Although this approach has generated vast progress in relation to at least a number of mental disorders, more and more voices have been calling for a radical paradigm shift for validity reasons (Lilienfeld & Treadway, 2016; Markon et al., 2011). The arguments in favor of such a paradigm shift have been variously arranged by a number of authors. Lilienfeld and Treadway (2016) provide a more elaborate review.

Overlap in Diagnostic Criteria/Multimorbidity

A first problem with the DSM–ICD assumptions is that a lot of the descriptive syndromes share common observational symptoms. Aggressive behavior, for example, can be a symptom of posttraumatic stress disorder, intermittent explosive disorder, major neurocognitive disorder, or of a number of the currently adopted personality disorder (PD) categories (e.g., borderline PD, antisocial PD). Clusters of observational symptoms are labeled as distinct syndromes but can show overlap to the extent that the validity of the classification (and its subsequent operationalization) becomes problematic (Trull & Durrett, 2005).

Algorithms for Syndrome Diagnosis/Heterogeneity

Research into the origins and mechanisms of DSM-5/ICD-11 syndromes typically compares participants who meet the criteria for a specific syndrome with a reference group (which can consist of a nonclinical sample or a group of participants meeting the criteria for another syndrome) in relation to the variable(s) under examination. This is problematic because it incorporates the assumption that the syndrome diagnoses are classical categories (Wittgenstein, 1958) while they are, in fact, polythetic: members share a number of features but none of these features is in itself necessary or sufficient for category membership (Needham, 1975). For example, unlike the classical category of triangles of which membership can be defined in terms of necessary and sufficient conditions ("closed plane figures with three straight sides"; Irzik & Nola, 2011, p. 594), the three sisters on the right in figure 12.1 share common features without one feature common to all members

Figure 12.1 Three triangles as an example of a classical category (left), versus three sisters as an example of a polythetic category (right). Unlike the triangles, the sisters share common features without one feature common to all members of the category. The category "sisters" is defined as meeting two out of four criteria: (1) dark eyes, (2) oval face, (3) light mouth, (4) light eyebrows.

of the sister category. Like the three sisters, the DSM-5/ICD-11 syndromes are polythetic. For example, the DSM-5 borderline personality disorder (BPD) can be diagnosed if the subject fits any five of the nine comprising criteria, thereby leaving room for no less than 9x8x7x6x5 variants. As a consequence, this creates heterogeneity right at the construct level, on which subsequent research intended to advance our understanding gets built.

Lack of Dimensionality

A third problem with the DSM–ICD is that both classification systems define mental disorders as categories, distinct from normal functioning. Therefore, they are ill-equipped to integrate the growing insights stemming from research that conceptualizes psychopathology as extreme positions on a dimensionally distributed function. In the field of personality pathology, for example, research has shown no evidence for the existence of discontinuities in the distributions of personality traits, and has documented a highly similar personality trait factor structure in nonclinical and clinical groups (e.g., Livesley, 2003; Trull & Durrett, 2005). In addition, the official 10 DSM-5 personality disorder categories fall short of exhaustively representing the forms of personality pathology we encounter in daily clinical practice (Shedler & Westen, 2004). Moreover, Lilienfeld and Treadway (2016) argued that even for a taxonomic system, a dimensional instead of a categorical measurement would be preferable as the latter is unable to include an individual's proximity to the cutoff point.

The RDoC Project

As an answer to the shortcomings of the ICD/DSM model, the RDoC project research is guided by three principles (Casey et al., 2014). First, it advocates a dimensional approach as opposed to a categorical system to be able to connect brain circuits with observable behavior and experienced symptoms. Second, RDoC starts from behavior-brain relationships as a guiding principle to understand clinical phenomena, rather than investigating the correlates and etiology of a priori defined, discrete disease entities. Third, RDoC outlines its research through a number of constructs (e.g., Negative Valence Systems and Positive Valence Systems) that are put forward as the elemental organizing principles of clinical symptomatology, and that are studied at subsequent levels of analysis—ranging from genes to subjective experience (Insel et al., 2010).

The RDoC Matrix

Figure 12.2 displays the first two of the four RDoC matrix dimensions. The rows consist of the constructs, each representing a convergent line of ongoing empirical data. Higher-order research domains align the constructs based on their interrelatedness. The columns denote the level of analysis at which each construct can be studied. Starting from the center column (specific Brain Circuits) and moving to the left, we find Cells and Molecules. As of May 2017, references to specific genes have been removed from the RDoC Genes column, awaiting genome-wide association studies as opposed to previous candidate gene approaches. Moving to the right from the center column, we encounter Physiology, Behavior, and Self-Reports. The third dimension of the matrix (not depicted in fig. 12.2) represents the developmental course of the research dimensions at their various levels of analysis as they move through time and maturation (or, for that matter, time and decline). The fourth and final dimension of the matrix (not depicted in fig. 12.2) represents environmental influences affecting the research dimensions again at their various levels of analysis. The next sections concisely address each of the four RDoC dimensions. A full description can be found on the NIMH website.

First Dimension: Higher-Order Research Domains and Comprising Constructs

Negative Valence Systems react to aversive stimuli. Acute threat (Fear) motivates protection from unconditioned as well as conditioned threat stimuli, which can be exteroceptive or interoceptive. Potential threat (Anxiety) involves enhanced vigilance in response to potential but distant, ambiguous or low/uncertain probability threats. Sustained threat represents reactions to an actual or anticipated prolonged exposure to negative stimuli (internal or external), which persist after their disappearance. *Loss* involves an episodic (e.g., grief) or sustained state of deprivation, responding to permanent or sustained loss of resources. Frustrative nonreward denotes reactions following from prevention or withdrawal of reward despite sustained effort.

Positive Valence Systems react to positive stimuli. Reward responsiveness motivates hedonistic responses to impending or possible reward. Subconstructs are (1) Reward Anticipation, (2) Initial Response to Reward, and (3) Reward Satiation. Reward Learning involves learning what predicts positive outcomes and the modification of behavior when a novel or unexpectedly high reward takes place. Subconstructs are (1) Probabilistic and Reinforcement Learning, (2) Reward Prediction Error, and (3) Habit. Reward Valuation is the computation of probability and benefits of anticipated reward using prior experience,

The RDoC matrix

DOMAINS/CONSTRUCTS	UNITS OF ANALYSIS							
	[Genes]*	Molecules	Cells	Circuits	Physiology	Behavior	Self-Reports	Paradigms
Negative Valence Systems								
Acute Threat ("Fear")								
Potential Threat ("Anxiety")								
Sustained threat								
Loss								
Frustrative Nonreward								
Positive Valence Systems								
Reward Responsiveness								
Reward Learning								
Reward Valuation								
Cognitive Systems								
Attention								
Perception								
Working Memory								
Declarative Memory								
Language								
Cognitive Control								
Systems for Social Processes								
Affiliation and Attachment								
Social Communication								
Perception and Understanding of Self								
Perception and Understanding of Others								
Arousal/Modulatory Systems								
Arousal								
Circadian Rhythms								
Sleep-Wakefulness								
Sensi-motor Systems								
Motor Actions								
Agency and Ownership								
Habit-Sensi-motor								
Innate Motor Patterns								

The RDoC matrix representing the first two dimensions of the RDoC system, available from https://www.nimh.nih.gov/research/research-funded-by-nimh/rdoc/constructs/rdoc-matrix.shtml.
*Removed from the matrix since May 2017 pending robust evidence of association from genome wide association studies

Figure 12.2 The RDoC matrix. The RDoC matrix representing the first two dimensions of the RDoC system, available from https://www.nimh.nih.gov/research/research-funded-by-nimh/rdoc/constructs/rdoc-matrix.shtml. *Removed from the matrix since May 2017 pending robust evidence of association from genome wide association studies.

social context, and other information. Subconstructs are (1) Reward (probability), (2) Delay, and (3) Effort.

Cognitive systems involve various cognitive functions. Selective and divided attention regulate access to ongoing perceptual or motor processes that are limited in capacity and can be in competition with each other. Perception performs computations on sensory data to construct predictive representations of the external world. Working memory actively maintains and updates goal-relevant information in an ongoing, flexible manner, resisting interference but also limited in capacity. Declarative memory encodes, stores, and retrieves representations and the spatial, temporal, or other contextual relations between them. Language abstracts concrete representations into a shared system of symbolic representatives that enables thought and communication. Cognitive control modulates competition between various cognitive and emotional systems as a function of goal-directed behavior, including goal selection, response selection through inhibition processes, and performance monitoring.

Systems for social processes regulate interpersonal functioning. Affiliation is the engagement in positive, social interactions, with Attachment as the selective affiliation through the development of a social bond. Social communication is the exchange of socially relevant information in order to integrate in the social environment. This informational exchange can be explicit or implicit, including receptive affect or facial recognition, as well as productive eye contact, gaze-following or expressive reciprocity. Perception and understanding of self governs self-awareness, self-monitoring and self-knowledge. Perception and understanding of others is the ability to perceive others as animate agents who have their own mental states from which behavior can be interpreted or predicted.

Arousal/Regulatory systems generate activation in function of homeostatic regulation of energy balance and sleep/wake cycles. Arousal denotes a continuum of sensitivity to internal and external stimuli, which can be regulated by homeostatic drives like thirst, hunger, sex, and sleep. Circadian rhythms are endogenous and self-sustaining oscillations that organize the timing of biological systems to optimize physiology, behavior, and health. Sleep-wakefulness is a special representative of these.

Sensorimotor systems control and execute and refine motor behavior. Motor actions comprise all processes relating to planning and execution of a motor action in accordance with the context. Subconstructs are (1) Action Planning and Selection, (2) Sensorimotor Dynamics, (3) Initiation, (4) Execution, and (5) Inhibition and Termination. Agency and Ownership is the sense that one's actions, body (parts) and senses belong to oneself. Habit—Sensorimotor refers to learned stimulus-response mappings that are independent of the current value of the goal. Innate motor patterns are built-in action plans.

Second Dimension: Levels of Analysis

The central column, Circuits, can be investigated through neuroimaging technology or by measuring responses that have been documented as direct one-on-one recordings of circuit indices (e.g., fear-potentiated startle reflex; Morris & Cuthbert, 2012). Moving to the left, "cells" might, for example, include research on alpha Motor neurons or Pyramidal cells; "Molecules," the study of GABA or dopamine molecules; and "Genes" the future input of genome wide association studies. Moving to the right, "Physiology" refers to documented effects of circuit activation that do not measure circuit activity directly. Examples include heart rate, heart rate variability, or skin conductance. "Behavior" can include discrete observable motor responses on, for example, performance-based assessment tasks, or any systematically occurring, organized set of behavioral responses. "Self-reports" comprise reports of subjective experiences, which can be examined through, for example, questionnaires or interviews. The "Paradigms" column lists specific methodologies that can be used to study specific domains, like, for example, the CO_2 Challenge Test (e.g., Klein, 1993) to investigate the Acute Threat (Fear) construct of the Negative Valence Systems domain, or the *Reading the Mind in the Eyes* paradigm (Baron-Cohen et al., 2001) to study the Perception and Understanding of Others construct of the Social Processes domain.

Third Dimension: Developmental Course

Inherent to the RDoC is the study of the research domains and constructs at the different levels of analysis as they mature, develop, or degenerate through time. Examples might include the study of emergent circuit abnormalities and synaptic pruning in adolescent brain maturation in relation to the onset of delusions and hallucinations, or the investigation of the longitudinal effect of cortical activation levels during task performance on the onset or evolution of mental disorders in elderly subjects. Importantly, the RDoC approach allows for research into risk factors as well as the study of developmental patterns leading to resilience. Casey et al. (2014) suggested three areas of RDoC neurodevelopmental research: (1) the study of neuroanatomic development in relation to psychopathology, (2) research into specifically sensitive periods during maturation with regard to specific RDoC domains and constructs, and (3) the study of causal pathways between impairment in different brain systems through time.

Fourth Dimension: Environmental Influences

The fourth and final dimension of the matrix represents environmental influences that bidirectionally affect the research domains and constructs at their various levels of analysis. Examples include research on the effect of child abuse on mental problems in children, or the effect of parental caregiving behavior at home on the exploratory and attachment behavior of young children in experimental laboratory situations (Ainsworth et al., 1975). Importantly, RDoC also comprises the bidirectional effect of environmental factors on the developmental course (i.e., the third dimension of the RDoC). This includes, for example, genetic differences explaining differential susceptibility to environmental effects, but also the mediating role of environment factors on gene expression, with an impact that can last throughout the lifetime, and can even be transmitted to the next generation (Rakyan & Beck, 2006).

RDoC General Implications and Case Example

Adopting the RDoC perspective implies the departure from psychiatric categorization as the organizing principle for (1) scientific research, (2) future clinical diagnostic assessment, and (3) future clinical treatment.

RDoC General Implications

With regard to scientific research, RDoC stands for a transdiagnostic delineation of experimental and control groups, as opposed to a delineation based on DSM or ICD categories. The RDoC framework promotes the study of any phenomenon, regardless of its traditional overarching diagnostic category (if existing), within any RDoC domain/construct (the rows of the matrix) and at any level of analysis (the columns of the matrix). In accordance with its principle of left-to-right columns of cascading causality, RDoC conceptualizes phenomena through their neurobiological mechanics.

With regard to future clinical diagnostic assessment, it is important to underline that the RDoC framework at this point in its development does not offer an alternative to the current way of diagnosing mental disorders. However, it is hoped that the use of its paradigm, which fosters the investigation of normal range functions rather than a priori definitions of clinical syndromes, will inform future nosologies based on neurobiological underpinnings (Cuthbert, 2020). As a proof of principle, Cuthbert (2020) referred to the anxiety program by Lang et al. (2016), who defined a transdiagnostic dimension of low-to-high psychophysiology, using a composite measure of startle reflex and heart rate reactivity to patient-specific fear cues. Independent of specific DSM diagnoses within the anxiety spectrum, Lang et al. (2016) found a direct correspondence between an increasing psychophysiological blunting and a stepwise increase in anxiety symptomatology and functional impairment. Other than informing future nosologies in the general sense, the vision of RDoC also entails the future possibility for person-tailored treatments based on neurobiological parameters. For example, elaborating on Lang et al. (2016), Cuthbert (2020) suggested the use of physiological reactivity as a prognostic biomarker informative for the choice of therapy (e.g., which patients are best helped with medication vs. exposure therapy vs. cognitive therapy). Similarly, De Raedt (2020) envisioned a future patient-specific assessment of neurocognitive processes to set up a personalized medicine approach to the treatment of depression, although admittedly, the current reliability and validity of neurobiological measures does not allow for such yet.

With regard to clinical treatment itself, RDoC fosters mechanistic interventions to adjust or remediate aberrations in normal range functions. Examples are the reinstatement of reward processing in anhedonic adults through neurofeedback interventions using functional magnetic resonance imaging (Mao & Yuang, 2021), but also (the study of the neurobiological mechanisms of) more classic mindfulness interventions as a treatment for chronic stress (Garland et al., 2017). As another example, interventions using heart rate variability feedback have proven to significantly lower self-reported stress and anxiety in treatment populations (Goessl et al., 2017) to the degree of more traditional treatment (Tolin et al., 2020).

Case Example

In their 2014 article, Alexopoulos and Arean argued for the departure from available psychotherapies, stating that their comprising interventions are too complex to directly connect to brain circuits. As an alternative, the authors propose the development of new psychotherapies that get built upon the RDoC perspective. As a case example, the authors put forward their engage approach to the treatment of late-onset depression. While the components of the engage approach are similar to the ingredients of traditional cognitive behavioral therapy for depression, the key difference lies in its bottom-up, neurobiologically based compilation. Starting from RDoC research that has identified disruptions in the Positive Valence Systems domain in depression (e.g., Russo & Nestler, 2013), the patient spends the first three Engage sessions on selecting, choosing, and implementing rewarding activities. Simultaneously, the therapist identifies barriers associated with documented impairments in specific RDoC domains, and subsequently tries to alleviate these.

A first barrier to target is negative bias, or selective attention to negativity, the behavioral expression of the loss construct within the RDoC Negative Valence Systems domain (e.g., Gordon et al., 2008). Possible interventions include classic cognitive strategies like documenting one's negative thoughts and writing more positive alternative explanations for them. A second barrier to address is apathy, or the behavioral manifestation of a disruption in the RDoC Arousal and Regulatory Systems domain (Alexopoulos et al., 2013). Apathy is expressed as difficulties with initiating activity and maintaining interest. Again in accordance with the traditional approach, possible interventions are the use of prompts like classical checklists, audiovisual tools, or the mobilizing of family and friends to get and to keep the patient on task. A third barrier to overcome is emotional dysregulation, or the behavior associated with a disruption in the RDoC Cognitive Control construct of the Cognitive Systems domain (e.g., Etkin et al., 2011). Interventions that can be used to modulate overwhelming negative emotions are for example the use of meditation or relaxation, or deep-breathing techniques. Using a stepped-care principle, the Engage approach also offers evaluation tools to rate the patient on the four behavioral expressions of the RDoC domains involved in late-onset depression. As examples, Alexopoulos and Arean (2014) named the Behavioral Activation for Depression Scale (Kanter et al., 2007) in relation to reward exposure, the Brief Risk-Resilience Index for Screening (BRISC; Williams et al., 2012) in relation to negative bias, the Apathy Evaluation Scale (Marin et al., 1991) in relation to apathy, and again the BRISC (Williams et al., 2012) in relation to emotional dysregulation.

RDoC and Nonsuicidal Self-Injury

In contrast to traditional research subsuming nonsuicidal self-injury (NSSI) as a symptom of a specific DSM categorical diagnosis, RDoC research is particularly well placed to examine causal pathways with regard to the phenomenon itself, relying on neurobiological evidence. The importance of this is difficult to overstate; NSSI has been documented as a potential precursor to suicide attempts, sometimes but not always part of a mood disorder (Asarnow et al., 2011), as co-occurring with eating disorders and substance abuse disorders (Hasking & Claes, 2020), or as a defining characteristic of BPD. Like other transdiagnostic phenomena, limiting its investigation to the study of the overarching category runs the risk of impeding a more precise understanding. As will become apparent in the following chapters, the RDoC Positive Valence, Negative Valence, Cognitive, and Social Processes systems all prove most relevant to the reasons for NSSI to occur and reoccur.

With regard to the Negative Valence Systems domain, research shows that negative affect often precedes self-injury, and that the act of NSSI commonly creates a momentary relief from negative affect (Klonsky, 2007). In the following section of this book, Swerdlow, Pearlstein, Sandel, and Johnson (see chapter 13, this volume) document converging evidence for the relevance of negative affect to NSSI onset, frequency, as well as severity. The authors explain how within-person variation in negative affect coincides with acts of NSSI, describe neural indices shared by both, and discuss the short- versus long-term effects of NSSI. In line with the literature gap described by Schreiner et al. (2015), Swerdlow et al. further delve into sophisticated models that operationalize temporal dynamic fluctuations in negative affect and NSSI (more on positive valence systems specific to NSSI can be found in chapter 15, this volume).

Within the Threat system, studies focusing on the Acute Threat construct have found evidence for greater amygdala activation in both patients and nonpatients with versus without histories of NSSI (Niedtfeld et al., 2010; Plener et al., 2012). Studies focusing on the Sustained Threat construct have highlighted hyperreactivity of the Stress Response System in persons with histories of NSSI (Jovev et al., 2008). Carosella et al. (chapter 14, this volume) specifically address how in individuals with NSSI, the HPA (hypothalamic–pituitary–adrenal) axis response to environmental stressors might have developed over time in response to prolonged stress exposure. The authors provide an overview of the neuroendocrine and the neural threat system, discuss developmental changes in it, and how this relates to NSSI.

With regard to the Positive Valence Systems domain, studies have suggested orbitofrontal overactivation in the reward processing of NSSI patients independent of their diagnosis of BPD (Vega et al., 2018), or have focused on potential differences in endogenous opioids in NSSI versus non-NSSI patients (Sandman et al., 1997; Stanley et al., 2010). In chapter 15 (this volume), Claes et al. empirically review different theoretical models on NSSI and Positive Valence Systems. Second, they review the role of the Positive Valence Systems in the relation between NSSI and other adverse emotion-regulating behaviors, like substance use and eating disorder behavior, and discuss possible transdiagnostic interventions.

Within the Cognitive Systems domain, research on the Perception construct has suggested the possibility of abnormalities in pain perception (Franklin et al., 2013). With regard to future research, Schreiner et al. (2015) recommend more studies focusing on the general NSSI population, as opposed to specific patient groups, and the inclusion of longitudinal designs that can investigate the time course in the pathophysiology of, for example, pain perception.

Of special interest as well are studies tying NSSI to the Effortful Control construct, with, for example, findings by Glenn and Klonsky (2010) showing that confrontation with negative emotions prompts people with NSSI to make hasty and ill-advised decisions more so than it does people without NSSI. Browning and Muehlenkamp (chapter 16, this volume) summarize what is currently known about transdiagnostic cognitive processes that activate NSSI, namely, rumination, attentional bias, and cognitive control deficits, and those that maintain and increase it, namely, rule-governed behavior and expectancies.

Social processes have also proven to be of vital importance in explaining NSSI behavior. For example, a history of poor attachment quality, mediated by poor emotion regulation and identity problems, has been known to predict NSSI (Gandhi et al., 2019). As another example, a positive perception of self has proven to protect against NSSI, while a negative perception of self increases the risk for NSSI (Hooley & Franklin, 2018). Using the four constructs of the RDoC systems for social processes, Zetterqvist and Johan Bjureberg (chapter 17, this volume) look at the effects of social exclusion, rejection sensitivity and negative social bias, including a clinical case example.

To date, research connecting NSSI with the Arousal and Regulatory Systems domain or the Sensorimotor domain remains sparse. As a general directive, Schreiner et al. (2015) acknowledge that the different RDoC domains and constructs interact heavily with each other, requiring future NSSI research to examine the interfacing of multiple constructs and to include temporal dynamics, prolonged effects, and, finally, the remaining units of analysis of the RDoC matrix.

RDoC as an Avenue to the (Re)Conceptualization of Psychopathology

Moving away from DSM personality categories, the RDoC system is particularly well placed to (re)conceptualize (personality) pathology and describe a number of its causal pathways through five of the current six research domains and their constituting constructs. Rather than an exhaustive overview, we briefly discuss five lines of transdiagnostic personality pathology research as proof of concept, mapping them on the consecutive RDoC domains and constructs. As an alternative approach, Koudys et al. (2019) have successfully aligned the individual criteria of the polythetic categorical personality disorders in DSM-5 onto the RDoC constructs.

Negative and Positive Valence Systems: Reinforcement Sensitivity Theory Research

Landmark personality pathology research by Gray (1976) on his reinforcement sensitivity theory (RST) directly addresses RDoC's Negative and Positive Valence Systems. The original RST is as an interplay between three neurobiological systems: a Behavioral Inhibition System (BIS; Gray, 1976, 1982), a Behavioral Approach System (BAS; Gray, 1987), and a Fight/Flight System (FFS; Gray, 1987). The BIS responds to conditioned aversive stimuli, to unconditioned fear stimuli, and to extreme novel/high intensity stimuli. The BAS reacts to conditioned appetitive stimuli. The FFS responds to unconditioned aversive stimuli eliciting anger or panic (Gray, 1987). According to RST, individuals high on BIS are more sensitive to aversive signals relative to low-BIS persons, and individuals high on BAS are more responsive to (potential) reward in comparison to low-BAS persons (Corr, 2001; see also Pickering et al., 1997). In the revised form of RST (Corr, 2008; Gray & McNaughton, 2000), FFS is elaborated into the Fight/Flight/Freeze System (FFFS). The BIS now stands for the resolution of goal conflict: in situations that include both threat (RDoC's Negative Valence Systems; activating the FFFS) and reward (RDoC's Positive Valence Systems; activating the BAS), the BIS will inhibit one of both (the FFFS if reward outweighs threat, resulting in approach behavior, versus the BAS if threat outweighs reward, resulting in avoidance behavior). Both high and low BIS and BAS reactivity have been associated with different personality disorders in predictable ways (e.g., Caseras et al., 2001; Pastor et al., 2007). Of note, high BIS reactivity also corresponds to depression, eating disorders, and alcoholism (Bijttebier et al., 2009), low BIS reactivity to psychopathy (Fowles, 1980; Uzieblo et al., 2007), high BAS reactivity to conduct problems, substance abuse and mania (Bijttebier et al., 2009), and low BAS reactivity to depression (Campbell-Sills et al., 2004).

Cognitive Systems: Adding Effortful Control Research

In 1989, Rothbart coined "effortful control" (EC; Evans & Rothbart, 2007; Nigg, 2017; Rothbart, 1989), or the capacity to actively self-regulate behavioral and emotional reactions. EC is a product of brain maturation and comprises behavioral control and attentional control. Behavioral control includes the capacity to actively inhibit behavior (Inhibitory control) as well as to activate behavior (Activation control), both in accordance with appropriate circumstances. Attentional control represents the ability to guide attention to where it is needed—that is, the capacity to focus or shift attention in accordance of situational (external or internal) demands. Rothbart's behavioral control maps onto the RDoC Cognitive Systems Cognitive Control construct, while his attentional control relates to the RDoC Cognitive Systems Attention construct. Combining the reactive BIS/BAS constellations with EC, Claes et al. (2009) found that high BIS only relates to severe personality pathology if EC is low. Low EC has been associated with other forms of psychopathology as well, like anxiety and depression (Gulley et al. 2016) and externalizing problems (Meehan et al., 2013).

Introducing a Proximity Dimension

McNaughton (2020) renamed the BIS to the Goal Inhibition System (GIS), the BAS to the Goal Attraction System (GAS), and the FFFS of the revised RST (Corr, 2008) to the Goal Repulsion System (GRS). In addition, he introduces a defensive/appetitive distance dimension that denotes the proximity of the repulsive/attractive object. This now allows for a hierarchical reformulation of the three systems, with different neuronal modules working at lower versus higher levels of each of the three systems (fig. 12.3). The lowest (i.e., most proximal level) represents the most immediate, reactive, and object-specific responses of the GAS/GRS/GIS. The highest (i.e. most distal level) represents the higher-order planning circuits of each of the GAS/GRS/GIS, and, according to McNaughton (2020), constitutes motivation-related (personality) traits. Higher serotonin levels shift the control from lower to higher levels of the three systems (fig. 12.3). Other neuromodulators and hormonal compounds influence the hierarchically organized modules of the GAS/GRS/GIS as well, with some (e.g., benzodiazepine ligands) affecting all the modules of a specific system (i.e., the GIS), and others (e.g., noradrenaline and dopamine) all the modules of the three systems (McNaughton, 2020).

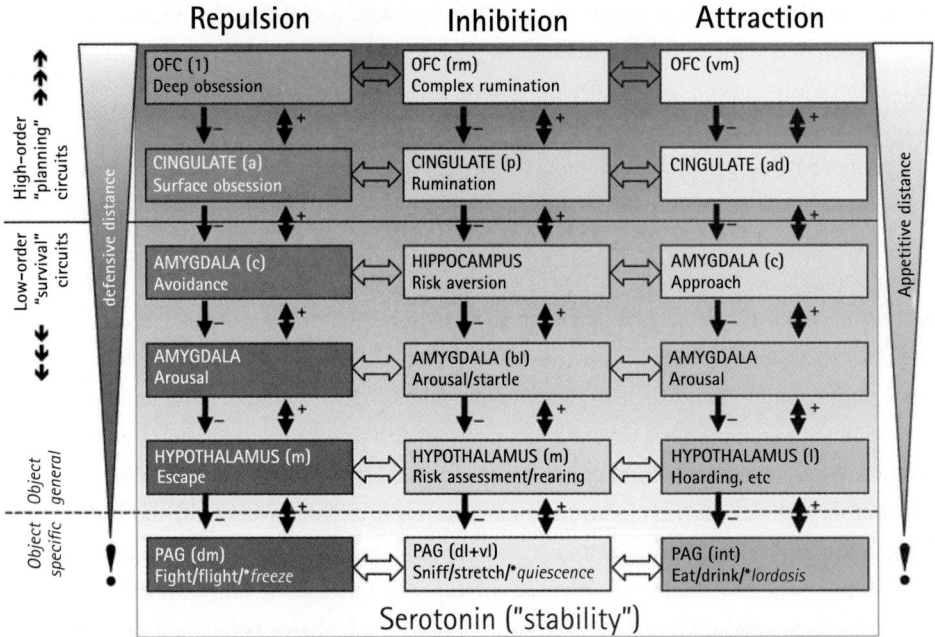

Figure 12.3 McNaughton's hierarchy: Goal Attraction System (GAS), Goal Repulsion System (GRS), and Goal Inhibition System (GIS). McNaughton's hierarchically organized GAS, GRS, and GIS, activated by conflict between goals, with comprising modules in relation to motivational distance (contacting-distant) and neural location (caudal-rostral). McNaughton, 2020, p. 12. We thank the author for his kind permission to use this figure. Figure reproduced under the terms of a CC BY 4.0 license.

Social Systems: Research on Mentalizing and Epistemic Trust

Difficulties in the RDoC Social Systems domain are arguably synonymous with personality pathology. The ongoing personality pathology research on "mentalizing" provides a strong example. Introduced by Fonagy in 1989, "mentalizing" is the ability to be aware of the subjectivity of one's own and other's experiences, and to see behavior as driven by personal feelings, desires, wishes, attitudes, and goals (Fonagy, 1989; Luyten & Fonagy, 2015). As a result, mentalizing greatly strengthens one's capacity for affect regulation and regulation of interpersonal relationships (Balestrieri, 2015). In their overview of the neurobiology involved in mentalizing, Luyten and Fonagy (2015) distinguish between automatic and controlled mentalizing, each involving different neural circuits. Automatic mentalizing is fast, is reflexive, and demands little effort. Brain structures involved include the amygdala, basal ganglia, ventromedial prefrontal cortex, lateral temporal cortex, and dorsal anterior cingulate cortex (Luyten & Fonagy, 2015; Satpute & Lieberman, 2006). Controlled mentalizing requires reflective, verbal, and conscious effort. Brain structures involved include the lateral prefrontal cortex, medial prefrontal cortex, the lateral and medial parietal cortex, the medial temporal lobe, and the rostral anterior cingulate cortex (Luyten & Fonagy, 2015; Uddin et al., 2007). Within the RDoC frame of reference, mentalizing relates directly to the RDoC Social Systems

Social Communication, Perception and Understanding of Self, and Perception and Understanding of Others constructs. Personality pathology as well as other mental disorders have been associated with temporary or permanent impairment in the ability for controlled mentalizing (Fonagy et al., 2015; Luyten et al., 2020). Examples other than personality pathology include depression (Ladegaard et al., 2014), autism and psychosis (Chung et al., 2014), and posttraumatic stress disorder (Allen, 2001). Mapping directly on the constituents of the RDoC Social systems social communication, affiliation, and attachment constructs, is the investigation into the concept of epistemic trust, or the "trust in the authenticity and personal relevance of interpersonally transmitted knowledge about how the social environment works and how best to navigate it" (Fonagy et al., 2017, p. 177).

Sensorimotor Systems: Research on Self–Other Distinction
Current personality pathology research by De Meulemeester et al. (2021a, 2021b) translates directly to the Sensorimotor Systems agency and ownership construct. Further investigating the mechanisms involved in the process of mentalizing, the authors study problems in so-called self–other distinction (SOD) in BPD, with SOD referring to the capacity to discriminate between one's own body, motor actions, and mental representations versus those of others (Lamm et al., 2016). De Meulemeester et al. (2021b) find BPD to evidence decreased agency over one's own motor actions, decreased ownership over one's own body, and difficulties in *shifting between self and other representations. Research shows SOD to be related to the* medial prefrontal cortex and the temporo-parietal junction (Uddin et al., 2007; Van Overwalle, 2009).

RDoC Limitations and Alternative Approaches
The RDoC framework has clearly opened up promising opportunities. Through its neurobiological paradigm, it has the capacity to tie together and further advance a plethora of findings stemming from different lines of research. There are three related, current limitations of the RDoC frame of reference. The first consideration pertains to properties emerging from interactions between RDoC Domains/Constructs/Subconstructs. The second consideration pertains to emergent properties at higher levels of hierarchical systems. The third consideration deals with the assumed unidirectionality in the current RDoC research. Although we believe these current limitations are amendable, acknowledging them is important, in order to avoid a future obstacle not unlike the current hampering publication requirement of DSM/ICD categorical delineation of research groups, which the RDoC approach sets out to overcome (see, e.g., Hershenberg & Goldfried, 2015). Indeed, Clarkson et al. (2020) cited both Reardon (2017) and Teachman et al. (2018) when stating that in youth research, "NIMH funding for psychosocial intervention research without clear biological outcome measures has decreased by 45%" (Clarkson et al., 2020, p. 298).

Properties Emerging From Interaction Between RDoC Domains/Constructs/Subconstructs
Clarkson et al. (2020) state that the RDoC framework stimulates dimensional research across units of analysis and diagnoses, but within a domain/construct/subconstruct. While this is indeed where business has to start, it is important to consider that in the course of time we will probably need to take into account many interaction effects between domains/constructs/subconstructs in order to advance our scientific understanding of observable phenomena. To name but one example, one can consider the putative interaction between the Positive Valence Systems construct Reward Valuation, the Negative Valence Systems construct Loss, and the Systems for Social Processes construct of Attachment in case of the gene-silencing effect of nonresponsive mothering during the critical period in early infancy (e.g., Stolzenberg & Mayer, 2019). Indeed, identical brain regions are involved in different domains/constructs/subconstructs. Studying the Social systems domain, Jarcho et al. (2016), for example, described highly active amygdala (a key region in the Negative Systems Domain) in high social reticence preadolescents in receipt of unpredictable negative peer evaluation.

Emergent Properties at Higher Levels of Hierarchical Systems
In accordance with its position that mental disorders ultimately result from dysfunctional neurobiological mechanisms, RDoC has mainly fostered research in which conditions in one column of the matrix (fig. 12.2) get explained by looking at conditions in a preceding column. As such, its approach is reductionistic; that is, it looks for conclusive explanations at the most basic level possible. Borsboom et al. (2019) argues that this approach might not be sufficient, as symptoms can also "arise from relations between multiple realizable mental states, and hence resist reduction to underlying biology" (Borsboom et al., 2019, p. 5). Or as formulated by McNaughton (2020, p. 14) in the case of personality pathology, a neural-level approach "will clearly not explain all personality traits," although "it will provide a solid foundation on which to build understanding of traits that emerge at higher levels." Figure 12.4 illustrates the predicament in principle: the properties and functionalities of the LEGO® lion on the right as fig. 12.4b and building blocks on the left as fig. 12.4a but emerge from their arrangement.

ASSUMED UNIDIRECTIONALITY

In addition to the previous point, an important question regards the status of the subjective experience at the far right of the RDoC units of analysis. While current RDoC research largely focuses on subjective experience as an endpoint in the causal chain, research does show that feedback loops do exist, with the ability to reshape the very start of the cascading phenomena (Seth & Friston, 2016). Even if this would be limited to a retroactive reshaping (i.e., taking place within a closed circuit and with mental states as an initial endpoint phenomenon), subjective experience remains a therapeutic point of entry with the capacity to even partly correct epigenetic attachment gene-silencing in adult

Figure 12.4 Properties emerging from a higher level: the functionalities of the LEGO® lion.

patients (Liggan & Kay, 1999). Beauregard (2007) demonstrates convincingly that mental processes like metacognition and beliefs exert causal influence on brain plasticity at the molecular, cellular, and neural circuit level. Similarly, the conceptual framework put forward by Kalisch et al. (2015), the positive appraisal style theory of resilience (PASTOR), considers resilience as the product of top-down appraisal of stressful stimuli. In sum, future RDoC practice will undoubtedly be enriched by research that reinstates subjective experience as a potential significant contributor as opposed to an inert epiphenomenon of neural processes.

OTHER TRANSDIAGNOSTIC APPROACHES

Two examples of other transdiagnostic approaches are the network approach (e.g., Persson, 2019), and the Hierarchical Taxonomy of Psychopathology (HiTOP; Kotov et al., 2017). The Network approach does not look for latent causes for presenting symptoms (e.g., the latent construct "depression" causing observable symptoms like sleep loss, loss of interest, suicidal ideation etc.; Persson, 2019, p. 262), but conceptualizes pathology constructs as states of systems that emerge from the presenting symptoms (e.g., depression as the system state that emanates from sleep loss, loss of interest, and suicidal ideation; Persson, 2019, p. 262). The HiTOP (Kotov et al., 2017) is a dimensional classification system based on empirical symptom and maladaptive trait covariation. It uses factor analysis and latent class analysis to come up with transdiagnostic dimensions that are in line with the dimensional nature of psychopathology, and that address the problem of comorbidity, the within-disorder heterogeneity, and the symptom overlap that plague the traditional a priori DSM/ICD categories Michelini et al. (2021). Most interestingly, Michelini et al. (2021) have recently produced an interface that links RDoC and HiTOP, with HiTOP as an invaluable aid to RDoC-informed research by supplying "psychometrically robust clinical targets" (Michelini et al., 2021, p. 4).

Conclusion

This introductory chapter has familiarized the reader with the RDoC and the paradigm shift it represents toward a new conceptualization of psychopathology. We believe the RDoC framework provides an answer to the problems currently encountered in the present classification systems of mental disorders, advocated by either the DSM-5 (American Psychiatric Association, 2013) or the ICD-11 (World Health Organization, 2019). The RDoC approach holds great promise as the organizing principle for (1) scientific research, (2) future clinical diagnostic assessment, and (3) future clinical treatment. With regard to NSSI specifically, studies along at least four of RDoC's domains and comprising constructs have already generated most encouraging contributions to the field. Importantly however, we also see three limitations of the RDoC approach in its current form that can subsequently be addressed to advance future research. These are (1) the need for future studies to investigate interactions between the RDoC domains/constructs instead of within domain/construct studies, (2) the future inclusion of system properties emerging at higher levels of hierarchical systems, and (3) the inclusion of research into the bidirectionality of the RDoC columns, in addition to the current left-to-right causality studies.

References

Ainsworth M. D., Blehar, M. C., Waters, E., & Wall, S. (1975). *Patterns of attachment: A psychological study of the Strange Situation*. Erlbaum.

Alexopoulos, G. S., & Arean, P. (2014). A model for streamlining psychotherapy in the RDoC era: The example of "Engage." *Molecular Psychiatry, 19*, 14–19. https://doi.org/10.1038/mp.2013.150

Alexopoulos, G. S., Hoptman, M. J., Yuen, G., Kanellopoulos, D., Seirup, J. K., Lim, K. O., & Gunning, F. M. (2013). Functional connectivity in apathy of late-life depression: A preliminary study. *Journal of Affective Disorders, 149*, 398–405. https://doi.org/10.1016/j.jad.2012.11.023

Allen, J. G. (2001). *Traumatic relationships and serious mental disorders*. Wiley.

American Psychiatric Association. (2013). *Diagnostic and statistical manual of mental disorders*. 5th ed.

Asarnow, J. R., Porta, G., Spirito, A., Emslie, G., Clarke, G., Wagner, K. D., Vitiello, B., Keller, M., Birmaher, B., McCracken, J., Mayes, T., Berk, M., & Brent, D. A. (2011). Suicide attempts and nonsuicidal self-injury in the treatment of resistant depression in adolescents: Findings from the TORDIA study. *Journal of the American Academy of Child & Adolescent Psychiatry, 50*, 772–781. https://doi.org/10.1016/j.jaac.2011.04.003

Balestrieri, M., Zuanon, S., Pellizzari, J., Zappoli-Thyrion, E., & Ciano, R. (2015). Mentalization in eating disorders: A preliminary trial comparing mentalization-based treatment (MBT) with a psychodynamic-oriented treatment. *Eating and Weight Disorders-Studies on Anorexia, Bulimia and Obesity, 20*, 525–528. https://doi.org/10.1007/s40519-015-0204-1

Baron-Cohen, S., Wheelwright, S., Hill, J., Raste, Y., & Plumb, I. (2001). The "Reading the Mind in the Eyes" Test revised version: A study with normal adults, and adults with Asperger syndrome or high-functioning autism. *Journal of Child Psychology and Psychiatry, 42*, 241–251. https://doi.org/10.1111/1469-7610.00715

Beauregard, M. (2007). Mind does really matter: Evidence from neuroimaging studies of emotional self-regulation, psychotherapy, and placebo effect. *Progress in Neurobiology, 81*, 218–236. https://doi.org/10.1016/j.pneurobio.2007.01.005

Bijttebier, P., Beck, I., Claes, L., & Vandereycken, W. (2009). Gray's Reinforcement Sensitivity Theory as a framework for research on personality–psychopathology associations. *Clinical Psychology Review, 29*, 421–430. https://doi.org/10.1016/j.cpr.2009.04.002

Borsboom, D., Cramer, A. O., & Kalis, A. (2019). Brain disorders? Not really: Why network structures block reductionism in psychopathology research. *Behavioral and Brain Sciences, 42*, 1–63. https://doi.org/10.1017/S0140525X17002266

Campbell-Sills, L., Liverant, G. I., & Brown, T. A. (2004). Psychometric evaluation of the behavioral inhibition/behavioral activation scales in a large sample of outpatients with anxiety and mood disorders. *Psychological Assessment, 16*, 244–254. https://doi.org/10.1037/1528-3542.6.4.587

Caseras, X., Torrubia, R., & Farré, J. M. (2001). Is the Behavioural Inhibition System the core vulnerability for cluster C personality disorders? *Personality and Individual Differences, 31*, 349–359. https://doi.org/10.1016/S0191-8869(00)00141-0

Casey, B. J., Oliveri, M. E., & Insel, T. (2014). A neurodevelopmental perspective on the research domain criteria (RDoC) framework. *Biological Psychiatry, 76*, 350–353. https://doi.org/10.1016/j.biopsych.2014.01.006

Chung, Y. S., Barch, D., & Strube, M. (2014). A meta-analysis of Mentalizing impairments in adults with schizophrenia and autism spectrum disorder. *Schizophrenia Bulletin, 40*, 602–616. https://doi.org/10.1093/schbul/sbt048

Claes, L., Vertommen, S., Smits, D., & Bijttebier, P. (2009). Emotional reactivity and self-regulation in relation to personality disorders. *Personality and Individual Differences, 47*, 948–953. https://doi.org/10.1016/j.paid.2009.07.027

Clarkson, T., Kang, E., Capriola-Hall, N., Lerner, M. D., Jarcho, J., & Prinstein, M. J. (2020). Meta-analysis of the RDoC social processing domain across units of analysis in children and adolescents. *Journal of Clinical Child & Adolescent Psychology, 49*, 297–321. https://doi.org/10.1080/15374416.2019.1678167

Corr, P. J. (2001). Testing problems in JA Gray's personality theory: A commentary on. *Personality and Individual Differences, 30*, 333–352. https://doi.org/10.1016/S0191-8869(00)00028-3

Corr, P. J. (2008). Reinforcement sensitivity theory (RST): Introduction. In P. J. Corr (Ed.), *The reinforcement sensitivity theory of personality* (pp. 1–43). Cambridge University Press.

Cuthbert, B. N. (2014). The RDoC framework: Facilitating transition from ICD/DSM to dimensional approaches that integrate neuroscience and psychopathology. *World Psychiatry, 13*, 28–35. https://doi.org/10.1002/wps.20087

Cuthbert, B. N. (2020). The role of RDoC in future classification of mental disorders. *Dialogues in Clinical Neuroscience, 22*, 81–85. https://doi.org/10.31887/DCNS.2020.22.1/bcuthbert

De Meulemeester, C., Lowyck, B., & Luyten, P. (2021a). The role of impairments in self–other distinction in borderline personality disorder: A narrative review of recent evidence. *Neuroscience & Biobehavioral Reviews, 127*, 242–254. https://doi.org/10.1016/j.neubiorev.2021.04.022

De Meulemeester, C., Lowyck, B., Panagiotopoulou, E., Fotopoulou, A., & Luyten, P. (2021b). Self–other distinction and borderline personality disorder features: Evidence for egocentric and altercentric bias in a self–other facial morphing task. *Personality Disorders: Theory, Research, and Treatment, 2*(4):377–388. https://doi.org/10.1037/per0000415

De Raedt, R. (2020). Contributions from neuroscience to the practice of Cognitive Behaviour Therapy: Translational psychological science in service of good practice. *Behaviour Research and Therapy, 125*, 103545. https://doi.org/10.1016/j.brat.2019.103545

Etkin, A., Egner, T., & Kalisch, R. (2011). Emotional processing in anterior cingulate and medial prefrontal cortex. *Trends in Cognitive Sciences, 15*, 85–93. https://doi.org/10.1016/j.tics.2010.11.004

Evans, D. E., & Rothbart, M. K. (2007). Developing a model for adult temperament. *Journal of Research in Personality, 41*, 868–888. https://doi.org/10.1016/j.jrp.2006.11.002

Fonagy P. (1989). On tolerating mental states: Theory of mind in borderline patients. *Bulletin of the Anna Freud Centre, 12*, 91–115.

Fonagy, P., Campbell, C., & Bateman, A. (2017). Mentalizing, attachment, and epistemic trust in group therapy. *International Journal of Group Psychotherapy, 67*, 176–201. https://doi.org/10.1080/00207284.2016.1263156

Fonagy, P., Luyten, P., & Bateman, A. (2015). Translation: Mentalizing as treatment target in borderline personality disorder. *Personality Disorders: Theory, Research, and Treatment*, 6, 380–392. https://doi.org/10.1037/per0000113

Fowles, D. C. (1980). The three arousal model: Implications of Gray's two-factor learning theory for heart rate, electrodermal activity, and psychopathy. *Psychophysiology*, 17, 87–104. https://doi.org/10.1111/j.1469-8986.1980.tb00117.x

Franklin, J. C., Puzia, M. E., Lee, K. M., Lee, G. E., Hanna, E. K., Spring, V. L., & Prinstein, M. J. (2013). The nature of pain offset relief in nonsuicidal self-injury: A laboratory study. *Clinical Psychological Science*, 1, 110–119. https://doi.org/10.1177/2167702612474440

Garland, E. L., Hanley, A. W., Baker, A. K., & Howard, M. O. (2017). Biobehavioral mechanisms of mindfulness as a treatment for chronic stress: An RDoC perspective. *Chronic Stress*, 1, 1–14. https://doi.org/10.1177/2470547017711912.

Gandhi, A., Luyckx, K., Molenberghs, G., Baetens, I., Goossens, L., Maitra, S., & Claes, L. (2019). Maternal and peer attachment, identity formation, and non-suicidal self-injury: A longitudinal mediation study. *Child and Adolescent Psychiatry and Mental Health*, 13, 7. https://doi.org/10.1186/s13034-019-0267-2

Glenn, C. R., & Klonsky, E. D. (2010). A multimethod analysis of impulsivity in nonsuicidal self-injury. *Personality Disorders: Theory, Research, and Treatment*, 1, 67–75. https://doi.org/10.1037/a0017427

Goessl, V. C., Curtiss, J. E., & Hofmann, S. G. (2017). The effect of heart rate variability biofeedback training on stress and anxiety: A meta-analysis. *Psychological medicine*, 47, 2578–2586. https://doi.org/10.1017/S0033291717001003

Gordon, E., Barnett, K. J., Cooper, N. J., Tran, N., & Williams, L. M. (2008). An "integrative neuroscience" platform: Application to profiles of negativity and positivity bias. *Journal of Integrative Neuroscience*, 7, 345–366. https://doi.org/10.1142/S0219635208001927

Gray, J. A. (1976). The Behavioural Inhibition System: A possible substrate for anxiety. In M. P. Feldman, & A. M. Broadhurst (Eds.), *Theoretical and experimental bases of behaviour modification* (pp. 3–41). Wiley.

Gray, J. A. (1982). *The neuropsychology of anxiety: An enquiry into the functions of the septo-hippocampal system*. Oxford University Press.

Gray, J. A. (1987). *The psychology of fear and stress*. Cambridge University Press.

Gray, J. A., & McNaughton, N. (2000). *The neuropsychology of anxiety*. Oxford University Press.

Gulley, L. D., Hankin, B. L., & Young, J. F. (2016). Risk for depression and anxiety in youth: The interaction between negative affectivity, effortful control, and stressors. *Journal of Abnormal Child Psychology*, 44, 207–218. https://doi.org/10.1007/s10802-015-9997-7

Hasking, P., & Claes, L. (2020). Transdiagnostic mechanisms involved in nonsuicidal self-injury, risky drinking and disordered eating: Impulsivity, emotion regulation and alexithymia. *Journal of American College Health*, 68, 603–609. https://doi.org/10.1080/07448481.2019.1583661

Hershenberg, R., & Goldfried, M. R. (2015). Implications of RDoC for the research and practice of psychotherapy. *Behavior Therapy*, 46, 156–165. https://doi.org/10.1016/j.beth.2014.09.014

Hooley, J. M., & Franklin, J. C. (2018). Why do people hurt themselves? A new conceptual model of nonsuicidal self-injury. *Clinical Psychological Science*, 6, 428–451. https://doi.org/10.1177/2167702617745641

Insel, T. R. (2014). The NIMH Research Domain Criteria (RDoC) project: Precision medicine for psychiatry. *American Journal of Psychiatry*, 171, 395–397. https://doi.org/10.1176/appi.ajp.2014.14020138

Insel, T. R., Cuthbert, B., Garvey, M., Heinssen, R., Pine, D.S., Quinn, K., Sanislow, C., & Wang, P. (2010). Research Domain Criteria (RDoC): Toward a new classification framework for research on mental disorders. *American Journal of Psychiatry*, 167, 748–751. https://doi.org/10.1176/appi.ajp.2010.09091379

Irzik, G., & Nola, R. (2011). A family resemblance approach to the nature of science for science education. *Science & Education*, 20, 591–607. https://doi.org/10.1007/s11191-010-9293-44

Jarcho, J. M., Davis, M. M., Shechner, T., Degnan, K. A., Henderson, H. A., Stoddard, J., Fox, N. A., Leibenluft, E., Pine, D. S., & Nelson, E. E. (2016). Early-childhood social reticence predicts brain function in preadolescent youths during distinct forms of peer evaluation. *Psychological science*, 27, 821–835. https://doi.org/10.1177/0956797616638319

Jovev, M., Garner, B., Phillips, L., Velakoulis, D., Wood, S. J., Jackson, H. J., Pantelis, C., McGorry, P. D., & Chanen, A. M. (2008). An MRI study of pituitary volume and parasuicidal behavior in teenagers with first-presentation borderline personality disorder. *Psychiatry Research: Neuroimaging*, 162, 273–277. https://doi.org/10.1016/j.pscychresns.2007.12.003

Kalisch, R., Müller, M. B., & Tüscher, O. (2015). A conceptual framework for the neurobiological study of resilience. *Behavioral and Brain Sciences, 38*, 1–79. https://doi.org/10.1017/S0140525X1400082X

Kanter, J. W., Mulick, P. S., Busch, A. M., Berlin, K. S., & Martell, C. R. (2007). The Behavioral Activation for Depression Scale (BADS): Psychometric properties and factor structure. *Journal of Psychopathology and Behavioral Assessment, 29*, 191–202. https://doi.org/10.1007/s10862-006-9038-5

Klein, D. F. (1993). False suffocation alarms, spontaneous panics and related conditions: An integrative hypothesis. *Archives of General Psychiatry, 50*, 306–317. https://doi.org/10.1001/archpsyc.1993.01820160076009

Klonsky, E. D. (2007). The functions of deliberate self-injury: A review of the evidence. *Clinical Psychology Review, 27*, 226–239. https://doi.org/10.1016/j.cpr.2006.08.002

Kotov, R., Krueger, R. F., Watson, D., Achenbach, T. M., Althoff, R. R., Bagby, R. M., Brown, T. A., Carpenter, W. T., Caspi, A., Clark, L. A., Eaton, N. R., Forbes, M. K., Forbush, K. T., Goldberg, D., Hasin, D., Hyman, S. E., Ivanova, M. Y., Lynam, D. R., Markon, K., . . . Zimmerman, M. (2017). The Hierarchical Taxonomy of Psychopathology (HiTOP): A dimensional alternative to traditional nosologies. *Journal of Abnormal Psychology, 126*, 454–477. https://doi.org/10.1037/abn0000258

Koudys, J. W., Traynor, J. M., Rodrigo, A. H., Carcone, D., & Ruocco, A. C. (2019). The NIMH Research Domain Criteria (RDoC) initiative and its implications for research on personality disorder. *Current Psychiatry Reports, 21*, 1–12. https://doi.org/10.1007/s11920-019-1023-2

Ladegaard, N., Larsen, E. R., Videbech, P., & Lysaker, P. H. (2014). Higher-order social cognition in first-episode major depression. *Psychiatry Research, 216*, 37–43. https://doi.org/10.1016/j.psychres.2013.12.010

Lamm, C., Bukowski, H., & Silani, G. (2016). From shared to distinct self–other representations in empathy: Evidence from neurotypical function and socio-cognitive disorders. *Philosophical Transactions of the Royal Society B: Biological Sciences, 371*, 1–7. https://doi.org/10.1098/rstb.2015.0083.

Lang, P. J., McTeague, L. M., & Bradley, M. M. (2016). RDoC, DSM, and the reflex physiology of fear: A biodimensional analysis of the anxiety disorders spectrum. *Psychophysiology, 53*, 336–347. https://doi.org/10.1111/psyp.12462

Liggan, D. Y., & Kay, J. (1999). Some neurobiological aspects of psychotherapy: A review. *The Journal of Psychotherapy Practice and Research, 8*, 103–114.

Lilienfeld, S. O., & Treadway, M. T. (2016). Clashing diagnostic approaches: DSM-ICD versus RDoC *Annual Review of Clinical Psychology, 12*, 435–463. https://doi.org/10.1146/annurev-clinpsy-021815-093122

Livesley, W. J. (2003). Diagnostic dilemmas in the classification of personality disorder. In K. Phillips, M. First, & H. Z. Pincus (Eds.), *Advancing DSM: Dilemmas in psychiatric diagnosis* (pp. 153–189). American Psychiatric Association.

Luyten, P., Campbell, C., Allison, E., & Fonagy, P. (2020). The mentalizing approach to psychopathology: State of the art and future directions. *Annual Review of Clinical Psychology, 16*, 297–325. https://doi.org/10.1146/annurev-clinpsy-071919-015355

Luyten, P., & Fonagy, P. (2015). The neurobiology of mentalizing. *Personality Disorders: Theory, Research, and Treatment, 6*, 366–377. https://doi.org/10.1037/per0000117

Mao, J., & Yuan, J. (2021). Anhedonia and its intervention in depressive adults: New developments based on Research Domain Criteria (RDoC) in mental illnesses. *Stress and Brain, 1*, 2–32. 10.26599/SAB.2020.9060002

Marin, R. S., Biedrzycki, R. C., & Firinciogullari, S. (1991). Reliability and validity of the Apathy Evaluation Scale. *Psychiatry research, 38*, 143–162. https://doi.org/10.1016/0165-1781(91)90040-V

Markon, K. E., Chmielewski, M., & Miller, C. J. (2011). The reliability and validity of discrete and continuous measures of psychopathology: A quantitative review. *Psychological Bulletin, 137*, 856–79. https://doi.org/10.1037/a0023678

McNaughton, N. (2020). Personality neuroscience and psychopathology: Should we start with biology and look for neural-level factors? *Personality Neuroscience, 3*, 1–16. https://doi.org/10.1017/pen.2020.5

Meehan, K. B., De Panfilis, C., Cain, N. M., & Clarkin, J. F. (2013). Effortful control and externalizing problems in young adults. *Personality and Individual Differences, 55*, 553–558. https://doi.org/10.1016/j.paid.2013.04.019

Michelini, G., Palumbo, I. M., DeYoung, C. G., Latzman, R. D., & Kotov, R. (2021). Linking RDoC and HiTOP: A new interface for advancing psychiatric nosology and neuroscience. *Clinical Psychology Review, 86*, Article 102025. https://doi.org/10.1016/j.cpr.2021.102025.

Morris, S. E., & Cuthbert, B. N. (2012). Research Domain Criteria: Cognitive systems, neural circuits, and dimensions of behavior. *Dialogues in Clinical Neuroscience, 14*, 29–37. https://doi.org/10.31887/DCNS.2012.14.1/smorris

Needham, R. (1975). Polythetic classification: Convergence and consequences. *Man, 10*, 349–369. https://www.jstor.org/stable/2799807

Niedtfeld, I., Schulze, L., Kirsch, P., Herpertz, S. C., Bohus, M., & Schmahl, C. (2010). Affect regulation and pain in borderline personality disorder: A possible link to the understanding of self-injury. *Biological Psychiatry, 68*, 383–391. https://doi.org/10.1016/j.biopsych.2010.04.015

Nigg, J. T. (2017). Annual Research Review: On the relations among self-regulation, self-control, executive functioning, effortful control, cognitive control, impulsivity, risk-taking, and inhibition for developmental psychopathology. *Journal of Child Psychology and Psychiatry, 58*, 361–383. https://doi.org/10.1111/jcpp.12675

Pastor, M. C., Ross, S. R., Segarra, P., Montañés, S., Poy, R., & Moltó, J. (2007). Behavioral inhibition and activation dimensions: Relationship to MMPI-2 indices of personality disorder. *Personality and Individual Differences, 42*, 235–245. https://doi.org/10.1016/j.paid.2006.06.015

Persson, B. N. (2019). Current directions in psychiatric classification: From the DSM to RDoC. In D. Garcia, T. Archer, & R. M. Kostrzewa (Eds.), *Personality and brain disorders* (pp. 253–268). Springer, Cham.

Pickering, A. D., Corr, P. J., Powell, J. H., Kumari, V., Thornton, J. C., & Gray, J. A. (1997). Individual differences in reactions to reinforcing stimuli are neither black nor white: To what extent are they gray?. In H. Nyborg (Ed.), *The scientific study of human nature: Tribute to Hans J. Eysenck at eighty* (pp. 36–67). Elsevier Sciences.

Plener, P. L., Bubalo, N., Fladung, A. K., Ludolph, A. G., & Lulé, D. (2012). Prone to excitement: Adolescent females with non-suicidal self-injury (NSSI) show altered cortical pattern to emotional and NSS-related material. *Psychiatry Research: Neuroimaging, 203*, 146–152. https://doi.org/10.1016/j.pscychresns.2011.12.012

Rakyan V. K., & Beck, S. (2006). Epigenetic variation and inheritance in mammals. *Current Opinion in Genetics & Development, 16*, 573–577. https://doi.org/10.1016/j.gde.2006.09.002.

Reardon, S. (2017). US mental-health agency's push for basic research has slashed support for clinical trials. *Nature, 546*, 338–339. https://doi.org/10.1038/546338a

Rothbart, M. K. (1989). Temperament and development. In: G. A. Kohnstamm, J. E. Bates, & M. K. Rothbart (Eds.), *Temperament in childhood*, pp. 187–247. Wiley.

Russo, S. J., & Nestler, E. J. (2013). The brain reward circuitry in mood disorders. *Nature Reviews Neuroscience, 14*, 609–625. https://doi.org/10.1038/nrn3381

Sandman, C. A., Hetrick, W., Taylor, D. V., & Chicz-DeMet, A. (1997). Dissociation of POMC peptides after self-injury predicts responses to centrally acting opiate blockers. *American Journal on Mental Retardation, 102*, 182–199. https://doi.org/10.1352/0895-8017(1997)102<0182:DOPPAS>2.0.CO;2

Satpute, A. B., & Lieberman, M. D. (2006). Integrating automatic and controlled processes into neurocognitive models of social cognition. *Brain Research, 1079*, 86–97. https://doi.org/10.1016/j.brainres.2006.01.005

Schreiner, M. W., Klimes-Dougan, B., Begnel, E. D., & Cullen, K. R. (2015). Conceptualizing the neurobiology of non-suicidal self-injury from the perspective of the Research Domain Criteria project. *Neuroscience & Biobehavioral Reviews, 57*, 381–391. https://doi.org/10.1016/j.neubiorev.2015.09.011

Seth, A. K., & Friston, K. J. (2016). Active interoceptive inference and the emotional brain. *Philosophical Transactions of the Royal Society B: Biological Sciences, 371*, 1708–1718. https://doi.org/10.1098/rstb.2016.0007

Shedler, J., & Westen, D. (2004). Refining DSM-IV personality disorder diagnosis: Integrating science and practice. *American Journal of Psychiatry, 161*, 1350–1365. https://doi.org/10.1176/appi.ajp.161.8.1350

Stanley, B., Sher, L., Wilson, S., Ekman, R., Huang, Y. Y., & Mann, J. J. (2010). Non-suicidal self-injurious behavior, endogenous opioids and monoamine neurotransmitters. *Journal of Affective Disorders, 124*, 134–140. https://doi.org/10.1016/j.jad.2009.10.028

Stolzenberg, D. S., & Mayer, H. S. (2019). Experience-dependent mechanisms in the regulation of parental care. *Frontiers in Neuroendocrinology, 54*, 1–12. https://doi.org/10.1016/j.yfrne.2019.04.002

Teachman, B. A., McKay, D., Barch, D. M., Prinstein, M. J., Hollon, S. D., & Chambless, D. L. (2018). How psychosocial research can help the National Institute of Mental Health achieve its grand challenge to reduce the burden of mental illnesses and psychological disorders. *American Psychologist, 74*, 415–431. https://doi.org/10.1037/amp0000361

Tolin, D. F., Davies, C. D., & Moskow, D. M. (2020). Biofeedback and neurofeedback for anxiety disorders: A quantitative and qualitative systematic review. *Advances in Experimental Medicine and Biology, 1191*, 265–289. https://doi.org/10.1007/978-981-32-9705-0_16

Trull, T., & Durrett, C. A. (2005). Categorical and dimensional models of personality disorder. *Annual Review of Clinical Psychology, 1*, 355–380. https://doi.org/10.1146/annurev.clinpsy.1.102803.144009

Uddin, L. Q., Iacoboni, M., Lange, C., & Keenan, J. P. (2007). The self and social cognition: The role of cortical midline structures and mirror neurons. *Trends in Cognitive Sciences, 11*, 153–157. https://doi.org/10.1016/j.tics.2007.01.001

Uzieblo, K., Verschuere, B., & Crombez, G. (2007). The Psychopathic Personality Inventory: Construct validity of the two-factor structure. *Personality and Individual Differences, 43*, 657–667. https://doi.org/10.1016/j.paid.2007.01.008

Van Overwalle, F. (2009). Social cognition and the brain: A meta-analysis. *Human Brain Mapping, 30*, 829–858. https://doi.org/10.1002/hbm.20547

Vega, D., Ripollés, P., Soto, À., Torrubia, R., Ribas, J., Monreal, J. A., Pascual, J. C., Salvador, R., Pomarol-Clotet, E., Rodríguez-Fornells, A., & Marco-Pallarés, J. (2018). Orbitofrontal overactivation in reward processing in borderline personality disorder: The role of non-suicidal self-injury. *Brain Imaging and Behavior, 12*, 217–228. https://doi.org/10.1007/s11682-017-9687-x

Williams, L. M., Cooper, N. J., Wisniewski, S. R., Gatt, J. M., Koslow, S. H., Kulkarni, J., DeVarney, S., Gordon, E., & John Rush, A. (2012). Sensitivity, specificity, and predictive power of the "Brief Risk-resilience Index for SCreening," a brief pan-diagnostic web screen for emotional health. *Brain and Behavior, 2*, 576–589. https://doi.org/10.1002/brb3.76

Wittgenstein, L. (1958). *Philosophical investigations*. Blackwell.

World Health Organization. (2019). *Clinical descriptions and diagnostic guidelines for mental and behavioral disorders*. https://gcp.network/eng/private/icd-11-guidelines/disorders.

CHAPTER 13

Negative Affect and Nonsuicidal Self-Injury

Benjamin A. Swerdlow, Jennifer G. Pearlstein, Devon B. Sandel, *and* Sheri L. Johnson

Abstract

Virtually all contemporary models of nonsuicidal self-injury (NSSI) emphasize negative affectivity as central to the phenomenology of NSSI. This chapter briefly illustrates the major points of divergence among these contemporary models before turning to the current state of the empirical literature. The focus, in particular, is on reviewing findings related to three facets of the negative affect-NSSI relationship: (a) negative affectivity as a risk factor for NSSI initiation and frequency, including trait-like individual differences, stressful life experiences, and central and peripheral neurophysiology; (b) heightened negative affect as a precursor to NSSI acts; and (c) short- and long-term consequences of NSSI engagement for negative affect. Several key takeaways emerge from this review. First, across multiple units of analysis, heightened negative affectivity and difficulties responding to negative affect are consistent risk factors for NSSI. Second, retrospective and ecological sampling studies converge on the conclusion that NSSI acts are typically preceded by higher-than-usual negative affect. Third, laboratory studies have demonstrated that pain offset is capable of reducing negative affect, arousal, and rumination in people with and without histories of NSSI, consistent with regulation of negative affect being the single most commonly endorsed function of NSSI. However, inconsistent findings from ecological sampling studies suggest that the affective consequences of NSSI are variable in practice, and evidence from longitudinal studies suggests that NSSI engagement is a harbinger of increased negative affectivity in the long run. These key findings are illustrated with a brief clinical vignette. Clinical implications and recommendations for future research conclude the chapter.

Key Words: negative affect, functions of nonsuicidal self-injury, affect regulation, emotion regulation, ecological momentary assessment, self-criticism

As increasing attention has been paid to nonsuicidal self-injury (NSSI), researchers have focused on understanding how and why this behavior is initiated and maintained. Apparent links between experiences of negative affect and the phenomenology of NSSI have been described in the clinical and research literatures for decades (e.g., Bennun, 1984; Feldman, 1988; Leibenluft et al., 1987; Pattison & Kahan, 1983). A rich set of models of NSSI has been developed, and virtually all these models emphasize that negative affect is central to the etiology of NSSI (Klonsky, 2007). These models differ, though, in the nature of the negative affective state considered to be primary, the temporal dynamics of the interplay between negative affect and NSSI, the affective functions and consequences ascribed to NSSI, and the contextual variables believed to be most central to triggering negative affect and amplifying its effects.

Alongside theories on negative affect as a trigger for NSSI, the Research Domain Criteria (RDoC) differentiate a rich array of negative affect-related constructs. More specifically, RDoC delineate subsystems of acute threat ("fear"), potential threat ("anxiety"), sustained threat, loss, and frustrative nonreward. For the most part, the literature on NSSI has not attended to these more specific subsystems driving negative affect. Where work fits one of these subsystems more directly, we will note that. At the same time, RDoC have provided a framework for considering the coordination of biological, psychological, and behavioral processes. Accordingly, we draw from multimodal work related to negative affect in NSSI. Before turning to the empirical literature on links between negative affect and NSSI, we briefly outline some of the contemporary models of NSSI to illustrate the various ways that they incorporate negative affect.

Theories of Negative Affect as a Trigger

At the broadest level, many theories focus on the intensity of negative emotions in those who engage in NSSI. Some models, though, are more specific about variables that might contribute to this intensity. For example, the emotional cascade theory (Selby & Joiner, 2009) focuses on processes that might lead to the intensification of negative emotion, such as tendencies toward rumination (this theoretical model and others are reviewed in Hird et al., this volume). Beyond general negative affect, some models have considered specific emotions that might be particularly tied to NSSI. For example, NSSI has been proposed to be more directly related to shame than to general negative affect, in that people who believe they deserve pain and punishment might find that the self-inflicted punishment involved in NSSI provides relief from shame and self-blame. In keeping with this, work by Hooley and colleagues (2002, 2010) suggests that tendencies toward self-criticism and self-hatred are key contextual factors in predicting the use of NSSI in response to negative emotions. Overall, then, multiple theories indicate that negative affect may trigger NSSI.

Theories Regarding the Function of NSSI in the Context of Negative Affect

Multiple theories describe a rich set of "functions" of NSSI specifically in relation to negative affect. Most contemporary models place some importance on the ways in which NSSI might regulate negative affect—that is, one salient consequence of NSSI acts may be short-term relief from negative affect. For example, the affect regulation function of NSSI was central in Linehan's clinical work on NSSI (Linehan, 1993). Critical to this account is the idea that people who experience their emotions as intolerable and who doubt their ability to regulate those emotions may find NSSI to be a particularly attractive strategy (see also Selby & Joiner, 2009; Spitzen et al., 2022).

According to the emotional cascade model, as negative emotions intensify and build on themselves, many common emotion regulation techniques and acts (e.g., going for a walk) may cease to be powerful enough to interrupt the emotional cascade. Indeed, as initially suggested by clinical observation (Linehan, 1993), several empirical articles have suggested that many emotion regulation techniques, such as cognitive reappraisal, may be more difficult to implement and less successful during periods of high arousal (see Sheppes, 2020). In this context, NSSI, with its powerful effects of refocusing attention on bodily pain and injury, is theorized to provide more immediate relief than other emotion regulation strategies.

There are multiple putative mechanisms through which NSSI has been theorized to contribute to affect regulation. For example, NSSI might relieve uncomfortable experiences of numbness by evoking some feeling—with the idea that even pain might be preferable to the absence of any feeling (Linehan, 1993). NSSI also could promote emotion regulation through distraction, in that pain may serve to break a focus on other negative stimuli and thoughts—one route to emotional avoidance (Chapman et al., 2006). Alternatively, the pain offset model suggests that by deliberately creating a temporary source of physical pain, NSSI can be reliably followed by relief from that pain—which alleviates negative affect and enhances positive affect. Pain offset is hypothesized to be mediated by activation followed by deactivation of neural regions involved in processing emotional and physical pain, such as the anterior cingulate and anterior insula (Muehlenkamp, 2014).

Beyond the direct affect regulation functions of NSSI, several other common functions have been ascribed to NSSI, and it is worth noting that several of these have relevance to negative affect. For example, perhaps the most commonly endorsed *inter*personal function of NSSI is communicating distress (cf. Nock & Prinstein, 2004)—again indicating the primacy of negative affect.

Finally, some models anticipate that the relationship between negative affect and NSSI will shift predictably over time. For example, in their description of the four functions model, Nock and Prinstein (2004) proposed that modeling of NSSI behavior and social communicative functions (e.g., communicating distress) may be particularly critical to the initiation of NSSI. Once initiated, though, individuals may begin to recognize and respond to the affect regulation functions, so that these are expected to become more central to the maintenance of NSSI (Nock & Prinstein, 2004; see also Hooley & Franklin, 2018). That is, relief from negative affect is expected to serve as a negative reinforcer, such that NSSI could become a conditioned response to negative emotional states over time (Selby & Joiner, 2009; Swerdlow et al., 2020). Consistent with the idea of the evolution of a conditioned response, some have suggested that with recurrent pairing of negative emotion and NSSI, engagement in NSSI in response to negative emotions may become habit-driven (Victor et al., 2012). Taken together, one possibility is that the affect regulating functions may be more related to the maintenance of NSSI than to initiation. Overall, a rich array of models focus on the functions of NSSI, and many of these functions directly implicate negative affect.

Summary of Theories of Negative Affect and NSSI

Negative affect occupies a central role in contemporary models of NSSI, including models involving affect regulation, self-punishment, and communication of distress to others (e.g., Hooley & Franklin, 2018; McKenzie & Gross, 2014; Nock & Prinstein, 2004). There is variation, though, in the specific roles that negative affective states are thought to play (e.g., trigger vs. functional reinforcer), the specific negative emotions that are thought to be most relevant (general negative affect vs. shame or other specific emotions), the developmental progression of whether negative affect is expected to be more predictive of the onset versus maintenance of NSSI, and the individual differences thought to be most relevant to vulnerability across these models.

Our focus in this chapter, then, will be on the current state of the evidence regarding links between negative affect and NSSI. Reflecting theory in this area, we will consider bidirectional links between negative affect and NSSI. First, we will survey the empirical literature related to risk factors for NSSI initiation and maintenance (i.e., frequency), with a specific focus on those related to negative affectivity. Then, we will consider proximal associations between negative affect and NSSI. That is, we outline evidence that heightened negative affect imminently precedes NSSI acts and then turn to evidence that NSSI provides short-term relief from general negative affect as well as specific negative emotions, such as shame. Finally, we turn our attention to clinical implications, recommendations for future research, and conclusions.

Negative Affectivity as a Risk Factor for NSSI

Considerable empirical evidence suggests that NSSI risk is heighted in the presence of chronically elevated negative affect and stress. In this section, we briefly review trait-based individual differences, environmental contributors, and biological processes (i.e., brain structure and function, neuroendocrine responses, and peripheral physiology) that may set the stage for the formation of a link between negative affect and NSSI.

Individual Differences in Tendencies toward Negative Affect and NSSI

In a pioneering meta-analysis of 20 longitudinal studies, hopelessness (weighted OR = 3.08), depressive symptoms (OR = 1.98), and affect dysregulation (OR = 1.05) all significantly predicted increased NSSI risk (Fox et al., 2015). Although affect dysregulation showed only a modest effect, the affect dysregulation index in this meta-analysis encompassed a very broad set of measures—specifically including laboratory indices of emotional reactivity alongside self-report measures of emotional suppression and negative affectivity. Of note, then, recent empirical evidence converges on the conclusion that self-perceptions of and beliefs about emotions and emotion dysregulation may be more central than observed emotional reactivity (cf. Hooley & Franklin, 2018).

NEUROTICISM

Consistent with this, measures of self-reported neuroticism have been found to be substantially elevated among those who engage in NSSI as compared to those who do not (d = .79 in Brown, 2009; see also Mullins-Sweatt et al., 2013). Neuroticism has also been tied to more frequent NSSI (Nicolai et al., 2015; You et al., 2016). Daily diary and ecological momentary assessment (EMA) studies have likewise found that people who engage in NSSI report higher daily negative affect, negative self-consciousness, stress, and affective instability compared to people without a history of NSSI (e.g., Bresin, 2014; Vansteelandt et al., 2017; Victor & Klonsky, 2014), although the magnitude of these between-group differences are often modest (see Hooley & Franklin, 2018). In a similar vein, various psychiatric syndromes associated with heightened negative affect, including not only major depression but also panic disorder and posttraumatic stress disorder, have been shown to be associated with NSSI engagement (see Bentley et al., 2015 for meta-analysis).

TRAIT RUMINATION, REJECTION SENSITIVITY, SHAME PRONENESS, NEGATIVE URGENCY, AND DISTRESS INTOLERANCE

Perhaps unsurprisingly, then, a wide array of traits tied to heightened negative affect, as well as those related to difficulty responding to negative affect, have likewise been found to be elevated among those who engage in NSSI compared to those who do not and to be associated with NSSI frequency. For example, trait rumination (e.g., Nicolai et al., 2015; Wolff et al., 2019), rejection sensitivity (e.g., Cawley et al., 2019), and shame-proneness (e.g., Mahtani et al., 2018; Sheehy et al., 2019) have all been found to be associated with NSSI.

Two traits that both involve difficulty responding to negative affect are distress intolerance, the tendency toward perceiving oneself as having a reduced capacity to withstand negative psychological states (Simons & Gaher, 2005; see also Selby & Joiner, 2009), and negative urgency, the tendency toward rash behavior in response to heightened negative emotions (Whiteside & Lynam, 2001). Distress intolerance has been found to be associated with lifetime NSSI history and frequency (e.g., Anestis et al., 2014), and evidence of difficulty tolerating distress using laboratory manipulations has been reported in adolescents with a history of NSSI compared to adolescents without an NSSI history (Nock & Mendes, 2008). In a similar fashion, meta-analytic evidence indicates that people with an NSSI history report higher negative urgency (Hamza et al., 2015), and negative urgency has been shown to predict NSSI over a 9-month period (Riley et al., 2015). Two recent laboratory studies suggest that this association between negative urgency and NSSI may be explained in part by poor response inhibition in the context of negative emotional stimuli (Allen & Hooley, 2015, 2019), a cognitive process that has been tied to poor emotion regulation. Taken together, traits that increase propensity toward negative affect and that involve difficulty responding to negative affect are associated with increased risk for NSSI.

Elevated Environmental and Interpersonal Stress

Beyond trait-like vulnerabilities, life experiences that evoke negative affect, especially in interpersonal contexts, are also associated with increased likelihood of engaging in NSSI (for review, see Liu et al., 2016). A full review of the links between social and environmental contributors to NSSI is beyond the scope of this chapter; however, a series of recent longitudinal investigations have converged on the conclusion that elevated stress and distress—including childhood adversity, childhood peer victimization, and recent stressors—are longitudinally associated with heightened risk for initiation and maintenance of NSSI (Buelens et al., 2019; Cassels et al., 2018; Hamza et al., 2021; Lereya et al., 2013; Miller et al., 2019; Victor, Scott, et al., 2019; Voon et al., 2014a) (see Zetterqvist & Bjureberg, this volume, for more on the social processes of NSSI). In a similar fashion, people with marginalized identities, such as those with minoritized sexual and gender identities, are at increased risk for NSSI, again in part due to increased likelihood of experiencing social exclusion, rejection, and discrimination (for review and meta-analysis, see Liu et al., 2019). In addition to direct effects on NSSI risk, environmental stressors are known to impact individual differences relevant for experiencing and responding to negative affect, including stress sensitivity, processing of reward and emotion, and emotion regulation (e.g., Krugers et al., 2017; Pechtel & Pizzagalli, 2011).

Aversion to NSSI as a Deterrent

Whereas global negative affectivity conveys increased risk, it should be noted that certain domain-specific manifestations of negative affect may actually be significant barriers to NSSI engagement. More specifically, aversion to NSSI and NSSI-related stimuli is highly prevalent and intense and has been proposed to be a critical deterrent (see Hooley & Franklin, 2018). Empirical evidence supports the claim that when aversion toward NSSI stimuli is low, risk for NSSI is elevated (e.g., Fox et al., 2018; Franklin, Puzia, et al., 2014; Burke, Allen, et al., 2021). It remains unsettled, though, whether this diminished aversion typically predates NSSI initiation or is a consequence of having previously engaged in NSSI. In support of the latter possibility, one study found that recent, frequent engagement in NSSI undermined aversion to NSSI (Franklin, Lee, et al., 2014).

Peripheral and Central Neurophysiology

Consistent with the focus of the RDoC initiative on multimodal measurement spanning multiple units of analysis, multiple investigations have tested links between NSSI and peripheral and central neurophysiology. For example, neural correlates of negative affectivity, including indices of brain structure and function, have been well-documented as correlates of NSSI (for reviews, see Auerbach et al., 2021; Groschwitz & Plener, 2012; Westlund Schreiner et al., 2015). Moreover, studies using emotional or NSSI-related stimuli indicate differential activation of key regions implicated in emotion responding between those with and without a history of NSSI. In response to negative emotional stimuli, those with a history of NSSI show significantly differentiated activation in the amygdala, hippocampus and anterior cingulate cortex as compared to those without a history of NSSI (Hooley et al., 2020; Plener et al., 2012; Westlund Schreiner et al., 2017). A similar pattern emerges in response to NSSI stimuli, with those with a history of NSSI exhibiting differential patterns in the amygdala, cingulate cortex, and orbitofrontal cortex (Hooley et al., 2020; Plener et al., 2012). For example, in social exclusion tasks, those with a history of NSSI show greater medial prefrontal cortex and ventrolateral prefrontal cortex activation compared to depressed adolescents (Groschwitz et al., 2016) and increased activation in the pregenual anterior cingulate cortex and the anterior insula compared to comparators (Malejko et al., 2020).

Congruent with findings on emotion responding and stress as risk factors, multiple studies have implicated the hypothalamic-pituitary axis (HPA) and processes tied to stress responsivity in NSSI. For example, structural functional magnetic resonance imaging (fMRI) work has found that in young adults with a history of NSSI, the number of NSSI episodes was positively associated with pituitary volume, which has been interpreted as an indicator of hyperreactivity of the stress response system (Jovev et al., 2008).

Notwithstanding these intriguing findings, results regarding cortisol blunting versus reactivity have varied among those who engage in NSSI, and may differ as a function of individual differences, such as gender. A study of female adolescents with histories of NSSI showed a reduced cortisol response, despite comparable self-reported affect, compared to healthy controls (Kaess et al., 2012). In a second study of conflict conversations in young adults, cortisol reactivity was impacted by both gender and coping styles: women who used emotional support had reduced cortisol reactivity, whereas women who used other forms of coping had heightened cortisol reactivity. Men with NSSI histories, on the other hand, consistently displayed higher cortisol reactivity (Powers & McArdle, 2003). Further research is warranted to ascertain how and when these HPA axis parameters are tied to NSSI. Overall, though, evidence spanning multiple units of analysis implicates multiple dimensions of negative affect as robust risk factors for NSSI.

NSSI Acts Are Typically Preceded by Heightened Negative Affect

Consistent with early and contemporary theorizing, considerable empirical evidence has accrued for the idea that acts of NSSI are often preceded by heightened negative affect and stress. In retrospective self-report studies, for example, one of the most reliable and robust findings is that overwhelming majorities of participants recall experiencing strong negative thoughts and feelings immediately before the act (e.g., 98.5% of participants in a large community sample; Zetterqvist et al., 2013; see also Klonsky, 2007). Several early laboratory studies using personalized guided NSSI imagery provided converging evidence (see Klonsky, 2007, for review). That is, when participants were guided through recall of the moments leading up to a memorable autobiographical act of NSSI, they tended to report heightened negative affect and to exhibit elevated physiological arousal (e.g., Haines et al., 1995). These early retrospective studies provided reason to believe that NSSI episodes could potentially be predicted from changes in negative affect and perhaps even that negative affect itself was a critical trigger for NSSI acts.

Findings from Ecological Sampling Studies

Following on this early work, ecological sampling methods have emerged over the last decade as an important tool for examining the role of negative affect as it relates to NSSI in daily life. To the extent, after all, that NSSI is thought to be triggered by negative affect and to relieve negative affect, this is a fundamentally dynamic, within-person model, which lends itself to intensive repeated measures data.

One relatively less granular approach to collecting and analyzing such data is to investigate whether daily negative affect is higher on days when people engaged in NSSI acts versus days when people did not. This approach has yielded mixed findings. Some studies have found evidence for the idea that people report greater negative affect on the days that they engage in NSSI (e.g., Turner et al., 2016; Victor & Klonsky, 2014). Other studies have concluded that increased likelihood of NSSI on a given day is not predicted by overall negative affect but is predicted by levels of specific negative emotions, potentially including hostility and fear (e.g., Lear et al., 2019). In one study, daily negative affect was related to same-day urges to engage in NSSI but not directly to NSSI acts (Bresin et al., 2013), although daily NSSI urges are themselves related to NSSI engagement (Ammerman et al., 2017).

A more temporally fine-grained approach is to examine negative affect at multiple time points preceding, coinciding with, and/or succeeding an NSSI act as opposed to only sampling once per day or aggregating observations at the daily level. EMA research using this approach has consistently yielded evidence that negative affect is typically elevated in the hours leading up to NSSI acts (Andrewes et al., 2017; Armey et al., 2011; Hepp et al., 2021; Houben et al., 2017; Koenig et al., 2021; Kranzler et al., 2018; Scala et al., 2018;, Scott, et al., 2019b; see Kuehn et al., 2022 for meta-analysis). This finding emerges not only in samples of participants with borderline personality disorder but also in other diagnosed and nondiagnosed samples, as well as when specifically controlling for borderline symptoms (Victor & Klonsky, 2014). As elsewhere, some investigations have found stronger evidence for specific negatively valenced states—variously including irritability and guilt (Law et al., 2016), anger (Humber et al., 2013), self-punishing and self-critical thoughts (Burke, Fox et al., 2021), and social rejection and isolation (Snir et al., 2015)—than for overall negative affect. Of note, the mean absolute magnitude of reported negative affect preceding NSSI acts is not necessarily extreme, consistent with emerging empirical evidence that NSSI thoughts and acts may be better predicted by within-person fluctuations in stress and negative affect (i.e., experiencing higher-than-usual stress) than by between-person differences (Kiekens et al., 2020; Miller et al., 2019; cf. Hooley & Franklin, 2018).

A small handful of EMA studies have investigated factors that may amplify the link between state negative affect and NSSI. One example is rumination or repetitive negative thinking. Not only do people who engage in NSSI tend to be higher in trait rumination as previously mentioned (see Wolff et al., 2019, for meta-analysis), but also momentary rumination has been found to moderate the association between state negative affect and NSSI in two studies. In the first, instability of moment-to-moment repetitive negative thinking was found to interact with instability of negative affect to predict NSSI, such that NSSI rates were higher when rumination and/or negative affect were more unstable than when rumination and negative affect were both relatively stable (Selby et al., 2013). In the second, momentary repetitive negative thinking was similarly found to moderate the association between feeling anxious and overwhelmed and NSSI in an adolescent community sample (Hughes et al., 2019). Alongside repetitive negative thinking, a second example of a potential amplifier comes from a recent study on response inhibition to NSSI stimuli. In that study, response inhibition (measured at baseline) was not found to be directly associated with NSSI urges, but was instead found to moderate the association between momentary negative affect and NSSI urges in daily life (Burke, Allen, et al., 2021), such that the association between momentary negative affect and NSSI urges was stronger when response inhibition was low. These three small studies (ns = 47-60) highlight the need for more research on individual and contextual differences that amplify the links between negative affect and NSSI.

Findings from Laboratory Studies
Regarding experimental studies, we were able to identify only a single laboratory study that investigated changes in NSSI urges after a negative affect-inducing manipulation. In that study, young adult women with a history of NSSI who were exposed to a personalized peer criticism induction experienced increased NSSI urges relative to baseline (Haliczer, 2020). This increase in NSSI urge was not observed among participants with an NSSI history who were randomized to peer praise or neutral conditions or among participants without an NSSI history. It is unclear, though, whether the observed effect was specific to experiences of criticism (consistent with conceptual models of NSSI that emphasize the role of self-criticism; cf. Fox et al., 2019) or whether it was a more general effect of negative affect, as neither of the comparison conditions entailed inducing negative affect.

In summary, negative affect is predictive of NSSI engagement across multiple timescales: not only can experiences associated with heightened negative affect and distress confer heightened risk for NSSI in the succeeding weeks, months, and years, but also individual acts of NSSI are typically imminently preceded by higher-than-usual negative affect. As outlined in the introduction, though, the relationship between negative affect and NSSI is thought to be bidirectional. Accordingly, in the next section we turn our attention to empirical research on the effects of NSSI acts on negative affect.

NSSI Regulates and Reduces Negative Affect in the Short Term

Consistent with early clinical observation, multiple lines of research support the idea that NSSI acts may function to relieve negative affect. To begin, escape or relief from negative affect is the single most commonly—albeit not universally—endorsed motive for NSSI (see Taylor et al., 2018 for meta-analysis), and endorsement of the affect regulation functions of NSSI appears tied to the frequency of NSSI engagement (Klonsky & Olino, 2008). Consistent with the apparent centrality of this affect regulation function, a meta-analysis of 48 cross-sectional and longitudinal studies, most of them using the Difficulties in Emotion Regulation Scale, found strong support for the claim that NSSI is associated with self-reported perceptions of difficulty with emotion regulation (meta-analytic bias-adjusted OR = 2.40) and especially with perceptions of having limited access to effective emotion regulation strategies (OR = 3.89; Wolff et al., 2019). That is, people with a history of NSSI engagement tend to report higher emotion dysregulation than those without, and among people with a history of NSSI engagement, higher emotion dysregulation is associated with greater NSSI severity and frequency. Beyond self-reported difficulties, one laboratory study found that people with a history of NSSI demonstrated lower cognitive reappraisal ability (Davis et al., 2014), suggesting that people who engage in NSSI may have more difficulty implementing potentially protective emotion regulation strategies. In other words, not only do people who engage in NSSI report that it helps them to regulate their affect, but also they report not having access to effective alternative strategies. A key question, though, is the extent to which NSSI is, in fact, capable of providing effective relief from negative affective states.

Findings from Laboratory Studies

Multiple laboratory studies have now demonstrated convincingly that administration of acutely painful stimuli (e.g., shocks and cold pressors) can effectively reduce negative affect, arousal, and rumination in people with and without NSSI histories (e.g., Bresin & Gordon, 2013; Franklin et al., 2010; Harmon-Jones et al., 2019; Schoenleber et al., 2014). In one particularly striking study of a nonclinical community sample that used a multitrial laboratory emotion regulation choice task, participants frequently *chose* to administer painful stimulation (instead of choosing to use cognitive reframing, cognitive avoidance, or nonpainful physical stimulation) to cope with viewing upsetting images, and doing so did provide short-term relief from negative affect (Doukas et al., 2020). Crucially, these studies suggest that the affect regulation functions of pain induction and offset are not limited to a small subset of the population but instead substantively generalize across people. In a small study that compared the induction of pain (by using a small incision with a scalpel on the forearm) to a sham after a stress induction (combining arithmetic with disappointing feedback), though, those with recent NSSI showed relatively greater decreases in subjective stress and amygdala activity as well as normalized functional connectivity with the superior frontal gyrus compared to those with no NSSI history (Reitz et al., 2015), suggesting that some people may experience a stronger pain offset response than others (see also Osuch et al., 2014 for a comparable finding).

One specific reason that pain could relieve negative affect would be that it provides punishment the individual believes to be warranted. In an experimental test of this idea, Hooley and St. Germain (2014) conducted experimental manipulations to enhance self-worth. For those with a history of NSSI, temporary self-worth improvement led to significantly decreased duration of tolerating pain, an effect not observed for those with no history of NSSI. This finding provides intriguing support for one specific mechanism through which affect regulation could occur.

In sum, laboratory studies have provided compelling evidence that the infliction and subsequent cessation of pain *can* fulfill short-term affect regulatory functions. That is, experiences of physical pain are indeed capable of providing short-term relief from aversive emotional and affective states in the general population and perhaps even more effectively for people with NSSI histories (see Selby & Hughes, this volume, for more on pain and its role in NSSI). In turn, we and others have argued that pain offset relief and concomitant amelioration of negative affect after acts of NSSI can serve as potent reinforcers that motivate, maintain, and potentially render habitual NSSI behavior (Swerdlow et al., 2020; see also Yarali et al., 2008, for evidence from a nonhuman animal model of pain offset learning).

Findings from Ecological Sampling Studies
Notwithstanding these insights, the ecological validity of these laboratory studies is limited. That is, titrated electrical shocks or incisions administered in controlled settings may not veridically reproduce the sensory, psychological, or contextual dynamics of NSSI. To understand if NSSI is reliably associated with downregulation of negative affect, EMA studies following people as they naturally engage in these behaviors have helped fill the gap. EMA research, though, has yielded mixed findings for whether acts of NSSI effectively subserve affect regulatory functions in practice. Multiple studies have found support for the affect-regulating properties of NSSI, such that NSSI acts were followed, on average, by near-term decreases in negative affect (e.g., Andrewes et al., 2017; Armey et al., 2011; Hepp et al., 2021; Kranzler et al., 2018; Snir et al., 2015; see Kuehn et al., 2022 for meta-analysis); however, other studies have observed no average change in negative affect after NSSI (e.g., Law et al., 2016), and others still have reported *increases* in negative affect after NSSI (e.g., Houben et al., 2017; Koenig et al., 2021).

There are several plausible explanations for these apparent discrepancies. One particularly thorny issue in measuring potential decreases in negative affect after NSSI acts is the timing of EMA surveys. To wit, the number of surveys sent per day varies greatly across studies of NSSI in daily life (ranging from 1 to 12+ per day; see Rodriguez-Blanco et al., 2018, for review). There is no clear evidence that different sampling frequencies yield different results on whether NSSI regulates affect; if anything, the studies that observed increased negative affect after NSSI had comparatively short measurement windows (less than 1.5 hours). Nonetheless, many short-term affect regulatory processes, potentially including those associated with NSSI, may unfold on the order of seconds or minutes, rather than close to an hour, the shortest window seen in most EMA work. In some cases, for example, rapid relief of negative affect following pain offset might quickly give way to regret or shame (cf. Power et al., 2015). As a result, EMA studies may "miss" potential hedonic consequences of NSSI, especially if they are not using event-contingent sampling strategies.

A second potential explanation is that even the short-term hedonic benefits of NSSI are only intermittently attained in practice. Mood-repairing benefits may vary or wane over time, perhaps because some acts of NSSI may be initiated via habit (see Swerdlow et al., 2020). In addition, the affect-regulating properties of NSSI may vary as a function of individual differences, as suggested previously. Although cross-diagnostic comparisons are not available, effects do not appear specific to diagnosis in the studies cited here, which have included samples with and without borderline personality disorder. Instead, the most compelling evidence that has emerged in the realm of individual differences to date relates to trait self-criticism. In a pair of laboratory studies, participants with and without a history of NSSI underwent negative mood inductions and subsequently completed a pain task. Regardless of NSSI history, participants who were higher in trait self-criticism experienced significant mood improvement *during* pain administration, whereas those who were lower in self-criticism tended to feel worse during pain administration and to only experience mood repair following pain offset (Fox et al., 2017; Fox et al., 2019).

Other work is also consistent with the idea that the mechanisms involved in the affect-regulating functions of NSSI will vary across persons. For example, we noted that one reason that NSSI could produce emotion regulation would be relief of numbness (Linehan, 1993). In one EMA study, only a small proportion of individuals described numbness preceding NSSI thoughts, and there was considerable variability in whether self-hatred versus other negative emotions preceded NSSI thoughts (Nock et al., 2009). These studies provide support for the idea that there are important individual differences in the motivators and mechanisms related to affect-regulating properties of NSSI.

In summary, understanding the reasons for the variability in EMA findings is of import. It remains the case that affect regulation is endorsed as a reason for engaging in NSSI by a majority of participants across adult, adolescent, inpatient, outpatient, and nonclinical samples (Klonsky, 2007), and understanding the sources of those beliefs is a key research goal. Taken together, though, there is evidence that affect-regulating functions and processes of NSSI vary within people over time, from episode to episode, and between people.

Long-Term Consequences of NSSI Engagement for Negative Affect

Whereas acts of NSSI may effectively meet short-term affect regulatory needs at least some of the time, considerable empirical evidence indicates that engaging in NSSI is also associated with long-term risks relevant to negative affectivity. First and foremost, a history of NSSI is among the most robust predictors of suicide attempts (see Franklin et al., 2017, for meta-analysis). More specifically, one study found that stronger perceptions of the efficacy of NSSI for meeting intrapersonal functions (prominently including affect regulation) were associated with greater likelihood of suicide plans and attempts (Brausch & Muehlenkamp, 2018). In a similar fashion, there is gathering evidence that NSSI engagement longitudinally predicts an array of variables related to heightened negative affect, including increased distress (Buelens et al., 2019), rumination (Buelens et al., 2019), life stress (Burke et al., 2015; Voon et al., 2014b), depressive symptoms (Burke, Fox, et al., 2019; Lundh et al., 2011; Mars et al., 2014), and difficulties with emotion regulation (Daukantaitė et al., 2021; Robinson et al., 2019), although null findings have also been reported for longitudinal associations with depressive symptoms (Marshall et al., 2013) and trait self-criticism (Burke, Fox, et al., 2019).

Tied to these negative affective outcomes is that NSSI is a highly stigmatized behavior (Burke, Piccirillo, et al., 2019; Staniland et al., 2020). Even among people who engage in NSSI, many report negative attitudes toward NSSI (Piccirillo et al., 2020; Sandel et al., 2021) and specifically that their scars frequently make them feel ashamed and weak (Burke et al., 2017). In fact, whereas a pair of laboratory studies reported that pain administration can acutely reduce shame (Schoenleber et al., 2014) and guilt (Bastian et al., 2011), respectively, the persistence or activation of self-conscious negative affect in the wake of NSSI has recently been proposed to be a potential factor motivating ongoing NSSI (Spitzen et al., 2020). In other words, although NSSI acts may be capable of regulating negative affect in the short term, they may simultaneously contribute to a vicious cycle in the long run. Given this—alongside the fact that NSSI can lead to lasting physical harm (e.g., infection) and even accidental death—there has been considerable interest in developing effective interventions to reduce NSSI frequency and severity. More specifically, there has been considerable emphasis on clinical targets related to negative affectivity, consistent with the empirical findings that we have reviewed. In the next section, therefore, we provide a brief, illustrative clinical vignette and reflection on the clinical implications of currently available research.

Clinical Vignette and Implications

Maria is a 24-year-old Latina woman who had a long-standing history of NSSI and depression. She began cutting herself as an adolescent, which she attributes partly to the fact that "some of my friends were doing it" and partly to the fact that she was "hopeless and miserable" due to conflicts at home and questioning of her sexual orientation. Being raised in a traditional religious community, her emerging questions about her sexual identity contributed to increases in shame and fears of social rejection. Maria describes herself as being emotionally sensitive, highly impulsive to her negative emotions (i.e., high in negative urgency), and unable to withstand the stresses of life (i.e., high in distress intolerance). Over time, Maria learned to rely on NSSI as a means of emotion regulation, and so this behavior persisted. After disclosing her self-harm to her primary care provider, Maria enrolled in dialectical behavior therapy (DBT), an intervention that focuses on teaching skills related to emotion regulation, distress tolerance, mindfulness, and interpersonal effectiveness (Linehan, 1993). As she gained skills to reduce and regulate her negative affect and manage her depression, Maria began to engage in NSSI less frequently and eventually her NSSI urges also became less frequent.

This vignette is broadly consistent with the available nomothetic evidence. Although we have described negative affect as a possible trigger for NSSI and relief from negative affect as a potential outcome of NSSI, we have also highlighted that these effects are not universal. People vary in the nature of the emotions that precede their NSSI and the degree to which NSSI provides effective short-term affect regulation. Given this, it will be important for clinicians to consider the idea that there may be considerable diversity in how negative affect relates to NSSI for any given person. Accordingly, we believe it is important to consider three goals in clinical assessment. First, we recommend assessing the extent to which fluctuations in negative affect trigger NSSI urges and behavior for a given client, and the nature of negative emotions involved (e.g., shame, sadness, loneliness, etc.). Here, we see innovative work using person-centered EMA approaches as a prelude to treatment planning (cf. Fisher et al., 2019) as a particularly fruitful tool in building a person-focused case conceptualization. Second, as illustrated in the vignette, we believe it is particularly important to consider the affect regulatory functions of NSSI with clients and to offer alternative strategies. Third, it is essential to understand problems related to self-worth, shame, and beliefs about deserving punishment. With clearer treatment targets in mind, early work suggests that skills focused around emotion identification, emotion regulation, and self-worth enhancement could be helpful, as we discuss in more detail below.

Challenges, Recommendations, and Future Directions in Research and Treatment

Taken together, the extant empirical literature provides extensive, multimodal evidence that negative affectivity traits and states predict NSSI onset, severity, and frequency and that NSSI acts have short-term and long-term effects on negative affectivity. The supportive findings stem from a rich array of research designs, including a variety of self-report and psychophysiological indices. Given this, we turn to a consideration of the challenges and future directions facing this field.

Despite considerable progress, it is worth highlighting that many different models of negative affectivity and NSSI are available. Some of these are rapidly accruing support, including the importance of rumination and self-criticism for understanding negative affectivity in NSSI. In other ways, though, it remains difficult to consider whether any one theory better explains NSSI. Some of this is because models often overlap in key predictions. Some models, though, provide differential hypotheses. For example, models of shame versus general negative affect as triggers for NSSI are particularly distinct. To date, however, findings of EMA research have varied in whether shame versus other negative emotions appears to be a more potent trigger for NSSI. Although it is unlikely that any one of these theories will eventually win a horse race against all others, we see more careful testing and differentiation of the specific forms of negative affect and processes involved in affect regulation as one goal for future research, while bearing in mind that risk variables and proposed processes will likely apply differentially across individuals.

Similarly, we highlighted that multiple theories emphasize negative affectivity as a contributor to maintenance as compared to initiation. Although negative affectivity appears clearly tied to the recurrence of NSSI, much work continues to focus on negative affectivity as a differentiator of those who do and do not engage in NSSI. To gain better understanding of the developmental course of NSSI initiation and maintenance, we recommend much greater attention to differentiation of these processes (cf. Klonsky & Olino, 2008; Muehlenkamp et al., 2013).

Perhaps of most import, many of the current findings regarding negative affectivity and NSSI do not appear to easily generalize across individuals or even across instances of NSSI within an individual. For example, EMA findings are mixed regarding the putative affect regulation benefits of NSSI, notwithstanding laboratory findings that suggest that pain offset relief is substantially generalizable. It seems highly likely that the affective triggers and the affective functions differ across and within individuals, highlighting the need to consider dynamic, person-specific models within this field. On the other hand, whereas one might expect that negative affect models would need to take into account factors such as borderline personality disorder, the findings we have reviewed here appear parallel for those with and without borderline personality disorder. Other, more refined individual differences may be important to consider, as illustrated by the promising work by Fox and colleagues (2017, 2019) on how self-criticism tendencies shape responses to pain.

From an RDoC perspective, the current literature has strengths and weaknesses. We have highlighted one strength: multimodal findings spanning self-report, behavioral, and neural indices indicating that negative affect is implicated in NSSI. On the other hand, RDoC has considerably more specificity than much of the present literature does, both in considering more levels (e.g., genes and molecules) and in delineating subsystems of the negative valence system (e.g., acute threat, potential threat, and sustained threat, loss). We have highlighted that neural responses to negative stimuli appear related to NSSI, suggesting the importance of ongoing work on responses to acute threat. At the same time, the findings noted regarding pituitary volume appear to implicate sustained threat responding. More work is needed to consider each of the negative valence subsystems and their relative involvement. Beyond a more refined focus on the subsystems of the negative valence system, current models point to the need to bridge between the negative affect systems and other RDoC domains, including social communication, pain, habit, and cognitive control (cf. Westlund Schreiner, et al., 2015).

It is hoped that refining these models can provide knowledge to improve treatment efficacy, particularly given that recent meta-analyses of randomized controlled trials have called into question the effectiveness of extant treatments (psychological or pharmacological) for NSSI (Calati & Courtet, 2016; Fox et al., 2020; Hetrick et al., 2016). Of relevance to this chapter, antidepressants and psychological treatments focused on emotion regulation have shown no systematic advantage compared to other forms of treatments when examined across suicidality and NSSI outcomes (Fox et al., 2020). Even DBT, which is designed to address NSSI and emotion regulation (among many other targets), has shown mixed effects when compared to control conditions (Turner et al., 2014). (See Section IX for a thorough review of various NSSI treatments.)

Some glimmers of hope have emerged, though, in considering whether negative affect is a potential treatment target for NSSI. First, several studies among adolescents have shown that DBT, compared to an active control condition, leads to moderate reductions in NSSI (meta-analytic d = .51; Kothgassner et al., 2020). It is not entirely clear why DBT may work better with adolescents than adults, but it is possible that interventions targeting the emotion regulation function of NSSI may be more successful when offered before repeated reinforcement and habitual responding become entrenched. At a broader level, NSSI is more normative among adolescents, such that adults who engage in NSSI may have more persistent or severe difficulties, making change more difficult to attain. Understanding more about who responds well to DBT is an important goal for future research, and one that could include careful examination of negative affectivity processes.

Although not all treatments involving emotion regulation appear particularly successful, a second source of hope is recent work on more specifically targeting emotion regulation. Whereas DBT covers many different types of skills training, two recently developed treatment approaches focus more specifically on emotion regulation skills, with early promising effects. First, drawing from the Unified Protocol for Transdiagnostic Treatment of Emotional Disorders, Bentley et al. (2017) tested mindful emotion awareness training and cognitive reappraisal skills. In a well-controlled repeated experimental single case design, 8 of 10 participants showed reductions in their NSSI behavior with the introduction of either strategy. Second, promising results also have emerged for a brief group approach specifically focused on emotion regulation: emotion regulation group therapy (ERGT). In two randomized controlled trials, patients who completed ERGT showed more reduction in the frequency of NSSI than did those who were engaged in treatment as usual (Gratz et al., 2012; Gratz & Tull, 2011). At the same time, one study found that changes in perceptions of the functions of NSSI, including affect regulation, may track treatment outcomes (Victor et al., 2016). In other words, there remains reason to think that interventions focused specifically on negative affectivity and emotion regulation may be effective for addressing NSSI—an important direction for future research.

A third source of hope stems from experimental laboratory research showing that bolstering self-worth can reduce the willingness to endure pain observed among those with NSSI (Hooley & St. Germain, 2014). Work like this suggests that laboratory research could suggest potent targets to reduce the chances of negative affect translating into NSSI. Along these lines, a recent study of a novel daily journaling intervention found support both for reduced self-criticism and for reduced NSSI episodes, although participants assigned to the self-enhancement journaling condition did not show greater reductions in NSSI frequency than those assigned to the general daily journaling active comparison condition (Hooley et al., 2018).

In sum, targeted interventions directed at negative affect as a trigger, functions of NSSI for reducing negative affect, and self-criticism have yielded promising effects, suggesting the possible translation of basic science to treatment development. Although we find this early work encouraging, we also hope that this chapter inspires others to conduct research to understand the diversity in links of negative affectivity with NSSI by considering for whom and when these models best apply.

Conclusion

Converging evidence indicates that traits relevant for experiencing and responding to negative affect predict NSSI onset and are associated with NSSI severity and frequency; that neural indices corresponding to negative affectivity are also elevated among those with NSSI; and that within-person fluctuations in negative affective states track with recurrence of NSSI acts. Negative affectivity, then, appears relevant to whether people initiate NSSI as well as whether the behavior continues over time. Multiple studies suggest that painful stimuli can relieve short-term negative affect, and may do so more robustly for those who engage in NSSI. Nonetheless, EMA studies suggest that the affect regulation benefits of NSSI may vary considerably across time and persons in practice. At the same time, NSSI can take a toll on emotional well-being and self-esteem over time, with evidence that it is a harbinger of increases in depression and suicidality. Findings regarding both affective reactivity and regulation appear not to differ according to diagnostic status. Taken together, researchers have developed and tested sophisticated models of the temporal dynamic fluctuations in negative affect and NSSI, and have used intriguing laboratory techniques to study negative affectivity and self-criticism in relation to NSSI.

References

Allen, K. J., & Hooley, J. M. (2015). Inhibitory control in people who self-injure: Evidence for impairment and enhancement. *Psychiatry Research, 225*(3), 631–637. https://doi.org/10.1016/j.psychres.2014.11.033

Allen, K. J., & Hooley, J. M. (2019). Negative emotional action termination (NEAT): Support for a cognitive mechanism underlying negative urgency in nonsuicidal self-injury. *Behavior Therapy, 50*(5), 924–937. https://doi.org/10.1016/j.beth.2019.02.001

Ammerman, B. A., Olino, T. M., Coccaro, E. F., & McCloskey, M. S. (2017). Predicting nonsuicidal self-injury in borderline personality disorder using ecological momentary assessment. *Journal of Personality Disorders, 31*(6), 844–855. https://doi.org/10.1521/pedi_2017_31_278

Andrewes, H. E., Hulbert, C., Cotton, S. M., Betts, J., & Chanen, A. M. (2017). Ecological momentary assessment of nonsuicidal self-injury in youth with borderline personality disorder. *Personality Disorders: Theory, Research, and Treatment, 8*(4), 357. https://doi.org/10.1037/per0000205

Anestis, M. D., Kleiman, E. M., Lavender, J. M., Tull, M. T., & Gratz, K. L. (2014). The pursuit of death versus escape from negative affect: An examination of the nature of the relationship between emotion dysregulation and both suicidal behavior and non-suicidal self-injury. *Comprehensive Psychiatry, 55*(8), 1820–1830. https://doi.org/10.1016/j.comppsych.2014.07.007

Armey, M. F., Crowther, J. H., & Miller, I. W. (2011). Changes in ecological momentary assessment reported affect associated with episodes of nonsuicidal self-injury. *Behavior Therapy, 42*(4), 579–588. https://doi.org/10.1016/j.beth.2011.01.002

Auerbach, R. P., Pagliaccio, D., Allison, G. O., Alqueza, K. L., & Alonso, M. F. (2021). Neural correlates associated with suicide and nonsuicidal self-injury in youth. *Biological Psychiatry, 89*(2), 119–133. https://doi.org/10.1016/j.biopsych.2020.06.002

Bastian, B., Jetten, J., & Fasoli, F. (2011). Cleansing the soul by hurting the flesh: The guilt-reducing effect of pain. *Psychological Science, 22*(3), 334. https://doi.org/10.1177/0956797610397058

Bennun, I. (1984). Psychological models of self-mutilation. *Suicide and Life-Threatening Behavior, 14*(3), 166–186. https://doi.org/10.1111/j.1943-278X.1984.tb00447.x

Bentley, K. H., Cassiello-Robbins, C. F., Vittorio, L., Sauer-Zavala, S., & Barlow, D. H. (2015). The association between nonsuicidal self-injury and the emotional disorders: A meta-analytic review. *Clinical Psychology Review, 37*, 72–88. https://doi.org/10.1016/j.cpr.2015.02.006

Bentley, K. H., Nock, M. K., Sauer-Zavala, S., Gorman, B. S., & Barlow, D. H. (2017). A functional analysis of two transdiagnostic, emotion-focused interventions on nonsuicidal self-injury. *Journal of Consulting and Clinical Psychology, 85*(6), 632–646. https://doi.org/10.1037/ccp0000205

Brausch, A. M., & Muehlenkamp, J. J. (2018). Perceived effectiveness of NSSI in achieving functions on severity and suicide risk. *Psychiatry Research, 265*, 144–150. https://doi.org/10.1016/j.psychres.2018.04.038

Bresin, K. (2014). Five indices of emotion regulation in participants with a history of nonsuicidal self-injury: A daily diary study. *Behavior Therapy, 45*(1), 56–66. https://doi.org/10.1016/j.beth.2013.09.005

Bresin, K., Carter, D. L., & Gordon, K. H. (2013). The relationship between trait impulsivity, negative affective states, and urge for nonsuicidal self-injury: A daily diary study. *Psychiatry Research, 205*(3), 227–231. https://doi.org/10.1016/j.psychres.2012.09.033

Bresin, K., & Gordon, K. H. (2013). Changes in negative affect following pain (vs. nonpainful) stimulation in individuals with and without a history of nonsuicidal self-injury. *Personality Disorders, 4*(1), 62–66. https://doi.org/10.1037/a0025736

Brown, S. A. (2009). Personality and non-suicidal deliberate self-harm: Trait differences among a non-clinical population. *Psychiatry Research, 169*(1), 28–32. https://doi.org/10.1016/j.psychres.2008.06.005

Buelens, T., Luyckx, K., Gandhi, A., Kiekens, G., & Claes, L. (2019). Non-suicidal self-injury in adolescence: Longitudinal associations with psychological distress and rumination. *Journal of Abnormal Child Psychology, 47*(9), 1569–1581. https://doi.org/10.1007/s10802-019-00531-8

Burke, T. A., Allen, K. J., Carpenter, R. W., Siegel, D. M., Kautz, M. M., Liu, R. T., & Alloy, L. B. (2021). Emotional response inhibition to self-harm stimuli interacts with momentary negative affect to predict nonsuicidal self-injury urges. *Behaviour Research and Therapy, 142*, Article 103865. https://doi.org/10.1016/j.brat.2021.103865

Burke, T. A., Fox, K., Kautz, M., Siegel, D. M., Kleiman, E., & Alloy, L. B. (2021). Real-time monitoring of the associations between self-critical and self-punishment cognitions and nonsuicidal self-injury. *Behaviour Research and Therapy, 137*, Article 103775. https://doi.org/10.1016/j.brat.2020.103775

Burke, T. A., Fox, K., Zelkowitz, R. L., Smith, D. M., Alloy, L. B., Hooley, J. M., & Cole, D. A. (2019). Does nonsuicidal self-injury prospectively predict change in depression and self-criticism?. *Cognitive Therapy and Research, 43*(2), 345–353. https://doi.org/10.1007/s10608-018-9984-8

Burke, T. A., Hamilton, J. L., Abramson, L. Y., & Alloy, L. B. (2015). Non-suicidal self-injury prospectively predicts interpersonal stressful life events and depressive symptoms among adolescent girls. *Psychiatry Research*, *228*(3), 416–424. https://doi.org/10.1016/j.psychres.2015.06.021

Burke, T. A., Olino, T. M., & Alloy, L. B. (2017). Initial psychometric validation of the non-suicidal self-injury scar cognition scale. *Journal of Psychopathology and Behavioral Assessment*, *39*(3), 546–562. https://doi.org/10.1007/s10862-017-9595-9

Burke, T. A., Piccirillo, M. L., Moore-Berg, S. L., Alloy, L. B., & Heimberg, R. G. (2019). The stigmatization of nonsuicidal self-injury. *Journal of Clinical Psychology*, *75*(3), 481–498. https://doi.org/10.1002/jclp.22713

Calati, R., & Courtet, P. (2016). Is psychotherapy effective for reducing suicide attempts and non-suicidal self-injury rates?: Meta-analysis and meta-regression of literature data. *Journal of Psychiatric Research*, *79*, 8–20. https://doi.org/10.1016/j.jpsychires.2016.04.003

Cassels, M., van Harmelen, A. L., Neufeld, S., Goodyer, I., Jones, P. B., & Wilkinson, P. (2018). Poor family functioning mediates the link between childhood adversity and adolescent nonsuicidal self-injury. *Journal of Child Psychology and Psychiatry and Allied Disciplines*, *59*(8), 881–887. https://doi.org/10.1111/jcpp.12866

Cawley, R., Pontin, E. E., Touhey, J., Sheehy, K., & Taylor, P. J. (2019). What is the relationship between rejection and self-harm or suicidality in adulthood? *Journal of Affective Disorders*, *242*, 123–134. https://doi.org/10.1016/j.jad.2018.08.082

Chapman, A. L., Gratz, K. L., & Brown, M. Z. (2006). Solving the puzzle of deliberate self-harm: The experiential avoidance model. *Behaviour Research and Therapy*, *44*(3), 371–394. https://doi.org/10.1016/j.brat.2005.03.005

Daukantaitė, D., Lundh, L. G., Wångby-Lundh, M., Claréus, B., Bjärehed, J., Zhou, Y., & Liljedahl, S. I. (2021). What happens to young adults who have engaged in self-injurious behavior as adolescents? A 10-year follow-up. *European Child & Adolescent Psychiatry*, *30*(3), 475–492. https://doi.org/10.1007/s00787-020-01533-4

Davis, T. S., Mauss, I. B., Lumian, D., Troy, A. S., Shallcross, A. J., Zarolia, P., Ford, B. Q.,& McRae, K. (2014). Emotional reactivity and emotion regulation among adults with a history of self-harm: Laboratory self-report and functional MRI evidence. *Journal of Abnormal Psychology*, *123*(3), 499–509. https://doi.org/10.1037/a0036962

Doukas, A. M., D'Andrea, W. M., Gregory, W. E., Joachim, B., Lee, K. A., Robinson, G., Freed, S. J., Khedari-DePierro, V., Pfeffer, K. A., Todman, M., & Siegle, G. J. (2020). Hurts so good: Pain as an emotion regulation strategy. *Emotion*, *20*(9), 1382–1389. https://doi.org/10.1037/emo0000656

Feldman, M. D. (1988). The challenge of self-mutilation: A review. *Comprehensive Psychiatry*, *29*(3), 252–269. https://doi.org/10.1016/0010-440X(88)90048-X

Fisher, A. J., Bosley, H. G., Fernandez, K. C., Reeves, J. W., Soyster, P. D., Diamond, A. E., & Barkin, J. (2019). Open trial of a personalized modular treatment for mood and anxiety. *Behavioral Research Therapy*, *116*, 69–79. https://doi.org/10.1016/j.brat.2019.01.010

Fox, K. R., Franklin, J. C., Ribeiro, J. D., Kleiman, E. M., Bentley, K. H., & Nock, M. K. (2015). Meta-analysis of risk factors for nonsuicidal self-injury. *Clinical Psychology Review*, *42*, 156–167. https://doi.org/10.1016/j.cpr.2015.09.002

Fox, K. R., Huang, X., Guzmán, E. M., Funsch, K. M., Cha, C. B., Ribeiro, J. D., & Franklin, J. C. (2020). Interventions for suicide and self-injury: A meta-analysis of randomized controlled trials across nearly 50 years of research. *Psychological Bulletin*, *146*(12), 1117–1145. https://doi.org/10.1037/bul0000305

Fox, K. R., O'Sullivan, I. M., Wang, S. B., & Hooley, J. M. (2019). Self-criticism impacts emotional responses to pain. *Behavior Therapy*, *50*(2), 410–420. https://doi.org/10.1016/j.beth.2018.07.008

Fox, K. R., Ribeiro, J. D., Kleiman, E. M., Hooley, J. M., Nock, M. K., & Franklin, J. C. (2018). Affect toward the self and self-injury stimuli as potential risk factors for nonsuicidal self-injury. *Psychiatry Research*, *260*, 279–285. https://doi.org/10.1016/j.psychres.2017.11.083

Fox, K. R., Toole, K. E., Franklin, J. C., & Hooley, J. M. (2017). Why does nonsuicidal self-injury improve mood? A preliminary test of three hypotheses. *Clinical Psychological Science*, *5*(1), 111–121. https://doi.org/10.1177/2167702616662270

Franklin, J. C., Hessel, E. T., Aaron, R. V., Arthur, M. S., Heilbron, N., & Prinstein, M. J. (2010). The functions of nonsuicidal self-injury: Support for cognitive–affective regulation and opponent processes from a novel psychophysiological paradigm. *Journal of Abnormal Psychology*, *119*(4), 850. https://doi.org/10.1037/a0020896

Franklin, J. C., Lee, K. M., Puzia, M. E., & Prinstein, M. J. (2014). Recent and frequent nonsuicidal self-injury is associated with diminished implicit and explicit aversion toward self-cutting stimuli. *Clinical Psychological Science*, *2*(3), 306–318. https://doi.org/10.1177/2167702613503140

Franklin, J. C., Puzia, M. E., Lee, K. M., & Prinstein, M. J. (2014). Low implicit and explicit aversion toward self-cutting stimuli longitudinally predict nonsuicidal self-injury. *Journal of Abnormal Psychology*, *123*(2), 463. https://doi.org/10.1037/a0036436

Franklin, J. C., Ribeiro, J. D., Fox, K. R., Bentley, K. H., Kleiman, E. M., Huang, X., Musacchio, K. M., Jaroszewski, A. C., Chang, B. P., & Nock, M. K. (2017). Risk factors for suicidal thoughts and behaviors: a meta-analysis of 50 years of research. *Psychological Bulletin*, *143*(2), 187. https://doi.org/10.1037/bul0000084

Gratz, K. L., Levy, R., & Tull, M. T. (2012). Emotion regulation as a mechanism of change in an acceptance-based emotion regulation group therapy for deliberate self-harm among women with borderline personality pathology. *Journal of Cognitive Psychotherapy*, *26*(4), 365–380. https://doi.org/10.1891/0889-8391.26.4.365

Gratz, K. L., & Tull, M. T. (2011). Extending research on the utility of an adjunctive emotion regulation group therapy for deliberate self-harm among women with borderline personality pathology. *Personality Disorders*, *2*(4), 316–326. https://doi.org/10.1037/a0022144

Groschwitz, R., & Plener, P. (2012). The neurobiology of non-suicidal self-injury (NSSI): A review. *Suicidology Online*, *3*, 24–32.

Groschwitz, R. C., Plener, P. L., Groen, G., Bonenberger, M., & Abler, B. (2016). Differential neural processing of social exclusion in adolescents with non-suicidal self-injury: An fMRI study. *Psychiatry Research-Neuroimaging*, *255*, 43–49. https://doi.org/10.1016/j.pscychresns.2016.08.001

Haines, J., Williams, C. L., Brain, K. L., & Wilson, G. V. (1995). The psychophysiology of self-mutilation. *Journal of Abnormal Psychology*, *104*(3), 471. https://doi.org/10.1037/0021-843X.104.3.471

Haliczer, L. (2020). *An experimental investigation of how peer criticism and praise affect urges for self-injury* [Master's thesis]. University of Massachusetts, Amherst. https://doi.org/10.7275/17887393

Hamza, C. A., Goldstein, A. L., Heath, N. L., & Ewing, L. (2021). Stressful experiences in university predict non-suicidal self-injury through emotional reactivity. *Frontiers in Psychology*, *12*, Article 1209. https://doi.org/10.3389/fpsyg.2021.610670

Hamza, C. A., Willoughby, T., & Heffer, T. (2015). Impulsivity and nonsuicidal self-injury: A review and meta-analysis. *Clinical Psychology Review*, *38*, 13–24. https://doi.org/10.1016/j.cpr.2015.02.010

Harmon-Jones, C., Hinton, E., Tien, J., Summerell, E., & Bastian, B. (2019). Pain offset reduces rumination in response to evoked anger and sadness. *Journal of Personality and Social Psychology*, *117*(6), 1189. https://doi.org/10.1037/pspp0000240

Hepp, J., Carpenter, R. W., Freeman, L. K., Vebares, T. J., & Trull, T. J. (2021). The environmental, interpersonal, and affective context of nonsuicidal self-injury urges in daily life. *Personality Disorders: Theory, Research, and Treatment*, *12*(1), 29–38. https://doi.org/10.1037/per0000456

Hetrick, S. E., Robinson, J., Spittal, M. J., & Carter, G. (2016). Effective psychological and psychosocial approaches to reduce repetition of self-harm: A systematic review, meta-analysis, and meta-regression. *BMJ Open*, *6*(9), Article e011024. https://doi.org/10.1136/bmjopen-2016-011024

Hooley, J. M., Dahlgren, M. K., Best, S. G., Gonenc, A., & Gruber, S. A. (2020). Decreased Amygdalar activation to NSSI-stimuli in people who engage in NSSI: A neuroimaging pilot study. *Frontiers in Psychiatry*, *11*(April), 1–14. https://doi.org/10.3389/fpsyt.2020.00238

Hooley, J. M., & Dominiak, G. M. (2002). Borderline personality disorder and the family. In A. Schaub (Ed.), *New family interventions and associated research in psychiatric disorders* (pp. 135–152). Springer, Vienna. https://doi.org/10.1007/978-3-7091-6148-7_8

Hooley, J. M., Fox, K. R., Wang, S. B., & Kwashie, A. (2018). Novel online daily diary interventions for nonsuicidal self-injury: A randomized controlled trial. *BMC Psychiatry*, *18*(1), 264. https://doi.org/10.1186/s12888-018-1840-6

Hooley, J. M., & Franklin, J. C. (2018). Why do people hurt themselves? A new conceptual model of nonsuicidal self-injury. *Clinical Psychological Science*, *6*(3), 428–451. https://doi.org/10.1177/2167702617745641

Hooley, J. M., Ho, D. T., Slater, J., & Lockshin, A. (2010). Pain perception and nonsuicidal self-injury: A laboratory investigation. *Personality Disorders: Theory, Research, and Treatment*, *1*(3), 170. https://doi.org/10.1037/a0020106

Hooley, J. M., & St. Germain, S. A. (2014). Nonsuicidal self-injury, pain, and self-criticism: Does changing self-worth change pain endurance in people who engage in self-injury? *Clinical Psychological Science*, *2*(3), 297–305. http://dx.doi.org/10.1177/2167702613509372

Houben, M., Claes, L., Vansteelandt, K., Berens, A., Sleuwaegen, E., & Kuppens, P. (2017). The emotion regulation function of nonsuicidal self-injury: A momentary assessment study in inpatients with borderline personality disorder features. *Journal of Abnormal Psychology*, *126*(1), 89. https://doi.org/10.1037/abn 0000229

Hughes, C. D., King, A. M., Kranzler, A., Fehling, K., Miller, A., Lindqvist, J., & Selby, E. A. (2019). Anxious and overwhelming affects and repetitive negative thinking as ecological predictors of self-injurious thoughts and behaviors. *Cognitive Therapy and Research*, *43*(1), 88–101. https://doi.org/10.1007/s10 608-019-09996-9

Humber, N., Emsley, R., Pratt, D., & Tarrier, N. (2013). Anger as a predictor of psychological distress and self-harm ideation in inmates: A structured self-assessment diary study. *Psychiatry Research*, *210*(1), 166–173.

Jovev, M., Garner, B., Phillips, L., Velakoulis, D., Wood, S. J., Jackson, H. J., Pantelis, C., McGorry, P. D., & Chanen, A. M. (2008). An MRI study of pituitary volume and parasuicidal behavior in teenagers with first-presentation borderline personality disorder. *Psychiatry Research-Neuroimaging*, *162*(3), 273–277. https://doi.org/10.1016/j.pscychresns.2007.12.003

Kaess, M., Hille, M., Parzer, P., Maser-Gluth, C., Resch, F., & Brunner, R. (2012). Alterations in the neuroendocrinological stress response to acute psychosocial stress in adolescents engaging in nonsuicidal self-injury. *Psychoneuroendocrinology*, *37*(1), 157–161. https://doi.org/10.1016/j.psyneuen.2011.05.009

Kiekens, G., Hasking P., Nock, M. K., Boyes, M., Kirtley, O., Bruffaerts, R., Myin-Germeys, I., & Claes, L. (2020). Fluctuations in affective states and self-efficacy to resist non-suicidal self-injury as real-time predictors of non-suicidal self-injurious thoughts and behaviors. *Frontiers in Psychiatry*, *11*, Article 214. https://doi.org/10.3389/fpsyt.2020.00214

Klonsky, E. D. (2007). The functions of deliberate self-injury: A review of the evidence. *Clinical Psychology Review*, *27*(2), 226–239. https://doi.org/10.1016/j.cpr.2006.08.002

Klonsky, E. D., & Olino, T. M. (2008). Identifying clinically distinct subgroups of self-injurers among young adults: A latent class analysis. *Journal of Consulting and Clinical Psychology*, *76*(1), 22–27. https://doi.org/10.1037/0022-006X.76.1.22

Koenig, J., Klier, J., Parzer, P., Santangelo, P., Resch, F., Ebner-Priemer, U., & Kaess, M. (2021). High-frequency ecological momentary assessment of emotional and interpersonal states preceding and following self-injury in female adolescents. *European Child & Adolescent Psychiatry*, *30*, 1299–1308. https://doi.org/10.1007/s00787-020-01626-0

Kothgassner, O. D., Robinson, K., Goreis, A., Ougrin, D., & Plener, P. L. (2020). Does treatment method matter? A meta-analysis of the past 20 years of research on therapeutic interventions for self-harm and suicidal ideation in adolescents. *Borderline Personality Disorder and Emotion Regulation*, *7*, Article 9. https://doi.org/10.1186/s40479-020-00123-9

Kranzler, A., Fehling, K. B., Lindqvist, J., Brillante, J., Yuan, F., Gao, X., Miller, A. L., & Selby, E. A. (2018). An ecological investigation of the emotional context surrounding nonsuicidal self-injurious thoughts and behaviors in adolescents and young adults. *Suicide and Life-Threatening Behavior*, *48*(2), 149–159.

Krugers, H. J., Arp, J. M., Xiong, H., Kanatsou, S., Lesuis, S. L., Korosi, A., Joels, M., & Lucassen, P. J. (2017). Early life adversity: Lasting consequences for emotional learning. *Neurobiology of Stress*, *6*, 14–21. https://doi.org/10.1016/j.ynstr.2016.11.005

Kuehn, K. S., Dora, J., Harned, M. S., Foster, K. T., Song, F., Smith, M. R., & King, K. M. (2022). A meta-analysis on the affect regulation function of real-time self-injurious thoughts and behaviours. *Nature Human Behaviour*, *6*(7), 964–974. https://doi.org/10.1038/s41562-022-01340-8

Law, M. K., Fleeson, W., Arnold, E. M., & Furr, R. M. (2016). Using negative emotions to trace the experience of borderline personality pathology: Interconnected relationships revealed in an experience sampling study. *Journal of Personality Disorders*, *30*(1), 52–70. https://doi.org/10.1521/pedi_2015_29_180

Lear, M. K., Wilkowski, B. M., & Pepper, C. M. (2019). A daily diary investigation of the defective self model among college students with recent self-injury. *Behavior Therapy*, *50*(5), 1002–1012. https://doi.org/10.1016/j.beth.2019.03.005

Leibenluft, E., Gardner, D. L., & Cowdry, R. W. (1987). The inner experience of the borderline self-mutilator. *Journal of Personality Disorders*, *1*(4), 317–324. https://doi.org/10.1521/pedi.1987.1.4.317

Lereya, S. T., Winsper, C., Heron, J., Lewis, G., Gunnell, D., Fisher, H. L., & Wolke, D. (2013). Being bullied during childhood and the prospective pathways to self-harm in late adolescence. *Journal of the American Academy of Child and Adolescent Psychiatry, 52*(6), 608–618. https://doi.org/10.1016/j.jaac.2013.03.012

Linehan, M. M. (1993). *Cognitive-behavioral treatment of borderline personality disorder.* Guilford Press.

Liu, R. T., Cheek, S. M., & Nestor, B. A. (2016). Non-suicidal self-injury and life stress: A systematic meta-analysis and theoretical elaboration. *Clinical Psychology Review, 47*, 1–14. https://doi.org/10.1016/j.cpr.2016.05.005.

Liu, R. T., Sheehan, A. E., Walsh, R. F. L., Sanzari, C. M., Cheek, S. M., & Hernandez, E. M. (2019). Prevalence and correlates of non-suicidal self-injury among lesbian, gay, bisexual, and transgender individuals: A systematic review and meta-analysis. *Clinical Psychology Review, 74*(October), Article 101783. https://doi.org/10.1016/j.cpr.2019.101783

Lundh, L. G., Wångby-Lundh, M., Paaske, M., Ingesson, S., & Bjärehed, J. (2011). Depressive symptoms and deliberate self-harm in a community sample of adolescents: A prospective study. *Depression Research and Treatment, 2011*, Article 935871. https://doi.org/10.1155/2011/935871

Mahtani, S., Melvin, G. A., & Hasking, P. (2018). Shame proneness, shame coping, and functions of non-suicidal self-injury (NSSI) among emerging adults: A developmental analysis. *Emerging Adulthood, 6*(3), 159–171. https://doi.org/10.1177/2167696817711350

Malejko, K., Brown, R., Plener, P., Bonenberger, M., Abler, B., & Graf, H. (2020). Neural correlates of social inclusion in borderline personality disorder and non-suicidal self-injury. *Pharmacopsychiatry, 53*(2), 92–93. https://doi.org/10.1055/s-0039-3403031

Mars, B., Heron, J., Crane, C., Hawton, K., Kidger, J., Lewis, G., Macleod, J., Tilling, K., & Gunnell, D. (2014). Differences in risk factors for self-harm with and without suicidal intent: Findings from the ALSPAC cohort. *Journal of Affective Disorders, 168*, 407–414. https://doi.org/10.1016/j.jad.2014.07.009

Marshall, S. K., Tilton-Weaver, L. C., & Stattin, H. (2013). Non-suicidal self-injury and depressive symptoms during middle adolescence: A longitudinal analysis. *Journal of Youth and Adolescence, 42*(8), 1234–1242. https://doi.org/10.1007/s10964-013-9919-3

McKenzie, K. C., & Gross, J. J. (2014). Nonsuicidal self-injury: An emotion regulation perspective. *Psychopathology, 47*(4), 207–219. https://doi.org/10.1159/000358097

Miller, A. B., Eisenlohr-Moul, T., Glenn, C. R., Turner, B. J., Chapman, A. L., Nock, M. K., & Prinstein, M. J. (2019). Does higher-than-usual stress predict nonsuicidal self-injury? Evidence from two prospective studies in adolescent and emerging adult females. *Journal of Child Psychology and Psychiatry, 60*(10), 1076–1084. https://doi.org/10.1111/jcpp.13072

Muehlenkamp, J. J. (2014). Distinguishing between suicidal and nonsuicidal self-injury. In M. K. Nock (Ed.), *The Oxford handbook of suicide and self-injury* (pp. 23–46). Oxford University Press.

Muehlenkamp, J., Brausch, A., Quigley, K., & Whitlock, J. (2013). Interpersonal features and functions of nonsuicidal self-injury. *Suicide and Life-Threatening Behavior, 43*(1), 67–80.

Mullins-Sweatt, S. N., Lengel, G. J., & Grant, D. M. (2013). Non-suicidal self-injury: The contribution of general personality functioning. *Personality and Mental Health, 7*, 56–68. https://doi.org/10.1002/pmh

Nicolai, K. A., Wielgus, M. D., & Mezulis, A. (2015). Identifying risk for self-harm: Rumination and negative affectivity in the prospective prediction of nonsuicidal self-injury. *Suicide and Life-Threatening Behavior, 46*(2), 223–233. https://doi.org/10.1111/sltb.12186

Nock, M. K., & Mendes, W. B. (2008). Physiological arousal, distress tolerance, and social problem-solving deficits among adolescent self-injurers. *Journal of Consulting and Clinical Psychology, 76*(1), 28–38. https://doi.org/10.1037/0022-006X.76.1.28

Nock, M. K., & Prinstein, M. J. (2004). A functional approach to the assessment of self-mutilative behavior. *Journal of Consulting and Clinical Psychology, 72*(5), 885. https://doi.org/10.1037/0022-006X.72.5.885

Nock, M. K., Prinstein, M. J., & Sterba, S. K. (2009). Revealing the form and function of self-injurious thoughts and behaviors: A real-time ecological assessment study among adolescents and young adults. *Journal of Abnormal Psychology, 118*(4), 816–827. https://doi.org/10.1037/a0016948

Osuch, E., Ford, K., Wrath, A., Bartha, R., & Neufeld, R. (2014). Functional MRI of pain application in youth who engaged in repetitive non-suicidal self-injury vs. psychiatric controls. *Psychiatry Research: Neuroimaging, 223*(2), 104–112. https://doi.org/10.1016/j.pscychresns.2014.05.003

Pattison, E. M., & Kahan, J. (1983). The deliberate self-harm syndrome. *The American Journal of Psychiatry, 140*(7), 867–872. https://doi.org/10.1176/ajp.140.7.867

Pechtel, P., & Pizzagalli, D. A. (2011). Effects of early life stress on cognitive and affective function: An integrated review of human literature. *Psychopharmacology, 214*(1), 55–70. https://doi.org/10.1007/s00 213-010-2009-2

Piccirillo, M. L., Burke, T. A., Moore-Berg, S. L., Alloy, L. B., & Heimberg, R. G. (2020). Self-stigma toward nonsuicidal self-injury: An examination of implicit and explicit attitudes. *Suicide and Life-Threatening Behavior, 50*(5), 1007–1024. https://doi.org/10.1111/sltb.12640

Plener, P. L., Bubalo, N., Fladung, A. K., Ludolph, A. G., & Lulé, D. (2012). Prone to excitement: Adolescent females with non-suicidal self-injury (NSSI) show altered cortical pattern to emotional and NSS-related material. *Psychiatry Research-Neuroimaging, 203*(2–3), 146–152. https://doi.org/10.1016/j.pscychresns.2011.12.012

Power, J., Usher, A. M., & Beaudette, J. N. (2015). Non-suicidal self-injury in male offenders: Initiation, motivations, emotions, and precipitating events. *International Journal of Forensic Mental Health, 14*, 147–160. https://doi.org/10.1080/14999013.2015.1073196

Powers, S. I., & McArdle, E. T. (2003). Coping strategies moderate the relation of hypothalamus-pituitary-adrenal axis reactivity to self-injurious behavior. *Annals of the New York Academy of Sciences, 1008*(1), 285–288. https://doi.org/10.1196/annals.1301.033

Reitz, S., Kluetsch, R., Niedtfeld, I., Knorz, T., Lis, S., Paret, C., Kirsch, P., Meyer-Lindenberg, A., Treede, R. D., Baumgärtner, U., Bohus, M., & Schmahl, C. (2015). Incision and stress regulation in borderline personality disorder: Neurobiological mechanisms of self-injurious behaviour. *British Journal of Psychiatry, 207*(2), 165–172. https://doi.org/10.1192/bjp.bp.114.153379

Riley, E. N., Combs, J. L., Jordan, C. E., & Smith, G. T. (2015). Negative urgency and lack of perseverance: Identification of differential pathways of onset and maintenance risk in the longitudinal prediction of nonsuicidal self-injury. *Behavior Therapy, 46*(4), 439–448. https://doi.org/10.1016/j.beth.2015.03.002

Robinson, K., Garisch, J. A., Kingi, T., Brocklesby, M., O'Connell, A., Langlands, R. L., Russell, L., & Wilson, M. S. (2019). Reciprocal risk: The longitudinal relationship between emotion regulation and non-suicidal self-injury in adolescents. *Journal of Abnormal Child Psychology, 47*(2), 325–332. https://doi.org/10.1007/s10802-018-0450-6

Rodriguez-Blanco, L., Carballo, J. J., & Baca-Garcia, E. (2018). Use of ecological momentary assessment (EMA) in non-suicidal self-injury (NSSI): A systematic review. *Psychiatry Research, 263*, 212–219. https://doi.org/10.1016/j.psychres.2018.02.051

Sandel, D. B., Jomar, K., Johnson, S. L., Dickson, J. M., Dandy, S., Forrester, R., & Taylor, P. J. (2021). Beliefs about one's non-suicidal self-injury: The Experiences of Self-Injury Questionnaire (ESIQ). *Archives of Suicide Research, 25*(3), 458–474. https://doi.org/10.1080/13811118.2020.1712285

Scala, J. W., Levy, K. N., Johnson, B. N., Kivity, Y., Ellison, W. D., Pincus, A. L., Wilson, S. J., & Newman, M. G. (2018). The role of negative affect and self-concept clarity in predicting self-injurious urges in borderline personality disorder using ecological momentary assessment. *Journal of Personality Disorders, 32*, 36–57. https://doi.org/10.1521/pedi.2018.32.supp.36

Schoenleber, M., Berenbaum, H., & Motl, R. (2014). Shame-related functions of and motivations for self-injurious behavior. *Personality Disorders: Theory, Research, and Treatment, 5*(2), 204. https://doi.org/10.1037/per0000035

Selby, E. A., Franklin, J., Carson-Wong, A., & Rizvi, S. L. (2013). Emotional cascades and self-injury: Investigating instability of rumination and negative emotion. *Journal of Clinical Psychology, 69*(12), 1213–1227. https://doi.org/10.1002/jclp.21966

Selby, E. A., & Joiner Jr., T. E. (2009). Cascades of emotion: The emergence of borderline personality disorder from emotional and behavioral dysregulation. *Review of General Psychology, 13*(3), 219–229. https://doi.org/10.1037/a0015687

Sheehy, K., Noureen, A., Khaliq, A., Dhingra, K., Husain, N., Pontin, E. E., Cawley, R., & Taylor, P. J. (2019). An examination of the relationship between shame, guilt and self-harm: A systematic review and meta-analysis. *Clinical Psychology Review, 73*(July), Article 101779. https://doi.org/10.1016/j.cpr.2019.101779

Sheppes, G. (2020). Transcending the "good & bad" and "here & now" in emotion regulation: Costs and benefits of strategies across regulatory stages. *Advances in Experimental Social Psychology, 61*, 185–236. https://doi.org/10.1016/bs.aesp.2019.09.003

Simons, J. S., & Gaher, R. M. (2005). The distress tolerance scale: Development and validation of a self-report measure. *Motivation and Emotion, 29*(2), 83–102. https://doi.org/10.1007/s11031-005-7955-3

Snir, A., Rafaeli, E., Gadassi, R., Berenson, K., & Downey, G. (2015). Explicit and inferred motives for non-suicidal self-injurious acts and urges in borderline and avoidant personality disorders. *Personality Disorders: Theory, Research, and Treatment*, *6*(3), 267. https://doi.org/10.1037/per0000104

Spitzen, T. L., Tull, M. T., Baer, M. M., Dixon-Gordon, K. L., Chapman, A. L., & Gratz, K. L. (2020). Predicting engagement in nonsuicidal self-injury (NSSI) over the course of 12 months: the roles of borderline personality disorder pathology and emotional consequences of NSSI. *Journal of Affective Disorders*, *277*, 631–639. https://doi.org/10.1016/j.jad.2020.08.049

Spitzen, T. L., Tull, M. T., & Gratz, K. L. (2022). The roles of emotion regulation self-efficacy and emotional avoidance in self-injurious thoughts and behaviors. *Archives of Suicide Research*, *26*(2), 595–613. https://doi.org/10.1080/13811118.2020.1818654

Staniland, L., Hasking, P., Boyes, M., & Lewis, S. (2021). Stigma and nonsuicidal self-injury: Application of a conceptual framework. *Stigma and Health*, *6*(3), 312–323. https://doi.org/10.1037/sah0000257

Swerdlow, B. A., Pearlstein, J. G., Sandel, D. B., Mauss, I. B., & Johnson, S. L. (2020). Maladaptive behavior and affect regulation: A functionalist perspective. *Emotion*, *20*(1), 75. https://doi.org/10.1037/emo0000660

Taylor, P. J., Jomar, K., Dhingra, K., Forrester, R., Shahmalak, U., & Dickson, J. M. (2018). A meta-analysis of the prevalence of different functions of non-suicidal self-injury. *Journal of Affective Disorders*, *227*, 759–769. https://doi.org/10.1016/j.jad.2017.11.073

Turner, B. J., Austin, S. B., & Chapman, A. L. (2014). Treating nonsuicidal self-injury: A systematic review of psychological and pharmacological interventions. *Canadian Journal of Psychiatry/Revue Canadienne de Psychiatrie*, *59*(11), 576–585. https://doi.org/10.1177/070674371405901103

Turner, B. J., Yiu, A., Claes, L., Muehlenkamp, J. J., & Chapman, A. L. (2016). Occurrence and co-occurrence of nonsuicidal self-injury and disordered eating in a daily diary study: Which behavior, when? *Psychiatry Research*, *246*, 39–47. https://doi.org/10.1016/j.psychres.2016.09.012

Vansteelandt, K., Houben, M., Claes, L., Berens, A., Sleuwaegen, E., Sienaert, P., & Kuppens, P. (2017). The affect stabilization function of nonsuicidal self injury in borderline personality disorder: An ecological momentary assessment study. *Behaviour Research and Therapy*, *92*, 41–50. https://doi.org/10.1016/j.brat.2017.02.003

Victor, S. E., Glenn, C. R., & Klonsky, E. D. (2012). Is non-suicidal self-injury an "addiction"? A comparison of craving in substance use and non-suicidal self-injury. *Psychiatry Research*, *197*(1-2), 73–77. https://doi.org/10.1016/j.psychres.2011.12.011

Victor, S. E., & Klonsky, E. D. (2014). Daily emotion in non-suicidal self-injury. *Journal of Clinical Psychology*, *70*(4), 364–375. https://doi.org/10.1002/jclp.22037

Victor, S. E., Scott, L. N., Stepp, S. D., & Goldstein, T. R. (2019). I want you to want me: Interpersonal stress and affective experiences as within-person predictors of nonsuicidal self-injury and suicide urges in daily life. *Suicide and Life-Threatening Behavior*, *49*(4), 1157–1177. https://doi.org/10.1111/sltb.12513

Victor, S. E., Styer, D., & Washburn, J. J. (2016). Functions of nonsuicidal self-injury (NSSI): Cross-sectional associations with NSSI duration and longitudinal changes over time and following treatment. *Psychiatry Research*, *241*, 83–90. https://doi.org/10.1016/j.psychres.2016.04.083

Voon, D., Hasking, P., & Martin, G. (2014a). Emotion regulation in first episode adolescent non-suicidal self-injury: What difference does a year make?. *Journal of Adolescence*, *37*(7), 1077–1087. https://doi.org/10.1016/j.adolescence.2014.07.020

Voon, D., Hasking, P., & Martin, G. (2014b). Change in emotion regulation strategy use and its impact on adolescent nonsuicidal self-injury: A three-year longitudinal analysis using latent growth modeling. *Journal of Abnormal Psychology*, *123*(3), 487. https://doi.org/10.1037/a0037024

Westlund Schreiner, M., Klimes-Dougan, B., Begnel, E. D., & Cullen K. R. (2015). Conceptualizing the neurobiology of non-suicidal self-injury from the perspective of the Research Domain Criteria Project. *Neuroscience & Biobehavioral Reviews*, *57*, 381–391. https://doi.org/10.1016/j.neubiorev.2015.09.011.

Westlund Schreiner, M., Klimes-Dougan, B., Mueller, B. A., Eberly, L. E., Reigstad, K. M., Carstedt, P. A., Thomas, K. M., Hunt, R. H., Lim, K. O., & Cullen, K. R. (2017). Multi-modal neuroimaging of adolescents with non-suicidal self-injury: Amygdala functional connectivity. *Journal of Affective Disorders*, *221*, 47–55. https://doi.org/10.1016/j.jad.2017.06.004

Whiteside, S. P., & Lynam, D. R. (2001). The five factor model and impulsivity: Using a structural model of personality to understand impulsivity. *Personality and Individual Differences*, *30*(4), 660–689. https://doi.org/10.1016/S0191-8869(00)00064-7

Wolff, J. C., Thompson, E., Thomas, S. A., Nesi, J., Bettis, A. H., Ransford, B., Scopelliti, K., Frazier, E. A., & Liu, R. T. (2019). Emotion dysregulation and non-suicidal self-injury: A systematic review and meta-analysis. *European Psychiatry, 59*, 25–36. https://doi.org/10.1016/j.eurpsy.2019.03.004

Yarali, A., Niewalda, T., Chen, Y. C., Tanimoto, H., Duerrnagel, S., & Gerber, B. (2008). "Pain relief" learning in fruit flies. *Animal Behaviour, 76*(4), 1173–1185. https://doi.org/10.1016/j.anbehav.2008.05.025

You, J., Lin, M., Xu, S., & Hu, W. (2016). Big Five personality traits in the occurrence and repetition of nonsuicidal self-injury among adolescents: The mediating effects of depressive symptoms. *Personality and Individual Differences, 101*, 227–231. https://doi.org/10.1016/j.paid.2016.05.057

Zetterqvist, M., Lundh, L. G., Dahlström, Ö., & Svedin, C. G. (2013). Prevalence and function of non-suicidal self-injury (NSSI) in a community sample of adolescents, using suggested DSM-5 criteria for a potential NSSI disorder. *Journal of Abnormal Child Psychology, 41*(5), 759–773. https://doi.org/10.1007/s10802-013-9712-5

CHAPTER 14

The Brain and Body's Threat System Functioning in Those with NSSI

Katherine A. Carosella, Andrea Wiglesworth, Zeynep Başgöze, Kathryn R. Cullen, and Bonnie Klimes-Dougan

Abstract

Non-suicidal self-injury (NSSI) defies the core purpose of the brain and body's threat processing and response system: self-preservation and protection from harm. The hypothalamic-pituitary-adrenal (HPA) axis coordinates the endocrine response to threats. Preliminary evidence suggests that individuals who engage in NSSI demonstrate blunted cortisol responses to stressors and possibly elevations in basal cortisol.
The neural threat system involves the amygdala, anterior cingulate cortex (ACC), prefrontal cortex (PFC), and insula. Individuals with a history of NSSI have been shown to have structural alterations in and between the ACC, insula, and amygdala. Functional connectivity between the amygdala and PFC has been shown to be altered in adolescents with a history of NSSI as well. Further, individuals with a history of NSSI have been shown to have increased amygdala activation in response to emotional stimuli. Work that integrates multiple modes of measuring stress response has shown discordance between the HPA axis response, experience of stress, and expression of stress among those with more severe NSSI. More work is needed to disentangle discordance within the threat processing system. Additionally, there is a need for more nuanced understanding of (a) environmental mechanisms of risk and protection, (b) implications of sustained engagement in NSSI, and (c) a broader array of pathology as it relates to biological threat-system disturbances for those who engage in NSSI. Future work on NSSI should explore ways to mitigate the impact of risk factors and leverage the protective factors and neurobiological and psychological underpinnings of NSSI to identify novel treatment modalities.

Key Words: NSSI, HPA axis, Endocrine, Brain, Threat Processing, Threat Response

Introduction

Exemplar Case

Jamie is a 17-year-old high school junior. She lives with her mother, her stepfather, and her younger brother in an affluent suburb. Her parents divorced when she was 8 years old and have joint custody of the teen. Prior to her parents separating, Jamie frequently witnessed loud arguments, which occasionally resulted in threats toward her mother and holes punched in the wall. During one argument, Jamie witnessed her father holding her mother in a chokehold, which left dark bruises on her mother's neck. Jamie was first seen for two sessions by mental health professionals when she was 5 years old to address separation anxiety. No other information from her early developmental, social, academic, or medical history was remarkable.

Jamie began engaging in non-suicidal self-injury (NSSI) at age 13, when she was in the eighth grade. Earlier in the year, she began having stomachaches, which resulted in her not being able to stay at her father's house on the weekends as per the custody arrangements and heightened the disputes between her parents about visitation. Although visits at her father's house were generally uneventful and he had never struck either of the children, she lived in fear that he would hit them when he was frustrated. Jamie also began worrying about her grades in school and about her mother's job, and because her social group had recently reorganized, she felt very anxious at lunchtime because she didn't have a regular group of friends to sit with. Within the next several months, she quit trying out for school plays (something she has always enjoyed) and complained about having to go to dance class after school. After a classmate posted on social media a list of classmates (which included her) who he would never invite to a party, her mood deteriorated further. She started crying almost every night, having trouble falling asleep, feeling very irritable in the mornings, and saying that no one at school liked her. It was around this time that Jamie overheard some classmates talking about cutting. She looked toward social media to learn more about cutting, where she saw posts saying that cutting helps some people relieve distress. She thought this could work for her because she had been having a really hard time. This behavior then became very common for her, where she would cut herself on her wrists and arms several times a week.

About a year later, Jamie's mother saw the cuts on her arms and was alarmed because she assumed her daughter was trying to end her life. She initiated treatment with a clinical psychologist for psychotherapy, and later a psychiatrist for medication assessments. During these treatment sessions, it became known that although Jamie had initially only self-harmed through cutting, she recently had begun biting and hitting herself as well because those behaviors are easier for her to do spontaneously in moments of distress. Since transitioning to these modalities of NSSI, Jamie reports that the behaviors feel almost like a habit, happening automatically without forethought. The frequency of NSSI has increased over the past four years despite a decrease in depressive and anxious symptoms. Since she began, several of Jamie's friends have also begun to self-harm. She reports feeling numb almost constantly, with NSSI being the only thing that "makes [her] feel something." Currently, Jamie is dealing with stressors including conflict with her parents regarding her sexual orientation, conflict within her friend group, and academic performance decline. Additionally, Jamie was the victim of sexual assault by a peer in the past year. Jamie finds herself checking social media constantly, trying to make sure she hasn't offended anyone in her friend group and keeping up with the lives of those in a popular group. Current concerns include ongoing self-harm and passive suicidal ideation; specifically, she states that she would not try to save her life if she found herself in danger and that she does not care if she dies. The current course of treatment has effectively addressed her depressive and anxious symptoms but has not been successful in treating her persistent NSSI. Through a systematic evaluation of the threat system, we may be able to gain insights into factors underlying persistent NSSI in cases like Jamie's, and with these insights guide strategies toward more efficacious intervention.

Background

NSSI is a complex maladaptive behavior that frequently develops during adolescence (Plener et al., 2015) and represents an important risk factor for future suicide attempts (Horwitz et al., 2015; Mars et al., 2019; Swannell et al., 2014; Tang et al., 2011; Victor & Klonsky, 2014). A striking feature of NSSI is that it goes against the most basic survival instinct of self-preservation. Human beings have multiple highly conserved biological systems in place geared toward interpreting and responding to threats to prevent injury and promote survival. Understanding the mechanisms that underlie the tendency for certain individuals to intentionally harm themselves is critical for gaining new insights into this concerning behavior, and in doing so advances the understanding of the developmental neurobiological mechanisms underlying NSSI, and developing effective interventions.

NSSI is a transdiagnostic phenomenon, frequently co-occurring with suicidal ideation and attempt, major depressive disorder (MDD), bipolar disorder (BP), and borderline personality disorder (BPD), all of which share overlapping clinical characteristics (Ando et al., 2018; Başgöze, Wiglesworth, et al., 2021; Brambilla et al., 2004). These co-occurrences point to the need for reconceptualizing these constructs, potentially in a dimensional way. Dimensional approaches recognize psychological phenomena as occurring on a spectrum across multiple domains as opposed to existing in distinct categories (Krueger, 1999). One such approach is the Research Domain Criteria (RDoC) framework (Insel et al., 2010), which also emphasizes the importance of incorporating multiple levels of analysis (e.g., brain, body, and behavior) to assess key domains of functioning that are implicated in clinical problems. Employing the RDoC framework holds promise for advancing our understanding of biological substrates of NSSI (e.g., Westlund Schreiner et al., 2015). The RDoC framework outlines domains of interest which include negative valence systems, positive valence systems, cognitive systems, social processes, arousal and regulatory systems, and sensorimotor systems (see Bastiaens & Claes, this volume, for more on the RDoC framework). The focus of this chapter is on the negative valence domain, and, even more specifically, on endocrine and neural threat responses that are central to NSSI engagement.

Overview of the Endocrine and Neural Threat Systems

The world is a dangerous place. This was especially true for our ancestors, for whom threats could be hiding around every corner. Through the course of natural selection, the genes coding for neural structures critical to detecting threats have been preserved. Today, threat elicits physiological activation of the autonomic nervous system (ANS; McCarty, 2016) and the hypothalamic-pituitary-adrenal (HPA) axis. The sympathetic branch of the ANS (which includes sensory, endocrine, vascular, and digestive organs) readies the body for action and engages the processes necessary to keep us alive in the face of imminent threat. The HPA axis provides metabolic resources to the organism to engage in these potentially life-saving functions. While the ANS and HPA axis responses are indispensable for survival, they are not able to adequately counter ambiguity or anticipate consequences of behavior; the brain is in command of these higher-order tasks. Understanding the interplay between the endocrine and neural systems along with their individual characteristics is important for grasping the role that threat processing plays in NSSI (e.g., Klimes-Dougan et al., 2014).

The endocrine response by the HPA axis is instrumental in eliciting a coordinated cognitive and behavioral response to threat. The release of cortisol from the HPA axis in reaction to a stressor elicits a cascade of signaling that enacts bodily responses to stressors and initiates a negative feedback loop that attenuates future responses (Herman et al., 2012; Meaney & Szyf, 2005). This negative feedback occurs over the course of a short time period via glucocorticoids that directly dampen the release of the corticotropin-releasing hormone (CRH) and inhibitory inputs from the hippocampus and medial prefrontal cortex. This process, in turn, further decreases the amount of CRH released. Over a longer period of time, increased levels of cortisol can lead to a destabilization of CRH messenger RNA in the HPA axis and subsequent decreased production of cortisol. Critically, when considering this longer time scale, chronic heightened cortisol levels produce an increase in CRH mRNA in the central amygdala, which leads to an increase in amygdala activity in response to stressors (Herman et al., 2012). Additionally, the glucocorticoids released in response to HPA activation also serve a role in providing negative feedback to the secretion of CRH. Glucocorticoid receptors translocate to the nucleus of the neuron after binding with glucocorticoid and modulates gene expression (Chrousos et al., 2009). These short- and long-term feedback mechanisms are likely to have a role in the production of abnormal HPA axis functioning in those with NSSI, particularly because these individuals are known to often have experienced an increased level of chronic stressors (Brown & Plener, 2017). Furthermore, NSSI is often a chronic behavior, pointing to lasting alterations in threat processing being implicated in its instantiation and maintenance (Liu et al., 2018).

Exposure to multiple threats, particularly sustained threats, can lead to allostatic overload. Allostatic overload is the "cost of chronic exposure to fluctuating or heightened neural or neuroendocrine response resulting from repeated or chronic environmental challenge that an individual reacts to as being particularly stressful" (McEwen & Stellar, 1993, p. 2093, para. 4). Each individual has a certain level of allostatic load which they can proficiently handle. When a person's stressors accumulate in excess of this level, they enter a state of allostatic overload which is characterized by dysregulation across multiple threat systems. Additionally, in allostatic overload, one's adaptive techniques for mitigating stressors fail, which can lead to adverse physical and mental health outcomes (Guidi et al., 2021; Lupien et al., 2006). One of these potential negative mental health outcomes is the engagement in NSSI as a maladaptive coping strategy (Hasking et al., 2017). Indeed, there is a growing body of literature that links NSSI engagement with current and past stressors (Guerry & Prinstein, 2009; Miller et al., 2018).

The brain's threat processing and response production are conducted through serial and parallel processing steps connected by feedback loops between critical regions. The amygdala is a core node for processing of negative emotion and threat (LeDoux 2000; Lindquist et al., 2016). Frontal regions such as the anterior cingulate cortex (ACC) and prefrontal cortex (PFC), including the medial (mPFC) and dorsolateral (dlPFC) subregions, are key for regulating responses in other regions (Banks et al., 2007). The hippocampus is responsible for emotional memory and HPA axis regulation (Lupien et al., 2009) and the insula is key in emotion salience processing (Seeley et al., 2007). Finally, the HPA axis works to regulate reactions to stressors, thus acting as the interface between the brain and body (Lupien et al., 2009; Zorn et al., 2017). This chapter discusses the endocrine and neural systems implicated in NSSI, a tool for coping with allostatic overload. These systems are subject to significant changes over the course of development and, as such, must be considered in the context of these processes.

Developmental Changes to the Endocrine and Neural Threat Systems

While engagement in NSSI may occur at any developmental stage, this behavior most commonly onsets during adolescence. Adolescence is a time of widespread change in the brain (Giedd et al., 1999; Giedd et al., 2009). It is posited that the increased neuroplasticity inherent to this period leads not only to an increased capacity for new learning and adaptation but also to a vulnerability for the onset of mental illness (Paus et al., 2008). Indeed, the areas of the brain and body that are implicated in threat response are changing in a variety of ways simultaneously; synaptic plasticity allows for the establishment and strengthening of connections between brain regions, whereas synaptic pruning eliminates connections that have not served the individual up to that point. The HPA axis also undergoes change across development; of particular note is the rise in cortisol reactivity to threats that occur in early- to mid-adolescence (Gunnar et al., 2009; Klimes-Dougan et al., 2001; Stroud et al., 2009). Additionally, the endocrine system introduces heightened hormone levels, including cortisol, though the magnitude of hormone increase differs between sexes (Gunnar et al., 2009; Klimes-Dougan et al., 2001; Stroud et al., 2009). Also of critical importance to NSSI are the changes that occur in the frontolimbic regions of the brain during this developmental period. In particular, the connections between the amygdala and the PFC mature across adolescence (Cunningham et al., 2002; Gee et al., 2013; Perlman & Pelphrey, 2011; Swartz et al., 2014). Simultaneously, there is an increase in PFC activation in response to stressful stimuli (Yurgelun-Todd & Killgore, 2006). From an evolutionary point of view, survival of our species and other mammals is enhanced by moving farther from the natal family unit (Spear, 2000), and while motivated to engage in novel experiences that may involve increased risk, this period may also include increased need of vigilance for threat (Casey et al., 2010). This context potentially accounts for the increased susceptibility of these processes to alterations, and thus the onset of psychopathology, during this period (Brown & Plener, 2017; Plener et al., 2015) (See Kiekens et al., this volume, for a review of adolescence and NSSI). The HPA axis undergoes changes in response to the hormone fluctuations characteristic of development and also demonstrates plasticity in the face of chronic and acute stressors.

The HPA Axis in NSSI

HPA axis functioning can be indexed using a variety of peripheral measures and in a variety of contexts (e.g., in the presence or absence of acute threat). Cortisol accumulates over time in hair, offering a route to measure cumulative HPA axis activation over long periods of time (i.e., months; Russell et al., 2012). Also of interest are more momentary fluctuations in HPA axis functioning such as those that naturally change over the course of a day and in response to stressors. Cortisol circulating in the body can be measured in a temporally specific fashion by sampling body fluids, including the saliva and blood plasma. The temporal specificity of these measures gives great insight into the daily fluctuations in cortisol levels, which are known to follow a common pattern over the course of the day. Additionally, these techniques are leveraged to follow specific phases of the HPA axis response to a stressor; they can track the baseline (e.g., pre-stress), immediate rise, and eventual fall of cortisol levels that normally occur in the minutes before, during and following exposure to an acute stressor (Pruessner et al., 2007). Examining cortisol through these different methods can allow us to quantify the patterns of functioning of the HPA axis across multiple timescales and conditions.

Diurnal cortisol, the pattern of cortisol level change that naturally fluctuates over the course of a day, is thought to index the general functioning of the HPA axis and is typically assessed by salivary cortisol. The diurnal slope refers to the pattern of decrease in cortisol levels that naturally occurs following a morning peak until an evening nadir, the lowest levels of the day. While research has not identified differences in diurnal slopes between individuals who engage in NSSI and healthy controls broadly, it does seem that childhood adversity moderates diurnal slopes (Reichl et al., 2016). That is, while healthy controls who had a history of adversity show flattened slopes, or less change over the course of the day, individuals with a history of NSSI and greater childhood adversity show steeper diurnal slopes (Reichl et al., 2016). Thus, there may be more variability in cortisol patterning throughout the day for those with a history of greater stressors.

Changes in cortisol levels during specific periods of the day are of particular interest. For instance, the steep rise and fall of cortisol levels in the 30 minutes after waking is called the cortisol awakening response (CAR). The CAR is thought to capture HPA axis functioning at a time when the neural regulatory systems are coming online after being at rest and show the shift from subcortical regulation (e.g., amygdala) to cortical regulation (e.g., PFC) (Clow et al., 2010; McEwen, 2007). Measuring the CAR may also give insight into the expectation of the upcoming day's stressors (Fries et al., 2009). Research suggests that individuals with a history of NSSI demonstrate heightened CAR as compared to healthy controls (Reichl et al., 2016), which may be indicative of alterations in threat processing or a heightened propensity to detect threat in their environment.

Little work thus far has focused on evaluating cortisol levels at bedtime, when cortisol levels are typically at their nadir, among those who engage in NSSI. However, extant research does not show differences in mean evening cortisol levels when comparing individuals with a history of NSSI compared to healthy controls (Reichl et al., 2016). This null effect could be because of within-individual fluctuations in bedtime cortisol levels. Indeed, one case study showed a great deal of variability in bedtime cortisol levels in an individual with BPD and NSSI and, importantly, found that heightened evening cortisol predicted NSSI engagement within the following 1 to 3 days (Sachsse et al., 2002).

Patterns of cortisol output over protracted periods of time are similarly understudied with respect to their association with NSSI, with extant research producing mixed results. First, research comparing individuals with a history of NSSI to healthy controls found no significant difference in hair cortisol levels (e.g., cumulative cortisol output) measured over 3 months (Reichl et al., 2016). However, the same group of researchers later examined sibling dyads, comparing those who engage in NSSI to their siblings who do not engage in NSSI, as a means of accounting for potential shared environmental stressors. In this study, the researchers found higher hair cortisol levels in those with a history of NSSI as compared to their siblings (Reichl et al., 2019). Together, the findings of these two studies suggest that those who engage in NSSI may perceive, encounter, or respond physiologically differently than other individuals to events in their daily life. However, careful consideration is needed in determining the most adequate comparison group for future research in this area.

Much of the work assessing HPA axis functioning is focused on reactivity to acute stressors. Repeated saliva and blood samples are most frequently used to index the HPA axis response to and recovery from a stressor. Several studies to date have used the well-validated Trier Social Stress Test (TSST) to measure stress reactivity. In the TSST, salivary samples are collected at intervals prior to and after an experimental paradigm in which participants prepare and then give a speech about themselves to a panel of impassive judges and then complete a difficult serial subtraction task verbally with corrective feedback (Kirschbaum et al., 1993). In adolescence, individuals with prior NSSI engagement show lower levels of cortisol output in response to the TSST than do agemates without a history of NSSI (Kaess et al., 2012; Plenar et al., 2017). These blunted responses to stress are thought to be the result of the aforementioned negative feedback processes in the HPA system that come into effect following chronic activation.

More recent work with larger samples has extended these studies by replicating group differences and demonstrating that the severity of self-harm may be reflected in the degree of cortisol blunting. In one such study by Klimes-Dougan et al. (2019), adolescents diagnosed with MDD and those with no clinical diagnoses were assessed in the context of the TSST. A subgroup of the adolescents with MDD had a history of engaging in NSSI. Adolescents with MDD and NSSI showed significantly lower cortisol levels in response to the TSST than those with MDD without NSSI as well as those with no diagnosis. This pattern of blunted cortisol was most pronounced in those with four or more episodes of NSSI as compared to those with one to three episodes of NSSI (Klimes-Dougan et al., 2019). This research was critical for starting to understand differential patterns of physiological stress responses among subgroups of depressed youth. This same research group replicated this finding of blunted salivary cortisol in another cohort of participants assigned female at birth who engaged in no/mild, moderate, or severe NSSI (Başgöze, Mirza, et al., 2021). Within the context of the TSST, salivary cortisol levels were significantly lower for those with severe NSSI than no/mild NSSI, but no differences were observed between those with a moderate history of NSSI and no/mild NSSI. This work highlights the need to evaluate NSSI along a spectrum of severity, and the importance of using statistical methods that are capable of demonstrating meaningful individual differences.

Assessing cortisol output under other potentially stressful conditions can give insight into different aspects of the threat processing system and alterations in individuals with a history of NSSI. Similar to the TSST findings, cortisol reactivity in response to the recall of childhood adversity in sibling dyads revealed that those with a history of NSSI showed decreased reactivity compared to their siblings without a history of NSSI (Reichl et al., 2019). Another study used exogenous dexamethasone to mimic a feedback mechanism that inhibits cortisol response following a stressor and found that individuals with a history of self-injury showed more suppressed cortisol levels than those without a history of self-injury (Beauchaine et al., 2015). By contrast, research examining responses to pain showed the opposite pattern. Koenig et al. (2017) used cold pain stimulation to elicit a threat response and found that those with a history of NSSI had a greater cortisol response than healthy controls, signaling that the neural response to threat and pain is likely distinct.

In summary, there is preliminary evidence that those with NSSI may demonstrate higher cortisol levels under non-reactive contexts (e.g., during awakening and over time), though these patterns are less clear. Further, there is consistent evidence that adolescents and young adults with a history of NSSI have lower cortisol levels in the context of a stressor than those with no history of NSSI. These findings are likely due to long-acting negative feedback mechanisms that are shaping the functioning of the HPA axis in response to a history of repeated stress. Specifically, chronic exposure to stress and resulting allostatic overload of the threat systems manifest in blunting of the HPA axis response. The endocrine response by the HPA axis works in concert with processing in the brain that governs the evaluation of and behavioral response to threatening situations. Understanding the ways in which the activity in and communication between brain regions can go awry when faced with a stressor is important to developing a more comprehensive conceptualization of NSSI.

The Neural Threat Systems in NSSI

As previously noted, key structures in the brain's threat system include the amygdala, ACC, mPFC, dlPFC, insula, and hippocampus. Advances in neuroimaging have enabled the characterization of structural and functional mechanisms of threat processing and response, which together facilitate our understanding of NSSI. In the following sections, we review the state of current knowledge according to the different types of neuroimaging approaches that have been used to date in the study of the neural underpinnings of NSSI, which has also been reviewed recently by Brañas et al. (2021) and Auerbach et al., 2021.

Brain Structure and NSSI

Structural (T1-weighted) MRI can provide measures of gray matter volume as well as cortical thickness and surface area. Findings to date regarding structural alterations in individuals who engage in NSSI have broadly implicated frontolimbic regions involved in threat processing. Most of the studies in the literature examining structural alterations in individuals with NSSI include samples that were primarily targeted for other clinical factors, such as a history of suicide attempts (SA), MDD, BD, or BPD. Even though recruitment for NSSI is not a primary aim for many of these studies, these populations typically include high numbers of individuals with a history of NSSI engagement. Reduced amygdala and hippocampal volumes have been demonstrated in adults with BPD (Nunes et al., 2009; Weniger et al., 2009). By contrast, in the previously described study that employed a dimensional, multilevel approach to explore the impact of sustained threat in female adolescents who exhibit a continuum of NSSI severity (no, mild, moderate, and severe), the findings failed to show differences in amygdala volume across groups (Başgöze, Mirza, et al., 2021). Structural neuroimaging studies in youth with NSSI have also demonstrated reduced gray matter volume associated with NSSI in the insula, a key region that processes pain and emotion (Ando et al., 2018; Beauchaine et al., 2019). Further, gray matter volume was found to be reduced in the inferior frontal gyrus in those with a history of NSSI (Beauchaine et al., 2019). When examining individuals with a history of NSSI and a history of SA, Ando et al. (2018) found a smaller ACC volume compared to those without this history.

Similar to other areas of neuroimaging in psychiatric disorders, the structural neuroimaging literature for NSSI has faced challenges related to replication. A recent meta-analysis including studies using various different imaging techniques (such as computed tomography, MRI, and diffusion tensor imaging) to look across several brain regions (such as PFC, ACC, and amygdala) found no significant structural differences associated with NSSI (Huang et al., 2020). Thus, the field is still in need of further work, likely with larger samples.

White Matter Connectivity and NSSI

Diffusion imaging studies can inform us about the integrity of white matter connections which make up the "wiring" in neural circuits (Pierpaoli & Basser, 1996). A study using diffusion MRI found evidence of disrupted white matter microstructure of the connections between the amygdala and ACC in adolescents who engaged in NSSI compared to healthy controls, indicating that youth with a history of NSSI had lower white matter connections between the amygdala and the ACC than their healthy counterparts (Westlund Schreiner et al., 2020). An earlier study employing diffusion imaging found that adult females with BPD and a history of NSSI had decreased white matter microstructure integrity in inferior frontal brain regions (Grant et al., 2007). These alterations in connectivity may be indicative of less efficient threat processing systems in those with a history of NSSI.

Resting-State Functional Connectivity and NSSI

Resting-state functional connectivity (RSFC) is a statistical approach derived from functional neuroimaging which allows researchers to gain insight into the strength of the connections that exist between brain regions by calculating the correlations between the spontaneously fluctuating signals measured in these regions during rest. In an effort to better understand the neural basis of NSSI, connectivity between brain regions critical to detecting threats, processing emotions, and producing behavioral outcomes has been investigated while the brain is at rest. To date, there are very few RSFC studies on individuals with NSSI. A notable exception is a study that compared adolescent females with a history of NSSI with healthy controls. Adolescents with NSSI demonstrated less negative amygdala-frontal connectivity both during resting state and during an emotion task compared to healthy controls, though the results did not remain significant after controlling for depressive symptoms (Westlund Schreiner et al., 2017). This finding was replicated by Santamarina-Perez et al. (2019) wherein they found reduced amygdala-mPFC RSFC in both male and female adolescents with NSSI compared to healthy controls. Recently, with the previously described cohort of participants assigned female at birth (Başgöze, Mirza, et al., 2021), lower bilateral amygdala-mPFC RSFC was found in individuals with severe NSSI as compared to their peers with no/mild NSSI. This larger sample allowed for tests of robustness to be conducted and this reported RSFC pattern remained significant on the left after correcting for age, medication status, depression and anxiety levels, and childhood trauma (Başgöze, Mirza, et al., 2021).

Task-Based Functional Imaging

Task fMRI allows researchers to identify which brain regions become activated or deactivated in response to specific stimuli of interest. For example, work has shown that in individuals with a history of NSSI, there is a relationship between limited internal emotion awareness and differential reactivity to masked faces in right frontal regions (Demers et al., 2019). Additionally, the amygdala has frequently been a region of interest in task-based NSSI research given its importance in negative emotion processing (e.g. Hariri et al., 2002). Thus far, there have been mixed findings with respect to amygdala activation during stress-inducing tasks in individuals who engage in NSSI. When comparing amygdala activation between those with and without a history of NSSI in reaction to NSSI-related stimuli, Plener et al. (2012) found increased activation in those with a history of NSSI, Mayo et al. (2021) found no difference between the those with and without a history of NSSI, and Hooley et al. (2020) found decreased activation in those with a history of NSSI compared to those who do not have such a history. In a task that involved negative emotion face-matching, no difference was found between adolescents with NSSI and healthy controls (Westlund Schreiner et al., 2017). Discrepancies across studies may stem from the variance in severity within participants with NSSI. Indeed, recent work showed that moderate, but not severe, NSSI showed elevated right amygdala activation compared to peers with less or no NSSI severity (Başgöze, Mirza, et al., 2021). This pattern indicates that it is possible that with time, initially elevated amygdala responses also undergo allostatic processes and become attenuated, as is seen in HPA axis functioning.

Multimodal Imaging

Although there is great value in research projects considering connectivity and activation separately, these measurements assess complementary underlying patterns of response at a systems level. Connectivity assesses the strength of the communication within a given network and often is examined at rest (e.g., RSFC) whereas activation assesses the potential co-activation of distinct regions under a particular condition of interest (e.g., stressful, emotional tasks). Employing multiple modes of measuring for neural functioning within the same mechanistic model could help elucidate the complex interactions implicated in NSSI. Indeed, Başgöze, Mirza et al. (2021) examined RSFC and task-based fMRI in the same sample and showed that lower amygdala-mPFC RSFC and higher right but lower left amygdala task activation toward threatening stimuli best predicted greater lifetime NSSI episodes.

In summary, across neuroimaging modalities, findings related to NSSI have broadly implicated dysfunction in the front-limbic circuits that are critical for emotion processing. Notably, findings to date from neuroimaging studies are mixed likely due to small samples (e.g., some results may potentially represent spurious findings), variability associated with neurodevelopment and sex differences within participant groups, and the likelihood of substantial neurobiological heterogeneity in the population of youth who engage in NSSI.

Concordance and Discordance across Levels of Threat-System Functioning

Although it is critical to understand how specific features of the threat system operate in those who engage in NSSI, understanding how these systems are coordinated across different levels of analysis is an important next step. Some studies that found blunted cortisol reactivity in those with a history of NSSI also found that these individuals self-reported equivalent (Kaess et al., 2012) or heightened distress (Klimes-Dougan et al., 2019) compared to those without a history of NSSI. More recent work suggests that this discordance may be driven by severity: those with a history of severe engagement in NSSI showed decreased cortisol reactivity and increased self-reports of stressors whereas those with moderate, mild, and no history of NSSI showed less discordance (Başgöze, Mirza, et al., 2021). This finding suggests that there may be a great deal of diversity of response to and perception of stressors among those with a history of NSSI.

Examining multiple levels of analysis of threat-system functioning has also involved examining concordance or discordance across critical brain systems and the HPA axis within the context of lab-based social stress paradigms (e.g., the Trier Social Stress Test [TSST]). Thai (2020) demonstrated that compared to their healthy counterparts, depressed adolescents showed minimal or negative association between frontolimbic connectivity and neuroendocrine system response toward stressors and that this result was even stronger for adolescents with both depression and NSSI. Başgöze, Mirza, et al. (2021) found that adolescent girls with severe NSSI showed a lower association between amygdala-mPFC RSFC and cortisol responses to acute stress compared to those with mild or no NSSI. More work exploring the interplay between systems is needed to better understand the scope of the biological alterations associated with NSSI.

More robust modes of investigation have begun to extend beyond traditional variable-centered approaches to person-centered approaches that identify clusters of individuals who share patterns of variability across numerous indices of threat response. Based on the previously discussed sample (see Klimes-Dougan et al., 2019), multi-trajectory modeling was used to detect four profiles of stress responses spanning the experience, expression, and physiological reactions of stress in the context of the TSST (Bendezú et al., 2022. Importantly, NSSI was more common in adolescents with discordance across systems (high ratings of experiences and expressions of stress but blunted cortisol reactivity) during the TSST, compared to the other three groups, including a group that was concordant across indices of high stress reactivity (high ratings of experience and expression of stress with high levels of cortisol). This study suggests that discordant stress responding across systems may be a mechanism of risk for those with NSSI. Further, the results highlight the importance of understanding individual-level variation across indices, as merely noting high stress experience or expression in this sample would not have differentiated those with NSSI from those without NSSI. Instead, this information is only salient when including physiological reactivity alongside these other indices of experience and expression of stress responding during the TSST.

Potential Avenues of Future Exploration

The field is just beginning to address foundational questions of threat-system functioning for those who engage in NSSI. Indeed, we need more nuanced work considering (a) environmental factors as mechanisms of risk and protection for the alterations in threat processing seen in those with NSSI, (b) implications of sustained engagement in NSSI, (c) how a systems approach would enable a more complete understanding of dynamic processes of the brain and physiological systems for those who engage in NSSI, and (d) a broader array of pathology as it relates to biological threat-system disturbances for those who engage in NSSI.

Environmental Factors as Mechanisms of Risk and Protection

As is true for many aspects of development, threat-system development occurs in the presence of inherited and environmental factors that interact to affect trajectories (e.g., Sumner et al., 2014). Inputs from the environment that are perceived as "stressful" impact neural and psychophysiological development within the threat system (McLaughlin et al., 2015), which may differ based on their intensity, chronicity, and timing. Such impacts may predispose an adolescent to experiment with, and potentially maintain, NSSI engagement. Indeed, work has shown that individuals who go on to engage in NSSI were significantly more likely to have experienced trauma during childhood compared to those who did not go on to engage in NSSI (Brown et al., 2018). However, there is little ultimately known about the nature of the relations between stress experiences, threat-system development, and NSSI.

Existing research has rarely bridged a gap between stress exposures and threat-system-functioning work and stress exposures and NSSI work within the same study. There is emerging evidence that the alterations in threat-system functioning are sculpted over time through extreme environmental adversity. The changes are most pronounced in neural and physiological systems that support threat detection, response, and regulation. More specifically, indices of threat (such as interpersonal violence or abuse) are most robustly associated with reduced cortical thickness in the medial/lateral PFC and medial/lateral temporal cortex, reduced amygdala volume, and heightened amygdala activation to threat (see McLaughlin et al., 2019, for review; see also Busso, McLaughlin, Brueck, et al., 2017; Gold et al., 2016). Threat is further associated with changes in the HPA axis across development. Heightened HPA axis activation has been observed following trauma in childhood (Trickett et al., 2010). Conversely, adolescents with a history of childhood adversity showed blunted sympathetic and HPA axis reactivity (Busso, McLaughlin, Brueck, et al., 2017). Additionally, past research has implicated larger pituitary gland volume as a moderator between childhood adversity and blunted morning cortisol trajectories (Kaess et al., 2018) (See Serafini et al., this volume, for more on the relationship between early childhood trauma and NSSI). By contrast, indices of deprivation (e.g., neglect and poverty) are associated with "accelerated neurodevelopment," including earlier synaptic pruning and limited myelination (McLaughlin et al., 2017), resulting most often in reduced volume and altered function of frontoparietal brain regions (McLaughlin et al., 2019, for review). Some evidence has found that deprivation experiences are not related to alterations in physiological reactivity to stress (Busso, McLaughlin, Brueck, et al., 2017). Any number of these neurobiological and physiological alterations might act as mechanisms underlying the relation between early adversity and NSSI, which has been well established within the literature (see Fox et al., 2015, for review). In addition to the experience of abuse, Fox's review also found that parental psychopathology, dysfunction in the family, internalizing and externalizing symptoms, hopelessness, and exposure to peer self-harm were all risk factors for NSSI engagement. More recent work by Esposito et al. (2019) also found that bullying and peer rejection are risk factors for NSSI engagement. Although we might hypothesize that these relationships exist in part due to threat-system functioning, the biological mechanisms of these associations have yet to be delineated in research.

The impact of minority stress (e.g., the impacts of discrimination, stigma, and prejudice; Meyer, 2003) on threat-system development and risk for NSSI may also be highly relevant to consider. A robust literature review has noted that youth who identify as sexual and gender minorities (SGM) are more likely than their heterosexual and cisgender counterparts to engage in NSSI (Liu & Mustanski, 2012; Reisner et al., 2014; Sornberger et al., 2013). Further, research has identified minority stress as a potential mechanism driving this association (Fehling, 2019; Muehlenkamp et al., 2015; Staples et al., 2018). Minority stress as it relates to racial identity has been less thoroughly examined with respect to NSSI, though some studies have found null associations (e.g., Chesin et al., 2013; Walls et al., 2010). Despite the lack of explicit findings linking racial discrimination and NSSI, work has shown that individuals who experience higher rates of racial discrimination as adolescents exhibit blunted diurnal and waking cortisol levels, suggesting that prolonged exposure to such stressors is taxing to their threat-response systems (Adam et al., 2015). This is in concert with extant research that generally shows that, across a variety of marginalized identities, discrimination is associated with changes in the HPA axis (see Busse et al., 2017, for review; Zeiders et al., 2017), but that the direction and degree of change appears to be related to the timing and chronicity of discrimination experiences. One notable example is that lesbian, gay, and bisexual young adults raised in environments high in structural stigma, defined in this case as states with policies that excluded sexual minorities from social institutions such as marriage, show blunted cortisol responding to acute stressors as compared to those individuals from low-stigma environments (Hatzenbuehler & McLaughlin, 2014). While neurobiological research on minority stress is limited, alterations in brain structure and function in regions underlying emotion regulation, similar to that seen in chronic stress exposure, have been associated with racial discrimination (Berger & Sarnyai, 2015; Fani et al., 2021; Wright et al., 2020). More research is needed to understand the mechanisms that place marginalized individuals at disproportionate risk for engaging in NSSI. As we work toward cultivating a more nuanced understanding of how minority stress is biologically embedded to impact NSSI, centering intersectionality theory, which emphasizes the unique minority stress experiences (e.g., stigma and prejudice), structural oppression, and associated distress of those who hold multiple marginalized identities (e.g., being a nonbinary person of color), may be critical (Crenshaw, 1989).

Environmental inputs from parents have the potential to modulate stress responses among offspring during childhood in ways that might set the stage for the later onset of NSSI in adolescence. Indeed, Gunnar et al. (2015) found that parental support elevated HPA axis responses to acute stressors in children but not in adolescents. However, there is evidence that parental support might still matter for adolescents who are susceptible to NSSI engagement. Research investigating the impact of unique environmental stressors, such as the COVID-19 pandemic, suggests that parental support may be protective against NSSI behavior (Carosella et al., 2021). Further, emotional socialization from parents (e.g., modeling of how to respond to emotions), may play a role in promoting processes that might protect youth from NSSI engagement. A recent study found that female youth whose mothers were more likely to provide supportive responses to negative emotions reported a fewer number of lifetime NSSI episodes than their peers whose mothers reported less supportive responses (White et al., 2021). While the domain of parental influence on threat-system functioning and NSSI is still in its nascency, these studies provide some preliminary evidence to support future investigation into this field (see James & Gibb, this volume, for more on parenting and NSSI).

Implications of Sustained Engagement in NSSI

NSSI is often chronic and difficult to treat, which may be due in part to the reinforcement learning that is thought to take place as individuals engage in this behavior. When an individual is experiencing extreme, untenable levels of stress, they may engage in NSSI, which can lead to a sense of calm or relief and can sometimes elicit attention from others (Klonsky, 2011; Lloyd-Richardson et al., 2007). Additionally, engagement in NSSI can provide short-term relief by resulting in removal from aversive social situations and reduction in negative affect (Klonsky, 2011; Bentley et al., 2014; Nock & Prinstein, 2004). The association between NSSI and relief is fortified with repeated engagement. NSSI typically starts in adolescence before more adaptive strategies of emotion regulation have been learned (Plener et al., 2015). In many individuals, these behaviors become habitual (Graybiel, 2008). Though the progression of NSSI over the lifetime has not been fully delineated, a large portion of those who begin engaging in NSSI in adolescence continue to do so into adulthood (Selby et al., 2015).

Understanding the impact of repeated NSSI is particularly of interest to understand why those with a history of NSSI have an increased risk for suicide. Joiner's interpersonal theory of suicide (Joiner, 2005; Van Orden et al., 2010) emphasizes the importance of an acquired capability for suicide. The patterns of blunted cortisol reactivity to stressors that have been found in individuals with a history of NSSI have also been found in individuals with a history of suicide attempt, suggesting shared risk factors (O'Connor et al., 2017). When self-injury becomes routine, the threshold for going through with a suicide attempt may be lowered. Taken together, the heightened pain tolerance (Koenig et al., 2016), dampened activation to external acute stressors, and habitual self-harming (discussed below) associated with NSSI lend themselves to the acquired capacity for suicide.

Considering a Broader Systems Approach
While it is useful to focus on a single system using multiple levels of analysis to understand how disruptions in that system contribute to NSSI, it is also important to recognize that an array of disruptions from multiple systems likely interact to result in the onset and maintenance of this behavior. For example, the threat system may interact with the neural system, which underlies self-knowledge. Repeated threats to a young person during critical years in which teenagers typically solidify their identities and gain competence in social relationships with peers likely has a detrimental impact on the brain mechanisms underlying self-representation (Groschwitz et al., 2016). In turn, impairments in how perceptions of self and others are processed in the brain could serve to amplify threat responses or could play a role in shutting down this system in the response to chronic perceived threats.

As a second example, alterations in the threat system may interact with the neurobiological systems underlying cognitive control. In this case, the need to frequently operate in survival mode due to chronic perceived threat (primarily relying on more primitive limbic brain regions as opposed to more highly evolved cortical regions) may interfere over time with normative development (reduced practice) of the cognitive control system. This interaction may vary across individuals, potentially explaining the variance across studies with respect to the role of impulsivity and other cognitive control deficits in NSSI (Glenn & Klonsky, 2010; Janis & Nock, 2009).

Third, the threat system may interact with the neural systems underlying habit. The cognitive neuroscience definition of habitual behaviors stipulates that they (a) must be innate, (b) must be evoked by specific contexts and stimuli, (c) must be repetitive and must become fixed over time, and (d) must occur with very little effort once acquired. Liu (2017) argues that NSSI meets all these criteria and, in particular, highlights the self-reinforcing characteristics of NSSI, as well as the increased pain tolerance seen in those with a history of NSSI (Koenig et al., 2016) and heightened cortisol reactivity to painful stimuli (Koenig et al., 2017). This theory is further supported by evidence that the supplementary motor area (SMA), a region traditionally activated by engagement in habitual behaviors, is more strongly functionally connected to the amygdala in adolescents with a history of NSSI than in those without a history of engagement, even when controlling for depression severity (Westlund Schreiner et al., 2017). The SMA is an area involved not only in planning complex movements but also in switching automatic responses to more controlled ones (Cunnington et al., 2005). These findings could be potentially explained by the habit-like characteristics of NSSI; these behaviors often happen repeatedly and can become automatic in response to negative emotions. The conceptualization of NSSI being a habitual behavior lends itself to important clinical implications. Preliminary work has raised the possibility that the amygdala-SMA network might be altered with treatment. After a 4-week open-label trial of n-acetylcysteine, adolescents with NSSI showed decreased RSFC between amygdala and SMA correlated with reduced frequency of NSSI episodes (Cullen et al., 2020). Following the insights of this research, new modes of treatment that are used to treat other habit-based psychopathologies, such as obsessive-compulsive disorder, may represent promising avenues for cessation of NSSI behaviors.

Abnormalities across multiple systems that are directly implicated in threat processing and are downstream impacts from prolonged exposure to threat likely have important implications for the instantiation and maintenance of NSSI. This suggests that multiple methods of analysis of NSSI may in some cases reveal divergent findings, highlighting the complexity of the threat system and the need for a multimodal approach. The role of development and chronicity of exposure and engagement in shaping these neurobiological systems underscores the need for the longitudinal analysis of these processes.

NSSI in the Context of a Broader Array of Psychopathology

While NSSI can be expressed in those without any clinical diagnoses and those with any number of disorders, the literature on other problems that are characterized by negative affect and emotional instability may be useful to examine as they may be relevant to NSSI. In particular, the more developed literature on depression, BPD, and other disorders that frequently co-occur with NSSI could give insight into facets of NSSI. While the literature to date has focused on populations in which the primary comorbidities with NSSI are disorders with alterations in mood and emotion regulation, there are many other populations in which behaviors with shared form (e.g., self-hitting) and function (e.g., coping) can occur including obsessive-compulsive disorder, eating disorders, and autism spectrum disorder (ASD; Cipriano et al., 2017; Maddox et al., 2017). For example, individuals with ASD and other neurodevelopmental disorders frequently demonstrate repetitive self-injurious behaviors, though the function and underlying pathophysiology may differ compared to those with mood and related disorders. Research has been conducted to investigate neural correlates of NSSI in those with ASD and found no differences in total gray matter, white matter, or cerebrospinal fluid volumes; thickness of the cingulate; or surface area of the prefrontal cortex, cingulate gyrus, or insulas of those engaging in NSSI (Duerden et al., 2012). However, this study demonstrated that within the ASD group, self-injurious behaviors (frequency of self-injury as reported by the parents) were negatively correlated with the thickness of somatosensory areas, the volume of thalamic nuclei, and the related white matter pathways (see Bradley et al., this volume, for more information on NSSI in individuals with developmental disabilities). Understanding the shared and distinct motivations and mechanisms implicated in NSSI engagement in those with other forms of psychopathology may give insight into underlying neural processes.

Clinical Implications of Alterations in the Threat System in NSSI

New insights into how threat-system processes are aberrant in those with NSSI give insight into why current treatments are effective and suggest avenues for conceptualizing, developing, and personalizing novel interventions. At this stage, the field is still conducting foundational research to gain knowledge about how neurodevelopmental trajectories go awry and underlie the onset and maintenance of NSSI in adolescence. More work is needed because of the heightened vulnerability of individuals with NSSI to enduring life-threatening physical harm due to the NSSI itself and their increased risk for suicide. Nevertheless, there are some promising avenues that may address threat-system functioning that are worthy of consideration.

The understanding of threat-system functioning in individuals who engage in NSSI may inform the employment and adaptation of established intervention programs. In a recent review of the available psychotherapy literature (Glenn et al., 2019), dialectical behavior therapy (DBT; Linehan et al., 2006) was classified as the only well-established therapy for adolescent NSSI. For example, in one study adolescents with recent NSSI were randomized to DBT or individual and group supportive therapy (IGST) for a 6-month course of therapy (McCauley et al., 2018). Results showed decreased self-harm and suicide attempts in the DBT versus the IGST group. Importantly, at the 12-month follow-up, none of the adolescents in the DBT group reported engaging in NSSI. DBT modules that might specifically target negative affect through techniques that include mindfulness, emotion regulation, and distress tolerance. Though not directly targeting NSSI, these techniques may work to decrease engagement through improvements in emotion regulation skills. This is an important advance. Only preliminary evidence is available for the efficacy of psychopharmacological or naturopathic interventions (e.g., Cullen et al., 2018), and as of now, no drug interventions have been identified that specifically address NSSI in adolescence (Plener et al., 2018), leaving much room for advances in this area.

A greater understanding of the neural markers signifying risk for NSSI will reveal treatment targets to optimize functioning. Validated approaches to personalize treatment are needed given the heterogeneity among those engaging in NSSI. In order to optimize treatment recommendations, more work will be needed to determine what works best for whom (Myin-Germeys et al., 2018). These recommendations will need to be tailored to the individual's neurobiology, possibly taking into account the function of NSSI and the individual's stage of illness or development. For example, Favazza (2012) suggested a framework for tailoring NSSI treatment. They suggested that compulsive NSSI might benefit from n-acetylcysteine (NAC), an antioxidant that is presently sold over the counter for a variety of purposes; stereotypical NSSI in the context of ASD might benefit from analgesics, antidepressants, or antipsychotics; compulsive NSSI (e.g., trichotillomania) might benefit from NAC; and impulsive NSSI (which may be commonly associated with depressive and borderline symptoms) might respond to psychotherapy, especially DBT, as well as other treatments with antipsychotic and mood stabilizers. While this framework has yet to be validated, it provides a starting place to consider how there may be individual variation in those who engage in NSSI, and treatments may be best served if they address this variation. Further, digital technologies are now beginning to be explored as potential strategies for tailoring treatment and monitoring treatment response (Arshad et al., 2020).

Finally, it is likely that advancing our understanding of biological correlates of threat-system functioning within the context of NSSI will provide avenues of development of new treatments. For example, in consideration of the HPA axis results discussed here, an intervention for a child or adolescent who is either in the very early stages or simply at risk for NSSI may be geared to providing tools to enhance strategies for coping with perceived threat with the goal of accelerating recovery and gaining confidence in one's ability to regulate negative affect. On the other hand, for an adolescent with severe and chronic NSSI, for whom the HPA axis has already undergone significant adaptation such that a robust cortisol response to threat is muted, interventions may be geared to enhancing flexibility within this system. Current work in other populations shows promising potential avenues by which such flexibility can be increased. For example, acceptance and commitment therapy has been shown to increase psychological flexibility among adults (Thompson et al., 2021). Additionally, novel pharmacological interventions that act on PFC-nucleus accumbens connections show promise in increasing cognitive flexibility in a preclinical model of anorexia nervosa (Milton et al., 2021). Finally, ketamine has been shown to decrease depressive symptoms and increase entropy, possibly a form of neural flexibility, in the nucleus accumbens (Roy et al., 2021). This is just a glimpse drawn from the insights discussed in this chapter, of what might be on the horizon of possibilities to help those who are suffering from NSSI.

Conclusions

Unfortunately, cases like Jamie's are relatively common. Jamie's NSSI began in response to distress caused by chronic and acute stressors that occurred during the sensitive period of adolescence. There are some contradictions. Dysregulation in Jamie's neurobiological stress system can be seen in her history of depression and anxiety symptoms. Additionally, Jamie's reports of feeling numb in the face of stressors and her engagement in NSSI also belie miscalibration in her threat-response processing system. The automatic, habit-like engagement in self-hitting and biting demonstrate the potential role that the SMA may play in maintaining NSSI behaviors. Finally, like many cases, Jamie's experience with therapeutic and pharmacological interventions, where depressive and anxiety symptoms improved but not NSSI, highlight the need for further work in this area.

NSSI is a maladaptive method of coping with stress or other forms of negative affect that frequently arises in adolescents. The threat system involves the HPA axis, which mounts an endocrine response to threat and coordinates multiple brain regions that, in turn, process the information and produce potential response behaviors. In the context of chronic stress, adolescents with NSSI may demonstrate heightened cumulative activation of the HPA axis over longer periods of time but dampened activation in response to specific stressors. This pattern likely indicates that those with NSSI perceive more stressors in their environments but that their HPA axis reacts less strongly to each individual instance. This blunted reaction may be a result of allostatic overload and negative feedback mechanisms that are set in motion in response to exposure to chronic stressors. Research to date investigating the neural structure, function, and connectivity of the frontolimbic brain systems underlying the threat response have revealed alterations in individuals who engage in NSSI, albeit with some mixed findings. Findings on the complex interplay between different elements of the threat system indicate some discordance across systems. Moving forward, advanced approaches (e.g., longitudinal designs and person-centered techniques) are needed to disentangle the complexities of how systems interact over the course of risk, onset, and maintenance of NSSI and to advance our understanding of the heterogeneity of neurobiological patterns across individuals with NSSI. The field is increasingly cognizant of how early experiences (including adversity, parental buffering, and emotional development influenced by important relationships) set the stage for an increased risk for psychopathology including the onset of NSSI. Advances are needed to better understand how neurobiological changes that evolve alongside the progression of NSSI as a habitual behavior may reflect adaptive mechanisms, which may in turn perpetuate risk. Continued advancements on these frontiers will be required for conceptualization, testing, and implementation of novel interventions that could be tailored to each individual's particular pattern of behavior and neurobiology.

References

Adam, E. K., Heissel, J. A., Zeiders, K. H., Richeson, J. A., Ross, E. C., Ehrlich, K. B., Levy, D. J., Kemeny, M., Brodish, A. B., Malanchuk, O., Peck, S. C, Fuller-Rowell, T. E., & Eccles, J. S. (2015). Developmental histories of perceived racial discrimination and diurnal cortisol profiles in adulthood: A 20-year prospective study. *Psychoneuroendocrinology*, *62*, 279–291.

Ando, A., Reichl, C., Scheu, F., Bykova, A., Parzer, P., Resch, F., Brunner, R., & Kaess, M. (2018). Regional grey matter volume reduction in adolescents engaging in non-suicidal self-injury. *Psychiatry Research: Neuroimaging*, *280*, 48–55.

Arshad, U., Gauntlett, J., Husain, N., Chaudhry, N., & Taylor, P. J. (2020). A systematic review of the evidence supporting mobile- and internet-based psychological interventions for self-harm. *Suicide and Life-Threatening Behavior*, *50*(1), 151–179.

Auerbach, R. P., Pagliaccio, D., Allison, G. O., Alqueza, K. L., & Alonso, M. F. (2021). Neural correlates associated with suicide and nonsuicidal self-injury in youth. *Biological Psychiatry*, *89*(2), 119–133.

Banks, S. J., Eddy, K. T., Angstadt, M., Nathan, P. J., & Phan, K. L. (2007). Amygdala–frontal connectivity during emotion regulation. *Social Cognitive and Affective Neuroscience, 2*(4), 303–312.

Başgöze, Z., Mirza, S. A., Silamongkol, T., Hill, D., Falke, C., Thai, M., Westlund Schreiner, M., Parenteau, A. M., Roediger, D. J., Hendrickson, T. J., Mueller, B. A., Fiecas, M. B., Klimes-Dougan, B., & Cullen, K. R. (2021). Multimodal assessment of sustained threat in adolescents with nonsuicidal self-injury. *Development and Psychopathology, 33*(5), 1774–1792.

Başgöze, Z., Wiglesworth, A., Carosella, K. A., Klimes-Dougan, B., & Cullen, K. R. (2021). Depression, non-suicidal self-injury, and suicidality in adolescents: Common and distinct precursors, correlates, and outcomes. *Journal of Psychiatry and Brain Science, 6*(5).

Beauchaine, T. P., Crowell, S. E., & Hsiao, R. C. (2015). Post-dexamethasone cortisol, self-inflicted injury, and suicidal ideation among depressed adolescent girls. *Journal of Abnormal Child Psychology, 43*(4), 619–632.

Beauchaine, T. P., Sauder, C. L., Derbidge, C. M., & Uyeji, L. L. (2019). Self-injuring adolescent girls exhibit insular cortex volumetric abnormalities that are similar to those seen in adults with borderline personality disorder. *Development and Psychopathology, 31*(4), 1203–1212.

Bendezú, J. J., Thai, M., Wiglesworth, A., Cullen, K. R., & Klimes-Dougan, B. (2022). Adolescent stress experience–expression–physiology correspondence: Links to depression, self-injurious thoughts and behaviors, and frontolimbic neural circuity. *Journal of Affective Disorders, 300*, 269–279.

Bentley, K. H., Nock, M. K., & Barlow, D. H. (2014). The four-function model of nonsuicidal self-injury: Key directions for future research. *Clinical Psychological Science, 2*(5), 638–656.

Berger, M., & Sarnyai, Z. (2015). "More than skin deep": Stress neurobiology and mental health consequences of racial discrimination. *Stress, 18*(1), 1–10.

Brambilla, P., Soloff, P. H., Sala, M., Nicoletti, M. A., Keshavan, M. S., & Soares, J. C. (2004). Anatomical MRI study of borderline personality disorder patients. *Psychiatry Research: Neuroimaging, 131*(2), 125–133.

Brañas, M. J., Croci, M. S., Ravagnani Salto, A. B., Doretto, V. F., Martinho, E., Macedo, M., Miguel., E. C., Roever, L., & Pan, P. M. (2021). Neuroimaging studies of nonsuicidal self-injury in youth: A systematic review. *Life, 11*(8), 729.

Brown, R. C., Heines, S., Witt, A., Braehler, E., Fegert, J. M., Harsch, D., & Plener, P. L. (2018). The impact of child maltreatment on non-suicidal self-injury: Data from a representative sample of the general population. *BMC Psychiatry, 18*(1), 1–8.

Brown, R. C., & Plener, P. L. (2017). Non-suicidal self-injury in adolescence. *Current Psychiatry Reports, 19*(3), 20.

Busse, D., Yim, I. S., Campos, B., & Marshburn, C. K. (2017). Discrimination and the HPA axis: Current evidence and future directions. *Journal of Behavioral Medicine, 40*(4), 539–552.

Busso, D. S., McLaughlin, K. A., Brueck, S., Peverill, M., Gold, A. L., & Sheridan, M. A. (2017). Child abuse, neural structure, and adolescent psychopathology: A longitudinal study. *Journal of the American Academy of Child & Adolescent Psychiatry, 56*(4), 321–328.

Busso, D. S., McLaughlin, K. A., & Sheridan, M. A. (2017). Dimensions of adversity, physiological reactivity, and externalizing psychopathology in adolescence: Deprivation and threat. *Psychosomatic medicine, 79*(2), 162.

Carosella, K. A., Wiglesworth, A., Silamongkol, T., Tavares, N., Falke, C. A., Fiecas, M. B., Cullen, K. R., & Klimes-Dougan, B. (2021). Non-suicidal self-injury in the context of COVID-19: The importance of psychosocial factors for female adolescents. *Journal of Affective Disorders Reports, 4*, Article 100137.

Casey, B. J., Jones, R. M., Levita, L., Libby, V., Pattwell, S. S., Ruberry, E. J., Soliman, F., & Somerville, L. H. (2010). The storm and stress of adolescence: Insights from human imaging and mouse genetics. *Developmental Psychobiology: The Journal of the International Society for Developmental Psychobiology, 52*(3), 225–235.

Chesin, M. S., Moster, A. N., & Jeglic, E. L. (2013). Non-suicidal self-injury among ethnically and racially diverse emerging adults: Do factors unique to the minority experience matter? *Current Psychology, 32*(4), 318–328.

Chrousos, G. P., Kino, T., & Charmandari, E. (2009). Evaluation of the hypothalamic-pituitary-adrenal axis function in childhood and adolescence. *Neuroimmunomodulation, 16*(5), 272–283.

Cipriano, A., Cella, S., & Cotrufo, P. (2017). Nonsuicidal self-injury: A systematic review. *Frontiers in Psychology, 8*, Article 1946.

Clow, A., Hucklebridge, F., Stalder, T., Evans, P., & Thorn, L. (2010). The cortisol awakening response: More than a measure of HPA axis function. *Neuroscience & Biobehavioral Reviews, 35*(1), 97–103.

Crenshaw, K. (1989). Demarginalizing the intersection of race and sex: A Black feminist critique of antidiscrimination doctrine, feminist theory, and antiracist politics [1989]. In K. T. Bartlett & R. Kennedy (Eds.), *Feminist legal theory* (pp. 57–80). Routledge.

Cullen, K. R., Klimes-Dougan, B., Westlund Schreiner, M., Carstedt, P., Marka, N., Nelson, K., Miller, M. J., Reigstad, K., Westervelt, A., Gunlicks-Stoessel, M., & Eberly, L. E. (2018). N-acetylcysteine for non-suicidal self-injurious behavior in adolescents: An open-label pilot study. *Journal of Child and Adolescent Psychopharmacology, 28*(2), 136–144.

Cullen, K. R., Schreiner, M. W., Klimes-Dougan, B., Eberly, L. E., LaRiviere, L. L., Lim, K. O., Camchong, J., & Mueller, B. A. (2020). Neural correlates of clinical improvement in response to N-acetylcysteine in adolescents with non-suicidal self-injury. *Progress in Neuro-Psychopharmacology and Biological Psychiatry, 99*, Article 109778.

Cunningham, M. G., Bhattacharyya, S., & Benes, F. M. (2002). Amygdalo-cortical sprouting continues into early adulthood: Implications for the development of normal and abnormal function during adolescence. *Journal of Comparative Neurology, 453*(2), 116–130.

Cunnington, R., Windischberger, C., & Moser, E. (2005). Premovement activity of the pre-supplementary motor area and the readiness for action: Studies of time-resolved event-related functional MRI. *Human Movement Science, 24*(5–6), 644–656.

Demers, L. A., Schreiner, M. W., Hunt, R. H., Mueller, B. A., Klimes-Dougan, B., Thomas, K. M., & Cullen, K. R. (2019). Alexithymia is associated with neural reactivity to masked emotional faces in adolescents who self-harm. *Journal of Affective Disorders, 249*, 253–261.

Duerden, E. G., Oatley, H. K., Mak-Fan, K. M., McGrath, P. A., Taylor, M. J., Szatmari, P., & Roberts, S. W. (2012). Risk factors associated with self-injurious behaviors in children and adolescents with autism spectrum disorders. *Journal of Autism and Developmental Disorders, 42*(11), 2460–2470.

Esposito, C., Bacchini, D., & Affuso, G. (2019). Adolescent non-suicidal self-injury and its relationships with school bullying and peer rejection. *Psychiatry Research, 274*, 1–6.

Fani, N., Carter, S. E., Harnett, N. G., Ressler, K. J., & Bradley, B. (2021). Association of racial discrimination with neural response to threat in Black women in the US exposed to trauma. *JAMA Psychiatry, 78*(9), 1005–1012.

Favazza, A. R. (2012). Nonsuicidal self-injury: How categorization guides treatment. *Current Psychiatry, 11*(3), 21–25.

Fehling, K. B. (2019). *An ecological momentary assessment study of sexual minority stress and nonsuicidal self-injury in sexual minority adults* [Unpublished doctoral dissertation]. Rutgers, The State University of New Jersey, School of Graduate Studies.

Fox, K. R., Franklin, J. C., Ribeiro, J. D., Kleiman, E. M., Bentley, K. H., & Nock, M. K. (2015). Meta-analysis of risk factors for nonsuicidal self-injury. *Clinical Psychology Review, 42*, 156–167.

Fries, E., Dettenborn, L., & Kirschbaum, C. (2009). The cortisol awakening response (CAR): Facts and future directions. *International Journal of Psychophysiology, 72*(1), 67–73.

Gee, D. G., Humphreys, K. L., Flannery, J., Goff, B., Telzer, E. H., Shapiro, M., Hare, T. A., Bookheimer, S. Y., & Tottenham, N. (2013). A developmental shift from positive to negative connectivity in human amygdala–prefrontal circuitry. *Journal of Neuroscience, 33*(10), 4584–4593.

Giedd, J. N., Blumenthal, J., Jeffries, N.O., Castellanos, F.X., Liu, H., Zijdenbos, A., Paus, T., Evans, A. C., & Rapoport, J. L. (1999). Brain development during childhood and adolescence: A longitudinal MRI study. *Nature Neuroscience, 2*(10), 861–863. https://doi.org/10.1038/13158

Giedd, J. N., Lalonde, F. M., Celano, M. J., White, S. L., Wallace, G. L., Lee, N. R., & Lenroot, R. K. (2009). Anatomical brain magnetic resonance imaging of typically developing children and adolescents. *Journal of the American Academy of Child and Adolescent Psychiatry, 48*(5), 465. https://doi.org/10.1097/CHI.0b013e31819f2715

Glenn, C. R., Esposito, E. C., Porter, A. C., & Robinson, D. J. (2019). Evidence base update of psychosocial treatments for self-injurious thoughts and behaviors in youth. *Journal of Clinical Child & Adolescent Psychology, 48*(3), 357–392.

Glenn, C. R., & Klonsky, E. D. (2010). A multimethod analysis of impulsivity in nonsuicidal self-injury. *Personality Disorders: Theory, Research, and Treatment, 1*(1), 67.

Gold, A. L., Sheridan, M. A., Peverill, M., Busso, D. S., Lambert, H. K., Alves, S., Pine, D. S., & McLaughlin, K. A. (2016). Childhood abuse and reduced cortical thickness in brain regions involved in emotional processing. *Journal of Child Psychology and Psychiatry, 57*(10), 1154–1164.

Grant, J. E., Correia, S., Brennan-Krohn, T., Malloy, P. F., Laidlaw, D. H., & Schulz, S. C. (2007). Frontal white matter integrity in borderline personality disorder with self-injurious behavior. *The Journal of Neuropsychiatry and Clinical Neurosciences, 19*(4), 383–390.

Graybiel, A. M. (2008). Habits, rituals, and the evaluative brain. *Annual Review of Neuroscience, 31*, 359–387.

Groschwitz, R. C., Plener, P. L., Groen, G., Bonenberger, M., & Abler, B. (2016). Differential neural processing of social exclusion in adolescents with non-suicidal self-injury: An fMRI study. *Psychiatry Research: Neuroimaging, 255*, 43–49.

Guerry, J. D., & Prinstein, M. J. (2009). Longitudinal prediction of adolescent nonsuicidal self-injury: Examination of a cognitive vulnerability-stress model. *Journal of Clinical Child & Adolescent Psychology, 39*(1), 77–89.

Guidi, J., Lucente, M., Sonino, N., & Fava, G. A. (2021). Allostatic load and its impact on health: A systematic review. *Psychotherapy and Psychosomatics, 90*(1), 11–27.

Gunnar, M. R., Hostinar, C. E., Sanchez, M. M., Tottenham, N., & Sullivan, R. M. (2015). Parental buffering of fear and stress neurobiology: Reviewing parallels across rodent, monkey, and human models. *Social Neuroscience, 10*(5), 474–478.

Gunnar, M. R., Wewerka, S., Frenn, K., Long, J. D., & Griggs, C. (2009). Developmental changes in hypothalamus–pituitary–adrenal activity over the transition to adolescence: Normative changes and associations with puberty. *Development and Psychopathology, 21*(1), 69–85.

Hariri, A. R., Tessitore, A., Mattay, V. S., Fera, F., & Weinberger, D. R. (2002). The amygdala response to emotional stimuli: A comparison of faces and scenes. *NeuroImage, 17*, 317–323. doi:10.1006/nimg.2002.1179

Hasking, P., Whitlock, J., Voon, D., & Rose, A. (2017). A cognitive-emotional model of NSSI: Using emotion regulation and cognitive processes to explain why people self-injure. *Cognition and Emotion, 31*(8), 1543–1556.

Hatzenbuehler, M. L., & McLaughlin, K. A. (2014). Structural stigma and hypothalamic–pituitary–adrenocortical axis reactivity in lesbian, gay, and bisexual young adults. *Annals of Behavioral Medicine, 47*(1), 39–47.

Herman, J. P., McKlveen, J. M., Solomon, M. B., Carvalho-Netto, E., & Myers, B. (2012). Neural regulation of the stress response: Glucocorticoid feedback mechanisms. *Brazilian Journal of Medical and Biological Research, 45*, 292–298.

Hooley, J. M., Dahlgren, M. K., Best, S. G., Gonenc, A., & Gruber, S. A. (2020). Decreased amygdalar activation to NSSI-stimuli in people who engage in NSSI: A neuroimaging pilot study. *Frontiers in Psychiatry, 11*, Article 238.

Horwitz, A. G., Czyz, E. K., & King, C. A. (2015). Predicting future suicide attempts among adolescent and emerging adult psychiatric emergency patients. *Journal of Clinical Child & Adolescent Psychology, 44*(5), 751–761.

Huang, X., Rootes-Murdy, K., Bastidas, D. M., Nee, D. E., & Franklin, J. C. (2020). Brain differences associated with self-injurious thoughts and behaviors: A meta-analysis of neuroimaging studies. *Scientific Reports, 10*(1), 1–13.

Insel, T., Cuthbert, B., Garvey, M., Heinssen, R., Pine, D. S., Quinn, K., Sanislow, C., & Wang, P. (2010). Research domain criteria (RDoC): Toward a new classification framework for research on mental disorders. *The American Journal of Psychiatry, 167*(7), 748–751. https://doi.org/10.1176/appi.ajp.2010.09091379

Janis, I. B., & Nock, M. K. (2009). Are self-injurers impulsive?: Results from two behavioral laboratory studies. *Psychiatry Research, 169*(3), 261–267.

Joiner, T. E. (2005). *Why people die by suicide*. Harvard University Press.

Kaess, M., Hille, M., Parzer, P., Maser-Gluth, C., Resch, F., & Brunner, R., 2012. Alterations in the neuroendocrinological stress response to acute psychosocial stress in adolescents engaging in nonsuicidal self-injury. *Psychoneuroendocrinology, 37*, 157–161. https://doi.org/10.1016/j.psyneuen.2011.05.009

Kaess, M., Whittle, S., O'Brien-Simpson, L., Allen, N. B., & Simmons, J. B., 2018. Childhood maltreatment, pituitary volume and adolescent hypothalamic-pituitary-adrenal axis–Evidence for a maltreatment-related attenuation. *Psychoneuroendocrinology, 98*, 39–45. https://doi.org/10.1016/j.psyneuen.2018.08.004

Kirschbaum, C., Pirke, K. M., & Hellhammer, D. H. (1993). The "Trier Social Stress Test"–A tool for investigating psychobiological stress responses in a laboratory setting. *Neuropsychobiology, 28*(1–2), 76–81.

Klimes-Dougan, B., Begnel, E., Almy, B., Thai, M., Schreiner, M. W., & Cullen, K. R. (2019). Hypothalamic-pituitary-adrenal axis dysregulation in depressed adolescents with non-suicidal self-injury. *Psychoneuroendocrinology, 102*, 216–224. https://doi.org/10.1016/j.psyneuen.2018.11.004

Klimes-Dougan, B., Eberly, L. E., Schreiner, M. W., Kurkiewicz, P., Houri, A., Schlesinger, A., Thomas, K. M., Mueller, B. A., Lim, K. O., & Cullen, K. R. (2014). Multilevel assessment of the neurobiological threat system in depressed adolescents: Interplay between the limbic system and hypothalamic–pituitary–adrenal axis. *Development and Psychopathology, 26*(4, Pt. 2), 1321–1335.

Klimes-Dougan, Hastings, P. D., Granger, D. A., Usher, B. A., & Zahn–Waxler, C. (2001). Adrenocortical activity in at-risk and normally developing adolescents: Individual differences in salivary cortisol basal levels, diurnal variation, and responses to social challenges. *Development and Psychopathology, 13*(3), 695–719.

Klonsky, E. D. (2011). Non-suicidal self-injury in United States adults: Prevalence, sociodemographics, topography and functions. *Psychological Medicine, 41*(9), 1981–1986.

Koenig, J., Rinnewitz, L., Warth, M., Hillecke, T. K., Brunner, R., Resch, F., & Kaess, M. (2017). Psychobiological response to pain in female adolescents with nonsuicidal self-injury. *Journal of Psychiatry and Neuroscience, 42*(3), 189–199. https://doi.org/10.1503/jpn.160074

Koenig, J., Thayer, J. F., & Kaess, M. (2016). A meta-analysis on pain sensitivity in self-injury. *Psychological Medicine, 46*(8), 1597–1612.

Krueger, R. F. (1999). The structure of common mental disorders. *Archives of General Psychiatry, 56*(10), 921–926.

LeDoux, J. E. (2000). Emotion circuits in the brain. *Annual Review of Neuroscience, 23*(1), 155–184. https://doi.org/10.1146/annurev.neuro.23.1.155

Lindquist, K. A., Satpute, A. B., Wager, T. D., Weber, J., & Barrett, L. F. (2016). The brain basis of positive and negative affect: Evidence from a meta-analysis of the human neuroimaging literature. *Cerebral Cortex, 26*(5), 1910–1922. https://doi.org/10.1093/cercor/bhv001

Linehan, M. M., Comtois, K. A., Murray, A. M., Brown, M. Z., Gallop, R. J., Heard, H. L., Korslund, K. E., Tutek, D. A., Reynolds, S. K., & Lindenboim, N. (2006). Two-year randomized controlled trial and follow-up of dialectical behavior therapy vs therapy by experts for suicidal behaviors and borderline personality disorder. *Archives of General Psychiatry, 63*(7), 757–766.

Liu, R. T. (2017). Characterizing the course of non-suicidal self-injury: A cognitive neuroscience perspective. *Neuroscience & Biobehavioral Reviews, 80*, 159–165.

Liu, R. T., & Mustanski, B. (2012). Suicidal ideation and self-harm in lesbian, gay, bisexual, and transgender youth. *American Journal of Preventive Medicine, 42*(3), 221–228.

Liu, R. T., Scopelliti, K. M., Pittman, S. K., & Zamora, A. S., 2018. Childhood maltreatment and non-suicidal self-injury: A systematic review and meta-analysis. *Lancet Psychiatry, 5*, 51–64. https://doi.org/10.1016/s2215-0366(17)30469-8

Lloyd-Richardson, E. E., Perrine, N., Dierker, L., & Kelley, M. L. (2007). Characteristics and functions of non-suicidal self-injury in a community sample of adolescents. *Psychological Medicine, 37*(8), 1183–1192.

Lupien, S. J., Lupien, S. J., McEwen, B. S., Gunnar, M. R., & Heim, C. (2009). Effects of stress throughout the lifespan on the brain, behaviour and cognition. *Nature Reviews Neuroscience, 10*(6), 434–445. https://doi.org/10.1038/nrn2639

Lupien, S. J., Ouellet-Morin, I., Hupbach, A., Tu, M. T., Buss, C., Walker, D., Pruessner, J., McEwen, B. S. (2006). Beyond the stress concept: Allostatic load—A developmental biological and cognitive perspective. In D. Cicchetti & D. J. Cohen (Eds.), *Developmental psychopathology: Developmental neuroscience* (pp. 578–628). John Wiley & Sons.

Maddox, B. B., Trubanova, A., & White, S. W. (2017). Untended wounds: Non-suicidal self-injury in adults with autism spectrum disorder. *Autism, 21*(4), 412–422.

Mars, B., Heron, J., Klonsky E. D., Moran, P., O'Connor, R. C., Tilling, K., Wilkinson, P., Gunnell, D. (2019). Predictors of future suicide attempt among adolescents with suicidal thoughts or non-suicidal self-harm: A population-based birth cohort study. *Lancet Psychiatry, 6*, 327–337. https://doi.org/10.1016/s2215-0366(19)30030-6

Mayo, L. M., Perini, I., Gustafsson, P. A., Hamilton, J. P., Kämpe, R., Heilig, M., & Zetterqvist, M. (2021). Psychophysiological and neural support for enhanced emotional reactivity in female adolescents with non-suicidal self-injury. *Biological psychiatry: Cognitive Neuroscience and Neuroimaging, 6*(7), 682–691.

McCarty, R. (2016). The fight-or-flight response: A cornerstone of stress research. In George Fink (Ed.), *Stress: Concepts, cognition, emotion, and behavior* (Handbook of stress series) (Vol. 1, pp. 33–37). Academic Press.

McCauley, E., Berk, M. S., Asarnow, J. R., Adrian, M., Cohen, J., Korslund, K., Avina, C., Hughes, J., Harned, M., Gallop, R., & Linehan, M. M. (2018). Efficacy of dialectical behavior therapy for adolescents at high risk for suicide: A randomized clinical trial. *JAMA Psychiatry, 75*(8), 777–785.

McEwen, B. S. (2007). Physiology and neurobiology of stress and adaptation: Central role of the brain. *Physiological Reviews, 87*(3), 873–904.

McEwen, B. S., & Stellar, E. (1993). Stress and the individual: Mechanisms leading to disease. *Archives of Internal Medicine, 153*(18), 2093–2101.

McLaughlin, K. A., Sheridan, M. A., & Nelson, C. A. (2017). Neglect as a violation of species-expectant experience: Neurodevelopmental consequences. *Biological Psychiatry, 82*(7), 462–471.

McLaughlin, K. A., Sheridan, M. A., Tibu, F., Fox, N. A., Zeanah, C. H., & Nelson, C. A. (2015). Causal effects of the early caregiving environment on development of stress response systems in children. *Proceedings of the National Academy of Sciences, 112*(18), 5637–5642.

McLaughlin, K. A., Weissman, D., & Bitrán, D. (2019). Childhood adversity and neural development: A systematic review. *Annual Review of Developmental Psychology, 1*, 277–312.

Meaney, M. J., & Szyf, M. (2005). Environmental programming of stress responses through DNA methylation: Life at the interface between a dynamic environment and a fixed genome. *Dialogues in Clinical Neuroscience, 7*(2), 103.

Meyer, I. H. (2003). Prejudice, social stress, and mental health in lesbian, gay, and bisexual populations: Conceptual issues and research evidence. *Psychological Bulletin, 129*(5), 674.

Miller, A. B., Linthicum, K. P., Helms, S. W., Giletta, M., Rudolph, K. D., Hastings, P. D., Nock, M. K., & Prinstein, M. J. (2018). Reciprocal associations between adolescent girls' chronic interpersonal stress and nonsuicidal self-injury: A multi-wave prospective investigation. *Journal of Adolescent Health, 63*(6), 694–700.

Milton, L. K., Mirabella, P. N., Greaves, E., Spanswick, D. C., van den Buuse, M., Oldfield, B. J., & Foldi, C. J. (2021). Suppression of corticostriatal circuit activity improves cognitive flexibility and prevents body weight loss in activity-based anorexia in rats. *Biological Psychiatry, 90*(12), 819–828.

Muehlenkamp, J. J., Hilt, L. M., Ehlinger, P. P., & McMillan, T. (2015). Nonsuicidal self-injury in sexual minority college students: A test of theoretical integration. *Child and Adolescent Psychiatry and Mental Health, 9*(1), 1–8.

Myin-Germeys, I., Kasanova, Z., Vaessen, T., Vachon, H., Kirtley, O., Viechtbauer, W., & Reininghaus, U. (2018). Experience sampling methodology in mental health research: New insights and technical developments. *World Psychiatry, 17*(2), 123–132.

Nock, M. K., & Prinstein, M. J. (2004). A functional approach to the assessment of self-mutilative behavior. *Journal of Consulting and Clinical Psychology, 72*(5), 885.

Nunes, P. M., Wenzel, A., Borges, K. T., Porto, C. R., Caminha, R. M., & De Oliveira, I. R. (2009). Volumes of the hippocampus and amygdala in patients with borderline personality disorder: A meta-analysis. *Journal of Personality Disorders, 23*(4), 333–345.

O'Connor, D. B., Green, J. A., Ferguson, E., O'Carroll, R. E., & O'Connor, R. C. (2017). Cortisol reactivity and suicidal behavior: Investigating the role of hypothalamic-pituitary-adrenal axis responses to stress in suicide attempters and ideators. *Psychoneuroendocrinology, 75*, 183–191.

Paus, T., Keshavan, M., & Giedd, J. N. (2008). Why do many psychiatric disorders emerge during adolescence? *Nature Reviews Neuroscience, 9*(12), 947–957. https://doi.org/10.1038/nrn2513

Perlman, S. B., & Pelphrey, K. A. (2011). Developing connections for affective regulation: Age-related changes in emotional brain connectivity. *Journal of Experimental Child Psychology, 108*(3), 607–620.

Pierpaoli, C., & Basser, P. J. (1996). Toward a quantitative assessment of diffusion anisotropy. *Magnetic Resonance in Medicine, 36*(6), 893–906.

Plener, P. L., Bubalo, N., Fladung, A. K., Ludolph, A. G., & Lulé, D. (2012). Prone to excitement: Adolescent females with non-suicidal self-injury (NSSI) show altered cortical pattern to emotional and NSS-related material. *Psychiatry Research: Neuroimaging, 203*(2–3), 146–152. https://doi.org/10.1016/j.pscychresns.2011.12.012

Plener, P. L., Kaess, M., Schmahl, C., Pollak, S., Fegert, J. M., & Brown, R. C. (2018). Nonsuicidal self-injury in adolescents. *Deutsches Ärzteblatt International, 115*(3), 23.

Plener, P. L., Schumacher, T. S., Munz, L. M., & Groschwitz, R. C. (2015). The longitudinal course of non-suicidal self-injury and deliberate self-harm: A systematic review of the literature. *Borderline Personality Disorder and Emotion Dysregulation, 2*(1), 1–11. https://doi.org/10.1186/s40479-014-0024-3

Plener, P. L., Zohsel, K., Hohm, E., Buchmann, A. F., Banaschewski, T., Zimmermann, U. S., & Laucht, M., 2017. Lower cortisol level in response to a psychosocial stressor in young females with self-harm. *Psychoneuroendocrinology, 76*, 84–87. https://doi.org/10.1016/j.psyneuen.2016.11.009

Pruessner, M., Pruessner, J. C., Hellhammer, D. H., Pike, G. B., & Lupien, S. J. (2007). The associations among hippocampal volume, cortisol reactivity, and memory performance in healthy young men. *Psychiatry Research: Neuroimaging, 155*(1), 1–10.

Reichl, C., Brunner, R., Bender, N., Parzer, P., Koenig, J., Resch, F., Kaess, M. (2019). Adolescent nonsuicidal self-injury and cortisol response to the retrieval of adversity: A sibling study. *Psychoneuroendocrinology, 110*, Article 104460. https://doi.org/10.1016/j.psyneuen.2019.104460

Reichl, C., Heyer, A., Brunner, R., Parzer, P., Völker, J. M., Resch, F., & Kaess, M. (2016). Hypothalamic-pituitary-adrenal axis, childhood adversity and adolescent nonsuicidal self-injury. *Psychoneuroendocrinology, 74*, 203–211. https://doi.org/10.1016/j.psyneuen.2016.09.011

Reisner, S. L., Biello, K., Perry, N. S., Gamarel, K. E., & Mimiaga, M. J. (2014). A compensatory model of risk and resilience applied to adolescent sexual orientation disparities in nonsuicidal self-injury and suicide attempts. *American Journal of Orthopsychiatry, 84*(5), 545.

Roy, A. V., Thai, M., Klimes-Dougan, B., Westlund Schreiner, M., Mueller, B. A., Albott, C. S., Lim, K. O., Fiecas, M., Tye, S. J., & Cullen, K. R. (2021). Brain entropy and neurotrophic molecular markers accompanying clinical improvement after ketamine: Preliminary evidence in adolescents with treatment-resistant depression. *Journal of Psychopharmacology, 35*(2), 168–177.

Russell, E., Koren, G., Rieder, M., & Van Uum, S. (2012). Hair cortisol as a biological marker of chronic stress: Current status, future directions and unanswered questions. *Psychoneuroendocrinology, 37*(5), 589–601.

Sachsse, U., Von Der Heyde, S., & Huether, G. (2002). Stress regulation and self-mutilation. *American Journal of Psychiatry, 159*(4), 672–672.

Santamarina-Perez, P., Romero, S., Mendez, I., Leslie, S. M., Packer, M. M., Sugranyes, G., Picado, M., Font, E., Moreno, E., Martinez, E., Morer, A., Romero, M., & Singh, M. K. (2019). Fronto-limbic connectivity as a predictor of improvement in nonsuicidal self-injury in adolescents following psychotherapy. *Journal of Child and Adolescent Psychopharmacology, 29*(6), 456–465.

Schreiner, M. W., Klimes-Dougan, B., Mueller, B. A., Eberly, L. E., Reigstad, K. M., Carstedt, P. A., Thomas, K. M., Hunt, R. H., Lim, K. O., & Cullen, K. R. (2017). Multi-modal neuroimaging of adolescents with non-suicidal self-injury: Amygdala functional connectivity. *Journal of Affective Disorders, 221*, 47–55.

Schreiner, M., Klimes-Dougan, B., Begnel, E. D., & Cullen, K. R. (2015). Conceptualizing the neurobiology of non-suicidal self-injury from the perspective of the Research Domain Criteria Project. *Neuroscience & Biobehavioral Reviews, 57*, 381–391.

Seeley, W. W., Menon, V., Schatzberg, A. F., Keller, J., Glover, G. H., Kenna, H., ... & Greicius, M. D. (2007). Dissociable intrinsic connectivity networks for salience processing and executive control. *Journal of Neuroscience, 27*(9), 2349–2356.

Selby, E. A., Kranzler, A., Fehling, K. B., & Panza, E. (2015). Nonsuicidal self-injury disorder: The path to diagnostic validity and final obstacles. *Clinical Psychology Review, 38*, 79–91.

Sornberger, M. J., Smith, N. G., Toste, J. R., & Heath, N. L. (2013). Nonsuicidal self-injury, coping strategies, and sexual orientation. *Journal of Clinical Psychology, 69*(6), 571–583.

Spear, L. P. (2000). The adolescent brain and age-related behavioral manifestations. *Neuroscience & Biobehavioral Reviews, 24*(4), 417–463.

Staples, J. M., Neilson, E. C., Bryan, A. E., & George, W. H. (2018). The role of distal minority stress and internalized transnegativity in suicidal ideation and nonsuicidal self-injury among transgender adults. *The Journal of Sex Research, 55*(4–5), 591–603.

Stroud, L. R., Foster, E., Papandonatos, G. D., Handwerger, K., Granger, D. A., Kivlighan, K. T., & Niaura, R. (2009). Stress response and the adolescent transition: Performance versus peer rejection stressors. *Development and Psychopathology, 21*(1), 47–68.

Sumner, J. A., McLaughlin, K. A., Walsh, K., Sheridan, M. A., & Koenen, K. C. (2014). CRHR1 genotype and history of maltreatment predict cortisol reactivity to stress in adolescents. *Psychoneuroendocrinology, 43*, 71–80.

Swannell, S. V., Martin, G. E., Page, A., Hasking, P., & St John, N. J. (2014). Prevalence of nonsuicidal self-injury in nonclinical samples: Systematic review, meta-analysis and meta-regression. *Suicide and Life-Threatening Behavior, 44*(3), 273–303. https://doi.org/10.1111/sltb.12070

Swartz, J. R., Carrasco, M., Wiggins, J. L., Thomason, M. E., & Monk, C. S. (2014). Age-related changes in the structure and function of prefrontal cortex–amygdala circuitry in children and adolescents: A multimodal imaging approach. *Neuroimage, 86*, 212–220.

Tang, J., Yu, Y., Wu, Y., Du, Y., Ma, Y., Zhu, H., Zhang, P., & Liu, Z. (2011). Association between non-suicidal self-injuries and suicide attempts in Chinese adolescents and college students: A cross-section study. *PloS One, 6*(4), Article17977.

Thai, M. (2020). Interplay *between frontolimbic resting state connectivity and hypothalamic-pituitary-adrenal axis functioning in adolescents with and without depression* [Unpublished doctoral dissertation]. University of Minnesota.

Thompson, E. M., Destree, L., Albertella, L., & Fontenelle, L. F. (2021). Internet-based acceptance and commitment therapy: A transdiagnostic systematic review and meta-analysis for mental health outcomes. *Behavior Therapy, 52*(2), 492–507.

Trickett, P. K., Noll, J. G., Susman, E. J., Shenk, C. E., & Putnam, F. W. (2010). Attenuation of cortisol across development for victims of sexual abuse. *Development and Psychopathology, 22*(1), 165–175. https://doi.org/10.1017/s0954579409990332

Van Orden, K. A., Witte, T. K., Cukrowicz, K. C., Braithwaite, S. R., Selby, E. A., & Joiner Jr., T. E. (2010). The interpersonal theory of suicide. *Psychological Review, 117*(2), 575.

Victor, S. E., & Klonsky, E. D. (2014). Correlates of suicide attempts among self-injurers: A meta-analysis. *Clinical Psychology Review, 34*(4), 282–297.

Walls, N. E., Laser, J., Nickels, S. J., & Wisneski, H. (2010). Correlates of cutting behavior among sexual minority youths and young adults. *Social Work Research, 34*(4), 213–226.

Weniger, G., Lange, C., Sachsse, U., & Irle, E. (2009). Reduced amygdala and hippocampus size in trauma-exposed women with borderline personality disorder and without posttraumatic stress disorder. *Journal of Psychiatry & Neuroscience: JPN, 34*(5), 383.

Westlund Schreiner, M., Mueller, B. A., Klimes-Dougan, B., Begnel, E. D., Fiecas, M., Hill, D., Lim, K. O., & Cullen, K. R. (2020). White matter microstructure in adolescents and young adults with non-suicidal self-injury. *Frontiers in Psychiatry, 10*, Article 1019.

White, H. V., Silamongkol, T., Wiglesworth, A., Labella, M. H., Goetz, E. R., Cullen, K. R., & Klimes-Dougan, B. (2021). Maternal emotion socialization of adolescent girls engaging in non-suicidal self-injury. *Research on Child and Adolescent Psychopathology, 49*(5), 683–695.

Wright, K. D., Jack, A. I., Friedman, J. P., Jones, L. M., Sattar, A., Fresco, D. M., & Moore, S. M. (2020). Neural processing and perceived discrimination stress in African Americans. *Nursing Research, 69*(5), 331–338.

Yurgelun-Todd, D. A., & Killgore, W. D. (2006). Fear-related activity in the prefrontal cortex increases with age during adolescence: A preliminary fMRI study. *Neuroscience Letters, 406*(3), 194–199.

Zeiders, K. H. (2017). Discrimination, daily stress, sleep, and Mexican-origin adolescents' internalizing symptoms. *Cultural Diversity and Ethnic Minority Psychology, 23*(4), 570.

Zorn, J. V., Schür, R. R., Boks, M. P., Kahn, R. S., Joëls, M., & Vinkers, C. H. (2017). Cortisol stress reactivity across psychiatric disorders: A systematic review and meta-analysis. *Psychoneuroendocrinology, 77*, 25–36.

CHAPTER 15

Positive Valence Systems and Nonsuicidal Self-Injury

Laurence Claes, Koen Luyckx, *and* Glenn Kiekens

Abstract

The present chapter focuses on reward sensitivity and positive emotionality in the development and maintenance of NSSI. The chapter discusses several theoretical models that explain specific mechanisms that may contribute to the positive reinforcement qualities of NSSI. Additionally, it considers whether the association between NSSI and other harmful emotion regulating behaviors—that is, eating disorder behaviors (EDs) and substance use behaviors (SUDs)—can be partially explained by different characteristics of the positive valence systems. The chapter concludes that NSSI, ED, and SUD have both shared and distinct correlations with measures of reward sensitivity. All three behaviors seem to be triggered by specific cues, and patients show attentional bias toward these cues. NSSI, ED, and SUD can be automatically/socially positively reinforced, which explains their continuation for some people. Furthermore, on the neurobiological level, all three behaviors seem—at the starting phase—to be related to a hyperreactivity of the reward-related systems in the brain that is driven by dopamine release. However, over time, dysregulation of the dopaminergic system leads to a hyporeactivity of the reward-related systems, which may increase susceptibility for the use of NSSI, ED, and SUD behaviors to increase positive emotional experiences. On the level of temperamental features, the findings are more mixed. It seems that NSSI and ED behaviors have more common temperamental features than SUD. Additionally, the chapter discusses transdiagnostic interventions. Finally, it provides suggestions for future research and summarizes the main findings here. To conclude, research on the reward system is challenging, and requires further research.

Keywords non-suicidal self-injury, sensitivity, positive emotionality, eating disorder behaviors, substance use behaviors, positive valence systems, transdiagnostic interventions, self-harming behaviors

Introduction

Although the idea of injuring oneself may feel rather scary (it may be expected to hurt), for individuals who engage in nonsuicidal self-injury (NSSI), it often feels rewarding and is used to cope with difficulties in life. Many studies show that NSSI may serve an emotion regulation function for those who engage in NSSI, by reducing negative emotions and increasing positive emotions, such as feeling cheerful or excited (Franz et al., 2019). The role of positive emotionality in emotion-regulating behaviors like self-injury has historically been understudied. The present chapter focuses on reward sensitivity and positive emotionality in the development and maintenance of NSSI (for more on the functions of NSSI, see Taylor et al., this volume).

To study the role of positive emotions in psychopathology, Gruber et al. (2019) developed a valuable two-dimensional framework that is useful when evaluating the role of positive emotions in psychopathology. The first dimension is the *level of analysis* which differentiates between units of emotion stability as positive emotions can be studied from momentary state responses (state markers), over longer-lasting positive mood to relatively stable temperamental dispositions in positive affectivity (trait markers) (Gruber et al., 2019). According to Kaess et al. (2021), a trait is a relatively stable, enduring pattern of behavioral/biological functioning, which plays an antecedent role in the pathophysiology of psychiatric conditions, whereas a state is a temporary psychological/biological way of being (e.g., the moments immediately before, during, and after NSSI or a proxy of NSSI—that is, the experimental exposure to pain/stress) (Kaess et al., 2021). A second dimension is the *temporal course* of positive emotions. Increases/decreases in positive emotionality can precede, occur during (e.g., excitement during NSSI due to an endorphin rush), or follow harmful behavior (e.g., pain-offset release after NSSI) (Gruber et al., 2019).

Positive Valence Systems

The need for identifying pathophysiological markers of altered responding to rewards (and related positive emotionality) in psychopathology has been put forward as an important direction for future research by the National Institute of Mental Health (Cuthbert & Kozak, 2013; Insel et al., 2010; Sanislow et al., 2010). The NIMH introduced the Research Domain Criteria (RDoC) in 2009 to guide research on the neurobiological bases of psychopathology organized around biobehavioral dimensions (RDoC; Insel et al., 2010). The RDoC framework was operationalized in the RDoC matrix (NIMH, 2011, 2018). The matrix columns represent eight units of analysis (genes, molecules, cells, circuits, physiology, behavior, paradigms, and self-reports). The rows represent domains (positive valence systems, negative valence systems, etc.), constructs, and subconstructs, representing functional dimensions (Michelini et al., 2021). "Positive Valence Systems are primarily responsible for responses to positive motivational situations or contexts, such as reward-seeking, consummatory behavior, and reward/habit learning" (NIMH, 2018, pp. 6–8). The domain "Positive Valence Systems" has three constructs (i.e., reward responsiveness, reward learning, and reward valuation) and nine subconstructs (NIMH, 2018, pp. 6–8; see table 15.1 for a detailed description). Khazanov et al. (2019) developed the 45-item Positive Valence Systems Scales (PVSS) to broadly assess the positive valence systems domain criteria as well as a short 21-item form of the PVSS (PVSS-21) which measures responses to a wide range of rewards (food, physical touch, social interactions, goals, hobbies, etc.).

Although the constructs of reward-seeking, consummatory behavior, and reward/habit learning are supposed to map onto particular neural circuits, only a limited number of studies have examined the extent to which this is the case for these different constructs

Table 15.1 Constructs and Subconstructs in the Positive Valence System	
Positive Valence Systems	Positive Valence Systems are primarily responsible for responses to positive motivational situations or contexts, such as reward seeking, consummatory behavior, and reward/habit learning.
1. Reward Responsiveness	Processes that govern an organism's hedonic response to impending or possible reward (as reflected in reward anticipation), the receipt of reward (as reflected in initial response to reward), and following repeated receipt of reward (as in reward satiation); across these subdomains, reward responsiveness primarily reflects neural activity to receipt of reward and reward cues and can also be measured in terms of subjective and behavioral responses.
1.1. *Reward Anticipation*	Processes associated with the ability to anticipate and/or represent a future incentive—as reflected in language expression, behavioral responses, and/or engagement of the neural systems to cues about a future positive reinforcer.
1.2. *Initial Response to Reward*	Processes evoked by the initial presentation of a positive reinforcer as reflected by indices of neuronal activity and verbal or behavioral responses.
1.3. *Reward Satiation*	Processes associated with the change in incentive value of a reinforcer over time as that reinforcer is consumed or experienced, as reflected in language expression, behavioral responses, and/or engagement of the neural systems.
2. Reward Learning	A process by which organisms acquire information about stimuli, actions, and contexts that predict positive outcomes, and by which behavior is modified when a novel reward occurs, or outcomes are better than expected. Reward learning is a type of reinforcement learning.
2.1. *Probabilistic and Reinforcement Learning*	The ability to learn which actions or stimuli are associated with obtaining a reinforcer, even when a particular action or stimulus is not always associated with obtaining the reinforcer.
2.2. *Reward Prediction Error*	Processes associated with the difference between anticipated and obtained rewards are important for reinforcement learning. The error can indicate that the reward received was either larger than expected (positive prediction error) or smaller than expected (negative prediction error).
2.3. *Habit*	Sequential, repetitive motor behaviors or cognitive processes elicited by external or internal triggers that, once initiated, can go to completion without continuous effortful oversight. Habits can be adaptive by virtue of freeing up cognitive resources. Habit formation is a frequent consequence of reward learning, but, over time, its expression can become resistant to changes in outcome value. Some habit-related behaviors could be pathological expressions of processes that under other circumstances subserve adaptive goals.

Table 15.1 *Continued*	
3. **Reward Valuation**	Processes by which the probability and benefits of a prospective outcome are computed by reference to external information, social context (e.g., group input), and/or prior experience. This computation is influenced by preexisting biases, learning, memory, stimulus characteristics, and deprivation states. Reward valuation may involve the assignment of incentive salience to stimuli.
3.1. *Reward (ambiguity/risk)*	Process by which the value of a reinforcer is computed as a function of its magnitude, valence, and predictability.
3.2. *Delay*	Processes by which the value of a reinforcer is computed as a function of its magnitude and the time interval prior to its expected delivery.
3.3. *Effort*	Processes by which the value of a reinforcer is computed as a function of its magnitude and the perceived costs of the physical or cognitive effort required to obtain it.

Source: NIMH (2018, pp. 6–8).

(Khazanov et al., 2019). Most studies have investigated neurobiological differences between "the motivation to pursue reward" ("wanting," involving dopamine signaling in the neurostriatal circuit) and "the pleasure experienced when a reward is attained" ("liking," involving endogenous opioids) (Khazanov et al., 2019). Particularly in adolescence, we see a sensitization of the brain's reward system due to alterations in the dopamine system (Galvan & Radhar, 2013). These dopaminergic alterations, coupled with heightened limbic activation and weak inhibitory control from prefrontal regions, make (especially younger) adolescents prone to risky/reward-seeking behaviors, such as NSSI (Franz et al., 2019). Indeed, researchers have consistently observed that individuals are most vulnerable to begin NSSI during early and mid-adolescence (Gandhi et al., 2018; Kiekens et al., 2021; Plener et al., 2015).

In the next sections, we discuss several theoretical models that explain specific mechanisms that may contribute to the positive reinforcement qualities of NSSI and review empirical evidence for each of these models. Additionally, we consider whether the association between NSSI and other harmful emotion regulating behaviors (i.e., eating disorder behaviors and substance use disorder behaviors) can be partially explained by different characteristics of the positive valence systems: (a) positive reinforcement, (b) reward-seeking temperament/personality, (c) cognitive biases, (d) over- and underactivation of the reward circuitry in the brain, and (e) psychophysiological reactivity toward positive affect. In doing so, we discuss transdiagnostic interventions, which focus on the reward-related triggers and consequences of self-harming behaviors. Finally, we summarize the main findings of this chapter and provide suggestions for future research.

Four-Function Model of NSSI: Automatic/Social Positive Reinforcement of NSSI

The empirically well-validated four-function model (Nock & Prinstein, 2004) postulates that the functions of NSSI differ along two dimensions. The first dimension refers to the positive and negative reinforcement of NSSI (i.e., NSSI is followed by a positive stimulus or the removal of a negative stimulus, respectively). The second dimension refers to the automatic (intrapersonal) versus social (interpersonal) function of NSSI. The crossing of both dimensions leads to four broad function domains: automatic negative reinforcement (e.g., NSSI to reduce negative affect), automatic positive reinforcement (e.g., NSSI to induce excitement), social negative reinforcement (e.g., NSSI to escape from social activities), and finally social positive reinforcement (e.g., getting support or attention following NSSI) (Bentley et al., 2014; Nock & Prinstein, 2004). For the scope of the present chapter, the automatic/social positive reinforcement functions are particularly relevant.

Similarly, the benefits and barriers model of NSSI developed by Hooley and Franklin (2018) suggests that NSSI engagement may provide both affective as well as self-punishment, affiliation and communication benefits. According to this model, an increase in positive mood can occur while experiencing pain or following the termination of pain (i.e., pain offset relief; Hooley et al., 2020). Several studies have shown that pain offset relief is related to positive affective states via neurobiological mechanisms (i.e., opioids; Franz et al., 2019) and may signal approach (Whiech & Tracy, 2013). The affiliation and communication benefits refer to the use of NSSI to improve the relationship with peers or to get attention and support when verbal forms of communication are not effective (Hooley & Franklin, 2018). Finally, the self-punishment benefit in this model indicates that NSSI may gratify self-punishment desires of people.

Several studies have tested the positive reinforcement function of NSSI in cross-sectional studies (for reviews, see Bentley et al., 2014; Taylor et al., 2018) as well as in longitudinal studies utilizing ecological momentary assessment (for a recent review, see Hepp et al., 2020). In what follows, we summarize the findings from these studies.

Automatic/Social Positive Reinforcement: Cross-Sectional and Prospective Survey Studies

Nock and Prinstein (2004) reported the following automatic positive reinforcement functions that NSSI served in adolescent inpatients: to punish oneself (31.8%), to feel relaxed (23.5%), and to feel something even if it was pain (34.1%). The social positive reinforcement functions with the highest prevalence rates were to give yourself something to do when alone (23.5%); to get control of a situation (15.3%); to try to get a reaction from someone, even if it is negative (15.3%); to get help (14.1%); to get attention (14.1%); to let others know how desperate you are (14.1%); and to receive more attention from parents or friends (14.1%). However, the function with the highest endorsement rate was still "to stop bad feelings" (52.9%), which refers to the automatic negative reinforcement function of NSSI. Taylor et al. (2018), in a meta-analytic review, reported similar findings. They found that the automatic negative reinforcement functions of NSSI "escaping a negative/unwanted state" (62–78%) and "emotion regulation" (63–78%) were the most frequently reported functions, followed by "inducing a positive state" (42–57%) and "punishing oneself" (41–62%), both automatic positive reinforcement functions. Within the interpersonal functions, "communicating levels of distress to others" (30–55%; social positive reinforcement) was the most frequently endorsed function (Taylor et al., 2018, pp. 762–763). Interestingly, Muehlenkamp et al. (2013) differentiated between initial motives for NSSI (onset) and functions of repeated NSSI (continuation) in undergraduate students. In their study, the most frequently reported automatic/social positive reinforcement functions of NSSI onset were the following: "It felt good" (16.4%) and "I wanted someone to notice me or my injuries" (10.9%). The function "angry at myself'" (39.9%) was most prevalent. In contrast, the most frequently automatic/social positive reinforcement functions for NSSI maintenance were "to feel something" (23.5%) and "hope others notice something is wrong" (13.1%) (Muehlenkamp et al., 2013). These findings suggest that the functions that underlie NSSI may change over time. In line with Muehlenkamp et al. (2013), several authors investigated the predictive utility of functions for the maintenance of NSSI. Among those with a history of NSSI, Yen et al. (2016) found that the automatic positive reinforcement function "to generate feelings or emotions" was related to the maintenance of NSSI in adolescents, whereas in adults, the function "to get a rush or surge of energy" was related to the maintenance of NSSI (Kiekens et al., 2017). Furthermore, Pollak et al. (2020) reported that automatic negative reinforcement was related to NSSI thoughts during hospitalization of adolescents, whereas automatic positive reinforcement was related to the maintenance of NSSI behavior during hospitalization. In this study, none of the NSSI functions predicted NSSI thoughts/behaviors after hospitalization among a subsample of 66 patients with follow-up data (Pollak et al., 2020). In sum, the generation of positive feelings and the communication of distress toward others are the most frequently endorsed intra/interpersonal positive reinforcers of NSSI. Preliminary evidence suggests that individuals who endorse automatic positive reinforcement may be at higher risk for the maintenance of NSSI. However, future prospective work is needed to clarify whether different function patterns predict the onset and maintenance of NSSI.

Automatic/Social Positive Reinforcement: Ecological Momentary Assessment Studies

Hepp et al. (2020) summarized 35 longitudinal ecological momentary assessment (EMA) studies that investigated whether positive affect decreased before NSSI and increased following NSSI. Two studies showed decreased positive affect before and increased positive affect following NSSI in youth with borderline personality disorder (BPD) and bulimia nervosa (Andrewes et al., 2017; Muehlenkamp et al., 2009). Kranzler et al. (2018) did not find decreased positive affect (PA) before NSSI but observed increased levels of PA following NSSI in youth with depression and BPD. Contrary to these findings, Armey et al. (2011) did not find a decrease in PA before NSSI or an increase in PA following NSSI, and Houben et al. (2017) even found decreased PA levels following NSSI in chronic inpatients with BPD features. One daily diary study also investigated the social positive reinforcement function of NSSI. Turner et al. (2016) assessed how social support related to the occurrence of NSSI in adults with mood disorders or BPD. The authors of this study found that social support increased on days that adults engaged in NSSI, which supports the idea that NSSI can evoke interpersonal positive reinforcement. Importantly, however, as most of these studies used different time frames, it is difficult to compare results across studies. Future EMA studies that add brief follow-up surveys to their protocol when people report NSSI thoughts provide a unique opportunity to unravel affective and social contingencies that happen in the minutes that lead up to and immediately follow NSSI as well as across longer time intervals (e.g., hours and days; Voelkle et al., 2018).

Temperament and Personality Traits Related to the Positive Valence Systems Based on Self-Report

The RDoC constructs of positive valence systems are assumed to manifest behaviorally through temperamental positive affectivity and personality traits related to reward sensitivity (Kessel et al., 2017; Poon et al., 2019).

Rothbart's Temperament Model: Positive Affectivity/Positive Reactivity

Three studies (Baetens et al., 2011; Claes et al., 2014; Cohen et al., 2015) compared positive affectivity/positive reactivity in adolescents and adults with and without NSSI by means of the Early Adolescents Temperament Questionnaire (EATQ; Ellis & Rothbart, 2001), the Adult Temperament Questionnaire (ATQ; Evans & Rothbart, 2007; Rothbart et al., 2000), and the Positive and Negative Affect Schedule (PANAS; Watson et al., 1988). Positive affectivity/reactivity discriminated between participants with and without NSSI in none of these studies.

Cloninger's Temperament and Character Model: Novelty Seeking and Reward Responsiveness

According to Cloninger's personality model (Cloninger et al., 1993; Cloninger et al., 1999), two of the four temperament dimensions are related to reward sensitivity, Being Novelty Seeking (i.e., marked exploratory activity in the face of novelty) and Reward Dependence (i.e., intense responses to rewards, including social rewards). Five cross-sectional studies used the Temperament and Character Inventory-(Revised) (TCI/TCI-R; Cloninger, 1994, 1999) to investigate temperamental differences in male (Claes et al., 2012) and female eating disorder (ED)/borderline personality disorder (BPD) patients with and without NSSI (Buelens et al., 2020; Chapman et al., 2009; Islam et al., 2015; Gomez-Exposito et al., 2016). Novelty Seeking differentiated between patients with and without lifetime NSSI in none of these studies; however, in the study by Buelens et al. (2020), Novelty Seeking differentiated patients with recent NSSI (last 12 months) from those with a history of NSSI but without recent self-injury. Patients with recent NSSI scored significantly lower than patients without recent NSSI on Novelty Seeking (indicating anhedonia in patients with recent NSSI). Concerning Reward Responsiveness, three studies showed that patients with lifetime NSSI scored significantly lower on Reward Responsiveness compared to patients without a history of NSSI (Chapman et al., 2009; Gomez-Exposito et al., 2016; Islam et al., 2015). Chapman et al. (2009) showed that patients with NSSI scored significantly lower on the Reward Responsiveness subscale Attachment compared with patients without NSSI (probably related to traumatic experiences in patients with NSSI).

In sum, individuals with a history of lifetime NSSI score significantly lower on Reward Responsiveness (Attachment) compared to patients without NSSI; however, they do not seem to score differently on Positive Affectivity/Reactivity and Sensation Seeking.

Lynam and Miller's UPPS-P Model: Sensation Seeking and Positive Urgency.
The multidimensional model of impulsivity (Lynam & Miller, 2004) consists of five dimensions: Negative Urgency, Lack of Perseverance, Lack of Premeditation, Sensation Seeking, and Positive Urgency (UPPS-P). Two of the five impulsivity dimensions are related to the Positive Valence Systems: Sensation Seeking (i.e., an individual's tendency to pursue activities that are exciting and novel) and Positive Urgency (i.e., an individual's tendency to act impulsively under conditions of heightened positive affect). We identified 10 cross-sectional studies in which the UPPS-(P) Impulsive Behavior scale (Whiteside & Lynam, 2001; Whiteside et al., 2005) was used to discriminate participants with and without NSSI in community (Ammerman et al., 2017; Claes & Muehlenkamp, 2013; Glenn & Klonsky, 2010, 2011; Peterson et al., 2020; Peterson & Fischer, 2012; Riley et al., 2015) and patient samples (Claes et al., 2015; Gomez-Exposito et al., 2016; Lynam et al., 2011). The results clearly show that Sensation Seeking does not significantly discriminate between participants with and without NSSI. Only in one study (Ammerman et al., 2017) was Sensation Seeking found to be significantly lower in participants with than without NSSI, but this difference was no longer significant when the authors controlled for sociodemographic variables and clinical comorbidity.

Positive Urgency has been included in 5 of these 10 studies (this dimension was later added to the scale; Ammerman et al., 2017; Claes et al., 2015; Claes & Muehlenkamp, 2013; Gomez-Exposito et al., 2016; Riley et al., 2015), and showed a positive association with the presence of lifetime NSSI in two studies (Claes et al., 2015; Claes & Muehlenkamp, 2013). To date, only two longitudinal studies assessed whether the UPPS dimensions (Positive Urgency was not included in both studies) could predict NSSI at 8-month (Peterson & Fischer, 2012) and 1-year follow-up (Glenn & Klonsky, 2011). The UPPS dimensions prospectively predicted NSSI in none of the studies.

Taken together, these studies suggest that individuals with a history of NSSI score significantly higher on the UPPS-Positive Urgency scale compared to individuals without NSSI but do not differ on the UPPS-Sensation Seeking scale. However, more longitudinal studies are needed to investigate the predictive utility of the UPPS-P dimensions for the onset and maintenance of NSSI.

The Big Five Personality Model: Extraversion

According to the Big Five Personality Model (Wiggins, 1996), the personality trait of Extraversion is related to reward sensitivity (Depue & Collins, 1999). Three studies used the Big Five Measure (B5; Perugini & Di Blas, 2002), the Quick Big Five (QBF; Vermulst & Gerris, 2005), and the NEO-Personality Inventory-Revised (NEO-PI-R; Costa & McCrae, 1992) to assess the Big Five personality traits in participants with and without NSSI in community samples (Cerutti et al., 2012; Kiekens et al., 2015; Robertson et al., 2013). These studies found that Extraversion was not significantly related with a history of NSSI (Cerutti et al., 2012; Kiekens et al., 2015) and the frequency/number of methods of lifetime NSSI.

Gray's Reinforcement Sensitivity Theory

According to Gray's reinforcement sensitivity theory (RST) (Gray, 1991; Gray & McNaughton, 2000), two motivational systems are driving our behaviors: the behavioral inhibition system (BIS) and the behavioral activation system (BAS). In the scope of the present chapter, the BAS is important given that it reacts to (un)conditioned stimuli of reward, elicits positive affectivity, and triggers approach behavior. In the literature, two questionnaires are used to assess BAS reactivity, being the BISBAS scales (BISBAS; Carver & White, 1994) and the Sensitivity to Punishment and Sensitivity to Reward Questionnaire (SPSRQ; Torrubia et al., 2001).

Four cross-sectional studies in community samples used the SPSRQ to investigate the association between the Sensitivity to Reward and NSSI characteristics (Ammerman et al., 2017; Cohen et al., 2015; Jenkins et al., 2013; Robertson et al., 2013). Robertson et al. (2013) and Jenkins et al. (2013) reported significant positive correlations between Sensitivity to Reward (SR) and the lifetime frequency of NSSI acts and number of NSSI methods. Cohen et al. (2015) and Ammerman et al. (2017) did not find significant associations between Sensitivity to Reward and a history of NSSI.

Six cross-sectional studies used the BISBAS scales to investigate the associations between BAS reactivity and NSSI in community samples (Burke et al., 2015; Cerutti et al., 2012; Cohen et al., 2015; Gandhi et al., 2016; Jenkins et al., 2013; Wu et al., 2021). Using the total BAS score, scholars did not find significant associations between BAS and NSSI (Cohen et al., 2015; Gandhi et al., 2016). Burke et al. (2015) divided their sample in adolescents with moderate and high BAS total scores and found positive associations between moderate/high BAS and lifetime NSSI ($r = .23$, $p < .01$) and

12-month NSSI ($r = .17$, $p < .05$). Three studies used the BAS subscales (BAS-Drive, BAS-Reward Responsiveness, BAS-Fun Seeking) to investigate the relations between BAS subfacets and NSSI.

BAS-Drive (i.e., the persistent pursuit of desired goals) correlated positively with the frequency of lifetime NSSI acts (Jenkins et al., 2013; Wu et al., 2021) but not with other NSSI characteristics (Cerutti et al., 2012). Also, BAS-Fun Seeking (i.e., the desire for new rewards and a willingness to approach potentially rewarding events) correlated positively with the frequency of lifetime NSSI acts (Jenkins et al., 2013; Wu et al., 2021) and the number of NSSI methods applied (Jenkins et al., 2013). BAS-Reward Responsiveness (i.e., the positive responsivity to reward) was not significantly related to NSSI parameters in two studies (Cerutti et al., 2012; Wu et al., 2021) and showed mixed results in the study of Jenkins et al. (2013). In sum, Sensitivity to Reward and BAS-Drive/Fun Seeking seem to be positively related to the frequency/versatility of lifetime NSSI in community samples, which suggests that it may be an underlying indicator of the severity of NSSI. However, again prospective studies are needed to investigate this possibility further. Finally, Burke et al. (2022) assessed the associations between BAS-Drive, Reward Responsiveness, and Fun Seeking and NSSI urge severity by means of an ecological momentary assessment protocol in a sample of 64 undergraduates with a history of repetitive NSSI. BAS-Drive and Reward Responsiveness were concurrently positively related to NSSI urge severity. However, no associations between BAS subscales and prospective NSSI urges were found.

Based on the overview about the relationship between lifetime NSSI and temperament/personality traits, we can tentatively conclude that Positive Reactivity (ATQ), Novelty Seeking (TCI), Sensation Seeking (UPPS), and Extraversion (NEO-FFI) do not appear to differentiate individuals with and without a history of NSSI. Sensitivity to Reward (SPSRQ) and BAS-Drive/Fun Seeking have been related to the frequency of lifetime NSSI acts in community samples. It should however be mentioned that some instruments were only used in community samples (SPSRQ, BISBAS scales, NEO), whereas others have been consistently used in clinical samples (e.g., TCI). Additionally, although some studies only focused on the presence/absence of lifetime NSSI, others also investigated different NSSI characteristics (e.g., frequency and versatility) among those with a history of NSSI. Finally, and perhaps most important, most reviewed studies were cross-sectional in nature. The only two studies that had a prospective design did not show a temporal relationship between temperament/personality traits and NSSI engagement.

Cognitive Biases Related to the Positive Valence Systems Based on Experimental Paradigms

Increased motivation to engage in NSSI (approach tendency) has also been associated with several cognitive biases. Employing a dot-probe task, Riquino et al. (2020) showed that young adults with a history of NSSI exhibited an attentional bias toward NSSI cues compared to negative and neutral cues. Additionally, NSSI urge increased and positive affect decreased following exposure to NSSI cues in the task. However, it remains to be explored whether young adults rely on NSSI to recover from a reduction in positive affect after exposure to NSSI-specific cues (Riquino et al., 2020). Furthermore, studies using the Self-Injury Implicit Association Task (SI-IAT; Nock & Banaji, 2007a, 2007b) found that people who engage in NSSI have implicitly a stronger positive attitude toward NSSI than individuals who do not self-injure (Glenn & Klonsky, 2011; Nock & Banaji, 2007a, 2007b). Responses to the SI-IAT also predicted concurrent NSSI status in adolescents (Cha et al., 2016; Nock & Banaji, 2007a, 2007b), but did not predict future NSSI in students (Glenn & Klonsky, 2011) and adolescent inpatients (Dickstein et al., 2015). For a detailed overview of cognitive biases in individuals who engage in NSSI, see Ammerman et al. (2018).

Brain Structures that Comprise the Positive Valence Systems

In the following paragraphs, we focus on (a) the reward circuitry in the brain based on fMRI studies, (b) neurotransmitters that are related to the positive valence systems, and finally (c) the psychophysiology of positive affective processing via reflexive and facial electromyography.

Reward Circuitry in the Brain Based on fMRI Studies

Although many regions in the brain react to reward, the frontostriatal neural circuit is the primary center of the reward system (Nusslock & Alloy, 2017). "This circuit involves dopaminergic projections from midbrain nuclei (the ventral tegmental area) to subcortical regions that are central to processing the rewarding properties of stimuli (the ventral striatum, including the nucleus accumbens) to cortical target regions (the orbitofrontal cortex, medial prefrontal cortex, anterior cingulate cortex (ACC))" (Nusslock & Alloy, 2017, p. 4). There is, however, limited evidence for the role of neural reward processing in NSSI as findings to date have shown mixed results.

Plener et al. (2012) performed a study in 18 adolescents with (N = 9; Mage = 15.2; SD = 1.5) and without a history of NSSI (N = 9) who had to look at pictures of the International Affective Picture System (IAPS) and NSSI-related pictures during a functional magnetic resonance imaging (fMRI). For the IAPS pictures, adolescents with NSSI showed a stronger brain response in the amygdala, hippocampus, and anterior cingulate cortex (ACC). For the NSSI-related pictures, adolescents with a history of NSSI showed increased activity in the middle orbitofrontal cortex and inferior and middle frontal cortex. According to Nusslock and Alloy (2017, p. 5), "the medial orbitofrontal cortex is very sensitive to the rewarding properties of stimuli and the generation of positive/approach-related affect."

Osuch et al. (2014) used a painfully cold stimulus (NSSI substitute) in 13 patients with a history of NSSI (Mage = 20.0; SD = 2.4) and 15 patients without a history of NSSI (Mage = 21.0; SD = 1.8) during an fMRI study. The cold stimulus could be administered by the experimenter or by the patients themselves. The results showed that both groups reported equivalent levels of pain in response to painfully cold stimuli, but the NSSI group reported greater relief following the self-administered pain stimuli. Within the NSSI group, relief after self-afflicted cold stimuli was positively related to blood oxygen level dependent (BOLD) signal within the dorsal striatum, a brain region involved in reward processing and habitual behavior formation (habit learning; Liu, 2017; Westlund Schreiner et al., 2015). "With repeated engagement in the NSSI, followed by reward (operant learning), the behavior will become relatively insensitive to reward (i.e., stimulus-response learning or habit learning). The transition from voluntary behavior (operant learning) to habitual behavior (stimulus-response learning) is reflected by the shift in striatal locus of control from the ventral to dorsal striatum" (Liu, 2017, pp. 4–5).

Sauder et al. (2016) investigated 19 female adolescents with NSSI and 19 adolescents without NSSI (age range 13–19 years) by means of a monetary incentive delay task during an fMRI. Contrary to the findings of Plener et al. (2012) and Osuch et al. (2014), adolescents with NSSI exhibited less activation in both striatal and orbitofrontal cortex regions and showed reduced bilateral amygdala activation during anticipation of reward compared to adolescents without NSSI.

In a study by Vega et al. (2018), borderline patients with ($n = 20$) and without ($n = 20$) a history of NSSI and individuals without BPD and NSSI ($n = 20$) underwent an fMRI while performing a gambling task (age range 18–45 years). Borderline patients with a history of NSSI exhibited enhanced activation of the orbitofrontal cortex following an unexpectedly high reward compared with borderline patients who did not self-injure and the control group.

Poon et al. (2019) investigated whether altered reward processing was also associated with adolescents' thoughts of NSSI. Seventy-one adolescents (Mage = 12.52; age range 12–14 years) underwent an fMRI while performing a reward paradigm (i.e., card-guessing task). Results showed that early adolescents with NSSI thoughts exhibited heightened activation in the bilateral putamen in response to monetary reward compared to adolescents without NSSI thoughts, indicating heightened neural sensitivity to reward (but no significant heightened activation in the nucleus accumbens [NAcc] and the ventromedial prefrontal cortex [vmPFC]). Haruno and Kawato (2006) reported that the putamen is important in learning stimulus-response associations and the preparation and execution of reward-oriented motor reactions.

Finally, in a study by Hooley et al. (2020), 15 adults who reported self-cutting and 15 adults without a history of self-cutting (age range 18–31 years) underwent an fMRI while viewing neutral, positive, and negative pictures of the IAPS and NSSI-related images. Compared to adults without a history of NSSI, adults with a history of NSSI showed decreased amygdala and increased cingulate cortex and orbitofrontal cortex (OFC) activation to NSSI and negative IAPS pictures. Adults with a history of NSSI also showed increased amygdala and OFC activation to positive images. None of the two groups demonstrated significant activation within regions more typically associated with reward (NAcc and ventral tegmental area) during any conditions (which was to be expected given the participants did not rate the neutral/negative/positive IAPS and NSSI-related pictures as rewarding).

These aforementioned mixed findings (i.e., hyper- vs. hypoactivation of rewards circuits in NSSI) can possibly be understood from a development perspective (Poon et al., 2019. In early adolescents, increased reward system activation (in the putamen) may be associated with thoughts about future NSSI. In contrast, heightened activity in the reward circuitry has been related to active NSSI engagement in mid- to late adolescents (Poon et al., 2019). Chronic engagement in NSSI may alter and desensitize the reactivity of the reward system in middle- to late adolescents, leading to a blunted response over time (Poon et al., 2019). Therefore, longitudinal studies are particularly needed to understand the changes in developmental trajectories of reward processing abnormalities preceding and following NSSI engagement over time (Kaess et al., 2021; Poon et al., 2019).

Besides age differences of the studied populations, the use of different types of rewards applied in the studies (e.g., monetary reward, picture of NSSI, and cold pain stimulus as substitute of NSSI) could explain why other areas of the reward circuitry were reactive. In future fMRI studies, researchers should not only take the presence/absence of NSSI into account but also characteristics of the behavior itself (e.g., chronicity, frequency, and number of NSSI methods).

Neurotransmitters and the Positive Valence Systems

Another mechanism that may reinforce the painful experience of NSSI is the release of endogenous opioids (e.g., β endorphins) following NSSI (Franz et al., 2019). The binding of increased opioids (e.g., β endorphins) with μ and δ receptors is related to pain reduction and feelings of euphoria (experienced as a rewarding "rush" or "high"; Stanley et al., 2010). Studies have shown that patients with a history of NSSI are characterized by lower levels of opioids than patients without a history of NSSI (Stanley et al., 2010), so the release of opioids after painful NSSI (which bind with μ and δ receptors) may have an analgesic and euphoric effect for patients with low levels of opioids (Bresin & Gordon, 2013; Störkel et al., 2021). Several authors have shown that β endorphins levels were higher in adults with developmental disorders and adolescents after NSSI engagement than their morning levels of β endorphins (see also Sandman et al., 1997; van der Venne et al., 2020; Westlund Schreiner et al., 2015). Empirical findings also showed that treatment with a long-lasting opioid antagonist (e.g., naltrexone or naloxone) blocks the reward of the increased endogenous opioids caused by NSSI and leads to the extinction of NSSI in individuals with developmental disorders (for a review, see Sher & Stanley, 2008).

Psychophysiology of Positive Affective Processing via Reflexive and Facial Electromyography

Mayo et al. (2021) investigated emotional reactivity toward positive and negative pictures via facial electromyography (EMG) and via self-reported ratings of valence and arousal of these pictures in 30 female adolescents with and without NSSI. Positive emotional stimuli activate the zygomatic muscle (i.e., smile), and negative emotional stimuli activate the corrugator muscle (i.e., frown; Mayo & de Wit, 2015). The adolescents with NSSI responded to the pictures with higher levels of positive (e.g., zygomatic) and negative (e.g., corrugator) reactivity compared to healthy controls. The authors did not find differences in self-reported valence and arousal of the pictures between adolescents with and without NSSI (Mayo et al., 2021). The lack of difference in self-reported positive reactivity between adolescents with and without NSSI confirms findings of previous studies (e.g., Boyes et al., 2020; Mettler et al., 2021). Further research is needed to investigate actual versus perceived positive emotional reactivity (Perini et al., 2021).

Franklin et al. (2013) investigated psychophysiological indices of positive affect (startle postauricular reactivity) and negative affect (startle eyeblink reactivity) after painful electric shocks (proxy of NSSI) to test the pain offset relief theory of NSSI in 21 self-cutters and 21 controls. They observed that the cessation of the electric shocks were associated with an increased positive affective response (postauricular reflex) and a reduced negative affective response (startle eye blink reflex) in both groups (but more pronounced in the NSSI group).

Reactivity of the Positive Valence Systems as a Transdiagnostic Mechanism?

NSSI constitutes a transdiagnostic behavior, which occurs in the context of a broad range of mental disorders (Kiekens, Hasking, Boyes, et al., 2018; Kiekens et al., 2021; Liu, 2021), including anxiety and mood disorders (Bentley et al., 2015), EDs (Cucchi et al., 2016), substance use disorders (SUDs) (Benjet et al., 2017), and personality disorders (Nock et al., 2006). Prospective research has shown that the presence of a mental disorder increases risk for NSSI (Fox et al., 2015; Kiekens et al., 2019), whereas recent findings suggest that NSSI is also a behavioral marker of newly emerging mental disorders (Daukantaitė et al., 2021; Kiekens et al., 2021; Wilkinson et al., 2018). Furthermore, NSSI often co-occurs with suicidal forms of self-injury (e.g., Benjet et al., 2017) and is a risk factor for later suicide attempts (Franklin et al., 2017; Kiekens, Hasking, Boyes, et al., 2018) (see Victor et al., this volume, for more on NSSI and suicide). In what follows, we will investigate whether the comorbidity between NSSI behaviors and ED behaviors (e.g., binge eating, and vomiting) and SUD (e.g., alcohol and cannabis) can partially be explained by shared characteristics of the positive valence systems. Are these behaviors driven by (a) positive reinforcement, (b) reward-seeking temperament, (c) cognitive biases, and/or (d) over/underactivation of the reward circuitry in the brain.

Comorbidity between NSSI and ED/SUD

Recent meta-analyses clearly show comorbidity between NSSI on the one hand and ED/SUD on the other hand (Bresin & Mekawi, 2020; Cucchi et al., 2016; Escelsior et al., 2021). Cucchi et al. (2016) reported that 27.3% (95% CI: [23.8–31%]) of ED patients reported a life-time history of NSSI, 21.8% for anorexia nervosa (95% CI: [18.5–25.6%]), and 32.7% for bulimia nervosa (95% CI: [26.9–39.1%]). The lifetime history of NSSI was significantly higher (OR = 1.77) for bulimia nervosa compared to anorexia nervosa patients. Furthermore, Nock et al. (2006) reported that 59.6% of adolescents inpatients who engaged in NSSI reported at least one SUD: alcohol abuse (18%)/dependence (16.8%), 38.6% nicotine dependence, marijuana abuse (12.6%)/dependence (29.5%), and other substance abuse (3.4%)/dependence (5.6%). Kiekens et al. (2021) investigated the prevalence of alcohol/drugs abuse disorders in 20,842 first-year college students, and found that 10.3% of students who engage in lifetime NSSI reported an alcohol use disorder; and 7.3% a drug use disorder (compared to 6.3% and 2.6%, respectively, in students with no history of NSSI). Also, Bresin and Mekawi (2020) found a significant positive association between NSSI and alcohol use, (OR [odds ratio] = 1.78, 95% CI [confidence interval]: [1.53–2.07]). Moderation analysis showed that this relation was stronger for younger participants and participants with more severe alcohol use (Bresin & Mekawi, 2020). Finally, Escelsior et al. (2021) showed that cannabinoid use was significantly positively related with (N)SSI cross-sectionally, (OR = 1.569, 95% CI = [1.167–2.108]) and longitudinally, (OR = 2.569, 95% CI = [2.207–3.256]).

Automatic/Social Positive Reinforcement as a Transdiagnostic Mechanism of NSSI, ED, and SUD

As described earlier in the four-function model of NSSI (Nock & Prinstein, 2004; Taylor et al., 2018), NSSI is clearly driven by automatic positive reinforcement (i.e., to feel relaxed) and social positive reinforcement (i.e., to get help, to get attention).

CROSS-SECTIONAL STUDIES

Wedig and Nock (2010) applied the four-function model of NSSI to the presence of binge eating/purging behaviors and found that both binge eating and purging were also reported to be positively reinforced. The most frequently endorsed automatic positive reinforcement functions of binge eating/purging were "to give yourself something to do when you are alone" (binge eating: 72.9%, purging: 46.4%), "to feel relaxed" (binge eating: 45%; purging: 56.5%), and "to feel something at all" (binge eating: 43.4%; purging: 44.7%). The most common social positive reinforcement functions were "to get a reaction from someone, even if it is negative" (binge eating: 18.1%, purging: 21.8%) and "to let others know how desperate you were feeling" (binge eating: 17%, purging: 21%). As is the case for NSSI, automatic positive reinforcement is more commonly reported by individuals with EDs than social positive reinforcement.

Finally, drinking motives have also been classified in four domains based on the dimensions (Cooper, 1994) positive-negative reinforcement and internal-external reinforcement: mood enhancement (positive-internal; i.e., drinking to increase positive affect), social (positive-external, i.e., drinking to gain social rewards or facilitation), emotional coping (negative-internal), and conformity (negative-external, i.e., drinking to avoid peer rejection; Pallavi & Klanecky, 2016). According to a review by Kuntsche et al. (2005), most adolescents drink for enhancement or social motives in the sense of enjoyment. Jerez and Covielle (1998), for example, reported that 80% of adolescents drink for enjoyment, 7% to improve bad mood, 4.6% to be accepted by peers, and 1% to relax. However, drinking to cope with negative emotional states is particularly related with alcohol problems/abuse (Kuntsche et al., 2005). The change from positive reinforcement to negative reinforcement functions of alcohol abuse, goes along with the neurobiological changes during the addiction process (Koob & Volkow, 2016). Koob and Volkow (2016) stated that earlier stages of addiction primarily involve pleasure-seeking or gratification, whereas later stages of addiction are characterized by relief of negative affect. Ross et al. (2018) investigated the motives of marijuana use in a sample of 41 participants (29.3% met criteria for cannabis dependence) and reported that almost one half (49.2%) used marijuana for pleasure, while 10.4% used marijuana to cope or to conform. Taken together, the positive reinforcement functions of substance use disorders seem to be more frequently endorsed than the positive reinforcement function of NSSI/ED.

LONGITUDINAL STUDIES: EMA STUDIES

EMA studies investigating the course of positive affect preceding and following NSSI showed a decrease of positive affect before NSSI and an increase in positive affect following NSSI in four of the six studies (Hepp et al., 2020). Several studies also investigated the course of positive affect preceding and following binge eating and vomiting behaviors in patients with anorexia nervosa and bulimia nervosa (e.g., Engel et al., 2013; Smyth et al., 2007). Positive affect has been found to decrease before binge-eating and vomiting and increase after engagement in bulimic behaviors (e.g., Engel et al., 2013; Smyth et al., 2007). Dvorak and Simons (2014) investigated the associations between positive mood and the likelihood/intensity of drinking in undergraduate students. Consistent with the enhancement motive of drinking, results showed that positive mood was consistently positively associated with both the likelihood and intensity of alcohol use (Dvorak & Simons, 2014). Similar results were reported in other EMA studies investigating positive mood preceding alcohol abuse (e.g., Hussong et al., 2001; Swendsen et al., 2000). Harder et al. (2014) investigated the association between the number of alcohol drinks and positive mood and showed that increased alcohol use significantly predicted decreased happiness the next day. Finally, Ross et al. (2018) investigated positive affect following marijuana use utilizing EMA and taking dependence status into account. Positive affect following marijuana use was higher for participants who met dependence criteria, whereas participants without dependence had no significant within-person change in positive affect following marijuana use (Ross et al., 2018).

Temperament/Personality Traits as a Common Mechanism of NSSI, ED, and SUD

In what follows, we describe various temperament and personality traits that underlie NSSI, ED and SUD. The following models will be taken into account: (a) the TCI model, (b) the UPPS-P model, (c) the Big Five Model, and finally (d) the BISBAS model as guiding frameworks.

TCI MODEL

As previously described, the presence/absence of lifetime NSSI was not significantly related to TCI Novelty Seeking and significantly negatively related to Reward Dependence (Attachment). In a systematic review of the association between TCI-dimensions and ED diagnoses, only bulimia patients reported significantly higher scores on Novelty Seeking compared to controls, and none of the ED groups differed significantly from the healthy controls on Reward Dependence (Atiye et al., 2015; Farstad et al., 2016). Several studies also investigated temperament and character differences between participants with and without alcohol/drug addiction using the TCI (Le Bon et al., 2004; Milivojevic et al., 2012). Results clearly showed that alcohol- and drug (heroin)-addicted participants scored significantly higher on Novelty Seeking than the control group. The three groups did not significantly differ from each other on Reward Dependence.

UPPS-P MODEL

Studies on the association between the UPPS-P model and NSSI found that NSSI is not related to Sensation-Seeking, and positively related to Positive Urgency in two of four studies. In a meta-analysis on the association between the UPPS-P model and psychopathology (Berg et al., 2015), the authors reported that both Sensation-Seeking and Positive Urgency were strongly related to the frequency of substance and alcohol use (e.g., Coskunpinar et al., 2013). Although some studies report a small positive correlation between Sensation Seeking and bulimic symptoms (Fischer et al., 2008), the overall effect size of this association was not significant (Berg et al., 2015). The authors noted that there were not enough studies available in the literature to draw firm conclusions about the association between eating disorders and Positive Urgency (Berg et al., 2015).

BIG FIVE

NSSI (characteristics) did not show significant associations with the Big Five trait of Extraversion. Similar findings were reported for the association between ED and Extraversion. Systematic reviews (Cassin & von Ranson, 2005; Farstad et al., 2016) reported weakly negative to nonexistent associations between extraversion and ED symptomatology in nonclinical and clinical samples. These findings were also confirmed in systematic reviews on the association between SUD and the Big Five trait of Extraversion (Kotov et al., 2010; Ruiz et al., 2008)

BISBAS MODEL

The frequency of NSSI and the number of methods used to engage in NSSI were significantly associated with BAS reactivity. In a review by Bijttebier et al. (2009), the associations between BAS reactivity and EDs showed that compared to controls, patients with bulimia nervosa (BN) reported higher levels of BAS reactivity. In contrast, restrictive anorexia nervosa (AN) patients showed lower levels of BAS reactivity (Claes et al., 2006). In patients with eating disorders, bulimic AN/BN patients reported significantly higher BAS reactivity scores than restrictive AN patients (Beck et al., 2009). Concerning the association between BAS reactivity and alcohol and other substance addictions, the literature consistently shows robust positive associations between BAS reactivity and alcohol and other substance addictions in both community (e.g., Franken & Muris, 2006) and clinical (Johnson et al., 2003) samples (for a detailed review, see Bijttebier et al., 2009).

Cognitive Biases Related to Positive Valence Systems

In the same vein that appetitive motivation toward NSSI is associated with an attentional bias toward NSSI-related cues, appetitive motivation in EDs and SUDs is also related to an attentional bias toward food- and drug-related stimuli, respectively (Field et al., 2016). In their review, Field et al. (2016) concluded that attentional bias for food/drugs in obesity/SUDs predicts future behaviors, exerts a causal influence on consummatory behavior, and reflects appetitive motivational processes, but only when the incentive value of the food/drug is high (Field et al., 2016). Through an associative learning process, food-/drug-related cues acquire strong motivational properties (because the consumption of food/drugs goes along with dopamine release in the reward-related brain areas), and as a consequence, these cues grab one's attention and guide behavior toward the incentive cue (Robinson & Berridge, 1993, cited in Field et al. 2016).

Reactivity of Reward System in the Brain as Common Mechanisms of NSSI, ED, and SUD

As described earlier, NSSI is related to hyper/hypoactivity of the reward areas in the brain, depending on the developmental stage of participants. These changes in the reactivity of the reward systems also go along with changes in dopamine regulation. Similar neurobiological findings have been described for both SUDs and ED behaviors (more specific, binge eating) in the three-stage addiction model of SUDs (see Koob & Volkow, 2016) and food addiction (Adams et al., 2019). When a substance/palatable food is consumed, the brain releases dopamine and positive feelings (binge/intoxication phase). Over time, this increase in dopamine leads to the downregulation of dopamine receptors, causing a reduction in positive feelings during substance/food consumption. This decrease in positive affect coupled/combined with other symptoms such as craving, withdrawal, and emotional and behavioral problems leads the person to engage in compensatory behaviors by increasing substance/food consumption (withdrawal/negative affect phase) (see Adams et al., 2019; Koob & Volkow, 2016).

Psychophysiology of Positive Affective Processing Related to NSSI, ED, and SUD

As described earlier, individuals with NSSI showed a heightened emotional reactivity to positive and negative pictures compared to individuals without NSSI by means of a facial EMG (Mayo et al., 2021). The adolescents with NSSI responded to the positive/negative pictures with higher levels of, respectively, zygomatic muscle (i.e., smile) and corrugator muscle (i.e., frown) reactivity compared to healthy controls. In reaction to the cessation of a painful stimulus (proxy of NSSI), individuals with NSSI and healthy controls showed psychophysiological indices of increased positive affect (startle postauricular reactivity) and decreased negative affect (startle eyeblink reactivity) (Franklin et al., 2013). In EDs, Racine et al. (2018) investigated the associations between psychophysiological responses (reflexive and facial EMG) to food versus neutral cues and ED symptoms in college students. Binge eating was related to an increased postauricular reflex, indicating a positive attitude toward food versus neutral images. Disturbed ED cognitions were related to more corrugator activity (i.e., frown) to food versus neutral cues, indicating a negative attitude toward food (Racine et al., 2018). Finally, in patients with drug abuse, drug cues triggered increased reactivity of the zygomatic muscle reactivity (i.e., smile) and decreased corrugator muscle reactivity (i.e., frown) (for a review, see Mayo & De Wit, 2015).

Transdiagnostic Treatment Focusing on Positive Valence Systems

Researchers have clearly shown that exposure to NSSI-related cues elicits attentional bias toward these NSSI cues, decreases positive affect, and increases NSSI urges, enhancing the risk of engaging in NSSI (classic conditioning). NSSI engagement can elicit positive affect immediately following the behavior (linked to release of opiates in the reward-related areas of the brain), which positively reinforces the behavior (operant conditioning). A similar behavioral chain can be described for engagement in eating/substance use behaviors.

At the start of treatment, it is important to assess the antecedents, functions, and consequences of the NSSI (and related behaviors) using functional analyses. Insight into the triggers (cues) that elicit the behavior and the consequences of the behavior (automatic/social reinforcers/punishers) will guide treatment. If more self-harm behaviors are present, it is essential to make functional analyses of the different self-harm behaviors to explore to what extent they share the same function (i.e., whether they are functional equivalent). In case they are functionally equivalent, the therapist needs to be vigilant for behavior shifts, which means that a decrease in one type of self-harming behavior (e.g., NSSI) can lead to an increase in another self-harming behavior (e.g., binge eating), which has the same function (e.g., Garke et al., 2019; Green et al., 2020). In that case, focusing on transdiagnostic mechanisms (e.g., emotional regulation and impulse regulation.) that tackle different types of self-harming behaviors at the same time will be the treatment of choice.

Given that attentional bias toward NSSI-related cues can trigger a decrease in PA and increase the urge to engage in NSSI behaviors, it is crucial that patients learn skills to manage cue-elicited urges and tolerate changes in affective states in reaction to NSSI cues. In the field of obesity/SUDs, it has already been shown that attentional bias modification training can lead to reduced food/substance intake (Adams et al., 2019). As far as we know, attentional bias modification training has not been applied yet in patients who engage in NSSI. Besides training attentional bias modification, patients can also learn skills to cope with distressing feelings and urges triggered by NSSI-related cues. This way, they become more equipped to deal with transdiagnostic processes that link exposure to NSSI-related cues to NSSI behaviors (Riquino et al., 2020). These transdiagnostic interventions (i.e., emotion regulation and impulse regulation) can also be used to target other self-harming behaviors.

Next, it is important that the patient learns how to replace self-harming behaviors with more self-caring behaviors that serve the same function(s), and have the same result (e.g., automatic/social positive reinforcement), as the self-harming behaviors. "No pain, no gain" needs to be translated into "Without pain, also gain." It is crucial that patients themselves look for alternative behaviors that can be applied when alone or in company and lead to fast emotional release but do not cause harm. In the cutting-down program, Taylor et al. (2015) advised selecting alternative behaviors that appeal to different senses, for instance, to look at the stars, to listen to music/to call a friend, to taste herbal tea, to pet a dog (touch), and to smell essential oils. Given that (rewarding) functions of self-harming behaviors are individual-specific, self-caring alternatives need to fit the individual patient. Evidence-based transdiagnostic interventions that deal with NSSI and other self-harming behaviors are dialectical behavioral therapy (Linehan, 1993) and the cutting-down program (Taylor et al., 2011; Taylor et al., 2015) for adolescents as well as adults.

Finally, if the opioid system is central to repetitive NSSI (e.g., in patients with developmental disorders), then treatment with an opioid antagonist (e.g., naloxone) can block the reward of the enhanced endogenous opioids that is caused by self-injury, thereby facilitating NSSI cessation in these patients (e.g., Sher & Stanley, 2008). However, it should be mentioned that evidence for the use of an opioid antagonist is scarce and mixed for patients without a development disorder (e.g., Sher & Stanley, 2008).

Case Illustration

Jane is a 16-year-old girl who describes herself as "outgoing" and "kick-seeking" (temperament/personality). Recently, her boyfriend broke up their relationship, which made Jane very sad. She felt the urge to cut herself with a razor blade. While engaging in NSSI, she felt high and her sadness faded away (automatic reinforcement). Although she felt pain when cutting her skin, the offset of pain when removing the razor blade made her feel good and relieved (pain offset release theory). Jane talks about NSSI with her friends, who also self-injure and understand her, which helps to battle her loneliness (social reinforcement). Jane also engages in binge eating to comfort herself, followed by purging behaviors to avoid weight gain. She mentions behavior shifts such that an increase in NSSI is accompanied by a reduction in binge eating and vice versa (functional equivalence). Engaging in less harmful behaviors to deal with emotions is difficult, as Jane reports that these are not as effective. Together with her therapist, Jane is working on practicing more self-care (therapy).

Suggestions for Future Research

Besides the strengths of the studies focusing on NSSI and reactivity of the positive valence systems, there are some valuable suggestions for future research. First, the characteristics of NSSI that were assessed varied across studies. Most studies focused on a lifetime history of NSSI and compared individuals who engaged in NSSI at least once in their lifetime with individuals who did not. Furthermore, current engagement in NSSI and frequency and versatility of NSSI acts were frequently not examined. Therefore, future studies are advised also to assess associations between reward sensitivity and NSSI characteristics among participants with a history of NSSI. The latter is a heterogeneous group, and variability within this group on severity indices (e.g., with and without DSM-5 NSSI disorder) may explain different patterns of reward sensitivity (and related comorbidity).

Second, the relationship between reward sensitivity and NSSI engagement can also be moderated by age and gender, but few studies considered sociodemographic differences. This may be because samples are typically composed of mainly female adolescents and young adults. Hence, to investigate this possibility in future research, studies are needed with more representative samples, which include sufficient males and (older) adults.

Third, many studies use self-report measures to assess the reactivity of the positive valence systems, whereas studies focusing on performance-based tasks and fMRI studies are scarce and often based on small samples. Additionally, the cues used to investigate the reactivity of the positive valence systems are often different, which may cause activation of different brain areas. For example, while some studies used pathology-specific cues (e.g., NSSI/food/drugs-related pictures), others relied on general rewarding stimuli (like money).

Fourth, most of the studies are based on a cross-sectional design, making it impossible to investigate the temporal relationship of the features under investigation. Therefore, more longitudinal studies focusing on reward system reactivity and NSSI (and related) behaviors are necessary to investigate the directionality of effect between these variables, the temporal development of these states/traits and behaviors, and possible behavior shifts that are driven by the same reward-related traits.

Finally, apart from investigating between-person variability in the associations between reward-related traits and NSSI/ED/SUD behaviors, it is equally important to investigate these relations on a within-person level with individuals serving as their own control (Piccirillo & Rodebaugh, 2019). From a therapeutic point of view, it is imperative to know—on an individual-level—how reward-related traits, temperamental features, and situational cues together increase risk for NSSI and related self-harming behaviors in daily life. Insight in this "individual signature" will facilitate personalized and more effective treatment for our patients so we can maximally help them resist harmful behaviors and stimulate self-care and support their recovery process.

Conclusions

In the present chapter, we investigated the association between (re)activity of the positive valence systems and NSSI based on different assessment methods (i.e., self-report, performance-based tasks, and fMRI studies). We also investigated whether the transdiagnostic mechanism of reward sensitivity could partially explain the comorbidity between NSSI and other self-harming behaviors (i.e., binge eating, purging, and substance (ab)use). Based on our narrative overview, we can conclude that NSSI, ED, and SUD have both shared and distinct correlations with measures of reward sensitivity. All three behaviors seem to be triggered by specific cues (i.e., NSSI materials, food, and drugs/alcohol) and patients show attentional bias toward these cues. NSSI, ED, and SUD can be automatically/socially positively reinforced, which explains the continuation of these behaviors for some people. Furthermore, on the neurobiological level, all three behaviors seem—at the starting phase—to be related to a hyperreactivity of the reward-related systems in the brain, which is driven by dopamine release. However, over time, dysregulation of the dopaminergic system leads to a hyporeactivity of the reward-related systems, which may increase susceptibility for the use of NSSI, ED, and SUD behaviors (habit learning) to increase positive emotional experiences (often by taking away negative affect).

However, more research is needed concerning attentional biases and neuroimaging techniques to confirm the preliminary conclusions. On the level of temperamental features, the findings are more mixed. It seems that NSSI and ED behaviors have more common temperamental features than substance (ab)use. Whereas NSSI/ED in EMA studies seem to be preceded by a decrease in positive affect, substance (ab)use seems to be preceded by an increase in positive affect (at least in the early stages). In the same vein, patients who engage in substance (ab)use are more prone to novelty seeking/sensation seeking than those without a history of substance abuse. Yet, individuals who engage in NSSI/ED show similar levels of novelty seeking/sensation seeking than peers without a history of NSSI. On the level of BAS reactivity/reward sensitivity, we found that NSSI, ED, and SUD are related to increased BAS reactivity/reward sensitivity, making individuals sensitive to the rewarding effect (positive reinforcement) of these behaviors. However, while patients with NSSI and ED also report elevated levels of BIS sensitivity (punishment sensitivity) besides BAS reactivity, this is not (or rarely) the case for individuals who engage in SUD. To conclude, research on the reward system remains inconclusive and requires further research (see also Kaess et al., 2021).

References

Adams, R. C., Sedgmond, J., Maizy, L., Chambers, C. D., & Lawrence, N. S. (2019). Food addiction: Implications for the diagnosis and treatment of overeating. *Nutrients*, *11*, Article 2086. https://doi.org/10.3390/nu11092086

Ammerman, B., Berman, M. E., & McCloskey, M. S. (2018). Assessing non-suicidal self-injury in the laboratory. *Archives of Suicide Research*, *22*, 193–223. https://doi.org/10.1080/13811118.2017.1319312

Ammerman, B. A., Kleiman, E. M., Jenkins, A. L., Berman, M. E., & McCloskey, M. S. (2017). Using propensity scores to examine the association between behavioral inhibition/activation and nonsuicidal and suicidal self-injury. *Crisis*, *38*, 227–236. https://doi.org/10.1027/0227-5910/a000436

Andrewes, H. E., Hulbert, C., Cotton, S. M., Betts, J., & Chanen, A. M. (2017). An ecological momentary assessment investigation of complex and conflicting emotions in youth with borderline personality disorder. *Psychiatry Research*, *252*, 102–110. https://doi.org/10.1016/j.psychres.2017.01.100

Armey, M. F., Crowther, J. H., & Miller, I. W. (2011). Changes in ecological momentary assessment reported affect associated with episodes of nonsuicidal self-injury. *Behavior Therapy*, *42*(4), 579–588. https://doi.org/10.1016/j.beth.2011.01.002

Atiye, M., Jouko, M., & Raevuori-Helkamaa, A. (2015). A meta-analysis of temperament in eating disorders. *European Eating Disorders Review*, *23*, 89–99. https://doi.org/10.1002/erv.2342

Baetens, I., Claes, L., Willem, L., Muehlenkamp, J. J., & Bijttebier, P. (2011). The relationship between nonsuicidal self-injury and temperament in male and female adolescents based on child- and parent-report. *Personality and Individual Differences*, *50*, 527–530. https://doi.org/10.1016/j.paid.2010.11.015

Beck, I., Smits, D. J. M., Claes, L., Vandereycken, W., & Bijttebier, P. (2009). Psychometric evaluation of the behavioural inhibition/behavioural activation system scales and the sensitivity to punishment and sensitivity to reward questionnaire in a sample of eating disordered patients. *Personality and Individual Differences*, *47*, 407–412. https://doi.org/10.1016/j.paid.2009.04.007

Benjet, C., González-Herrera, I., Castro-Silva, E., Méndez, E., Borges, G., Casanova, L., & Medina-Mora, M. E. (2017). Non-suicidal self-injury in Mexican young adults: Prevalence, associations with suicidal behavior and psychiatric disorders, and DSM-5 proposed diagnostic criteria. *Journal of Affective Disorders*, *215*, 1–8. https://doi.org/10.1016/j.jad.2017.03.025

Bentley, K. H., Cassiello-Robbins, C. F., Vittorio, L., Sauer-Zavala, S., & Barlow, D. H. (2015). The association between nonsuicidal self-injury and the emotional disorders: A meta-analytic review. *Clinical Psychology Review*, *37*, 72–88. https://doi.org/10.1016/j.cpr.2015.02.006

Bentley, K. H., Nock, M. K., & Barlow, D. H. (2014). The four-function model of non-suicidal self-injury: Key directions for future research. *Clinical Psychological Science*, *2*, 638–656. https://doi.org/10.1177/2167702613514563

Berg, J. M., Latzman, R. D., Bliwise, N. G., & Lilienfeld, S. O. (2015). Parsing the heterogeneity of impulsivity: A meta-analytic review of the behavioral implications of the UPPS for psychopathology. *Psychological Assessment*, *4*, 1129–1146. https://doi.org/10.1037/pas0000111

Bijttebier, P., Beck, I., Claes, L., & Vandereycken, W. (2009). Gray's reinforcement sensitivity theory as a framework for research on personality-psychopathology associations. *Clinical Psychology Review*, *29*, 421–430. https://doi.org/10.1016/j.cpr.2009.04.002

Boyes, M. E., Wilmot, A., & Hasking, P. A. (2020). Nonsuicidal self-injury-related differences in the experience of negative and positive emotion. *Suicide and Life-Threatening Behaviors*, *50*, 437–448. https://doi.org/10.1111/sltb.12599

Bresin, K., & Gordon, K. H. (2013). Endogenous opioids and nonsuicidal self-injury: A mechanism of affect regulation. *Neuroscience & Biobehavioral Reviews*, *37*, 374–383. https://doi.org/10.1016/j.neubiorev.2013.01.020

Bresin, K., & Mekawi, Y. (2020). Different ways to drown out the pain: A meta-analysis of the association between nonsuicidal self-injury and alcohol use. *Archives of Suicide Research*, *26*(2), 348–369. https://doi.org/10.1080/13811118.2020.1802378

Buelens, T., Luyckx, K., Verschueren, M., Schoevaerts, K., Dierckx, E., Depestele, L., & Claes, L. (2020). Temperament and character traits of female eating disorder patients with(out) non-suicidal self-injury. *Journal of Clinical Medicine*, *9*(4), Article 1207. https://doi.org/10.3390/jcm9041207

Burke, T. A., Shao, S., Jacobucci, R., Kautz, M., Alloy, L. B., & Ammerman, B. A. (2022). Examining momentary associations between behavioral approach system indices and nonsuicidal self-injury urges. *Journal of Affective Disorders*, *296*, 244–249. https://doi.org/10.1016/j.jad.2021.09.029

Burke, T. A., Stange, J. P., Hamilton, J. L., Cohen, J. N., O'Garro-Moore, J., Daryanani, I., Abramson, L. Y., & Alloy, L. B. (2015). Cognitive and emotion-regulatory mediators of the relationship between behavioral approach system sensitivity and non-suicidal self-injury frequency. *Suicide and Life-Threatening Behavior, 45*, 495–504. https://doi.org/10.1111/sltb.12145

Carver, C. S., & White, T. L. (1994). Behavioral inhibition, behavioral activation, and affective responses to impending reward and punishment: The BIS/BAS scales. *Journal of Personality and Social Psychology, 67*, Article 319. https://doi.org/10.1037/0022-3514.67.2.319

Cassin, S. E., & von Ranson, K. M. (2005). Personality and eating disorders: A decade in review. *Clinical Psychology Review, 25*, 895–916. https://doi.org/10.1016/j.cpr.2005.04.012

Cerutti, R., Presaghi, F., Manca, M., & Gratz, K. L. (2012). Deliberate self-harm behavior among Italian young adults: Correlations with clinical and nonclinical dimensions of personality. *American Journal of Orthopsychiatry, 82*, 298–308. https://doi.org/10.1111/j.1939-0025.2012.01169.x

Cha, C. B., Augenstein, T. M., Frost, K. H., Gallagher, K., D'Angelo, E. J., & Nock, M. K. (2016). Using implicit and explicit measure to predict non-suicidal self-injury among adolescent inpatients. *Journal of American Academy of Child and Adolescent Psychiatry, 55*, 62–68. https://doi.org/10.1016/j.jaac.2015.10.008

Chapman, A. L., Derbidge, C. M., Cooney, E., Hong, P. Y., & Linehan, M. M. (2009). Temperament as a prospective predictor of self-injury among patients with borderline personality disorder. *Journal of Personality Disorders, 23*, 122–140. https://doi.org/10.1521/pedi.2009.23.2.122

Claes, L., Islam, M. A. I., Fagundo, A. B., Jimenez-Murcia, S., Granero, R., Agüera, Z., Rossi, E., Menchon, J. M., & Fernandez-Aranda, F. (2015). The relationship between non-suicidal self-injury and the UPPS-P impulsivity facets in eating disorders and healthy controls. *PLoS One, 10*(5), Article e0126083. https://doi.org/10.1371/journal.pone.0126083

Claes, L., Jiménez-Murcia, S., Agüera, Z., Castro, R., Sanchez, I., Menchon, J. M., & Fernandez-Aranda, F. (2012). Male eating disorder patients with and without non-suicidal self-injury: A comparison of psychopathological and personality features. *European Eating Disorders Review, 20*, 335–338. https://doi.org/10.1002/erv.1161

Claes, L., & Muehlenkamp, J. (2013). The relationship between the UPPS-P impulsivity dimensions and non-suicidal self-injury characteristics in male and female high school students. *Psychiatry Journal, 2013*, Article 654847. https://doi.org/10.1155/2013/654847

Claes, L., Nederkoorn, C., Vandereycken, W., Guerrieri, R., & Vertommen, H. (2006). Impulsiveness and lack of inhibitory control in eating disorders. *Eating Behaviors, 7*, 196–203. https://doi.org/10.1016/j.eatbeh.2006.05.001

Claes, L., Norré, J., Van Assche, L., & Bijttebier, P. (2014). Non-suicidal self-injury (functions) in eating disorders: associations with reactive and regulative temperament. *Personality and Individual Differences, 57*, 65–69. https://doi.org/10.1016/j.paid.2013.09.022

Cloninger, C. R. (1994). *The Temperament and Character Inventory: A guide for its development and use*. Centre for Psychobiology of Personality, Washington University.

Cloninger, C. R. (1999). *The Temperament and Character Inventory-Revised (TCI-R)*. Centre for Psychobiology of Personality, Washington University.

Cloninger, C. R., Svrakic, D. M., Bayon, C., & Przybeck, T. R. (1999). Measurement of psychopathology as variants of personality. In C. R. Cloninger (Ed.), *Personality and psychopathology* (pp. 33–65). Psychiatric Press.

Cloninger, C. R., Svrakic, D. M., & Przybeck, T. R. (1993). A psychobiological model of temperament and character. *Archives of General Psychiatry, 50*, 975–990.

Cohen, J. N., Stange, J. P., Hamilton, J. L., Burke, T. A., Jenkins, A., Ong, M.-L., Heimberg, R. G., Abramson, L. Y., & Alloy, L. B. (2015). The interaction of affective states and cognitive vulnerabilities in the prediction of non-suicidal self-injury. *Cognition and Emotion, 29*, 539–547. https://doi.org/10.1080/02699931.2014.918872

Cooper, M. L. (1994). Motivations for alcohol use among adolescents: Development and validation of a four-factor model. *Psychological Assessment, 6*, 117–128. https://doi.org/10.1037/1040-3590.6.2.117

Coskunpinar, A., Dir, A. L., & Cyders, M. A. (2013). Multidimensionality in impulsivity and alohol use: A meta-analysis using the UPPS model of impulsivity. *Clinical and Experimental Research, 37*, 1441–1450. https://doi.org/10.1111/acer.12131

Costa, P. T., & McCrae, R. R. (1992). *Revised NEO Personality Inventory (NEO PI-R) and NEO Five-Factor Inventory (NEO-FFI)*. Psychological Assessment Resources.

Cucchi, A., Ryan, D., Konstantakopoulo, G., Stroumpa, S., Kacar, A. S., Renshaw, S., Landau, S., & Kravariti, E. (2016). Lifetime prevalence of non-suicidal self-injury in patients with eating disorders: A systematic review and meta-analysis. *Psychological Medicine, 46*, 1345–1358. https://doi.org/10.1017/S0033291716000027

Cuthbert, B. N., & Kozak, M. J. (2013). Constructing constructs for psychopathology: The NIMH research domain criteria. *Journal of Abnormal Psychology, 122*, 928–937. https://doi.org/10.1037/a0034028

Daukantaitė, D., Lundh, L. G., Wångby-Lundh, M., Claréus, B., Bjärehed, J., Zhou, Y., & Liljedahl, S. I. (2021). What happens to young adults who have engaged in self-injurious behavior as adolescents? A 10-year follow-up. *European Child & Adolescent Psychiatry, 30*, 475–492. https://doi.org/10.1007/s00787-020-01533-4

Depue, R. A., & Collins, P. F. (1999). Neurobiology of the structure of personality: Dopamine, facilitation of incentive motivation, and extraversion. *Behavioral and Brain Sciences, 22*(3), 491–569. https://doi.org/10.1017/s0140525x99002046

Dickstein, D. P., Puzia, M. E., Cushman, G. K., Weissman, A. B., Wegbreit, E., Kim, L., Nock, M. K., & Spirito, A. (2015). Self-injurious implicit attitudes among adolescent suicide attempters versus those engaged in nonsuicidal self-injury. *Journal of Child Psychology and Psychiatry, 10*, 1127–1136. https://doi.org/10.1111/jcpp.12385

Dvorak, R. D., & Simons, J. S. (2014). Daily associations between anxiety and alcohol use: Variation by sustained attention, set shifting, and gender. *Psychology of Addictive Behaviors, 28*(4), 969–979. https://doi.org/10.1037/a0037642

Ellis, L. K., & Rothbart, M. K. (2001). *Revision of the Early Adolescent Temperament Questionnaire* [Poster presentation]. 2001 biennial meeting of the Society for Research in Child Development, Minneapolis, MN.

Engel, S. G., Wonderlich, S. A., Crosby, R. D., & Mitchell, J. E., Crow, S., Peterson, C. B., Le Grange, D., Simonich, H. K., Cao, L., Lavender, J. M., & Gordon, K. (2013). The role of affect in the maintenance of anorexia nervosa: Evidence from a naturalistic assessment of momentary behaviors and emotion. *Journal of Abnormal Psychology, 122*, 709–719. https://doi.org/10.1037/a0034010

Escelsior, A., Murri, M. B., Corsini, G. P., Serafini, G., Aguglia, A., Zampogna, D., Cattedra, S., Nebbia, J., Trabucco, A., Prestia, D., Olcese, M., Barletta, E., Pereira da Silva, B., & Amore, M. (2021). Cannabinoid use of and self-injurious behaviours: A systematic review and meta-analysis. *Journal of Affective Disorders, 278*, 85–98. https://doi.org/10.1016/j.jad.2020.09.020

Evans, D. E., & Rothbart, M. K. (2007). Developing a model for adult temperament. *Journal of Research in Personality, 41*, 868–888. https://doi.org/10.1016/j.jrp.2006.11.002

Farstand, S. M., McGeown, L. M., & von Ranson, K. M. (2016). Eating disorders and personality, 2004-2016: A systematic review and meta-analysis. *Clinical Psychology Review, 46*, 91–105. https://doi.org/10.1016/j.cpr.2016.04.005

Field, M., Werthman, J., Franken, I., Hofmann, W., Hogarth, L., & Roefs, A. (2016). The role of attentional bias in obesity and addiction. *Health Psychology, 35*, 767–780. https://doi.org/10.1037/hea0000405

Franken, I. H. A., & Muris, P. (2006). BIS/BAS personality characteristics and college students' substance use. *Personality and Individual Differences, 40*, 1497–1503. https://doi.org/10.15288/jsad.2011.72.1028

Franklin, J. C., Puzia, M. E., Lee, K. M., Lee, G. E., Hanna, E. K., Spring, V. L., & Prinstein, M. J. (2013). The nature of pain offset relief in nonsuicidal self-injury: A laboratory study. *Clinical Psychological Science, 1*, 110–119. https://doi.org/10.1177/2167702612474440

Franklin, J. C., Ribeiro, J. D., Fox, K. R., Bentley, K. H., Kleiman, E. M., Huang, X., Musacchio, K. M., Jaroszewski, A. C., Chang, B. P., & Nock, M. K. (2017). Risk factors for suicidal thoughts and behaviors: A meta-analysis of 50 years of research. *Psychological Bulletin, 143*, Article 187. https://doi.org/10.1037/bul0000084

Franz, P. J., Kleiman, E. M., & Nock, M. K. (2019). Who do people hurt themselves? Self-harm as a means to attain positive emotion. In J. Gruber (Ed.), *The Oxford handbook of positive emotion and psychopathology*. Oxford University Press.

Fischer, S., Smith, G. T., & Cyders, M. A. (2008). Another look at impulsivity: A meta-analytic review comparing specific dispositions to rash action in their relationship to bulimic symptoms. *Clinical Psychology Review, 28*, 1413–1425. https://doi.org/10.1016/j.cpr.2008.09.001

Fox, K. R., Franklin, J. C., Ribeiro, J. D., Kleiman, E. M., Bentley, K. H., & Nock, M. K. (2015). Meta-analysis of risk factors for nonsuicidal self-injury. *Clinical Psychology Review, 42*, 156–167. https://doi.org/10.1016/j.cpr.2015.09.002

Galvan, A., & Rahdar, A. (2013). The neurobiological effects of stress on adolescent decision making. *Neuroscience, 249*, 223–231. https://doi.org/10.1016/j.neuroscience.2012.09.074

Gandhi A., Luyckx K., Baetens I., Kiekens G., Sleuwaegen E., Berens A., Maitra S., & Claes L. (2018). Age of onset of non-suicidal self-injury in Dutch-speaking adolescents and emerging adults: An event history analysis of pooled data. *Comprehensive Psychiatry, 80*, 170–178. https://doi.org/10.1016/j.comppsych.2017.10.007

Gandhi, A., Luyckx., K., Maitra, S., Kiekens, G., & Claes, L. (2016). Reactive and regulative temperament and non-suicidal self-injury in Flemish adolescents: The intervening role of identity formation. *Personality and Individual Differences, 99*, 254–259. https://doi.org/10.1016/j.paid.2016.05.007

Garke, M., Sörman, K., Jayaram-Lindström, N., Hellner, C., & Birgegård, A. (2019). Symptom shifting and associations with mental illness: A transdiagnostic approach applied to eating disorders. *Journal of Abnormal Psychology, 128*, 585–595. https://doi.org/10.1037/abn0000425

Glenn, C. R., & Klonsky, E. D. (2010). A multimethod analysis of impulsivity in nonsuicidal self-injury. *Personality Disorders: Theory, Research, and Treatment, 1*, 67–75. https://doi.org/10.1037/a0017427

Glenn, C. R., & Klonsky, E. D. (2011). Prospective prediction of nonsuicidal self-injury: A 1-year longitudinal study in young adults. *Behavior Therapy, 42*, 751–762. https://doi.org/10.1016/j.beth.2011.04.005

Gomez-Exposito, A., Wolz, I., Fagundo, A. B., Granero, R., Steward, T., Jimenez-Murcia, S., Aguera, Z., & Fernandez-Aranda, F. (2016). Correlates of non-suicidal self-injury and suicide attempts in bulimic spectrum disorders. *Frontiers in Psychology, 7*, Article 1244. https://doi.org/10.3389/fpsyg.2016.01244

Gray, J. A. (1991). The neuropsychology of temperament. In J. Stelau & A. Angleiter (Eds.), *Explorations in temperament* (pp. 105–128). Plenum Press.

Gray, J. A., & McNaughton, N. (2000). *The neuropsychology of anxiety: An enquiry into the functions of the septo-hippocampal system* (2nd ed.). Oxford University Press.

Greene, D., Boyes, M., & Hasking, P. (2020). The association between alexithymia and non-suicidal self-injury and risky drinking. A systematic review and meta-analysis. *Journal of Affective Disorders, 260*, 140–166. https://doi.org/10.1016/j.jad.2019.08.088

Gruber, J., Tobias, M. R., Flux, M. C., & Gilbert, K. E. (2019). An introduction to positive emotion and psychopathology. In J. Gruber (Ed.), *The Oxford handbook of positive emotion and psychopathology*. Oxford University Press. https://doi.org/10.1093/oxfordhb/9780190653200.013.1

Harder, V. S., Ayer, L. A., Rose, G. L., Naylor, M. R., & Helzer, J. E. (2014). Alcohol, moods and male-female differences: Daily interactive voice response over 6 months. *Alcohol and Alcoholism, 49*, 60–65. https://doi.org/10.1093/alcalc/agt069

Haruno, M., & Kawato, M. (2006). Different neural correlates of reward expectation and reward expectation error in the putamen and caudate nucleus during stimulus-action-reward association learning. *Journal of Neurophysiology, 95*, 948–959. https://doi.org/10.1152/jn.00382.2005

Hepp, J., Carpenter, R. W., Störkel, L. M., Schmitz, S. E., Schmahl, C., & Niedtfeld, I. (2020). A systematic review of daily life studies on non-suicidal self-injury based on the four-function model. *Clinical Psychology Review, 82*, 1–21. https://doi.org/10.1016/j.cpr.2020.101888

Hooley, J. M., & Franklin, J. C. (2018). Why do people hurt themselves? A new conceptual model of nonsuicidal self-injury. *Clinical Psychological Science, 6*, 428–451. https://doi.org/10.1177/2167702617745641

Hooley, J. M., Dahlgren, M. K., Best, S. G., Gonenc, A., & Gruber, S. A. (2020). Decreased amygdalar activation to NSSI-stimuli in people who engage in NSSI: A neuroimaging pilot study. *Frontiers in Psychiatry, 11*, Article 238. https://doi.org/10.3389/fpsyt.2020.00238

Houben, M., Claes, L., Vansteelandt, K., Berens, A., Sleuwaegen, E., & Kuppens, P. (2017). The emotion regulation function of nonsuicidal self-injury: A momentary assessment study in inpatients with borderline personality disorder features. *Journal of Abnormal Psychology, 126*, 89–95. https://doi.org/10.1037/abn0000229

Hussong, A. M., Hick, R. E., Levy, S. A., & Curran, P. J. (2001). Specifying the relations between affect and heavy alcohol use among young adults. *Journal of Abnormal Psychology, 110*, 449–461. https://doi.org/10.1037/0021-843X.110.3.449

Insel, T., Cuthbert, B., Garvey, M., Heinssen, R., Kozak, M., Pine, D. S., Quinn, K., Sanislow, C., & Wang, P. (2010). Research Domain Criteria (RDoC): Toward a new classification framework for research on mental disorders. *American Journal of Psychiatry, 167*, 748–751. https://doi.org/10.1176/appi.ajp.2010.09091379

Islam, M. A., Steiger, H., Jimenez-Murcia, S., Israel, M., Granero, R., Agüera, Z., Castro, R., Sánchez, I., Riesco, N., & Menchón, J. M., & Fernández-Aranda, F. (2015). Non-suicidal self-injury in different eating disorder types: Relevance of personality traits and gender. *European Eating Disorders Review*, 23, 553–560. https://doi.org/10.1002/erv.2374

Jenkins, A. L., Seelbach, A. C., Bradley, T. C., & Alloy, L. B. (2013). The roles of behavioral activation and inhibition among young adults engaging in self-injury. *Personality and Mental Health*, 7, 39–55. https://doi.org/10.1002/pmh.1200

Jerez, S. J., & Coviello, A. (1998). Alcohol drinking and blood pressure among adolescents. *Alcohol*, 16, 1–5. https://doi.org/10.1016/s0741-8329(97)00152-3

Johnson, S. L., Turner, R. J., & Iwata, N. (2003). BIS/BAS Levels and psychiatric disorder: An epidemiological study. *Journal of Psychopathology and Behavioral Assessment*, 25, 25–36.

Kaess, M., Hooley, J. M., Klimes-Dougan, B., Koenig, J., Plener, P. L., Reichl, C., Robinson, K., Schmahl, C., Sicorello, M., Westlund Scheiner, M., & Cullen, K. R. (2021). Advancing a temporal framework for understanding the biology of nonsuicidal self-injury: An expert review. *Neuroscience and Biobehavioral Reviews*, 130, 228–239.

Kessel, E. M., Kujawa, A., Goldstein, B., Hajcak, G., Bufferd, S. J., Dyson, M., & Klein, D. N. (2017). Behavioral observations of positive and negative valence systems in early childhood predict physiological measures of emotional processing three years later. *Journal of Affective Disorders*, 216, 70–77. https://doi.org/10.1016/j.jad.2016.10.044

Khazanov, G. K., Ruscio, A. M., & Forbes, C. N. (2019). The Positive Valence Systems Scale: Development and validation. *Assessment*, 27, 1045–1069. https://doi.org/10.1177/1073191119869836

Kiekens, G., Bruffaerts, R., Nock, M. K., Van de Ven, M., Witteman, C., Mortier, P., Demyttenaere, K., & Claes, L. (2015). Non-suicidal self-injury among Dutch and Belgian adolescents: Personality, stress, and coping. *European Psychiatry*, 30, 743–749. https://doi.org/10.1016/j.eurpsy.2015.06.007

Kiekens, G., Hasking, P., Boyes, M., Claes, L., Mortier, P., Auerbach, R. P., Cuijpers, P., Demyttenaere, K., Green, J. G., Kessler, R. C., Myin-Germeys, I., Nock, M. K., & Bruffaerts, R. (2018). The associations between non-suicidal self-injury and first onset suicidal thoughts and behaviors. *Journal of Affective Disorders*, 239, 171–179. https://doi.org/10.1016/j.jad.2018.06.033

Kiekens, G., Hasking, P., Bruffaerts, R., Alonso, J., Auerbach, R. P., Bantjes, J., Benjet, C., Boyes, M., Chiu, W. T., Claes, L., Cuijpers, P., Ebert, D. D., Mak, A., Mortier, P., O'Neill, S., Sampson, N. A., Stein, D. J., Vilagut, G., Nock, M. K., & Kessler, R. C. (2021). Non-suicidal self-injury among first-year college students and its association with mental disorders: Results from the World Mental Health International College Student (WMH-ICS) Initiative. *Journal of the American Academy of Child & Adolescent Psychiatry*. Advance online publication. https://doi.org/10.1017/S0033291721002245

Kiekens, G., Hasking, P., Claes, L., Boyes, M., Mortier, P., Auerbach, R. P., Cuijpers, P., Demyttenaere, K., Green, J. G., Kessler, R. C., Myin-Germeys, I., Nock, M. K., & Bruffaerts, R. (2019). Predicting the incidence of non-suicidal self-injury in college students. *European Psychiatry*, 59, 44–51. https://doi.org/10.1016/j.eurpsy.2019.04.002

Kiekens, G., Hasking, P., Bruffaerts, R., Claes, L., Baetens, I., Boyes, M., Mortier, P., Demyttenaere, K., & Whitlock, J. (2017). What predicts ongoing nonsuicidal self-injury?: A comparison between persistent and ceased self-injury in emerging adults. *The Journal of Nervous and Mental Disease*, 205, 762–770. https://doi.org/10.1097/NMD.0000000000000726

Kiekens, G., Hasking, P., Claes, L., Mortier, P., Auerbach, R. P., Boyes, M., Cuijpers, P., Demyttenaere, K., Green, J. G., Kessler, R. C., Nock, M. K., & Bruffaerts, R. (2018). The DSM-5 nonsuicidal self-injury disorder among incoming college students: Prevalence and associations with 12-month mental disorders and suicidal thoughts and behaviors. *Depression and Anxiety*, 35, 629–637. https://doi.org/10.1002/da.22754

Koob, G. F., & Volkow, N. D. (2016). Neurobiology of addiction: A neurocircuitry analysis. *Lancet Psychiatry*, 3, 673–760. https://doi.org/10.1016/S2215-0366(16)00104-8

Kotov, R., Gamez, W., Schmidt, F., & Watson, D. (2010). Linking Big Personality traits to anxiety, depressive, and substance use disorders: A meta-analysis. *Psychological Bulletin*, 136, 768–821. https://doi.org/10.1037/a0020327

Kranzler, A., Fehling, K. B., Lindqvist, J., Brillante, J., Yuan, F., Gao, X., Miller, A. L., & Selby, E. A. (2018). An ecological investigation of the emotional context surrounding nonsuicidal self-injurious thoughts and behaviors in adolescents and young adults. *Suicide and Life-Threatening Behavior*, 48(2), 149–159. https://doi.org/10.1111/sltb.12373

Kuntsche, E., Knibbe, R., Gmel, G., & Engels, R. (2005). Why do young people drink? A review of drinking motives. *Clinical Psychology Review*, 25, 841–861. https://doi.org/10.1016/j.cpr.2005.06.002

Le Bon, O., Basiaux, P., Streel, E., Tecco, J., Hanak, C., Hansenne, M., Ansseau, M., Pelc, I., Verbanck, P., & Dupont, S. (2004). Personality profile and drug of choice: a multivariate analys using Cloninger's TCI on heroin addicts, alcoholics, and a random population. *Drug and Alcohol Dependence, 73*, 175–182. https://doi.org/10.1016/j.drugalcdep.2003.10.006

Linehan, M. M. (1993). *Skills training manual for treating borderline personality disorder*. Guilford Press.

Liu, R. T. (2017). Characterizing the course of non-suicidal self-injury: A cognitive neuroscience perspective. *Neuroscience & Biobehavioral Reviews, 80*, 159–165. https://doi.org/10.1016/j.neubiorev.2017.05.026

Liu, R. T. (2021). The epidemiology of non-suicidal self-injury: lifetime prevalence, sociodemographic and clinical correlates, and treatment use in a nationally representative sample of adults in England. *Psychological Medicine, 7*, 1–9. https://doi.org/10.1017/S003329172100146X

Lynam, D. R., & Miller, J. D. (2004). Personality pathways to impulsive behavior and their relations to deviance: Results from three samples. *Journal of Quantitative Criminology, 20*, 319–341.

Lynam, D. R., Miller, J. D., Miller, D. J., Bornovalova, M. A., & Lejuez, C. W. (2011). Testing the relations between impulsivity-related traits, suicidality, and nonsuicidal self-injury: A test of the incremental validity of the UPPS model. *Personality Disorders: Theory, Research, and Treatment, 2*, 151–160. https://doi.org/10.1037/a0019978

Mayo, L. M., & de Wit, H. (2015). Acquisition of responses to a methamphetamine-associated cue in healthy humans: Self-report, behavioral, and psychophysiological measures. *Neuropsychopharmacology, 40*, 1734–1741. https://doi.org/10.1002/erv.2567

Mayo, L. M., Perini, I., Gustafsson, P. A., Hamilton, J. P., Kämpe, R., Heilig, M., & Zetterqvist, M. (2021). Psychophysiological and neural support for enhanced emotional reactivity in adolescent females with nonsuicidal self-injury. *Biological Psychiatry: Cognitive Neuroscience and Neuroimaging, 6*, 682–691. https://doi.org/10.1016/j.bpsc.2020.11.004

Mettler, J., Stern, M., Lewis, S. P., & Heath, N. L. (2021). Perceived vs. actual emotion reactivity and regulation in individuals with and without a history of NSSI. *Frontiers in Psychology, 12*, Article 612792. https://doi.org/10.3389/fpsyg.2021.612792

Michelini, G., Palumbo, I. M., DeYoung, C. G., Latzman, R. D., & Kotov, R. (2021). Linking RDoC and HiTOP: A new interface for advancing psychiatric nosology and neuroscience. *Clinical Psychology Review*. Advance online publication. https://doi.org/10.1016/j.cpr.2021.102025

Milivojevic, D., Milovanovic, S. D., Jovanovic, M., Svrakic, D. M., Svrakic, N. M., Svrakic, S. M., & Cloninger, C. R. (2012). Temperament and Character modify risk of drug addiction and influence choice of drugs. *The American Journal on Addictions, 21*, 462–467. https://doi.org/10.1111/j.1521-0391.2012.00251.x

Muehlenkamp, J., Brausch, A., Quigley, K., & Whitlock, J. (2013). Interpersonal features and functions of nonsuicidal self-injury. *Suicide and Life-Threatening Behavior, 43*, 67–80. https://doi.org/10.1111/j.1943-278X.2012.00128.x

Muehlenkamp, J. J., Scot, S. G., Wadeson, A., Crosby, R. D., Wonderlich, S. A., Simonich, H., & Mitchell, J. E. (2009). Emotional states preceding and following acts of non-suicidal self-injury in bulimia nervosa patients. *Behaviour Research and Therapy, 47*, 83–87. https://doi.org/10.1016/j.brat.2008.10.011

National Institute of Mental Health. (2011). *Positive valence systems: Workshop proceedings*. Retrieved from https://www.nimh.nih.gov/research/research-funded-by-nimh/rdoc/positive-valence-systems-workshop-proceedings.shtml

National Institute of Mental Health. (2018). *RDoC Changes to the Matrix (CMAT) workgroup update: Proposed positive valence domain revisions*. Retrieved from https://www.nimh.nih.gov/about/advisory-boards-and-groups/namhc/reports/cmat-pvs-report-508_157003.pdf

Nock, M. K., & Banaji, M. R. (2007a). Assessment of self-injurious thoughts using a behavioral test. *American Journal of Psychiatry, 164*, 820–823. https://doi.org/10.1176/ajp.2007.164.5.820

Nock, M. K., & Banaji, M. R. (2007b). Prediction of suicide ideation and attempts among adolescents using a brief performance-based test. *Journal of Consulting and Clinical Psychology, 75*, 707–715. https://doi.org/10.1037/0022-006X.75.5.707

Nock, M. K., Joiner Jr, T. E., Gordon, K. H., Lloyd-Richardson, E., & Prinstein, M. J. (2006). Non-suicidal self-injury among adolescents: Diagnostic correlates and relation to suicide attempts. *Psychiatry Research, 144*, 65–72. https://doi.org/10.1016/j.psychres.2006.05.010

Nock, M. K., & Prinstein, M. J. (2004). A functional approach to the assessment of self-mutilative behavior. *Journal of Consulting and Clinical Psychology, 72*, 885–890. https://doi.org/10.1037/0022-006X.72.5.885

Nusslock, R., & Alloy, L. B. (2017). Reward processing and mood-related symptoms: An RDoC and translational neuroscience perspective. *Journal of Affective Disorders*, *216*, 3–16. https://doi.org/10.1016/j.jad.2017.02.001

Osuch, E., Ford, K., Wrath, A., Bartha, R., & Neufeld, R. (2014). Functional MRI of pain application in youth who engaged in repetitive non-suicidal self-injury vs. psychiatric controls. *Psychiatry Research*, *223*, 104–112. https://doi.org/10.1016/j.pscychresns.2014.05.003

Pallavi, A., & Klanecky, A. K. (2016) Drinking motives mediate emotion regulation difficulties and problem drinking in college students. *The American Journal of Drug and Alcohol Abuse*, *42*, 341–350. https://doi.org/10.3109/00952990.2015.1133633

Perini, I., Zetterqvist, M., & Mayo, L. M. (2021). Beyond distress: A role for positive affect in nonsuicidal self-injury. *Current Opinion in Behaivoral Sciences*, *39*, 209–215.

Perugini, M., & Di Blas, L. (2002). The Big Five Marker Scales (BFMS) and the Italian AB5C taxonomy: Analyses from an emic-ethic perspective. In B. De Raad & M. Perugini (Eds.), *Big five assessment* (pp. 153–165). Hogrefe & Huber.

Peterson, C. M., & Fischer, S. (2012). A prospective study of the influence of the UPPS model of impulsivity on the co-occurrence of bulimic symptoms and non-suicidal self-injury. *Eating Behaviors*, *13*, 335–341. https://doi.org/10.1016/j.eatbeh.2012.05.007

Peterson, C. M., Mara, C. A., Conard, L. A. E., & Grossoehmee, D. (2020). The relationship of the UPPS model of impulsivity on bulimic symptoms and non-suicidal self-injury in transgender youth. *Eating Behaviors*, *39*, Article 101416. https://doi.org/10.1016/j.eatbeh.2020.101416

Piccirillo, M. L., & Rodebaugh, T. L. (2019). Foundations of idiographic methods in psychology and applications for psychotherapy. *Clinical Psychology Review*, *71*, 90–100. https://doi.org/10.1016/j.cpr.2019.01.002

Plener, P. L., Bubalo, N., Fladung, A. K., Ludolph, A. G., & Lule´, D. (2012). Prone to excitement: Adolescent females with non-suicidal self-injury (NSSI) show altered cortical pattern to emotional and NSS-related material. *Psychiatry Research Neuroimaging*, *203*, 146–152. https://doi.org/10.1016/j.pscychresns.2011.12.012

Plener, P. L., Schumacher, T. S., Munz, L. M., & Groschwitz, R. C. (2015). The longitudinal course of non-suicidal self-injury and deliberate self-harm: A systematic review of the literature. *Borderline Personality Disorder and Emotion Dysregulation*, *2*, 1–11. https://doi.org/10.1186/s40479-014-0024-3

Pollak, O. H., D'Angelo, E. J., & Cha, C. B. (2020). Does function predict persistence? Nonsuicidal self-injury among adolescents during and after hospitalization. *Psychiatry Research*, *286*, Article 112839. https://doi.org/10.1016/j.psychres.2020.112839

Poon, J. A., Thompson, J. C., Forbes, E. E., & Chaplin, T. M. (2019). Adolescents' reward-related neural activation: Links to thoughts of non-suicidal self-injury. *Suicide and Life-Threatening Behavior*, *49*, 76–89. https://doi.org/10.1111/sltb.12418

Racine, S. E., Hebert, K. R., & Benning, S. D. (2018). Cognitions and behaviors: Evidence to support the motivational conflict hypothesis. *European Eating Disorders Review*, *26*, 3–10. https://doi.org/10.1002/erv.2567

Riley, E. N., Combs, J. L., Jordan, C. E., & Smith, G. T. (2015). Negative urgency and Lack of Perseverance: Identification of Differential pathways of onset and maintenance risk in the longitudinal prediction of non-suicidal self-injury. *Behavior Therapy*, *46*, 439–448. https://doi.org/10.1016/j.beth.2015.03.002

Riquino, M. R., Reese, S. E., & Garland, E. L. (2020). Assessing attentional bias toward nonsuicidal self-injury cues in young adults with histories of engaging in self-harm. *Child and Adolescent Social Work Journal*, *8*, 641–650. https://doi.org/10.1007/s10560-020-00692-2

Robertson, C. D., Miskey, H., Mitchell, J., & Nelson-Gray, R. (2013). Variety of self-injury: Is the number of different methods of non-suicidal self-injury related to personality, psychopathology, or functions of self-injury. *Archives of Suicide Research*, *17*, 33–40. https://doi.org/10.1080/13811118.2013.748410

Robinson, T. E., & Berridge, K. C. (1993). The neural basis of drug craving: An incentive-sensitization theory of addiction. *Brain Research Reviews*, *18*, 247–291. https://doi.org/10.1016/0165-0173(93)90013-p

Ross, C. S., Brooks, D. R., Aschengrau, A., Siegel, M. B., Weinberg, J., & Shrier, L. A. (2018). Positive and negative affect following marijuana use in naturalistic settings: An ecological momentary assessment study. *Addictive Behaviors*, *76*, 61–67. https://doi.org/10.1016/j.addbeh.2017.07.020

Rothbart, M. K., Ahadi, S. A., & Evans, D. E. (2000). Temperament and personality: Origins and outcomes. *Journal of Personality and Social Psychology*, *78*, 122–135. https://doi.org/10.1037//0022-3514.78.1.122

Ruiz, M. A., Pincus, A. L., & Schinka, J. A. (2008). Externalizing pathology and the five-factor model: A meta-analysis of personality traits associated with antisocial personality disorder, substance use disorder, and their co-occurrence. *Journal of Personality Disorders, 22*, 365–388. https://doi.org/10.1521/pedi.2008.22.4.365

Sandman, C. A., Hetrick, W., Taylor, D. V., & Chicz-DeMet, A. (1997). Dissociation of POMC peptides after self-injury predicts responses to centrally acting opiate blockers. *American Journal of Mental Retardation, 102*, 182–199. https://doi.org/10.1352/0895-8017(1997)102<0182:DOPPAS>2.0.CO;2

Sanislow, C. A., Pine, D. S., Quinn, K. J., Kozak, M. J., Garvey, M. A., Heinssen, R. K., Sung-en Wang, F., & Cuthbert, B. N. (2010). Developing constructs for psychopathology research: Research domain criteria. *Journal of Abnormal Psychology, 119*, 631–639. https://doi.org/10.1037/a0020909

Sauder, C. L., Derbidge, C. M., & Beauchaine, T. P. (2016). Neural responses to monetary incentives among self-injuring adolescent girls. *Development and Psychopathology, 28*, 277–291. https://doi.org/10.1017/S0954579415000449

Sher, L., & Stanley, B. H. (2008). The role of endogenous opioids in the pathophysiology of self-injurious and suicidal behavior. *Archives of Suicide Research, 12*, 299–308. https://doi.org/10.1080/13811110802324748

Smyth, J. M., Wonderlich, S. A., Heron, K. E., Sliwinski, M. J., Crosby, R. D., Mitchell, J. E., & Engel, S. G. (2007). Daily and momentary mood and stress are associated with binge eating and vomiting in bulimia nervosa patients in the natural environment. *Journal of Consulting and Clinical Psychology, 75*, 629–638. https://doi.org/10.1037/0022-006X.75.4.629

Stanley, B., Sher, L., Wilson, S., Ekman, R., Huang, Y., & Mann, J. J., 2010. Non-suicidal self-injurious behavior, endogenous opioids and monoamine neurotransmitters. *Journal of Affective Disorders, 124*, 134–140. https://doi.org/10.1016/j.jad.2009.10.028

Störkel, L. M., Karabatsiakis, A., Hepp, J., Kolassa, I. T., Schmahl, C., & Niedtfeld, I. (2021). Salivary Beta-Endorphin in non-suicidal self-injury: An ambulatory assessment study. *Neuropsychopharmacology, 46*, 1357–1363. https://doi.org/10.1038/s41386-020-00914-2

Swendsen, J. D., Tennen, H., Carney, M. A., Affleck, G., Willard, A., & Hromi, A. (2000). Mood and alcohol consumption: An experience sampling test of the self-medication hypothesis. *Journal of Abnormal Psychology, 109*, 198–204. https://doi.org/10.1037/0021-843X.109.2.198

Taylor, L. M. W., Oldershaw, A., Richards, C., Davidson, K., Schmidt, U., & Simic, M. (2011). Development and pilot evaluation of a manualized cognitive-behavioural treatment package for adolescent self-harm. *Behavioural and Cognitive Psychotherapy, 39*, 619–625. https://doi.org/10.1017/S1352465811000075

Taylor, L., Simic, M., & Schmidt, U. (2015). *Cutting Down. A CBT workbook for treating young people who self-harm*. Routledge.

Taylor, P. J., Jomar, K. Dhingra, K., Forrester, R., Shahmalak, U., & Dickson, J. M. (2018). A meta-analysis of the prevalence of different functions of non-suicidal self-injury. *Journal of Affective Disorders, 227*, 759–769. https://doi.org/10.1016/j.jad.2017.11.073

Torrubia, R., Avila, C., Molto, J., & Caseras, X. (2001). The Sensitivity to Punishment and Sensitivity to Reward Questionnaire (SPSRQ) as a measure of Gray's anxiety and impulsivity dimensions. *Personality and Individual Difference, 31*, 837–862. https://doi.org/10.1016/S0191-8869(00)00183-5

Turner, B. J., Cobb, R. J., Gratz, K. L., & Chapman, A. L. (2016). The role of interpersonal conflict and perceived social support in nonsuicidal self-injury in daily life. *Journal of Abnormal Psychology, 125*, 588–598. https://doi.org/10.1037/abn0000141

Van der Venne, P., Balint, A., Drews, E., Parzer, P., Resch, F., Koenig, J., & Kaess, M. (2020). Pain sensitivity and plasma beta-endorphin in adolescent non-suicidal self-injury. *Journal of Affective Disorders, 278*, 199–208. https://doi.org/10.1016/j.jad.2020.09.036.

Vega, D., Ripolles, P., Soto, A., Torrubia, R., Ribas, J., Monreal, J. A., Pascual, J. C., Salvador, R., Pomarol-Clotet, E., Rodriguez-Fornells, A., & Marco-Pallares, J. (2018). Orbitofrontal overactivation in reward processing in borderline personality disorder: The role of non-suicidal self-injury. *Brain Imaging and Behavior, 12*, 217–228. https://doi.org/10.1007/s11682-017-9687-x

Vermulst, A. A., & Gerris, J. (2005). *QBF: Quick Big Five Persoonlijkheidstest Handleiding*. [Quick Big Five personality test manual]. LDC Publications.

Voelkle, M. C., Gische, C., Driver, C. C., & Lindenberger, U. (2018). The role of time in the quest for understanding psychological mechanisms. *Multivariate Behavioral Research, 53*, 782–805. https://doi.org/10.1080/00273171.2018.1496813

Watson, D., Clark, L. A., & Tellegen, A. (1988). Development and validation of brief measures of positive and negative affect: The PANAS scales. *Journal of Personality and Social Psychology*, *54*, 1063–1070. https://doi.org/10.1037//0022-3514.54.6.1063

Wedig, M. M., & Nock, M. K. (2010). The functional assessment of maladaptive behaviors: A preliminary evaluation of binge eating and purging among women. *Psychiatry Research*, *178*, 518–524. https://doi.org/10.1016/j.psychres.2009.05.010

Westlund Schreiner, M., Klimes-Dougan, B., Begnel, E. D., & Cullen, K. R. (2015). Conceptualizing the neurobiology of non-suicidal self-injury from the perspective of the Research Domain Criteria Project. *Neuroscience and Biobehavioral Reviews*, *57*, 381–391. https://doi.org/10.1016/j.neubiorev.2015.09.011

Wiggins, J. S. (1996). *The five-factor model of personality: Theoretical perspectives*. Guilford Press.

Wilkinson, P. O., Qiu, T., Neufeld, S., Jones, P. B., & Goodyer, I. M. (2018). Sporadic and recurrent non-suicidal self-injury before age 14 and incident onset of psychiatric disorders by 17 years: prospective cohort study. *The British Journal of Psychiatry*, *212*, 222–226. https://doi.org/10.1192/bjp.2017.45

Whiteside, S. P., & Lynam, D. R. (2001). The five factor model and impulsivity: Using a structural model of personality to understand impulsivity. *Personality and Individual Differences*, *30*, 669–689. https://doi.org/10.1016/S0191-8869(00)00064-7

Whiteside, S. P., Lynam, D. R., Miller, J. D., & Reynolds, S. K. (2005). Validation of the UPPS impulsive behaviour scale: A four-factor model of impulsivity. *European Journal of Personality*, *19*, 559–574. https://doi.org/10.1002/per.556

Wiech, K., & Tracy, I. (2013). Pain, decisions, and actions. A motivational perspective. *Frontiers in Neuroscience*, *7*, Article 46. https://doi.org/10.3389/fnins.2013.00046

Wu, R., Huang, J., Ying, J., Gao, Q., Guo, J., & You, J. (2021). Behavioral inhibition/approach systems and adolescent nonsuicidal self-injury: The chain mediating effects of difficulty in emotion regulation and depression. *Personality and Individual Differences*, *175*, Article 110718 https://doi.org/10.1016/j.paid.2021.110718

Yen, S., Kuehn, K., Melvin, C., Weinstock, L. M., Andover, M. S., Selby, E. A., Solomon, J. B., & Spirito, A. (2016). Predicting persistence of nonsuicidal self-injury in suicidal adolescents. *Suicide and Life-Threatening Behavior*, *46*, 13–22. https://doi.org/10.1111/sltb.12167

CHAPTER 16

Cognitive Systems in NSSI and Co-Occurring Conditions

Morgan E. Browning *and* Jennifer J. Muehlenkamp

Abstract

Nonsuicidal self-injury (NSSI) is conceptualized as an emotion-avoidant behavior similar to other co-occurring maladaptive behaviors such as substance abuse, disordered eating, and obsessive-compulsive behaviors. Although all these behaviors are motivated by emotion avoidance resulting in short-term benefits, a variety of cognitive processes are vital to understanding the onset and maintenance of these behaviors. This chapter overviews current research on the cognitive processes and related neurobiological features believed to increase vulnerability to NSSI. The chapter provides an integrative summary proposing that NSSI originates from a cognitive control dysfunction, rumination, and attentional biases toward negative emotions that result in the use of NSSI or other maladaptive regulation strategies. Continued use of the behavior leads to a cyclical pattern of reward that increases positive expectancies, attentional biases, development of rule-governed behavior, and cognitive inflexibility, and reliance on NSSI for coping is exacerbated. The integrated cycle of cognitive processes discussed in this chapter complements recent transdiagnostic models of emotion-avoidant disorders and helps to expand current emotion-focused theoretical understandings of NSSI.

Key Words: Rumination, attention, cognitive control, values, rule-governed behavior, comorbidity

Nonsuicidal self-injury (NSSI) is often conceptualized as a behavior that falls along a continuum of maladaptive actions ranging from indirect to direct physical damage to the body. Indirect self-harmful behaviors tend to include behaviors involved with disordered eating, repetitive compulsive actions (e.g., severe washing), and substance use where the damaging physical consequences emerge over time and may not be immediately observable. Direct self-harm refers to behaviors that result in immediate physical harm and are representative of NSSI and suicidal behaviors. Although NSSI is studied as an independent behavior (see Muehlenkamp & Tillotson, this volume), it co-occurs at high rates with eating disorders (EDs), substance use disorders (SUDs), and obsessive-compulsive disorder (OCD); all of which also show high comorbidity (Bahji et al., 2019; Bentley et al., 2015; Cucchi et al., 2016). All these behaviors are conceptualized as dysfunctional avoidant strategies used to achieve short-term benefits (e.g., escaping unpleasant emotions) that are hard to control and are associated with long-term distress and impairment (Bresin, 2020). The extensive overlap and avoidant features among these disorders suggest that similar transdiagnostic processes contribute to the onset and maintenance of the dysfunctional behaviors core to each disorder and therefore, should be studied together. Indeed, independent theoretical models (see Hird et al., this volume) explaining mechanisms that contribute to the onset, maintenance, and exacerbation of NSSI, EDs, SUDs, and OCD all describe the dysfunctional behavior as serving an avoidance function in response to distress. While emphasized to differing degrees, each of these theories also acknowledges cognitive processes as being critical to the emotion-distress-avoidance cycle.

Cognitive processes are integral to understanding psychopathology, representing a core dimension with multiple subdomains having differential impacts on the severity or type of disorder (Abramovitch et al., 2021). A handful of cognitive constructs, some of which fall under The Research Domain Criteria (RDoC) cognitive systems domain (e.g., attention and cognitive control) have consistently been identified as mechanisms contributing to the activation and maintenance of dysfunctional behaviors such as NSSI. However, these studies tend to examine single cognitive processes within NSSI, failing to account for the intersection among processes or co-occurring behavioral pathologies. Given the prominence of cognitive processes in understanding vulnerability for psychopathology and significant theoretical and phenomenological overlap among NSSI and related behaviors such as EDs, SUDs, and OCD, the purpose of this chapter is to integrate what is currently known about transdiagnostic cognitive processes likely to play a central role in NSSI behaviors. Specifically, we focus on cognitive processes likely to activate the behavior (i.e., rumination, attentional bias, and cognitive control deficits) and those contributing to the maintenance or exacerbation of the behavior (i.e., rule-governed behavior and expectancies). Potential neurobiological features influencing these processes will be reviewed where possible and the chapter concludes with recommendations for future study and clinical practice implications.

Rumination

Rumination is thought to be a core cognitive process underlying the behaviors of NSSI, ED, SUD, and OCD because of the role it can play in escalating emotion dysregulation and inhibited problem-solving. The emotional cascade theory (Selby et al., 2013) articulates this process, describing how rumination on negative emotion and experiences increasingly intensifies negative affect to overwhelming levels that only cease once a dysregulated behavior (e.g., NSSI and binge-purge) is engaged in. Research aligns with the idea that behaviors including substance use, binge eating/purging, and NSSI are used to escape from or stop the cascades of negative emotion (Hughes et al., 2019; Watkins & Roberts, 2020). For example, in their 7-week diary study, Nicolai et al. (2015) found that high negative affect co-occurring with high rumination predicted NSSI, and rumination moderated the relationship between negative affect and frequency of NSSI. Studies have also identified rumination as having a robust association with other avoidant-focused behaviors, linking it to increased negative affect (Smith et al., 2020) and compulsive habit formation (Kollárik et al., 2020; Wahl et al., 2021; Watkins & Roberts, 2020). While there is a solid body of evidence indicating that rumination is a transdiagnostic process contributing to dysregulated and avoidant-coping behaviors such as NSSI, the research is limited by cross-sectional studies. Additionally, few studies have examined the underlying mechanisms of rumination or how rumination interacts with other transdiagnostic processes to impact pathology which may be one reason it is excluded from the current RDoCs framework.

Watkins and Roberts (2020) propose the "H-EX-A-GO-N" model to represent how rumination onsets and is maintained as a habitual cognitive process that then contributes to dysfunctional escape behaviors. According to Watkins and Roberts (2020), rumination develops as a habitual way of processing negatively biased information resulting from poor cognitive control (see below). They further explain that rumination intensifies and extends negative mood states, making it challenging for someone to take in new information and make decisions, which then leads to increased stress responses and risks for psychopathology or avoidant-coping behaviors. There is a growing body of evidence from neurobiological studies supporting this process and the observed impact rumination has on producing emotional cascades that lead to NSSI and other dysfunctional behaviors.

Some studies have found that rumination is related to elevated activity in the amygdala, hippocampus, and cingulate cortex which sustain and contribute to intensified emotional experiences (Disner et al., 2011). Furthermore, altered functioning of the rostral anterior cingulate cortex (ACC) prevents the inhibition of attention to negative emotional stimuli and blocks attention to positive stimuli, which when combined with observed hypoactivity in the left dorso- and ventral-lateral prefrontal cortex lowers the ability to block out negative thoughts fueling rumination and subsequently intensifying emotional distress. Emerging evidence also suggests that compulsive behavior as well as repetitive negative thinking may occur due to reduced activity in the medial orbitofrontal cortex (OFC; responsible for goal-directed behavior) and increased activity in the caudate, which is responsible for habit formation (Gillan & Robbins, 2014; Gillan et al., 2016). The overactivity in this neurocognitive circuit has been correlated with habit formation, which may increase tendencies to overprocess negative information in an abstract way (i.e., rumination), impairing effective problem-solving (Watkins & Roberts, 2020). Finally, there is evidence that rumination impairs parasympathetic flexibility, preventing individuals from calming physiological arousal which further perpetuates experiences of distress (Ottaviani et al., 2016).

The research indicates that rumination on negative emotion and experiences partially occurs because of struggles with cognitive inhibition or the inability to choose adaptive emotion regulation skills, leading to the use of avoidant coping behaviors to take the focus off the negative experience. Consequently, individuals who engage in avoidant coping behaviors have a heightened sensitivity to negative emotion (e.g., overactive amygdala and cingulate), which is easily activated and intensified through an inability to cognitively disengage from the stimuli (e.g., altered rostral ACC functioning) and impairments in working memory and goal selection (e.g., hippocampus and medial prefrontal cortex [MPFC] dysfunction). The aversive negative stimuli continue to be intensified through overactivity in the OFC and caudate circuitry further interfering with access to and use of cognitive control or adaptive coping strategies, leading to an intense aversive state the individual wishes to escape from using NSSI, substances, binge/purge/restricting, or compulsions. Rumination, therefore, appears to be a central cognitive facet for understanding dysfunctional avoidant behaviors, primarily through its impact on emotional processes and problem-solving or coping. It is important for future work to build on the strong literature examining emotional dysfunction in NSSI and related behaviors with an increased understanding of the role of cognitions, so that the interaction between the two can be better addressed within interventions and prevention programming. It also seems important for the RDoCs (see Bastiaens & Claes, this volume) framework to consider rumination as a transdiagnostic dimension within cognitive control, given its salience to understanding a wide range of psychopathology and dysfunctional behavior (see Watkins & Roberts, 2020).

Attentional Bias

Attentional bias occurs when a person differentially focuses their attention on a particular stimulus, and it is viewed as another key cognitive process in maintaining avoidant behaviors. When individuals repeatedly engage in a behavior, like NSSI, a variety of internal and environmental cues become associated with the behavior and its effects. As a result, the associated cues capture attention more quickly, receive more time in attention, and are harder to disengage from, disproportionately increasing the salience of the cues to the person over time. The difficulty redirecting attention away from the stimuli suggests that attentional bias also contributes to rumination (see above) and difficulties in goal redirection or task switching (see below), making behavioral engagement more likely. A large body of research supports a powerful role of attentional bias in perpetuating substance use and disordered eating behaviors (Stojek et al., 2018; Zhang et al., 2018), with evidence that attentional biases are stronger the more severe the disorder is (O'Neil et al., 2020; Zhang et al., 2018), although the biases may only be weakly associated with cravings. Similar patterns have been observed for NSSI, with studies focusing on cue engagement using the implicit association test. In the largest study to date, Glenn et al. (2017) reported that those with a history of NSSI showed stronger attentional bias to NSSI-relevant stimuli, and the bias was highest among those with persistent and severe NSSI. In a small experimental study using the dot-probe test, Riquino et al. (2021) found that those with NSSI showed strong attentional bias to NSSI cues versus neutral cues, and the strength of the attentional bias was significantly related to increased urges to engage in NSSI. Participants also showed attentional bias toward negative emotion cues, but this bias was not related to increased behavioral urges.

Attentional bias may be partially driven by reward responses whereby an individual is more likely to attend to, and engage in, behaviors that produce positive internal experiences. Neurobiological processes suggest that the dopaminergic release ("feel good" neurotransmitters) within the frontostriatal network and mesolimbic system following engagement in a behavior underlies the strong reward learning that occurs to promote attentional biases (Halicka-Maslowska et al., 2020; Leeman et al., 2014). The increased activation of the putamen, amygdala, and nucleus accumbens in response to cues observed among those with NSSI, ED, and SUD further supports the observed hypersensitivity toward reward-based cues underlying these behaviors (e.g., Auerbach et al., 2021; Leeman et al., 2014). The powerful biological reward response that is elicited from behaviorally relevant cues and subsequent attentional bias interferes with inhibitory control, resulting in activation of automatic bottom-up cognitive processing, and leaves the person fewer cognitive resources to apply adaptive coping or problem-solving strategies. The increased use of automatic processing contributes to stronger tendencies to approach the cues and thus engage in the behavior, which further strengthens both the reward and the attentional salience of the cues, resulting in habit formation and repeated acts.

Emerging research also suggests that there are strong interactions between emotional states and attentional bias to cues such that when in emotional distress, stimuli related to a reward-valued behavior, such as NSSI, become even more salient, making it harder for the person to disengage and consider an alternative action. Neurobiological studies support these interacting processes among individuals with NSSI, ED, and SUD, consistently documenting increased activation within frontal cortical regions including the prefrontal cortex (PFC), dorsal ACC, and limbic system structures such as the amygdala, insula, and gyrus, indicating greater attentional processing of behavior-relevant stimuli especially when under emotional stress (see Auerbach et al., 2021; Ralph-Nearman et al., 2019). The congruency of findings across study populations and methods suggests attentional biases are a central cognitive process impacting avoidant behaviors such as NSSI. However, data specific to NSSI are limited by the number of studies conducted, restricted attentional bias assessments utilized, and overreliance on nonclinical young adult populations. Furthermore, exploration of the neurobiological correlates involved in attentional processing among those engaging in NSSI is scarce and represents an important avenue of research to pursue (see Auerbach et al., 2021).

Expectancies and Rule-Governed Behavior

Outcome expectancy theory suggests that individuals engage in behaviors according to their beliefs about the anticipated outcome of the behavior such that positive outcome beliefs (i.e., positive expectancies) result in increased behavioral action and negative expectancies result in decreased action. It is well established that NSSI, as well as SUDs, EDs, and OCD are understood as behaviors maintained and exacerbated by the reinforcing outcomes experienced. The reinforcing experiences of these behaviors provide powerful reward learning whereby the person comes to anticipate a positive outcome from engaging in the NSSI or other behaviors, creating a cognitive expectancy. A solid body of research has established that alcohol expectancies play a critical role in the development and maintenance of alcohol use, with interventions that challenge positive expectancies showing significant effects for reducing or preventing alcohol use (see Gesualdo & Pinquart, 2021). Similarly, two recent studies have found that eating expectancies mediated the relationship between emotion regulation/distress and binge/purge behaviors (Della Longa & DeYoung, 2018; Smith et al., 2020), meaning that expectancies of relief explained why emotion dysregulation was linked to binge/purge behavior. While research on expectancies and NSSI is limited, in a study validating diagnostic criteria for NSSI disorder, 82% of participants in the study reported expecting the NSSI would make their negative state feel better (Washburn et al., 2015).

The data strongly point to the fact that holding positive expectancies about an act of NSSI, use of a substance, and so on, contributes to increased likelihood the behavior will occur again when encountering an aversive experience. Positive expectancies about the outcome of a specific behavior may also contribute to the creation of rule-governed behavioral processes that can lead to habit formation, further perpetuating the behaviors. Rule-governed behavior (RGB) sets up an "if-then" context for behavioral engagement that is created from the learned function of the behavior and internalized through human's language abilities (Törneke et al., 2008). RGBs occur when rules imposed by society or oneself are internalized and begin to act as an antecedent for an action: "If I experience significant negative affect, then I will binge/purge to feel better." In the example of NSSI, someone may hold the verbal rule that "if I do not cut myself, those around me will not understand my suffering," or "I must cut myself to be able to tolerate this difficult emotion. I cannot otherwise tolerate difficult feelings" (Lynch & Cozza, 2009). Such rules limit flexible responding and perpetuate engagement in avoidant behaviors that can become habitual responses to aversive internal states. RGBs are understood in the context of relational frame theory, which serves as the basis for acceptance and commitment therapy (ACT; Hayes et al., 2006).

Neurobiological studies have found that habit formation is rooted within the dopamine-reward circuits in the striatum. Floods of dopamine strengthen connections within the striatal regions, intensifying associations between a behavior (NSSI) and positive outcome (relief). Furthermore, disruptions in the dorsal lateral striatum appear to increase sensitivity to the outcome value of a behavior and enhance reliance on automatized, goal-directed behavior (Amaya & Smith, 2018; Antons et al., 2020). Thus, it appears that cognitive expectancies may be formed in conjunction with the dopamine floods produced by behavioral engagement that lead to increased sensitivity to reward within the striatum (e.g., emotional relief), thereby promoting rule-governed behavioral habits. Consequently, expectancies may then activate the dopaminergic striatal pathways that enhance attentional salience of a stimulus and initiate reliance on goal-directed behavioral response to distress, perpetuating engagement in avoidance behaviors like NSSI, substance use, disordered eating, and compulsions. Additional work is needed to map these neurobiological processes (for more on how biology informs NSSI treatments, see Plener, this volume).

Cognitive Control

Cognitive control is understood to be a cornerstone of psychopathology and is a central focus of the RDoC matrix. Cognitive control consists of three primary executive function processes of impulsivity (e.g., inhibition/suppression of behavioral response), shifting between goal-directed tasks (e.g., task-shifting), and controlling or monitoring the content of working memory (Hofmann et al., 2012). Recent research suggests that all mental disorders may originate from some amount of cognitive control dysfunction, proposed as the "c" factor of psychopathology (Abramovitch et al., 2021). Additionally, some current research suggests that situational experiences such as elevated emotional distress may temporarily reduce the efficiency of cognitive control processes, especially among individuals with preexisting deficits, contributing to failures in self-regulatory behaviors (Hofmann et al., 2012). While NSSI was not included in the meta-analysis of cognitive dysfunction in psychopathology, EDs, substance use, and OCD all showed medium effect sizes for deficits across cognitive-control processes including set-shifting, response inhibition, and working memory (Abramovitch et al., 2021). Individual studies of select cognitive control processes such as response inhibition/impulsivity, effortful control, and task-shifting suggest that individuals who engage in NSSI may also have deficits in these cognitive functions (Buelens et al., 2020; Gifuni et al., 2021; Lockwood et al., 2017).

Research has demonstrated that individuals who are low in behavioral inhibition (e.g., high in impulsivity) are more strongly influenced by reward-based cues, making it hard for them to shift a behavioral response away from the reward (Hofmann et al., 2012). This process is believed to contribute to the experiential avoidance influencing NSSI, disordered eating behavior, substance use, and compulsions because it becomes hard for the individual to shift attention or goals away from engaging in the behavior to alleviate distress (reward-based goal). Neurobiologically, the PFC is related to values-based decision-making, and the rostral ACC is related to set-shifting (Dixon & Christoff, 2014; Gläscher et al., 2012). Studies among those with NSSI and OCD have identified increased activation in the dorsal and rostral ACC and decreased activity in the dorsal PFC which then correlated with challenges in set-shifting and values-based decision-making (Dahlgren et al., 2018, Kaess et al., 2021). These observed biological dysfunctions interfere with emotional and impulse control. Across numerous studies, trait and state impulsivity, especially negative urgency, or the perceived need to immediately alleviate an aversive state, has been implicated in both the initiation and maintenance of NSSI (Lockwood et al., 2017;

McHugh et al., 2019; Westlund Schreiner et al., 2015). In addition, the construct of cognitive fusion, or taking thoughts literally as truth and forming behavioral rules from them (Hayes et al., 2011), interferes with one's ability to shift actions based on new information, impairing adaptive goal selection and problem-solving. Cognitive fusion is believed to perpetuate engagement in avoidant behaviors due to both the distress it may generate and by limiting flexible problem-solving. Primarily studied within OCD, cognitive fusion has been found to differentially predict compulsive symptoms above and beyond obsessive beliefs (Hellberg et al., 2020). However, recent studies are finding relationships between cognitive fusion and NSSI (Callahan et al., 2021), ED symptoms (Zucchelli et al., 2020), and SUDs (Ii et al., 2019), suggesting this may be a transdiagnostic cognitive feature as well. Exploration of cognitive fusion as an element of cognitive control or a contributor to problem-solving deficits within these behaviors is relatively new, so additional research is needed.

Hofmann et al. (2012) also make a strong argument for the salience of working-memory deficits in poor self-regulation. Specifically, they suggest that limited working-memory capacity can make it challenging to direct attention away from tempting stimuli (e.g., drug cues) and leading to additional processing that subsequently makes the stimuli more emotionally salient, which contributes to the attentional biases discussed earlier. Furthermore, limited working memory interferes with one's ability to sustain attention toward a self-regulatory goal or task in the presence of a competing goal or tempting distraction. This working-memory deficit makes automatic and impulsive responding to immediately rewarding actions, like NSSI, more likely, especially when under emotional strain (Hofmann et al., 2012). Deficits in working memory also impair individuals' ability to redirect their focus to alternative contents perpetuating ruminative processes, which can further escalate emotion dysregulation due to a lack of cognitive "working space" to engage in reappraisal processes for regulating emotions. Many of the neurobiological disruptions already discussed correspond to and are also implicated in these working-memory deficits, including breakdown in the circuitry between the PFC, ACC, and precentral gyrus. A growing amount of research provides clear support that working memory may be an essential cognitive control process important for successful self-regulation (Abramovitch et al., 2021; Hofmann et al., 2012), but research on the role of working memory and its impacts on other cognitive control functions within NSSI is limited.

It is evident that the cognitive processing literature contains a wide array of constructs and studies that highlight similar themes of cognitive control deficits that contribute to difficulties in shifting attention from unhelpful thoughts or behaviors to more adaptive ones that could contribute to more adaptive behavioral responses to distress. In their review, Gillan et al. (2016) describe how the behaviors underlying avoidant disorders such as OCD, addiction, and binge-eating disorder result from deficits in activating adaptive goal-directed behaviors coupled with strong stimulus response associations, leading to a reliance on habits (e.g., automatic processing) instead of top-down executive function cognitive processes. Studies show that cognitive control is managed through a neurobiological network including frontal-cingulate-parietal-insular pathways. This network is responsible for "multiple demand" cognitive tasks, and dysfunctions in cognitive control have been predicted by reduced gray matter across regions in this network (McTeague et al., 2016). Aspects of this network, especially frontal brain regions, have been implicated in NSSI behaviors (Westlund Schreiner et al., 2015), but additional imaging and longitudinal studies are needed to draw firm conclusions about the contribution to the cognitive control deficits believed to underlie NSSI and its related avoidant behaviors.

Integrated Conceptualization and Model

Based on the literature reviewed, it is clear that NSSI shares transdiagnostic cognitive biases and dysfunction that contribute to and maintain emotion-avoidant behaviors. We propose that explanatory models of these behaviors need to integrate how cognitive processes influence and interact with emotional processes to develop a transdiagnostic understanding of risk (e.g., Barlow et al., 2021; Jarecki et al., 2020). We suggest that maladaptive regulation strategies such as NSSI are automatically chosen after a reaction to negative emotions interacting with rumination, positive outcome expectancies, and cognitive control deficits that interfere with the ability to redirect attention to adaptive coping and self-regulate (Villalobos et al., 2021). The reinforcing properties of the avoidant behaviors activate strong reward processes that intensify the salience of behavior-relevant cues, thereby increasing attentional biases to internal, interpersonal, and environmental stimuli that easily activate the negative emotional cascades prompting the avoidant behavior. These interacting cognitive and emotional processes create a powerful feedback loop contributing to repeated and habitual engagement in the avoidant behavior. Reviews of the neurobiological processes involved further support these processes, suggesting dysfunction within neural circuits related to the approach (striatum, ACC), avoidance (amygdala), and regulatory (PFC) systems (Auerbach et al., 2021). These dysfunctions may potentiate avoidant behaviors given their roles in exacerbating attentional bias to negative emotional contents, rumination, impulsivity, cognitive inflexibility, and reduced capacity for decision-making.

Although the behaviors reviewed in this chapter are all maladaptive avoidance strategies and influenced by similar processes, they are diverse in their manifestation, which suggests that additional factors, or moderators, may impact what drives engagement in a compulsive symptom versus another behavior. An additive model may be relevant to consider when conceptualizing all these behaviors and their underlying relationships, given that the distinction between compulsive and dysregulated behaviors can blur as they are all driven by experiences of distress and attempts to avoid such experiences (Bresin, 2020; Den Ouden et al., 2020). Alternatively, Barlow et al. (2021) argue that avoidant behaviors stem from a neurotic temperament (including cortical and autonomic system reactivity) that interacts with life stressors to create overreactions to emotional experiences that are perceived as uncontrollable and unpredictable. The emotion-motivated avoidant behavior (e.g., NSSI) provides a false sense of control over the aversive emotional arousal that paradoxically ends up perpetuating reactivity to future aversive emotional cascades resulting in a more ingrained overreliance on the avoidant coping behavior (Barlow et al., 2021). It will be important for future studies of NSSI to consider how this model can enhance our understanding of the behavior, as well as what unique processes distinguish compulsive (OCD), addictive (SUD), and dysregulated behaviors (ED) and where NSSI falls along this behavioral continuum.

Challenges, Limitations, and Recommendations

The increasing focus on cognitive processes contributing to NSSI and related avoidant behaviors represents a strength in the development of models for understanding these behaviors and opens opportunities for enhanced understanding beyond emotional processing regulation models. However, much of the cognitive process research is guided by the RDoCs framework which provides a narrow conceptualization of transdiagnostic cognitive processes involved in avoidant behaviors. For example, there is clear evidence that rumination and attentional biases are salient cognitive processes impacting multiple disorders, suggesting they may be transdiagnostic features (e.g., Wahl et al., 2019), but neither is currently included within the RDoCs. Another example would be to consider compulsivity, given there is growing support for a neurocognitive model of compulsivity that shares features with existing neurocognitive deficits observed across dysfunctional behaviors (Fineberg et al., 2016). In addition, it will be important to examine the impact of the identified cognitive processes within co-occurring diagnoses or in relation to each other. Currently, understanding of cognitive processes has been restricted to single-factor or single-disorder examination. To fully capture the complexities of NSSI and other avoidant behaviors we need studies that evaluate whether the observed cognitive processes are similar, stronger, or weaker among comorbid and co-occurring diagnostic groups (e.g., NSSI + ED diagnosis; SUD + OCD diagnosis).

Examining potential interactive relationships among the cognitive processes identified within RDoCs and evaluating cognitive processing strengths would enrich the field's conceptualization of these behaviors while also addressing the complexities likely to be involved. Also, the RDoC could work with existing schools of psychological science so that all parties can align research, clinical, and logistical priorities and establish a common set of terms and structures. For example, the Association for Contextual Behavioral Science (ACBS) recently published a white paper of their research recommendations, emphasizing multiple dimensions and levels of analysis priorities for psychological research while emphasizing the role of context (Hayes et al., 2021) that overlaps with and complements the existing RDoC framework. Integrating priorities could streamline efforts to efficiently advance our understanding of numerous processes involved in psychopathology. Moving forward, research will need to continue to clarify neural and cognitive abnormalities, commonalities, and differences across avoidant behaviors to determine whether they represent vulnerability markers or direct causal pathways. Including a focus on identifying potential moderators of the cognitive processes implicated in self-regulation could help guide treatment interventions. Emphasizing cognitive control strengths and how they may relate to things like value-based decision-making will also be important to promoting interventions that can support full recovery. Essentially, it is important that the cognitive influencers of NSSI and related behaviors are not overlooked within research and theoretical or clinical intervention models given their impactful role on both emotional and behavioral processes underlying their occurrence.

Implications for Treatment

It is important that adequate treatment for NSSI and any co-occurring conditions properly accounts for both cognitive processes and emotion regulation, considering that cognitive processes are frequent antecedents to negative affect processes that lead to maladaptive behaviors. While there is support for the effectiveness of dialectical behavior therapy (DBT) and cognitive behavioral therapy (CBT) in reducing NSSI, disordered eating symptoms, substance abuse, and symptoms of OCD (DeCou, et al., 2019; Magill et al., 2019; Öst, et al., 2015; Vogel et al., 2021), other treatment approaches that directly target the cognitive processes reviewed in this chapter may represent a fruitful avenue to pursue. For example, a growing number of studies have found that attentional bias modification training, similar to habit reversal or cue retraining, has been successful in reducing NSSI acts, cravings and use of substances, binge/purge episodes, and compulsive behaviors (e.g., Aulbach et al., 2019; Cristea et al., 2016; Franklin et al., 2016). Incorporating these strategies with emotion regulation interventions may enhance the effectiveness and speed of the effects in reducing the problematic behaviors.

Another promising treatment that may help through its impact on cognitive control processes and promotion of values-based (top-down) decision-making is ACT (Hayes et al., 2011). ACT has shown effectiveness in reducing symptoms of a variety of avoidant and impulsive behaviors and disorders (Gloster et al., 2020; Morrison et al., 2020), and it may be particularly useful for NSSI given it also emphasizes reducing life-interfering behaviors and acceptance of internal and external experiences. In addition, clinicians may want to consider the unified protocol for transdiagnostic treatment of emotional disorders which has consistently shown effectiveness in reducing symptom severity across many emotional disorders including NSSI (Bentley, 2017; Cassiello-Robbins et al., 2020). Although heavily emphasizing emotion regulation processes, the unified protocol also addresses underlying cognitive and physiological experiences contributing to reliance on dysfunctional avoidant emotion regulation strategies and teaching adaptive regulation skills.

Treatments such as these, including DBT, ACT, and CBT, are believed to reduce NSSI and related behaviors because they teach adaptive skills but also because they affect the neurobiological dysfunctions underlying the emotional and cognitive processes contributing to the problem behaviors (see Kinley & Reyno, 2016). Specifically, treatments such as DBT, appear to work by helping to regulate and reestablish functional homeostasis within the limbic (amygdala, insula) and PFC, ACC regions (for more on behavioral approaches to NSSI treatment, see Chapman et al., this volume). Therapeutic changes have also been shown to correlate with improved integration and connectivity between the prefrontal cortical and frontolimbic circuitry, dampening arousal and attentional bias, and enhancing both self-awareness and decision-making (Kinley & Reyno, 2016). The observed neurobiological improvements resulting from specific treatment strategies directly map onto the regions of dysfunction observed in the cognitive processes reviewed above. As such, integrating treatments that address the dysfunctional cognitive processes underlying these behaviors is an important next step.

Case Example

We can consider the case of "Alex," a 25-year-old female. She has experienced generalized worries since she was a child, and around age 11 she developed OCD centered around contamination, finding a "just right" feeling, and distress related to intrusive violent and sexual images. While initial treatment for the OCD helped, as puberty onset, Alex started to have increased difficulty regulating emotions, would become easily overwhelmed, and had occasional reoccurrences of her OCD symptoms. During these times, Alex would lash out or shut down and feel tense, anxious, and guilty for perceived faults in relationships; the emotions were often a result of rumination on the perceived faults and inability to relieve her emotional distress. After experiencing some relief from scratching her wrists during an emotional lashing-out, Alex began to scratch her wrists more frequently and severely when distressed or feeling guilt about social interactions. She began to scratch herself anytime she perceived herself to cause interpersonal stress for others and to help distract from her anxiety, although she noticed she had to injure herself until she experienced the "just right feeling" like her past obsessions. The emotional relief Alex experienced from her severe scratching began to generalize to additional experiences such as when she was prevented from finishing a compulsion or when she could not finish to the point where she felt "just right." After one particularly tough day that included an argument with her guardians, Alex could not get intrusive thoughts of cutting herself out of her mind and saw potential tools for cutting all around her, so she cut herself. A couple of days later, her guardians learned that Alex had cut herself and they responded with additional concern, seeming to finally understand the increased frequency, severity, and distress her obsessions were causing.

After this event, Alex began to cut herself more frequently and sometimes in anticipation of a negative experience or to "ward off" obsessive thoughts. Over time, Alex found that once an urge to self-injure appeared, she could not resist it and would injure herself almost immediately. Alex came to "trust" the self-injury as her primary coping tool and she often would rub or stare at her scars, which provided her with peace and relief. When she entered college, Alex's anxiety intensified along with feelings of social isolation, so she began drinking alcohol and smoking marijuana with some peers to fit in. Alex discovered these substances provided the same quiet in her mind as the cutting so she began to increase her use, especially on days when cutting was less feasible due to living with roommates in the residence halls. However, after drinking or smoking marijuana, Alex's anxiety and self-critical thoughts would be stronger the next day, so she often ended up cutting herself. Alex confided in a friend that she felt out of control and unable to cope with her distress without cutting or using substances, which led to Alex seeking treatment at the university behavioral health center.

If we consider Alex's case, we can see that her self-injury and later substance use emerge from a desire to control her environment and to cope with her aversive internal experiences. Alex's tendency to ruminate on faults as well as her obsessions and the resulting distress exacerbates her negative emotions to the point where they feel overwhelming and out of control. To regain a sense of control, Alex engages in NSSI, which quickly leads to the development of positive outcome expectancies that the scratching and cutting will provide relief, strengthening the use of NSSI as a coping strategy. Possibly due to the positive expectancies of relief generated from the self-injury, when under distress, Alex has heightened awareness of both her urges to self-injure and things in her environment that could serve as tools for the NSSI. We also saw that Alex comes to develop anticipatory distress for both interpersonal difficulties and obsessive thoughts, which also activates NSSI behavior as a preemptive attempt to self-regulate. This attentional bias toward self-injury and her distress makes it hard for Alex to resist her urges and she ends up cutting herself. Alex's narrow reliance on NSSI and then substances to cope, along with quick engagement in the behaviors once the urge appeared, suggests that some cognitive control deficits and impulsivity are likely influencing her use of these emotion-avoidant behaviors. Further assessment uncovered examples of RGB, such that Alex believed she could not cope without the NSSI and that she was a bad person because of the behaviors, which further justified their use via self-punishment motives. She also came to believe that she did not deserve help unless her distress was severe, creating additional "if-then" rules which led to reliance on NSSI and substances to cope rather than seeking help earlier.

Treatment for Alex would be multifaceted and first focus on establishing safety while teaching additional strategies to regulate extreme distress (see Kinley & Reyno, 2016). Conducting a thorough functional analysis will help to determine the core cognitions and rumination patterns driving Alex's distress as well as any expectancies further maintaining the self-injury. Psychoeducation about the adaptive components of emotions and strategies to improve cognitive flexibility that challenge RGBs and other maladaptive thoughts would likely help reduce Alex's fear of negative emotions and help her separate herself, and her behavior, from the cognitions driving it. Cue-retraining strategies may also help Alex reduce her anxiety and weaken NSSI urges by assisting her in noticing adaptive coping and calming cues in her environment (e.g., Cristea et al., 2016). Behavioral techniques that expose Alex to experiences of negative emotion and use of adaptive coping strategies would also likely help to reduce her reliance on the emotion-avoidance behaviors. Further exploring Alex's values and goals and teaching her how to separate cognitions from actions may be helpful in providing her a forward-thinking and values-focused way to view her world and make choices on how to manage distress. Overall, a combination of evidence-based therapies such as DBT, ACT, and CBT would likely assist Alex in coping with her OCD symptoms while also reducing her reliance on NSSI and substances for coping. Given the overlap and likely need to utilize strategies from multiple therapies, it could be more efficient to begin with using the unified protocol for emotional disorder as this treatment has been effective in reducing aversive reactivity to emotional experiences and subsequent emotion-avoidant behaviors, like NSSI, across a variety of emotional disorders (see Cassiello-Robbins et al., 2020). The promising news for Alex is that there are a variety of treatments available to treat the underlying cognitive and emotional processes contributing to her self-injury with likely success.

Conclusion

The research reviewed in this chapter provides strong evidence that a variety of cognitive processes impact vulnerability to and maintenance of NSSI behaviors. Many of these cognitive processes are similarly implicated in additional behavioral disorders such as EDs, substance use, and OCD, all of which co-occur at high rates with NSSI. All these behaviors are conceptualized as emotion-avoidant strategies designed to help self-regulate but result in short-term relief, which reinforces further dysfunctional engagement. The underlying cognitive control process deficiencies, rumination on negative emotions, and cognitions that orient toward a desire to avoid negative emotions fuel the emotion-avoidant cycle exacerbating the NSSI and other dysfunctional behaviors. Although each of these cognitive processes has demonstrated reliable connections to NSSI, most have been studied in isolation from each other and the synergistic influence of these processes needs further study. More research is also needed to identify and understand potential moderators of the observed relationships to determine factors impacting why someone might engage in NSSI versus another behavior, or different behaviors at different time points. Longitudinal studies using experimental designs to evaluate changes in cognitive processes would be highly valuable for advancing our knowledge of NSSI vulnerability. Integrating a neurobiological focus into the studies of cognitive processes underlying NSSI, especially within longitudinal designs, would be an innovative and desirable way to expand current understanding of how cognitive processes impact the onset and maintenance of NSSI.

For clinicians, the data in this chapter highlight the importance of integrating cognitive therapies and cognitive retraining strategies into the treatment of NSSI and related avoidant behaviors. The use of functional analysis is a recommended tool given its ability to understand the nuances of each symptom and behavior, and the function they serve, along with elaborating how cognitive processes such as attentional bias, impulsivity, rumination, expectancies, and cognitive inflexibility contribute to the behavioral patterns. Clinical studies that examine the relevance and effectiveness of adding treatments such as ACT and attention/cue-retraining to existing protocols would expand current interventions for NSSI, as would additional studies examining the use of transdiagnostic treatment approaches like the unified protocol (e.g., Bentley, 2017). Overall, the current review indicates that interventions need to take a multifaceted approach to the treatment of NSSI that can address the interacting influences of cognitive processes on the emotional pathways leading to self-injury. Future research needs to consider, more extensively, the cognitive processes described in the RDoCs contributing to NSSI, along with other cognitive factors like compulsivity and rumination given the strong role these seem to play in NSSI and among co-occurring emotion-avoidant behaviors.

References

Abramovitch, A., Short, T., & Schweiger, A. (2021). The C factor: Cognitive dysfunction as a transdiagnostic dimension in psychopathology. *Clinical Psychology Review*, *86*, Article 102007. https://doi.org/10.1016/j.cpr.2021.102007

Amaya, K. A., & Smith, K. S. (2018). Neurobiology of habit formation. *Current Opinion in Behavioral Sciences*, *20*, 145–152.

Antons, S., Brand, M., & Potenza, M. N. (2020). Neurobiology of cue-reactivity, craving, and inhibitory control in non-substance addictive behaviors. *Journal of the Neurological Sciences*, *415*, Article 116952. https://doi.org/10.1016/j.jns.2020.116952

Auerbach, R. P., Pagliaccio, D., Allison, G. O., Alqueza, K. L., & Alonso, M. F. (2021). Neural correlates associated with suicide and nonsuicidal self-injury in youth. *Biological Psychiatry*, *89*, 119–133. https://doi.org/10.1016/j.biopsych.2020.06.002

Aulbach, M. B., Knittle, K., & Haukkala, A. (2019). Implicit process interventions in eating behaviour: A meta-analysis examining mediators and moderators. *Health Psychology Review*, *13*(2), 179–208. https://doi.org/10.1080/17437199.2019.1571933

Bahji, A., Mazhar, M. N., Hudson, C. C., Nadkarni, P., MacNeil, B. A., & Hawken, E. (2019). Prevalence of substance use disorder comorbidity among individuals with eating disorders: A systematic review and meta-analysis. *Psychiatry Research*, *273*, 58–66. https://doi.org/10.1016/j.psychres.2019.01.007

Barlow, D. H., Curreri, A. J., & Woodard, L. S. (2021). Neuroticism and disorders of emotion: A new synthesis. *Current Directions in Psychological Science*, *305*(5), 410–417. https://doi.org/10.1177/09637214211030253

Bentley, K. H. (2017). Applying the unified protocol transdiagnostic treatment to nonsuicidal self-injury and co-occurring emotional disorders: A case illustration. *Journal of Clinical Psychology*, *73*(5), 547–558. https://doi.org/10.1002/jclp.22452

Bentley, K. H., Cassiello-Robbins, C. F., Vittorio, L., Sauer-Zavala, S., & Barlow, D. H. (2015). The association between nonsuicidal self-injury and the emotional disorders: A meta-analytic review. *Clinical Psychology Review*, *37*, 72–88. https://doi.org/10.1016/j.cpr.2015.02.006

Bresin, K. (2020). Toward a unifying theory of dysregulated behaviors. *Clinical Psychology Review*, *80*, 101885–101885. https://doi.org/10.1016/j.cpr.2020.101885

Buelens, T., Luyckx, K., Verschueren, M., Schoevaerts, K., Dierckx, E., Depestele, L., & Claes, L. (2020). Temperament and character traits of female eating disorder patients with(out) non-suicidal self-injury. *Journal of Clinical Medicine*, *9*(4), Article 1207. https://doi.org/10.3390/jcm9041207

Callahan, K. E., Stori, S. A., & Donahue, J. J. (2021). Psychological inflexibility processes and nonsuicidal self-injury: Concurrent and prospective associations. *Journal of Clinical Psychology*, *77*(6), 1394–1411. https://doi.org/10.1002/jclp.23086

Cassiello-Robbins, C., Southward, M. W., Tirpak, J. W., & Sauer-Zavala, S. (2020). A systematic review of unified protocol applications with adult populations: Facilitating widespread dissemination via adaptability. *Clinical Psychology Review*, *78*, Article 101852. https://doi.org/10.1016/j.cpr.2020.101852

Cristea, I. A., Kok, R. N., & Cuijpers, P. (2016). The effectiveness of cognitive bias modification interventions for substance addictions: A meta-analysis. *PloS One, 11*(9), Article e0162226. https://doi.org/10.1371/journal.pone.0162226

Cucchi, A., Ryan, D., Konstantakopoulos, G., Stroumpa, S., Kaçar, A., Renshaw, S., Landau, S., & Kravariti, E. (2016). Lifetime prevalence of non-suicidal self-injury in patients with eating disorders: A systematic review and meta-analysis. *Psychological Medicine, 46*(7), 1345–1358. https://doi.org/10.1017/S0033291716000027

DeCou, C. R., Comtois, K. A., & Landes, S. J. (2019). Dialectical behavior therapy is effective for the treatment of suicidal behavior: A meta-analysis. *Behavior Therapy, 50*(1), 60–72. https://doi.org/10.1016/j.beth.2018.03.009

Della Longa, N. M., & De Young, K. P. (2018). Experiential avoidance, eating expectancies, and binge eating: A preliminary test of an adaption of the acquired preparedness model of eating disorder risk. *Appetite, 120*, 423–430. https://doi.org/10.1016/j.appet.2017.09.022

Den Ouden, L., Tiego, J., Lee, R. S., Albertella, L., Greenwood, L.-M., Fontenelle, L., Yücel, M., & Segrave, R. (2020). The role of experiential avoidance in transdiagnostic compulsive behavior: A structural model analysis. *Addictive Behaviors, 108*, 106464–106464. https://doi.org/10.1016/j.addbeh.2020.106464

Disner, S. G., Beevers, C. G., Haigh, E. A., & Beck, A. T. (2011). Neural mechanisms of the cognitive model of depression. Nature *Reviews Neuroscience, 12*(8), 467–477.

Dahlgren, M. K., Hooley, J. M., Best, S. G., Sagar, K. A., Gonenc, A., & Gruber, S. A. (2018). Prefrontal cortex activation during cognitive interference in nonsuicidal self-injury. *Psychiatry Research. Neuroimaging, 277*, 28–38. https://doi.org/10.1016/j.pscychresns.2018.04.006

Dixon, M. L., & Christoff, K. (2014). The lateral prefrontal cortex and complex value-based learning and decision making. *Neuroscience and Biobehavioral Reviews, 45*, 9–18. https://doi.org/10.1016/j.neubiorev.2014.04.011

Fineberg, N., Menchon, J., Zohar, J., & Veltman, D. (2016). Compulsivity—A new trans-diagnostic research domain for the roadmap for Mental Health Research in Europe (ROAMER) and Research Domain Criteria (RDoC) initiatives. *European Neuropsychopharmacology, 26*(5), 797–799. https://doi.org/10.1016/j.euroneuro.2016.04.001

Franklin, J. C., Fox, K. R., Franklin, C. R., Kleiman, E. M., Ribeiro, J. D., Jaroszewski, A. C., Hooley, J. M. & Nock, M. K. (2016). A brief mobile app reduces nonsuicidal and suicidal self-injury: Evidence from three randomized controlled trials. *Journal of Consulting and Clinical Psychology, 84*, 544–557. http://dx.doi.org.proxy.uwec.edu/10.1037/ccp0000093

Gesualdo, C., & Pinquart, M. (2021). Expectancy challenge interventions to reduce alcohol consumption among high school and college students: A meta-analysis. *Psychology of Addictive Behaviors, 35*(7), 817–828. http://dx.doi.org.proxy.uwec.edu/10.1037/adb0000732

Gifuni, A. J., Perret, L. C., Lacourse, E., Geoffroy, M. C., Mbekou, V., Jollant, F., & Renaud, J. (2021). Decision-making and cognitive control in adolescent suicidal behaviors: A qualitative systematic review of the literature. *European Child & Adolescent Psychiatry, 30*(12), 1839–1855. https://doi.org/10.1007/s00787-020-01550-3

Gillan, C. M., & Robbins, T. W. (2014). Goal-directed learning and obsessive–compulsive disorder. *Philosophical Transactions of the Royal Society B: Biological Sciences, 369*(1655), Article 20130475. https://doi.org/10.1098/rstb.2013.0475

Gillan, C. M., Robbins, T. W., Sahakian, B. J., van den Heuvel, O. A., & van Wingen, G. (2016). The role of habit in compulsivity. *European Neuropsychopharmacology, 26*(5), 828–840. https://doi.org/10.1016/j.euroneuro.2015.12.033

Gläscher, J., Adolphs, R., Damasio, H., Bechara, A., Rudrauf, D., Calamia, M., Paul, L. K., & Tranel, D. (2012). Lesion mapping of cognitive control and value-based decision making in the prefrontal cortex. *Proceedings of the National Academy of Sciences, 109*(36), 14681–14686. https://doi.org/10.1073/pnas.1206608109

Glenn, J. J., Werntz, A. J., Slama, S. J., Steinman, S. A., Teachman, B. A., & Nock, M. K. (2017). Suicide and self-injury-related implicit cognition: A large-scale examination and replication. *Journal of Abnormal Psychology, 126*(2), 199–211. https://doi.org/10.1037/abn0000230

Gloster, A. T., Walder, N., Levin, M. E., Twohig, M. P., & Karekla, M. (2020). The empirical status of acceptance and commitment therapy: A review of meta-analyses. *Journal of Contextual Behavioral Science, 18*, 181–192. https://doi.org/10.1016/j.jcbs.2020.09.009

Halicka-Masłowska, J., Szewczuk-Bogusławska, M., Adamska, A., & Misiak, B. (2020). Neurobiology of the association between non-suicidal self-injury, suicidal behavior and emotional intelligence: A review. *Archives of Psychiatry and Psychotherapy*, *2*, 25–35. https://doi.org/10.12740/APP/117705

Hayes, S., Luoma, J., Bond, F., Masuda, A., & Lillis, J. (2006). Acceptance and commitment therapy: Model, processes and outcomes. *Behaviour Research and Therapy*, *44*(1), 1–25. https://doi.org/10.1016/j.brat.2005.06.006

Hayes, S. C., Merwin, R. M., McHugh, L., Sandoz, E. K., A-Tjak, J. G., Ruiz, F. J., Barnes-Holmes, D., Bricker, J. B., Ciarrochi, J., Dixon, M. R., Fung, K. P.-L., Gloster, A. T., Gobin, R. L., Gould, E. R., Hofmann, S. G., Kasujja, R., Karekla, M., Luciano, C., & McCracken, L. M. (2021). Report of the ACBS Task Force on the strategies and tactics of contextual behavioral science research. *Journal of Contextual Behavioral Science*, *20*, 172–183. https://doi.org/10.1016/j.jcbs.2021.03.007

Hayes, S., Strosahl, K., & Wilson, K. (2011). *Acceptance and commitment therapy: The process and practice of mindful change*. 2nd ed. Guilford Press.

Hellberg, S., Buchholz, J., Twohig, M., & Abramowitz, J. (2020). Not just thinking, but believing: Obsessive beliefs and domains of cognitive fusion in the prediction of OCD symptom dimensions. *Clinical Psychology and Psychotherapy*, *27*(1), 69–78. https://doi.org/10.1002/cpp.2409

Hofmann, W., Schmeichel, B. J., & Baddeley, A. D. (2012). Executive functions and self-regulation. *Trends in Cognitive Sciences*, *16*(3), 174–180. https://doi.org/10.1016/j.tics.2012.01.006

Hughes, C. D., King, A. M., Kranzler, A., Fehling, K., Miller, A., Lindqvist, J., & Selby, E. A. (2019). Anxious and overwhelming affects and repetitive negative thinking as ecological predictors of self-injurious thoughts and behaviors. *Cognitive Therapy and Research*, *43*(1), 88–101. https://doi.org/10.1007/s10608-019-09996-9

Ii, T., Sato, H., Watanabe, N., Kondo, M., Masuda, A., Hayes, S. C., & Akechi, T. (2019). Psychological flexibility-based interventions versus first-line psychosocial interventions for substance use disorders: Systematic review and meta-analyses of randomized controlled trials. *Journal of Contextual Behavioral Science*, *13*, 109–120. https://doi.org/10.1016/j.jcbs.2019.07.003

Jarecki, J. B., Tan, J. H., & Jenny, M. A. (2020). A framework for building cognitive process models. *Psychonomic Bulletin & Review*, *27*(6), 1218–1229. https://doi.org/10.3758/s13423-020-01747-2

Kaess, M., Hooley, J. M., Klimes-Dougan, B., Koenig, J., Plener, P. L., Reichl, C., Robinson, K., Schmahl, C., Sicorello, M., Westlund Schreiner, M., & Cullen, K. R. (2021). Advancing a temporal framework for understanding the biology of nonsuicidal self-injury: An expert review. *Neuroscience and Biobehavioral Reviews*, *130*, 228–239. https://doi.org/10.1016/j.neubiorev.2021.08.022

Kinley, J. L., & Reyno, S. M. (2016). Project for a scientific psychiatry: A neurobiologically informed, phasic, brain-based model of integrated psychotherapy. *Journal of Psychotherapy Integration*, *26*(1), 61–73. https://doi.org/10.1037/a0039636

Kollárik, van den Hout, M., Heinzel, C. V., Hofer, P. D., Lieb, R., & Wahl, K. (2020). Effects of rumination on unwanted intrusive thoughts: A replication and extension. *Journal of Experimental Psychopathology*, *11*(1), 204380872091258. https://doi.org/10.1177/2043808720912583

Leeman, R. F., Robinson, C. D., Waters, A. J., & Sofuoglu, M. (2014). A critical review of the literature on attentional bias in cocaine use disorder and suggestions for future research. *Experimental and Clinical Psychopharmacology*, *22*, 469–483. https://doi.org/10.1037/a0037806

Lockwood, J., Daley, D., Townsend, E., & Sayal, K. (2017). Impulsivity and self-harm in adolescence: A systematic review. *European Child & Adolescent Psychiatry*, *26*(4), 387–402. https://doi.org/10.1007/s00787-016-0915-5

Lynch, T. R., & Cozza, C. (2009). Behavior therapy for nonsuicidal self-injury. In M. K. Nock (Ed.), *Understanding nonsuicidal self-injury: Origins, assessment, and treatment* (pp. 211–250). American Psychological Association. https://doi.org/10.1037/11875-012

Magill, M., Ray, L., Kiluk, B., Hoadley, A., Bernstein, M., Tonigan, J. S., & Carroll, K. (2019). A meta-analysis of cognitive-behavioral therapy for alcohol or other drug use disorders: Treatment efficacy by contrast condition. *Journal of Consulting and Clinical Psychology*, *87*, 1093–1105. https://doi.org/10.1037/ccp0000447

McHugh, C. M., Chun Lee, R. S., Hermens, D. F., Corderoy, A., Large, M., & Hickie, I. B. (2019). Impulsivity in the self-harm and suicidal behavior of young people: A systematic review and meta-analysis. *Journal of Psychiatric Research*, *116*, 51–60. https://doi.org/10.1016/j.jpsychires.2019.05.012

McTeague, L. M., Goodkind, M. S., & Etkin, A. (2016). Transdiagnostic impairment of cognitive control in mental illness. *Journal of Psychiatric Research*, *83*, 37–46. https://doi.org/10.1016/j.jpsychires.2016.08.001

Morrison, K. L., Smith, B. M., Ong, C. W., Lee, E. B., Friedel, J. E., Odum, A., Madden, G. J., Ledermann, T., Rung, J., & Twohig, M. P. (2020). Effects of acceptance and commitment therapy on impulsive decision-making. *Behavior Modification, 44*(4), 600–623. https://doi.org/10.1177/0145445519833041

Nicolai, K. A., Wielgus, M. D., & Mezulis, A. (2015). Identifying risk for self-harm: Rumination and negative affectivity in the prospective prediction of nonsuicidal self-injury. *Suicide and Life-Threatening Behavior, 46*(2), 223–233. https://doi.org/10.1111/sltb.12186

O'Neill, A., Bachi, B., & Bhattacharyya, S. (2020). Attentional bias towards cannabis cues in cannabis users: A systematic review and meta-analysis. *Drug and Alcohol Dependence, 206*, Article 107719. https://doi.org/10.1016/j.drugalcdep.2019.107719

Öst, L.-G., Havnen, A., Hansen, B., & Kvale, G. (2015). Cognitive behavioral treatments of obsessive–compulsive disorder. A systematic review and meta-analysis of studies published 1993–2014. *Clinical Psychology Review, 40*, 156–169. https://doi.org/10.1016/j.cpr.2015.06.003

Ottaviani, C., Thayer, J. F., Verkuil, B., Lonigro, A., Medea, B., Couyoumdjian, A., & Brosschot, J. F. (2016). Physiological concomitants of perseverative cognition: A systematic review and meta-analysis. *Psychological Bulletin, 142*(3), 231. http://dx.doi.org.proxy.uwec.edu/10.1037/bul0000036

Ralph-Nearman, C., Achee, M., Lapidus, R., Stewart, J. L., & Filik, R. (2019). A systematic and methodological review of attentional biases in eating disorders: Food, body, and perfectionism. *Brain and Behavior, 9*(12), Article e01458. https://doi.org/10.1002/brb3.1458

Riquino, M. R., Reese, S. E., & Garland, E. L. (2021). Assessing attentional bias toward nonsuicidal self-injury cues in young adults with histories of engaging in self-harm. *Child and Adolescent Social Work Journal, 38*(6), 641–650. https://doi.org/10.1007/s10560-020-00692-2

Selby, E. A., Franklin, J., Carson-Wong, A., & Rizvi, S. L. (2013). Emotional cascades and self-injury: Investigating instability of rumination and negative emotion. *Journal of Clinical Psychology, 69*(12), 1213–1227. https://doi.org/10.1002/jclp.21966

Smith, K. E., Mason, T. B., Juarascio, A., Weinbach, N., Dvorak, R., Crosby, R. D., & Wonderlich, S. A. (2020). The momentary interplay of affect, attention bias, and expectancies as predictors of binge eating in the natural environment. *International Journal of Eating Disorders, 53*(4), 586–594. https://doi.org/10.1002/eat.23235

Stojek, M., Shank, L. M., Vannucci, A., Bongiorno, D. M., Nelson, E. E., Waters, A. J., Engel, S. G., Boutelle, K. N., Pine, D. S., Yanovski, J. A., & Tanofsky-Kraff, M. (2018). A systematic review of attentional biases in disorders involving binge eating. *Appetite, 123*, 367–389. https://doi.org/10.1016/j.appet.2018.01.019

Törneke, N., Luciano, C., & Salas, S. V. (2008). Rule-governed behavior and psychological problems. *Revista Internacional de Psicología y Terapia Psicológica, 8*(2), 141–156. https://doi.org/10.1007/978-1-4757-0447-1_3

Villalobos, D., Pacios, J., & Vázquez, C. (2021). Cognitive control, cognitive biases and emotion regulation in depression: A new proposal for an integrative interplay model. *Frontiers in Psychology, 12*, 628416–628416. https://doi.org/10.3389/fpsyg.2021.628416

Vogel, E.N., Singh, S., & Accurso, E.C. (2021). A systematic review of cognitive behavior therapy and dialectical behavior therapy for adolescent eating disorders. *Journal of Eating Disorders, 9*(1), 1–131. https://doi.org/10.1186/s40337-021-00461-1

Wahl, K., Ehring, T., Kley, H., Lieb, R., Meyer, A., Kordon, A., Heinzel, C. V., Mazanec, M., & Schönfeld, S. (2019). Is repetitive negative thinking a transdiagnostic process? A comparison of key processes of RNT in depression, generalized anxiety disorder, obsessive-compulsive disorder, and community controls. *Journal of Behavior Therapy and Experimental Psychiatry, 64*, 45–53. https://doi.org/10.1016/j.jbtep.2019.02.006

Wahl, K., van den Hout, M., Heinzel, C. V., Kollárik, M., Meyer, A., Benoy, C., Berberich, G., Domschke, K., Gloster, A., Gradwohl, G., Hofecker, M., Jähne, A., Koch, S., Külz, A. K., Moggi, F., Poppe, C., Riedel, A., Rufer, M., Stierle, C., . . . Lieb, R. (2021). Rumination about obsessive symptoms and mood maintains obsessive-compulsive symptoms and depressed mood: An experimental study. *Journal of Abnormal Psychology, 130*(5), 435–442. https://doi-org.libproxy.umassd.edu/10.1037/abn0000677

Washburn, J. J., Potthoff, L. M., Juzwin, K. R., & Styer, D. M. (2015). Assessing DSM-5 nonsuicidal self-injury disorder in a clinical sample. *Psychological Assessment, 27*(1), 31–41. http://dx.doi.org/10.1037/pas0000021

Watkins, E. R., & Roberts, H. (2020). Reflecting on rumination: Consequences, causes, mechanisms and treatment of rumination. *Behaviour Research and Therapy, 127*, 103573–. https://doi.org/10.1016/j.brat.2020.103573

Westlund Schreiner, M., Klimes-Dougan, B., Begnel, E. D., & Cullen, K. R. (2015). Conceptualizing the neurobiology of non-suicidal self-injury from the perspective of the Research Domain Criteria Project. *Neuroscience and Biobehavioral Reviews, 57*, 381–391. https://doi.org/10.1016/j.neubiorev.2015.09.011

Zhang, M. W., Ying, J., Wing, T., Song, G., Fung, D. S., & Smith, H. E. (2018). Cognitive biases in cannabis, opioid, and stimulant disorders: A systematic review. *Frontiers in Psychiatry, 9*, 376–393. https://doi.org/10.3389/fpsyt.2018.00376

Zucchelli, F., White, P., & Williamson, H. (2020). Experiential avoidance and cognitive fusion mediate the relationship between body evaluation and unhelpful body image coping strategies in individuals with visible differences. *Body Image, 32*, 121–127. https://doi.org/10.1016/j.bodyim.2019.12.002

CHAPTER 17

Social Processes in Nonsuicidal Self-Injury

Maria Zetterqvist *and* Johan Bjureberg

Abstract

Social interactions are critical for the health and well-being of all group-living primates, including humans, across the lifespan. Social stressors, such as perceived criticism and rejection, are common triggers of nonsuicidal self-injury (NSSI). Social processes may thus have a central role in the etiology and maintenance of NSSI. Using the Research Domain Criteria (RDoC) framework for systems for social processes, the chapter presents recent findings on NSSI, mapping them onto the four constructs: affiliation and attachment, social communication, perception and understanding of self, and perception and understanding of others. The chapter also discusses available research related to NSSI for the respective units of analysis (genes and molecules, physiology, neurocircuitry, behavior, and self-report), focusing on the effects of social exclusion, rejection sensitivity, and negative social bias. The chapter also includes an overview of overlapping features related to social exclusion and rejection sensitivity between NSSI and borderline personality disorder, a condition characterized by interpersonal difficulties. This chapter provides an account of evidence-based assessment and intervention areas of social processes in NSSI together with recommendations and future directions. The chapter concludes that social processes are relevant to NSSI across the RDoC constructs and units of analyses. Social difficulties, social problem-solving, and experiences and interpretations of social situations need to be included in the conceptualization of how NSSI is developed and maintained and ultimately assessed and treated. In an effort to bring such conceptualization to life, a case example illustrates how an understanding of social processes may guide assessment and treatment of NSSI.

Key Words: nonsuicidal self-injury, Research Domain Criteria, social processes, social stressors, units of analysis, assessment, intervention

Introduction

Social interactions are critical for the health and well-being of all group-living primates, including humans, across the lifespan. Humans strive to interact with others, and establishing and maintaining social connections are essential parts of their existence. Social exclusion has a profound effect on afflicted individuals and leads to detrimental emotional, cognitive, and behavioral consequences, as well as significant public health costs (Heinz et al., 2019). Interference and difficulties in social functioning and navigating the social world occur across a wide range of behavioral and psychological problems and disorders

(Cotter et al., 2018). Social difficulties have therefore been recognized as a key priority for a mental health research agenda (National Institute of Mental Health [NIMH], 2020).

Nonsuicidal Self-Injury

One behavioral problem that has received increased attention during the past decade is nonsuicidal self-injury (NSSI). NSSI is defined as the deliberate, self-inflicted destruction of body tissue without suicidal intent and for purposes not socially sanctioned; it includes behaviors such as cutting, burning, biting, and scratching skin (Nock, 2010). Adolescents with NSSI have more experience with social stressors and adverse life events compared to adolescents without NSSI (Zetterqvist et al., 2013), and they also rate themselves as more interpersonally sensitive (Kim et al., 2015). Social stressors, such as perceived criticism and rejection, are common triggers of NSSI (Nock et al., 2009; Turner et al., 2016). In addition to regulating internal states, NSSI is also sometimes performed—implicitly or explicitly—to change the external environment (Turner et al., 2012). It has been argued that people escalate to NSSI as a means of influencing others when less drastic forms of social communication have not been successful (Nock, 2008). Social processes thus have a central role in NSSI and need to be included in the conceptualization of how NSSI is developed and maintained. This has been noted in the proposed criteria for the potential NSSI disorder according to the fifth edition of *Diagnostic and Statistical Manual of Mental Disorders* (DSM-5), which describes interpersonal difficulties and the expectation of resolving them by harming oneself (American Psychiatric Association, 2013).

The Research Domain Criteria

The Research Domain Criteria (RDoC) is an integrated research framework developed to increase the understanding and treatment of mental disorders (NIMH, 2020). The RDoC consider a range of behaviors from normal to abnormal rather than presenting specific diagnostic categories. The RDoC recognize social processes as one of their six domains, containing a set of constructs that include elements, processes, mechanisms, and responses. The RDoC also refer to units of analysis, which, for example, can be physiological or behavioral. The domain Systems for Social Processes is concerned with how individuals relate to one another, including how they perceive and interpret social events, as well as how they relate to and act in the social world. Four constructs—affiliation and attachment, social communication, perception and understanding of self, and perception and understanding of others—have been detailed in this domain (further information on the RDoC can be found in Bastiaens & Claes, this volume).

Using the RDoC framework for Systems for Social Processes, we first present recent findings on NSSI and map them onto the four constructs. We then present available research related to NSSI for the respective units of analysis. Throughout the chapter we focus in particular on the effects of social exclusion, rejection sensitivity, and negative social bias. We include a discussion on the overlapping features between NSSI and borderline personality disorder (BPD) and finally give an account of evidence-based assessment and intervention areas of social processes in NSSI.

Recent Findings within the RDoC Systems for Social Processes Related to NSSI

Below we present recent findings on NSSI within the RDoC constructs for social processes: Affiliation and attachment, Social communication, and Perception and understanding of self, and Perception and understanding of others.

NSSI within the Construct Affiliation and Attachment

Affiliation refers to positive engagement with others, and attachment is a type of selective affiliation that evolves once social bonds have been developed. Affiliation and attachment are moderated by a range of processes, such as processing social cues and social motivation. Disruptions in affiliation and attachment may be manifested as social withdrawal, indifference, and overattachment (NIMH, 2020). Experiencing nurturing relationships and social proximity can moderate reactions to social stressors. Attachment figures have the potential to reduce not only subjective but also physiological and neural responses to social exclusion (Coan et al., 2006; Karremans et al., 2011; Liddell & Courtney, 2018).

A history of poor attachment quality—thought to be the result of repeated experiences of social conflict, parental invalidation, and criticism—predicts NSSI, often through mediating variables such as emotion regulation difficulties and disturbed identity formation (Gandhi et al., 2019; Victor, Hipwell, et al., 2019). Also in adults, insecure attachment states of mind, especially preoccupied attachment, are associated with NSSI, while a dismissive state of mind is not (Martin et al., 2017).

Positive social interactions and social support have generally been shown to have a beneficial effect on NSSI, whereas perceived low social support, especially in the face of adversities, is associated with increased risk for NSSI (Wan et al., 2019). Studies using ecological momentary assessment (EMA) have shown that individuals with NSSI have less contact with family and friends, perceive less support, and are less likely to seek support to cope (Turner et al., 2017). Also, talking to others after thoughts of NSSI have been shown to potentially prevent actual engagement in NSSI (Fitzpatrick et al., 2020). The role of perceived social support, especially from family, as contributing to the cessation of NSSI, has been confirmed in self-report studies (Tatnell et al., 2014). Interestingly, however, although Hasking et al. found that telling peers about NSSI did not result in a perceived increase in social support (Hasking et al., 2015), another EMA study showed that perceived social support was indeed increased after NSSI was disclosed to others, and this perceived social support was associated with an increased risk of subsequent NSSI episodes (Turner et al., 2016). It would thus seem that when examining consequences of social support in NSSI, it is important to consider when and from whom the social support comes. To summarize, positive engagement with others and close social bonds have shown to moderate reactions to social stressors and function as a buffer against NSSI.

NSSI within the Construct Social Communication

Social communication refers to both productive and receptive transactions of socially relevant information. This involves both explicit and implicit processes, such as recognizing affect, facial recognition, eye contact, and reciprocal behavior (NIMH, 2020). Accurate perception of facial emotions is a central part of social communication. A few studies have examined facial emotion in relation to NSSI. In two studies of clinical samples of adolescents with NSSI, no behavioral group differences were found for recognition and accuracy of facial expression compared to clinical and healthy controls, using a dynamically developing emotion task (In-Albon et al., 2015; Perini et al., 2019), nor were there any physiological differences, as assessed with facial electromyography (EMG), between healthy controls and adolescents with NSSI in reaction to emotional faces (Perini et al., 2019). Seymour et al. (2016) did, however, find deficits in emotion identification in an NSSI sample, but they used static emotion images as opposed to dynamic, which could potentially explain the difference in results. Another psychophysiological study using facial EMG (Ziebell et al., 2020) found attenuated modulation in the corrugator response in individuals with a history of NSSI when watching dynamic angry and happy faces. The corrugator is the facial muscle ("frown"), which is more active when an individual experiences a negative internal state and less so in response to a positive emotion. Less mimicry was associated with self-reported social functions of NSSI.

In a study by Lutz et al. (2020), individuals with depression and NSSI rated neutral faces as more sad and also gave higher sad ratings to sad faces compared to the clinical controls with depression and no NSSI, indicating a bias in the perception of the emotional expression in others with implications for social communication. In their study, adolescents with NSSI also showed less neural activation in the occipital lobe and cerebellum to happy faces versus neutral faces, compared to the clinical controls, but there were no group differences in limbic activity in the emotion processing task (Lutz et al., 2020). An earlier study found atypical amygdala-frontal connectivity with, for example, lower connectivity between amygdala and the bilateral frontal pole, medial frontal cortex, and paracingulate in individuals with NSSI compared to healthy controls during an emotion face-matching functional magnetic resonance imaging (fMRI) task (Westlund Schreiner et al., 2017).

Although findings are not conclusive, a negative bias in interpreting others' facial emotional reactions and a potential risk of perceiving others as signaling criticism or disappointment could potentially increase social stressors and heighten the emotional reaction during social interactions in individuals with NSSI.

NSSI within the Construct Perception and Understanding of Self and Others

Perception and understanding of self involve being aware of, accessing knowledge about, and/or making judgments about the self (NIMH, 2020). A positive view of self is suggested to be a barrier against NSSI, and a negative view of self is associated with NSSI (Hooley & Franklin, 2018). High levels of self-criticism are reported in those who self-injure, and self-punishment is a common reason for engaging in NSSI (Hooley & Germain, 2014). Adolescents with NSSI report more negative affect before a social stressful situation compared to healthy controls (Kaess et al., 2012), which perhaps can be interpreted as a potential negative bias in the perception of competence and skills. Adolescents with NSSI further reported significantly lower perception of self-efficacy for solving social problems than controls without NSSI (Nock & Mendes, 2008). Self-report studies show that young people with NSSI rate themselves as less attractive and skilled than their healthy controls (Claes et al., 2010), and a review supports generally lower self-reported self-esteem in those with NSSI (Forrester et al., 2017). For example, adolescents with NSSI reported significantly lower liking when seeing a photo of their own face compared to healthy controls (Perini et al., 2019). Self-reported poorer social self-worth and self-competence have also been shown to predict NSSI (Victor, Hipwell, et al., 2019). However, young adults with NSSI did not differ from those without NSSI on self-perceived social competence (Turner et al., 2017). Neural basis of social processing has also been investigated using a social self-processing task in clinical adolescents with depression and NSSI, with results supporting a disruption in self- and emotional processing with greater limbic and anterior and posterior cortical midline structure activity in those with NSSI compared to both clinically depressed controls and healthy controls (Quevedo et al., 2016). Taken together, these data support a potential negative bias in self-processing, suggesting that NSSI might be an expression of and way to deal with negative perception of the self and confused self-processing (Gandhi et al., 2019; Quevedo et al., 2016) (see Swerdlow et al., this volume, for more on negative affect and NSSI).

Perception and understanding of others refer to individuals' understanding and judgments about other individuals (NIMH, 2020). Individuals with NSSI perceive their parents as less supportive and more critical than those without NSSI (Ammerman & Brown, 2018). There is also support for high limbic activity (i.e., activity in the area of the brain involved in the process of emotion and memory) during an fMRI task of self-processing in depressed adolescents with NSSI when they took the perspective of their mother during a self-reflection task. The elevated limbic activity correlated with lower maternal emotional support (Quevedo et al., 2016). The authors interpret the findings as evidence of a "disruption in self- and emotion-processing and conflicted social relationships in the neurobiology of NSSI" (Quevedo et al., 2016, p. 145) when comparing depressed adolescents with NSSI to control groups of both depressed and healthy adolescents.

The next section presents research related to NSSI for the respective units of analysis, focusing in particular on the effects of social exclusion, rejection sensitivity, and negative social bias.

NSSI and Social Stressors: Genes and Molecules as Units of Analyses

Hankin et al. (2015) found a significant gene-environment effect in their study of NSSI in a community sample, where those with at least one short carrier of Serotonin Transporter-Linked Polymorphic Region (5-HTTLPR) in combination with severe and long-lasting social stressors were at heightened risk for NSSI (Hankin et al., 2015). A recent study that investigated the role of the 5-HTT genotype variation and early parental neglect in rhesus monkeys that were exposed to social stressors found a significant interaction effect on the 5-HTT genotype by NSSI status on stress-induced behaviors (Wood et al., 2021). Data on genetic susceptibility for NSSI, specifically in relation to social processes, are sparse and more studies are needed.

The intensity of the stressful reactions to real or perceived social exclusion can be associated with dysregulated neuropeptides, such as oxytocin, vasopressin, and opioids (Stanley & Siever, 2010). Oxytocin is implicated in social affiliative behavior and stress reduction, and opioids are implicated in both soothing and distress during social exclusion, suggesting that these peptides are relevant in social processes. The relationship between oxytocin and social exclusion has, for example, been examined in BPD, depression, and also suicidality (Chu et al., 2020; Jobst et al., 2014), and it is most likely also of interest for NSSI, but it has to our knowledge not specifically been looked into. The role of opioids has been discussed in models of NSSI, suggesting a vulnerability in this system with reduced levels of beta-endorphin (BE) and enkephalins in individuals with NSSI and BPD with self-injury (Bresin & Gordon, 2013; Stanley & Siever, 2010). Opioids play a part in separation distress and relief when separation is ended, in comfort during caring, as well as in pain associated with social exclusion and rejection. Reduced levels of opioids alter these experiences, and altered µ-opioid receptors are implicated in sensitivity to rejection. It is proposed that lower levels of opioids are a consequence of both environmental and genetic factors (Stanley & Siever, 2010). One recent study investigated BE levels in adolescents with NSSI who were exposed to pain and found lower plasma BE levels compared to controls, supporting earlier results of an opioid deficiency (Venne et al., 2021). The idea of lower baseline levels of endogenous opioids in NSSI has also been questioned (see, e.g., Hooley & Franklin, 2018), and more longitudinal and experimental work is needed. Some earlier work has been done using genes and molecules as units of analysis for understanding NSSI and social stressors, but more research is needed to further examine these constructs.

NSSI and Social Stressors: Physiology as Unit of Analysis

Studies have investigated (altered) stress responses, and a possible dysfunction of the hypothalamic-pituitary-adrenal (HPA) axis, in NSSI. The HPA axis is the body's response system to stress. Self-injury (with unclear intent) is associated with lower cortisol levels after administration of dexamethasone in adolescent girls with depressive symptomatology, using a dexamethasone suppression test (Beauchaine et al., 2015). Kaess et al. (2012)

investigated salivary cortisol levels in adolescents with NSSI after the Trier Social Stress Test (TSST), in which social stress is induced through socially evaluative tasks performed in front of a panel of judges, and found support for an attenuated stress response in those with NSSI compared to controls. A later study of young females with self-injury with unclear intent also showed lower blood cortisol during the TSST (Plener et al., 2017), which has shown to be especially pronounced for those with repetitive NSSI (Klimes-Dougan et al., 2019). Nonstimulated HPA-axis functioning has also been investigated in a clinical sample of adolescents with NSSI compared to healthy controls. Results suggest that there may be alterations in the HPA-stress system in those with NSSI (Reichl et al., 2016). Taken together, these results tentatively indicate preliminary support for a blunted cortisol level during psychosocial stress in young people with NSSI. A potential explanation for this altered stress reaction is that repeated adverse experiences and stress have led to habituation and desensitization of the stress response.

Although skin conductance levels (SCL) increased during TSST for young adults both with and without NSSI, Tatnell et al. (2018) found no differences between groups. An earlier study by Nock and Mendes (2008) did find physiological group differences in response to a distressing task with greater SCL changes in adolescents with NSSI. Their stress trigger was, however, less social in nature. Respiratory sinus arrhythmia (RSA) has also been examined experimentally in response to social stressors (Wielgus et al., 2016), with greater RSA withdrawal to social stressors significantly predicting recent NSSI (Crowell et al., 2005; Fox et al., 2018). Kaess et al. (2012) found no differences, however, between controls and NSSI in heart rate response to the TSST.

Difficulties regulating physiological reactions when exposed to social stressors might make some individuals more susceptible to regulate emotions through NSSI (Fox et al., 2018; Wielgus et al., 2016). Further experimental settings using social stressors for assessing physiological responses are needed.

NSSI and Social Stressors: Neurocircuitry as Unit of Analysis

Neural processes in relation to social rejection have mainly been investigated using the cyberball task (Williams & Jarvis, 2006) with fMRI. In this paradigm, the participant engages in a ball-tossing game with other virtual players, during which the participant initially is included and then becomes increasingly excluded. Earlier studies have consistently shown that the cyberball task results in distress following rejection (Radke et al., 2018), and clinical groups typically report higher levels of distress than healthy controls (Olié et al., 2017).

The regions of the insula; anterior cingulate cortex (ACC); frontal gyrus; and temporal, occipital, and prefrontal cortex (PFC) are usually activated during cyberball (Mwilambwe-Tshilobo & Spreng, 2021; Wang et al., 2017). In particular, activity in the dorsal ACC has previously been suggested to be implicated in social exclusion, with a potential neural overlap between social and physical pain (Eisenberger et al., 2003).

However, recent meta-analytic evidence of cyberball findings prompts to a reinterpretation of the specificity of dorsal ACC activity during social rejection and highlights the role of the default mode network in social exclusion (Mwilambwe-Tshilobo & Spreng, 2021; Vijayakumar et al., 2017). The neurobiology of social exclusion has also been investigated in individuals with NSSI using the cyberball paradigm (Brown et al., 2017; Groschwitz et al., 2016). Brown et al. (2017) found an increased activation in the ventral ACC in both adults with BPD + NSSI and adolescents with NSSI compared to healthy controls during social exclusion. Depressed adolescents with NSSI showed greater activation of the medial PFC and the ventrolateral PFC compared to depressed adolescents without NSSI and healthy controls during cyberball (Groschwitz et al., 2016). Using a recently developed paradigm consisting of a simulated online game (Perini et al., 2018) to increase the real-world validity of social rejection in experimental settings, participants experienced evaluative social feedback with likes and dislikes resembling social media. Perini et al. (2019) identified significant brain differences in processing social information in adolescents with NSSI (independent of psychiatric diagnosis) compared to healthy controls. A multivoxel pattern analysis identified brain regions that robustly classified NSSI subjects and controls, over and beyond symptoms of BPD and depression. These regions included dorsomedial PFC and subgenual ACC, a region implicated in mood control. Furthermore, the classification scores correlated with behavioral sensitivity to negative feedback from others (Perini et al., 2019). Although studies are few and samples small, results tentatively support a higher neural responsiveness to social rejection in individuals with NSSI. Thus, neural signatures of social stressors and NSSI have been identified, but neurobiological studies need to be replicated using larger samples as well as clinical controls without NSSI (see Carosella et al., this volume, for detailed overview of the brain and body's threat system function and NSSI).

NSSI and Social Stressors: Behavior and Self-Report as Units of Analysis

During the fMRI studies in adolescents with NSSI, behavioral and self-report data on experiences of social exclusion were also collected. Adolescents with NSSI reported being disliked during the online interaction game in the magnetic resonance scanner significantly more often than controls, and they also misjudged the number of social rejections, expressing a negative bias. Adolescents with NSSI also reported a significantly worse reaction to being disliked in the online social game setting than did healthy controls (Perini et al., 2019). Results from this study further showed an association between NSSI recency and rejection; that is, the more recent the NSSI episodes, the more the participant felt rejected. Results in this study suggested a negative bias in the perception of rejection in adolescents with NSSI (Perini et al., 2019).

Similarly, both adults with BPD + NSSI and adolescents with NSSI self-reported significantly higher sensitivity for social exclusion compared to their matched healthy controls. Adults with BPD + NSSI also reported significantly higher ratings of social exclusion following cyberball. Adolescents with NSSI, however, did not differ from healthy controls in this aspect (Brown et al., 2017). Similarly, an earlier study of adolescents with NSSI did not show behavioral differences between groups of adolescents (NSSI, depression, and healthy controls) on self-reported feelings of exclusion during the cyberball fMRI experiment (Groschwitz et al., 2016). Adults with NSSI did not report feeling more excluded during a social exclusion task than did healthy controls (Schatten et al., 2015). Thus, although all groups tend to report feelings of social exclusion during cyberball, differences between groups vary somewhat.

Studies using EMA have found that experiences of criticism and rejection were common, and especially perceived rejection increased risk of engaging in NSSI (Gee et al., 2020; Nock et al., 2009; Victor, Scott, et al., 2019). Also, adolescents with NSSI experienced more social instability in relation to both mother and friends compared to healthy controls (Santangelo et al., 2017), and feelings of being left out and excluded were strongly associated with NSSI (Victor, Scott, et al., 2019). Adolescents with NSSI experienced more stress during a social stressful task compared to both healthy controls and adolescents with a suicide attempt. They also self-reported higher levels of social sensitivity (Kim et al., 2015). Thus, experience of rejection seems to be closely related to NSSI, at least among adolescents. The findings from self-report and behavioral tasks consistently show a relationship between social stressors and NSSI.

To summarize, social stressors have been found to be closely related to NSSI across different units of analyses. Self-report is to date the most examined unit of analysis. Future studies are therefore needed to increase our understanding of social processes and the development and maintenance of NSSI, using several units of analyses. Social stressors, such as interpersonal difficulties and rejection sensitivity, also play a central role in BPD, a construct connected to NSSI. The relationship between NSSI and BPD in the context of social stressors therefore deserves special attention.

Overlapping Features between NSSI and BPD

NSSI is listed in DSM-5 as a criterion for BPD. In addition to self-injurious and impulsive behaviors, BPD is characterized by emotional instability and rejection sensitivity (American Psychiatric Association, 2013). Compared to both healthy and clinical controls, participants with BPD have demonstrated increased neural activation within the dorsomedial prefrontal cortex (dmPFC) when presented with a situation characterized by social exclusion (Domsalla et al., 2014). The dmPFC is suggested to be involved in emotional conflict monitoring (Etkin et al., 2011; Ochsner et al., 2004) and self-referential mentalization (Powers et al., 2013). Interestingly, participants with BPD also seem to display similar neural reactivity during social inclusion, suggesting that individuals with BPD have difficulties discriminating between situations characterized by social inclusion and exclusion (Malejko et al., 2018). As previously noted, individuals with NSSI have also been shown to have a heightened sensitivity to perceived social rejection.

However, in direct comparison of individuals with NSSI (without BPD) and individuals with BPD, individuals with BPD have shown relatively increased activation in the dmPFC under social inclusion (Brown et al., 2017; Malejko et al., 2019). These results add to a growing body of literature suggesting that NSSI may not always be equated with BPD, potentially lending support for NSSI disorder as a distinct psychiatric disorder, beyond BPD (Malejko et al., 2019). Further, as previously mentioned, individuals with both BPD and NSSI have demonstrated enhanced activation in the ventral ACC under social exclusion compared to healthy controls (Brown et al., 2017), and in the right pregenual anterior cortex and anterior insula compared to healthy controls (Malejko et al., 2019). Some of these areas are part of the salience network that has been associated with emotional appraisals of social situations, such as when experiencing social judgment (Perini et al., 2018). Researchers have suggested a hypothesis that NSSI and BPD may exist on a developmental continuum, beginning with an enhanced neural sensitivity to social exclusion in youth with NSSI that later generalizes to all situations, even neutral or positive social situations in adults with BPD, with or without NSSI (Brown et al., 2017; Malejko et al., 2019).

Evidence-Based Assessment and Intervention: Recommendations for Clinical Practice

This section presents recommendations for assessment and interventions, and includes a case example to illustrate how social processes may guide the assessment and treatment of NSSI.

Assessment

The literature offers a wide selection of self-report questionnaires, interviews, behavioral performance tests, and paradigms to assess social processes described in the RDoC matrix of relevance to NSSI. Many of these assessment methods are in need of further study to determine psychometric properties, as norms and utility of the behavioral tests and paradigms within clinics are not known. Although innovative measures that are insensitive to social desirability and degree of self-knowledge show promise, this review only describes a selection of the self-report questionnaires that have been applied in clinical practice.

The extent to which NSSI serves social functions for an individual may be, for example, assessed by the Inventory of Statements About Self-injury (ISAS; Klonsky & Glenn, 2009) or the Functional Assessment of Self-Mutilation (FASM; Lloyd et al., 1997). ISAS has been grouped into two factors: intrapersonal and interpersonal. The interpersonal subscale assesses functions such as creating boundaries, letting others know the extent of the pain, and fitting in with others (Klonsky & Glenn, 2009). The FASM has in factor analysis been shown to assess four factors, of which two are within the social domain: social-negative reinforcement and social-positive reinforcement. Examples of the former include avoiding doing something unpleasant. Examples of the latter include getting a reaction from someone, and feeling more a part of a group (Nock & Prinstein, 2004). The ISAS and the FASM have shown sound psychometric properties in a range of different samples (Klonsky et al., 2015) and can be used in clinical practice to screen for social functions of NSSI, relevant to treatment planning. Both ISAS and FASM were developed to assess functions in individuals who engage in NSSI and do not lend themselves to be used to assess anticipated outcomes of NSSI in individuals who are at risk of NSSI but have not yet engaged in the behavior, or for those who have ceased to harm themselves but are at risk of relapse. The Non-Suicidal Self-Injury Expectancy Questionnaire (NEQ; Hasking & Boyes, 2018) is a 49-item self-report questionnaire that assesses NSSI outcome expectancies (e.g., "I would get care from others") and has demonstrated preliminary evidence for reliable reliability and validity. The NEQ may be relevant in clinical practice to understand who is at risk of debuting or relapsing in NSSI.

Experiences of being socially rejected and ignored have predominantly been assessed in laboratory settings, with a few exceptions. The Ostracism Experience Scale for Adolescents (OES-A; Gilman et al., 2013) is a 19-item self-report measure that may be used to measure feelings of social exclusion in adolescents (e.g., "In general, others treat me as if I am invisible"). For adults, the four-item Ostracism Short Scale (OSS; Rudert et al., 2019) can be used to assess general subjective frequency that a person felt ostracized within the past two months (e.g., "Others shut me out from the conversation"). Both scales have demonstrated good internal consistency and concurrent validity (Gilman et al., 2013; Rudert et al., 2019). The responses on these measures may serve as a discussion point to differentiate between actual and perceived social rejection and exclusion, which may require different interventions.

Feelings of inadequacy and inferiority in relation to other people (e.g., "feeling that people are unfriendly or dislike you") can be measured by the nine-item interpersonal sensitivity subscale of the Symptom Checklist-90 Revised (SCL-90-R; Derogatis & Unger, 2010). Interpersonal difficulties can be assessed by the 15-item interpersonal chaos subscale (e.g., "many of my relationships have been full of intense arguments") of the Life Problem Inventory (LPI; Rathus, Wagner, et al., 2015). Both the SCL-90-R and the LPI are self-report measures that have shown good psychometric properties and could be used to screen for social sensitivity/difficulties and monitor treatment outcome.

Self-criticism can be measured using 22-item Forms of Self-Criticizing/Attacking and Self-Reassuring Scale (FSCRS; Gilbert et al. 2004). The FSCRS includes statements about perception of oneself being inadequate, the tendency to reassure oneself, and self-hatred (e.g., "I have a sense of disgust with myself"). Self-esteem may be assessed by the 10-item Rosenberg Self-Esteem Scale (RSES; Rosenberg, 1965), which measures self-perceived global self-worth (e.g., "All in all, I am inclined to feel that I am a failure"). Both the FSCRS and RSES have demonstrated sound psychometric properties and may be used to assess perception of self and changes during the course of therapy. A related construct is Expressed Emotions, encompassing critical or emotionally overinvolved attitudes expressed by caregivers (e.g., spouse and parents) toward a significant other. A simple way to assess aspects of expressed emotions is by using a one-item version of the Perceived Criticism Measure (PCM; Hooley & Teasdale, 1989). The respondents rate how critical they think an identified emotionally important individual is of them ("How critical is your relative of you?"). The PCM appears to have good reliability and validity and has shown clinical utility in terms of its associations to NSSI and in its capacity to predict relapse in a range of mental health problems; it may thus be relevant to use both prior and posttreatment intervention.

Attachment-related anxiety and avoidance, as defined in attachment theory, can be measured by the Experiences in Close Relationships Inventory–Revised (ECR; Brennan et al., 1998). The ECR is a self-report measure directed to adults that assesses insecure attachment (e.g., "I don't feel comfortable opening up to romantic partners") using 12 or 36 items, depending on version. There is also a modified version of the scale for children and adolescents. The ERQ has demonstrated good reliability and validity in both adolescents (Brenning et al., 2014) and adults (Brennan et al., 1998) and may be used to screen for attachment-related problems and change in attachment security during treatment.

Social skills and problem-solving abilities may be assessed by the Social Problem-Solving Inventory-Revised (SPSI-R; D'Zurilla et al., 2002). The SPSI-R consists of a short (25 items) and a long (52 items) version and has been evaluated in different age groups from 13 years of age. Respondents are asked to rate their general approach toward solving bothersome problems in everyday living. The SPSI-R inventory could help determine patients' social problem-solving strengths and difficulties so that deficits can be addressed and treatment progress can be tracked.

Subjective appraisal of social support received from others, including friends, family, and significant others (e.g., "I can talk about my problems with my friends"), may be assessed by the 12-item questionnaire Multidimensional Scale of Perceived Social Support (MSPS; Zimet et al., 1988). The MSPS has demonstrated good reliability and validity (Zimet et al., 1988) and could be used to screen for social support and assess change following partner/parental interventions.

Finally, NSSI has an impact on the individual's life, often socially. Social consequences of NSSI may be measured by the 10-item questionnaire Impact NSSI Scale (INS; Burke et al., 2017). The INS assesses social and other consequences of engaging in NSSI (e.g., "I think my social life would be better if I didn't self-harm"). The INS may be used to screen for the presence of social NSSI-related distress or interference.

Interventions

We have shown how a range of social features are relevant to the development and/or maintenance of NSSI, suggesting that preventive programs and treatment intervention may benefit from including a focus on the social context and social skills of the individual; strengthening social skills; and supporting network, social information processing, and attachment style. To date, intervention research on self-injurious behavior has been dominated by evaluating large treatment packages such as cognitive behavior therapy (CBT), dialectical behavior therapy (DBT), emotion regulation group treatment, mentalization-based treatment (MBT), and schema-focused therapy (the two latter treatments have been evaluated for self-injury with unclear intent, but not specifically for NSSI). Only evaluating an integrated delivery of a wide range of different strategies and processes precludes understanding their respective effects. Although the strategies mentioned below are derived from evidence-based treatments for NSSI (for a comprehensive review of common NSSI treatments, see section IX: Treatment, this volume), the reader should bear in mind that the effect of any particular strategy, treatment component, or process reviewed is not known when implemented as a separate intervention.

Considering that NSSI also serves social functions, clinicians may carefully consider the immediate antecedents and contingencies of NSSI, to decrease its occurrence either by addressing triggers or by reinforcing consequences. Once the clinician and client understand the potential social functions of the client's NSSI, they may work together to modify the context and/or develop other alternative and incompatible behaviors to replace the behavior. This is central to both CBT and DBT. DBT therapists use daily diary cards to help the client analyze the context in which NSSI occurs to increase their understanding of their behaviors, develop a plan to modify the triggers and consequences, and identify and practice more adaptive strategies that can be used in similar subsequent situations. It is sometimes helpful to modify the client's environment to achieve behavior change. This could involve working with a partner, close friends, parents, and school personnel. Although the support for specific family-centered treatments for self-injurious behaviors is limited (Kothgassner et al., 2020), it is usually recommended that treatments for NSSI, in particular in youth, should consider the family and social-environmental context (Asarnow & Mehlum, 2019). DBT for adolescents (DBT-A), for example, includes a strong family component (Iyengar et al., 2018; Kothgassner et al., 2020; Rathus, Campbell, et al., 2015). In addition to sharing the treatment philosophy and plan with the family, the DBT-A clinician works to modify maladaptive interactions in the family. The whole family practices skills in how to resolve conflicts, how to make a request in a respectful and effective manner (Rathus & Miller, 2014), as well as how to acknowledge the validity in what someone else is saying or feeling (Rathus, Campbell, et al., 2015). Increased social skills can help both the adolescents and parents to express their needs and desires in more adaptive ways, potentially changing both antecedents and contingencies of NSSI. Similarly, validation can decrease conflicts and social distress in families, among friends, and in school, thus decreasing the likelihood of NSSI being triggered. Indeed, preliminary evidence suggests that DBT-A may not only lead to a decrease in self-injurious behavior but also to reductions in social sensitivity and difficulties (Rathus & Miller, 2002).

According to recent developments of attachment theory, mentalization (e.g., "the process by which we make sense of each other and ourselves, implicitly and explicitly, in terms of subjective states and mental processes"; Bateman & Fonagy, 2010, p. 11) is a precondition of social skills and empathy. MBT for adolescents (MBT-A) with self-injurious behavior (with unclear intent) has been shown to decrease attachment avoidance (but not attachment anxiety) and mediate reduction in self-injury (with unclear intent) following treatment. In the final phase of MBT-A, the therapist addresses separation issues and how to manage anticipated challenges using mentalization (Rossouw & Fonagy, 2012). Thus, clinicians might consider addressing capacity to mentalize and target attachment avoidance in adolescents with NSSI.

A potential negative bias in interpreting social situations and a heightened sensitivity to rejection, combined with less adaptive strategies for social problem-solving, most likely result in reoccurring distress following social interactions. Addressing rigid, judgmental, maladaptive appraisals of social situations could reduce potential triggers of NSSI. Social information processing and interpretations of social situations need to be addressed, helping individuals who struggle with NSSI become aware of a potential negative social bias and promoting more favorable interpretations of both their own competence and the behavior of others. Most treatment approaches for NSSI include a component aiming at making individuals with NSSI more aware of their affective biases, which can help make social interactions less difficult and facilitate more favorable interpretations of social feedback. Social problem-solving skills—that is, the ability to generate, select, and enact adaptive behavioral responses to social situations—are, for example, practiced both in DBT (Rathus & Miller, 2014) and in CBT for NSSI (Kaess et al., 2020; Weinberg & Klonsky, 2009).

To conclude, social processes are crucial in understanding the development and maintenance of NSSI. Including important others such as parents and spouses in treatment is essential to decrease social stressors and model adaptive social behaviors. Social difficulties, social problem-solving, and experiences and interpretations of social situations need to be targeted in treatment.

Case Example

Rebecca is a 17-year-old adolescent who has struggled with depression, social anxiety, and NSSI for several years. Rebecca grew up as an only child living with her mother who also suffered from depression. Rebecca's father left the family when Rebecca was 8 years old and seldom kept in touch after that. Rebecca described herself as being shy and cautious as a child. She had the experience of being bullied during middle school. Rebecca has recently changed school, which she only attends sporadically, and she was recently referred to therapy by the school counselor. Rebecca spends most of her time at home by her computer and rarely meets friends in person. She has occasional social interactions on an online forum but often does not join the online discussion out of fear of being perceived as incompetent. During initial assessment, Rebecca was diagnosed with social anxiety disorder and depression, and she also met criteria for NSSI disorder.

Due to her impairments in social interaction, autism spectrum disorder (ASD) was also considered a differential and/or comorbid condition, but Rebecca did not meet full criteria for ASD. She had previously been prescribed selective serotonin reuptake inhibitors (SSRIs) for her symptoms. Rebecca's main concerns were anhedonia, loneliness, difficulties making friends, severe discomfort in social interactions, and low self-esteem. Her mother was worried that Rebecca was becoming more and more socially isolated. During the assessment interview, it became clear that Rebecca thought she had nothing to offer others and she was constantly afraid of being socially excluded. She felt unsafe during interpersonal interactions and experienced extreme fear of being judged or criticized by others, which often triggered NSSI. In session, Rebecca displayed little emotional expression, she tended to avoid eye contact and it was difficult to engage her in social interaction. In addition to assessment of depression and anxiety, Rebecca completed self-report questionnaires measuring functions of NSSI, attachment, emotional awareness and expression, self-criticism and self-esteem, and experiences of ostracism and social support. It was conceptualized that Rebecca had disruptions in affiliation and attachment, which manifested as social withdrawal, anhedonia, and low engagement in positive social interactions. She also displayed low social motivation and approach behaviors. She often experienced anxiety during social interaction but displayed very little behavioral expression of this. Based on her past experiences, she had negative expectations of other people's behavior toward her and interpreted most social communication as threatening. Rebecca therefore often kept her distance, masked her feelings to others, and avoided most social interactions. Based on the assessment, it was suggested that Rebecca's underlying vulnerability in the domain of social processes should be targeted, and deficits in social signaling were addressed using a skills-based approach. Rebecca's mother was involved in therapy, and parental skills of validation, behavioral activation, emotional expression, and communication were also included. To begin with, Rebecca was given extensive psychoeducation, increasing her knowledge of how her biological vulnerability in combination with her learning history have affected her current problems with social interactions. Based on the skills Rebecca was taught in therapy, she practiced mindfulness and increased awareness of her physiological, cognitive, and emotional processes as well as avoidance behavior, using observing and describing skills. Verbal and nonverbal social communication was practiced in session to facilitate Rebecca's social approach behaviors. Behavioral activation with gradual exposure to social interactions was introduced where Rebecca practiced self-disclosure in social relationships, becoming more emotionally open and increasing her emotional expression to facilitate connectedness with others. As Rebecca began using the skills in her everyday life and opening up to friends at school and connecting with her mother, her extensive fear and negative interpretation of others during social interaction gradually subsided, as did her need to engage in NSSI.

Challenges, Recommendations, and Future Directions

The RDoC initiative within the social processing domain across units of analysis needs to be examined further, as does the relationship between social processes and other RDoC domains (Clarkson et al., 2020). Future studies examining underlying mechanisms related to social processes in NSSI are needed, including several units of analyses (other than just self-report), using longitudinal, prospective designs to increase our understanding of the development and maintenance of NSSI over time (Westlund Schreiner et al., 2015). Especially the biological processes that contribute to the relationship between NSSI and social exclusion need to be explored, such as the neurobiological systems implicated in social processes (Westlund Schreiner et al., 2015), as does research on biomarkers for assessing risk. There is also a need for experimental paradigms that are more realistic and ecologically valid (Quevedo et al., 2016) and development of sound measures for social stressors (Tatnell et al., 2018). With regard to treatment research, studies with a dismantling design that contribute further information on specific mechanisms of change are needed. Improving responses to disclosure of NSSI is also necessary to promote communication about this behavior and the perceived helpfulness of such conversations. The possible varying effects of social support following disclosure, depending on when and from whom the social support is given, also need to be examined further. More research should study the types of responses individuals with NSSI would find to be most helpful. These findings could then be integrated into treatment programs.

References

American Psychiatric Association. (2013). *Diagnostic and statistical manual of mental disorders* (5th ed.). Author.

Ammerman, B. A., & Brown, S. (2018). The mediating role of self-criticism in the relationship between parental expressed emotion and NSSI. *Current Psychology, 37*(1), 325–333. https://doi.org/10.1007/s12144-016-9516-1

Asarnow, J. R., & Mehlum, L. (2019). Practitioner review: Treatment for suicidal and self-harming adolescents—Advances in suicide prevention care. *Journal of Child Psychology and Psychiatry, 60*(10), 1046–1054. https://doi.org/10.1111/jcpp.13130

Bateman, A., & Fonagy, P. (2010). Mentalization based treatment for borderline personality disorder. *World Psychiatry, 9*(1), 11–15. https://doi.org/10.1002/j.2051-5545.2010.tb00255.x

Beauchaine, T. P., Crowell, S. E., & Hsiao, R. C. (2015). Post-dexamethasone cortisol, self-inflicted injury, and suicidal ideation among depressed adolescent girls. *Journal of Abnormal Child Psychology, 43*(4), 619–632. https://doi.org/10.1007/s10802-014-9933-2

Brennan, K. A., Clark, C. L., & Shaver, P. R. (1998). Self-report measurement of adult attachment: An integrative overview. In J. A. Simpson & W. S. Rholes (Eds.), *Attachment theory and close relationships* (pp. 46–76). Guilford Press.

Brenning, K., Petegem, S. V., Vanhalst, J., & Soenens, B. (2014). The psychometric qualities of a short version of the Experiences in Close Relationships Scale–Revised Child version. *Personality and Individual Differences, 68*(C), 118–123. https://doi.org/10.1016/j.paid.2014.04.005

Bresin, K., & Gordon, K. H. (2013). Aggression as affect regulation: Extending catharsis theory to evaluate aggression and experiential anger in the laboratory and daily life. *Journal of Social and Clinical Psychology, 32*, 400–423. https://doi.org/https://doi.org/10.1521/jscp.2013.32.4.400

Brown, R. C., Plener, P. L., Groen, G., Neff, D., Bonenberger, M., & Abler, B. (2017). Differential neural processing of social exclusion and inclusion in adolescents with non-suicidal self-injury and young adults with borderline personality disorder. *Frontiers in Psychiatry*, *8*, Article 267. https://doi.org/10.3389/fpsyt.2017.00267

Burke, T. A., Ammerman, B. A., Hamilton, J. L., & Alloy, L. B. (2017). Impact of non-suicidal self-injury scale: Initial psychometric validation. *Cognitive Therapy and Research*, *41*(1), 130–142. https://doi.org/10.1007/s10608-016-9806-9

Chu, C., Hammock, E. A. D., & Joiner, T. E. (2020). Unextracted plasma oxytocin levels decrease following in-laboratory social exclusion in young adults with a suicide attempt history. *Journal of Psychiatric Research*, *121*, 173–181. https://doi.org/10.1016/j.jpsychires.2019.11.015

Claes, L., Houben, A., Vandereycken, W., Bijttebier, P., & Muehlenkamp, J. (2010). Brief report: The association between non-suicidal self-injury, self-concept and acquaintance with self-injurious peers in a sample of adolescents. *Journal of Adolescence*, *33*(5), 775–778. https://doi.org/10.1016/j.adolescence.2009.10.012

Clarkson, T., Kang, E., Capriola-Hall, N., Lerner, M. D., Jarcho, J., & Prinstein, M. J. (2020). Meta-analysis of the RDoC social processing domain across units of analysis in children and adolescents. *Journal of Clinical Child & Adolescent Psychology*, *49*(3), 1–25. https://doi.org/10.1080/15374416.2019.1678167

Coan, J. A., Schaefer, H. S., & Davidson, R. J. (2006). Lending a hand. *Psychological Science*, *17*(12), 1032–1039. https://doi.org/10.1111/j.1467-9280.2006.01832.x

Cotter, J., Granger, K., Backx, R., Hobbs, M., Looi, C. Y., & Barnett, J. H. (2018). Social cognitive dysfunction as a clinical marker: A systematic review of meta-analyses across 30 clinical conditions. *Neuroscience & Biobehavioral Reviews*, *84*, 92–99. https://doi.org/10.1016/j.neubiorev.2017.11.014

Crowell, S. E., Beauchaine, T. P., McCauley, E., Smith, C. J., Stevens, A. L., & Sylvers, P. (2005). Psychological, autonomic, and serotonergic correlates of parasuicide among adolescent girls. *Development and Psychopathology*, *17*(4), 1105–1127. https://doi.org/10.1017/s0954579405050522

Derogatis, L. R., & Unger, R. (2010). Symptom Checklist-90-Revised. In I. B. Weiner & W. E. Craighead (Eds.), *The Corsini encyclopedia of psychology* (pp. 1–2). American Cancer Society. https://doi.org/10.1002/9780470479216.corpsy0970

Domsalla, M., Koppe, G., Niedtfeld, I., Vollstädt-Klein, S., Schmahl, C., Bohus, M., & Lis, S. (2014). Cerebral processing of social rejection in patients with borderline personality disorder. *Social Cognitive and Affective Neuroscience*, *9*(11), 1789–1797. https://doi.org/10.1093/scan/nst176

D'Zurilla, T. J., Nezu, A. M., & Maydeu-Olivares, A. (2002). *Social Problem-Solving Inventory-Revised*. Multi-Health Systems.

Eisenberger, N. I., Lieberman, M. D., & Williams, K. D. (2003). Does rejection hurt? An fMRI study of social exclusion. *Science*, *302*(5643), 290–292. https://doi.org/10.1126/science.1089134

Etkin, A., Egner, T., & Kalisch, R. (2011). Emotional processing in anterior cingulate and medial prefrontal cortex. *Trends in Cognitive Sciences*, *15*(2), 85–93. https://doi.org/10.1016/j.tics.2010.11.004

Fitzpatrick, S., Kranzler, A., Fehling, K., Lindqvist, J., & Selby, E. A. (2020). Investigating the role of the intensity and duration of self-injury thoughts in self-injury with ecological momentary assessment. *Psychiatry Research*, *284*, Article 112761. https://doi.org/10.1016/j.psychres.2020.112761

Forrester, R. L., Slater, H., Jomar, K., Mitzman, S., & Taylor, P. J. (2017). Self-esteem and non-suicidal self-injury in adulthood: A systematic review. *Journal of Affective Disorders*, *221*, 172–183. https://doi.org/10.1016/j.jad.2017.06.027

Fox, A. R., Hammond, L. E., & Mezulis, A. H. (2018). Respiratory sinus arrhythmia and adaptive emotion regulation as predictors of nonsuicidal self-injury in young adults. *International Journal of Psychophysiology*, *133*, 1–11. https://doi.org/10.1016/j.ijpsycho.2018.09.006

Gandhi, A., Luyckx, K., Molenberghs, G., Baetens, I., Goossens, L., Maitra, S., & Claes, L. (2019). Maternal and peer attachment, identity formation, and non-suicidal self-injury: A longitudinal mediation study. *Child and Adolescent Psychiatry and Mental Health*, *13*(1), 7. https://doi.org/10.1186/s13034-019-0267-2

Gee, B. L., Han, J., Benassi, H., & Batterham, P. J. (2020). Suicidal thoughts, suicidal behaviours and self-harm in daily life: A systematic review of ecological momentary assessment studies. *Digital Health*, *6*, Article 2055207620963958. https://doi.org/10.1177/2055207620963958

Gilbert, P., Clarke, M., Hempel, S., Miles, J. N. V., & Irons, C. (2004). Criticizing and reassuring oneself: An exploration of forms, styles and reasons in female students. *British Journal of Clinical Psychology*, *43*, 31–50. http://doi.org/10.1348/014466504772812959

Gilman, R., Carter-Sowell, A., DeWall, C. N., Adams, R. E., & Carboni, I. (2013). Validation of the Ostracism Experience Scale for Adolescents. *Psychological Assessment*, *25*(2), 319–330. https://doi.org/10.1037/a0030913

Groschwitz, R. C., Plener, P. L., Groen, G., Bonenberger, M., & Abler, B. (2016). Differential neural processing of social exclusion in adolescents with non-suicidal self-injury: An fMRI study. *Psychiatry Research: Neuroimaging, 255*(C), 43–49. https://doi.org/10.1016/j.pscychresns.2016.08.001

Hankin, B. L., Barrocas, A. L., Young, J. F., Haberstick, B., & Smolen, A. (2015). 5-HTTLPR×interpersonal stress interaction and nonsuicidal self-injury in general community sample of youth. *Psychiatry Research, 225*(3), 609–612. https://doi.org/10.1016/j.psychres.2014.11.037

Hasking, P., & Boyes, M. (2018). The non-suicidal self-injury expectancy questionnaire: Factor structure and initial validation. *Clinical Psychologist, 22*(2), 251–261. https://doi.org/10.1111/cp.12127

Hasking, P., Rees, C. S., Martin, G., & Quigley, J. (2015). What happens when you tell someone you self-injure? The effects of disclosing NSSI to adults and peers. *BMC Public Health, 15*(1), Article 1039. https://doi.org/10.1186/s12889-015-2383-0

Heinz, A., Zhao, X., & Liu, S. (2019). Implications of the association of social exclusion with mental health. *JAMA Psychiatry, 77*(2), 113–114. https://doi.org/10.1001/jamapsychiatry.2019.3009

Hooley, J. M., & Franklin, J. C. (2018). Why do people hurt themselves? A new conceptual model of non-suicidal self-injury. *Clinical Psychological Science, 6*(3), 428–451. https://doi.org/10.1177/2167702617745641

Hooley, J. M., & St. Germain, S. A. (2014). Nonsuicidal self-injury, pain, and self-criticism. *Clinical Psychological Science, 2*(3), 297–305. https://doi.org/10.1177/2167702613509372

Hooley, J. M., & Teasdale, J. D. (1989). Predictors of relapse in unipolar depressives: Expressed emotion, marital distress, and perceived criticism. *Journal of Abnormal Psychology, 98*(3), 229–235. https://doi.org/10.1037/0021-843X.98.3.229

In-Albon, T., Ruf, C., & Schmid, M. (2015). Facial emotion recognition in adolescents with nonsuicidal self-injury. *Psychiatry Research, 228*(3), 332–339. https://doi.org/10.1016/j.psychres.2015.05.089

Iyengar, U., Snowden, N., Asarnow, J. R., Moran, P., Tranah, T., & Ougrin, D. (2018). A further look at therapeutic interventions for suicide attempts and self-harm in adolescents: An updated systematic review of randomized controlled trials. *Frontiers in Psychiatry, 9*, 1–16. https://doi.org/10.3389/fpsyt.2018.00583

Jobst, A., Albert, A., Bauriedl-Schmidt, C., Mauer, M. C., Renneberg, B., Buchheim, A., Sabass, L., Falkai, P., Zill, P., & Padberg, F. (2014). Social exclusion leads to divergent changes of oxytocin levels in borderline patients and healthy subjects. *Psychotherapy and Psychosomatics, 83*(4), 252–254. https://doi.org/10.1159/000358526

Kaess, M., Edinger, A., Fischer-Waldschmidt, G., Parzer, P., Brunner, R., & Resch, F. (2020). Effectiveness of a brief psychotherapeutic intervention compared with treatment as usual for adolescent nonsuicidal self-injury: A single-centre, randomised controlled trial. *European Child & Adolescent Psychiatry, 29*(6), 881–891. https://doi.org/10.1007/s00787-019-01399-1

Kaess, M., Hille, M., Parzer, P., Maser-Gluth, C., Resch, F., & Brunner, R. (2012). Alterations in the neuroendocrinological stress response to acute psychosocial stress in adolescents engaging in nonsuicidal self-injury. *Psychoneuroendocrinology, 37*(1), 157–161. https://doi.org/10.1016/j.psyneuen.2011.05.009

Karremans, J. C., Heslenfeld, D. J., van Dillen, L. F., & Van Lange, P. A. (2011). Secure attachment partners attenuate neural responses to social exclusion: An fMRI investigation. *International Journal of Psychophysiology, 81*(1), 44–50. https://doi.org/10.1016/j.ijpsycho.2011.04.003

Kim, K. L., Cushman, G. K., Weissman, A. B., Puzia, M. E., Wegbreit, E., Tone, E. B., Spirito, A., & Dickstein, D. P. (2015). Behavioral and emotional responses to interpersonal stress: A comparison of adolescents engaged in non-suicidal self-injury to adolescent suicide attempters. *Psychiatry Research, 228*(3), 899–906. https://doi.org/10.1016/j.psychres.2015.05.001

Klimes-Dougan, B., Begnel, E., Almy, B., Thai, M., Westlund Schreiner, M., & Cullen, K. R. (2019). Hypothalamic-pituitary-adrenal axis dysregulation in depressed adolescents with non-suicidal self-injury. *Psychoneuroendocrinology, 102*, 216–224. https://doi.org/10.1016/j.psyneuen.2018.11.004

Klonsky, E. D., & Glenn, C. R. (2009). Assessing the functions of non-suicidal self-injury: psychometric properties of the Inventory of Statements About Self-injury (ISAS). *Journal of Psychopathology and Behavioral Assessment, 31*(3), 215–219. https://doi.org/10.1007/s10862-008-9107-z

Klonsky, E. D., Glenn, C. R., Styer, D. M., Olino, T. M., & Washburn, J. J. (2015). The functions of nonsuicidal self-injury: Converging evidence for a two-factor structure. *Child and Adolescent Psychiatry and Mental Health, 9*(1), 44. https://doi.org/10.1186/s13034-015-0073-4

Kothgassner, O. D., Robinson, K., Goreis, A., Ougrin, D., & Plener, P. L. (2020). Does treatment method matter? A meta-analysis of the past 20 years of research on therapeutic interventions for self-harm and suicidal ideation in adolescents. *Borderline Personality Disorder and Emotion Dysregulation*, *7*(1), Article 9. https://doi.org/10.1186/s40479-020-00123-9

Liddell, B. J., & Courtney, B. S. (2018). Attachment buffers the physiological impact of social exclusion. *PLoS One*, *13*(9), Article e0203287. https://doi.org/10.1371/journal.pone.0203287

Lloyd, E. E., Kelley, M. L., & Hope, T. (1997, April). Self-mutilation in a community sample of adolescents: Descriptive characteristics and provisional prevalence rates [Poster presentation]. Annual meeting of the Society for Behavioral Medicine, New Orleans, LA.

Lutz, N., Villa, L., Jassim, N., Goodyer, I., Suckling, J., & Wilkinson, P. (2020). Neurobiological underpinnings of social-emotional impairments in adolescents with non-suicidal self-injury. *medRxiv*, 2020.11.12.20229138. https://doi.org/10.1101/2020.11.12.20229138

Malejko, K., Neff, D., Brown, R., Plener, P. L., Bonenberger, M., Abler, B., & Graf, H. (2018). Neural correlates of social inclusion in borderline personality disorder. *Frontiers in Psychiatry*, *9*, Article 653. https://doi.org/10.3389/fpsyt.2018.00653

Malejko, K., Neff, D., Brown, R. C., Plener, P. L., Bonenberger, M., Abler, B., & Graf, H. (2019). Neural signatures of social inclusion in borderline personality disorder versus non-suicidal self-injury. *Brain Topography*, *32*(5), 753–761. https://doi.org/10.1007/s10548-019-00712-0

Martin, J., Raby, K. L., Labella, M. H., & Roisman, G. I. (2017). Childhood abuse and neglect, attachment states of mind, and non-suicidal self-injury. *Attachment & Human Development*, *19*(5), 1–22. https://doi.org/10.1080/14616734.2017.1330832

Mwilambwe-Tshilobo, L., & Spreng, R. N. (2021). Social exclusion reliably engages the default network: A meta-analysis of cyberball. *NeuroImage*, *227*, Article 117666. https://doi.org/10.1016/j.neuroimage.2020.117666

National Institute of Mental Health. (2020, December 26). *Research Domain Criteria (RDoC)*. https://www.nimh.nih.gov/research/research-funded-by-nimh/rdoc/index.shtml

Nock, M. K. (2008). Actions speak louder than words: an elaborated theoretical model of the social functions of self-injury and other harmful behaviors. *Applied and Preventive Psychology*, *12*(4), 159–168. https://doi.org/10.1016/j.appsy.2008.05.002

Nock, M. K. (2010). Self-injury. *Annual Review of Clinical Psychology*, *6*(1), 339–363. https://doi.org/10.1146/annurev.clinpsy.121208.131258

Nock, M. K., & Mendes, W. B. (2008). Physiological arousal, distress tolerance, and social problem-solving deficits among adolescent self-injurers. *Journal of Consulting and Clinical Psychology*, *76*(1), 28–38. https://doi.org/10.1037/0022-006x.76.1.28

Nock, M. K., & Prinstein, M. J. (2004). A functional approach to the assessment of self-mutilative behavior. *Journal of Consulting and Clinical Psychology*, *72*(5), 885–890. https://doi.org/10.1037/0022-006x.72.5.885

Nock, M. K., Prinstein, M. J., & Sterba, S. K. (2009). Revealing the form and function of self-injurious thoughts and behaviors: A real-time ecological assessment study among adolescents and young adults. *Journal of Abnormal Psychology*, *118*(4), 816–827. https://doi.org/10.1037/a0016948

Ochsner, K. N., Knierim, K., Ludlow, D. H., Hanelin, J., Ramachandran, T., Glover, G., & Mackey, S. C. (2004). Reflecting upon feelings: An fMRI study of neural systems supporting the attribution of emotion to self and other. *Journal of Cognitive Neuroscience*, *16*(10), 1746–1772. https://doi.org/10.1162/0898929042947829

Olié, E., Jollant, F., Deverdun, J., Champfleur, N. M. de, Cyprien, F., Bars, E. L., Mura, T., Bonafé, A., & Courtet, P. (2017). The experience of social exclusion in women with a history of suicidal acts: a neuroimaging study. *Scientific Reports*, *7*(1), Article 89. https://doi.org/10.1038/s41598-017-00211-x

Perini, I., Gustafsson, P. A., Hamilton, J. P., Kämpe, R., Mayo, L. M., Heilig, M., & Zetterqvist, M. (2019). Brain-based classification of negative social bias in adolescents with nonsuicidal self-injury: Findings from simulated online social interaction. *EClinicalMedicine*, *13*, 81–90. https://doi.org/10.1016/j.eclinm.2019.06.016

Perini, I., Gustafsson, P. A., Hamilton, J. P., Kämpe, R., Zetterqvist, M., & Heilig, M. (2018). The salience of self, not social pain, is encoded by dorsal anterior cingulate and insula. *Scientific Reports*, *8*(1), 6165. https://doi.org/10.1038/s41598-018-24658-8

Plener, P. L., Zohsel, K., Hohm, E., Buchmann, A. F., Banaschewski, T., Zimmermann, U. S., & Laucht, M. (2017). Lower cortisol level in response to a psychosocial stressor in young females with self-harm. *Psychoneuroendocrinology*, *76*, 84–87. https://doi.org/10.1016/j.psyneuen.2016.11.009

Powers, K. E., Wagner, D. D., Norris, C. J., & Heatherton, T. F. (2013). Socially excluded individuals fail to recruit medial prefrontal cortex for negative social scenes. *Social Cognitive and Affective Neuroscience, 8*(2), 151–157. https://doi.org/10.1093/scan/nsr079

Quevedo, K., Martin, J., Scott, H., Smyda, G., & Pfeifer, J. H. (2016). The neurobiology of self-knowledge in depressed and self-injurious youth. *Psychiatry Research: Neuroimaging, 254,* 145–155. https://doi.org/10.1016/j.pscychresns.2016.06.015

Radke, S., Seidel, E. M., Boubela, R. N., Thaler, H., Metzler, H., Kryspin-Exner, I., Moser, E., Habel, U., & Derntl, B. (2018). Immediate and delayed neuroendocrine responses to social exclusion in males and females. *Psychoneuroendocrinology, 93,* 56–64. https://doi.org/10.1016/j.psyneuen.2018.04.005

Rathus, J., Campbell, B., Miller, A., & Smith, H. (2015). Treatment acceptability study of Walking the Middle Path, a new DBT skills module for adolescents and their families. *American Journal of Psychotherapy, 69*(2), 163–178. https://doi.org/10.1176/appi.psychotherapy.2015.69.2.163

Rathus, J. H., & Miller, A. L. (2002). Dialectical behavior therapy adapted for suicidal adolescents. *Suicide and Life-Threatening Behavior, 32*(2), 146–157. https://doi.org/10.1521/suli.32.2.146.24399

Rathus, J. H., & Miller, A. L. (2014). *DBT skills manual for adolescents.* Guilford Press.

Rathus, J. H., Wagner, D., & Miller, A. L. (2015). Psychometric evaluation of the life problems inventory, a measure of borderline personality features in adolescents. *Journal of Psychology & Psychotherapy, 5,* 198. https://doi.org/10.4172/2161-0487.1000198

Reichl, C., Heyer, A., Brunner, R., Parzer, P., Völker, J. M., Resch, F., & Kaess, M. (2016). Hypothalamic-pituitary-adrenal axis, childhood adversity and adolescent nonsuicidal self-injury. *Psychoneuroendocrinology, 74,* 203–211. https://doi.org/10.1016/j.psyneuen.2016.09.011

Rosenberg, M. (1965). *Society and the adolescent self-image.* Princeton University Press.

Rossouw, T. I., & Fonagy, P. (2012). Mentalization-based treatment for self-harm in adolescents: a randomized controlled trial. *Journal of the American Academy of Child & Adolescent Psychiatry, 51*(12), 1304–1313. https://doi.org/10.1016/j.jaac.2012.09.018

Rudert, S. C., Keller, M. D., Hales, A. H., Walker, M., & Greifeneder, R. (2019). Who gets ostracized? A personality perspective on risk and protective factors of ostracism. *Journal of Personality and Social Psychology, 118*(6), 1247–1268. https://doi.org/10.1037/pspp0000271

Santangelo, P. S., Koenig, J., Funke, V., Parzer, P., Resch, F., Ebner-Priemer, U. W., & Kaess, M. (2017). Ecological momentary assessment of affective and interpersonal instability in adolescent non-suicidal self-injury. *Journal of Abnormal Child Psychology, 45*(7), 1429–1438. https://doi.org/10.1007/s10802-016-0249-2

Schatten, H. T., Andover, M. S., & Armey, M. F. (2015). The roles of social stress and decision-making in non-suicidal self-injury. *Psychiatry Research, 229*(3), 983–991. https://doi.org/10.1016/j.psychres.2015.05.087

Seymour, K. E., Jones, R. N., Cushman, G. K., Galvan, T., Puzia, M. E., Kim, K. L., Spirito, A., & Dickstein, D. P. (2016). Emotional face recognition in adolescent suicide attempters and adolescents engaging in non-suicidal self-injury. *European Child & Adolescent Psychiatry, 25*(3), 247–259. https://doi.org/10.1007/s00787-015-0733-1

Stanley, B., & Siever, L. J. (2010). The interpersonal dimension of borderline personality disorder: toward a neuropeptide model. *American Journal of Psychiatry, 167*(1), 24–39. https://doi.org/10.1176/appi.ajp.2009.09050744

Tatnell, R., Hasking, P., Lipp, O. V., Boyes, M., & Dawkins, J. (2018). Emotional responding in NSSI: Examinations of appraisals of positive and negative emotional stimuli, with and without acute stress. *Cognition and Emotion, 32*(6), 1–13. https://doi.org/10.1080/02699931.2017.1411785

Tatnell, R., Kelada, L., Hasking, P., & Martin, G. (2014). Longitudinal analysis of adolescent NSSI: The role of intrapersonal and interpersonal factors. *Journal of Abnormal Child Psychology, 42*(6), 885–896. https://doi.org/10.1007/s10802-013-9837-6

Turner, B. J., Chapman, A. L., & Layden, B. K. (2012). Intrapersonal and interpersonal functions of non suicidal self-injury: Associations with emotional and social functioning. *Suicide and Life-Threatening Behavior, 42*(1), 36–55. https://doi.org/10.1111/j.1943-278x.2011.00069.x

Turner, B. J., Cobb, R. J., Gratz, K. L., & Chapman, A. L. (2016). The role of interpersonal conflict and perceived social support in nonsuicidal self-injury in daily life. *Journal of Abnormal Psychology, 125*(4), 588–598. https://doi.org/10.1037/abn0000141

Turner, B. J., Wakefield, M. A., Gratz, K. L., & Chapman, A. L. (2017). Characterizing interpersonal difficulties among young adults who engage in nonsuicidal self-injury using a daily diary. *Behavior Therapy*, *48*(3), 366–379. https://doi.org/10.1016/j.beth.2016.07.001

Venne, P. van der, Balint, A., Drews, E., Parzer, P., Resch, F., Koenig, J., & Kaess, M. (2021). Pain sensitivity and plasma beta-endorphin in adolescent non-suicidal self-injury. *Journal of Affective Disorders*, *278*, 199–208. https://doi.org/10.1016/j.jad.2020.09.036

Victor, S. E., Hipwell, A. E., Stepp, S. D., & Scott, L. N. (2019). Parent and peer relationships as longitudinal predictors of adolescent non-suicidal self-injury onset. *Child and Adolescent Psychiatry and Mental Health*, *13*(1), Article 1. https://doi.org/10.1186/s13034-018-0261-0

Victor, S. E., Scott, L. N., Stepp, S. D., & Goldstein, T. R. (2019). I want you to want me: interpersonal stress and affective experiences as within-person predictors of nonsuicidal self-injury and suicide urges in daily life. *Suicide and Life-Threatening Behavior*, *49*(4), 1157–1177. https://doi.org/10.1111/sltb.12513

Vijayakumar, N., Cheng, T. W., & Pfeifer, J. H. (2017). Neural correlates of social exclusion across ages: A coordinate-based meta-analysis of functional MRI studies. *NeuroImage*, *153*, 359–368. https://doi.org/10.1016/j.neuroimage.2017.02.050

Wan, Y., Chen, R., Ma, S., McFeeters, D., Sun, Y., Hao, J., & Tao, F. (2019). Associations of adverse childhood experiences and social support with self-injurious behaviour and suicidality in adolescents. *The British Journal of Psychiatry*, *214*(3), 146–152. https://doi.org/10.1192/bjp.2018.263

Wang, H., Braun, C., & Enck, P. (2017). How the brain reacts to social stress (exclusion)—A scoping review. *Neuroscience & Biobehavioral Reviews*, *80*, 80–88. https://doi.org/10.1016/j.neubiorev.2017.05.012

Weinberg, A., & Klonsky, E. D. (2009). Measurement of emotion dysregulation in adolescents. *Psychological Assessment*, *21*(4), 616–621. https://doi.org/10.1037/a0016669

Westlund Schreiner, M., Klimes-Dougan, B., Begnel, E. D., & Cullen, K. R. (2015). Conceptualizing the neurobiology of non-suicidal self-injury from the perspective of the Research Domain Criteria Project. *Neuroscience & Biobehavioral Reviews*, *57*, 381–391. https://doi.org/10.1016/j.neubiorev.2015.09.011

Westlund Schreiner, M., Klimes-Dougan, B., Mueller, B. A., Eberly, L. E., Reigstad, K. M., Carstedt, P. A., Thomas, K. M., Hunt, R. H., Lim, K. O., & Cullen, K. R. (2017). Multi-modal neuroimaging of adolescents with non-suicidal self-injury: Amygdala functional connectivity. *Journal of Affective Disorders*, *221*, 47–55. https://doi.org/10.1016/j.jad.2017.06.004

Wielgus, M. D., Aldrich, J. T., Mezulis, A. H., & Crowell, S. E. (2016). Respiratory sinus arrhythmia as a predictor of self-injurious thoughts and behaviors among adolescents. *International Journal of Psychophysiology*, *106*, 127–134. https://doi.org/10.1016/j.ijpsycho.2016.05.005

Williams, K. D., & Jarvis, B. (2006). Cyberball: A program for use in research on interpersonal ostracism and acceptance. *Behavior Research Methods*, *38*(1), 174–180. https://doi.org/10.3758/bf03192765

Wood, E. K., Kruger, R., Day, J. P., Day, S. M., Hunter, J. N., Neville, L., Lindell, S. G., Barr, C. S., Schwandt, M. L., Goldman, D., Suomi, S. J., Harris, J. C., & Higley, J. D. (2021). A nonhuman primate model of human non-suicidal self-injury: Serotonin-transporter genotype-mediated typologies. *Neuropsychopharmacology*, *47*(6), 1256–1262. https://doi.org/10.1038/s41386-021-00994-8

Zetterqvist, M., Lundh, L.-G., & Svedin, C. G. (2013). A comparison of adolescents engaging in self-injurious behaviors with and without suicidal intent: Self-reported experiences of adverse life events and trauma symptoms. *Journal of Youth and Adolescence*, *42*(8), Article 1257. https://doi.org/10.1007/s10964-012-9872-6

Ziebell, L., Collin, C., Mazalu, M., Rainville, S., Weippert, M., & Skolov, M. (2020). Electromyographic evidence of reduced emotion mimicry in individuals with a history of non-suicidal self-injury. *PLoS One*, *15*(12), Article e0243860. https://doi.org/10.1371/journal.pone.0243860

Zimet, G. D., Dahlem, N. W., Zimet, S. G., & Farley, G. K. (1988). The Multidimensional Scale of Perceived Social Support. *Journal of Personality Assessment*, *52*(1), 30–41. https://doi.org/10.1207/s15327752jpa5201_2

CHAPTER 18

Autonomic Nervous System Function in Nonsuicidal Self-Injury—A Research Domain Criteria Perspective on the Arousal/Regulatory Systems

Christine Sigrist, Michael Kaess, *and* Julian Koenig

Abstract

This chapter addresses autonomic nervous system (ANS) function in nonsuicidal self-injury (NSSI) from the perspective of the Research Domain Criteria (RDoC). Based on the RDoC framework, the ANS, as a major stress-regulatory system in humans, is primarily considered to be implicated in the domain of arousal/regulatory systems, while it shows associations also to other domains. Drawing on recent theoretical models providing a framework for understanding the neurobiology of NSSI, it is suggested that NSSI may result from failures in physiological and socioemotional stress regulation. In the present chapter, after introducing ANS function under the RDoC framework and outlining a potential rationale for an involvement of the ANS in NSSI, central mechanisms and concepts will be presented that help to understand how ANS function in NSSI is typically considered in the context of psychophysiological research studies. Further, an overview of indices that are frequently derived in the lab to quantify ANS function is provided. The chapter then reviews existing research studies where the respective indices have been measured to study the involvement of ANS function in NSSI from different temporal angles (i.e., ANS function under resting state, in response to stress, as well as considering its diurnal rhythmicity). On the basis of the evidence reviewed, the chapter discusses the current state of the research field and concludes with a short summary and outlook highlighting avenues for future NSSI research.

Key Words: nonsuicidal self-injury, Research Domain Criteria, RDoC, stress regulation, emotion regulation, cardiac autonomic activity, developmental psychopathology

ANS Function under the RDoC Framework

As detailed in the preceding chapters of this handbook, the Research Domain Criteria (RDoC; Insel et al., 2010; see Bastiaens & Claes, this volume, for an overview) present a new approach to the classification and characterization of psychiatric disorders and phenomena. The present chapter addresses autonomic nervous system (ANS) function in nonsuicidal self-injury (NSSI) from an RDoC perspective. Within the RDoC framework, the ANS is primarily implicated in the domain of arousal/regulatory systems but shows associations also to other domains, such as, for example, the negative valence systems. As defined in the RDoC framework arousal/regulatory systems domain:

> [A]rousal is a continuum of sensitivity of the organism to stimuli, both external and internal. [It] facilitates interaction with the environment in a context-specific manner (e.g., under conditions of threat, some stimuli must be ignored while sensitivity to and responses to others is enhanced, as exemplified in the startle reflex); can be evoked by either external/environmental stimuli or internal stimuli (e.g., emotions and cognition); can be modulated by the physical characteristics and motivational significance of stimuli; varies along a continuum that can be quantified in any behavioral state, including wakefulness and low-arousal states including sleep, anesthesia, and coma; is distinct from motivation and valence but can covary with intensity of motivation and valence; may be associated with increased or decreased locomotor activity, and can be regulated by homeostatic drives (e.g., hunger, sleep, thirst, sex).
>
> *(National Institute of Mental Health, 2022)*

Concerning the units of analyses as defined within the RDoC framework, we will predominantly focus on the level of *physiology*, defined as "measures that are well-established indices of certain constructs [. . .] (e.g., heart rate [. . .])" (Morris & Cuthbert, 2022, p. 31). Concerning these indices, we limit the present review on measures with clear implications for ANS functioning, as detailed further below. It is well understood that other indices and constructs show ANS involvement or at least associations with ANS function (i.e., inflammatory processes and hypothalmic-pituitary-adrenal axis activity). However, we will stick to classic psychophysiological indices frequently derived in the lab to directly quantify ANS function.

To narrow down ANS involvement in NSSI, we further discuss findings in the field in light of a temporal framework for understanding the biology of NSSI (Kaess et al., 2021; see Westlund Schreiner et al., this volume). In brief, the respective framework distinguishes between trait and state markers on the biological level associated with NSSI. Distal biological traits (predictors) of NSSI, proximal biological traits (correlates) of NSSI, and biological states directly preceding or following NSSI are distinguished. More specifically,

> according to [the] model, the biological characteristics related to the development, onset, execution, and maintenance of NSSI can be divided into: distal biological traits (i.e., genetic factors or risk factors that predict the development of NSSI), proximal biological traits defined as underlying biological alterations observed among individuals who engage in NSSI (i.e., alterations in brain structure and functioning as well as endocrine and physiological systems), and biological states that directly precede or follow NSSI (i.e., changes in brain functioning as well as reactivity of endocrine and physiological systems).
>
> *(Kaess et al., 2021, p. 230)*

Concerning the ANS, some of the questions at hand are: Does ANS function (early in development) predict the development of NSSI? Do patients engaging in NSSI differ as compared to controls (or other patients) concerning their ANS function? Is ANS activity altered during actual acts of NSSI?

Rationale for ANS Involvement in NSSI

Concerning the principal rationale for involvement of ANS function in the phenomenology of NSSI, one may justify such perspective based on the strong association between stress and NSSI—NSSI may (according to such view), represent a dysfunctional strategy to regulate stress. Alongside the hypothalamic-pituitary-adrenal (HPA) axis, the ANS is the most prominent endogenous stress system; thus, ANS dysfunction can be hypothesized to be altered in patients presenting with NSSI disorder or other disorders associated with NSSI and acts of NSSI should interfere with ANS activity. From another perspective, ANS activity is in principle implicated in pain processing. The ANS is responsive to painful experiences (e.g., Koenig et al., 2014), and furthermore, ANS activity is directly linked to pain processing via vagal-nociceptive networks and descending inhibitory pathways from cerebral structures to the dorsal horn, which suppress or potentiate the processing of nociceptive information, as we have previously detailed elsewhere (Koenig, Falvay, et al., 2016; Koenig, Loerbroks, et al., 2016). Given that patients engaging in NSSI show altered sensitivity to painful stimulation (Koenig, Loerbroks, et al., 2016), ANS involvement in pain processing provides another rationale, alongside the stress hypothesis, concerning a general involvement of ANS function in NSSI. Finally, it is important to acknowledge that NSSI is frequently associated with psychiatric comorbidity—in particular, personality disorders such as borderline personality disorder (BPD) and affective disorders such as depression. Both BPD and depression have been associated with altered ANS function (Koenig, Kemp, Beauchaine, et al., 2016; Koenig, Kemp, Feeling, et al., 2016). These different lines of reasoning illustrate the complexity of issues that research on the involvement of the ANS in NSSI is facing. ANS function is not a specific marker but is broadly implicated in NSSI and associated phenomena.

Studying ANS Function

As indicated above, the assessment and study of ANS function are subspecialties in the field of psychophysiology—and led to important insights considering the role of this major physiological-regulatory system in the etiology and maintenance of diverse psychopathological phenomena. In this and the subsequent sections, we provide a short and introductory overview of the ANS followed by a short review of strategies that have been widely adopted—and are sufficiently valid and suitable in the context of psychopathology research—to measure its function. An overview of studies that specifically examined ANS function in the context of NSSI (and/or related conditions) is presented subsequently, across the different subunits of analysis reviewed below.

Introductory Overview of ANS Function

In brief, the main function of the ANS is coordinating bodily functions to ensure homeostasis and performing adaptive responses when faced with changes in the external and internal environment, such as those that arise from physical activity, posture change, food consumption, or infection. Furthermore, the ANS can prepare the body for anticipated threats to the homeostatic state even in the absence of actual (environmental or internal) changes, as is the case when faced with stressors that are purely symbolic (or psychological) in nature. The corresponding response is generally known as the physiological stress response. The normative stress response involves activation of the two major stress axes, that is, activation of the ANS, which is followed by activation of the HPA axis which produces cortisol in humans, and subsequent deactivation of the ANS. Timely activation and deactivation of the stress response allow an individual to manage stressful situations and to return to normal resting baseline (i.e., normal functioning) following stress cessation.

In many textbook definitions, the term "ANS" is introduced synonymous with its sympathetic and parasympathetic branches, while the sympathetic nervous system (SNS) is characterized by its key role in the fight-or-flight response. As such, increased activity of the SNS will cause an increase in heart rate and contractility, blood pressure, breathing rate, bronchodilation, sweat production, epinephrine secretion, and a redistribution of blood flow favoring the muscles (De Geus et al., 2013). Somehow in contrast, the parasympathetic nervous system (PNS) is typically characterized as promoting maintenance of the body, acquiring energy from food, and disposing of wastes. Accordingly, PNS activity will cause slowing of the heart, constriction of the pupils, stimulation of the gut and salivary glands, and other responses that help restore energy, which is why the PNS is often labeled the "rest and digest" branch of the ANS.

Importantly, when considering the study of ANS function, one should also bear in mind the actual neuroanatomical and neurophysiological complexity it inherently entails. The ANS might be thought of as a complex system of hierarchically organized feedback loops, constituting neuronal circuits and autonomic reflex arcs from end-organ receptors (Nahm & Freeman, 2017). Signals arising from these structures are directed to central autonomic structures, via unmyelinated and myelinated autonomic nerves. The nucleus tractus solitarius, located in the dorsal medulla, receives much of this afferent peripheral autonomic input and has reciprocal connections to central regions regulating both sympathetic and parasympathetic functions, which play an important role in feedback regulatory circuits (De Geus et al., 2013). Since the anatomic location of the ANS has rendered its direct physiological assessment difficult in humans, different techniques have been developed to measure ANS function indirectly, by measuring end-organ activity (Freeman, 2006). Each of these indices itself presents an incomplete indicator of the functioning of this complex system of central autonomic control and continual feedback between the brain and peripheral organ systems (Benarroch, 1993; Eddie et al., 2018).

Most organs in the human body are innervated by both the sympathetic and the parasympathetic branches of the ANS (i.e., dual innervation), and an increase in the activity of these branches is often assumed to exert opposing actions. However, some organs are not dually innervated by the ANS, and even for organ systems innervated by sympathetic and parasympathetic nerve fibers, these two branches of the ANS may function in a complex relationship, including *antagonistic*, *complementary*, or *cooperative* functions, while their relative balance may be set by genetics and largely modified by internal and environmental influences (Wulsin et al., 2018). Partly due to this complexity, the activity of the ANS is characterized by large interindividual differences in in the basal resting state (Bernston, Cacioppo, Binkley, et al., 1994; Bernston, Cacioppo, & Quigley, 1994; Grossman & Kollai, 1993; Light et al., 1998; Salomon et al., 2000), and these interindividual differences are further enhanced when the ANS is activated in response to stress (De Geus et al., 2007; Houtveen & Rietveld, 2002; Lucini et al., 2002; Wang et al., 2009)—also including prolonged psychosocial stress (Riese et al., 2000; Vrijkotte et al., 2004). Of note, the characterization of the autonomic stress response includes both responsivity to stress exposure and subsequent recovery—that is, returning to the resting baseline, after stress exposure has ceased (Eddie et al., 2018). Like most physiological systems of the human body, ANS activity is also characterized by large variations unfolding intraindividually over the course of 24 hours, commonly referred to as "circadian variation" or "circadian rhythmicity" of ANS activity—another important domain covered by the RDoC.

Measures of ANS Function

As detailed in the previous section, measures of ANS activity can be differentiated based on the specific end-organ activity measured, but also based on measurement techniques that are applied to measure it. Furthermore, measurement of ANS function is differentiated by the organismic state of activity at the time of measurement (i.e., resting state and responsivity–recovery), while long-term or ambulatory measurement will allow the quantification of circadian variation patterns. The next sections provide an overview of different ANS measures as reviewed here; for more details regarding the measurement and analysis of each signal, we refer the reader to table 18.1 for the respective resources (i.e., reviews and guidelines).

STUDYING ELECTRODERMAL ACTIVITY

Electrodermal activity (EDA), sometimes also referred to as galvanic skin responses or skin conductance (SC), presents a measure of ANS activity that has a fairly long history in psychophysiological research. EDA is a noninvasive measure of the variations in electrical conductance of the respective skin and depends on the changes in the level of sweat in the ducts (Cacioppo et al., 2007). Given the absence of parasympathetic innervation on eccrine sweat glands, SC has been suggested to reflect sole influence of sympathetic modulation—and thus has been largely used to assess sympathetic activity

Table 18.1 Overview of Common Measures and Metrics of ANS Function in Psychopathology Research

Signal	Principle	Measures	Reviews—Guidelines
Electrodermal Activity (EDA)	Measurement of activity or responses in the eccrine sweat glands via electrodes attached to the skin	Skin conductance (SC) Skin potential (SP)	(Geršak, 2020; Posada-Quintero & Chon, 2020; Shaffer et al., 2016; Topoglu et al., 2020)
Cardiovascular Activity	Cardiovascular system includes the heart and the vessels through which oxygenated and deoxygenated blood is delivered away from the heart to the periphery and vice versa	Heart rate (HR) Heart rate variability (HRV)	(Quintana & Heathers, 2014; Shaffer & Ginsberg, 2017; Task Force of the European Society of Cardiology, 1996)
		Systolic blood pressure (SBP) Diastolic blood pressure (DBP)	(TRUE Consortium, 2017; Stergiou et al., 2018)
		Measures of Respiration	(Porges & Byrne, 1992; Wientjes, 1992)
Pupillometry	Measurement of pupil size in response to different kinds of stimuli	Pupil Size	(Winn et al., 2018)

during challenging situations (Jacobs et al., 1994). However, recent evidence points to noradrenergic and cholinergic innervation of sweat glands in humans, questioning this popular belief (Weihe et al., 2005). EDA signals are commonly measured via measuring the SC or the skin potential (SP). SC can be quantified reciprocally to the resistance to a small current that is passed through the skin, via a bipolar placement of Ag/AgCl sensors placed on the fingers, palms, or soles of the feet. SP is collected using unipolar placement of sensors without the use of an external current, while one sensor is placed at an active and one on an inactive site, typically including the palm of the hand and the forearm. SC and SP can be measured during tonic (i.e., levels) and phasic (i.e., responses) states, resulting in SC level (SCL) and SC response (SCR), and SP level (SPL) and SP response (SPR), respectively (Mendes, 2009). Finally, rapid phasic elements of the signal can occur as a consequence of stimulation or as spontaneous activity, referred to as non-specific SC response.

STUDYING CARDIOVASCULAR ACTIVITY

The cardiovascular system includes the heart and the vessels through which oxygenated and deoxygenated blood are delivered away from the heart to the periphery and vice versa. Next, we review only the most prominent indices in this field of research—although many other measures (e.g., cardiac output and left ventricular ejection time) are available and can provide valuable insights.

Heart Rate and Heart Rate Variability
Different measurement techniques exist to quantify the cardiac cycle, including electrocardiogram (ECG) and photoplethysmography (PPG). ECG devices measure the electrical signal that is produced by the heart, resulting in a recording of ECG curves as typically used for standard short-term measurement. Ambulatory ECG devices (e.g., attached to a textile chest belt with dry electrodes) allow for long-term ECG measurement, typically over a period of 24 hours or more. Furthermore, different kinds of wearables based on PPG (i.e., continuous monitoring of changes in blood volume in a portion of the peripheral microvasculature) allow for short- and long-term assessment of the cardiac cycle. Comparative studies report PPG to be a fairly accurate proxy of ECG, particularly under resting conditions and in healthy participants (Bolanos et al., 2006; Ghamari, 2018; Lu et al., 2009; Weiler et al., 2017). Various measures indexing sympathetic or parasympathetic activity (or a mix of both) can be derived from the short- and long-term ECG and PPG signals, based on various techniques for analyses.

Heart rate, which presents a mix of both sympathetic and parasympathetic influences, is calculated by counting the number of systolic peaks (or R-peaks) in the cardiac cycle per minute, as visible in ECG or PPG signals. Besides, in normal resting conditions and a healthy heart, the time intervals between systolic peaks are characterized by normal fluctuations over time, which are also due to the interplay of sympathetic and parasympathetic nerves at the sino-atrial node of the heart (Nolte et al., 2017; Saul, 1990; Smith et al., 2017; Thayer & Lane, 2000). This results in a complex variability in the heart rate time series, commonly referred to as heart rate variability (HRV). HRV can be quantified and displayed using various techniques of analysis, such as time domain, frequency domain, or nonlinear methods (for a review and respective guidelines, see, e.g., Shaffer & Ginsberg, 2017; Task Force of the European Society of Cardiology, 1996). Here, we commonly refer to HRV as a measure of vagal (parasympathetic) activity.

Studying Breathing
Measurement of respiratory responses requires techniques that provide sufficient precision with regard to respiratory timing and volume. In terms of analysis, relevant response dimensions must be assessed and several artifact problems need to be managed (Wientjes, 1992). Based on these prerequisites, breathing can be assessed in several ways. Measurement of pressure during inspiration and expiration using a strain gauge placed on the torso and immediately under the arms, which allows measurement of upper respiration, can be used to extract rate and depth of breath. Respiration rate can also be extracted from impedance cardiography, which is a noninvasive technique to estimate blood flow changes, and other techniques may be used to assess additional variables associated with breathing, such as oxygen saturation—however, these are not covered here (for further reading, we refer to, e.g., Chan et al., 2013; Harskamp et al., 2021; Jubran, 2015; Mendes, 2009).

Studying Blood Pressure

Blood pressure (BP) refers to the amount of pressure that is put on the vessel walls during the cardiac cycle and is measured in millimeters of mercury pressure (mmHg). Typically, systolic blood pressure (SBP), representing peak pressure, and diastolic blood pressure (DBP), representing lowest pressure, are provided. These two measures are correlated but provide unique information regarding cardiovascular health (Chobanian et al., 2003) and physiological responsivity (Brownley et al., 2000; Wright & Kirby, 2001). BP can be obtained from various places of the body including the brachial artery (upper arm), radial artery (wrist), or the finger. In research settings, continuous measures are preferred, since intermittent measures might be too distractive in the context of many experimental paradigms. Yet, with increasing distance of the place of measurement from the heart, measurement accuracy will be somewhat reduced.

PUPILLOMETRY AND STUDYING PUPIL DILATION

Pupillometry, the measurement of changes in pupil diameter, has become a widely used psychophysiological research tool providing valuable insights into the mechanisms underlying diverse cognitive and affective processes, and even possible disruptions in clinical populations (Kret & Sjak-Shie, 2019). In general, the pupil changes its size in response to three different kinds of stimuli, that is, brightness, near fixation, and increased cognitive activity, such as increased levels of arousal or mental effort. While the two former processes imply pupil contraction, the latter generally induces a dilation of the pupil (Mathôt, 2018).

Pupillary movements are controlled by the action of smooth muscles, which are associated with sympathetic and parasympathetic activity (Kret & Sjak-Shie, 2019). Pupil dilation is regulated by the SNS and mediated almost exclusively via norepinephrine (NE) from the locus coeruleus (LC), which is distinct from the strong contractions exhibited during the pupillary light reflex as mediated by acetylcholine (parasympathetic innervation). Under constant low light levels, pupil size thus presents an accessible measure of the LC-NE complex (Aston-Jones & Cohen, 2005; Koss, 1986; Nieuwenhuis et al., 2005; Yu et al., 2004). One of the most frequently applied standardized measuring methods of pupil size is the pupillometer, consisting of a lens system with a built-in millimeter scale that estimates the pupil diameter (Schmitz et al., 2003). Yet, researchers are increasingly using eye trackers to explore changes in pupil size. Such computerized techniques allow for dynamic and binocular measurement of pupil diameter by use of infrared light (Schmitz et al., 2003). Detailed guidelines on preprocessing of pupil size data are also available (e.g., Kar, 2019).

The measures outlined above present a selection of prominent ANS measures widely used in research studies with clinical populations, but there are actually many more possibilities for monitoring ANS activity. This also applies in terms of measurement settings and conditions, which are further outlined below.

Studying ANS Activity during Resting State, Responsivity, and Recovery
Psychophysiological research focusing on ANS function generally involves the measurement of one or more physiological signals such as these reviewed above, during one or more periods of resting state, as well as during mental or physical challenges. As stated earlier, such studies have been instrumental in establishing the existence of stable interindividual differences in ANS function and have provided valuable insights on the mechanisms of ANS responsivity and recovery. Resting ANS (and specifically vagal or parasympathetic) activity has been the focus of a particularly large number of studies in the field of psychophysiology. "Resting" thereby refers to a baseline activity measured under standardized conditions, typically in a seated position and with a standard duration of 5 min, as recommended in official guidelines (e.g., Task Force of the European Society of Cardiology, 1996). Furthermore, many studies have investigated the role of "ANS responsivity," which reflects a change from ANS activity at rest to activity under conditions of challenge, with physiological signals exhibiting a typical decrease or increase from baseline to challenge, respectively. For example, heart rate becomes faster and more regular, and such vagal withdrawal (i.e., decreased HRV) indicates reduced parasympathetic control over sympathetic activation, facilitating the mounting of a stress response to cope with challenges. Besides increased heart rate (HR) and decreased HRV, ANS response under conditions of challenge is indicated by increased blood pressure (especially SBP), activity of the sweat glands (increased SC and SP), and pupil size (increased pupil dilation). Of note, sympathetic activation and vagal withdrawal have been found to contribute relatively equally to cardiovascular stress reactivity (Brindle et al., 2014). "ANS recovery" finally refers to the process of returning to initial resting-state levels and reestablishing homeostasis after a stressor has ceased—a process equally central to the adaptation of the organism.

Besides the investigation of resting state, responsivity, and recovery of ANS activity, interest in the circadian variation of cardiac autonomic activity recently arose.

Diurnal Variation of ANS Activity
Within the RDoC matrix, the arousal and regulatory systems domain also comprises the construct of circadian rhythms, referring to the body's ability to regulate and time biological systems (Westlund Schreiner et al., 2015). In humans and other mammalian species, physiology and behavior are subject to daily cycles that are driven by endogenous clocks and characterized by a periodicity approximating 24 hours (i.e., circadian) (Hastings & Maywood, 2000). The circadian master-clock, which lies in the suprachiasmatic nuclei (SCN) of the hypothalamus and is sensitive to exogenous environmental cycles such as light, sound, posture, physical activity, and mental and emotional stress (Smolensky et al., 2016), is driving activity and rest as well as neuroendocrine and autonomic rhythms. Autonomic activity therefore follows a pattern of diurnal variation with a frequency of an approximate solar day, while it might show peak levels during nighttime (Huikuri et al., 1994; Jarczok et al., 2018; Li et al., 2011). The diurnal variation of BP, for example, is

affected by other endogenous rhythms such as sleep-wake patterns, blood volume variation, melatonin variation, and the renin-angiotensin-aldosterone system, and along with HR, blood pressure has been found to rapidly increase in the morning (Muller et al., 1989). Among the physiological markers of ANS activity reviewed here, the diurnal variation of cardiac autonomic activity is probably most actively studied. Diurnal variation of cardiac autonomic activity indexed by HR and HRV has been observed in children already from 1 year of age but not in neonates (Massin et al., 2000; Weinert et al., 1994), and it continues throughout adolescence (Schubert et al., 1995) and adulthood (Furlan et al., 1990; Huikuri et al., 1994; Lombardi et al., 1992; Malpas & Purdie, 1990; Nakagawa et al., 1998), although it might diminish in older age (Thayer et al., 2010). EDA might show diurnal variation with resistance reaching a minimum between 3 and 5 pm (Kim et al., 2018).

As has been illustrated in this section, ANS function can be studied in diverse ways. The next section looks at research focusing on ANS involvement in NSSI and provides a comprehensive review of existing studies in this evolving field.

ANS Function in NSSI

As outlined in another chapter of this handbook (see Westlund Schreiner et al., this volume), most research studies on the involvement of biological systems in NSSI to date have been focusing on neural systems and the HPA axis. Focusing on the involvement of the ANS in NSSI, most studies have investigated ANS activity over measures of cardiac and electrodermal activity (Kaess et al., 2021). In this section, we aim to provide an overview of existing studies in which the involvement of ANS activity in NSSI has been investigated across one or multiple subunits of analysis as previously introduced. Results are presented for each subunit separately, while an overview of all studies reviewed here can be seen in table 18.2.

Findings on Electrodermal Activity

Haines et al. (1995) and Brain and colleagues (1998, 2002) reported initial evidence on ANS function in NSSI from a series of studies conducted in Australia. The task paradigm used in these studies was a guided imagery task of NSSI and control events (accidental injury, anger, neutral), which examined various indices of ANS activity. The first study (Haines et al., 1995) was conducted in incarcerated male individuals. In the second study (Brain et al., 1998), individuals engaging in NSSI ($N = 35$; $N = 20$ females) and a control group ($N = 35$, matched based on age, sex, and imagery ability) were examined, while the third study (Brain et al., 2002) included a sample of individuals who engaged in NSSI either frequently ($N = 29$) or infrequently ($N = 14$). SCL was also measured in these studies, via two 10-mm Ag/AgCl cup electrodes connected to the fingertips of the first and third fingers of the nondominant hand. In all three studies, SCL remained high across stages 1 and 2 of the imagery task, significantly decreased at stage 3, and remained low throughout stage 4. In a study conducted in Germany by Bohus et al. (2000), SCL was reported to be similar in 12 female patients with BPD compared to 19 controls before, during, and after a cold pain stimulation task. In a study conducted in the United States by Crowell et al. (2005), EDA was recorded continuously, and nonspecific SC responses (fluctuations exceeding 0.5 μs) were derived. The authors found no differences in SC between a group of parasuicidal adolescent girls with lifetime NSSI ($N = 23$) and age-matched controls ($N = 23$) during an experimental paradigm including an initial 1-min resting baseline, sadness induction via a 3-min video clip, and 3 min of subsequent recovery. In another study conducted in the United States, Nock and Mendes (2008) examined physiological arousal during a frustrating and distressing task in the context of an attention task. SC data were collected during the distress tolerance and problem-solving portions of the experimental procedure with Biopac transducers placed on the distal phalanges of the middle and ring fingers of the participant's nondominant hand. They compared a sample of adolescents and young adults with NSSI ($N = 62$) to healthy controls ($N = 30$; matched for age, sex, and ethnicity), finding that the NSSI group exhibited greater changes in SCL over time than the control group. Notably, this difference became especially pronounced in the later minutes (14 min) of the distress tolerance test, when participants were informed that their answers were consistently incorrect. Furthermore, there were indications of a positive relationship between higher scores on an item measuring engagement in NSSI for the purpose of decreasing aversive arousal and greater increases in SC during a frustration task. In a study also conducted in the United States, Welch et al. (2008) in a sample of ($N = 38$) adults fulfilling diagnostic criteria for BPD examined psychophysiological and emotional responses during a personally relevant imagery script involving an NSSI incident (as previously introduced by Brain et al., 1998, 2002; Haines et al., 1995). A statistically significant decrease in SCL was found only between the incident and consequence stages. In another study conducted by Crowell et al. (2012), groups of adolescent girls with NSSI alone ($N = 25$), NSSI and depression ($N = 25$), or typical controls ($N = 25$) were compared with respect to nonspecific SCR (see above). The authors reported lower SCR during resting state among self-injuring participants, but no significant between-group differences emerged during a sadness induction paradigm. Tatnell et al. (2018) in a study conducted in Australia examined differences in SCL, measured via two disposable electrodes (Biopac) attached to the thenar and hypothenar eminences of the nondominant hand, in an NSSI group ($N = 25$) compared to individuals without a history of NSSI ($N = 53$). Differences in SCL between the two study groups were examined during a resting baseline, and while viewing images and rating them concerning perceived image valence and arousal two times, that is, before and after the administration of a stress task (i.e., Trier Social Stress Test, or TSST). No significant differences in SCL for participants who did and did not report NSSI were observed during baseline or any phase of the TSST, and no main effects of image valence, arousal, time (pre–post stress), or NSSI group on SCL responses to images were observed. However, following the TSST administration,

Table 18.2 Summary of Studies included in the Present Review of ANS Function in NSSI*

Study	Study Groups	Mean Age (SD)	Resting Condition	Rec. Length	Stress Paradigm	ANS Measures	Main ANS Findings
Haines et al., 1995	NSSI: $N = 15$ (incarcerated males); prisoner controls without NSSI: $N = 11$; non-prisoner controls without NSSI: $N = 12$	21.3 (5.1)	Eyes-open	30 sec (rest); 1 min (task stages)	Guided imagery	Respiration SCL HR	Reduction in psychophysiological arousal in NSSI group during depiction of NSSI
Brain et. al, 1998	NSSI: $N = 35$ (20 females); controls: $N = 35$	n.r.	Eyes-closed	1 min (rest); 1 min (task stages)	Guided imagery	Respiration SCL HR	Reduction in psychophysiological arousal in NSSI group during depiction of NSSI
Bohus et al., 2000	NSSI: $N = 12$ (females with BPD); controls: $N = 19$	29.1 (8.4)	Seated position	n.r.	Cold Pressor Test; Tourniquet Pain Test	SCL HR	During painful stimulation, there were no significant differences in autonomic activity, potentially owing to individual response patterns
Brain et al., 2002	NSSI: $N = 43$ (25 females)	23.5 (1.23)	Eyes-closed	1 min (rest); 1 min (task stages)	Guided imagery	Respiration SCL HR	No differences in psychophysiological response to imagery between repetitive and infrequent NSSI
Crowell et al., 2005	NSSI: $N = 23$ females; controls: $N = 23$	15.3 (1.1)	Seated position	1 min (rest); 3 min (video clip); 3 min (recovery)	3-min sadness evoking film clip	SCL HRV	Reduced resting RSA as well as during sadness induction and recovery in the NSSI compared to the control group; No differences in SCL
Nock & Mendes, 2008	NSSI: $N = 62$ (49 females); controls: $N = 30$	17.4 (1.8)	Seated position	n.r.	Distress Tolerance Test (administered via Wisconsin Card Sort Test); Social Problem-Solving Skills Test	SCL	Compared to noninjurious adolescents, those with a history of NSSI displayed an increased physiological reactivity to a stressful task

Cowell et al., 2012	NSSI: $N = 25$ females; controls: $N = 25$	16.3 (1.0)	Seated position	1 min (rest); 3 min (video clip); 3 min (recovery)	3-min sadness evoking film clip	SCL	Self-injuring adolescents exhibited lower SCL at rest than depressed and typical control groups
Kaess et al., 2021	NSSI: $N = 14$ females; controls: $N = 14$ females	16.6 (1.7); 16.3 (2.2)	n.a.	5 min (task)	Trier Social Stress Test (TSST)	HR	Similar increase in HR during TSST in both groups
Wielgus et al., 2016	$N = 108$ (community sample)	12.82 (0.82)	"vanilla" baseline	4 min (rest); 5 min (stress); 2 min (recovery)	Anagram task	HRV	HRV recovery after a stressor prospectively predicted engagement in NSSI
Giner-Bartolome et al., 2017	NSSI: $N = 12$ (with eating disorder); non-NSSI: $N = 32$ (with eating disorder); controls: $N = 22$	31.77 (9.70); 26.83 (8.78); 28.55 (7.88)	n.a.	n.r.	Serious videogame	HRV	No significant differences in HRV throughout the task were found between any of the groups
Koenig et al., 2017	NSSI: 30 females	15.27 (1.36)	Seated position	5 min (rest); max. 4 min (task)	Cold Pain Stimulation	HR HRV BP	HR increased and HRV decreased during painful stimulation indicating increased physiological arousal, while this response did not differ between the NSSI and control group
Scott et al., 2017	$N = 57$ female adolescents (urban community sample)	n.r.	Seated position	30 sec (rest); 30 sec (clips)	Maternal Feedback Task	Pupil size	Greater pupillary reactivity to maternal criticism predicted a worsening course of BPD symptoms over time

(continued)

Table 18.2 Continued

Study	Study Groups	Mean Age (SD)	Resting Condition	Rec. Length	Stress Paradigm	ANS Measures	Main ANS Findings
Tatnell et al., (2018)	NSSI: N = 25	20.5 (1,74)	Seated position	5 min (rest); n.r. (tasks)	Exposure to and rating of emotional stimuli; TSST	SCL	groups did not differ in ANS arousal across the TSST, although changes in SCL from baseline indicate that the stressor was effective; Participants not reporting NSSI responded more to positive images and rated these as more pleasant after the stressor, while participants reporting NSSI physiologically responded less to positive images after the stressor
Gratz et al., 2019	NSSI and BPD: N = 21; NSSI without BPD: N = 18; No NSSI/BPD: N = 25	23.94 (4.79)	Seated position (vanilla Baseline)	5 min (rest); 5 min (task)	Audio-recorded, 5-min, imaginal social rejection scenario	SCL HRV	No significant differences in psychophysiological parameters between study groups were observed in response to the negative emotion induction
Fitzpatrick et al., 2020	NSSI and BPD: N = 22	n.r.	Seated position	5 min (rest); n.r. (task)	Emotion induction via images	SCL HRV	higher baseline vagally-mediated HRV and higher baseline SCR predicted greater frequency of lifetime NSSI

Kaufman et al., 2020	NSSI female adolescent + mother dyads: $N = 30$; control dyads: $N = 30$	NSSI group: 15.47 (1.48); control group: 14.77 (1.33)	Individual + dyadic	5 min (individual—dyadic rest); n.r. (task)	Conflict discussion task	HRV	Self-harming teens and their mothers generally had lower baseline RSA compared with controls; mothers of self-injuring teens demonstrated RSA increases in the context of sitting quietly with their child; RSA increased during the conflict condition relative to baseline across all participants
Nelson et al., 2021	147 adolescents (community sample)	12.34 (0.58)	Participants were asked to sit up straight with their legs uncrossed and their feet flat on the floor	n.r.	n.a.	HR	Interaction between assessed peer conflict and resting HR at baseline significantly predicted increased NSSI at follow-up
Tuna & Gençöz, 2021	NSSI group: $N = 34$; controls: $N = 36$	total sample: 21.07 (1.58)	Seated position	2 min (rest); n.r. (tasks)	cold pain stimulation; distressing card-sorting task	SCL	No significant differences in baseline SCL or reactivity during the task paradigm between study groups

*Focus is put on results pertaining to ANS measures. *Note.* *n.a.* = not applicable; *n.r.* = not reported.

participants who did report NSSI showed a smaller SCL response to positive images compared to participants who did not report NSSI; in other words, participants who did not report NSSI showed stronger arousal in response to positive images after the stressor had ceased. No between-group differences with regard to negative images or based on arousal were observed. In a study conducted in the United States, Gratz et al. (2019) examined SCL, acquired with Ag/AgCl electrodes on the medial phalanges of two fingers on the nondominant hand via Biopac Systems, in response to social rejection emotion induction (relative to a neutral emotion induction) in three groups of young adults with either NSSI and BPD ($N = 21$) or NSSI but not fulfilling diagnostic criteria for BPD ($N = 18$) and control participants with neither NSSI nor BPD ($N = 25$). In this study, no significant differences in SCL between any of the groups were observed in response to the negative emotion induction. Fitzpatrick et al. (2020) in a study conducted in Canada derived SCL at baseline and during emotion induction based on emotionally valenced images and found higher resting-state SCL to be significantly linked with a higher frequency of lifetime NSSI in participants (age not reported) engaging in NSSI and diagnosed BPD ($N = 22$).

Findings on Blood Pressure

In a study conducted in Germany, Koenig et al. (2017) reported the psychophysiological response to cold pain as a physiological stressor in 30 female adolescents fulfilling DSM-5 research diagnostic criteria for NSSI disorder and 30 matched healthy controls. Koenig et al. (2015) had previously hypothesized that female adolescents with NSSI would exhibit an altered ANS (and HPA axis) responsivity to experimentally induced pain compared to healthy control participants, and specifically, it was expected that sympathetic response would be decreased, while parasympathetic response would be increased, in the NSSI group in response to cold pain. Various measures of ANS activity were recorded before and immediately after exposure to painful stimulation. BP was measured via an automated digital device, and SBP and DBP were derived as respective indices. In this study, no statistically significant difference in SBP or DBP at resting state between the NSSI group and healthy controls was observed, and the groups showed no differences regarding SBP and DBP responsivity in unadjusted or adjusted (smoking, body-mass index, alcohol consumption, drug consumption, medication, and contraceptives) analyses.

Findings on Breathing

In the studies conducted by Brain et al. (1998, 2002) as a replication of a previous study (Haines et al., 1995), as cited above, respiration was measured using a Pneumotrace respiration sensor band fitted around the upper torso. The authors found a significant increase in respiration rate from stage 1 of the imagery task (description of the general scene) to stage 2 (description of events preceding NSSI), and a significant decrease at stage 3 (details of actual NSSI)—which was maintained at stage 4 (immediate consequences of NSSI).

Findings on Heart Rate and Heart Rate Variability

In the studies by Haines et al. (1995) and Brain et al. (1998, 2002), ECG was also measured, using two Gereonics 7-mm Ag/AgCI electrodes fitted at the second rib on both sides of the torso, and HR was derived. A significant increase in HR was observed between stages 1 (scene) and 2 (preceding events) of the guided imagery, and HR significantly decreased at stage 3 (actual NSSI) and was maintained at stage 4 (consequences). In the study by Bohus et al. (2000), a significant difference in resting HR was found between 12 female BPD patients and 19 age-matched controls before conducting a cold pain stimulation task, while no task effects were observed between or within groups. In another study cited earlier (Crowell et al., 2005), ECG was recorded using a Biopac system and vagally mediated HRV derived via spectral analysis. Parasuicidal adolescent girls with lifetime NSSI showed lower HRV (respiratory sinus arrhythmia, or RSA) compared to age-matched controls at resting baseline, during mood induction, and at subsequent recovery, and no group x task interaction effects were observed.

In another study conducted in Germany, Kaess et al. (2021) collected HR (among other measures) throughout a standardized psychosocial stress paradigm (TSST) in a sample of adolescent girls engaging in NSSI ($N = 14$) and healthy controls ($N = 14$). They found no statistically significant difference in HR between study groups, while HR showed significant increases during the TSST in both groups. In the United States, Wielgus et al. (2016), in one of the few longitudinal studies, examined whether HRV at rest and during as well as after a stress task (responsivity and recovery), respectively, would predict risk of NSSI during the following 6 months in a sample of ($N = 108$) community adolescents. The authors measured ECG via disposable pre-gelled Ag/AgCl electrodes placed on the chest and abdomen (Lead II), using a Biopac System, and derived HRV (RSA) throughout a task paradigm, including a 4-min "vanilla" baseline, a 5-min stress task, and a 2-min recovery period. While HRV at rest and HRV responsivity percentage did not significantly predict engagement in NSSI at a 6-month follow-up, interestingly, HRV recovery percentage did significantly predict NSSI engagement, such that lower HRV during the recovery period was associated with increased risk for NSSI, above and beyond the effect of depressive symptoms and lifetime history of NSSI.

In another study by our group investigating psychophysiological responsivity to cold pain (Koenig et al., 2017), ECG was recorded using a Polar device with electrodes attached to an elastic belt affixed to the chest, and both HR and HRV were derived. No statistically significant differences in resting-state HR or HRV were observed between the NSSI and control group, and the groups did not significantly differ regarding changes in HR or HRV in response to cold pain stimulation. Exploratory analyses of ultra-short-term HRV measured before (pain anticipation) and after (ANS recovery) painful stimulation revealed significant group differences between the NSSI and matched control group, such that the NSSI group had significantly higher HRV 60 sec before (pain anticipation), and significantly lower HRV 30 sec after exposure to cold pain, while the respective group difference was no longer present 60 sec after cold pain exposure. In a follow-up analysis of the respective study, we found that greater childhood adversity was associated with prolonged autonomic arousal following pain induction (Rinnewitz et al., 2018).

In a study conducted in Spain, Giner-Bartolome et al. (2017) examined HRV in a sample of adult female patients with either disordered eating and NSSI ($N = 12$) or disordered eating alone ($N = 32$) as well as in psychologically healthy controls ($N = 22$). ECG was acquired through an amplifier sensor system throughout a serious videogame task. No significant differences in HRV throughout the task between any of the groups were observed. In a study conducted in the United States, Fox et al. (2018) examined whether and how resting-state vagally mediated HRV and HRV in response to stress predicted NSSI in a sample of ($N = 70$) young adults, half of whom had a recent history of NSSI while the other half had never engaged in NSSI. Respective results indicated that resting HRV did not predict recent NSSI engagement, whereas greater decreases in HRV in response to social stress significantly predicted recent NSSI. Moreover, individuals with greater decreases in HRV in response to stress were significantly more likely to engage in NSSI if they also reported low problem-solving skills. In a study previously cited by Gratz et al. (2019), ECG data were acquired using Ag/AgCl electrodes via a Biopac System, and the high-frequency component of HRV (0.15–0.40 Hz) was derived from the electrocardiogram via spectral analysis. In this study, no significant differences in HRV between the study groups of BPD and NSSI ($N = 21$), NSSI without BPD ($N = 18$), and controls with neither BPD nor NSSI ($N = 25$) were observed in response to the negative emotion induction. In another study previously cited (Fitzpatrick et al., 2020), ECG was acquired as well (Biopac System), and the authors found higher resting HRV to predict greater lifetime frequency of NSSI in a sample of BPD patients (sample age not reported). In a study conducted in Canada, Kaufman et al. (2020) included a sample of female adolescents engaging in NSSI and their mothers ($N = 30$ dyads), as well as control mother-daughter dyads ($N = 30$). They examined HRV measured via Mindware hardware with a standard spot electrode configuration at a resting baseline (5-min individual and 5-min dyadic baselines), during a conflict discussion task, and during subsequent rediscussion of the conflictual topics after watching an instructional video on validation. They found lower resting vagally mediated HRV in mothers of adolescents engaging in NSSI during individual baseline, whereas HRV increased during dyadic baseline compared to control-dyad mothers. There was no group differences between mothers' HRV during subsequent conflict tasks, while HRV generally increased during conflict. Considering adolescents, those engaging in NSSI had lower vagally mediated HRV during both individual and dyadic resting baseline compared to control adolescents. Also here, although HRV generally increased during conflict, there was no group effect.

Finally, in another prospective study in the United States, Nelson et al. (2021) examined the potential role of the ANS (and in interaction with socioemotional stressors) in NSSI risk, in a sample of ($N = 147$) community adolescents. The authors tested whether experiences of social conflict (i.e., parent and peer conflict) would interact with resting HR to predict adolescent NSSI (and suicidal ideation) across one year. Respective analyses revealed that although neither greater social conflict nor higher HR at baseline alone was associated with NSSI at follow-up, adolescents experiencing both greater peer conflict and higher HR at baseline showed significant longitudinal increases in NSSI from baseline to follow-up.

Findings on Pupil Size

Although not directly addressing NSSI, in a prospective study conducted in the United States, Scott et al. (2017) in a sample of ($N = 57$) adolescent girls examined pupillary (and affective) responses to maternal feedback as predictors of BPD symptom development over 18 months. Pupillary data was acquired using a table-mounted ISCAN RK464 video-based infrared pupillometer while participants heard recorded clips of their own mothers making critical or praising statements about them, as well as neutral statements that did not pertain to them. In this study, greater pupillary response to maternal criticism predicted increases in BPD symptoms over time.

Reviewing the existing evidence on altered ANS function in NSSI, it became apparent that the respective results are mixed. Independent of measurement conditions, some studies reported evidence for lower SNS/greater PNS activity (Brain et al., 1998; Cowell et al., 2012; Fitzpatrick et al., 2020; Haines et al., 1995)) (only HRV), while other studies found no evidence for altered ANS activity in patients engaging in NSSI (Bohus et al., 2000; Brain et al., 2002; Giner-Bartolome et al., 2017; Gratz et al., 2019; Kaess et al., 2021; Tatnell et al., 2018; Tuna & Gençöz, 2021)—and still other studies reported greater SNS/lower PNS activity (Crowell et al., 2005; Fitzgerald et al., 2020 [only SCR]; Kaufman et al., 2020; Koenig et al., 2017; Nock & Mendes, 2008). A synthesis of the existing evidence is hindered, given that experimental conditions across studies are not comparable. Although different research groups were interested in different experimental paradigms (i.e., ANS response to emotion induction and ANS response to pain induction), the field would do well to agree on minimal standards (e.g., baseline recordings of standardized length) to enable meta-analytical approaches.

Findings on the Diurnal Variation of ANS Activity in NSSI

In a first and recent study conducted in Germany including female adolescents with NSSI disorder and healthy controls ($N = 30$ each), Sigrist et al. (2022) found that the NSSI group was characterized by altered diurnal variation of ANS activity, indexed by a greater HR MESOR (rhythm adjusted mean), Amplitude (extent of predictable variation within a cycle), and Acrophase (time of overall high values recurring in each cycle), as well as a lower Amplitude and MESOR, and greater Acrophase, of vmHRV—although the latter findings were not robust when adjusting for important confounds. Further, diurnal variation of ANS activity in the NSSI group was characterized by a general shift in rhythmicity of about one hour, as indexed by higher Acrophases.

Although the results presented here are preliminary and will need further replication with rigorous control of exogenous stressors and further confounders, they suggest potential disruptions in the maturation of ANS function associated with impairments in stress-regulatory domains in adolescents, and further highlight the importance of future research concerned with the physiology and pathology of diurnal rhythmicity in the etiology of NSSI.

Discussion and Future Directions

Addressing an ANS involvement in NSSI is a psychophysiological research topic of increasing interest. Given the association between stress and NSSI, research methods of quantifying ANS activity have been broadly applied, predominantly in classic case-control studies including patients with NSSI. Unsurprisingly, the majority of studies focused on measures to quantify cardiovascular activity. In contrast to measures of EDA or pupillometry, the respective techniques (e.g., ECG) are easily implemented at low costs and pose only moderate challenges to the research setting.

Most of the existing studies on ANS activity in NSSI addressed ANS activity as *proximal biological traits* (Kaess et al., 2021), with only a few studies addressing how ANS activity may be associated with later onset of NSSI or the longitudinal prediction of its severity (see table 18.2). Although some studies induced pain in the laboratory setting to study ANS response to the respective procedures, studies addressing ANS response to actual acts of NSSI in everyday life (i.e., biological states that directly precede or follow NSSI) are currently missing and present an interesting avenue for future research. Research on circadian rhythms underlying ANS activity in NSSI is rare. These real-world applications of the psychophysiological research methodology in quantifying ANS activity seem fruitful to advance the current state of art in the field, which is predominantly focusing on lab-based settings that allow for a better control of confounding factors and experimental conditions. However, recent advances in wearable technology allow for a broader application of the respective methods that may help to maximize the generalizability of findings beyond the lab. Further, a broader consensus in the field seems warranted, as it is currently characterized by small individual studies without proper replication and great heterogeneity in measurement conditions, derived measures and different approaches in analytical processing, and statistical analyses.

As outlined in a previous chapter (see Zetterqvist & Bjureberg, this volume), social processes have a central role in NSSI and thus need to be included in the conceptualization of how NSSI is developed and maintained. In this chapter, the focus has been on the psychophysiological underpinnings of NSSI as a means of regulating internal states, yet the psychophysiology of social regulatory functions of NSSI as one unit of analysis within the RDoC framework is an important topic of inquiry and merits further investigation. Most probably, understanding who engages in NSSI will likely involve multiple interacting constructs, such that dysfunctions or disruptions across several functional domains are implicated in the onset of NSSI. In particular, future research is also needed to investigate functional interactions between different physiological regulatory systems under various conditions of functioning (i.e., under resting state, stress exposure, as well as circadian influences). In this context, as one example, research focusing on potential biological aberrations linked with early life adversity, which is often also implicated in the history of individuals engaging in NSSI, found asymmetries between HPA axis and ANS activity response patterns under psychosocial stress exposure (Gordis et al., 2008), with absent associations between peripheral markers of HPA axis and sympathetic activity in the group exposed to severe early life adversity. Discordance across RDoC systems (e.g., subjective experience divergent from HPA-axis response to stress) might be more common in adolescents engaging in NSSI, as will in the chapter by Westlund Schreiner et al. (this volume).

Beyond the foregoing challenges, it remains questionable whether existing findings reflect specific phenomena associated with NSSI or if these are better explained by comorbidity (i.e., affective of personality disorders), associated health behavior (i.e., smoking, drug and alcohol consumption, and immobility), or joint mechanisms (i.e., trauma and adversity) that are infrequently covered with great rigor in existing primary studies. Researchers are encouraged to adopt an RDoC approach and move beyond case-control studies, contrasting patients with different clinical presentations as a function of severity and consider innovative real-world applications of the psychophysiological research methodology to tackle potential specifics of NSSI in association with actual acts of NSSI. Psychophysiological research methods hold considerable advances in comparison to other quantitative methods, concerning, for example, costs associated with their implementation (e.g., MRI) and a lesser degree of complexity. Although their specific utility to deepen our understanding of the etiology of NSSI may be limited, they hold great potential to study actual events of NSSI in the open field.

Indeed, over the past few years, multistream data collection, consisting of a combination of biometric measures and experience sampling techniques such as ecological momentary assessment (EMA), has enabled the development and implementation of predictive algorithms to detect activities, emotional states, or social contexts an individual may be engaged with momentarily, which has already informed the development of promising interventions in clinical populations (including, e.g., anxiety, depression, substance abuse, sleep, eating, stress, and gambling disorders as well as suicidal behavior) (Donker et al., 2013). When translating to the present context of NSSI, insights from multistream data collection, concretely, the assessment of the covariation between autonomic and NSSI-related states, might assist the identification of at-risk states for engagement in NSSI (Calati & Courtet, 2016; Liu et al., 2018; Ougrin et al., 2015; Westlund Schreiner et al., 2015). For example, based on a relatively high temporal resolution—which is possible with ECG—ambulatory assessment of cardiac autonomic states via long-term ECG recordings might present an initial, practical, and accessible means to detect states that are potentially linked with emotional processes that precede NSSI incidents—which could ultimately help to expand the currently available treatment options for NSSI.

Conclusion

In sum, this chapter underlines ANS involvement in NSSI as a psychophysiological research topic of increasing interest. Existing studies are centered around specific approaches to quantify ANS function and report mixed and inconclusive results. The heterogeneity between studies in the field hinders further advances such as metascience, which would help to derive higher levels of confidence in the reported findings. All in all, the field would do well to agree on minimal research standards when it comes to the assessment of ANS function, while on the clinical end, more diverse NSSI samples with differing psychiatric conditions and varying levels of disease severity should be considered and contrasted against. In the years ahead, overcoming these and many further difficulties will be a complex challenge to the study of NSSI, but increasing possibilities in terms of psychophysiological research methods and applications as well as a growing awareness of the usefulness of more innovative approaches such as the RDoC will continue to advance this emerging field of inquiry.

Acknowledgments

We would like to thank our research assistant, Ms. Roxana Rothe, for her great help in identifying potentially relevant studies investigating ANS activity in NSSI.

References

Aston-Jones, G., & Cohen, J. D. (2005). Adaptive gain and the role of the locus coeruleus-norepinephrine system in optimal performance. *The Journal of Comparative Neurology*, *493*(1), 99–110. https://doi.org/10.1002/cne.20723

Benarroch, E. E. (1993). The central autonomic network: Functional organization, dysfunction, and perspective. *Mayo Clinic Proceedings*, *68*(10), 988–1001.

Bernston, G. G., Cacioppo, J. T., Binkley, P. F., Uchino, B. N., Quigley, K. S., & Fieldstone, A. (1994). Autonomic cardiac control. III. Psychological stress and cardiac response in autonomic space as revealed by pharmacological blockades. *Psychophyisiology*, *31*, 599–608.

Bernston, G. G., Cacioppo, J. T., & Quigley, K. S. (1994). Autonomic cardiac control. I. Estimation and validation from pharmacological blockades. *Psychophysiology*, *31*, 572–585.

Bohus, M., Limberger, M., Ebner, U., Glocker, F. X., Schwarz, B., Wernz, M., & Lieb, K. (2000). Pain perception during self-reported distress and calmness in patients with borderline personality disorder and self-mutilating behavior. *Psychiatry Research*, *95*(3), 251–260. https://doi.org/10.1016/S0165-1781(00)00179-7

Bolanos, M., Nazeran, H., & Haltiwanger, E. (2006). Comparison of heart rate variability signal features derived from lectrocardiography and photoplethysmography in healthy Individuals. *International Conference of the IEEE Engineering in Medicine and Biology Society*, *2006*, 4289–4294. https://doi.org/10.1109/IEMBS.2006.260607

Brain, K. L., Haines, J., & Williams, C. L. (1998). The psychophysiology of self-mutilation: Evidence of tension reduction. *Archives of Suicide Research*, *4*(3), 227–242. https://doi.org/10.1080/13811119808258298

Brain, K. L., Haines, J., & Williams, C. L. (2002). The psychophysiology of repetitive self-mutilation. *Archives of Suicide Research*, *6*(3), 199–210. https://doi.org/10.1080/13811110214140

Brindle, R. C., Ginty, A. T., Phillips, A. C., & Carroll, D. (2014). A tale of two mechanisms: A meta-analytic approach toward understanding the autonomic basis of cardiovascular reactivity to acute psychological stress: Autonomic basis of cardiovascular reactivity. *Psychophysiology, 51*(10), 964–976. https://doi.org/10.1111/psyp.12248

Brownley, K. A., Hurwitz, B. E., & Schneiderman, N. (2000). Cardiovascular psychophysiology. Cardiovascular psychophysiology. In J. T. Cacioppo, L. G. Tassinary, & G. G. Berntson (Eds.), *Handbook of psychophysiology* (pp. 224–264). Cambridge University Press.

Cacioppo, J. T., Tassinary, L. G., & Bernston, G. G. (2007). Psychophysiological science: Interdisciplinary approaches to classic questions about the mind. In J. T. Cacioppo, L. G. Tassinary, & G. G. Berntson (Eds.), *Handbook of psychophysiology* (Vol. 1–3, pp. 1–16). Cambridge University Press.

Calati, R., & Courtet, P. (2016). Is psychotherapy effective for reducing suicide attempt and non-suicidal self-injury rates? Meta-analysis and meta-regression of literature data. *Journal of Psychiatric Research, 79*, 8–20. https://doi.org/10.1016/j.jpsychires.2016.04.003

Chan, E. D., Chan, M. M., & Chan, M. M. (2013). Pulse oximetry: Understanding its basic principles facilitates appreciation of its limitations. *Respiratory Medicine, 107*(6), 789–799. https://doi.org/10.1016/j.rmed.2013.02.004

Chobanian, A. V., Bakris, G. L., Black, H. R., Cushman, W. C., Green, L. A., Izzo, J. L., Jones, D. W., Materson, B. J., Oparil, S., Wright, J. T., Roccella, E. J., & National High Blood Pressure Education Program Coordinating Committee. (2003). Seventh report of the joint national committee on prevention, detection, evaluation, and treatment of high blood pressure. *Hypertension, 42*(6), 1206–1252. https://doi.org/10.1161/01.HYP.0000107251.49515.c2

Crowell, S. E., Beauchaine, T. P., Hsiao, R. C., Vasilev, C. A., Yaptangco, M., Linehan, M. M., & McCauley, E. (2012). Differentiating adolescent self-injury from adolescent depression: Possible implications for borderline personality development. *Journal of Abnormal Child Psychology, 40*(1), 45–57. https://doi.org/10.1007/s10802-011-9578-3

Crowell, S. E., Beauchaine, T. P., McCauley, E., Smith, C. J., Stevens, A. L., & Sylvers, P. (2005). Psychological, autonomic, and serotonergic correlates of parasuicide among adolescent girls. *Development and Psychopathology, 17*(4), 1105–1127. https://doi.org/10.1017/S0954579405050522

De Geus, E. J. C., Kupper, N., Boomsma, D. I., & Snieder, H. (2007). Bivariate genetic modeling of cardiovascular stress reactivity: Does stress uncover genetic variance? *Psychosomatic Medicine, 69*(4), 356–364. https://doi.org/10.1097/PSY.0b013e318049cc2d

De Geus, E., Van Lien, R., Neijts, M., & Willemsen, G. (2013). Genetics of autonomic nervous system activity. In T. Canli (Ed.), *The Oxford handbook of molecular psychology* (pp. 357–390). Oxford University Press.

Donker, T., Petrie, K., Proudfoot, J., Clarke, J., Birch, M.-R., & Christensen, H. (2013). Smartphones for smarter delivery of mental health programs: A systematic review. *Journal of Medical Internet Research, 15*(11), Article e247. https://doi.org/10.2196/jmir.2791

Eddie, D., Bates, M. E., Vaschillo, E. G., Lehrer, P. M., Retkwa, M., & Miuccio, M. (2018). Rest, reactivity and recovery: A psychophysiological assessment of borderline personality disorder. *Frontiers in Psychiatry, 9*, Article 505. https://doi.org/10.3389/fpsyt.2018.00505

Fitzpatrick, S., Zeifman, R., Krantz, L., McMain, S., & Kuo, J. R. (2020). Getting specific about emotion and self-inflicted Injury: An examination across emotion processes in borderline personality disorder. *Archives of Suicide Research, 24*(Suppl.1), 102–123. https://doi.org/10.1080/13811118.2019.1586605

Fox, A. R., Hammond, L. E., & Mezulis, A. H. (2018). Respiratory sinus arrhythmia and adaptive emotion regulation as predictors of nonsuicidal self-injury in young adults. *International Journal of Psychophysiology, 133*, 1–11. https://doi.org/10.1016/j.ijpsycho.2018.09.006

Freeman, R. (2006). Assessment of cardiovascular autonomic function. *Clinical Neurophysiology, 117*(4), 716–730. https://doi.org/10.1016/j.clinph.2005.09.027

Furlan, R., Guzzetti, S., & Crivellaro, W. (1990). Continuous 24-hour assessment of the neural regulation of systemic arterial pressure and RR variabilities in ambulant subjects. *Circulation, 81*, 537–547.

Geršak, G. (2020). Electrodermal activity—A beginner's guide. *Elektrotehniski Vestnik, 87*(4), 175–182.

Ghamari, M. (2018). A review on wearable photoplethysmography sensors and their potential future applications in health care. *International Journal of Biosensors & Bioelectronics, 4*(4), 195–202. https://doi.org/10.15406/ijbsbe.2018.04.00125

Giner-Bartolome, C., Mallorquí-Bagué, N., Tolosa-Sola, I., Steward, T., Jimenez-Murcia, S., Granero, R., & Fernandez-Aranda, F. (2017). Non-suicidal self-injury in eating disordered patients: Associations with heart rate variability and state-trait anxiety. *Frontiers in Psychology, 8*, Article 1163. https://doi.org/10.3389/fpsyg.2017.01163

Gordis, E. B., Granger, D. A., Susman, E. J., & Trickett, P. K. (2008). Salivary alpha amylase–cortisol asymmetry in maltreated youth. *Hormones and Behavior*, *53*(1), 96–103. https://doi.org/10.1016/j.yhbeh.2007.09.002

Gratz, K. L., Richmond, J. R., Dixon-Gordon, K. L., Chapman, A. L., & Tull, M. T. (2019). Multimodal assessment of emotional reactivity and regulation in response to social rejection among self-harming adults with and without borderline personality disorder. *Personality Disorders: Theory, Research, and Treatment*, *10*(5), 395–405. https://doi.org/10.1037/per0000334

Grossman, P., & Kollai, M. (1993). Respiratory sinus arrhythmia, cardiac vagal tone, and respiration: Within- and between-individual relations. *Psychophysiology*, *30*, 486–495.

Haines, J., Williams, C. L., & Brain, K. L. (1995). The psychopathology of incarcerated self-mutilators. *The Canadian Journal of Psychiatry*, *40*(9), 514–522.

Harskamp, R. E., Bekker, L., Himmelreich, J. C. L., De Clercq, L., Karregat, E. P. M., Sleeswijk, M. E., & Lucassen, W. A. M. (2021). Performance of popular pulse oximeters compared with simultaneous arterial oxygen saturation or clinical-grade pulse oximetry: A cross-sectional validation study in intensive care patients. *BMJ Open Respiratory Research*, *8*(1), Article e000939. https://doi.org/10.1136/bmjresp-2021-000939

Hastings, M., & Maywood, E. S. (2000). Circadian clocks in the mammalian brain. *BioEssays*, *22*(1), 23–31. https://doi.org/10.1002/(SICI)1521-1878(200001)22:1<23::AID-BIES6>3.0.CO;2-Z

Houtveen, J. H., & Rietveld, S. (2002). Contribution of tonic vagal modulation of heart rate, central respiratory drive, respiratory depth, and respiratory frequency to respiratory sinus arrhythmia during mental stress and physical exercise. *Psychophyisiology*, *44*(2), 203–215.

Huikuri, H. V., Niemelä, M. J., Ojala, S., Rantala, A., Ikäheimo, M. J., & Airaksinen, K. E. (1994). Circadian rhythms of frequency domain measures of heart rate variability in healthy subjects and patients with coronary artery disease. Effects of arousal and upright posture. *Circulation*, *90*(1), 121–126. https://doi.org/10.1161/01.CIR.90.1.121

Insel, T., Cuthbert, B., Garvey, M., Heinssen, R., Pine, D. S., Quinn, K., Sanislow, C., & Wang, P. (2010). Research Domain Criteria (RDoC): Toward a new classification framework for research on mental disorders. *The American Journal of Psychiatry*, *167*(7), 748–751. https://doi.org/10.1176/appi.ajp.2010.09091379

Jacobs, S. C., Friedman, R., Parker, J. D., Tofler, G. H., Jimenez, A. H., Muller, J. E., Benson, H., & Stone, P. H. (1994). Use of skin conductance changes during mental stress testing as an index of autonomic arousal in cardiovascular research. *American Heart Journal*, *128*(6), 1170–1177. https://doi.org/10.1016/0002-8703(94)90748-X

Jarczok, M. N., Aguilar-Raab, C., Koenig, J., Kaess, M., Borniger, J. C., Nelson, R. J., Hall, M., Ditzen, B., Thayer, J. F., & Fischer, J. E. (2018). The heart's rhythm "n" blues: Sex differences in circadian variation patterns of vagal activity vary by depressive symptoms in predominantly healthy employees. *Chronobiology International*, *35*(7), 896–909. https://doi.org/10.1080/07420528.2018.1439499

Jubran, A. (2015). Pulse oximetry. *Critical Care*, *19*(1), 272. https://doi.org/10.1186/s13054-015-0984-8

Kaess, M., Hooley, J. M., Klimes-Dougan, B., Koenig, J., Plener, P. L., Reichl, C., Robinson, K., Schmahl, C., Sicorello, M., Westlund Schreiner, M., & Cullen, K. R. (2021). Advancing a temporal framework for understanding the biology of nonsuicidal self-injury: An expert review. *Neuroscience and Biobehavioral Reviews*, *130*, 228–239. https://doi.org/10.1016/j.neubiorev.2021.08.022

Kar, S. K. (2019). Predictors of response to repetitive transcranial magnetic stimulation in depression: A review of recent updates. *Clinical Psychopharmacology and Neuroscience*, *17*(1), 25–33. https://doi.org/10.9758/cpn.2019.17.1.25

Kaufman, E. A., Puzia, M. E., Godfrey, D. A., & Crowell, S. E. (2020). Physiological and behavioral effects of interpersonal validation: A multilevel approach to examining a core intervention strategy among self-injuring adolescents and their mothers. *Journal of Clinical Psychology*, *76*(3), 559–580. https://doi.org/10.1002/jclp.22902

Kerryn L. Brain, Janet Haines & Christopher L. Williams (1998) The psychophysiology of self-mutilation: Evidence of tension reduction, Archives of Suicide Research, 4:3, 227–242, DOI: 10.1080/13811119808258298

Kim, J., Ku, B., Bae, J.-H., Han, G.-C., & Kim, J. U. (2018). Contrast in the circadian behaviors of an electrodermal activity and bioimpedance spectroscopy. *Chronobiology International*, *35*(10), 1413–1422. https://doi.org/10.1080/07420528.2018.1486852

Koenig, J., Falvay, D., Clamor, A., Wagner, J., Jarczok, M. N., Ellis, R. J., Weber, C., & Thayer, J. F. (2016). Pneumogastric (vagus) nerve activity indexed by heart rate variability in chronic pain patients compared to healthy controls: A systematic review and meta-analysis. *Pain Physician*, *19*(1), E55–E78. https://doi.org/10.36076/ppj/2016.19.E55

Koenig, J., Jarczok, M. N., Ellis, R. J., Hillecke, T. K., & Thayer, J. F. (2014). Heart rate variability and experimentally induced pain in healthy adults: A systematic review. *European Journal of Pain*, *18*(3), 301–314. https://doi.org/10.1002/j.1532-2149.2013.00379.x

Koenig, J., Kemp, A. H., Beauchaine, T. P., Thayer, J. F., & Kaess, M. (2016). Depression and resting state heart rate variability in children and adolescents—A systematic review and meta-analysis. *Clinical Psychology Review*, *46*, 136–150. https://doi.org/10.1016/j.cpr.2016.04.013

Koenig, J., Kemp, A. H., Feeling, N. R., Thayer, J. F., & Kaess, M. (2016). Resting state vagal tone in borderline personality disorder: A meta-analysis. *Progress in Neuro-Psychopharmacology and Biological Psychiatry*, *64*, 18–26. https://doi.org/10.1016/j.pnpbp.2015.07.002

Koenig, J., Loerbroks, A., Jarczok, M. N., Fischer, J. E., & Thayer, J. F. (2016). Chronic pain and heart rate variability in a cross-sectional occupational sample: Evidence for impaired vagal control. *The Clinical Journal of Pain*, *32*(3), 218–225. https://doi.org/10.1097/AJP.0000000000000242

Koenig, J., Rinnewitz, L., Warth, M., Hillecke, T. K., Brunner, R., Resch, F., & Kaess, M. (2017). Psychobiological response to pain in female adolescents with nonsuicidal self-injury. *Journal of Psychiatry & Neuroscience*, *42*(3), 189–199. https://doi.org/10.1503/jpn.160074

Koenig, J., Rinnewitz, L., Warth, M., & Kaess, M. (2015). Autonomic nervous system and hypothalamic–pituitary–adrenal axis response to experimentally induced cold pain in adolescent non-suicidal self-injury—Study protocol. *BMC Psychiatry*, *15*(1), Article 150. https://doi.org/10.1186/s12888-015-0544-4

Koss, M. C. (1986). Pupillary dilation as an index of central nervous system α2-adrenoceptor activation. *Journal of Pharmacological Methods*, *15*(1), 1–19.

Kret, M. E., & Sjak-Shie, E. E. (2019). Preprocessing pupil size data: Guidelines and code. *Behavior Research Methods*, *51*(3), 1336–1342. https://doi.org/10.3758/s13428-018-1075-y

Li, X., Shaffer, M. L., Rodriguez-Colon, S., He, F., Wolbrette, D. L., Alagona, P., Wu, C., & Liao, D. (2011). The circadian pattern of cardiac autonomic modulation in a middle-aged population. *Clinical Autonomic Research*, *21*(3), 143–150. https://doi.org/10.1007/s10286-010-0112-4

Light, K. C., Kothandapani, R. V., & Allen, M. T. (1998). Enhanced cardiovascular and catecholamine responses in women with depressive symptoms. *International Journal of Psychophysiology*, *28*, 157–166.

Liu, R. T., Scopelliti, K. M., Pittman, S. K., & Zamora, A. S. (2018). Childhood maltreatment and nonsuicidal self-injury: A systematic review and meta-analysis. *The Lancet Psychiatry*, *5*(1), 51–64. https://doi.org/10.1016/S2215-0366(17)30469-8

Lombardi, F., Sandrone, G., & Mortara, A. (1992). Circadian variation of spectral indices of heart rate variability after myocardial infarction. *American Heart Journal*, *123*, 1521–1529.

Lu, G., Yang, F., Taylor, J. A., & Stein, J. F. (2009). A comparison of photoplethysmography and ECG recording to analyse heart rate variability in healthy subjects. *Journal of Medical Engineering & Technology*, *33*(8), 634–641. https://doi.org/10.3109/03091900903150998

Lucini, D., Norbiato, G., Clerici, M., & Pagani, M. (2002). Hemodynamic and autonomic adjustments to real life stress conditions in humans. *Hypertension*, *39*(1), 184–188. https://doi.org/10.1161/hy0102.100784

Malpas, S., & Purdie, G. (1990). Circadian variation of heart rate variability. *Cardiovascular Research*, *24*, 210–213.

Massin, M. M., Maeyns, K., Withofs, N., Ravet, F., & Gérard, P. (2000). Circadian rhythm of heart rate and heart rate variability. *Archives of Disease in Childhood*, *83*, 179–182.

Mathôt, S. (2018). Pupillometry: Psychology, physiology, and function. *Journal of Cognition*, *1*(1), Article 16. https://doi.org/10.5334/joc.18

Morris, S. E., & Cuthbert, B. N. (2022). Research Domain Criteria: cognitive systems, neural circuits, and dimensions of behavior. Dialogues in Clinical Neuroscience, *14*, 31.

Mendes, W. B. (2009). Assessing autonomic nervous system activity. *Methods in Social Neuroscience*, *118*, 147.

Muller, J. E., Tofler, G. H., & Stone, P. H. (1989). Circadian variation and triggers of onset of acute cardiovascular disease. *Circulation*, *79*(4), 733–743. https://doi.org/10.1161/01.CIR.79.4.733

Nahm, F. K., & Freeman, R. (2017). Autonomic nervous system testing. In A. S. Blum & S. B. Rutkove (Eds.), *The clinical neurophysiology primer* (pp. 447–460). Humana Press.

Nakagawa, M., Iwao, T., & Ishida, S. (1998). Circadian rhythm of the signal averaged electrocardiogram and its relation to heart rate variability in healthy subjects. *Heart, 79*, 493–496.

National Institute of Mental Health. (2022). Definitions of the RDoC domains and constructs. *Research Domain Criteria (RDoC)*. https://www.nimh.nih.gov/research/research-funded-by-nimh/rdoc/definitions-of-the-rdoc-domains-and-constructs

Nelson, B., Pollak, O., Clayton, M., Telzer, E., & Prinstein, M. (2021). *An RDoC-based approach to adolescent self-injurious thoughts and behaviors: The interactive role of social affiliation and cardiac arousal.* [Preprint]. psyarxiv.com

Nieuwenhuis, S., Aston-Jones, G., & Cohen, J. D. (2005). Decision making, the P3, and the locus coeruleus—Norepinephrine system. *Psychological Bulletin, 131*(4), 510–532. https://doi.org/10.1037/0033-2909.131.4.510

Nock, M. K., & Mendes, W. B. (2008). Physiological arousal, distress tolerance, and social problem-solving deficits among adolescent self-injurers. *Journal of Consulting and Clinical Psychology, 76*(1), 28–38. https://doi.org/10.1037/0022-006X.76.1.28

Nolte, I. M., Munoz, M. L., Tragante, V., Amare, A. T., Jansen, R., Vaez, A., von der Heyde, B., Avery, C. L., Bis, J. C., Dierckx, B., van Dongen, J., Gogarten, S. M., Goyette, P., Hernesniemi, J., Huikari, V., Hwang, S.-J., Jaju, D., Kerr, K. F., Kluttig, A., . . . de Geus, E. J. C. (2017). Genetic loci associated with heart rate variability and their effects on cardiac disease risk. *Nature Communications, 8*(1), Article 15805. https://doi.org/10.1038/ncomms15805

Ougrin, D., Tranah, T., Stahl, D., Moran, P., & Asarnow, J. R. (2015). Therapeutic Interventions for suicide attempts and Self-harm in adolescents: Systematic review and meta-analysis. *Journal of the American Academy of Child & Adolescent Psychiatry, 54*(2), 97–107. https://doi.org/10.1016/j.jaac.2014.10.009

Porges, W., & Byrne, E. A. (1992). Research methods for measurement and respiration. *Biological Psychology, 34*, 93–130.

Posada-Quintero, H. F., & Chon, K. H. (2020). Innovations in electrodermal activity data collection and signal processing: A systematic review. *Sensors, 20*(2), Article 479. https://doi.org/10.3390/s20020479

Quintana, D. S., & Heathers, J. A. J. (2014). Considerations in the assessment of heart rate variability in biobehavioral research. *Frontiers in Psychology, 5*, 1–10. https://doi.org/10.3389/fpsyg.2014.00805

TRUE Consortium. (2017). Recommended standards for assessing blood pressure in human research where blood pressure or hypertension is a major focus. (2017). *Kidney International Reports, 2*(4), 733–738. https://doi.org/10.1016/j.ekir.2017.02.009

Riese, H., van Doornen, L. J., & de Geus, E. J. (2000). Job strain and risk indicators for cardiovascular disease in young female nurses. *Health Psychology, 19*, 429–440.

Rinnewitz, L., Koenig, J., Parzer, P., Brunner, R., Resch, F., & Kaess, M. (2018). Childhood adversity and psychophysiological reactivity to pain in adolescent nonsuicidal self-injury. *Psychopathology, 51*(5), 346–352. https://doi.org/10.1159/000491702

Salomon, K., Matthews, K. A., & Allen, M. T. (2000). Patterns of sympathetic and parasympathetic reactivity in a sample of children and adolescents. *Psychophysiology, 37*, 842–849.

Saul, J. (1990). Beat-to-beat variations of heart rate reflect modulation of cardiac autonomic outflow. *Physiology, 5*(1), 32–37. https://doi.org/10.1152/physiologyonline.1990.5.1.32

Schmitz, S., Krummenauer, F., Henn, S., & Dick, H. B. (2003). Comparison of three different technologies for pupil diameter measurement. *Graefe's Archive for Clinical and Experimental Ophthalmology, 241*(6), 472–477. https://doi.org/10.1007/s00417-003-0669-x

Schubert, E., Kannenberg, A., Unbehaun, A., Lewinsohn, D., & Patzak, D. (1995). Circadian rhythms in the spectrum of heart rate variability. *Wien Med Wochenschr, 145*, 460–462.

Scott, L. N., Zalewski, M., Beeney, J. E., Jones, N. P., & Stepp, S. D. (2017). Pupillary and affective responses to maternal feedback and the development of borderline personality disorder symptoms. *Development and Psychopathology, 29*(3), 1089–1104. https://doi.org/10.1017/S0954579416001048

Shaffer, F., Combatalade, D., Peper, E., & Meehan, Z. M. (2016). A guide to cleaner electrodermal activity measurements. *Biofeedback, 44*(2), 90–100. https://doi.org/10.5298/1081-5937-44.2.01

Shaffer, F., & Ginsberg, J. P. (2017). An overview of heart rate variability metrics and norms. *Frontiers in Public Health, 5*, Article 258. https://doi.org/10.3389/fpubh.2017.00258

Sigrist, C., Jakob, H., Beeretz, C. J., Schmidt, S. J., Kaess, M., Koenig, J. (2022). Diurnal variation of cardiac autonomic activity in adolescent non-suicidal self-injury. (Under Review).

Smith, R., Thayer, J. F., Khalsa, S. S., & Lane, R. D. (2017). The hierarchical basis of neurovisceral integration. *Neuroscience & Biobehavioral Reviews, 75*, 274–296. https://doi.org/10.1016/j.neubiorev.2017.02.003

Smolensky, M. H., Hermida, R. C., Reinberg, A., Sackett-Lundeen, L., & Portaluppi, F. (2016). Circadian disruption: New clinical perspective of disease pathology and basis for chronotherapeutic intervention. *Chronobiology International, 33*(8), 1101–1119. https://doi.org/10.1080/07420528.2016.1184678

Stergiou, G. S., Parati, G., McManus, R. J., Head, G. A., Myers, M. G., & Whelton, P. K. (2018). Guidelines for blood pressure measurement: Development over 30 years. *The Journal of Clinical Hypertension, 20*(7), 1089–1091. https://doi.org/10.1111/jch.13295

Task Force of the European Society of Cardiology. (1996). Heart rate variability, standards of measurement, physiological interpretation, and clinical use. *Circulation, 93*(5), 1043–1065.

Tatnell, R., Hasking, P., Lipp, O. V., Boyes, M., & Dawkins, J. (2018). Emotional responding in NSSI: Examinations of appraisals of positive and negative emotional stimuli, with and without acute stress. *Cognition and Emotion, 32*(6), 1304–1316. https://doi.org/10.1080/02699931.2017.1411785

Thayer, J. F., & Lane, R. D. (2000). A model of neurovisceral integration in emotion regulation and dysregulation. *Journal of Affective Disorders, 61*(3), 201–216. https://doi.org/10.1016/S0165-0327(00)00338-4

Thayer, J. F., Yamamoto, S. S., & Brosschot, J. F. (2010). The relationship of autonomic imbalance, heart rate variability and cardiovascular disease risk factors. *International Journal of Cardiology, 141*(2), 122–131. https://doi.org/10.1016/j.ijcard.2009.09.543

Topoglu, Y., Watson, J., Suri, R., & Ayaz, H. (2020). Electrodermal activity in ambulatory settings: A narrative review of literature. In H. Ayaz (Ed.), *Advances in neuroergonomics and cognitive engineering* (Vol. 953, pp. 91–102). Springer International. https://doi.org/10.1007/978-3-030-20473-0_10

Tuna, E., & Gençöz, T. (2021). Pain perception, distress tolerance and self-compassion in Turkish young adults with and without a history of non-suicidal self-injury. *Current Psychology, 40*(8), 4143–4155.

Vrijkotte, T. G. M., van Doornen, L. J. P., & de Geus, E. J. C. (2004). Overcommitment to work is associated with changes in cardiac sympathetic regulation. *Psychosomatic Medicine, 66*(5), 656–663. https://doi.org/10.1097/01.psy.0000138283.65547.78

Wang, X., Ding, X., Su, S., Li, Z., Riese, H., Thayer, J. F., Treiber, F., & Snieder, H. (2009). Genetic influences on heart rate variability at rest and during stress. *Psychophysiology, 46*(3), 458–465. https://doi.org/10.1111/j.1469-8986.2009.00793.x

Weihe, E., Schütz, B., Hartschuh, W., Anlauf, M., Schäfer, M. K., & Eiden, L. E. (2005). Coexpression of cholinergic and noradrenergic phenotypes in human and nonhuman autonomic nervous system. *The Journal of Comparative Neurology, 492*(3), 370–379. https://doi.org/10.1002/cne.20745

Weiler, D. T., Villajuan, S. O., Edkins, L., Cleary, S., & Saleem, J. J. (2017). Wearable heart rate monitor technology accuracy in research: A comparative study between PPG and ECG technology. *Proceedings of the Human Factors and Ergonomics Society Annual Meeting, 61*(1), 1292–1296. https://doi.org/10.1177/1541931213601804

Weinert, D., Sitka, U., Minors, D. S., & Waterhouse, J. M. (1994). The development of circadian rhythmicity in neonates. *Early Human Development, 36*(2), 117–126. https://doi.org/10.1016/0378-3782(94)90039-6

Welch, S. S., Linehan, M. M., Sylvers, P., Chittams, J., & Rizvi, S. L. (2008). Emotional responses to self-injury imagery among adults with borderline personality disorder. *Journal of Consulting and Clinical Psychology, 76*(1), 45–51. https://doi.org/10.1037/0022-006X.76.1.45

Westlund Schreiner, M., Klimes-Dougan, B., Begnel, E. D., & Cullen, K. R. (2015). Conceptualizing the neurobiology of non-suicidal self-injury from the perspective of the Research Domain Criteria Project. *Neuroscience & Biobehavioral Reviews, 57*, 381–391. https://doi.org/10.1016/j.neubiorev.2015.09.011

Wielgus, M. D., Aldrich, J. T., Mezulis, A. H., & Crowell, S. E. (2016). Respiratory sinus arrhythmia as a predictor of self-injurious thoughts and behaviors among adolescents. *International Journal of Psychophysiology, 106*, 127–134. https://doi.org/10.1016/j.ijpsycho.2016.05.005

Wientjes, C. J. E. (1992). Respiration in psychophysiology: Measurement issues and applications. *Biological Psychology, 34*, 179–203.

Winn, M. B., Wendt, D., Koelewijn, T., & Kuchinsky, S. E. (2018). Best practices and advice for using pupillometry to measure listening effort: An introduction for those who want to get started. *Trends in Hearing, 22*, Article 233121651880086. https://doi.org/10.1177/2331216518800869

Wright, R. A., & Kirby, L. D. (2001). Effort determination of cardiovascular response: An integrative analysis with applications in social psychology. In M. P. Zanna (Ed.), *Advances in experimental social psychology* (Vol. 33, pp. 255–307). Elsevier. https://doi.org/10.1016/S0065-2601(01)80007-1

Wulsin, L., Herman, J., & Thayer, J. F. (2018). Stress, autonomic imbalance, and the prediction of metabolic risk: A model and a proposal for research. *Neuroscience & Biobehavioral Reviews, 86*, 12–20. https://doi.org/10.1016/j.neubiorev.2017.12.010

Yu, Y., Ramage, A. G., & Koss, M. C. (2004). Pharmacological studies of 8-OH-DPAT-induced pupillary dilation in anesthetized rats. *European Journal of Pharmacology, 489*(3), 207–213. https://doi.org/10.1016/j.ejphar.2004.03.007

CHAPTER 19

Bridging Brain and Behavior: Using Biology to Inform NSSI Interventions

Mindy Westlund Schreiner, Summer B. Frandsen, Nicolette C. Molina, *and* Alina K. Dillahunt

Abstract

Although research is increasingly considering neurobiological processes underlying psychopathology, there is a lack of a comprehensive bridge to clinical practice. One way to bridge this gap is through personalized or precision medicine. This involves using an individual's unique biological characteristics to inform treatment rather than a traditional one-size-fits-all approach to intervention. This goal can be furthered by the Research Domain Criteria (RDoC) initiative, which aims to use multiple units of analyses (e.g., circuits, physiology, and self-report) to study discrete maladaptive behaviors that are separated into domains (e.g., negative and positive valence systems and systems for social processes). One important but understudied focus is nonsuicidal self-injury (NSSI), the overall prevalence of which has shown no reduction using conventional therapeutic and pharmaceutical interventions. The current treatments for NSSI show some modest success with a top-down approach of using existing interventions to target neurobiology but would also benefit from a bottom-up approach of creating interventions to specifically target neurobiological targets. Likewise, the field would benefit from an integration of biological and clinical trials to translate findings and move more quickly toward precision medicine. This chapter discusses prior findings of the association between NSSI and neurocircuitry, heart rate variability, and other psychophysiological markers and suggests future directions to integrate treatment targets and intervention innovations to move toward alleviating distress associated with NSSI.

Key Words: nonsuicidal self-injury, intervention, biology, research domain criteria, precision medicine

Introduction

With the continued and rapid developments in our ability to assess neurobiological processes associated with behavior, there has been increased focus on the application of these methods in a way that is clinically meaningful. The field of precision medicine within psychiatry aims to develop an understanding of biomarkers and psychosocial characteristics that underlie psychopathology, including nonsuicidal self-injury (NSSI), and predict effectiveness of treatment for any one individual. Relatedly, the Research Domain Criteria (RDoC; see Bastiaens & Claes, this volume, for RDoC overview) initiative aims to further this agenda by gathering a more comprehensive picture of psychopathology using multiple units of analyses (e.g., circuits, physiology, and self-report) to study discrete behaviors that may fall into one or more domains (e.g., negative valence systems—see Swerdlow et al., this volume), positive valence systems (see Claes et al., this volume), and systems for social processes (see Zetterqvist & Bjureberg, this volume).

By considering each individual patient's unique characteristics and symptom profiles, treatment can be tailored based on what will be most successful for the individual rather than arbitrarily following the trends of treatment efficacy within the field. This is particularly salient when considering the heterogeneity of diagnoses and the relatively stagnant progress in reducing the burden of mental illness. For instance, major depressive disorder (MDD) theoretically can have 227 symptom combinations, and in a sample of more than 1,500 patients, 170 different symptom combinations were present (Zimmerman et al., 2015).

In addition to providing a prime example of the heterogeneity of psychiatric disorders, MDD provides a lesson in the importance of developing a better understanding of neurobiological underpinnings to optimize interventions. Data from the Sequenced Treatment Alternatives to Relieve Depression (STAR*D) trial have shown that roughly 37% of individuals with MDD experience remission after their first medication trial, with fewer individuals responding to each successive medication trial (Rush et al., 2006). Taken together, the remission rate of individuals who participated in one to four medication trials was less than 70% (Rush et al., 2006). Of the utmost concern, while research has failed to conclusively support the serotonin theory of depression, the theory persists in clinical practice with many providers and media sources perpetuating the "chemical imbalance" theory in explaining MDD to patients (Cowen & Browning, 2015; Lacasse & Leo, 2005; Liu et al., 2017). This has likely contributed to a failure to develop effective interventions that bring relief to a substantial number of individuals. By investing more in not just understanding the neurobiological underpinnings of psychopathology but also in understanding the mechanisms of change associated with improvement in psychopathology, we can make greater strides in alleviating the burden of disorders such as MDD and maladaptive behaviors such as NSSI.

Given that NSSI is well suited for exploration from an RDoC framework, prior work has reviewed neurobiological research using this approach (Westlund Schreiner et al., 2015) with a more recent review providing an update and summarizing work that goes beyond neuroimaging and emphasizes developmental context (Kaess et al., 2021). Although still in the early stages, strides in understanding the neurobiological features of NSSI hold promise in the ability to use this information to guide the development and selection of interventions to optimize outcomes. Research to date has begun to apply this approach with other forms of psychopathology, including disorders in which prevalence of NSSI is high, such as MDD and borderline personality disorder (BPD). As this research is more developed than that of NSSI, we review some examples of how research has investigated ways in which symptom profiles may guide intervention.

Symptom-Guided Intervention

Some studies have capitalized on the heterogeneity of psychiatric illnesses to demonstrate how different features of the same illness can be used to guide treatment selection. In MDD, for instance, individuals who have psychotic features are more likely to respond to electroconvulsive therapy (ECT; Van Diermen et al., 2018), while higher levels of appetitive symptoms predicted greater treatment response to fluoxetine and light therapy (Levitan et al., 2018). Also in MDD, insomnia and sleep duration have been associated with lack of response to psychotherapy and/or pharmacological interventions (Troxel et al., 2012).

Even beyond symptoms, seemingly unrelated characteristics such as attachment styles can predict treatment response. Attachment avoidance in MDD has been associated with greater symptom reduction following cognitive behavioral therapy (CBT) or acceptance and commitment therapy (ACT; A-Tjak et al., 2020). The international Study to Predict Optimized Treatment for Depression (iSPOT-D) found that trauma characteristics in adults with MDD predict treatment response, with abuse occurring at age 7 years or younger predicting poor outcomes to antidepressant medications (escitalopram, sertraline, and venlafaxine), and abuse between the ages of 4 and 7 predicting the poorest response to sertraline (Williams et al., 2016). Studies that demonstrate characteristics that predict poor treatment response highlight the need to consider more varied intervention strategies that may yield treatment response in individuals with these characteristics (e.g., trauma history, insomnia, and sleep duration).

Tools Used to Study Biological Factors Associated with NSSI

Before reviewing literature examining the association between intervention and biology within disorders associated with NSSI, we provide a brief description of commonly used biological measures. To study circuits in NSSI, the most used method is neuroimaging, particularly magnetic resonance imaging (MRI) and functional magnetic resonance imaging (fMRI). fMRI measures blood oxygen level dependent (BOLD) response to evaluate activation in the brain. This has since grown to include functional connectivity, which evaluates the temporal correlation of BOLD response between various brain regions. Although less frequently seen in the NSSI literature, MRI can also provide information about brain structure including volume of brain region, cortical thickness, and structural connectivity. Structural connectivity is assessed using diffusion weighted imaging (DWI) techniques, which measure the movement of water molecules within the brain to provide an estimate of white matter organization. This can reflect the level of efficiency in neuronal communication.

Other physiological components of NSSI are studied using a greater variety of methods. This includes cortisol, heart rate variability (HRV), respiratory sinus arrhythmia (RSA), and skin conductance response (SCR). Cortisol is considered a stress hormone that is most commonly collected via saliva or hair. It provides information about the functioning of the hypothalamic-pituitary-adrenal axis, which becomes engaged in response to stressors. HRV is the time between each heartbeat and is regulated by the autonomic nervous system (ANS) consisting of the parasympathetic (inhibitory) and sympathetic (excitatory) nervous systems. RSA examines the synchronicity between respiration and HRV.

Biological Indices of Treatment Response in NSSI-Adjacent Disorders

Our current understanding of individual differences in biological mechanisms maintaining depressive symptoms is facilitating precision medicine approaches (Beijers et al., 2019; Lynch et al., 2020). In a recent study, Yang et al. (2021) found two MDD subtypes based on structural covariance networks, which included the default mode network (DMN), ventromedial prefrontal cortex (vmPFC), and salience network. Distinguishing clinical features of these groups were driven by one group demonstrating earlier age of onset and depression severity while also demonstrating poorer performance on cognitive tasks (Yang et al., 2021). Identification of neurobiologically informed subtypes of depression may be leveraged for clinical decision-making and determining individual prognosis. For instance, a growing body of research is investigating how biological indices may provide a framework for personalized treatment (Arnow et al., 2015; Dunlop et al., 2017; Gyurak et al., 2016; Pizzagalli et al., 2018; Schatzberg et al., 2015). In one of these studies, Arnow et al. (2015) found resting-state functional connectivity differentially identified probability of remission or treatment following randomization to selective serotonin reuptake inhibitors (SSRIs), serotonin and norepinephrine reuptake inhibitors (SNRIs), or cognitive behavioral therapy (CBT; Arnow et al., 2015). Another pathophysiological prognostic marker of treatment outcome for depression includes rostral anterior cingulate cortex activity as measured by electroencephalography (EEG) and positron emission tomography (PET), a link that has been replicated several times (Mayberg et al., 1997; Pizzagalli et al., 2001; Pizzagalli et al., 2018).

Ongoing work to discover biologically-driven approaches to uncovering dimensions and subtypes of depression show meaningful promise in facilitating precision medicine (Buch & Liston, 2021). One such study measured NSSI, suicidal ideation (SI), and suicide attempts (SA) in an adolescent sample with treatment-resistant depression, finding that participants who were given CBT and changed medications had a more positive outcome in a 24-week follow-up than either treatment alone (Asarnow et al., 2011). This highlights important considerations when deciding course of treatment, including self-injurious thoughts and behaviors (SITBs). When co-occurring with MDD, borderline personality disorder (BPD) can often be overlooked, as an antidepressant medication or CBT is given; however, it is recommended that these disorders be treated concurrently, especially since CBT alone does not have favorable outcomes in BPD (Beatson & Rao, 2013).

NSSI, particularly when it presents in adults, is commonly associated with BPD due to "recurrent suicidal behavior, gestures, or threats, or self-mutilating behavior" being an explicit diagnostic criterion for the disorder (American Psychiatric Association, 2013, p. 663). Although a diagnosis of BPD includes 256 symptom combinations, Hawkins et al. (2014) used multiple different methods yielding a one-factor structure for BPD, as individuals with elevations in one symptom typically have elevations in the other eight symptoms. Although this provides support for BPD as being a strong starting point in understanding the biological correlates of NSSI and intervention, it should be noted that self-harm was one of the lowest loading symptoms, at least based on immediate and weekly reports (it had higher loading for retrospective reporting) (Hawkins et al., 2014). However, given the paucity of research on the biology of NSSI and interventions, studies examining the biological mechanisms of change in BPD are still valuable in guiding future work.

When considering BPD symptom change broadly, improvements in cognitive disturbance have been associated with an increase in amygdala-temporal fusiform and parahippocampal gyri functional connectivity at rest in a sample of adults with BPD who completed MRI scanning approximately 8 weeks apart (Westlund Schreiner, Klimes-Dougan, Mueller, et al., 2019). Also in this study, improvements in disturbed relationships were associated with increased negative amygdala-frontal pole connectivity at rest (Westlund Schreiner, Klimes-Dougan, Mueller, et al., 2019). Additional regions demonstrating change over the course of treatment include the anterior and posterior cingulate cortex, temporal cortex, and insula, as adult female BPD patients showed a reduction in activation of these regions over the course of a 12-week inpatient dialectical behavior therapy (DBT) program (Schnell & Herpertz, 2007). Schnell and Herpertz also found reduced activation in the amygdala and hippocampi among patients who showed adequate treatment response, defined as meeting at least two of three treatment goals that were outlined at the beginning of treatment (2007). Aside from biological indices identified using neuroimaging, HRV has also been identified as a potential marker of treatment response. Particularly, greater clinical improvement was associated with greater pretreatment (DBT-Adolescent) resting HRV in adolescents with at least subthreshold BPD criteria (Weise et al., 2021).

Emotion dysregulation is a common treatment target in BPD, which is exemplified in DBT as it is one of the four treatment modules for this intervention (emotion regulation, distress tolerance, interpersonal effectiveness, and mindfulness; Linehan, 1993). In a study of adults with BPD, patients who completed 12 weeks of a DBT-based residential treatment program showed reduced activation in the right inferior parietal lobe and supramarginal gyrus during a distraction task in the context of negative stimuli (Winter et al., 2017). Further, the magnitude of this decrease was associated with greater improvement in BPD symptoms (Winter et al., 2017). After 12 months of DBT, adults with BPD demonstrated greater emotion regulation and decreased amygdala reactivity in response to viewing negative, positive, and neutral images (Goodman et al., 2014).

Preliminary Findings of Biological Factors Associated with NSSI Intervention

Although many related disorders have tried and tested biological indicators of treatment response, much less is known about NSSI. The biological units of analysis most typically utilized in studying NSSI are circuits and physiology, often used in tangent with self-report and behavioral measures. Since reviewed in detail elsewhere, we begin with a brief summary of the biological correlates of NSSI, followed by a discussion of the existing work that incorporates NSSI intervention.

Biological Correlates of NSSI

Neuroimaging studies of NSSI focused on brain activation and functional connectivity have implicated the amygdala, anterior cingulate cortex (ACC), dorsolateral prefrontal cortex, and supplementary motor area (SMA) relative to controls (Dahlgren et al., 2018; Demers et al., 2019; Groschwitz et al., 2016; Osuch et al., 2014; Reitz et al., 2015; Thai et al., 2021; Westlund Schreiner et al., 2017). Preliminary work has also shown compromised white matter microstructure of the cingulum and uncinate fasciculus in NSSI (Westlund Schreiner et al., 2020).

Due to the associations between NSSI and reduced pain sensitivity, many studies focus on HRV before and after painful stimuli. One such study found that compared to controls, females who have engaged in NSSI showed less arousal in the ANS, or higher HRV, before the stimulus but lower HRV and less arousal in ANS for longer after the pain stimuli (Koenig et al., 2017). This suggests that anticipating painful stimuli elicits less aversion for those who engage in NSSI and increased arousal afterward which may work to stimulate the ANS and reduce negative affect and perhaps promote stress relief.

Unfortunately, the growing number of neurobiological NSSI studies does not necessarily translate to clinically useful NSSI interventions. Although these studies aid in hypothesis generation for future clinical trials, they predominantly use cross-sectional designs, which do not allow for attributing cause and effect or what may be problematic neurobiological processes versus adaptive compensatory responses. These limitations of the existing research are likely a major factor in the limited research on neurobiological changes during and after treatment. To date, the only interventions with any empirical evidence of change in neurobiological mechanisms for NSSI specifically are DBT (see Chapman et al., this volume, for a review) and limited pharmacological options, such as a dietary supplement (Cullen et al., 2019; Goodman et al., 2014; Santamarina-Perez et al., 2019).

Biology of Psychotherapeutic Approaches to NSSI

Although DBT and pharmacology have some neurobiological evidence to support them, the research is still very sparse. Currently, DBT is the most commonly recommended treatment for NSSI, showing significant decreases in symptoms posttreatment in both adults and adolescents (Cook & Gorraiz, 2016; Koons et al., 2001; Linehan et al., 1991; Linehan et al., 2006; Linehan et al., 1993; van den Bosch et al., 2005; Verheul et al., 2003). Although not yet fully supported empirically, there is a strong theoretical underpinning to the make-up of DBT which likely maps to the circuitry believed to be involved in NSSI. For example, as described earlier, a central module of DBT is emotion regulation, a skill frequently associated with the amygdala, insula, dorsolateral prefrontal cortex (dlPFC), and ACC (Allman et al., 2001; Banks et al., 2007; Stein, 2008). A series of studies involving adults with BPD have indicated that greater emotional regulation is successfully targeted by DBT and that increases in regulation (and decreases in reactivity) are correlated with changes in amygdala, ACC, posterior cingulate cortex (PCC), and insula activity (Goodman et al., 2014; Schnell & Herpertz, 2007). Regarding studies directly targeting NSSI, Ruocco et al. (2016) showed that the greatest NSSI response to DBT was predicted by low dlPFC activity, which increased after 7 months of therapy. As an important side note, this work also offers a potential preexisting biological characteristic on which to base individualized treatment. Another study with comorbid BPD and NSSI showed dysregulated connectivity between the amygdala and dorsal ACC along with decreased activity in the amygdala during both physically and emotionally negative stimuli (Niedtfeld et al., 2017).

Despite DBT not being originally developed with neurobiological targets in mind, research to date offers some support for the hypothesis that DBT may target anomalous neurocircuitry associated with NSSI behaviors. However, more evidence is needed to definitively state what neurobiological mechanisms DBT works through, and the strongest factors that lead to positive change, whether that be emotion regulation, pain-mediated affect regulation, impulsivity, or cognitive reappraisals. To date, one study has examined neurobiological predictors of NSSI improvement in response to 6 months of DBT-A (Santamarina-Perez et al., 2019). Santamarina-Perez et al. (2019) identified that in adolescents ages 12–17, participants who showed greater negative connectivity between the amygdala and PFC had greater improvement in NSSI posttreatment. This work provides preliminary evidence for the value of understanding biological mechanisms of change associated with intervention and reduction in NSSI.

Other emerging treatments have shown efficacy in the literature but have unclear neurobiological mechanisms of change, including two psychotherapies that share commonalities with DBT—emotion regulation group therapy and individual therapy for adolescents (ERGT and ERITA, respectively), which focus on building emotion regulation and goal-setting skills (Bjureberg et al., 2017; Sahlin et al., 2017)—manual-assisted cognitive therapy (MACT), a structured, six-session treatment involving self-help booklets and individual cognitive therapy (Evans et al., 1999); and treatment for self-injurious behaviors (T-SIB), which focuses on the functions of NSSI and how it is reinforced (Andover et al., 2015). These psychotherapies have resulted in significant reductions in NSSI frequency, and due to their links with DBT, it could be posited that they may have similar neurobiological mechanisms. Nonetheless, research evaluating the biological mechanisms of these interventions has yet to be completed.

Biology of Psychopharmacological Approaches to NSSI
Unlike DBT, pharmacological interventions are developed specifically to impact neurobiology, which means that improvements in NSSI due to medication use can be more directly linked to neurobiological changes. Medications shown to improve NSSI symptoms are selective serotonin reuptake inhibitors (SSRIs); atypical antipsychotics such as ziprasidone and aripiprazole; opioid antagonists such as naltrexone and buprenorphine; and, finally, dietary supplements such as n-acetylcysteine (NAC; Cullen et al., 2019; Westlund Schreiner, Klimes-Dougan, Mueller, et al., 2019; Turner et al., 2014). Although we know that medications are directly impacting neurobiology, often acting as antagonists or agonists, inhibiting or enhancing specific neurotransmitter receptors (e.g., clozapine blocks norepinephrine alpha 2 receptors, among several others), and, incidentally, associated with reduced suicidality (see Khokhar et al., 2018 for review), the exact mechanisms by which these are translated to changes in neurocircuitry, physiology, and ultimately NSSI are not completely clear. However, some studies have begun to look at the implicated circuitry associated with pharmacological improvements (e.g., Nord et al., 2021; Ionescu et al., 2018, for review; Herpertz et al., 2018; Paret et al., 2021). The majority of these have looked at disorders commonly comorbid with NSSI, many of which show overlap with the circuitry we would expect to be implicated in improvements of NSSI.

More recently, a study by Cullen et al. (2019) looked specifically at the neural circuitry associated with NSSI improvement from the dietary supplement NAC. NSSI improvement was correlated with decreased connectivity between the amygdala and supplementary motor area and increased connectivity between the amygdala and frontal cortex (Cullen et al., 2019). Unfortunately, this is the extent of research to date that explicitly examines the direct impact of medications on NSSI neurobiological changes. Better understanding how successful pharmacological treatments mitigate NSSI could provide greater insight into the neurobiology of NSSI and assist in developing or improving current medications to better target NSSI circuitry.

Looking Ahead
With very little existing research evaluating the neurobiological mechanisms of change related to NSSI, advancements in this area are sorely needed. The importance of this is further highlighted when considering that the prevalence and incidence of NSSI continue to escalate. This also emphasizes the wealth of possibilities for future exploration in this

area. Fortunately, some groups are already seizing this opportunity, with ongoing data collection to derive a better understanding of how intervention can disrupt problematic, or enhance helpful, neurocircuitry and other aspects of physiology that may otherwise predispose and maintain NSSI. This includes studies investigating NAC, online interventions, and rumination-focused CBT.

Existing opportunities for future research include the evaluation of existing interventions, such as larger studies investigating mechanisms of change associated with DBT and some commonly prescribed psychiatric medications. Additional interventions worthy of consideration include mentalization-based therapy, rumination-focused cognitive behavioral therapy (RF-CBT), and single-session therapeutic and neuromodulation approaches such as transcranial magnetic stimulation. With the existing knowledge of the neurobiological characteristics of NSSI and intervention mechanisms individually, researchers can form hypotheses as to how certain treatments may target aberrant neural processes that have been demonstrated in NSSI to date. Table 19.1 provides some examples of potentially fruitful targets for NSSI and interventions that may correspond with those targets based on Westlund Schreiner, Klimes-Dougan, Mueller, et al. 2019.

Table 19.1 provides a brief overview of biological findings associated with NSSI, the context in which those findings occur, and examples of interventions that may be effective given this information. For example, Osuch et al. (2014) found that hyperactivation of the dorsal striatum was associated with relief following the experience of a painful stimulus in patients with NSSI. The dorsal striatum integrates cognitive, emotional, and reward-related information to contribute to the early stages of decision-making (Balleine

Table 19.1 Example of Possible Biologically Based Strategies and Interventions to Target NSSI

Target	Reference Implicating Target	Context*	Possible Interventions
Amygdala hyperactivation (fMRI)	• Plener et al., 2012	• Emotional images	• Emotion regulation and distress tolerance modules of DBT
Dorsal striatum hyperactivation (fMRI)	• Osuch et al., 2014	• Relief after painful stimulus	• MBT • Opioid antagonists/partial agonists
HPA axis/cortisol blunting	• Kaess et al., 2012 • Plener et al., 2017 • Klimes-Dougan et al., 2019	• Acute social stressor	• Interpersonal effectiveness and emotion regulation modules of DBT • SSRIs
RSA reactivity	• Crowell et al., 2005	• Negative mood induction	• MBT • Mindfulness, distress tolerance, and emotion regulation modules of DBT

*Context: The circumstances in which the characteristic in the "Target" column occurs (e.g., amygdala hyperactivation in NSSI has been demonstrated in the context of emotional imagery).

et al., 2007). The relationship between feelings of relief and dorsal striatum activation suggests the presence of a heightened reward response following a painful stimulus. One possible way to target this response is through the use of opioid antagonists or partial agonists (e.g., naltrexone or naloxone), which work by reducing the brain's production of dopamine, the neurotransmitter responsible for the experience of pleasure. Whereas there has been some success in using this approach to treat NSSI, particularly in patients with developmental disorders (Symons et al., 2004), it is not effective for everyone (Sandman et al., 2000), and significantly more research is needed. Further, disorders commonly co-occurring with NSSI, specifically MDD, are associated with already reduced presence of dopamine (Kapur & Mann, 1992), suggesting that for at least some individuals, this strategy could be contraindicated. However, at least among patients with opioid dependence, treatment with naltrexone was not associated with an increase in depressive symptoms (Dean et al., 2006). The complexities of this relationship underscore the importance of developing a nuanced neurobiologically informed decision-making model in determining the most appropriate interventions for NSSI.

Hypothetical Case Example

Following is a case example of how knowledge of biological mechanisms associated with NSSI and treatment response can be leveraged to guide more effective treatment selection:

Sonya is a 16-year-old female who has a history of NSSI beginning at the age of 12, which is when she was first prescribed an antidepressant due to co-occurring symptoms of MDD. After five months of taking the antidepressant, she ceased engaging in NSSI and experienced a remission of MDD symptoms. At this time, she discontinued the antidepressant medication. This improvement in symptoms also corresponded to the end of the school year and persisted until the age of 16, when she experienced a recurrence of MDD symptoms in addition to NSSI. She began weekly supportive therapy and was again prescribed an antidepressant but only exhibited a partial response after three months. She continued experiencing depressed mood, feelings of worthlessness, and NSSI. Sonya and her parents enrolled in a research study investigating the use of resting-state fMRI in clinical decision-making. Neuroimaging results indicated strong negative resting-state functional connectivity between the amygdala and prefrontal cortex. Based on previous work on predictors of treatment response (Santamarina-Perez et al., 2019). *Sonya was referred to a DBT-A program in the area, where she demonstrated a significant improvement in NSSI and other symptoms over the course of the next few months.*

In the case example, the patient received intervention based not just on her presenting problem (NSSI) but on her biological profile. Had this not been the case, the patient would likely have continued treatment as usual with the possibility of additional medication trials, which may or may not prove helpful. Given the lack of feasibility of routinely having patients complete MRI scans, characteristics will ideally be reliably mapped to more accessible measures in the future.

Conclusion

Research to date captures the top-down approach in using existing interventions to target neurobiology based on its potential effects on biological targets for NSSI. The field would also benefit from applying a bottom-up approach, which would entail the creation of new interventions that are explicitly designed to address the biological target. Novel interventions that capitalize on what we know thus far from cross-sectional studies of biological correlates of NSSI may also be of importance. Future approaches may be benefited by using the integration of neuroimaging, physiological measures, and more causal neural approaches. Whereas better understanding current treatments is a crucial step in developing future treatments as well as understanding NSSI behaviors more fully, other approaches are also necessary. We posit that future treatment development will rely on (a) more studies looking at the direct link between current interventions, NSSI, and the changes in neurobiology; (b) the creation of treatments based on the neurobiological knowledge of NSSI we currently have; and (c) modifying existing treatments for comorbid disorders that have potential utility for NSSI.

The importance of engaging in a neurobiologically informed personalized medicine approach is underscored by the lack of reduction seen in NSSI over the years despite efforts to understand the behavior. It can be argued that at least some of this stagnation is the result of biological and clinical trials research typically being siloed from one another, leading to delays in performing truly translational work. Research that integrates these approaches is urgently needed to move forward in addressing the challenge in reducing suffering associated not with just NSSI but with all mental health difficulties.

Summary

NSSI is a complex behavior that transcends the boundaries placed by traditional psychiatric diagnoses. Such a complex behavior requires what may be an even more complex understanding of the biological correlates of this behavior and how they relate to treatment targets. Research to date has been limited in its investigation of NSSI-focused interventions, which has subsequently led to a lack of reduction of this behavior in the general population. To be most effective, NSSI intervention research will require greater collaboration, creativity, and careful consideration and integration of the biopsychosocial factors that influence this behavior. Although existing studies provide only a modest foundation, they provide preliminary direction for future work. Importantly, NSSI has been associated with neurocircuitry, HRV, and other psychophysiological phenomena that can be used to inform interventions and serve as possible treatment targets. Additional research that builds on this knowledge, ideally while integrating a promising intervention, is necessary to make larger and more rapid strides toward alleviating the distress associated with NSSI and fostering adaptive outcomes.

References

Allman, J. M., Hakeem, A., Erwin, J. M., Nimchinsky, E., & Hof, P. (2001). The anterior cingulate cortex. The evolution of an interface between emotion and cognition. *Annals of the New York Academy of Sciences, 935*, 107–117. https://pubmed.ncbi.nlm.nih.gov/11411161/

American Psychiatric Association. (2013). *Diagnostic and statistical manual of mental disorders* (5th ed.). American Psychiatric Association Press.

Andover, M. S., Schatten, H. T., Morris, B. W., & Miller, I. W. (2015). Development of an intervention for nonsuicidal self-injury in young adults: An open pilot trial. *Cognitive and Behavioral Practice, 22*(4), 491–503. https://doi.org/10.1016/j.cbpra.2014.05.003

Arnow, B. A., Blasey, C., Williams, L. M., Palmer, D. M., Rekshan, W., Schatzberg, A. F., Etkin, A., Kulkarni, J., Luther, J. F., & Rush, A. J. (2015). Depression subtypes in predicting antidepressant response: A report from the iSPOT-D Trial. *The American Journal of Psychiatry, 172*(8), 743–750. https://doi.org/10.1176/APPI.AJP.2015.14020181

Asarnow, J. R., Porta, G., Spirito, A., Emslie, G., Clarke, G., Wagner, K. D., Vitiello, B., Keller, M., Birmaher, B., McCracken, J., Mayes, T., Berk, M., & Brent, D. A. (2011). Suicide attempts and nonsuicidal self-injury in the treatment of resistant depression in adolescents: Findings from the TORDIA study. *Journal of the American Academy of Child and Adolescent Psychiatry, 50*(8), 772–781. https://doi.org/10.1016/j.jaac.2011.04.003

A-Tjak, J. G. L., Morina, N., Boendermaker, W. J., Topper, M., & Emmelkamp, P. M. G. (2020). Explicit and implicit attachment and the outcomes of acceptance and commitment therapy and cognitive behavioral therapy for depression. *BMC Psychiatry, 20*(1), Article 155. https://doi.org/10.1186/S12888-020-02547-7

Balleine, B. W., Delgado, M. R., & Hikosaka, O. (2007). The role of the dorsal striatum in reward and decision making. *Journal of Neuroscience, 27*(31), 8161–8165. https://doi.org/10.1523/JNEUROSCI.1554-07.2007

Banks, S. J., Eddy, K. T., Angstadt, M., Nathan, P. J., & Phan, K. L. (2007). Amygdala–frontal connectivity during emotion regulation. *Social Cognitive and Affective Neuroscience, 2*(4), 303–312. https://doi.org/10.1093/scan/nsm029

Beatson, J. A., & Rao, S. (2013). Depression and borderline personality disorder. *Medical Journal of Australia, 199*(6), S24–S27. https://doi.org/10.5694/MJA12.10474

Beijers, L., Wardenaar, K. J., van Loo, H. M., & Schoevers, R. A. (2019). Data-driven biological subtypes of depression: Systematic review of biological approaches to depression subtyping. *Molecular Psychiatry, 24*(6), 888–900. https://doi.org/10.1038/S41380-019-0385-5

Bjureberg, J., Sahlin, H., Hellner, C., Hedman-Lagerlöf, E., Gratz, K. L., Bjärehed, J., Jokinen, J., Tull, M. T., & Ljótsson, B. (2017). Emotion regulation individual therapy for adolescents with nonsuicidal self-injury disorder: A feasibility study. *BMC Psychiatry, 17*(1), Article 411. https://doi.org/10.1186/s12888-017-1527-4

Buch, A. M., & Liston, C. (2021). Dissecting diagnostic heterogeneity in depression by integrating neuroimaging and genetics. *Neuropsychopharmacology: Official Publication of the American College of Neuropsychopharmacology, 46*(1), 156–175. https://doi.org/10.1038/S41386-020-00789-3

Cook, N. E., & Gorraiz, M. (2016). Dialectical behavior therapy for nonsuicidal self-injury and depression among adolescents: Preliminary meta-analytic evidence. *Child and Adolescent Mental Health, 21*(2), 81–89. https://doi.org/10.1111/camh.12112

Cowen, P. J., & Browning, M. (2015). What has serotonin to do with depression? *World Psychiatry, 14*(2), 158. https://doi.org/10.1002/WPS.20229

Crowell, S. E., Beauchaine, T. P., McCauley, E., Smith, C. J., Stevens, A. L., & Sylvers, P. (2005). Psychological, autonomic, and serotonergic correlates of parasuicide among adolescent girls. *Development and Psychopathology, 17*(4), 1105–1127. https://doi.org/10.1017/s0954579405050522

Cullen, K. R., Schreiner, M. W., Klimes-Dougan, B., Eberly, L. E., LaRiviere, L., Lim, K. O., Camchong, J., & Mueller, B. A. (2019). Neural correlates of clinical improvement in response to N-acetylcysteine in adolescents with non-suicidal self-injury. *Progress in Neuro-Psychopharmacology & Biological Psychiatry, 99*, Article 109778. https://doi.org/10.1016/j.pnpbp.2019.109778

Dahlgren, M. K., Hooley, J. M., Best, S. G., Sagar, K. A., Gonenc, A., & Gruber, S. A. (2018). Prefrontal cortex activation during cognitive interference in nonsuicidal self-injury. *Psychiatry Research-Neuroimaging, 277*, 28–38. https://doi.org/10.1016/J.PSCYCHRESNS.2018.04.006

Dean, A. J., Saunders, J. B., Jones, R. T., Young, R. M., Connor, J. P., & Lawford, B. R. (2006). Does naltrexone treatment lead to depression? Findings from a randomized controlled trial in subjects with opioid dependence. *Journal of Psychiatry and Neuroscience, 31*(1), 38–45.

Demers, L. A., Westlund Schreiner, M., Hunt, R. H., Mueller, B. A., Klimes-Dougan, B., Thomas, K. M., & Cullen, K. R. (2019). Alexithymia is associated with neural reactivity to masked emotional faces in adolescents who self-harm. *Journal of Affective Disorders, 249*, 253–261. https://doi.org/10.1016/J.JAD.2019.02.038

Dunlop, B. W., Rajendra, J. K., Craighead, W. E., Kelley, M. E., McGrath, C. L., Choi, K. S., Kinkead, B., Nemeroff, C. B., & Mayberg, H. S. (2017). Functional connectivity of the subcallosal cingulate cortex and differential outcomes to treatment with cognitive-behavioral therapy or antidepressant medication for major depressive disorder. *The American Journal of Psychiatry, 174*(6), 533–545. https://doi.org/10.1176/APPI.AJP.2016.16050518

Evans, K., Tyrer, P., Catalan, J., Schmidt, U., Davidson, K., Dent, J., Tata, P., Thornton, S., Barber, J., & Thompson, S. (1999). Manual-assisted cognitive-behaviour therapy (MACT): A randomized controlled trial of a brief intervention with bibliotherapy in the treatment of recurrent deliberate self-harm. *Psychological Medicine, 29*(1), 19–25. https://doi.org/10.1017/S003329179800765X

Goodman, M., Carpenter, D., Tang, C. Y., Goldstein, K. E., Avedon, J., Fernandez, N., Mascitelli, K. A., Blair, N. J., New, A. S., Triebwasser, J., Siever, L. J., & Hazlett, E. A. (2014). Dialectical behavior therapy alters emotion regulation and amygdala activity in patients with borderline personality disorder. *Journal of Psychiatric Research, 57*, 108–116. https://doi.org/10.1016/j.jpsychires.2014.06.020

Groschwitz, R. C., Plener, P. L., Groen, G., Bonenberger, M., & Abler, B. (2016). Differential neural processing of social exclusion in adolescents with non-suicidal self-injury: An fMRI study. *Psychiatry Research: Neuroimaging, 255*, 43–49. https://doi.org/10.1016/j.pscychresns.2016.08.001

Gyurak, A., Patenaude, B., Korgaonkar, M. S., Grieve, S. M., Williams, L. M., & Etkin, A. (2016). Frontoparietal activation during response inhibition predicts remission to antidepressants in patients with major depression. *Biological Psychiatry, 79*(4), 274–281. https://doi.org/10.1016/J.BIOPSYCH.2015.02.037

Hawkins, A. A., Furr, R. M., Arnold, E. M., Law, M. K., Mneimne, M., & Fleeson, W. (2014). The structure of borderline personality disorder symptoms: A multi-method, multi-sample examination. *Personality Disorders, 5*(4), 380–389. https://doi.org/10.1037/per0000086

Herpertz, S. C., Schneider, I., Schmahl, C., & Bertsch, K. (2018). Neurobiological mechanisms mediating emotion dysregulation as targets of change in borderline personality disorder. *Psychopathology, 51*, 96–104. https://doi.org/10.1159/000488357

Ionescu, D. F., Felicione, J. M., Gosai, A., Cusin, C., Shin, P., Shapero, B. G., & Deckersbach, T. (2018). Ketamine-associated brain changes: A review of the neuroimaging literature. *Harvard Review of Psychiatry, 26*(6), 320–339. https://doi.org/10.1097/HRP.0000000000000179

Kaess, M., Hille, M., Parzer, P., Maser-Gluth, C., Resch, F., & Brunner, R. (2012). Alterations in the neuroendocrinological stress response to acute psychosocial stress in adolescents engaging in nonsuicidal self-injury. *Psychoneuroendocrinology, 37*(1), 157–161. https://doi.org/10.1016/j.psyneuen.2011.05.009

Kaess, M., Hooley, J. M., Klimes-Dougan, B., Koenig, J., Plener, P. L., Reichl, C., Robinson, K., Schmahl, C., Sicorello, M., Westlund Schreiner, M., & Cullen, K. R. (2021). Advancing a temporal framework for understanding the biology of nonsuicidal self-injury: An expert review. *Neuroscience & Biobehavioral Reviews, 130*, 228–239. https://doi.org/10.1016/J.NEUBIOREV.2021.08.022

Kapur, S., & Mann, J.J. (1992). Role of the dopaminergic system in depression. *Biological Psychiatry, 31*(1), 1–17. https://doi.org/10.1016/0006-3223(92)90137-o

Khokhar, J. Y., Henricks, A. M., Sullivan, E. D. K., & Green, A. I. (2018). Unique effects of clozapine: A pharmacological perspective. In G. W. Pasternak & J. T. Coyle (Eds.), *Advances in pharmacology* (pp. 137–162). Academic Press. https://doi.org/10.1016/bs.apha.2017.09.009

Klimes-Dougan, B., Begnel, E., Almy, B., Thai, M., Schreiner, M. W., & Cullen, K. R. (2019). Hypothalamic-pituitary-adrenal axis dysregulation in depressed adolescents with non-suicidal self-injury. *Psychoneuroendocrinology, 102*, 216–224.

Koenig, J., Rinnewitz, L., Warth, M., Hillecke, T. K., Brunner, R., Resch, F., & Kaess, M. (2017). Psychobiological response to pain in female adolescents with nonsuicidal self-injury. *Journal of Psychiatry & Neuroscience, 42*(3), 189–199. https://doi.org/10.1503/jpn.160074

Koons, C. R., Robins, C. J., Lindsey Tweed, J., Lynch, T. R., Gonzalez, A. M., Morse, J. Q., Bishop, G. K., Butterfield, M. I., & Bastian, L. A. (2001). Efficacy of dialectical behavior therapy in women veterans with borderline personality disorder. *Behavior Therapy*, *32*(2), 371–390. https://doi.org/10.1016/S0005-7894(01)80009-5

Lacasse, J. R., & Leo, J. (2005). Serotonin and depression: A disconnect between the advertisements and the scientific literature. *PLoS Medicine*, *2*(12), Article e392. https://doi.org/10.1371/JOURNAL.PMED.0020392

Levitan, R. D., Levitt, A. J., Michalak, E. E., Morehouse, R., Ramasubbu, R., Yatham, L. N., Tam, E. M., & Lam, R. W. (2018). Appetitive symptoms differentially predict treatment response to fluoxetine, light, and placebo in nonseasonal major depression. *The Journal of Clinical Psychiatry*, *79*(4), Article 17m11856. https://doi.org/10.4088/JCP.17M11856

Linehan, M. M. (1993). *Cognitive-behavioral treatment of borderline personality disorder*. Guilford Press.

Linehan, M. M., Armstrong, H. E., Suarez, A., Allmon, D., & Heard, H. L. (1991). Cognitive-behavioral treatment of chronically parasuicidal borderline patients. *Archives of General Psychiatry*, *48*(12), 1060–1064. https://doi.org/10.1001/archpsyc.1991.01810360024003

Linehan, M. M., Comtois, K. A., Murray, A. M., Brown, M. Z., Gallop, R. J., Heard, H. L., Korslund, K. E., Tutek, D. A., Reynolds, S. K., & Lindenboim, N. (2006). Two-year randomized controlled trial and follow-up of dialectical behavior therapy vs therapy by experts for suicidal behaviors and borderline personality disorder. *Archives of General Psychiatry*, *63*(7), 757–766. https://doi.org/10.1001/archpsyc.63.7.757

Linehan, M. M., Heard, H. L., & Armstrong, H. E. (1993). Naturalistic follow-up of a behavioral treatment for chronically parasuicidal borderline patients. *Archives of General Psychiatry*, *50*(12), 971–974. https://doi.org/10.1001/archpsyc.1993.01820240055007

Liu, B., Liu, J., Wang, M., Zhang, Y., & Li, L. (2017). From serotonin to neuroplasticity: Evolvement of theories for major depressive disorder. *Frontiers in Cellular Neuroscience*, *11*, Article 305. https://doi.org/10.3389/FNCEL.2017.00305/BIBTEX

Lynch, C. J., Gunning, F. M., & Liston, C. (2020). Causes and consequences of diagnostic heterogeneity in depression: Paths to discovering novel biological depression subtypes. *Biological Psychiatry*, *88*(1), 83–94. https://doi.org/10.1016/J.BIOPSYCH.2020.01.012

Mayberg, H. S., Brannan, S. K., Mahurin, R. K., Jerabek, P. A., Brickman, J. S., Tekell, J. L., Silva, J. A., McGinnis, S., Glass, T. G., Martin, C. C., & Fox, P. T. (1997). Cingulate function in depression: A potential predictor of treatment response. *Neuroreport*, *8*(4), 1057–1061. https://doi.org/10.1097/00001756-199703030-00048

Niedtfeld, I., Schmitt, R., Winter, D., Bohus, M., Schmahl, C., Sabine, C., & Herpertz. (2017). Pain-mediated affect regulation is reduced after dialectical behavior therapy in borderline personality disorder: A longitudinal fMRI study. *Social Cognitive and Affective Neuroscience*, *12*(5), Article nsw183. https://doi.org/10.1093/scan/nsw183

Nord, C.L., Feldman Barrett, L., Lindquist, K.A., Ma, Y., Marwood, L., Satpute, A.B., & Dalgleish, T. (2021). Neural effects of antidepressant medication and psychological treatments: A quantitative synthesis across three meta-analyses. *The British Journal of Psychiatry*, *219*(4), 546–550. https://doi.org/10.1192/bjp.2021.16

Osuch, E., Ford, K., Wrath, A., Bartha, R., & Neufeld, R. (2014). Functional MRI of pain application in youth who engaged in repetitive non-suicidal self-injury vs. psychiatric controls. *Psychiatry Research*, *223*(2), 104–112. https://doi.org/10.1016/j.pscychresns.2014.05.003

Paret, C., Niedtfeld, I., Lotter, T., Wunder, A., Grimm, S., Mennes, M., Okell, T., Beckmann, C., & Schmahl, C. (2021). Single-dose effects of citalopram on neural responses to affective stimuli in borderline personality disorder: A randomized clinical trial. *Biological Psychiatry: Cognitive Neuroscience and Neuroimaging*, *6*(8), 837–845. https://doi.org/10.1016/j.bpsc.2021.02.002

Pizzagalli, D., Pascual-Marqui, R. D., Nitschke, J. B., Oakes, T. R., Larson, C. L., Abercrombie, H. C., Schaefer, S. M., Koger, J. V., Benca, R. M., & Davidson, R. J. (2001). Anterior cingulate activity as a predictor of degree of treatment response in major depression: Evidence from brain electrical tomography analysis. *The American Journal of Psychiatry*, *158*(3), 405–415. https://doi.org/10.1176/APPI.AJP.158.3.405

Pizzagalli, D. A., Webb, C. A., Dillon, D. G., Tenke, C. E., Kayser, J., Goer, F., Fava, M., McGrath, P., Weissman, M., Parsey, R., Adams, P., Trombello, J., Cooper, C., Deldin, P., Oquendo, M. A., McInnis, M. G., Carmody, T., Bruder, G., & Trivedi, M. H. (2018). Pretreatment rostral anterior cingulate cortex theta activity in relation to symptom improvement in depression: A randomized trial. *JAMA Psychiatry*, *75*(6), 547–554. https://doi.org/10.1001/JAMAPSYCHIATRY.2018.0252

Plener, P. L., Bubalo, N., Fladung, A. K., Ludolph, A. G., & Lulé, D. (2012). Prone to excitement: adolescent females with Non-suicidal self-injury (NSSI) show altered cortical pattern to emotional and NSS-related material. *Psychiatry Research*, *203*(2–3), 146–152. https://doi.org/10.1016/j.pscychresns.2011.12.012

Plener, P. L., Zohsel, K., Hohm, E., Buchmann, A. F., Banaschewski, T., Zimmermann, U. S., & Laucht, M. (2017). Lower cortisol level in response to a psychosocial stressor in young females with self-harm. *Psychoneuroendocrinology*, *76*, 84–87. https://doi.org/10.1016/j.psyneuen.2016.11.009

Reitz, S., Kluetsch, R., Niedtfeld, I., Knorz, T., Lis, S., Paret, C., Kirsch, P., Meyer-Lindenberg, A., Treede, R.-D., Baumgärtner, U., Bohus, M., & Schmahl, C. (2015). Incision and stress regulation in borderline personality disorder: Neurobiological mechanisms of self-injurious behaviour. *British Journal of Psychiatry*, *207*(2), 165–172. https://doi.org/10.1192/bjp.bp.114.153379

Ruocco, A. C., Rodrigo, A. H., McMain, S. F., Page-Gould, E., Ayaz, H., & Links, P. S. (2016) Predicting treatment outcomes from prefrontal cortex activation for self-harming patients with borderline personality disorder: A preliminary study. *Frontiers in Human Neuroscience*, *10*, Article 220. https://doi.org/10.3389/fnhum.2016.00220

Rush, A. J., Trivedi, M. H., Wisniewski, S. R., Nierenberg, A. A., Stewart, J. W., Warden, D., Niederehe, G., Thase, M. E., Lavori, P. W., Lebowitz, B. D., McGrath, P. J., Rosenbaum, J. F., Sackeim, H. A., Kupfer, D. J., Luther, J., & Fava, M. (2006). Acute and longer-term outcomes in depressed outpatients requiring one or several treatment steps: A STAR*D report. *American Journal of Psychiatry*, *163*(11), 1905–1917. https://doi.org/10.1176/AJP.2006.163.11.1905/ASSET/IMAGES/LARGE/R114F4.JPEG

Sahlin, H., Bjureberg, J., Gratz, K. L., Tull, M. T., Hedman, E., Bjärehed, J., Jokinen, J., Lundh, L.-G., Ljótsson, B., & Hellner, C. (2017). Emotion regulation group therapy for deliberate self-harm: A multi-site evaluation in routine care using an uncontrolled open trial design. *BMJ Open*, *7*(10), e016220–e016220. https://doi.org/10.1136/bmjopen-2017-016220

Sandman, C. A., Hetrick, W., Taylor, D. V., Marion, S. D., Touchette, P., Barron, J. L., Martinezzi, V., Steinberg, R. M., & Crinella, F. M. (2000). Long-term effects of naltrexone on self-injurious behavior. *American Journal of Mental Retardation*, *105*(2), 103–117. https://doi.org/10.1352/0895-8017(2000)105<0103:LEONOS>2.0.CO;2

Santamarina-Perez, P., Romero, S., Mendez, I., Leslie, S. M., Packer, M. M., Sugranyes, G., Picado, M., Font, E., Moreno, E., Martinez, E., Morer, A., Romero, M., & Singh, M. K. (2019). Fronto-limbic connectivity as a predictor of improvement in nonsuicidal self-injury in adolescents following psychotherapy. *Journal of Child and Adolescent Psychopharmacology*, *29*(6), 456–465. https://doi.org/10.1089/cap.2018.0152

Schatzberg, A. F., DeBattista, C., Lazzeroni, L. C., Etkin, A., Murphy, G. M., & Williams, L. M. (2015). ABCB1 genetic effects on antidepressant outcomes: A report from the iSPOT-D trial. *The American Journal of Psychiatry*, *172*(8), 751–759. https://doi.org/10.1176/APPI.AJP.2015.14050680

Schnell, K., & Herpertz, S. C. (2007). Effects of dialectic-behavioral-therapy on the neural correlates of affective hyperarousal in borderline personality disorder. *Journal of Psychiatric Research*, *41*(10), 837–847. https://doi.org/10.1016/j.jpsychires.2006.08.011

Stein, D. (2008). Emotional regulation: Implications for the psychobiology of psychotherapy. *CNS Spectrums*, *13*(3), 195–201. https://doi.org/10.1017/s1092852900028431

Symons, F. J., Thompson, A., & Rodriguez, M. C. (2004). Self-injurious behavior and the efficacy of naltrexone treatment: A quantitative synthesis. *Mental Retardation and Developmental Disabilities Research Reviews*, *10*(3), 193–200. https://doi.org/10.1002/mrdd.20031

Thai, M., Schreiner, M. W., Mueller, B. A., Cullen, K. R., & Klimes-Dougan, B. (2021). Coordination between frontolimbic resting state connectivity and hypothalamic–pituitary–adrenal axis functioning in adolescents with and without depression. *Psychoneuroendocrinology*, *125*, Article 105123. https://doi.org/10.1016/j.psyneuen.2020.105123

Troxel, W. M., Kupfer, D. J., Reynolds, C. F., Frank, E., Thase, M. E., Miewald, J. M., & Buysse, D. J. (2012). Insomnia and objectively measured sleep disturbances predict treatment outcome in depressed patients treated with psychotherapy or psychotherapy-pharmacotherapy combinations. *The Journal of Clinical Psychiatry*, *73*(4), 478–485. https://doi.org/10.4088/JCP.11M07184

Turner, B. J., Austin, S. B., & Chapman, A. L. (2014). Treating nonsuicidal self-injury: A systematic review of psychological and pharmacological interventions. Canadian journal of psychiatry. *Revue canadienne de psychiatrie*, *59*(11), 576–585. https://doi.org/10.1177/070674371405901103

van den Bosch, L. M. C., Koeter, M. W. J., Stijnen, T., Verheul, R., & van den Brink, W. (2005). Sustained efficacy of dialectical behaviour therapy for borderline personality disorder. *Behaviour Research and Therapy*, *43*(9), 1231–1241. https://doi.org/10.1016/j.brat.2004.09.008

Van Diermen, L., Van Den Ameele, S., Kamperman, A. M., Sabbe, B. C. G., Vermeulen, T., Schrijvers, D., & Birkenhäger, T. K. (2018). Prediction of electroconvulsive therapy response and remission in major depression: Meta-analysis. *The British Journal of Psychiatry: The Journal of Mental Science*, *212*(2), 71–80. https://doi.org/10.1192/BJP.2017.28

Verheul, R., van den Bosch, L. M. C., Koeter, M. W. J., de Ridder, M. A. J., Stijnen, T., & van den Brink, W. (2003). Dialectical behaviour therapy for women with borderline personality disorder: 12-month, randomised clinical trial in the Netherlands. *British Journal of Psychiatry*, *182*(2), 135–140. https://doi.org/10.1192/bjp.182.2.135

Weise, S., Parzer, P., Fürer, L., Zimmermann, R., Schmeck, K., Resch, F., Kaess, M., & Koenig, J. (2021). Autonomic nervous system activity and dialectical behavioral therapy outcome in adolescent borderline personality pathology. *The World Journal of Biological Psychiatry*, *22*(7), 535–545. https://doi.org/10.1080/15622975.2020.1858155

Westlund Schreiner, M., Klimes-Dougan, B., Begnel, E. D., & Cullen, K. R. (2015). Conceptualizing the neurobiology of non-suicidal self-injury from the perspective of the Research Domain Criteria Project. *Neuroscience and Biobehavioral Reviews*, *57*, 381–491. https://doi.org/10.1016/j.neubiorev.2015.09.011

Westlund Schreiner, M., Klimes-Dougan, B., Mueller, B. A., Eberly, L. E., Reigstad, K. M., Carstedt, P. A., Thomas, K. M., Hunt, R. H., Lim, K. O., & Cullen, K. R. (2017). Multi-modal neuroimaging of adolescents with non-suicidal self-injury: Amygdala functional connectivity. *Journal of Affective Disorders*, *221*, 47–55. https://doi.org/10.1016/j.jad.2017.06.004

Westlund Schreiner, M., Klimes-Dougan, B., Mueller, B. A., Nelson, K. J., Lim, K. O., & Cullen, K. R. (2019). Neurocircuitry associated with symptom dimensions at baseline and with change in borderline personality disorder. *Psychiatry Research: Neuroimaging*, *290*, 58–65. https://doi.org/10.1016/j.pscychresns.2019.07.001

Westlund Schreiner, M., Klimes-Dougan, B., Parenteau, A., Hill, D., & Cullen, K. R. (2019). A framework for identifying neurobiologically based intervention targets for NSSI. *Current Behavioral Neuroscience Reports*, *6*(4), 177–187. https://doi.org/10.1007/s40473-019-00188-z

Westlund Schreiner, M., Mueller, B. A., Klimes-Dougan, B., Begnel, E. D., Fiecas, M., Hill, D., Lim, K. O., & Cullen, K. R. (2020). White matter microstructure in adolescents and young adults with non-suicidal self-injury. *Frontiers in Psychiatry*, *10*, 1019. https://doi.org/10.3389/fpsyt.2019.01019

Williams, L. M., Debattista, C., Duchemin, A. M., Schatzberg, A. F., & Nemeroff, C. B. (2016). Childhood trauma predicts antidepressant response in adults with major depression: Data from the randomized international study to predict optimized treatment for depression. *Translational Psychiatry*, *6*(5), e799–e799. https://doi.org/10.1038/tp.2016.61

Winter, D., Niedtfeld, I., Schmitt, R., Bohus, M., Schmahl, C., & Herpertz, S. C. (2017). Neural correlates of distraction in borderline personality disorder before and after dialectical behavior therapy. *European Archives of Psychiatry and Clinical Neuroscience*, *267*(1), 51–62. https://doi.org/10.1007/s00406-016-0689-2

Yang, X., Kumar, P., Nickerson, L. D., Du, Y., Wang, M., Chen, Y., Li, T., Pizzagalli, D. A., & Ma, X. (2021). Identifying subgroups of major depressive disorder using brain structural covariance networks and mapping of associated clinical and cognitive variables. *Biological Psychiatry Global Open Science*, *1*(2), 135–145. https://doi.org/10.1016/J.BPSGOS.2021.04.006/ATTACHMENT/34122F29-9915-4B92-B5EA-1FB113D0CCC5/MMC1.PDF

Zimmerman, M., Ellison, W., Young, D., Chelminski, I., & Dalrymple, K. (2015). How many different ways do patients meet the diagnostic criteria for major depressive disorder? *Comprehensive Psychiatry*, *56*, 29–34. https://doi.org/10.1016/J.COMPPSYCH.2014.09.007

CHAPTER 20
Lived Experience Perspectives on Self-Injury: Current Evidence and Practical Applications

Penelope Hasking, Therese E. Kenny, *and* Stephen P. Lewis

> **Abstract**
>
> Although there have been many important gains in our understanding of self-injury over the past couple of decades, the majority of this research has emerged from the perspective of clinicians and researchers, overlooking the important insights provided by individuals who have lived experience of nonsuicidal self-injury (NSSI). To date, research has typically asked participants about their experiences rather than involving them as active participants in the research. While this has yielded a better understanding of NSSI, recovery, disclosure, and stigma, giving individuals with lived NSSI experience a more active role in research may inform what and how we study NSSI and may also benefit participants themselves (e.g., by fostering greater insight or feelings of contribution). There is a moral imperative to involve individuals with lived experience at all stages of research, as well as in clinical care and advocacy settings. In doing so, this chapter acknowledges the ethical challenges that may emerge, primarily protection of vulnerable persons and peoples and inclusion/representation of diverse experiences. These challenges, however, should not be a barrier to centering lived experience perspectives but, rather, should be acknowledged in order to improve the quality of NSSI research, treatment approaches, and advocacy initiatives.
>
> **Key Words:** self-injury, lived experience, participatory action research, advocacy, inclusion

Many gains have been made in the understanding of self-injury over the past few decades, some of which are outlined in great detail throughout this book. The majority of our knowledge has emerged from researchers and clinicians. Less attention, however, has been paid to what can be learned from individuals with lived self-injury experience. In this chapter, we discuss the importance of integrating lived experience perspectives in self-injury research, clinical practice, and advocacy/outreach work. The chapter begins with an overview of the rationale for including lived experience perspectives, followed by a review of the extant literature incorporating such views. The final section provides an overview of the applications of lived experience perspectives in research, clinical, and advocacy/outreach initiatives.

Rationale

Across numerous disciplines and areas of mental health, there are well-established initiatives for people with lived experience to be involved in research, outreach, and service provision endeavors. Indeed, the World Health Organization (WHO) has long advocated for such efforts given their promise to empower individuals with mental health difficulties. Although researchers often include individuals with lived experience as research participants, a more active role in the research process would give individuals a voice in setting the research agenda, actually conducting research, and providing expert views that inform best practice (Lewis & Hasking, 2020). Work concerning the experience of self-injury (e.g., work focused on topics such as stigma, disclosure, the effects of scarring, and recovery) is best conducted from the vantage point of individuals with lived experience, rather than examining topics that researchers deem to be relevant. By involving people with lived experience in service delivery, for example, individuals who have been historically marginalized are granted opportunities to become actively involved in decision-making and thus have greater access to resources and treatment. This can, in turn, foster greater social connectedness and promote both self-esteem and self-efficacy. Similarly, many professional organizations have dedicated membership sections for people with lived experience (e.g., Academy for Eating Disorders and American Association for Suicidology). Here, individuals can connect with other organizational members to engage in needed advocacy and to ensure lived experience voices are accounted for in organizational agenda setting and decision-making.

Similarly, efforts to formally involve people with lived experience in research are increasingly being prioritized. In Canada, for instance, federal granting agencies (e.g., Canadian Institute of Health Research) have allocated funds to support projects that are patient-oriented and participatory in design. These initiatives afford the opportunity to directly involve people with lived experience in the research process—as researchers. Inasmuch as involvement in clinical care decision-making can empower people with lived experience, the same applies in research.

Barriers to Lived Experience Initiatives

Until recently (Lewis & Hasking, 2019), little effort had been made to advocate for the formal inclusion of people with lived experience of self-injury in research, clinical care provision, outreach, and membership in discipline-based organizations and societies. A major impediment to progress in the field has been stigma. Stigma associated with mental health difficulties (e.g., depression) is certainly pervasive and profound in impact (Corrigan & Watson, 2002, Corrigan, 2005). Nevertheless, anti-stigma efforts have helped to shape and at least, in part, improve public discourses and understandings of mental illness and mental health difficulties (Corrigan et al., 2012; Thornicroft et al., 2016). Indeed, mental health difficulties are not nearly as frequently viewed as the product of personal failure, and there is greater recognition that people cannot just "get over it" and that individuals with lived experience are not weak.

Unfortunately, these views do not typically generalize to self-injury. By its very nature, self-injury is a self-effected act which often results in physically visible marks in the form of injuries and scarring. Accordingly, laypeople may be less able to fathom why someone might deliberately injure themselves, which, in turn, can foment negative and otherwise unhelpful attitudes, reactions, assumptions, and stereotypes. The stigmatization of self-injury is indeed widespread and substantive (Staniland et al., 2021), with countless reports of stigma in lay, school, university, and even healthcare settings (Berger et al., 2014; Heath et al., 2011; Karman et al., 2015; Mitten et al., 2016; Saunders et al., 2012). It should be no surprise then that many individuals with lived experience are hesitant, if not outright unwilling, to disclose their experience and seek support (Mitten et al., 2016; Rosenrot & Lewis, 2020). Not circumscribed to support-seeking contexts, the stigma associated with self-injury also likely thwarts the focus and progress of research as individuals with lived experience are rarely included in the research process, with the obvious exception of their involvement as participants.

Another reason that may account for the lag in efforts to include people with lived experience of self-injury in research is the perceived risk such involvement may have. For example, some self-injury research may involve the induction of difficult emotional states (e.g., anxiety) or exposure to content (e.g., images related to self-injury) that may be distressing or inadvertently triggering to participants. In line with this view is concern that by taking part in research on self-injury, participants will be inclined to self-injure. The aspect of iatrogenic risk may thus deter researchers from involving participants in the research process beyond their traditional role as participants. These risks notwithstanding, several studies have examined iatrogenic risk and the extent to which being asked about self-injury provokes engagement in the behavior. Results indicate that individuals do not report engaging in self-injury immediately or several days after taking part in these studies (e.g., Muehlenkamp et al., 2015).

Taken together, the field of self-injury is behind with respect to the formal inclusion of people with lived experience. We contend that this equates to a critical missed opportunity. Inclusion of people with lived experience in all facets of the field would arguably contribute to (a) the development, carrying out, and dissemination of research; (b) greater promotion of awareness and destigmatization of people who self-injure; and (c) encouragement of support seeking and enhancement of service delivery when needed. Indeed, we argue that inclusion of lived experience voices is not only necessary to advance the field as a whole but also represents a moral imperative.

Reasons to Include Lived Experience Voices

There are many reasons to involve lived experience voices in self-injury research, outreach and advocacy, as well as provision of service. First, individuals who have engaged in self-injury are often very willing to undertake these initiatives. In research contexts, there are ample data to suggest that many people take part in self-injury research for altruistic reasons and are very self-motivated to play a role in research (e.g., Hasking et al., 2015; Lewis & Hasking, 2019). Outside research contexts, there are numerous examples of individuals with lived experience who use social media and other media platforms (e.g., The Mighty and podcasts) to advocate for individuals who have self-injured and to spread greater awareness in an effort to combat the undue stigma linked to self-injury. Indeed, it seems that many people with lived experience of self-injury are ready to take on a variety of roles in the field.

Involvement of people with lived experience in the field represents a critical albeit overdue step toward priority-driven research. To ensure the needs of people with lived experience are met, research agendas must align with lived experience priorities. This does not imply that the research conducted to date has not significantly advanced our collective understanding of self-injury. Rather, we argue that by positioning lived experience perspectives in the context of undertaking research initiatives, we can augment both the focus and the impact of research in the field. For example, several areas remain that would benefit from greater research, including but not limited to understanding and addressing barriers and facilitators to healthcare, ascertaining the optimal means of service provision, ensuring greater inclusivity and diversity in NSSI research more broadly, enhancing the training required for health professionals who provide treatment, addressing NSSI stigma, and fostering recovery. Lived experience views could shed needed light on ways to achieve these critical aims—among many others.

Arguably, adopting a lived experience approach in research settings can also enhance the experience of research for people with lived experience. Indeed, it can work toward fostering more appropriate and person-centered language. For example, value-laden terms (e.g., "maladaptive" behavior; Hasking et al., 2019) or using labels (e.g., "cutter" or "self-injurer"; Lewis, 2017) can be hurtful for people with lived experience and ought to be outright avoided. Thus, approaching research through a lived experience lens (i.e., through the perspective of the person who has self-injured) can yield more sensitively and respectfully worded questions, interactions (e.g., in interview-based studies), and thus experiences for people with lived experience who take part in self-injury research.

Beyond the above reasons for the formal inclusion of lived experience perspectives in research, there are also several direct benefits to individuals themselves. For instance, it has been found that taking part in research can bring about deeper reflection on one's own experience and thus more insight and understanding into one's lived experience (e.g., Blades et al., 2018). Additionally, including people with lived experience in research affords an opportunity and platform for individuals to share their story when stigma may have previously silenced them. A review of the literature indicates that sharing one's experience with mental illness may work to reduce self-stigma, foster supportive relationships, and encourage formal help-seeking (Corrigan et al., 2013). Thus, the same may transpire for people with lived experience of self-injury. Finally, there is some evidence to suggest that by taking part in research, people with lived experience may feel more empowerment and thus greater self-esteem, self-confidence, and a heightened sense of meaning (Hasking et al., 2015). It is conceivable that this may have particular salience for individuals who take on leadership roles on research projects.

In the context of clinical care and service delivery, perspectives of people with lived experience would also be beneficial. Learning from and elevating these views can work toward ensuring that intervention approaches are sufficiently tailored to meet the needs of the individuals who receive them. Importantly, such work would help to avoid generalizations about the use of a particular approach for all individuals who self-injure. Indeed, no two experiences of self-injury are completely alike, and it should not be assumed that an approach that works well for one person by default works for the next. Accounting for the uniqueness of people's lived experiences in clinical practice thus ensures that people's individual needs and concerns are met. As discussed later in the chapter, a critical part of this approach is adopting a person-centered framework (Lewis & Hasking, 2021a).

Lived experience voices can also enhance outreach and advocacy. As noted, self-injury is unfortunately shrouded in much stigma. Hence, efforts are needed to combat this stigma. Commensurate with anti-stigma efforts in the field of mental illness more broadly, it is essential that lived experience voices be woven into the fabric of all anti-stigma initiatives (Corrigan et al., 2012, 2013, 2014). Indeed, these contact-based approaches have the double benefit of empowering people with lived experience while concurrently addressing stigmatizing attitudes and stereotypes (e.g., Corrigan et al., 2014). Although similar calls have been made in the context of self-injury (e.g., Lewis & Hasking, 2019; Lewis et al., 2022), this work has not yet been realized. By way of incorporating lived experience voices in advocacy, we also have an opportunity to support individuals who wish to pursue different roles in the field of self-injury (e.g., graduate school, research, or clinical careers; Victor et al., 2022). This has the potential of ensuring that lived experience perspectives continue to be heard and can inspire future generations to take on a variety of roles, including leadership positions, in the field (Lewis & Hasking, 2019; Victor et al., 2020).

Finally, beyond direct inclusion of people with lived experience (i.e., individuals who have self-injured), it will be important to ensure that a broad scope is used when operationalizing "individuals with lived experience." In particular, this should include family, friends, romantic partners, school personnel, and mental health professionals, among many others. Doing so is conducive to ensuring that the various needs of all relevant stakeholders across different contexts are accounted for and that relevant research findings and resources are widely and appropriately disseminated to the most relevant stakeholders.

Literature on Including Lived Experience Perspectives

Traditionally, the focus of much NSSI research has been on exploring factors that might be associated with the onset or maintenance of self-injury—identifying risk factors and correlates of the behavior. Although this research has provided us with foundational knowledge about why someone may engage in self-injury, it largely fails to provide an understanding of what it means to self-injure—from the perspective of individuals with lived experience of NSSI. Over the past few years, there has been significant growth in research that seeks to explore the experience of self-injury, moving away from the study of risk factors and seeking to better understand how individuals with a history of NSSI navigate their self-injury experiences.

NSSI goes well beyond the experience or regulation of emotions, although this is an important aspect of why someone may self-injure. Lived experience voices are critical to understanding the process of recovery, how disclosures (voluntary and not) are navigated, the stigma associated with NSSI, the central role of language in perpetuating myths and fostering NSSI stigma, the importance of adopting a person-centered approach when talking about NSSI, and even how NSSI should be conceptualized and assessed. In this section, we outline the latest work incorporating lived experience voices to understand (a) the conceptualization of NSSI; (b) the experience of NSSI recovery; (c) navigating disclosures; (d) the experience of NSSI stigma; and (e) the importance of adopting a person-centered approach to understanding NSSI.

Conceptualization of NSSI
The inclusion of NSSI in the *Diagnostic and Statistical Manual for Mental Disorders* (DSM-5; American Psychiatric Association, 2013) has led to much debate about how much we understand NSSI and at what point it might be considered "pathological." When asking clinicians and researchers their opinions of the definition and conceptualization of NSSI, Lengel et al. (2022) noted significant disagreement among the field regarding what is considered NSSI. Not surprisingly, then, Criterion A—that the individual has self-injured on five or more days in the last year—has been met with significant criticism, with many finding that this criterion is too lax to indicate a mental disorder (Andover, 2014; Muehlenkamp et al., 2017; Washburn et al., 2015). Ammerman et al. (2021) noted that many considered NSSI in the last month to be more clinically meaningful than NSSI in the last year.

When asking individuals with lived experience about the potential inclusion of NSSI in the DSM, individuals express divided opinions (Lewis et al., 2017). Some could see advantages in terms of validation of their experience and facilitating treatment; others expressed reservations about an NSSI diagnosis (e.g., potential to exacerbate stigma and dismissing other concerns). If NSSI does become a clinical diagnosis, we urge clinicians to consider the needs of the client and how they view their own self-injury, and whether a formal psychiatric diagnosis may be helpful or harmful for that client.

NSSI Recovery
In previous literature, researchers have often conceptualized recovery from NSSI as complete cessation of the behavior or as not having engaged in the behavior for at least one year (Andrews et al., 2013). The transtheoretical model (TTM; Kamen, 2009; Prochaska

& DiClemente, 1983) is one that has been suggested to have promise in conceptualizing NSSI recovery. The TTM considers behavior change to occur across a series of temporally dependent stages, from not considering behavior change to maintenance of behavior change. Behavior change is facilitated by consideration of its pros and cons, cognitive and behavioral processes that facilitate change, and self-efficacy to change (Kruzan & Whitlock, 2019; Kruzan et al., 2020). While consideration of the processes underlying change can be insightful, within a TTM framework the ultimate aim of "recovery" is to stop self-injuring (Kamen, 2009).

Whereas identifying correlates of behavioral cessation is important and provides valuable insights into potential intervention targets, talking to individuals with lived experience gives us a much more nuanced view of NSSI recovery (Lewis et al., 2019). In early work, adolescents told us that they viewed recovery as no longer having the urge to self-injure (Kelada et al., 2018). However, participants also reported significant ambivalence about engaging in NSSI, reporting ongoing thoughts and urges to self-injure but also expressing that they believed they had stopped, or liked to think they had stopped.

This ambivalence about recovery is not uncommon (Gray et al., 2021) and underscores the need to adopt a broader lens than behavior cessation when conceptualizing NSSI recovery. In addition to behavioral cessation, individuals with lived experience have told us that recovery can involve ongoing thoughts and urges to self-injure, that recovery is a nonlinear process, that recovery involves developing resilience, and that recovery means different things to different people (Lewis et al., 2019). For more on recovery and models of change, see Whitlock et al., this volume.

Based on work with individuals with lived NSSI experience, we recently proposed a new framework for NSSI recovery that emphasizes that recovery is a nonlinear and an individualized process; that ongoing thoughts and urges are common; that recovery involves fostering self-efficacy both to resist urges to self-injure and to practice alternative strategies; that individuals who self-injure possess many strengths that can be harnessed in recovery; that for individuals who have visible scarring as a result of their self-injury, acceptance of scars may be an important consideration; and that a plan for navigating disclosures of NSSI may be pertinent (Lewis & Hasking, 2019, 2021b).

Rather than being based on existing theoretical frameworks and existing treatment approaches, our new framework has been developed by listening to people with lived experience. We believe the central role of people with lived experience in formulating our conceptualization of recovery will help foster rapport and lead to more positive treatment outcomes than an exclusive focus on NSSI cessation. Indeed, in presenting this framework to individuals with lived experience, there has been universal support and a sense of validation among these individuals, who are encouraged that we are acknowledging that NSSI recovery is more than simply stopping the behavior. Naturally, further work is needed to see how effective this framework is in action.

Navigating Disclosures

For individuals with a lived experience of self-injury, the decision to disclose this to others can be a difficult one. All too often, individuals with a history of NSSI choose, or feel the need, to hide this behavior and not reveal it to anyone. If they do reveal it, it is more likely that individuals disclose to friends and family members rather than health professionals (Simone & Hamza, 2020). Although disclosure to informal sources may increase the likelihood of sourcing professional support (Hasking et al., 2015), individuals with lived experience tell us that anticipated stigma, shame, and a concern that they will be a burden to others are barriers to disclosing their self-injury (Rosenrot & Lewis, 2020; Simone & Hamza, 2020). A review of the disclosure literature revealed that individuals often receive negative reactions to disclosure, which further reduces the likelihood that they will talk about their experiences (Park et al., 2021). Individuals are more likely to reveal their self-injury if the injuries are medically severe, or if accompanied by suicidal ideation (Armiento et al., 2014); this may indicate a need for disclosure (e.g., to get medical attention) rather than a considered choice to disclose what self-injury means for them.

Of course, not all disclosures of self-injury are voluntary. For individuals with visible scarring, this may lead to inadvertent disclosure to others, without an explicit vocalization of the experience. Likewise, individuals may learn of another's lived experience from a third party. These discoveries, or involuntary disclosures, of self-injury can be harder to manage than voluntary disclosures, as the individual has less control over how the disclosure occurs or who the recipient of the disclosure is. Consideration of how an individual may respond to involuntary disclosures warrants consideration within the context of NSSI recovery (Lewis & Hasking, 2021a). Further work with individuals with lived experience—both those who have disclosed to others and those who have not—will inform consideration of the factors that lead to the decision to disclose NSSI and how to navigate experiences of discovery or involuntary disclosure of NSSI.

NSSI Stigma

NSSI is often described as a highly stigmatized behavior (Staniland et al, 2021), and one that people go to great lengths to conceal from others (Burke et al., 2020). Indeed, people display more stigma toward NSSI than other forms of injury (Burke et al., 2019) and are more dismissive of individuals who disclose their NSSI than those who do not, suggesting they view disclosure as attention seeking (Lloyd et al., 2018). This public stigma can become internalized, leading an individual to believe they are inferior, weak, or not deserving of help (Burke et al., 2020; Staniland et al., 2021). People tell us that a deep sense of shame associated with NSSI is a salient barrier to disclosing NSSI, as is the fear that others may perceive them to be a burden if they disclose their NSSI (Rosenrot & Lewis, 2020; Tan et al., 2019).

One area in which stigma may be particularly felt is when a researcher or clinician has their own lived experience of self-injury. For a researcher, the notion of "me-search," or conducting research with which one has a personal experience or a close connection to, is associated with negative connotations of unprofessionalism, lack of scientific credibility, and personal bias (Devendorf, 2022). And yet, there are several advantages to people with lived experience conducting their own research, including contributing to setting the research agenda and being a role model for students who may also have lived experience (Lewis & Hasking, 2020). In clinical work, individuals may fear that disclosing NSSI would preclude them from admission to graduate programs, or that they would be perceived as incompetent to undertake clinical practice (Victor et al., 2022). Such stigma runs the risk of excluding exceptional clinicians from clinical practice. Open discussion of the strengths and considerations to be made by including people with lived experience in both research and practice may help reduce some of this stigma.

A further consideration when exploring the views of individuals with lived experience is the language we use to talk about self-injury and individuals who engage in the behavior. Language is a powerful form of communication that allows us to develop shared meanings and understandings of the world around us. Importantly, the way we use language can give value to people, objects, and ideas—denoting them as "good" or "bad." In this way, inappropriate language can perpetuate stigma and reinforce stereotypes about self-injury. Over the last few decades, there has been an active movement toward using person-centered language in the mental health field. We recognize that labeling someone by a condition or behavior is reductionist and does not do justice to the person as a whole (e.g., calling someone a self-injurer or cutter; Lewis, 2017).

Recently, we conducted a survey with individuals with lived experience, researchers, and clinicians (noting that these are not mutually exclusive groups) to understand which words or phrases they deemed appropriate when discussing NSSI and individuals who engage in the behavior. Not surprisingly, we observed some differences in language that people with lived experience find appropriate and language that researchers and clinicians find appropriate. We also asked researchers and clinicians which words and phrases they typically use to discuss NSSI. It was encouraging to observe that researchers and clinicians do not typically use terminology they deem inappropriate (e.g., manipulative), but they were less likely to use language that was considered most appropriate by individuals with lived experience (e.g., individuals with a history of NSSI; Hasking et al., 2021). These findings led us to call on researchers and clinicians to be mindful of the language they use to discuss self-injury and consider its impact on individuals with lived experience.

Adopting a Person-Centered Approach
Bringing all these considerations together, we argue the need to adopt a person-centered approach to understanding an individual's experience of NSSI. Each individual is an expert in their own story, and each of these stories will be different. Making assumptions about why someone self-injures and what their experience is like minimizes rapport and risks invalidating that experience. For individuals who already feel misunderstood and

isolated, this can exacerbate their feelings and further silence them. In moving our understanding of self-injury forward, it will be imperative to continue to listen to individuals with lived experience of self-injury, to hear their stories, and make active efforts to involve them in all phases of research and practice (Lewis & Hasking, 2020).

Practical Applications

Having described the rationale for including lived experience voices and reviewed the extant research in the field, we now turn to the practical applications of integrating lived experience perspectives across research, clinical, and advocacy domains. Notably, working toward greater inclusion of lived experience perspectives requires consideration of the ethical implications incumbent in such inclusion, particularly the protection of vulnerable persons and the need for representation of diverse experiences. Thus, the final section of this chapter describes the practical applications of integrating lived experience perspectives into research, clinical, and advocacy work, highlighting ethical challenges that may arise and providing possible solutions. In doing so, we acknowledge that people may occupy one or more of these identities/spaces.

Research Applications

The importance of integrating lived experience perspectives in research has been outlined elsewhere (Lewis & Hasking, 2020). Briefly, and as should be evident from the previous sections in this chapter, individuals with lived experience have expertise in the experience of NSSI that can augment our understanding of NSSI and associated factors. Historically, these perspectives have been accessed through research that asks individuals about their lived experience with the goal of better understanding the experience of self-injury. As described in the section "Literature on Including Lived Experience Perspectives," this has yielded information about conceptualizations of NSSI (Lewis et al., 2017), recovery (Kelada et al., 2018; Lewis et al., 2019), disclosures (Rosenrot & Lewis, 2020; Simone & Hamza, 2020), and stigma (Rosenrot & Lewis, 2020; Tan et al., 2019). The value of this research notwithstanding, such an approach engages individuals with lived experience in later stages of research (i.e., data collection), and there may be merit in engaging individuals with lived experience at all stages of the research process. By having individuals with lived experience involved at the conceptualization, analyses, and dissemination stages, it may guide the nature of the questions being asked, how data is understood, and the reach of research findings.

There are multiple ways that individuals with lived experience may be involved at earlier stages in the research process. Perhaps most simply, it is possible to consult with individuals who have lived experience when developing research questions and methodologies. Of course, this should involve proper compensation for their time and expertise. More formally, methods such as participatory action research have been described (e.g., Baum et al., 2006). Participatory action research comprises a range of methodological approaches that involve people with lived experience in the planning, implementation, and dissemination of research (Cabassa et al., 2013; Ferrari et al., 2015; Flanagan et al., 2016; Gubrium & Harper, 2016; Sitter, 2012). There is well-documented evidence that marginalized individuals who take part in these types of studies experience a reclamation of voice and greater empowerment, among many other positive outcomes (Buchanan & Murray, 2012; Carmichael et al., 2019; Cabassa et al., 2013; Ferrari et al., 2015). Although there are calls for the use of these approaches in the context of self-injury research (Lewis et al., 2022), their use remains conspicuously sparse. To our knowledge, only two participatory action research studies have been conducted in the field. These focused on staff development and training in prison (Ward & Bailey, 2013) and physician general practice (Bailey et al., 2019) settings. The absence of such research again points to barriers preventing the integration of lived experience voices in research, particularly at stages where their experiences may influence the research design or analysis.

How individuals are involved in participatory action research will depend on the aims of the research and the research question. Notably, individuals may be at different stages in their self-injury and/or recovery experiences. For example, some projects may require that individuals have some distance from their self-injury to minimize any potential for upset or retraumatization. Other projects may seek to actively involve individuals who still self-injure, in order to capture more proximal concerns around the experience of self-injury. Other stakeholders (e.g., caregivers and clinicians) may also be involved in participatory action research exploring the impact of self-injury on others, or evaluating care approaches. While such research may raise issues such as duty of care and the need for self-care, people get more benefit out of being actively involved and having their voices heard than from being excluded (Lewis & Hasking, 2020).

In addition to the concerns noted earlier (i.e., stigma and worry about iatrogenic effects), the exclusion of individuals with lived experience from the planning, conceptualization, and analysis stages of research is likely a function of the dominant positivist paradigm in psychology (Tolman, 1992). Positivism holds that knowledge can only be known if it is reducible to sensory or observable experiences; that researchers must be separate from their research; and that objectivity is imperative (Park et al., 2020). Because of this paradigmatic approach, research that employs experimental methods has been privileged over qualitative approaches in psychology (Mitchell, 2003). Part of the hesitancy then to engage individuals with lived experience in the research process (as well as concerns about "me-search") seems to be related to a view that subjectivity is inherently negative and that we must be "completely objective" to engage in good research. In line with arguments that positivism limits the understanding of clinical psychology (Miller, 1999) and that there is a need to move beyond this paradigm (Breen & Darlston-Jones, 2010), we suggest that research can never be truly objective, as it is impossible to separate past experiences, research, and knowledge from current work. Moreover, we contend that there is value to be gleaned from research that takes a more subjective approach. For example, research stemming from a qualitative paradigm, in which knowledge is constructed, often focuses on process rather than outcome (Patton, 2001). This has great relevance in understanding the development and progression of self-injury.

The barriers to engaging individuals with lived experience at all stages of the research notwithstanding, research asking individuals about their lived experience has grown in recent years. It is important to acknowledge, however, that the majority of research that has employed this approach has focused on white, cis-women recruited from a university setting. The generalizability of these findings is therefore limited, and we *must* work to include diverse experiences. In doing so, there may be additional ethical considerations in order to protect vulnerable and/or marginalized individuals. Providing safe, trauma-sensitive spaces and appropriate reimbursement is an example. Furthermore, there is a need to consult with (and compensate) individuals from diverse backgrounds to ensure that questions are being asked in a sensitive and trauma-sensitive way. Thus, not only is it incumbent on researchers to *do* lived experience research, it is also incumbent on researchers to make sure this research is ethical, generalizable, and meaningful. For a summary of lived experience applications as well as challenges to implementation and solutions for research, see table 20.1.

Clinical Applications

In clinical practice, lived experience perspectives suggest a person-centered approach to NSSI and recovery. From this perspective, each individual is viewed as unique, experiencing different factors that contribute to the onset and maintenance of NSSI (Lewis & Hasking, 2021b). Recovery is viewed as comprising nine related but distinct elements (e.g., normalizing thoughts and urges, addressing, and accepting scarring) which individuals may move through at different times and to different degrees (Lewis & Hasking, 2021a). In clinical settings, this suggests a bottom-up approach in which clinicians gather information about each individual and develop a conceptualization of their unique challenges rather than applying a single model (e.g., emotion regulation) or treatment modality (e.g., dialectical behavior therapy). Notably, this involves viewing individuals holistically rather than simply focusing on the self-injury. Understanding the whole person can help to support the individual in returning to a state of general well-being. Finally, adopting a person-centered approach involves acknowledging that treatment may not be appropriate for everyone. Some individuals may do better without treatment or by engaging in holistic practices not conventional in Western culture. The take-away here is that individuals may have different needs in their recovery process, and it is their decision whether treatment fits their needs at a given point in their journey.

This of course leads to challenges, given that traditional interventions for NSSI typically involve formal treatment (e.g., Walsh, 2012). Helping professionals typically enter the field because they want to help. Allowing individuals to dictate their own trajectory in recovery seemingly goes against clinical training. Moreover, helping professionals often have an idea of what "recovery" looks like. This can result in these professionals pushing individuals toward a goal or outcome that may not resonate with the individual. Returning to the person-centered model, it is important to check in with what the individual wants and needs out of therapy and to respect any and all responses. This does not mean refraining from sharing a clinical opinion but rather doing so in a kind and compassionate way which communicates understanding of the individual's experience. Ultimately, whether to take part in treatment and which modality of treatment to use are up to the individual, and lived experience research suggests that there are some individuals who may benefit from different approaches from those conventionally offered to individuals seeking support for NSSI.

Additionally, it may be difficult for helping professionals to move away from dominant approaches in the field. For example, although numerous functions of NSSI have been cited (e.g., Nock, 2009), emotion regulation, in which NSSI is viewed as a means of coping with intense or uncomfortable emotions, tends to be highlighted (Andover & Morris, 2014). Though this framework provides greater understanding of self-injury generally, it should not be applied to every individual or forced when an individual indicates that this conceptualization does not fit (see Taylor et al., this volume, to review the constellation of functions that may be associated with NSSI). Similarly, it may be hard for professionals to let go of the narrative that "recovery equals cessation." This is not surprising given the possible dangerous outcomes associated with NSSI; however, perspectives presented by individuals with lived experience suggest that recovery is much more than cessation (e.g., Lewis et al., 2019). Being truly person-centered in clinical practice then involves being cognizant of, but ultimately letting go of, existing narratives around self-injury and recovery to view each individual as unique. This is not to say that extant paradigms and understandings do not have value but rather to suggest that these should be applied consciously, judiciously, and mindfully after gathering sufficient information about the individual's unique experience of self-injury.

Of note, when considering the application of lived experience perspectives in clinical practice, we need to acknowledge that access to assessment/treatment is not equal for all individuals and that some individuals may be more likely to receive support than others. For example, a survey of adults with autism revealed that they face unique challenges accessing treatment for self-injury (Camm-Crosbie et al. 2018). We would also expect challenges in accessing treatment among Black, Indigenous, and People of Color, as well as LGBTQ+ individuals, among whom rates of NSSI are elevated (Gholamrezaei et al., 2017; Reisner et al. 2014; Rojas-Velasquez et al., 2021; Whitlock et al., 2011). The lack of research into treatment accessibility and appropriateness for individuals inhabiting one or more marginalized identities again points to the limitations of extant research, even that which incorporates lived experience voices. In line with this, when considering individuals from a holistic perspective, we need to be open to the fact that racial trauma and other forms of oppression are likely to be very real aspects of the individual's NSSI story. Having trauma-sensitive and culturally humble providers will be essential in providing support to individuals who have marginalized identities. Perhaps more important, the clinical field needs to work to make it safe and accessible for marginalized individuals to become clinical providers. For a summary of lived experience applications as well as challenges to implementation and solutions for clinical applications, see table 20.1.

Advocacy and Outreach Applications

Finally, in addition to research and clinical applications, lived experience perspectives of NSSI have relevance in advocacy and outreach work. This includes highlighting lived experience perspectives in outreach efforts in order to increase awareness, understanding,

Table 20.1 Lived Experience Applications as well as Challenges to Implementation and Solutions

	Practical Application	Ethical Challenges	Solutions
Research	Involve people with lived experience in all research stages	Historical lack of appropriate compensation	Establish appropriate compensation
		Stigma	Ensure trauma sensitive, safe spaces for individuals with lived experience; engage in consultation as needed
		Iatrogenic Risk	Ensure appropriate resources are readily available. Draw on extant guidelines for ethical NSSI research
Clinical	Adopt a person-centered approach, guided by people with lived experience	This may go against traditional treatment approaches; clinicians and clients may hold different goals or views (e.g., on recovery). Paucity of research in this space, especially when working with diverse and historically marginalized people	Engage in regular check-ins with clients to ascertain their preferences/goals; frame clinical views compassionately. Adopt an open, holistic, and culturally humble approach; consider historical/systemic considerations
Advocacy & Outreach	Highlighting people's lived experience in outreach projects	Historically different value placed on involvement of people with lived experience vs. clinicians/researchers. Reliance on particular (often dominant) narratives/experiences	Appropriate compensation for people with lived experience. Inclusion of diverse and often untold stories. Ensuring safe, trauma sensitive spaces; having appropriate supports for individuals and tailoring efforts to their preferences/needs

and destigmatization of NSSI, as well as looking and deferring to people with lived experience to inform these initiatives. As highlighted earlier and is discussed again, appropriate compensation is imperative in these initiatives, particularly among individuals who are marginalized.

Though seemingly simple, there are a number of barriers that make it difficult to center lived experience voices in advocacy work. First, when individuals with lived experience are included in these events, there tends to be an emphasis on individuals who are "recovered" because it provides a story of hope. In doing so, however, this negates the challenges and difficulties inherent in self-injury, which, according to individuals with lived experience, are a natural part of the recovery process (Kelada et al., 2018; Lewis et al., 2019). Furthermore, lived experience tends not to be valued to the same degree as clinical or research expertise, and thus individuals with lived experience are often not compensated for their work. This is not only an ethical issue but leads to speakers and advocates being people who can afford to do labor for free. Typically, these are individuals from privileged backgrounds who can continue to do pro bono work because of their ongoing privilege. This limits who is seen as someone with self-injury and also narrows the image of what recovery "should" look like. It is easy to center accessible voices (e.g., white and cis-women) in advocacy and outreach efforts. If integrating lived experience perspectives is truly going to be effective, we need to do the work to include people whose stories are not often told, even when this means confronting difficult topics such as the role of white supremacy, colonization, or oppression in self-injury.

Extending from this, advocacy and outreach work can put people in vulnerable positions, and we need to consider the ethical obligations we have in mobilizing these efforts. This includes creating spaces where people feel safe to share their stories, including respecting wishes about the event, including who can attend and how big the event should be. This also includes having supports available if necessary and plans for how to intervene should there be inappropriate, triggering, or discriminatory comments. This is particularly important for individuals who have previously experienced marginalization and oppression. Individuals with lived experience are not a token for advocacy work. They are people with full lives, experiences, and emotions. Similar to considering individuals from a clinical perspective, outreach and advocacy initiatives should strive to see these individuals holistically and from a person-centered framework. For a summary of lived experience applications as well as challenges to implementation and solutions for advocacy and outreach, see table 20.1.

Conclusion

Commensurate with calls to action in other areas of mental health, there is an urgent need to integrate lived experience perspectives with research, clinical, and advocacy efforts related to self-injury. While a review of the extant literature highlights what has been gleaned from integrating lived experience perspectives, this research has included individuals with lived experience primarily as participants. We contend that while valuable, such an approach still limits the lived experience involvement in ways that are consistent with a positivist approach, rather than turning to these individuals as experts in the experience of self-injury. Deference to individuals with lived experience is needed in all stages of research planning, execution, and dissemination, as well as clinical and advocacy efforts. In doing so, we highlight the need for ethical and equitable inclusion of lived experience voices, as opposed to the status quo of recruiting accessible voices. We acknowledge that this represents a shift from the way that the role of lived experience has traditionally been viewed in psychology, and that it will involve more effort on the part of researchers, clinicians, and advocates. Nevertheless, it is imperative that if we want to better understand self-injury, we need to look to individuals who have diverse expertise in its experience.

Acknowledgment

The authors of this chapter are listed alphabetically. All authors contributed equally to the chapter.

References

American Psychiatric Association. (2013). *Diagnostic and statistical manual of mental disorders: diagnostic and statistical manual of mental disorders* (5th ed.). American Psychiatric Association.

Ammerman, B. A., Lengel, G. J., & Washburn, J. J. (2021). Consideration of clinician and researcher opinions on the parameters of nonsuicidal self-injury disorder diagnostic criteria. *Psychiatry Research*, *296*, Article 113642.

Andover, M. S. (2014). Non-suicidal suicidal self-injury disorder in a community sample of adults. *Psychiatry Research*, *219*(2), 305–310.

Andover, M. S., & Morris, B. W. (2014). Expanding and clarifying the role of emotion regulation in nonsuicidal self-injury. *The Canadian Journal of Psychiatry*, *59*(11), 569–575.

Andrews, T., Martin, G., Hasking, P., & Page, A. (2013). Predictors of continuation and cessation of nonsuicidal self-injury. *Journal of Adolescent Health*, *53*(1), 40–46.

Armiento, J. S., Hamza, C. A., & Willoughby, T. (2014). An examination of disclosure of nonsuicidal self-injury among university students. *Journal of Community and Applied Social Psychology*, *24*(6), 518–533.

Bailey, D., Kemp, L., Wright, N., & Mutale, G. (2019). Talk about self-harm (TASH): Participatory action research with young people, GPs and practice nurses to explore how the experiences of young people who self-harm could be improved in GP surgeries. *Family Practice*, *36*(5), 621–626.

Baum, F., MacDougall, C., & Smith, D. (2006). Participatory action research. *Journal of Epidemiology and Community Health*, *60*(10), 854–857.

Berger, E., Hasking, P., & Reupert, A. (2014). "We're working in the dark here": Knowledge, attitudes and response of school staff towards adolescents' self-injury. School Mental Health, 6, 201–212.

Blades, C. A., Stritzke, W. G., Page, A. C., & Brown, J. D. (2018). The benefits and risks of asking research participants about suicide: A meta-analysis of the impact of exposure to suicide-related content. *Clinical Psychology Review*, *64*, 1–12.

Breen, L. J., & Darlston-Jones, D. (2010). Moving beyond the enduring dominance of positivism in psychological research: Implications for psychology in Australia. *Australian Psychologist*, *45*(1), 67–76.

Buchanan, A., & Murray, M. (2012). Using participatory video to challenge the stigma of mental illness: A case study. *International Journal of Mental Health Promotion*, *14*(1), 35–43.

Burke, T. A., Piccirillo, M. L., Moore-Berg, S. L., Alloy, L. B., & Heimberg, R. G. (2019). The stigmatization of nonsuicidal self-injury. *Journal of Clinical Psychology*, *75*(3), 481–498.

Burke, T. A., Ammerman, B. A., Hamilton, J. L., Stange, J. P., & Piccirillo, M. (2020). Nonsuicidal self-injury scar concealment from the self and others. *Journal of Psychiatric Research*, *130*, 313–320.

Cabassa, L. J., Nicasio, A., & Whitley, R. (2013). Picturing recovery: A photovoice exploration of recovery dimensions among people with serious mental illness. *Psychiatric Services*, *64*(9), 837–842.

Camm-Corsbie, L., Bradley, L., Shaw, R., Baron-Cohon, S., & Cassidy, S. (2018). "People like me don't get support": Autistic adults' experiences of support and treatment for mental health difficulties, self-injury and suicidality. *Autism*, *23*(6), 1431–1441.

Carmichael V, Adamson G, Sitter KC, & Whitley R. (2019). Media coverage of mental illness: a comparison of citizen journalism vs. professional journalism portrayals. *Journal of Mental Health*, *28*(5), 520–526.

Corrigan, P. W. (2005). On the stigma of mental illness: Practical strategies for research and social change. American Psychological Association.

Corrigan, P. W., Kosyluk, K. A., & Rüsch, N. (2013). Reducing self-stigma by coming out proud. American Journal of Public Health, 103, 794–800.

Corrigan, P. W., Michaels, P. J., Vega, E., Gause, M., Larson, J., Krzyzanowski, R., & Botcheva, L. (2014). Key ingredients to contact-based stigma change: A cross-validation. *Psychiatric Rehabilitation Journal*, *37*(1), 62.

Corrigan, P. W., Morris, S. B., Michaels, P. J., Rafacz, J. D., & Rüsch, N. (2012). Challenging the public stigma of mental illness: A meta-analysis of outcome studies. Psychiatric Services, 63, 963–973.

Corrigan, P.W., & Watson, A.C. (2002). Understanding the impact of stigma on people with mental illness. World Psychiatry, 1, 16–20.

Devendorf, A. R. (2022). Is "me-search" a kiss of death in mental health research? *Psychological Services*, 19, 49–54.

Ferrari, M., Rice, C., & McKenzie, K. (2015). ACE Pathways Project: Therapeutic catharsis in digital storytelling. *Psychiatric Services*, *66*(5), 556–556.

Flanagan, E. H., Buck, T., Gamble, A., Hunter, C., Sewell, I., & Davidson, L. (2016). "Recovery speaks": A photovoice intervention to reduce stigma among primary care providers. *Psychiatric Services*, *67*(5), 566–569.

Gray, N., Hasking, P., & Boyes, M. (2021). The impact of ambivalence on recovery from non-suicidal self-injury: Considerations for health professionals. *Journal of Public Mental Health*, 20, 251–258.

Gholamrezaei, M., De Stefano, J., & Heath, N. L. (2017). Nonsuicidal self-injury across cultures and ethnic and racial minorities: A review. *International Journal of Psychology*, *52*(4), 316–326. https://doi.org/10.1002/ijop.12230

Gubrium, A., & Harper, K. (2016). *Participatory visual and digital methods (Vol. 10)*. Routledge.

Hasking, P., Lewis, S. P., & Boyes, M. (2019). When language is maladaptive: Recommendations for discussing self-injury. Journal of Public Mental Health, 18, 148–152.

Hasking, P., Lewis, S.P., & Boyes, M. (2021). The language of self-injury: A data-informed commentary. *Journal of Nervous and Mental Disease*, *209*(4), 233–236.

Hasking, P., Rees, C., Martin, G., & Quigley, J. (2015). What happens when you tell someone you self-injure? The effects of disclosing NSSI to adults and peers. *BMC Public Health*, *15*(1), Article 1039.

Heath, N. L., Toste, J. R., Sornberger, M. J., & Wagner, C. (2011). Teachers' perceptions of non-suicidal self-injury in the schools. *School Mental Health*, *3*, 35–43.

Kamen, D. G. (2009). How can we stop our children from hurting themselves? Stages of change, motivational interviewing, and exposure therapy applications for nonsuicidal self-injury in children and adolescents. *International Journal of Behavioral Consultation and Therapy 5*(1), 106–123.

Karman, P., Kool, N., Gamel, C., & van Meijel, B. (2015). From judgment to understanding. *Archives of Psychiatric Nursing*, *29*, 401–406.

Kelada, L., Hasking, P., Melvin, G., Whitlock, J., & Baetens, I. (2018). "I do want to stop, at least I think I do": An international comparison of recovery from nonsuicidal self-injury among young people. *Journal of Adolescent Research*, *33*(4), 416–441.

Kruzan, K. P., & Whitlock, J. (2019). Processes of change and nonsuicidal self-injury: A qualitative interview study with individuals at various stages of change. Global Qualitative Nursing Research, 6, 2333393619852935.

Kruzan, K. P., Whitlock, J., & Hasking, P. (2020). Development and initial validation of scales to assess decision balance (NSSI-DB), processes of change (NSSI-POC) and self-efficacy (NSSI-SE) in a population of young adults engaging in non-suicidal self-injury. Psychological Assessment, 32, 635–648.

Lengel, G. J., Ammerman, B. A., & Washburn, J. J. (2022). Clarifying the definition of nonsuicidal self-injury: Clinician and researcher perspectives. *Crisis*, 43(2), 119.

Lewis, S. P. (2017). I cut therefore I am? Avoiding labels in the context of self-injury. *Medical Humanities*, 43(3), 204.

Lewis, S. P., Bryant, L. A., Schaefer, B. M., & Grunberg, P. H. (2017). In their own words: Perspectives on nonsuicidal self-injury disorder among those with lived experience. *Journal of Nervous and Mental Disease*, 205 (10), 771–779.

Lewis, S. P., & Hasking, P. (2019). Rethinking self-injury recovery: A commentary and conceptual reframing. *BJPsych Bulletin*, 44(2), 44–46.

Lewis, S. P., & Hasking, P. (2020). Putting the self in self-injury research: Inclusion of people with lived experience in research. *Psychiatric Services*, 70(11), 1058–1060.

Lewis, S. P., & Hasking, P. (2021a). Self-injury recovery: A person-centred framework. *Journal of Clinical Psychology*, 77(4), 884–895.

Lewis, S. P., & Hasking, P. (2021b). Understanding self-injury: A person-centered approach. *Psychiatric Services*. Advance online publication.

Lewis, S. P., Heath, N. L., & Whitley, R. (2022). Addressing self-injury stigma: The promise of innovative digital and video action-research methods. *Canadian Journal of CommunityMental Health*, 40(3), 45–54.

Lewis, S. P., Kenny, T. E., Whitfield, K., & Gomez, J. (2019). Understanding self-injury recovery: Views from individuals with lived experience. *Journal of Clinical Psychology*, 75(12), 2119–2139.

Lloyd, B., Blazely, A., & Phillips, L. (2018). Stigma towards individuals who self-harm: Impact of gender and disclosure. *Journal of Public Mental Health*, 17(4), 184–194.

Miller, E. (1999). Positivism and clinical psychology. *Clinical Psychology & Psychotherapy*, 6(1) 1–6.

Mitchell, J. (2003). The quantitative imperative: Positivism, naive realism and the place of qualitative methods in psychology. *Theory and Psychology*, 13(1), 5–31.

Mitten, N., Preyde, M., Lewis, S., Vanderkooy, J., & Heintzman, J. (2016). The perceptions of adolescents who self-harm on stigma and care following inpatient psychiatric treatment. *Social Work in Mental Health*, 14(1), 1–21.

Muehlenkamp, J. J., Brausch, A. M., & Washburn, J. J. (2017). How much is enough? Examining frequency criteria for NSSI disorder in adolescent inpatients. *Journal of Consulting and Clinical Psychology*, 85(6), 611–619.

Muehlenkamp, J. J., Swenson, L. P., Batejan, K. L., & Jarvi, S. M. (2015). Emotional and behavioral effects of participating in an online study of nonsuicidal self-injury: An experimental analysis. *Clinical Psychological Science*, 3, 26–37.

Nock, M. K. (2009). Why do people hurt themselves?: New insights into the nature and function of self-injury. *Current Directions in Psychological Science*, 18(2), 78–83.

Park, Y., Konge, L., & Artino, A. (2020). The positivism paradigm of research. *Academic Medicine*, 95(5), 690–694.

Park, Y., Mahdy, J. C., & Ammerman, B. A. (2021). How others respond to non-suicidal self-injury disclosure: A systematic review. *Journal of Community and Applied Psychology*, 31, 107–119.

Patton, M. Q. (2001). *Qualitative research & evaluation methods*. (3rd ed.). St. Paul, MN: SAGE.

Prochaska, J. O., & DiClemente, C. C. (1983). Stages and processes of self-change of smoking: toward an integrative model of change. *Journal of Consulting and Clinical Psychology*, 51(3), 390.

Reisner, S. L., Biello, K., Perry, N. S., Gamarel, K. E., & Mimiaga, M. J. (2014). A compensatory model of risk and resilience applied to adolescent sexual orientation disparities in nonsuicidal self-injury and suicide attempts. *American Journal of Orthopsychiatry*, 84 (5), 545–556.

Rojas-Velasquez, D. A., Pluhar, E. I., Burns, P. A., & Burton, E. T. (2021). Nonsuicidal self-injury among African American and Hispanic adolescents and young adults: A systematic review. *Prevention science*, 22(3), 367–377.

Rosenrot, S. A., & Lewis, S. P. (2020). Barriers and responses to the disclosure of self-injury: A thematic analysis. *Counselling Psychology Quarterly*, 33(2), 121–141.

Saunders, K. E. A., Hawton, K., Fortune, S., & Farrell, S. (2012). Attitudes and knowledge of clinical staff regarding people who self-harm: A systematic review. *Journal of Affective Disorders*, 139(3), 205–216.

Simone, A. C., & Hamza, C. A. (2020). Examining the disclosure of nonsuicidal self-injury to informal and formal sources: A review of the literature. *Clinical Psychology Review*, 82, Article 101907.

Sitter, K. C. (2012). Participatory video: Toward a method, advocacy and voice (MAV) framework. *Intercultural Education, 23*(6), 541–554.

Staniland, L., Hasking, P., Boyes, M., & Lewis, S.P. (2021). Stigma and nonsuicidal self-injury: Application of a conceptual framework. *Stigma and Health, 6*, 312–323.

Tan, S. C., Tam, C. L., & Bonn, G. (2019). Feeling better or worse? The lived experience of non-suicidal self-injury among Malaysian university students. *Asia Pacific Journal of Counselling and Psychotherapy, 10*(7), 1–18.

Thornicroft, G., Mehta, N., Clement, S., Evans-Lacko, S., Doherty, M., Rose, D., . . . & Henderson, C. (2016). Evidence for effective interventions to reduce mental-health-related stigma and discrimination. *Lancet, 387*(10023), 1123–1132.

Tolman, C. W. (Ed.). (1992). *Recent research in psychology. Positivism in psychology: Historical and contemporary problems.* Springer-Verlag.

Victor, S. E., Lewis, S. P., & Muehlenkamp, J. J. (2022). Psychologists with lived experience of non-suicidal self-injury: Priorities, obstacles, and recommendations for inclusion. *Psychological Services, 19*(1), 21.

Walsh, B. W. (2012). *Treating self-injury: A practical guide* (2nd ed.). Guilford Press.

Ward, J., & Bailey, D. (2013). A participatory action research methodology in the management of self-harm in prison. *Journal of Mental Health, 22*(4), 306–316.

Washburn, J. J., Potthoff, L. M., Juzwin, K. R., & Styer, D. M. (2015). Assessing DSM-5 nonsuicidal self-injury disorder in a clinical sample. *Psychological Assessment, 27*(1), 31–41.

Whitlock, J., Muehlenkamp, J., Purington, A., Eckenrode, J., Barreira, P., Baral Abrams, G., Marchell, T., Kress, V., Girard, K., Chin, C. & Knox, K. (2011). Nonsuicidal self-injury in a college population: General trends and sex differences. *Journal of American College Health, 59*, 691–698.

CHAPTER 21

Beyond "Stopping": Reconceptualizing NSSI Recovery in Favor of Healing and Growth

Janis L. Whitlock, Elizabeth E. Lloyd-Richardson, *and* Josie Woolsen

> **Abstract**
>
> This chapter considers recovery from nonsuicidal self-injury (NSSI) under the notion of healing and growth. It looks into how recovery has been operationalized in mental health and NSSI-specific literature. Historically, recovery originated from pathology-based paradigms that assume the need for intervention and are closely aligned with behavioral conformity to accepted norms and mores. Moreover, recovery includes dimensions of wellness, growth, dynamic, intentional, relational, policies, individually situated, community-supported, and spiritually supporting. The chapter discusses the clinical implications of recovery and practitioners using approaches such as identifying underlying psychological processes and creating short-term meetable goals. It highlights full cessation as a common therapeutic goal when concerned with self-injury.
>
> **Key Words:** NSSI recovery, growth, pathology, full cessation, mental health, intervention, behavioral conformity, healing

What Is Recovery? and Why Is It Important?

The idea of "recovery" is at the heart of almost all medical and health science. Medical professionals understand the core of their profession to revolve around the healing and promotion of health for all patients. Within mental health, application of the idea can be traced to John Perceval, son of a British prime minister, who wrote about his recovery from living with psychosis for three years, for which he was institutionalized in the 1830s (Bateson, 1961).

As a heuristic idea, "recovery" is accessible and meaning rich, and most of us can quickly pull up a general idea of what it means. Yet, these subjective renderings lead to considerable variability, depending on the individual and condition being discussed. For example, when speaking about a short-term or acute physical illness, all affected individuals would likely agree that "recovery" means complete resolution of the disease/pathogen and full return of the physical body to its preaffected state. For chronic physical disease, what recovery means is often unclear or may not be used at all. If it is used in this context, it will likely imply short- or long-term remission of symptoms.

When it comes to mental health, these gray areas of recovery are even murkier. What did John Perceval, for example, mean when he wrote about recovery from psychosis? Did he mean that after years of experiencing psychotic episodes, he believed that he would never experience psychosis again? Or, did he perceive that after a period of frequent psychotic events, the severity and chronicity had appreciably reduced and was now manageable? And, what about when the mental health challenge manifests largely as a behavior rather than as an internal condition with few outward behavioral demonstrations? This last question is the most germane here since nonsuicidal self-injury (NSSI) most often fits into this last category. While the idea of recovery in NSSI research has been loosely operationalized as cessation of the behavior for a significant amount of time, calls for more nuanced and robust conceptualizations are increasingly common (Lewis et al., 2017; Lewis & Hasking, 2021; Victor et al., 2022).

The remainder of this chapter is dedicated to reviewing literature germane to the question of how recovery has been theoretically and empirically operationalized in mental health, how it has been operationalized in NSSI-specific literature, and an exploration of how NSSI recovery conceptualization and operationalization might be broadened to better capture the various processes at play. We then apply some of the core concepts reviewed to two case studies and advance recommendations for research and clinical practice.

Models of "Recovery" and Their Dimensions

As heuristically accessible as it is, clearly conceptualizing and measuring recovery is more complex. Applied to the areas of mental health and alcohol and other drug (AOD) abuse, recovery has historically been rooted in pathology-based paradigms that assume the need for intervention and are closely aligned with behavioral conformity to accepted norms and mores (White, 2007). Modeled on traditional approaches to AOD addictions, the earliest recovery models assumed there were clear etiologies to problem behaviors that could be solved with professional treatment focused on assisting individuals to overcome cravings and problem behaviors (Ashford et al., 2019; White, 2007). The primary goal of recovery in this model was identified most simply as the elimination or reduction of symptoms. Similarly, evidence-based cognitive and behavioral therapies have long focused on planning for "maintenance" through such intervention approaches as relapse prevention.

In response to calls for more nuanced and growth-oriented paradigms, a number of key mental health-focused agencies took up the call to fashion a definition of recovery that comports to the more modern strength-based sensibilities. Perhaps the most comprehensive and purposeful of these efforts was the initiative undertaken by the Recovery Science Research Collaborative (RSRC) as part of their 2017 inaugural meeting. The RSRC represents a collaboration among university researchers, practitioners, public health professionals, and policy advisors from institutions across the United States. The goal of the inaugural meeting was to review definitions of recovery used by leading stakeholder institutions and groups such as the Substance Abuse and Mental Health Services

Administration (SAMSHA, 2011), the American Society of Addiction Medicine (ASAM; American Society of Addiction Medicine, 2013), and the Betty Ford Institute Consensus Panel (BFICP; the Betty Ford Institute Consensus Panel, 2007). Although each of the definitions they considered (see Ashford et al., 2019, for details) captured important and somewhat distinct facets of recovery, the aim was to reach consensus on a robust and nuanced operationalization of "recovery" after a rigorous and consensus-based review of extant definitions and literature.

The resulting RSRC consensus definition of recovery reads, "Recovery is an individualized, intentional, dynamic, and relational process involving sustained efforts to improve wellness" (Ashford et al., 2019, p. 183). Included in this definition are several key ideas. One of these is the idea that recovery is dynamic and involves a process of change that unfolds over time in ways that reflect individual character and context. As such, what "recovery" looks like at any given moment is likely to be quite variable and may not include a particular outcome or appearance. The overall trend, however, should reflect a clear movement from disordered to more harmonious and life-supporting states. One across-person feature of this dynamic improvement arc is evidence of clear, sustained effort reflective of a commitment to wellness across the life spheres negatively affected by the condition from which one is recovering, even if the sphere is seemingly not directly related (Ashford et al., 2019).

Notably, absence of clinically relevant behavior, such as substance use or, in our case, NSSI, is not a key feature of the RSRC definition, although the definition does not exclude this either. The refined definition focuses on prioritizing diversity in recovery paths and suggests that abstinence may be considered a clinical or aspirational outcome rather than a requisite evidential pillar of recovery. Although steady movement away from what the RSRC authors characterize as "pathological bondage" is part of the universal recovery process, robust conceptualization and measurement of *sustained movement toward wellness*, within an individualized context, is a more valuable and useful measure of recovery than simple tallies of symptom abatement (Ashford et al., 2019). This can be seen in newer clinical conceptual models, such as that reflected in process-based therapy (Hayes et al., 2020; Hofmann et al., 2021), which acknowledges the importance of successful maintenance strategies while also purposely fostering growth and resilience. By eschewing a problem-focused approach, process-based therapy promotes a vision of "problems to prosperity" that emphasizes human growth and resilience through structured process-based functional analysis in a broad model, termed the extended evolutionary metamodel (EEMM), which explores maladaptive and adaptive processes that derive from multiple individual-level dimensions as well as biophysiological and sociocultural considerations (Hofmann et al., 2021). Models such as this span research and clinical domains as they help to reshape our conceptualization of recovery.

These efforts are a positive step in moving from a deficit-focused paradigm to a growth-oriented paradigm that captures individual variation in recovery processes and supports. It also offers important and useful guidance relative to conceptualizing and measuring recovery in mental health-linked conditions, such as NSSI. Taken as a whole, previously identified and RSRC-identified domains emphasize the importance of recognizing, supporting, and, when applicable, measuring multiple core recovery domains. More specifically, and of relevance here, recovery includes the following dimensions:

1. **Wellness and growth focused.** One of the primary messages to emerge from efforts to more broadly conceptualize and support "recovery" processes is the understanding that recovery is less about returning to a former state, even a healthy former state, than it is about actively promoting new capacity for growth, centeredness, and wholeness. In this way, recovery is best conceptualized as steady progress toward improved quality of life and psychological functioning. Within this framework, cessation of health and growth challenging behaviors, cravings, and/or other detrimental cognitive and emotional patterns, are likely to be a *byproduct* of growth rather than the main point of growth and wellness (see also ASAM, 2013; SAMHSA, 2011).

2. **Dynamic.** Recovery is a dynamic process and reflects cognitive, emotional, and behavioral changes that occur as a result of time and interactions with the environment. It also reflects the foundational idea that recovery is marked by individuals' desire to move from chaos and/or pain into greater cohesion and meaning.

3. **Intentional.** Forward, intentional motion in the recovery process is agentic and self-directed. Steady goal-directed behavior reflects a sense of hope and purpose and relies on personal recovery capital (Granfield & Cloud, 1999). In this way, it is best identified as an autonomous process in which individuals are self-directing active partners, intrinsically engaged in collaboratively crafting recovery process goals and outcomes in formal exchange with mental health providers and/or through informal networks of family, friends, and other loved ones (Ashford et al., 2019).

4. **Relational.** Humans are wired to connect (Badenoch & Cox, 2013; Turkle, 2016) and experience both hurt and healing embedded within relationships with individuals, families, peer groups, and organizations and institutions. Health and recovery, in particular, are closely yoked to the social context within which each individual develops and functions. Individuals in recovery-supportive relationships and social environments are much better positioned to make and achieve recovery/growth goals than those in recovery-inhibiting environments, such as environments with high levels of stress or tension, mental health related stigma, and/or low tolerance for authentic connection and sharing.

5. **Policy and program affected**. In addition to interpersonal and relational resources salient in supporting (or hindering) recovery and growth processes, sustained movement toward wellness is strongly influenced by extra-individual contextual factors, such as organizational- and community-level policies (e.g., advocacy efforts, workplace policies, and employee assistance programs), availability of support institutions and programs (support groups, resource aids etc.), and any other community-level resources available to individuals in recovery.
6. **Individually situated.** Individual history (trauma, abuse, attachment, etc.), internal assets (resilience, cognitive reframing capacity, persistence, etc.), and demographic and/or health-linked influences (e.g., gender, sex, ethnicity, age, discrimination/disenfranchisement, and overall health). Without considering demographic and historical context, recovery frameworks cannot be applied to historically disenfranchised people, as it will not meet their specific needs.
7. **Community-supported and aligned.** Best understood as an intrinsic part of the relational element of the recovery process, the RSRC review highlights the role that institutions, groups, and other structures in local communities play in providing both support systems and networks as well as norms, mores, and social expectations important in serving as a "north star" for identifying socially aligned ways of behaving and living. Provision of formal and informal spaces and forums for coming together with individuals who share similar challenges or who otherwise support positive engagement fosters healthy and prosocial relationship development. Beyond this, however, it provides individuals with psychological signposts for coming into alignment with prosocial values, actions, and behavioral norms.
8. **Spirituality-supporting**. Some conceptualizations of mental health struggles and recovery processes incorporate a spiritual dimension (ASAM, 2013; Ashford et. al., 2019), such as viewing substance addictions as a spiritual malady and as a pathway to healing (Cook, 2004). Although understudied, research suggests that spirituality may play a role in recovery processes by facilitating a sense of connectedness to something larger than the self, enhancing self-awareness and understanding, and providing a sense of coherence in linking the past, present, and future (Cook, 2004; Drobin, 2014). For many individuals, spirituality is an essential aspect of recovery (Kelly et al., 2017).

Overall, in strong alliance with Bronfenbrenner's model of human development (Bronfenbrenner & Morris, 2006), the RSRC report situates both illness/disease and healing and recovery in multiple broad, interlinked contexts that include the individual but also the larger contexts within which they reside:

> Relationships between individuals, relationships with oneself, and relationships to institutions, ideas, and cultural social systems are the chief wellspring from which the pathological manifestations of substance use disorder and related mental health pathologies tend to manifest. . . Thus, the chief platform or stage where recovery emerges is in these same realms, but more importantly, in the recovering individual's relationships to themselves, others, and society. Recovery is very much a pro-social process whereby individuals become more synchronized in values, thoughts, actions, and beliefs through their relationships to the world around them. This is a mutually beneficial and reciprocal arrangement which builds the multi-directionality needed for stable social capital.
>
> *(Ashford et al., 2019, p 184)*

How Has NSSI "Recovery" Been Conceptualized?

Research dedicated to exploring recovery definitions and pathways in NSSI are relatively nascent. What has emerged over the past decade elucidates key processes even as it highlights the complexity and need for reformulated assumptions as illustrated in the RSRC document (Ashford et al., 2019) reviewed above. It was not until 2013 that NSSI was included in the *Diagnostic and Statistical Manual of Mental Disorders* (DSM-5; American Psychiatric Association, 2013). Although identified as a condition in need of additional research, NSSI disorder was preliminarily operationalized as (a) not socially sanctioned (e.g., tattooing or piercing) or only causing minor injury or occurring only in the context of psychosis, delirium, substance use, or another psychiatric or medical condition, and characterized by (b) engaging in NSSI on five or more days in the past year, with the expectation that (c) NSSI will provide relief from a negative emotional state or induce a positive mood state or will remedy an interpersonal challenge, and is (d) accompanied by one or more of the following: frequent thoughts of preoccupation with NSSI, presence of distress, and/or interference in life functioning (American Psychiatric Association, 2022, p. 923). This set of criteria reflected literature on NSSI function, periodicity, and general phenomenological contours (e.g., distinct from both suicidal thoughts and behaviors and not inclusive of socially sanctioned behaviors).

Case Studies

Using the two case studies that follow, we reflect on how recovery has been currently constructed, what that means to these individuals, and how a broader formulation of recovery expands the roles of healing and growth across dimensions of case conceptualization and intervention planning.

Case Study 1: Tanya

Tanya is 20 years old and enrolled in her junior year in college. She is majoring in psychology and has done well in school so far. She's noticed recently, however, that the urge to cut herself when she feels stressed has started to grow stronger again. She began using self-injury to control stress when she was about 15 and tended to use it often, whenever she needed to reduce high levels of tension quickly. It's been two years, though, since she last injured and she's a little surprised by the intensity of the urges. When the urges first showed up a few weeks ago, she gave in a couple of times because she knew it would help alleviate her sense of fear and apprehension. She's been able to resist since then, but has sought out therapy on campus to help her figure out what's going on. She's had two meetings with a campus counselor and believes it's helping, but she sometimes worries that she'll never fully stop wanting to self-injure when she's stressed. (The next time she meets with her therapist she wants to talk about what to expect and how to know when she has recovered and can move on from these urges and this period of her life.)

Case Study 2: Mario

Mario is 27 and works as an accountant for a small firm in Texas. As a teenager, Mario noticed that he would pick fights with people so that he could experience pain and vent emotion. Sometimes feelings of anger and frustration would well up so strongly that he just needed a way to get it out. He didn't always pick fights, sometimes he punched walls or used a lighter on his skin. He didn't feel great about it, but it did offer a short-term relief. He always assumed that he would stop when he got a little older, but he finds that he still really likes to punch things when he's very angry or upset. He took up mixed martial arts as a way to vent his emotions and to feel physical pain in a more healthy, socially acceptable way. He has stopped picking fights and he doesn't tend to damage property anymore, but he does sometimes end up with injuries that last for days or weeks after a vigorous mixed martial arts session.

In keeping with broadly accepted convention, the earliest waves of research on NSSI and recovery focused on processes of change and largely conceptualized "recovery" as cessation of NSSI for significant periods of time (Andrews et al., 2013; Brown et al., 2007; Rotolone & Martin, 2012; Whitlock et al., 2015). This simple marker paralleled other mental health conditions where full recovery has historically been conceptualized by cessation of the damaging or otherwise problematic behavior (alcohol, drug use, binging/purging cycles, etc.). This is also in alignment with most stages of change models, such as the transtheoretical model (TTM) of stages of change (Prochaska et al., 1992), which recognizes various stages of readiness and actualizes change, all in service of full cessation: contemplation (intent to stop behavior in the next six months), preparation (intent to take steps to stop behavior within next month), action (taken steps to stop behavior), maintenance (taken steps to stop behavior for more than six months), and termination (cessation of behavior for past three years) (Prochaska et al., 1992). Although limited by a narrow definition of recovery, this line of research has been fruitful in identifying key change mechanisms (see table 21.1), all of which have important implications for prevention, intervention, and treatment.

Use of cessation as a key recovery marker has been standard until recently, when the larger mental health field, including but not limited to NSSI scholars and professionals, began grappling with calls to reconceptualize what recovery means in research, clinical practice, and from both emic and etic vantage points. These come from within the academic and professional community (e.g., Ashford et al., 2019; Lewis et al., 2017; Rogers, 2017; Victor et al., 2022) as well as from those with lived experience (e.g., Bergner, 2022). Regardless of the communication vector, the charge is to move beyond cessation as the primary marker of recovery in favor of a broader, more flexible set of markers identified using person-centered approaches (Lewis & Hasking, 2020).

Also contributing to the need for a larger conversation about how to best conceptualize and track NSSI recovery is the fact that NSSI cessation is a rare outcome of any current therapeutic modality (see Fox et al., 2020, for review). This largely stems from the fact that NSSI is widely regarded as challenging to treat. However, since virtually all indices of treatment success lean heavily on NSSI cessation as the primary marker of success, "success" may be artificially constrained. In fact, as much of the qualitative literature demonstrates, individuals with lived NSSI experience describe a wide array of perceptions, changes, and, often, growth in the course of living with and through NSSI experiences (also see Kress et al., this volume) (Lewis et al., 2017; Lewis & Hasking, 2021; Victor et al., 2022). Little of this is reflected in studies employing purely quantitative and/or randomized controlled trial designs where NSSI cessation is the default measure of recovery.

Defining and Measuring the Process of NSSI Recovery: A Review of Emerging Themes

It is difficult to imagine that behavioral cessation will cease to be at least one important marker of NSSI recovery, but calls to approach conceptualization and measurement of NSSI recovery differently have generated a small but growing number of high-yield empirical studies that add important dimensionality to the larger question of what NSSI recovery means from the vantage point of those who have lived through its unfolding in real time (see table 21.1 for list of NSSI recovery-focused studies). Review of existing work in this area reveals a few notable themes:

1. ***NSSI recovery is nonlinear and relapse is common, so "cessation" is an unrealistic measure of recovery.***
   One of the reasons for using NSSI cessation as the primary measure of recovery is that relapse is very common (Degenstein, 2018; Kelada et al., 2018; Lewis et al., 2019) and so designation of cessation as something achieved after a period of "sobriety" (as it would be considered in the AOD

literature) is challenging. Indeed, even among studies that use NSSI cessation as the primary recovery marker, there is significant variation in how long participants needed to have been NSSI-free to be considered "recovered." For example, Lewis et al. (2019) document and extend the need for broader definition in a qualitative study designed to explore the meaning of recovery among those with lived experience. While many of their respondents identified cessation as a key element of recovery, they also highlighted the need to (a) *identify NSSI as a process* that may involve slips and setbacks, (b) recognize that *NSSI is more than a behavior*—it also involves repetitive thoughts and urges, and (c) recovery involves *enhancing psychological capacity* through improved resilience, self-acceptance, and coping.

In another recovery-focused qualitative study, Wadman et al. (2017) found that complete NSSI cessation may prove impossible for some. Several of their respondents doubted that they would ever be able to fully stop. Similarly, many of the participants in qualitative research on the recovery process (Degenstein, 2018) also indicated that even if they were to reduce NSSI frequency, full cessation may be impossible. NSSI is known to be cyclical in nature for many people, with months or years in between episodes (Whitlock & Selekman, 2014) and NSSI urges remain present for years whether the behavior is performed or not (Kelada et al., 2018; Lewis et al., 2019). In cases like this, where NSSI activity is sporadic and where incidents may be separated by years, we must ask, what is "recovery" and how useful is sustained NSSI cessation as *the* critical therapeutic goal? Should someone who has experienced a small number of NSSI incidents over a long window of time be considered in the same "nonrecovered" category as someone who is engaging in NSSI more regularly? Nevertheless, despite valid objections to cessation as a singular and primary NSSI recovery marker, there have been few alternatives employed in empirical operationalization.

2. **NSSI recovery is not just behavioral; it requires sustained shifts in a variety of intrapsychic areas.**

   As noted above, one of the most consistent criticisms of existing recovery-focused literature is the use of behavioral markers, including but not limited to NSSI frequency. While parsimony in development and deployment of recovery indicators is understandable, it is inadequate and limiting. For example, in a cross-national study of young adults interviewed about their perspectives on NSSI recovery, young adults consistently defined recovery as no longer having the urge to self-injure when feeling distressed. They also reported ambivalence when recovery was framed as complete cessation (Kelada et al., 2018). They asserted that conceptualization of NSSI recovery needed to include broader consideration of unobservable experiences and qualities, like urges. Further, respondents indicated that reducing emphasis on behavioral cessation and expanding consideration of nonbehavioral indicators, like urges, would reduce the pressure they often felt for failing to reach and sustain full NSSI cessation.

While behavioral markers will likely always play a role in assessing progress toward recovering from a psychologically constricted and health-compromising state, like NSSI, a growing body of literature indicates a need for a more progressive approach to tracking progress toward healthier states of being, along with development of a broader suite of non-behaviorally focused indicators for use in research and clinical assessment. Both general and NSSI-specific recovery literature suggest that these indicators will need to include a variety of cognitive, emotional, relational, and contextual dimensions (specific examples of these domains will be explored more fully below). This is reflected in recent models such as process-based therapy's EEMM model, which refers to a multidimensional and holistic approach to examining root causes and effective treatment approaches (Hofmann et al., 2021). The specific themes that may prove useful in creating a set of recovery-linked progress and growth markers are discussed at greater length below.

3. **NSSI recovery and the processes that facilitate it are multidimensional and whole person-situated; this must be reflected in conceptualization and measurement.**

Lessons drawn from the lived experience perspective require finding ways to fuse at least two distinct vantage points: recovery processes are both intrapsychic and contextually situated. That is, they take place both within dynamically engaged internal contexts, such as thoughts and emotions, as well as external social and relational contexts, such as experiences with loved ones and daily life. Demands for better understanding and representing these dimensions have grown considerably over the past half decade and have begun to proliferate across a number of mental health domains, including but not limited to alcohol and substance use (Ashford et al., 2019), schizophrenia (Bergner, 2022), and NSSI (Lewis et al., 2017; Lewis & Hasking 2021; Victor et al., 2022).

Creating universally applicable ways of capturing and comparing markers of change favored by science (e.g., averages, trends, and categories) is often at odds with the personal, dynamic experience of each individual represented in a single datapoint (Degenstein, 2018; Lewis & Hasking, 2021). Science favors and is heavily dependent on clear distinctions, aggregates, and discrete boxes that can be compared, contrasted, and otherwise manipulated. While understandable, the very nature of its angularity mandates minimizing and/or obscuring any singular data point within its boundaried boxes. Contained in each datapoint, however, is a multifaceted and unique human story; stories that when distilled to only the elements easy to compare, contrast, or manipulate quickly lose the features reflective of the rich human journey they signal. This leaves the person behind any one datapoint hidden; it also limits the capacity of the science to meaningfully capture and speak to the tender realness of any one or more human experience(s). The consequences of this preference are more significant than inadequate representation. Since it is the findings and methods of science that largely determine (a) subsequent research questions and studies, (b) clinical tracking and treatment approaches, and (c) the way the larger community understands a phenomenon of interest, then *how* NSSI recovery is operationalized, understood, and used in research practice and policy matters a lot. Reducing nuanced stories to simple elements for the sake of scientific parsimony means sacrificing a much needed holistic understanding of how individuals move into, though, and out of constricted states of health. As Degenstein (2018) has pointed out in her rich doctoral work on NSSI recovery:

This statement was echoed implicitly and explicitly in the other narratives as well—that

recovery from NSSI wasn't just about stopping the cutting, the burning, the pinching or the banging, and it wasn't just about connection received or being mentally healthy now or in the future – it was about all of these things. It was a sum that was greater than its parts. Recovery from self-harm took time, patience, and an appreciation of things changing in all the wounded and yet to be fulfilled aspects of their lives. It was not merely a choice, but rather a process, a holistic process, and it could not be forced. (p. 127)

This is one of the reasons why current thinking surrounding recovery includes calls for integrating multidimensional measures reflective of both clinical remission and social outcomes (e.g., Lewis et al., 2019). Resnick et al. (2004) proposed that recovery be assessed using both objective measures of behavioral symptoms *and* positive changes in the subjective life domains linked to personal confidence, hope, sense of meaning and purpose in life; taking responsibility for one's life and recovery; willingness to ask for help; and healthy interdependence on others. For instance, Probst et al. (2020) designed a process-based measure to capture internalization of healthy processes of change that develop across therapy sessions in service of strengthening psychological flexibility (e.g., "The last psychotherapy session helped me to accept unpleasant feelings, thoughts, or body sensations rather than fight them.").

4. ***NSSI engagement and agency are critical in recovery processes and need to play a more central role in (understanding and) establishing markers of progress and outcomes.***

   One of the more central elements of all recent discourse related to recovery frameworks and approaches is the demand for greater voice, agency, and active engagement of individuals with lived NSSI experience. This is applicable in both research and clinical domains. It is, perhaps, most readily accessible in the clinical domain where clients can be included in setting personal recovery aims that reflect their own goals and definitions of recovery. As articulated in the RSRC document:

   > Recovery as an intentional process relates to the autonomy of the individual in choosing to engage in the process—that they are an active partner, self-directing the desired outcomes through formal partnership with professionals, peer-driven communities, and fellowships, or through informal, organic networks such as family, friends, and/or faith. (p. 184)

   Such an approach is not entirely novel, it is a core part of collaborative therapeutic processes (see Selekman, this volume), but centering lived-experience perspectives in defining and setting criteria for NSSI recovery remains a fairly rare approach (see Hasking et al., this volume, on lived-experience perspectives). Nevertheless, while better supporting client agency and engagement in establishing recovery targets is reasonably viable in clinical settings, it is more challenging in research endeavors where modular, comparable measures are important in allowing for identifying trends and comparing findings across population and setting. Mandating inclusion of lived-experience perspectives in individual studies, however, has become an increasingly common expectation of funders and will likely engender creative and potent approaches over time.

Beyond Cessation: Conceptualizing and Measuring Recovery as a Process

In addition to the "what constitutes recovery" questions discussed above, there is a problem with the term itself.

Is "Recovery" the Right Concept?

The term "recovery" implies a return to a prior, presumably healthy state of being—a conceptualization that is problematic for several reasons. For example, the Cambridge Dictionary defines recovery as: (a) *the process of becoming well again after an illness or injury*, (b) *the process of becoming successful or normal again after problems*, and (c) *the process of getting something back*. Thus, embedded in the idea of "recovery" is a return to some prior state of assumed health or "normality." While recovery as a construct makes sense when applied to many physical health ailments (e.g., recovering from a cold or flu does mean returning to a prior state of health), relying on it as a marker of health or normalcy in areas intrinsically reflective of psychological functioning is limiting because it completely neglects experience and indelible changes that occur as part of a dynamic set of lived moments that affect perceptions, understanding, and desires. Indeed, as discussed above, individuals with NSSI lived experience (and their loved ones) do not see themselves as returning to a prior state of being but as having taken a journey that unfolds over time and which often leaves them changed in some way—positively, negatively, or often a mix of both (e.g., Whitlock et al., 2018).

In this way, recovery would be better framed as a process and not simply as an endpoint or as a process that "returns" one to a previous state of health. Moving beyond simplistic endpoint ideas of recovery to more multifaceted measures of progress would assist in expanding options for conceptualizing and measuring movement from a place of psychological suffering toward or into a place of sustained integration, psychological spaciousness, and health across multiple life dimensions. Indeed, such an inquiry opens interesting and important considerations of the assumptions that underlie NSSI (and other mental health conditions) recovery. Rather than being so cessation driven, it is likely to be more accurate and helpful to conceptualize what happens in the course of NSSI or other mental health conditions as a "journey" with a number of personalized turning points and challenges to be experienced and, ideally, integrated as enhanced self-awareness and knowledge in personally meaningful ways. What this means for creation of universally applicable markers requires thoughtful consideration, of course, but invites a shift toward meaningful fusion of professional perspectives and uses (e.g., research and clinical indices) and the more qualitative and dynamic insights and experiences that emerge from lived experience.

How Does Existing Research Inform Broadening the Conceptualization of Recovery Milestones?

Despite the narrow way in which NSSI recovery has been operationalized in all studies, there is broad consensus that measuring it as no NSSI activity for some designated period of time, usually 6 to 12 months, is arbitrary and inadequate (Lewis & Hasking, 2021). The need for a fundamentally different framework for considering recovery is the subject of articles by Lewis and Hasking (e.g., Lewis & Hasking, 2020; Lewis & Hasking, 2021). In general, they call for an end to use of "disease-based language" in describing NSSI since it contributes to increased stigma and may have an othering effect by inadvertently placing individuals with lived experience in a group of people with disease.

But what would an extended bench of recovery markers/indices look like? As Whitlock and Lloyd-Richardson (2019) point out in their book for parents of youth who self-injure, the most obvious place to start is to consider what kinds of inner shifts in "psychological architecture" generally take place before behavioral cessation occurs. In creating a checklist for parents to use as they track a youth's progress without fixating on NSSI behavior, they lean on their knowledge of recovery trajectories and, in particular, factors most often associated with movement toward recovery. The tool consists of indices that help parents pay attention to subtle changes in behavior, emotions, cognition, engagement in activities, and relationships.

The general approach advocated by Whitlock and Lloyd-Richardson (2019), nevertheless, is useful. In service to generating a more empirically grounded set of domains that may serve as markers for progress toward recovery goals, table 21.1 presents a broad array of NSSI-recovery focused empirical articles along with factors identified in each article as key turning points or influential factors in the recovery process. Without exception, all studies included in the table identify NSSI cessation for some period of time, as the key recovery marker (or as the factor which differentiates past vs. present self-injury status used as the grouping variable for comparative analysis). Although not meant to be an exhaustive review of all relevant studies or constructs, we hope that it will provide a starting point for considering how researchers and clinicians might begin constructing a more multifaceted bench/set of markers for assessing progress and/or growth over the course of the NSSI journey. Each of these areas offer potential domains for building recovery-related markers that could be used in research and clinically, ideally using client driven/collaborative approaches.

Markers of Progress Toward NSSI Recovery

Table 21.1 provides an overview of factors associated with NSSI cessation, measured in a variety of ways. Referenced studies vary in structure and approach, population, and measures. But, since the goal here is to identify broad domains that facilitate progress toward NSSI recovery (however defined by the authors), it is a useful starting place for thinking about areas in which an array of outcomes may be developed for assessing progress toward NSSI recovery goals.

From table 21.1 we can derive at least seven broad domains for action: (a) NSSI behavior (frequency, severity, multiplicity of form and function), (b) professional support, (c) informal relationships and support, (d) engagement and sense of mastery, (e) self-awareness linked skills (cognition and emotion), (f) coping skills and capacity, and (g) shifts in environmental contexts. Since these are the areas that regularly emerge as influential in moving toward NSSI cessation, they individually and collectively offer areas to assess as markers of progress. A brief summary of each domain follows. Note that, in service to keeping summaries below concise, no citations are included unless referencing material is not available in table 21.1; consult the table for domain correspondent references:

NSSI BEHAVIOR (FREQUENCY, SEVERITY, FORM, URGES, FUNCTION)

While cessation is the most common NSSI behavioral marker of recovery, studies (quantitative studies, in particular) aimed at exploring contributors to cessation find a number

Table 21.1 NSSI Recovery-Focused Articles and Factors Associated With NSSI Recovery (Primarily Defined as NSSI Cessation)

Study	NSSI Recovery (Cessation) Associated With:
Andrews et al. (2013)	• Reduction in NSSI severity (lethality, frequency, and number of methods significantly increased) • Increased capacity for cognitive reappraisal • Reduced emotional suppression
Buser et al. (2014)	• Recognition of serious physical damage • Social influence (perceived disapproval) • Positive social connection • Moving from unhealthy to healthy environments
Claréus et al. (2021)	Identified key turning points that increased: • Sense of agency • Belonging • Freedom from perceived contextual constraints • Heightened perspective taking ability
Degenstein (2018)	• Connectedness to others • Self-love and acceptance • Broadened vision and understanding of self and NSSI • Enhanced coping capacity • Enhanced experience of joy and other positive emotion • Understanding self-injury recovery in the context of the whole person
Deliberto & Nock (2008)	• To reduce unwanted attention from others • To prevent scarring • To reduce shame caused from engaging in NSSI • To enhance relationships with family and friends
Gelinas & Wright (2013)	• Development of positive coping behaviors/decrease in negative coping behaviors • Professional support • Positive social support / relationships • Positive self-talk, self-worth
Halpin & Duffy (2020)	• Being older in age • Having received previous mental health treatment • Using of NSSI to serve interpersonal functions • Reduction in symptoms of depression, stress and anxiety • Greater satisfaction with life • Higher employment rates and educational attainment
Kelada et al. (2018)	• Supportive, understanding and nonjudgmental responses from parents • Positive experiences with mental health professionals
Kiekens et al. (2017)	• Decrease in NSSI frequency • Decrease in number of methods • Less likely to report self-injuring to get a rush or surge of energy or because of an uncontrollable urge • Absence of current psychological distress • Lower academic stress • Emotion regulation capacity

Table 21.1 Continued	
Study	NSSI Recovery (Cessation) Associated With:
Kruzan & Whitlock (2019)	• Informal support • Professional help/therapists • Connection to similar others • Not wanting to let others down • Increased consciousness of social stigma • Opportunity to be role model • Meaningful engagement in life / school / professional work
Meheli et al. (2021)	• Increased sense of agency and control • Increased self-awareness and regard (reduction of negative emotions and inadequacy, increased self-worth and self-compassion) • Increased capacity for self-control/self-efficacy • Enhanced body regard/desire to care for body; making peace with scars • Healthy interpersonal relationships • Moving away from negative contexts • Concern about social stigma • Meaningful life engagement
Mummé et al. (2017)	• Family support • Self-esteem • Emotional regulation • Professional help
Rissanen et al. (2013)	• Meaning of NSSI had changed: they found self-cutting useless and unhelpful and to have no sense at all • Maturation or the personal will to stop self-cutting, may have contributed to this change • Support from significant others in caring relationships and in caring environment that enabled help-seeking • Improvement in one's life situation • Personal will to stop self-cutting and the negative physical sequels of self-cutting
Rotolone & Martin (2012)	• Social connectedness/family support • Self-esteem • Resilience • Satisfaction with life
Shaw (2006)	• Decrease in comorbid conditions that heighten distress • Decrease in contextual factors that trigger NSSI • Increase in positive engagement • Positive therapeutic engagement and support • Decrease in NSSI-linked identification • Experience with and quality of disclosure • Increase in self-awareness, self-efficacy, and agency • Magnitude of desire to change NSSI behavior Positive relationships with others

(continued)

Table 21.1 Continued	
Study	NSSI Recovery (Cessation) Associated With:
Tofthagen et al. (2017)	• Actively choose life • Increased capacity to verbally express inner pain • Increased self-acceptance / reconciliation with life histories • Increased coping capacity • More positive relationships • Positive connections to and experiences with professional mental health providers
Turner, Helps, & Ames (2022)	• Short term increase in alcohol, cannabis and tobacco use followed by gradual reductions in alcohol and tobacco use • Gradual improvement in comorbid depression, anxiety, and externalizing symptoms • Reduction in peer victimization • Greater involvement in work • Receiving needed medical treatment • Greater environmental mastery • Greater self-acceptance
Whitlock et al. (2015)	• Lower NSSI frequency • Lower number of NSSI forms • Number of NSSI functions • Lower scores on current psychological distress • Less likely to identity as "self-injurer" • Presence of therapeutic support • Perceiving social support • Having a sense of meaning in life • Emotion regulation capacity • Life satisfaction • Acknowledgement that NSSI interfered with their lives

of other important behavioral factors, including presence and intensity of NSSI urges and thoughts (Kelada et al., 2018; Lewis & Hasking, 2021). In addition to thoughts and urges, the number of forms used and number of functions served differentiate between individuals who have sustained NSSI cessation and those who have not.

PROFESSIONAL SUPPORT

Working with a mental health professional emerges as a factor discriminating between those who have and have not stopped self-injuring in multiple studies. For many, it is a necessary ingredient in moving toward resolution of underlying challenges and toward development of a healthier life. That said, other than presence/absence of professional support, most extant research is silent on other dimensions that may matter. We know, for example, that many individuals with lived NSSI experience do not ever participate in therapy, find therapy unhelpful, or start and stop therapy (Fortune et al., 2008; Nixon et al., 2008), but the more nuanced relationship of therapy involvement, satisfaction, and the broader role of therapeutic alliance, as they contribute to NSSI recovery is unclear (also see Rockstroh & Kaess, this volume).

INFORMAL RELATIONSHIPS AND SUPPORT

Nearly all studies that explore recovery processes surface the critical role of positive informal support in the recovery process. These typically occur in several ways: (a) a decrease of negative/unhealthy relationships, b) an increase in positive/healthy relationships, (c) enhanced capacity for the individual who self-injures to see and care about the negative impact on others they care about, and (d) feeling cared about and understood rather than judged. Improvement in one or more of these areas is likely to be present in many cases. Informal relationships are most often present in physical life, but judicious use of online communities for support can also be helpful (Kruzan et al., 2022).

ENGAGEMENT AND SENSE OF MASTERY

Changes in investment and engagement in life emerge as important indicators of health, growth, and progress toward NSSI recovery goals. This is usually reported in terms of breadth of involvement in activities (e.g., hobbies, school, and work) as well as in subjective satisfaction, enjoyment, mastery, and/or sense of purpose. Notably, one of the fairly consistent subthemes in this area is the healing that results from having the opportunity to support others on a similar healing trajectory. Including markers of engagement and mastery in indices of progress is likely to be helpful.

ENHANCED SELF-AWARENESS SKILLS

A cornerstone of healing, and a critical element of the psychological architecture that contributes to both NSSI behavior as well as healing is the role of self-awareness. Of all of the domains, this area is the broadest and most nuanced. Indeed, this may be best unpacked into several subdomains, such as cognition (e.g., increased positive thoughts/skew and decreased negative thoughts/skew); emotion (e.g., emotion identification and labeling, adverse emotion tolerance, emotional agility, and reduced negative emotion and increased positive emotion); increased sense of self-love, compassion, and/or worth; enhanced understanding of oneself and meaning attached to NSSI; and enhanced self-efficacy.

One particular area reflective of the diversity in developing self-awareness skills relates to an individual's relationship with their scars (e.g., Lewis & Hasking, 2021). Unlike many mental health conditions, NSSI can produce lasting imprints of its presence on a body. This means that many individuals with lived NSSI experience can and do come to have a relationship with their wounds and scars, which can and does change over time. While understanding natural variation in this relationship and, in particular, what constitutes a healthy relationship with scars is nascent, this domain offers another opportunity for measuring progress toward recovery/healing goals.

ENHANCED COPING CAPACITY AND EFFICACY

Viable alternatives to NSSI when one is triggered or experiencing significant distress is another common theme in the recovery literature. Qualitative studies nearly always surface learning new coping mechanisms as an important component of progress toward recovery goals. Coinciding with this is the role that self-efficacy and self-control play in the healing process (Lewis & Hasking, 2021). Indeed, some research has found that perceived emotional regulation trumps other emotion-related features in the downregulation process (Kiekens et al., 2020). Understanding an individual's self-efficacy and confidence to use alternative coping strategies may further knowledge of how coping and self-efficacy manifest in NSSI recovery (Hasking et al., 2018).

SHIFTS IN ENVIRONMENTAL CONTEXTS

Moving from more stressful to less stressful environments is often cited as a contributor to NSSI recovery and resolution, as well as increased sense of life satisfaction. In some cases, this is actively engineered, and in other cases it is a by-product of natural life changes, such as moving from one school or work setting to another, or the active inclusion of additional social supports. Shifts in the environmental contexts may be particularly useful if they also serve the purpose of supporting healthy processes of change (for instance, volunteering to help others also experiencing challenges may serve to enhance self-awareness skills while also fostering compassion and decreasing social isolation). Items designed to measure decreases in external stress and increases in external conditions that introduce or augment a sense of support or ease are useful elements.

Growth and Healing Stemming from Adversity

Calls for broadening the recovery aperture to include growth come from a variety of areas/sectors (Ashford et al., 2019; Whitlock et al., 2018; Whitlock et al., 2015; Witkiewitz et al., 2020) and are grounded in the science of positive psychology (Seligman & Csikszentmihalyi, 2000). For example, in a study of NSSI cessation and growth, Whitlock et al. (2015) found that 33% of the past self-injury sample perceived at least one benefit to the experience. Notably, the contributors to growth included conversations with others about NSSI experience, having felt a high dependence on NSSI and experience with suicide-behavior, leading the authors to suggest that there may be something about the adversity experience itself, perhaps a result of processing difficult experiences with others, that sets the stage for growth. Their findings support the idea that enhanced self-awareness and social support are primary drivers of the healing and growth process. In a study of the recovery process and secondary stress in families (Whitlock et al., 2018), researchers found that more than half (53.3%) of the parent respondents indicated that their child's experience with NSSI had led to personal psychological growth and another half (51%) indicated that they had witnessed their child grow psychologically as a result of their experience with NSSI, as well. Additionally, a quarter of respondents indicated that their experience had brought them closer as a family and another quarter said they were still in the throes of the experience but expected that it would bring their family closer. Similarly, in a study of agency and psychological growth in youth who have discontinued self-injury in adolescence, researchers find that NSSI discontinuation was accompanied by psychological growth when participants experienced themselves as agentic across multiple domains of life (Claréus et al., 2021).

Summary

The process for developing a bank of usable recovery/healing and growth indices is well beyond the scope of this chapter, but each of the above domains represents areas in which measures of positive progress toward recovery/healing can be developed for research and clinical purposes. There are a number of existing NSSI-specific tools that may already go some distance in providing relevant information relating to stages of change, decisional balance, processes of change, and self-efficacy, such as the three tools developed by Kruzan et al. (2020) based on the TTM stages of change (Prochaska et al., 1992). As an alternative to evidence-based scales, it may be useful, particularly in clinical settings, to offer a simple weekly self-report checklist that individuals with lived experience, parents, or others who support them can complete to broaden their perspective on the process of healing, and to document changes across a range of areas, including NSSI behavior, emotions/mood, thoughts/statements, engagement in activities and social relationships, which can then be discussed in session For example, Whitlock and Lloyd-Richardson (2019) created a checklist for youth and their parents to use in informal assessments of non-NSSI behavior linked change with a number of different areas (NSSI behavior, emotion and mood, thoughts/statements, engagement in activity, and social relationships) in which parents/guardians may note the degree of improvement before seeing clear reduction in self-injury behavior.

Unfortunately, the English language does not include a single word that simultaneously captures both a sense of health after challenge *and* growth/advancement that is a result of our challenges. Although the element of growth is not likely to be a universal component of NSSI experience from onset to some subjective or objective endpoint, adoption of a term or phrase that captures a broader bundle of experience would yield pathways to a more robust, nuanced, and respectfully representative experience. We propose that the term "healing" may be a reasonable alternative to recovery. The Merriam-Webster dictionary defines healing in the following ways: "(1) to make free from injury or disease: to make sound or whole; to make well again, to restore to health; (2) to cause (an undesirable condition) to be overcome; to patch up or correct (a breach or division); (3) to restore to original purity or integrity." These various definitions do not imply restoration to a previous state but nevertheless suggest being able to achieve wholeness and resolution and embrace the notion of growth that is born out of adversity.

While accommodating the idea that psychological adversity can inspire growth, it is crucial to assure that a focus on health, well-being, and growth is not viewed as an essential part of the recovery process, since it may be too high a bar for some and does not take into account differences in the situational and daily contexts of people's lives (Witkiewitz et al., 2020). Assuming that all individuals live in environments that support thriving and well-being is erroneous and may stigmatize or diminish individuals facing sustained disadvantage or discriminatory challenges.

Case Study Consideration: Intervention Planning with Healing Goals

How is recovery/healing best measured? Should measurement needs and approaches vary by contexts (e.g., research vs. clinical)? How are recovery goals and targets set? How flexible can these be to accommodate lived-experience perspectives and desires? While ultimately these questions are setting and case specific, the onus is on researchers and clinicians to both develop and use a more varied, representative, and collaboratively designated set of progress markers. For example, although research relies on psychometrically validated measures that can be compared across study design, population, region, and other research-relevant dimensions, within clinical practice working collaboratively with clients to identify a diverse set of markers that align with healing goals and foci can be a powerful way to (a) set therapeutic goals, (b) enhance client and clinician awareness of the various but personal internal and external factors at play in supporting the onset, maintenance and cessation of NSSI behavior, and (c) regularly assess meaningful healing and growth along a variety of client-relevant dimensions. In the cases of Tanya and Mario, these questions would be applied with the following outcomes:

Tanya

The provider who worked with Tanya through her college counseling office was aware that self-injury can be challenging to fully stop and that urges can be powerful. She started by making sure that she fully understood Tanya's history and, most especially, Tanya's current stress and support landscape. Together they identified what Tanya identified as the early warning signs that stress was becoming overwhelming and reviewed what Tanya knew about some of the areas she needed to focus on to strengthen her resolve not to self-injure when the urge became strong. The therapist guided Tanya through a goal-setting activity in which Tanya identified several areas that she wanted to strengthen over the next few weeks. They decided to start with three areas that Tanya thought were likely to be the easiest to modify:

1. Speaking up when she had something to say, despite feeling concerned about how it would be received.
2. Using art to express the emotional turbulence she was feeling so regularly.
3. Using a process-based functional analysis (e.g., Hofmann et al., 2021) strategy that engaged Tanya in identifying the relevant characteristics of herself,

her thoughts and behaviors, subjective experiences, and the context in which these occur.

This helped Tanya to better understand her relevant strengths and weaknesses, such as her willingness to reach out for professional support; her artistic, creative, and resilient nature; and her close family bonds. Together they created a progress marker chart to help Tanya recognize small but meaningful progress in each area. They agreed to meet weekly for a few sessions to talk about what Tanya was noticing. Tanya felt supported but not hand-held and was able to successfully implement her three goals. In addition to meeting to gauge progress, the therapist helped Tanya to recognize a number of collateral areas of growth and development that she noticed as they worked together. Tanya reported significant reduction of urges, one of her primary therapeutic goals, after a few weeks of focused work together.

Mario

Mario returned to a therapist with whom he had worked after he punched a wall as a means of experiencing pain. He was concerned that he might be backsliding and wanted to figure out how to balance the strong feelings that needed an outlet without hurting himself or others. Considering a broader process of recovery, Mario and his therapist used a process-based functional analysis and the EEMM. Mario and his therapist together mapped out the emotional, cognitive, and contextual challenges working for and against him. Mario knew that a lot of his anger was rooted in interpersonal relationship dynamics that frustrated and confused him. His urges and behaviors were conceptualized as not simply expressions of an underlying disease process but, instead, challenges occurring across a variety of dimensions (e.g., affect, cognition, attention, self, motivation, and overt behavior) and levels (biophysiological, sociocultural) that reflect his strong emotional urges, in adaptive and maladaptive forms. The goal of therapy thus became considering how these dimensions connected with one another and to notice the underlying patterns. Mario also recognized, with therapeutic support, that having a group of other men to talk to about how he was feeling might help him both understand his feelings better and process options for effectively meeting relationship challenges. His therapist helped him to find a group to join. In addition to drawing on support available in the community, they worked together to identify several short-term goals that would help Mario figure out the early signs of growing frustration. They created strategies to help him recognize his emotions and emotional triggers and progress roadmap that Mario could use to track weekly ups and downs and changes. He knew he needed to keep engaging in intense physical workouts, but he also wanted to learn how to do brief meditations so he could work on learning to quiet his mind when needed. His therapist focused their sessions on skills and insights for helping Mario meet his own goals; stopping all self-injury was not a target.

His therapist also kept detailed notes on other areas of growth he noticed as they worked together so Mario could see how his efforts were paying off in multiple ways.

Research Implications

The above review contains several implications for research. One implication leads to a question about whether "recovery" is the right concept for describing the process or "journey" that characterizes so much of the qualitative literature in this area. "Recovery" is a term used to connote a return to a prior state of health, an idea that is not resonant with the reality of lived experiences. Nor does recovery as a concept leave space for the idea of change and growth, both of which feature prominently in lived experience stories.

The second implication for research is related to the need to broaden the scope and menu of measures for assessing healing/recovery processes. One of the major takeaways from all reviews is that using NSSI cessation as the primary measure of "recovery" is sorely inadequate—both because NSSI can be so cyclical and relapse so common and because it fails to encompass other significant features of the phenomenon, such as persistent urges and intrusive NSSI-related thoughts. Beyond the behavioral component, however, it is very clear from review of recovery literature that NSSI develops, progresses, and/or ceases in several larger contexts and that positive change is often visible in a number of areas before NSSI behavior itself has changed. In particular, development of versatile assessments that tap salient dimensions of growth is needed, such as the roles of professional support, informal support and relationship quality, self-awareness (emotion regulation, cognition), engagement and sense of self-mastery, enhanced coping capacity and self-efficacy, and positive shifts in environmental contexts (e.g., moving to a new location and ending a negative relationship). While developing a menu of usable recovery-focused measures may complicate comparison across study, a menu of such measures would offer progress toward broadening endpoints for how we come to represent "recovery."

A primary challenge, as pointed out by Ashford et al. (2019), is to find ways of measuring the dynamic interplay of salient domains over time. They suggest that longitudinal, daily diary, and ecological momentary assessment (EMA) designs are likely to be the most fruitful in capturing the unique and dynamic processes of change (for more information on EMA, see Legg et al., this volume). These designs are currently seldomly used in recovery-focused research, which tends to rely on single timepoint assessments. Clinicians who work with individual clients are intrinsically motivated and well positioned to monitor client progress across a variety of personalized domains over time, but use of abstinence-focused frameworks for marking recovery processes continue to dominate clinical measures of progress. Also, there is evidence to suggest that regular self-assessment of change is helpful in facilitating customized approaches in psychotherapy (Smits et al., 2016).

A final implication for research is the need to increase and improve the lived-experience perspective in recovery-focused research. Incorporating individuals with lived experience in the development, selection, and testing of a more comprehensive set of healing-linked measures offers one meaningful avenue for accomplishing this. Endeavoring to find ways to assess similarities and differences in each person's healing journey, one that includes trials and tribulations, moments of broadened understanding, revelation, and new resilience-enhancing skills, is important especially since there is also variation in how individuals with lived experience perceive recovery (Lewis et al., 2019).

Clinical Implications

Clinically, many practitioners are already using approaches consistent with what we have identified here. Identifying underlying psychological processes, creating short-term meetable goals, assessing contextual risks and supports, leveraging environmental opportunities for enhancing social connection, building new skills, and providing some of the wraparound supports that clients may not have readily accessible are common therapeutic approaches. When it comes to self-injury, however, full cessation remains a common therapeutic goal, even if unstated. This may be at odds with client goals (full cessation may not be a short- or even long-term goal) and capacities. While assessing behavioral NSSI frequency and patterns is likely to be useful and important, clinical focus on cessation as a key or even eventual endpoint, if not in clear alignment with client perceptions of what is desirable and possible, may inadvertently undermine therapeutic effectiveness and alliance. So, the importance of collaboratively setting realistic and achievable goals is paramount when working with individuals who self-injure (see Selekman, this volume). As part of this, it will be important for clinical professionals to clearly signal that they understand that experiencing sustained urges and periodic self-injury incidents are a part of the self-injury journey for many individuals and the goal is not behavioral cessation or elimination of urges but enhanced self-understanding (emotionally, cognitively, contextually), increased coping capacity in areas of interest to the client, and forward-looking plans for navigating anticipated challenges, such as disclosures related to scarring (Lewis, 2016; Lewis & Mehrabkhani, 2016). What "recovery" means, then, should be jointly considered, applied, and modified as needed. Therapeutic focus on strengths and progress in client-defined areas is a core part of this approach.

If the goal is not about arriving at a particular endpoint, such as behavioral cessation, then more focus can be placed on creating narrative coherence, the idea of a "journey" that moves well beyond that of recovery viewed as a return to a presumed prior state of health. Narrative coherence, in which one creates a coherent story of self that engenders self-understanding and, ideally, self-compassion, has been longitudinally shown to increase agency and to improve mental health and well-being in therapy (Adler, 2012). The process of developing coherent life storylines requires understanding of how adversity, setbacks, and even perceived character flaws fit into a larger story of oneself within context and across time. This experience may be particularly useful for individuals who self-injure because they often carry negative, unagentic, and incoherent stories of their past and present (Claréus et al., 2021). Using narrative coherence and life as journey-focused conceptualizations of the healing process are likely to be fruitful and to inspire development of growth-focused orientations.

Finally, one of the clear implications of the work reviewed here is that clinical assessments of progress need to include subjective reflections on progress toward collaboratively defined goals. These can be interview based and/or based on measures such as the Anamnestic Comparative Self-Assessment (ACSA), a self-anchoring rating scale for subjective well-being (SWB) that has been demonstrated to reduce bias in the measurement of SWB in patients suffering from a number of medical conditions (Bernheim et al., 2006).

References

Adler, J. M. (2012). Living into the story: Agency and coherence in a longitudinal study of narrative identity development and mental health over the course of psychotherapy. *Journal of Personality and Social Psychology, 102*(2), 367–389.

American Psychiatric Association. (2013). *Diagnostic and statistical manual of mental disorders* (5th ed.). https://doi.org/10.1176/appi.books.9780890425596

American Psychiatric Association. (2022). *Diagnostic and statistical manual of mental disorders* (5th ed., text rev.). https://doi.org/10.1176/appi.books.9780890425787

American Society of Addiction Medicine. (2013). *Terminology related to addiction, treatment, and recovery.*

Andrews, T., Martin, G., Hasking, P., & Page, A. (2013). Predictors of continuation and cessation of nonsuicidal self-injury. *Journal of Adolescent Health, 53*(1), 40–46. https://doi.org/10.1016/j.jadohealth.2013.01.009

Ashford, R. D., Brown, A., Brown, T., Callis, J., Cleveland, H. H., Eisenhart, E., Groover, H., Hayes, N., Johnston, T., Kimball, T., Manteuffel, B., McDaniel, J., Montgomery, L., Phillips, S., Polacek, M., Statman, M., & Whitney, J. (2019). Defining and operationalizing the phenomena of recovery: A working definition from the recovery science research collaborative. *Addiction Research & Theory, 27*(3), 179–188. https://doi.org/10.1080/16066359.2018.1515352

Badenoch, B., & Cox, P. (2013). We human beings are hardwired to connect with one another throughout life, to seek the most attuned attachments avail. *The Interpersonal Neurobiology of Group Psychotherapy and Group Process, 60*(4), 1.

Bateson, G. (Ed.). (1961). *Perceval's narrative: A patient's account of his psychosis, 1830–1832.* Stanford University Press.

Bergner, (2022, May 17). Doctors gave her antipsychotics. She decided to live with her voices. *The New York Times.* https://www.nytimes.com/2022/05/17/magazine/antipsychotic-medications-mental-health.html

Bernheim, J. L., Theuns, P., Mazaheri, M., Hofmans, J., Fliege, H., & Rose, M. (2006). The potential of anamnestic comparative self-assessment (ACSA) to reduce bias in the measurement of subjective well-being. *Journal of Happiness Studies, 7*(2), 227–250. https://doi.org/10.1007/s10902-005-4755-0

Betty Ford Institute Consensus Panel. (2007). What is recovery? A working definition from the Betty Ford Institute. *Journal of Substance Abuse Treatment, 33*(3), 221–228. https://doi.org/10.1016/j.jsat.2007.06.001

Bronfenbrenner, U., & Morris, P. A. (2006). The bioecological model of human development. In R. M. Lerner (Ed.), Handbook of *child psychology* (pp. 793–828). John Wiley & Sons.

Brown, S. A., Williams, K., & Collins, A. (2007). Past and recent deliberate self-harm: Emotion and coping strategy differences. *Journal of Clinical Psychology, 63*(9), 791–803. https://doi.org/10.1002/jclp.20380

Buser, T. J., Pitchko, A., & Buser, J. K. (2014). Naturalistic recovery from nonsuicidal self-injury: A phenomenological inquiry. *Journal of Counseling & Development, 92*(4), 438–446. https://doi.org/10.1002/j.1556-6676.2014.00170.x

Claréus, B., Lundberg, T., & Daukantaité, D. (2021). "What I couldn't do before, I can do now": Narrations of agentic shifts and psychological growth by young adults reporting discontinuation of self-injury since adolescence. *International Journal of Qualitative Studies on Health and Well-being, 16*(1), Article 1986277. https://doi.org/10.1080/17482631.2021.1986277

Cook, C. C. (2004). Addiction and spirituality. *Addiction, 99*(5), 539–551. https://doi.org/10.1111/j.1360-0443.2004.00715.x

Degenstein, C. (2018). *Young adults' accounts of recovery from youth non-suicidal self-injury: An interpretive phenomenological analysis* [Unpublished doctoral dissertation]. University of Toronto.

Deliberto, T. L., & Nock, M. K. (2008). An exploratory study of correlates, onset, and offset of non-suicidal self-injury. *Archives of Suicide Research*, *12*(3), 219–231. https://doi.org/10.1080/13811110802101096

Drobin, F. (2014). Recovery, spirituality and psychotherapy. *Journal of Religion and Health*, *53*(3), 789–795. https://doi.org/10.1007/s10943-013-9800-4

Fortune, S., Sinclair, J., & Hawton, K. (2008). Help-seeking before and after episodes of self-harm: A descriptive study in school pupils in England. *BMC Public Health*, *8*(369), 1–13. https://doi.org/10.1186/1471-2458-8-369

Fox, K. R., Huang, X., Guzmán, E. M., Funsch, K. M., Cha, C. B., Ribeiro, J. D., & Franklin, J. C. (2020). Interventions for suicide and self-injury: A meta-analysis of randomized controlled trials across nearly 50 years of research. *Psychological Bulletin*, *146*(12), 1117. https://doi.org/10.1037/bul0000305

Gelinas, B. L., & Wright, K. D. (2013). The cessation of deliberate self-harm in a university sample: The reasons, barriers, and strategies involved. *Archives of Suicide Research*, *17*(4), 373–386.

Granfield, R., & Cloud, W. (1999). *Coming clean: Overcoming addiction without treatment*. New York University Press.

Halpin, S. A., & Duffy, N. M. (2020). Predictors of non-suicidal self-injury cessation in adults who self-injured during adolescence. *Journal of Affective Disorders Reports*, *1*, Article 100017. https://doi.org/10.1016/j.jadr.2020.100017

Hasking, P., Boyes, M., & Greves, S. (2018). Self-efficacy and emotionally dysregulated behaviour: An exploratory test of the role of emotion regulatory and behaviour-specific beliefs. *Psychiatry Research*, *270*, 335–340.

Hayes, S., Hofmann, S. & Ciarrochi, J. (2020). A process-based approach to psychological diagnosis and treatment: The conceptual and treatment utility of an extended evolutionary meta model. *Clinical Psychology Review*, *82*, 101908. https://doi.org/10.1016/j.cpr.2020.101908

Hofmann, S. G., Hayes, S. C., & Lorscheid, D. N. (2021). *Learning process-based therapy: A skills training manual for targeting the core processes of psychological change in clinical practice*. New Harbinger.

Kelada, L., Hasking, P., Melvin, G., Whitlock, J., & Baetens, I. (2018). "I do want to stop, at least i think i do": An international comparison of recovery from nonsuicidal self-injury among young people. *Journal of Adolescent Research*, *33*(4), 416–441. https://doi.org/10.1177/0743558416684954

Kelly, J. F., Bergman, B., Hoeppner, B. B., Vilsaint, C., & White, W. L. (2017). Prevalence and pathways of recovery from drug and alcohol problems in the United States population: Implications for practice, research, and policy. *Drug & Alcohol Dependence*, *181*, 162–169. https://doi.org/10.1016/j.drugalcdep.2017.09.028

Kiekens, G., Hasking, P., Bruffaerts, R., Claes, L., Baetens, I., Boyes, M., Mortier, P., Demyttenaere, K., & Whitlock, J. (2017). What predicts ongoing nonsuicidal self-injury?: A comparison between persistent and ceased self-injury in emerging adults. *Journal of Nervous and Mental Disease*, *205*(10), 762–770. https://doi.org/10.1097/NMD.0000000000000726

Kiekens, G., Hasking, P., Nock, M. K., Boyes, M., Kirtley, O., Bruffaerts, R., . . . & Claes, L. (2020). Fluctuations in affective states and self-efficacy to resist non-suicidal self-injury as real-time predictors of non-suicidal self-injurious thoughts and behaviors. *Frontiers in Psychiatry*, *11*, Article 214.

Kruzan, K. P., & Whitlock, J. (2019). Processes of change and non-suicidal self-injury: A qualitative interview study with individuals at various stages of change. *Global Qualitative Nursing Research*, *6*, Article 2333393619852935. https://doi.org/10.1177/2333393619852935

Kruzan, K. P., Whitlock, J., Bazarova, N. N., Bhandari, A., & Chapman, J. (2022). Use of a mobile peer support app among young people with nonsuicidal self-injury: Small-scale randomized controlled trial. *JMIR Formative Research*, *6*(1), Article e26526. https://doi.org/10.2196/26526

Kruzan, K. P., Whitlock. J, & Hasking, P. (2020). Development and initial validation of scales to assess decisional balance (NSSI-DB), processes of change (NSSI-POC), and self-efficacy (NSSI-SE) in a population of young adults engaging in non-suicidal self-injury. *Psychological Assessment*, *32*(7), 635–648. https://doi.org/10.1037/pas0000821

Lewis, S. P. (2016). The overlooked role of self-injury scars: Commentary and suggestions for clinical practice. *The Journal of Nervous and Mental Disease*, *204*(1), 33–35. https://doi.org/10.1097/NMD.0000000000000436

Lewis, S. P., Bryant, L. A., Schaefer, B. M., & Grunberg, P. H. (2017). In their own words: Perspectives on nonsuicidal self-injury disorder among those with lived experience. *The Journal of Nervous and Mental Disease*, *205*(10), 771–779. https://doi.org/10.1097/NMD.0000000000000733

Lewis, S. P., & Hasking, P. A. (2020). Rethinking self-injury recovery: A commentary and conceptual reframing. *British Journal of Psychiatry Bulletin*, *44*(2), 44–46. https://doi.org/10.1192/bjb.2019.51

Lewis, S. P., & Hasking, P. A. (2021). Self-injury recovery: A person-centered framework. *Journal of Clinical Psychology*, *77*(4), 884–895. https://doi.org/10.1002/jclp.23094

Lewis, S. P., Kenny, T. E., Whitfield, K., & Gomez, J. (2019). Understanding self-injury recovery: Views from individuals with lived experience. *Journal of Clinical Psychology*, *75*(12), 2119–2139. https://doi.org/10.1002/jclp.22834

Lewis, S. P., & Mehrabkhani, S. (2016). Every scar tells a story: Insight into people's self-injury scar experiences. *Counselling Psychology Quarterly*, *29*(3), 296–310. https://doi.org/10.1080/09515070.2015.1088431

Meheli, S., Bhola, P., & Murugappan, N. P. (2021). From self-injury to recovery: A qualitative exploration with self-injuring youth in India. *Journal of Psychosocial Rehabilitation and Mental Health*, *8*(2), 147–158.

Merriam-Webster. (n.d.). Heal. Retrieved September 19, 2022, from https://www.merriam-webster.com/dictionary/heal

Mummé, T. A., Mildred, H., & Knight, T. (2017). How do people stop non-suicidal self-injury? A systematic review. *Archives of Suicide Research*, *21*(3), 470–489. https://doi.org/10.1080/13811118.2016.1222319

Nixon, M. K., Cloutier P., & Jansson, S. M. (2008). Nonsuicidal self-harm in youth: A population-based survey. *Canadian Medical Association Journal CMAJ*, *178* (3), 306–312. https://doi.org/10.1503/cmaj.061693

Probst, T., Muhlberger, A., Kuhner, J., Eifert, G. H., Pieh, C., Hackbarth, T. & Mander, J. (2020). Development and initial validation of a brief questionnaire on the patients' view of the in-session realization of the six core components of acceptance and commitment therapy. *Clinical Psychology in Europe*, *2*(3), 1–23. https://doi.org/10.32872/cpe.v2i3.3115

Prochaska, J. O., DiClemente, C. C., & Norcross, J. C. (1992). In search of how people change: Applications to addictive behaviors. *American Psychologist*, *47*(9), 1102–1114. https://doi.org/10.1037/0003-066X.47.9.1102

Resnick, S. G., Rosenheck, R. A. & Lehman, A. F. (2004). An exploratory analysis of correlates of recovery. *Psychiatric Services*, *55*(5), 540–547. https://doi.org/10.1176/appi.ps.55.5.540

Rissanen, M. L., Kylma, J., Hintikka, J., Honkalampi, K., Tolmunen, T., & Laukkanen, E. (2013). Factors helping adolescents to stop self-cutting: Descriptions of 347 adolescents aged 13–18 years. *Journal of Clinical Nursing*, *22*(13–14), 2011–2019. https://doi.org/10.1111/jocn.12077

Rogers, A (2017). Star neuroscientist Tom Insel leaves the google-spawned verily for . . . a startup? Wired [website]. https://www.wired.com/2017/05/star-neuroscientist-tominsel-leaves-google-spawned-verily-startup/

Rotolone, C., & Martin, G. (2012). Giving up self injury: A comparison of everyday social and personal resources in past versus current self-injurers. *Archives of Suicide Research*, *16*(2), 147–158. https://doi.org/10.1080/13811118.2012.667333

Seligman, M. E. & Csikszentmihalyi, M. (2000). Positive psychology: An introduction. *American Psychologist*, *55*(1), 5–14. https://doi.org/10.1037//0003-066x.55.1.5

Shaw, S. N. (2006). Certainty, revision, and ambivalence: A qualitative investigation into women's journeys to stop self-injuring. *Women & Therapy*, *29*(1–2), 153–177.

Smits, D., Stinckens, N., Luyckx, K., & Claes, L. (2016). Early symptom change in adult outpatients: Relationship with patient characteristics and therapeutic alliance. *Psychology and Psychotherapy: Theory, Research and Practice*, *89*(4), 402–417. https://doi.org/10.1111/papt.12086

Substance Abuse and Mental Health Services Administration. (2011). *Results from the 2010 national survey on drug use and health: Summary of national findings*. NSDUH Series H-41 (HHS Publication No. (SMA) 11–4658).

Tofthagen, R., Talseth, A. G., & Fagerstrøm, L. M. (2017). Former patients' experiences of recovery from self-harm as an individual, prolonged learning process: A phenomenological hermeneutical study. *Journal of Advanced Nursing*, *73*(10), 2306–2317. https://doi-org.proxy.library.cornell.edu/10.1111/jan.13295

Turkle, S. (2016). Reclaiming conversation: The power of talk in a digital age. *Perspectives on Science and Christian Faith*, *68*(4), 278.

Turner, B. J., Helps, C. E., & Ames, M. E. (2022). Stop self-injuring, then what? Psychosocial risk associated with initiation and cessation of nonsuicidal self-injury from adolescence to early adulthood. *Journal of Psychopathology and Clinical Science*, *131*(1), 45. https://doi.org/10.1037/abn0000718

Victor, S. E., Lewis, S. P., & Muehlenkamp, J. J. (2022). Psychologists with lived experience of non-suicidal self-injury: Priorities, obstacles, and recommendations for inclusion. *Psychological Services*, *19*(1), 21–28. https://doi.org/10.1037/ser0000510

Wadman, R., Clarke, D., Sayal, K., Vostanis, P., Armstrong, M., Harroe, C., Majumder, P., & Townsend, E. (2017). An interpretative phenomenological analysis of the experience of self-harm repetition and recovery in young adults. *Journal of Health Psychology, 22*(13), 1631–1641. https://doi.org/10.1177/1359105316631405

White, W. L. (2007). Addiction recovery: Its definition and conceptual boundaries. *Journal of Substance Abuse Treatment, 33*(3), 229–241. https://doi.org/10.1016/j.jsat.2007.04.015

Whitlock, J., & Lloyd-Richardson, E. (2019). *Healing self-injury: A compassionate guide for parents and other loved ones.* Oxford University Trade Press.

Whitlock, J., Lloyd-Richardson, E., Fisseha, F., & Bates, T. (2018). Parental secondary stress: The often hidden consequences of non-suicidal self-injury in youth. *Journal of Clinical Psychology, 74*(1), 178–196. https://doi.org/10.1002/jclp.22488

Whitlock, J., Prussien, K., & Pietrusza, C. (2015). Predictors of self-injury cessation and subsequent psychological growth: Results of a probability sample survey of students in eight universities and colleges. *Child and Adolescent Psychiatry and Mental Health, 9*(1), 1–12. https://doi.org/10.1186/s13034-015-0048-5

Whitlock, J. L., & Selekman, M. (2014). Non-suicidal self-injury (NSSI) across the lifespan. In M. Nock (Ed.), *The Oxford handbook of suicide and self-injury.* Oxford Library of Psychology. Oxford University Press.

Witkiewitz, K., Montes, K. S., Schwebel, F. J., & Tucker, J. A. (2020). What is recovery?. *Alcohol Research: Current Reviews, 40*(3). https://doi.org/10.35946/arcr.v40.3.01

CHAPTER 22

The Dynamics and Perception of Pain During Self-Injury

Edward A. Selby *and* Christopher Hughes

> **Abstract**
>
> This chapter looks into the dynamics and perception of pain during nonsuicidal self-injury (NSSI). It cites that the dynamics of pain are essential for understanding the NSSI's etiology and adaptation of treatment. One of the key issues in the field of self-injury research is the presence, nature, and stability of pain experiences during NSSI. Thus, etiological relevance, research relevance, treatment relevance, and public health policy are four primary ways to understand the role of pain during NSSI improves overall NSSI research and treatment. The chapter covers methodological approaches to research the role of pain in NSSI while considering some theoretical motivations for self-injury such as self-punishment motivation and pain analgesia.
>
> **Key Words:** NSSI, etiology, pain, treatment, self-punishment motivation, pain analgesia, public health policy

Does Nonsuicidal Self-Injury Hurt?

On its face, the question of whether nonsuicidal self-injury (NSSI) is physically painful might seem rhetorical, with the average response being, "Of course, it has to be painful!" Yet, as it turns out, the answer is not so simple. In fact, the presence, nature, and stability of pain experiences during NSSI remains one of the central issues in the field of self-injury research today. Variable pain responses during self-injury is also part of what makes NSSI such a paradoxical behavior, in that people are purposely choosing to hurt themselves, when most people prefer to avoid pain.

NSSI has always engendered an enigmatic quality, as in the behavior people purposely inflict physical injury, tissue damage, and/or pain upon themselves. Yet, the very nature of most animals is to prioritize avoiding pain and injury (Sneddon et al., 2014). Therefore, although humans may tolerate or endure low to moderate levels of pain in the service of accomplishing a desired goal, most would prefer to avoid pain, especially high-intensity pain, if at all possible. So why do those who self-injure damage bodily tissue and potentially experience pain in the process? Well, we don't know whether everyone who self-injures feels pain during the injury process, with at least some self-injurers reporting no pain during NSSI (Selby et al., 2019), a phenomenon known as pain analgesia (or sometimes known as anti-nociception). However, for those that do feel pain during NSSI, the question remains as to why they would voluntarily experience physical pain. The purpose of this chapter is to explore the experience and dynamics of pain during NSSI and discuss what the implications of pain experience versus pain analgesia indicate for NSSI in clinical settings. As will be seen, pain experiences in NSSI can be quite diverse and can vary over time—even for the same individual—and understanding the role of pain in NSSI can help us understand the psychological function of this unsettling, paradoxical behavior.

Why Does Understanding Pain Experience and Perception During NSSI Matter?

Before delving into the nuances of pain responses surrounding NSSI, it is important to consider the larger implications of this topic. Those new to the topic of NSSI may wonder, "what does it matter if someone engaging in NSSI feels pain or not during the injury, we just need to stop the behavior!" While helping a patient cease and refrain from NSSI is undoubtedly the goal of clinical practice, we would argue that reaching such a goal will be impeded or delayed by neglecting to understand and address the dynamics and role of pain during NSSI. This is because there are four primary ways in which understanding the role of pain during NSSI improves overall NSSI research and treatment.

Etiological Relevance

Pain experience is an integral part of NSSI behavior, both at the initiation of the behavior as well as the longer-term maintenance of the behavior. Indeed, when lay audiences are confronted with accounts of NSSI behavior, it is not unusual to hear voices of confusion about why people would purposely want to feel pain. This reaction is telling and highlights why most people do not engage in NSSI—most people inherently avoid such behavior precisely because they instinctively do not wish to feel pain. However, this may not be true of self-injuring individuals, who are either not deterred by the pain, purposely seek out pain sensations, or simply don't feel pain during the experience. So pain experiences serve to deter most from NSSI but also play a significant psychological role in the onset and function of NSSI. Likewise, there may be key differences in pain perception and physiology that distinguish self-injuring from noninjuring populations. Only by understanding the experience of pain during NSSI, and pain responses specific to those who self-injure, can we most effectively assess, study, and intervene on NSSI behavior.

Research Relevance

Better comprehending pain during NSSI is also essential for effective clinical research on NSSI. While the topic of pain during NSSI is itself a major research question, we argue that understanding how pain perceptions shape NSSI behavior is necessary to accurately define, assess, and track NSSI across research paradigms. Having a proper conceptualization of NSSI (including the role of pain) influences everything from the research questions asked, to assessment methods (self-report vs. interview), to overall study design (e.g., cross-section, case-control, and naturalistic vs. experimental designs). If incorrect assumptions are made about self-injury (e.g., all who self-injure feel pain, or none feel pain), this can affect the reliability and validity of research findings.

Treatment Relevance
Empirically supported treatments for NSSI continue to remain in preliminary stages, and although several promising approaches have been piloted and tested in smaller-scale designs, there is no current, gold-standard treatment for NSSI. Challenges with treating self-injurious populations are numerous, but when focusing on the topic of pain and NSSI it's plain to see why some treatments may run into challenges. Take, for example, the growing evidence (which will be described in more detail below) that those who self-injure can have very different pain experiences. How does a comprehensive treatment accurately attend to the needs of those who self-injure who report having no physical pain during the experience, while also addressing the functions of self-injury for those specifically self-injuring to feel pain? Although one strategy, such as identifying alternative physical sensations (e.g., holding an ice cube), may work for the latter group, the same strategy may be completely ineffective for the former group that doesn't feel pain during NSSI. Accordingly, a precise understanding of pain experiences and how they can differ is likely to make our treatments techniques more effective when applied under the appropriate context.

Public Health Policy
Finally, understanding pain during NSSI is necessary for implementing public health policies and strategies. By better understanding key risk factors for NSSI (including atypical pain responses), we can create and improve primary and secondary prevention programs. For example, if assessing individual differences in pain perceptions highlights essential differences for those at most risk for NSSI, advanced screening tools can be used across clinical or school settings to identify potential high-risk NSSI cases early on or even before the behavior starts. On the other hand, inclusion of psychoeducation about self-injury and the role of pain experience in youth health education materials may be effective in disseminating crucial information that encourages help-seeking behavior.

Thus, there are several, clear benefits to improving our understanding of pain experience during NSSI. However, as will be seen below, the role of pain experiences during NSSI are actually complex and challenging to study. This is because many self-injury patients have very different pain experiences, and even beyond this, there are a number of methodological challenges that arise as well.

Methodological Approaches to Study the Role of Pain in NSSI

Before delving into the complexities of pain experiences during NSSI, it is important to understand the various methodological approaches that have been used when studying NSSI, and associated challenges and limitations. Only by teasing apart what findings may be a function of research limitations versus actual patient responses can we begin to sort out what people who self-injure are experiencing during NSSI.

Defining Pain

Part of the challenge of studying pain processes is that pain is a highly subjective experience. One individual's experience of discomfort during a situation may be experienced as outright painful by another. For the purposes of this chapter, we define *pain* as the aversive, noxious, or unpleasant internal experience resulting from one's cognitive and affective interpretation of signals received by the central nervous system when sensory receptors in the peripheral nervous system, nociceptors, are stimulated (Kirtley et al., 2016, p. 349). Although this definition of pain is generally comprehensive and inclusive of most forms of painful stimuli, and serves as a conceptual description of how pain is viewed in this chapter, there are alternative ways of defining pain that are more amenable to empirical study and have been used in many studies of NSSI. *Pain threshold*, for example, is operationally defined as the lowest intensity of stimulation that one perceives as painful (Hooley et al., 2010). This definition of pain is helpful for studying pain onset and sensitivity but is less helpful for studying responses to more painful stimuli. *Pain tolerance*, on the other hand, is the greatest intensity or duration of painful stimuli that one is able to endure (Hooley et al., 2010). This definition of pain may be more helpful for understanding severe NSSI behaviors, such as deep cutting, which require someone to experience pain far beyond initial pain onset.

Measuring and Assessing Pain in Self-Injury Research

The bulk of NSSI research has been conducted with retrospective, self-report methods such as completing psychological measures or clinical interviews. However, in more recent years alternative laboratory designs have also been explored, with both self-report methods and laboratory methods having important benefits and limitations.

Cross-Sectional Self-Report and Interview Methods

Self-report and clinical interview methods typically assess self-injuring individuals about the average pain experiences during NSSI in general, whether any pain was felt and if so, what level of pain was experienced (Selby et al., 2019). Self-report measures and interview methods have the benefit of getting direct, clear information and NSSI experiences and pain surrounding NSSI, with semistructured interviews even allowing for follow-up/clarifying questions. Such self-report studies were the first to uncover the surprising finding that whereas many who self-injure do so to purposely feel pain (Osuch et al., 1999), others do not appear to feel pain during NSSI (Russ et al., 1996). However, although retrospective self-report studies are numerous and span decades, and they challenged potential assumptions that those who self-injure feel pain when they do so, these methods are substantially limited by various heuristics and sources of bias (e.g., recall bias, over general memory, limited insight, social desirability, and demand characteristics). Indeed, retrospective self-report assessments of NSSI frequency are inconsistent at times, with self-injury participants reporting substantially different self-injury rates and lifetime frequency at follow-up assessment months apart (Daukantaitė et al., 2020). Self-report methods are also limited in that they reduce self-injury experiences to an "average" experience, and do not allow for variability of pain during NSSI. This is particularly important because pain experiences may differ as a function of self-injury frequency (e.g., cutting once during a session vs. multiple times), method of injury (e.g., cutting vs. pinching), severity of the injury, and location of the injury (e.g., leg vs. arm). It is also possible that pain experience may change over time and the frequency of NSSI (Daukantaitė et al., 2020). Although clinical interviews are likely to improve the general characterization of NSSI pain experiences through more detailed questioning, they are still limited by many of these same considerations. Thus, the challenges of these reporting issues alone make pain during NSSI particularly difficult to study.

A second, related challenge to self-report assessment of pain during NSSI is assessing the very nature of pain in itself. Pain is a notoriously subjective and difficult experience to standardize and study (Reed & Van Nostran, 2014). Although one individual may report an experience as highly painful, another may only list the same experience as moderately or mildly painful. Individuals also differ substantially in their pain onset (the point at which pain is noticed) and their pain threshold (the amount of pain they can endure). Such effects differ by age and gender, with women tending to be more tolerant of pain than men, and pain tolerance increasing as a function of life experiences (e.g., trauma and childbirth). Because of this interpersonal variability in pain responding, those who study pain experiences have worked to include "anchors" for pain assessment (Reed & Van Nostran, 2014), wherein an individual uses a standardized anchor that allows for improved interpersonal comparison of pain experiences, such as having a rater identify a ceiling via labels such as "unbearable pain." Another method to address this variability of pain measurement includes collecting more frequent ratings from participants, which may reduce intrapersonal variability when averaged, as well as the use of person-centered measurement of pain (e.g., an individual's personal mean pain rating), which compares pain reports to an individual's average experience, rather than comparing to the average individual experience (e.g., group mean). Such nuanced approaches to studying pain are particularly amenable to daily diary or experience sampling research, discussed next.

Experience Sample Methods
Because of the challenges with studying pain during NSSI with self-report, in more recent years researchers have begun studying the issue with novel analytic methods such as

experience sample methods (ESM) and experimental methodology. In ESM, participants are repeatedly assessed in their daily lives over the course of one to four weeks, by responding to surveys assessing their NSSI experiences either daily (daily diary) or multiple times per day (ecological momentary assessment). The benefit to this approach is it allows for more accurate assessment of real experiences in a more ecologically valid context, it improves estimation of the frequency of events (like NSSI, which is frequently overestimated in standard self-report measures; Daukantaitė et al., 2020), and variables can be studied in a longitudinal fashion over shorter periods of time (e.g., hours or days). However, ESM is not without its challenges. Even when studying pain during NSSI, it can be difficult to obtain an actual report of pain during the NSSI act. Most studies that have attempted this approach have still been shortly after the NSSI occurred (Selby et al., 2019), making the recordings an improved yet still retrospectively biased result. Other ESM approaches have attempted to collect psychophysiological data during the *actual* occurrence of self-injuries. However, physiological measures of stress during actual self-injury are also limited with regard to assessing pain, as pain is only partially correlated with activation of the sympathetic nervous system (e.g., the part connected to both pain and emotional stress), and this system is frequently emotionally activated surrounding NSSI behavior (Koenig, Rinnewitz, Warth, et al., 2017a). Essentially, there is still no way to objectively measure pain, and all methods involve some degree of subjective assessment. Finally, there are also ethical challenges that arise with ESM research on self-injury, particularly actively monitoring an individual who is engaging in self-injury without intervening if such behaviors may lead to severe injuries or involve simultaneous suicide ideation.

Laboratory-Based Methods

In addition to self-report and ESM methods, in more recent years novel laboratory designs and assessments have emerged to enhance the study of pain responding during NSSI. These laboratory measures can include picture-/image-based designs, computer designs, psychophysiological designs, and somatic sensory designs meant to serve as NSSI proxies during laboratory-based pain inductions. Some of the designs compare self-injuring individuals to those who don't self-injure and compare factors like pain sensitivity, tolerance, and endurance, whereas others are meant to examine pain during actual, imagined, or proxy-based injuries. For example, NSSI studies have frequently examined patient pain threshold and tolerance with pain pressure algometers or tools like the cold pressor (Russ et al., 1992), which submits patients to freezing thermal stimuli to the point that pain is detected. Just like these tasks can be used to measure overall pain perception potential, they can also be used to elicit pain responses during experimental designs. Laboratory-based pain analogues used for studying NSSI can include self-guided imagery, cold pressor task, heat thermode exposure, pressure-based pain algometers, surgical blade insertion, and electric shock (Ammerman et al., 2018). Although there are multiple analogues that have been used, at present there is not yet consensus regarding which pain task is preferable or ideal for studying pain responses in NSSI, and further work in this area is still needed. Finally, a particularly challenging laboratory approach to studying NSSI in recent years has included the actual infliction of injury/pain meant to fully simulate NSSI in the laboratory. For example, Magerl et al. (2012) examined patient responses to actual pinpricks versus intradermal capsaicin injection (capsaicin is the noxious substance found in spicy peppers), while Schloss et al. (2019) made actual incisions on the skin. However, such physically invasive approaches can pose potential ethical challenges to research on pain during NSSI and must be done with high attention to safety precautions.

Developmental Assessment Considerations

The final methodological note with regard to studying pain in NSSI involves developmental considerations. NSSI typically begins in adolescence (Wang et al., 2017), and although many youth mature out of the behavior, for others NSSI can continue well into adulthood. This creates a particular challenge for studying pain in NSSI, as the experience of pain may be different for a youth versus an adult. People in general experience changes in pain perception during their lifetimes (Lautenbacher et al., 2017), and depending on when they enroll in a study, their pain experiences may have changed over a matter of years. Questions about the validity and reliability of some youth self-injury assessments can also arise, making assessment of factors like NSSI frequency and pain perceptions even more challenging than with adult populations. Finally, it is also particularly difficult to study NSSI in youth samples, who may be attempting to hide such behavior from family and friends, potentially complicating research findings or providing ethical challenges to such studies. Likewise, most laboratory-based pain induction research is on adults because of the extra logistical and ethical challenges of having youth participate in potentially painful and/or physically invasive research.

But Why Would Someone Intentionally Cause Themselves Physical Injury or Pain?

Here we briefly discuss theoretical motivations for self-injury that directly pertain to the experience of pain. Of note, other theoretical motivations for self-injury exist, but they will not be discussed here if they do not expressly specify a functional role for pain. However, even if those other theoretical NSSI models do not explicitly address pain as a motivation for NSSI, pain may still be a relevant issue. For example, one of the most commonly cited motivations for self-injury is the "self-punishment" motivation, in which an individual is self-directing anger and frustration onto themselves via the injury (Burke et al., 2021). In such a model, although pain is not the key purpose of the behavior, pain remains a related consequence. Similarly, some NSSI models view pain as either absent from NSSI behavior or completely masked during the behavior (Stanley et al., 2010).

Thus, pain during NSSI can be viewed as a transtheoretical issue with NSSI, and while it may be functional, a secondary consequence, or even absent, pain plays an important role in the NSSI phenomenon.

Regarding the various theoretical approaches to NSSI that specify a key role for pain, we can divide theoretical motivations into three general views: (a) pain is felt and performs a reinforcing function during NSSI (pain onset), (b) pain is felt during NSSI but it is the removal of pain that reinforces NSSI (pain offset), and (c) no pain is actually felt during NSSI (pain analgesia). Although each of these perspectives on pain during NSSI will be covered in more detail subsequently, it is helpful to have a brief orientation to each here to set the context for discussion of the complex role of pain in NSSI.

Pain Onset

The first set of theoretical approaches to NSSI involves "pain onset" viewpoints. This viewpoint involves a number of theoretical approaches to understanding NSSI, primarily with focus on the emotion regulation functions of NSSI (Nock, 2009). According to this view, pain and other experiences associated with NSSI have a functional role in that they help provide potent distraction from other aversive experiences, such as emotional distress or interpersonal rejection. Accordingly, during a distressing experience, a self-injuring individual would turn to NSSI specifically to feel physical pain, with the anticipation that the physical pain would provide relief from the emotional state. Why such relief is provided differs based on the theoretical viewpoint, and the relieving effects may be a function of general distraction (Chapman et al., 2006), cognitive distraction (Selby et al., 2008), or even endogenous opioid release (Stanley et al., 2010). In all viewpoints, the swapping of the aversive emotional stimulus for the more tolerable physical pain leads to negative reinforcement of NSSI behavior.

Pain Offset

The pain offset view of self-injury and pain pertains to a phenomenon related to the pain-onset viewpoint, but instead of focusing on the direct pain that arises from NSSI, the pain-offset approach focuses on the self-injury experience after NSSI ceases and pain reduces (Franklin et al., 2013b). The premise of the pain-offset perspective is that pain is such a naturally aversive experience, that the very removal of pain is itself rewarding or relieving. Franklin and colleagues (2013b) also suggest that there is a neurophysiological coupling between emotional and physical perceptions of pain versus reward that may drive this seemingly counterintuitive mechanism of NSSI. In this way, it may be that when those who self-injure enact an injury, the cessation of the injury may lead to immediate relief from pain, which may subsequently positively reinforce NSSI behaviors. Of note, the pain-offset viewpoint inherently assumes that there is initial pain onset during the NSSI.

Pain Analgesia

The final view is that pain is not actually felt during NSSI, or that it is blocked by biological processes such as release of endogenous endorphins (Stanley et al., 2010). The pain-analgesia view is perhaps one of the most parsimonious resolutions to NSSI's paradoxical phenomenology of hurting oneself to feel better, in that those individuals who engage in NSSI do not actually experience self-injury as painful because of concomitant opioid release. More detail will be provided on the pain-analgesia viewpoint shortly, but for now suffice it to say that NSSI has been described by many individuals with clinically severe behavior as having either reduced pain or being totally absent of pain (Koenig, Rinnewitz, Niederbäumer, et al., 2017b; Nock, 2009; Selby et al., 2019). However, it is important to note that this is not expressly the case for all individuals who self-injure, most of whom report feeling pain at least to some extent during at least some instances of their NSSI behavior.

Thus, there are multiple etiological views on why people might do something as potentially painful as self-injury, and how individuals who engage in NSSI experience pain differently. However, as will be seen, common to each of these etiological theories is that the individual is experiencing emotional distress and/or other pain, from which the NSSI-caused pain serves as a distractor, thereby either positively or negatively reinforcing the behavior.

So, Is NSSI Actually Painful?

At this point we can return our attention to the primary focus of this chapter, exploring published research regarding whether people who self-injure find their self-inflicted injures painful or not. As will be seen, findings are quite mixed, with many reporting pain but others reporting no experience of pain. It is this inconsistency that makes studying self-injury so challenging.

Pain Onset During NSSI

The pain-onset scenario for NSSI explicitly suggests that pain is elicited by self-injurious behavior, potentially as a function of the self-injury method and severity (e.g., more severe methods and behavior may lead to increased pain at the time of the injury). At this point in the literature, the evidence is clear that NSSI is physically painful for at least some if not most of those who self-injure, at least some of the time. However, whether all who self-injure feel physical pain at some point during their experience with the behavior remains unclear, and it is certainly possible that a subset of individuals engaging in self-injury never felt or feel pain during NSSI. There are a number of factors that may separate those who feel pain during NSSI from those who do not, including NSSI frequency and severity as well as possible physiological differences, but these will be discussed in more detail in the subsequent section on pain analgesia.

For many, perhaps most of those with a history of NSSI, at least some NSSI episodes are or were painful. Numerous case studies and cross-sectional, self-report studies make this clear. For example, in one case study, an individual who engaged in self-injury stated: "Right after I hurt myself, I felt physical pain, but my mind and body were much more at ease than before" (Leibenluft et al., 1987, p. 320). Based on this kind of patient description, it is not surprising that in a large sample of adolescents endorsing active self-injury, Laye-Gindhu and Schonert-Reichl (2005) found that 34% self-injured because they "wanted to feel pain" (37% of girls and 23% of boys endorse this item, suggesting possible gender differences as well).

These findings were consistent with ESM investigations of NSSI as well. Selby et al. (2014) found via daily ESM monitoring that 24% of youth in a clinical setting who self-injure reported doing so specifically to feel pain (and 10% of all NSSI behaviors were attributed to this motivation). Even more interesting was that this same study found that regardless of initial NSSI motivation, 31% of the sample felt pain during NSSI. In another study of self-injuring youth who underwent two weeks of ESM and reported on NSSI and pain experiences, Selby et al. (2019) found that when measured at baseline, 62% of participants reported feeling pain during NSSI "often," as opposed to 36% who felt pain only sometimes. With ESM measurement of NSSI, 72% of 442 NSSI behaviors (more than 143 episodes) were rated as resulting in a net increase in pain, relative to before the injury occurred.

Laboratory findings also indicate that pain is felt by a number of individuals who engage in NSSI during the self-injury. In a laboratory-based shock simulation study, Weinberg and Klonsky (2012) found that participants with a history of NSSI who were expected to self-administer varying intensity shocks during an anger induction exhibited intact pain responding during the task. Furthermore, although moderate shocks reduced emotional arousal from the anger induction, if the shocks became too painful any benefits in reduced emotional arousal were lost. These findings suggest that pain is not only likely felt during many self-injury episodes, but that if pain becomes too great, the emotion regulation benefits of self-injury may be diminished, if not lost entirely. In another study, Schloss et al. (2019) implemented an injury/pain experience in the lab, during which participants were compared with regard to their experience with a small incision on the forearm versus a noninvasive seven-second blade application. Again, patients in both the self-injury and control conditions reported the incision as painful relative to the noninvasive blade stimulus, although the self-injury group demonstrated a faster reduction in pain after the incision than did control participants.

Does Pain Continue After Self-Injury Ceases?

Patient experiences of pain during the self-injury event do not necessarily end at the cessation of self-injurious behavior (e.g., the patient stops cutting), and variable pain sensations may continue for quite some time even after the behavior ends. For example, in one clinical case report, the patient described her pain after NSSI as being "intense at first, then mellowed out and lasted long" (Gill et al., 2021, p. 25). The ongoing experience of pain after NSSI is also likely to vary depending on the method utilized and the severity of the self-injury method.

Unfortunately, the high variability and role of pain experiences after NSSI only serves to further complicate the topic of pain during NSSI. However, recognizing the trajectories of pain after NSSI ceases is highly informative. If an individual feels no pain during NSSI, and does not feel any pain from the injury later on, that may provide important information about that individual's physiological pain responses. Alternatively, if an individual feels pain for an extended period after the NSSI ceases, that may change the frequency of NSSI behavior in important ways.

The concept of whether pain perceptions continue after NSSI ends has only been addressed in a few studies. For example, Selby et al. (2019) also found that pain did not cease after the behavior ended. On average, self-injury episodes were rated as having elevated pain after the episode had ended, relative to pain experienced prior to the occurrence of the behavior (a medium effect size d = 0.51). Laboratory findings also indicate long-lasting pain effects from NSSI proxies with self-injuring individuals. Naoum et al. (2016) had patients engage in stress induction tasks, which were then followed by a non-invasive pain stimulus via a blade that lasted for seven seconds. Both healthy controls and the self-injuring group reported feeling similar levels of pain during the task, and even after completion of the task pain ratings remained elevated.

But Why Would Physical Pain Experience During Self-Injury Improve Mood?

Although it is beyond the scope of this chapter to delve into all theoretical models explaining NSSI, it is important here to discuss those models that highlight physical pain as a key function of NSSI behavior. Later, additional etiological models of NSSI will also be addressed, including pain-offset models (Franklin et al., 2013b) and the opioid hypothesis of pain analgesia during NSSI (Stanley et al., 2010).

Emotion Dysregulation Theories of NSSI

Generally, the NSSI literature supports the notion that many who self-injure report engaging in NSSI specifically to reduce feelings of emotional distress (Bentley et al., 2014). Experience sampling data also support this effect, with participants reporting significant decreases in negative emotion immediately following NSSI (Kranzler et al., 2018). As paradoxical as it may seem, physical pain felt during NSSI may be "helpful" to an individual in that it may distract from more aversive emotional and cognitive experiences (Selby et al., 2008), potentially increasing the utility and frequency of the behavior as a coping mechanism.

Although some emotion regulation models of NSSI have suggested that NSSI may provide distraction from upsetting internal experiences and emotions (Chapman et al., 2006; Hasking et al., 2017), one model in particular has focused specifically on the role of physical pain: the Emotional Cascade Model (ECM) proposed by Selby and colleagues (Selby & Joiner, 2013; Selby et al., 2009). The ECM proposes that NSSI is used specifically to distract from self-perpetuating and progressively intensifying cycles of distressing thoughts, rumination, and negative emotion, and that the physical pain elicited by NSSI is a potent physical sensation that allows an individual to short-circuit an emotional cascade, thus eliciting feelings of relief and negatively reinforcing the self-injurious behavior. Importantly, rumination and emotional cascades have been cross-sectionally and prospectively linked to NSSI behavior (Pelta, in press; Selby et al., 2013; Selby & Joiner, 2013; Selby et al., 2021; Tuna & Bozo, 2014). The emotional cascade phenomenon is also consistent with qualitative descriptions of self-injury, such as one patient who reported, "The pain . . . gives my mind a concrete feeling that is logical to focus on, rather than the abstract feelings" (Horne & Csipke, 2009, p. 661). Thus, initial research supports the possibility that pain elicited by NSSI may contribute to the paradoxical effects of the behavior by contributing to distraction from emotional distress.

Although there is still much debate regarding the specific mechanisms through which NSSI reduces negative emotion, there are clearly a large portion of those who self-injure specifically to feel pain (Gee et al., 2020; Nock et al., 2006; Selby et al., 2019). Laboratory findings also support the emotion regulation function of pain during NSSI. One study that enacted thermal pain during a negative emotion induction with self-injuring participants found that greater experiences of pain during the task resulted in greater reductions in negative affect (Bresin & Gordon, 2013). In another study that involved actual laboratory-based tissue damage with a mild incision, Reitz et al. (2015) demonstrated decreased activity in the amygdala in the self-injuring BPD group relative to control participants, who in contrast showed an increase. These findings suggest that the simulated injury was mildly stress inducing for controls, it was stress reducing for those who self-injured.

Self-Punishment Model of NSSI

The self-punishment model of NSSI (Hooley & Franklin, 2018) is, in some ways, an emotion regulation model of NSSI, but it is also unique in that its primary view is that NSSI is engaged in specifically to enact punishment on oneself for various reasons. Although punishment does not explicitly mean pain, pain is often a part of punishment and may be viewed as consistent with punishment of a self-injuring individual. Therefore, pain may be either more tolerable or even viewed as having positive qualities if NSSI is engaged in for self-punishment motivations. This is in line with Hamza et al. (2014), who found that those who identified using self-punishment as a motivation for NSSI also reported diminished pain during NSSI, when compared to those endorsing alternative motivations. Although some studies have examined NSSI for self-punishment motivations using laboratory-induced pain (Schoenleber et al., 2014), most such studies have examined emotional reactions to the pain induction while few studies have examined differential pain perception experiences as a function of self-punishment. Further research is needed to determine if pain is present or absent during NSSI with self-punishment motivations, and whether pain responses during NSSI (present or absent) alter the perceived effectiveness of NSSI for self-punishment.

Regardless of the nuances of various emotion regulation theories of NSSI, a clear takeaway is that pain may serve to help reduce negative emotion during NSSI via potential mechanisms of distraction and/or enactment of self-punishment. However, until now we have primarily focused on the role of initial pain onset during NSSI. There may be additional characteristics of pain during NSSI that arise upon cessation of the behavior, as well as with long-term engagement in NSSI.

Can Pain During Self-Injury Be "Rewarding"?

Although most of this chapter has focused on the aversive aspects of pain experienced during self-injury, there may also be potentially unexpected positive experiences that arise during the self-injury process as well. Such positive experiences may mask or muddle the experience of pain.

Pain-Offset Theory

While we have previously discussed that a large portion of individuals who engage in self-injury feel at least some pain during NSSI, and that pain can linger after the behavior ceases, the experience of pain at the immediate cessation of NSSI may be particularly important to consider. This is because pain may be at the highest intensity right before the injury is finished, and immediately after the painful stimulus is withdrawn there may be experiences of relief simply from the removal of pain. This pain relief vis-à-vis pain removal (i.e., pain offset) may actually be interpreted by the individual as a positive or rewarding experience. In one case study of a young woman who would burn herself, the woman indicated that self-injury was her way of "getting high" and that the onset of self-injury felt "sharp and good" (Gill et al., 2021, p. 25). Through pain offset, self-injury may also produce a hedonic contrast where the positive perception or "rewarding" aspect of NSSI is a function of feeling better relative to a prior aversive reference point (Voichek & Novemsky, 2021). Therefore, in the pain-offset theory of NSSI, it is not the pain itself that has an emotion regulatory effect but rather the subsequent subsiding of the pain (Franklin et al., 2013b).

The average individual reports experiencing relief or pleasantness when a pain stimulus is removed (Leknes, et al., 2008), and that relief from pain can itself be experienced as rewarding (Navratilova et al., 2013). As described earlier, the natural inclination of most animals is to avoid pain for self-preservation purposes (Sneddon et al., 2014). It is interesting, then, that some individuals might come to find pain during NSSI as a rewarding experience. But that is the primary focus of the pain-offset model of NSSI, in that pain is first applied during the active injury phase of NSSI, but upon removal of the painful stimulus a positive or rewarding emotional state arises. According to this model, pain offset is a normative experience, wherein because of the high overlap between physical and emotional pain, the removal of one form of pain offsets or reduces the other. Those who self-injure do not differ from those absent from NSSI history in their experience of this phenomenon but rather in their intentional engagement in physically painful behaviors in order to access this effect. Finally, pain is also more contrast dependent than pleasure (Voichek & Novemsky, 2021), which means that the shift from experiencing pain to the cessation of pain may be more profound at the sensory level as compared to the shift from a neutral feeling to a positive feeling (e.g., taste reward sensation).

Evidence Supporting Pain-Offset Theories
In one of the first examinations of pain-offset theory, Franklin et al. (2013a) found that after painful shocks, self-injuring participants demonstrated simultaneous decreases in physiologically indexed negative affect as well as increases in physiologically indexed positive affect (i.e., relief). Additional experimental psychophysiological evidence with self-injuring participants also supports the notion that positive emotion may increase after NSSI (Franklin et al., 2010), as does experience sampling data demonstrating increases in discrete positive emotions after NSSI (Kranzler et al., 2018). Both findings may potentially be a function of pain offset. Accordingly, there appears to be growing evidence that the removal of the painful stimulus following NSSI results in both a reduction in pain and an increase in associated relief. However, relatively few studies have specifically examined pain offset following NSSI, or investigated whether magnitude of pain offset predicts frequency of NSSI behavior.

Selby et al. (2019) also found some support for the pain-offset model with ESM data, in that most self-injuring youth participants reported a significant reduction in physical pain after NSSI behavior had ended, relative to peak pain reported during the injury. However, the pain-offset effect identified in this study was somewhat small and did not hold when key covariates were included in the model. But also noteworthy is that this study did not examine the degree of pain offset relative to emotional responses reported during NSSI, which is a fundamental component of the pain-offset model.

Other findings relevant to pain-offset theory emerged from the Selby et al. (2019) ESM data as well. After the injury was completed, many indicated that their reported physical pain level remained at a substantially higher level than before the NSSI started (though it was lower than peak pain during the injury). This finding indicates that residual pain may continue to occur after self-injury ends. In consideration of these findings, it remains unclear what degree of physical pain offset is required to obtain the hypothesized emotional negatively reinforcing contrast: is a small-medium reduction from the peak physical pain enough to generate this emotional effect, or is a close to total reduction in physical pain necessary? It is also important to distinguish pain-offset effects from other potential effects. For example, if self-injuring individuals do feel pain during NSSI, is it possible that when pain subsides it is followed by the experience of relief via either pain offset *or* reduction of the preexisting negative emotional state (or both)? Indeed, Franklin et al. (2013b) also suggest that with pain offset there is a neurophysiological coupling between emotional and physical perceptions of pain versus reward, which if true may make it difficult to tease apart which phenomenon drives NSSI behavior more: physical pain offset or negative emotion reduction via pain as a distraction.

Finally, it is important to note that the many functions and theories of NSSI are not necessarily mutually exclusive. It may not be a simple matter of whether a pain-onset viewpoint versus a pain-offset viewpoint is the primary function of NSSI but rather that these motives and functions likely work in unison to motivate and reinforce the complex behavior that is NSSI. Pain-onset and -offset functions likely work in unison, probably contributing to the reinforcing qualities of NSSI and the ongoing challenges of treating NSSI. For example, pain offset in one study of non-self-injuring individuals was found to reduce rumination (Harmon-Jones et al., 2019), which would suggest that perhaps both pain onset and pain offset may play a role in the emotion regulation functions of NSSI.

Pain Analgesia During NSSI

Prior to the early 1990s, the general perspective of clinicians was along the lines of "certainly self-injury must hurt." However, since then researchers have found consistent evidence that many who engage in NSSI report either no or diminished pain during the behavior (Selby et al., 2019). Meta-analytic studies have also found those with a history of NSSI tend to show moderate to large increases in pain threshold and tolerance and lower pain intensity than healthy controls (Koenig et al., 2016). Therefore, questions arise pertaining to whether a preexisting elevated tolerance to pain is what facilitates an individual's willingness to engage in NSSI, or if pain analgesia is a state phenomenon that arises as a function of NSSI behavior.

Pain Analgesia Findings

Some of the earliest studies of pain in NSSI uncovered the possibility that some participants experience a pain analgesia effect. For example, Russ et al. (1992) found that participants that self-injure who reported feeling *no* pain during NSSI also reported lower ratings of pain during a cold pressor task than participants who self-injure who *did* feel pain during NSSI. Additional experimental studies then found evidence for specific psychological and biological characteristics among those who report pain analgesia during self-injury (Bohus et al., 2000). In a small sample of women with borderline personality disorder (BPD), Russ et al. (1996) found that those who do not experience pain during NSSI discriminated poorly between imaginary painful and actual mildly painful situations, and that pain analgesia responses may have been a function of dissociative experiences. Kemperman et al. (1997) used signal detection theory and thermal pain stimuli with self-injuring patients with BPD and found that those who reported no pain during

NSSI discriminated poorly between stimuli of similar intensity that those who did not feel pain during NSSI or did not self-injure. Finally, Glenn et al. (2014) found that enhanced pain tolerance was also present in adolescents with a history of self-injury, who were also found to have a higher pain threshold and greater pain endurance than individuals absent NSSI history.

Laboratory findings are also supported by self-report measurements. Using an adolescent psychiatric sample, cross-sectional self-reported data indicated that 47% of those who self-injured reported experiencing no pain at all during the behavior (Nock et al., 2006). ESM studies also provide real-world evidence for the pain analgesia effect of NSSI. Selby et al. (2014) found that among a clinical sample of youth who reported actively engaging in self-injury, approximately 47% of the sample reported feeling no sensation of any kind during NSSI, and that 77% of all NSSI episodes were characterized as having no sensations. These findings suggest a sizable minority of self-injuring individuals experienced no pain during NSSI, which is consistent with the pain analgesia model of NSSI. In a separate ESM study of self-injuring youth, Selby et al. (2019) similarly found that only 28% of self-injuring youth reported feeling either no pain or even a pain decrease during at least one NSSI episode. However, among those who'd felt no pain during one or more episodes, all but one had reported feeling pain during other NSSI episodes. This finding is particularly important, as the experience of pain analgesia may actually be an intermittent phenomenon, and it likely depends on the method and severity of the injury enacted.

Despite increasing attention in research, the pain analgesia effect of NSSI is still not well understood, and potential etiological explanations for this effect vary. It may be that diminished pain perception in general initially leads to increased risk for developing NSSI behavior, as more recent research indicates that those who self-injure regularly are more likely to exhibit higher pain thresholds and endure pain longer (Bohus et al., 2000; Glenn et al., 2014; Hooley et al., 2010). Alternatively, it is possible that pain perception may change as a function of self-injury, with repeated self-injury leading to habituation to pain over time (Glenn et al., 2014).

Endogenous Opioid Release Hypothesis

One potential explanation for pain analgesia during NSSI is the release of endorphins, endogenous opioids that reduce pain (Bresin & Gordon, 2013). In this model of NSSI, a key component of self-injury is the body's release of natural endorphins in response to the injury, which can cause both pain analgesia as well as secondary euphoric characteristics (Stanley et al., 2010). Accordingly, some self-injuring individuals may feel no pain because the resultant endorphins mask the pain, and even more, the release of endorphins could become the primary purpose of the injurious behavior. It may also be that self-injury is engaged in to remediate preexisting deficits in endogenous opioids, and the injury raises levels in a preferable manner. In support of this hypothesis, Stanley et al. (2010) examined the cerebrospinal fluid of NSSI and non-NSSI adults and found that the NSSI group had significantly lower levels of β-endorphin and met-enkephalin. In a similar study of adolescents, those reporting self-injury found that they exhibited lower pain sensitivity and decreased intravenous β-endorphin levels relative to controls (van der Venne et al., 2021).

Additional support for endogenous opioids in NSSI has been found outside the laboratory. During an ambulatory assessment with adult endorsing active NSSI behavior during which routine samples of salivary β-endorphin levels were assessed before and after NSSI, findings indicated that β-endorphin levels were lower before self-injury, relative to levels measured afterward (Störkel et al., 2021). Furthermore, there were significant associations between the severity of the injury and β-endorphin levels. These findings are essential in supporting the potential role of endogenous opioids in the experience of NSSI, and evidence that they may reduce pain during or after NSSI. However, the study did not find a correlation between subjective pain level and endorphin level, which makes it unclear whether endorphins actually reduced the pain or may play a more complex role in NSSI.

Although the endogenous opioid release function of NSSI seems intuitive, particularly for explaining why pain is absent for many who self-injure, it also faces several scientific challenges. The biggest challenge is that efforts at administering opioid antagonists, such as naloxone and naltrexone, to patients exhibiting self-injury appears to have mixed effects on reducing self-injury behavior (Barrett et al., 1989; Kelty et al., 2018; Roth et al., 1996). Opiate antagonists block the binding of opiate receptors, and if a major function of NSSI pertains to opiate release and potential positive reinforcement of the behavior, the behavior should diminish upon blocking of opiate effects. But this has not yet been shown to be the case. Likewise, there are numerous other behaviors thought to release endogenous opiates, such as smoking (Kishioka et al., 2014) or food consumption (Mathes et al., 2009), making it unclear why self-injury might be preferentially selected over other opioid release alternatives. While few studies have found a reduction of NSSI in response to opiate antagonists, some recent studies have found that opiate antagonists provide other general beneficial effects in patient recovery (Timäus et al., 2021). Clearly, the role of endogenous opioids in NSSI pain-analgesia effects is complex and in need of further study.

Alternative Hypotheses
Although release of endogenous opioids may explain the pain-analgesia effect in NSSI, there are some additional, non-pharmacological hypotheses worth noting. First is the potential for pain analgesia during NSSI to be related to dissociation effects that are known to occur during NSSI (Calati et al., 2017). A subset of self-injuring individuals report that they either dissociate during the NSSI episode, or sometimes they use NSSI as a way of halting a dissociative episode. Although the connection between pain analgesia and dissociation has not received much research attention, it is possible that the diminished perception of pain is affected or driven by dissociative experiences. A second

possible explanation for the pain-analgesia effect is what's known as the "habituation" model, where with extended engagement in NSSI, an individual experiences diminishing levels of pain via habituation to pain stimuli (Glenn et al., 2014; Stacy et al., 2018). This effect is possibly supported by research highlighting that greater frequency of NSSI is correlated with increased pain sensitivity and threshold (Glenn et al., 2014; Koenig et al., 2016). Similarly, starting NSSI at a younger age is predictive of increased NSSI frequency and severity (Muehlenkamp et al., 2018) and patient reports of having to injure more severely due to diminishing effectiveness of NSSI (Taliaferro et al., 2019).

Challenges With the Developmental Dynamics of Pain During Self-Injury
One of the biggest problems with the study of self-injury is that self-injurious behavior is not static, and patients exhibit substantial variability in frequency and severity of behavior when followed over long time frames (Daukantaitė et al., 2020). That means that a self-injuring participant may report different experiences with NSSI and pain at different time points, as well as across developmental stages, given most self-injury starts in adolescence but can carry over into adulthood for many. Likewise, pain perceptions can change over time and with age (Lautenbacher et al., 2017). The primary purpose of this section is to frame the previous findings in a developmental context wherein examining any single episode of NSSI is insufficient for understanding the dynamics of pain in NSSI. Rather, NSSI may have different pain experiences at the start of the behavior that change over time. Pain experience in NSSI is best viewed as ever-changing as a function of NSSI form and frequency, as well as potential emotional considerations driving the behavior.

Pain During Initial Self-Injury Onset
Unfortunately, there is very little empirical research on the initial onset conditions surrounding first experiences with self-injury. Even case studies tend to be with individuals who have been self-injuring for a notable length of time, and those who have only engaged in NSSI between once and a handful of times tend not to be the focus of either case studies or empirical investigations. Issues with sample power also emerge, which, given the difficulty of enrolling actively self-injuring individuals into studies, means that we now have to identify an even lower base-rate group of individuals who are relatively new to self-injury. Yet, understanding what initial experiences with self-injury are like, especially for those who go on to more severe behavior, is particularly important, especially before initial perceptions of the experience are altered by later experiences. As noted, part of the challenge with studying NSSI onset is that the behavior tends to begin in adolescence (Wang et al., 2017), which makes it particularly challenging to study with research parental consent requirements and tendencies for youth to hide NSSI.

The very first NSSI behaviors are most likely to provide the best answer to what pain perceptions exist with the onset of self-injury: Did the first injuries hurt (or not)? How did the individual generate the idea to self-injure? What was the anticipated or desired outcome of the behavior? If we can better answer these questions, then we can better map out the trajectory of NSSI behavior across the lifespan (for those who do not naturally cease NSSI). With more information we may see that self-injury is painful at first, but perhaps pain diminishes over time, age, or self-injury frequency. On the other hand, perhaps some people feel no pain during NSSI from the very start, and it's the absence of pain during the behavior that encourages its use as a coping mechanism. Regardless of how NSSI begins, however, we have a better understanding of some trajectories after NSSI becomes more fully engrained.

Pain Perception as Self-Injury Continues
Another one of the key challenges with studying NSSI is that many who self-injure do so infrequently, and the majority of those who self-injure as adolescents appear to mature out of the behavior during the transition to adulthood. For example, one longitudinal study of Chinese adolescents identified that roughly 87% of the sample could be classified as exhibiting negligible NSSI (74.6%) or experimenting with NSSI (12.8%; Wang et al., 2017). The other 13% of the sample included those with a decreasing trajectory of NSSI over time (10.8%) or having a high fluctuating rate of NSSI (1.9%). These findings indicated that while self-injury rates may be decreasing with age for many, for a subset of individuals endorsing NSSI the rate increases. Although the modal self-injuring individual only engages in the behavior a few times, those who continue to self-injury in the long term tend to exhibit important characteristics. For those individuals which NSSI becomes an ongoing problem, the clinical trajectory tends to be toward more frequent NSSI and more severe NSSI with a rising potential for major physical injury (Buser et al., 2017).

So, what role does pain perception play for those who continue NSSI for long periods of time? Meta-analytic research has found that those who engage in NSSI have been well documented to exhibit higher pain thresholds and tolerance along with decreased pain sensitivity (Koenig et al., 2016). However, in general research on pain trajectories have indicated mixed findings. For example, in one study those endorsing more severe NSSI histories were more likely to report more pain during NSSI (Lloyd-Richardson et al., 2007). On the other hand, length of NSSI history has been found to be inversely related to pain threshold and tolerance (Claes et al., 2006; Hooley et al., 2010), meaning that those with the longest history reported the least pain with the behavior. Self-reported experience of decreased pain during NSSI also predicts increased likelihood of suicidal behavior (Ammerman et al., 2016).

Although there are likely many trajectories of pain and NSSI frequency and severity among individuals with NSSI histories, a couple of major trajectories have been hypothesized. First, is the trajectory associated with those who do not feel pain during NSSI. Generally, this group is known to have increased NSSI frequency and worse long-term outcomes, and these negative outcomes may be precisely because of pain analgesia effects

(Case et al., 2020). Either the absence of pain during NSSI serves to facilitate and drive the behavior to worse outcomes, and in this sense pain provides a protective barrier from NSSI wherein those who feel pain self-injure less precisely because it hurts.

Second, the other major hypothesis with NSSI trajectories is the previously discussed "habituation" model, where when self-injury is engaged in, many participants will develop increased pain tolerance and habituation to pain over time (Glenn et al., 2014; Stacy et al., 2018), combined with the posited emotion regulation effects of pain during NSSI (Selby et al., 2013; Selby et al., 2019), this habituation to pain results in a decreased effectiveness of NSSI, necessitating more frequent and severe NSSI (see Walsh et al., this volume for more on atypical or severe cases of NSSI). Consistent with this suggestion, with ESM data Selby et al. (2019) found that instances of NSSI where less or no pain was felt also included a higher number of injurious behaviors during the episode, and there were even more NSSI behaviors under conditions of high negative emotion during the injury. Although such findings cannot rule out that more injuries were occurring because little pain was felt, the combination of more behaviors during high negative emotion episodes where low pain was felt may suggest the NSSI was less effective, thus requiring more of it to obtain the desired emotion regulatory effects.

Some researchers have suggested these progressively more severe effects of long-term NSSI to be akin to "addiction" to NSSI (Buser et al., 2017), and there is growing evidence to support this conceptualization. For example, Whitlock et al. (2014) developed the Nonsuicidal Self-Injury Assessment Test (NSSI-AT), which includes a "habituation" subscale meant to conceptually model resistance or tolerance of NSSI in a similar fashion as substance use disorders. Interestingly, the habituation scale appears to be strongly correlated with NSSI severity and approximately 33% of respondents endorse experiencing habituation with NSSI (Whitlock et al., 2014; Whitlock et al., 2008). Furthermore, two items from the NSSI-AT scale are called "perceived dependence" to NSSI, and between 25% and 37% of one sample endorsed these items as well, with women endorsing the items significantly more than men (Whitlock et al., 2011). Thus, the conceptualization of NSSI as an addition is intriguing, especially when considering the dynamics of pain during the behavior. However, there are also challenges to conceptualizing NSSI as addiction, including potentially stigmatizing an already stigmatized behavior further and determining whether a potential NSSI addiction arises from emotion regulation effects of NSSI or other biological responses to NSSI (such as opioid release). Relatedly, future research should also work to determine if worsening trajectories of NSSI are a function, or result, of diminished pain perception, which may not necessarily arise as a function of addiction but other habituation processes instead. For example, potential addiction-like qualities of NSSI may instead reflect the diminishing effectiveness of NSSI as a coping behavior over time, potentially as a function of changing pain perceptions and perceived effectiveness of the behavior in relation to coping with a stressful environment (see Blasco-Fontecilla, this volume for further discussion on the addictive nature of NSSI).

Clinical Implications: How Understanding Pain Experiences During Self-Injury Can Improve Treatment

The preceding discussions of pain experiences during NSSI are important not only for understanding the etiology of NSSI but for providing clear, direct relevance to the treatment of NSSI. First, it is important to note that since pain perceptions are so important to understanding the etiology of NSSI, the better we can understand how NSSI develops, the better our treatments are likely to be. Second, at present, most NSSI treatments are concerned with important considerations such as developing healthy emotion regulation and coping skills; however, few current treatments for NSSI address the function or utility of pain during NSSI. Furthermore, few interventions have been explored with regard to differential pain responding during NSSI, and it may be that those who exhibit pain analgesia, for example, are more responsive to one treatment than another. Thus, future studies should examine differential responding to NSSI intervention as a function of NSSI pain perception, and they should also examine pain responding as a potential clinical outcome during treatment, where perhaps we may see pain response (e.g., threshold or tolerance) move closer to the level exhibited by non-self-injuring individuals. But for now, we will clarify where NSSI pain is addressed or modified in current treatments.

Psychotherapy

As mentioned, interventions for NSSI are focused very heavily on the establishment of new coping and emotion regulation skills, and appropriately so (e.g., see Bentley & Jaroszewski, this volume on unified protocol for treatment of NSSI). However, given the potential functional role of pursuing pain (either consciously or subconsciously) as a way of distracting from negative emotions (Selby et al., 2008; Selby et al., 2019), there may be room to improve current treatments by integrating this conceptualization of pain. It may be beneficial, for example, to improve psychoeducation about how pain contributes to self-injury reinforcement via both negative reinforcement (e.g., distraction) and positive reinforcement (e.g., pain offset; Franklin et al., 2013b). A better understanding of NSSI pain effects is likely to empower patients to choose healthy coping strategies instead of NSSI. Likewise, pain has been suggested as a potent distractor of negative emotion (Selby et al., 2008) where other intervention distractors or strategies may be less effective (e.g., NSSI is effective at regulating emotion, whereas alternative healthy skills may not be as effective even if healthy and preferable). This point is essential to helping patients understand that even if pain is effective for coping with distress, it must not be viewed as a reasonable alternative, and the patient and provider should brainstorm several alternative behaviors to NSSI with varying levels of sensory intensity. Finally, in some cases patients may need to identify an effective sequence of coping skills to emulate desired NSSI effects, such as utilizing healthy sensation effects to distract from upsetting thoughts and emotions then followed by self-soothing or relaxing activities to lower stress further.

Pain Substitution Intervention Strategies

The only therapy we are aware of that incorporates alternative sensory experience in lieu of NSSI is dialectical behavior therapy (DBT; Linehan, 2014). DBT includes the "TIPP" skill, which helps patients bring down emotional intensity via *t*emperature, *i*ntense exercise, *p*aced breathing, and *p*aired muscle relaxation. In particular, the temperature part of the skill describes potential activities such as dipping one's face in cold water or placing an ice pack on one's face. Another DBT skill that is meant to provide alternative sensations during emotional distress is the "ACCEPTS" skill, which includes pursuit of intense sensations as a coping skill (e.g., holding ice, squeezing a rubber ball, taking a hot shower, eating spicy food(s), sucking on a lemon, listening to loud music, and sex/self-pleasuring). Little research has examined the relative effectiveness of these sensory substitutions for pain in reducing NSSI urges, but based on the theoretical roles of pain in driving NSSI, additional research seems warranted. In fact, identifying alternative sensations to replace NSSI with during distress may be a key avenue for future intervention research. Finally, although DBT demonstrates effectiveness at reducing NSSI and other suicidal behaviors, DBT is also limited in terms of geographical access, amount of time commitment required for treatment, and a long-prescribed treatment length. Future studies may benefit from identifying more efficient and accessible ways of packaging useful DBT strategies directly to those with NSSI concerns (see more on DBT and NSSI in Chapman et al., this volume).

Future Directions in the Science of Pain During Self-Injury

Based on the preceding discussion, our understanding of pain experiences during NSSI are still far from complete. Further research is needed with laboratory and experimental designs, but also with methods such as ESM and qualitative interviews to address many of the nuanced questions surrounding pain and NSSI. Accordingly, a number of important directives emerge from this chapter to guide future research on pain responding during NSSI.

Qualitative Research

Additional qualitative and idiographic research on NSSI is necessary. In the early days of NSSI research, most approaches were quantitative and led to key hypotheses and more intensive quantitative research on self-injury. However, major questions still exist about the developmental trajectories of NSSI, such as regarding whether all participants feel pain during NSSI or if some have always experienced pain analgesia during the behavior. In the absence of longitudinal studies that follow youth for many years, some of the developmental questions surrounding NSSI will remain elusive in quantitative research designs. Instead, qualitative designs with careful, semistructured interviews may be able to help self-injury patients recall what pain experiences they had with their initial self-injurious behavior and whether those pain experiences changed over time.

Other questions about pain during NSSI may be informed by qualitative designs, such as determining what levels of pain are present, acceptable, or tolerated during NSSI and whether a patient can experience too much pain during NSSI (and if pain levels alter the effectiveness of desired outcome of the injury). Finally, the area of pain in NSSI has high potential for the integration of atypical study designs in which researchers might aim to recruit a large youth sample and follow them for a long enough time frame (e.g., years) to track who goes on to develop NSSI behaviors versus the rest of the sample; the "Pittsburgh Girls Study" is a good example of a similar methodological approach (Keenan et al., 2010).

Dose-Effect Functions of NSSI Pain Severity and Method

Several viewpoints discussed in this chapter have proposed that NSSI serves a specific function (e.g., distraction, pain offset, and opioid release); however it is unclear whether these functions work in a dose-effect manner where a larger dose of self-injury results in a more potent functional outcome, relative to a lower dose of self-injury. For example, pain-onset emotion regulation models (Selby et al., 2009) propose self-injury is enacted to feel pain for distraction purposes, yet what degree of pain is necessary for effect and can there be too much pain? Horne and Csipke (2009) actually have a patient describe the very issue of dose-effect, stating, "a certain level of damage has to be reached before I can feel 'ouch' and re-integrate" (p. 661). Likewise, Koenig, Rinnewitz, Niederbäumer, et al. (2017b) suggest that, "NSSI may be terminated due to a loss of effectiveness once pain tolerance gets too high" (p. 83). Does this mean that either pain or pain offset only have functional benefits at low to moderate levels of pain, versus high levels of pain? Similarly, should the opioid hypothesis predict linear increases in endogenous opioids in response to severe self-injury? Likewise, exploring dose-effect functions of NSSI may be problematic if only linear functions are examined, and instead there may exist exponential or logarithmic relationships between self-injury and expected outcomes (Selby et al., 2016), all of which should be considered and explored. Finally, self-injury method and differential pain outcomes should be explored, as some NSSI methods may inherently be more painful than others, something that no studies to date have examined.

Is Pain Analgesia About Local or Global Maxima in Pain Tolerance?

While research on pain-analgesia effects in NSSI continues to grow, a key question that should be answered is whether the pain-analgesia effect is effectively a local maximum in pain tolerance established by the ethical or practical limitations of a study (e.g., to increase the pain stimulus too high would violate study ethical requirements). It may be that participants would feel pain in a research protocol if a more severe stimulus were to be applied, in which what the field terms "pain analgesia" may really be more of a local pain maximum or ceiling effect than a global maximum effect where literally no pain can be felt. This question is also important to understanding the etiological functions of

NSSI. For example, if the NSSI pain habituation model is accurate, then individual local maximum pain tolerance may progressively increase without becoming a global maximum. Alternatively, pain tolerance may hit an individual global maximum if the behavior is driven by endogenous opioids, the function of which may be so strong that no pain is felt even during the most severe NSSI behaviors. Thus, future research should explore these issues in creative yet ethical ways and potentially through safe but evocative patient imaginary simulations where they would consider NSSI responses to highly variable pain scenarios.

Novel Sensory Interventions

As discussed previously, certain interventions relevant to NSSI (e.g., DBT) include alternative sensory options as replacements for NSSI in emotion regulation (e.g., holding ice and taking a cold shower). Based on this chapter, those techniques should be explored in more detail to determine their actual effectiveness. Also, there may be room to expand NSSI interventions beyond the psychotherapy office by exploring the utility and effectiveness of novel sensory apparatuses that deliver safe but engaging physical sensations as an alternative to NSSI. Potential options could include the use of textured devices, weighted blankets, deep tissue massage, or stretching. Physical activities that involve intense exertion or focus on physical body position and sensations (e.g., yoga) may also serve as sensory alternatives to NSSI.

Conclusion

There is no one singular pain experience during NSSI, with patient samples reporting a variety of mixed experiences that range from feeling pain during NSSI to pain analgesia. Some studies even find alternating pain experiences for the same patient across different NSSI episodes. Yet, understanding the dynamics of pain during NSSI is essential for understanding the etiology of NSSI and adapting treatments to be more effective. While future work should continue to examine the more basic question of what pain experiences occur during NSSI, additional work should be done to examine differential patient histories, developmental processes, and clinical outcomes among those who report differential pain experiences, including work on potential dose-effect associations between NSSI method/severity and pain (or its absence). Novel methodologies such as laboratory-based pain inductions and ESM should be further embraced, and treatment modalities that specifically address pain during NSSI should be explored.

References

Ammerman, B. A., Berman, M. E., & McCloskey, M. S. (2018). Assessing non-suicidal self-injury in the laboratory. *Archives of Suicide Research*, *22*(2), 193–223. https://doi.org/10.1080/13811118.2017.1319312

Ammerman, B. A., Burke, T. A., Alloy, L. B., & McCloskey, M. S. (2016). Subjective pain during NSSI as an active agent in suicide risk. *Psychiatry Research*, *236*, 80–85. https://doi.org/10.1016/j.psychres.2015.12.028

Barrett, R. P., Feinstein, C., & Hole, W. T. (1989). Effects of naloxone and naltrexone on self-injury: A double-blind, placebo-controlled analysis. *American Journal on Mental Retardation*, *93*, 644–651.

Bentley, K. H., Nock, M. K., & Barlow, D. H. (2014). The four-function model of nonsuicidal self-injury key directions for future research. *Clinical Psychological Science, 2*(5), 638–656. https://doi.org/10.1177/2167702613514563

Bohus, M., Limberger, M., Ebner, U., Glocker, F. X., Schwarz, B., Wernz, M., & Lieb, K. (2000). Pain perception during self-reported distress and calmness in patients with borderline personality disorder and self-mutilating behavior. *Psychiatry Research, 95*(3), 251–260. https://doi.org/10.1016/S0165-1781(00)00179-7

Bresin, K., & Gordon, K. H. (2013). Changes in negative affect following pain (vs. nonpainful) stimulation in individuals with and without a history of nonsuicidal self-injury. *Personality Disorders: Theory, Research, and Treatment, 4*(1), 62–66.

Burke, T. A., Fox, K., Kautz, M., Siegel, D. M., Kleiman, E., & Alloy, L. B. (2021). Real-time monitoring of the associations between self-critical and self-punishment cognitions and nonsuicidal self-injury. *Behaviour Research and Therapy, 137*, Article 103775. https://doi.org/10.1016/j.brat.2020.103775

Buser, T. J., Buser, J. K., & Rutt, C. C. (2017). Predictors of unintentionally severe harm during nonsuicidal self-injury. *Journal of Counseling & Development, 95*(1), 14–23. https://doi.org/10.1002/jcad.12113

Calati, R., Bensassi, I., & Courtet, P. (2017). The link between dissociation and both suicide attempts and non-suicidal self-injury: Meta-analyses. *Psychiatry Research, 251*, 103–114. https://doi.org/10.1016/j.psychres.2017.01.035

Case, J. A., Burke, T. A., Siegel, D. M., Piccirillo, M. L., Alloy, L. B., & Olino, T. M. (2020). Functions of nonsuicidal self-injury in late adolescence: A latent class analysis. *Archives of Suicide Research, 24*, S165–S186. https://doi.org/10.1080/13811118.2019.1586607

Chapman, A. L., Gratz, K. L., & Brown, M. Z. (2006). Solving the puzzle of deliberate self-harm: The experiential avoidance model. *Behaviour Research and Therapy, 44*(3), 371–394. https://doi.org/10.1016/j.brat.2005.03.005

Claes, L., Vandereycken, W., & Vertommen, H. (2006). Pain experience related to self-injury in eating disorder patients. *Eating Behaviors, 7*(3), 204–213.

Daukantaitė, D., Lantto, R., Liljedahl, S. I., Helleman, M., & Westling, S. (2020). One-year consistency in lifetime frequency estimates and functions of non-suicidal self-injury in a clinical sample. *Frontiers in Psychiatry, 11*, Article 538. https://doi.org/10.3389/fpsyt.2020.00538

Franklin, J. C., Hessel, E. T., Aaron, R. V., Arthur, M. S., Heilbron, N., & Prinstein, M. J. (2010). The functions of nonsuicidal self-injury: Support for cognitive–affective regulation and opponent processes from a novel psychophysiological paradigm. *Journal of Abnormal Psychology, 119*(4), 850–862.

Franklin, J. C., Lee, K. M., Hanna, E. K., & Prinstein, M. J. (2013a). Feeling worse to feel better pain-offset relief simultaneously stimulates positive affect and reduces negative affect. *Psychological Science, 24*, 521–529. https://doi.org/10.1177/0956797612458805

Franklin, J. C., Puzia, M. E., Lee, K. M., Lee, G. E., Hanna, E. K., Spring, V. L., & Prinstein, M. J. (2013b). The nature of pain offset relief in nonsuicidal self-injury: A laboratory study. *Clinical Psychological Science, 1*, 110–119. https://doi.org/10.1177/2167702612474440

Gee, B. L., Han, J., Benassi, H., & Batterham, P. J. (2020). Suicidal thoughts, suicidal behaviours and self-harm in daily life: A systematic review of ecological momentary assessment studies. *Digital Health, 6*, Article 2055207620963958. https://doi.org/10.1177/2055207620963958

Gill, G., Tran, K., Mitra, S., & Korenis, P. (2021). "I burn myself to get high": A case report on how pain can be an addiction. *Journal of Scientific Innovation in Medicine, 4*(2), 25. https://doi.org/10.29024/jsim.121

Glenn, J. J., Michel, B. D., Franklin, J. C., Hooley, J. M., & Nock, M. K. (2014). Pain analgesia among adolescent self-injurers. *Psychiatry Research, 220*, 921–926. https://doi.org/10.1016/j.psychres.2014.08.016

Hamza, C. A., Willoughby, T., & Armiento, J. (2014). A laboratory examination of pain threshold and tolerance among nonsuicidal self-injurers with and without self-punishing motivations. *Archives of Scientific Psychology, 2*(1), 33–42. https://doi.org/10.1037/arc0000008

Harmon-Jones, C., Hinton, E., Tien, J., Summerell, E., & Bastian, B. (2019). Pain offset reduces rumination in response to evoked anger and sadness. *Journal of Personality and Social Psychology, 117*(6), 1189–1202. https://doi.org/10.1037/pspp0000240

Hasking, P., Whitlock, J., Voon, D., & Rose, A. (2017). A cognitive-emotional model of NSSI: Using emotion regulation and cognitive processes to explain why people self-injure. *Cognition and Emotion, 31*(8), 1543–1556. https://doi.org/10.1080/02699931.2016.1241219

Hooley, J. M., & Franklin, J. C. (2018). Why do people hurt themselves? A new conceptual model of non-suicidal self-injury. *Clinical Psychological Science, 6*(3), 428–451. https://doi.org/10.1177/2167702617745641

Hooley, J. M., Ho, D. T., Slater, J., & Lockshin, A. (2010). Pain perception and nonsuicidal self-injury: A laboratory investigation. *Personality Disorders: Theory, Research, and Treatment, 1*(3), 170–179. https://doi.org/10.1037/a0020106

Horne, O., & Csipke, E. (2009). From feeling too little and too much, to feeling more and less? A nonparadoxical theory of the functions of self-harm. *Qualitative Health Research, 19*(5), 655–667. https://doi.org/10.1177/1049732309334249

Keenan, K., Hipwell, A., Chung, T., Stepp, S., Stouthamer-Loeber, M., Loeber, R., & McTigue, K. (2010). The Pittsburgh Girls Study: Overview and initial findings. *Journal of Clinical Child & Adolescent Psychology, 39*(4), 506–521. https://doi.org/10.1080/15374416.2010.486320

Kelty, E., & Hulse, G. (2018). Self-injuring behavior and mental illness in opioid-dependent patients treated with implant naltrexone, methadone, and buprenorphine in Western Australia. *International Journal of Mental Health and Addiction, 16*(1), 187–198. https://doi.org/10.1007/s11469-017-9856-6

Kemperman, I., Russ, M. J., Clark, W. C., Kakuma, T., Zanine, E., & Harrison, K. (1997). Pain assessment in self-injurious patients with borderline personality disorder using signal detection theory. *Psychiatry Research, 70*, 175–183. https://doi.org/10.1016/S0165-1781(97)00034-6

Kirtley, O. J., O'Carroll, R. E., & O'Connor, R. C. (2016). Pain and self-harm: A systematic review. *Journal of Affective Disorders, 203*, 347–363. https://doi.org/10.1016/j.jad.2016.05.068

Kishioka, S., Kiguchi, N., Kobayashi, Y., & Saika, F. (2014). Nicotine effects and the endogenous opioid system. *Journal of Pharmacological Sciences, 125*(2), 117–124. https://doi.org/10.1254/jphs.14R03CP

Koenig, J., Rinnewitz, L., Warth, M., Hillecke, T. K., Brunner, R., Resch, F., & Kaess, M. (2017a). Psychobiological response to pain in female adolescents with nonsuicidal self-injury. *Journal of Psychiatry & Neuroscience: JPN, 42*(3), 189–199. https://doi.org/10.1503/jpn.160074

Koenig, J., Rinnewitz, L., Niederbäumer, M., Strozyk, T., Parzer, P., Resch, F., & Kaess, M. (2017b). Longitudinal development of pain sensitivity in adolescent non-suicidal self-injury. *Journal of Psychiatric Research, 89*, 81–84. https://doi.org/10.1016/j.jpsychires.2017.02.001

Koenig, J., Thayer, J. F., & Kaess, M. (2016). A meta-analysis on pain sensitivity in self injury. *Psychological Medicine, 46*(8), 1597–1612. https://doi.org/10.1017/S0033291716000301

Kranzler, A., Fehling, K. B., Lindqvist, J., Brillante, J., Yuan, F., Gao, X., Miller, A. L., & Selby, E. A. (2018). An ecological investigation of the emotional context surrounding nonsuicidal self-injurious thoughts and behaviors in adolescents and young adults. *Suicide and Life-Threatening Behavior, 48*(2), 149–159. https://doi.org/10.1111/sltb.12373

Lautenbacher, S., Peters, J. H., Heesen, M., Scheel, J., & Kunz, M. (2017). Age changes in pain perception: A systematic-review and meta-analysis of age effects on pain and tolerance thresholds. *Neuroscience & Biobehavioral Reviews, 75*, 104–113. https://doi.org/10.1016/j.neubiorev.2017.01.039

Laye-Gindhu, A., & Schonert-Reichl, K. A. (2005). Nonsuicidal self-harm among community adolescents: Understanding the "whats" and "whys" of self-harm. *Journal of Youth and Adolescence, 34*, 447–457. https://doi.org/10.1007/s10964-005-7262-z

Leibenluft, E., Gardner, D. L., & Cowdry, R. W. (1987). Special feature the inner experience of the borderline self-mutilator. *Journal of Personality Disorders, 1*, 317–324. https://doi.org/10.1521/pedi.1987.1.4.317

Leknes, S., Brooks, J. C., Wiech, K., & Tracey, I. (2008). Pain relief as an opponent process: A psychophysical investigation. *European Journal of Neuroscience, 28*, 794–801. https://doi.org/10.1111/j.1460-9568.2008.06380.x

Linehan, M. (2014). *DBT skills training manual*. Guilford Press.

Lloyd-Richardson, E. E., Perrine, N., Dierker, L., & Kelley, M. L. (2007). Characteristics and functions of non-suicidal self-injury in a community sample of adolescents. *Psychological Medicine, 37*(8), 1183–1192. https://doi.org/10.1017/S003329170700027X

Magerl, W., Burkart, D., Fernandez, A., Schmidt, L. G., & Treede, R. D. (2012). Persistent antinociception through repeated self-injury in patients with borderline personality disorder. *Pain, 153*(3), 575–584. https://doi.org/10.1016/j.pain.2011.11.021

Mathes, W. F., Brownley, K. A., Mo, X., & Bulik, C. M. (2009). The biology of binge eating. *Appetite, 52*(3), 545–553. https://doi.org/10.1016/j.appet.2009.03.005

Muehlenkamp, J. J., Xhunga, N., & Brausch, A. M. (2018). Self-injury age of onset: A risk factor for NSSI severity and suicidal behavior. *Archives of Suicide Research, 23,* 551–563. https://doi.org/10.1080/13811118.2018.1486252

Naoum, J., Reitz, S., Krause-Utz, A., Kleindienst, N., Willis, F., Kuniss, S., Mancke, F., Treede, R., & Schmahl, C. (2016). The role of seeing blood in non-suicidal self-injury in female patients with borderline personality disorder. *Psychiatry Research, 246,* 676–682. https://doi.org/10.1016/j.psychres.2016.10.066

Navratilova, E., Xie, J. Y., King, T., & Porreca, F. (2013). Evaluation of reward from pain relief. *Annals of the New York Academy of Sciences, 1282,* 1–11. https://doi.org/10.1111/nyas.12095

Nock, M. K. (2009). Why do people hurt themselves? New insights into the nature and functions of self-injury. *Current Directions in Psychological Science, 18*(2), 78–83. https://doi.org/10.1111/j.1467-8721.2009.01613.x

Nock, M. K., Joiner Jr, T. E., Gordon, K. H., Lloyd-Richardson, E., & Prinstein, M. J. (2006). Non-suicidal self-injury among adolescents: Diagnostic correlates and relation to suicide attempts. *Psychiatry Research, 144*(1), 65–72. https://doi.org/10.1016/j.psychres.2006.05.010

Osuch, E. A., Noll, J. G., & Putnam, F. W. (1999). The motivations for self-injury in psychiatric inpatients. *Psychiatry, 62*(4), 334–346. https://doi.org/10.1080/00332747.1999.11024881

Pelta, C. (in press). Emotional cascade model and deep learning. *International Journal of Advanced Computer Science and Applications, 12*(8), 363–367.

Reed, M. D., & Van Nostran, W. (2014). Assessing pain intensity with the visual analog scale: A plea for uniformity. *The Journal of Clinical Pharmacology, 54*(3), 241–244. https://doi.org/10.1002/jcph.250

Reitz, S., Kluetsch, R., Niedtfeld, I., Knorz, T., Lis, S., Paret, C., Kirsch, P., Meyer-Lindenberg, A., Treede, R., Baumgärtner, U., Bohus, M., & Schmahl, C. (2015). Incision and stress regulation in borderline personality disorder: Neurobiological mechanisms of self-injurious behaviour. *The British Journal of Psychiatry, 207*(2), 165–172. https://doi.org/10.1192/bjp.bp.114.153379

Roth, A. S., Ostroff, R. B., & Hoffman, R. E. (1996). Naltrexone as a treatment for repetitive self-injurious behavior: An open-label trial. *The Journal of Clinical Psychiatry, 57,* 233–237.

Russ, M. J., Clark, W. C., Cross, L. W., Kemperman, I., Kakuma, T., & Harrison, K. (1996). Pain and self-injury in borderline patients: Sensory decision theory, coping strategies, and locus of control. *Psychiatry Research, 63*(1), 57–65. https://doi.org/10.1016/0165-1781(96)02808-9

Russ, M. J., Roth, S. D., Lerman, A., Kakuma, T., Harrison, K., Shindledecker, R. D., Hull, J., & Mattis, S. (1992). Pain perception in self-injurious patients with borderline personality disorder. *Biological Psychiatry, 32*(6), 501–511. https://doi.org/10.1016/0006-3223(92)90218-O

Schloss, N., Shabes, P., Kuniss, S., Willis, F., Treede, R. D., Schmahl, C., & Baumgärtner, U. (2019). Differential perception of sharp pain in patients with borderline personality disorder. *European Journal of Pain, 23*(8), 1448–1463. https://doi.org/10.1002/ejp.1411

Schoenleber, M., Berenbaum, H., & Motl, R. (2014). Shame-related functions of and motivations for self-injurious behavior. *Personality Disorders: Theory, Research, and Treatment, 5*(2), 204. https://doi.org/10.1037/per0000035

Selby, E. A., Anestis, M. D., Bender, T. W., & Joiner Jr, T. E. (2009). An exploration of the emotional cascade model in borderline personality disorder. *Journal of Abnormal Psychology, 118*(2), 375–387. https://doi.org/10.1037/a0015711

Selby, E. A., Anestis, M. D., & Joiner, T. E. (2008). Understanding the relationship between emotional and behavioral dysregulation: Emotional cascades. *Behaviour Research and Therapy, 46*(5), 593–611. https://doi.org/10.1016/j.brat.2008.02.002

Selby, E. A., Franklin, J., Carson-Wong, A., & Rizvi, S. L. (2013). Emotional cascades and self-injury: Investigating instability of rumination and negative emotion. *Journal of Clinical Psychology, 69*(12), 1213–1227. https://doi.org/10.1002/jclp.21966

Selby, E. A., & Joiner Jr, T. E. (2013). Emotional cascades as prospective predictors of dysregulated behaviors in borderline personality disorder. *Personality Disorders: Theory, Research, and Treatment, 4*(2), 168–174.

Selby, E. A., Kondratyuk, S., Lindqvist, J., Fehling, K., & Kranzler, A. (2021). Temporal Bayesian Network modeling approach to evaluating the emotional cascade model of borderline personality disorder. *Personality Disorders: Theory, Research, and Treatment, 12*(1), 39–50.

Selby, E. A., Kranzler, A., Lindqvist, J., Fehling, K. B., Brillante, J., Yuan, F., X. Gao, & Miller, A. L. (2019). The dynamics of pain during nonsuicidal self-injury. *Clinical Psychological Science, 7*(2), 302–320. https://doi.org/10.1177/2167702618807147

Selby, E. A., Kranzler, A., Panza, E., & Fehling, K. B. (2016). Bidirectional-compounding effects of rumination and negative emotion in predicting impulsive behavior: Implications for emotional cascades. *Journal of Personality*, *84*(2), 139–153. https://doi.org/10.1111/jopy.12147

Selby, E. A., Nock, M. K., & Kranzler, A. (2014). How does self-injury feel? Examining automatic positive reinforcement in adolescent self-injurers with experience sampling. *Psychiatry Research*, *215*(2), 417–423. https://doi.org/10.1016/j.psychres.2013.12.005

Sneddon, L. U., Elwood, R. W., Adamo, S. A., & Leach, M. C. (2014). Defining and assessing animal pain. *Animal Behaviour*, *97*, 201–212. https://doi.org/10.1016/j.anbehav.2014.09.007

Stacy, S. E., Bandel, S. L., Lear, M. K., & Pepper, C. M. (2018). Before, during, and after self injury: The practice patterns of nonsuicidal self injury. *The Journal of Nervous and Mental Disease*, *206*(7), 522–527. https://doi.org/10.1097/NMD.0000000000000846

Stanley, B., Sher, L., Wilson, S., Ekman, R., Huang, Y. Y., & Mann, J. J. (2010). Non-suicidal self-injurious behavior, endogenous opioids and monoamine neurotransmitters. *Journal of Affective Disorders*, *124*, 134–140. https://doi.org/10.1016/j.jad.2009.10.028

Störkel, L. M., Karabatsiakis, A., Hepp, J., Kolassa, I. T., Schmahl, C., & Niedtfeld, I. (2021). Salivary beta-endorphin in nonsuicidal self-injury: An ambulatory assessment study. *Neuropsychopharmacology*, *46*(7), 1357–1363. https://doi.org/10.1038/s41386-020-00914-2

Taliaferro, L. A., Almeida, J., Aguinaldo, L. D., & McManama O'Brien, K. H. (2019). Function and progression of non-suicidal self-injury and relationship with suicide attempts: A qualitative investigation with an adolescent clinical sample. *Clinical Child Psychology and Psychiatry*, *24*(4), 821–830. https://doi.org/10.1177/1359104519862340

Timäus, C., Meiser, M., Wiltfang, J., Bandelow, B., & Wedekind, D. (2021). Efficacy of naltrexone in borderline personality disorder: A retrospective analysis in inpatients. *Human Psychopharmacology: Clinical and Experimental*, *36*(6), Article e2800. https://doi.org/10.1002/hup.2800

Tuna, E., & Bozo, Ö. (2014). Exploring the link between emotional and behavioral dysregulation: A test of the emotional cascade model. *The Journal of General Psychology*, *141*(1), 1–17. https://doi.org/10.1080/00221309.2013.834289

van der Venne, P., Balint, A., Drews, E., Parzer, P., Resch, F., Koenig, J., & Kaess, M. (2021). Pain sensitivity and plasma beta-endorphin in adolescent non-suicidal self-injury. *Journal of Affective Disorders*, *278*, 199–208. https://doi.org/10.1016/j.jad.2020.09.036

Voichek, G., & Novemsky, N. (2021). Asymmetric hedonic contrast: Pain is more contrast dependent than pleasure. *Psychological Science*, *32*(7), 1038–1046. https://doi.org/10.1177/0956797621991140

Wang, B., You, J., Lin, M. P., Xu, S., & Leung, F. (2017). Developmental trajectories of nonsuicidal self-injury in adolescence and intrapersonal/interpersonal risk factors. *Journal of Research on Adolescence*, *27*(2), 392–406. https://doi.org/10.1111/jora.12273

Weinberg, A., & Klonsky, E. D. (2012). The effects of self-injury on acute negative arousal: A laboratory simulation. *Motivation and Emotion*, *36*(2), 242–254. https://doi.org/10.1007/s11031-011-9233-x

Whitlock, J., Exner-Cortens, D., & Purington, A. (2014). Assessment of nonsuicidal self-injury: Development and initial validation of the Non-Suicidal Self-Injury–Assessment Tool (NSSI-AT). *Psychological Assessment*, *26*(3), 935–946. https://doi.org/10.1037/a0036611

Whitlock, J., Muehlenkamp, J., & Eckenrode, J. (2008). Variation in nonsuicidal self-injury: Identification and features of latent classes in a college population of emerging adults. *Journal of Clinical Child & Adolescent Psychology*, *37*(4), 725–735. https://doi.org/10.1080/15374410802359734

Whitlock, J., Muehlenkamp, J., Purington, A., Eckenrode, J., Barreira, P., Baral Abrams, G., Marchell, T., Kress, V., Girard, K., Calvin, C., & Knox, K. (2011). Nonsuicidal self-injury in a college population: General trends and sex differences. *Journal of American College Health*, *59*(8), 691–698. https://doi.org/10.1080/07448481.2010.529626

CHAPTER 23

The Role of Self and Blood in Ritual and Nonritual Self-Injury

Annette Hornbacher, William Sax, Janina Naoum, *and* Christian Schmahl

Abstract

This chapter covers the role of self and blood in ritual and nonritual self-injury (SI). It considers a socioanthropological perspective to describe and compare ritualized SI in particular cultural settings in South and Southeast Asia with nonritualized SI. Individual agency is vital for both ritual and nonritual SI as it signifies a person's self-control or faith. Generally, the interpretation of ritual SI depends largely on the sociocultural context. Even though SI is mostly regarded negatively in Europe or North America, certain ritual contexts in South and Southeast Asia view SI as examples of heroic devotion and manifestations of divine presence and bliss that miraculously protect the human body.

Key Words: ritual self-injury, nonritual self-injury, sociocultural context, South Asia, Southeast Asia, heroic devotion

Introduction

In this chapter, we describe and compare ritualized self-injury (SI) in South and Southeast Asia, which is usually seen in a positive light, with nonritualized SI in Europe and North America, where it is generally regarded as pathological (Muehlenkamp et al., 2012) even though there are "subcultures," in which it is considered as normative behavior (Bowes et al., 2015; Young et al., 2014). We focus in particular on the meaning and function of cutting and bleeding. Although the ritualized and nonritualized forms look similar at the phenomenological level, there are fundamental differences in motives, agents, and meanings (see Wilson, this volume).

For nonritual SI, the first-person perspective is important (e.g. "I am cutting to feel myself"), since regaining self-control is often a decisive motive for SI. In most forms of ritual SI in South Asia, individual agency is also important. One walks on burning coals, carries red-hot iron objects, pierces oneself with sharp objects, and so on, but is (normally) not injured, thus demonstrating the intensity of one's devotion. To come through the ordeal unharmed, without severe burning or excessive bleeding, is to "prove" the power of divine protection in response to this dramatic demonstration of faith, determination, and stamina. Excessive bleeding, like severe burning or inability to withstand the pain, would mean that the ritual was ineffective, either because of insufficient faith on the devotee's part, or for some other reason, such as impurity.

By contrast, in examples of ritual SI from Indonesia, discussed below, the human self or individual agency is not particularly important: What looks like "self-injury" to an external observer is considered to be the act of an otherwise invisible agent, a spirit, deity, or ancestor that usually dwells in certain places in the environment but enters a human body to articulate wishes, anger or to leave blessings. Such states of possession are sometimes violent—according to the nature and mood of the spirit—but the intention is not to heroically endure emotional or physical pain or bleeding, nor is SI a form of self-control (Belo, 1960). On the contrary, the apparently self-injurious acts are performed by a spiritual being during states of deep trance-possession, and the human subject neither remembers these acts nor ascribes them to themselves. The (often rather violent) behavior is not interpreted and controlled in terms of individual faith but by the ritual community and priests, who communicate with the nonhuman agents that have entered another human body (Belo, 1960; Hornbacher, 2011). Such acts of SI are therefore never performed privately, or in order to release subjective feelings, but only in public settings and highly ritualized frameworks of public care and interpretation, and as manifestation of an otherwise invisible reality for the sake of the community.

The role of (seeing) blood as well as the relation between SI and bleeding is complex: Some but not all ritual forms of SI avoid bleeding at any cost while others emphasize the importance of bleeding as an act of emulation or embodied memorialization or scarification (Christian crucifixion in the Philippines, flagellation in Christianity and Islam, certain ritual battles in Bali). It seems that there is even variation in nonritual SI: while in Europe seeing one's own blood flow leads to an improvement of symptoms, flowing blood seems to be of less importance to female Indonesian university students, for whom nonritual forms of SI that do not involve bleeding (e.g., burning the skin and ripping out the hair) have been reported (Maidah, 2013). In the next section, we will give examples of nonritual and ritual self-injury.

Descriptive Examples of Nonritual and Ritual Self-Injury
AN ADOLESCENT GIRL WITH BORDERLINE PERSONALITY DISORDER FROM GERMANY
An adolescent girl describes how she cuts herself, feeling relief after seeing her blood flow over her arm, and reports,

> Everything is turning around in my head, my thoughts go head over heels. My feelings are so extreme that I am nearly cracking. I have the impression I cannot stand this tension. It is as if I were in trance. When I come to a drugstore, I walk inside without looking left or right. My arm reaches out to get the razor blades. I walk to the counter and pay like a robot. Once I am at home, I close the curtains, listen to my favorite music and lay down on the sofa. I prepare a few compresses and bandages. I take out one of the razor blades and put it down

on my arm and close my eyes. I press on the blade, but it does not hurt. I open my eyes and realize that it was not very deep. This time I cut deeper. When I open my eyes I see the red blood streaming over my skin. While watching the blood I feel myself calming down. Slowly I feel the pain and with it, my head becomes clearer, my thoughts are sorted out again. My tension slowly decreases.

RITUAL SELF-INJURY IN SOUTH ASIA

Austerities are practiced at many religious shrines and festivals in South Asia. Some of these involve heat: firewalking, grasping or carrying heated metal objects, retrieving coins from a pot of boiling oil, and so on. The devotee's faith is thought to please the deity, who prevents him/her from being burned. Elsewhere, people pierce various parts of their bodies with skewers, knives, rods, and hooks, to which ropes are often attached by means of which they pull carts or hang suspended, with little evidence of bleeding or pain. "There is also no bleeding—this is ascribed to the protection of the deity, who is said to control the bleeding and pain in devotees with sufficient *namikkai* (faith) in her/him" (Derges, 2013). Typically, such "mortification of the flesh" is part of a vow, performed either as thanks for blessings received, or in anticipation of blessings to be given after its successful completion. Perhaps the best-known such rituals are associated with the Hindu god Murugan (Skanda), who is particularly venerated by Tamil-speaking Hindus in India, Sri Lanka, Malaysia, Singapore, and Mauritius (Collins, 1997; Krishnan, 2021; Ward, 1984).

In these piercing rituals, the absence of excessive bleeding and the ability to withstand pain is thought to demonstrate both the faith of the devotee and the favor of the deity, who protects him and/or grants him a boon. The absence of blood can be contrasted with Christian practices of flagellation, where bleeding is an integral part of the "imitation of Christ" and usually conceived as an act of penance or the fulfillment of a vow. It also differs from Shia Muslim self-flagellation in memory of the martyrdom of Husain, a practice intended to cause bleeding and which, in recent decades, has come to be ever more frequently banned in the Muslim world (Bräunlein, 2010). Muslim rituals involving cutting and bleeding are also performed by Bawa fakirs of the Rifai Sufi order in Sri Lanka, who enter a state of ecstasy, then slash their heads and faces with knives. This sect is well-known for such practices, which are regarded as forms of spiritual healing (Çizmeci, 2018; McGilvray, 2004). The head and hands are slashed with sharp instruments to show that Allah can disrupt the natural processes of the world: in this case, bleeding. The anthropologist Dennis McGilvray (personal communication) suggests that the local force of such practices may have to do with Tamilians' cultural aversion to blood and bleeding, such that merely uttering the Tamil word for blood (*irattam*) "causes many Tamilians to cringe."

Piercing rituals performed by Tamil Hindus increased dramatically in the north Sri Lankan city of Jaffna during a lull in the country's civil war in the 1970s. Social psychologist Jane Derges (2013) analyzed them as forms of healing, where language was insufficient to express the trauma (often imprisonment and torture) that the actors had experienced, so that they instead used their bodies as media of communication. "The devotees I spoke to," writes Derges (2013), "unanimously dismissed the physical aspect of the ritual and referred instead to their feelings of peace (amaithi) and strength (valimai) and sense of a new beginning—of having undertaken a trial of devotion (or challenge) and emerging transformed and renewed, both within their selves and as members of their community of fellow sufferers" (169). Xygalatas et al. (2019) have also argued that such rituals may provide significant physical and mental health benefits via "two potential mechanisms: . . . a bottom-up process triggered by neurological responses to pain and a top-down process related to increased social support and self-enhancement. These mechanisms may buffer stress-induced pressures and positively affect quality of life" (cf. Jegindø et al., 2013).

VIOLENT AND POTENTIALLY SELF-INJURING ACTS ALSO PART OF MANY RITUALS IN INDONESIA AND OTHER PARTS OF SOUTHEAST ASIA

But whereas public flagellation and piercing among Hindus, Christians, or Muslims in South Asia often demonstrate personal faith and heroic devotion, Indonesian rituals of SI differ in several respects. It is important to note that SI as well as the performative enactment of extreme emotional intensity, including SI, during states of trance-possession represent the opposite of the Javano-Balinese ideal of social harmony and complete control of emotions. Most ritual enactments of SI are performed during states of trance-possession, and considered to be the expression of a deity that has entered a human body rather than of personal agency, devotion or strength (Belo, 1960; Christensen, 2014; Geertz, 1960; Hughes-Freeland, 2008; Rapoport, 2018; Spies & de Zoete, 1938). During possession, divine agents are thought to transfigure a human body, which thereby becomes invulnerable and is temporarily able to endure different forms of trauma without being injured. But while ritual SI and bleeding are sometimes embodied memorializations of a religious salvation history in Christianity, Islam, or Hinduism, this does not apply to Indonesia. On the predominantly Muslim island of Java, rituals involving SI are mostly performed during Islamic transition rituals like circumcision by young men, but they follow a certain script informed by folk traditions rather than Islam: Kuda Lumping or Jathilan dancers are trained performers who are possessed by a horse spirit, or a spirit from the local environs, who is invoked by the ritual master (Pawang), who controls the spirits and thus the performance without ever going into trance himself (Burridge, 1961; Christensen, 2014; Geertz, 1960; Rapoport, 2018). The spirit is summoned into a flat hobby horse made of bamboo, from which it enters the bodies of dancers while the gamelan orchestra is playing. Performances include relatively controlled dance movements as well as wild jumps, acrobatic stunts, ritual fights, screaming, and various forms of SI. Depending on the context, performers are considered to be warriors, animal spirits from the jungle, or horses. They are beaten by a Pawang who directs the scene with his long, thick whip, several meters in length, while the possessed dance and leap and chew and swallow live chickens, coconut husks, and above all large amounts of broken glass or even dozens of razor blades, ostensibly without being hurt during or after the performance. Even though bleeding wounds in the mouth after a performance have been reported, they are ignored both by the performers and the audience. Similar combinations of trance-possession and SI occur on the neighboring island of Bali in the context of Hindu temple rituals. There, too, horse spirit mediums (*sanghyang jaran*) and spirits from the wilderness (tigers, turtles, snakes, and demons) as well as ancestral gods are considered to enter human bodies, and their enactment is usually part of a temple ritual controlled by a local priest. The aspect of SI applies particularly to a ritual drama (*calonarang*) representing a cosmic battle between destructive and benevolent powers and deities who appear in mask costumes and trigger violent forms of possession cum SI both in dancers and parts of the audience (Bandem & De Boer, 1995; Belo, 1949, 1960; Hornbacher, 2011; Spies & de Zoete, 1938). During a performance, actors as well as members of the audiences may be possessed and start acting violently: They—or rather the gods—demand to touch, embrace, and even swallow burning coals and bundles of incense, which from the divine perspective are perceived as a purifying shower. Others demand sharp daggers or knives, which they press forcefully against their chest or eyes without hurting themselves, because the god in their body resists human weapons. In all these cases, the possessed do not feel or remember pain, and there should be no visible wounds. In those rare cases where someone is indeed wounded or starts bleeding, it is taken as a sign the ritual has failed, and the performer may be blamed for being ritually polluted, merely simulating possession, and so on. This is different from what self-injurers from Europe or North America report, where the sight of blood appears necessary for the desired effect of stress reduction or emotion regulation (see below).

On the other hand, there are a small number of ritualized battles in old Balinese villages that do not imply trance-possession but bleeding. These battles involve beating with thorny pandanus leaves or sticks, resulting in pain and wounds, and this is indeed the goal of the ritual.

Apart from such ritual settings, nonritual forms of individual SI (slashing hands and/or wrists, plucking out hair) have been observed more recently among university students and in response to dysfunctional family dynamics and emotional suffering, but while cutting and the plucking out of hair are described as comparable forms of SI, the role of bleeding was not highlighted (Maidah, 2013).

In the following section, we compare the methodological approaches of anthropology and experimental psychopathology.

Methodological Approaches
ANTHROPOLOGY
Much anthropological writing on self-harm and trance-possession analyzes these acts in terms of an external (non-indigenous) theory, which might be symbolic, sociological, or psychoanalytic. Derges's (2013) book on the body as a medium of symbolic communication

is an example. More recently, psychological and psychiatric interpretations of trance-possession and SI have begun referring to such behaviors as "cultural idioms of distress" (Antze, 1992; Hecker et al., 2015; Suryani & Jensen, 1993) or as somehow related to multiple personality disorder (Suryani & Jensen, 1993). The two anthropologists contributing to this article take a different approach, seeking instead to understand actors' motivations and experiences "from the inside" and especially within the conceptual framework of the societies, where different forms of ritual SI are institutionalized and practiced. They do this by asking practitioners what they are doing and why, by observing and reflecting on these practices and discussing their understanding further with practitioners so that, ideally, a collaborative interpretation in terms of local categories is reached, rather than an external explanation in terms of a completely different epistemic framework.

Formal interviews with quantifiable results play a very reduced role in this methodology, experiments are practically impossible during ritual performances, and in any case they would be ethically problematic, since SI is regarded as a sacred act. From an anthropological point of view, quantification is not very helpful in understanding the relation between individual motivation, local theory, and social practices. One tries to conduct qualitative interviews, but they are not always helpful, since actors merely say what they think they are expected to say, or they are unable to articulate their motivations, or have no memory of a performance in which they were, according to local beliefs, literally not present. Answers vary according to numerous factors like shifting mood or one's relationship to the interviewer, and are sometimes inconsistent with actual behavior. When local explanations of ritual SI are available, they may vary from place to place and according to individual interpretations. In fact, this is usually the case when rituals are not prescribed by doctrinal religions with a systematic theology, as they are in Christianity or Islam. For us, it is not important to find a single consistent explanation of SI (and in fact we think that there is none) but rather to show the multiple ways in which it is understood: sometimes as a beneficial manifestation of deities, sometimes as a demonstration of heroic faith, sometimes as a kind of collective healing, but rarely and only recently and from the point of view of outsiders as a pathological act. When we grasp these local understandings, we may well find that they are at odds with typical "Western" assumptions about the body, self-harm, therapeutic efficacy, and so on, so that what we unreflectively assume to be pathological (e.g., various forms of self-injury) turn out to be regarded as beneficial actions. In this respect, it is interesting to note that a recent, multidisciplinary study with a significant biomedical component and published in a prominent scientific journal concluded that "[e]xtreme ritual practices involving pain and suffering" are "associated with subjective health improvements, and these improvements were greater for those who engaged in more intense forms of participation" (Xygalatas et al., 2019). This rather unusual attempt to measure the results of ritual SI and analyze them according to a psychophysiological paradigm tends to "depathologize" them and to confirm important aspects of local understandings, while at the same time facilitating a comparison of them with nonritual SI among psychiatric patients in Europe.

EXPERIMENTAL PSYCHOPATHOLOGY

Even though many patients in the clinical setting emphasize the importance of seeing blood during nonritual self-injury, it is an aspect which has barely been examined. The role of seeing blood was first mentioned in a paper by Favazza and Conterio (1989) in which behavioral, attitudinal, and emotional aspects of nonritual self-injury in a group of 240 female self-injurers was assessed via questionnaire. The role of seeing blood was only assessed marginally in one item; however, 47% stated that it is comforting for them to see their own blood during self-injury, whereas 25% reported that they liked to taste their blood.

Over two decades later, Glenn and Klonsky (2010) published the first empirical study examining the prevalence, function, and clinical correlates of the role of blood during nonritual self-injury. For this study, 64 college students (53 female and 11 male) with a history of skin cutting were interviewed via questionnaire and structured clinical interview. Half of the participants (51.6%) reported that it was important for them to see blood during self-injury. However, 84.8% of the participants reported that seeing blood during self-injury served multiple functions. The most common result of seeing blood during self-injury was tension relief (84.8%), followed by feeling calm (72.7%), feeling real (51.5%), showing that self-injury is real (42.4%), helping to focus (33.3%), and showing that self-injury has been performed correctly (15.2%). The group of participants who stated that blood was important for them, engaged in eight times as much self-injury and used self-injury for a significantly more intrapersonal function, (e.g., affect regulation; see Taylor et al., this volume) as the "blood is not important" group. In any case, no differences were shown in age of onset, gender, ethnicity, number of self-injury methods used, or time since last engaged in self-injury. Participants in the "blood important" group were more likely to fulfill criteria for bulimia nervosa and borderline personality disorder (BPD) according to the fourth edition of *Diagnostic and Statistical Manual for Mental Disorders* (DSM-IV; American Psychiatric Association, 1994).

The first experimental approach to the role of seeing blood during nonritual self-injury was by Naoum et al. (2016). In this pilot study, 20 females with BPD and self-injury in the past six months prior to the study, as well as 20 healthy controls were examined and their level of arousal, pain, urge for self-injury and heart rate were assessed. Participants completed two sessions of stress induction through forced mental arithmetic and white noise, followed by a seven-second noninvasive pain stimulus on the volar forearm. One session only contained the painful stimulus; in the other session, the painful stimulus and artificial blood were combined. The stimulus was followed by a 31.5-minute relaxation phase, in which the parameters arousal, pain, and urge for self-injury were assessed every 3.5 minutes, whereas heart rate was continuously measured.

The results showed a tendency to a faster decrease of arousal early on when artificial blood was added in the patient group. However, the BPD patients showed higher arousal levels toward the end of the experiment in the blood condition, compared to the non-blood condition. These findings lead to the assumption that seeing blood during self-injury has an immediate effect in arousal reduction, which is only temporary and results in higher arousal levels over time. The authors assume that the long-term increase of arousal after seeing blood during self-injury, might be a result of secondary feelings of disgust, guilt, and shame. Also, the decrease in the urge for self-injury was greater when artificial blood was added to the painful stimulus in the patient group.

Three to six seconds after the painful stimulus was applied, a significant acceleration of the heart rate was shown during the blood condition in the BPD patient group; however, no long-term differences in heart rate were shown. This early heart rate acceleration in BPD patients after seeing blood signals a sympathetic activation and might explain why seeing blood is so important for many who self-injure. Preliminary experimental data from our group also point to stronger reduction of stress levels when pain stimulus is applied by oneself rather than by an experimenter.

Indigenous Motives and Explanations and the Role of Blood

The motives and explanations of ritual self-injury are quite consistent with the corresponding practices: throughout South Asia, successful ritual piercing (that is, piercing without excessive bleeding and without permanent harm to the piercer) "proves" the devotion of the piercer and/or the protective benevolence of the God. By contrast, Javanese and Balinese ritual forms of SI during trance possession are not considered to be demonstrations of individual faith, personal heroism, devotion of the believer or expressions of the trancer's religion. Rather, such practices are place-based traditions, considered to manifestat invisible local deities or ancestors who choose whomever they find fitting or "pure." This may be a child or an adult, and in Balinese temples it may even be a Muslim from Java or a Westerner, because trancers are regarded as external mediums or literally "sitting places" (pelinggihan) of local deities, spirits, or ancestors who choose their own mediums, not according to human beliefs but according to their own intentions. Hence, even though trance-possession cum SI occurs in ritual settings of Muslim or Hindu societies in Southeast Asia they are not direct expressions of any particular religion. They are better understood as elements of older pre-Islamic and even pre-Hindu traditions related not to doctrinal belief systems but to practices of communication with the spiritual or ancestral dimension of the reality.

In any case, the performance of SI in such settings is thought of as a form of selfless service (ngayah) to local deities and their human community that does not change the status of the performer. Neither the pain nor the acts of SI are remembered or heroized after the ritual, and this makes it difficult or rather impossible to describe this as SI (*strictu sensu*). Trancers have to ask the audience what the god has done. This may also explain why in many cases there is a floating gap between SI, injuries by ritual leaders (whipping) or mutual injuries (ritual fights): What matters is not the subjective intention or ego of the trancer but the public manifestation of an invisible deity, or the blood sacrifice for the deity. This corresponds to the fact that the trancers are never possessed in their private lives but only in ritual settings. And because such performances are physically exhausting, some performers withdraw from the rituals when they get older. They feel they can no longer "serve" (ngayah) the god and the community.

The role of blood is highly ambivalent. In South Asia and Indonesia, although human blood is inherently impure, various forms of animal sacrifice are said to be "purifying." In Bali, even if trance possession takes violent forms and involves SI, the possessed are not supposed to show wounds or blood. In fact, if somebody starts bleeding excessively, or (even worse) if someone dies (which happens now and then) he or she will be accused of only "faking" the presence of the god, or of not obeying the rules of ritual purity. Bleeding in particular is regarded as a failure of authentic possession for which the performer can be slapped during the performance because if he would be transfigured into a god, he would be invulnerable. It is worth noting in this respect that human blood is regarded as a highly ambiguous essence. Whereas Balinese spill the blood of sacrificial animals for the ambivalent gods of the earth and wilderness (which explains why some of the possessed devour live animals when such a deity has entered them), by the same token their bodies have become invulnerable (i.e., human bleeding is strictly taboo). Moreover, human blood is not only a vital essence but also associated with transitional states of birth and death which are considered to be extremely polluting. That is why temples are strictly taboo for menstruating women or anybody with a bleeding wound.

Significantly different from this general rule are the few rituals in remote villages at the eastern end of the island, which have hardly been influenced by the Hindu-Javanese court culture of the classical kingdom of Majapahit that shifted the center of its political and cultural power to Bali during the 14th century. The *Bali aga* or "original Balinese" villages in East Bali have preserved different and more East-Austronesian traditions where blood is essential and, indeed, the apex of a ritual battle. In one case, young men beat each other once a year with thorny pandanut leaves until they bleed. In another case, near the end of the dry season, men beat each other with hard sticks until they bleed. In both cases, human blood is regarded as the essential sacrifice to the local gods. It is closely related to rain in the very dry environment of East Bali, or to the worship of Indra, the god of war.

Finally, there are recent reports about SI among Indonesian urban college girls, which emphasize the connection between self-harm and emotional relief, but this does not seem to depend on blood alone because SI involves the cutting of wrists as well as burning and the plucking of hair.

Similarities and Differences between Ritual and Nonritual SI

From a phenomenological point of view, there are some obvious similarities between these two forms of SI: Both include a voluntary destruction of body tissue (e.g., by cutting into or through the skin). Subjective reports of stress relief by European or North American patients resemble reports by South Indians and Sri Lankans that the piercing rituals induce a sense of "peace" and "strength." However, in the former case, seeing one's own blood flow is an important and empirically proven aspect of the effectiveness of SI for stress and emotion regulation (Glenn & Klonsky, 2010; Naoum et al., 2016) while in the latter cases, the positive effects are associated with reduced or nearly absent bleeding. SI is mostly regarded negatively in Europe or North America but positively in certain ritual contexts in South and Southeast Asia, where they are seen as examples of heroic devotion and/or manifestations of divine presence and bliss that "miraculously" protect the human body from harm, pain, and the destruction of body tissue. Derges (2013) argued that a temporary, dramatic increase in piercing rituals in the 1970s was a therapeutic response to a pathological context (civil war and the use of torture by the opposed factions); however, neither she nor her subjects regarded piercing as pathological per se. Recent examples of individual SI among young Indonesian university students who find emotional release in different forms of SI can be regarded as pathological because they express the emotional suffering and because it only takes place in the private life of an individual. While these forms of SI in Indonesia are responses to feelings of depression and anxiety, psychological studies do not report the importance of seeing blood but rather its communicative dimension: Maidah (2013), for example, describes a case where the blood is used to write the sentence "I hate my life," similar to what can be found in European or North American psychiatric contexts.

In nearly all cases of ritual SI discussed above, bleeding is regarded negatively, because to bleed would indicate insufficient faith, or suggest that the embodiment of a god is nothing but a subjective pretension or that it has failed due to the pollution of sacred spaces. In the Hindu cases of Sri Lanka and in the Javanese as well as Balinese cases where SI is embedded in trance-possession, bleeding is associated with ritual failure. But in Christian and Muslim ritual SI, blood must flow as a sign of emulation and identification, and blood is also crucial for old-Balinese rituals but for a different reason: human blood is the paradigmatic sacrificial gift for fierce deities.

When SI is part of trance-possession rituals, as in Java and Bali, the human self or subject is not considered to be in any way involved in acts of self-harm. Rather the human self is said to have left the body, which is temporarily inhabited by another being that can be a deity, a demon or an ancestor. If human mediums don't attend rituals, they don't get possessed, and several tests by Dutch and American psychiatrists during the 1930s found that in their everyday life trancers were not significantly different from other people, which suggests that the SI is not performed for the sake of the individual but rather as a service for the gods and the community (Belo, 1960; van Wulfften Palthe, 1940) In Sri Lanka, too, the rituals discussed are public, and the support of the temple community or the ritual masters and priests is an integral part of them. SI as well as trance-possession is often part of public rituals but doesn't happen privately—with the important exception of modern urban contexts, where SI among girls has become an issue in recent years. This stands in contrast to nonritual SI in Europe or North America, which is mostly done alone and considered a private and subjective act. However, SI is often not only reinforced intrapersonally but also on an interpersonal level (e.g., by changing relationships or other peoples' behavior) (Hepp et al., 2020).

In South Asian rituals, piercing and other forms of ritual self-injury are overwhelmingly male activities, and the same applies to Balinese ritual battles that involve bleeding. In Sri Lanka, women or children rarely engage in piercing, and when they do so, it is with very small skewers. More often, they play important supporting roles. But such gender patterns do not apply to SI in Indonesian trance-possession rituals. In Bali, there is no significant difference between men and women regarding SI during states of trance-possession; indeed, it seems that women are even more active in this field. And whereas Javanese Jathilan was mainly performed by young boys and men in recent years, young girls also participate, and they too perform SI during trance-possession. But there are two exceptions to this rule: Balinese ritual battles involving bleeding are performed only by young men. On the other hand, reports about the more recent nonritual forms of SI among university students are only referring to young women using SI as an outlet for feelings of depression, despair, and helplessness. This resembles findings for nonritual SI, where prevalence in females is higher than in males (Bresin & Schoenleber, 2015).

While nonritual SI is intended to reduce aversive states or trance-like dissociative states (Kleindienst et al., 2008), ritual SI in the Indonesian examples is performed in a state of trance-possession and is often regarded as proof for the temporary manifestation of divine presence or supernatural power in human shape. Trance media are therefore called "kulit" or "skin" or "pelinggihan" or "sitting place." And whereas it has been argued that for a brief period in the 1970s, certain piercing rituals in the northern part of Sri Lanka had a therapeutic effect for the entire society, they are usually regarded not as therapeutic responses to illness, but rather as techniques for bringing about health and well-being for individual persons and their societies, by attracting the blessings of God or the gods. Other forms of SI during trance possession are not necessarily related to individual or social healing or to the negotiation of conflicts. In many villages, they are rather part of an annual ritual attended by a god, and in more recent times, some of these performances (e.g., Javanese Jathilan) have also become forms of entertainment.

In general, the interpretation of ritual SI depends largely on the sociocultural context: the South Asian examples emphasize the connection of SI to certain religious beliefs and traditions of piety, while the Javanese and Balinese examples are better understood as parts of theatrical performances ranging from entertainment to the manifestations of divine presence that allow transgressive behavior and hence innovation.

For all trance-possession rituals, pain and physical harm are not intended even though performers may feel exhausted and have physical pain when they are again conscious. Yet for rituals that involve bleeding, to endure pain and bleeding is very important and regarded as heroic.

Summary

In many industrialized countries, self-injury is experienced as deviating from normality not only by health experts but also by most of the affected, and the sight of blood contributes to stress relief. In contrast, there are many ritual contexts throughout the world where apparent self-injury is understood as positive, something that promotes health and well-being of the individual or the community. These contexts are, however, quite diverse. For Christians and Muslims in many different societies, rituals involving bleeding are agentive (purposeful) acts of imitation/memory in which blood flow is essential. In the rituals from South and Southeast Asia involving piercing and bleeding discussed above, it is important that bleeding should be minimal or entirely absent. In some rituals, the fact that the "injured" body does not bleed is understood to demonstrate the heroic agency of the devotee who is protected from harm by a benevolent deity. In others, the one doing SI is not even the person whose body is harmed but rather a local god or ancestor who temporarily inhabits his body. In general, the sight of blood is negatively valued because flowing blood would mean that the ritual has failed. This stands in sharp contrast to nonritual SI, where a frequent motive of SI is to see one's own blood flow, and empirical research demonstrated a stress-reducing effect of seeing (artificial) blood.

Taken together, there are similarities as well as differences between ritual and nonritual forms of self-injury, and blood plays an important role in differentiating the two. Emerging empirical research in both forms of SI, however, reveals interesting similarities on a psychophysiological level. Furthermore, cultural changes in South and South East Asian societies (e.g., students moving from rural areas into larger cities) seem to lead to mixed patterns of ritual and nonritual forms.

References

American Psychiatric Association. (1994). *Diagnostic and Statistical Manual of Mental Disorders*. 4th ed. APA.
Antze, P. (1992). Possession trance and multiple personality: Psychiatric disorders or idioms of distress?. *Transcultural Psychiatric Research Review, 29*(4), 319–323.
Bandem, I. M., & De Boer, F. E. (1995). *Balinese dance in transition. Kaja and Kelod*. Oxford University Press.
Belo, J. (1949). *Bali: Rangda and barong* (Vol. 16). JJ Augustin.
Belo, J. (1960). *Trance in Bali*. Columbia University Press.
Bowes, L., Carnegie, R., Pearson, R., Mars, B., Biddle, L., Maughan, B., Lewis, G., Fernyhough, C., & Heron, J. (2015). Risk of depression and self-harm in teenagers identifying with goth subculture: A longitudinal cohort study. *Lancet Psychiatry, 2*, 793–800.
Bräunlein, P. J. (2010). "Flagellation." In M. Baumann & J. Gordon Melton (Eds.), *Religions of the world. A comprehensive encyclopedia of beliefs and practices* (pp. 1120–1122). 2nd ed. ABL-CLIO.
Bresin, K., & Schoenleber, M. (2015). Gender differences in the prevalence on non-suicidal self-injury: A meta-analysis. *Clinical Psychology Review, 38*, 55–64.
Burridge, K. O. L. (1961). Kuda Kepang in Batu Pahat, Johore. *Man* 61, 33–36.
Christensen, P. (2014). Modernity and spirit possession in Java. Horse dance and its contested magic. In V. Gottowik (Ed.), *Dynamics of religion in Southeast Asia: Magic and modernity* (pp. 91–112). Amsterdam University Press.
Çizmeci, E. (2018). Performing Sufi disfiguration: Transformation of the self. *Performance Research, 23*(8), 74–82.

Collins, E. F. (1997). *Pierced by Murugan's lance: Ritual, power, and moral redemption among Malaysian Hindus*. Northern Illinois University Press.

Derges, J. (2013). *Ritual and recovery in post-conflict Sri Lanka*. Routledge.

Favazza, A. R., & Conterio, K. (1989). Female habitual self-mutilators. *Acta Psychiatrica Scandinavica, 79*(3), 283–289.

Geertz, C. (1960). *The religion of Java*. University of Chicago Press.

Glenn, C. R., & Klonsky, E. D. (2010). The role of seeing blood in non-suicidal self-injury. *Journal of Clinical Psychology, 66*(4), 466–473.

Hecker, T., Braitmayer, L., & Van Duijl, M. (2015). Global mental health and trauma exposure: The current evidence for the relationship between traumatic experiences and spirit possession. *European Journal of Psychotraumatology, 6*(1), Article 29126.

Hepp, J., Carpenter, R. W., Stoerkel, S., Schmitz, S., Schmahl, C., & Niedtfeld, I. (2020). Non-suicidal self-injurious acts and urges in daily life: A systematic review of ambulatory assessment studies based on the four functions model. *Clinical Psychological Review, 82*, Article 101888.

Hornbacher, A. (2011). The withdrawal of the gods: Remarks on ritual trance-possession and its decline in Bali. In M. Picard & R. Madinier (Eds.), *The politics of religion in Indonesia* (pp. 167–191) Routledge.

Hughes-Freeland, F. (2008). "Becoming a puppet": Javanese dance as spiritual art. *The Journal of Religion and Theatre, 7*(1), 35–54.

Jegindø, E., Elmholdt, M., Vase, L., Jegindø, J., & Geertz, A. W. (2013). Pain and sacrifice: Experience and modulation of pain in a religious piercing ritual. *International Journal for the Psychology of Religion, 23*(3), 171–187.

Kleindienst, N., Bohus, M., Ludascher, P., Limberger, M. F., Kuenkele, K., Ebner-Priemer, U. W., Chapman, A. L., Reicherzer, M., Stieglitu, R. D., & Schmahl, C. (2008). Motives for nonsuicidal self-injury among women with borderline personality disorder. *Journal of Nervous and Mental Disease, 196*(3), 230–236.

Krishnan, G.P. (2021). *Following Murukan: Tai Pucam in Singapore. Krishnan GP. Following Murukan: Tai Pucam in Singapore*. First International Conference on Skanda-Murukan, held at the Institute of Asian Studies, University of Chennai, India. Accessed May 23, 2021. http://murugan.org/research/gauri_krishnan.htm.

Maidah, D. (2013). Self injury pada mahasiswa. *Development and Clinical Psychology, 2*(1), 6–8.

McGilvray, D. (2004). Jailani: A Sufi shrine in Sri Lanka. In I. Ahmad & H. Reifield (Eds.), *Lived Islam in South Asia: Adaptation, accommodation & conflict* (pp. 273–290). Berghahn.

Muehlenkamp, J. J., Claes, L., Havertape, L., & Plener, P. L. (2012). International prevalence of adolescent non-suicidal self-injury and deliberate self-harm. *Child and Adolescent Psychiatry and Mental Health, 6*, Article 10.

Naoum, J., Reitz, S., Krause-Utz, A., Kleindienst, N., Willis, F., Kuniss, S., & Baumgärtner, U., Mancke, F., Treede, R. D., & Schmahl, C. (2016). The role of seeing blood in non-suicidal self-injury in female patients with borderline personality disorder. *Psychiatry Research, 246*, 676–682.

Rapoport, E. (2018). Jathilan horse dance: Spirit possession beliefs and practices in present-day Java. IKAT: *The Indonesian Journal of Southeast Asian Studies, 2*(1), 1–17.

Spies, W., & de Zoete, B. (1938). *Dance and drama in Bali*. London.

Suryani, L. K., & Jensen, G. D. (1993). *Trance and possession in Bali: A window on Western multiple personality, possession disorder, and suicide*. Oxford University Press.

van Wulfften Palthe, P. M. (1940). Over de Bezetenheid. *Geneesk T. Ned.-Ind.*, 36, 2123–2153.

Ward, C. (1984). Thaipusam in Malaysia: A psycho-anthropological analysis of ritual trance, ceremonial possession and self-mortification practices. *Ethos, 12*(4), 307–334.

Xygalatas, D., Khan, S., Lang, M., Kundt, R., Kundtová-Klocová, E., Krátký, J., & Shaver, J. (2019). Effects of extreme ritual practices on psychophysiological well-being. *Current Anthropology, 60*(5), 699–707.

Young, R., Sproeber, N., Groschwitz, R. C., Preiss, M., & Plener, P. L. (2014). Why alternative teenagers self-harm: Exploring the link between non-suicidal self-injury, attempted suicidNe and adolescent identity. *BMC Psychiatry, 14*, Article 137.

CHAPTER 24

The Significance of Location of Self-Injury

Kathryn Jane Gardner, Caroline Clements, Harriet Bickley, Gillian Rayner, *and* Peter James Taylor

> **Abstract**
>
> This chapter examines whether location of injury may have meaning for people with lived experience of nonsuicidal self-injury (NSSI), and what research to date reveals about possible meanings, implications, and correlates of the location of self-injury on the body. It begins by reviewing the prevalence of different self-injury locations and the role of culture, followed by functional, cognitive, and psychodynamic perspectives. Studies suggest a preference for self-injury on the arms and legs, followed by the torso. Yet, within these largely Caucasian samples there is variation in reported percentages for common locations across studies and sample types. Moreover, there is a knowledge gap on NSSI in non-Western and minority groups. The chapter then considers research and clinical implications that stem directly from an improved understanding of the relevance of location of the injury.
>
> **Key Words:** nonsuicidal self-injury, self-injury locations, culture, minority groups, psychodynamic perspective, cognitive perspective, functional perspective

Introduction

In recent years our understanding of the presenting clinical features and contextual characteristics of nonsuicidal self-injury (NSSI) has advanced, identifying important psychological and clinical implications. The location of injury (i.e., where on the body an injury is directed) could be important, potentially providing valuable insight into the drivers behind self-injury, its personal meaning, or the context within which this behavior occurs. However, empirical and theoretical work in this area are limited. In this chapter we explore whether location of injury may have meaning for people with lived experience of NSSI, and what research to date tells us about possible meanings, implications, and correlates of the location of self-injury on the body. We begin by reviewing the prevalence of different self-injury locations and the role of culture, followed by functional, cognitive, and psychodynamic perspectives. We conclude by considering research and clinical implications that stem directly from an improved understanding of the relevance of location of the injury.

Perspectives on Self-Injury Location

While work focused on understanding location of self-injury is scarce, information about injury location is available from some broader epidemiological, survey, and interview studies. Here we explore the prevalence of NSSI in different locations on the body according to international studies in Western and non-Western countries, including how location might vary by demographic characteristics such as gender.[1]

Prevalence and Cultural Perspectives of Injury Location

Studies of hospital presenting self-injury in different countries, including the UK (Gardner et al., 2020; Geulayov et al., 2023; Horrocks et al., 2003) and New Zealand (Taylor & Cameron, 1998), typically find a high proportion of injuries to the wrists and arms. A paper on the significance of location in self-cutting among young people (Gardner et al., 2020) presented broad category figures for the distribution of injury locations across the body, based on a large clinical dataset of young people who attended emergency departments. The most common locations for self-injury by cutting were the wrist and forearm (54%); upper arm (33%); leg (7%); followed by head, neck, and torso (2% each). Similar distributions were found in a larger multisite study of all ages (Geulayov et al., 2023). The latter study looked at location by gender and age and found that injuries on the neck, head and torso were more common in men, while injuries to the leg and wrist or arm were more often seen in women (though total numbers in some categories e.g. "neck" were small). Locations other than the wrist or arm were more common among people ages 55 years and older; and self-injury to areas other than the wrist/arm, especially the neck, elevates suicide risk (Geulayov et al., 2023).

These above studies did not differentiate NSSI from suicidal self-injury, though studies of NSSI in community settings have found similar patterns of injury locations. A study using data mining techniques in U.S. university students included a more granular list of 18 injury locations, with less common locations including the neck (7%), breasts (3%), genitals (1%), and feet/toes (4%; Burke et al., 2018). The most common sites remained consistent with other work, with injuries on the arms/wrists (62%), upper arm (18%), hands (26%), lower limbs (34% thigh, 12% lower leg/ankle, 7% knee), abdomen (17%) and hips (16%). In a survey of U.S. college students, Whitlock (2006) similarly found that arms and wrists were the most common NSSI locations; however, there were differences by gender with men, who were more likely to injure their hands, and women with their wrists and legs. In students in New Zealand, Fitzgerald and Curtis (2017) found that women were more likely to injure their wrists and legs but less likely to injure their head compared to males, but there were no differences for injury to hands and arms. In a U.S. study, girls and young women had more injuries to legs *and* arms in comparison to boys/young men, but less to their chest, face, or genitals (Sornberger et al., 2012). And in Finnish adolescents in the community, 67.2% injured only their arms (Laukkanen et al.,

2013) with girls significantly more likely to injure in other locations. The lower limbs were a common injury location (13.4% thigh; 14.6% shin; 13.4% ankles), followed by the abdomen (7.7%), and a range of other sites (e.g., genitals, breasts, scalp). Inconsistencies in gender differences between studies may, however, be due to the different categorization systems used (e.g., separating vs. not separating the wrist from the arm).

These studies suggest a preference for self-injury on the arms and legs, followed by the torso. Yet, within these largely Caucasian samples there is variation in reported percentages for common locations across studies and sample types. One Flemish interview study of adolescents found that hands, legs, breasts, and the neck were most common (Rissanen et al., 2008). The prevalence of more sensitive regions such as the genitals remains low across studies irrespective of data collection methods. However, as noted by Conde et al. (2017), perceived embarrassment associated with the sexual nature of the location could mean that injury to the genitals is underreported. People may be less likely to present to services for medical treatment for the same reason.

BEYOND WESTERN-BASED STUDIES

With extant work conducted primarily on Caucasian-majority samples there is a knowledge gap on NSSI in non-Western and minority groups (Brown et al., 2019; Verroken et al., 2018). A small body of international literature shows that rates and characteristics of NSSI may differ due to cultural influences (Chang et al., 2015; Chesin et al., 2013; Wester et al., 2015), but the inclusion of information on location of injury that would enable cross-cultural comparisons is rare. Where location is included, findings are broadly consistent with those discussed above, suggesting little difference between Western and non-Western cultures in the most common injury locations. A small-scale interview study of nine Turkish women living in a traditional society primarily cut themselves on their forearms and legs (Medina, 2011), though the study did not differentiate NSSI from suicidal behavior. In a study of NSSI in refugee minors in Belgium (e.g., many being sole representatives from countries such as Syria, Afghanistan, Somalia, Albania, and Bangladesh), the most common locations were hands, followed by wrists and arms (Verroken et al., 2018).

Work from China demonstrates possible differences in NSSI location that may reflect cultural differences *within* a country. Children from mainland China most often cut on the hands, scalp, and lips (Zhang et al., 2019), and two thirds (152/227) reported injuring more than one body part. In contrast, a Hong Kong study of 42 Chinese adolescents found that all participants cut their arms or wrists, with only four also cutting on the legs (You et al., 2015). The authors speculate that differences may lie in cultural differences in relationships and individualism in Hong Kong (previously a British colony) whereas mainland China emphasizes collectivism (You et al., 2013). But differences in data collection methods make direct comparison of the results difficult.

Functional Perspectives

NSSI is typically functional in nature (see Taylor et al., this volume), occurring in response to individual need. Possible functions vary widely, and while individuals may endorse multiple functions, these commonly relate to regulation of aversive emotional states (Edmondson et al., 2016; Taylor et al., 2018). In considering the meaning behind the location of self-injury, the function the behavior serves is likely to be important. Functions of NSSI can be divided into the intrapersonal (to do with internal states and experiences) and the interpersonal (to do with external, often social experiences; Dahlström et al., 2015; Klonksy et al., 2015). The latter group of functions can include NSSI as a way to bond with peers or fit into a peer group, to communicate distress, vulnerability, strength, or the need for help/care (Edmondson et al., 2016; Nock, 2008; Klonsky et al., 2015; Taylor et al., 2018), and it may be that more visible locations of injury are chosen (Nock, 2008). Gambetta (2009) discusses how in prison environments, acts of self-injury in more noticeable locations (e.g., self-injury to the face or hands) may be used to signal that one is strong, unpredictable, or dangerous, a finding supported by one qualitative study (Morales, 2013). However, the extent to which interpersonal functions influence decisions around where to self-injure is unclear, as direct evidence is scarce. It is possible that the self-injury served other emotion-laden functions at the time and the location was selected for a different reason, but that visibility also helped the individual to meet interpersonal needs after the self-injury has taken place.

Individuals who self-injure with primarily intrapersonal motivations (e.g., to regulate distressing feelings) might self-injure in a concealed location to meet affective needs while avoiding notice (Austin, 2004), or negative reactions from others. While self-injury is typically a very personal behavior that occurs in private (O'Loughlin et al., 2021), our review of the literature shows that locations that are more easily concealed (e.g., torso) are not as common as potentially visible sites such the wrist/arm. In our study comparing the characteristics of episodes of concealed and visible self-cutting in young people who presented to emergency departments, we found that more episodes were in visible sites, which included the head, neck, forearm or wrist (56%), compared to concealed locations such as the torso and leg (40%; 4% were in mixed locations; Gardner et al., 2020; fig. 1). Our work illustrates a simple empirical approach to the study of self-injury location by using two broad conceptual categories of concealed and visible self-injury. We explored whether the location of self-injury (irrespective of the presence/absence of suicidal intent) was related to a range of clinical and psychological characteristics, including clinically derived intent-related variables. Location was not associated with suicidal thoughts or plans, but self-cutting in a concealed location was associated with a greater likelihood of past self-harm, premeditation, and current psychiatric treatment. The association with premeditation suggests that concealed cutting might be underpinned by more controlled decision-making whereas visible cutting might reflect an impulsive situational response (Gardner et al., 2020). People with a history of self-injury and/or psychiatric treatment may be more likely to injure in more concealed locations due to previous negative reactions from others, perceived shame or stigma (Long, 2017), or concern about attempts by clinical staff to stop them self-injuring, thereby removing their coping method. If so, there might be a simple trajectory of progressing from a visible to concealed site. However, Gardner and colleagues found that switching from a visible to a concealed location occurred at a similar frequency (44%) as switching from concealed to visible locations in later episodes (39%). Although it is possible to speculate that the latter shift reflects a progression to self-injuring in visible areas to meet an interpersonal need, it is equally possible that such shifts are driven by other factors, including the ongoing practicalities of cutting in certain areas. An excess of scar tissue in a preferred concealed site for example, could result in a change to less preferred visible sites. Reasons for changing location have not been empirically investigated, however, and many people continue to injure the same location across episodes of self-injury, suggestive of ritualistic patterns of behavior (Gardner et al., 2020; Stacy et al., 2018). These issues highlight the complex, dynamic, fluid, and contradictory nature of self-injury, both between and within individuals.

The complexities of self-injury and its functions highlight the need to exercise caution in adopting overly simplistic interpretations of the meaning behind the location of an injury. The hands or face are the most visible sites for many people but may not necessarily be driven by a social function, while self-injury in a concealed location such as the genitals or stomach does not preclude a social function; an individual may choose to tell others about their self-injury, or consciously display initially concealed injuries as a form of active communication (e.g., by turning up sleeves to reveal arms, wearing shorts to show the thigh area, or not covering up when changing in front of others; Gambetta, 2009; Griller, 2013). The wrist/forearm can also be difficult to interpret when considering whether location has functional relevance, since this area might be best considered one of "ambivalent visibility," that is, the wrist/forearm can be easily hidden with clothing, or revealed, giving the individual control over whether others see their injuries and when (Seko, 2013).

The possible relationships between NSSI function and location of injury remain largely speculative given the scarcity of research investigating these hypotheses. Yet, there is work examining the psychological significance of specific body sites, from which we can generalize. Evidence from a study of Japanese young people in a juvenile detention center suggests NSSI for emotion regulation may be linked to locations of ambivalent visibility (arm vs. wrist; Matsumoto et al., 2004). In this study, self-cutting due to feelings of anger was more common in those who cut their arm compared to those who cut their wrists. There were no differences between location for the endorsement of other functions (e.g., "To obtain emotional release"), though the small sample ($n = 33$) is a limitation of this study (Matsumoto et al., 2004). Laukkanen et al.'s (2013) study of Finnish adolescents similarly suggests that injury to particular areas might be underpinned by affective difficulties, as well as a more complex psychological presentation; they found that cutting on locations other than the upper arms was associated with greater depression, more dissociative experiences, suicidal ideation, and other emotional and social difficulties. From a functional perspective, therefore, it is possible that more complex presentations (e.g., both affective and social difficulties) might be associated with multiple intra- and interpersonal functions, which could manifest as injuring multiple sites of the body. However, irrespective of presentation, many individuals endorse multiple NSSI functions simultaneously (e.g., Klonsky, 2011; Klonsky & Glenn, 2009) and this might inform location, depending on the functions and their interaction with other factors.

Visibility of the injury is just one characteristic of location and may be driven by a range of environmental, contextual, clinical, and psychological factors and interact with NSSI functions in other ways. Seeing the injury or the blood appears important for many who self-injure (e.g. 52% of participants in Glenn & Klonksy, 2010); therefore, location may be based on the ease of visibility of blood loss; for others it may be the pain (e.g., Selby et al., 2019), physical sensation, or some other quality of the experience that informs location.

Cognitive Perspectives

Cognitive approaches to NSSI center around how constructs such as beliefs, attitudes, or expectations may contribute to the occurrence of self-injury. In the cognitive-emotional model of NSSI (Hasking et al., 2017), *expectations* an individual holds about NSSI, the anticipated or imagined consequences of the behavior, play a role in determining whether someone engages in NSSI. There is emerging evidence that expectations about self-injury (e.g., if I self-injure, I will feel calm; or if I self-injure, my friends will be disgusted) and beliefs in one's ability to perform NSSI (self-efficacy beliefs) are associated with the behavior (Dawkins et al., 2021; Hasking & Boyes, 2018). Likewise, the general beliefs individuals hold about self-injury are potentially important, with positive beliefs (viewing self-injury as protective or necessary) being associated with the frequency of NSSI (Sandel et al., 2021). It is possible these cognitive constructs extend to location. When a person thinks about self-injury, specific methods and locations may come to mind. Expectancies may relate to self-injury at a particular location (i.e., "If I cut here, I will feel better"), and could also be driven by prior experience of self-injury being effective in this location (e.g., whether injury to the wrist provided the desired relief from distress). The perceived effectiveness of NSSI in achieving a particular function has been studied by Brausch and Muehlenkamp (2018) but has yet to be explored in relation to location-based expectancies.

Mental imagery may also contain information about location of self-injury. In a sample of university students with experience of NSSI, the majority described some form of mental imagery relating to self-injury (74%) with images relating to blood or the injury itself being common (e.g., "blood running down my arm"; Hasking et al., 2018). Mental imagery surrounding NSSI may in part determine the location of NSSI, but we are not aware of any research exploring this.

Psychodynamic Perspectives

Psychodynamic literature includes a range of concepts that help us understand NSSI. We consider here several concepts discussed within the context of location, despite limited empirical work. Case examples and qualitative work remain subjective in nature and those included here are intended to widen the discussion rather than allow for broad generalizations.

INTRAPERSONAL PROCESSES AND REENACTMENT

Unconscious drives and meaning are at the heart of the psychodynamic perspective of self-injury, where self-injury can be also understood within a relational context and attachment framework (Yakeley & Burbridge-James, 2018; as discussed in James and Gibb, this volume). There is certainly evidence that NSSI is related to insecure attachment (Tatnell et al., 2014, 2016), abuse (Liu et al., 2018), and dissociation (Černis et al., 2019; Karpel et al., 2015), as well as evidence to suggest that attachment impacts NSSI via self-identify formation (Gandhi et al., 2019). Decisions about NSSI might operate at an unconscious automatic level (Glenn et al., 2016; Glenn et al., 2017), and this level of processing could influence self-injury location.

Dissociation is a disruption, interruption, or discontinuity of the integration of behavior, memory, identity, consciousness, emotions, and perceptions (*Diagnostic and Statistical Manual of Mental Disorders* [DSM-5], American Psychiatric Association, 2013). An empirical review by Holmes et al. (2005) suggests that dissociation includes both detachment type experiences (depersonalization and derealization) which have been described as feeling numb by those who self-injure (Tantam & Hubband, 2009); and compartmentalization (amnesia, hallucination, dissociative identities, which is typically experienced as a loss of conscious awareness and behavioral control, that is, the person may not realize what they are doing when they self-injure (Tantam & Huband, 2009). Studies have found that self-injury can function to terminate dissociation (a commonly reported function of NSSI; Klonsky, 2007; Klonsky & Glenn, 2009); or in some cases, induce a dissociative state (Tantam & Huband, 2009). In relation to location, the timing of these dissociative experiences could be important. If dissociation is experienced *prior* to the self-injury, the individual may have little or no conscious recollection of why they have injured in a specific location while dissociated and may be unaware they are causing significant physical damage (Tantam & Huband, 2009). If, however, dissociation is experienced as compartmentalization, or a process of numbing (detachment) that *follows* self-injury, individuals might be able to discuss the location selected and the reason for this, because they had conscious control and awareness when the self-injury occurred. These relationships are important to understand because higher levels of dissociation have been associated with more severe self-injury (e.g., Černis et al., 2019), and location could be an important factor here (i.e., unintentionally injuring in more medically risky locations during a dissociative state).

The relationship between NSSI and dissociation appears to be complex (Karpel et al., 2015) interacting with other factors to determine location. Miller (1994) describes how dissociation from one's body while abuse is happening could result in self-injury to locations that represent physical expressions of anger at the person who abused them (Miller, 1994). Within this perspective, self-injury is a behavioral form of abuse re-enactment, which Collins (1996) describes as an unconscious or conscious way of retrieving the past and expressing it either to the self or others. Re-enactment can be conceptualized in a multitude of ways (Levy, 1998) however, and in addition to dissociation there are likely to be multiple mechanisms that could inform location when abuse is re-enacted through self-injury.

The role of past abuse in self-injury location has been discussed in relation to genital self-injury (e.g., Hymen, 1999), though this is less common and there is some evidence it is associated with the presence of other risk factors such as psychosis (Conde et al., 2017; Martin & Gattaz, 1991). Using case examples, Collins (1996) illustrates how individuals might also connect experiences of abuse to other self-injury sites, including an individual who injured their hands and knees and "could recall no details of the abuse except 'He would push me down on my hands and knees'. This screen memory persisted for her and was re-enacted traumatically in the present." (p.470). According to Collins (1996) self-injury is a "symbolic representation. . . expressed in the act and chosen body site" (p.469). Yakeley and Burbridge-James (2018) further describe how sexual abuse could lead to feelings of disgust about any part of one's body, and the self-injury provides relief by cleansing these toxic parts of the body. Though, the idiographic nature of these case examples precludes generalizations to wider populations, and many who self-injure have not experienced abuse (Gratz, 2003), hence other past experiences or factors may drive location choice.

SELF-IDENTITY AND THE COMMUNICATIVE AND SCARRED BODY

The communicative nature of self-injury is central to functional models and location could be important here, as we have discussed above, yet this concept can be traced back to earlier writings in the psychodynamic literature (e.g., Freud, 1920) and is explicitly addressed in recent discussion papers (e.g., Yakeley & Burbridge-James, 2018). It has been suggested that the body is a canvas on which self-injury and resulting scars are written as a symbolic form of signaling to others (Collins, 1996; Reece, 2005), but also to the self as a mark of self-identity (e.g., "this is who I am"; Hymen, 1999). Self-injury and self-identity are empirically associated (Breen et al., 2013) and qualitative studies also suggest that self-injury can be used to represent the self and form an identity (Stänicke et al., 2021). Straker (2006) refers to this as "signing with a scar," positioning self-injury as an attempt to repair a fragile self-structure (e.g., by creating a shared point of attention on the wrist for self and others to focus on). Whether self-identity guides decisions around which *specific* body sites to self-injure is unclear as this is seldom the focus of research, though work tangential to location has addressed whether scars in fully visible locations impact how individuals view their bodies. One study found no differences in perceived body image relative to individuals with scars in partially or fully concealed locations such as the legs and torso, yet these findings are tentative given the small group sizes (Dyer et al., 2015). Given the general salience of scars, their potential permanency, ability to act as constant reminders of traumatic events and evoke strong feelings from self and others, and relevance to self-identity formation (Brown et al., 2008; Lewis & Mehrabkhani, 2016), it is possible that scars in clearly visible locations play a unique role in self-identity formation if they are more noticeable to self and others.

Studies have shown that some individuals implement scar-related stigma management strategies such as only injuring in concealed locations and/or concealing by using clothing or tattoos (Chandler, 2014; Hodgson, 2004; Seko, 2013). These concealment practices are underpinned by negative beliefs about the self (Burke et al., 2020), and can help individuals manage what is conceivably a stigmatized and alienated identity as "self-injurer" (Hodgson, 2004; Straker, 2006). However, the individual meaning attached to scars is variable with many individuals viewing their scars positively, as a sign of strength or a resilient self (Bachtelle et al., 2015; Lewis & Mehrabkhani, 2016). Irrespective of whether scars are perceived negatively or positively, visible scars in locations such as the hands, wrist or arms could connect the individual with their present or past identity as someone who self-injures, without the need to fully remove clothing. While qualitative studies show that self-injury scars are important to how people view their past, present and future selves (Gandhi et al., 2019; Kendall et al., 2021; Lewis & Mehrabkhani, 2016), they have yet to explore whether visible or specific locations are salient to the individual and their self-identity.

Summary and Discussion of Factors That Might Determine Location and Its Meaning

There is limited empirical literature on the location of self-injury and especially in relation to non-western cultures and non-white ethnicities. Based on data currently available, many individuals injure in multiple locations and injury patterns are relatively consistent across cultural and ethnic groups, with the extremities (arms, hands, and legs) being the most common locations identified across studies. Yet, self-injury also occurs in less common areas of the body. Location choice could be symbolic for some individuals or driven by a range of psychological processes that can change over time, such as interpersonal need or abuse reenactment; different perspectives can be used to understand this, though a lack of evidence cuts across all theoretical perspectives we have considered. The functional approach provides a framework for understanding why individuals might self-injure in visible or concealed locations, though it is less clear how functions might be differentially associated with self-injury in specific sites. Notably, the theoretical explanations for NSSI location choice reviewed in this chapter are a starting point to stimulate discussion and debate, a consideration of other perspectives, and research in this area that explores factors associated with location choice. While it is possible to speculate about the deeper meaning and relevance of location of self-injury, location choice may be driven by more parsimonious explanations such as avoiding tattoos that could be damaged, social exposure to common locations, or curiosity about what it feels like to injure in that area. Some literature suggests that exposure to other people's NSSI (e.g., through direct observation, or via online media) may increase the risk of a person engaging in self-injury themselves, with the potential relevance of location being speculated (e.g., Jarvi et al., 2013). Online platforms such as YouTube for example, expose individuals to common self-injury sites as they disproportionately include videos of self-injury to the wrists (Lewis et al., 2011).

The ease and convenience of injuring in a specific location might also explain location choice. Forearms are easily accessible, often without the need to remove clothing, and this may explain why they are the most common location of injuries. Moreover, the forearm can be readily covered, and injuries here do not have the same potential to hamper day-to-day functioning in the way that injury to the hands or digits might. A high proportion of injuries occur on the left wrist or forearm, possibly reflecting the high proportion of right-handed individuals (Ersen et al., 2017). However, given the practical convenience of the forearms, an important question is why some people switch self-injury location (Gardner et al., 2020), perhaps moving to less convenient locations. As discussed, a range of factors, including concerns about injuries becoming noticeable to others, may be relevant. Thus, location of self-injury may reflect an interaction between a variety of factors, including, but not necessarily limited to, the practical convenience of the location.

Implications for Practice

Prevention and Initial Detection of NSSI

Consideration of the location of self-injury may be beneficial for the primary prevention of NSSI. Some authors recommend that school-based primary prevention programs that aim to prevent young people from beginning to engage in NSSI, could focus on reduction of visible injuries or scars (Wester et al., 2017) because exposure to NSSI can increase the risk of others beginning to self-injure (Jarvi et al., 2013). While specific location may not be crucial, visibility could be key, with some locations being naturally more difficult to conceal (e.g. hands, face). However, asking those who self-injure to conceal their scars could lead to negative beliefs about their scars and psychological distress (Burke et al., 2020). Primary prevention programs must therefore mitigate against potential iatrogenic effects both in those who do as well as those who do not self-injure. While schools appear to be appropriate grounds for running prevention programs, these are scarce, and any positive effects usually relate to broader outcomes such as help-seeking (see Baetens et al., this volume, and Petrovic et al., this volume for discussion).

Choice of NSSI location could also determine how easily and quickly self-injury is detected (Whitlock, 2010), which can facilitate early intervention. If injuries are in concealed locations and the individual does not seek help, the self-injury can go undetected for many years and early detection must rely on other indicators and risk factors, with schools potentially playing a role in early prevention as self-injury typically begins during adolescence (Wilkinson, 2011). Training for school staff could include information on the range of locations that young people self-injure, while remaining aware of other signs and risk factors for self-injury. Training that encourages staff to ask the young person about their self-injury with "respectful curiosity" may help avoid automatic assumptions about meaning or level of distress based on external cues such as location (Gardner et al., in preparation; Lloyd-Richardson et al., 2020; Lewis et al., 2019). Such recommendations to any preventative context and age group.

Clinical Assessment
Asking about location as part of broader psychosocial assessments may help develop a deeper understanding of patterns to the self-injury (Walsh, 2007), personal meaning behind an individual's self-injury, links to earlier traumas, adversities or psychological difficulties, or the function behind the self-injury such as whether there is a communicative aspect. Assessments should adopt an individualized, collaborative and consultative approach that empowers service users to actively self-assess and engage in formulation of the risk posed by their self-injury (Markham, 2020) in specific locations and within the context of other characteristics such as function and meaning. Reason for location choice also may not be clear to the individual; hence, comprehensive assessment may assist understanding for both parties.

Considering location of self-injury as part of clinical assessments, in tandem with clinical characteristics such as extent of physical damage (Walsh, 2007), may also be important to understanding the individuals' risk and needs. For example, injuries to areas other than the arm/wrist (e.g., the neck) may elevate suicide risk (Carroll et al., 2016; Geulayov et al., 2023), and severe wrist/arm cutting can significantly damage arteries, tendons or nerves and can lead to permanent sensory or motor dysfunction (Ersen et al., 2017; Kisch et al., 2019). Staff training around high-risk areas and the potential damage and lasting consequences to specific body parts appears essential here, yet, it is important to hold in mind that injury to any location increases suicide risk and thorough assessments should be conducted regardless of location (Gardner et al., 2020; Geulayov et al., 2023).

Intervention and Recovery
If location has meaning for an individual and relates to clinical risk, it will be important to integrate knowledge of these into therapeutic work and interventions to co-design safer ways of coping. The nature of the intervention will depend on the significance of location for the individual but could include raising the individual's awareness and understanding of the immediate clinical risks, potential lethality, and potential long-term damage associated with injuring in each location (e.g., risk of damage to wrist tendons or to specific

facial structures); and exploring how past experiences (e.g., trauma), specific psychological factors (e.g., dissociative states), and self-injury functions could precipitate a decision to self-injure in a certain location. Conversations need to be managed carefully given the potential for clinicians to appear blaming and judging when discussing the negative physical consequences of self-injury. Aiming for a collaborative conversation that centers on the clients' needs and their concerns, is likely to be of most value.

The potential for NSSI scarring might also be important to explore with clients since scars could be important not only to an individual's self-identity, as discussed above, but also to their recovery (Lewis & Mehrabkhani, 2016). It has been argued that self-acceptance is key to recovery (Lewis & Hasking, 2020), and location could be one of many factors that impacts scar acceptance. A study of facial laceration scars found they were associated with social self-consciousness of appearance (e.g., feeling judged or embarrassed) and anxiety up to six months later (Tebble et al., 2006), though the study did not include a comparison with scars in other locations. Self-injury and scars, especially when located on the forearm, can be identifiable to others and some studies suggest these public displays can be misunderstood and pejoratively labeled as "attention-seeking," while hidden self-harm is seen to be underpinned by authentic distress and psychological pain (Chandler, 2018; Crouch & Wright, 2004; Scourfield et al., 2011). Location, especially whether the injury is on a potentially visible site of the body, therefore seems an important factor in perpetuating stigma, determining how individuals feel about themselves and their appearance, and allowing individuals control over whether others see their self-injury, all of which can impact recovery. Indeed, stigmatizing attitudes toward self-injury and self-injury scars are well documented (Rayner & Warne, 2015; Rayner et al., 2019) and can lead to a self-perpetuating cycle of shame (Bachtelle et al., 2015; Sheehy et al., 2019). Changing public attitudes and reducing the stigma that surrounds these difficulties is imperative, with programs being co-designed with people with lived experience of self-injury. On an individual basis, empirically supported therapeutic interventions that adopt a compassion-focused approach or which focus on individuals' processing and acceptance of scar-related emotions and cognitions with a view toward promoting acceptance (e.g., van Vliet & Kalnins, 2011; Tighe, 2018) may be helpful. Arguably, injuries and scars in some locations could for some people be easier to accept than others.

Implications for Research

This chapter has discussed a range of perspectives that provide a platform for further empirical work on the location of NSSI, but our current understanding has been derived largely in the absence of robust empirical studies. Given the potential clinical implications, location should be an important focus of future quantitative and qualitative studies and considered in terms of both between- and within-person variance.

More large-scale studies on the prevalence of self-injury in different locations are needed to inform future research and systematic reviews in this area. These studies could identify trends in location of the injury and reflect on the cultural meaning of location, both within and between cultures.

Studies exploring the correlates of location in conjunction with theoretically relevant covariates are needed as these are scarce and some existing studies lack statistical power (e.g., Matsumoto et al., 2004). Correlates include the wider characteristics of self-injury such as severity, frequency, and recency, which may work alongside location to determine whether the self-injury is detected by others. Functions is a key psychological correlate and should be operationalized using a standardized psychometric tool (e.g., the Inventory of Statements about Self-Injury; Klonsky & Glenn, 2009), and investigated alongside constructs outlined in comprehensive etiological models of NSSI (e.g., Nock, 2009) to understand whether location is also correlated with theoretically pertinent distal (e.g., childhood abuse) and proximal (e.g., poor communication skills and specific psychological disorders) vulnerability factors that cut across multiple theoretical perspectives. This is key to understanding the conceptual basis of location choice and whether location can be functionally, cognitively, or psychodynamically represented. For example, research into individual differences in the way self-injury is cognitively represented, encompassing beliefs, expectations, and images, could further examine how location forms part of this representation. Studies could also examine whether more visible self-injury, or less typical locations, are associated with the presence of specific psychological presentations. Stroehmer et al. (2015) found that individuals diagnosed with BPD were more likely to self-injure in multiple areas relative to those without BPD, including in visible locations such as the hands, while psychosis is often present in cases of extreme acts of self-injury to the genitals (Conde et al., 2017; Martin & Gattaz, 1991) and face (Jones, 1990). There are many psychological factors that may influence NSSI location and which extend beyond the perspectives considered within this chapter.

Associations between functions and changes in location could be investigated using within-person approaches to capture whether location changes across time and situations. This could include identifying whether changes in functions over time (Gardner et al., 2021) coincide with changes in visible to concealed locations, or vice versa. Within-person approaches could also capture shifts toward characteristically different or more medically severe self-injury, such as from less painful to more painful sites, or clinically risky to less risky locations. These conceptually meaningful yet simplistic dichotomous categories can be problematic if self-injury episodes or individuals do not fall neatly into one group (e.g., injuring both concealed and visible areas), or they conceal a potential third group (e.g., injuring areas of ambivalent/partial visibility). Sensitivity analyses can determine the robustness of results based on different input parameters (e.g., relocating "forearm" from a visible concealed), as demonstrated by Gardner et al. (2020) and explained in Thabane et al. (2013). In the absence of evidence-based decision rules however, location could simply be operationalized in terms of general bodily locations (e.g., face, hands, arms, torso, and legs), or specific regions within these general locations (e.g., inner and outer thigh), as captured by measures such as the Self-Injury Trauma Scale (SIT; Iwata et al., 1990).

Qualitative research about experiences relating to location, meaning, and function could provide detailed accounts of in-depth and personal experiences relating to the site chosen and the context to this decision, such as connections to the past and previous adversity. Mixed-methods designs (qualitative and quantitative) could also provide a triangulated conceptualization of these issues and also in relation to professionals' responses. For example, mixed-methods studies of hospital staff responses to self-injury cases could extend the work of Gardner et al. (2020) and identify whether location of the injury impacts on clinical management via staff assumptions about clinical risk.

Conclusion

Evidence suggests that location of self-injury could be psychologically and clinically meaningful, but there are many facets to location and different processes in play. There is a dearth of supporting empirical evidence in this field, and the underrepresentation of non-Western cultures in the NSSI literature further impacts an evidence-based perspective. The complex and idiosyncratic nature of individuals' choice of injury location underscores the need for lived-experience research in this area that can contextualize location choice and consider it alongside pertinent contextual, psychological, and clinical factors. It is important that individuals who self-injure fully understand all aspects of their self-injury, including why they injure particular body parts and the possible intrapersonal and interpersonal consequences of this, and are aware of the associated immediate and long-term clinical risks of injuring in a specific region. Location choice, whether consciously selected or not, could be important to consider alongside other characteristics when preventing, detecting, understanding, and treating self-injury.

Note

1. As studies do not typically distinguish between gender which is socially constructed and biological sex, it is not possible to draw conclusions about how each of these may be differentially associated with self-injury in specific sites

References

American Psychiatric Association. (2013). *Diagnostic and statistical manual of mental disorders*. 5th ed.
Austin, L., & Kortum, J. (2004). Self-injury: The secret language of pain for teenagers. *Education, 124*(3), 517–527.
Bachtelle, S. E., & Pepper, C. M. (2015). The physical results of nonsuicidal self-injury. *Journal of Nervous & Mental Disease, 203*(12), 927–933. https://doi.org/10.1097/nmd.0000000000000398
Breen, A. V., Lewis, S. P., & Sutherland, O. (2013). Brief report: Non-suicidal self-injury in the context of self and identity development. *Journal of Adult Development, 20*(1), 57–62. https://doi.org/10.1007/s10804-013-9156-8
Brown, B., McKenna, S., Siddhi, K., McGrouther, D., & Bayat, A. (2008). The hidden cost of skin scars: Quality of life after skin scarring. *Journal of Plastic, Reconstructive & Aesthetic Surgery, 61*(9), 1049–1058. https://doi.org/10.1016/j.bjps.2008.03.020

Brown, R. C., & Witt, A. (2019). Social factors associated with non-suicidal self-injury (NSSI). Child and Adolescent *Psychiatry and Mental Health*, *13*(1), 23. https://doi.org/10.1186/s13034-019-0284-1

Burke, T. A., Ammerman, B. A., Hamilton, J. L., Stange, J. P., & Piccirillo, M. (2020). Nonsuicidal self-injury scar concealment from the self and others. *Journal of Psychiatric Research*, *130*, 313–320. https://doi.org/10.1016/j.jpsychires.2020.07.040

Burke, T. A., Jacobucci, R., Ammerman, B. A., Piccirillo, M., McCloskey, M. S., Heimberg, R. G., & Alloy, L. B. (2018). Identifying the relative importance of non-suicidal self-injury features in classifying suicidal ideation, plans, and behavior using exploratory data mining. *Psychiatry Research*, *262*, 175–183. https://doi.org/10.1016/j.psychres.2018.01.045

Brausch, A. M., & Muehlenkamp, J. J. (2018). Perceived effectiveness of NSSI in achieving functions on severity and suicide risk. *Psychiatry Research*, *265*, 144–150. https://doi.org/10.1016/j.psychres.2018.04.038

Carroll, R., Thomas, K., Bramley, K., Williams, S., Griffin, L., Potokar, J., & Gunnell, D. (2016). Self-cutting and risk of subsequent suicide. *Journal of Affective Disorders*, *192*, 8–10. http://doi.org/10.1016/j.jad.2015.12.007

Černis, E., Chan, C., & Cooper, M. (2019). What is the relationship between dissociation and self-harming behaviour in adolescents? *Clinical Psychology & Psychotherapy*, *26*(3), 328–338. https://doi.org/10.1002/cpp.2354

Chandler, A. (2014). Narrating the self-injured body. *Medical Humanities*, *40*(2), 111–116. https://doi.org/10.1136/medhum-2013-010488

Chandler, A. (2018). Seeking secrecy. *YOUNG*, *26*(4), 313–331. https://doi.org/10.1177/1103308817717367

Chang, S. S., Steeg, S., Kapur, N., Webb, R. T., Yip, P. S., & Cooper, J. (2015). Self-harm amongst people of Chinese origin versus White people living in England: A cohort study. *BMC Psychiatry*, *15*(1). https://doi.org/10.1186/s12888-015-0467-0

Chesin, M. S., Moster, A. N., & Jeglic, E. L. (2013). Non-suicidal self-injury among ethnically and racially diverse emerging adults: Do factors unique to the minority experience matter? *Current Psychology*, *32*(4), 318–328. https://doi.org/10.1007/s12144-013-9185-2

Collins, D. (1996). Attacks on the body: How can we understand self-harm? *Psychodynamic Counselling*, *2*(4), 463–475. https://doi.org/10.1080/13533339608402471

Conde, E., Santos, T., Leite, R., Vicente, C., & Figueiredo, A. M. (2017). A case of genital self-mutilation in a female—Symptom choice and meaning. *Journal of Sex & Marital Therapy*, *43*(6), 560–566. https://doi.org/10.1080/0092623x.2016.1208699

Crouch, W., & Wright, J. (2004). Deliberate self-harm at an adolescent unit: A qualitative investigation. *Clinical Child Psychology and Psychiatry*, *9*(2), 185–204. https://doi.org/10.1177/1359104504041918

Dahlström, R., Zetterqvist, M., Lundh, L. G., & Svedin, C. G. (2015). Functions of nonsuicidal self-injury: Exploratory and confirmatory factor analyses in a large community sample of adolescents. *Psychological Assessment*, *27*(1), 302–313. https://doi.org/10.1037/pas0000034

Dawkins, J., Penelope A. Hasking & Mark E. Boyes (2021) Thoughts and beliefs about nonsuicidal self-injury: An application of social cognitive theory, *Journal of American College Health*, *69*(4), 428–434. https://doi.org/10.1080/07448481.2019.1679917

Dyer, A., Mayer-Eckhard, L., White, A. J., & Alpers, G. W. (2015). The role of scar origin in shaping men's body image. *American Journal of Men's Health*, *9*(2), 115–123. https://doi.org/10.1177/1557988314531446

Edmondson, A. J., Brennan, C. A., & House, A. O. (2016). Non-suicidal reasons for self-harm: A systematic review of self-reported accounts. *Journal of Affective Disorders*, *191*, 109–117. https://doi.org/10.1016/j.jad.2015.11.043

Ersen, B., Kahveci, R., Saki, M. C., Tunali, O., & Aksu, I. (2017). Analysis of 41 suicide attempts by wrist cutting: A retrospective analysis. *European Journal of Trauma and Emergency Surgery*, *43*(1), 129–135. https://doi.org/10.1007/s00068-015-0599-4

Fitzgerald, J., & Curtis, C. (2017). Non-suicidal self-injury in a New Zealand student population: Demographic and self-harm characteristics. *New Zealand Journal of Psychology*, *46*(3), 156–163.

Freud, S. (1920). Beyond the pleasure principle. In J. Strachey (Ed.), *Standard edition of the complete psychological works of Sigmund Freud* (Vol. 18, pp 1–64). Hogarth.

Gardner, K. J., Paul, E., Selby, E. A., Klonsky, E. D., & Mars, B. (2021). Intrapersonal and interpersonal functions as pathways to future self-harm repetition and suicide attempts. *Frontiers in Psychology*, *12*, Article 688472 https://doi.org/10.3389/fpsyg.2021.688472

Gratz, K. L. (2003). Risk factors for and functions of deliberate self-harm: An empirical and conceptual review. *Clinical Psychology: Science and Practice, 10*(2), 192–205. https://doi.org/10.1093/clipsy.bpg022

Gambetta, D. (2009). *Codes of the underworld: How criminals communicate*. Princeton University Press.

Gandhi, A., Luyckx, K., Molenberghs, G., Baetens, I., Goossens, L., Maitra, S., & Claes, L. (2019). Maternal and peer attachment, identity formation, and non-suicidal self-injury: A longitudinal mediation study. *Child and Adolescent Psychiatry and Mental Health, 13*(1), 7. https://doi.org/10.1186/s13034-019-0267-2

Gardner, K. J., Bickley, H., Turnbull, P., Kapur, N., Taylor, P., & Clements, C. (2020). The significance of site of cut in self-harm in young people. *Journal of Affective Disorders, 266*, 603–609. https://doi.org/10.1016/j.jad.2020.01.093

Geulayov, G., Casey, D., Bale, E., Brand, F., Clements, C., Farooq, B., Kapur, N., Ness, J., Waters, K., Patel, A., & Hawton, K. (2023). Risk of suicide in patients who present to hospital after self-cutting according to site of injury: Findings from the Multicentre Study of Self-harm in England. *Psychological Medicine, 53*(4), 1400–1408. https://doi.org/10.1017/s0033291721002956

Glenn, C. R., Kleiman, E. M., Cha, C. B., Nock, M. K., & Prinstein, M. J. (2016). Implicit cognition about self-injury predicts actual self-injurious behavior: Results from a longitudinal study of adolescents. *Journal of Child Psychology and Psychiatry, and Allied Disciplines, 57*(7), 805–813. https://doi.org/10.1111/jcpp.12500

Glenn, C. R., & Klonsky, E. D. (2010). The role of seeing blood in non-suicidal self-injury. *Journal of Clinical Psychology*, n/a. https://doi.org/10.1002/jclp.20661

Glenn, J. J., Werntz, A. J., Slama, S. J. K., Steinman, S. A., Teachman, B. A., & Nock, M. K. (2017). Suicide and self-injury-related implicit cognition: A large-scale examination and replication. *Journal of Abnormal Psychology, 126*(2), 199–211. https://doi.org/10.1037/abn0000230

Griller, J. (2013). *The paradox of self-harm in prison: Psychopathy or an evolved coping strategy?* Anchor Academic Publishing.

Hasking, P., & Boyes, M. (2018). The Non-Suicidal Self-Injury Expectancy Questionnaire: Factor structure and initial validation. *Clinical Psychologist, 22*(2), 251–261. https://doi.org/10.1111/cp.12127

Hasking, P. A., Simplicio, M. D., McEvoy, P. M., & Reesa, C. S. (2018). Emotional cascade theory and non-suicidal self-injury: The importance of imagery and positive affect. *Cognition and Emotion, 32*(5), 941–952. https://doi.org/10.1080/02699931.2017.1368456

Hasking, P., Whitlock, J., Voon, D., & Rose, A. (2017). A cognitive-emotional model of NSSI: Using emotion regulation and cognitive processes to explain why people self-injure. *Cognition and Emotion, 31*(8), 1543–1556. https://doi.org/10.1080/02699931.2016.1241219

Hodgson, S. (2004). Cutting through the silence: A sociological construction of self-injury. *Sociological Inquiry, 74*(2), 162–179. https://doi.org/10.1111/j.1475-682x.2004.00085.x

Holmes, E. A., Brown, R. J., Mansell, W., Fearon, R. P., Hunter, E. C. M., Frasquilho, F., & Oakley, D. A. (2005). Are there two qualitatively distinct forms of dissociation? A review and some clinical implications. *Clinical Psychology Review, 25*(1), 1–23. https://doi.org/10.1016/j.cpr.2004.08.006

Horrocks, J., Price, S., House, A., & Owens, D. (2003). Self-injury attendances in the accident and emergency department: Clinical database study. *British Journal of Psychiatry, 183*(1), 34–39. https://doi.org/10.1192/bjp.183.1.34

Hymen, J.W. (1999). *Women living with self-injury*. Temple University Press.

Iwata B. A., Pace G. M., Kissel R. C., Nau P. A. & Farber J. M. (1990). The Self-Injury Trauma (SIT) Scale: A method for quantifying surface tissue damage caused by self injurious behavior. *Journal of Applied Behavior Analysis, 23*, 99–110. https://doi.org/10.1901/jaba.1990.23-99

Jarvi, S., Jackson, B., Swenson, L., & Crawford, H. (2013). The impact of social contagion on non-suicidal self-injury: A review of the literature. *Archives of Suicide Research, 17*(1), 1–19. https://doi.org/10.1080/13811118.2013.748404

Jones N. P. (1990). Self-enucleation and psychosis. *The British Journal of Ophthalmology, 74*(9), 571–573. https://doi.org/10.1136/bjo.74.9.571

Karpel, M. G., & Jerram, M. W. (2015). Levels of dissociation and nonsuicidal self-injury: A quartile risk model. *Journal of Trauma & Dissociation, 16*(3), 303–321. https://doi.org/10.1080/15299732.2015.989645

Kendall, N., MacDonald, C., & Binnie, J. (2021). Blogs, identity, stigma and scars: The legacy of self-injury. *Mental Health Review Journal, 26*(3), 258–278. https://doi.org/10.1108/mhrj-06-2020-0041

Kisch, T., Matzkeit, N., Waldmann, A., Stang, F., Krämer, R., Schweiger, U., Mailänder, P., & Westermair, A. L. (2019). The reason matters: Deep wrist injury patterns differ with intentionality (accident versus suicide attempt). *Plastic and Reconstructive Surgery: Global Open, 7*(5), Article e2139. https://doi.org/10.1097/GOX.0000000000002139

Klonsky, E. D. (2007). The functions of deliberate self-injury: A review of the evidence. *Clinical Psychology Review, 27*(2), 226–239. https://doi.org/10.1016/j.cpr.2006.08.002

Klonsky, E. D. (2011). Non-suicidal self-injury in United States adults: Prevalence, sociodemographics, topography and functions. *Psychological Medicine, 41*(9), 1981–1986. https://doi.org/10.1017/s0033291710002497

Klonsky, E. D., & Glenn, C. R. (2009). Assessing the functions of non-suicidal self-injury: Psychometric properties of the Inventory of Statements About Self-injury (ISAS). *Journal of Psychopathology & Behavioral Assessment, 31*(3), 215–219. https://doi.org/10.1007/s10862-008-9107-z

Klonsky, E. D., Glenn, C. R., Styer, D. M., Olino, T. M., & Washburn, J. J. (2015). The functions of nonsuicidal self-injury: Converging evidence for a two-factor structure. *Child and Adolescent Psychiatry and Mental Health, 9*, 44–53. https://doi.org/10.1186/s13034-015-0073-4

Laukkanen, E., Rissanen, M. L., Tolmunen, T., Kylmä, J., & Hintikka, J. (2013). Adolescent self-cutting elsewhere than on the arms reveals more serious psychiatric symptoms. *European Child & Adolescent Psychiatry, 22*(8), 501–510. https://doi.org/10.1007/s00787-013-0390-1

Levy M. S. (1998). A helpful way to conceptualize and understand reenactments. *The Journal of Psychotherapy Practice and Research, 7*(3), 227–235.

Lewis, S. P., & Hasking, P. A. (2020). Rethinking self-injury recovery: A commentary and conceptual reframing. *Bjpsych Bulletin, 44*(2), 44–46. https://doi.org/10.1192/bjb.2019.51

Lewis, S. P., Heath, N. L., Hasking, P. A., Whitlock, J. L., Wilson, M. S., & Plener, P. L. (2019). Addressing self-injury on college campuses: Institutional recommendations. *Journal of College Counseling, 22*(1), 70–82. https://doi.org/10.1002/jocc.12115

Lewis, S. P., Heath, N. L., St Denis, J. M., & Noble, R. (2011). The scope of nonsuicidal self-injury on YouTube. *Pediatrics, 127*(3), e552–e557. https://doi.org/10.1542/peds.2010-2317.

Lewis, S. P., & Mehrabkhani, S. (2016). Every scar tells a story: Insight into people's self-injury scar experiences. *Counselling Psychology Quarterly, 29*(3), 296–310. https://doi.org/10.1080/09515070.2015.1088431

Liu, R. T., Scopelliti, K. M., Pittman, S. K., & Zamora, A. S. (2018). Childhood maltreatment and nonsuicidal self-injury: A systematic review and meta-analysis. *The lancet. Psychiatry, 5*(1), 51–64. https://doi.org/10.1016/S2215-0366(17)30469-8

Lloyd-Richardson, E. E., Hasking, P., Lewis, S., Hamza, C., McAllister, M., Baetens, I., & Muehlenkamp, J. (2020). Addressing self-injury in schools, part 1: Understanding nonsuicidal self-injury and the importance of respectful curiosity in supporting youth who engage in self-injury. *NASN School Nurse, 35*(2), 92–98. https://doi.org/10.1177/1942602x19886381

Long, M. (2017). "We're not monsters . . . we're just really sad sometimes:" hidden self-injury, stigma and help-seeking. *Health Sociology Review, 27*(1), 89–103. https://doi.org/10.1080/14461242.2017.1375862

Markham S. (2020). Collaborative risk assessment in secure and forensic mental health settings in the UK. *General Psychiatry, 33*(5), Article e100291. https://doi.org/10.1136/gpsych-2020-100291

Martin, T., & Gattaz, W. F. (1991). Psychiatric aspects of male genital self-mutilation. *Psychopathology, 24*(3), 170–178. https://doi.org/10.1159/000284711

Matsumoto, T., Yamaguchi, A., Chiba, Y., Asami, T., Iseki, E., & Hirayasu, Y. (2004). Patterns of self-cutting: A preliminary study on differences in clinical implications between wrist- and arm-cutting using a Japanese juvenile detention center sample. *Psychiatry and Clinical Neurosciences, 58*(4), 377–382. https://doi.org/10.1111/j.1440-1819.2004.01271.x

Medina M. (2011). Physical and psychic imprisonment and the curative function of self-cutting. *Psychoanalytic Psychology 28*(1), 2–12. https://psycnet.apa.org/doi/10.1037/a0022557

Miller, D. (1994). *Women who hurt themselves: A book of hope and understanding.* Basic Books.

Morales, Y. (2013). *Exploring the phenomenon of self-mutilation among adult males in a correctional setting: A quantitative and qualitative inquiry.* [Doctoral dissertation, University of New Mexico]. ProQuest Dissertations and Theses Global.

Nock, M. K. (2008). Actions speak louder than words: An elaborated theoretical model of the social functions of self-injury and other harmful behaviors. *Applied and Preventive Psychology, 12*(4), 159–168. https://doi.org/10.1016/j.appsy.2008.05.002

Nock, M. K. (2009). Why do people hurt themselves? New insights into the nature and functions of self-injury. *Current Directions in Psychological Science, 18*, 78–83. https://doi.org/10.1111/j.1467-8721.2009.01613.x

O'Loughlin, C. M., Gomer, B., & Ammerman, B. A. (2021). The social context of nonsuicidal self-injury: Links to severity, suicide risk, and social factors. *Journal of Clinical Psychology*, *77*(4), 1004–1017. https://doi.org/10.1002/jclp.23073

Rayner, G., Blackburn, J., Edward, K. L., Stephenson, J., & Ousey, K. (2019). Emergency department nurse's attitudes towards patients who self-harm: A meta-analysis. *International Journal of Mental Health Nursing*, *28*(1), 40–53. https://doi.org/10.1111/inm.12550

Rayner, G., & Warne, T. (2015). Interpersonal processes and self-injury: A qualitative study using Bricolage. *Journal of Psychiatric and Mental Health Nursing*, *23*(1), 54–65. https://doi.org/10.1111/jpm.12277

Reece, J. (2005). The language of cutting: Initial reflections on a study of the experiences of self-injury in a group of women and nurses. *Issues in Mental Health Nursing*, *26*(6), 561–574. https://doi.org/10.1080/01612840590959380

Rissanen, M. L., Kylmä, J., & Laukkanen, E. (2008). Descriptions of self-mutilation among Finnish adolescents: A qualitative descriptive inquiry. *Issues in Mental Health Nursing*, *29*(2), 145–163. https://doi.org/10.1080/01612840701792597

Sandel, D. B., Jomar, K., Johnson, S. L., Dickson, J. M., Dandy, S., Forrester, R., & Taylor, P. J. (2021). Beliefs about one's non-suicidal self-injury: The experiences of self-injury questionnaire (ESIQ). *Archives of Suicide Research*, *25*(3), 458–474. https://doi.org/10.1080/13811118.2020.1712285

Scourfield J., Roen K. & McDermott E. (2011). The non-display of authentic distress: Public-private dualism in young people's discursive construction of self-harm. *Sociology of Health and Illness 33*(5), 777–791. https://doi.org/10.1111/j.1467-9566.2010.01322.x.

Seko. (2013). Picturesque wounds: A multimodal analysis of self-injury photographs on Flickr. *Forum Qualitative Research*, *14*(2), article 22. https://doi.org/10.17169/fqs-14.2.1935

Selby, E. A, Kranzler A, Lindqvist J, Fehling, K. B., Brillante, J., Yuan, F., Gao, X., & Miller, A. L. (2019). The dynamics of pain during nonsuicidal self-injury. *Clinical Psychological Science*, *7*(2), 302–320. https://doi.org/10.1177/2167702618807147

Sheehy, K., Noureen, A., Khaliq, A., Dhingra, K., Husain, N., Pontin, E. E., Cawley, R., & Taylor, P. J. (2019). An examination of the relationship between shame, guilt and self-harm: A systematic review and meta-analysis. *Clinical Psychology Review*, *73*, Article 101779. https://doi.org/10.1016/j.cpr.2019.101779

Sornberger, M. J., Heath, N. L., Toste, J. R. & McLouth, R. (2012). Non-suicidal self-injury and gender: Patterns of prevalence, methods, and locations among adolescents. *Suicide and Life-Threatening Behavior*, *42*, 266–278. https://doi.org/10.1111/j.1943-278X.2012.00088.x

Stacy, S. E., Bandel, S. L., Lear, M. K., & Pepper, C. M. (2018). Before, during, and after self injury: The practice patterns of nonsuicidal self injury. *The Journal of Nervous and Mental Disease*, *206*(7), 522–527. https://doi.org/10.1097/NMD.0000000000000846

Stänicke L. I. (2021). The punished self, the unknown self, and the harmed self —Toward a more nuanced understanding of self-harm among adolescent girls. *Frontiers in Psychology*, *12*, Article 543303. https://doi.org/10.3389/fpsyg.2021.543303

Straker, G. (2006). Signing with a scar: Understanding self-harm. *Psychoanalytic Dialogues*, *16*, 93–112. https://doi.org/10.2513/s10481885pd1601_6

Stroehmer, R., Edel, M. A., Pott, S., Juckel, G., & Haussleiter, I. S. (2015). Digital comparison of healthy young adults and borderline patients engaged in non-suicidal self-injury. *Annals of General Psychiatry*, *14*(1), 47. https://doi.org/10.1186/s12991-015-0088-5

Tantam, D. & Huband, N. (2009). *Understanding repeated self-injury: A multidisciplinary approach*. Palgrave Macmillan.

Tatnell, R., Hasking, P., Newman, L., Taffe, J., & Martin, G. (2016). Attachment, emotion regulation, childhood abuse and assault: Examining predictors of NSSI among adolescents. *Archives of Suicide Research*, *21*, 610–620. https://doi.org/10.1080/13811118.2016.1246267

Tatnell, R., Kelada, L., Hasking, P., & Martin, G. (2014). Longitudinal analysis of adolescent NSSI: The role of intrapersonal and interpersonal factors. *Journal of Abnormal Child Psychology*, *42*, 885–896. https://doi.org/10.1007/s10802-013-9837-6

Taylor, D. M., & Cameron, P. A. (1998). Deliberate self-inflicted trauma: Population demographics, the nature of injury and a comparison with patients who overdose. *Australian and New Zealand Journal of Public Health*, *22*(1), 120–125. https://doi.org/10.1111/j.1467-842x.1998.tb01155.x

Taylor, P. J., Jomar, K., Dhingra, K., Forrester, R., Shahmalak, U., & Dickson, J. M. (2018). A meta-analysis of the prevalence of different functions of non-suicidal self-injury. *Journal of Affective Disorders*, 227: 759–769.

https://doi.org/10.1016/j.jad.2017.11.073. Epub 2017 Nov 21. Erratum in: *Journal of Affective Disorders*, 2019 Dec 1;259: 440. PMID: 29689691.

Tebble, N. J., Adams, R., Thomas, D. W., & Price, P. (2006). Anxiety and self-consciousness in patients with facial lacerations one week and six months later. *British Journal of Oral and Maxillofacial Surgery*, *44*(6), 520–525. https://doi.org/10.1016/j.bjoms.2005.10.010

Thabane, L., Mbuagbaw, L., Zhang, S., Samaan, Z., Marcucci, M., Ye, C., Thabane, M., Giangregorio, L., Dennis, B., Kosa, D., Debono, V. B., Dillenburg, R., Fruci, V., Bawor, M., Lee, J., Wells, G., & Goldsmith, C. H. (2013). A tutorial on sensitivity analyses in clinical trials: The what, why, when and how. *BMC Medical Research Methodology*, *13*(1), Article 92. https://doi.org/10.1186/1471-2288-13-92

Tighe, J., Nicholas, J., Shand, F., & Christensen, H. (2018). Efficacy of acceptance and commitment therapy in reducing suicidal ideation and deliberate self-harm: Systematic review. *JMIR Mental Health*, *5*(2), Article e10732. https://doi.org/10.2196/10732

van Vliet, K. J., & Kalnins, G. R. C. (2011). A compassion-focused approach to nonsuicidal self-injury. *Journal of Mental Health Counseling*, *33*(4), 295–311. https://doi.org/10.17744/mehc.33.4.j7540338q223t417

Verroken, S., Schotte, C., Derluyn, I., & Baetens, I. (2018). Starting from scratch: Prevalence, methods, and functions of non-suicidal self-injury among refugee minors in Belgium. *Child and Adolescent Psychiatry and Mental Health*, *12*(1), 51. https://doi.org/10.1186/s13034-018-0260-1

Walsh B. (2007). Clinical assessment of self-injury: A practical guide. *Journal of clinical Psychology*, *63*(11), 1057–1068. https://doi.org/10.1002/jclp.20413

Wester, K. L., & Trepal, H. C. (2015) Non-suicidal self-injury: Exploring the correlations among race, ethnic identity, and ethnic belonging. *Journal of College Student Development*, *56*(2), 127–139.

Wester, K. L., Wachter Morris, C., & Williams, B. (2017). Nonsuicidal self-injury in the schools: A tiered prevention approach for reducing social contagion. *Professional School Counseling*, *21*(1), 1096–2409. https://doi.org/10.5330/1096-2409-21.1.142

Whitlock, J. (2006). Self-injurious behaviors in a college population. *Pediatrics*, *117*(6), 1939–1948. https://doi.org/10.1542/peds.2005-2543

Whitlock, J. (2010). self-injurious behavior in adolescents. *PLoS Medicine*, *7*(5), Article e1000240. https://doi.org/10.1371/journal.pmed.1000240

Wilkinson, B. (2011). Current trends in remediating adolescent self-injury. *The Journal of School Nursing*, *27*(2), 120–128. https://doi.org/10.1177/1059840510388570

Yakeley, J., & Burbridge-James, W. (2018). Psychodynamic approaches to suicide and self-harm. *BJPsych Advances*, *24*(1), 37–45. https://doi.org/10.1192/bja.2017.6

You, J., Lin, M. P., & Leung, F. (2013). Functions of nonsuicidal self-injury among Chinese community adolescents. *Journal of Adolescence*, *36*(4), 737–745. https://doi.org/10.1016/j.adolescence.2013.05.007

You, J., Ma, C., Lin, M. P., & Leung, F. (2015). Comparing among the experiences of self-cutting, hitting, and scratching in Chinese adolescents attending secondary schools: An interview study. *Behavioral Disorders*, *40*(2), 122–137. https://doi.org/10.17988/bd-14-9.1

Zhang, F., Cloutier, P. F., Yang, H., Liu, W., Cheng, W., & Xiao, Z. (2019). Non-suicidal self-injury in Shanghai inner bound middle school students. *General Psychiatry*, *32*(4), Article e100083. https://doi.org/10.1136/gpsych-2019-100083

CHAPTER 25

NSSI in Elementary School

Lisa Van Hove, Imke Baetens, Amanda Simundic, Elana Bloom, *and* Nancy Heath

Abstract

This chapter discusses nonsuicidal self-injury (NSSI) found among children of elementary age, referencing the research on Belgian and Canadian elementary school staff's experiences with children who engage in NSSI. Suicide ideation was associated with elevated levels of study anxiety, self-accusation, impulsivity, and loneliness across all age groups. In terms of NSSI methods, interfering with wound healing, head banging, and cutting were reported frequently by both Belgian and Canadian school staff. The chapter explains the most perceived reasons for engaging in NSSI were frustration, difficulty in communicating emotions, and managing stress. Most Belgian and Canadian school staff expressed that they felt ill-prepared to deal with NSSI situations, which resulted in the suggestion for NSSI professional development for elementary educators and school professionals.

Key Words: NSSI, elementary, children, Belgian school staff, Canadian school staff, suicide ideation

Introduction

Thus far, most studies on nonsuicidal self-injury (NSSI) focus on adolescent and young adult samples, due to the observed peak in NSSI onset and prevalence during these important transition years (e.g., Gandhi et al., 2018; Kiekens et al., 2019) and the heightened risk for suicidality (Griep & MacKinnon, 2022). Furthermore, most interventions and treatments are focused on these age groups (Beauchaine et al., 2019; Gilbert et al., 2020; Plener, 2020; Turner et al., 2014).

Although research regarding NSSI among elementary-school-age children is scarce, a few studies suggest that NSSI may occur in this age group (e.g., Barrocas et al., 2012; Hankin & Abela, 2011) and that a younger age of onset may be associated with more severe/frequent NSSI (Ammerman et al., 2018; Muehlenkamp & Brausch, 2012) and elevated suicide risk (Muehlenkamp & Brausch, 2012). This underlines the importance of investigating NSSI in elementary schools and exploring educators' experiences with NSSI.

The first part of this chapter outlines the limited current knowledge in the field of NSSI in elementary age children. Next, we summarize the findings of a recent study

(Simundic et al., submitted), which addresses the minimal NSSI research in elementary school children by studying Belgian and Canadian elementary school staffs' experiences with children who engage in NSSI. Finally, we discuss the gaps and hurdles in studying NSSI in elementary age children. Implications for clinical practice, policies, and future research will also be outlined. Two vignettes illustrate best-practice approaches in this area for school staff.

Research on NSSI in Elementary School Children

Recent studies have indicated that NSSI lifetime prevalence rates vary between 7% and 9% in children ages 6–12 years. For example, Deville et al. (2020) conducted a cross-sectional study in which 11,814 children (ages 9–10 years) were included. In total, 9.1% of the children reported current and/or past NSSI. This corresponds with the 7% NSSI lifetime prevalence found by researchers who investigated NSSI among community samples of 7- to 11-year-olds (Barrocas et al., 2012; James & Gibb, 2019). Similar yearly prevalence rates (8%) were found among slightly older children (10–14 years; Hankin & Abela, 2011).

Although research has shown that retrospective evaluations may lead to biases (e.g., Hardt & Rutter, 2004; Klimes-Dougan et al., 2007) and larger variability, most studies up to date report on individuals' retrospective self-reported estimations of the age of NSSI onset. Several retrospective studies indicate that 1% to 5% of individuals recall engaging in NSSI for the first time before the age of 10 (Nock & Prinstein, 2004; Whitlock et al., 2006). Moreover, Gandhi et al. (2018) found in their retrospective study that some Flemish adolescents and emerging adults recalled their first NSSI episode by the age of 6 and that the risk for onset of NSSI increased exponentially after the age of 9 years. This exponential increase was also reported by Martin et al. (2010). Also, a paucity of studies has examined NSSI in elementary school age via multi-informant reports. For example, Resch et al. (2008) questioned parents about NSSI behaviors of their child (ages 11–17 years). Although 2.9% of the adolescents reported NSSI within the last six months, only 1.4% of the parents indicated that their child had engaged in NSSI. Also, Baetens et al. (2015) found that 1.5% of the parents were aware of their child's NSSI at age 13, whereas a yearly incidence rate of 2.8% was reported by the children themselves. This discrepancy was also reported by Deville et al. (2020), who found a parent-child discordance of 84%. This highlights the secrecy of NSSI behavior. No study up to date has examined prevalence rates of NSSI via teacher report. Although school staff tends to underestimate NSSI prevalence, they may be reliable informants on the nature of NSSI (Berger et al., 2014). This important gap in research emphasizes the need to investigate prevalence both directly with students and in the school context. Therefore, one of the challenges that accompanies research on NSSI in children is how to more accurately capture NSSI activity and details.

Regarding risk and protective factors of NSSI in elementary school children, few have been identified thus far. However, Tan and et al. (2018) recently uncovered a significant difference between risk factors for suicidal ideation that apply to primary school students (ages 9–12 years), middle school students (13–15 years), and high school students (ages 16–18 years). For example, suicide ideation was associated with elevated levels of study anxiety, self-accusation, impulsivity, and loneliness across all age groups. Additionally, higher levels of hypersensitivity and physical symptoms were associated with suicide ideation only in middle and high school students specifically. These differences might also be present for NSSI, as NSSI is an important precursor of suicidal behaviors (e.g., Kiekens et al., 2018; Muehlenkamp & Gutierrez, 2007) and would imply that some identified risk factors in adolescent samples may no longer be applicable. Vice versa, some factors found to be "insignificant" in older samples, may be significantly associated with NSSI in children specifically.

Currently, to the best of our knowledge only three studies focused on risk and protective factors in a sample of children ages 12 years and younger. First, James and Gibb (2019) found in a community sample of 7- to 11-year-olds that being exposed to greater levels of maternal expressed emotion-criticism (i.e., level of expressed hostility and criticism by a mother toward her child; Hooley et al., 1986) was a significant risk factor for girls, not boys. Borschmann et al. (2020) found persistent depressive and anxious symptoms, frequent bullying victimization, and recent alcohol consumption at age 8/9 to be predictive for self-harm at age 11/12. Also, self-harm at age 11/12 was associated with having few friends, poor emotional control, and antisocial behavior. Deville et al. (2020) found in a cross-sectional study with 11,814 children (ages 9–10 years) that NSSI engagement was associated with high family conflict and low parental monitoring.

Finally, some studies have identified an earlier onset of NSSI as a potential risk factor for more severe and frequent NSSI in adolescence. This increase in severity was also reflected in the number of hospital visits due to NSSI (Ammerman et al., 2018; Muehlenkamp & Brausch, 2012). In addition, researchers suggested that a younger age of NSSI onset might be associated with an increased risk for suicidality (Muehlenkamp & Brausch, 2012), although this was not confirmed by Ammerman et al. (2018).

The cases in the next sections highlight the common experiences and what the literature outlines in NSSI among elementary students. Throughout the chapter it will be helpful to pay attention to the core elements of the cases captured in the literature. In the section "Clinical Implications," a follow-up on the cases will be provided via school response principles and appropriate resolutions.

Case 1: Jasmine
Jasmine is a grade 2 student who lives at home with her parents. She is well liked by adults and peers. Jasmine performs extremely well academically and takes her school work very seriously. She has a strong sense of fairness and justice, which can at times lead to peer conflict and not feeling heard in the classroom. Jasmine has difficulty with transitions and change, when she feels as though her performance is subpar, or when she doesn't

understand/follow the instructions. This often leads to her feeling extremely worried, stressed, and overwhelmed. In these situations, Jasmine will either hide under her desk or remain unresponsive. Recently, she has begun using her scissors and paper clips to frequently scratch her wrist and hands. In some instances, the scratches have started to bleed.

Case 2: Joey

Joey is a grade 6 student diagnosed with attention deficit/hyperactivity disorder (ADHD). He has struggled in school, both socially and academically since grade 2. Although a recent psychological report and a consultation with Joey's pediatrician suggested that Joey begin a trial of medication, his parents refuse. Joey has difficulty managing his emotions and has daily physical and verbal conflicts with peers. He often feels rejected by others and has challenges joining a peer group. When particularly frustrated, Joey punches hard objects and sometimes cuts his arm with the blade from his pencil sharpener.

NSSI in School Settings

NSSI has a detrimental impact on the school setting (e.g., school staff and classmates). Some studies have focused on needs assessment of school staff with regard to NSSI in school settings. For example, 57% of secondary school teachers felt unknowledgeable about this behavior (Heath et al., 2011). This lack of NSSI knowledge and feelings of being ill-equipped to support students who self-injure was also reported by school counselors. Furthermore, a lack of professional development and school policies on how to deal with NSSI among students was mentioned (De Riggi et al., 2016; Duggan et al., 2011).

However, despite evidence that NSSI exists in elementary age children as noted above, and therefore elementary school educators may be encountering students with NSSI, to our knowledge there have been no studies of educators understanding of NSSI in this context. Consequently, it is unclear whether elementary school educators encounter NSSI and how they respond to it, if they do. This is critical information for supporting appropriate professional development and training programs for schools.

In summary, some studies (e.g., James & Gibb, 2019; MacPherson et al., 2018) have indicated the presence of NSSI among young children and its disturbing association with suicidal behavior (e.g., MacPherson et al., 2018; Muehlenkamp & Brausch, 2012). Moreover in a secondary school setting, the majority of school staff feel ill-equipped to deal with this behavior (Heath et al., 2011). To address this gap, Baetens et al. conducted a study investigating Belgian and Canadian elementary school staff's perceptions and experiences with NSSI in elementary school settings. When interpreting school staff's responses, one must be aware of the potential biases that may impact the results (e.g., Baetens et al., 2015) and interpret them solely as teacher-reports. Their needs assessment can be ground for the development of a school policy to address NSSI in elementary schools.

Brief Report of the Experiences of Elementary School Staff With Children Who Engage in NSSI

In the next sections, the study by Baetens et al. regarding elementary school staff's perceptions and experiences with NSSI is discussed.

Method

In total, 118 Belgian (85.6% female) and 63 Canadian (87.3% female) staff members of elementary schools participated in this study. Staff members who took part in the present study were asked to report on (a) their perceptions and beliefs about NSSI engagement in elementary students and (b) previous encounters they have had with NSSI engagement among students, independent of their professional role within the institution. In the Belgian sample, the age ranged from 24 to 60 years old ($M = 43.2$, $SD = 10.7$) and the total years of service from 0 to 41 ($M = 20.9$, $SD = 11.6$). This is similar to the Canadian sample, in which the age range was 23–63 years old ($M = 41.2$, $SD = 10.8$) and the total years of service was 1 to 39 ($M = 15.1$, $SD = 9.2$).

At both sites, participants responded to demographic questions regarding age, gender, education, and their role within the school. Thereafter, they responded to researcher-developed questions that included both open- and close-ended questions. Questions asked school staff about their knowledge of NSSI among elementary students (e.g., "How often do you think typically developing students in elementary school engage in NSSI?"), their professional experiences with NSSI among elementary school students (e.g., "In your experience, do students who engage in NSSI appear to have a common pattern of family and/or peer circumstances, or not?"), in addition to questions regarding professional development they want to receive in this area (e.g., "What, if any, professional development do you as an educator feel you need in this area?"). The online survey questions were originally developed in English and then translated to Dutch and French. The French version was only administered as an option in Canada and the Dutch version only in Belgium.

In Canada, elementary school staff were recruited through social media advertisements, teacher association listservs, and directly through school principals who distributed the study information to their school staff. In Belgium, schools were contacted via their general email addresses which were retrieved from a governmental website. The administrative staff and/or school principal were then asked to forward the information letter and access to the study to the elementary school staff. Before agreeing to participate, participants were able to view the consent form and received all information regarding the study. Participants were provided with an anonymous link to the consent form (to provide their formal consent), followed by the online demographic and researcher-developed questions. Following completion of the online survey, participants received debriefing information along with downloadable resources on the topic of NSSI. Moreover, participants were provided with the opportunity to enter their email address separately from the survey, to be entered in a raffle for a chance to win 50 dollars (Canada) or a gift certificate of 50 euros (Belgium).

Results

In total, 28% of Belgian participants indicated having personal/private experiences with NSSI (e.g., self, family members, and loved ones) and 47.5% had been in contact with one or multiple student(s) who engaged in NSSI. In Canada, 50.8% of participants had experiences with NSSI personal/private experiences with NSSI and 65.1% had encountered students who engage in NSSI. Of those school personnel who had encountered and responded to students who engaged in NSSI, 12.7% of the Belgian and 15.9% of Canadian participants indicated that the students they had dealt with also verbalized a wish to die.

PERSPECTIVES OF ELEMENTARY SCHOOL STAFF REGARDING NSSI

First, most Belgian and Canadian participants estimated NSSI engagement in elementary school to be a "very rare" (Belgium: 58.5%, Canada: 31.7%) to "rare" (Belgium: 30.5%, Canada: 38.1%) phenomenon. The remaining participants reported that NSSI occurs "sometimes" (Belgium: 8.5%, Canada: 20.6%), "never" (Belgium: 1.7%, Canada: 6.3%), and "often" (Belgium: 0.8%, Canada: 6.3%). Furthermore, in both samples NSSI engagement was estimated to be least frequent in grade 1 (Belgium: 8.5%, Canada: 23.8%) and most frequent in level 6 (Belgium: 94.9%, Canada: 98.4%) (see table 25.1).

The majority of Belgian (54.2%) and almost half of the Canadian participants (46.0%) perceived NSSI to be more often present among girls than boys. In Belgium, the most frequently observed method of NSSI engagement reported by school staff who have responded to NSSI in their schools was carving skin (46.6%), whereas in Canada it was interfering with wound healing (e.g., scab picking; 47.6%). For the five most frequently

Table 25.1 School Staff's Estimation of NSSI Across All Grades

Grade	Belgium ($n = 118$) %	Canada ($n = 63$) %
Kindergarten	n/a	20.6
Grade level 1	8.5	23.8
Grade level 2	9.3	30.2
Grade level 3	19.5	42.9
Grade level 4	44.9	57.1
Grade level 5	79.7	92.1
Grade level 6	94.9	98.4

Note: Participants were asked to report all the grades in which they believe NSSI engagement to occur.

Table 25.2 Five Most Frequent Methods of Engagement in NSSI

Belgium (n = 118)		Canada (n = 63)	
NSSI method	%	NSSI method	%
Carving skin	46.6	Interfering with wound healing	47.6
Head banging	33.1	Severe scratching	46
Interfering with wound healing	25.4	Cutting	44.4
Cutting	23.7	Head banging	42.9
Hair pulling	23.7	Self-hitting	33.3

Note: School staff who have responded to NSSI in their schools were asked to select all the methods of NSSI engagement they have observed in students.

observed methods of engagement in NSSI by school staff who have responded to NSSI in their school, estimated by Belgian and Canadian school staff, refer to table 25.2.

Finally, school staff were asked to report reasons for engaging in NSSI that they perceive apply to elementary students. The three most commonly perceived reasons for engaging in NSSI by school staff were frustration (Belgium: 61.9%, Canada: 87.3%), difficulty in communicating emotions (Belgium: 57.6%, Canada: 88.9%), and managing stress (Belgium: 52.2%, Canada: 82.5%). In Belgium, attention (45.8%) and redirecting anger (43.2%) were also perceived as frequent reasons for engaging in NSSI. This was not in line with the Canadian sample, which perceived self-hatred (73.0%) and self-punishment (68.3%) as common reasons. When participants were asked to elaborate on their beliefs about other reasons elementary students may engage in NSSI, the majority reported believing that stressors at home (Belgium: 34.9%, Canada: 31.7%) were a contributor to NSSI. Other reasons mentioned by both samples were stress in general (Belgium: 24.1%, Canada: 19.0%); negative self-image (Belgium: 21.7%, Canada, 11.1%); to get attention (Belgium: 3.2%, Canada: 20.6%); mental health difficulties (Belgium: 18.1%), such as anxiety (Canada: 27.0%), depression (Canada: 7.9%), and trauma (Canada: 6.4%); difficulty with emotions (Belgium: 12.0%, Canada: 11.1%); and stressors at school (Canada: 7.9%), such as being bullied (Belgium: 10.8%).

SUPPORTIVE NEEDS OF SCHOOL STAFF

Only 7.8% of Belgian and 9.5% of Canadian participants felt equipped to deal with students who engage in NSSI. Some participants indicated that this is due to a lack of training and support (Belgium: 58.5%, Canada: 51.9%). Participants were asked about the professional development they believe they need in the area. In response, a need for NSSI training (e.g., how to respond to and support students who engage in NSSI) and psychoeducation (e.g., being made aware of the signs) was reported (Belgium: 57.7%, Canada: 50.8%). Furthermore, some participants (Belgium: 5.6%, Canada: 11.1%) also reported the need for a specific protocol to follow when NSSI is suspected or occurs. In Belgium specifically, participants needed the involvement of external mental health care services (31.0%), fluent referrals to external mental health care workers (e.g., psychologists, pediatricians, and psychiatrists; 14.1%), and a contact person/confidant (9.9%). Finally, some participants (Belgium: 12.7%, Canada: 9.5%) indicated that, as educators, they felt this was outside their responsibility and they should not be expected to respond. Specifically, these participants expressed that professional development and training was not needed (Canada: 9.5%).

Conclusion

One in two staff members have been in contact with one or multiple elementary student(s) who engage(d) in NSSI. In both countries, the majority of sampled school staff reported having dealt with NSSI at least once in the past. Despite this prior experience reported by many school staff, the majority perceived the prevalence of NSSI among this age group to be quite rare. This divergence may be a result of school staff reporting their personal experience over a period of years whereas the prevalence is understood as occurring at a single time point. Additionally, school staff thought NSSI was systematically more prevalent with increasing age. In terms of the methods of NSSI, interfering with wound healing (e.g., picking scabs), head banging, and cutting were reported frequently by both Belgian and Canadian and school staff. In both Belgium and Canada, the most cited perceived reasons for engaging in NSSI were frustration, difficulty in communicating emotions, and managing stress. Importantly, most Belgian and Canadian school staff expressed that they felt ill prepared to deal with NSSI situations. Consequently, a need for psychoeducation and training was suggested. Some would also like to have a NSSI school protocol, in which external mental health professionals to whom they can refer are listed, an internal contact person is appointed, and strategies to help students emotionally, are described. Finally, a small minority of participants questioned the extent to which it is their job to handle NSSI situations.

Discussion

A review of literature shows a lack in research on experiences and needs of involved stakeholders (e.g., parents, school staff, professional health care workers) on how to deal with NSSI. Simundic et al. (submitted) show that more than 50% of elementary school staff have been confronted with one or more elementary school students that engage in NSSI and feel ill-equipped in responding to these students' needs. This finding implies, in line with Beauchaine et al. (2019), a lack of prevention/intervention that is adjusted to this younger population. Due to a lack in research and availability of resources, school staff and clinicians are forced to use models and approaches that were developed for adolescents or adults. Future research should focus on adapted interventions and preventions for NSSI at an elementary school level.

Furthermore, in light of the present chapter's preliminary findings of elementary educators' experiences and beliefs about NSSI, it is evident there is a pressing need for more in-depth, qualitative explorations of educators' understanding and, more critically, of their response to NSSI.

Existing studies (e.g., Barrocas et al., 2012) estimate a prevalence of 7% to 9% of NSSI in elementary-school-age children, although further studies are needed in the area. However, an important hurdle to overcome in the study of NSSI in a population of elementary school children is the ethical dilemma. Research should consider potential iatrogenic consequences of examining risk behavior such as NSSI in elementary school children, and determine which forms of research (e.g., self-report, interviews, and ecological momentary assessment) are most suitable in this population. Prior research (e.g., Baetens et al., 2020) has shown no iatrogenic effects of examining NSSI in (pre-) adolescent and adult populations (both in clinical and community samples), and future research focusing on NSSI in elementary age children should be aligned with ethical considerations as mentioned in Hasking et al. (2019) and Lloyd-Richardson et al. (2015). Another important hurdle is the development of validated NSSI questionnaires that are adjusted to a developmentally appropriate child level without losing valuable nuances. Also, researchers should consider whether different scientific approaches affect receptivity to studying NSSI in age 11 or 12 (i.e., grade 5 and 6) in comparison to studying NSSI under the age of 10, as visual and digital methods, as well as observational research are more favorable research methodology for children (Christensen et al., 2017).

Implications for Clinical Practice

With regard to clinical implications, there is a clear need for NSSI professional development for elementary educators and school professionals. As noted above, because understanding of underlying mechanisms of NSSI in this age group remain largely unexamined, recommendations around clinical intervention are necessarily limited. However, as the present survey of elementary educators revealed, school professionals will be most focused on minimizing potential harm in their response to self-injury. This may best be accomplished through professional development (see Baetens et al., this volume, for guidelines on responding to NSSI in secondary schools and universities) for elementary school professionals. The primary professional development goal must include current information about NSSI with a particular focus on challenging common misperceptions (e.g., NSSI is the result of a harmful family environment, NSSI's relationship to suicide). Additional essential elements in professional development would include (a) appropriate first response to self-injury by educators and other school professionals, (b) the need for a school protocol with guidelines for school wide response and support, and (c) the importance of confidentiality in educators' response to self-injury and mechanisms for consultation with the school mental health professional(s).

Further, school mental health professionals will need to adapt interventions aimed at early adolescents to this younger age group, as interventions specifically aimed at elementary schools do not yet exist. Adaptations to intervention approaches designed for secondary school settings will need to be guided by the clinical judgment of mental health taking into account the developmental stage of elementary students. For older elementary students (ages 11–12 years) little change is needed; however, to adapt interventions for younger children, differing abilities in emotional regulation, attention, and communication will require simplification of existing intervention materials. Most importantly, elementary school mental health professionals must ensure that they are informed of current best-practice response to self-injury in younger populations and not assume that NSSI rarely occurs in this context. It is important at a minimum for the mental health professionals to be up to date with the literature in the field, seek clinical supervision, and connect with the community of practice focused in this area (e.g., see International Society for the Study of Self-Injury). Understanding the developmental context as it relates to NSSI in schools is significant in being able to provide resources to, and support students, parents, and school staff. In addition, the mental health professionals (MHP) plays an instrumental role in the school in providing resources for parents and school staff. Ensuring they are suggesting current, and evidence-based approaches as part of their clinical practice role within the school is necessary. Further, the MHP plays a pivotal role in educating school boards and informing policies. It is essential that MHPs be aware of and adopt best-practice approaches to be able to inform policy.

School Response Principles
The cases and resolutions below illustrate there are key elements of response for school staff to consider in support of students who engage in NSSI:

1. Refrain from making assumptions about why a student self-injures. The literature shows that the most common reason for self-injury is difficulty communicating emotions. As illustrated by the case, there was a widely held assumption that Jasmine's self-injury was a function of parenting practices. Further information would be needed to assess the accuracy of this assumption as discussed in more detail in the conclusion and analysis sections of the case.
2. Have an open mind in understanding and approaching students who engage in NSSI. Although the act of self-injury can be upsetting and disturbing for many teachers and paraprofessionals, professional development and information from the MHP can be valuable in decreasing these common feelings. Openness to NSSI among elementary students can significantly impact a first response from a school staff and subsequently a student's comfort in help-seeking behaviors and treatment.
3. Refrain from adopting the common misconceptions of NSSI, such that it is more common among females, it is a cry for attention or that cutting is the

only method of self-injury. This can lead to students who are engaging in NSSI not receiving timey intervention.
4. Support the family and refrain from adopting biases and judgments. As depicted in the first vignette, there was a common held view that Jasmine's self-injury was a result of parenting practices. More information would be needed to draw such a conclusion. Given the developmental context of elementary age students, involving parents, such as by providing them with information, resources, and support, will be critical as part of an intervention plan.
5. Maintain confidentiality and refrain from discussing sensitive information as it relates to a students' engagement in NSSI or mental health with others who are not directly involved with the student. Should discussions need to occur, they should be in a confidential, supportive space.
6. Understand the complexity of NSSI, that it is the best a child can do in the moment to cope with intense emotions. They need support in learning alternative ways of coping in these situations.
7. Seek support from colleagues. Having to respond to and support elementary-age students who engage in NSSI can be distressing. It is important to seek support from the MHP designated to your school and create mentorship as needed. Professional development, information sharing and communities of practice can also be of benefit.

Vignette 1: Grade 2

Conclusion: One time in class, Jasmine's teacher sees her using the scissors to scratch her wrist. Upon seeing this, the teacher becomes extremely distressed not knowing how to intervene or to support Jasmine. She seeks support from colleagues and her principal, strongly feeling that Jasmine's self-injury is a function of her home situation. The teacher questions the quality of parenting and the need for direct parent intervention. The principal is also concerned about the home situation and Jasmine's risk of suicidality and contacts youth protection. Meanwhile many colleagues are discussing Jasmine's situation and awareness of her condition is growing among school staff.

Analysis: Jasmine's case is a common occurrence and illustrates how harmful a lack of understanding of appropriate NSSI responses and false assumptions can be. Confidentiality should have been respected and the teacher should have consulted the MHP who could have better interpreted the self-injury and included the principal as needed.

Vignette 2: Grade 6

Conclusion: One of Joey's friends notices that his knuckles are all bruised and sees him punching the brick wall. The friend tells this to Joey's classroom teacher, who watches Joey closely and "catches" Joey cutting his arm. Feeling extremely overwhelmed, the teacher reaches out to the school mental health professional (MHP) for support. He tells the MHP that he and his colleagues need more training in this area, and that Joey's difficulties are too much for a classroom teacher to be able to manage. Additionally, the teacher mentions that this is not his role and Joey needs a specialized classroom and treatment, and that he isn't a psychologist. He asks that Joey be removed from his classroom in the meantime as he says it is too upsetting for the other students.

Analysis: Joey's teacher's response is characteristic of how many elementary teachers feel. They find the act of self-injury very disturbing and upsetting which then results in their not wanting to engage with the student at all. This response can be mitigated through professional development where educators can learn about self-injury and how to respond effectively within the constraints of the educator's role. Joey's teacher did reach out to the MHP as would be recommended but not for additional support for Joey but with the goal of having the student removed. In contrast, best practice would suggest that the MHP would consult with the teacher to help him support Joey in the classroom. In addition, the MHP would directly support Joey and his parents as well as suggest community resources.

Conclusion

Although little is known about the prevalence and etiology of NSSI in children, the current state of the field clearly underpins that NSSI is prevalent among children, with prevalence rates around 7%. Onset of NSSI can be seen in a paucity of children from 6 years onward, although research indicated a heightened risk for onset of NSSI at age 9. Future research should consider ethical guidelines in examining prevalence and etiology of NSSI in young children, and consider suitable research methodologies to examine this gap in research, with for example focusing on multi-informant reports. This chapter has briefly summarized results of the study by Simundic et al. (submitted), showing that the majority of elementary school staff have encountered one or more elementary school students that engage in NSSI and feel ill-equipped in responding to these students' needs. Future research should focus on adapted interventions and preventions for NSSI at an elementary school level, as well as adapted professional development to educators, MHPs, and administrators at this level to decrease false assumptions and poor response.

We hope that this chapter increases the awareness of the presence of NSSI in elementary schools and boosts this domain of research.

References

Ammerman, B. A., Jacobucci, R., Kleiman, E. M., Uyeji, L. L., & McCloskey, M. S. (2018). The relationship between nonsuicidal self-injury age of onset and severity of self-harm. *Suicide and Life-Threatening Behavior*, *48*(1), 31–37. https://doi.org/10.1111/sltb.12330

Baetens, I., Claes, L., Onghena, P., Van Leeuwen, K., Pieters, C., Wiersema, J. R., & Griffith, J. W. (2015). The effects of nonsuicidal self-injury on parenting behaviors: A longitudinal analyses of the perspective of the parent. *Child and Adolescent Psychiatry and Mental Health*, *9*, 24. https://doi.org/10.1186/s13034-015-0059-2

Baetens, I., Decruy, C., Vatandoost, S., Vanderhaegen, B., & Kiekens, G. (2020). School-based prevention targeting non-suicidal self-injury: a pilot study. *Frontiers in psychiatry*, *11*, 437. https://doi.org/10.3389/fpsyt.2020.00437

Barrocas, A. L., Hankin, B. L., Young, J. F., & Abela, J. R. (2012). Rates of non-suicidal self-injury in youth: Age, sex and behavioral methods in a community sample. *Pediatrics*, *130*(1), 39–45. https://doi.org/10.1542/peds.2011-2094

Beauchaine, T., Hinshaw, S., & Bridge, J. (2019). Nonsuicidal self-injury and suicidal behaviors in girls: The case for targeted prevention in preadolescence. *Clinical Psychological Science*, *7*(4), 643–667. https://doi.org/10.1177/2167702618814744

Berger, E., Hasking, P., & Reupert, A. E. (2014). "We're working in the dark here": Education needs of teachers and school staff regarding student self-injury. *School Mental Health*, *6*(3), 201–212. https://doi.org/10.1007/s12310-013-9114-4

Borschmann, R., Mundy, L. K., Canterford, L., Moreno-Betancur, M., Moran, P.A., Allen, N. B., Viner, R. M., Degenhardt, L., Kosola, S., Fedyszyn, I., & Patton, G. C. (2020). Self-harm in primary school-aged children: Prospective cohort study. *PLoS One*, *15*(11), Article e242802. https://doi.org/10.1371/journal.pone.0242802

Christensen, P., & James, A. (2017). *Research with children*. Taylor & Francis.

De Riggi, M.E., Moumne, S., Heath, N. L., & Lewis, S. P. (2016). Non-suicidal self-injury in our schools: A review and research-informed guidelines for school mental health professionals. *Canadian Journal of School Psychology*, *32*(2), 1–22. https://doi.org/10.1177/0829573516645563

DeVille, D. C., Whalen, D., Breslin, F. J., Morris, A. S., Khalsa, S. B., Paulus, M. P., & Barch, D. M. (2020). Prevalence and family-related factors associated with suicidal ideation, suicide attempts, and self-injury in children aged 9 to 10 years. *JAMA Network Open*, *3*(2), Article e1920956. https://doi.org/10.1001/jamanetworkopen.2019.20956

Duggan, J. M., Heath, N. L., Toste, J. R., & Ross, S. (2011). School counsellors' understanding of non-suicidal self-injury: Experiences and international variability. *Canadian Journal of Counselling and Psychotherapy*, *45*(4), 327–348.

Gandhi, A., Luyckx, K., Baetens, I., Kiekens, G., Sleuwaegen, E., Berens, A., Maitra, S., & Claes, L. (2018). Age of onset of non-suicidal self-injury in Dutch-speaking adolescents and emerging adults: An event history analysis of pooled data. *Comprehensive Psychiatry*, *80*(1), 170–178. https://doi.org/10.1016/j.comppsych.2017.10.007

Gilbert, A. C., DeYoung, L. L., Barthelemy, C. M., Jenkins, G. A., MacPherson, H. A., Kim, K. L., Kudinova, A. Y., Radoeva, P. D., & Dickstein, D. P. (2020). The treatment of suicide and self-injurious behaviors in children and adolescents. *Current Treatment Options in Psychiatry*, *7*(1), 39–52. https://doi.org/10.1007/s40501-020-00201-3

Griep, S. K., & MacKinnon, D. F. (2022). Does nonsuicidal self-injury predict later suicidal attempts? A review of studies. *Archives of Suicide Research*, *26*(2), 428–446. https://doi.org/10.1080/13811118.2020.1822244

Hankin, B., & Abela, J. (2011). Nonsuicidal self-injury in adolescence: Prospective rates and risk factors in a 2 ½ year longitudinal study. *Psychiatry Research*, *186*(1), 65–70. https://doi.org/10.1016/j.psychres.2010.07.056

Hasking, P. A., Lewis, S. P., Robinson, K., Heath, N. L., & Wilson, M. S. (2019). Conducting research on nonsuicidal self-injury in schools: Ethical considerations and recommendations. *School Psychology International*, *40*(3), 217–234. https://doi.org/10.1177/0143034319827056

Hardt, J., & Rutter, M. (2004). Validity of adult retrospective reports of adverse childhood experiences: Review of the evidence. *Journal of Child Psychology and Psychiatry*, *45*(2), 260–273. https://doi.org/10.1111/j.1469-7610.2004.00218.x

Heath, N. L., Toste, J. R., Sornberger, M. J., & Wagner, C. (2011). Teachers' perceptions of non-suicidal self-injury in the schools. *School Mental Health*, *3*, 35–43. https://doi.org/10.1007/s12310-010-9043-4

Hooley J. M., Orley, J., & Teasdale, J. D. (1986). Levels of expressed emotion and relapse in depressed patients. *The British Journal of Psychiatry*, *14*(6), 642–647. https://doi.org/10.1192/bjp.148.6.642

James, K. M., & Gibb, B. E. (2019). Maternal criticism and non-suicidal self-injury in school-aged children. *Psychiatry Research*, *273*, 89–93. https://doi.org/10.1016/j.psychres.2019.01.019

Kiekens, G., Hasking, P., Boys, M., Claes, L., Mortier, P., Auerbach, R. P., Cuijpers, P., Demyttenaere, K., Green, J. G., Kessler, R. C., Myin-Germeys, I., Nock, M. K., & Bruffaerts, R. (2018). The associations between non-suicidal self-injury and first onset suicidal thoughts and behaviors. *Journal of Affective Disorders*, *239*, 171–179. https://doi.org/10.1016/j.jad.2018.06.033

Kiekens, G., Hasking, P., Claes, L., Boyes, M., Mortier, P., Auerbach, R.P., Cuijpers, P., Demyttenaere, K., Green, J.G., Kessler, R.C., Myin-Germeys, I., Nock, M.K., & Bruffaerts, R. (2019). Predicting the incidence of non-suicidal self-injury in college students. *European Psychiatry*, *59*, 44–51. https://doi.org/10.1016/j.eurpsy.2019.04.002 0924-9338

Klimes-Dougan, B., Safer, M. A., Ronsaville, D., Tinsley, R., & Harris, S. J. (2007). The value of forgetting suicidal thoughts and behavior. *Suicide and Life-Threatening Behavior*, *37*(4). https://doi.org/10.1521/suli.2007.37.4.431

Lloyd-Richardson, E. E., Lewis, S. P., Whitlock, J. L., Rodham, K., & Schatten, H. T. (2015). Research with adolescents who engage in non-suicidal self-injury: Ethical considerations and challenges. *Child and Adolescent Psychiatry and Mental Health*, *9*(1), 1–14. https://doi.org/10.1186/s13034-015-0071-6

MacPherson, H. A., Weinstein, S. M., & West, A. E. (2018). Non-suicidal self-injury in pediatric bipolar disorder: Clinical correlates and impact on psychosocial treatment outcomes. *Journal of Abnormal Child Psychology*, *46*(4), 857–870. https://doi.org/10.1007/s10802-017-0331-4

Martin, G., Swannell, S. V., Hazell, P. L., Harrison, E., & Taylor, A. W. (2010). Self-injury in Australia: A community survey. *The Medical Journal of Australia*, *193*(9), 506–510. https://doi.org/10.5694/j.1326-5377.2010.tb04033.x

Muehlenkamp, J., & Brausch, A. (2012). Body image as a mediator of non-suicidal self-injury in adolescents. *Journal of Adolescence*, *35*(1), 1–9. https://doi.org/10.1016/j.adolescence.2011.06.010

Muehlenkamp, J., & Gutierrez, P. M. (2007). Risk for suicide attempts among adolescents who engage in non-suicidal self-injury. *Archives of Suicide Research*, *11*(1), 69–82. https://doi.org/10.1080/13811110600992902

Nock, M. K., & Prinstein, M. J. (2004). A functional approach to the assessment of self mutilative behavior. *Journal of Consulting and Clinical Psychology*, *72*(1), 885–890. https://doi.org/10.1037/022-006X.72.5.885

Plener, P. L. (2020). Tailoring treatments for adolescents with nonsuicidal self-injury. *European Child & Adolescent psychiatry*, *29*(6), 893–895. https://doi.org/10.1007/s00787-020-01523-6

Resch, F., Parzer, P., & Brunner, R. (2008). Self-mutilation and suicidal behaviour in children and adolescents: Prevalence and psychosocial correlates: Results of the BELLA study. *European Child & Adolescent Psychiatry*, *17*, 92–98. https://doi.org/10.1007/s00787-008-1010-3

Simundic, A., Van Hove, L., Baetens, I., Bloom, E., & Heath, N. L. (submitted). *NSSI in elementary school: School personnel's knowledge and supportive needs.* Psychology in the Schools.

Tan, L., Xia, T., & Reece, C. (2018). Social and individual risk factors for suicide ideation among Chinese children and adolescents: A multilevel analysis. *International Journal of Psychology*, *53*(2), 117–125. https://doi.org/10.1002/ijop.12273

Turner, B. J., Austin, S. B., & Chapman, A. L. (2014). Treating nonsuicidal self-injury: A systematic review of psychological and pharmacological interventions. *The Canadian Journal of Psychiatry*, *59*(11), 576–585. https://doi.org/10.1177/070674371405901103

Whitlock, J., Eckenrode, J., & Silverman, D. (2006). Self-injurious behaviors in a college population. *Pediatrics*, *117*(6), 1939–1948. https://doi.org/10.1542/peds.2005-2543

CHAPTER 26

NSSI in Adolescence and Emerging Adulthood

Glenn Kiekens, Penelope Hasking, *and* Laurence Claes

> **Abstract**
>
> This chapter considers why adolescence and emerging adulthood are the most sensitive life periods for nonsuicidal self-injury (NSSI) and summarizes the knowledge about the course and developmental risk and protective factors of NSSI. This includes a literature review on the associations between NSSI and early life trauma, personality and identity development, emotion regulation, cognitive vulnerabilities, mental disorders, parenting and family relationships, and peer relationships. The authors then evaluate the possible consequences of engaging in NSSI as an adolescent or emerging adult and discuss how we can intervene to address NSSI among young people. Finally, the authors formulate recommendations to further our understanding as we move into the next decade of research. One of the main suggestions is to consider developmental variation in future prospective studies as well as an increased focus on prevention and intervention.
>
> **Key Words:** nonsuicidal self-injury, NSSI, adolescence, emerging adulthood, development

Introduction

Nonsuicidal self-injury (NSSI), defined as the direct and deliberate damage of one's body tissue without suicidal intent (e.g., cutting and hitting oneself; International Society for the Study of Self-Injury, 2022), is a significant mental health concern among young people worldwide. NSSI can occur as early as childhood and persist into adulthood, but typically has its onset during adolescence (11–18 years) and emerging adulthood (18–29 years). This chapter takes a developmental perspective to advance our understanding of NSSI during adolescence and emerging adulthood. First, we describe how biopsychosocial changes in adolescence and emerging adulthood may increase susceptibility for NSSI. Next, we summarize recent findings regarding the epidemiology and normative course of NSSI, risk and protective factors, as well as potential consequences of NSSI. Because few studies take developmental variation into account, we discuss studies of adolescents and emerging adults together. Finally, we consider how to respond appropriately to NSSI among young people and conclude the chapter with several recommendations for future research.

Why Are Adolescence and Emerging Adulthood Sensitive Periods for NSSI?

Adolescence is characterized by significant biological, psychological, and social changes that start at the onset of puberty around 10–13 years. In a recent review, Cummings et al. (2021) argue that two neurodevelopmental mechanisms increase the risk of NSSI during adolescence: a socioaffective pain pathway and a reward sensitivity pathway. While the former increases sensitivity to socioemotional stressors, such as perceived social rejection and exclusion that contribute to the onset of NSSI, the latter amplifies reinforcement learning about socioaffective benefits of self-injury and contributes to its maintenance (Cummings et al., 2021). On the psychosocial level, there is a shift toward more autonomy from parents, frequent interaction with same-age peers, and exploration of romantic relationships, making adolescents more susceptible to peer influences (see Zetterqvist & Bjureberg, this volume). Adolescents also become more self-focused as they gradually explore and establish an independent sense of self. Importantly, however, the developmental tasks that characterize adolescence are, for many individuals, not resolved by age 18.

The 20th century has been characterized by a shift from manufacturing toward information-based economies that require postsecondary education for most professions in industrialized societies. As a result, many adolescents now enter college to seek higher education before entering the workforce, getting married, and having children. To capture the period between adolescence and adulthood, Arnett (2015) introduced "emerging adulthood" as a new life stage between 18 and 29 years, which describes a time of continued transition, exploration, and evaluation. While many emerging adults enjoy this life period's relative freedom and possibilities, it is like adolescence, also a time of change and heightened instability and uncertainty. From a developmental perspective, emerging adults are caught in the middle—no longer adolescents but not yet in a position to fulfill adulthood's responsibilities (Arnett, 2015). The lack of structure and stability can increase isolation and leave someone feeling ambivalent, lost and unsure of who they are and where they fit in the world. In addition, academic pressure, relationship concerns, and uncertainty about future employment can make emerging adulthood stressful and enhance vulnerability and psychosocial risk.

Evidencing that adolescence and emerging adulthood are sensitive developmental periods for mental health difficulties, a recent meta-analysis revealed that 48% and 63% of mental disorders begin before 18 and 25 years, respectively (Solmi et al., 2021). Unfortunately, professional treatment is often not sought because most adolescents and emerging adults prefer to handle problems alone and are afraid of stigmatization (e.g., Aguirre Velasco et al., 2020). Accordingly, many young people are left behind with high levels of distress and are at risk of engaging in emotion-regulating behaviors. NSSI is perhaps one of the most puzzling of these emotion-regulation behaviors, including behaviors such as cutting, scratching, and hitting oneself.

What Is the Normative Course of NSSI in Adolescence and Emerging Adulthood?

Understanding the normative course of NSSI is a prerequisite for identifying developmental factors that may alter the progression of NSSI through adolescence and emerging adulthood. Therefore, we first review the current knowledge on the prevalence and features of NSSI, the age of onset and incidence, and persistence and cessation of NSSI.

Prevalence and Features of NSSI (Disorder)

NSSI is most prevalent during adolescence and emerging adulthood. Approximately 13% to 23% report a lifetime history of NSSI (Gillies et al., 2018; Swannell et al., 2014), with 12-month prevalence rates in the 8–19% range (Gillies et al., 2018; Kiekens et al., 2023). Females are slightly more likely to engage in NSSI than males, with a larger gender difference in clinical samples (Bresin & Schoenleber, 2015). A group of young people with higher rates of NSSI are sexual and gender minority individuals. A recent meta-analysis found that 36.5% of those identifying as lesbian, gay, bisexual, or transgender (LGBT) reported lifetime NSSI compared to 14.5% for people identifying as heterosexual or cisgender. Of note, the highest pooled estimates were observed for bisexual and transgender individuals, with lifetime rates estimated as high as 41–47% (Liu et al., 2019).

Approximately three quarters of young people report repeated NSSI (> 1 episode), with nearly half reporting five or more episodes in their lifetime (Heath et al., 2008). Most also use more than one NSSI method (Sornberger et al., 2012), with an average of five methods endorsed among clinical samples (Victor et al., 2018). Cutting, scratching, and hitting are the most frequently used methods (Bresin & Schoenleber, 2015) and occur mostly on arms, wrists/hands, and legs (Sornberger et al., 2012). In 2013, the fifth edition of *Diagnostic and Statistical Manual of Mental Disorders* (DSM-5) included NSSI disorder as a condition requiring further study (American Psychiatric Association, 2013). To meet NSSI disorder necessitates NSSI on at least five days in the past year, significant distress due to NSSI, and several other conditions (e.g., intense urges, and expecting a favorable outcome following NSSI). While few studies have assessed all criteria, the prevalence of NSSI disorder is close to 7% among community adolescents (Buelens et al., 2020b) and ranges between 0.2% and 2% among emerging adults (Benjet et al., 2017; Kiekens, Hasking, Claes, et al., 2018; Kiekens et al., 2023). However, females are more likely to meet NSSI disorder criteria than males (Buelens et al., 2020b; Kiekens, Hasking, Claes, et al., 2018).

Age of Onset and Incidence

Gandhi and colleagues have investigated the onset pattern of NSSI among 4,379 adolescents and (emerging) adults from community and clinical samples (Gandhi et al., 2018). Their findings suggest that the onset of NSSI may have a bimodal peak, as NSSI started to emerge in late childhood and early adolescence (9–12 years), peaked in mid-adolescence

(14–15 years), declined again into late adolescence (16–18 years), and then had a second lower peak of onset when transitioning into emerging adulthood (19–21 years). However, it should be mentioned that this study relied on retrospective recall, which may be prone to recall bias. Therefore, prospective studies are needed to clarify incidence rates (i.e., onset among those without lifetime NSSI in a discrete period).

In prospective studies of adolescents (Andrews et al., 2014; Huang et al., 2017; Marin et al., 2020), the one-year incidence rate of NSSI is estimated in the 3.6–4% range. Recently, Victor et al. (2019) investigated incidence rates across different age groups in a one-year prospective study among female adolescents. As expected, higher rates (although consistently lower than the other studies) were observed in younger than older age groups: one-year incidence rates were estimated around 2.1% at ages 14–15, 1.5% at age 16, and 1% at age 17. Among emerging adults, mean one-year incidence rates of NSSI have been observed in the 2.2–4.1% range (Hamza & Willoughby, 2014; Riley et al., 2015). Researchers have also investigated onset rates of sporadic (< 5 episodes) and repetitive NSSI (≥5 episodes) separately. For example, Daukantaite et al. (2021) found that 14.7% of 13–14-year-olds report sporadic NSSI (1–4 episodes) and 9.8% repetitive NSSI in a one-year follow-up assessment. Recently, scholars also examined NSSI onset among emerging adults entering college (Kiekens et al., 2019). Findings indicate that 7% start to engage in repetitive NSSI (≥5 episodes) and 8.6% in sporadic NSSI (one to four episodes), with the highest one-year incidence rate observed in the first year of college (10.3%).

Persistence and Cessation

Few studies have examined the persistence and cessation patterns of NSSI among adolescents and emerging adults. In one cross-sectional study among adolescents, researchers found that 56.5% of those with a history of NSSI reported 12-month NSSI (Halpin & Duffy, 2020). Similar rates have been observed among emerging adults, with rates of NSSI persistence in the 44–59% range (Kiekens et al., 2023; Whitlock et al., 2015). Prospective studies observed that 25–63% of adolescents with adolescent-onset NSSI report persistent NSSI in emerging adulthood (Glenn & Klonsky, 2011; Hamza & Willoughby, 2014; Kiekens et al., 2022). In the earlier mentioned study by Daukantaite et al. (2021), two-thirds of adolescents reporting engagement in any lifetime NSSI behavior reported persistent NSSI one year later. Of those reporting repetitive NSSI (≥5 episodes) in year 1, more than half (56%) indicated ongoing repetitive NSSI in year 2, whereas 21% reported sporadic NSSI, and 23% did not report recent NSSI. Repetitive NSSI also decreased from approximately 18% at ages 13–16 to 10% by age 25 (Daukantaite et al., 2021). While Turner et al. (2021) recently observed that 75% of adolescents ceased NSSI between ages 18–21, Kiekens et al. (2022) found that 56% of individuals with a history of NSSI report persistent self-injury during their college years. Although most students reported a sporadic course (27.9%) or a low-frequency repetitive pattern (12.9%), 15.6% reported a high-frequency repetitive pattern (annually ≥5 episodes). These authors observed that NSSI persistence (especially the high-frequency repetitive pattern) predicted an increased risk for 12-month mental disorders, role impairment, and suicidal thoughts and behaviors later in college. Young people who engage in NSSI more frequently, use more methods, and make more medically serious wounds, are most likely to report persistent NSSI (Andrews et al., 2013; Glenn & Klonsky, 2011; Kiekens et al., 2017; Kiekens et al., 2022). However, as most studies have relatively short follow-up periods, more work is needed to clarify the developmental course of NSSI as well as the implications of following a "normative" (i.e., onset in adolescence and offset by emerging adulthood) relative to an "atypical" course (i.e., onset and ongoing NSSI in emerging adulthood).

What Are Developmental Risk and Protective Factors?

Next, we provide an overview of risk and protective factors of NSSI in adolescence and emerging adulthood. We focus here on developmental factors for which empirical research has provided substantial evidence in either adolescents, emerging adults, or both. This includes childhood-adolescent trauma, personality and identity development, emotion regulation, cognitive vulnerabilities, psychopathology and mental disorders, parenting and family influences, and peer influences.

Early Life Trauma

Liu et al. (2018) conducted a comprehensive meta-analysis on the association between childhood trauma (i.e., sexual abuse, physical abuse and neglect, and emotional abuse and neglect) and NSSI. Across 71 publications, people who reported some form of maltreatment were more likely to report a history of NSSI, with the strongest effect observed for childhood emotional abuse (Liu et al., 2018). As this is also the most prevalent form of childhood maltreatment (Stoltenborgh et al., 2015), preventing emotional abuse may hold potential to decrease the incidence of NSSI (Kiekens et al., 2019). Notably, scholars have observed that the association between several childhood trauma subtypes and NSSI is stronger in the community than in clinical samples (Liu et al., 2018), which implies that assessing trauma is essential when determining risk for NSSI in the general population.

Several studies have investigated the mediational pathways through which trauma may pose a risk for NSSI, providing initial evidence that proximal factors including emotional dysregulation, dissociation, distress intolerance, identity issues, self-criticism, and psychopathology are implicated in explaining the trauma-NSSI relationship (Gu et al., 2020; Horowitz & Stermac, 2018; Kang et al., 2018; Liu et al., 2018). However, these studies are primarily cross-sectional (as was most data in the systematic review by Liu and colleagues). Thus, prospective work is warranted to clarify which aspects of early trauma (i.e., type, severity, and frequency) increase the risk of NSSI, as well as studies explaining the underlying mechanisms of such temporal associations.

Personality and Identity Development

Researchers have also investigated the relationship between personality traits and NSSI. A consistent finding is that young people who are predisposed to experience negative emotions (e.g., trait neuroticism and negative affectivity) while reporting disinhibition (e.g., low effortful control), particularly in handling negative emotion (i.e., negative urgency), show elevated rates of NSSI (Gromatsky et al., 2017; Turner et al., 2018). In addition, some studies also found a positive relationship between antagonism-related traits, such as lower trait agreeableness and higher trait aggression, and NSSI (Kiekens et al., 2015; Kleiman et al., 2015). While NSSI is included as a symptom of Borderline Personality Disorder (BPD), research shows that the relationship between NSSI and BPD is complex. For instance, while 95% of adolescents with a diagnosis of BPD report a history of NSSI and more than half meet NSSI-D criteria (as self-injury is a symptom of BPD), only 7% of those with a history of NSSI and 11% with NSSI-D meet BPD criteria (Buelens et al., 2020a; Goodman et al., 2017). There is evidence that the presence of NSSI in early adolescence may signal risk for BPD in emerging adulthood (Biskin et al., 2021). Conversely, researchers have also prospectively linked BPD to the maintenance of NSSI (Glenn & Klonsky, 2011), with recent work drawing attention to identity problems (as a core feature of BPB) to account for this relationship (Spitzen et al., 2020).

Forming a stable identity is a core developmental challenge of adolescence and emerging adulthood. Research has shown that some young people may use NSSI to tackle disturbances in identity formation through self-injury (i.e., identifying as a self-injurer; Breen et al., 2013). Adolescents who engage in NSSI report lower levels of identity synthesis and more identity confusion (Verschueren et al., 2020). Using longitudinal data, researchers have shown that the association between identity synthesis/confusion and NSSI is likely bidirectional (Gandhi et al., 2017). Furthermore, research indicates that identity processes may operate as a proximal factor, linking dysfunctional maternal and peer attachment to the development of NSSI (Gandhi et al., 2019; Taliaferro et al., 2020). These findings show that problems in identity formation and NSSI are closely linked and imply that targeting identity issues may be a beneficial treatment strategy for young people engaging in NSSI. This is especially relevant for those identifying as a gender or sexual minority as they may experience additional distress over their identity in addition to discrimination and victimization, putting them at greater risk of NSSI (Liu et al., 2019).

Emotion Regulation

Emotion regulation, defined as managing and responding effectively to emotion, is perhaps the most examined risk factor of NSSI. Meta-analytic findings suggest that 63–78% of individuals report engaging in NSSI for its emotion-regulatory ability (Taylor et al., 2018). In addition, studies have consistently found an association between emotion dysregulation and NSSI (Wolff et al., 2019), with the strongest effects observed for impulse control difficulties and limited access to emotion-regulation strategies (Wolff et al., 2019; Zelkowitz et al., 2016). Emotion regulation is also associated prospectively with NSSI persistence (Kiekens et al., 2017). Cummings et al. (2021) suggest that emotion-regulation ability is crucial in determining whether NSSI continues past adolescence. The emotion-regulatory properties of NSSI have also been evaluated using ecological momentary assessment (EMA; also known as experience sampling methodology). In their recent review, Hepp et al. (2020) found evidence for increased negative emotion before NSSI. However, although most studies also report decreased negative emotion following NSSI, no study has examined whether the propensity of NSSI to reduce negative emotion (i.e., the decrease from pre- to post-NSSI) increases the likelihood of future self-injury. Future work using EMA schedules with sufficient temporal granularity promise to examine this and provide better insight into the contingencies of NSSI that unfold across shorter and longer time intervals.

Cognitive Vulnerabilities

Contemporaneous theoretical models posit the *joint* influence of emotion and cognitive vulnerabilities in explaining why some individuals engage in NSSI. According to the emotional cascade model (ECM; Selby et al., 2013), reinforcing cyclic cascades of rumination and negative emotion lead to intolerable states that require behaviors with intense physical sensations, such as NSSI, short-circuiting these cascades of high negative intensity. In support of the ECM, young people with a history of NSSI experience greater initial increases in negative affect following rumination than peers who do not self-injure (Arbuthnott, Lewis, & Bailey, 2015). Trait rumination—especially brooding and depressive rumination—is also associated with NSSI history and frequency (Coleman et al., 2021), and researchers have observed that rumination might exacerbate or mediate the relationship of other risk factors (e.g., emotional abuse; Gu et al., 2020). For example, Nicolai et al. (2016) found that trait negative affect and rumination predicted engagement and frequency of NSSI, such that emerging adults who scored high on both traits were more likely to self-injure and did so more frequently across an eight-week follow-up period than peers scoring low on either trait. Recently, Hughes et al. (2019) showed in an EMA study that the risk of NSSI thoughts and behavior was heightened when adolescents and emerging adults experienced high levels of negative emotion (i.e., feeling anxious and overwhelmed) and repetitive negative thinking.

The cognitive-emotional model of NSSI argues for an expanded role of NSSI-related cognitions (Hasking et al., 2017). This model suggests that whether someone will self-injure partially depends on NSSI-related outcome expectancies and self-efficacy expectancies. Researchers, for instance, observed that emerging adults who self-injure—compared to peers who do not—hold more favorable outcome expectancies from NSSI (i.e., affect regulation, less pain) and have the perception of being less able to resist NSSI (Dawkins et al., 2019). These cognitions have also been shown to interact (Dawkins et al., 2021), such that belief in the ability to resist self-injury can counter expectations that self-injury will result in emotion regulation. Recent evidence from an EMA study indicates that low self-efficacy to resist NSSI was predictive of NSSI even when NSSI thoughts were taken into account (Kiekens et al., 2020). Together, these findings suggest that focusing on NSSI-related cognitions might have clinical utility in preventing NSSI among adolescents and emerging adults.

Finally, the benefits and barriers model of NSSI argues for a unique role of self-criticism in explaining NSSI (Hooley & Franklin, 2017). Negative self-beliefs are suggested to erode barriers to NSSI, making NSSI a more viable option to regulate negative emotion as it is congruent with an internal negative self-view. Research confirms that young people who engage in NSSI are more self-critical and less self-compassionate than those with no history of NSSI (Burke, Fox, Kautz, Siegel, et al., 2021; Zelkowitz & Cole, 2019). In addition, prospective work has shown that high self-criticism and body image dissatisfaction predict engagement in NSSI (Black et al., 2019; Burke, Fox, Kautz, Rodriguez-Seijas, et al., 2021; Fox et al., 2018). Furthermore, experimental work has shown that young people who are highly self-critical can endure pain longer (Glenn et al., 2014) and experience it as rewarding compared to peers lower in self-criticism (Fox et al., 2016).

Psychopathology and Mental Disorders

Internalizing, externalizing, and psychotic symptoms and disorders have all been prospectively related to the onset of NSSI (Fox et al., 2015; Hielscher et al., 2021; Kiekens et al., 2019). Eating-disordered behaviors are also frequently present together with NSSI (Cucchi et al., 2016; Kiekens & Claes, 2020) and prospectively predict NSSI (e.g., Micali et al., 2017; Turner et al., 2015). Researchers have also linked psychiatric symptoms and mental disorders to the persistence of NSSI (Kiekens, et al., 2023; Steinhoff et al., 2021). Of note, there appears to be a dose-response relationship between the number of mental disorders and the likelihood of NSSI engagement (Kiekens et al., 2023), with the incremental odds of NSSI increasing at a decreasing rate with the number of mental disorders. This suggests that the effect of a single mental disorder on the future likelihood of NSSI is strongest among those without any prior disorder but has an upper limit in predictive utility for adolescents and emerging adults with several existing disorders. One reason for this ceiling effect may be shared pathways through which disorders govern risk for NSSI (Bentley et al., 2015).

Parenting and Family Influences

The association between family and parental relationships and NSSI has been well-studied (Arbuthnott & Lewis, 2015). Jiang et al. (2017) found that low quality of current attachment with parents distinguished adolescents who engaged in NSSI from those without a history of NSSI (see James & Gibb, this volume, on the parent-child dyad and other family factors associated with youth NSSI). Longitudinal studies have also linked low family support and difficulties in parent-child relationships (e.g., poor quality of attachment and low parental warmth) with the onset and continuation of NSSI (Arbuthnott & Lewis, 2015; Tatnell et al., 2014; Victor et al., 2019). For instance, Hamza and Willoughby (2014) found that college students who experienced increased problems with parents were more likely to report a trajectory characterized by recent NSSI (i.e., onset, relapse, or persistence).

Several recent studies have investigated how family relationships may govern risk for NSSI—finding preliminary evidence for alexithymia and communication difficulties (Cerutti et al., 2018; Claes et al., 2016), identity issues (Gandhi et al., 2019), behavioral problems (Cassels et al., 2019), and emotional reactivity and emotional dysregulation as mediational pathways (Hasking, Dawkins, et al., 2020). Conversely, there is evidence that positive connections to parents and supportive familial relationships can safeguard against NSSI (Claes et al., 2015; Taliaferro et al., 2020). Research, for instance, suggests that being able to make use of family support is protective of NSSI onset and facilitates NSSI cessation (Tatnell et al., 2014; Whitlock et al., 2015). Interestingly, social motivations are endorsed more frequently for initiating NSSI than repeating the behavior, and family support has been found to differentiate college students who reported a single episode of self-injury from those peers who engaged in repeated NSSI (Muehlenkamp et al., 2013). This shows that boosting family support remains important after NSSI is initiated. For example, a recent study found that female adolescents who experienced more stress and lower levels of family support in the early months of the COVID-19 pandemic were more likely to report persistent NSSI (Carosella et al., 2021).

Peer Influences
Adolescents and emerging adults with negative attitudes or connections toward peers are more likely to report engaging in NSSI. Of all peer experiences, bully victimization has consistently been associated with a history of NSSI (van Geel et al., 2015; Serafini et al., 2021). Victor et al. (2019) recently observed that peer victimization predicted NSSI onset among adolescent girls during the following year. Similarly, Kiekens et al. (2019) found that bully victimization before the age of 17 predicted the onset of both sporadic (< 5 episodes) and repetitive NSSI (≥5 episodes) during the first two years of college (when controlling for other adversities). There is evidence for a dose-response relationship, such that adolescents who experienced repetitive bullying are more likely to report recent NSSI than peers who experienced occasional bullying (Jantzer et al., 2015). Bully perpetration appears equally associated with NSSI (Serafini et al., 2021), and research suggests that depressive symptoms may partially explain the link between bully victimization/perpetration and NSSI (Baiden et al., 2017).

Knowing a friend who engages in NSSI has also been associated with the likelihood of NSSI (Syed et al., 2020), particularly among young people experiencing high levels of distress (Hasking et al., 2013). For example, Schwartz-Mette and Lawrence (2019) observed that the frequency of NSSI of friends was associated with the number of times adolescents self-injured over a six-month follow-up period (see Jarvi Steele et al., this volume, on social contagion of NSSI). This effect was strongest among young people reporting emotion-regulation difficulties, highlighting the interplay between interpersonal and intrapersonal factors underlying NSSI. Similar to family relationships, findings underscore the importance of drawing upon the protective effects of peer relationships in preventing NSSI among adolescents and emerging adults. For example, in a prospective study by Giletta et al. (2015), support from friends was associated with a reduced likelihood of experiencing a chronic NSSI trajectory. Similarly, Wu et al. (2019) observed that peer acceptance is related to reduced NSSI one year later through enhanced self-compassion and reduced depressive symptoms. Finally, among a large statewide US sample ($n = 73{,}648$), it was recently found that adolescents who experienced family adversity were less likely to report past-year NSSI when they experienced social support from peers (Forster et al., 2020).

What Are the Potential Consequences of Engaging in NSSI as an Adolescent/Emerging Adult?

While the previous section illustrates that we have acquired substantial knowledge about developmental factors that may increase or buffer risk of NSSI, several researchers have also investigated possible consequences of engaging in NSSI. Therefore, in what follows, we provide an update on the literature concerning the risk of suicidal thoughts and behaviors and psychosocial outcomes more broadly following NSSI.

NSSI as a Risk Factor for Suicidal Thoughts and Behaviors

NSSI is engaged without the desire to end one's life and should be differentiated from a suicide attempt. However, both forms of self-injury frequently co-occur (Grandclerc et al., 2016), and research suggests that young people who engage in NSSI are at increased risk for a future suicide attempt (Griep & MacKinnon, 2020; Ribeiro et al., 2016). According to the gateway theory, NSSI directly increases the risk for a suicide attempt among people experiencing high levels of intrapersonal distress (Hamza et al, 2012). Yet, NSSI has also been associated with an increased risk of a future suicide attempt independently from mental disorders (Kiekens, Hasking, Claes, et al., 2018). Alternatively, the interpersonal theory of suicide (IPTS) posits that a young person will only attempt suicide if there is the desire to attempt suicide—originating from thwarted belongingness and perceived burdensomeness—*and* the capability to attempt suicide (Joiner, 2005; Van Orden et al., 2010). According to this theory, NSSI may pose a risk to suicide because repeated tissue damage would prepare an individual to make a suicide attempt by building up a capability for suicide. Willoughby et al. (2015) tested this theory among college students and found that more frequent NSSI predicted an increase in the capability for suicide one year later. However, recent studies suggests that acquired capability for suicide alone may not fully explain the NSSI-suicide attempt relationship (Brackman et al., 2016; Matney et al., 2018). Therefore, future studies are needed, especially those assessing acquired capability for suicide and incorporating belongingness and burdensomeness in investigating the relationship between NSSI and suicide attempts (Mbroh et al., 2018).

Importantly, emerging evidence suggests that NSSI may increase not only the capability to end one's own life but also the desire to die (Hamza & Willoughby, 2016) and the probability to transition from suicide ideation or a plan to a first suicide attempt (Kiekens, Hasking, Claes, et al., 2018). These findings highlight the importance of screening and treatment efforts in preventing suicidal thoughts and behaviors among adolescents and emerging adults who engage in NSSI. Hence, to better enable clinicians to gauge risk, several scholars have investigated NSSI characteristics that may explain which young people with a history of NSSI are more vulnerable to developing suicidal thoughts and behaviors. Findings from this line of work suggest that an earlier onset, greater frequency, use of multiple methods, medical treatment for self-injury, reporting self-cutting, NSSI scars, and self-injuring to avoid thoughts of suicide are all associated with higher odds of suicidal thoughts and behaviors (Burke et al., 2018; Kiekens, Hasking, Claes, et al., 2018; Muehlenkamp et al., 2019; Victor et al., 2015). Prospective studies are needed to evaluate the clinical utility of NSSI characteristics together with psychosocial factors (e.g., depression, hopelessness, and social relationships) in gauging suicide risk. Worth mentioning in this context, Whitlock et al. (2013) identified meaning in life and support from parents as prospective factors that—above and beyond NSSI frequency—decreased the likelihood to move from NSSI to suicidal thoughts and behaviors, which implies that reducing hopelessness and boosting social relationships are essential treatment targets.

NSSI as a Risk Factor for Adverse Psychosocial Outcomes

Taking a broader lifespan perspective, there is increased understanding that NSSI is associated with a variety of adverse psychosocial outcomes during adolescence and emerging adulthood, including reduced academic functioning (Kiekens et al., 2016), difficulties in identity formation (Gandhi et al., 2017), increased risk for mental disorders (Kiekens, Hasking, et al., 2018; Wilkinson et al., 2018), and stigmatization (Burke et al., 2019; Staniland et al., 2020). For instance, among 1,762 university students, staff, and student-staff, a recent study revealed that university stakeholders reported greater stigma toward NSSI than mental illness in general (Hamza et al., 2021). In addition, recent studies have linked NSSI to increased interpersonal stressors and conflict (Burke et al., 2015; Turner et al., 2017), and adverse trajectories in emotional and cognitive functioning (Buelens et al., 2019). For example, Robinson et al. (2019) examined the temporal relationship between NSSI and emotion regulation over three years throughout adolescence, finding evidence for a reciprocal risk relationship. Poor emotion regulation was confirmed as a risk factor for NSSI; however, NSSI also predicted reduced emotion-regulation competencies one year later (Robinson et al., 2019). The authors suggest that NSSI may increase emotion sensitivity, install negative self-beliefs about one's ability to regulate emotion, and provide less opportunity to learn emotion-regulation skills. In support of these findings, scholars found that young people who engaged in repetitive NSSI during adolescence had more emotion-regulation difficulties and increased impulsivity in emerging adulthood (Daukantaite et al., 2021).

Turner et al. (2021) recently investigated how the course of NSSI is related to changes in psychosocial outcomes across adolescence and emerging adulthood. While many of the developmental factors considered in the section "What Are Developmental Risk and Protective Factors?" (e.g., anxiety, depression, self-concept, and peer and family victimization) were associated with the onset, persistence, and cessation of NSSI, it was found that at least four to eight years of sustained NSSI cessation is required to abate psychosocial deteriorations that accumulated during NSSI (Turner et al., 2021). Cessation of NSSI was also associated with temporal increases in heavy drinking and other substance use behaviors. However, individuals with persistent NSSI were most vulnerable to experience adverse long-term psychosocial functioning in emerging adulthood, such as decreased subjective well-being, working fewer hours, and delaying medical treatment for financial reasons. These findings imply that the need for care and interventions does not stop following the cessation of NSSI and clarify that much could be learned from future investigations adopting a broader transactional framework in which psychosocial and NSSI outcomes might influence each other reciprocally throughout adolescence and emerging adulthood. Better clarification of developmental cascades and providing insight into the mechanisms that account for such relationships would aid scientific understanding and offer useful information for prevention and intervention efforts.

How Can We Intervene to Prevent NSSI?

Considering the potential adverse consequences of NSSI, one of the most valuable questions to address is how to prevent young individuals from engaging in self-injury. In what follows, we discuss the central role of schools and postsecondary institutions and the importance of evidence-based assessment and intervention in addressing NSSI among young people.

Schools and Postsecondary Institutions

Schools and colleges/universities are well-placed and critical stakeholders in preventing NSSI as they constitute a primary access point of care for young people. The prevention of NSSI in educational settings necessitates a holistic multilayered approach that promotes mental health literacy (Hasking et al., 2016; Lewis et al., 2019). Schools and colleges must be made aware of the extent of NSSI in their institution and the probability of poor outcomes if NSSI is not appropriately addressed. There should be guidelines for identifying students at risk for NSSI, a protocol for responding to NSSI, and procedures for making appropriate referrals (Hasking et al., 2016; Lewis et al., 2019). A clear protocol outlines the various roles of all staff and students (including academics, professional staff, mental health professionals, and students; Hasking et al., 2016; Lewis et al., 2019). Given that NSSI is often kept secret, there should also be guidelines for involving parents (Hasking et al., 2016). Similarly, resources should be provided to peer networks, romantic partners, and residence hall staff in higher education settings (Lewis et al., 2019), who are most likely to be the confidants of students who self-injure (Simone & Hamza, 2020). Peers can learn to adopt a "respectful curiosity" when talking to students who self-injure, avoiding stigmatizing or hurtful language, and offering to help seek support from counseling services.

A positive commitment must be made to addressing NSSI in the school context, potentially as part of a more comprehensive mental health agenda (Hasking et al., 2016; Lewis et al., 2019), and professional training should be offered to school staff (Hasking, Bloom, et al., 2020). For example, gatekeeper interventions have been used effectively to train staff and students to respond to students in distress and make appropriate referrals (Rallis et al., 2018). Provision of information specific to NSSI can be incorporated into existing programs (e.g., Baetens et al., 2020) but should include a basic understanding of NSSI, how to talk with people who self-injure, knowledge of appropriate referral options, and the importance of self-care. Generally, experts recommend that rather than discussing details of NSSI, including methods, that the conversation focuses on coping strategies in general or on the issues underlying NSSI. In this way, the focus remains positive, and students are less likely to be triggered by graphic details of NSSI.

Evidence-Based Assessment and Intervention

Addressing NSSI among young people who self-injure necessitates identifying the appropriate level of services and care that is needed. Prior to providing interventions, a thorough clinical assessment of NSSI should occur, including NSSI history and severity, functions of NSSI, antecedents and consequences, risk factors, and comorbidities (Lengel & Styer, 2019). Westers et al. (2016) developed the SOARS model to help clinicians screen for self-injury among young individuals by inventorying suicidal ideation; onset, frequency, and methods of NSSI; aftercare; reasons for self-injury; and stage of change. This assessment (and potential wound care) must occur in a nonjudgmental way using a respectful curiosity and dispassionate tone. Scholars have argued that brief routine screening for NSSI (and suicidality) should occur in primary and emergency care settings (Westers & Plener, 2020). Screening in primary care has the advantage of picking up people who might otherwise be missed and minimizing the burden on emergency services. On the other hand, when someone presents to emergency services because of injuries, a full assessment (including suicide) should always be conducted (Franzen et al., 2019). Some countries developed treatment guidelines for NSSI and suicidal behaviors. The German guidelines, for instance, outline the importance of building commitment for treatment, psychoeducation, identifying risk factors that trigger NSSI, attention for comorbidities, and providing alternative skills and problem-solving strategies (Plener et al., 2016). Importantly, as NSSI recovery will typically involve NSSI (re)lapses (Steinhoff et al., 2021), realistic expectations regarding cessation of NSSI should be set.

In recent years, there has been an increase in randomized control trials (RCTs) that assess evidence-based interventions for NSSI. A preliminary meta-analysis (containing six studies) found that Dialectical Behavior Therapy (DBT) had a large positive effect on the frequency of NSSI among adolescents (Cook & Gorraiz, 2016). However, given substantial heterogeneity in NSSI severity and a growing lack of mental health care resources, there have been calls for a stepped-care approach in responding to NSSI, such that specialized resource-intensive treatments are available for those who need them most (Westers & Plener, 2020). In response to this, several brief low-intensity interventions have recently been developed showing promising results. The cutting down program (CDP) is a low-intensity psychotherapeutic intervention of 8–12 sessions based on DBT, with RCTs showing that this program effectively reduced NSSI and achieved faster recovery compared with an intensive treatment as usual among adolescents (Kaess et al., 2020). In a similar vein, a low-intensity emotion-regulation individual therapy showed promising results in reducing NSSI with effects maintained or even further improved at six-month follow-up in two pilot studies with adolescents (Bjureberg et al., 2017) and emerging adults (Sahlin et al., 2017). Recently, Bjureberg et al. (2018) developed an online version that also reduced the frequency and methods of NSSI. Another behavioral intervention, the treatment for self-injurious behaviors (T-SIB) consists of nine sessions designed to assess the function of NSSI and develop alternative strategies that serve a similar function (Andover et al., 2017). Initial findings supported feasibility and acceptability of this intervention, with medium effects in decreasing NSSI frequency. Finally, a daily diary intervention (Hooley et al., 2018) involving autobiographical self-enhancement training to help emerging adults focus on positive personal attributes has shown a comparable decline in NSSI frequency relative to active control conditions. However, these general effects were not maintained at 4- and 12-week follow-up assessments.

Recommendations for Future Research

The work presented in this chapter advances our understanding of NSSI among adolescents and emerging adults but also leaves many important questions unanswered. Therefore, we formulate four critical directions for future research.

Broaden the Focus Epidemiologically

An important direction for future research is the differentiation of meaningful epidemiological outcomes (i.e., prevalence of NSSI, onset, persistence, and remission). Even though research on NSSI among adolescents and emerging adults has increased dramatically, there is a lack of detailed information on patterns of risk associated with NSSI incidence and persistence, changes over time, and the course of NSSI in different cultures.

Some initial studies found NSSI may be equally prevalent in developing and developed countries but found preliminary evidence that the features, phenomenology, and explanations of NSSI may be culturally influenced (Gandhi et al., 2020). Importantly, studies suggest that the prevalence of NSSI among adolescents and emerging adults has increased during the past decade (Duffy et al., 2019) as well as more recently during COVID-19 (Zetterqvist et al., 2021). However, an important caveat is that it is currently unclear to what extent these apparent differences are accurate or potentially due to methodological artifacts, such as decreasing response rates or different assessment procedures resulting in higher prevalence estimates (Robinson & Wilson, 2020). Addressing these questions in future studies will be pivotal in shaping a more nuanced picture of the epidemiology of NSSI in adolescence and emerging adulthood.

Broaden the Focus Developmentally
To date, few studies span both adolescence and emerging adulthood or even include samples of adolescents and emerging adults together. As such, there is a need to conduct studies that account for developmental variation in explaining risk. Although there is some evidence that the salience of primary psychological symptoms (e.g., depression) for NSSI may not change (Victor et al., 2019), developmental tasks vary as a young person transitions from adolescence to emerging adulthood. Furthermore, research has shown substantial variation in intra- and interpersonal processes, such as body image, self-esteem, emotion regulation, rumination, and social support seeking, with generally improved outcomes for emerging adults (e.g., Nelson et al., 2018; Zimmermann & Iwanski, 2014). Emerging adulthood also represents an accelerated period of independence from parents and a further increased interest in social relationships (especially romantic relationships; Arnett, 2015). However, future studies are required to address this lack of specificity in current knowledge by moving toward a developmentally informed model of NSSI. In doing so, it will be valuable to take a holistic approach in which developmental factors discussed in this chapter are considered simultaneously for explaining the course of NSSI in adolescence and emerging adulthood.

Increase the Focus on Prevention, Barriers to Care, and Novel Treatment Modalities
There is a need for more research on the prevention and treatment of NSSI among adolescents and emerging adults. Although some existing studies demonstrate the feasibility of prevention programs in school settings, there is limited research in this area (Kruzan & Whitlock, 2019). Muehlenkamp et al. (2010) developed the signs of self-injury program (SOSI), providing education about NSSI and its warning signs to school staff and offering adolescents skills to respond to NSSI disclosures from peers. Results indicated that SOSI was well received, increased knowledge of NSSI and openness to help-seeking attitudes, and decreased discomfort and avoidance of discussing NSSI with friends. Recently, Baetens et al. (2020) added a psychoeducation module about NSSI to an existing

prevention program that aims to enhance general mental well-being and resilience among adolescents, providing evidence that incorporating NSSI-specific modules is feasible and does not lead to iatrogenic effects. To date, however, no NSSI prevention program has shown efficacy in reducing rates of NSSI. An important question to address in future work is whether a universal (i.e., everyone receives the intervention), targeted (i.e., at-risk individuals receive the intervention), or a stepped program (combination of universal and indicated interventions) has the most potential in preventing NSSI. Scholars are encouraged to consider developing programs that adopt a multilevel approach that involves societal, community, relational, and individual levels (Kruzan & Whitlock, 2019). For instance, as not everyone attends tertiary education, including services outside a school context, such as workplaces and general practitioners, will be required to avoid leaving groups of young people without resources.

At the same time, it is equally important to understand better the barriers to help-seeking and effective treatment modalities for NSSI. Help-seeking for NSSI is often low, and many young people do not find their way to (or need) conventional therapy (Steinhoff et al., 2021; Whitlock et al., 2011). Emerging work suggests that there is also a delay of 1.5–2 years before adolescents who have NSSI thoughts and behavior access care, with longer delay durations observed for those with more severe psychopathology (Lustig et al., 2021). Given the ubiquity of technology use (especially among young people; Statista, 2020), making better use of mobile technologies' growing capacities will be pivotal in the prevention and intervention of NSSI. There are currently a variety of mobile apps for NSSI (Vieira & Lewis, 2018), yet most have not been theoretically grounded or evaluated empirically (for exceptions see Franklin et al., 2016; Kruzan et al., 2021). However, more future work is needed to investigate the clinical potential and the effectiveness of these novel treatment modalities. Research co-design and qualitative studies to capture young people's expectations and preferences offer promise here (Hetrick et al., 2018).

Increase the Focus on the Individual

Finally, a last important direction for future research is to adopt a person-centered approach in NSSI research and treatment (Lewis & Hasking, 2021). Such an approach recognizes young individuals as experts in their own lived experience. Therefore, scientist-practitioners are encouraged to adopt an idiographic approach in their research in which within-person knowledge is generated with individuals serving as their own control (Piccirillo & Rodebaugh, 2019). To date, researchers have taken mainly a nomothetic approach in which respondents report on their history of NSSI and are then divided into groups that are compared against each other—typically lifetime or 12-month NSSI versus no NSSI history. Although this helps clarify profiles of individuals who are on average at greater risk, such between-group knowledge does not translate to the here and now at the individual level. Retrospectively aggregating data over months to years (e.g., "Have you self-injured since last year?") also lacks temporal precision to gauge acute risk of NSSI.

However, this is precisely what clinicians working with young people must consider. For them, what matters is the story of each client and their risk of both self-injury within the next hours, days, and weeks. EMA and real-time monitoring offers potential here, as it could help people take an active role in treatment and offers highly specific information on NSSI-related cognitions, urges, and behaviors as well as the factors and situations that trigger or prevent against NSSI cognitions and behaviors in daily life (for a review of the opportunities and challenges of real-time monitoring, see Kiekens, Robinson, et al., 2021). This could ultimately provide valuable information to better tailor treatment according to young people's dynamic therapy needs and client-defined outcomes.

Conclusion

In this chapter, we described adolescence and emerging adulthood as critical periods for NSSI and provided an update on the course, risk and protective factors, and possible consequences of NSSI during these life phases. This revealed that NSSI is a behavior that warrants research and clinical attention as many young people engage in NSSI at some point, with considerable proportions reporting NSSI for some years. A range of developmental factors was reviewed to consider when working with young individuals at risk for NSSI. We have learned that NSSI should always be taken seriously, as those who self-injure are at risk for various adverse psychosocial outcomes. To effectively address NSSI, the role of schools and colleges was discussed as well as evidence-based assessments and interventions. Finally, we provided some directions for future work to increase our understanding of NSSI among adolescents and emerging adults. We are hopeful that the next generation of research will build constructively on the strengths and limitations of the existing studies to translate these findings into developmentally appropriate prevention and intervention strategies.

Acknowledgment

Dr. Kiekens is supported by a postdoctoral fellowship from Research Foundation Flanders (12ZZM21N). The authors have no conflict of interest to declare concerning the publication of this chapter.

References

Aguirre Velasco, A., Cruz, I. S. S., Billings, J., Jimenez, M., & Rowe, S. (2020). What are the barriers, facilitators and interventions targeting help-seeking behaviours for common mental health problems in adolescents? A systematic review. *BMC Psychiatry, 20*(1), 293. https://doi.org/10.1186/s12888-020-02659-0

American Psychiatric Association. (2013). *The diagnostic and statistical manual of mental disorders* (5th ed.).

Andover, M. S., Schatten, H. T., Morris, B. W., Holman, C. S., & Miller, I. W. (2017). An intervention for nonsuicidal self-injury in young adults: A pilot randomized controlled trial. *Journal of Consulting and Clinical Psychology, 85*(6), 620–631. https://doi.org/10.1037/ccp0000206

Andrews, T., Martin, G., Hasking, P., & Page, A. (2013). Predictors of continuation and cessation of nonsuicidal self-injury. *Journal of Adolescent Health, 53*(1), 40–46. https://doi.org/10.1016/j.jadohealth.2013.01.009

Andrews, T., Martin, G., Hasking, P., & Page, A. (2014). Predictors of onset for non-suicidal self-injury within a school-based sample of adolescents. *Prevention Science, 15*(6), 850–859. https://doi.org/10.1007/s11121-013-0412-8

Arbuthnott, A. E., Lewis, S. P., & Bailey, H. N. (2015). Rumination and emotions in nonsuicidal self-injury and eating disorder behaviors: A preliminary test of the emotional cascade model. *Journal of Clinical Psychology, 71*(1), 62–71. https://doi.org/10.1002/jclp.22115

Arbuthnott, A. E., & Lewis, S. P. (2015). Parents of youth who self-injure: A review of the literature and implications for mental health professionals. *Child and Adolescent Psychiatry and Mental Health, 9*, 35. https://doi.org/10.1186/s13034-015-0066-3

Arnett, J. J. (2015). *Emerging adulthood: The winding road from the late teens through the twenties* (2nd ed.). Oxford University Press.

Baetens, I., Decruy, C., Vatandoost, S., Vanderhaegen, B., & Kiekens, G. (2020). School-based prevention targeting non-suicidal self-injury: A pilot study. *Frontiers in Psychiatry, 11*, Article 437. https://doi.org/10.3389/fpsyt.2020.00437

Baiden, P., Stewart, S. L., & Fallon, B. (2017). The mediating effect of depressive symptoms on the relationship between bullying victimization and non-suicidal self-injury among adolescents: Findings from community and inpatient mental health settings in Ontario, Canada. *Psychiatry Research, 255*, 238–247. https://doi.org/10.1016/j.psychres.2017.05.018

Benjet, C., González-Herrera, I., Castro-Silva, E., Méndez, E., Borges, G., Casanova, L., & Medina-Mora, M. E. (2017). Non-suicidal self-injury in Mexican young adults: Prevalence, associations with suicidal behavior and psychiatric disorders, and DSM-5 proposed diagnostic criteria. *Journal of Affective Disorders, 215*, 1–8. https://doi.org/10.1016/j.jad.2017.03.025

Bentley, K. H., Cassiello-Robbins, C. F., Vittorio, L., Sauer-Zavala, S., & Barlow, D. H. (2015). The association between nonsuicidal self-injury and the emotional disorders: A meta-analytic review. *Clinical Psychology Review, 37*, 72–88. https://doi.org/10.1016/j.cpr.2015.02.006

Biskin, R. S., Paris, J., Zelkowitz, P., Mills, D., Laporte, L., & Heath, N. (2021). Nonsuicidal self-injury in early adolescence as a predictor of borderline personality disorder in early adulthood. *Journal of Personality Disorders, 35*(5), 764–775. https://doi.org/10.1521/pedi_2020_34_500

Bjureberg, J., Sahlin, H., Hedman-Lagerlof, E., Gratz, K. L., Tull, M. T., Jokinen, J., Hellner, C., & Ljotsson, B. (2018). Extending research on Emotion Regulation Individual Therapy for Adolescents (ERITA) with nonsuicidal self-injury disorder: Open pilot trial and mediation analysis of a novel online version. *BMC Psychiatry, 18*(1), Article 326. https://doi.org/10.1186/s12888-018-1885-6

Bjureberg, J., Sahlin, H., Hellner, C., Hedman-Lagerlöf, E., Gratz, K. L., Bjärehed, J., Jokinen, J., Tull, M. T., & Ljótsson, B. (2017). Emotion regulation individual therapy for adolescents with nonsuicidal self-injury disorder: A feasibility study. *BMC Psychiatry, 17*(1), 411. https://doi.org/10.1186/s12888-017-1527-4

Black, E. B., Garratt, M., Beccaria, G., Mildred, H., & Kwan, M. (2019). Body image as a predictor of nonsuicidal self-injury in women: A longitudinal study. *Comprehensive Psychiatry, 88*, 83–89. https://doi.org/10.1016/j.comppsych.2018.11.010

Brackman, E. H., Morris, B. W., & Andover, M. S. (2016). Predicting risk for suicide: A preliminary examination of non-suicidal self-injury and the acquired capability construct in a college sample. *Archives of Suicide Research, 20*(4), 663–676. https://doi.org/10.1080/13811118.2016.1162247

Breen, A. V., Lewis, S. P., & Sutherland, O. (2013). Brief report: Non-suicidal self-injury in the context of self and identity development. *Journal of Adult Development, 20*(1), 57–62. https://doi.org/10.1007/s10804-013-9156-8

Bresin, K., & Schoenleber, M. (2015). Gender differences in the prevalence of nonsuicidal self-injury: A meta-analysis. *Clinical Psychology Review, 38*, 55–64. https://doi.org/10.1016/j.cpr.2015.02.009

Buelens, T., Costantini, G., Luyckx, K., & Claes, L. (2020a). Comorbidity between non-suicidal self-injury disorder and borderline personality disorder in adolescents: A graphical network approach. *Frontiers in Psychiatry, 11*, Article 580922. https://doi.org/10.3389/fpsyt.2020.580922

Buelens, T., Luyckx, K., Gandhi, A., Kiekens, G., & Claes, L. (2019). Non-suicidal self-injury in adolescence: Longitudinal associations with psychological distress and rumination. *Journal of Abnormal Child Psychology, 47*(9), 1569–1581. https://doi.org/10.1007/s10802-019-00531-8

Buelens, T., Luyckx, K., Kiekens, G., Gandhi, A., Muehlenkamp, J. J., & Claes, L. (2020b). Investigating the DSM-5 criteria for non-suicidal self-injury disorder in a community sample of adolescents. *Journal of Affective Disorders, 260*, 314–322. https://doi.org/10.1016/j.jad.2019.09.009

Burke, T. A., Fox, K., Kautz, M. M., Rodriguez-Seijas, C., Bettis, A. H., & Alloy, L. B. (2021). Self-critical and self-punishment cognitions differentiate those with and without a history of nonsuicidal self-injury:

An ecological momentary assessment study. *Behavior Therapy, 52*(3), 686–697. https://doi.org/10.1016/j.beth.2020.08.006

Burke, T. A., Fox, K., Kautz, M., Siegel, D. M., Kleiman, E., & Alloy, L. B. (2021). Real-time monitoring of the associations between self-critical and self-punishment cognitions and nonsuicidal self-injury. *Behaviour Research and Therapy, 137*, 103775. https://doi.org/10.1016/j.brat.2020.103775

Burke, T. A., Hamilton, J. L., Abramson, L. Y., & Alloy, L. B. (2015). Non-suicidal self-injury prospectively predicts interpersonal stressful life events and depressive symptoms among adolescent girls. *Psychiatry Research, 228*(3), 416–424. https://doi.org/10.1016/j.psychres.2015.06.021

Burke, T. A., Jacobucci, R., Ammerman, B. A., Piccirillo, M., McCloskey, M. S., Heimberg, R. G., & Alloy, L. B. (2018). Identifying the relative importance of non-suicidal self-injury features in classifying suicidal ideation, plans, and behavior using exploratory data mining. *Psychiatry Research, 262*, 175–183. https://doi.org/10.1016/j.psychres.2018.01.045

Burke, T. A., Piccirillo, M. L., Moore-Berg, S. L., Alloy, L. B., & Heimberg, R. G. (2019). The stigmatization of nonsuicidal self-injury. *Journal of Clinical Psychology, 75*(3), 481–498. https://doi.org/10.1002/jclp.22713

Carosella, K. A., Wiglesworth, A., Silamongkol, T., Tavares, N., Falke, C. A., Fiecas, M. B., Cullen, K. R., & Klimes-Dougan, B. (2021). Non-suicidal self-injury in the context of COVID-19: The importance of psychosocial factors for female adolescents. *Journal of Affective Disorders Reports, 4*, Article 100137. https://doi.org/10.1016/j.jadr.2021.100137

Cassels, M., Baetens, I., Wilkinson, P., Hoppenbrouwers, K., Wiersema, J. R., Van Leeuwen, K., & Kiekens, G. (2019). Attachment and non-suicidal self-injury among young adolescents: The indirect role of behavioral problems. *Archives of Suicide Research, 23*(4), 688–696. https://doi.org/10.1080/13811118.2018.1494651

Cerutti, R., Zuffiano, A., & Spensieri, V. (2018). The role of difficulty in identifying and describing feelings in non-suicidal self-Injury behavior (NSSI): Associations with perceived attachment quality, stressful life events, and suicidal ideation. *Frontiers in Psychology, 9*, Article 318. https://doi.org/10.3389/fpsyg.2018.00318

Claes, L., De Raedt, R., Van de Walle, M., & Bosmans, G. (2016). Attentional bias moderates the link between attachment-related expectations and non-suicidal self-injury. *Cognitive Therapy and Research, 40*(4), 540–548. https://doi.org/10.1007/s10608-016-9761-5

Claes, L., Luyckx, K., Baetens, I., Van de Ven, M., & Witteman, C. (2015). Bullying and victimization, depressive mood, and non-suicidal self-injury in adolescents: The moderating role of parental support. *Journal of Child and Family Studies, 24*(11), 3363–3371. https://doi.org/10.1007/s10826-015-0138-2

Coleman, S. E., Dunlop, B. J., Hartley, S., & Taylor, P. J. (2021). The relationship between rumination and NSSI: A systematic review and meta-analysis. *British Journal of Clinical Psychology.* https://doi.org/10.1111/bjc.12350

Cook, N. E., & Gorraiz, M. (2016). Dialectical behavior therapy for nonsuicidal self-injury and depression among adolescents: Preliminary meta-analytic evidence. *Child and Adolescent Mental Health, 21*(2), 81–89. https://doi.org/10.1111/camh.12112

Cucchi, A., Ryan, D., Konstantakopoulos, G., Stroumpa, S., Kacar, A. S., Renshaw, S., Landau, S., & Kravariti, E. (2016). Lifetime prevalence of non-suicidal self-injury in patients with eating disorders: A systematic review and meta-analysis. *Psychological Medicine, 46*(7), 1345–1358. https://doi.org/10.1017/S0033291716000027

Cummings, L. R., Mattfeld, A. T., Pettit, J. W., & McMakin, D. L. (2021). Viewing nonsuicidal self-injury in adolescence through a developmental neuroscience lens: The impact of neural sensitivity to socioaffective pain and reward. *Clinical Psychological Science, 9*(5), 767–790. https://doi.org/10.1177/2167702621989323

Daukantaite, D., Lundh, L. G., Wangby-Lundh, M., Clareus, B., Bjarehed, J., Zhou, Y., & Liljedahl, S. I. (2021). What happens to young adults who have engaged in self-injurious behavior as adolescents? A 10-year follow-up. *European Child & Adolescent Psychiatry, 30*, 475–492. https://doi.org/10.1007/s00787-020-01533-4

Dawkins, J. C., Hasking, P. A., & Boyes, M. E. (2021). Thoughts and beliefs about nonsuicidal self-injury: An application of social cognitive theory. *Journal of American College Health, 69*(4), 428–434. https://doi.org/10.1080/07448481.2019.1679817

Dawkins, J. C., Hasking, P. A., Boyes, M. E., Greene, D., & Passchier, C. (2019). Applying a cognitive-emotional model to nonsuicidal self-injury. *Stress & Health, 35*(1), 39–48. https://doi.org/10.1002/smi.2837

Duffy, M. E., Twenge, J. M., & Joiner, T. E. (2019). Trends in mood and anxiety symptoms and suicide-related outcomes among U.S. undergraduates, 2007-2018: Evidence from two national surveys. *Journal of Adolescent Health, 65*(5), 590–598. https://doi.org/10.1016/j.jadohealth.2019.04.033

Forster, M., Grigsby, T. J., Gower, A. L., Mehus, C. J., & McMorris, B. J. (2020). The role of social support in the association between childhood adversity and adolescent self-injury and suicide: Findings from a statewide sample of high school students. *Journal of Youth and Adolescence, 49*(6), 1195–1208. https://doi.org/10.1007/s10964-020-01235-9

Fox, K. R., Franklin, J. C., Ribeiro, J. D., Kleiman, E. M., Bentley, K. H., & Nock, M. K. (2015). Meta-analysis of risk factors for nonsuicidal self-injury. *Clinical Psychology Review, 42*, 156–167. https://doi.org/10.1016/j.cpr.2015.09.002

Fox, K. R., Ribeiro, J. D., Kleiman, E. M., Hooley, J. M., Nock, M. K., & Franklin, J. C. (2018). Affect toward the self and self-injury stimuli as potential risk factors for nonsuicidal self-injury. *Psychiatry Research, 260*, 279–285. https://doi.org/10.1016/j.psychres.2017.11.083

Fox, K. R., Toole, K. E., Franklin, J. C., & Hooley, J. M. (2016). Why does nonsuicidal self-injury improve mood? A preliminary test of three hypotheses. *Clinical Psychological Science, 5*(1), 111–121. https://doi.org/10.1177/2167702616662270

Franklin, J. C., Fox, K. R., Franklin, C. R., Kleiman, E. M., Ribeiro, J. D., Jaroszewski, A. C., Hooley, J. M., & Nock, M. K. (2016). A brief mobile app reduces nonsuicidal and suicidal self-injury: Evidence from three randomized controlled trials. *Journal of Consulting and Clinical Psychology, 84*(6), 544–557. https://doi.org/10.1037/ccp0000093

Franzen, M., Keller, F., Brown, R. C., & Plener, P. L. (2019). Emergency presentations to child and adolescent psychiatry: Nonsuicidal self-injury and suicidality. *Frontiers in Psychiatry, 10*, Article 979. https://doi.org/10.3389/fpsyt.2019.00979

Gandhi, A., Luyckx, K., Adhikari, A., Parmar, D., Desousa, A., Shah, N., Maitra, S., & Claes, L. (2020). Non-suicidal self-injury and its association with identity formation in India and Belgium: A cross-cultural case-control study. *Transcultural Psychiatry, 58*(1), 52–62. https://doi.org/10.1177/1363461520933759

Gandhi, A., Luyckx, K., Baetens, I., Kiekens, G., Sleuwaegen, E., Berens, A., Maitra, S., & Claes, L. (2018). Age of onset of non-suicidal self-injury in Dutch-speaking adolescents and emerging adults: An event history analysis of pooled data. *Comprehensive Psychiatry, 80*, 170–178. https://doi.org/10.1016/j.comppsych.2017.10.007

Gandhi, A., Luyckx, K., Maitra, S., Kiekens, G., Verschueren, M., & Claes, L. (2017). Directionality of effects between non-suicidal self-injury and identity formation: A prospective study in adolescents. *Personality and Individual Differences, 109*, 124–129. https://doi.org/10.1016/j.paid.2017.01.003

Gandhi, A., Luyckx, K., Molenberghs, G., Baetens, I., Goossens, L., Maitra, S., & Claes, L. (2019). Maternal and peer attachment, identity formation, and non-suicidal self-injury: A longitudinal mediation study. *Child and Adolescent Psychiatry and Mental Health, 13*, Article 7. https://doi.org/10.1186/s13034-019-0267-2

Giletta, M., Prinstein, M. J., Abela, J. R., Gibb, B. E., Barrocas, A. L., & Hankin, B. L. (2015). Trajectories of suicide ideation and nonsuicidal self-injury among adolescents in mainland China: Peer predictors, joint development, and risk for suicide attempts. *Journal of Consulting and Clinical Psychology, 83*(2), 265–279. doi:10.1037/a0038652

Gillies, D., Christou, M. A., Dixon, A. C., Featherston, O. J., Rapti, I., Garcia-Anguita, A., Villasis-Keever, M., Reebye, P., Christou, E., Kabir, N. A., & Christou, P. A. (2018). Prevalence and characteristics of self-harm in adolescents: Meta-analyses of community-based studies 1990-2015. *Journal of the American Academy of Child & Adolescent Psychiatry, 57*(10), 733–741. https://doi.org/10.1016/j.jaac.2018.06.018

Glenn, C. R., & Klonsky, E. D. (2011). Prospective prediction of nonsuicidal self-injury: A 1-year longitudinal study in young adults. *Behavior Therapy, 42*(4), 751–762. https://doi.org/10.1016/j.beth.2011.04.005

Glenn, J. J., Michel, B. D., Franklin, J. C., Hooley, J. M., & Nock, M. K. (2014). Pain analgesia among adolescent self-injurers. *Psychiatry Research, 220*(3), 921–926. https://doi.org/10.1016/j.psychres.2014.08.016

Goodman, M., Tomas, I. A., Temes, C. M., Fitzmaurice, G. M., Aguirre, B. A., & Zanarini, M. C. (2017). Suicide attempts and self-injurious behaviours in adolescent and adult patients with borderline personality disorder. *Personality and Mental Health, 11*(3), 157–163. https://doi.org/10.1002/pmh.1375

Grandclerc, S., De Labrouhe, D., Spodenkiewicz, M., Lachal, J., & Moro, M. R. (2016). Relations between nonsuicidal self-injury and suicidal behavior in adolescence: A Systematic review. *PLoS One, 11*(4), Article e0153760. https://doi.org/10.1371/journal.pone.0153760

Griep, S. K., & MacKinnon, D. F. (2020). Does nonsuicidal self-injury predict later suicidal attempts? A review of studies. *Archives of Suicide Research, 26*(2), 428–446. https://doi.org/10.1080/13811118.2020.1822244

Gromatsky, M. A., Waszczuk, M. A., Perlman, G., Salis, K. L., Klein, D. N., & Kotov, R. (2017). The role of parental psychopathology and personality in adolescent non-suicidal self-injury. *Journal of Psychiatric Research*, *85*, 15–23. https://doi.org/10.1016/j.jpsychires.2016.10.013

Gu, H., Ma, P., & Xia, T. (2020). Childhood emotional abuse and adolescent nonsuicidal self-injury: The mediating role of identity confusion and moderating role of rumination. *Child Abuse & Neglect*, *106*, Article 104474. https://doi.org/10.1016/j.chiabu.2020.104474

Halpin, S. A., & Duffy, N. M. (2020). Predictors of non-suicidal self-injury cessation in adults who self-injured during adolescence. *Journal of Affective Disorders Reports*, *1*, Article 100017. https://doi.org/10.1016/j.jadr.2020.100017

Hamza, C. A., Robinson, K., Hasking, P. A., Heath, N. L., Lewis, S. P., Lloyd-Richardson, E., Whitlock, J., & Wilson, M. S. (2021). Educational stakeholders' attitudes and knowledge about nonsuicidal self-injury among university students: A cross-national study. *Journal of American College Health*, 1–11. https://doi.org/10.1080/07448481.2021.1961782

Hamza, C. A., Stewart, S. L., & Willoughby, T. (2012). Examining the link between nonsuicidal self-injury and suicidal behavior: A review of the literature and an integrated model. *Clinical Psychology Review*, *32*(6), 482–495. https://doi.org/10.1016/j.cpr.2012.05.003

Hamza, C. A., & Willoughby, T. (2014). A longitudinal person-centered examination of nonsuicidal self-injury among university students. *Journal of Youth and Adolescence*, *43*(4), 671–685. https://doi.org/10.1007/s10964-013-9991-8

Hamza, C. A., & Willoughby, T. (2016). Nonsuicidal self-injury and suicidal risk among emerging adults. *Journal of Adolescent Health*, *59*(4), 411–415. https://doi.org/10.1016/j.jadohealth.2016.05.019

Hasking, P., Andrews, T., & Martin, G. (2013). The role of exposure to self-injury among peers in predicting later self-injury. *Journal of Youth and Adolescence*, *42*(10), 1543–1556. https://doi.org/10.1007/s10964-013-9931-7

Hasking, P. A., Bloom, E., Lewis, S. P., & Baetens, I. (2020). Developing a policy, and professional development for school staff, to address and respond to nonsuicidal self-injury in schools. *International Perspectives in Psychology*, *9*(3), 176–179. https://doi.org/10.1037/ipp0000143

Hasking, P., Dawkins, J., Gray, N., Wijeratne, P., & Boyes, M. (2020). Indirect effects of family functioning on non-suicidal self-injury and risky drinking: The roles of emotion reactivity and emotion regulation. *Journal of Child and Family Studies*, *29*(7), 2070–2079. https://doi.org/10.1007/s10826-020-01722-4

Hasking, P. A., Heath, N. L., Kaess, M., Lewis, S. P., Plener, P. L., Walsh, B. W., Whitlock, J., & Wilson, M. S. (2016). Position paper for guiding response to non-suicidal self-injury in schools. *School Psychology International*, *37*(6), 644–663. https://doi.org/10.1177/0143034316678656

Hasking, P., Whitlock, J., Voon, D., & Rose, A. (2017). A cognitive-emotional model of NSSI: Using emotion regulation and cognitive processes to explain why people self-injure. *Cognition and Emotion*, *31*(8), 1543–1556. https://doi.org/10.1080/02699931.2016.1241219

Heath, N., Toste, J., Nedecheva, T., & Charlebois, A. (2008). An examination of nonsuicidal self-injury among college students. *Journal of Mental Health Counseling*, *30*(2), 137–156. https://doi.org/10.17744/mehc.30.2.8p879p3443514678

Hepp, J., Carpenter, R. W., Störkel, L. M., Schmitz, S. E., Schmahl, C., & Niedtfeld, I. (2020). A systematic review of daily life studies on non-suicidal self-injury based on the four-function model. *Clinical Psychology Review*, *82*, Article 101888. https://doi.org/10.1016/j.cpr.2020.101888

Hetrick, S. E., Robinson, J., Burge, E., Blandon, R., Mobilio, B., Rice, S. M., Simmons, M. B., Alvarez-Jimenez, M., Goodrich, S., & Davey, C. G. (2018). Youth codesign of a mobile phone app to facilitate self-monitoring and management of mood symptoms in young people with major depression, suicidal ideation, and self-harm. *JMIR Mental Health*, *5*(1), Article e9. https://doi.org/10.2196/mental.9041

Hielscher, E., DeVylder, J., Hasking, P., Connell, M., Martin, G., & Scott, J. G. (2021). Can't get you out of my head: Persistence and remission of psychotic experiences in adolescents and its association with self-injury and suicide attempts. *Schizophrenia Research*, *229*, 63–72. https://doi.org/10.1016/j.schres.2020.11.019

Hooley, J. M., Fox, K. R., Wang, S. B., & Kwashie, A. N. D. (2018). Novel online daily diary interventions for nonsuicidal self-injury: A randomized controlled trial. *BMC Psychiatry*, *18*(1), 264. https://doi.org/10.1186/s12888-018-1840-6

Hooley, J. M., & Franklin, J. C. (2017). Why do people hurt themselves? A new conceptual model of nonsuicidal self-injury. *Clinical Psychological Science*, *6*(3), 428–451. https://doi.org/10.1177/2167702617745641

Horowitz, S., & Stermac, L. (2018). The relationship between interpersonal trauma history and the functions of non-suicidal self-injury in young adults: An experience sampling study. *Journal of Trauma & Dissociation*, *19*(2), 232–246. https://doi.org/10.1080/15299732.2017.1330228

Huang, Y. H., Liu, H. C., Sun, F. J., Tsai, F. J., Huang, K. Y., Chen, T. C., Huang, Y., & Liu, S. I. (2017). Relationship between predictors of incident deliberate self-harm and suicide attempts among adolescents. *Journal of Adolescent Health*, *60*(5), 612–618. https://doi.org/10.1016/j.jadohealth.2016.12.005

Hughes, C. D., King, A. M., Kranzler, A., Fehling, K., Miller, A., Lindqvist, J., & Selby, E. A. (2019). Anxious and overwhelming affects and repetitive negative thinking as ecological predictors of self-injurious thoughts and behaviors. *Cognitive Therapy and Research*, *43*(1), 88–101. https://doi.org/10.1007/s10608-019-09996-9

International Society for the Study of Self-injury (2022). *What is self-injury?* https://itriples.org/about-self-injury/what-is-self-injury/

Jantzer, V., Haffner, J., Parzer, P., Resch, F., & Kaess, M. (2015). Does parental monitoring moderate the relationship between bullying and adolescent nonsuicidal self-injury and suicidal behavior? A community-based self-report study of adolescents in Germany. *BMC Public Health*, *15*, Article 583. https://doi.org/10.1186/s12889-015-1940-x

Jiang, Y., You, J., Zheng, X., & Lin, M. P. (2017). The qualities of attachment with significant others and self-compassion protect adolescents from non-suicidal self-injury. *School Psychology Quarterly*, *32*(2), 143–155. https://doi.org/10.1037/spq0000187

Joiner, T. E. (2005). *Why people die by suicide*. Harvard University Press.

Kaess, M., Edinger, A., Fischer-Waldschmidt, G., Parzer, P., Brunner, R., & Resch, F. (2020). Effectiveness of a brief psychotherapeutic intervention compared with treatment as usual for adolescent nonsuicidal self-injury: A single-centre, randomised controlled trial. *European Child & Adolescent Psychiatry*, *29*(6), 881–891. https://doi.org/10.1007/s00787-019-01399-1

Kang, N., Jiang, Y., Ren, Y., Gong, T., Liu, X., Leung, F., & You, J. (2018). Distress intolerance mediates the relationship between child maltreatment and nonsuicidal self-injury among Chinese adolescents: A three-wave longitudinal study. *Journal of Youth and Adolescence*, *47*(10), 2220–2230. https://doi.org/10.1007/s10964-018-0877-7

Kiekens, G., Bruffaerts, R., Nock, M. K., Van de Ven, M., Witteman, C., Mortier, P., Demyttenaere, K., & Claes, L. (2015). Non-suicidal self-injury among Dutch and Belgian adolescents: Personality, stress and coping. *European Psychiatry*, *30*(6), 743–749. https://doi.org/10.1016/j.eurpsy.2015.06.007

Kiekens, G., & Claes, L. (2020). Non-suicidal self-injury and eating disordered behaviors: An update on what we do and do not know. *Current Psychiatry Reports*, *22*(12), 68. https://doi.org/10.1007/s11920-020-01191-y

Kiekens, G., Claes, L., Demyttenaere, K., Auerbach, R. P., Green, J. G., Kessler, R. C., Mortier, P., Nock, M. K., & Bruffaerts, R. (2016). Lifetime and 12-month nonsuicidal self-injury and academic performance in college freshmen. *Suicide and Life-Threatening Behavior*, *46*(5), 563–576. https://doi.org/10.1111/sltb.12237

Kiekens, G., Claes, L., Hasking, P., Mortier, P., Bootsma, E., Boyes, M., Myin-Germeys, I., Demyttenaere, K., Cuijpers, P., Kessler, R. C., Nock, M. K., & Bruffaerts, R. (2022). A longitudinal investigation of non-suicidal self-injury persistence patterns, risk factors, and clinical outcomes during the college period. *Psychological Medicine*. Advance online publication. https://doi.org/10.1017/S0033291722003178

Kiekens, G., Hasking, P., Boyes, M., Claes, L., Mortier, P., Auerbach, R. P., Cuijpers, P., Demyttenaere, K., Green, J. G., Kessler, R. C., Myin-Germeys, I., Nock, M. K., & Bruffaerts, R. (2018). The associations between non-suicidal self-injury and first onset suicidal thoughts and behaviors. *Journal of Affective Disorders*, *239*, 171–179. https://doi.org/10.1016/j.jad.2018.06.033

Kiekens, G., Hasking, P., Bruffaerts, R., Alonso, J., Auerbach, R. P., Bantjes, J., Benjet, C., Boyes, M., Chiu, W. T., Claes, L., Cuijpers, P., Ebert, D. D., Mak, A., Mortier, P., O'Neill, S., Sampson, N. A., Stein, D. J., Vilagut, G., Nock, M. K., & Kessler, R. C. (2023). Non-suicidal self-injury among first-year college students and its association with mental disorders: Results from the World Mental Health International College Student (WMH-ICS) initiative. *Psychological Medicine*, *53*, 875–886. https://doi.org/10.1017/S0033291721002245

Kiekens, G., Hasking, P., Bruffaerts, R., Claes, L., Baetens, I., Boyes, M., Mortier, P., Demyttenaere, K., & Whitlock, J. (2017). What predicts ongoing nonsuicidal self-injury? A comparison between persistent and ceased self-injury in emerging adults. *Journal of Nervous and Mental Disease, 205*(10), 762–770. https://doi.org/10.1097/NMD.0000000000000726

Kiekens, G., Hasking, P., Claes, L., Boyes, M., Mortier, P., Auerbach, R. P., Cuijpers, P., Demyttenaere, K., Green, J. G., Kessler, R. C., Myin-Germeys, I., Nock, M. K., & Bruffaerts, R. (2019). Predicting the incidence of non-suicidal self-injury in college students. *European Psychiatry, 59*, 44–51. https://doi.org/10.1016/j.eurpsy.2019.04.002

Kiekens, G., Hasking, P., Claes, L., Mortier, P., Auerbach, R. P., Boyes, M., Cuijpers, P., Demyttenaere, K., Green, J. G., Kessler, R. C., Nock, M. K., & Bruffaerts, R. (2018). The DSM-5 nonsuicidal self-injury disorder among incoming college students: Prevalence and associations with 12-month mental disorders and suicidal thoughts and behaviors. *Depression & Anxiety, 35*(7), 629–637. https://doi.org/10.1002/da.22754

Kiekens, G., Hasking, P., Nock, M. K., Boyes, M., Kirtley, O., Bruffaerts, R., Myin-Germeys, I., & Claes, L. (2020). Fluctuations in affective states and self-Efficacy to resist non-suicidal self-injury as real-time predictors of non-suicidal self-injurious thoughts and behaviors. *Frontiers in Psychiatry, 11*, 214. https://doi.org/10.3389/fpsyt.2020.00214

Kiekens, G., Robinson, K., Tatnell, R., & Kirtley, O. J. (2021). Opening the black box of daily life in nonsuicidal self-injury research: With great opportunity comes great responsibility. *JMIR Mental Health, 8*(11), Article e30915. https://doi.org/10.2196/30915

Kleiman, E. M., Ammerman, B. A., Kulper, D. A., Uyeji, L. L., Jenkins, A. L., & McCloskey, M. S. (2015). Forms of non-suicidal self-injury as a function of trait aggression. *Comprehensive Psychiatry, 59*, 21–27. https://doi.org/10.1016/j.comppsych.2014.12.004

Kruzan, K. P., & Whitlock, J. (2019). Prevention of nonsuicidal self-Injury. In J. J. Washburn (Ed.), *Nonsuicidal self-injury: Advances in research and practice* (pp. 215–239). Routledge.

Kruzan, K. P., Whitlock, J., & Bazarova, N. N. (2021). Examining the relationship between the use of a mobile peer-support app and self-injury outcomes: Longitudinal mixed methods study. *JMIR Mental Health, 8*(1), Article e21854. https://doi.org/10.2196/21854

Lengel, G. J., & Styer, D. (2019). Comprehensive assessment of nonsuicidal self-injury. In J. J. Washburn (Ed.), *Nonsuicidal self-injury: Advances in research and practice* (pp. 127–147). Routledge.

Lewis, S. P., & Hasking, P. A. (2021). Self-injury recovery: A person-centered framework. *Journal of Clinical Psychology, 77*, 884–895. https://doi.org/10.1002/jclp.23094

Lewis, S. P., Heath, N. L., Hasking, P. A., Whitlock, J. L., Wilson, M. S., & Plener, P. L. (2019). Addressing self-injury on college campuses: Institutional recommendations. *Journal of College Counselling, 22*, 70–82. https://doi.org/10.1002/jocc.12115

Liu, R. T., Scopelliti, K. M., Pittman, S. K., & Zamora, A. S. (2018). Childhood maltreatment and non-suicidal self-injury: A systematic review and meta-analysis. *Lancet Psychiatry, 5*(1), 51–64. https://doi.org/10.1016/S2215-0366(17)30469-8

Liu, R. T., Sheehan, A. E., Walsh, R. F. L., Sanzari, C. M., Cheek, S. M., & Hernandez, E. M. (2019). Prevalence and correlates of non-suicidal self-injury among lesbian, gay, bisexual, and transgender individuals: A systematic review and meta-analysis. *Clinical Psychology Review, 74*, Article 101783. https://doi.org/10.1016/j.cpr.2019.101783

Lustig, S., Koenig, J., Resch, F., & Kaess, M. (2021). Help-seeking duration in adolescents with suicidal behavior and non-suicidal self-injury. *Journal of Psychiatric Research, 140*, 60–67. https://doi.org/10.1016/j.jpsychires.2021.05.037

Marin, S., Hajizadeh, M., Sahebihagh, M. H., Nemati, H., Ataeiasl, M., Anbarlouei, M., Pashapour, H., Mahmoodi, M., & Mohammadpoorasl, A. (2020). Epidemiology and determinants of self-injury Among high school students in Iran: A longitudinal study. *Psychiatry Quarterly, 91*(4), 1407–1413. https://doi.org/10.1007/s11126-020-09764-z

Matney, J., Westers, N. J., Horton, S. E., King, J. D., Eaddy, M., Emslie, G. J., Kennard, B. D., & Stewart, S. M. (2018). Frequency and methods of nonsuicidal self-injury in relation to acquired capability for suicide among adolescents. *Archives of Suicide Research, 22*(1), 91–105. https://doi.org/10.1080/13811118.2017.1283266

Mbroh, H., Zullo, L., Westers, N., Stone, L., King, J., Kennard, B., Emslie, G., & Stewart, S. (2018). Double trouble: Nonsuicidal self-injury and its relationship to suicidal ideation and number of past suicide attempts in clinical adolescents. *Journal of Affective Disorders, 238*, 579–585. https://doi.org/10.1016/j.jad.2018.05.056

Micali, N., Horton, N. J., Crosby, R. D., Swanson, S. A., Sonneville, K. R., Solmi, F., Calzo, J. P., Eddy, K. T., & Field, A. E. (2017). Eating disorder behaviours amongst adolescents: Investigating classification, persistence and prospective associations with adverse outcomes using latent class models. *European Child & Adolescent Psychiatry*, *26*(2), 231–240. https://doi.org/10.1007/s00787-016-0877-7

Muehlenkamp, J., Brausch, A., Quigley, K., & Whitlock, J. (2013). Interpersonal features and functions of nonsuicidal self-injury. *Suicide and Life-Threatening Behavior*, *43*(1), 67–80. https://doi.org/10.1111/j.1943-278X.2012.00128.x

Muehlenkamp, J. J., Walsh, B. W., & McDade, M. (2010). Preventing non-suicidal self-injury in adolescents: The signs of self-injury program. *Journal of Youth and Adolescence*, *39*(3), 306–314. https://doi.org/10.1007/s10964-009-9450-8

Muehlenkamp, J. J., Xhunga, N., & Brausch, A. M. (2019). Self-injury age of onset: A risk factor for NSSI severity and suicidal behavior. *Archives of Suicide Research*, *23*(4), 551–563. https://doi.org/10.1080/13811118.2018.1486252

Nelson, S. C., Kling, J., Wangqvist, M., Frisen, A., & Syed, M. (2018). Identity and the body: Trajectories of body esteem from adolescence to emerging adulthood. *Developmental Psychology*, *54*(6), 1159–1171. https://doi.org/10.1037/dev0000435

Nicolai, K. A., Wielgus, M. D., & Mezulis, A. (2016). Identifying risk for self-harm: Rumination and negative affectivity in the prospective prediction of nonsuicidal self-injury. *Suicide and Life-Threatening Behavior*, *46*(2), 223–233. https://doi.org/10.1111/sltb.12186

Piccirillo, M. L., & Rodebaugh, T. L. (2019). Foundations of idiographic methods in psychology and applications for psychotherapy. *Clinical Psychology Review*, *71*, 90–100. https://doi.org/10.1016/j.cpr.2019.01.002

Plener, P. L., Brunner, R., Fegert, J. M., Groschwitz, R. C., In-Albon, T., Kaess, M., Kapusta, N. D., Resch, F., & Becker, K. (2016). Treating nonsuicidal self-injury (NSSI) in adolescents: Consensus based German guidelines. *Child and Adolescent Psychiatry and Mental Health*, *10*, 46. https://doi.org/10.1186/s13034-016-0134-3

Rallis, B. A., Esposito-Smythers, C., Disabato, D. J., Mehlenbeck, R. S., Kaplan, S., Geer, L., Adams, R., & Meehan, B. (2018). A brief peer gatekeeper suicide prevention training: Results of an open pilot trial. *Journal of Clinical Psychology*, *74*(7), 1106–1116. https://doi.org/10.1002/jclp.22590

Ribeiro, J. D., Franklin, J. C., Fox, K. R., Bentley, K. H., Kleiman, E. M., Chang, B. P., & Nock, M. K. (2016). Self-injurious thoughts and behaviors as risk factors for future suicide ideation, attempts, and death: A meta-analysis of longitudinal studies. *Psychological Medicine*, *46*(2), 225–236. https://doi.org/10.1017/S0033291715001804

Riley, E. N., Combs, J. L., Jordan, C. E., & Smith, G. T. (2015). Negative urgency and lack of perseverance: Identification of differential pathways of onset and maintenance risk in the longitudinal prediction of nonsuicidal self-injury. *Behavior Therapy*, *46*(4), 439–448. https://doi.org/10.1016/j.beth.2015.03.002

Robinson, K., Garisch, J. A., Kingi, T., Brocklesby, M., O'Connell, A., Langlands, R. L., Russell, L., & Wilson, M. S. (2019). Reciprocal risk: The longitudinal relationship between emotion regulation and non-suicidal self-injury in adolescents. *Journal of Abnormal Child Psychology*, *47*(2), 325–332. https://doi.org/10.1007/s10802-018-0450-6

Robinson, K., & Wilson, M. S. (2020). Open to interpretation? Inconsistent reporting of lifetime nonsuicidal self-injury across two common assessments. *Psychological Assessment*, *32*(8), 726–738. https://doi.org/10.1037/pas0000830

Sahlin, H., Bjureberg, J., Gratz, K. L., Tull, M. T., Hedman, E., Bjärehed, J., Jokinen, J., Lundh, L., Ljótsson, B., & Hellner, C. (2017). Emotion regulation group therapy for deliberate self-harm: A multi-site evaluation in routine care using an uncontrolled open trial design. *BMJ Open*, *7*(10), Article e016220. https://doi.org/10.1136/bmjopen-2017-016220

Schwartz-Mette, R. A., & Lawrence, H. R. (2019). Peer socialization of non-suicidal self-injury in adolescents' close friendships. *Journal of Abnormal Child Psychology*, *47*(11), 1851–1862. https://doi.org/10.1007/s10802-019-00569-8

Selby, E. A., Franklin, J., Carson-Wong, A., & Rizvi, S. L. (2013). Emotional cascades and self-injury: Investigating instability of rumination and negative emotion. *Journal of Clinical Psychology*, *69*(12), 1213–1227. https://doi.org/10.1002/jclp.21966

Serafini, G., Aguglia, A., Amerio, A., Canepa, G., Adavastro, G., Conigliaro, C., Nebbia, J., Franchi, L., Flouri, E., & Amore, M. (2021). The relationship between bullying victimization and perpetration and non-suicidal self-injury: A systematic review. *Child Psychiatry & Human Development*, *54*(1), 154–175. https://doi.org/10.1007/s10578-021-01231-5

Simone, A. C., & Hamza, C. A. (2020). Examining the disclosure of nonsuicidal self-injury to informal and formal sources: A review of the literature. *Clinical Psychology Review, 82*, Article 101907. https://doi.org/10.1016/j.cpr.2020.101907

Solmi, M., Radua, J., Olivola, M., Croce, E., Soardo, L., Salazar de Pablo, G., Il Shin, J., Kirkbride, J. B., Jones, P., Kim J. H., Kim, J. Y., Carvalho, A. F., Seeman, M. V., Correll, C. U., & Fusar-Poli, P. (2021). Age at onset of mental disorders worldwide: Large-scale meta-analysis of 192 epidemiological studies. *Molecular Psychiatry, 27*(1), 281–295. https://doi.org/10.1038/s41380-021-01161-7

Sornberger, M. J., Heath, N. L., Toste, J. R., & McLouth, R. (2012). Nonsuicidal self-injury and gender: Patterns of prevalence, methods, and locations among adolescents. *Suicide and Life-Threatening Behavior, 42*(3), 266–278. https://doi.org/10.1111/j.1943-278X.2012.0088.x

Spitzen, T. L., Tull, M. T., Baer, M. M., Dixon-Gordon, K. L., Chapman, A. L., & Gratz, K. L. (2020). Predicting engagement in nonsuicidal self-injury (NSSI) over the course of 12 months: The roles of borderline personality disorder pathology and emotional consequences of NSSI. *Journal of Affective Disorders, 277*, 631–639. https://doi.org/10.1016/j.jad.2020.08.049

Staniland, L., Hasking, P., Boyes, M., & Lewis, S. (2020). Stigma and nonsuicidal self-injury: Application of a conceptual framework. *Stigma and Health, 6*, 312–323. https://doi.org/10.1037/sah0000257

Statista. (2020). *Smartphones–Statistics & facts*. https://www.statista.com/topics/840/smartphones/

Steinhoff, A., Ribeaud, D., Kupferschmid, S., Raible-Destan, N., Quednow, B. B., Hepp, U., Eisner, M., & Shanahan, L. (2021). Self-injury from early adolescence to early adulthood: Age-related course, recurrence, and services use in males and females from the community. *European Child & Adolescent Psychiatry, 30*, 937–951. https://doi.org/10.1007/s00787-020-01573-w

Stoltenborgh, M., Bakermans-Kranenburg, M. J., Alink, L. R., & van IJzendoorn, M. H. (2015). The prevalence of child maltreatment across the globe: Review of a series of meta-analyses. *Child Abuse Review, 24*(1), 37–50. https://doi.org/10.1002/car.2353

Swannell, S. V., Martin, G. E., Page, A., Hasking, P., & St John, N. J. (2014). Prevalence of nonsuicidal self-injury in nonclinical samples: Systematic review, meta-analysis and meta-regression. *Suicide and Life-Threatening Behavior, 44*(3), 273–303. https://doi.org/10.1111/sltb.12070

Syed, S., Kingsbury, M., Bennett, K., Manion, I., & Colman, I. (2020). Adolescents' knowledge of a peer's non-suicidal self-injury and own non-suicidal self-injury and suicidality. *Acta Psychiatrica Scandinavica, 142*(5), 366–373. https://doi.org/10.1111/acps.13229

Taliaferro, L. A., Jang, S. T., Westers, N. J., Muehlenkamp, J. J., Whitlock, J. L., & McMorris, B. J. (2020). Associations between connections to parents and friends and non-suicidal self-injury among adolescents: The mediating role of developmental assets. *Clinical Child Psychology and Psychiatry, 25*(2), 359–371. https://doi.org/10.1177/1359104519868493

Tatnell, R., Kelada, L., Hasking, P., & Martin, G. (2014). Longitudinal analysis of adolescent NSSI: The role of intrapersonal and interpersonal factors. *Journal of Abnormal Child Psychology, 42*(6), 885–896. https://doi.org/10.1007/s10802-013-9837-6

Taylor, P. J., Jomar, K., Dhingra, K., Forrester, R., Shahmalak, U., & Dickson, J. M. (2018). A meta-analysis of the prevalence of different functions of non-suicidal self-injury. *Journal of Affective Disorders, 227*, 759–769. https://doi.org/10.1016/j.jad.2017.11.073

Turner, B. J., Helps, C. E., & Ames, M. E. (2021). Stop self-injuring, then what? Psychosocial risk associated with initiation and cessation of nonsuicidal self-injury from adolescence to early adulthood. *Journal of Abnormal Psychology, 131*(1), 45–57. https://doi.org/10.1037/abn0000718

Turner, B. J., Jin, H. M., Anestis, M. D., Dixon-Gordon, K. L., & Gratz, K. L. (2018). Personality pathology and intentional self-harm: Cross-cutting insights from categorical and dimensional models. *Current Opinion in Psychology, 21*, 55–59. https://doi.org/10.1016/j.copsyc.2017.09.009

Turner, B. J., Wakefield, M. A., Gratz, K. L., & Chapman, A. L. (2017). Characterizing interpersonal difficulties among young adults who engage in nonsuicidal self-injury using a daily diary. *Behavior Therapy, 48*(3), 366–379. https://doi.org/10.1016/j.beth.2016.07.001

Turner, B. J., Yiu, A., Layden, B. K., Claes, L., Zaitsoff, S., & Chapman, A. L. (2015). Temporal associations between disordered eating and nonsuicidal self-injury: Examining symptom overlap over 1 year. *Behavior Therapy, 46*(1), 125–138. https://doi.org/10.1016/j.beth.2014.09.002

van Geel, M., Goemans, A., & Vedder, P. (2015). A meta-analysis on the relation between peer victimization and adolescent non-suicidal self-injury. *Psychiatry Research, 230*(2), 364–368. https://doi.org/10.1016/j.psychres.2015.09.017

Van Orden, K. A., Witte, T. K., Cukrowicz, K. C., Braithwaite, S. R., Selby, E. A., & Joiner, T. E., Jr. (2010). The interpersonal theory of suicide. *Psychological Review, 117*(2), 575–600. https://doi.org/10.1037/a0018697

Verschueren, M., Claes, L., Gandhi, A., & Luyckx, K. (2020). Identity and psychopathology: Bridging developmental and clinical research. *Emerging Adulthood, 8*, 319–332. https://doi.org/10.1177/2167696819870021

Victor, S. E., Hipwell, A. E., Stepp, S. D., & Scott, L. N. (2019). Parent and peer relationships as longitudinal predictors of adolescent non-suicidal self-injury onset. *Child and Adolescent Psychiatry and Mental Health, 13*, 1. https://doi.org/10.1186/s13034-018-0261-0

Victor, S. E., Muehlenkamp, J. J., Hayes, N. A., Lengel, G. J., Styer, D. M., & Washburn, J. J. (2018). Characterizing gender differences in nonsuicidal self-injury: Evidence from a large clinical sample of adolescents and adults. *Comprehensive Psychiatry, 82*, 53–60. https://doi.org/10.1016/j.comppsych.2018.01.009

Victor, S. E., Styer, D., & Washburn, J. J. (2015). Characteristics of nonsuicidal self-injury associated with suicidal ideation: Evidence from a clinical sample of youth. *Child and Adolescent Psychiatry and Mental Health, 9*, 20. https://doi.org/10.1186/s13034-015-0053-8

Vieira, A. M., & Lewis, S. P. (2018). Mobile apps for self-injury: A content analysis. *Cyberpsychology, Behavior, and Social Networking, 21*(5), 333–337. https://doi.org/10.1089/cyber.2017.0535

Westers, N. J., Muehlenkamp, J. J., & Lau, M. (2016). SOARS model: Risk assessment of nonsuicidal self-injury. *Contemporary Pediatrics, 33*(7), 25–31.

Westers, N. J., & Plener, P. L. (2020). Managing risk and self-harm: Keeping young people safe. *Clinical Child Psychology and Psychiatry, 25*(3), 610–624. https://doi.org/10.1177/1359104519895064

Whitlock, J., Muehlenkamp, J., Eckenrode, J., Purington, A., Baral Abrams, G., Barreira, P., & Kress, V. (2013). Nonsuicidal self-injury as a gateway to suicide in young adults. *Journal of Adolescent Health, 52*(4), 486–492. https://doi.org/10.1016/j.jadohealth.2012.09.010

Whitlock, J., Muehlenkamp, J. J., Purington, A., Eckenrode, J., Barreira, P., Baral Abrams, G., Marchell, T., Kress, V., Girard, K., Chin, C., & Knox, K. (2011). Nonsuicidal self-injury in a college population: General trends and sex differences. *Journal of American College Health, 59*(8), 691–698. https://doi.org/10.1080/07448481.2010.529626

Whitlock, J., Prussien, K., & Pietrusza, C. (2015). Predictors of self-injury cessation and subsequent psychological growth: Results of a probability sample survey of students in eight universities and colleges. *Child and Adolescent Psychiatry and Mental Health, 9*, 19. https://doi.org/10.1186/s13034-015-0048-5

Wilkinson, P. O., Qiu, T., Neufeld, S., Jones, P. B., & Goodyer, I. M. (2018). Sporadic and recurrent non-suicidal self-injury before age 14 and incident onset of psychiatric disorders by 17 years: Prospective cohort study. *British Journal of Psychiatry, 212*(4), 222–226. https://doi.org/10.1192/bjp.2017.45

Willoughby, T., Heffer, T., & Hamza, C. A. (2015). The link between nonsuicidal self-injury and acquired capability for suicide: A longitudinal study. *Journal of Abnormal Psychology, 124*(4), 1110–1115. https://doi.org/10.1037/abn0000104

Wolff, J. C., Thompson, E., Thomas, S. A., Nesi, J., Bettis, A. H., Ransford, B., Scopelliti, K., Frazier, E. A., & Liu, R. T. (2019). Emotion dysregulation and non-suicidal self-injury: A systematic review and meta-analysis. *European Psychiatry, 59*, 25–36. https://doi.org/10.1016/j.eurpsy.2019.03.004

Wu, N., Hou, Y., Chen, P., & You, J. (2019). Peer acceptance and nonsuicidal self-injury among Chinese adolescents: A longitudinal moderated mediation model. *Journal of Youth and Adolescence, 48*(9), 1806–1817. https://doi.org/10.1007/s10964-019-01093-0

Zelkowitz, R. L., & Cole, D. A. (2019). Self-criticism as a transdiagnostic process in nonsuicidal self-injury and disordered eating: Systematic review and meta-analysis. *Suicide and Life-Threatening Behavior, 49*(1), 310–327. https://doi.org/10.1111/sltb.12436

Zelkowitz, R. L., Cole, D. A., Han, G. T., & Tomarken, A. J. (2016). The incremental utility of emotion regulation but not emotion reactivity in nonsuicidal self-injury. *Suicide and Life-Threatening Behavior, 46*(5), 545–562. https://doi.org/10.1111/sltb.12236

Zetterqvist, M., Jonsson, L. S., Landberg, A., & Svedin, C. G. (2021). A potential increase in adolescent nonsuicidal self-injury during covid-19: A comparison of data from three different time points during 2011–2021. *Psychiatry Research, 305*, Article 114208. https://doi.org/10.1016/j.psychres.2021.114208

Zimmermann, P., & Iwanski, A. (2014). Emotion regulation from early adolescence to emerging adulthood and middle adulthood. *International Journal of Behavioral Development, 38*(2), 182–194. https://doi.org/10.1177/0165025413515405

CHAPTER 27

Understanding and Working with Adults with NSSI

Margaret Andover, Hae-Joon Kim, Vincent Corcoran, Michelle Hiner, Ana Rabasco, *and* Joshua DeSon

Abstract

This chapter elaborates on the prevalence of nonsuicidal self-injury (NSSI) among adults. NSSI severity can be characterized in different ways, including increased versatility, increased frequency, need for medical attention due to the physical harm caused by NSSI, or self-reported subjective severity. Moreover, NSSI commonly co-occurs with other psychiatric disorders. According to NSSI research focused on adult samples, the functions of NSSI primarily reduce unwanted negative emotions, which is similar to other age groups. The chapter clarifies how critical it is to recognize that NSSI is not limited to the youth so prevention and intervention must be accessible to people of all ages.

Key Words: nonsuicidal self-injury, adults, youth, NSSI severity, psychiatric disorders, negative emotions, prevention, intervention

Although nonsuicidal self-injury (NSSI) is often associated with adolescent and young adult populations, adults also engage in the behavior, albeit at decreased rates. Clinicians may encounter adults who engage in NSSI, some of whom may be disclosing their behavior for the first time. Further, some adults may have a history of NSSI beginning in adolescence or young adulthood, some may have recently engaged in NSSI for the first time, and still others may not be injuring currently but may be living with scars from NSSI. Much of our understanding of NSSI comes from research with adolescent and young adult samples; this chapter adds to the literature focused on NSSI in adults and reviews research with adult samples on age of onset, prevalence and course, severity of the behavior, comorbidity with psychopathology, functions of NSSI, and assessment and treatment of NSSI among adults.

Age of Onset

NSSI is largely considered to onset during adolescence, although research has shown that nearly 8% of third-graders (approximately 7 years of age) report engaging in NSSI (Barrocas et al., 2012). Mean age of onset is often reported between 14 and 15 years of age (e.g., Heath et al., 2008; Muehlenkamp et al., 2019; Whitlock et al., 2006), although women often report their first episode of NSSI at a younger age than men (e.g., O'Connor et al., 2018). Younger age of onset is associated with increased severity of NSSI and self-injury in general. For instance, earlier age of onset, such as before 12 years of age, is associated with frequency of NSSI, even when statistically controlling for duration of the behavior (Ammerman et al., 2018; Muehlenkamp et al., 2019; O'Connor et al., 2018), and a greater number of hospital visits (Ammerman et al., 2018). Individuals with a younger age of onset are also more likely to have planned or attempted suicide (Ammerman et al., 2018; Muehlenkamp et al., 2019).

However, researchers have also reported the onset of NSSI later in adolescence and into adulthood. Samples including participants in middle adulthood and later report a mean age of onset of 16 to 17 years of age (Klonsky, 2011; O'Connor et al., 2018; Plener et al., 2016). Nearly 40% of individuals who engage in NSSI report beginning after age 17 (Heath et al., 2008; Klonsky, 2011; Whitlock et al., 2006), but ranges of reported age of onset have been as high as 54 years old (Plener et al., 2016). In fact, a recent meta-analysis found a bimodal distribution for age of onset, with one peak in probability of NSSI onset at 14 years of age, and a second, smaller peak around age 20 (Gandhi et al., 2018).

Our understanding of age of onset is likely to be influenced by the age of the samples studied; studies focusing on adolescent and young adult samples are going to have an earlier age of onset by virtue of the sample composition, while samples including participants across adulthood allow for greater variability in older reported ages of onset (e.g., Plener et al., 2016)—but also the potential for recall bias (Gandhi et al., 2018). However, even research with young adult samples finds a notable increase in onset of the behavior in late adolescence/early adulthood (e.g., Gandhi et al., 2018; Heath et al., 2008; Klonsky, 2011; Whitlock et al., 2006). Although factors influencing this second peak have not yet been identified, researchers suggest that it may be secondary to unaddressed concerns that arose during adolescence, such as mental illness or issues with identity formation, or that the age of NSSI onset may in fact be bimodal, similar to other psychiatric diagnoses (Gandhi et al., 2018). Additional research with individuals spanning adulthood is necessary to more fully understand factors contributing to the later onset of NSSI. Further, research on the course of and outcomes associated with later onset NSSI is nascent; although some research suggests older age of NSSI onset is associated with less suicidality (Muehlenkamp et al., 2019), additional research in this area is necessary.

NSSI Prevalence and Course

Included under "Conditions for Further Study" in the *Diagnostic and Statistical Manual of Mental Disorders* (DSM-5; American Psychiatric Association, 2013), little is written about NSSI's course and development. DSM-5 simply states that NSSI most often starts in early adolescence and can continue for years, and that hospital admissions due to NSSI peak in young adulthood (20–29 years old; American Psychiatric Association, 2013). However, most NSSI research continues to focus on adolescent and young adult populations. There is limited understanding regarding the true prevalence and course of NSSI in adults.

A meta-analysis and metaregression of nonclinical samples estimated a lifetime pooled prevalence rate of NSSI in adults (age ≥ 25 years) to be 5.5% (Swannell et al., 2014). This rate is much lower than the 17.2% prevalence the same study estimated for adolescents (ages 10–17 years) and the 13.2% for young adults (ages 18–24 years). Further, a systematic review highlights the wide range of prevalence estimates found among studies investigating adult NSSI, with rates varying from 4% to 23% (Cipriano et al., 2017). For example, 3.1% of participants in a representative German sample (ages 14–94) reported engaging in NSSI at least once in their lifetime. Examined by age group, adolescents/young adults 14–24 years old had the highest prevalence rate (7.6%), compared with 5.9% for adults 25–34 years old, 3.8% for adults 35–44 years old, 1.7% for adults 45–54 years old, and 2.2% for adults 55–64 years old (Plener et al., 2016). Comparatively, an online community sample of adults (ages 18–73) reported a higher 23% prevalence of individuals engaging in NSSI at least once in their lifetime (Andover, 2014). Nonetheless, most studies find the lifetime prevalence of NSSI to be lower among adults compared with adolescents and young adults (Cipriano et al., 2017; Plener et al. 2016; Swannell et al., 2014).

The lower lifetime prevalence estimates of NSSI found among adults compared with adolescents and young adults may be suggestive of increasing rates of NSSI, because if rates of NSSI were stagnant, lifetime prevalence rates reported by adults would be more comparable (Swannell et al., 2014). Although there are some data to support an increase in NSSI prevalence among younger cohorts (Griffin et al., 2018), there remain several factors which may be contributing to artificially higher lifetime estimates in adolescent and young adult samples compared to that reported in adult samples. One factor that influences the variability observed in prevalence rates between age groups is the use of different measurement methodologies (Muehlenkamp, Claes, et al., 2012a; Swannell et al., 2014). Checklist assessments likely yield higher and more accurate NSSI estimates than single yes or no items; they are considered recognition tasks which likely result in more accurate estimates compared to free recall "yes" or "no" items. Data on young adult NSSI may be inflated due to the high utilization of checklist assessments in studies of university samples; 87% of data on NSSI among young adults is derived from college samples. Recall bias may impact NSSI reporting among adults more than among younger populations, particularly if studies are using yes or no items in their NSSI assessment rather than checklists (Swannell et al., 2014).

In addition, there is a paucity of research regarding lifetime NSSI in clinical adult populations. For example, those diagnosed with eating disorders report elevated rates of NSSI, with one meta-analysis finding a 27.3% lifetime prevalence (Cucchi et al., 2016). However, of the 29 studies included in the meta-analysis, only three had samples in which the mean age was 30 or older, highlighting again that most data likely skew toward representing adolescents and young adults. Additionally, those living with autism spectrum disorder (ASD) represent another adult population in which data regarding NSSI are scarce. The lack of research in adult ASD is of concern, given that one study of adults living with ASD reported a lifetime NSSI history of 50% (Maddox et al., 2017).

Regarding the course of NSSI, there is limited longitudinal data investigating the evolution of the behavior in adolescence and young adulthood. A meta-analysis of 32 longitudinal studies assessing for either NSSI or deliberate self-harm (DSH) concluded that while highly inconsistent, incidents of both NSSI and DSH increase in adolescence and then decrease during the transition to young adulthood (Plener et al., 2015). However, the meta-analysis made no general conclusions about the course of NSSI into adulthood or how the behavior persists, ceases, or changes in adults who self-injure. Only three studies in the meta-analysis followed a baseline sample of adults for multiple years, all of which were clinical samples (McGlashan et al., 2005; Sinclair et al., 2010; Wedig et al., 2012). The longest study was a 16-year prospective follow-up in patients with borderline personality disorder (BPD); the cohort had a mean age of 26.9 years at baseline, with assessment occurring every two years. From baseline to year 16, the prevalence of self-injury in the sample decreased from 90.3% to 14.3% (Wedig et al., 2012). Although this provides evidence for a decrease in NSSI incidence over an individual's adult years, the focus on a clinical sample of individuals with BPD limits its generalizability to the larger population of adults who self-injure.

NSSI is understood to be a behavior that can have multiple underlying transdiagnostic mechanisms (Hasking & Claes, 2020) and occur across different clinical presentations (Ose et al., 2021). For example, a recent national Norwegian study found that about 7% of adult psychiatric outpatients (30–59 years old) with diagnoses ranging from anxiety to psychotic disorders had engaged in at least one instance of NSSI over a four-week period (Ose et al., 2021). Overall, more longitudinal research in both nonclinical and clinical adult samples is greatly needed to clarify the course of NSSI during the adult decades of life, particularly in those 30 years and older. Questions around the trajectory of adult onset NSSI or the course of NSSI that does not remit in young adulthood remain underexplored in the current literature.

NSSI Severity in Adults

NSSI severity can be characterized in a number of different ways, including increased versatility (number of different methods an individual uses to engage in NSSI), increased frequency, need for medical attention due to the physical harm caused by NSSI, or self-reported subjective severity (see Walsh, Doerfler, & Van Hove, this volume, on atypical severe NSSI). NSSI severity is underexamined in the literature; this is especially true for research conducted with adult samples.

Previous research has found that NSSI versatility rates among adults are slightly lower than those found among adolescents or college students. For example, Klonsky (2011) found that among a sample of adults with a mean age of 55 years old, approximately half of respondents reported using multiple methods of engaging in NSSI. Another study conducted with adult survivors of military sexual trauma found that 55% of participants used multiple methods of NSSI (Holliday et al., 2018). In comparison, reports of multiple NSSI methods among adolescents and young adults have ranged from 58% to 63.3% (Lloyd-Richardson et al., 2007; Whitlock et al., 2011). Taken together, these studies suggest that NSSI versatility does not differ drastically between adolescents or young adults and adults. Limited research has examined frequency of NSSI specifically among adults. Among Klonsky's (2011) sample of adults who engaged in NSSI ($n = 26$), 54% reported a lifetime NSSI frequency of 1–4 times, 24% reported a lifetime NSSI frequency of 5–9 times, and 22% reported a lifetime NSSI frequency of 10 or more times. This is a somewhat lower NSSI frequency than found in a sample of college students, where 29% of the sample reported engaging in NSSI 11 or more times over their lifetime (Whitlock et al., 2011).

Requiring medical attention for one's NSSI can reflect increased severity of the behavior. Rates of receiving medical attention or treatment for NSSI among adults varies based on the sample. Klonsky's (2011) epidemiological study of NSSI among United States adults found that only one participant (3.8%) reported requiring medical treatment as a result of the physical harm caused by NSSI. A nationally representative study of adults in England, however, found that approximately 31% of respondents with a lifetime history of NSSI reported receiving medical attention for their NSSI (Liu, 2021). This discrepancy in receipt of medical attention for NSSI may be because England provides free public health care through the National Health Service, while the United States does not (Thorlby, 2020). In addition, previous research conducted with college students in the United States found that 11.6% of those who engaged in NSSI sought medical treatment for NSSI injuries, while 27% reported hurting themselves so badly that they *should have* been seen by a medical professional (Whitlock et al., 2014). This suggests that there may be barriers to accessing medical treatment for NSSI, especially in the United States. This underscores the importance of using multiple measures of NSSI severity, including subjective self-report.

Finally, in a sample of incarcerated adults, 93% of participants required medical attention or hospitalization due to NSSI behaviors (Morales & Guarnero, 2014). Conditions specific to incarceration, such as solitary confinement, have been found to confer increased risk for NSSI, which may explain the high rates of NSSI severity among this sample (Kaba et al., 2014). Overall, the rates of requiring medical attention for physical harm caused by NSSI vary greatly across adult samples, with incarcerated adults appearing to be at particularly high risk for requiring medical treatment due to NSSI.

There is a distinct lack of research on other metrics of NSSI severity, such as self-reported NSSI severity, among adults. In sum, NSSI severity differs depending on how severity is conceptualized (e.g., NSSI versatility, NSSI frequency, and medical attention needed due to NSSI) and the specific adult sample assessed (e.g., community and prison). In general, NSSI versatility appears to be comparable between adults and adolescents and college students, while research on NSSI frequency has found that rates are slightly lower among adults compared with college students. Furthermore, rates of receiving medical attention for NSSI appear to be higher among certain populations of adults.

Comorbidity among Adults

NSSI commonly co-occurs with other psychiatric disorders; the rate of comorbidity can exceed 50%, particularly in clinical samples (Dulit et al., 1994; Shearer, 1994). The most robust associations have been found for BPD, depressive disorders, anxiety disorders, eating disorders/disordered eating behaviors, substance use disorders, and posttraumatic stress disorder (PTSD) (Nitkowski & Petermann, 2011). The shared mechanism for comorbidity may be emotion regulation; one of the most common functions of NSSI is to reduce unwanted negative emotions and regulate emotions, and many disorders which frequently co-occur with NSSI are linked to increased emotion dysregulation (see Swerdlow et al., this volume, on NSSI and negative affectivity; Andover & Morris, 2014; Wolff et al., 2019).

Up to 80% of individuals diagnosed with BPD report a history of NSSI, and NSSI is one of the diagnostic criteria for BPD in the DSM-5 (American Psychiatric Association, 2013; Zanarini et al., 2003). Although the onset of BPD traits may occur in childhood or adolescence, the disorder is typically only diagnosed in individuals over 18 years of age (American Psychiatric Association, 2013). Both NSSI and BPD symptoms tend to abate over time (Zanarini et al., 2005), thus it is possible that while co-occurring BPD and NSSI are only formally diagnosed in adulthood, this comorbidity becomes less frequent over the lifespan.

NSSI is also associated with higher levels of depressive symptoms. In a study of adults who engage in NSSI, 32.5% screened positive for a probable depressive disorder; these individuals were more likely to report NSSI than those who did not screen positive (Gollust et al., 2008). Research has also shown that depressive symptoms are associated with greater severity of NSSI in adults (Hamza & Willoughby, 2013).

Between 25% and 54% of adults who engage in NSSI report comorbid disordered eating behaviors (Gollust et al., 2008; Muehlenkamp et al., 2012b). Although no studies on comorbid disordered eating and NSSI distinguish between adults and other age groups, research shows that levels of disordered eating and body dissatisfaction tend to increase from adolescence to adulthood (Slane et al., 2014). However, another study found that engaging in both NSSI and disordered eating was associated with younger age (Islam et al., 2015).

Studies suggest that adults who engage in NSSI are more likely to have an anxiety disorder than those without an NSSI history. In one study, 88.3% of adults who engaged in NSSI met criteria for any anxiety disorder; 40.3% met criteria for social phobia and

23.9% met criteria for generalized anxiety disorder, 19.6% met criteria for panic disorder, and 10.4% met criteria for agoraphobia (Chartrand et al., 2012). Similarly, there is a high degree of association between substance use and NSSI in both clinical and nonclinical samples (Moller et al., 2013). One study found that for adults with a single act of NSSI, 27.3% reported a history of drug or alcohol use and 15% reported using substances while engaging in NSSI; 42.1% of participants with multiple acts of NSSI reported current substance use and 23.6% reported using substances while engaging in NSSI (Kakhnovets et al., 2010). Another study found that among adult prescription drug abusers, 19% reported a lifetime frequency of NSSI between 1 and 10 times, and 25% reported engaging in NSSI more than 10 times (MacLaren & Best, 2010). However, comorbid substance use and NSSI may decrease over the lifespan; one study found that comorbid substance use and NSSI were significantly associated with younger age (Gupta et al., 2019).

Studies have also found a strong association between NSSI and PTSD among adults. A study of male veterans with PTSD found that more than half (58.8%) were engaging in NSSI (Cunningham et al., 2019). Comorbidities between NSSI and PTSD often involve a BPD diagnosis; in adult samples, comorbid BPD and PTSD were associated with increased risk of NSSI (Heffernan & Cloitre, 2000; Pagura et al., 2010).

Regulation of negative emotions or affect instability may be the mechanism underlying the co-occurrence of NSSI and other disorders. Although research on age-based differences in emotion dysregulation among individuals who self-injure is mixed (Wolff et al., 2019; You et al., 2018), in the general population, older adults report greater ability to engage in goal-directed coping behaviors and greater ability to refrain from impulsive behaviors (Orgeta & Phillips, 2008). Although adults who self-injure may experience continued difficulties with emotion regulation, evidence suggests that overall, both NSSI and co-occurring disorders tend to decrease in adulthood. However, there are few studies investigating how comorbidities of NSSI may change over the lifespan or research which compares adults to other age groups, and more research is needed in order to draw meaningful conclusions.

Functions of NSSI in Adults

NSSI is explained by a variety of different functions, the most common of which is to relieve or reduce unwanted negative emotions. Research focused on adult samples suggests that the functions of NSSI are similar in adults as in other age groups (Taylor et al., 2018). However, a few differences between adults and other age groups have emerged in the literature.

A two-factor structure has been proposed for understanding the functions of NSSI; these factors are intrapersonal and interpersonal. Intrapersonal functions include self-focused functions such as emotion regulation, antidissociation, and self-punishment, while interpersonal functions encompass other-related functions such as interpersonal influence, peer bonding, and revenge (see Taylor et al., this volume, on functions of NSSI)

(Klonsky et al., 2015). Intrapersonal functions—particularly emotion regulation—are more frequently endorsed as a reason for engaging in NSSI compared to interpersonal functions, and this is true of both adult and child and adolescent samples (Taylor et al., 2018). However, adults may differ from children and adolescents in intensity of emotion dysregulation and specific mechanisms for the use of NSSI in emotion regulation. Although one meta-analysis reported that age did not significantly moderate the association between overall emotion dysregulation and NSSI, another meta-analysis reported significant differences between adults and adolescents who self-injure; specifically, that adolescents who self-injure experience more difficulty in engaging in goal-directed behaviors in response to negative emotions (Wolff et al., 2019; You et al., 2018). This may be due to the fact that adolescents generally engage in more impulsive behaviors, and NSSI serves as a more immediate means of coping with emotion dysregulation for adolescents who have difficulty engaging in goal-directed activity, as compared with adults (You et al., 2018). Finally, NSSI functions may change over the course of adulthood; when comparing older (60 + years old) and younger adults, NSSI is more associated with high suicidal intent among older adults (Conwell, 1997; Sakinofsky, 2000).

Studies have also shown that NSSI may be less associated with psychopathology in adults than in adolescents. In a study of adults with BPD, younger age was a predictor of a BPD diagnosis and engaging in NSSI. Additionally, whereas 81% of adults in the study engaged in NSSI within the past two years, only 26% reported doing so at a six-year follow-up (Zanarini et al., 2003). As BPD symptoms improve over time, NSSI may become less necessary as a means of emotion regulation.

Overall, NSSI in adulthood functions very similarly to NSSI in adolescence in reducing intense negative emotions and regulating affective instability. Although there are changes in adulthood in terms of increased ability to regulate emotions and impulsive behaviors, which may explain the lower prevalence rate of NSSI in adults, the functions of the behavior in those who continue to self-injure in adulthood are similar as in adolescence.

NSSI Scarring

Scarring from NSSI behaviors is a prevalent issue, as 56% of individuals who have engaged in NSSI in their lifetime have at least one self-injury scar (SIS; Burke et al., 2020), defined here as a scar resulting from an act of NSSI. Uniquely, unlike other mental health concerns that do not leave an observable marker when resolved or treated, an SIS remains even after an individual has stopped engaging in NSSI (Lewis & Mehrabkhani, 2015). Due to the potentially high visibility of scars from NSSI, many individuals living with SISs are diligent about concealing their scars (Lewis, 2016), more so than individuals with scars from accidents or surgery (Stacy et al., 2017). Concealment is often accomplished through physically covering SIS and through avoiding situations where their scars may be made visible (e.g., intimacy and swimming), indicating that the presence of SISs impacts daily functioning (Hodgson, 2004). The act of concealing SISs from both the self and others is strongly associated with negative scar-specific beliefs (e.g., "having scars makes me weak") and psychological distress (Burke et al., 2020).

Although research investigating the psychological effects of SISs is limited, one in four people with SISs have a negative perception of their scars, which persist even after NSSI has ceased (Lewis & Mehrabkhani, 2015), and individuals who had previously engaged in NSSI who report feelings of shame, emphasize regret over having SISs rather than the act of self-injury itself (Bachtelle & Pepper, 2015). The self-stigma associated with NSSI may be associated with the development of psychopathology, such as depression or decreased self-worth (Garisch & Wilson, 2015). Further, the presence of SISs is associated with both suicidal ideation and suicide attempt in adults (Burke et al., 2016).

Individuals with SISs may experience stigma from others based on misconceptions about NSSI and self-injury, such as that they are actively suicidal (e.g., Kumar et al., 2004), attention-seeking (e.g., Caicedo & Whitlock, 2009), or victims of abuse (e.g., Klonsky et al., 2014), which may further concealment efforts and psychological distress or result in external consequences such as missed employment opportunities (Rosenrot, 2015). Individuals without NSSI history report more anger and callousness toward people who engage in NSSI who they feel are responsible for their own behavior and consequent scarring (Lloyd et al., 2018). SISs and NSSI injuries may also be met with negative perceptions from healthcare professionals (e.g., Armiento et al., 2014), impacting the likelihood of seeking professional help and medical care. For example, medical students who believed that patients were to blame for their own self-injury often labeled these patients as manipulative and suggested that they do not deserve support (Law et al., 2009). Similarly, when doctors perceived patients engaged in NSSI to gain attention, they believed that the person who had harmed themself to be unworthy of receiving treatment (Hadfield et al., 2009), potentially impacting the individuals' willingness to receive care for NSSI or other conditions or resulting in inadequate care because of biases.

Assessment

Assessments for NSSI that have been developed with adolescent and young adult samples are applicable to adults, and no assessments have been validated exclusively in adult samples. Methods of evaluation include self-report, structured interview, and unstructured interview. For example, the Inventory of Statements About Self-Injury (ISAS; Klonsky & Glenn, 2009), the Functional Assessment of Self-Mutilation (FASM; Lloyd et al., 1997), and the Nonsuicidal Self-Injury Assessment Tool (NSSI-AT; Whitlock et al., 2014) are all commonly used self-report measures used to assess different aspects of NSSI. Each measure assesses for form, frequency, and function of NSSI behaviors, in addition to other details depending on measure.

Structured and unstructured clinical interviews are a recommended method of assessing NSSI (Klonsky & Weinberg, 2009). Two such structured interviews are the

Suicide Attempt Self-Injury Interview (SASII; Linehan et al., 2006) and the Self-Injurious Thoughts and Behaviors Interview (SITBI; Nock et al., 2007). The SASII assesses both suicidal and nonsuicidal self-injury with 31 items. Form, function, frequency, lethality, medical treatment, and topography are among the domains assessed (Linehan et al., 2006). The SITBI is a 169-item interview (or a 72-item short form) that can be administered by trained bachelor's-level personnel and takes up to 15 minutes to complete. Like the SASII, it assesses both suicidal and nonsuicidal thoughts and behavior and includes questions regarding methods, frequency, functions, severity, precipitants, impulsivity, and likelihood of future occurrence (Nock et al., 2007). One difference between the measures is the SASII's focus on acquiring detailed accounts of each self-injurious act endorsed (Klonsky & Weinberg, 2009). Besides these structured interview forms, general recommendations for unstructured interviews also exist. Unstructured NSSI assessments should include the form, versatility (the number of different methods used), frequency, and medical severity of NSSI behaviors. Each of these domains has literature indicating their importance in determining the overall severity or future risk of the behavior (Ammerman et al., 2020; Andrewes et al., 2019; Turner et al., 2013). Additionally, due to the relationship between NSSI and suicidality (e.g., Kiekens et al., 2018; Whitlock et al., 2013), suicidal thoughts and behaviors should also be assessed.

Treatment

Although NSSI can be difficult to treat, it does respond to intervention (e.g., Turner et al., 2014). Several manualized interventions have demonstrated success at decreasing rates of NSSI in adults, including dialectical behavior therapy (DBT; Linehan, 1993), manual-assisted cognitive therapy (MACT; Tyrer et al., 2003), and emotion regulation group therapy (ERGT; Gratz et al., 2006). However, research on NSSI interventions often focuses on individuals with BPD symptoms or diagnoses (Turner et al., 2014), though not every person who self-injures has a personality disorder. Interventions for NSSI developed for non-BPD samples would be beneficial (e.g., Andover et al., 2015). Further, research on the efficacy of many of these treatments is limited, and more research is needed in both adolescent and adult samples (see Turner et al. (2014) for review). Adults who stop engaging in NSSI without intervention may be a critical population for research, as factors associated with NSSI cessation may indicate novel targets for treatment development.

Implications for Clinicians and Community Advocates

For clinicians and community advocates, it is critical to recognize that NSSI is not limited to youth. Those working with adults should assess for NSSI behaviors regardless of client age and recognize that some may be disclosing their behavior for the first time. Prevention and intervention efforts should be accessible to individuals of all ages and not limited or exclusively targeted to youth. In addition to the concerns related to the behavior itself, NSSI is often comorbid with other mental health concerns, and the behavior is known to be associated with increased suicide risk. In addition, unlike other mental health concerns, NSSI scars serve as a lasting reminder—even if an adult no longer engages in NSSI, they may experience lasting distress or stigma due to scarring.

Conclusions

Although NSSI is often thought of as behavior of adolescence and young adulthood, it is also prevalent among adults. However, much of our understanding of NSSI is derived from research with younger samples, and differences between the age groups are not well understood. Research suggests similarities in factors related to NSSI between youth and adults, but more research with adult samples is needed to determine if and how the behavior differs, factors influencing adult onset of NSSI, and the course of NSSI.

References

American Psychiatric Association. (2013). *Diagnostic and statistical manual of mental disorders* (5th ed.). https://doi.org/10.1176/appi.books.9780890425596

Ammerman, B. A., Jacobucci, R., Kleiman, E. M., Uyeji, L. L., & McCloskey, M. S. (2018). The relationship between nonsuicidal self-injury age of onset and severity of self-harm. *Suicide and Life-Threatening Behavior*, *48*(1), 31–37. https://doi.org/10.1111/sltb.12330

Ammerman, B. A., Jacobucci, R., Turner, B. J., Dixon-Gordon, K. L., & McCloskey, M. S. (2020). Quantifying the importance of lifetime frequency versus number of methods in conceptualizing nonsuicidal self-injury severity. *Psychology of Violence*, *10*(4), 442–451. https://doi.org/10.1037/vio0000263

Andover, M. S. (2014). Non-suicidal self-injury disorder in a community sample of adults. *Psychiatry Research*, *219*(2), 305–310. https://doi.org/10.1016/j.psychres.2014.06.001

Andover, M. S., & Morris, B. W. (2014). Expanding and clarifying the role of emotion regulation in nonsuicidal self-injury. *Canadian Journal of Psychiatry*, *59*(11), 569–575. https://doi.org/10.1177/070674371405901102

Andover, M. S., Schatten, H. T., Morris, B. W., & Miller, I. W. (2015). Development of an intervention for nonsuicidal self-injury in young adults: An open pilot trial. *Cognitive and Behavioral Practice*, *22*(4), 491–503. https://doi.org/10.1016/j.cbpra.2014.05.003

Andrewes, H. E., Hulbert, C., Cotton, S. M., Betts, J., & Chanen, A. M. (2019). Relationships between the frequency and severity of non-suicidal self-injury and suicide attempts in youth with borderline personality disorder. *Early Intervention in Psychiatry*, *13*(2), 194–201. https://doi.org/10.1111/eip.12461

Armiento, J. S., Hamza, C. A., & Willoughby, T. (2014). An examination of disclosure of nonsuicidal self-injury among university students. *Journal of Community & Applied Social Psychology*, *24*(6), 518–533. https://doi.org/10.1002/casp.2190

Bachtelle, S. E., & Pepper, C. M. (2015). The physical results of nonsuicidal self-injury: The meaning behind the scars. *Journal of Nervous & Mental Disease*, *203*(12), 927–933. https://doi.org/10.1097/NMD.0000000000000398

Barrocas, A. L., Hankin, B. L., Young, J. F., & Abela, J. R. (2012). Rates of nonsuicidal self-injury in youth: Age, sex, and behavioral methods in a community sample. *Pediatrics*, *130*(1), 39–45. https://doi.org/10.1542/peds.2011-2094

Burke, T. A., Ammerman, B. A., Hamilton, J. L., Stange, J. P., & Piccirillo, M. (2020). Nonsuicidal self-injury scar concealment from the self and others. *Journal of Psychiatric Research*, *130*(1), 313–320. https://doi.org/10.1016/j.jpsychires.2020.07.040

Burke, T. A., Hamilton, J. L., Cohen, J. N., Stange, J. P., & Alloy, L. B. (2016). Identifying a physical indicator of suicide risk: Non-suicidal self-injury scars predict suicidal ideation and suicide attempts. *Comprehensive Psychiatry*, *65*(1), 79–87. https://doi.org/10.1016/j.comppsych.2015.10.008

Caicedo, S., & Whitlock, J. L. (2009). *Top misconceptions about self-injury*. Cornell Research Program on Self-Injury and Recovery, Cornell University. http://selfinjury.bctr.cornell.edu/perch/resources/15-misconceptions-1.pdf

Chartrand, H., Sareen, J., Toews, M., & Bolton, J. M. (2012). Suicide attempts versus nonsuicidal self-injury among individuals with anxiety disorders in a nationally representative sample. *Depression and Anxiety*, *29*(3), 172–179. https://doi.org/10.1002/da.20882

Cipriano, A., Cella, S., & Cotrufo, P. (2017). Nonsuicidal self-injury: A systematic review. *Frontiers in Psychology*, *8*(1), Article 1946. https://doi-org/10.3389/fpsyg.2017.01946

Conwell, Y. (1997). Management of suicidal behavior in the elderly. *Psychiatric Clinics of North America*, *20*(3), 667–683. https://doi.org/10.1016/S0193-953X(05)70336-1

Cucchi, A., Ryan, D., Konstantakopoulos, G., Stroumpa, S., Kaçar, A. Ş., Renshaw, S., Landau, S., & Kravariti, E. (2016). Lifetime prevalence of non-suicidal self-injury in patients with eating disorders: A systematic review and meta-analysis. *Psychological Medicine*, *46*(7), 1345–1358. https://doi-org/10.1017/S0033291716000027

Cunningham, K. C., Grossmann, J. L., Seay, K. B., Dennis, P. A., Clancy, C. P., Hertzberg, M. A., Berlin, K., Ruffin, R. A., Dedert, E. A., Gratz, K. L., Calhoun, P. S., Beckham, J. C., & Kimbrel, N. A. (2019). Nonsuicidal self-injury and borderline personality features as risk factors for suicidal ideation among male veterans with posttraumatic stress disorder. *Journal of Traumatic Stress*, *32*(1), 141–147. https://doi.org/10.1002/jts.22369

Dulit, R. A., Fyer, M. R., Leon, A. C., Brodsky, B. S., & Frances, A. J. (1994). Clinical correlates of self-mutilation in borderline personality disorder. *American Journal of Psychiatry*, *151*(9), 1305–1311. https://doi.org/10.1176/ajp.151.9.1305

Gandhi, A., Luyckx, K., Baetens, I., Kiekens, G., Sleuwaegen, E., Berens, A., Maitra, S., & Claes, L. (2018). Age of onset of non-suicidal self-injury in Dutch-speaking adolescents and emerging adults: An event history analysis of pooled data. *Comprehensive Psychiatry*, *80*(1), 170–178. https://doi.org/10.1016/j.comppsych.2017.10.007

Garisch, J. A., & Wilson, M. S. (2015). Prevalence, correlates, and prospective predictors of non-suicidal self-injury among New Zealand adolescents: Cross-sectional and longitudinal survey data. *Child and Adolescent Psychiatry and Mental Health*, *9*(1), 1–11. https://doi.org/10.1186/s13034-015-0055-6

Gollust, S. E., Eisenberg, D., & Golberstein, E. (2008). Prevalence and correlates of self-injury among university students. *Journal of American College Health*, *56*(5), 491–498. https://doi.org/10.3200/JACH.56.5.491-498

Gratz, K. L., & Gunderson, J. G. (2006). Preliminary data on an acceptance-based emotion regulation group intervention for deliberate self-harm among women with borderline personality disorder. *Behavior Therapy*, *37*(1), 25–35. https://doi.org/10.1016/j.beth.2005.03.002

Griffin, E., McMahon, E., McNicholas, F., Corcoran, P., Perry, I. J., & Arensman, E. (2018). Increasing rates of self-harm among children, adolescents and young adults: A 10-year national registry study 2007–2016. *Social Psychiatry and Psychiatric Epidemiology*, *53*(7), 663–671. https://doi.org/10.1007/s00127-018-1522-1

Gupta, R., Narnoli, S., Das, N., Sarkar, S., & Balhara, Y. P. S. (2019). Patterns and predictors of self-harm in patients with substance-use disorder. *Indian Journal of Psychiatry*, *61*(5), 431–438. https://doi.org/10.4103/psychiatry.IndianJPsychiatry_578_18

Hadfield, J., Brown, D., Pembroke, L., & Hayward, M. (2009). Analysis of accident and emergency doctors' responses to treating people who self-harm. *Qualitative Health Research*, *19*(6), 755–765. https://doi.org/10.1177/1049732309334473

Hamza, C. A., & Willoughby, T. (2013). Nonsuicidal self-injury and suicidal behavior: A latent class analysis among young adults. *PLoS One*, *8*(3), Article e59955. https://doi.org/10.1371/journal.pone.0059955

Hasking, P., & Claes, L. (2020). Transdiagnostic mechanisms involved in nonsuicidal self-injury, risky drinking and disordered eating: Impulsivity, emotion regulation and alexithymia. *Journal of American College Health*, *68*(6), 603–609. https://doi-org/10.1080/07448481.2019.1583661

Heath, N. L., Toste, J. R., Nedecheva, T., & Charlebois, A. (2008). An examination of nonsuicidal self-injury among college students. *Journal of Mental Health Counseling*, *30*(2), 137–156. https://doi.org/10.17744/mehc.30.2.8p879p3443514678

Heffernan, K., & Cloitre, M. (2000). A comparison of posttraumatic stress disorder with and without borderline personality disorder among women with a history of childhood sexual abuse. *Journal of Nervous and Mental Disease*, *188*(9), 589–595. https://doi.org/10.1097/00005053-200009000-00005

Hodgson, S. (2004). Cutting through the silence: A sociological construction of self-injury. *Sociological Inquiry*, *74*(2), 162–179. https://doi.org/10.1111/j.1475-682X.2004.00085.x

Holliday, R., Smith, N. B., & Monteith, L. L. (2018). An initial investigation of nonsuicidal self-injury among male and female survivors of military sexual trauma. *Psychiatry Research, 268*(1), 335–339. https://doi.org/10.1016/j.psychres.2018.07.033

Islam, M. A., Steiger, H., Jimenez-Murcia, S., Israel, M., Granero, R., Agüera, Z., Castro, R., Sánchez, I., Riesco, N., Menchón, J. M., & Fernández-Aranda, F. (2015). Non-suicidal self-injury in different eating disorder types: Relevance of personality traits and gender. *European Eating Disorders Review, 23*(6), 553–560. https://doi.org/10.1002/erv.2374

Kaba, F., Lewis, A., Glowa-Kollisch, S., Hadler, J., Lee, D., Alper, H., Selling, D., MacDonald, R., Solimo, A., Parsons, A., & Venters, H. (2014). Solitary confinement and risk of self-harm among jail inmates. *American Journal of Public Health, 104*(3), 442–447. https://doi.org/10.2105/AJPH.2013.301742

Kakhnovets, R., Young, H., Purnell, A., Huebner, E., & Bishop, C. (2010). Self-reported experience of self-injurious behavior in college students. *Journal of Mental Health Counseling, 32*(4), 309–323. https://doi.org/10.17744/mehc.32.4.a7370773244lq808

Kiekens, G., Hasking, P., Boyes, M., Claes, L., Mortier, P., Auerbach, R. P., Cuijpers, P., Demyttenaere, K., Green, J. G., Kessler, R. C., Myin-Germeys, I., Nock, M. K., & Bruffaerts, R. (2018). The associations between non-suicidal self-injury and first onset suicidal thoughts and behaviors. *Journal of Affective Disorders, 239*(1), 171–179. https://doi.org/10.1016/j.jad.2018.06.033

Klonsky, E. D. (2011). Non-suicidal self injury in United States adults: Prevalence, sociodemographics, topography and functions. *Psychological Medicine, 41*(9), 1981–1986. https://doi.org/10.1017/S0033291710002497

Klonsky, E. D., & Glenn, C. R. (2009). Assessing the functions of non-suicidal self-injury: Psychometric properties of the Inventory of Statements About Self-injury (ISAS). *Journal of Psychopathology and Behavioral Assessment, 31*(3), 215–219. https://doi.org/10.1007/s10862-008-9107-z

Klonsky, E. D., Glenn, C. R., Styer, D. M., Olino, T. M., & Washburn, J. J. (2015). The functions of nonsuicidal self-injury: Converging evidence for a two-factor structure. *Child and Adolescent Psychiatry and Mental Health, 9*(1), 1–9. https://doi.org/10.1186/s13034-015-0073-4

Klonsky, E. D., Victor, S. E., & Saffer, B. Y. (2014). Nonsuicidal self-injury: What we know, and what we need to know. *Canadian Journal of Psychiatry, 59*(11), 565–568. https://doi.org/10.1177/070674371405901101

Klonsky, E. D., & Weinberg, A. (2009). Assessment of nonsuicidal self-injury. In M. K. Nock (Ed.), *Understanding nonsuicidal self-injury: Origins, assessment, and treatment* (pp. 183–199). American Psychological Association.

Kumar, G., Pepe, D., & Steer, R. A. (2004). Adolescent psychiatric inpatients' self-reported reasons for cutting themselves. *The Journal of Nervous and Mental Disease, 192*(12), 830–836. https://doi.org/10.1097/01.nmd.0000146737.18053.d2

Law, G. U., Rostill-Brookes, H., & Goodman, D. (2009). Public stigma in health and non-healthcare students: Attributions, emotions and willingness to help with adolescent self-harm. *International Journal of Nursing Studies, 46*(1), 108–119. https://doi.org/10.1016/j.ijnurstu.2008.08.014

Lewis, S. P. (2016). The overlooked role of self-injury scars: Commentary and suggestions for clinical practice. *Journal of Nervous & Mental Disease, 204*(1), 33–35. https://doi.org/10.1097/NMD.0000000000000436

Lewis, S. P., & Mehrabkhani, S. (2015). Every scar tells a story: Insight into people's self-injury scar experiences. *Counselling Psychology Quarterly, 29*(3), 296–310. https://doi.org/10.1080/09515070.2015.1088431

Linehan, M. M. (1993). *Cognitive-behavioral treatment of borderline personality disorder*. Guilford Press.

Linehan, M. M., Comtois, K. A., Brown, M. Z., Heard, H. L., & Wagner, A. (2006). Suicide Attempt Self-Injury Interview (SASII): Development, reliability, and validity of a scale to assess suicide attempts and intentional self-injury. *Psychological Assessment, 18*(3), 303–312. https://doi.org/10.1037/1040-3590.18.3.303

Liu, R. T. (2021). The epidemiology of non-suicidal self-injury: Lifetime prevalence, sociodemographic and clinical correlates, and treatment use in a nationally representative sample of adults in England. *Psychological Medicine*. Advance online publication. https://doi.org/10.1017/S003329172100146X

Lloyd, B., Blazely, A., & Phillips, L. (2018). Stigma towards individuals who self harm: Impact of gender and disclosure. *Journal of Public Mental Health, 17*(4), 184–194. https://doi.org/10.1108/JPMH-02-2018-0016

Lloyd, E. E., Kelley, M. L., & Hope, T. (1997). *Self-mutilation in a community sample of adolescents: Descriptive characteristics and provisional prevalence rates* [Poster presentation]. Annual meeting of the Society for Behavioral Medicine, New Orleans, LA.

Lloyd-Richardson, E. E., Perrine, N., Dierker, L., & Kelley, M. L. (2007). Characteristics and functions of non-suicidal self-injury in a community sample of adolescents. *Psychological Medicine, 37*(8), 1183–1192. https://doi.org/10.1017/S003329170700027X

MacLaren, V. V., & Best, L. A. (2010). Nonsuicidal self-injury, potentially addictive behaviors, and the Five Factor Model in undergraduates. *Personality and Individual Differences, 49*(5), 521–525. https://doi.org/10.1016/j.paid.2010.05.019

Maddox, B. B., Trubanova, A., & White, S. W. (2017). Untended wounds: Non-suicidal self-injury in adults with autism spectrum disorder. *Autism, 21*(4), 412–422. https://doi.org/10.1177/1362361316644731

McGlashan, T. H., Grilo, C. M., Sanislow, C. A., Ralevski, E., Morey, L. C., Gunderson, J. G., Skodol, A. E., Shea, M. T., Zanarini, M. C., Bender, D. B., Stout, R. L., Yen, S., & Pagano, M. (2005). Two-year prevalence and stability of individual DSM-IV criteria for schizotypal, borderline, avoidant, and obsessive-compulsive personality disorders: Toward a hybrid model of axis II disorders. *American Journal of Psychiatry, 162*(5), 883–889. https://doi-org/10.1176/appi.ajp.162.5.883

Moller, C. I., Tait, R. J., & Byrne, D. G. (2013). Deliberate self-harm, substance use, and negative affect in nonclinical samples: A systematic review. *Substance Abuse, 34*(2), 188–207. https://doi.org/10.1080/08897077.2012.693462

Morales, Y. M., & Guarnero, P. A. (2014). Non-suicidal self-injury among adult males in a correctional setting. *Issues in Mental Health Nursing, 35*(8), 628–634. https://doi.org/10.3109/01612840.2014.927943

Muehlenkamp, J. J., Claes, L., Havertape, L., & Plener, P. L. (2012a). International prevalence of adolescent non-suicidal self-injury and deliberate self-harm. *Child and Adolescent Psychiatry and Mental Health, 6*(1), 1–9. https://doi.org/10.1186/1753-2000-6-10

Muehlenkamp, J. J., Peat, C. M., Claes, L., & Smits, D. (2012b). Self-injury and disordered eating: Expressing emotion dysregulation through the body. *Suicide and Life-Threatening Behavior, 42*(4), 416–425. https://doi.org/10.1111/j.1943-278X.2012.00100.x

Muehlenkamp, J. J., Xhunga, N., & Brausch, A. M. (2019). Self-injury age of onset: A risk factor for NSSI severity and suicidal behavior. *Archives of Suicide Research, 23*(4), 551–563. https://doi.org/10.1080/13811118.2018.1486252

Nitkowski, D., & Petermann, F. (2011). Non-suicidal self-injury and comorbid mental disorders: A review. *Fortschritte Der Neurologie-Psychiatrie, 79*(1), 9–20. https://doi.org/10.1055/s-0029-1245772

Nock, M. K., Holmberg, E. B., Photos, V. I., & Michel, B. D. (2007). Self-injurious thoughts and behaviors interview: Development, reliability, and validity in an adolescent sample. *Psychological Assessment, 19*(3), 309–317. https://doi.org/10.1037/1040-3590.19.3.309

O'Connor, R. C., Wetherall, K., Cleare, S., Eschle, S., Drummond, J., Ferguson, E., O'Connor, D. B., & O'Carroll, R. E. (2018). Suicide attempts and non-suicidal self-harm: National prevalence study of young adults. *BJPsych Open, 4*(3), 142–148. https://doi.org/10.1192/bjo.2018.14

Orgeta, V., & Phillips, L. H. (2008). Effects of age and emotional intensity on the recognition of facial emotion. *Experimental Aging Research, 34*(1), 63–79. https://doi.org/10.1080/03610730701762047

Ose, S. O., Tveit, T., & Mehlum, L. (2021). Non-suicidal self-injury (NSSI) in adult psychiatric outpatients– A nationwide study. *Journal of Psychiatric Research, 133*(1), 1–9. https://doi-org/10.1016/j.jpsychires.2020.11.031

Pagura, J., Stein, M. B., Bolton, J. M., Cox, B. J., Grant, B., & Sareen, J. (2010). Comorbidity of borderline personality disorder and posttraumatic stress disorder in the U.S. population. *Journal of Psychiatric Research, 44*(16), 1190–1198. https://doi.org/10.1016/j.jpsychires.2010.04.016

Plener, P. L., Allroggen, M., Kapusta, N. D., Brähler, E., Fegert, J. M., & Groschwitz, R. C. (2016). The prevalence of Nonsuicidal Self-Injury (NSSI) in a representative sample of the German population. *BMC Psychiatry, 16*(1), 1–7. https://doi.org/10.1186/s12888-016-1060-x

Plener, P. L., Schumacher, T. S., Munz, L. M., & Groschwitz, R. C. (2015). The longitudinal course of non-suicidal self-injury and deliberate self-harm: A systematic review of the literature. *Borderline Personality Disorder and Emotion Dysregulation, 2*(1), 1–11. https://doi.org/10.1186/s40479-014-0024-3

Rosenrot, S. (2015). *Talking about non-suicidal self-injury: The identification of barriers, correlates, and responses to NSSI disclosure* [Unpublished doctoral dissertation]. University of Guelph.

Sakinofsky, I. (2000). Repetition of suicidal behavior. In K. Hawton & K. van Heeringen (Eds.), *The international handbook of suicide and attempted suicide* (pp. 385–404). Wiley.

Shearer, S. L. (1994). Phenomenology of self-injury among inpatient women with borderline personality disorder. *Journal of Nervous and Mental Disease, 182*(9), 524–526.

Sinclair, J. M., Hawton, K., & Gray, A. (2010). Six year follow-up of a clinical sample of self-harm patients. *Journal of Affective Disorders, 121*(3), 247–252. https://doi.org/10.1016/j.jad.2009.05.027

Slane, J. D., Klump, K. L., McGue, M., & Iacono, W. G. (2014). Developmental trajectories of disordered eating from early adolescence to young adulthood: A longitudinal study. *International Journal of Eating Disorders, 47*(7), 793–801. https://doi.org/10.1002/eat.22329

Stacy, S. E., Lear, M. K., & Pepper, C. M. (2017). The importance of origin: Differences in interpretation of self-inflicted versus environmentally-inflicted scars. *Personality and Individual Differences, 116*(1), 92–95. https://doi.org/10.1016/j.paid.2017.04.035

Swannell, S. V., Martin, G. E., Page, A., Hasking, P., & St John, N. J. (2014). Prevalence of nonsuicidal self-injury in nonclinical samples: Systematic review, meta-analysis and meta-regression. *Suicide and Life-Threatening Behavior, 44*(3), 273–303. https://doi-org/10.1111/sltb.12070

Taylor, P. J., Jomar, K., Dhingra, K., Forrester, R., Shahmalak, U., & Dickson, J. M. (2018). A meta-analysis of the prevalence of different functions of non-suicidal self-injury. *Journal of Affective Disorders, 227*, 759–769. https://doi.org/10.1016/j.jad.2017.11.073

Thorlby, R. (2020, June 6). *International health care system profiles: England.* The Commonwealth Fund. https://www.commonwealthfund.org/international-health-policy-center/countries/england

Turner, B. J., Austin, S. B., & Chapman, A. L. (2014). Treating nonsuicidal self-injury: A systematic review of psychological and pharmacological interventions. *The Canadian Journal of Psychiatry, 59*(11), 576–585. https://doi.org/10.1080/13811118.2013.802660

Turner, B. J., Layden, B. K., Butler, S. M., & Chapman, A. L. (2013). How often, or how many ways: Clarifying the relationship between non-suicidal self-injury and suicidality. *Archives of Suicide Research, 17*(4), 397–415. https://doi.org/10.1080/13811118.2013.802660

Tyrer, P., Thompson, S., Schmidt, U., Jones, V., Knapp, M. Davidson, K., Catalan, J., Airlie, J., Baxter, S., Byford, S., Byrne, G., Cameron, S., Caplan, R., Cooper, S., Ferguson, B., Freeman, C., Frost, S., Godley, J., Greenshields, J., . . . Wessely, S. (2003). Randomized controlled trial of brief cognitive behavior therapy versus treatment as usual in recurrent deliberate self-harm: The POPMACT study. *Psychological Medicine, 33*(1), 969–976. https://doi.org/10.1017/S0033291703008171

Wedig, M. M., Silverman, M. H., Frankenburg, F. R., Reich, D. B., Fitzmaurice, G., & Zanarini, M. C. (2012). Predictors of suicide attempts in patients with borderline personality disorder over 16 years of prospective follow-up. *Psychological Medicine, 42*(11), Article 2395. https://doi-org/10.1017/S0033291712000517

Whitlock, J., Eckenrode, J., & Silverman, D. (2006). Self-injurious behaviors in a college population. *Pediatrics, 117*(6), 1939–1948. https://doi.org/10.1542/peds.2005-2543

Whitlock, J., Exner-Cortens, D., & Purington, A. (2014). Assessment of nonsuicidal self-injury: Development and initial validation of the Non-Suicidal Self-Injury–Assessment Tool (NSSI-AT). *Psychological Assessment, 26*(3), 935–946. https://doi.org/10.1037/a0036611

Whitlock, J., Muehlenkamp, J., Eckenrode, J., Purington, A., Baral Abrams, G., Barreira, P., & Kress, V. (2013). Nonsuicidal self-injury as a gateway to suicide in young adults. *Journal of Adolescent Health, 52*, 486–492. https://doi.org/10.1016/j.jadohealth.2012.09.010

Whitlock, J., Muehlenkamp, J., Purington, A., Eckenrode, J., Barreira, P., Baral Abrams, G., Marchell, T., Kress, V., Girard, K., Chin, C., & Knox, K. (2011). Nonsuicidal self-injury in a college population: General trends and sex differences. *Journal of American College Health, 59*(8), 691–698. https://doi.org/10.1080/07448481.2010.529626

Wolff, J. C., Thompson, E., Thomas, S. A., Nesi, J., Bettis, A. H., Ransford, B., Scopelliti, K., Frazier, E. A., & Liu, R. T. (2019). Emotion dysregulation and non-suicidal self-injury: A systematic review and meta-analysis. *European Psychiatry, 59*(3), 25–36. https://doi.org/10.1016/j.eurpsy.2019.03.004

You, J., Ren, Y., Zhang, X., Wu, Z., Xu, S., & Lin, M. P. (2018). Emotional dysregulation and nonsuicidal self-injury: A meta-analytic review. *Neuropsychiatry, 8*(2), 733–748. https://doi.org/10.4172/neuropsychiatry.1000399

Zanarini, M. C., Frankenburg, F. R., Hennen, J., Reich, D. B., & Silk, K. R. (2005). The McLean Study of Adult Development (MSAD): Overview and implications of the first six years of prospective follow-up. *Journal of Personality Disorders, 19*(5), 505–523. https://doi.org/10.1521/pedi.2005.19.5.505

Zanarini, M. C., Frankenburg, F. R., Hennen, J., & Silk, K. R. (2003). The longitudinal course of borderline psychopathology: 6-year prospective follow-up of the phenomenology of borderline personality disorder. *American Journal of Psychiatry, 160*(2), 274–283. https://doi.org/10.1176/appi.ajp.160.2.274

CHAPTER 28

Understanding and Treating Atypical, Severe Nonsuicidal Self-Injury

Barent W. Walsh, Leonard Doerfler, *and* Lisa Van Hove

Abstract

This chapter focuses on an outlier in the field of nonsuicidal self-injury (NSSI): atypical, severe NSSI. The definition consists of three types of behavior: (a) NSSI requiring medical attention such as sutures, staples, glue, bandages; (b) NSSI to unusual body areas: face, eyes, breasts, genitals, and anus; and (c) foreign body ingestion. Although at first look, these behaviors may not appear to have a great deal in common, they share several features. This chapter contends that atypical, severe NSSI may be a distinct, clinically important category. A study reviewed in this chapter examined whether atypical, severe NSSI was related to other self-destructive and self-defeating behaviors in a sample of 467 male and female adults living in intensive community-based group homes or supported housing programs. Analysis using general linear models showed that clients with a lifetime history of atypical, severe NSSI had a significantly higher number of risk indicators than clients without a lifetime history of atypical, severe NSSI. More important, clients with a history of atypical, severe NSSI also had significantly more risk indicators than clients with a history of common NSSI only. The study also found that individuals with a history of atypical, severe NSSI demonstrated more severe psychopathology than clients with common NSSI only. Based on these findings, it may be clinically useful to consider individuals with an atypical, severe NSSI history to be a high-risk subgroup. The chapter concludes with a description of the psychological functions of atypical, severe NSSI, treatment recommendations, two client examples, and suggestions for future research.

Key Words: Atypical, severe, NSSI, NSSI requiring medical attention, NSSI to unusual body areas, Foreign body ingestion

Introduction

This chapter focuses on an outlier in the field of nonsuicidal self-injury (NSSI): atypical, severe NSSI, which consists of three types of behavior:

- NSSI requiring medical attention such as sutures, staples, glue, bandages;
- NSSI to unusual body areas: face, eyes, breasts, genitals, and anus; and
- Foreign body ingestion.

See the section "Atypical, Severe NSSI" for an explanation of why these types are included in this category.

Background

The history of publications on NSSI has been rather dichotomous. About 30 to 40 years ago, research and published reports on the topic largely came from clinical settings. Study samples often consisted of psychiatric inpatients or persons in residential treatment with serious psychological challenges (e.g., Favazza & Conterio, 1989; Pao, 1969; Pattison & Kahan, 1983; Walsh & Rosen, 1988). The reason for this clinical focus was that, at the time, NSSI was largely confined to such intensive treatment settings.

This all changed around the beginning of the 21st century, when self-injury surfaced as a public health problem in the general population (e.g., Briere & Gil, 1998; Ross & Heath, 2002). In a seminally influential paper, Whitlock et al. (2006) reported an NSSI rate of 17% in an Ivy League college sample of more than 3,000 students. Ever since, the overwhelming majority of publications on NSSI have focused on relatively mild forms of the behavior, including cutting, scratching, abrading, burning, or self-hitting, often inflicted on the extremities. Moreover, community-based research also found the prevalence of NSSI-onset peaks around the age of 14 to 20 years (Ammerman et al., 2018; Gandhi et al., 2018; Muehlenkamp et al., 2012; Plener et al., 2015). Therefore, these studies have generally employed community samples from high schools (e.g., Lin et al., 2017; Muehlenkamp et al., 2012; Plener et al., 2015) or universities (e.g., Ammerman et al., 2018; Gandhi et al., 2018; Kiekens et al., 2019; Klonsky, 2009; Muehlenkamp et al., 2018). Often, these studies have reported NSSI that did not require medical attention. For example, in study by Klonsky (2009) using college undergraduates, 5% of the sample required medical attention for their NSSI. In another study, Muehlenkamp et al. (2018) reported that 15% of their university sample indicated having sought medical attention for their NSSI. These prevalence rates—and the rather high likelihood that these rates will be even greater in inpatient samples—indicate the need to take a closer look at severe forms of NSSI. For a systematic review of this literature across the decades, see Cipriano et al. (2017).

Although severe forms of NSSI are discussed in this chapter, the focus is *not* on "major self-mutilation" as originally formulated by Favazza (1992). Favazza included in this category extremely rare, catastrophic forms of self-mutilation such as autocastration and self-enucleation (i.e., self-inflicted eye removal). As an example of the rarity of such behaviors, Chechko et al. (2020) reported that self-enucleation occurs in only 1 among 30 million people. Also, this chapter does not discuss other rare and idiosyncratic forms of NSSI such as mutilation of the tongue (see Moriya et al., 2020) or self-castration or penile amputation (see Boyer & Tucker, 2020).

Atypical Severe NSSI

This chapter represents a return of sorts to focusing on individuals from clinical settings. As noted above, atypical, severe NSSI involves three subtypes. Although at first look these behaviors may not appear to have a great deal in common, in actuality they share several features:

1. They are not suicidal behaviors. Almost no one dies from these acts and few individuals indicate suicidal intent.
2. They are nonetheless seriously self-destructive. They often require far more medical intervention than the common, low lethality forms of NSSI reported in the studies using community samples cited above.
3. They are largely found in persons with histories of sustained, complex mental health challenges.
4. They generally require intensive, multimodal psychological treatments for the persons to fully recover.
5. They are all profoundly socially stigmatizing.

NSSI Involving Medical Intervention

Why are wounds that require medical attention important? When persons injure themselves requiring medical attention, the behavior is not only unusual but is also suggestive of a greater level of self-perceived distress (e.g., Klonsky et al., 2015; Messer & Fremouw, 2008; Nock & Cha, 2009; Nock & Prinstein, 2004; Taylor et al., 2018). For example, reflect on a time—perhaps in childhood—when you were accidentally injured, involving a wound that required medical treatment. This is an event that we naturally want to avoid. Now imagine individuals *intentionally* inflicting a wound that requires 10 or 100 sutures to repair. This example illustrates that it is not extreme to speculate that such persons must be experiencing profound distress. The amount of damage can be viewed—like an equation—as *directly* related to the intensity and degree of distress and an inability to manage such.

Unusual Body Locations for NSSI

Second, the location of NSSI on the body matters (see Kathryn Gardner et al., this volume, for a review of the significance of body location in NSSI). Most people who self-injure damage wrists, forearms, shoulders, legs, or abdomen (for reviews, see Klonsky 2007; Nock 2010; Whitlock et al., 2014). In contrast, few individuals wound the face. For example, in a college sample of 11,529 young adults, Whitlock et al. (2014) said that only 8.2% of those who self-injured reported damaging their face. It was the least prevalent wound location. The other bodily locations reported were arms, hands, wrists, thighs, stomach or chest, calves or ankles, fingers, and head.

Why is damaging the face both unusual and especially alarming? As humans we present to and recognize each other first and foremost via our faces, instead of our hands, feet, or shoulders. We also use facial characteristics to detect emotions and communicate nonverbally (e.g., Bruce, 1996; Jack & Schyns, 2015). Therefore, when persons intentionally injure the face, it suggests an alarming level of social disconnection. People seem to be thinking, "I don't care how I look or how I impact others" and "I'm willing to 'de-face' myself." One female inpatient had a door-knob-sized callous on her forehead due to extreme, repetitive head-banging. She had endured years of sexual abuse by her biological father. When asked if she was concerned about the effect of her scar/wound on her appearance, she said, "I want to look ugly so no one will approach me."

Wounding the eyes is even more alarming. Eyes are sensitive organs that provide the fundamentally important function of sight. Because wounds to the eye have no guarantee of fully healing, people risk permanent impairment (Negrél & Thylefors, 1998). Persons who intentionally wound their eyes are generally in very grave crisis mode. On the extreme end of the continuum are those who self-enucleate. Often, persons who engage in this behavior are psychotic (Amiri et al., 2015; Ananth et al., 1984; Chechko et al., 2020; Field & Waldfogel, 1995; Harish et al., 2012; Large & Nielssen, 2012; Walsh & Rosen, 1988). These extreme cases are not reviewed here (see Fan, 2007; Patton, 2004, for a review). But other individuals hurt their eyes in ways that can compromise sight and/or affect appearance in less major ways (e.g., causing damage that heals quickly or does not impair sight long term). Fortunately, in a study by Grossman (2001) only 90 cases of ocular self-injury have been identified in the psychology literature since the late 1800s. Similar alarm is appropriate for those who damage the breasts (in females) or genitals (in either gender). Fortunately, this behavior also appears to be quite rare. For example, Grossman (2001, p. 53) noted that only "115 cases of male genital self-mutilation have been reported in English, German, and Japanese literature since the end of the nineteenth century." There are numerous reasons why harming the breasts or genitals is especially concerning. First of all, these body areas are replete with nerve endings (e.g., Lemaine & Simmons, 2012). Thus, persons deliberately damaging these areas appear to have very unusual relationships with physical pain. Often such persons deny pain at the time of their acts. This may be due to desensitization of the pain response (due to marked repetition of NSSI) or dissociation (Franklin et al., 2012; Koenig et al., 2016; McCoy et al., 2010; Nock & Prinstein, 2005; Tuna & Gençöz, 2020; see Selby & Hughes, this volume, for review of pain perception during NSSI).

In addition, when clinicians encounter individuals who assault breasts or genitals, they should carefully assess for either posttraumatic stress disorder (PTSD) and/or psychotic decompensation. These body areas have obvious real-world importance and symbolic significance as to sexuality. It is not unusual that such persons report "punishing" their sexual organs for past "involvement" in sexually abusive, traumatic experiences or due to command hallucinations about "sinful" aspects of sexuality (Walsh, 2012).

A related topic can be NSSI involving the anus (e.g., inserting objects into it or intentionally damaging the anus). But this appears to be a rare location for NSSI. Those who have presented with this behavior have had a psychotic preoccupation with constipation/disimpaction or had been repeating and/or attempting to resolve some sort of previous sexual assault. It can be difficult to elicit accurate information about NSSI involving the anus with clients due to their shame or avoidance. Indicating a "nonjudgmental" attitude about such actions, and that it is "another form of human behavior," can be helpful in obtaining accurate disclosures.

Foreign Body Ingestion as a Form of Atypical, Severe NSSI

Foreign body ingestion (FBI) is an especially puzzling form of NSSI. It involves people deliberately ingesting inedible objects such as screws, nails, shards of plastic or glass, coins, pebbles, razor blades, toothbrushes, tools, eating utensils, and so on (see Poynter et al., 2011; Robertson, 2018; Walsh, 2012, for review articles). Many have asked the question: Is FBI an example of suicidal behavior, NSSI, or some other form of self-harm? We believe it to be *a form of atypical, severe NSSI* because:

- It is intentionally self-destructive, yet most individuals deny suicidal intent (Walsh, 2012).
- Consistent with these reports (Walsh, 2012), very few individuals die from FBI.
- Although not suicidal, it is much more alarming than common, low lethality NSSI, which most often does not involve such levels of physical damage.
- Similar to other forms of self-injury, it can result in direct bodily harm, most frequently gastritis, esophagitis, gastroesophageal reflux disease (GERD), and, much more rarely, blockage, perforation, peritonitis, and so on (American Society for Gastrointestinal Endoscopy, 2002). In some cases, the amount of damage can be microscopic.

However, and contrary to most other forms of self-injury for which wounds on extremities or other body areas are instantly evident, bodily harm caused by FBI is *not immediately visible to the perpetrator or others*. In fact, with FBI the behavior can be invisible to self and others for hours, days, and even weeks. Nonetheless, FBI does adhere to the definition of self-injury provided in Walsh (2017). It is "intentional, non-life-threatening, self-effected bodily harm . . . of a socially unacceptable nature, performed to reduce psychological distress and/ or effect change in others."

Atypical, Severe NSSI: Is It a Distinct, Clinically Important Category?

After five decades of such experience, Walsh notes that scores of clinical encounters in highly supervised community-based group homes or state psychiatric hospitals have suggested that those who present with atypical, severe NSSI represent a clinically distinct group of individuals. They appear to have greater and more sustained levels of psychological distress. And they often present with multiple self-destructive behavioral problems in combination. The complexity and severity of their self-destructive acts appear to be far greater than those presenting with common, low lethality NSSI. However, clinical experiences are one thing; empirical data are another.

A Study with Findings re Atypical NSSI

These clinical impressions led Walsh et al. to examine whether atypical, severe NSSI is related to other self-destructive and self-defeating behaviors in a sample of 467 male and female adults living in intensive community-based group homes or supported housing programs (Hom et al., 2018; Walsh & Doerfler, 2016). A broad range of self-destructive and risk behaviors, including atypical, severe NSSI, was examined to discover which behaviors could serve as markers of severe psychopathology. These risk indicators covered the following domains.

- Self-destructive behaviors—including suicide thoughts, plans, actions; atypical severe NSSI; common, low lethality NSSI; eating disorders; substance abuse; risk-taking behaviors; and recurrent psychotropic medication noncompliance;
- Physical health and longevity—including coping with/managing serious medical illness; physical mobility challenges; and inability to avoid danger;
- Trauma—including experiencing physical and/or sexual abuse during childhood and/or experiencing recent physical and/or sexual abuse; and
- Public safety—including violence toward others; problematic sexual behavior; fire-setting; unwarranted 911 calls; other illegal behavior.

For this sample, 33 (7.1%) clients reported a lifetime history of atypical, severe NSSI; only 7 clients (1.5% of the total sample) were reported to engage in atypical, severe NSSI in the prior 6-month period. Analysis using general linear models showed that clients with a lifetime history of atypical, severe NSSI had a significantly higher number of risk indicators than clients without a lifetime history of atypical, severe NSSI. More important, clients with a history of atypical, severe NSSI also had significantly more risk indicators than clients with a history of common NSSI only. Contrary to expectation, individuals with a lifetime history of atypical, severe NSSI were not found to have significantly higher rates of recent suicidal ideation discloses, plans disclosed, or suicidal actions than individuals with a lifetime history of common NSSI only (Hom et al., 2018). This finding suggests that atypical, severe NSSI does not differentially increase suicide risk in this client population.

Walsh and Doerfler (2016) also calculated descriptive statistics to identify specific risk indicators that were associated with elevated numbers or clusters of risk indicators for this sample. The mean number of risk indicators for individuals in this sample was 2.4. Results indicated that five individual risk indicators each were associated with especially high numbers (clusters) of risk indicators. Each of the following risk indicators was associated with at least three times the overall mean number of risk indicators for the entire sample: (1) atypical, severe NSSI, (2) recent physical or sexual abuse, (3) suicidal actions, (4) physical restraint in the program, and (5) unwarranted 911 calls. Among these risk indicators, atypical, severe NSSI stood out as being associated with almost four times the sample mean for risk indicators/behaviors. The findings of these descriptive analyses converge with the findings reported by Hom et al. (2018) to indicate that individuals with a history of atypical, severe NSSI demonstrate more severe psychopathology than clients with common NSSI only. Based on these findings, Hom et al. (2018, p. 586) concluded that "it may be clinically useful to consider individuals with an atypical/severe history to be a high-risk subgroup."

Functions of Atypical, Severe NSSI

How do we understand the psychological functions of atypical/severe NSSI? In their four-component model, Nock and Prinstein (2004) provided a well-accepted strategy for analyzing such functions. As shown in table 28.1, the model includes positive and negative *intrapersonal* functions and positive and negative *interpersonal* functions. Since there are no studies of atypical severe NSSI that address functions in detail yet, the content in tables 28.1, 28.2 and 28.3 come from clinical experience (from Walsh, the first author). As a result, these functions need to be viewed as clinically informed *speculations*. The functions provided in table 28.1 pertain to self-injury involving damage that requires medical attention. Table 28.2 addresses injury to unusual body areas, and table 28.3 looks at FBI.

Note that in table 28.1, the reinforcers provided are all in the intrapersonal realm. In Walsh's experience, it is very rare that NSSI requiring medical intervention is reinforced socially or in an environment. Persons mainly seem to engage in this behavior because of profound, unmanageable emotional distress. Also, other persons tend to recoil at the damage. And caregivers may find the "cleanup" in the environment after such actions to be extremely aversive.

Table 28.2 presents speculations about atypical NSSI involving unusual body areas. For these behaviors, the functions fall into both the intrapersonal and the interpersonal realms, although no concrete speculation could be provided for the positive interpersonal

Table 28.1 Functions for Atypical NSSI Requiring Medical Attention

Positive Intrapersonal Reinforcers	Negative Intrapersonal Reinforcers
"I deserve extensive damage. Superficial cuts don't do the job. That's for wimps."	"I have to cut deep to get relief from my intense emotional distress"
"It's a positive relief to inflict pain and damage on myself. The pain feels good."	"Superficial damage doesn't work."
"I feel exhilarated or high when I do more serious damage."	"What used to work doesn't work anymore. I have to do more damage to get relief."

Table 28.2 Functions for Atypical NSSI of Unusual Body Areas	
Positive Intrapersonal Reinforcers	*Negative Intrapersonal Reinforcers*
Face: "I deserve to be disfigured." "I'm already ugly; why not make it more so?" Sexual organs: "I know this sounds weird, but hurting my genitals can be a turn on."	Eyes: "My voices are so loud and demanding, I have to obey them." Sexual organs: "I know it's crazy but when I hurt my genitals, I feel relief from guilt and shame about my abuse." Anus: "I feel relief when I insert things in my anus. It reminds me of my abuse and punishes me for having been part of that. Then I feel calm."
Positive Interpersonal Reinforcers	*Negative Interpersonal Reinforcers*
	Face: "People will avoid me. I prefer social isolation." Sexual organs: "I avoid people sexually because I know am disfigured, unattractive. For me that's a relief."

realm specifically. Items in quotation are direct quotes from clients who have presented with NSSI inflicted on unusual body areas.

Table 28.3 refers to FBI. The functions provided in this table come from a qualitative study by Walsh et al. (2012, cited in in Walsh, 2012). The study involved interviewing nine individuals who had presented with recurrent FBI and were residing in state hospitals or correctional facilities. Subjects were asked, "What does ingesting do for you?" The responses in table 28.3 are taken verbatim from the nine individuals.

What is especially striking about the functions of FBI for these persons is that the *social reinforcers were generally much more important than the internal reinforcers*. This finding is very different from that in most other studies of self-injury (e.g., Klonsky, 2007; Nock, 2010), where the primary motivations for FBI have been internal affect regulation. Only two of the nine patients cited internal affect regulation as a reason for their FBI and these were of secondary importance (Walsh, 2012).

The most common explanation voiced by these patients was that they ingested in order to be transferred from their psychiatric wards or correctional cellblock to medical facilities. In some cases, they sought this transfer because they found the medical staff to be more nurturing and compassionate. Other patients indicated they "liked the scopes" or sedatives associated with endoscopies. And many of the patients expressed a desire to escape their psychiatric wards due to ongoing interpersonal conflicts with staff and other patients (Walsh, 2012).

For those working with individuals who present with atypical severe NSSI, the four-function model can be very useful in understanding the behavior and designing treatment strategies.

Treating Individuals with Atypical Severe NSSI

If individuals with these atypical NSSI behaviors are prone to clusters of other risk behaviors, including suicide thoughts and behaviors, how do we treat them? While there are certainly no rigorous studies that have examined the effectiveness of such treatment, we

Table 28.3 Functions of FBI for Nine Individuals	
Positive self-reinforcement	Negative self-reinforcement
"To have a sensation of food in my stomach"	"Sense of relief" "I thought the battery would explode & kill me" "Same function as cutting"
Positive social reinforcement	Negative social reinforcement
"I was jealous of someone who got to go to the ER" "I like the scopes at the medical unit" "I get high off the sedatives they give me for the endoscopies" "I want control of my treatment" "It's like playing Russian roulette and slapping God in the face"	"I don't want to be here (state hospital): I want to go to the medical hospital" "When I swallow objects, I get transferred off the cellblock to a medical unit." "I get transferred from a psych ward to a medical hospital" "I want a sharp object lodged in my anus so that when someone rapes me, he will get his dick shredded.

can at least propose reasonable clinical guidelines, partially based on Walsh's clinical experience with persons presenting with severe, atypical NSSI.

Hierarchy of Risk

In treating persons who engage in severe, atypical NSSI, it is logical to employ a "hierarchy of risk" (Walsh, 2012). These are individuals who present with multiple self-harm behaviors in combination. It is neither practical nor reasonable to expect these individuals to overcome *all* these self-destructive acts at the same time. Yet, we often see treatment plans in programs or inpatient facilities that read "client (or patient) will refrain from self-harm behaviors for the next 30 days." Such treatment goals are generally a prescription for failure. A more realistic strategy is to employ a hierarchy that targets the most potentially lethal behaviors first and then moves to the next most alarming behavior, and so on. For example, a poly-self-destructive individual might merit a treatment plan with hierarchical goals of reducing/eliminating

1. Suicide plans and rehearsal regarding overdose;
2. Abuse of a prescribed opiate;
3. Atypical severe self-injury via cutting involving sutures and occasional FBI;
4. Moderate binge eating; and
5. Common, low lethality self-injury on extremities not requiring medical attention.

An individual with a simpler (but not unchallenging) combination of problems might employ a hierarchy like this:

1. Atypical severe NSSI—reopening sutured wounds;
2. Episodic binging on alcohol; and
3. Cutting of extremities not requiring medical attention.

Sequential, Multimodal Treatments

A second clinical principle is to employ a *series* of evidence-based treatment sequentially. We have done this with many clients at The Bridge (now Open Sky). A common place to start is providing dialectical behavior therapy (DBT; Linehan, 2015) *according to protocol*. Learning the DBT skills of mindfulness, distress tolerance, emotion regulation, and interpersonal effectiveness provides the bedrock toolkit for other subsequent treatments. The intense emotional distress that generally triggers atypical severe NSSI must become manageable if clients are to give up the behaviors. In addition, clients need to master the interpersonal effectiveness skills that allow individuals to ask for help before self-injuring and learn conflict resolution skills which can reduce triggers for subsequent NSSI. Once clients have participated in one to two rounds of DBT (generally lasting six months each), they can move into more specialized treatments. An outcome study of DBT with adolescents conducted at The Bridge showed significant reductions in suicidal behavior, NSSI, and psychiatric hospitalizations for the study subjects who had completed one to two rounds compared to individuals who had completed less than one round (Walsh et al., 2012, cited in Walsh, 2012).

A common second treatment is cognitive restructuring (CR) for PTSD (Mueser et al., 2009; Walsh, 2012). The large majority of clients who have presented with atypical self-injury have histories of trauma. For example, in the qualitative study of nine individuals who presented with FBI referenced above (Walsh, 2012), all nine had been sexually abused as children. In addition, six of nine (67%) had been physically abused. These individuals had clearly experienced extremely problematic childhoods. We selected CR for PTSD as the evidence-based treatment to use because it is a *nonexposure* treatment (Mueser et al., 2009; Walsh, 2012). We have found that many Bridge clients are unable to tolerate treatments that involve prolonged exposure (e.g., Foa et al., 2007). Instead, their self-destructive behaviors are often exacerbated during treatment. CR for PTSD is a 12- to 16-week, manualized treatment that teaches breathing retraining and provides psychoeducation about PTSD symptoms. The heart of the treatment is CR and action planning. Rather than requiring detailed discussion of past traumatic events (exposure), the treatment targets the thoughts and beliefs *derived from the trauma*. For example, the treatment focuses on inaccurate, unhelpful beliefs that are common in individuals with PTSD such as, "the abuse must have been my fault because it went on so long," or "I broke up the family when I told someone," or "my body is contaminated by the abuse." According to Mueser et al. (2015), in addition to empirical support as the efficacy of CR for PTSD, The Bridge has data for the first 88 clients served with CR. The results indicated significant reductions in both PTSD and depression scores for the study subjects (Walsh, 2017).

Illness, management, and recovery (IMR; McGuire et al., 2014; Mueser et al., 2006) is a third evidence-based treatment provided by The Bridge to individuals who present with atypical severe NSSI and other related self-harm behaviors. This treatment is designed for persons with serious mental illness (especially psychosis) who are prone to decompensation and relapse. It is a better match for persons with psychosis than DBT—which emphasizes dealing with emotion dysregulation. IMR is quite useful in reducing self-harm behaviors in this population because of its very structured, manualized approach—which is helpful for cognitively disorganized individuals. The manual for IMR has 10 modules which cover the topics of recovery strategies; practical facts about mental illness; stress-vulnerability model; building social support; using medication effectively; reducing relapse; coping with stress; coping with symptoms; getting your needs met in the mental health system; and finally drug and alcohol use. Moreover, IMR is based on a recovery model that emphasizes personal choice and self-determination (Mueser et al., 2006) (a free copy of the IMR manual is available at http://store.samhsa.gov/product/Illness-Management-and-Recovery-Evidence-Based-Practices-EBP-KIT/SMA09-4463).

Other specialized evidence-based treatments that The Bridge has offered individuals with atypical NSSI have included:

- CBT for eating disorders (Fairburn, 2008);
- CBT for aggression (Reilly & Shopshire, 2002); and
- CBT for psychosis (Turkington & Kingdon, 2005).

Two Client Examples Regarding Treatment

As discussed, treating people who present with atypical severe NSSI may require both a hierarchy of risk and a sequence of evidence-based treatments. Two client examples demonstrate a case with a complicated, unresolved outcome, one with a decidedly positive conclusion.

Client Example 1

Ms. M is a 38-year-old woman with a long history of institutionalization. She has presented with 19 of the 28 risk behaviors described above (Walsh & Doerfler, 2016), including suicide attempts, atypical severe NSSI (i.e., cutting with many sutures and FBI), common NSSI, substance abuse, eating disorder, failure to take prescribed medication, and so on. She has been attempting to live in the community in a highly supervised group home; however, she has been chronically unstable with many emergency room visits per month and several psychiatric hospitalizations per quarter. Her insurance payor assumed $30,000 in ambulance charges within the past six months. She has potential damage to her esophagus due to frequent FBI, related scopes, and x-rays. She also recurrently expresses specific suicidal plans. Her major treatment challenge is that she has been unable to engage in evidence-based treatments. When she has attempted to engage, her community tenures have been so short due to hospitalizations that she has missed an excessive number of sessions. Her ability to reside in the community is tenuous at best. She is likely to return to a state hospital for an extended stay. When she was asked, "What is the safest place you have ever lived?" she replied, "The state hospital." No wonder she prefers to return.

Client Example 2

This 26-year-old woman entered a community-based residential treatment program three and a half years ago, having been discharged from a state hospital. The program offered on-site IMR with which she immediately engaged. She identified her recovery goals as (a) reducing suicide and self-injury behaviors and (b) moving to her own apartment. Prior to entering in the program, she had presented with 16 of the 28 aforementioned risk behaviors, including suicide attempts, atypical NSSI (cutting with sutures, FBI), extensive superficial cutting, obesity, alcohol abuse, noncompliance with medications, elopements, sexual risk-taking, and so on. Over the first six months of treatment, she made progress on her "hierarchy of risk." She became adept at communicating suicide urges with staff in the program and was able to cease suicide attempts. She also had no instances of atypical severe NSSI, although she continued to occasionally cut her skin superficially. These behaviors were managed within the program without resorting to psychiatric hospitalizations. Within six months in the program, she also began attending off-site DBT groups offered by the agency. This treatment taught her emotion regulation and distress tolerance skills. These prepared her to do trauma work related to her history of being sexually and physically abused as a child. After a year of DBT, she began CR for PTSD with an accompanying coach from her residential program. The treatment proved an excellent match for her, resulting in notable reductions in her PTSD and depression scores. A year later she graduated to her own apartment and is now receiving intensive supported housing services. She has several enduring friendships in the community and works part-time in a bakery. She remains stable and safe!

Implications for Research

As can be observed throughout this chapter, research on severe, atypical NSSI is scarce. Yet, studies have found that 5% to 15% of young adults who self-injure require medical attention as a consequence of their NSSI (Klonsky, 2009; Muehlenkamp et al., 2018). This implies that severe NSSI forms might be more prevalent than researchers currently assume. Such assumptions may be due to the severity of NSSI being overlooked in prior research and therefore remaining unrevealed.

Furthermore, the prevalence of severe NSSI may be underreported because most studies post-20th century have focused on community-based samples (e.g., Ammerman et al., 2018; Gandhi et al., 2018; Muehlenkamp et al., 2012; Plener et al., 2015). Walsh (2012) found that severe, atypical NSSI most commonly goes hand in hand with serious psychopathology. This indicates a higher presence of such severe forms among clinical samples. Thus, to examine such forms more closely, epidemiological studies composed of inpatient and community-based, intensive treatment settings are necessary.

To enable researchers to examine this phenomenon in the future, a clear and consistent definition of severe, atypical NSSI should first be established. For example, Ammerman and colleagues (2018, 2019) distinguished common, less lethal NSSI from severe NSSI by NSSI frequency, the number of methods used, and the amount of hospital visits as a consequence of NSSI. Walsh proposed three subtypes, which can be summarized as NSSI (a) to unusual body parts; (b) by foreign body ingestion; and/or (c) requiring medical attention. Future research can validate this definition and perhaps lead to the inclusion of severe, atypical NSSI in commonly used screening tools.

Finally, although the prevalence rate of severe, atypical NSSI is relatively low in comparison to common, less lethal NSSI (Hom et al., 2018), it is crucial for clinicians to find effective ways to treat severe, atypical NSSI for a number of reasons. First, severe, atypical NSSI is characterized by a higher degree of physical damage. Next, the social stigma associated with these behaviors can be extreme (Walsh, 2017). Finally, although NSSI is frequently used to diminish perceived distress (e.g., Klonsky et al., 2015; Messer & Fremouw, 2008), engaging in NSSI also leads to increased levels of psychological distress over time (Kiekens et al., 2018). In its turn, this high amount of distress may have a detrimental effect on NSSI cessation (Andrews et al., 2013; Whitlock et al., 2015). Now, clinicians often feel astray, which can possibly lead to mistreatment or overlooking of severe atypical NSSI. For example, clinicians may simply pass over its presence because they used a screening tool that did not include such severe forms. Also, severe atypical NSSI might be overlooked due to the lack of visibility on the body of some severe forms (i.e., FBI). Because these forms are not yet recognized in the general population as NSSI, clinicians often do not explicity inquire about such severe forms.

Based on Walsh's clinical experience, a hierarchy of risk (Walsh, 2012) in combination with sequential evidence-based treatments (e.g., DBT; Linehan, 2015) may be effective. Yet, thus far there are no intervention studies that empirically support these treatments for severe, atypical NSSI. Such studies can further help clinicians find effective ways to adequately treat such forms. Finally, findings suggest that an earlier onset of NSSI (i.e., 12 years of age) is a marker of a more severe NSSI course (Ferrara et al., 2012; Muehlenkamp & Brausch, 2012). Hence, an earlier age of onset may also be an important precursor of severe NSSI and may consequently help clinicians to prevent an increase of NSSI severity. Future research should more closely examine this predictive association.

Conclusion

Atypical, severe NSSI can be conceptualized as comprising three subgroups: (1) NSSI requiring medical attention; (2) injury to unusual body parts including face, eyes, breasts, genitals, and anus; and (3) foreign body ingestion. These three subgroups may have different functions, ranging from intrapersonal to interpersonal or both. Research has indicated that these different subtypes of atypical severe NSSI may be a key marker for severe psychopathology, other risk behaviors, and suicide attempts (Walsh & Doerfler, 2016).

Atypical, severe NSSI is vastly underresearched and merits significantly more attention because of the clinical risks posed by the behavior. Even with the limited research available, clinicians still must find ways to treat atypical, severe NSSI effectively. A reasonable approach may be to employ a hierarchy of risk in combination with sequential evidence-based treatments.

References

American Society for Gastrointestinal Endoscopy. (2002). Guideline for the management of ingested foreign bodies. *Gastrointestinal Endoscopy*, 55(7), 802–806. https://doi.org/10.1016/s0016-5107(02)70407-0

Amiri, S., Arfaei, A., & Farhang, S. (2015). Self-inflicted needle injuries to the eye: A curing pain. *Case Reports in Psychiatry*, *2015*, Article 960579. https://doi.org/10.1155/2015/960579

Ammerman, B. A., Hong, M., Sorgi, K., Park, Y., Jacobucci, R., & McCloskey, M. S. (2019). An examination of individual forms of nonsuicidal self-injury. *Psychiatry Research*, *278*, 268–274. https://doi.org/10.1016/j.psychres.2019.06.029

Ammerman, B. A., Jacobucci, R., Kleiman, E. M., Uyeji, L., & McCloskey, M. S. (2018). The relationship between nonsuicidal self-injury age of onset and severity of self-harm. *Suicide and Life-Threatening Behavior*, *48*(1), 31–37. https://doi.org/10.1111/sltb.12330

Ananth, J., Kaplan, H. S., & Lin, K. M. (1984). Self-inflicted enucleation of an eye: Two case reports. *Canadian Journal of Psychiatry*, *29*(2), 145–146. https://doi.org/10.1177/070674378402900213

Andrews, T., Martin, G., Hasking, P., & Page, A. (2013). Predictors of continuation and cessation of nonsuicidal self-injury. *Journal of Adolescent Health*, *53*, 40–46. https://doi.org/10.1016/j.jadohealth.2013.01.009

Boyer, E. R., & Tucker, P. (2020). Genital self-mutilation, a cutting conundrum. *Psychiatric Times*, *37*(7), 1–10.

Briere, J., & Gil, E. (1998). Self-mutilation in clinical and general population samples: Prevalence, correlates, and functions. *American Journal of Orthopsychiatry*, *68*(4), 609–620. https://doi.org/10.1037/h0080369

Bruce, V. (1996). The role of the face in communication: Implications for videophone design. *Interacting with Computers*, *8*(2), 166–176. https://doi.org/10.1016/0953-5438(96)01026-0

Chechko, N., Stormanns, E., Podoll, K., Stickel, S., & Neuner, I. (2020). Self-enucleation of the right eye by a 38-year-old woman diagnosed with schizoaffective disorder: A case report. *BMC Psychiatry*, *20*, Article 563. https://doi.org/10.1186/s12888-020-02974-6

Cipriano, A., Cella, S., & Cotrufo, P. (2017). Nonsuicidal self-injury: A systematic review. *Frontiers in Psychology*, *8*, Article 1946. https://doi.org/10.3389/fpsyg.2017.01946

Fairburn, C. G. (2008). *Cognitive behavior therapy and eating disorders*. Guilford Press.

Fan, A. H. (2007). Autoenucleation: A case report and literature review. *Psychiatry (Edgmont)*, *4*(10), 60–62.

Ferrara, M., Terrinoni, A., & Williams, R. (2012). Non-suicidal self-injury (NSSI) in adolescent inpatients: Assessing personality features and attitude toward death. *Child and Adolescent Psychiatry and Mental Health*, *6*, 1–8. https://doi.org/10.1186/1753-2000-6-12

Favazza, A. R. (1992). Repetitive self-mutilation. *Psychiatric Annals*, *22*(2), 60–63. https://doi.org/10.3928/0048-5713-19920201-06

Favazza, A. R., & Conterio, K. (1989). Female habitual self-mutilators. *Acta Psychiatrica Scandinavica*, *79*(3), 283–289. https://doi.org/10.1111/j.1600-0447.1989.tb10259.x

Field, H. L., & Waldfogel, S. (1995). Severe ocular self-injury. *General Hospital Psychiatry*, *17*(3), 224–227. https://doi.org/10.1016/0163-8343(95)00031-l

Foa, E., Hembree, E., & Rothbaum, B. O. (2007). *Prolonged exposure therapy for PTSD: Emotional processing of traumatic experiences therapist guide*. Oxford University Press.

Franklin, J. C., Aaron, R. V., Arhurt, M. S., Shorkey, S. P., & Prinstein, M. J. (2012). Nonsuicidal self-injury and diminished pain perception: The role of emotion dysregulation. *Comprehensive Psychiatry*, *53*(6), 691–700. https://doi.org/10.1016/j.comppsych.2011.11.008

Gandhi, A., Luyckx, K., Baetens, I., Kiekens, G., Sleuwaegen, E., Berens, A., Maitra, S., & Claes, L. (2018). Age of onset of non-suicidal self-injury in Dutch-speaking adolescents and emerging adults: An event history analysis of pooled data. *Comprehensive Psychiatry*, *80*, 170–178. https/doi.org/10.1016/j.comppsych.2017.10.007

Grossman, R. (2001). Psychotic self-injurious behaviors: Phenomenology, neurobiology, and treatment. In D. Simeon & E. Hollander (Eds.), *Self-injurious behaviors: Assessment and treatment* (pp. 49–70). American Psychiatric Association.

Harish, T., Chawan, N., Rajkumar, R. P., & Chaturvedi, S.K. (2012). Bilateral self-enucleation in acute transient psychotic disorder: The influence of sociocultural factors on psychopathology. *Comprehensive Psychiatry*, *53*(5), 576–578. https://doi.org/10.1016/j.comppsych.2011.07.001

Hom, M. A., Rogers, M. L., Schneider, M. E., Chiurliza, B., Doerfler, L., Walsh, B. W., & Joiner, T. E. (2018). Atypical and severe non-suicidal self-injury as an indicator of severe psychopathology: Findings from a sample of high-risk community mental health clients. *The Journal of Nervous and Mental Disease*, *206*(8), 582–588. https://doi.org/10.1097/NMD.0000000000000865

Jack, R. E., & Schyns, P. G. (2015). The human face as a dynamic tool for social communication. *Current Biology*, *25*(14), 621–634. https://doi.org/10.1016/j.cub.2015.05.052

Kiekens, G., Hasking, P., Claes, L., Boyes, M., Mortier, P., Auerbach, R. P., Cuijpers, P., Demyttenaere, K., Green, J. G., Kessler, R. C., Myin-Germeys, I., Nock, M. K., & Bruffaerts, R. (2019). Predicting the incidence of non-suicidal self-injury in college students. *European Psychiatry*, *59*, 44–51. https://doi.org/10.1016/j.eurpsy.2019.04.002

Kiekens, G., Hasking, P., Claes, L., Mortier, P., Auerbach, R. P., Boyes, M., Cuijpers, P., Demyttenaere, K., Green, J. G., Kessler, R. C., Nock, M. K., & Bruffaerts, R. (2018). The DSM-5 nonsuicidal self-injury disorder among incoming college students: Prevalence and associations with 12-month mental disorders and suicidal thoughts and behaviors. *Depression and Anxiety*, *35*(7), 629–637. https://doi.org/10.1002/da.22754

Klonsky, E. D. (2007). The functions of deliberate self-injury: A review of the evidence. *Clinical Psychology Review*, *27*(2), 226–239. https://doi.org/10.1016/j.cpr.2006.08.002

Klonsky, E.D., & Glenn, C.R. (2009). Assessing the functions of non-suicidal self-injury: Psychometric properties of the Inventory of Statements About Self-injury (ISAS). *Journal of Psychopathology and Behavioral Assessment*, *31*(3), 215–219. https://doi.org/10.1007/s10862-008-9107-z

Klonsky, E. D., Glenn, C. R., Styer, D. M., Olino, T. M., & Washburn, J. J. (2015). The functions of nonsuicidal self-injury: Converging evidence for a two-factor structure. *Child and Adolescent Psychiatry and Mental Health*, *9*, Article 44. https://doi.org/10.1186/s13034-015-0073-4

Koenig, J., Thayer, J. F., & Kaess, M. (2016). A meta-analysis on pain sensitivity in self-injury. *Psychological Medicine*, *46*(8), 1597–1612. https://doi.org/10.1017/S0033291716000301

Large, M. M., & Nielssen, O. B. (2012). Self-enucleation: Forget Freud and Oedipus, it's all about untreated psychosis. *British Journal of Ophthalmology*, *96*(8), 1056–1057. https://doi.org/10.1136/bjophthalmol-2012-301531

Lemaine, V., & Simmons, P. S. (2012). The adolescent female: Breast and reproductive embryology and anatomy. *Clinical Anatomy*, *26*(1), 22–28. https://doi.org/10.1002/ca.22167

Lin, M., You, J., Ren, Y., Wu, J. Y., Hu, W., Yen, C., & Zhang, X. (2017). Prevalence of nonsuicidal self-injury and its risk and protective factors among adolescents in Taiwan. *Psychiatry Research*, *255*, 119–127. https://doi.org/10.1016/j.psychres.2017.05.028

Linehan, M. M. (2015). *DBT Skills training manual* (2nd ed.). Guilford Press.

McCoy, K., Fremouw, W., & McNeil, D. W. (2010). Thresholds and tolerance of physical pain among young adults who self-injure. *Pain Research and Management*, *15*(6), 371–377. https://doi.org/10.1155/2010/326507

McGuire, A. B., Kukla, M., Green, A., Gilbride, D., Mueser, K.T., & Salyers, M. P. (2014). Illness management and recovery: A review of the literature. *Psychiatric Services*, *65*(2), 171–170. https://doi.org/10.1176/appi.ps.201200274

Messer, J. M., & Fremouw, W. J. (2008). A critical review of explanatory models for self-mutilating behaviors in adolescents. *Clinical Psychology Review*, *28*(1), 162–178. https://doi.org/10.1016/j.cpr.2007.04.006

Muehlenkamp, J. J, & Brausch, A. M. (2012). Body image as a mediator of non-suicidal self-injury in adolescents. *Journal of Adolescence*. *35*, 1–9. https://doi.org/10.1016/j.adolescence.2011.06.010

Muehlenkamp, J. J., Claes, L., Havertape, L., & Plener, P. L. (2012). International prevalence of adolescent non-suicidal self-injury and deliberate self-harm. *Child and Adolescent Psychiatry and Mental Health*, *6*(1), Article 10. https://doi.org/10.1186/17530-2000-6-10

Muehlenkamp, J. J., Xhunga, N., & Brausch, A. (2018). Self-injury age of onset: A risk factor for NSSI severity and suicidal behavior. *Archives of Suicidal Research*, *23*(4), 551–563. https://doi.org/10.1080/13811118.2018.1486252

Moriya, T., Sato, H., Takeda, K., Ikezaki, K., Katada, R., & Shirota, T. (2020). Two cases of nonsuicidal self-injury comprising partial autoamputation of the apex of the tongue. *Case Reports in Dentistry, 2020*, Article 8691270. https://doi.org/10.1155/2020/8691270

Mueser, K. T., Gottlieb, J. D., Xie, H., Yanos, P. T., Rosenberg, S. D. Silverstein, S. M., Duva, S. M., Minsky, S. Wolfe, R. S., & McHugo, G. J. (2015). *British Journal of Psychiatry, 205*(6), 501–508. https://doi.org/10.21203/rs.3.rs-149400/v1

Mueser, K. T., Meyer, P. S., Penn, D. L., Clancy, R., Clancy, D. M., & Salyers, M. P. (2006). The illness management and recovery program: Rationale, development, and preliminary findings. *Schizophrenia Bulletin, 32*(1), 32–43. https://doi.org/10.1093/schbul/sbl022

Mueser, K. T., Rosenberg, S. D., & Rosenberg, H. J. (2009). *Treatment of posttraumatic stress disorder in special populations: A cognitive restructuring program*. American Psychological Association.

Négrel, A. D., & Thylefors, B. (1998). The global impact of eye injuries. *Ophthalmic Epidemiology, 5*(3), 143–169. https://doi.org/10.1076/opep.5.3.143.8364

Nock, M. K. (2010). Self-injury. *Annual Review of Clinical Psychology, 6*, 339–363. https://doi.org/10.1146/annurev.clinpsy.121208.131258

Nock, M. K., & Cha, C. B. (2009). Psychological models of nonsuicidal self-injury. In M.K. Nock (Ed.), *Understanding nonsuicidal self-injury: Origins, assessment, and treatment* (pp. 65–77). American Psychological Association. https://doi.org/10.1037/11875-004

Nock, M. K., & Prinstein, M. J. (2004). A functional approach to the assessment of self-mutilative behavior. *Journal of Consulting and Clinical Psychology, 72*(5), 885–890. https://doi.org/10.1037/0022-006X.72.5.885

Nock, M. K., & Prinstein, M. J. (2005). Contextual features and behavioral functions of self-mutilation among adolescents. *Journal of Abnormal Psychology, 114*(1), 140–146. https://doi.org/10.1037/0021-843X.114.1.140

Pao, P. N. (1969). The syndrome of delicate self-cutting. *British Journal of Medical Psychology, 42*(3), 195–206. https://doi.org/10.1111/j.2044-8341.1969.tb02071.x

Pattison, E. M., & Kahan, J. (1983). The deliberate self-harm syndrome. *The American Journal of Psychiatry, 140*(7), 867–872. https://doi.org/10.1176/ajp.140.7.867

Patton, N. (2004). Self-inflicted eye injuries: A review. *Eye, 18*(9), 867–872. https://doi.org/10.1038/sj.eye.6701365

Plener, P. L., Schumacher, T. S., Munz, L. M., & Groschwitz, R. C. (2015). The longitudinal course of non-suicidal self-injury and deliberate self-harm: A systematic review of the literature. *Borderline Personality Disorder and Emotion Dysregulation, 2*(2), Article 2. https://doi.org/186/s40479-014-0024-3

Poynter, B. A., Hunter, J. J., Coverdale, M. D., & Kampinsky, C. A. (2011). Hard to swallow: A systematic review of deliberated foreign body ingestion. *General Hospital Psychiatry, 33*(5), 518–524. https://doi.org/10.1016/j.genhosppsych.2011.06.011

Reilly, P. M., & Shopshire, M. S. (2002) *Anger management for substance abuse and mental health clients, a CBT manual*. SAMHSA.

Robertson, A. R. (2018). Self-harm by sharp foreign body ingestion. *Suicide and Life-Threatening Behavior, 49*(3), 735–738. https://doi.org/10.1111/sltb.12474

Ross, S., & Heath, N. (2002). A study of the frequency of self-mutilation in a community sample of adolescents. *Journal of Youth and Adolescence, 31*, 67–77. https://doi.org/10.1023/A:1014089117419

Taylor, P. J., Jomar, K., Dhingra, K., Forrester, R., Shahmalak, U., & Dickson, J. M. (2018). A meta-analysis of the prevalence of different functions of non-suicidal self-injury. *Journal of Affective Disorders, 227*, 759–769. https://doi.org/10.1016/j.jad.2017.11.073

Tuna, E., & Gençöz, T. (2020). Pain perception, distress tolerance and self-compassion in Turkish young adults with and without a history of non-suicidal self-injury. *Current Psychology, 40*(8), 4143–4155. https://doi.org/10.1007/s12144-020-00634-2

Turkington, D. G., & Kingdon, D. (2005). *Cognitive therapy of schizophrenia*. Guilford Press.

Walsh, B. W. (2012). *Treating self-injury: A practical guide* (2nd ed.). Guilford Press.

Walsh, B. W. (2017, April). *Workshop on "Understanding, Managing and Treating Non-Suicidal Self-Injury"* [Conference presentation]. American Association of Suicidology annual meeting, Phoenix, AZ.

Walsh, B. W., & Doerfler, L. (2016, December). *Van Gogh's ear: Why atypical, severe self-injury is an especially alarming form of self-harm* [Paper presentation]. Harvard Medical School/ Cambridge Health Alliance conference on Treating Self-Destructive Behavior, Boston, MA.

Walsh, B. W., Doerfler, L. A., & Perry, A. (2012). Residential treatment for adolescents targeting self-injury and suicidal behavior. In B. W. Walsh (Ed.), *Treating self-injury: A practical guide* (pp. 253–268) (2nd ed.). Guilford Press.

Walsh, B. W., & Rosen, P. M. (1988). *Self-mutilation: Theory, research and treatment*. Guilford Press.

Whitlock, J., Eckenrode, J., & Silverman, D. (2006). Self-injurious behaviors in a college population. *Pediatrics, 117*(6), 1939–1948. https://doi.org/10.1542/peds.2005-2543

Whitlock, J., Exner-Cortens, D., & Purington, A. (2014). Assessment of nonsuicidal self-injury: Development and initial validation of the Non-Suicidal Self-Injury—Assessment Tool (NSSI-AT). *Psychological Assessment, 26*(3), 935–946. http://dx.doi.org/10.1037/a0036611

Whitlock, J., Prussien, K., & Pietrusza, C. (2015). Predictors of self-injury cessation and subsequent psychological growth: results of a probability sample survey of students in eight universities and colleges. *Child and Adolescent Psychiatry and Mental Health, 9*, Article 19. https://doi.org/10.1186/s13034-015-0048-5

CHAPTER 29

NSSI in Older Adults

Lisa Van Hove, Imke Baetens, Chloe A. Hamza, Eva Dierckx, An Haekens, Lila Fieremans, *and* Steven Vanderstichelen

> **Abstract**
>
> This chapter explores the epidemiology of nonsuicidal self-injury (NSSI) in older adults. It explains how a systematic review presents the risk and protective factors of NSSI among the elderly population, referencing the selection process of the Meta-Analyses and Systematic Reviews of Observational Studies in Epidemiology. Even though some findings are similar to NSSI research on adolescents and young adults, the experience of loss is specific to NSSI-related behaviors among older adults. The chapter then considers the distinction between suicidal intent and the directness of self-harm within the elderly population. It suggests conducting a longitudinal, cross-cultural design that distinguishes between the specific forms of self-harm to conduct an early intervention and prevent NSSI repetition.
>
> **Key Words:** epidemiology, NSSI, elderly population, experience of loss, suicidal intent, self-harm, systematic review, early intervention

Introduction

Mia (75 years old) was recently admitted to an emergency unit for a suicide attempt. There she was referred to a psychiatric hospital for further treatment and diagnostics. The team of the psychogeriatric ward notices several scars on the patient's forearms. Upon inquiry, it appears that, when she was younger, Mia injured herself to deal with high tension but not with suicidal intent. This form of self-injury disappeared when she was given "depressant" medication from her psychiatrist. Nowadays, she has a new doctor who reduced her medication resulting in greater tensions at home and with her partner. Furthermore, the team also notes that the patient is unable to follow the therapeutic sessions due to language and memory problems (later diagnosed as frontotemporal dementia). Despite the fact that she worked a whole career as a teacher, she currently is no longer able to remember appointments and to bring structure in her daily activities. This feeling of loss of control, together with a recent change in her medication may have led to an increase in stress, resulting in the suicide attempt.

Over the past two decades, an increasing number of researchers have shown interest in studying self-harm. This includes behaviors that are deliberately performed with intent (i.e., suicidal self-harm) or with no intent to die (i.e., nonsuicidal self-harm; Nock, 2010). Some of these behaviors cause physical damage indirectly (i.e., indirect self-harm), such as alcohol abuse or eating disorders, while other behaviors cause direct damage to the bodily tissue (i.e., direct self-harm), such as cutting. Although many studies have since researched self-harm, only few focus on this phenomenon in older adults (age 60 years and older). This is especially the case for nonsuicidal self-injury (NSSI).

In this chapter, we describe the epidemiology of NSSI in older adults. As there is almost no research on risk and protective factors of NSSI in this population, we present a systematic review of the existing literature on NSSI-linked behaviors in older adults (considering literature on indirect self-harm and suicidal thoughts and behaviors in older adults). We conclude by reviewing implications for clinicians and researchers.

Epidemiology and Etiology of NSSI (and Self-Harm) in Older Adults

Martin and Swannell (2016) were among the first to study NSSI specifically across age groups (N = 12,006). Of the 219 persons who had engaged in NSSI the preceding year, 6.8% were 60 years old or over (n = 15). These older adults were predominantly female (73.5%). They found that NSSI was more strongly associated with a psychiatric diagnosis, higher psychological distress, and lifetime suicide attempts among older adults in comparison to younger adults. However, for the execution of their analyses, they defined older adults upward of age 40. Therefore these results may not be applicable to older adults age 60 years and above.

Choi et al. (2016) also researched NSSI among older adults. They conducted a retrospective study in which they investigated emergency department (ED) visits of older adults age 50 years and older (N = 26,142,903) caused by any form of injury. Of these patients, 3% (n = 789,516) visited the ED after a suicidal attempt or NSSI episode. Although 76.9% of these patients presented with suicidal attempts, NSSI was the cause of the ED visit in the remaining 23.1% of these cases. Among patients age 65 years and older specifically, NSSI accounted for 25% of the cases. Choi et al. (2016) also found this reflected in the slightly higher odds for older adults age 65 years and older to be admitted for NSSI rather than a suicidal attempt, in comparison to adults age 50 to 64 years. Regarding gender, males (55%) seemed to engage more often in suicidal attempts in comparison to females (45%), while more females (56%) presented with NSSI than males (44%). Moreover, multi-injury, anxiety disorder and drug use disorder were more strongly associated with NSSI than suicidal attempts. Surprisingly, older adults who visited the ED after a NSSI episode were more likely to be admitted to the hospital, in comparison to those whose visit was caused by a suicidal attempt (Choi et al., 2016).

Most recently, Ose et al. (2021) examined the incidence of NSSI and SSI (i.e., suicidal self-injury) in a national adult psychiatric outpatient sample (N = 23,124) via clinician's report. In the age group of 60- to 69-year-olds, 6.3% of the patients had engaged in NSSI in the past four weeks, 13.6% showed suicidal thoughts, and 0.4% attempted suicide. For adults age 70 years and older, clinicians registered NSSI for 2.9%, and 9.2% exhibited SSI thoughts in the past four weeks, whereas 0.8% attempted suicide.

Although the above-mentioned prevalence rates seem to suggest that NSSI does occur among older adults, literature on risk and protective factors of NSSI in this special population is scarce (except for sociodemographic features, and the link with SSI/SA/indirect self-harm). Moreover, the risk and protective factors found in younger populations (adults, young adults/adolescents) might not always apply to this population. This was also suggested by Crocker et al. (2006), who interviewed 15 older adults, ages 65 years to 91 years old, who had recently attempted suicide. They found that few well-established risk factors in (N)SSI literature were mentioned by the older adults.

Systematic Review on Risk and Protective Factors of NSSI-Linked Behaviors among Older Adults

To address this gap of research in elderly population, a systematic review was executed to present risk and protective factors of NSSI among this age group specifically. Since literature on NSSI in older adults is sparse, we also drew from literature on indirect self-harm and suicidal thoughts and behaviors in older adults throughout the past 20 years. This literature was used to identify needs for future research and practical implications for NSSI among older adults. Although prior systematic reviews have been performed on self-harm among older adults in general (e.g., Fässberg et al., 2016; Troya, Babatunde et al., 2019), no review has examined risk and protective factors divided according to their intent and directness.

Method

As this systematic review primarily included observational studies, the selection process of the Meta-Analyses and Systematic Reviews of Observational Studies in Epidemiology (MOOSE; Stroup et al., 2000) was used (see fig. 29.1). On September 1, 2020, four electronic databases, namely, EBSCOHost, PubMed, Scopus, and Web of Science, were systematically searched on title and abstract with the search string: ([elder* OR "older adults" OR "older people"] AND ["self-directed violence" OR self-injur* OR nssi OR self-harm* OR suicid* OR "indirect harm" OR "self-inflicted self-injury" OR self-mutilation OR automutilation] AND [risk OR protective OR epidemiology OR etiology]).

The applied eligibility criteria can be found in figure 29.1. As NSSI was not often delineated from suicidal behaviors before 2000, this systematic review searched for articles that were published during the past 20 years. Because a cut-off age of 60 years is applied in other studies among older adults (e.g., Lapierre et al., 2011; Troya, Babatunde et al., 2019), we defined an older adult as being 60 years or older. A protective and risk factor was defined as *"a measurable characterization of each subject in a specified population that precedes the outcome of interest and which can be used to divide the population into two groups (the high-risk and the low-risk groups that comprise the total population)"* (Kraemer et al.,

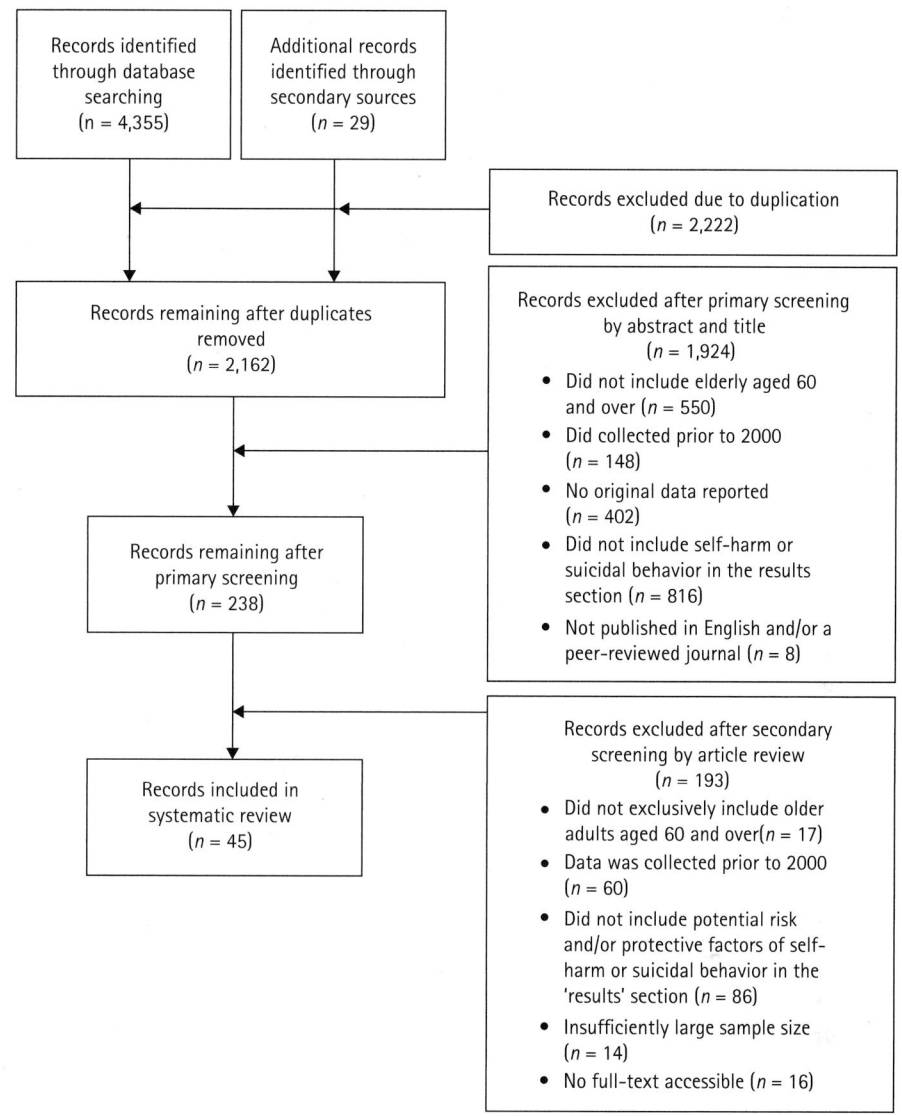

Figure 29.1 MOOSE Flow Chart of the Selection Process

1997, p. 338). For quantitative studies, the cut-off sample size was 30 cases (per group if comparing groups) based on the central limit theorem, which suggests that quantitative studies only require 30 cases to withstand violations of normality (Field, 2013; Rosenblatt, 1956). For qualitative studies, an inclusion criterion for the sample size was not applied due to the enormous difficulties researchers experience when determining an exact sample size a priori (Sim et al., 2018). Further, sample sizes are often absent or inconsistently/incompletely reported and inadequately assessed in qualitative studies (Vasileiou et al., 2018). To heighten the interrater reliability, studies were screened and selected independently by two researchers. Disagreements regarding the selection of studies were resolved through consensus.

Results

In the results section, the included studies are discussed in light of their methodological designs and outcomes.

Included Studies

In total, 45 articles were included (see Table 29.1). Of these articles, 34 were quantitative studies and 11 were qualitative studies. Regarding the quantitative studies, the majority applied a retrospective methodology ($n = 37$). Of these studies, 15 applied a case-control psychological autopsy design. Further, eight articles described a cohort or nationwide study, of which two were population-based and four articles contained a community-based study. Finally, only two studies used a longitudinal design. Of the 45 included articles, 19 studies took place in Asian countries, 11 in Europe, and 7 in North America. The majority of studies ($n = 22$) included suicide cases in community samples of older adults ($n = 12$). The remaining studies were primarily patient samples (i.e., Eds, general hospitals, and/or primary care facilities). Ages 60 ($n = 21$) and 65 years old ($n = 18$) were most frequently applied as the cut-off age. Because some articles did not explicitly mention the maximum age, this could not be reviewed. Regarding gender, 24 samples were predominantly male (i.e., > 50%) compared to 20 samples that mostly comprised females.

There were no studies found that specifically focused on NSSI or indirect self-injury among older adults. In total, 29 included articles discussed completed suicide, of which 29 studies analyzed risk factors and four protective factors. Suicide attempts among older adults were studied in 11 articles, of which 9 included risk factors and 3 protective factors. Six articles were retrieved that did not distinguish in intent and directness. Importantly, no factors were found for indirect suicidal behaviors specifically. This was also the case for direct and indirect nonsuicidal behaviors (see table 29.1).

Based upon the examination of the included studies, we can conclude that few researchers have made a distinction in suicidal intent and directness of self-harm. This is especially alarming in regard to NSSI, as NSSI has been repeatedly reported as an important precursor of suicidal behaviors, including death by suicide (Nock et al., 2008; Whalen et al., 2015). Due to the lack of researching this behavior specifically, barely anything is known about the etiology and epidemiology of NSSI among older adults. Moreover, Sher (2011) has raised the question whether suicide is predictable, as the event is both context and time dependent. Findings by Hung et al. (2015) support this questionability and especially the ability to identify high suicide risk groups in need of interventions. What has been studied however, is the ability to identify groups that are at high risk to engage in NSSI (Somer et al., 2015). Consequently, it is a necessity that future research among older adults focuses on NSSI specifically. This will also allow us to prevent the development of

Table 29.1 Characteristics of Included Studies

Author, year	N	Female (%)	Age (years)	Country	Type of behavior	Method and sample type	Risk (RF) and/or protective factors (PF)
(In) direct (non-)suicidal self-harm							
Cheung et al. (2017)	339	55.2	65–96: M = 75.0 SD = 7.6	New Zealand	Self-harm (i.e., act of intentional self-injury irrespective of intent)	Retrospective study; patients presented to seven EDs after a self-harm episode	History of self-harm; positive blood alcohol reading (RF)
Morgan et al. (2018)	2,854	58	65+:65–74 = 41.7% 75–84 = 37.4% 85+ = 20.9%	England	Suicidal and nonsuicidal self-injury	Retrospective study; primary care cohort of older adults with a self-harm episode	Diagnosed previous mental illness; previous physical health condition (RF)
Murphy et al. (2012)	1,777	56	60–97	England	Repeated self-harm (i.e., act of intentional self-injury irrespective of intent)	Prospective, population-based study; self-harm cohort presenting to general hospitals	Previous self-harm; previous psychiatric treatment; age 60–74 years (RF)
Troya, Dikomitis et al. (2019)	9	66.7	60–72:M = 63.4 SD = 3.7	England	Self-harm (i.e., act of intentional self-injury irrespective of intent)	Qualitative study; older adults engaging in self-harm	Accumulating stressors throughout the life-course (i.e., health problems, adverse childhood events, loss, loneliness, and interpersonal problems) (RF)
Wand et al. (2018)	30	50.0	80–102:M = 86.5	Australia	Self-harm (i.e., (in)direct act of intentional self-injury irrespective of intent)	Qualitative study; people recruited from two teaching hospitals and associated community services ages 80 years and over who had self-harmed within the previous month	Enough is enough; loneliness; disintegration of self; being a burden; cumulative adversity; hopelessness and endless suffering; helplessness with rejection; untenable situation (RF)

(continued)

Table 29.1 Continued

Author, year	N	Female (%)	Age (years)	Country	Type of behavior	Method and sample type	Risk (RF) and/or protective factors (PF)
Wand et al. (2019)	19	63.2	81–94; M = 86.2	Australia	Self-harm (i.e., (in)direct act of intentional self-injury irrespective of intent)	Qualitative study; patients at two teaching hospitals and associated community services who self-harmed	Denial and secrets; endless suffering; more invalidation; being heard; miserable in care (RF)
Direct Suicidal Self-harm							
Cao et al. (2019)	484	44.2	60+	China	Completed suicide	Case-control psychological autopsy study; suicide cases and community controls	Severely impaired capability of DLA; low family functioning; mental disorder; low social support; more than two life events in the last year (RF)
Carlsten et al. (2009)	238	16.4	65+; M = 75.0	Sweden	Completed suicide	Case-control study: suicide cases and population-based comparison subjects	Sedatives and hypnotics (RF)
Cheung et al. (2015)	212	25.5	65+; M = 76.0	New Zealand	Completed suicide	Qualitative study; suicide cases that had left a suicide note	Reduced QoL; life as a struggle; physical health problems; inability to function independently; fear of having to live at a rest home
Chiu et al. (2004)	170	Suicide cases: 54.3 Control subjects: 57.0	60+; Suicide cases: M = 74.6 SD = 7.7 Control subjects: M = 72.1 SD = 8.0	China	Completed suicide	Case-controlled psychological autopsy study; suicide cases and community-dwelling control subjects	Psychiatric problems (i.e., major depression, adjustment disorder, dysthymic disorder); non-affective psychotic disorders (i.e., schizophrenia); consulting a doctor within one month of suicide; history of suicidal attempt (RF)

Choi & Park (2020)	259,688	43.6	62–115:60–74 = 60.7% 75+ = 39.3%	South Korea	Completed suicide	Nationwide retrospective cohort study; outpatients	Cancer (i.e., bladder, head and neck, liver, lung, and stomach cancers), especially if a mental disorder diagnosis preceded cancer diagnosis (RF)
Choi, Kim et al. (2019)	558,147	58.7	60–119:60–74 = 79.0% 75+ = 21.0%	South Korea	Completed suicide	Nationwide retrospective cohort study; outpatients	Poverty, especially among males and young-old adults (RF)
Choi, Lee et al. (2019)	128,286	57.4	63–114:60–74 = 55.3% 75+ = 44.7%	South Korea	Completed suicide	Nationwide retrospective cohort study; outpatients	Poststroke patients during 1 year following discharge, especially patients who were diagnosed with depression (RF)
Choi, DiNitto et al. (2019)	16,924	16.37	65+:65–74 = 51.7% 75–84 = 34.2% 85+ = 14.1%	United States	Completed suicide	Retrospective study; death records	Physical health problems (i.e., suffering from bodily pain and cancer) (RF)
De Leo et al. (2013)	152	29.60	60–95	Australia	Completed suicide	Case-control psychological autopsy study; suicide cases and sudden death cases	Hopelessness in the past 12 months; history of previous suicide attempts; living alone; better self-maintenance (RF)
Hedna et al. (2020)	1 413 806	57.80	75–112:M = 80.5 SD = 6	Sweden	Completed suicide	National population-based study; Swedish residents	Being unmarried; being a woman who was born outside of Nordic countries (and who did not use ADs); being a man who did not use ADs and had a blue-collar job (RF); having had a blue-collar job in women who used ADs (BF)
Hung et al. (2015)	101,764	49.1	65+:65–74 = 60.1% 75–84 = 33.6% 85+ = 6.2%	Taiwan	Completed suicide	Community-based cohort study; Taipei City residents	Male sex; lower educational attainment; lower income; psychological distress (i.e., depressive mood and insomnia) (RF)

(*continued*)

Table 29.1 Continued

Author, year	N	Female (%)	Age (years)	Country	Type of behavior	Method and sample type	Risk (RF) and/or protective factors (PF)
Jang et al. (2020)	34,431	73.81	60+: M = 75 SD = 6.86	Korea	Completed suicide	Nationwide cohort study; patients with hip fracture and matched controls	Hip fracture (RF)
Kjølseth et al. (2010)	23	17.4	65–90: M = 78.0	Norway	Completed suicide	Psychological autopsy study; 63 informants	Experiences of life (i.e., this life has been lived and life as a burden); perception of themselves (i.e., losing oneself); conceptions of death (i.e., acknowledgement/acceptance and death is better than life) (RF)
Liu et al. (2017)	104	40.4	60+: M = 74.0 SD = 8.1	China	Completed suicide	Case-controlled psychological autopsy study	Greater tendency to experience negative life events; not living with a spouse (RF)
Ngui et al. (2015)	3,396	56.4	65–99: M = 74.3 SD = 5.9	Canada	Completed suicide	Case-control psychological autopsy study; suicide cases and control cases	*At the individual level*: male; aged 65–69; use of ED; hospitalization; mental disorder; dispense of psychoactive drug (RF)*At the area level*: higher population density; highest concentration of men and persons without any diploma; highest rate of unemployment (RF); higher concentration of lone families (BF)
Niu, Jia et al. (2020)	484	43.8	60+: Suicide cases: M = 74.4 SD = 8.2 Living controls: M = 74.1 SD = 8.2	China	Completed suicide	Case-control psychological autopsy study; suicide cases and living community controls	Unemployment; lower subjective social support; living alone; depressive symptoms; higher hopelessness; both higher levels of hopelessness and loneliness (RF)

Study	N	%	Age	Country	Outcome	Study type	Risk factors
Niu, Ma et al. (2020)	484	43.8	60+: Suicide cases: M = 74.4 SD = 8.2 Living controls: M = 74.1 SD = 8.2	China	Completed suicide	Case-control psychological autopsy study; suicide cases and living community controls	Depressive symptoms; hopelessness (RF)
Paraschakis et al. (2012)	118	30.5	60–97: M = 73.6 SD = 8.9	Greece	Completed suicide	Two-year psychological autopsy study; suicide cases	Psychiatric history, more specifically depression; physical illness (RF)
Seyfried et al. (2011)	294,952	2.8	60+: 60–69 = 14.3% 70–79 = 42.9% 80–89 = 40.1% 90+ = 2.7%	United States	Completed suicide	National, retrospective, cohort study; suicide cases of veterans diagnosed with dementia	White race; depression; younger age; history of inpatient psychiatric hospitalizations; prescription fills of antidepressants or anxiolytics (RF); nursing home admission (BF)
Schmutte & Wilkinson (2019)	26,884	30.9	65+: 65–69 = 29.4% 70–74 = 22.5% 75–79 = 18.3% 80–84 = 15.2% 85+ = 14.6%	United States	Completed suicide	National retrospective study; suicide cases	Physical illness (RF)
Torresani et al. (2014)	191	23.8	60+: 60–64 = 21.5% 65–69 = 18.8% 70–74 = 19.4% 75–79 = 15.7% 80–84 = 13.1% 85+ = 11.5%	Italy	Completed suicide	Psychological autopsy study; South Tyrolians in various residential settings	Low educational level; living in a one-person household; having seen a doctor in the past month; living in a residential facility (RF)
Vasiliadis et al. (2017)	2,987	61.7	64+:64–69 = 35.8% 70–74 = 26.0% 75–79 = 22.1% 80–84 = 11.6% 85–89 = 3.7% 90+ = 0.8%	Canada	Completed suicide	Case-control psychological autopsy study; suicide cases and control subjects	Presence of a psychiatric illness (RF)

(continued)

Table 29.1 Continued

Author, year	N	Female (%)	Age (years)	Country	Type of behavior	Method and sample type	Risk (RF) and/or protective factors (PF)
Wang et al. (2018)	15	46.7	65+	New Zealand	Completed suicide	Qualitative study; older Asians who lived in New Zealand	Suicide occurring in the context of a family (i.e., isolation, loss and adjustment and communication); declining health; violent suicide method (RF)
Wanta et al. (2009)	534	15.0	65–100: 65–74 = 47.6 75–84 = 37.4 85+ = 15.0	United States	Completed suicide	Retrospective study; Wisconsin residents who died by suicide	Being single; male; male in advancing age (RF)
Wei et al. (2020)	484	44.2	60+: $M = 74.0$ $SD = 8.2$	China	Completed suicide	Case-control psychological autopsy study; suicide cases and control subjects	Family dysfunction (RF)
Yeh et al. (2017)	2,528	34.8	65+: 65–74 = 50.1% 75–84 = 36.8% 85+ = 13.1%	Taiwan	Completed suicide	National pair-matched case-control study	Higher level of psychiatric contact in the preceding year; depression; bipolar disorder; physical illnesses; low-income households (RF)
Yeh et al. (2020)	2,528	34.8	65+: 65–74 = 50.1% 75–84 = 36.8% 85+ = 13.1%	Taiwan	Completed suicide	National pair-matched case-control study	Psychiatric and physical illnesses, especially depression, cancer and schizophrenia (RF)
Zhou et al. (2019)	484	44.2	60+: $M = 74.0$ $SD = 8.0$	China	Completed suicide	Matched case-control psychological autopsy study	Unstable marital status; unemployment; depressive symptoms; mental disorder (RF)

Study	N	%	Age	Country	Focus	Design	Key findings
Tsoh et al. (2005)	224	58.0	65+: Suicide completers: M = 77.2 SD = 7.2 Suicide attempters: M = 75.5 SD = 7.0 Comparison subjects: M = 74.8 SD = 7.3	China	Suicide attempt and completed suicide	Multi-group, case-controlled study; older adults who attempted suicide or completed suicide and comparison subjects	*Suicide attempt*: major depression; past suicide attempt(s); poorer function of self-care; arthritis; low Conscientiousness (RF) *Completed suicide*: major depression; past suicide attempt(s); arthritis; malignancy; change in abode; number of life events (RF) *Suicide attempt and completed suicide*: co-residence with children (BF)
Bonnewyn et al. (2014)	8	75.0	66–85: M = 71.8 SD = 7.0	Belgium	Suicide attempt	Qualitative study; inpatients of a psychiatric ward after making a suicide attempt	Experiencing life and self as disrupted after a loss; loneliness; loss of control: unwillingness to continue living the current live (RF)
Chen et al. (2014)	31	58.1	65–74: M = 70.3 SD = 2.71	Taiwan	Suicide attempt	Qualitative descriptive study; outpatients	Satisfied with one's life; suicide cannot resolve problems; fear of humiliating one's children; religious beliefs, never thought about suicide; living in harmony with nature (BF)
Crocker et al. (2006)	15	60.0	65–91: M = 69.5	United Kingdom	Suicide attempt	Qualitative study; older adults who had recently made a suicide attempt	Experiencing life as a struggle; trying to maintain control over life; feeling invisible or disconnected from others (RF)
Deuter et al. (2020)	7	71.43	60–82	Australia	Suicide attempt	Qualitative, multiple-case study; older adults who attempted suicide	Seeing value and meaning in surviving; focused decision-making; self-care; self-awareness, self-acceptance; spiritual faith; sense of responsibility and accountability; interpersonal relationships, meaningful activities and interests; community engagement; involvement of mental health services staff (BF)

(*continued*)

Table 29.1 Continued

Author, year	N	Female (%)	Age (years)	Country	Type of behavior	Method and sample type	Risk (RF) and/or protective factors (PF)
Kim et al. (2016)	78	42.3	65+: M = 72.3 SD = 6.8	Korea	Suicide attempt	Retrospective, comparative study; (non-)older patients who visited an ED	Chronic disease; depression; unemployment; cohabitation; high lethality (RF)
Ku et al. (2009)	19	0	73–85: M = 80.1 SD = 3.3	Taiwan	Suicide attempt	Qualitative study; older male residents who live in veterans' homes	Illness and pain; death of close relatives or friends; conflicts with family members; disputes with friends or workers; difficulty adopting to institutional life (RF)
Neufeld et al. (2015)	180,891	63.3	60+: 60–74 = 25.0% 75–84 = 42.0% 85+ = 33.0%	Canada	Suicide attempt	Longitudinal study; rural and urban home recipients with a hospital or ED visit for suicide attempts	Psychiatric diagnosis; alcohol use and dependence; loneliness, depression; more impairment in ADL and cognition (RF)
Oh et al. (2015)	655	57.7	60+: 60–79 = 86.6% 80+ = 13.4%	South Korea	Suicide attempt	Longitudinal study; community-dwelling older adults	Suicidality; living alone; problem drinking (RF)
Van Orden et al. (2015)	101	54.4	70–91: M = 79.7 SD = 5.3	Sweden	Suicide attempt	Prospective cohort study; older adults who presented to EDs for suicide attempts	Desire to escape; reduced functioning and autonomy; psychological problems including depression, somatic problems and physical pain; perceived burdensomeness; social problems that reflected either thwarted belongingness or family conflict; lack of meaning in life (RF)
Wiktorsson et al. (2016)	101	45.5	70–91: M = 79.6	Sweden	Suicide attempt	Study using an open-ended question; hospitalized older adults who attempted suicide	Somatic distress (RF)

or intervene at an earlier stage of the suicidal process and as NSSI is an important risk factor of suicidal behavior, disruption of NSSI may also lead to a disruption of SI.

In total, 34 quantitative studies and 11 qualitative studies were included in the outlined systematic review, of which a vast majority was conducted retrospectively (e.g., case-control psychological autopsy studies). Further, the majority solely included older adults living in an Asian country. Protective factors were included in only five studies. Regarding NSSI, no studies could be retrieved. This is due to the lack of applying a distinction (i.e., suicidal vs. nonsuicidal and direct vs. indirect) within studies. Consequently, no specific risk or protective factors for these behaviors can be reported. This is an important gap in the literature as studies show that NSSI is indeed prevalent among older adults (e.g., Martin & Swannell, 2016). Moreover, Parks and Fieldman (2006) hypothesized that NSSI methods and functions may be different in older adults.

No studies were retrieved regarding indirect self-injurious behaviors with or without suicidal intent. Concerning retrieved risk factors for completed suicide, the following themes apply: a lower socioeconomic status (e.g., Niu, Jia et al., 2020), indices of social isolation (e.g., Hedna et al., 2020), functional impairment caused by physical or mental illnesses (e.g., Yeh et al., 2020), and family discord (e.g., Wei et al., 2020). These themes corresponded with those of the included studies that focused on suicide attempts specifically (e.g., Van Orden et al., 2015). Some of these themes can be linked to and explained by the *Interpersonal Theory of Suicide* (Joiner, 2005). First, social isolation is an important indicator of thwarted belongingness, that can be found in older adults who live alone (e.g., Torresani et al., 2014), are unwed or single (e.g., Hedna et al., 2020), report a lower social support (e.g., Niu, Jia et al., 2020), and more loneliness (Niu, Jia et al., 2020). This was in line with the findings of the included studies that solely focused on suicide attempts (e.g., Bonnewyn et al., 2018; Crocker et al., 2006; Kim et al., 2016; Neufeld et al., 2015; Oh et al., 2015; Van Orden et al., 2015). These findings also align with protective factors for suicide attempts, such as the involvement of mental health services staff, community engagement, engaging in meaningful activities and interests, and interpersonal relationships (Deuter et al., 2020). Next, perceived burdensomeness also represents a key factor in Joiner's (2005) tripartite model of suicide. This was confirmed repeatedly by the included studies in this review (Kjølseth et al., 2010; Van Orden et al., 2015). Perceived burdensomeness arises when the need for social competence is unmet (Ryan & Deci, 2000; Van Orden et al., 2012) and was found to be associated with functional impairment (Conwell et al., 2010) caused by physical health problems (e.g., Yeh et al., 2020), mental problems (e.g., Niu, Jia et al., 2020), and family discord (Duberstein et al., 2004; Heikkinen et al., 1994). This was supported by the identification of low family functioning and family dysfunction as risk factors for completed suicide (e.g., Wei et al., 2020) and co-residence with children (Tsoh et al., 2005) as a protective factor. Yet again, the above-mentioned risk factors for completed suicide are congruous with the predictors of suicide attempts that were reported in the included studies (see Victor et al., this volume) (e.g., Bonnewyn et al., 2018; Wiktorsson et al., 2016). Six studies focused on (in)direct self-harm irrespective of intent among older adults. These studies identified adverse and/or stressful life events over the life-course (Troya, Dikomitis et al., 2019), interpersonal problems (Troya, Dikomitis et al., 2019; Wand et al., 2018), and physical (e.g., Morgan et al., 2018) and/or mental problems (Morgan et al., 2018; Troya, Dikomitis et al., 2019) as risk factors. As can be expected, most of these older adults also had a mental health services, psychiatric, or self-harm history (Cheung et al., 2017; Murphy et al., 2012).

Overarchingly, three themes arose: physical (e.g., declining physical health), psychological (e.g., psychiatric disorder), and social loss/difficulties (e.g., loneliness). (See Fox, this volume, and James & Gibb, this volume, for an overview on inter- and intrapersonal risk factors.) Further, few studies made a distinction in suicidal intent and directness of self-harm. Compared to risk and protective factors of NSSI among adolescents and (young) adults, some of these findings were compatible (e.g., family conflict and close friends) (e.g., Aggarwal et al., 2017). However, one theme seemed to be specific for NSSI-related behaviors among older adults, namely, experiences of loss (e.g., Bonnewyn et al., 2018).

Our findings indicate that few studies make a distinction in suicidal intent and directness of self-harm. This highlights the need for studies that do apply a clear distinction, as this will allow us to determine overlapping and/or unique risk and protective factors of specific forms of self-harm among older adults (see Burke et al., this volume). Moreover, it would provide the opportunity to better understand the role that NSSI plays in suicidal self-harm. Furthermore, this systematic review applied the MOOSE method, which is a standardized selection process for observational studies (Brooke et al., 2021; Stroup et al., 2000). Our search strategies were provided in detail and the applied in- and exclusion criteria were predetermined. This heightens the replicability of the systematic review. Also, multiple databases were systematically searched to ensure the minimalization of missing studies that complied to the in- and exclusion criteria. The eligibility of the studies was assessed by two independent reviewers as to ensure interrater reliability (Belur et al., 2018).

Aside from these strengths, some limitations should also be taken into account. First, not all included studies exhaustively defined the behaviors included. Second, the validity of systematic reviews may be subverted by a publication and reporting bias (Dwan et al., 2013; Song et al., 2010). Next, the assessment of the quality of the included studies was limited to an unstandardized, subjective judgment by both reviewers and the employment of a cut-off sample size as an inclusion criterion. Further, this systematic review did not set out to quantify the magnitude of the identified risk factors. Finally, most included studies were conducted retrospectively. Therefore, caution is warranted regarding causation.

Implications for Future Research

Definitions applied to self-harm are often inconsistent across studies. Consequently, future research should focus on constructing a valid, reliable definition of these behaviors.

Furthermore, most studies include a wide age range. It has been observed that NSSI patterns are age group-dependent among older adults. Researchers believe these differences will further increase as the life expectancy is gradually rising (Choi et al., 2016; Waern et al., 2003). Future studies should bear these differences in mind and execute age-specific analyses.

In regard to the systematic review's methodology, a vast majority of the included studies were conducted retrospectively. This can lead to recall bias, which signifies the effect of the period of time between the event and assessment of the event on the response reliability (Niu, Ma et al., 2020; Torresani et al., 2014; Wei et al., 2020). This is especially the case for studies that collect data by proxy informants (Conner et al., 2012; Heikkinen et al., 1992), although Conner et al. (2001) found support for the validity of proxy informant-based data in suicide research specifically. Consequently, a need for longitudinal studies arises. Most included studies collected data in hospital settings or via a psychological autopsy design, but such data are often characterized by multiple limitations. For example, reported mental health problems are often based on clinical judgment instead of validated questionnaires (Cheung et al., 2017) and therefore potentially mislabel NSSI behaviors (Rhodes et al., 2002; Wanta et al., 2009). Additionally, stigma regarding NSSI may cause an underestimation of these behaviors. Finally, no studies that were included in the systematic review applied a cross-cultural design. Most were conducted in Asian countries, suggesting future studies might be able to uncover cross-cultural differences.

Implications for Clinicians

The few studies that have investigated NSSI among older adults thus far indicate that NSSI does occur in this population (i.e., Choi et al., 2016; Martin & Swannell, 2016). As NSSI has been significantly associated with suicidal behaviors (Hamza et al., 2012; Ose et al., 2021), the current gap in the literature is alarming. Consequently, clinicians should be attentive for NSSI among older adults. Alertness for such behaviors may be heightened by inquiring about NSSI engagement in their screening. As NSSI often finds its onset in adolescence (Nock, 2010), lifetime engagement should also be assessed. Furthermore, as stigma often arises when talking about NSSI (e.g., Burke et al., 2019), clinicians should approach this topic systematically and respectfully and use adequate language (Hasking & Boyes, 2018). Finally, although the risk and protective factors found in the systematic review do not specifically apply to NSSI, research has shown a strong overlap between risk and protective factors of NSSI and those of suicidal behaviors. Clinicians may rely on the factors identified by the systematic review to assess NSSI risk in older adults.

Conclusion

This chapter evaluated the current research field of NSSI among older adults specifically by reporting a recent systematic review that distinguished between suicidal intent and directness of self-harm. First, few studies thus far have applied this distinction. This may lead to biased findings regarding prevalence rates, risk and protective factors, and interventions. Next, no studies zoomed in on NSSI, which calls for NSSI studies among this age group. Finally, most studies applied a retrospective study design and were performed in Asian countries. Future research should apply a longitudinal, cross-cultural design that distinguishes between the specific forms of self-harm. This will not only allow us to intervene at an earlier stage in the suicidal process but also help to prevent NSSI repetition.

References

Aggarwal, S., Patton, G., Reavley, N., Sreenivasan, S. A., & Berk, M. (2017). Youth self-harm in low- and middle-income countries: Systematic review of the risk and protective factors. *International Journal of Social Psychiatry*, *63*(4), 359–375. https://doi.org/10.1177/0020764017700175

Belur, J., Tompson, L., Thornton, A., & Simon, M. (2018). Interrater reliability in systematic review methodology: Exploring variation in coder decision-making. *Sociological Methods & Research*, *50*(2), 837–865. https://doi.org/10.1177/0049124118799372

Bonnewyn, A., Shah, A., Bruffaerts, R., Schoevaerts, K., Rober, P., Van Parys, H., & Demyttenaere, K. (2014). Reflections of older adults on the process preceding their suicide attempt: A qualitative approach. *Death Studies*, *38*(9), 612–618. https://doi.org/10.1080/07481187.2013.835753

Bonnewyn, A., & Voshaar, R. C. O. (2018). Suïcidaliteit en suïcide bij ouderen [Suicidality and suicide in elderly]. In R. C. O. Voshaar, R. van der Mast, M. Stek, F. Verhey and M. Vandenbulcke (Eds.). *Handboek ouderenpsychiatrie* [*Handbook geriatric psychiatry*] (pp. 669–680). De Tijdstroom.

Brooke, B. S., Schwartz, T. A., & Pawlik, T. M. (2021). MOOSE reporting guidelines for meta-analyses of observational studies. *JAMA Surgery*, *156*(8), 787–788. https://doi.org/10.1001/jamasurg.2021.0522

Burke, T. A., Piccirillo, M. L., Moore-Berg, S. L., Alloy, L. B., & Heimberg, R. G. (2019). The stigmatization of non-suicidal self-injury. *Journal of Clinical Psychology*, *75*(3), 481–498. https://doi.org/10.1002/jclp.22713

Cao, R., Jia, C., Ma, Z., & Zhou, L. (2019). Disability in daily living activities, family disfunction, and late-life suicide in rural China: A case-control psychological autopsy study. *Frontiers in Psychiatry*, *10*, Article 827. https://doi.org/10.3389/fpsyt.2019.00827

Carlsten, A., & Waern, M. (2009). Are sedatives and hypnotics associated with increased suicide in the older adults? *BMC Geriatrics*, *9*, Article 20. https://doi.org/10.1186/1471-2318-9-20

Chen, Y., Tsai, Y., Lee, S., & Lee, H. (2014). Protective factors against suicide among young-old Chinese outpatients. *BMC Public Health*, *14*, Article 372. https://doi.org/10.1186/1471-2458-14-372

Cheung, G., Foster, G., de Beer, W., Gee, S., Hawkes, T., Rimkeit, S., Tan, Y. M., Merry, S., & Sundram, F. (2017). Predictors for repeat self-harm and suicide among older people within 12 months of a self-harm presentation. *International Psychogeriatrics*, *29*(8), 1237–1245. https://doi.org/10.1017/S1041610217000308

Cheung, G., Merry, S., & Sundram, F. (2015). Late-life suicide: Insight on motives and contributors derived from suicide notes. *Journal of Affective Disorders*, *185*, 17–23. https://doi.org/10.1016/j.jad.2015.06.035

Chiu, H. F. K., Yip, P. S. F., Chi, I., Chan, S., Tsoh, J., Kwan, C. W., Li, S. F., Conwell, Y., & Caine, E. (2004). Older adults suicide in Hong Kong—A case-controlled psychological autopsy study. *Acta Psychiatrica Scandinavica*, *109*, 299–305. https://doi.org/10.1046/j.1600-0447.2003.00263.x

Choi, J. W., Kim, T. H., Shin, J., & Han, E. (2019). Poverty and suicide risk in older adults: A retrospective longitudinal cohort study. *Geriatric Psychiatry*, *34*, 1565–1571. https://doi.org/10.1002/gps.5166

Choi, J. W., Lee, S. G., Kim, T. H., & Han, E. (2019). Poststroke suicide risk among older adults in South Korea: A retrospective longitudinal cohort study. *Geriatric Psychiatry*, *35*, 282–289. https://doi.org/10.1002/gps.5245

Choi, J. W., & Park, E. (2020). Suicide risk after cancer diagnosis among older adults: A nationwide retrospective cohort study. *Journal of Geriatric Oncology*, *11*, 814–819. https://doi.org/10.1016/j.jgo.2019.11.006

Choi, N. G., DiNitto, D. M., Marti, C. N., & Choi, B. Y. (2016). Nonsuicidal self-injury and suicide attempts among ED patients older than 50 years: Comparison of risk factors and ED visit outcomes. *American Journal for Emergency Medicine*, *34*(6), 1016–1021. https://doi.org/10.1016/j.ajem.2016.02.058

Choi, N. G., DiNitto, D. M., Marti, N., & Conwell, Y. (2019). Physical health problems as a late-life suicide precipitant: Examination of coroner/medical examiner and law enforcement reports. *The Gerontologist*, *59*(2), 356–367. https://doi.org/10.1093/geront/gnx143

Conner, K. R., Beautrais, A. L., Brent, D. A., Conwell, Y., Philips, M. R., & Schneider, B. (2012). The next generation of psychological autopsy studies. Part I. Interview content. *Suicide and Life-Threatening Behavior*, *41*(6), 594–613. https://doi.org/10.1111/j.1943-278X.2011.00057.x

Conner, K. R., Duberstein, P. R., & Conwell, Y. (2001). The validity of proxy-based data in suicide research: A study of patients 50 years of age and older who attempted suicide. I. Psychiatric diagnoses. *Acta Psychiatrica Scandinavica*, *104*(3), 204–209. https://doi.org/10.1034/j.1600-0447.2001.00405.x

Conwell, Y., Duberstein, P. R., Hirsch, J. L., Conner, K. R., Eberly, S., & Caine, E. D. (2010). Health status and suicide in the second half of life. *International Journal of Geriatric Psychiatry*, *25*, 271–379. https://doi.org/10.1002/gps.2348

Crocker, L., Clare, L., & Evans, K. (2006). Giving up or finding a solution? The experience of attempted suicide in later life. *Aging and Mental Health*, *10*(6), 638–647. https://doi.org/10.1080/13607860600640905

De Leo, D., Draper, B. M., Snowdon, J., & Kõlves, K. (2013). Suicides in older adults: A case-control psychological autopsy study in Australia. *Journal of Psychiatric Research*, *47*(7), 980–988. https://doi.org/10.1016/j.jpsychires.2013.02.009

Deuter, K., Procter, N., & Evans, D. (2020). Protective factors for older suicide attempters: Findings reasons and experiences to live. *Death Studies*, *44*(7), 430–439. https://doi.org/10.1080/07481187.2019.1578303

Duberstein, P. R., Conwell, Y., Conner, K. R., Eberly, S., & Caine, E. D. (2004). Suicide at 50 years of age and older: perceived physical illness, family discord and financial strain. *Psychological Medicine*, *34*(1), 137–146. https://doi.org/10.1017/s0033291703008584

Dwan, K., Gamble, C., Williamson, P. R., & Kirkham, J. J. (2013). Systematic review of the empirical evidence of study publication bias and outcome reporting bias—An updated review. *PLoS One*, *8*(7), Article e66844. https://doi.org/10.1371/journal.pone.0066844

Fässberg, M. M., Cheung, G., Canetto, S. S., Erlangsen, A., Lapierre, S., Lindner, R., Draper, B., Gallo, J. J., Wong, C., Wu, J., Duberstein, P., & Waern, M. (2016). A systematic review of physical illness, functional disability, and suicidal behaviour among older adults. *Aging & Mental Health*, *20*(2), 166–194. https://doi.org/10.1080/13607863.2015.1083945

Field, A. (2013). *Discovering statistics using IBM SPSS statistics*. SAGE.

Hamza, C. A., Stewart, S. L., & Willoughby, T. (2012). Examining the link between nonsuicidal self-injury and suicidal behavior: A review of the literature and an integrated model. *Clinical Psychology Review*, *32*(6), 482–495. https://doi.org/10.1016/j.cpr.2012.05.003

Hasking, P., & Boyes, M. (2018). Cutting words: A commentary on language and stigma in the context of nonsuicidal self-injury. *The Journal of Nervous and Mental Disease*, *206*(11), 829–833. https://doi.org/10.1097/NMD.0000000000000899

Hedna, K., Hensing, G., Skoog, I., Fastbom, J., & Waern, M. (2020). Sociodemographic and gender determinants of late-life suicide in users and non-users of antidepressants. *European Journal of Public Health*, *30*(5), 958–964. https://doi.org/10.1093/eurpub/ckaa114

Heikkinen, M., Aro, H., & Lonnqvist, J. (1992). The partner's views on precipitant stressors in suicide. *Acta Psychiatrica Scandinavica*, *85*(5), 380–384. https://doi.org/10.1111/j.1600-0447.1992.tb10323.x

Heikkinen, M., Aro, H., & Lönnqvist, J. (1994). Recent life events, social support and suicide. *Acta Psychiatrica Scandinavica*, *89*, 65–72. https://doi.org/10.1111/j.1600-0447.1994.tb05805.x

Hung, G. C., Kwok, C., Yip, P. S. F., Gunnell, D., & Chen, Y. (2015). Predicting suicide in older adults—A community-based cohort study in Taipei City, Taiwan. *Journal of Affective Disorders*, *172*, 165–170. https://doi.org/10.1016/j.jad.2014.09.037

Jang, S., Yang, D., Cha, Y., Yoo, H., Kim, K., & Choy, W. (2020). Suicide in elderly patients with hip fracture. *The Journal of Bone and Joint Surgery*, *102*, 1059–1065. https://doi.org/10.2106/JBJS.19.01436

Joiner, T. E. (2005). *Why people die by suicide*. Harvard University Press.

Kim, K. H., Jeong, K. Y., Lee, J. S., Choi, H. S., Hong, H. P., & Ko, Y. G. (2016). The characteristics of older adults patients with suicide attempts: A comparative study with non-older adults patients. *Annals of Geriatric Medicine and Research*, *20*(4), 209–220. https://doi.org/10.4235/agmr.2016.20.4.209

Kjølseth, I., Øivind, E., & Steihaug, S. (2010). Why suicide? Elderly people who committed suicide and their experience of life in the period before their death. *International Psychogeriatrics*, *22*(2), 209–2018. https://doi.org/10.1017/S1041610209990949

Kraemer, H. C., Kazdin, A. E., Offord, D. R., Kessler, R. C., Jensen, P. S., & Kupfer, D. J. (1997). Coming to terms with the terms of risk. *Archives of General Psychiatry, 54*(4), 337–343. https://doi.org/10.1001/archpsyc.1997.01830160065009

Ku, Y., Tsai, Y., Lin, Y., & Lin, Y. (2009). Suicide experiences among institutionalized older veterans in Taiwan. *The Gerontologist, 49*(6), 746–754. https://doi.org/10.1093/geront/gnp114

Lapierre, S., Erlangsen, A., Waern, M., De Leo, D., Oyama, H., Scocco, P., Gallo, J., Szanto, K., Conwell, Y., Draper, B., & Quinnett, P. (2011). A systematic review of older adults suicide prevention programs. *Crisis, 32*(2), 88–98. https://doi.org/10.1027/0227-5910/a000076

Liu, B., Qin, P., & Jia, C. (2017). Behavior characteristics and risk factors for suicide among the older adults in rural China. *The Journal of Nervous and Mental Disease, 206*(3), 195–201. https://doi.org/10.1097/NMD.0000000000000728

Martin, G., & Swannell, S. (2016). Non-suicidal self-injury in the over 40s: Results from a large national epidemiological survey. *Epidemiology (Sunnyvale), 6*(5), Article 266. https://doi.org/10.4172/2161-1165.1000266

Morgan, C., Webb, R. T., Carr, M. J., Kontopantelis, E., Chew-Graham, C. A., Kapur, N., & Ashcroft, D. M. (2018). Self-harm in a primary care cohort of older people: Incidence, clinical management, and risk of suicide and other causes of death. *The Lancet Psychiatry, 5*(11), 905–912. https://doi.org/10.1016/S2215-0366(18)30348-1

Murphy, E., Kapur, N., Webb, R., Purandare, N., Hawton, K., Bergen, H., Waters, K., & Cooper, J. (2012). Risk factors for repetition and suicide following self-harm in older adults: Multicentre cohort study. *British Journal of Psychiatry, 200*, 399–404. https://doi.org/10.1192/bjp.bp.111.094177

Neufeld, E., Hirdes, J. P., Perlman, C. M., & Rabinowitz, T. (2015). A longitudinal examination of rural status and suicide risk. *Healthcare Management Forum, 28*(4), 129–133. https://doi.org/10.1177/0840470415581233

Ngui, A.N., Vasiliadis, H., & Préville, M. (2015). Individual and area-level factors correlated with death by suicide in older adults. *Preventive Medicine, 75*, 44–48. https://doi.org/10.1016/j.ypmed.2015.03.015

Niu, L., Jia, C., Ma, Z., Wang, G., Sun, B., Zhang, D., & Zhou, L. (2020). Loneliness, hopelessness and suicide in later life: A case–control psychological autopsy study in rural China. *Epidemiology and Psychiatric Sciences, 29*, 1–7. https://doi.org/10.1017/S2045796020000335

Niu, L., Ma, Z., Jia, C., & Zhou, L. (2020). Gender-specific risk for late-life suicide in rural China: A case-control psychological autopsy study. *Age and Ageing, 49*(4), 683–687. https://doi.org/10.1093/ageing/afaa036

Nock, M. K. (2010). Self-injury. *Annual Review of Clinical Psychology, 6*, 339–363. https://doi.org/10.1146/annurev.clinpsy.121208.131258

Nock, M. K., Borges, G., Bromet, E. J., Cha, C. B., Kessler, R. C., & Lee, S. (2008). Suicide and suicidal behavior. *Epidemiologic Reviews, 30*(1), 133–154. https://doi.org/10.1093/epirev/mxn002

Oh, D. J., Park, J. Y., Oh, M., Kim, K., Hong, J., Kim, T., Han, J. W., Kim, T. H., & Kim, K. W. (2015). Suicidality-based prediction of suicide attempts in a community-dwelling older adults population: Results from the Osan Mental Health Survey. *Journal of Affective Disorders, 184*, 286–292. https://doi.org/10.1016/j.jad.2015.06.010

Ose, S. O., Tveit, T., & Mehlum, L. (2021). Non-suicidal self-injury (NSSI) in adult psychiatric outpatients—A nationwide study. *Journal of Psychiatric Research, 133*, 1–9. https://doi.org/10.1016/j.jpsychires.2020.11.031

Paraschakis, A., Douzenis, A., Michopoulos, I., Christodoulou, C., Vassilopoulou, K., Koutsaftis, F., & Lykouras, L. (2012). Archives of Gerontology *and Geriatrics, 54*, 136–139. https://doi.org/10.1016/j.archger.2011.02.011

Parks, S., & Feldman, S. (2006). Self-injurious behavior in the elderly. *The Consultant Pharmacist, 21*(11), 905–910. https://doi.org/10.4140/TCP.n.2006.905

Rhodes, A. E., Links, P. S., Streiner, D. L., Dawe, I., Cass, D., & Janes, S. (2002). Do hospital E-codes consistently capture suicidal behaviour? *Chronic Disease and Cancer, 23*(4), 139–145.

Rosenblatt, M. (1956). A central limit theorem and a strong mixing condition. *Proceedings of the National Academy of Sciences of the United States of America, 42*(1), 42–47. https://doi.org/10.1073/pnas.42.1.43

Ryan, R. M., & Deci, E. L. (2000). Self-determination theory and the facilitation of intrinsic motivation, social development, and well-being. *American Psychologist, 55*(1), 68–78. https://doi.org/10.1037110003-066X.55.1.68

Schmutte, T. J., & Wilkinson, S. T. (2019). Suicide in older adults with and without known mental illness: Results from the National Violent Death Reporting System, 2003-2016. *American Journal of Preventive Medicine*, *58*(4), 584–590. https://doi.org/10.1016/j.amepre.2019.11.001

Seyfried, L. S., Kales, H. C., Ignacio, R. V., Conwell, Y., & Valenstein, M. (2011). Predictors of suicide in patients with dementia. *Alzheimer's & Dementia*, *7*, 567–573. https://doi.org/10.1016/j.jalz.2011.01.006

Sher, L. (2011). Is it possible to predict suicide? *Australian & New Zealand Journal of Psychiatry*, *45*(4), Article 341. https://doi.org/10.3109/00048674.2011.560136

Sim, J., Saunders, B., Waterfield, J., & Kingstone, T. (2018). Can sample size in qualitative research be determined a priori? *International Journal of Social Research Methodology*, *21*(5), 619–634. https://doi.org/10.1080/13645579.2018.1454643

Somer, O., Bildik, T., Kabukçu-Başay, B., Güngör, D., Başay, Ö., & Farmer, R. F. (2015). Prevalence of non-suicidal self-injury and distinct groups of self-injurers in a community sample of adolescents. *Social Psychiatry and Psychiatric Epidemiology*, *50*, 1163–1171. https://doi.org/10.1007/s00127-015-1060-z

Song, F., Parekh, S., Hooper, L., Loke, Y. K., Ryder, J., Sutton, A. J., Hing, C., Kwok, C. S., Pang, C., & Harvey, I. (2010). Dissemination and publication of research findings: An updated review of related biases. *Health Technology Assessment*, *14*(8), 1–193. https://doi.org/10.3310/hta14080

Stroup, D. F., Berlin, J. A., Morton, S. C., Olkin, I., Williamson, G. D., Rennie, D., Moher, D., Becker, B. J., Sipe, T. A., & Thacker, S. B. (2000). Meta-analysis of observational studies in epidemiology. A proposal for reporting. *JAMA*, *283*(15), 2008–2012. https://doi.org/10.1001/jama.283.15.2008

Torresani, S., Toffol, E., Scocco, P., & Fanolla, A. (2014). Suicide in older adults South Tyroleans in various residential settings at the time of death: A psychological autopsy study. *Psychogeriatrics*, *14*, 101–109. https://doi.org/10.1111/psyg.12046

Troya, M., Babatunde, O. O., Polidano, K., Bartlam, B., McCloskey, E., Dikomitis, L., & Chew-Graham, C. A. (2019). Self-harm in older adults: A systematic review. *British Journal of Psychiatry*, *214*(4), 186–200. https://doi.org/10.1192/bjp.2019.11

Troya, M. I., Dikomitis, L., Babatunde, O. O., Bartlam, B., & Chew-Graham, C. A. (2019). Understanding self-harm in older adults: A qualitative study. *EClinical Medicine*, *12*, 52–61. https://doi.org/10.1016/j.eclinm.2019.06.002

Tsoh, J., Chiu, H., Duberstein, P. R., Chan, S. S. M., Chi, I., Yip, P. S. F., & Conwell, Y. (2005). Attempted suicide in older adults Chinese persons: A multi-group, controlled study. *American Journal of Geriatric Psychiatry*, *13*(7), 562–571. https://doi.org/10.1176/appi.ajgp.13.7.562

Van Orden, K. A., Cukrowicz, K. C., Witte, T. K., & Joiner, T. E. (2012). Thwarted belongingness and perceived burdensomeness: Construct validity and psychometric properties of the Interpersonal Needs Questionnaire. *Psychological Assessment*, *24*(1), 197–215. https://doi.org/10.1037/a0025358

Van Orden, K. A., Wiktorsson, S., Duberstein, P., Berg, A. I., Fässberg, M. M., & Waern, M. (2015). Reasons for attempted suicide in later life. *American Journal of Geriatric Psychiatry*, *23*(5), 536–544. https://doi.org/10.1016/j.jagp.2014.07.003

Vasileiou, K., Barnett, J., Thorpe, S., & Young, T. (2018). Characterising and justifying sample size sufficiency in interview-based studies: Systematic analysis of qualitative health research over a 15-year period. *BMC Medical Research Methodology*, *18*, 148. https://doi.org/10.1186/s12874-018-0594-7

Vasiliadis, H., Lamoureux-Lamarche, C., & Gontijo Guerra, S. (2017). Gender and age group differences in suicide risk associated with co-morbid physical and psychiatric disorders in older adults. *International Psychogeriatrics*, *29*(2), 249–257. https://doi.org/10.1017/S1041610216001290

Waern, M., Rubenowitz, E., & Wilhelmson, K. (2003). Predictors of suicide in the old elderly. *Gerontology*, *49*, 328–334. https://doi.org/10.1159/000071715

Wand, A. P. F., Draper, B., Brodaty, H., & Peisah, C. (2019). Self-harm in the very old one year later: Has anything changed? *International Psychogeriatrics*, *31*(11), 1559–1568. https://doi.org/10.1017/S1041610219000632

Wand, A. P. F., Peisah, C., Draper, B., & Brodaty, H. (2018). Why do the very old self-harm? A qualitative study. *American Journal of Geriatric Psychiatry*, *26*(8), 862–871. https://doi.org/10.1016/j.jagp.2018.03.005

Wang, J., Ho, E., Au, P., & Cheung, G. (2018). Late-life suicide in Asian people living in New Zealand: A qualitative study of coronial records. *Psychogeriatrics*, *18*, 259–267. https://doi.org/10.1111/psyg.12318

Wanta, B. T., Schlotthauer, A. E., Guse, C. E., & Hargarten, S. W. (2009). The burden of suicide in Wisconsin's older adult population. *Wisconsin Medical Journal*, *108*(2), 87–93.

Wei, Y., Liu, B., Ma, Z., Zhou, L., & Jia, C. (2020). Family functioning and suicide among the older adults in rural China: A case-control psychological autopsy study. *The Journal of Nervous and Mental Disease, 208*(2), 131–137. https://doi.org/10.1097/NMD.0000000000001116

Whalen, D. J., Dixon-Gordon, K., Belden, A. C., Barch, D., & Luby, J. L. (2015). Correlates and consequences of suicidal cognitions and behaviors in children ages 3-7. *Journal of American Academy of Child and Adolescent Psychiatry, 54*(11), 926–937. https://doi/org/10.1080/13811118.2017.1413468

Wiktorsson, S., Berg, A.I., Wilhelmson, K., Fässberg, M. M., Van Orden, K., Duberstein, P., & Waern, M. (2016). Assessing the role of physical illness in young old and older suicide attempters. *International Journal of Geriatric Psychiatry, 31*, 771–774. https://doi.org/10.1002/gps.4390

Yeh, S., Ng, Y., & Wu, S. (2017). Risk of suicide according to the level of psychiatric contact in the older people: Analysis of national health insurance databases in Taiwan. *Comprehensive Psychiatry, 74*, 189–195. https://doi.org/10.1016/j.comppsych.2017.01.016

Yeh, S., Ng, Y., & Wu, S. (2020). Association of psychiatric and physical illnesses with suicide in older adults in Taiwan. *Journal of Affective Disorders, 264*, 425–429. https://doi.org/10.1016/j.jad.2019.11.070

Zhou, L., Wang, G., Jia, C., & Ma, Z. (2019). Being left-behind, mental disorder, and older adults suicide in rural China: A case–control psychological autopsy study. *Psychological Medicine, 49*, 458–464. https://doi.org/10.1017/S003329171800106X

CHAPTER 30

What Do NCI Data Tell Us About People Who Need Support for Self-Injurious Behavior

Valerie J. Bradley, Dorothy Hiersteiner, David A. Rotholz, *and* Henan Li

> **Abstract**
>
> This chapter provides an overview of the data from the National Core Indicators (NCI) In-Person Survey (IPS) regarding people who need support for self-injurious behavior (SIB). It primarily focuses on the characteristics of people who require support for SIB who receive services from state intellectual and developmental disabilities (IDD) systems and the community. SIB poses challenges when it comes to planning for and supporting a person to live and participate in their community. Thus, supporting people who require support for SIB entails a significant investment of staff and financial resources. The chapter states that the NCI captured the reported need for SIB-related supports, but the provisions and quality of those supports remain unknown.
>
> **Key Words:** National Core Indicators, self-injurious behavior, support, intellectual and developmental disabilities systems, provisions, financial resources

Overview

For people with intellectual and developmental disabilities (IDD), self-injurious behavior (SIB) can have serious negative effects on both health and quality of life (Symons et al., 1999). It can also pose challenges when it comes to planning for and supporting a person to live and participate in their community. Not only can the presence of SIB lead to permanent physical harm, but it can also lead to social isolation, anxiety, the imposition of caretaking challenges on families, and, ultimately, institutionalization. Finally, supporting people who require support for SIB entails a significant investment of staff and financial resources.

Knowledge about the characteristics and etiology of self-injurious behavior continues to grow as researchers and clinicians seek to isolate and describe the distinct set of behaviors that compose SIB and to identify the individuals most likely to exhibit SIB (Richman et al., 2013; Rojahn et al., 2007). However, many of the studies of SIB were focused on people with IDD residing in institutions. The purpose of this chapter is to shed light on the characteristics of people who require support for SIB who receive services from state developmental disabilities (DD) systems and by and large live in the community. To provide this unique insight, the authors will use data from the National Core Indicators® (NCI®) In-Person Survey (IPS) (2018–2019)—data that also make it possible to assess a range of quality of life and other outcomes experienced by people who receive services from state DD systems and need support for SIB.

Definition and Characteristics of SIB

It is important to note which behaviors are outside the definition of SIB. Over the years, there has been a tendency among some to cluster SIB with aggressive, destructive, or stereotypical behaviors (Rojahn et al., 2007). However, SIB may be relatively independent of aggressive and stereotyped behaviors. In a meta-analysis of the characteristics of individuals with a range of behavioral challenges, the authors found that "from a psychometric view . . . self-injurious behavior topographies formed a separate and independent construct" (p. 15). They note, however, that the construct is still not tightly defined. SIB in people with IDD is also distinguished from instances of self-injurious or self-mutilation associated with psychiatric disorders in the general population—including cutting, burning, or ingestion of toxic substances (Rojahn et al., 2007).

For people with IDD, Rojahn et al. assert that self-injurious behavior is "pathological" in that it requires significant clinical intervention, recurs frequently and uniformly, may cause cumulative physical damage, and typically includes behaviors such as "self-biting, head hitting, . . . self-scratching, self-induced vomiting, and other behaviors leading to a wide range of self-induced injuries" (p. 3).

Prevalence and Etiology

Because of differences in assessment methods, sampling strategies, and the nature of the population surveyed, estimates of the prevalence of SIB among adults with IDD vary widely. Rojahn et al. (2007) reviewed large-scale surveys of individuals with IDD in the United States and in some European countries in both community settings and institutions and found that estimated rates of SIB ranged from 4% to 9%. Emerson et al. (2001) conducted a national study in the United Kingdom and found that 4% of the sample of individuals with IDD receiving services in a variety of venues were diagnosed with SIB. For the population with a diagnosis of autism, estimates vary even more widely—ranging from 33% to 71% (Richards et al., 2012)—because of variations in the definitions of both autism spectrum disorder (ASD) and self-injury as well as variations in the level of disability among the samples. Self-injury is more common among people with severe epilepsy, restricted mobility, severe hearing impairment, severe intellectual disability, severe communication difficulties, reduced self-care skills, greater problems with continence and more stereotypical behaviors (Emerson et al., 2001). Several studies have shown a higher incidence of mental health disorders among people with SIB than among those without (Borthwick-Duffy, 1994; Rojahn et al., 2004).

In 1976, Carr et al. demonstrated that SIB can occur for specific reasons (e.g., to escape from undesired demands) and that it can be decreased by changing the social environment in ways that address those conditions. Carr (1977) also provided a review of some hypotheses on the motivation of SIB that proved to be a seminal contribution. Over the next few decades, Carr's contributions provided the basis for research and treatment of SIB exhibited by individuals with IDD. Subsequent applied research studies extended the hypothesis of Carr (1977) regarding the environmental and other triggers of SIB with empirical examination of the broader possible motivations for the behavior (Iwata et al., 1994).

Carr and Durand (1985) provided an example of the application of functional analysis methods to the challenging behavior of children in classroom settings. They demonstrated that similar problem behaviors can occur for different reasons (motivations) across children. Also of great importance was their demonstration that when problem behavior serves a communicative function (e.g., to gain attention or escape a demand), appropriate communication skills can be taught that both remediate the problem behavior *and* benefit the child's education and quality of life from that point forward. Although there may be a variety of reasons for SIB—including pain, seizure disorder, biochemical factors, specific genetic syndromes, arousal, self-stimulation, frustration, and inability to communicate (Edelson, 2016), practitioners of applied behavior analysis argue that SIB has a strong environmental/contextual component even when biological factors are present. The functional assessment is a key component for reducing self-injurious behavior (Iwata et al., 1994; Carr & Durand, 1985).

Impact on Individuals and Families
Prolonged self-injury can lead to serious health risks such as lacerations, bone damage, intestinal disorders, infection, and vision problems such as a detached retina. As Symons et al. (1999) noted, individuals with SIB also "have significant problems in daily living" which can result in reduced opportunities for employment, education, and social interaction (p. 304). Further, the need to control these behaviors leads in many instances to the use of psychoactive medications that have their own health and quality-of-life problems.

Parents of individuals with IDD with co-occurring behavior problems report higher levels of stress and depression than do parents of children with IDD only (Baker et al., 2003; McIntyre & Brown, 2013). Such caregiving challenges may eventually lead to costly crisis intervention and potentially to out-of-home placement (Minshawi et al., 2015).

Therapeutic Interventions and Public Policies
There is a comparatively limited evidence base of effective approaches to support people with SIB; more recent advances have focused on addressing the *cause* or *function* served by the behavior, such as the inability to express oneself. Though very infrequently, some people diagnosed with SIB are still subjected to aversive and painful interventions including

electric shock.[1] Even today, people with SIB are often restrained. Because of the intensity of need of individuals with SIB, the societal costs in terms of public and private resources are also significant. Further, Taylor et al. (2010) have suggested that the longer the behavior continues, the more the behavior becomes chronic and the more difficult it becomes to reduce that incidence.

The development of a treatment plan for SIB begins with a careful assessment of the nature, frequency, and potential causes of these behaviors—biological, psychological, genetic, or some combination thereof—as well as a functional assessment. The results of the assessment may lead to a range of behavioral supports, medication regimens, communication aids, speech therapy, visual aids, healthcare (for pain or other health issues related to the behavior), mental health treatment, and potentially the use of physical restraints. Treatment approaches have increasingly moved away from the use of punishment and aversive interventions, with the most extreme examples such as electric shock rarely used and typically prohibited in most state regulations (Rotholz et al., 2013). As Rotholz et al. (2013) have noted, "The application of behavioral supports, particularly positive behavior supports, has resulted in significant behavioral and quality of life changes in the lives of many people with IDD" (p. 433).

Policies and practices related to behavioral supports for persons supported by state and federally funded services are determined by the developmental disability agency in the state where the person lives. With no national standards for behavioral supports, the result has been policies and practices that vary considerably across states and in ways that have significant implications for persons who exhibit SIB (Rotholz et al., 2013). The policies and practices of concern include, but are not limited to, those that cover key variables that impact quality of supports such as required, promoted and prohibited practices, qualifications of providers, continuing education and quality assurance.

Methods

This review provides information on a subsample of individuals who are identified as needing some or extensive support for self-injurious behavior in the NCI survey sample of individuals with IDD. Many of the studies of SIB in the last several decades have been focused on individuals living in institutions; this review includes information on the characteristics of individuals needing support for SIB outside institutional settings—including individuals living with their families and in their own homes. Given the breadth of the NCI sample, the authors can compare the characteristics and outcomes of individuals who need support for SIB with those who do not need support for SIB. The review concludes with recommendations for enhancements in public policy, research and clinical practice to ensure an evidence-based and person-centered approach to supporting individuals who need support for SIB.

NCI is a collaboration among state public developmental disability agencies, the National Association of State Directors of Developmental Disabilities Services, and the

Human Services Research Institute to generate a national database on the outcomes and personal characteristics of the population of people with IDD who receive public supports. NCI provides state public managers with the ability to track the performance of state systems by examining the outcomes experienced by individuals and families receiving long-term services and supports (LTSS). Each year, participating states can elect to conduct the NCI IPS with a random sample of adults to gain insights into key domains of their lives—including employment, rights, service planning, community inclusion, choice, health, and safety. For the purposes of reporting, the data are aggregated to produce state averages and a national average.

The data for this analysis come from states that participated in the 2018–2019 cycle of NCI In-Person Survey. The total IPS sample for 2018–2019 was 22,009 individuals from 37 states.[2] All participating states are instructed to select a random sample of 400 adults (age 18 and over) with IDD who receive at least one publicly funded service (such as institutional, community, or home-based services) in addition to case management. The sample size must be large enough to meet power requirements of 95% confidence level and 5% margin of error. By randomizing the sample, every person in the state or service area who meets the sample eligibility criteria has an equal opportunity to be interviewed. There are no a priori prescreening or exclusion procedures. Individuals selected as part of the sample are offered the opportunity to participate and may choose to refuse. Data on refusals and participation rates in every state are not available.

The IPS is composed of three parts. The first part is the "Background Information Section" and is used to collect information on the demographic and personal characteristics of the individual being surveyed; this information is usually drawn from individual, agency, or case management records. In some instances, when the information is unavailable in the records, it may be obtained during the second part of the survey—the face-to-face interview with the individual. The second and third parts of the survey are collected via an in-person interview only. The second part of the survey is named "Section I" and contains questions on the individual's personal subjective opinions; it can only be answered by the individual receiving services themselves. The third part of the survey is named "Section II" and contains questions that pertain to more directly observable, measurable occurrences, such as how often the person participates in specific community events; consequently, proxy responses are permitted for this portion. A proxy respondent can be a family member, staff person, or someone else who knows the individual well. To avoid potential conflict of interest, case managers or service coordinators are not allowed to respond on an individual's behalf.

The Background Information Section contains a subsection titled Behavioral Support Needs. Surveyors are asked to identify the level of support needed for three types of behavior: self-injurious, disruptive (refers to behavior that interferes with the activities of others—e.g., by laughing or crying without apparent reason, yelling or screaming, cursing, or threatening), and destructive (refers broadly to externally directed, defiant behavior—e.g., taking other people's property, destroying property, stealing, or assaulting/injuring others). The response options are "no support needed," "some support needed; requires only occasional assistance or monitoring," "extensive support needed; frequent or severe enough to require regular assistance," and "don't know." The definition of SIB in the survey is: "attempts to cause harm to one's own body—e.g., by hitting or biting self, banging head, scratching or puncturing skin, ingesting inedible substances."

The following analysis excludes "don't know" and missing responses from the denominator. Of the 20,025 valid responses to the question regarding SIB, the total number of cases indicating a need for some support to manage SIB was 3,348, or 16.7%. The total number of records indicating need for extensive support to manage SIB was 1111, or 5.5%. And the total number of records indicating that no support is needed for SIB was 15,566, or 77.7%. A binary variable was created in which the response options "some support needed to manage SIB" and "extensive support needed to manage SIB" were collapsed. Based on the resulting variable, 4,459 cases, or 22.3% of the total cases needed some or extensive support for SIB.

Chi-squared analyses were conducted to assess whether significant relationships existed between the groups of individuals with and without SIB support needs regarding variables of interest. The N displayed for each analysis demonstrates the number of cases for which data on the independent and dependent variable were both available.

Results

Incidence by State

State-by-state data on incidence showed a wide range in the proportions of individuals in the state samples identified as needing some or extensive support for SIB. Proportions ranged from 11.7% of valid responses from Florida to 51.5% of the valid responses from Kansas, with an overall sample mean of 22.3%.

Personal Characteristics

The data indicate significant differences in the attributes and personal characteristics of individuals who need support for SIB and those who need no support for SIB. Table 30.1 shows the data on personal characteristics.

Respondent Race/Ethnicity

In the Background Information Section of the IPS, respondents are asked to identify the race/ethnicity of the respondent receiving LTSS. Of the list of response options, the respondent is asked to check all that apply, allowing for multiple responses. The response options include American Indian or Alaska Native, Asian (Asian Indian, Chinese, Filipino, Japanese, Korean, Vietnamese, or Other Asian), Black or African American, Pacific Islander (Native Hawaiian, Guamanian or Chamorro, Samoan, or Other Pacific Islander), White, Hispanic/Latino (Mexican, Mexican American, Chicano, Puerto Rican,

Table 30.1 Personal Characteristics by Need for Support for Self-Injurious Behavior

		No SIB support needs	Some or extensive SIB support needs	p-value	N
Age	18–22	6.0%	8.6%	< 0.001	19,906
	23–34	31.2%	35.1%		
	35–54	36.1%	34.1%		
	55–074	24.2%	20.4%		
	75+	2.5%	1.8%		
Gender	Male	57.3%	58.2%	.463	19,956
Race	White	71.3%	74.7%	< 0.001	19,554
	African American	16.3%	12.1%		
	Hispanic	6.0%	5.1%		
	American Indian or Alaska Native	1.2%	1.0%		
	Asian	1.8%	2.7%		
	Pacific Islander	0.3%	0.2%		
Guardianship	Has a legally appointed guardian/conservator	50.0%	67.0%	< 0.001	19,460
Level of ID	N/A- no ID diagnosis on file	8.9%	6.2%	< 0.001	18,056
	Mild ID	41.8%	27.0%		
	Moderate ID	30.7%	30.3%		
	Severe ID	10.7%	18.4%		
	Profound ID	6.5%	12.9%		
	Unspecified level	9.4%	10.4%		
	ID level unknown	1.0%	1.0%		
Mental Health	Mood disorder	29.4%	48.3%	< 0.001	18,806
	Anxiety disorder	24.5%	44.1%	< 0.001	18,443
	Behavior challenges	19.3%	73.0%	< 0.001	19,049
	Psychotic disorder	9.5%	19.2%	< 0.001	18,651
Diagnoses	Autism spectrum disorder	16.1%	35.5%	< 0.001	19,220
	Seizure disorder/neurological problem	26.7%	35.8%	< 0.001	18,632
	Down syndrome	10.4%	5.8%	< 0.001	19,360
	Limited or no vision	9.4%	11.7%	< 0.001	19,209
	Hearing loss, severe or profound	6.0%	7.0%	0.012	19,059
	Prader Willi Syndrome	0.4%	1.5%	< 0.001	19,226
	Fetal alcohol syndrome	0.8%	1.7%	< 0.001	19,056

(continued)

Table 30.1 *Continued*

		No SIB support needs	Some or extensive SIB support needs	p-value	N
Mobility	Moves self around environment without aids	76.2%	77.6%	0.103	19,771
	Moves self around environment with aids or uses wheelchair independently	14.6%	13.9%		
	Nonambulatory, always needs assistance	9.2%	8.4%		
Self-reported health status ‡	Fairly good or poor	32.4%	35.1%	0.330	19,314
Preferred means of expression	Spoken	83.5%	68.4%	< 0.001	19,835
	Gestures/body language	12.2%	23.4%		
	Sign language/finger spelling	1.5%	3.0%		
	Communication aid	1.1%	1.7%		
	Other	1.7%	3.6%		
Additional services needed ‡	Communication technology	4.6%	7.3%	< 0.001	18,628
Other behavior support needs	Needs some or extensive support for destructive behavior[a]	15.2%	66.5%	< 0.001	17,486
	Needs some or extensive support for disruptive behavior[b]	26.8%	81.8%	< 0.001	17,528
Medications to treat behavior	Yes	16.3%	54.9%	< 0.001	17,321
Has behavior plan	Yes	18.3%	57.2%	< 0.001	17,924
Residential setting	ICF/IID, nursing facility or other institutional setting	5.2%	8.4%	< 0.001	19,651
	Group residential setting (e.g., group home)	26.3%	41.0%		
	Own home or apartment	19.4%	11.9%		
	Parents/relatives home	41.6%	28.7%		

Note: Questions that occur in Section II, for which a proxy is allowed, are indicated with ‡.

[a] Refers broadly to externally directed, defiant behavior; for example, taking other people's property, destroying property, stealing, or assaulting/injuring others.

[b] Refers to behavior that interferes with the activities of others; for example, by laughing or crying without apparent reason, yelling or screaming, cursing, or threatening.

Cuban or Other Spanish/Hispanic/Latino) or Other race not listed. Though Hispanic ethnicity is not considered a "race," including it as a response option along with the race options aligns with the changes to the Census 2020 questions on race and ethnicity (Cohn, 2017).

There are significant differences in the need for SIB support by race ($p \leq 0.001$). Those who need some or extensive support for SIB were more likely to be White (74.7% of those who needed some or extensive support were reported to be White, compared to 71.3% of those who did not need support). Those who need some or extensive support were significantly less likely to be Black/African American (12.1% of those who needed some or extensive support were reported to be Black/African American, while 16.3% of those who did not need support were reported to be Black/African American). There do not appear to be significant differences in American Indian/Alaska Native, Asian, Pacific Islander race for those with and without SIB support needs. In addition, there do not appear to be differences in Hispanic ethnicity.

AGE

Individuals requiring some or extensive support for SIB were more likely to be younger. Around two-fifths (43.7%) of respondents needing some or extensive support for SIB were between 18 and 34, compared to 37.2% of those needing no support for SIB. Conversely, 56.3% of respondents needing some or extensive support for SIB were age 35+, while 62.8% of those needing no support were in the 35+ age group ($p \leq 0.001$; $N = 19,906$).

LEVEL OF ID

Consistent with research on individuals with SIB, NCI data indicate that individuals with support needs for SIB and with ID are more likely to have a diagnosis of severe or profound intellectual disability: 31.3% of those who needed some or extensive support for SIB were reported to have severe or profound ID as compared to 17.2% of those without SIB support needs ($p \leq 0.001$; $N = 18,056$).

MENTAL ILLNESS AS A CO-OCCURRING CONDITION

Again, consistent with previous reviews, individuals requiring some or extensive support for SIB were significantly more likely to have a mood disorder diagnosis (e.g., depression, mania, and bipolar disorder) than those without SIB support needs (48.3% vs. 29.4%; $p \leq 0.001$; $N = 18,806$). Similarly, those requiring support were more likely to have a diagnosis of anxiety disorder (e.g., obsessive disorders and panic disorders) (44.1% vs. 24.5%; $p \leq 0.001$; $N = 18,443$) and/or psychotic disorder (schizophrenia, hallucinations, etc.) (19.2% vs. 9.5%; $p \leq 0.001$; $N = 18,651$). Perhaps surprisingly, 27.0% of those with some or extensive support needs for SIB were not reported to have a diagnosis of behavioral challenges ($N = 19,049$).

PRESENCE OF GUARDIANSHIP

Respondents needing some or extensive support for SIB were more likely to have a legally appointed guardian/conservator. Over two thirds of respondents needing some or extensive support for SIB (67.0%) were in such guardian relationships, while 50.0% of those not needing support for SIB had guardians ($p \leq 0.001$; $N = 19,460$).

OTHER DIAGNOSES/CONDITIONS

Consistent with the literature on SIB, individuals needing some or extensive support for SIB were more likely to have a diagnosis of autism spectrum disorder (e.g., autism, Asperger's syndrome, or pervasive developmental disorder) (35.5% vs. 16.1% of those without SIB support needs; $p \leq 0.001$; $N = 19,220$). According to the National Core Indicators data, 38.5% of adults with an ASD diagnosis were reported to need some or extensive support for SIB. Among those without ASD, 18.0% needed some or extensive support for SIB ($p \leq 0.001$; $N = 19,220$).

Individuals needing some or extensive support for SIB were more likely to have a seizure disorder and/or neurological problem (35.8% vs. 26.7%; $p \leq 0.001$; $N = 18,632$). Individuals with SIB were less likely to have a diagnosis of Down syndrome (5.8% vs. 10.4%; $p \leq 0.001$; $N = 19,360$). Individuals with SIB were more likely to have a diagnosis of limited or no vision (11.7% vs. 9.4%; $p \leq 0.001$; $N = 19,209$) and severe or profound hearing loss (7.0% vs. 6.0%; $p = 0.012$; $N = 19,059$). Individuals with SIB were also more likely to have a diagnosis of fetal alcohol syndrome (1.7% vs. 0.8%; $p \leq 0.001$; $N = 19,056$) and Prader Willi syndrome (1.5% vs. 0.4%; $p \leq 0.001$; $N = 19,226$).

There were no significant differences in mobility (22.4% of those needing some or extensive support for SIB were reported to use a wheelchair independently or be nonambulatory vs. 23.8% of those who didn't need support for SIB; $p = 0.103$; $N = 19,771$) between those with and without need for support for SIB.

Interestingly, there were significant differences in self-reported/proxy reported overall health—35.1% of those who needed some or extensive support for SIB reported having fairly good or poor health versus 32.4% of those not needing support for SIB ($p \leq 0.001$; $N = 19,314$).

MODE OF COMMUNICATION

Carr and Durand (1985) have argued that problem behavior serves a communicative function. To underscore that observation, there were significant differences in preferred means of expression between those who need some or extensive support for SIB and those who need no support for SIB ($p \leq 0.001$; $N = 19,835$). Individuals with support needs for SIB were reported to be less likely to communicate by speaking (68.4% vs. 83.5%) and were significantly more likely to prefer to communicate via gestures/body language or sign language or finger spelling (23.4% vs. 12.2%). In addition, those with support needs for

SIB were more likely to report needing additional communication technology supports and services from the state (7.3% vs. 4.6%; $p < 0.001$; $N = 18,628$).

OTHER BEHAVIOR SUPPORT AND MEDICATION NEEDS

Individuals needing support for SIB were more likely to be reported to also need support for disruptive behavior (refers to behavior that interferes with the activities of others—e.g., by laughing or crying without apparent reason, yelling or screaming, cursing, or threatening) (81.7% vs. 26.8%; $p \leq 0.001$; $N = 17,528$) and/or destructive behavior (refers broadly to externally directed, defiant behavior—e.g., taking other people's property, destroying property, stealing, or assaulting/injuring others) (66.5% vs. 15.2%; $p \leq 0.001$; $N = 17,486$). They were also significantly more likely to be reported to take medications to treat behavior problems (54.9% vs. 16.3%; $p \leq 0.001$; $N = 17,321$). Similarly, they were significantly more likely to have a behavior plan in place (57.2% vs. 18.3%; $p < 0=.001$; $N = 17,924$). Notably, the data also show that 42.8% of those who need support for SIB do not have a behavior plan in place.[3]

WHERE PEOPLE LIVE

Because of the level of their level of supports needs, it is not surprising that there were significant differences in residence type between people who need some or extensive support for SIB and those who do not need support ($p \leq 0.001$; $N = 19,651$). Individuals needing some or extensive support for SIB were significantly more likely to be reported to be living in a group living setting. Namely, 49.4% requiring such support live in a group residential setting such as an ICF/IID or group home, compared to 31.5% of those who do not need support for SIB. Conversely, those who need support for SIB were significantly less likely to be living in their own home/apartment or in a parent or relative's home when compared to those who do not need support for SIB (40.6% vs. 61.0%).

Outcomes of Respondents with Support Needs for SIB

The data presented in this section come from all three parts of the IPS—the Background Information Section, Section I (which must be answered by the individual), and Section II in which a proxy may have helped with some responses. In the following results, we indicate which part of the survey each outcome element was derived from.

If the individual is unable or unwilling to complete Section I, the section is skipped or deemed invalid. Individuals with some or extensive support needs for SIB were less likely to have Section I recorded as "valid" (57.2% vs. 76.4%; $p <= 0.001$; $N = 19,817$). Those responses marked as invalid were excluded from analysis for questions occurring in Section I. For questions in Section II, individuals who needed some or extensive support for SIB were more likely to have a proxy respond than individuals who did not need such support (see table 30.2).

Table 30.2 Outcomes by Need for Support for Self-Injurious Behavior

	Outcome	No SIB support needs	Some or extensive SIB support needs	p-value	N
Satisfaction	Likes where lives†	90.9%	87.1%	< 0.001	13,987
	Wants to live somewhere else†	24.8%	29.8%	< 0.001	13,536
	Goes to day program or workshop†	57.5%	63.4%	< 0.001	13,741
	Would like to go to day program/workshop less†	15.1%	19.3%	< 0.001	7,653
	Services and supports are helping to live a good life†	82.3%	82.1%	0.833	13,386
Safety	Feels afraid in home, day program, work, community, transport, and/or other situation†	19.9%	23.4%	< 0.001	13,127
Relationships	Has friends who are not family or staff†	80.4%	75.6%	< 0.001	13,651
	Needs more help to make friends or keep in contact with friends†	48.7%	55.9%	< 0.001	13,050
	Has other ways of communicating with friends when they cannot see them†	82.3%	75.2%	< 0.001	11,973
	Can communicate with family when wanted†	82.5%	78.7%	< 0.001	8,060
	Can communicate with friends when wanted†	82.3%	75.2%	0.002	11,973
	Can date without restrictions, or is married/living with partner†	75.5%	68.6%	< 0.001	10,930
	Often feels lonely†	10.7%	14.7%	< 0.001	13,251
Community inclusion, participation, and leisure	Has enough things likes to do at home†	84.9%	81.6%	< 0.001	13,504
	Participates in community groups and/or activities†	36.9%	30.7%	< 0.001	19,172
Choice and decision-making	Chose or had some input in choosing home‡	60.8%	44.6%	< 0.001	10,965
	Chose or had some input in choosing who lives with (if not living in family home)‡	48.9%	34.2%	< 0.001	10,896

	Outcome	No SIB support needs	Some or extensive SIB support needs	p-value	N
Table 30.2 Continued					
	Chose or had some input in choosing staff‡	69.1%	64.0%	< 0.001	17,301
	Chose or had some input in choosing daily schedule‡	85.1%	78.2%	< 0.001	19,321
	Chose or had some input in choosing what to do in free time‡	93.1%	91.8%	< 0.001	19,217
	Chose or had some input in choosing day activity‡	62.8%	50.6%	< 0.001	10,649
	Chose or had some input in choosing what to buy with spending money‡	91.4%	86.0%	< 0.001	18,660
	Chose or had some input in choosing case manager‡	87.0%	84.8%	< 0.001	16,432
	Chose or had some input in choosing job‡	84.0%	76.4%	< 0.001	4,916
Rights and respect	Has a place to be alone at home†	96.4%	95.4%	0.019	13,666
	Has key to home‡	53.8%	35.1%	< 0.001	19,246
	Can lock bedroom‡	54.3%	46.8%	< 0.001	17,790
	Has voted in a federal, state, or local election or had opportunity to register to vote but chose not to‡	41.0%	27.1%	< 0.001	18,707
	Staff always treats with respect†	92.9%	89.8%	< 0.001	12,293
	Can be alone with visitors without restrictions†	85.5%	78.3%	< 0.001	12,282
	There are rules around having visitors in home†	34.7%	45.4%	< 0.001	11,816
	Can use phone or internet whenever wanted†	90.1%	85.9%	< 0.001	12,784
Service coordination	Took part in last service planning meeting†	96.3%	95.5%	< 0.001	12,609
	At last service planning meeting, knew what was being talked about†	80.6%	76.5%	< 0.001	11,396
	Was able to choose the services that were received†	74.9%	69.3%	< 0.001	10,327

(continued)

Table 30.2 *Continued*

	Outcome	No SIB support needs	Some or extensive SIB support needs	*p*-value	N
Employment	Had paid, community-based job in the past two weeks¶	23.5%	12.5%	< 0.001	18,293
	Had unpaid, facility-based activity in the past two weeks¶	39.9%	45.4%	< 0.001	16,032
	Those without community employment who would like community employment*	45.7%	55.0%	< 0.001	8,949
	Community employment is goal in service plan¶	30.7%	23.2%	< 0.001	16,989

Note: Questions that occur in the Background Information Section are indicated with a ¶. Those that occur in Section I are indicated with †, and those that occur in Section II, where proxies are allowed, are indicated with ‡.

SATISFACTION WITH SUPPORTS

Individuals with support needs for SIB were less likely to report that they like where they live compared to those without SIB support needs (87.1% vs. 90.9%; $p \leq .001$; $N = 13,987$). They were more likely to report that they want to live somewhere else (29.8% vs. 24.8%; $p \leq 0.001$; $N = 13,536$). Individuals with support needs for SIB were more likely to report that they go to a day program or workshop during the day (63.4% vs. 57.5%; $p \leq 0.001$; $N = 13,741$) and that they would like to go to the day program less than they currently go (19.3% vs. 15.1%; $p \leq 0.001$; $N = 7,653$).

PERCEPTION OF PERSONAL SAFETY

Individuals with support needs for SIB were more likely to report that they feel afraid in their home, at their day program, in their workplace, in their community, when taking transportation, and/or in other situations (23.4% vs. 19.9%; $p \leq 0.001$; $N = 13,127$). This is a troubling finding given that the literature has shown that people with communication limitations and those who live in segregated facilities are more likely to be subjects of abuse (Disability Justice, n.d.).

RELATIONSHIPS WITH FRIENDS AND FAMILY

Individuals with some or extensive SIB support needs were less likely to report having friends beyond family members or staff (75.6% vs. 80.4%; $p \leq 0.001$; $N = 13,651$) and were more likely to report that they need more help to make friends or keep in contact with friends (55.9% vs. 48.7%; $p \leq 0.001$; $N = 13,050$). Those with some or extensive SIB support needs were less likely to report that they have other ways of communicating with friends when they cannot see them (75.2% vs. 82.3%; $p \leq 0.001$; $N = 11,973$). They were also less likely to report that they can see or communicate with family when they want to (78.7%% vs. 82.5%; $p \leq 0.001$; $N = 8,060$), can see or communicate with friends when they want to (75.2% vs. 82.3%; $p = 0.002$; $N = 11,973$) and that they can go on dates or are married and living with their partner (68.6% vs. 75.5%; $p \leq 0.001$; $N = 10,930$). In addition, they were more likely to report often feeling lonely (14.7% vs. 10.7%; $p \leq 0.001$; $N = 13,251$).

COMMUNITY INCLUSION, PARTICIPATION, AND LEISURE

Individuals with support needs for SIB were less likely to report having enough things they like to do at home (81.6% vs. 84.9%; $p \leq 0.001$; $N = 13,504$). In addition, they were less likely to report that they participate in community groups or activities (30.7% vs. 36.9%; $p = 0.001$; $N = 19,172$).

CHOICE AND CONTROL

When compared to those who did not need support for SIB, individuals who require support for SIB were significantly less likely to report having been involved in choosing:

- their home (44.6% vs. 60.8%; $p \leq 0.001$; $n = 10,965$)
- their housemates (34.2% vs. 48.9%; $p \leq 0.001$; $n = 10,896$)
- their staff (64.0% vs. 69.1%; $p \leq 0.001$; $n = 17,301$)
- their daily schedule (78.2% vs. 85.1%; $p \leq 0.001$; $n = 19,321$)
- what to do in their free time (91.8% vs. 93.1%; $p \leq 0.001$; $n = 19,217$)
- their job (among those with a paid job in the community) (76.4% vs. 84.0%; $p \leq 0.001$; $n = 4,916$)
- their day activity (50.6% vs. 62.8%; $p \leq 0.001$; $n = 10,649$)
- what to buy with their spending money (86.0% vs. 91.4%; $p \leq 0.001$; $n = 18,660$)
- their case manager (84.8% vs. 87.0%; $p \leq 0.001$; $N = 16,432$)

RIGHTS AND RESPECT

Contrary to the requirements of the Center for Medicare and Medicaid Services Setting Rule (2015), that laid out a series of rights that all individuals in residential arrangements supported by HCBS waivers should enjoy, those with some or extensive SIB support needs were less likely to report having a key to their home (35.1% vs. 53.8%; $p \leq 0.001$; $N = 19,246$) or being able to lock their bedrooms (46.8% vs. 54.3%; $p \leq 0.001$; $N = 17,790$). They were also less likely to report that they had a place to be alone in their home (95.4% vs. 96.4%; $p = 0.019$; $N = 13,666$). They were less likely to report that they can be alone with their friends or visitors in their home (78.3% vs. 85.5%; $p \leq 0.001$; $N = 12,282$) and more likely to report that there are rules about having friends or visitors in their home (45.4% vs. 34.7%; $p \leq 0.001$; $N = 11,816$). They were also less likely to report being able to use the phone or Internet whenever they wanted (85.9% vs. 90.1%; $p \leq 0.001$; $N = 12,784$).

With respect to involvement in civic life, those who need support for SIB were significantly less likely to report having voted in a federal, state, or local election or having had the opportunity to do so (27.1% vs. 41.0%; $p \leq 0.001$; $N = 18,707$). Further, those with support needs for SIB were significantly less likely to report that their staff always treat them with respect (89.8% vs. 92.9%; $p \leq 0.001$; $N = 12,293$).

EXPERIENCE WITH SERVICE COORDINATION

Respondents with need for some or extensive support for SIB were less likely than those without SIB support needs to have experienced the following:

- Took part in last service planning meeting (95.5% vs. 96.3%; $p \leq 0.001$; $N = 12,609$)
- Understood what was being talked about at the last service planning meeting (76.5% vs. 80.6%; $p \leq 0.001$; $N = 11,396$)
- Able to choose the services that were received as part of the service plan (69.3% vs. 74.9%; $p \leq 0.001$; $N = 10,327$)

EMPLOYMENT

While the numbers of people with IDD receiving public supports who are employed in a community job (an individual or group job in a local business alongside peers who do not have disabilities) is relatively low, respondents with some or extensive SIB support needs were even less likely to have a paid job in the community than those individuals who do not require support for SIS (12.5% vs. 23.5%; $p \leq 0.001$; $N = 18,293$). Those with SIB support needs who did not have a paid community job were significantly more likely to say that they would like a paid community job, when compared to those with a paid community job and no SIB support needs (55.0% vs. 45.7%; $p \leq 0.001$; $N = 8,949$).

Those with SIB support needs were more likely to have an unpaid facility-based activity during the day (45.4% vs. 39.9%; $p \leq 0.001$; $N = 16,032$). Those with SIB support needs were significantly less likely to have community-based employment as a goal in their service plan (23.2% vs. 30.7%; $p \leq 0.001$; $N = 16,989$).

Summary

The National Core Indicators data from 2018–2019 demonstrate significant differences in the demographics and personal characteristics of those who need some or extensive support for self-injurious behavior compared to those who do not.

DEMOGRAPHICS/PERSONAL CHARACTERISTICS

When compared to survey respondents who do not need support for SIB, those who do need support for SIB were more likely to be White and have severe or profound ID. They were significantly more likely to have a diagnosis of a mood disorder, anxiety disorder, behavior challenge, or psychotic disorder. Interestingly, however, 32.8% were not reported as having a diagnosis of behavior challenges. Individuals who need support for SIB were more likely to have an ASD diagnosis or a seizure or neurological problem and were less likely to have a diagnosis of Down syndrome.

Individuals needing support for SIB were less likely to use spoken language to communicate, significantly more likely to need some or extensive support for destructive behavior and/or disruptive behavior, and more likely to take medications for behavior challenges. However, a significant proportion, 47.0%, were not taking medications for behavior challenges. Similarly, those who need some or extensive support for SIB were significantly more likely to be reported as having a behavior plan in place. However, NCI data suggest that 44.2% of those who need some or extensive support for SIB did not have a behavior plan in place.

With regard to living situation, people needing support for SIB were more likely to be living in a group residential setting than those who did not need support for SIB.

OUTCOMES

Compared with those in the sample who did not need support for SIB, those needing some or extensive support for SIB were less likely to like where they live, to be employed (or to have employment as part of their service plan), to have friends, to go on dates, and to participate in their communities. They were more likely to be afraid—especially in their homes. They were also more likely to need help to communicate with friends and family and were more likely to often feel lonely.

Individuals needing support for SIB were less likely to report having had at least some involvement in critical life decisions such as where to live and with whom, who to employ as staff, and who their case manager would be. They were also less likely to report having had input into their own daily schedule, their free-time activities, their day activity, and what to buy with their spending money. In their homes, they were less likely to have a key to their home, to be able to lock their bedroom if they would like, to be alone with visitors, and to be able to use the phone or internet when they want. Finally, they were less like to say that they are treated with respect or to have voted in an election.

Limitations

There are several limitations to the findings. First, the information taken from the Background Information section of the survey—which includes the key variable of interest: support for self-injurious behavior—comes from existing data sources such as state developmental disability agency records, case records, or provider records. Consequently, the quality of the data is reliant on the completeness of the state data source and whether the data source is up to date.

Furthermore, the National Core Indicators dataset includes a random sample of people who are receiving services from state systems that serve people with intellectual and developmental disabilities. Therefore, this sample only represents those who have sought out, are eligible for, and have been successful in achieving access to services in their state. There is some variation in eligibility requirements by state; for example, some states include ASD as a qualifying condition while others do not. That said, the dataset does represent a significant number of people who need support and receiving public services, and it demonstrates gaps in outcomes when compared to others who are receiving supports.

The findings are not adjusted for differences in demographics between the population identified as needing support for SIB and those who do not need such support. Further research is required to understand the nature of supports received and how they align with outcomes for people with SIB support needs. Further, the variation across states in terms of the proportion of individuals who need some or extensive support for SIB may signify that the outcomes of those who need such support in specific states are disproportionately represented in the data presented here.

The NCI survey does not ask whether the individual engages in SIB—instead, it asks whether the individual needs supports for such behaviors. This may exclude those who engage in infrequent or mild SIB whose support needs for such are minimal. Additionally, the survey does not set forth any definition of what is meant by "support" for the purposes of this question. Therefore, there may be variation in the interpretation of the term "support" among those providing responses to this question.

Conclusions

Directions for Future Research

Approximately 22% of the 2018–2019 random sample of more than 20,000 adults receiving support from public DD agencies in the United States needed some or intensive support related to their self-injurious behavior. The data show that this portion of population of people with IDD receiving services experiences a diminished quality of life compared to their peers who don't need support for SIB. To address the challenges identified in this analysis, enhanced and accelerated research should be considered, including:

- *Race*: NCI data show that those who need some or extensive support for SIB are significantly more likely to be White and significantly less likely to be Black/African American than those who do not need support for SIB. With the information currently available, this is a noteworthy result, but without explanation. Since most respondents live in community settings, this raises the question of cultural influence. Do some communities or cultures seek less help for SIB? Could this be due to self-reliance, inequality of service provision, assistance from sources other than that reflected in the survey, or other unknown factors?

- *Quality of services*: Do localities that supply high-quality positive behavior supports and/or mental health services see less extensive needs for SIB-related services? Are there particular system components that are related to better outcomes—such as implementation of person-centered planning, employment first policies, and the broad use of positive behavior supports?
- *Influence of demographic factors*: This analysis did not control for specific variables, such as level of ID, presence of other diagnoses, or living arrangement. Further researchers should explore the role these other factors have on outcomes aside from the presence of SIB.
- *Experiences during the COVID-19 pandemic*: There should be an examination of the experiences of people who need support for SIB during the weeks of isolation. Did the incident of SIB increase? Decrease? What are the implications?

Considerations for Public Policy

The data presented here strongly suggest that there may be a widely divergent conception and definition of self-injurious behavior from state to state. Previous research suggests that the prevalence rate of individuals who need *extensive support* for SIB is somewhere between 4% and 9%—and significantly higher for people with autism: 33% to 71%. However, the NCI data indicate a wide range across states, from 12% to 52%. Even allowing for differences in eligibility criteria, these variations are still difficult to reconcile. There is clearly a need for a more standardized construct to facilitate the accurate assessment of self-injurious behavior. Further, some of the possible overidentification may be the result of inadequate assessment protocols and a failure to identify antecedent health, communication, or environmental causes that could be contributing to the behavior.

The NCI survey results regarding the use of behavior plans and those who need support for SIB also suggest the need for a review of existing state-level policies regarding behavior support plans. Rotholz et al. (2013) note that there is variation among states in behavior plan training, design, and review. Jurisdictions should examine their behavior plan processes and examine gaps such as, for example, the lack of required qualifications of those charged with creating behavior plans, the absence of a behavior support committee, and the lack of qualification requirements for members of such committees. Well-designed, well-monitored, person-centered behavior plans informed by evidence and research may serve to improve the outcomes of individuals who need some or extensive support for SIB (Kincaid & Fox, 2002).

States should also work to develop and maintain high standards regarding qualification, training, and quality assurance of those who provide support for SIB. Rotholz et al. (2013) noted the variety in qualification standards across states and asserted that "the lack of a rigorous, professionally endorsed national standard such as medical licensure that applies to behavior supports for people with IDD raises significant questions regarding the ability of states and provider agencies to set practice criteria and assure the quality and appropriateness of the services being provided" (p. 443). States should work to ensure that the workforce providing supports for individuals with self-injurious behavior is well trained in person-centered planning and supports. Administrative entities should also work to determine a qualification standard that applies to behavior supports.

States should also consider expanding family crisis and respite services for families with a family member who has SIB support needs. Parent and family stress have been shown to impact individuals with disabilities and can reduce positive effects of interventions (Karst & Van Hecke, 2012). Increasing the availability of crisis and respite supports could serve to reduce caregiver stress (Norton et al., 2016; Whitmore, 2016) and translate to higher quality of caregiving and enhanced outcomes for individuals with disabilities (Rotholz et al., 2013).

Finally, the number of individuals with autism being served by state DD agencies is growing nationally. The NCI survey data suggest that individuals who need support for SIB are more likely to also have an ASD diagnosis than those who do not need such support. Therefore, it will become increasingly important for public managers and providers to understand the idiosyncratic needs of these individuals and the types of evidence-based interventions most likely to ameliorate the behavior.

Clinical and Treatment Reforms
To improve outcomes for individuals with support needs for SIB, public managers and providers need to reinforce the importance of a functional assessment and/or analysis of individuals displaying self-injurious behavior. Such assessments are critical to identifying potential causes (e.g., pain, communication challenges, seizure disorder, biochemical factors, specific genetic syndromes, arousal, self-stimulation, or frustration) and consequences of the behavior. Both antecedents and consequence information are essential to determine the best way to replace the problem behavior with a functionally related appropriate alternative. Similarly, the results regarding the co-occurrence of SIB and other mental health diagnoses such as mood disorders and anxiety disorders may prompt public managers and providers to examine the availability of mental health interventions and supports for those receiving public services.

The need to improve the well-being of individuals who exhibit self-injurious behavior underscores the importance of employing evidence-based practices, such as positive behavior supports, to ameliorate the intensity or presence of SIB. The adoption of evidence-based interventions also necessitates expanded training—both in the field and in universities—for individuals who design and implement behavior supports (Symons, 2012). Positive behavior supports (PBS) have been found to enhance quality of life for individuals with SIB (Carr & Horner, 2007; Rotholz et al., 2013). Given the disparity in outcomes noted in this analysis between individuals who need extensive support for

SIB and those who do not, expansion of evidence-based practices could offer those with SIB the promise of improved quality of life. Similarly, public managers should look at their policies regarding aversive treatments. In their review of state policies and practices in behavior supports, Rotholz et al. (2013) found that of the 45 states that responded to their survey, 9 reported that they allow the use of aversive interventions "designed to cause discomfort or pain for behavior reduction" (p. 439). States may examine their policies on such interventions and determine whether these policies align with desired quality of life outcomes.

As noted by Rotholz et al. (2013), and still unchanged, there is no national standard or certification in PBS. While the board certification in behavior analysis (see bacb.com) goes a long way toward this in that PBS builds upon a foundation of applied behavior analysis, but it is not equivalent to PBS and does not necessarily include (training or implementation of) key components of PBS (e.g., person-centered planning and other interventions and therapies as needed by the individual).

Many states suffer from insufficient provider capacity to implement PBS for their service recipients who exhibit SIB. Compounding this problem is the reality that in many cases, state agency and university efforts to train/develop professionals in ABA and PBS are focused primarily on serving children with ASD and not adults with IDD who exhibit SIB. The recent requirement by Centers for Medicare and Medicaid Services (CMS) for state Medicaid plans to include ASD services, while potentially beneficial to children, youth and adults with ASD, may well be detracting from the ability of state IDD service systems to increase availability of high-quality supports for those with SIB.

An issue that compounds the concern with provider capacity to serve people with IDD who exhibit SIB is the quality of those services. The first concern is that the training, experience and skills needed to develop, implement and supervise appropriate supports to address SIB are not necessarily addressed in a qualification process. For example in recent years the federal CMS required states to include services for persons with ASD in individual state Medicaid plans. The qualifications to provide Medicaid-funded services and supports for this population are not typically specific to addressing the severe behavioral challenges posed by those exhibiting SIB, instead focusing on having earned an educational degree or certification.

Final Thoughts

We face the challenge of unknown and likely varied quality of supports for people with IDD who exhibit SIB. While NCI effectively captures the reported need for supports related to SIB, the provision and quality of those supports is not known. It is hoped that policies and practices of state IDD service systems will shift to a greater focus on PBS as recommended by National Association of State Directors of Developmental Disabilities Services (i.e., that "PBS is recommended as the most appropriate approach for state service system use in supporting people with I/DD to address problem behavior"). Few states, at last report (Rotholz et al., 2013), had specific policies, qualifications, training, technical assistance, and/or quality assurance efforts focused on positive behavior supports.

Ideally, this examination of the status and outcomes of individuals needing support for SIB in the United States will provide a national and international framework for continued clinical research, more targeted public policy on the needs and outcomes of these individuals.

Author's Note

This chapter contains updated data conclusions from a previously published journal article (see Bradley et al., 2018).

Notes

1. As of this writing, a federal appeals court vacated a Food and Drug Administration rule banning electric shock devices to treat self-harming behavior (Setty, 2021).
2. Participating states were Alabama, Arkansas, Arizona, Colorado, Connecticut, Delaware, Florida, Georgia, Hawaii, Indiana, Kansas, Kentucky, Maine, Michigan, Minnesota, Missouri, North Carolina, Nebraska, New Hampshire, New Jersey, Nevada, New York, Ohio, Oklahoma, Oregon, Pennsylvania, Rhode Island, South Carolina, South Dakota, Tennessee, Texas, Utah, Virginia, Vermont, Washington, Wisconsin, and Wyoming.
3. "A behavior plan is based on an assessment of an individual's challenging behavior. The plan includes a description of the individual's strengths, preferences, and interests; the goal(s) related to diminishing and/or eliminating the behavior; and applicable information about the nature of the behavior and potential triggering events. The plan should describe the interventions and accommodations that will contribute to the goal(s). It should also include the ways in which progress will be monitored, the staff who will be responsible for the interventions, and the length of time that the plan will be in place."

References

Baker, B. L., McIntyre, L. L., Blacher, J., Crnic, K., Edelbrok, C., & Low, C. (2003). Pre-school children with and without developmental delay: Behavior problems and parenting over time. *Journal of Intellectual Disabilities Research*, *47*(4–5), 217–230.

Borthwick-Duffy, S. A. (1994). Prevalence of "destructive behaviors." In T. Thompson & D. B. Gray (Eds.), *Destructive behavior in developmental disabilities: Diagnosis and treatment* (pp. 3–23). SAGE.

Bradley, V., Hiersteiner, D., Rotholz, D., Maloney, J., Li, H., Bonardi, A., & Bershadsky, J. (2018). Personal characteristics and outcomes of individuals with developmental disabilities who need support for self-injurious behaviour. *Journal of Intellectual Disability Research*, *62*(12), 1043–1057. https://doi.org/10.1111/jir.12518

Carr, E. G. (1977). The motivation of self-injurious behavior: a review of some hypotheses. *Psychological Bulletin*, *84*(4), 800–816. https://doi.org/10.1037/0033-2909.84.4.800

Carr, E. G., & Horner, R. H. (2007). The expanding vision of positive behavior support: research perspectives on happiness, helpfulness, hopefulness. *Journal of Positive Behavior Interventions*, *9*(1), 3–14. https://doi.org.ezproxy.neu.edu/10.1177/10983007070090010201

Carr, E. G., & Durand, V. M. (1985). Reducing behavior problems through functional communication training. *Journal of Applied Behavior Analysis*, *18*(2), 111–126. https://doi.org/10.1901/jaba.1985.18-111

Carr, E. G., Newsom, C. D., & Binkhoff, J. A. (1976). Stimulus control of self-destructive behavior in a psychotic child. *Journal of Abnormal Child Psychology*, *4*(2), 139–153. https://doi.org/10.1007/BF00916518

Centers for Medicare & Medicaid Services (CMS) & U.S. Department of Health and Human Services. (2015). *Home and community-based settings, excluded settings, and the heightened scrutiny process*. https://www.nmhealth.org/publication/view/policy/3784/

Cohn, D. (2017). *Seeking better data on Hispanics, Census Bureau may change how it asks about race*. Pew Research Center. https://www.pewresearch.org/short-reads/2017/04/20/seeking-better-data-on-hispanics-census-bureau-may-change-how-it-asks-about-race/

Disability Justice. (n.d.). Abuse and exploitation of people with developmental disabilities. https://disabilityjustice.org/justice-denied/abuse-and-exploitation/

Edelson, S.M. (2016). *Understanding and treating self-injurious behavior*. Available from https://www.autism.com/symptoms_self-injury

Emerson, E., Kiernan, C., Alborz, C., Reeves, D., Mason, H., Swarbrick, R., Mason, L., & Hatton, C. (2001). The prevalence of challenging behaviors: a total population study. *Developmental Disabilities, 22*(2), 77–93.

Iwata, B. A., Dorsey, M. F., Slifer, K. J., Bauman, K. E., & Richman, G. S. (1994). Toward a functional analysis of self-injury. *Journal of Applied Behavior Analysis, 27*(2), 197–209.

Karst, J., & Van Hecke, A. (2012). Parent and family impact of autism spectrum disorders: a review and proposed model for intervention evaluation. *Clinical Child and Family Psychology Review, 15*(3), 247–277.

Kincaid, D., & Fox, L. (2002). Person-centered planning and positive behavior support. In S. Holburn & P. Vietze (Eds.), *Research and practice in person-centered planning* (pp. 29–50). Paul H. Brookes.

McIntyre, L. L., & Brown, M. (2013). Involving families in the prevention and intervention of behavior problems in individuals with intellectual and developmental disabilities. In D. D. Reed, F. D. DiGennaro Reed, & J. K. Luiselli (Eds.), *Handbook of crisis intervention and developmental disabilities* (pp. 248–260). Springer.

Minshawi, N. F., Hurwitz, S., Morriss, D., & McDougle, C. J. (2015). Multidisciplinary assessment and treatment of self-injurious behavior in autism spectrum disorder and intellectual disability: integration of psychological and biological theory and approach. *Journal of Autism and Developmental Disorders, 45*(6), 1541–1568. https://doi.org/10.1007/s10803-014-2307-3

Norton, M., Dyches, T., Harper, J., Roper, S. & Caldarella, P. (2016). Respite care, stress, uplifts and marital quality in parents of children with Down syndrome. *Journal of Autism and Developmental Disorders, 46*(12), 3700–3711.

Richards, C., Oliver, C., Nelson L., & Moss, J. (2012). Self-injurious behavior in individuals with autism spectrum disorder and intellectual disability. *Journal of Research in Intellectual Disability, 56*(5), 476–489.

Richman, D., Barnard-Brak, L., Bosch, A., Thompson, S., Grubb, L., & Abby, L. (2013). Predictors of self-injurious behavior exhibited by individuals with autism spectrum disorder. *Journal of Intellectual Disability Research, 57*(5), 429–439.

Rojahn, J., Matson, J. L., Naglieri, J. A., & Mayville, E. (2004). Relationships between psychiatric conditions and behavior problems among adults with mental retardation. *American Journal of Mental Retardation, 109*(1), 21–33.

Rojahn, J., Schroeder, S. R., & Hoch, T. A. (2007). *Self-Injurious Behavior in Intellectual Disabilities*. Elsevier Science.

Rotholz, D. A., Moseley, C. R., & Carlson, K. R. (2013). State policies and practices in behavior supports for persons with intellectual and developmental disabilities in the United States: a national survey. *Intellectual and Developmental Disabilities, 51*(6), 433–445. https://doi.org/10.1352/1934-9556-51.6.433

Setty, G. (2021, July). Federal appeals court vacates FDA rule banning electric shock devices to treat self-harming behavior. CNN health. https://keyt.com/health/cnn-health/2021/07/16/federal-appeals-court-vacates-fda-rule-banning-electric-shock-devices-to-treat-self-harming-behavior/

Symons, F. J. (2012). Editorial: Self-injurious behavior in people with intellectual disability. *Journal of Intellectual Disability Research, 56*(5), 421–426.

Symons, F. J., Koppekin, A., & Wehby, J. H. (1999). Treatment of self-injurious behavior and quality of life for persons with mental retardation. *Mental Retardation, 37*(4 0), 297–307. https://doi.org/10.1352/0047-6765(1999)037<0297:TOSBAQ=2.0.CO;2

Taylor, L., Oliver, C., & Murphy, G. (2010). The chronicity of self-injurious behaviour: A long-term follow-up of a total population study. *Journal of Applied Research in Intellectual Disabilities, 24*, 105–117

Whitmore, K. (2016). Respite care and stress among caregivers of children with autism spectrum disorder: An integrative review. *Journal of Pediatric Nursing, 31*(6), 630–652.

CHAPTER
31

Self-Injury in Prison Populations

Natalie Winicov

> **Abstract**
>
> This chapter discusses the common phenomenon of self-injury in prison populations. It notes that rates of self-injury are significantly higher among the detainees compared to the general population, referencing that self-injurious behavior is one of the primary causes of morbidity in correctional facilities. One of the most pressing concerns surrounding self-harm in prisons is the strong link between nonsuicidal self-injury (NSSI) and the risk of suicide attempts and completions. The chapter explains how prison deprives its detainees of the freedom to cope with healthy strategies, leading to consequential feelings of loneliness and hopelessness. Numerous research calls for improved prison mental health care and advancement in treatments focusing on NSSI.
>
> **Key Words:** self-injury, prison, NSSI, correctional facilities, loneliness, hopelessness, treatment, suicide

Introduction

Rates of self-injury are significantly higher among the incarcerated population compared to the general population, and self-injurious behavior is one of the primary causes of morbidity in correctional facilities. The highest estimates report that up to 48% of offenders and up to 61% of offenders living with mental illnesses have engaged in nonsuicidal self-injury (NSSI) (Dixon-Gordon et al., 2012). In comparison, research estimates self-harm rates of 4% in the general population and 21% in the mental health population (Dixon-Gordon et al., 2012). With the prison population reaching 1,311,100 people in 2020, this issue is of particular significance (Kang-Brown et al., 2021). The issue of prison NSSI is not exclusive to American prisons—among many studies conducted internationally, Gu et al.'s (2020) study demonstrated that 14.8% of incarcerated individuals in a China prison engaged in NSSI at least once over the course of one year. Similar findings have emerged from studies in England, Wales, Belgium, Canada, and Japan (Favril, 2019; Hawton et al., 2014; Martin et al., 2014; Matsumoto et al., 2005).

One of the most pressing concerns surrounding self-harm in prisons is the strong link between NSSI and the risk of suicide attempts and completions. While NSSI is defined by its lack of suicidal intent, those who engage in NSSI are at a higher risk of accidental death, and often have a poor ability to judge the lethality of their self-harming behavior. A group of studies has demonstrated that NSSI was the strongest predictor of suicide among the prison population, both during one's incarceration and following release, implying that the absence of intent to die should not lead to a conclusion that suicide is unlikely (Dixon-Gordon et al., 2012; Fagan et al., 2010). Fazel et al. (2017) found that among male prisoners, suicide rates were 3 to 8 times higher than in the general population, while the rates among female prisoners were more than 10 times higher. Prison NSSI places a strain on the entire prison system, consumes significant resources for its treatment, and is not only a serious public health issue but a liability concern for the facilities. Correctional institutions are responsible for the protection of those in their custody, and correctional officers are expected to uphold this responsibility. However, relevant research is lacking, and the existing studies provide inconsistent data, leaving a need for further exploration of screening tools, interventions, and policy-level changes that would prevent NSSI in forensic settings (Winicov, 2019).

In most cases, the literature does not differentiate between self-injury and "suicidal behavior." For the purposes of this chapter, NSSI refers to "a direct behavior that causes minor to moderate physical injury, that is undertaken without conscious suicidal intent, and that occurs in the absence of psychoses and/or organic intellectual impairment" (Fagan et al., 2010). The relevant research clarifies that "biologically driven" self-injury is fundamentally distinct from other forms of NSSI. "Biologically driven" NSSI refers to self-injury that occurs among individuals living with developmental disabilities or experiencing command hallucinations or delusions related to psychosis. This distinctness comes from the lack of conscious control over self-injurious behaviors (Dixon-Gordon et al., 2012; Fagan et al., 2010).

In prison settings, the most used methods for NSSI include cutting, burning, scratching, reopening previous wounds, biting the insides of mouths, and inserting materials into old wounds or orifices (Appelbaum et al., 2011; DeHart et al., 2009; Dixon-Gordon et al., 2012; Fagan et al., 2010). Ritualistic or culturally based self-mutilation that frequently occurs in prisons, such as tattooing, branding, and piercing, is not considered NSSI due to its distinctness in intent.

It is important to distinguish the risks, implications, and challenges of NSSI in prisons from NSSI in the general population for several reasons. The unique structural and procedural limitations of correctional facilities impact risk, treatment, and research in this area. Incarcerated people have few means by which they can cope with distress and the lack of options for mitigating one's suffering makes self-harm a particularly appealing coping method. Prison deprives its detainees of the freedom to cope with many healthy strategies, offering limited to no contact with the outside world including their support system of family and friends. Later in this chapter, we will further elaborate on isolation from support systems and the consequential feelings of loneliness and hopelessness.

Tight prison budgets leave little opportunity for paying trained treatment professionals and treatment programs and thus afford detainees very limited access to adequate mental health treatment. Owing to limited resources, correctional officers, not trained to respond using trauma-informed intervention, are often the first responders. Even in facilities that employ an adequate number of mental health professionals, prisons rarely implement even the most promising interventions, and the treatment of NSSI can be uneven, frustrating, demanding, and exhausting. Staff exposure to frequent episodes of NSSI can significantly increase staff risk of vicarious trauma, burnout, and apathy and contribute to staffs' negative perceptions about detainees who engage in NSSI and high turnover rates (Dehart et al., 2009; Fagan et al., 2010).

The means by which incarcerated individuals self-injure makes prison NSSI particularly risky for lethality (also see Walsh et al., this volume): Detainees often rely on unsterile tools such as broken glass, staples, screws, and plastic to self-injure, as well as the swallowing of objects such as batteries and pens (Dehart et al., 2009). More severe acts of NSSI include facial mutilation, amputation, and eye enucleation, requiring outside medical attention. Due to the limited space in prison facilities, these incidents increase the risk of the spread of blood-borne pathogens among other detainees and correctional staff (Dehart et al., 2009).

The human costs involved in NSSI are enormous, but there are also substantial monetary consequences. Keeping one person incarcerated in an American prison costs an average of $33,274 per person per year (The Price of Prisons, 2015). When a single episode of NSSI occurs, the basic cost of incarceration can be amplified by hundreds of thousands of dollars due to the cost of transportation to medical facilities, doctors, medication, and specialized medical services as well as additional covering staff, interruption and rescheduling of daily routines, and subsequent increases in staff monitoring and safety measures. (Dehart et al., 2009).

Theoretical Model for Prison-Specific NSSI

Dear (2008) conducted research on self-harm in prison between 1996 and 2006 to understand the relationship between self-harm, personal distress, personal vulnerability (one's psychological features, such as inflexible thinking or impulsivity), and prison vulnerability (lack of procedural fairness, supportive staff, and engaging activities) (Dear et al., 2000). This research illustrates that in the worst case, a person with high personal vulnerability (i.e., poor coping skills) incarcerated in an institution with poor crisis management (i.e., unsafe conditions and untrained staff) will have significantly higher potential for NSSI.

To counter such vulnerability, Dear (2008) recommends several prevention strategies. First, the authors suggest evaluating and improving the culture of the prison environment to create a "moral climate," which as further defined elsewhere by Liebling (2006) as having "integrity, procedural fairness, justice, and genuine focus on providing for prisoners' legitimate psychological needs." Dear's (2008) second recommendation is to conduct screening upon prison entry to detect factors associated with greater risk for self-harm and subsequently provide resilience-building interventions. Last, and most important, the authors suggest that prison systems develop a comprehensive approach to identifying prisoner distress and supporting individuals in communicating their distress to prison staff (Dear, 2008) without which all other intervention and response become negligible. Notably, Dear (2008) shifts the focus away from the current approach to NSSI of restraining or punishing self-injuring prisoners and toward minimizing damage caused by the prison environment while implementing methods to recognize individual distress.

This chapter explores the current state of the empirical evidence on NSSI in prisons, including risk factors, functions, and the consequences of pervasive self-injury. Cited studies will include offender samples from prisons in Australia, Russia, Pakistan, Greece, Japan, Canada, Belgium, England/Wales, the United States, and China. Following this, we review evaluation studies of interventions aimed at preventing and reducing incidents of suicide and self-harm among incarcerated individuals. Finally, the chapter discusses limitations, conclusions, and recommendations for future research.

Function of NSSI in Prisons

NSSI is a complex behavior that serves many functions for the self-injuring individual, including distress response, emotional regulation, environmental change, and self-punishment (Jeglic et al., 2005).

Distress Response and Emotional Regulation

NSSI in the prison system is unique from NSSI in the general population in that it serves many functions in an environment that offers little autonomy or bodily integrity, in an environment of unparalleled shame, hopelessness, isolation, violence, and injustice (Riaz & Agha, 2012). Distress, Dear (2008) theorizes, is the key component of prison NSSI, where self-injury is one of the few tools available to regulate painful emotions. Gu et al. (2020) demonstrated a positive correlation between negative life events during incarceration and NSSI, suggesting that NSSI is conducted to cope with negative emotions caused by life events, a finding supported by Gallagher and Sheldon's (2010) interview of a similar population that resulted in 79% reporting emotion regulation as their motive for NSSI. While the relief provided by self-injury is very short term, the immediate gratification and physiological arousal serve as a strong behavioral reinforcement can also serve as a form of nonverbal expression of anger or distress in prisons (also see Claes et al., this volume) (Kenning et al., 2010; Mangnall & Yurkovich, 2008). However, Sakelliades et al. (2010) found that a much smaller percentage (31.6%) of their participants were responding to distress and that for 21.1%, the goal of self-injurious behavior was anger release (incarcerated female participants labeled anger as the most common emotional trigger for NSSI) (Chapman & Dixon-Gordon, 2007).

Influencing the Environment

There is a resounding consensus among prison staff that self-injury is perceived as manipulative in nature, and it appears to be true that prisoners use NSSI as a means for cell change, removal from solitary confinement or lockup, placement into a hospital facility, break from harassment, the obtaining of medication, or transfer to a different prison facility. Yaroshevsky (1975) highlights this function, citing examples in Soviet prisons of individuals committing high-lethality acts of NSSI to be moved to a hospital or protective custody, sometimes to escape the threat of attack from others. Incarcerated individuals have also used NSSI to punish those who have wronged the self-injurer.

NSSI serves as a particularly accessible means for communication or goal achievement in the prison environment, where prisoners have minimal control over their situation, and verbal requests or appeals are seldom regarded with seriousness.

In Dear et al.'s (2000) study, detainees cited manipulation as "the third most common reason for a recent incident of NSSI," endorsed by up to 41% of participants. In fact, Holmqvist et al. (2008) found that NSSI as a function of interpersonal influence occurs significantly more frequently among the prison population compared to community samples. However, Dear et al. (2000) warned against regarding NSSI with manipulative intent as any less serious than NSSI for other reasons. In his 2000 study, his team found that individuals who used NSSI to manipulate or communicate presented with the same degree of suicidal intent as others who engaged in NSSI for other reasons (Dear et al., 2000). Moreover, the focus on intention distracts from the larger issue that failure to treat any NSSI, regardless of intent, is morally and legally irresponsible on the part of the facility.

The literature suggests that in general, intrapersonal objectives, such as emotional regulation, are primary to interpersonal objectives, such as environmental manipulation (Klonsky, 2007).

Self-Punishment

Though less research supports this theory, some studies suggest that incarcerated folks use NSSI to punish themselves. According to Milligan and Andrews (2005), incarcerated individuals who employ NSSI report higher levels of shame compared to those who do not self-injure. Incarceration after committing a crime could certainly induce an overwhelming urge to self-punish and in a study, participants most often selected self-punishment as their secondary reason for NSSI, following emotional regulation (Klonsky, 2007). Dixon-Gordon et al. (2012) posit that self-derogation may be "ego-syntonic for those who already have a negative view of self, particularly those who have been "raised in an invalidating environment."

Prison-Specific Risk Factors for NSSI

Among the literature is a set of clinical, demographic, and situational characteristics that are widely accepted as risk factors for NSSI in community samples. Although these factors are applicable to the prison population, incarcerated individuals also carry a unique set of risk factors for self-injury.

Facility Characteristics

The media has recently directed attention to the conditions of state prisons in the Southern United States and their impact on the mental health and behaviors of detainees. As a result of litigation against prisons over extremely hot conditions, it was revealed that in the hottest states in the United States (i.e., Texas, Kansas, Louisiana, Mississippi, and Alabama), fewer than half the prisons have air conditioning in the housing quarters. Almost 75% of Texas prisons lack air conditioning, with the indoor heat index reaching 150 degrees Fahrenheit (Grobar, 2021).

The Vera Institute of Justice reports that during the summer months, rates of self-harm incidents in prisons spike when the heat index exceeds 100 degrees with a significant positive correlation of 0.791 ($p < 0.01$) (Cloud et al., 2019). Almost all psychotropic medications can impair one's ability to regulate body temperature, and in hot weather conditions, this can lead to heat exhaustion and heatstroke. Excessive heat forces prisoners to decide whether to continue psychiatric medication and risk a heat stroke or protect one's physical health by ceasing pharmacological treatment.

Dangerous heat conditions are typically even more severe in restrictive cell blocks, or solitary confinement, where ventilation is limited, and the occupant has little to no access to cooler air. In Louisiana state prisons, where 17.4% of detainees are in solitary confinement, the average summer temperatures are above 90 degrees Fahrenheit, on average (Toohey, 2019). The unbearable heat becomes a particularly strong motive for segregated detainees to self-harm as a means of removal to an air-conditioned hospital or psychiatrist's office. Further, sweltering conditions interfere with staff's ability to conduct routine wellness checks and provide appropriate monitoring.

Demographic Factors

There is a consensus that detained females have a heightened risk for NSSI, accounting for almost half of all reported episodes of self-injury, despite only representing 6% of the prison population (Casiano et al., 2013; Dear et al., 2000; Dixon-Gordon et al., 2012; Matsumoto et al., 2005). These data appear to be consistent with community sample data, however, but there is some conflicting data suggesting that there are no gender differences among offender samples (Briere & Gil, 1998; Klonsky et al., 2003).

There is further discrepancy regarding race and NSSI among incarcerated individuals. A group of studies provides data that indicate higher rates of NSSI among Caucasians (Alessi et al., 1984; Dixon-Gordon et al., 2012; Hawton et al., 2014; Kempton & Forehand, 1992); however, Borrill et al. (2003) reported that while self-harm was more common among White females, "Black/mixed-race women dependent on drugs had the highest proportion of women reporting self-harm."

Studies on criminal history as a risk factor have produced mixed results. In one study, female detainees were at a higher risk of self-harm if they had a previous violent offense (Hawton et al., 2014), and correspondingly, Gu et al. (2020) found a positive correlation between NSSI and violent crime.

Despite the body of evidence focusing on risk factors for NSSI in prison, Fagan et al. (2010) cautioned that some studies have found conflicting evidence against all demographic risk factor hypotheses, and therefore, there is "no clear consensus on risk factors associated with self-injury."

Psychological Distress

According to Dear's (2008) model, the key ingredient for NSSI in prison populations is the presence of psychological distress. There are several unique precipitants to severe distress that are worth discussing. Studies have demonstrated a relationship between longer prison sentences and higher rates of self-injury. Kaba et al. (2014) noted that the risk ratio for NSSI significantly increased with time in detainment, and similarly, Hawton et al.'s (2014) data suggested that a life sentence significantly heightened the NSSI risk.

Other sentence-specific contributors to psychological distress include denial of parole or bail, concerns about upcoming court appearances or parole board hearings, and subjectively unjust trial outcomes. The commonality among these events is the prevalence of hopelessness, guilt, and shame. Fagan et al. (2010) suggested that, over time, hopelessness increases as one "finds it progressively more difficult to cope with the incarceration environment or just gives up hope of a different life." The study of Gu et al. (2020) on 1,042 Chinese male prisoners found a connection between hopelessness, belief in a just world, negative life events, and NSSI. Their findings suggest that a higher belief in a just world weakens the extent to which negative life events contribute to hopelessness and, consequently weakens the relationship between negative life events and NSSI. The mediator, belief in a "just world," seems to impact one's appraisal of the daily stressors of prison life, where one with a strong "just world" belief views these as challenges as opposed to threats.

Another major contributor to psychological distress among prisoners is interpersonal conflicts among both peers and staff (Riaz & Agha, 2012). Mannion's (2009) study in a high-security hospital suggested that conflict is the most cited stressful event preceding NSSI, accounting for 42% of incidents. Dear (2008) found an even higher figure, claiming that 71% of precipitating factors to NSSI were stressful events that included conflicts with peers and conflict with staff.

Isolation from established support systems only exacerbates an individual's risk of experiencing psychological distress. Dear (2008) notes that 43% of prisoners noted missing their support system or worrying about the consequences of their incarceration on their families, and 42% regarded relationships ending, or stopped visits from family, as primarily contributing to distress. For incarcerated women, separation from one's child and/or the fear of losing custody is particularly distressing (Riaz & Agha, 2012).

Individual Coping Styles and Temperament

There is some evidence to suggest that self-injury within the prison context is related to an individual's ability to cope and the way in which they approach conflict or challenges. Dear et al.'s (2001) work on prisoner coping response indicated that self-injuring detainees used coping strategies more likely to increase stress, supporting Liebling's (1995) "poor-coper" model of prisoners who self-harm. In both Dear (2008) and Dixon-Gordon et al.'s (2012), self-injuring prisoners demonstrated poorer cognitive coping resources in comparison to those who did not self-harm, including exhibit higher avoidance, lower approach styles, and inflexible thinking patterns during stressful situations. It is not clear whether these individuals have an inherent deficit in coping abilities or simply fail to use effective coping strategies in moments of crisis or high arousal. These authors also found that those engaged in NSSI were more likely to have deficits in problem-solving abilities, including fewer attempts to change their situation, more avoidance of their problems, and lower perceived control in challenging situations. Some of the research states that NSSI-engaging individuals achieved lower scores on a problem-solving task and are more likely to exhibit higher avoidance, lower approach styles, and inflexible thinking patterns (Casiano et al., 2013; Dear, 2008; Dixon-Gordon et al., 2012).

Self-harming detainees also demonstrate baseline aggression and impulsivity. Hillbrand et al. (1996) found they were rated as more aggressive by the staff, though these data carry little weight due to their highly subjective nature. However, prisoners' self-report of aggression was a "unique predictor" of self-harm (Sakelliadis et al., 2010). Favril (2019) suggested that while susceptibility to aggression may explain the reason for the higher risk of suicide among folks charged with violent crimes, the correlation between violent offenders, aggression, and self-harm requires much more exploration to be conclusive. The relationship between impulsivity and NSSI among prisoners is also worth exploring; Dear (2008) posited that high impulsivity contributes to an individual's vulnerability to NSSI, fuels both peer-to-peer and peer-to-staff conflict. Several other bodies of literature have supported impulsivity as an NSSI risk factor (Rohde et al., 2004; Sanislow et al., 2003).

Mental Health Disorders

The research on NSSI as a symptom of a mental health disorder among the prison population is consistent with similar research on the general population. This is a particularly relevant area of study, given that in the United States, correctional facilities are the leading provider of mental health treatment. The National Alliance on Mental Illness (NAMI) estimates that 25%–40% of all mentally ill Americans will be detained in a correctional facility in their lifetime (Ford, 2021). Among those incarcerated with serious mental illness (SMI), an estimated 61% engage in self-injurious behavior (Gray et al., 2003).

Research suggests that of the mental health disorders associated with NSSI, there is a higher risk for those with Axis II personality disorder diagnoses, particularly borderline personality disorder (BPD) (Dixon-Gordon et al., 2012; Casiano et al., 2013). Estimates state that BPD is often more prevalent in prisons and jails than it is in psychiatric hospitals, and about twice as prevalent in correctional facilities than it is in outpatient clinics (Conn et al., 2010). Among female detainees with BPD, Chapman et al. (2005) found a 73% prevalence of NSSI. However, diagnostic measures used in correctional facilities are often less rigorous than those used in more traditional mental health settings (see Cliffe et al., this volume).

Although most of the related research distinguishes psychosis-induced self-injury as being "biologically driven" and distinct from typical NSSI, the strong association is still worth noting. O'Brien et al.'s (2003) study found that 33% of female detainees with psychotic disorder self-harmed, compared to 10% of females without psychotic disorder. In Dear's (2008) research in Australian prisons, 31% reported psychological symptoms as a precipitating factor for NSSI, largely psychotic symptoms, drug withdrawal, and intrusive, traumatic memories.

Other mental health disorder diagnoses mentioned as precipitants for NSSI include major depressive disorder and substance use disorders, although further research is needed in this area.

Interventions

Prison clinicians and researchers have tried to implement and evaluate a variety of interventions to prevent NSSI and treat its underlying contributing factors. Many published interventions center on training staff to identify risk and provide direct supervision to those deemed susceptible to suicidal tendencies. However, the vast majority of facilities simply respond to episodes of NSSI with punitive measures such as detainment and seclusion.

Solitary Confinement

The most common responses to NSSI include isolation (use of a "crisis-intervention cell"), confiscation of objects, physical restraint, first aid, and report filing (Dehart et al., 2009). Solitary confinement typically involves a detainee being removed from the general population, placed in an isolation cell with a paper gown or no clothing, and subjected to constant or interval monitoring. In one study, 80.8% of correctional staff surveyed reported that seclusion or monitoring was a part of their NSSI prevention strategy (Marzano & Adler, 2007). Professionals in Dehart et al.'s (2009) research reported that these seclusion and detainment approaches did not initiate long-term change or target the underlying issue but, rather, served to "get to the next day." Further, constant observation and use of restraints require significant staff time and energy, resulting in higher costs for the prison system.

Appelbaum et al. (2011) conducted a study on the prevalence, management, and epidemiology of NSSI throughout 39 state prison systems in the United States and found that 63% of these prison systems treat NSSI as a rule violation. One of the dangers of utilizing solitary confinement as a punishment for NSSI is that seclusion often exacerbates urges to self-injure. Raymond Bonner, chief psychologist at the Federal Correctional Institution in Allenwood, Pennsylvania, stated that "by and large, most self-harm behavior in prison is exhibited by individuals who are confined in conditions of segregation, social isolation, and/or psychosocial deprivation." And thus, begins a self-perpetuating cycle of self-harm: one self-injures to cope with distress, is then placed in solitary confinement which increases distress, continues to self-injure to cope, and is then sentenced to even longer periods in lockdown. In fact, detainees in segregation units or lockdown exhibited the highest rates of self-injury in 76% of the systems studied by Appelbaum et al. (2011). Kaba et al. (2014) published similar findings: detainees who were placed in solitary confinement as penalization were at a 6.9 times higher likelihood of engaging in NSSI, even after controlling for mental illness, age, race, and length of stay. It is evident that segregation does not prevent individuals from harming themselves; on the contrary, it can significantly worsen symptoms of an existing mental illness and contribute to the onset of acute mental illness among those who did not previously experience any symptoms (Grassian, 2006). Regarding rule 30B in the prison matrix, which defines "direct or indirect harm to oneself" as a rule infraction, the Vera Institute of Justice recommends that facilities should immediately prohibit punishment for NSSI and "respond to such behavior with clinical approaches" (Cloud et al., 2019).

Ironically, detainees commonly engage in self-injury as a means of escaping solitary confinement, perhaps through transfer to a hospital facility. As Kaba noted, "many inmates report to us that they have and will continue to do anything to escape these settings" (Kaba et al., 2014, p. 446). Research suggests that NSSI occurs more frequently in maximum-security settings, and 48% of prison systems reported that the first or second highest rates of NSSI occurred in the maximum-security units (Appelbaum et al., 2011) which seems to question if increased surveillance and restrictions leads to increased prisoner safety.

Medication

In both correctional and community samples, the evidence is lacking in pharmacological interventions as a treatment for NSSI. Appelbaum et al. (2011) found that of the 39 studied state prison systems, 36% report that "most of the time" they prescribe selective serotonin reuptake inhibitors (SSRIs) for the treatment self-harm, while fewer reported the use of beta blockers (5%), antipsychotics (5%), and anticonvulsants (4%). Other studies suggest that prison clinicians do not use medication to treat NSSI but rather to treat underlying mental health conditions (Dixon-Gordon et al., 2012). (More information on pharmacological intervention can be found in Plener, this volume.)

Cognitive Behavioral Therapy

While in both correctional and community samples, the evidence is lacking in pharmacological interventions as a treatment for NSSI, in community samples, there is some evidence to suggest that cognitive behavioral therapy (CBT) interventions are effective in reducing the frequency and severity of self-harm (Slee et al., 2008). Three studies test this effectiveness in correctional settings (Mitchell et al., 2011; Pratt et al., 2015; Riaz & Agha, 2012). In all three CBT studies, the treatment was manualized and combined psychoeducation, cognitive restructuring, problem-solving, and relaxation techniques. Topics included identifying triggers, recognizing the consequent thoughts and feelings, identifying thought distortions, changing distorted thinking, and adopting new, more rational thoughts and coping skills.

Pratt et al. (2015) applied a CBT intervention called "cognitive–behavioral suicide prevention" (CBSP) therapy, which targets suicidal ideation/behavior. The curriculum addresses "(i) information-processing biases, (ii) appraisals and (iii) a suicide schema to be the main components contributing to an individual's experience of suicidality" (Pratt et al., 2015, p. 3443). The results are promising. At the six-month assessment, the CBSP treatment group demonstrated a decrease in the mean number of self-injury behaviors (SIB) of almost 50% and no participants reported an increase of SIBs relative to baseline. In contrast, there was a negligible change in SIB rates among the treatment as usual (TAU) group, and six TAU participants reported an increase in SIBs. At the endpoint of treatment, 56% of CBSP participants achieved a "clinically significant recovery" in comparison to the 23% of TAU group participants, although this improvement was not maintained at the six-month follow-up.

The results of Riaz and Agha (2012) and Mitchell et al. (2011) imply that standard CBT may suffice in reducing incidents of self-harm in prisons. In a Pakistani women's prison, Riaz and Agha (2012) applied a group-based CBT intervention to nine incarcerated women for four months and observed a reduction in the number of deliberate self-harm episodes. Between the end of the intervention and the one-month follow-up, there was an absence of self-harming events among the participants. The women reported improved use of adaptive coping methods post-therapy (i.e., increased religious involvement), while some participants also reported an increase in avoidant behaviors, such as cigarette use or self-distraction. Of note, this sample only included nine participants, and only one follow-up was conducted at one month posttreatment due to institutional constraints. More information on CBT can be found in Chapman et al., this volume.

Dialectical Behavioral Therapy
Dialectical behavioral therapy (DBT) was initially designed to address suicidal behavior and BPD, making it a viable contender as an intervention for chronic NSSI. That said, there is only one study, to this author's knowledge, that applies DBT to target NSSI in a carceral setting. In their study on adolescent females in a Juvenile Rehabilitation Administration facility, Trupin et al. (2002) administered a DBT intervention to one experimental group and two control groups. The treatment approach included training in five skill categories: core mindfulness, interpersonal effectiveness, emotion regulation,

distress tolerance, and self-management. In this study, the treatment group was the only group that demonstrated a significant reduction in "serious" behavior. However, the effects did not show in the post-study data from the same group in the prior year (Trupin et al., 2002). More information on DBT can be found in Chapman et al. (this volume).

Peer Prevention Program

Peer prevention programs have gained popularity in prison settings with the hope that detainees would be more likely to disclose distress to peers, compared to correctional staff. These programs are designed to train fellow detainees on various clinical concepts, such as effective and active listening, suicide prevention and intervention, nonverbal communications, the nature of mental illness, and the concept of befriending. The trainees are available to serve as "peer listeners" to their distressed peers. Junker et al. (2005) implemented one such program, called the Inmate Observer Program. The results indicated a decrease in the mean number of hours that individuals were on "suicide watch," and that when peer listeners were employed, significantly fewer watches were required for individuals with personality disorder diagnoses. Hall and Gabor (2004) examined a similar peer program in a Canadian correctional facility; however, the sample size was too small to offer any conclusions.

Behavioral Management Plans

Fagan et al. (2010) recommend the use of a behavioral management plan, using positive reinforcement and limitations to encourage more desirable behaviors. The authors endorse a cooperative approach in which the self-harming individual can provide input into their plan, with options from which they can choose. The authors point out that many self-harming individuals struggle with delayed reinforcement and would therefore benefit from time-limited, short-term plans. Fagan et al. (2010) also emphasized the importance of making behavioral management plans multidisciplinary efforts, agreed upon and understood by all correctional staff and the self-injurer. Of note, many behavioral management programs in correctional facilities are ineffective due to a shortage of mental health staff, leaving general correctional staff to create and manage the programs with minimal training and supervision (Appelbaum et al., 2011).

Risk Screening

In a comprehensive review of detainee safety needs, Fagan et al. (2010) concluded that "there is no clear consensus on risk factors associated with self-injury for other, nonlethal reasons" (p. 55). Nevertheless, much of the literature on this issue calls for increased use and refinement of NSSI risk assessments upon one's entry into a facility, guided by research-informed NSSI predictive variables. At the same time, most researchers agree that due to the heterogeneous nature of self-injury, and the fact that many of these risk factors are highly common among the population at baseline, most current risk measures have extremely poor predictive power. At baseline, the prison population demonstrates inflated rates of risk factors, such as a diagnosis of a psychiatric illness or history of violent crime increasing the likelihood of screening instruments being overly inclusive, and. In fact, across the literature, most detainees who were flagged for NSSI risk factors did not experience any episodes of self-injury (Martin et al., 2014).

While further research is needed to identify reliable assessments for usable predictive factors, the literature suggests that efforts should be focused on helping train correctional staff to identify an individual's psychological distress in real time, rather than during designated screening period.

Institution-Level Interventions

A large contributor to the prevention and management of NSSI within prisons is the moral culture of the facility. Although somewhat of an oxymoron, Her Majesty's Inspectorate of Prisons (1999) proposed the term "healthy prison" in which mental health services and rehabilitation are provided, and a culture of fairness is shared among correctional staff. Liebling (2006) has found some support that an improvement in an institution's "moral climate" results in fewer incidences of self-harm. Gu et al. (2020) recommended that prison staff participate in training focused on treating detainees with respect, dignity, and procedural fairness and contribute to a culture in which detainees feel comfortable asking for help. This highlights the significant distrust that exists between detainees and prison staff, and the widely held belief among detainees that disclosure to staff will be met with punishment, shaming, or nonresponse. Evidence points to the use of rehabilitative methods—focus on minimizing distress and improving regulation skills long term—rather than the use of punishment and physical barriers as a "band-aid" solution to the problem.

The Vera Institute for Justice has identified safe alternatives to segregation to reduce self-harm incidents. Recommendations include enacting policies that would prevent young people, and people with serious mental illness, from being placed in solitary confinement and eliminating the loss of visitation and/or phone access as a disciplinary measure. Evidence clearly points to the strong impact of isolation from supports on one's mental well-being, particularly those with higher baseline risk for serious mental illness (SMI). In the same vein, detainment centers should minimize the use of recreation restrictions to allow exercise and outdoor time to be used as a coping strategy as often as possible (Cloud et al., 2019).

Special Considerations for Youth in Custody

In both community and incarcerated samples, young people exhibit higher rates of NSSI. Hawton et al.'s (2014) study illustrated that individuals less than 20 years of age accounted for 21%–23% of the self-injuring prison sample, despite only making up 13% of the prison population. A six-month study showed that 5% of male juveniles (ages 15–18) and

7% of male young offenders (ages 18–21) self-injured, compared to 1.5% of adult males (Muehlenkamp & Gutierrez, 2007; Welfare & Mitchell, 2005).

Most of the research agrees that young people who find themselves in detention centers have, at baseline, experienced higher rates of cumulative exposure and complex traumatic experiences. Those who have the misfortune of being sent to prisons and jails are subjected to further humiliation, abuse, and depersonalization; deprived of age-appropriate educational, medical, or rehabilitative services; and denied basic human rights. Detention facilities bear a deeply ingrained culture of violence, and gang activity flourishes within the walls of detention facilities. There are frequent accounts of staff brutality toward detainees, and reporting abuse from a correctional officer often leads to even more abuse, perpetuating a silence and self-inflicted harm as means for coping. For young people who already experience cumulative exposure, increased vulnerability to poor coping skills, and psychological adversity, the culture of a detention facility runs completely counter to any rehabilitative goals.

Youth-Specific Risk Factors

There appear to be some unique risks for NSSI among the juvenile detainee population. While some adult studies have discussed substance withdrawal and its exacerbation of NSSI risk, youth studies highlight more specific relationships between drugs and NSSI. Studies of incarcerated youth report that self-harming youth are more likely to have injected drugs, have a diagnosis of substance use disorder, and/or have a history of illicit drug use (Kenny et al., 2008; Penn et al., 2003; McReynolds et al., 2017). Casiano et al. (2013) found that "after controlling for depression and impulsivity, drug abuse remained associated only with self-harm among detainees" (p. 121).

Kenny et al.'s (2008) study investigates history of head injury as a possible indicator of risk-taking and, consequently, self-harm. The connection between head injuries, risk-taking, impulsivity, and NSSI is an overlooked topic worth further exploration.

Dehart et al. (2009) raised the issue of "copycat" self-injurious behavior. The cluster effect of self-harm incidents in prisons, described as "contagious," are even more relevant in studies focused on incarcerated youth, given a young person's increased susceptibility to peer influence (McReynolds et al., 2017). Some young people may observe their peers' positive outcomes of NSSI (i.e., cell transfer) and feel further motivated to engage in NSSI. Segal et al. (1963) have characterized a series of self-inflicted ocular injuries among a group of prisoners as an "epidemic," in which the participants were attempting to seek status or respect from peers for their ability to self-inflict and endure pain.

Youth-Specific Interventions

Rohde et al. (2004) developed a unique program intervention called "Coping Course." The treatment involved 16 sessions provided over the course of eight weeks, during which the group clinician taught emotional regulation skills. Sessions included social skills training, relaxation techniques, cognitive restructuring, communication improvement, and problem-solving. In a comparison of pre- and post-intervention scores, study participants demonstrated a statistically significant decrease in Life Attitudes Schedule (LAS) death-related scores.

In an adolescent correctional facility, Mitchell et al. (2011) provided weekly CBT to a group of self-harming adolescents, while the control group received TAU. Among the CBT group, scores on the Difficulties and Coping Profiles Questionnaire (DCP) indicated a decrease in self-harm and suicidal ideation and significant increases in the coping ability for depression and anxiety. There were no significant changes among the TAU group. At the 12-month follow-up, researchers found no statistically significant outcomes for key measures in either group.

The "Access Program" is an intervention designed for adolescents, applied in a youth correctional facility in the United Kingdom (Welfare & Mitchell, 2005). The program aims to reduce the incidence of self-injury and improve participant hopelessness, self-esteem, locus of control, and assertiveness. This intervention is unique in its incorporation of physical activity, which is intended to promote teamwork and improve self-esteem. For 12 sessions, subjects participated in an hour of emotional skills work, including problem-solving and emotion management, and an hour of gymnasium activity. Records of self-harm incidents indicate that the outcomes for participants were significantly better than for those in the wait-list group who did not receive the intervention. Staff reports indicate a decrease in participant actual and threatened self-injury that was maintained at the six-week follow-up (Welfare & Mitchell, 2005).

Limitations of Existing Research

The existing studies provide important groundwork for future risk assessment and intervention design, and the results suggest that peer support programs and CBT treatments for NSSI in prisons are worth researching more extensively. Despite this, the integrity of the included studies on NSSI treatment is compromised by definitional variances, missing comparison groups, and inconsistency in behavioral outcome measures (Pratt et al., 2015). Further, the sample sizes within studies widely vary, harming the validity of any direct comparison made between interventions.

Definitional Variances

Self-injury is described by a wide variety of terms in the research literature, including self-harm, NSSI, self-injury, SIB, suicidal behavior, and deliberate self-harm (DSH). Some studies involving prisoner populations condense all forms of self-injury, both suicidal and nonsuicidal, under one blanket term, such as "suicidal behavior" or "problem behavior" (Mitchell et al., 2011; Trupin et al., 2002), and one study broadly observed "death-related thoughts" (Rohde et al., 2004). This inconsistency points to the need for a stronger differentiation between "suicidal behavior" and "self-injury" in the literature. Although there is a high rate of co-occurrence between NSSI and suicide attempts, NSSI is decisively marked by the lack of intent to die.

Differences in Behavioral Outcome Measures
There are significant differences in the measurement tools used in intervention studies, even among those measuring the same target behavior. Mitchell et al. (2011), for example, used the SAVRY assessment, the Youth Self-Report and the Difficulties and Coping Profile. These tools place more emphasis on the risk of violence and rely on participant self-report, which provides a greater opportunity for bias. Conversely, Trupin et al. (2002) measured overall problem behavior through community risk assessment scores and assessed self-harm incidents via qualitative information from daily behavior logs and staff reports. The results of each study certainly have clinical significance and implications for practice, but this discrepancy affects the ability to truly synthesize study results and accurately compare interventions.

Nature of Self-Harm
It is challenging to assess an intervention for a behavior that serves so many functions, particularly in a correctional facility. Further, self-harm is uniquely difficult to study because "studying risk for self-injury through randomized controlled trials or without any intervention is almost always unethical" (Martin et al., 2014, p. 265).

In view of the research on functionality, it is impractical to treat self-injury as one uniform problem and subsequently apply one blanket treatment. Although it can be difficult to assess and identify the intent behind one's self-harming behaviors, researchers ought to study interventions that target risk assessment and distress identification.

Study Design
Researchers face a particularly challenging task when assessing the effectiveness of NSSI prevention. While unfortunately, NSSI occurs at a higher rate in forensic settings compared to the general population, it is still a relatively rare occurrence. The authors caution against drawing conclusions from data with such low absolute frequency. Other factors that were unaccounted for may have led to underestimates of NSSI rates. For example, Kenny et al. (2008) excluded those with serious mental illness, severe violence, or substance use withdrawal from the sample.

Significant variance in sample size and study design among the published research threatens the internal and external validity of the research. Additionally, the inconsistency of follow-up periods among studies also weakens the validity of comparisons between results; short follow-up times allow more opportunity for bias and do not convey whether the initial improvements made post-intervention are enduring or short-lived.

Barriers to Conducting Clinical Research in Correctional Facilities

As with any research conducted in correctional facilities, researchers in this field face a gamut of systemic obstacles that can compromise treatment delivery and data collection. Thanks to frequent facility transfers and/or high rates of treatment refusal, attrition rates are fairly high—that is, 64% among eligible prisoners in Pratt et al.'s (2015) study. This opens the possibility that those who completed the studies differ in study-based characteristics at baseline, compared to those who did not complete or refused.

Prison settings typically offer limited facility access to researchers and therefore interfere with their ability to conduct the full series of treatment sessions. Riaz and Agha (2012) were limited to six months of access to the facility, and one of these months was devoted to recruitment. This left only five months for the therapeutic intervention and a follow-up at one-month post-intervention, a time frame that is far too brief to accurately evaluate any impact of CBT on DSH (Riaz & Agha, 2012). The therapist in this study was prohibited from conducting the sessions in the same room as participants, and the spaces made available for treatment offered very limited privacy. Correctional staff's occasional attendance at sessions often resulted in reserved behavior from participants, unable to express staff-related complaints or share incidents of rule-breaking. Further, research in correctional facilities is often interrupted or prevented by frequent lockdowns, which requires participants to return to their cells, causing a loss of treatment time and major disruptions in the flow during therapeutic sessions.

The validity of facility reports and self-reports in correctional facilities also comes into question. Other researchers reviewed prison medical records to track the number of episodes of suicidal or self-injurious behavior. However, correctional facilities may benefit from underreporting incidences of self-injury, particularly ones that can be attributed to staff negligence. Incarcerated participants are often reluctant to disclose potentially damning information such as self-harm or possession of a sharp implement, considering the potential consequences. Therefore, there is an increased chance of inaccurate information in studies that relied on self-reports (Mitchell et al., 2011). Limited fiscal resources create additional challenges for researchers by limiting their access to additional mental health staff and appropriate psychometric tools. Moreover, due to changes in policy, public opinion, and public and/or private funding, these budgets are constantly changing and require frequent adjustments from clinical staff.

Conclusions

NSSI is a relatively common phenomenon within correctional facilities internationally, presenting the risk for prisoner injury or death, staff burnout, elevated costs, and the overall functioning of a prison. Many studies call for improved prison mental health care and advancement in treatments that specifically target NSSI. While research can speculate about the many associated risk factors, functions, consequences, and treatments of NSSI in the prison context, it is crucial that we examine the role that the modern carceral system plays in perpetuating maladaptive behaviors. The nature of the prison system is punitive and was not designed to rehabilitate or to serve as a comprehensive mental health treatment. And yet, prisons and jails are the *largest* mental health care providers in the United States. Published findings indicate the occurrence of the same phenomenon in countries across the globe, including Russia, (Bobrik et al., 2005; Burgermeister, 2003), Australia (Mental Health Council of Australia, 2010), and the UK where "prison has become a 'catch-all' social and mental healthcare service, and a breeding ground for poor mental health" (Brooker & Ullmann, 2008, p. 6).

This author cautions against the attribution of prison NSSI to psychological disorders, which are often secondary to the stressful prison environment's role in the use of self-injury as a coping mechanism for distress. Perhaps, self-injury is a fairly "normal" response to an extremely abnormal living condition.

Some critics highlight the need for the reform of prison culture and a progression toward "healthy prisons" (Her Majesty's Inspectorate of Prisons, 1999). However, we must examine the meaning of a "healthy prison" and the viability of the terms "healthy" and "prison" ever truly co-occurring within the U.S. industrial prison complex. The called-upon strategy of "reform" implies that only certain aspects of the institution are flawed but the institution itself is not. This is not the case. By virtue of a prison being a prison, correctional facilities are in perpetual crisis and thus generate a state of ongoing, psychological distress among their occupants, including staff.

The monetary and human cost of prison NSSI is significant enough for us to reexamine the upstream factors contributing to the issue, rather than directing resources and attention toward mitigating the negative impact of the prison environment. At the same time, although movement toward prison reform and alternatives to incarceration may be on the horizon, the reality is that approximately 10.35 million people are incarcerated worldwide, with the United States reporting the highest incarceration rate in the world (BBC, 2005). Thus, the need for further investigation of effective strategies to manage detainee distress and reduce incidents of NSSI is still relevant and will continue to be for the foreseeable future.

The literature concedes that areas for strategic intervention include correctional staffs' ability to identify psychological distress among prisoners, the relationships between staff and prisoners to allow for more open and willing communication, and prisoners' coping abilities. The current research explores several angles for intervention; however, the many logistical barriers involved in empirical studies in prisons and the heterogeneous nature of NSSI necessitate further comprehensive studies.

References

Alessi, N. E., McManus, M., Brickman, A., & Grapentine, L. (1984). Suicidal behavior among serious juvenile offenders. *American Journal of Psychiatry, 141*(2), 286–287.

Appelbaum, K. L., Savageau, J. A., Trestman, R. L., Metzner, J. L., & Baillargeon, J. (2011). A national survey of self-injurious behavior in American prisons. *Psychiatric Services, 62*, 285–290. https://doi.org/10.1176/ps.62.3.pss6203_0285

BBC. (2005, June 20). *In depth*. BBC News. http://news.bbc.co.uk/2/shared/spl/hi/uk/06/prisons/html/nn2page1.stm.

Bobrik A., Danishevski K., Eroshina K., & McKee, M. (2005). Prison health in Russia: The larger picture. *Journal of Public Health Policy*, *26*(1), 30–59. https://doi.org/10.1057/palgrave.jphp.3200002

Borrill, J., Burnett, R., Atkins, R., Miller, S., Briggs, D., Weaver, T., & Maden, A. (2003). Patterns of self-harm and attempted suicide among white and black/mixed race female prisoners. *Criminal Behaviour and Mental Health*, *13*(4), 229–240. https://doi.org/10.1002/cbm.549

Briere, J., & Gil, E. (1998). Self-mutilation in clinical and general population samples: Prevalence, correlates, and functions. *American Journal of Orthopsychiatry*, *68*(4), 609–620. https://doi.org/10.1037/h0080369

Brooker, C., & Ullmann, B. (2008). *Out of sight, out of mind. The state of mental healthcare in prison. Policy exchange*. Clutha House.

Burgermeister J. (2003). Three quarters of Russia's prisoners have serious diseases. *BMJ*, *327*(7423), 1066. https://doi.org/10.1136/bmj.327.7423.1066-b

Casiano, H., Katz, L. Y., Globerman, D., & Sareen, J. (2013). Suicide and deliberate self-injurious behavior in juvenile correctional facilities: A review. *Journal of the Canadian Academy of Child and Adolescent Psychiatry*, *22*(2), 118–124.

Chapman, A., Specht, M. W., & Cellucci, T. (2005). Borderline personality disorder and deliberate self-harm: Does experiential avoidance play a role? *Suicide and Life-Threatening Behavior*, *35*, 388–399. doi:10.1521/suli.2005.35.4.388

Chapman, A. L., & Dixon-Gordon, K. L. (2007). Emotional antecedents and consequences of deliberate self-harm and suicide attempts. *Suicide and Life-Threatening Behavior*, *37*(5), 543–552. https://doi.org/10.1521/suli.2007.37.5.543

Cloud, D., LaChance, J., Smith, L., & Galarza, L. (2019). *The safe alternatives to segregation initiative: Findings and recommendations for the Louisiana Department of Public Safety and Corrections, and progress toward implementation*. https://www.vera.org/downloads/publications/safe-alternatives-segregation-initiative-findings-recommendations-ldps.pdf

Conn, C., Warden, R., Stuewig, J., Kim, E. H., Harty, L., Hastings, M., & Tangney, J. P. (2010). Borderline personality disorder among jail inmates: How common and how distinct? *Corrections Compendium*, *35*(4), 6–13.

Dear, G. E. (2008). Ten years of research into self-harm in the Western Australian prison system: Where to next? *Psychiatry, Psychology and Law*, *15*(3), 469–481. https://doi.org/10.1080/13218710802101613

Dear, G. E., Slattery, J. L., & Hillan, R. J. (2001). Evaluations of the quality of coping reported by prisoners who have self-harmed and those who have not. *Suicide and Life-Threatening Behavior*, *31*(4), 442–450. https://doi.org/10.1521/suli.31.4.442.22039

Dear, G. E., Thomson, D., & Hills, A. (2000). Self-harm in prison. *Criminal Justice and Behavior*, *27*(2), 160–175. https://doi.org/10.1177/0093854800027002002

DeHart, D. D., Smith, H. P., & Kaminski, R. J. (2009). Institutional responses to self-injurious behavior among inmates. *Journal of Correctional Health Care*, *15*, 129–141.

Dixon-Gordon, K., Harrison, N., & Roesch, R. (2012). Non-suicidal self-injury within offender populations: A systematic review. *International Journal of Forensic Mental Health*, *11*(1), 33–50. https://doi.org/10.1080/14999013.2012.667513

Fagan, T. J., Cox, J., Helfand, S. J., & Aufderheide, D. (2010). Self-injurious behavior in correctional settings. *Journal of Correctional Health Care*, *16*(1), 48–66. https://doi.org/10.1177/1078345809348212

Favril, L. (2019). Non-suicidal self-injury and co-occurring suicide attempt in male prisoners. *Psychiatry Research*, *276*, 196–202. https://doi.org/10.1016/j.psychres.2019.05.017

Fazel, S., Ramesh, T., & Hawton, K. (2017). Suicide in prisons: An international study of prevalence and contributory factors. *The Lancet Psychiatry*, *4*(12), 946–952. https://doi.org/10.1016/s2215-0366(17)30430-3

Ford, M. (2021, February 16). America's largest mental hospital is a jail. *The Atlantic*. https://www.theatlantic.com/politics/archive/2015/06/americas-largest-mental-hospital-is-a-jail/395012/.

Gallagher, J., & Sheldon, K. (2010). Assessing the functions of self-harm behaviours for danger and severely personality disordered males in a high secure hospital. *British Journal of Forensic Practice*, *12*, 22–32. doi:10.5042/bjfp.2010.0035

Grassian, S. (2006). Psychiatric effects of solitary confinement. *The Journal of Law and Policy*, *22*, 325–383. https://openscholarship.wustl.edu/law_journal_law_policy/vol22/iss1/24

Gray, S. G., McGleish, A., MacCulloch, M. J., Hill, C., Timmons, D., & Snowden, R. (2003). Prediction of violence and self-harm in mentally disordered offenders: A prospective study of the efficacy of HCR-20, PCL–R, and psychiatric symptomatology. *Journal of Clinical Psychology, 182*, 443–451. https://doi.org/10.1037/0022-006X.71.3.443

Grobar, M. (2021, June 13). *"Last Week Tonight": John Oliver slams U.S. prisons "Cooking prisoners to death" through lack of air conditioning.* https://deadline.com/2021/06/john-oliver-tackles-issue-of-prison-heat-last-week-tonight-1234774450/

Gu, H., Lu, Y., & Cheng, Y. (2020). Negative life events and nonsuicidal self-injury in prisoners: The mediating role of hopelessness and moderating role of belief in a just world. *Journal of Clinical Psychology, 77*(1), 145–155. https://doi.org/10.1002/jclp.23015

Hall, B., & Gabor, P., (2004). Peer suicide prevention in a prison. *Crisis, 25*, 19–26.

Hawton, K., Linsell, L., Adeniji, T., Sariaslan, A., & Fazel, S. (2014). Self-harm in prisons in England and Wales: An epidemiological study of prevalence, risk factors, clustering, and subsequent suicide. *The Lancet, 383*(9923), 1147–1154. https://doi.org/10.1016/s0140-6736(13)62118-2

Her Majesty's Inspectorate of Prisons. (1999). *Suicide is everyone's concern: A thematic review by HM Chief Inspector of Prisons for England and Wales.* Home Office.

Hillbrand, M., Young, J. L., & Krystal, J. H. (1996). Recurrent self-injurious behavior in forensic patients. *Psychiatric Quarterly, 67*(1), 33–45. https://doi.org/10.1007/bf02244273

Holmqvist, R., Carlberg, M., & Hellgren, L. (2008). Deliberate selfharm behaviour in Swedish adolescent girls reports from public assessment and treatment agencies. *Child Youth Care Forum, 37*, 1–13. doi:10.1007/s10566-007-9044-0

Jeglic, E., Vanderhoff, H., & Donovick, P. (2005). The function of self-harm behavior in a forensic population. *International Journal of Offender Therapy and Comparative Criminology, 49*(2), 131–142. https://doi.org/10.1177/0306624X04271130

Junker, G., Beeler, A., & Bates, J. (2005). Using trained offender observers for suicide watch in a federal correctional setting: A win-win solution. *Psychological Services, 2*(1), 20–27. https://doi.org/10.1037/1541-1559.2.1.20

Kaba, F., Lewis, A., Glowa-Kollisch, S., Hadler, J., Lee, D., Alper, H., Selling, D., MacDonald, R., Solimo, A., Parsons, A., & Venters, H. (2014). Solitary confinement and risk of self-harm among jail inmates. *American Journal of Public Health, 104*(3), 442–447. https://doi.org/10.2105/ajph.2013.301742

Kang-Brown, J., Montagnet, C., & Heiss, J. (2021, January). *People in jail and prison in 2020.* https://www.vera.org/downloads/publications/people-in-jail-and-prison-in-2020.pdf.

Kempton, T., & Forehand, R. L. (1992). Suicide attempts among juvenile delinquents: The contribution of mental health factors. *Behaviour Research and Therapy, 30*(5), 537–541. https://doi.org/10.1016/0005-7967(92)90038-I

Kenning, C., Cooper, J., Short, V., Shaw, J., Abel, K., & Chew-Graham, C. (2010). Prison staff and women prisoner's views on self-harm; their implications for service delivery and development: A qualitative study. *Criminal Behavior and Mental Health, 20*, 274–284. doi:10.1002/cbm.777

Kenny, D. T., Lennings, C. J., & Munn, O. A. (2008). Risk factors for self-harm and suicide in incarcerated young offenders: Implications for policy and practice. *Journal of Forensic Psychology Practice, 8*(4), 358–382. https://doi.org/10.1080/15228930802199317

Klonsky, E. D. (2007). The functions of deliberate self-injury: A review of the evidence. *Clinical Psychology Review, 27*(2), 226–239. https://doi.org/10.1016/j.cpr.2006.08.002

Klonsky, E. D., Oltmanns, T. F., & Turkheimer, E. (2003). Deliberate self-harm in a nonclinical population: Prevalence and psychological correlates. *American Journal of Psychiatry, 160*(8), 1501–1508. https://doi.org/10.1176/appi.ajp.160.8.1501

Liebling, A. (1995). Vulnerability and Prison Suicide. *The British Journal of Criminology, 35*(2), 173–187. http://www.jstor.org/stable/23638549

Liebling, A. (2006). Prisons in transition. *International journal of Law and Psychiatry, 29*(5), 422–430. https://doi.org/10.1016/j.ijlp.2006.03.002

Mangnall, J., & Yurkovich, E. (2008). A Literature review of deliberate self-harm. *Perspectives in Psychiatric Care, 44*(3), 175–184. https://doi.org/10.1111/j.1744-6163.2008.00172.x

Mannion, A. (2009). Self-harm in a dangerous and severely personality disordered population, *The Journal of Forensic Psychiatry & Psychology, 20*(2), 322–331. DOI: 10.1080/14789940802377106

Martin, M. S., Dorken, S. K., Colman, I., McKenzie, K., & Simpson, A. I. (2014). The incidence and prediction of self-injury among sentenced prisoners. *The Canadian Journal of Psychiatry, 59*(5), 259–267. https://doi.org/10.1177/070674371405900505

Marzano, L., & Adler, J. R. (2007). Supporting staff working with prisoners who self-harm: A survey of support staff dealing with self-harm in prisons in England and Wales. *International Journal of Prisoner Health, 3*, 268–282. 10.1192/bjp.bp.109.075424

Matsumoto, T., Yamaguchi, A., Chiba, Y., Asami, T., Iseki, E., & Hirayasu, Y. (2005). Self-burning versus self-cutting: Patterns and implications of self-mutilation. A preliminary study of differences between self-cutting and self-burning in a Japanese juvenile detention center. *Psychiatry and Clinical Neurosciences, 59*(1), 62–69. https://doi.org/10.1111/j.1440-1819.2005.01333.x

McReynolds, L. S., Wasserman, G., & Ozbardakci, E. (2017). Contributors to nonsuicidal self-injury in incarcerated youth. *Health & Justice, 5*(1), Article 13. https://doi.org/10.1186/s40352-017-0058-x

Mental Health Council of Australia. (2010, January 19). *Lack of services mean mentally ill sent to prison, not treated* [Press release]. https://mhaustralia.org/media-releases/lack-services-mean-mentally-ill-sent-prison-not-treated-january-2010

Milligan, R. J., & Andrews, B. (2005). Suicidal and other self-harming behaviour in offender women: The role of shame, anger and childhood abuse. *Legal and Criminological Psychology, 10*(1), 13–25. https://doi.org/10.1348/135532504x15439

Mitchell, P., Smedley, K., Kenning, C., Mckee, A., Woods, D., Rennie, C. E., Dolan, M. (2011). Cognitive behaviour therapy for adolescent offenders with mental health problems in custody. *Journal of Adolescence, 34*(3), 433–443. https://doi.org/10.1016/j.adolescence.2010.06.009

Muehlenkamp, J. J., & Gutierrez, P. M. (2007). Risk for suicide attempts among adolescents who engage in non-suicidal self-injury. *Archives of Suicide Research, 11*(1), 69–82. https://doi.org/10.1080/13811110600992902

O'Brien, M., Mortimer, L., Singleton, N., & Meltzer, H. (2003). Psychiatric morbidity among women prisoners in England and Wales. *International Review of Psychiatry, 15*, 153–157.

Penn, J. V., Esposito, C. L., Schaeffer, L. E., Fritz, G. K., & Spirito, A. (2003). Suicide attempts and self-mutilative behavior in a juvenile correctional facility. *Journal of the American Academy of Child & Adolescent Psychiatry, 42*(7), 762–769. https://doi.org/10.1097/01.chi.0000046869.56865.46

Pratt, D., Tarrier, N., Dunn, G., Awenat, Y., Shaw, J., Ulph, F., & Gooding, P. (2015). Cognitive–behavioural suicide prevention for male prisoners: A pilot randomized controlled trial. *Psychological Medicine, 45*(16), 3441–3451. https://doi.org/10.1017/S0033291715001348

Riaz, R., & Agha, S. (2012). Efficacy of cognitive behavior therapy with deliberate self-harm in incarcerated women. *Pakistan Journal of Psychological Research, 27*(1), 21–35.

Rohde, P., Jorgensen, J. S., Seeley, J. R., & Mace, D. E. (2004). Pilot evaluation of the coping course: A cognitive-behavioral intervention to enhance coping skills in incarcerated youth. *Journal of the American Academy of Child & Adolescent Psychiatry, 43*(6), 669–678. https://doi.org/10.1097/01.chi.0000121068.29744.a5

Sakelliadis, E. I., Papadodima, S. A., Sergentanis, T. N., Giotakos, O., & Spiliopoulou, C. A. (2010). Self-injurious behavior among Greek male prisoners: Prevalence and risk factors. *The Journal of Association of European Psychiatrists, 25*, 151–158. https://doi.org/10.1016/j.eurpsy.2009.07.014

Sanislow, C., Chapman, J., & McGlashan, T. (2003). *Crisis Intervention Services in Juvenile Detention Centers*. Psychiatry Online. https://ps.psychiatryonline.org/doi/full/10.1176/appi.ps.54.1.107

Segal, P., Mrzyglod, S., Alichniewicz-Czaplicka, H., Dunin-Horkawicz, W., & Zwyrzykowski, E. (1963). Self-inflicted eye injuries. *American Journal of Ophthalmology, 55*(2), 349–362. https://doi.org/10.1016/0002-9394(63)92695-3

Slee, N., Garnefski, N., van der Leeden, R., Arensman, E., & Spinhoven, P. (2008). Cognitive-behavioural intervention for self-harm: Randomised controlled trial. *British Journal of Psychiatry, 192*(3), 202–211. https://doi.org/10.1192/bjp.bp.107.037564

Vera Institute of Justice. (2015). *The price of prisons—Prison spending in 2015*. https://www.vera.org/publications/price-of-prisons-2015-state-spending-trends/price-of-prisons-2015-state-spending-trends/price-of-prisons-2015-state-spending-trends-prison-spending.

Toohey, G. (2019, May 27). Self-harm spikes in Louisiana prisons in hot summer months, advocates say; "it's unconscionable." https://www.theadvocate.com/baton_rouge/news/crime_police/article_a222bb3e-7d92-11e9-bf1d-57767ce4f72d.html.

Trupin, E. W., Stewart, D. G., Beach, B., & Boesky, L. (2002). Effectiveness of a dialectical behaviour therapy program for incarcerated female juvenile offenders. *Child and Adolescent Mental Health*, *7*(3), 121–127. https://doi.org/10.1111/1475-3588.00022

Welfare, H., & Mitchell, J. (2005). Addressing vulnerability amongst imprisoned juvenile offenders: An evaluation of the Access course. *International Journal of Prisoner Health*, *1*, 171–181. https://doi.org/10.1080/17449200600552912

Winicov, N. (2019). A systematic review of behavioral health interventions for suicidal and self-harming individuals in prisons and jails. *Heliyon*, *5*(9), Article e02379. https://doi.org/10.1016/j.heliyon.2019.e02379

Yaroshevsky, F. (1975). Self-Mutilation in Soviet Prisons. *Canadian Psychiatric Association Journal*, *20*(6), 443–446. https://doi.org/10.1177/070674377502000603

CHAPTER 32

NSSI Among Military Service Members and Veterans

Molly Gromatsky, Adam J. Mann, Nathan A. Kimbrel, *and* Kirsten H. Dillon

Abstract

This chapter discusses nonsuicidal self-injury (NSSI) among military service members and veterans. Though NSSI typically emerges and is most prevalent during adolescence and young adulthood, research examining NSSI in service members—who represent a younger demographic of military personnel—is limited in quantity. Existing literature reporting NSSI prevalence rates among service members varies, and initial lifetime estimates among nonclinical samples are low. As with rates of suicidal thoughts and behaviors, NSSI prevalence rates tend to be higher among veterans or combined military personnel samples compared to service members alone. The chapter then looks at demographic differences in NSSI rates among military service members and veterans, considering gender, sexual and gender minority status, age and military service era, and race and ethnicity. It studies the relationship between NSSI and affect-related conditions, suicide risk, trauma exposure, substance use, obsessive-compulsive disorder (OCD), and attention-deficit/hyperactivity disorder (ADHD). The chapter also assesses the forms and functions of NSSI in service members and veterans before exploring future directions for assessment and treatment of NSSI in military personnel.

Key Words: nonsuicidal self-injury, military service members, military veterans, military personnel, suicide risk, trauma exposure, substance use, obsessive-compulsive disorder, attention-deficit/hyperactivity disorder

Introduction

Military service members and veterans represent a group vulnerable to suicide and related behaviors. Despite political legislation and clinical initiatives aimed at reducing suicide rates among military personnel (Executive Order No. 13861, 2019), young and enlisted service members evidence elevated suicide risk and veterans account for 13.8% of all suicide deaths nationally with 18 dying by suicide daily (Department of Defense, 2020; Department of Veterans Affairs, 2020). Converging evidence indicates that nonsuicidal self-injury (NSSI) constitutes one of the most robust predictors of suicidal thoughts and behavior among military service members and veterans (Baer, LaCroix, Browne, Hassen, Perera, Soumoff, et al., 2018; Franklin et al., 2017; Kimbrel et al., 2016; Villatte et al., 2015), making its study and treatment a pivotal component of suicide prevention.

Furthermore, NSSI alone is a valuable treatment target as it is associated with significant distress, impairment, and potential for serious physical injury (Doshi et al., 2005; Selby et al., 2012). In more recent years, NSSI has been recognized as a distinct diagnostic entity with the creation of NSSI disorder (American Psychiatric Association, 2013). While the extant literature has substantially increased our knowledge and understanding of NSSI among civilians—especially adolescents and young adults (Fox et al., 2015; Swannell et al., 2014)—there is presently a relative paucity of data exploring NSSI in military samples.

Prevalence

Though NSSI typically emerges and is most prevalent during adolescence and young adulthood (Klonsky, 2011; Swannell et al., 2014), research examining NSSI in service members—who represent a younger demographic of military personnel—is limited in quantity. In the existing literature reporting on NSSI, prevalence rates among service members vary, and initial lifetime estimates among nonclinical samples are low (e.g., 4% of U.S. military recruits completing basic training; Klonsky et al., 2003); however, rates of lifetime NSSI in subsequent studies of nonclinical service members are generally comparable to civilian counterparts or higher: 6.3% of soldiers and 7.9% of new recruits (Turner et al., 2019); 7% of National Guard members (May et al., 2018); 15.9% of service members broadly (Bandel & Anestis, 2020). Rates are higher among clinical samples of service members (e.g., 17.2% of those with broad mental health difficulties, Jones et al., 2019) and, as expected, even greater among service members at increased risk for suicide. For example, Bryan, Rudd, et al. (2015) found nearly a third (30.3%) of service members seeking outpatient treatment for suicide risk reported NSSI history, and Nock et al. (2017) found 22.6% of service members who died by suicide evidenced NSSI history per family member report.

As with rates of suicidal thoughts and behaviors, NSSI prevalence rates tend to be higher among veteran or combined military personnel samples compared to service members alone (Jones et al., 2019). For example, rates of lifetime NSSI in service members and veterans enrolled in college courses range from 12.3% to 14% (Bryan & Bryan, 2014; Bryan, Bryan, et al., 2015; Bryan et al., 2014) and 6% to 16.4% in non-treatment-seeking veterans (Bryan & Bryan, 2014; Bryan et al., 2014; Kimbrel et al., 2015; Lear et al., 2021; Pinder et al., 2012). Comparatively lower rates in service members may be due, in part, to fear of real or perceived career repercussions of reporting about traditionally stigmatized topics (e.g., suicide and mental health difficulties) and/or seeking treatment, including potential discharge or changes to military duties (Zinzow et al., 2013). It is less likely that lower rates are due to NSSI emerging after the start or conclusion of military service, as NSSI typically precedes military service among those endorsing history (i.e., 63.5% of service members and veterans, Bryan et al., 2014; 75% of service members, Turner et al., 2019). This may also account for significantly lower rates of recent NSSI (i.e., occurring in the last year) evidenced among college students with military service (7.5%) versus those without (9.6%, Pease et al., 2015). Nonetheless, service members and veterans with even remote NSSI history are at greater risk for suicidal thoughts and behaviors (Turner et al., 2019).

Rates of NSSI appear to be highest among service members and veterans actively seeking or receiving mental health treatment (e.g., Gromatsky et al., 2021; Kimbrel, Thomas, et al., 2018; Villatte et al., 2015). For example, Villatte et al. (2015) examined suicide attempt characteristics of high-risk military personnel (i.e., reporting either current suicidal ideation or lifetime history of suicide attempt). This pooled analysis found lifetime NSSI prevalence among service members receiving mental health treatment for acute suicide risk (34%) was double the rate of lifetime NSSI observed among veteran peers (17%). However, a more recent study conducted by Gromatsky et al. (2021) that recruited veterans receiving mental health services who were at higher risk for suicide (i.e., those who either presented to the emergency room for suicidal thoughts or behaviors; had been hospitalized for suicidal thoughts or behaviors; had experienced chronic suicidal ideation; and/or had been assigned to a "high risk for suicide" list during the past three months) found the overall rate of lifetime NSSI was approximately 26%. Furthermore, evidence also suggests that soldiers with recent (i.e., past-year) NSSI are more likely to report recent mental health service utilization compared to those with a more remote history of NSSI (Turner et al., 2019).

Interestingly, the highest rates of NSSI observed among treatment-seeking service members or veterans to date come not from a study of suicidal patients but from a series of studies of veterans seeking treatment for PTSD at the Durham Veterans Administration (VA) Medical Center PTSD Clinic (Calhoun et al., 2017; Kimbrel et al., 2014; Kimbrel, Thomas, et al., 2018; Sacks et al., 2008). These studies utilized overlapping samples, so we will only discuss the largest analysis of this sample to date (n = 1,143 veterans seeking PTSD treatment) conducted by Kimbrel, Meyer, et al. and Kimbrel, Thomas, et al. (2018). Notably, this study found 62% of veterans seeking treatment for PTSD endorsed a lifetime history of engaging in one or more "traditional" forms of NSSI, including scratching, cutting, burning, or hitting oneself; however, when the operational definition of NSSI was modified to also include punching walls and objects, the lifetime prevalence increased to 82%. While independent replication is necessary, findings strongly suggest veterans seeking treatment for PTSD may be especially likely to engage in NSSI behaviors.

In sum, while initial reports of NSSI among service members and veterans may have underestimated its prevalence, converging evidence supports NSSI rates at least comparable and generally higher than those for civilian counterparts—particularly among treatment-seeking samples. Disparities in reported NSSI rates over time among service members and veterans may be due to rising prevalence rates. For example, among a United Kingdom mental health research cohort of military personnel, NSSI prevalence rates increased from 2% to 5% (service members) between 2004 and 2006, and from 4.2% to 6.6% (veterans) between 2014 and 2016 (Jones et al., 2019). Other possible explanations include improvement in measurement and more inclusive operationalization of NSSI behaviors, as well as increased awareness of certain demand characteristics present that inhibit disclosure of traditionally stigmatized topics (i.e., suicide and NSSI). For example, Klonsky et al. (2003) excluded recruits endorsing suicide attempt history and assessed only *repeated* self-injury or self-harm performed to regulate affect—which may not encompass all NSSI history. Furthermore, data were collected during basic training when new recruits often receive military assignments and, consequently, may be more reticent to disclose NSSI history in fear of negative career consequences. Thus, prevalence rates, particularly of active-duty service members with the most to lose by disclosing NSSI, are likely to vary based on circumstances of reporting.

Demographic Differences

Prevalence and characteristics of NSSI among military personnel may differ based on certain demographic characteristics including gender, sexual and gender minority status, age and military service era, and race and ethnicity.

Gender

Military personnel are predominantly male, and many studies of their NSSI include exclusively male samples. While population-based studies have not found gender differences in NSSI rates among adults in the general population (Briere & Gil, 1998; Klonsky, 2011), some literature suggests women (particularly in clinical settings) may be more likely to engage in NSSI (Bresin & Schoenlber, 2015). However, NSSI rates in men may be underestimated due to engagement in different forms of NSSI not typically assessed or recognized as self-injury. For example, in a study of veterans seeking PTSD treatment (97% male), researchers found men were more than twice as likely to have engaged in wall/object punching during the past two weeks (44.0% vs. 21.7%), whereas there were no gender differences found for the other forms of NSSI in the same time frame (Kimbrel, Calhoun, & Becker, 2017). In a large sample of male service members, NSSI history was associated with greater adherence to masculine norms (i.e., self-reliance, emotional control, and less aversion to violence), highlighting the need to further understand sex differences in NSSI among military personnel (Bandel & Anestis, 2020).

Whereas several studies explore NSSI among male veterans, far fewer have focused exclusively on females (Monteith et al., 2020). Studies comparing gender differences in NSSI rates among service members and veterans generally find women are more likely to engage in NSSI than men. In an anonymous online survey of service members and veterans enrolled in college classes, 22.1% of women versus 11.4% of men reported a history of NSSI (Bryan & Bryan, 2014). In secondary analyses of two representative surveys, the odds of lifetime and 12-month NSSI were greater in female active-duty and newly enlisted soldiers than male counterparts (Turner et al., 2019). Findings are similar among clinical samples of service members and veterans. For example, in a sample of psychiatric inpatients at military treatment facilities, women (66%) were more likely than men (39%) to report a history of NSSI (Baer, LaCroix, Browne, Hassen, Perera, Soumoff, et al., 2018). Similar results have been found among female military personnel (67.6%) with suicide attempt history compared to men (44.0%; Baer, LaCroix, Browne, Hassen, Perera, Weaver, et al., 2018). However, in a study of military sexual trauma (MST) survivors, NSSI history was comparable by gender suggesting MST may especially increase risk for male service members and veterans (Holliday et al., 2018).

Sexual and Gender Minority Status
There is a dearth of research on NSSI and sexual and gender minority status among service members and veterans. To our knowledge, only one study has examined the relationship to these constructs. Ray-Sannerud et al. (2015) investigated NSSI prevalence among service members and veterans enrolled in college courses with a history of same-sex behavior. They found sexual minority participants were twice as likely to report NSSI than their sexual majority peers. This association remained significant when considering age and gender, but not when trauma exposure was included. However, only other-sex versus same-sex behavior (vs. attraction or identity) was assessed highlighting the need for additional research into the relationship between NSSI and other sexual orientations. Among a sample of both veterans and nonveterans, transgender/gender diverse (TGD) participants were more likely to endorse NSSI behavior (Aboussouan et al., 2019). While NSSI prevalence was lower among veterans, they were more likely to report seeking medical care and a history of hospitalization due to NSSI. These findings suggest service members and veterans identifying as TGD may engage in more serious or potentially life-threatening NSSI compared to civilian counterparts, or TGD veterans may be more likely to trust and engage with VA care than nonveterans with community care.

Age and Military Service Era
Though rates of NSSI are highest during adolescence and young adulthood (Klonsky, 2011; Swannell et al., 2014), there are conflicting results regarding the association between age and NSSI in service members and veterans. Compared to peers without a history of NSSI disorder, evidence suggests service members and veterans with NSSI disorder tend to be significantly younger (Cunningham et al., 2021; Patel et al., 2021; Sacks et al., 2008; Turner et al., 2019). However, Bryan and Bryan (2014) found a positive association between age and NSSI engagement among a sample of college students with military service history. Finally, other researchers have found no significant association between age and NSSI. In a study of veterans, age was unrelated to the presence of NSSI history or NSSI methods used (i.e., scratching/skin picking vs. cutting, hitting, and burning; Calhoun et al., 2017). As noted previously, this discordance may be influenced by varied circumstances of reporting (e.g., demand characteristics, varying measurement, and operationalizations).

Rates of lifetime and recent NSSI among clinical veteran samples appear to be similar across military service era. Sacks et al. (2008) found lifetime NSSI was reported by 66% of primarily Vietnam-era treatment-seeking veterans, with 55% reporting NSSI within the previous two weeks. Similar NSSI prevalence rates are evidenced among Operation Enduring Freedom (OEF) and Operation Iraqi Freedom (OIF) veterans seeking treatment for PTSD, with 57% endorsing lifetime history and 45% engaging in NSSI in the past two weeks (Kimbrel et al., 2014). Direct comparisons among clinical veteran samples have not evidenced differences in rates of lifetime NSSI endorsement by veteran service era, or differences in the form of NSSI engaged in (Calhoun et al., 2017). However, a more recent study of NSSI among a community sample of veterans found that those serving during the OEF/OIF era were overrepresented in the NSSI group, accounting for 82% of the NSSI group yet only 65% of the total sample (Lear et al., 2021). These findings support existing literature evidencing increasing prevalence rates of NSSI in service members and veterans over time (Jones et al., 2019) and suggest that potential generational or service-era differences may exist among the broader military personnel population.

Race and Ethnicity
The association between racial and ethnic identity and NSSI among service members and veterans is also unclear. Among military personnel college students, NSSI history was only related to Native American racial identity (Bryan & Bryan, 2014). However, in a later study of outpatient active-duty soldiers, individuals endorsing a history of both NSSI and suicide attempt were more likely to identify as Hispanic but less likely to identify as either Native American or Caucasian (Bryan, Rudd, et al., 2015). In contrast, another study found that newly enlisted and active-duty soldiers identifying as African American were less likely to endorse NSSI history compared to those identifying as non-Hispanic white identity (Turner et al., 2019). At the same time, others have found no significant association between race, ethnicity, and NSSI disorder (Calhoun et al., 2017; Patel et al., 2021).

Comorbidities
Certain comorbidities are especially relevant to understanding NSSI among service members and veterans, namely affect-related conditions, suicidal thoughts and behaviors, trauma exposure, substance use, obsessive-compulsive disorder, and attention-deficit/hyperactivity disorder.

Affect-Related Conditions
One of the most commonly reported functions of NSSI is regulation of strong affective experiences (Zetterqvist et al., 2013; see Taylor et al., this volume, on the functions of NSSI). Anger is particularly prevalent among veterans and can be difficult to regulate (Sayer et al., 2010; Sippel et al., 2016). Recent findings have directly explored the relationship between anger and veteran NSSI. In one study, anger was the most common

emotional antecedent to NSSI among veterans reporting NSSI in the past year (Cassiello-Robbins et al., 2021). In fact, 85% of participants reported anger was one of the most common emotions that preceded NSSI, and 57% said that anger *always* preceded NSSI. Anger was associated with many methods of NSSI, including burning oneself with a cigarette, skin carving, severe scratching, sticking sharp objects into skin, head banging, punching oneself, and punching walls or objects. Furthermore, when controlling for the presence of other negative emotions, anger was associated with NSSI to relieve tension, stop feeling numb, communicate with others, feel alive, get help from others, and prove to oneself how bad things are. Further support for the importance of anger comes from an ecological momentary assessment (EMA) study which found anger/hostility predicted subsequent NSSI urges and behaviors, but not vice versa, in a sample of veterans with NSSI disorder (Dillon et al., 2021).

NSSI has also been linked to interpersonal aggression. In a study of male veterans seeking treatment for PTSD, those with recent NSSI were more likely to report making violent threats and behaving violently in the past year than those without NSSI (Calhoun et al., 2017). Notably, this association persisted even after controlling for a variety of risk factors for violence (i.e., PTSD severity, depression, substance use, and combat exposure).

Although NSSI is a behavior highly prevalent among those meeting criteria for borderline personality disorder (BPD), little research has explored this relationship in military populations. Existing literature suggests that the presence of BPD is a significant risk factor for NSSI in service members and veterans. In one study of service members with significant suicidal ideation, the number of BPD criteria met was significantly associated with the presence and amount of NSSI reported (Fruhbauerova et al., 2021). Additionally, BPD was the diagnosis most strongly associated with NSSI disorder among a sample of veterans with psychiatric disorders (Patel et al., 2021). Furthermore, Cunningham et al. (2019) found that co-occurring NSSI, BPD, and PTSD significantly increased the odds of experiencing suicidal ideation. However, their more recent work found that NSSI disorder is a stronger diagnostic predictor of lifetime suicide attempts than BPD, PTSD, and major depressive disorder (MDD), highlighting the need for additional research to understand this relationship (Cunningham et al., 2021).

NSSI and Suicide Risk

Consistent with research from civilians (e.g., Franklin et al., 2017; Klonsky et al., 2013), NSSI is also strongly associated with risk for suicidal thoughts and behaviors in service members and veterans (e.g., Bryan, Rudd, et al., 2015; Cunningham et al., 2021; Cunningham et al., 2019; Gromatsky et al., 2021; Kiekens et al., 2018; Kimbrel et al., 2016; Kimbrel et al., 2015; Kimbrel et al., 2014; Kimbrel, Meyer, et al., 2018; Turner et al., 2019; see Victor et al., this volume, on the link between NSSI and suicide). For example, Turner et al. (2019) recently reported that NSSI was associated with subsequent onset of both suicidal ideation and suicide attempts among service members; furthermore, those with NSSI history were more likely than those without to report a history of suicide attempt(s). Kimbrel et al. (2016) have reported similar findings among veterans, finding that those with a lifetime history of NSSI were far more likely to have a lifetime history of suicide attempts (and multiple suicide attempts) than veterans without NSSI history. Furthermore, lifetime NSSI history in service members and veterans has been found to be associated with greater exposure to suicide, closeness to a suicide decedent, and negative impact from suicide death—particularly among women (Hom et al., 2017). Though additional work is necessary to understand the temporal relationship, these findings highlight the potential impact of suicide in the military community on NSSI risk.

In addition, several studies have found that NSSI is associated with lifetime history of suicidal thoughts and behaviors in military personnel, over and above a wide array of demographic and diagnostic correlates (e.g., Cunningham et al., 2021, Cunningham et al., 2019; Kimbrel et al., 2016; Kimbrel et al., 2015; Kimbrel et al., 2014; Kimbrel, Meyer, et al., 2018). Most notable are findings by Bryan, Rudd, et al. (2015) among service members with a recent history of suicidal ideation or attempt(s) which revealed NSSI may be a stronger predictor of future suicide attempt than lifetime history of suicide attempts. While more work is necessary in this area, most findings to date suggest that NSSI is strongly associated with increased risk for suicidal thoughts and behaviors among both service members and veterans.

Trauma Exposure

Trauma exposure (particularly childhood maltreatment; see Serafini et al., this volume, on early childhood and NSSI) is strongly associated with risk of NSSI in civilians (Ford & Gómez, 2015; Serafini et al., 2017). Given their high levels of exposure to potentially traumatic experiences (e.g., combat, death, and MST; Magruder et al., 2009; Wilson et al., 2018), it is imperative to understand how these events may confer risk for NSSI in service members and veterans. As discussed above, many studies exploring NSSI in military personnel have done so in samples that all meet criteria for PTSD (e.g., Calhoun et al., 2017; Cunningham et al., 2019; Kimbrel et al., 2015; Kimbrel et al., 2014; Kimbrel, Calhoun, & Beckham, 2017; Sacks et al., 2008) or with high rates of comorbid PTSD (e.g., Dillon et al., 2021; Cassiello-Robbins et al., 2021). Patel et al. (2021) found NSSI disorder was not associated with PTSD; however, this was likely due to a lack of a large enough comparison group (approximately 93% met criteria for PTSD). To better explore this potential relationship, researchers examined the role of emotion dysregulation in the association between PTSD and NSSI among trauma-exposed veterans (Raudales et al., 2020). They found that the relationship between PTSD severity and NSSI was mediated by two specific aspects of negative emotion regulation—difficulty controlling impulsive behavior when distressed and lack of emotional clarity. The authors also identified the role of positive emotion regulation in this association and highlighted the need to target emotion regulation issues among veterans to address both PTSD symptoms and NSSI.

Research has begun to explore the association between NSSI and MST. In a sample of veterans with MST history, Holliday et al. (2018) found that 25% of participants endorsed a lifetime history of NSSI. Of them, 67% reported first engaging in NSSI after their MST, while 85% had engaged in NSSI at least once post-MST. These findings contrast with existing literature that NSSI tends to predate military service and suggests that MST may be an important prospective risk factor for NSSI onset. Furthermore, most veterans with MST history reported engaging in multiple methods of NSSI, most often cutting/carving oneself and hitting oneself. In addition, White et al. (2018) investigated the association between MST and NSSI in a sample of National Guard members and concluded that individuals with MST were more than four times more likely to endorse NSSI history than members without MST history. These associations remained significant when accounting for gender, age, and race but were no longer significant when psychiatric disorders (i.e., PTSD, MDD, and alcohol use disorder) were included in analyses. Further, a recent study found no significant differences in MST between NSSI-only, suicide attempt-only, concurrent NSSI and suicide attempt, and no self-directed violence groups (Lear et al., 2021).

Substance Use

Despite the shared association with impulsivity, there has been only limited research on the association between service member and veteran NSSI and substance use to date. For example, NSSI history has been significantly associated with alcohol and drug misuse among OEF/OIF veterans with deployment history (Forkus et al., 2019). Cannabis use, specifically, appears associated with NSSI among veterans (Kimbrel, Meyer, et al., 2018; Patel et al., 2021). Patel et al. (2021) observed that lifetime history of NSSI disorder in veterans was associated with cannabis use disorder at the bivariate level, but unrelated to each of the other substance use disorders examined; however, the association between cannabis use disorder and NSSI disorder did not remain significant in a logistic regression in which a wide range of demographic variables and diagnoses were included as predictors of lifetime NSSI disorder. In contrast, Kimbrel, Meyer, et al. (2018) observed that cannabis use disorder did remain predictive of lifetime NSSI ($AOR = 5.12$, $p = 0.009$) after accounting for a wide range of covariates, including sex, age, sexual orientation, combat exposure, traumatic life events, traumatic brain injury, PTSD, depression, alcohol use disorder (AUD), and non-cannabis drug use disorder. These findings suggest cannabis use disorder may represent a unique risk factor for NSSI in veterans.

Obsessive-Compulsive Disorder

To our knowledge, only one study to date has examined the association between obsessive-compulsive disorder (OCD) and NSSI in veterans. Patel et al. (2021) examined a wide range of psychiatric diagnoses in relation to lifetime NSSI disorder and observed a strong bivariate association between the two diagnoses. Furthermore, when they used logistic regression to identify the top diagnostic predictors of lifetime NSSI disorder, they found OCD (AOR = 3.4, p = 0.008) and BPD (AOR = 10.1, p < 0.001) were the only diagnostic predictors associated with NSSI disorder in the final model. While further replication in independent veteran and service member samples is necessary, OCD has been consistently associated with NSSI in civilian samples (Bentley et al., 2015) and may be substantially more common in veterans than civilians (Barrera et al., 2019; Patel et al., 2021). Thus, future research on the association between OCD and NSSI in military personnel is necessary at the present time.

Attention-Deficit/Hyperactivity Disorder

Despite consistent associations between attention-deficit/hyperactivity disorder (ADHD) and NSSI in civilian samples (e.g., Meszaros et al., 2017), only one study examines the association between ADHD and NSSI in veterans. Specifically, Kimbrel, Wilson, et al. (2017) found that 25% of male veterans screened positive for clinically significant ADHD symptoms. They further observed that ADHD was associated with increased risk for both PTSD and NSSI. Importantly, they found ADHD remained significantly associated with NSSI among male veterans (AOR = 3.509, p = 0.031) even after accounting for PTSD, depression, AUD, and demographic variables. Given that ADHD frequently occurs among veterans with PTSD (Harrington et al., 2012) and veterans with PTSD are at substantially increased risk for NSSI (Kimbrel, Thomas, et al., 2018), future research exploring the association between ADHD and NSSI among veterans is also clearly warranted.

Forms and Functions of NSSI in Service Members and Veterans

Certain characteristics of NSSI in service members and veterans are similar to those observed in civilians, including late adolescent onset (15 to 17.5 years old) and generally low median frequency of behavior (e.g., 6 to 12 lifetime occurrences; Bandel & Anestis, 2020; Bryan & Bryan, 2014; Lear et al., 2021; May et al., 2018). Significant improvements in the broader NSSI field have contributed to our understanding of the varied forms NSSI can take in addition to or instead of cutting oneself (a traditionally studied NSSI method). There is mixed evidence regarding the number of NSSI methods service members and veterans typically use, with some studies finding evidence for one method (Bandel & Anestis, 2020; Lear et al., 2021) and others finding evidence of several (Bryan & Bryan, 2014; Holliday et al., 2018; May et al., 2018).

Evidence suggests that the form NSSI takes among service members and veterans has both similarities and differences to what is typically observed in civilians. For example, evidence supports the presence of common NSSI behaviors among military samples, including cutting oneself, especially among females (Bandel & Anestis, 2020; Bryan & Bryan, 2014; Lear et al., 2021; May et al., 2018). However, several other methods of NSSI less common among civilians are also frequently endorsed, including burning oneself (e.g., with cigarettes and/or lighters, 20.2% to 34%) and hitting oneself and/or head banging (38.1% to 44.7%; Bandel & Anestis, 2020; Bryan & Bryan, 2014; Lear et al., 2021; May et al., 2018). Furthermore, a case study of three veterans engaging in behavior (scab-picking, nail-biting, and tattooing) qualifying as NSSI based on intent, function, and distress/impairment support the presence and inclusion of various NSSI methods when considering a diagnosis of NSSI disorder for service members and veterans (Mann et al., 2020). Evidence suggests that examination of NSSI in these samples should consider more "indirect" methods of self-injury more prevalent among predominantly male military personnel compared to typically female civilian counterparts (Lear et al., 2021). For example, wall/object punching appears to be a prevalent but underrecognized form of NSSI in veterans. Its association with other traditional forms of NSSI, relief from negative affect, and suicidal ideation support its conceptualization as an NSSI behavior (Kimbrel, Wilson, et al., 2017).

While extant literature has examined the various functions NSSI serves in civilians, particularly for exerting influence over internal (e.g., affect regulation) and to a lesser degree external (e.g., social) environments (Taylor et al., 2018), there is a paucity of literature directly examining prevalent functions of NSSI among service members and veterans. Evidence suggests that NSSI almost always occurs in military personnel prior to suicide attempt but following suicidal ideation onset (Bryan, Bryan, et al., 2015). Furthermore, while repeated engagement (especially) is associated with higher risk of future suicide attempt (Bryan, Rudd, et al., 2015), a similar proportion of service members and veterans with NSSI history following suicidal ideation onset do not attempt suicide. Together, these findings suggest that NSSI can either act as a steppingstone between suicidal ideation to action or somehow delay the transition (e.g., by serving an emotion regulation function).

To that end, preliminary research supports NSSI functioning as a means of self-regulation in the face of negative emotions among service members and veterans (Klonsky et al., 2003). Findings of antecedents and consequences of NSSI among veterans further support the possibility that NSSI may be used by military personnel as a strategy to cope with distress (particularly anger) and reinforced by a sense of relief (Cassiello-Robbins et al., 2021; Dillon et al., 2021; Kimbrel, Thomas, et al., 2018; Sacks et al., 2008). Male service members and veterans, especially, with NSSI history tend to exhibit similar difficulties as civilian counterparts with regard to greater emotion dysregulation, impulsivity, personality pathology, depression, and anxiety symptom severity (Baer, LaCroix, Browne, Hassen, Perera, Soumoff, et al., 2018; Bandel & Anestis, 2020; Klonsky et al., 2003). They also exhibit unique characteristics of adherence to masculine norms (i.e., self-reliance, emotional control) and pathological narcissism (Bandel & Anestis, 2020). Evidence also supports NSSI engagement by service members and veterans for interpersonal reasons, including communicating and getting help from others (Cassiello-Robbins et al., 2021). These findings support evidence of emotional suppression and independence ("hegemonic masculinity") valued in military culture (Chen & Dognin, 2017) which may hinder prophylactic, effective means of help-seeking that could prevent NSSI or encourage earlier cessation (Ganzini et al., 2013).

Future Directions

Existing literature highlights advances in the field of NSSI among service members and veterans. However, there remain several important avenues for future research and development among military personnel including advances in the assessment and treatment of NSSI, incorporating innovative methodological approaches to study NSSI, and understanding implications of current knowledge for clinical practice and research efforts.

Assessment of NSSI in Military Personnel

A significant barrier to improved understanding of NSSI among service members and veterans is a lack of thorough and uniform assessment. Most large-scale studies of military personnel utilize screeners which focus on the assessment of suicide risk alone (a major research priority of the Department of Defense and Veterans Health Administration) and often neglect other forms of self-harm. NSSI is rarely a primary outcome of funded studies of military personnel, and data collected are consequently often abbreviated (e.g., as a single dichotomous "yes" or "no" variable). In addition to nonvalidated screening tools, far fewer studies leverage comprehensive self-report or interview instruments for NSSI. Moreover, these are typically developed in female and civilian samples and not validated in military samples. Consequently, exploration of the nuances of NSSI behavior among service members and veterans remains difficult. Furthermore, screeners and clinical assessment tools may use stigmatizing language (e.g., "self-mutilative" behavior and "self-harm") that results in underreporting of behavior. This has led to the development of the Direct and Indirect Self-Harm Inventory (DISH; Green et al., 2017). The DISH is the first measure designed to detect both direct and indirect means of self-harm (including NSSI) among veterans without the use of potentially stigmatizing language. As previously noted, service members and veterans (especially males) may be more likely to engage in "indirect" methods of NSSI (e.g., wall/object punching) highlighting the DISH's value. Further validation of this and other existing measures of NSSI in military samples and/or the creation of new assessment tools is necessary to capture the unique experiences of military personnel.

Innovative Methodological Approaches to Study of NSSI

EMA gathers data in real time as emotions, cognitions, and behaviors occur in participants' natural environments (Bolger et al., 2003). In addition to combatting reporting biases that may be more prevalent among service members and veterans, EMA is also a promising methodology for the assessment of immediate antecedents and consequences of NSSI. Despite its potential value, EMA has been underutilized in military personnel to study mental health outcomes (Gromatsky et al., 2020). Only one study to date has leveraged EMA to study NSSI in veterans, results from which support its safety and acceptability (Gromatsky et al., 2022). In fact, many veterans reported benefits to participating including a therapeutic quality to assessments, greater awareness and insight into one's emotions and behaviors, and social/communication improvements. Recent findings from this study also suggest anger and hostility preceded and predicted NSSI urges and behavior in this sample (Dillon et al., 2021) and highlight the importance of assessing anger to understand short-term risk for NSSI in service members and veterans.

No study to date has expanded on existing civilian literature examining biological and neuroanatomical underpinnings of NSSI to explore their applicability among service members and veterans (Bunderla & Gregorič Kumperščak, 2015; Domínguez-Baleón et al., 2018; Groschwitz & Plener, 2012). Such endeavors are especially important among military personnel who are more likely to experience traumatic brain injury (TBI) that can result in neuroanatomical changes, contribute to behavioral disinhibition, and subsequently increase risk for suicide and NSSI (Yurgelun-Todd et al., 2011). Preliminary evidence suggests that NSSI independently differentiates veterans along the suicide ideation-to-action framework; however, this effect was no longer significant when introducing affect-modulated startle to negative stimuli, a proxy for amygdala dysfunction and emotion reactivity (Gromatsky et al., 2021). While findings highlight the importance of NSSI in the study of veteran suicide risk, further research is necessary to better understand its relationship with potential psychophysiological and/or neuroanatomical differences.

Additional research is also necessary which leverages cognitive and/or behavioral tasks to study NSSI risk in service members and veterans. This methodology examines implicit associations, making it a valuable tool for use among populations that may be less likely to explicitly endorse mental health concerns with self-report or interview methods. This may include military personnel who evidence greater distrust toward mental health professionals (Kim et al., 2011) and fear repercussions of disclosure (Bryan & Morrow, 2011). For example, among veterans with PTSD and AUD, self-harm was associated with self-reported impulsivity but not a behavioral measure of impulsivity (Hausman et al., 2020). As is often the case, self-directed violence was broadly defined (with either suicidal or nonsuicidal intent), limiting interpretation and application of findings to understanding of NSSI in service members and veterans. However, results support further investigation of differences in measures of impulsivity and NSSI among military personnel and, more broadly, examination of differences in symptomatology by assessment method.

Treatment for NSSI in Military Personnel

The only empirically supported treatment directly targeting NSSI is dialectical behavior therapy (DBT; Linehan et al., 2015; see Chapman et al., this volume), which has been largely studied in the context of BPD among female civilians (Harned et al., 2014). DBT aims to address broader emotion regulation, impulsivity, and interpersonal difficulties common among those meeting criteria for BPD. Treatment targets include a range of target behaviors that may or may not include NSSI. Several VA hospitals in the United States have begun to implement DBT (Landes et al., 2017). Findings from studies leveraging DBT in veteran samples are mixed: some evidence supports its efficacy for decreasing suicidal thoughts (Decker et al., 2019) and self-directed violence (either suicidal or nonsuicidal; Koons et al., 2001) whereas one study found its utility comparable to treatment as usual (Goodman et al., 2016). However, veterans participating in these trials were selected on the basis of their suicide risk or presence of BPD. The collaborative assessment and management of suicidality (CAMS; Jobes, 2012) is an intervention developed to target suicidal thoughts and behaviors in veterans and has been found to be as effective as DBT for reducing NSSI in civilians with BPD (Andreasson et al., 2016). Thus, further research is needed to explore the efficacy of both DBT and CAMS for the treatment of NSSI, specifically, in military personnel.

Implications for Clinical Practice

Existing literature highlights the importance of an inclusive conceptualization and assessment of behavior that may represent NSSI by clinicians working with service members and veterans. Findings suggest their NSSI may take the form of indirect methods to hurt oneself like punching walls or objects, especially among males. Preliminary findings suggest NSSI evidenced among service members and veterans serving a variety of interpersonal and intrapersonal functions. Particularly salient is the use of NSSI as a means of coping with, escaping from, or reducing distress that may be associated with strong affective experiences—namely, anger (Cassiello-Robbins et al., 2021; Dillon et al., 2021). Clinical interventions for NSSI among military personnel would be best targeted at addressing impulsivity and emotional regulation deficits, especially encouraging a sense of control when distressed (Baer, LaCroix, Browne, Hassen, Perera, Soumoff, et al., 2018; Raudales et al., 2020). These deficits may increase vulnerability for NSSI to cope with strong emotions—including that which is associated with comorbid conditions.

Rates of NSSI are strikingly high among trauma-exposed veterans and those with PTSD (Cunningham et al., 2019; Kimbrel et al., 2015; Kimbrel et al., 2014; Raudales et al., 2020; Sacks et al., 2008); however, many evidence-based treatment (EBT) trials for PTSD exclude those with significant NSSI. Literature supports the development or adaptation of interventions specifically aiming to address NSSI in PTSD populations which may seek to improve overall emotion regulation ability and in turn improve one's ability to cope with PTSD symptoms. Furthermore, interoceptive deficits and lack of emotional clarity reported by service members and veterans endorsing NSSI highlight the need to first aid in labeling emotions and psychoeducation about common associated physical sensations (Raudales et al., 2020; Smith et al., 2020). In lieu of the endorsement of interpersonal functions NSSI can serve in military personnel (e.g., communicating to others), treatment efforts would also benefit from encouraging emotional expression and fostering interpersonal effectiveness skills. Clinicians should explore beliefs and values about help-seeking and disclosure that may develop during military service that may impede NSSI cessation and treatment efforts.

Most service members and veterans endorsing NSSI history report onset and resolution predating their military service but which, nonetheless, confers subsequent suicide risk (Turner et al., 2019). However, accuracy of these rates may be occluded by efforts to conceal one's NSSI history or onset during military service. As of August 2020, armed force applicants may request a waiver for psychiatric and behavioral health conditions (e.g., personality disorder, mood disorder, suicide attempt, or self-directed violence) except for instances involving "self-mutilation." Thus, NSSI and suicide prevention efforts for service members and veterans may include adding NSSI to a list of waiverable conditions to encourage disclosure at the beginning and throughout the course of one's military service without risk of discharge. Relief from strong emotions is often reported after NSSI, which may maintain NSSI and make it challenging to treat. Thus, service members may benefit from ongoing instruction beginning in basic training to encourage development of coping skills to manage negative affect (particularly anger) and prevent NSSI onset.

Future Research Priorities

Despite recent advances made in the burgeoning field of NSSI among service members and veterans, many questions remain to be addressed by future research efforts, and methodological considerations would improve interpretation of findings. As is the case with all NSSI research, the field would benefit from greater specificity about the intent of self-injury (i.e., with/without suicidal intent) when designing or implementing assessment measures. A plethora of empirical findings highlight important distinctions between NSSI and suicidal behavior (Klonsky et al., 2014), supporting the creation of NSSI disorder in the most recent version of the DSM (American Psychiatric Association, 2013). Thus, NSSI should be independently and more expansively assessed as an important treatment target among military personnel, in addition to its utility as a predictor for other clinical outcomes. Comprehensive assessment efforts would benefit from further exploration of the varied functions NSSI serves in service members and veterans to guide treatment approaches. In addition to its application as a means of regulating strong, negative emotions, NSSI also appears to serve a communicative function (Baer, LaCroix, Browne, Hassen, Perera, Soumoff, et al., 2018; Cassiello-Robbins et al., 2021). Furthermore, it is imperative to better understand short-term mechanisms contributing to NSSI urges and engagement, as well as immediate antecedents and consequences as these represent important treatment targets.

Additional research should expand on the extremely limited literature exploring the etiology, course, and relationship of NSSI with other psychopathology among service members and veterans. Particularly important is to better understand the mechanisms behind how NSSI confers risk for subsequent suicide, as prevention and reduction efforts are VA and DoD priorities. Efforts to understand differing trajectories of NSSI onset and cessation could aid in developing treatment approaches delivered throughout the course of and following military service.

References

Aboussouan, A., Snow, A., Cerel, J., & Tucker, R. P. (2019). Non-suicidal self-injury, suicide ideation, and past suicide attempts: Comparison between transgender and gender diverse veterans and non-veterans. *Journal of Affective Disorders, 259*, 186–194. https://doi.org/10.1016/j.jad.2019.08.046

American Psychiatric Association. (2013). *Diagnostic and statistical manual of mental disorders* (5th ed.; DSM-5).

Andreasson, K., Krogh, J., Wenneberg, C., Jessen, H. K., Krakauer, K., Gluud, C., Thomsen, R. R., Randers, L., & Nordentoft, M. (2016). Effectiveness of dialectical behavior therapy versus collaborative assessment and management of suicidality treatment for reduction of self-harm in adults with borderline personality traits and disorder—A randomized observer-blinded clinical trial. *Depression and Anxiety, 33*(6), 520–530. https://doi.org/10.1002/da.22472

Baer, M. M., LaCroix, J. M., Browne, J. C., Hassen, H. O., Perera, K. U., Soumoff, A., Weaver, J., & Ghahramanlou-Holloway, M. (2018). Impulse control difficulties while distressed: A facet of emotion dysregulation links to non-suicidal self-injury among psychiatric inpatients at military treatment facilities. *Psychiatry Research, 269*, 419–424. https://doi.org/10.1016/j.psychres.2018.08.082

Baer, M. M., LaCroix, J. M., Browne, J. C., Hassen, H. O., Perera, K. U., Weaver, J., Soumoff, A., & Ghahramanlou-Holloway, M. (2018). Non-suicidal self-injury elevates suicide risk among United States military personnel with lifetime attempted suicide. *Archives of Suicide Research, 22*(3), 453–464. https://doi.org/10.1080/13811118.2017.1358225

Bandel, S. L., & Anestis, M. D. (2020). Non-suicidal self-injury among male service members: Descriptive information and a preliminary examination of external correlates. *Psychiatry Research, 285*, Article 112815. https://doi.org/10.1016/j.psychres.2020.112815

Barrera, T. L., McIngvale, E., Lindsay, J. A., Walder, A. M., Kauth, M. R., Smith, T. L., Van Kirk, N., Teng, E. J., & Stanley, M. A. (2019). Obsessive-compulsive disorder in the Veterans Health Administration. *Psychological Services, 16*(4), Article 605. https://doi.org/10.1037/ser0000249

Bentley, K. H., Cassiello-Robbins, C. F., Vittorio, L., Sauer-Zavala, S., & Barlow, D. H. (2015). The association between nonsuicidal self-injury and the emotional disorders: A meta-analytic review. *Clinical Psychology Review, 37*, 72–88. https://doi.org/10.1016/j.cpr.2015.02.006

Bolger, N., Davis, A., & Rafaeli, E. (2003). Diary methods: Capturing life as it is lived. *Annual Review of Psychology, 54*(1), 579–616. https://doi.org/10.1146/annurev.psych.54.101601.145030

Bresin, K., & Schoenleber, M. (2015). Gender differences in the prevalence of nonsuicidal self-injury: A meta-analysis. *Clinical Psychology Review, 38*, 55–64. https://doi.org/10.1016/j.cpr.2015.02.009

Briere, J., & Gil, E. (1998). Self-mutilation in clinical and general population samples: Prevalence, correlates, and functions. *American Journal of Orthopsychiatry, 68*(4), 609–620. https://doi.org/10.1037/h0080369

Bryan, C., & Bryan, A. (2014). Nonsuicidal self-injury among a sample of united states military personnel and veterans enrolled in college classes. *Journal of Clinical Psychology, 70*(9), 874–885. https://doi.org/10.1002/jclp.22075

Bryan, C. J., Bryan, A. O., May, A. M., & Klonsky, E. D. (2015). Trajectories of suicide ideation, nonsuicidal self-injury, and suicide attempts in a nonclinical sample of military personnel and veterans. *Suicide and Life-Threatening Behavior, 45*(3), 315–325. https://doi.org/10.1111/sltb.12127

Bryan, C. J., & Morrow, C. E. (2011). Circumventing mental health stigma by embracing the warrior culture: Lessons learned from the Defender's Edge program. *Professional Psychology: Research and Practice, 42*(1), 16. https://doi.org/10.1037/a0022290

Bryan, C. J., Rudd, M. D., Wertenberger, E., Young-McCaughon, S., & Peterson, A. (2015). Nonsuicidal self-injury as a prospective predictor of suicide attempts in a clinical sample of military personnel. *Comprehensive Psychiatry, 59*, 1–7. https://doi.org/10.1016/j.comppsych.2014.07.009

Bryan, C. J., Rudd, M. D., Wertenberger, E., Etienne, N., Ray-Sannerud, B. N., Morrow, C. E., Peterson, A. L., & Young-McCaughon, S. (2014). Improving the detection and prediction of suicidal behavior among military personnel by measuring suicidal beliefs: An evaluation of the suicide cognitions scale. *Journal of Affective Disorders, 159*, 15–22. https://doi.org/10.1016/j.jad.2014.02.021

Bunderla, T., & Gregorič Kumperščak, H. (2015). Altered pain perception in self-injurious behavior and the association of psychological elements with pain perception measures: A systematic review. *Psychiatria Danubina*, *27*(4), 346–354.

Calhoun, P. S., Van Voorhees, E. E., Elbogen, E. B., Dedert, E. A., Clancy, C. P., Hair, L. P., Hertzberg, M., Beckham, J. C., & Kimbrel, N. A. (2017). Nonsuicidal self-injury and interpersonal violence in U.S. veterans seeking help for posttraumatic stress disorder. *Psychiatry Research*, *247*, 250–256. https://doi.org/10.1016/j.psychres.2016.11.032

Cassiello-Robbins, C., Dillon, K. H., Blalock, D. V., Calhoun, P. S., Beckham, J. C., & Kimbrel, N. A. (2021). Exploring the role of anger in nonsuicidal self-injury in veterans. *Journal of Psychiatric Research*, *137*, 55–65. https://doi.org/10.1016/j.jpsychires.2021.02.026

Chen, C. K., & Dognin, J. S. (2017). Addressing the influence of hegemonic masculinity on veterans through brief dynamic interpersonal therapy. *Psychology of Men & Masculinity*, *18*(3), 238–242. https://doi.org/10.1037/men0000118

Cunningham, K. C., Aunon, F. M., Patel, T. A., Mann, A. J., DeBeer, B. B., Meyer, E. C., Morissette, S. B., Silvia, P. J., Gratz, K. L., Calhoun, P. S., Beckham, J. C., & Kimbrel, N. A. (2021). Nonsuicidal self-injury disorder, borderline personality disorder, and lifetime history of suicide attempts among male and female veterans with mental health disorders. *Journal of Affective Disorders*, *287*, 276–281. https://doi.org/10.1016/j.jad.2021.03.033

Cunningham, K. C., Grossmann, J. L., Seay, K. B., Dennis, P. A., Clancy, C. P., Hertzberg, M. A., Berlin, K., Ruffin, R. A., Dedert, E. A., Gratz, K. L., Calhoun, P. S., Beckham, J. C., & Kimbrel, N. A. (2019). Nonsuicidal self-injury and borderline personality features as risk factors for suicidal ideation among male veterans with posttraumatic stress disorder. *Journal of Traumatic Stress*, *32*(1), 141–147. https://doi.org/10.1002/jts.22369

Decker, S. E., Adams, L., Watkins, L. E., Sippel, L. M., Presnall-Shvorin, J., Sofuoglu, M., & Martino, S. (2019). Feasibility and preliminary efficacy of dialectical behaviour therapy skills groups for Veterans with suicidal ideation: Pilot. *Behavioural and Cognitive Psychotherapy*, *47*(5), 616–621. https://doi.org/10.1017/s1352465819000122

Department of Defense. (2020). Annual suicide report: Calendar year 2019. Department of Defense, Secretary of Defense for Personnel and Readiness. Available at https://www.dspo.mil/Portals/113/Documents/CY2019%20Suicide%20Report/DoD%20Calendar%20Year%20CY%202019%20Annual%20Suicide%20Report.pdf?ver=YOA4IZVcVA9mzwtsfdO5Ew%3D%3D#:~:text=The%20CY%202019%20suicide%20rate,100%2C000%20Active%20Component%20Service%20members

Department of Veterans Affairs. (2020). *2020 national veteran suicide prevention annual report*. Department of Veterans Affairs, Office of Mental Health And Suicide Prevention. Available at https://www.mentalhealth.va.gov/suicide_prevention/data.asp

Dillon, K. H., Glenn, J. J., Dennis, P. A., LoSavio, S. T., Cassiello-Robbins, C., Gromatsky, M. A., Beckham, J. C., Calhoun, P. S., & Kimbrel, N. A. (2021). Anger precedes and predicts nonsuicidal self-injury in veterans: Findings from an ecological momentary assessment study. *Journal of Psychiatric Research*, *135*, 47–51. https://doi.org/10.1016/j.jpsychires.2021.01.011

Domínguez-Baleón, C., Gutiérrez-Mondragón, L. F., Campos-González, A. I., & Rentería, M. E. (2018). Neuroimaging studies of suicidal behavior and non-suicidal self-injury in psychiatric patients: A systematic review. *Frontiers in Psychiatry*, *9*, Article 500. https://doi.org/10.3389/fpsyt.2018.00500

Doshi, A., Boudreaux, E. D., Wang, N., Pelletier, A. J., & Camargo Jr, C. A. (2005). National study of US emergency department visits for attempted suicide and self-inflicted injury, 1997-2001. *Annals of Emergency Medicine*, *46*(4), 369–375. https://doi.org/10.1016/j.annemergmed.2005.04.018

Executive Order No. 13861, 84 Fed. Reg. 8585 (2019).

Ford, J. D., & Gómez, J. M. (2015). The relationship of psychological trauma and dissociative and posttraumatic stress disorders to nonsuicidal self-injury and suicidality: A review. *Journal of Trauma & Dissociation*, *16*(3), 232–271. https://doi.org/10.1080/15299732.2015.989563

Forkus, S. R., Breines, J. G., & Weiss, N. H. (2019). Morally injurious experiences and mental health: The moderating role of self-compassion. *Psychological Trauma: Theory, Research, Practice, and Policy*, *11*(6), Article 630. https://doi.org/10.1037/tra0000446

Fox, K. R., Franklin, J. C., Ribeiro, J. D., Kleiman, E. M., Bentley, K. H., & Nock, M. K. (2015). Meta-analysis of risk factors for nonsuicidal self-injury. *Clinical Psychology Review*, *42*, 156–167. https://doi.org/10.1016/j.cpr.2015.09.002

Franklin, J. C., Ribeiro, J. D., Fox, K. R., Bentley, K. H., Kleiman, E. M., Huang, X., Musacchio, K. M., Jaroszewski, A. C., Chang, B. P., & Nock, M. K. (2017). Risk factors for suicidal thoughts and behaviors: A meta-analysis of 50 years of research. *Psychological Bulletin*, *143*(2), 187–232. https://doi.org/10.1037/bul0000084

Fruhbauerova, M., DeCou, C. R., Crow, B. E., & Comtois, K. A. (2021). Borderline personality disorder and self-directed violence in a sample of suicidal army soldiers. *Psychological Services*, *18*(1), 104–115. https://doi.org/10.1037/ser0000369

Ganzini, L., Denneson, L. M., Press, N., Bair, M. J., Helmer, D. A., Poat, J., & Dobscha, S. K. (2013). Trust is the basis for effective suicide risk screening and assessment in veterans. *Journal of General Internal Medicine*, *28*(9), 1215–1221. https://doi.org/10.1007/s11606-013-2412-6

Goodman, M., Banthin, D., Blair, N. J., Mascitelli, K. A., Wilsnack, J., Chen, J., Messenger, J. W., Perez-Rodriguez, M. M., Triebwasser, J., Koenigsberg, H. W., Goetz, R. R., Hazlett, E. A., & New, A. S. (2016). A randomized trial of dialectical behavior therapy in high-risk suicidal veterans. *The Journal of Clinical Psychiatry*, *77*(12), 1591–1600. https://doi.org/10.4088/jcp.15m10235

Green, J. D., Hatgis, C., Kearns, J. C., Nock, M. K., & Marx, B. P. (2017). The Direct and Indirect Self-Harm Inventory (DISH): A new measure for assessing high-risk and self-harm behaviors among military veterans. *Psychology of Men & Masculinity*, *18*(3), 208–214. https://doi.org/10.1037/men0000116

Gromatsky, M., Edwards, E. R., Sullivan, S. R., Goodman, M., & Hazlett, E. A. (2021). Distinguishing veterans with suicidal ideation from suicide attempt history: The role of emotion reactivity. *Suicide and Life-Threatening Behavior*, *51*(3), 572–585. https://doi.org/10.1111/sltb.12744

Gromatsky, M., Patel, T. A., Wilson, S. M., Mann, A. J., Aho, N., Carpenter, V. L., Calhoun, P. S., Beckham, J. C., Goodman, M., Kimbrel, N. A. (2022). Qualitative analysis of participant experiences during an ecological momentary assessment study of nonsuicidal self-injury among veterans. *Psychiatry Research*, *310*, 114437. https://doi.org/10.1016/j.psychres.2022.114437

Gromatsky, M., Sullivan, S. R., Spears, A. P., Mitchell, E., Walsh, S., Kimbrel, N. A., & Goodman, M. (2020). Ecological momentary assessment (EMA) of mental health outcomes in veterans and servicemembers: A scoping review. *Psychiatry Research*, Article 113359. https://doi.org/10.1016/j.psychres.2020.113359

Groschwitz, R. C., & Plener, P. L. (2012). The neurobiology of non-suicidal self-injury (NSSI): A review. *Suicidology Online*, *3*(1), 24–32.

Harned, M. S., Korslund, K. E., & Linehan, M. M. (2014). A pilot randomized controlled trial of dialectical behavior therapy with and without the dialectical behavior therapy prolonged exposure protocol for suicidal and self-injuring women with borderline personality disorder and PTSD. *Behaviour Research and Therapy*, *55*, 7–17. tps://doi.org/10.1016/j.brat.2014.01.008

Harrington, K. M., Miller, M. W., Wolf, E. J., Reardon, A. F., Ryabchenko, K. A., & Ofrat, S. (2012). Attention-deficit/hyperactivity disorder comorbidity in a sample of veterans with posttraumatic stress disorder. *Comprehensive Psychiatry*, *53*(6), 679–690. https://doi.org/10.1016/j.comppsych.2011.12.001

Hausman, C., Meffert, B. N., Mosich, M. K., & Heinz, A. J. (2020). Impulsivity and cognitive flexibility as neuropsychological markers for suicidality: A multi-modal investigation among military veterans with alcohol use disorder and PTSD. *Archives of Suicide Research*, *24*(3), 313–326. https://doi.org/10.1080/13811118.2019.1635930

Holliday, R., Smith, N. B., & Monteith, L. L. (2018). An initial investigation of nonsuicidal self-injury among male and female survivors of military sexual trauma. *Psychiatry Research*, *268*, 335–339. https://doi.org/10.1016/j.psychres.2018.07.033

Hom, M. A., Stanley, I. H., Gutierrez, P. M., & Joiner Jr, T. E. (2017). Exploring the association between exposure to suicide and suicide risk among military service members and veterans. *Journal of Affective Disorders*, *207*, 327–335. https://doi.org/10.1016/j.jad.2016.09.043

Jobes, D. A. (2012). The Collaborative Assessment and Management of Suicidality (CAMS): An evolving evidence-based clinical approach to suicidal risk. *Suicide and Life-Threatening Behavior*, *42*(6), 640–653. https://doi.org/10.1111/j.1943-278x.2012.00119.x

Jones, N., Sharp, M. L., Phillips, A., & Stevelink, S. A. (2019). Suicidal ideation, suicidal attempts, and self-harm in the UK armed forces. *Suicide and Life-Threatening Behavior*, *49*(6), 1762–1779. https://doi.org/10.1111/sltb.12570

Kiekens, G., Hasking, P., Boyes, M., Claes, L., Mortier, P., Auerbach, R. P., Cuijpers, P., Demyttenaere, K., Green, J. G., Kessler, R. C., Myin-Germeys, I., Nock, M. K., & Bruffaerts, R. (2018). The associations between non-suicidal self-injury and first onset suicidal thoughts and behaviors. *Journal of Affective Disorders, 239*, 171–179. https://doi.org/10.1016/j.jad.2018.06.033

Kim, P. Y., Britt, T. W., Klocko, R. P., Riviere, L. A., & Adler, A. B. (2011). Stigma, negative attitudes about treatment, and utilization of mental health care among soldiers. *Military Psychology, 23*(1), 65–81. https://doi.org/10.1080/08995605.2011.534415

Kimbrel, N. A., Calhoun, P. S., & Beckham, J. C. (2017). Nonsuicidal self-injury in men: A serious problem that has been overlooked for too long. *World Psychiatry, 16*(1), 108–109. https://doi.org/10.1002/wps.20358

Kimbrel, N. A., DeBeer, B. B., Meyer, E. C., Gulliver, S. B., & Morissette, S. B. (2016). Nonsuicidal self-injury and suicide attempts in Iraq/Afghanistan war veterans. *Psychiatry Research, 243*, 232–237. https://doi.org/10.1016/j.psychres.2016.06.039

Kimbrel, N. A., Gratz, K. L., Tull, M. T., Morissette, S. B., Meyer, E. C., DeBeer, B. B., Silvia, P. J., Calhoun, P. C., & Beckham, J. C. (2015). Non-suicidal self-injury as a predictor of active and passive suicidal ideation among Iraq/Afghanistan war veterans. *Psychiatry Research, 227*(2-3), 360–362. https://doi.org/10.1016/j.psychres.2015.03.026

Kimbrel, N. A., Johnson, M. E., Clancy, C., Hertzberg, M., Collie, C., Van Voorhees, E. E., Dennis, M. F., Calhoun, P. S., & Beckham, J. C. (2014). Deliberate self-harm and suicidal ideation among male Iraq/Afghanistan-era veterans seeking treatment for PTSD. *Journal of Traumatic Stress, 27*(4), 474–477. https://doi.org/10.1002/jts.21932

Kimbrel, N. A., Meyer, E. C., DeBeer, B. B., Gulliver, S. B., & Morissette, S. B. (2018). The impact of cannabis use disorder on suicidal and nonsuicidal self-injury in Iraq/Afghanistan-era veterans with and without mental health disorders. *Suicide and Life-Threatening Behavior, 48*(2), 140–148. https://doi.org/10.1111/sltb.12345

Kimbrel, N. A., Thomas, S. P., Hicks, T. A., Hertzberg, M. A., Clancy, C. P., Elbogen, E. B., Meyer, E. C., DeBeer, B. B., Gross, G. M., Silvia, P. J., Morissette, S. B., Gratz, K. L., Calhoun, P. S. & Beckham, J. C. (2018). Wall/object punching: An important but under-recognized form of nonsuicidal self-injury. *Suicide and Life-Threatening Behavior, 48*(5), 501–511. https://doi.org/10.1111/sltb.12371

Kimbrel, N. A., Wilson, L. C., Mitchell, J. T., Meyer, E. C., DeBeer, B. B., Silvia, P. J., Gratz, K. L., Calhoun, P. S., Beckham, J. C., & Morissette, S. B. (2017). ADHD and nonsuicidal self-injury in male veterans with and without PTSD. *Psychiatry Research, 252*, 161–163. https://doi.org/10.1016/j.psychres.2017.02.015

Klonsky, E. D. (2011). Non-suicidal self-injury in United States adults: Prevalence, sociodemographics, topography and functions. *Psychological Medicine, 41*(9), 1981–1986. https://doi.org/10.1017/s0033291710002497

Klonsky, E. D., May, A. M., & Glenn, C. R. (2013). The relationship between nonsuicidal self-injury and attempted suicide: Converging evidence from four samples. *Journal of Abnormal Psychology, 122*(1), 231–237. https://doi.org/10.1037/a0030278

Klonsky, E. D., Oltmanns, T. F., & Turkheimer, E. (2003). Deliberate self-harm in a nonclinical population: Prevalence and psychological correlates. *American Journal of Psychiatry, 160*(8), 1501–1508. https://doi.org/10.1176/appi.ajp.160.8.1501

Klonsky, E. D., Victor, S. E., & Saffer, B. Y. (2014). Nonsuicidal self-injury: What we know, and what we need to know. *The Canadian Journal of Psychiatry, 59*(11), 565–568. https://doi.org/10.1177/070674371405901101

Koons, C. R., Robins, C. J., Tweed, J. L., Lynch, T. R., Gonzalez, A. M., Morse, J. Q., Bishop, G. K., Butterfield, M. I., & Bastian, L. A. (2001). Efficacy of dialectical behavior therapy in women veterans with borderline personality disorder. *Behavior Therapy, 32*(2), 371–390. https://doi.org/10.1016/s0005-7894(01)80009-5

Landes, S. J., Rodriguez, A. L., Smith, B. N., Matthieu, M. M., Trent, L. R., Kemp, J., & Thompson, C. (2017). Barriers, facilitators, and benefits of implementation of dialectical behavior therapy in routine care: Results from a national program evaluation survey in the Veterans Health Administration. *Translational Behavioral Medicine, 7*(4), 832–844. https://doi.org/10.1007/s13142-017-0465-5

Lear, M. K., Penzenik, M. E., Forster, J. E., Starosta, A., Brenner, L. A., & Nazem, S. (2021). Characteristics of nonsuicidal self-injury among veterans. *Journal of Clinical Psychology, 77*(1), 286–297. https://doi.org/10.1002/jclp.23027

Linehan, M. M., Korslund, K. E., Harned, M. S., Gallop, R. J., Lungu, A., Neacsiu, A. D., McDavid, J., Comtois, K. A., & Murray-Gregory, A. M. (2015). Dialectical behavior therapy for high suicide risk in individuals with borderline personality disorder: A randomized clinical trial and component analysis. *JAMA Psychiatry, 72*(5), 475–482. https://doi.org/10.1001/jamapsychiatry.2014.3039

Magruder, K. M., & Yeager, D. E. (2009). The prevalence of PTSD across war eras and the effect of deployment on PTSD: A systematic review and meta-analysis. *Psychiatric Annals, 39*(8). https://doi.org/10.3928/00485713-20090728-04

Mann, A. J., Van Voorhees, E. E., Patel, T. A., Wilson, S. M., Gratz, K. L., Calhoun, P. S., Beckham, J. C., & Kimbrel, N. A. (2020). Nail-biting, scab-picking, and tattooing as nonsuicidal self-injury (NSSI): A deviant case series analysis of the proposed NSSI disorder diagnostic criteria. *Journal of Clinical Psychology, 76*(12), 2296–2313. https://doi.org/10.1002/jclp.23008

May, A. M., Lawson, W. C., Bryan, A., & Bryan, C. J. (2018). Nonsuicidal self-injury, suicide ideation and suicide attempts in the National Guard. *Comprehensive Psychiatry, 86*, 115–118. https://doi.org/10.1016/j.comppsych.2018.08.003

Meszaros, G., Horvath, L. O., & Balazs, J. (2017). Self-injury and externalizing pathology: A systematic literature review. *BMC Psychiatry, 17*(1), 1–21. https://doi.org/10.1186/s12888-017-1326-y

Monteith, L. L., Holliday, R., Miller, C., Schneider, A. L., Hoffmire, C. A., Bahraini, N. H., & Forster, J. E. (2020). Suicidal ideation, suicide attempt, and non-suicidal self-injury among female veterans: Prevalence, timing, and onset. *Journal of Affective Disorders, 273*, 350–357. https://doi.org/10.1016/j.jad.2020.04.017

Nock, M. K., Dempsey, C. L., Aliaga, P. A., Brent, D. A., Heeringa, S. G., Kessler, R. C., Stein, M. B., Ursano, R. J., & Benedek, D. (2017). Psychological autopsy study comparing suicide decedents, suicide ideators, and propensity score matched controls: Results from the study to assess risk and resilience in service members (Army STARRS). *Psychological Medicine, 47*(15), 2663–2674. https://doi.org/10.1017/s0033291717001179

Patel, T. A., Mann, A. J., Blakey, S. M., Aunon, F. M., Calhoun, P. S., Beckham, J. C., & Kimbrel, N. A. (2021). Diagnostic correlates of nonsuicidal self-injury disorder among veterans with psychiatric disorders. *Psychiatry Research, 296*, 113672. https://doi.org/10.1016/j.psychres.2020.113672

Pease, J. L., Monteith, L. L., Hostetter, T. A., Forster, J. E., & Bahraini, N. H. (2015). Military service and suicidal thoughts and behaviors in a national sample of college students. *Crisis, 36*(2), 117–125. https://doi.org/10.1027/0227-5910/a000300

Pinder, R. J., Iversen, A. C., Kapur, N., Wessely, S., & Fear, N. T. (2012). Self-harm and attempted suicide among UK Armed Forces personnel: Results of a cross-sectional survey. *International Journal of Social Psychiatry, 58*(4), 433–439. https://doi.org/10.1177/0020764011408534

Raudales, A. M., Weiss, N. H., Goncharenko, S., Forkus, S. R., & Contractor, A. A. (2020). Posttraumatic stress disorder and deliberate self-harm among military veterans: Indirect effects through negative and positive emotion dysregulation. *Psychological Trauma: Theory, Research, Practice, and Policy, 12*(7), 707–715. https://doi.org/10.1037/tra0000962

Ray-Sannerud, B. N., Bryan, C. J., Perry, N. S., & Bryan, A. O. (2015). High levels of emotional distress, trauma exposure, and self-injurious thoughts and behaviors among military personnel and veterans with a history of same sex behavior. *Psychology of Sexual Orientation and Gender Diversity, 2*(2), 130–137. https://doi.org/10.1037/sgd0000096

Sacks, M. B., Flood, A. M., Dennis, M. F., Hertzberg, M. A., & Beckham, J. C. (2008). Self-mutilative behaviors in male veterans with posttraumatic stress disorder. *Journal of Psychiatric Research, 42*(6), 487–494. https://doi.org/10.1016/j.jpsychires.2007.05.001

Sayer, N. A., Noorbaloochi, S., Frazier, P., Carlson, K., Gravely, A., & Murdoch, M. (2010). Reintegration problems and treatment interests among Iraq and Afghanistan combat veterans receiving VA medical care. *Psychiatric Services, 61*(6), 589–597. https://doi.org/10.1176/ps.2010.61.6.589

Selby, E. A., Bender, T. W., Gordon, K. H., Nock, M. K., & Joiner Jr, T. E. (2012). Non-suicidal self-injury (NSSI) disorder: A preliminary study. *Personality Disorders: Theory, Research, and Treatment, 3*(2), 167–175. https://doi.org/10.1037/a0024405

Serafini, G., Canepa, G., Adavastro, G., Nebbia, J., Belvederi Murri, M., Erbuto, D., Pocai, B., Fiorillo, A., Pompili, M., Flouri, E., & Amore, M. (2017). The relationship between childhood maltreatment and non-suicidal self-injury: A systematic review. *Frontiers in Psychiatry, 8*, Article 149. https://doi.org/10.3389/fpsyt.2017.00149

Sippel, L. M., Mota, N. P., Kachadourian, L. K., Krystal, J. H., Southwick, S. M., Harpaz-Rotem, I., & Pietrzak, R. H. (2016). The burden of hostility in US Veterans: Results from the National Health and Resilience in Veterans Study. *Psychiatry Research, 243*, 421–430. https://doi.org/10.1016/j.psychres.2016.06.040

Smith, A. R., Dodd, D. R., Ortiz, S., Forrest, L. N., & Witte, T. K. (2020). Interoceptive deficits differentiate suicide groups and associate with self-injurious thoughts and behaviors in a military sample. *Suicide and Life-Threatening Behavior*, *50*(2), 472–489. https://doi.org/10.1111/sltb.12603

Swannell, S. V., Martin, G. E., Page, A., Hasking, P., & St John, N. J. (2014). Prevalence of nonsuicidal self-injury in nonclinical samples: Systematic review, meta-analysis and meta-regression. *Suicide and Life-Threatening Behavior*, *44*(3), 273–303. https://doi.org/10.1111/sltb.12070

Taylor, P. J., Jomar, K., Dhingra, K., Forrester, R., Shahmalak, U., & Dickson, J. M. (2018). A meta-analysis of the prevalence of different functions of non-suicidal self-injury. *Journal of Affective Disorders*, *227*, 759–769. https://doi.org/10.1016/j.jad.2017.11.073

Turner, B. J., Kleiman, E. M., & Nock, M. K. (2019). Non-suicidal self-injury prevalence, course, and association with suicidal thoughts and behaviors in two large, representative samples of US Army soldiers. *Psychological Medicine*, *49*(9), 1470–1480. https://doi.org/10.1017/s0033291718002015

Villatte, J. L., O'Connor, S. S., Leitner, R., Kerbrat, A. H., Johnson, L. L., & Gutierrez, P. M. (2015). Suicide attempt characteristics among veterans and active-duty service members receiving mental health services: A pooled data analysis. *Military Behavioral Health*, *3*(4), 316–327. https://doi.org/10.1080/21635781.2015.1093981

White, K. L., Harris, J. A., Bryan, A. O., Reynolds, M., Fuessel-Herrmann, D., & Bryan, C. J. (2018). Military sexual trauma and suicidal behavior among National Guard personnel. *Comprehensive Psychiatry*, *87*, 1–6. https://doi.org/10.1016/j.comppsych.2018.08.008

Wilson, L. C. (2018). The prevalence of military sexual trauma: A meta-analysis. *Trauma, Violence, & Abuse*, *19*(5), 584–597. https://doi.org/10.1177/1524838016683459

Yurgelun-Todd, D. A., Bueler, C. E., McGlade, E. C., Churchwell, J. C., Brenner, L. A., & Lopez-Larson, M. P. (2011). Neuroimaging correlates of traumatic brain injury and suicidal behavior. *The Journal of Head Trauma Rehabilitation*, *26*(4), 276–289. https://doi.org/10.1097/htr.0b013e31822251dc

Zetterqvist, M., Lundh, L. G., Dahlström, Ö., & Svedin, C. G. (2013). Prevalence and function of non-suicidal self-injury (NSSI) in a community sample of adolescents, using suggested DSM-5 criteria for a potential NSSI disorder. *Journal of Abnormal Child Psychology*, *41*(5), 759–773. https://doi.org/10.1007/s10802-013-9712-5

Zinzow, H. M., Britt, T. W., Pury, C. L., Raymond, M. A., McFadden, A. C., & Burnette, C. M. (2013). Barriers and facilitators of mental health treatment seeking among active-duty army personnel. *Military Psychology*, *25*(5), 514–535. https://doi.org/10.1037/mil0000015

CHAPTER
33

NSSI Among Sexual and Gender Diverse Youth

Lucas Zullo, Megan L. Rogers, *and* Lindsay A. Taliaferro

> **Abstract**
>
> This chapter considers the frequency of nonsuicidal self-injury (NSSI) among sexual and gender diverse (SGD) youth. Compared to their heterosexual and cisgender counterparts, SGD youth report higher rates of NSSI within the past year and across the lifespan. The chapter looks into the Minority Stress Model, which highlights the SGD youth's experiences of stigma, discrimination, victimization, violence, rejection, and prejudice. The most powerful reductions in minority stress will likely occur once SGD youth have regular access to safe and affirming environments. The chapter clarifies that no evidence-based interventions are currently available to target this specific population aside from Attachment-Based Family Therapy (ABFT) for Lesbian, Gay, and Bisexual (LGB) Youth, which was designed for suicidal sexual minority youth.
>
> **Key Words:** NSSI, sexual and gender diverse youth, discrimination, victimization, violence, environment, Minority Stress Model

Introduction

Sexual and gender diverse (SGD) youth, defined as youth who experience a sexual orientation other than solely heterosexual attraction and/or youth who identify with a gender other than the gender assigned at birth, demonstrate significantly elevated risk for NSSI, compared to their heterosexual and cisgender counterparts. According to a recent systematic review by Rogers and Taliaferro (2020), SGD youth report higher rates of NSSI within the past year and across the lifespan than their heterosexual and cisgender counterparts. Specifically, rates of NSSI are approximately 2.25 to 5.80 times higher among sexual minority youth than among heterosexual youth (Amos et al., 2020; DeCamp & Bakken, 2016; Fox et al., 2020; Fraser et al., 2018; Goodin et al., 2019; Hirschtritt et al., 2018; Irish et al., 2019; Li et al., 2019; Liu, 2019; Monto et al., 2018). Likewise, approximately half (49.0%–54.8%) of gender diverse youth report NSSI in the past year (Katz-Wise et al., 2018; Ross-Reed et al., 2019; Taliaferro et al., 2018), with 40.3% reporting repetitive NSSI (i.e., 10+ times) within the past year (Taliaferro et al., 2018), and 55.7% reporting lifetime NSSI (Nahata et al., 2017). Thus, compared to cisgender youth, gender diverse youth are more than 20% more likely to report past-year NSSI (Clark et al., 2014;

Spack et al., 2012) and more than 10% more likely to report lifetime NSSI (Reisner et al., 2015). Thus, rates of NSSI among SGD youth far exceed those among youth in the general population, where approximately 18.0% of adolescents report engaging in NSSI (Muehlenkamp et al., 2012), and are comparable to those of sexual (29.7%) and gender (46.7%) diverse adults (Liu et al., 2019), underscoring the magnitude and lasting impact of this major public health problem among SGD populations.

Given the high rates and increased risk of NSSI among SGD youth, we must understand potential intrapersonal, interpersonal, community, and societal mechanisms underlying this problem. Greater understanding of factors contributing to NSSI among these populations may aid in the development and implementation of evidence-based assessments and interventions to decrease the prevalence of this public health concern among SGD youth. In this chapter, we first describe relevant theoretical frameworks and empirical literature that guide current evidence regarding risk for NSSI among SGD youth. We then provide a case example and recommendations for clinical practice, discuss potential implications for intervention and prevention in community/upstream settings, and elaborate on future directions broadly to better understand, predict, and prevent NSSI among SGD youth. Finally, we highlight challenges, recommendations, and implications related to NSSI research within SGD youth populations.

Theoretical Models and Empirically Supported Risk and Protective Factors

Although researchers have developed numerous models for NSSI more generally (described elsewhere in this book), researchers have applied few identity-specific theoretical models to the study of NSSI among SGD individuals. One exception is the Minority Stress Model (Meyer, 1995, 2003)/Gender Minority Stress and Resilience Model (Testa et al., 2015), which represents the primary framework through which risk for adverse mental health outcomes, including NSSI, has been examined among SGD individuals. The Minority Stress Model proposes that experiences of stigma, discrimination, victimization, violence, rejection, and prejudice (i.e., distal minority stressors) due to negative and hostile community and societal attitudes about SGD identities increase risk of negative mental health outcomes among SGD individuals (Meyer, 2003). In particular, distal minority stressors may generate several internalized minority stress processes—internalized homophobia/transphobia, negative expectancies for future events, and concealment of one's sexual orientation and/or gender identity—that serve as mechanisms driving disparities in mental health outcomes and NSSI among sexual and gender minorities (Hatzenbuehler, 2009). However, the model also allows for a resilience framework by incorporating protective factors that can buffer the impact of stressors on mental health outcomes. The presence of identity strengths, coping skills, and social supports serve as important moderating and mitigating factors on poor mental health outcomes (Meyer, 2003).

The Minority Stress Model can be understood through the lens of the socioecological model of risk and resilience across individual, interpersonal, community, and societal levels (Dahlberg & Krug, 2002). Although researchers have predominantly explored the Minority Stress Model among adult or young adult populations (Kelleher, 2009; Shilo & Savaya, 2012), the model's appropriateness and applicability to youth populations has also been noted (Goldbach & Gibbs, 2017). Specifically, results from a thematic analysis of interviews with 48 sexual minority adolescents highlighted the utility of the Minority Stress Model, as well as a need to emphasize unique developmental processes related to identity development during adolescence, social contexts, and coping resources among youth (Goldbach & Gibbs, 2017). Adolescence represents a critical period for the development of one's sexuality and/or gender identity (Erikson, 1968), and invalidating experiences, such as exposure to homophobia/transphobia, during this time period may have lasting negative impacts on mental health (e.g., increased depression/anxiety) into adulthood (Gibbs & Rice, 2016). Moreover, given the importance of myriad social contexts on both minority stress and coping among SGD adolescents—spanning familial, peer, school, religious, and other domains (Goldbach & Gibbs, 2017)—integrating interpersonal and structural (i.e., community and society) risk and resilience factors with intrapersonal factors within the Minority Stress Model seems paramount in youth populations.

Individual

Individual-level risk and resilience factors for NSSI include cognitive, affective, physiological, and behavioral responses that occur as reactions to more distal minority stressors (i.e., interpersonal, community, and societal) and influence one's risk for negative outcomes, including NSSI. Specifically, the Minority Stress Model highlights three stress factors—internalized homophobia/transphobia, negative expectancies/rejection sensitivity, and nondisclosure/concealment of one's sexual orientation and/or gender identity (Hatzenbuehler, 2009; Meyer, 2003). Internalized homophobia/transphobia reflects the internalization of negative societal attitudes toward one's sexual orientation and/or gender identity and has been consistently associated with negative mental health outcomes, including NSSI (Batejan et al., 2015; Jackman et al., 2016; Liu et al., 2019), among SGD individuals (Newcomb & Mustanski, 2010; Rogers et al., 2021; Testa et al., 2017). Negative expectations for future events represent the belief that one will experience discrimination, prejudice, and rejection based on prior experiences and/or awareness of societal stigma against SGD individuals (Meyer, 2003; Testa et al., 2015). Negative expectancies toward future events were associated with suicidal ideation among a sample of gender diverse adults (Testa et al., 2017), but researchers have not specifically examined these expectations among youth or in relation to NSSI. Sensitivity to potential rejection and negative expectancies may become particularly salient during adolescence (Westenberg et al., 2004) and may have long-lasting effects spanning into adulthood (Lev-Wiesel et al., 2006) for SGD youth. Finally, SGD individuals may not disclose or choose to conceal their sexual and/or gender identities to protect themselves from discrimination, victimization, or rejection (Testa et al., 2015). However, SGD adults who do not disclose their identities demonstrate increased risk of suicidal ideation (Michaels et al., 2016; Testa et al., 2017). Researchers have not examined the effects of identity nondisclosure among SGD youth or in relation to NSSI.

Potential positive individual factors include possessing positive attitudes about one's sexual and/or gender identity (Lehavot & Simoni, 2011; Mohr & Sarno, 2016; Riggle et al., 2017), as well as utilizing effective coping strategies, especially SGD-specific coping strategies, that facilitate belongingness and access to SGD community support systems (Singh, 2013; Toomey et al., 2018). In particular, thoughts and behaviors consistent with being ashamed of one's identity (e.g., identity concealment) are associated with lower psychological well-being, whereas living authentically with one's SGD identity is linked with enhanced psychological well-being (Riggle et al., 2017). Thus, thoughts and behaviors associated with pride regarding one's SGD identity represent protective factors for emotional well-being (Graham et al., 2017).

Interpersonal

As part of the Minority Stress Model, interpersonal factors are often referred to as external minority stressors, or interactions between a sexual and/or gender minority individual and someone else in the environment driven by discrimination, victimization, and/or rejection based on one's sexual and/or gender identity (Meyer, 2003; Testa et al., 2015). According to Meyer's (2003) and Testa et al.'s (2015) adaptation of the Minority Stress Model, identity-based discrimination refers to difficulties obtaining housing, employment, medical care, and legal documents because of one's sexual and/or gender identity. Victimization involves physical or verbal acts of violence or hatred committed against a person or their property due to their sexual and/or gender identity. Rejection may include multiple forms of nonaffirmation and/or rejection from close others, other individuals, institutions, and/or communities as a result of one's sexual and/or gender identity (Meyer, 2003; Testa et al., 2015). These interpersonal stressors (see Zetterqvist & Bjureberg, this volume) take the form of overt actions, such as hate crimes, as well as covert actions, such as microaggressions (e.g., making heteronormative assumptions about partners and assuming pronouns based on physical appearance). Within the Minority Stress Model, these external minority stressors may generate internal minority stress processes, as described above, that have pernicious impacts on mental health outcomes (Hatzenbuehler, 2009; Meyer, 2003). Among SGD adolescents specifically, the effects of external minority stressors on NSSI have focused predominantly on (1) peer victimization and bullying and (2) parental rejection. Specifically, recent systematic reviews and meta-analyses highlighted 28 and 40 published studies, respectively, that examined the relation between bullying and victimization, including LGBT-specific victimization, on self-injurious thoughts and behaviors in samples of SGD youth

(Rogers & Taliaferro, 2020; Williams et al., 2021). One of these reviews (Rogers & Taliaferro, 2020) also highlighted the potential protective role of connection and support, both broadly (Katz-Wise et al., 2018; Ross-Reed et al., 2019; Smith et al., 2020) and specifically within families (Gower et al., 2018; Taliaferro et al., 2018; Taliaferro & Muehlenkamp, 2017), against engagement in NSSI. Connections to nonparental adults (Taliaferro et al., 2019a; Taliaferro & Muehlenkamp, 2017) and SGD peers (Russell & Fish, 2016; Singh, 2013) have also proven protective for SGD youth, who may need to create a "chosen family" of affirming adults and peers when they lack support from their families of origin. Recent research indicates SGD youth who have the support of at least one accepting adult were 40% less likely to report a suicide attempt in the past year (The Trevor Project, 2019).

Community

Community-level factors include characteristics and the culture of settings in which interpersonal relationships occur, such as schools, neighborhoods, and home environments, which may foster negative experiences that contribute to internalized minority stressors and negative mental health outcomes, or positive experiences that promote resilience, among SGD youth. Although researchers have examined the effects of various community contexts on psychopathology more broadly, they have not focused on NSSI as an outcome, except when examining school environments and societal markers of SGD acceptance. A systematic review of recent research (Rogers & Taliaferro, 2020) highlighted seven studies that examined characteristics of school environments in relation to self-injurious thoughts and behaviors among SGD youth. In particular, perceptions of school violence, feeling less safe at school, and perceptions of a homonegative climate at school (e.g., that it is challenging being a sexual and/or gender minority student at their school) were each positively associated with NSSI (Espelage et al., 2018; Goldbach et al., 2017; Gower et al., 2018). Additionally, although predominantly explored in relation to suicide-related outcomes, rather than NSSI, several school-based protective factors indicating cultural affirmation of SGD youth were associated with reduced risk of suicidality among SGD youth, including the presence of a school-based health center (Zhang et al., 2020), LGBTQ-specific educational presentations (Burk et al., 2018), LGBTQ-inclusive sex education (Proulx et al., 2019), and youth development opportunities more generally (Gower et al., 2018). Further, an examination of the relationship between supportive social environments (i.e., operationalized as the greater proportion of same-sex couples, the presence of gender-sexuality alliances in schools, and school-level nondiscrimination and antibullying policies that specifically protect sexual minority students) surrounding sexual minority youth and risk of suicide attempts among LGB youth revealed that the risk of attempting suicide was 20% higher in unsupportive environments than in supportive environments, controlling for a multitude of sociodemographic characteristics and risk factors (Hatzenbuehler, 2011).

The Gay, Lesbian & Straight Education Network (GLSEN) regularly emphasizes the critical importance of SGD-affirming school groups and safe spaces in their annual national School Climate Survey (Kosciw et al., 2010). In this annual report, an abundance of data demonstrates relationships between school culture (presence/absence of harassment, clubs for SGD youth, supportive teachers, etc.) and emotional well-being of SGD youth. Quotes from youth highlight the important, positive effect an affirming school club can provide students frequently bullied or harassed for their SGD identities. Similarly, affirming adult mentors in schools who support SGD-affirming groups or provide emotional support to SGD students have shown to have a meaningful impact on the resilience and well-being of SGD youth (Asakura, 2017; Bird et al., 2012; Jones & Hillier, 2013).

Religion represents another powerful influence in the community setting. Although religiosity and religious engagement are usually protective against mental health problems (Braam & Koenig, 2019; Kleiman & Liu, 2018; Koenig, 2009; Koenig et al., 2015; Unterrainer et al., 2014), for SGD individuals, the positive effects are less clear (Hall, 2018; Longo et al., 2013; McCann et al., 2020). Researchers found two thirds of SGD individuals reported experiencing internalized homophobia from religious messages that preached sinfulness of same-sex sexual attraction and the need for repentance (Sherry et al., 2010). This internalized homophobia/transphobia could lead to anxiety, depression, and suicidality arising from feelings of guilt, shame, and self-blaming (McCann et al., 2020; Schuck & Liddle, 2001; Sowe et al., 2017). Religious affiliation that results in internalized homophobia/transphobia could represent a major stressor affecting mental well-being among SGD youth, especially for those whose cultures prioritize religion (Meyer, 2003).

Societal

Several macro-level societal factors contribute to a climate in which the aforementioned interpersonal and community risk factors, including violence, discrimination, harassment, and rejection, are more likely to occur against SGD individuals (Mallory & Sears, 2020). To our knowledge, no studies specifically examine direct relationships between social policies and engagement in NSSI among SGD youth. However, social policies (e.g., protection against workplace discrimination on the basis of SGD identity and lack of access to gender neutral bathrooms) that influence perceptions and treatment of SGD people, whether through marginalization or support/protection, may have considerable impact on the general social and cultural climates that SGD youth experience. For instance, SGD youth living in states where positive portrayals of LGBTQ people are prohibited are less likely to have access to LGBTQ resources at school or effective interventions from school staff when bullying and harassment occur (Kosciw et al., 2010). Another potential consequence of these environments is internalized homophobia/transphobia (Hendricks & Testa, 2012; Meyer, 1995). Thus, whereas direct associations between broad state-level anti-bullying laws, anti-LGBTQ discrimination policies, and same-sex marriage policies, and suicidal thoughts and suicide attempts may be modest (Proulx et al., 2019; Raifman et al., 2017; Seelman & Walker, 2018), large indirect effects may exist through the cultivation of supportive and inclusive environments that reduce the presence and effects of other distal and proximal minority stressors on mental health. Advocacy for social services, resources, and policies that benefit SGD youth development may, in turn, reduce the likelihood of these youth engaging in NSSI.

Summary

SGD youth are at a much higher risk of engaging in NSSI than their heterosexual and cisgender peers. The primary framework through which this discrepancy is explained in the extant literature is the Minority Stress Model. This model identifies four main sources of potential invalidation and stress that may contribute to the manifestation of NSSI: individual; interpersonal; community; and society. Conversely, positive messaging and affirmation from these domains are protective against NSSI.

To facilitate the translation from research to practice, the following section highlights a clinical vignette to illustrate the real-life application of material covered in this chapter.

Clinical Considerations, Implications, and Recommendations

Ash is a 14-year-old, Indian-American, nonbinary youth (pronouns: he/him, they/them) living in Boston, Massachusetts. He recently started questioning his gender identity and sexual orientation, but has felt too scared to tell anyone because he has never met another person who is part of the LGBTQ community. His parents are devout Muslims, and he has experienced a conservative upbringing. Ash's local faith community openly condemns SGD people, and he is struggling with thoughts of self-hate. Recently, Ash has wanted to explore his gender expression with the clothing he wears to school, but he feels too ashamed and embarrassed to do so. He has become increasingly upset that he is not "normal" like his classmates and has started to cut himself with a shaving razor in the shower. One of Ash's teachers noticed he appears down lately and referred him to see the school psychologist.

As we present the following information, we ask the reader to place themselves in the shoes of the school psychologist from this vignette and consider possible clinical implications of the research summarized as it pertains to the case example.

Treatments for NSSI among SGD Youth

Despite the clear disparity in rates of NSSI among SGD youth, when compared to their heterosexual, cisgender peers, no evidence-based interventions are currently available to target this specific population. Only one intervention has been specifically designed for suicidal sexual minority youth: Attachment-Based Family Therapy (ABFT) for Lesbian, Gay, and Bisexual (LGB) Youth (Diamond et al., 2013). Notably, this intervention was not developed while incorporating the needs of gender diverse youth, making the treatment only applicable to a portion of individuals in the SGD community.

This notable lack of tailored interventions targeting NSSI and suicidal ideation and suicide attempts among SGD youth has led to calls for prioritizing research that adapts existing evidence-based treatments to better meet the needs of SGD youth (Mustanski & Espelage, 2020). For example, DBT recently was the first treatment to meet the "Level 1 criteria for a Well-Established Treatment" for reducing self-harm, including NSSI, among youth (Glenn et al., 2019; McCauley et al., 2018; Mehlum et al., 2014), making DBT an ideal treatment for adaptation for SGD youth. Thus, researchers/clinicians may not need to build a new intervention from the ground up, but instead engage in quality improvement efforts to customize strong and promising NSSI treatments for the needs of SGD youth.

A quality improvement initiative that tailors evidence-based self-harm treatments for SGD youth can come in two forms: (1) incorporating key components of existing evidence-based treatments for SGD youth that are not specific to NSSI, but target essential transdiagnostic aspects of working with these youth (i.e., minority stress) and/or (2) implementing a participatory action approach by eliciting qualitative feedback from stakeholders, especially SGD youth themselves, to obtain information regarding needed modifications to current evidence-based care. Both approaches have clear strengths. The former utilizes evidence-based techniques with established empirical support, and the latter embraces a more open-ended and flexible framework that ensures SGD youth voices are heard and their needs are understood and may highlight perspectives not featured in the extant literature.

To provide an example of the first approach, we can consider current evidence-based treatments, such as Project Youth Affirm (Craig et al., 2019), an affirmative cognitive behavioral therapy. Treatments such as Project Youth Affirm do not target NSSI specifically, but they address salient stressors, such as maladaptive thoughts and beliefs around minority stress and SGD identity, that could contribute significantly to the manifestation of NSSI behavior. As such, these SGD-specific interventions may be ideally suited to enhance and complement the delivery of NSSI-specific interventions. When considering option (2) of going to youth stakeholders directly, published studies, such as those by Eisenberg and colleagues (2020), Taliaferro and colleagues (2019b), and Zullo and colleagues (2021), offer perspectives from SGD youth on how to enhance the delivery of evidence-based care in a variety of settings. A summary of these suggestions, sorted by setting, is described below. The term 'clinic' represents any setting where care takes place (e.g., primary care, school counselor, etc.).

Linking to Care

Youth have described feeling apprehensive about seeking care, if they feel unsure whether or not a clinic/provider is SGD-friendly (Zullo et al., 2021). Thus, clinic messaging to prospective patients is critical to help youth feel comfortable with the first step of reaching out to learn more about a provider/clinic or schedule an initial appointment. This messaging can take different forms, including clear, affirming language on a clinic website or advertising flyer. This language can include training in SGD topics providers have completed or specific areas of expertise providers possess relevant to the SGD community.

For youth with little or no caregiver support due to their SGD identity, healthcare systems and clinics will need to consider policies that improve access to care. For example, youth may experience transportation barriers, potentially addressed by telehealth, or financial barriers if caregivers are unwilling to pay for services from a SGD-affirming provider, potentially addressed by sliding scale or pro bono work. Overall, healthcare systems and individual providers need to identify barriers and become more flexible to decrease these barriers to ensure SGD youth who lack support from caregivers can obtain quality care and have their needs met.

Clinic Environment

Once youth feel comfortable entering the clinic space, visible markers indicating the space is safe for SGD youth are essential to set an affirming and welcoming tone prior to the very first interaction with healthcare staff. These markers should convey the message that providers in this setting are educated about SGD-affirming care and committed to providing this type of care to patients. Examples of affirming markers include rainbow flag imagery, pictures of same-sex couples, and pamphlets on SGD-specific healthcare in public areas such as the waiting room, or items worn by staff such as lanyards. Additionally, providers might wear pins indicating preferred pronouns. Affirming markers can extend to telehealth video backgrounds as well. Youth shared that these symbols are especially helpful when used by clinic staff or providers who are part of demographic groups for which youth may make assumptions around levels of SGD acceptance. For example, SGD youth may assume an older, white, male provider working in a conservative region of the country might possess homophobic or transphobic views (Zullo et al., 2021). However, seeing a symbol, such as a rainbow flag lanyard, could assuage a youth's concerns and increase their feelings of comfort and safety.

Assessment and Intervention

Evidence is mixed regarding the best way to initially assess SGD identity among youth. Some youth want providers to directly ask about SGD identity (Eisenberg et al., 2020), whereas others feel hesitant to disclose this information if asked due to concerns about confidentiality or acceptance from the provider (Zullo et al., 2021). However, despite possibly feeling uncomfortable disclosing this information, youth prefer providers who initiate conversations about SGD identity, rather than relying on the youth to bring up this information themselves (Taliaferro et al., 2019b). Other youth described indirect methods, such as intake forms asking about SGD identity, as more comfortable than direct verbal communication because this method does not involve direct disclosure to a new adult (Zullo et al., 2021). Still, clinic staff and providers must familiarize themselves with and incorporate information listed on intake forms during clinical encounters such as using youth's preferred names and pronouns and asking about intimate relationships and behavior appropriately.

Youth also want staff and providers to show signs of affirmative interest in them by engaging in ongoing assessment of their SGD identities in various ways during a therapeutic relationship, past the intake session, such as with questions around romantic interests and support systems (Zullo et al., 2021). Ongoing assessment strengthens rapport with a provider and allows youth to expand upon nuances of their identities such as their coming out process (to themselves and others) or internalized feelings of stigma they may feel.

A significant concern to youth involves a potential misunderstanding regarding confidentiality related to disclosure of SGD identity and thoughts of NSSI or suicide. Specifically, youth report feeling unsure about what information providers may share with their caregivers, and what type of self-disclosure may lead to a visit to the emergency department or inpatient hospitalization (Zullo et al., 2021). These two factors have been described as a "double barrier" to feeling comfortable sharing certain information with a provider (Zullo et al., 2021). To address these fears, providers should clearly explain the limits of confidentiality at the outset of a visit, providing specific examples of information they must disclose to a caregiver, such as clear and imminent plans to kill oneself, and information they will not disclose such as a patient's SGD identity.

Additionally, youth report significant damage to rapport and the therapeutic relationship when providers make assumptions about a connection between a SGD identity and thoughts of NSSI or suicide (Zullo et al., 2021). Therefore, providers need to work with youth to understand what, if any, role an SGD identity plays in their NSSI and how the influence of a SGD identity may impact the plan for care. For example, youth may benefit from being connected to SGD community support services and identifying a SGD adult mentor who can provide affirmation and support. Additionally, a provider might suggest linkage to affirming resources, such as the online Trevor Space forum, or provide affirming books on SGD identity development, if minority stress and internalized stigma are primary stressors.

Additional Considerations

Unfortunately, SGD youth can experience significant variability in the level of support they receive from their caregivers. Therefore, providers must collaborate with youth when deciding the degree to which caregivers should be involved in their treatment. Some caregivers will need time alone to receive psychoeducation on appropriate language to use in relation to SGD people or how to best support their child. The child should not be put in the position of providing this psychoeducation to their caregivers. Some caregivers may need coaching from providers before they can effectively participate in family sessions with youth. Specifically, some caregivers may have especially strong emotional reactions to learning about their child's SGD identity and might need time alone with a provider to process these emotions. Youth should not be present in a therapeutic session before caregivers can express themselves in a supportive and constructive manner, especially if a caregiver's initial reaction includes anger or rejection.

A common treatment goal for SGD youth involves meeting other members of the SGD community (Zullo et al., 2021). Providers can support youth with this goal by knowing about and linking them to LGBTQ-supportive and -affirming centers, support groups, and so on in their communities. Discussing involvement in prosocial, online SGD communities and making new friends through the internet in a safe way that aligns with treatment goals may represent another helpful strategy. For instance, in a report by the Gay, Lesbian & Straight Education Network (GLSEN et al., 2013), the internet was described as an opportunity for SGD youth to foster healthy sexual/gender identity development, social support, and civic engagement. Hillier and Harrison (2007) report on how the internet allows SGD youth who have limited in-person opportunities to experience romantic socialization to reach out and forge meaningful relationships through online communities. Aside from romantic socialization, Ybarra et al. (2015) describe how online social support can serve as a buffer for SGD youth against bullying that may occur both online and in person.

Putting Everything Together

We now return to the case vignette of Ash and highlight how the material covered in this chapter can be used to inform care for SGD youth who engage in NSSI.

During the "Introduction" and "Epidemiology" sections of the chapter, we learned that approximately half of gender diverse youth report NSSI in the past year, with about 40% reporting repetitive NSSI during the past year (Taliaferro et al., 2018). With regards to Ash, who identifies as nonbinary, this information suggests his NSSI behavior is likely to repeat without access to evidence-based care. In the "Theoretical Models" section, the importance of minority stress was covered. The second sentence of the vignette illustrates the role of minority stress in Ash's fear to come out to anyone, feeling of not being "normal" in comparison to his peers, and internalized stigma related to his gender identity. In addition, he lacks any support from members of the SGD community, which could represent a protective factor for NSSI urges and behavior. These factors are helpful for the school psychologist to consider in deciding how to help Ash manage his NSSI by informing specific salient treatment targets (i.e., minority stress in relation to peers and self-image, fear of coming out, and importance of linkage to SGD peers), as well as understanding the likelihood of Ash repeating his NSSI without adequate care.

Risk and resilience factors were discussed in the context of the socioecological model. The information described in this section of the chapter is especially useful when designing a treatment plan. For Ash, the following factors can be considered:

- Individual/intrapersonal—views of self-hate, does not view self as "normal," resulting in feeling ashamed and embarrassed, fear of coming out;

- Interpersonal/relationships—parents are devout Muslims and raised Ash with a conservative upbringing, and he is uncomfortable going to them for support;
- Community—Ash's local faith community condemns SGD people and contributes significantly to his feelings of self-hate and internalized transphobia/homophobia; and
- Societal—Ash lives in Massachusetts, a state that has frequently led the country in implementing affirming policies for SGD individuals

Possible treatment plan: Significant contributing factors to Ash's distress involve negative messaging he received from his parents and faith community and lack of positive messaging due to an absence of a SGD-affirming support network. Therefore, Ash may benefit from exposure to social groups with other SGD youth and adults, either online or in person. The school psychologist might try to link Ash to a SGD-supportive group, which may be relatively straightforward if Ash's school has a Gender-Sexualities Alliance Club. Ash might also appreciate books or handouts on navigating one's own religious identity as it relates to a SGD identity. Overall, the school psychologist should strive to provide a strong affirming environment for Ash where his SGD identity is regularly normalized and supported during treatment for NSSI.

Considering the quality improvement suggestions, the school psychologist's clinic/office environment must demonstrate to Ash she represents a safe person who will provide SGD-affirming care. Ash will likely feel apprehensive and possibly fearful during his first meeting with her due to negative messaging he received from his parents and religious community about SGD individuals, which he internalized. A rainbow pride/blue and pink transgender flag or similar indication of SGD support will help Ash feel comfortable and perceive the psychologist's clinic/office as a safe space. Similarly, carefully reviewing the limits of confidentiality will help Ash remain open and forthcoming, without fear the psychologist will share their conversation with his parents. Regarding disclosure of his SGD identity, Ash will likely need to build some rapport with the school psychologist before initiating a disclosure and may feel too scared to share this information on an intake form.

As the school psychologist learns more about Ash's situation, she should appreciate that his SGD identity likely represents just one contributing factor to his NSSI behavior. The psychologist should complete a comprehensive assessment of his behavior to fully understand the contributing factors (Westers et al., 2016). Moreover, the psychologist must involve Ash in decision-making related to sharing information with his parents. Ash may prefer to focus solely on the NSSI behavior and wait until much later in care before discussing his SGD identity with his family. Sharing both Ash's NSSI and SGD identity with his parents at the same time may overwhelm them and lead to an extremely stressful family dynamic that may increase distress and risk of other adverse outcomes (e.g., victimization and abandonment) for Ash.

Since minority stress represents a key component of Ash's distress, he may appreciate learning ways to meet other SGD youth for the first time. Although creating a safety plan for suicidal behavior and NSSI (including providing several alternative coping behaviors to NSSI or a suicide attempt) will represent the priority for an initial session, bringing up an opportunity for social connection may inspire hope for the future and allow Ash to take a first step in combating his maladaptive thoughts around his SGD identity. To conclude our chapter, we present different priority areas for future research to address the disproportionate prevalence of NSSI among SGD youth.

Future Research Directions

Based on a recent review of the literature on self-injurious thoughts and behavior among SGD youth (Rogers & Taliaferro, 2020), we recommend several areas of research to enhance the body of rigorous research on NSSI among this population. First, we need more research on representative samples of SGD youth from the general community. Most studies on NSSI among SGD youth have been epidemiological in nature, using data from statewide surveys (Rogers & Taliaferro, 2020). These surveys allow researchers to examine NSSI among population-based or representative samples of youth. However, without an item assessing NSSI on the national Youth Risk Behavior Surveillance System, we only have data from individual states, which limits the generalizability of the findings and conclusions we can draw from these studies. Further, epidemiological surveys lack items assessing SGD identity-specific factors such as minority stressors. Assessing identity-specific factors among large, representative samples of SGD youth could yield data that enables researchers to delineate factors underlying rates of NSSI among this population. In addition, most state YRBS surveys do not assess gender identity. Thus, we have little data on NSSI among representative samples of gender minority adolescents.

Second, we need longitudinal studies on NSSI among SGD youth. Most research on NSSI among this population used cross-sectional designs, which does not allow for an examination of causality among study variables. Longitudinal designs would help clarify the nature of individual, interpersonal, community, and societal risk and resilience factors associated with NSSI; provide an opportunity to study the initiation and persistence of NSSI over time; and identify possible sensitive developmental periods during which youth show increased risk for engaging in NSSI. Research across adolescence is needed because sensitive developmental periods, when the effects of particular experiences can be particularly deleterious, are important to study due to their strong influence on brain development and behavior (Casey et al., 2014; Glenn et al., 2017). Studying sensitive periods is important for understanding the temporal impact of environmental events, such as changes in social connectedness or the correlates and consequences of identity nondisclosure, on adolescents' development and windows of opportunity to change behavior (Casey et al., 2014). This research is also important for understanding environmental components in the etiology of mental health and when an intervention may prove most effective (Casey et al., 2014). Thus, longitudinal research during adolescence can provide needed evidence for intervention development and implementation.

Third, we need studies that include protective factors, especially identity-specific protective factors. Most studies examining factors associated with NSSI among SGD youth emphasized risk factors. In contrast to a risk-focused approach, strengths-based, resilience research focuses on protective factors and positive features of development. We need more research examining factors that enhance resilience, especially identity-specific individual and interpersonal protective factors, among SGD youth. Examining factors protecting against the processes underpinning NSSI aligns with public health approaches that seek to understand potential "upstream" prevention targets and employ early preventive interventions (Caine, 2013; Caine et al., 2018; O'Connor & Nock, 2014). A strengths-based, asset-building approach would allow researchers to identify malleable positive identity-specific factors clinicians and public health program planners can address to prevent NSSI among SGD youth. This approach aligns with initiatives to enhance resilience within the SGD community rather than focus on problems that can pathologize this population.

Fourth, we need research that examines differences across subgroups of SGD youth. Limited research shows health disparities across subgroups of SGD youth (Green et al., 2021; Rogers & Taliaferro, 2020). However, a weakness of the extant literature is the tendency to combine different sexual and gender minority groups (Bostwick et al., 2010), obscuring important disparities in risk and protective factors, as well as NSSI outcomes, across subpopulations. Research that includes a sufficient number of participants across subgroups to perform stratified analyses remains essential for understanding disparities and developing tailored interventions.

Fifth, future research should include an intersectional approach when studying NSSI among SGD youth. Racial/ethnic minority and LGBTQ youth each face unique challenges related to their marginalized identities, yet researchers most often study these risks using an independent rather than intersectional approach (Mallory & Russell, 2021; Miller, 2011). Thus, we need more intersectionality research to understand how SGD identity intersects with racial and ethnic identities to affect mental health (Green et al., 2021), including NSSI (Russell & Fish, 2016). This intersection of identities may present distinct stressors for some SGD youth, compared to others, and minority stress may be most persistent and problematic for youth who occupy multiple marginalized social positions and experience multiple forms of discrimination or victimization (Cyrus, 2017; Grollman, 2012). The limited research suggests SGD youth of color experience mental health disparities, compared to their White SGD counterparts (The Trevor Project, 2019). Intersectionality research is also needed to examine the relative contribution of sexuality/gender- versus race/ethnicity-specific factors on NSSI risk and protection. Researchers most frequently examined sexuality/gender-based and race/ethnicity-based stressors as separate domains (Cheref et al., 2019; Hatchel et al., 2019; Taliaferro et al., 2019a). A better understanding of the intersection of sexuality/gender- and race/ethnicity-based minority stressors could aid in the development of interventions targeting both specific and multiple domains of minority stressors with the goal of attenuating relationships between minority stressors and adverse mental health outcomes (Moradi et al., 2010).

Sixth, given the dearth of research on NSSI among SGD youth, particularly unique identity-specific factors associated with this behavior, future research should include qualitative methods to identify novel factors that may remain unknown to investigators. Qualitative research represents the preferred approach for investigating intersectionality (Bowleg, 2008; Jackson, 2017). Qualitative methods encourage participants to expand on responses to provide in-depth and nuanced understanding of complex phenomena, such as NSSI, and can uncover new topics of relevance not initially considered (Merriam, 2019). Qualitative data also are essential for developing tailored interventions (Jackson, 2017).

Finally, future research should be informed or guided by SGD youth with lived experience of NSSI (see Hasking et al., this volume). A youth participatory action approach, where researchers learn from SGD adolescents, would help move the science in this area forward.

Conclusion

NSSI among SGD youth constitutes a public health crisis. However, despite a recent increase in the number of studies examining NSSI in this vulnerable population, the needs of SGD youth around NSSI prevention are still severely understudied. We have outlined numerous potential avenues for future work and demonstrated how to translate findings from the current literature into clinical practice. We hope advances made by future research and public policy and in the social climate across the country will enhance affirmation of SGD youth. While tailored interventions specific to minority stress will be of great value in targeting NSSI among SGD youth, the most powerful reductions in minority stress will likely occur once SGD youth have regular access to safe and affirming environments.

Authors' Note

This work was supported by a National Institute for Mental Health Diversity Supplement (Dr. Zullo) under Award Number R01MH112147. The authors do not report any conflicts of interest.

References

Amos, R., Manalastas, E. J., White, R., Bos, H., & Patalay, P. (2020). Mental health, social adversity, and health-related outcomes in sexual minority adolescents: A contemporary national cohort study. *The Lancet Child & Adolescent Health, 4*, 36–45. https://doi.org/10.1016/S2352-4642(19)30339-6

Asakura, K. (2017). Paving pathways through the pain: A grounded theory of resilience among lesbian, gay, bisexual, trans, and queer youth. *Journal of Research on Adolescence, 27*, 521–536. https://doi.org/10.1111/jora.12291

Batejan, K. L., Jarvi, S. M., & Swenson, L. P. (2015). Sexual orientation and non-suicidal self-injury: A meta-analytic review. *Archives of Suicide Research, 19*, 131–150. https://doi.org/10.1080/13811118.2014.957450

Bird, J. D. P., Kuhns, L., & Garofalo, R. (2012). The impact of role models on health outcomes for lesbian, gay, bisexual and transgender youth. *Journal of Adolescent Health, 50*, 353–357. https://doi.org/10.1016/j.jadohealth.2011.08.006

Bostwick, W. B., Boyd, C. J., Hughes, T. L., & McCabe, S. E. (2010). Dimensions of sexual orientation and the prevalence of mood and anxiety disorders in the United States. *American Journal of Public Health, 100*, 468–475. https://doi.org/10.2105/AJPH.2008.152942

Bowleg, L. (2008). When black + lesbian + woman ≠ black lesbian woman: The methodological challenges of qualitative and quantitative intersectionality research. *Sex Roles, 59*, 312–325. https://doi.org/10.1007/s11199-008-9400-z

Braam, A. W., & Koenig, H. G. (2019). Religion, spirituality and depression in prospective studies: A systematic review. *Journal of Affective Disorders, 257*, 428–438. https://doi.org/10.1016/j.jad.2019.06.063

Burk, J., Park, M., & Saewyc, E. M. (2018). A media-based school Intervention to reduce sexual orientation prejudice and its relationship to discrimination, bullying, and the mental health of lesbian, gay, and bisexual adolescents in western Canada: A population-based evaluation. *International Journal of Environmental Research and Public Health, 15*(11), Article 2447. https://doi.org/10.3390/ijerph15112447

Caine, E. D. (2013). Forging an agenda for suicide prevention in the United States. *American Journal of Public Health, 103*, 822–829. https://doi.org/10.2105/AJPH.2012.301078

Caine, E. D., Reed, J., Hindman, J., & Quinlan, K. (2018). Comprehensive, integrated approaches to suicide prevention: Practical guidance. *Injury Prevention, 24*, i38–i45. https://doi.org/10.1136/injuryprev-2017-042366

Casey, B. J., Oliveri, M. E., & Insel, T. (2014). A neurodevelopmental perspective on the research domain criteria (RDoC) framework. *Biological Psychiatry, 76*, 350–353. https://doi.org/10.1016/j.biopsych.2014.01.006

Cheref, S., Talavera, D., & Walker, R. L. (2019). Perceived discrimination and suicide ideation: Moderating roles of anxiety symptoms and ethnic identity among Asian American, African American, and Hispanic emerging adults. *Suicide & Life-Threatening Behavior, 49*, 665–677. https://doi.org/10.1111/sltb.12467

Clark, T. C., Lucassen, M. F. G., Bullen, P., Denny, S. J., Fleming, T. M., Robinson, E. M., & Rossen, F. V. (2014). The health and well-being of transgender high school students: Results from the New Zealand adolescent health survey (Youth'12). *Journal of Adolescent Health, 55*, 93–99. https://doi.org/10.1016/j.jadohealth.2013.11.008

Craig, S. L., McInroy, L. B., Eaton, A. D., Iacono, G., Leung, V. W., Austin, A., & Dobinson, C. (2019). An affirmative coping skills intervention to improve the mental and sexual health of sexual and gender minority youth (Project Youth AFFIRM): Protocol for an implementation study. *JMIR Research Protocols, 8*, Article e13462. https://doi.org/10.2196/13462

Cyrus, K. (2017). Multiple minorities as multiply marginalized: Applying the minority stress theory to LGBTQ people of color. *Journal of Gay & Lesbian Mental Health, 21*, 194–202. https://doi.org/10.1080/19359705.2017.1320739

Dahlberg, L. L., & Krug, E. G. (2002). Violence: A global public health problem. In E. Krug, L. L. Dahlberg, J. A. Mercy, A. B. Zwi, & R. Lozano (Eds.), *World Report on Violence and Health* (pp. 1–21). World Health Organization.

DeCamp, W., & Bakken, N. W. (2016). Self-injury, suicide ideation, and sexual orientation: Differences in causes and correlates among high school students. *Journal of Injury and Violence Research, 8*, 15–24. https://doi.org/10.5249/jivr.v8i1.545

Diamond, G. M., Diamond, G. S., Levy, S., Closs, C., Ladipo, T., & Siqueland, L. (2013). Attachment-based family therapy for suicidal lesbian, gay, and bisexual adolescents: A treatment development study and open trial with preliminary findings. *Psychology of Sexual Orientation and Gender Diversity, 1*, 91–100. https://doi.org/10.1037/2329-0382.1.S.91

Eisenberg, M. E., McMorris, B. J., Rider, G. N., Gower, A. L., & Coleman, E. (2020). "It's kind of hard to go to the doctor's office if you're hated there." A call for gender-affirming care from transgender and gender diverse adolescents in the United States. *Health & Social Care in the Community, 28*, 1082–1089. https://doi.org/10.1111/hsc.12941

Erikson, E. H. (1968). *Identity: Youth and crisis*. W. W. Norton.

Espelage, D. L., Merrin, G. J., & Hatchel, T. (2018). Peer victimization and dating violence among LGBTQ youth: The impact of school violence and crime on mental health outcomes. *Youth Violence and Juvenile Justice, 16*, 156–173. https://doi.org/10.1177/1541204016680408

Fox, K. R., Choukas-Bradley, S., Salk, R. H., Marshal, M. P., & Thoma, B. C. (2020). Mental health among sexual and gender minority adolescents: Examining interactions with race and ethnicity. *Journal of Consulting and Clinical Psychology*, *88*, 402–415. https://doi.org/10.1037/ccp0000486

Fraser, G., Wilson, M. S., Garisch, J. A., Robinson, K., Brocklesby, M., Kingi, T., O'Connell, A., & Russell, L. (2018). Non-suicidal self-injury, sexuality concerns, and emotion regulation among sexually diverse adolescents: A multiple mediation analysis. *Archives of Suicide Research: Official Journal of the International Academy for Suicide Research*, *22*(3), 432–452. https://doi.org/10.1080/13811118.2017.1358224

Gibbs, J. J., & Rice, E. (2016). The social context of depression symptomology in sexual minority male youth: Determinants of depression in a sample of Grindr users. *Journal of Homosexuality*, *63*, 278–299. https://doi.org/10.1080/00918369.2015.1083773

Glenn, C. R., Cha, C. B., Kleiman, E. M., & Nock, M. K. (2017). Understanding suicide risk within the Research Domain Criteria (RDoC) framework: Insights, challenges, and future research considerations. *Clinical Psychological Science*, *5*, 568–592. https://doi.org/10.1177/2167702616686854

Glenn, C. R., Esposito, E. C., Porter, A. C., & Robinson, D. J. (2019). Evidence base update of psychosocial treatments for self-injurious thoughts and behaviors in youth. *Journal of Clinical Child and Adolescent Psychology*, *48*, 357–392. https://doi.org/10.1080/15374416.2019.1591281

GLSEN, CiPHR, & CCRC. (2013). *Out online: The experiences of lesbian, gay, bisexual and transgender youth on the Internet*. GLSEN.

Goldbach, J. T., & Gibbs, J. J. (2017). A developmentally informed adaptation of minority stress for sexual minority adolescents. *Journal of Adolescence*, *55*, 36–50. https://doi.org/10.1016/j.adolescence.2016.12.007

Goldbach, J. T., Schrager, S. M., & Mamey, M. R. (2017). Criterion and divergent validity of the Sexual Minority Adolescent Stress Inventory. *Frontiers in Psychology*, *8*, Article 2057. https://doi.org/10.3389/fpsyg.2017.02057

Goodin, A., Elswick, A., & Fallin-Bennett, A. (2019). Mental health disparities and high-risk alcohol use among non-heterosexual high school students. *Perspectives in Psychiatric Care*, *55*, 570–575. https://doi.org/10.1111/ppc.12394

Gower, A. L., Rider, G. N., Brown, C., McMorris, B. J., Coleman, E., Taliaferro, L. A., & Eisenberg, M. E. (2018). Supporting transgender and gender diverse youth: Protection against emotional distress and substance use. *American Journal of Preventive Medicine*, *55*, 787–794. https://doi.org/10.1016/j.amepre.2018.06.030

Graham, K., Treharne, G. J., Ruzibiza, C., & Nicolson, M. (2017). The importance of health(ism): A focus group study of lesbian, gay, bisexual, pansexual, queer and transgender individuals' understandings of health. *Journal of Health Psychology*, *22*, 237–247. https://doi.org/10.1177/1359105315600236

Green, A., Taliaferro, L. A., & Price-Feeney, M. (2021). Risk and protective factors to improve well-being and prevent suicide among LGBTQ youth. In R. Miranda & E. L. Jeglic (Eds.), *Handbook of youth suicide prevention: Integrating research into practice* (pp. 177–194). Springer International.

Grollman, E. A. (2012). Multiple forms of perceived discrimination and health among adolescents and young adults. *Journal of Health and Social Behavior*, *53*, 199–214. https://doi.org/10.1177/0022146512444289

Hall, W. J. (2018). Psychosocial risk and protective factors for depression among lesbian, gay, bisexual, and queer youth: A systematic review. *Journal of Homosexuality*, *65*, 263–316. https://doi.org/10.1080/00918369.2017.1317467

Hatchel, T., Ingram, K. M., Mintz, S., Hartley, C., Valido, A., Espelage, D. L., & Wyman, P. (2019). Predictors of suicidal ideation and attempts among LGBTQ adolescents: The roles of help-seeking beliefs, peer victimization, depressive symptoms, and drug use. *Journal of Child and Family Studies*, *28*, 2443–2455. https://doi.org/10.1007/s10826-019-01339-2

Hatzenbuehler, M. L. (2009). How does sexual minority stigma "get under the skin"? A psychological mediation framework. *Psychological Bulletin*, *135*, 707–730. https://doi.org/10.1037/a0016441

Hatzenbuehler, M. L. (2011). The social environment and suicide attempts in lesbian, gay, and bisexual youth. *Pediatrics*, *127*, 896–903. https://doi.org/10.1542/peds.2010-3020

Hendricks, M. L., & Testa, R. J. (2012). A conceptual framework for clinical work with transgender and gender nonconforming clients: An adaptation of the Minority Stress Model. *Professional Psychology: Research and Practice*, *43*, 460–467. https://doi.org/10.1037/a0029597

Hillier, L., & Harrison, L. (2007). Building realities less limited than their own: Young people practising same-sex attraction on the internet. *Sexualities*, *10*, 82–100. https://doi.org/10.1177/1363460707072956

Hirschtritt, M. E., Dauria, E. F., Marshall, B. D. L., & Tolou-Shams, M. (2018). Sexual minority, justice-involved youth: A hidden population in need of integrated mental health, substance use, and sexual health services. *The Journal of Adolescent Health*, *63*, 421–428. https://doi.org/10.1016/j.jadohealth.2018.05.020

Irish, M., Solmi, F., Mars, B., King, M., Lewis, G., Pearson, R. M., Pitman, A., Rowe, S., Srinivasan, R., & Lewis, G. (2019). Depression and self-harm from adolescence to young adulthood in sexual minorities compared with heterosexuals in the UK: A population-based cohort study. *The Lancet Child & Adolescent Health*, *3*, 91–98. https://doi.org/10.1016/S2352-4642(18)30343-2

Jackman, K., Honig, J., & Bockting, W. (2016). Nonsuicidal self-injury among lesbian, gay, bisexual and transgender populations: An integrative review. *Journal of Clinical Nursing*, *25*, 3438–3453. https://doi.org/10.1111/jocn.13236

Jackson, J. W. (2017). Explaining intersectionality through description, counterfactual thinking, and mediation analysis. *Social Psychiatry and Psychiatric Epidemiology*, *52*, 785–793. https://doi.org/10.1007/s00127-017-1390-0

Jones, T., & Hillier, L. (2013). Comparing trans-spectrum and same-sex-attracted youth in Australia: Increased risks, increased activisms. *Journal of LGBT Youth*, *10*, 287–307. https://doi.org/10.1080/19361653.2013.825197

Katz-Wise, S. L., Ehrensaft, D., Vetters, R., Forcier, M., & Austin, S. B. (2018). Family functioning and mental health of transgender and gender-nonconforming youth in the Trans Teen and Family Narratives Project. *Journal of Sex Research*, *55*, 582–590. https://doi.org/10.1080/00224499.2017.1415291

Kelleher, C. (2009). Minority stress and health: Implications for lesbian, gay, bisexual, transgender, and questioning (LGBTQ) young people. *Counselling Psychology Quarterly*, *22*, 373–379. https://doi.org/10.1080/09515070903334995

Kleiman, E. M., & Liu, R. T. (2018). An examination of the prospective association between religious service attendance and suicide: Explanatory factors and period effects. *Journal of Affective Disorders*, *225*, 618–623. https://doi.org/10.1016/j.jad.2017.08.083

Koenig, H. G. (2009). Research on religion, spirituality, and mental health: A review. *Canadian Journal of Psychiatry*, *54*, 283–291. https://doi.org/10.1177/070674370905400502

Koenig, H. G., Al Zaben, F. N., & Al Shohaib, S. (2015). Religion and health: Clinical considerations and applications. In J. D. Wright (Ed.), *International encyclopedia of the social & behavioral sciences* (2nd ed., pp. 263–268). Elsevier. https://doi.org/10.1016/B978-0-08-097086-8.14026-7

Kosciw, J. G., Greytak, E. A., Diaz, E. M., & Bartkiewicz, M. J. (2010). *The 2009 National School Climate Survey: The experiences of lesbian, gay, bisexual, and transgender youth in our nation's schools*. Gay, Lesbian and Straight Education Network.

Lehavot, K., & Simoni, J. M. (2011). The impact of minority stress on mental health and substance use among sexual minority women. *Journal of Consulting and Clinical Psychology*, *79*, 159–170. https://doi.org/10.1037/a0022839

Lev-Wiesel, R., Nuttman-Shwartz, O., & Sternberg, R. (2006). Peer rejection during adolescence: Psychological long-term effects. *Journal of Loss and Trauma*, *11*, 131–142. https://doi.org/10.1080/15325020500409200

Li, X., Zheng, H., Tucker, W., Xu, W., Wen, X., Lin, Y., Jia, Z., Yuan, Z., & Yang, W. (2019). Research on relationships between sexual identity, adverse childhood experiences and non-suicidal self-injury among rural high school students in less developed areas of China. *International Journal of Environmental Research and Public Health*, *16*(17), Article 3158. https://doi.org/10.3390/ijerph16173158

Liu, R. T. (2019). Temporal trends in the prevalence of nonsuicidal self-injury among sexual minority and heterosexual youth from 2005 through 2017. *JAMA Pediatrics*, *173*(8), 790–791. https://doi.org/10.1001/jamapediatrics.2019.1433

Liu, R. T., Sheehan, A. E., Walsh, R. F. L., Sanzari, C. M., Cheek, S. M., & Hernandez, E. M. (2019). Prevalence and correlates of non-suicidal self-injury among lesbian, gay, bisexual, and transgender individuals: A systematic review and meta-analysis. *Clinical Psychology Review*, *74*, 101783. https://doi.org/10.1016/j.cpr.2019.101783

Longo, J., Walls, N. E., & Wisneski, H. (2013). Religion and religiosity: Protective or harmful factors for sexual minority youth? *Mental Health, Religion & Culture*, *16*, 273–290. https://doi.org/10.1080/13674676.2012.659240

Mallory, A. B., & Russell, S. T. (2021). Intersections of racial discrimination and LGB victimization for mental health: A prospective study of sexual minority youth of color. *Journal of Youth and Adolescence*, *50*, 1353–1368. https://doi.org/10.1007/s10964-021-01443-x

Mallory, C., & Sears, B. (2020). LGBT discrimination, subnational public policy, and law in the United States. *Oxford research encyclopedia of politics*. https://doi.org/10.1093/acrefore/9780190228637.013.1200

McCann, E., Donohue, G., & Timmins, F. (2020). An exploration of the relationship between spirituality, religion and mental health among youth who identify as LGBT+: A systematic literature review. *Journal of Religion and Health, 59*, 828–844. https://doi.org/10.1007/s10943-020-00989-7

McCauley, E., Berk, M. S., Asarnow, J. R., Adrian, M., Cohen, J., Korslund, K., Avina, C., Hughes, J., Harned, M., Gallop, R., & Linehan, M. M. (2018). Efficacy of dialectical behavior therapy for adolescents at high risk for suicide: A randomized clinical trial. *JAMA Psychiatry, 75*, 777–785. https://doi.org/10.1001/jamapsychiatry.2018.1109

Mehlum, L., Tørmoen, A. J., Ramberg, M., Haga, E., Diep, L. M., Laberg, S., Larsson, B. S., Stanley, B. H., Miller, A. L., Sund, A. M., & Grøholt, B. (2014). Dialectical behavior therapy for adolescents with repeated suicidal and self-harming behavior: A randomized trial. *Journal of the American Academy of Child and Adolescent Psychiatry, 53*, 1082–1091. https://doi.org/10.1016/j.jaac.2014.07.003

Merriam, S. (2019). *Qualitative research in practice: Examples for discussion and analysis*. Jossey-Bass.

Meyer, I. H. (1995). Minority stress and mental health in gay men. *Journal of Health and Social Behavior, 36*, 38–56. https://doi.org/10.2307/2137286

Meyer, I. H. (2003). *Minority stress and mental health in gay men*. In L. D. Garnets & D. C. Kimmel (Eds.), *Psychological perspectives on lesbian, gay, and bisexual experiences* (pp. 699–731). Columbia University Press.

Michaels, M. S., Parent, M. C., & Torrey, C. L. (2016). A minority stress model for suicidal ideation in gay men. *Suicide and Life-Threatening Behavior, 46*, 23–34. https://doi.org/10.1111/sltb.12169

Miller, S. J. (2011). African-American lesbian identity management and identity development in the context of family and community. *Journal of Homosexuality, 58*, 547–563. https://doi.org/10.1080/00918369.2011.556937

Mohr, J. J., & Sarno, E. L. (2016). The ups and downs of being lesbian, gay, and bisexual: A daily experience perspective on minority stress and support processes. *Journal of Counseling Psychology, 63*, 106–118. https://doi.org/10.1037/cou0000125

Monto, M. A., McRee, N., & Deryck, F. S. (2018). Nonsuicidal self-injury among a representative sample of US adolescents, 2015. *American Journal of Public Health, 108*, 1042–1048. https://doi.org/10.2105/AJPH.2018.304470

Moradi, B., Wiseman, M. C., DeBlaere, C., Goodman, M. B., Sarkees, A., Brewster, M. E., & Huang, Y. (2010). LGB of color and white individuals' perceptions of heterosexist stigma, internalized homophobia, and outness: Comparisons of levels and links. *The Counseling Psychologist, 38*, 397–424. https://doi.org/10.1177/0011000009335263

Muehlenkamp, J. J., Claes, L., Havertape, L., & Plener, P. L. (2012). International prevalence of adolescent non-suicidal self-injury and deliberate self-harm. *Child and Adolescent Psychiatry and Mental Health, 6*, Article 10. https://doi.org/10.1186/1753-2000-6-10

Mustanski, B., & Espelage, D. L. (2020). Why are we not closing the gap in suicide disparities for sexual minority youth? *Pediatrics, 145*, Article e20194002. https://doi.org/10.1542/peds.2019-4002

Nahata, L., Quinn, G. P., Caltabellotta, N. M., & Tishelman, A. C. (2017). Mental health concerns and insurance denials among transgender adolescents. *LGBT Health, 4*, 188–193. https://doi.org/10.1089/lgbt.2016.0151

Newcomb, M. E., & Mustanski, B. (2010). Internalized homophobia and internalizing mental health problems: A meta-analytic review. *Clinical Psychology Review, 30*, 1019–1029. https://doi.org/10.1016/j.cpr.2010.07.003

O'Connor, R. C., & Nock, M. K. (2014). The psychology of suicidal behaviour. *The Lancet Psychiatry, 1*, 73–85. https://doi.org/10.1016/S2215-0366(14)70222-6

Proulx, C. N., Coulter, R. W. S., Egan, J. E., Matthews, D. D., & Mair, C. (2019). Associations of lesbian, gay, bisexual, transgender, and questioning-inclusive sex education with mental health outcomes and school-based victimization in U.S. high school students. *The Journal of Adolescent Health, 64*, 608–614. https://doi.org/10.1016/j.jadohealth.2018.11.012

Raifman, J., Moscoe, E., Austin, S. B., & McConnell, M. (2017). Difference-in-differences analysis of the association between state same-sex marriage policies and adolescent suicide attempts. *JAMA Pediatrics, 171*, 350–356. https://doi.org/10.1001/jamapediatrics.2016.4529

Reisner, S. L., Vetters, R., Leclerc, M., Zaslow, S., Wolfrum, S., Shumer, D., & Mimiaga, M. J. (2015). Mental health of transgender youth in care at an adolescent urban community health center: A matched retrospective cohort study. *Journal of Adolescent Health*, *56*, 274–279. https://doi.org/10.1016/j.jadohealth.2014.10.264

Riggle, E. D. B., Rostosky, S. S., Black, W. W., & Rosenkrantz, D. E. (2017). Outness, concealment, and authenticity: Associations with LGB individuals' psychological distress and well-being. *Psychology of Sexual Orientation and Gender Diversity*, *4*, 54–62. https://doi.org/10.1037/sgd0000202

Rogers, M. L., Hom, M. A., Janakiraman, R., & Joiner, T. E. (2021). Examination of minority stress pathways to suicidal ideation among sexual minority adults: The moderating role of LGBT community connectedness. *Psychology of Sexual Orientation and Gender Diversity*, *8*, 38–47. https://doi.org/10.1037/sgd0000409

Rogers, M. L., & Taliaferro, L. A. (2020). Self-injurious thoughts and behaviors among sexual and gender minority youth: A systematic review of recent research. *Current Sexual Health Reports*, *12*, 335–350. https://doi.org/10.1007/s11930-020-00295-z

Ross-Reed, D. E., Reno, J., Peñaloza, L., Green, D., & FitzGerald, C. (2019). Family, school, and peer support are associated with rates of violence victimization and self-harm among gender minority and cisgender youth. *Journal of Adolescent Health*, *65*, 776–783. https://doi.org/10.1016/j.jadohealth.2019.07.-013

Russell, S. T., & Fish, J. N. (2016). Mental health in lesbian, gay, bisexual, and transgender (LGBT) youth. *Annual Review of Clinical Psychology*, *12*, 465–487. https://doi.org/10.1146/annurev-clinpsy-021815-093153

Schuck, K. D., & Liddle, B. J. (2001). Religious conflicts experienced by lesbian, gay, and bisexual individuals. *Journal of Gay & Lesbian Psychotherapy*, *5*, 63–82. https://doi.org/10.1300/J236v05n02_07

Seelman, K. L., & Walker, M. B. (2018). Do anti-bullying laws reduce in-school victimization, fear-based absenteeism, and suicidality for lesbian, gay, bisexual, and questioning youth? *Journal of Youth and Adolescence*, *47*, 2301–2319. https://doi.org/10.1007/s10964-018-0904-8

Sherry, A., Adelman, A., Whilde, M. R., & Quick, D. (2010). Competing selves: Negotiating the intersection of spiritual and sexual identities. *Professional Psychology: Research and Practice*, *41*, 112–119. https://doi.org/10.1037/a0017471

Shilo, G., & Savaya, R. (2012). Mental health of lesbian, gay, and bisexual youth and young adults: Differential effects of age, gender, religiosity, and sexual orientation. *Journal of Research on Adolescence*, *22*, 310–325. https://doi.org/10.1111/j.1532-7795.2011.00772.x

Singh, A. A. (2013). Transgender youth of color and resilience: Negotiating oppression and finding support. *Sex Roles*, *68*, 690–702. https://doi.org/10.1007/s11199-012-0149-z

Smith, D. M., Wang, S. B., Carter, M. L., Fox, K. R., & Hooley, J. M. (2020). Longitudinal predictors of self-injurious thoughts and behaviors in sexual and gender minority adolescents. *Journal of Abnormal Psychology*, *129*, 114–121. https://doi.org/10.1037/abn0000483

Sowe, B. J., Taylor, A. J., & Brown, J. (2017). Religious anti-gay prejudice as a predictor of mental health, abuse, and substance use. *American Journal of Orthopsychiatry*, *87*, 690–703. https://doi.org/10.1037/ort0000297

Spack, N. P., Edwards-Leeper, L., Feldman, H. A., Leibowitz, S., Mandel, F., Diamond, D. A., & Vance, S. R. (2012). Children and adolescents with gender identity disorder referred to a pediatric medical center. *Pediatrics*, *129*, 418–425. https://doi.org/10.1542/peds.2011-0907

Taliaferro, L. A., Harder, B. M., Lampe, N. M., Carter, S. K., Rider, G. N., & Eisenberg, M. E. (2019a). Social connectedness factors that facilitate use of healthcare services: Comparison of transgender and gender non-conforming and cisgender adolescents. *The Journal of Pediatrics*, *211*, 172–178. https://doi.org/10.1016/j.jpeds.2019.04.024

Taliaferro, L. A., McMorris, B. J., & Eisenberg, M. E. (2018). Connections that moderate risk of non-suicidal self-injury among transgender and gender non-conforming youth. *Psychiatry Research*, *268*, 65–67. https://doi.org/10.1016/j.psychres.2018.06.068

Taliaferro, L. A., Mishtal, J., Chulani, V. L., Acevedo, M., Middleton, T. C., & Eisenberg, M. E. (2019b). Communicating effectively with sexual minority youth: Perspectives of young people and healthcare providers. *Acta Scientific Paediatrics*, *2*, 32–39. https://doi.org/10.31080/ASPE.2019.02.0144

Taliaferro, L. A., & Muehlenkamp, J. J. (2017). Nonsuicidal self-injury and suicidality among sexual minority youth: Risk factors and protective connectedness factors. *Academic Pediatrics*, *17*, 715–722. https://doi.org/10.1016/j.acap.2016.11.002

Testa, R. J., Habarth, J., Peta, J., Balsam, K., & Bockting, W. (2015). Development of the Gender Minority Stress and Resilience Measure. *Psychology of Sexual Orientation and Gender Diversity*, *2*, 65–77. https://doi.org/10.1037/sgd0000081

Testa, R. J., Michaels, M. S., Bliss, W., Rogers, M. L., Balsam, K. F., & Joiner, T. E. (2017). Suicidal ideation in transgender people: Gender minority stress and interpersonal theory factors. *Journal of Abnormal Psychology, 126*, 125–136. https://doi.org/10.1037/abn0000234

The Trevor Project (2019). *The Trevor Project research brief: Suicide attempts among LGBTQ youth of color.*

Toomey, R. B., Ryan, C., Diaz, R. M., & Russell, S. T. (2018). Coping with sexual orientation-related minority stress. *Journal of Homosexuality, 65*, 484–500. https://doi.org/10.1080/00918369.2017.1321888

Unterrainer, H. F., Lewis, A. J., & Fink, A. (2014). Religious/spiritual well-being, personality and mental health: A review of results and conceptual issues. *Journal of Religion and Health, 53*, 382–392. https://doi.org/10.1007/s10943-012-9642-5

Westenberg, P. M., Drewes, M. J., Goedhart, A. W., Siebelink, B. M., & Treffers, P. D. A. (2004). A developmental analysis of self-reported fears in late childhood through mid-adolescence: Social-evaluative fears on the rise? *Journal of Child Psychology and Psychiatry, 45*, 481–495. https://doi.org/10.1111/j.1469-7610.2004.00239.x

Westers, N., Muehlenkamp, J., & Lau, M. (2016). SOARS Model: Risk assessment of nonsuicidal self-injury. *Contemporary Pediatrics, 33*, 25–31.

Williams, A. J., Jones, C., Arcelus, J., Townsend, E., Lazaridou, A., & Michail, M. (2021). A systematic review and meta-analysis of victimisation and mental health prevalence among LGBTQ+ young people with experiences of self-harm and suicide. *PloS One, 16*, Article e0245268. https://doi.org/10.1371/journal.pone.0245268

Ybarra, M. L., Mitchell, K. J., Palmer, N. A., & Reisner, S. L. (2015). Online social support as a buffer against online and offline peer and sexual victimization among U.S. LGBT and non-LGBT youth. *Child Abuse & Neglect, 39*, 123–136. https://doi.org/10.1016/j.chiabu.2014.08.006

Zhang, L., Finan, L. J., Bersamin, M., & Fisher, D. A. (2020). Sexual orientation–based depression and suicidality health disparities: The protective role of school-based health centers. *Journal of Research on Adolescence, 30*, 134–142. https://doi.org/10.1111/jora.12454

Zullo, L., Seager van Dyk, I., Ollen, E., Ramos, N., Asarnow, J., & Miranda, J. (2021). Treatment recommendations and barriers to care for suicidal LGBTQ youth: A quality improvement study. *Evidence-Based Practice in Child and Adolescent Mental Health, 6*, 393–409. https://doi.org/10.1080/23794925.2021.1950079

CHAPTER 34

Understanding the Link Between Direct and Indirect Self-Injurious Behavior

Bo Møhl *and* Lotte Rubæk

Abstract

In this chapter, the authors examine the factors that might explain why individuals who engage in direct self-injurious behavior (SIB) have a higher likelihood of also engaging in indirect SIB, and vice versa. As there are no general models to describe a transdiagnostic understanding of the potential underlying mechanisms of both direct and indirect SIB, the authors rely on a modified version of the "Conceptual model of interactive risk factors for both NSSI and ED" to describe the etiological factors underlying direct and indirect SIB more broadly. The model distinguishes between distal risk factors (e.g., temperament, family environment, and traumatic experiences) and proximal risk factors (e.g., emotional dysregulation, body disregard, and psychiatric disorders) and their mutual interaction.

In both direct and indirect SIB, the motivation to self-injure is related to the function (benefits) of the behaviors. Hence, the behaviors are largely controlled by events that immediately precede and follow them (i.e., antecedents and consequences). In the authors' review of the shared functions and functional equivalence of direct and indirect SIB, they find that they often serve the same purpose (e.g., affect regulation) and thus may replace or stand in for one another (symptom shifting). Although the two forms of the behavior largely share etiology and functions, the authors still find it useful to maintain the separation between the two phenomena.

Key Words: direct self-injurious behavior, indirect self-injurious behavior, distal risk factors, proximal risk factors, motivation, etiology

Introduction

Generally, self-injurious behavior (SIB) can be divided into direct SIB, defined by being self-inflicted, intentional, direct, and with immediate physical effect (e.g., cutting), and indirect SIB, in which the damage typically accumulates over time and in which the indirect self-injury episodes often are not harmful in themselves. With indirect SIB, such as heavy drinking or smoking, the actual harm stemming from the behavior is unclear, and in many cases, the harmful effects are a matter of chance. Earlier in this volume, we proposed a categorization of indirect nonsuicidal SIB as follows: (a) indirect self-injury (active or passive), (b) self-injury by proxy, and (c) risk-taking behavior. A recently introduced form of indirect SIB is self-injury by proxy, in which the person self-injures by provoking another person or an animal to inflict the injuries (Møhl, 2019). Several studies have documented a positive correlation between direct and indirect SIB. Individuals who engage in direct SIB have a higher likelihood of also engaging in indirect SIB, and vice versa. Thus, indirect SIBs, such as eating disorders (ED) (Ahn et al., 2021; Cucchi et al., 2016; Warne et al., 2021), alcohol abuse (Bresin & Mekawi, 2022), cannabis use (Escelsior et al., 2021), substance misuse (Klassen et al., 2018; Monto et al., 2018; Richardson et al., 2020), sexual risk-taking behaviors (Brown et al., 2005; Zetterqvist et al., 2018), cigarette smoking (Korhonen et al., 2018), and general reckless and risk-taking behaviors (Duggan & Heath, 2014), occur more frequently in adolescents and young adults with a history of nonsuicidal self-injury (NSSI).

In addition to the co-occurrence of direct and indirect SIB (also see Rubæk & Møhl, this volume, for more information), research has also found that the two forms share similar etiological pathways (e.g., childhood trauma, emotion dysregulation, impulsivity, and alexithymia) (also see Serafini et al., this volume) (Hasking & Claes, 2020), are motivated by similar functions, and thus may promote and substitute for each other and result in symptom shifting or substitution (Garke et al., 2019).

No general models have been developed to describe a transdiagnostic understanding of the potential underlying mechanisms of both direct and indirect SIB, which may be related to the fact that indirect SIB is a highly heterogeneous constellation of phenomena that cannot be treated as a whole. Svirko and Hawton (2007) formulated an integrative model for the co-occurrence of eating disorders and NSSI, which, among other aspects, identifies a number of common factors (impulsivity, obsessive-compulsive characteristics, affect dysregulation, dissociation, self-criticism and self-punishment, control, family environment, and traumas). Similarly, Krug et al. (2021) find that emotion dysregulation, impulsivity, self-esteem, and body dissatisfaction are mediators in the relationship between insecure attachment and subsequent eating disorder and self-harm symptoms. As a key point, these researchers are not suggesting a causal link but, instead, propose potential mediators. Bresin (2019) focuses on various forms of dysregulated behaviors (e.g., drinking, self-injury, and risky sex) that commonly co-occur and thus likely share common etiologies. He discusses dysregulated behaviors in relation to (a) research domain criteria (RDoC) (Cuthbert, 2022; also see Bastiaens & Claes, this volume), finding that RDoC provides a framework for developing an etiological theory of dysregulated behaviors, and (b) a hierarchical taxonomy of psychopathology (Hi-TOP) (Kotov et al., 2017) that similarly looks at psychopathologies in spectrums as an alternative to the categorical understanding in the fifth edition of *Diagnostic and Statistical Manual of Mental Disorders* (DSM-5; American Psychiatric Association, 2013). Although both RDoC and Hi-TOP contain constructive potential for understanding SIBs as manifestations of dysregulated behaviors, additional research is required.

Most of the research into the connection between direct and indirect SIB deals with EDs and NSSI. Based on these respective forms of SIB, Kiekens and Claes (2020) pointed to two research lines which have contributed to our understanding of direct and indirect SIB, namely, the identification of (a) the shared etiology and (b) the shared functions (*functional equivalence*) of direct and indirect SIB.

In this chapter, we use a modified version of the "conceptual model of interactive risk factors for both NSSI and ED" (Claes & Muehlenkamp, 2014b; see fig. 34.1) as a *matrix* for understanding risk factors and underlying mechanisms for the development and maintenance of direct and indirect SIB. Subsequently, we provide a description of the motivation and function of direct and indirect SIB, respectively, within the framework of the four-function model (FFM; Nock & Prinstein, 2004) (also see Hird et al., this volume).

Shared Etiology

In recent years, there has been a gradual shift toward a transdiagnostic understanding of psychological symptoms that searches for common underlying mechanisms of NSSI and different forms of indirect SIB (Hasking & Claes, 2020). According to this way of thinking, different forms of direct and indirect SIB are multidetermined by a range of similar individual, social, and cultural risk factors that interact with each other. This involves both distal risk factors (at the individual level: temperament and personality; at the social level: family environment, traumatic experiences, and cultural pressures) and proximal risk factors (e.g., emotional dysregulation, vulnerable cognitions, body disregard, dissociation, peer influence, and psychiatric disorders). It is assumed that certain interactions, both within a given category and between the categories, increase the person's risk of developing both direct and indirect SIB, just as stressful life events may also play a key role in triggering the problem behavior, which in turn should be understood as an attempt at downregulating painful inner states. Proximal risk factors may both trigger and perpetuate direct SIB and indirect SIB, both of which act as coping strategies, and the mutual reinforcement between behavior and risk factors will often set off a negative cycle that makes the behavior self-reinforcing (Claes & Muehlenkamp, 2014b).

The distal and proximal risk factors offer a broad explanation of the link between NSSI and different forms of indirect SIB.

Distal Risk Factors

Distal risk factors at the individual level refer to such aspects as temperament and personality. Several studies have found that persons with both direct and indirect SIB (e.g., ED behaviors, substance abuse, and risk-taking behaviors) are characterized by a *temperament* that makes them emotionally reactive, which, generally, causes them to experience more difficult emotions and to experience them with greater intensity and persistence (Kiekens & Claes, 2020; Mayo et al., 2021; Smith et al., 2018). In their "experiential

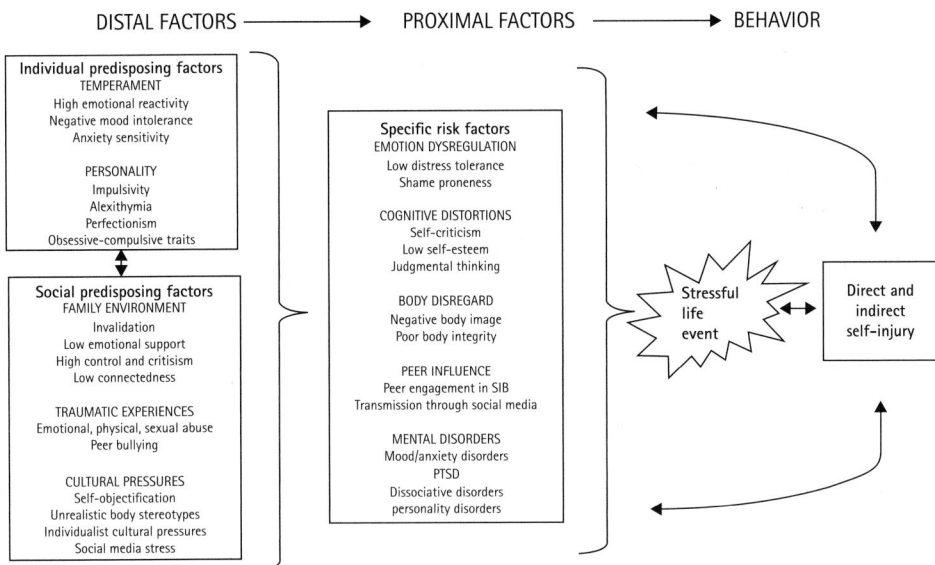

Figure 34.1 *Model of Interactive Risk Factors for Direct and Indirect Self-Injury.* Based on Nock (2010) and Claes and Muehlenkamp (2014b).

avoidance model" Chapman et al. (2006; see Hird et al., this volume) described how a temperament characterized by avoidance of negative emotions can lead to self-injury, just as others have found a link between direct and indirect self-injury forms and avoidance (Anderson et al., 2018).

In terms of *personality*, studies have found that impulsivity (Hamza et al., 2015; Lockwood et al., 2017), perfectionism (Gyori & Balazs, 2021; Tonta et al., 2022), alexithymia (Greene et al., 2020; Sleuwaegen et al., 2017; Westwood et al., 2017), and emotion dysregulation (Haynos et al., 2018; Puttevils et al., 2021) play an underlying dynamic role (Hasking & Claes, 2020) in relation to NSSI, risky drinking, and disordered eating. It is not inconceivable that other forms of indirect SIB (e.g., substance abuse) might be added to this list. With regard to impulsivity, several studies have documented that NSSI is associated with negative urgency and lack of premeditation (Claes & Muehlenkamp, 2013; Glenn & Klonsky, 2010), and similar results have been found in relation to eating disorders (especially bulimia nervosa [BN]) (Cassin & von Ranson, 2005; Claes et al., 2005), substance abuse (Moeller & Dougherty, 2002), and risk-taking behavior (Kentopp et al., 2021). Obsessive-compulsive features have been found in persons with NSSI (Claes et al., 2012), ED (Boone et al., 2010; Halmi et al., 2005) and substance abuse (Blom et al., 2011).

Although common dynamics have been found to underlie NSSI, risky drinking, risk-taking behavior, and eating disorders, it is important to note that the association between the specific form of SIB and the underlying dynamic may vary. For example, Greene et al. (2020) found a significant positive association between alexithymia (difficulties identifying and describing feelings) and both NSSI and risky drinking. However, they also found indications that individuals may engage in NSSI in order to regulate negative feelings and consume alcohol to gain more confidence in expressing their feelings.

Distal risk factors at the social level are environmental factors that might predispose a person for both direct and indirect SIB (e.g., family environment, traumatic experiences, and cultural pressures).

The *family environment* for persons with both NSSI and eating disorders is characterized by low emotional support and a high level of psychological and behavioral control (Claes et al., 2012). A similar link exists between insecure attachment or parenting style and both NSSI and ED (Baetens et al., 2014; Hampshire et al., 2022). Claes et al. (2004) found that persons with both ED and NSSI describe their family environment as less cohesive and expressive and more conflictual than persons with ED alone; in a related finding, Claes et al. (2012) identified high self-criticism as a mediating factor. A link has also been found between family environment and risk-taking behavior (e.g., Hill et al., 2008), sex as self-injury (SASI) (Fredlund et al., 2017), and substance abuse (e.g., Johnson & Pandina, 1991). Cipriano et al. (2020) found that parental rejection has a significant positive correlation with both self-cutting and substance use, mediated through anger-in (redirecting anger inward) for self-cutting and anger-out (expressing anger outward) for substance use.

A link has been found between *traumatic experiences* in childhood (e.g., physical or sexual abuse) and the development of both direct (e.g., NSSI) (Fox et al., 2015; Yates et al., 2008; also see Serafini et al., this volume) and indirect SIB, such as ED (Johnson et al., 2002; Neumark-Sztainer et al., 2000), substance abuse (Wu et al., 2010), and SASI (Fredlund et al., 2017). Claes and Muehlenkamp (2014a) suggested that the relationship between abuse and NSSI or ED may be better understood in light of mediators, such as emotion regulation, dissociation, and attachment style, while Zelkowitz and Cole (2019) added self-criticism as a mediator. Non-heterosexual persons are more likely to report adverse childhood experiences (ACEs) than heterosexual persons (Andresen et al., 2022); along with minority stress, this may be the reason why they have a heightened risk of both direct and indirect SIB (Liu et al., 2019; Parker & Harriger, 2020). Other scholars have pointed out that peer victimization is related to the development of both NSSI (Victor et al., 2018) and ED (Lee & Vaillancourt, 2019), and Afifi et al. (2020) found that the risk of developing substance abuse increases if a person with adverse childhood events also experiences peer victimization.

The impact of *cultural pressures* refers, for example, to the perceived pressure to have a perfect physical appearance that many young people experience, which plays a crucial role for the development of both direct and indirect SIB. The term also describes how mass media, social media (SoMe), and the fashion and entertainment industries reinforce unrealistic and sexually objectivizing body stereotypes that have a huge influence on individuals' body dissatisfaction and self-objectification (viewing one's own body as an object and from an "other" perspective) (Calogero et al., 2011). Self-objectification is associated with increased bodily disconnection, which may explain the link with both NSSI (Nelson & Muehlenkamp, 2012) and ED (Muehlenkamp & Saris-Baglama, 2002). Similarly, a negative body image and body disconnection would predispose the person for other self-destructive behaviors. There is a close connection between traumas that lead to dissociation and a severely disordered body image and indirect SIB, such as substance use, SASI, abusive relationships, and risk-taking behaviors (Liechty, 2019; Silveira et al., 2020; Stupiggia, 2019; Zetterqvist et al., 2018).

Proximal Risk Factors

Proximal risk factors can both trigger the development of the problem behavior and contribute to its perpetuation (Claes & Muehlenkamp, 2014a; Kiekens & Claes, 2020). Specific risk factors include, for example, emotion dysregulation, vulnerable cognitions, body disregard, peer influence, and mental disorders.

As described above, *emotion dysregulation* is one of the most important proximal risk factors for SIB, and emotion regulation is often mentioned as a primary motivation for SIB (Fox et al., 2015; Taylor et al., 2018). Whitlock et al. (2011) found that 81% of college students who reported NSSI endorsed that the behavior served an emotion regulation function. According to Garke et al. (2019), there is support for the assumption that emotional dysregulation may be the underlying dynamic that precipitates NSSI (Kranzler et al., 2018), eating disorder symptoms (Haynos et al., 2018; Prefit et al., 2019; Puttevils et al., 2021), and substance and alcohol use (Garofalo & Velotti, 2015; Greene et al., 2020; Hasking & Claes, 2020; Weiss et al., 2022), such that any of them may substitute for any other one and downregulate or distract from negative emotions. Similarly, affect regulation has been identified as one of the main drivers of SASI (Fredlund et al., 2017). Intense emotions often precede acts of direct and indirect SIB (Crosby et al., 2009; Hasking et al., 2017), and the specific behaviors effectively reduce the intensity of the negative emotions and sometimes increase positive emotions, such as relief and relaxation (Andrewes et al., 2017; Muehlenkamp et al., 2009).

Both increased self-criticism and diminished self-esteem are examples of *vulnerable cognitions* that increase the risk of direct (NSSI) and indirect SIB (Baetens et al., 2012; Zelkowitz & Cole, 2020). In a longitudinal study, Lee et al. (2018) found self-esteem to be a predictor of binge drinking, marijuana use, and cocaine use at the age of 15 years (but not at the age of 21 years). In a community sample, St. Germain and Hooley (2012) found that persons with direct or indirect SIB compared to non-self-injuring controls were more impulsive, experienced more problems with negative emotions and aggression, tended to be more undercontrolled in their behavior (disinhibition), and had a lower level of self-esteem. They were similarly more likely to display psychopathology and aberrant pain perception (St. Germain & Hooley, 2013; Hooley & St. Germain, 2014). Persons who engaged in direct SIB reported higher levels of self-criticism, higher levels of suicide proneness, and more past suicidal attempts compared to people who only engaged in indirect SIB (e.g., disordered eating, substance abuse, staying in abusive relationships, reckless behaviors) (Hooley & St. Germain, 2014). These findings have been discussed by, among others, Zelkowitz and Cole (2019), who found that NSSI and ED behaviors show similarly strong associations with self-criticism. Claes and Muehlenkamp (2014a) describe that persons with both NSSI and ED report that they use SIB as self-punishment, which confirms the presence of a self-critical and judgmental cognitive style (Svirko & Hawton, 2007).

Body disregard, or a negative body image, plays a major role in all forms of SIB. Several studies have identified negative body attitude as a factor that both precipitates and perpetuates SIB (Stice et al., 2017), while a positive body attitude is a protective factor (Hooley & Franklin, 2018; Muehlenkamp & Wagner, 2022). A longitudinal study found that body dissatisfaction was also a predictor of NSSI, even in the absence of comorbid ED (Black et al., 2019). Persons with a negative body attitude are more inclined and able to damage their own body because poor overall body regard increases the likelihood that they will objectify and mistreat their body, which in turn increases the risk of NSSI and disordered eating (Claes & Muehlenkamp, 2014a). Numerous studies suggest that body image and body regard play a key role for emotionally dysregulated persons to become self-injurious (Gattario et al., 2020; Kruzan et al., 2022; Muehlenkamp, 2012; Muehlenkamp & Brausch, 2012; Oktan, 2017). Similarly, Nieri et al. (2005) found that poor body image correlates with drug and alcohol use among young people. As mentioned earlier, Fredlund et al. (2017) found that persons who use SASI are highly likely to have experienced earlier traumas, such as sexual and physical abuse. Persons who have experienced traumas will often use SIB as self-punishment (Kaess et al., 2013), and Muehlenkamp (2012) found that body regard mediates the link between self-punishment as motivation and the frequency of NSSI. Other theorists have addressed how SIB may be associated with reclaiming control or feeling alive for someone who otherwise feels empty, dead, or detached from reality (Weierich & Nock, 2008).

Peer influence happens in both physical and virtual arenas. Young people increasingly live their lives through SoMe, such as Instagram, Facebook, and Snapchat, where they are constantly "on" and subject to others' assessments (e.g., number of likes and comments) (Beyens et al., 2016; Brown et al., 2018; Lewis & Seko, 2016; Memon et al., 2018). Thus, young persons must constantly perform in all arenas of life and never have any time off. Hence, fear of missing out (FOMO) and demands for perfection are extremely stressful to many young people (Fabris et al., 2020); the mindset that "*perfect is the new normal*" is enhanced by the fact that most selfies posted on SoMe are retouched (Mills et al., 2018; Overholser & Dimaggio, 2020). In addition, several studies document harmful effects of cyberbullying (Viner et al., 2019) and that young people with various problem behaviors can influence and inspire each other and thus transfer or affirm each other's problem behavior. This applies to young people with

NSSI (Conigliaro & Ward-Ciesielski, 2021; Schwartz-Mette & Lawrence, 2019), ED (Allison et al., 2014), substance use and abuse (Allen et al., 2012), and risk-taking behavior (van Hoorn et al., 2016; Siraj et al., 2021).

Mental disorders are an important risk factor for developing NSSI, and links have been found between NSSI and most mental disorders (Glenn & Klonsky, 2013; Kiekens et al., 2018; Peters et al., 2018), while the reverse link also applies, with NSSI being a risk factor for the development of mental illness (Wilkinson et al., 2018). A similar connection exists for mental disorders and substance abuse, where clear links have also been found, with the temporality going both ways (Groenman et al., 2017). In a meta-analysis, Groenman et al. (2017) found that attention deficit/hyperactivity disorder (ADHD), oppositional defiant disorder (ODD), conduct disorder (CD), and depression in childhood constitute particularly heightened risk of developing substance-related disorders. Similarly, comorbidity has been found between eating disorders and other mental disorders, such as major depression, anxiety disorders, posttraumatic stress disorder (PTSD), alcohol/substance-related disorders, and personality disorders (Nock et al., 2006; Udo & Grilo, 2019). In a recent study of a sample of adult psychiatric patients, D'Agostino et al. (2020) found that patients presenting both direct and indirect SIB compared to healthy controls showed higher clinically significant levels of somatization, interpersonal sensitivity, depression, and anxiety along with greater severity, intensity, and number of symptoms. They also presented more symptoms of personality disorders, psychosis, and depression as well as higher, albeit not significantly higher, levels of basic deficits in personal identity (low self-esteem and sense of emptiness). Thus, they have "something more" compared to patients with only indirect self-harm. Finally, Fredlund et al. (2017) found that trauma symptoms, suicide attempts, depression, and eating disorders are common among adolescents who engage in SASI.

There is a well-documented connection between SIB and dissociation (Calati et al., 2017). Levenkron (1998) distinguished between "non-dissociative cutting," using self-injury to escape a dissociative state, and "dissociative cutting," using the behavior to achieve a dissociative state as a defense against an unbearable reality. Similarly, a link has been found between dissociation and eating disorders (Vanderlinden & Palmisano, 2017). Several studies point to dissociation as a mediating factor between traumatic childhood experiences (such as sexual, physical, and emotional abuse and emotional and physical neglect) and eating disorders (Vanderlinden & Palmisano, 2017) or NSSI (Franzke et al., 2015). One study of patients with PTSD and substance use disorder found that the "high-dissociation" group reported a stronger expectation that substances would help them manage their psychiatric symptoms than the "low dissociation" group, while another study found dissociation to be relatively uncommon in alcohol-dependent patients and that when it does occur, dissociation is associated with emotional abuse in childhood (Schäfer et al., 2007). Studies have found a link between trauma, dissociation, and high-risk behavior (Kianpoor & Bakhshani, 2012; Ross et al., 2004), and Zetterqvist et al. (2018) found that persons who use SASI are more likely to have trauma symptoms, such as dissociation.

It is important to see the above-mentioned relationships between distal and proximal risk factors in a vulnerability-stress perspective (Hankin & Abela, 2005). Thus, a person with a large distal vulnerability due to, for example, an attachment disorder will in principle respond with the development of SIB when faced with less stressful life events, while others with a less distal vulnerability may handle major stressful life events without engaging in SIB. Similarly, several smaller risk factors together could contribute to a high level of vulnerability. Thus, as a result of distal risk factors, individuals prone to negative emotions and self-negative thoughts who also have lower distress tolerance and a tendency to act impulsively are developmentally predisposed for both direct and indirect SIB.

Functional Equivalence

Several of the forms of direct and indirect SIB mentioned in Rubæk and Møhl (this volume) serve the same purpose (e.g., affect regulation) and may thus replace or stand in for one another, known as symptom shifting or symptom substitution. Symptom shifting is defined as a decrease in one symptom matched by an increase in another over time (Garke et al., 2019) and appears to be particularly common in connection with SIB (Farber, 1997; Sansone & Sansone, 2007). An example of symptom shifting is that 19% were found to shift from an eating disorder-related behavior to direct SIB or substance use over the course of one year (Garke et al., 2019). This is in line with findings that individuals who give up NSSI tend to shift to other problem behaviors, such as substance use or ED. Bresin (2019) offered another example when he pointed out that alcohol consumption tends to increase at the ages when NSSI decreases (e.g., transition between high school and college), possibly suggesting that alcohol may eventually replace NSSI as an emotion regulation strategy (Bresin & Mekawi, 2022). An example of symptom shifting is offered in the case vignette that follows.

> *A 24-year-old university student is referred to treatment for cutting, burning, and scratching herself, to the point of drawing blood, for the past 10 years, at times almost daily. When she is stressed, she commonly also exhibits a bulimic eating pattern with overeating followed by self-induced vomiting, but she has this behavior under control at the time of referral. However, her bulimic eating pattern returns in connection with a stressful exam and problems with her boyfriend at a time when DBT skills training has (finally) enabled her to stop cutting, burning, and scratching herself. The patient too sees this as a clear example of symptom shifting.*

Functional equivalence may explain why the severity of direct and indirect SIB are often closely related. Sorgi et al. (2021) found that binge eating and purging behaviors among college students who have engaged in NSSI were associated with a greater variety of NSSI methods, which is an indicator of a more severe disorder (Kiekens et al., 2017;

Turner et al., 2013). Similarly, a higher frequency of NSSI, a greater variety of NSSI methods, and a history of medical treatment of NSSI were associated with a greater severity of eating disorders (Turner et al., 2015; Yiu et al., 2015). Turner et al. (2015) further found that an increase in NSSI frequency predicted greater ED severity three months later, which might be interpreted as an indication that both forms of SIB increase when the person struggles more. In a Swedish community sample of adolescents, Zetterqvist et al. (2013) similarly found that increased frequency of NSSI is related to increased substance use (smoking, alcohol, drugs); This finding is confirmed by a study involving American high school students, which found that adolescents who use NSSI more frequently also seem to use disordered eating behaviors and substances more frequently to serve similar functions (Brausch & Boone, 2015).

In both direct and indirect SIB, the motivation to self-injure is related to the function of the behaviors. The functional approach is based on the assumption that behaviors are largely controlled by events that immediately precede and follow them (i.e., antecedents and consequences). From a functional perspective, SIB should be understood as goal-directed behavior performed to obtain some desired end (Claes & Vandereycken, 2007).

The four-function model (Nock & Prinstein, 2004. Also see Taylor et al., this volume) is based on the notion that the behavior is maintained by four distinct functional reinforcement processes. Each process falls along two dichotomous dimensions: negative versus positive and automatic (i.e., intrapersonal) versus social (i.e., interpersonal) contingencies. However, the same behavior may serve different functions in different situations. The four processes include:

1. Automatic negative reinforcement, where SIB reduces aversive affective or cognitive states (e.g., anxiety, depression, shame, feelings of inadequacy, loneliness, anger) is the most reported motive for SIB (Taylor et al., 2018).
2. Automatic positive reinforcement, where SIB generates positive feelings or physiological stimulation. Both direct and indirect SIB can generate positive feelings (e.g., alcohol or drug use) (Bresin & Gordon 2013; Franklin et al., 2013).
3. Social negative reinforcement, where SIB facilitates escape from unwanted social situations or removes interpersonal demands. For example, visible physical damage can signal suffering and thus serve to reduce social demands.
4. Social positive reinforcement, where SIB elicits attention, facilitates access to resources, or promotes help-seeking behavior. For example, alcohol consumption may facilitate positive relations with others because it helps the person relax, and a picture of a wound from self-injury on SoMe generates likes and caring comments.

The relationship between positive and negative reinforcement and between automatic and social reinforcement may vary for different forms of SIB. For example, in the early stages, alcohol will mainly be used to obtain a positive feeling (automatic positive reinforcement), while its role later in the dependency process will be to reduce negative emotions or abstinence states (automatic negative reinforcement) (Koob, 2013). The transition from positive to negative reinforcement of alcohol can be explained by neuronal adaptations that occur with repeated exposure (Bresin & Mekawi, 2022). Furthermore, both drugs and, especially, alcohol are often used in company with others and may thus be motivated by social positive reinforcement because it helps the person relax and facilitates interpersonal communication, which in turn helps the person make friends.

Other behaviors that subsequently develop in a compulsive direction (e.g., compulsive exercise) (Dalle Grave et al., 2008), may initially be motivated by a desire to generate positive emotions (automatic positive reinforcement), but over time, once the behavior has become compulsive, the desire to avoid withdrawal symptoms or feeling guilty may become the actual motivation (automatic negative reinforcement) (Lichtenstein et al., 2017). This process may be reversed for NSSI, which is often initially used to downregulate negative emotions (automatic negative reinforcement), but due to the reward function of the endogenous opioid system, some also experience positive emotions and a physiological "high" in connection with NSSI (automatic positive reinforcement), which may at a later state become the actual motivation for self-injuring (Franklin et al, 2013). SASI, compulsive exercise, sensation-seeking, and risk-taking behavior all seem to be driven by automatic positive reinforcement by activating dopamine, among other neurochemicals (Norbury et al., 2013). However, they may also be motivated by automatic negative reinforcement, driven by an urge to downregulate or find distraction from negative emotions (Lichtenstein et al., 2017; Zetterqvist et al., 2018). To illustrate this, we briefly mention the case of a young woman:

> *A 19-year-old woman with restrictive eating (anorexia) is during the early stage of her eating disorder motivated by social negative reinforcement: her parents argue less as their concern for her weight loss increases. Later, automatic negative reinforcement plays an increasing role, as hunger dampens her difficult emotions, along with social positive reinforcement because she begins to get more "likes" on Instagram as she gets thinner.*

Muehlenkamp et al. (2019) compared a broad range of functions in direct (NSSI) and indirect SIB (ED). They found that the same function–factor structure exists for direct (NSSI) and indirect (ED behaviors) SIB, which supports the use of a transdiagnostic conceptualization of functions that contribute to engagement in direct (NSSI) and indirect (ED behaviors) SIB. However, they also found differences: affect regulation, antidissociation, marking distress, and interpersonal influence were rated as more relevant to NSSI than to ED in the study, while interpersonal boundaries, peer bonding, and autonomy were rated as more relevant to ED than to NSSI. The four-function model is empirically supported for NSSI (Hepp et al., 2020) and has been used for various forms of indirect SIB although the evidence base for this latter use is less well documented than for NSSI. Additional studies are needed of the specific functions of different forms of SIB.

The functional approach has been used to understand various forms of SIB, including NSSI (Bentley et al., 2014; Nock & Prinstein, 2004; Nock, 2010), substance use (McHugh et al., 2010), alcohol use (Bresin & Mekawi, 2022), eating disorders (Muehlenkamp et al., 2019; Wedig, 2014), risky sexual behavior (Cooper et al., 1998), and compulsive exercise (Dalle Grave et al., 2008). However, it undoubtedly also applies to other forms of SIB, such as risk-taking behavior or SASI and staying in an abusive relationship (Bastian, 2019; Karakurt et al., 2022).

Discussion of Challenges

The fact that SIB covers such a wide range of behaviors is in itself a great challenge, as it makes it both theoretically and therapeutically difficult to approach them as one. The balance between benefits and barriers (Hooley & Franklin, 2018) for different forms of SIB varies because some forms of indirect SIB border on widely culturally accepted behaviors, including the use of stimulants such as tobacco, alcohol, or cannabis, which generally have a lower barrier, while other forms, for example, bulimic behavior, are categorized as psychiatric disorders with a higher barrier.

Another challenge is to develop treatment models that include modern technology, such as online solutions and smartphone apps. Several of these forms of SIB are associated with a high level of shame, which is why an internet-based and thus less stigmatizing and confrontational treatment format may be appealing (Berger et al., 2005).

Recommendations for Clinical Practice

The main challenge in clinical practice is to develop effective prevention and feasible short-term treatment models that take into account the fact that SIB constitutes a wide range of behaviors.

To prevent symptom shifting and to ensure effective treatment of patients with a wider range of SIBs, it is necessary to have a transdiagnostic approach (Garke et al., 2019) that addresses underlying dynamic factors and the common functions of the behaviors. Treatment focus could, for example, address the following topics: affect regulation (Hasking & Claes, 2020), perfectionism (Gyori & Balazs, 2021), self-criticism (Zelkowitz & Cole, 2019), self-esteem (Duarte et al., 2016; Fox et al., 2018; Oktan, 2017), alexithymia (Greene et al., 2020; Raffagnato et al., 2020), shame (Cameron et al., 2020), impulsivity (Hasking & Claes, 2020; Lockwood et al., 2017), and negative body image (Muehlenkamp & Wagner, 2022). Also, treatment models should address common functions of the behaviors and provide the client with new skills that fulfill the same function as the SIB (e.g., interpersonal effectiveness skills such as asking for help or care). A common feature of different forms of SIB is that the body is used to regulate the individual's psychosocial state here and now; thus, the treatment of SIB may benefit from a focus on improving body satisfaction (e.g., through yoga and mindfulness), and it is conceivable that other forms of body therapy could be integrated into the treatment of SIB.

Conclusion

In this chapter, we have described a positive correlation between direct and indirect SIB, which means that persons who engage in direct self-injury have a higher likelihood of also engaging in indirect SIB, and vice versa. In particular, indirect SIB consists of a series of diverse behaviors, some of which border on normal cultural behaviors (e.g., tobacco, alcohol, or cannabis use), and it does not make sense to describe indirect SIB as a uniform and well-defined phenomenon. Direct and indirect SIB may have the same function (functional equivalence) as well as a number of common distal and proximal risk factors, which increase the risk that the individual acts by engaging in SIB and uses the body in a maladaptive way rather than engaging in mentalization or relating to other people in order to regulate their mental state.

There is evidence that both direct (NSSI) and indirect SIB have both intrapersonal and interpersonal functions (Hepp et al., 2020; Mason et al., 2021), and that persons who use direct and/or indirect SIB do so because they achieve a positive effect here and now, even though it is at the cost of their physical integrity in the short or long term.

Even though the categorical distinction between direct and indirect SIB has been challenged we would advocate continuing to distinguish between direct SIB, which causes immediate physical damage (e.g., burning or cutting), although we cannot define a precise time limit for "immediate" (cf. Lengel et al., 2021), and indirect SIB, which increases the risk of physical damage but in which such damage is inherently a matter of chance. This also helps us understand the correlation and interaction between direct and indirect SIB and how we can develop transdiagnostic treatment approaches that prevent symptom shifting.

The key points in this chapter are the following:

1. It remains meaningful to distinguish between direct and indirect SIB despite the lack of clear-cut boundaries and the many commonalities in etiology and function.
2. Further research must be initiated into the connection between direct and indirect SIB to understand causality, mediators, and course of development.
3. Short-term transdiagnostic treatment models that include modern technology, such as online solutions and smartphone apps, must be developed and investigated with regard to feasibility and effect.

References

Afifi, T. O., Taillieu, T., Salmon, S., Davila, I. G., Stewart-Tufescu, A., Fortier, J., Struck, S., Asmundson, G. J. G., Sareen, J., & MacMillan, H. L. (2020). Adverse childhood experiences (ACEs), peer victimization, and substance use among adolescents. *Child Abuse & Neglect, 106*, Article 104504. https://doi.org/10.1016/j.chiabu.2020.104504

Ahn, J., Lee, J. H., & Jung, Y. C. (2021). Identifying predictors of non-suicidal self-injuries in individuals with eating disorders. *Yonsei Medical Journal, 62*(2), 159–163. https://doi.org/10.3349/ymj.2021.62.2.159

Allen, J. P., Chango, J., Szwedo, D., Schad, M., & Marston, E. (2012). Predictors of susceptibility to peer influence regarding substance use in adolescence. *Child Development, 83*(1), 337–350. https://doi.org/10.1111/j.1467-8624.2011.01682.x

Allison, S., Warin, M., & Bastiampillai, T. (2014). Anorexia nervosa and social contagion: Clinical implications. *Australian & New Zealand Journal of Psychiatry, 48*(2), 116–120. https://doi.org/10.1177/0004867413502092

American Psychiatric Association. (2013). *Diagnostic and statistical manual of mental disorders* (5th ed.).

Anderson, N. L., Smith, K. E., Mason, T. B., & Crowther, J. H. (2018). Testing an integrative model of affect regulation and avoidance in non-suicidal self-injury and disordered eating. *Archives of Suicide Research, 22*(2), 295–310. https://doi.org/10.1080/13811118.2017.1340854

Andresen, J. B., Graugaard, C., Andersson, M., Bahnsen, M. K., & Frisch, M. (2022). Adverse childhood experiences and mental health problems in a nationally representative study of heterosexual, homosexual and bisexual Danes. *World psychiatry, 21*(3), 427–435. https://doi.org/10.1002/wps.21008

Andrewes, H. E., Hulbert, C., Cotton, S. M., Betts, J., & Chanen, A. M. (2017). Ecological momentary assessment of non-suicidal self-injury in youth with borderline personality disorder. *Personality Disorders: Theory, Research, and Treatment, 8*(4), 357–365. https://doi.org/10.1037/per0000205

Baetens, I., Claes, L., Martin, G., Onghena, P., Grietens, H., Van Leeuwen, K., Pieters, C., Wiersema, J. R., & Griffith, J. W. (2014). Is non-suicidal self-injury associated with parenting and family factors?. *The Journal of Early Adolescence, 34*(3), 387–405. https://doi.org/10.1177/0272431613494006

Baetens, I., Claes, L., Muehlenkamp, J., Grietens, H., & Onghena, P. (2012). Differences in psychological symptoms and self-competencies in non-suicidal self-injurious Flemish adolescents. *Journal of Adolescence, 35*(3), 753–759. https://doi.org/10.1016/j.adolescence.2011.11.001

Bastian B. (2019). A dehumanization perspective on dependence in low-satisfaction (abusive) relationships. *Journal of Social and Personal Relationships, 36*(5), 1421–1440. https://doi.org/10.1177/0265407519835978

Bentley, K. H., Nock, M. K., & Barlow, D. H. (2014). The four-function model of non-suicidal self-injury: Key directions for future research. *Clinical Psychological Science, 2*(5), 638–656. https://doi.org/10.1177/2167702613514563

Berger, M., Wagner, T. H., & Baker, L. C. (2005). Internet use and stigmatized illness. *Social Science & Medicine, 61*(8), 1821–1827. https://doi.org/10.1016/j.socscimed.2005.03.025

Beyens, I., Frison, E., & Eggermont, S. (2016). "I don't want to miss a thing": Adolescents' fear of missing out and its relationship to adolescents' social needs, Facebook use, and Facebook related stress. *Computers in Human Behavior, 64*, 1–8. https://doi.org/10.1016/j.chb.2016.05.083

Black, E. B., Garratt, M., Beccaria, G., Mildred, H., & Kwan, M. (2019). Body image as a predictor of non-suicidal self-injury in women: A longitudinal study. *Comprehensive Psychiatry, 88*, 83–89. https://doi.org/10.1016/j.comppsych.2018.11.010

Blom, R. M., Koeter, M., van den Brink, W., de Graaf, R., Ten Have, M., & Denys, D. (2011). Co-occurrence of obsessive-compulsive disorder and substance use disorder in the general population. *Addiction, 106*(12), 2178–2185. https://doi.org/10.1111/j.1360-0443.2011.03559.x

Boone, L., Soenens, B., Braet, C., & Goossens, L. (2010). An empirical typology of perfectionism in early-to-mid adolescents and its relation with eating disorder symptoms. *Behaviour Research and Therapy, 48*(7), 686–691. https://doi.org/10.1016/j.brat.2010.03.022

Brausch, A. M., & Boone, S. D. (2015). Frequency of non-suicidal self-injury in adolescents: Differences in suicide attempts, substance use, and disordered eating. *Suicide and Life-Threatening Behavior, 45*(5), 612–622. https://doi.org/10.1111/sltb.12155

Bresin, K. (2019). A meta-analytic review of laboratory studies testing the alcohol stress response dampening hypothesis. *Psychology of Addictive Behaviors, 33*(7), Article 581. https://doi.org/10.1037/adb0000516

Bresin, K., & Gordon, K. H. (2013). Endogenous opioids and nonsuicidal self-injury: A mechanism of affect regulation. *Neuroscience & Biobehavioral Reviews, 37*(3), 374–383.

Bresin, K., & Mekawi, Y. (2022). Different ways to drown out the pain: A meta-analysis of the association between non-suicidal self-injury and alcohol use. *Archives of Suicide Research, 26*(2), 348–369. https://doi.org/10.1080/13811118.2020.1802378

Brown, L. K., Houck, C. D., Hadley, W. S., & Lescano, C. M. (2005). Self-cutting and sexual risk among adolescents in intensive psychiatric treatment. *Psychiatric Services, 56*(2), 216–218. https://doi.org/10.1176/appi.ps.56.2.216

Brown, R. C., Fischer, T., Goldwich, A. D., Keller, F., Young, R., & Plener, P. L. (2018). # cutting: Non-suicidal self-injury (NSSI) on Instagram. *Psychological Medicine, 48*(2), 337–346. https://doi.org/10.1017/S0033291717001751

Calati, R., Bensassi, I., & Courtet, P. (2017). The link between dissociation and both suicide attempts and non-suicidal self-injury: Meta-analyses. *Psychiatry Research, 251*, 103–114. https://doi.org/10.1016/j.psychres.2017.01.035

Calogero, R. M., Tantleff-Dunn, S., & Thompson, J. K. (Eds.). (2011). *Self-objectification in women. Causes, consequences, and counteractions*. American Psychological Association. https://doi.org/10.1037/12304-000

Cameron, A. Y., Erisman, S., & Palm Reed, K. (2020). The relationship among shame, non-suicidal self-injury, and suicidal behaviors in borderline personality disorder. *Psychological Reports, 123*(3), 648–659. https://doi.org/10.1177/0033294118818091

Cassin, S. E., & von Ranson, K. M. (2005). Personality and eating disorders: A decade in review. *Clinical Psychology Review, 25*(7), 895–916. https://doi.org/10.1016/j.cpr.2005.04.012

Chapman, A. L., Gratz, K. L., & Brown, M. Z. (2006). Solving the puzzle of deliberate self-harm: The experiential avoidance model. *Behaviour Research and Therapy, 44*(3), 371–394. https://doi.org/10.1016/j.brat.2005.03.005

Cipriano, A., Claes, L., Gandhi, A., Cella, S., & Cotrufo, P. (2020). Does anger expression mediate the relationship between parental rejection and direct and indirect forms of non-suicidal self-injury? *Journal of Child and Family Studies, 29*(12), 3575–3585. https://doi.org/10.1007/s10826-020-01844-9

Claes, L., & Muehlenkamp, J. (2013). The relationship between the UPPS-P impulsivity dimensions and non-suicidal self-injury characteristics in male and female high-school students. *Psychiatry Journal, 2013*, Article 654847. https://doi.org/10.1155/2013/654847

Claes, L., & Muehlenkamp J. J. (Eds.). (2014a). *Non-suicidal self-injury in eating disorders: Advancements in etiology and treatment*. Springer-Verlag. https://doi.org/10.1007/978-3-642-40107-7

Claes, L., & Muehlenkamp J. J. (2014b). Non-suicidal self-injury and eating disorders: Dimensions of self-harm. In L. Claes & J. J. Muehlenkamp (Eds.), *Non-suicidal self-injury in eating disorders: Advancements in etiology and treatment* (pp. 3–18). Springer. https://doi.org/10.1007/978-3-642-40107-7_1

Claes, L., Soenens, B., Vansteenkiste M., & Vandereycken, W. (2012). The scars of the inner critic: Perfectionism and non-suicidal self-injury in eating disorders. *European Eating Disorders Review, 20*, 196–202. https://doi.org/10.1002/erv.1158

Claes, L., & Vandereycken, W. (2007). Self-injurious behavior: Differential diagnosis and functional differentiation. *Comprehensive Psychiatry, 48*(2), 137–144. https://doi.org/10.1016/j.comppsych.2006.10.009

Claes, L., Vandereycken, W., & Vertommen, H. (2004). Family environment of eating-disordered patients with and without self-injurious behaviors. *European Psychiatry, 19*(8), 494–498. https://doi.org/10.1016/j.eurpsy.2004.09.001

Claes, L., Vandereycken, W., & Vertommen, H. (2005). Impulsivity-related traits in eating disorder patients. *Personality and Individual Differences, 39*(4), 739–749. https://doi.org/10.1016/j.paid.2005.02.022

Conigliaro, A., & Ward-Ciesielski, E. (2021). Associations between social contagion, group conformity characteristics, and non-suicidal self-injury. *Journal of American College Health*. 1–9. Advance online publication. https://doi.org/10.1080/07448481.2021.1928141

Cooper, M. L., Shapiro, C. M., & Powers, A. M. (1998). Motivations for sex and risky sexual behavior among adolescents and young adults: A functional perspective. *Journal of Personality and Social Psychology, 75*(6), Article 1528. https://doi.org/10.1037/0022-3514.75.6.1528

Crosby, R. D., Wonderlich, S. A., Engel, S., Simonich, H., Smyth, J., & Mitchell, J. E. (2009). Daily mood patterns and bulimic behaviors in the natural environment. *Behaviour Research and Therapy, 47*(3), 181–188. https://doi.org/10.1016/j.brat.2008.11.006

Cucchi, A., Ryan, D., Konstantakopoulos, G., Stroumpa, S., Kaçar, A. Ş., Renshaw, S., Landau, S., & Kravariti, E. (2016). Lifetime prevalence of non-suicidal self-injury in patients with eating disorders: A systematic review and meta-analysis. *Psychological Medicine, 46*(7), 1345–1358. https://doi.org/10.1017/S0033291716000027

Cuthbert, B. N. (2022). Research Domain Criteria (RDoC): Progress and potential. *Current Directions in Psychological Science, 31*(2), 107–114. https://doi.org/10.1177/09637214211051363

D'Agostino, A., Boni, M., Aportone, A., Pepi, R., & Monti, M. R. (2020). Direct and indirect self-injury: Is it really all the same?. *Mediterranean Journal of Clinical Psychology, 8*(2). https://doi.org/10.6092/2282-1619/mjcp-2434

Dalle Grave, R., Calugi, S., & Marchesini, G. (2008). Compulsive exercise to control shape or weight in eating disorders: Prevalence, associated features, and treatment outcome. *Comprehensive Psychiatry, 49*(4), 346–352. https://doi.org/10.1016/j.comppsych.2007.12.007

Duarte, C., Ferreira, C., & Pinto-Gouveia, J. (2016). At the core of eating disorders: Overvaluation, social rank, self-criticism and shame in anorexia, bulimia and binge eating disorder. *Comprehensive Psychiatry, 66*, 123–131. https://doi.org/10.1016/j.comppsych.2016.01.003

Duggan, J. M., & Heath, N. L. (2014). Co-occurring health-risk behaviors of non-suicidal self-injury and eating disorders. In L. Claes & J. J. Muehlenkamp (Eds.), *Non-suicidal self-injury in eating disorders* (pp. 217–236). Springer-Verlag. https://doi.org/10.1007/978-3-642-40107-7_13

Escelsior, A., Murri, M. B., Corsini, G. P., Serafini, G., Aguglia, A., Zampogna, D., Cattedra, S., Nebbia, J., Trabucco, A., Prestia, D., Olcese, M., Barletta, E., da Silva, B. P., & Amore, M. (2021). Cannabinoid use and self-injurious behaviours: A systematic review and meta-analysis. *Journal of Affective Disorders, 278*, 85–98. https://doi.org/10.1016/j.jad.2020.09.020

Fabris, M. A., Marengo, D., Longobardi, C., & Settanni, M. (2020). Investigating the links between fear of missing out, social media addiction, and emotional symptoms in adolescence: The role of stress associated with neglect and negative reactions on social media. *Addictive Behaviors, 106*, Article 106364. https://doi.org/10.1016/j.addbeh.2020.106364

Farber, S. K. (1997). Self-medication, traumatic reenactment, and somatic expression in bulimic and self-mutilating behavior. *Clinical Social Work Journal, 25*(1), 87–107. https://doi.org/10.1023/A:1025785911606

Fox, K. R., Franklin, J. C., Ribeiro, J. D., Kleiman, E. M., Bentley, K. H., & Nock, M. K. (2015). Meta-analysis of risk factors for non-suicidal self-injury. *Clinical Psychology Review, 42*, 156–167. https://doi.org/10.1016/j.cpr.2015.09.002

Fox, K. R., Ribeiro, J. D., Kleiman, E. M., Hooley, J. M., Nock, M. K., & Franklin, J. C. (2018). Affect toward the self and self-injury stimuli as potential risk factors for nonsuicidal self-injury. *Psychiatry Research, 260*, 279–285. https://doi.org/10.1016/j.psychres.2017.11.083

Franklin, J. C., Lee, K. M., Hanna, E. K., & Prinstein, M. J. (2013). Feeling worse to feel better: Pain-offset relief simultaneously stimulates positive affect and reduces negative affect. *Psychological Science, 24*(4), 521–529. https://doi.org/10.1177/0956797612458805

Franzke, I., Wabnitz, P., & Catani, C. (2015). Dissociation as a mediator of the relationship between childhood trauma and non-suicidal self-injury in females: A path analytic approach. *Journal of Trauma & Dissociation, 16*(3), 286–302. https://doi.org/10.1080/15299732.2015.989646

Fredlund, C., Svedin, C. G., Priebe, G., Jonsson, L., & Wadsby, M. (2017). Self-reported frequency of sex as self-injury (SASI) in a national study of Swedish adolescents and association to sociodemographic factors, sexual behaviors, abuse and mental health. *Child and Adolescent Psychiatry and Mental Health, 11*(1), 1–11. https://doi.org/10.1186/s13034-017-0146-7

Garke, M., Sörman, K., Jayaram-Lindström, N., Hellner, C., & Birgegård, A. (2019). Symptom shifting and associations with mental illness: A transdiagnostic approach applied to eating disorders. *Journal of Abnormal Psychology, 128*(6), 585–595. https://doi.org/10.1037/abn0000425

Garofalo, C., & Velotti, P. (2015). Alcohol misuse in psychiatric patients and nonclinical individuals: The role of emotion dysregulation and impulsivity. *Addiction Research and Theory, 23*(4), 294–300. https://doi.org/10.3109/16066359.2014.987758

Gattario, K. H., Frisén, A., Teall, T. L., & Piran, N. (2020). Embodiment: Cultural and gender differences and associations with life satisfaction. *Body Image, 35*, 1–10. https://doi.org/10.1016/j.bodyim.2020.07.005

Glenn, C. R., & Klonsky, E. D. (2010). A multimethod analysis of impulsivity in non-suicidal self-injury. *Personality Disorders: Theory, Research, and Treatment, 1*(1), 67. https://doi.org/10.1037/a0017427

Glenn, C. R., & Klonsky, E. D. (2013). Non-suicidal self-injury disorder: An empirical investigation in adolescent psychiatric patients. *Journal of Clinical Child and Adolescent Psychology, 42*(4), 496–507. https://doi.org/10.1080/15374416.2013.794699

Greene, D., Boyes, M., & Hasking, P. (2020). The associations between alexithymia and both non-suicidal self-injury and risky drinking: A systematic review and meta-analysis. *Journal of Affective Disorders, 260*, 140–166. https://doi.org/10.1016/j.jad.2019.08.088

Groenman, A. P., Janssen, T. W., & Oosterlaan, J. (2017). Childhood psychiatric disorders as risk factor for subsequent substance abuse: A meta-analysis. *Journal of the American Academy of Child & Adolescent Psychiatry, 56*(7), 556–569. https://doi.org/10.1016/j.jaac.2017.05.004

Gyori, D., & Balazs, J. (2021). Non-suicidal self-injury and perfectionism: A systematic review. *Frontiers in Psychiatry, 12*, Article 1076. https://doi.org/10.3389/fpsyt.2021.691147

Halmi, K. A., Tozzi, F., Thornton, L. M., Crow, S., Fichter, M. M., Kaplan, A. S. & Bulik, C. M. (2005). The relation among perfectionism, obsessive-compulsive personality disorder and obsessive-compulsive disorder in individuals with eating disorders. *International Journal of Eating Disorders, 38*(4), 371–374. https://doi.org/10.1002/eat.20190

Hampshire, C., Mahoney, B., & Davis, S. K. (2022). Parenting styles and disordered eating among youths: A rapid scoping review. *Frontiers in Psychology, 12*, Article 802567. https://doi.org/10.3389/fpsyg.2021.802567

Hamza, C. A., Willoughby, T., & Heffer, T. (2015). Impulsivity and non-suicidal self-injury: A review and meta-analysis. *Clinical Psychology Review, 38*, 13–24. https://doi.org/10.1016/j.cpr.2015.02.010

Hankin, B. L., & Abela, J. R. (Eds.). (2005). *Development of psychopathology: A vulnerability-stress perspective.* SAGE. https://doi.org/10.4135/9781452231655

Hasking, P., & Claes, L. (2020). Transdiagnostic mechanisms involved in non-suicidal self-injury, risky drinking and disordered eating: Impulsivity, emotion regulation and alexithymia. *Journal of American College Health, 68*(6), 603–609. https://doi.org/10.1080/07448481.2019.1583661

Hasking, P., Whitlock, J., Voon, D., & Rose, A. (2017). A cognitive-emotional model of NSSI: Using emotion regulation and cognitive processes to explain why people self-injure. *Cognition and Emotion, 31*(8), 1543–1556. https://doi.org/10.1080/02699931.2016.1241219

Haynos, A. F., Wang, S. B., & Fruzzetti, A. E. (2018). Restrictive eating is associated with emotion regulation difficulties in a non-clinical sample. *Eating Disorders, 26*(1), 5–12. https://doi.org/10.1080/10640266.2018.1418264

Hepp, J., Carpenter, R. W., Störkel, L. M., Schmitz, S. E., Schmahl, C., & Niedtfeld, I. (2020). A systematic review of daily life studies on non-suicidal self-injury based on the four-function model. *Clinical Psychology Review, 82*, Article 101888. https://doi.org/10.1016/j.cpr.2020.101888

Hill, E. M., Jenkins, J., & Farmer, L. (2008). Family unpredictability, future discounting, and risk taking. *The Journal of Socio-Economics, 37*(4), 1381–1396. https://doi.org/10.1016/j.socec.2006.12.081

Hooley, J. M., & Franklin, J. C. (2018). Why do people hurt themselves? A new conceptual model of non-suicidal self-injury. *Clinical Psychological Science, 6*(3), 428–451. https://doi.org/10.1177/2167702617745641

Hooley, J. M., & St. Germain, S. A. (2014). Should we expand the conceptualization of self-injurious behavior? Rationale, review, and recommendations. In M. K. Nock (Ed.), *The Oxford handbook of suicide and self-injury* (pp. 47–58). Oxford University Press. https://doi.org/10.1093/oxfordhb/9780195388565.013.0006

Johnson, J. G., Cohen, P., Kasen, S., & Brook, J. S. (2002). Childhood adversities associated with risk for eating disorders or weight problems during adolescence or early adulthood. *American Journal of Psychiatry, 159*(3), 394–400. https://doi.org/10.1176/appi.ajp.159.3.394

Johnson, V., & Pandina, R. J. (1991). Effects of the family environment on adolescent substance use, delinquency, and coping styles. *The American Journal of Drug and Alcohol Abuse, 17*(1), 71–88. https://doi.org/10.3109/00952999108992811

Kaess, M., Parzer, P., Mattern, M., Plener, P. L., Bifulco, A., Resch, F., & Brunner, R. (2013). Adverse childhood experiences and their impact on frequency, severity, and the individual function of nonsuicidal self-injury in youth. *Psychiatry Research, 206*(2–3), 265–272. https://doi.org/10.1016/j.psychres.2012.10.012

Karakurt, G., Ayluçtarhan, Z., Ergüner-Tekinalp, B., & Köse, Ö. (2022). Regaining courage to leave abusive relationships: Theoretical framework. *The American Journal of Family Therapy, 50*(2), 144–158. https://doi.org/10.1080/01926187.2021.1877208

Kentopp, S. D., Conner, B. T., Fetterling, T. J., Delgadillo, A. A., & Rebecca, R. A. (2021). Sensation seeking and non-suicidal self-injurious behavior among adolescent psychiatric patients. *Clinical Child Psychology and Psychiatry, 26*(2), 430–442. https://doi.org/10.1177/1359104521994627

Kianpoor, M., & Bakhshani, N. M. (2012). Trauma, dissociation, and high-risk behaviors. *International Journal of High-Risk Behaviors and Addiction, 1*(1), 9–13. https://doi.org/10.5812/ijhrba.4624

Kiekens, G., & Claes, L. (2020). Non-suicidal self-injury and eating disordered behaviors: An update on what we do and do not know. *Current Psychiatry Reports, 22*(12), 1–11. https://doi.org/10.1007/s11920-020-01191-y

Kiekens, G., Hasking, P., Bruffaerts, R., Claes, L., Baetens, I., Boyes, M., Mortier, P., Demyttenaere, K., & Whitlock, J. (2017). What predicts ongoing non-suicidal self-injury?: A comparison between persistent and ceased self-injury in emerging adults. *The Journal of Nervous and Mental Disease, 205*(10), 762–770. https://doi.org/10.1097/NMD.0000000000000726

Kiekens, G., Hasking, P., Claes, L., Mortier, P., Auerbach, R. P., Boyes, M., & Bruffaerts, R. (2018). The DSM-5 non-suicidal self-injury disorder among incoming college students: Prevalence and associations with 12-month mental disorders and suicidal thoughts and behaviors. *Depression and Anxiety, 35*(7), 629–637. https://doi.org/10.1002/da.22754

Klassen, J. A., Hamza, C. A., & Stewart, S. L. (2018). An examination of correlates for adolescent engagement in non-suicidal self-injury, suicidal self-injury, and substance use. *Journal of Research on Adolescence, 28*(2), 342–353. https://doi.org/10.1111/jora.12333

Koob, G. F. (2013). Theoretical frameworks and mechanistic aspects of alcohol addiction: alcohol addiction as a reward deficit disorder. *American Journal of Psychiatry, 164*(8), 1149–1159. https://doi.org/10.1007/978-3-642-28720-6_129

Korhonen, T., Sihvola, E., Latvala, A., Dick, D. M., Pulkkinen, L., Nurnberger, J., Rose, R. J., & Kaprio, J. (2018). Early-onset tobacco use and suicide-related behavior—A prospective study from adolescence to young adulthood, *Addictive Behaviors, 79*, 32–38. https://doi.org/10.1016/j.addbeh.2017.12.008

Kotov, R., Krueger, R. F., Watson, D., Achenbach, T. M., Althoff, R. R., Bagby, R. M., Brown, T. A., Carpenter, W. T., Caspi, A., Clark, L. A., Eaton, N. R., Forbes, M. K., Forbush, K. T., Goldberg, D., Hasin, D., Hyman, S. E., Ivanova, M. Y., Lynam, D. R., Markon. K. . . . Zimmerman, M. (2017). The Hierarchical Taxonomy of Psychopathology (HiTOP): A dimensional alternative to traditional nosologies. *Journal of Abnormal Psychology, 126*(4), 454. https://doi.org/10.1037/abn0000258

Kranzler, A., Fehling, K. B., Lindqvist, J., Brillante, J., Yuan, F., Gao, X., & Selby, E. A. (2018). An ecological investigation of the emotional context surrounding non-suicidal self-injurious thoughts and behaviors in adolescents and young adults. *Suicide & Life-Threatening Behavior, 48*(2), 149–159. https://doi.org/10.1111/sltb.12373

Krug, I., Arroyo, M. D., Giles, S., Dang, A. B., Kiropoulos, L., De Paoli, T., Buck, K., Treasure, J., & Fuller-Tyszkiewicz, M. (2021). A new integrative model for the co-occurrence of non-suicidal self-injury behaviours and eating disorder symptoms. *Journal of Eating Disorders, 9*(1), 1–17. https://doi.org/10.1186/s40337-021-00508-3

Kruzan, K. P., Muehlenkamp, J. J., & Claes, L. (2022). Identity, self-blame, and body regard in NSSI: A test of moderated-mediation. *Comprehensive Psychiatry, 116*, Article 152322. https://doi.org/10.1016/j.comppsych.2022.152322

Lee, C. G., Seo, D. C., Torabi, M. R., Lohrmann, D. K., & Song, T. M. (2018). Longitudinal trajectory of the relationship between self-esteem and substance use from adolescence to young adulthood. *Journal of School Health, 88*(1), 9–14. https://doi.org/10.1111/josh.12574

Lee, K. S., & Vaillancourt, T. (2019). A four-year prospective study of bullying, anxiety, and disordered eating behavior across early adolescence. *Child Psychiatry & Human Development, 50*(5), 815–825. https://doi.org/10.1007/s10578-019-00884-7

Lengel, G. J., Ammerman, B. A., & Washburn, J. J. (2021). Clarifying the definition of non-suicidal self-injury: Clinician and researcher perspectives. *Crisis: The Journal of Crisis Intervention and Suicide Prevention*. Advance online publication. https://doi.org/10.1027/0227-5910/a000764

Levenkron, S. (1998). *Cutting: Understanding and Overcoming Self-Mutilation*. W. W. Norton.

Lewis, S. P., & Seko, Y. (2016). A double-edged sword: A review of benefits and risks of online non-suicidal self-injury activities. *Journal of Clinical Psychology, 72*(3), 249–262. https://doi.org/10.1002/jclp.22242

Lichtenstein, M. B., Hinze, C. J., Emborg, B., Thomsen, F., & Hemmingsen, S. D. (2017). Compulsive exercise: Links, risks and challenges faced. *Psychology Research and Behavior Management, 10*, 85. https://doi.org/10.2147/PRBM.S113093

Liechty, J. M. (2019). Promoting a resistant Stance Toward Media Images. In N. Piran (Ed.), *Handbook of positive body image and embodiment. Construct, protective factors and interventions* (pp 201–213). Oxford University Press. https://doi.org/10.1093/med-psych/9780190841874.003.0020

Liu, R. T., Sheehan, A. E., Walsh, R. F., Sanzari, C. M., Cheek, S. M., & Hernandez, E. M. (2019). Prevalence and correlates of non-suicidal self-injury among lesbian, gay, bisexual, and transgender individuals: A systematic review and meta-analysis. *Clinical Psychology Review*, *74*, Article 101783. https://doi.org/10.1016/j.cpr.2019.101783

Lockwood, J., Daley, D., Townsend, E., & Sayal, K. (2017). Impulsivity and self-harm in adolescence: A systematic review. *European Child & Adolescent Psychiatry*, *26*(4), 387–402. https://doi.org/10.1007/s00787-016-0915-5

Mason, T. B., Smith, K. E., Crosby, R. D., Engel, S. G., & Wonderlich, S. A. (2021). Examination of momentary maintenance factors and eating disorder behaviors and cognitions using ecological momentary assessment. *Eating Disorders*, *29*(1), 42–55. https://doi.org/10.1080/10640266.2019.1613847

Mayo, L. M., Perini, I., Gustafsson, P. A., Hamilton, J. P., Kämpe, R., Heilig, M., & Zetterqvist, M. (2021). Psychophysiological and neural support for enhanced emotional reactivity in female adolescents with non-suicidal self-injury. *Biological Psychiatry: Cognitive Neuroscience and Neuroimaging*, *6*(7), 682–691. https://doi.org/10.1016/j.bpsc.2020.11.004

McHugh, R. K., Hearon, B. A., & Otto, M. W. (2010). Cognitive behavioral therapy for substance use disorders. *Psychiatric Clinics*, *33*(3), 511–525. https://doi.org/10.1016/j.psc.2010.04.012

Memon, A. M., Sharma, S. G., Mohite, S. S., & Jain, S. (2018). The role of online social networking on deliberate self-harm and suicidality in adolescents: A systematized review of literature. *Indian Journal of Psychiatry*, *60*(4), Article 384. https://doi.org/10.4103/psychiatry.IndianJPsychiatry_414_17

Mills, J. S., Musto, S., Williams, L., & Tiggemann, M. (2018). "Selfie" harm: Effects on mood and body image in young women. *Body Image*, *27*, 86–92. https://doi.org/10.1016/j.bodyim.2018.08.007

Moeller, F. G. D., & Dougherty, D. M. (2002). Impulsivity and substance abuse: What is the connection? *Addictive Disorders & Their Treatment*, *1*(1), 3–10. https://doi.org/10.1097/00132576-200205000-00002

Møhl, B. (2019). *Assessment and treatment of non-suicidal self-injury: A clinical perspective*. Routledge. https://doi.org/10.4324/9780429296352

Monto, M. A., McRee, N., & Deryck, F. S. (2018). Non-suicidal self-injury among a representative sample of US adolescents. *American Journal of Public Health*, *108*(8), 1042–1048. https://doi.org/10.2105/AJPH.2018.304470

Muehlenkamp, J. J. (2012). Body regard in non-suicidal self-injury: Theoretical explanations and treatment directions. *Journal of Cognitive Psychotherapy*, *26*(4), 331–347. https://doi.org/10.1891/0889-8391.26.4.331

Muehlenkamp, J. J., & Brausch, A. M. (2012). Body image as a mediator of non-suicidal self-injury in adolescents. *Journal of Adolescence*, 35(1), 1–9. https://doi.org/10.1016/j.adolescence.2011.06.010

Muehlenkamp, J. J., Engel, S. G., Wadeson, A., Crosby, R. D., Wonderlich, S. A., Simonich, H., & Mitchell, J. E. (2009). Emotional states preceding and following acts of non-suicidal self-injury in bulimia nervosa patients. *Behaviour Research and Therapy*, *47*(1), 83–87. https://doi.org/10.1016/j.brat.2008.10.011

Muehlenkamp, J. J., & Saris-Baglama, R. N. (2002). Self-objectification and its psychological outcomes for college women. *Psychology of Women Quarterly*, *26*(4), 371–379. https://doi.org/10.1111/1471-6402.t01-1-00076

Muehlenkamp, J. J., Suzuki, T., Brausch, A. M., & Peyerl, N. (2019). Behavioral functions underlying NSSI and eating disorder behaviors. *Journal of Clinical Psychology*, *75*(7), 1219–1232. https://doi.org/10.1002/jclp.22745

Muehlenkamp, J. J., & Wagner, E. M. (2022). Yoga and nonsuicidal self-injury: Mediational effects of self-compassion and body appreciation. *Body Image*, *43*, 17–24. https://doi.org/10.1016/j.bodyim.2022.08.001

Nelson, A., & Muehlenkamp, J. J. (2012). Body attitudes and objectification in non-suicidal selfinjury: Comparing males and females. *Archives of Suicide Research*, *16*(1), 1–12. https://doi.org/10.1080/13811118.2012.640578

Neumark-Sztainer, D., Story, M., Hannan, P. J., Beuhring, T., & Resnick, M. D. (2000). Disordered eating among adolescents: Associations with sexual/physical abuse and other familial/psychosocial factors. *International Journal of Eating Disorders*, *28*(3), 249–258. https://doi.org/10.1002/1098-108X(200011)28:3

Nieri, T., Kulis, S., Keith, V. M., & Hurdle, D. (2005). Body image, acculturation, and substance abuse among boys and girls in the Southwest. *The American Journal of Drug and Alcohol Abuse*, *31*(4), 617–639. https://doi.org/10.1081/ADA-200068418

Nock, M. K. (2010). Self-injury. *Annual Review of Clinical Psychology, 6*(1), 339–363. https://doi.org/10.1146/annurev.clinpsy.121208.131258

Nock, M. K., Joiner, T. E., Gordon, K. H., Lloyd-Richardson, E., & Prinstein, M. J. (2006). Non-suicidal self-injury among adolescents: Diagnostic correlates and relation to suicide attempts. *Psychiatry Research, 144*(1), 65–72. https://doi.org/10.1016/j.psychres.2006.05.010

Nock, M. K., & Prinstein, M. (2004). A functional approach to the assessment of self-mutilative behavior. *Journal of Consulting and Clinical Psychology, 72*(5), 885–890. https://doi.org/10.1037/0022-006X.72.5.885

Norbury, A., Manohar, S., Rogers, R. D., & Husain, M. (2013). Dopamine modulates risk-taking as a function of baseline sensation-seeking trait. *Journal of Neuroscience, 33*(32), 12982–12986. https://doi.org/10.1523/JNEUROSCI.5587-12.2013

Oktan, V. (2017). Self-harm behaviour in adolescents: Body image and self-esteem. *Journal of Psychologists and Counsellors in Schools, 27*(2),177–189. https://doi.org/10.1017/jgc.2017.6

Overholser, J., & Dimaggio, G. (2020). Struggling with perfectionism: When good enough is not good enough. *Journal of Clinical Psychology, 76*(11), 2019–2027. https://doi.org/10.1002/jts.20081

Parker, L. L., & Harriger, J. A. (2020). Eating disorders and disordered eating behaviors in the LGBT population: A review of the literature. *Journal of Eating Disorders, 8*(1), 1–20. https://doi.org/10.1186/s40337-020-00327-y

Peters, E. M., John, A., Baetz, M., & Balbuena, L. (2018). Examining the role of borderline personality traits in the relationship between major depression and non-suicidal self-injury. *Comprehensive Psychiatry, 86*, 96–101. https://doi.org/10.1016/j.comppsych.2018.07.008

Prefit, A. B., Cândea, D. M., & Szentagotai-Tătar, A. (2019). Emotion regulation across eating pathology: A meta-analysis. *Appetite, 143*, Article 104438. https://doi.org/10.1016/j.appet.2019.104438

Puttevils, L., Vanderhasselt, M. A., Horczak, P., & Vervaet, M. (2021). Differences in the use of emotion regulation strategies between anorexia and bulimia nervosa: A systematic review and meta-analysis. *Comprehensive Psychiatry, 109*, Article 152262. https://doi.org/10.1016/j.comppsych.2021.152262

Raffagnato, A., Angelico, C., Valentini, P., Miscioscia, M., & Gatta, M. (2020). Using the body when there are no words for feelings: Alexithymia and somatization in self-harming adolescents. *Frontiers in Psychiatry, 11*, Article 262. https://doi.org/10.3389/fpsyt.2020.00262

Richardson, E., DePue, M. K., Therriault, D. J., Alli, S., & Liu, R. (2020). The influence of substance use on engagement in non-suicidal self-injury (NSI) in adults. *Substance Use & Misuse, 55*(1), 89–94. https://doi.org/10.1080/10826084.2019.1656254

Ross, C. A., Farley, M., & Schwartz, H. L. (2004). Dissociation among women in prostitution. *Journal of Trauma Practice, 2*(3–4), 199–212. https://doi.org/10.1300/J189v02n03_11

Sansone, R. A., & Sansone, L. A. (2007). Childhood trauma, borderline personality, and eating disorders: A developmental cascade. *Eating Disorders, 15*(4), 333–346. https://doi.org/10.1080/10640260701454345

Schäfer, I., Reininghaus, U., Langeland, W., Voss, A., Zieger, N., Haasen, C., & Karow, A. (2007). Dissociative symptoms in alcohol-dependent patients: associations with childhood trauma and substance abuse characteristics. *Comprehensive Psychiatry, 48*(6), 539–545. https://doi.org/10.1016/j.comppsych.2007.05.013

Schwartz-Mette, R. A., & Lawrence, H. R. (2019). Peer socialization of non-suicidal self-injury in adolescents' close friendships. *Journal of Abnormal Child Psychology, 47*(11), 1851–1862. https://doi.org/10.1007/s10802-019-00569-8

Silveira, S., Shah, R., Nooner, K. B., Nagel, B. J., Tapert, S. F., De Bellis, M. D., & Mishra, J. (2020). Impact of childhood trauma on executive function in adolescence-mediating functional brain networks and prediction of high-risk drinking. *Biological Psychiatry: Cognitive Neuroscience and Neuroimaging, 5*(5), 499–509. https://doi.org/10.1016/j.bpsc.2020.01.011

Siraj, R., Najam, B., & Ghazal, S. (2021). Sensation seeking, peer influence, and risk-taking behavior in adolescents. *Education Research International*, Article 2021. https://doi.org/10.1155/2021/8403024

Sleuwaegen, E., Houben, M., Claes, L., Berens, A., & Sabbe, B. (2017). The relationship between non-suicidal self-injury and alexithymia in borderline personality disorder: "Actions instead of words". *Comprehensive Psychiatry, 77*, 80–88. https://doi.org/10.1016/j.comppsych.2017.06.006

Smith, S. G., Zhang, X., Basile, K. C., Merrick, M. T., Wang, J., Kresnow, M. J., & Chen, J. (2018). *The national intimate partner and sexual violence survey: 2015 Data brief-updated release*. National Center for Injury Prevention and Control, Centers for Disease Control and Prevention.

Sorgi, K. M., Ammerman, B. A., Cheung, J. C., Fahlgren, M. K., Puhalla, A. A., & McCloskey, M. S. (2021). Relationships between non-suicidal self-injury and other maladaptive behaviors: Beyond difficulties in emotion regulation. *Archives of Suicide Research*, *25*(3), 530–551. https://doi.org/10.1080/13811118.2020.1715906

St. Germain, S. A., & Hooley, J. M. (2012). Direct and indirect forms of non-suicidal self-injury: Evidence for a distinction. *Psychiatry Research*, *197*(1-2), 78–84. https://doi.org/10.1016/j.psychres.2011.12.050

St. Germain, S. A., & Hooley, J. M. (2013). Aberrant pain perception in direct and indirect non-suicidal self-injury: An empirical test of Joiner's interpersonal theory. *Comprehensive Psychiatry*, *54*(6), 694–701. https://doi.org/10.1016/j.comppsych.2012.12.029

Stice, E., Gau, J. M., Rohde, P., & Shaw, H. (2017). Risk factors that predict future onset of each DSM-5 eating disorder: Predictive specificity in high-risk adolescent females. *Journal of Abnormal Psychology*, *126*(1), Article 38. https://doi.org/10.1037/abn0000219

Stupiggia, M. (2019). Traumatic dis-embodiment: Effects of trauma on body perception and body image. In H. Payne, S. Koch, J. Tantia, & T. Fuchs (Eds.), *The Routledge international handbook of embodied perspectives in psychotherapy* (pp. 389–396). Routledge. https://doi.org/10.4324/9781315159416-40

Svirko, E., & Hawton, K. (2007). Self-injurious behavior and eating disorders: The extent and nature of the association. *Suicide and Life-Threatening Behavior*, *37*(4), 409–421. https://doi.org/10.1521/suli.2007.37.4.409

Taylor, P. J., Jomar, K., Dhingra, K., Forrester, R., Shahmalak, U., & Dickson, J. M. (2018). A meta-analysis of the prevalence of different functions of non-suicidal self-injury. *Journal of Affective Disorders*, *227*, 759–769. https://doi.org/10.1016/j.jad.2017.11.073

Tonta, K. E., Boyes, M., Howell, J., McEvoy, P., Johnson, A., & Hasking, P. (2022). Modeling pathways to non-suicidal self-injury: The roles of perfectionism, negative affect, rumination, and attention control. *Journal of Clinical Psychology*, *78*(7):1463–1477. https://doi.org/10.1002/jclp.23315

Turner, B. J., Layden, B. K., Butler, S. M., & Chapman, A. L. (2013). How often, or how many ways: Clarifying the relationship between non-suicidal self-injury and suicidality. *Archives of Suicide Research*, *17*(4), 397–415. https://doi.org/10.1080/13811118.2013.802660

Turner, B. J., Yiu, A., Layden, B. K., Claes, L., Zaitsoff, S., & Chapman, A. L. (2015). Temporal associations between disordered eating and non-suicidal self-injury: Examining symptom overlap over 1 year. *Behavior Therapy*, *46*(1), 125–138. https://doi.org/10.1016/j.beth.2014.09.002

Udo, T., & Grilo, C. M. (2019). Psychiatric and medical correlates of DSM-5 eating disorders in a nationally representative sample of adults in the United States. *International Journal of Eating Disorders*, *52*(1), 42–50. https://doi.org/10.1002/eat.23004

van Hoorn, J., Crone, E. A., Crone, & Van Leijenhorst, L. (2016). Hanging out with the right crowd: Peer influence on risk-taking behavior in adolescence. *Journal of Research on Adolescence*, *27*(1), 189–200. https://doi.org/10.1111/jora.12265

Vanderlinden, J., & Palmisano, G. (2017). Trauma and the eating disorders: The state of the art (chapter 2). In A. Seubert & P. Virdi (Eds.), *Trauma-informed approaches to eating disorders* (pp. 13–30). Springer.

Victor, S. E., Muehlenkamp, J. J., Hayes, N. A., Lengel, G. J., Styer, D. M., & Washburn, J. J. (2018). Characterizing gender differences in non-suicidal self-injury: Evidence from a large clinical sample of adolescents and adults. *Comprehensive Psychiatry*, *82*, 53–60. https://doi.org/10.1016/j.comppsych.2018.01.009

Viner, R. M., Gireesh, A., Stiglic, N., Hudson, L. D., Goddings, A. L., Ward, J. L., & Nicholls, D. E. (2019). Roles of cyberbullying, sleep, and physical activity in mediating the effects of social media use on mental health and wellbeing among young people in England: A secondary analysis of longitudinal data. *The Lancet Child & Adolescent Health*, *3*(10), 685–696. https://doi.org/10.1016/S2352-4642(19)30186-5

Warne, N., Heron, J., Mars, B., Moran, P., Stewart, A., Munafò, M., Biddle, L., Skinner, A., Gunnell, D., & Bould, H. (2021). Comorbidity of self-harm and disordered eating in young people: Evidence from a UK population-based cohort. *Journal of Affective Disorders*, *282*, 386–390. https://doi.org/10.1016/j.jad.2020.12.053

Wedig, M. M. (2014). Psychological meanings and functions of non-suicidal self-injury and eating disorders. In L. Claes & J. J. Muehlenkamp (Eds.), *Non-suicidal self-injury in eating disorders: Advancements in etiology and treatment* (pp. 73–84). Springer. https://doi.org/10.1007/978-3-642-40107-7_5

Weierich, M. R., & Nock, M. K. (2008). Posttraumatic stress symptoms mediate the relation between childhood sexual abuse and non-suicidal self-injury. *Journal of Consulting and Clinical Psychology*, *76*(1), 39. https://doi.org/10.1037/0022-006X.76.1.39

Weiss, N. H., Kiefer, R., Goncharenko, S., Raudales, A. M., Forkus, S. R., Schick, M. R., & Contractor, A. A. (2022). Emotion regulation and substance use: A meta-analysis. *Drug and Alcohol Dependence, 230*, Article 109131. https://doi.org/10.1016/j.drugalcdep.2021.109131

Westwood, H., Kerr-Gaffney, J., Stahl, D., & Tchanturia, K. (2017). Alexithymia in eating disorders: Systematic review and meta-analyses of studies using the Toronto Alexithymia Scale. *Journal of Psychosomatic Research, 99*, 66–81. https://doi.org/10.1016/j.jpsychores.2017.06.007

Whitlock, J., Muehlenkamp, J., Purington, A., Eckenrode, J., Barreira, P., Baral Abrams, G., & Knox, K. (2011). Nonsuicidal self-injury in a college population: General trends and sex differences. *Journal of American College Health, 59*(8), 691–698. https://doi.org/10.1080/07448481.2010.529626

Wilkinson, P. O., Qiu, T., Neufeld, S., Jones, P. B., & Goodyer, I. M. (2018). Sporadic and recurrent non-suicidal self-injury before age 14 and incident onset of psychiatric disorders by 17 years: Prospective cohort study. *The British Journal of Psychiatry, 212*(4), 222–226. https://doi.org/10.1192/bjp.2017.45

Wu, N. S., Schairer, L. C., Dellor, E., & Grella, C. (2010). Childhood trauma and health outcomes in adults with comorbid substance abuse and mental health disorders. *Addictive Behaviors, 35*(1), 68–71. https://doi.org/10.1016/j.addbeh.2009.09.003

Yates, T. M., Carlson, E. A., & Egeland, B. (2008). A prospective study of child maltreatment and self-injurious behavior in a community sample. *Development and Psychopathology, 20*(2), 651–671. https://doi.org/10.1017/S0954579408000321

Yiu, A., Turner, B. J., Layden, B. K., Chapman, A. L., & Zaitsoff, S. L. (2015). Prevalence and correlates of eating disorder symptoms in a community sample with non-suicidal self-injury. *Journal of Psychopathology and Behavioral Assessment, 37*(3), 504–511. https://doi.org/10.1007/s10862-014-9470-x

Zelkowitz, R. L., & Cole, D. A. (2019). Self-criticism as a transdiagnostic process in nonsuicidal self-injury and disordered eating: Systematic review and meta-analysis. *Suicide and Life-Threatening Behavior, 49*(1), 310–327. https://doi.org/10.1111/sltb.12436

Zelkowitz, R. L., & Cole, D. A. (2020). Longitudinal relations of self-criticism with disordered eating behaviors and non-suicidal self-injury. *International Journal of Eating Disorders, 53*(7), 1097–1107. https://doi.org/10.1002/eat.23284

Zetterqvist, M., Lundh, L. G., Dahlström, Ö., & Svedin, C. G. (2013). Prevalence and function of non-suicidal self-injury (NSSI) in a community sample of adolescents, using suggested DSM-5 criteria for a potential NSSI disorder. *Journal of Abnormal Child Psychology, 41*(5), 759–773. https://doi.org/10.1007/s10802-013-9712-5

Zetterqvist, M., Svedin, C. G., Fredlund, C., Priebe, G., Wadsby, M., & Jonsson, L. S. (2018). Self-reported nonsuicidal self-injury (NSSI) and sex as self-injury (SASI): Relationship to abuse, risk behaviors, trauma symptoms, self-esteem and attachment. *Psychiatry Research, 265*, 309–316. https://doi.org/10.1016/j.psychres.2018.05.013

CHAPTER 35

An Integrated Cognitive-Emotional Perspective of NSSI

Kate Tonta, Danyelle Greene, Penelope Hasking, *and* Mark Boyes

Abstract

This chapter covers an integrated cognitive-emotional perspective of nonsuicidal self-injury (NSSI). Recent understandings of NSSI highlight the importance of emotions in the experience of NSSI. Transdiagnostic cognitive processes associated with the onset, maintenance, and recovery of NSSI range between rumination, distress tolerance, self-criticism, and perfectionism. Thus, therapists must consider from a range of therapeutic approaches how to best target emotional difficulties, transdiagnostic processes, and behavior-specific thoughts and beliefs. The chapter details how patterns of cognition can amplify emotional distress. It then mentions how future research could use ecological momentary assessment methodology to track emotion, cognitive processes, and behavior-specific thoughts and beliefs.

Key Words: NSSI, emotions, transdiagnostic cognitive processes, therapists, behavior-specific thoughts, ecological momentary assessment, rumination, self-criticism, perfectionism

Introduction

Throughout this chapter, we will explore the importance of both emotional and cognition processes in the context of nonsuicidal self-injury (NSSI). Current understandings of NSSI emphasize the role of emotion in the experience of NSSI, but given what we know about the cognitive-behavioral conceptualization of emotional problems, it is also important to consider how cognitive processes (also see Browning & Muehlenkamp, this volume) may be involved. These cognitions include transdiagnostic cognitive processes, such as rumination and perfectionism, as well as NSSI-specific cognitions, such as what an individual expects will happen if they engage in NSSI, and their belief in their ability to resist engaging in NSSI. We first review the evidence on how an individual's experience of emotion (e.g., emotion reactivity, alexithymia, and avoidance) can lead to engagement in self-injury. Second, we review research on specific transdiagnostic cognitive processes which have been linked to NSSI, and we review how patterns of cognitions can amplify emotional distress. Third, we outline how behavior-specific outcome expectancies and self-efficacy beliefs work together to predict engagement in NSSI. Next, we discuss theoretical implications of integrating cognitive and emotional perspectives in the context of NSSI. Finally, we outline clinical implications and integrate the emotion and cognitive perspectives of NSSI using case examples. This format will highlight the interactions between emotion, thoughts, and beliefs and emphasize that these factors do not exist in isolation. Further, we utilize case examples to offer insight into how these processes may be modifiable from a cognitive-behavioral therapy (CBT) perspective.

Emotional Processing

A large section of the research attempting to explain engagement in NSSI has focused on an individual's experience of their emotions. The majority of models used to predict NSSI advocate an important role for emotional experience and the ability to regulate one's emotions in the onset and maintenance of self-injury (e.g., Emotional Cascade Theory, Selby et al., 2008; Nock's Integrated Model of NSSI, Nock, 2010; the Experiential Avoidance Model, Chapman et al., 2006; see Hird et al., this volume). Theoretically, individuals who self-injure are more reactive and more sensitive to emotions, experience emotions more intensely, and do not quickly recover from an emotional experience (Linehan, 2018). Indeed, the most reported motive for self-injury is to regulate negative emotions (Taylor et al., 2018; see Taylor et al., this volume). Much of the current literature has focused on the role of negative emotions in predicting engagement in self-injury, with little focus given to the role of positive emotions in predicting self-injury (e.g., Jenkins & Schmitz, 2012). Yet, studying the role of positive emotion is also important in the context of NSSI, with evidence suggesting that high levels of positive affect could be a protective factor that reduces the odds of NSSI (Hasking et al., 2018). Further, research indicates that self-injury is often used to downregulate strong negative emotions and upregulate low levels of positive emotions (Claes et al., 2010). On the contrary, similar to difficulties processing negative emotions, difficulties processing positive emotions has been associated with poor emotion regulatory skills and engagement in NSSI (Greene et al., 2021; Greene, Hasking, Boyes et al., 2020; Jenkins & Schmitz, 2012).

Emotion Reactivity

Being highly emotionally reactive might be a key factor in an individual's ability to process and regulate their emotions (Gross, 2015). Emotion reactivity relates to how strongly and persistently an individual experiences their emotions in response to a wide variety of situations (Cole et al., 1994; Eisenberg et al., 1995). Emotion reactivity is thought to be synonymous across valence, implying that if an individual experiences strong negative emotions, they will also experience strong positive emotions (Larsen et al., 1987). Unsurprisingly, past research implies that individuals who engage in NSSI experience negative emotions more strongly than individuals who have never engaged in NSSI (Anderson & Crowther, 2012; Boyes et al., 2020; Jenkins & Schmitz, 2012; Mettler et al., 2021; Nock et al., 2008). In regard to positive reactivity, research is limited and mixed. Unexpectedly, Boyes et al. (2020) found that individuals with a history of NSSI were less reactive to positive emotions than individuals without a history of NSSI. Yet, Mettler et al. (2021) found that there was no difference in positive reactivity between individuals who have and individuals who have not engaged in NSSI. Nevertheless, poor emotion regulation skills appear to predict NSSI beyond that of emotion reactivity (Zelkowitz & Cole, 2016). Thus, we should consider what might hamper an individual's ability to regulate their emotions.

Alexithymia

Beyond emotional reactivity, several authors (Gross, 2015; Preece et al., 2017; Taylor, 1994), consider an individual's inability to attend to and appraise their feelings (alexithymia) to be a rate-limiting factor for effective emotion regulation. Alexithymia is a multifaceted personality trait that encompasses three key facets of poor emotional processing: (a) difficulties identifying personal emotions, (b) difficulties describing one's emotions to others, and (c) a tendency to place one's attention on the external world as opposed to one's internal emotional states (Bagby et al., 1994; Preece et al., 2017). Specifically, individuals who have elevated levels of alexithymia rarely orient their attention to internal feelings and find it difficult to accurately appraise those very feelings (Preece et al., 2017). Theoretically, having difficulties appraising and attending to one's feelings will greatly impair a person's capacity to respond to and regulate adverse emotional states (Gross, 2015; Preece et al., 2017) which, in turn, may lead an individual to respond by engaging in self-injury to help regulate adverse emotions. Furthermore, people with elevated alexithymia have a tendency to confuse bodily sensations with emotions and overemphasize physical sensations (Lumley et al., 1996). Thus, self-injury might help orient one's attention away from the feelings they are having problems appraising, onto the physical sensations associated with NSSI (e.g., pain) that individuals with high levels of alexithymia have less difficulties processing and understanding (Lumley et al., 1996).

Recent systematic reviews and meta-analyses (Greene, Boyes, & Hasking, 2020; Norman et al., 2020) suggest that individuals who have difficulties identifying and describing their feelings are more likely to engage in NSSI than individuals who do not have difficulties identifying and describing their feelings. Yet, an individual's tendency to focus on the external world opposed to their personal thoughts and feelings seems to not influence engagement in NSSI (Greene, Boyes, & Hasking, 2020; Norman et al., 2020). The majority of the work focuses on an individual's ability to identify and describe negative emotions (Preece et al., 2020), with little focus on an individual's ability to appraise positive emotions.

The importance of considering valence-specific alexithymia has been highlighted in the literature. Specifically, Van der Velde et al. (2013) highlight that neural associates of alexithymia were conditional on valence of the feelings that were being appraised. When individuals were processing negative content, alexithymia was associated with a reduced response of the amygdala, indicating that the individual was placing less attention on the content. Whereas when individuals were processing positive content, alexithymia was related to reduced activation of the precuneus and right insula, precluding reduced emotional awareness. Furthermore, individuals typically have more difficulties appraising negative emotions than positive emotions (Preece et al., 2018). In relation to NSSI, recent research (Greene, Hasking, Boyes et al., 2020; Greene, Hasking, Boyes, & Preece, 2020) has found that, compared to individuals who have no history of NSSI, individuals with a history of NSSI not only have more difficulties identifying and describing negative emotions but also have more difficulties identifying and describing positive emotions.

Experiential Avoidance

Considering that NSSI is often engaged in to regulate adverse emotional states (Klonsky, 2007), individuals who engage in NSSI often have elevated levels of experiential avoidance (Chapman et al., 2006). Experiential avoidance is the propensity to escape, control, suppress, and modify adverse emotional states (Hayes et al., 2004). Thus, NSSI might be used to avoid an adverse experience (e.g., emotions, thoughts, images, and memories) when an individual is unwilling or unable to sit with the experience. Relatedly, Anderson and Crowther (2012) reported that individuals who either had a history of NSSI or had recently engaged in NSSI had a greater tendency toward avoidant behaviors. Likewise, Nielsen et al. (2016) found that individuals who had engaged in NSSI during their lifetime had a stronger propensity to avoid internal thoughts, feelings, and other internal experiences. Further, the suppression of unwanted negative emotions, and higher levels of cognitive avoidance have been associated with self-injury (Anderson & Crowther, 2012; Claes et al., 2010). In a recent systematic review, Brereton and McGlinchey (2019) found a consistent association between experiential avoidance and self-injury in the literature.

The relationships between emotional difficulties (e.g., regulation, reactivity, processing, and avoidance), and NSSI are well documented and are reflected in theories used to explain the onset and maintenance of NSSI. Current understandings of NSSI emphasize the role of emotion in the experience of NSSI but pay less attention to verbal cognitions (i.e., thoughts) and how these thoughts might interact with emotional processes. Important cognitions include transdiagnostic cognitive processes (e.g., rumination) as well as NSSI-specific cognitions, such as what an individual anticipates from engaging in NSSI and their belief in their ability to resist self-injury.

Transdiagnostic Cognitive Processes

There are a range of transdiagnostic cognitive processes that have been associated with NSSI, including rumination, distress tolerance, self-criticism, and perfectionism. Here we review how these cognitive processes are related to the onset, maintenance, and recovery of NSSI.

Distress Tolerance

Distress tolerance is a transdiagnostic process that includes an individual's perceived capacity and behavioral ability to tolerate negative or unwanted emotional states (Leyro et al.,

2010). As a transdiagnostic process, distress tolerance is implicated in the onset and maintenance of a range of psychopathologies and behavioral outcomes including eating disorders, alcohol use, and NSSI. An individual with a low capacity to tolerate distress may engage in dysregulated behaviors (such as alcohol misuse, restrictive or binge eating, and NSSI) as a way of avoiding unwanted or unpleasant emotional experiences. Individuals with poor distress tolerance may have beliefs or cognitions about how they cannot experience negative emotions and may feel a strong need to engage in strategies that alleviate or distract from those feelings. When an individual successfully distracts themselves from or alters their negative emotional state by engaging in NSSI, that behavior becomes a negatively reinforced response to distress which is more likely to be utilized in future.

Distress tolerance has been conceptualized as comprised of four domains: tolerability and aversiveness, appraisal and acceptability, tendency to absorb attention and disrupt functioning, and regulation of emotions (action tendencies; Simons & Gaher, 2005). According to this definition, individuals with lower distress tolerance will report that distress is intolerable or unbearable; they will assess their distress as unacceptable and potentially shameful, will find that their attention is more absorbed by their distress, and will make attempts to engage in behaviors which assist with avoidance or alleviation of their distress (such as NSSI).

There is a range of evidence supporting the role of distress tolerance in NSSI. Individuals who have a history of self-injury consistently report lower levels of distress tolerance than individuals who do not self-injure (e.g., Lin et al., 2018; Slabbert et al., 2020), and these differences are found across all four facets (tolerance, appraisal, absorption, and regulation) as well as the higher-order distress tolerance factor (Slabbert et al., 2021). Lower distress tolerance is also significantly associated with increased frequency of self-injury among those who have a history of the behavior (Anestis et al., 2013).

Rumination

Rumination is a cognitive process where, in response to distress, an individual thinks repetitively about the nature, causes, and consequences of their negative emotional experience. This involves repetitive thinking about past problems, current stressors, and worries about the future and about emotional states. Individuals engage in rumination in an attempt to cognitively regulate affect—in other words, repetitive thinking is an ineffective problem-solving strategy that appears to intensify and prolong distress. Engagement in rumination is associated with increased intensity and duration of negative affect (McIntosh, 1996; Nolen-Hoeksema, 1991). Given understanding of NSSI as a behavior to regulate unwanted or unpleasant emotions, rumination may increase the risk of engaging in NSSI by increasing intensity and duration of negative emotions. It is therefore no surprise that theoretical models suggest that ruminative cognitions in NSSI are an important part of the experience (e.g., the Emotional Cascade Model, Selby et al., 2008; Cognitive-Emotional Model of NSSI, Hasking et al., 2017).

Rumination has been positively related to NSSI in a range of studies (e.g., Dawkins, et al., 2019; Nicolai et al., 2016), and there is self-report and experimental evidence that elevated rumination is associated with NSSI (Arbuthnott et al., 2015; Selby et al., 2010; Slabbert et al., 2018). Individuals who engage in NSSI consistently report higher levels of trait rumination, and daily fluctuations in rumination are also predictive of daily NSSI episodes (Selby et al., 2013). There has been some exploration of which content of rumination may be more or less related to episodes of NSSI—one study using ecological momentary assessment (EMA) found that individual episodes of NSSI were prospectively related to increased rumination on past problems but the relationship was inverse for rumination on concerns about the future and about emotional states (Selby et al., 2013).

Self-Criticism
Self-criticism is another transdiagnostic process which is associated with increased risk of NSSI as well as other adverse outcomes such as eating disorders. Self-criticism is the tendency to respond to oneself and one's attributes in a negative way. It has been consistently positively associated with engagement in NSSI (Zelkowitz & Cole, 2019), such that higher levels of self-criticism are associated with higher risk for NSSI. Theoretical models of NSSI suggest a role for aversive cognitions, such as self-criticism (Hasking et al., 2017; Nock, 2010), as risk factors for engaging in NSSI, and this is supported by empirical findings across adolescent (e.g., Baetens et al., 2015) and adult samples (e.g., Gilbert et al., 2010) and across clinical (e.g., Itzhaky et al., 2016) and nonclinical samples (e.g., Hooley & St. Germain, 2014).

Perfectionism
Perfectionism is also a transdiagnostic process that has been implicated in nonsuicidal self-injury. Perfectionism is the setting of personally demanding high standards and overly critical evaluation of self-worth in relation to attainment of those standards (Shafran et al., 2002). Perfectionism is related to the onset and maintenance of a wide range of psychopathologies including eating disorders, anxiety, mood disorders, and obsessive-compulsive disorders. Perfectionism has also been associated with other outcomes related to psychopathology, including suicidal ideation, and psychological distress (Limburg et al., 2017). There is evidence that perfectionism is associated with NSSI in a range of demographic groups (Gyori & Balazs, 2021) including adolescents (Luyckx et al., 2015), adults (Claes et al., 2012), and clinical (Claes et al., 2012) and nonclinical samples (Hoff & Muehlenkamp, 2009). However, there is limited evidence for mechanisms that may explain the relationship between perfectionism and NSSI.

NSSI Specific Cognitions: Outcome Expectancies and Self-Efficacy Beliefs

According to social cognitive theory, our personal thoughts and feelings, behaviors, and environment interact with each other in reciprocal relationships (Bandura, 1986).

Bandura (1986) implies that behaviors are initiated and maintained by two thought processes, outcome expectancies and self-efficacy beliefs. Outcome expectancies are an individual's anticipated outcomes of a given behavior, and self-efficacy beliefs are an individual's beliefs about their ability to successfully engage in a behavior. If an individual believes the behavior will result in a positive outcome, and they can successfully perform the behavior, they will be more likely to engage in that behavior. Anticipating positive outcomes facilitates engagement, whereas anticipating negative outcomes is protective against engaging in a behavior (Bandura, 1986). Refusal self-efficacy, defined as a person's belief in their ability to resist a behavior, is a salient predictor of engagement in risky behaviors, including NSSI (Dawkins, Hasking, & Boyes, 2021b; Dawkins et al., 2019; Hasking & Rose, 2016).

Research into NSSI-specific outcome expectancies is relatively new, but there are several relevant studies that have been published in Australia over the past few years. Unsurprisingly, anticipating emotion regulatory outcomes from NSSI is associated with an increased likelihood of self-injury (Dawkins, Hasking, & Boyes, 2021a; Dawkins et al., 2019; Greene et al., 2021; Greene, Hasking, & Boyes, 2021; Hasking & Rose, 2016). Conversely, anticipating that self-injury will be painful decreases the likelihood of NSSI. Further, individuals who have a history of NSSI are unlikely to anticipate that self-injury will help them to communicate their distress to others. The anticipation of negative self-beliefs (e.g., hatred of self and seeing oneself as a failure) from engagement in NSSI is associated with a decreased likelihood of self-injury (Dawkins, Hasking, & Boyes, 2021a; Dawkins et al., 2019; Greene, Hasking, & Boyes, 2021; Hasking & Rose, 2016).

Individuals are more likely to engage in NSSI if they believe they do not have the capacity to resist the behavior (Dawkins, Hasking, & Boyes, 2021a, 2021b; Greene, Hasking, & Boyes, 2021). The majority of this work was conducted with a general measure of NSSI refusal self-efficacy, yet Bandura highlighted the importance of considering how different contexts may impact an individual's behavior-specific beliefs. Dawkins, Hasking, and Boyes (2021a) recently developed a measure of self-efficacy to resist NSSI across three different contexts: risk contexts (e.g., when feeling distressed), protective contexts (e.g., when another reassures me), and contexts where the individual is reminded of NSSI (e.g., seeing images of NSSI). Unsurprisingly, reduced ability to resist NSSI in risk contexts was a stronger predictor of NSSI than reduced ability to resist NSSI in protective contexts and in contexts when the individual is reminded of NSSI (Dawkins, Hasking, & Boyes, 2021a).

Bandura (1986) suggests that outcome expectancies and self-efficacy beliefs should be considered in tandem. Even if an individual anticipates a positive outcome from self-injury, they may be less likely to engage in self-injury if they hold strong beliefs in their ability to resist NSSI (Dawkins et al., 2019; Dawkins, Hasking, & Boyes, 2021a, 2021b). Further, even individuals who anticipate that engaging in NSSI will be painful have a high chance of engaging in NSSI if they believe they are unlikely to resist NSSI in protective contexts (e.g., when someone reassures me; Dawkins, Hasking, & Boyes, 2021a) and in general (Dawkins, Hasking, & Boyes, 2021b). Consistent with social cognitive theory, a combination of negative outcome expectancies (e.g., pain and communication) and strong self-efficacy to resist NSSI appear to be salient protective factors against engaging in NSSI (Dawkins, Hasking, & Boyes, 2021a, 2021b).

A few studies have integrated emotional processes and NSSI-specific verbal cognitions (i.e., thoughts) in predicting/explaining engagement in self-injury. Specifically, Dawkins, Hasking, and Boyes (2021a) found that a combination of low self-efficacy to resist NSSI and heightened emotional reactivity predicted engagement in NSSI. Specifically, individuals who are emotionally reactive might be at increased risk of experiencing emotions that they believe they cannot control, and thus believe they cannot resist self-injury. These individuals will be more likely to self-injure to regulate their emotions. Further, a combination of heightened emotion reactivity and anticipating that self-injury would increase negative self-beliefs predicted recent engagement in NSSI (Dawkins, Hasking, & Boyes, 2021a).

Emotional processing difficulties (e.g., alexithymia) may be indirectly associated with self-injury through NSSI-specific thoughts and beliefs. Specifically, individuals who have difficulties identifying and describing their emotions might engage in NSSI because they believe it will help them to regulate their emotions (Greene et al., 2021; Greene, Hasking, & Boyes, 2021). Further, individuals who have emotion processing difficulties might believe they are unable to resist engaging in NSSI under circumstances where they are required to appraise their feelings, which in turn might lead them to engaging in NSSI to regulate their emotions. However, work integrating emotional processes and NSSI specific thoughts and beliefs is limited, and further work is needed. Yet, the few studies that have integrated the two perspectives are promising and highlight the importance of considering behavior-specific thoughts and beliefs during emotionally charged experiences in the context of NSSI.

Theoretical Implications

The current body of literature prompts other ways of conceptualizing NSSI beyond emotion regulation. Specifically, our theoretical understanding of NSSI should shift away from solely emotion-focused theories and move toward an integrated cognitive-emotional understanding. The cognitive-emotional model of NSSI (Hasking et al., 2017) combines aspects from emotion regulatory models and cognitive processes outlined by social cognitive theory to provide a more thorough perspective on the occurrence and maintenance of NSSI. This model can be used as a basis for future research avenues.

From a cognitive-emotional perspective, individuals hold specific thoughts and beliefs about the functions various behaviors might serve (e.g., exercise, drinking, and smoking), and under what circumstances each behavior(s) could be used to achieve a desirable outcome. Theoretically, simply conceptualizing NSSI as a result of poor emotion regulation does not allow us to understand why an individual might engage in NSSI over a range of other behaviors that might serve a similar function (e.g., alcohol use and restrictive/binge eating). Further, by taking an integrated perspective we can determine under what circumstances an individual may or may not engage in NSSI, and when they might choose to employ an alternative behavior. Thus, future research could take a broader approach and evaluate under what circumstances an individual might engage in NSSI and under what circumstances they might choose to engage in another behavior.

For example, a student might exhibit high levels of perfectionism and a tendency to strongly react to emotionally volatile situations. The individual believes that both self-injury and consuming alcohol could help relieve intense emotions. However, they have high self-efficacy to resist NSSI in public but do not have the skills to resist consuming alcohol. When with a group of friends, the student receives a mark on an assignment that does not meet their high standards and finds this emotionally distressing. In this situation, this individual is likely to drink alcohol to reduce distress rather than engage in self-injury. Alternatively, if the individual was alone when they found out their score on the assignment they might self-injure instead of consuming alcohol as they believe that self-injury relieves tension faster than drinking. Yet another individual might anticipate that both NSSI and risky drinking can regulate adverse emotional experiences and believe they can effectively engage in both behaviors, but also have other emotion regulation strategies they can access in the situation to prevent them from engaging in either behavior. Thus, many combinations of contextually specific emotional and cognitive factors can determine whether or not an individual might self-injure in an emotionally volatile situation. The cognitive-emotional perspective lends itself perfectly to EMA research. Therefore, the next step would be EMA research that tracks emotion, cognitive processes, and behavior-specific thoughts and beliefs in real time to determine under which circumstances someone might or might not self-injure.

Clinical Implications

In considering the clinical implications of the current understanding of emotional and cognitive perspectives of NSSI, it is important to consider which of these factors may be more readily modified in therapeutic interventions. By considering transdiagnostic processes for intervention, we may be able to reduce NSSI behaviors in the context of a protective mental health intervention. The advantage of this is that interventions are not primarily focused on reducing behavioral outcomes—rather, those reductions are the logical consequence of reducing harmful transdiagnostic cognitive and emotional processes that contribute more globally to the experience of distress. This person-centered approach aims to improve the psychological health of the individual holistically rather than simply reducing self-injurious behavior. For example, providing an individual with alternative ways of regulating intense emotions and helping to reduce rumination through CBT or another evidence-based intervention may theoretically reduce the drive to engage in NSSI as the individual has alternative strategies to self-regulate.

First, with respect to outcome expectancies and self-efficacy beliefs, it is worth considering how these may be modified in therapy. Clinicians may wish to consider the role of self-efficacy beliefs to resist engaging in NSSI as well as self-efficacy to engage in alternative behaviors. Self-efficacy beliefs can be fostered or supported using motivational interviewing techniques. Although there have been no explicit tests of this intervention in the context of NSSI, motivational interviewing is a behavior-change technique that specifically aims to address self-efficacy beliefs of individuals (Miller & Rollnick, 1991). This technique has effectively modified self-efficacy beliefs and subsequent behavioral outcomes for a range of health behaviors including alcohol and substance use, smoking, diet, and exercise (e.g., Bein et al., 1993; Berman et al., 2010; Burke et al., 2003). Motivational interviewing has also been suggested as an intervention in the context of NSSI to encourage readiness for change (Kress & Hoffman, 2008) and treatment seeking (Kamen, 2009). It is plausible that motivational interviewing may be used to bolster an individual's self-efficacy to resist engaging in NSSI (e.g., by prompting the individual to think of instances where they may have had urges to engage in NSSI but did not engage), and this may impact future NSSI behaviors.

Another potential avenue for intervention is with respect to perfectionism, which can be effectively reduced through CBT (Lloyd et al., 2015). CBT for perfectionism has been efficacious in a range of ages (including adolescents and adults) in different settings (clinical samples including eating disorders, major depression, obsessive-compulsive disorder, as well as nonclinical samples). These interventions are effective when delivered individually and in groups, as well as face to face and online (Suh et al., 2019). Further, these interventions demonstrate the transdiagnostic benefits of reducing perfectionism on outcomes including mood, anxiety, stress, eating disorder symptoms, and obsessive-compulsive symptoms (Limburg et al., 2017). CBT for perfectionism is also effective in an unguided online self-help format (Galloway et al., 2022; Shu et al., 2019), demonstrating a cost-effective potential direction for support.

Rumination may also be effectively modified using evidence-based interventions. Interventions known to be effective for reducing rumination include rumination-focused CBT, mindfulness-based CBT, and metacognitive therapy (Watkins & Roberts, 2020; Wells & Papageorgiou, 2003). Interventions for rumination are effective at reducing rumination as well as associated psychological distress (Watkins & Roberts, 2020), although no studies have explored the direct effects of these interventions on NSSI behaviors.

Arguably, most psychological interventions aim to improve emotional regulation. Some specific examples of this include dialectical behavior therapy (DBT; Linehan, 2014)—one of the four key modules is targeted at emotion regulation and aims to increase understanding of and reduce vulnerability to intense emotions as well as changing unwanted emotions (Neacsiu et al., 2014). DBT is an intervention that was specifically designed to address suicidal and nonsuicidal behaviors, and there is meta-analytic evidence that it is effective in reducing the incidence of NSSI (Hunnicutt Hollenbaugh & Lenz, 2018; see Chapman et al., this volume) as well as other symptoms of psychological distress. CBT encompasses a range of techniques that aim to alter cognitions that drive unpleasant or unwanted emotions, such as cognitive restructuring with thought diaries and identifying and modifying unhelpful thinking styles. Evidence suggests that CBT can improve cognitive reappraisal (Forkmann et al., 2014), an emotion regulation strategy consistently associated with reduced engagement in NSSI (Richmond et al., 2017).

Distress tolerance is another construct that may also benefit from a range of intervention techniques. The DBT skills program has a core module on distress tolerance which aims to provide clients with skills to tolerate their distress by encouraging acceptance of emotions and to prevent behaviors and cognitions that may worsen the experience of emotions. As mentioned previously, trials of DBT have been demonstrated as effective in improving distress tolerance (McMain et al., 2017) and in reducing self-injury (Hunnicutt Hollenbaugh & Lenz, 2018).

An interesting avenue for future research is in the efficacy of emotion-focused therapy for people who engage in NSSI. Emotion-focused therapy (EFT) involves building understanding and acceptance of emotions (Greenberg, 2010) and four of the six core principles map directly onto the domains of distress tolerance. Although this has not been specifically applied in populations who engage in NSSI, EFT has effectively reduced distress tolerance in other populations and contexts (e.g., Faghih & Kazemi, 2018).

Alexithymia is another transdiagnostic process that may benefit from interventions that seek to improve the individual's awareness and understanding of emotions. There is evidence that mindfulness-based interventions are effective at reducing alexithymia by increasing awareness of bodily sensations and the associated emotions. These interventions may be individual or group-based sessions (Norman et al., 2019). There is also evidence that DBT may improve alexithymia (Linehan, 2014) with an initial focus on how to identify, accept, and express one's thoughts, feelings, and physical sensations. Although there is no research exploring the impact of DBT on alexithymia, there is theoretical justification for its utility in this application and evidence that DBT has positive impacts on reducing self-injury. Finally, one other possible intervention which may, in theory, be useful for individuals high in alexithymia is EFT. As noted earlier, EFT psychoeducation provides training around awareness and understanding of emotions (Greenberg, 2010). However, it is worth noting that individuals higher in alexithymia may find EFT to be an unappealing or unacceptable option given the nomenclature.

In this section, we have reviewed a number of cognitive and emotional processes that may be targeted in therapeutic interventions. Importantly, these suggestions are unique in that we make recommendations about transdiagnostic processes that are known to predispose a range of symptoms of psychological distress, including low mood and anxiety as well as a range of behavioral outcomes. We made suggestions for interventions at a transdiagnostic level—these interventions may help to support the overall psychological functioning of individuals and reduce NSSI behaviors because of increased coping and psychological well-being. However, many of these suggestions have not yet been formally studied in clinical trials, indicating an important direction for future research.

Case Examples

Emotions, thoughts, and beliefs must be considered dynamic processes, meaning that emotions, thoughts, and beliefs continually influence one other and should not be considered in isolation. From a cognitive-emotional perspective, an individual brings their emotional processing skills, cognitive thought processes, and any behavior-specific thoughts and beliefs to a given situation (Hasking et al., 2017). In this section we highlight the interactions between emotions, thoughts, and beliefs and NSSI using two case examples. Further, we provide insight into how these processes may be modifiable from a CBT perspective.

Example One

Taylor is seeking therapy to help them understand their engagement in self-injury. Taylor describes that during and after arguments with their parents they felt intense negative emotions which lasted for a long time (high levels of reactivity and perseveration) and tended to ruminate on the situation and the associated emotions they were feeling. When asked what strategies they used to regulate their emotions when experiencing adverse situations, they responded that they tended to engage in NSSI when the emotions became too intense. Taylor stated that during these situations, they believed that self-injury would help them to achieve emotional relief and escape the volatile emotional situation (i.e., positive outcome expectancies) and because of this, they believed they would be unable to resist self-injury during the situation.

The clinical implications for this example may include supporting Taylor's self-efficacy to resist engaging in NSSI through motivational interviewing, as well as considering the possible negative outcome expectancies (e.g., pain and negative self-beliefs, if they exist). A clinician may wish to assist Taylor to build skills disengaging from repetitive negative thoughts by using interventions for rumination such as CBT, mindfulness-based cognitive therapy, or metacognitive therapy. The choice of intervention style for this should be guided by the clinical judgment about which theoretical orientation is likely to resonate with Taylor.

Example Two

Darren, a man in his early 30s, is seeking counseling because he is having difficulties communicating his emotions to his partner (high levels of alexithymia), and she often becomes frustrated with him due to the lack of communication. The therapist gathers from talks with Darren that he feels as though he is an invalid and a worthless partner due to these difficulties (high levels of self-criticism). Furthermore, when asked how he feels when his wife becomes frustrated with him, Darren answers that he "doesn't know" and always finds the situation to be too much and is unable to resist burning himself with his cigarette or drinking a beer to distract him from the situation.

In this situation, a clinician has a number of therapeutic directions (the prioritization of which should be guided by the client's preference and clinician's recommendations). With respect to the interpersonal difficulties exacerbated by Darren's alexithymia, EFT for couples may help the client to identify and understand his emotions and how they may provide important information about the interpersonal challenges. It may also be worthwhile engaging in CBT around unhelpful thinking styles (self-criticism about his value as a partner). Darren's low tolerance of distress (feeling things are "too much") may benefit from DBT skills training or other elements of EFT or CBT, while the client's alexithymia may also be supported by DBT skills training or CBT around awareness of emotions.

Conclusion

From a cognitive-emotional perspective, behaviors such as NSSI are maintained not only by emotional processing difficulties but also by transdiagnostic thought processes, as well as behavior-specific thoughts and beliefs. Future research could use ecological momentary assessment methodology to track emotion, cognitive processes, and behavior-specific thoughts and beliefs to highlight how emotion and thought processes interact in real time. Furthermore, more clinical research is required that investigates how targeting transdiagnostic and behavior-specific thought processes could be beneficial for NSSI recovery. There is ample support for CBT for perfectionism in reducing symptoms of eating disorders, and thus given the association between perfectionism and NSSI, CBT for perfectionism may be also beneficial for treating NSSI. Likewise, targeting self-efficacy to resist drinking through motivational interviewing is well researched; research investigating a similar therapeutic approach in the context of NSSI would also be beneficial. In conclusion, while considering the client's preference, it may be valuable for a therapist to consider from a range of therapeutic approaches how best to target emotional difficulties, transdiagnostic processes, and behavior-specific thoughts and beliefs.

References

Anderson, N. L., & Crowther, J. H. (2012). Using the experiential avoidance model of non-suicidal self-injury: Understanding who stops and who continues. *Archives of Suicide Research*, *16*(2), 124–134. https://doi.org/10.1080/13811118.2012.667329.

Anestis, M. D., Pennings, S. M., Lavender, J. M., Tull, M. T., & Gratz, K. L. (2013). Low distress tolerance as an indirect risk factor for suicidal behavior: Considering the explanatory role of non-suicidal self-injury. *Comprehensive Psychiatry*, *54*(7), 996–1002. https://doi.org/10.1016/j.comppsych.2013.04.005

Arbuthnott, A. E., Lewis, S. P., & Bailey, H. N. (2015). Rumination and emotions in nonsuicidal self-injury and eating disorder behaviors: A preliminary test of the Emotional Cascade Model. *Journal of Clinical Psychology*, *71*(1), 62–71. https://doi.org/10.1002/jclp.22115

Baetens, I., Claes, L., Hasking, P., Smits, D., Grietens, H., Onghena, P., & Martin, G. (2015). The relationship between parental expressed emotions and non-suicidal self-injury: The mediating roles of self-criticism and depression. *Journal of Child and Family Studies*, *24*(2), 491–498. https://doi.org/10.1007/s10826-013-9861-8

Bagby, R. M., Parker, J. D., & Taylor, G. J. (1994). The twenty-item Toronto Alexithymia Scale--I. Item selection and cross-validation of the factor structure. *Journal of Psychosomatic Research*, *38*(1), 23–32. https://doi.org/10.1016/0022-3999(94)90005-1

Bandura, A. (1986). *Social foundations of thought and action*. Prentice-Hall.

Bein, T. H., Miller, W. R., & Boroughs, J. M. (1993). Motivational interviewing with alcohol outpatients. *Behavioural and Cognitive Psychotherapy*, *21*(4), 347–356. https://doi.org/10.1017/S135246580001167X

Berman, A. H., Forsberg, L., Durbeej, N., Källmén, H., & Hermansson, U. (2010). Single-session motivational interviewing for drug detoxification inpatients: Effects on self-efficacy, stages of change and substance use. *Substance Use & Misuse*, *45*(3), 384–402. https://doi.org/10.3109/10826080903452488

Boyes, M. E., Wilmot, A., & Hasking, P. A. (2020). Nonsuicidal self-injury-related differences in the experience of negative and positive emotion. *Suicide and Life-Threatening Behavior*, *50*(2), 437–448. https://doi.org/10.1111/sltb.12599

Brereton, A., & McGlinchey, E. (2019). Self-harm, emotion regulation, and experiential avoidance: A systematic review. *Archives of Suicide Research*, *24*(Supp. 1), 1–24. https://doi.org/10.1080/13811118.2018.1563575

Burke, B. L., Arkowitz, H., & Menchola, M. (2003). The efficacy of motivational interviewing: A meta-analysis of controlled clinical trials. *Journal of Consulting and Clinical Psychology*, *71*(5), 843–861. https://doi.org/10.1037/0022-006X.71.5.843

Chapman, A. L., Gratz, K. L., & Brown, M. Z. (2006). Solving the puzzle of deliberate self-harm: The experiential avoidance model. *Behaviour Research and Therapy*, *44*(3), 371–394. https://doi.org/https://doi.org/10.1016/j.brat.2005.03.005

Claes, L., Klonsky, E. D., Muehlenkamp, J., Kuppens, P., & Vandereycken, W. (2010). The affect-regulation function of nonsuicidal self-injury in eating-disordered patients: Which affect states are regulated? *Comprehensive Psychiatry*, *51*(4), 386–392. https://doi.org/10.1016/j.comppsych.2009.09.001

Claes, L., Soenens, B., Vansteenkiste, M., & Vandereycken, W. (2012). The scars of the inner critic: Perfectionism and nonsuicidal self-injury in eating disorders. *European Eating Disorder Review*, *20*(3), 196–202. https://doi.org/10.1002/erv.1158

Cole, P. M., Michel, M. K., & Teti, L. O. D. (1994). The development of emotion regulation and dysregulation: A clinical perspective. *Monographs of the Society for Research in Child Development*, *59*(2–3), 73–102.

Dawkins, J. C., Hasking, P. A., & Boyes, M. E. (2021a). Applying social cognitive theory to nonsuicidal self-injury: Interactions between expectancy beliefs. *Journal of American College Health*, *70*(7), 1990–1998. https://doi.org/10.1080/07448481.2020.1841771

Dawkins, J. C., Hasking, P. A., & Boyes, M. E. (2021b). Thoughts and beliefs about nonsuicidal self-injury: An application of social cognitive theory. *Journal of American College Health*, *69*(4), 428–434. https://doi.org/10.1080/07448481.2019.1679817

Dawkins, J. C., Hasking, P. A., Boyes, M. E., Greene, D., & Passchier, C. (2019). Applying a cognitive-emotional model to nonsuicidal self-injury. *Stress and Health: Journal of the International Society for the Investigation of Stress*, *35*(1), 39–48. https://doi.org/10.1002/smi.2837

Eisenberg, N., Fabes, R. A., Murphy, B., Maszk, P., Smith, M., & Karbon, M. (1995). The role of emotionality and regulation in children's social functioning: A longitudinal study. *Child Development*, *66*(5), 1360–1384.

Faghih, S., Kazemi, H. (2018). The effectiveness of emotionally focused therapy on distress tolerance in infertile couples in Isfahan. *Community Health Journal*, *12*(1), 22–29. https://doi.org/10.22123/chj.2018.110652.1068

Forkmann, T., Scherer, A., Pawelzik, M., Mainz, V., Drueke, B., Boecker, M., & Gauggel, S. (2014). Does cognitive behavior therapy alter emotion regulation in inpatients with a depressive disorder? *Psychology Research and Behavior Management*, *7*, 147–153. https://doi.org/10.2147/PRBM.S59421

Galloway, R., Watson, H., Greene, D., Shafran, R., & Egan, S. J. (2022). The efficacy of randomised controlled trials of cognitive behaviour therapy for perfectionism: A systematic review and meta-analysis. *Cognitive Behaviour Therapy*, *51*(2), 170–184. https://doi.org/10.1080/16506073.2021.1952302

Gilbert, P., McEwan, K., Irons, C., Bhundia, R., Christie, R., Broomhead, C., & Rockliff, H. (2010). Self-harm in a mixed clinical population: The roles of self-criticism, shame, and social rank. *British Journal of Clinical Psychology*, *49*(4), 563–576. https://doi.org/10.1348/014466509X479771

Greenberg, L. S. (2010). Emotion-focused therapy: A clinical synthesis. *FOCUS*, *8*(1), 32–42. https://doi.org/10.1176/foc.8.1.foc32

Greene, D., Boyes, M., & Hasking, P. (2020). The associations between alexithymia and both non-suicidal self-injury and risky drinking: A systematic review and meta-analysis. *Journal of Affective Disorders, 260*, 140–166. https://doi.org/10.1016/j.jad.2019.08.088

Greene, D., Hasking, P., & Boyes, M. (2021). A comparison of the associations between alexithymia and both non-suicidal self-injury and risky drinking: The roles of explicit outcome expectancies and refusal self-efficacy. *Stress and Health: Journal of the International Society for the Investigation of Stress, 37*(2), 272–284. https://doi.org/10.1002/smi.2991

Greene, D., Hasking, P., Boyes, M., & Preece, D. (2020). Measurement invariance of two measures of alexithymia in students who do and who do not engage in non-suicidal self-injury and risky drinking. *Journal of Psychopathology and Behavioral Assessment, 42*(4), 808–825. https://doi.org/10.1007/s10862-020-09806-7

Gross, J. J. (2015). Emotion regulation: Current status and future prospects. *Psychological inquiry, 26*(1), 1–26. https://doi.org/10.1080/1047840X.2014.940781

Gyori, D., & Balazs, J. (2021). Nonsuicidal self-injury and perfectionism: A systematic review. *Frontiers in Psychiatry, 12*, Article 691147. https://doi.org/10.3389/fpsyt.2021.691147

Hasking, P., & Rose, A. (2016). A preliminary application of social cognitive theory to nonsuicidal self-injury. *Journal of Youth and Adolescence, 45*(8), 1560–1574. https://doi.org/10.1007/s10964-016-0449-7

Hasking, P. A., Di Simplicio, M., McEvoy, P. M., & Rees, C. S. (2018). Emotional cascade theory and non-suicidal self-injury: The importance of imagery and positive affect. *Cognition and Emotion, 32*(5), 941–952. https://doi.org/10.1080/02699931.2017.1368456

Hasking, P., Whitlock, J., Voon, D., & Rose, A. (2017). A cognitive-emotional model of NSSI: Using emotion regulation and cognitive processes to explain why people self-injure. *Cognition and Emotion, 31*(8), 1543–1556. https://doi.org/10.1080/02699931.2016.1241219

Hayes, S. C., Strosahl, K., Wilson, K. G., Bissett, R. T., Pistorello, J., Toarmino, D., Polusny, M. A., Dykstra, T. A., Batten, S. V., & Bergan, J. (2004). Measuring experiential avoidance: A preliminary test of a working model. *The Psychological Record, 54*(4), 553–578. https://doi.org/10.1007/BF03395492

Hoff, E. R., & Muehlenkamp, J. J. (2009). Nonsuicidal self-injury in college students: The role of perfectionism and rumination. *Suicide and Life-Threatening Behavior, 39*(6), 576–587. https://doi.org/10.1521/suli.2009.39.6.576

Hooley, J. M., & St. Germain, S. A. (2014). Nonsuicidal self-injury, pain, and self-criticism: Does changing self-worth change pain endurance in people who engage in self-injury? *Clinical Psychological Science, 2*(3), 297–305. https://psycnet.apa.org/doi/10.1177/2167702613509372

Hunnicutt Hollenbaugh, K. M., & Lenz, A. S. (2018). Preliminary evidence for the effectiveness of Dialectical Behavior Therapy for adolescents. *Journal of Counseling & Development, 96*(2), 119–131. https://psycnet.apa.org/doi/10.1002/jcad.12186

Itzhaky, L., Shahar, G., Stein, D., & Fennig, S. (2016). In eating-disordered inpatient adolescents, self-criticism predicts nonsuicidal self-injury. *Suicide and Life-Threatening Behavior, 46*(4), 385–397. https://doi.org/10.1111/sltb.12223

Jenkins, A. L., & Schmitz, M. F. (2012). The roles of affect dysregulation and positive affect in non-suicidal self-injury. *Archives of Suicide Research, 16*(3), 212–225. https://doi.org/10.1080/13811118.2012.695270

Kamen, D. G. (2009). How can we stop our children from hurting themselves? Stages of change, motivational interviewing, and exposure therapy applications for non-suicidal self-injury in children and adolescents. *International Journal of Behavioral Consultation and Therapy, 5*(1), 106–123. http://dx.doi.org/10.1037/h0100874

Klonsky, E. D. (2007). The functions of deliberate self-injury: A review of the evidence. *Clinical Psychology Review, 27*(2), 226–239. http://doi.org/10.1016/j.cpr.2006.08.002

Kress, V. E., & Hoffman, R. M. (2008). Non-suicidal self-injury and motivational interviewing: Enhancing readiness for change. *Journal of Mental Health Counseling, 30*(4), 311–329. https://psycnet.apa.org/doi/10.17744/mehc.30.4.n2136170r5732u6h

Larsen, R. J., Diener, E., & Cropanzano, R. S. (1987). Cognitive operations associated with individual differences in affect intensity. *Journal of Personality and Social Psychology, 53*(4), 767–774. http://doi.org/10.1037//0022-3514.53.4.767

Leyro, T. M., Zvolensky, M. J., & Bernstein, A. (2010). Distress tolerance and psychopathological symptoms and disorders: A review of the empirical literature among adults. *Psychological Bulletin, 136*(4), 576–600. https://psycnet.apa.org/doi/10.1037/a0019712

Limburg, K., Watson, H. J., Hagger, M. S., & Egan, S. J. (2017). The relationship between perfectionism and psychopathology: A meta-analysis. *Journal of Clinical Psychology, 73*(10), 1301–1326. https://psycnet.apa.org/doi/10.1002/jclp.22435

Lin, M. P., You, J., Wu, Y. W., & Jiang, Y. (2018). Depression mediates the relationship between distress tolerance and nonsuicidal self-injury among adolescents: One-year follow-up. *Suicide and Life-Threatening Behavior, 48*(5), 589–600. https://doi.org/10.1111/sltb.12382

Linehan, M. (2014). *DBT skills training manual*. Guilford Press.

Linehan, M. M. (2018). *Cognitive-behavioral treatment of borderline personality disorder*. Guilford Press.

Lloyd, S., Schmidt, U., Khondoker, M., & Tchanturia, K. (2015). Can psychological interventions reduce perfectionism? A systematic review and meta-analysis. *Behavioural and Cognitive Psychotherapy, 43*(6), 705–731. https://doi.org/10.1017/S1352465814000162

Lumley, M. A., Stettner, L., & Wehmer, F. (1996). How are alexithymia and physical illness linked? A review and critique of pathways. *Journal of Psychosomatic Research, 41*(6), 505–518. https://doi.org/10.1016/S0022-3999(96)00222-X

Luyckx, K., Gandhi, A., Bijttebier, P., & Claes, L. (2015). Non-suicidal self-injury in female adolescents and psychiatric patients: A replication and extension of the role of identity formation. *Personality and Individual Differences, 77*, 91–96. https://psycnet.apa.org/doi/10.1016/j.paid.2014.12.057

McIntosh, W. D. (1996). When does goal nonattainment lead to negative emotional reactions, and when doesn't it? The role of linking and rumination. In L. L. Martin & A. Tesser (Eds.), *Striving and feeling: Interactions among goals, affect, and self-regulation* (pp. 53–77). Erlbaum.

McMain, S. F., Guimond, T., Barnhart, R., Habinski, L., & Streiner, D. L. (2017). A randomized trial of brief dialectical behaviour therapy skills training in suicidal patients suffering from borderline disorder. *Acta Psychiatrica Scandinavica, 135*(2), 138–148. https://doi.org/10.1111/acps.12664

Mettler, J., Stern, M., Lewis, S. P., & Heath, N. L. (2021). Perceived vs. actual emotion reactivity and regulation in individuals with and without a history of NSSI. *Frontiers in Psychology, 12*, Article e612792. https://doi.org/10.3389/fpsyg.2021.612792

Miller, W. R., & Rollnick, S. (1991). *Motivational interviewing: Preparing people to change addictive behaviour*. Guildford Press.

Neacsiu, A. D., Bohus, M., & Linehan, M. M. (2014). Dialectical behavior therapy: An intervention for emotion dysregulation. In J. J. Gross (Ed.), *Handbook of emotion regulation* (2nd ed., pp. 491–507). Guilford Press.

Nicolai, K. A., Wielgus, M. D., & Mezulis, A. (2016). Identifying risk for self-harm: Rumination and negative affectivity in the prospective prediction of nonsuicidal self-injury. *Suicide and Life-Threatening Behavior, 46*(2), 223–233. https://doi.org/10.1111/sltb.12186

Nielsen, E., Sayal, K., & Townsend, E. (2016). Exploring the relationship between experiential avoidance, coping functions and the recency and frequency of self-harm. *PloS One, 11*(7), Article e0159854. https://doi.org/10.1371/journal.pone.0159854

Nock, M. K. (2010). Self-injury. *Annual Review of Clinical Psychology, 6*(1), 339–363. https://doi.org/10.1146/annurev.clinpsy.121208.131258

Nock, M. K., Wedig, M. M., Holmberg, E. B., & Hooley, J. M. (2008). The emotion reactivity scale: Development, evaluation, and relation to self-injurious thoughts and behaviors. *Behavior Therapy, 39*(2), 107–116. https://doi.org/10.1016/j.beth.2007.05.005

Nolen-Hoeksema, S. (1991). Responses to depression and their effects on the duration of depressed mood. *Journal of Abnormal Psychology, 100*(4), 569–582.

Norman, H., Marzano, L., Coulson, M., & Oskis, A. (2019). Effects of mindfulness-based interventions on alexithymia: A systematic review. *Evidence Based Mental Health, 22*(1), 36–43. http://dx.doi.org/10.1136/ebmental-2018-300029

Norman, H., Oskis, A., Marzano, L., & Coulson, M. (2020). The relationship between self-harm and alexithymia: A systematic review and meta-analysis. *Scandinavian Journal of Psychology, 61*(6), 85–876. https://doi.org/10.1111/sjop.12668

Preece, D., Becerra, R., Allan, A., Robinson, K., & Dandy, J. (2017). Establishing the theoretical components of alexithymia via factor analysis: Introduction and validation of the attention-appraisal model of alexithymia. *Personality and Individual Differences, 119*, 341–352. https://doi.org/10.1016/j.paid.2017.08.003

Preece, D. A., Becerra, R., Boyes, M. E., Northcott, C., McGillivray, L., & Hasking, P. A. (2020). Do self-report measures of alexithymia measure alexithymia or general psychological distress? A factor analytic examination across five samples. *Personality and Individual Differences, 155*, Article 109721. https://doi.org/10.1016/j.paid.2019.109721

Preece, D., Becerra, R., Robinson, K., Dandy, J., & Allan, A. (2018). The psychometric assessment of alexithymia: Development and validation of the Perth Alexithymia Questionnaire. *Personality and Individual Differences*, *132*, 32–44. https://doi.org/10.1016/j.paid.2018.05.011

Richmond, S., Hasking, P., & Meaney, R. (2017). Psychological distress and non-suicidal self-injury: The mediating roles of rumination, cognitive reappraisal, and expressive suppression. *Archives of Suicide Research*, *21*(1), 62–72. https://doi.org/10.1080/13811118.2015.1008160

Selby, E. A., Anestis, M. D., & Joiner, T. E. (2008). Understanding the relationship between emotional and behavioral dysregulation: Emotional cascades. *Behaviour Research and Therapy*, *46*(5), 593–611. https://psycnet.apa.org/doi/10.1016/j.brat.2008.02.002

Selby, E. A., Connell, L. D., & Joiner, T. E. (2010). The pernicious blend of rumination and fearlessness in non-suicidal self-injury. *Cognitive Therapy and Research*, *34*(5), 421–428. https://psycnet.apa.org/doi/10.1007/s10608-009-9260-z

Selby, E. A., Franklin, J., Carson-Wong, A., & Rizvi, S. L. (2013). Emotional cascades and self-injury: Investigating instability of rumination and negative emotion. *Journal of Clinical Psychology*, *69*(12), 1213–1227. https://doi.org/10.1002/jclp.21966

Shafran, R., Cooper, Z., & Fairburn, C. (2002). Clinical perfectionism: A cognitive–behavioural analysis. *Behaviour Research and Therapy*, *40*(7), 773–791. https://doi.org/10.1016/s0005-7967(01)00059-6

Shu, C. Y., Watson, H. J., Anderson, R. A., Wade, T. D., Kane, R. T., & Egan, S. J. (2019). A randomized controlled trial of unguided internet cognitive behaviour therapy for perfectionism in adolescents: Impact on risk for eating disorders. *Behaviour Research and Therapy*, *120*, Article 103429. https://psycnet.apa.org/doi/10.1016/j.brat.2019.103429

Simons, J. S., & Gaher, R. M. (2005). The distress tolerance scale: Development and validation of a self-report measure. *Motivation and Emotion*, *29*(2), 83–102. https://doi.org/10.1007/s11031-005-7955-3

Slabbert, A., Hasking, P., & Boyes, M. (2018, Nov). Riding the emotional roller coaster: The role of distress tolerance in non-suicidal self-injury. *Psychiatry Research*, *269*, 309–315. https://doi.org/10.1016/j.psychres.2018.08.061

Slabbert, A., Hasking, P., Greene, D., & Boyes, M. (2021). Measurement invariance of the distress tolerance scale among university students with and without a history of non-suicidal self-injury. *PeerJ*, *9*, Article e10915. https://doi.org/10.7717/peerj.10915

Slabbert, A., Hasking, P., Notebaert, L., & Boyes, M. (2020). The role of distress tolerance in the relationship between affect and NSSI. *Archives of Suicide Research*, *26*(2), 761–775. https://doi.org/10.1080/13811118.2020.1833797

Suh, H., Sohn, H., Kim, T., & Lee, D. (2019). A review and meta-analysis of perfectionism interventions: Comparing face-to-face with online modalities. *Journal of Counseling Psychology*, *66*(4), 473–486. https://doi.org/10.1037/cou0000355

Taylor, G. (1994). The alexithymia construct: Conceptualization, validation, and relationship with basic dimensions of personality. *New Trends in Experimental & Clinical Psychiatry*, *10*(2), 61–74.

Taylor, P. J., Jomar, K., Dhingra, K., Forrester, R., Shahmalak, U., & Dickson, J. M. (2018). A meta-analysis of the prevalence of different functions of non-suicidal self-injury. *Journal of Affective Disorders*, *227*, 759–769. http://doi.org/10.1016/j.jad.2017.11.073

van der Velde, J., Servaas, M. N., Goerlich, K. S., Bruggeman, R., Horton, P., Costafreda, S. G., & Aleman, A. (2013). Neural correlates of alexithymia: A meta-analysis of emotion processing studies. *Neuroscience & Biobehavioral Reviews*, *37*(8), 1774–1785. https://doi.org/10.1016/j.neubiorev.2013.07.008

Watkins, E. R., & Roberts, H. (2020). Reflecting on rumination: Consequences, causes, mechanisms and treatment of rumination. *Behaviour Research and Therapy*, *127*, Article 103573. https://doi.org/10.1016/j.brat.2020.103573

Wells, A., & Papageorgiou, C. (2003). Metacognitive therapy for depressive rumination. In C. Papageorgiou & A. Wells (Eds.), *Depressive rumination: Nature, theory and treatment* (pp. 259–274). Wiley. https://doi.org/10.1002/9780470713853.ch13

Zelkowitz, R. L., & Cole, D. A. (2016). Measures of emotion reactivity and emotion regulation: Convergent and discriminant validity. *Personality and Individual Differences*, *102*, 123–132. https://doi.org/10.1016/j.paid.2016.06.045

Zelkowitz, R. L., & Cole, D. A. (2019). Self-criticism as a transdiagnostic process in nonsuicidal self-injury and disordered eating: Systematic review and meta-analysis. *Suicide and Life-Threatening Behavior*, *49*(1), 310–327. https://doi.org/10.1111/sltb.12436

CHAPTER
36 Intrapersonal Risk and Protective Factors for NSSI

Saskia Jorgensen, Erica A. Hart, Emily Burns, *and* Kathryn R. Fox

Abstract

This chapter begins by defining risk and protective factors, with a focus on their use in the context of nonsuicidal self-injury (NSSI). Theoretically, risk factor constructs should both be observable prior to the onset of NSSI and differentiate those who do and do not develop NSSI over time. Whereas risk factors are constructs that increase risk, protective factors are those that decrease risk. There are several additional critical considerations when reviewing risk factors, such as the variation of risk factor potency across populations and the implications of different types of risk factors (fixed risk factors, variable risk factors, and causal risk factors). The chapter then describes the barriers to research on NSSI risk and protective factors; among the most critical includes NSSI measurement. Risk factor research requires that the outcome of interest can be defined and measured clearly and consistently. Unfortunately, definitions and measures of NSSI vary widely across researchers. The chapter also summarizes the current state of research on intrapersonal (i.e., factors that occur within someone) NSSI risk and protective factors.

Key Words: risk factors, protective factors, nonsuicidal self-injury, risk factor potency, fixed risk factors, variable risk factors, causal risk factors, NSSI measurement, intrapersonal NSSI risk factors, intrapersonal NSSI protective factors

Introduction

The ultimate goal of most nonsuicidal self-injury (NSSI) research is to reduce suffering, to reduce NSSI engagement, and to find ways to prevent these behaviors from occurring from the start. Unfortunately, despite the proliferation of research on NSSI in the past few decades, treatment and prevention programs for these behaviors have not improved. A recent meta-analysis of 591 studies over the past 50 years examining treatment efficacy for self-injurious thoughts and behaviors, including NSSI, found that intervention effects were small across all outcomes, and that they were particularly weak for NSSI, despite more randomized control trial research in recent decades (Fox et al., 2020). This meta-analysis also found that no intervention proved consistently more efficacious than others. These disappointing results indicate that our existing treatments may not target the core processes underlying NSSI.

Improving NSSI treatment and prevention programs may require a better understanding of core mechanisms underlying NSSI. Experimental designs are needed to identify causes of a given behavior, yet, it is not ethical or desirable to intentionally manipulate factors thought to increase NSSI. Instead, risk factor studies that examine how cognitive, social, and/or environmental variables predict NSSI risk are most commonly used to approximate NSSI causes.

Identifying strong risk factors is critical for accurate prediction of a given behavior, and can highlight malleable states and traits that may be ideal treatment and prevention targets. It is important to note that the term "risk factor" is often applied incorrectly (Kraemer et al., 1997). In this chapter, we first define risk and protective factors, with a focus on their use in the context of NSSI; second, we describe the barriers to research on NSSI risk and protective factors; third, we summarize the current state of research on intrapersonal (i.e., factors that occur within someone) NSSI risk and protective factors; finally, we discuss future directions for this research.

Defining Risk and Protective Factors

As defined by Kraemer et al. (1997), risk factors are measurable constructs that occur in an individual or group prior to an outcome of interest (in this case NSSI). Theoretically, risk factor constructs should both be observable prior to the onset of NSSI and differentiate those who do and do not develop NSSI over time. In addition to statistically differentiating those who do and do not engage in NSSI, it is critical to find those risk factors that are not only statistically significant but also clinically meaningful. In other words, in addition to statistical significance, risk factors should provide meaningful information. Whereas risk factors are constructs that increase risk, protective factors are those that decrease risk. Below, we'll use the term "risk factor" in describing key components of both risk and protective factors.

There are several additional critical considerations when reviewing risk factors. For example, risk factor potency may vary across populations (consider, for example, the association between NSSI engagement and strength of parent relationships in youth vs. older adults); it is therefore important to consider and define a population of interest in advance of a given study. Additionally, there are several types of risk factors, each with different implications for prediction and treatment. Fixed markers, or fixed risk factors, refer to immutable factors (e.g., race, year of birth, genetics); in contrast, variable risk factors (e.g., age, depressive symptoms) can be changed, either intentionally (e.g., via targeted treatment) or unintentionally (e.g., with time). Most relevant to treatments, causal risk factors are a specific type of variable risk factor that, when manipulated, change the risk of the outcome of interest (NSSI). Finally, identification of risk factors, and even causal risk factors, does not necessarily clarify the underlying causes or mechanisms of a given outcome. For example, having access to sharps may be a causal risk factor for NSSI, but this access does not help to understand *why* someone chooses to engage in NSSI.

Concurrently measuring factors (e.g., depressive symptoms) with an outcome of interest (e.g., NSSI) may erroneously highlight a consequence and/or a simple correlate of the outcome itself rather than a risk factor. These consequences and correlates tend to be much more strongly associated with an outcome than true risk factors, which must occur prior to the outcome. Most, but not all, studies of NSSI risk factors have measured all variables at a single timepoint, making it impossible to know whether relationships reflect correlates, consequences, or true risk factors. We caution here that these existing studies likely overestimate and even misrepresent these relationships; results from such studies should instead be considered distinct from risk factors. As an exception to this pattern, often fixed and stable traits (like race and genetics) could be measured concomitantly while still representing risk factors, as these theoretically always occur prior to the outcome itself.

Research highlighting casual risk factors (factors increasing the likelihood) and protective factors (factors decreasing the likelihood) of NSSI may help to identify targets for treatment and prevention programs. Although NSSI risk factor research has proliferated in the past decade, far fewer studies have examined protective factors. This is problematic, as protective characteristics that confer resilience may play a critical role in effective treatment and prevention strategies.

Risk Factors

The following section summarizes the current state of the literature on intrapersonal risk factors for NSSI engagement. This chapter highlights several limitations in existing work examining risk factors, including inconsistencies across definitions and measures of NSSI, as well as methodological constraints within the body of research. These limitations may partially help to explain the relatively low predictive ability of identified risk factors, as discussed below.

Barriers to Risk Factor Research

Before discussing the current state of research on NSSI risk factors, it is important to highlight a critical barrier to this research: NSSI measurement. Risk factor research requires that the outcome of interest can be defined and measured clearly and consistently (Kraemer et al., 1997). Unfortunately, definitions and measures of NSSI vary widely across researchers. For example, whereas some definitions and measures require that NSSI cause moderate harm and skin damage, others allow for more mild forms of self-harm (e.g., picking at wounds) to be categorized as NSSI. Such differences are meaningful, given that more moderate forms of self-harm are less common, and they are associated with greater levels of psychopathology and poorer outcomes compared to milder forms (Lloyd-Richardson et al., 2007; Tang et al., 2011). Similarly, some NSSI definitions and measures clarify that more severe behaviors (e.g., breaking bones), stereotypical self-harm (e.g., head banging), and hair pulling (e.g., trichotillomania) are not considered NSSI, whereas others lump across all forms of self-harm despite evidence of distinct etiologies. Perhaps even more critically, some NSSI measures clearly state that the harm self-inflicted must be nonsuicidal (i.e., zero intent to die as a result of the behavior) in nature whereas others do not include this distinction, likely including suicidal forms of self-harm and forms of self-harm where suicidal intent was ambivalent, as well as nonsuicidal.

A distinct but related issue involves the operationalization of NSSI as the dependent variable of interest. Whereas some studies assess NSSI engagement as binary, requiring only a single episode, others require repeated NSSI engagement (e.g., 5 + episodes) for a participant to be categorized as self-harming, and others still assess NSSI frequency continuously. Such differences are meaningful, as different relationships may be expected, making it difficult if not impossible to summarize findings across studies and even across time.

Current State of Evidence for Intrapersonal NSSI Risk Factors

Despite the barriers mentioned above, a growing body of research has examined risk and protective factors for NSSI. Unfortunately, research conducted to date on these factors has provided weak results at best. A meta-analysis published by Fox et al. (2015) indicated that across 20 longitudinal studies, there were no strong, single risk factors for NSSI. Instead, numerous significant risk factors emerged, showing weak NSSI prediction (odds ratios averaging around 1.5). Since then, several qualitative reviews have emerged to summarize NSSI and self-harm risk factors (e.g., Plener et al., 2018; Valencia-Agudo et al., 2018). Similar factors continue to emerge weakly, without strong support for any one or handful of factors.

Most research on NSSI risk and protective factors has focused on intrapersonal risk factors. This focus is consistent with theories of NSSI that highlight that NSSI is most commonly engaged in to help to improve mood (e.g., Hooley & Franklin, 2018; Nock 2010). Indeed, from the meta-meta-analysis and reviews described above, the most consistent risk factors that emerged were all intrapersonal level factors (e.g., Cluster B personality symptoms, hopelessness, a prior history of NSSI). Despite evidence for the potential importance of intrapersonal risk factors, overall effects were weaker than expected and suggested weak overall prediction of future NSSI. In other words, although many risk factors, and particularly intrapersonal-level risk factors emerged as "significant" NSSI predictors, most would not be considered clinically meaningful, as they would not substantially improve the prediction or understanding of NSSI on their own. Perhaps contributing to this lower overall convergence, extreme heterogeneity across NSSI measurement emerged. As described previously, this heterogeneity in measurement may contribute to heterogeneity in risk factor magnitude across studies, thus negatively impacting clinical short-term risk identification and intervention.

Most studies of NSSI risk factors focus on single or a handful of risk factors when examining their relationships with NSSI. When thinking about research exploring individual risk factors for NSSI, it is important to consider that different individuals may have unique risk profiles. Whereas depression may be a strong predictor for one person's engagement in NSSI, it may be entirely unrelated to another. Such distinct risk factor profiles may lead to weak relationships on average. Indeed, research suggests that there are myriad reasons people engage in NSSI; although emotion regulation is the most common function for these behaviors, it is not the only function and different people endorse different NSSI functionality (Taylor et al., 2018). Consistent with these diverse functions, Wang et al. (2017) noted the importance of considering heterogeneity in NSSI etiology; others argue that there is likely no single profile to describe individuals who engage in nonsuicidal self-harm and that researchers should further consider potential complex interactions across risk factors (Stanford et al., 2018). Consistent with these arguments, complex combinations of dozens of risk factors may significantly improve predictive power (e.g., Fox et al., 2019b).

Intrapersonal NSSI Risk Factors

Numerous longitudinal studies examining potential risk factors for NSSI have been conducted. Paralleling previous findings, a review of this literature highlights that most emerging significant risk factors are also relatively weak predictors of NSSI. Despite these weak effects, this next part of the chapter will describe the intrapersonal-level risk factors and risk profiles that consistently emerge as NSSI risk factors. This section will end with discussion of more complicated models that may be better suited for NSSI prediction.

PSYCHOPATHOLOGY

In line with current NSSI theories that primarily link NSSI to emotion regulation difficulties, numerous NSSI risk factor studies focus on internalizing symptoms (e.g., depression, hopelessness, anxiety), emotion regulation deficits, and prior self-injurious thoughts and behaviors (including NSSI as well as suicidal thoughts and behaviors) as NSSI risk factors. The idea of internalizing symptoms as a risk factor for NSSI is consistent with research on NSSI functions, which demonstrate that most people who engage in NSSI most commonly say it helps them to decrease negative feelings (e.g., negative or depressed mood, anxiety) and/or increase positive feelings (or any feelings, in the case of numbness; Taylor et al., 2018). Consistent with these theories and NSSI functions, there are dozens of studies linking NSSI to internalizing psychopathology, including depression, anxiety, and emotion regulation difficulties (see the following for thorough review: Fox et al., 2015; Plener et al., 2018; Valencia-Agudo et al., 2018). However, the relationship between internalizing psychopathology and NSSI is weaker than one may assume from these theories. Indeed, meta-analytic work suggests that depression, anxiety, eating pathology, and broader internalizing symptoms, for example, predict NSSI with an average odds ratio across studies below 2; surprisingly, even emotion regulation, which is considered central to NSSI, shows an average odds ratio of 1.05.

Other NSSI theories suggest that impulse control problems, like impulsivity and negative urgency, underlie NSSI engagement (e.g., Glenn & Klonsky, 2010; Hamza et al., 2015). According to such theories, NSSI may provide an easily accessible form of emotion regulation in the context of negative emotion, particularly for people who want to feel better quickly, regardless of their longer-term goals and values. Although the relationship between self-reported (but not behavioral) impulsivity, negative urgency, and NSSI has been strong when considered cross-sectionally (e.g., Hamza et al., 2015), effects are inconsistent and quite weak when considered prospectively (e.g., Fox et al., 2015; Hamza et al., 2015). Future research that seeks to disentangle self-reported versus behavioral and different facets of impulsivity (e.g., impulsivity in the context of specific negative emotions) may be better suited to clarify the potential for impulsivity as a risk factor for NSSI.

Finally, NSSI was traditionally understood primarily as a problem occurring in the context of borderline personality disorder (BPD). Although today NSSI is more widely understood as transdiagnostic, many believe BPD may be a strong risk factor for NSSI engagement. Indeed, several studies have observed significant relationships between BPD and NSSI, with average odds ratios higher than any other risk factors aside from a prior history of NSSI (odds ratio = 5.93; Fox et al., 2015). Although notable, this finding is limited in two key ways: First, effects observed are inconsistent, with some studies showing weak and null effects, and others showing very large effects that likely skew this effect to be higher than would otherwise be the case (as highlighted by a large confidence interval). Second, NSSI is listed as a symptom of BPD, and therefore research using symptom measurements and or diagnoses of BPD as predictors may unintentionally inflate the relationship between BPD and NSSI.

SELF-CRITICISM AND SELF-PUNISHMENT DESIRE

Other NSSI theories, like the Self-Punishment Hypothesis (Favazza, 1996; Walsh & Rosen, 1988), the Defective Self Model (Hooley et al., 2010), and the Benefits and Barriers Model (Hooley & Franklin, 2018) propose that NSSI may serve as a form of self-punishment. Indeed, behind emotion regulation, self-punishment is among the most commonly endorsed NSSI functions (Taylor et al., 2018). Laboratory and self-report studies both support this theory, demonstrating that self-punishment desires increase a desire to self-inflict pain, decrease sensitivity to pain, and increase positive consequences from pain among people with and without NSSI histories (e.g., Bastian et al., 2011; Fox et al., 2019a; Fox et al., 2017; Schoenleber et al., 2014). Moreover, numerous studies show moderate to large elevations in self-criticism and self-hatred among people who engage in NSSI compared to people who do not (Zelkowitz & Cole, 2019). However, the longitudinal relationship between self-criticism, self-punishment desire, and NSSI is weaker. Although several studies show that self-criticism and desire to self-punish are significant NSSI risk factors (e.g., Fox et al., 2018; Lear et al., 2019; Perkins et al., 2020), other studies do not show this effect (e.g., Daly & Willoughby, 2019; You et al., 2017).

Thus, research to date suggests that these factors are likely weak risk factors for future NSSI, at best.

LIFETIME HISTORY OF NSSI AND OTHER FORMS OF SELF-INJURIOUS THOUGHTS AND BEHAVIOR
Perhaps the strongest and most consistent risk factor for NSSI is prior NSSI. Indeed, in prior meta-analytic work examining all NSSI risk factors studied to date, NSSI emerged as the strongest risk factor for future NSSI (Fox et al., 2015). This is perhaps unsurprising, and parallels other research showing that prior behavior tends to best predict future behavior. Interestingly, in the same meta-analysis, suicidal thoughts and behaviors also emerged as significant risk factors for NSSI (average odds ratio = 2.21). Although this latter relationship was weaker, results suggest that all forms of self-injurious thoughts and behaviors may be candidate risk factors for future NSSI. This is particularly important given that NSSI is often examined as a risk factor for future suicidal thoughts and behaviors (Ribeiro et al., 2016), but the reverse remains less studied and less commonly discussed in research and clinical care.

DEMOGRAPHIC AND IDENTITY CHARACTERISTICS
In addition to the intrapersonal-level risk factors described above, demographic and identity characteristics have also emerged as NSSI risk factors. Prior to discussing these demographic factors, it is critical to conceptualize what it means when demographic differences reflect "risk" for a given outcome, like NSSI. It is a misnomer to say that demographics like race/ethnicity, sex, gender diversity, sexual orientation, and so on are risk factors for NSSI. Instead, it is the interpersonal- and structural-level stressors faced by minority groups that impact their risk for health risk behaviors like NSSI.

The typical onset for NSSI is during adolescence (13–16 years), yet, earlier age of onset of NSSI behaviors is associated with more severe NSSI (Muehlenkamp et al., 2019). For example, Muehlenkamp and colleagues found participants who engaged in NSSI behaviors at or before age 12 reported significantly more lifetime NSSI, greater method versatility, and medically severe NSSI than those who began engaging in NSSI behaviors at older ages (17 years). Although notable, it is important to consider that these reports tend to be retrospective and age of onset emerged as only weak predictors of severity and engagement in future NSSI when summarizing across studies (Fox et al., 2015).

Adolescent Risk Factors. Moreover, risk factors for NSSI may be unique for adolescents and adults given their unique life stressors, developmental stages, and experiences. In light of potential differences, Valencia-Agudo and colleagues (2018) conducted a systematic review of risk factors for NSSI among community samples of adolescents. Results of their work highlighted that peer victimization and bullying were each risk factors for NSSI (emerging in five of seven studies), and that sexual trauma, but not physical abuse, was a consistently observed NSSI risk factor. Moreover, peer NSSI emerged as a significant predictor of NSSI in four of six studies, suggesting that peer contagion may also play a role for adolescents (See Jarvi Steele et al., this volume, on social contagion of NSSI).

Previous research shows inconsistency in sex and gender differences in NSSI risk. Notably, most research in this area conflates sex and gender, with more recent research highlighting important differences in this domain. In this section, we primarily discuss sex differences. Early research on NSSI indicated that NSSI was substantially more common among females than males; however, more recent research has challenged these findings. Indeed, two meta-analyses to date have reviewed sex differences in NSSI with one demonstrating no significant differences across males and females drawing on only community-based samples (Swannell et al., 2014) and the other showing a small effect (female-to-male NSSI ratio: 1.5) that was stronger among clinical compared to community samples (Bresin & Schoenleber, 2015). Together, this work suggests that female sex may be a weak but significant NSSI risk factor, particularly when considering clinical samples.

People identifying as transgender and gender expansive (i.e., gender non-conforming, gender diverse) include anyone who identifies with a gender distinct from their birth-assigned sex (i.e., non-cisgender). Research increasingly suggests that gender diversity is associated with higher rates of NSSI (for more information, see Taliaferro et al., this volume, on NSSI in gender and sexually diverse youth). For example, in their meta-analysis, Surace et al. (2021) found the mean prevalence of NSSI for people with gender expansive identities was 28%, much higher than the ~17–18% prevalence in the general adolescent population consisting predominantly of cisgender youth (Muehlenkamp et al., 2012; Swannell et al., 2014). This elevated risk should be understood in the context of the minority stress model (Brooks, 1981; Hendricks & Testa, 2012; Meyer, 2003, 2015), which highlights the excess experiences of stressors across interpersonal and structural levels faced by transgender and gender expansive people.

Sexuality is also related to NSSI risk. An increasing number of studies have demonstrated elevated rates of NSSI among lesbian, gay, bisexual, queer, and questioning people, and this work often includes transgender and gender expansive people (e.g., for meta-analyses on this topic, see Batejan et al., 2015; Liu et al., 2019). For example, in their meta-analysis, Liu et al. (2019) showing elevated NSSI rates among lesbian, gay, bisexual, queer, and questioning as well as transgender and gender expansive youth (46.65%) compared to their heterosexual and/or cisgender peers (14.57%). Transgender and bisexual individuals were found to have the greatest risk for NSSI engagement compared to peers with diverse sexualities and genders, as well as heterosexual, cisgender peers.

Like many risk factors discussed thus far, findings on patterns of prevalence of NSSI among minority ethnic and racial groups have been inconsistent. For example, in their review of NSSI prevalence across race/ethnicities in Western countries, Gholamrezaei et al. (2015) highlighted some general trends. Briefly, incidence rates of NSSI are sometimes found to be lower among Asian/Asian American, African American, and Hispanic youth, whereas other studies find no differences or even higher rates among African American youths. Helping to make sense of these discrepant findings, there may be important interactions across race and gender and race and socioeconomic status. Though this area of study is underexplored, Gholamrezaei et al. (2015) noted that sociocultural and structural factors such as perceived discrimination, immigration, acculturation stress, bicultural identity, and systematic oppression all impact mental health and likely play a role in NSSI risk for ethnic and racial minority populations. Educational attainment was another noted factor that may impact NSSI risk for minority populations (Gholamrezaei et al., 2015). For example, NSSI was found to be more prevalent among African American high school students from both high- and low-socioeconomic-status families but less prevalent among university students. Gholamrezaei and colleagues suggest that educational achievement is likely a social and economic advantage that may provide a buffer to risk; however, researchers have yet to study this potential role in NSSI risk. For more information, see Wilson, this volume, on cross-cultural representations of NSSI.

Protective Factors

Identification of protective factors may play an important role in understanding who engages in NSSI and why, while simultaneously highlighting useful treatment and prevention targets. Unfortunately, protective factors for NSSI are understudied and underemphasized. Most commonly, protective factors are examined in conjunction with risk factors, and inverse relationships between variables and risk are labeled protective factors because they are associated with decreased odds of NSSI. Although technically correct, this often precludes a deeper understanding of promotive factors that may help to reduce NSSI risk. Further, as with most risk factor studies, most research on protective factors relies on cross-sectional designs.

Supportive social networks are among the strongest and most replicated protective factors for NSSI onset and continuation (Aggarwal et al., 2017; Blasco et al., 2019; Nixon & Heath, 2009; Tabaac et al., 2016; Wu et al., 2019). For example, family support and connection have been found to protect against NSSI in adolescent populations (Aggarwal et al., 2017; Nixon & Heath, 2009; Reisner et al., 2014; Tatnell et al., 2014), supporting a compensatory model of resilience. Similarly, parent or adult connectedness may buffer against adolescent NSSI engagement (Taliaferro et al., 2019). Outside the family, perceived school competence and sense of university membership were each negatively correlated with NSSI risk in a sample of Spanish young adults (Blasco et al., 2019). Similarly, sense of belongingness and safety in school were each negatively correlated with NSSI onset and continuation in youth from low- and middle-income countries and transgender and gender expansive adolescents (Aggarwal et al., 2017; Taliaferro et al., 2019).

Just as self-criticism and self-hatred may be an NSSI risk factor, self-compassion may protect against NSSI. Indeed, the Benefits and Barriers Model (Hooley & Franklin, 2018) posits that a positive self-view may serve as a key barrier to NSSI engagement (for theoretical models for NSSI, see Hird et al., this volume). Self-compassion, in which someone views themselves, their thoughts, and their feelings nonjudgmentally, is associated with more positive self-views, lower levels of self-criticism, and lower levels of shame (Gilbert & Irons, 2009). Prior research shows that higher levels of self-compassion are concurrently associated with lower levels of NSSI (e.g., Boyne & Hamza, 2021; Hankin & Abela, 2011; Kiekens et al., 2015; Kokaliari et al., 2017; Lathren et al., 2019). However, few longitudinal studies have examined this relationship, with inconsistent demonstration of this effect (e.g., Boyne & Hamza, 2021).

Although not yet studied as an isolated variable potentially able to buffer against NSSI, use of positive coping strategies during emotional distress has been found to decrease risk of the dangerous behaviors (Stanford et al., 2018). Often examined in conjunction with coping, lower levels of affective instability, defined as the tendency to experience quick and intense mood swings, is linked to lower likelihood of NSSI in youth (You et al., 2012). That is, when experiencing more stable affect and emotional regulation in response to distress, adolescents are more likely to cease NSSI.

As research on protective factors for NSSI grows, it is worth mentioning variables that are relatives to protective factors. These include instances where low levels of a risk factor are associated with lower likelihood of NSSI and, conversely, low levels of a promotive factor are associated with higher levels of NSSI. For example, higher levels of self-esteem (Lin et al., 2017) and lower levels of anxiety (Stanford et al., 2018) are each associated with reduced risk for NSSI engagement. Similarly, low affect instability protects against NSSI onset and continuation, and reducing emotional and environmental instability decreases NSSI likelihood, with medication and gender moderating differences (Peters et al., 2016; You et al., 2012). Finally, lower impulsivity is found to be a distant protective factor for NSSI due to its negative association with NSSI rates in adolescents (Stanford et al., 2018; Wu et al., 2019).

Future Directions: Research and Clinical Practice

Once a consistent definition of NSSI is established and used across studies, research capturing a wider range of potential variables, NSSI at multiple time points over time, controlling for attrition may help to build a better understanding of intrapersonal risk and protective factors. Moreover, although studies looking at individual or a handful of risk factors using longitudinal design have merit, individual, group-level risk factors will likely never be sufficient on their own to predict or understand NSSI, two key goals of many NSSI researchers.

A Call for Novel Methods

Methods moving beyond examining one or several risk factors may be needed for stronger NSSI prediction; similarly, gaining a strong explanatory understanding may require the use of experimental methods. This section briefly discusses alternative research methods to improve our prediction and understanding of NSSI methods, beyond risk and protective factor models dominating the field to date.

PREDICTION

As highlighted above, research examining single variables and small combinations of variables have resulted in weak NSSI prediction. New approaches are likely needed. One such approach involves real-time assessment of NSSI and potential risk factors. Until recently, NSSI research primarily relied on retrospective self-report measures, which ask participants to think back to times when they have engaged in NSSI and to consider their motivations or precursors to that behavior. This was even the case in longitudinal studies, where participants were asked to think back over the past week, month, or year since prior study assessments. These methods are limited in a number of ways, including possible discrepancies between the way a person remembers or perceives a past event and way that they felt and behaved in the moment itself (Stone et al., 1999), as well as the often-brief onset and duration of self-injurious thoughts and behaviors, lending themselves to being forgotten across time (Kleiman & Nock, 2018). A promising direction for NSSI research is the use of real-time assessments (i.e., ecological momentary assessments), which ask participants to respond to questions about their moods, experiences, behaviors, and thoughts in the moment (e.g., prompted to respond at a random time in their day) and within their natural environment across a period of days, weeks, or months. Recent research has highlighted the importance of looking at individual "state" factors that confer risk based on specific circumstances and emotions rather than "trait" factors that suggest personalities or patterns inherent to a person or group that put them at elevated risk. Due to the complex nature of SITBs, there is evidence to suggest that looking at within-person factors, rather than or in addition to averaging across people, in a given moment, within a given situation, or in response to a given event, may provide stronger predictive power than looking only at between-person factors assessed via retrospective self-report. By using these real-time methods in research, the field may be better able to understand changes within an individual that confer risk for NSSI at a given time (Rodriguez-Blanco et al., 2018).

Additionally, advanced statistical methods examining complex combinations across a multitude of factors may be more effective than traditional single-factor approaches. Providing support for this possibility, Fox et al. (2019b) compared model fit in the prediction of NSSI engagement across short-term (3, 14, and 28 days) follow-up periods using univariate logistic regression, multiple logistic regression, and random forest machine learning algorithms incorporating all study variables. Results of this work leveraging a large (n = 1,021) and high-risk sample (i.e., past-year engagement in some form of self-injurious thought or behavior) demonstrated the random forest algorithm, incorporating complex combinations across all study variables, produced the strongest NSSI prediction across each time point. Moreover, multiple logistic regression, incorporating each variable individually (without interactions), outperformed univariate logistic regression models. Interestingly, even when the strongest predictors from the random forest model were removed, prediction accuracy remained nearly equivalent. Results highlighted that complex statistical models (i.e., random forest) resulted in the most accurate NSSI over short-term, clinically relevant periods. Results provide support for theories that NSSI engagement is complex, and likely cannot be understood or predicted from a small set of factors. Instead, results suggest that a large set of factors and sophisticated statistical modeling may be needed for more accurate NSSI risk detection.

CAUSES AND EXPLANATIONS

Although many infer NSSI causes from this risk factor literature, prospective studies are not suited for causal inference; experimental paradigms are needed to identify cause. To date, most researchers have avoided experimental paradigms in the study of SITBs as it is not ethical to intentionally manipulate factors that could increase the likelihood of these dangerous outcomes. However, other fields interested in the causes of harmful outcomes, like disease, illness, or injury, have overcome this limitation by using proxies for their outcome of interest. For example, to understand the influence of alcohol on unsafe driving and accidents, researchers use alcohol and driving simulations in controlled laboratory settings to draw inferences about how alcohol influences real-world driving (Marczinski et al., 2008).

Following these approaches, NSSI proxies (e.g., safe pain induction paradigms) can be used to approximate NSSI in experimental designs. Critically, pain induction methods, like the pressure algometer, have been safely used in many previous studies, including studies of children and adolescents, and many of these methods are deemed to pose no more than minimal risk (see Birnie et al., 2014, for a review of evidence that it is safe and ethical to use experimental pain approaches in children and adolescents). These methods have been successfully used to test emotion regulation theories of NSSI and have revealed that pain and pain offset relief help to regulate mood, particularly in the context of negative affect (e.g., Bresin & Gordon, 2013; Franklin et al., 2010; Hooley et al., 2010). Leveraging these approaches has also allowed researchers to examine factors that do and do not impact mood improvements from pain in samples both with and without NSSI histories (e.g., Fox et al., 2017; Hamza et al., 2015). For example, another study examined the role of boredom and negative emotions in the choice to self-inflict pain using a randomized experimental design (Nederkoorn et al., 2016). Interestingly, in this study, participants assigned to the monotonous condition were more likely to shock themselves at a higher intensity than those assigned to watch a sad or neutral film. Moreover, those participants in the study with NSSI histories were more susceptible to the effects of boredom. These findings suggest that, contrary to many NSSI theories, boredom may be a key motivational factor for NSSI that could be targeted in treatment programs. Continued creativity in experimental design will allow for examination of myriad factors and constructs that may underlie NSSI engagement.

Discussion

There is still much work to be done across research and clinical approaches to better understand, prevent, and treat NSSI, and identification of intrapersonal risk factors is a cornerstone of these goals. Previous research supports the contribution of several individual-level risk and protective factors for NSSI; however, most of these factors are only weakly related to prospective NSSI. Among the strongest and most commonly replicated intrapersonal risk factors include prior NSSI and self-injury engagement, Cluster B Personality symptoms (including borderline personality symptoms), and hopelessness. There is far less research on protective factors against NSSI, and many of the proposed possible protective factors are inferred reverse relationships with risk factors (e.g., self-esteem vs. self-criticism and poor emotion regulation vs. strong emotion regulation). Moreover, few studies to date have examined protective factors longitudinally. That said, several significant protective factors have emerged, including strong interpersonal networks and belongingness, positive coping skills, lower levels of affect instability, low levels of impulsivity, and low levels of anxiety. As with risk factors, these protective factors tend to show weak prospective relationships with NSSI.

We argue that one of the most important and consistent findings in the research around NSSI is that there is no single profile to describe people who engage in NSSI, and perhaps relatedly, there is no single risk factor for NSSI. Rather, there is a wide array of possible risk and protective factors that combine in unique ways to put people at risk. Going forward, both researchers and clinicians should consider moving away from a single-factor approach to conceptualize or predict NSSI. Instead, psychologists should consider examining complex models that combine various individual-level characteristics to better understand and predict NSSI risk. Additionally, psychologists should consider studying idiographic motivations for engaging in NSSI, rather than a continued focus on finding clear-cut, universal predictors, as this approach has been shown to be ineffective.

Along with more complex research and statistical approaches to identifying NSSI risk, there are important implications and recommendations for mental health care providers to consider. Results of research on NSSI correlates and risk factors unambiguously suggest that NSSI is not a behavior that can be explained solely by a diagnosis of BPD or depression. NSSI occurs across psychiatric diagnoses, and even in the absence of any psychiatric diagnosis. Moreover, NSSI is not a behavior that occurs only in females. Mental health providers should consider asking all clients about their NSSI engagement, rather than asking only those who fit a certain profile. Historically, there have been concerns that asking about NSSI may give clients the idea to engage in NSSI (i.e., suggesting iatrogenic effects of asking about NSSI engagement); however, these concerns are not supported by empirical research. Instead, approaches that avoid asking about NSSI are likely more harmful than helpful (e.g., Cha et al., 2016; Lloyd-Richardson et al., 2015; Whitlock et al., 2013). Considering this, best practice involves clinicians asking clients directly about possible NSSI engagement. Similar implications exist in prevention domains. For example, school-based prevention programs should consider moving away from overly simplistic explanations for NSSI. Instead, school-based programs should educate teachers and parents on NSSI behaviors, including discussion of how to best encourage open dialogue about NSSI with students. It is important that these settings also emphasize the inaccuracies of the single-profile model of NSSI engagement to avoid missing students who do not fit these profiles. In other words, teachers and school counselors, like clinicians and researchers, should understand that NSSI could impact any of their students, not only those with depression or BPD. Additionally, school-based programs should develop awareness, prevention, and intervention campaigns as well as work to teach young people healthy coping skills and resource awareness.

Conclusion

As outlined in the chapter, there is still much to be done to understand intrapersonal risk and protective factors for NSSI. Existing literature suggests an array of possible factors, though many show only weak significance in predicting engagement in NSSI. As research continues to expand and evolve, it is important that psychologists recognize that although the current state of the literature is not necessarily clear-cut does not mean that it is not valuable. Taking what we already know, researchers and clinicians alike can work towards increasingly complex models and understandings of NSSI risk and protective factors. In research, this should include using increasingly complex statistical modeling (e.g., multiple factor approaches) and more intensive methodological design that examines within-person "state" factors (e.g., using ecological momentary assessment) and those that mimic NSSI (e.g., pain induction methods). It should also include methods and questions that directly target NSSI rather than outcomes or correlates that have been presumed to be associated with NSSI (e.g., depression and BPD). In clinical practice, future efforts similarly should work to increase understanding that NSSI is complex and multidimensional, rather than basing treatment and prevention efforts on assumptions of single risk factors, traits, or psychiatric diagnoses associated with NSSI.

By using complex models, accepting and leaning into complexities, and allocating resources in a way that reflects the importance of this work, we can continue to move toward increased predictive ability with the eventual goal of prevention, treatment, and overall decreased rates of nonsuicidal self-injury.

References

Aggarwal, S., Patton, G., Reavley, N., Sreenivasan, S. A., & Berk, M. (2017). Youth self-harm in low-and middle-income countries: Systematic review of the risk and protective factors. *International Journal of Social Psychiatry, 63*(4), 359–375. https://doi.org/10.1177/0020764017700175

Bastian, B., Jetten, J., & Fasoli, F. (2011). Cleansing the soul by hurting the flesh: The guilt-reducing effect of pain. *Psychological Science, 22*(3), 334–335. https://doi.org/10.1177/0956797610397058

Batejan, K. L., Jarvi, S. M., & Swenson, L. P. (2015). Sexual orientation and non-suicidal self-injury: A meta-analytic review. *Archives of Suicide Research, 19*(2), 131–150. https://doi.org/10.1080/13811118.2014.957450

Birnie, K. A., Caes, L., Wilson, A. C., Williams, S. E., & Chambers, C. T. (2014). A practical guide and perspectives on the use of experimental pain modalities with children and adolescents. *Pain Management*, *4*(2), 97–111. https://doi.org/10.2217/pmt.13.72

Blasco, M. J., Vilagut, G., Alayo, I., Almenara, J., Cebrià, A. I., Echeburúa, E., Gabilondo, A., Gili, M., Lagares, C., Piqueras, J. A., Roca, M., Soto-Sanz, V., Ballester, L., Urdangarin, A., Bruffaerts, R., Mortier, P., Auerbach, R. P., Nock, M. K., Kessler, R. C., & Alonso, J. (2019). First-onset and persistence of suicidal ideation in university students: A one-year follow-up study. *Journal of Affective Disorders*, *256*, 192–204. https://doi.org/10.1016/j.jad.2019.05.035

Boyne, H., & Hamza, C. A. (2021). Depressive symptoms, perceived stress, self-compassion and nonsuicidal self-injury among emerging adults: An examination of the between and within-person associations over time. *Emerging Adulthood*, *10*(5). https://doi.org/10.1177/21676968211029768

Bresin, K., & Gordon, K. H. (2013). Changes in negative affect following pain (vs. Nonpainful) stimulation in individuals with and without a history of nonsuicidal self-injury. *Personality Disorders: Theory, Research, and Treatment*, *4*(1), 62–66. https://doi.org/10.1037/a0025736

Bresin, K., & Schoenleber, M. (2015). Gender differences in the prevalence of nonsuicidal self-injury: A meta-analysis. *Clinical Psychology Review*, *38*, 55–64. https://doi.org/10.1016/j.cpr.2015.02.009

Brooks, Virginia R. (1981). *Minority stress and lesbian women*. Lexington Books.

Cha, C. B., Augenstein, T. M., Frost, K. H., Gallagher, K., D'Angelo, E. J., & Nock, M. K. (2016). Using implicit and explicit measures to predict nonsuicidal self-injury among adolescent inpatients. *Journal of the American Academy of Child & Adolescent Psychiatry*, *55*(1), 62–68. https://doi.org/10.1016/j.jaac.2015.10.008

Daly, O., & Willoughby, T. (2019). A longitudinal study investigating bidirectionality among nonsuicidal self-injury, self-criticism, and parental criticism. *Psychiatry Research*, *271*, 678–683. https://doi.org/10.1016/j.psychres.2018.12.056

Favazza, A.R. (1996). *Bodies under siege: Self-mutilation and body modification in culture and psychiatry* (2nd ed.). John Hopkins University Press.

Fox, K. R., Franklin, J. C., Ribeiro, J. D., Kleiman, E. M., Bentley, K. H., & Nock, M. K. (2015). Meta-analysis of risk factors for nonsuicidal self-injury. *Clinical Psychology Review*, *42*, 156–167. https://doi.org/10.1016/j.cpr.2015.09.002

Fox, K. R., Huang, X., Guzmán, E., Funsch, K., Cha, C., Ribeiro, J., & Franklin, J. (2020). Interventions for suicide and self-injury: A meta-analysis of randomized controlled trials across nearly 50 years of research. *Psychological Bulletin*, *146*. https://doi.org/10.1037/bul0000305

Fox, K. R., Huang, X., Linthicum, K. P., Wang, S. B., Franklin, J. C., & Ribeiro, J. D. (2019a). Model complexity improves the prediction of nonsuicidal self-injury. *Journal of Consulting and Clinical Psychology*, *87*(8), 684–692. https://doi.org/10.1037/ccp0000421

Fox, K. R., O'Sullivan, I. M., Wang, S. B., & Hooley, J. M. (2019b). Self-criticism impacts emotional responses to pain. *Behavior Therapy*, *50*(2), 410–420. https://doi.org/10.1016/j.beth.2018.07.008

Fox, K. R., Ribeiro, J. D., Kleiman, E. M., Hooley, J. M., Nock, M. K., & Franklin, J. C. (2018). Affect toward the self and self-injury stimuli as potential risk factors for nonsuicidal self-injury. *Psychiatry Research*, *260*, 279–285. https://doi.org/10.1016/j.psychres.2017.11.083

Fox, K. R., Toole, K. E., Franklin, J. C., & Hooley, J. M. (2017). Why does nonsuicidal self-injury improve mood? A preliminary test of three hypotheses. *Clinical Psychological Science*, *5*(1), 111–121. https://doi.org/10.1177/2167702616662270

Franklin, J. C., Hessel, E. T., Aaron, R. V., Arthur, M. S., Heilbron, N., & Prinstein, M. J. (2010). The functions of nonsuicidal self-injury: Support for cognitive–affective regulation and opponent processes from a novel psychophysiological paradigm. *Journal of Abnormal Psychology*, *119*(4), 850–862. https://doi.org/10.1037/a0020896

Gholamrezaei, M., Stefano, J., & Heath, N. (2015). Nonsuicidal self-injury across cultures and ethnic and racial minorities: A review. *International Journal of Psychology: Journal International de Psychologie*, *52*. https://doi.org/10.1002/ijop.12230

Gilbert, P., & Irons, C. (2009). Shame, self-criticism, and self-compassion in adolescence. In N. Allen & L. Sheeber (Eds.), *Adolescent emotional development and the emergence of depressive disorders* (pp. 195–214). Cambridge University Press. doi:10.1017/CBO9780511551963.011

Glenn, C. R., & Klonsky, E. D. (2010). A multimethod analysis of impulsivity in nonsuicidal self-injury. *Personality Disorders: Theory, Research, and Treatment*, *1*(1), 67–75. https://doi.org/10.1037/a0017427

Hamza, C. A., Willoughby, T., & Heffer, T. (2015). Impulsivity and nonsuicidal self-injury: A review and meta-analysis. *Clinical Psychology Review*, *38*, 13–24. https://doi.org/10.1016/j.cpr.2015.02.010

Hankin, B. L., & Abela, J. R. Z. (2011). Nonsuicidal self-injury in adolescence: Prospective rates and risk factors in a 2 1/2 year longitudinal study. *Psychiatry Research*, *186*(1), 65–70. https://doi.org/10.1016/j.psychres.2010.07.056

Hendricks, M. L., & Testa, R. J. (2012). A conceptual framework for clinical work with transgender and gender nonconforming clients: An adaptation of the minority stress model. *Professional Psychology: Research and Practice*, *43*(5), 460–467. https://doi.org/10.1037/a0029597

Hooley, J. M., & Franklin, J. C. (2018). Why do people hurt themselves? A new conceptual model of nonsuicidal self-injury. *Clinical Psychological Science*, *6*(3), 428–451. https://doi.org/10.1177/2167702617745641

Hooley, J. M., Ho, D. T., Slater, J., & Lockshin, A. (2010). Pain perception and nonsuicidal self-injury: A laboratory investigation. *Personality Disorders: Theory, Research, and Treatment*, *1*(3), 170–179. https://doi.org/10.1037/a0020106

Kiekens, G., Bruffaerts, R., Nock, M. K., Van de Ven, M., Witteman, C., Mortier, P., Demyttenaere, K., & Claes, L. (2015). Non-suicidal self-injury among Dutch and Belgian adolescents: Personality, stress, and coping. *European Psychiatry*, *30*, 743–749. https://doi.org/10.1016/j.eurpsy.2015.06.007

Kleiman, E. M., & Nock, M. K. (2018). Real-time assessment of suicidal thoughts and behaviors. *Current Opinion in Psychology*, *22*, 33–37. https://doi.org/10.1016/j.copsyc.2017.07.026

Kokaliari, E. D., Roy, A. W., & Koutra, K. (2017). A cross-sectional study comparing predictors of non-suicidal self-injury among college students in the United States and Greece. *International Journal of Culture and Mental Health*, *10*(1), 50–61. https://doi.org/10.1080/17542863.2016.1259339

Kraemer, H. C., Kazdin, A. E., Offord, D. R., Kessler, R. C., Jensen, P. S., & Kupfer, D. J. (1997). Coming to terms with the terms of risk. *Archives of General Psychiatry*, *54*(4), 337–343. https://doi.org/10.1001/archpsyc.1997.01830160065009

Lathren, C., Bluth, K., & Parnk, J. (2019). Adolescent self-compassion moderates the relationship between perceived stress and internalizing symptoms. *Personality and Individual Differences*, *143*, 36–41. https://doi.org/10.1016/j.paid.2019.02.008

Lear, M. K., Wilkowski, B. M., & Pepper, C. M. (2019). A daily diary investigation of the defective self model among college students with recent self-injury. *Behavior Therapy*, *50*(5), 1002–1012. https://doi.org/10.1016/j.beth.2019.03.005

Lin, M.-P., You, J., Ren, Y., Wu, J. Y.-W., Hu, W.-H., Yen, C.-F., & Zhang, X. (2017). Prevalence of nonsuicidal self-injury and its risk and protective factors among adolescents in Taiwan. *Psychiatry Research*, *255*, 119–127. https://doi.org/10.1016/j.psychres.2017.05.028

Liu, R. T., Sheehan, A. E., Walsh, R. F. L., Sanzari, C. M., Cheek, S. M., & Hernandez, E. M. (2019). Prevalence and correlates of non-suicidal self-injury among lesbian, gay, bisexual, and transgender individuals: A systematic review and meta-analysis. *Clinical Psychology Review*, *74*, 101783. https://doi.org/10.1016/j.cpr.2019.101783

Lloyd-Richardson, E. E., Lewis, S. P., Whitlock, J. L., Rodham, K., & Schatten, H. T. (2015). Research with adolescents who engage in non-suicidal self-injury: Ethical considerations and challenges. *Child and Adolescent Psychiatry and Mental Health*, *9*(1), 37. https://doi.org/10.1186/s13034-015-0071-6

Lloyd-Richardson, E. E., Perrine, N., Dierker, L., & Kelley, M. L. (2007). Characteristics and functions of non-suicidal self-injury in a community sample of adolescents. *Psychological Medicine*, *37*(8), 1183–1192. https://doi.org/10.1017/S003329170700027X

Marczinski, C.A., Harrison, E.L. and Fillmore, M.T. (2008), Effects of alcohol on simulated driving and perceived driving impairment in binge drinkers. *Alcoholism: Clinical and Experimental Research*, *32*, 1329–1337. https://doi.org/10.1111/j.1530-0277.2008.00701.x

Meyer, I. H. (2003). Prejudice, social stress, and mental health in lesbian, gay, and bisexual populations: Conceptual issues and research evidence. *Psychological Bulletin*, *129*, 674–697.

Meyer, I. H. (2015). Resilience in the study of minority stress and health of sexual and gender minorities. *Psychology of Sexual Orientation and Gender Diversity*, *2*(3), 209–213. https://doi.org/10.1037/sgd0000132

Muehlenkamp, J. J., Claes, L., Havertape, L., & Plener, P. L. (2012). International prevalence of adolescent non-suicidal self-injury and deliberate self-harm. *Child and Adolescent Psychiatry and Mental Health*, *6*(1), 10. https://doi.org/10.1186/1753-2000-6-10

Muehlenkamp, J. J., Xhunga, N., & Brausch, A. M. (2019). Self-injury age of onset: A risk factor for NSSI severity and suicidal behavior. *Archives of Suicide Research: Official Journal of the International Academy for Suicide Research, 23*(4), 551–563. https://doi.org/10.1080/13811118.2018.1486252

Nederkoorn, C., Vancleef, L., Wilkenhöner, A., Claes, L., & Havermans, R. C. (2016). Self-inflicted pain out of boredom. *Psychiatry Research, 237*, 127–132. https://doi.org/10.1016/j.psychres.2016.01.063

Nixon, M. K., & Heath, N. L. (Eds.). (2009). *Self-injury in youth: The essential guide to assessment and intervention*. Routledge/Taylor & Francis Group.

Nock, M. K. (2010). Self-injury. *Annual Review of Clinical Psychology, 6*(1), 339–363. https://doi.org/10.1146/annurev.clinpsy.121208.131258

Perkins, N. M., Ortiz, S. N., & Smith, A. R. (2020). Self-criticism longitudinally predicts nonsuicidal self-injury in eating disorders. *Eating disorders, 28*(2), 157–170. https://doi.org/10.1080/10640266.2019.1695450

Peters, E. M., Balbuena, L., Marwaha, S., Baetz, M., & Bowen, R. (2016). Mood instability and impulsivity as trait predictors of suicidal thoughts. *Psychology and Psychotherapy, 89*(4), 435–444. https://doi.org/10.1111/papt.12088

Plener, P. L., Kaess, M., Schmahl, C., Pollak, S. M., Fegert, J., & C. Brown, R. (2018). Nonsuicidal self-injury in adolescents. *Deutsches Ärzteblatt International, 115*(3), 23–30. https://doi.org/10.3238/arztebl.2018.0023

Reisner, S. L., Biello, K., Perry, N. S., Gamarel, K. E., & Mimiaga, M. J. (2014). A compensatory model of risk and resilience applied to adolescent sexual orientation disparities in nonsuicidal self-injury and suicide attempts. *American Journal of Orthopsychiatry, 84*(5), 545–556. https://doi.org/10.1037/ort0000008

Ribeiro, J. D., Franklin, J. C., Fox, K. R., Bentley, K. H., Kleiman, E. M., Chang, B. P., & Nock, M. K. (2016). Self-injurious thoughts and behaviors as risk factors for future suicide ideation, attempts, and death: A meta-analysis of longitudinal studies. *Psychological Medicine, 46*(2), 225–236. https://doi.org/10.1017/S0033291715001804

Rodríguez-Blanco, L., Carballo, J. J., & Baca-García, E. (2018). Use of ecological momentary assessment (EMA) in non-suicidal self-injury (NSSI): A systematic review. *Psychiatry Research, 263*, 212–219. https://doi.org/10.1016/j.psychres.2018.02.051

Schoenleber, M., Berenbaum, H., & Motl, R. (2014). Shame-related functions of and motivations for self-injurious behavior. *Personality Disorders: Theory, Research, and Treatment, 5*(2), 204–211. https://doi.org/10.1037/per0000035

Stanford, S., Jones, M. P., & Hudson, J. L. (2018). Appreciating complexity in adolescent self-harm risk factors: Psychological profiling in a longitudinal community sample. *Journal of Youth and Adolescence, 47*(5), 916–931. http://dx.doi.org.du.idm.oclc.org/10.1007/s10964-017-0721-5

Stone, A. A., Bachrach, C. A., Jobe, J. B., Kurtzman, H. S., & Cain, V. S. (1999). *The science of self-report: Implications for research and practice*. Psychology Press.

Surace, T., Fusar-Poli, L., Vozza, L., Cavone, V., Arcidiacono, C., Mammano, R., Basile, L., Rodolico, A., Bisicchia, P., Caponnetto, P., Signorelli, M. S., & Aguglia, E. (2021). Lifetime prevalence of suicidal ideation and suicidal behaviors in gender non-conforming youths: A meta-analysis. *European Child & Adolescent Psychiatry, 30*(8), 1147–1161. https://doi.org/10.1007/s00787-020-01508-5

Swannell, S. V., Martin, G. E., Page, A., Hasking, P., & St John, N. J. (2014). Prevalence of nonsuicidal self-injury in nonclinical samples: Systematic review, meta-analysis and meta-regression. *Suicide and Life-Threatening Behavior, 44*(3), 273–303. https://doi.org/10.1111/sltb.12070

Tabaac, A. R., Perrin, P., & Rabinovitch, A. (2016). The relationship between social support and suicide risk in a national sample of ethnically diverse sexual minority women. *Journal of Gay & Lesbian Mental Health*. https://doi.org/10.1080/19359705.2015.1135842

Taliaferro, L. A., McMorris, B. J., Rider, G. N., & Eisenberg, M. E. (2019). Risk and protective factors for self-harm in a population-based sample of transgender youth. *Archives of Suicide Research, 23*(2), 203–221. https://doi.org/10.1080/13811118.2018.1430639

Tang, J., Yu, Y., Wu, Y., Du, Y., Ma, Y., Zhu, H., Zhang, P., & Liu, Z. (2011). Association between non-suicidal self-injuries and suicide attempts in Chinese adolescents and college students: A cross-section study. *PLoS One, 6*(4), Article e17977. https://doi.org/10.1371/journal.pone.0017977

Tatnell, R., Kelada, L., Hasking, P., & Martin, G. (2014). Longitudinal analysis of adolescent NSSI: The role of intrapersonal and interpersonal factors. *Journal of Abnormal Child Psychology, 42*(6), 885–896. https://doi.org/10.1007/s10802-013-9837-6

Taylor, P. J., Jomar, K., Dhingra, K., Forrester, R., Shahmalak, U., & Dickson, J. M. (2018). A meta-analysis of the prevalence of different functions of non-suicidal self-injury. *Journal of Affective Disorders, 227*, 759–769. https://doi.org/10.1016/j.jad.2017.11.073

Valencia-Agudo, F., Burcher, G. C., Ezpeleta, L., & Kramer, T. (2018). Nonsuicidal self-injury in community adolescents: A systematic review of prospective predictors, mediators and moderators. *Journal of Adolescence, 65*, 25–38. https://doi.org/10.1016/j.adolescence.2018.02.012

Walsh, B. W., & Rosen, P. M. (1988). *Self-mutilation: Theory, research, and treatment*. Guilford Press.

Wang, B., You, J., Lin, M.-P., Xu, S., & Leung, F. (2017). Developmental trajectories of nonsuicidal self-injury in adolescence and intrapersonal/interpersonal risk factors. *Journal of Research on Adolescence, 27*(2), 392–406. https://doi.org/10.1111/jora.12273

Whitlock, J., Muehlenkamp, J., Eckenrode, J., Purington, A., Baral Abrams, G., Barreira, P., & Kress, V. (2013). Nonsuicidal self-injury as a gateway to suicide in young adults. *Journal of Adolescent Health, 52*(4), 486–492. https://doi.org/10.1016/j.jadohealth.2012.09.010

Wu, N., Hou, Y., Chen, P., & You, J. (2019). Peer acceptance and nonsuicidal self-injury among Chinese adolescents: A longitudinal moderated mediation model. *Journal of Youth and Adolescence, 48*(9), 1806–1817. https://doi.org/10.1007/s10964-019-01093-0

You, J., Jiang, Y., Zhang, M., Du, C., Lin, M.-P., & Leung, F. (2017). Perceived parental control, self-criticism, and nonsuicidal self-injury among adolescents: Testing the reciprocal relationships by a three-wave cross-lag model. *Archives of Suicide Research, 21*(3), 379–391. https://doi.org/10.1080/13811118.2016.1199989

You, J., Leung, F., Lai, C. M., & Fu, K. (2012). The associations between non-suicidal self-injury and borderline personality disorder features among Chinese adolescents. *Journal of Personality Disorders, 26*(2), 226–237. https://doi.org/10.1521/pedi.2012.26.2.226

Zelkowitz, R. L., & Cole, D. A. (2019). Self-criticism as a transdiagnostic process in nonsuicidal self-injury and disordered eating: Systematic review and meta-analysis. *Suicide and Life-Threatening Behavior, 49*(1), 310–327. https://doi.org/10.1111/sltb.12436

CHAPTER 37

Early Childhood Trauma and Nonsuicidal Self-Injury

Gianluca Serafini, Nicolò Cipriani, Laura Costanza De Angelis, *and* Mario Amore

> **Abstract**
>
> This chapter discusses the interplay between early childhood trauma and nonsuicidal self-injury. It defines early childhood trauma as the experience of a traumatic event by children aged 0–6 years. A traumatic event primarily refers to an emotionally painful, distressful, or violent event that poses a threat to a child's life, bodily integrity, or sense of safety. The chapter elaborates on different types of childhood trauma, citing how maltreatment consistently presents as the antecedent to psychopathology. It then looks into several childhood trauma prevention and trauma-focused therapeutic approaches, which include trauma-informed care, Dialectical Behavior Therapy, and Acceptance and Commitment Therapy.
>
> **Key Words:** childhood trauma, nonsuicidal self-injury, traumatic event, maltreatment, psychopathology, trauma-informed care, Dialectical Behavior Therapy, Acceptance and Commitment Therapy

Childhood Trauma: Different Types of Childhood Trauma

Early childhood trauma is defined as the experience of a traumatic event by children ages 0–6 years. A traumatic event is an emotionally painful, distressful, or violent event which poses a threat to the child's life, bodily integrity, or sense of safety. It encompasses several domains that share an underlying exposure to variable degree of threat or deprivation (defined as the absence of age-expectant cognitive and social inputs) and includes both unintentional traumatic events and different forms of childhood maltreatment.

Among the different types of traumatic events experienced by a child, maltreatment rather than exposure to other stressors consistently presents as the antecedent to psychopathology. In addition, regardless of the type, severity, and chronicity of trauma, the psychopathological consequences of a traumatic event rely on the actual meaning attributed by the child to the event. For instance, the perception of the threat may be significantly different from the one experienced by adults or older children. While fear of death and physical injury characterize the majority of adult traumas, most children younger than five years may not understand the profound meaning of death and the potential consequences of physical harm. On the other hand, an almost universal childhood fear is the loss of caregivers, especially the primary attachment figure, and what is recognized as "home" (Terr, 2013).

As a consequence, as children are profoundly aware of their dependence on caregivers for survival, they may endure significant adversities as long as they feel protected and cared for. Conversely, when the adversity directly comes from their caretakers, the psychological consequences of a traumatic event may be far more complex.

Childhood Trauma Stress Response Systems

The exposure to a traumatic event results in the physiological activation of the stress-mediating systems, which primarily include the hypothalamic-pituitary-adrenocortical axis and the sympathetic-adreno-medullary system. This activation leads to a significant release of stress-related hormones, including cortisol, corticotropin-releasing hormone, epinephrine, and norepinephrine. In addition, the release of inflammatory cytokines and the sympathetic nervous system activation are also involved in the response to stressful events. While transient increases in these stress mediators are protective and possibly essential for survival, a prolonged and sustained overactivation of these systems may lead to physiological harm and long-term consequences for health.

On the basis of their potential long-term physiological consequences, the National Scientific Council on the Developing Child identified three main stress-response patterns in young children: the positive, the tolerable stress response, and the toxic stress (Shonkoff et al., 2012).

The positive stress response is the exposure to a brief and mild traumatic event (e.g., first day of school, medical visit, vaccine administration, and dealing with frustration). This stress response is experienced in the presence of a caring, stable, and responsive adult who helps the child cope with the stressor, thus facilitating the return of the stress response systems back to baseline status. In this context, positive stress responses are a growth-promoting element of normal development, in which adaptive responses to adverse experiences are reinforced.

The tolerable stress response is associated with exposure to events characterized by a high degree of adversity or threat, usually defined as unintentional traumatic events. Despite the highly stressful event, in the presence of a supportive and protective environment provided by loving caregivers, the long-term physical and psychological consequences can be generally attenuated by the child's adaptive coping strategies.

Conversely, the toxic stress response results from intense, frequent, or enduring activation of the body's stress response systems in the absence of the buffering protection of a supportive, adult relationship. The archetype of toxic stress is childhood maltreatment, a traumatic event characterized by the perception of intentionality to inflict harm and the absence of the buffering protection of a nurturing caregiver. As a consequence, an overactivation of the physiological stress responses in young children can cause stress-induced changes in brain architecture and function, leading to long-term anatomic changes and/

or physiological dysregulation, precursors of later learning a behavioral impairments, and stress-related physical and mental illness.

Childhood Maltreatment

Childhood maltreatment is defined by the World Health Organization (WHO; 2006) as "physical and/or emotional ill-treatment, sexual abuse, neglect or negligence and commercial or other exploitation, which results in actual or potential harm to the child's health, survival, development or dignity in the context of a relationship of responsibility, trust or power" (p. 9). Estimated prevalence rates differ substantially by maltreatment definition and category, gender, and geographical region, and though it is increasingly recognized as a global public health concern, it still remains underrecorded.

Childhood maltreatment comprises two main domains: abuse and neglect. Child abuse is further subdivided in three main categories: physical abuse (deliberate physical harm), emotional abuse (verbal aggression, or behaviors that may humiliate, embarrass, or seriously threaten the child), and sexual abuse (any type of sexual contact/behavior between an adult and the child). Worldwide median prevalence of sexual abuse is around 20%, with wide variation across continents; physical abuse varies from 19% in Europe to 55% in Africa; while emotional abuse varies between 21.1% and 9.5% in the United States and Europe, respectively (Moody et al., 2018).

Although less investigated, child neglect represents the most common form of childhood maltreatment, accounting for about 70% of reported cases of maltreatment with a stable prevalence across countries. It may be further classified as physical neglect, a failure to adequately meet the physical needs of a child, and emotional neglect. The latter represents a failure to satisfy vital emotional and psychological needs such as love and support leading to behavioral, cognitive, and emotional disorders in the child. Unlike physical or sexual abuse, which are usually incident specific, neglect often involves more chronic situations that may not be easily identified as specific incidents due to the lack of visible injuries and their delayed impact on development and psychopathological tracts.

Child maltreatment results from a complex interaction of child, caregiver, and environmental factors, and the co-occurrence of two or more forms of maltreatment is often reported. Though it affects children of all ages, ethnicities, and sociodemographic backgrounds, the presence of coexisting factors increases maltreatment vulnerability. Among these factors, child characteristics that predispose to maltreatment include propensity to physical aggression, poor emotional regulation, distractibility, or oppositive behaviors as well as the presence of special healthcare needs, chronic illnesses, and physical or developmental disabilities. In addition, some circumstances may acutely trigger potential maltreatment, including crying, toilet training, or nighttime awakenings.

On the other hand, several parental factors may reduce their ability to cope with stress thus increasing the potential for maltreatment: low self-esteem, poor impulse control, substance abuse, young age, low educational level, absent social support, mental illness, poverty, unemployment, and personal history of child maltreatment. As a consequence, the combination of unfavorable child, parent, and environmental factors may precipitate abusive behaviors toward children.

The association between childhood maltreatment and the subsequent development of mental and physical health problems throughout the lifespan has been largely demonstrated. One of the largest and most famous investigations is the Adverse Childhood Experiences (ACE) study (Felitti et al., 1998) which assessed the association between childhood maltreatment and later health and well-being. The study, involving more than 17,000 people in the United States, found a high prevalence of exposure to at least one form of abuse or household dysfunction during childhood, and a strong relationship between childhood maltreatment and multiple risk factors for several of the leading causes of death in adults. The original ACE study was subsequently replicated in many other countries, confirming the link between adverse childhood experience and negative health outcomes.

Although not all maltreated children will develop psychopathological disorders, maltreatment occurring during the early years of life may contribute to the emergence of various psychiatric symptoms, including depressive disorders, suicide attempts, posttraumatic stress disorder, anxiety, personality disorder, dissociation, and substance abuse. Childhood maltreatment also impacts economic and social outcomes, including low school attendance, welfare dependency, addiction, at-risk sexual behaviors, and involvement in violence. In addition, an increased risk of death in young adulthood after exposure to child maltreatment has been recently highlighted, particularly for suicide or circumstances involving poisonings, alcohol, drugs, other substances, or mental illness (Schilling & Christian, 2014).

Due to its frequency and the negative lifelong consequences on physical and mental health, child maltreatment represents a concerning public health issue, and despite the identification of many modifiable risk factors, it remains a serious and widespread phenomenon.

Childhood Maltreatment and Nonsuicidal Self-Injury

Childhood maltreatment negatively affects developmental processes across multiple levels, including self-concept, neurophysiology, and emotional regulation, which may contribute to self-injurious behavior. Besides its relevant influence on suicide, exposure to childhood maltreatment has been largely recognized as the most salient factor for nonsuicidal self-injury (NSSI) across a range of age groups and populations, even beyond the effect of other risk factors for self-injury (Gratz et al., 2002). In a large population study, prevalence of child maltreatment has been reported in nearly 55% and 72% of males and females with NSSI, respectively, and three quarter of adults maltreated as children reported NSSI (Swannell et al., 2012).

NSSI, defined as the deliberate destruction of bodily tissue without suicidal intent, is increasingly recognized as a common issue in adolescence, with a prevalence ranging from

10% to 40% (Nock, 2010; see Kiekens et al., this volume). NSSI is typically intentional, deliberate, and directly aimed to alter or destroy bodily tissues, in the absence of conscious suicidal intent. NSSI serves two main functions: an affective/cognitive regulation function in which self-injury leads to an immediate decrease in an aversive internal state or increase in a desired state, and a social regulation function in which self-injury leads to a desired increase in social support or removal of some undesired social situation (see Taylor et al., this volume). In this context, disadaptive skill development secondary to childhood maltreatment may lead to self-injurious behavior as a compensatory strategy for affective and relational regulation.

In the last decades, a significant body of research investigated the complex relationship between childhood maltreatment and self-injury, and despite the high heterogeneity of studies, maltreatment emerged as a strong predictor of NSSI. The nature and the strength of the relationship between childhood trauma and self-injury seems to depend on the type of childhood maltreatment (Liu et al., 2016). A recent meta-analysis systematically reviewed findings from 71 studies examining the association between childhood maltreatment subtypes and NSSI. The authors found a positive association with sexual abuse, physical abuse, physical neglect, emotional abuse, and emotional neglect, with most pronounced effects in community compared with clinical samples. The association was strongest for emotional abuse and weakest for emotional neglect, in spite of the paucity of studies on emotional neglect.

Generally, multiple and repeated maltreatments and familial association with the abuser are predictive for increased frequency and duration of self-injury. Gender differences have also been observed. When compared to males, females who experienced childhood traumatic experiences (particularly sexual abuse) seem to be more vulnerable to NSSI and suicidal behaviors. On the other hand, when physical and sexual abuse co-occurs or when the experience of abuse is prolonged, both males and females were at risk of NSSI and suicidal behaviors (Serafini et al., 2017).

Childhood Sexual Abuse

The direct relationship between childhood sexual abuse and self-injury has been extensively observed across studies. While this association is specific for this type of abuse, the co-occurrence of nonsexual trauma and sexual trauma is high and the contribution of the single trauma on the subsequent risk of NSSI may be variable (Yates et al., 2008). Abuse and perpetrator characteristics may play a role in determining the magnitude of NSSI. More invasive abuse (e.g., abuse involving penetration), abuse involving physical violence, and abuse among those who lacked family or social support (Plunkett et al., 2001) are more likely to increase the risk of subsequent NSSI (Fergusson et al., 2013; Rabinovitch et al., 2015).

Childhood Physical Abuse

Although few studies examined the association between physical abuse and self-injurious behavior, most findings support this relationship. A strong correlation emerged for child physical abuse and cutting, self-destructive behaviors, and intermittent rather than recurrent self-injurious behavior, with onset at around 15–16 years of age, in both general and clinical samples (Chapman et al., 2006).

Child Neglect and/or Emotional Abuse

A positive association between self-reported child physical and/or emotional neglect and suicidal behavior and self-injury has been observed. Nevertheless, mixed results emerged, especially for emotional neglect. The contradictory nature of these results may be due to differences in how neglect, a multidimensional and complex trauma, is operationalized across studies.

In order to clarify the causal role of childhood maltreatment in NSSI and to improve therapeutic strategies of self-injury, important efforts have been made to identify the potential mediators of this relationship. Above all, emotion dysregulation, self-criticism, alexithymia, posttraumatic stress disorder symptoms, and depression emerged as the main moderators.

Emotional Reactivity and Regulation

Described as a pattern of emotional experience and/or expression interfering with adaptive goal-directed behaviors, dysregulation of emotional processes confers vulnerability to a wide range of psychopathological disorders and represents a pivotal mechanism underlying the relationship between childhood trauma and NSSI (Ford & Gómez, 2015). Emotional processes may be defined as emotion reactivity, which is the subjective feeling, the behavioral manifestations, and the bodily responses in reaction to an emotion, and emotion regulation, which refers to the modulation of emotional experience and expression.

The presence of a caregiver providing both an emotionally supportive environment and adaptive models to deal with challenging situations is a critical step for developing adaptive emotion reactivity and regulations skills. Due to the early and significant influence of caregivers, emotional maltreatment has the potential to negatively impact the foundation of socioemotional development. It has been observed that maltreated children display several impairments in recognition, expression, and understanding of emotions, showing high levels of sadness, anger, and hostility and low levels of joy and happiness. To explain the effect of childhood maltreatment on the development of affective processing abilities, multiple theoretical models have been postulated.

The first model, focusing on attachment, addresses the impact of insecure and disturbed parent-child bond on emotion reactivity and regulation (Rom et al., 2003). Maltreatment increases the probability of insecure and disorganized attachment due to the rejecting behavior of parents who punish the child for proximity seeking and expression of needs and emotions, possibly leading to hyporeactivity to both negative and positive emotions, coupled with an inability to regulate emotions when these are activated. In addition, intruding parents may enhance the sense of helplessness and deficits in self-regulation, so that the child develops hyperreactivity to negative emotions and hyporeactivity to positive emotions.

The second theoretical model is based on the social information-processing theory, which describes the cognitive processing and behavioral stages of response execution. According to this model, maltreatment leads to dysfunctional encoding and interpretation of external cues, resulting in high levels of child hostility, anger, and aggression (Crick & Dodge, 1994). Physically abused children demonstrate a more accurate detection of facial expressions of anger compared to other emotions, suggesting that early adverse experiences influence maltreated children's selective attention to threat-related signals (Koizumi & Takagishi, 2014). Maltreated preschool- and school-age children show disruptive and aggressive behaviors and react to peer distress with poorly regulated and inappropriate emotions and behavior, including anger, fear, and aggression rather than empathy and concern (Huang et al., 2022).

A third model linking maltreatment to emotion reactivity and regulation suggests that maltreated children learn dysfunctional reactivity and regulation from their parents. The lack of environmental input about emotions and the compromised emotion regulation profile of caregivers may further compromise the acquisition of appropriate emotion regulation strategies. Several studies reported that maltreated children tend to have parents who display ineffective regulation strategies, low facial expressions of emotions, and greater expression of negative emotions and are less accurate in recognizing facial expressions. These types of parents may fail to teach their children effective ways to reduce distress and negative feelings, invalidating their children's feelings or neglecting them in emotional situations (Shipman et al., 2007).

On the other hand, a large body of evidence suggests that emotion dysregulation confers a significant vulnerability to NSSI. Theoretical models of self-injury (see Hird et al., this volume) suggest that NSSI may occur as a means of handling negative feelings, serving as a maladaptive method to regulate affective experiences (Klonsky, 2007; Nock, 2010). NSSI typically occurs when the person is alone, experiencing negative feelings or thoughts in response to a stressful event, and this behavior is frequently followed by an immediate decrease or cessation of aversive thoughts or feelings (Nock, 2009). In this framework, individuals with deficits in emotion reactivity and regulation are assumed to use self-injury to alter the experience of distress.

Dissociation

Dissociation is defined by DSM-5 as "disruption of and/or discontinuity in the normal integration of consciousness, memory, identity, emotion, perception, body representation, motor control, and behavior" (American Psychiatric Association, 2013, p. 291). The most relevant forms of dissociation are dissociative amnesia, which describes the inability to recall autobiographical information, and depersonalization/derealization disorders which comprises experiences of feeling disconnected or estranged from one's body, thoughts, or emotions (American Psychiatric Association, 2013).

Serving as a method of "escaping" the experience of highly traumatic events, dissociation may represent a coping skill, but when overly reinforced, it may lead to maladaptive functioning and enhancing symptom severity in several psychiatric disorders (Gratz et al., 2002; Nester et al., 2022). Dissociation is strongly associated with self-injury. Dissociative individuals engage in self-injury more frequently, use more methods of self-injury, and began to self-injure at an earlier age when compared to individuals who did not dissociate (Saxe et al., 2002). Recent studies suggest that dissociation may play a mediating role between trauma and self-injury (Ford & Gómez, 2015; Franzke et al., 2015).

Posttraumatic Stress Disorder

Maltreatment occurring during developmentally vulnerable periods of childhood has been strongly associated with an increased risk of posttraumatic stress disorder (PTSD) symptoms (Kolk, 2009). PTSD is a multifaceted syndrome encompassing both trauma-related symptoms and personality disturbance, and it is characterized by the development and the persistence of reexperiencing, avoidant, and hyperarousal symptoms following direct or indirect exposure to a traumatic event (Blake et al., 1990). Co-occurrence of PTSD and NSSI exceeds 50% (Dyer et al., 2009), and evidence from clinical studies support the role of PTSD symptoms in the development and maintenance of self-injury (Bornovalova et al., 2011). Specifically, it has been observed that two episodic symptoms of PTSD, reexperiencing symptoms and avoidance/numbing symptoms, constitute specific mediating mechanisms through which childhood maltreatment, especially sexual abuse, may be associated with subsequent presence and severity of NSSI. The control/suppression of reexperiencing symptoms, which include recurrent, distressing, and intrusive thoughts or images associated with a traumatic event, is more difficult in patients who engage in NSSI (Najmi et al., 2007). In addition, avoidance numbing symptoms, including efforts to avoid reminders of trauma and difficulty feeling positive emotions, has been significantly associated with NSSI above and beyond depressive symptoms (Weierich & Nock, 2008).

Studies on the possible moderating role of personality disorders in the association between PTSD and self-injury is limited, but emerging research suggests that avoidant personality disorder, common among patients with PTSD, is significantly present in patients with PTSD engaging in NSSI. To explain this association, it has been speculated that avoidant personality disorder is strongly linked to an intolerance of emotional distress and difficulties in regulating such distress, which are two of the mechanisms implicated in the development and maintenance of self-injury, and for this reason a considerable influence on NSSI engagement is plausible (Chapman et al., 2006; Gratz & Tull, 2012).

Depression and Psychache

The role of depression as a risk factor of NSSI has been confirmed by multiple studies. At the same time, depression is also known to be a frequent consequence of childhood maltreatment. Maltreated individuals, especially those exposed to childhood emotional abuse, are twice as likely to develop depression in adulthood, display an earlier depression onset, and more frequently develop chronic or treatment-resistant depression (Nanni et al., 2012). A recent study found that depression and anxiety symptoms represent important mediating factors between childhood maltreatment and NSSI, especially for sexual abuse and physical neglect (Brown et al., 2018).

First proposed by Shneidman (1993), psychache refers to "the hurt, anguish, soreness, aching, psychological pain in the psyche, the mind" arising when vital psychological needs are blocked or unmet (p. 145). Evidence suggests psychache to be a strong predictor of suicide (Mento et al., 2020), but literature on its possible mediating role is currently lacking. One recent study demonstrated the effect of psychache as a distinct independent factor mediating the effect of parental invalidation on NSSI during adolescence, even after controlling for the presence of major depression (Holden et al., 2021).

Self-Criticism

Self-criticism is the tendency toward constant and harsh self-scrutiny, excessively critical evaluations of one's own behavior, and negative reactions to perceived failures. It has been associated with various mental disorders, including eating-disordered behavior and suicidal behavior (Werner et al., 2019). Given the directly self-abusive nature of self-injury, self-criticism is also proposed as one of the mechanisms through which early childhood maltreatment is associated with subsequent NSSI, with higher evidence for emotional abuse (Glassman et al., 2007). It has been observed that children who are excessively criticized and verbally or emotionally abused could internalize critical thinking toward the self, developing a self-critical cognitive style. According to this model, to face stressful events, adolescents with such a cognitive style may be more prone to engage in excessive self-criticism and to use NSSI as a form of direct self-punishment (Glassman et al., 2007).

Neurobiological Factors

The marked brain plasticity during the fetal and early childhood periods makes it particularly sensitive to chemical influences, and several animal and human studies demonstrated that persistently high levels of stress hormones alter its developing architecture (Musazzi & Marrocco, 2016; also see Westlund Schreiner et al., this volume). The neural circuits for dealing with stress are particularly malleable (or "plastic") during the fetal and early childhood periods. Early experiences shape how readily they are activated and how well they can be contained and turned off.

The examination of the neurobiological correlates and sequelae of child maltreatment has recently received more attention. Different components of brain functioning have been assessed, using diverse methods, such as neuroendocrine regulation and magnetic resonance imaging. It has been hypothesized that maltreatment may initiate neurobiological alterations and physiological cascades that contribute to self-injury through its influences on the structure, organization, and function of neurobiological stress response systems (Teicher & Samson, 2016). This theory is supported by the finding of a consistent association between childhood abuse and brain alterations, both in clinical and preclinical animal studies (Kelly et al., 2013). Exposure to specific types of abuse seems to selectively target sensory pathways processing the traumatic experience, enhancing neuroplastic adaptive responses to the trauma itself. Not only may the type of abuse have an important role in determining the type of brain alterations, but the age of exposure may be significant, following a different vulnerability period of brain structures, including hippocampus, amygdala, prefrontal and occipital cortex, and the gender of the abused individual (Wan et al., 2022). Nevertheless, the potential reversibility of neurobiological consequences of childhood maltreatment, the high incidence of comorbidities in these patients, as well as the presence of similar findings in apparently resilient individuals with a history of maltreatment render the interpretation of neurobiological studies rather complex.

Neuroendocrine Regulation

The functioning of the hypothalamic-pituitary-adrenal (HPA) axis, an important stress-response physiological system, has been largely investigated in childhood maltreatment settings (Schär et al., 2022). Several brain areas, such as the amygdala, hippocampus, and prefrontal cortex, display a large number of glucocorticoid receptors, which, if exposed to a persistent activation due to stressful experiences, may lead to an alteration of the size and architecture of these areas, as well as to a compromission in learning, memory, and executive functions (McEwen et al., 2016).

In particular, the amygdala and orbitofrontal cortex seem to undergo hypertrophy and overactivity after chronic stress, while the hippocampus and medial prefrontal cortex undergo hypotrophy and reduction in neural connections. This may lead to anxiety symptoms and mood dysregulation due to a loosening in the top-down control system and to hippocampal reduction (McEwen, 2006).

While brief elevations in corticosteroids following acute stressors may improve the ability to physiologically manage stressful experiences, chronic hyperactivity of the HPA axis may lead to higher loss of hippocampal neurons, inhibition of neurogenesis, defective myelination, abnormalities in synaptic pruning, and impaired affective and cognitive ability (Teicher et al., 2002). A number of studies indicate atypical regulation of the HPA axis in some maltreated children, with noteworthy variations among different types of trauma.

Magnetic Resonance Imaging

Increased amygdala volume has been reported specifically in individuals exposed to caregiver neglect, raised with chronically depressed mothers, or who experienced disrupted attachments, while childhood abuse was reported to be associated with reductions in amygdala and hippocampal volume (Tottenham et al., 2010). The amygdala plays an important role in mediating fear and anxiety (Šimić et al., 2021). It activates physiological stress response by stimulating sympathetic activity and promoting the release of corticotropin-releasing hormone (CRH) in the hypothalamus, which lead to increased levels of serum cortisol.

Significant stress in early childhood may trigger amygdala hypertrophy resulting in a hyperresponsive or chronically activated physiological stress response. In addition, alteration in corpus callosus structures were detected both in neglected males and in sexually abused females.

The prefrontal cortex also has a role in mitigating the cortisol response, suppressing amygdala activity, and regulating the autonomic balance (i.e., sympathetic vs. parasympathetic effects) (Zhang et al., 2021). In addition, it plays a role in the development of executive functions, such as decision-making, working memory, behavioral self-regulation, and mood and impulse control (Cisler, 2017). It has been observed that the exposure to stress and elevated cortisol levels result in significant changes in the connectivity within the prefrontal cortex, which may impair its ability to inhibit amygdala activity and adaptive responses to stress (Shonkoff et al., 2012).

Genetic Vulnerability

The association between childhood trauma and the later development of NSSI may also be mediated by epigenetic alterations. Early-life stress and adverse childhood experiences, such as emotional maltreatment, disorganized attachment, parental neglect, or parental abuse seem to lead to an increased risk for psychiatric conditions and ineffective coping strategies due to hyperactivity in the HPA response system (Kundakovic & Champagne, 2015; Nagy et al., 2018). Glucocorticoids receptors in certain brain areas, in particular the hippocampus, may undergo hypoactivation leading to an impairment of the HPA negative-feedback response system (e.g., increase in corticotropin-releasing factor, or CRF) after prolonged exposure to traumatic events in childhood. The epigenetic mechanisms involved in this dysfunction in stress-response after childhood trauma may take place at methylation level (e.g., hypermethylation of the NR3C1 gene), posttranslational histone modifications (e.g., H3 acetylation), and altered miRNAs expression (Mourtzi et al., 2021).

Childhood Trauma Prevention and Trauma Focused Therapeutic Approach

Emerging data suggest that maltreatment can be prevented, and that when it occurs, its negative sequelae can be treated, particularly when intervention is theoretically informed and provided early in development. To decrease the likelihood of NSSI among adolescents, an effective surveillance for significant risk factors in the primary healthcare setting is of paramount importance. Given the high prevalence of early trauma exposure and the role of pediatric providers in facilitating healthy child development, pediatric healthcare networks are an ideal setting to implement a trauma-informed approach to medical care, thus mitigating negative effects of exposure to trauma.

In this context, trauma-informed care (TIC) is a recent and evolving approach which specifically addresses the potential impact of trauma within healthcare and emphasizes physical, psychological, and emotional safety. Originally designed for adult patients with identified previous trauma, TIC is increasingly suggested as a key component of pediatric general practice. The trauma-informed approach includes four key elements: (a) realizing the widespread impact of trauma, (b) recognizing how trauma may affect everyday life, (c) applying knowledge about trauma into practice, and (d) preventing retraumatization. Family interventions directed at decreasing child maltreatment and psychosocial interventions aimed at decreasing adolescent self-criticism may be effective in treating or preventing NSSI (Marsac et al., 2016).

Despite the robust association between childhood trauma and NSSI, pharmacological and psychosocial treatments specifically designed for NSSI following early childhood trauma are still lacking. However, some psychosocial approaches seem to exert beneficial effects on NSSI secondary to trauma exposure, such as dialectical behavior therapy and acceptance and commitment therapy, given their established efficacy in treating self-injury as well as other trauma sequelae, and the common aim to develop more effective affect regulation skills (Mehlum et al., 2016). Dialectical behavioral therapy focuses on the treatment of pervasive emotion dysregulation causing impulsive and maladaptive behaviors, including self-directed violence, as well as the inability to adequately respond to life events (DeCou et al., 2019). Acceptance and commitment therapy has shown to be effective in treating PTSD symptoms and self-injury (Ost, 2014). It prioritizes experiential avoidance and emotional numbing favoring the acceptance and tolerance of painful internal events without resorting to self-injury as a way to avoid or distort them (Orsillo & Batten, 2005). In addition, trauma-focused cognitive-behavioral therapy represents the only intervention thus far indicated for the treatment of posttraumatic stress symptoms related to maltreatment history in children and adolescents (Silverman et al., 2008).

Originally designed to address PTSD symptoms associated with sexual abuse, this model has been adapted to treat various types of abuse and other traumas, such as experiencing physical or emotional abuse or neglect and witnessing community or domestic violence, traumatic loss, war, or natural disasters. Key elements of this intervention include psychoeducation, gradual exposure, behavior modeling, coping strategies, and body safety skills training, that should be adjusted according to the treatment needs of the child and family involved (de Arellano et al., 2014).

Challenges and Future Directions

Even though not all children who have been abused or neglected develop mental illnesses, the burden of psychopathology resulting from child maltreatment is significant. At the same time, NSSI has been identified as one of the strongest predictors for future suicide attempts, highlighting the need for a deeper comprehension of its etiology and its mediating factors (Fox et al., 2015; see Victor et al., this volume). Research on the association between childhood maltreatment and NSSI is characterized by a lack of studies that focus on early adolescence, considered the peak period of NSSI onset. A high heterogeneity in both childhood maltreatment and self-injury evaluation and definitions could explain the rather mixed results among studies. In addition, there still are few studies assessing the moderating factors between different forms of childhood maltreatment and NSSI. Despite the high co-occurrence between maltreatment and self-injury, the cross-sectional nature of most studies makes the causal relationship hard to establish.

For these reasons, there is an urgent need for longitudinal studies assessing the relation between childhood maltreatment subtypes, especially the poorly considered emotional abuse and NSSI, particularly in community settings. In addition, a comprehensive delineation of moderators and mediational pathways through which childhood maltreatment is associated with NSSI may enhance both risk stratification strategies and targeted interventions.

References

American Psychiatric Association. (2013). *Diagnostic and statistical manual of mental disorders* (5th ed.). https://doi.org/10.1176/appi.books.9780890425596

Blake, D. D., Weathers, F. W., Nagy, L. M., Kaloupek, D. G., Klauminzer, G., Charney, D. S., & Keane, T. M. (1990). A clinician rating scale for assessing current and lifetime PTSD: The CAPS-1. *The Behavior Therapist*, *13*, 187–188

Bornovalova, M. A., Tull, M. T., Gratz, K. L., Levy, R., & Lejuez, C. W. (2011). Extending models of deliberate self-harm and suicide attempts to substance users: Exploring the roles of childhood abuse, posttraumatic stress, and difficulties controlling impulsive behavior when distressed. *Psychological Trauma: Theory, Research, Practice, and Policy*, *3*(4), 349–359. https://doi.org/10.1037/a0021579

Brown, R. C., Heines, S., Witt, A., Braehler, E., Fegert, J. M., Harsch, D., & Plener, P. L. (2018). The impact of child maltreatment on non-suicidal self-injury: Data from a representative sample of the general population. *BMC Psychiatry*, *18*(1), 1–8. https://doi.org/10.1186/s12888-018-1754-3

Chapman, A. L., Gratz, K. L., & Brown, M. Z. (2006). Solving the puzzle of deliberate self-harm: The experiential avoidance model. *Behaviour Research and Therapy*, *44*(3), 371–394. https://doi.org/10.1016/j.brat.2005.03.005

Cisler, J. M. (2017, May). Childhood trauma and functional connectivity between amygdala and medial prefrontal cortex: A dynamic functional connectivity and large-scale network perspective. *Frontiers in Systems Neuroscience*, *11*, 1–11. https://doi.org/10.3389/fnsys.2017.00029

Crick, N. R., & Dodge, K. A. (1994). A Review and reformulation of social information-processing mechanisms in children's social adjustment. *Psychological Bulletin*, *115*(1), 74–101. https://doi.org/10.1037/0033-2909.115.1.74

de Arellano, M. A., Lyman, D. R., Jobe-Shields, L., George, P., Dougherty, R. H., Daniels, A. S., Ghose, S. S., Huang, L., & Delphin-Rittmon, M. E. (2014). Trauma-focused cognitive-behavioral therapy for children and adolescents: Assessing the evidence. *Psychiatric Services (Washington, D.C.)*, *65*(5), 591–602. https://doi.org/10.1176/appi.ps.201300255

DeCou, C. R., Comtois, K. A., & Landes, S. J. (2019). Dialectical behavior therapy is effective for the treatment of suicidal behavior: A meta-analysis. *Behavior Therapy*, *50*(1), 60–72. https://doi.org/10.1016/j.beth.2018.03.009

Dyer, K. F., Dorahy, M. J., Hamilton, G., Corry, M., Shannon, M., MacSherry, A., McRobert, G., Elder, R., & McElhill, B. (2009). Anger, aggression, and self-harm in PTSD and complex PTSD. *Journal of Clinical Psychology*, *65*(10), 1099–1114. https://doi.org/10.1002/jclp.20619

Felitti, V. J., Anda, R. F., Nordenberg, D., Williamson, D. F., Spitz, A. M., Edwards, V., Koss, M. P., & Marks, J. S. (1998). Relationship of childhood abuse and household dysfunction to many of the leading causes of death in adults. The Adverse Childhood Experiences (ACE) study. *American Journal of Preventive Medicine*, *14*(4), 245–258. https://doi.org/10.1016/s0749-3797(98)00017-8

Fergusson, D. M., McLeod, G. F. H., & Horwood, L. J. (2013). Childhood sexual abuse and adult developmental outcomes: Findings from a 30-year longitudinal study in New Zealand. *Child Abuse and Neglect, 37*(9), 664–674. https://doi.org/10.1016/j.chiabu.2013.03.013

Ford, J. D., & Gómez, J. M. (2015). The relationship of psychological trauma and dissociative and posttraumatic stress disorders to nonsuicidal self-injury and suicidality: A review. *Journal of Trauma and Dissociation, 16*(3), 232–271. https://doi.org/10.1080/15299732.2015.989563

Fox, K. R., Franklin, J. C., Ribeiro, J. D., Kleiman, E. M., Bentley, K. H., & Nock, M. K. (2015). Meta-analysis of risk factors for nonsuicidal self-injury. *Clinical Psychology Review, 42*, 156–167. https://doi.org/10.1016/j.cpr.2015.09.002

Franzke, I., Wabnitz, P., & Catani, C. (2015). Dissociation as a mediator of the relationship between childhood trauma and nonsuicidal self-injury in females: A path analytic approach. *Journal of Trauma & Dissociation: The Official Journal of the International Society for the Study of Dissociation (ISSD), 16*(3), 286–302. https://doi.org/10.1080/15299732.2015.989646

Glassman, L. H., Weierich, M. R., Hooley, J. M., Deliberto, T. L., & Nock, M. K. (2007). Child maltreatment, non-suicidal self-injury, and the mediating role of self-criticism. *Behaviour Research and Therapy, 45*(10), 2483–2490. https://doi.org/10.1016/j.brat.2007.04.002

Gratz, K. L., Conrad, S. D., & Roemer, L. (2002). Risk factors for deliberate self-harm among college students. *American Journal of Orthopsychiatry, 72*(1), 128–140.

Gratz, K. L., & Tull, M. T. (2012). Exploring the relationship between posttraumatic stress disorder and deliberate self-harm: The moderating roles of borderline and avoidant personality disorders. *Psychiatry Research, 199*(1), 19–23. https://doi.org/10.1016/j.psychres.2012.03.025

Holden, R. R., Lambert, C. E., La Rochelle, M., Billet, M. I., & Fekken, G. C. (2021). Invalidating childhood environments and nonsuicidal self-injury in university students: Depression and mental pain as potential mediators. *Journal of Clinical Psychology, 77*(3), 722–731. https://doi.org/10.1002/jclp.23052

Huang, Y., Zhang, S., Zhong, S., Gou, N., Sun, Q., Guo, H., Lin, R., Guo, W., Chen, H., Wang, J., Zhou, J., & Wang, X. (2022). The association of childhood adversities and mental health problems with dual-harm in individuals with serious aggressive behaviors. *BMC Psychiatry, 22*(1), Article 385. https://doi.org/10.1186/s12888-022-04027-6

Kelly, P. A., Viding, E., Wallace, G. L., Schaer, M., De Brito, S. A., Robustelli, B., & McCrory, E. J. (2013). Cortical thickness, surface area, and gyrification abnormalities in children exposed to maltreatment: Neural markers of vulnerability?. *Biological Psychiatry, 74*(11), 845–852. https://doi.org/10.1016/j.biopsych.2013.06.020

Klonsky, E. D. (2007). The functions of deliberate self-injury: A review of the evidence. *Clinical Psychology Review, 27*(2), 226–239. https://doi.org/10.1016/j.cpr.2006.08.002

Koizumi, M., & Takagishi, H. (2014). The relationship between child maltreatment and emotion recognition. *PloS One, 9*(1), Article e86093. https://doi.org/10.1371/journal.pone.0086093

Kundakovic, M., & Champagne, F. A. (2015). Early-life experience, epigenetics, and the developing brain. *Neuropsychopharmacology, 40*(1), 141–153. https://doi.org/10.1038/npp.2014.140

Liu, R. T., Scopelliti, K. M., Pittman, S. K., & Zamora, A. S. (2016). Childhood maltreatment and non-suicidal self-injury: A systematic review and meta-analysis. *Physiology & Behavior, 176*(1), 100–106. https://doi.org/10.1016/S2215-0366(17)30469-8.Childhood

Marsac, M. L., Kassam-Adams, N., Hildenbrand, A. K., Nicholls, E., Winston, F. K., Leff, S. S., & Fein, J. (2016). Implementing a trauma-informed approach in pediatric health care networks. *JAMA Pediatrics, 170*(1), 70–77. https://doi.org/10.1001/jamapediatrics.2015.2206

McEwen, B. S. (2006). Protective and damaging effects of stress mediators: Central role of the brain. *Dialogues in Clinical Neuroscience, 8*(4), 367–381. https://doi.org/10.31887/dcns.2006.8.4/bmcewen

McEwen, B. S., Nasca, C., & Gray, J. D. (2016). Stress effects on neuronal structure: Hippocampus, amygdala, and prefrontal cortex. *Neuropsychopharmacology: Official Publication of the American College of Neuropsychopharmacology, 41*(1), 3–23. https://doi.org/10.1038/npp.2015.171

Mehlum, L., Ramberg, M., Tørmoen, A. J., Haga, E., Diep, L. M., Stanley, B. H., Miller, A. L., Sund, A. M., & Grøholt, B. (2016). Dialectical behavior therapy compared with enhanced usual care for adolescents with repeated suicidal and self-harming behavior: Outcomes over a one-year follow-up. *Journal of the American Academy of Child and Adolescent Psychiatry, 55*(4), 295–300. https://doi.org/10.1016/j.jaac.2016.01.005

Mento, C., Silvestri, M. C., Muscatello, M., Rizzo, A., Celebre, L., Bruno, A., & Zoccali, A. R. (2020). Psychological pain and risk of suicide in adolescence. *International Journal of Adolescent Medicine and Health, 34*(3). https://doi.org/10.1515/ijamh-2019-0270

Moody, G., Cannings-John, R., Hood, K., Kemp, A., & Robling, M. (2018). Establishing the international prevalence of self-reported child maltreatment: A systematic review by maltreatment type and gender. *BMC Public Health, 18*(1), 1–15. https://doi.org/10.1186/s12889-018-6044-y

Mourtzi, N., Sertedaki, A., & Charmandari, E. (2021). Glucocorticoid signaling and epigenetic alterations in stress-related disorders. *International Journal of Molecular Sciences, 22*(11), Article 5964. https://doi.org/10.3390/ijms22115964

Musazzi, L., & Marrocco, J. (2016). Stress response and perinatal reprogramming: Unraveling (mal)adaptive strategies. *Neural Plasticity, 2016*, Article 6752193. https://doi.org/10.1155/2016/6752193

Nagy, C., Vaillancourt, K., & Turecki, G. (2018). A role for activity-dependent epigenetics in the development and treatment of major depressive disorder. *Genes, Brain and Behavior, 17*(3), 1–9. https://doi.org/10.1111/gbb.12446

Najmi, S., Wegner, D. M., & Nock, M. K. (2007). Thought suppression and self-injurious thoughts and behaviors. *Behaviour Research and Therapy, 45*(8), 1957–1965. https://doi.org/10.1016/j.brat.2006.09.014

Nanni, V., Uher, R., & Danese, A. (2012). Childhood maltreatment predicts unfavorable course of illness and treatment outcome in depression: A meta-analysis. *American Journal of Psychiatry, 169*(2), 141–151. https://doi.org/10.1176/appi.ajp.2011.11020335

Nester, M. S., Brand, B. L., Schielke, H. J., & Kumar, S. (2022). An examination of the relations between emotion dysregulation, dissociation, and self-injury among dissociative disorder patients. *European Journal of Psychotraumatology, 13*(1), Article 2031592. https://doi.org/10.1080/20008198.2022.2031592

Nock, M. K. (2009). Why do people hurt themselves?: New insights into the nature and functions of self-injury. *Current Directions in Psychological Science, 18*(2), 78–83. https://doi.org/10.1111/j.1467-8721.2009.01613.x

Nock, M. K. (2010). Self-injury. *Annual Review of Clinical Psychology, 6*, 339–363. https://doi.org/10.1146/annurev.clinpsy.121208.131258

Orsillo, S. M., & Batten, S. V. (2005). Acceptance and commitment therapy in the treatment of posttraumatic stress disorder. *Behavior Modification, 29*(1), 95–129. https://doi.org/10.1177/0145445504270876

Ost, L. G. (2014). The efficacy of acceptance and commitment therapy: An updated systematic review and meta-analysis. *Behaviour Research and Therapy, 61*, 105–121. https://doi.org/10.1016/j.brat.2014.07.018

Plunkett, A., O'Toole, B., Swanston, H., Oates, R. K., Shrimpton, S., & Parkinson, P. (2001). Suicide risk following child sexual abuse. *Ambulatory Pediatrics, 1*(5), 262–266. https://doi.org/10.1367/1539-4409(2001)001<0262:SRFCSA>2.0.CO;2

Rabinovitch, S. M., Kerr, D. C. R., Leve, L. D., & Chamberlain, P. (2015). Suicidal behavior outcomes of childhood sexual abuse: Longitudinal study of adjudicated girls. *Suicide and Life-Threatening Behavior, 45*(4), 431–447. https://doi.org/10.1111/sltb.12141

Rom, E., & Mikulincer, M. (2003). Attachment theory and group processes: The association between attachment style and group-related representations, goals, memories, and functioning. *Journal of Personality and Social Psychology, 84*(6), 1220–1235. https://doi.org/10.1037/0022-3514.84.6.1220

Saxe, G. N., Chawla, N., & van der Kolk, B. (2002). Self-destructive behavior in patients with dissociative disorders. *Suicide and Life-Threatening Behavior, 32*(3), 313–320. https://doi.org/10.1521/suli.32.3.313.22174

Schär, S., Mürner-Lavanchy, I., Schmidt, S. J., Koenig, J., & Kaess, M. (2022). Child maltreatment and hypothalamic-pituitary-adrenal axis functioning: A systematic review and meta-analysis. *Frontiers in Neuroendocrinology, 66*, Article 100987. Advance online publication. https://doi.org/10.1016/j.yfrne.2022.100987

Schilling, S., & Christian, C. W. (2014). Child physical abuse and neglect. *Child and Adolescent Psychiatric Clinics of North America, 23*(2), 309–319. https://doi.org/10.1016/j.chc.2014.01.001

Serafini, G., Canepa, G., Adavastro, G., Nebbia, J., Murri, M. B., Erbuto, D., Pocai, B., Fiorillo, A., Pompili, M., Flouri, E., & Amore, M. (2017, August). The relationship between childhood maltreatment and non-suicidal self-injury: A systematic review. *Frontiers in Psychiatry, 8*, Article 149. https://doi.org/10.3389/fpsyt.2017.00149

Shipman, K. L., Schneider, R., Fitzgerald, M. M., Sims, C., Swisher, L., & Edwards, A. (2007). Maternal emotion socialization in maltreating and non-maltreating families: Implications for children's emotion regulation. *Social Development, 16*(2), 268–285. https://doi.org/10.1111/j.1467-9507.2007.00384.x

Shneidman, E. S. (1993). Commentary: Suicide as psychache. *Journal of Nervous and Mental Disease, 181*(3), 145–147. https://doi.org/10.1097/00005053-199303000-00001

Shonkoff, J. P., Garner, A. S., Siegel, B. S., Dobbins, M. I., Earls, M. F., McGuinn, L., Pascoe, J., Wood, D. L., High, P. C., Donoghue, E., Fussell, J. J., Gleason, M. M., Jaudes, P. K., Jones, V. F., Rubin, D. M., Schulte, E. E., Macias, M. M., Bridgemohan, C., Fussell, J.. . . Wegner, L. M. (2012). The lifelong effects of early childhood adversity and toxic stress. *Pediatrics*, *129*(1), e232–e246. https://doi.org/10.1542/peds.2011-2663

Silverman, W. K., Pina, A. A., & Viswesvaran, C. (2008). Evidence-based psychosocial treatments for phobic and anxiety disorders in children and adolescents. *Journal of Clinical Child and Adolescent Psychology*, *37*(1), 105–130. https://doi.org/10.1080/15374410701817907

Šimić, G., Tkalčić, M., Vukić, V., Mulc, D., Španić, E., Šagud, M., Olucha-Bordonau, F. E., Vukšić, M., & Hof, P. R. (2021). Understanding emotions: Origins and roles of the amygdala. *Biomolecules*, *11*(6), Article 823. https://doi.org/10.3390/biom11060823

Swannell, S., Martin, G., Page, A., Hasking, P., Hazell, P., Taylor, A., & Protani, M. (2012). Child maltreatment, subsequent non-suicidal self-injury and the mediating roles of dissociation, alexithymia and self-blame. *Child Abuse and Neglect*, *36*(7–8), 572–584. https://doi.org/10.1016/j.chiabu.2012.05.005

Teicher, M. H., Andersen, S. L., Polcari, A., Anderson, C. M., & Navalta, C. P. (2002). Developmental neurobiology of childhood stress and trauma. *Psychiatric Clinics of North America*, *25*(2), 397–426.

Teicher, M. H., & Samson, J. A. (2016). Annual research review: Enduring neurobiological effects of childhood abuse and neglect. *Journal of Child Psychology and Psychiatry, and Allied Disciplines*, *57*(3), 241–266. https://doi.org/10.1111/jcpp.12507

Terr, L. C. (2013). Treating childhood trauma. *Child and Adolescent Psychiatric Clinics of North America*, *22*(1), 51–66. https://doi.org/10.1016/j.chc.2012.08.003

Tottenham, N., Hare, T. A., Quinn, B. T., McCarry, T. W., Nurse, M., Gilhooly, T., Millner, A., Galvan, A., Davidson, M. C., Eigsti, I. M., Thomas, K. M., Freed, P. J., Booma, E. S., Gunnar, M. R., Altemus, M., Aronson, J., & Casey, B. J. (2010). Prolonged institutional rearing is associated with atypically large amygdala volume and difficulties in emotion regulation. *Developmental Science*, *13*(1), 46–61. https://doi.org/10.1111/j.1467-7687.2009.00852.x

van der Kolk, B. A. (2009). Entwicklungstrauma-störung: Auf dem weg zu einer sinnvollen diagnostik für chronisch traumatisierte kinder. *Praxis Der Kinderpsychologie Und Kinderpsychiatrie*, *58*(8), 572–586. https://doi.org/10.13109/prkk.2009.58.8.572

Wan, Z., Rolls, E. T., Feng, J., & Cheng, W. (2022). Brain functional connectivities that mediate the association between childhood traumatic events, and adult mental health and cognition. *EBioMedicine*, *79*, Article 104002. https://doi.org/10.1016/j.ebiom.2022.104002

Weierich, M. R., & Nock, M. K. (2008). Posttraumatic stress symptoms mediate the relation between childhood sexual abuse and nonsuicidal self-injury. *Journal of Consulting and Clinical Psychology*, *76*(1), 39–44. https://doi.org/10.1037/0022-006X.76.1.39

Werner, A. M., Tibubos, A. N., Rohrmann, S., & Reiss, N. (2019). The clinical trait self-criticism and its relation to psychopathology: A systematic review—Update. *Journal of Affective Disorders*, *246*, 530–547. https://doi.org/10.1016/j.jad.2018.12.069

World Health Organization. (2006). *Preventing child maltreatment: A guide to taking action and generating evidence*.

Yates, T. M., Carlson, E. A., & Egeland, B. (2008). A prospective study of child maltreatment and self-injurious behavior in a community sample. *Development and Psychopathology*, *20*(2), 651–671. https://doi.org/10.1017/S0954579408000321

Zhang, W. H., Zhang, J. Y., Holmes, A., & Pan, B. X. (2021). Amygdala circuit substrates for stress adaptation and adversity. *Biological Psychiatry*, *89*(9), 847–856. https://doi.org/10.1016/j.biopsych.2020.12.026

CHAPTER 38

The Parent-Child Dyad and Other Family Factors Associated with Youth Nonsuicidal Self-Injury

Kiera M. James *and* Brandon E. Gibb

Abstract

Nonsuicidal self-injury (NSSI) is a significant public health concern with clear negative consequences for the individual and their families. NSSI is most prevalent during adolescence—a developmental period during which youth navigate normative interpersonal stressors and developmental challenges. Although elevated rates of NSSI during adolescence are likely due to a combination of genetic, environmental, and contextual factors, this chapter focuses specifically on the influence of parents and the parent-child relationship on risk. To this end, we outline relevant theoretical frameworks in the context of developmental trajectories of NSSI. We review risk factors involving parents and the parent-child dyad, including parent-related factors that perpetuate risk in the context of parental awareness or youth disclosure of NSSI. We discuss protective factors within the parent-child dyad that reduce risk for youth NSSI, and provide an overview of interventions for youth NSSI that involve strong parental components, including parent training and parent education programs.

Key Words: parent, youth, parent-child relationships, NSSI, parent training, communication, psychoeducation

Nonsuicidal self-injury (NSSI), which involves intentional self-inflicted harm without the intent to die (cutting, scratching, burning, hitting self, inserting objects under nails, etc.), is a transdiagnostic behavior that occurs in the presence of many psychiatric diagnoses as well as in the absence of any diagnosis (Nock et al., 2006). Nonetheless, NSSI and suicidal thoughts and behaviors are highly comorbid, and there is clear evidence that NSSI heightens risk not only for future engagement in NSSI but also for suicide attempts (Ribeiro et al., 2016). There are clear age differences in NSSI, with adolescents reporting higher rates of NSSI than children or adults. More specifically, studies suggest a lifetime NSSI prevalence of approximately 8% in children, 18% in adolescents, and 6% in adults (Barrocas et al., 2012; Muehlenkamp et al., 2012; Swannell et al., 2014). There is also a small but significant sex difference in NSSI, with women across all age groups being one and a half times as likely to have a history of NSSI as men (Bresin & Schoenleber, 2015). Moreover, there is also evidence that rates of NSSI are significantly elevated in gender and sexual minority groups. For example, 45%–55% of transgender or gender nonconforming teens reported NSSI within the last year (Clark et al., 2014; Eisenberg et al., 2017). In addition, in a large sample of children, those identifying as gay or bisexual were 4.7 times more likely than children identifying as heterosexual to report a history of NSSI (21.6% vs. 5.5%; Blashill et al., 2021).

The precise reasons for these high rates of NSSI in youth are unclear and are likely due to a combination of genetic, environmental, and contextual factors. In this chapter, we focus specifically on the influence of parents and the parent-child relationship. Although this overview includes a focus on parental characteristics and parent-child relational risk factors for NSSI, we also discuss the reciprocal nature of youth NSSI and factors involved in parent-child interactions. Therefore, we first outline relevant theoretical frameworks in the context of developmental trajectories of NSSI and then review risk factors involving parents and the parent-child dyad. Third, we review parent-related factors that perpetuate risk in the context of parental awareness or youth disclosure of NSSI. Fourth, we discuss protective factors within the parent-child dyad that reduce the risk for youth NSSI. Fifth, we provide an overview of interventions for youth NSSI that involve strong parental components, including parent education programs. The sixth section presents a case example that illustrates some of the relations described in this chapter. Finally, we propose important areas for future research in these areas.

Theoretical Frameworks of NSSI

Theoretical frameworks for NSSI are still evolving. Many of these theories focus on the role of emotional reactivity and emotion regulation. For example, according to many classic theories of NSSI, elevated levels of negative affect and increased reactivity to emotional stimuli play key roles in risk for NSSI (Chapman et al., 2006; Hasking et al., 2016; Linehan, 1993; Selby & Joiner, 2009). In contrast, more recent models include a more explicit focus on interpersonal influences.

In their four functions model of NSSI, Nock and Prinstein (2004) hypothesize four processes that reinforce NSSI (see Hird et al., this volume). These processes fall along two separate dimensions: positive versus negative and automatic (intrapersonal) versus social (interpersonal). The intrapersonal functions (i.e., automatic negative and automatic positive reinforcement) build from earlier emotion regulation models of NSSI, suggesting that self-injury is preceded by emotion dysregulation and can function as an emotion regulation strategy. However, the interpersonal functions (i.e., social negative reinforcement and social positive reinforcement) represent novel additions and highlight interpersonal processes in NSSI risk. Specifically, they suggest that engagement in NSSI may help to modify the individual's social environment (e.g., increase attention or reduce punishment). This model, therefore, highlights the potential role of an individual's social environment in the decision to engage in NSSI, presuming that individuals with undesirable or negative social environments may be more motivated to change their social environment than individuals without such social stress. Further, it is important to note that the interpersonal and intrapersonal factors underscored in this model may be concurrently present and correlated given that the perception of a negative or stressful social environment may be exacerbated by a propensity for emotion dysregulation or heightened reactivity to emotional situations.

Hooley and Franklin (2018) built upon earlier models but proposed that, despite evidence that NSSI is often preceded by increased negative affect and emotion dysregulation, those who engage in NSSI do not necessarily experience higher levels of negative affect or emotion dysregulation compared to individuals who do not engage in NSSI. Rather, these theorists propose that NSSI is a behavioral strategy employed by individuals for whom the benefits of NSSI—which can include emotion regulation, self-punishment, peer group affiliation, and/or communication—outweigh the physiological, psychological, and social barriers of such behavior. Thus, in addition to NSSI being reinforced through emotion regulation or self-punishment, social influences are hypothesized to play a key role either in terms of closer perceived ties to a desired social group or through its perceived utility in communicating distress (or strength) to others.

Finally, the family distress cascade theory (Waals et al., 2018) focuses specifically on dynamic cycles of risk within families. Waals et al. proposed that following disclosure of NSSI, parents may demonstrate increased hypervigilance and heightened efforts to control their child's behavior because of their own experience of guilt, fear, or shame, which, in turn, perpetuates risk. This model is unique in that it underscores the reciprocal relation between parental factors and youth NSSI, particularly following the parental discovery of youth NSSI. As such, this model may provide a particularly relevant theoretical framework for NSSI risk across childhood and adolescence given compounding interpersonal stressors (e.g., balancing relationships with peers and parents) and normative developmental challenges (e.g., desire for more independence) that occur during this period.

Parental and Parent-Child Relational Risk Factors

Evidence for relations between youth NSSI and numerous parental factors has been growing over the last two decades (Arbuthnott & Lewis, 2015; Bean et al., 2021; Fortune et al., 2016). This line of research comprises efforts to understand the role of parental characteristics (e.g., psychopathology), as well as factors related to the parent-child relationship and interactions, including relationship quality, relational conflict, perceived lack of parental support, invalidation, rejection, parental control, and perceived parental criticism. Importantly, there is also growing theoretical and empirical support for additional parent-related factors that emerge and perpetuate risk following youth disclosure or parental awareness of NSSI (i.e., parental well-being and access to accurate information about NSSI). Relevant findings are reviewed and discussed below.

Parental Self-Injury and Psychopathology

There is strong empirical support for the intergenerational transmission of suicidal thoughts and behaviors (Brent & Melhem, 2008), which is likely due to both genetic and environmental influences. Although much less work has focused on NSSI specifically, evidence from a twin study suggests that genetic influences account for 46% and 62% of the variance in NSSI for men and women, respectively (MacIejewski et al., 2014). Regarding the behavior itself, however, only two studies of which we are aware have examined the link between parent and offspring NSSI. One of these, which focused on offspring of parents with a history of mood disorders, found that neither parental NSSI nor suicide attempts prospectively predicted youth engagement in NSSI over a one- to eight-year follow-up (Cox et al., 2012). In contrast, a study of college students found that those who reported a history of NSSI in their parents were more likely to have a history of NSSI themselves than were those who denied any history of NSSI in their parents (Dawkins et al., 2019). Although the reason for this difference in findings is not clear, it is possible that intergenerational transmission of NSSI risk is more likely when offspring are directly exposed to NSSI in their parents or are at least aware of its occurrence.

Research regarding the impact of parent psychopathology on youth NSSI is similarly sparse and has also yielded mixed results. For example, maternal and paternal depression have been linked to youth history of NSSI (Wilcox et al., 2012), and one study found that onset of maternal depression predicted subsequent NSSI in youth (Hankin & Abela, 2011). In contrast, however, other research found no association between parental mood and anxiety disorders and youth NSSI and suggested, instead, that parental substance use disorders and attention deficit/hyperactivity disorder (ADHD) are associated with youth NSSI (Gromatsky et al., 2017; Gromatsky et al., 2020). Clearly, more research is needed in this area.

Parent-Child Relationship and Interactions

Research examining factors related to the parent-child relationship and interactions provides clear evidence that perceived lack of parental support, perceived invalidation/rejection, and general conflict within the parent-child relationship are associated with youth engagement in NSSI (Arbuthnott & Lewis, 2015; Bean et al., 2021; Fortune et al., 2016). This research comprises both cross-sectional (Adrian et al., 2011; Ammerman & Brown, 2018; Claes et al., 2015; Liu et al., 2020) and longitudinal (Andrews et al., 2013; Hilt et al., 2008; Victor et al., 2019; You & Leung, 2012; Zhu et al., 2020) studies that employ a variety of self-report measures of the parent-child relational and interaction factors. For instance, a perceived lack of parental support is associated with prior engagement in NSSI among youth (Ammerman & Brown, 2018), and prospectively predicts youth engagement in NSSI over a 12-month follow-up (Andrews et al., 2013; Tatnell et al., 2014). Similarly, parental invalidation predicts youths' future engagement in NSSI in research involving self-report assessment (You & Leung, 2012) and behavioral coding of invalidation during parent-child interactions (Adrian et al., 2018). Finally, still other research suggests that harsh parental punishment, low parental monitoring, and poor parent-child attachment quality are associated with first occurrence of NSSI within the next year (Victor et al., 2019), which further supports earlier findings that youth who self-injure report poorer parent-child relationship quality than youth who do not (Hilt et al., 2008). There is also evidence that these relations persist into adulthood, such that adults who endorsed NSSI within the previous six months also described experiencing increased parental control, parental alienation, and fear or concern related to their parents' care (or lack thereof) during childhood (Bureau et al., 2010).

Notably, a small but growing line of research focused specifically on the relation between parental criticism and youth NSSI has emerged from the larger body of literature examining parent-child relational factors and NSSI. Research in this area has employed measures of youths' perceived levels of parental criticism (Ammerman & Brown, 2018; Baetens et al., 2015a; Yates et al., 2008) and interviewer-coded levels of parental criticism (James & Gibb, 2019; Wedig & Nock, 2007), with both cross-sectional (Ammerman & Brown, 2018; Wedig & Nock, 2007; Yates et al., 2008) and longitudinal (Yates et al., 2008) designs. Taken together, these studies suggest that youths' perceptions of parental criticism as well as interviewer-coded levels of parental criticism are linked to youth NSSI. Specifically, youth of parents exhibiting high, compared to low, levels of criticism are more likely to have a past history of NSSI (Ammerman & Brown, 2018; James & Gibb, 2019; Wedig & Nock, 2007) and are more likely to engage in NSSI in the future (Yates et al., 2008). Support for the link between parental criticism and NSSI across these two levels of analysis is important as youths' perceptions of parental criticism may be susceptible to response or recall bias. It is also important to note that, like other parent-child relational and interaction factors, there is preliminary evidence that parental criticism during childhood continues to be associated with engagement in NSSI into adulthood (Daly & Willoughby, 2019; Hack & Martin, 2018).

Thus far, we have focused on the impact of parent factors on youth NSSI. However, as noted above, this relation is hypothesized to be reciprocal (Waals et al., 2018). Supporting this transactional model of risk, one qualitative study synthesizing interviews from 20 parents of youth who engage in NSSI underscores how parental awareness of youth NSSI can alter parenting and communication styles within a family in an effort to reduce risk of additional NSSI (Fu et al., 2020). Also consistent with transactional models, findings from one recent longitudinal study suggest that parental rejection predicts prospective NSSI engagement and that youth NSSI engagement predicts prospective parental rejection (Zhu et al., 2020). Another study similarly suggests reciprocal relations between parental control and youth NSSI such that higher levels of parental control were associated with youth NSSI six months later and youth NSSI predicted prospective increases in parental control (You et al., 2017). These efforts to better understand the relation between these parent-child factors and risks are critical to reducing risk and offer support for a dynamic cycle of risk.

Finally, we want to briefly acknowledge that although this chapter is focused specifically on the role of parental and parent-child relational factors on risk for NSSI in youth, at a broader level, myriad family factors are also associated with youth NSSI (e.g., Baetens et al., 2015b; DeVille et al., 2020; Hack & Martin, 2018; Hasking et al., 2020; Jiang et al., 2016; Kelada et al., 2016; Webster & King, 2018). Further, the impact of youth NSSI on parents' well-being (described below) can dramatically impact the dynamic and functioning of a family (e.g., Byrne et al., 2008). Indeed, factors such as family functioning (Baetens et al., 2015b; Hasking et al., 2020a; Kelada et al., 2018), cohesion (Cruz et al., 2014; Liang et al., 2014), conflict (DeVille et al., 2020), and communication patterns (Hack & Martin, 2018; Latina et al., 2015; Webster & King, 2018) have each been linked to risk for NSSI in youth. Of note, although poor communication may increase risk for NSSI, communication competence within a family may also serve as a protective factor with risk for NSSI decreasing as competence increases (Latina et al., 2015; Webster & King, 2018). It is likely that many of these family factors encompass, and are fed by, the parental and parent-child relational factors previously described. Nonetheless, these factors may also provide additional and important system-level context for youth risk.

Parental Awareness and NSSI Disclosure

It is not uncommon for youth to hide their engagement in NSSI from others (Fortune et al., 2008b; Rossow & Wichstrøm, 2010). Furthermore, many parents of youth who self-injure are never aware of their child's engagement in NSSI (Baetens et al., 2014; Kelada et al., 2016; Mojtabai & Olfson, 2008). Because youth are more likely to disclose their NSSI to a friend than to a parent (Fortune et al., 2008b; Rossow & Wichstrøm, 2010; Watanabe et al., 2012), parents are sometimes made aware of youth NSSI by their child's school or medical provider (Oldershaw et al., 2008). Moreover, youth who choose to disclose their NSSI directly to a parent are more likely to disclose after an episode of NSSI rather than in the process of seeking help from a parent to prevent NSSI (Evans et al., 2005). To this end, factors that contribute to initial and ongoing parental responses to NSSI disclosure, including parental well-being and psychological education, may play an integral role in future help-seeking prior to NSSI engagement and NSSI cessation.

Parental Well-Being

Managing the distress and safety of youth who self-injure can be a terrifying, exhausting, and traumatic experience that takes a toll on parental well-being, which, in turn, can impact parental capacity to effectively support youth (Byrne et al., 2008; McDonald et al., 2007; Oldershaw et al., 2008; Rissanen et al., 2009). Guilt, shame, fear, anxiety, anger, and helplessness are common emotional experiences following NSSI disclosure that are intensified by the stigma associated with the behavior, and can make parents reluctant to access resources or seek support (Byrne et al., 2008; Fu et al., 2020; Krysinska et al., 2020). These emotional experiences can also lead parents to feel isolated and alone in the process of supporting their child. Similarly, many parents may exhibit difficulties prioritizing their own needs and well-being when supporting youth who engage in NSSI (Oldershaw et al., 2008). Therefore, with NSSI awareness, parents may deny their own self-care or experience difficulty modeling effective emotion regulation due to the fatigue and secondary stress that frequently accompanies supporting a youth who engages in NSSI (Krysinska et al., 2020; Whitlock et al., 2018). Finally, financial strain can impact parental time and resources to access professional services to support their own emotional well-being. Moreover, parents' financial strain can be exacerbated by changes in employment that sometimes result from supporting youth who self-injure (i.e., working fewer hours, taking unpaid leave) (Fu et al., 2020; McDonald et al., 2007).

Parental Education about NSSI

Parental responses to NSSI may be informed by stigma associated with the behavior and commonly held misconceptions, including those that minimize the behavior (e.g., "cutting is a normative adolescent behavior" or "if I ignore it then it will stop") and those that catastrophize it (e.g., "NSSI indicates imminent death by suicide" or "NSSI occurs exclusively in the context of a psychiatric disorder") (Arbuthnott & Lewis, 2015; Byrne et al., 2008; Fu et al., 2020; Oldershaw et al., 2008; Rissanen et al., 2009). Although some parents may recognize their child's NSSI as a sign of distress, such misinformation can make it difficult for parents to understand their child's engagement in NSSI and respond effectively (Oldershaw et al., 2008; Rissanen et al., 2009). To this end, parental access to, and understanding of, accurate information about the etiology, implications, and treatment of NSSI may be critical to reducing risk (Curtis et al., 2018). Indeed, parents of youth who self-injure have highlighted the need for access to digestible and accurate information about the behavior, including written recommendations and examples, to assist with supporting youth who self-injure (Krysinska et al., 2020; Stewart et al., 2018).

Protective Factors

Although research often focuses upon parental characteristics and parent-child relational factors associated with risk, many components of the parent-child relationship function as protective factors, buffering against youth NSSI. For instance, the presence of positive parenting behaviors, such as parental support, comfort, and warmth have all been linked to reduced risk for NSSI in youth (Claes et al., 2015; Tatnell et al., 2014; Victor et al., 2019). Indeed, it is possible that when youth feel cared for and supported by their parents, they are more likely to engage in help-seeking behaviors from their parents, or to openly communicate their distress and thoughts about NSSI with their parents (Arbuthnott & Lewis, 2015; Fortune et al., 2008a, 2008b; Rissanen et al., 2009). Moreover, these familial factors, as well as family cohesion and adaptability, play a key role in prevention and intervention efforts to decrease the likelihood that youth will initiate, or reengage in, NSSI (Brent et al., 2013; Glenn et al., 2015, 2019; Tompson et al., 2012). To this end, parental resources, including awareness of and access to psychological resources and educational materials that offer accurate information about NSSI and treatment, are also pertinent considerations in youth risk (Arbuthnott & Lewis, 2015; Byrne et al., 2008). As described above, these factors may be especially relevant for protecting against future risk following youth disclosure of NSSI and facilitating help-seeking behaviors. Indeed, educational resources can shape parental responses to NSSI disclosure, thereby preventing or interrupting the dynamic cycle of risk proposed by the NSSI family distress cascade theory (Waals et al., 2018).

Interventions

Although there is clear support for links between youth NSSI and parental, parent-child relational, and parent-child interaction factors, efforts to empirically validate treatments of NSSI in youth have largely focused on individualistic treatment approaches, like cognitive behavioral therapy (CBT) and dialectical behavior therapy (DBT) (Bean et al., 2021). Importantly, however, treatments with strong parental components and parental education or training programs have been identified as some of the most effective approaches for reducing NSSI in youth (Glenn et al., 2015, 2019; Ougrin et al., 2015). To this end, in a recent review focused on family factors involved in youth NSSI and the use and utility of family therapy in reducing risk for self-injury, Bean et al. (2021) proposed that interpersonal contextual factors should be a primary target of treatment for NSSI and that empirically validated individualistic interventions for NSSI (e.g., CBT and DBT) may be enhanced by efforts to incorporate increased attention to interpersonal factors and considerations of the family environment. For example, these treatments could be updated and improved through integration of specific interventions targeting parental support/invalidation, parental criticism/shame, family rigidity/parental control, and conflict within the parent-child relationship.

Within this line of research, there is growing support for two-clinician treatment models, which offer individual support to youth and their parents as well as joint family interventions. Specifically, programs such as Safe Alternatives for Teens and Youth (SAFETY; Asarnow et al., 2015) strive to improve youths' protective interpersonal supports through CBT- and DBT-informed intervention with both the teen and their parents and demonstrate promising reductions in NSSI and suicide attempts three months after treatment (Asarnow et al., 2017). Similarly, attachment-based family therapy (Diamond, 2014; Ewing et al., 2015) seeks to improve the parent-child relationship by addressing relationship ruptures to rebuild trust within the relationship and foster positive parent involvement. This type of intervention is designed to reduce risk by increasing youth willingness to seek parental support and training parents to respond effectively (Amoss et al., 2016). It is important to note, however, that these interventions are currently designed to target suicidality. Nonetheless, they also appear well suited to address and reduce youth

NSSI risk by addressing individual and dyadic influences of risk, thereby supporting parents' ability to effectively manage youth NSSI risk.

Parent education and training programs are also effective in reducing risk by helping parents appropriately respond to episodes of NSSI and support the safety of their child (Glenn et al., 2019). As previously described, misconceptions about NSSI can influence parental response to NSSI disclosure (Arbuthnott & Lewis, 2015; Byrne et al., 2008; Fu et al., 2020; Oldershaw et al., 2008; Rissanen et al., 2009). These programs, therefore, can support parents in the process of caring for their children by disseminating accurate information about the etiology, implications, and treatment of youth NSSI (Curtis et al., 2018; Krysinska et al., 2020; Stewart et al., 2018). These parent training programs should also include information about interpersonal influences, family conflict resolution strategies, training in skills for emotion regulation, communication, and problem-solving (Bean et al., 2021). Finally, the programs may be strengthened through the inclusion of information pertaining to parental self-care.

Case Example

To help illustrate many of these considerations in practice, a clinical example may be useful. Zo was a 14-year-old nonbinary teen who lived with their parents and younger brother. Zo presented to the emergency department following an intentional Tylenol ingestion in a suicide attempt with recent cuts on their arms and scarring on their upper thighs and stomach. Thus, although NSSI does not always occur in the context of suicidal thoughts and behaviors, Zo's suicide attempt illustrates the increased risk for suicide attempts among youth who self-injure (Ribeiro et al., 2016). During their initial psychological evaluation, Zo reported having experienced symptoms of depression, including sadness, anhedonia, difficulty concentrating, disrupted sleep, and feelings of worthlessness, for approximately one year. They reported experiencing suicidal thoughts for approximately six months and denied any suicidal behavior prior to this attempt. They first engaged in NSSI (i.e., cutting, initially with a pencil sharpener blade, and more recently with a razor) about nine months prior to admission and had been self-injuring several times a week for the last month. They denied any use of tobacco, alcohol, or substances. They also denied any experiences of trauma or abuse.

During the interview, Zo stated that they first expressed their preference for they/them pronouns to their parents six months ago. Zo's parents expressed support for Zo's pronoun preference, yet Zo shared that they sometimes misgender them when talking to others. Zo expressed that these errors are invalidating. Zo reported that their parents apologize when they make mistakes and explained that it was hard to adjust to the change. Their parents also occasionally talk about missing their "daughter." Zo reported feeling like an inconvenience and that they have let their parents down. Zo described feeling hesitant to ask their parents for support, including help for NSSI, and identified being misgendered and thoughts of inconveniencing their parents as frequent precipitants to NSSI.

Zo reported that when their parents first learned about their NSSI a couple of months ago after seeing some marks on their arm, they "freaked out." Their parents immediately began looking for a therapist, and they lost their right to privacy. Zo shared that they can no longer be in their room alone and that their parents now closely monitor their phone and social media use after reading texts between Zo and a friend about the self-injury. Their parents worried that Zo's friend was influencing them to engage in NSSI. Zo shared that this friend is one of the only people they feel comfortable talking to about their urges to self-injure. Zo expressed feeling overwhelmed and frustrated by their parents' reaction, which exacerbated their symptoms of depression, suicidality, and urges to self-harm.

This case highlights a number of points raised in this chapter. As noted earlier, rates of NSSI are elevated in adolescents, particularly among gender-nonconforming teenagers (Clark et al., 2014; Eisenberg et al., 2017). As noted above, a perceived lack of parental support is a risk factor for NSSI (Andrews et al., 2013; Tatnell et al., 2014), and, in this case, Zo's parents' intermittent use of she/her pronouns was perceived as invalidating their identity and autonomy. This negatively affected Zo's relationship with their parents and likely amplified Zo's desire for accepting social connection (e.g., from peers). This case also clearly illustrates the dynamic cycle of risk for NSSI proposed in the NSSI family distress cascade theory (Waals et al., 2018) and is consistent with prior research demonstrating transactional relations between youth NSSI and parent control over time (Bureau et al., 2010). Indeed, upon learning about Zo's engagement in NSSI, Zo's parents increased their supervision and monitoring of Zo's behaviors for fear of future incidents of NSSI and, perhaps, suicide attempts. This increase in parental control could be perceived by Zo as a punishment as it resulted in limits to Zo's developmentally normative desire for independence and a barrier to supportive social connections. Though well-meaning, this type of parental response is likely to reinforce Zo's desire to hide their distress from their parents and reduce their willingness to seek help, which perpetuates their risk. Building from the empirically supported treatments reviewed earlier, it appears that Zo would benefit from treatment with a strong parental component or a two-clinician intervention model to enhance communication within the family from both Zo and their parents (i.e., around the impact of misgendering, emotional distress, and risk for NSSI), particularly as Zo's parents verbally expressed their desire to support Zo's gender identity and responded to their engagement in NSSI with concern. In addition to targeting communication, treatment should focus on increasing Zo's help-seeking behavior from their parents, helping Zo's parents to learn to appropriately respond to their NSSI, and teaching Zo skills to more effectively tolerate the emotional distress they experience.

Future Directions

A review of research examining parent-child dyads and youth NSSI illuminates several important directions for future studies. One key area for future research is the examination of developmental differences in youth NSSI risk and protective factors. As noted at the outset, there are clear developmental differences in the prevalence of NSSI, with rates more than twice as high in adolescents compared to children (Barrocas et al., 2012; Muehlenkamp et al., 2012; Swannell et al., 2014). However, the reasons for this increase are not well understood. The transition to adolescence is characterized by significant hormonal and neural changes associated with increased stress reactivity and reward sensitivity (Casey et al., 2008; Gunnar et al., 2009; Paus et al., 2008; Rudolph, 2014) as well as changing relationships with parents and peers that can lead to increases in interpersonal stress (see Zetterqvist & Bjureberg, this volume). In terms of these social changes, adolescents begin to experiment with new social roles that often inform their self-concept (Casey et al., 2008; Chein et al., 2011; Collins & Repinski, 1994; Somerville, 2013). They develop heightened awareness of societal expectations and nurture greater emotional intimacy in platonic and romantic peer relationships as peer relationships take on more central roles (Nesi et al., 2018; Rose & Rudolph, 2006; Steinberg & Morris, 2001). During adolescence, youth—particularly girls—also experience an increase in negative life events and interpersonal stress to which they exhibit increased reactivity (Ge et al., 1994; Rose & Rudolph, 2006; Rudolph, 2014; Rudolph & Hammen, 1999). These developmental changes underscore a need for research examining how parents can help to buffer these effects. Thus, adolescence is characterized by heightened emotional reactivity and need for emotion regulation, an increased salience of peer influences, and a normative desire for more independence, which lead to new negotiations to balance peer and familial relationships to meet adolescents' needs of both autonomy and connectedness. These changes result in a normative escalation in the emotional intensity of parent-child conflict (Laursen et al., 1998). What remains unclear, however, is the extent to which these factors help explain the dramatic rise in NSSI observed during adolescence.

A second key area for future research is the increased diversity of the samples studied, in terms of both the youth and the parents included. In terms of parents, the vast majority of studies reviewed in this chapter focus specifically on mothers and the mother-child relationship. Continued efforts to examine whether findings from this extant research generalize to fathers and the father-child relationship, as well as caretaker relationships in nontraditional families, are critical. In turn, it will be important to examine whether these processes differ depending upon the nature of the dyadic relationship (mother-daughter, mother-son, father-daughter, father-son, mother-nonbinary youth, etc.). Indeed, these processes may be most salient within certain relationships (at certain developmental stages) than others. Future research on diverse youth samples is also needed to determine how family factors may be similar versus different for different minority samples. Specifically, despite lack of clear evidence for racial/ethnic differences in the prevalence of NSSI (Gholamrezaei et al., 2017), and only relatively small sex differences (Bresin & Schoenleber, 2015), there are significantly higher rates of NSSI in gender and sexual minority youth (Blashill et al., 2021; Clark et al., 2014; Eisenberg et al., 2017; Fox et al., 2020; see Zullo et al., this volume). Additional research is needed to determine how parents and the parent-child relationship can either exacerbate or mitigate the stress these youth experience that can increase NSSI risk. This type of research is also a critical step toward cultural humility and the development of culturally informed adaptations of evidence-based care.

The third need for future research is the increasingly sophisticated research design. With growing evidence that the relation between parent-child dyadic factors and youth NSSI is reciprocal, there is an increasing need for multimethod research with multiple informants (i.e., parents and youth) with longitudinal designs. Despite important contributions, the vast majority of research to date has focused on self-report assessments of either the parent or youth. It will be important for future research to obtain reports from both the parent and the child to better understand the specific nature of this dynamic cycle of risk and identify points of intervention to prevent or interrupt this cycle. Moreover, given that self-report data are susceptible to reporter bias, such research would be enhanced by additional, more objective methods of assessment. For instance, interviewer-coded paradigms (e.g., five minute speech sample; Magaña et al., 1986) and behavioral coding systems are seldom employed in this area of research and could provide a more robust picture of processes occurring during parent-child interactions that increase risk for NSSI. These methodological approaches have greater ecological validity than self-report measures and could be augmented by other fine-grained assessments during interactions (e.g., moment-to-moment changes in facial affect assessed with electromyography). Finally, research involving intensive longitudinal designs (e.g., through ecological momentary assessment) have the capacity to capture real-time fluctuations in this cycle of risk to better pinpoint specific targets and opportunities for intervention.

Finally, additional research is needed to determine the incremental validity of family-based interventions versus individual therapy and to determine when one approach may be preferable to the other. There is also a need for additional emphasis on psychoeducation and support for parents of youth who engage in NSSI. Another significant question for intervention research is whether interventions that target self-injury broadly are most effective or whether outcomes would be improved by a specific focus on NSSI among youth with no history of suicidal ideation or attempt. This targeted approach might allow a greater focus on factors thought to maintain NSSI specifically rather than self-injury more broadly. To this end, there is a need for more research that specifically aims to better understand how risk and protective factors for NSSI may differ from those involved in youth suicidality.

Conclusions

In summary, NSSI is a significant public health concern with clear negative consequences for the individual and their families. Although not uncommon in children, rates increase dramatically during adolescence, particularly for gender and sexual minority youth. Across childhood and adolescence, specific family influences have been shown to increase or buffer risk for NSSI, with parent and youth influences likely to be reciprocal. Consistent with these effects, there is growing support for family-based interventions, which not only include a focus on parent training and improved communication but also general psychoeducation for parents so that they can respond effectively to occurrences of NSSI in their family. It is important to note, however, that much of the extant research in this area examines risk for both suicidal and nonsuicidal self-injury. Therefore, there is a pressing need to identify predictors of risk that are specific to NSSI. Building from the strengths of this body of work, the next phase of research in this area will seek to increase the diversity of the samples studied, in terms of both parents and youth, and will benefit from increasingly sophisticated research designs to provide a more fine-grained understanding of family-based cycles of risk so that even more effective prevention and intervention efforts can be developed.

References

Adrian, M., Berk, M. S., Korslund, K., Whitlock, K., McCauley, E., & Linehan, M. (2018). Parental validation and invalidation predict adolescent self-harm. *Professional Psychology: Research and Practice*, *49*(4), 247–281. https://doi.org/10.1037/pro0000200

Adrian, M., Zeman, J., Erdley, C., Lisa, L., & Sim, L. (2011). Emotional dysregulation and interpersonal difficulties as risk factors for nonsuicidal self-injury in adolescent girls. *Journal of Abnormal Child Psychology*, *39*(3), 389–400. https://doi.org/10.1007/s10802-010-9465-3

Ammerman, B. A., & Brown, S. (2018). The mediating role of self-criticism in the relationship between parental expressed emotion and NSSI. *Current Psychology*, *37*(1), 325–333. https://doi.org/10.1007/s12144-016-9516-1

Amoss, S., Lynch, M., & Bratley, M. (2016). Bringing forth stories of blame and shame in dialogues with families affected by adolescent self-harm. *Journal of Family Therapy*, *38*(2), 189–205. https://doi.org/10.1111/1467-6427.12101

Andrews, T., Martin, G., Hasking, P., & Page, A. (2013). Predictors of onset for non-suicidal self-injury within a school-based sample of adolescents. *Prevention Science*, *15*(6), 850–859. https://doi.org/10.1007/s11121-013-0412-8

Arbuthnott, A. E., & Lewis, S. P. (2015). Parents of youth who self-injure: A review of the literature and implications for mental health professionals. *Child and Adolescent Psychiatry and Mental Health*, *9*(1), Article 35. https://doi.org/10.1186/s13034-015-0066-3

Asarnow, J. R., Berk, M., Hughes, J. L., & Anderson, N. L. (2015). The SAFETY program: A treatment-development trial of a cognitive-behavioral family treatment for adolescent suicide attempters. *Journal of Clinical Child and Adolescent Psychology*, *44*(1), 194–203. https://doi.org/10.1080/15374416.2014.940624

Asarnow, J. R., Hughes, J. L., Babeva, K. N., & Sugar, C. A. (2017). Cognitive-behavioral family treatment for suicide attempt prevention: A randomized controlled trial. *Journal of the American Academy of Child and Adolescent Psychiatry*, *56*(6), 506–514. https://doi.org/10.1016/j.jaac.2017.03.015

Baetens, I., Claes, L., Hasking, P., Smits, D., Grietens, H., Onghena, P., & Martin, G. (2015a). The relationship between parental expressed emotions and non-suicidal self-injury: The mediating roles of self-criticism and depression. *Journal of Child and Family Studies*, *24*(2), 491–498. https://doi.org/10.1007/s10826-013-9861-8

Baetens, I., Andrews, T., Claes, L., & Martin, G. (2015b). The association between family functioning and NSSI in adolescence: The mediating role of depressive symptoms. *Family Science*, *6*(1), 330–337. https://doi.org/10.1080/19424620.2015.1056917

Baetens, I., Claes, L., Onghena, P., Grietens, H., Van Leeuwen, K., Pieters, C., Wiersema, J. R., & Griffith, J. W. (2014). Non-suicidal self-injury in adolescence: A longitudinal study of the relationship between NSSI, psychological distress and perceived parenting. *Journal of Adolescence*, *37*(6), 817–826. https://doi.org/10.1016/j.adolescence.2014.05.010

Barrocas, A. L., Hankin, B. L., Young, J. F., & Abela, J. R. Z. (2012). Rates of nonsuicidal self-injury in youth: Age, sex, and behavioral methods in a community sample. *Pediatrics, 130*(1), 39–45. https://doi.org/10.1542/peds.2011-2094

Bean, R. A., Keenan, B. H., & Fox, C. (2021). Treatment of adolescent non-suicidal self-injury: A review of family factors and family therapy. *American Journal of Family Therapy*. Advance online publication. https://doi.org/10.1080/01926187.2021.1909513

Blashill, A. J., Fox, K., Feinstein, B. A., Albright, C. A., & Calzo, J. P. (2021). Nonsuicidal self-injury, suicide ideation, and suicide attempts among sexual minority children. *Journal of Consulting and Clinical Psychology, 89*(2), 73–80. https://doi.org/10.1037/ccp0000624

Brent, D. A., McMakin, D. L., Kennard, B. D., Goldstein, T. R., Mayes, T. L., & Douaihy, A. B. (2013). Protecting adolescents from self-harm: A critical review of intervention studies. *Journal of the American Academy of Child and Adolescent Psychiatry, 52*(12), 1260–1271. https://doi.org/10.1016/j.jaac.2013.09.009

Brent, D. A., & Melhem, N. (2008). Familial transmission of suicidal behavior. *Psychiatric Clinics of North America, 31*(2), 157–177. https://doi.org/10.1016/j.psc.2008.02.001

Bresin, K., & Schoenleber, M. (2015). Gender differences in the prevalence of nonsuicidal self-injury: A meta-analysis. *Clinical Psychology Review, 38*, 55–64. https://doi.org/10.1016/j.cpr.2015.02.009

Bureau, J. F., Martin, J., Freynet, N., Poirier, A. A., Lafontaine, M. F., & Cloutier, P. (2010). Perceived dimensions of parenting and non-suicidal self-injury in young adults. *Journal of Youth and Adolescence, 39*, 484–494. https://doi.org/10.1007/s10964-009-9470-4

Byrne, S., Morgan, S., Fitzpatrick, C., Boylan, C., Crowley, S., Gahan, H., Howley, J., Staunton, D., & Guerin, S. (2008). Deliberate self-harm in children and adolescents: A qualitative study exploring the needs of parents and carers. *Clinical Child Psychology and Psychiatry, 13*(4), 493–504. https://doi.org/10.1177/1359104508096765

Casey, B. J., Jones, R. M., & Hare, T. A. (2008). The adolescent brain. *Annals of the New York Academy of Sciences, 1124*, 111–126. https://doi.org/10.1196/annals.1440.010

Chapman, A. L., Gratz, K. L., & Brown, M. Z. (2006). Solving the puzzle of deliberate self-harm: The experiential avoidance model. *Behaviour Research and Therapy, 44*(3), 371–394. https://doi.org/10.1016/j.brat.2005.03.005

Chein, J. M., Albert, D., O'Brien, L., Uckert, K., & Steinberg, L. (2011). Peers increase adolescent risk taking by enhancing activity in the brain's reward circuitry. *Developmental Science, 14*(2), F1–F10. https://doi.org/10.1111/j.1467-7687.2010.01035.x

Claes, L., Luyckx, K., Baetens, I., Van de Ven, M., & Witteman, C. (2015). Bullying and victimization, depressive mood, and non-suicidal self-injury in adolescents: The moderating role of parental support. *Journal of Child and Family Studies, 24*(11), 3363–3371. https://doi.org/10.1007/s10826-015-0138-2

Clark, T. C., Lucassen, M. F. G., Bullen, P., Denny, S. J., Fleming, T. M., Robinson, E. M., & Rossen, F. V. (2014). The health and well-being of transgender high school students: Results from the New Zealand adolescent health survey (youth' 12). *Journal of Adolescent Health, 55*, 93–99. https://doi.org/10.1016/j.jadohealth.2013.11.008

Collins, W. A., & Repinski, D. J. (1994). Relationships during adolescence: Continuity and change in interpersonal perspective. In R. Montemayor, G. R. Adams, & T. P. Gullotta (Eds.), *Personal relationships during adolescence* (pp. 7–36). SAGE. https://doi.org/10.1016/j.celrep.2011.1011.1001.7

Cox, L. J., Stanley, B. H., Melhem, N. M., Oquendo, M. A., Birmaher, B., Burke, A., Kolko, D. J., Zelazny, J. M., Mann, J. J., Porta, G., & Brent, D. A. (2012). A longitudinal study of nonsuicidal self-injury in offspring at high risk for mood disorder. *Journal of Clinical Psychiatry, 73*(6), 821–828. https://doi.org/10.4088/JCP.11m07250

Cruz, D., Narciso, I., Pereira, C. R., & Sampaio, D. (2014). Risk trajectories of self-destructiveness in adolescence: Family core influences. *Journal of Child and Family Studies, 23*(7), 1172–1181. https://doi.org/10.1007/s10826-013-9777-3

Curtis, S., Thorn, P., McRoberts, A., Hetrick, S., Rice, S., & Robinson, J. (2018). Caring for young people who self-harm: A review of perspectives from families and young people. *International Journal of Environmental Research and Public Health, 15*(5), Article 950. https://doi.org/10.3390/ijerph15050950

Daly, O., & Willoughby, T. (2019). A longitudinal study investigating bidirectionality among nonsuicidal self-injury, self-criticism, and parental criticism. *Psychiatry Research, 271*, 678–683. https://doi.org/10.1016/j.psychres.2018.12.056

Dawkins, J., Hasking, P., & Boyes, M. (2019). Knowledge of parental nonsuicidal self-injury in young people who self-injure: The mediating role of outcome expectancies. *Journal of Family Studies, 27*(4), 479–490. https://doi.org/10.1080/13229400.2019.1633385

DeVille, D. C., Whalen, D., Breslin, F. J., Morris, A. S., Khalsa, S. S., Paulus, M. P., & Barch, D. M. (2020). Prevalence and family-related factors associated with suicidal ideation, suicide attempts, and self-injury in children aged 9 to 10 years. *JAMA Network Open, 3*(2), Article e1920956. https://doi.org/10.1001/jamanetworkopen.2019.20956

Diamond, G. M. (2014). Attachment-based family therapy interventions. *Psychotherapy, 51*(1), 15–19. https://doi.org/10.1037/a0032689

Eisenberg, M. E., Gower, A. L., McMorris, B. J., Rider, G. N., Shea, G., & Coleman, E. (2017). Risk and protective factors in the lives of transgender/gender nonconforming adolescents. *Journal of Adolescent Health, 61*(4), 521–526. https://doi.org/10.1016/j.jadohealth.2017.04.014

Evans, E., Hawton, K., & Rodham, K. (2005). In what ways are adolescents who engage in self-harm or experience thoughts of self-harm different in terms of help-seeking, communication and coping strategies? *Journal of Adolescence, 28*(4), 573–587. https://doi.org/10.1016/j.adolescence.2004.11.001

Ewing, E. S. K., Diamond, G., & Levy, S. (2015). Attachment-based family therapy for depressed and suicidal adolescents: Theory, clinical model and empirical support. *Attachment and Human Development, 17*(2), 136–156. https://doi.org/10.1080/14616734.2015.1006384

Fortune, S., Cottrell, D., & Fife, S. (2016). Family factors associated with adolescent self-harm: A narrative review. *Journal of Family Therapy, 38*, 226–256. https://doi.org/10.1111/1467-6427.12119

Fortune, S., Sinclair, J., & Hawton, K. (2008a). Adolescents' views on preventing self-harm. A large community study. *Social Psychiatry and Psychiatric Epidemiology, 43*(2), 96–104. https://doi.org/10.7748/phc.18.2.29.s23

Fortune, S., Sinclair, J., & Hawton, K. (2008b). Help-seeking before and after episodes of self-harm: A descriptive study in school pupils in England. *BMC Public Health, 8*(1), 1–13. https://doi.org/10.1186/1471-2458-8-369

Fox, K. R., Choukas-Bradley, S., Salk, R. H., Marshal, M. P., & Thoma, B. C. (2020). Mental health among sexual and gender minority adolescents: Examining interactions with race and ethnicity. *Journal of Consulting and Clinical Psychology, 88*(5), 402–415. https://doi.org/10.1037/ccp0000486

Fu, X., Yang, J., Liao, X., Lin, J., Peng, Y., Shen, Y., Ou, J., Li, Y., & Chen, R. (2020). Parents' attitudes toward and experience of non-suicidal self-injury in adolescents: A qualitative study. *Frontiers in Psychiatry, 11*, Article 651. https://doi.org/10.3389/fpsyt.2020.00651

Ge, X., Lorenz, F. O., Conger, R. D., Elder, G. H., & Simons, R. L. (1994). Trajectories of stressful life events and depressive symptoms during adolescence. *Developmental Psychology, 30*(4), 467–483. https://doi.org/10.1037/0012-1649.30.4.467

Gholamrezaei, M., De Stefano, J., & Heath, N. L. (2017). Nonsuicidal self-injury across cultures and ethnic and racial minorities: A review. *International Journal of Psychology, 52*(4), 316–326. https://doi.org/10.1002/ijop.12230

Glenn, C. R., Esposito, E. C., Porter, A. C., & Robinson, D. J. (2019). Evidence base update of psychosocial treatments for self-injurious thoughts and behaviors in youth. *Journal of Clinical Child and Adolescent Psychology, 48*(3), 357–392. https://doi.org/10.1080/15374416.2019.1591281

Glenn, C. R., Franklin, J. C., & Nock, M. K. (2015). Evidence-based psychosocial treatments for self-injurious thoughts and behaviors in youth. *Journal of Clinical Child & Adolescent Psychology, 44*(1), 1–29. https://doi.org/10.1080/15374416.2014.945211

Gromatsky, M. A., He, S., Perlman, G., Klein, D. N., Kotov, R., & Waszczuk, M. A. (2020). Prospective prediction of first onset of nonsuicidal self-injury in adolescent girls. *Journal of the American Academy of Child and Adolescent Psychiatry, 59*(9), 1049–1057. https://doi.org/10.1016/j.jaac.2019.08.006

Gromatsky, M. A., Waszczuk, M. A., Perlman, G., Salis, K. L., Klein, D. N., & Kotov, R. (2017). The role of parental psychopathology and personality in adolescent non-suicidal self-injury. *Journal of Psychiatric Research, 85*, 15–23. https://doi.org/10.1016/j.jpsychires.2016.10.013

Gunnar, M. R., Wewerka, S., Frenn, K., Long, J. D., & Griggs, C. (2009). Developmental changes in hypothalamus-pituitary-adrenal activity over the transition to adolescence: Normative changes and associations with puberty. *Development and Psychopathology, 21*(1), 69–85. https://doi.org/10.1017/S0954579409000054

Hack, J., & Martin, G. (2018). Expressed emotion, shame, and non-suicidal self-injury. *International Journal of Environmental Research and Public Health*, *15*(5), Article 890. https://doi.org/10.3390/ijerph15050890

Hankin, B. L., & Abela, J. R. Z. (2011). Nonsuicidal self-injury in adolescence: Prospective rates and risk factors in a 2 1/2 year longitudinal study. *Psychiatry Research*, *186*(1), 65–70. https://doi.org/10.1016/j.psychres.2010.07.056

Hasking, P., Dawkins, J., Gray, N., Wijeratne, P., & Boyes, M. (2020). Indirect effects of family functioning on non-Suicidal self-injury and risky drinking: The roles of emotion reactivity and emotion regulation. *Journal of Child and Family Studies*, *29*(7), 2070–2079. https://doi.org/10.1007/s10826-020-01722-4

Hasking, P., Whitlock, J., Voon, D., & Rose, A. (2016). A cognitive-emotional model of NSSI: Using emotion regulation and cognitive processes to explain why people self-injure. *Cognition and Emotion*, *22*(2), 161–171. https://doi.org/10.1080/02699931.2016.1241219

Hilt, L. M., Nock, M. K., Lloyd-Richardson, E. E., & Prinstein, M. J. (2008). Longitudinal study of nonsuicidal self-injury among young adolescents: Rates, correlates, and preliminary test of an interpersonal model. *Journal of Early Adolescence*, *28*(3), 455–469. https://doi.org/10.1177/0272431608316604

Hooley, J. M., & Franklin, J. C. (2018). Why do people hurt themselves? A new conceptual model of non-suicidal self-injury. *Clinical Psychological Science*, *6*(3), 428–451. https://doi.org/10.1177/2167702617745641

James, K. M., & Gibb, B. E. (2019). Maternal criticism and non-suicidal self-injury in school-aged children. *Psychiatry Research*, *273*, 89–93. https://doi.org/10.1016/j.psychres.2019.01.019

Jiang, Y., You, J., Hou, Y., Du, C., Lin, M. P., Zheng, X., & Ma, C. (2016). Buffering the effects of peer victimization on adolescent non-suicidal self-injury: The role of self-compassion and family cohesion. *Journal of Adolescence*, *53*, 107–115. https://doi.org/10.1016/j.adolescence.2016.09.005

Kelada, L., Hasking, P., & Melvin, G. (2016). The relationship between nonsuicidal self-injury and family functioning: Adolescent and parent perspectives. *Journal of Marital and Family Therapy*, *42*(3), 536–549. https://doi.org/10.1111/jmft.12150

Kelada, L., Hasking, P., & Melvin, G. (2018). Adolescent NSSI and recovery: The role of family functioning and emotion regulation. *Youth & Society*, *50*(8), 1056–1077. https://doi.org/10.1177/0044118X16653153

Krysinska, K., Curtis, S., Lamblin, M., Stefanac, N., Gibson, K., Byrne, S., Thorn, P., Rice, S. M., McRoberts, A., Ferrey, A., Perry, Y., Lin, A., Hetrick, S., Hawton, K., & Robinson, J. (2020). Parents' experience and psychoeducation needs when supporting a young person who self-harms. *International Journal of Environmental Research and Public Health*, *17*(10), Article 3662. https://doi.org/10.3390/ijerph17103662

Latina, D., Giannotta, F., & Rabaglietti, E. (2015). Do friends' co-rumination and communication with parents prevent depressed adolescents from self-harm?. *Journal of Applied Developmental Psychology*, *41*, 120–128. http://dx.doi.org/10.1016/j.appdev.2015.10.001

Laursen, B., Coy, K. C., & Collins, W. A. (1998). Reconsidering changes in parent-child conflict across adolescence: A meta-analysis. *Child Development*, *69*(3), 817–832. https://doi.org/10.1111/j.1467-8624.1998.tb06245.x

Liang, S., Yan, J., Zhang, T., Zhu, C., Situ, M., Du, N., & Huang, Y. (2014). Differences between non-suicidal self-injury and suicide attempt in Chinese adolescents. *Asian Journal of Psychiatry*, *8*, 76–83. https://doi.org/10.1016/j.ajp.2013.11.015

Linehan, M. M. (1993). Cognitive-behavioral treatment of borderline personality disorder. In *Cognitive-behavioral treatment of borderline personality disorder*. Guilford Press. https://doi.org/10.1017/CBO9781107415324.004

Liu, Y., Xiao, Y., Ran, H., He, X., Jiang, L., Wang, T. L., Yang, R. X., Xu, X., Yang, G., & Lu, J. (2020). Association between parenting and non-suicidal self-injury among adolescents in Yunnan, China: A cross-sectional survey. *PeerJ*, *8*, Article e10493. https://doi.org/10.7717/peerj.10493

MacIejewski, D. F., Creemers, H. E., Lynskey, M. T., Madden, P. A. F., Heath, A. C., Statham, D. J., Martin, N. G., & Verweij, K. J. H. (2014). Overlapping genetic and environmental influences on nonsuicidal self-injury and suicidal ideation: Different outcomes, same etiology? *JAMA Psychiatry*, *71*(6), 699–705. https://doi.org/10.1001/jamapsychiatry.2014.89

Magaña, A. B., Goldstein, M. J., Karno, M., Miklowitz, D. J., Jenkins, J., & Falloon, I. R. H. (1986). A brief method for assessing expressed emotion in relatives of psychiatric patients. *Psychiatry Research*, *17*(3), 203–212. https://doi.org/10.1016/0165-1781(86)90049-1

McDonald, G., O'Brien, L., & Jackson, D. (2007). Guilt and shame: Experiences of parents of self-harming adolescents. *Journal of Child Health Care*, *11*(4), 298–310. https://doi.org/10.1177/1367493507082759

Mojtabai, R., & Olfson, M. (2008). Parental detection of youth's self-harm behavior. *Suicide and Life-Threatening Behavior, 38*(1), 60–73. https://doi.org/10.1521/suli.2008.38.1.60

Muehlenkamp, J. J., Claes, L., Havertape, L., & Plener, P. L. (2012). International prevalence of adolescent non-suicidal self-injury and deliberate self-harm. *Child and Adolescent Psychiatry and Mental Health, 6*(1), 10. https://doi.org/10.1186/1753-2000-6-10

Nesi, J., Choukas-Bradley, S., & Prinstein, M. J. (2018). Transformation of adolescent peer relations in the social media context: Part 1—A theoretical framework and application to dyadic peer relationships. *Clinical Child and Family Psychology Review, 21*(3), 267–294. https://doi.org/10.1007/s10567-018-0261-x

Nock, M. K., Joiner, T. E., Gordon, K. H., Lloyd-Richardson, E., & Prinstein, M. J. (2006). Non-suicidal self-injury among adolescents: Diagnostic correlates and relation to suicide attempts. *Psychiatry Research, 144*(1), 65–72. https://doi.org/10.1016/j.psychres.2006.05.010

Nock, M. K., & Prinstein, M. J. (2004). A Functional Approach to the Assessment of Self-Mutilative Behavior. *Journal of Consulting and Clinical Psychology, 72*(5), 885–890. https://doi.org/10.1037/0022-006X.72.5.885

Oldershaw, A., Richards, C., Simic, M., & Schmidt, U. (2008). Parents' perspectives on adolescent self-harm: Qualitative study. *British Journal of Psychiatry, 193*(2), 140–144. https://doi.org/10.1192/bjp.bp.107.045930

Ougrin, D., Tranah, T., Stahl, D., Moran, P., & Asarnow, J. R. (2015). Therapeutic interventions for suicide attempts and self-harm in adolescents: Systematic review and meta-analysis. *Journal of the American Academy of Child and Adolescent Psychiatry, 54*, 97–107. https://doi.org/10.1016/j.jaac.2014.10.009

Paus, T., Keshavan, M., & Giedd, J. N. (2008). Why do many psychiatric disorders emerge during adolescence? *Nature Reviews Neuroscience, 9*(12), 947–957. https://doi.org/10.1038/nrn2513

Ribeiro, J. D., Franklin, J. C., Fox, K. R., Bentley, K. H., Kleiman, E. M., Chang, B. P., & Nock, M. K. (2016). Self-injurious thoughts and behaviors as risk factors for future suicide ideation, attempts, and death: A meta-analysis of longitudinal studies. *Psychological Medicine, 46*(02), 225–236. https://doi.org/10.1017/S0033291715001804

Rissanen, M. L., Kylmä, J., & Eila Laukkanen, E. (2009). Descriptions of help by Finnish adolescents who self-mutilate. *Journal of Child and Adolescent Psychiatric Nursing, 22*, 7–15. https://doi.org/10.1111/j.1744-6171.2008.00164.x

Rose, A. J., & Rudolph, K. D. (2006). A review of sex differences in peer relationship processes: Potential tradeoffs for the emotional and behavioral development of girls and boys. *Psychological Bulletin, 132*(1), 98–131. https://doi.org/10.1037/0033-2909.132.1.98

Rossow, I., & Wichstrøm, L. (2010). Receipt of help after deliberate self-harm among adolescents: Changes over an eight-year period. *Psychiatric Services, 61*(8), 783–787. https://doi.org/10.1176/ps.2010.61.8.783

Rudolph, K. D. (2014). Puberty as a developmental context of risk for psychopathology. In M. Lewis & K. D. Randolph (Eds.), *Handbook of developmental psychopathology* (3rd ed., pp. 331–354). Springer. https://doi.org/10.1007/978-1-4614-9608-3_17

Rudolph, K. D., & Hammen, C. (1999). Age and gender as determinants of stress exposure, generation, and reactions in youngsters: A transactional perspective. *Child Development, 70*(3), 660–677. https://doi.org/10.1111/1467-8624.00048

Selby, E. A., & Joiner, T. E. (2009). Cascades of emotion: The emergence of borderline personality disorder from emotional and behavioral dysregulation. *Review of General Psychology, 13*(3), 219–229. https://doi.org/10.1037/a0015687

Somerville, L. H. (2013). Special issue on the teenage brain: Sensitivity to social evaluation. *Current Directions in Psychological Science, 22*(2), 121–127. https://doi.org/10.1177/0963721413476512

Steinberg, L., & Morris, A. S. (2001). Adolescent development. *Annual Review of Psychology, 52*, 83–110. https://doi.org/10.1146/annurev.psych.52.1.83

Stewart, A., Hughes, N. D., Simkin, S., Locock, L., Ferrey, A., Kapur, N., Gunnell, D., & Hawton, K. (2018). Navigating an unfamiliar world: How parents of young people who self-harm experience support and treatment. *Child and Adolescent Mental Health, 23*(2), 78–84. https://doi.org/10.1111/camh.12205

Swannell, S. V., Martin, G. E., Page, A., Hasking, P., & St John, N. J. (2014). Prevalence of nonsuicidal self-injury in nonclinical samples: Systematic review, meta-analysis and meta-regression. *Suicide and Life-Threatening Behavior, 44*(3), 273–303. https://doi.org/10.1111/sltb.12070

Tatnell, R., Kelada, L., Hasking, P., & Martin, G. (2014). Longitudinal analysis of adolescent NSSI: The role of intrapersonal and interpersonal factors. *Journal of Abnormal Child Psychology, 42*(6), 885–896. https://doi.org/10.1007/s10802-013-9837-6

Tompson, M. C., Boger, K. D., & Asarnow, J. R. (2012). Enhancing the developmental appropriateness of treatment for depression in youth: Integrating the family in treatment. *Child and Adolescent Psychiatric Clinics of North America*, *21*(2), 345–384. https://doi.org/10.1016/j.chc.2012.01.003

Victor, S. E., Hipwell, A. E., Stepp, S. D., & Scott, L. N. (2019). Parent and peer relationships as longitudinal predictors of adolescent non-suicidal self-injury onset. *Child and Adolescent Psychiatry and Mental Health*, *13*, Article 1. https://doi.org/10.1186/s13034-018-0261-0

Waals, L., Baetens, I., Rober, P., Lewis, S., Van Parys, H., Goethals, E. R., & Whitlock, J. (2018). The NSSI family distress cascade theory. *Child and Adolescent Psychiatry and Mental Health*, *12*(1), Article 52. https://doi.org/10.1186/s13034-018-0259-7

Watanabe, N., Nishida, A., Shimodera, S., Inoue, K., Oshima, N., Sasaki, T., Inoue, S., Akechi, T., Furukawa, T. A., & Okazaki, Y. (2012). Help-seeking behavior among Japanese school students who self-harm: Results from a self-report survey of 18,104 adolescents. *Neuropsychiatric Disease and Treatment*, *8*, 561–569. https://doi.org/10.2147/NDT.S37543

Wester, K. L., & King, K. (2018). Family communication patterns and the mediating role of communication competence and alexithymia in relation to nonsuicidal self-injury. *Journal of Mental Health Counseling*, *40*(3), 226–239. https://doi.org/10.17744/mehc.40.3.04

Wedig, M. M., & Nock, M. K. (2007). Parental expressed emotion and adolescent self-injury. *Journal of the American Academy of Child & Adolescent Psychiatry*, *46*(9), 1171–1178. https://doi.org/10.1097/chi.0b013e3180ca9aaf

Whitlock, J., Lloyd-Richardson, E., Fisseha, F., & Bates, T. (2018). Parental secondary stress: The often hidden consequences of nonsuicidal self-injury in youth. *Journal of Clinical Psychology*, *74*(1), 178–196. https://doi.org/10.1002/jclp.22488

Wilcox, H. C., Arria, A. M., Caldeira, K. M., Vincent, K. B., Pinchevsky, G. M., & O'Grady, K. E. (2012). Longitudinal predictors of past-year non-suicidal self-injury and motives among college students. *Psychological Medicine*, *42*(4), 717–726. https://doi.org/10.1017/S0033291711001814

Yates, T. M., Tracy, A. J., & Luthar, S. S. (2008). Nonsuicidal self-injury among "privileged" youths: Longitudinal and cross-sectional approaches to developmental process. *Journal of Consulting and Clinical Psychology*, *76*(1), 52–62. https://doi.org/10.1037/0022-006X.76.1.52

You, J., Jiang, Y., Zhang, M., Du, C., Lin, M. P., & Leung, F. (2017). Perceived parental control, self-criticism, and nonsuicidal self-injury among adolescents: Testing the reciprocal relationships by a three-wave cross-lag model. *Archives of Suicide Research*, *21*(3), 379–391. https://doi.org/10.1080/13811118.2016.1199989

You, J., & Leung, F. (2012). The role of depressive symptoms, family invalidation and behavioral impulsivity in the occurrence and repetition of non-suicidal self-injury in Chinese adolescents: A 2-year follow-up study. *Journal of Adolescence*, *35*(2), 389–395. https://doi.org/10.1016/j.adolescence.2011.07.020

Zhu, J., Chen, Y., & Su, B. (2020). Non-suicidal self-injury in adolescence: Longitudinal evidence of recursive associations with adolescent depression and parental rejection. *Journal of Adolescence*, *84*, 36–44. https://doi.org/10.1016/j.adolescence.2020.08.002

CHAPTER 39

Media Representations of Nonsuicidal Self-Injury

Nicholas J. Westers

Abstract

This chapter reviews the extant literature on the relationship between representations of nonsuicidal self-injury (NSSI) in media and NSSI engagement. It places this discussion within the context of the cognitive-emotional model of NSSI and begins by looking at the risk and protective factors of exposure to NSSI content in traditional forms of media, including films, television, news, music, and print novels and comics. Consistent with the Werther and Papageno effects, it summarizes media depictions of NSSI as increasing or decreasing the likelihood someone will experience NSSI urges, behaviors, and stigma. It then discusses how framing of NSSI matters in terms of perpetuating stigma and unhelpful narratives or promoting new and more helpful narratives, highlighting its bidirectional association with cultural narratives and public perceptions of the behavior. It references guidelines for responsibly depicting NSSI in media and then focuses on challenges, recommendations, and future considerations related to researching NSSI and media. Finally, it discusses ethical concerns and clinical implications. Key takeaways include: the way in which NSSI is represented in media may increase or decrease the risk for NSSI, although research is limited and causal relationships cannot be inferred; use of trigger warnings in media to warn audiences of potentially disturbing content related to NSSI may be ineffective or problematic; referencing NSSI media guidelines as flexible and aspirational "principles of conduct" may increase their uptake among media professionals; cinematherapy and bibliotherapy using exemplar NSSI portrayals may help individuals self-reflect on their own NSSI from a safe distance and consider alternative coping behaviors.

Key Words: nonsuicidal self-injury, media representation, Werther effect, Papageno effect, cognitive-emotional model, traditional media, social media, Mental Health Media Guide

In 1774 Europe, Johann Wolfgang von Goethe published the fictional book *The Sorrows of Young Werther*, in which the hero, named Werther, died by suicide. It reportedly sparked a wave of suicides across Europe in which individuals imitated Werther's method of suicide, leading several countries to ban the book. Two hundred years later, the same effect can be noted when real stories of suicide are featured in the news (Phillips, 1974). That is, when a suicide is publicized, rates of suicide among similar individuals acutely increase within the subsequent days and weeks. Phillips (1974) coined this phenomenon the "Werther effect." Indeed, since Phillips' seminal paper, decades of social psychology research have demonstrated that the link between publicizing stories of suicide and acute increases in actual suicide deaths is real, particularly when such stories include the suicide of a celebrity (Domaradzki, 2021). Modern examples include the fictional Netflix series *13 Reasons Why* (Bridge et al., 2020; Feuer & Havens, 2017) and the prominent coverage of the suicides of Robin Williams (Fink et al., 2018), Kate Spade, and Anthony Bourdain (Sinyor et al., 2021).

Although media reporting of suicide can be a risk factor for suicide, responsible media coverage can play a protective role against suicide. In 2010, researchers in Austria showed that when media coverage of individuals struggling with thoughts of suicide focused on reporting how these individuals coped positively, there was a negative association with suicide (Niederkrotenthaler et al., 2010). The researchers named this protective role the "Papageno effect," drawing from Mozart's opera *The Magic Flute* in which Papageno, a character contemplating suicide, refrains from suicide when he is directed by three boys to use alternative coping strategies.

It is clear that certain types of media representations of suicide can place individuals at risk for suicide or serve a protective function in directing individuals experiencing suicidal thoughts toward healthy coping strategies. Are there similar risk and protective factors associated with media representations of nonsuicidal self-injury (NSSI)? Preliminary evidence suggests that, yes, there are similar factors at play, where improper depictions may lead to similar NSSI behavior and where careful depictions may lead to decreased NSSI behavior and increased help-seeking (Westers et al., 2021). However, these relationships are complex and much more research is needed. In this chapter, we examine the extant literature on the relationship between NSSI engagement and exposure to NSSI content in traditional forms of media, including films, television, news, music, and print novels and comics (see Pritchard & Lewis, this volume, for discussion of NSSI and online forums).

Risk and Protective Factors of NSSI Media Representations

Understanding the risk and protective factors of media representations of NSSI is relevant because there has been a clear increase in NSSI content across media platforms over time. Depictions of NSSI in movies, news, and music were rare before 1990 and nearly nonexistent prior to 1980 (Purington & Whitlock, 2010; Whitlock et al., 2009). Examining the period between 1966 and 1980, Whitlock et al. (2009) found no references to NSSI in songs, just 2 clear references or scenes depicting NSSI in movies, and 14 references to NSSI in print news media. By 2007, those numbers increased to 89 songs, 47 movies, and more than 4,000 print news stories (Whitlock et al., 2009). With the proliferation of the internet, access to media in which NSSI is depicted is now easy and ubiquitous.

Consistent with the Werther and Papageno effects, the cognitive-emotional model of NSSI (Hasking et al., 2017; also see Hird et al., this volume for theoretical models of NSSI) provides an explanatory framework for how media representations of NSSI may increase or decrease the likelihood someone will engage in NSSI. Drawing from models of emotion regulation (e.g., experiential avoidance; Chapman et al., 2006) and models of cognition (e.g., social cognitive theory; Bandura, 1986), the cognitive-emotional model of NSSI describes how cognitions and regulation of emotions together determine if and when an individual self-injures. More specifically, individuals who tend to experience emotional reactivity and/or deploy attention to negative or NSSI-related stimuli may develop thoughts and beliefs about themselves and NSSI which, in turn, influence what those individuals expect in terms of outcomes of engaging in NSSI (i.e., outcome expectancies) and their ability to engage, or refrain from engaging, in NSSI (i.e., self-efficacy expectancies). For instance, when experiencing an emotionally charged situation, someone who holds positive outcome expectancies about NSSI (e.g., "self-injuring will help me feel relieved") and their self-efficacy to resist engaging in NSSI is low, then they are more likely to engage in NSSI in that moment. On the other hand, if someone holds negative outcome expectancies (e.g., "my friends will be disgusted if I self-injure" or "I will feel ashamed") and their self-efficacy to resist any urges to self-injure is high, they may be less likely to engage in NSSI.

Risk Factors of NSSI Media Representations: Evidence of a Werther Effect

Exposure to NSSI content in the media may inform one's outcome expectancies as well as influence their self-efficacy expectancies (Hasking & Rose, 2016; Hasking et al., 2017). Here, when media portray individuals or characters engaging in NSSI with whom audience members (i.e., viewers, readers, and listeners) can identify or relate, audience members may be inclined to adopt those very behaviors themselves, depending on how the behavior and outcome are depicted. Social cognitive theory, from which the cognitive-emotional model of NSSI draws, posits that behavior is learned in the context of the social environment through observation, and that individuals, influenced by cognitive processes such as outcome and self-efficacy expectancies, are more likely to emulate observed behaviors when they identify with the person modeling the behavior, especially if the model is similar to themselves (Bandura, 1986).

Research has demonstrated support for the application of social cognitive theory to NSSI and peer influence, where individuals who know someone who has self-injured are more likely to also report having self-injured (Jarvi et al., 2013) and to do so more frequently if their self-efficacy to resist NSSI is low (Hasking & Rose, 2016). Relatedly, if media representations of NSSI suggest a positive outcome, then audiences may expect similar positive outcomes. If media portrayals include someone effectively resisting urges to self-injure, then audiences may come to believe that they, too, can resist urges to self-injure. Indeed, Radovic and Hasking (2013) found that the more films depicting NSSI that individuals viewed, the more likely they were to report having self-injured, especially if they identified with the character. Results from a similar study by Hasking and Rose (2016), however, did not replicate these findings. A closer look at this latter study reveals that the relationship between exposure and identification with characters who self-injure was moderated by self-efficacy and outcome expectancies of social cognitive theory. That is, viewing more films depicting NSSI was associated with increased likelihood of having engaged in NSSI when self-efficacy to resist NSSI was low (Hasking & Rose, 2016). Recent research by Kirtley et al. (2021) also indicated an indirect relationship between exposure to self-harm in movies and television and one's own engagement in the behavior, although they did not differentiate between NSSI and suicide attempts.

Other forms of media, such as music, have suggested a similar indirect relationship. For instance, undergraduate college students in the United Kingdom who identified as fans of "problem music," defined as alternative hard rock, punk, rap, or hip-hop music, were more likely to also report engaging in NSSI, but this was largely mediated by low self-esteem and "delinquent" behavior, which was defined as antisocial behavior like intentionally hurting the feelings of other people and carrying weapons in public (North & Hargreaves, 2006). These authors and others (e.g., Baker & Brown, 2016) caution against interpreting results as indicative of a causal relationship between certain types of music and NSSI and argue that the relationship is more complex than is often portrayed by both fans and protesters of such music.

There is currently no research examining the causal link between any form of traditional media and NSSI. For instance, do individuals with low self-efficacy to resist NSSI seek out more movies in which NSSI is depicted, or does viewing more movies in which NSSI is depicted lead to lower self-efficacy (Hasking & Rose, 2016)? Additionally, evidence suggests that youth with a history of NSSI who seek out self-injury content in the media, regardless of the type of media, are more likely to report more frequently engaging in self-injury than those who self-injure but do not seek out NSSI content (Zhu et al., 2016). Does this mean that seeking out NSSI content increases the likelihood of engaging in NSSI more frequently, or does it indicate that engaging in NSSI more frequently increases the likelihood of seeking out NSSI content, or both?

Regardless, few characters portrayed in media pursue help or receive treatment for their NSSI. Analyses of films in which NSSI is depicted reveal that most characters who self-injure do not seek or receive medical or mental health treatment for their NSSI (Purington & Whitlock, 2010; Trewavas et al., 2010; Whitlock et al., 2009). Similarly, a recent content analysis of NSSI depicted in Japanese manga, a form of comic or graphic novel, found that the majority of characters who self-injure were not participating in any mental health treatment at the time of their self-injury or after engaging in it (Seko & Kikuchi, 2021). About half of characters in motion pictures and manga receive support from romantic partners and friends, but parents and family are rarely depicted as sources of support (Seko & Kikuchi, 2021; Trewavas et al., 2010). Even when news stories cover NSSI, most do not offer resources for where individuals can obtain mental health treatment or help. On the contrary, nearly two-thirds of news media articles published between 2007 and 2018 detailed specific methods of NSSI in their coverage of the behavior, and many frequently included images that convey sadness or hopelessness (Staniland et al., 2023). Research indicates that individuals with a history of NSSI are more likely to use methods of self-injury to which they have been exposed in the media and to use them more frequently the greater number of times they are exposed to them (Radovic & Hasking, 2013; Zhu et al., 2016).

Media depictions of NSSI also rarely show long-term consequences of engaging in the behavior. Portrayals often highlight the utility of NSSI in the short term but rarely show unintended consequences such as unexpectedly needing medical treatment for wounds or receiving lasting, unwanted scars (Purington & Whitlock, 2010). Likewise, most scenes involving NSSI behavior in manga do not show the immediate consequences of self-injury or if medical treatment is needed or received (Seko & Kikuchi, 2021). Media interviews with celebrities who have a history of NSSI frequently focus on the self-injurious behavior but do not paint the full picture of the celebrity's experience or offer resolution. Audiences are often left with incomplete understanding of NSSI and its immediate or long-term consequences which can mystify, glamorize, or even romanticize the behavior (Purington & Whitlock, 2010). Such representations of NSSI in the media risk normalizing the behavior, as if it is typical behavior with little hope for change. One study found that, compared to those with no history of NSSI, individuals who self-injure were more likely to report that films normalized NSSI and even triggered their own engagement in it (Radovic & Hasking, 2013).

Media representations of NSSI may also indirectly increase risk of NSSI via perpetuation of myths and stigmatization of the behavior and those who engage in it. In their analysis of 41 movies in which NSSI is depicted, Trewavas et al. (2010) found that representations of NSSI were moderately consistent with actual empirical research about the behavior, but NSSI was more frequently associated with suicide than it is in the general community. Conflating NSSI with suicide behavior perpetuates misinformation, risks invalidating and dismissing individual phenomenological experiences, and may result in inappropriate treatment and/or psychiatric inpatient admissions when unnecessary (Staniland et al., 2022; Westers et al., 2021; Westers & Plener, 2020). News articles rarely define NSSI and most often use the word "self-harm," a term that typically encompasses both suicidal and nonsuicidal behavior and potentially leads readers to further misunderstand a behavior that is already frequently misunderstood (Staniland et al., 2023).

Additional myths that have been shown to be reinforced by some media include the incorrect assumption that individuals who engage in NSSI must also have significant mental health difficulties (Staniland et al., 2022; Trewavas et al., 2010; Whitlock et al., 2009) and are adolescent White females of middle to high socioeconomic status who cut (Bareiss, 2017; Seko & Kikuchi, 2021; Whitlock et al., 2009). Through Spring 2007, of 36 movies depicting 43 characters who had engaged in NSSI, all were White (Whitlock et al., 2009). This may influence viewers to conclude that only people who are White engage in NSSI, as if individuals of other races and cultures do not, or could not, engage in the behavior. This framing of NSSI could lead to overlooking differences across cultures and ethnicities related to NSSI function and purpose (Gholamrezaei et al., 2017; Westers & Plener, 2020) and further stigmatize individuals of other races who self-injure.

Both motion pictures and news media often sensationalize NSSI, which can also stigmatize those who engage in self-injury (Staniland et al., 2022; Trewavas et al., 2010) and consequently decrease their likelihood of seeking help (Burke et al., 2019; Pumpa & Martin, 2015; Staniland et al., 2021; Westers et al., 2021). Movies can foster negative attitudes toward self-injury and those who engage in it (Radovic & Hasking, 2013), and news media have sometimes depicted individuals who engage in NSSI as violent, dangerous, or manipulative (Staniland et al., 2022). News accounts of NSSI among youth often place blame on adolescents for engaging in what some consider a socially unacceptable behavior and direct all responsibility on the youth to stop self-injuring rather than addressing the social context or conditions that may be triggering or influencing the behavior (Bareiss, 2014). These negative attitudes and misinformation can foment public stigma of NSSI that may become internalized self-stigma among those who self-injure and thereby decrease their likelihood of seeking help (Staniland et al., 2021).

Protective Factors of NSSI Media Representations: Evidence of a Papageno Effect

It is clear that how media frame NSSI matters. How media construct messages, including about NSSI, informs public opinions, which, in turn, can reinforce those very opinions, attitudes, beliefs, and behaviors (Bareiss, 2014, 2017; Entman, 1993). In other words, there is a bidirectional relationship between narratives of NSSI and public perceptions of the behavior. People shape culture and culture shapes people. In a narrative analysis of NSSI depicted in popular motion pictures, Bareiss (2017) explains that media portrayals serve as both models of NSSI (i.e., they educate audiences about NSSI) and models for NSSI (i.e., they teach what should be done about NSSI). Just as poor media framing of NSSI can lead to the variety of risk factors for NSSI described above, research has shown that hopeful messages related to NSSI can build self-efficacy toward recovery and help-seeking (Lewis et al., 2018). Although it is true that motion pictures depicting NSSI can normalize the behavior in a negative way, Radovic and Hasking (2013) revealed that many individuals who self-injure also endorse that they feel seen and less alone and abnormal. Consistent with the Papageno effect and cognitive-emotional model of self-injury, Radovic and Hasking found that when movie characters modeled alternative, healthier coping strategies and sought treatment to address their NSSI, many viewers reported similar improvements in outcome and self-efficacy expectancies such that they, too, shared hope for ceasing self-injury. They also found that motion pictures can cultivate positive attitudes toward individuals who self-injure, and therefore decrease stigma, as many viewers reported learning more about NSSI and developing greater empathy for those who self-injure.

Similar to research on the protective effects of responsible reporting of suicide in the media, there is little research examining the protective role media may play in decreasing or preventing NSSI behavior. Nevertheless, researchers have highlighted the potential protective effects that media may have, especially when carefully depicting NSSI in film and news. Movies, for example, have the ability to foster empathy for those who self-injure, reduce stigma, and include storylines of hope and recovery (Radovic & Hasking, 2013; Trewavas et al., 2010). News stories that portray NSSI as a complex issue and in ways that also contextualize NSSI as a coping response to societal pressures, as opposed to framing the behavior as a problem inherent within individuals who are to blame for their difficulties, are more helpful and hopeful ways of framing NSSI (Bareiss, 2014). Prioritizing narratives of NSSI that are strengths-based and focused on journeys of recovery, accompanied by stories of lived experience that highlight the nuanced reasons someone might engage in NSSI, may also have a protective effect as they promote hope rather than sensationalism (Bareiss, 2014; Staniland et al., 2022). It is narratives like these that may lead audiences to develop more accurate and complete outcome expectancies in addition to greater self-efficacy expectancies to resist NSSI.

Guidelines for Appropriate Representation of NSSI in Media

Many countries have published media guidelines for responsibly reporting on suicide, grounding them in research evidence of the Werther effect, facts about suicide, and general professionalism (Pirkis et al., 2006). With a growing body of research showing how responsible reporting of suicide in media can also have a protective effect and inspire individuals at risk for suicide to seek help or utilize safer, healthier coping strategies (e.g., Domaradzki, 2021; Niederkrotenthaler & Till, 2019; Niederkrotenthaler et al., 2010), the World Health Organization (WHO; 2017) updated their media guide for reporting on suicide by adding a recommendation based on the Papageno effect. The WHO now recommends that media report stories about how to cope well amid stress and thoughts of suicide. They also moved to the top of the list the importance of media providing information where individuals can seek help (World Health Organization, 2017).

The International Society for the Study of Self-Injury (ISSS) has set forth similar guidelines for responsibly reporting and depicting NSSI in media (Westers et al., 2021). These recommendations are grounded in the growing body of NSSI research demonstrating potential Werther and Papageno effects related to both traditional media, as described in this chapter, and social media. Because media have the ability to inform and shape public opinion about NSSI, depending on what aspects of NSSI they choose to depict and how they position such aspects to be more salient than others (Entman, 1993), there is great potential to increase the likelihood of a Papageno effect. Again, messaging matters. Yet, even creators and communicators of media, such as producers or journalists, are influenced by their own outcome and self-efficacy expectancies. Their beliefs about NSSI, whether conscious or unconscious, may influence the framing of the behavior and how it is depicted in media (Entman, 1993). For instance, they may highlight certain pieces of information when depicting NSSI that will become more salient in the minds of audience members, such as repeatedly using sensationalized words like "self-mutilation" or "cutter," which could cultivate greater stigma (Lewis, 2017; Westers et al., 2021), or focusing on a mental health diagnosis that may lead audiences to incorrectly believe NSSI is always related to mental illness (e.g., Trewavas et al., 2010; Whitlock et al., 2009). This is important because mental health conditions, when depicted, are often dehumanized in movies and television (Smith et al., 2019).

To improve how mental health is portrayed in media, experts have published the *Mental Health Media Guide* for media creators, which includes a section with specific tips for depicting NSSI (Moutier et al., 2021). These tips complement the current media guidelines for appropriately portraying and reporting NSSI (Westers et al., 2021). To minimize the Werther effect and stigma and to promote the Papageno effect and help-seeking, the NSSI media recommendations include six core guidelines:

1. Avoiding use of NSSI-related images and detailed text descriptions of the behavior and its methods;
2. Highlighting treatment, recovery narratives, and healthy coping strategies;
3. Avoiding communication of misinformation by presenting facts and differentiating NSSI from suicide;
4. Avoiding sensationalizing NSSI by presenting information neutrally;
5. Separating individuals who engage in NSSI from the behavior of NSSI by using nonstigmatizing language; and
6. Ensuring responsible moderating of online article comments that could be harmful.

Challenges, Recommendations and Future Directions for Researching Media and NSSI

Despite the increase in media representations of NSSI in recent years, much is still unknown about the association between media and NSSI. One challenge in researching this relationship is measuring the temporal relationship of exposure to NSSI and engagement in NSSI to determine if media exposure is causally associated in any way to one's own engagement in the behavior, or vice versa. Chronology of exposure to and engagement in NSSI can be difficult when asking participants to retrospectively recall when they saw NSSI portrayed in media and when they engaged in NSSI or thought about engaging in NSSI. This could be especially true if exposure and engagement occurred around the same time or even years ago (Zhu et al., 2016). For similar reasons, it can be difficult to determine whether individuals intentionally seek out such content or stumble upon it before engaging in NSSI (Kirtley et al., 2021; Zhu et al., 2016). Research has yet to examine whether there is a difference in how intentional or unintentional exposure to

NSSI content in media affects individuals with lived experience of NSSI or how such differences in exposure may influence outcome expectancies. Likewise, media depictions of NSSI could include both negative elements (e.g., a graphic image in a film) and positive elements (e.g., a character in the film sought help and learned to resist urges to self-injure), which could conceal any direct relationships (Hasking & Rose, 2016).

An additional research challenge is that certain types of exposure could be more closely associated with NSSI, but because media is multifaceted and can take many forms (e.g., video, photographic images, comics, text, and audio), differentiating what elements of which forms of media are related to NSSI is difficult. For instance, if a news article includes a graphic image depicting NSSI accompanied by an attention-grabbing, sensational headline with detailed text descriptions of the self-injurious act, the implement(s) used, and the nature of the wound, it may be difficult to determine which element, or elements, of the news article is most problematic and for whom. One reader could identify with the individual who is being described in the news report but not with the method of NSSI used. Another reader could have an experience similar to the text-based description of the NSSI method and resultant wound, whereas a third reader could simply experience an urge to self-injure simply by viewing the graphic image at the start of the article. In each case, each reader could be triggered differently than other readers and, depending on their outcome and self-efficacy expectancies, may or may not be influenced to subsequently engage in NSSI.

Challenges related to researching representations of NSSI specifically in news media and how they might directly or indirectly affect individuals with and without a history of NSSI include counting which news articles are read and shared more often than others (Staniland et al., 2023). Print and television news are now made available online and can be accessed multiple times a day and at any hour, so determining if the advent of online media sources has impacted NSSI attitudes and behaviors differently than in the past is difficult to assess.

Research using longitudinal and experimental designs may provide additional insight into how depictions of NSSI in media relate to audience attitudes toward NSSI and their actual engagement in it. For instance, to better assess the effects that motion pictures have on viewer attitudes and beliefs about NSSI, research participants could complete measures before and after viewing such films (Trewavas et al., 2010). This method could also be used for examining other forms of media. Another step could be to experimentally manipulate what types of NSSI-related media research participants are exposed to and assess changes in cognitions such as anticipated consequences (i.e., outcome expectancies) and beliefs about behavior change (i.e., self-efficacy expectancies; Hasking et al., 2017; Staniland et al., 2022). This might also assist with assessing differences between fictional and nonfictional portrayals of NSSI and their relationship to NSSI attitudes and behaviors. Furthermore, future research should include individuals with lived experience of NSSI as contributors to all stages of the research process related to media and NSSI (see Hasking et al., this volume, for a review of lived experience and NSSI), such as the development of research questions and study designs and extending to prevention and intervention efforts (Lewis & Hasking, 2019).

With the newly released media guidelines for the responsible reporting and depicting of NSSI (Westers et al., 2021), it will be important to empirically evaluate how these guidelines are perceived by media creators such as journalists, editors, writers, and producers. It is likely that some media professionals have lived experience of self-injury, so understanding their perspective of the media recommendations will be important as well as assessing if their media depictions of NSSI are different than those of media professionals without lived experience. Much of media, especially news media, is fast-paced and driven by deadlines, so assessing the feasibility of implementing guidelines is important. For instance, research on suicide reporting guidelines in Canada found that media professionals believe the recommendations are helpful but difficult to implement based on media climate and culture. Despite research evidence that the Werther effect is a real phenomenon, some journalists are not convinced and, therefore, are reluctant to follow guidelines they perceive to be cumbersome, unnecessary, and a form of censorship (Gandy & Terrion, 2015). It will be important to understand if NSSI media recommendations are perceived similarly.

Future directions related to researching the awareness, uptake, and feasibility of NSSI media guidelines should also explore cultural differences. For example, some Asian societies are more prone to view sensationalized reporting of suicide in the media as acceptable but other forms of reporting as unacceptable, such as describing individuals who die by suicide as having escaped problems (Bohanna & Wang, 2012; Chang & Freedman, 2018). This latter portrayal of suicide may be particularly problematic because certain Asian cultures emphasize responsibility to family, and portraying suicide as decreasing burden on family could place individuals at greater risk for suicide (Chang & Freedman, 2018). Like suicide reporting guidelines, it is possible that each of the six recommendations outlined in the media guidelines for NSSI could also be viewed differently depending on cultural variables. Understanding these perspectives will inform the likelihood of guideline uptake and dissemination and how to better frame important media messaging related to NSSI. More broadly, learning how cultural interpretations of NSSI may protect against or exacerbate risk for engaging in NSSI is a gap in self-injury research in general (Seko & Kikuchi, 2021). Few studies examine how reasons for engaging in NSSI and related mental health issues are conceptualized across cultures (Bohanna & Wang, 2012; Gholamrezaei et al., 2017; Seko & Kikuchi, 2021).

Ethical Considerations

Requesting that media creators follow guidelines may be perceived as an infringement on values of free speech and the belief that portrayals of NSSI narratives should be honest and objective, even if it is difficult for audiences to view, read, or listen (Bohanna & Wang, 2012; Gandy & Terrion, 2015; Westers et al., 2021). However, with evidence demonstrating a Werther effect for suicide and the potential for a similar effect for NSSI, it can be argued that graphic and gratuitous depictions or portrayals of NSSI are unnecessary at best and unethical at worst. A collaborative approach with media professionals is essential to increasing the likelihood that self-injury is appropriately represented in media (Abbott et al., 2018; Bohanna & Wang, 2012; Gandy & Terrion, 2015; Westers et al., 2021). Efforts should aim to balance preserving media's freedom of speech with promoting a Papageno effect by reporting and depicting NSSI sensitively (Bohanna & Wang, 2012; Westers et al., 2021). Referring to media guidelines as flexible and aspirational "principles of conduct" (Abbott et al., 2018) may increase the likelihood that media professionals will portray NSSI in a safer, more ethical manner.

It is possible to balance accurate depictions of NSSI with nongratuitous representations (for examples, see Westers et al., 2021). When potentially graphic or disturbing material is presented, whether in media or educational settings, trigger warnings are often used so that individuals who might be uncomfortable with the content or have lived experience related to the material can feel prepared to be exposed to it or excuse themselves (Kimble et al., 2021). In the case of NSSI, media professionals may feel justified in portraying NSSI graphically if they use a trigger warning to let audiences know of the impending content. After all, this would seem to resolve the ethical conundrum of depicting an honest and detailed account of NSSI without fear of a Werther effect. However, some argue that trigger warnings prime individuals to experience the subsequent content more intensely and for longer duration (Bellet et al., 2020; Bridgland & Takarangi, 2021; Kimble et al., 2021). Perhaps more importantly, one recent study discovered that 96% of participants bypassed trigger warnings and exposed themselves to the content anyway, even when provided alternative content and even if the triggering content was relevant to their own trauma (Kimble et al., 2021).

At best, it appears that trigger warnings have little or no effect and may be neither significantly harmful nor helpful (Sanson et al., 2019). Nevertheless, parents may appreciate the use of trigger warnings in order to determine if they will allow their child to read about or view NSSI content. These results highlight the importance of the ethical use of nonsensational headlines and neutral titles so that individuals can be informed of the general content to which they will be exposed should they choose to engage further, and thereby decrease the need for a trigger warning that could inadvertently sensationalize the content that follows and prime audiences for emotional distress. In short, use of trigger warnings alone does not justify use of triggering content, especially if such content is shared carelessly or gratuitously. Careful depictions of NSSI accompanied by debriefing audiences and offering resources during or immediately following media exposure to NSSI-related content may be more important and helpful than trigger warnings.

Implications for Clinical Practice

Given the potential protective effects that media representations of NSSI can have, especially if framed in such a way that they improve outcome and self-efficacy expectancies, media have the ability to be utilized positively in the treatment of those seeking to address NSSI behavior. Cinematherapy, or carefully using motion pictures in therapy that portray NSSI, may help individuals who self-injure to safely explore their own problems from a distance and develop more objective perspectives or consider additional coping strategies, especially if they are able to identify with the character (Radovic & Hasking, 2013; Trewavas et al., 2010). Bibliotherapy may be used in a similar way, such as using written or graphic novels like manga to help individuals better understand themselves and receive support (Seko & Kikuchi, 2021). Anders (2021) suggests that the novel *Fight Club*, later produced as a major motion picture, can be used to conceptualize how NSSI interferes with genuine relationships with others, and what must be done to establish and heal relationships. Although NSSI is defined more liberally here than is typically done (i.e., the internal struggle between the main character and his alter ego as a metaphorical violence toward the self that also serves as a way to establish communication and relationships with others), Anders argues that the text of *Fight Club* reveals that learning to communicate with others and establish nonviolent healthy relationships is required for one to effectively cease NSSI and vice versa (i.e., cessation of NSSI is required to establish nonviolent healthy relationships). Identifying exemplar media depictions of NSSI may prove challenging, but even this could be a point of clinical discussion in treatment.

Building mental health literacy (Bohanna & Wang, 2012) and media literacy skills (Purington & Whitlock, 2010) may also prove useful. That is, teaching individuals how to critically evaluate that which is viewed, read, or heard in media by carefully examining media messaging and media framing can help audiences unearth content that is biased, incorrect, or incomplete (Purington & Whitlock, 2010; Zhu et al., 2016). Additional strategies for building mental health and media literacy include pointing out media portrayals of NSSI that omit depictions of both short- and long-term consequences, discussing how these portrayals could be viewed by others, exploring actual or probable consequences to NSSI engagement depicted, considering the goals and intentions of media creators, brainstorming healthier strategies for coping, and discussing how characters can seek help or find resources even if it is not shown.

Finally, returning to the cognitive-emotional model of self-injury (Hasking et al., 2017), modifying cognitive variables like outcome expectancies and self-efficacy may help buffer the influence of unhelpful or problematic NSSI expectancies depicted in media. Hasking and Rose (2016) proposed a two-stage process in which beliefs about outcome (e.g., NSSI will be helpful or unhelpful in a given moment) are more relevant when individuals first start self-injuring whereas beliefs about self-efficacy (e.g., I can or cannot resist NSSI urges) are more relevant later, after NSSI urges and behavior become more conditioned responses to emotionally distressing experiences or situations. For individuals with recent onset of NSSI engagement, interventions might address outcome expectancies by validating short-term helpful consequences of the behavior but emphasizing short- and long-term unpleasant consequences. For those who have engaged in repeated NSSI and use it as a primary coping strategy, interventions might focus on skills building and cultivation of self-efficacy (Hasking & Rose, 2016). Addressing outcome and self-efficacy expectancies can also include building media literacy skills described above, critically evaluating media representations of NSSI as models in some cases for what is present (e.g., help-seeking, stories of recovery) and what is missing (e.g., actual consequences of NSSI, hope), reviewing media guidelines, and advocating for appropriate representations of NSSI in media.

Conclusion

In summary, although research is limited and causal relationships cannot be inferred, certain representations of NSSI in media may increase risk for NSSI whereas others may be protective. Media may normalize the behavior, introduce new methods of NSSI, decrease likelihood of seeking help or support and offer few resources, paint incomplete pictures of the behavior and its consequences, fail to depict positive problem-solving or resolution, perpetuate myths and misinformation, sensationalize and stigmatize NSSI and those who engage in it, inadvertently cast blame on those who self-injure, erroneously portray NSSI as suicidal behavior, and, in some cases, directly trigger NSSI urges and acts. In line with the Werther effect and the cognitive-emotional model of self-injury, these problematic representations of NSSI could influence individuals to expect similar outcomes related to NSSI (e.g., a normalized and helpful coping behavior with no negative consequences) and beliefs about their ability to resist urges to self-injure. Audiences who tend to experience emotional volatility may come to expect positive short-term outcomes of NSSI, lack a model of how to seek help or treatment, feel hopeless about change (i.e., have low self-efficacy expectancies), and, in some cases, be inclined to self-injure using the very methods to which they have been exposed.

On the other hand, media can carefully frame messages about NSSI and depict stories of hope and recovery, promote help-seeking, model healthy coping, help individuals with lived experience of self-injury feel less abnormal and less alone, foster more positive attitudes and empathy for those who self-injure, decrease stigma, and educate audiences about the complex nature of and reasons for NSSI. In line with the Papageno effect and the cognitive-emotional model of NSSI, these more appropriate representations of self-injury could lead individuals to collect more complete pictures of the consequences of the behavior and so have more realistic and complete outcome expectancies. Audiences who are prone to emotion dysregulation may view positive models in the media about resisting NSSI and be influenced to conclude that they, too, have the self-efficacy to resist urges. In conclusion, working collaboratively with media professionals is imperative to mitigate any Werther effect and maximize any Papageno effect related to NSSI.

Author's Note

Nicholas J. Westers ORCID iD https://orcid.org/0000-0002-1602-6155

I have no conflict of interest to disclose. Correspondence concerning this article should be addressed to Nicholas J. Westers, Department of Psychiatry, Children's Health, 1341 W Mockingbird Lane, Suite 1200E, Dallas, TX 75247. Email: nicholas.westers@childrens.com

References

Abbott, M., Ramchand, R., Chamberlin, M., & Marcellino, W. (2018). Detecting changes in newspaper reporting of suicide after a statewide social marketing campaign. *Health Communication*, *33*(6), 674–680. https://doi.org/10.1080/10410236.2017.1298198

Anders, L., (2021). Fighting the self: Interpersonal and intrapersonal communicative violence in Chuck Palahniuk's *Fight Club*. In W. J. Bareiss (Ed.), *Communicating with, about, and through self-harm: Scarred discourse* (pp. 161–181). Lexington Books.

Baker, C., & Brown, B. (2016). Suicide, self-harm and survival strategies in contemporary heavy metal music: A cultural and literary analysis. *Journal of Medical Humanities*, *37*(1), 1–17. https://doi.org/10.1007/s10912-014-9274-8

Bandura, A. (1986). *Social foundations of thought and action: A social cognitive theory*. Prentice Hall.

Bareiss, W. (2014). "Mauled by a bear": Narrative analysis of self-injury among adolescents in US news, 2007–2012. *Health*, *18*(3), 279–301. https://doi.org/10.1177/1363459313497608

Bareiss, W. (2017). Adolescent daughters and ritual abjection: Narrative analysis of self-injury in four US films. *Journal of Medical Humanities*, *38*(3), 319–337. https://doi.org/10.1007/s10912-015-9353-5

Bellet, B. W., Jones, P. J., Meyersburg, C. A., Brenneman, M. M., & Morehead, K. E. (2020). Trigger warnings and resilience in college students: A preregistered replication and extension. *Journal of Experimental Psychology: Applied*, *26*(4), 717–723. https://doi.org/10.1037/xap0000270

Bohanna, I., & Wang, X. (2012). Media guidelines for the responsible reporting of suicide: A review of effectiveness. *Crisis*, *33*(4), 190–198. https://doi.org/10.1027/0227-5910/a000137

Bridge, J. A., Greenhouse, J. B., Ruch, D., Stevens, J., Ackerman, J., Sheftall, A. H., Horowitz, L. M., Kelleher, K. J., & Campo, J. V. (2020). Association between the release of Netflix's 13 Reasons Why and suicide rates in the United States: An interrupted time series analysis. *Journal of the American Academy of Child & Adolescent Psychiatry*, *59*(2), 236–243. https://doi.org/10.1016/j.jaac.2019.04.020

Bridgland, V. M. E., & Takarangi, M. K. T. (2021). Danger! Negative memories ahead: The effect of warnings on reactions to and recall of negative memories. *Memory*, *29*(3), 319–329. https://doi.org/10.1080/09658211.2021.1892147

Burke, T. A., Piccirillo, M. L., Moore-Berg, S. L., Alloy, L. B., & Heimberg, R. G. (2019). The stigmatization of nonsuicidal self-injury. *Journal of Clinical Psychology*, *75*(3), 481–498. https://doi.org/10.1002/jclp.22713

Chang, K.-K., & Freedman, E. (2018). WHO's media guidelines in the press and in public perception. *Journal of Media Ethics*, *33*(1), 14–25. https://doi.org/10.1080/23736992.2017.1401930

Chapman, A. L., Gratz, K. L., & Brown, M. Z. (2006). Solving the puzzle of deliberate self-harm: The experiential avoidance model. *Behaviour Research and Therapy*, *44*(3), 371–394. https://doi.org/10.1016/j.brat.2005.03.005

Domaradzki, J. (2021). The Werther effect, the Papageno effect or no effect? A literature review. *International Journal of Environmental Research and Public Health*, *18*(5), Article3 2396. https://doi.org/10.3390/ijerph18052396

Entman, R. M. (1993). Framing: Toward clarification of a fractured paradigm. *Journal of Communication*, *43*(4), 51–58. https://doi.org/10.1111/j.1460-2466.1993.tb01304.x

Feuer, V., & Havens, J., (2017). Teen suicide: Fanning the flames of a public health crisis. *Journal of the American Academy of Child & Adolescent Psychiatry*, *56*(9), 723–724. https://doi.org/10.1016/j.jaac.2017.07.006

Fink, D. S., Santaella-Tenorio, J., & Keyes, K. M. (2018). Increase in suicides the months after the death of Robin Williams in the US. *PLoS One*, *13*(2), Article e0191405. https://doi.org/10.1371/journal.pone.0191405

Gandy, J., & Terrion, J. L. (2015). Journalism and suicide reporting guidelines in Canada: Perspectives, partnerships, and processes. *International Journal of Mental Health Promotion, 17*(5), 249–260. https://doi.org/10.1080/14623730.2015.1077613

Gholamrezaei, M., De Stefano, J., & Heath, N. L. (2017). Nonsuicidal self-injury across cultures and ethnic and racial minorities: A review. *International Journal of Psychology, 52*(4), 316–326. https://doi.org/10.1002/ijop.12230

Hasking, P., & Rose, A. (2016). A preliminary application of social cognitive theory to nonsuicidal self-injury. *Journal of Youth and Adolescence, 45*(8), 1560–1574. https://doi.org/10.1007/s10964-016-0449-7

Hasking, P., Whitlock, J., Voon, D., & Rose, A. (2017). A cognitive-emotional model of NSSI: Using emotion regulation and cognitive processes to explain why people self-injure. *Cognition and Emotion, 31*(8), 1543–1556. https://doi.org/10.1080/02699931.2016.1241219

Jarvi, S., Jackson, B., Swenson, L., & Crawford, H. (2013). The impact of social contagion on non-suicidal self-injury: A review of the literature. *Archives of Suicide Research 17*(1), 1–19. https://doi.org/10.1080/13811118.2013.748404

Kimble, M., Flack, W., Koide, J., Bennion, K., Brenneman, M., & Meyersburg, C. (2021). Student reactions to traumatic material in literature: Implications for trigger warnings. *PLoS One, 16*(3), Article e0247579. https://doi.org/10.1371/journal.pone.0247579

Kirtley, O. J., Hussey, I., & Marzano, L. (2021). Exposure to and experience of self-harm and self-harm related content: An exploratory network analysis. *Psychiatry Research, 295*, 113572. https://doi.org/10.1016/j.psychres.2020.113572

Lewis, S. P. (2017). I cut therefore I am? Avoiding labels in the context of self-injury. *Medical Humanities, 43*(3), 204. https://doi.org/10.1136/medhum-2017-011221

Lewis, S. P., & Hasking, P. (2019). Putting the "self" in self-injury research: Inclusion of people with lived experience in the research process. *Psychiatric Services, 70*(11), 1058–1060. https://doi.org/10.1176/appi.ps.201800488

Lewis, S. P., Seko, Y., & Joshi, P. (2018). The impact of YouTube peer feedback on attitudes toward recovery from non-suicidal self-injury: An experimental pilot study. *Digital Health, 4*, 1–7. https://doi.org/10.1177/2055207618780499

Moutier, C. Y., Smith, S., Gold, J., Lindsey, M. A., Bradford, J. H., & Knowles, C. (2021). *Mental health media guide*. Viacom International. (https://mentalhealthmediaguide.com/guide-front-page/tips-by-theme-or-topic/self-injury-suicide-and-overdose/self-injury/)

Niederkrotenthaler, T., & Till, B. (2019). Suicide and the media: From Werther to Papageno effects-a selective literature review. *Suicidologi, 24*(2), 4–12. https://doi.org/10.5617/suicidologi.7398

Niederkrotenthaler, T., Voracek, M., Herberth, A., Till, B., Strauss, M., Etzersdorfer, E., Eisenwort, B., & Sonneck, G. (2010). Role of media reports in completed and prevented suicide: Werther v. Papageno effects. *The British Journal of Psychiatry, 197*(3), 234–243. https://doi.org/10.1192/bjp.bp.109.074633

North, A. C., & Hargreaves, D. J. (2006). Problem music and self-harming. *Suicide and Life-Threatening Behavior, 36*(5), 582–590. https://doi.org/10.1521/suli.2006.36.5.582

Phillips, D. P. (1974). The influence of suggestion on suicide: Substantive and theoretical implications of the Werther effect. *American Sociological Review, 39*(3), 340–354. https://doi.org/10.2307/2094294

Pirkis, J., Blood, R. W., Beautrais, A., Burgess, P., & Skehan, J. (2006). Media guidelines on the reporting of suicide. *Crisis, 27*(2), 82–87. https://doi.org/10.1027/0227-5910.27.2.82

Pumpa, M., & Martin, G. (2015). The impact of attitudes as a mediator between sense of autonomy and help-seeking intentions for self-injury. *Child Adolescent Psychiatry and Mental Health, 9*, 27. https://doi.org/10.1186/s13034-015-0058-3

Purington, A. P., & Whitlock, J. (2010). Non-suicidal self-injury in the media. *The Prevention Researcher, 17*(1), 11–13.

Radovic, S., & Hasking, P. (2013). The relationship between portrayals of nonsuicidal self-injury, attitudes, knowledge, and behavior. *Crisis, 34*(5), 324–334. https://doi.org/10.1027/0227-5910/a000199

Sanson, M., Strange, D., & Garry, M. (2019). Trigger warnings are trivially helpful at reducing negative affect, intrusive thoughts, and avoidance. *Clinical Psychological Science, 7*(4), 778–793. https://doi.org/10.1177/2167702619827018

Seko, Y., & Kikuchi, M. (2021). Self-injury in Japanese manga: A content analysis. *Journal of Medical Humanities, 42*(3), 355–369. https://doi.org/10.1007/s10912-019-09602-9

Sinyor, M., Tran, U. S., Garcia, D., Till, B., Voracek, M., & Niederkrotenthaler, T. (2021). Suicide mortality in the United States following the suicides of Kate Spade and Anthony Bourdain. *Australian & New Zealand Journal of Psychiatry, 55*(6), 613–619. https://doi.org/10.1177/0004867420976844

Smith, S. L., Choueiti, M., Choi, A., Pieper, K., & Moutier, C. (2019). *Mental health conditions in film & TV: Portrayals that dehumanize and trivialize characters.* USC Annenberg Inclusion Initiative.

Staniland, L., Hasking, P., Boyes, M., & Lewis, S. (2021). Stigma and nonsuicidal self-injury: Application of a conceptual framework. *Stigma and Health, 6*(3), 312–323. https://doi.org/10.1037/sah0000257

Staniland, L., Hasking, P., Lewis, S. P., & Boyes, M. (2022). News media framing of self-harm in Australia. *Stigma and Health, 7*(1), 35–44. https://doi.org/10.1037/sah0000350

Staniland, L., Hasking, P., Lewis, S. P., Boyes, M., & Mirichlis, S. (2023). Crazy, weak, and incompetent: A directed content analysis of self-injury stigma experiences. *Deviant Behavior, 44*(2), 278–295. https://doi.org/10.1080/01639625.2022.2038022

Trewavas, C., Hasking, P., & McAllister, M. (2010). Representations of non-suicidal self-injury in motion pictures. *Archives of Suicide Research, 14*(1), 89–103. https://doi.org/10.1080/13811110903479110

Westers, N. J., Lewis, S. P., Whitlock, J., Schatten, H. T., Ammerman, B., Andover, M. S., & Lloyd-Richardson, E. E. (2021). Media guidelines for the responsible reporting and depicting of non-suicidal self-injury. *The British Journal of Psychiatry, 219*(2), 415–418. https://doi.org/10.1192/bjp.2020.191

Westers, N. J., & Plener, P. L. (2020). Managing risk and self-harm: Keeping young people safe. *Clinical Child Psychology and Psychiatry, 25*(3), 610–624. https://doi.org/10.1177/1359104519895064

Whitlock, J., Purington, A., & Gershkovich, M. (2009). Media, the internet, and nonsuicidal self-injury. In M. K. Nock (Ed.), *Understanding nonsuicidal self-injury: Origins, assessment, and treatment* (pp. 139–155). American Psychological Association.

World Health Organization. (2017). *Preventing suicide: A resource for media professionals, update 2017.* WHO Press.

Zhu, L., Westers, N. J., Horton, S. E., King, J. D., Diederich, A., Stewart, S. M., & Kennard, B. D. (2016). Frequency of exposure to and engagement in nonsuicidal self-injury among inpatient adolescents. *Archives of Suicide Research, 20*(4), 580–590. https://doi.org/10.1080/13811118.2016.1162240

CHAPTER 40

Understanding Online Self-Injury Activity: Implications for Research, Practice, and Outreach

Tyler R. Pritchard *and* Stephen P. Lewis

> **Abstract**
>
> This chapter considers the implications of online self-injury activity for research, practice, and outreach. It acknowledges how social media and online platforms have become highly salient means of connecting individuals and obtaining information around the world. Thus, online communication has emerged as particularly relevant among people who have lived experience of nonsuicidal self-injury (NSSI). The chapter looks into the motives of individuals with lived experience of NSSI to go online, such as acceptance, validation, curiosity, understanding, self-expression, help-seeking, and help-giving. It discusses the incorporation of online NSSI activity into assessment and intervention potential in an effort to augment treatment outcomes.
>
> **Key Words:** online self-injury, research, practice, outreach, NSSI, self-expression, assessment, intervention, treatment

Social media and online platforms have become a highly salient means of connecting individuals and obtaining information around the world. People frequently go online for myriad reasons including but certainly not limited to expressing themselves, sharing content with others (e.g., images and video), accessing news, learning about different topics, and playing a role in social movements and advocating for different causes. In a similar manner, online communication has emerged as particularly relevant among people who have lived experience of nonsuicidal self-injury (NSSI). This may be particularly the case for youth and emerging adults who not only report the highest rates of NSSI (e.g., Lewis & Heath, 2015; Swannell et al., 2014) but also report the most use of the internet and social media. Indeed, almost all teens in the United States going online multiple times daily (Pew Research Centre, 2018); almost one half of emerging adults are likewise online daily (Pew Research Center, 2021). Interestingly, a small but growing research base suggests that individuals who self-injure may be more active online than individuals who do not self-injure (De Riggi et al., 2017; Mitchell & Ybarra, 2007), pointing to the importance of online activity for people with lived NSSI experience (see Lewis & Seko, 2015).

Given the above, researchers and clinicians can benefit from understanding the nature of online NSSI, what motivates individuals to engage in online NSSI activity, as well as the potential positive and negative impacts of such activity. This is conducive to better supporting individuals by illuminating the strengths and benefits of online NSSI activity while putting safeguards in place to minimize potential risks. Indeed, the unique risks and benefits associated with online NSSI activity (e.g., Lewis & Seko, 2015) may impact people's functioning and thus play a role in the effectiveness of NSSI intervention. Accordingly, it may be beneficial to incorporate online NSSI activity into clinical practice and consider clients' online activity in assessment and relevant treatment plans (Lewis, Heath, Michal et al., 2012; Lewis et al., 2018). Thus, the current chapter unpacks what we know regarding online NSSI activity including the nature of what is communicated online, what motivates online NSSI activity, and what impact (benefits and risks) this may have. We also discuss implications for researchers and clinicians, as well as opportunities for outreach and training.

Types of Online NSSI Activity

There are a multitude of ways to be active online, just as there are many forms of online NSSI activity. Thus, before discussing individuals' motives to engage in online NSSI activity and what benefits and risks it may have, it is first important to articulate what online NSSI activity comprises. In general, such activity involves any content posted or accessed that pertains to NSSI, as well as any interactions about NSSI that happen between people in an online context. Interestingly, these activities occur on a wide range of platforms. In some cases, websites are developed specifically for NSSI (e.g., a stand-alone NSSI website or discussion forum). In other instances, NSSI represents a specific topic or focus within a broader website (e.g., a platform centered on mental health challenges). However, NSSI is also mentioned and discussed on more general platforms such as major social networks (e.g., Facebook and Instagram) that were not initially developed for that purpose.

Across these platforms, the nature of what is posted and discussed varies considerably. It can involve text-based content (e.g., sharing one's story, posing a question, and providing information about NSSI) as well as imagery (e.g., photography and created images), animations, and videos. In some instances, the nature of material available online may not permit interaction with people who access the site (e.g., someone posting material on a blog that does not permit comments or someone creating a static website that provides facts about NSSI). In others, however, interaction between individuals is permitted (e.g., via comments and online chat functions). Ultimately, what is shared on a given platform and the extent to which interaction transpires hinges on the nature of that platform.

Motives for Engaging in Online NSSI Activity

Understanding why individuals engage in online NSSI activity is paramount to understanding the appeal of the internet and social media among people with lived experience.

To date, there have been numerous empirical investigations focused on the motives for, or reasons why, individuals with lived experience of NSSI go online. These motives/reasons include (a) acceptance and validation, (b) curiosity and understanding, and (c) and help-seeking and help-giving.

Acceptance and Validation

Researchers have suggested that a primary motivation to go online for individuals who self-injure is to find acceptance and validation that may be lacking in their daily offline lives (see Lewis & Seko, 2015). Indeed, individuals who self-injure sometimes report that others, such as family, friends, and professionals, fail to understand their self-injury or act in stigmatizing ways toward them (Brown et al., 2020; Lewis, Heath, Michal et al., 2012; Pritchard et al., 2021; Rowe et al., 2014; Whitlock et al., 2006). In a recent study investigating posts on a social network focused on youth mental health, researchers found that some individuals posted messages that sought validation from other members or expressed feeling misunderstood (e.g., "No one understands what I'm going through"; Pritchard et al., 2021, p. 534). This aligns with prior work that has found that a preponderance of posts in some online contexts involve people seeking a sense of belonging and validation that they are not alone in their NSSI experience (Lewis, Heath, Michal et al., 2012). Commensurate with this, Jones et al. (2011) asked users of self-injury discussion forums about their online activity. Their findings suggested a strong consensus that it is often easier to talk about NSSI to people online than to find offline support. Thus, it seems clear that seeking online support has appeal for many people who self-injure.

Notably, an appealing feature of online activity concerning NSSI is its potential to offer anonymity, which may provide a sense of safety when sharing personal experiences related to self-injury. Indeed, such safety may be perceived as absent offline. This notion is supported by the results of a recent study wherein researchers interviewed Instagram users to better understand their motives for posting NSSI-related content (Brown et al., 2020). Here, participants explained that they felt safe posting content on Instagram, including disclosing their self-injury, due to the anonymity the platform afforded. Along these lines, posting online may be especially appealing as one's posted experience is often validated by other, like-minded users (Lewis, Heath, Sornberger, et al., 2012; Brown et al., 2017). As many online platforms contain built-in feedback features, such as likes and retweets, in addition to more personalized comments or responses, having others respond with acceptance, understanding, and empathy may encourage subsequent posting through reciprocal support (e.g., Brown et al., 2020).

Curiosity and Understanding

In addition to seeking support and validation, many people may use the internet due to curiosity about self-injury and a desire to better understand it and their own experience (Haberstroh & Moyer, 2012; Jacob et al., 2017; Johnson et al., 2009; Lewis & Michal,

2014). For example, in a study asking people with lived experience why they went online, some individuals noted that they first used online NSSI platforms to better understand self-injury (Lewis & Michal, 2014). In line with this, a study examining the content of a popular app-based mental health community for youth found that users of the platform posted questions about NSSI, such as "Why do people cut themselves?" (Pritchard et al., 2021, p. 534). The use of the internet to find information about NSSI has also been documented elsewhere, with one study finding that annually, tens of millions of searches are conducted on Google to find information about NSSI (Lewis et al., 2014). Interestingly, individuals do not search only for general information about NSSI. Sometimes, individuals may seek alternative NSSI methods, ways to hide scars, or how to increase the pain of self-injury (Jacob et al., 2017). In this way, the nature of what is retrieved online may differentially impact individuals who self-injure; we address this further in the section "Potential Impact of NSSI Activity."

Help-Seeking and Help-Giving

Individuals with lived experience may also go online to obtain help from others (Haberstroh & Moyer, 2012; Johnson et al., 2009; Lewis & Michal, 2014; Murray & Fox, 2006; Rodham et al., 2013; Sternudd, 2012). Here, a primary aim is to find help that is conducive to addressing NSSI (e.g., coping with urges) and facilitating recovery (Lewis & Seko, 2015). The dynamics of recovery from NSSI are discussed further in Whitlock et al., this volume. In some cases, people who engage in NSSI activity receive unhelpful or stigmatizing reactions from others about their NSSI or feel a sense or mistrust with offline supports, including mental health professionals, and, therefore, they may prefer obtaining help online (Haberstroh & Moyer, 2012; Lewis & Seko, 2015; Pritchard et al., 2021; Whitlock et al., 2006). At the same time, some people will access NSSI platforms to actively find help (e.g., coping strategies) that complements formal mental health services (Haberstroh & Moyer, 2012). Reliance on the internet to obtain help can also stem from a lack of access to formal mental health services (e.g., during the COVID-19 pandemic; Hasking et al., 2020). Indeed, the nature of seeking help for NSSI via online platforms may be context dependent (see Brausch & Clapham, this volume, for more on NSSI and self-harming behaviors during the COVID-19 pandemic).

The research conducted to date demonstrates that individuals may go online to seek help for an array of NSSI-related concerns, including a desire to learn about ways to reduce self-harm, find medical advice for self-injury outcomes (e.g., infections), or obtain social support that can motivate recovery (e.g., Pritchard et al., 2021). A recent study investigating responses to users' NSSI-related posts on Instagram suggested that about 40% of posters were offered help from other individuals (Brown et al., 2020). Indeed, help-giving is another cited reason for engaging in online NSSI activity (Brown et al., 2017; Brown et al., 2020; Pritchard et al., 2021; Rodham et al., 2013; Sternudd, 2012). Some people make themselves available as a support/resource to others, provide general encouragement to all members, or offer helpful resources external to the platform (e.g., phone apps) (Pritchard et al., 2021). This may result from a place of readiness to offer help (e.g., if one views oneself as recovered); however, some individuals offer help to others despite their own ongoing NSSI challenges (Rodham et al., 2013). Indeed, when people view NSSI content posted by others with lived experience, they may feel a desire to reach out and help (Brown et al., 2020). Thus there is evidence for both help-seeking and -providing as reasons for online NSSI activity, and this may indicate a sense of community among people who engage in NSSI (Lewis & Seko, 2015).

Self-Expression
Finally, online NSSI activity may provide a preferred way for people to express themselves. Given the stigma associated with NSSI (see Hasking & Boyes, 2018; Staniland et al., 2021), this is understandable. Aware of this stigma and perhaps driven by prior stigmatizing encounters, many individuals are motivated to share their NSSI experiences and thus use the internet as a vehicle of expression. For example, some individuals post about their experience monitoring their attempts to stop self-injuring and working toward recovery; likewise, some people share changes in NSSI (e.g., recurrences after a time of not self-injuring) over time (Brown et al., 2020; Pritchard et al., 2021; Rodham et al., 2013). Interestingly, the nature of this content is not always posted with the intent to connect with others; rather, it may be posted for personal documentation (e.g., Brown et al., 2020; Rodham et al., 2013). The anonymity of many online platforms may also hold appeal in this regard as people can express themselves in a safe manner—that is, without concern that someone they know will see what is posted.

Although the above motives outline the core themes identified across the literature, these are not an exhaustive representation of reasons for online NSSI activity. For example, some individuals may engage in online NSSI activity to ride out self-injury urges (Pritchard et al., 2021) and to avoid engaging in NSSI. In other cases, individuals may inadvertently discover NSSI content or platforms (Lewis & Michal, 2014).

There are many reasons for online NSSI activity. Accordingly, it is important to avoid assumptions about why one might engage in these kinds of behaviors in research and clinical contexts.

Potential Impact of NSSI Activity

There are numerous potential risks and benefits associated with online NSSI activity. Below, we discuss what these involve based on current evidence in the field.

Potential Benefits
Several reviews of the evidence suggests that there are four major benefits linked with engaging in online NSSI activity, including (a) reduced social isolation, (b) disclosing NSSI experiences, (c) improving NSSI outcomes, and (d) resource provision (Dyson et

al., 2016; Lewis & Seko, 2015; Marchant et al., 2017). These are presented in more detail below.

REDUCED SOCIAL ISOLATION

Perhaps unsurprisingly, many individuals report feeling isolated or misunderstood by their offline supporters and offline interactions (Klonsky et al., 2014) and, thus, may seek refuge through online platforms. Indeed, fear of being misunderstood or stigmatized can serve as a barrier to self-injury disclosure (e.g., Rosenrot & Lewis, 2018; Rowe et al., 2014). As a result, by going online and connecting with like-minded others (who also have lived experience of NSSI) people may experience reduced isolation and a greater sense of connection and a corresponding sense of community (Haberstroh & Moyer, 2012; Johnson et al., 2009; Murray & Fox, 2006; Pritchard et al., 2021). More information on social support can be found in Jarvi Steele et al., this volume. Along these lines, online communication about NSSI may afford a safe space to disclose, inquire, or connect with others about self-injury (Brown et al., 2020) and provide a sense of acceptance (Lewis & Seko, 2015), as well as validation that people are not alone in their own NSSI experience (Baker & Lewis, 2013; Rodham et al., 2007). Ultimately, individuals who access NSSI platforms or content may feel less isolated by being understood, making connections, and getting support from others who have similar experiences.

IMPROVING NSSI OUTCOMES

A few papers have investigated the association between online NSSI activity and NSSI outcomes. To this end, some individuals who use broader self-harm or suicide websites have noted that online activity serves as an alternate coping mechanism to self-harm engagement (Baker & Fortune, 2008). Given that self-injury can be used to regulate challenging emotions and thoughts (Taylor et al., 2018), the internet may serve as a suitable alternative by allowing individuals to express challenging emotions and thoughts while potentially receiving support. Supporting this are findings from two studies suggesting that many users of NSSI message boards or discussion groups report a reduction of NSSI severity and/or frequency pursuant to engaging with these online communities (Johnson et al., 2019; Murray & Fox, 2006).

Relatedly, some people use online platforms to reduce or distract themselves from NSSI urges. For instance, a recent study examining posts on a mental health social media network found that some people explicitly mentioned using the platform to curb an urge to self-injure (Pritchard et al., 2021). Further, some individuals have reported that viewing NSSI images online may reduce associated urges to hurt themselves (Baker & Lewis, 2013; Rodham et al., 2013; Sternudd, 2012). As imagery can also carry risk (also the "Triggering Effects" section for more information), more research is needed to ascertain the mechanisms involved and who may be differentially affected by exposure to NSSI imagery. Likewise, more research is needed to better understand how and why engaging online NSSI activity may reduce NSSI frequency and urges.

RESOURCE PROVISION AND RECOVERY ENCOURAGEMENT

Several studies have suggested that providing resources and encouraging recovery may be a benefit of online NSSI activity (see Lewis & Seko, 2015). The need for empirically informed supported resources is paramount to effectively support people searching for help when online. Resource provision can occur directly on a specific platform or indirectly through a platform's members (e.g., as a comment to a post). Many websites directly provide resources to help people engaging in NSSI or offer ways that people can support individuals who engage in self-injury. One study investigated the quality of content that is likely accessed by someone searching for self-injury information online (Swannell et al., 2010). Of the websites investigated, all contained information for individuals and families. Most websites provided crisis support information (80%) or information for professionals who can offer help (60%). However, another study that comprehensively examined websites that populated from NSSI-related Google searches suggested that many websites provide questionable content and resources (Lewis et al., 2014). For example, there was an average of one NSSI myth per website. Further, only a small number of sites (11%) referenced the information present, making it unclear if the content was research informed. Taken together, online NSSI content is pervasive and easily accessed, yet its quality varies considerably. Therefore, there is an opportunity to ensure people have access to high-quality information, which we touch on later in the section, "Outreach and Training."

Some online NSSI content and interactions encourage help-seeking and promote recovery. Encouragement and support are sometimes provided indirectly from other platform members. For example, results from a recent study indicated that posts on a mental health-focused social media platform sometimes contained resources to external content or apps (Pritchard et al., 2021). Additional reports note that when online, people receive encouragement to seek offline support from mental health or other professionals (Niwa & Mandrusiak, 2012; Whitlock et al., 2006). Resources and support are also offered through less interactive websites. Here, the empirically informed resources and messages that emphasize recovery are posted directly on the website for easy access (e.g., self-injury outreach and support; Lewis, Heath, Michal et al., 2012).

Potential Risks

In addition to potential benefits, evidence from the literature also suggests that there are several potential risks associated with online NSSI activity (e.g., Dyson et al., 2016; Lewis & Seko, 2015). Specifically, online NSSI activity may contribute to (a) NSSI reinforcement, (b) triggering effects, and (c) stigma.

NSSI REINFORCEMENT

Several studies that suggest that individuals may be at increased risk of continued NSSI as a result of their online NSSI activities. Specifically, individuals may be exposed to hopeless messaging. For example, an investigation of YouTube videos found that NSSI video content often carried hopeless tones (Lewis et al., 2012) and a follow-up study likewise found that comments were often hopeless and seldom mentioned recovery or encouraged help-seeking (Lewis, Heath, Sornberger, et al., 2012). Similar reports have been found on NSSI websites, in which most websites seemed to have melancholic themes and hopeless messages concerning recovery (Lewis & Baker, 2011). More recently, more than 20% of posts on the self-injury section of a popular mental health-focused social network contained themes of hopelessness (Pritchard et al., 2021). A comprehensive review of the literature has suggested that repeated exposure to these types of messages may communicate that recovery is impossible, which, in turn, may reduce people's willingness to seek help or work on their own recovery (Lewis & Seko, 2015).

The reinforcement of NSSI may also occur through other means. Of note, researchers have found that some content online involves sharing ways to hide NSSI from others (e.g., parents) as well as sharing NSSI methods. In some cases, people may actively seek out this content. Indeed, some users post questions about how or where to self-injure (e.g., "what are some good places to cut"; Pritchard et al., 2021, p. 534) or post content that discusses information about self-injury methods that are less likely to be discovered by others (e.g., Whitlock et al., 2006). Consistent with these reports, more than half of the NSSI websites identified in one study shared NSSI concealment strategies (Lewis & Baker, 2011). Relatedly, sharing first-aid tips regarding NSSI may be another avenue through which NSSI is maintained. Reports of this nature are not uncommon (e.g., Lewis & Baker, 2011; Lewis & Knoll, 2015). For example, in a study of NSSI first aid shared through videos on YouTube, the video content rarely encouraged seeking professional medical help for NSSI (Lewis & Knoll, 2015). Thus, NSSI may be reinforced when people are exposed to strategies that deter formal help-seeking or otherwise present strategies that maintain the behavior.

TRIGGERING EFFECTS

Researchers have also highlighted the potential triggering content that exists online. In particular, this pertains to graphic NSSI imagery, video, or text in which details of NSSI are explicitly shared (Lewis & Seko, 2015). In these instances, individuals engaging in online NSSI activity may experience distress and NSSI urges after accessing such content. One study highlighted that readers and authors of NSSI websites reported NSSI activity being triggered upon accessing NSSI content via the internet; in some cases, individuals reported engagement in NSSI (Lewis & Baker, 2011). Similarly, in another study, about one third of individuals who viewed NSSI images online reported the experience as triggering (Sternudd, 2012).

Despite their pervasive use, trigger warnings may largely be ineffective because individuals in distress or other vulnerable states may ignore them (Baker & Lewis, 2013). However, it is important to consider the individual characteristics of who is accessing the content. A review of the literature indicates that not everyone who accesses NSSI material online will be triggered or upset by it. Specifically, viewing NSSI content can curb urges for some while it may be triggering for others (Lewis & Seko, 2015). Looking ahead, it will therefore be important to disentangle the unique individual and contextual factors that differentially impact people who access potentially triggering material.

Recently, the link between NSSI outcomes and uploading or viewing triggering content was examined (Kruzan et al., 2021). To do this, researchers used survey data examining NSSI outcomes alongside people's naturally occurring log activity on a popular social network dedicated to mental health discussion and support for youth. It was found that posting triggering content related to a higher probability of people engaging in or having thoughts about NSSI. Interestingly, viewing triggering content was associated with an increased intent to engage in NSSI but also more capacity to resist urges. These findings cohere with some of the aforementioned research indicating that viewing triggering content may carry risks, but this will not apply to everyone (e.g., Baker & Lewis, 2013). This underscores the need for more work in to ascertain why individuals are differentially affected by viewing triggering material.

STIGMA

Individuals who self-injure report that others often misunderstand their NSSI and it is not uncommon for people with lived experience to report NSSI-related stigma (e.g., Pritchard et al., 2021; Rosenrot & Lewis, 2018). And, although the internet may hold appeal as a means to share one's experiences and communicate about NSSI, people can still be exposed to NSSI stigma when online (Niwa & Mandrusiak, 2012). Specifically, stigma may take the form of bullying/trolling; however, it can also manifest through accessing misinformation and content about NSSI that perpetuates myths and misconceptions about the behavior and people who enact it (Lewis & Seko, 2015).

People who engage in online NSSI activity are sometimes responded to by cyberbullies or trolls. While cyberbullying and trolling represent complex behaviors (e.g., Sanfillipo et al., 2017), these generally refer to instances when individuals communicate messages (e.g., posting comments/photos) that are intentionally cruel, minimizing, or inciting (e.g., pushing people to engage in self-harm) to individuals with lived experience of NSSI. Some users of NSSI platforms report having experienced negative and stigmatizing comments from other members. One study reported that 21% of a NSSI-focused Facebook group had comments that were critical of or which mocked and condemned users, including posts encouraging people to attempt suicide (Niwa & Mandrusiak, 2012). Similar reports come from other studies also examining popular social media (e.g., YouTube), wherein harsh comments and responses toward people who self-injure are posted (Lewis,

Heath, Sornberger et al., 2012). Although it is the case that some platforms are moderated to ensure that posted content is relevant and supportive, this is not always the case. In larger and highly used platforms, it can be more difficult to moderate posted material given the sheer number of users. In the future, it will be important to examine the short- and long-term impact of being exposed to stigmatizing messages when online and to identify ways to mitigate these risks.

Finally, individuals engaging in online NSSI activity may experience stigma when viewing inaccurate information that propagates NSSI myths or dissuades individuals from seeking offline support. For example, many websites contain NSSI myths (e.g., NSSI being portrayed as attention-seeking and NSSI being an indicator of mental illness; Lewis et al., 2014). Thus, when exposed to such content it may leave individuals who self-injure feeling more misunderstood and invalidated. Indeed, such messaging may reinforce a commonly shared sentiment that those with lived experience have, namely, that other people do not understand NSSI. Ensuring that individuals struggling with self-injury can access empirically supported evidence is thus paramount.

Research Implications

Although there have been many advances in our understanding of online NSSI activity in recent years, several important avenues remain outstanding. As described earlier, although several possible benefits and risks of online NSSI activity have been documented, few efforts have directly examined the extent to which engaging in online NSSI activity directly impacts individuals with lived experience. In particular, there is a paucity of research examining the temporal nature of this link, with a few exceptions (Kruzan et al., 2021; Lewis et al., 2018). More research that investigates how people are affected by their online activity when it occurs would elucidate who is most impacted by their online activity, what kinds of online material are influential, and what mechanisms may be involved in this process. Importantly, efforts that consider both risks (e.g., triggering and reinforcement) and benefits (e.g., reductions in NSSI and greater recovery motivation) are recommended.

Researching how online activities associate with treatment outcomes merits attention. For example, it remains unclear whether access to online recovery-oriented content while seeking NSSI treatment is associated with better outcomes. Knowing how to augment extant treatment approaches would be ideal, especially given the appeal that online activity has for many people who self-injure. It will also be important to consider how online activity can impede treatment moving forward.

Given the ever-changing nature of online technology and social media, it is incumbent on researchers to consider how new platforms are used for online NSSI activity and whether existing platforms change how NSSI is communicated. This is important for a few reasons. First, certain kinds of online activity may change in their popularity and level of salience among people with lived experience. Knowing which platforms are most germane to people who self-injure is critical to our understanding of how their online behavior may impact NSSI-related outcomes. Second, this is relevant for clinical work. Indeed, as discussed later, clinicians need to know what kinds of online activity their clients may use and how they may impact their client's NSSI and overall well-being.

The above outlines some of the key questions to be answered as the field evolves. To meet these aims, a broad range of research approaches are needed. Although a majority of NSSI research in general draws on quantitative methods, and these approaches will certainly be useful moving forward, the nature of online data comes in many forms. For example, online material can be text, image, or video based and platforms often rely on all of these in tandem. In this way, it will be important to draw on qualitative and mixed-method approaches to ensure that the richness of certain data (e.g., in-depth text descriptions or detailed video) is not overlooked. Along these lines, consideration of text-based analysis and the use of Big Data should also be used. Finally, beyond relying on the use of online data itself, engaging with people who have lived experience is recommended. This includes interview-based studies, the use of surveys, and even involving people who self-injure in the early stages of research to ensure that the nature of questions pursued by a research agenda are indeed relevant to people with lived experience (Lewis & Hasking, 2019).

Clinical Implications

For clinicians working with clients who engage in NSSI, it is important that online activity be considered when assessing a client's NSSI and, as needed, when conducting intervention. As a first step, becoming familiar with the nature of online NSSI activity (described earlier in the chapter), including its motives and potential impacts, is critical. This knowledge is key in terms of recognizing how online activity *may* affect a client's NSSI engagement and overall well-being.

Congruent with this is the import of adopting a person-centered and balanced approach regarding the way that a client's online activity may impact them. Despite there being both risks and benefits linked with online NSSI activity, there is arguably more emphasis placed on risks in research and in the broader media, as discussed in Westers, this volume (Lewis, Heath, Michal et al., 2012; Lewis et al., 2014). Thus, viewing each client's situation as unique and refraining from assumptions that all (or even most) online activity related to NSSI is harmful is key. Doing so is conducive to fostering a stronger case formulation and collaborative alliance with the client.

Assessment

Building on the above, and commensurate with recommendations for assessing NSSI more broadly (Klonsky & Lewis, 2014; Klonsky et al., 2011), as well as published guidelines for addressing online NSSI activity in clinical contexts (Lewis, Heath, Michal et al., 2012; Lewis & Arbuthnott, 2014; Lewis et al., 2019), we recommend the use of a functional assessment to gain insight into a client's online NSSI activity. A functional log focuses on the temporal nature of a client's online activities and any related impact that may have on them. To this end, the following domains should be included in a log: (a) precursors to a client's online activity, which includes life events, social interactions, thoughts, and emotions that led to online NSSI activity; (b) what occurred when the client went online, which includes the nature of the online activity and any associated thoughts and feelings (e.g., those evoked by the online activity); and (c) the (potential) outcomes that stemmed from the online activity; this includes thoughts, and feelings as well as NSSI-specific factors such as urges and NSSI engagement.

To employ a functional assessment, it can be helpful to engage the client in a discussion about what a functional log entails and the way it can be utilized to record their online activity outside of sessions. Importantly, clients should be afforded opportunities to address questions and concerns through this process. It may also be helpful to work on a sample log collaboratively with a client to troubleshoot areas of uncertainty; from here, clients can complete their log between subsequent treatment sessions. Regular check-ins about the content of the log (i.e., what one's online activity involved, how it affected them) can then help identify whether there are changes in the association between online NSSI activity, NSSI engagement (e.g., reductions and increases), and well-being (e.g., distress levels). The use of check-ins also provides collaborative opportunities to troubleshoot issues (e.g., forgetting to complete the log). As clinicians better understand the way that their clients' online activity affects them, they will be better positioned to incorporate this in their treatment plan. Along these lines, Box 40.1 offers a series of practical questions that may be useful when asking about a client's online NSSI activity; these may also be useful when broaching the topic of online activity related to NSSI and engaging in discussion about this with clients.

Finally, it should be noted that functional logs can benefit clients by allowing them to become more aware of what impact their online activity may be having on their own functioning. For example, in some cases, clients may be unaware that what they do online is having a negative effect (e.g., reading stories that are hopeless in nature impacting their own views on recovery). Thus, through continued use of a functional log, greater insight into how online activity affects NSSI can be obtained.

Treatment Approaches

Should it be determined that a client's online activity is having an adverse effect, many clients may nonetheless be unready to stop their online activity. As such, demands or even requests to do so are not recommended when working with clients. This kind of messaging may indicate to the client that the clinician does not fully understand the importance of the online activity or presumes that it is easy to stop when it may not be. Doing so may also inadvertently signal that what the client is doing online is wrong or that if they engage forms of online activity, this should not be raised in future sessions. Consequently, this may

Box 40.1. Questions for Use with Clients When Asking about Online NSSI Activity

When asking about a client's type and frequency of online NSSI activity

- Some people who self-injure will use the internet to access material related to self-injury or to interact with people who also self-injure. I'm wondering if this is something you've done?
- What kinds of things do you view related to self-injury when you're online?
- What kinds of things do you talk about with others about self-injury when you're online?
- Can you help me understand what kinds of things you view/access when you're online? What do the websites look like? Do you have any favorite ones?
- Do you tend to go to websites specifically about self-injury or do you more use social media or other sites like that? Are there any in particular that you tend to use?
- When you're on these websites (mention specific one if relevant), what do you typically do there? (e.g., reading/browsing, posting material, and communicating with people directly)?
- Are you a member of an online group related to self-injury (e.g., message board and forum)?
- Approximately how often would you say you do this? (e.g., daily, weekly, or monthly)?
- Some people say that they go online more at certain times of day. Is there a typical time of day that you think you do this more often?
- Have you noticed any change in how often you've done this from when you first did it? More? Less? About the same?

When asking about the nature of information on a website

- When you go online, do you look for any particular kinds of information or resources?
- What type of resources/information do you tend to access when online?
- Do you know who makes the website (e.g., a hospital, university, someone with lived experience, a charity)?
- Do you know if the website is moderated? If so, do you know who does this? (e.g., a professional or someone in the online community)?
- When you access information online, what kind of things do you view? Do you find this is helpful? I'm wondering if you can help me understand what makes it helpful/unhelpful?
- How would you describe the overall theme of the website? (e.g., supportive, unhelpful)

When asking about a client's media sharing (viewing/posting with others)

- When you look at content online, are there particular kinds of material you tend to view? (e.g., photos, videos)?
- Do you develop and post/share content as well (e.g., photos, videos)? What kind of content do you post online? How might you describe the theme of what you post? Can you help me to understand why you post this material?
- When you're online, do you look for pictures or videos about self-injury? Are there trigger warnings? Do you use them?
- Do you look for triggering content? Do you find material triggering? Can you help me understand what makes it triggering for you? (explore to what degree and intensity)

> **When using a functional assessment**
>
> - If you could think back, when would you say you started going online to find content about/talk about self-injury?
> - Have you noticed any change in your own self-injury since this time? For example, some people will say that they self-injure more or less often? What do you think may be the reason for that?
> - Do you ever self-injure before or after engaging in online activity related to self-injury? Can you help me understand that a bit more (e.g., how long before/after, where are you when this happens)?
> - Can you help me understand what going online about self-injury does for you? Is it helpful? How so? Is it ever unhelpful? How so?

lead to secrecy, inaccurate completion of functional logs, or disengagement from the therapeutic process altogether. It should be recognized that much like someone may be unready to stop self-injuring, they may similarly be unready to stop certain kinds of online activity. As noted, many people view online NSSI activity as highly salient (e.g., as a means of not feeling alone and feeling validated in their experience; Lewis, Heath, Michal et al., 2012; Lewis & Seko, 2015). Thus, letting go of this is bound to be difficult for many people.

Consistent with recommendations for addressing online NSSI activity (Lewis, Heath, Michal et al., 2012), motivational interviewing can be helpful as it explicitly considers and addresses the potential for client reluctance or ambivalence about ceasing any potentially harmful online activity. Hence, a main goal is to foster agency on part of the client, so they are motivated to make changes in online activity that is having an adverse effect. Therefore, with time, and as individuals become more engaged in the therapeutic process, they are likely to become more open to changing aspects of their online activity. At this juncture, clinicians can encourage clients to identify alternative behaviors that can take the place of online activities that were having adverse effects. Examples of alternative activities include exercise, socializing with a friend, spending time with family, using mindfulness, and engaging in a creative activity (e.g., art or music) among countless others. When working toward use an alternative behavior, having a list of options can be fruitful. This way, if one alternative is not viable another can be used instead. Drawing on alternatives may be especially useful when one's tendency to go online coincides with NSSI thoughts or urges to self-injure. Indeed, clients will likely have strategies to use in these contexts already as a part of therapy.

Although the use of offline alternatives is likely to be preferable, it can be useful to consider helpful online activities. In this regard, introducing and directing individuals to reputable, research-informed, and recovery-focused websites would be important. In concert with this, clients can also be encouraged to use their functional log to assess how these activities affect them. By virtue of doing this, clients recognize how using these kinds of websites may be beneficial to them. However, as research indicates that many websites

> **Box 40.2.** NSSI Resources
>
> **Self-Injury Outreach and Support (SiOS)**
>
> www.sioutreach.org
>
> SiOS offers a suite of research-informed resources about self-injury. All content is recovery-oriented, which includes research-informed coping guides (e.g., how to manage urges to self-injure) and an array of recovery stories from individuals with lived experience. In addition, SiOS offers research-informed guides for people who play key supportive roles in the lives of individuals with lived experience. This includes families, friends, romantic partners, schools, and various health and mental professionals.
>
> **Cornell Research Program on Self-injury and Recovery**
>
> www.selfinjury.bctr.cornell.edu
>
> Situated at Cornell University, this website provides a series of research-informed resources about self-injury. This includes recovery-based information for people who self-injure as well as a series of other practical resources (e.g., content on disclosures). In addition, this website has guides and research-informed content for families, schools, and professionals.
>
> **SAFE Alternatives**
>
> www.selfinjury.com
>
> SAFE Alternatives is a treatment approach and service located in the United States. Their website also houses educational resources for individuals engaging in NSSI, caregivers, families, and educational and health professionals.
>
> **Shedding Light on Self-injury**
>
> www.self-injury.org.au
>
> On this website, visitors will have access to research-informed material meant for health professionals. Also on this website is general information for all individuals wishing to learn more about self-injury.
>
> **The Mighty's Guide to Understanding Self-harm**
>
> https://themighty.com/2019/06/what-is-self-harm/#addiction-self-harm
>
> This webpage from The Mighty, an e-community that aims to shed light on people's lived experience of physical and mental health difficulties, presents an integrated series of resources about self-injury recovery. The material is research informed and stems from consultation with leading experts in the field. The content on this is for individuals with lived experience of self-injury and concerned loved ones.

promote questionable content, knowing what websites to suggest in these instances is imperative. Box 40.2 presents recommended websites to suggest to clients.

Outreach and Training

Beyond needing more research examining online NSSI activity and the relevance of such activity in clinical settings, the internet also represents a powerful means to provide outreach. This can take on many forms. At a basic level, given the ubiquity and reach of the internet, there is an opportunity to use online platforms to disseminate high-quality information to address common myths (e.g., NSSI only occurs among teenage girls) and, thus, increase NSSI literacy for the public. This information should also be practical in nature and offer recommendations about how various individuals can support people with lived experience. For example, several websites—including those outlined in Box 40.2—offer guidance for family and friends of people who self-injure. Likewise, many will also target various stakeholders (e.g., schools) in outreach initiatives.

Commensurate with the above is the use of the internet to tackle NSSI stigma. Although this may organically occur to some degree through broader knowledge dissemination efforts, this is just one component of effective anti-stigma work. Indeed, many leading stigma scholars advocate for contact-based sessions wherein messages are delivered by people with lived experience (e.g., Corrigan et al., 2012; Thornicroft et al., 2016). While such efforts have been called for in the context of combatting NSSI stigma they are yet to be fully realized (Lewis et al., 2022; Lewis & Hasking, 2019; Lewis & Hasking, 2023). In this way, anti-stigma approaches that center on people's lived experience are needed.

The internet can also be used to reach specific stakeholder groups who work with and support people with lived experience (e.g., school personnel and mental health professionals). This has perhaps become especially relevant amid the COVID-19 global pandemic. Given the public health measures needed to curtail disease spread, countless individuals worldwide have had to rely on the internet to hold work-based meetings, attend conferences, and offer education. In a similar vein, training workshops that provide knowledge and practical guidance for use when working with individuals with lived experience could be similarly implemented. Indeed, efforts of this nature have already begun with pioneering work by Janis Whitlock at Cornell University who has developed a suite of e-trainings for individuals in support roles, including training for parents of youth who self-injure. As the field continues to evolve, such novel approaches to training are bound to become more common given their appeal and accessibility. Hence, efforts to evaluate their impact to ensure that people's informational and practical needs are fully met ought to be prioritized as this happens.

Conclusion

For many individuals with lived experience of NSSI, social media and online communication represent salient ways to connect with others, obtain support, and access information and recovery-oriented resources. Yet, researchers have found that online NSSI activity is a "double-edged sword" and may carry both benefits and risks (Lewis & Seko, 2015). Given this mixed evidence, it is imperative to adopt a balanced approach when considering the impact of online NSSI activity—one that avoids generalizations and assumptions that online NSSI activity is either all "harmful" or all "helpful." While research in this area has grown, there are many outstanding questions for researchers to address. It will be important to address these avenues to further propel the field and to optimize the support available to individuals who have lived experience and who engage in online NSSI activity. In keeping with this, it is important for mental health practitioners to consider the online activity of their clients who self-injure. Ultimately, incorporating online NSSI activity into assessment and intervention has potential to augment treatment outcomes. Finally, the internet and use of social media has much promise as an effective means of outreach and may work to provide needed training to stakeholders who work with and support people with lived experience. Taken together, there is much potential to harness the use of the internet to make significant and lasting impacts in the lives of people with lived NSSI experience.

References

Baker, D., & Fortune, S. (2008). Understanding self-harm and suicide websites: A qualitative interview study of young adult website users. *Crisis, 29*(3), 118–122. https://doi.org/10.1027/0227-5910.29.3.118

Baker, T. G., & Lewis, S. P. (2013). Responses to online photographs of non-suicidal self-injury: A thematic analysis. *Archives of Suicide Research, 17*(3), 223–235. https://doi.org/10.1080/13811118.2013.805642

Brown, R. C., Fischer, T., Goldwich, A. D., Keller, F., Young, R., & Plener, P. L. (2017). #cutting: Non-suicidal self-injury (NSSI) on Instagram. *Psychological Medicine, 48*(2), 337–346. https://doi.org/10.1017/s0033291717001751

Brown, R. C., Fischer, T., Goldwich, D. A., & Plener, P. L. (2020). "I just finally wanted to belong somewhere"—Qualitative analysis of experiences with posting pictures of self-injury on Instagram. *Frontiers in Psychiatry, 11*, Article 274. https://doi.org/10.3389/fpsyt.2020.00274

Corrigan, P. W. (2012). Research and the elimination of the stigma of mental illness. *The British Journal of Psychiatry, 201*, 7–8. http://dx.doi.org/10.1192/bjp.bp.111.103382

De Riggi, M. E., Moumne, S., Heath, N. L., & Lewis, S. P. (2017). Non-suicidal self-injury in our schools: A review and research-informed guidelines for school mental health professionals. *Canadian Journal of School Psychology, 32*(2), 122–143. https://doi.org/10.1177/0829573516645563

Dyson, M. P., Hartling, L., Shulhan, J., Chisholm, A., Milne, A., Sundar, P., Scott, S. D., & Newton, A. S. (2016). A systematic review of social media use to discuss and view deliberate self-harm acts. *PLoS One, 11*(5), Article e0155813. https://doi.org/10.1371/journal.pone.0155813

Haberstroh, S., & Moyer, M. (2012). Exploring an online self-injury support group: Perspectives from group members. *The Journal for Specialists in Group Work, 37*(2), 113–132. https://doi.org/10.1080/01933922.2011.646088

Hasking, P., & Boyes, M. (2018). Cutting words: A commentary on language and stigma in the context of nonsuicidal self-injury. *Journal of Nervous & Mental Disease, 206*(11), 829–833. https://doi.org/10.1097/nmd.0000000000000899

Hasking, P., Lewis, S. P., Bloom, E., Brausch, A., Kaess, M., & Robinson, K. (2020). Impact of the COVID-19 pandemic on students at elevated risk of self-injury: The importance of virtual and online resources. *School Psychology International, 42*(1), 57–78. https://doi.org/10.1177/0143034320974414

Jacob, N., Evans, R., & Scourfield, J. (2017). The influence of online images on self-harm: A qualitative study of young people aged 16–24. *Journal of Adolescence, 60*, 140–147. https://doi.org/10.1016/j.adolescence.2017.08.001

Johnson, G. M., Zastawny, S., & Kulpa, A. (2009). E-message boards for those who self-injure: Implications for e-health. *International Journal of Mental Health and Addiction, 8*(4), 566–569. https://doi.org/10.1007/s11469-009-9237-x

Jones, R., Sharkey, S., Ford, T., Emmens, T., Hewis, E., Smithson, J., Sheaves, B., & Owens, C. (2011). Online discussion forums for young people who self-harm: User views. *The Psychiatrist, 35*(10), 364–368. https://doi.org/10.1192/pb.bp.110.033449

Klonsky, E. D., & Lewis, S. P. (2014). Assessment of non-suicidal self-injury. In M. K. Nock (Ed.), *The Oxford handbook of suicide and self-injury* (pp. 337–351). Oxford University Press.

Klonsky, E. D., Muehlenkamp, J. J., Lewis, S. P., & Walsh, B. (2011). *Non-suicidal self-injury*. Hogrefe & Huber.

Klonsky, E. D., Victor, S. E., & Saffer, B. Y. (2014). Nonsuicidal self-injury: What we know, and what we need to know. *The Canadian Journal of Psychiatry, 59*(11), 565–568. https://doi.org/10.1177/070674371405901101

Kruzan, K. P., Whitlock, J., & Bazarova, N. N. (2021). Examining the relationship between the use of a mobile peer-support app and self-injury outcomes: Longitudinal mixed methods study. *JMIR Mental Health, 8*(1), Article e21854. https://doi.org/10.2196/21854

Lewis, S. P., & Arbuthnott, A. E. (2014). Non-suicidal self-injury, eating disorders: The influence of the internet and social media. In L. Claes & J. Muehlenkamp (Eds.), *Non- suicidal self-injury in eating disorders* (pp. 273–293). Springer.

Lewis, S. P., & Baker, T. G. (2011). The possible risks of self-injury web sites: A content analysis. *Archives of Suicide Research, 15*(4), 390–396. https://doi.org/10.1080/13811118.2011.616154

Lewis, S. P., & Hasking, P. (2019). Putting the "self" in self-injury research: Inclusion of people with lived experience in the research process. *Psychiatric Services, 70*(11), 1058–1060. https://doi.org/10.1176/appi.ps.201800488

Lewis, S. P., & Hasking, P. A. (2023). *Understanding self-injury: A person-centered approach*. Oxford University Press.

Lewis, S. P., & Heath, N. L. (2015). Nonsuicidal self-injury among youth. *The Journal of Pediatrics, 166*(3), 526–530. https://doi.org/10.1016/j.jpeds.2014.11.062

Lewis, S. P., Heath, N. L., Michal, N. J., & Duggan, J. M. (2012). Non-suicidal self-injury, youth, and the Internet: What mental health professionals need to know. *Child and Adolescent Psychiatry and Mental Health, 6*(1), Article 13. https://doi.org/10.1186/1753-2000-6-13

Lewis, S. P., Heath, N. L., Sornberger, M. J., & Arbuthnott, A. E. (2012). Helpful or harmful? An examination of viewers' responses to nonsuicidal self-injury videos on YouTube. *Journal of Adolescent Health, 51*(4), 380–385. https://doi.org/10.1016/j.jadohealth.2012.01.013

Lewis, S. P., Heath, N. L., & Whitley, R. (2022). Addressing self-injury stigma: The promise of innovative digital and video action-research methods. *Canadian Journal of Community Mental Health, 40*(3), 45–54.

Lewis, S. P., Kenny, T. E., & Pritchard, T. R. (2019). Toward an understanding of online self-injury activity: Review and recommendations for researchers and clinicians. In. J. Washburn (Ed.), *Nonsuicidal self-injury: Advances in research and practice* (pp. 195–214). Routledge

Lewis, S. P., & Knoll, A. K. (2015). Do it yourself: Examination of self-injury first aid tips on YouTube. *Cyberpsychology, Behavior, and Social Networking, 18*(5), 301–304. https://doi.org/10.1089/cyber.2014.0407

Lewis, S. P., Mahdy, J. C., Michal, N. J., & Arbuthnott, A. E. (2014). Googling self-injury: The state of health information obtained through online searches for self-injury. *JAMA Pediatrics, 168*(5), 443–449. https://doi.org/10.1001/jamapediatrics.2014.187

Lewis, S. P., & Michal, N. J. (2014). Start, stop, and continue: Preliminary insight into the appeal of self-injury e-communities. *Journal of Health Psychology, 21*(2), 250–260. https://doi.org/10.1177/1359105314527140

Lewis, S. P., & Seko, Y. (2015). A double-edged sword: A review of benefits and risks of online nonsuicidal self-injury activities. *Journal of Clinical Psychology, 72*(3), 249–262. https://doi.org/10.1002/jclp.22242

Lewis, S. P., Seko, Y., & Joshi, P. (2018). The impact of YouTube peer feedback on attitudes toward recovery from non-suicidal self-injury: An experimental pilot study. *Digital Health, 4*, Article 2055207618780499.

Marchant, A., Hawton, K., Stewart, A., Montgomery, P., Singaravelu, V., Lloyd, K., Purdy, N., Daine, K., & John, A. (2017). A systematic review of the relationship between internet use, self-harm and suicidal behaviour in young people: The good, the bad and the unknown. *PLoS One, 12*(8), Article e0181722. https://doi.org/10.1371/journal.pone.0181722

Mitchell, K. J., & Ybarra, M. L. (2007). Online behavior of youth who engage in self-harm provides clues for preventive intervention. *Preventive Medicine, 45*(5), 392–396. https://doi.org/10.1016/j.ypmed.2007.05.008

Murray, C. D., & Fox, J. (2006). Do internet self-harm discussion groups alleviate or exacerbate self-harming behaviour? *Australian E-Journal for the Advancement of Mental Health, 5*(3), 225–233. https://doi.org/10.5172/jamh.5.3.225

Niwa, K. D., & Mandrusiak, M. N. (2012). Self-injury groups on Facebook. *Canadian Journal of Counseling and Psychotherapy, 46*, 1–20.

Pew Research Center. (2018). Accessed September 14, 2021. https://www.pewresearch.org/internet/2018/05/31/teens-social-media-technology-2018/)

Pew Research Center. (2021). Accessed September 14, 2021. https://www.pewresearch.org/fact-tank/2021/03/26/about-three-in-ten-u-s-adults-say-they-are-almost-constantly-online/).

Pritchard, T. R., Lewis, S. P., & Marcincinova, I. (2021). Needs of youth posting about nonsuicidal self-injury: A time-trend analysis. *Journal of Adolescent Health*, *68*(3), 532–539. https://doi.org/10.1016/j.jadohealth.2020.06.038

Rodham, K., Gavin, J., Lewis, S. P., St. Denis, J. M., & Bandalli, P. (2013). An investigation of the motivations driving the online representation of self-injury: A thematic analysis. *Archives of Suicide Research*, *17*(2), 173–183. https://doi.org/10.1080/13811118.2013.776459

Rodham, K., Gavin, J., & Miles, M. (2007). I hear, I listen and I care: A qualitative investigation into the function of a self-harm message board. *Suicide and Life-Threatening Behavior*, *37*(4), 422–430. https://doi.org/10.1521/suli.2007.37.4.422

Rosenrot, S. A., & Lewis, S. P. (2018). Barriers and responses to the disclosure of non-suicidal self-injury: A thematic analysis. *Counselling Psychology Quarterly*, *33*(2), 121–141. https://doi.org/10.1080/09515070.2018.1489220

Rowe, S. L., French, R. S., Henderson, C., Ougrin, D., Slade, M., & Moran, P. (2014). Help-seeking behaviour and adolescent self-harm: A systematic review. *Australian & New Zealand Journal of Psychiatry*, *48*(12), 1083–1095. https://doi.org/10.1177/0004867414555718

Sanfilippo, M. R., Fichman, P., & Yang, S. (2017). Multidimensionality of online trolling behaviors. *The Information Society*, *34*(1), 27–39. https://doi.org/10.1080/01972243.2017.1391911

Staniland, L., Hasking, P., Boyes, M., & Lewis, S. (2021). Stigma and nonsuicidal self-injury: Application of a conceptual framework. *Stigma and Health*, *6*(3), 312–323. https://doi.org/10.1037/sah0000257

Sternudd, H. T. (2012). Photographs of self-injury: Production and reception in a group of self-injurers. *Journal of Youth Studies*, *15*(4), 421–436. https://doi.org/10.1080/13676261.2012.663894

Swannell, S., Martin, G., Krysinska, K., Kay, T., Olsson, K., & Win, A. (2010). Cutting on-line: Self-injury and the internet. *Advances in Mental Health*, *9*(2), 177–189. https://doi.org/10.5172/jamh.9.2.177

Swannell, S. V., Martin, G. E., Page, A., Hasking, P., & St. John, N. J. (2014). Prevalence of nonsuicidal self-injury in nonclinical samples: Systematic review, meta-analysis and meta-regression. *Suicide and Life-Threatening Behavior*, *44*(3), 273–303. https://doi.org/10.1111/sltb.12070

Taylor, P. J., Jomar, K., Dhingra, K., Forrester, R., Shahmalak, U., & Dickson, J. M. (2018). A meta-analysis of the prevalence of different functions of non-suicidal self-injury. *Journal of Affective Disorders*, *227*, 759–769. https://doi.org/10.1016/j.jad.2017.11.073

Thornicroft, G., Mehta, N., Clement, S., Evans-Lacko, S., Doherty, M., Rose, D., Koschorke, M., Shidhaye, R., O'Reilly, C., & Henderson, C. (2016). Evidence for effective interventions to reduce mental-health-related stigma and discrimination. *The Lancet*, *387*(10023), 1123–1132. https://doi.org/10.1016/s0140-6736(15)00298-6

Whitlock, J. L., Powers, J. L., & Eckenrode, J. (2006). The virtual cutting edge: The Internet and adolescent self-injury. *Developmental Psychology*, *42*(3), 407–417. https://doi.org/10.1037/0012-1649.42.3.407

CHAPTER 41

Understanding the Social Context of NSSI: Interpersonal Stress in Romantic and Peer Relationships and Peer Socialization of NSSI

Olivia H. Pollak, Matthew G. Clayton, Benjamin W. Nelson, *and* Mitchell J. Prinstein

Abstract

This chapter assesses recent research examining social and interpersonal factors in relation to nonsuicidal self-injury (NSSI), with a focus on peer relationships and peer influence processes, particularly among adolescents. It begins by discussing several domains of peer-related experiences that have been shown to cross-sectionally or longitudinally predict NSSI engagement in adolescents. These include romantic relationships, peer friendships, and experiences of peer victimization. The chapter then reviews emerging work on biophysiological responses to socially themed stress that may characterize those who engage in NSSI, and which may shed light on intraindividual mechanisms linking peer-related experiences of stress and NSSI. It also considers how exposure to others' engagement in NSSI, particularly in peer networks, may be a potent environmental-level factor within adolescents' social milieu that may moderate risk for NSSI. Finally, the chapter describes social—including family, peer, and romantic partner—protective factors, with important clinical implications for prevention and treatment of NSSI.

Key Words: nonsuicidal self-injury, peer relationships, adolescents, romantic relationships, peer friendships, peer victimization, socially themed stress, peer networks, social protective factors

Introduction

In the past two decades, research has made notable advances in furthering theoretical models of nonsuicidal self-injury (NSSI) and identifying NSSI correlates and risk factors, reflecting an interest among researchers in better understanding NSSI as a distinct outcome among the broader class of self-injurious (i.e., nonsuicidal and suicidal) thoughts and behaviors. Much of this research has focused on intrapersonal or intraindividual factors associated with NSSI, including deficits in affective or emotion regulation processes that may precipitate NSSI engagement (e.g., Chapman et al., 2006; Selby & Joiner, 2009), as described in Fox (this volume). However, a smaller but growing body of work has explored the role of interpersonal or socially themed factors that may interact with intrapersonal processes to heighten risk for NSSI.

Aligned with developmental psychopathology and systems theory perspectives (Bronfenbrenner, 1977), examining interpersonal or social factors is critical to understanding the emergence and maintenance of psychopathology, including NSSI. Indeed, NSSI-specific theoretical work provides support for associations between NSSI and social factors that may either precipitate and maintain these behaviors or otherwise characterize the interpersonal contexts in which NSSI behaviors are more likely to emerge. For example, functional models of NSSI (e.g., Nock & Prinstein, 2004), which conceptualize NSSI behaviors according to their immediate antecedents and consequences, articulate several social functions that NSSI may serve (alongside automatic functions more specifically associated with emotion or affect regulation). Such models posit that NSSI may serve, for example, to influence or communicate with others, and consequent reactions from others (e.g., attention, increased support) in response to NSSI may reinforce these behaviors (Nock, 2008).

Empirical work also implicates interpersonally themed factors in the pathogenesis of NSSI and provides support for interpersonal deficits among those who engage in these behaviors. For example, NSSI is associated with impaired interpersonal problem-solving and poor communication skills (Hilt et al., 2008; Nock & Mendes, 2008). Experimental studies suggest that individuals who engage in NSSI may be less willing to tolerate emotional distress specifically after recalling negative interpersonal interactions, suggesting that affective distress may be linked to interpersonally themed stress among those with a history of NSSI (Gratz et al., 2011). Taken together, theoretical and empirical research to date suggests that NSSI may, for some individuals or in certain contexts, represent a behavioral response to interpersonally themed stress—to be understood in combination with more distal risk factors (e.g., parenting styles and peer victimization) and proximal, maladaptive responses to stress conceptualized across multiple domains (e.g., affective and physiological).

Interpersonal and social factors may be especially relevant to understanding the etiology of NSSI among adolescents, specifically. First, NSSI behaviors most commonly begin in adolescence (Nock et al., 2013), a developmental period also characterized by significant changes in peer relations and increases in peer-related stress (Prinstein & Giletta, 2016). Studies further suggest that interpersonal or social problems, such as peer victimization and peer relationship conflict, are among the most commonly cited precipitants of self-injurious behaviors in adolescence, including both suicidal behavior (Brent et al., 1999; Brent et al., 1993; Bridge et al., 2006; Gould et al., 1996) and NSSI (Hawton et al., 1996). Indeed, peer-related factors—including both negative peer experiences and peer influence processes—may be particularly potent risk factors for NSSI. Given the heightened importance of peers in adolescence, as well as marked increases in rates of NSSI during this period, peer-related experiences represent a critical domain of interpersonal factors that have shown associations with onset, presence, or maintenance of NSSI.

This chapter reviews recent research examining social and interpersonal factors in relation to NSSI, with a focus on peer relationships and peer influence processes, particularly among adolescents. In framing this chapter, we borrow from developmental psychopathology and systems theory perspectives to propose that adolescents' experiences of interpersonal stress across multiple domains are associated with NSSI, and that particular responses to these stressors may act as a mechanism that further increases NSSI risk. Indeed, recent work examining acute stress responses offers preliminary, empirical tests of biopsychosocial models of NSSI, which build on diathesis-stress frameworks to emphasize the interaction of biological vulnerabilities with social-ecological risk factors to precipitate self-injurious behaviors—perhaps most immediately following occurrence of acute social stress, such as peer relationship conflict (Bridge et al., 2006; Miller & Prinstein, 2019). Additionally, exposure to others' engagement in NSSI, particularly in peer networks, may be a potent environmental-level factor within adolescents' social milieu that may moderate risk for NSSI. Indeed, the broader interpersonal context is critical to a complete understanding of a developmental-transactional model of NSSI in adolescents. While NSSI may be related to specific experiences of interpersonal stress (e.g., interpersonal loss and victimization), the ways in which NSSI behaviors are learned about or socialized suggest that reciprocal processes among multiple interpersonal factors within adolescents' social contexts may heighten risk for NSSI. Relatedly, interpersonal processes operating at the ecological level—such as social support within peer, family, or school networks—may attenuate NSSI risk and should also be considered when discussing the interpersonal context of NSSI. Figure 41.1 shows an interpersonal model depicting key interpersonal and social factors associated with NSSI.

In line with this conceptualization, we begin by discussing several domains of peer-related experiences that have been shown to cross-sectionally or longitudinally predict

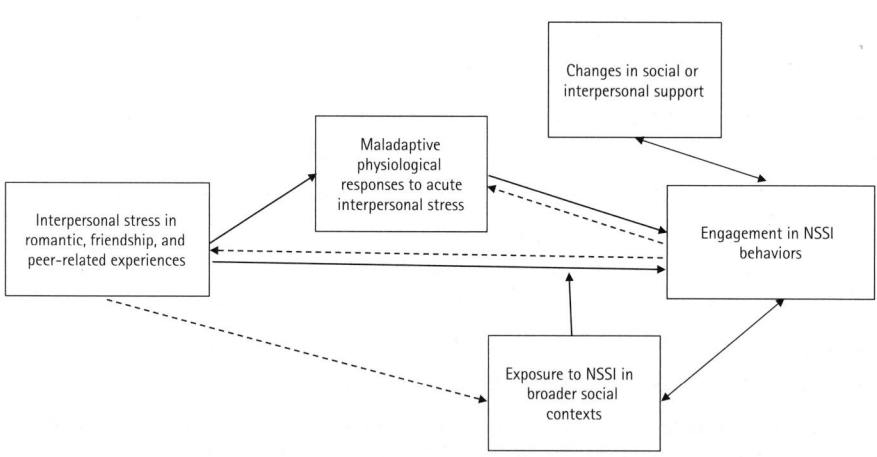

Note. Heuristic model depicting interpersonal constructs associated with NSSI, with arrows indicating unidirectional and bidirectional associations. Solid lines indicate associations with more robust empirical support, while dashed lines indicate associations with more preliminary empirical support.

Figure 41.1 Heuristic model depicting extant research support for interpersonal constructs associated with NSSI.

NSSI engagement in adolescents. We then review emerging work on biophysiological responses to socially themed stress that may characterize those who engage in NSSI, and which may shed light on intraindividual mechanisms linking peer-related experiences of stress and NSSI. While preliminary, we briefly review these findings and note their potential for better understanding the interplay of interpersonal and individual-level risk factors for NSSI. We then discuss studies that adopt a broader social context perspective to consider the role of peer influence processes in initiation and spread of NSSI behaviors. Finally, whereas some peer relations processes within social networks (e.g., peer influence) may act as risk factors, others may act as protective factors (e.g., peer social support). Thus, this chapter concludes by briefly describing social—including family, peer, and romantic partner—protective factors, with important clinical implications for prevention and treatment of NSSI.

We summarize these lines of research by specifically discussing NSSI in the context of the following interpersonal and peer domains: (a) interpersonal or socially themed correlates and risk factors, with a focus on romantic relationship stress, friendship stress, and peer victimization; (b) acute interpersonal stress responses and NSSI; (c) peer influence and socialization of NSSI within peer groups; and (d) familial, romantic partner, and peer social support as protective factors. Of note, given the unique importance of peers and peer relationships to adolescent development, a majority of the studies cited in this chapter focus on adolescents. However, we note several investigations among adults that, although not specific to adolescence or adolescent peer relationships, nevertheless contribute important or novel findings regarding social or interpersonally themed factors (e.g., physiological responses to social stress) that may be associated with NSSI, or otherwise confer heightened risk for engagement in these behaviors.

Interpersonal Stress and Socially Themed Correlates and Risk Factors for NSSI

Adolescence is characterized by dramatic changes in social systems. Such changes encompass both alterations in the nature, frequency, and quality of interpersonal relationships as well as individual-level changes in adolescents' orientation toward, and sensitivity to, social experiences (Casey et al., 2008; Somerville, 2013; Steinberg & Morris, 2001). In the transition to adolescence, youth spend more time with peers and increasingly turn to interpersonal relationships to fulfill different intrapersonal functions (e.g., reflected appraisal and social support). As dyadic peer experiences become more frequent and emotionally intimate, adolescents begin to develop new types of relationships, including close friendships and romantic relationships. This section discusses several interpersonal contexts that take on increased salience in adolescence—contexts in which exposure to interpersonal stressors associated with NSSI may be heightened. Specifically, we discuss NSSI within the context of adolescents' participation in romantic relationships, peer friendships, and experiences of peer victimization.

Romantic Relationship Stress and Breakups

While interpersonal factors are explicitly or implicitly central to many theoretical models of NSSI, relatively little empirical work has examined NSSI in the specific context of romantic relationships. Given robust evidence that relational stressors—such as interpersonal rejection, loss, or conflict—are associated with NSSI, it is surprising that few studies have explored adolescents' intimate relationship functioning in relation to NSSI. While further work is needed in this area, both individual-level attachment vulnerabilities and poor-quality romantic relationships have been shown to predict NSSI (e.g., Levesque et al., 2010; Miller et al., 2018; Tatnell et al., 2017). Specifically, studies examining adolescents' romantic relationships and NSSI have primarily focused on three facets of romantic relationships: romantic attachment styles; relationship quality, including stress, violence, and abuse within romantic partnerships; and dyadic processes between romantic partners that may increase the risk for NSSI. We expand on each area and discuss relevant findings below.

Borrowing from attachment theory as an explanatory framework for NSSI, several studies have shown associations between adolescents' NSSI and abandonment anxiety, attachment anxiety, and avoidance in the context of romantic relationships (e.g., Levesque et al., 2010). This work is premised on the hypothesis that both NSSI and certain attachment styles, such as insecure or avoidant attachment, are associated with emotion dysregulation and negative representations of self or others, and that particular attachment styles may therefore characterize those who engage in NSSI (Levesque et al., 2010; Yates, 2004, 2009). Of note, despite findings supporting links between NSSI and attachment anxiety and avoidance (Caron et al., 2017), no empirical studies to our knowledge have directly tested associations between NSSI and termination of romantic relationships, though related work has demonstrated associations between romantic breakups and suicide-related outcomes (Donald et al., 2006; Paul, 2018). Studies examining whether termination of romantic relationships represents a proximal risk factor for NSSI, including in the context of particular attachment styles, would meaningfully contribute to this literature.

Other work focusing on the quality of adolescents' romantic relationships demonstrates that stress, violence, or abuse within relationships may be associated with one or both partners' engagement in NSSI. Importantly, recent longitudinal studies suggest that romantic partnership stress may represent a risk factor for future NSSI. Among adolescents, a combination of elevated interpersonal stress, including romantic partner stress, and negative attributional style has been shown to predict trajectories of increased NSSI engagement over 9- to 18-month follow-up (Guerry & Prinstein, 2010). Similarly, a recent investigation in adolescent females found evidence for reciprocal associations between chronic interpersonal stress, including romantic stress, and NSSI (Miller et al., 2018). Genetic vulnerabilities may also exacerbate risk for NSSI among those experiencing romantic relationship stress: higher levels of chronic interpersonal stress (i.e., a composite measure of both romantic and peer stress), in conjunction with genetic vulnerabilities, have been shown to be cross-sectionally associated with NSSI engagement in adolescents, providing preliminary support for a gene-environment interaction in predicting NSSI risk in the context of interpersonal (including romantic relationship) stress (Hankin et al., 2015). In addition to romantic partnership stress, NSSI is also associated with low levels of romantic partnership support. In a longitudinal investigation in adolescents, lower levels of relationship quality with romantic partners, peers, and family predicted NSSI assessed six months later, suggesting that less interpersonal support, including in romantic relationships, may be a prospective predictor of NSSI (Hankin & Abela, 2011). While more research is needed, recent longitudinal work provides important preliminary support for specific characteristics of poor-quality romantic relationships, including elevated stress and low levels of support, as risk factors for adolescents' subsequent NSSI (Miller et al., 2018).

Additionally, studies examining more acute manifestations of intimate partner stress consistently show associations between NSSI and both physical and psychological intimate partner abuse or violence in young adult and adult samples (Levesque et al., 2010; Sansone et al., 2007). Being a victim of dating violence is associated with NSSI in the context of elevated trait anger among male adolescents and indirect aggression in female adolescents (Rizzo et al., 2014). Other work suggests that associations between NSSI and romantic relationship violence may be bidirectional, such that NSSI engagement is associated with both intimate partner violence perpetration and victimization (Carranza et al., 2020). Future studies are needed to further identify which specific aspects of romantic relationship stress are associated with NSSI, and to differentiate whether stress, violence, and abuse in romantic domains represent correlates, risk factors, and/or consequences of NSSI engagement.

Finally, several studies have examined intimate partner dyads to better understand the mechanisms through which romantic relationship dynamics, including those that may contribute to relationship stress, are associated with NSSI. Studies suggest that emotion regulation difficulties may mediate associations between insecure romantic attachment and both maladaptive dyadic coping and NSSI (Levesque et al., 2017). Specifically, emotion regulation deficits among individuals with high attachment anxiety or avoidance may be associated with poor dyadic coping strategies, which may increase the likelihood of NSSI engagement. Indeed, emotion regulation has been implicated as a mediator of associations between multiple subdomains of romantic relationships (e.g., romantic attachment and intimate partner violence) and NSSI (e.g., Silva et al., 2017). Other work suggests that individuals with NSSI endorse more frequent contact with romantic partners, which may reflect an overreliance on romantic partners to provide support or reassurance or to fulfill emotion regulation functions (Turner et al., 2017). Studies employing real-time measures of emotion regulation and incorporating both relationship partners are needed to further understand the mechanisms and temporal dynamics by which romantic partner interactions may influence an individual's NSSI engagement.

Friendship Stress and Peer Relationship Quality

Adolescents' difficulties with peers may represent significant experiences of social stress closely associated with NSSI. While adolescence is marked by increases in interactions with peers and the formation of new friendships, these changes, including initiation of new dyadic relationships, can be significant sources of stress. Further, adolescents may be particularly vulnerable to stress resulting from changes in peer experiences: compared to adults, adolescents report greater levels of, and emotional reactivity to, peer-related interpersonal stressors (Rudolph, 2014; also see Kiekens et al., this volume for a review of NSSI in adolescence and emerging adulthood). Indeed, research suggests that both elevated distress within friend and peer relationships as well as deficits in the number or quality of these relationships (e.g., lack of friends or poor friendship support) are related to NSSI risk. Of note, advances in real-time monitoring technologies have permitted increasingly fine-grained analyses of peer-related stressors in relation to NSSI engagement in daily life. Given the novelty and ecological validity of these data, we primarily highlight these findings demonstrating associations between NSSI and multiple types of aversive peer-related experiences, including peer- or friendship-related stress, poor-quality peer relationships, and lack of social support.

Individuals, including adolescents, often endorse NSSI urges while socializing or experiencing interpersonal conflict. These associations are supported by both retrospective self-report as well as more recent ambulatory assessment and experience sampling studies, which provide real-time, ecological data on the social, including peer-related, contexts in which NSSI may be most likely to occur (Andrewes et al., 2017; Nock et al., 2009; Turner et al., 2016). One such study reported that adolescents' thoughts of NSSI frequently occurred when socializing. Descriptive analyses further showed that NSSI thoughts were more often experienced when with peers and friends and less often with family or strangers, suggesting that peer-specific interpersonal experiences may be particularly salient to NSSI risk among adolescents (Nock et al., 2009). Similarly, investigations in adults show that feelings of rejection or experiences of interpersonal conflict (i.e., including, but not specific to, conflict with peers) are associated with same-day NSSI urges and greater likelihood of NSSI behaviors (Turner et al., 2016). These novel data provide tentative support for a potential causal effect between social-contextual factors, including interpersonal stress, and proximal NSSI risk by demonstrating that NSSI thoughts or behaviors may be more likely to occur on days when individuals experience greater interpersonal stress or conflict.

The relationship between social- or peer-related stress and NSSI may be reciprocal. A study in adults showed that perceptions of rejection and isolation were elevated prior to NSSI engagement and diminished following NSSI, suggesting that interpersonal factors influence, and are influenced by, NSSI (Snir et al., 2015). While results require replication in adolescent samples, these data provide compelling support for theories of NSSI as occurring in the context of aversive interpersonal experiences, whereby these behaviors may then be engaged in to regulate distress related to aversive interpersonal experiences or to achieve interpersonally relevant goals (e.g., interpersonal communication or avoidance; Nock & Prinstein, 2004, 2005). Other longitudinal investigations, while few, support similar conclusions. A study in adults found that NSSI engagement that was disclosed to others was associated with subsequent increases in perceived social support, which in turn predicted greater likelihood of future NSSI (Turner et al., 2016). In adolescent girls, not only has interpersonal stress been shown to predict subsequent NSSI, but NSSI may also predict subsequent increases in interpersonal stress (Miller et al., 2018). Of note, associations between interpersonal stress and subsequent NSSI were observed specifically among girls with more advanced pubertal development, suggesting that puberty may exacerbate the risk for maladaptive behaviors, such as NSSI, in contexts of interpersonal stress. Taken together, these results suggest a bidirectional transaction between environment and behavior, in line with developmental psychopathology perspectives of NSSI as both occurring in response to, and contributing to, individuals' social environment.

In addition to elevated stress within peer relationships, deficits in the number, availability, or supportiveness of adolescents' friendships are also associated with NSSI. Compared to non-self-injuring peers, adolescents who engage in NSSI endorse lower levels of perceived social support and report having fewer individuals to seek advice from (Heath et al., 2009; Muehlenkamp et al., 2013). Loneliness and social isolation are correlates of NSSI, and adolescents with a lifetime history of NSSI endorse greater peer-related loneliness and more positive attitudes toward (i.e., stronger affinity for) aloneness compared to those without NSSI histories (Gandhi et al., 2018). Daily diary and real-time monitoring studies reveal similar patterns: adolescents who engage in NSSI report less social support and report less frequent contact with peers, compared to those without NSSI (Turner et al., 2017). These differences may be partly explained by higher levels of social anxiety, negative attributional style, or greater reliance on maladaptive coping strategies, in line with cognitive vulnerability-stress models of NSSI (Guerry & Prinstein, 2010; see Hird et al., this volume, for a review of theoretical models). Notably, poor social support may be a risk factor for later NSSI onset. Lack of social support has been shown to prospectively predict NSSI, including new onset of both sporadic and repetitive NSSI, among adolescents and young adults (Hankin & Abela, 2011; Kiekens et al., 2019). Multiwave longitudinal designs with repeated assessments of NSSI and peer-related experiences (e.g., frequency and quality of peer interactions) will be important to further understand how experiences of peer-related distress or poor peer support relate to initiation and maintenance of NSSI, and over what timescales such risk may unfold.

Peer Victimization

Extensive work has suggested that peer victimization—defined as excluding, attacking, or humiliating a peer—is associated with multiple, negative psychological and physical health outcomes, including NSSI. Among children and adolescents in particular, experiences of peer victimization are consistently linked to the occurrence and severity of NSSI (for reviews, see Cheek et al., 2020; Van Geel et al., 2015). Importantly, associations between peer victimization and NSSI appear to be consistent across cultures, as demonstrated in work in samples from the United States, China, the Netherlands, and Italy, among others (Giletta et al., 2012; Jiang et al., 2016; Mossige et al., 2016).

Although many studies have shown associations between peer victimization and NSSI, fewer have examined whether these associations differ based on specific types of victimization. Distinguishing between types and contexts of victimization may be important for understanding NSSI risk; for example, prevalence of overt victimization (i.e., physical behaviors, such as hitting or pushing) and relational victimization (i.e., behaviors targeting relationships and peer status, such as social exclusion or spreading rumors) has been shown to vary by age and gender (Heilbron & Prinstein, 2010). For example, sexual and gender minority youth have higher rates of victimization than heterosexual peers, and this group has been shown to be at heightened risk for engagement in NSSI as a coping strategy when experiencing homophobic victimization (i.e., targeted victimization of LGBTQ individuals; Sang et al., 2020; see Taliaferro et al., this volume, for a review of NSSI in gender and sexually diverse youth). Meanwhile, other research has shown that homophobic victimization may predict the severity, but not likelihood, of NSSI engagement, suggesting that certain types of victimization may be associated with particular patterns of NSSI engagement but may not distinguish *who* will engage (Esposito et al., 2021). Bullying, or repeated acts of victimization in the context of a power imbalance (Salmivalli, 2010), also appears to function distinctly in the context of NSSI risk. For example, both bullying victims and perpetrators are at higher risk for engagement in NSSI (Claes et al., 2015; Esposito et al., 2019; Vergara et al., 2019), suggesting that both those who perpetrate and those who experience victimization may be at elevated risk for NSSI. Future work should explore whether and how mechanisms of NSSI risk vary among those implicated in experiences of peer victimization.

Other recent work has examined protective factors that may mitigate the deleterious effects of peer victimization on risk for NSSI engagement. High levels of parental support have been shown to buffer associations between victimization and risk for NSSI (Claes et al., 2015), while associations between homophobic victimization and NSSI may be modulated by adequate classmate support (Esposito et al., 2021). In a community sample of Chinese adolescents, self-compassion reduced the association between victimization and risk for NSSI (Jiang et al., 2016), and self-control may serve as a protective factor against experiences of cyberbullying and risk for subsequent NSSI (Zhu et al., 2021). Additional work in this area will be important to further identify both vulnerability and protective factors, which can serve as critical targets for intervention and treatment.

Importantly, the proliferation of social media, the ubiquity of smartphones, and increases in online interconnectedness have created new platforms and opportunities for perpetration and exposure to negative peer experiences, such as victimization. As noted in recent research on social media and adolescent self-injurious thoughts and behaviors (for a review, see Nesi et al., 2021), cyber victimization has been repeatedly shown to confer risk for self-injurious behaviors, including NSSI (Faura-Garcia et al., 2021; John et al., 2018; Zhu et al., 2021), and may be particularly deleterious for adolescents (see Pritchard & Lewis, this volume, for a review of NSSI, online forums and cyberbullying). Future work should continue to distinguish between different types of cyber victimization experiences in the context of NSSI risk, especially as new online platforms create additional avenues for perpetration of, or exposure to, peer victimization. Given that experiences of victimization increase in adolescence (Nansel et al., 2004), addressing peer victimization and related negative peer experiences (e.g., bullying and cyber victimization) in adolescence may meaningfully mitigate risk for NSSI.

Acute Interpersonal Stress Responses and NSSI

While adolescence is characterized by increases in the frequency, intensity, and salience of peer experiences, biological development during puberty may also render adolescents more reactive to these changes in the social environment. As mentioned previously, NSSI is closely tied to experiences of interpersonal (including peer-related) stress, and co-occurring biological changes may help explain why or how these interpersonal stressors confer heightened risk for NSSI during this period. Here, we review literature suggesting that particular *responses*—specifically, physiological responses—to acute interpersonal stressors may further contribute to risk for adolescent self-injurious thoughts and behaviors, including NSSI.

Adolescence is a developmental period during which there is a recalibration of stress-response systems, and recent work has posited that such changes may increase vulnerability to stressful experiences and heighten risk for psychopathology (Gunnar & Quevedo, 2007; Nelson et al., 2021; Stroud et al., 2009). Stress-response systems activate interconnected biological processes spanning the autonomic nervous system (ANS), hypothalamic-pituitary-adrenal (HPA) axis, and the inflammatory system, which act on different timescales to enable adaptation to environmental demands through allostasis (Nelson et al., 2021). Repeated activation in the form of exposure to higher-frequency, longer-duration, and/or greater-intensity environmental and psychological stress can compromise these systems and lead to allostatic load (i.e., "wear and tear"), which may be associated with negative mental and physical health outcomes (Lupien et al., 2009; McEwen, 2017).

Recent theoretical work has proposed that adolescent self-injurious thoughts and behaviors may be associated with failures in stress regulation, particularly in response to interpersonally themed stress (Miller & Prinstein, 2019). Given that rates of self-injurious thoughts and behaviors increase dramatically in the transition to adolescence (Nock et al., 2013), these recent theoretical models attempt to explain adolescent self-injurious thoughts and behaviors through a developmental lens that accounts for the social and physiological changes that partly characterize this developmental period. In particular, these models propose that adolescents with dysregulated stress responses may be particularly susceptible to acute social stressors, which may lower thresholds for engaging in self-injurious thoughts or behaviors, such as NSSI (Beauchaine et al., 2019; Miller & Prinstein, 2019). Indeed, studies testing these theoretical models in the context of suicidal outcomes have found that adolescent females' maladaptive physiological responses to socially themed stress are associated with increased risk for suicidal ideation and suicide attempts over 9- to 18-month follow-up (Eisenlohr-Moul et al., 2018; Giletta et al., 2017).

Regarding NSSI, cross-sectional investigations provide preliminary support for associations between NSSI and altered stress responses. Compared to controls, adolescent females with a history of NSSI show attenuated cortisol responses following simulation of acute social stress, providing support for patterns of maladaptive stress responses (i.e., attenuated cortisol response) following psychosocial stress among self-injuring adolescents (Kaess et al., 2012). During parent-child dyadic interactions involving conflict, self-injuring adolescents have also been shown to exhibit heightened physiological (e.g., sympathetic and parasympathetic nervous system) reactivity to maternal behaviors—an effect not observed in depressed but non-self-injuring adolescents (Crowell et al., 2017). Although not specific to interpersonal stress, other work has shown that adolescent girls with histories of NSSI exhibit differential patterns in ANS responses, including reduced respiratory sinus arrhythmia (RSA) at baseline and elevated RSA reactivity during negative mood induction, compared to non-self-injuring peers (Crowell et al., 2005).

Cross-sectional results leave uncertain whether maladaptive stress responses represent risk factors for NSSI, or whether such responses are correlates or consequences of NSSI. Of note, some research in adolescents suggests that NSSI desensitizes neurobiological stress response systems (Beauchaine et al., 2015), which may underlie reinforcement of these behaviors over time. Nevertheless, preliminary longitudinal work suggests that some maladaptive stress response patterns may temporally precede NSSI. While not specific to interpersonal stress, poorer RSA recovery following a stressful cognitive task has been shown to predict engagement in self-injurious thoughts or behaviors, including NSSI and/or suicidal outcomes, over a 6-month follow-up (Wielgus et al., 2016). Regarding interpersonal stress, one recent longitudinal study showed that heightened resting cardiac arousal, in the context of higher peer stress, was associated with significant increases in NSSI over follow-up during the transition to adolescence (Nelson et al., 2023). While preliminary, these findings call for further examination of the biophysiological processes underlying responses to stress in the psychosocial environment to better understand who is at heightened risk for NSSI, as well as when these behaviors may be most likely to occur.

Socialization of NSSI Within Friendships and Peer Networks

Above, we have discussed interpersonal stress and physiological responses to interpersonal stress as two risk factors for NSSI. The multifinality of these risk factors should be noted, however; both are relevant to a variety of deleterious outcomes. While many adolescents experience interpersonal stress and exhibit maladaptive stress responses, only some adolescents engage in NSSI. Decisions to engage in NSSI among distressed adolescents with atypical or maladaptive stress responses may depend in part on a third interpersonal factor: exposure to NSSI among peers or close friends. In the past several decades, the role of peer influence in the initiation or spread of NSSI behaviors has garnered increasing attention in both the empirical research literature and mainstream (e.g., popular media) discussions of self-injury. As noted previously, rates of NSSI are particularly high among adolescents, leading to concerns over whether exposure to or affiliation with self-injuring peers may confer risk for NSSI engagement.

Peer influence in the context of NSSI has been conceptualized across behavioral, social, and cognitive theoretical perspectives. Building on social learning theories (Bandura, 1973) and empirical studies of status and engagement in other high-risk behaviors (Prinstein et al., 2003; Rose, 2002), individuals may be more likely to emulate behaviors, such as NSSI, that close friends or higher-status peers perceive as socially acceptable. Emulation of such behaviors may serve to garner higher social standing and avoid ostracization (Heilbron & Prinstein, 2008). From a social psychology perspective, initiation of NSSI behaviors in order to conform to peer group norms may be related to identity-formation processes. Indeed, social theorists (e.g., Markus & Wurf, 1987; Schlenker, 1985) contend that individuals are motivated to behave in ways that uphold a positive sense of self, which is partly determined by alignment with accepted behaviors exhibited by respected peers (e.g., close friends). Both conceptualizations are consistent with social motivations for NSSI articulated in functional models (Nock & Prinstein, 2004, 2005).

Importantly, research in developmental psychology has demonstrated that an adolescent's perceptions of others' engagement in a given behavior are one of the most potent predictors of an adolescent's own behavior (Brechwald & Prinstein, 2011; Prinstein et al., 2001), including self-injurious behaviors (Heilbron & Prinstein, 2008; Kiuru et al., 2012). Regarding NSSI, studies suggest that peer influence processes may play a role in promoting NSSI engagement for some individuals, as demonstrated in both clinical and non-clinical samples of youth and young adults. Studies in psychiatric inpatient units, for example, have provided tentative evidence of "contagion effects" among groups of patients, whereby one patient's engagement in NSSI is associated with others' subsequent engagement in NSSI, including among those with no prior NSSI history (Ghaziuddin et al., 1992; Taiminen et al., 1998; Walsh & Rosen, 1985). Similar patterns have been demonstrated in nonclinical populations (Hasking et al., 2013; Prinstein et al., 2010), particularly in close friendship dyads (Schwartz-Mette & Lawrence, 2019). To date, a majority of research on peer influence and self-injurious thoughts and behaviors has focused on examining occurrence of clusters (i.e., higher rates of self-injurious thoughts and behaviors among temporally or geographically proximal groups of individuals; Insel & Gould, 2008; Joiner, 2003) and contagion effects (Joiner Jr., 1999).

More recently, research has aimed to delineate the specific mechanisms by which peer influence processes may promote NSSI engagement. According to seminal work by Kandel (1978), two tenets of "homophily" may underlie similarities between an individual's and his or her friends' attitudes and behaviors: "selection effects," whereby individuals choose to affiliate with peers whom they regard as similar to themselves; and "socialization effects," whereby peer attitudes and behaviors may increase the likelihood of similar attitudes and behaviors within a group of peers or friends. While "socialization effects," including potential indirect socialization via shared characteristics associated with NSSI (e.g., depression and emotion dysregulation), have received increased attention in the past decade, research has found support for concurrent selection and socialization effects in the context of NSSI. In a study among clinically elevated and community-based adolescents, longitudinal evidence of both mechanisms was observed, even after controlling for prior depressive symptoms (Prinstein et al., 2010). Other school-based studies of adolescents have found similar effects (You et al., 2013), with some evidence that socialization becomes more pronounced under conditions of high psychological distress (Hasking et al., 2013). Among friendship dyads, research suggests that adolescents with higher levels of emotion dysregulation may be most susceptible to potential socialization effects of NSSI (Schwartz-Mette & Lawrence, 2019). Interestingly, a school-based study of adolescents—which used models that controlled for several network and selection effects—did not find evidence of direct socialization over a four-year period, but did find support for indirect socialization effects of NSSI via friends' depressive symptoms (Giletta et al., 2013). This and other work (Brechwald & Prinstein, 2011) underscores the need for new or updated conceptualizations of how peer influence processes function dynamically over time and across peer group contexts, perhaps especially as social media continues to transform the availability and frequency of peer group communication and social interactions (e.g., online-only friendships and parasocial relationships; Nesi et al., 2018).

While not new to the psychology literature, propinquity has recently been proposed as a mechanism by which individuals may be cognitively primed to consider self-injurious behaviors as viable options to manage emotional distress (Abrutyn & Mueller, 2014). Propinquity theory suggests that, under duress, individuals become more likely to consider behaviors, such as NSSI, to which they have been repeatedly exposed and/or with which they identify. While some individuals may never consider engaging in NSSI in response to chronic stress, those who have repeatedly observed or heard of others (e.g., friends, family members, celebrities, and public figures) engaging in NSSI may be more likely to engage in these behaviors themselves. As NSSI becomes more socially acceptable, or even more publicized, it may be that individuals become cognitively predisposed to regard NSSI as a viable behavioral response to psychological distress (Miller & Prinstein, 2019).

The role of peer influence processes in understanding the initiation and socialization of NSSI behaviors is complex. Such processes are likely dynamic, and conceptually and functionally multifaceted. While an individual may initially engage in NSSI to conform to perceived social norms, for example, maintenance over time may be better explained by alternative mechanisms, such as emotion regulation processes or motivations to reduce psychological distress. Additional research is needed to examine whether and how peer influence is related to initiation, reinforcement, or maintenance of NSSI behaviors to better understand how these and related social influence phenomena may be implicated in the etiology of NSSI.

Protective Factors: Family, Peer, and Romantic Partner Support

The broader literature on self-injurious behaviors has largely focused on risk factors. Indeed, associations between NSSI and aversive interpersonal or peer-related experiences, such as those described in prior sections, are well-supported by prior work. Comparatively less attention, however, has been given to protective factors that may just as critically influence the likelihood of NSSI onset or maintenance in adolescence (Gallagher & Miller, 2018). As adolescents navigate changing social landscapes, which may increase opportunities for exposure to negative interpersonal experiences, social protective factors may operate at the ecological level to buffer against NSSI risk (Luthar et al., 2000). Here, we briefly review research on protective factors within adolescents' social context, with a specific focus on cohesion, connectedness, and support in family, peer, and romantic partner domains.

Adaptive family functioning has been shown to predict reduced likelihood of engaging in NSSI. Lower levels of parental support and higher levels of parental control are associated with increased risk for NSSI, while greater parental support has been shown to buffer associations between multiple NSSI risk factors (i.e., bullying, victimization, and depressive mood) and NSSI in adolescents (Baetens et al., 2014; Claes et al., 2015). Among youth with no history of NSSI, positive parenting has been shown to predict reduced odds of NSSI engagement one year later, suggesting that adaptive parenting may protect against the onset of NSSI in adolescence (Victor et al., 2019). Similarly, other longitudinal studies reveal the importance of family support in protecting against both initiation and maintenance of NSSI. Compared to other interpersonal factors (e.g., peer support), perceived family support may be a particularly potent protective factor against NSSI (Kaminski et al., 2010; Tatnell et al., 2014).

Peer support and connectedness show similar protective effects. Studies comparing those with and without histories of NSSI demonstrate that those without NSSI report higher social connectedness (Rotolone & Martin, 2012). Given longitudinal evidence for associations between specific negative peer experiences, including peer victimization and low social self-worth, and subsequent development of NSSI, the presence of supportive peer relationships and higher social self-worth are likely to buffer against risk for NSSI onset, perhaps especially in adolescence (Victor et al., 2019). Meanwhile, research suggests that higher friendship quality and greater romantic partner support are associated with NSSI disclosure (Ammerman et al., 2021; Armiento et al., 2014), pointing to the potential benefits of supportive peer and intimate partner relationships for increasing the likelihood of help-seeking behaviors.

Perhaps somewhat paradoxically, and in contrast to work on peer influence and NSSI mentioned previously, affiliation with self-injuring peers in certain contexts may provide protective benefits, or otherwise serve to reduce NSSI. Studies have found that individuals who frequently visit self-injury online message boards or engage with NSSI-related content online reported decreases in NSSI engagement or frequency, as well as reduced feelings of isolation and loneliness (Corcoran & Andover, 2020; Johnson et al., 2010; Whitlock et al., 2007). These effects may be due to a sense of positive social support afforded by membership in internet communities (Frost & Casey, 2016; Whitlock et al., 2006). Such communities may also promote disclosure, which may in turn promote help-seeking behaviors or yield other positive psychological benefits (Lewis & Seko, 2016). Additionally, while interpersonal support has been shown to protect against NSSI, NSSI engagement itself has also been shown to increase interpersonal support. One investigation found that adolescent girls who engaged in NSSI reported significant improvements in relationships with their fathers over time (Hilt et al., 2008). These findings align with interpersonal functional models of NSSI, whereby NSSI may serve to elicit desired responses from others in the environment. Indeed, as noted previously, an experience sampling investigation found support for bidirectional associations between social support and NSSI, such that perceived support increased following engagement in NSSI, and perceived support was then associated with a greater likelihood of future NSSI (Turner et al., 2016). These findings suggest that associations between interpersonal support and NSSI engagement may be nuanced, such that associations may be neither unidirectional nor always beneficial. Future research might explore the circumstances in which interpersonal support may promote versus protect against NSSI engagement, as well as whether particular sources of support (e.g., family, romantic partner, and peer) yield stronger protective benefits.

Conclusions and Recommendations for Clinical Practice and Future Research

The empirical findings presented in this chapter have important clinical implications for understanding associations between aversive interpersonal, including peer-related, experiences and NSSI risk. These implications are discussed below alongside recommendations for future research to better understand how interpersonal factors may increase risk for future NSSI.

Implications for Clinical Practice and Community-Based Prevention and Intervention

First, the negative impact of stress within romantic and peer relationships highlights the importance of assessing romantic and peer relationship functioning when treating individuals who engage in, or who are at risk for, NSSI. Given preliminary support for links between maladaptive biophysiological responses to social stress and NSSI, future research might continue to test the extent to which treatments that build self-regulation skills—perhaps especially those that focus on biophysiological regulation (e.g., mindfulness)—are effective in reducing engagement in NSSI (Bentley et al., 2017; Rees et al., 2015).

Second, findings from studies using methodologies such as ambulatory assessment or experience sampling provide novel, ecological data that may be clinically relevant. In particular, these studies have provided a more fine-grained, temporally precise picture of the interpersonal processes that may precipitate and reinforce NSSI behaviors, which may point to important treatment targets. For example, studies using electronic daily surveys of individuals with NSSI show that disclosure of NSSI to others is associated with increases in support, which in turn is associated with increased NSSI urges and likelihood of future NSSI (Turner et al., 2016). Such results not only support theoretical models of NSSI as serving interpersonal functions (e.g., to communicate distress and elicit support) for some individuals, but also suggest that interpersonal events, including positive social feedback, may reinforce NSSI. In light of these findings, clinicians might help clients identify the interpersonal consequences of NSSI engagement, including whether and how such consequences may motivate continued NSSI behaviors. Indeed, recent ambulatory assessment research suggests that individuals may often be unaware of the motives and environmental precipitants of their NSSI behaviors as they occur in real time (Andrewes et al., 2017). Further, given evidence to suggest that individuals may underestimate the frequency of interpersonal (vs. affective or intrapersonal) motivations for NSSI (Snir et al., 2015), clinicians might employ daily diary or self-monitoring exercises to increase awareness of situational or interpersonal precipitants of NSSI. Behavior chain analysis (Linehan, 1993) and further exploration of interpersonal functions (e.g., to signal distress and elicit support) fulfilled by NSSI may help clients transition to other adaptive behaviors that may serve similar functions. Treatments that adopt an interpersonal focus and focus on social skills development may also help target interpersonal deficits and contingencies underlying NSSI.

Community-based prevention and intervention efforts for NSSI might also attend to the social and peer-related factors addressed in this chapter. Given the evidence that peer victimization may be a particularly robust correlate of (and risk factor for) NSSI, school-based programs aimed at reducing victimization may be especially effective in protecting against NSSI onset, perhaps especially in the transition to adolescence. Community- or school-based initiatives might consider addressing the ways that health risk behaviors such as NSSI may be socialized within peer groups. Such programs might also incorporate psychoeducation for parents and teachers to increase awareness that adolescents who know of peers' or friends' NSSI may themselves be at increased risk for NSSI. Finally, as social media use becomes widespread among youth, new prevention programs aimed at reducing the incidence of aversive peer experiences online will be critical. Such programs might train youth to identify and intervene in cyberbullying behaviors, while promoting social support-seeking or other coping strategies for victims of cyberbullying or cyber victimization. Other efforts may reduce the incidence of NSSI by teaching parents how to effectively monitor adolescents' engagement in NSSI-related content online, including whether and how frequently youth post about, discuss, or view NSSI-related material online.

Recommendations for Future Research

Additional longitudinal work is needed to more robustly test whether interpersonal factors, such as those discussed in this chapter, specifically represent *risk* factors for future NSSI. A meta-analysis revealed relatively few robust NSSI risk factors, and estimates of effect magnitude across the broader "social factors" category of risk factors were not significant (Fox et al., 2015). However, as many as 33%–56% of individuals report engaging in NSSI for interpersonal functions at least some of the time (Taylor et al., 2018), pointing to the need for more investigations of social functions and interpersonal risk factors of NSSI. Future studies should also prioritize longitudinal designs examining the interaction of multiple social or interpersonal domains for the prediction of NSSI, including among individuals with no prior NSSI history in order to better understand risk factors for NSSI onset (Victor et al., 2019).

Micro-longitudinal or ambulatory assessment studies would further elucidate the temporal and contextual nature of NSSI, including timescales over which interpersonally themed precipitants of NSSI behaviors unfold, immediate interpersonal consequences of NSSI, and social contexts in which NSSI may be most likely to occur. Continuous monitoring and use of multiple assessments daily may better capture NSSI-related phenomena of interest (e.g., social interactions and interpersonal conflict) that occur or change quickly. Indeed, ambulatory assessment studies suggest that NSSI functions themselves, including social functions, vary considerably within individuals and over time, highlighting the importance of continuous measurement of NSSI behaviors, correlates, and risk factors across finer timescales and real-world contexts (Coppersmith et al., 2021). Such investigations might also incorporate multiple informants' reports—including peers, friends, and romantic partners—to provide a more comprehensive picture of the interpersonal dynamics (e.g., within-peer networks and romantic partner dyads) that may increase the risk for NSSI. Finally, studies might consider assessing NSSI urges, in addition to behaviors. Basic descriptive research on NSSI urges—including their phenomenology and the contexts in which they frequently occur—would further elucidate interpersonally relevant factors associated with NSSI. NSSI urges are predictive of NSSI engagement and may be more likely than NSSI behaviors to actually occur in interpersonal contexts (Hepp et al., 2020).

A comprehensive understanding of NSSI requires considering the interaction of intraindividual factors (e.g., psychological, affective, and biological processes) with an individual's broader social context and experiences. Multiple facets of interpersonal experiences have been implicated in risk for NSSI, including stress in romantic and peer relationships, as well as aversive peer experiences like victimization. Recent work also suggests that particular physiological responses to these and similar experiences of interpersonal stress may characterize those who engage in NSSI, highlighting potential mechanisms linking social stress and individual-level vulnerabilities in relation to NSSI. Further, NSSI behaviors may be sensitive to social influence processes within the social environment, perhaps especially in adolescent peer networks. Indeed, the peer-related experiences and influence processes discussed in this chapter may be particularly relevant to understanding NSSI engagement among adolescents, given the salience of peer relations to this age group, and notable increases in rates of NSSI in the transition to adolescence (Nock et al., 2013; Prinstein & Giletta, 2016). Finally, in contrast to the large body of work demonstrating associations between negative interpersonal experiences and heightened NSSI risk, a growing number of studies have shown that positive interpersonal experiences, including familial, romantic partner, and peer support, may yield protective benefits. Beyond the research literature, the findings discussed in this chapter have important clinical implications. Reducing the incidence of relationship stress and peer victimization, building awareness of links between aversive interpersonal contingencies and NSSI behaviors, and enhancing sources of social support may be important targets when addressing NSSI in clinical practice, as well as in school- or community-based intervention and prevention programs.

References

Abrutyn, S., & Mueller, A. S. (2014). Are suicidal behaviors contagious in adolescence? Using longitudinal data to examine suicide suggestion. *American Sociological Review, 79*(2), 211–227. https://doi.org/10.1177/0003122413519445

Ammerman, B. A., Wilcox, K. T., O'Loughlin, C. M., & McCloskey, M. S. (2021). Characterizing the choice to disclose nonsuicidal self-injury. *Journal of Clinical Psychology, 77*(3), 683–700. https://doi.org/10.1002/jclp.23045

Andrewes, H. E., Hulbert, C., Cotton, S. M., Betts, J., & Chanen, A. M. (2017). Ecological momentary assessment of nonsuicidal self-injury in youth with borderline personality disorder. *Personality Disorders: Theory, Research, and Treatment, 8*(4), 357–365. https://doi.org/10.1037/per0000205

Armiento, J. S., Hamza, C. A., & Willoughby, T. (2014). An examination of disclosure of nonsuicidal self-injury among university students. *Journal of Community & Applied Social Psychology, 24*(6), 518–533. https://doi.org/10.1002/casp.2190

Baetens, I., Claes, L., Martin, G., Onghena, P., Grietens, H., Van Leeuwen, K., Pieters, C., Wiersema, J.R., & Griffith J.W. (2014). Is nonsuicidal self-injury associated with parenting and family factors? *Journal of Early Adolescence, 34*(3), 387–405. https://doi.org/10.1177/0272431613494006

Bandura, A. (1973). *Aggression: A social learning analysis*. Prentice-Hall.

Beauchaine, T. P., Crowell, S. E., & Hsiao, R. C. (2015). Post-dexamethasone cortisol, self-inflicted injury, and suicidal ideation among depressed adolescent girls. *Journal of Abnormal Child Psychology, 43*(4), 619–632. https://doi.org/10.1007/s10802-014-9933-2

Beauchaine, T. P., Hinshaw, S. P., & Bridge, J. A. (2019). Nonsuicidal self-injury and suicidal behaviors in girls: The case for targeted prevention in preadolescence. *Clinical Psychological Science: A Journal of the Association for Psychological Science, 7*(4), 643–667. https://doi.org/10.1177/2167702618818474

Bentley, K. H., Nock, M. K., Sauer-Zavala, S., Gorman, B. S., & Barlow, D. H. (2017). A functional analysis of two transdiagnostic, emotion-focused interventions on nonsuicidal self-injury. *Journal of Consulting and Clinical Psychology, 85*(6), 632–646. https://doi.org/10.1037/ccp0000205

Brechwald, W. A., & Prinstein, M. J. (2011). Beyond homophily: A decade of advances in understanding peer influence processes. *Journal of Research on Adolescence: The Official Journal of the Society for Research on Adolescence, 21*(1), 166–179. https://doi.org/10.1111/j.1532-7795.2010.00721.x

Brent, D. A., Baugher, M., Bridge, J., Chen, T., & Chiappetta, L. (1999). Age- and sex-related risk factors for adolescent suicide. *Journal of the American Academy of Child and Adolescent Psychiatry, 38*(12), 1497–1505. https://doi.org/10.1097/00004583-199912000-00010

Brent, D. A., Perper, J. A., Moritz, G., Baugher, M., Roth, C., Balach, L., & Schweers, J. (1993). Stressful life events, psychopathology, and adolescent suicide: A case control study. *Suicide & Life-Threatening Behavior, 23*(3), 179–187.

Bridge, J. A., Goldstein, T. R., & Brent, D. A. (2006). Adolescent suicide and suicidal behavior. *Journal of Child Psychology and Psychiatry, and Allied Disciplines, 47*(3–4), 372–394. https://doi.org/10.1111/j.1469-7610.2006.01615.x

Bronfenbrenner, U. (1977). Toward an experimental ecology of human development. *American Psychologist, 32*(7), 513–531. https://doi.org/10.1037/0003-066X.32.7.513

Caron, A., Lafontaine, M.-F., & Bureau, J.-F. (2017). Linking romantic attachment and self-injury: The roles of the behavioural systems. *Journal of Relationships Research, 8*. http://dx.doi.org.libproxy.lib.unc.edu/10.1017/jrr.2017.5

Carranza, A. B., Wallis, C. R. D., Jonnson, M. R., Klonsky, E. D., & Walsh, Z. (2020). Nonsuicidal self-injury and intimate partner violence: Directionality of violence and motives for self-injury. *Journal of Interpersonal Violence, 37*(3–4):1688–1707. https://doi.org/10.1177/0886260520922372

Casey, B. J., Jones, R. M., & Hare, T. A. (2008). The adolescent brain. *Annals of the New York Academy of Sciences, 1124*, 111–126. https://doi.org/10.1196/annals.1440.010

Chapman, A. L., Gratz, K. L., & Brown, M. Z. (2006). Solving the puzzle of deliberate self-harm: The experiential avoidance model. *Behaviour Research and Therapy, 44*(3), 371–394. https://doi.org/10.1016/j.brat.2005.03.005

Cheek, S. M., Reiter-Lavery, T., & Goldston, D. B. (2020). Social rejection, popularity, peer victimization, and self-injurious thoughts and behaviors among adolescents: A systematic review and meta-analysis. *Clinical Psychology Review, 82*, Article 101936. https://doi.org/10.1016/j.cpr.2020.101936

Claes, L., Luyckx, K., Baetens, I., Van de Ven, M., & Witteman, C. (2015). Bullying and victimization, depressive mood, and non-suicidal self-injury in adolescents: The moderating role of parental support. *Journal of Child and Family Studies, 24*(11), 3363–3371. https://doi.org/10.1007/s10826-015-0138-2

Coppersmith, D. D. L., Bentley, K. H., Kleiman, E. M., & Nock, M. K. (2021). Variability in the functions of non-suicidal self-injury: Evidence from three real-time monitoring studies. *Behavior Therapy, 52*(6):1516–1528. https://doi.org/10.1016/j.beth.2021.05.003

Corcoran, V. P., & Andover, M. S. (2020). Online disinhibition and internet communication of non-suicidal self-injury. *Suicide & Life-Threatening Behavior, 50*(6), 1091–1096. https://doi.org/10.1111/sltb.12659

Crowell, S. E., Beauchaine, T. P., McCauley, E., Smith, C. J., Stevens, A. L., & Sylvers, P. (2005). Psychological, autonomic, and serotonergic correlates of parasuicide among adolescent girls. *Development and Psychopathology, 17*(4), 1105–1127. https://doi.org/10.1017/s0954579405050522

Crowell, S. E., Butner, J. E., Wiltshire, T. J., Munion, A. K., Yaptangco, M., & Beauchaine, T. P. (2017). Evaluating emotional and biological sensitivity to maternal behavior among self-injuring and depressed adolescent girls using nonlinear dynamics. *Clinical Psychological Science, 5*(2), 272–285. https://doi.org/10.1177/2167702617692861

Donald, M., Dower, J., Correa-Velez, I., & Jones, M. (2006). Risk and protective factors for medically serious suicide attempts: A comparison of hospital-based with population-based samples of young adults. *The Australian and New Zealand Journal of Psychiatry, 40*(1), 87–96. https://doi.org/10.1080/j.1440-1614.2006.01747.x

Eisenlohr-Moul, T. A., Miller, A. B., Giletta, M., Hastings, P. D., Rudolph, K. D., Nock, M. K., & Prinstein, M. J. (2018). HPA axis response and psychosocial stress as interactive predictors of suicidal ideation and behavior in adolescent females: A multilevel diathesis-stress framework. *Neuropsychopharmacology: Official Publication of the American College of Neuropsychopharmacology, 43*(13), 2564–2571. https://doi.org/10.1038/s41386-018-0206-6

Esposito, C., Affuso, G., Amodeo, A. L., Dragone, M., & Bacchini, D. (2021). Bullying victimization: Investigating the unique contribution of homophobic bias on adolescent non-suicidal self-injury and the buffering role of school support. *School Mental Health, 13*(2), 420–435. https://doi.org/10.1007/s12310-021-09434-w

Esposito, C., Bacchini, D., & Affuso, G. (2019). Adolescent non-suicidal self-injury and its relationships with school bullying and peer rejection. *Psychiatry Research, 274*, 1–6. https://doi.org/10.1016/j.psychres.2019.02.018

Faura-Garcia, J., Orue, I., & Calvete, E. (2021). Cyberbullying victimization and nonsuicidal self-injury in adolescents: The role of maladaptive schemas and dispositional mindfulness. *Child Abuse & Neglect, 118*, Article 105135. https://doi.org/10.1016/j.chiabu.2021.105135

Fox, K. R., Franklin, J. C., Ribeiro, J. D., Kleiman, E. M., Bentley, K. H., & Nock, M. K. (2015). Meta-analysis of risk factors for nonsuicidal self-injury. *Clinical Psychology Review, 42*, 156–167. https://doi.org/10.1016/j.cpr.2015.09.002

Frost, M., & Casey, L. (2016). Who seeks help online for self-injury? *Archives of Suicide Research, 20*(1), 69–79. https://doi.org/10.1080/13811118.2015.1004470

Gallagher, M. L., & Miller, A. B. (2018). Suicidal thoughts and behavior in children and adolescents: An ecological model of resilience. *Adolescent Research Review, 3*(2), 123–154. https://doi.org/10.1007/s40894-017-0066-z

Gandhi, A., Luyckx, K., Goossens, L., Maitra, S., & Claes, L. (2018). Association between non-suicidal self-injury, parents and peers related loneliness, and attitude towards aloneness in Flemish adolescents: An empirical note. *Psychologica Belgica, 58*(1), 3–12. https://doi.org/10.5334/pb.385

Ghaziuddin, M., Tsai, L., Naylor, M., & Ghaziuddin, N. (1992). Mood disorder in a group of self-cutting adolescents. *Acta Paedopsychiatrica, 55*(2), 103–105.

Giletta, M., Burk, W. J., Scholte, R. H. J., Engels, R. C. M. E., & Prinstein, M. J. (2013). Direct and indirect peer socialization of adolescent nonsuicidal self-injury. *Journal of Research on Adolescence, 23*(3), 450–463. https://doi.org/10.1111/jora.1203

Giletta, M., Hastings, P. D., Rudolph, K. D., Bauer, D. J., Nock, M. K., & Prinstein, M. J. (2017). Suicide ideation among high-risk adolescent females: Examining the interplay between parasympathetic regulation and friendship support. *Development and Psychopathology, 29*(4), 1161–1175. https://doi.org/10.1017/S0954579416001218

Giletta, M., Scholte, R. H. J., Engels, R. C. M. E., Ciairano, S., & Prinstein, M. J. (2012). Adolescent non-suicidal self-injury: A cross-national study of community samples from Italy, the Netherlands and the United States. *Psychiatry Research, 197*(1–2), 66–72. https://doi.org/10.1016/j.psychres.2012.02.009

Gould, M. S., Fisher, P., Parides, M., Flory, M., & Shaffer, D. (1996). Psychosocial risk factors of child and adolescent completed suicide. *Archives of General Psychiatry, 53*(12), 1155–1162. https://doi.org/10.1001/archpsyc.1996.01830120095016

Gratz, K. L., Hepworth, C., Tull, M. T., Paulson, A., Clarke, S., Remington, B., & Lejuez, C. W. (2011). An experimental investigation of emotional willingness and physical pain tolerance in deliberate self-harm: The moderating role of interpersonal distress. *Comprehensive Psychiatry, 52*(1), 63–74. https://doi.org/10.1016/j.comppsych.2010.04.009

Guerry, J. D., & Prinstein, M. J. (2010). Longitudinal prediction of adolescent nonsuicidal self-injury: Examination of a cognitive vulnerability-stress model. *Journal of Clinical Child and Adolescent Psychology: The Official Journal for the Society of Clinical Child and Adolescent Psychology, American Psychological Association, Division 53, 39*(1), 77–89. https://doi.org/10.1080/15374410903401195

Gunnar, M., & Quevedo, K. (2007). The neurobiology of stress and development. *Annual Review of Psychology, 58*, 145–173. https://doi.org/10.1146/annurev.psych.58.110405.085605

Hankin, B. L., & Abela, J. R. Z. (2011). Nonsuicidal self-injury in adolescence: Prospective rates and risk factors in a 2½ year longitudinal study. *Psychiatry Research, 186*(1), 65–70. https://doi.org/10.1016/j.psychres.2010.07.056

Hankin, B. L., Barrocas, A. L., Young, J. F., Haberstick, B., & Smolen, A. (2015). 5-HTTLPR×interpersonal stress interaction and nonsuicidal self-injury in general community sample of youth. *Psychiatry Research, 225*(3), 609–612. https://doi.org/10.1016/j.psychres.2014.11.037

Hasking, P., Andrews, T., & Martin, G. (2013). The role of exposure to self-injury among peers in predicting later self-injury. *Journal of Youth and Adolescence, 42*(10), 1543–1556. https://doi.org/10.1007/s10964-013-9931-7

Hawton, K., Fagg, J., & Simkin, S. (1996). Deliberate self-poisoning and self-injury in children and adolescents under 16 years of age in Oxford, 1976-1993. *The British Journal of Psychiatry: The Journal of Mental Science, 169*(2), 202–208. https://doi.org/10.1192/bjp.169.2.202

Heath, N. L., Ross, S., Toste, J. R., Charlebois, A., & Nedecheva, T. (2009). Retrospective analysis of social factors and nonsuicidal self-injury among young adults. *Canadian Journal of Behavioural Science [Revue Canadienne Des Sciences Du Comportement]*, *41*(3), 180–186. https://doi.org/10.1037/a0015732

Heilbron, N., & Prinstein, M. J. (2008). Peer influence and adolescent nonsuicidal self-injury: A theoretical review of mechanisms and moderators. *Applied and Preventive Psychology*, *12*(4), 169–177. https://doi.org/10.1016/j.appsy.2008.05.004

Heilbron, N., & Prinstein, M. J. (2010). Adolescent peer victimization, peer status, suicidal ideation, and nonsuicidal self-injury: Examining concurrent and longitudinal associations. *Merrill-Palmer Quarterly (Wayne State University. Press)*, *56*(3), 388–419. https://doi.org/10.1353/mpq.0.0049

Hepp, J., Carpenter, R. W., Störkel, L. M., Schmitz, S. E., Schmahl, C., & Niedtfeld, I. (2020). A systematic review of daily life studies on non-suicidal self-injury based on the four-function model. *Clinical Psychology Review*, *82*, Article 101888. https://doi.org/10.1016/j.cpr.2020.101888

Hilt, L. M., Nock, M. K., Lloyd-Richardson, E. E., & Prinstein, M. J. (2008). Longitudinal study of nonsuicidal self-injury among young adolescents: Rates, correlates, and preliminary test of an interpersonal model. *The Journal of Early Adolescence*, *28*(3), 455–469. https://doi.org/10.1177/0272431608316604

Insel, B. J., & Gould, M. S. (2008). Impact of modeling on adolescent suicidal behavior. *The Psychiatric Clinics of North America*, *31*(2), 293–316. https://doi.org/10.1016/j.psc.2008.01.007

Jiang, Y., You, J., Hou, Y., Du, C., Lin, M.-P., Zheng, X., & Ma, C. (2016). Buffering the effects of peer victimization on adolescent non-suicidal self-injury: The role of self-compassion and family cohesion. *Journal of Adolescence*, *53*, 107–115. https://doi.org/10.1016/j.adolescence.2016.09.005

John, A., Glendenning, A. C., Marchant, A., Montgomery, P., Stewart, A., Wood, S., Lloyd, K., & Hawton, K. (2018). Self-harm, suicidal behaviours, and cyberbullying in children and young people: Systematic review. *Journal of Medical Internet Research*, *20*(4), Article e129. https://doi.org/10.2196/jmir.9044

Johnson, G. M., Zastawny, S., & Kulpa, A. (2010). E-message boards for those who self-injure: Implications for e-health. *International Journal of Mental Health and Addiction*, *8*(4), 566–569. https://doi.org/10.1007/s11469-009-9237-x

Joiner Jr., T. E. (1999). The clustering and contagion of suicide. *Current Directions in Psychological Science*, *8*(3), 89–92. https://doi.org/10.1111/1467-8721.00021

Joiner, T. E. (2003). Contagion of suicidal symptoms as a function of assortative relating and shared relationship stress in college roommates. *Journal of Adolescence*, *26*(4), 495–504. https://doi.org/10.1016/s0140-1971(02)00133-1

Kaess, M., Hille, M., Parzer, P., Maser-Gluth, C., Resch, F., & Brunner, R. (2012). Alterations in the neuroendocrinological stress response to acute psychosocial stress in adolescents engaging in nonsuicidal self-injury. *Psychoneuroendocrinology*, *37*(1), 157–161. https://doi.org/10.1016/j.psyneuen.2011.05.009

Kaminski, J. W., Puddy, R. W., Hall, D. M., Cashman, S. Y., Crosby, A. E., & Ortega, L. A. G. (2010). The relative influence of different domains of social connectedness on self-directed violence in adolescence. *Journal of Youth and Adolescence*, *39*(5), 460–473. https://doi.org/10.1007/s10964-009-9472-2

Kandel, D. B. (1978). Homophily, selection, and socialization in adolescent friendships. *American Journal of Sociology*, *84*(2), 427–436. https://doi.org/10.1086/226792

Kiekens, G., Hasking, P., Claes, L., Boyes, M., Mortier, P., Auerbach, R. P., Cuijpers, P., Demyttenaere, K., Green, J. G., Kessler, R. C., Myin-Germeys, I., Nock, M. K., & Bruffaerts, R. (2019). Predicting the incidence of non-suicidal self-injury in college students. *European Psychiatry*, *59*, 44–51. https://doi.org/10.1016/j.eurpsy.2019.04.002

Kiuru, N., Burk, W. J., Laursen, B., Nurmi, J.-E., & Salmela-Aro, K. (2012). Is depression contagious? A test of alternative peer socialization mechanisms of depressive symptoms in adolescent peer networks. *The Journal of Adolescent Health*, *50*(3), 250–255. https://doi.org/10.1016/j.jadohealth.2011.06.013

Levesque, C., Lafontaine, M.-F., & Bureau, J.-F. (2017). The mediating effects of emotion regulation and dyadic coping on the relationship between romantic attachment and non-suicidal self-injury. *Journal of Youth and Adolescence*, *46*(2), 277–287. https://doi.org/10.1007/s10964-016-0547-6

Levesque, C., Lafontaine, M.-F., Bureau, J.-F., Cloutier, P., & Dandurand, C. (2010). The influence of romantic attachment and intimate partner violence on non-suicidal self-injury in young adults. *Journal of Youth and Adolescence*, *39*(5), 474–483. https://doi.org/10.1007/s10964-009-9471-3

Lewis, S. P., & Seko, Y. (2016). A double-edged sword: A review of benefits and risks of online nonsuicidal self-injury activities. *Journal of Clinical Psychology*, *72*(3), 249–262. https://doi.org/10.1002/jclp.22242

Linehan, M. M. (1993). *Cognitive behavioural treatment of borderline personality disorder*. Guilford Press.

Lupien, S. J., McEwen, B. S., Gunnar, M. R., & Heim, C. (2009). Effects of stress throughout the lifespan on the brain, behaviour and cognition. *Nature Reviews. Neuroscience, 10*(6), 434–445. https://doi.org/10.1038/nrn2639

Luthar, S. S., Cicchetti, D., & Becker, B. (2000). The construct of resilience: A critical evaluation and guidelines for future work. *Child Development, 71*(3), 543–562. https://doi.org/10.1111/1467-8624.00164

Markus, H., & Wurf, E. (1987). The dynamic self-concept: A social psychological perspective. *Annual Review of Psychology, 38*(1), 299–337. https://doi.org/10.1146/annurev.ps.38.020187.001503

McEwen, B. S. (2017). Allostasis and the epigenetics of brain and body health over the life course: The brain on stress. *JAMA Psychiatry, 74*(6), 551–552. https://doi.org/10.1001/jamapsychiatry.2017.0270

Miller, A. B., Linthicum, K. P., Helms, S. W., Giletta, M., Rudolph, K. D., Hastings, P. D., Nock, M. K., & Prinstein, M. J. (2018). Reciprocal associations between adolescent girls' chronic interpersonal stress and nonsuicidal self-injury: A multi-wave prospective investigation. *Journal of Adolescent Health, 63*(6), 694–700. https://doi.org/10.1016/j.jadohealth.2018.06.033

Miller, A. B., & Prinstein, M. J. (2019). Adolescent suicide as a failure of acute stress-response systems. *Annual Review of Clinical Psychology, 15*(1), 425–450. https://doi.org/10.1146/annurev-clinpsy-050718-095625

Mossige, S., Huang, L., Straiton, M., & Roen, K. (2016). Suicidal ideation and self-harm among youths in Norway: Associations with verbal, physical and sexual abuse. *Child & Family Social Work, 21*(2), 166–175. https://doi.org/10.1111/cfs.12126

Muehlenkamp, J., Brausch, A., Quigley, K., & Whitlock, J. (2013). Interpersonal features and functions of nonsuicidal self-injury. *Suicide and Life-Threatening Behavior, 43*(1), 67–80. https://doi.org/10.1111/j.1943-278X.2012.00128.x

Nansel, T. R., Craig, W., Overpeck, M. D., Saluja, G., Ruan, W. J., & Health Behaviour in School-aged Children Bullying Analyses Working Group. (2004). Cross-national consistency in the relationship between bullying behaviors and psychosocial adjustment. *Archives of Pediatrics & Adolescent Medicine, 158*(8), 730–736. https://doi.org/10.1001/archpedi.158.8.730

Nelson, B. W., Pollak, O., Clayton, M., Telzer, E., & Prinstein, M. J. (2023). An RDoC-based approach to adolescent self-injurious thoughts and behaviors: The interactive role of social affiliation and cardiac arousal. *PsyArXiv preprint* [Manuscript under review]. https://doi.org/10.31234/osf.io/rma69

Nelson, B. W., Sheeber, L., Pfeifer, J., & Allen, N. B. (2021). Psychobiological markers of allostatic load in depressed and nondepressed mothers and their adolescent offspring. *Journal of Child Psychology and Psychiatry, and Allied Disciplines, 62*(2), 199–211. https://doi.org/10.1111/jcpp.13264

Nesi, J., Burke, T. A., Bettis, A. H., Kudinova, A. Y., Thompson, E. C., MacPherson, H. A., Fox, K. A., Lawrence, H. R., Thomas, S. A., Wolff, J. C., Altemus, M. K., Soriano, S., & Liu, R. T. (2021). Social media use and self-injurious thoughts and behaviors: A systematic review and meta-analysis. *Clinical Psychology Review, 87*, Article 102038. https://doi.org/10.1016/j.cpr.2021.102038

Nesi, J., Choukas-Bradley, S., & Prinstein, M. J. (2018). Transformation of adolescent peer relations in the social media context: Part 1-A Theoretical framework and application to dyadic peer relationships. *Clinical Child and Family Psychology Review, 21*(3), 267–294. https://doi.org/10.1007/s10567-018-0261-x

Nock, M. K. (2008). Actions speak louder than words: An elaborated theoretical model of the social functions of self-injury and other harmful behaviors. *Applied & Preventive Psychology: Journal of the American Association of Applied and Preventive Psychology, 12*(4), 159–168. https://doi.org/10.1016/j.appsy.2008.05.002

Nock, M. K., Green, J. G., Hwang, I., McLaughlin, K. A., Sampson, N. A., Zaslavsky, A. M., & Kessler, R. C. (2013). Prevalence, correlates, and treatment of lifetime suicidal behavior among adolescents: Results from the National Comorbidity Survey Replication Adolescent Supplement. *JAMA Psychiatry, 70*(3), 300–310. https://doi.org/10.1001/2013.jamapsychiatry.55

Nock, M. K., & Mendes, W. B. (2008). Physiological arousal, distress tolerance, and social problem-solving deficits among adolescent self-injurers. *Journal of Consulting and Clinical Psychology, 76*(1), 28–38. https://doi.org/10.1037/0022-006X.76.1.28

Nock, M. K., & Prinstein, M. J. (2004). A functional approach to the assessment of self-mutilative behavior. *Journal of Consulting and Clinical Psychology, 72*(5), 885–890. https://doi.org/10.1037/0022-006X.72.5.885

Nock, M. K., & Prinstein, M. J. (2005). Contextual features and behavioral functions of self-mutilation among adolescents. *Journal of Abnormal Psychology, 114*(1), 140–146. https://doi.org/10.1037/0021-843X.114.1.140

Nock, M. K., Prinstein, M. J., & Sterba, S. K. (2009). Revealing the form and function of self-injurious thoughts and behaviors: A real-time ecological assessment study among adolescents and young adults. *Journal of Abnormal Psychology, 118*(4), 816–827. https://doi.org/10.1037/a0016948

Paul, E. (2018). Proximally-occurring life events and the first transition from suicidal ideation to suicide attempt in adolescents. *Journal of Affective Disorders, 241*, 499–504. https://doi.org/10.1016/j.jad.2018.08.059

Prinstein, M. J., Boergers, J., & Spirito, A. (2001). Adolescents' and their friends' health-risk behavior: Factors that alter or add to peer influence. *Journal of Pediatric Psychology, 26*(5), 287–298. https://doi.org/10.1093/jpepsy/26.5.287

Prinstein, M. J., & Giletta, M. (2016). Peer relations and developmental psychopathology. In D. Cicchetti (Ed.), *Developmental Psychopathology* (pp. 527–579). Wiley.

Prinstein, M. J., Heilbron, N., Guerry, J. D., Franklin, J. C., Rancourt, D., Simon, V., & Spirito, A. (2010). Peer influence and nonsuicidal self injury: Longitudinal results in community and clinically-referred adolescent samples. *Journal of Abnormal Child Psychology, 38*(5), 669–682. https://doi.org/10.1007/s10802-010-9423-0

Prinstein, M. J., Meade, C. S., & Cohen, G. L. (2003). Adolescent oral sex, peer popularity, and perceptions of best friends' sexual behavior. *Journal of Pediatric Psychology, 28*(4), 243–249. https://doi.org/10.1093/jpepsy/jsg012

Rees, C. S., Hasking, P., Breen, L. J., Lipp, O. V., & Mamotte, C. (2015). Group mindfulness based cognitive therapy vs group support for self-injury among young people: Study protocol for a randomised controlled trial. *BMC Psychiatry, 15*, 154. https://doi.org/10.1186/s12888-015-0527-5

Rizzo, C. J., Esposito-Smythers, C., Swenson, L., Hower, H. M., Wolff, J., & Spirito, A. (2014). Dating violence victimization, dispositional aggression, and nonsuicidal self-injury among psychiatrically hospitalized male and female adolescents. *Suicide and Life-Threatening Behavior, 44*(3), 338–351. https://doi.org/10.1111/sltb.12081

Rose, A. J. (2002). Co-rumination in the friendships of girls and boys. *Child Development, 73*(6), 1830–1843. https://doi.org/10.1111/1467-8624.00509

Rotolone, C., & Martin, G. (2012). Giving up self-injury: A comparison of everyday social and personal resources in past versus current self-injurers. *Archives of Suicide Research, 16*(2), 147–158. https://doi.org/10.1080/13811118.2012.667333

Rudolph, K. D. (2014). Puberty as a developmental context of risk for psychopathology. In M. Lewis & K. D. Rudolph (Eds.), *Handbook of developmental psychopathology* (pp. 331–354). Springer US. https://doi.org/10.1007/978-1-4614-9608-3_17

Salmivalli, C. (2010). Bullying and the peer group: A review. *Aggression and Violent Behavior, 15*(2), 112–120. https://doi.org/10.1016/j.avb.2009.08.007

Sang, J. M., Louth-Marquez, W., Henderson, E. R., Egan, J. E., Chugani, C. D., Hunter, S. C., Espelage, D., Friedman, M. S., & Coulter, R. W. S. (2020). "It's not okay for you to call me that": How sexual and gender minority youth cope with bullying victimization. *Journal of Homosexuality, 0*(0), 1–20. https://doi.org/10.1080/00918369.2020.1826831

Sansone, R. A., Chu, J., & Wiederman, M. W. (2007). Self-inflicted bodily harm among victims of intimate-partner violence. *Clinical Psychology & Psychotherapy, 14*(5), 352–357. https://doi.org/10.1002/cpp.528

Schlenker, B. R. (1985). *The self and the social life*. McGraw-Hill.

Schwartz-Mette, R. A., & Lawrence, H. R. (2019). Peer socialization of non-suicidal self-injury in adolescents' close friendships. *Journal of Abnormal Child Psychology, 47*(11), 1851–1862. https://doi.org/10.1007/s10802-019-00569-8

Selby, E. A., & Joiner, T. E. (2009). Cascades of emotion: The emergence of borderline personality disorder from emotional and behavioral dysregulation. *Review of General Psychology, 13*(3), 219–229. https://doi.org/10.1037/a0015687

Silva, E., Machado, B. C., Moreira, C., Ramalho, S., & Gonçalves, S. (2017). Romantic relationships and non-suicidal self-injury among college students: The mediating role of emotion regulation. *Journal of Applied Developmental Psychology, 50*, 36–44. https://doi.org/10.1016/J.APPDEV.2017.04.001

Snir, A., Rafaeli, E., Gadassi, R., Berenson, K., & Downey, G. (2015). Explicit and inferred motives for non-suicidal self-injurious acts and urges in borderline and avoidant personality disorders. *Personality Disorders, 6*(3), 267–277. https://doi.org/10.1037/per0000104

Somerville, L. H. (2013). Special issue on the teenage brain: Sensitivity to social evaluation. *Current Directions in Psychological Science, 22*(2), 121–127. https://doi.org/10.1177/0963721413476512

Steinberg, L., & Morris, A. S. (2001). Adolescent development. *Annual Review of Psychology, 52*, 83–110. https://doi.org/10.1146/annurev.psych.52.1.83

Stroud, L. R., Foster, E., Papandonatos, G. D., Handwerger, K., Granger, D. A., Kivlighan, K. T., & Niaura, R. (2009). Stress response and the adolescent transition: Performance versus peer rejection stressors. *Development and Psychopathology, 21*(1), 47–68. https://doi.org/10.1017/S0954579409000042

Taiminen, T. J., Kallio-Soukainen, K., Nokso-Koivisto, H., Kaljonen, A., & Helenius, H. (1998). Contagion of deliberate self-harm among adolescent inpatients. *Journal of the American Academy of Child and Adolescent Psychiatry, 37*(2), 211–217. https://doi.org/10.1097/00004583-199802000-00014

Tatnell, R., Hasking, P., Newman, L., Taffe, J., & Martin, G. (2017). Attachment, emotion regulation, childhood abuse and assault: Examining predictors of NSSI among adolescents. *Archives of Suicide Research, 21*(4), 610–620. https://doi.org/10.1080/13811118.2016.1246267

Tatnell, R., Kelada, L., Hasking, P., & Martin, G. (2014). Longitudinal analysis of adolescent NSSI: The role of intrapersonal and interpersonal factors. *Journal of Abnormal Child Psychology, 42*(6), 885–896. https://doi.org/10.1007/s10802-013-9837-6

Taylor, P. J., Jomar, K., Dhingra, K., Forrester, R., Shahmalak, U., & Dickson, J. M. (2018). A meta-analysis of the prevalence of different functions of non-suicidal self-injury. *Journal of Affective Disorders, 227*, 759–769. https://doi.org/10.1016/j.jad.2017.11.073

Turner, B. J., Cobb, R. J., Gratz, K. L., & Chapman, A. L. (2016). The role of interpersonal conflict and perceived social support in nonsuicidal self-injury in daily life. *Journal of Abnormal Psychology, 125*(4), 588–598. https://doi.org/10.1037/abn0000141

Turner, B. J., Wakefield, M. A., Gratz, K. L., & Chapman, A. L. (2017). Characterizing interpersonal difficulties among young adults who engage in nonsuicidal self-injury using a daily diary. *Behavior Therapy, 48*(3), 366–379. https://doi.org/10.1016/j.beth.2016.07.001

van Geel, M., Goemans, A., & Vedder, P. (2015). A meta-analysis on the relation between peer victimization and adolescent non-suicidal self-injury. *Psychiatry Research, 230*(2), 364–368. https://doi.org/10.1016/j.psychres.2015.09.017

Vergara, G. A., Stewart, J. G., Cosby, E. A., Lincoln, S. H., & Auerbach, R. P. (2019). Non-Suicidal self-injury and suicide in depressed Adolescents: Impact of peer victimization and bullying. *Journal of Affective Disorders, 245*, 744–749. https://doi.org/10.1016/j.jad.2018.11.084

Victor, S. E., Hipwell, A. E., Stepp, S. D., & Scott, L. N. (2019). Parent and peer relationships as longitudinal predictors of adolescent non-suicidal self-injury onset. *Child and Adolescent Psychiatry and Mental Health, 13*(1), Article 1. https://doi.org/10.1186/s13034-018-0261-0

Walsh, B. W., & Rosen, P. (1985). Self-mutilation and contagion: An empirical test. *The American Journal of Psychiatry, 142*(1), 119–120. https://doi.org/10.1176/ajp.142.1.119

Whitlock, J. L., Lader, W., & Conterio, K. (2007). The internet and self-injury: What psychotherapists should know. *Journal of Clinical Psychology, 63*(11), 1135–1143. https://doi.org/10.1002/jclp.20420

Whitlock, J. L., Powers, J. L., & Eckenrode, J. (2006). The virtual cutting edge: The internet and adolescent self-injury. *Developmental Psychology, 42*(3), 407–417. https://doi.org/10.1037/0012-1649.42.3.407

Wielgus, M. D., Aldrich, J. T., Mezulis, A. H., & Crowell, S. E. (2016). Respiratory sinus arrhythmia as a predictor of self-injurious thoughts and behaviors among adolescents. *International Journal of Psychophysiology, 106*, 127–134. https://doi.org/10.1016/j.ijpsycho.2016.05.005

Yates, T. M. (2004). The developmental psychopathology of self-injurious behavior: Compensatory regulation in posttraumatic adaptation. *Clinical Psychology Review, 24*(1), 35–74. https://doi.org/10.1016/j.cpr.2003.10.001

Yates, T. M. (2009). Developmental pathways from child maltreatment to nonsuicidal self-injury. In M. K. Nock (Ed.), *Understanding nonsuicidal self-injury: Origins, assessment, and treatment* (pp. 117–137). American Psychological Association. https://doi.org/10.1037/11875-007

You, J., Lin, M. P., Fu, K., & Leung, F. (2013). The best friend and friendship group influence on adolescent nonsuicidal self-injury. *Journal of Abnormal Child Psychology, 41*(6), 993–1004. https://doi.org/10.1007/s10802-013-9734-z

Zhu, J., Chen, Y., Su, B., & Zhang, W. (2021). Anxiety symptoms mediates the influence of cybervictimization on adolescent non-suicidal self-injury: The moderating effect of self-control. *Journal of Affective Disorders, 285*, 144–151. https://doi.org/10.1016/j.jad.2021.01.004

CHAPTER 42

Social Contagion of Nonsuicidal Self-Injury

Stephanie Jarvi Steele, Nigel Jaffe, *and* Grace Murray

Abstract

This chapter explores the social contagion of nonsuicidal self-injury (NSSI) via interpersonal, media and online exposure among both youths and adults by referencing social learning theory and the Social Exposure to Non-Suicidal Self-Injury Scale. According to social learning theory, people imitate and learn certain behaviors by identifying with people who act as models. The chapter elaborates on the concepts of social learning, modeling, and imitation, and general recommendations for the assessment and treatment of clinical practice addressing social contagion factors. It then suggests utilizing ecological momentary assessment (EMA) and single-case experimental design (SCED) for future studies on social contagion of NSSI.

Key Words: NSSI, social contagion, interpersonal, media, social learning theory, behaviors, social learning, modeling, ecological momentary assessment, single-case experimental design

Research in recent years has made significant advances toward a more thorough understanding of major risk factors and predictors of nonsuicidal self-injury (NSSI). Most studies have focused on correlates of NSSI at the level of the individual (e.g., related psychopathology), but promising results have also been achieved in the study of interpersonal processes (e.g., peer and family support) that impact the risk of NSSI. The social contagion of NSSI, or the process by which one person's self-injurious behaviors can promote the same behaviors in others, is an underexplored topic in the study of NSSI and adds an important dimension when it comes to both onset and maintenance of NSSI.

One of the primary aims of this chapter is to review empirical studies that focus on social contagion via interpersonal, media, and online exposure to NSSI among both youths and adults. Research suggests that people are exposed to NSSI through a diverse range of sources, including peers, social media, and the internet, and that being exposed to NSSI through these avenues may then predispose individuals to engage in NSSI themselves. One way of understanding this relationship, drawing on social learning theory (Bandura, 1977), is to view exposure as a means through which individuals learn to model their own behavior on what they observe in others. This theoretical viewpoint complicates the role of social factors in NSSI, as social learning may promote NSSI (Jarvi et al., 2013) at the same time as peer support acts to protect against it (Heath et al., 2009).

Defining Key Terms

In line with the nomenclature used by Jarvi et al. (2013), we define *social contagion* primarily as the occurrence of NSSI in two or more people from the same group within a short time period. Further, social contagion also refers specifically to the process by which one individual's behavior can increase the occurrence of the same behavior in other people, distinguishing social contagion from the related notion of *clusters*, which is commonly used to describe a significantly high frequency of suicidal or self-injurious behavior among members of a group (Heilbron et al., 2014). The process of social contagion necessarily involves one person being exposed to someone else's NSSI in some way, so it is worth clarifying what is meant by *exposure* to NSSI; this definition has been operationalized in the literature in various ways. The term accommodates many different pathways by which someone can encounter NSSI; indeed, the Social Exposure to Non-Suicidal Self-Injury Scale (Zelkowitz et al., 2017), which aims to capture key constructs in the literature, includes items ranging from indirect sources, such as music lyrics, to highly direct sources, like witnessing someone engage in NSSI. Finally, phrases such as *social learning*, *modeling*, and *imitation* draw on Bandura's (1977) social learning theory, which suggests that people imitate—and thereby learn—certain behaviors by identifying with people who, by displaying those behaviors, act as models.

What follows is our review of the existing literature that has explored some form of exposure and related social contagion of NSSI across various demographic groups and platforms (e.g., in person vs. online). In addition to reviewing the empirical literature, we attempt to bridge the gap between research and clinical practice in this area. We introduce a case study that involved treatment of a patient impacted by social contagion in her initial onset of NSSI as a young adult, and review some clinical implications to consider when it comes to identifying, assessing, and addressing possible social contagion factors in treatment and intervention. Finally, we conclude with a discussion of limitations to the current empirical base and recommendations for future work in this important area of study.

Brief Description of the Issue

Social contagion processes have been associated with the onset and maintenance of NSSI well before the more recent uptick in both research and clinical interest in NSSI; the first documented acknowledgment of this relationship in the literature appears to date back to the 1960s (Matthews, 1968). Although further research is needed to determine and elucidate this relationship, it is likely that social contagion factors serve as both distal and proximal risk factors for NSSI. The identification of distal and proximal risk factors has been at the center of NSSI research in recent years, as researchers have posed questions and designed studies to better understand who self-injures, why, and what puts one individual at risk of engaging in NSSI compared to any other. Like the suicide literature, the NSSI literature has identified more distal risk factors for NSSI than proximal indicators that *immediately* precede episodes of NSSI. Yet these proximal factors are of course of primary concern to both researchers and clinicians alike, as identification of these risk factors would allow for the possibility of the prevention of NSSI among individuals most at risk for future occurrences of these behaviors (see Kiekens et al., 2020).

In sum, studies to date suggest that many individuals who have or who are currently engaging in NSSI endorse exposure to NSSI through various sources. Evidence suggests that interpersonal (which we define as direct, explicit, in person exposure) and media exposure to NSSI is associated with the occurrence of NSSI. Data suggest that exposure to NSSI can serve as a social learning process, and that NSSI is a learned behavior in some instances, for certain individuals (Jarvi et al., 2013). A number of associated risk factors and characteristics have been identified in the literature elucidating who is most likely to be impacted by social contagion of NSSI (e.g., adolescents, individuals with more adverse life events; Hasking et al., 2013). Social transmission of NSSI has been documented most frequently among adolescent participants, supporting the significant influence that interpersonal relationships have on adolescents during this developmental stage. Of course, social contagion is not a necessary factor or the only predisposing risk factor for NSSI, and onset and maintenance of NSSI are certainly influenced by a variety of both proximal and distal indicators.

Social Contagion in Adolescent Samples

Research regarding NSSI in adolescents supports the frequent co-occurrence of individuals and their friends engaging in self-injury (Hasking et al., 2013; Victor & Klonksy, 2018). Furthermore, data have shown social contagion of NSSI between two best friends, but not among groups of friends (You et al., 2013). Further research is needed to clarify the moderators of this effect, and especially among adolescents in inpatient and residential treatment settings, an understudied population in social contagion research.

Data suggest that peers are a common source of initial exposure to NSSI, and that adolescents who self-injure often have peers or family members who do as well. In a study of 94 adolescents, investigators assessed a wide range of factors potentially associated with NSSI, including a family history of psychopathology, sexual orientation, comorbid psychopathology, and noninjurious repetitive behaviors, as well as qualitative information regarding the source of the adolescent's idea to begin engaging in NSSI, and their reason for stopping, if applicable (Deliberto & Nock, 2008). The most frequently endorsed source that led to the idea of engaging in NSSI was from peers (38.3%), followed by coming up with the idea independently (20.0%), and from the media (13.3%). The desire to stop engaging in NSSI due to a social reason (e.g., unwanted attention or because it upsets family and friends) was more common among individuals who learned about NSSI from a peer. In another study, 3,757 students in 10th and 11th grade in Queensland, Australia responded to a battery of self-report measures assessing "deliberate self-harm behavior" and psychopathological symptoms (De Leo & Heller, 2004). The strongest associations with self-harm were exposure to self-harm in friends and exposure to self-harm in family members. Additionally, in a study that included 89 adolescents, Victor and Klonsky (2018) investigated several social aspects of NSSI. They found that 71.6% of participants had friends who also self-injured, and half of the participants reported discussing NSSI with their friends. On the other hand, very few participants reported either assisting their friends in engaging in NSSI, suggesting NSSI to someone, feeling that their friends play a role in their NSSI, or engaging in NSSI with friends. Those adolescents who reported knowing that a friend engaged in NSSI tended to also report engaging in more NSSI methods, an accepted proxy for severity, than other adolescents (Victor & Klonsky, 2018). Together, these studies suggest the importance of social relationships and social learning for adolescent NSSI, which may be particularly relevant factors to consider and assess in relation to initial NSSI onset.

Research has consistently established exposure to NSSI in a friend as a predictive factor for later engagement in NSSI. You et al. (2013) conducted a longitudinal study of high school students involving two assessments, six months apart. Specifically, they investigated the effects of a best friend's behavior and a friend group's behavior on an individual's engagement in NSSI. To match participants' data to their friends' data, the authors instructed participants to identify their five best friends. They found negligible, but statistically significant, associations between the participant's NSSI status and their best friend's NSSI status at both Time 1 ($r = 0.12$) and Time 2 ($r = 0.15$). Within the same time frame, there was a slight tendency for best friends to have the same NSSI status. A stronger correlation existed between the best friend's NSSI status at Time 1 and the participant's status at Time 2 ($r = 0.44$). A logistic regression indicated a predictive relationship, suggesting that an individual is more likely to begin engaging in NSSI if their best friend already does (i.e., increased risk due to socialization). Conversely, the participant's Time 1 status did not predict their best friend's Time 2 status, which may indicate the lack of a selection effect (i.e., adolescents who already self-injure are not more likely to select a best friend who self-injures as well). In another set of analyses examining frequency, the results indicated that the participant's NSSI frequency at Time 1 did not predict their best friend's frequency; nor did the best friend's frequency predict the participant's. Thus, additional questions remain about the role of social contagion of NSSI in NSSI onset, as well as whether and how social contagion may impact maintenance of NSSI and related factors, such as frequency and methods used.

In another longitudinal study of 186 adolescents (93 nested friendship dyads; Schwartz-Mette & Lawrence, 2019), results provided further evidence for the socialization effect between friends. Participants' Time 2 and Time 3 NSSI frequency scores were predicted by both their own and their friend's Time 1 and Time 2 scores, respectively. In a novel exploration of emotion regulation ability and friendship quality as moderators, the authors also found that high levels of emotion regulation difficulty were associated with greater socialization effects between friends, but that friendship quality was not a significant moderator. It is important to note that an additional study conducted by Hasking et al. (2013) yielded a discrepant finding. In the year-long study, knowing a friend who self-injured at baseline predicted NSSI at follow-up only for those adolescents who also reported more adverse life events. However, this study relied on participants' knowledge and accurate reporting of their friends' behavior because it did not match participants' data to their friends' data, as other studies did. This study also reported the novel finding that the primary methods for self-injury tended to be consistent across friendship, while motives did not. Taken together, these longitudinal studies support the idea that adolescents are more at risk for NSSI onset if they have a close friend who engages in NSSI, with the caveat that certain additional factors, such as emotion regulation difficulty or adverse life events, may impact the risk level.

Of note are You et al.'s (2013) additional analyses regarding characteristics and patterns of NSSI behavior within friend groups of three to five adolescents. They found that independent of depressive or impulsive characteristics, there was less within-group variance regarding NSSI status than a between-group variance. In other words, adolescents were more likely to share NSSI status with members of their friend group than with other adolescents generally. Furthermore, multiple regression analyses indicated that a participant's NSSI status at Time 1 predicted their friend group's NSSI status at Time 2, but a friend group's status at Time 1 did not predict the participant's status at Time 2. The authors interpreted this finding to indicate a selection process whereby adolescents who had a history of NSSI behavior chose to join friend groups of peers who also engaged in NSSI (You et al., 2013). This process is notably distinct from that which has been observed to occur between two best friends, highlighting the complexity of the social processes at play (Schwartz-Mette & Lawrence, 2019; You et al., 2013).

Although most studies on social contagion of NSSI among adolescents were conducted in the general community, two studies investigated inpatients. Consistent with findings in the community, in one study, a large majority of the patients (87%) reported exposure to NSSI before they began engaging in NSSI (Zhu et al., 2016). The researchers found mixed results regarding the association between exposure to a specific method of NSSI and engagement in that method. Some methods, such as scratching, hitting, and pinching, were associated with frequency of use, while others were not. Although exposure to cutting was not related to engagement in cutting, individuals who used this method of NSSI tended to do so more frequently if they had more frequent exposure to it. There was also a significant correlation between exposure to NSSI in the media (overall, traditional, or social media) and engagement in NSSI (see Westers, this volume). Furthermore, participants who intentionally sought NSSI content in the media tended to report engaging in NSSI more frequently than others (Zhu et al., 2016). In a qualitative study, researchers interviewed eight residents from two adolescent inpatient units (Smith-Gowling et al.,

2018). Two key themes across the interviews were "pre-admission exposure to self-harm" and "exposure on the inside." Participants described pre-admission exposure to NSSI from family members, friends/peers, and on social media. They also discussed the difficulty of being "surrounded" by others in distress and the difficulties that arose when a patient self-injured on the unit, which included both physical consequences (e.g., room searches) and emotional consequences (e.g., being reminded of their own history of NSSI). Further research is needed among adolescents in inpatient or residential settings, as these individuals may experience distinct or more intense socialization processes regarding social contagion of NSSI.

One might expect that, due to the relationship between NSSI and suicidal behavior, the socialization of NSSI may translate into suicidal behavior. However, there is no evidence to support this notion, and there is in fact some evidence against it. In a population-based birth cohort study, Mars et al. (2019) investigated predictors of suicide attempts by age 21 among participants who endorsed suicidal thoughts ($n = 456$) and "nonsuicidal self-harm" ($n = 569$) at age 16. The researchers found that among adolescents who experienced suicidal thoughts and engaged in NSSI, exposure to NSSI in a friend or family member did not predict future suicide attempts. This finding underscores the distinct processes underlying NSSI and suicidality.

In sum, the literature to date supports the social contagion of NSSI among adolescents. Data suggest that adolescents learn about NSSI from external sources, such as the media or a friend, before the initial onset of the behavior. Longitudinal studies have captured the increased risk of NSSI for adolescents who have a close friend who already engages in NSSI, and the socialization process of choosing to surround oneself with a group of friends with a shared NSSI status. Additional factors such as difficulty with emotion regulation and adverse life events may increase risk level, but further research is needed to replicate and clarify these effects and their impact on the uptake of NSSI behavior. The body of literature regarding social contagion of NSSI among adolescents is relatively small, and further research in a wider variety of settings (e.g., residential or inpatient treatment) and closely examining mediating and moderating factors is warranted.

Social Contagion of NSSI in College Samples

Many college students are socially well connected with other people their age, and some are living independently and/or away from home for the first time in their lives. Although these factors make college students less representative of the broader population, they also make college samples important and convenient participants for the study of social influences and NSSI. To date, studies have shown that social and media exposure are highly prevalent among college students, particularly through friends, movies, and television (Heath et al., 2009). Moreover, findings suggest social exposure to NSSI is a better predictor of NSSI risk than both media exposure to NSSI and social exposure to suicide (Muehlenkamp et al., 2008). Some research in this area has focused on potential moderators (e.g., NSSI outcome expectancies; Hasking & Rose, 2016) of the relationship between social exposure and NSSI risk, but further work, particularly longitudinal research, is needed.

To date, research in college samples suggests the importance of social motivations in NSSI. For example, Heath et al. (2009) examined social influences on initiation, disclosure, methods, and motivations for NSSI in a small ($n = 23$) sample of college students with a lifetime history of NSSI. A total of 22% of participants reported that they first thought about engaging in NSSI because they knew someone else who had engaged in it, while another 22% learned to engage in self-injury through the media or the internet. The importance of direct interpersonal influence was clear, as 65% of participants reported talking to their friends about NSSI and 74% reported knowing at least one friend who had self-injured. More than half of participants (59%) within the latter group reported that their friend had engaged in NSSI before they did, while 65% used some or all of the same methods as their peers who had self-injured. Finally, participants from a matched comparison group of 23 students who did not self-injure reported significantly higher levels of peer support than participants who did self-injure. Although this study was primarily descriptive with a small sample size and only two male participants, Heath et al. (2009) illustrated the influence of social connections on NSSI in college students.

Muehlenkamp et al. (2008) investigated whether exposure to NSSI or suicidal behavior in acquaintances was associated with an increased risk of NSSI. Participants ($N = 1,965$), of whom 21.2% ($n = 417$) endorsed lifetime NSSI, were asked whether they knew someone who had engaged in NSSI or suicidal behavior and were divided into four groups accordingly: suicide-only exposure ($n = 380$), NSSI-only exposure ($n = 229$), suicide and NSSI exposure ($n = 1028$), and no exposure ($n = 328$). Participants in the NSSI-only exposure group were significantly more likely than controls to engage in NSSI themselves, while participants in the suicide-only exposure group were *not* more likely than controls to engage in NSSI. Further, the rate of NSSI in the group who had exposure to both NSSI and suicide was not significantly different from the NSSI-only exposure group, suggesting that exposure to NSSI specifically—and not suicide—may be a factor heightening risk for NSSI. This cross-sectional study does not allow for an analysis of the temporal influence of exposure on NSSI risk, and the method of assessing exposure leaves little room for nuance in the types of exposure accounted for. However, these findings from Muehlenkamp et al. (2008) fall in line with a social learning theory of NSSI (Bandura, 1977), showing that exposure to NSSI *specifically* is associated with the risk of engaging in NSSI.

In a sample of 340 U.S. college students, Zelkowitz et al. (2017) more thoroughly examined the social learning theory of NSSI, clarifying the relationship between NSSI history and social exposure to NSSI while testing the interaction between social exposure and emotion dysregulation in relation to NSSI. The authors assessed the prevalence of exposure via personal relationships with people engaging in NSSI (38%), the internet

(24%), and movies and TV (71% and 64%), finding that both social and media exposure were common. Participants with a history of NSSI reported significantly higher levels of both social and media exposure to NSSI compared to those with no NSSI history. Social exposure and emotion dysregulation were each significantly associated with NSSI history and frequency when controlling for the other, but media exposure was not significant. Although social exposure did not moderate the impact of emotion dysregulation, greater social exposure to NSSI was associated with increased NSSI frequency—as well as the likelihood of reporting lifetime NSSI history—at both low and high levels of emotion dysregulation. These findings align with the idea that, as expressed in the social learning hypothesis of NSSI, risk factors like emotion dysregulation might exacerbate risk in the context of social exposure to NSSI. Zelkowitz et al. (2017) offered a thorough account of the prevalence of different types of exposure in this college sample, and provided support for a social learning and interpersonal influence-based model of NSSI.

In a study aimed to further explore the mechanisms through which social exposure leads to increased NSSI risk, Hasking and Rose (2016) tested whether core cognitions (e.g., self-efficacy expectancies), as well as knowledge about and attitudes toward NSSI, work as moderators or otherwise influence this relationship. They drew on social cognitive theory, which states that the relationship between external influences and behavior can be explained partly in terms of individual cognitions—or expectancies—about the outcomes of a behavior and one's perceived ability to perform the behavior (Bandura, 1986). In line with findings from Zelkowitz et al. (2017), social and media exposure were common in the sample, which included 389 undergraduate students at an Australian university. Although knowing at least one friend who self-injured was not directly related to the frequency of NSSI, participants' self-efficacy to resist NSSI was inversely related to frequency. Hasking and Rose's (2016) findings support social cognitive theory as a framework for understanding NSSI, and they add further nuance to the question of how exactly social exposure to NSSI increases the probability of engaging in future NSSI.

The studies reviewed here present several key insights into the social contagion of NSSI among college studies, but a few broader methodological shortcomings also stand out. Interpersonal influence is clearly highly common among college students (Heath et al., 2009; Zelkowitz et al., 2017), but studies that aim to assess the prevalence of NSSI and different vectors of exposure to it must prioritize recruiting larger samples with greater racial and gender diversity. Research suggests that social exposure to NSSI is strongly associated with NSSI risk (Zelkowitz et al., 2017), and studies suggest that it performs better as a predictor of NSSI than either media exposure to NSSI or social exposure to suicide specifically (Muehlenkamp et al., 2008). While Bandura's (1977) social learning theory and social cognitive theory (Bandura, 1986) apply usefully to the study of moderators of the relationship between exposure to NSSI and risk of NSSI (Hasking & Rose, 2016; Muehlenkamp et al., 2008), researchers may also consider examining potential mediators in this relationship.

Social Contagion of NSSI in Online Samples

Despite widespread usage of smartphones and social media among young people, and the common appearance of NSSI-related content online, few studies have rigorously examined online exposure to NSSI as a vector for social contagion above and beyond interpersonal exposure (Jarvi et al., 2017; Lewis et al., 2012). The precise influence social media has on children and adolescents is difficult to predict, as the posts users encounter on these platforms may be created and shared by peers, high-profile celebrities, or various other sources, exposing users to a wide range of content with little official oversight or censoring. As such, some forms of online exposure to NSSI may at times operate in a similar way to interpersonal exposure, but digitally mediated, while other forms of online exposure are less directly targeted and meant for a broad audience. Further, there is little consensus among researchers as to what counts as social exposure via the internet (see Pritchard & Lewis, this volume). Some studies (e.g., Heath et al., 2009) consider it social exposure when people learn about NSSI in the media or online, but these forms of exposure do not necessarily involve communicating with another person, casting doubt on whether they should be thought of as "social." Research on social contagion in online samples has found that exposure to NSSI over social media is tied to negative outcomes whether or not users intend to view NSSI content (Arendt et al., 2019), but further research is needed to elucidate the broader ways that NSSI impacts people online, and how (e.g., communicating/posting about NSSI vs. scrolling through others' content/pictures/stories).

In a recent study, Arendt et al. (2019) focused on online exposure to NSSI over Instagram, one of the most popular social media platforms among youth today, aiming to assess the relationship between exposure to NSSI or suicidality-related outcomes. Young adults were recruited from internet gaming websites to complete surveys at two time points (one month apart) assessing exposure to NSSI on Instagram, suicidal thoughts and behaviors, and emotional well-being. The authors measured exposure to NSSI by asking participants if they had seen posts showing someone who intentionally self-injures, for example, by cutting. They found that exposure to NSSI on Instagram was significantly associated with suicidal ideation, NSSI, and emotional disturbance. Further, exposure to NSSI at the first time point predicted NSSI and suicidality-related outcomes at the second time point, and exposure to NSSI was related to negative outcomes even for participants who accidentally (rather than intentionally) encountered NSSI content (Arendt et al., 2019). These findings point to the potentially contagious nature of online exposure to NSSI as distinct from but similar to in person social exposure.

According to a study by Whitlock et al. (2006), hundreds of forums exist on the internet for the purpose of anonymously discussing NSSI, hosting communities populated primarily by users who are female and between 14 and 20 years old. The authors located more than 400 such forums (in the early 2000s) and selected 10 of the most popular for a more in-depth content analysis, which involved coding almost 3,000 posts. The most common themes in the message board posts were support for others, motivation and triggers for NSSI, concealing NSSI, and addiction-like elements, where users discussed NSSI as if it were a drug they were trying to quit using. Most communication on the forums was supportive and involved sharing personal experiences, suggesting a high level of trust despite the anonymity. The researchers found that some of the conversations on the message boards normalized or encouraged NSSI, and sometimes involved sharing new methods for self-injuring (Whitlock et al., 2006). It is clear that online forums are not necessarily a positive environment for adolescents, and even when content is supportive, users may still be exposed to accounts of NSSI in stark detail. More research is needed on different kinds of online exposure (e.g., visual vs. textual references to NSSI, social media vs. other media) in order to capture the nuanced ways in which individuals can encounter NSSI online. This is a challenging area of research to keep updated due to the fast pace and always evolving nature of social media.

It is worth noting that different online forums and social networking sites vary widely in their approaches to monitoring and censoring NSSI-related content (Lewis & Baker, 2011). Whitlock et al. (2006) divided the message boards they analyzed into three levels according to the extent to which each forum's moderators blocked or labeled potentially triggering posts. High-moderation boards completely prohibited potentially triggering or "disruptive" posts, whereas medium-moderation boards allowed such posts but clearly labeled them, and low-moderation message boards did not attempt to block or label any posts. Among the 10 message boards the researchers examined, four were low-moderation, another four were medium-moderation, and one was high-moderation. In general, forums that choose to moderate their content often employ volunteers to do so, who may be unreliable or inconsistent. Moreover, users may find ways around censorship in more strictly monitored online settings, such as by using euphemisms or other coded languages to refer to NSSI.

Challenges, Recommendations, and Future Directions in Research

The body of literature presented in this chapter has several limitations that represent directions for future work. At the most basic level, standard and consistent definitions of the different types of NSSI exposure are needed to enhance the study of these complex social processes. Studies have investigated exposure in a variety of forms: knowing that an acquaintance/friend/family member self-injures, talking about NSSI with another person, seeing images of NSSI in movies or on TV, being in the company of another person engaging in NSSI, and reading about or seeing images of NSSI on social media. Each type of exposure may contribute differently to the social contagion of NSSI, and the broad term "exposure" cannot necessarily be compared across studies. We also face the challenge of prior use of different terms and definitions of NSSI. For example, researchers who use the term "NSSI" typically refer very specifically to the definition presented at the beginning of this chapter, while researchers who use the broader term "self-harm" often include participants in their studies who endorse both nonsuicidal and suicidal self-injurious behaviors, potentially further complicating the overall picture. While NSSI and suicidality often co-occur and share conceptual overlaps, these behaviors are indeed distinct with unique risk factors (Andover et al., 2012; Ferrera et al., 2012) and are thus best studied and defined separately. NSSI researchers have made concerted efforts to clarify precise terminology regarding self-injury (e.g., Nock & Favazza, 2009), and the distinction between self-harm and NSSI has become more mainstream. However, researchers today are still left to contend with imprecise terminology in past publications, which muddle findings related to NSSI and complicate the process of building on or replicating prior research.

A further complication worth noting is the variety of measures that have been employed in research to date. Even studies that investigate the same type of exposure frequently use different modes of measurement (e.g., semistructured interviews, self-report surveys, items from larger validated surveys on general psychiatric symptoms, and stand-alone nonvalidated questions). Increasing the use of standardized measures will benefit the field of NSSI research in general, but work remains to be done with regard to social contagion research. Although there are a number of widely used and well-validated measures to assess NSSI history and severity (e.g., the Self-Injurious Thoughts and Behaviors Interview; Nock et al., 2007), there are no existing measures that capture social contagion that we are aware of. The development and validation of such a measure is another important area of future work in this area of NSSI research. Furthermore, the generalizability of results is limited by narrow study populations. Individuals who engage in NSSI may be in inpatient or residential psychiatric treatment, outpatient psychotherapy, or receiving no treatment at all. Social contagion processes may operate differently in treatment versus nontreatment settings. Similarly, differences in age, gender and sex, socioeconomic status, and adverse life events may impact social contagion. Standard operational definitions of exposure and NSSI, consistent measurement strategies, and diverse samples and settings will increase the reliability of results and allow cross-study comparisons.

Social contagion is necessarily a longitudinal process by which an individual becomes more susceptible to NSSI after exposure. Still, a large portion of the literature reports cross-sectional or retrospective research. Retrospective reports can be useful, but they are limited by human error and participant bias. Existing longitudinal research is largely limited to two or three time points, with lapses of several months to a year between data collection. These initial longitudinal investigations are valuable, but they lack the density and duration needed to understand how exposure influences NSSI trajectory across an individual's development. Without longitudinal data that captures real-time exposure to NSSI and its impact on future NSSI thoughts and behaviors, we remain unable to determine whether exposure to NSSI (and in what form) leads to higher risk for future NSSI. Related to this point, inclusion of younger participants, such as children and preteens, in longitudinal designs may increase the chance that we are able to capture first exposure to NSSI in real time, allowing us to understand and draw some preliminary conclusions about initial exposure and NSSI onset.

Finally, we suggest consideration of two critical methodologies in future studies on social contagion of NSSI: ecological momentary assessment (EMA) and single-case experimental design (SCED). EMA captures temporally dense, naturalistic data in real time that is impossible to replicate in retrospective or even traditional longitudinal studies. More recent advances in EMA technology and the use of smartphones, apps, and/or other wearable devices like smartwatches may allow researchers to capture incidences of exposure that immediately precede episodes of NSSI. This information would contribute significantly to our understanding of NSSI exposure and social contagion as a proximal risk factor for NSSI. Second, SCEDs (see Barlow et al., 2009) are powerful and cost-efficient tools to explore mechanisms, and have been generally underutilized in NSSI research to date. SCEDs involve quantitative examination of changes in behavior among a small group of participants; although these designs are typically used to explore the impact of an intervention on behavior, they offer a unique opportunity in the case of social contagion to explore the occurrence of NSSI over time in the context of a dose-response relationship (e.g., Does frequency or duration of exposure lead to severity or frequency of NSSI behavior? When direct exposure to NSSI is removed from the environment, does NSSI behavior decrease or remit?). Additional advantages of SCEDs include high internal validity and the opportunity to explore reasons for intersubject variability using flexible and responsive experimental strategies (Barlow et al., 2009).

Case Example

Greta is a 26-year-old female who identifies as biracial and heterosexual. She is currently single and lives with roommates in a major East Coast city where she is working on a graduate degree in social work, and works currently with child and family services doing in-home visits with children between the ages of 12 and 17. Greta is presenting for treatment to address her depression, recent diagnosis of borderline personality disorder (BPD), and NSSI in the context of a partial hospital program.

Yesterday, Greta was taken to the emergency room by a colleague for evaluation after making several concerning statements about hurting herself during the workday; the emergency room staff determined that Greta was not at acute risk of harming herself, did not have a suicide plan or intent in mind, had no history of suicidality, and was willing to work on a safety plan during the evaluation. Staff recommended that Greta seek further treatment in the local partial hospital program, and she was willing and able to start the program the next day.

In the six months leading up to Greta's partial hospitalization admission, she had been struggling with long-standing depression and seeing an outpatient therapist each week. The therapist had recently talked to Greta about BPD and presented it to her as an explanation to understand many of her persistent and long-standing issues in relationships, difficulty in regulating emotions, impulsivity, lack of a sense of self, and NSSI. Greta thought this was a fitting and validating diagnosis and has been attempting to learn more about her symptoms and coping skills to manage them. She has not received any evidence-based treatments for BPD.

Greta had first been directly exposed to NSSI in her role as a mental health care worker for child and family services about three months ago. She reported first engaging in NSSI herself after what she described as a very stressful day at work; she completed a home visit with a 13-year-old child whose family had been on her caseload for about eight months. The child, a female with a significant trauma history and long-standing NSSI with intermittent suicidal ideation, had shown Greta several recent cuts on her forearms and thighs. Greta, aware that this child had a history of NSSI, had never seen the cuts in person and was struck by the number and depth of the cuts. She reported leaving the home visit, getting in her car, feeling "out of control," and punching her dashboard and windows. She reported back to work and met with her supervisor (a licensed clinician) to discuss the case and how best to address the child's safety moving forward. That night after work, Greta cut herself repeatedly on the inside of her upper arms. She stated, "It [NSSI] wasn't a part of me at all, and then suddenly, it was. I always knew that some people hurt themselves in this way, but never understood it until I did it myself." Since this episode, Greta has been engaging in NSSI to manage emotional reactions primarily in the context of her role at work. She continues to cut her arms, where she can hide the wounds with clothing, and has not disclosed her NSSI to anyone but her therapist.

Clinical Considerations

A number of important factors likely contributed to the onset of Greta's NSSI in addition to the social learning that appears to have occurred in her response to her work with child and family services. These include, but are not limited to, a recent diagnosis of BPD (65%–80% of individuals diagnosed with BPD are estimated to have engaged in NSSI; see Brickman et al., 2014), comorbid depression, and general deficits in adaptive skills in emotion regulation. However, Greta seemed to be particularly influenced by exposure to her 13-year-old client's NSSI, indicated by her almost immediate response of engaging in NSSI herself following witnessing the client's cuts during the home visit.

This experience with the client, therefore, became a central component of Greta's early treatment, which included admission to a partial hospital program after she expressed suicidal ideation and intent to harm herself more seriously. During her seven-day treatment in the program, Greta's treatment team completed a structured diagnostic interview and confirmed diagnoses of BPD and major depressive disorder (moderate, recurrent). Greta started attending daily group therapy in the program, which involved skills training consistent with cognitive behavioral (e.g., cognitive restructuring) and dialectical behavioral practices (e.g., distress tolerance). Greta also saw an individual therapist for three, 50-minute sessions to expand the skill sets from group therapy and personalize her coping and safety plan in preparation for discharge. One meaningful aspect of individual therapy included discussion of Greta's lack of a stable sense of self (consistent with her

BPD diagnosis), which may have been a contributing factor to her vulnerability to the impact of social contagion in NSSI onset.

A notable difficulty in this case for Greta's treatment team at the partial hospital program and her outpatient therapist was whether—and if so, when—Greta could and should return to work with child and family services in the context of her own mental health challenges, recent hospitalization, and recent increased safety risk. At the time of Greta's discharge from the program, she decided to take a leave of absence from work for a period of time to focus on her treatment and to reassess her capacity to continue to work with high-risk clients in this context. Although she had not decided whether she would disclose any of the details of her hospitalization with her supervisor at work, Greta and the treatment team discussed ways in which Greta might work with her outpatient therapist in the future to have these conversations to manage her own safety and the safety of her clients (e.g., request that she see clients with an experienced therapist for home visits; request not to see clients with known, current NSSI or suicidality). Greta also continued her graduate studies in the social work program, and was hopeful that further education and clinical training would help her garner the necessary skills to work with patients presenting with high-risk behaviors.

General Recommendations for Clinical Practice

Perhaps the most important note to make regarding the assessment of possible social contagion factors in a patient presenting with NSSI is simply to ask about exposure to NSSI related to both onset and continuation of the behavior (e.g., knowledge of/exposure to friends, family, or peers and use of social media sites related to NSSI). Further assessment questions might include attempts to learn more about current exposure, and how the patient views its impact on NSSI thoughts, urges, and actions. Finally, explicit assessment of online behavior may be particularly useful in understanding social contagion factors, such as asking patients about usage, posting, frequency of engagement with others online who engage in discussion of NSSI, and how the individual sees online behavior impacting incidences of NSSI (e.g., does engagement with social media groups about NSSI increase or decrease NSSI behavior?).

After learning more about social contagion factors during the assessment phase, clinicians may then use this information to tailor interventions specific to the patient's presenting treatment targets related to NSSI (e.g., consider ways to reduce or eliminate exposure, and/or ways to cope when faced with NSSI exposure when/if it is unavoidable). Simple and straightforward psychoeducation about the impact of social learning and contagion on NSSI behavior may also be of use in treatment and allow for a collaborative approach to better understanding antecedents of NSSI in therapy. More targeted research is certainly needed to test existing science-based approaches for NSSI in the context of specifically addressing issues related to social contagion. However, established science-based approaches (cognitive-behavioral and/or dialectical behavior therapy) are well suited to include social contagion considerations as part of a treatment plan, for example, using cognitive-behavioral strategies to track and monitor the role that exposure to NSSI has on NSSI behavior (e.g., through exercises identifying antecedents, behaviors, and consequences of NSSI and/or using chain analysis exercises in the context of DBT; see Linehan, 2015). Finally, standard approaches to regulating risk behaviors should be utilized in group settings, such as discouraging discussion in the group about specific incidences of NSSI (e.g., the method used) and asking participants with recent lacerations/burns/etc. and/or scars to keep them covered while attending treatment in the group setting.

Conclusion

The study of social contagion factors in the development and maintenance of NSSI is a fascinating area of research, and one that certainly will benefit from continued examination. Research in this area can be advanced through more expansive views/definitions of social contagion and should include interdisciplinary collaborations between clinical researchers and, for example, researchers in the fields of public health, social psychology, and school psychology, among others. Additionally, the ever-expanding reach and impact of social media on our daily lives and behaviors, particularly among children and adolescents, cannot be underestimated in this particular case, while online exposure to NSSI remains a particular area of concern for those who may seek information and support in these somewhat less stigmatized and more anonymous forums, which to date remain largely unexplored and unregulated.

References

Andover, M. S., Morris, B. W., Wren, A., & Bruzese, M. (2012). The co-occurrence of non-suicidal self-injury among adolescents: Distinguishing risk factors and psychosocial correlates. *Child and Adolescent Psychiatry and Mental Health*, *6*(11), 11–17. https://doi.org/10.1186/1753-2000-6-11

Arendt, F., Scherr, S., & Romer, D. (2019). Effects of exposure to self-harm on social media: Evidence from a two-wave panel study among young adults. *New Media & Society*, *21*(11–12), 2422–2442. https://doi.org/10.1177%2F1461444819850106

Bandura, A. (1977). *Social learning theory*. Prentice Hall.

Bandura, A. (1986). *Social foundations of thought and action: A social cognitive theory*. Prentice Hall.

Barlow, D. H., Nock, M. K., & Hersen, M. (2009). *Single case experimental designs: Strategies for studying behavior change* (3rd ed.). Pearson.

Brickman, L. J., Ammerman, B. A., Look, A. E., Berman, M. E., & McCloskey, M. S. (2014). The relationship between non-suicidal self-injury and borderline personality disorder symptoms in a college sample. *Borderline Personality Disorder and Emotion Dysregulation*, *1*(14), 1–8. https://doi.org/10.1186/2051-6673-1-14

De Leo, D., Heller, T. (2004). Who are the kids who self-harm? An Australian self-report school survey. *Medical Journal of Australia*, *181*(3), 140–144. https://doi.org/10.5694/j.1326-5377.2004.tb06204.x

Deliberto, T. L., & Nock, M. K. (2008). Exploratory study of the correlates, onset, and offset of non-suicidal self-injury. *Archives of Suicide Research*, *12*(3), 219–231. https://doi.org/10.1080/13811110802101096

Ferrara, M., Terrinoni, A., & Williams, R. (2012). Non-suicidal self-injury (NSSI) in adolescent inpatients: Assessing personality features and attitude toward death. *Child and Adolescent Psychiatry and Mental Health*, *6*, Article 12. https://doi.org//10.1186/1753-2000-6-12

Hasking, P., Andrews, T., & Martin, G. (2013). The role of exposure to self-injury among peers in predicting later self-injury. *Journal of Youth and Adolescence, 42*(10), 1543–1556. https://doi.org/10.1007/s10964-013-9931-7

Hasking, P., & Rose, A. (2016). A preliminary application of social cognitive theory to nonsuicidal self-injury. *Journal of Youth and Adolescence, 14*(8), 1560–1574. https://dx.doi.org/10.1007/s10964-016-0449-7

Heath, N. L., Ross, S., Toste, J. R., Charlebois, A., & Nedecheva, T. (2009). Retrospective analysis of social factors and nonsuicidal self-injury among young adults. *Canadian Journal of Behavioural Science, 41*(3), 180–186. https://doi.org/10.1037/a0015732

Heilbron, N., Franklin, J. C., Guerry, J. D., & Prinstein, M. J. (2014). Social and ecological approaches to understanding suicidal behaviors and nonsuicidal self-injury. In M. K. Nock (Ed.), *The Oxford handbook of suicide and self-injury* (pp. 206–234). Oxford University Press.

Jarvi, S., Jackson, B., Swenson, L., & Crawford, H. (2013). The impact of social contagion on non-suicidal self-injury: A review of the literature. *Archives of Suicide Research, 17*(1), 1–19. https://doi.org/10.1080/13811118.2013.748404

Jarvi, S. M., Swenson, L. P., & Batejan, K. L. (2017). Motivation for and use of social networking sites: Comparisons among college students with and without histories of non-suicidal self-injury. *Journal of American College Health, 65*(5), 306–312. https://doi.org/10.1080/07448481.2017.1312410

Kiekens, G., Hasking, P., Nock, M. K., Boyes, M., Kirtley, O., Bruffaerts, R., Myin-Germeys, I., & Claes, L. (2020). Fluctuations in affective states and self-efficacy to resist non-suicidal self-injury as real-time predictors of non-suicidal self-injurious thoughts and behaviors. *Frontiers in Psychiatry, 11*, Article 214. https://doi.org/10.3389/fpsyt.2020.00214

Lewis, S. P., & Baker, T. (2011). The possible risks of self-injury websites: A content analysis. *Archives of Suicide Research, 15*(4), 390–396. https://doi.org/10.1080/13811118.2011.616154

Lewis, S. P., Heath, N. L., Michal, N. J., & Duggan, J. M. (2012). Non-suicidal self-injury, youth, and the Internet: What mental health professionals need to know. *Child and Adolescent Psychiatry and Mental Health, 6*(13), e1–e13. https://doi.org/10.1186/1753-2000-6-13

Linehan, M. M. (2015). *DBT skills training manual* (2nd ed.). Guilford Press.

Mars, B., Heron, J., Klonsky, E. D., Moran, P., O'Connor, R. C., Tilling, K., Wilkinson, P., & Gunnell, D. (2019). Predictors of future suicide attempt among adolescents with suicidal thoughts or non-suicidal self-harm: A population-based birth cohort study. *The Lancet Psychiatry, 6*(4), 327–337. https://doi.org/10.1016/S2215-0366(19)30030-6

Matthews, P. C. (1968). Epidemic self-injury in an adolescent unit. *International Journal of Social Psychiatry, 14*(2), 125–133. https://doi.org/10.1177/002076406801400206

Muehlenkamp, J. J., Hoff, E. R., Licht, J. G., Azure, J. A., & Hasenzahl, S. J. (2008). Rates of non-suicidal self-injury: A cross-sectional analysis of exposure. *Current Psychology, 27*(4), 234–241. https://doi.org/10.1007/s12144-008-9036-8

Nock, M. K., & Favazza, A. R. (2009). Non-suicidal self-injury: Definition and classification. In M. K. Nock (Ed.), *Understanding nonsuicidal self-injury* (pp. 9–18). American Psychological Association.

Nock, M. K., Holmberg, E. B., Photos, V. I., & Michel, B. D. (2007). Self-Injurious Thoughts and Behaviors Interview: Development, reliability, and validity in an adolescent sample. *Psychological Assessment, 19*(3), 309–317. https://doi.org/10.1037/1040-3590.19.3.309

Schwartz-Mette, R. A., & Lawrence, H. R. (2019). Peer socialization of non-suicidal self-injury in adolescents' close friendships. *Journal of Abnormal Child Psychology, 47*(11), 1851–1862. https://doi.org/10.1007/s10802-019-00569-8

Smith-Gowling, C., Knowles, S., & Hodge, S. (2018). Understanding experiences of the self-harm of others: A qualitative exploration of the views of young people with complex mental health needs. *Clinical Child Psychology and Psychiatry, 23*(4), 528–541. https://doi.org/10.1177/1359104518755216

Victor, S., & Klonsky, E. D. (2018) Understanding the social context of adolescent nonsuicidal self-injury. *Journal of Clinical Psychology, 74*(12), 2107–2116. https://doi.org/10.1002/jclp.22657

Whitlock, J. L., Powers, J. L., & Eckenrode, J. (2006). The virtual cutting edge: The internet and adolescent self-injury. *Developmental Psychology, 42*(3), 407–417. https://doi.org/10.1037/0012-1649.42.3.407

You, J., Lin, M. P., Fu, K., & Leung, F. (2013). The best friend and friendship group influence on adolescent nonsuicidal self-injury. *Journal of Abnormal Child Psychology, 41*(6), 993–1004. https://doi.org/10.1007/s10802-013-9734-z

Zelkowitz, R. L., Porter, A. C., Heiman, E. R., & Cole, D. A. (2017). Social exposure and emotion dysregulation: Main effects in relation to nonsuicidal self-injury. *Journal of Adolescence, 60*, 94–103. https://doi.org/10.1016/j.adolescence.2017.07.015

Zhu, L., Westers, N. J., Horton, S. E., King, J. D., Diederich, A., Stewart, S. M., & Kennard, B. D. (2016). Frequency of exposure to and engagement in non-suicidal self-injury among inpatient adolescents. *Archives of Suicide Research, 20*(4), 580–590. https://doi.org/10.1080/13811118.2016.1162240

CHAPTER 43

Assessing NSSI in Clinical and Community Settings

Charlotte Cliffe, Rosemary Sedgwick, Sophie Epstein, Catherine Polling, *and* Dennis Ougrin

> **Abstract**
>
> This chapter explores the assessment of non-suicidal self-injury (NSSI) in clinical and community settings. It mentions how NSSI is still subject to stigma and misunderstanding that could impair assessment if not adequately considered. Since NSSI is prevalent amongst all ages, professionals in community settings such as schools, universities, primary care or mental health settings will come into contact with NSSI. Assessment can take various forms, could include structured tools, and may be conducted by a range of professionals. Community detection and assessment of NSSI play a vital role in the identification of NSSI, which subsequently provides valuable opportunities to intervene. The chapter looks into the factors of engagement, confidentiality, suicidal intent and suicide risk.
>
> **Key Words:** non-suicidal self-injury, assessment, clinical settings, community settings, professionals, engagement, confidentiality, suicidal intent, suicide risk

Introduction to the Assessment of NSSI

This chapter focuses on the assessment of nonsuicidal self-injury (NSSI) in clinical and community settings. Depending on the exact setting, there may be existing guidelines to support this assessment, but given that it is still an emerging area, the evidence to support these guidelines maybe limited, therefore consistency between settings maybe challenging to navigate. NSSI is common, but still subject to stigma and misunderstanding, which could impair assessment if not adequately considered from the outset. NSSI is prevalent across the age span but is most common in adolescents and young adults (Plener et al., 2016). This means that professionals in community settings, be it school, university, primary care, or mental health settings will come into contact with NSSI.

NSSI is often described as a "direct and deliberate destruction of one's own body tissue in the absence of lethal intent"; examples include cutting, head banging and burning (Nock et al., 2010). One challenge with this definition, in both clinical and community settings, is separating those with and without intent of suicide, as some regard NSSI on a continuum with suicide (Selby et al., 2015). This is particularly supported by studies that demonstrate that both suicide attempt and NSSI frequently coexist (Nock et al., 2006). It has been argued that NSSI is associated with obtaining emotional relief, repetitively, rather than death-orientated thoughts, and that it is possible to separate and distinguish the two (Selby et al., 2015). Despite this, there is the practical challenge of determining intent within clinical settings, as individuals may report ambiguously (Selby et al., 2015), and reported intent for the same episode may fluctuate over time (Kapur et al., 2013).

Across Europe and Australia, The World Health Organisation's *International Classification of Diseases* definition of self-harm is most commonly adopted. Its criteria do not attempt to distinguish suicidal from nonsuicidal self-harm. UK national clinical guidance uses a definition of self-harm that includes both self-poisoning or self-injury and similarly does not distinguish types by presence of suicidal intent (National Institute for Health Care and Excellence, 2022). NSSI, as outlined in the *Diagnostic Statistical Manual of Mental Disorders* (DSM) does not include self-poisoning or self-harm with any level of suicidal intent, this being defined as a suicide attempt. For this chapter, we will refer to "NSSI" throughout. However, we have drawn on evidence relating to both NSSI and self-harm where this has relevance to NSSI assessment. This reflects the fact that in clinical practice, the distinction is often ambiguous. In addition, when we refer to NSSI, we have taken a broad definition as described above rather than the specific DSM-5 (fifth edition; American Psychiatric Association, 2013) definition which requires a certain frequency and relates to specific functions of the behavior, which may not be known at the point of assessment. We will be excluding content referring to self-injurious behavior in the context of intellectual disability or autism spectrum disorder (ASD), as this is considered outside the scope of this book.

NSSI in the Community

Community professionals may be the first to interact with an individual after NSSI and have a vital role in its detection. Much of the self-harming behavior occurring in the community does not result in any contact with hospital services and so remains largely undetected. This is described by the "Iceberg Model" of self-harm, which has three levels: fatal self-harm, hospital-presenting self-harm, and community-occurring self-harm. A large study of English adolescents found that in 12–14-year-olds, the rate ratio of hospital-presenting self-harm to community self-harm was 1:28 for males and 1:18 for females (Geulayov et al., 2018). This high prevalence of community occurring self-harm has also been echoed in the English Adult Psychiatric Morbidity survey, which found that one in four 16–24-year-old women have self-harmed at some point (twice the male rate), but the majority did not seek professional help afterward (McManus et al., 2016). Evidence such as this may not distinguish self-harm with suicidal intent from NSSI, but it remains a valuable illustration for the overall burden of self-harming behaviors.

Primary care professionals in the community such as general practitioners, pediatricians, and family doctors may be the first point of contact when an individual presents with NSSI. They may have the benefit of a preexisting relationship with the individual and a broader understanding of the context. There may also be additional challenges, for example, if individuals may be more secretive, or there are limitations on the time available for the assessment. If the assessment is not specifically for NSSI, professionals may incidentally identify concerns (e.g., through physical examination). Community detection and assessment of NSSI can play a vital role in the identification of NSSI and provide valuable opportunities to intervene. It is also important to note that a healthcare worker may not be the first person to interact with someone after NSSI and the information in this chapter may also be of relevance to other professionals when utilized within the scope of their role and setting. While it is unlikely for it to be possible or appropriate for a non-mental health professional to conduct a full psychosocial assessment, the information below will hopefully inform decision-making, such as when referral for more specialist assessment or a more appropriate setting may be required.

Engagement

A collaborative approach to the assessment of NSSI is important. NSSI is transdiagnostic and related to many dynamic psychological and social factors. To understand these and the presenting issue for an individual, rapport and freedom from judgment are essential. A curious, calm, and nonjudgmental approach is key. This will aid the collecting of information, formulation, or diagnosis and how the situation will be managed. Service users may have had previous poor, or even hostile, experiences of healthcare and it is important to be sensitive to this, as it may impact their willingness to engage or even contribute to the risk of repetition (MacDonald et al., 2020). Psychosocial assessment may include collecting a large amount of factual information but can also be an opportunity to provide a positive experience. Qualitive research has found that feeling judged during assessment impacted willingness to be open and seek help, whereas when professionals legitimized their distress there was potential for it to be a positive and cathartic experience, improving self-worth and confidence to seek help in future (Hunter et al., 2013).

Confidentiality

Confidentiality is a complex area in the assessment of NSSI. As a guiding principle, assessors should seek to assess the risk of imminent and serious harm to self and consider breaking confidentiality if these conditions are met. Acute risks could include further serious, but not life-threatening injury requiring medical attention, risk to others, or escalation to suicide. This is the reason for the importance of the assessment of intent and future plans. When assessing whether confidentiality may need to be broken, the patient's self-report of their intent and other objective factors (such as the severity of the harm inflicted and the social context) should be considered on balance.

When conducting an assessment, it is important to be clear and transparent with the individual about the limits of confidentiality. This will likely be impacted greatly by age, but in any circumstance, it is important to involve the individual in this process if confidentiality does need to be broken. It can be helpful to discuss this early in the assessment process and identify who might need to be included in the discussion (e.g., a parent, carer, partner or therapist). It is also important for the assessor to be aware of local safeguarding policies and the potential for other statutory services, such as social services, to be involved when a young person or adult with children presents with NSSI. This should be discussed with the individual, as fear of social services involvement may be a barrier to seeking mental health support (Polling et al., 2021).

Suicidal Intent and Suicide Risk

As the lack of suicidal intent may not be clear until assessment has begun, there may be some overlap with an assessment of suicidal behaviors. We are therefore including discussion of suicide risk in this chapter.

As mentioned above, determining whether an act of self-harm was carried out with or without suicidal intent can be challenging, and assessors should not be clouded by their own assumptions. For example, self-poisoning is a behavior often assumed to have suicidal intent and perceived as conferring greater risk of suicide than superficial NSSI. In an observational study by Geulayov et al. carried out in England, nonfatal self-harm (defined as "any act of intentional self-poisoning or self-injury, irrespective of the nature of the motivation including degree of suicidal intent") was measured, and clinical episodes were grouped and linked to mortality register data for up to 15 years following presentation. In those presenting to the hospital after self-cutting, the likelihood of later suicide was found to be comparable with self-poisoning when involving the arm/wrist. Cutting of other body parts posed even greater risk of suicide, particularly the neck, which caried a fourfold greater chance of subsequent suicide relative to self-poisoning (Geulayov et al., 2021). We cannot infer the role of intent from these findings, though it does underline the importance of not underestimating risk associated with self-cutting and also suggests that there may be important differences between various presentations of self-cutting, which should be considered along with the self-reported intent and context of the presentation. This might be particularly relevant in cases where the individual is struggling, or not willing to discuss their behavior in detail.

NSSI can serve various functions, one of which may be to alleviate negative affect (Plener et al., 2016). For those engaging in regular NSSI, there may also be a habituation to pain, increasing the risk of more violent or severe attempts at harming oneself (Anestis et al., 2013). Method of NSSI is an important component of assessment, as certain methods (e.g., cutting) and certain subgroups (e.g., those with substance use disorders) have shown greater association with suicide attempt (Baer et al., 2020). An individual who has one or more psychiatric disorders, has received treatment for mental health problems, and/or has been a victim of childhood maltreatment is more likely to report NSSI (Brown et al., 2018; Liu, 2021; Plener et al., 2016). This highlights the importance of thorough assessment, both of NSSI itself and the wider social and psychological context. Importantly, there is a higher risk of suicide or attempt following NSSI (Guan et al., 2012). Prior history of NSSI was associated with a significantly increased risk of suicide attempts, emerging as the strongest known risk factor in a large meta-analysis which also included suicidal ideation (Ribeiro et al., 2016). Rates are estimated as high as a 30–50 fold increased risk of death within the year after a hospital presentation for self-harm(National Institute for Health Care and Excellence, 2022. However, it is important to remember that despite these high relative risks, because suicide remains a rare event these factors are still only marginally better than chance at predicting suicide when taken in isolation. All of the above are important aspects of a comprehensive assessment and are described in more detail below.

Professional Guidance

The United Kingdom's (UK), National Health Service (NHS) aims to set a consistent approach to recommendations around assessment and treatment of self-harm in the UK, including NSSI. Current UK guidelines on assessment are produced by the National Institute for Health and Care Excellence (NICE) and are relevant to children, young people and adultswho have self-harmed (National Institute for Health Care and Excellence, 2022). These guidelines are freely available and are utilized by professionals in a variety of settings. The key components of the assessment in both clinical and community settings are applicable to primary care (i.e., general practitioners) staff in educational settings, the criminal justice system and accident and emergency (A&E) and hospital settings. Table 43.1 highlights the quality statements that are deemed essential to the assessment and treatment of patients presenting with self-injury. Most pertinent to this guide is the acknowledgement that assessment should consider physical, psychological, and social circumstances and treat patients with compassion and dignity, this last point acknowledging the fact that patients presenting with NSSI are often subject to stigma from both within and outside the mental health profession.

Table 43.1 Summary of Assessment Questions	
History of NSSI	Age onset, duration, frequency
Triggers	Relationship conflict, emotional distress, social triggers
Outline NSSI	Method, body location, damage, psychological function
Consequences	Biological, psychological, and social (i.e., help-seeking, remorse)
Psychiatric comorbidity	Mood, anxiety, eating patterns, drug and alcohol history, personality disorder screening
Coping mechanisms	Social support, safety plans, harm minimization, distraction
Safeguarding	Children at home, domestic conflict or abuse
Risk assessment	Suicidal intent, hopelessness, depression, physical health, male

The UK guidelines do not recommend the use of any structured tools or any global risk stratification to either predict future NSSI or determine who should be discharged (National Institute for Health Care and Excellence, 2022). Risk assessment tools for self-harm used in practice in the UK are often developed locally. Graney et al included more than 150 tools used across the NHS in their mixed methods study, though none of these specifically looked at NSSI, and no one was considered more reliable than others. These tools mostly aimed to predict future behavior, stratify risk, and guide management, and although almost all included self-harm and suicide, only 47% collected data on suicidal intent (Graney et al., 2020). Similarly in child and adolescent services, predictive risk assessment tools varied significantly and no one tool has been identified as superior or more accurate (Harris et al., 2019). These will be explored in the chapter under the heading title: "Structured assessment tools."

Psychosocial Assessment

An assessment must be undertaken by a healthcare worker to assess the risk and needs of anyone who has engaged in NSSI; however, such an assessment may also be informative to non-mental health professionals who come into contact with individuals following NSSI and who need to offer support and make decisions about onwards referral. This assessment is important to not only understand and engage the individual but also to manage risk, in view of the high risk of suicide or a suicide attempt after NSSI (National Institute for Health Care and Excellence, 2012). At assessment, it is important to determine the relationship of NSSI with suicidal thoughts or intentions, but first it is important to discuss the clinician approach, as building a therapeutic relationship is key to the assessment of NSSI.

Clinician Approach

The challenge for a clinician can be balancing an informal response, which will promote trust, with assessing the details of the NSSI. It has been recommended that clinicians respond without causing the patient to feel judged, criticized, or condemned for the NSSI to ensure they do not worsen the patient's distress (Walsh, 2007). For the patient to feel comfortable to provide information, it is important not to respond with shock or disgust. It has been suggested that responding with a "non-judgmental, respectfully curious tone with a low-key demeanour" provides the most therapeutic approach (Walsh, 2007, p. 1061). Once this has been established, there are several key topics to be explored to gather details.

Detailed Assessment of NSSI Episode

This section outlines in detail areas to be covered when undertaking psychosocial assessment of NSSI. The information in this chapter is designed to be of use in a variety of settings and applicable across the age range, though some elements will be of more relevance than others depending on the experience of the assessor, the setting, and the individual being assessed.

First, it is important to detail the most recent episode of NSSI.

PSYCHOLOGICAL FUNCTION

Understanding the *psychological function* of NSSI is important as it will determine the intervention required by the clinician. There is considerable evidence some people use NSSI to regulate emotional distress and interpersonal relationships; in particular at reducing intense feelings of anxiety, anger, sadness, depression, guilt, or shame. The most common reason cited is internal emotional regulation, and others cite interpersonal motivation, such as communicating distress to peers, to resolve conflicts or generate intimacy in relationships (Nock & Prinstein, 2004; Walsh, 2007). A four-function model has been suggested (see Hird et al., this volume), incorporating reasons for NSSI into the following four categories: automatic intrapersonal positive reinforcement (NSSI results in a positive thought or emotions), automatic intrapersonal negative reinforcement (where NSSI results in reduction in unpleasant thoughts or emotions), interpersonal (or "social") positive reinforcement (NSSI elicits care and support from others), and social negative reinforcement (where NSSI results in someone reducing their negative behavior [e.g., bullying]) (Nock et al., 2010; Nock & Prinstein, 2004). It should not, however, be assumed that NSSI is to regulate emotions as it could also relate to underlying mental disorder—for example, NSSI in response to delusional thought content or hallucinatory experiences or in relation to compulsions associated with obsessive compulsive disorder (OCD). Understanding the psychological function and purpose the NSSI serves and its relation to other psychiatric symptoms will help target treatment and support.

METHOD

It is important to enquire about the *method* of NSSI and extent of physical injury. More violent methods or severe wounds may indicate a higher level of distress, but this is not always the case. Individuals may move from the low-lethality methods to the higher-lethality methods, or use multiple methods concurrently. It has been suggested that repetitive NSSI increases the risk by habituation to pain (Selby et al., 2015). Methods may also convey something about the nature of the NSSI. For example, self-injury requiring access to means of harm, such as blades, lighters, or ligatures, may indicate a degree of premeditation. More spontaneous actions such as punching, scratching, or head banging could indicate higher levels of impulsivity. As clinicians may most commonly encounter NSSI by cutting and the majority of research in NSSI is in this method, there is a risk that alternative or less common methods may be overlooked, or considered less significant. The acceptability of being identified as having mental health problems might also be an influence in the method of NSSI; for example, young men might find provoking violence from others as a means of making NSSI more acceptable, especially if it might impact their standing in the community (Polling et al., 2021). In order to detect self-harm in groups less commonly thought of in connection to NSSI (e.g., young men), it may be useful for assessors to think and ask about a wider range of behaviors and approach atypical presentations with an open mind and curiosity about potential causes. It is also important to fully assess and document each specific form of NSSI and not to assume that their self-injurious behavior is limited to the presenting act or form.

BODY SITE

Another important question is *body location*; it is more common for NSSI to be on the extremities or abdomen. NSSI presentations to hospital are most commonly due to lacerations to the arm or wrist. Other body sites, particularly the neck, have been associated with higher risk of suicide (Geulayov et al., 2021). Gender does seem to have an impact; females more commonly opt for arms and legs. Injuries to the chest, genitals, and face are more common in males than in females (Sornberger et al., 2012). It is also possible that the site of NSSI may relate to underlying pathology. This could be specific, such as NSSI to an area such as the face, eyes, breasts, or genitals representing some connection to the underlying pathology (i.e., psychosis, trauma, or dysphoria about elements of physical appearance). In more general terms, NSSI in concealed locations may indicate greater levels of risk and is more commonly in direct response to psychiatric symptoms, physical health problems, or being the victim of crime or abuse (Gardner et al., 2020). It is also worth considering that people may engage with different types of NSSI, and may switch between concealed and visible sites, so thorough history is essential (Gardner et al., 2020). The significance of self-injury site is further described in Gardner et al. (this volume).

TIMING

Other details that must be included would be the *timing* of the episode—for example, the duration of the episode, time of day, and gaps between recent episodes. Being aware of the high-risk times of the day, such as nighttime, or common proximal triggers might allow an opportunity to intervene.

LOCATION OF NSSI

Finally, inquiring about *where the NSSI takes place*—for example, NSSI undertaken alone in a locked bedroom in secret—is important, as it may allow for interventions such as keeping the door open with a view to facilitate behavior change (Walsh, 2007). Whether there are other people around may also be of relevance to understanding the episode.

History of NSSI

Past history of NSSI includes questions about age of onset, the methods of NSSI (cutting, burning, hitting, etc.), duration, frequency, and physical damage (National Institute for Health Care and Excellence, 2011). Inquiry about duration is important as longer duration of NSSI would be more difficult to challenge and stop (Fox et al., 2015; Walsh, 2007). In terms of age of onset, there is some evidence that those who begin self-harming at a younger age may have a higher risk of suicide attempt or recurrent severe NSSI in the future (Muehlenkamp et al., 2019). Furthermore, repetitive methods that cause more physical damage, such as scars, indicate a higher risk of suicide (Burke et al., 2016).

TRIGGERS AND ANTECEDENTS

It is important to understand the antecedents that lead to an incident of NSSI, otherwise known as "triggers," which could be divided broadly into biological, psychological, and social factors. Social "triggers" (e.g., relationship conflict, breakup, disappointment, or reminders of past trauma) may result in NSSI and may coexist with biological factors such as intoxication, fatigue, insomnia, or illness (Walsh, 2007). However, intrapersonal factors could also be important and the trigger could be unrelated to environmental factors but associated with unwanted internal states or sensations (Taylor et al., 2018). Identifying these antecedents could provide opportunities to therapeutically target high-risk periods, circumstances, or thoughts, and will aid management planning around risk.

CONSEQUENCES

The assessment could again be divided into biological, psychological, and social questions, which may, or may not, relate to the antecedent. A biological assessment involves questions about the physical sensation post NSSI—for example, any pain? Was the pain pleasant or unpleasant? Were the wounds tended to (e.g., cleaned and bandaged) (Walsh, 2007)? If the desired outcome was to relieve distressing thoughts or sensations or to regulate emotions, was this achieved? If the function of the NSSI was interpersonal (i.e., to communicate distress or elicit support), it is important to explore how others reacted and the impact of their reaction. Cognitions following the episode such as remorse and neutral or positive thoughts are important as they may also indicate the likelihood of repetition. NSSI as a means of hurting or punishing others is uncommon, but, as the management of this type would differ from the type primarily related to emotional regulation, it is important to detect (Taylor et al., 2018). In conditions such as OCD, the relationship may be complex, particularly if repeated NSSI is compulsive and associated with relief from obsessional thoughts (Palombini et al., 2021). This would also be a situation where the management would differ significantly.

Psychiatric Comorbidity

Research demonstrates that those who have psychiatric comorbidities such as depression, in particular, thoughts of hopelessness, have an increased risk of a subsequent suicide attempt (Fox et al., 2015; National Institute for Health Care and Excellence, 2004). It is also important to screen for comorbidity as another target for intervention, as this could increase the risk of NSSI, or subsequent risk of suicide attempt. In particular, mood symptoms, disturbed eating patterns, concerns around body image, and anxiety should all be screened for as depression, anxiety disorders, eating disorders, and personality disorders are all strongly associated with NSSI (Bentley et al., 2015; Cliffe et al., 2020). It is also crucial to inquire about any alcohol or drug misuse; these have also been associated with an increased risk of repetitive NSSI and an eventual suicide attempt (Ames, 2017; Borges et al., 2017; National Institute for Health Care and Excellence, 2011).

Coping Mechanisms and Social Networks in Place

It is important to assess social support networks in place already and any need for occupational rehabilitation, social care, or support with any personal or financial problems. This can ensure that "safety plans" (Stanley & Brown, 2012) or treatment pathways can include the appropriate social support (National Institute for Health Care and Excellence, 2011). It is also worth exploring what mechanisms the patient has developed to cope with NSSI; for example, some may find distraction or techniques to minimize harm from NSSI helpful (National Institute for Health Care and Excellence, 2011; Shaw, 2012).

Safeguarding and Social Circumstances

This may relate to the individual if they are a child or considered a vulnerable adult. It is important also to inquire about any children in the house such as siblings or dependent children of the individual, again to determine whether extra support from social care is required (National Institute for Health Care and Excellence, 2022). As well, research has demonstrated that those presenting to services, particularly in the emergency room, are more likely to have experienced domestic abuse (Boyle et al., 2006).

Suicide Risk

Assessing risk of suicide or suicide attempt is a key component to the psychosocial assessment of NSSI. It may also be covered in other contexts such as past psychiatric history and in exploration of the NSSI episode at presentation, but it should also be explored in its own right. Assessment of suicide risk should include consideration of clinical and demographic features associated with further NSSI, suicide attempts, and suicide. Factors such as male gender and physical health problems increase the risk of completed suicide in men who self-harm (Chan et al., 2016). Other psychological factors such as depression, hopelessness, or suicidal intent must also be screened for, as they may indicate an increase in risk (Fox et al., 2015; National Institute for Health Care and Excellence, 2004). Burke et al. (this volume) discuss differentiating assessments for suicide risk as well as NSSI behaviors.

Risk Management Planning

An important aspect of the assessment of NSSI is risk management planning. Safety planning interventions have been found to reduce suicidal behaviors and improve engagement (Stanley et al., 2018). Examples of elements that may be included in a risk management plan, sometimes referred to as a "safety plan" or "crisis plan," are reducing access to means of self-harm; distraction techniques, which could be used when the individual experiences the urge to harm themselves; and developing a plan with the patient regarding sources of help and support in the case of distress or crisis, including friends and family as well as formal services (Stanley & Brown, 2012). Identifying carers or people who can support the person who has presented with NSSI is an important part of safety planning. When discussing reducing access to means this may depend on the age and environment the patient is in but should include keeping sharps (or any means by which NSSI is inflicted) away from easy access or, in the case of children, locked away by caregivers. Even a few minutes may allow time for the emotion to pass and provide some time to reflect or seek out distraction or an alternative coping strategy. When discussing distraction techniques, this can be a nice way to explore the patients' hobbies and interests, or they may find techniques such as breathing exercises or meditation more helpful.

Risk management plans can come in many forms, but the key is for it to be personal to the patient and their circumstances and to consider factors that have been explored in the assessment, such as common triggers, the function of the NSSI, and the methods used. The UK NICE guidance states that a risk management plan should include the following components (National Institute for Health Care and Excellence, 2012):

- Address each of the long-term and more immediate risks identified in the risk assessment.
- Address the specific factors (psychological, pharmacological, social, and relational) identified in the assessment as associated with increased risk, with the agreed aim of reducing the risk of repetition of self-harm and/or the risk of suicide.
- Include a crisis plan outlining self-management strategies and how to access services during a crisis when self-management strategies fail.
- Ensure that the risk management plan is consistent with the long-term treatment strategy.

Structured Assessment Tools

A number of structured assessment tools have been developed to aid in the assessment of NSSI. The purpose of some tools is to provide a framework for the thorough assessment of a recent or past episode or episodes of NSSI. These tools may contain questions relating to any or all the domains described in relation to clinical assessment, such as the details of the episode itself, triggers, functions, and lethality. Many of these tools assess both suicidal and nonsuicidal self-harm and include questions to help distinguish the two. These tools can be in interview or questionnaire format.

The Self-injurious Thoughts and Behaviors Interview (SITBI) (Nock et al., 2007) is an example of a structured assessment tool that aims to assess details of a range of self-injurious thoughts and behaviors including NSSI. It has been evaluated on a sample of adolescents and young adults and includes questions on several domains including frequency, functions, severity, precipitants, and characteristics such as peer influence and drug and alcohol use. There are also tools that specifically assess the functions of NSSI, to aid the understanding of the reasons why an individual may harm themselves. An example is the Inventory of Statements about Self-injury (ISAS), which assesses 13 potential functions of NSSI: affect regulation, antidissociation, antisuicide, autonomy, interpersonal boundaries, interpersonal influence, marking distress, peer-bonding, self-care, self-punishment, revenge, sensation seeking, and toughness (Klonsky & Glenn, 2009).

Another group of structured assessment tools, rather than aiding a comprehensive assessment, is specifically for the purpose of assessing risk of repeat NSSI, suicide attempts, or completed suicide. Some tools may serve both purposes simultaneously—providing a framework for conducting a thorough assessment and understanding future risk. An example of this is the Self-Harm Behavior Questionnaire (Gutierrez et al., 2001), a structured self-report questionnaire which assesses a range of self-harm and suicide-related behaviors including NSSI and includes questions on frequency, methods, history, intent, and risk of future episodes.

In terms of assessment of risk, neither NICE nor Cochrane, two main sources of clinical guidance in the UK, recommends using structured tools to replace clinical decision-making on risk assessment and management after an episode of NSSI (National Institute for Health Care and Excellence, 2012). Similarly, the advice in New Zealand and Australia is to focus on clinical assessment rather than relying on one tool (Carter et al., 2016). Guidelines in the United States suggest that if a tool is valid and reliable it can be a useful component of a full evaluation but that there is not one simple scale leading to a score that would substitute clinical judgment (Office of the Surgeon General & National Action Alliance for Suicide Prevention, 2012).

Risk Assessment Tools

Systematic reviews that have compared the content of tools that assess risk of future NSSI or suicidal behavior have demonstrated a lack of consistency between them (Quinlivan et al., 2014) and that scores are poor at predicting future NSSI or suicide (Carter et al., 2017; Quinlivan et al., 2016).

In adults, there are several tools that have been developed to assess risk and determine clinical management post NSSI. The performance of these tools is commonly assessed using measures of diagnostic accuracy including sensitivity and positive predictive value (PPV) (see table 43.2 for further explanation). Recent systematic reviews of studies assessing the performance of these tools have determined that there is not one tool superior to another (Carter et al., 2017; Quinlivan et al., 2016). The difficulties in using the tools

Table 43.2 Explanation of Terms

Terms	Explanation
Sensitivity	Proportion of individuals who are identified as high risk of repeating self-harm by the test and then repeat self-harm
Specificity	Proportion of people who are identified as low risk of repeating self-harm and do not repeat self-harm
Positive predictive value (PPV)	The probability a person who is identified at risk of repeat self-harm then goes on to repeat self-harm
Negative predictive value (NPV)	The probability a person identified as low risk of repeat self-harm then does not repeat self-harm
Odds ratio	The likelihood of the outcome of self-harm as identified by the tool. Scores over 1 identify an increase in likelihood
Hazards ratio	The likelihood of an event such as self-harm when compared to a control group as identified by the tool

are consistently reported as generating scores that either produce too many false positives (leading to overtreatment and overuse of resources) or lack sensitivity (meaning high numbers of false negatives, leading to misclassifying individuals as low risk who then go onto self-harm).

Findings from a large systematic review and meta-analysis of tools to predict risk of suicidal behaviors, which included 24 tools in use in the United States, 13 in the UK, 12 in Europe, and 3 across Australia/New Zealand, found that the pooled PPVs were low for suicide at 5.5% (95% CI 3.9%–7.9%), self-harm 26.3% (95% CI 21.8%–31.3%) and self-harm with suicide 35.9% (95% CI 25.8%–47.4%) (Carter et al., 2017). Tools were evaluated for a range of different populations, mostly high-risk clinical samples, including many with a history of self-harm. Such tools could potentially be used to assess risk of future suicidal behavior in those who present with NSSI; however, the conclusion was that in view of such low predictive values, a clinical assessment with appropriate follow-up is much safer and more productive, particularly focusing on a "needs-based approach" (Carter et al., 2017). This would focus on reducing exposures to any potential risk factors and ensuring that appropriate interventions such as focused treatment, family support, and therapeutic interventions are provided regardless of predicted risk.

Another systematic review, focusing on 11 tools specific to the prediction of repeat self-harm, determined that there were significant differences between the tools in terms of accuracy in relation to their sensitivity and PPV ranging from 6% (95% CI 5–6%) to 97% (95% CI 94%–98%) in sensitivity and from 5% (95% CI 3% to 9%) to 84% (95% CI 80% to 87%) in PPV (Quinlivan et al., 2016). These studies were conducted in Canada, Australia, the UK, and Sweden, mostly emergency room settings.

Within this review, the tools with the highest PPVs such as the Barratt Impulsivity Scale (BIS) (Randall et al., 2012) and Global Severity Index (GSI) (Randall et al.,

2011) had the lowest sensitivity in detecting repeat self-harm; therefore, they were more likely to miss those potentially at risk. However, the most sensitive tools such as Manchester Self-Harm Rule (MSHR) (Cooper et al., 2007) and ReACT Self-Harm Rule (ReACT) (Steeg et al., 2012) had the lowest PPV so were more likely to overtreat those at risk.

There are also risk assessment tools specifically developed for young people. A recent review identified 10 different tools being used by clinicians among patients aged between 10 and 25 years, in clinical settings such as inpatient and outpatient facilities or home treatment programs (Harris et al., 2019). The ability of the tools to predict a further self-harm or even suicide attempt varied significantly from 27% to 95.8% in sensitivity (Harris et al., 2019). However, the tools varied in the setting, outcome measures, length of follow-up, and method for evaluation of effectiveness. As for the adult tools, a particular challenge is that the tools with the highest sensitivity had lower PPVs.

One might argue that it would be preferable to have more sensitive tools to avoid missing anyone who might be at risk, but this could also lead to overtreatment for those not at risk. Equally important, evidence from the UK suggests that services already struggle to provide adequate psychosocial assessment and therapeutic follow-up to many of those presenting to health services following self-harm and felt to be at risk. Given this, thought needs to be given to what purpose is served by tools identifying an expanded group of at-risk individuals within resource contexts where already overstretched health systems may not be able to offer them any additional input.

A UK-based mixed-method study more recently aimed to understand the views of patients, clinicians, and family members on the use of structured tools to predict self-harm and suicide. There were 156 tools included across various trusts (Graney et al., 2020). Similar concerns around lack of consistency among the tools was highlighted. Other concerns included a risk of false reassurance, the tools being time-consuming, a risk of dehumanizing the interaction between clinician and patient as well as focusing on a cross-sectional risk rather than assessing the risk over time, which is preferable as risk fluctuates (Graney et al., 2020). However, there were some positive aspects such as facilitating communication in difficult circumstances (Graney et al., 2020). In conclusion, when assessing NSSI, the key is to integrate multiple approaches, considering the setting, the patient, and the background of the assessor. Risk assessment tools may have a role in particular settings and situations but are unlikely to be a substitute for a good history, as outlined earlier in this chapter.

Alternative Approaches to the Assessment of NSSI

It has been argued that a dynamic approach to risk assessment over time, while the patient is engaged in treatment, rather than reliance on a tool that captures a "snapshot" in time, is the most accurate approach (National Institute for Health Care and Excellence, 2022). This has been described as a "needs-based approach"—encouraging personalization and modifying risk factors (Graney et al., 2020). There are a number of possible therapeutic approaches that would facilitate this.

Ecological Momentary Assessment

Ecological momentary assessment (EMA) is an approach to assessment which specifically aims to collect information on individuals' behaviors and experiences in real time using repeated sampling. By doing this, rather than a single-point-in-time retrospective report, EMA aims to minimize recall bias and to tries to understand processes that influence behavior in real-world contexts. EMA uses a range of approaches including written and electronic diaries and physiological sensors. (Shiffman et al., 2008).

A systematic review identified 23 studies using EMA in those engaged in NSSI. Most studies investigated daily life factors which might influence the occurrence of NSSI. Of these, the majority have focused on the emotional context, but others have investigated the cognitive and situational context of NSSI (Rodríguez-Blanco et al., 2018). By using EMA, it may be possible to identify warning signals for NSSI which could be used by clinicians or other professionals to guide management and intervene to reduce risk. The studies of EMA in NSSI populations, however, have so far been short term, with small samples and mainly in adults (Rodríguez-Blanco et al., 2018). It also may be the case that sophisticated data analysis methods such as machine learning are required in order to interpret the complex longitudinal data gathered by an EMA approach (Gee et al., 2020). Therefore, further research is needed to gain a better understanding of the utility of this approach to NSSI assessment.

Implicit Associations

The Implicit Association Test (IAT) is an approach that assesses individual's implicit associations with NSSI, death, and suicide methods (Glenn et al., 2019). The Death IAT for example, measures reaction times when classifying words to measure implicit associations between death and self. For example, a study in psychiatric ED patients found that those who had attempted suicide hold significantly stronger implicit associations between death and self than those without a history of suicide attempt (Nock et al., 2010). IATs also exist for self-injury by cutting and suicide. A study in the United States found that those with a history of suicide attempt and NSSI had stronger implicit associations for self and cutting, self and suicide, and self and death compared to those with no history of self-harm. The self-injury IAT for example, performed with a sensitivity of 53% and positive predictive value of 82% in predicting the presence of lifetime NSSI (Glenn et al., 2017).

IATs are therefore a potential tool for clinicians to aid an ongoing risk assessment for repeat NSSI, suicide, and suicide attempts in those with a history of NSSI. A potential advantage of this approach is that it could provide additional data about NSSI risk in situations where individuals may lack insight into their difficulties or future risk, or where they may feel there are reasons to conceal their intent to harm themselves for fear of negative consequences such as stigma or they wish to avoid hospital admission (Dickstein et al., 2015; Millner et al., 2019). However, this should be considered a potential supplement to careful exploration of individuals' own accounts. Future utility of IAT-based tools is not yet clear in view of a number of limitations including the cross-sectional nature of many studies used to test implicit associations, and therefore their ability to predict future events needs further investigation (Glenn et al., 2017).

Therapeutic Assessment

This approach to assessment combines information gathering with a brief intervention, aimed to improve engagement with follow-up. Follow-up is particularly important since there are high rates of nonadherence with follow-up and treatment in those who self-harm (Trautman, Stewart, & Morishima, 1993), and non-adherence is in turn associated with poor outcomes (Votta & Manion, 2004). Therapeutic assessment (TA) is based on the cognitive analytic therapy paradigm. It consists of several components, first conducting a standard psychosocial history and risk assessment, then a 30-minute intervention which includes consideration of reciprocal roles, core pain, and maladaptive procedures, identifying a target problem, considering and enhancing motivation for change, and exploring ways of breaking vicious cycles identified (Ougrin, Ng, & Low, 2008). This process is manualized and has been tested in a randomized controlled trial of 70 participants, with controls receiving a standard psychosocial assessment only. This trial showed that the TA group were significantly more likely to attend their first follow-up appointment 83% versus 49%, OR 5.12, 95% CI (1.49 to 17.55) and more likely to attend four or more treatment sessions: 40% versus 11%, OR 5.19, 95% CI (2.22 to 12.10) compared to the assessment-as-usual group (Ougrin et al., 2011).

Other Therapeutic Modalities

The main treatment modalities for NSSI include cognitive behavioral therapy (CBT), dialectical behavioral therapy (DBT), mentalization-based therapy (MBT), and motivational interviewing (MI) and all contain aspects of ongoing assessment including risk assessment during the course of therapy. CBT and DBT, for example, use tools such a diary cards to monitor risk and risk events and MBT includes ongoing assessment focusing on the interpersonal space between the therapist and the patient. MI specifically for NSSI has not been widely evaluated, but it is acknowledged as a useful tool for a variety of problem behaviors (Burke et al., 2003). MI uses tools such as scales to perform ongoing assessment and aid therapy. For example, an individual may be asked to rate on a scale of 1 to 10 "how important is living to you right now?" (Britton et al., 2011). Where the risk of further NSSI or suicide attempts is detected at assessment, MI could be useful at assessing risk while evoking protective motivation to reduce it (Hoy et al., 2016).

Assessing NSSI in Different Settings and in Specific Groups

Clinical assessment guidance for NSSI is largely developed for mental health professionals conducting assessments in clinical settings such as EDs or outpatient clinics. Similarly, most structured tools have been developed and tested in ED settings. There are developments to improve validity of measures across different ages and populations. An example of this is evidence from a nonreferred community sample, which showed strong validity for both in-person and online assessment of suicide and self-harming thoughts and behaviors, using a revised version of the Self-Injurious Thoughts and Behaviors Interview (SITBI-R) (Fox et al., 2020). Time permitting, much of the content of the clinical assessment and the structured tools described above can be applied to assessment of NSSI in multiple settings and by a range of professionals. This could include physical and mental health inpatient settings, primary care, social care, and schools.

An important group to consider in the assessment of NSSI is children and adolescents. In particular, this is due to the fact that NSSI is most common among adolescents and young adults, with the most common age of onset between 12 and 14 years (Cipriano et al., 2017). In the assessment of NSSI in young people, particularly those under the age of 18, it is important to consider others who should be involved in the assessment, such as parents/caregivers, other trusted adults, or friends. It is important, however, to conduct at least part of the assessment with the young person alone, to provide an opportunity for them to voice issues they may be uncomfortable or feel unsafe discussing with someone else present, particularly if there are safeguarding issues. As discussed above, the distinction between suicidal and nonsuicidal self-harm is often difficult to determine, and this is particularly challenging for children and adolescents who may not have a clear idea of the motivation for an act of NSSI. There are a number of other specific settings outside of healthcare settings that guidance in the UK is available for ((National Institute for Health Care and Excellence, 2022)

Primary care/family medicine (National Institute for Health Care and Excellence, 2022)

If a person presents to primary care after an episode of self-harm a referral to mental health services for a full assessment with consent should be considered. This should be prioritized when:

1. Distress or concerns are rising, high or sustained
2. Frequency or degree of self harm is increasing
3. The assessor in primary care is concerned
4. The person asks for support from mental health services
5. Distress amongst family members are rising, high or sustained

The primary care assessor should offer regular appointments with their GP for review of NSSI, a medicine review, information given to the person about voluntary and social care sector support and any care for comorbid illness.

Professionals in other sectors (National Institute for Health Care and Excellence, 2022
This section is particularly useful for non healthcare professionals such as a teacher or staff in the criminal justice system where NSSI behavior is also prevalent.

- Work collaboratively with the person to ensure their views are understood
- Address immediate physical needs and call for emergency services if necessary or external medical support
- Seek advice from healthcare professional or social care practitioners, including a referral if necessary
- Ensure the person is aware of sources of support such as charities and mental health helplines available to them locally
- Address any safeguarding issues and refer to the correct team for safeguarding if necessary

It is also advised the professional determines how severe the injury is and how urgent the treatment required is, the person's emotional and mental state, any immediate concern to the person's safety, whether the person already has a care or safety plan in place and any safeguarding concerns.

Schools and educational settings (National Institute for Health Care and Excellence, 2022

Educational settings are advised to have policies and procedures in place for staff supporting students who self harm. This includes

- How to identify NSSI
- How to assess the students needs
- What to do if a student self harms
- How to support the student's friends and peer group

It is recommended a designated lead is responsible to ensure the policies are implemented and support staff individually who may need to implement them.

Future Directions for Research, Based on Current Evidence

Co-production
Given that, as mentioned above, NSSI is often misunderstood and remains subject to stigma within health professions as well as wider society, the involvement in research of those with lived experience of NSSI is crucial. Even regardless of stigma, in order to gain a detailed and accurate understanding of NSSI, the evidence base requires contributions that are led by and co-produced with those with experience of NSSI. Such research helps to ensure that the research questions most relevant and important to those with lived experience of NSSI are being investigated.

Implementation Science and Health Services Research

Another important area of research is to understand to what extent policies and guidelines for the assessment of NSSI are implemented in practice. For example, a qualitative survey with patients and carers in Australia and New Zealand found that many reported not receiving a psychosocial assessment following self-harm. Reasons reported included patients themselves declining an assessment due to long waiting times or feeling unsafe in the ED as well as not being offered an assessment, being excluded due to being intoxicated, or not reaching clinical thresholds. (Millner et al., 2019) Understanding the reasons why certain individuals, groups, or populations are not receiving appropriate assessment for NSSI and identifying the aspects of health systems which contribute to the deficiencies in provision will provide important information on which to base service improvement initiatives or implementation strategies to improve NSSI assessment.

Implementation of evidence-based assessment tools for NSSI must be based on the principles of generalizability of the available evidence; applicability of the evidence to diverse patients; involvement of multiple stakeholders; relying on detailed, step-by-step implementation plan; identifying barriers to implementation; and using implementation strategies such as quality improvement, structured feedback, training, and supervision to achieve sustainability.

Machine Learning

The complex nature of factors likely to contribute to the occurrence of NSSI makes it difficult to design a universal assessment tool both for understanding causes, triggers, or functions and for predicting risk. In terms of risk prediction in NSSI, as described in the section "Structured Assessment Tools," none have so far succeeded in achieving an accurate and clinically significant prediction of NSSI or other risk behaviors. Machine learning, rather than relying on relatively simple, theoretically driven models, where several predictors of importance are chosen by researchers, has the potential to create much more complex models (Fox et al., 2019; Yarkoni & Westfall, 2017). More detail on this approach can be found in Wang et al, this volume.

Digital Monitoring Technologies

Another area of work in developing new ways to help identify and predict NSSI is through the use of smartphones, wearable devices, and other digital monitoring technologies. (Melbye et al., 2020) Research in this area remains in its fairly early stages, with some studies exploring the feasibility and acceptability of such approaches. Kleiman and colleagues, for example, tested the acceptability of using wearable physiological monitors among suicidal adolescent inpatients, with a view to the possibility of such technology being used to identify physiological changes associated with suicidal thoughts (Kleiman et al., 2019). Malott et al. conducted a study on a small number of individuals ($N = 4$) to test whether wearable accelerometer devices could identify self-harming behavior and distinguish this from other nonharmful activities. The device had a preliminary classification accuracy of 80% (Malott et al., 2015). Kennard and colleagues used a smartphone app to help participants discharged from hospital monitor their emotions and provide personalized strategies, and although this pilot study did not show a significant reduction in further suicide attempts, interventions such as this do show promise and warrant further investigation (Kennard et al., 2018). Future directions for research could therefore include the testing of wearable devices or similar technologies in those with a history of NSSI to identify physiological changes such as changes in heart rate or changes in patterns of movement or activity which could predict imminent episodes of NSSI. There may also be a role for psychological monitoring and interventions using already owned devices such as smartphones.

Neurobiological Correlates and Pain Perception

Advances in neurobiological research have explored patterns of physiological abnormalities which may be associated with NSSI. One of the more widely researched aspects of this is the possibility of an increased pain threshold in those who self-harm compared to the general population. A systematic review by Kirtley and colleagues reported strong evidence for an increased pain tolerance in NSSI (Kirtley et al., 2016). Similarly a meta-analysis by Koenig and colleagues found that individuals engaging in self-injurious behavior had greater pain threshold and tolerance and reported less pain intensity compared to healthy controls (Koenig et al., 2016). However, both reviews identified only cross-sectional studies, and therefore longitudinal studies are needed in order to understand whether altered pain tolerance leads to an increased risk of NSSI or whether it is a consequence of NSSI (Kirtley et al., 2016; Koenig et al., 2016). In addition, and perhaps of relevance for understanding this association, there is some evidence that adolescents with self-harm also show hyposensitivity to nonpainful stimuli (Cummins et al., 2021).

Anomalies in other neurobiological domains have also been investigated in the context of NSSI. Studies have examined and provide some evidence of the relevance of processes such as sustained threat, reward learning, and cognitive control in NSSI behavior (Schreiner et al., 2015). A study by Poon and colleagues explored reward-related neural activation in adolescents and found that having thoughts of NSSI was associated with heightened activation in the bilateral putamen in response to a monetary reward (Poon et al., 2019). Again, much of the research has been cross-sectional, and therefore further research is needed in order to understand which factors may be predisposing versus those which may precipitate or maintain NSSI (Schreiner et al., 2015).

Future directions for research could therefore include longitidinal studies to help identify neurobiological factors which may predict future NSSI in those with a history of this behavior, and could be a component of an ongoing dynamic assessment following NSSI.

Implications for Clinical Practice

One of the challenges in assessment of NSSI is the distinction between self-harm with and without suicidal intent. As discussed above, this is an essential component of the assessment; however, it will not always be possible to definitively determine the presence or absence of suicidal intent. All the above components of the assessment are important regardless of the intent behind the act, largely due to the similar outcomes associated with both behaviors.

In terms of the use of structured tools to predict future NSSI or suicide attempts after an episode of NSSI, no tool has an accuracy sufficient to inform clinical decision-making with regard to risk management, with each tool lacking in either sensitivity (thus underidentifying those at risk) or PPV (misclassifying low-risk individuals as being at high risk of NSSI or suicide attempt). Detailed structured interviews or questionnaires designed to help guide a comprehensive clinical assessment, could, however, be a useful tool, particularly in situations where professionals are less experienced in NSSI assessment.

Alternative methods of assessment and recent advances such as EMA, digital monitoring technologies, and the use of neurobiological markers are not yet incorporated into routine clinical practice. For some of these, a sufficient evidence base already exists; however, the method cannot feasibly be rolled out into routine care. For others, further research is still needed.

Even for the well-established aspects of NSSI assessment, there are numerous practical and logistical challenges with conducting an ideal assessment. This may vary across settings in terms of time and resource pressures and the skills, knowledge, and training of professionals.

Conclusions

This chapter has outlined components of the assessment of NSSI in clinical and community settings. The main essential component of assessment of NSSI, in any setting, is a thorough psychosocial assessment, utilizing a nonjudgmental approach. Assessment can take various forms, could include structured tools, and may be conducted by a range of professionals. In most cases, this will be the mental health professional, but in certain situations assessment may be conducted by other groups such as educators (also see Baetens et al., this volume) or social care professionals. Key components to this assessment include a detailed history of the current and previous episodes of NSSI, other self-harm or suicidal thoughts or behaviors, as well as an assessment of risk of future NSSI or suicide attempts and agreeing an ongoing management plan including management of risk. While undertaking assessment, there may be opportunities to address and change behaviors, increase the likelihood of future engagement with support, and reduce risk. Assessment should therefore be considered a valuable opportunity and potentially therapeutic experience for those who have engaged in NSSI.

References

American Psychiatric Association. (2013). *Diagnostic and Statistical Manual of Mental Disorders*, Fifth Edition. American Psychiatric Association.

Ames, D. (2017). Intoxication with alcohol at the time of self-harm and pre-existing involvement with mental health services are associated with a pre-disposition to repetition of self-harming behavior in a large cohort of older New Zealanders presenting with an index episode of self-harm. *International Psychogeriatrics, 29*(8), pp.1235. https://doi.org/10.1017/s104161021700093x

Anestis, M. D., Knorr, A. C., Tull, M. T., Lavender, J. M., & Gratz, K. L. (2013). The importance of high distress tolerance in the relationship between nonsuicidal self-injury and suicide potential. *Suicide and Life-Threatening Behavior, 43*(6), 663–675. https://doi.org/10.1111/sltb.12048

Baer, M. M., Tull, M. T., Forbes, C. N., Richmond, J. R., & Gratz, K. L. (2020). Methods matter: Nonsuicidal self-injury in the form of cutting is uniquely associated with suicide attempt severity in patients with substance use disorders. *Suicide and Life-Threatening Behavior, 50*(2), 397–407. https://doi.org/10.1111/sltb.12596

Bentley, K. H., Cassiello-Robbins, C. F., Vittorio, L., Sauer-Zavala, S., & Barlow, D. H. (2015). The association between nonsuicidal self-injury and the emotional disorders: A meta-analytic review. *Clinical Psychology Review, 37*, 72–88. https://doi.org/10.1016/j.cpr.2015.02.006

Borges, G., Bagge, C. L., Cherpitel, C. J., Conner, K. R., Orozco, R., & Rossow, I. (2017). A meta-analysis of acute use of alcohol and the risk of suicide attempt. *Psychological Medicine, 47*(5), 949–957. https://doi.org/10.1017/s0033291716002841

Boyle, A., Jones, P., & Lloyd, S. (2006). The association between domestic violence and self harm in emergency medicine patients. *Emergency Medicine Journal, 23*(8), 604–607. https://doi.org/10.1136/emj.2005.031260

Britton, P. C., Patrick, H., Wenzel, A., & Williams, G. C. (2011). Integrating motivational interviewing and self determination theory with cognitive behavioral therapy to prevent suicide. *Cognitive and Behavioral Practice, 18*(1), 16–27. https://doi.org/10.1016/j.cbpra.2009.06.004

Brown, R. C., Heines, S., Witt, A., Braehler, E., Fegert, J. M., Harsch, D., & Plener, P. L. (2018). The impact of child maltreatment on non-suicidal self-injury: Data from a representative sample of the general population. *BMC Psychiatry, 18*(1), Article 181. https://doi.org/10.1186/s12888-018-1754-3

Burke, B. L., Arkowitz, H., & Menchola, M. (2003). The efficacy of motivational interviewing: A meta-analysis of controlled clinical trials. *Journal of Consulting and Clinical Psychology, 71*(5), 843–861. https://doi.org/10.1037/0022-006X.71.5.843

Burke, T. A., Hamilton, J. L., Cohen, J. N., Stange, J. P., & Alloy, L. B. (2016). Identifying a physical indicator of suicide risk: Non-suicidal self-injury scars predict suicidal ideation and suicide attempts. *Comprehensive Psychiatry, 65*, 79–87. https://doi.org/10.1016/j.comppsych.2015.10.008

Carter, G., Milner, A., McGill, K., Pirkis, J., Kapur, N., & Spittal, M. J. (2017). Predicting suicidal behaviours using clinical instruments: Systematic review and meta-analysis of positive predictive values for risk scales. *British Journal of Psychiatry, 210*(6), 387–395. https://doi.org/10.1192/bjp.bp.116.182717

Carter, G., Page, A., Large, M., Hetrick, S., Milner, A. J., Bendit, N., Walton, C., Draper, B., Hazell, P., Fortune, S., Burns, J., Patton, G., Lawrence, M., Dadd, L., Robinson, J., & Christensen, H. (2016). Royal Australian and New Zealand College of Psychiatrists clinical practice guideline for the management of deliberate self-harm. *Australian & New Zealand Journal of Psychiatry, 50*(10), 939–1000. https://doi.org/10.1177/0004867416661039

Chan, M. K., Bhatti, H., Meader, N., Stockton, S., Evans, J., O'Connor, R. C., Kapur, N., & Kendall, T. (2016). Predicting suicide following self-harm: Systematic review of risk factors and risk scales. *British Journal of Psychiatry, 209*(4), 277–283. https://doi.org/10.1192/bjp.bp.115.170050

Cipriano, A., Cella, S., & Cotrufo, P. (2017). Nonsuicidal self-injury: A systematic review. *Frontiers in Psychology, 8*, 1946–1946. https://doi.org/10.3389/fpsyg.2017.01946

Cliffe, C., Shetty, H., Himmerich, H., Schmidt, U., Stewart, R., & Dutta, R. (2020). Suicide attempts requiring hospitalization in patients with eating disorders: A retrospective cohort study. *International Journal of Eating Disorders, 53*(5), 458–465. https://doi.org/10.1002/eat.23240#

Cooper, J., Kapur, N., & Mackway-Jones, K. (2007). A comparison between clinicians' assessment and the Manchester Self-Harm Rule: A cohort study. *Emergency Medicine Journal, 24*(10), 720–721. https://doi.org/10.1136/emj.2007.048983

Cummins, T. M., English, O., Minnis, H., Stahl, D., O'Connor, R. C., Bannister, K., McMahon, S. B., & Ougrin, D. (2021). Assessment of somatosensory function and self-harm in adolescents. *JAMA Network Open, 4*(7), Article e2116853. https://doi.org/10.1001/jamanetworkopen.2021.16853

Dickstein, D. P., Puzia, M. E., Cushman, G. K., Weissman, A. B., Wegbreit, E., Kim, K. L., & Nock, M. K., Spirito, A. (2015). Self-injurious implicit attitudes among adolescent suicide attempters versus those engaged in nonsuicidal self-injury. *Journal of Child Psychology & Psychiatry*, *56*(10), 1127–1136. https://doi.org/10.1111/jcpp.12385

Fox, K. R., Harris, J. A., Wang, S. B., Millner, A. J., Deming, C. A., & Nock, M. K. (2020). Self-Injurious Thoughts and Behaviors Interview—Revised: Development, reliability, and validity. *Psychological Assessment*, *32*(7), 677–689. https://doi.org/10.1037/pas0000819

Fox, K. R., Franklin, J. C., Ribeiro, J. D., Kleiman, E. M., Bentley, K. H., & Nock, M. K. (2015). Meta-analysis of risk factors for nonsuicidal self-injury. *Clinical Psychology Review*, *42*, 156–167. https://doi.org/10.1016/j.cpr.2015.09.002

Fox, K. R., Huang, X., Linthicum, K. P., Wang, S. B., Franklin, J. C., & Ribeiro, J. D. (2019). Model complexity improves the prediction of nonsuicidal self-injury. *Journal of Consulting and Clinical Psychology*, *87*(8), 684–692. https://doi.org/10.1037/ccp0000421

Gardner, K. J., Bickley, H., Turnbull, P., Kapur, N., Taylor, P., & Clements, C. (2020). The significance of site of cut in self-harm in young people. *Journal of Affective Disorders*, *266*, 603–609. https://doi.org/10.1016/j.jad.2020.01.093

Gee, B. L., Han, J., Benassi, H., & Batterham, P. J. (2020). Suicidal thoughts, suicidal behaviours and self-harm in daily life: A systematic review of ecological momentary assessment studies. *Digital health*, *6*, Article 2055207620963958. https://doi.org/10.1177/2055207620963958

Geulayov, G., Casey, D., Bale, E., Brand, F., Clements, C., Farooq, B., Kapur, N., Ness, J., Waters, K., Patel, A., & Hawton, K. (2021). Risk of suicide in patients who present to hospital after self-cutting according to site of injury: Findings from the Multicentre Study of Self-harm in England. *Psychological Medicine*. Advance online publication. https://doi.org/10.1017/S0033291721002956

Geulayov, G., Casey, D., McDonald, K. C., Foster, P., Pritchard, K., Wells, C., Clements, C., Kapur, N., Ness, J., Waters, K., & Hawton, K. (2018). Incidence of suicide, hospital-presenting non-fatal self-harm, and community-occurring non-fatal self-harm in adolescents in England (the iceberg model of self-harm): A retrospective study. *The Lancet. Psychiatry*, *5*(2), 167–174. https://doi.org/10.1016/S2215-0366(17)30478-9

Glenn, C. R., Millner, A. J., Esposito, E. C., Porter, A. C., & Nock, M. K. (2019). Implicit identification with death predicts suicidal thoughts and behaviors in adolescents. *Journal of Clinical Child and Adolescent Psychology: The Official Journal for the Society of Clinical Child and Adolescent Psychology, American Psychological Association, Division 53*, *48*(2), 263–272. https://doi.org/10.1080/15374416.2018.1528548

Glenn, J. J., Werntz, A. J., Slama, S. J., Steinman, S. A., Teachman, B. A., & Nock, M. K. (2017). Suicide and self-injury-related implicit cognition: A large-scale examination and replication. *Journal of Abnormal Psychology*, *126*(2), 199–211. https://doi.org/10.1037/abn0000230

Graney, J., Hunt, I. M., Quinlivan, L., Rodway, C., Turnbull, P., Gianatsi, M., Appleby, L., & Kapur, N. (2020). Suicide risk assessment in UK mental health services: A national mixed-methods study. *The lancet. Psychiatry*, *7*(12), 1046–1053. https://doi.org/10.1016/S2215-0366(20)30381-3

Guan, K., Fox, K. R., & Prinstein, M. J. (2012). Nonsuicidal self-injury as a time-invariant predictor of adolescent suicide ideation and attempts in a diverse community sample. *Journal of Consulting and Clinical Psychology*, *80*(5), 842–849. https://doi.org/10.1037/a0029429

Gutierrez, P. M., Osman, A., Barrios, F. X., & Kopper, B. A. (2001). Development and initial validation of the Self-harm Behavior Questionnaire. *Journal of Personal Assessment*, *77*(3), 475–490. https://doi.org/10.1207/s15327752jpa7703_08

Harris, I. M., Beese, S., & Moore, D. (2019). Predicting future self-harm or suicide in adolescents: A systematic review of risk assessment scales/tools. *BMJ Open*, *9*(9), Article e029311. https://doi.org.10.1136/bmjopen-2019-029311

Hoy, J., Natarajan, A., & Petra, M. M. (2016). Motivational interviewing and the transtheoretical model of change: Under-explored resources for suicide intervention. *Community Mental Health Journal*, *52*(5), 559–567. https://doi.org/10.1007/s10597-016-9997-2

Hunter, C., Chantler, K., Kapur, N., & Cooper, J. (2013). Service user perspectives on psychosocial assessment following self-harm and its impact on further help-seeking: A qualitative study. *Journal of Affective Disorders*, *145*(3), 315–323. https://doi.org/10.1016/j.jad.2012.08.009

Kapur, N., Cooper, J., O'Connor, R. C., & Hawton, K. (2013). Non-suicidal self-injury v. attempted suicide: New diagnosis or false dichotomy?. *The British Journal of Psychiatry: The Journal of Mental Science*, *202*(5), 326–328. https://doi.org/10.1192/bjp.bp.112.116111

Kennard, B. D., Goldstein, T., Foxwell, A. A., McMakin, D. L., Wolfe, K., Biernesser, C., Moorehead, A., Douaihy, A., Zullo, L., Wentroble, E., Owen, V., Zelazny, J., Iyengar, S., Porta, G., & Brent, D. (2018). As Safe as Possible (ASAP): A brief app-supported inpatient intervention to prevent postdischarge suicidal behavior in hospitalized, suicidal adolescents. *The American Journal of Psychiatry, 175*(9), 864–872. https://doi.org/10.1176/appi.ajp.2018.17101151

Kirtley, O. J., O'Carroll, R. E., & O'Connor, R. C. (2016). Pain and self-harm: A systematic review. *Journal of Affective Disorders, 203*, 347–363. doi:https://doi.org/10.1016/j.jad.2016.05.068

Kleiman, E., Millner, A. J., Joyce, V. W., Nash, C. C., Buonopane, R. J., & Nock, M. K. (2019). Using wearable physiological monitors with suicidal adolescent inpatients: Feasibility and acceptability study. *Journal of Medical Internet Research: Mhealth uHealth, 7*(9), Article e13725. https://doi.org/10.2196/13725

Klonsky, E. D., & Glenn, C. R. (2009). Assessing the functions of non-suicidal self-injury: Psychometric properties of the Inventory of Statements About Self-injury (ISAS). *Journal of Psychopathology and Behavioral Assessment, 31*(3), 215–219. https://doi.org/10.1007/s10862-008-9107-z

Koenig, J., Thayer, J. F., & Kaess, M. (2016). A meta-analysis on pain sensitivity in self-injury. *Psychological Medicine, 46*(8), 1597–1612. https://doi.org/10.1017/S0033291716000301

Liu R. T. (2021). The epidemiology of non-suicidal self-injury: Lifetime prevalence, sociodemographic and clinical correlates, and treatment use in a nationally representative sample of adults in England. *Psychological Medicine*. Advance online publication. https://doi.org/10.1017/S003329172100146X

MacDonald, S., Sampson, C., Turley, R., Biddle, L., Ring, N., Begley, R., & Evans, R. (2020). Patients' experiences of emergency hospital care following self-harm: Systematic review and thematic synthesis of qualitative research. *Qualitative Health Research, 30*(3), 471–485. https://doi.org/10.1177/1049732319886566

Malott, L., Bharti, P., Hilbert, N., Gopalakrishna, G., & Chellappan, S. (2015, 23-27 March 2015). Detecting self-harming activities with wearable devices. [Paper presentation]. 2015 IEEE International Conference on Pervasive Computing and Communication Workshops (PerCom Workshops, St Louis, MO, USA). https://doi.org/10.1109/PERCOMW.2015.7134105

McManus, S., B. P., Jenkins, R., & Brugha, T. (Eds.). (2016). *Mental health and well-being in England: Adult Psychiatric Morbidity Survey 2014*. NHS Digital.

Melbye, S., Kessing, L. V., Bardram, J. E., & Faurholt-Jepsen, M. (2020). Smartphone-Based Self-Monitoring, Treatment, and Automatically Generated Data in Children, Adolescents, and Young Adults With Psychiatric Disorders: Systematic Review. *JMIR mental health, 7*(10), e17453. https://doi.org/10.2196/17453

Millner, A. J., Augenstein, T. M., Visser, K. H., Gallagher, K., Vergara, G. A., D'Angelo, E. J., & Nock, M. K. (2019). Implicit cognitions as a behavioral marker of suicide attempts in adolescents. *Archives of Suicide Research, 23*(1), 47–63. https://doi.org/10.1080/13811118.2017.1421488

Muehlenkamp, J. J., Xhunga, N., & Brausch, A. M. (2019). Self-injury age of onset: A risk factor for NSSI severity and suicidal behavior. *Archives of Suicide Research, 23*(4), 551–563. https://doi.org/10.1080/13811118.2018.1486252

National Institute for Health Care and Excellence. (2004). *Self-harm in over 8s: Shorter-term management*. 1.7. https://www.nice.org.uk/guidance/cg16/chapter/1-Guidance#psychosocial-assessment

National Institute for Health Care and Excellence. (2011). *Self-harm (longer-term management) (CG133) Paragraph number:1.3, 22*. https://www.nice.org.uk/guidance/CG133/chapter/1-Guidance#psychosocial-assessment-in-community-mental-health-services-and-other-specialist-mental-health

National Institute for Health Care and Excellence. (2012). *Self-harm in over 8s: Long-term management*. www.nice.org.uk/guidance/CG133

National Institute for Health Care and Excellence. (2022). *Self-harm assessment, management and preventing recurrence*. www.nice.org.uk/guidance/ng225

Nock, M. K. (2010). Self-injury. *Annual Review of Clinical Psychology, 6*, 339–363. https://doi.org/10.1146/annurev.clinpsy.121208.131258

Nock, M. K., Holmberg, E. B., Photos, V. I., & Michel, B. D. (2007). Self-Injurious Thoughts and Behaviors Interview: Development, reliability, and validity in an adolescent sample. *Psychological Assessment, 19*(3), 309–317. https://doi.org/10.1037/1040-3590.19.3.309

Nock, M. K., Joiner, T. E., Jr., Gordon, K. H., Lloyd-Richardson, E., & Prinstein, M. J. (2006). Non-suicidal self-injury among adolescents: Diagnostic correlates and relation to suicide attempts. *Psychiatry Research, 144*(1), 65–72. https://doi.org/10.1016/j.psychres.2006.05.010

Nock, M. K., Park, J. M., Finn, C. T., Deliberto, T. L., Dour, H. J., & Banaji, M. R. (2010). Measuring the suicidal mind: Implicit cognition predicts suicidal behavior. *Psychological Science*, *21*(4), 511–517. https://doi.org/10.1177/0956797610364762

Nock, M. K., & Prinstein, M. J. (2004). A functional approach to the assessment of self-mutilative behavior. *Journal of Consulting and Clinical Psychology*, *72*(5), 885–890. https://doi.org/10.1037/0022-006x.72.5.885

Office of the Surgeon General & National Action Alliance for Suicide Prevention. (2012). *National strategy for suicide prevention: Goals and objectives for action: A report of the U.S. Surgeon General and of the National Action Alliance for Suicide Prevention*. U.S. Department of Health & Human Services. https://www.ncbi.nlm.nih.gov/books/NBK109917/

Ougrin, D., Ng, A. V., & Low, J. (2008). Therapeutic assessment based on cognitive-analytic therapy for young people presenting with self-harm: Pilot study. *Psychiatric Bulletin*, *32*(11), 423–426. https://doi.org/10.1192/pb.bp.107.018473

Ougrin, D., Zundel, T., Ng, A., Banarsee, R., Bottle, A., & Taylor, E. (2011). Trial of therapeutic assessment in London: Randomised controlled trial of therapeutic assessment versus standard psychosocial assessment in adolescents presenting with self-harm. *Archives of Disease in Childhood*, *96*(2), 148–153. https://doi.org/10.1136/adc.2010.188755

Palombini, E., Richardson, J., McAllister, E., Veale, D., & Thomson, A. B. (2021). When self-harm is about preventing harm: Emergency management of obsessive–compulsive disorder and associated self-harm. *BJPsych Bulletin*, *45*(2), 109–114. https://doi.org/10.1192/bjb.2020.70

Plener, P. L., Allroggen, M., Kapusta, N. D., Brähler, E., Fegert, J. M., & Groschwitz, R. C. (2016). The prevalence of nonsuicidal self-injury (NSSI) in a representative sample of the German population. *BMC Psychiatry*, *16*(1), Article 353. https://doi.org/10.1186/s12888-016-1060-x

Polling, C. A.-O., Woodhead, C., Harwood, H., Hotopf, M., & Hatch, S. L. (2021). "There is so much more for us to lose if we were to kill ourselves": Understanding paradoxically low rates of self-harm in a socioeconomically disadvantaged community in London. *Qualitative Health Research*, *31*(1), 122–136. https://doi.org/10.1177%2F1049732320957628

Poon, J. A., Thompson, J. C., Forbes, E. E., & Chaplin, T. M. (2019). Adolescents' reward-related neural activation: Links to thoughts of nonsuicidal self-injury. *Suicide and Life-Threatening Behavior*, *49*(1), 76–89. https://doi.org/10.1111/sltb.12418

Quinlivan, L., Cooper, J., Davies, L., Hawton, K., Gunnell, D., & Kapur, N. (2016). Which are the most useful scales for predicting repeat self-harm? A systematic review evaluating risk scales using measures of diagnostic accuracy. *BMJ Open*, *6*(2), Article e009297. https://doi.org/10.1136/bmjopen-2015-009297

Quinlivan, L., Cooper, J., Steeg, S., Davies, L., Hawton, K., Gunnell, D., & Kapur, N. (2014). Scales for predicting risk following self-harm: An observational study in 32 hospitals in England. *BMJ Open*, *4*(5), Article e004732. https://doi.org/10.1136/bmjopen-2013-004732

Randall, J. R., Colman, I., & Rowe, B. H. (2011). A systematic review of psychometric assessment of self-harm risk in the emergency department. *Journal of Affective Disorders*, *134*(1), 348–355. https://doi.org/10.1016/j.jad.2011.05.032

Randall, J. R., Rowe, B. H., & Colman, I. (2012). Emergency department assessment of self-harm risk using psychometric questionnaires. *Canadian Journal of Psychiatry*, *57*(1), 21–28. https://doi.org/10.1177/070674371205700105

Ribeiro, J. D., Franklin, J. C., Fox, K. R., Bentley, K. H., Kleiman, E. M., Chang, B. P., & Nock, M. K. (2016). Self-injurious thoughts and behaviors as risk factors for future suicide ideation, attempts, and death: A meta-analysis of longitudinal studies. *Psychological Medicine*, *46*(2), 225–236. https://doi.org/10.1017/S0033291715001804

Rodríguez-Blanco, L., Carballo, J. J., & Baca-García, E. (2018). Use of ecological momentary assessment (EMA) in non-suicidal self-injury (NSSI): A systematic review. *Psychiatry Research*, *263*, 212–219. https://doi.org/10.1016/j.psychres.2018.02.051

Selby, E. A., Kranzler, A., Fehling, K. B., & Panza, E. (2015). Nonsuicidal self-injury disorder: The path to diagnostic validity and final obstacles. *Clinical Psychology Review*, *38*, 79–91. https://doi.org/10.1016/j.cpr.2015.03.003

Shaw C. (2012). Harm-minimisation for self-harm. *Mental Health Today (Brighton, England)*, pp. 19–21.

Shiffman, S., Stone, A. A., & Hufford, M. R. (2008). Ecological momentary assessment. *Annual REVIEW of Clinical Psychology*, *4*, 1–32. https://doi.org/10.1146/annurev.clinpsy.3.022806.091415

Schreiner, W. M., Klimes-Dougan, B., Begnel, E. D., & Cullen, K. R. (2015). Conceptualizing the neurobiology of non-suicidal self-injury from the perspective of the Research Domain Criteria Project. *Neuroscience & Biobehavioral Reviews, 57*, 381–91. https://doi.org/10.1016/j.neubiorev.2015.09.011.

Sornberger, M. J., Heath, N. L., Toste, J. R., & McLouth, R. (2012). Nonsuicidal self-injury and gender: PATTERNS of prevalence, methods, and locations among adolescents. *Suicide and Life-Threatening Behavior, 42*(3), 266–278. https://doi.org/10.1111/j.1943-278X.2012.0088.x

Stanley, B., & Brown, G. K. (2012). Safety planning intervention: A brief intervention to mitigate suicide risk. *Cognitive and Behavioral Practice, 19*(2), 256–264. https://doi.org/10.1016/j.cbpra.2011.01.001

Stanley, B., Brown, G. K., Brenner, L. A., Galfalvy, H. C., Currier, G. W., Knox, K. L., Chaudhury, S. R., Bush, A. L., & Green, K. L. (2018). Comparison of the safety planning intervention with follow-up vs usual care of suicidal patients treated in the emergency department. *JAMA Psychiatry, 75*(9), 894–900. https://doi.org/10.1001/jamapsychiatry.2018.1776

Steeg, S., Kapur, N., Webb, R., Applegate, E, Stewart, S. L., Hawton, K., Bergen, H., Waters, K., & Cooper, J. (2012). The development of a population-level clinical screening tool for self-harm repetition and suicide: The ReACT Self-Harm Rule. *Psychological Medicine, 42*(11), 2383–2394. https://doi.org/10.1017/S0033291712000347

Taylor, P. J., Jomar, K., Dhingra, K., Forrester, R., Shahmalak, U., & Dickson, J. M. (2018). A meta-analysis of the prevalence of different functions of non-suicidal self-injury. *Journal of Affective Disorders, 227*, 759–769. https://doi.org/10.1016/j.jad.2017.11.073

Trautman, P. D., Stewart, N., & Morishima, A. (1993). Are adolescent suicide attempters noncompliant with outpatient care? *Journal of the American Academy of Child and Adolescent Psychiatry, 32*(1), 89–94. https://doi.org/10.1097/00004583-199301000-00013

Votta, E., & Manion, I. (2004). Suicide, high-risk behaviors, and coping style in homeless adolescent males' adjustment. *The Journal of Adolescent Health: Official Publication of the Society for Adolescent Medicine, 34*(3), 237–243. https://doi.org/10.1016/j.jadohealth.2003.06.002

Walsh B. (2007). Clinical assessment of self-injury: A practical guide. *Journal of Clinical Psychology, 63*(11), 1057–1068. https://doi.org/10.1002/jclp.20413

Yarkoni, T., & Westfall, J. (2017). Choosing prediction over explanation in psychology: Lessons from machine learning. *Perspectives on Psychological Science: A Journal of the Association for Psychological Science, 12*(6), 1100–1122. https://doi.org/10.1177/1745691617693393

CHAPTER 44

Risk Assessment, Intervention, and Guidance for First Responders and Medical Settings

Nicholas J. Westers *and* Brittany Tinsley

> **Abstract**
>
> Healthcare providers in medical settings often serve as first responders in treating individuals who engage in nonsuicidal self-injury (NSSI). This chapter highlights the importance of interpersonal style, self-awareness, and how medical professionals can and should screen for NSSI. It then introduces risk assessment models and highlights important questions for first responders to integrate into their interviews with patients to determine next steps in care. This chapter offers sample questions to use in clinical practice and extends these to a discussion about how first responders can effectively intervene, care for wounds, and provide brief, targeted medical advice to those who self-injure. It discusses challenges, recommendations, and future considerations related to NSSI risk assessment research and ends with a discussion about ethical concerns. This chapter considers the perspective of individuals with lived experience of NSSI and encourages first responders to reflect on how their clinical care may be perceived by those who self-injure at all points of the medical encounter. Key takeaways include:
>
> **Key Words:** healthcare providers, first responders, nonsuicidal self-injury, interpersonal style, self-awareness, risk assessment models, interviews, ethical concerns, medical professionals, medical education

- Medical professionals should routinely screen for NSSI at standard intake appointments and annual checkups.
- Risk assessments should include an evaluation of wounds and provision of proper care, a respectful discussion about the reasons for engaging in the behavior, and questions about co-occurring suicidal ideation.
- First responders should consider how those with lived experience interpret their care.
- Concern for liability is an inadequate reason to refer to a higher level of care or refer out to a mental health professional without completing a good risk assessment.

Risk Assessment, Intervention, and Guidance for First Responders and Medical Settings

As primary care clinics and emergency departments (EDs) see increasing numbers of individuals presenting with mental health concerns, they have become the de facto source of primary mental health care (Gray et al., 2005; Larkin et al., 2009). Consequently, medical professionals are frequently the first to learn about an individual's engagement in NSSI (Kerr et al., 2010). That is, they are likely to serve as "first responders," a term we broadly use in this chapter to include any healthcare provider who is among the first to learn of an individual's recent engagement in NSSI. First responders may have a short-term relationship with an individual who has engaged in NSSI, such as clinicians in the ED who are triaging patients or providing direct clinical care, or a long-term relationship with them, such as family medicine physicians, pediatricians, or nurse practitioners, among others.

Visits to the ED for self-harm (i.e., suicidal self-injury and NSSI) among youth have trended upward over the past two decades (Bell et al., 2016; Mercado et al., 2017), and individuals who visit the ED for pain-related physical complaints are at significant risk for returning to the ED for the treatment of self-harm within the following six months (Wang et al., 2019). Nevertheless, many medical professionals in both the ED and primary care feel inadequately prepared to address NSSI behavior and only 22%–27% routinely inquire about NSSI (Taliaferro et al., 2013; Westers et al., 2023). The majority have expressed a need for more training in addressing NSSI (Taliaferro et al., 2013) and believe that such training is important (Westers et al., 2023). When healthcare professionals do receive training in how to best assess and respond to NSSI, they not only report greater competence in treating individuals who self-injure (Muehlenkamp et al., 2013; Taliaferro et al., 2023; Westers et al., 2023) but also experience greater empathy and positive attitudes toward those who engage in the behavior (Muehlenkamp et al., 2013).

Cultivating Safety: First Responders as Conduits of Health

The manner in which healthcare professionals react to NSSI is crucial (Brickell & Jellinek, 2014; Kameg et al., 2013; Walsh, 2012; Westers et al., 2016). Because NSSI is often a highly secretive behavior, any attempts by medical professionals to address NSSI can feel threatening and intrusive. Those with lived experience of NSSI often fear the reaction of others to their self-injurious behaviors and can be highly sensitive to the tone or perceived assumptions made through the nature of language used when assessing the behavior (Westers & Plener, 2020). Therefore, an important first step in assessing and providing care to individuals who self-injure is to engage in honest self-reflection of one's own values and beliefs about the behavior. Doing so places first responders in a position to better manage their immediate verbal and emotional responses in the moment and thereby provide better clinical care to their patients and create an emotionally safe environment (Kameg et al., 2013; Westers et al., 2016).

For instance, if first responders believe that individuals typically engage in NSSI as a form of attention-seeking or a way to manipulate other people, two beliefs that reflect negative attitudes toward those who self-injure, they may provide lower quality of care (Muehlenkamp et al., 2013). Although it is true that some individuals self-injure to communicate with others or to get attention, it is one of the least commonly endorsed reasons for engaging in NSSI for both adolescents (Nock & Prinstein, 2004) and adults (Klonsky, 2011). If an individual feels so distressed that they would harm themselves in order to obtain the support or attention they need, an empathic response would be to kindly give them attention. After all, as Brickell and Jellinek (2014) noted, wanting attention is normal. Furthermore, treatment for NSSI typically involves developing alternative coping strategies that often include reaching out to others for emotional support. Recommending that someone reach out for support when they self-injure or experience the urge to self-injure but then calling them attention-seeking when they do reach out creates a double bind, a conflicting message laden with judgment. Similarly, labeling NSSI as "manipulative" or "gamey," which are inherently pejorative terms (Westers & Plener, 2020), decreases first responders' ability to empathize and fails to recognize the complexity of NSSI. Research has confirmed that we cannot accurately infer the intent of someone's behavior (Willett et al., 2017). Conducting a thorough functional analysis of NSSI behavior in these cases will likely reveal reinforcing consequences of the self-injury (e.g., obtaining emotional relief and/or support) that may adequately explain why it is perceived as manipulative. In other words, a good assessment will eliminate the need for descriptors like "manipulative" and "gamey," terms that may more accurately reflect a clinician's anxiety or frustration about the behavior than it does the behavior itself. In short, prescribing motives to a patient's NSSI should be avoided.

First responders may also have their own lived experience of NSSI. Although little research has examined NSSI among first responders, recent data reveal approximately 16% of students and faculty within schools of applied psychology have a history of NSSI (Victor, Devendorf et al., 2022) and 14% of medical students report having self-injured at least once in their life (Allroggen et al., 2014). Nevertheless, first responders with lived experience, too, should engage in self-reflection about their own values and experiences related to NSSI and avoid making assumptions about why someone else self-injures. Overidentifying with patients who engage in NSSI and generalizing one's own engagement in NSSI as representative of that of others with lived experience may lead to personal bias and unhelpful responses (Victor, Lewis, & Muehlenkamp, 2022).

After healthcare professionals evaluate their beliefs and assumptions about NSSI and modify them as needed, the next step in creating a safe environment for an effective risk assessment is to ensure one utilizes a low-key, dispassionate demeanor and a respectful curiosity when speaking to patients (Walsh, 2012). Rarely would a clinician intentionally judge a patient for their behavior, but again, individuals who engage in NSSI readily pick up on subtleties in language that convey disapproval or even unconscious negative bias (Westers & Plener, 2020).

Starting the Conversation: Screening for Nonsuicidal Self-Injury

Within primary care settings in which patients expect to have an ongoing relationship with their provider, medical professionals should routinely screen for NSSI at standard intake appointments and annual checkups (Cama & Fosbenner, 2021; Vijay et al., 2018; Westers & Plener, 2020). In settings in which patients will have a short-term relationship with medical professionals, such as in the ED, patients should be screened for NSSI particularly if they present for a behavioral health-related concern such as depression, hopelessness, disordered eating, or suicidal thoughts or behaviors, as these are risk factors for NSSI (Fox et al., 2015; see Fox, this volume). Just as there are no iatrogenic effects when asking about suicidal thoughts and behaviors (Blades et al., 2018), evidence shows that there are no iatrogenic effects when asking about NSSI (Muehlenkamp et al., 2010). Even if a patient denies ever having engaged in NSSI (i.e., screens negative) but later begins engaging in the behavior, the way in which their healthcare provider initially asked about NSSI may influence their decision to disclose their self-injury at subsequent visits. Relatedly, how clinicians pose the NSSI screening question matters. Using a broad, single-item assessment with a dichotomous yes/no response option tends to result in lower prevalence rates of NSSI than using a checklist format in which respondents indicate if they have engaged in specific NSSI behaviors (Gillies et al., 2018). Recent research suggests that single-item measures best capture those who specifically engage in self-cutting and/or identify as someone who self-injures but may miss individuals who engage in other forms of NSSI, do not necessarily identify with the behavior, or even those who are male (Robinson & Wilson, 2020).

The best time to screen for NSSI is during the standard psychosocial assessment (Cama & Fosbenner, 2021; Westers et al., 2016). The HEEADSSS psychosocial interview (Klein et al., 2014) is an exceptional model because it begins with more benign questions about home life, education, and leisure activities and then builds up to questions about sexuality, suicidality, and now, NSSI. Using a matter-of-fact, neutral tone, medical professionals can state, "I know some people who experience stressors similar to yours think about hurting themselves on purpose without intending suicide," and then respectfully ask, "Have you ever hurt yourself on purpose without intending to end your life or attempt suicide . . . like cutting, biting, burning, hitting, severely scratching yourself . . . ?" (Westers et al., 2016; see Table 44.1 for a variety of example statements and responses that can be used throughout an assessment). Because understanding intent of self-harm is important in differentiating NSSI from suicidal behavior and determining if they co-occur simultaneously, it is best to screen for NSSI just after or just before screening for suicidal thoughts and behaviors (Westers et al., 2016).

Another way healthcare professionals can routinely screen for NSSI, specifically past-year NSSI, is to utilize the newly developed 10-item Screen for Nonsuicidal Self-Injury (SNSI; Halverson et al., 2022), a measure created to be used in primary care and other clinical settings as a brief screen for identifying individuals who meet criteria for NSSI Disorder, a condition proposed for further study in the fifth edition of the *Diagnostic and Statistical Manual of Mental Disorders* (DSM-5; American Psychiatric Association, 2013). The SNSI has sound psychometric properties, with those endorsing 2 or more of the 10 items suggested to likely meet criteria for NSSI Disorder (sensitivity = 0.93), and is considered fair at ruling out those who do not meet NSSI Disorder criteria (specificity = 0.78; Halverson et al., 2022).

Considering the Perspective of Those with Lived Experience of Self-Injury

From the perspective of an individual with lived experience, when a first responder who will have an ongoing relationship with a patient is made aware of their NSSI, they should make it clear that they are willing to discuss and treat the behavior. The reaction of the first responder and their communication regarding the discovery of any self-injurious behaviors sets the tone for the remainder of the medical experience. Gentle interest and compassion paired with statements of fact (e.g., "I noticed a wound/some scars and I'm interested to know more") create space for a conversation upon which a positive ongoing relationship between medical professional and patient can be built. First responders' willingness to openly discuss NSSI in a casual and confident manner will allow the patient to feel more comfortable bringing up on their own any concerns related to their NSSI. A medical professional might state, for example, "I'd like you to know that I'm willing to discuss your self-injury at any point and I am willing to provide referrals and/or resources when you're ready." Additionally, setting up procedural expectations for the patient regarding future visits may lessen a patient's anxiety as they move forward with seeking routine medical care. Statements such as, "When I see you again, I'd like to hear a little more about your self-injury. Would that be okay?" or, during follow-up appointments, "Has there been any change in your self-injury in terms of frequency or severity you'd like to tell me about since we last spoke?" can foster a sense of safety and respect with clear expectations. As long as no emergent action is required, building a relationship with someone who engages in NSSI is more important than securing every piece of information with each interaction.

When it is expected that a first responder will have a short-term relationship with a patient, and the first responder learns of the patient's self-injury, they should make it a point of discussion if it appears to need immediate medical attention. If medical attention is required, the first responder should also conduct a thorough risk assessment. However, if there is another, more pressing medical issue at hand, the patient will unlikely be prepared to discuss NSSI and any attempts to discuss it are likely to be rebuffed. When the

Table 44.1 Sample Statements/Responses

Topic	Sample statements/responses
Screening	• I know some people think about hurting themselves on purpose without intending suicide. Have you ever hurt yourself on purpose without intending to end your life or attempt suicide, like cutting, biting, burning, hitting, severely scratching yourself, . . .?
Starting the conversation	• I noticed some scars/wounds. Would you like to tell me about that? • I noticed a wound/some scars and I'm interested to know more. • I'd like you to know that I'm willing to discuss your self-injury at any point and am willing to provide referrals and/or resources when you're ready. • When I see you again, I'd like to hear more about your self-injury. Would that be okay? • Has there been any change in your self-injury in terms of frequency or severity you'd like to tell me about since we last spoke?
Examining wounds	• What do you typically do to take care of your wounds? • I am concerned about what I'm seeing/what you're describing and would like to assess your wounds in order to determine if you need additional medical attention. • I do need to assess your wounds so we can provide proper care and avoid infection.
When needing to inform a minor's caregiver(s)	• I am concerned about your self-injury and think it's important your parent knows. Would you like to tell them, or would you prefer that I tell them? What details would you like to share with your parent?
Informing caregivers	• During our visit, I became aware that your child is engaging in self-injurious behaviors. This does not mean your child is suicidal. I'm sure you have dozens of questions you'd like to ask your child and that this could be an overwhelming situation. • *If the child is present and engaged:* Right now, this is what they would like you to know. [Provide details the child shared or give the child the space to share themselves.] • *If the child is not present or is disengaged*: As you begin to discuss this at home, I'd encourage you to ask open-ended questions and listen to the answers your child gives, whether or not you agree with what is being said. If you feel the conversation is becoming too much for either of you, take a step back and revisit the topic when everyone has had a chance to calm down.
Suggesting a higher level of care	• I think it would be beneficial for you to have someone who can provide more specialized care as part of your health team. I'm going to give you a referral for . . ./I'd like you to be seen by . . . • Based on what I'm seeing/hearing, I think a good next step for you would be X because . . .

patient's presenting medical concern has been addressed, the first responder may then ask if they would like to discuss it further or be given information regarding resources available to them. If the patient refuses to discuss their NSSI but clearly requires medical attention for it, the first responder can state in a matter-of-fact, kind manner, "I do need to assess your wounds so we can be sure to provide the proper care and avoid infection" (Westers et al., 2016).

Continuing the Conversation: Nonsuicidal Self-Injury Risk Assessment

If a patient screens positive for NSSI, healthcare providers can then conduct a risk assessment in order to evaluate the severity of the self-injury as well as the risk for suicide attempt (Heath & Nixon, 2009; Kerr et al., 2010; Westers et al., 2016). This should be completed even if the patient screened negative for suicidal thoughts and behaviors because levels of risk may change over time (Heath & Nixon, 2009), and while NSSI behavior is distinct from suicide behavior, NSSI is one of the strongest risk factors for attempting suicide (Franklin et al., 2017). Rather than immediately refer to the ED or to a higher level of care because of a positive screen for NSSI, a good risk assessment can, in a short amount of time, determine the next steps in care.

First responders who have ample time to conduct a comprehensive risk assessment of NSSI may find the STOPS FIRE mnemonic strategy particularly helpful (Kerr et al., 2010). It was developed to be implemented in primary care settings as a way to recall important domains of NSSI assessment, including: Suicidal ideation, Types, Onset, Place/location, Severity of damage, Functions, Intensity of self-injury urges, Repetition, and Episodic frequency (Kerr et al., 2010). The STOPS FIRE assessment overlaps with the briefer, more targeted SOARS model (Westers et al., 2016) which was specifically developed for busy medical professionals who work with adolescents but is also applicable to the assessment of adults who engage in NSSI and as a tool for other first responders like mental health clinicians (Westers & Plener, 2020). The SOARS model is intended to be administered in the context of a larger psychosocial interview (e.g., the HEEADSSS assessment) and includes examples of validating statements followed by assessment questions grounded in research that examines factors that, if present, increase risk for suicide attempt. If first responders have just five minutes to conduct a good NSSI risk assessment, SOARS delineates (1) what questions to ask, (2) why to ask these specific questions (grounded in theory and research), and (3) how to ask them in a way that validates the patient and optimizes the likelihood of honest report (Westers et al., 2016). To assist with recall of important assessment domains, SOARS stands for: Suicidal ideation; Onset, frequency, and methods; Aftercare; Reasons; and Stage of change. In cases where medical professionals only have time for three questions, the model can be shortened to SAR to highlight the most important questions in medical settings: Suicidal ideation, Aftercare, and Reasons (Westers et al., 2016).

The order in which assessment questions are asked is flexible. Based on the perspective of those with lived experience, we suggest flipping the Ss in SOARS so that questions about suicide occur at the end of the interview. For some, asking about co-occurring suicidal thoughts at the outset could feel like a setup and lead them to shut down: "If I say yes, I set off a series of events; if I say no, I worry they won't believe me or they'll think self-injury with no suicidal ideation is attention-seeking." If rapport is first established using the other questions in the model, it may prove that the first responder understands NSSI and is open to hearing what the patient has to say. Those with lived experience are then more likely to be honest about any suicidal thoughts and behaviors. Next, we discuss each domain of SOARS, starting with stage of change.

Stage of Change

Not everyone who engages in NSSI considers it a problem or believes discontinuation is possible should they have the desire to stop. First responders can begin by exploring a patient's openness to or thoughts about NSSI cessation by asking, "Is this something you'd like to stop, or have you ever considered stopping?" (Westers et al., 2016). How individuals respond to this question may indicate how receptive they will be to a referral for psychotherapy and what role first responders will have moving forward. After completing the full SOARS assessment, an individual who endorses multiple factors associated with suicide risk but is ambivalent about change may need sooner follow-up than one who expresses a clear desire to stop. Applying the transtheoretical model of behavior change (Prochaska & DiClemente, 1983) to NSSI, those who self-injure and have never considered cessation as a possibility might move from precontemplation to contemplation simply by being presented with the idea of discontinuing.

Onset, Frequency, and Methods

Key characteristics of NSSI behavior, such as onset and duration, lifetime number of episodes (i.e., frequency), and number of methods used also inform level of risk for suicide (Kerr et al., 2010; Westers et al., 2016). The Interpersonal Theory of Suicide (IPTS; Joiner, 2005; see Victor et al., this volume) provides a useful framework for understanding why. The theory posits that, over time, people acquire the capability to act on suicidal ideation when they are exposed to painful and provocative experiences such as abuse, military combat, substance misuse, past suicide attempts, and NSSI. Each painful and provocative experience increases one's capability to act on any suicidal desire because such experiences, especially if repeated, lead to a habituation to pain and a decreased fear of death over time.

Consistent with the IPTS, some research has shown that a longer history of NSSI is associated with attempting suicide (Nock et al., 2006) and that individuals with an early age of onset of the behavior (i.e., at or before age 12) are more likely than those with later onset to report having made a suicide plan (Ammerman et al., 2018) and endorse having experienced suicidal thoughts and attempted suicide (Muehlenkamp et al., 2019). Therefore, clinicians should assess when individuals first began self-injuring and for how long they have engaged in the behavior (Kerr et al., 2010; Westers et al., 2016). Research has also demonstrated that greater lifetime number of NSSI episodes is associated with increased risk over time of attempting suicide and that more frequent NSSI is related to greater number of suicide attempts among both adults (Andover & Gibbs, 2010) and adolescents (Matney et al., 2018), where 11–50 episodes of NSSI indicate moderate risk and more than 50 episodes indicate high risk (Kerr et al., 2010). Other research has found a curvilinear relationship between NSSI frequency and suicide attempts such that risk for attempting suicide increases as number of NSSI episodes increases, peaks around 21–50 episodes and declines afterward, yet remains high (Paul et al., 2015; Whitlock & Knox, 2007). For this reason, clinicians should assess frequency and number of NSSI episodes during a risk assessment.

Most individuals who engage in NSSI use more than one method (Kerr et al., 2010), but research has consistently shown that the greater number of methods used, especially when NSSI frequency is high, the greater risk for attempting suicide (Anestis et al., 2015; Matney et al., 2018; Turner et al., 2013). In line with the IPTS, different methods of NSSI are affiliated with different types of pain and may increase one's capability for suicide. For instance, tearing pain may be caused by cutting, carving (i.e., cutting words or symbols into the skin), or excoriating and severely scratching oneself; burning pain may be caused by burning oneself or using an eraser to cause an abrasion; and bruising pain may be caused by self-hitting or biting (Turner et al., 2013). Engaging in NSSI using three or more different methods may indicate high risk (Kerr et al., 2010). Hence, first responders should assess what methods and how many methods patients use and be sure to keep in mind methods of NSSI beyond self-cutting.

Aftercare

As medical professionals, first responders should always assess the severity and nature of any new or recent wounds as well as how patients provide care to them. Taking a respectfully curious approach, clinicians can ask, "How do you typically take care of the wounds afterward?" (Westers et al., 2016). Most wounds do not raise concern for safety (Washburn, 2014), but some individuals may injure themselves more severely than intended. Before performing an objective physical assessment of wounds, first responders may assess their subjective severity by eliciting the patient's perspective and asking, "Have you ever hurt yourself so badly that you needed medical attention, like stitches, even if you never got it?" (Westers et al., 2016).

Injuries may be categorized into three levels: (1) minimal severity, in which no medical attention is required other than basic wound care, such as cleaning and bandaging; (2) moderate severity, in which the wound is open and/or infected; and (3) high severity, in which major medical attention is required, the patient has embedded objects under their skin, and/or they have engaged in NSSI on their face, neck, breasts, or genitals (Washburn, 2014). First responders should always ensure provision of high-quality medical care, including using pain medication and numbing agents when treating self-injury wounds as well as achieving the best esthetic/cosmetic outcomes possible when providing surgical treatment (Malaga et al., 2016; Plener et al., 2016; Washburn, 2014). Likewise, if the patient presents for an issue directly related to their NSSI, first responders should offer treatment in the same way they would for any other presenting issue, making no mention of wasted time or effort on a self-inflicted wound (Plener et al., 2016).

Reasons

It is also important that first responders assess the reasons patients give for self-injuring; that is, what function(s) NSSI may serve for them (see Taylor et al., this volume). Most individuals engage in NSSI for multiple reasons, and these reasons can change over time with each NSSI episode, and often one episode of NSSI serves multiple functions (Coppersmith et al., 2021). However, as the number of different reasons for NSSI increases, so does risk for attempting suicide (Paul et al., 2015). Self-injuring specifically to avoid suicide or self-injuring because of self-hatred or to end experiences of dissociation are functions most closely related to suicide attempts (Paul et al., 2015). When assessing reasons for NSSI, first responders should refrain from asking patients "why" they self-injure because this can easily come across as judgmental. Instead, medical professionals should first demonstrate their understanding that people self-injure for many different reasons, typically because it is helpful in managing emotions, and then ask for motivations underlying the behavior. We highly recommend that clinicians, therefore, first make a statement of observation and validation (e.g., "It seems like self-injury has been helpful to you at times") and then proceed with an inquiry of the functions of the behavior (e.g., "In what ways does it help you?") (Westers et al., 2016).

Suicidal Ideation

When completing an NSSI risk assessment, first responders should clearly delineate between NSSI and suicidal self-injury but recognize that they may co-occur. Treating NSSI as a suicide attempt may invalidate a patient's experience and intent of the behavior and lead to improper responses such as unnecessary referrals to the ED or unnecessary costly psychiatric hospitalizations (Muehlenkamp, 2005; Westers & Plener, 2020; for evidence-based guidelines for treatment see Plener, this volume). However, research has shown that individuals who engage in NSSI as a way to cope with concurrent suicidal thoughts are at high risk for attempting suicide (Paul et al., 2015). That is, first responders should take note of elevated suicide risk if a patient endorses self-injuring specifically to avoid suicide (Westers et al., 2016). Likewise, risk is elevated when patients who engage in NSSI experience co-occurring major depressive disorder (Asarnow et al., 2011; Tuisku et al., 2014; Wilkinson et al., 2011). Hence, it is important to neither overreact by assuming NSSI is always accompanied by suicidal ideation nor underreact by presuming NSSI will not lead to suicidal thoughts or attempts. First responders should verbally acknowledge to patients that they understand NSSI is not the same as a suicide attempt (e.g., "I know self-injury isn't usually about suicide, but some people may think about suicide when they self-injure") and then ask directly, "Do you ever think about suicide when you [NSSI behavior]?" (Kerr et al., 2010; Westers et al., 2016). Making known to patients that their NSSI behavior will not be conflated with suicidal behavior, but acknowledging they do sometimes co-occur, will demonstrate first responder competence and likely increase patient honesty and confidence that they will receive proper treatment.

Considering the Perspective of Those with Lived Experience of Self-Injury

First responders should always consider the perspective of individuals with lived experience and what emotions a physical exam and interview about their NSSI may bring up during a visit. While a medical professional may be most concerned about risk, a person with a history of NSSI is often most concerned about being understood. Any verbal acknowledgement of wounds during an exam, either that they are worse than expected or better than expected, is not helpful. If a medical professional is shocked by the extent or severity of wounds, the patient may interpret their reaction as judgment and experience a shame deep enough that it could prevent them from seeking needed medical treatment in the future. Although their intention may be to offer reassurance, when a medical professional describes the patient's wounds as "not that bad," "surface-level," "not too serious," "better than expected," or the like, their words negate the patient's experience with NSSI and may inadvertently challenge the individual to harm more severely in the future in an effort to prove their emotional pain is valid.

Allowing first responders to examine a wound related to self-injury puts the individual engaging in NSSI in a vulnerable position, more so than would the examination of most other kinds of wounds. As such, medical professionals should be sensitive to the personal nature of the examination. We recommend implementing a "tell-show-do" approach when assessing wounds. That is, medical professionals offer a verbal explanation and rationale of what to expect from the exam, demonstrate how they will care for it (e.g., using a diagram/picture on the exam room wall, demonstrating or pantomiming in the air), and then deliver the actual medical care. This can be especially true if the patient has a history of trauma and has self-injured in more personal/private areas. Employing a tell-show-do approach to wound care, including for NSSI, is congruent with trauma-informed care (Raja et al., 2014).

In preparation for medical visits, routine or otherwise, those with lived experience may be anxiously anticipating how their NSSI will be addressed. As they think through their visit, they may attempt to mentally prepare for a reaction to or conversation around NSSI by working through a series of questions and considerations similar to the following:

1. *Is this a medical professional I have seen before who is aware of my NSSI?* If so, a medical professional will likely react similarly to the manner in which they reacted initially. If a previous reaction was negative, those with lived experience may feel significantly anxious, avoid or cancel their appointment, or even minimize or deny any recent NSSI behavior during screening so they can regain a sense of emotional safety. If a previous reaction was professional and appropriate, patients may feel safe to disclose any recent NSSI. If the medical professional is unaware of the NSSI, then individuals with lived experience may naturally ask themselves the next question.

2. *If the medical professional is unaware of my NSSI, will they see evidence of it over the course of the visit naturally?* If a medical professional will likely not discover the NSSI during the visit naturally, there may be lower probability that a conversation about NSSI will be held and patients may feel more relaxed. However, a visit to the dermatologist or to a primary care provider for an annual physical may lead to anxiety about wounds or scars and lead to the next question.

3. *Do I want to wait and see if the medical professional brings up NSSI or would I prefer to address my NSSI up front?* In the event an individual decides not to bring up their NSSI, they will likely follow the medical professional's lead regarding any discussion of NSSI rather than preemptively volunteer any information. Waiting for medical providers to bring up the topic if they see wounds or scars can be anxiety-provoking, but so can addressing it up front. If patients with lived experience decide to initiate the conversation rather than wait for their provider to ask about it, they may ask themselves the final question.

4. *What do I want to say?* If an individual decides to address their NSSI up front, they may say something like, "I have struggled with self-injury and you may notice some wounds/scars today." They may also choose to inform their healthcare provider that they are currently in therapy to address this or they participated in therapy in the past. This is an attempt to take control of the delivery of the information in an effort to mitigate a negative or fear-based reaction from the medical professional. In preparation for their conversation with a first responder, individuals with lived experience of self-injury may have spent significant amounts of time scripting what they want to say and even practicing in front of a mirror so that it feels more natural and less anxiety-provoking.

Intervention in Medical Settings: Implications for Clinical Practice

Intervention for NSSI in medical settings can include wound care, brief medical counsel, motivational interviewing, and a referral to a mental health professional. We have already discussed the importance of assessing and providing good clinical care of NSSI wounds, including engaging in honest self-reflection about one's own beliefs and assumptions related to NSSI (i.e., exploring one's own stigma toward the behavior) in order to provide optimal care. Rather than immediately default to referring out for therapy, first responders can provide brief, targeted medical counsel and advice, especially if they are able to spend a few extra minutes with a patient. If using the SOARS model, the best time to provide this brief intervention and develop a treatment plan is when assessing the reasons for engaging in the behavior (Westers et al., 2016). It is here that first responders can discuss with patients specific targeted advice based on function(s) of the behavior.

The most commonly endorsed function of NSSI is to find relief from aversive emotional states (Coppersmith et al., 2021), so most brief interventions will focus on assisting individuals who self-injure to build adaptive strategies for regulating their emotions. Since first responders will likely have already conducted a psychosocial interview in which they will have previously asked about activities the patient enjoys, one of the simplest ways they can begin exploring alternative healthy coping strategies is to circle back to the psychosocial interview and encourage the patient to consider doing more of what they already enjoy doing but as a replacement strategy for NSSI. For example, if journaling or drawing or exercising are enjoyable and stress-reducing, and the individual also engages in NSSI to cope with stress and bring about emotional relief, clinicians can discuss with them how engaging in these very activities may help reduce emotional tension in a safer, healthier way than self-injuring. It is important for first responders to verbally acknowledge, however, that they understand NSSI typically leads to immediate emotional relief. That is, NSSI is most often instantly reinforced, whereas other coping strategies typically take time to bring relief. Clinicians can inquire, "What are some other ways you can manage when you're feeling overwhelmed, even if they don't work as quickly as self-injury?" (Westers et al., 2016).

Another frequently endorsed function of NSSI is to generate desirable emotional states, or to feel something because of feeling numb or empty. First responders can begin targeting this function by exploring other strategies in which individuals can generate feelings, such as taking a cold shower, eating spicy foods, or simply learning to sit with numbness or undesirable emotional states (Westers et al., 2016). For individuals who self-injure to communicate their emotional needs, first responders can teach interpersonal skills, such as articulating to others how they are feeling and making clear requests for support or encouragement rather than turning to NSSI. Clinicians can ask, "How might you ask your friends and family for emotional support without turning to self-injury or immediately telling them you're going to hurt yourself?" (Westers et al., 2016). In general, adding healthy coping strategies is prioritized over removing unhealthy ones because cultivating healthy strategies often leads to relinquishing unhealthy ones. In this way, addition is better than subtraction (Gerle et al., 2019; Walsh, 2012).

A unique, yet common, function of NSSI is to punish oneself, a function that requires more than replacement skills and likely a referral to a skilled mental health professional. Here, first responders can use Socratic questioning as a way to widen perspective and collaboratively explore evidence that one must injure themselves as penitence or payment for the perceived transgression at hand. Assuming there is good rapport, clinicians can gently and respectfully ask, "Does this apply to everyone? Would you say that everyone who misses a deadline, like you did, is bad and deserves to be punished?" or, "Are there ever times when negative natural consequences are punishment enough?" or, "Is it possible that cutting yourself will make no difference in preventing you from messing up again?" This approach assumes patients already possess the knowledge but simply need someone to walk alongside to help them see the evidence for themselves, enabling them to come to their own conclusions. However, this strategy may be too advanced for most first responders. Introducing concepts of self-forgiveness and self-compassion may be easier. For instance, to begin discussion about self-forgiveness, clinicians may ask, "I wonder what it would be like to extend forgiveness toward yourself and allow space for mistakes rather than punishing yourself?" (Westers et al., 2016). To introduce self-compassion and its three core components, clinicians can explore with patients how they might allow themselves to experience their unpleasant emotions without avoiding them or overidentifying with them (i.e., mindfulness), reflect on the fact that everyone makes mistakes or fails on occasion (i.e., shared humanity vs. isolation), and discuss how they can be kind to themselves rather than engage in NSSI to punish themselves (i.e., self-kindness vs. self-judgment) (Neff, 2003).

Once first responders have validated, assessed, and listened carefully to the reasons for which a patient self-injures (i.e., the benefits of NSSI), the conversation ought to naturally flow into a thoughtful discussion about the costs of NSSI. In other words, if a first responder effectively acknowledges and validates how NSSI helps their patient in the moment (i.e., the "R" in SOARS), their patient will likely be more open to having a conversation about the negative short- and long-term consequences of the behavior and thereby foster increased motivation for change (i.e., an "S" in SOARS). Clinicians may find motivational interviewing (Rollnick et al., 2008) particularly helpful here. Collaborating with patients by exploring the advantages and disadvantages of life with and without NSSI may help guide them through the stages of change and build motivation for learning healthier, safer coping strategies (Westers et al., 2016).

Finally, after first responders have provided care for any new or open wounds and provided brief medical counsel as intervention, a referral to a mental health professional with experience treating NSSI may be warranted. They will likely need to lean on their clinical judgment and the patient's responses to the risk assessment to determine what level of care is needed. It is generally recommended that medical professionals refer all patients who self-injure to a mental health professional even if there is no diagnosable co-occurring mental health disorder (Brickell & Jellinek, 2014; Vijay et al., 2018; Westers et al., 2016). When NSSI is mild and infrequent, others (e.g., Møhl, 2020) may recommend a wait-and-see approach in which no formal treatment is indicated. If NSSI is more severe and frequent and done in isolation with co-occurring suicidal ideation, Møhl (2020) suggests outpatient treatment. If a referral to therapy is made, we recommend that first responders follow up by phone within two to three weeks as a way to demonstrate care, foster motivation for follow-through, and identify and address barriers keeping them from treatment (Washburn, 2014; Westers et al., 2016). A referral to psychiatry may also be warranted, especially to address any co-occurring mental health diagnoses (Washburn, 2014). Inpatient hospitalization or day treatment may be recommended if NSSI urges and behaviors are nearly constant, involve multiple methods, and co-occur with suicidal thoughts or impulses (Møhl, 2020).

Considering the Perspective of Those with Lived Experience of Self-Injury
When referring an individual engaging in NSSI to therapy, the individual may be apprehensive or resistant to the idea. Within the community of those with lived experience, there is ample anecdotal evidence of therapists who do not understand NSSI and, therefore, react poorly to admissions of self-injury. Because self-injury is an effective coping mechanism and serves a purpose for those utilizing it, there is often a fear that a therapist will immediately demand cessation of the behavior, something many individuals are not ready to consider. Assurance that the therapist to whom the individual is being referred is experienced in treating NSSI may alleviate some concerns associated with seeking therapeutic support.

Challenges, Recommendations, and Future Directions for Research

There is a lack of research examining NSSI risk assessment and intervention in medical settings. One challenge in researching this area is the lack of clinically focused standardized screening measures specifically for NSSI beyond those used in research settings. The SNSI (Halverson et al., 2022) may be helpful in identifying those who meet criteria for NSSI Disorder and who would benefit from a referral to therapy but not for determining risk for severe injury or suicide. The SOARS model is a useful risk assessment tool but currently lacks dichotomized items and criteria that would allow clinicians to predict risk for attempting suicide with high specificity and sensitivity. Future research should seek to modify questions on the SOARS to include dichotomized response options or to develop a separate brief screening instrument in which assessment questions can be numerically calculated so that a cutoff score can be used to detect elevated risk for attempting suicide.

Because current tools such as the SNSI, STOPS FIRE, and SOARS models may not yet be used as part of standard care across all medical settings, how first responders screen, assess, and respond to individuals who self-injure varies greatly. This variability in how medical professionals screen and assess for NSSI, if they do at all, leads to another research challenge: objectively measuring the clinical abilities of medical professionals in treating individuals who engage in NSSI (i.e., objective competence) beyond just their general comfort level (i.e., subjective competence). Medical professionals who receive education about responding to NSSI typically learn about it as a side note within broader training on screening for suicide, and very few receive any formal training in assessing and responding to NSSI (Westers et al., 2023). Formal training on NSSI should be made widely available to medical professionals. For hospital settings, we recommend integrating it into the annual competency and refresher trainings required for ongoing credentialing within the hospital system.

We also recommend integrating this training into medical residency and nursing school curricula. A one-hour didactic in the SOARS model has been shown to increase NSSI risk assessment knowledge and subjective competence among pediatric medical residents (Westers et al., 2023). To better assess and foster objective competence, Ingraham et al. (2019) created a virtual learning environment (VLE) in which pediatric resident learners could practice using the SOARS model while participating in a virtual reality simulation with a live avatar of a patient who self-injures. The patient avatar is "puppeteered" by a human operator and educator in real time to provide verbal and nonverbal feedback to learners. Research combining training in the SOARS model with use of this VLE has demonstrated increased confidence and knowledge about NSSI and greater likelihood of screening for and addressing NSSI in the future among pediatric residents (Taliaferro et al., 2023).

There are many times when a referral to the ED is necessary. However, with consideration of high volumes in the ED and increasing rates of those who self-injure seeking care in the ED even when not necessarily needed, future research should examine the source of ED referrals for NSSI. Clarifying if individuals who engage in NSSI are self-referring to the ED, being brought by a family member (e.g., a parent bringing a child to the ED for NSSI without a formal referral), or being sent by a medical professional or school staff is important in understanding where training is needed. For example, if increases in referrals to the ED for NSSI are coming from schools, whether primary, secondary, or institutes of higher education, then efforts should be made to educate first responders within educational settings. On the other hand, if increases in referrals are because of unprepared first responders in primary care settings, then clinicians and educators can focus on training and equipping medical professionals in primary care about completing more thorough NSSI risk assessments.

Ethical Considerations

It is possible that first responders who do not feel equipped to care for individuals who self-injure or are unsure of how to conduct an NSSI risk assessment also have concern about liability. That is, they may misinterpret NSSI as suicide behavior, believe that NSSI will inevitably lead to a suicide attempt, or fear that they are not properly trained to provide care. These concerns may lead them to refer these individuals to a higher level of care, like the ED, for further evaluation even when unneeded. Liability of inadequately assessing risk because of discomfort and lack of knowledge must be weighed against liability of referring out and hoping someone else will provide care. With ample information about caring for individuals who self-injure available, there may be greater liability in referring patients out simply because of personal or professional discomfort.

Another dilemma that some first responders may face, particularly those who have an ongoing relationship with a patient who self-injures, is determining if every wound requires examination and if every visit requires reassessment of past wounds. Healthcare professionals generally take a patient's word at face value. If a patient states they superficially self-injured a week ago, did not need medical treatment, and prefer their medical provider not assess the wound, first responders must consider respecting a patient's autonomy and determine if it is necessary to still examine the wound. Relatedly, when a risk assessment results in a recommendation to a higher level of care, it is important to involve the patient in decisions regarding their own care and avoid coercion, power struggles, and threats such as "If you don't stop harming yourself, you'll have to go to inpatient" (Gerle et al., 2019; Westers & Plener, 2020). From the perspective of individuals with lived experience, medical professionals should first listen with authentic interest, involve them in treatment decisions, and provide information about treatment to increase predictability of what they can expect (Gerle et al., 2019).

One of the most common dilemmas for first responders in pediatric medical settings is determining when to disclose NSSI behavior to a caregiver. Do the parents of a 14-year-old need to know that their child engaged in superficial self-cutting three times one month ago, especially if there are no other risk factors and the teen does not want their parents to know? Perhaps the first responder chooses to respect the teen's autonomy by referring them to therapy for NSSI but, instead of disclosing the NSSI to parents, tells the parent the recommendation for therapy is to learn healthier coping strategies. First responders must use their clinical judgment conjointly with a good risk assessment to determine if parental involvement is indicated. However, if a minor discloses that they engage in NSSI to cope with suicidal thoughts and to avoid suicide, a clear risk factor for attempting suicide (Paul et al., 2015), first responders should disclose this to caregivers for at least two reasons. First, a conversation about safety and limits to confidentiality about suicidal thoughts and behaviors will likely have already occurred during consent for treatment, so caregivers will appropriately expect to learn about any safety concerns. Second, it is possible that in the time between the current and follow-up visits, NSSI could become insufficient in preventing a suicide attempt. Functions of NSSI often vary over time within the same individual (Coppersmith et al., 2021), so someone who self-injures to avoid suicide may later attempt suicide if the function becomes ineffective (Westers et al., 2016).

Conclusion

To summarize, because medical professionals are on the frontlines of healthcare, they are often the first people to whom individuals who self-injure disclose their NSSI or the first to learn of an individual's NSSI due to a physical exam. As first responders, they play an invaluable role both in supporting those who self-injure and in completing a good risk assessment before defaulting to making a referral to a mental health professional. First responders ought to examine their own beliefs and assumptions about NSSI and those who engage in the behavior in preparation to provide quality healthcare. They should screen for NSSI at intake and annual checkups and may find risk assessment tools such as the SOARS model as helpful guides for specific assessment questions. All good assessments validate how NSSI serves a useful purpose for the patient, reflect a respectful curiosity accompanied by expression of concern, include exploration of healthier coping strategies, and discuss a referral for therapy (Westers et al., 2016). Finally, first responders should always keep in mind how the questions they are asking and the care they are providing are interpreted by individuals with lived experience of NSSI.

References

Allroggen, M., Kleinrahm, R., Rau, T. A. D., Weninger, L., Ludolph, A. G., & Plener, P. L. (2014). Nonsuicidal self-injury and its relation to personality traits in medical students. *The Journal of Nervous and Mental Disease, 202*(4), 300–304. https://doi.org/10.1097/NMD.0000000000000122

American Psychiatric Association. (2013). *Diagnostic and statistical manual of mental disorders* (5th ed.). https://doi.org/10/1176/appi.books.9780890425596

Ammerman, B. A., Jacobucci, R., Kleiman, E. M., Uyeji, L. L., & McCloskey, M. S. (2018). The relationship between nonsuicidal self-injury age of onset and severity of self-harm. *Suicide and Life-Threatening Behavior, 48*(1), 31–38. https://doi.org/10.1111/sltb.12330

Andover, M. S., & Gibb, B. E. (2010). Non-suicidal self-injury, attempted suicide, and suicidal intent among psychiatric inpatients. *Psychiatry Research, 178*(1), 101–105. https://doi.org/10.1016/j.psychres.2010.03.019

Anestis, M. D., Khazem, L. R., & Law, K. C. (2015). How many times and how many ways: The impact of number of nonsuicidal self-injury methods on the relationship between nonsuicidal self-injury frequency and suicidal behavior. Suicide and Life-Threatening *Behavior, 45*(2), 164–177. https://doi.org/10.1111/sltb.12120

Asarnow, J. R., Porta, G., Spirito, A., Emslie, G., Clarke, G., Wagner, K. D., Vitiello, B., Keller, M., Birmaher, B., McCracken, J., Mayes, T., Berk, M., & Brent, D. A. (2011). Suicide attempts and nonsuicidal self-injury in the treatment of resistant depression in adolescents: Findings from the TORDIA study. *Journal of the American Academy of Child and Adolescent Psychiatry, 50*(3), 772–781. https://doi.org/10.1016/j.jaac.2011.04.003

Bell, T. M., Qiao, N., Jenkins, P. C., Siedlecki, C. B., & Fecher, A. M. (2016). Trends in emergency department visits for nonfatal violence-related injuries among adolescents in the United States, 2009-2013. *Journal of Adolescent Health, 58*(5), 573–575. https://doi.org/10.1016/j.jadohealth.2015.12.016

Blades, C. A., Stritzke, W. G. K., Page, A. C., & Brown, J. D. (2018). The benefits and risks of asking research participants about suicide: A meta-analysis of the impact of exposure to suicide-related content. *Clinical Psychology Review, 64*, 1–12. https://doi.org/10.1016/j.cpr.2018.07.001

Brickell, C. M., & Jellinek, M. S. (2014). Self-injury: Why teens do it, how to help. *Contemporary Pediatrics, 31*(3), 22–27.

Cama, S. F., & Fosbenner, S. (2021). Nonsuicidal self-injury in youth: A primer for pediatricians. *Pediatric Annals, 50*(2), e72–e76. https://doi.org/10.3928/19382359-20210121-01

Coppersmith, D. D., Bentley, K. H., Kleiman, E. M., & Nock, M. K. (2021). Variability in the functions of nonsuicidal self-injury: Evidence from three real-time monitoring studies. *Behavior Therapy, 52*(6), 1516–1528.

Fox, K. R., Franklin, J. C., Ribeiro, J. D., Kleiman, E. M., Bentley, K. H., & Nock, M. K. (2015). Meta-analysis of risk factors for nonsuicidal self-injury. *Clinical Psychology Review, 42*, 156–167. https://doi.org/10.1016/j.cpr.2015.09.002

Franklin, J. C., Ribeiro, J. D., Fox, K. R., Bentley, K. H., Kleiman, E. M., Huang, Xieyining, Musacchio, K. M., Jaroszewksi, A. C., Chang, B. P., & Nock, M. K. (2017). Risk factors for suicidal thoughts and behaviors: A meta-analysis of 50 years of research. *Psychological Bulletin, 143*(2), 187–232. https://doi.org/10.1037/bul0000084

Gerle, E., Fischer, A., & Lundh, L.G. (2019). "Voluntarily admitted against my will": Patient perspectives on effects of, and alternatives to, coercion in psychiatric care for self-injury. *Journal of Patient Experience, 6*(4), 265–270. https://doi.org/10.1177/2374373518800811

Gillies, D., Christou, M. A., Dixon, A. C., Featherston, O. J., Rapti, I., Garcia-Anguita, A., Villasis-Keever, M., Reebye, P., Christou, E., Al Kabir, N., & Christou, P. A. (2018). Prevalence and characteristics of self-harm in adolescents: Meta-analyses of community-based studies 1990–2015. *Journal of the American Academy of Child and Adolescent Psychiatry, 57*(10), 733–741. https://doi.org/10.1016/j.jaac.2018.06.018

Gray, G. V., Brody, D. S., & Johnson, D. (2005). The evolution of behavioral primary care. *Professional Psychology: Research and Practice, 36*(2), 123–129. https://doi.org/10.1037/0735-7028.36.2.123

Halverson, T. F., Patel, T. A., Mann, A. J. D., Evans, M. K., Gratz, K. L., Beckham, J. C., Calhoun, P. S., & Kimbrel, N. A. (2022). The Screen for Nonsuicidal Self-Injury: Development and initial validation among veterans with psychiatric disorders. *Suicide and Life-Threatening Behavior, 52*(4), 615–630. https://doi.org/10.1111/sltb.12847

Heath, N. L., & Nixon, M. K. (2009). Assessment of nonsuicidal self-injury in youth. In M. K. Nixon & N. L. Heath (Eds.), *Self-injury in youth: The essential guide to assessment and intervention* (pp. 143–170). Routledge.

Ingraham, K., Hughes, C., Taliaferro, L., Westers, N. J., Dieker, L., & Hynes, M. (2019). Using digital puppetry to prepare physicians to address non-suicidal self-injury among teens. In M. Antona & C. Stephanidis (Eds.), *Universal access in human-computer interaction. Theory, methods and tools* (pp. 555–568). Springer. https://doi.org/10.1007/978-3-030-23560-4

Joiner, T. E. (2005). *Why people die by suicide.* Harvard University Press.

Kameg, K. M., Woods, A. S., Szpak, J. L., & McCormick, M. (2013). Identifying and managing nonsuicidal self-injurious behavior in the primary care setting. *Journal of the American Association of Nurse Practitioners, 25*(4), 167–172. https://doi.org/10.1111/1745-7599.12006

Kerr, P. L., Muehlenkamp, J. J., & Turner, J. M. (2010). Nonsuicidal self-injury: A review of current research for family medicine and primary care physicians. *Journal of the American Board of Family Medicine, 23*(2), 240–259. https://doi.org/10.3122/jabfm.2010.02.090110

Klein, D. A., Goldenring, J. M., & Adelman, W. P. (2014). HEEADSSS 3.0: The psychosocial interview for adolescents updated for a new century fueled by media. *Contemporary Pediatrics, 31*(1), 16–28.

Klonsky, E. D. (2011). Non-suicidal self-injury in United States adults: Prevalence, sociodemographics, topography and functions. *Psychological Medicine, 41*(9), 1981–1986. https://doi.org/10.1017/S0033291710002497

Larkin, G. L., Beautrais, A. L., Spirito, A., Kirrane, B. M., Lippmann, M. J., & Milzman, D. P. (2009). Mental health and emergency medicine: A research agenda. *Academic Emergency Medicine, 16*(11), 1110–1119. https://doi.org/10.1111/j.1553-2712.2009.00545.x

Malaga, E. G., Aguilera, E. M. M., Eaton, C., & Ameerally, P. (2016). Management of self-harm injuries in the maxillofacial region: A report of 2 cases and review of the literature. *Journal of Oral and Maxillofacial Surgery, 74*(6), 1198.e1–1198.e9. https://doi.org/10.1016/j.joms.2016.02.018.

Matney, J., Westers, N. J., Horton, S. E., King, J. D., Eaddy, M., Emslie, G. J., Kennard, B. D., & Stewart, S. M. (2018). Frequency and methods of nonsuicidal self-injury in relation to acquired capability for suicide among adolescents. *Archives of Suicide Research, 22*(1), 91–105. https://doi.org/10.1080/13811118.2017.1283266

Mercado, M. C., Holland, K., Leemis, R. W., Stone, D. M., & Wang, J. (2017). Trends in emergency department visits for nonfatal self-inflicted injuries among youth aged 10 to 24 years in the United States, 2001–2015. *JAMA, 318*(19), 1931–1933. https://doi.org/10.1001/jama.2017.13317

Møhl, B. (2020). *Assessment and treatment of non-suicidal self-injury: A clinical perspective.* Routledge.

Muehlenkamp, J. J. (2005). Self-injurious behavior as a separate clinical syndrome. *American Journal of Orthopsychiatry, 75*(2), 324–333. https://doi.org/10.1037/0002-9432.75.2.324

Muehlenkamp, J. J., Claes, L., Quigley, K., Prosser, E., Claes, S., & Jans, D. (2013). Association of training on attitudes towards self-injuring clients across health professionals. *Archives of Suicide Research, 17*(4), 462–468. https://doi.org/10.1080/13811118.2013.801815

Muehlenkamp, J. J., Walsh, B. W., & McDade, M. (2010). Preventing non-suicidal self-injury in adolescents: The signs of self-injury program. *Journal of Youth and Adolescence, 39*, 306–314. https://doi.org/10.1007/s10964-009-9450-8

Muehlenkamp, J. J., Xhunga, N., & Brausch, A. M. (2019). Self-injury age of onset: A risk factor for NSSI severity and suicidal behavior. *Archives of Suicide Research, 23*(4), 551–563. https://doi.org/10.1080/13811118.2018.1486252

Neff, K. D. (2003). The development and validation of a scale to measure self-compassion. *Self and Identity, 2*(3), 223–250. https://doi.org/10.1080/15298860309027

Nock, M. K., Joiner, T. E., Gordon, K. H., Lloyd-Richardson, E., & Prinstein, M. J. (2006). Non-suicidal self-injury among adolescents: Diagnostic correlates and relation to suicide attempts. *Psychiatry Research*, *144*(1), 65–72. https://doi.org/10.1016/j.psychres.2006.05.010

Nock, M. K., & Prinstein, M. J. (2004). A functional approach to the assessment of self-mutilative behavior. *Journal of Consulting and Clinical Psychology*, *72*, 885–890. https://doi.org/10.1037/0022-006X.72.5.885

Paul, E., Tsypes, A., Eidlitz, L., Emhout, C., & Whitlock, J. (2015). Frequency and functions of non-suicidal self-injury: Associations with suicidal thoughts and behaviors. *Psychiatry Research*, *225*(3), 276–282. https://doi.org/10.1016/j.psychres.2014.12.026

Plener, P. L., Brunner, R., Fegert, J. M., Groschwitz, R. C., In-Albon, T., Kaess, M., Kapusta, N. D., Resch, F., & Becker, K. (2016). Treating nonsuicidal self-injury (NSSI) in adolescents: Consensus based German guidelines. *Child and Adolescent Psychiatry and Mental Health*, *10*, 46. https://doi.org/10.1186/s13034-016-0134-3

Prochaska, J. O., & DiClemente, C. C. (1983). Stages and processes of self-change of smoking: Toward an integrative model of change. *Journal of Consulting and Clinical Psychology*, *51*(3), 390–395. https://doi.org/10.1037//0022-006x.51.3.390

Raja, S., Hoersch, M., Rajagopalan, C. F., & Chang, P. (2014). Treating patients with traumatic life experiences. *The Journal of the American Dental Association*, *145*(3), 238–245. https://doi.org/10.14219/jada.2013.30

Robinson, K., & Wilson, M. S. (2020). Open to interpretation? Inconsistent reporting of lifetime nonsuicidal self-injury across two common assessments. *Psychological Assessment*, *32*(8), 726–738.https://doi.org/10.1037/pas0000830

Rollnick, S., Miller, W. R., & Butler, C. C. (2008). *Motivational interviewing in health care: Helping patients change behavior*. Guilford Press.

Taliaferro, L. A., Muehlenkamp, J. J., Hetler, J., Edwall, G., Wright, C., Edwards, A., & Borowsky, I. W. (2013). Nonsuicidal self-injury among adolescents: A training priority for primary care providers. *Suicide and Life-Threatening Behavior*, *43*(3), 250–261. https://doi.org/10.1111/sltb.12001

Taliaferro, L. A., Westers, N. J., Matsumiya, B., Ingraham, K., Muehlenkamp, J. J., & Hughes, C. E. (2023). Improving capacity to identify, assess, and manage adolescents engaging in non-suicidal self-injury using patient avatars. *Medical Teacher*. Advance online publication. https://doi.org/10.1080/0142159X.2023.2216861

Tuisku, V., Kiviruusu, O., Pelkonen, M., Karlsson, L., Strandholm, T., & Marttunen, M. (2014). Depressed adolescents as young adults—Predictors of suicide attempt and non-suicidal self-injury during an 8-year follow-up. *Journal of Affective Disorders*, *152–154*, 313–319. https://doi.org/10.1016/j.jad.2013.09.031

Turner, B. J., Layden, B. K., Butler, S. M., & Chapman, A. L. (2013). How often, or how many ways: Clarifying the relationship between nonsuicidal self-injury and suicidality. *Archives of Suicide Research*, *17*(4), 397–415. https://doi.org/10.1080/13811118.2013.802660

Victor, S. E., Devendorf, A. R., Lewis, S. P., Rottenberg, J., Muehlenkamp, J. J., Stage, D. L., & Miller, R. H. (2022). Only human: Mental health difficulties among clinical, counseling, and school psychology faculty and trainees. *Perspectives on Psychological Science*, *17*(6), 1576–1590. https://doi.org/10.31234/osf.io/xbfr6

Victor, S. E., Lewis, S. P., & Muehlenkamp, J. J. (2022). Psychologists with lived experience of non-suicidal self-injury: Priorities, obstacles, and recommendations for inclusion. *Psychological Services*, *19*(1), 21–28. https://doi.org/10.1037/ser0000510

Vijay, A., Salmon, M. R., & Stewart, C. E. (2018). Suicide and non-suicidal self-injury. In S. Y. Vinson & E. S. Vinson (Eds.), *Pediatric mental health for primary care providers: A clinician's guide* (pp. 33–46). Springer. https://doi.org/10.1007/978-3-319-90350-7_4

Walsh, B. W. (2012). *Treating self-injury: A practical guide* (2nd ed.). Guilford Press.

Wang, J., Xie, H., Holland, K. M., Sumner, S. A., Balaji, A. B., David-Ferdon, C. F., & Crosby, A. E. (2019). Self-directed violence after medical emergency department visits among youth. *American Journal of Preventive Medicine*, *56*(2), 205–214. https://doi.org/10.1016/j.amepre.2018.09.014

Washburn, J. J. (2014). *Self-injury: Simple answers to complex questions*. Alexian Brothers Press.

Westers, N. J., Muehlenkamp, J. J., & Lau, M. (2016). SOARS model: Risk assessment of nonsuicidal self-injury. *Contemporary Pediatrics*, *33*(7), 25–31.

Westers, N. J., Needham, H. E., & Walsh, J. B. (2023). Effectiveness of a nonsuicidal self-injury curriculum on improving pediatric residents' knowledge and competence in caring for adolescents who self-injure. *Academic Psychiatry*, *47*(1), 18–24. https://doi.org/10.1007/s40596-022-01684-3

Westers, N. J., & Plener, P. L. (2020). Managing risk and self-harm: Keeping young people safe. *Clinical Child Psychology and Psychiatry, 25*(3), 610–624. https://doi.org/10.1177/1359104519895064

Whitlock, J., & Knox, K. L. (2007). The relationship between self-injurious behavior and suicide in a young adult population. *Archives of Pediatrics and Adolescent Medicine, 161*(7), 634–640. https://doi.org/10.1001/archpedi.161.7.634.

Willett, A. B. S., Marken, R. S., Parker, M. G., & Mansell, W. (2017). Control blindness: Why people can make incorrect inferences about the intentions of others. *Attention, Perception & Psychophysics, 79*(3), 841–849. https://doi.org/10.3758/s13414-016-1268-3

Wilkinson, P., Kelvin, R., Roberts, C., Dubicka, B., & Goodyer, I. (2011) Clinical and psychosocial predictors of suicide attempts and nonsuicidal self-injury in the Adolescent Depression Antidepressants and Psychotherapy Trial (ADAPT). *The American Journal of Psychiatry, 168*(5), 495–501. https://doi.org/10.1176/appi.ajp.2010.10050718

CHAPTER 45

Novel Assessment Methods for Differentiating Those at Risk for Suicidal and Nonsuicidal Self-Injurious Behaviors

Taylor A. Burke, Brooke A. Ammerman, *and* Richard T. Liu

Abstract

This chapter reviews novel assessment methods for differentiating risk for suicidal and nonsuicidal self-injurious behaviors. An overview is provided of several prominent conceptualizations of how these distinct clinical phenomena interrelate. The chapter discusses the measurement of NSSI and related processes, with a focus on self-report questionnaires and interviews, as well as laboratory-based behavioral measures and neuroimaging paradigms that may inform our understanding of NSSI and its similarity to and distinction from suicidal behaviors. The chapter also presents emerging approaches that seem particularly promising for the purpose of differentiating risk for NSSI and suicidal behavior. It concludes with a review of the challenges and limitations of methodological paradigms aimed at differentiating risk for NSSI and suicidal behavior.

Key Words: NSSI, assessment, suicidal behavior, virtual reality, digital phenotyping, wearable technology, medical lethality, frequency

Introduction

Although NSSI has historically been viewed as existing along a continuum of severity with suicidal behaviors (Brent, 2011; Liu et al., 2016), it has received growing recognition as a distinct phenomenon and clinically important behavior in its own right (e.g., Muehlenkamp, 2005). Reflecting this shift, early terms commonly adopted to describe NSSI behavior (e.g., self-mutilation, deliberate self-harm, and self-destructive behavior) did not differentiate between forms of self-injury based on the presence versus absence of suicidal intent (Angelotta, 2015; Prinstein, 2008), whereas the term "NSSI" is now commonly used to describe behavior that differs from suicidal behavior in its complete absence of any suicidal intent (Nock, 2010). Indeed, the very basis of this distinction is inherent in the term "NSSI" itself.

Beyond the underlying intent of the behavior, NSSI also differs notably in its phenomenology from suicidal behavior in terms of general frequency and medical lethality. Specifically, NSSI tends to occur much more frequently than suicidal behavior, with this difference being particularly noticeable in clinical samples. For example, in a sample of psychiatric inpatients, the mean frequency for suicide attempts was found to be 2.14 (SD = 2.76), and, in contrast, the mean frequency for NSSI was 156.92 (SD = 680.81) over the same time period (Andover & Gibb, 2010). As for medical lethality, NSSI typically involves lower-lethality methods (e.g., physically superficial cutting) than is often the case for suicidal behavior (e.g., self-inflicted gun shots; Muehlenkamp, 2005; Muehlenkamp & Gutierrez, 2004). This is, in part, due to the fact that NSSI occurs in the absence of suicide intent and, in some cases, is adopted specifically as a method to cope with suicidal thoughts (i.e., antisuicide function; Klonsky, 2007).

With greater recognition of NSSI as a distinct and clinically important outcome, there has been a corresponding increase in the measures available for assessing this behavior, as well as a growing body of theoretical and empirical literature devoted to disambiguating risk for non\suicidal and suicidal self-injury. In the current chapter, we begin first with a focus on the nature of the relationship between NSSI and suicidal self-injury, including an overview of several prominent conceptualizations of how these two clinical phenomena may interrelate. Next, we provide a discussion of the measurement of NSSI and related processes, with a focus on self-report questionnaires and interviews, as well as laboratory-based behavioral measures and neuroimaging paradigms that may inform our understanding of NSSI and its similarity to and distinction from suicidal behaviors. As part of this discussion, we will also present relatively more recent methodological developments in the study of self-injurious behaviors, including unique opportunities provided by virtual reality, digital phenotyping, and wearables to differentiate between NSSI and suicidal behaviors. This discussion will also include reflections on the challenges and potential limitations of methodological paradigms aimed at differentiating risk for NSSI and suicidal behavior. Finally, we end with a focus on considerations and implications for the assessment of NSSI in research and across different clinical contexts.

Empirical and Theoretical Considerations for Differentiating Nonsuicidal from Suicidal Self-Injury

As context for describing current theoretical conceptualizations of NSSI in relation to suicidal behavior, it should be acknowledged that although now generally viewed as clinically distinct behaviors, these two forms of self-injury nevertheless share significant overlap in their occurrence and underlying etiologies (Brent, 2011; Knorr et al., 2019). For example, a history of suicide attempts accompanied 36.94% of NSSI cases in a clinical sample of adolescents (Asarnow et al., 2011). This closely matches the rate observed in a recent epidemiological study of young adults, with 39.6% of those with lifetime history of NSSI also having a history of suicidal behavior and 66.3% of those with lifetime suicide attempt history also having previously engaged in NSSI (Voss et al., 2020). Regarding overlapping etiologies, both NSSI and suicidal behavior have been observed to be characterized by poor social problem-solving (Brent, 2011; Nock, 2010; Pollock & Williams, 2004), difficulties with emotion regulation (Gratz et al., 2020; Neacsiu et al., 2018; Nock, 2009), negative cognitive tendencies (Abramson et al., 2000; Nock, 2010; Wenzel & Beck, 2008), as well as adverse childhood experiences (e.g., child maltreatment; Ammerman et al., 2018; Liu et al., 2018; Turecki & Brent, 2016). Furthermore, both NSSI and suicidal behavior feature some of the same psychiatric comorbidities (Nock, 2010).

These commonalities between NSSI and suicidal behavior, however, do not invalidate the current view of these phenomena as distinct from each other, supported by empirical evidence of the existence of distinct differences in underlying characteristics (e.g., neurobiological and motivational processes; Brent, 2011). Indeed, this degree of overlap and comorbidity is not uncharacteristic of other forms of psychopathology commonly held to be distinct (e.g., depression and anxiety; Anderson & Hope, 2008; Clark & Watson, 1991; Cole et al., 1998), and instead, these commonalities speak to the current challenge of differentiating risk for NSSI from risk for suicidal behaviors.[1] Several conceptual models, some discussed in Victor et al., this volume, have been proposed in part to address this challenge, to attempt to account for the relationship between NSSI and suicidal behavior. Some of these are briefly presented below: a third variable hypothesis, the gateway theory, the interpersonal theory of suicide, and an integrated model.

Perhaps the simplest of these conceptualizations of the association between NSSI and suicidal behavior is that these clinical outcomes may not have a direct causal association with each other and are instead better accounted for by shared risk factors that preexist both outcomes—that is, a third variable hypothesis (Klonsky et al., 2013; Hamza et al., 2012). Several of the aforementioned characteristics associated with both NSSI and suicidal behavior (e.g., emotion regulation difficulties, child maltreatment experiences, or a preexisting psychiatric disorder, such as borderline personality disorder) may serve as potential third variable candidates within this conceptual framework. Although it is possible that there may be some explanatory causal third variables, there is much evidence to support the view of a unique association between NSSI and suicidal behavior, independent of overlapping characteristics. That is, NSSI has been found to predict suicidal behavior after accounting for variables that share an association with both (Klonsky et al., 2013; Hamza et al., 2012).

Another conceptualization that has received empirical attention is the gateway theory (Whitlock et al., 2013). According to this perspective, NSSI may serve as a gateway behavior that potentiates future initiation of more severe forms of self-injury (i.e., suicidal behavior), in much the same manner that certain drugs have been perceived as serving as gateways for future use of harder drugs (Kandel, 1975; Kirby & Barry, 2012).[2] Consistent with this theory, NSSI has been found to be a robust predictor of future suicidal behavior. In fact, it appears to be an even stronger predictor of future suicide attempts than is a past history of attempted suicide (Ribeiro et al., 2016). This theory may also account for the high co-occurrence of NSSI and suicidal behavior described above. Also, as previously mentioned, the evidence countering the third variable hypothesis is supportive of a unique association between NSSI and suicidal behavior. Additional findings consistent with the possibility that NSSI may serve as a gateway for suicidal behavior is that NSSI typically has an earlier age of onset than does suicidal behavior (Hamza et al., 2012).

What is unclear in the gateway theory, however, is *how* NSSI might lead to increased risk of future suicidal behavior; potential mechanistic pathways underlying the relationship between these two phenomena are not described. The interpersonal theory of suicide (Joiner, 2005; Joiner et al., 2012; Van Orden et al., 2010) provides one such account. According to this theory, not everyone who experiences suicidal thoughts acts on those thoughts because they lack the capability for suicide. That is, they would need to overcome intrinsic self-preserving barriers to engaging in potentially medically serious or lethal self-injury (i.e., the pain and fear associated with death). Engagement in NSSI may therefore weaken the fear and attenuate the pain associated with death, and thus through engagement in this behavior, individuals may acquire the capability for suicide. Although there is evidence that NSSI is associated with reduced pain sensitivity (Koenig et al., 2016), whether this pain tolerance temporally precedes, and thus predisposes certain individuals to engage in NSSI, or occurs as a consequence of NSSI engagement remains unclear. More broadly, although NSSI is now firmly established as a risk factor for suicidal behavior, there is currently a paucity of longitudinal studies directly evaluating mediators of this association.

Finally, it is important to note that these conceptualizations of NSSI and suicidal behavior should not be regarded as mutually exclusive. Rather, they may be complementary. It may be that certain risk factors are indeed third variables accounting for risk for both NSSI and suicidal behavior, and NSSI may nonetheless also serve as a causal risk factor for future suicidal behavior through the processes outlined in the gateway theory and the interpersonal theory of suicide. That is, according to this view, NSSI and suicidal behavior share overlapping diatheses but also have processes of risk unique to each form of self-injury. Indeed, this possibility of nonmutual exclusivity has been recently proposed within an integrated theoretical model (Hamza et al., 2012). According to this model, NSSI may be associated with suicidal behavior through several means. First, these two forms of self-injury may have shared etiological factors (i.e., third variable hypothesis). Furthermore, NSSI may confer risk for suicidal behavior in the presence of interpersonal stress (i.e., a diathesis-stress model), and NSSI severity may lead to an acquired capability for suicide, which interacts with perceived burdensomeness and thwarted belongingness (other key components of the interpersonal theory of suicide) to result in risk for suicidal behavior (i.e., a moderated mediation model within the interpersonal theory of suicide).

Assessment Approaches in Differentiating Suicidal and Nonsuicidal Self-Injury

Given the extensive literature supporting the distinction between nonsuicidal and suicidal self-injury, several assessment methodologies have been implemented with the aim of differentiating NSSI and suicidal behavior risk. These assessment methods may be characterized on a continuum from direct assessments (i.e., via self-reported non-suicidal and suicidal behaviors) to indirect or implicit processes thought to be closely linked to NSSI and suicidal behaviors (i.e., utilizing laboratory tasks). While numerous studies examining risk for NSSI and/or suicidal behaviors are in existence, this chapter focuses on methodologies that are most directly relevant to the assessment of NSSI and suicidal behavior.

Self-Report Assessments

Self-report questionnaires are the most common assessments of NSSI and suicidal behavior, reliant on an individual's report of their behavior and associated motivations. While numerous self-report questionnaires of NSSI and suicidal behavior exist (for reviews, see Batterham et al., 2015; Chávez-Flores et al., 2019; Cloutier & Humphreys, 2009), they almost exclusively assess NSSI and suicidal behaviors independent from one another (i.e., in separate self-report questionnaires, which may or may not be administered in the same battery). Thus, while NSSI is consistently defined as being a behavior engaged without associated suicidal intent (e.g., American Psychiatric Association, 2013; International Society for the Study of Self-injury, 2018; Nock, 2009), it is dependent on the individual to accurately describe their behavior as occurring with or without suicidal intent, in the absence of direct behavioral comparisons. Self-report questionnaires that assess for both NSSI and suicidal behavior concurrently are used infrequently and have largely been replaced with shorter versions that no longer offer a simultaneous assessment (i.e., Suicidal Behavior Questionnaire vs. Suicidal Behavior Questionnaire—Revised; Linehan & Nielsen, 1981; Osman et al., 2001). However, given the potential advantages of this approach, there have been self-reports designed, or revised (e.g., Self-Injurious Thoughts and Behaviors Interview; Fox et al., 2020; Nock et al., 2007), that concurrently assess for NSSI and suicidal behavior, and are growing in popularity. Self-report tools that allow for the concurrent assessment of both NSSI and suicidal behavior may be superior, as they may offer greater clarity to the respondent about how to differentiate between their own self-injurious behaviors. However, no studies to our knowledge have examined whether the use of self-report questionnaires that measure both NSSI and suicide outperform tools that measure these behaviors independent of one another.

Over the past decade, there has been a surge of research utilizing experience sampling methods (e.g., ecological momentary assessment [EMA]) to assess self-injurious behaviors. Experience sampling methods, such as EMA, can be used to gather data about an individual's thoughts, feelings, or behaviors, in real time, using repeated assessment within one's natural environment. This approach can provide information about the context and possible proximal predictors of NSSI and suicidal behavior. Employing self-report assessments via experience sampling methods may be particularly useful for distinguishing between NSSI and suicidal behavior with greater ecological validity. With these methods, individuals can document their self-injurious behaviors as well as their associated intent (i.e., nonsuicidal vs. suicidal) in real time (i.e., immediately after the behavior), thus reducing recall bias and increasing classification accuracy. Notably, given the frequency of daily assessments, experience sampling methods require very brief assessments to ensure respondents are not overburdened. As a result, with the increasing popularity of such methodologies in both research and clinical contexts, validated batteries of single items that assess for NSSI and suicidal behavior have become available (Forkmann et al., 2018). These single items are most commonly intended to be completed within a singular assessment window, and thus likely benefit from increasing respondents' accuracy through reminding them how to classify NSSI and suicidal self-injury simultaneously (for more information, see Legg et al., this volume).

As the potential of under- *and* overreporting behavioral frequency for both NSSI and suicidal behaviors on self-report questionnaires has been highlighted (Lungu et al., 2019), the past decade has seen a greater emphasis on the use of interviews for assessing, and differentiating between, NSSI and suicidal behaviors. While interviews that independently assess for NSSI and suicidal behaviors exist, simultaneous assessment is more common. The majority of these interviews have been around for over a decade (e.g., Suicide Attempt Self-Injury Interview; Self-Injurious Thoughts and Behaviors Interview; Linehan et al., 2006; Nock et al., 2007) but are now being utilized across diverse (i.e., emergency medicine) and widespread (i.e., among state-level screening initiatives; i.e., Columbia—Suicide Severity Rating Scale; Posner et al., 2011) settings (for more information, see Westers & Tinsley, this volume). In addition to allowing respondents to discuss differences in intent among their self-injurious behaviors, many of these interviews are also semistructured in format. This allows the interviewer to flexibly ask follow-up questions about each behavior, resulting in increased accuracy of behavior categorization (e.g., Millner et al., 2015).

While both self-report questionnaires and interviews differentiate NSSI from suicidal behaviors based on reported behavioral intentions, their advantages and disadvantages should be considered when deciding to employ one or both forms of assessment for research and clinical purposes.

Laboratory-Based Methods

While self-report assessments are most commonly used to assess for and differentiate between NSSI and suicidal behavior, they are limited by individuals' willingness to disclose (e.g., Ammerman et al., 2021; Drum et al., 2009), their interpretation of the definitions of NSSI and suicidal behavior, and their awareness and ability to accurately communicate their behavioral intentions. To address these weaknesses, self-reports are often used in conjunction with laboratory-based methods to assess indirect or implicit differential risk processes of NSSI and suicidal behaviors.

Implicit Association Tests (IATs) are computer-based categorization tasks that permit the assessment of automatic, cognitive self-associations through measuring reaction times when associating the self with another construct. IATs have gained traction in the field of self-injury risk assessments given their ability to capture one's self-associations that may be outside conscious awareness. For example, IATs have been used among those with a history of NSSI and/or suicide attempts to assess implicit self-identification with, or attitudes toward, NSSI, suicide, and/or death by utilizing a range of stimuli, including NSSI-related images, NSSI-relevant words, suicide-related words, and death-related words (Cha et al., 2016; Nock et al., 2010; Nock & Banaji, 2007b, 2007a). Just as with self-report assessments, the majority of studies utilizing IATs have studied NSSI and suicidality separately. The self-injury IAT (which utilizes NSSI-related images and words) has demonstrated great utility in informing NSSI risk. Task performance predicted NSSI status (Nock & Banaji, 2007b), as well as self-cutting behavior during psychiatric hospitalization (Cha et al., 2016) above and beyond demographic and psychiatric factors. Similarly, IATs related to suicide/death were found to distinguish between individuals with lifetime and past-year suicide attempts (Millner et al., 2018) and prospectively predict the experience of suicidal ideation over the subsequent year (Glenn et al., 2019). While limited, the research that has concurrently examined IAT performance in relation to NSSI and suicidal behavior has been informative with regard to overlapping and unique risk processes. Performance on the self-injury IAT (i.e., NSSI-specific IAT) differentiated between individuals with a prior suicide attempt, those with prior suicide ideation but no attempt, and those with no history of ideation or attempt (Nock & Banaji, 2007b). Further, individuals with an NSSI history without a history of suicide attempts more strongly identified with NSSI on the self-injury IAT than those with only suicide attempt history (Dickstein et al., 2015). There has been one large-scale study examining the specificity of the various self-injury IATs in differentiating between those with NSSI and/or suicidal behavior histories (Glenn et al., 2017). Individuals with both NSSI and suicide attempt histories demonstrated a stronger identification with self-injury than noninjury (on the self-injury IAT) and a weaker identification with life but not a stronger identification with death (suicide and death related IATs). Further, the observed effects for the IAT were the strongest when the stimuli matched specific target behaviors: those with only a history of NSSI were found to have an implicit identification with NSSI but not with death or suicide and, alternatively, among individuals with a history of suicidal ideation or attempts, findings suggest differences on the death and suicide IAT but not on the SI-IAT (Glenn et al., 2017). This research highlights the potential utility of utilizing IAT performance in differentiating NSSI versus suicidal behavior risk.

Another laboratory-based method, guided imagery, directs individuals to visualize the step-by-step process leading up to an act of NSSI or a suicide attempt. Several studies have utilized guided imagery specific to NSSI (e.g., Brain et al., 1998, 2002), demonstrating decreases in subjective and physiological measures of negative emotion immediately after an imagined NSSI event. These findings are in contrast to those using guided imagery for suicide attempts; individuals exhibited no changes in negative emotion during or after suicide attempt imagery (Welch et al., 2008). While the co-examination of NSSI and suicide attempt has been limited, guided imagery methods have promise in differentiating NSSI and suicidal behavior risk processes. For example, existing literature provides partial support for an escape conditioning model of NSSI but suggests it may not be an appropriate explanatory model for suicide attempts.

Methods used to examine processes related to the experience of pain, as detailed in Selby & Hughes, this volume, including pain threshold (i.e., the first point of experiencing pain), tolerance (i.e., the duration that pain can be tolerated) and persistence (i.e., the difference between pain threshold and tolerance), have also been utilized among self-injury samples. A meta-analysis of 32 studies underscores the consistency of results utilizing these methods to examine pain processes in relation to NSSI (Koenig et al., 2016). Across different stimuli types used to induce pain (e.g., cold, heat, pressure, and electric shock), individuals engaging in NSSI show greater pain threshold and tolerance and report less pain intensity (i.e., lower subjective reports of a set pain level) compared to healthy controls (Koenig et al., 2016). These methods have also been used to examine different regulatory processes associated with NSSI, with results suggesting that NSSI may not only serve an affect regulation function but also a cognitive regulation function (Franklin et al., 2010). Although pain processes are relevant to engagement in suicidal behavior, including the relationship between NSSI and suicidal behavior, given the theorized role in developing the capability for suicide (Joiner et al., 2012), there has been very limited research to utilize these tasks in relation to suicidal behavior. For example, prior research found that the relationship between physically painful and fear-provoking events (a mechanism by which NSSI may increase suicide risk) and acquired capability for suicide is mediated by pain tolerance (Franklin, Hessel, & Prinstein, 2011); however, NSSI and suicide attempts were not directly assessed in this study. In a more targeted investigation, it was found that pain persistence strengthens the relationship between NSSI and suicidal behaviors (Law et al., 2017). Despite this work, it is still unclear how those with NSSI versus suicidal behavior histories may differ in their perceptions and experiences of pain. Given the relevance of pain processes to both NSSI and suicidal behavior, and yet the distinct differences that pain sensitivity may play in each form of self-injury, future research delineating these processes may be fruitful.

Neuroimaging
Several of the aforementioned laboratory-based methods have been utilized in conjunction with neuroimaging to examine potential neural correlates associated with self-injury, with research centering on NSSI being more prominent than that related to suicidal behavior. For example, utilizing NSSI-related pictures similar to those of the self-injury IAT, individuals with a history of NSSI reported NSSI-related photos to be more arousing and showed increased activation in the limbic system and prefrontal cortex for NSSI-related (vs. neutral) pictures (Plener et al., 2012). Heat stimuli (i.e., from pain processes paradigms) have also been used to examine neural activation among those with NSSI

history at both fixed and idiographic heat levels (Schmahl et al., 2006). Upon exposure to the fixed temperature, those with a NSSI history (vs. without) perceived the stimuli as more painful and demonstrated lower activity in the right posterior parietal cortex. When exposed to individualized pain thresholds, those with a NSSI history showed lower activity in the parietal cortex, greater activity in the left dorsolateral prefrontal cortex, and deactivation in the right amygdala and perigenual portion of the anterior cingulate cortex, areas thought to evaluate pain intensity and be involved in the affective evaluation of pain (Schmahl et al., 2006). A recent study has used a different paradigm to mimic the NSSI experience by carrying out a small incision on an individual's forearm with a razor blade; the primary goal of this laboratory method is to increase the ecological validity of the lab task. Using this method, it was found that following the incision, those with a NSSI history demonstrated greater decreased amygdala activity and normalized functional connectivity in the superiorfrontal gyrus (Reitz et al., 2015).

Integrating findings from the above studies, as well as other lab-based research focused on indirect processes related to self-injury (i.e., self-referential processes), a recent review of the neural correlates associated with NSSI versus suicidality has provided insights into potential similar and unique processes (Auerbach et al., 2021). Authors highlight three primary areas of findings. First, results suggest reduced volume in the ventral prefrontal and orbitofrontal cortices among those with suicidal behavior histories, as well as reduced anterior cingulate cortex volume related to both suicidal behaviors and NSSI. It was also found that blunted striatal activation may characterize those with both suicidal behaviors and NSSI, whereas reduced frontolimbic task-based connectivity is found among only those with suicide attempts. Finally, whereas resting state analyses find there is reduced positive connectivity between the default mode network and salience network among those with a history of suicide attempts, those with a NSSI history exhibit frontolimbic alterations (Auerbach et al., 2021). While much of this work has limited integration of lab-based methods specific to self-injurious behavior (e.g., pain paradigms), this research provides foundational knowledge regarding potential neurobiological differences between those with NSSI and suicide attempt history.

The Assessment Horizon: Emerging Approaches and Opportunities

There are a wide range of emerging approaches that may allow us to differentiate those at risk for suicidal and nonsuicidal behaviors. Acknowledging that it is beyond the scope of this chapter to outline all such emerging approaches, we highlight several that seem particularly promising for the purpose of differentiating risk for NSSI and suicidal behavior: virtual reality; digital phenotyping; linguistic, acoustic, and visual analysis; and wearable monitoring of autonomic processes.

Franklin et al. (2019) recently developed virtual reality (VR) approaches to allow tests of causal hypotheses related to suicidal behavior risk, with the goal of augmenting our understanding of suicide causes. Notably, there is some evidence to support the safety of this paradigm (Franklin et al., 2019; Huang et al., 2021). Demonstrating the validity of this methodological approach, preliminary studies suggest that enacting VR suicide is associated with traditional suicidal behavior risk factors, including male sex, suicide desire, and prior suicidality (Franklin et al., 2019). This research has been extended, finding that experimentally manipulated anticipated consequences of VR suicide (i.e., providing instructions to participants outlining that enacting VR suicide will allow them to avoid a stressor) are associated with engaging in VR suicide (Huang et al., 2020). VR technologies hold promise as a future avenue for differentiating risk for NSSI and suicidal behavior via experimental approaches that examine risk, as well as manipulate risk conditions, for these outcomes, in a safe and controlled environment.

Greater attention is being paid to digital phenotyping, or the passive sensing of smartphones and/or social media to assess risk indices for self-injurious behaviors. Advances in natural language processing for text data and computer vision methodology for image and video data may offer opportunities to distinguish both public (e.g., publicly posted data on social media) and private (e.g., messages, posts, and accessed online content) data as being related to self-injury (Ramírez-Cifuentes et al., 2020; Sawhney et al., 2020; Scherr et al., 2020). As these techniques become more sophisticated, there will be opportunities for assessing more detailed features of risk. For example, there is promise that this technology may be able to assess whether an individual is messaging others or posting content about self-injury with and/or without suicidal intent, and similarly, whether an individual is viewing text, image, or video content depicting self-harm with and/or without suicidal intent. In addition to accessing social media application data, text logs, and search histories, there is opportunity for the real-time collection and analysis of data from a wide range of smartphone sensors, such as GPS and accelerometers, given the numerous smartphone applications that collect an almost limitless amount of user data. Thus, beyond the more direct assessment of whether an individual is communicating about or accessing information regarding NSSI versus suicidal behavior, passive sensing of smartphones may also be able to assess real-time risk factors for self-injurious behaviors, including the identification of risk factors that differentiate self-injurious behaviors based on intent.

Significant advancements in linguistic, acoustic, and visual data analysis also have promise in distinguishing between those at risk for NSSI and suicidal behavior. Recent evidence supports the feasibility and potential success of analyzing linguistic and acoustic speech patterns to automate suicide risk quantification, based on read-aloud sentence tasks (Stasak et al., 2021), spontaneous or naturalistic speech (e.g., Chakravarthula et al., 2020; Gideon et al., 2019), and speech recorded during routine clinical tasks, such as during clinical interviews or in response to clinical tasks (e.g., Belouali et al., 2021; Pestian et al., 2020; Scherer, et al., 2013; Venek, et al., 2014). The application of computer vision, or the automated analysis of visual markers (e.g., facial and body posture), may also be able to quantify self-injury risk based on video data from clinical interviews or a live feed (Laksana et al., 2017). There is substantial opportunity to simultaneously leverage linguistic, acoustic, and visual analysis through employing multimodal assessment (e.g., Shah et al., 2019); these data may then be used to increase the predictive validity of machine learning methods to differentiate those at risk for self-injurious behaviors with and without suicidal intent.

Advancements in wearable technology that allow for real-time autonomic monitoring (i.e., heart rate) may also enhance our ability to differentiate risk for NSSI and suicidal behavior. Indeed, prior literature suggests that autonomic processes such as those measured via electrodermal activity and heart rate are associated with the experience of distress (Kreibig, 2010; Lazarus et al., 1962; Nock & Mendes, 2008). Given that NSSI and suicidal behavior are often engaged in during periods of high distress, autonomic monitoring wearables have promise in detecting their occurrence. These wearables may be able to shed light on whether there are different physiological processes before, during, and after engagement in self-injurious behaviors, based on behavior intent. Despite the availability of such wearable technologies, and thus the ability to assess the autonomic processes associated with self-injury in real time, there has been little published empirical research in this area. However, recent work highlights the feasibility and acceptability of wearing autonomic monitoring devices, including utilizing an "event marker" function, among individuals at high risk for self-injury (Kleiman et al., 2019). Kleiman et al. (2019) found that psychiatrically hospitalized youth used this event marker during periods of time that they were instructed to do so and did so without prompting. These feasibility data suggest that this technology could be used to monitor psychophysiological profiles during episodes of NSSI and suicidal behavior; with enough data, machine learning algorithms could theoretically identify psychophysiological risk states associated with NSSI versus suicidal behavior.

Assessment Challenges

Despite the significant opportunity for advancements in technology and future research to illuminate how we may be able to distinguish risk for self-injurious behaviors engaged in with versus without intent to die, there are notable challenges to conducting this research that apply across the reviewed methodologies. For all ecologically valid methods aiming to assess self-injury and associated behavioral risk states in real time, the low base rate of self-injurious behaviors is limiting. While both NSSI and suicidal behavior occur relatively infrequently, the particularly infrequent nature of suicidal behavior makes it especially challenging to assess in real time. Given the particularly infrequent occurrence of suicidal behavior, very large samples of high-risk participants need to be monitored for long periods of time to obtain an adequate sample of self-injurious behaviors with and without suicide intent for analysis. Further, real-time assessment methods, even those that are passive in nature and thus do not require active engagement from participants, often require a participatory component (e.g., EMA) in order to assess whether a behavior has occurred. Unfortunately, requiring a long period of active participation presents many feasibility challenges. Additionally, given that many, if not all, of the methods outlined ultimately rely on the self-report of NSSI and suicidal behavior for their own validation, it is important to acknowledge (a) the inherent limitations of self-report and (b) that these limitations will necessarily influence the validity of even the most innovative and powerful of indirect assessment methods.

Recommendations for Research and Clinical Practice

While the outlined laboratory-based assessment methods and emerging approaches are exciting and represent great possibility, these methods are not yet validated to be used as a sole assessment for NSSI or suicidal behavior risk within clinical or research settings. Moreover, they are even further from being validated to be able to differentiate risk for NSSI and suicidal behavior, given that many of these methodologies have yet to be utilized among samples reporting NSSI and suicidal behavior. Thus, it is recommended that researchers, as well as clinicians across outpatient, emergency and psychiatric, and school/other settings, rely on self-report questionnaires and interview methods to differentiate these self-injurious behaviors.

Evidence indicates that some people may be more comfortable reporting self-injurious thoughts and behaviors in a self-report questionnaire format as compared to a face-to-face interview format, with rates sometimes being higher in the former (Kaplan et al., 1994; Lungu et al., 2019; Yigletu et al., 2004). However, individuals may sometimes find it difficult to classify and thus differentiate their own self-injurious behaviors. This may be particularly true for individuals who engage in NSSI while simultaneously experiencing suicidal ideation, or for individuals who engage in suicidal behavior with only minor suicidal intent. Thus, using both self-report and interview-based assessment may be considered best practice, as using both may augment the likelihood of identifying all cases while incorporating a check for accuracy (e.g., Millner et al., 2015). For screening purposes, we recommend a first step of using self-report measures that assess for both suicidal and nonsuicidal self-injury and following up positive cases with interview assessments whenever possible. For clinical practice, we recommend that all high-risk patients are assessed for both suicidal and nonsuicidal self-injury on a continual basis, as risk for these behaviors fluctuates significantly over both long and short periods of time (Kleiman et al., 2017). Clinicians should consider *frequently* assessing for both NSSI and suicidal behavior risk among clinically high-risk patients, and this may be particularly important among patients with a history of either NSSI or suicidal behavior given the strength of prior history of self-injury in predicting future suicidal behavior (Franklin et al., 2017).

Conclusion

Nonsuicidal and suicidal self-injurious behaviors are distinct, yet related, high-risk clinical behaviors. Although self-report questionnaire and interview-based assessment methods are currently the gold standard assessment methods for differentiating NSSI and suicidal behavior, a range of laboratory-based methods has been developed, demonstrating initial evidence that they may aid in this pursuit. Technological advancements including the use of virtual reality, digital phenotyping, and wearables have significant promise in moving this effort forward and yet are in their infancy in development and application to distinguishing risk for NSSI and suicidal behavior.

Notes

1. It is interesting to note that much of this discussion regarding the relationship between NSSI and suicidal behavior mirrors the focus several decades ago on the relationship between anxiety and depression (cf. Cole et al., 1998; Dobson, 1985; Kendler et al., 1987), doubtless a reflection of the respective state of depression and anxiety research at the time and the relatively still-nascent stage of NSSI research currently.
2. It should be noted, however, that gateway theory as applied to drug use is not without controversy (Kirby & Barry, 2012).

References

Abramson, L. Y., Alloy, L. B., Hogan, M. E., Whitehouse, W. G., Gibb, B. E., Hankin, B. L., & Cornette, M. M. (2000). The hopelessness theory of suicidality. In T. E. Joiner & M. D. Rudd (Eds.), *Suicide science: Expanding boundaries* (pp. 17–32). Kluwer Academic.

American Psychiatric Association. (2013). *Diagnostic and statistical manual of mental disorders* (5th ed.). https://doi.org/10.1176/appi.books.9780890425596.744053

Ammerman, B. A., Serang, S., Jacobucci, R., Burke, T. A., Alloy, L. B., & McCloskey, M. S. (2018). Exploratory analysis of mediators of the relationship between childhood maltreatment and suicidal behavior. *Journal of Adolescence*, 69, 103–112. https://doi.org/10.1016/j.adolescence.2018.09.004

Ammerman, B. A., Wilcox, K. T., O'Loughlin, C. M., & McCloskey, M. S. (2021). Characterizing the choice to disclose nonsuicidal self-injury. *Journal of Clinical Psychology*, 77(3), 683–700. https://doi.org/10.1002/jclp.23045

Anderson, E., & Hope, D. A. (2008). A review of the tripartite model for understanding the link between anxiety and depression in youth. *Clinical Psychology Review*, 28, 275–287. https://doi.org/10.1016/j.cpr.2007.05.004

Andover, M. S., & Gibb, B. E. (2010). Non-suicidal self-injury, attempted suicide, and suicidal intent among psychiatric inpatients. *Psychiatry Research*, 178, 101–105. https://doi.org/10.1016/j.psychres.2010.03.019

Angelotta, C. (2015). Defining and refining self-harm: A historical perspective on nonsuicidal self-injury. *Journal of Nervous and Mental Disease*, 203, 75–80. https://doi.org/10.1097/NMD.0000000000000243

Asarnow, J. R., Porta, G., Spirito, A., Emslie, G., Clarke, G., Wagner, K. D., Vitiello, B., Keller, M., Birmaher, B., McCracken, J., Mayes, T., Berk, M., & Brent, D. A. (2011). Suicide attempts and nonsuicidal self-injury in the treatment of resistant depression in adolescents: Findings from the TORDIA study. *Journal of the American Academy of Child and Adolescent Psychiatry*, 50, 772–781. https://doi.org/10.1016/j.jaac.2011.04.003

Auerbach, R. P., Chase, H. W., & Brent, D. A. (2021). The elusive phenotype of preadolescent suicidal thoughts and behaviors: Can neuroimaging deliver on its promise? *American Journal of Psychiatry*, 78(4), 285–287. https://doi.org/10.1176/appi.ajp.2020.21010022

Batterham, P. J., Ftanou, M., Pirkis, J., Brewer, J. L., Mackinnon, A. J., Beautrais, A., Kate Fairweather-Schmidt, A., & Christensen, H. (2015). A systematic review and evaluation of measures for suicidal ideation and behaviors in population-based research. *Psychological Assessment*, 27(2), 501–512. https://doi.org/10.1037/pas0000053

Belouali, A., Gupta, S., Sourirajan, V., Yu, J., Allen, N., Alaoui, A., Dutton, M. A., & Reinhard, M. (2021). Acoustic and language analysis of speech for suicide ideation among US veterans. *BioData Mining*, 14, Article 11. https://doi.org/10.1101/2020.07.08.20147504

Brain, K. L., Haines, J., & Williams, C. L. (1998). The psychophysiology of self-mutilation: Evidence of tension reduction. *Archives of Suicide Research*, 4(3), 227–242. https://doi.org/10.1080/13811119808258298

Brain, K. L., Haines, J., & Williams, C. L. (2002). The psychophysiology of repetitive self-mutilation. *Archives of Suicide Research*, 6(3), 199–210. https://doi.org/10.1080/13811110214140

Brent, D. (2011). Nonsuicidal self-injury as a predictor of suicidal behavior in depressed adolescents. *American Journal of Psychiatry, 168*, 452–454. https://doi.org/10.1176/appi.ajp.2011.11020215

Cha, C. B., Augenstein, T. M., Frost, K. H., Gallagher, K., D'Angelo, E. J., & Nock, M. K. (2016). Using implicit and explicit measures to predict nonsuicidal self-injury among adolescent inpatients. *Journal of the American Academy of Child and Adolescent Psychiatry, 55*(1), 62–68. https://doi.org/10.1016/j.jaac.2015.10.008

Chakravarthula, S. N., Nasir, M., Tseng, S. Y., Li, H., Park, T. J., Baucom, B., Bryan, C. J., Narayanan, S., & Georgiou, P. (2020, May). Automatic prediction of suicidal risk in military couples using multimodal interaction cues from couples conversations. *ICASSP, IEEE International Conference on Acoustics, Speech and Signal Processing—Proceedings*. Barcelona, Spain. https://doi.org/10.1109/ICASSP40776.2020.9053246

Chávez-Flores, Y. V., Hidalgo-Rasmussen, C. A., & Yanez-Peñúñuri, L. Y. (2019). Assessment tools of non-suicidal self-injury in adolescents 1990-2016: A systematic review. *Ciencia e Saude Coletiva, 24*(8), 2871–2882. https://doi.org/10.1590/1413-81232018248.18502017

Clark, L. A., & Watson, D. (1991). Tripartite model of anxiety and depression: Psychometric evidence and taxonomic implications. *Journal of Abnormal Psychology, 100*, 316–336. https://doi.org/10.1037/0021-843X.100.3.316

Cloutier, P., & Humphreys, L. (2009). Measurement of nonsuicidal self-injury in adolescents. In M. K. Nixon & N. L. Heath (Eds.), *Self-Injury in youth*: The *essential guide to assessment and intervention* (pp. 115–142). Routledge/Taylor & Francis Group. https://doi.org/10.4324/9780203892671

Cole, D. A., Peeke, L. G., Martin, J. M., Truglio, R., & Seroczynski, A. D. (1998). A longitudinal look at the relation between depression and anxiety in children and adolescents. *Journal of Consulting and Clinical Psychology, 66*, 451–460. https://doi.org/10.1037/0022-006X.66.3.451

Dickstein, D. P., Puzia, M. E., Cushman, G. K., Weissman, A. B., Wegbreit, E., Kim, K. L., Nock, M. K., & Spirito, A. (2015). Self-injurious implicit attitudes among adolescent suicide attempters versus those engaged in nonsuicidal self-injury. *Journal of Child Psychology and Psychiatry and Allied Disciplines, 56*(10): 1127–1136. https://doi.org/10.1111/jcpp.12385

Dobson, K. S. (1985). The relationship between anxiety and depression. *Clinical Psychology Review, 5*, 307–324. https://doi.org/10.1016/0272-7358(85)90010-8

Drum, D. J., Brownson, C., Denmark, A. B., & Smith, S. E. (2009). New data on the nature of suicidal crises in college students: Shifting the paradigm. *Professional Psychology: Research and Practice, 40*(3), 213–222. https://doi.org/10.1037/a0014465

Forkmann, T., Spangenberg, L., Rath, D., Hallensleben, N., Hegerl, U., Kersting, A., & Glaesmer, H. (2018). Assessing suicidality in real time: A psychometric evaluation of self-report items for the assessment of suicidal ideation and its proximal risk factors using ecological momentary assessments. *Journal of Abnormal Psychology, 127*(8), 758–769. https://doi.org/10.1037/abn0000381

Fox, K. R., Harris, J. A., Wang, S. B., Millner, A. J., Deming, C. A., & Nock, M. K. (2020). Self-injurious thoughts and behaviors interview-revised: Development, reliability, and validity. *Psychological Assessment, 32*, 677–689. https://doi.org/10.1037/pas0000819

Franklin, J. C., Hessel, E. T., Aaron, R. V., Arthur, M. S., Heilbron, N., & Prinstein, M. J. (2010). The functions of nonsuicidal self-injury: Support for cognitive-affective regulation and opponent processes from a novel psychophysiological paradigm. *Journal of Abnormal Psychology, 119*(4), 850–862. https://doi.org/10.1037/a0020896

Franklin, J. C., Hessel, E. T., & Prinstein, M. J. (2011). Clarifying the role of pain tolerance in suicidal capability. *Psychiatry Research, 189*, 362–367. https://doi.org/10.1016/j.psychres.2011.08.001

Franklin, J. C., Huang, X., & Bastidas, D. (2019). Virtual reality suicide: Development of a translational approach for studying suicide causes. *Behaviour Research and Therapy, 120*, Article 103360. https://doi.org/10.1016/j.brat.2018.12.013

Franklin, J. C., Ribeiro, J. D., Fox, K. R., Bentley, K. H., Kleiman, E. M., Huang, X., Musacchio, K. M., Jaroszewski, A. C., Chang, B. P., & Nock, M. K. (2017). Risk factors for suicidal thoughts and behaviors: A meta-analysis of 50 years of research. *Psychological Bulletin, 143*(2), 187–232. https://doi.org/10.1037/bul0000084

Gideon, J., Schatten, H. T., McInnis, M. G., & Provost, E. M. (2019, September 15–19). Emotion recognition from natural phone conversations in individuals with and without recent suicidal ideation. *Proceedings of the Annual Conference of the International Speech Communication Association, INTERSPEECH*. Graz, Austria. https://doi.org/10.21437/Interspeech.2019-1830

Glenn, C. R., Millner, A. J., Esposito, E. C., Porter, A. C., & Nock, M. K. (2019). Implicit identification with death predicts suicidal thoughts and behaviors in adolescents. *Journal of Clinical Child and Adolescent Psychology, 48*(2), 263–272. https://doi.org/10.1080/15374416.2018.1528548

Glenn, J. J., Werntz, A. J., Slama, S. J. K., Steinman, S. A., Teachman, B. A., & Nock, M. K. (2017). Suicide and self-injury-related implicit cognition: A large-scale examination and replication. *Journal of Abnormal Psychology, 126*(2), 199–211. https://doi.org/10.1037/abn0000230

Gratz, K. L., Spitzen, T. L., & Tull, M. T. (2020). Expanding our understanding of the relationship between nonsuicidal self-injury and suicide attempts: The roles of emotion regulation self-efficacy and the acquired capability for suicide. *Journal of Clinical Psychology, 76*, 1653–1667. https://doi.org/10.1002/jclp.22950

Hamza, C. A., Stewart, S. L., & Willoughby, T. (2012). Examining the link between nonsuicidal self-injury and suicidal behavior: A review of the literature and an integrated model. *Clinical Psychology Review, 32*(6), 482–495. https://doi.org/10.1016/j.cpr.2012.05.003

Huang, X., Funsch, K. M., Park, E. C., Conway, P., Franklin, J. C., & Ribeiro, J. D. (2021). Longitudinal studies support the safety and ethics of virtual reality suicide as a research method. *Scientific Reports, 11*(1), Article 9653. https://doi.org/10.1038/s41598-021-89152-0

Huang, X., Funsch, K. M., Park, E. C., & Franklin, J. C. (2020). Anticipated consequences as the primary causes of suicidal behavior: Evidence from a laboratory study. *Behaviour Research and Therapy, 134*, Article 103726. https://doi.org/10.1016/j.brat.2020.103726

International Society for the Study of Self-injury. (2018, May). *What is self-injury?* Retrieved from https://itriples.org/about-self-injury/what-is-self-injury.

Joiner, T. E. (2005). *Why people die by suicide*. Harvard University Press.

Joiner, T. E., Ribeiro, J. D., & Silva, C. (2012). Nonsuicidal self-injury, suicidal behavior, and their co-occurrence as viewed through the lens of the interpersonal theory of suicide. *Current Directions in Psychological Science, 21*, 342–347. https://doi.org/10.1177/0963721412454873

Kandel, D. (1975). Stages in adolescent involvement in drug use. *Science, 190*, 912–914. https://doi.org/10.1126/science.1188374

Kaplan, M. L., Asnis, G. M., Sanderson, W. C., Keswani, L., de Lecuona, J. M., & Joseph, S. (1994). Suicide assessment: Clinical interview vs. self-report. *Journal of Clinical Psychology, 50*(2), 294–298. https://doi.org/10.1002/1097-4679(199403)50:2<294::AID-JCLP2270500224>3.0.CO;2-R

Kendler, K. S., Heath, A. C., Martin, N. G., & Eaves, L. J. (1987). Symptoms of anxiety and symptoms of depression: Same genes, different environments? *Archives of General Psychiatry, 44*, 451–457. https://doi.org/10.1001/archpsyc.1987.01800170073010

Kirby, T., & Barry, A. E. (2012). Alcohol as a gateway drug: A study of US 12th graders. *Journal of School Health, 82*, 371–379. https://doi.org/10.1111/j.1746-1561.2012.00712.x

Kleiman, E. M., Turner, B. J., Fedor, S., Beale, E. E., Huffman, J. C., & Nock, M. K. (2017). Examination of real-time fluctuations in suicidal ideation and its risk factors: Results from two ecological momentary assessment studies. *Journal of Abnormal Psychology, 126*(6), 726–738. https://doi.org/10.1037/abn0000273

Kleiman, E., Millner, A. J., Joyce, V. W., Nash, C. C., Buonopane, R. J., & Nock, M. K. (2019). Using wearable physiological monitors with suicidal adolescent inpatients: Feasibility and acceptability study. *JMIR mHealth and uHealth, 7*(9), e13725.

Klonsky, E. D. (2007). The functions of deliberate self-injury: A review of the evidence. In *Clinical Psychology Review, 27*(2), 226–239. https://doi.org/10.1016/j.cpr.2006.08.002

Klonsky, E., May, A. M., & Glenn, C. R. (2013). The relationship between nonsuicidal self-injury and attempted suicide: Converging evidence from four samples. *Journal of Abnormal Psychology, 122*(1), 231–237. https://doi.org/10.1037/a0030278

Knorr, A. C., Ammerman, B. A., Hamilton, A. J., & McCloskey, M. S. (2019). Predicting status along the continuum of suicidal thoughts and behavior among those with a history of nonsuicidal self-injury. *Psychiatry Research, 273*, 514–522. https://doi.org/10.1016/j.psychres.2019.01.067

Koenig, J., Thayer, J. F., & Kaess, M. (2016). A meta-analysis on pain sensitivity in self-injury. *Psychological Medicine, 46*(8), 1597–1612. https://doi.org/10.1017/S0033291716000301

Kreibig, S. D. (2010). Autonomic nervous system activity in emotion: A review. *Biological Psychology, 84*(3), 394–421. https://doi.org/10.1016/j.biopsycho.2010.03.010

Laksana, E., Baltrušaitis, T., Morency, L. P., & Pestian, J. P. (2017, May). Investigating facial behavior indicators of suicidal ideation. In *2017 12th IEEE International Conference on Automatic Face & Gesture Recognition (FG 2017)* (pp. 770–777). IEEE.

Law, K. C., Khazem, L. R., Jin, H. M., & Anestis, M. D. (2017). Non-suicidal self-injury and frequency of suicide attempts: The role of pain persistence. *Journal of Affective Disorders, 209*, 254–261 https://doi.org/10.1016/j.jad.2016.11.028

Lazarus, R. S., Speisman, J. C., Mordkoff, A. M., & Davison, L. A. (1962). A laboratory study of psychological stress produced by a motion picture film. *Psychological Monographs: General and Applied, 76*(34), 1–35. https://doi.org/10.1037/h0093861

Linehan, M. M., Comtois, K. A., Brown, M. Z., Heard, H. L., & Wagner, A. (2006). Suicide Attempt Self-Injury Interview (SASII): Development, reliability, and validity of a scale to assess suicide attempts and intentional self-injury. *Psychological Assessment, 18*(3), 303–312. https://doi.org/10.1037/1040-3590.18.3.303

Linehan, M. M., & Nielsen, S. L. (1981). Assessment of suicide ideation and parasuicide: Hopelessness and social desirability. *Journal of Consulting and Clinical Psychology, 49*(5), 773–775. https://doi.org/10.1037/0022-006X.49.5.773

Liu, R. T., Cheek, S. M., & Nestor, B. A. (2016). Non-suicidal self-injury and life stress: A systematic meta-analysis and theoretical elaboration. *Clinical Psychology Review, 47*, 1–14. https://doi.org/10.1016/j.cpr.2016.05.005

Liu, R. T., Scopelliti, K. M., Pittman, S. K., & Zamora, A. S. (2018). Childhood maltreatment and non-suicidal self-injury: A systematic review and meta-analysis. *Lancet Psychiatry, 5*, 51–64. https://doi.org/10.1016/S2215-0366(17)30469-8

Lungu, A., Wilks, C. R., Coyle, T. N., & Linehan, M. M. (2019). assessing suicidal and nonsuicidal self-injury via in-depth interview or self-report: Balancing assessment effort and results. *Suicide and Life-Threatening Behavior, 49*(5), 1347–1359. https://doi.org/10.1111/sltb.12526

Millner, A. J., Coppersmith, D. D. L., Teachman, B. A., & Nock, M. K. (2018). The brief death implicit association test: Scoring recommendations, reliability, validity, and comparisons with the Death Implicit Association Test. *Psychological Assessment, 30*(10), 1356–1366. https://doi.org/10.1037/pas0000580

Millner, A. J., Lee, M. D., & Nock, M. K. (2015). Single-item measurement of suicidal behaviors: Validity and consequences of misclassification. *PLoS ONE, 10*(10), Article e0141606. https://doi.org/10.1371/journal.pone.0141606

Muehlenkamp, J. J. (2005). Self-injurious behavior as a separate clinical syndrome. *American Journal of Orthopsychiatry, 75*, 324–333. https://doi.org/10.1037/0002-9432.75.2.324

Muehlenkamp, J. J., & Gutierrez, P. M. (2004). An investigation of differences between self-injurious behavior and suicide attempts in a sample of adolescents. *Suicide and Life-Threatening Behavior, 34*, 12–23. https://doi.org/10.1521/suli.34.1.12.27769

Neacsiu, A. D., Fang, C. M., Rodriguez, M., & Rosenthal, M. Z. (2018). Suicidal behavior and problems with emotion regulation. *Suicide and Life-Threatening Behavior, 48*, 52–74. https://doi.org/10.1111/sltb.12335

Nock, M. K. (2009). Why do people hurt themselves?: New insights into the nature and functions of self-injury. *Current Directions in Psychological Science, 18*, 78–83. https://doi.org/10.1111/j.1467-8721.2009.01613.x

Nock, M. K. (2010). Self-Injury. *Annual Review of Clinical Psychology, 6*, 339–363. https://doi.org/10.1146/annurev.clinpsy.121208.131258

Nock, M. K., & Banaji, M. R. (2007a). Assessment of self-injurious thoughts using a behavioral test. *American Journal of Psychiatry, 164*(5), 820–823. https://doi.org/10.1176/ajp.2007.164.5.820

Nock, M. K., & Banaji, M. R. (2007b). Prediction of suicide ideation and attempts among adolescents using a brief performance-based test. *Journal of Consulting and Clinical Psychology, 75*, 707–715. https://doi.org/10.1037/0022-006X.75.5.707

Nock, M. K., Holmberg, E. B., Photos, V. I., & Michel, B. D. (2007). self-injurious thoughts and behaviors interview: Development, reliability, and validity in an adolescent sample. *Psychological Assessment, 19*, 309–317. https://doi.org/10.1037/1040-3590.19.3.309

Nock, M. K., & Mendes, W. B. (2008). Physiological arousal, distress tolerance, and social problem-solving deficits among adolescent self-injurers. *Journal of Consulting and Clinical Psychology, 76*, 28–38. https://doi.org/10.1037/0022-006X.76.1.28

Nock, M. K., Park, J. M., Finn, C. T., Deliberto, T. L., Dour, H. J., & Banaji, M. R. (2010). Measuring the suicidal mind: Implicit cognition predicts suicidal behavior. *Psychological Science, 21*, 511–517. https://doi.org/10.1177/0956797610364762

Osman, A., Bagge, C. L., Gutierrez, P. M., Konick, L. C., Kopper, B. A., & Barrios, F. X. (2001). The Suicidal Behaviors Questionnaire-Revised (SBQ-R): Validation with clinical and nonclinical samples. *Assessment, 8*(4), 443–454. https://doi.org/10.1177/107319110100800409

Pestian, J., Santel, D., Sorter, M., Bayram, U., Connolly, B., Glauser, T., DelBello, M., Tamang, S., & Cohen, K. (2020). A machine learning approach to identifying changes in suicidal language. *Suicide and Life-Threatening Behavior*, *50*(5), 939–947. https://doi.org/10.1111/sltb.12642

Plener, P. L., Bubalo, N., Fladung, A. K., Ludolph, A. G., & Lulé, D. (2012). Prone to excitement: Adolescent females with non-suicidal self-injury (NSSI) show altered cortical pattern to emotional and NSS-related material. *Psychiatry Research—Neuroimaging*, *203*(2–3), 146–152. https://doi.org/10.1016/j.pscychresns.2011.12.012

Pollock, L. R., & Williams, J. M. G. (2004). Problem-solving in suicide attempters. *Psychological Medicine*, *34*, 163–167. https://doi.org/10.1017/S0033291703008092

Posner, K., Brown, G. K., Stanley, B., Brent, D. A., Yershova, K. V., Oquendo, M. A., Currier, G. W., Melvin, G. A., Greenhill, L., Shen, S., & Mann, J. J. (2011). The Columbia-suicide severity rating scale: Initial validity and internal consistency findings from three multisite studies with adolescents and adults. *American Journal of Psychiatry*, *168*, 1266–1277. https://doi.org/10.1176/appi.ajp.2011.10111704

Prinstein, M. J. (2008). Introduction to the special section on suicide and nonsuicidal self-injury: A review of unique challenges and important directions for self-injury science. *Journal of Consulting and Clinical Psychology*, *76*, 1–8. https://doi.org/10.1037/0022-006X.76.1.1

Ramírez-Cifuentes, D., Freire, A., Baeza-Yates, R., Puntí, J., Medina-Bravo, P., Velazquez, D. A., Gonfaus, J. M., & Gonzàlez, J. (2020). Detection of suicidal ideation on social media: Multimodal, relational, and behavioral analysis. *Journal of Medical Internet Research*, *22*(7), Article e17758. https://doi.org/10.2196/17758

Reitz, S., Kluetsch, R., Niedtfeld, I., Knorz, T., Lis, S., Paret, C., Kirsch, P., Meyer-Lindenberg, A., Treede, R. D., Baumgärtner, U., Bohus, M., & Schmahl, C. (2015). Incision and stress regulation in borderline personality disorder: Neurobiological mechanisms of self-injurious behaviour. *British Journal of Psychiatry*, *207*(2), 165–172. https://doi.org/10.1192/bjp.bp.114.153379

Ribeiro, J. D., Franklin, J. C., Fox, K. R., Bentley, K. H., Kleiman, E. M., Chang, B. P., & Nock, M. K. (2016). Self-injurious thoughts and behaviors as risk factors for future suicide ideation, attempts, and death: a meta-analysis of longitudinal studies. *Psychological Medicine*, *46*, 225–236. https://doi.org/10.1017/S0033291715001804

Sawhney, R., Joshi, H., Gandhi, S., & Shah, R. R. (2020). *A time-aware transformer based model for suicide ideation detection on social media*. https://doi.org/10.18653/v1/2020.emnlp-main.619

Scherer, S., Pestian, J., & Morency, L. P. (2013, 26–31). Investigating the speech characteristics of suicidal adolescents. *2013 IEEE International Conference on Acoustics, Speech and Signal Processing*, Vancouver, BC. https://doi.org/10.1109/ICASSP.2013.6637740

Scherr, S., Arendt, F., Frissen, T., & Oramas M. J. (2020). Detecting intentional self-harm on Instagram: Development, testing, and validation of an automatic image-recognition algorithm to discover cutting-related posts. *Social Science Computer Review*, *38*(6), 673–685. https://doi.org/10.1177/0894439319836389

Schmahl, C., Bohus, M., Esposito, F., Treede, R. D., Di Salle, F., Greffrath, W., Ludaescher, P., Jochims, A., Lieb, K., Scheffler, K., Hennig, J., & Seifritz, E. (2006). Neural correlates of antinociception in borderline personality disorder. *Archives of General Psychiatry*, *63*(6), 659–667. https://doi.org/10.1001/archpsyc.63.6.659

Shah, A., Vaibhav, Sharma, V., Al-Ismail, M., Girard, J., & Morency, L. P. (2019, October 14–18). Multimodal behavioral markers exploring suicidal intent in social media videos. *ICMI 2019—Proceedings of the 2019 International Conference on Multimodal Interaction*, Suzhou, China. https://doi.org/10.1145/3340555.3353718

Stasak, B., Epps, J., Schatten, H. T., Miller, I. W., Provost, E. M., & Armey, M. F. (2021). Read speech voice quality and disfluency in individuals with recent suicidal ideation or suicide attempt. *Speech Communication*, *132*, 10–20. https://doi.org/10.1016/j.specom.2021.05.004

Turecki, G., & Brent, D. A. (2016). Suicide and suicidal behaviour. *Lancet*, *387*, 1227–1239. https://doi.org/10.1016/S0140-6736(15)00234-2

Van Orden, K. A., Witte, T. K., Cukrowicz, K. C., Braithwaite, S. R., Selby, E. A., & Joiner, T. E. (2010). The interpersonal theory of suicide. *Psychological Review*, *117*, 575–600. https://doi.org/10.1037/a0018697

Venek, V., Scherer, S., Morency, L. P., Rizzo, A. S., & Pestian, J. (2014). Adolescent suicidal risk assessment in clinician-patient interaction: A study of verbal and acoustic behaviors. *Proceedings of the 2014 IEEE*

Workshop on Spoken Language Technology (*SLT*) (pp. 277–282), South Lake Tahoe, NV. https://doi.org/10.1109/SLT.2014.7078587

Voss, C., Hoyer, J., Venz, J., Pieper, L., & Beesdo-Baum, K. (2020). Non-suicidal self-injury and its co-occurrence with suicidal behavior: An epidemiological-study among adolescents and young adults. *Acta Psychiatrica Scandinavica, 142*, 496–508. https://doi.org/10.1111/acps.13237

Welch, S. S., Linehan, M. M., Sylvers, P., Chittams, J., & Rizvi, S. L. (2008). Emotional responses to self-injury imagery among adults with borderline personality disorder. *Journal of Consulting and Clinical Psychology, 76*(1), 45–51. https://doi.org/10.1037/0022-006X.76.1.45

Wenzel, A., & Beck, A. T. (2008). A cognitive model of suicidal behavior: Theory and treatment. *Applied and Preventive Psychology, 12*, 189–201. https://doi.org/10.1016/j.appsy.2008.05.001

Whitlock, J., Muehlenkamp, J., Eckenrode, J., Purington, A., Baral Abrams, G., Barreira, P., & Kress, V. (2013). Nonsuicidal self-injury as a gateway to suicide in young adults. *Journal of Adolescent Health, 52*(4), 486–492. https://doi.org/10.1016/j.jadohealth.2012.09.010

Yigletu, H., Tucker, S., Harris, M., & Hatlevig, J. (2004). Assessing suicide ideation: Comparing self-report versus clinician report. *Journal of the American Psychiatric Nurses Association, 10*(1), 9–15. https://doi.org/10.1177/1078390303262655

CHAPTER 46

Fine-Grained Assessment of Nonsuicidal Self-Injury

Nicole K. Legg, Andrew C. Switzer, *and* Brianna J. Turner

Abstract

This chapter focuses on the use of fine-grained assessment approaches in nonsuicidal self-injury (NSSI) research. Fine-grained assessment has enabled researchers to collect near real-time information about the proximal precipitants, consequences, and correlates of NSSI; test theoretical models in ecologically valid contexts; and further our understanding of the temporal sequencing of NSSI-related events. The chapter begins by discussing the need to balance benefits against the potential costs in the context of choosing the frequency, timing, and duration of study assessments, as well as measurement strategies for NSSI and other variables. It then considers some of the unique ethical and technical challenges that are inherent within fine-grained assessment studies. The chapter also offers recommendations for maximizing participant compliance and retention, navigating technological challenges, limiting recruitment or selection biases, and implementing effective risk assessments. Finally, this chapter explores frontiers in the area of fine-grained NSSI assessment, providing recommendations for future work and summarizing potential clinical applications of these methods.

Key Words: fine-grained assessment, nonsuicidal self-injury, measurement strategies, participant compliance, selection biases, risk assessments

Nonsuicidal self-injury (NSSI) has traditionally been assessed in both clinical and research settings by asking a person about their history of NSSI: for instance, whether they have ever engaged in NSSI, approximately how many times they have done so, and what reasons or motives drive this behavior (Cipriano et al., 2017). Although these retrospective methods are useful in understanding many important features of NSSI, they are limited in their ability to provide fine-grained information about the real-time circumstances that surround NSSI. Moreover, because NSSI is a discrete behavior that rarely occurs in laboratory or clinical settings, it is difficult to directly observe the proximal factors and microprocesses that may influence NSSI using solely retrospective methods (Shiffman et al., 2008). Recent surges in portable technologies such as smartphones, compact biosensing, and wearable technologies offer exciting opportunities to observe the contexts of NSSI much nearer in time to when it occurs, and closer to the real-world settings in which it occurs, than was previously possible. This chapter provides a brief overview of the use of "fine-grained assessment"[1] methods to understand NSSI, including some of the key logistical and ethical issues in their application to NSSI.

To understand the potential of fine-grained assessment designs, it is helpful to contrast them with traditional longitudinal designs. Longitudinal designs use repeated assessments of the same individuals to examine within-person changes in behaviors, emotions, or other phenomena of interest, typically over periods of months or years. These designs have particular value in clinical psychology where experimental manipulation of putative causal factors is often impractical and/or ethically problematic, as they allow researchers an alternative means of evaluating causal claims. However, longitudinal studies are often costly and labor intensive (Anderson et al., 2016). Moreover, even an interval of weeks or months may not be well suited to understanding proximal inter- and intraindividual processes that influence behavior, particularly when these processes are not easily or accurately recalled (Ebner-Priemer & Trull, 2009). Fine-grained assessment circumvents some limitations of traditional longitudinal designs because (a) assessments are repeated over much shorter intervals (e.g., minutes, hours, or days); (b) assessment occurs as an individual goes about their everyday life; and (c) assessment focuses on recent or immediate experiences, for instance, asking participants to describe events, emotions, and behaviors that occurred within the past several hours or collecting data continuously through biosensors or other technologies (Ebner-Priemer & Trull, 2009). Because of these features, fine-grained assessments in the context of NSSI are well suited to answering important questions about *when* and *why* individuals engage in such behaviors.

The use of fine-grained assessment approaches in NSSI research has enabled researchers to collect near real-time information about the proximal precipitants, consequences, and correlates of NSSI, test theoretical models in ecologically valid contexts, and further our understanding of the temporal sequencing of NSSI-related events (Rodriguez-Blanco et al., 2018).

Several recent reviews have summarized the substantive knowledge gleaned from these studies (see Gee et al., 2020; Hepp et al., 2020; Rodriguez-Blanco et al., 2018), and as such, we will not repeat those findings here. Instead, this chapter aims to provide practical guidance to help researchers implement fine-grained assessment methods. We begin by describing key decisions in undertaking a fine-grained assessment study, using existing studies to illustrate some of the benefits and drawbacks of various design choices. Next, we discuss technical and ethical challenges that are associated with these methods, and the ways in which these challenges may be addressed. We conclude by briefly reviewing some exciting frontiers in this area, providing recommendations for future work, and summarizing some clinical applications of fine-grained assessment.

Key Decision Points in Designing Fine-Grained Assessment Studies

The major benefits of fine-grained assessment are the ability to collect information on dynamic processes as they unfold, and the ability to examine these processes or behaviors of interest in their natural settings. However, employing frequent sampling requires careful consideration to balance its benefits against the potential costs to both researchers and participants. The following sections discuss this balance in the context of choosing the frequency, timing, and duration of study assessments, as well as measurement strategies for NSSI and other variables.

Frequency of Assessment in Fine-Grained Studies

A primary decision in fine-grained study design is *how often* relevant constructs will be assessed. Two common approaches include daily diary designs, which use a single daily assessment (e.g., Turner et al., 2016; Victor & Klonsky, 2014), and ecological momentary assessment (EMA) designs, which include multiple assessments per day (e.g., Armey et al., 2011; Nock et al., 2009; Snir et al., 2015). Each approach offers unique benefits and drawbacks that affect its ability to answer a given research question.

Researchers have harnessed daily diary designs to examine emotional experiences, interpersonal conflict, and social support surrounding episodes of NSSI (Turner et al., 2016; Victor & Klonsky, 2014). For example, Victor and Klonsky (2014) asked young adults who did and did not report a history of NSSI to describe the duration, frequency, and intensity of various emotions they experienced throughout the day every night before going to bed for 14 days. Relative to young people with no history of NSSI, those with a history of NSSI reported more negative emotions on average, and particularly more self-dissatisfaction, over a two-week period (for more information on negative affectivity, see Swerdlow et al., this volume).

Compared to EMA designs, daily diary designs tend to confer lower participant burden (e.g., fewer daily interruptions and less need to remember and respond to prompts) and to be technologically easier to implement (e.g., using online survey software or paper-and-pencil questionnaires). Relative to longitudinal designs, daily diary designs can offer enhanced ecological validity, improved reliability in assessing dynamic constructs, and greater participant retention (Bolger & Laurenceau, 2013). Daily diary designs are well suited for collecting information about experiences that are easily and accurately recalled several hours later, such as the presence/absence of an event, the amount of time spent engaged in certain activities, or the highest or lowest point of a particular emotional experience or urge. These designs may be less well suited to understanding highly dynamic experiences that are prone to reconstructive, recall, or mood-state biases (Conner & Feldman Barrett, 2012). Moreover, daily diary designs may be limited in their ability to answer questions regarding the precise temporal ordering of events or experiences (e.g., whether feelings of rejection preceded or followed an increase in NSSI urges). Adaptations to daily diary designs include the day reconstruction method (which ties reports to discrete episodes or periods within the day; Kahneman et al., 2004), and time-use diaries (which focus on assessing the duration of engagement in daily activities; e.g., van der Ploeg et al., 2010). These methods can enhance the validity and reliability of data collected in daily diary studies.

EMA methods offer some advantages over other designs due to their more frequent assessment schedules; however, EMA requires more participant time and effort, and often generates complex data with increased requirements for appropriate cleaning and analysis. As such, careful consideration of added advantages versus complexities must be given before adopting EMA approaches. One unique feature of EMA is the focus on assessing immediate or very recent experiences, which minimizes the potential for recall biases and confounds (Ebner-Priemer & Trull, 2009). It is this feature that gives rise to the "*momentary*" component of EMA. For instance, EMA studies of emotion commonly ask participants to rate how they are feeling *right now* or *in this moment,* or to report their average mood within a short recall window (e.g., within the last two hours). This may be especially helpful for capturing affective and emotional experiences that surround NSSI, as certain clinical features that correlate with NSSI, such as emotion dysregulation (Wolff et al., 2019), can increase state-dependent, mood-congruent, and peak-end recall biases that diminish the accuracy of retrospective emotion ratings (Ebner-Priemer et al., 2006; Fredrickson, 2000; Stone et al., 2006). Moreover, because experiences can be assessed shortly before and after an event of interest (e.g., immediately following an episode of NSSI or a moment of strong NSSI urges), data derived from EMA designs may be less vulnerable to well-known cognitive biases that affect narrative reconstructions of events, such as confirmation, hindsight, or negativity biases, and actor-observer effects (Conner & Feldman Barrett, 2012). In this way, EMA may be especially helpful for understanding internal and environmental features that predict whether a person does or doesn't engage in NSSI.

In light of these advantages, it is unsurprising that applications of EMA methods have expanded to examine dynamics of thoughts, urges, emotions, and motives that surround NSSI (Armey et al., 2011; Nock et al., 2009; Snir et al., 2015). Illustrating the unique benefits of EMA methods, Armey et al. (2011) asked participants to rate their emotions six times per day, as well as immediately following any engagement in NSSI. This frequency of assessment provided in-depth information about the in vivo changes in affect that preceded and followed NSSI. However, illustrating the increased participant burden, participants in this study completed an average of 2.26 assessments a day (each of which took an average of 4.82 minutes to complete) across the seven days, representing 38% of the total possible assessments in the study. This demonstrates that while EMA methods *can* provide in-depth information, participant compliance may be lower, which can substantially attenuate the unique benefits of using EMA methods. We provide recommendations on promoting participant engagement in EMA studies later in this chapter.

When deciding on frequency of assessment, researchers must carefully balance (a) the constructs being assessed, including how much and how quickly they are expected to vary and how accurately they are likely to be recalled after a delay; with (b) the potential for added participant burden to result in incomplete or missing data. Static variables, such as the occurrence of specific events, may be less susceptible to recall errors and necessitate less frequent assessment, while dynamic variables, such as affective states and subjective experiences, may be more prone to biases and necessitate more frequent assessment. Consulting basic and clinical literature and completing pilot testing can help to inform these decisions.

Timing and Duration of Assessment
In addition to deciding how often participants will be assessed, researchers must also decide *when*, and for *how long*, participants will be assessed. When deciding on the timing of assessment, researchers should consider when the phenomena of interest are most likely to occur, and when an assessment would provide maximum informativeness. For example, given diurnal deterioration of mood (Stone et al., 2006) and clinical accounts that NSSI commonly occurs later in the day, daily diary studies examining NSSI often prompt participants to complete their daily report as close to bedtime as possible (e.g., Turner et al., 2016; Victor & Klonsky, 2014). In addition to considering the timing of reports, researchers must also consider what contingencies should prompt data collection. For example, assessments may be event-contingent (i.e., after an event or behavior of interest has occurred), interval-contingent (i.e., at a certain time [e.g., 10 p.m. every day], or after a certain period has elapsed [e.g., every 3 hours]), signal-contingent (i.e., using a random or semi-random schedule to deliver prompts), or a mix of multiple contingencies (Bolger & Laurenceau, 2013). Event-contingent sampling is often used when researchers are interested in collecting information that is specific to a pre-identified event. While event-contingencies can greatly reduce participant frequency and burden of responding, this method relies on participants remembering to report after the event occurs. Interval-contingent sampling ensures consistency of when participants will be sampled, which may be important when time elapsed, or time of day, is relevant to the research question and may reduce participant burden associated with responding to unexpected prompts. However, if participants know when they will be sampled, this may introduce participant reactivity. Finally, signal-contingent sampling may increase the likelihood of capturing a representative and unbiased sample of the phenomena of interest, as participants will not know when to expect the prompt. Most studies of NSSI combine either signal- or interval-contingent reports with NSSI event-contingent reports. For example, Snir et al. (2015) combined signal- and event-contingent assessments to examine explicit and implicit motives for engaging in NSSI. The researchers asked participants to complete a survey after an NSSI episode and utilized software that divided participants' typical waking hours into five equal time intervals and sampled participants at random times within each interval. Accordingly, researchers were able to examine explicit motives for NSSI reported after each episode, and use ratings of emotions and cognitions before and after NSSI episodes to infer implicit motives for engagement.

Finally, researchers must decide on the duration of their fine-grained assessment protocol. At present, most fine-grained assessment studies last between 7 and 21 days (see

Rodriguez-Blanco et al., 2018, for a review). When deciding on the duration of the study, a key consideration is the number of observations needed to detect an effect. Power calculations, along with a review of past literature to determine base rates and/or variability of the phenomena of interest, will help to determine how many observations per participant (and how many participants) are required and how long may be needed to accrue such observations. The duration of time needed to accrue the required observations will greatly depend on the nature of the constructs being observed, as well as the type of sample (i.e., clinical vs. nonclinical). Studies examining engagement in NSSI, versus NSSI thoughts and urges, may require longer study protocols to ensure one or more episodes of NSSI per participant are observed. For example, to examine engagement in NSSI acts, Muehlenkamp et al. (2009) employed 7 assessments per day for a total of 14 days (resulting in a maximum of 98 observations per person) among a community sample of 19 women with bulimia nervosa and observed 55 reports of NSSI. Houben et al. (2017) used 10 assessments per day for 8 days (resulting in a maximum of 80 observations per person) among a sample of psychiatric inpatients with borderline personality disorder (BPD) and observed 134 reports of NSSI by 18 participants. Thus, although these studies had a similar number of possible observations per participant, the study durations and number of NSSI episodes varied considerably, reflecting the higher base rates of NSSI among psychiatric patients with BPD. Reviewing past research that approximates the researchers' intended sample, setting, and design can elucidate the optimal timing, frequency, and duration of assessments for a fine-grained study.

Assessment of NSSI and Other Variables

As with all research, the quality of fine-grained NSSI assessment studies hinges upon the reliable and valid assessment of the key constructs. Fine-grained assessment studies have examined many aspects of NSSI including engagement in NSSI acts (e.g., Armey et al., 2011; Koenig et al., 2020), thoughts or urges related to NSSI (e.g., Kiekens et al., 2020; Victor et al., 2019), inferred and explicit motives for NSSI (e.g., Snir et al., 2015), and coping strategies that help individuals avoid or resist NSSI (e.g., Kiekens et al., 2020; Nock et al., 2009; Turner et al., 2019). The aspects(s) of NSSI that should be assessed depend, of course, on the research question(s), the type of sample and corresponding base rates of NSSI, as well as the theoretical associations of these NSSI aspects to other variables included in the study. For example, Vansteelandt et al. (2017) opted to assess NSSI acts using a single, dichotomous question (yes/no) in order to examine whether NSSI helps to stabilize negative affect. In contrast, Kiekens et al. (2020) asked participants to rate the intensity of their NSSI thoughts on a 7-point Likert scale at each sampling timepoint to examine pathways from NSSI thoughts to behaviors. Different still, Fitzpatrick et al. (2020) collected detailed information about the intensity and duration of NSSI thoughts and characteristics (duration, frequency methods used) of NSSI acts to characterize variability in NSSI experiences. As these examples illustrate, assessment of NSSI can be accomplished in many ways, using single- or multi-item assessments comprised of dichotomous or Likert-type items. The examples above also illustrate the potential of fine-grained assessments to describe NSSI, ranging from experiential (e.g., when and where are adolescents most likely to experience NSSI thoughts; Nock et al., 2009) to causal (e.g., does self-efficacy to resist NSSI predict inhibition of NSSI; Kiekens et al., 2020). Researchers must carefully consider what aspects of NSSI need to be assessed, and to what level of granularity, to address their research question efficiently but comprehensively. Decisions about how, and what aspects of NSSI should be assessed, must be balanced against other aspects of the study design that contribute to participant burden (single vs. multiple daily assessments, length and breadth of other assessments, etc.). On one end of this spectrum, for instance, Nock et al. (2009) employed a broad survey, multiple times a day, to examine the perceived functions of NSSI thoughts and acts, as well as the emotional, situational, and social contexts that surround these behaviors. The researchers balanced this breadth by employing skip logic so that participants did not read nor complete irrelevant questions and used dichotomous and multiple-choice response formats instead of free-response formats. Conversely, Santangelo et al. (2017) used EMA methods to test a well-established theoretical model of NSSI (i.e., regulatory function) and examined if affective and interpersonal instability were related to NSSI. The nature of the study facilitated the creation of an EMA survey that was in depth but narrow in scope: it employed visual analog scales to assess momentary affect and attachment (12 items total). The brevity of the survey, and its ease of completion, enabled researchers to administer the survey approximately every 60 minutes for four days. These examples illustrate key themes of balancing breadth against depth, and balancing validity and reliability against participant and researcher burden, when deciding how to structure fine-grained assessments.

Resolving Ethical and Technical Issues

In planning a fine-grained assessment study, it is worth considering some of the unique ethical and technical challenges that are inherent within these studies. Below, we offer recommendations for maximizing participant compliance and retention, navigating technological challenges, limiting recruitment or selection biases, and implementing effective risk assessments.

Compliance and Retention

Because fine-grained assessment studies require considerable effort on the part of participants (e.g., responding to prompted or unprompted surveys; monitoring whether apps or technologies are functioning correctly; and/or charging, wearing, or maintaining special equipment), promoting compliance is a key concern. Recent meta-analytic reviews document good compliance with EMA designs in varied populations, including people who use substances (median compliance = 75%; Jones et al., 2019), people with chronic pain (mean compliance = 85%; Ono et al., 2019), children and adolescents (mean compliance

= 78%; Wen et al., 2017), and general community samples (mean compliance = 77%; Degroote et al., 2020). While some analyses suggest that compliance is not associated with survey prompt frequency, study duration, or type of device used (Jones et al., 2019), others find that compliance tends to decrease over time (Ono et al., 2019) and when six or more survey prompts are administered per day (Wen et al., 2017).

When it comes to promoting compliance, we know that participants are more likely to engage with procedures that are easy to use, clear, and intrinsically rewarding or interesting (Doherty et al., 2020). Thus, choosing software and/or hardware with good user-experience design qualities (e.g., intuitive to navigate and limited action options), pilot testing survey items to ensure they are easy to understand, providing participants with training and support in learning the procedures, providing real-time feedback on response rates, and ensuring that study goals and incentives are meaningful to participants, can help to increase participant motivation and reduce frustration or fatigue (Doherty et al., 2020).

Many studies provide incentives to participants to recognize the effort, inconvenience, risk and benefits, and potential discomfort associated with participating in fine-grained assessment research. However, we wish to be clear that this is only one of many possible tools in a researcher's compliance toolkit. Monetary incentives for fine-grained assessment studies commonly combine a flat-rate participation award with one or more bonus amounts if a participant achieves certain compliance thresholds (e.g., completing 80% or more of the study prompts; uploading data for 70% or more of the study days; Degroote et al., 2020). Incentive structures can be "gamified," such that participants can earn prizes or rewards based on their achievement of certain "levels" of engagement. If using monetary incentives, it is important to be mindful that incentives should not be coercive, undermining a person's ability or willingness to freely refuse to participate, nor should they be exploitative, failing to fairly recognize a person's contributions to the research effort. Different models for establishing an appropriate rate of pay include the free market, appreciation, reimbursement, and wage-payment approaches (Resnik, 2015). Nonmonetary incentives may include course credit, access to personalized data summaries or study reports, and/or support for mental health resources or organizations. Whether monetary or nonmonetary, too high an incentive can bias the sample and limit generalizability, while too small an incentive can slow recruitment and contribute to attrition. Researchers may wish to consider engaging in stakeholder consultations to identify strategies that would be most appropriate and acceptable to their intended study population and design.

Technological Challenges

It is important for researchers to be aware of some of the technological nuances inherent in collecting high-quality fine-grained assessment data. Surveys, which require user input, are typically delivered via an application (an "app") that participants download to their mobile device (e.g., Koenig et al., 2020), a personal data assistant (PDA) device such as a Palm Pilot computer (e.g., Houben et al., 2017), or an online survey platform (e.g., SurveyMonkey, Qualtrics, Redcap) that participants access through a web browser (e.g., Victor et al., 2019). In the former two systems, survey prompts can be delivered via push notifications or alerts (including sounds or vibrations) to the device's home screen, while online survey platforms typically send reminders through external communication systems such as email or text message. As long as there is a linkage to the database that records responses, these systems can resend notifications periodically (i.e., "reminder" alerts) until a survey is completed or expires. However, these systems have important differences with respect to technical complexity. Generally, smartphone applications are more time-consuming to develop and maintain because they need to be compatible with multiple operating systems (which may be frequently updated, resulting in significant upkeep requirements) and are subject to technical and privacy reviews to ensure compliance with third-party policies (e.g., Apple App or Google Play store). For this reason, teams without substantial technical expertise may be tempted to choose an "off the shelf" application that supports the intended functionality; these solutions, however, tend to be costly, and must be carefully reviewed to ensure compliance with local privacy regulations and legislation. On the other end of the spectrum, using online survey platforms can offer a solution with fewer technical requirements where linkages with passive sensing, described below, is not required. At a minimum, informing oneself of how data will be collected, stored, retrieved and secured on local and cloud-based databases, the most up-to-date capabilities and requirements of desired operating systems and devices, and what customization options and integrations with external databases or sources are available can help inform this decision. Because NSSI researchers may not have the necessary expertise to keep up with the rapidly changing landscape of mobile technology which can impact feasibility, data quality, and regulatory compliance, we recommend that researchers seek out consultation from technical and legal experts before committing to a particular platform or device.

Recruitment and Selection Bias
Balancing internal and external validity is a core consideration in research design. To maximize internal validity as well as statistical power, researchers may wish to limit their sample to participants who are likely to be highly adherent to fine-grained assessment protocols, technically savvy, and insightful into their own psychological processes. To maximize external validity, however, researchers aim to recruit diverse participants who approximate the population of interest on as many demographic and clinical characteristics as possible. Previous fine-grained assessment studies of NSSI demonstrate the feasibility of engaging psychiatric inpatients and outpatients (e.g., Houben et al., 2017), adolescents (e.g., Koenig et al., 2020), and community adults (e.g., Kiekens et al., 2020) who engage in NSSI, with excellent participant compliance. However, researchers should consider potential sources of bias that may result from various design choices (e.g., Apple

users tend to be younger, female, and more image-conscious relative to Android users; Shaw et al., 2016; smartphone ownership is more common in younger, higher-income people who live in urban or suburban settings and attended postsecondary schools relative to older, lower-income people who live in rural settings and left school after high school; Pew Research, 2021). Moreover, researchers should consider the types of clinical concerns that may co-occur with NSSI (Nock et al., 2006) and how this can impact user experience, and ensure they are prepared to support participants. Tailoring inclusion and exclusion criteria to match the study characteristics and supports is crucial. We explore this issue next.

Risk Assessment and Response

Research ethics boards tasked with protecting the safety and well-being of research participants will justifiably want to know how researchers, who are conducting a fine-grained assessment study of NSSI, will assess and respond to any indications that a participant is at risk of causing serious harm to themself or someone else. While NSSI is, by definition, not intended to cause death, thoughts of NSSI often co-occur with thoughts of suicide (Ose et al., 2021). Moreover, while the majority of NSSI behaviors do not result in life-threatening injuries, some individuals may require immediate medical attention (Walsh, 2019). At the same time, available evidence suggests that asking people about self-harm does not increase their likelihood of engaging in these behaviors (Blades et al., 2018), that online or remote studies are no more risky than in-person studies of self-injury experiences (Smith et al., 2021), and that participating in NSSI research is often experienced as neutral or positive by participants (Whitlock et al., 2013), indicating that fine-grained assessment studies are unlikely to directly elevate a person's risk. Still, researchers should have a plan to mitigate and actively address risk should it arise.

Researchers hold substantial responsibilities to both participants and the public to safeguard individuals from harm, support autonomy, protect confidentiality, and act in a manner that promotes public trust and confidence in scientific endeavors. Researchers also have a responsibility to take actions to safeguard a participant they believe to be at imminent risk of serious harm (e.g., by disclosing confidential information to a third party who can reduce risk), and participants must be informed of these responsibilities as a part of the consent process. We recommend that researchers consider what types of support could be feasibly offered to participants to reduce imminent risk without compromising the study's objectives. Risk mitigation plans should be informed by the local context (e.g., does a local mental health clinic typically have a weeks-long waiting list that would prevent a participant from accessing urgent care?), competencies and training of the research team (e.g., are study staff available and competent to conduct brief risk assessments, if needed?), availability of clinicians to support risk mitigation (e.g., will all participants have an identified therapist who could be contacted in the event they experience a mental health crisis?), and preferences of the study's target population, if known.

Recent consensus guidelines recommend that researchers conducting fine-grained assessment studies with people who are at risk of suicide: (a) collect contact information for each participant, along with a corresponding emergency contact who can be mobilized to reach the participant (e.g., a family member, friend, therapist, or doctor) if the researcher believes that there is imminent risk; (b) complete an individualized safety plan with each participant at enrolment, including coping strategies and resources that could be engaged if a crisis emerged; and (c) screen incoming responses at least once per day for indications of imminent risk and contact the participant and/or their emergency contact as soon as possible if imminent risk is identified (Nock et al., 2020). Both the researcher and the participant should have a clear understanding of what indicators will be used to signal imminent risk, along with the resulting risk management protocols that will be followed before data collection begins.

The questions of whether to assess suicidal thoughts and/or exclude participants who are at high risk for suicide from fine-grained assessment studies of NSSI are controversial (e.g., Kiekens et al., 2021). In our view, given that we know suicidal thoughts are relatively common in people who experience NSSI (Ose et al., 2021) and that participation in a fine-grained NSSI assessment study creates an opportunity for intervention that might not otherwise exist (Kiekens et al. 2021), we recommend that researchers assess suicidal thoughts and intent. However, we also recommend that researchers think carefully about whether there are people who might not be adequately protected by the risk monitoring and response protocol; where this is the case, these people might be excluded from participating and instead referred to an appropriate community support.

Future Directions and "Frontiers"

As technology evolves, so do the ways in which technology can be harnessed to enhance fine-grained assessments of NSSI. In turn, increasingly advanced fine-grained assessment methods provide new avenues for how these methods can be applied in clinical settings. The following section outlines some exciting frontiers in the area of fine-grained NSSI assessment, provides recommendations for future work, and summarizes some clinical applications of fine-grained assessment.

Implications for Research

Novel methods are constantly being incorporated into fine-grained assessment studies in the service of increasing the ecological validity of behavioral science. One exciting "frontier" in fine-grained assessments of NSSI involves using non-self-report modalities (e.g., biosensing and wearable technologies, passive and active audio recordings, and passive smartphone data), sometimes referred to as "passive sensing" because, unlike surveys, they do not require direct input from the user. Instead, data are generated automatically as an individual interacts with an electronic device (an accelerometer is worn on the wrist to generate information about movement; logs of device state changes [screen on/

off] provide information about technology use patterns, etc.). Passive sensing allows researchers to collect information that may be inaccurate, burdensome, or undetectable via self-report methods alone, such as physiological, interpersonal, and environmental information. Used in combination with self-reports, these passive sensing methods may uncover links between NSSI and moment-to-moment processes that were previously unknown. Here, we describe the benefits and challenges of collecting multimodal data in fine-grained assessment studies.

While researchers have used portable biosensing and wearable technologies for more than two decades, these technologies are now more affordable and accessible than ever before (Hilty et al., 2021). As a result, wearables are proliferating in research contexts; passive sensing is incorporated into about half of existing fine-grained assessment studies (Ono et al., 2019; Wen et al., 2017). The defining purpose of biosensing wearables are to record some aspect of the wearer's behaviors (e.g., physical movements and sleep; Rothney et al., 2008) or physiological processes (e.g., heart rate; Nelson et al., 2020; autonomic arousal via electrodermal activity; Poh et al., 2010; brain activity via electroencephalogram; Levendowski et al., 2017) with minimal burden or involvement from the wearer. Specific passive sensing devices and methods vary widely, particularly in the extent that they have been validated against "gold standard" assessments and their provisions for researchers to access raw data in addition to data summaries (many of which are generated by proprietary algorithms which may or may not meet transparency expectations in research contexts).

Passive and active audio recordings can be used to assess or infer a range of environmental and interpersonal constructs, such as ambient noise levels, presence of human voices, affective qualities of human interactions, and daily activities (Mehl, 2017). These approaches typically involve the collection and analysis of short audio samples (e.g., 5–30-second recordings) that are recorded at random or predetermined intervals (e.g., every 5–12 minutes) as an individual goes about their daily activities. Samples can then be subjected to either manual or automated coding, analysis, or transcription (see Kaplan et al., 2020, for best practices) to build a comprehensive, ecologically valid picture of the contexts in which NSSI occurs.

Most smartphones now come equipped with various native sensors and hardware (e.g., accelerometers and gyroscopes; ambient light, sound, and temperature sensors; Global Positioning Systems [GPS]; cameras; and microphones) and can generate phone usage summaries (e.g., time and duration of screen state changes, application, or hardware [e.g., camera, microphone] usage; incoming/outgoing phone and SMS communications; signal strength of nearby WiFi networks or Bluetooth beacons). This information can be combined to make accurate inferences regarding theoretically important constructs (e.g., physical activity and sleep, social interaction patterns, and mood states; Narziev et al., 2020; Saeb et al., 2017). Several smartphone applications facilitate integrated collection of self-report and passive data garnered from these sensors (e.g., mEMA, AWARE, and StudentLife), allowing researchers to harness smartphone technology to collect multiple indicators of behavior, while reducing participant burden, recall bias, and missing data, within fine-grained assessment studies. Researchers seeking to gather smartphone-generated data should be aware that the ability to do so differs substantially depending on the device's operating system, with much greater openness offered by Android-compatible devices versus devices running Apple's iOS.

When designing a study involving any of these technologies, researchers must consider possible challenges in data collection, management, and analysis, as well as the unique ethical considerations related to privacy and consent that are inherent in collecting data without user input or action. While each of these technologies is passive in some way, they are not burden-free. Wearable devices may require frequent charging and active logging of their use by the wearer. Some participants may worry that a wearable device could signify their participation in a study to others, or they may find the device uncomfortable or irritating. Participants may also experience a psychological burden, knowing that different aspects of their lives are being recorded. Researchers must be especially careful to clearly communicate how potentially sensitive and identifying information, especially geographic location or audio recordings, are being safeguarded. As our lives are increasingly entwined with technology platforms and devices, it is becoming more and more clear that collecting huge volumes of device- or interface-generated data comes with unique risks, including inadvertent (or intentional) reidentification of deidentified data (e.g., Meyer, 2018), as well as the potential to infer various characteristics about a user (some of which may fall outside the scope of a researcher's scientific aims or what the participant would like to have known about themselves). Researchers should reflect on such issues and have a clear plan regarding whether and how participants should be informed of these potentials, how and by whom the data will be used and shared, and what uses of the data are or are not acceptable.

Implications for Clinical Practice

Principles of self-monitoring have been used for decades within clinical contexts, underpinning many psychotherapeutic interventions. For instance, cognitive behavioral therapy (CBT; see Chapman et al., this volume) uses daily activity and mood monitoring diaries, behavioral schedules, and thought records to build clients' awareness of their thoughts, feelings, and behaviors and to help them recognize their maladaptive processes in order to enact change (Chen et al., 2017). Similarly, dialectical behavior therapy (see Chapman et al., this volume) harnesses interval-contingent assessments in the form of diary cards that ask clients to track their NSSI engagement, emotions, and skills use (Linehan, 1993). Unsurprisingly, there has been substantial interest in using fine-grained assessment methodologies, as well as emerging portable and wearable technologies, in clinical contexts. Indeed, a recent report by the American Psychological Association (APA) found that more than 20,000 mobile applications purporting to support mental health (so called "mobile health", or mHealth, apps) were available through Google and Apple app stores (APA, 2021). People often rate technology-assisted self-monitoring favorably, whether used in research (van Os et al., 2017) or clinical contexts (Grist et al., 2018). Moreover, disclosing NSSI and connecting with supportive communities, which may be facilitated by technology, can promote self-reflection, help-seeking, and growth (Whitlock et al., 2013). To meet mental health service demands, mental health care increasingly emphasizes client self-management and monitoring (Kazdin & Blase, 2011). Still, issues related to quality control, fidelity to evidence-based principles, and access, are ongoing concerns in this sphere. Researchers have an important role to play in developing high-quality, effective, and equitable solutions to meet clinical needs.

One area of active development is the use of technology-assisted fine-grained assessment to create individualized risk predictions that could alert people when they are likely to experience strong NSSI urges and provide tailored supports, such as automated alerts to encourage the use of coping skills or practical strategies for avoiding NSSI. Machine learning (see Wang et al., this volume) and smart algorithms use "big data" garnered from fine-grained assessments and passive sensing data to predict future behaviors, such as suicide attempts among military personnel (Rozek et al., 2020) and psychiatric inpatients (Haines-Delmont et al., 2020). While these methods may have potential to offer individualized, intensive, and ongoing care to at-risk patients, they are not without controversy, including concerns regarding privacy, autonomy, and professional liability (Tiffin & Paton, 2018).

Conclusions

Fine-grained assessments have facilitated major advances in NSSI research by circumventing many of the limitations of traditional repeated measures designs and offering researchers the opportunity to examine the proximal, dynamic circumstances surrounding NSSI. Researchers are tasked with making several key decisions in designing their fine-grained assessment study that balance informativeness, reliability and accuracy, internal and external validity, and participant and researcher burden. Moreover, researchers must be aware of the ethical challenges that are inherent within active monitoring and sampling of NSSI and related constructs, along with the technical challenges that accompany the use of new technologies. Despite some of these challenging decisions and considerations, fine-grained assessments, particularly when combined with multimodal assessments, provide opportunities to examine the real- and near-time, within-person processes that influence NSSI in the natural settings where it occurs. Fine-grained assessments are particularly suited to examining when, why, and under what circumstances NSSI occurs, thereby advancing our theoretical models and informing tailored and targeted interventions. The rapidly evolving landscape of mobile technologies and "mobile health" applications highlights the potentiality to bolster accessibility of prevention and targeted intervention efforts.

Note

1. The authors acknowledge that multiple terms have been used to describe these methods, including "intensive longitudinal designs," "ambulatory assessment," "real-time monitoring," and "experience sampling." We use fine-grained assessment to refer to any research design that collects repeated observations of the same person many times per day or week. This term subsumes more specific designs, such as "ecological momentary assessment" (characterized by multiple daily assessments of immediate or current psychological states), "daily diaries" (characterized by a single retrospective daily report of events, activities and psychological states), and "passive sensing" (characterized by the inclusion of data sources that do not require direct user input, such as wearable accelerometers or voice recorders). Where possible, we will use narrower terms to describe specific study designs and the more general "fine-gained assessment" to apply to the broader category.

References

American Psychological Association. (2021). Mental health apps are gaining traction. *APA Monitor on Psychology, 2021*(1). Retrieved May 31, 2021, from https://www.apa.org/monitor/2021/01/trends-mental-health-apps

Anderson, A. L., Clinkinbeard, S. S., Barnum, T. C., & Augustyn, R. J. (2016). Examining behaviors using respondents' cell phones and a burst design: Drinking and activities across the first year of college among transitioning freshmen. *Journal of Developmental and Life-Course Criminology, 2*(1), 64–84. https://doi.org/10.1007/s40865-016-0027-4

Armey, M. F., Crowther, J. H., & Miller, I. W. (2011). Changes in ecological momentary assessment reported affect associated with episodes of nonsuicidal self-injury. *Behavior Therapy, 42*(4), 579–588. https://doi.org/10.1016/j.beth.2011.01.002

Blades, C. A., Stritzke, W., Page, A. C., & Brown, J. D. (2018). The benefits and risks of asking research participants about suicide: A meta-analysis of the impact of exposure to suicide-related content. *Clinical Psychology Review, 64*, 1–12. https://doi.org/10.1016/j.cpr.2018.07.001

Bolger, N., & Laurenceau, J. P. (2013). *Intensive longitudinal methods: An introduction to diary and experience sampling research*. Guilford Press.

Chen, J. A., Fearey, E., & Smith, R. E. (2017). "That which is measured improves": A theoretical and empirical review of self-monitoring in self-management and adaptive behavior change. *Journal of Behavior Therapy and Mental Health, 1*(4), 19–38. https://doi.org/10.14302/issn.2474-9273.jbtm-16-1180

Cipriano, A., Cella, S., & Cotrufo, P. (2017). Nonsuicidal self-injury: A systematic review. *Frontiers in Psychology, 8*, 1946–1946. https://doi.org/10.3389/fpsyg.2017.01946

Conner, T. S., & Feldman Barrett, L. (2012). Trends in ambulatory self-report: The role of momentary experience in psychosomatic medicine. *Psychosomatic Medicine, 74*(4), 327–337. https://doi.org/10.1097/psy.0b013e3182546f18

Degroote, L., DeSmet, A., De Bourdeaudhuij, I., Van Dyck, D., & Crombez, G. (2020). Content validity and methodological considerations in ecological momentary assessment studies on physical activity and sedentary behavior: A systematic review. *International Journal of Behavioral Nutrition and Physical Activity, 17*, 35. https://doi.org/10.1186/s12966-020-00932-9

Doherty, K., Balaskas, A., & Doherty, G. (2020). The design of ecological momentary assessment technologies. *Interacting with Computers, 32*(3), 257–278. https://doi.org/10.1093/iwcomp/iwaa019

Ebner-Priemer, U. W., Kuo, J., Welch, S. S., Thielgen, T., Witte, S., Bohus, M., & Linehan, M. M. (2006). A valence-dependent group-specific recall bias of retrospective self-reports: A study of borderline personality disorder in everyday life. *Journal of Nervous & Mental Disease, 194*(10), 774–779. https://doi.org/10.1097/01.nmd.0000239900.46595.72

Ebner-Priemer, U. W., & Trull, T. J. (2009). Ecological momentary assessment of mood disorders and mood dysregulation. *Psychological Assessment, 21*(4), 463–475. https://doi.org/10.1037/a0017075

Fitzpatrick, S., Kranzler, A., Fehling, K., Lindqvist, J., & Selby, E. A. (2020). Investigating the role of the intensity and duration of self-injury thoughts in self-injury with ecological momentary assessment. *Psychiatry Research, 284*, Article 112761. https://doi.org/10.1016/j.psychres.2020.112761

Fredrickson, B. L. (2000). Extracting meaning from past affective experiences: The importance of peaks, ends, and specific emotions. *Cognition & Emotion, 14*(4), 577–606. https://doi.org/10.1080/026999300402808

Gee, B. L., Han, J., Benassi, H., & Batterham, P. J. (2020). Suicidal thoughts, suicidal behaviors and self-harm in daily life: A systematic review of ecological momentary assessment studies. *Digital Health*, *6*, Article 2055207620963958. https://doi.org/10.1177/2055207620963958

Grist, R., Porter, J., & Stallard, P. (2018). Acceptability, use, and safety of a mobile phone app (BlueIce) for young people who self-harm: Qualitative study of service users' experience. *Journal of Medical Internet Research Mental Health*, *5*(1), Article e8779. https://doi.org/10.2196/mental.8779

Haines-Delmont, A., Chahal, G., Bruen, A. J., Wall, A., Khan, C. T., Sadashiv, R., & Fearnley, D. (2020). Testing suicide risk prediction algorithms using phone measurements with patients in acute mental health settings: Feasibility study. *Journal of Medical Internet Research MHealth & UHealth*, *8*(6). https://doi.org/10.2196/15901

Hepp, J., Carpenter, R. W., Störkel, L. M., Schmitz, S. E., Schmahl, C., & Niedtfeld, I. (2020). A systematic review of daily life studies on non-suicidal self-injury based on the four-function model. *Clinical Psychology Review*, *82*, 101888–101888. https://doi.org/10.1016/j.cpr.2020.101888

Hilty, D. M., Armstrong, C. M., Luxton, D. D., Gentry, M. T., & Krupinski, E. A. (2021). A Scoping review of sensors, wearables, and remote monitoring for behavioral health: Uses, Outcomes, clinical competencies, and research directions. *Journal of Technology in Behavioral Science*. https://doi.org/10.1007/s41347-021-00199-2

Houben, M., Claes, L., Vansteelandt, K., Berens, A., Sleuwaegen, E., & Kuppens, P. (2017). The emotion regulation function of nonsuicidal self-injury: A momentary assessment study in inpatients with borderline personality disorder features. *Journal of Abnormal Psychology*, *126*(1), 89–95. https://doi.org/10.1037/abn0000229

Jones, A., Remmerswaal, D., Verveer, I., Robinson, E., Franken, I. H. A., Wen, C. K. F., & Field, M. (2019). Compliance with ecological momentary assessment protocols in substance users: A meta-analysis. *Addiction*, *114*(4), 609–619. https://doi.org/10.1111/add.14503

Kahneman, D., Krueger, A. B., Schkade, D. A., Schwarz, N., & Stone, A. A. (2004). A survey method for characterizing daily life experience: The day reconstruction method. *Science*, *306*(5702), 1776–1780. https://doi.org/10.1126/science.1103572

Kaplan, D. M., Rentscher, K. E., Lim, M., Reyes, R., Keating, D., Romero, J., Shah, A., Smith, A. D., York, K., Milek, A., Tackman, A., & Mehl, M. R. (2020). Best practices for Electronically Activated Recorder (EAR) research: A practical guide to coding and processing EAR data. *Behavior Research Methods*, *52*(4), 1538–1551. https://doi.org/10.3758/s13428-019-01333-y

Kazdin, A. E., & Blase, S. L. (2011). Rebooting psychotherapy research and practice to reduce the burden of mental illness. *Perspectives on Psychological Science*, *6*(1), 21–37. https://doi.org/10.1177/1745691610393527

Kiekens, G., Hasking, P., Nock, M. K., Boyes, M., Kirtley, O., Bruffaerts, R., Myin-Germeys, I., & Claes, L. (2020). Fluctuations in affective states and self-efficacy to resist non-suicidal self-injury as real-time predictors of non-suicidal self-injurious thoughts and behaviors. *Frontiers in Psychiatry*, *11*, 214. https://doi.org/10.3389/fpsyt.2020.00214

Kiekens, G., Robinson, K., Tatnell, R., & Kirtley, O. J. (2021). Opening the black box of daily life in nonsuicidal self-injury research: With great opportunity comes great responsibility. *JMIR Mental Health*, *8*(11), Article e30915. https://doi.org/10.2196/30915

Koenig, J., Klier, J., Parzer, P., Santangelo, P., Resch, F., Ebner-Priemer, U., & Kaess, M. (2020). High-frequency ecological momentary assessment of emotional and interpersonal states preceding and following self-injury in female adolescents. *European Child & Adolescent Psychiatry*, *30*(8), 1299–1308. https://doi.org/10.1007/s00787-020-01626-0

Levendowski, D. J., Ferini-Strambi, L., Gamaldo, C., Cetel, M., Rosenberg, R., & Westbrook, P. R. (2017). The Accuracy, night-to-night variability, and stability of frontopolar sleep electroencephalography biomarkers. *Journal of Clinical Sleep Medicine*, *13*(6), 791–803. https://doi.org/10.5664/jcsm.6618

Linehan, M. M. (1993). *Cognitive behavioral therapy for borderline personality disorder*. Guilford Press.

Mehl, M. R. (2017). The electronically activated recorder (EAR): A method for the naturalistic observation of daily social behavior. *Current Directions in Psychological Science*, *26*(2), 184–190. https://doi.org/10.1177/0963721416680611

Muehlenkamp, J. J., Engel, S. G., Wadeson, A., Crosby, R. D., Wonderlich, S. A., Simonich, H., & Mitchell, J. E. (2009). Emotional states preceding and following acts of non-suicidal self-injury in bulimia nervosa patients. *Behavior Research & Therapy*, *47*(1), 83–87. https://doi.org/10.1016/j.brat.2008.10.011

Meyer, M. N. (2018). Practical tips for ethical data sharing. *Advances in Methods and Practices in Psychological Science, 1*(1), 131–144. https://doi.org/10.1177/2515245917747656

Narziev, N., Goh, H., Toshnazarov, K., Lee, S. A., Chung, K.-M., & Noh, Y. (2020). STDD: Short-term depression detection with passive sensing. *Sensors, 20*(5), Article 1396. https://doi.org/10.3390/s20051396

Nelson, B. W., Low, C. A., Jacobson, N., Areán, P., Torous, J., & Allen, N. B. (2020). Guidelines for wrist-worn consumer wearable assessment of heart rate in biobehavioral research. *Digital Medicine, 3*(1), Article 90. https://doi.org/10.1038/s41746-020-0297-4

Nock, M. K., Joiner, T. E., Gordon, K. H., Lloyd-Richardson, E., & Prinstein, M. J. (2006). Non-suicidal self-injury among adolescents: Diagnostic correlates and relation to suicide attempts. *Psychiatry Research, 144*(1), 65–72. https://doi.org/10.1016/j.psychres.2006.05.010

Nock, M. K., Kleiman, E.M., Abraham, M., Bentley, K.H., Brent, D.A., Buonopane, R. J., Castro-Ramirez, F., Cha, C. B., Dempsey, W., Draper, J., Glenn, C. R., Harkavy-Friedman, J., Hollander, M. R., Huffman, J. C., Lee, H. I. S., Millner, A. J., Mou, D., Onnela, J., Picard, R. W., ... & Pearson, J. L. (2020), Consensus statement on ethical & safety practices for conducting digital monitoring studies with people at risk of suicide and related behaviors. *Psychiatric Research Clinical Practice, 3*(2), 57–66. https://doi.org/10.1176/appi.prcp.20200029

Nock, M. K., Prinstein, M. J., & Sterba, S. K. (2009). Revealing the form and function of self-injurious thoughts and behaviors: A real-time ecological assessment study among adolescents and young adults. *Journal of Abnormal Psychology, 118*(4), 816–827. https://doi.org/10.1037/a0016948

Ono, M., Schneider, S., Junghaenel, D. U., & Stone, A. A. (2019). What affects the completion of ecological momentary assessments in chronic pain research? An individual patient data meta-analysis. *Journal of Medical Internet Research, 21*(2), Article e11398. https://doi.org/10.2196/11398

Ose, S. O., Tveit, T., & Mehlum, L. (2021). Non-suicidal self-injury (NSSI) in adult psychiatric outpatients – A nationwide study. *Journal of Psychiatric Research, 133*, 1–9. https://doi.org/10.1016/j.jpsychires.2020.11.031

Pew Research Center. (2021). Mobile fact sheet. Retrieved May 31, 2021, from https://www.pewresearch.org/internet/fact-sheet/mobile/

Poh, M., Swenson, N. C., & Picard, R. W. (2010). A wearable sensor for unobtrusive, long-term assessment of electrodermal activity. *IEEE Transactions on Biomedical Engineering, 57*(5), 1243–1252. https://doi.org/10.1109/TBME.2009.2038487

Resnik, D. B. (2015). Bioethical issues in providing financial incentives to research participants. *Medicolegal and Bioethics, 5*, 35–41. https://doi.org/10.2147/mb.s70416

Rodríguez-Blanco, L., Carballo, J. J., & Baca-García, E. (2018). Use of ecological momentary assessment (EMA) in non-suicidal self-injury (NSSI): A systematic review. *Psychiatry Research, 263*, 212–219. https://doi.org/10.1016/j.psychres.2018.02.051

Rothney, M. P., Schaefer, E. V, Neumann, M. M., Choi, L., & Chen, K. Y. (2008). Validity of physical activity intensity predictions by ActiGraph, Actical, and RT3 accelerometers. *Obesity, 16*(8), 1946–1952. https://doi.org/10.1038/oby.2008.279

Rozek, D. C., Andres, W. C., Smith, N. B., Leifker, F. R., Arne, K., Jennings, G., Dartnell, N., Bryan, C.J., & Rudd, M. D. (2020). Using machine learning to predict suicide attempts in military personnel. *Psychiatry Research, 294*, 113515–113515. https://doi.org/10.1016/j.psychres.2020.113515

Saeb, S., Cybulski, T. R., Schueller, S. M., Kording, K. P., & Mohr, D. C. (2017). Scalable passive sleep monitoring using mobile phones: Opportunities and obstacles. *Journal of Medical Internet Research, 19*(4). https://doi.org/10.2196/jmir.6821

Santangelo, P. S., Koenig, J., Funke, V., Parzer, P., Resch, F., Ebner-Priemer, U. W., & Kaess, M. (2017). Ecological momentary assessment of affective and interpersonal instability in adolescent non-suicidal self-injury. *Journal of Abnormal Child Psychology, 45*(7), 1429–1438. https://doi.org/10.1007/s10802-016-0249-2

Shaw, H., Ellis, D. A., Kendrick, L.-R., Ziegler, F., & Wiseman, R. (2016). Predicting smartphone operating system from personality and individual differences. *Cyberpsychology, Behavior and Social Networking, 19*(12), 727–732. https://doi.org/10.1089/cyber.2016.0324

Shiffman, S., Stone, A. A., & Hufford, M. R. (2008). Ecological momentary assessment. *Annual Review of Clinical Psychology, 4*, 1–32. https://doi.org/10.1146/annurev.clinpsy.3.022806.091415

Smith, D. M., Lipson, S. M., Wang, S. B., & Fox, K. R. (2021). Online methods in adolescent self-injury research: Challenges and recommendations. *Journal of Clinical Child & Adolescent Psychology*. https://doi.org/10.1080/15374416.2021.1875325

Snir, A., Rafaeli, E., Gadassi, R., Berenson, K., & Downey, G. (2015). Explicit and inferred motives for nonsuicidal self injurious acts and urges in borderline and avoidant personality disorders. *Personality Disorders*, *6*(3), 267–277. https://doi.org/10.1037/per0000104

Stone, A. A., Schwartz, J. E., Schkade, D., Schwarz, N., Krueger, A., & Kahneman, D. (2006). A population approach to the study of emotion: Diurnal rhythms of a working day examined with the day reconstruction method. *Emotion*, *6*(1), 139–149. https://doi.org/10.1037/1528-3542.6.1.139

Tiffin, P. A., & Paton, L. W. (2018). Rise of the machines? Machine learning approaches and mental health: Opportunities and challenges. *The British Journal of Psychiatry: The Journal of Mental Science*, *213*(3), 509–510. https://doi.org/10.1192/bjp.2018.105

Turner, B. J., Baglole, J. S., Chapman, A. L. & Gratz, K. L. (2019). Experiencing and resisting nonsuicidal self-injury thoughts and urges in everyday life. *Suicide & Life-Threatening Behavior*, *49*(5), 1332–1346. https://doi.org/10.1111/sltb.12510

Turner, B. J., Cobb, R. J., Gratz, K. L., & Chapman, A. L. (2016). The role of interpersonal conflict and perceived social support in nonsuicidal self-injury in daily life. *Journal of Abnormal Psychology (1965)*, *125*(4), 588–598. https://doi.org/10.1037/abn0000141

van der Ploeg, H. P., Merom, D., Chau, J. Y., Bittman, M., Trost, S.G., & Bauman, A. E. (2010). Advances in population surveillance for physical activity and sedentary behavior: Reliability and validity of time use surveys. *American Journal of Epidemiology*, *172*(10), 1199–1206. https://doi.org/10.1093/aje/kwq265

van Os, J., Verhagen, S., Marsman, A., Peeters, F., Bak, M., Marcelis, M., Drukker, M., Reininghaus, U., Jacobs, N., Lataster, T., Simons, C., Lousberg, R., Gülöksüz, S., Leue, C., Groot, P. C., Viechtbauer, W., & Delespaul, P. (2017). The experience sampling method as an mHealth tool to support self-monitoring, self-insight, and personalized health care in clinical practice. *Depression and Anxiety*, *34*(6), 481–493. https://doi.org/10.1002/da.22647

Vansteelandt, K., Houben, M., Claes, L., Berens, A., Sleuwaegen, E., Sienaert, P., & Kuppens, P. (2017). The affect stabilization function of nonsuicidal self-injury in borderline personality disorder: An ecological momentary assessment study. *Behavior Research & Therapy*, *92*, 41–50. https://doi.org/10.1016/j.brat.2017.02.003

Victor, S. E., & Klonsky, E. D. (2014). Daily emotion in non-suicidal self-injury. *Journal of Clinical Psychology*, *70*(4), 364–375. https://doi.org/https://doi.org/10.1002/jclp.22037

Victor, S. E., Scott, L. N., Stepp, S. D., & Goldstein, T. R. (2019). I want you to want me: Interpersonal stress and affective experiences as within-person predictors of nonsuicidal self-injury and suicide urges in daily life. *Suicide & Life-Threatening Behavior*, *49*(4), 1157–1177. https://doi.org/10.1111/sltb.12513

Walsh, B. W. (2019). Atypical, severe self-injury: How to understand and treat it. In J. J. Washburn (Ed.), *Nonsuicidal self-injury*. Routledge.

Wen, C., Schneider, S., Stone, A., & Spruijt-Metz, D. (2017). Compliance with mobile ecological momentary assessment protocols in children and adolescents: A systematic review and meta-analysis. *Journal of Medical Internet Research*, *19*(4), Article e132. https://doi.org/102196/jmir/6641

Whitlock, J., Pietrusza, C., & Purington, A. (2013). Young adult respondent experiences of disclosing self-injury, suicide-related behavior, and psychological distress in a web-based survey. *Archives of Suicide Research*, *17*(1), 20–32. https://doi.org/10.1080/13811118.2013.748405

Wolff, J. C., Thompson, E., Thomas, S. A., Nesi, J., Bettis, A. H., Ransford, B., Scopelliti, K., Frazier, E. A., & Liu, R. T. (2019). Emotion dysregulation and non-suicidal self-injury: A systematic review and meta-analysis. *European Psychiatry*, *59*, 25–36. https://doi.org/10.1016/j.eurpsy.2019.03.004

CHAPTER 47

Guidelines, Policies, and Recommendations for Responding to NSSI in Schools and Universities

Imke Baetens, Elizabeth E. Lloyd-Richardson, Elana Bloom, Chloe A. Hamza, Penelope Hasking, Stephen P. Lewis, Dariya Bezugla, Esther Meers, *and* Lisa Van Hove

Abstract

Nonsuicidal self-injury (NSSI; e.g., self-directed cutting, burning, or bruising without lethal intent) is a commonly occurring behavior among students in secondary and postsecondary school. Academic stressors, in addition to challenges associated with navigating adolescence and emerging adulthood, may contribute to heightened risk for NSSI among students. NSSI is associated with increased vulnerability for other mental health concerns and increased risk for suicidality, suggesting that providing early support and intervention for students who engage in NSSI is critically important. Despite the widespread prevalence of this behavior, students and staff often report feeling ill-equipped to respond and address NSSI in school-based contexts. The authors of this chapter, all members of the International Consortium on Self-injury in Educational Settings (ICSES), aim to provide the readers some guidelines and recommendations for NSSI policies in educational settings, due to the lack of research-informed policy guidelines and recommendations. Here, the authors underscore the importance of developing a school-based policy on NSSI to ensure consistent and effective identification, response, and support for students who self-injure. The authors describe the roles and responsibilities of each stakeholder (e.g., students, teachers, parents, administrators, and school mental health practitioners) in implementing a policy on NSSI. Finally, the authors provide an example of a policy specifically developed and piloted for a university in Brussels, to serve as a template that can be used across a variety of educational settings. The chapter concludes with several suggested resources and links for additional information on supporting students who self-injure in schools.

Key Words: nonsuicidal self-injury, students, academic stressors, mental health, International Consortium on Self-injury in Educational Settings, school-based policy, suicidality

Introduction

Nonsuicidal self-injury (NSSI), the direct and deliberate damage or alteration of bodily tissue in the absence of lethal intent (International Society for the Study of Self-injury, 2018), is a widely occurring behavior among school-age adolescents and young adults. As many as 20% of secondary and postsecondary students engage in NSSI (Muehlenkamp et al., 2012; Swannell et al., 2014). NSSI most often begins during early adolescence, but another peak period of onset also may occur in early adulthood (Gandhi et al., 2018). Navigating increasing independence and new social relationships in adolescence and early adulthood, in addition to academic stressors in school, may be challenging for some students (Arnett et al., 2014; Shulman et al., 2016) and may lead to NSSI as a form of coping (Taylor et al., 2018). In line with this, research has shown that students who engage in NSSI report greater intra- and interpersonal distress (e.g., depressive symptoms, bullying, lack of social connectedness, and other school-based stressors) relative to students without a history of NSSI (Hamza, Goldstein, et al., 2021; Madjar et al., 2017; Xavier et al., 2017). With regard to school-based stressors, Baetens et al. (2021) found that unsatisfactory academic performance predicted future engagement in NSSI, but not vice versa. Similarly, Kiekens et al. (2016) found that university students who engaged in NSSI were at increased risk for poor academic performance. School-related attitudes may also be important mechanisms that maintain NSSI behaviors. In a longitudinal study with community-based adolescents, Baetens et al. (2021) found a bidirectional relation between negative attitudes toward school and NSSI; having a negative attitude toward school predicted NSSI at age 13, and engagement in NSSI at age 13 predicted a negative attitude toward school at age 14.

School-related factors not only influence NSSI but may also be impacted by students' NSSI engagement. Often classmates report feeling overwhelmed by NSSI disclosures from peers. Further, most teachers express uncertainty and helplessness when it comes to addressing NSSI with students (Hamza, Goldstein, et al., 2021). Due to the high prevalence of NSSI in secondary schools and higher education, most school staff have encountered at least one student who engages in NSSI in their career (Berger et al., 2015), and as they are in daily contact with students, school staff may play a central role in responding to NSSI. In this chapter we will review the role of school staff in responding to NSSI, describe recommendations and guidelines, and present a sample protocol for responding to NSSI in a university setting.

Addressing NSSI in Schools

While school staff are generally empathic and somewhat knowledgeable about NSSI, they still report a knowledge-practice gap and a desire for additional NSSI training (Berger et al., 2014). University staff similarly report a lack of knowledge and resources for responding to NSSI (Whitlock et al., 2011). In our experience training school and university stakeholders, we routinely see the uncertainty, and often outright fear, that school and university staff have when thinking about appropriately addressing and responding to NSSI in these educational contexts. Of greatest concern to schools are how to assess suicide risk and NSSI, what to do if risk is ambiguous, how to manage socialization effects, and how and when to contact parents or caregivers. Given these concerns, it is not uncommon for school principals and staff to consider their roles as primarily administrative and often defer responsibility of NSSI to school mental health staff.

Academic institutions may also face the challenge of a lack of mental health resources (Auerbach et al., 2018). This calls for innovative solutions, such as a streamlined and multilayered approach involving numerous stakeholders, such as peers, staff with adjacent and support roles, and the wider social network to address NSSI (Lewis et al., 2019). NSSI may be revealed to or witnessed by friends, romantic partners, and dormitory/residence staff among others. Lewis et al. (2019) cautioned that this wider group of stakeholders may also require psychological and informational support. While the involvement of trainees and volunteers can offer additional valuable points of contact, these individuals often lack relevant experience and specialization (Lewis et al., 2019).

Through training and access to quality information, school and postsecondary staff can gain knowledge and acquire skills to provide an effective response when witnessing NSSI, which, in turn, leaves staff feeling better prepared and equipped for the task (Kelada et al., 2017). Training regarding the use of an NSSI protocol, engagement of various stakeholders, and support from the administration are key to a consistent and an effective response to NSSI (Berger et al., 2015; McAllister et al., 2010). A well-constructed, research-informed policy that incorporates these elements is critical to the success of managing NSSI in educational settings.

Research-Informed NSSI Policy in Educational Settings

Many researchers in the field of NSSI have joined efforts to offer support in designing and implementing NSSI policies in educational settings by sharing the best evidence-informed practices for effective prevention and early intervention. Educational settings may organize NSSI prevention and early intervention in primary, secondary, and tertiary levels in accordance with the Heath et al.'s (2020) school consultation model for NSSI school response (see Petrovic et al., this volume, and Morena et al., this volume). Primary prevention/intervention aims to prevent the onset of NSSI through universal intervention, as, for example, *Happyles* (Baetens et al., 2020) or the *Youth Aware of Mental Health Program* (YAM; Lindow et al., 2020). Universal programs usually target group norms, as well as group- or individual-level knowledge and/or practices (Heath et al., 2020), to have an impact on all pupils involved. Effect sizes of universal programs are often lower than secondary/tertiary interventions; however, some scholars have argued that these lower effect sizes may reflect a challenge in obtaining a large enough sample to detect "cases" in a universal sample, rather than a superior efficacy of targeted interventions at secondary/tertiary level (Werner-Seidler et al., 2017). A benefit of universal programs versus targeted secondary/tertiary interventions is that there is no need for screening, which also limits a duty-of-care issue (i.e., what to do when acute suicidality is detected in a screening?) and decreases the potential stigmatization of targeted students at risk (i.e., no "special/differential" handling, all students get the program). With regard to the latter, in a pilot study with 800 students, Baetens et al. (2020) showed that adding NSSI specific psychoeducational information (in combination with a universal approach) has a positive impact in terms of decreased stigmatization and increased help-seeking.

At a secondary level, education settings may aim to prevent the onset of a behavior for individuals at risk (more targeted intervention). For example, programs such as DBT in Schools (Mazza et al., 2016) show promising results as a school-based intervention to prevent the onset of NSSI. This program teaches youth skills in emotion regulation, distress tolerance, and interpersonal effectiveness, drawing on principles of dialectical behavior therapy. In sum, interventions for at-risk groups often have larger effect sizes compared to universal programs (Werner-Seidler et al., 2017), although targeted interventions are often more time and cost intensive.

At the tertiary level, schools can aim to respond to NSSI once it has emerged to reduce its negative impacts on the pupil, as well as others in the school-based context (Heath et al., 2020). Little to no evidence-based tertiary interventions have been examined to date, except for the SOSI program (Muehlenkamp et al., 2010). In a small pilot evaluation of this program, Muehlenkamp et al. (2010) reported general improvement of students' awareness and understanding of NSSI but did not measure benefits for students already engaging in NSSI (such as increased help-seeking or decreased rates of NSSI engagement).

Due to the lack of empirical data, some scholars have published research-informed guidelines to support schools in how to adequately respond to and address NSSI engagement in school-based contexts (Berger et al., 2014, 2015; De Riggi et al., 2016; Hasking et al., 2016; Hasking et al., 2020; Kelada et al., 2017). Lewis et al. (2019) were among the first to formulate recommendations for addressing NSSI on college campuses specifically. There is strong consensus in the field that addressing NSSI in educational settings requires the timely identification, response, and referral for students. In the following sections, we highlight various roles stakeholders may have in addressing NSSI in schools and identify some key elements for an NSSI policy in secondary and postsecondary educational settings.

Recommendations and Guidelines

An effective NSSI policy should include best practice approaches for supporting students who self-injure, as well as detailed procedural information that includes various stakeholder roles and responsibilities (i.e., administrators, faculty, staff, students, and caregivers) (Hasking et al., 2020). At each level of the policy, the stakeholder's role and responsibilities will vary based on key factors such as student's reaction and further help-seeking behavior, suicide risk, and need for medical intervention (Hamza & Heath, 2018; Hasking et al., 2019). For an NSSI policy to be effectively implemented and adhered to, information sharing, professional development, and resources should be shared with all educational stakeholders in an ongoing process. The policy should be viewed as a fluid document that is guided by experience and changes with information and best practice knowledge in the field. Our website www.icsesgroup.org contains freely available online content that may be useful to inform development of protocols for educational settings (in different languages).

Administrators

Administrators play an important role in systemic policy implementation, which is supported through a professional development strategic plan. Specifically, training that focuses on increasing the understanding of NSSI, in terms of what it is, its prevalence, at-risk groups, underlying functions, and addressing often-held myths, will help to increase awareness and knowledge. As the role of an administrator is to support their staff, it is important that they have high knowledge in this area to provide information and demystify erroneous beliefs about NSSI. This will help to ensure timely and effective referrals of students to the appropriate resources (Lloyd-Richardson et al., 2020).

School and University Staff

School and university staff, such as teachers and faculty, require ongoing professional development that focuses on how best to respond to students who engage in NSSI and to recognize appropriate referral paths. Lack of knowledge regarding the methods and different functions of NSSI, accompanied by student secrecy and reluctance to disclose the behavior, may contribute to the difficulty of identifying students engaging in NSSI (De Riggi et al., 2016). Lewis et al. (2020) stressed the importance of continuing education and training devoted to improving understanding of NSSI behaviors, functions, and their possible evolution over time; risk factors; frequent comorbidity with other mental health problems; NSSI in online communities; the socialization effect; and the link between NSSI and suicidal behaviors (Lewis et al., 2020). Moreover, being aware of students' behaviors and the specific warning signs related to NSSI, such as wearing irregular clothing (e.g., long sleeves in hot weather) or bandages to cover injuries and scars, reluctance to change clothes during sports activities, or a noticeably heightened need for privacy and secrecy could help identify current engagement in NSSI (Hasking et al., 2016). While this education and training on NSSI is important, it is equally important for staff members to be aware of their own beliefs and biases toward NSSI and other forms of self-injury, and work to adopt a framework of empathy and compassion. Students deserve to be met with responses that are nonjudgmental and caring.

Students and Caregivers

Students and caregivers within the school/university setting are critical stakeholders in the development and maintenance of an effective NSSI policy. They should be provided with information as it relates to NSSI. There should be clear guidelines about to whom and how to refer a peer or student of concern, as well as how to reach out if support is needed. Resources and information should be made available to students and caregivers and shared regularly via various fora. Further, if more direct support is needed, there should be a section in the policy regarding how best to respond and the referral process (Hamza & Heath, 2018; Hasking et al., 2020). We recommend keeping resources up to date. Ready-to-use psychoeducation or informational materials have been developed and are freely available (Berger et al., 2014; ICSES).

Mental Health Professionals

Mental health professionals (MHPs) play a key role in supporting the implementation of an NSSI policy at the institutional level. MHPs must be trained on best practice approaches in the assessment of and intervention with students who engage in NSSI. However, the role of an MHP goes beyond direct service delivery with students, as they must also act as a resource for faculty, staff, and caregivers. A comprehensive NSSI policy should clearly lay out the roles and responsibilities of the MHP in providing information, resources, workshops, sessions, and support to the various stakeholders. In order for MHPs to serve as a resource for others, they will need to have ongoing professional development and training and create a supportive community for learning from and sharing with one another. Having a clear strategy within a policy that specifies how to accomplish this is highly recommended. For instance, Hasking et al. (2016) propose integrating a coordination team for case management of NSSI occurrences. Similarly, mental health professionals will likely benefit from the formation of small mentorship and support groups designed to allow them to connect with one another and feel supported in these efforts (Kelada et al., 2017).

RISK ASSESSMENT BY MH PROFESSIONAL

Risk assessment includes severity of injury and if medical help is required, and if the student has disclosed the NSSI to anyone from their network so that the person could be involved in further treatment (De Riggi et al., 2016). A variety of tools have been developed to assist clinicians in determining level of risk (see Chávez-Flores et al., 2019, for a review). Also, given that NSSI is the most reliable predictor of suicidality (Franklin et al., 2017), any protocol must establish clear suicide risk assessment guidelines that offer clear guidance on suicide risk assessment and the ability to distinguish between these (Whitlock et al., 2019).

SOCIAL ANTECEDENTS AND CONSEQUENCES

Risk for social contributors must also be addressed in any NSSI protocol. Specifically, how, when, and to whom communications about NSSI are delivered should be outlined in order to adequately handle social factors that contribute to NSSI or result from NSSI. The main goal of successful communication regarding NSSI would be to position MHPs as an available source of support for NSSI and for any form of distress. Providing information regarding NSSI and alternative coping strategies could contribute to reducing NSSI stigma and normalizing help-seeking for NSSI (De Riggi et al., 2016). Nonetheless, making information regarding NSSI available requires caution. Giving too much of a specific focus or providing graphic details may adversely affect more vulnerable students. Instead of focusing on NSSI actions as such, the authors encourage touching upon the underlying causes of NSSI. It is recommended that NSSI be mentioned as one form of coping, which comprises methods that are likely beneficial (e.g., exercise, talking to someone, and journaling) and those that may carry risks (e.g., substance misuse and NSSI). This framing situates coping within a broader context, rather than portraying NSSI as simply "unhealthy" or "wrong," which may contribute to feelings of guilt and shame on the part of the student (Hasking et al., 2019).

CULTURAL CONSIDERATIONS

Because studies that address NSSI policies and guidelines may be enacted in different countries, generalizing their findings requires caution. Cultural aspects may also play an important role in responding to NSSI on university campuses and should be taken into account when implementing an NSSI policy in educational settings. In sum, taking into account the broader framework of the policies, culture, and available resources of the school or university setting is important in the development of school policy on NSSI (Hasking et al., 2016; Lewis et al., 2019). Tailored policies (taking into account cultural considerations, local policies, and legal settings) will provide clarity, thus reducing all stakeholders' stress and anxiety when facing NSSI, particularly for the less experienced among them (Kelada et al., 2017).

Case Example of a University-Based NSSI Policy

Designing an effective NSSI policy begins with identifying the support needs of university staff and the resources required to provide an effective NSSI response on the university campus (Lewis et al., 2019). For example, Hamza, Robinson, et al. (2021) recently reported on attitudes toward NSSI in a college sample and found that stakeholders reported significantly greater stigma toward NSSI than mental illness in general. Students employed by the university reported greater perceived knowledge and comfort, and demonstrated greater knowledge of NSSI, than students and university staff. As a case example, the authors (members of the International Consortium on Self-injury in Educational Settings, ICSES) developed a NSSI policy for universities, specifically tailored for the Vrije Universiteit Brussel (VUB). Prior to developing the policy, we investigated university staff's knowledge about NSSI, their attitudes toward NSSI, and level of stigma regarding NSSI.

Participants were recruited at VUB (Brussels, Belgium). All university staff members (e.g., teaching staff, on-campus security, medical staff, and student psychologists) were invited via email to fill out an online survey consisting of demographic questions (e.g., age and gender); questions concerning their professional and personal experiences with

NSSI; and questions regarding stigma, their attitude toward NSSI, and their knowledge about NSSI.

In total, 93 university staff participated in this study, and of these, 63 responses were considered valid and included in the analyses. Fifteen participants (22.4%) were men and 47 (70.1%) were women; one participant identified as nonbinary. Ages ranged from less than 25 to greater than 65 years, although most were between 25 and 45 years. Several occupations were reported, including 12 psychologists. Almost half (41.3%) of the participants had personal experiences with NSSI (engaged in NSSI themselves or knew somebody who engaged in NSSI in their personal life, such as family, friends); and only 11.1% had encountered NSSI in their professional experiences.

We found a general lack of knowledge about NSSI among university staff. In addition, stigma toward NSSI was identified but not among all university staff. Almost half of the sample had a rather positive attitude toward NSSI. Another important finding was that participants reported a lack of knowledge and the feeling that they did not know how to handle or react effectively when encountering NSSI. Noteworthy was the positive correlation between lack of knowledge and a negative attitude, underscoring the need for training of university staff. Taken together, the results underscore the need for an NSSI protocol to aid in guiding and supporting university staff in how to react effectively, when to refer, and to whom.

Based on this needs assessment, an NSSI protocol was made for VUB, together with an online training of one hour for staff, one hour for students, and three hours of online training in assessment and how to respond mental health MH staff. The NSSI protocol for universities, tailored for the Vrije Universiteit Brussels, can be found in the Appendix.

Summary and Future Directions for Research and Clinical Practice

The development of an NSSI school policy allows for consistency in response; provides clarity regarding the legal obligations; and offers a set of best practices for administrators, staff, students, and families. Whereas educational programs have been designed to increase knowledge of NSSI and educators, administrators, staff, parents, and students, schools and universities are too often left on their own to develop policies on issues such as suicide or NSSI, creating them with little guidance. Collaborative efforts that join the expertise of researchers, clinicians experienced in NSSI work, and other educational stakeholders would allow for the development of school NSSI policies that take into account best available practices, while also aligning with the culture of the school community. The VUB NSSI Policy (see Appendix) offers one example of how policy can be shaped by existing research on best practices, offers guidance and support for all stakeholders that is tailored to the specific needs of the situation and individual, and is communicated in a clear, approachable form for staff to implement. Future research is needed that evaluates the short- and long-term effectiveness of these programs and how they impact NSSI-specific knowledge, NSSI and mental health stigma, and NSSI rates.

Appendix VUB NSSI Policy

Introduction

AIM

This NSSI Policy has been developed in order to address Nonsuicidal Self-Injury (NSSI) at VUB. The policy supports all the involved parties including students, peers, college staff, health services, and mental health professionals.

WHAT IS NONSUICIDAL SELF-INJURY?

Nonsuicidal self-injury is *"the direct, deliberate damage to one's own body tissue without suicidal intent"* (ISSS, 2018) and typically includes behaviors such as cutting, burning, and hitting oneself. As has been well established (e.g., Nock & Prinstein, 2004), NSSI is best understood as a coping strategy that assists those who use it to find relief when experiencing difficult/painful emotions, to self-punish for perceived wrongdoings, or just to feel something when feeling numb. NSSI is recognized as a widespread and important mental health concern among adolescents and emerging adults (Kiekens et al., 2019; Lewis & Heath, 2015). Numerous studies have identified associations between NSSI and psychological distress and mental health difficulties, such as depression and anxiety (Kiekens, Hasking, Claes, et al., 2018; Klonsky et al., 2014; Lewis & Heath, 2015).

NSSI is not one and the same as suicide and research has shown clear distinctions between NSSI and suicidality (American Psychiatric Association, 2013). However, students who self-injure are at increased risk for suicide and NSSI is a reliable predictor of suicidality (Asarnow et al., 2011; Franklin et al., 2017; Guan et al., 2012; Hamza et al., 2012; Ribeiro et al., 2016; Wilkinson & Goodyer, 2011).

WHY DO PEOPLE SELF-INJURE?

There are several reasons people report engaging in NSSI. The most commonly mentioned reason people self-injure is to regulate intense emotions; self-injury is often a means of coping that provides relief when feeling difficult/painful emotions. The second most common reason people report self-injury is as a way to punish themselves or release/express self-directed anger. Self-injury can also be a form of communication, a way to connect with someone or to communicate a need for help. Intentionally seeking attention is hardly ever a reason for NSSI.

NSSI AMONG COLLEGE STUDENTS

The lifetime prevalence rate of NSSI among college students is 23% (Swannell et al., 2014), indicating a high rate of prevalence in student populations. While the overall average age of onset is in early adolescence, Kiekens et al. (2019) found that the risk of onset increased around the age of 20, when many youth were in college. Recent studies have shown an association between NSSI and poor academic performance (Baetens et al., 2021; Kiekens et al., 2016; Kiekens, Hasking, Claes, et al., 2018).

In terms of sex differences, the results of epidemiological studies are inconsistent; although there are studies reporting higher prevalence rates among females in comparison to males, the other studies found no differences. A moderator analysis reported by Bresin and Schoenleber (2015) revealed that these gender differences in the clinical samples are bigger than college/community samples.

Identifying NSSI among College Students

Prior to responding to NSSI within a college campus, it is important to correctly identify students who self-injure. However, the identification can be a challenging process because most students decide not to reveal NSSI. Therefore, it is crucial to take actions sensitively. Furthermore, students who self-injure often feel misunderstood and are reluctant to seek help (Lewis & Michal, 2016; Rosenrot & Lewis, 2020). Thus, it is important that students do not perceive these actions as intrusive or embarrassing. There are several possible signs of NSSI that are important to be aware of:

> Unexplained cuts, burns, and/or bruises.
> Inappropriate clothing for weather, such as wearing bulky clothes when it is hot or long sleeves for sport activities and/or avoiding activities that may affect the removal of clothing (e.g., swimming and gym).

It is important to bear in mind that there is no single specific or consistent sign of NSSI and the presence of any of those listed above does not necessarily mean that the student is engaging in self-injury. Indeed, many of these signs will not become visible until the emerging adult is motivated to seek help.

General Mental Health Promotion

Although school-based NSSI prevention programs are growing gradually, they are often not specific for colleges. Generally, there are several suggested prevention strategies including improving emotion-regulation strategies and encouraging social connectedness. VUB actively invests in both social connectedness and emotion-regulation strategies via the student psychologist services (SBC-Studiebegeleiding |Vrije Universiteit Brussel (vub.be)). Our student VUB mental health policy explicitly encourages openness to talk about distress and mental health concerns. "Leave no one behind" is a resource for VUB students that provides them with multiple types of support; if they need to chat or are feeling not well, they can contact different professional health care services, or if they want to talk to fellow students there are several initiatives for and by students. Students can reach these and more via the VUB student website or MoodSpace. Next to a general policy for mental health of students, an enhancement of understanding of NSSI at all levels (students, staff, mental health professionals) is needed. All mental health staff of VUB received online training on NSSI, and resources (including this VUB protocol) for VUB staff are available via VUB intranet (both in Dutch and English). The best prevention program for campus students is to let them know there are people available to talk with them safely (also about NSSI) via VUB staff, VUB mental health staff, and social media campaigns (at least four campaigns per academic year).

Promoting Disclosures and Help-Seeking Behavior

Despite the high rates of NSSI, most self-injury remains hidden. Research indicates that 30%–57% of people who engage in self-injury have never disclosed it to others (Armiento et al., 2014; Martin et al., 2010; Michelmore & Hindley, 2012; Nixon et al., 2008; Whitlock et al., 2006) and most of them talk about their NSSI only once or twice (Heath et al., 2009). In addition, studies estimate that 9%–16% of individuals seek professional support (Baetens et al., 2012; Whitlock et al., 2011). Disclosure of self-injury may provide the opportunity of getting support and help from others and increase the chance to access professional help (Baetens et al., 2012; Whitlock et al., 2011). A central reason for unwillingness to disclose NSSI is the stigma associated with it (Rosenrot & Lewis, 2020; Staniland et al., 2020). As such, the destigmatization of NSSI may help to increase corresponding help-seeking behavior. Enhancing NSSI literacy therefore represents a significant step toward reducing stigma and promoting disclosure.

The advantages of mental health concerns and risk behaviors disclosure have been recognized widely (e.g., Chaudoir & Quinn, 2010; Corrigan & Rao, 2012). Even if the students disclose their behavior to friends, they can be a mediator to seeking professional help. Therefore, targeting peer networks increases the chance of disclosure.

Previous research has identified the reaction of the confidante as the most powerful factor in willingness to disclose NSSI (Chaudoir & Fisher, 2010; Derlega et al., 2011). When an individual is considering whether they want to talk about self-injury with someone else, they are likely to consider the reaction of that person and the consequences of the disclosure itself. This highlights the importance of ensuring students about confidentiality and being nonjudgmental, and empathic. Another important factor in disclosure is the quality of relationships. Armiento et al. (2014) suggested that as romantic relationships mostly are based on high levels of trust, support, and emotional intimacy, romantic partners can significantly facilitate the disclosure. Particularly since romantic relationships are an important part of emerging adults' lives (Roisman et al., 2004), having strategies and training for students' partners would be helpful in treating NSSI in the campus. Also, the degree of distress that the individual is experiencing influences their decision to talk about it with others or not. Some individuals who engage in NSSI want to keep this behavior private as something that helps them. In sum, for those students who do want to talk about it and reach out for help, it is important to lower the barriers to seeking and obtaining support.

Improving NSSI Literacy at All Levels

College settings provide opportunities for NSSI identification and services for students who engage in self-injury. Taking steps to decrease stigma and improve staff effectiveness in responding to NSSI disclosure is especially important. Although college staff report an increase of self-injury among college students, they also report low knowledge and skill in addressing NSSI effectively (Whisenhunt et al., 2015; Whitlock et al., 2009).

A health promotion training program should emphasize understanding why students self-injure, responding effectively, and knowing what appropriate referral options are available. Psychoeducational training programs should guide constructive and effective responding and referrals for students involved in self-injury as these are essential steps to enhancing mental health knowledge at all institutional levels (Lewis et al., 2019). Important points to keep in mind:

- Implementation of the policy would require widespread support of campus staff;
- There is a wide range of self-injurious behaviors;
- NSSI does not equal suicide, but students who self-injure are at increased risk for suicide;
- Yearly risk screening is a good opportunity to identify students at a risk of NSSI; and
- Talking about NSSI does not encourage or provoke NSSI.

How to Respond Effectively?

When it is learned that a student engages in self-injury, the initial reaction is highly important because it may influence whether the student will seek help in the future. Students who engage in NSSI are often worried and uncertain about the disclosure (if it is a good or bad idea, how the other person will respond, etc.). If a supportive response is given, the likelihood of future help-seeking will be increased.

General recommendations for supportive, effective responses include (adapted from Lewis et al., 2019):

- Interact with the student in a calm, nonjudgmental and empathic way, allowing the student to feel supported. In contrast, overreactive responses could alienate the student. For example: *"it seems you are experiencing a hard time lately, thank you for sharing."*
- Take a "respectful curiosity" approach in talking with self-injuring students. Show that you are interested in understanding their experiences. For example: *"I'd like to understand it better. Could you let me know what self-injury is like for you?"*

- Use the student's language. If the student refers to it as "cutting" rather than self-injury, follow their language and convey active listening. For example: "*Can you tell me more about the stressors leading up to the cutting?*"
- Validate the student's experience. Show you understand the motivation for self-injury. For example: "*So when you feel distressed, self-injury helps you feel calm again?*"
- Focus on overall well-being. For example: "*Several personal and relationship difficulties can trigger self-injury in students. I would like to know more about how you have been doing and what you are going through.*"
- Recommend referral/connections to those who can help. "*I know there are people who you can talk to. Can I help you with finding a time to meet with them?*"

COLLEGE ADMINISTRATION/FACULTY

Self-injury is a common concern among college students, with up to one in five students reporting self-injury (Swanell et al., 2014). Self-injury increases the risk for suicide and must be taken seriously (Franklin et al., 2017). Not addressing self-injury on campus can significantly impact students' academic performance and adversely affect their well-being. Administrators can play a key role by addressing stigma and ensuring supportive resources, including crisis resources, are available on campus. Addressing self-injury and related concerns can situate campuses as leaders in addressing student well-being (Lewis et al., 2019).

College administration and faculty staff are sometimes the first points of contact to disclose distress related to their academic performance. It is always a good idea to keep in mind that some students engage in NSSI to cope with stress or intensive thoughts and emotions. If you see one or more signs that might indicate NSSI, please address your concern in an empathic, nonjudgmental way. You do not have to actively promote help-seeking or indicate that the student has to stop with the self-injury, but acknowledge this is their way of coping and let them know that they can contact Studiebegeleidingcentrum (SBC; Study Guidance Center) / Brussels University Consultation Center (BRUCC) if they would like to. Other suggestions for how and when you engage with students include:

- Keep in touch with students who engage in NSSI, or those for whom you have a gut feeling they might be at risk.
- Listen actively to students and validate their experience, including the reasons they may have for self-injury.
- Use a calm, empathic, and nonjudgmental tone.
- Be aware of on- and off-campus resources, which is essential to ensuring students can access ongoing support after the initial encounter. For more information, see VUB SharePoint NSSI.

The process of referring can be challenging for campus staff. The student who discloses their self-injury is vulnerable and might be reluctant to trust or share this information with others. The important point is to show them you really care about them and that you are worried about their well-being and you want to support them to feel better. You can offer to accompany them to the mental health service on campus and stay there during the assessment session. You can even help the student (who is hesitant and not secure) to begin the process of getting mental health help if they want.

PEER SUPPORT NETWORKS AND VUB BUDDIES

Given that many students prefer to discuss self-injury with same-age peers (Armiento et al., 2014), students may seek support at on-campus peer support networks. Peer support workers can help by:

- Actively listening to peers of students who engage in NSSI. Being a friend of somebody who self-injures can evoke an array of negative feelings (such as guilt and worries) and may contribute to secondary distress.
- Validate the important support they offer to students who engage in NSSI, and validate their experience.
- Peer support workers should have opportunities to debrief as needed, and self-care strategies for both students and peer support workers should also be emphasized.

DORMS/STUDENT HOUSES

Many students live away from home and in the residence halls when attending college. Due to the high rates of self-injury on campuses, residence hall staff may encounter students who self-injure. Residence hall staff can help by:

- Being aware of on- and off-campus resources for ensuring students have access to support services after their initial encounter.
- Providing opportunities to debrief as needed and engage in self-care.
- Being aware of the impact of social contagion and how people may be more likely to begin to self-injure if they are around others who self-injure.

One of the main challenges in dorms/student housing emerges when a student shows their wounds or no longer wants to hide their recent injuries/scars. This might upset other students, or it may have a suggestive effect on other students, especially in students' dormitories. Typically this pertains to open wounds and recent injuries, which can be triggering for other students. This tends to not be the case with regard to old wounds or scars. Making the decision to show scars and not hiding them anymore is not necessarily negative but can sometimes be helpful for the student's recovery process because it indicates that the person is open to accepting their scars and that phase of their life. Therefore, for responding to students who are struggling with self-injuries recently, there are a few suggestions, as follows:

- As showing recent injuries/wounds may raise a risk for infections and upset other students, it is important to ask students who have recently self-injured to cover the recent injuries. Explain to them that showing their injuries might also trigger self-injury among other students with lived experience of NSSI.
- For students who do not want to hide their scars, validate their experiences and feelings. Talking about scars and one's willingness to not conceal them no longer, can be a positive step in acceptance. Therefore we should respond empathetically and support them, while bearing the following points in mind:
  1. Realize that it is the students' choice and it may contribute to a positive outcome for the student;
  2. Discuss with the student how they will respond to and cope with the possible overwhelming/negative reactions and questions from others; and
  3. Make sure there will be a regular check-in plan to be updated about the students' situation and keep supporting them.

HEALTH SERVICES

Physicians, nurses, and other professionals who work in on-campus health clinics may encounter students who self-injure. These professionals can help by:

- During interactions with students who self-injure, using a calm, nonjudgmental, and empathic approach;
- Validating that self-injury serves a purpose and using respectful curiosity to understand the student's experience;
- Being aware that although students do not self-injure to die by suicide, self-injury is associated with increased risk of suicide. All students who self-injure must be assessed for suicide risk;
- Recognizing that students who self-injure may not be ready to stop yet; and
- Being aware of on- and off-campus resources when referring students for additional ongoing support and care. For more information, see VUB SharePoint NSSI.

COLLEGE MENTAL HEALTH PROFESSIONALS

Although students do not engage in NSSI because they want to die by suicide, engaging in NSSI is associated with suicidal thoughts and behaviors (Kiekens, Hasking, Boyes, et al., 2018; Mars et al., 2019). Therefore, all students who self-injure must be assessed for suicide risk. When talking to students, college mental health professionals can help by:

- Using a calm, nonjudgmental, and empathic approach;
- Validating that self-injury serves a purpose and using respectful curiosity to understand the student's experience;
- Recognizing that they may not be ready to stop yet, or might never want to stop;
- Using approaches grounded in motivational interviewing, which may help to foster readiness to work on self-injury;
- Working with students collaboratively to find other ways to meet their needs or cope;
- Using approaches that emphasize emotion regulation;
- Seeking more information; for example, see VUB SharePoint risk assessment for NSSI (also see Westers & Tinsley, this volume).

NSSI Protocol for VUB

This NSSI protocol is embedded in a tiered approach of mental health promotion in educational settings, where tier 1 is a general policy for well-being of students with an active promotion of mental health, ways of coping with stress, and mental health and NSSI literacy, via social media campaigns, trainings/webinars, websites. Tier 2 focuses on students at risk by providing extra resources and interventions (scholarships, resilience based trainings for those students who perceive a severe academic stress, etc.). In a third tier, a more specific protocol for NSSI is embedded, in line with a suicide protocol, and protocols for psychiatric diagnoses and crisis situations. The guidelines for NSSI protocols focus on students who are actively engaging in NSSI. Students who self-injure could be guided in getting help from mental health services (e.g., counselor, psychologist, or consultation center), which then can conduct an initial risk assessment.

A first key issue to address concerns determining the role of each person involved, as stipulated above. Trainings should be organized for all stakeholders (e.g., Campus staff, MH staff, and students). This also includes the appointment of a point person (i.e., campus contact person) whom staff can reach out to in case they suspect a student is engaging in self-injury or if they have any questions on how to handle NSSI in educational settings. An alternative option, with consent of the student, is a direct referral to MH services or student psychologists (see fig. 47.1), without risk assessment of the campus contact person. Another key element in the protocol is to lay out clear guidelines about risk assessment and the referral process of students who engage in self-injury (see fig. 47.2), which is usually handled by the campus contact person, who is preferably a psychologist or MH professional. This should include a plan of actions to assess suicide risk and mental health

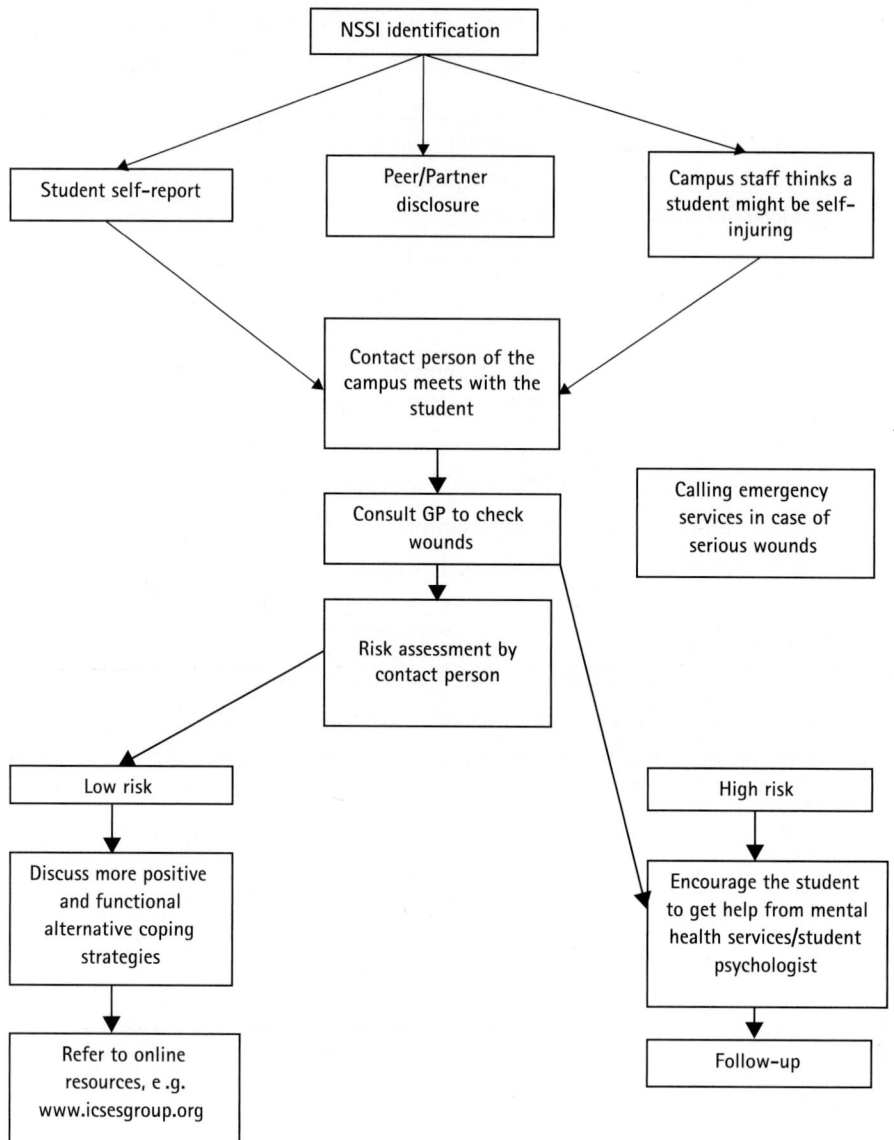

Figure 47.1 Roles in the Referral Process

screening, to refer both in- and outside mental health services, and to deal with crisis situations.

Useful Online Resources
- Self-Injury Outreach and Support (SiOS)
- International Consortium on Self-Injury in Educational Settings
- Shedding Light on Self-Injury

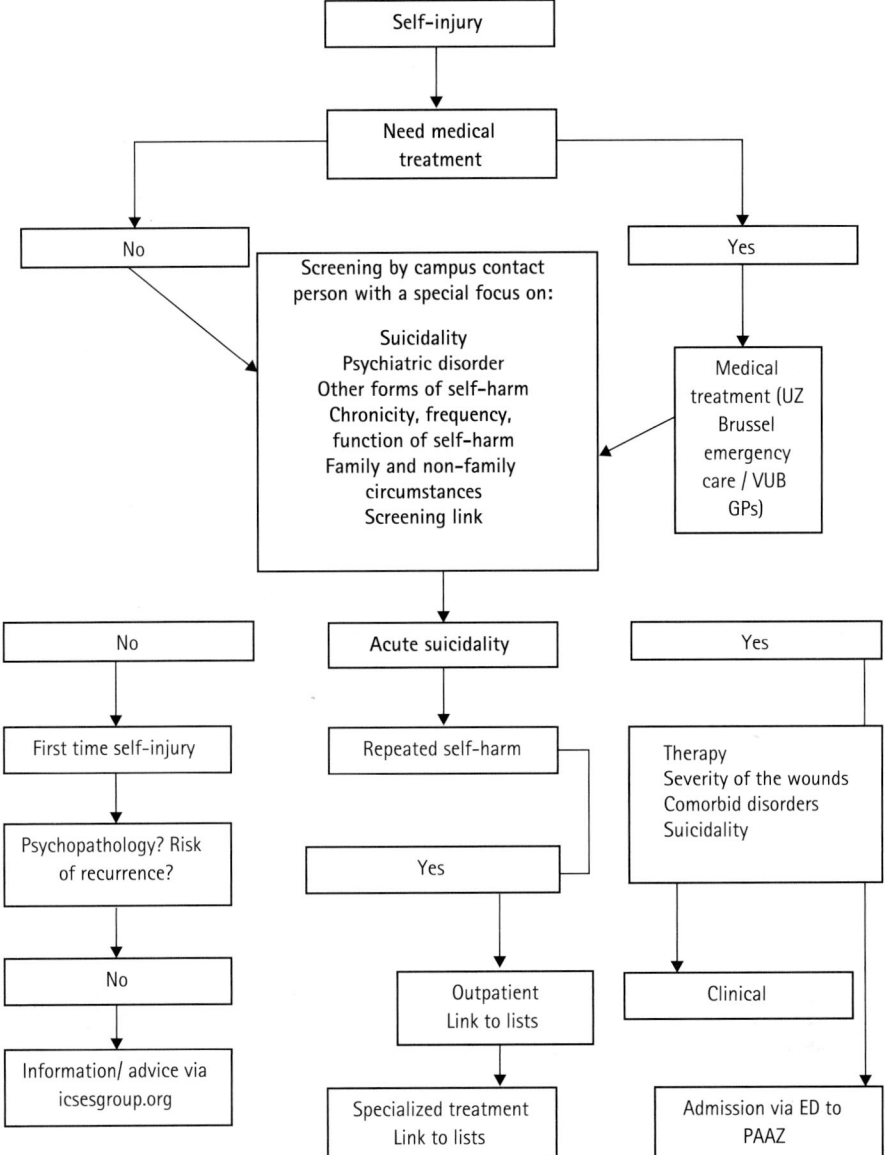

Figure 47.2 Referral Process

- Self-Injury and Recovery Research and Resources
- Safe Alternatives

References

American Psychiatric Association. (2013). *Diagnostic and statistical manual of mental disorders* (5th ed.).

Armiento, J. S., Hamza, C. A., & Willoughby, T. (2014). An examination of disclosure of nonsuicidal self-injury among university students. *Journal of Community & Applied Social Psychology, 24*(6), 518–533. https://doi.org/10.1002/casp.2190

Arnett, J. J., Žukauskienė, R., & Sugimura, K. (2014). The new life stage of emerging adulthood at ages 18–29 years: Implications for mental health. *The Lancet Psychiatry*, *1*(7), 569–576. https://doi.org/10.1016/s2215-0366(14)00080-7

Asarnow, J. R., Porta, G., Spirito, A., Emslie, G., Clarke, G., Wagner, K. D., Vitiello, B., Keller, M., Birmaher, B., McCracken, J., Mayes, T., Berk, M., & Brent, D. A. (2011). Suicide attempts and nonsuicidal self-injury in the treatment of resistant depression in adolescents: Findings from the TORDIA study. *Journal of the American Academy of Child and Adolescent Psychiatry*, *50*(8), 772–781. https://doi.org/10.1016/j.jaac.2011.04.003

Auerbach, R. P., Mortier, P., Bruffaerts, R., Alonso, J., Benjet, C., Cuijpers, P., Demyttenaere, K., Ebert, D. D., Green, J. G., Hasking, P., Murray, E., Nock, M. K., Pinder-Amaker, S., Sampson, N. A., Stein, D. J., Vilagut, G., Zaslavsky, A. M., & Kessler, R. C. (2018). WHO world mental health surveys international college student project: Prevalence and distribution of mental disorders. *Journal of Abnormal Psychology*, *127*(7), 623–638. https://doi.org/10.1037/abn0000362

Baetens, I., Claes, L., Muehlenkamp, J., Grietens, H., & Onghena, P. (2012). Differences in psychological symptoms and self-competencies in non-suicidal self-injurious Flemish adolescents. *Journal of Adolescence*, *35*(3), 753–759. https://doi.org/10.1016/j.adolescence.2011.11.001

Baetens, I., Decruy, C., Vatandoost, S., Vanderhaegen, B., & Kiekens, G. (2020). School-based prevention targeting non-suicidal self-injury: A pilot study. *Frontiers in Psychiatry*, *11*, Article 437. https://doi.org/10.3389/fpsyt.2020.00437

Baetens, I., Greene, D., Van Hove, L., Van Leeuwen, K., Wiersema, J. R., Desoete, A., & Roelants, M. (2021). Predictors and consequences of non-suicidal self-injury in relation to life, peer, and school factors. *Journal of Adolescence*, *90*, 100–108. https://doi.org/10.1016/j.adolescence.2021.06.005

Berger, E., Hasking, P., & Reupert, A. (2014). "We're working in the dark here": Education needs of teachers and school staff regarding student self-injury. *School Mental Health*, *6*(3), 201–212. https://doi.org/10.1007/s12310-013-9114-4

Berger, E., Hasking, P., & Reupert, A. (2015). Developing a policy to address nonsuicidal self-injury in schools. *Journal of School Health*, *85*(9), 629–647. https://doi.org/10.1111/josh.12292

Bresin, K., & Schoenleber, M. (2015). Gender differences in the prevalence of nonsuicidal self-injury: A meta-analysis. *Clinical Psychology Review*, *38*, 55–64. https://doi.org/10.1016/j.cpr.2015.02.009

Chaudoir, S. R., & Fisher, J. D. (2010). The disclosure processes model: Understanding disclosure decision making and postdisclosure outcomes among people living with a concealable stigmatized identity. *Psychological Bulletin*, *136*(2), 236–256. https://doi.org/10.1037/a0018193

Chaudoir, S. R., & Quinn, D. M. (2010). Revealing concealable stigmatized identities: The impact of disclosure motivations and positive first disclosure experiences on fear of disclosure and well-being. *The Journal of Social Issues*, *66*(3), 570–584. https://doi.org/10.1111/j.15404560.2010.01663.x

Chávez-Flores, Y. V., Hidalgo-Rasmussen, C. A., Yanez-Peñúñuri, L. Y. (2019). Assessment tools of non-suicidal self-injury in adolescents 1990-2016: A systematic review. *Ciencia & Saude Coletiva*, *24*(8), 2871–2882. https://doi.org/10.1590/1413-81232018248.18502017

Corrigan, P. W., & Rao, D. (2012). On the self-stigma of mental illness: Stages, disclosure, and strategies for change. *Canadian Journal of Psychiatry*, *57*(8), 464–469. https://doi.org/10.1177/070674371205700804

De Riggi, M. E., Moumne, S., Heath, N. L., & Lewis, S. P. (2016). Non-suicidal self-injury in our schools: A review and research-informed guidelines for school mental health professionals. *Canadian Journal of School Psychology*, *32*(2), 122–143. https://doi.org/10.1177/0829573516645563

Derlega, V. J., Anderson, S., Winstead, B. A., & Greene, K. (2011). Positive disclosure among college students: What do they talk about, to whom, and why? *The Journal of Positive Psychology*, *6*(2), 119–130. https://doi.org/10.1080/17439760.2010.545430

Franklin, J. C., Ribeiro, J. D., Fox, K. R., Bentley, K. H., Kleiman, E. M., Huang, X., Musacchio, K. M., Jaroszewski, A. C., Chang, B. P., & Nock, M. K. (2017). Risk factors for suicidal thoughts and behaviors: A meta-analysis of 50 years of research. *Psychological Bulletin*, *143*(2), 187–232. https://doi.org/10.1037/bul0000084

Gandhi, A., Luyckx, K., Baetens, I., Kiekens, G., Sleuwaegen, E., Berens, A., Maitra, S., & Claes, L. (2018). Age of onset of non-suicidal self-injury in Dutch-speaking adolescents and emerging adults: An event history analysis of pooled data. *Comprehensive Psychiatry*, *80*, 170–178. https://doi.org/10.1016/j.comppsych.2017.10.007

Guan, K., Fox, K. R., & Prinstein, M. J. (2012). Nonsuicidal self-injury as a time-invariant predictor of adolescent suicide ideation and attempts in a diverse community sample. *Journal of Consulting and Clinical Psychology*, *80*(5), 842–849. https://doi.org/10.1037/a0029429

Hamza, C. A., Goldstein, A. L., Heath, N. L., & Ewing, L. (2021). Stressful experiences in university predict non-suicidal self-injury through emotional reactivity. *Frontiers in Psychology*, *12*, Article 610670. https://doi.org/10.3389/fpsyg.2021.610670

Hamza, C. A., & Heath, N. L. (2018). Nonsuicidal self-injury: What schools can do. In A. Leschied, D. Saklofske, & G. Flett (Eds.), *Handbook of school-based mental health promotion* (pp. 237–260). Springer. https://doi.org/10.1007/978-3-319-89842-1_14

Hamza, C. A., Robinson, K., Hasking, P. A., Heath, N. L., Lewis, S. P., Lloyd-Richardson, E., Whitlock, J., & Wilson, M. S. (2021). Educational stakeholders' attitudes and knowledge about nonsuicidal self-injury among university students: A cross-national study. *Journal of American College Health*. Advance online publication. https://doi.org/10.1080/07448481.2021.1961782

Hamza, C. A., Stewart, S. L., & Willoughby, T. (2012). Examining the link between nonsuicidal self-injury and suicidal behavior: A review of the literature and an integrated model. *Clinical Psychology Review*, *32*(6), 482–495. https://doi.org/10.1016/j.cpr.2012.05.003

Hasking, P., Baetens, I., Bloom, E., Heath, N., Lewis, S. P., Lloyd-Richardson, E., & Robinson, K. (2019). Addressing and responding to nonsuicidal self-injury in the school context. In J. J. Washburn (Ed.), *Nonsuicidal self-injury* (pp. 175–194). Routledge. https://doi.org/10.4324/9781315164182-11

Hasking, P. A., Bloom, E., Lewis, S. P., & Baetens, I. (2020). Developing a policy, and professional development for school staff, to address and respond to nonsuicidal self-injury in schools. *International Perspectives in Psychology*, *9*(3), 176–179. https://doi.org/10.1037/ipp0000143

Hasking, P. A., Heath, N. L., Kaess, M., Lewis, S. P., Plener, P. L., Walsh, B. W., Whitlock, J., & Wilson, M. S. (2016). Position paper for guiding response to non-suicidal self-injury in schools. *School Psychology International*, *37*(6), 644–663. https://doi.org/10.1177/0143034316678656

Heath, N. L., Bastien, L., Mettler, J., Bloom, E., & Hamza, C. (2020). School response to non-suicidal self-injury. In E. Cole & M. Kokai (Eds.), *Consultation and mental health interventions in school settings: A scientist-practitioner's guide* (pp. 145–172). Hogrefe GmbH.

Heath, N. L., Ross, S., Toste, J. R., Charlebois, A., & Nedecheva, T. (2009). Retrospective analysis of social factors and nonsuicidal self-injury among young adults. *Canadian Journal of Behavioral Science*, *41*(3), 180–186. https://doi.org/10.1037/a0015732

International Society for the Study of Self-injury (ISSS). (2018). What is self-injury? https://itriples.org/about-self-injury/what-is-selfinjury

Kelada, L., Hasking, P., & Melvin, G. A. (2017). School response to self-injury: Concerns of mental health staff and parents. *School Psychology Quarterly*, *32*(2), 173–187. https://doi.org/10.1037/spq0000194

Kiekens, G., Claes, L., Demyttenaere, K., Auerbach, R. P., Green, J. G., Kessler, R. C., Mortier, P., Nock, M. K., & Bruffaerts, R. (2016). Lifetime and 12-month nonsuicidal self-injury and academic performance in college freshmen. *Suicide and Life-Threatening Behavior*, *46*, 563–576. https://doi.org/10.1111/sltb.12237

Kiekens, G., Hasking, P., Boyes, M., Claes, L., Mortier, P., Auerbach, R. P., Cuijpers, P., Demyttenaere, K., Green, J. G., Kessler, R. C., Myin-Germeys, I., Nock, M. K., & Bruffaerts, R. (2018). The associations between non-suicidal self-injury and first onset suicidal thoughts and behaviors. *Journal of Affective Disorders*, *239*, 171–179. https://doi.org/10.1016/j.jad.2018.06.033

Kiekens, G., Hasking, P., Claes, L., Boyes, M., Mortier, P., Auerbach, R. P., Cuijpers, P., Demyttenaere, K., Green, J. G., Kessler, R. C., Myin-Germeys, I., Nock, M. K., & Bruffaerts, R. (2019). Predicting the incidence of non-suicidal self-injury in college students. *European Psychiatry*, *59*, 44–51. https://doi.org/10.1016/j.eurpsy.2019.04.002

Kiekens, G., Hasking, P., Claes, L., Mortier, P., Auerbach, R. P., Boyes, M., Cuijpers, P., Demyttenaere, K., Green, J. G., Kessler, R. C., Nock, M. K., & Bruffaerts, R. (2018). The DSM-5 nonsuicidal self-injury disorder among incoming college students: Prevalence and associations with 12-month mental disorders and suicidal thoughts and behaviors. *Depression and Anxiety*, *35*(7), 629–637. https://doi.org/10.1002/da.22754

Klonsky, E. D., Victor, S. E., & Saffer, B. Y. (2014). Nonsuicidal self-injury: What we know, and what we need to know. *The Canadian Journal of Psychiatry*, *59*(11), 565–568. https://doi.org/10.1177/070674371405901101

Lewis, S. P., & Heath, N. L. (2015). Nonsuicidal self-injury among youth. *The Journal of Pediatrics*, *166*(3), 526–530. https://doi.org/10.1016/j.jpeds.2014.11.062

Lewis, S. P., Heath, N. L., Hasking, P. A., Hamza, C. A., Bloom, E. L., Lloyd-Richardson, E. E., & Whitlock, J. (2020). Advocacy for improved response to self-injury in schools: A call to action for school psychologists. *Psychological Services*, *17*(S1), 86–92. https://doi.org/10.1037/ser0000352

Lewis, S. P., Heath, N. L., Hasking, P. A., Whitlock, J. L., Wilson, M. S., & Plener, P. L. (2019). Addressing self-injury on college campuses: Institutional recommendations. *Journal of College Counseling*, *22*(1), 70–82. https://doi.org/10.1002/jocc.12115

Lewis, S. P., & Michal, N. J. (2016). Start, stop, and continue: Preliminary insight into the appeal of self-injury e-communities. *Journal of Health Psychology*, *21*(2), 250–260. https://doi.org/10.1177/1359105314527140

Lindow, J. C., Hughes, J. L., South, C., Gutierrez, L., Bannister, E., Trivedi, M. H., & Byerly, M. J. (2020). Feasibility and acceptability of the Youth Aware of Mental health (YAM) intervention in US adolescents. *Archives of Suicide Research*, *24*(2), 269–284. https://doi.org/10.1080/13811118.2019.1624667

Lloyd-Richardson, E. E., Hasking, P., Lewis, S., Hamza, C., McAllister, M., Baetens, I., & Muehlenkamp, J. (2020). Addressing self-injury in schools, part 2: How school nurses can help with supporting assessment, ongoing care, and referral for treatment. *NASN School Nurse*, *35*(2), 99–103. https://doi.org/10.1177/1942602x19887353

Madjar, N., Ben Shabat, S., Elia, R., Fellner, N., Rehavi, M., Rubin, S., Segal, N., & Shoval, G. (2017). Nonsuicidal self-injury within the school context: Multilevel analysis of teachers' support and peer climate. *European Psychiatry*, *41*(1), 95–101. https://doi.org/10.1016/j.eurpsy.2016.11.003

Mars, B., Heron, J., Klonsky, E. D., Moran, P., O'Connor, R. C., Tilling, K., Wilkinson, P., & Gunnell, D. (2019). Predictors of future suicide attempt among adolescents with suicidal thoughts or non-suicidal self-harm: A population-based birth cohort study. *The Lancet Psychiatry*, *6*(4), 327–337. https://doi.org/10.1016/s2215-0366(19)30030-6

Martin, G., Swannell, S. V., Hazell, P. L., Harrison, J. E., & Taylor, A. W. (2010). Self-injury in Australia: A community survey. *The Medical Journal of Australia*, *193*(9), 506–510. https://doi.org/10.5694/j.1326-5377.2010.tb04033.x

Mazza, J. J., Dexter-Mazza, E. T., Miller, A. L., Rathus, J. H., Murphy, H. E., & Linehan, M. M. (2016). *DBT® skills in schools: Skills training for emotional problem solving for adolescents (DBT STEPS-A)*. Guilford Press.

McAllister, M., Hasking, P., Estefan, A., McClenaghan, K., & Lowe, J. (2010). A strengths-based group program on self-harm. *The Journal of School Nursing*, *26*(4), 289–300. https://doi.org/10.1177/1059840510368801

Michelmore, L., & Hindley, P. (2012). Help-seeking for suicidal thoughts and self-harm in young people: A systematic review. *Suicide & Life-Threatening Behavior*, *42*(5), 507–524. https://doi.org/10.1111/j.1943-278X.2012.00108.x

Muehlenkamp, J. J., Claes, L., Havertape, L., & Plener, P. L. (2012). International prevalence of adolescent non-suicidal self-injury and deliberate self-harm. *Child and Adolescent Psychiatry and Mental Health*, *6*(1), Article 10. https://doi.org/10.1186/1753-2000-6-10

Muehlenkamp, J. J., Walsh, B. W., & McDade, M. (2010). Preventing non-suicidal self-injury in adolescents: The Signs of Self-Injury Program. *Journal of Youth and Adolescence*, *39*(3), 306–314. https://doi.org/10.1007/s10964-009-9450-8

Nixon, M. K., Cloutier, P., & Jansson, S. (2008). Nonsuicidal self-harm in youth: A population-based survey. *Canadian Medical Association Journal*, *178*(3), 306–312. https://doi.org/10.1503/cmaj.061693

Nock, M. K., & Prinstein, M. J. (2004). A functional approach to the assessment of self-mutilative behavior. *Journal of Consulting and Clinical Psychology*, *72*(5), 885–890. https://doi.org/10.1037/0022-006X.72.5.885

Ribeiro, J. D., Franklin, J. C., Fox, K. R., Bentley, K. H., Kleiman, E. M., Chang, B. P., & Nock, M. K. (2016). Self-injurious thoughts and behaviors as risk factors for future suicide ideation, attempts, and death: A meta-analysis of longitudinal studies. *Psychological Medicine*, *46*(2), 225–236. https://doi.org/10.1017/S0033291715001804

Roisman, G. I., Masten, A. S., Coatsworth, J. D., & Tellegen, A. (2004). Salient and emerging developmental tasks in the transition to adulthood. *Child Development*, *75*(1), 123–133. https://doi.org/10.1111/j.1467-8624.2004.00658.x

Rosenrot, S. A., & Lewis, S. P. (2020). Barriers and responses to the disclosure of non-suicidal self-injury: A thematic analysis. *Counseling Psychology Quarterly, 33*(2), 121–141. https://doi.org/10.1080/09515070.2018.1489220.

Shulman, E. P., Smith, A. R., Silva, K., Icenogle, G., Duell, N., Chein, J., & Steinberg, L. (2016). The dual systems model: Review, reappraisal, and reaffirmation. *Developmental Cognitive Neuroscience, 17*, 103–117. https://doi.org/10.1016/j.dcn.2015.12.010

Staniland, L., Hasking, P., Boyes, M., & Lewis, S. (2020). Stigma and nonsuicidal self-injury: Application of a conceptual framework. *Stigma and Health. 6*(3), 312–323. https://doi.org/10.1037/sah0000257

Swannell, S. V., Martin, G. E., Page, A., Hasking, P., & St John, N. J. (2014). Prevalence of nonsuicidal self-injury in nonclinical samples: Systematic review, meta-analysis and meta-regression. *Suicide & Life-Threatening Behavior, 44*(3), 273–303. https://doi.org/10.1111/sltb.12070

Taylor, P. J., Jomar, K., Dhingra, K., Forrester, R., Shahmalak, U., & Dickson, J. M. (2018). A meta-analysis of the prevalence of different functions of non-suicidal self-injury. *Journal of Affective Disorders, 227*, 759–769. https://doi.org/10.1016/j.jad.2017.11.073

Werner-Seidler, A., Perry, Y., Calear, A. L., Newby, J. M., & Christensen, H. (2017). School-based depression and anxiety prevention programs for young people: A systematic review and meta-analysis. *Clinical Psychology Review, 51*, 30–47. https://doi.org/10.1016/j.cpr.2016.10.005

Whisenhunt, J. L., Chang, C. Y., Brack, G. L., Orr, J., Adams, L. G., Paige, M. R., McDonald, P. L., & O'Hara, C. (2015). Self-injury and suicide: Practical information for college counselors. *Journal of College Counseling, 18*(3), 275–288. https://doi.org/10.1002/jocc.12020

Whitlock, J., Eckenrode, J., & Silverman, D. (2006). Self-injurious behaviors in a college population. *Pediatrics, 117*, 1939–1948. https://doi.org/10.1542/peds.2005-2543.

Whitlock, J., Lewis, S. P., Baetens, I., & Hasking, P. (2019). Non-suicidal self-injury on college campuses. *Higher Education Today*. Blog post by American Council on Education. https://www.higheredtoday.org/2019/02/06/non-suicidal-self-injury-college-campuses/

Whitlock, J., Muehlenkamp, J., Purington, A., Eckenrode, J., Barreira, P., Baral Abrams, G., Marchell, T., Kress, V., Girard, K., Chin, C., & Knox, K. (2011). Nonsuicidal self-injury in a college population: General trends and sex differences. *Journal of American College Health, 59*(8), 691–698. https://doi.org/10.1080/07448481.2010.529626

Whitlock, J., Purington, A., & Gershkovich, M. (2009). Media, the internet, and nonsuicidal self-injury. In M. K. Nock (Ed.), *Understanding nonsuicidal self-injury: Origins, assessment, and treatment* (pp. 139–155). American Psychological Association. https://doi.org/10.1037/11875-008.

Wilkinson, P., & Goodyer, I. (2011). Non-suicidal self-injury. *European Child & Adolescent Psychiatry, 20*(2), 103–108. https://doi.org/10.1007/s00787-010-0156-y0

Xavier, A., Pinto-Gouveia, J., Cunha, M., & Dinis, A. (2017). Longitudinal pathways for the maintenance of non-suicidal self-injury in adolescence: The pernicious blend of depressive symptoms and self-criticism. *Child & Youth Care Forum, 46*(6), 841–856. https://doi.org/10.1007/s10566-017-9406-1

CHAPTER 48

Promising Approaches in Prevention and Intervention in Secondary School Settings

Julia Petrovic, Laurianne Bastien, Jessica Mettler, Elana Bloom, Chloe A. Hamza, *and* Nancy Heath

Abstract

Self-injury is not an unusual occurrence in adolescence and thus arises in secondary school settings with some frequency. However, as discussed in this chapter, the complexity of the behavior and the importance of school involvement cannot be underestimated. This chapter begins with a brief overview of the occurrence of NSSI in secondary school students, contextualizing it in terms of its prevalence, functions, stigmatization, and risk and protective factors. The developmental and contextual significance of addressing NSSI in secondary schools will then be highlighted. Following this, a review of the literature surrounding NSSI prevention/intervention approaches within secondary school settings is discussed. Recommendations for NSSI prevention and intervention in secondary school settings will then be organized by level (i.e., primary, secondary, and tertiary). Elements of both prevention and intervention are embedded within each level; specifically, (a) primary prevention/intervention aims to prevent the onset of a behavior through universal intervention; (b) secondary prevention/intervention aims to prevent the onset of a behavior in individuals at-risk; and (c) tertiary prevention/intervention aims to respond to a behavior once it has emerged to reduce its negative impacts. The chapter then concludes by discussing the challenges to NSSI prevention/intervention in secondary school settings, recommendations for navigating such challenges should they arise, and suggestions for future research in this area.

Key Words: NSSI, self-injury, secondary school settings, students, stigmatization, prevention, intervention, adolescence

Case 1. *E.L. is a 16-year-old female who has a history of engaging in self-cutting that spans over three years. She is highly perfectionistic and self-critical. Although she has very supportive family and friends, they are unaware of her self-injury. She is connected to an online self-injury community. She finds self-injury helps her focus and deal with the stress of exams. A friend noticed her cuts and spoke to the school mental health professional about it. However, the student refuses all treatment.*

Case 2. *M.P. is a 15-year-old male who has occasional suicidal thoughts. He feels stressed and hopeless about academics, and feels as though he cannot measure up to family pressure. Out of*

frustration, he began by banging himself to the point of bruising before exams; this progressed to cutting over time. He refuses treatment due to stigma, stating that his family would be so ashamed.

Case 3. *A.J. is a 16-year-old nonbinary student. They frequently burnt themself with cigarettes in front of their peers, who did not take it seriously. Subsequently, they attempted suicide and were hospitalized. They have returned to the school while continuing to receive outpatient services. They are withdrawn, appear to be depressed, and continue to burn themself. The parents are unsupportive of their gender identity, and are noncooperative and unavailable. The school mental health professional is having difficulty accessing information from the hospital and is unsure how to proceed.*

Background/Context

NSSI is a common mental health concern among adolescents, both in clinical and subclinical settings, and is linked to a host of negative outcomes (e.g., Biskin et al., 2020; Brown & Plener, 2017; Heath et al., 2016; Walsh, 2012). Among adolescents who engage in self-injury, the most common methods include cutting, severe scratching, hitting or banging, carving, and burning (Brown & Plener, 2017; Doyle et al., 2015; Garisch & Wilson, 2015). Furthermore, the most common functions of NSSI in adolescence include the downregulation of negative thoughts and emotions, self-punishment, and communication with or influencing others (Brown & Plener, 2017; Cipriano et al., 2017; Taylor et al., 2018) (see Taylor et al., this volume). Despite the prevalence of NSSI in adolescence, this behavior is stigmatized and often misunderstood (Staniland et al., 2020). Its stigmatization may be attributed to the associations between NSSI and mental illness, the self-inflicted nature of self-injury which defies the human instinct of self-preservation, and the wounds and scars that often remain following engagement. Unfortunately, stigmatization and misconceptions surrounding NSSI may serve as barriers to adolescents' help-seeking for this behavior (Hasking et al., 2016; Toste & Heath, 2010), as illustrated by Case 2, whereby M.P. refuses treatment due to stigma, stating that his family would be deeply ashamed of him. In addition to the challenges that adolescents face with respect to NSSI stigmatization and help-seeking, school personnel often express uncertainty and helplessness when it comes to addressing self-injury among their students (e.g., De Riggi et al., 2017; Hasking et al., 2016). Thus, the provision of specific, evidence-informed guidelines for addressing NSSI prevention and intervention in secondary school settings is warranted.

A variety of risk and protective factors for NSSI in adolescence have been documented (See Fox, this volume, and James & Gibb, this volume) and contribute to its elevated prevalence during this developmental period (e.g., Brown & Plener, 2017; Tatnell et al., 2017). Psychological risk factors for NSSI during adolescence include depressive symptoms, high self-criticism, and low self-esteem (Baetens et al., 2015; Tatnell et al., 2017), as reported in Cases 3, 1, and 2, respectively. Demographic risk factors include adolescent age, gender minority status, and nonheterosexual orientation (Brown & Plener, 2017; Doyle et al., 2015; Liu et al., 2019; Smith et al., 2020). There are notable social risk factors for NSSI during adolescence as well (See Jarvi Steele et al., this volume), such as knowing someone who engages in self-injury; being the victim of bullying; and having experienced emotional, physical, or sexual abuse as a child (Brown & Plener, 2017; Doyle et al., 2015; Garisch & Wilson, 2015; Tatnell et al., 2017). On the other hand, protective factors for NSSI include emotion regulation, high self-esteem, secure attachment, and perceived support in relationships with friends and family (e.g., Garisch & Wilson, 2015; Tatnell et al., 2017).

There are also a number of risk factors for engaging in NSSI that are specific to the secondary school context. For instance, decreased academic performance and negative attitudes toward school have both been found to positively predict subsequent engagement in NSSI among secondary school students (Baetens et al., 2021). In addition, lower perceived teacher support, a decreased sense of school belongingness, and a more negative peer climate have also emerged as risk factors for NSSI during adolescence (Madjar, Ben Shabat, et al., 2017; Madjar, Zalsman, et al., 2017). All these school-related risk factors likely lead to heightened distress among students, who then engage in NSSI to cope with this distress, as the most commonly reported function of NSSI during adolescence is to regulate negative thoughts and emotions (Cipriano et al., 2017; Taylor et al., 2018). Thus, as is evidenced above, numerous psychosocial and school-related factors may predispose adolescents to engage in NSSI, and prevention efforts should take these risk factors into consideration where possible.

Furthermore, the primary justifications for addressing NSSI prevention and intervention within secondary school settings in particular are twofold. First, addressing NSSI within secondary schools is of great developmental importance (Evans et al., 2019). Adolescence is a vulnerable period for the onset of NSSI, partly due to elevated levels of impulsivity and emotion reactivity during this developmental period (Brown & Plener, 2017). Accordingly, research has repeatedly documented an average age of onset for NSSI around 14 years of age (e.g., Heath et al., 2009b; Morey et al., 2017), and engaging in NSSI from a young age is associated with a greater frequency of self-injury, the use of more diverse and dangerous methods, and an increased risk of hospitalization (Ammerman et al., 2018), as shown in Case 3. The occurrence of NSSI among adolescents has been of growing concern, with prevalence rates spanning from 10%–20% during this developmental period (Swannell et al., 2014; Tatnell et al., 2017). Engaging in NSSI during adolescence is a significant mental health concern as it has been associated with increased depressive symptoms, anxiety, suicidality, substance use, and engagement in risk-taking behaviors; a higher risk for the development of borderline personality disorder symptoms and impaired psychosocial functioning in adulthood; as well as unfavorable academic outcomes including a lack of school engagement and absenteeism (Biskin et al., 2020; Brown & Plener, 2017; Garisch & Wilson, 2015; Heath et al., 2016; Walsh, 2012). In light of all of these concerns, addressing NSSI prevention and intervention during adolescence is warranted.

Additionally, addressing NSSI prevention within the school setting is of notable contextual importance. Given the proportion of adolescents' time that is spent in school, schools are uniquely well positioned to provide students with strategies and support related to NSSI prevention and intervention (Tatnell et al., 2017; Wester et al., 2018). Particularly given the stigmatization surrounding—and resultant hesitation to seek help for—NSSI behaviors (Hasking et al., 2016; Toste & Heath, 2010), providing psychoeducation and strategies within the school context permits a universal preventative approach, thereby ensuring that this information reaches all students whether they actively seek it out or not. Moreover, the multilevel support that is available to adolescents within their school is critical to NSSI prevention efforts (Heath et al., 2014; Heath et al., 2020) but is unlikely to be as readily accessible elsewhere. Finally, schools have the opportunity to deliver prevention and intervention programs in large group settings, such as in classrooms and assemblies, therefore providing a more cost-effective means with a broader reach than most clinical and community models of service delivery. Thus, for all of the reasons outlined above, addressing NSSI in secondary school settings is strongly recommended.

Relative to clinical, community, and even postsecondary settings, there is a notable uniqueness to secondary school settings in terms of addressing NSSI. For instance, as illustrated by the diverse cases described at the beginning of this chapter, schools may be expected to provide support (a) for a student who is engaging in NSSI but refuses all treatment yet still needs to be monitored for suicidality, (b) where the demands of the academic setting together with parental expectations may trigger the self-injury, or (c) where the school needs to navigate shared care with a hospital setting. Thus, the school must take on a wide range of roles when responding to such a diversity of experiences, and these settings may face the challenge of responding effectively despite having access to very limited resources relative to clinical and postsecondary settings (Evans et al., 2019). In addition, secondary schools often lack personnel with training and experience in responding to NSSI (De Riggi et al., 2017; Hasking et al., 2016). This is problematic given the frequency with which their personnel might encounter students who engage in NSSI, which is likely to be elevated as a result of rotating classes whereby educators encounter hundreds of students each day, combined with the well-documented elevated prevalence of NSSI during adolescence (Swannell et al., 2014; Tatnell et al., 2017).

Current State of the Empirical Evidence

Despite the timely importance of addressing NSSI prevention and intervention efforts in secondary school settings, this still represents a limited area of research. This section thus outlines previous NSSI prevention and intervention approaches within secondary school settings, several of which include elements relevant across all levels of prevention/intervention.

Currently, there are very few school-based programs that are known to effectively prevent or reduce NSSI behaviors among adolescents (Heath et al., 2014). One of these programs is HappylesPLUS (Baetens et al., 2020), an adaptation of the Happyles program (a school-based program aimed at enhancing general mental health and social connectedness; van der Zanden & van der Linden, 2013) with an added NSSI-focused psychoeducation module. This program was recently piloted with secondary school students and evaluated in terms of its potential effectiveness at preventing NSSI before it has occurred (i.e., at the *primary and secondary levels of prevention*). Results from this pilot study revealed no iatrogenic effects of the program (i.e., it did not increase NSSI thoughts or behaviors). In addition, following program completion, students reported a reduced likelihood of future NSSI engagement and increased help-seeking intentions. While these results are promising, an important limitation of this pilot study is that it spanned only six weeks, and the program's long-term effects on NSSI-related outcomes remain unknown. Thus, additional longitudinal research is needed to establish the long-term benefits of the HappylesPLUS prevention program.

To our knowledge, the only other school-based NSSI prevention program that has demonstrated efficacy is the Signs of Self-Injury (SOSI) program, created by Screening for Mental Health, Inc. (Jacobs et al., 2009) as an expansion of a widely used school-based suicide prevention program. The SOSI program involves psychoeducation provided to school personnel, focusing on response to student disclosure of NSSI, as well as guidelines for developing school policy. It should be noted that this program is a *tertiary prevention* program (i.e., intervening when NSSI has occurred to minimize its negative impacts), rather than a primary or secondary prevention program with the intent of preventing NSSI before it occurs. Furthermore, although initial evaluations of the SOSI program (i.e., Muehlenkamp et al., 2010) in secondary school settings have demonstrated some promise for improving student awareness and understanding of NSSI, it remains unclear whether the SOSI program actually results in increased help-seeking, or decreased rates of NSSI engagement, among students who engage in NSSI.

While there are currently very few school-based NSSI prevention programs, several prevention programs and gatekeeping workshops that target suicidality among secondary school students have also been evaluated, although the generalizability of these findings to NSSI prevention remains unclear. For instance, the Saving and Empowering Young Lives in Europe (SEYLE; Wasserman et al., 2015) study tested the effectiveness of a blended *primary and secondary prevention* program targeting suicidality among adolescents. Within this study, the universal (i.e., primary) prevention program for suicidality demonstrated the highest level of efficacy at reducing suicide ideation and attempts among students, although the program's potential impacts on NSSI engagement were not evaluated. Moreover, school-based gatekeeping programs, which train school staff to identify students at risk and help them acquire the support they need, have also gained popularity in recent years. For example, Brown et al. (2018) evaluated a gatekeeper training for suicidality, delivered to educators and school-based mental health professionals (MHPs) and found that it was effective at enhancing knowledge and confidence in school staff surrounding suicidality. The adaptation of this suicide prevention approach to NSSI may be worthwhile, particularly in terms of its potential to train school staff to appropriately respond to students at risk for NSSI.

Notably, there has also been an increasing recognition of the need to implement social and emotional learning (SEL) in school settings, in an effort to improve students' emotion regulation, social skills, coping abilities, and overall well-being (e.g., Yeager, 2017). While a variety of SEL-based programs have been developed, the Dialectical Behavior Therapy Skills in Schools: Skills Training for Emotional Problem Solving for Adolescents (DBT STEPS-A; Mazza et al., 2016) program, which is a SEL-based universal program, is particularly promising for the prevention of unhealthy coping behaviors such as NSSI. DBT STEPS-A is a manualized adaptation of DBT (Mazza et al., 2016) and has been adapted for use in secondary school settings. Its SEL-based curriculum centers on skill-building in the four core areas of standard DBT: emotion regulation, interpersonal effectiveness, distress tolerance, and mindfulness (Mazza et al., 2016). While its curriculum was developed to be implemented primarily at the universal (i.e., primary prevention and intervention) level, its manual also includes supplemental guidelines for working with students who might require further support at the secondary or tertiary levels of prevention and intervention (Mazza & Dexter-Mazza, 2019). Although there is currently only preliminary evidence supporting the effectiveness of DBT STEPS-A in secondary school settings and further research is needed to establish its effectiveness at preventing and reducing NSSI engagement among students, it remains one of the most promising approaches for addressing NSSI in schools for a number of reasons discussed below.

Taken together, the empirical evidence to date suggests that a universal, school-based adaptation of DBT may be a promising route for NSSI prevention and intervention in secondary school settings. Additional support at the secondary and tertiary levels of prevention/intervention is also needed for students at risk of engaging in NSSI, including school involvement in effective referral to external supports for students with more intensive needs. Importantly, implementing programs such as DBT STEPS-A (Mazza et al., 2016) into secondary school curricula requires a careful consideration of the uniqueness of secondary school settings in terms of addressing NSSI prevention and intervention. Specifically, the diversity of students' potential experiences with NSSI should be considered, as should the resource limitations that many schools are faced with (e.g., Evans et al., 2019). Thus, program implementation at all levels of NSSI prevention/intervention should take into account feasibility considerations (e.g., resource limitations) and the sheer diversity of NSSI experiences within secondary school settings, as illustrated by the highly diverse cases presented at the beginning of this chapter.

Prevention and Intervention in Secondary School Settings

In order to effectively develop and implement NSSI prevention programs in secondary school settings, it is paramount that such programs incorporate prevention science best-practice considerations (e.g., Durlak, 1997). In addition, three levels of prevention/intervention should be considered. These best-practice considerations and levels of prevention/intervention are described in detail below.

Prevention Science Best-Practice Considerations

First, programs should be evidence-based, drawing from research and theory on factors contributing to NSSI engagement (Heath et al., 2014), such as emotion dysregulation, distress tolerance, self-derogation, and ineffective communication skills (Brown & Plener, 2017; Cipriano et al., 2017; Taylor et al., 2018). Programs should thus focus on enhancing overall wellness and mental health resilience in the school, while specifically targeting the same skills that have demonstrated effectiveness in treatment for NSSI (Heath et al., 2014). Programs should also be socially and culturally relevant to the target group (Durlak, 1997); in this case, they should be developmentally appropriate for adolescents and should take into consideration the sociocultural context. Finally, prevention and intervention efforts should be collaborative and multipronged; besides the students themselves, such approaches should involve educators, MHPs, and other school personnel, as well as the families and/or caregivers of students (Arbuthnott & Lewis, 2015; Hasking et al., 2016).

As proposed by Heath et al. (2020), and in line with Cole and Siegel's (2003) comprehensive model, three levels of prevention/intervention should be considered when developing school-wide programs to ultimately reduce NSSI in secondary schools, as each level may be tailored to the experiences and needs of different students. While these levels may be accessed sequentially, whereby a student participating at the primary level may voluntarily choose to seek out further support at the secondary or tertiary levels, the ultimate goal of implementing this model is to have all three levels of prevention/intervention functioning simultaneously within the school. Detailed recommendations for each of the three levels are provided below (see Heath et al. 2020 for further detail regarding each level).

Primary Prevention and Intervention

At the primary level of prevention/intervention, the main goal is to prevent the emergence of NSSI behaviors in all students. To this end, a universal, school-wide approach is optimal wherein the aim is to (a) improve overall capacity for healthy coping, (b) decrease stigmatization, and (c) develop a community of support and help-seeking within the school (Heath et al., 2020), through general stress management and coping skills-building. This universal primary prevention/intervention should be provided to all students in large group settings such as classrooms or assemblies. Importantly, teachings from these "workshops," delivered by school MHPs, should be integrated across multiple stakeholders (e.g., family/caregivers, educators, and school administrators) through school, community, and online resource provision.

Provided that the goal of primary prevention/intervention is to decrease the likelihood that students will engage in NSSI, instruction at this level should be relevant to the commonly reported functions of self-injury. For instance, the most commonly reported function of NSSI during adolescence is to regulate intense or recurring negative thoughts and emotions (e.g., Brown & Plener, 2017; Cipriano et al., 2017; Taylor et al., 2018; see Taylor et al., this volume). As such, psychoeducation related to effective coping in order to enhance emotion regulation and reactivity should be a central component of primary prevention/intervention. Another common function of NSSI in adolescence is self-punishment (Cipriano et al., 2017; Taylor et al., 2018). Accordingly, psychoeducation related to fostering self-compassion and the management of self-criticism should be included in these universal workshops as well. Finally, a less common, but nonetheless persistently reported, function of NSSI is to communicate with or influence others (Cipriano et al., 2017; Taylor et al., 2018). Thus, primary prevention/intervention workshops should address effective interpersonal communication as well.

As mentioned earlier, a central goal of these universal workshops is to improve students' overall capacity for healthy coping while actively decreasing stigmatization in the school. Therefore, at the primary level, workshops should have a broad appeal and be contextualized as general stress management and coping skills-building. Numerous healthy and unhealthy coping behaviors should be addressed within these workshops, with NSSI contextualized as merely one example of an unhealthy coping behavior (e.g., Lewis et al., 2019), in order to decrease stigma surrounding NSSI and avoid sensationalizing it. Moreover, information pertaining to help-seeking and help-giving should be embedded in workshops at the primary level of prevention/intervention. The aim of this approach is to enhance students' willingness to seek help for NSSI and other coping behaviors (which would be beneficial in Cases 1 and 2 where treatment is otherwise refused by the students), as well as to improve students' ability to respond appropriately and supportively to their peers' disclosures of unhealthy coping.

Secondary schools may benefit from referring to the DBT STEPS-A manual (Mazza et al., 2016) in order to develop universal workshops that share relevant psychoeducation and healthy coping strategies to enhance resilience among all students. Although other SEL programs exist, we encourage the use of DBT STEPS-A given its suitability to the reduction of unhealthy coping behaviors such as NSSI in secondary school settings. The teachings of these universal sessions should be integrated across all relevant stakeholders, including educators, MHPs, and other school personnel, as well as the families and/or caregivers of students (Arbuthnott & Lewis, 2015; Hasking et al., 2016). This may be achieved through the development and dissemination of pamphlets, infographics, or emails (see International Consortium on Self-injury in Educational Settings, n.d., for sample resources), should in-person workshops or information sessions not be feasible. Furthermore, educators should be informed of the skills that students are being taught in the workshops and how they may be applicable in the classroom, and parents should be provided with the contact information of a designated person within the school for questions or concerns related to the content being taught in these workshops. This collaborative approach is highly beneficial to the development of a school culture of wellness and will ensure that students feel supported and that a sense of community is developed within the school. Finally, school, community, and online resources and support should be provided to students, such that students may feel equipped to seek help if they find themselves struggling, or to help a friend or peer who may be engaging in unhealthy coping.

Secondary Prevention and Intervention
Additional targeted support may be required for students who are struggling with some aspects of coping or for whom the support and resources offered at the primary level of prevention/intervention are insufficient. Thus, at the secondary level of prevention/intervention, the main goal is to prevent or delay the onset of NSSI behaviors in at-risk students. This can be accomplished through a series of school MHP-led independent small-group sessions (i.e., of up to 15 students) which students would ideally self-select to attend following participation at the primary level, or to which they may be recommended or referred (e.g., by school MHPs or their caregivers; Heath et al., 2020). While the number of sessions held may vary depending upon students' needs and the school's resources, each session should focus on the further development of specific skills and strategies that are known to be potential risk factors or precursors to the emergence of NSSI, and should provide an opportunity for more guided strategy practice than is possible in the universal workshops. Similarly to the universal workshops offered at the primary level, small-group sessions at the secondary level may be structured using the DBT STEPS-A manual (Mazza et al., 2016), as this manual provides detailed group session outlines and may thus be used even by MHPs who are lacking formalized DBT training.

In general, sessions should review the psychoeducational content taught within the primary-level workshops. In addition, given that students who self-select to attend the secondary-level sessions would likely benefit from more practice in coping with difficult situations and/or emotions, an in-depth practice of skills should be embedded within these sessions. Furthermore, discussion periods should be included throughout to discuss daily life application of strategies taught and to problem-solve for anticipated obstacles. Students who attend these sessions would also benefit from the provision of additional resources for the implementation of the skills taught, as well as to encourage students' overall help-seeking.

Moreover, at the secondary level of prevention/intervention, the primary focus should remain on resilience-building and building students' capacity for healthy coping, rather than on describing and/or exploring less healthy coping behaviors such as NSSI. If a student discloses NSSI engagement at any time during their participation in the primary- and/or secondary-level sessions, they should be offered tertiary support as outlined below. Nevertheless, the three levels of prevention/intervention and the sessions and resources they encompass are not mutually exclusive; as such, students may voluntarily choose to participate in both the secondary and tertiary levels, if they feel that it is of benefit to them. Finally, communication between the school and caregivers is needed at this level of prevention/intervention, taking into account matters of confidentiality as needed, to encourage at-home use of the strategies taught in these sessions.

Tertiary Prevention and Intervention

At the tertiary level of prevention/intervention, the primary aim is to appropriately and effectively respond to NSSI once it has emerged to reduce negative impacts. As described below, an effective response at the tertiary level includes elements such as the development of an NSSI-specific school protocol, widespread knowledge surrounding an appropriate and effective first response to NSSI, the necessity of conducting a risk assessment, and effective referral (Heath et al., 2020).

It can be challenging to identify students who self-injure, particularly since they are often reluctant to disclose and/or seek help for their NSSI (Hasking et al., 2016). This is illustrated in Case 1, whereby E.L.'s supportive family and friends remain unaware of her self-injury. This reluctance may stem from the anticipated response to disclosure, which is often met with fear, judgment, or horror (Lewis et al., 2019). As such, efforts to identify or confirm the occurrence of NSSI should be managed with extreme sensitivity, as students may find such efforts intrusive or humiliating (Hasking et al., 2016). Ultimately, the identification of NSSI may occur through multiple pathways, including from the student themselves or from a peer, caregiver, or educator who may know or have reason to believe that the student is engaging in self-injury.

The first step in being prepared to respond to students who engage in NSSI involves the development, distribution, monitoring, and routine evaluation of an NSSI-specific school protocol (also see Baetens et al., this volume) that provides clear guidelines on effective and appropriate first response to NSSI engagement among students (De Riggi et al., 2017; Hamza & Heath, 2018; Hasking et al., 2016). This protocol should clearly outline the roles and responsibilities of all school personnel and establish a designated MHP to coordinate case management for students who self-injure (e.g., to conduct suicide risk assessments, make necessary referrals) as well as to provide school-wide staff education around NSSI (Hasking et al., 2016). Additionally, it should provide guidelines for when caregivers of students are to be informed of their child's NSSI (Hasking et al., 2016), as will be described later in this chapter.

It is important to note that the first response to a disclosure of NSSI will play a critical role in the student's future help-seeking behavior (Toste & Heath, 2010). All school personnel must understand the importance of a supportive, empathic, and nonjudgmental demeanor when responding, as implicitly or explicitly communicating judgment or disgust can exacerbate internalized stigma, thwart help-seeking, and reinforce NSSI (Hasking et al., 2016; Lewis et al., 2019; Toste & Heath, 2010). Validating the student's feelings or thoughts associated with the NSSI is also important (Hasking et al., 2016). If NSSI is identified by, or disclosed to, nontrained staff, the staff member should recommend that the student seek help from the school's designated MHP. If the student refuses, the staff member must notify the MHP themselves but should communicate to the student that they are initiating this support as part of the school protocol and because they are concerned for the student's well-being (De Riggi et al., 2017). Although it may be challenging for the MHP to build rapport with the student, this rapport is integral to building a therapeutic alliance, and MHPs should therefore approach first conversations with students in a calm, patient, and supportive manner.

Once an appropriate first response to NSSI disclosure has been made, an assessment of risk by a school MHP is necessary. Risk assessments should include sensitive inquiries about any suicide ideation, the age of onset and duration of the NSSI, the frequency of engagement, the number of methods used, the potential need for medical attention, and the reasons behind the NSSI (Westers et al., 2016). For some students (i.e., certain low-risk students), school-based NSSI intervention will be sufficient; for others (i.e., certain high-risk students), external support may be needed in conjunction with school-based support (Hasking et al., 2016; Toste & Heath, 2010).

If a student is of legal age to refuse treatment, it is not unlikely for them to do so (as demonstrated by two of the three cases described earlier, wherein the students had refused all treatment), particularly out of fear of being asked to stop engaging in NSSI altogether or to share emotional details underlying their engagement (Heath et al., 2020). It should be communicated that the goal is simply to learn additional coping strategies which may be used in moments of distress, rather than immediately halting NSSI, and that they will not be forced to stop this behavior or commit to treatment. School personnel, caregivers, and peers need to be aware that as students learn healthier coping and their NSSI diminishes, there should not be excessive focus on "recovery" or NSSI cessation. NSSI recovery is often nonlinear, and schools may have either a primary or supportive role in this process depending on the needs and preferences of the student, as well as on the resources available within the school.

NSSI in Secondary Schools: Summary of Recommendations
In summary, a review of existing approaches to NSSI prevention/intervention among adolescents suggests that school-based interventions should (a) be offered universally to all students, (b) be collaborative and multipronged, incorporating school personnel and caregivers at every level, (c) encompass three levels of prevention and intervention to respond to the diversity of NSSI experiences that is likely to be encountered in a secondary school

setting, and (d) be evidence-based, drawing particularly from SEL-based skills building programs such as DBT STEPS-A (Mazza et al., 2016) and incorporating modules on mindfulness, emotion regulation, distress tolerance, and interpersonal effectiveness.

Challenges to NSSI Prevention and Intervention in Schools

There are a number of challenges that are unique to addressing NSSI prevention/intervention in secondary school settings. Three examples of such challenges are outlined and recommendations are provided.

Response to Wounds or Scarring

Another challenge in schools is the demonstration of an appropriate response to wounds or scarring. Schools are often concerned that viewing scars or wounds can be triggering for vulnerable students. Although there is evidence that viewing fresh wounds carries a likelihood of being triggering (Baker & Lewis, 2013), research has suggested that choosing to stop concealing one's scars can be very therapeutic and an important step in recovery (Lewis, 2016; Lewis & Mehrabkhani, 2016). The school's response should thus differ depending upon whether fresh wounds or scars are revealed (Hasking et al., 2016). It is recommended that fresh wounds should be kept concealed to prevent potential infection, and it should be explained to students that there is some evidence that the sight of wounds by those who may be still struggling with their recovery around NSSI can be triggering. On the other hand, as previously noted, a student's choice to stop concealing scars can be a positive step toward recovery (Lewis, 2016; Lewis & Mehrabkhani, 2016). Nevertheless, school MHPs should have a sensitive and compassionate discussion with the student that involves acknowledging that this is the student's choice and may be a positive step for them, but also discussing the potential negative consequences that may arise (e.g., intrusive questions, negative comments, and bullying) and how these potential challenges may be addressed, as well as how the student can be supported in facing such challenges.

NSSI Online Activities

Research has demonstrated that adolescents who self-injure are more likely to seek peer, rather than professional, help (e.g., Doyle et al., 2015). As such, internet use, and specifically the use of social media, has increased in recent years for discussion and help-seeking surrounding NSSI (e.g., De Riggi et al., 2018), as illustrated in Case 1 at the start of this chapter. In fact, one third of youth with a history of self-injury reported online help-seeking for NSSI (Frost & Casey, 2016). While NSSI online activities may be beneficial for decreasing social isolation, encouraging recovery, and providing a platform for emotional self-disclosure, they also have the potential to be harmful. Specifically, NSSI online activities may trigger urges to self-injure and provide social reinforcement of the behavior, as well as ideas for concealing NSSI (De Riggi et al., 2018; Lewis & Seko, 2016; Murray & Fox, 2006). Furthermore, some websites display content such as images and videos that may cause distress or trigger urges to self-injure, and while certain websites provide trigger warnings for such content, others do not (Duggan et al., 2012). In any case, it appears that the majority of NSSI-related online searches are primarily seeking supportive, recovery-oriented information (Swannell et al., 2010), and thus have a positive underlying motivation.

Recommendations for secondary schools in responding to NSSI online activities are as follows. First, an open discussion of students' online NSSI activities should be incorporated into the tertiary level of school-based NSSI prevention/intervention programs (Berger et al., 2017). MHPs can provide guidance regarding appropriate websites and/or discussion forums for NSSI (Swannell et al., 2010), in an effort to steer students away from potentially harmful websites. Finally, as part of the tertiary intervention discussed earlier, schools should help adolescents become aware of the potential benefits and risks associated with online activities and/or online NSSI disclosure (Christofides et al., 2012), helping them to become informed consumers of digital supports rather than simply recommending that they stay offline.

Social "Contagion" (Influence)

Although frequently referred to as social "contagion" (see Jarvi Steele et al., this volume), we do not endorse this terminology as it is stigmatizing in its disease-based connotation; thus, we will henceforth refer to this construct as social influence. Social influence may be defined as the presence and spread of behavior (i.e., NSSI) in at least two people in the same group within a short period of time (Rosen & Walsh, 1989) or a significant number of individuals engaging in NSSI within the same group (Walsh & Rosen, 1985). As noted earlier, the increased use of social media, particularly among adolescents, may serve to normalize NSSI by disseminating instances of it to a large number of individuals in a short period of time. Social influence has also been suggested to increase when NSSI serves a social or interpersonal function (Jarvi et al., 2013). In fact, individuals who self-injure largely report learning about NSSI through peers and/or some form of media (Heath et al., 2009a; Hodgson, 2004). Thus, the social influence of NSSI has been proposed as a potential reason for its rising prevalence (White Kress et al., 2004) and has been identified as an ongoing concern in schools (Toste & Heath, 2010; Wester et al., 2018).

Recommendations for secondary schools in responding to the potential social influence of NSSI are as follows. First, tiered NSSI prevention/intervention approaches, as outlined in this chapter, have been identified as central to preventing and/or diminishing social influence of NSSI (Wester et al., 2018). Specifically, preventing the onset of NSSI behaviors before they occur, as is the goal at the primary level of prevention/intervention, can effectively eliminate the possibility of social influence. At the secondary level, the social influence of NSSI may be reduced through the targeted instruction of healthy coping strategies within small-group sessions. Any group discussions of coping behaviors should be contextualized within a healthy/unhealthy coping framework, as group discussions that are centered on NSSI may be triggering, exacerbate social influence, and should thus be avoided (Wester et al., 2018). Nevertheless, despite past recommendations to reduce social influence by avoiding or prohibiting all discussions surrounding NSSI in schools (e.g., Walsh, 2012), this is no longer recommended (e.g., Hasking et al., 2016). However, discussions surrounding NSSI should take place on an individual basis (Wester et al., 2018). Importantly, these discussions should include information about the potential harm in supporting or encouraging self-injury within peer groups.

Informing Caregivers

For secondary schools, helping caregivers respond productively to their youth's NSSI is a vital part of effectively addressing it (Arbuthnott & Lewis, 2015; Whitlock et al., 2018). However, a challenge for schools involves knowing when, and how, to involve caregivers in a discussion of their child's self-injury (Berger et al., 2013). MHPs must carefully weigh the adolescent's risk profile along relevant legal and clinical obligations (Hasking et al., 2016). Moreover, MHPs in schools have a duty to break confidentiality and notify a students' caregiver of their NSSI when the student is at risk for suicidality (Lloyd-Richardson et al., 2015). Otherwise, MHPs should use clinical judgment while relying on school protocol and professional order guidelines. Notably, they should take into account what is known about the student, the family, and how they are likely to react to NSSI disclosures (Hasking et al., 2016). When feasible, the student should be actively involved in decision-making; this might include obtaining their consent to contact caregivers, allowing the student to be present when caregivers are informed, and being actively involved in decisions regarding treatment (Hasking et al., 2016; Whitlock et al., 2018). Finally, caregivers should be provided with support and information when notified of their child's NSSI. Specifically, MHPs should help caregivers navigate first conversations by encouraging them to know what to expect in terms of the NSSI recovery process, and understanding and addressing safety concerns (Whitlock et al., 2018). It may also be beneficial to encourage caregivers to seek informal or formal support for themselves, in order for them to feel adequately supported throughout their efforts to support their child.

Recommendations for Future Research

Despite the prevalence of NSSI in secondary school settings, to date, very few school-based programs have demonstrated efficacy at preventing and/or reducing NSSI behaviors among adolescents (Heath et al., 2014). Therefore, there is a need for future research on NSSI prevention in secondary school settings to rigorously evaluate existing school-based prevention programs across all three levels of prevention/intervention (e.g., Baetens et al., 2020; Muehlenkamp et al., 2010), particularly in terms of their long-term efficacy at preventing NSSI and promoting greater levels of help-seeking in secondary school students at risk. In addition, we have proposed that a multipronged approach as well as prevention science best-practice considerations should be incorporated into prevention programs to optimize their efficacy (Arbuthnott & Lewis, 2015; Durlak, 1997; Hasking et al., 2016). Future research should thus consider evaluating NSSI prevention/intervention programs on the basis of their inclusion of these proposed essential elements. Finally, there is also a need to continue developing, distributing, monitoring, and evaluating the effectiveness of NSSI-specific school protocols that support students across all three levels of care.

Conclusion

Although addressing NSSI prevention/intervention in secondary school settings is of paramount developmental and contextual importance, school personnel often feel ill-equipped to respond to this rising mental health concern. This challenge is further exacerbated by a lack of research empirically evaluating school-based NSSI prevention/intervention programs. Specifically, there is evidence to suggest that existing programs can be implemented in a manner that is feasible in schools (e.g., Mazza & Dexter-Mazza, 2019), although at this time, they have not been rigorously evaluated. Nevertheless, the provision of education and information surrounding NSSI can serve as a beneficial foundation for addressing its incidence in secondary school settings, and may even be similarly impactful as implementing comprehensive prevention programs. Schools are uniquely positioned to respond to adolescents' NSSI and to pioneer for the destigmatization of this coping behavior; they may take on a number of highly important roles in their students' journeys with NSSI, as outlined below.

Case 1. Resolution: *Despite refusing treatment, E.L. participated in her school's universal prevention program, attending sessions at the primary and secondary level, and completed regular check-ins. As a result, her coping abilities improved and her self-injury decreased.* Analysis: E.L.'s case highlights the importance of having primary and secondary interventions available for those who decline intervention for self-injury but would benefit from learning healthier coping.

Case 2. Resolution: *M.P. took part in class-wide primary-level activities to learn better emotion regulation skills. His self-injury decreased over time as a result, and his suicidality is monitored on an ongoing basis through check-ins with the school counselor.* Analysis: Similar to E.L., albeit for different reasons, M.P. benefited from the primary program and, over time, was more open to considering the secondary-level groups. The use of safety/wellness check-ins also ensured that changes in suicide risk were being monitored. M.P.'s case highlights the challenges of involving caregivers without a well-considered evaluation of the potential benefits and drawbacks.

Case 3. Resolution: *The school struggled to collaborate with A.J.'s hospital care. Liability issues around risk level continued and were never fully resolved. Ultimately, the student dropped out of high school and is still in and out of the hospital.* Analysis: A.J.'s case is illustrative of the continued difficulties in coordinating care between hospitals and schools. The need for school MHPs to be well informed and proactive in working to establish the needed collaboration for supporting students as they transition back to the school is critical.

Summary

There is a notable uniqueness to secondary school settings in terms of addressing NSSI prevention and intervention. Central to being able to effectively respond to students who engage in NSSI is the development, distribution, ongoing monitoring, and routine evaluation of an NSSI-specific school protocol that clearly delineates the roles of all relevant stakeholders. Furthermore, while the ultimate goal is to prevent NSSI, early intervention (i.e., once NSSI has been disclosed) is also imperative, but neither can occur without the involvement of educators, MHPs, and other school personnel, as well as the families and/or caregivers of students. Therefore, school-based NSSI prevention programs should be collaborative and multipronged, in addition to incorporating prevention science best-practice considerations. Additionally, three levels of prevention/intervention should be incorporated in NSSI prevention programs (i.e., primary, secondary, and tertiary), with each level being uniquely tailored to the experiences and needs of different subsets of students. To date, there is a lack of research rigorously evaluating the immediate and long-term effectiveness of NSSI prevention programs in secondary school settings. Nonetheless, the provision of evidence-informed, NSSI-focused psychoeducation can serve as an important first step for addressing its occurrence in secondary school settings. While the implementation of a universal, school-wide approach to NSSI prevention is the ultimate aim, every effort to reduce stigmatization around NSSI and improve the school response can have a notable impact on all members of a secondary school community.

References

Ammerman, B. A., Jacobucci, R., Kleiman, E. M., Uyeji, L., & McCloskey, M. S. (2018). The relationship between nonsuicidal self-injury age of onset and severity of self-harm. *Suicide and Life-Threatening Behavior*, 48, 31–37. https://doi.org/10.1111/sltb.12330

Arbuthnott, A. E., & Lewis, S. P. (2015). Parents of youth who self-injure: A review of the literature and implications for mental health professionals. *Child and Adolescent Psychiatry and Mental Health*, 9(1), 35. https://doi.org/10.1186/s13034-015-0066-3

Baetens, I., Claes, L., Hasking, P., Smits, D., Grietens, H., Onghena, P., & Martin, G. (2015). The relationship between parental expressed emotions and non-suicidal self-injury: The mediating roles of self-criticism and depression. *Journal of Child and Family Studies*, 24, 491–498. https://doi.org/10.1007/s10826-013-9861-8

Baetens, I., Decruy, C., Vatandoost, S., Vanderhaegen, B., & Kiekens, G. (2020). School-based prevention targeting non-suicidal self-injury: A pilot study. *Frontiers in Psychiatry*, 11, Article 437. https://doi.org/10.3389/fpsyt.2020.00437

Baetens, I., Greene, D., Van Hove, L., Van Leeuwen, K., Wiersema, J. R., Desoete, A., & Roelants, M. (2021). Predictors and consequences of non-suicidal self-injury in relation to life, peer, and school factors. *Journal of Adolescence*, 90, 100–108. https://doi.org/10.1016/j.adolescence.2021.06.005

Baker, T. G., & Lewis, S. P. (2013). Responses to online photographs of non-suicidal self- injury: A thematic analysis. *Archives of Suicide Research*, 17, 223–235. https://doi.org/10.1080/13811118.2013.805642

Berger, E., Hasking, P., & Martin, G. (2013). 'Listen to them': Adolescents' views on helping young people who self-injure. *Journal of Adolescence*, 36(5), 935–945. https://doi.org/10.1016/j.adolescence.2013.07.011

Berger, E., Hasking, P., & Martin, G. (2017). Adolescents' perspectives of youth non-suicidal self-injury prevention. *Youth & Society*, 49(1), 3–22. https://doi.org/10.1177/0044118X13520561

Biskin, R. S., Paris, J., Zelkowitz, P., Mills, D., Laporte, L., & Heath, N. L. (2020). Nonsuicidal self-injury in early adolescence as a predictor of borderline personality disorder in early adulthood. *Journal of Personality Disorders*, 35(5), 764–775. https://doi.org/10.1521/pedi_2020_34_500

Brown, R. C., & Plener, P. L. (2017). Non-suicidal self-injury in adolescence. *Current Psychiatry Reports, 19*(3), 20.

Brown, R. C., Straub, J., Bohnacker, I., & Plener, P. L. (2018). Increasing knowledge, skills, and confidence concerning students' suicidality through a gatekeeper workshop for school staff. *Frontiers in Psychology, 9*, Article 1233. https://doi.org/10.3389/fpsyg.2018.01233

Christofides, E., Muise, A., & Desmarais, S. (2012). Risky disclosures on Facebook: The effect of having a bad experience on online behavior. *Journal of Adolescent Research, 27*(6), 714–731. https://doi.org/10.1177/0743558411432635

Cipriano, A., Cella, S., & Cotrufo, P. (2017). Nonsuicidal self-injury: A systematic review. *Frontiers in Psychology, 8*, Article 1946. https://doi.org/10.3389/fpsyg.2017.01946

Cole, E., & Siegel, J. A. (Eds.). (2003). *Effective consultation in school psychology* (2nd ed.). Hogrefe & Huber.

De Riggi, M. E., Lewis, S. P., & Heath, N. L. (2018). Brief report: Non-suicidal self-injury in adolescence: Turning to the Internet for support. *Counselling Psychology Quarterly, 31*(3), 397–405. https://doi.org/10.1080/09515070.2018.1427556

De Riggi, M. E., Moumne, S., Heath, N. L., & Lewis, S. P. (2017). Non-suicidal self-injury in our schools: A review and research-informed guidelines for school mental health professionals. *Canadian Journal of School Psychology, 32*, 122–143. https://doi.org/10.1177/0829573516645563

Doyle, L., Treacy, M. P., & Sheridan, A. (2015). Self-harm in young people: Prevalence, associated factors and help-seeking in school-going adolescents. *International Journal of Mental Health Nursing, 24*(6), 485–494. https://doi.org/10.1111/inm.12144

Duggan, J. M., Heath, N. L., Lewis, S. P., & Baxter, A. L. (2012). An examination of the scope and nature of non-suicidal self-injury online activities: Implications for school mental health professionals. *School Mental Health, 4*(1), 56–67. https://doi.org/10.1007/s12310-011-9065-6

Durlak, J. A. (1997). *Successful prevention programs for children and adolescents*. Plenum Press. https://doi.org/10.1007/978-1-4899-0065-4

Evans, R., Parker, R., Russell, A. E., Mathews, F., Ford, T., Hewitt, G., Scourfield, J., & Janssens, A. (2019). Adolescent self-harm prevention and intervention in secondary schools: A survey of staff in England and Wales. *Child and Adolescent Mental Health, 24*(3), 230–238. https://doi.org/10.1111/camh.12308

Frost, M., & Casey, L. (2016). Who seeks help online for self-injury? *Archives of Suicide Research, 20*(1), 69–79. https://doi.org/10.1080/13811118.2015.1004470

Garisch, J. A., & Wilson, M. S. (2015). Prevalence, correlates, and prospective predictors of non-suicidal self-injury among New Zealand adolescents: Cross-sectional and longitudinal survey data. *Child and Adolescent Psychiatry and Mental Health, 9*, 28. https://doi.org/10.1186/s13034-015-0055-6

Hamza, C. A., & Heath, N. L. (2018). Nonsuicidal self-injury: What schools can do. In A. W Leschied, D. H. Saklofske, & G. L. Flett (Eds.), *The handbook of school-based mental health promotion: An evidence informed framework for implementation* (pp. 237–260). Springer International.

Hasking, P. A., Heath, N. L., Kaess, M., Lewis, S. P., Plener, P. L., Walsh, B. W., Whitlock, J., & Wilson, M. S. (2016). Position paper for guiding response to non-suicidal self-injury in schools. *School Psychology International, 37*(6), 644–663. https://doi.org/10.1177/0143034316678656

Heath, N. L., Bastien, L., Mettler, J., Bloom, E., & Hamza, C. (2020). School response to non-suicidal self-injury. In E. Cole & M. Kokai (Eds.), *Consultation and mental health interventions in school settings: A scientist-practitioner's guide* (pp. 147–172). Hogrefe GmbH.

Heath, N. L., Carsley, D., De Riggi, M. E., Mills, D., & Mettler, J. (2016). The relationship between mindfulness, depressive symptoms, and non-suicidal self-injury amongst adolescents. *Archives of Suicide Research, 20*(4), 635–649. https://doi.org/10.1080/13811118.2016.1162243

Heath, N. L., Ross, S., Toste, J., Charlebois, A., & Nedecheva, T. (2009a). Retrospective analysis of social factors and nonsuicidal self-injury among young adults. *Canadian Journal of Behavioral Science, 41*, 180–186. https://doi.org/10.1037%2Fa0015732

Heath, N. L., Schaub, K., Holly, S., & Nixon, M. K. (2009b). Self-injury today: Review of population and clinical studies in adolescents. In M. K. Nixon & N. L. Heath (Eds.), *Self-injury in youth: The essential guide to assessment and intervention* (pp. 9–27). Routledge Taylor & Francis Group.

Heath, N. L., Toste, J. R., & MacPhee, S.-D. (2014). Prevention of nonsuicidal self-injury. In M. K. Nock (Ed.), *The Oxford handbook of suicide and self-injury* (pp. 397–408). Oxford University Press. https://doi.org/10.1093/oxfordhb/9780195388565.013.0022

Hodgson, S. (2004). Cutting through the silence: A sociological construction of self-injury. *Sociological Inquiry, 74*(2), 162–179. https://doi.org/10.1111/j.1475-682X.2004.00085.x

International Consortium on Self-injury in Educational Settings (ICSES). (n.d.). *General resources*. http://icsesgroup.org/general-resources

Jacobs, D., Walsh, B. W., McDade, M., & Pigeon, S. (2009). *Signs of self-injury prevention manual*. Screening for Mental Health.

Jarvi, S., Jackson, B., Swenson, L., & Crawford, H. (2013). The impact of social contagion on non-suicidal self-injury: A review of the literature. *Archives of Suicide Research, 17*, 1–19. https://doi.org/10.1080/13811118.2013.748404

Lewis, S. P. (2016). The overlooked role of self-injury scars: A commentary and suggestions for clinical practice. *Journal of Nervous and Mental Disease, 204*, 33–35. https://doi.org/10.1097/NMD.0000000000000436

Lewis, S. P., Heath, N. L., Hasking, P. A., Hamza, C. A., Bloom, E. L., Lloyd-Richardson, E. E., & Whitlock, J. (2019). Advocacy for improved response to self-injury in schools: A call to action for school psychologists. *Psychological Services, 17*(1), 86–92. https://doi.org/10.1037/ser0000352

Lewis, S. P., & Mehrabkhani, S. (2016). Every scar tells a story: Insight into people's self- injury scar experiences. *Counselling Psychology Quarterly, 29*, 296–310. https://doi.org/10.1080/09515070.2015.1088431

Lewis, S. P., & Seko, Y. (2016). A double-edged sword: A review of benefits and risks of online nonsuicidal self-injury activities. *Journal of Clinical Psychology, 72*(3), 249–262. https://doi.org/10.1002/jclp.22242

Liu, R. T., Sheehan, A. E., Walsh, R. F., Sanzari, C. M., Cheek, S. M., & Hernandez, E. M. (2019). Prevalence and correlates of non-suicidal self-injury among lesbian, gay, bisexual, and transgender individuals: A systematic review and meta-analysis. *Clinical Psychology Review, 74*, Article 101783. https://doi.org/10.1016/j.cpr.2019.101783

Lloyd-Richardson, E., Lewis, S. P., Whitlock, J., Rodham, K., & Schatten, H. (2015). Research with adolescents at risk for non-suicidal self-injury: Ethical considerations and challenges. *Child and Adolescent Psychiatry and Mental Health, 9*(1), 37. https://doi.org/10.1186/s13034-015-0071-6

Madjar, N., Ben Shabat, S., Elia, R., Fellner, N., Rehavi, M., Rubin, S. E., Segal, N., & Shoval, G. (2017). Non-suicidal self-injury within the school context: Multilevel analysis of teachers' support and peer climate. *European Psychiatry, 41*, 95–101. https://doi.org/10.1016/j.eurpsy.2016.11.003

Madjar, N., Zalsman, G., Ben Mordechai, T. R., & Shoval, G. (2017). Repetitive vs. occasional non-suicidal self-injury and school-related factors among Israeli high school students. *Psychiatry Research, 257*, 358–360. https://doi.org/10.1016/j.psychres.2017.07.073

Mazza, J. J., & Dexter-Mazza, E. T. (2019). DBT skills in schools: Implementation of the DBT steps- A social emotional curriculum. In M. A. Swales (Ed.), *The Oxford handbook of dialectical behaviour therapy* (pp. 719–733). Oxford University Press.

Mazza, J. J., Dexter-Mazza, E. T., Miller, A. L., Rathus, J. H., & Murphy, H. E. (2016). *DBT skills in schools: Skills training for emotional problem solving for adolescents*. Guilford Press.

Morey, Y., Mellon, D., Dailami, N., Verne, J., & Tapp, A. (2017). Adolescent self-harm in the community: An update on prevalence using a self-report survey of adolescents aged 13-18 in England. *Journal of Public Health, 39*(1), 58–64. https://doi.org/10.1093/pubmed/fdw010

Muehlenkamp, J. J., Walsh, B. W., & McDade, M. (2010). Preventing non-suicidal self-injury in adolescents: The signs of self-injury program. *Journal of Youth and Adolescence, 39*(3), 306–314. https://doi.org/10.1007/s10964-009-9450-8

Murray, C. D., & Fox, J. (2006). Do Internet self-harm discussion groups alleviate or exacerbate self-harming behaviour? Australian e-Journal for the Advancement of Mental *Health, 5*(3), 225–233. https://doi.org/10.5172/jamh.5.3.225

Rosen, P., & Walsh, B. (1989). Patterns of contagion in self-mutilation epidemics. *The American Journal of Psychiatry, 146*(5), 656–658. https://doi.org/10.1176/ajp.146.5.656

Smith, D. M., Wang, S. B., Carter, M. L., Fox, K. R., & Hooley, J. M. (2020). Longitudinal predictors of self-injurious thoughts and behaviors in sexual and gender minority adolescents. *Journal of Abnormal Psychology, 129*(1), 114–121. https://doi.org/10.1037/abn0000483

Staniland, L., Hasking, P., Boyes, M., & Lewis, S. (2020). Stigma and nonsuicidal self-injury: Application of a conceptual framework. *Stigma and Health, 6*(3), 312–323. https://doi.org/10.1037/sah0000257

Swannell, S., Martin, G., Krysinska, K. E., Kay, T., Olsson, K., & Win, A. (2010). Cutting on-line: Self-injury and the Internet. *Advances in Mental Health, 9*, 177–189. https://doi.org/10.5172=jamh.9.2.177

Swannell, S. V., Martin, G. E., Page, A., Hasking, P., & St John, N. J. (2014). Prevalence of nonsuicidal self-injury in nonclinical samples: Systematic review, meta-analysis and meta-regression. *Suicide and Life-Threatening Behavior*, *44*(3), 273–303. https://doi.org/10.1111/sltb.12070

Tatnell, R., Hasking, P., Newman, L., Taffe, J., & Martin, G. (2017). Attachment, emotion regulation, childhood abuse and assault: Examining predictors of NSSI among adolescents. *Archives of Suicide Research*, *21*(4), 610–620. https://doi.org/10.1080/13811118.2016.1246267

Taylor, P. J., Jomar, K., Dhingra, K., Forrester, R., Shahmalak, U., & Dickson, J. M. (2018). A meta-analysis of the prevalence of different functions of non-suicidal self-injury. *Journal of Affective Disorders*, *227*, 759–769. https://doi.org/10.1016/j.jad.2017.11.073

Toste, J. R., & Heath, N. L. (2010). School response to non-suicidal self-injury. *The Prevention Researcher*, *17*(1), 14–17. https://cemh.lbpsb.qc.ca/Portals/cemh/NSSI/School-Response-NSSI.pdf

van der Zanden, R., & van der Linden, D. (2013). *Evaluatieonderzoek Happyles Den Haag. Implementatie van Happyles in het VMBO en de Jeugdzorgketen ter bevordering van de mentale veerkracht van jongeren*. Trimbos-Instituut. http://docplayer.nl/16500233-Evaluatieonderzoek-happyles-den-haag.html.

Walsh, B. W. (2012). *Treating self-injury: A practical guide*. Guilford Press.

Walsh, B., & Rosen, P. (1985). Self-mutilation and contagion: An empirical test. *American Journal of Psychiatry*, *142*(1), 119–120. https://doi.org/10.1176/ajp.142.1.119

Wasserman, D., Hoven, C. W., Wasserman, C., Wall, M., Eisenberg, R., Hadlaczky, G., Kelleher, I., Sarchiapone, M., Apter, A., Balazs, J., Bobes, J., Brunner, R., Corcoran, P., Cosman, D., Guillemin, F., Haring, C., Iosue, M., Kaess, M., Kahn, J. P., & Carli, V. (2015). School-based suicide prevention programmes: The SEYLE cluster-randomised, controlled trial. *Lancet*, *385*(9977), 1536–1544. https://doi.org/10.1016/S0140-6736(14)61213-7

Wester, K. L., Morris, C. W., & Williams, B. (2018). Nonsuicidal self-injury in the schools: A tiered prevention approach for reducing social contagion. *Professional School Counseling*, *21*(1), 142–151. https://doi.org/10.5330/1096-2409-21.1.142

Westers, N. J., Muehlenkamp, J. J., & Lau, M. (2016). SOARS model: Risk assessment of nonsuicidal self-injury. *Contemporary Pediatrics*, *33*(7), 25–31. https://www.contemporarypediatrics.com/view/soars-model-risk-assessment-nonsuicidal-self-injury

White Kress, V. E., Gibson, D. M., & Reyonds, C. A. (2004). Adolescents who self-injure: Implications and strategies for school counselors. *Professional School Counseling*, *7*, 195–201. https://doi.org/10.5330/prsc.10.2.x238gl581p74236q

Whitlock, J. L., Baetens, I., Lloyd-Richardson, E., Hasking, P., Hamza, C., Lewis, S., Franz, P., & Robinson, K. (2018). Helping schools support caregivers of youth who self-injure: Considerations and recommendations. *School Psychology International*, *39*(3), 312–328. https://doi.org/10.1177/0143034318771415

Yeager, D. (2017). Social and emotional learning programs for adolescents. *The Future of Children*, *27*(1), 73–94. http://www.jstor.org/stable/44219022

CHAPTER 49

Promising Approaches to Prevention and Intervention in Higher Education

Alexandra L. Morena, Akshay V. Trisal, *and* Elizabeth E. Lloyd-Richardson

Abstract

This chapter aims to briefly summarize existing research examining NSSI among those attending university, highlighting the prevalence and other significant descriptive characteristics of NSSI on college campuses, risk factors, and the key characteristics linking NSSI and suicidal behavior. The authors acknowledge a wide range of prevention and intervention strategies that can and should be employed for university students and that capitalize on the strengths offered by integrating key stakeholders (e.g., peers, faculty, and campus counseling services). The authors explore and describe brief peer- and classroom-based intervention strategies that are currently implemented in the university context. Additionally, the authors offer recommendations for improving existing strategies to more explicitly include NSSI-specific content along with future considerations for improving prevention and universal interventions in the university context, and how doing so can directly target and promote NSSI prevention among university students. Although the research in the area of individual-level intervention approaches is limited, university settings offer promising opportunities to deliver multifaceted approaches designed to offer multiple "doses" of intervention to support students' mental health throughout their years attending university and beyond.

Key Words: NSSI, university, suicidal behavior, classroom-based intervention strategies, peer-based intervention strategies, prevention, intervention

Rates of NSSI on College Campuses are Significant

Historically, research exploring NSSI prevalence has focused mainly on adolescents, with rates ranging widely from 7% to upward of 47% (Hilt et al., 2008; Klonsky & Muehlenkamp, 2007; Lloyd-Richardson et al., 2007; Whitlock et al., 2011). Emerging adults, in particular university students, are also at high risk for engaging in NSSI (Kiekens et al., 2019; Whitlock et al., 2011; see Kiekens et al., this volume) given the preponderance of mental health challenges and risk behaviors engaged in during this developmental period (Arnett, 2015; Lipson et al., 2022). Understanding the prevalence of NSSI within this population is imperative to implementing various intervention efforts, as NSSI engagement within university students is associated with low help-seeking and poor academic performance (Kiekens et al., 2019).

Among 36,900 U.S. university students, 15% endorsed lifetime NSSI engagement and 6.8% reported engagement within the past 12 months (Whitlock et al., 2011). Among this sample, the mean age of self-injurers was 20 years old and the average onset was approximately 15 years old. However, 22.7% of self-injurers reported onset occurring during typical ages of university attendance (e.g., 18 to 22 years). Such findings are congruent indications that there are two peaks of onset that exist for NSSI, one during adolescence and a second peak at around 20 years of age (Kiekens et al., 2019; Whitlock et al., 2011). Kiekens et al. (2019) found that over a two-year period, 12-month incidence of NSSI among university samples was approximately 10% in the first year, and 6% during the second year. NSSI onset during this two-year period was approximately 7%, with the most commonly reported methods being scraping skin, smashing walls or objects, and hitting oneself.

Consistent with this, Kiekens et al. (2023) examined the 12-month prevalence of nonsuicidal self-injury-disorder (NSSI-D) according to the fifth edition of *Diagnostic and Statistical Manual of Mental Disorders* (DSM-5; American Psychiatric Association, 2013), recognized as a "condition requiring further study," in a large, representative sample of incoming first-year university students participating in the World Mental Health International College Student initiative (n = 20,842). Approximately 18% reported lifetime NSSI engagement and 8.4% reported past 12-month engagement, with 2.3% meeting 12-month DSM-5 NSSI disorder criteria (Kiekens et al., 2023). Further, those reporting lifetime NSSI were likely (59.6%) to meet criteria for at least one DSM-5 disorder, and engaging in NSSI also predicted later onset of other mental disorders, even after controlling for preexisting mental disorders (Kiekens et al., 2023).

With more research focusing on NSSI in the university context, it has become evident that NSSI prevalence is increasing among university students. A study involving three university student cohorts found that lifetime engagement of NSSI almost doubled between 2008 and 2011, and tripled between 2008 and 2015, with around 50% of freshmen participants in the 2015 cohort endorsing lifetime NSSI engagement (Wester et al., 2018). Current NSSI engagement in 2008 was approximately 2.6%, with a sevenfold increase of 19.4% observed in 2015 (Wester et al., 2018).

With respect to demographic characteristics, women are generally more likely to engage in NSSI than men (1.5 x as likely), although this gender disparity varies based on population being studied, with a greater disparity seen in clinical samples (1.8 x more likely) than in college (1.2 x) or community (1.5 x) samples (Bresin & Schoenleber, 2015). Rates of NSSI-D are significantly higher in females than males (Kiekens et al., 2018). Other potential demographic correlates include religion (those with higher religious convictions are less likely to report engaging in NSSI; Westers et al., 2014), age (younger college students are more likely to engage in NSSI; Kuentzel et al., 2012); and sexual orientation (see Zullo et al., this volume). Students who described themselves as anything other than straight were more likely to engage in NSSI, with women facing an increased impact from their sexuality (Whitlock et al., 2011).

Much of the current NSSI literature is made up of participants who are primarily White and from Western countries. A review conducted by Gholamrezaei et al. (2017) found that, across multiple studies involving samples from Eastern countries, prevalence rates of NSSI in students were similar to studies from Western countries. Results from this review also suggested that strong attachment to racial or ethnic identities may be a protective factor from NSSI engagement (Gholamrezaei et al., 2017). Indeed, recent survey of students across 373 U.S. college campuses found that students of color had the lowest rates of mental health service utilization compared to White students (Lipson et al., 2022). For a review of developmental risk and protective factors during the emerging adult years, see Kiekens et al. (this volume).

Risk Factors for NSSI among University Students

Students who struggle to adapt to the university environment are often at heightened risk of mental health challenges (such as anxiety and depression) as well as risky behaviors (e.g., binge drinking, self-harm, and substance use (Boke et al., 2019; Jao et al., 2019; Kwan et al., 2016; Serras et al., 2010; Wilcox et al, 2012). Indeed, a recent national sample of U.S. college students found that greater than 60% of students met criteria for one or more mental health challenges (most commonly depression, anxiety, and suicide ideation), amounting to a 50% increase from 2013 (Lipson et al., 2022). Young adults who are subject to significant stress (e.g., sexual minority stress, trauma, and academic and social pressures) and/or struggling with psychosocial difficulties are at greater risk for self-injury (Fox et al., 2015; see Fox, this volume). Common cognitive processes may underlie these risk behaviors. For instance, NSSI, disordered eating, and alcohol abuse in university students all share a common association with impulsivity (Berg et al., 2015; Hamza et al., 2015); alexithymia, or difficulties in describing and identifying emotions (Greene et al., 2020; Herman et al., 2020; Mazzeo & Espelage, 2002); emotion dysregulation (Hasking & Claes, 2020); perfectionism and rumination (Hoff & Muehlenkamp, 2009); and maladaptive coping (Borrill et al., 2009). Trait mindfulness has also received recent attention and been found to be negatively associated with emotion dysregulation and difficulties with impulse control, both of which are associated with higher rates of engaging in NSSI (Calvete et al., 2022). These findings indicate the complexity of cognitive factors associated with NSSI and other common risk behaviors in those attending university. Strategies that both address the NSSI behaviors as well as build strong cognitive coping skills that target associated cognitive risk factors will assist students in navigating their university years and reduce poor academic performance and attrition (Mahmoud et al., 2012; Mandracchia & Pendleton, 2015), as well as provide skills that can be used throughout adulthood when navigating life's challenges.

The Relationship between NSSI and Suicide Is Complex

Much attention has been paid to suicide and suicide prevention among university students, given that suicide is the second leading cause of death among people ages 15–29 (World Health Organization, 2021). Although NSSI and suicide risk differ in multiple areas (e.g., prevalence, methods used, and intent to die), they are also significantly related to one another (Zareian & Klonsky, 2019). For instance, similar to NSSI, suicidality tends to progress over time, with suicidal ideation starting as early as adolescence and attempts developing later in adolescence or adulthood (Hamza et al., 2012).

Two theories can further explain the relationship between NSSI and suicidality: gateway theory and acquired capability. Gateway theory states that NSSI and suicidality exists along the same self-injury continuum, both at opposite ends of the spectrum (Glenn & Klonsky, 2011; Hamza et al., 2012). The primary assumption made by this theory is that NSSI *must* proceed suicidality, and suicide attempts stem from an escalation of NSSI behaviors (Hamza et al., 2012). Thus, gateway theory posits that NSSI severity will increase prior to the development of ideation and attempt behavior, and that NSSI can be predicted over periods of time (Zareian & Klonsky, 2019).

In contrast, acquired capability, one of three constructs present in Joiner's interpersonal theory of suicide (IPTS; Joiner, 2007) is conceptualized as a desensitization to one's own death as well as enhanced pain tolerance, both of which are necessary for someone to transition from suicidal ideation (cognition) to suicide attempt (action) (Joiner, 2007; Van Orden et al., 2010). Attempting suicide requires the individual to override inherent self-preservation instincts, which is only facilitated through acquired capability (Joiner, 2007; Van Orden et al., 2010; Willoughby et al., 2015). Acquired capability often develops over time and is thought to develop due to exposure to painful provocative events, such as experiencing abuse, active military duty, or sexual trauma (Joiner, 2007; Van Orden et al., 2010; Willoughby et al., 2015). NSSI can be considered a painful provocative event, as it effectively increases one's pain tolerance while also desensitizing someone to their own death as they are inflicting pain and serious harm to themselves (Joiner, 2007; Willoughby et al., 2015). A study conducted by Willoughby et al. (2015) found that NSSI had a significant link to acquired capability over time, even when controlling for other factors like age and sex. Results from Willoughby et al. (2015) also suggest the relationship between NSSI and acquired capability is a positive unidirectional relationship—as NSSI frequency increases, higher acquired capability is predicted over time.

In sum, it is essential that any individual working within a university system be familiar with the concepts of gateway theory and acquired capability, the range of self-injurious behaviors, signs of heightened risk, similarities and distinctions between NSSI and suicidal thoughts and behaviors, and how to refer students for support (Whisenhunt et al., 2015).

Understanding Typologies and Latent Classes of NSSI Has Implications for Intervention Efforts

With empirical research focusing on both clinical and nonclinical populations, variations among those who engage in NSSI have been observed across studies (Klonsky & Olino, 2008; Whitlock et al., 2008). Differences have been noted across clinical symptomatology (e.g., anxiety, borderline personality disorder, and posttraumatic stress disorder), NSSI methods used, functions served, injury severity, race, and gender (Klonsky & Olino, 2008; Whitlock et al., 2008), as well as risk for suicidality (Joiner, 2007; Whitlock et al., 2008).

Klonsky and Olino (2008) identified four distinct subgroups of individuals attending university who engaged in NSSI: an experimental NSSI group, a mild NSSI group, a "multiple functions/anxious" group, and an autonomic function/suicidality group (Klonsky & Olino, 2008). Class 1 (termed the "experimental NSSI" group) consisted of those who had engaged in NSSI on only a few occasions and had the fewest clinical symptoms. Class 2 (termed the "mild NSSI" group) had an earlier onset of symptoms (an average of 11 years old), and engaged in more NSSI behaviors, especially biting, pinching, and scratching. Class 3 (termed the "multiple functions/anxious" group) endorsed a larger variety of NSSI behaviors and had much higher depression, anxiety, and borderline personality disorder scores than class 1 or 2. Class 4 (termed the "automatic functions/suicidal" groups) predominantly featured those whose only NSSI act was cutting themselves in private (usually to reduce negative emotions), and reported high levels of suicidal ideation and attempts. Interestingly, some groups (e.g., experimental) did not meet criteria for a psychological disorder whereas others (e.g., autonomic function/suicidality) displayed significantly more symptoms of a variety of clinical disorders including depression, borderline personality disorder, anxiety, and suicidality.

Whitlock et al. (2008) observed three distinct subgroups among those endorsing self-injury, who varied along several key dimensions of NSSI method and frequency, as well as psychosocial correlates, past NSSI engagement, and treatment history. Class 1 (termed "superficial NSSI") consisted largely of women (74%) with fewer than 11 lifetime NSSI incidents, typically employing one form of NSSI that resulted in largely superficial damage. Class 2 (termed "moderate severity NSSI") contained more men (59%) than women, reporting fewer than 11 lifetime NSSI incidents and commonly using two to three NSSI forms to cause a moderate to high degree of tissue damage. Class 3 (termed "high severity NSSI") consisted largely of women (71%) who reported higher numbers of NSSI incidents, more than three forms of NSSI, with a high degree of tissue damage. Of the three groups, those in the high severity NSSI group were found to be more distinct from the other two classes, reporting greater rates of severe NSSI, addiction, friends who self-injure, disordered eating, twice the risk of suicidality, a history of abuse, and having received a clinical diagnosis and therapy (Whitlock et al., 2008).

Results from both studies have direct implications for NSSI intervention design and implementation. Not all individuals who engage in self-injury will meet criteria for a psychiatric diagnosis and may not benefit from psychiatric intervention compared to other groups. In fact, some may benefit from behaviorally based interventions that are focused more on skills training, psychoeducation, and stigma reduction. Understanding the different types of self-injury in each university population will help inform what levels of intervention need to be available for students.

Reasons for Engaging in NSSI and for Quitting Inform Intervention Strategies
NSSI is most commonly engaged in to self-regulate intense emotional distress (e.g., to reduce stress and to feel something), although self-punishment motives are very common as well (Hooley & Franklin, 2018; Taylor et al., 2018; see also Taylor et al., this volume). While endorsed less frequently, interpersonally oriented reasons (e.g., to communicate distress and influence others) also motivate acts of NSSI, with some suggestion that these may be more salient to initiating NSSI whereas the self-regulating motives may be more relevant to maintaining the behavior, resulting in repeat acts (e.g., Muehlenkamp et al., 2013). While NSSI is often described as an effective means of alleviating distress, this serves to also reinforce its use further (also see Swerdlow et al., this volume). Nevertheless, those who engage in NSSI report higher levels of daily distress (Kiekens et al., 2015) and may also be hyperreactive to stress (Reichl et al., 2016) and more tolerant of certain types of pain (Franklin et al., 2013).

Among a sample of university students who had successfully discontinued their self-harm, Gelinas and Wright (2013) noted that intrapersonal motives of affect regulation, self-punishment, and antidissociation were more commonly endorsed than interpersonal motives. Six themes for reasons for cessation emerged: realization of deliberate self-harm stupidity/futility; distress regarding scarring and negative attention; change for interpersonal reasons; receipt of help/support; desire for wellness; and development of alternate coping strategies. Common strategies used to discontinue self-harm included positive coping behaviors (29%; e.g., journaling and poetry); seeking professional help (26%); negative coping behaviors (17%; e.g., drug use, vomiting, and hair pulling); seeking social support from family and friends (17%); and rationalization/self-talk (12%; e.g., talked self down from self-harm). A number of important barriers to quitting were also identified, namely, the experience of mental illness; ongoing interpersonal issues and other sources of stress; and the ease, addictive properties, and functionality of self-harm (Gelinas & Wright, 2013). Acknowledging these directly in intervention programming is critical (e.g., Turner et al., 2014, 2022).

The College Environment and How It Contributes to NSSI
Transitioning to university is often considered an exciting but tumultuous time (Arnett, 2015). For many young adults, the university years are marked by identity exploration, moving away from family and friends for the first time, and increased autonomy (Arnett,

2015; Mahmoud et al., 2012). Along with such transitions, attending university also requires students to manage heavy academic loads, maintain and establish new relationships and social support, and navigate pressures of on-campus living (e.g., lack of alone time and increased availability of alcohol and illicit substances) (Mandracchia & Pendleton, 2015; Srivastava et al., 2009). Experimenting with risky behaviors, such as substance use and abuse, unhealthy eating patterns, and risky sexual encounters, is common and often associated with NSSI (Serras et al., 2010).

In 2020, 40.9% of university students reported being diagnosed with at least one mental health condition within the previous year, while only 27.7% of these reported receiving mental health care (American College Health Association, 2021). Students experiencing mental health challenges are more likely to have poorer academic performance and attrition (Mandracchia & Pendleton, 2015). Moreover, issues that develop during these years are more likely to persist into adulthood, thus further increasing risk for negative health outcomes (Daw et al., 2017).

Given the confluence of high rates of NSSI among university students plus the important role that peers play in adolescence and emerging adulthood, the role of social contagion must also be acknowledged. Jarvi et al. (2013; see also Jarvi Steele et al., this volume) defined social contagion as the presence of a specific behavior in at least two people within the same group for at least 24 hours. Previous research suggests that NSSI is impacted by social contagion in clinical settings (e.g., inpatient psychiatric facilities and group homes) (Jarvi et al., 2013). Students who know someone who engages in NSSI thus may be at increased risk of engaging in NSSI themselves, as they may perceive the behavior as an effective coping strategy (Jarvi et al., 2013). Undergraduates who are exposed to NSSI through friends are more likely to engage in NSSI themselves, with some research suggesting this may be influenced by interpersonal overdependence and need-to-belong (Conigliaro & Ward-Ciesielski, 2021).

Lack of Knowledge, NSSI Stigma, and Their Role in Preventing Seeking Support

LUniversity staff report an increase in NSSI-related concerns in their work with students, yet also report low knowledge and/or confidence to effectively address or manage NSSI (Whisenhunt et al., 2015; Whitlock et al., 2011). Similarly, commonly reported barriers to treatment seeking among university students include stigma and a lack of awareness-related attitudes (Downs & Eisenberg, 2012). Students perceived their needs as not serious, felt they did not have time for treatment, and believed they could manage their challenges on their own without treatment (Downs & Eisenberg, 2012). Education on mental health can reduce mental health stigma, with encouragement from friends, family, and university staff helping to facilitate treatment seeking (Corrigan et al., 2001; DeVylder et al., 2022; Pompeo-Fargnoli, 2022).

Building Multifaceted Intervention Efforts That Target NSSI on University Campuses

There are several frameworks to consider in building a comprehensive response to NSSI. Considerations need to be made for *who* should be targeted, and *how* they will be targeted. Universal prevention programs target everyone in a specified setting, such as campus-wide initiatives, while targeted programs devote energy to a specific subpopulation based on demographics or risk level. Stepped programs are created from a hybrid of both universal and targeted approaches and based on the specific needs of the organization. Given the high rates of NSSI among emerging adults, in comparison with the relatively low rates of students who may meet full criteria for NSSI-D (American Psychiatric Association, 2013; Hooley et al., 2020), this suggests opportunities for offering a range of services that are both targeted and tailored to the college population and the commonly observed rates of stress, anxiety, and depressive symptoms.

To date, mental health intervention efforts have been successfully implemented for two general purposes among university students: (a) to prevent psychiatric crises, and (b) to promote overall well-being among students with various mental health challenges (and, to a lesser extent, to serve as universal, primary prevention strategies aimed at preventing future mental health challenges) (see Conley et al., 2015; Conley et al., 2017 for general reviews). As is the case with any risky or problematic behavior, not every person is ready to take action to change their behavior. Considering the transtheoretical model and its proposed stages of change, Grunberg and Lewis (2015) offer a cautionary note that, among users of an NSSI e-community forum, most posts were coded as being in the contemplation stage (52.1%), followed by the precontemplation stage (39.7%), with recovery commonly viewed as a disadvantage as it meant the absence of being able to rely on NSSI as a coping strategy. Thus, as interventions are developed and implemented, it is likely that many individuals engaging in NSSI are aware that engaging in NSSI may be a problem, but they have no desire or commitment to change and so may require different skills-building and educational intervention approaches.

Theoretically, the college years are an excellent period for implementing an effective, multitiered response to NSSI (and other risky health behaviors) given the length of time students are attending university and the multiple opportunities to engage across various educational and social platforms, offering resources through various campus venues, in classrooms, and in counseling centers. Several valuable resources are available for developing a multifaceted approach to managing self-injury risk and supporting university student needs. For instance, Baetens et al. (this volume) offers an example model of university policies that can be implemented (with similar offerings outlined for secondary school counselors in Stargell et al., 2018), as well as resources posted on the International Consortium on Self-Injury in Educational Settings website. Lewis et al. (2019) also provide a review of university institutional-level responses to self-injury, including guidelines for responding by various stakeholders.

For purposes of this chapter, we focus on promising university-based opportunities for targeting students in novel ways, through gatekeeper interventions and classroom-based interventions, as well as novel services being offered at campus counseling centers. Given the dearth of literature available specifically devoted to NSSI, where appropriate we also refer to intervention research that is designed to reduce suicide risk or improve the overall mental health of emerging adults attending university.

Intervention Strategies in the University Context

Counseling Center-Based Interventions

Although most existing treatments for NSSI were not originally designed specifically for NSSI, several treatments have now been explored for their utility in reducing NSSI urges and behaviors, as well as associated reductions in suicidal intent. Pistorello et al. (2012) applied dialectical behavior therapy (DBT) to a sample of college students reporting current suicidal ideation, a history of NSSI, and at least three borderline personality disorder (BPD) symptoms and found that those who received DBT reported greater decreases in NSSI than those who received treatment as usual. Nevertheless, individuals who engage in NSSI do not always meet criteria for a psychiatric diagnosis, as noted in research exploring subgroups of NSSI (e.g., Klonsky & Olino, 2008; Whitlock et al., 2008) and, in an environment with commonly scarce mental health resources, DBT is a time- and resource-intensive therapy that many students may not be able or willing to complete or university counseling centers able to fully deliver.

Andover et al. (2015) developed a brief intervention specifically for NSSI in young adults attending university (treatment for self-injurious behaviors, T-SIB). Consisting of nine weekly individual sessions, T-SIB covers the following: psychoeducation on NSSI, addressing ambivalence, identifying antecedents and consequences of NSSI behaviors and urges, identifying alternative behaviors to differentially reinforce, functional assessment of skills deficits and strengths, and relapse prevention. While small, the initial open pilot trial was promising and suggested clinically meaningful change in depression, number of days engaged in NSSI, and number of NSSI urges at posttreatment and three-month follow-up. A more recent study examined moderators of T-SIB and found that the treatment may be more effective for individuals with greater NSSI frequency, as well as those with higher levels of anxiety (Andover et al., 2020).

Bentley (2017) applied the unified protocol (UP) to a clinical case of a young woman attending college who met criteria for NSSI-D, social anxiety disorder, and generalized anxiety disorder. Despite her mental health symptoms, the client was functioning at a high level, earning good grades, and maintaining a part-time job and a small group of friends, although she reported a strained relationship with her family. Given the client's central experience of negative perceptions of the experience of emotion, frequent and intense negative affect, and a high degree of negative reactivity to intense emotions, the UP was selected over other evidence-based treatment approaches as it focused on the emotional symptoms underlying each of the client's diagnoses; integrated an approach-oriented stance toward intense emotions; and offered a structured, time-limited protocol that was less intensive than other therapies, such as DBT. The UP for transdiagnostic treatment of emotional disorders (Barlow et al., 2017; Barlow et al., 2020) is a cognitive-behavioral intervention designed to directly address core temperamental factors that maintain emotional disorders—specifically, frequent/acute negative affect and the perception of negative emotion as intolerable. Accordingly, the aim of the UP is to *extinguish distress in response to the experience of strong emotion*. The UP consists of eight treatment modules, and while generally administered in order, each module can function independently; thus, clinicians are able to flexibly reorder and repeat individual UP modules as needed. Bentley began with 4 weekly sessions of mindful emotion awareness training followed by 12 sessions that focused on motivation enhancement, the functional nature of emotion, cognitive flexibility, countering emotional behaviors, emotion exposure, and relapse prevention. Over the course of the 16 individual treatment sessions, the client experienced significant reductions in NSSI urges and behaviors (maintained over a five-month window of time), self-reported ability to respond adaptively to intense emotions, showed and moderate reductions in anxiety symptoms. For more information on UP, see Bentley and Jaroszewski (this volume).

Gatekeeper Interventions

Gatekeeper interventions have become a commonly utilized suicide prevention model implemented at the university level, as they are highly recommended by the American Foundation for Suicide Prevention (AFSP) to reduce psychological crisis and suicide risk in this setting (Rallis et al., 2018; Ross et al., 2021; Yonemoto et al., 2019). A gatekeeper is defined as an individual who has frequent direct contact with fellow community members (Mo et al., 2018). Gatekeeper training aims to prepare individuals to engage with distressed or at-risk students by teaching them skills on how to identify warning signs of mental health distress and how to engage with distressed students effectively (Mo et al., 2018; Rallis et al., 2018). Engagement skills include active listening, effective questions to assess risk, and how to initiate contact with counseling services (Mo et al., 2018; Rallis et al., 2018). Additionally, gatekeeper trainings also target and promote mental health literacy and typically teach students about common mental health problems, including stress, anxiety, depression, and suicide risk (Liu et al., 2021).

Commonly Implemented Gatekeeper Trainings in University Settings

Due to the growing support for these interventions, multiple gatekeeper interventions have emerged over the last two decades (Mo et al., 2018; Yonemoto et al., 2019).

QUESTION, PERSUADE, REFER

One of the most well-established gatekeeper models is the question, persuade, refer (QPR) model (Quinnett & Bratcher, 1996). QPR teaches trainees to recognize warning signs, assess suicidal ideation, employ active listening, and refer others to counseling across several two-hour sessions. Multiple studies documenting modest but significant increases in both suicide knowledge and gatekeeper behaviors (i.e., questioning about suicidality and referral to counseling services) have been observed, but it is less known how well these changes are maintained over time (Cross et al., 2007; Wyman et al., 2008).

CAMPUS CONNECT

Campus Connect (Wallack & Pasco, 2006) is a nationally recognized university-based gatekeeper intervention that is specifically tailored to and designed for college/university community members (Pasco et al., 2012). While the content covered in this three-hour, gatekeeper training is comparable to QPR and other gatekeeper trainings (e.g., enhancing active listening/communication skills, increasing mental health literacy, and disseminating knowledge on how to identify warning signs and ask direct questions pertaining to risk), a unique aspect of Campus Connect is its interactive learning format (Muehlenkamp & Quinn-Lee, 2023; Pasco et al., 2012). Campus Connect emphasizes the importance of not only disseminating knowledge about gatekeeper skills, but also strengthening application of these skills (e.g., assessing risk and referring to services) through interactive role-play and case-based scenarios (Morton et al., 2021; Muehlenkamp & Quinn-Lee, 2023). Studies evaluating Campus Connect have observed improvements in trainees' responsiveness to crisis situations, increased self-efficacy, increase in identification of at-risk students, and referral to counseling services (Morton et al., 2021; Pasco et al., 2012). However, a potential limitation to implementing Campus Connect is its format. As this training takes a minimum of three hours to complete, implementing Campus Connect university-wide or in classroom settings may not be feasible (Muehlenkamp & Quinn-Lee, 2023).

KOGNITO

Kognito is a brief virtual avatar-based gatekeeper intervention with various population-specific training modules (e.g., veterans, college students, and LGBTQ folks) (Coleman et al., 2019; Smith-Millman et al., 2022). Kognito has developed two gatekeeper trainings for the university context targeting either university staff (e.g., At-risk for University/College Faculty & Staff) or university students (e.g., At-risk for College Students) (see Kognito.com). Each module takes approximately 30 to 45 minutes to complete, and trainees are immersed in a virtual environment where they interact with students who are experiencing depression, anxiety, and suicide risk (Coleman et al., 2019; Smith-Millman et al., 2022). To progress through each scenario, trainees must select the appropriate response to the distressed student and refer them to counseling services. Studies evaluating the effectiveness of Kognito's university-based training observed significant increases in identification of at-risk students, as well as students referred to university counseling centers (Coleman et al., 2019; Smith-Millman et al., 2022). Increases in trainees' own help-seeking behavior was also observed (Coleman et al., 2019). See below for additional information regarding Kognito's efficacy when comparing students to faculty trainees.

Who Makes the Most Impactful/Effective Gatekeeper?

At the university level, gatekeeper interventions have been primarily tailored toward targeting campus staff (e.g., professors), with fewer gatekeeper interventions targeting students (Rallis et al., 2018). University staff may be well positioned to serve as gatekeepers, given their frequent engagement with the student body as a whole (Rallis et al., 2018; Smith-Millman et al., 2022), and there is evidence to suggest these interventions have yielded improvements in the perceived preparedness and knowledge of staff (Rein et al., 2018; Smith-Millman et al., 2022). Nevertheless, targeting peers as gatekeepers may ultimately be a more impactful strategy to improve mental health outcomes in university settings, as college students are significantly more likely to disclose suicide risk or mental health distress to a peer (i.e., romantic partner, roommate, friend) compared to a professor or other campus staff) (Brownson et al., 2011; Drum et al., 2009; Westefeld et al., 2005).

The benefits and utility in training and preparing peers to become gatekeepers has been demonstrated in previous research. For instance, Smith-Millman et al. (2022) implemented and evaluated Kognito and its artificial intelligence-driven platform with college student and university staff gatekeeper training. While both groups reported significant improvements in perceived preparedness, self-efficacy, and likelihood to engage in gatekeeper behaviors, only the student trainee group reported significant gains in gatekeeper behaviors (e.g., referring students to counseling and number of students asked about suicide risk) at follow-up. Interestingly, faculty and staff were able to maintain their new levels of preparedness and self-efficacy more so than students at three-month follow-up (Smith-Millman et al., 2022). Results from this study suggest that while university faculty are feeling prepared to engage in these behaviors, there are barriers in converting these thoughts into actions. Similar results were also observed in a study conducted by Zinzow et al. (2020) which implemented and evaluated an in-person 90-minute training based on elements from various gatekeeper programs (e.g., Applied Suicide Intervention Skill Training and QPR) delivered to students, faculty, and staff. Results found that students benefited the most from participating in this training, with a significant increase in gatekeeper behavior engagement being observed between pre- and post-training. Compared to nonstudents (e.g., faculty and staff), students engaged in more gatekeeper behaviors at three-month follow-up. In sum, students have more frequent opportunities to execute gatekeeper behaviors with peers compared to staff (Smith-Millman et al., 2022; Zinzow et al., 2020), suggesting that students may be well suited to participating in gatekeeper trainings and engaging with students in need of support (Rein et al., 2018).

Gatekeeper Interventions and Applicability to NSSI

While gatekeeper interventions have become a highly utilized intervention strategy in university settings, NSSI-related content has not explicitly been incorporated (Berger et al., 2014; Hamza et al., 2021). Previous research has consistently demonstrated that NSSI among university students remains poorly understood (Lewis et al., 2019), is highly stigmatized (Downs & Eisenberg, 2012), and is increasing on college campuses (Kiekens et al., 2019), incorporating NSSI-specific content is a necessary step to promote broad mental health literacy, NSSI-specific literacy, reduce stigma, and increase identification of students engaging in NSSI. Additionally, given that NSSI is a significant predictor of future suicidality (Zareian & Klonsky, 2019), and the complex relationship between these two behaviors, emphasizing the relationship between them allows for a more comprehensive suicide prevention curriculum and improves strength and breadth of gatekeeper trainings. Table 49.1 offers recommendations for incorporating NSSI-specific content into current gatekeeper training areas, and reflects content derived from Westers et al. (2016) and resources available from the Cornell Self-Injury and Recovery Resources website.

Considerations and Recommendations for Improving Gatekeeper Trainings in University Settings

Incorporating those with lived experience, often referenced as peer specialists in other contexts, may be particularly relevant to this gatekeeper, peer-support-based training

Table 49.1 Recommendations for Applying NSSI-Specific Content to Focus Areas Of Gatekeeper Interventions

Content area of training	NSSI content to include
Mental health literacy	NSSI definition, common forms, functions, and prevalence of NSSI among college/university students; NSSI and its relationship to suicide risk (e.g., differences in intent, frequency, and lethality; similarities across both behaviors), and other common mental health problems
Identifying warning signs	Emotions/behaviors that could indicate self-injury is occurring, including but not limited to unexplainable cuts/marks/burns, feeling overwhelmed or other negative feelings, wearing clothes considered "seasonally inappropriate" (e.g., long pants/shirts in the summer)
Conversation skills to employ	Showing "respectful curiosity" (e.g., "How does self-injury make you feel?" or "What does NSSI do for you?"), utilize "I" statements (e.g., "I have noticed cuts on your arm recently")
What to avoid	Avoid using accusatory language or language that perpetuates common NSSI-related stigma (e.g., "you're not just cutting yourself because you want attention, right?"); do not agree to keep secrets.

(Fuhr et al., 2014; O'Connor & Portzky, 2018). Lived experience in the suicide prevention space has been defined as "having experienced suicidal thoughts, survived a suicide attempt, cared for someone through suicide crisis, or been bereaved by suicide" (Roses in the Ocean, 2016, pg 1). Not only does incorporating those with lived experience into these peer-support based interventions directly benefit at-risk students, doing so also yields benefits to the individual with lived experience by including paid work, being in a cooperative environment, and promoting continual recovery (Hawgood et al., 2022). Per a study by Hawgood et al. (2022), those with lived experience engaging in suicide prevention work stated that doing so enhanced their reasons for living due to fostering strong connections, being engaged in service, and strengthening their orientation for the future.

Additionally, it is possible that those with lived experience have already established relevant gatekeeper behaviors, including knowledge, identifying warning signs, and assessing risk. A study by Milkin et al. (2019) interviewed 50 individuals who were exposed to suicide (e.g., cared for someone through suicidal crisis) and found that 77% of participants reported increased awareness following exposure, recognizing that suicide is something that "actually happens" along with increased concern for others' mental health and safety. Milkin et al. (2019) assert that individuals with this specific form of lived experience (e.g., exposure) may be particularly amenable to participating in planning, disseminating, or participating in suicide prevention/interventions. With this information in mind, it is plausible that those with exposure may be well-suited for the gatekeeper role, due to previous engagement in relevant behaviors.

However, it is important to note that while exposure can lead to increased concern for others well-being, it may also instill negative attitudes or stigma toward others who have engaged in suicidality or NSSI behaviors (Milkin et al., 2019). More research is needed to explore the roles of individuals with lived experience and their effectiveness as gatekeepers specifically. Incorporating those in recovery from or with other NSSI-specific lived experience may be an important first-step to emphasizing NSSI-related content in current university-based gatekeeper interventions.

Assessment and Evaluation Challenges of Gatekeeper Trainings and Other Novel Interventions

Gatekeeper interventions come with their own challenges with respect to targeted outcomes to measure "success," whether referring to increased NSSI knowledge of those receiving the training, how newly acquired engagement skills may be used in real life, whether referrals are made to the university counseling center, and so on. Examples exist of hypothetical scenarios being used as an alternative strategy to self-report questionnaires, particularly when it comes to topic areas that individuals may be unwilling to share. For instance, Borrill et al. (2012) used hypothetical case scenarios tailored to the nationality and gender of participating students to elicit how perceptions of NSSI, its severity, intent, secretiveness, and whether considered "abnormal" based on cultural values might influence perspectives on nondisclosure. For instance, male participants were more likely to discuss the negative consequences that might occur if those in the scenarios were to disclose, with the authors suggesting that prevalence studies using structured self-report measures may underestimate self-injury behaviors in those whose culture or gender strongly frowns upon self-injury. Use of these hypothetical scenarios as an alternative to traditional quantitative surveys offers an important new perspective that suggests there may be a greater risk of nondisclosure by certain populations, which could in turn be contributing to the reduced effectiveness of interventions designed to date (Borrill et al., 2012).

Morena et al. (in preparation) compared the interactive Kognito (Coleman et al., 2019; Smith-Millman et al., 2022) gatekeeper intervention At-risk for College Students to a brief prerecorded presentation on skills development (e.g., identifying warning signs, utilizing active listening, asking questions about psychological distress, and referring to services). University students were randomly assigned to receive the Kognito intervention, a prerecorded training on suicidal behaviors and NSSI, or the wait-list control group. Two open-response case scenarios were created to assess indirect behavior change postintervention by examining participants' abilities to intervene through assessing practical and conceptual knowledge (see table 49.2 for coding criteria). Case vignettes described scenarios of peers in distress who were experiencing suicidal ideation or NSSI, and asked participants to describe how they would handle each situation. Participant responses were coded for (a) their ability to identify a distressed peer, (b) how they would ask about suicide and NSSI in each scenario, and (c) whether they would refer the peer for mental health services and how they would do so. Responses were coded by three reviewers blind to participants' assigned condition. Design of the vignettes was based on guidelines recommended by the Suicide Prevention Resource Center (SPRC) and included two counterbalanced vignettes of similar length and detail, each with a different protagonist (male vs. female), as well as different stressor types (academic vs. social). To score the vignettes, point values were assigned (0, 1, or 2 depending on the question) based on the response provided by participants. Negative point values were assigned if a participant provided an inappropriate response (e.g., responses that perpetuated myths or were damaging) or failed to ask pertinent questions about NSSI and suicide risk (Suicide Prevention Resource Center, 2009). All coders were trained by the primary investigator to ensure interrater reliability greater than 85% agreement across vignettes. An example vignette is included below:

Peer Vignette One—Jessica [academic stressors w/ self-injury]
You first met Jessica your freshman year in your Residence Hall, as you both live on the same floor. Jessica is a nursing student, and when she isn't studying, she's hanging out with you and your friends, and she is very kind and sociable. However, with finals around the corner, Jessica has been noticeably stressed. She becomes tearful seemingly at random and is always worrying about all the work she has to do before the semester ends. Lately she has been pulling all-nighters to get her work done and hasn't been sleeping much. She's stopped hanging out with everyone as much and

Table 49.2 Qualitative Scoring Convention for Open-Ended Peer Vignette Activity

Response themes example questions	−1 point	0 point	1 point	2 points	Example response
Empathic concern: How likely are you to express empathic concern to this person? Why or why not?	N/A	Description only, mechanical nonvalidating advice	Expresses concern OR offers hope	Expresses concern AND offers hope, offers some sort of example	"I would tell her that she is young and has a lot to live for, and that breaking up with a guy isn't the end of the world"
Active listening: How likely are you to engage in active listening with this person? Why or why not?	N/A	Description only, mechanical, nonvalidating advice	Listens by paying attention, attention, acknowledges importance of listening and showing you're listening	Along with 1, uses some form of reflection/validation, such as summarizing, asking questions that foster respect and understanding.	"I would try to connect with what they're going through" "It sounds like you've been feeling this way for a while, is that right?"
Questioning: How likely are you to discuss risks of nonsuicidal self-injury with this person?	Explicitly states they would not ask about these behaviors	No questions about suicide or NSSI—states they're worried or concerned	No questions about risk, but does not ask explicit questions about NSSI/suicide	Asks explicit questions about suicide and NSSI, assesses risk, intent/plan, etc.	"It worries me that you're harming yourself" "How do you feel after you cut yourself"
Referral to service: How likely are you to refer this person to counselling services?	N/A	No effort to encourage person to seek/accept professional help	Effort at having peer consider help from mental health professional	Actively encourages peer to receive help and follow-up with peer	"Are you open to getting help?" "Are you open to going to counselling services? We can go together."

it seems like she's almost always studying or doing work. One night you and Jessica go to the cafe for dinner, and she tells you that she's feeling really down and is feeling overwhelmed. She tells you she's been having difficulty sleeping and is losing interest in things she typically enjoys doing, like yoga and hanging out with friends. She tells you she's been scratching at her skin and has even cut herself, "just so I could feel something. But I've only done that a few times. It wasn't a big deal."

Results indicated that participants receiving either interactive Kognito or the recorded presentation scored significantly higher in active listening as compared to the control group. For instance, example quotes demonstrating active listening for intervention participants included statements such as: "*I would let Adam know that I am here to listen to him talk about what's going on and how he's feeling and make sure to ask if he wants or needs advice. Sometimes, people who are going through something really only want someone to listen to their thoughts and validate their feelings. I would make sure to let Adam know that his feelings are valid and that he has people around him who love and support him*" and "*I would show that I am listening by nodding my head and clarifying the things she says by repeating what she says back to her, and I would also ask further questions if she gives me open ended responses.*" In contrast, responses regarding active listening among wait-list control participants were generally less detailed and demonstrative of key active listening components (e.g., maintaining eye contact, using body language to communicate engagement in conversation, and restating what the person has communicated to them), examples include: "*I would basically listen to him and encourage him to keep pushing through because things will get better*" and "*Keep pushing you can do it.*"

Of the 106 responses coded across two vignette scenarios ($N = 71$), a total of 12 (11.3%) inappropriate responses were noted, 11 of which (92%) were responses made by participants from the wait-list control group. Ten (83%) of these were indicative of perpetuating myths about NSSI or suicidality (e.g., discussing NSSI or suicide would give their peer ideas about engaging in these behaviors). No significant group differences were noted between groups on dimensions of empathic concern, questioning, and referral to service.

Brief Classroom- and Campus-Based Interventions

Classroom-based delivery of brief, transdiagnostic skills-based interventions are an important avenue for offering training, outreach, and mental health skills development and support for university students. These interventions can be embedded in traditional college classes and seminars, societies, clubs, or teams, and provided in person or asynchronously. They serve to offer students entry into emotional and cognitive skills development that expands coping strategies, diminishes mental health stigma, and facilitates future willingness to seek counseling services if needed. For those students struggling with mental health challenges, classroom-based interventions afford them access to mental health supports they might not have otherwise had access to outside therapy. Further, they offer skills training with multiple opportunities for supervised practice, which further promotes long-term behavior change and has been found to improve self-perceptions, stress, and anxiety (Conley et al., 2015).

Acceptance and commitment therapy (ACT) has been successfully delivered to university students embedded in first-year experience courses and in psychology courses, as well as in workshops and senior psychology seminars, and as a stand-alone online curriculum, with results yielding improvements in student acceptance; stress, anxiety, and depression levels; increased values-based motivations toward school; improved attitudes toward mental health treatment; and improved psychological flexibility (Barrasso-Catanzaro, 2015; Browning et al., 2022; Danitz et al., 2016; Mullen et al., 2021; Pistorello et al., 2016; Viskovich & Pakenham, 2020).

Christodoulou et al. (2021) implemented a one-day ACT skills training for university students that focused on "learning how to untangle from internal barriers to pursue values-based action" through developing mindfulness (present-moment awareness, defusion, and acceptance), and values-based action (clarification of personal values and values-based goal and action planning). Participants were randomized to receive either the ACT training or wait-list control, and the training resulted in reduced general psychological distress and negative emotions (depression, anxiety, stress composite score), with changes influenced by psychological flexibility and mindfulness. Those receiving ACT continued to improve over time and maintained at the two-month follow-up. Embedding interventions in university courses is an ideal next step that allows for greater reach and for the potential to deliver both universal prevention and targeted intervention efforts (Chugani et al., 2020; Conley et al., 2013; Petersen et al., 2022).

Browning et al. (2022) piloted a brief, four-session ACT intervention with undergraduate students enrolled in a psychology seminar. The intervention incorporated didactic presentations, discussion, and experiential exercises and was delivered by graduate students. Nearly half (45.2%) of the sample met clinical criteria for depression and/or anxiety. Significant reductions in stress and anxiety were found at the end of the intervention and at five-week follow-up; no significant changes in depression levels were noted. Students reported the most common skills practiced outside class were grounded in ACT processes: mindfulness techniques (59%), practicing acceptance (45.5%), and taking committed action (36.4%). Coupled with brief stress management strategies like mindfulness, the interactive format and supportive classroom culture may have provided short-term immediate relief to reduce stress, anxiety, and mental health stigma. This study offers a promising example of using existing classroom settings as platforms for efficiently delivering accessible and affordable mental health treatment to students (Pistorello et al., 2016).

Chugani et al. (2020) have extended this model of education as prevention and developed a college course entitled "Wellness and Resilience for College and Beyond." Primarily grounded in DBT (Mazza, et al., 2016) with additional elements from positive psychology and ACT, the course was designed to partially address the high rates of suicidality among college students by offering content that can benefit students already living with mental health disorders, while also general enough to aid in prevention for those without symptoms. Four skill domains are targeted: mindfulness, emotion regulation, distress tolerance, and interpersonal effectiveness. Importantly, the curriculum is designed for a broad range of general education instructors to teach and requires no special mental health training. The course materials are freely available, including content covering 14 weekly class sessions, reflective homework posts, skills practice "diary cards," and examination materials (Chugani et al., 2020). At present, clinical trial data collection is ongoing, with measures of adaptive and dysfunctional coping, emotion dysregulation, as well as lifetime and past-30-day suicide ideation and behaviors assessed at baseline, end of semester, and three-month follow-up. Although final results are not yet available, this work highlights creative efforts to embed interventions in existing or new college courses and offers promising approaches to target widespread prevention and intervention efforts to reduce NSSI and associated mental health risk factors. Nevertheless, while education efforts such as these are extremely popular on college campuses, research evaluating college courses focused on well-being is struggling to keep up with their increasing availability. Thus, future research efforts must continue to evaluate the efficacy of these programs to reduce mental health problems, develop healthy coping practices, offer access to support and treatment services, and reduce mental health stigma.

While not evaluated specifically with college populations, the use of bibliotherapy, journaling, and creative writing to improve mental health has been explored. Hooley et al. (2018) recruited participants from an online forum who had engaged in NSSI at least twice within the past month, randomizing them to engage in one of three journaling conditions, writing for five minutes each day: autobiographical self-enhancement training (ASET) focused on reducing self-criticism and enhancing positive self-worth (asked to write about something that happened that day that made them feel good about themselves); expressive writing (asked to write about something that bothered them or was on their mind); or journaling (asked to write about the events of the day in a general and factually descriptive way). While the ASET journaling condition did lead to reduced self-criticism and suicide ideation, overall, all three of the writing-based approaches provided clinical benefits and reduced NSSI episodes. Franz et al. (2022) employed a digital bibliotherapy intervention among adults visiting a social media platform. Participants were randomized to read one suicide narrative a day for 14 days, or to a wait-list control condition, theorizing that reading first-person narratives about working through suicidal thoughts would lead to reduced desire to die, mediated by increased perceived shared experience and optimism. Indeed, participants in the treatment condition reported lower desire to die than participants in the control condition during the 14-day trial and at two-week follow-up, with increased perceived shared experience and optimism mediating the effect of treatment on desire to die. These findings suggest that the benefits of regular, consistent journaling or bibliotherapy may offer opportunities as highly scalable and disseminable treatments among university populations.

Future Implications for University Mental Health Services

In the midst of a mental health crisis among emerging adults attending university, we believe that university stakeholders are well positioned to aid students. How can we get universities to take more responsibility for building resources to support student mental health awareness generally, and NSSI education and intervention more specifically? Campus counseling centers were traditionally designed to care for a relatively small proportion of students and not the large numbers of students currently needing mental health support. A shift in conceptualizing who is responsible for the mental health of students must move from a *them* mindset (i.e., counseling center) to an *us* mindset (i.e., *everyone* has varied roles to play).

University stakeholders must recognize that more is needed to move beyond efforts that simply normalize stress (e.g., campus events designed to relieve stress during high stress time periods, such as final exams), and instead aim to scaffold a multilevel approach that addresses and manages mental health stigma and discomfort and develops universal and targeted prevention and intervention approaches that both capitalize on the skills of various stakeholders (e.g., peers as gatekeepers), and also offer students multiple "doses" of intervention during their university years. Routine check-ins by peer gatekeepers, residence hall assistants, faculty, and counseling center staff who ask about mental health, stress levels, and self-harm could offer risk screening and provision of educational materials in various spaces and places around campus. Efforts such as these allow for more attention to be paid to NSSI and suicide risk, and when to get additional help. They also serve to destigmatize mental health challenges. Through engaging in regular "doses" of conversation and learning about mental health, windows of opportunities open for sharing, disclosing, and paying attention to those around you who may be in need, teaching students to be informed consumers of what it means to be mentally healthy, and how mental health services can support them, which benefits individuals well into adulthood.

Research supports the valuable role that gatekeepers can play in a university community's mental health through building social networks and strengthening community outreach to mental health professionals (Shtivelband et al., 2015). Nevertheless, gatekeepers remain an underutilized resource. Incorporating NSSI into gatekeeper training for peers and staff members alike is a necessary next step for the dissemination of knowledge and the provision of support to students.

Worth noting is the consistent incorporation of mindfulness training across all the described interventions. Indeed, Argento et al., (2020) documented the use of a 10-minute body scan mindfulness training among those with a history of engaging in NSSI and found a significant increase in state mindfulness and reduced stress levels following a stress induction task. Mindfulness training has long been incorporated into clinical therapy sessions, but it offers many ways to build in small "doses" of practice in classroom settings, and so on. While research is limited to date, the addition of mindfulness-based skills and practice may be a key element for future treatment of NSSI in assisting to increase self-awareness and recognize early signs of heightened negative arousal and engaging in reduced emotion regulation difficulties, adaptive coping, and management of urges (Thew, et al., 2018).

Efforts to expand the breadth and depth of universal and targeted intervention efforts should continue to creatively embed interventions in existing college courses, such as required freshmen or upperclassmen seminars, or classes in diverse subject areas. Work with brief interventions will help facilitate future support and mental health treatment of university students. A meta-analysis conducted by Conley et al. (2015) indicates that skills-based interventions are strongly preferred over psychoeducational interventions alone, with supervised practice (under supervision or with feedback from a trained peer support, staff member, etc.) essential for promoting longer-lasting effects.

Future Research Directions

Research is that specifically targets NSSI among emerging adults attending university is quite limited. Exploration of various typologies and risk profiles for NSSI among university students suggests that a variety of universal and targeted approaches are needed that serve to improve global mental health challenges as well as to educate, destigmatize, and provide support for those engaging in NSSI and other forms of self-harm. Future research must continue to explore novel approaches to delivering interactive, hands-on intervention such as the ones described here. While this is challenging work that takes time and resources, the need is great.

Utilizing peer vignettes as a proxy for assessment of behavior change and intervention skills learned may be an effective strategy for understanding indirect behavior change in the university context. Future research should continue to explore vignettes as a novel data collection method to ascertain how well participants are adapting and utilizing skills learned in brief interventions.

Universal approaches must strive to capitalize on the strengths of a university community through embedding NSSI education into classroom-based curricula and providing multiple "doses" of mental health screening and wellness initiatives through campus-based initiatives, peer gatekeepers, and so on. Regarding targeted efforts, current health research suggests that personalized treatments that explore what individual characteristics predict responsiveness or resistance to therapy (e.g., Itzhaky et al., 2022) are an important future research direction. Approaches such as these would then afford tailoring treatment approaches to best fit individual characteristics. This is not a particularly novel idea, as clinicians routinely do this in therapy sessions, taking into account psychosocial factors, family dynamics, and biological factors. What *is* novel about this recommendation is the notion of research imitating clinical work, with the challenge being tailoring individual interventions while still maintaining a structured research protocol. Given the limited empirical work examining intervention frameworks designed for the college mental health crisis, recommendations for the development of novel partnerships such as broad practice-research networks are warranted (Kirsch et al., 2014).

References

American College Health Association. (2021). *American College Health Association-National College Health Assessment III: Undergraduate Student Reference Group Executive Summary Fall 2020*. https://www.acha.org/documents/ncha/NCHA-III_Fall_2020_Undergraduate_Reference_Group_Executive_Summary.pdf

American Psychiatric Association. (2013). *Diagnostic and statistical manual of mental disorders*. 5th ed.

Andover, M. S., Schatten, H. T., Holman, C. S., & Miller, I. W. (2020). Moderators of treatment response to an intervention for nonsuicidal self-injury in young adults. *Journal of Consulting and Clinical Psychology*, *88*(11), 1032–1038.

Andover, M. S., Schatten, H. T., Morris, B. W. & Miller, I. W. (2015). Development of an intervention for nonsuicidal self-injury in young adults: An open pilot trial. *Cognitive and Behavioral Practice*, *22*, 491–503.

Argento, A., Simundic, A., Mettler, J., Mills, D. J., & Heath, N.L. (2020). Evaluating the effectiveness of a brief mindfulness activity in university settings with non-suicidal self-injury engagement. *Archives of Suicide Research*, *26*(2), 871–885.

Arnett, J. J. (2015). *Emerging adulthood: The winding road from the late teens through the twenties*. Oxford University Press.

Barlow, D. H., Farchione, T. J., Bullis, J. R., Gallagher, M. W., Murray-Latin, H., Sauer-Zavala, S., Bentley, K. H., Thompson-Hollands, J., Conklin, L. R., Boswell, J. F., Ametaj, A., Carl, J. R., Boettcher, H. T., & Cassiello-Robbins, C. (2017). The unified protocol for transdiagnostic treatment of emotional disorders compared with diagnosis-specific protocols for anxiety disorders: A randomized clinical trial. *JAMA Psychiatry*, *74*(9), 875–884.

Barlow, D. H., Harris, B. A., Eustis, E. H., & Farchione, T. J. (2020). The unified protocol for transdiagnostic treatment of emotional disorders. *World Psychiatry*, *19*(2), 245–246.

Barrasso-Catanzaro, C. (2015). *Integrating mindfulness and acceptance-based practice into the college curriculum: Examining receptivity in undergraduate students* [Doctoral dissertation, Kean University]. ProQuest Dissertations & Theses Global.

Bentley, K.H. (2017). Applying the unified protocol transdiagnostic treatment to nonsuicidal self-injury and co-occurring emotional disorders: A case illustration. *Journal of Clinical Psychology: In Session*, *73*(5), 547–558.

Berg, J. M., Latzman, R. D., Bliwise, N. G., & Lilienfeld, S. O. (2015). Parsing the heterogeneity of impulsivity: A meta-analytic review of the behavioral implications of the UPPS for psychopathology. *Psychological Assessment*, *27*(4), 1129–1146.

Berger, E., Hasking, P., & Reupert, A. (2014). "We're working in the dark here": Education needs of teachers and school staff regarding student self-injury. *School Mental Health*, *6*(3), 201–212.

Böke, B. N., Mills, D. J., Mettler, J., & Heath, N. L. (2019). Stress and coping patterns of university students. *Journal of College Student Development*, *60*(1), 85–103.

Borrill, J., Fox, P., Flynn, M., & Roger, D. (2009). Students who self-harm: Coping style, rumination and alexithymia. *Counselling Psychology Quarterly*, *22*(4), 361–372.

Borrill, J., Lorenz, E., Abbasnejad, A. (2012). Using qualitative methods to explore non-disclosure: The example of self-injury. *International Journal of Qualitative Methods*, *11*(4), 384–398.

Bresin, K., & Schoenleber, M. (2015). Gender differences in the prevalence of nonsuicidal self-injury: A meta-analysis. *Clinical Psychology Review*, *38*, 55–64.

Browning, M. E., Morena, A., Gould, E. R. & Lloyd-Richardson, E. E. (2022). Brief ACT for undergraduates: A mixed-methods pilot investigation of acceptance and commitment therapy delivered over zoom. *Journal of College Student Psychotherapy*. Advance online publication. https://doi.org/10.1080/87568225.2022.2029659

Brownson, C., Drum, D. J., Smith, S. E., & Burton Denmark, A. (2011). Differences in suicidal experiences of male and female undergraduate and graduate students. *Journal of College Student Psychotherapy*, *25*(4), 277–294.

Calvete, E., Royuela-Colomer, E. & Maruottolo, C. (2022). Emotion dysregulation and mindfulness in non-suicidal self-injury. *Psychiatry Research*, *314*, Article 114691.

Christodoulou, V., Flaxman, P. E., & Lloyd, J. (2021). Acceptance and commitment therapy in group Format for college students. *Journal of College Counseling*, *24*(3), 210–223.

Chugani, C. D., Fuhrman, B., Abebe, K. Z., Tallis, J., Miller, E., & Coulter, R. W. S. (2020). Wellness and resilience for college and beyond: Protocol for a quasi-experimental pilot study investigating a dialectical behaviour therapy skill-infused college course. *BMJ Open*, *10*, 1–7.

Coleman, D., Black, N., Ng, J., & Blumenthal, E. (2019). Kognito's avatar-based suicide prevention training for college students: Results of a randomized controlled trial and a naturalistic evaluation. *Suicide and Life-Threatening Behavior*, *49*(6), 1735–1745. https://doi.org/10.1111/sltb.12550

Conigliaro, A., & Ward-Ciesielski, E. (2021). Associations between social contagion, group conformity characteristics, and non-suicidal self-injury. *Journal of American College Health*. Advance online publication.

Conley, C. S., Durlak, J. A., & Dickson, D. A. (2013). An evaluative review of outcome research on universal mental health promotion and prevention programs for higher education students. *Journal of American College Health*, *61*(5), 286–301. https://doi.org/10.1080/07448481.2013.802237

Conley, C. S., Durlak, J. A., & Kirsch, A. C. (2015). A meta-analysis of universal mental health prevention programs for higher education students. *Prevention Science*, *16*, 487–507.

Conley, C. S., Shapiro, J. B., Kirsch, A. C., & Durlak, J. A. (2017). A meta-analysis of indicated mental health prevention programs for at-risk higher education students. *Journal of Counseling Psychology*, *64*(2), 121–140. https://doi.org/10.1037/cou0000190

Corrigan, P. W., River, L. P., Lundin, R. K., Penn, D. L., Uphoff-Wasowski, K., Campion, J., Mathisen, J., Gagnon, C., Bergman, M., Goldstein, H., & Kubiak, M. A. (2001). Three strategies for changing attributions about severe mental illness. *Schizophrenia Bulletin*, *27*(2), 187–195.

Cross, W., Matthieu, M. M., Cerel, J., & Knox, K. L. (2007). Proximate outcomes of gatekeeper training for suicide prevention in the workplace. *Suicide and Life-Threatening Behavior*, *37*(6), 659–670.

Danitz, S., Suvak, M., & Orsillo, S. (2016). The mindful way through the semester: Evaluating the impact of integrating an acceptance-based behavioral program into a first-year experience course for undergraduates. *Behavior Therapy*, *47*(4), 487–499.

Daw, J., Margolis, R., & Wright, L. (2017). Emerging adulthood, emergent health lifestyles: Sociodemographic determinants of trajectories of smoking, binge drinking, obesity, and sedentary behavior. *Journal of Health and Social Behavior*, *58*(2), 181–197.

DeVylder, J., Yang, L. H., Goldstein, R., Ross, A. M., Oh, H., Zhou, S., Horowitz, L., & Bridge, J. A. (2022). Mental health correlates of stigma among college students with suicidal ideation: Data from the 2020–2021 Healthy Minds Study. *Stigma and Health (Washington, D.C.)*, *7*(2), 247–250.

Downs, M. F., & Eisenberg, D. (2012). Help seeking and treatment use among suicidal college students. *Journal of American College Health*, *60*(2), 104–114.

Drum, D. J., Brownson, C., Burton Denmark, A., & Smith, S. E. (2009). New data on the nature of suicidal crises in college students: Shifting the paradigm. *Professional Psychology: Research and Practice*, *40*(3), 213–222.

Fox, K. R., Franklin, J. C., Ribeiro, J. D., Kleiman, E. M., Bentley, K. H., & Nock, M. K. (2015). Meta-analysis of risk factors for nonsuicidal self-injury. *Clinical Psychology Review*, *42*, 156–167.

Franklin, J. C., Lee, K. M., Hanna, E. K., & Prinstein, M. J. (2013). Feeling worse to feel better: Pain-offset relief simultaneously stimulates positive affect and reduces negative affect. *Psychological Science*, *24*(4), 521–529.

Franz, P. J., Mou, D., Kessler, D. T., Stubbing, J., Jaroszewski, A. C., Ray, S., Cao-Silveira, V. B., Bachman, S., Schuster, S., Graupensperger, D., Alpert, J. E., Porath, M., & Nock, M. K. (2022). Digital bibliotherapy as a scalable intervention for suicidal thoughts: A randomized controlled trial. *Journal of Consulting and Clinical Psychology*, *90*(8), 626–637.

Fuhr, D. C., Salisbury, T. T., De Silva, M. J., Atif, N., van Ginneken, N., Rahman, A., & Patel, V. (2014). Effectiveness of peer-delivered interventions for severe mental illness and depression on clinical and psychosocial outcomes: A systematic review and meta-analysis. *Social Psychiatry and Psychiatric Epidemiology*, *49*(11), 1691–1702.

Gelinas, B. L., & Wright, K. D. (2013). The cessation of deliberate self-harm in a university sample: The reasons, barriers, and strategies involved. *Archives of Suicide Research*, *17*(4), 373–386.

Gholamrezaei, M., De Stefano, J., & Heath, N. L. (2017). Nonsuicidal self-injury across cultures and ethnic and racial minorities: A review. *International Journal of Psychology, 52*(4), 316–326.

Glenn, C. R., & Klonsky, D. E. (2011). Prospective prediction of nonsuicidal self-injury: A 1-year longitudinal study in young adults. *Behavior Therapy, 42*, 751–762.

Greene, D., Boyes, M., & Hasking, P. (2020). The associations between alexithymia and both non-suicidal self-injury and risky drinking: A systematic review and meta-analysis. *Journal of Affective Disorders, 260*, 140–166.

Grunberg, P. H., & Lewis, S. P. (2015). Self-injury and readiness to recover: Preliminary examination of components of the stages of change model. *Counseling Psychology Quarterly, 28*(4), 361–371.

Hamza, C. A., Robinson, K., Hasking, P. A., Heath, N. L., Lewis, S. P., Lloyd-Richardson, E., Whitlock, J., & Wilson, M. S. (2021). Educational stakeholders' attitudes and knowledge about nonsuicidal self-injury among university students: A cross-national study. *Journal of American College Health, 11*, 1–11.

Hamza, C. A., Stewart, S. L., & Willoughby, T. (2012). Examining the link between nonsuicidal self-injury and suicidal behavior: A review of the literature and an integrated model. *Clinical Psychology Review, 32*(6), 482–495.

Hamza, C. A., Willoughby, T., & Heffer, T. (2015). Impulsivity and nonsuicidal self-injury: A review and meta-analysis. *Clinical Psychology Review, 38*, 13–24.

Hasking, P., & Claes, L. (2020). Transdiagnostic mechanisms involved in nonsuicidal self-injury, risky drinking and disordered eating: Impulsivity, emotion regulation and alexithymia. *Journal of American College Health, 68*(6), 603–609.

Hawgood, J., Rimkeviciene, J., Gibson, M., McGrath, M., & Edwards, B. (2022). Reasons for living among those with lived experience entering the suicide prevention workforce. *Death Studies, 46*(4), 1009–1014.

Herman, A. M., Pilcher, N., & Duka, T. (2020). Deter the emotions: Alexithymia, impulsivity and their relationship to binge drinking. *Addictive Behaviors Reports, 12*, Article 100308.

Hilt, L. M., Nock, M. K., Lloyd-Richardson, E.E., & Prinstein, M. J. (2008). Longitudinal study of nonsuicidal self-injury among young adolescents: Rates, correlates, and preliminary test of an interpersonal model. *Journal of Early Adolescence, 28*, 455–469.

Hoff, E. R., & Muehlenkamp, J. J. (2009). Nonsuicidal self-injury in college students: The role of perfectionism and rumination. *Suicide and Life-Threatening Behavior, 39*(6), 576–587.

Hooley, J. M., Fox, K. R., & Boccagno, C. (2020). Nonsuicidal self-injury: Diagnostic challenges and current perspectives. *Neuropsychiatric Disorders and Treatment, 16*, 101–112.

Hooley, J. M., Fox, K. R., Wang, S. B., & Kwashie, A. (2018). Novel online daily diary interventions for nonsuicidal self-injury: A randomized controlled trial. *BMC Psychiatry, 18*(1), 264.

Hooley, J. M., & Franklin, J. C. (2018). Why do people hurt themselves? A new conceptual model of nonsuicidal self-injury. *Clinical Psychological Science, 6*(3), 428–451.

Itzhaky, L., Davaasambuu, S., Ellis, S. P., Cisneros-Trujillo, S., Hannett, K., Scolaro, K., Stanley, B. H., Mann, J. J., Wainberg, M. L., Oquendo, M. A., & Sublette, M. E. (2022). Twenty-six years of psychosocial interventions to reduce suicide risk in adolescents: Systematic review and meta-analysis. *Journal of Affective Disorders, 300*, 511–531.

Jao, N. C., Robinson, L. D., Kelly, P. J., Ciecierski, C. C., & Hitsman, B. (2019). Unhealthy behavior clustering and mental health status in United States college students. *Journal of American College Health, 67*(8), 790–800.

Jarvi, S., Jackson, B., Swenson, L., & Crawford, H. (2013). The impact of social contagion on non-suicidal self-injury: A review of the literature. *Archives of Suicide Research, 17*(1), 1–19.

Joiner, T. (2007). *Why people die by suicide* (paperback ed). Harvard University Press.

Kiekens, G., Bruffaerts, R., Nock, M. K., Van de Ven, M., Witteman, C., Mortier, P., Demyttenaere, K., & Claes, L. (2015). Non-suicidal self-injury among Dutch and Belgian adolescents: Personality, stress, and coping. *European Psychiatry: The Journal of the Association of European Psychiatrists, 30*(6), 743–749.

Kiekens, G., Hasking, P., Bruffaerts, R., Alonso, J., Auerbach, R. P., Bantjes, J., Benjet, C., Boyes, M., Chiu, W. T., Claes, L., Cuijpers, P., Ebert, D. D., Mak, A., Mortier, P., O'Neill, S., Sampson, N. A., Stein, D. J., Vilagut, G., Nock, M. K., & Kessler, R. C. (2023). Non-suicidal self-injury among first-year college students and its association with mental disorders: Results from the World Mental Health International College Student (WMH-ICS) initiative. *Psychological Medicine, 53*(3), 875–886.

Kiekens, G., Hasking, P., Claes, L., Boyes, M., Mortier, P., Auerbach, R. P., Cuijpers, P., Demyttenaere, K., Green, J. G., Kessler, R. C., Myin-Germeys, I., Nock, M. K., & Bruffaerts, R. (2019). Predicting the incidence of non-suicidal self-injury in college students. *European Psychiatry, 59*, 44–51.

Kiekens, G., Hasking, P., Claes, L., Mortier, P., Auerbach, R. P., Boyes, M., Cuijpers, P., Demyttenaere, K., Green, J. G., Kessler, R. C., Nock, M. K., & Bruffaerts, R. (2018). The DSM-5 nonsuicidal self-injury disorder among incoming college students: Prevalence and associations with 12-month mental disorders and suicidal thoughts and behaviors. *Depression & Anxiety, 35*, 629–637.

Kirsch, D. J., Pinder-Amaker, S. L., Morse, C., Ellison, M. L., Doerfler, L. A., & Riba, M. B. (2014). Population-based initiatives in college mental health: Students helping students to overcome obstacles. *Current Psychiatry Reports, 16*(12), 525.

Klonsky, E. D., & Muehlenkamp, J. J. (2007). Self-injury: A research review for the practitioner. *Journal of Clinical Psychology, 63*(11), 1045–1056.

Klonsky, E. D., & Olino, T. M. (2008). Identifying clinically distinct subgroups of self-injurers among young adults: A latent class analysis. *Journal of Consulting and Clinical Psychology, 76*(1), 22.

Kuentzel, J. G., Arble, E., Boutros, N., Chugani, D., & Barnett, D. (2012). Nonsuicidal self-injury in an ethnically diverse college sample. *The American Journal of Orthopsychiatry, 82*(3), 291–297.

Kwan, M. Y., Arbour-Nicitopoulos, K. P., Duku, E., & Faulkner, G. (2016). Patterns of multiple health risk-behaviours in university students and their association with mental health: Application of latent class analysis. *Health Promotion and Chronic Disease Prevention in Canada: Research, Policy and Practice, 36*(8), 163.

Lewis, S. P., Heath, N. L., Hasking, P. A., Whitlock, J. L., Wilson, M. S., & Plener, P. L. (2019). Addressing self-injury on college campuses: Institutional recommendations. *Journal of College Counseling, 22*(1), 70–82.

Lipson, S.K., Zhou, S., Abelson, S., Heinze, J., Jirsa, M., Morigney, J., Patterson, A., Singh, M. & Eisenberg, D. (2022). Trends in college student mental health and help-seeking by race/ethnicity: Findings from the national healthy minds study, 2013-2021. *Journal of Affective Disorders, 306*, 138–147.

Liu, Y., Yue, S., Hu, X., Zhu, J., Wu, Z., Wang, J., & Wu, Y. (2021). Associations between feelings/behaviors during COVID-19 pandemic lockdown and depression/anxiety after lockdown in a sample of Chinese children and adolescents. *Journal of Affective Disorders, 284*, 98–103.

Lloyd-Richardson, E. E., Perrine, N., Dierker, L., & Kelley, M. L. (2007). Characteristics and functions of non-suicidal self-injury in a community sample of adolescents. *Psychological Medicine, 37*(8), 1183–1192.

Mahmoud, J. S. R., Staten, R. "Topsy," Hall, L. A., & Lennie, T. A. (2012). The relationship among young adult college students' depression, anxiety, stress, demographics, life satisfaction, and coping styles. *Issues in Mental Health Nursing, 33*(3), 149–156.

Mandracchia, J. T., & Pendleton, S. (2015). Understanding college students' problems: Dysfunctional thinking, mental health, and maladaptive behavior. *Journal of College Student Retention: Research, Theory & Practice, 17*(2), 226–242.

Mazza, J., Dexter-Mazza, E., Miller, A., Rathus, J.H. & Murphy, H.E. (2016). *DBT skills in schools: Skills training for emotional problem solving for adolescents (DBT STEPS-A)*. Guilford Press.

Mazzeo, S. E., & Espelage, D. L. (2002). Association between childhood physical and emotional abuse and disordered eating behaviors in female undergraduates: An investigation of the mediating role of alexithymia and depression. *Journal of Counseling Psychology, 49*(1), 86–100.

Miklin, S., Mueller, A. S., Abrutyn, S., & Ordonez, K. (2019). What does it mean to be exposed to suicide?: Suicide exposure, suicide risk, and the importance of meaning-making. *Social Science & Medicine, 233*, 21–27.

Mo, P. K. H., Ko, T. T., & Xin, M. Q. (2018). School-based gatekeeper training programmes in enhancing gatekeepers' cognitions and behaviours for adolescent suicide prevention: A systematic review. *Child and Adolescent Psychiatry and Mental Health, 12*(1), 29.

Morena, A.L., Browning, M.E., & Lloyd-Richardson, E. E., (in preparation). Evaluation of a brief online gatekeeper intervention for college students: A mixed-methods approach.

Morton, M., Wang, S., Tse, K., Chung, C., Bergmans, Y., Ceniti, A., Flam, S., Johannes, R., Schade, K., Terah, F., & Rizvi, S. (2021). Gatekeeper training for friends and family of individuals at risk of suicide: A systematic review. *Journal of Community Psychology, 49*(6), 1838.

Muehlenkamp, J. J., Brausch, A., Quigley, K., & Whitlock, J. (2013). Interpersonal features and functions of nonsuicidal self-injury. *Suicide and Life-Threatening Behavior, 43*, 67–80.

Muehlenkamp, J. J., & Quinn-Lee, L. (2023). Effectiveness of a peer-led gatekeeper program: A longitudinal mixed-method analysis. *Journal of American College Health, 71*(1), 282–291.

Mullen, R. A., Tracy, P., Block-Lerner, J., Marks, D., Sandoz, E., & Ricardo, P. (2021). Curriculum-based yoga and acceptance and commitment training intervention for undergraduate students: Mixed-methods investigation. *Journal of Contextual Behavioral Science*, *19*, 92–99.

O'Connor, R. C., & Portzky, G. (2018). Looking to the future: A synthesis of new developments and challenges in suicide research and prevention. *Frontiers in Psychology*, *9*, 2139.

Pasco, S., Wallack, C., Sartin, R. M., & Dayton, R. (2012). The impact of experiential exercises on communication and relational skills in a suicide prevention gatekeeper-training program for college resident advisors. *Journal of American College Health*, *60*(2), 134–140.

Petersen, J. M., Davis, C. H., Renshaw, T. L., Levin, M. E., & Twohig, M. P. (2022). School-based acceptance and commitment therapy for adolescents with anxiety: A pilot trial. *Cognitive and Behavioral Practice*.

Pistorello, J., Fruzzetti, A. E., MacLane, C., Gallop, R., & Iverson, K. M. (2012). Dialectical behavior therapy (DBT) applied to college students: A randomized clinical trial. *Journal of Consulting and Clinical Psychology*, *80*(6), 982.

Pistorello, J., Hayes, S. C., Seeley, J., Biglan, T., Long, D. M., Levin, M. E., Kosty, D., Lillis, J., Villatte, J., MacLane, C., Vilardaga, R., Daflos, S., Hammonds, S., Locklear, A., & Hanna, E. (2016). ACT-based first year experience seminars. In J. BlockLerner & L. Cardaciotto (Eds.), *The mindfulness-informed educator: Building acceptance & psychological flexibility in higher education* (pp. 101–120). Routledge.

Pompeo-Fargnoli, A. (2022). Mental health stigma among college students: Misperceptions of perceived and personal stigmas. *Journal of American College Health*, *70*(4), 1030–1039.

Quinnett, P. G., & Bratcher, K. (1996). *Question, persuade, refer, treat: Suicide risk management inventory user's manual*. Greentree Behavioral Health.

Rallis, B. A., Esposito-Smythers, C., Disabato, D. J., Mehlenbeck, R. S., Kaplan, S., Geer, L., Adams, R., & Meehan, B. (2018). A brief peer gatekeeper suicide prevention training: Results of an open pilot trial. *Journal of Clinical Psychology*, *74*(7), 1106–1116.

Reichl, C., Heyer, A., Brunner, R., Parzer, P., Völker, J. M., Resch, F., & Kaess, M. (2016). Hypothalamic-pituitary-adrenal axis, childhood adversity and adolescent nonsuicidal self-injury. *Psychoneuroendocrinology*, *74*, 203–211.

Rein, B. A., McNeil, D. W., Hayes, A. R., Hawkins, T. A., Ng, H. M., & Yura, C. A. (2018). Evaluation of an avatar-based training program to promote suicide prevention awareness in a college setting. *Journal of American College Health*, *66*(5), 401–411.

Roses in the Ocean. (2016). *Lived experience of suicide*. https://rosesintheocean.com.au/livedexperience-suicide/

Ross, S. G., DeHay, T., & Deiling, M. (2021). The Suicide Prevention for College Student Gatekeepers Program: A pilot study. *Crisis*, *42*(1), 48–55.

Serras, A., Saules, K. K., Cranford, J. A., & Eisenberg, D. (2010). Self-injury, substance use, and associated risk factors in a multi-campus probability sample of college students. *Psychology of addictive behaviors*, *24*(1), 119.

Shtivelband, A., Aloise-Young, P. A., & Chen, P. Y. (2015). Sustaining the effects of gatekeeper suicide prevention training: A qualitative study. *Crisis: The Journal of Crisis Intervention and Suicide Prevention*, *36*(2), 102–109. https://doi.org/10.1027/0227-5910/a000304

Smith-Millman, M., Bernstein, L., Link, N., Hoover, S., & Lever, N. (2022). Effectiveness of an online suicide prevention program for college faculty and students. *Journal of American College Health*, *70*(5), 1457–1464.

Srivastava, S., Tamir, M., McGonigal, K. M., John, O. P., & Gross, J. J. (2009). The social costs of emotional suppression: A prospective study of the transition to college. *Journal of Personality and Social Psychology*, *96*(4), 883–897.

Stargell, N. A., Zoldan, C. A., Kress, V. E., Walker-Andrews, L., & Whisenhunt, J. L. (2018). Student nonsuicidal self-injury: A protocol for school counselors. *Professional School Counseling*, *21*(1), 37–46.

Suicide Prevention Resource Center. (2009). *Evaluating gatekeeper effectiveness: Use of case vignettes*. Retrieved from https://sprc.org/system/files/private/event training/C4EChrisAlbertSAMSHAGKTcasescenarios.pdf

Taylor, P. J., Jomar, K., Dhingra, K., Forrester, R., Shahmalak, U., & Dickson, J. M. (2018). A meta-analysis of the prevalence of different functions of non-suicidal self-injury. *Journal of Affective Disorders*, *227*, 759–769.

Thew, H., McDermott, D., & Willmott, D. (2018). *Mindfulness as a psychological approach to managing self-harming behaviours: Application and review within clinical settings*. Crime, Security and Society. http://eprints.hud.ac.uk/journal/css/

Turner, B. J., Chapman, A. L., & Gratz, K. L. (2014). Why stop self-injuring? Development of the Reasons to Stop Self-Injury Questionnaire. *Behavior Modification, 38*(1), 69–106. https://doi.org/10.1177/0145445513508977

Turner, B. J., Helps, C. E., & Ames, M. E. (2022). Stop self-injuring, then what? Psychosocial risk associated with initiation and cessation of nonsuicidal self-injury from adolescence to early adulthood. *Journal of Psychopathology and Clinical Science, 131*(1), Article 45.

Van Orden, K., Witte, T., Cukrowicz, K., Braithwaite, S., Selby, E., Joiner, T. (2010). The interpersonal theory of suicide. *Psychological Review, 117*(2), 575–600.

Viskovich, S., & Pakenham, K. I. (2020). Randomized controlled trial of a web-based acceptance and commitment therapy (ACT) program to promote mental health in university students. *Journal of Clinical Psychology, 76*(6), 929–951.

Wallack, C., & Pasco, S. (2006). *Campus Connect: A suicide prevention training for gatekeepers*. Syracuse University.

Westefeld, J. S., Homaifar, B., Spotts, J., Furr, S., Range, L., & Werth, J. L. (2005). Perceptions concerning college student suicide: Data from four universities. *Suicide and Life-Threatening Behavior, 35*(6), 640–645.

Wester, K., Trepal, H., & King, K. (2018). Nonsuicidal self-injury: Increased prevalence in engagement. *Suicide and Life-Threatening Behavior, 48*(6), 690–698.

Westers, N. J., Muehlenkamp, J., & Lau, M. (2016). SOARS model: Risk assessment of nonsuicidal self-injury. *Contemporary Pediatrics*.

Westers, N. J., Rehfuss, M., Olson, L., & Wiemann, C. M. (2014). An exploration of adolescent nonsuicidal self-injury and religious coping. *International Journal of Adolescent Medicine and Health, 26*(3), 345–349.

Whisenhunt, J. L., Chang, C. Y., Brack, G. L., Orr, J., Adams, L. G., Paige, M. R., McDonald, C. P. L., & O'Hara, C. (2015). Self-injury and suicide: Practical information for college counselors. *Journal of College Counseling, 18*, 275–288.

Whitlock, J., Muehlenkamp, J., & Eckenrode, J. (2008). Variation in nonsuicidal self-injury: Identification and features of latent classes in a college population of emerging adults. *Journal of Clinical Child and Adolescent Psychology, 37*(4), 725–735.

Whitlock, J., Muehlenkamp, J., Purington, A., Eckenrode, J., Barreira, P., Baral Abrams, G., Marchell, T., Kress, V., Girard, K., Chin, C., & Knox, K. (2011). Nonsuicidal self-injury in a college population: General trends and sex differences. *Journal of American College Health, 59*(8), 691–698.

Wilcox, H. C., Arria, A. M., Caldeira, K. M., Vincent, K. B., Pinchevsky, G. M., & O'Grady, K. E. (2012). Longitudinal predictors of past-year non-suicidal self-injury and motives among college students. *Psychological Medicine, 42*(4), 717–726.

Willoughby, T., Heffer, T., & Hamza, C. A. (2015). The link between nonsuicidal self-injury and acquired capability for suicide: A longitudinal study. *Journal of Abnormal Psychology, 124*(4), 1110–1115.

World Health Organization. (2021). *Suicide*. https://www.who.int/news-room/fact-sheets/detail/suicide

Wyman, P. A., Brown, C. H., Inman, J., Cross, W., Schmeelk-Cone, K., Guo, J., & Pena, J. B. (2008). Randomized trial of a gatekeeper program for suicide prevention: 1-year impact on secondary school staff. *Journal of Consulting and Clinical Psychology, 76*(1), 104–115.

Yonemoto, N., Kawashima, Y., Endo, K., & Yamada, M. (2019). Gatekeeper training for suicidal behaviors: A systematic review. *Journal of Affective Disorders, 246*, 506–514.

Zareian, B., & Klonsky, E. D. (2019). Nonsuicidal and suicidal self-injury. In J. J. Washburn (Ed.), *Nonsuicidal self-injury: Advances in research and practice* (pp. 109–124). Routledge.

Zinzow, H. M., Thompson, M. P., Fulmer, C. B., Goree, J., & Evinger, L. (2020). Evaluation of a brief suicide prevention training program for college campuses. *Archives of Suicide Research, 24*(1), 82–95.

CHAPTER 50

Digital Interventions for Nonsuicidal Self-Injury

Kaylee P. Kruzan *and* Janis L. Whitlock

Abstract

This chapter focuses on digital interventions for nonsuicidal self-injury. In line with the presence and influence of new media in daily life, Internet-based websites and applications have become popular places for clinical and broader public health interventions. The proliferation of new digital technologies has resulted in considerations about how to best design resources capable of meeting people in online spaces and how to augment the accessibility of existing evidence-based interventions. Thus, researchers, clinicians, and other health service professionals must be aware of how to assess the strengths and limitations of digital offerings. The chapter discusses existing clinical trials of digital interventions, such as Autobiographical Self-Enhancement Training (ASET) and Self-injury: Treatment, Assessment and Recovery (STAR). It also considers user engagement, safety, privacy, risk management, ethics, and the accessibility of digital interventions.

Key Words: internet, media, digital interventions, accessibility, clinical trials, safety, privacy, risk management, ethics, evidence-based interventions

Introduction

The rise of media influence in human life has evolved in ways that would have been unthinkable even a century ago. More than 90% of American adults have internet access in their home and 85% of them go online daily (Perrin & Atske, 2021a, 2021b). Moreover, nearly all U.S. adolescents (95%) have a smartphone, with 45% reporting almost constant use as a way to pass time (Schaeffer, 2019). For adults and youth alike, contemporary internet affordances have rendered it a go-to for pretty much everything including connecting to others (known and unknown), being entertained, learning new things, and exchanging support.

It is not surprising, then, that internet-based websites and applications have become a popular place for clinical and broader public health interventions. This is especially salient since not only has the internet become a default resource for mental health information, but it has also become a standard resource for individuals looking for help, informally through support groups and other forums, and more formally through online or app-based clinical interventions. The tendency is even more pronounced for younger users, who have grown up alongside the internet and reflexively turn there for resources and support (see Pritchard & Lewis, this volume). Interventions and resources delivered through online and mobile technologies are thus promising as they are capable of meeting people where they are and may more seamlessly fit within their daily routines and lifestyles.

While there is strong evidence for the efficacy of digital interventions, when compared to standard treatment for common mental health conditions like depression and anxiety (Firth, Torous, Nicholas, Carney, Pratap, et al., 2017; Firth, Torous, Nicholas, Carney, Rosenbaum, et al., 2017; Linardon et al., 2019), there has been much less work focused on the potential of digital interventions and resources for nonsuicidal self-injury (NSSI). This is surprising given low rates of treatment among individuals who engage in NSSI for reasons including, but not limited to, stigma, fears of disclosure, not perceiving NSSI to be an issue, and structural barriers such as cost, time, and geography (Fortune et al., 2008; Michelmore & Hindley, 2012; Whitlock et al., 2011; Whitlock et al., 2006). Moreover, current evidence-based treatments for NSSI are frequently resource and time intensive, making them inaccessible to those who could otherwise reap benefit (Gratz & Gunderson, 2006; Linehan, 1993). Digital interventions and resources for NSSI represent a promising potential pathway to provide evidence-based support and resources to individuals who otherwise may not be able, or willing, to engage with traditional treatments.

Brief Chapter Overview

The goal of the present chapter is to provide an entry into digital interventions for NSSI. First, the chapter reviews the current state of empirical evidence supporting the use of digital interventions for NSSI. It then turns to a review of existing clinical trials of digital interventions, including randomized controlled trials (RCTs) and pilot trials. This is followed by formative work highlighting the needs and preferences of this population as they relate to digital interventions and resources. These two early sections provide necessary background for the remainder of the chapter, which focuses on practical and ethical considerations for researchers developing digital interventions for, and clinicians working with, individuals who engage in NSSI. The chapter outlines an affordance framework useful in thinking through different modalities and delivery mechanisms for digital intervention (DI). Finally, the chapter concludes with challenges and recommendations for future work in this area.

Part I: Current State of Empirical Evidence on NSSI Digital Intervention

Interest in the use of technologies to deliver and enhance mental health treatment is not novel. However, the proliferation of new digital technologies, many of which are mobile and internet-accessible, has led to considerations about how to best design resources capable of meeting people in online spaces visited daily and about how to improve or augment accessibility of evidence-based interventions. This is an important line of inquiry because, as mentioned, individuals with lived NSSI experience are often hesitant to disclose their behaviors or seek face-to-face help (Ammerman et al., 2021; Armiento et al., 2014; Fox et al., 2022) (see Hasking et al., this volume). Many also face other significant structural barriers such as cost and physical accessibility, as well as attitudinal barriers to help-seeking, such as perceived stigma, reluctance to disclose, and fear of giving up effective, but maladaptive, coping strategies (Fortune et al., 2008; Michelmore & Hindley, 2012; Whitlock et al., 2011; Whitlock et al., 2006).

Despite these barriers, many individuals report being open to receiving help and resources through online and digital platforms. Research has shown that people often use the internet to seek information about NSSI, to connect with others with shared NSSI experiences, and access coping resources (Frost & Casey, 2016; Gould et al., 2002; Horgan & Sweeney, 2010; Ybarra & Eaton, 2005). In one study, one third of young people with a history of NSSI reported seeking help online, and those who engaged in online help-seeking were younger, reported more frequent and recent NSSI behaviors, and were significantly more distressed than those who had not sought help online (Frost & Casey, 2016). This suggests that, along with increasing access, digital interventions may be able to reach those *at highest risk of serious harm.*

Digital interventions offer a promising alternative to address unmet needs, intervention hesitancy, and structural barriers. They can also be used to augment in-person therapeutic modalities, such as for use between visits. For example, prior work has shown that an app (DBT Coach) focused on dialectical behavior therapy (DBT) skills was perceived to be useful to patients with NSSI who were enrolled in traditional in-person DBT therapy (Rizvi et al., 2016). Additionally, a new web-based treatment for adolescents who engage in NSSI (emotion regulation individual therapy for adolescents; ERITA) includes an app as a complement to facilitate tracking and skills practice, and was perceived to be a useful and flexible way to engage in treatment in recent qualitative work (Simonsson et al., 2021).

In addition to offering a greater range of access opportunities to evidence-based interventions, digital spaces are ripe for the development and implementation of novel, light touch, or low intensity, interventions and resources (Baumel et al., 2020). The ubiquity of different internet-based technologies in daily life, including mobile devices and wearables, makes it possible to consider interventions that are delivered across several technological platforms. These interventions may have no clear analogue to offline offerings but can be used to support individuals in self-directed management of NSSI impulses, behaviors, and underlying contributors either as a low-risk prelude to more formal interventions or therapy or as an addendum to other approaches.

Finally, emerging algorithm-driven risk detection and monitoring capabilities provide opportunities for highly personalized, targeted digital NSSI prevention, awareness campaigns, and delivery of just-in-time adaptive interventions (JITAIs) (Coppersmith et al., 2022). These new technical affordances are increasingly capable of integrating complex and in-the-moment data gathered by smartphones or wearable devices. The result is rapid detection and response interventions that are likely to be increasingly responsive to a variety of user characteristics, including, but not limited to, user motivation and readiness to change, and modality and delivery preferences.

This is a growing area of research, so at present there is limited evidence for the efficacy of digital interventions for NSSI. However, the studies that have been conducted are promising. There is also strong preliminary support for the feasibility and acceptability of digital interventions among individuals with NSSI.

Efficacy Trials of Digital Interventions for NSSI

In a recent review of 22 trials for digital (web- and mobile-) interventions for self-injurious thoughts and behaviors, broadly defined, the majority of the work focused on suicidal ideation, with just four trials examining NSSI specifically, and two trials focused on self-injurious behaviors without distinguishing between those with or without suicidal intent (i.e., henceforth referred to as "self-harm") (Arshad et al., 2020). Of the 22 trials, most involved adult samples (k = 16) and the majority used mobile phones as the main delivery platform (nine apps, four text-messaging based interventions). Seven interventions translated established therapies to internet-based websites, while others were designed for specific purposes such as skills practice or used an experimental paradigm. This chapter focuses on trials explicitly examining NSSI or self-harm outcomes, although DIs that tap into targets of particular relevance for NSSI may also illuminate promising intervention components.

Digital Interventions: NSSI

Trials of DIs assessing NSSI as a primary outcome include two DIs based on psychotherapeutic principles from existing treatments, namely, DBT and ERGT, and two that focus on more experimental targets (e.g., aversive conditioning, self-criticism) derived from theoretical models of NSSI or suicide. We include a final DI which was not included in the Arshad et al. (2020) review, but is currently being trialed and is based on cognitive behavioral therapy (CBT) and DBT principles.

DBT Coach is a mobile app designed to promote skills generalization (e.g., practicing skills in real life and applying them outside therapy) as an adjunct to treatment for individuals with borderline personality disorder (BPD). The app includes content from the four primary evidence-based DBT modules (e.g., mindfulness, distress tolerance, emotion regulation, and interpersonal effectiveness) and is intended to assist users in choosing and applying DBT skills in moments of distress. The app was introduced as an adjunct to six months of standard DBT, in a small pilot trial of 16 individuals with BPD and NSSI or recent suicide attempts (Rizvi et al., 2016). After just three months, app use was associated with reductions in urges to self-harm, NSSI frequency, and subjective distress. In an earlier quasi-experimental study of the same platform, 22 individuals with co-occurring substance use and BPD used the app for around two weeks. Findings showed that app use was associated with improved self-efficacy and emotion regulation (Rizvi et al., 2011); however, participants self-rated interest in the app waned over time. These studies provide preliminary evidence of this adjunctive app-based DI to improve both targets relevant to NSSI, and NSSI outcomes.

The second DI, ERITA (Olsen et al., 2021; Simonsson et al., 2021), is a 12-week web-based intervention adapted from a manualized treatment for adults with BPD (Emotion Regulation Group Therapy, Gratz & Gunderson, 2006). The treatment targets emotion regulatory capacity to reduce NSSI frequency in adolescents, through web-based modules that provide skills training in emotional awareness, acceptance, impulse control, validation, and valued directions. The modules consist of psychoeducational texts, audio, short films, and weekly homework. In addition to the web modules, ERITA includes light-touch support from a therapist (e.g., brief reminders and check-ins), a parent-facing psychoeducation program, and a complementary mobile app. The app is intended to facilitate daily reports of NSSI behaviors and impulses, and it reminds users to do at home skill exercises. In a preliminary open trial of this intervention, 25 adolescents showed improvements in global functioning and emotion dysregulation as well as a significant pre-post reduction of 69% in NSSI over 6 months (Bjureberg et al., 2018). Qualitative interviews with adolescents and their caregivers following treatment suggest that it was generally accepted by both stakeholder groups, with adolescents completing 9 of 11 modules on average (Simonsson et al., 2021). A full RCT of this intervention is underway.

The next two interventions focus on novel or experimental targets derived from the Benefits and Barriers Model (Hooley & Franklin, 2018). Therapeutic Evaluative Conditioning (TEC) is an experimental DI wherein adults with self-injurious thoughts and behaviors (SITBs) are asked to pair self-related words (e.g., my and I) with images depicting self-injury, suicide, and death in one- to two-minute sessions (Franklin et al., 2016). This app, which is based on aversive conditioning, is meant to decrease aversion to the self and increase aversion to SITBs. Across three RCTs, TEC produced mixed results for NSSI. In one trial, TEC was associated with reductions in NSSI over the course of four weeks, relative to a control condition. However, no effects were observed in the other two RCTs, and results were not sustained at follow-up periods. The app is not available to the public and the researchers note challenges with engagement including low adherence (29% of TEC participants never opened the app) and low use rates. Rigorous future testing would be needed to determine whether this brief DI is useful for NSSI and in what contexts.

Next, Hooley et al. (2018) examined Autobiographical Self-Enhancement Training (ASET), an online daily diary intervention. This was a cognitive expressive writing intervention aimed at enhancing positive self-worth and reducing self-criticism in adults with NSSI. In a three-arm RCT comparing ASET to expressive writing (EW) and active control (journaling), participants were asked to write for five minutes a day about something that made them feel good about themselves (ASET condition), something that bothered them (EW condition), or events of the day in a factual manner (journaling condition). Significant reductions in NSSI were noted across all groups; however, there were no significant differences between treatment and control conditions (Hooley et al., 2018). Additionally, effects on self-criticism and NSSI were not sustained at three-month follow up. Interestingly, the authors described that the ASET condition was perceived to be less enjoyable, and participants completed fewer overall sessions than either of the controls, pointing again to challenges of engagement with digital tools.

Finally, Self-injury: Treatment, Assessment and Recovery (STAR) is a DI for adolescents and young adults who engage in NSSI, and is currently in trial (Kaess et al., 2019). STAR is derived from the Cutting Down Program (CDP), which is a form of manualized cognitive behavioral therapy for adolescents. Although there are currently no published data from the trial of the online intervention (Kaess et al., 2019), an RCT of the face-to-face treatment showed promise. STAR includes 10 modules focused on (1) information about CBT and NSSI, (2) reasons for engaging in NSSI, (3) testing alternative behaviors, and (4) maintenance of alternative behaviors. The program is to be completed in 8 to 12 sessions and includes once-weekly contact with a case manager through email or phone, as well as a moderated online group chat, and between session homework and exercises. Findings from the in-person RCT ($n = 74$) showed equally significant reductions of NSSI frequency (past six months) across the treatment and control groups, with a large effect size for treatment (d = .99). Moreover, quicker reductions were observed in the treatment group, suggesting the efficiency of the intervention.

Digital Interventions: Self-Harm

Two additional digital interventions target self-harm (self-injury with *and* without suicidal intent). BlueIce is a mobile app designed as an adjunct face-to-face therapy for young people who self-harm (Stallard et al., 2018). The app contains coping strategies rooted in CBT and DBT, including activities meant to improve mood, a mood diary, and safety checks. A preliminary 12-week open trial with 44 adolescents, showed post-use improvement on depression and anxiety symptoms, and 73% of users reported having stopped or decreased self-injury over the course of the trial. Additionally, qualitative feedback from participants following the trial suggest that among perceived benefits of the app were facilitating mood tracking, trigger identification, and distraction (Grist et al., 2018). Similar to DBT Coach, findings from BlueIce point to the promise of adjunctive digital interventions focused on skill development.

Finally, a small open trial investigated a supportive text-messaging service for psychiatric outpatients with mental illness and high suicidal ideation. Self-injurious behaviors were included as an outcome measure given high co-occurrence in this population (Kodama et al., 2016). The service specifically aimed to promote help-seeking behaviors through informative texts sent twice per week over a six-month period. Messages were developed by clinicians and discussed managing stress, mental health maintenance, medication adherence, sleep hygiene, getting help, and connections to local sources. In a pilot uncontrolled experiment, the intervention was associated with reductions in frequency of self-injurious behaviors, suicidal ideation, and increases in social service engagement posttreatment. This model of intervention is consistent with Caring Contacts—wherein patients receive follow-up communication, sometimes via digital technologies, upon discharge from hospitalization after suicide attempt (Larsen et al., 2017).

In summary, existing research on DI for NSSI is limited, but results thus far have shown promise. The trials above provide preliminary evidence for the feasibility and acceptability of DIs for NSSI. Notably, of the interventions reviewed most were mobile apps, with just one texting and two web-based module interventions, suggesting that we have yet to tap into the many different modalities that may have promise (described later). Many interventions with preliminary support focus on skill building and are informed by evidence-based treatments. However, more novel/experimental targets also produced promising, albeit inconsistent results.

Challenges with Digital Interventions

A noted challenge characterizing most DIs, including those mentioned above, is promoting sustained engagement with the intervention over time (Andrews, 2018; Baumel et al., 2019). Many studies reported early dropout or limited use patterns. Several factors are thought to contribute to user engagement. For example, a recent systematic review of studies focused on barriers and facilitators of user engagement with DIs, 208 studies were identified (Borghouts et al., 2021). Identified barriers included technical issues and a lack of perceived personalization. Facilitators were DIs that provided insights into health and social connectedness and allowed users to feel in control of their health. Since improving user engagement is likely contingent upon developing a resource that meets a user's needs, preferences, and lifestyle, formative work with the target population (individuals with lived experience of NSSI) is critical. In the next section we describe some studies aimed at understanding the role digital interventions may have in their recovery journeys.

Formative Research to Understand Digital Intervention Needs and Preferences

In addition to the clinical trials of DIs described above, there have been qualitative studies focused on how the needs of individuals with lived experience of NSSI can be met through the design of digital tools. Much of this work comes from the field of human computer interaction (HCI) and employs user-centered design (UCD) methodologies including formative elicitation activities such as interviews and focus groups, needs assessments, and design feedback studies as well as usability testing (For a more detailed overview on user-centered design for NSSI DIs, see Kruzan, Meyerhoff, et al., 2021).

In HCI, it is common to approach the development of new tech-based interventions (or products) from a person-centered approach, by directly engaging potential users in the research and design process. This grounds the development of DIs in the specific needs, challenges, and preferences of the individuals they are ultimately meant to serve. Indeed, several co-design studies have solicited feedback from individuals with lived experience of NSSI, clinicians, and other stakeholders to identify preferences in regard to digital tools for this population (Birbeck et al., 2017; Hetrick et al., 2018).

Table 50.1 displays a list of desired content and features. This list is not comprehensive but provides a general overview of common findings across studies. Young people often report the value of tools that help them develop or reinforce positive coping skills, which is aligned with the coping skill features already incorporated in many of the current DIs for NSSI. Findings also surface several design challenges. For example, young people often report wanting to engage with digital tools autonomously but note the value of social support and sharing of experiences. This suggests the value of including shared stories or peer support as an optional, but not required, feature. Additionally, personalization and perceived resonance with individual NSSI experiences is critical to engagement. Finally, while study findings often referenced a desire for a digital tool to highlight personal patterns of relevance, they also acknowledge potential harms from tracking NSSI over time (e.g., exacerbate symptoms). Several formative studies and their key findings are discussed below.

A 2018 co-design workshop hosted by researchers focused on designing a self-monitoring app to provide young people and their clinician feedback and information between in-person visits. Sixteen clinicians and eight young adults with depression and suicidal ideation, including those with NSSI, gathered to provide feedback on their needs. The workshops involved participants sketching ideas, discussing with the group, and group prioritization of features. Real-time distractions, mood-tracking capabilities that were linked to brief coping interventions, and easy access to emergency services in moments of crisis were the most important services identified by the young people (Hetrick et al., 2018). As such, the final tool included features for mood-monitoring, brief interventions based on distress tolerance, and distraction resources.

Table 50.1 Summary of Desired Content or Platform Features From Formative Research

Desired content or platform feature	Examples
Brief on demand coping skills exercises	Real-time distractions, mindfulness, distress tolerance
Psychoeducation on NSSI	Information about NSSI, alternatives to NSSI coping strategies
Self-knowledge about patterns	Identification of triggers, mood tracking
Opportunity for social connection	Opportunities to exchange helpful strategies and get support
Features that address NSSI, as well as related concerns	Resources for comorbid mental health concerns, help-seeking options

Similarly, a co-design study by Birbeck et al. (2017) gathered young people with NSSI and clinicians to participate in an NSSI-focused hackathon. All stakeholders were provided several "challenges," among them: developing a technology that (a) might be used by people who self-injure to support them in times of need and (b) will improve our understanding of NSSI. Stakeholders were divided into teams to brainstorm and make prototypes of such a tool. In this work, features that enabled coping, including active distraction, mindfulness, self-reflection, and distress tolerance activities, were identified as particularly desired components (Birbeck et al., 2017).

A three-part study including interviews with 4 counselors, and a survey and elicitation workshop with 11 young people with lived NSSI experience produced similar themes (Honary et al., 2020). Counselors emphasized the potential for digital tools to facilitate identification of triggers, distraction, psychoeducation about NSSI, and emotion regulation. Young people similarly expressed a desire for features that helped with distraction, and use of coping strategies, and added the importance of the intervention providing them with a greater sense of control, nudges, and social connection. Given the relevance of self-tracking as a digital intervention for mental health (Murnane et al., 2016; Rooksby et al., 2014), young people were also asked how they felt about the potential app's tracking capabilities. Interestingly, many participants expressed ambivalence, with some describing how tracking may actually exacerbate their symptoms (Honary et al., 2020). This finding is in general alignment with the broader literature on self-tracking, which indicates that a pitfall with common self-tracking technologies like mood apps is delivering useful next steps. Generally, participants want to become aware of their struggles so they can take action, which requires the tool to offer suggestions on how to move forward (Schueller et al., 2021).

In an interview study with 15 adolescent girls (12–18) meeting criteria for NSSI disorder, researchers assessed participants' perceived needs and preferences for smartphone-based interventions. Since engagement is a consistent issue in DIs, the study aimed to develop a framework for designing engaging DI for adolescents with NSSI (Čuš et al., 2021). Some of the key findings from these interviews were the importance of easy-to-implement emotion regulation strategies and coping strategies for managing urges to self-injure—particularly complete distraction. Many young people also reported difficulties reaching out for support and interest in customization and psychoeducation around alternatives to NSSI.

In another project focused on developing a DI for young people who engage in NSSI, researchers conducted semistructured interviews with seven young people. The interviews were meant to identify young peoples' experiences of NSSI urges and triggers, and to understand how a technology may be useful. Two key recommendations surfaced in these preliminary interviews (Hetrick et al., 2020). First, young people felt that an app-based intervention could be useful if it allowed them to store things that would make them feel good, and improve mood, in moments when they were experiencing an urge to self-injure. Second, they wanted to be able to share or exchange helpful strategies with others who have similar experiences. This second component of peer exchange, points to the need to find ways to safely allow for peer exchange—be that through peer stories, vignettes, or a forum.

While the above studies focus on app-based tools, text-messaging services have also been developed. Owens and colleagues designed a text-messaging based intervention for adolescents who engage in self-harm (Owens et al., 2011). In this project, researchers engaged adolescents with lived NSSI experience, caregivers, and clinical stakeholders in a series of six elicitation workshops aimed at understanding user needs and preferences and developing and refining messages. In workshops, potential users were presented with messages that were co-developed in the first workshop and asked whether they felt the messages would influence their urges to self-harm. This early elicitation work revealed broad support for a text-messaging service as an adjunct to clinical treatment. Texting was seen as a private and comfortable method for contact and perceived as less intrusive than phone calls. However, this work also revealed that a generic and predetermined bank of messages was unlikely to be perceived as caring or useful by all users. Researchers thus refined the intervention to enable individual tailoring by supporting individuals in authoring their own self-efficacy messages to be stored and sent during predetermined times throughout the day.

A final study focuses on help-seeking among young people with recent (within 12 month) self-harm (Rowe et al., 2018). In this work, researchers solicited feedback from young people and clinicians on the needs and help-seeking preferences of this population. In turn, they developed a web-based decisional aid (DA) that walks young people through a series of help-seeking options, help-seeking attributes of importance (e.g., confidentiality), and concerns, which users provide ratings on, and then the DA suggests options based on those self-ratings. In a feasibility and acceptability trial, wherein 10 youths between 12 and 18 years old received the decisional aid or were in a control group (n = 13) the DA produced good acceptability, with all 10 participants reporting that they would follow the DA advice, that it changed their attitudes toward help-seeking, and that they would likely recommend it to others. Qualitative interviews after the trial revealed a preference for the tool to address multiple mental health conditions (e.g., depression and anxiety) in addition to help-seeking for self-harm. This finding highlights a potential need to focus on transdiagnostic features, as well as coping skills that are relevant for managing urges and other symptoms associated with mental health and well-being.

In summary, formative work focused on understanding the needs and preferences of this population has provided insights into what is, and is not, perceived to be valuable. Overwhelmingly, these studies demonstrate a clear need for access to coping skills for use in moments when an urge to self-injure arises for both individuals in treatment and those not treatment-engaged who were self-managing their NSSI. Several studies pointed to the need to be able to customize or make the tool personally relevant, with user-generated content or options for users to choose from. These studies also provide support for further development of technologies targeting NSSI, and related aspects of mental health or well-being. Tools that went through usability tests all provide early evidence for their acceptability and desirability among people with lived experience of NSSI.

Part 2: Future Directions in Digital Intervention for NSSI
Like the broader field of digital mental health, most existing DIs for NSSI have sought to translate elements of evidence-based treatments (e.g., DBT and CBT) into digital formats. Doing so has the potential to increase the accessibility and scalability of these treatments, yet, proceeding to do so without also considering and adjusting for the fact that formal treatments are optimized for face-to-face contexts, and for individuals who encounter formal in-person mental healthcare, can be inadvertently limiting. Digital interventions designed with attention to the unique benefits, constraints, and affordances of the platform can offer new paths for the delivery of evidence-based services, and may also enable researchers to identify novel treatment targets, a widely noted need in the field of NSSI and SITB intervention (Fox et al., 2020). The following section is meant to provide a brief overview of key considerations for scholars working with digital NSSI interventions. It includes a review of benefits and constraints of different platforms and highlights some promising directions for future work.

Affordances of Digital Technologies and Their Relation to NSSI Intervention
An affordance lens can be useful when thinking through what digital format is most appropriate for a given intervention target. The affordances framework originated in the work of ecological psychologist Gibson (1977), and was later adapted by the information technologies and design field to explain features and functions of technological platforms, as they relate to perceived uses of technology (Gibson, 1977; Norman, 1988). An affordance relates to actual possibilities for action with technology. For example, at the most basic level, a chair affords sitting because it has a flat surface and is appropriately tall to accommodate an average size human. Perceived affordances, an expansion of the term, relate to actions a user perceives to be possible which informs how they are likely to interact, and thus what benefit they can derive. For example, a technology may have the capacity to facilitate social connection but be designed in a way that this possibility is not readily perceived by users.

Affordances represent the benefits or possibilities of the technology, as well as constraints. This framework can be especially useful when thinking through what type of platform might be best matched for a specific intervention (or intervention component). For example, a virtual reality (VR) intervention might not be the best match for a purely psychoeducational program because some of its key affordances are full immersion and embodiment, but this can come at the cost of ease and accessibility. Psychoeducational content can be easily delivered through a web-based program, which requires less complexity, is easily accessible, and may have a shallower learning curve. In contrast, the affordances of full immersion and embodiment may make VR an excellent choice for interventions that are meant to engage targets such as interoceptive capacity, body regard, and self-compassion. Indeed, the properties of immersion and embodiment have been leveraged in prior research on VR's clinical utility in engaging these targets (for comprehensive reviews, see Ferrer-García & Gutiérrez-Maldonado, 2012; Valmaggia et al., 2016) yet the therapeutic value of VR for NSSI has not yet been extensively considered (with some formative exceptions Kruzan et al., 2020; Nararro-Haro et al., 2016).

In the following section we detail five categories of technological affordances that can be informative in making decisions about digital interventions for NSSI: social, cognitive, identity-based, affective, and functional (Gibson, 1977; Hartson, 2003; Sutcliffe et al., 2011). A brief description of each and every examples is provided below. For more on affordances in the context of digital technologies, please see: (Moreno & D'Angelo, 2019; Wong et al., 2020). Table 50.2 displays benefits, constraints, and opportunities for NSSI DI design.

Social affordances refer to the degree to which technologies facilitate social connection and social exchange through their structure or perceived use. By their nature, communication technologies usually afford some socialization and connection with others. Social media are high in social affordances as they have specific features that facilitate connection and exchange, as well as features that quantify and make sociability highly visible and explicit. In contrast, mobile apps can range from completely self-guided (low social) to tools that share prerecorded, structured peer stories (moderate social) to fully interactive with groups (high social). Text-messaging interventions also allow for connection, but the medium is limited to an asynchronous back-and-forth exchange between two or more people. Text-messaging offers a more controlled way to deliver content, potentially mitigate risks of larger peer support platforms where young people may be exposed to harmful NSSI content. However, texting requires the individual to respond, and does not allow for "lurking"—or simply reading posts for resonance. Since interpersonal dynamics are frequently related to NSSI (Prinstein et al., 2009; Tatnell et al., 2014) and social support is critically important in recovery from NSSI (Kruzan & Whitlock, 2019; Lewis et al., 2019), the degree to which a technology has social affordances is important to consider.

Cognitive affordances refer to the ability of the technology to connect users with information and direct attention and provide opportunities for further skill building. A cognitive affordance of a web-based psychoeducation program is that it facilitates the delivery of information in a straightforward way. Web programs may be less cognitively taxing than technologies with many different inputs such as mobile apps with modules, a central hub, and a chat agent. Another consideration is the balance of "push" or "pull" elements within a technology. Pull elements require a user to initiate interaction with the technology, whereas push elements initiate the interaction for user response. Naturally, pull elements such as notifications and alerts are good at capturing attention but can

Table 50.2 Possible Benefits and Constraints of Digital Intervention Formats/Platforms

Intervention formats/Platforms	Possible benefits	Possible constraints	NSSI opportunities
Web-based interventions and resources	• Very efficient at delivering information; ease of use (Cognitive) • Ubiquitous, Relative ease of access and use (Functional) • Capable of supporting content in a variety of different formats (e.g., video, text, and interactive features) (Functional, Affective) • Often allows users to move back and forth freely and repeat content (Functional)	• Usually does not include many opportunities for identity formation/experimentation (Identity) • Can include features that enable social connection and exchange; but usually limited (Social) • Affective (Moderate): Emotions can be induced through graphics, stories, etc. (Affective) • Primarily a "pull" technology; quality of internet connection can vary significantly; requires a person to be at the location of the computer, sometimes at a specific time, perhaps limiting accessibility and/or privacy (Functional)	• Structured delivery of psychoeducation; structured practice of NSSI coping skills; most easily adapted for manualized intervention • NSSI example: • 12- week ERITA program (Bjureberg et al., 2018) • NSSI informational websites (CRPSIR, SOIS)
Mobile applications (apps) (Franklin et al., 2016; Rizvi et al., 2016; Rizvi & Steffel, 2014; Stallard et al., 2018)	• Mobile enables possibilities for just in time intervention (Functional) • Ability to use push and pull elements for engagement (Functional, Cognitive) • Opportunities with passive sensing (audio, location, keystrokes) (Cognitive) • Can be made easily accessible through app store (Functional) • Emotions can be induced through graphics, stories (Affective) • Can include features that enable social connection and exchange, or the sharing of peer stories (Social)	• Data capacity and storage limitations, which could result in increased likelihood of technical difficulties (Functional) • Must compete with other attentional demands on phone (e.g., notifications); Most apps are used a few times and disregarded (Cognitive) • Space constraints due to smaller display (Functional) • Usually limited, can include the development of a profile. (Identity)	• Delivery of psychoeducation; structured practice of NSSI coping skills; EMA integration and push elements for greater engagement and just-in-time intervention (urges) • NSSI examples: • TEC (Franklin et al., 2016; Rizvi et al., 2016; Rizvi & Steffel, 2014; Stallard et al., 2018) • DBT Coach (Rizvi et al., 2016; Rizvi & Steffel, 2014) • BlueIce (Stallard et al., 2018)

Platform	Strengths	Limitations	Notes / NSSI Examples
Text-messaging (SMS)	• Ease of use; users likely engage with texting daily, thus it may fit more seamlessly into their routines and fit with existing heuristics (Cognitive, Functional) • More accessible and less dependent on data storage (Functional) • Connection with one or more persons (Social)	• Interaction format makes it difficult for users to keep text message track of content within a thread—particularly if the service includes links to external sites (Functional) • Easy to ignore (Functional) • Space constraints due to small display (Functional) • Limited in terms of opportunities for identity development, beyond expression (Functional) • Ways of expressing emotions are dependent on data plan (e.g., emojis, gifs) (Affective)	• Providing social support; small bits of psychoeducation; good for reminders/ checking in; possibilities with automation and push or pull elements • NSSI examples: • (Kodama et al., 2016; Owens et al., 2010; Owens & Charles, 2016)
Chatbots (web and mobile)	• Can be highly engaging facilitate a natural feeling interaction (Functional) • Ability to be mobile or web-based and can be a feature in other intervention formats (Functional) • Capable of using basic and complex logic (Functional) • "Push and "pull" opportunities (Cognitive)	• Not all bots are sophisticated, and this can lead to unnatural exchanges (Functional) • Can be perceived to be inauthentic (Functional)	• Conveying empathy (support, validation); conversational to allow for reflection and deeper thinking (build self-knowledge); can facilitate decision-making processes (help-seeking, coping strategies) • NSSI Examples: • Pocket Skills (Schroeder et al., 2018) • Web-based decisional aid (Rowe et al., 2018)
Online forums/social media	• Capable of facilitating exchange of social and peer support (Social) • Many ways of building, sharing, reflecting on identity (Identity) • Fits with existing/natural use so it is accessible (Functional) • Ability to detect individuals at risk and message to person at the right time (Functional, Cognitive) • Ability to use existing forums or build platforms/groups for social element of intervention (Functional) • Ability to reach a lot of people at once (e.g., campaigns) (Functional)	• Social media is not a controlled environment, so there are many other people that can impact intervention, or intervention delivery (Functional) • Possibilities for inadvertent exposure to harmful content (Functional) • Possibilities for over or under detection of risk (Functional)	• Social support; knowledge acquisition; exchange of peer stories; ability to learn from others without the requirement of direct engagement; ability to meet young people where they already congregate to discuss NSSI and related topics • NSSI Examples: • TalkLife (Kruzan, Whitlock, et al., 2021) • Online communities (Baker & Lewis, 2013; Lewis & Michal, 2016)

(continued)

Table 50.2 Continued

Intervention formats/Platforms	Possible benefits	Possible constraints	NSSI opportunities
Virtual reality	• Highly engaging; capable of distraction, immersion, and embodiment (Functional, Affective) • Can involve opportunities for identity creation, experimentation (Identity) • Ability to shift internal perceptions and attitudes toward body (Cognitive)	• Not as easily accessible due to cost (Functional) • Requires person to commit to being in a time and place where VR is accessible (Functional) • Can be technically confusing and/or frustrating (Cognitive, Functional) • Side effects such as motion sickness—particularly if the graphics are not well designed (Cognitive, Functional) • May be best used as a complement to therapy with monitoring (Cognitive)	• Facilitating embodied practices (e.g., yoga, mindfulness); inducing perceptual shifts useful for targets such as interoception, body regard; highly immersive, facilitating distraction • NSSI Examples: • Affect modification (Kruzan et al., 2020) • DBT skills practice—meditation (Nararro-Haro et al., 2016)

be cognitive taxing when the user has many other things on the device competing with their attention (Moreno & D'Angelo, 2019). In contrast, passive sensing can collect data without burdening the user, thereby reducing the cognitive load. Cognitive affordances are an important consideration for sustained engagement with NSSI interventions. While push elements can be useful in tracking patterns over time, as in intervention incorporating ecological momentary assessments (EMA), young people often appreciate a sense of autonomy, so allowing them to initiate actions (pull elements) may be important.

Identity affordances refer to the ability for users to co-construct and reflect on their identity when interacting with a technology. Social media sites are probably richest in this affordance, but there is significant variability between sites. For example, Facebook requires users to sign up with their real name, and usually a profile is associated with a photo (or photos), and information about the person's likes or dislikes. In contrast, Reddit allows users to engage anonymously so "identity" affordances may be less rich on Reddit, allowing the user to preserve or conceal aspects of their identity, making it a preferred but it is resource for individuals with stigmatized conditions. Platforms with high-identity affordances may be particularly suited to tap into NSSI targets such as identity distress and self-concept clarity (Claes et al., 2014; Lear & Pepper, 2016).

Affective affordances refer to the ability of the technology to connect users with emotional support, to generate affect, and to express emotional states. Emotional support can be conveyed through any peer-based medium, but some technologies facilitate this better than others. For example, many young people with NSSI have expressed emotional support when engaging in online communication through forums. In these spaces users share their stories and experience and relate with one another (Kruzan, Bazarova, et al., 2021; Lewis & Michal, 2016). Web-based programs may convey emotional support through empathetic language or the sharing of peer stories—but this is less direct than a one-on-one or one-to-many connection afforded through social spaces. Chatbots offer a relatively dynamic framework for conveying emotional support and responding to user emotions in a human-like manner. In terms of affect generation, VR has been used specifically to invoke certain emotional states which make it suited to exposure therapies. In other technologies, emotions are conveyed through words, emojis, and gifs in text. Since the ability to manage emotions through reducing or inducing emotional states is often cited as self-management strategies among young people engaging in NSSI, it is worth considering the range of affective features in a technology to be used for DI.

Functional affordances refer to the functional elements of the platform, including accessibility, permanence of content, and dissemination avenues. This includes things like whether the technology can be readily accessed outside the home in daily life or whether it requires an individual to be in a specific location, at a specific time. Other functional affordances include ability to replicate content, how individuals navigate and engage with content, and searchability, for example. Functional affordances are perhaps the most obvious considerations for researchers when choosing a platform for an intervention. Because most existing programs focus on delivering psychoeducation and skills, mobile apps and web-based programs have been among the common formats for NSSI intervention. These two platforms are easily accessible, allow for searchability, and provide scalable options for services.

In sum, a nuanced understanding of the affordances of technologies being considered for the delivery of an NSSI DI can help researchers determine their appropriateness for engaging specific targets and achieving specific outcomes.

Challenges, Recommendations, and Future Directions in DI Research

Digital interventions are broadly accessible and prior work has demonstrated their acceptability to individuals who engage in NSSI in preliminary work. Digital interventions will not be acceptable to all users, however, as many studies reviewed in the chapter emphasized the importance of being able to customize or personalize aspects of the intervention to meet their preferences and needs. Such personalization may also help with the challenge of digital mental health interventions to maintain user engagement with resources over time. Notably, all trials reviewed above noted a decline in use over time. Several key challenges related to the development and implementation of DIs for NSSI are described below, including: (1) user engagement, (2) safety, privacy, and risk management, and (3) ethics and accessibility.

USER ENGAGEMENT

One of the most significant and consistent challenges with DIs is user engagement. Sustained engagement in *any* supportive treatment is further complicated with NSSI since most individuals do not disclose or engage in treatment, and those who do rarely complete a full course of treatment (Ammerman et al., 2021; Armiento et al., 2014; Fox et al., 2020). Part of this may be due to access barriers as well as the length of common treatments for NSSI (e.g., DBT). For example, shorter interventions that fit more seamlessly into an individual's life may be more manageable. Even short internet-based CBT programs note problems with attrition however (Perski et al., 2017; Wilks et al., 2020). The following paragraphs highlight two methods that may improve engagement in DIs: early investment in formative research on user needs (user-centered design) and the inclusion of human coaching.

Involving users with lived experience in the DI design and development process is thought to increase the relevance and likelihood of an DI being engaging for the target use. Perceived usefulness and ease of use are the two most important factors for technology adoption and sustained engagement, and can only really be addressed by understanding the unique needs of the individuals who will ultimately use the technology (Davis, 1989). The customizability of an intervention is frequently described as a need across technological platforms when research involves young people who engage in NSSI. Though customizability likely adds to cost and maintenance of the intervention, formative work understanding the various needs, preferences, and receptivity of key stakeholders can be a useful step towards developing interventions that are acceptable and have real-world efficacy.

Additionally, research has shown that engagement is often higher for DIs with some form of human support (Torous et al., 2020). While one of the appeals of DI is that they can be autonomous or require little human support, some degree of human support may be necessary. Lightweight coaching, wherein a human coach provides some motivational and reminder feedback, has been shown to improve DI use and mental health outcomes, relative to self-guided DIs in many studies (Linardon et al., 2019). However, this effect for coaching has not been universally observed. Some studies evaluating apps designed with user-centered design processes have produced strong results for self-guided apps, with the addition of coaching producing no significant, or only small, effects (Mohr et al., 2013; Mohr et al., 2019) This again underscores the importance involving stakeholder experience in the research process including the design of apps and the evaluation of the value of coaching, such as through user-centered design (UCD).

SAFETY, PRIVACY, AND RISK MANAGEMENT

User comfort and safety are important in the design of any DI for NSSI but may be especially so in digital tools that involve the collection of large amounts of data and allow users to interact with the system relatively autonomously. A discussion on the responsibilities of researchers utilizing active and passive EMA data, which is likely to be a common feature in DI work, can be found in Kiekens et al. (2021). In general, proper risk management and safety protocols require early planning, best practice, and integration of stakeholders' perspectives to determine what is acceptable and practical. Involving stakeholders, including individuals with lived experience, in the design of appropriate risk management and safety protocols is one way to ensure that all voices are heard and considered (Kruzan, Meyerhoff, et al., 2021). For example, people may feel resistant to using technology if they feel that the platform allows them little agency in moments of distress. As an example, the Trans Lifeline adapted their risk protocols and services based on concerns from their target population on nonconsensual rescues and involuntary psychiatric hospitalization (Gould et al., 2018; Green, 2018). As this example highlights, while crisis hotlines can provide highly effective coping skills and emotion regulation tools that reduce the risk of suicide attempt, certain aspects of an intervention can reduce engagement and efficacy or be harmful.

Risk management and safety protocols extend to the management of data and data privacy. Users are often concerned with the privacy of their data, with some preferring to interact with devices, or peers, anonymously. Privacy issues are among the most critical requirements for technology and engagement, because if users do not feel safe they are unlikely to engage (Doherty et al., 2010). Additionally, many individuals who may engage with a DI may otherwise not be involved in treatment. As such, they may be especially hesitant to share data that could signal risk and subsequent intervention deployment, leading to questions of user autonomy and ethics.

ETHICS AND ACCESSIBILITY

While digital spaces are contexts where interventions can be readily deployed and have the potential to increase accessibility, a careful consideration of ethics is necessary. Some of the intervention formats outlined earlier (e.g., chatbots and web-based interventions) can be integrated for deployment in existing online settings. Social media platforms have algorithmic risk protocols built into the platforms, as well as moderation. While these features are necessary to prevent the spread of harmful content and provide at-risk users with appropriate crisis contacts, such programming can also inadvertently make a space feel less safe and undercut the possibility of free expression. Thus, at every stage of the research process for DIs there must be careful consideration of the pros and cons of certain features and the duty of beneficence.

Though digital interventions offer new opportunities to reach individuals who may not otherwise be engaged in traditional face-to-face treatments for NSSI, they come with their own unique set of barriers which can further compound power asymmetries. Researchers and designers must be attuned to the ways a technological format may constrain use for certain members and be aware of the variations in digital literacy in their population of interest. For example, young people may be less likely to use a web-based intervention for NSSI if they share a computer with other family members for fear that others will find out. Mobile phones may be a more private option but they are also associated with additional costs and data plans. In sum, although there is great potential for digital interventions to help address NSSI, they are not a perfect solution. Just as digital interventions have the potential to resolve some common challenges with getting people engaged in treatment, they are also likely to create others.

Implications for Researchers

Research interested in using technologies to better understand the epidemiology of NSSI and predict NSSI behaviors and thoughts, through machine learning, artificial intelligence, and use of EMA, has grown significantly in recent years. Advancing these lines of inquiry, along with appropriate considerations of DI utility, uptake, and ethics, is critically important. Given the fast pace of technology development, there is a similar need for research focused on leveraging technologies to provide greater access to evidence-based resources and to tap into, or identify, novel treatment targets. To do so, researchers must consider specific platform affordances in the design of resources and weigh the pros and cons of different delivery mechanisms.

There are many opportunities for advancement in this field. Some of the most promising opportunities are outlined below.

1. **EMA, passive sensing, and just in time.** As a field we have begun to understand the value, and leverage, of EMA for understanding individual experiences with NSSI and the connection between NSSI and risk factors

(Rodríguez-Blanco et al., 2018). However, we have not yet tapped into the value of EMA for DI work. As research on EMA and passive sensing accrues, attention to DIs capable of intervening just-in-time using this technique will likely be an important inquiry. Just-in-time technologies may be particularly attractive for intervening with NSSI since many individuals who NSSI experience significant in-the-moment distress with urges or NSSI thoughts. Such methods can also be used to help individuals implement or practice coping skills between therapy visits. For more information also see Legg et al., this volume.

2. **Virtual reality.** Although there is a body of literature on the use of virtual reality (VR) in clinical contexts for other mental health disorders, there is less work focused on VR for NSSI. This may be a direction for future research efforts as VR has impressive capacity for exposure therapies, emotion regulation, skill introduction, and practice. Additionally, the embodied and immersive nature of VR make it a compelling platform to intervene in clinical targets dealing with perceptions, sensations, or attitudes about the body, including interoception, self-criticism, self-compassion, and emotion regulation.

3. **Artificial intelligence, machine learning and algorithms.** This area of work has already received much attention and has promise to address a number of challenges with NSSI detection and intervention (see Wang et al., this volume). Prevention and intervention efforts at a universal as well as individual scale can incorporate these methods into their programming to adapt the delivery of information to perceived needs of the community. Other opportunities include DIs informed by machine learning or artificial intelligence to reduce stigma, create awareness about NSSI, and dispel NSSI myths and inaccuracies.

4. **Social platforms built to reduce the risk and increase the benefit of engagement.** Social actors make safeguarding social media sites very difficult. However, we know how important these resources are for young people with lived experience of NSSI. Work is needed to identify and balance safe moderation with support for social media users and peer supporters.

Implications for Clinicians

Given the ubiquity of digital technologies and their effects on mental health, an awareness of the client's digital landscape is essential for clinicians who work with individuals who engage in NSSI. This includes an openness to discussing preferred platforms, patterns of social media use, and candid consideration of the ways in which technologies intersect with client experiences of NSSI. Having a list of questions to assess at intake or as therapy progresses can be helpful (see Lewis et al., 2012; Whitlock et al., 2007). Clinicians may be rightfully hesitant to adopt DIs as part of their practice, given the limited evidence that exists today; however, the growth of DIs for other common and complex mental health conditions suggests that there may be significant progress on DIs for NSSI in the coming decade. Although many of the existing technologies lack robust evaluation, preliminary research already suggests the ability of DIs to augment treatment as a between care aid and perhaps as a stepped-care option. Researcher-clinicians need to create good partnerships with colleagues in direct clinical practice because more research is needed on how DIs work (and do not work) within therapeutic environments.

Conclusion

Individuals with NSSI lived experience increasingly seek online and/or app-based options for understanding and managing NSSI-related impulses and behaviors. Since there are a growing number of digital affordances for meeting these needs, it is imperative that researchers, clinicians, and other health service professionals be aware of how to assess strengths and limitations of digital offerings. Understanding how to leverage online affordances to enhance self-awareness, set and meet NSSI intervention goals, and augment formal treatment approaches is important, and promising areas of DI development are being investigated. As the digital landscape expands, it will offer a growing array of tools that can act as stand-alone and adjunctive supports. Preliminary evidence regarding the efficacy of app-based, and other digital interventions to date is limited but promising. More research in this space has the potential to address a very real and growing need.

References

Ammerman, B. A., Wilcox, K. T., O'Loughlin, C. M., & McCloskey, M. S. (2021). Characterizing the choice to disclose nonsuicidal self-injury. *Journal of Clinical Psychology, 77*(3), 683–700. https://doi.org/10.1002/jclp.23045

Andrews, G. (2018). Computer therapy for the anxiety and depression disorders is effective, acceptable and practical health care—An updated meta-analysis. *Journal of Anxiety Disorders, 55*, 70–78. https://doi.org/10.1016/j.janxdis.2018.01.001

Armiento, J. S., Hamza, C. A., & Willoughby, T. (2014). An examination of disclosure of nonsuicidal self-injury among university students. *Journal of Community & Applied Social Psychology, 24*(6), 518–533. https://doi.org/10.1002/casp.2190

Arshad, U., Farhat-Ul-Ain, null, Gauntlett, J., Husain, N., Chaudhry, N., & Taylor, P. J. (2020). A systematic review of the evidence supporting mobile- and internet-based psychological interventions for self-harm. *Suicide & Life-Threatening Behavior, 50*(1), 151–179. https://doi.org/10.1111/sltb.12583

Baker, T. G., & Lewis, S. P. (2013). Responses to online photographs of non-suicidal self-injury: A thematic analysis. *Archives of Suicide Research, 17*(3), 223–235. https://doi.org/10.1080/13811118.2013.805642

Baumel, A., Fleming, T., & Schueller, S. M. (2020). Digital micro interventions for behavioral and mental health gains: Core components and conceptualization of digital micro intervention care. *Journal of Medical Internet Research, 22*(10), Article e20631. https://doi.org/10.2196/20631

Baumel, A., Muench, F., Edan, S., & Kane, J. M. (2019). Objective user engagement with mental health apps: Systematic search and panel-based usage analysis. *Journal of Medical Internet Research, 21*(9), Article e14567. https://doi.org/10.2196/14567

Birbeck, N., Lawson, S., Morrissey, K., Rapley, T., & Olivier, P. (2017). Self-harmony: Rethinking hackathons to design and critique digital technologies for those affected by self-harm. *CHI '17: Proceedings of the 2017*

CHI Conference on Human Factors in Computing Systems (pp. 146–157). Denver, CO. https://doi.org/10.1145/3025453.3025931

Bjureberg, J., Sahlin, H., Hedman-Lagerlöf, E., Gratz, K. L., Tull, M. T., Jokinen, J., Hellner, C., & Ljótsson, B. (2018). Extending research on emotion regulation individual therapy for adolescents (ERITA) with nonsuicidal self-injury disorder: Open pilot trial and mediation analysis of a novel online version. *BMC Psychiatry*, *18*(1), 326. https://doi.org/10.1186/s12888-018-1885-6

Borghouts, J., Eikey, E., Mark, G., De Leon, C., Schueller, S. M., Schneider, M., Stadnick, N., Zheng, K., Mukamel, D., & Sorkin, D. H. (2021). Barriers to and facilitators of user engagement with digital mental health interventions: Systematic review. *Journal of Medical Internet Research*, *23*(3), Article e24387. https://doi.org/10.2196/24387

Claes, L., Luyckx, K., & Bijttebier, P. (2014). Non-suicidal self-injury in adolescents: Prevalence and associations with identity formation above and beyond depression. *Personality and Individual Differences*, *61–62*, 101–104. https://doi.org/10.1016/j.paid.2013.12.019

Coppersmith, D., Dempsey, W., Kleinman, E. M., Bentley, K. H., Murphy, S. A., & Nock, M. N. (2022). Just-in-time adaptive interventions for suicide prevention: Promise, challenges, and future directions. *Psychiatry*, *85*(4), 317–333. https://doi.org/10.1080/00332747.2022.2092828.

Čuš, A., Edbrooke-Childs, J., Ohmann, S., Plener, P. L., & Akkaya-Kalayci, T. (2021). "Smartphone apps are cool, but do they help me?": A qualitative interview study of adolescents' perspectives on using smartphone interventions to manage nonsuicidal self-injury. *International Journal of Environmental Research and Public Health*, *18*(6), Article 3289. https://doi.org/10.3390/ijerph18063289

Davis, F. D. (1989). Perceived usefulness, perceived ease of use, and user acceptance of information technology. *MIS Quarterly*, *13*(3), 319–340. https://doi.org/10.2307/249008

Doherty, G., Coyle, D., & Matthews, M. (2010). Design and evaluation guidelines for mental health technologies. *Interacting with Computers*, *22*(4), 243–252. https://doi.org/10.1016/j.intcom.2010.02.006

Ferrer-García, M., & Gutiérrez-Maldonado, J. (2012). The use of virtual reality in the study, assessment, and treatment of body image in eating disorders and nonclinical samples: A review of the literature. *Body Image*, *9*(1), 1–11. https://doi.org/10.1016/j.bodyim.2011.10.001

Firth, J., Torous, J., Nicholas, J., Carney, R., Pratap, A., Rosenbaum, S., & Sarris, J. (2017). The efficacy of smartphone-based mental health interventions for depressive symptoms: A meta-analysis of randomized controlled trials. *World Psychiatry: Official Journal of the World Psychiatric Association (WPA)*, *16*(3), 287–298. https://doi.org/10.1002/wps.20472

Firth, J., Torous, J., Nicholas, J., Carney, R., Rosenbaum, S., & Sarris, J. (2017). Can smartphone mental health interventions reduce symptoms of anxiety? A meta-analysis of randomized controlled trials. *Journal of Affective Disorders*, *218*, 15–22. https://doi.org/10.1016/j.jad.2017.04.046

Fortune, S., Sinclair, J., & Hawton, K. (2008). Help-seeking before and after episodes of self-harm: A descriptive study in school pupils in England. *BMC Public Health*, *8*, Article 369. https://doi.org/10.1186/1471-2458-8-369

Fox, K. R., Bettis, A. H., Burke, T. A., Hart, E. A., & Wang, S. B. (2022). Exploring adolescent experiences with disclosing self-injurious thoughts and behaviors across settings. *Research on Child and Adolescent Psychopathology*, *50*(5), 669–681. https://doi.org/10.1007/s10802-021-00878-x

Fox, K. R., Huang, X., Guzmán, E. M., Funsch, K. M., Cha, C. B., Ribeiro, J. D., & Franklin, J. C. (2020). Interventions for suicide and self-injury: A meta-analysis of randomized controlled trials across nearly 50 years of research. *Psychological Bulletin*, *146*(12), 1117–1145. https://doi.org/10.1037/bul0000305

Franklin, J. C., Fox, K. R., Franklin, C. R., Kleiman, E. M., Ribeiro, J. D., Jaroszewski, A. C., Hooley, J. M., & Nock, M. K. (2016). A brief mobile app reduces nonsuicidal and suicidal self-injury: Evidence from three randomized controlled trials. *Journal of Consulting and Clinical Psychology*, *84*(6), 544–557. https://doi.org/10.1037/ccp0000093

Frost, M., & Casey, L. (2016). Who seeks help online for self-injury? *Archives of Suicide Research: Official Journal of the International Academy for Suicide Research*, *20*(1), 69–79. https://doi.org/10.1080/13811118.2015.1004470

Gibson, J. J. (1977). The theory of affordances. In R. Shaw & J. Bransford (Eds.), *Perceiving, acting, and knowing* (pp. 127–137). Erlbaum.

Gould, M. S., Lake, A. M., Galfalvy, H., Kleinman, M., Munfakh, J. L., Wright, J., & McKeon, R. (2018). Follow-up with callers to the National Suicide Prevention Lifeline: Evaluation of callers' perceptions of care. *Suicide and Life-Threatening Behavior*, *48*(1), 75–86. https://doi.org/10.1111/sltb.12339

Gould, M. S., Munfakh, J. L. H., Lubell, K., Kleinman, M., & Parker, S. (2002). Seeking help from the internet during adolescence. *Journal of the American Academy of Child & Adolescent Psychiatry*, *41*(10), 1182–1189. https://doi.org/10.1097/00004583-200210000-00007

Gratz, K. L., & Gunderson, J. G. (2006). Preliminary data on an acceptance-based emotion regulation group intervention for deliberate self-harm among women with borderline personality disorder. *Behavior Therapy*, *37*(1), 25–35. https://doi.org/10.1016/j.beth.2005.03.002

Green. (2018, June 2). *Why no non-consensual active rescue?* Trans Lifeline. https://translifeline.org/why-no-non-consensual-active-rescue/

Grist, R., Porter, J., & Stallard, P. (2018). Acceptability, use, and safety of a mobile phone app (BlueIce) for young people who self-harm: Qualitative study of service users' experience. *JMIR Mental Health*, *5*(1), Article e16. https://doi.org/10.2196/mental.8779

Hartson, R. (2003). Cognitive, physical, sensory, and functional affordances in interaction design. *Behaviour & Information Technology*, *22*(5), 315–338. https://doi.org/10.1080/01449290310001592587

Hetrick, S. E., Robinson, J., Burge, E., Blandon, R., Mobilio, B., Rice, S. M., Simmons, M. B., Alvarez-Jimenez, M., Goodrich, S., & Davey, C. G. (2018). Youth codesign of a mobile phone app to facilitate self-monitoring and management of mood symptoms in young people with major depression, suicidal ideation, and self-harm. *JMIR Mental Health*, *5*(1), Article e9. https://doi.org/10.2196/mental.9041

Hetrick, S. E., Subasinghe, A., Anglin, K., Hart, L., Morgan, A., & Robinson, J. (2020). Understanding the needs of young people who engage in self-harm: A qualitative investigation. *Frontiers in Psychology*, *10*, Article 2916. https://doi.org/10.3389/fpsyg.2019.02916

Honary, M., Bell, B., Clinch, S., Vega, J., Kroll, L., Sefi, A., & McNaney, R. (2020). Shaping the design of smartphone-based interventions for self-harm. *CHI '20: Proceedings of the 2020 CHI Conference on Human Factors in Computing Systems* (pp. 1–14). Honolulu, Hawaii. https://doi.org/10.1145/3313831.3376370

Hooley, J. M., Fox, K. R., Wang, S. B., & Kwashie, A. N. D. (2018). Novel online daily diary interventions for nonsuicidal self-injury: A randomized controlled trial. *BMC Psychiatry*, *18*(1), 264. https://doi.org/10.1186/s12888-018-1840-6

Hooley, J. M., & Franklin, J. C. (2018). Why Do People Hurt Themselves? A New Conceptual Model of Nonsuicidal Self-Injury. *Clinical Psychological Science*, *6*(3), 428–451. https://doi.org/10.1177/2167702617745641

Horgan, Á., & Sweeney, J. (2010). Young students' use of the internet for mental health information and support. *Journal of Psychiatric and Mental Health Nursing*, *17*(2), 117–123. https://doi.org/10.1111/j.1365-2850.2009.01497.x

Kaess, M., Koenig, J., Bauer, S., Moessner, M., Fischer-Waldschmidt, G., Mattern, M., Herpertz, S. C., Resch, F., Brown, R., In-Albon, T., Koelch, M., Plener, P. L., Schmahl, C., Edinger, A., & STAR Consortium. (2019). Self-injury: Treatment, Assessment, Recovery (STAR): Online intervention for adolescent non-suicidal self-injury—Study protocol for a randomized controlled trial. *Trials*, *20*(1), 425. https://doi.org/10.1186/s13063-019-3501-6

Kiekens, G., Robinson, K., Tatnell, R., & Kirtley, O. J. (2021). Opening the black box of daily life in nonsuicidal self-injury research: With great opportunity comes great responsibility. *JMIR Mental Health*, *8*(11), Article e30915. https://doi.org/10.2196/30915

Kodama, T., Syouji, H., Takaki, S., Fujimoto, H., Ishikawa, S., Fukutake, M., Taira, M., & Hashimoto, T. (2016). Text messaging for psychiatric outpatients: Effect on help-seeking and self-harming behaviors. *Journal of Psychosocial Nursing and Mental Health Services*, *54*(4), 31–37. https://doi.org/10.3928/02793695-20160121-01

Kruzan, K. P., Bazarova, N. N., & Whitlock, J. (2021). Investigating self-injury support solicitations and responses on a mobile peer support application. *Proceedings of the ACM on Human-Computer Interaction*, *5*(CSCW2), 1–23. https://doi.org/10.1145/3479498

Kruzan, K. P., Meyerhoff, J., Biernesser, C., Goldstein, T., Reddy, M., & Mohr, D. C. (2021). Centering lived experience in developing digital interventions for suicide and self-injurious behaviors: User-centered design approach. *JMIR Mental Health*, *8*(12), Article e31367. https://doi.org/10.2196/31367

Kruzan, K. P., & Whitlock, J. (2019). Processes of change and nonsuicidal self-injury: A qualitative interview study with individuals at various stages of change. *Global Qualitative Nursing Research*, *6*, Article 2333393619852935. https://doi.org/10.1177/2333393619852935

Kruzan, K. P., Whitlock, J., & Bazarova, N. N. (2021). Examining the relationship between the use of a mobile peer-support app and self-injury outcomes: Longitudinal mixed methods study. *JMIR Mental Health*, *8*(1), Article e21854. https://doi.org/10.2196/21854

Kruzan, K. P., Whitlock, J., Bazarova, N. N., Miller, K. D., Chapman, J., & Won, A. S. (2020). Supporting self-injury recovery: The potential for virtual reality intervention. *CHI '20: Proceedings of the 2020 CHI Conference on Human Factors in Computing Systems* (pp. 1–14). Honolulu, Hawaii. https://doi.org/10.1145/3313831.3376396

Larsen, M. E., Shand, F., Morley, K., Batterham, P. J., Petrie, K., Reda, B., Berrouiguet, S., Haber, P. S., Carter, G., & Christensen, H. (2017). A mobile text message intervention to reduce repeat suicidal episodes: Design and development of reconnecting after a Suicide attempt (RAFT). *JMIR Mental Health, 4*(4), Article e56. https://doi.org/10.2196/mental.7500

Lear, M. K., & Pepper, C. M. (2016). Self-concept clarity and emotion dysregulation in nonsuicidal self-injury. *Journal of Personality Disorders, 30*(6), 813–827. https://doi.org/10.1521/pedi_2015_29_232

Lewis, S. P., Heath, N. L., Michal, N. J., & Duggan, J. M. (2012). Non-suicidal self-injury, youth, and the internet: What mental health professionals need to know. *Child and Adolescent Psychiatry and Mental Health, 6*(1), Article 13. https://doi.org/10.1186/1753-2000-6-13

Lewis, S. P., Kenny, T. E., Whitfield, K., & Gomez, J. (2019). Understanding self-injury recovery: Views from individuals with lived experience. *Journal of Clinical Psychology, 75*(12), 2119–2139. https://doi.org/10.1002/jclp.22834

Lewis, S. P., & Michal, N. J. (2016). Start, stop, and continue: Preliminary insight into the appeal of self-injury e-communities. *Journal of Health Psychology, 21*(2), 250–260. https://doi.org/10.1177/1359105314527140

Linardon, J., Cuijpers, P., Carlbring, P., Messer, M., & Fuller-Tyszkiewicz, M. (2019). The efficacy of app-supported smartphone interventions for mental health problems: A meta-analysis of randomized controlled trials. *World Psychiatry: Official Journal of the World Psychiatric Association (WPA), 18*(3), 325–336. https://doi.org/10.1002/wps.20673

Linehan, M. (1993). *Skills training manual for treating borderline personality disorder* (Vol. 29). Guilford Press.

Michelmore, L., & Hindley, P. (2012). Help-seeking for suicidal thoughts and self-harm in young people: A systematic review. *Suicide & Life-Threatening Behavior, 42*(5), 507–524. https://doi.org/10.1111/j.1943-278X.2012.00108.x

Mohr, D. C., Duffecy, J., Ho, J., Kwasny, M., Cai, X., Burns, M. N., & Begale, M. (2013). A randomized controlled trial evaluating a manualized telecoaching protocol for improving adherence to a web-based intervention for the treatment of depression. *PloS One, 8*(8), Article e70086. https://doi.org/10.1371/journal.pone.0070086

Mohr, D. C., Schueller, S. M., Tomasino, K. N., Kaiser, S. M., Alam, N., Karr, C., Vergara, J. L., Gray, E. L., Kwasny, M. J., & Lattie, E. G. (2019). Comparison of the effects of coaching and receipt of app recommendations on depression, anxiety, and engagement in the Intellicare platform: Factorial randomized controlled trial. *Journal of Medical Internet Research, 21*(8), Article e13609. https://doi.org/10.2196/13609

Moreno, M. A., & D'Angelo, J. (2019). Social media intervention design: Applying an affordances framework. *Journal of Medical Internet Research, 21*(3), Article e11014. https://doi.org/10.2196/11014

Murnane, E. L., Cosley, D., Chang, P., Guha, S., Frank, E., Gay, G., & Matthews, M. (2016). Self-monitoring practices, attitudes, and needs of individuals with bipolar disorder: Implications for the design of technologies to manage mental health. *Journal of the American Medical Informatics Association, 23*(3), 477–484. https://doi.org/10.1093/jamia/ocv165

Nararro-Haro, M. V., Hoffman, H. G., Garcia-Palacios, A., Sampaio, M., Alhalabi, W., Hall, K., & Linehan, M. (2016). The use of virtual reality to facilitate mindfulness skills training in dialectical behavioral therapy for borderline personality disorder: A case study. *Frontiers in Psychology, 7*, Article 1573. https://doi.org/10.3389/fpsyg.2016.01573

Norman, D. A. (1988). *The psychology of everyday things*. Basic Books.

Olsen, M. H., Morthorst, B., Pagsberg, A. K., Heinrichsen, M., Møhl, B., Rubæk, L., Bjureberg, J., Simonsson, O., Lindschou, J., Gluud, C., & Jakobsen, J. C. (2021). An internet-based emotion regulation intervention versus no intervention for non-suicidal self-injury in adolescents: A statistical analysis plan for a feasibility randomised clinical trial. *Trials, 22*(1), 456. https://doi.org/10.1186/s13063-021-05406-2

Owens, C., & Charles, N. (2016). Implementation of a text-messaging intervention for adolescents who self-harm (TeenTEXT): A feasibility study using normalisation process theory. *Child and Adolescent Psychiatry and Mental Health, 10*(1), 14. https://doi.org/10.1186/s13034-016-0101-z

Owens, C., Farrand, P., Darvill, R., Emmens, T., Hewis, E., & Aitken, P. (2010). Involving service users in intervention design: A participatory approach to developing a text-messaging intervention to reduce repetition of self-harm. *Health Expectations, 14*(3), 285–295. https://doi.org/10.1111/j.1369-7625.2010.00623.x

Owens, C., Farrand, P., Darvill, R., Emmens, T., Hewis, E., & Aitken, P. (2011). Involving service users in intervention design: A participatory approach to developing a text-messaging intervention to reduce repetition of self-harm: Involving service users in intervention design. *Health Expectations*, *14*(3), 285–295. https://doi.org/10.1111/j.1369-7625.2010.00623.x

Perrin, R., & Atske, S. (2021a). 7% of Americans don't use the internet. Who are they? *Pew Research Center*. https://www.pewresearch.org/fact-tank/2021/04/02/7-of-americans-dont-use-the-internet-who-are-they/

Perrin, R., & Atske, S. (2021b). About three-in-ten U.S. adults say they are "almost constantly" online. *Pew Research Center*. https://www.pewresearch.org/fact-tank/2021/03/26/about-three-in-ten-u-s-adults-say-they-are-almost-constantly-online/

Perski, O., Blandford, A., West, R., & Michie, S. (2017). Conceptualising engagement with digital behaviour change interventions: A systematic review using principles from critical interpretive synthesis. *Translational Behavioral Medicine*, *7*(2), 254–267. https://doi.org/10.1007/s13142-016-0453-1

Prinstein, M. J., Guerry, J. D., Browne, C. B., & Rancourt, D. (2009). Interpersonal models of nonsuicidal self-injury. In M. K. Nock (Ed.), *Understanding nonsuicidal self-injury: Origins, assessment, and treatment* (pp. 79–98). American Psychological Association.

Rizvi, S. L., Dimeff, L. A., Skutch, J., Carroll, D., & Linehan, M. M. (2011). A pilot study of the DBT Coach: An interactive mobile phone application for individuals with borderline personality disorder and substance use disorder. *Behavior Therapy*, *42*(4), 589–600. https://doi.org/10.1016/j.beth.2011.01.003

Rizvi, S. L., Hughes, C. D., & Thomas, M. C. (2016). The DBT Coach mobile application as an adjunct to treatment for suicidal and self-injuring individuals with borderline personality disorder: A preliminary evaluation and challenges to client utilization. *Psychological Services*, *13*(4), 380–388. https://doi.org/10.1037/ser0000100

Rizvi, S. L., & Steffel, L. M. (2014). A pilot study of 2 brief forms of dialectical behavior therapy skills training for emotion dysregulation in college students. *Journal of American College Health*, *62*(6), 434–439. https://doi.org/10.1080/07448481.2014.907298

Rodríguez-Blanco, L., Carballo, J. J., & Baca-García, E. (2018). Use of ecological momentary assessment (EMA) in non-suicidal self-injury (NSSI): A systematic review. *Psychiatry Research*, *263*, 212–219. https://doi.org/10.1016/j.psychres.2018.02.051

Rooksby, J., Rost, M., Morrison, A., & Chalmers, M. (2014). Personal tracking as lived informatics. *CHI '14: Proceedings of the SIGCHI Conference on Human Factors in Computing Systems* (pp. 1163–1172). Toronto, Canada. https://doi.org/10.1145/2556288.2557039

Rowe, S. L., Patel, K., French, R. S., Henderson, C., Ougrin, D., Slade, M., & Moran, P. (2018). Web-based decision aid to assist help-seeking choices for young people who self-harm: Outcomes from a randomized controlled feasibility trial. *JMIR Mental Health*, *5*(1), e10. https://doi.org/10.2196/mental.8098

Schaeffer, K. (2019). Most U.S. teens who use cellphones do it to pass time, connect with others, learn new things. *Pew Research Center*. https://www.pewresearch.org/fact-tank/2019/08/23/most-u-s-teens-who-use-cellphones-do-it-to-pass-time-connect-with-others-learn-new-things/

Schroeder, J., Wilkes, C., Rowan, K., Toledo, A., Paradiso, A., Czerwinski, M., Mark, G., & Linehan, M. M. (2018). Pocket Skills: A conversational mobile web app to support dialectical behavioral therapy. *CHI '18: Proceedings of the 2018 CHI Conference on Human Factors in Computing Systems* (pp. 1–15). Montreal, Canada. https://doi.org/10.1145/3173574.3173972

Schueller, S. M., Neary, M., Lai, J., & Epstein, D. A. (2021). Understanding people's use of and perspectives on mood-tracking apps: Interview study. *JMIR Mental Health*, *8*(8), Article e29368. https://doi.org/10.2196/29368

Simonsson, O., Engberg, H., Bjureberg, J., Ljótsson, B., Stensils, J., Sahlin, H., & Hellner, C. (2021). Experiences of an online treatment for adolescents with nonsuicidal self-injury and their caregivers: Qualitative study. *JMIR Formative Research*, *5*(7), Article e17910. https://doi.org/10.2196/17910

Stallard, P., Porter, J., & Grist, R. (2018). A smartphone app (BlueIce) for young people who self-harm: Open phase 1 pre-post trial. *JMIR MHealth and UHealth*, *6*(1), Article e32. https://doi.org/10.2196/mhealth.8917

Sutcliffe, A. G., Gonzalez, V., Binder, J., & Nevarez, G. (2011). Social mediating technologies: Social affordances and functionalities. *International Journal of Human-Computer Interaction*, *27*(11), 1037–1065. https://doi.org/10.1080/10447318.2011.555318

Tatnell, R., Kelada, L., Hasking, P., & Martin, G. (2014). Longitudinal analysis of adolescent NSSI: The role of intrapersonal and interpersonal factors. *Journal of Abnormal Child Psychology*, *42*(6), 885–896. https://doi.org/10.1007/s10802-013-9837-6

Torous, J., Lipschitz, J., Ng, M., & Firth, J. (2020). Dropout rates in clinical trials of smartphone apps for depressive symptoms: A systematic review and meta-analysis. *Journal of Affective Disorders, 263*, 413–419. https://doi.org/10.1016/j.jad.2019.11.167

Valmaggia, L. R., Latif, L., Kempton, M. J., & Rus-Calafell, M. (2016). Virtual reality in the psychological treatment for mental health problems: A systematic review of recent evidence. *Psychiatry Research, 236*, 189–195. https://doi.org/10.1016/j.psychres.2016.01.015

Whitlock, J., Lader, W., & Conterio, K. (2007). The internet and self-injury: What psychotherapists should know. *Journal of Clinical Psychology, 63*(11), 1135–1143. https://doi.org/10.1002/jclp.20420

Whitlock, J., Muehlenkamp, J., Purington, A., Eckenrode, J., Barreira, P., Baral Abrams, G., Marchell, T., Kress, V., Girard, K., Chin, C., & Knox, K. (2011). Nonsuicidal self-injury in a college population: General trends and sex differences. *Journal of American College Health: J of ACH, 59*(8), 691–698. https://doi.org/10.1080/07448481.2010.529626

Whitlock, J. L., Powers, J. L., & Eckenrode, J. (2006). The virtual cutting edge: The internet and adolescent self-injury. *Developmental Psychology, 42*(3), 407–417. https://doi.org/10.1037/0012-1649.42.3.407

Wilks, C. R., Yin, Q., & Zuromski, K. L. (2020). User experience affects dropout from internet-delivered dialectical behavior therapy. *Telemedicine and E-Health, 26*(6), 794–797. https://doi.org/10.1089/tmj.2019.0124

Wong, C. A., Madanay, F., Ozer, E. M., Harris, S. K., Moore, M., Master, S. O., Moreno, M., & Weitzman, E. R. (2020). Digital health technology to enhance adolescent and young adult clinical preventive services: Affordances and challenges. *Journal of Adolescent Health, 67*(2), S24–S33. https://doi.org/10.1016/j.jadohealth.2019.10.018

Ybarra, M. L., & Eaton, W. W. (2005). Internet-based mental health interventions. *Mental Health Services Research, 7*(2), 75–87. https://doi.org/10.1007/s11020-005-3779-8

… CHAPTER

51 Machine Learning for Detection, Prediction, and Treatment of Nonsuicidal Self-Injury: Challenges and Future Directions

Shirley B. Wang, Walter Dempsey, Rowan A. Hunt, *and* Matthew K. Nock

Abstract

This chapter describes current progress, challenges, and future directions in machine learning (ML) for the detection, prediction, and treatment of nonsuicidal self-injury (NSSI). It highlights the importance of identifying individuals at risk for NSSI for prevention and early intervention efforts. ML methods are increasingly accurate at the task of detection, which expanded into the mental health domains. Additionally, researchers have begun to harness ML algorithms to improve clinical decision-making in predicting treatment outcomes for depression, anxiety, smoking cessation, and substance disorders. The chapter also notes the issues of ethics behind ML, such as data leakage that could occur when researchers fail to make a-priori decision during the model training and evaluation stage.

Key Words: machine learning, detection, prediction, treatment, nonsuicidal self-injury, ethics, clinical decision-making, prevention, early intervention

Introduction

Nonsuicidal self-injury (NSSI) refers to the direct and deliberate destruction of bodily tissue that is enacted without suicidal intent (e.g., self-cutting and self-burning; Nock, 2010). These behaviors are alarmingly common, with lifetime prevalence rates ranging between 5% and 17% in community samples (see Staring et al., this volume) and up to 50% in clinical samples (Cucchi et al., 2016; Glenn & Klonsky, 2013; Swannell et al., 2014; see Muehlenkamp & Tillotson, this volume). Beyond the inherent harm associated with NSSI, these high rates are concerning because NSSI is a strong predictor of future suicidal behavior (Andover et al., 2012; Ribeiro et al., 2016).

Identifying individuals at risk for NSSI is crucial for prevention and early intervention efforts, and there have been significant efforts to detect and predict NSSI over the past several decades of research. A large body of literature has identified many theoretically important variables that are associated with future NSSI engagement, such as higher levels of self-criticism (Fox et al., 2018) and impulsivity (Riley et al., 2015) and lower levels of emotion regulation ability (Adrian et al., 2011; Voon et al., 2014) and social support (Tatnell et al., 2014). However, prior studies have largely taken the form of null-hypothesis statistical testing of the association between NSSI and various putative correlates and/or risk factors (e.g., multiple linear or logistic regression analyses to identify predictors that are significantly associated with NSSI engagement). Whereas such traditional statistical methods are useful for making *inferences* about why people engage in NSSI, they are not designed to provide accurate *predictions* about future NSSI engagement. Rather, machine learning (ML) methods are better suited to optimize the prediction and detection of NSSI.

As described in several recent papers (Dwyer et al., 2018; Wang, 2021; Yarkoni & Westfall, 2017), ML methods differ from traditional inferential statistics in two important ways. First, ML algorithms (e.g., elastic net, random forests, and neural networks) tend to be more complex and better able to account for nonlinear associations than traditional statistical models often used in NSSI research (e.g., OLS regression). Second, whereas traditional statistical methods involve fitting a model using an entire dataset, ML methods often include splitting a single dataset into smaller datasets for model training, validation, and testing. Given the focus on prediction (over explanation) in ML, this allows researchers to obtain an estimate of how accurately a model *might* be able to predict important outcomes in new, unseen data.

In the past decade, there has been growing enthusiasm for the potential of ML in clinical psychology, with dozens of papers demonstrating the potential of ML to advance our detection, prediction, prevention, and treatment of psychopathology (Bokma et al., 2022; Chekroud et al., 2016; Haynos et al., 2021; Kessler et al., 2017). Perhaps most relevant to NSSI, there has been a proliferation of papers using ML to predict and detect suicidal thoughts and behaviors, using data from electronic health records (Barak-Corren et al., 2016; Su et al., 2020), large-scale population-based databases (de la Garza et al., 2021), real-time monitoring data (Wang et al., 2021), and social media platforms (Cheng et al., 2017; Roy et al., 2020). Many of these methods hold similar promise for NSSI research. Indeed, a smaller (but growing) number of papers are beginning to apply ML methods to the study of NSSI (Fox et al., 2019; Franz et al., 2020; Xian et al., 2019). However, there are also some significant differences between suicide and NSSI research that make ML research more challenging when studying NSSI. For instance, healthcare professionals may be less likely to conduct regular NSSI screenings, and thus NSSI may be less regularly documented in electronic medical records. When it is documented, it is most likely done with an ICD code for "self-inflicted injury," but those codes do not have a specifier to indicate whether there was suicidal intent (conflating suicidal and nonsuicidal self-injury). Similarly, large, population-based or epidemiological studies may be less likely to assess NSSI. Taken together, researchers may have less immediate access to large-scale databases with regular screening and documentation of NSSI and thus may be constrained to working with smaller sample sizes (e.g., data collected by individual research teams). Despite these limitations, there are myriad exciting opportunities for ML applications in NSSI research, including detection, prediction, and treatment of NSSI. This chapter reviews existing research in each of these domains, highlights challenges in these areas, and discusses future directions for ML in NSSI research.

Machine Learning Applications in NSSI Research

This section reviews applications of machine learning for the detection, prediction, and treatment of NSSI.

Detection of NSSI

ML methods are increasingly accurate at the task of detection. Such methods have been used to detect and accurately identify images, sounds, and spoken and written words. Recently, this has expanded into the mental health domains as well—a growing body of research uses ML models to detect current mental health. For instance, many studies have used ML methods with social media texts (e.g., from Facebook or Twitter) to measure and detect major depression (Chiong et al., 2021; Islam et al., 2018). A smaller but growing number of studies are taking a similar approach to detecting NSSI. For instance, Franz et al. (2020) used topic modeling applied to posts from a teen online forum to detect posts about suicidal and nonsuicidal self-injury with a high degree of accuracy. The approach used, Latent Dirichlet Allocation (LDA) (Blei et al., 2003), uses a probabilistic statistical model to infer the topics of documents (e.g., online posts, texts, and journal articles) based on the clustering of specific terms that appear in them. This approach not only finds posts about NSSI or suicide but also about other related latent topics, such as depression, social stress, family problems, and so on.

Approaches such as these can be used to make advances in the understanding, prediction, and prevention of NSSI; and many do so using natural language processing (NLP). NLP extracts the meaning of words and structure of sentences in textual data (e.g., qualitative responses, social media posts, and electronic health records). Such extraction generates NLP-based algorithms, which can then be used as inputs into ML models to classify and predict psychiatric symptoms. While NLP is a promising method that allows us to harness public data and social media sites for the detection of psychiatric concerns, there are limitations of the methods as used currently. For example, many NLP models are trained on general language (e.g., excerpts about mental health and broadly rather than more applicable and relevant text) and negative instances (i.e., cases where individuals *without* psychiatric concerns), thus contributing to unreliable models (Zhang et al., 2022). As such, future work utilizing NLP methods would benefit from building more mental health-specific models trained on more relevant text. The potential to capture those at risk for engagement in NSSI through social media posts can be used to push help-seeking resources to those unaware of them or without access to them. However, this requires better (and more nuanced) detection methods than those widely used.

Prediction of NSSI

In addition to detection of when people are *currently* engaging in NSSI, ML methods hold significant promise in *predicting* who is at risk for engaging in NSSI in the future, as well as when people may be at highest risk for NSSI. Regarding methods, supervised ML methods are best suited for predictive modeling tasks. Supervised learning refers to algorithms that use labeled data (e.g., "NSSI-present vs. NSSI-absent") to learn functions that map input to output variables (e.g., using baseline variables to predict whether someone will engage in NSSI at follow-up). In addition, supervised learning methods can be framed as classification problems (e.g., predicting presence of NSSI engagement) or regression problems (e.g., predicting the number of NSSI episodes or severity of NSSI). Common supervised learning algorithms include regularized regression models (e.g., lasso, ridge, and elastic net), tree-based methods (e.g., decision trees, bagging, boosting, and random forests), support vector machines, and neural networks. For greater technical, mathematical, and computational details, we refer the interested reader to recent tutorial papers (Dwyer et al., 2018; Strobl et al., 2009; Yarkoni & Westfall, 2017) and textbooks (James et al., 2013; Kuhn & Johnson, 2013).

Several papers to date have applied supervised ML methods to predict engagement in NSSI. In one of the first papers in this area, Fox et al. (2019) found that ML models (specifically random forests) outperformed univariate and multivariate logistic regression models in predicting short-term risk for NSSI in a sample of more than 1,000 participants. Interestingly, ML model performance remained strong even when models were rerun *without* the top-performing predictor in the original model. Although this should not be interpreted to mean that individual factors (e.g., history of self-injurious thoughts and behaviors, psychopathology, and demographics) have no relevance for NSSI, results do suggest that each individual factor *alone* is not sufficient for predicting future NSSI. Rather, a complex combination of factors may be necessary for accurate prediction of future NSSI (Fox et al., 2019). Paralleling this finding, compared to simple univariate and multivariate logistic regression models, ML models provide more accurate classification of individuals engaging in NSSI and/or suicide attempts (Huang et al., 2020).

When considering the promise of ML methods for predicting psychopathology outcomes (including NSSI), it is important to note that not all studies comparing ML to "traditional" statistical methods have found superior performance of ML models. Indeed, several studies in related fields (e.g., suicide) have found no advantage of ML models over simpler logistic or linear regression models (Zuromski et al., 2019). Similarly, a systematic review of 71 studies in the broader clinical prediction modeling literature (across a range of medical fields, including psychiatry, endocrinology, cardiology, oncology, primary care, geriatrics, critical care, and surgery) found no evidence for superior performance of ML compared to logistic regression (Christodoulou et al., 2019). Taken together, these findings suggest that while ML methods have the *potential* to advance prediction of NSSI, they are not *guaranteed* to do so. ML should not be viewed as a one-size-fits-all solution in NSSI research, but rather as a useful method that may optimize prediction in some studies and datasets but not in others. Indeed, identifying specific characteristics of predictive problems (e.g., nonlinearity, sample size, feature space, signal-to-noise ratio, and data missingness) for which ML methods (as well as specific algorithms) are best suited is an interesting area for future research.

Regarding future applications of ML for NSSI prediction, we echo recommendations from Christodoulou et al. (2019) on the importance of following best reporting practices (e.g., TRIPOD guidelines; Collins et al., 2015), using rigorous resampling and validation procedures, reporting results from model training and validation (in addition to model testing), and assessing model calibration.

Treatment of NSSI

Despite the recent proliferation of interventions for NSSI, a meta-analysis of randomized control trials for self-injurious thoughts and behaviors over the past 50 years reveals that there has been little to no improvement in intervention efficacy (Fox et al., 2020). In fact, many interventions produce only small intervention effects, highlighting a dire need for improved treatment for NSSI. However, these stalled improvements in mental health interventions are not exclusive to NSSI; across psychopathology, efforts to improve outcomes have led to a renewed interest in precision medicine (i.e., identifying *which* treatments work for *whom*) (DeRubeis, 2019). More recently, researchers have begun to harness ML algorithms to improve clinical decision-making; for example, ML-devised models have been used to predict treatment outcomes in depression (Lee et al., 2018), anxiety (Hornstein et al., 2021), smoking cessation (Coughlin et al., 2020), and substance disorders (Barenholtz et al., 2020). Accordingly, ML could also be used to improve treatment outcomes in NSSI by using ML-informed algorithms to identify patient characteristics that predict treatment outcomes, and match patients with treatments that may be the most effective for their particular constellation of symptoms.

Beyond traditional, therapist-delivered interventions, ML may also be useful in informing scalable, technology-based interventions. Just-in-time adaptive interventions (JITAIs) use mobile technology to deliver support and prompt skill use based on ongoing information about the individual's contexts and vulnerabilities (Nahum-Shani et al., 2018). JITAIs have been employed to treat many addictive behaviors (e.g., alcohol use and smoking) in which momentary, proximal factors may contribute to increased risk of lapse (Carpenter et al., 2020). Most JITAIs include four components: decision points (i.e., specific points of time in which an intervention can be delivered), intervention options (i.e., possible interventions that can be delivered at any given decision point), tailoring variables (i.e., information about the individual that is used to further adapt the intervention), and decision rules (i.e., rules that specify which intervention option to offer in response to tailoring variables; Carpenter et al., 2020). Often, these interventions function by using real-time monitoring data to inform ML algorithms that can identify tailoring variables and inform decision rules. JITAIs are currently being used to address various mental health concerns. For example, Juarascio et al. (2021) developed a JITAI to serve as an adjunct to cognitive behavioral therapy for bulimia nervosa. The JITAI system was developed with a starting algorithm informed by cognitive behavioral theory and used ML to trigger interventions when data from participants' self-monitoring logs suggested that they could use prompting to practice cognitive behavioral skills learned in therapy (Juarascio et al., 2021). This improved skill utilization as individuals were taught skills in the therapy room and then prompted to use them in their daily lives at the optimal times. Although no studies (to date) have used JITAIs in the treatment of NSSI, these methods could provide a promising avenue for intervening upon NSSI in real-time. As a flexible and dynamic method of intervention, JITAIs could be used to identify periods of elevated risk for engagement in NSSI and deliver treatments based on individuals' personalized triggers.

Theory and Researcher Choices

This next section discusses the importance of strong theory and impact of researcher choices for ML applications in NSSI research.

Developing Good Models and Testing Theory

ML methods are highly data driven, and their ability to automatically learn from data is often contrasted against traditional statistical methods which rely more explicitly on theory and researcher decision-making (Breiman, 2001). For instance, whereas a researcher working with traditional statistical methods (the "data modeling culture") might choose a specific model with predefined parameters (e.g., as in a linear regression model), a researcher working in ML (the "algorithmic modeling culture") assumes that the processes relating input x variables to output y variables are complex and partially unknown. In the algorithmic modeling culture of ML and predictive modeling, the goal is to find an algorithm $f(x)$ to predict future y s from future x s.

This difference between data modeling and algorithmic modeling cultures is often described as a shift from *explanation* to *prediction* (Yarkoni & Westfall, 2017). However, this should not be assumed to indicate that ML is an *atheoretical* approach. ML methods (and any other scientific or analytical method) are not applied in the absence of theory. Rather, theory impacts decision-making at every step of the research process, from study design to interpretation of results—whether researchers are explicitly aware of their theories or not. For instance, choosing to frame a problem as a regression (e.g., predicting the number of NSSI episodes someone will engage in over the next month) versus a classification (e.g., predicting whether or not someone will engage in *any* NSSI over the next month), the problem relies on researchers' theories about whether the *presence* or *severity* of NSSI is more theoretically and/or clinically meaningful. Such decisions have important downstream consequences—for instance, by determining whether future interventions based on ML model predictions should be targeted toward reducing severity of NSSI or preventing any NSSI engagement. Given the importance of theory in ML research and application, this section of the chapter aims to describe the importance of all data collection and modeling decisions being guided by strong theory, to the largest extent possible.

Study Design and Data Collection

Before any ML models can be built, data must be collected. There are myriad decisions to be made throughout the study design process that rely on strong theory. For instance, researchers' choice of features (i.e., independent variables and predictors) to include in a ML model is driven by their theoretical understanding of which variables are likely to be important for predicting or detecting NSSI. We encourage researchers to think beyond standard questionnaire- or interview-based measures, while these provide important information and should be included where necessary, emerging evidence suggests that other measurement approaches, such as behavioral tasks assessing implicit self-criticism and aversion to NSSI (Fox et al., 2018) and emotional response inhibition (Burke et al., 2021) may provide important information for predicting NSSI.

Theory is similarly important for identifying a target study population. Whereas research questions about predicting NSSI severity may be best suited to data collected from clinical samples, questions about predicting *first onset* of NSSI may be better suited to data collected from the general population. However, a key factor to consider for classification problems (e.g., predicting if participants will start engaging in NSSI) is the expected base rate of the outcome variable. While the prevalence of NSSI in nonclinical samples ranges from 5% to 17%, the incidence of NSSI within a specified research time frame will be much lower. Such *class imbalance* can pose significant challenges for building classification models. For instance, if 99% of participants in a dataset do *not* develop NSSI during a specified time period, a ML model could achieve 99% accuracy by simply predicting that no participants engage in NSSI—but this would not be a useful or informative model. These challenges can be addressed by carefully considering factors such as the time frame for data collection, frequency of data collection, and population characteristics (e.g., age).

Feature Engineering

In ML, feature engineering refers to the preprocessing steps of encoding, representing, and transforming *features* (i.e., independent variables) from raw data before building a model. Common issues to navigate in feature engineering include managing features that were measured on different scales have extreme outliers, missing values, zero or near-zero variance, or are highly correlated or redundant with other features in the dataset. To manage these and other issues, common steps for feature engineering include transforming features (e.g., centering and scaling), reducing the number of features (e.g., removing those with zero or near-zero variance), or creating new features (e.g., interaction terms).

While many feature engineering steps are governed by model assumptions (e.g., many models require features to be rescaled to the same measurement scale prior to analysis), theory can also inform features constructed from the data collected. For example, in the neighboring field of suicide prediction, prior research and theory suggested that suicidal thinking can fluctuate rapidly over time within people, and that variability in suicidal thought severity might be an important risk factor for future suicide attempts (Kleiman et al., 2017; Witte et al., 2005). Given this, Wang et al. (2021) constructed features from ecological momentary assessment data that indexed the likelihood of patients experiencing rapid fluctuations in suicidal thinking; these features emerged as the most important variables in a ML model to predict future suicide attempts. Thus, using theory to guide feature engineering may not only improve the accuracy of ML models but also inform future measurement, study design, and potential targets for intervention.

Outcome Measurement

Just as effective study design requires thoughtful consideration of theory, building accurate and useful ML models requires (a) a rigorous understanding of the outcome that we are predicting and (b) precise measurement of said outcome. Practically, this means that the predictive power of our ML models is limited by our current issues in measurement; without accurate and thorough measurement, even our most well-constructed model will be predicting a lot of noise. The fifth edition of *Diagnostic and Statistical Manual of Mental Disorders* (DSM-5; American Psychiatric Association, 2013) defines NSSI as intentional, deliberate, and self-inflicted damage to bodily tissue without suicidal intent. Therefore, it is important that self-report or interview-based measures of NSSI are well aligned with this definition (e.g., assessing behaviors such as self-cutting and self-burning while avoiding ambiguous behaviors such as pinching oneself or wearing shoes that are too tight) and are validated and psychometrically sound. Furthermore, it is also important to consider whether the measures have been validated for the *method* of data collection (i.e., online vs. in person). For example, the revised version of the Self-Injurious Behavior Interview-Revised (SITBI-R; Fox et al., 2020) provides a clear, precise definition of NSSI while also specifying that socially sanctioned (e.g., tattooing), minor (e.g., scab picking), and indirect (e.g., disordered eating) forms of self-injurious behavior should not be considered NSSI. Additionally, the measure has been validated for adolescents, adults, online and in-person. The use of the SITBI-R—or similar measures—to measure NSSI would provide rich, specific data likely to contribute to improved accuracy in ML models.

Finally, it is also important to consider whether validated measures will generalize to all individuals in a target population. For instance, if a measure has only been validated in samples of White, cisgender, heterosexual, and wealthy individuals, researchers should consider whether the measure can adequately capture the outcome of interest in more diverse populations. Otherwise, resulting ML models may be biased in under- or overpredicting NSSI for individuals from various backgrounds.

Missing Data

Ideally, when a researcher performs individual-level data collection, the individual provides all requested information. Practically, however, individuals may not complete all questionnaire or interview-based measures, perform every behavioral task assignment, or complete the study outcome NSSI questionnaire. Handling nonresponse within the ML data-analytic pipeline is critical to avoid biased predictions. Survey and task participation may be impacted by sociodemographic and psychological considerations as well as survey/task design. Survey design includes length and difficulty of the survey, interviewer abilities/attributes, and format—that is, face-to-face, telephone, or automated assessment via electronic device (Dillman, 2011). Moreover, participation can be impacted by researcher-chosen incentives which can include monetary and nonmonetary options (Church, 1993).

Missing data are often classified into three categories (Little & Rubin, 2019): (a) missing completely at random (MCAR), (b) missing at random (MAR), and (c) missing not at random (MNAR). MCAR refers to the missing data mechanism being entirely independent of the data. In this case, rows with complete data can be considered a random subset and thus listwise deletion of rows with missing data will not cause bias. In this case, ML models and evaluation can be performed within a complete-case framework with only a potential loss in predictive accuracy due to data loss and not due to bias. Analyzing complete data is problematic when missingness may depend on observed or unobserved covariates (i.e., MAR and MNAR, respectively). Given the observed data, it is impossible to test MAR versus MNAR (Enders, 2022). Researchers must assess whether MAR (i.e., missingness is conditionally independent of the outcome given the other observed variables) is a reasonable assumption. Data collection may be designed to ensure MAR is a reasonable starting point.

Many statistical imputation techniques exist and are common in social science research including unconditional mean imputation, multiple imputation (MI), k-nearest neighbor (KNN) imputation, and decision-tree algorithms. Regardless of which technique is employed, it is recommended to follow best practices of the missing-data literature to include as many auxiliary variables as possible and any variables that will be used in the subsequent ML predictive models (Enders, 2022; Little & Rubin, 2019). Imputation is performed within the standard training/test framework of evaluating ML models. Given the training sample, imputation is part of k-fold cross-validation when choosing the optimal hyperparameters as well as when training the complete predictive model. Even when performing imputation, missing data indicators can be used as features in the predictive model, which may be important if missingness is seen as an indicator of NSSI risk.

Ethics

In recent years, there has been an increased interest in replicability, research transparency, and open science across the field of psychological science—and for good reason. The ability to conduct rigorous, reproducible research is not only of methodological concern but an ethical concern as well. Our ability to improve conditions for those with mental health conditions and to responsibly use government resources (i.e., funding) requires that we, as a field, conduct research that is rigorous, reproducible, and open (Tackett et al., 2019). However, as discussed above, theory (or lack thereof) and researcher choices (e.g., study design and measurement) can contribute to findings that are difficult to reproduce; ML is not immune to these issues. While concerns about reproducibility have been primarily applied to traditional, inferential statistical methods, the same concerns apply to ML (Jacobson et al., 2020). Researcher degrees of freedom can contribute to multiple choices along the research process that can contribute to issues of replicability. One common example in ML is data leakage (i.e., training the ML model using information that would not typically be available in the training set), which can inadvertently occur when researchers fail to make a priori decisions during the model training and evaluation stage. As such, ML can benefit from the same recommendations suggested to improve reproducibility in inferential statistics: clear and public documentation of analytic decisions (i.e., preregistration) and methodological transparency (i.e., open materials and open data).

As is the nature of most psychological research, working with high-risk and vulnerable populations carries an ethical responsibility. Often, ML models are informed by real-time physiological and self-report data, and although this data may work to improve the accuracy of our models, it also introduces a new ethical conundrum: *what do we do when we, as researchers, gain information about someone's engagement in NSSI?* Furthermore, given the predictive power of ML models, another question arises: *What do we do when our model predicts someone's at elevated risk for NSSI? Who do we notify (e.g., the participant, their clinician—or, in the case of minors—their parents) when we detect risk of NSSI?* A recently published consensus statement on best practices for ethics and safety in digital monitoring studies with high-risk populations (e.g., suicidal individuals) offers various considerations that likely apply to NSSI as well (Nock et al., 2021); however, ultimately, decisions about intervening upon potential NSSI should also be made with the input of those with lived experience (e.g., through community-based participatory research and focus groups). Importantly, we can only intervene upon detected NSSI if we have effective interventions; the ability to detect and predict NSSI is only useful insofar as we have effective, scalable interventions to provide. Therefore, alongside this predictive research, there needs to be a simultaneous focus on the development of interventions for NSSI.

Implications

ML models are rapidly emerging across psychopathology research, including for NSSI prediction and detection. There are several important implications of ML implementations for NSSI, including for research and clinical practice. First, all ML models in NSSI research to date have solely relied on *internal* validation (e.g., splitting a single dataset into multiple training and testing subsets to examine model performance). Ultimately, we hope to see the field invest in large-scale collaborations to facilitate *external* validation, which can provide more useful information about the ability of models to accurately predict and detect NSSI in new situations. In addition, when building ML models, it is crucial to consider whether training datasets are representative of the population for which they will ultimately be used for. The field of NSSI research—not unlike psychopathology research in general—is limited by predominantly White samples. Individuals from racial and ethnic minority backgrounds may be less likely to seek and receive treatment, or develop NSSI due to different risk factors (e.g., racism and discrimination) (Polanco-Roman et al., 2014; Rojas-Velasquez et al., 2021). Relying on models developed from nondiverse and nonrepresentative samples, which do not consider factors relevant to individuals from various racial and ethnic groups, may *worsen* existing disparities in NSSI research and treatment. Thus, it is crucial to collect larger, more representative datasets in future projects aiming to harness ML for NSSI research.

Second, and relatedly, ML models have significant implications for clinical practice. Even if researchers were able to optimize a ML model to detect and predict NSSI with near-perfect accuracy, what would we do with that information? A recent meta-analysis of the past 50 years of research found that effect sizes for all NSSI interventions (and interventions for self-injurious thoughts and behaviors more broadly) are small, and that there has been no significant improvement in treatment efficacy over time (Fox et al., 2020). Further, no intervention to date appears consistently stronger than others (Fox et al., 2020). As described above, ML methods hold significant promise for identifying promising treatments for individuals; however, we also believe that new treatments are needed. A greater focus on theory development and elucidating the causes of NSSI—including in ML research—may facilitate more effective, scalable interventions which are sorely needed.

This chapter described the shift from *explanatory* to *predictive* modeling, reviewed ML applications in NSSI research to date, discussed the importance of theory for informing research choices throughout the ML process, and considered ethical challenges inherent in this work. Continued research in these areas, alongside treatment and intervention research, can provide crucial information to advance the understanding, prediction, and prevention of NSSI.

Acknowledgments

Shirley Wang is supported by the National Science Foundation Graduate Research Fellowship under Grant No. DGE-1745303 and the National Institute of Mental Health under Grant F31MH125495.

References

Adrian, M., Zeman, J., Erdley, C., Lisa, L., & Sim, L. (2011). Emotional dysregulation and interpersonal difficulties as risk factors for nonsuicidal self-injury in adolescent girls. *Journal of Abnormal Child Psychology*, *39*(3), 389–400. https://doi.org/10.1007/s10802-010-9465-3

American Psychiatric Association. (2013). *Diagnostic and statistical manual of mental disorders* (5th ed.).

Andover, M. S., Morris, B. W., Wren, A., & Bruzzese, M. E. (2012). The co-occurrence of non-suicidal self-injury and attempted suicide among adolescents: Distinguishing risk factors and psychosocial correlates. *Child and Adolescent Psychiatry and Mental Health*, *6*(1), 1–7. https://doi.org/10.1186/1753-2000-6-11

Barak-Corren, Y., Castro, V. M., Javitt, S., Hoffnagle, A. G., Dai, Y., Perlis, R. H., Nock, M. K., Smoller, J. W., & Reis, B. Y. (2016). Predicting suicidal behavior from longitudinal electronic health records. *American Journal of Psychiatry*, *174*(2), 154–162. https://doi.org/10.1176/appi.ajp.2016.16010077

Barenholtz, E., Fitzgerald, N. D., & Hahn, W. E. (2020). Machine-learning approaches to substance-abuse research: Emerging trends and their implications. *Current Opinion in Psychiatry*, *33*(4), 334–342. https://doi.org/10.1097/YCO.0000000000000611

Blei, D. M., Ng, A. Y., & Jordan, M. I. (2003, January). Latent dirichlet allocation. *Journal of Machine Learning Research*, *3*, 993–1022.

Bokma, W. A., Zhutovsky, P., Giltay, E. J., Schoevers, R. A., Penninx, B. W. J. H., van Balkom, A. L. J. M., Batelaan, N. M., & van Wingen, G. A. (2022). Predicting the naturalistic course in anxiety disorders using clinical and biological markers: A machine learning approach. *Psychological Medicine*, *52*(1), 57–67. https://doi.org/10.1017/S0033291720001658

Breiman, L. (2001). Statistical modeling: The two cultures (with comments and a rejoinder by the author). *Statistical Science*, *16*(3), 199–231. https://doi.org/10.1214/ss/1009213726

Burke, T. A., Allen, K. J. D., Carpenter, R. W., Siegel, D. M., Kautz, M. M., Liu, R. T., & Alloy, L. B. (2021). Emotional response inhibition to self-harm stimuli interacts with momentary negative affect to predict nonsuicidal self-injury urges. *Behaviour Research and Therapy*, *142*, Article 103865. https://doi.org/10.1016/j.brat.2021.103865

Carpenter, S. M., Menictas, M., Nahum-Shani, I., Wetter, D. W., & Murphy, S. A. (2020). Developments in mobile health just-in-time adaptive interventions for addiction science. *Current Addiction Reports*, *7*(3), 280–290. https://doi.org/10.1007/s40429-020-00322-y

Chekroud, A. M., Zotti, R. J., Shehzad, Z., Gueorguieva, R., Johnson, M. K., Trivedi, M. H., Cannon, T. D., Krystal, J. H., & Corlett, P. R. (2016). Cross-trial prediction of treatment outcome in depression: A machine learning approach. *The Lancet Psychiatry*, *3*(3), 243–250. https://doi.org/10.1016/S2215-0366(15)00471-X

Cheng, Q., Li, T. M., Kwok, C.-L., Zhu, T., & Yip, P. S. (2017). Assessing suicide risk and emotional distress in Chinese social media: A text mining and machine learning study. *Journal of Medical Internet Research*, *19*(7), Article e7276. https://doi.org/10.2196/jmir.7276

Chiong, R., Budhi, G. S., Dhakal, S., & Chiong, F. (2021). A textual-based featuring approach for depression detection using machine learning classifiers and social media texts. *Computers in Biology and Medicine*, *135*, Article 104499. https://doi.org/10.1016/j.compbiomed.2021.104499

Christodoulou, E., Ma, J., Collins, G. S., Steyerberg, E. W., Verbakel, J. Y., & Van Calster, B. (2019). A systematic review shows no performance benefit of machine learning over logistic regression for clinical prediction models. *Journal of Clinical Epidemiology*, *110*, 12–22. https://doi.org/10.1016/j.jclinepi.2019.02.004

Church, A. H. (1993). Estimating the effect of incentives on mail survey response rates: A meta-analysis. *Public Opinion Quarterly*, *57*(1), 62–79. https://doi.org/10.1086/269355

Collins, G. S., Reitsma, J. B., Altman, D. G., & Moons, K. G. (2015). Transparent reporting of a multivariable prediction model for individual prognosis or diagnosis (TRIPOD): The TRIPOD statement. *Circulation*, *131*(2), 211–219.

Coughlin, L. N., Tegge, A. N., Sheffer, C. E., & Bickel, W. K. (2020). A machine-learning approach to predicting smoking cessation treatment outcomes. *Nicotine and Tobacco Research*, *22*(3), 415–422. https://doi.org/10.1093/ntr/nty259

Cucchi, A., Ryan, D., Konstantakopoulos, G., Stroumpa, S., Kaçar, A. Ş., Renshaw, S., Landau, S., & Kravariti, E. (2016). Lifetime prevalence of non-suicidal self-injury in patients with eating disorders: A systematic review and meta-analysis. *Psychological Medicine*, *46*(7), 1345–1358. https://doi.org/10.1017/S0033291716000027

de la Garza, Á. G., Blanco, C., Olfson, M., & Wall, M. M. (2021). Identification of suicide attempt risk factors in a national US survey using machine learning. *JAMA Psychiatry, 78*(4), 398–406. https://doi.org/10.1001/jamapsychiatry.2020.4165

DeRubeis, R. J. (2019). The history, current status, and possible future of precision mental health. *Behaviour Research and Therapy, 123*, Article 103506. https://doi.org/10.1016/j.brat.2019.103506

Dillman, D. A. (2011). *Mail and Internet surveys: The tailored design method–2007 Update with new Internet, visual, and mixed-mode guide*. John Wiley & Sons.

Dwyer, D. B., Falkai, P., & Koutsouleris, N. (2018). Machine learning approaches for clinical psychology and psychiatry. *Annual Review of Clinical Psychology, 14*(1), 91–118. https://doi.org/10.1146/annurev-clinpsy-032816-045037

Enders, C. K. (2022). *Applied missing data analysis*. Guilford Press.

Fox, K. R., Huang, X., Guzmán, E. M., Funsch, K. M., Cha, C. B., Ribeiro, J. D., & Franklin, J. C. (2020). Interventions for suicide and self-injury: A meta-analysis of randomized controlled trials across nearly 50 years of research. *Psychological Bulletin, 146*(12), 1117–1145. https://doi.org/10.1037/bul0000305

Fox, K. R., Huang, X., Linthicum, K. P., Wang, S. B., Franklin, J. C., & Ribeiro, J. D. (2019). Model complexity improves the prediction of nonsuicidal self-injury. *Journal of Consulting and Clinical Psychology, 87*(8), 684–692. https://doi.org/10.1037/ccp0000421

Fox, K. R., Ribeiro, J. D., Kleiman, E. M., Hooley, J. M., Nock, M. K., & Franklin, J. C. (2018). Affect toward the self and self-injury stimuli as potential risk factors for nonsuicidal self-injury. *Psychiatry Research, 260*, 279–285. https://doi.org/10.1016/j.psychres.2017.11.083

Franz, P. J., Nook, E. C., Mair, P., & Nock, M. K. (2020). Using topic modeling to detect and describe self-injurious and related content on a large-scale digital platform. *Suicide and Life-Threatening Behavior, 50*(1), 5–18. https://doi.org/10.1111/sltb.12569

Glenn, C. R., & Klonsky, E. D. (2013). Non-suicidal self-injury disorder: An empirical investigation in adolescent psychiatric patients. Journal of Clinical Child and Adolescent Psychology: The Official *Journal for the Society of Clinical Child and Adolescent Psychology, American Psychological Association, Division 53, 42*(4), 496–507. https://doi.org/10.1080/15374416.2013.794699

Haynos, A. F., Wang, S. B., Lipson, S., Peterson, C. B., Mitchell, J. E., Halmi, K. A., Agras, W. S., & Crow, S. J. (2021). Machine learning enhances prediction of illness course: A longitudinal study in eating disorders. *Psychological Medicine, 51*(8), 1392–1402. https://doi.org/10.1017/S0033291720000227

Hornstein, S., Forman-Hoffman, V., Nazander, A., Ranta, K., & Hilbert, K. (2021). Predicting therapy outcome in a digital mental health intervention for depression and anxiety: A machine learning approach. *Digital Health, 7*, Article 20552076211060660. https://doi.org/10.1177/20552076211060659

Huang, X., Ribeiro, J. D., & Franklin, J. C. (2020). The differences between individuals engaging in nonsuicidal self-injury and suicide attempt are complex (vs. complicated or simple). *Frontiers in Psychiatry, 11*, Article 239. https://www.frontiersin.org/article/10.3389/fpsyt.2020.00239

Islam, M., Kabir, M. A., Ahmed, A., Kamal, A. R. M., Wang, H., & Ulhaq, A. (2018). Depression detection from social network data using machine learning techniques. *Health Information Science and Systems, 6*(1), 1–12. https://doi.org/10.1007/s13755-018-0046-0

Jacobson, N. C., Bentley, K. H., Walton, A., Wang, S. B., Fortgang, R. G., Millner, A. J., Coombs, G., Rodman, A. M., & Coppersmith, D. D. L. (2020). Ethical dilemmas posed by mobile health and machine learning in psychiatry research. *Bulletin of the World Health Organization, 98*(4), 270–276. https://doi.org/10.2471/BLT.19.237107

James, G., Witten, D., Hastie, T., & Tibshirani, R. (2013). *An introduction to statistical learning* (Vol. 103). Springer. https://doi.org/10.1007/978-1-4614-7138-7

Juarascio, A., Srivastava, P., Presseller, E., Clark, K., Manasse, S., & Forman, E. (2021). A clinician-controlled just-in-time adaptive intervention system (CBT+) designed to promote acquisition and utilization of cognitive behavioral therapy skills in bulimia nervosa: Development and preliminary evaluation study. *JMIR Formative Research, 5*(5), Article e18261. https://doi.org/10.2196/18261

Kessler, R. C., Stein, M. B., Petukhova, M. V., Bliese, P., Bossarte, R. M., Bromet, E. J., Fullerton, C. S., Gilman, S. E., Ivany, C., Lewandowski-Romps, L., Bell, A. M., Naifeh, J. A., Nock, M. K., Reis, B. Y., Rosellini, A. J., Sampson, N. A., Zaslavsky, A. M., & Ursano, R. J. (2017). Predicting suicides after outpatient mental health visits in the Army Study to Assess Risk and Resilience in Servicemembers (Army STARRS). *Molecular Psychiatry, 22*(4), 544–551. https://doi.org/10.1038/mp.2016.110

Kleiman, E. M., Turner, B. J., Fedor, S., Beale, E. E., Huffman, J. C., & Nock, M. K. (2017). Examination of real-time fluctuations in suicidal ideation and its risk factors: Results from two ecological momentary assessment studies. *Journal of Abnormal Psychology*, *126*(6), 726–738. https://doi.org/10.1037/abn0000273

Kuhn, M., & Johnson, K. (2013). *Applied predictive modeling*. Springer-Verlag. https://doi.org/10.1007/978-1-4614-6849-3

Lee, Y., Ragguett, R.-M., Mansur, R. B., Boutilier, J. J., Rosenblat, J. D., Trevizol, A., Brietzke, E., Lin, K., Pan, Z., & Subramaniapillai, M. (2018). Applications of machine learning algorithms to predict therapeutic outcomes in depression: A meta-analysis and systematic review. *Journal of Affective Disorders*, *241*, 519–532. https://doi.org/10.1016/j.jad.2018.08.073

Little, R. J., & Rubin, D. B. (2019). *Statistical analysis with missing data* (Vol. 793). John Wiley & Sons.

Nahum-Shani, I., Smith, S. N., Spring, B. J., Collins, L. M., Witkiewitz, K., Tewari, A., & Murphy, S. A. (2018). Just-in-time adaptive interventions (JITAIs) in mobile health: Key components and design principles for ongoing health behavior support. *Annals of Behavioral Medicine*, *52*(6), 446–462. https://doi.org/10.1007/s12160-016-9830-8

Nock, M. K. (2010). Self-injury. *Annual Review of Clinical Psychology*, *6*(1), 339–363. https://doi.org/10.1146/annurev.clinpsy.121208.131258

Nock, M. K., Kleiman, E. M., Abraham, M., Bentley, K. H., Brent, D. A., Buonopane, R. J., Castro-Ramirez, F., Cha, C. B., Dempsey, W., Draper, J., Glenn, C. R., Harkavy-Friedman, J., Hollander, M. R., Huffman, J. C., Lee, H. I. S., Millner, A. J., Mou, D., Onnela, J.-P., Picard, R. W., . . . Pearson, J. L. (2021). Consensus statement on ethical & safety practices for conducting digital monitoring studies with people at risk of suicide and related behaviors. *Psychiatric Research and Clinical Practice*, *3*(2), 57–66. https://doi.org/10.1176/appi.prcp.20200029

Polanco-Roman, L., Tsypes, A., Soffer, A., & Miranda, R. (2014). Ethnic differences in prevalence and correlates of self-harm behaviors in a treatment-seeking sample of emerging adults. *Psychiatry Research*, *220*(3), 927–934. https://doi.org/10.1016/j.psychres.2014.09.017

Ribeiro, J. D., Franklin, J. C., Fox, K. R., Bentley, K. H., Kleiman, E. M., Chang, B. P., & Nock, M. K. (2016). Self-injurious thoughts and behaviors as risk factors for future suicide ideation, attempts, and death: A meta-analysis of longitudinal studies. *Psychological Medicine*, *46*(2), 225–236. http://dx.doi.org/10.1017/S0033291715001804

Riley, E. N., Combs, J. L., Jordan, C. E., & Smith, G. T. (2015). Negative urgency and lack of perseverance: Identification of differential pathways of onset and maintenance risk in the longitudinal prediction of nonsuicidal self-injury. *Behavior Therapy*, *46*(4), 439–448. https://doi.org/10.1016/j.beth.2015.03.002

Rojas-Velasquez, D. A., Pluhar, E. I., Burns, P. A., & Burton, E. T. (2021). Nonsuicidal self-injury among African American and Hispanic adolescents and young adults: A systematic review. *Prevention Science*, *22*(3), 367–377. https://doi.org/10.1007/s11121-020-01147-x

Roy, A., Nikolitch, K., McGinn, R., Jinah, S., Klement, W., & Kaminsky, Z. A. (2020). A machine learning approach predicts future risk to suicidal ideation from social media data. *NPJ Digital Medicine*, *3*(1), 1–12. https://doi.org/10.1038/s41746-020-0287-6

Strobl, C., Malley, J., & Tutz, G. (2009). An introduction to recursive partitioning: Rationale, application and characteristics of classification and regression trees, bagging and random forests. *Psychological Methods*, *14*(4), 323–348. https://doi.org/10.1037/a0016973

Su, C., Aseltine, R., Doshi, R., Chen, K., Rogers, S. C., & Wang, F. (2020). Machine learning for suicide risk prediction in children and adolescents with electronic health records. *Translational Psychiatry*, *10*(1), 1–10. https://doi.org/10.1038/s41398-020-01100-0

Swannell, S. V., Martin, G. E., Page, A., Hasking, P., & St John, N. J. (2014). Prevalence of nonsuicidal self-injury in nonclinical samples: Systematic review, meta-analysis and meta-regression. *Suicide and Life-Threatening Behavior*, *44*(3), 273–303. https://doi.org/10.1111/sltb.12070

Tackett, J. L., Brandes, C. M., King, K. M., & Markon, K. E. (2019). Psychology's replication crisis and clinical psychological science. *Annual Review of Clinical Psychology*, *15*, 579–604. https://doi.org/10.1146/annurev-clinpsy-050718-095710

Tatnell, R., Kelada, L., Hasking, P., & Martin, G. (2014). Longitudinal analysis of adolescent NSSI: The role of intrapersonal and interpersonal factors. *Journal of Abnormal Child Psychology*, *42*(6), 885–896. https://doi.org/10.1007/s10802-013-9837-6

Voon, D., Hasking, P., & Martin, G. (2014). Change in emotion regulation strategy use and its impact on adolescent nonsuicidal self-injury: A three-year longitudinal analysis using latent growth modeling. *Journal of Abnormal Psychology, 123*(3), 487–498. https://doi.org/10.1037/a0037024

Wang, S. B. (2021). Machine learning to advance the prediction, prevention and treatment of eating disorders. *European Eating Disorders Review, 29*(5), 683–691.

Wang, S. B., Coppersmith, D. D. L., Kleiman, E. M., Bentley, K. H., Millner, A. J., Fortgang, R., Mair, P., Dempsey, W., Huffman, J. C., & Nock, M. K. (2021). A pilot study using frequent inpatient assessments of suicidal thinking to predict short-term postdischarge suicidal behavior. *JAMA Network Open, 4*(3), Article e210591. https://doi.org/10.1001/jamanetworkopen.2021.0591

Witte, T. K., Fitzpatrick, K. K., Joiner, T. E., & Schmidt, N. B. (2005). Variability in suicidal ideation: A better predictor of suicide attempts than intensity or duration of ideation? *Journal of Affective Disorders, 88*(2), 131–136. https://doi.org/10.1016/j.jad.2005.05.019

Xian, L., Vickers, S. D., Giordano, A. L., Lee, J., Kim, I. K., & Ramaswamy, L. (2019). *# selfha rm on Instagram: Quantitative analysis and classification of non-suicidal self-injury* [Paper presentation]. 2019 IEEE First International Conference on Cognitive Machine Intelligence (CogMI) (pp. 61–70). https://doi.org/10.1109/CogMI48466.2019.00017

Yarkoni, T., & Westfall, J. (2017). Choosing prediction over explanation in psychology: Lessons from machine learning. *Perspectives on Psychological Science: A Journal of the Association for Psychological Science, 12*(6), 1100–1122. https://doi.org/10.1177/1745691617693393

Zhang, T., Schoene, A. M., Ji, S., & Ananiadou, S. (2022). Natural language processing applied to mental illness detection: A narrative review. *npj Digital Medicine, 5*(1), 1–13. https://doi.org/10.1038/s41746-022-00589-7

Zuromski, K. L., Bernecker, S. L., Gutierrez, P. M., Joiner, T. E., King, A. J., Liu, H., Naifeh, J. A., Nock, M. K., Sampson, N. A., Zaslavsky, A. M., Stein, M. B., Ursano, R. J., & Kessler, R. C. (2019). Assessment of a risk index for suicide attempts among US army soldiers with suicide ideation: Analysis of data from the Army Study to Assess Risk and Resilience in Servicemembers (Army STARRS). *JAMA Network Open, 2*(3), Article e190766. https://doi.org/10.1001/jamanetworkopen.2019.0766

CHAPTER 52

Managing NSSI Across Different Treatment Contexts

Franziska Rockstroh *and* Michael Kaess

Abstract

Nonsuicidal self-injury (NSSI) is a common transdiagnostic behavior which can be observed in different clinical contexts and is associated with phenomena such as severe emotion dysregulation, suicidality, and other high-risk behaviors. This chapter gives an overview of the common challenges before and in treatment, and presents recent research on treatment programs on different interventional levels. Core elements and goals of treating NSSI are outlined. In order to gain a clear understanding of the behavior and to establish a transparent treatment plan, the importance of a thorough diagnostic evaluation is discussed. After patients present with self-injuries and acute wound care is provided, an assessment of the behavior itself but also comorbid psychopathology and (acute) suicidality by specifically trained clinicians is always indicated. This chapter presents guidelines for assessing and working with NSSI across different settings to facilitate clinical decision-making. Over the past years, efforts have been made by clinicians and researchers to advance the treatment of NSSI with a particular focus on reaching a wider at-risk population through low-threshold interventions and stepped-care approaches, developing evidence-based treatment programs, and improving recommendations for handling NSSI in inpatient settings. The last section discusses current challenges and future directions for managing NSSI, and a clinical case report sets the chapter's content into context.

Key Words: nonsuicidal self-injury, treatment, comorbid psychopathology, suicidality, clinical decision-making, emotion dysregulation

Treatment of NSSI Across Different Treatment Contexts

NSSI in Different Treatment Contexts

Nonsuicidal self-injury (NSSI) has become a widespread and common phenomenon in recent years that is not exclusive to psychiatric populations (see Staring, Kiekens, & Kirtley, this volume, on NSSI epidemiology in nonclinical samples). It occurs with increasing frequency in the general public (between 4% and 5.9%) and particularly among adolescents (around 17% in adolescents with 3%–4% showing repetitive NSSI) (Klonsky, 2011; Plener et al., 2014; Swannell et al., 2014). In addition to physical complications like scarring and infections, people engaging in NSSI often experience limitations in social relationships, employment, or education, as well as reduced well-being and quality of life (Kaess et al., 2017; Üstün & Kennedy, 2009; Victor et al., 2019). Further, NSSI occurs alongside various psychiatric disorders, such as mood disorders, eating disorders, anxiety disorders, substance abuse disorders, or posttraumatic stress disorder, and is highly associated with suicide attempts (Chesin et al., 2017; Ghinea et al., 2020; see Victor, Christensen, & Trieu, this volume, on the link between NSSI and suicide). Considering its clinical significance, it is not surprising that incidents of NSSI are common on psychiatric inpatient units: from 4% (Bowers et al., 2003) up to 70% (Swinton et al., 1998) of inpatients have been reported to engage in NSSI. In a study of adult psychiatric inpatients, 45.3% of the sample had engaged in NSSI (Andover & Gibb, 2010). Among adult inpatients, 1 of 10 patients will likely self-injure and most acts of suicidal and nonsuicidal self-injury occur shortly after inpatient admission (Stewart et al., 2012). Studies report that NSSI episodes in inpatients often follow adverse events, such as change in therapist or when the usual therapist is not available (e.g., due to vacation or staffing turnover) (Ulke et al., 2014). In turn, self-injuring patients who are hospitalized often have a prolonged length of stay with a resultant increased likelihood of therapist turnover (Timberlake et al., 2020). A study in adolescents found more than 50% of inpatients showing experiences with at least one suicidal or nonsuicidal self-injury in the past while 38.5% fulfilled criteria according to the fifth edition of *Diagnostic and Statistical Manual of Mental Disorders* (DSM-5; American Psychiatric Association, 2013) for NSSI (Sevecke et al., 2017). This is in line with previous findings that point to rates between 30% and 61% of psychiatric patients engaging in NSSI (Jacobson et al., 2008; Kaess et al., 2013; Klonsky & Muehlenkamp, 2007; Nock & Prinstein, 2004; Washburn et al., 2012).

The prevalence and comorbidity of NSSI with psychiatric disorders indicate a public health problem that requires effective intervention strategies. As NSSI occurs in various forms, severities, and contexts, it is important to determine the optimal treatment setting for individuals who self-injure and set up an individualized intervention strategy. General recommendations in the literature suggest that hospitalizations should be brief and that NSSI is best managed in structured outpatient psychotherapy (Linehan, 1993; Paris, 2004). Inpatient treatment should be highly specialized and reserved for the treatment of patients with the most severe psychiatric disorders.

Studies have shown that longer inpatient admissions might be associated with increased risk of self-injury (Bowers et al., 2008; Stewart et al., 2009). There are several factors that are proposed to be distressing for patients on inpatient units, and may thus contribute to incidents of self-injury: patients may be distressed by the interaction with other inpatients or staff, by the rules and routines of life on the ward including diagnostic or treatment procedures such as blood sampling, as well as restrictions of involuntary admission (de Kloet et al., 2011; Spencer et al., 2019). Feelings of loneliness and isolation from significant others as well as a lack of stimulation are further potential triggers of suicidal or nonsuicidal self-injury on inpatient units (Haynes et al., 2011; Nijman &

à Campo, 2002). It also might be that patients use NSSI as a way of seeking help when they do not feel supported by the staff on inpatient wards (Klonsky et al., 2015). NSSI has shown to be associated with regression (Bresin, 2014; Selby et al., 2013). Since patients engaging in NSSI tend to regress quickly during hospitalization, this will also contribute to an increased frequency of NSSI. Given the potential adverse consequences of hospitalization alongside the increased costs of inpatient care, current guidelines for managing self-injury suggest, ideally, avoiding inpatient admissions. However, the dilemma is that NSSI remains a symptom of many psychiatric patients who require admission for other reasons. Currently, there is no consensus on the most appropriate means of reducing and managing suicidal and non-suicidal self-injury during inpatient admissions (Nawaz et al., 2021). In the following sections, we give an overview of challenges commonly faced by clinicians and patients with NSSI and elaborate further on recent findings regarding the efficacy of NSSI treatment across settings.

General Challenges in the Treatment of NSSI

There are two major challenges in the treatment of NSSI. Most adolescents who suffer from NSSI and associated mental health problems have neither been competently diagnosed or adequately counseled nor are even undergoing treatment. Previous research illustrated that adolescents usually show an extremely low rate of help-seeking behavior, especially in the context of NSSI (Doyle et al., 2015; Pumpa & Martin, 2015; Rowe et al., 2014). One reason for this is the short-term but effective function of NSSI to manage emotional distress (Klonsky et al., 2015). It provides a quick relief from acutely intense negative mood or tension reduction which occur either in the context of specific life events or as a result of psychiatric disorders such as depression or, in particular, borderline personality disorder. NSSI is therefore highly reinforcing in adolescents with problematic emotion regulation while other emotion regulation strategies are not resorted to (Robinson et al., 2019). A second reason for low help-seeking among adolescents with NSSI are the negative attitudes toward professional help and treatment for adolescents who self-injure. In order to seek and accept help, adolescents need to be open and ready to self-disclose which often constitutes a substantial first barrier. Positive attitudes toward help and treatment are significantly related to greater willingness to seek help. Adolescents who currently report NSSI express significantly more negative attitudes toward help-seeking compared to adolescents who either never experienced suicidal and nonsuicidal self-injury or stopped the behavior in the past (Pumpa & Martin, 2015). These negative attitudes toward treatment and help arise from interpersonal barriers, such as negative reactions from the environment, and the accompanied stigma parents, peers, and mental health professionals often have toward self-harming behaviors (Hasking et al., 2015). Third, if adolescents with NSSI seek help, they are more likely to approach an informal, nonprofessional setting, such as friends and family, or turn to the internet in order to find peer support (Harris & Roberts, 2013; Rowe et al., 2014).

Additionally, there is still an enormous lack of knowledge of where to find help, which prevents help-seeking behavior.

The second major objective in the treatment of NSSI is the lack of specifically developed effective treatments for NSSI. Although there are effective treatments that include or expand on the treatment of NSSI, most of these are not specifically developed for NSSI but primarily for the treatment of, for example, personality disorders, such as mentalization-based treatment for adolescents (MBT-A) or dialectical behavior therapy for adolescents (DBT-A; see Chapman et al., this volume) (Turner et al., 2014). Treatments might not be accessible for many individuals, due to geographical (living in rural areas with limited mental health resources, travel distance to appointments), social (e.g., barriers related to stigma), organizational (e.g., waiting times or service availability), or even financial reasons (e.g., in healthcare contexts where clients must pay for their treatment).

Thus, treatments are comprehensive, are time-consuming, and usually require an intensive training for therapists. It is not desirable to treat all adolescents with borderline- or other disorder-specific therapeutic programs as financial resources in public mental health services are usually scarce (McMain et al., 2017). Therefore, research calls for less intensive but effective treatment programs that focus specifically on the treatment of NSSI to overcome these structural and individual challenges in the treatment of NSSI. These interventions should increase motivation to access therapy and decrease the fear of being stigmatized while being time- and cost-efficient. Plener (2020) summarized these challenges and presented potential solutions for tailoring treatment more specifically to adolescents with NSSI. The proposed framework (see fig. 52.1) includes common barriers currently in place and illustrates many aspects presented in this chapter.

One promising step in line with this framework includes the development of brief interventions with a low threshold and a short time frame as specific treatment approaches for NSSI. Andover et al. (2017) investigated a brief behavioral intervention for NSSI in young adults (treatment for self-injurious behaviors, T-SIB) and found medium effects for decreased NSSI frequency after treatment. Another brief psychotherapeutic program for treating NSSI is "The Cutting Down Program" (CDP). CDP consists of 8 to 12 sessions of individual CBT in two to four months and is based on cognitive behavioral therapy (CBT) and dialectical behavior therapy (DBT) (see Chapman, Hood, & Turner, this volume, for more details on CBT and DBT). In four modules, treatment focuses on enhancing treatment motivation, identifying reasons for NSSI, trying alternative behaviors to NSSI, and consolidation of these alternative behaviors (Taylor et al., 2011). Preliminary data showed that CDP was efficacious in reducing NSSI, suicidality, comorbid depression, and trait anxiety. In a single-centered randomized control trial (RCT), Kaess et al. (2020) found that CDP was equally effective and achieved faster recovery in NSSI frequency, suicide attempts, and depression as well as a significant improvement in quality of life compared to a significantly more intensive treatment as usual (TAU) in treating adolescents with NSSI. These data clearly show the potential of a brief psychotherapeutic

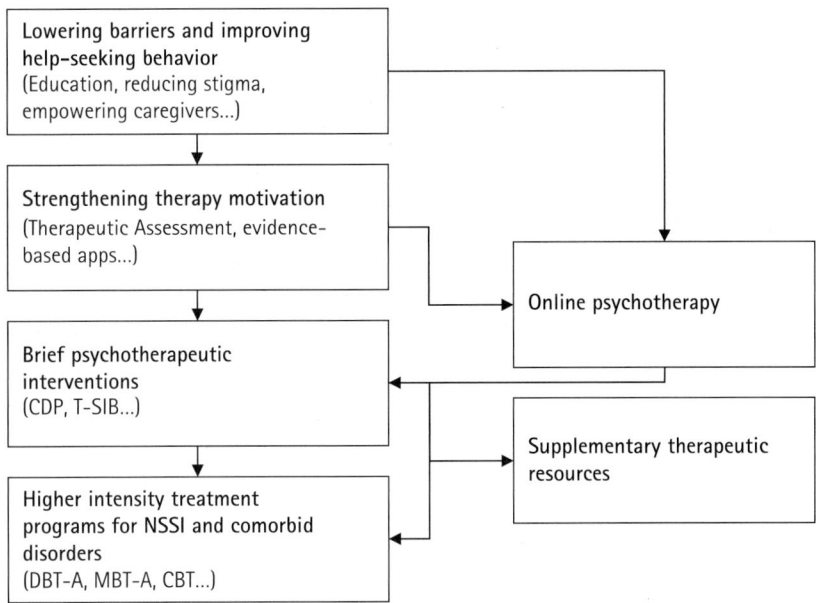

Figure 52.1 Proposed Stepped-Care Approach to Treat NSSI in Adolescents Adapted from Plener, P. L. (2020). Tailoring Treatments for Adolescents with Nonsuicidal Self-Injury. *European Child & Adolescent Psychiatry, 29*(6), 893–895. Reproduced with permission from Springer Nature.

program specifically developed for treating NSSI in help-seeking adolescents. The shorter time span further promotes accessibility for a more diverse target group compared to longer treatment options (Plener, 2020).

As most treatments are based on face-to-face contact, the accessibility to treatment is limited due to geographical reasons among others. Mobile- and internet-based therapeutic interventions have the potential in overcoming structural barriers, such as the accessibility of treatment or required effort needed like waiting times, for example, for adolescents in rural regions with limited mental health resources (please also see Hooley & Fox, this volume, for online therapy for NSSI). The larger the geographical distance to adequate treatment offers, the lower the actual help-seeking behavior (Kaess et al., 2014). Mobile Health refers to therapeutic interventions that are delivered or supported via remote devices, such as mobile phones or computers and has been increasingly considered a fitting medium for mental health interventions (Andersson, 2016). A systematic review showed promising evidence on mobile- and internet-based psychological interventions for self-injury, including NSSI and suicidal behavior, though RCTs are scarce (Arshad et al., 2019). Considering the frequent use of mobile and internet technologies in adolescence, low-threshold online interventions for adolescents engaging in NSSI might be a promising way to overcome low help-seeking behavior and other obstacles, especially as studies have shown that a significant percentage of adolescents and young adults (45%–93%) with risk behavior, including NSSI, prefer a technology-based format over an in-person face-to-face intervention (Ranney et al., 2013; Younes et al., 2015). The STAR Consortium (self-injury: treatment, assessment, recovery) developed an intervention for adolescents engaging in NSSI based on CDP, which is currently investigated in the first RCT comparing an intervention group to online psychoeducation in a sample of 700 participants (Kaess et al., 2019). The intervention targets adolescents who have engaged in NSSI on at least five days in the past year who are currently in neither inpatient nor outpatient psychotherapy. NSSI, comorbid symptoms, and quality of life are assessed at baseline and three follow-up evaluations after 4, 12, and 18 months. Both groups receive access to online psychoeducation containing information on NSSI, emotions, development, and treatment options. In the intervention group, 10 add-on online CDP modules are available on topics such as reasons for NSSI, thoughts, feelings, and behaviors linked to NSSI as well as strategies and skills for coping with NSSI. A fully automatic online content including exercises, quizzes, videos, sessions, and weekly feedback are complemented by personal chats or phone calls with clinical psychologists as well as the option to participate in a moderated group chat. All content is available for four months. Participants are made aware that their answers are not monitored in real time and emergency numbers are provided for acute crises and suicidality. Recruitment is ongoing and first results of the RCT are expected for 2024.

Efficacy of the Different Treatment Settings in Treating NSSI

There are effective psychotherapeutic treatment options for NSSI in adolescents. In order to maintain a daily structure and to sustain psychosocial functioning of patients, outpatient treatment options are generally the setting of choice for NSSI, which also facilitates integration of treatment objectives in daily routines of adolescents with typical challenges and interpersonal difficulties. Across all settings, adequate safety measures are a fundamental prerequisite in the treatment of self-injury, but it is important to note that in general, NSSI itself does not automatically necessitate inpatient treatment.

In the current literature, most evidence is available for specific therapy programs such as DBT-A (Mehlum et al., 2016; Tørmoen et al., 2014), CBT (Kaess et al., 2020; Taylor et al., 2011), and MBT-A (Rossouw & Fonagy, 2012), which was confirmed in a meta-analysis on therapeutic interventions for NSSI: Among 19 RCTs examining psychotherapeutic as well as pharmacological and social interventions, the largest effect sizes for NSSI reduction were detected among these psychotherapeutic treatment programs (Ougrin et al., 2015). All three interventions were not developed specifically for NSSI but rather for treating personality disorders. This results in comprehensive and therefore lengthy and cost-intense programs that require immense resources, and specialized treatment centers are scarce. Good evidence for more focused and lower-threshold programs such as CDP has been reported in recent years (see section "General Challenges in the Treatment of NSSI"), and further optimization of NSSI treatment programs is a main goal for further research.

Particularly for patients with severe or highly repetitive NSSI, traditional outpatient care with weekly therapy sessions may not be sufficient, and modifications to the treatment setting can be necessary. In order to maintain as much of the psychosocial environment as possible and to minimize costs, day care facilities should be considered a balance between strict out- and inpatient settings. Also referred to as partial hospitalization or intensive outpatient care, such programs allow more thorough monitoring of self-injurious and co-occurring risk behaviors during the day while patients remain in their known surroundings. Day care has been found to be effective in the treatment of a range of psychiatric disorders in youth (Frensch & Cameron, 2002; Thatte et al., 2013), but to date only one study examined treatment effects of a partial hospitalization program specifically designed for patients with NSSI (Slesinger et al., 2021). In a large sample of mostly adolescent patients, a significant decrease in NSSI frequency was reported and quality of life was significantly improved from admission to discharge. These findings are encouraging and more studies, especially RCTs, examining NSSI rates and other clinically relevant outcomes in intense psychiatric outpatient settings are necessary.

In some cases, if neither outpatient nor day care settings are adequate, inpatient treatment may be required. Criteria for inpatient admission are presented in the section "Algorithm on the Treatment of NSSI in Adolescents Across Different Treatment Contexts." Generally, treatment needs a clear concept regarding time frame and content such as crisis management, and shorter, more focused interventions should always be preferred over poorly structured long-term therapies (Linehan, 1993; Paris, 2004). Most research on inpatient treatment of NSSI has been conducted in patients with borderline personality disorder (BPD) (Fowler et al., 2018) and similar to day care settings, studies on NSSI-specific inpatient treatment are extremely rare. In an early controlled trial, Bohus et al. (2004) compared DBT in an inpatient setting to outpatient TAU in adult patients meeting BPD criteria. Although there was no significant change in the TAU group, patients receiving DBT showed significant improvement in most variables such as depression, anxiety, and self-injury after three months of treatment. Remission rates and clinically significant improvement remained stable over a two-year follow-up period (Kleindienst et al., 2008). Not many specialized inpatient programs exist for adolescents with NSSI. A German research group published their experiences from a DBT-A therapy inpatient unit for adolescent girls with BPD symptomatology. The concept was adapted structurally from inpatient DBT wards for adults and content-wise from outpatient DBT-A programs. Detailed qualitative information on the program including treatment steps, handling of NSSI, and particular challenges can be found in von Auer et al. (2015). The first year after establishment of the unit was evaluated quantitatively: BPD-specific psychopathology and NSSI frequency was reduced significantly from pre- to posttreatment but, in contrast to findings in adult populations and outpatient DBT-A, general psychopathology remained stable on a high level. The authors called for RCTs and the collection of longitudinal follow-up data to further adapt and improve treatment of NSSI in inpatient settings. In a recent study, DBT-A was evaluated in an acute inpatient unit and patients receiving TAU before implementation of DBT-A were analyzed as a historical control group (Tebbett-Mock et al., 2020). Compared to TAU, self-injury and suicide attempts were significantly reduced in the DBT-A condition. Further, hospitalization days and observation hours were decreased which led to considerably lower staff time and savings of more than $250,000. Boege et al. (2022) developed a program for treating NSSI in adolescent inpatients called "Cut the cut" (CTC) and recently published data from a pilot study. CTC combines well-known and effective psychotherapeutic elements, such as psychoeducation, emotion regulation, and skills training and treats patients in intervals by alternating inpatient treatment and periods at home. Duration of inpatient intervals was steadily decreased and discharge periods increased. By administering CTC in intervals, regression and increases in NSSI frequency are supposed to be minimized while improving self-responsibility. Patients in the CTC group reported a significant reduction in NSSI frequency, severity of NSSI was slightly decreased, and patient as well as parent satisfaction was high. They found no superiority or inferiority over TAU, though, and data from a larger, randomized sample are necessary to validate these findings.

Even though there is consent among mental health professionals that inpatient stays should be avoided among patients with NSSI, admissions are common and research on effective treatment programs is urgently needed. In general, clearly structured treatment programs such as DBT showed good results in reducing NSSI in inpatient settings, particularly among patients who fulfill BPD criteria. In future studies, new and economic programs with a clearer focus on NSSI reduction should be investigated with the overall goal of supporting clinical decision-making among staff working with patients showing suicidal and non-suicidal self-injurious behavior.

Aims and General Elements in the Psychotherapeutic Treatment of NSSI

The shared primary aim of psychotherapeutic interventions for patients with NSSI is the reduction or remission of self-injury. As described above, there are few interventions that seem to be successful in treating self-injury across different treatment contexts, but efficacious interventions share certain components and core elements of psychotherapeutic treatment that are highlighted in the following section (see Box 52.1).

> **Box 52.1 Core Elements across Psychotherapeutic Treatment of NSSI**
>
> - Reaching a clear agreement on how to manage suicidality and NSSI
> - Developing motivation to begin and building commitment to continue treatment of NSSI
> - Providing detailed and comprehensible psychoeducation on NSSI
> - Learning behavioral skills and coping strategies as an alternative to NSSI
> - Treating comorbid disorders and handling accompanying high-risk behaviors according to a dynamic treatment hierarchy
> - Identifying risk factors and resources in the interpersonal system
>
> *Note.* Adapted from Plener et al. (2016).

One of the most important elements in the psychotherapeutic treatment of NSSI is the establishment of a clear understanding and agreement regarding the handling of suicidality, crisis interventions or disruptions of the therapeutic framework as well as self-injurious behavior. These agreements are usually set as part of therapy contracts between therapists and patients during the first therapy sessions. Further, psychotherapeutic programs work with crisis plans that describe the exact procedures and steps to be taken if necessary and in case defined framework conditions are no longer met.

As lack of motivation for treatment is considered a fundamental problem in psychotherapy with NSSI (Fortune et al., 2008), the second major element in the treatment of NSSI is to develop a motivation and commitment to undergo treatment and to reduce or even terminate NSSI. Using a manualized assessment process and intervention during the first encounter with the patient, such as the Therapeutic Assessment, can lead to higher rates of treatment receivers (Ougrin et al., 2011): the Therapeutic Assessment is a short-term intervention in which the assessment is used collaboratively with the patients to help them understand themselves better and find initial solutions to their persistent problems.

Another important factor in the motivation and commitment process of NSSI treatment is extensive patient education. Understanding the nature of self-injurious behaviors, as well as problems and conflicts triggering or accompanying it, is a key element of psychoeducation, followed by recognizing possibilities for change. Learning about the functions of NSSI and understanding the potential of alternative, nonharming coping strategies may be an additional incentive for entering treatment. Thus, extensive patient education not only helps with developing and encouraging insight into the behavior, but it also breaks the taboo of speaking freely about NSSI.

A core element that was included in all efficacious treatments in NSSI is some sort of skills training component (Glenn et al., 2019). The most common shared skills training across treatments includes emotion regulation skills or distress tolerance (Asarnow et al., 2017; Esposito-Smythers et al., 2011; McCauley et al., 2018; Mehlum et al., 2016). Mindfulness, interpersonal effectiveness, and problem-solving skills are used frequently even though specific mechanisms explaining the efficacy of skills training still need to be investigated (Glenn et al., 2019).

As self-injury is accompanied by comorbid disorders in most cases, efficacious treatments focus and treat the comorbid psychiatric disorders as suggested in evidence-based guidelines (Plener et al., 2018). Therefore, so-called dynamic hierarchies are appropriate in the treatment of NSSI. These have proven particularly effective in the treatment of personality disorders such as BPD. The idea is that treatment focuses on the current situation and the needs of the patient but follows a hierarchical order. Priority is always given to suicidal ideation and other damaging and dangerous behaviors, such as NSSI as well as behavior that threatens therapy (e.g., frequent absence or tardiness to therapy sessions). Next, acute, particularly stressful events or conflicts in the patient's life and environment are addressed. By following this hierarchy, a certain stability can be built as a crucial basis for actual treatment. After a stable foundation has been established, therapy can begin or be continued according to the respective treatment manual (Kaess & Edinger, 2019). Such a dynamic hierarchy serves both the therapist and the patient as an orientation and guide for the various problem areas and focuses addressed in therapy.

Self-injurious behavior is often part of a complex interpersonal system, especially in adolescents who are dependent on family, teachers, and institutional helpers but also on the peer group. Therefore, another central component of the treatment of NSSI is the inclusion of the patient's environment in the therapeutic process. The main goal is to identify conflicts and problem areas of the system in therapy and to work on them with the patients as well as the important attachment figures. At the same time, the system can also be used as a resource and the coordination of the various caregivers and support systems can be promoted. Although there are multiple studies that included some sort of family therapy, such as parent psychoeducation or communication skills, additional research is needed to identify the optimal amount of family components and therapy needed to improve family functioning among patients with self-injurious behavior as well as to identify the relevant components of family interventions that are efficacious (Glenn et al., 2019).

Algorithm on the Treatment of NSSI in Adolescents across Different Treatment Contexts

Guidelines for managing NSSI have been provided by different stakeholders and research groups. In one of the first attempts to find consensus on first aid guidelines for supporting individuals with NSSI, Kelly et al. (2008) adopted the Delphi methodology to reach agreement between different organizations. In addition to a literature search, experts including professionals, people who had themselves engaged in NSSI, and people who cared for others with NSSI gave statements on a variety of questions across different relevant domains which were examined for consistency. The items most frequently and consistently endorsed were extracted and used to establish guidelines for members of the public dealing with a person showing self-injurious behavior. These statements can give specific assistance to people from the general public on how to handle current NSSI and how to deal with a person they suspect is self-injuring, and they include tips on minimizing NSSI and harm as well as ways to seek professional help. These guidelines do not include recommendations on specific treatment options, though, and are not designed for professionals in the mental health sector.

Closing this gap, the National Institute for Health and Care Excellence (NICE) presented a quality standard including eight statements for treating self-injury which was recently updated (National Institute for Health and Care Excellence, 2022). They describe general recommendations of action in the healthcare context for working with people who have self-injured independent of a suicidal or nonsuicidal motivation of the behavior. Statements include information on assessment and observation of self-injury, safety and care plans, and benefits of psychological interventions, as well as the importance of treating patients who present with NSSI with compassion, dignity and respect. Each statement is structured into subchapters and the relevance of the guideline is highlighted for different audiences such as patients as well as healthcare and service providers. Furthermore, an outcome measure is defined for every statement to allow specific assessment of change. A particular focus of the NICE guidelines lies on thorough psychosocial and risk assessments provided by healthcare professionals for all patients with self-injurious behaviors. The latest version of the guidelines was published in 2022 and updated with information for professionals in the education and criminal justice system.

These recommendations are all in line with the current and comprehensive German guidelines regarding NSSI in childhood and adolescence (Plener et al., 2016) by the Association of the Scientific Medical Societies in Germany (AWMF). They were developed by a consensus group with the shared goal of improving assessment and treatment of NSSI and providing a basis for future research. One particular strength of this consensus- and evidence-based guideline is the development of a treatment algorithm that can inform decision-making in managing NSSI across different treatment contexts. The following flow chart (see fig. 52.2) guides through different stages in the process of working with children and adolescents who present with NSSI and addresses critical steps to be taken by professionals under various conditions.

Self-injuries can take on different forms and functions and vary from person to person depending on severity. Self-injurious behaviors should always be taken seriously and examined adequately by health professionals in order to initiate appropriate measures. If an individual presents with injuries that appear to be self-inflicted, a thorough physical examination is always indicated to determine the need for further somatic care. Depending on injury severity and (potential) physical harm, a referral to emergency care or other somatic specialists has priority as a first step. In addition to wound care, potential risk factors such as vaccination status or infectious diseases should be explored.

After general physical integrity is ensured, a thorough diagnostic assessment should be conducted by a professional for child and adolescent psychiatry. Most importantly, suicide risk and urgency of immediate intervention need to be examined. Additionally, the self-injurious behavior should be characterized according to frequency, form, and function as well as maintaining elements. Even though NSSI does not necessarily need to be accompanied by psychopathology, many participants suffer from mental health issues without ever having received any treatment, which should be assessed in a comprehensive way in this setting. The exploration of family and social factors is clearly indicated and a detailed medical history should be obtained by integrating parent reports, but the diagnostic interviews themselves should be conducted with the patient alone to ensure privacy and create a calm, neutral, and unbiased atmosphere.

In case of acute suicidality and self-endangerment, an admission to a psychiatric inpatient unit specialized in childhood and adolescence is indicated. Ideally, a common

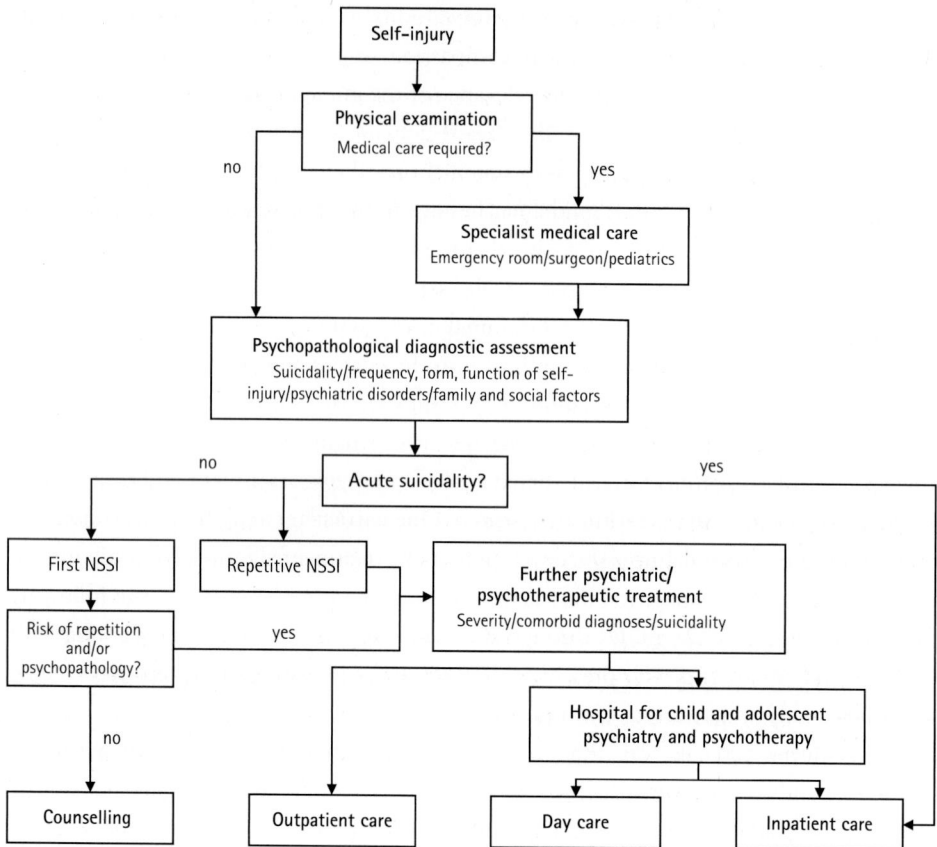

Figure 52.2 Proposed Treatment Algorithm for Nonsuicidal Self-Injury in Childhood and Adolescence. Adapted from the Association of the Scientific Medical Societies in Germany (AWMF) Guidelines. Plener, P. L., Fegert, J. M., Kaess, M., Kapusta, N. D., Brunner, R., Groschwitz, R. C., In-Albon, T., Resch, F., & Becker, K. (2016). Nicht-suizidales selbstverletzendes Verhalten (NSSV) im Jugendalter: Klinische Leitlinie zur Diagnostik und Therapie. *Zeitschrift für Kinder- und Jugendpsychiatrie und Psychotherapie, 45*(6), 463–474. https://doi.org/10.1024/1422-4917/a000463

understanding of the risk and need for emergency psychiatric care can be reached with the patient and all individuals involved and a forced admission can be avoided, which further emphasizes the importance of building a trusting and understanding relationship between a person suffering from self-injurious behavior and a clinician at first contact.

If an immediate risk of suicide or severe harm can be ruled out, several options may be taken into consideration for further support. Patients presenting after a first instance and with a mild form of NSSI and no comorbid psychopathology tend to have a low risk of repetition and aggravation. Counseling can be the fitting low-threshold point of contact for these patients and caregivers and depending on the situation, educational or family counseling centers may be recommended.

If NSSI is a recurring behavior and a psychiatric disorder is diagnosed during psychosocial assessment, further psychiatric or psychotherapeutic evaluation and potential treatment should be discussed. For underaged patients, a transfer to a mental health professional specializing in children and adolescents is strongly recommended. Even though acute suicidality may have been denied at the point of first contact, the exploration of suicidal thoughts and behaviors should be repeated and deepened in this context. In addition to acquiring alternative coping strategies to NSSI, comorbid psychiatric disorders need to be addressed and treated in accordance with evidence-based guidelines. As stated in the section "Aims and General Elements in the Psychotherapeutic Treatment of NSSI," a dynamic treatment hierarchy provides a sound basis for a successful integration of treatment goals and helps set shared priorities. In line with the superordinate goal of maintaining daily structure, outpatient settings are the first choice of treatment for most patients. Requirements for outpatient therapy include sufficient psychosocial functioning and the ability to cooperate in this therapeutic context.

In certain cases, an outpatient setting may not be the adequate form of care and a more intensive setting should be considered. If outpatient therapy did not achieve acceptable improvement or even a deterioration is observed, day care may be a more fitting surrounding. Also, severe impairment in psychosocial functioning due to comorbid psychiatric disorders may call for partial inpatient care as long as no acute risk of suicidality is observed. A main condition for day care programs is the ability to autonomously arrive on time every morning and to uphold a certain level of structure. Furthermore, even though day care settings provide far more intense treatment compared to outpatient offers, in contrast to inpatient unit patients need to adhere to official opening hours and there is, for example, no evening program. If neither outpatient nor day care is available, no sufficient treatment progress could be achieved or additional diagnostic examinations are necessary, the initiation of inpatient treatment needs to be evaluated. Box 52.2 summarizes potential indicators for inpatient treatment. Inpatient units may be the appropriate environment and necessary setting for certain patients with NSSI to provide adequate safety measures. In order to minimize the risk of increased frequency of NSSI and regressive behaviors, inpatient stays need to follow clearly predefined treatment targets and have a specific focus regarding content and time.

Box 52.2 Indicators for Inpatient Treatment of Patients with NSSI

- Acute suicidality
- Severe physical harm requiring close monitoring
- Environmental factors that may hinder positive treatment outcome (e.g., family and social environment)
- Acute endangerment and aggressive behaviors against others
- Severe comorbid disorders (e.g., depression, eating disorders, and addiction)
- Recurring and severe, potentially dangerous dissociative states
- Increasingly frequent and severe delinquency or other high-risk behaviors (e.g., unprotected sexual promiscuity)

Note. Adapted from Kaess and Edinger (2019).

Psychotherapeutic interventions mainly differ in regard to intensity when comparing outpatient, partial inpatient, and inpatient settings. As discussed before, therapy programs such as DBT-A are implemented in different treatment settings, and although inpatients normally receive more therapy sessions per week, the content itself remains the same. The main difference is the interdisciplinary care provided to inpatients: Whereas outpatients are primarily treated by psychological and/or medical healthcare professionals, (partial) inpatient staff additionally consists of nurses, pedagogues, and social workers. Close interdisciplinary work can be a vital aspect of providing adequate care to particularly vulnerable patients. Due to patients spending their days and/or nights on a unit, they should have a comprehensive day structure in addition to psychotherapeutic treatment. In such settings, the focus should not solely lie on the treatment of psychiatric disorders but on the improvement (or at least even maintenance) of psychosocial functioning, including potential first steps into rehabilitation. This may typically include a clinic school that consists of smaller classes where more individual and, if necessary, one-on-one teaching can take place. In addition, supporting programs such as group sessions and leisure activities may complement daily routines. Also, inpatients typically have one specific reference person among nursing staff who can provide additional support in different problem areas which can be of particular importance for reducing self-injury in this setting. This person can help with the application of skills outside therapy sessions and support adolescents in a moment of crisis.

As a transdiagnostic phenomenon, many mental health professionals will encounter NSSI in their work. While prevalence and severity vary, certain factors apply to the treatment of NSSI across all treatment settings. Suicidality must be assessed at first contact and reevaluated on a regular basis even if patients deny suicidal intention at the beginning. An emergency plan needs to be in place and patients need to know the points of contact for potential crises. The aim of all interventions should be the reduction and, ultimately, cessation of NSSI, but depending on comorbid psychopathology, hierarchical treatment goals are set. Skills training is a common part of psychotherapeutic interventions on all treatment levels, and the implementation differs depending on the setting: Whereas outpatients learn new skills in weekly therapy sessions and apply them as autonomously as possible in their daily life, (partial) inpatients receive more guidance. The transition into life after a clinic stay is particularly difficult and patients need to be prepared early and thoroughly. Finding the balance between guidance and autonomy is a common challenge in psychiatric treatment that particularly applies to the topic of NSSI. Although patients need to reclaim responsibility, the transfer after inpatient discharge is often supported by subsequent outpatient sessions. The management of NSSI therefore involves many stages and requires close cooperation between professional settings and disciplines.

Challenges, Recommendations, and Future Directions in Optimizing Treatment Strategies for NSSI

Despite its prevalence and high risk for severe comorbid mental disorders, physical complications, and suicidal behavior, the treatment of NSSI remains an understudied research area. One issue concerning the study of NSSI in general is the lack of consistency in terminology. Umbrella terms such as parasuicide, deliberate self-harm, and self-injurious behavior are often used to describe the act of self-injury, irrespective of the suicidal or nonsuicidal character of the behavior. This interferes with comparability across studies, making it difficult to determine treatment effects for different kinds of behaviors. The inclusion of "Nonsuicidal self-injury" in section 3 of the DSM-5 (American Psychiatric Association, 2013) as a diagnosis in need of further research is a chance for researchers to facilitate consistency and precision of terminology across future studies. In line with terminology, a clear understanding of NSSI as an independent entity and its delimitation from BPD needs to be strengthened. This is especially important with regard to treatment options that need to be tailored to the patient and a broad range of potential comorbidities.

Moreover, different forms of psychotherapy and treatment settings need to be examined further in order to determine an evidence-based gold standard for treating NSSI in different contexts. Therapy programs such as DBT-A and MBT-A have been studied and compared meta-analytically, but no superiority of treatment options for reducing NSSI has been established so far and existing study results need to be replicated by independent researchers (Gilbert et al., 2020; Glenn et al., 2019; Ougrin et al., 2015). On the path to finding the optimal treatment for NSSI, identifying mediators and moderators of treatment success is indispensable. The concept of personalized medicine has been introduced into psychotherapy (Cuijpers et al., 2016) and the need for more customizable treatment offers is evident, particularly for vulnerable groups like adolescents. Patients with NSSI may profit specifically from individualized interventions due to the transdiagnostic character of NSSI and examining which intervention works for who and why not only improves patient care but also leads to more efficient and economical treatment.

In line with these challenges in the field of psychotherapy research, there is a lack of research on different treatment settings for NSSI. Even though international consensus exists about avoiding psychiatric inpatient stays among patients with NSSI, prevalence numbers show frequent admissions. Inpatient units can be highly stressful environments and they bare the risk of aggravation of NSSI or an escalation into suicidal acts, as well as contagion onto other patients (see Jarvi Steele et al., this volume, on social contagion) (Timberlake et al., 2020; Tishler & Reiss, 2009). On the clinical side, more training needs to go into the handling of NSSI on psychiatric wards and commonly applied interventions such as constant observation and rigorous removal of objects potentially used for self-injury should be reassessed, since they can have iatrogenic effects (James et al., 2012). As for other disorders, the therapeutic relationship between staff and patients seems to be key in the reduction of NSSI on inpatient units (Timberlake et al., 2020). From a research perspective, more knowledge needs to be generated to support clinical decision-making regarding general care of patients who self-injure and the ideal form of treatment. In some cases, (partial) inpatient treatment is inevitable and we need more information on how to find the ideal interventional structure for these particularly vulnerable patients. This calls for RCTs comparing different treatment programs in outpatient and most importantly inpatient and day care settings (Boege et al., 2022; Slesinger et al., 2021). To ensure optimal recruitment and data collection as well as implementation of findings into the clinical context, close collaboration between researchers and clinicians is key.

A main and overarching goal of treating NSSI is the establishment of stepped-care approaches to provide adequate and efficient support to those affected by it (see fig. 52.1). Subgroups of patients have individual needs that require diverse actions. A stepped-care approach should therefore enable interventions on different levels, depending on severity of self-injury, comorbidities, and other environmental factors. Most importantly and before any interventions can take effect, general barriers to treatment need to be lowered in particular for adolescents. Reduced help-seeking behavior is common in adolescent populations, and NSSI is an additional hindering factor (Doyle et al., 2015; Pumpa & Martin, 2015; Rowe et al., 2014). To overcome this obstacle and reach more people affected by NSSI, online treatment offers bear potential to lower initial reluctance to seek help and maintain motivation once first contact has been established.

On this basis, low-threshold and brief interventions against NSSI can be offered to a larger population. By establishing such a stepped-care approach, many individuals can access help without the necessity of receiving extensive psychiatric care. Low-intensity interventions can be provided via online tools like evidence-based mobile apps or as in-person short-term programs, such as the CDP (Kaess et al., 2019, 2020). If further support is necessary, therapy can be increased in frequency, length, and intensity and structured programs such as DBT-A or MBT-A could be introduced. This way, more resources remain for a smaller group of vulnerable patients in need of intense and time-consuming psychotherapeutic interventions as well as treatment for comorbid psychiatric disorders. To implement this strategy on a larger scale, brief efficacious treatments that have the potential to fit into a stepped-care approach and reach at-risk youth while being based on thorough research are urgently needed (Glenn et al., 2019; Plener, 2020). By adopting a patient-centered strategy and focusing on adolescents' needs, early detection of mental health issues can be advanced, and patients can receive the support they need.

Clinical Case

Sarah was a 13-year-old girl living with both of her parents and her little brother. She had recently moved to Bern, and her problems had started due to being bullied at her new school. For a few months, she had been feeling sad and lonely most of the time but sometimes she also became very angry. Three months ago, she had started to cut herself and this really had given her a relief for her inner tension. Currently, Sarah almost cuts herself daily with a razor blade, a knife, or a scissor. Sarah had her first contact with the healthcare system after a severe incident of self-injury. She knew that she might have cut too deep and finally saw her teacher to ask for help. Her teacher brought her to the emergency department, where she received surgical wound revision. In addition, the surgeon asked the child and adolescent psychiatrist on call to see Sarah. It appeared that Sarah showed symptoms of a depressive episode alongside repetitive NSSI. In addition, she reported suicidal thoughts that had not yet turned into plans or actions. Thus, the child and adolescent psychiatrists asked Sarah (and her parents who had been called by the hospital) to attend the outpatient clinic within the next days. During the first outpatient treatment phase (brief psychotherapeutic intervention), Sarah was struggling with her chronic suicidality and her increasing difficulties to attend school. While she attended her psychotherapy sessions regularly, she finally presented with increased suicide risk and a loss of psychosocial functioning. In addition, her NSSI incidents resulted in regular visits at the emergency department for surgical care. After two months, Sarah and her therapist agreed that inpatient treatment was the best option to get Sarah back into day structure and work intensively on the NSSI and suicidal thoughts. She was referred to a specialized inpatient unit for DBT-A. From the beginning, treatment was limited to a duration of three months and the ultimate goal was to get Sarah back into regular outpatient treatment including a functional daily routine. Sarah underwent the highly structured DBT-A program, which helped her to learn how to reduce NSSI, how to stick to a nonsuicide commitment, and how to regulate herself to be able to participate in school and other daily routines. She practiced her acquired skills together with the staff and even other patients. Prior to discharge, she managed to change to another school and even had some days in her new class, which gave her some confidence. After her inpatient stay, Sarah was included in the outpatient DBT-A program, where she continued working on her skills and finally stopped injuring herself completely. This case shows how different treatment contexts may be beneficial in an adequate and successful pathway of care for young individuals with NSSI.

Conclusion

Nonsuicidal self-injury is a highly prevalent phenomenon among adolescents that often, but not exclusively, co-occurs with different forms of psychopathology. In line with the spectrum of comorbidity, adolescents who present with NSSI have highly individual needs and present to different treatment contexts. Early detection is key to prevent further aggravation, but barriers to receiving initial support are high and help-seeking behavior is particularly limited in this population. Low-threshold interventions are an important element in reaching a larger proportion of individuals with NSSI while reserving resources for those in need of more intense and expensive treatment forms. A stepped-care approach—with intensity varying from evidence-based online tools to efficacious psychotherapy programs and clearly structured inpatient treatment—is therefore recommended to provide adequate care on different levels of a treatment concept. To advance treatment of NSSI on all levels, challenges for future clinical research include further development and evaluation of low-threshold services and brief outpatient interventions as well as improved conditions for treating and reducing NSSI in inpatient settings.

References

American Psychiatric Association. (2013). *Diagnostic and statistical manual of mental disorders* (5th ed.).

Andersson, G. (2016). Internet-delivered psychological treatments. *Annual Review of Clinical Psychology, 12*(1), 157–179. https://doi.org/10.1146/annurev-clinpsy-021815-093006

Andover, M. S., & Gibb, B. E. (2010). Non-suicidal self-injury, attempted suicide, and suicidal intent among psychiatric inpatients. *Psychiatry Research, 178*(1), 101–105. https://doi.org/10.1016/j.psychres.2010.03.019

Andover, M. S., Schatten, H. T., Morris, B. W., Holman, C. S., & Miller, I. W. (2017). An intervention for nonsuicidal self-injury in young adults: A pilot randomized controlled trial. *Journal of Consulting and Clinical Psychology, 85*(6), 620–631. https://doi.org/10.1037/ccp0000206

Arshad, U., Gauntlett, J., Husain, N., Chaudhry, N., & Taylor, P. J. (2019). A systematic review of the evidence supporting mobile-and internet-based psychological interventions for self-harm. *Suicide and Life-Threatening Behavior, 50*(1), 151–179. https://doi.org/10.1111/sltb.12583

Asarnow, J., Hughes, J., Babeva, K., & Sugar, C. (2017). Cognitive-behavioral family treatment for suicide attempt prevention: A randomized controlled trial. *Journal of the American Academy of Child and Adolescent Psychiatry, 56*(6), 506–514. https://doi.org/10.1016/J.JAAC.2017.03.015

Boege, I., Schubert, N., Scheider, N., & Fegert, J. M. (2022). Pilot study: Cut the Cut—A treatment program for adolescent inpatients with nonsuicidal self-injury. *Child Psychiatry & Human Development, 53*, 928–940. https://doi.org/10.1007/s10578-021-01174-x

Bohus, M., Haaf, B., Simms, T., Limberger, M. F., Schmahl, C., Unckel, C., Lieb, K., & Linehan, M. M. (2004). Effectiveness of inpatient dialectical behavioral therapy for borderline personality disorder: A controlled trial. *Behaviour Research and Therapy, 42*(5), 487–499. https://doi.org/10.1016/S0005-7967(03)00174-8

Bowers, L., Simpson, A., & Alexander, J. (2003). Patient-staff conflict: Results of a survey on acute psychiatric wards. *Social Psychiatry and Psychiatric Epidemiology, 38*(7), 402–408. https://doi.org/10.1007/S00127-003-0648-X

Bowers, L., Whittington, R., Nolan, P., Parkin, D., Curtis, S., Bhui, K., Hackney, D., Allan, T., & Simpson, A. (2008). Relationship between service ecology, special observation and self-harm during acute in-patient care: City-128 study. *The British Journal of Psychiatry: The Journal of Mental Science, 193*(5), 395–401. https://doi.org/10.1192/BJP.BP.107.037721

Bresin, K. (2014). Five indices of emotion regulation in participants with a history of nonsuicidal self-injury: A daily diary study. *Behavior Therapy, 45*(1), 56–66. https://doi.org/10.1016/j.beth.2013.09.005

Chesin, M. S., Galfavy, H., Sonmez, C. C., Wong, A., Oquendo, M. A., Mann, J. J., & Stanley, B. (2017). Nonsuicidal self-injury is predictive of suicide attempts among individuals with mood disorders. *Suicide and Life-Threatening Behavior, 47*(5), 567–579. https://doi.org/10.1111/sltb.12331

Cuijpers, P., Ebert, D. D., Acarturk, C., Andersson, G., & Cristea, I. A. (2016). Personalized psychotherapy for adult depression: A meta-analytic review. *Behavior Therapy, 47*(6), 966–980. https://doi.org/10.1016/j.beth.2016.04.007

de Kloet, L., Starling, J., Hainsworth, C., Berntsen, E., Chapman, L., & Hancock, K. (2011). Risk factors for self-harm in children and adolescents admitted to a mental health inpatient unit. *The Australian and New Zealand Journal of Psychiatry, 45*(9), 749–755. https://doi.org/10.3109/00048674.2011.595682

Doyle, L., Treacy, M. P., & Sheridan, A. (2015). Self-harm in young people: Prevalence, associated factors, and help-seeking in school-going adolescents. *International Journal of Mental Health Nursing, 24*(6), 485–494. https://doi.org/10.1111/inm.12144

Esposito-Smythers, C., Spirito, A., Kahler, C. W., Hunt, J., & Monti, P. (2011). Treatment of co-occurring substance abuse and suicidality among adolescents: A randomized trial. *Journal of Consulting and Clinical Psychology, 79*(6), 728. https://doi.org/10.1037/A0026074

Fortune, S., Sinclair, J., & Hawton, K. (2008). Help-seeking before and after episodes of self-harm: A descriptive study in school pupils in England. *BMC Public Health, 8*, Article 369. https://doi.org/10.1186/1471-2458-8-369

Fowler, J. C., Clapp, J. D., Madan, A., Allen, J. G., Frueh, B. C., Fonagy, P., & Oldham, J. M. (2018). A naturalistic longitudinal study of extended inpatient treatment for adults with borderline personality disorder: An examination of treatment response, remission and deterioration. *Journal of Affective Disorders, 235*, 323–331. https://doi.org/10.1016/j.jad.2017.12.054

Frensch, K. M., & Cameron, G. (2002). Treatment of choice or a last resort? A review of residential mental health placements for children and youth. *Child and Youth Care Forum, 31*(5), 307–339. https://doi.org/10.1023/A:1016826627406

Ghinea, D., Edinger, A., Parzer, P., Koenig, J., Resch, F., & Kaess, M. (2020). Non-suicidal self-injury disorder as a stand-alone diagnosis in a consecutive help-seeking sample of adolescents. *Journal of Affective Disorders, 274*, 1122–1125. https://doi.org/10.1016/j.jad.2020.06.009

Gilbert, A. C., DeYoung, L. L. A., Barthelemy, C. M., Jenkins, G. A., MacPherson, H. A., Kim, K. L., Kudinova, A. Y., Radoeva, P. D., & Dickstein, D. P. (2020). The treatment of suicide and self-injurious behaviors in children and adolescents. *Current Treatment Options in Psychiatry, 7*(1), 39–52. https://doi.org/10.1007/s40501-020-00201-3

Glenn, C. R., Esposito, E. C., Porter, A. C., & Robinson, D. J. (2019). Evidence base update of psychosocial treatments for self-injurious thoughts and behaviors in youth. *Journal of Clinical Child and Adolescent Psychology, 48*(3), 357–392. https://doi.org/10.1080/15374416.2019.1591281

Harris, I. M., & Roberts, L. M. (2013). Exploring the use and effects of deliberate self-harm websites: An internet-based study. *Journal of Medical Internet Research, 15*(12), Article e2802. https://doi.org/10.2196/jmir.2802

Hasking, P., Rees, C. S., Martin, G., & Quigley, J. (2015). What happens when you tell someone you self-injure? The effects of disclosing NSSI to adults and peers. *BMC Public Health, 15*(1), 1–9. https://doi.org/10.1186/s12889-015-2383-0

Haynes, C., Eivors, A., & Crossley, J. (2011). "Living in an alternative reality": Adolescents' experiences of psychiatric inpatient care. *Child and Adolescent Mental Health, 16*(3), 150–157. https://doi.org/10.1111/j.1475-3588.2011.00598.x

Jacobson, C. M., Muehlenkamp, J. J., Miller, A. L., & Turner, J. B. (2008). Psychiatric impairment among adolescents engaging in different types of deliberate self-harm. *Journal of Clinical Child and Adolescent Psychology, 37*(2), 363–375. https://doi.org/10.1080/15374410801955771

James, K., Stewart, D., & Bowers, L. (2012). Self-harm and attempted suicide within inpatient psychiatric services: A review of the literature. *International Journal of Mental Health Nursing, 21*(4), 301–309. https://doi.org/10.1111/j.1447-0349.2011.00794.x

Kaess, M., Brunner, R., Parzer, P., Carli, V., Apter, A., Balazs, J. A., Bobes, J., Coman, H. G., Cosman, D., Cotter, P., Durkee, T., Farkas, L., Feldman, D., Haring, C., Iosue, M., Kahn, J.-P., Keeley, H., Podlogar, T., Postuvan, V., & Wasserman, D. (2014). Risk-behaviour screening for identifying adolescents with mental health problems in Europe. *European Child & Adolescent Psychiatry, 23*(7), 611–620. https://doi.org/10.1007/s00787-013-0490-y

Kaess, M., & Edinger, A. (2019). Selbstverletzendes Verhalten: Entwicklungsrisiken erkennen und behandeln [*Self-injurious behavior: Recognizing and treating development risks*] Ed. M. Schulte-Markwort & F. Resch. 2nd ed. Beltz.

Kaess, M., Edinger, A., Fischer-Waldschmidt, G., Parzer, P., Brunner, R., & Resch, F. (2020). Effectiveness of a brief psychotherapeutic intervention compared with treatment as usual for adolescent nonsuicidal self-injury: A single-centre, randomised controlled trial. *European Child & Adolescent Psychiatry, 29*(6), 881–891. https://doi.org/10.1007/s00787-019-01399-1

Kaess, M., Fischer-Waldschmidt, G., Resch, F., & Koenig, J. (2017). Health related quality of life and psychopathological distress in risk taking and self-harming adolescents with full-syndrome, subthreshold and without borderline personality disorder: Rethinking the clinical cut-off? *Borderline Personality Disorder and Emotion Dysregulation, 4*(1), 7. https://doi.org/10.1186/s40479-017-0058-4

Kaess, M., Koenig, J., Bauer, S., Moessner, M., Fischer-Waldschmidt, G., Mattern, M., Herpertz, S. C., Resch, F., Brown, R., In-Albon, T., Koelch, M., Plener, P. L., Schmahl, C., Edinger, A., & STAR Consortium. (2019). Self-injury: Treatment, Assessment, Recovery (STAR): Online intervention for adolescent non-suicidal self-injury - study protocol for a randomized controlled trial. *Trials, 20*(1), 425. https://doi.org/10.1186/s13063-019-3501-6

Kaess, M., Parzer, P., Mattern, M., Plener, P. L., Bifulco, A., Resch, F., & Brunner, R. (2013). Adverse childhood experiences and their impact on frequency, severity, and the individual function of nonsuicidal self-injury in youth. *Psychiatry Research, 206*(2), 265–272. https://doi.org/10.1016/j.psychres.2012.10.012

Kelly, C. M., Jorm, A. F., Kitchener, B. A., & Langlands, R. L. (2008). Development of mental health first aid guidelines for deliberate non-suicidal self-injury: A Delphi study. *BMC Psychiatry, 8*(1), 62. https://doi.org/10.1186/1471-244X-8-62

Kleindienst, N., Limberger, M. F., Schmahl, C., Steil, R., Ebner-Priemer, U. W., & Bohus, M. (2008). Do improvements after inpatient dialectical behavioral therapy persist in the long term?: A naturalistic follow-up in patients with borderline personality disorder. *The Journal of Nervous and Mental Disease, 196*(11), 847–851. https://doi.org/10.1097/NMD.0b013e31818b481d

Klonsky, E. D. (2011). Non-suicidal self-injury in United States adults: Prevalence, sociodemographics, topography and functions. *Psychological Medicine, 41*(9), 1981–1986. https://doi.org/10.1017/S0033291710002497

Klonsky, E. D., Glenn, C. R., Styer, D. M., Olino, T. M., & Washburn, J. J. (2015). The functions of nonsuicidal self-injury: Converging evidence for a two-factor structure. *Child and Adolescent Psychiatry and Mental Health, 9*(1), 1–9. https://doi.org/10.1186/S13034-015-0073-4

Klonsky, E. D., & Muehlenkamp, J. J. (2007). Self-injury: A research review for the practitioner. *Journal of Clinical Psychology, 63*(11), 1045–1056. https://doi.org/10.1002/JCLP.20412

Linehan, M. M. (1993). *Cognitive-behavioral treatment of borderline personality disorder*. Guilford Press.

McCauley, E., Berk, M., Asarnow, J., Adrian, M., Cohen, J., Korslund, K., Avina, C., Hughes, J., Harned, M., Gallop, R., & Linehan, M. M. (2018). Efficacy of dialectical behavior therapy for adolescents at high risk for suicide: A randomized clinical trial. *JAMA Psychiatry, 75*(8), 777–785. https://doi.org/10.1001/JAMAPSYCHIATRY.2018.1109

McMain, S. F., Guimond, T., Barnhart, R., Habinski, L., & Streiner, D. L. (2017). A randomized trial of brief dialectical behaviour therapy skills training in suicidal patients suffering from borderline disorder. *Acta Psychiatrica Scandinavica, 135*(2), 138–148. https://doi.org/10.1111/ACPS.12664

Mehlum, L., Ramberg, M., Tørmoen, A. J., Haga, E., Diep, L. M., Stanley, B. H., Miller, A. L., Sund, A. M., & Grøholt, B. (2016). Dialectical behavior therapy compared with enhanced usual care for adolescents with repeated suicidal and self-harming behavior: Outcomes over a one-year follow-up. *Journal of the American Academy of Child and Adolescent Psychiatry, 55*(4), 295–300. https://doi.org/10.1016/j.jaac.2016.01.005

National Institute for Health and Care Excellence. (2022). *Self-harm quality standard*. https://www.nice.org.uk/guidance/qs34/resources/selfharm-pdf-2098606243525

Nawaz, R. F., Reen, G., Bloodworth, N., Maughan, D., & Vincent, C. (2021). Interventions to reduce self-harm on in-patient wards: Systematic review. *BJPsych Open, 7*(3). https://doi.org/10.1192/bjo.2021.41

Nijman, H. L., & à Campo, J. M. (2002). Situational determinants of inpatient self-harm. *Suicide & Life-Threatening Behavior, 32*(2), 167–175. https://doi.org/10.1521/SULI.32.2.167.24401

Nock, M. K., & Prinstein, M. J. (2004). A functional approach to the assessment of self-mutilative behavior. *Journal of Consulting and Clinical Psychology, 72*(5), 885–890. https://doi.org/10.1037/0022-006X.72.5.885

Ougrin, D., Tranah, T., Stahl, D., Moran, P., & Asarnow, J. R. (2015). Therapeutic interventions for suicide attempts and self-harm in adolescents: Systematic review and meta-analysis. *Journal of the American Academy of Child & Adolescent Psychiatry, 54*(2), 97–107. https://doi.org/10.1016/j.jaac.2014.10.009

Ougrin, D., Zundel, T., Ng, A., Banarsee, R., Bottle, A., & Taylor, E. (2011). Trial of therapeutic assessment in London: Randomised controlled trial of therapeutic assessment versus standard psychosocial assessment in adolescents presenting with self-harm. *Archives of Disease in Childhood, 96*(2), 148–153. https://doi.org/10.1136/adc.2010.188755

Paris, J. (2004). Is hospitalization useful for suicidal patients with borderline personality disorder? *Journal of Personality Disorders, 18*(3), 240–247. https://doi.org/10.1521/pedi.18.3.240.35443

Plener, P. L. (2020). Tailoring treatments for adolescents with nonsuicidal self-injury. *European Child & Adolescent Psychiatry, 29*(6), 893–895. https://doi.org/10.1007/s00787-020-01523-6

Plener, P. L., Fegert, J. M., Kaess, M., Kapusta, N. D., Brunner, R., Groschwitz, R. C., In-Albon, T., Resch, F., & Becker, K. (2016). Nicht-suizidales selbstverletzendes Verhalten (NSSV) im Jugendalter: Klinische Leitlinie zur Diagnostik und Therapie [Non-suicidal self-injury (NSSI) in adolescence: Clinical guidelines for diagnostic assessment and therapy]. *Zeitschrift Für Kinder- Und Jugendpsychiatrie Und Psychotherapie, 45*(6), 463–474. https://doi.org/10.1024/1422-4917/a000463

Plener, P. L., Kaess, M., Schmahl, C., Pollak, S., Fegert, J. M., & Brown, R. C. (2018). Non-suicidal self-injury in adolescents. *Deutsches Arzteblatt International, 115*(3), 23–30. https://doi.org/10.3238/arztebl.2018.0023

Plener, P. L., Kapusta, N. D., Brunner, R., & Kaess, M. (2014). Nicht-suizidales Selbstverletzendes Verhalten (NSSV) und suizidale Verhaltensstörung (SVS) im DSM-5 [Non-suicidal self-injury (NSSI) and suicidal behavior disorder (SBD) in the DSM-5]. *Zeitschrift Für Kinder- Und Jugendpsychiatrie Und Psychotherapie*, *42*(6), 405–413. https://doi.org/10.1024/1422-4917/a000319

Pumpa, M., & Martin, G. (2015). The impact of attitudes as a mediator between sense of autonomy and help-seeking intentions for self-injury. *Child and Adolescent Psychiatry and Mental Health*, *9*, Article 27. https://doi.org/10.1186/s13034-015-0058-3

Ranney, M. L., Choo, E. K., Spirito, A., & Mello, M. J. (2013). Adolescents' preference for technology-based emergency department behavioral interventions: Does it depend on risky behaviors? *Pediatric Emergency Care*, *29*(4), 475–481. https://doi.org/10.1097/PEC.0b013e31828a322f

Robinson, K., Garisch, J. A., Kingi, T., Brocklesby, M., O'Connell, A., Langlands, R. L., Russell, L., & Wilson, M. S. (2019). The longitudinal relationship between emotion regulation and non-suicidal self-injury in adolescents. *Journal of Abnormal Child Psychology*, *47*(2), 325–332. https://doi.org/10.1007/S10802-018-0450-6

Rossouw, T. I., & Fonagy, P. (2012). Mentalization-Based Treatment for self-harm in adolescents: A randomized controlled trial. *Journal of the American Academy of Child & Adolescent Psychiatry*, *51*(12), 1304–1313.e3. https://doi.org/10.1016/j.jaac.2012.09.018

Rowe, S. L., French, R. S., Henderson, C., Ougrin, D., Slade, M., & Moran, P. (2014). Help-seeking behaviour and adolescent self-harm: A systematic review. *Australian and New Zealand Journal of Psychiatry*, *48*(12), 1083–1095. https://doi.org/10.1177/0004867414555718

Selby, E. A., Franklin, J., Carson-Wong, A., & Rizvi, S. L. (2013). Emotional cascades and self-injury: Investigating instability of rumination and negative emotion. *Journal of Clinical Psychology*, *69*(12), 1213–1227. https://doi.org/10.1002/jclp.21966

Sevecke, K., Bock, A., Fenzel, L., Gander, M., & Fuchs, M. (2017). Nonsuicidal self-injury in a naturalistic sample of adolescents undergoing inpatient psychiatric treatment: Prevalence, gender distribution and comorbidities. *Psychiatria Danubina*, *29*, 522–528. https://doi.org/10.24869/psyd.2017.522

Slesinger, C., Hayes, N. A., & Washburn, J. J. (2021). Understanding predictors of change in a day treatment setting for non-suicidal self-injury. *Psychology and Psychotherapy: Theory, Research and Practice*, *94*, 517–535. https://doi.org/10.1111/papt.12295

Spencer, S., Stone, T., Kable, A., & McMillan, M. (2019). Adolescents' experiences of distress on an acute mental health inpatient unit: A qualitative study. *International Journal of Mental Health Nursing*, *28*(3), 712–720. https://doi.org/10.1111/inm.12573

Stewart, D., Bowers, L., & Warburton, F. (2009). Constant special observation and self-harm on acute psychiatric wards: A longitudinal analysis. *General Hospital Psychiatry*, *31*(6), 523–530. https://doi.org/10.1016/J.GENHOSPPSYCH.2009.05.008

Stewart, D., Ross, J., Watson, C., James, K., & Bowers, L. (2012). Patient characteristics and behaviours associated with self-harm and attempted suicide in acute psychiatric wards. *Journal of Clinical Nursing*, *21*(7–8), 1004–1013. https://doi.org/10.1111/J.1365-2702.2011.03832.X

Swannell, S. V., Martin, G. E., Page, A., Hasking, P., & John, N. J. S. (2014). Prevalence of nonsuicidal self-injury in nonclinical samples: Systematic review, meta-analysis and meta-regression. *Suicide and Life-Threatening Behavior*, *44*(3), 273–303. https://doi.org/10.1111/sltb.12070

Swinton, M., Hopkins, R., & Swinton, J. (1998). Reports of self-injury in a maximum security hospital. *Criminal Behaviour and Mental Health*, *8*(1), 7–16. https://doi.org/10.1002/CBM.207

Taylor, L. M. W., Oldershaw, A., Richards, C., Davidson, K., Schmidt, U., & Simic, M. (2011). Development and pilot evaluation of a manualized cognitive-behavioural treatment package for adolescent self-harm. *Behavioural and Cognitive Psychotherapy*, *39*(5), 619–625. https://doi.org/10.1017/S1352465811000075

Tebbett-Mock, A. A., Saito, E., McGee, M., Woloszyn, P., & Venuti, M. (2020). Efficacy of Dialectical Behavior Therapy versus treatment as usual for acute-care inpatient adolescents. *Journal of the American Academy of Child & Adolescent Psychiatry*, *59*(1), 149–156. https://doi.org/10.1016/j.jaac.2019.01.020

Thatte, S., Makinen, J. A., Nguyen, H. N. T., Hill, E. M., & Flament, M. F. (2013). Partial hospitalization for youth with psychiatric disorders: Treatment outcomes and 3-month follow-up. *The Journal of Nervous and Mental Disease*, *201*(5), 429–434. https://doi.org/10.1097/NMD.0b013e31828e1141

Timberlake, L. M., Beeber, L. S., & Hubbard, G. (2020). Nonsuicidal self-injury: Management on the inpatient psychiatric unit. *Journal of the American Psychiatric Nurses Association*, *26*(1), 10–26. https://doi.org/10.1177/1078390319878878

Tishler, C., & Reiss, N. (2009). Inpatient suicide: Preventing a common sentinel event. *General Hospital Psychiatry*, *31*(2), 103–109. https://doi.org/10.1016/J.GENHOSPPSYCH.2008.09.007

Tørmoen, A. J., Grøholt, B., Haga, E., Brager-Larsen, A., Miller, A., Walby, F., Stanley, B., & Mehlum, L. (2014). Feasibility of dialectical behavior therapy with suicidal and self-harming adolescents with multi-problems: Training, adherence, and retention. *Archives of Suicide Research*, *18*(4), 432–444. https://doi.org/10.1080/13811118.2013.826156

Turner, B. J., Austin, S. B., & Chapman, A. L. (2014). Treating nonsuicidal self-injury: A systematic review of psychological and pharmacological interventions. *The Canadian Journal of Psychiatry*, *59*(11), 576–585. https://doi.org/10.1177/070674371405901103

Ulke, C., Klein, A. M., & Klitzing, K. (2014). Effects of ward interventions on repeated critical incidents in child and adolescent psychiatric inpatient care. *Praxis Der Kinderpsychologie Und Kinderpsychiatrie*, *63*(8), 616–634. https://doi.org/10.13109/PRKK.2014.63.8.616

Üstün, B., & Kennedy, C. (2009). What is "functional impairment"? Disentangling disability from clinical significance. *World Psychiatry*, *8*(2), 82–85. https://doi.org/10.1002/j.2051-5545.2009.tb00219.x

Victor, S. E., Hipwell, A. E., Stepp, S. D., & Scott, L. N. (2019). Parent and peer relationships as longitudinal predictors of adolescent non-suicidal self-injury onset. *Child and Adolescent Psychiatry and Mental Health*, *13*(1), 1. https://doi.org/10.1186/s13034-018-0261-0

von Auer, A. K., Kleindienst, N., Ludewig, S., Soyka, O., Bohus, M., & Ludäscher, P. (2015). Zehn Jahre Erfahrung mit der Dialektisch-Behavioralen Therapie für Adoleszente (DBT-A) unter stationären Bedingungen—die Station Wellenreiter. *Zeitschrift Für Kinder—Und Jugendpsychiatrie Und Psychotherapie*, *43*(5), 301–315. https://doi.org/10.1024/1422-4917/a000371

Washburn, J. J., Richardt, S. L., Styer, D. M., Gebhardt, M., Juzwin, K. R., Yourek, A., & Aldridge, D. (2012). Psychotherapeutic approaches to non-suicidal self-injury in adolescents. *Child and Adolescent Psychiatry and Mental Health*, *6*(1), 1–8. https://doi.org/10.1186/1753-2000-6-14

Younes, N., Chollet, A., Menard, E., & Melchior, M. (2015). E-mental health care among young adults and help-seeking behaviors: A transversal study in a community sample. *Journal of Medical Internet Research*, *17*(5), e123. https://doi.org/10.2196/jmir.4254

CHAPTER 53

Medical and Pharmaceutical Interventions in NSSI

Paul L. Plener

> **Abstract**
> There is growing evidence for the efficacy of psychotherapeutic interventions to target nonsuicidal self-injury (NSSI), yet fewer studies have investigated psychopharmacological treatment of NSSI. Although several agents such as selective serotonin reuptake inhibitors (SSRIs), antipsychotics, mood stabilizers, and benzodiazepines have been tested, the evidence for pharmaceutical interventions remains limited. This is especially true for the treatment of minors. There is a general lack of randomized controlled trials in this field of research, with the limited evidence often building on case series and open trials. To date, there is not a licensed psychopharmacological treatment for NSSI. With regard to other "biologically oriented" treatment methods, different modes of stimulation have been tested in populations showing NSSI. These methods include transcranial repetitive magnetic stimulation, transcranial direct current stimulation, and transauricular vagal nerve stimulation. However, evidence for these methods is scarce and reports are mostly based on open label trials. In summary, psychotherapeutic interventions remain the primary method of intervention in NSSI, which can be supported by psychopharmacological interventions to treat comorbid conditions (e.g., depression). There is to date not enough evidence to support specific treatment of NSSI using primarily biologically oriented therapeutic approaches.
>
> **Key Words:** Nonsuicidal Self-Injury, psychotherapeutic interventions, psychopharmacological treatment, Selective Serotonin Reuptake Inhibitors (SSRIs), antipsychotics, mood stabilizers, benzodiazepines, stimulation

Overview

Although recent years have seen an increase in treatment studies for NSSI using several psychotherapeutic interventions, there is still a paucity of data concerning other modes of treatment. This is especially true for the scarce literature on psychopharmacological interventions or other more "biologically oriented" treatment methods that aim to alter neurocircuitry and brain activation by directly targeting neurochemical or other neurobiological processes. Apart from psychopharmacological approaches, these methods include neurostimulation approaches such as electroconvulsive therapy (ECT), repetitive transcranial magnetic stimulation (rTMS), transcranial direct current stimulation (tDCS), or transcutaneous auricular vagus nerve stimulation (taVNS).

Broadening the field of "biological" treatments, one might also want to take a closer look at other bodily behaviors that have an influence on mood and emotion regulations, such as sleep or physical activity. Nevertheless, the literature on such interventions is limited. It is of interest to further explore new treatment avenues for their potential to augment existing psychotherapeutic strategies in certain patients who show a heightened severity of NSSI or remain treatment resistant to an evidence-based approach. Following clinical guidelines from other fields of mental health, such an augmentation approach would follow a stepped-care procedure in which "biologically oriented" interventions aid and support an ongoing psychotherapeutic treatment. Furthermore, increasing knowledge on the importance of regular sleep and physical activity in NSSI can inform our understanding of basic mechanisms of mental health and resilience that need to be included in psychoeducation and may serve as therapeutic targets in psychosocial interventions for NSSI.

This chapter first aims to briefly summarize findings on the neurobiology of NSSI with a clear focus of identifying possible treatment targets that can broaden our understanding of underlying processes. In a second step, the chapter reviews existing literature on psychopharmacological treatments in order to support evidence-based clinical decision-making on whether psychopharmacological agents might be considered. In a third step, the chapter reviews existing literature on the applicability of several interventions that directly try to interfere with neural functioning.

Neurobiological Background of NSSI

The neurobiology of NSSI has gained significant interest, given that the process that leads to NSSI is often influenced by an altered perception of events, a decreased ability to regulate emotions, as well as an altered pain threshold, all of which can also be understood as alterations in underlying neurobiological systems. The process of injury in itself leads to a rapid decrease of stress, is often accompanied by little or even no pain, and often leads to a soothing effect in the aftermath. Looking into the process of NSSI from a neurobiological perspective therefore includes the identification of distal risk factors, which can lead to situations in which the likelihood of NSSI is increased as well as an understanding for the process unfolding during and after NSSI (Kaess et al., 2021).

With regard to distal risk factors, one of the most stable findings in the literature concludes that a history of maltreatment or abuse increases the odds for engaging in NSSI later on (also see Serafini et al., this volume) (Serafini et al. 2017). These potential traumatic events also include bullying as another form of interpersonal aggression. From a neurobiological point of view, potentially traumatic events can lead to alterations in the hypothalamus-pituitary-adrenal (HPA) axis, therefore changing an individual's central stress response (see Carosella et al., this volume). Other changes include inflammatory processes, as well as several alterations in functional (and sometimes structural) changes in the brain. These changes in the brain often result in alterations in frontal-limbic circuitry, which can be broken down in high activation of limbic centers (such as the amygdala) and a decreased bottom-down control by (pre-)frontal regions (Nemeroff, 2004; Sherin & Nemeroff, 2011; Weis et al., 2021). Although the link between potentially traumatic events and NSSI has often been made in the empirical literature on risk factors (Brown et al., 2018; Fox et al., 2015), it is less clear how the exact neurobiological mechanisms behind this link can unfold. However, alterations in the mechanisms of the HPA axis have been observed, with findings of an elevated morning cortisol level as well as a blunted cortisol response in situations of social stress in patients with NSSI (see Kaess et al., 2021).

While these findings help our understanding of changes in the stress response, they can also serve as a part of a puzzle to understand the heightened need for emotion regulation. Emotional dysregulation is one of the core problems of why people engage in NSSI (Taylor et al., 2018), a finding strengthened by data from real-world settings using ecological momentary assessment (Santangelo et al., 2017), as well as from neuroimaging data. Adolescents with NSSI seem to show higher activation in their limbic structures while viewing pictures with emotional content (Plener et al., 2012), therefore fostering the finding that a higher need to counter extreme emotional states might arise in patients with NSSI.

Whereas the mechanisms mentioned here could serve as an explanation leading to the act of NSSI, it seems worthwhile to focus on the act of NSSI itself. One of the best validated and also one of the most intriguing findings has been reported with regard to pain. Several studies have found an increased pain threshold and an increased pain tolerance with people who engage in NSSI (Koenig et al., 2016). While the elevated pain threshold seems to be habitual, the underlying processes are still poorly understood, but they point in the direction of intact sensible pathways of pain (Bekrater-Bodman et al., 2015), with an altered subjective perception (Bonenberger et al., 2015). As pain can be understood as a barrier to NSSI (Hooley & Franklin, 2018), the absence of pain can also be viewed as a maintaining factor of NSSI. Interlinked with the signal of pain is the opioidergic system, which has recently attracted attention among those researching NSSI. A first study in patients with personality disorders has reported decreased levels of beta-endorphin and met-enkephalin in the cerebrospinal fluid of patients with NSSI (Stanley et al., 2010), and recent research was able to replicate this finding in more peripheral measures, showing lower beta-endorphin levels in the saliva and blood before NSSI (Störkel et al., 2021; van der Venne et al., 2021). These findings altogether add further support to the longstanding endogenous opioid hypothesis (Sher & Stanley, 2008). This hypothesis builds on the idea that individuals with NSSI show lower levels of certain opioid receptor agonists. Whenever these individuals encounter a demanding situation, there is an increasing need to achieve opioid homeostasis. Given that endogenous opioids are released in injuries, NSSI is used to increase levels of endogenous opioids. In summary, NSSI is seen as an act to restore opioidergic homeostasis in times of stress in patients. Looking in the emotion regulatory aspect of the actual act of NSSI, there is evidence for a decreased activity in the amygdala after administering pain, an effect that is even more pronounced if tissue is destroyed (Reitz et al., 2015; Schmahl et al., 2006). In summary, the decrease of arousal and negative emotions and getting back in control, which is often reported by patients with NSSI, is supported by neurobiological mechanisms of decreased limbic activity, increased (pre)frontal activity and an altered functional connection between these two regions.

The aftermath of NSSI is characterized by a stabilization of emotions, with some patients reporting feeling better, ranging from a neutral to a positive valence (see Claes et al., this volume). While seeing blood seems to add to a soothing effect (Naoum et al., 2016), there has also been a discussion on the effect of pain-offset relief (Franklin et al., 2013) (see Selby & Hughes, this volume). It has been shown in a sample of adolescents that a stronger signal was observable in areas associated with reward processing in pain-offset relief in participants with a history of NSSI (Osuch et al., 2014). This finding may additionally provide further support for a positive after-effect of NSSI (Osuch et al., 2014).

Although these neurobiological mechanisms only provide rough explanations and we are currently missing many bits and pieces from this picture, being far away from an overarching explanatory model, it has to be pointed out that these findings are very much in line with the clinical picture of NSSI. Patients report an unbearable emotional situation that can be (at least in the short term) "resolved" by injuring oneself. Findings from neurobiology provide support for this process, showing an altered stress regulatory system, in which emotions are perceived as more extreme and can be countered by injuring oneself without suffering from a great amount of pain, with a feeling of a neutral or even positive state after NSSI. It therefore could be helpful to think about other ways to deal with stressful situations or aversive emotional states without injuring oneself. Although it has to be repeated that psychotherapeutic interventions have shown their efficacy in decreasing NSSI and therefore need to be the first treatments of choice, there are also other possibilities to influence stress or help to regulate emotions, which shall be discussed further.

Psychotherapeutic Interventions as First Treatment of Choice

There is strong and increasing evidence for the efficacy of specific psychotherapeutic interventions to decrease the frequency of NSSI. Two meta-analyses have focused on the efficacy of psychotherapeutic interventions in NSSI (or, more specifically, self-harm). Ougrin et al. (2015) reported data from 19 randomized controlled trials (RCTs) in adolescents, showing a number needed to treat of 10 for NSSI, with all effect sizes being significantly different from 0. Dialectical behavior therapy (DBT), cognitive behavioral therapy (CBT), and mentalization-based therapy (MBT) showed the largest effect sizes. Altogether, studies with strong family components and studies with multiple sessions showed a significant reduction of self-harm (Ougrin et al., 2015). In a recent meta-analysis of 25 RCTs on self-harm, Kothgassner et al. (2020) reported a significant reduction of self-harm in minors

(d = 0.13, 95% CI [0.04–0.22], p = .004), with DBT-A showing the highest reduction of self-harm (d = 0.51, 95% CI [0.18–0.85], p = .002).

Based on the content of successful psychotherapeutic treatment options for NSSI, these treatments often involve emotion regulation strategies, social problem-solving, and mindfulness skills as well as cognitive techniques such as working with automatic thoughts and core beliefs. Given that the majority of patients describe an emotion regulation function as the primary motive for NSSI (Taylor et al., 2018), it seems central to address this specific treatment target when working with patients.

There are still some unresolved issues involving access and barriers to treatment, stepped-care approaches, as well as the question of how to help treatment-resistant patients in whom psychotherapeutic interventions, so far, have failed to show sufficient success. Several fields need further exploration. Although we know that effective treatments do exist, they are often not easily accessible, either because resources offering specialized treatment are limited or because they present a high barrier for individuals in need of support. The issue of scalability could be targeted by digitalizing interventions, while other approaches need to focus on lowering the threshold to enter treatment. This could involve school counselors or gatekeeper trainings. Nevertheless, even if psychotherapeutic interventions are available and accessible in a far broader range than at present, there will be a number of individuals with treatment-resistant NSSI, who do not respond to evidence-based treatment approaches. Therefore, alternative treatment strategies to support existing evidence-based approaches in severe cases are urgently needed.

Psychopharmacological Interventions

As NSSI is seen within the context of different mental health conditions, one possible way to influence NSSI behavior would be to target the underlying condition, such as depression or anxiety. This approach could also include psychopharmacological interventions, for example, the administration of selective serotonin reuptake inhibitors (SSRIs) for the treatment of depression, anxiety disorders, or bulimia or the use of stimulants in attention deficit/hyperactivity disorder (ADHD). While this approach should follow the recommended treatment guidelines of the respective disorders, there has so far been little support for the use of psychopharmacological interventions either alone or in combination with psychotherapeutic approaches to target NSSI specifically. A couple of options have been tested in NSSI, with patient populations often showing NSSI as a symptom of borderline personality disorder (BPD), or as part of stereotypical self-harm in pervasive developmental disorders. The latter represents a subgroup of patients who would not fit within the framework of the proposed NSSI disorder in the fifth edition of *Diagnostic and Statistical Manual of Mental Disorders* (DSM-5; American Psychiatric Association, 2013), so that a detailed discussion is beyond the scope of this chapter. Although the populations under treatment do differ, substances that have been discussed in the context of NSSI (i.e., atypical antipsychotics, naltrexone, or N-Acetylcysteine) are also encountered in the literature of pervasive developmental disorders (Sabus et al., 2019). On the other hand, studies on the group of patients with BPD, showing NSSI as a symptom in the context of controlling intense aversive emotions, could help to inform our understanding of psychopharmacological interventions. Psychopharmacological agents that have been tested for their efficacy to decrease NSSI in one or the other patient groups include SSRIs, antipsychotics, mood stabilizers, benzodiazepines, opiate receptor blockers, stimulants, and a variety of other drugs (most of these on the level of case studies). While SSRIs aim at increasing serotonin levels in the synaptic cleft by reuptake inhibition in the presynaptic neuron, their mode of action is still not fully understood, with newer data pointing to the role of SSRIs in increasing synaptic plasticity and an ability to alter negative cognitive bias (Godlewska & Harmer, 2021). Following a different mechanism, antipsychotics (both the older conventional and the newer atypical antipsychotics) aim to block dopamine receptors on the postsynaptic neuron and also to interfere with the serotonergic system. While the main idea behind the use of SSRIs is the potential influence on decreasing impulsivity, decreasing anxiety and elevating mood, antipsychotics have been used with the hope of stabilizing mood and also influencing impulsivity. The use of benzodiazepines, which are sedatives with an addictive potential as one of their adverse side effects, was guided by the thought that sedation could be helpful in emotional aversive states leading to NSSI. Opiate receptor antagonists, which block possible addiction-like mechanisms via the opioidergic system, have been used with the idea of blocking the addiction-like maintenance factors in persons with repetitive and severe NSSI (see Blasco-Fontecilla, this volume). There are several problems with regard to the evidence of these psychopharmacological options available for NSSI. There are a very limited number of studies designed to evaluate NSSI as a primary outcome marker. Of these, a couple of studies use self-harm terminology, and thus are also including suicidal behaviors, which makes it hard to address which differential effects these substances might have on NSSI. Sometimes NSSI has been used as a secondary or tertiary outcome marker in studies focusing on other fields of interest. Nevertheless, those studies have the potential to also inform clinical practice. However, based on the low number of studies and the lack of efficacy measures in these studies, clear recommendations for a psychopharmacological treatment approach that are based on solid research data cannot be given (Plener et al., 2013; Plener et al., 2016; Turner et al., 2014).

A recent systematic review and meta-analysis on psychopharmacological treatment for NSSI in adolescents concluded that SSRIs were unable to show an effect in RCTs (Eggart et al., 2022). Only a few more studies were available, which focused on other substances, such as a retrospective chart review reporting a good effect of the atypical antipsychotic Ziprasidone in a case series of adolescent psychiatric inpatients and missing effects of benzodiazepines (such as clonazepam and lorazepam) as well as trazodone and methylphenidate (Eggart et al., 2022). The most recent version of the Cochrane review on interventions for self-harm in children and adolescents underlines these findings by suggesting that no group of drugs that have been researched (including antidepressants, antipsychotics, anxiolytics, mood stabilizers, and natural products) were able to show an effect on self-harm in adolescents (Witt et al., 2021). As a new development (stemming from use in treating excoriation disorder), N-Acetylcysteine has been described as potentially capable of reducing NSSI in a case series of adolescents (Cullen et al., 2018), and it will be interesting to see whether this effect could be observed in future RCTs. In summary, although we have seen a strong increase in studies on the efficacy of psychotherapy, little is still known regarding specific psychopharmacological treatment options. Therefore, the use of psychopharmacology should be confined as a guideline-based treatment approach to target underlying mental health disorders. In addition, sedating psychopharmacological components (mostly conventional antipsychotics) could be used as the last part of a skill chain in an inpatient setting, in a way in which the patients with NSSI can choose medication to stop states of aversive high arousal after they have tried several other skills that don't lead to the necessary reduction of these negative states (Plener et al., 2016). It has to be noted that this would mean an off-label use of the aforementioned conventional antipsychotics which prescribers will have to keep in mind.

NonPharmaceutical "Biological" Interventions

Given the paucity of psychopharmacological interventions, it seems crucial to explore further options to target NSSI, which involve a direct alteration of biological states but without the focus on chemical imbalances (which are the primary target of psychopharmacological interventions) while still trying to influence circuits of stress and emotion regulation. This involves at a very basal level a focus on fostering sleep and physical activity, as both are known to stabilize individuals, improve mental health, and support emotion regulation.

Sleep and Physical Activity

A great number of adolescents who engage in NSSI report different kinds of sleep problems, which are also associated with suicidal attempts in this group *and* predict NSSI. In NSSI, higher rates of irregular sleep patterns have been reported (Asarnow et al., 2020; Burke et al., 2022), and a longitudinal study has shown links between insomnia, depression, and NSSI (Latina et al., 2021). Therefore, sleep should be assessed and, in the case of sleep problems, therapy needs to specifically address these issues with the aim of reinstating a better quality of sleep, either by using psychoeducation with regard to sleep hygiene, or—if insufficient—psychotherapeutic approaches like CBT for insomnia (CBT-I) (Asarnow & Manber, 2019). Should these strategies not improve the problem sufficiently, there are also several psychopharmacological treatment options available, which could support psychotherapeutic first-line approaches (Kansagra, 2020).

Another basic process receiving more attention with regard to NSSI is physical activity. Whereas the first single case study on the efficacy of physical activity for decreasing NSSI was demonstrated in an on-off design (Wallenstein & Nock, 2007), further studies have found that adolescents who identified themselves as athletes had lower levels of NSSI (Young et al., 2014), and the rate of NSSI found to be negatively related to levels of physical activity (Boone & Brausch, 2016). A study on adults in a partial hospitalization program clearly showed the link between lower physical activity and higher levels of NSSI (Jarvi et al., 2017), and a more recent study looked into the interplay between sleep, physical activity, and NSSI, reporting a modulation of the effect of negative emotion regulation ability on NSSI via sleep, while a direct effect on positive emotion regulation ability has been observed through physical activity (Lan et al., 2022).

Although these findings point to a need to take care of basic biological functions, such as sleep or physical activity, when targeting NSSI, so far studies showing an effect of sleep or exercise altering interventions to decrease NSSI are still missing, While the gap in the existing literature is waiting to be filled, clinicians should nevertheless keep in mind to thoroughly assess sleep and physical activity and aim to support these factors by motivation and behavioral planning or as parts of a skills list.

Vagal Stimulation

Among the mechanisms to influence stress, stimulation of the vagus nerve has gained increasing awareness recently. The vagus nerve is the tenth cranial nerve, directly starting in the brain and branching throughout the body. The vagus nerve plays a crucial role in the regulation of the parasympathetic, responsible for our "tend and befriend" system (in contrast to the sympathetic "fight or flight" system). Given that NSSI is often used in aversive states of high arousal, it makes sense to look at the somewhat "soothing" effect of vagal activity.

Whereas a lower vagal activity can be observed in states of high arousal, a higher vagal activity accompanies states of low arousal. To assess the function of the vagal system, proxy parameters such as heart rate variability (HRV), which is influenced by vagal activity, are often used. A lower HRV is observed in individuals with higher levels of stress and a decreased HRV has also been observed in BPD and patients with emotional dysregulation (Weise et al., 2020; Weise et al., 2022) and could be linked to a history of childhood trauma (Back et al., 2022). It can be hypothesized that NSSI and the act of seeing blood in the aftermath acts in a way that can be understood as vagal stimulation (van Hoorn, 2020), which raises the question of whether this effect can also be achieved by using other modes of stimulation. Although there are invasive techniques to implant vagal nerve stimulators, which require surgery, the peripheral use of vagal nerve stimulators has gained attention, since it is more easily accessible. As one of the branches of the vagus nerve reaches up to the body's outer surface just below the skin in the ear region, transcutaneous auricular vagal nerve stimulation (taVNS) has been used to target the nerve. It has even shown in a short, single-session study that healthy controls got better in cognitive reappraisal in an emotion regulation task (De Smet et al., 2021), while it has to be pointed out that the literature on effects of taVNS is mixed (Wolf et al., 2021).

With regard to auricular stimulation, the use of auricular acupuncture needs to be mentioned. In an open trial of nine adolescents with NSSI, auricular acupuncture was shown to be effective in decreasing frequency of NSSI (Nixon et al., 2003). It has to be noted that although parasympathetic effects of acupuncture were reported by the participants (such as feeling calm), acupuncture aims to target distinct points on channels in which chi is thought to be flowing, thus being not necessarily in line with the theory behind vagus nerve stimulation. In another study, self-acupuncture was taught to 10 adult patients with NSSI, also leading to a decrease in NSSI (Davies et al., 2011). However, apart from these case series, no further studies have looked into acupuncture and NSSI, thus not allowing for further recommendations on the use of acupuncture apart from experimental designs.

Repetitive Transcranial Magnetic Stimulation

With regard to the emotion regulation function of NSSI, it is worthwhile to think about possible mechanisms of influencing emotion. Based on the model of cognitive control of emotion (MCCE) by Tracy et al. (2015), a stimulus needs to be perceived before attention is drawn to the stimulus. This is followed by appraisal and a response, all of which offer processes in which cognitive control could change our emotional and behavioral response. We could choose situations by avoidance or selection, could modify the situation, decide whether the stimulus attracts further attention, or decide whether to choose distraction or stimulus reappraisal. On a behavioral level, we could alter our behavioral answer and modulate our behavior consciously. These decisions involve cognitive control, all of which are built on neurobiological processes. Structures involved in cognitive control of emotional situations often include regions of the prefrontal and frontal cortex.

rTMS describes the application of a strong magnetic field on certain areas of the brain from the outside with the aim of stimulating these regions and altering their activity. As magnetic fields quickly lose power throughout tissue, subcortical regions (like the amygdala) are hard to reach; however, cortical regions can be modulated in their activity by this stimulation, which explains, why rTMS has been discussed as a possibility to alter cortical control of emotional responses. It has been shown that rTMS has the potential to increase activity in the dorsolateral prefrontal cortex (Konstantinou et al., 2021). Furthermore, single case studies in BPD show decreased levels of impulsivity and better emotion control (Lisoni et al., 2022; Rachid, 2019). A recent systematic review provided the first hints for efficacy of rTMS in BPD; however, to date no double-blind placebo controlled RCT has been conducted to further substantiate this claim (Schmausser et al., 2022).

Transcranial Direct Current Stimulation

Following up on the literature on rTMS, another stimulation technique has gained increasing attention in recent years. Transcranial direct current stimulation is a noninvasive method in which cortical areas are stimulated with electric current to elicit neuronal excitability without eliciting action potentials. Using either anodal or cathodal stimulation, neuronal excitability can be reduced or increased (Prillinger et al., 2021). First studies on tDCS were able to report an enhanced frontolimbic connectivity after tDCS, but it has to be mentioned that these are still pilot studies (Lisoni et al., 2020, 2022). Connecting the findings to the aforementioned processes in the autonomic nervous system, tDCS has shown potential to alter HRV (Schmausser et al., 2022). In a recent RCT in patients with BPD, 10 sessions of tDCS were compared to sham stimulation, showing an increased cognitive reappraisal in those receiving tDCS (Molavi et al., 2020).

Conclusions

Although the evidence for the efficacy of psychotherapeutic interventions is strong and increasing, there are still gaps in our knowledge of other/augmented treatment options for NSSI. Given the high prevalence of NSSI, one needs to think about accessibility of treatment. As treatments showing efficacy for NSSI (such as DBT-A and MBT-A) need a high level of commitment in terms of motivation and invested time from the patients, it might seem unattractive to patients seeking faster solutions. Therefore, adding short-term treatment programs to the portfolio of available treatment options adds to the accessibility of interventions. So far, several brief, manualized, specific psychotherapeutic interventions are available (Calvo et al., 2022), starting from therapeutic assessment, which has proven successful in structuring the first encounter and engaging adolescents in further treatment (Ougrin et al., 2011). The short-term CBT approach "Cutting Down" is able to offer specific help for adolescents with NSSI within a very limited number of sessions (Kaess et al., 2020). These brief therapeutic interventions could be supplemented by the use of apps or online diaries, which have shown promising results as long as they are used regularly (Franklin et al., 2016; Hooley et al., 2018). This sort of blended therapy allows for fast accessibility and integration into patients' everyday lives, thus potentially increasing generalizability of therapy to daily life settings. Another way to increase accessibility is the idea of offering therapeutic programs online. While pilot studies have shown promise (Bjureberg et al., 2018), and RCTs are under way (Kaess et al., 2019; Olsen et al., 2021), future years may see an increasing number of online programs available and offering a first line of contact to treatment-seeking patients.

Although this is promising, there is still a need for further actions in the field oftherapeutic alternatives that can be offered to treatment resistant patients. In this realm, biologically informed treatment approaches could potentially offer new alternatives, such as augmenting treatment effects of psychotherapy with psychopharmacological options or providing stimulation techniques for training of emotional control via rTMS, tDCS, or taVNS. These alternatives could also be helpful for patients who refuse to enter psychotherapeutic treatment but would accept other ways of delivering care. Increasing research on these treatment models could inform our understanding of which treatments might offer help and where other models might fall short, all in service of creating an individualized and tailored approach to offering therapy for NSSI (Plener et al., 2020). Future research needs to build on existing knowledge and focus on hard-to-reach populations and situations in which the options that are available so far are not working sufficiently. Including biologically oriented methods in the therapeutic portfolio could offer gains in knowledge for a vulnerable population.

References

American Psychiatric Association. (2013). *Diagnostic and statistical manual of mental disorders* (5th ed.). https://doi.org/10.1176/appi.books.9780890425596

Asarnow, J. R., Bai, S., Babeva, K. N., Adrian, M., Berk, M. S., Asarnow, L. D., Senturk, D., Linehan, M. M., & McCauley, E. (2020). Sleep in youth with repeated self-harm and high suicidality: Does sleep predict self-harm risk? *Suicide and Life-Threatening Behavior, 50*(6), 1189–1197. https://doi.org/10.1111/sltb.12658

Asarnow, L. D., & Manber, R. (2019). Cognitive behavioral therapy for insomnia in depression. *Sleep Medicine Clinics, 14*(2), 177–184. https://doi.org/10.1016/j.jsmc.2019.01.009

Back, S. N., Schmitz, M., Koenig, J., Zettl, M., Kleindienst, N., Herpertz, S. C., & Bertsch, K. (2022). Reduced vagal activity in borderline personality disorder is unaffected by intranasal oxytocin administration, but predicted by the interaction between childhood trauma and attachment insecurity. *Journal of Neural Transmission, 129*(4), 409–419. https://doi.org/10.1007/s00702-022-02482-9

Bekrater-Bodmann, R., Chung, B.Y., Richter, I., Wicking, M., Foell, J., Mancke, F., Schmahl, C., & Flor, H. (2015). Deficits in pain perception in borderline personality disorder: Results from the thermal grill illusion. *Pain, 156*(10), 2084–2092. https://doi.org/10.1097/j.pain.0000000000000275

Bjureberg, J., Sahlin, H., Hedman-Lagerlöf, E., Gratz, K. L., Tull, M. T., Jokinen, J., Hellner, C., & Ljótsson, B. (2018). Extending research on emotion regulation individual therapy for adolescents (ERITA) with nonsuicidal self-injury disorder: Open pilot trial and mediation analysis of a novel online version. *BMC Psychiatry, 18*(1), 1–13. https://doi.org/10.1186/s12888-018-1885-6

Bonenberger, M., Plener, P. L., Groschwitz, R. C., Grön, G., & Abler, B. (2015). Differential neural processing of unpleasant haptic sensations in somatic and affective partitions of the insula in non-suicidal self-injury (NSSI). *Psychiatry Research: Neuroimaging, 234*(3), 298–304. https://doi.org/10.1016/j.pscychresns.2015.10.013

Boone, S. D., & Brausch, A. M. (2016). Physical activity, exercise motivations, depression, and nonsuicidal self-injury in youth. *Suicide and Life-Threatening Behavior, 46*(5), 625–633. https://doi.org/10.1111/sltb.12240

Brown, R. C., Heines, S., Witt, A., Braehler, E., Fegert, J. M., Harsch, D., & Plener, P. L. (2018). The impact of child maltreatment on non-suicidal self-injury: Data from a representative sample of the general population. *BMC Psychiatry, 18*(1), 1–8. https://doi.org/10.1186/s12888-018-1754-3

Burke, T. A., Hamilton, J. L., Seigel, D., Kautz, M., Liu, R. T., Alloy, L. B., & Barker, D. H. (2022). Sleep irregularity and nonsuicidal self-injurious urges and behaviors. *Sleep, 45*(6), Article zsac084. https://doi.org/10.1093/sleep/zsac084

Calvo, N., García-González, S., Perez-Galbarro, C., Regales-Peco, C., Lugo-Marin, J., Ramos-Quiroga, J. A., & Ferrer, M. (2022). Psychotherapeutic interventions specifically developed for NSSI in adolescence: A systematic review. *European Neuropsychopharmacology, 58*, 86–98. https://doi.org/10.1016/j.euroneuro.2022.02.009

Cullen, K. R., Klimes-Dougan, B., Westlund Schreiner, M., Carstedt, P., Marka, N., Nelson, K., Miller, M. J., Reigstad, K., Westervelt, A., Gunlicks-Stoessel, M., & Eberly, L. E. (2018). N-acetylcysteine for non-suicidal self-injurious behavior in adolescents: An open-label pilot study. *Journal of Child and Adolescent Psychopharmacology, 28*(2), 136–144. https://doi.org/10.1089/cap.2017.0032

Davies, S., Bell, D., Irvine, F., & Tranter, R. (2011). Self-administered acupuncture as an alternative to deliberate self-harm: A feasibility study. *Journal of Personality Disorders, 25*(6), 741–754. https://doi.org/101521pedi2011256741

De Smet, S., Baeken, C., Seminck, N., Tilleman, J., Carrette, E., Vonck, K., & Vanderhasselt, M. A. (2021). Non-invasive vagal nerve stimulation enhances cognitive emotion regulation. *Behaviour Research and Therapy, 145*, Article 103933. https://doi.org/10.1016/j.brat.2021.103933

Eggart, V., Cordier, S., Hasan, A., & Wagner, E. (2022). Psychotropic drugs for the treatment of non-suicidal self-injury in children and adolescents: A systematic review and meta-analysis. *European Archives of Psychiatry and Clinical Neuroscience, 272*(8), 1559–1568. https://doi.org/10.1007/s00406-022-01385-w

Fox, K. R., Franklin, J. C., Ribeiro, J. D., Kleiman, E. M., Bentley, K. H., & Nock, M. K. (2015). Meta-analysis of risk factors for nonsuicidal self-injury. *Clinical Psychology Review, 42*, 156–167. https://doi.org/10.1016/j.cpr.2015.09.002

Franklin, J. C., Fox, K. R., Franklin, C. R., Kleiman, E. M., Ribeiro, J. D., Jaroszewski, A. C., Hooley, J. M., & Nock, M. K. (2016). A brief mobile app reduces nonsuicidal and suicidal self-injury: Evidence from three randomized controlled trials. *Journal of Consulting and Clinical Psychology, 84*(6), 544–557. https://doi.org/10.1037/ccp0000093

Franklin, J. C., Puzia, M. E., Lee, K. M., Lee, G. E., Hanna, E. K., Spring, V. L., & Prinstein, M. J. (2013). The nature of pain offset relief in nonsuicidal self-injury: A laboratory study. *Clinical Psychological Science, 1*(2), 110–119. https://doi.org/10.1177/2167702612474440

Godlewska, B. R., & Harmer, C. J. (2021). Cognitive neuropsychological theory of antidepressant action: A modern-day approach to depression and its treatment. *Psychopharmacology, 238*(5), 1265–1278. https://doi.org/10.1007/s00213-019-05448-0

Hooley, J. M., Fox, K. R., Wang, S. B., & Kwashie, A. N. (2018). Novel online daily diary interventions for nonsuicidal self-injury: A randomized controlled trial. *BMC Psychiatry, 18*(1), 1–11. https://doi.org/10.1186/s12888-018-1840-6

Hooley, J. M., & Franklin, J. C. (2018). Why do people hurt themselves? A new conceptual model of nonsuicidal self-injury. *Clinical Psychological Science, 6*(3), 428–451. https://doi.org/10.1177/2167702617745641

Jarvi, S. M., Hearon, B. A., Batejan, K. L., Gironde, S., & Björgvinsson, T. (2017). Relations between past-week physical activity and recent nonsuicidal self-injury in treatment-seeking psychiatric adults. *Journal of Clinical Psychology, 73*(4), 479–488. https://doi.org/10.1002/jclp.22342

Kaess, M., Edinger, A., Fischer-Waldschmidt, G., Parzer, P., Brunner, R., & Resch, F. (2020). Effectiveness of a brief psychotherapeutic intervention compared with treatment as usual for adolescent nonsuicidal self-injury: A single-centre, randomised controlled trial. *European Child & Adolescent Psychiatry, 29*(6), 881–891. https://doi.org/10.1007/s00787-019-01399-1

Kaess, M., Hooley, J. M., Klimes-Dougan, B., Koenig, J., Plener, P. L., Reichl, C., Robinson, K., Schmahl, C., Sicorello, M., Westlund Schreiner, M., & Cullen, K. R. (2021). Advancing a temporal framework for understanding the biology of nonsuicidal self-injury: An expert review. *Neuroscience & Biobehavioral Reviews, 130*, 228–239. https://doi.org/10.1016/j.neubiorev.2021.08.022

Kaess, M., Koenig, J., Bauer, S., Moessner, M., Fischer-Waldschmidt, G., Mattern, M., Herpertz, S. C., Resch, F., Brown, R., In-Albon, T., Koelch, M., Plener, P. L., Schmahl, C., & Edinger, A. (2019). Self-injury: Treatment, Assessment, Recovery (STAR): Online intervention for adolescent non-suicidal self-injury-study protocol for a randomized controlled trial. *Trials, 20*(1), 1–10. https://doi.org/10.1186/s13063-019-3501-6

Kansagra, S. (2020). Sleep disorders in adolescents. *Pediatrics, 145*(Supp. 2), S204–S209. https://doi.org/10.1542/peds.2019-2056I

Koenig, J., Thayer, J. F., & Kaess, M. (2016). A meta-analysis on pain sensitivity in self-injury. *Psychological Medicine, 46*(8), 1597–1612. https://doi.org/10.1017/S0033291716000301

Konstantinou, G. N., Trevizol, A. P., Downar, J., McMain, S. F., Vila-Rodriguez, F., Daskalakis, Z. J., & Blumberger, D. M. (2021). Repetitive transcranial magnetic stimulation in patients with borderline personality disorder: A systematic review. *Psychiatry Research, 304*, Article 114145. https://doi.org/10.1016/j.psychres.2021.114145

Kothgassner, O. D., Robinson, K., Goreis, A., Ougrin, D., & Plener, P. L. (2020). Does treatment method matter? A meta-analysis of the past 20 years of research on therapeutic interventions for self-harm and suicidal ideation in adolescents. *Borderline Personality Disorder and Emotion Dysregulation, 7*(1), 1–16. https://doi.org/10.1186/s40479-020-00123-9

Lan, Z., Pau, K., Yusof, H. M., & Huang, X. (2022). The effect of emotion regulation on non-suicidal self-injury among adolescents: The mediating roles of sleep, exercise, and social support. *Psychology Research and Behavior Management*, *15*, 1451–1463. https://doi.org/10.2147/PRBM.S363433

Latina, D., Bauducco, S., & Tilton-Weaver, L. (2021). Insomnia symptoms and non-suicidal self-injury in adolescence: Understanding temporal relations and mechanisms. *Journal of Sleep Research*, *30*(1), Article e13190. https://doi.org/10.1111/jsr.13190

Lisoni, J., Barlati, S., Deste, G., Ceraso, A., Nibbio, G., Baldacci, G., & Vita, A. (2022). Efficacy and tolerability of Brain Stimulation interventions in Borderline Personality Disorder: State of the art and future perspectives–A systematic review. *Progress in Neuro-Psychopharmacology and Biological Psychiatry*, *116*, Article 110537. https://doi.org/10.1016/j.pnpbp.2022.110537

Lisoni, J., Miotto, P., Barlati, S., Calza, S., Crescini, A., Deste, G., Sacchetti, E., & Vita, A. (2020). Change in core symptoms of borderline personality disorder by tDCS: A pilot study. *Psychiatry Research*, *291*, Article 113261. https://doi.org/10.1016/j.psychres.2020.113261

Molavi, P., Aziziaram, S., Basharpoor, S., Atadokht, A., Nitsche, M. A., & Salehinejad, M. A. (2020). Repeated transcranial direct current stimulation of dorsolateral-prefrontal cortex improves executive functions, cognitive reappraisal emotion regulation, and control over emotional processing in borderline personality disorder: A randomized, sham-controlled, parallel-group study. *Journal of Affective Disorders*, *274*, 93–102. https://doi.org/10.1016/j.jad.2020.05.007

Naoum, J., Reitz, S., Krause-Utz, A., Kleindienst, N., Willis, F., Kuniss, S., Baumgärtner, U., Mancke, F., Treede, R. D., & Schmahl, C. (2016). The role of seeing blood in non-suicidal self-injury in female patients with borderline personality disorder. *Psychiatry Research*, *246*, 676–682. https://doi.org/10.1016/j.psychres.2016.10.066

Nemeroff, C. B. (2004). Neurobiological consequences of childhood trauma. *Journal of Clinical Psychiatry*, *65*, Article 1828. https://doi.org/10.1016/j.neuron.2016.01.019

Nixon, M. K., Cheng, M., & Cloutier, P. (2003). An open trial of auricular acupuncture for the treatment of repetitive self-injury in depressed adolescents. *The Canadian Child and Adolescent Psychiatry Review*, *12*(1), 10–12.

Olsen, M. H., Morthorst, B., Pagsberg, A. K., Heinrichsen, M., Møhl, B., Rubæk, L., Bjureberg, J., Simonsson, O., Lindschou, J., Gluud, C., & Jakobsen, J. C. (2021). An Internet-based emotion regulation intervention versus no intervention for non-suicidal self-injury in adolescents: A statistical analysis plan for a feasibility randomised clinical trial. *Trials*, *22*(1), 1–8. https://doi.org/10.1186/s13063-021-05406-2

Osuch, E., Ford, K., Wrath, A., Bartha, R., & Neufeld, R. (2014). Functional MRI of pain application in youth who engaged in repetitive non-suicidal self-injury vs. psychiatric controls. *Psychiatry Research: Neuroimaging*, *223*(2), 104–112. https://doi.org/10.1016/j.pscychresns.2014.05.003

Ougrin, D., Tranah, T., Stahl, D., Moran, P., & Asarnow, J. R. (2015). Therapeutic interventions for suicide attempts and self-harm in adolescents: Systematic review and meta-analysis. *Journal of the American Academy of Child & Adolescent Psychiatry*, *54*(2), 97–107. https://doi.org/10.1016/j.jaac.2014.10.009

Ougrin, D., Zundel, T., Ng, A., Banarsee, R., Bottle, A., & Taylor, E. (2011). Trial of therapeutic assessment in London: Randomised controlled trial of therapeutic assessment versus standard psychosocial assessment in adolescents presenting with self-harm. *Archives of Disease in Childhood*, *96*(2), 148–153. http://dx.doi.org/10.1136/adc.2010.188755

Plener, P. L. (2020). Tailoring treatments for adolescents with nonsuicidal self-injury. *European Child & Adolescent Psychiatry*, *29*(6), 893–895. https://doi.org/10.1007/s00787-020-01523-6

Plener, P. L., Brunner, R., Fegert, J. M., Groschwitz, R. C., In-Albon, T., Kaess, M., Kapusta, N. D., Resch, F., & Becker, K. (2016). Treating nonsuicidal self-injury (NSSI) in adolescents: Consensus based German guidelines. *Child and Adolescent Psychiatry and Mental Health*, *10*(1), 1–9. https://doi.org/10.1186/s13034-016-0134-3

Plener, P. L., Bubalo, N., Fladung, A.K., Ludolph, A.G., & Lulé, D. (2012). Prone to excitement: Adolescent females with Non-suicidal self-injury (NSSI) show altered cortical pattern to emotional and NSS-related material. *Psychiatry Research*, *203*(2–3), 146–152. https://doi.org/10.1016/j.pscychresns.2011.12.012. Epub 2012 Aug 16. PMID: 22901627

Plener, P. L., Libal, G., Fegert, J. M., & Kölch, M. G. (2013). Psychopharmakologische Behandlung von nicht suizidalem selbstverletzendem Verhalten. *Nervenheilkunde*, *32*(01/02), 38–41. https://doi.org/10.1055/s-0038-1628475

Prillinger, K., Radev, S. T., Amador de Lara, G., Klöbl, M., Lanzenberger, R., Plener, P. L., Poustka, L., & Konicar, L. (2021). Repeated sessions of transcranial direct current stimulation on adolescents with autism spectrum disorder: Study protocol for a randomized, double-blind, and sham-controlled clinical trial. *Frontiers in Psychiatry, 12*, Article 680525. https://doi.org/10.3389/fpsyt.2021.680525.

Rachid, F. (2019). Repetitive transcranial magnetic stimulation in the treatment of a difficult to treat condition, borderline personality disorder. *Journal of Psychiatric Practice®, 25*(1), 14–21. https://doi.org/10.1097/PRA.0000000000000350

Reitz, S., Kluetsch, R., Niedtfeld, I., Knorz, T., Lis, S., Paret, C., Kirsch, P., Meyer-Lindenberg, A., Treede, R. D., Baumgärtner, U., Bohus, M., & Schmahl, C. (2015). Incision and stress regulation in borderline personality disorder: Neurobiological mechanisms of self-injurious behaviour. *The British Journal of Psychiatry, 207*(2), 165–172. https://doi.org/10.1192/bjp.bp.114.153379

Sabus, A., Feinstein, J., Romani, P., Goldson, E., & Blackmer, A. (2019). Management of self-injurious behaviors in children with neurodevelopmental disorders: A pharmacotherapy overview. *Pharmacotherapy: The Journal of Human Pharmacology and Drug Therapy, 39*(6), 645–664. https://doi.org/10.1002/phar.2238

Santangelo, P. S., Koenig, J., Funke, V., Parzer, P., Resch, F., Ebner-Priemer, U. W., & Kaess, M. (2017). Ecological momentary assessment of affective and interpersonal instability in adolescent non-suicidal self-injury. *Journal of Abnormal Child Psychology, 45*(7), 1429–1438. https://doi.org/10.1007/s10802-016-0249-2

Schmahl, C., Bohus, M., Esposito, F., Treede, R. D., Di Salle, F., Greffrath, W., Ludaescher, P., Jochims, A., Lieb, K., Scheffler, K., Hennig, J., & Seifritz, E. (2006). Neural correlates of antinociception in borderline personality disorder. *Archives of General Psychiatry, 63*(6), 659–666. https://doi.org/10.1001/archpsyc.63.6.659

Schmausser, M., Hoffmann, S., Raab, M., & Laborde, S. (2022). The effects of noninvasive brain stimulation on heart rate and heart rate variability: A systematic review and meta-analysis. *Journal of Neuroscience Research, 100*(9), 1664–1694. https://doi.org/10.1002/jnr.25062

Serafini, G., Canepa, G., Adavastro, G., Nebbia, J., Belvederi Murri, M., Erbuto, D., Pocai, B., Fiorillo, A., Pompili, M., Flouri, E., & Amore, M. (2017). The relationship between childhood maltreatment and nonsuicidal self-injury: A systematic review. *Front Psychiatry, 8*, 149. https://doi.org/10.3389/fpsyt.2017.00149.

Sher, L., & Stanley, B. H. (2008). The role of endogenous opioids in the pathophysiology of self-injurious and suicidal behavior. *Archives of Suicide Research, 12*(4), 299–308. https://doi.org/10.1080/13811110802324748

Sherin, J. E., & Nemeroff, C. B. (2011). Post-traumatic stress disorder: The neurobiological impact of psychological trauma. *Dialogues in Clinical Neuroscience, 13*(3), 263–278. https://doi.org/10.31887/DCNS.2011.13.2/jsherin

Stanley, B., Sher, L., Wilson, S., Ekman, R., Huang, Y. Y., & Mann, J. J. (2010). Non-suicidal self-injurious behavior, endogenous opioids and monoamine neurotransmitters. *Journal of Affective Disorders, 124*(1–2), 134–140. https://doi.org/10.1016/j.jad.2009.10.028

Störkel, L. M., Karabatsiakis, A., Hepp, J., Kolassa, I. T., Schmahl, C., & Niedtfeld, I. (2021). Salivary beta-endorphin in nonsuicidal self-injury: An ambulatory assessment study. *Neuropsychopharmacology, 46*(7), 1357–1363. https://doi.org/10.1038/s41386-020-00914-2

Taylor, P. J., Jomar, K., Dhingra, K., Forrester, R., Shahmalak, U., & Dickson, J. M. (2018). A meta-analysis of the prevalence of different functions of non-suicidal self-injury. *Journal of Affective Disorders, 227*, 759–769. https://doi.org/10.1016/j.jad.2017.11.073

Tracy, D. K., Shergill, S. S., David, A. S., Fonagy, P., Zaman, R., Downar, J., Eliott, E., & Bhui, K. (2015). Self-harm and suicidal acts: A suitable case for treatment of impulsivity-driven behaviour with repetitive transcranial magnetic stimulation (rTMS). *BJPsych Open, 1*(1), 87–91. https://doi.org/10.1192/bjpo.bp.115.000315

Turner, B. J., Austin, S. B., & Chapman, A. L. (2014). Treating nonsuicidal self-injury: A systematic review of psychological and pharmacological interventions. *The Canadian Journal of Psychiatry, 59*(11), 576–585. https://doi.org/10.1177/070674371405901103

van der Venne, P., Balint, A., Drews, E., Parzer, P., Resch, F., Koenig, J., & Kaess, M. (2021). Pain sensitivity and plasma beta-endorphin in adolescent non-suicidal self-injury. *Journal of Affective Disorders, 278*, 199–208. https://doi.org/10.1016/j.jad.2020.09.036

van Hoorn, A. C. (2020). Could affect regulation via vagal nerve self-stimulation be a maintaining factor in non-suicidal self-harm? *Medical Hypotheses, 136*, Article 109498. https://doi.org/10.1016/j.mehy.2019.109498

Wallenstein, M. B., & Nock, M. K. (2007). Physical exercise as a treatment for non-suicidal self-injury: Evidence from a single-case study. *American Journal of Psychiatry, 164*(2), 350–351. https://doi.org/10.1176/ajp.2007.164.2.350a

Weis, C. N., Webb, E. K., deRoon-Cassini, T. A., & Larson, C. L. (2021). Emotion dysregulation following trauma: Shared neurocircuitry of traumatic brain injury and trauma-related psychiatric disorders. *Biological Psychiatry, 91*(5), 470–477. https://doi.org/10.1016/j.biopsych.2021.07.023

Weise, S., Parzer, P., Fürer, L., Zimmermann, R., Schmeck, K., Resch, F., Kaess, M., & Koenig, J. (2022). Autonomic nervous system activity and dialectical behavioral therapy outcome in adolescent borderline personality pathology. *The World Journal of Biological Psychiatry, 22*(7), 535–545. https://doi.org/10.1080/15622975.2020.1858155

Weise, S., Parzer, P., Zimmermann, R., Fürer, L., Resch, F., Kaess, M., & Koenig, J. (2020). Emotion dysregulation and resting-state autonomic function in adolescent borderline personality disorder—A multimodal assessment approach. *Personality Disorders: Theory, Research, and Treatment, 11*(1), 46–53. https://doi.org/10.1037/per0000367

Witt, K. G., Hetrick, S. E., Rajaram, G., Hazell, P., Taylor Salisbury, T. L., Townsend, E., & Hawton, K. (2021). Interventions for self-harm in children and adolescents. *The Cochrane Database of Systematic Reviews, 3*(3), Article CD013667. https://doi.org/10.1002/14651858.CD013667.pub2

Wolf, V., Kühnel, A., Teckentrup, V., Koenig, J., & Kroemer, N. B. (2021). Does transcutaneous auricular vagus nerve stimulation affect vagally mediated heart rate variability? A living and interactive Bayesian meta-analysis. *Psychophysiology, 58*(11), Article e13933. https://doi.org/10.1111/psyp.13933

Young, R., Sproeber, N., Groschwitz, R. C., Preiss, M., & Plener, P. L. (2014). Why alternative teenagers self-harm: Exploring the link between non-suicidal self-injury, attempted suicide and adolescent identity. *BMC Psychiatry, 14*(1), 1–14. https://doi.org/10.1186/1471-244X-14-137

CHAPTER 54

Online Approaches to NSSI Treatment

Jill M. Hooley *and* Kathryn R. Fox

> **Abstract**
>
> This chapter evaluates the online treatment of nonsuicidal self-injury (NSSI). Online interventions or mobile apps for the treatment of NSSI are still very much in their infancy. Some are based on existing treatment approaches such as dialectical behavioral therapy (DBT) and are designed to improve emotion regulation skills, interpersonal effectiveness, mindfulness, and/or distress tolerance. Others seek to modify more novel treatment targets that have been implicated in the development and maintenance of NSSI. Online treatments also vary in how they are designed and used; whereas some are designed to be adjunctive to traditional forms of treatment, others are designed as stand-alone treatments. The chapter looks at the DBT Coach mobile application, the online emotion regulation individual therapy for adolescents (ERITA), therapeutic evaluative conditioning (TEC), and autobiographic self-enhancement training (ASET). It then highlights the ethical issues and challenges raised by online approaches to NSSI.
>
> **Key Words:** nonsuicidal self-injury, online treatments, dialectical behavioral therapy, DBT Coach, online ERITA, therapeutic evaluative conditioning, autobiographic self-enhancement training

Introduction

Despite efforts to better understand and prevent nonsuicidal self-injury (NSSI), much remains to be learned. There are currently very few specific treatments designed to target NSSI and the effects of traditional interventions targeting self-injurious thoughts and behaviors, including NSSI, tend to be small and inconsistent (Fox et al., 2020). Moreover, the most strongly supported and most popular treatments for NSSI typically involve weekly (or more frequent) in-person interactions with one or more licensed mental health providers in a clinical office or other clinical settings.

Such approaches tend to be resource-intensive in terms of time and money. Many people who engage in NSSI live in parts of the country (or parts of the world) where mental health treatment is hard to access or, in some cases, almost nonexistent. Other factors, such as long wait lists, may create further barriers to help-seeking. For minors (including the age group where NSSI is the most common), treatment-seeking may be further complicated by a requirement for consent of a parent or guardian. This brings with it the fear of having to disclose NSSI to parents and of having parents (or other caretakers) judge, misunderstand, or otherwise punish NSSI behaviors. All this highlights the importance of developing new, inexpensive, and efficacious treatment approaches that can be easily accessed by those whose treatment needs are currently unmet by more traditional approaches.

Treatments leveraging the internet may be particularly well suited for NSSI. First, unlike traditional forms of treatment that require transportation to a clinic or other treatment site (which could be a considerable distance away), mobile or internet-based interventions are, for most people, as close as their smartphone or laptop. In the United States, 93% of adults report that they use the internet and 85% of adults own smartphones. Among those ages 18 to 49 years, the rate of smartphone ownership is even higher at 95% (Pew Research Center, 2021). Most adolescents have similar access to the internet either via their phones or computers (Anderson & Jiang, 2018). What this means is that the majority of people in the United States (and, indeed, in many other developed or developing parts of the world) can immediately access online forms of mental healthcare. Online treatments also help to increase feelings of anonymity, which may increase willingness to disclose difficulties with NSSI (Swannell et al., 2014). This is important because NSSI is a highly stigmatized behavior; only approximately half the number of people who engage in these behaviors choose to disclose their NSSI engagement to *anyone* (e.g., Ammerman et al., 2021) for a range of reasons but often due to shame (Rosenrot & Lewis, 2020). Additionally, online treatments lend themselves to reduced costs compared to traditional, brick-and-mortar care. Although some online treatment modalities may involve costs that are similar to traditional forms of care (e.g., teletherapy provided one on one by a licensed mental health professional, requiring HIPAA-compliant video software), other forms of online treatment may be self-guided in whole or in part, thus reducing financial burdens. Finally, in many cases, online interventions may be accessible immediately and on demand and at a time that is most convenient or emotionally necessary to the user. All this makes online forms of treatment especially well suited for NSSI.

In this chapter, we consider the issues raised by recent developments in the online treatment of NSSI. We begin, however, with a review of the current state of research in this area, highlighting the broad range of approaches that have been examined to date.

Online Treatments for NSSI

Online interventions or mobile apps for the treatment of NSSI are still very much in their infancy. Some are based on existing treatment approaches such as dialectical behavioral therapy (DBT) and are designed to improve emotion regulation skills, interpersonal effectiveness, mindfulness, and/or distress tolerance (see Chapman et al., this volume, for a review of cognitive behavioral therapy and DBT approaches). Others seek to modify more novel treatment targets that have been implicated in the development and maintenance of

NSSI. Online treatments also vary in how they are designed and used; whereas some are designed to be adjunctive to traditional forms of treatment, others are designed as stand-alone treatments.

DBT Coach

In an example of the former approach, Rizvi et al. (2016) sought to test the feasibility and immediate effects of using a mobile app to provide DBT skills coaching on demand. The app was designed as a supplemental treatment to regular in-person DBT. The participants were 16 adults with borderline personality disorder (BPD) who had a history of NSSI or a suicide attempt in the past six months, as well as a second instance of NSSI or suicide attempt in the previous five years. Of these participants, 75% were female and 94% had engaged in NSSI, with a median number of 60 lifetime acts of NSSI. The majority of the sample (84%) had also attempted suicide at some point in their lives. In addition to receiving weekly in-person DBT and weekly group skills training for a period of six months, participants were given access to a DBT Coach mobile application. This app, which was installed on participants' smartphones, included all four modules from Linehan's revised skills manual (Linehan, 2015). As such it provided skills coaching in mindfulness, distress tolerance, emotion regulation, and interpersonal effectiveness.

Over the course of this uncontrolled study, 15 of the 16 participants used the coach, although participants used the app less often than they had initially predicted. The median number of uses was 11.5 over a period of nine months (six months of treatment and three-month follow-up period). As might be expected, the use of the app also decreased over time. Use of the app was not associated with any changes in psychopathology, suicide attempts, or self-reported skills. However, greater use of the app was predictive of a greater reduction in NSSI over time. There was also a significant decrease in urges to engage in self-harm (broadly defined) following app use, although urges to engage in self-harm were relatively low overall. It is also not clear if use of the app decreased instances of NSSI in the moment because information about self-harm actions was not collected.

Overall, the results of this pilot study are best regarded as mixed. The app was not accessed as often as expected. Participants were also ambivalent about how helpful they felt the app was (mean rating of 3.08 on a scale of 1–5, not helpful–extremely helpful scale) or how enjoyable they found using it to be (mean = 2.5 on a scale of 1–5; not enjoyable–extremely enjoyable scale). That said, heavier users of the app reported greater reductions in distress and in urges to self-harm. Although the small sample size and the lack of a placebo app control group limit the conclusions that can be drawn, the results suggest that DBT skills can be incorporated into a mobile app format and used as an adjunct to standard treatment for people with BPD who engage in self-injurious behavior.

Emotion Regulation Individual Therapy for Adolescents

Another example of an online intervention based on an existing face-to-face clinical approach is online emotion regulation individual therapy for adolescents (ERITA; Bjureberg et al., 2018). Adapted from emotion regulation group therapy for adults with NSSI (Gratz et al., 2014), ERITA is a 12-week acceptance-based individual therapy. It is designed to decrease NSSI through the improvement of emotion regulation skills. In an initial pilot study, ERITA was delivered to 17 adolescents with NSSI disorder (NSSID) in a traditional in-person, face-to-face format (Bjureberg et al., 2017). Parents of the adolescents also participated through an online program developed to help them better interact with their adolescent offspring. Based on the positive results of the open trial, and the decrease in NSSI frequency from pre- to posttreatment, ERITA was subsequently adapted to an online intervention format. This was offered to 25 Swedish adolescents ages 13 to 17 who met diagnostic criteria for NSSID and who also had one or more episodes of NSSI in the past month. A parent program (also delivered online) was offered to their parents (Bjureberg et al., 2018).

The treatment period lasted 12 weeks. During this time, the adolescents were asked to complete 11 different treatment modules (one module per week with one extra floating week) via a web-based treatment platform. These covered topics such as functions of NSSI, impulse control, and emotional avoidance and were delivered via educational texts, animated films, case examples, and interactive exercises. A mobile app for adolescents was also developed to complement the online treatment. The program for parents involved six modules concerning such topics as psychoeducation, emotional awareness, validation, and invalidation. Parents completed a different module every other week. Of note, the adolescents and their parents were assigned to a clinical psychologist for the duration of the 12-week treatment period. This psychologist was responsible for helping guide participants through the program, as well as reviewing responses and providing written feedback via the platform. In cases where an increase in suicidality was observed (via weekly assessments of NSSI and suicidality), the adolescent and/or the parent was contacted immediately.

It must be pointed out that this was not a randomized controlled study and there was no control group. Ten of the 25 participants also reported some additional face-to-face treatment while receiving online ERITA. However, the results provide preliminary support for this approach. Only one participant dropped out during the treatment and the average number of treatment modules completed by the adolescents was 9.7 (of a maximum of 11) with parents completing an average of 5.2 of 6 modules. Therapists spent a total of 309.6 minutes working with each family on average and the therapeutic alliance was rated as good even though participants had no face-to-face contact with their assigned psychologist.

Importantly, there was a 55% decrease in NSSI frequency from pre- to posttreatment. NSSI frequency decreased an additional 52% from the posttreatment assessment to the three-month follow-up assessment, and this was maintained at the six-month follow-up. Overall, NSSI frequency declined by 69% from pretreatment to the six-month follow-up point with the mean frequency of NSSI decreasing from an average of 10.0 episodes in the past month to 3.1 past month episodes by six months. NSSI abstinence increased significantly from 0% at baseline to 28% at posttreatment. Significant posttreatment improvements were also noted in emotion regulation and global functioning, with these gains being improved at three months and maintained at six-month follow-up. Despite this, however, no significant changes in BPD symptoms were observed.

Given the design of the study, it is not possible to conclude that the clinical gains reported by the adolescent participants are a result of the treatment they received. Nonetheless, the preliminary results are promising and worthy of further investigation. What is needed now is a randomized controlled trial to establish the efficacy of ERITA in a more methodologically rigorous way.

Therapeutic Evaluative Conditioning

The online approaches just described represent adaptations of traditional interventions. therapeutic evaluative conditioning on the other hand, is a novel approach that was developed specifically to be delivered by a mobile app without the involvement of any clinician. Built from the ground up and based on fundamental principles of psychology combined with experimental data about self-injurious behaviors, TEC is delivered via a brief matching game that can be played multiple times. Each game takes one to two minutes to play, and points are given for speed and matching accuracy (Franklin et al., 2016). The TEC app can be downloaded for free and works on both Apple and Android devices (Franklin et al., 2017, n. 1 for details).

TEC seeks to modify two key variables. The first is how people feel about self-injury, suicide, and death. In people who engage in self-injurious behaviors, the instinct to avoid pain or injury as well as the fear of death tends to be diminished (Franklin et al., 2014). Accordingly, TEC is designed to reinstate an aversion to stimuli associated with death, injury, or suicide. The second variable that TEC is designed to modify is how people feel about themselves. People who engage in NSSI are highly self-critical and hold extremely negative views of themselves (Hooley et al., 2010; Hooley & St. Germain, 2014; see Swerdlow et al., this volume, for a review of negative affect and NSSI). TEC aims to reduce the high levels of self-criticism, self-hatred, and self-disgust that characterize people with NSSI by training them to feel more positively about themselves.

All this is accomplished in the context of an active evaluative conditioning paradigm. Within trials, stimuli associated with self-harm (e.g., a picture of a scalpel) are paired with unpleasant picture stimuli (such as an image of a snake or an infected toenail). Over time this creates negative associations with self-injury related stimuli. In contrast, pleasant stimuli (e.g., the word "good") are paired with self-related words such as "me."

Franklin et al. (2016) conducted three randomized controlled trials to test the effects of an active version of TEC versus a control version that included only neutral pictures or word pairings. Participants with histories of NSSI or suicidal behaviors were recruited from web-based forums focusing on self-injury. Across three different samples (involving 114, 131, and 163 participants) providing people with one month of access to TEC was associated with significant reductions in self-cutting, and suicidal behaviors compared to the control version of the game.

As encouraging as these results are, it must be noted that most participants only used TEC for about 10 minutes per week. The beneficial effects of TEC were also not sustained beyond the month-long treatment period. Going forward it will be important to add additional elements to the game to motivate more frequent use. Modifications to the format may also result in more enduring therapeutic gains. Finally, it is worth keeping in mind that even though TEC was designed to be a highly accessible, scalable, and anonymous stand-alone intervention, it can also be integrated into traditional face-to-face therapeutic approaches as an adjunctive treatment (Franklin et al., 2017). As such it provides a valuable additional tool for therapists working with individuals who engage in self-injury.

Autobiographic Self-Enhancement Training

As we have already noted, extreme self-criticism or self-hatred is implicated in the development and maintenance of NSSI (Hooley & Franklin, 2018). TEC uses a form of Pavlovian conditioning to decrease this aversion to the self. In the approach developed by Hooley et al. (2018), self-worth is again the treatment target. However, with autobiographic self-enhancement training (ASET), a more explicit approach is used.

Prior research by Hooley and St. Germain (2014) demonstrated that a very brief (five-minute) experimental cognitive intervention encouraging participants with NSSI histories to elaborate on positive self-traits changed both their self-worth and their willingness to endure physical pain. Building on this approach, Hooley and colleagues created an online daily diary intervention. This required participants to write for five minutes every day about something positive that they did that day that reflected one of their positive traits and values (e.g., helping a friend confront a challenging situation or helping a neighbor take a heavy suitcase up a flight of stairs). All study participants remained anonymous, and all writing assignments were submitted to the study team via an online portal. Participants were asked to write each day for a total of 28 days. Following the month of active treatment, participants completed follow-up assessments at one month and three months posttreatment.

In this randomized controlled trial, adult participants who reported at least two past-month episodes of NSSI were randomly assigned to ASET or one of two other conditions. One of these involved expressive writing (EW). This condition, which was based on the work of Pennebaker and Beall (1986), required participants to write for five minutes each day about something that had occurred that day that was upsetting or worrisome. The third condition involved journaling (JNL) about the factual events of the day (e.g., what the participant had done that day) without any emotional content.

At the end of the month-long daily writing intervention, participants who received ASET were significantly less self-critical than participants who engaged in JNL. However, contrary to expectation, levels of self-criticism and NSSI declined significantly in all participants, regardless of whether they received ASET or EW or were assigned to the JNL conditions. There were also significant pre- to posttreatment declines in depression and suicide ideation. Desire to discontinue NSSI remained unchanged, however, as did the likelihood of future NSSI, suicidal plans, and suicidal behaviors.

Although ASET, EW, and JNL all resulted in clinical benefits for participants, most of these were not sustained after treatment ended. The significant decreases in self-criticism and frequency of NSSI episodes were not maintained at follow-up. However, at the three-month follow-up, participants who had received ASET reported significantly less suicide ideation than those who had engaged in expressive writing. JNL was also associated with less suicide ideation at posttreatment and the three-month follow-up compared to the EW group. Another unexpected finding was that participants found writing about upsetting events (EW condition) more enjoyable and less annoying than writing about the positive things they had done (ASET condition). This may speak to the difficulties people who engage in NSSI face when they are asked to focus on positive aspects of themselves. Although contact with study staff was deliberately minimized in the design of this online intervention, going forward, having more access to a supportive coach could perhaps provide additional and more enduring benefits for those assigned to ASET. In future work, the potential therapeutic benefits of non-emotional JNL should also be more fully explored. Finally, given the importance of a highly negative sense of self in the development of NSSI (Hooley & Franklin, 2018), the possible benefits of using ASET as a preventative treatment for young people at risk should be investigated. As the following case example illustrates, when NSSI and highly negative beliefs about the self are firmly established, changing these beliefs and behaviors may require more than five minutes of daily writing for one month.

Anna (not her real name because all participants were anonymous) was a 34-year-old heterosexual woman whose NSSI began when she was seven years old. Anna reported an extensive history of self-cutting, hitting, burning, and scraping her skin to the point of drawing blood, with 1,000 lifetime and 126 NSSI episodes in the past year. She also had a history of suicidal thoughts and several suicide attempts. At baseline, Anna reported that she had engaged in 10 episodes of NSSI in the past month. On the scale used to assess self-criticism (which has a maximum score of 56), she scored 50.

Anna completed all 28 days of the online diary assignments. Her responses often centered on themes of being kind and caring. She wrote about complimenting people such as store clerks, giving a friend a ride to the train station, taking the time to listen to a friend who was struggling, and taking good care of her pets. These activities made her feel good about herself.

Across the four weeks of treatment, Anna showed modest reductions in self-criticism from her baseline score of 50. She scored 43 at week one, 45 at week two, 42 at week three, and 46 at week four. At the one-month and three-month follow-up assessments, Anna's self-criticism scores were 46 and 42, respectively. At baseline, Anna reported two past-week NSSI episodes. This was followed by 1, 3, 0, and 2 NSSI episodes across the four weeks of active treatment. Another six episodes occurred between the end of active treatment and the one-month follow up. In the month before the final three-month follow-up assessment, no episodes of NSSI occurred.

Overall, Anna was quite engaged with the ASET treatment. She reported finding the intervention moderately enjoyable. Although no large reductions in NSSI or self-criticism were observed, Anna showed modest reductions in self-criticism. Her engagement in NSSI also decreased compared to baseline.

Project SAVE

Project SAVE (Stop Adolescent Violence Everywhere; Dobias et al., 2021) is the first randomized controlled trial testing online interventions for NSSI (and suicide ideation) in adolescents. As with TEC and ASET, and building on that work, this intervention was designed as a stand-alone treatment; however, unlike these approaches, SAVE was designed as a single-session intervention. Single-session interventions include core elements of evidence-based treatments that are packaged into a ~30-minute online program. In addition to most youth being unable to access traditional forms of mental health care, nearly 60% of youth who do access mental health treatments drop out early (Harpaz-Rotem et al., 2004; Kataoka et al., 2002). Single-session interventions are particularly accessible compared to traditional treatments, and prior research shows that they can reduce diverse mental health difficulties in youth, including both internalizing and externalizing symptoms (e.g., Schleider & Weisz, 2018; Schleider et al., 2020). Project SAVE adopted this single-session format to include two targets relevant to NSSI and suicide ideation: self-punishment and emotion regulation.

In this treatment trial, 565 adolescents (ages 13–16 years) endorsing past month NSSI engagement and negative self-beliefs were randomly assigned to Project SAVE or an attention-matched control program encouraging participants to identify and express their feelings. Briefly, Project SAVE includes the following content sections: (a) psychoeducation about how changing your actions (e.g., decreasing self-injurious behaviors) can positively impact thoughts and emotions; (b psychoeducation and testimonials from other teens who had successfully decreased their self-injurious behaviors and noticed positive changes as a result; (c) evidence-based tips to overcome barriers to reducing self-injurious behaviors; and (d) allowing youth to share their own thoughts and advice on what they learned with other teenagers.

Results of the trial demonstrated that Project SAVE is a feasible and acceptable intervention—it was rated as highly acceptable among participants, and 80% of participants assigned to SAVE completed the full program. Moreover, relative to the control treatment, Project SAVE predicted greater desires to stop future NSSI and significantly reduced self-hatred from pre- to immediately posttreatment. However, limiting enthusiasm, Project SAVE did not significantly reduce the perceived likelihood of future NSSI, or decrease NSSI or suicide ideation frequency three months posttreatment. Reductions in self-hatred were also not significantly greater at three months posttreatment compared to the control group (although both groups demonstrated significant decreases in self-hate at follow-up).

Results of Project SAVE provide preliminary evidence that online interventions can be safely administered to youth in the absence of parental consent, and that they can be perceived as acceptable and enjoyable for youth. Moreover, although treatment efficacy was modest at best, results parallel much of the research on traditional forms of treatment for NSSI, which tend to be weaker among youth compared to adults (Fox et al., 2020).

Challenges and Opportunities

Online interventions offer many advantages. They also introduce new ethical issues. In the sections that follow, we consider two important challenges raised by online approaches and offer some preliminary recommendations. We also highlight a major opportunity the Internet creates for online research.

Managing Risk

NSSI and suicidal thoughts and behaviors are highly comorbid. For this reason, NSSI research often includes an assessment of suicidal thoughts and behaviors as well as a protocol for risk assessment and safety planning if a participant reports recent suicidal thoughts or behaviors. Risk assessment concerns make all research on NSSI and suicidal thoughts and behaviors more difficult (Lakeman & Fitzgerald, 2009). This difficulty is pronounced when conducting studies online. As mentioned previously, one advantage to online interventions for NSSI is the potential to provide a degree of anonymity that is impossible with in-person treatment approaches. However, one downside of this anonymity is the complexity it creates with respect to suicide risk assessments.

Smith et al. (2022) provide several recommendations for safe and ethical approaches to facilitate participant safety when using online methods. First, just as with in-person research approaches, collecting information concerning suicide and self-harm risk (e.g., past-month suicidal thoughts or behaviors) should be standard practice. When online treatments involve personalized teletherapy and/or individual- and group-level work that includes a therapist, risk assessments should mirror those used for in-person risk assessments. If clients endorse past-week suicidal thoughts, behaviors, or plans, risk assessments should be conducted over video or phone, and relevant steps (e.g., safety planning and providing crisis resources) should be followed.

When conducting research with anonymous participants, Smith et al. (2022) advise that researchers ask only about recent suicidal thoughts and behaviors, rather than including questions typically used to indicate imminent risk (e.g., current suicidal intent and current plan with access to the method). This approach is undoubtedly less comprehensive than traditional risk assessment approaches and precludes calling 911 or accompanying someone to a hospital emergency department in cases of imminent risk. However, no research has examined the effectiveness of these more extreme "risk mitigation strategies" in comparison to approaches that provide people with more autonomy and control over their own personal safety. It is also increasingly clear that researchers and clinicians are not able to determine who is at high risk for suicide with any degree of certainty (e.g., Large et al., 2017). Moreover, many traditional approaches (such as calling 911 or involuntary hospitalization) may be harmful (Wang et al., 2022) and may reduce trust in clinicians and researchers alike.

An alternative approach is to flag those who meet predetermined risk criteria and then follow up with them in a standardized and thorough manner. For example, one option involves sending automatic ("push") emails, text messages, or survey blocks that provide a range of accessible crisis and electronic resources, as well as additional information about these resources. These might include how to find local emergency or urgent care facilities, information about how to access suicide and crisis hotlines, warmlines (which provide free and confidential support for *anyone* and particularly people struggling with mental health difficulties), and other crisis services. In these instances, participants can also complete self-guided and electronic safety plans (see, e.g., https://osf.io/rwktm/). Although such safety plans are currently being tested for acceptability and utility, they very much mirror safety plans conducted in person. Alternatively, particularly in situations where participants provide phone numbers, researchers can follow up by phone or text to check in when higher-risk responses are reported. Using this approach, individualized safety plans can be created and/or referenced. Local crisis resources can also be discussed.

When treatments are administered anonymously and/or via a structured and predetermined format (e.g., Dobias et al., 2021; Franklin et al., 2016; Hooley et al., 2018) without a designated primary therapist, the approaches suggested above should be followed. It may also be appropriate to provide clients with the contact information (e.g., email address, phone number with limited work hours of a trained and licensed therapist, and/or to ask clients to provide their own contact information so that a trained and licensed therapist can contact them directly). With this approach, clients can then choose to contact and talk to a professional if they feel unsafe and need additional support.

Obtaining Consent

For research, online studies with adults (age 18+) can obtain electronic signatures and/or tacit informed consent after participants read a consent form and proceed to a given study. However, this becomes more difficult with minors (i.e., youth under 18) where parental consent and youth assent are typically required. It is very difficult (if not impossible) to determine the veracity of parent/guardian consent online. Therefore, another key ethical consideration for online NSSI treatment research is whether and when it may be appropriate to waive parental consent so that youth can participate.

Although issues here are far from resolved, when adolescents are capable of understanding study risks and benefits, many researchers maintain that waiving the requirement for parental/guardian consent may be appropriate and ethical (e.g., Coyne, 2010; Goredema-Braid, 2010). Smith et al. (2022) describe how research on NSSI and other forms of self-injurious thoughts and behaviors in youth may be eligible for waived parental consent requirements. Briefly, federal research regulations allow for parental consent waivers when (a) the research involves no greater than minimal risk, (b) the waiver does not impact the rights or welfare of participants, (c) the research cannot happen without the waiver, and (d) participants are provided with debriefing materials poststudy (General Requirements for Informed Consent, 2007). Many online studies of NSSI meet these requirements, particularly those that involve treatment and intervention programs. For example, a large-scale trial of an online intervention to reduce NSSI in adolescents is currently being conducted in Germany (Kaess et al., 2019). A waiver for parental consent was obtained for this study because of the potential for benefits to participants and the fact that the study could not be conducted without such a waiver.

Outside the research realm, clinical interventions with youth in the absence of parental consent remains a contentious topic. In the United States, laws differ across states. As of 2015, only seven states and Washington, DC, specifically required parent/guardian consent for outpatient youth mental health treatment. In other states, there was no specific law, allowing youth and/or a parent/guardian to consent to outpatient mental health treatment for the minor (Kerwin et al., 2015). However, the age range required for youth consent varies between states, with some allowing youth as young as 12 to consent to mental health outpatient treatment without a parent/guardian and others not permitting this until the minor is at least age 16. Mental health professionals seeking to provide online therapy for youth via more traditional modalities (e.g., one-on-one teletherapy) should follow their state guidelines to clarify the age at which youth consent is permitted and to determine if parent/guardian consent is needed. Alternative forms of mental health treatment for NSSI that are self-guided or brief likely do not fall under traditional state guidelines for mental healthcare, as no direct provider is seen. As such, interventionists should consider the risk level of a given intervention (it should be minimal) and the ability of clients to understand the treatment requirements, mandated reporting, and data safety involved in their intervention.

Inclusion of Minoritized Populations

Most NSSI treatment studies involve participants who identify as White and as female. Few have intentionally targeted adolescents and children. Most also fail to assess gender diversity and sexual orientation, despite the higher rates of NSSI observed in these populations (Fox et al., 2020; see Taliaferro et al., this volume). The internet provides an opportunity to recruit participants much more cheaply and easily across a range of race/ethnicities, sexualities, genders, ability and disability statuses, socioeconomic statuses, and intersections across these groups. Intervention research including, and centering, people from minority populations represents a critical step toward improving NSSI intervention research. Such research should prioritize recruitment of racial and ethnically representative populations, child and adolescent populations, and LGBTQ + populations. Going forward, research in this area would also benefit from testing whether these interventions are similarly efficacious across identities.

Related to this greater inclusivity, involving people with lived experience of NSSI into the design and dissemination of novel treatments, into the risk assessment and safety planning process, and into other parts of the recruitment process will represent a critical step for online interventions for NSSI. These voices and perspectives will ensure that treatments are maximally inclusive and relevant and will increase the likelihood that people will pursue these treatments in the future.

A Blueprint for the Future

Online interventions for NSSI range from an individual clinical practitioner seeing a client via Zoom to approaches such as TEC, which can be accessed privately, on demand, and without the involvement of any clinical professional. Although research in this area (particularly with regard to NSSI as opposed to suicidality) is still new, the range of methods that have been used to date is encouraging. Approaches such as ERITA have shown promising preliminary results, although conclusions about the efficacy of the intervention overall are premature in the absence of a randomized controlled trial. The randomized controlled trial by Hooley et al. (2018) involving ASET also yielded the unexpected finding that what was intended to be an inert control condition (non-emotional daily JNL) led to a reduction in NSSI. One possibility here is that non-emotional JNL facilitates the development of emotional distancing (Nook et al., 2017). This idea warrants further examination. Future modifications to the TEC mobile app may also increase engagement and lead to treatment effects that are more enduring and sustained.

Despite the promise of internet-based interventions, we remain far from having an effective and durable treatment for NSSI. To make true progress we need a much better understanding of the underlying causes of NSSI. Recognizing that there likely is not one or even a handful of factors that cause these behaviors may be a key step in designing novel and more effective NSSI interventions. However, while this more basic research is being conducted, and as we await innovations in treatment, it is essential to remember that people are struggling with NSSI now. Even if current treatment approaches are not ideal, we must do all we can to respond to people's needs for mental healthcare using the clinical tools that we have.

An increased focus on developing and testing online NSSI interventions should be a major priority for researchers. There is a pressing need for research testing the equivalence and/or superiority of online methods for treatment access and treatment efficacy using randomized control trials. More specifically, we need answers to the following research questions:

1. Do teletherapy and other forms of traditional therapy retrofitted for the online format perform at least as well as traditional, brick-and-mortar therapy formats for reducing NSSI?
2. Do self-guided interventions or interventions requiring fewer resources (time, money, personnel) perform at least as well as more traditional approaches (both brick-and-mortar and/or therapies retrofitted for the online format)?
3. When using sufficiently powered studies (i.e., those with a large enough sample to detect small effect sizes) and randomized control trials, do certain online intervention approaches outperform others?

Concluding Remarks

Online approaches reflect the pressing need to provide timely and effective interventions for NSSI. Yet it is important to emphasize that online methods are not meant to be a substitute for in-person treatment. Rather, such approaches simply make it more likely that we can reach people who might otherwise not be able to access treatment. Online approaches also do not preclude the involvement of clinicians. It is possible that having a clinical contact or clinical coach might provide additional benefits to those using online methods of treatment. The advantages of having some access to a clinician cannot be underestimated. This is especially so when dealing with high-risk treatment populations. Going forward, hybrid formats might represent a sweet spot, maximizing outreach while providing structure and clinical support in a cost-effective manner. Finally, the role of online interventions in the prevention of NSSI needs to be explored. Most of the work to date has involved adult participants with established histories of NSSI. Yet adolescence is the time of greatest risk for the development of NSSI. Most adolescents use the internet constantly. Widely available, inexpensive, and on-demand treatments that can be accessed privately by young people offer a valuable opportunity. If accessed early, such approaches may be one way to provide young people with the skills and resources they need to change what might otherwise be a trajectory toward more severe and chronic problems with NSSI.

Acknowledgements

We thank Emma Edenbaum for her assistance in the preparation of this chapter.

References

Ammerman, B. A., Wilcox, K. T., O'Loughlin, C. M., & McCloskey, M. S. (2021). Characterizing the choice to disclose nonsuicidal self-injury. *Journal of Clinical Psychology, 77*(3), 683–700. https://doi.org/10.1002/jclp.23045

Anderson, M., & Jiang, J. (2018). Teens, social media & technology 2018. *Pew Research Center, 31*, 1673–1689.

Coyne, I. (2010). Research with children and young people: The issue of parental (proxy) consent. *Children & Society, 24*(3), 227–237.

Bjureberg, J., Sahlin, H., Hellner, C., Hedman-Lagerlöf, E., Gratz, K. L., Bjärehed, J., Jokinen, J., Tull, M. T., & Ljótsson, B. (2017). Emotion regulation individual therapy for adolescents with nonsuicidal self-injury disorder: a feasibility study. *BMC Psychiatry, 17*, 411.

Bjureberg, J., Sahlin, H., Hedman-Lagerlöf, E., Gratz, Tull, Jokinen, Hellner, C., & Ljótsson, B. (2018). Extending research on emotion regulation individual therapy for adolescents (ERITA) with nonsuicidal self-injury disorder: Open pilot trial and mediation analysis of a novel online version. *BMC Psychiatry, 18*, 326. https://doi,org/10.1186/s12888-0181885-6

Dobias, M., Schleider, J. L., Jans, L., & Fox, K. (2021, April 20). An online, single-session intervention for adolescent self-injurious thoughts and behaviors: Results from a randomized trial. https://doi.org/10.31234/osf.io/jprcg

Fox, K. R., Huang, X., Guzmán, E. M., Funsch, K. M., Cha, C. B., Ribeiro, J. D., & Franklin, J. C. (2020). Interventions for suicide and self-injury: A meta-analysis of randomized controlled trials across nearly 50 years of research. *Psychological Bulletin, 146*(12), 1117–1145. https://doi.org/10.1037/bul0000305

Franklin, J. C., Fox, K. R., Franklin, C. R., Kleiman, E. M., Ribeiro, J. D., Jaroszewski, A. C., Hooley, J. M., & Nock, M. K. (2016). A brief mobile app reduces nonsuicidal and suicidal self-injury: Evidence from three randomized controlled trials. *Journal of Consulting and Clinical Psychology, 84*(6), 544–557. https://doi.org/10.1037/ccp0000093

Franklin, J. C., Fox, K. R., & Ribeiro, J. D. (2017). How to implement therapeutic evaluative conditioning in a clinical setting. *Journal of Clinical Psychology, 73*(5), 559–569. https://doi.org/10.1002/jclp.22453

Franklin, J. C., Lee, K. M., Puzia, M. E., & Prinstein, M. J. (2014). Recent and frequent nonsuicidal self-injury is associated with diminished implicit and explicit aversion toward self-cutting stimuli. *Clinical Psychological Science, 2*, 306–318.

General Requirements for Informed Consent. (2007). 45 C.F.R. 46.116.

Gratz, K. L., Tull, M. T., & Levy, R. (2014). Randomized controlled trial and uncontrolled 9-month follow-up of an adjunctive emotion regulation group therapy for deliberate self-harm among women with borderline personality disorder. *Psychological Medicine, 44*(10), 2099–2112. https://doi.org/10.1017/S0033291713002134.

Goredema-Braid, B. (2010). Ethical research with young people. *Research Ethics, 6*(2), 48–52. https://doi.org/10.1177/174701611000600204

Harpaz-Rotem, I., Leslie, D., & Rosenheck, R. A. (2004). Treatment retention among children entering a new episode of mental health care. *Psychiatric Services, 55*(9), 1022–1028. https://doi.org/10.1176/appi.ps.55.9.1022

Hooley, J. M., Fox, K. R., Wang, S., & Kwashie, A. N. D. (2018). Novel online daily diary interventions for nonsuicidal self-injury: A randomized controlled trial. *BMC Psychiatry, 18*, 264, https://doi.org/10.1186/s12888-018-1840-6

Hooley, J. M., & Franklin, J. C. (2018). Why do people hurt themselves? A new conceptual model of nonsuicidal self-injury. *Clinical Psychological Science, 6*(3), 428–451. https://doi.org/10.1177/2167702617745641

Hooley, J. M., Ho, D. T., Slater, J., & Lockshin, A. (2010). Pain perception and nonsuicidal self-injury: A laboratory investigation. *Personality Disorders: Theory, Research, and Treatment, 1*(3), 170–179. https://doi.org/10.1037/a0020106

Hooley, J. M., & St. Germain, S. A. (2014). Nonsuicidal self-injury, pain, and self-criticism: Does changing self-worth change pain endurance in people who engage in self-injury? *Clinical Psychological Science, 2*(3), 297–305. https://doi.org/10.1177/2167702613509372

Kaess, M., Koenig, J., Bauer, S., Moessner, M., Fischer-Waldschmidt, G., Mattern, M., Herpertz, S. C., Resch, F., Brown, F., In-Albon, T., Koelch, M., Plener, P. L., Schmahl, C., Edinger, A., & the STAR Consortium. (2019). Self-injury: Treatment, assessment, recovery (STAR): Online intervention for adolescent non-suicidal self-injury–study protocol for a randomized controlled trial. *Trials*, *20*, 425. https://doi.org/10.1186/s13063-019-35-1-6

Kataoka, S. H., Zhang, L., & Wells, K. B. (2002). Unmet need for mental health care among US children: Variation by ethnicity and insurance status. *American Journal of Psychiatry*, *159*(9), 1548–1555. https://doi.org/10.1176/appi.ajp.159.9.1548

Kerwin, M. E., Kirby, K. C., Speziali, D., Duggan, M., Mellitz, C., Versek, B., & McNamara, A. (2015). What can parents do? A review of state laws regarding decision making for adolescent drug abuse and mental health treatment. *Journal of Child and Adolescent Substance Abuse*, *24*(3), 166–176. https://doi.org/10.1080/1067828X.2013.777380

Lakeman, R., & Fitzgerald, M. (2009). Ethical suicide research: A survey of researchers. *International Journal of Mental Health Nursing*, *18*(1), 10–17. https://doi.org/10.1111/j.1447-0349.2008.00569.x

Large, M., Galletly, C., Myles, N., Ryan, C. J., & Myles, H. (2017). Known unknowns and unknown unknowns in suicide risk assessment: Evidence from meta-analyses of aleatory and epistemic uncertainty. *BJPsych Bulletin*, *41*(3), 160–163 https://doi.org/10.1192/pb.bp.116.054940

Linehan, M. M. (2015). *DBT skills training manual* (2nd ed.). Guilford Press.

Nook, E. C., Schleider, J. L., & Somerville, L. H. (2017). A linguistic signature of psychological distancing in emotion regulation. *Journal of Experimental Psychology: General*, *146*(3), 337. https://doi.org/10.1037/xge0000263

Pennebaker, J. W., & Beall, S. K. (1986). Confronting a traumatic event: Toward an understanding of inhibition and disease. *Journal of Abnormal Psychology*, *95*, 274–281.

Pew Research Center. (2021). Internet/broadband fact sheet. https://www.pewresearch.org/internet/fact-sheet/internet-broadband/

Rizvi, S. L., Hughes, C. D., & Thomas, M. C. (2016). The DBT Coach mobile applications as an adjunct to treatment for suicidal and self-injuring individuals with borderline personality disorder: A preliminary evaluation and challenges to client utilization. *Psychological Services*, *13*(4), 380–388. https://doi.org/10.1037/ser0000100

Rosenrot, S. A., & Lewis, S. P. (2020). Barriers and responses to the disclosure of non-suicidal self-injury: A thematic analysis. *Counselling Psychology Quarterly*, *33*(2), 121–141. https://doi.org/10.1080/09515070.2018.1489220

Schleider, J., & Weisz, J. (2018). A single-session growth mindset intervention for adolescent anxiety and depression: 9-month outcomes of a randomized trial. *Journal of Child Psychology and Psychiatry*, *59*(2), 160–170. https://doi.org/10.1111/jcpp.12811

Schleider, J. L., Dobias, M., Sung, J., Mumper, E., & Mullarkey, M. C. (2020). Acceptability and Utility of an open-access, online single-session intervention platform for adolescent mental health. *JMIR Mental Health*, *7*(6), Article e20513. https://doi.org/10.2196/20513.

Smith, D. M., Lipson, S. M., Wang, S. B., & Fox, K. R. (2022). Online methods in adolescent self-injury research: Challenges and recommendations. *Journal of Clinical Child and Adolescent Psychology*, *3*, 1–12. https://doi.org/10.1080/15374416.2021.1875325

Swannell, S. V., Martin, G. E., Page, A., Hasking, P., & St John, N. J. (2014). Prevalence of nonsuicidal self-injury in nonclinical samples: Systematic review, meta-analysis and meta-regression. *Suicide and Life-Threatening Behavior*, *44*(3), 273–303. https://doi.org/10.1111/sltb.12070

Wang, S. B., Dempsey, W., Nock, M. K. (2022). Machine learning for suicide prediction and prevention: Advances, challenges, and future directions. In J. P. Ackerman & L. M. Horowitz (Eds.), *Youth suicide prevention and intervention: Current best practices and policy implications*. Springer.

CHAPTER 55

Application of the Unified Protocol for Treatment of Nonsuicidal Self-Injury

Kate H. Bentley *and* Adam C. Jaroszewski

Abstract

Nonsuicidal self-injury (NSSI) is a prevalent and clinically significant behavioral health problem. Novel therapeutic approaches to treating NSSI are needed, especially given the many well-established barriers to seeking and accessing evidence-based psychological treatment, including for self-injuring individuals specifically. The Unified Protocol for Transdiagnostic Treatment of Emotional Disorders (UP) is a cognitive-behavioral protocol designed to address underlying functional mechanisms of the full range of emotional disorders and related problems. This broadly applicable and flexible protocol was developed in part to facilitate dissemination of and training in evidence-based psychological treatment, as therapists have the potential to learn one set of therapeutic strategies that can be used across a wide range of presenting problems and comorbid disorders and symptoms. This chapter presents a rationale for using the UP to treat patients engaging with NSSI—including high rates of co-occurrence NSSI and the emotional disorders and shared functions of NSSI and key emotional disorder features—and the growing empirical support for the UP in the treatment of NSSI. An overview of the core UP therapeutic strategies is provided, with an emphasis on the applicability to targeting NSSI, followed by a detailed illustrative case example. The chapter also addresses significant clinical considerations and makes suggestions for future research on the UP for targeting NSSI.

Key Words: NSSI, Unified Protocol for Transdiagnostic Treatment of Emotional Disorders, emotional disorders, evidence-based psychological treatment, behavioral health problem

Brief Introduction to the Unified Protocol

The Unified Protocol for Transdiagnostic Treatment of Emotional Disorders (UP; Barlow et al., 2011b, 2018a) is a cognitive-behavioral treatment designed to address core temperamental factors that underlie the range of emotional disorders (e.g., anxiety, depressive, and related disorders). Specifically, the UP is applicable to any diagnosis or problem maintained by the following functional mechanism: (a) propensity to experience frequent and intense negative emotions (a temperamental style referred to as neuroticism), (b) aversive reactivity to the experience of emotion (driven by a diminished sense of control and negative appraisal of emotion); and (c) efforts to dampen, escape, or avoid negative emotion, either preemptively or in reaction to onset of the emotion (Barlow et al., 2014; Bullis et al., 2019). The overarching aim of the UP, which is made up of eight modules that each distills theoretically driven therapeutic strategies from existing cognitive-behavioral treatments (see Chapman et al., this volume), is to extinguish distress (and thus, associated problematic and/or harmful or risky behaviors; e.g., forms of behavioral or cognitive avoidance, including NSSI) in response to experiencing strong emotion. By identifying and modifying problematic reactions to emotion, it is expected that the frequency and intensity of negative affect and corresponding problematic behaviors will lessen over time.

The transdiagnostic UP approach was developed in part to address the long-standing challenges to training, dissemination, implementation, and access associated with the traditional cognitive-behavioral treatments that largely target single disorders or symptom sets (McHugh & Barlow, 2010). Such "single-diagnosis protocols"—of which there are more than 50 listed by the American Psychological Association (2019) with at least moderate research support—pose various challenges to large-scale dissemination and access, including the struggle that providers can face when selecting a single-treatment protocol for patients presenting with multiple comorbidities or subthreshold symptoms, as well as the difficulty accessing what is often time-intensive and costly training in multiple protocols to address the range of commonly presenting diagnoses. As we describe in the sections to follow, the transdiagnostic nature of the UP has the potential facilitate more efficient treatment for patients with a wide range of potentially complex "real-world" presentations, and potentially, improve access to existing evidence-based therapeutic strategies, including for individuals engaging in nonsuicidal self-injury (NSSI).

Applicability of the UP to NSSI

There are several reasons why the UP may be a relevant treatment approach for individuals engaging in NSSI.

Empirical Evidence and Clinical Theory
COMORBIDITY

First, most people who engage in NSSI meet criteria for at least one comorbid emotional disorder for which the UP was designed and shown to be effective in treating (Sakiris & Berle, 2019; see Lengel et al., this volume). For example, studies show that a majority of hospitalized adolescents with recent NSSI contemporaneously meet diagnostic criteria for a range of emotional disorders, including 51% to 66% for major depressive disorder (MDD; Auerbach et al., 2014; Glenn et al., 2013; Nock et al., 2006), 46% for panic disorder (Auerbach et al, 2014), 15% to 33% for generalized anxiety disorder (GAD; Auerbach et al., 2014; Nock et al, 2006), and 23% to 26% for posttraumatic stress disorder (PTSD; Auerbach et al., 2014; Nock et al, 2006). Among those with NSSI seeking outpatient psychiatric care, approximately 40% of adults and 70% of adolescents met criteria for a depressive disorder and 17% adults and 40% of adolescents for an anxiety disorder (Ghinea et al., 2020; Selby et al., 2012). Finally, in a sample of community-based adults with past-year NSSI, approximately 90% met criteria for lifetime MDD, 43% for GAD, 29% for PTSD, and 25% for social anxiety disorder (Turner et al., 2015).

FUNCTIONAL FRAMEWORK

A large body of evidence suggests that NSSI tends to fit within the UP's functional framework of emotional disorders and related problems. First, studies consistently demonstrate that people who engage in NSSI are prone to experiencing greater negative affect (NA) and/or neuroticism (for more information, see Swerdlow et al., this volume), core treatment targets of the UP. Young adults from community and university samples who have engaged in NSSI display higher levels of trait neuroticism (Brown et al., 2007) and propensity to experience NA than persons with no history of NSSI (Schoenleber et al., 2014). Levels of NA have also been shown to vary as a function of NSSI recency, with more recent NSSI associated with higher NA (Brown et al., 2007). Other studies indicate that frequent NSSI is also positively associated with higher levels of neuroticism (Maclaren & Best, 2010; You et al., 2016). Notably, data from clinical samples suggest that higher NA/neuroticism among people with NSSI is not merely due to higher rates of comorbid psychiatric disorders, as individuals with NSSI and co-occurring disorders display higher neuroticism than those with psychiatric disorders alone (Claes et al., 2004; Williams & Hassanyeh, 1983).

Second, not only do people with an NSSI history display higher levels of NA, but they also show greater aversive reactivity to experiencing NA. Higher aversive reactivity refers to differences in the intensity and temporal course of behavioral and/or physiological responses to emotionally evocative stimuli (Chapman et al., 2006). Recent meta-analytic findings on the links between dimensions of emotion dysregulation and NSSI suggest that one of the most robust differences between people with and without a NSSI history pertains to emotion reactivity (You et al., 2018). People engaging in NSSI have higher emotion reactivity on both psychophysiological (Nock & Mendes, 2008) and self-report measures (Liu et al., 2020), with one study finding higher emotion reactivity to a negative, but not positive, mood induction (Mettler et al., 2021). Interestingly, several studies suggest emotion reactivity plays an important intermediary role in the relationship between NSSI and a number of important correlates, including recent life stress (Hamza et al., 2021), depressive symptoms (Smith et al., 2015), and psychiatric symptoms more broadly (Nock et al., 2008).

Third, people who engage in NSSI display higher experiential avoidance compared to non-self-injurers. Experiential avoidance is characterized by an unwillingness to accept and remain in contact with certain experiences (emotions, physical sensations, thoughts, etc.), thus leading to altering these experiences or the context in which they arise (e.g., by avoiding; Gámez et al., 2011; Hayes et al., 2004). Recent meta-analytic findings demonstrate a link between NSSI and nonacceptance of emotional responses (You et al., 2018). More recent NSSI has also been associated with higher experiential avoidance

(Anderson & Crowther, 2012) as well as behavioral disengagement in relation to emotion (Brown et al., 2007). Studies also suggest that more frequent NSSI is correlated with higher experiential avoidance (Anderson et al., 2018; Howe-Martin et al., 2012) with experiential avoidance mediating the relationship between emotional distress and NSSI (Anderson et al., 2018).

Fourth, people who engage in NSSI report doing so primarily to regulate or reduce negative emotion/NA. A recent systematic review and meta-analysis on the functions of NSSI found that although people often have multiple (simultaneous) motives for engaging in NSSI (e.g., reduce NA, self-punish; Klonsky, 2007; Lloyd-Richardson et al., 2007; see Taylor et al., this volume), the most frequently reported NSSI function endorsed is to regulate/reduce NA (66% to 81% pooled prevalence; Taylor et al., 2018). A vast majority of these data comes from studies using retrospective self-report methods, potentially limiting the validity of their findings; however, data collected via experience sampling methods, which provide much finer-grained temporal resolution, indicate that most (50% to 65%) NSSI episodes are indeed motivated by efforts to regulate NA (Andrewes et al., 2017a; Nock et al., 2009; Shingleton et al., 2013). Also, most experience sampling studies measuring changes in affect before and after engagement in NSSI indicated that, prior to NSSI, people tend to experience higher NA and lower positive affect (PA) (Andrewes et al., 2017a), whereas after engaging in NSSI people tend to experience reduced NA (Andrewes et al., 2017a; Andrewes et al., 2017b; Armey et al., 2011) and increased PA (Muehlenkamp et al., 2009). Taken together, these data strongly suggest that the primary function of NSSI is consistent with the UP's theoretical model, which posits that emotional disorders are maintained, in part, through efforts to reduce or avoid negative emotion.

Overview of UP Treatment Modules and Relevance to NSSI

Six of the eight UP modules (2 through 7) are considered "core" in that they directly target shared underlying features of emotional disorders (e.g., neuroticism and experiential avoidance), some of which are highly relevant to NSSI. Typically, the UP is delivered in 16 to 20 weekly sessions, but due to its modular structure, this can be flexible and adapted as needed. Here, we highlight key tenets of each module with an emphasis on applicability to treating NSSI.

INITIAL SESSION(S)

Prior to the start of Module 1, it is expected that the therapist will have conducted (or received results from) a diagnostic intake, which will inform the case formulation and, in particular, an understanding of how the patient's diagnoses, symptoms, and behaviors may fit into the functional framework of (a) frequent and intense negative emotion, (b) negative reactions to emotion, and (c) maladaptive, avoidant responses. Thus, at this point the therapist already has reason to believe that the UP may be an appropriate approach (a point we elaborate upon in the section "Clinical Recommendations"). In an initial session or two, the therapist will provide a brief rationale for and overview of transdiagnostic, emotion-focused treatment, and collaboratively explore the ways that the patient may or may not identify with the three key features of emotional disorders. During this discussion, patients may spontaneously identify NSSI as a form of emotion avoidance for them or a behavior they would like to stop; if they do not, the therapist can consider posing the possibility that thinking about or engaging in NSSI may fit into the UP's functional framework. This can be accomplished simply by asking the patient if they tend to feel any better or different (e.g., less anxious or angry, more grounded, or "in control") after engaging in NSSI compared to how they felt before the episode, thus introducing and instantiating the emotion regulation function of this behavior. Patients are also oriented to the UP's symptoms monitoring forms and progress record used to track target symptoms and/or behaviors over the course of treatment (including NSSI urges or acts when relevant).

MOTIVATIONAL ENHANCEMENT (MODULE 1)

The overall aims of Module 1—based on motivational interviewing (Arkowitz et al., 2017)—are to increase self-efficacy and enhance and foster motivation for treatment. These aims are accomplished through two primary exercises, the first of which is goal setting. Patients identify key problems that overwhelming emotions may be causing in their lives. Next, they generate concrete and measurable, short- or long-term goals and objectives that correspond to each key problem. In our experience, patients may not present to therapy expressing a strong desire to work on NSSI; often they want to work on mood or anxiety concerns. Thus, letting the patient lead with their highest priority problems and goals (even if this does not include NSSI) is consistent with the motivational interviewing framework.

Next is a decision balance, during which patients are asked to identify the pros/benefits and cons/costs of change (or engagement in treatment) and staying the same. Ambivalence about making changes (including reducing or stopping NSSI) can be elicited, clarified, and normalized, and the therapist and patient can plan collaboratively for how to handle fluctuations in motivation that may arise later. Additionally, factors that serve to reinforce NSSI (e.g., short-term benefits of relief or distraction), any doubts the patient has about their ability to change, or other sources of ambivalence (e.g., shame about discussing NSSI in therapy) can be explored. Both the goal-setting and decision balance exercises can be reviewed and revisited during the course of treatment as indicated, if and when motivation or engagement decreases.

ADAPTIVE NATURE OF EMOTION (MODULE 2)

Module 2, the first core module, comprises psychoeducation on the adaptive and functional nature of emotions as well as an introduction to the three-component model of emotion. The therapist will start by using Socratic questioning to explore how all emotions, even those that feel most intense or uncomfortable, serve an important purpose, thus encouraging the patient to begin viewing their emotions as adaptive or functional, albeit painful at times. It can be noted that certainly, emotions can surge to such an intense or overwhelming level that they become interfering and are no longer helpful, but that eliminating them entirely would actually not be helpful either. When treating self-injuring individuals, this discussion provides an opportunity to address how the negative emotions that contribute to NSSI urges may be communicating important information to them. For example, NSSI urges may be framed as a response to overwhelming feelings of anger toward a loved one, possibly indicating the need to have a direct and honest conversation with that individual.

Patients are then taught the foundational cognitive-behavioral therapy (CBT) skill of breaking down emotional experience into three components (thoughts, feelings, and behaviors/urges). The therapist can emphasize that breaking down emotion in this way can make overwhelming emotional experiences feel more manageable and identify where/when interventions may be most helpful. The therapist will typically ask the patient to walk them through a recent intense emotional experience (potentially a recent episode in which they had strong urges to self-injure) to illustrate the interactive relationships between these three components (see fig. 55.1 for an example). The therapist will also encourage the patient to identify the antecedents leading up to the emotional experience, both distal and proximal, as well as the short- and long-term consequences of their responses (e.g., NSSI providing short-term relief from intense negative emotions, followed by longer-term shame about the behavior and embarrassment about resultant scars).

MINDFUL EMOTION AWARENESS (MODULE 3)

In (core) Module 3, patients build from the foundational skills of Module 2 by fostering a specific type of awareness of emotional experiences: *mindful (i.e., nonjudgmental, present-focused) awareness*. With increased mindful awareness of emotional experiences as they unfold, individuals can choose to engage more adaptively with their ongoing emotional experiences instead of getting carried away by or reflexively reacting to them. Over time, this reduces the reliance on avoidance (including NSSI) to relieve distressing emotions. During an initial discussion about mindful awareness, two main points are made: (1) responding judgmentally to emotion tends to intensify (or bring up new) negative emotions (e.g., urges to engage in NSSI for relief from distressing emotions); and (2) shifting one's attention to the present moment (rather than ruminating about past events or worrying about future possibilities) facilitates responding adaptively to the current situation.

Over the coming sessions, a series of mindfulness activities are practiced in and outside session: first, a guided mindfulness exercise using a script provided in the UP client workbook (Barlow et al., 2011a, 2018b); second, by a mood induction during which patients are encouraged to practice attending nonjudgmentally to their thoughts, feelings, and behaviors while listening to an emotion-provoking song; and, finally, a tangible "anchoring in the present" skill that can be used during emotional situations as they naturally occur. In our experience, when working with self-injuring individuals, it can be important to think through together *when* using anchoring in the present—or other mindfulness strategies—may be most appropriate. Research and accumulated clinical anecdotes suggest that patients view practicing mindful emotion awareness as a stand-alone emotion regulation strategy as somewhat inaccessible and/or ineffective when experiencing extremely strong, overwhelming urges to engage in NSSI (Bentley et al., 2017a); however, these techniques may be more helpful when used to observe and accept (instead of pushing away or suppressing) less intense emotional experiences as they occur on an ongoing basis in order to prevent emotions from escalating to a point where strong NSSI urges arise (also see Kress et al., this volume). Given that mindful emotion awareness strategies are challenging to master, perhaps especially so for self-injuring individuals who tend to feel their emotions very strongly, the therapist may choose to frame these skills as new "muscles" that require ongoing practice and strengthening.

COGNITIVE FLEXIBILITY (MODULE 4)

The focus of (core) Module 4 is on one specific component of emotional experience: cognitions. There are two key differences between the UP's cognitive module and that of most other CBT protocols. First and foremost, the UP emphasizes promoting *flexibility* rather than *changing* cognitions. Automatic interpretations are not considered *maladaptive* or *unhelpful*. Instead, consistent with the principles of Module 3, patients are encouraged to notice their automatic thoughts nonjudgmentally, considering them as one of many possible interpretations of a situation. Second, patients are guided toward noticing any discrepancies between their initial interpretation(s) of a situation (which are often tied to past events or future possibilities) and what is happening in the present.

This module begins with an "ambiguous picture" exercise in which patients are encouraged to first identify their initial, automatic interpretations about an ambiguous scene (provided in the UP workbook), followed by other potential interpretations. This exercise is used to illustrate that (a) there are often at least several different interpretations for the same situation, and (b) once an automatic interpretation has been formed, it can be difficult to consider other perspectives, especially when feeling moderate or strong emotions. Next, the concept of thinking traps is introduced, after which patients begin practicing generating alternative interpretations using a list of "challenging questions," with the therapist praising more balanced interpretations that take into account other possibilities and the demands of the current situation. When working with self-injuring patients, in addition to applying this cognitive flexibility strategy to thoughts about emotions themselves, the therapist can also aim to apply this strategy to automatic cognitions specifically about NSSI (e.g., "cutting is the only thing that makes me feel better").

COUNTERING EMOTIONAL BEHAVIORS (MODULE 5)

Module 5 (core) focuses on another specific component of emotional experience: behaviors (and urges). The goal in this module is to identify and begin countering "emotional behaviors," which refer to any strategy (e.g., avoidance) enacted in response to an uncomfortable emotion (or anticipation of such an emotion). By this point, the patient should have a solid understanding of the paradoxical effects of pushing away or suppressing emotions, though the therapist may explicitly highlight this again. The therapist and patient will then work together to identify the patient's "go-to" emotional behaviors in response to a range of emotions, potentially observing that some of the exact same behaviors may either be problematic or adaptive depending on the specific function the behavior is serving in the given context. NSSI can be framed explicitly as an emotional behavior that tends to result in desirable short-term but negative long-term effects.

After identifying emotional behaviors, the therapist and patient will then brainstorm (ideally accessible and realistic) "alternative actions" to emotion-driven urges. Alternative actions typically bring individuals into contact with the emotion they are attempting to avoid or escape, and though such behaviors may *increase* uncomfortable emotion in the short term, such actions serve to reduce the distressing nature of (or interference due to) emotion over time. Common alternative actions for NSSI may include seeking social support, physical exercise, or self-soothing. Note that some viable alternatives to NSSI (e.g., distraction) may not necessarily bring the patient immediately into closer contact with their uncomfortable emotion. For those who are actively self-injuring, however, safety is the priority. Thus, most alternative, non-self-injurious actions to NSSI that over the short term help the person avoid hurting themselves and over the long term have the potential to increase their ability to cope with and tolerate intense emotions are still encouraged. Patients then begin setting small, realistic goals toward implementing these new behavioral responses, potentially with the complementary use of skills learned thus far (e.g., mindful awareness) to increase the likelihood of behavior change.

INTEROCEPTIVE EXPOSURE (MODULE 6)

Module 6 (core) targets the remaining part of the three-component model: physical sensations. The goal of this module is to improve awareness and tolerance of uncomfortable physical sensations associated with emotion by repeatedly eliciting the uncomfortable physical sensations via interoceptive exposure exercises and facing/feeling them. The rationale is that by noticing the physical sensations that arise during an emotional experience without judgment or aversive responding (e.g., "I must stop this feeling"), patients will ultimately be better able to tolerate emotional experiences without avoiding or escaping them, for example, via NSSI. Historically, interoceptive exposure was reserved for panic disorder; however, the UP conceptualizes physical sensations as playing an important role in all emotional disorders and related problems and, therefore, Module 6 is applied regardless of primary diagnosis. High levels of distressing physical sensations (headaches, stomachaches, etc.) are common for self-injuring individuals (Hielscher et al., 2019); moreover, the desire to escape distressing emotions and accompanying physical sensations putatively plays a primary role in motivating people to engage in NSSI. Therefore, promoting mindful awareness and tolerance of these sensations may be particularly relevant for this population.

After providing a rationale for interoceptive exposure and goals of the exercises (namely, learning that uncomfortable physical sensations do not last forever and do not always escalate, and other people usually do not notice them), the therapist will guide the patient through a series of activities (e.g., straw breathing and hyperventilating), designed to elicit physical sensations commonly associated with anxiety, with the aim of identifying exercises that are at least moderately distressing and similar to the patient's real-life experiences of emotion. Depending on what emotions the patient finds problematic (and, for those with NSSI, which emotions tend to trigger self-injurious urges), the therapist can suggest other activities designed to elicit sensations that may arise with other distressing/unwanted emotions, such as anger (e.g., tensing muscles to elicit flushing/heat), sadness (e.g., wearing around a heavy backpack to feel slowed/weighted down), or guilt (e.g., drinking carbonated beverages quickly before vigorous exercise to elicit stomach distress). Patients continue practicing interoceptive exposures for homework, tracking levels of intensity, distress, and real-world similarity.

EMOTION EXPOSURE (MODULE 7)

The final core UP module focuses on identifying and engaging in tasks that are designed to bring on moderate to strong levels of emotion. The rationale for engaging in systematic "emotion exposures" is threefold: first, these exercises give patients the opportunity to put into practice the skills they have learned thus far (Modules 2–5) when they are most needed—during emotional experiences—thus promoting skills rehearsal and consolidation in the context of emotion. Second, emotion exposures also allow patients to test their (often negative) predictions about what may happen in emotion-provoking situations. Third, such exposures can provide patients with the opportunity for learning that emotions tend to be temporary and that they can cope with and tolerate uncomfortable emotions without avoidance.

After providing a rationale for emotion exposure, the therapist and patient will collaboratively develop an exposure hierarchy that may span situational, imaginal, and/or interoceptive (or combinations of situational/imaginal with interoceptive exercises). Consistent with the transdiagnostic framework of the UP, any activity that elicits moderate to strong emotion can be included on the hierarchy, including the full range of negative and positive emotions that the patient may find distressing. Once the hierarchy is drafted, the therapist will guide the patient through an initial emotion exposure together in session using the UP's "exposure practice" worksheet, which facilitates preparation for the activity, integration of recently acquired skills during the activity, and reviewing key take-aways and aspects to improve/build upon next time. Patients then continue practicing exposures on their own, recording key aspects of their experiences, for homework.

When conducting emotion exposures with self-injuring individuals, it is important to plan collaboratively for the possibility that urges to engage in NSSI may arise during such exercises even though this is *not* the explicit aim. The therapist may emphasize that if self-injurious thoughts arise during an exposure, this is an opportunity to practice responding differently and more adaptively to such urges, for example, by noticing the urges without judgment or implementing an adaptive alternative action. For patients engaging in more severe forms of NSSI or experiencing active suicidal thoughts or behaviors, the therapist must use their clinical judgment to help determine what tasks the patient can take on without compromising safety.

RELAPSE PREVENTION (MODULE 8)

The final UP module includes three main components: (1) reviewing the patient's progress, (2) reviewing and consolidating key treatment material, and (3) planning for future skills practice and criteria for treatment reinitiation. When reviewing progress, the therapist and patient can begin with the progress record worksheet used to track target symptoms and behaviors and emphasize the potential for continued gains if the patient continues to implement the strategies learned. The goal-setting exercise from Module 1 can also be revisited and updated for this next "phase" of (self-directed) treatment. Then, the therapist and patient will review core UP skills, reflecting on the ways in which the patient is using/not using and perceives to be benefiting (or not) from each skill, and collaboratively developing specific plans for continued skills practice, exposures (e.g., when and how often), and strategies for keeping helpful skills/tools fresh in their minds (e.g., keeping the list of challenging questions from Module 4 easily accessible on their phone). This last module typically culminates with identifying and troubleshooting common potential triggers for symptom increases. The therapist can help set the patient's expectations that symptoms will fluctuate naturally, encouraging a nonjudgmental stance toward such changes. Especially for individuals engaging in NSSI, specific "warning signs" that indicate a need for booster sessions or reinitiating weekly (or more intensive) treatment may be warranted (resumption of NSSI, etc.).

Empirical Evidence to Date

Evidence from multiple ($N > 75$) studies (e.g., randomized controlled trials [RCTs], open trials, and single-case experimental design studies) demonstrates the efficacy and adaptability of the UP for treating a wide-range of emotional disorders (Cassiello-Robbins et al., 2020). Two recent meta-analyses indicate that the UP substantially reduces anxiety and depressive symptoms, as well as symptoms of specific disorders (e.g., generalized anxiety disorder, panic disorder, social anxiety disorder, obsessive-compulsive disorder [OCD], and borderline personality disorder [BPD]), all with large to moderate effect sizes (Sakiris & Berle, 2019), with some presentations (depression plus anxiety) maintaining these substantial gains three to six months posttreatment (Carlucci et al., 2021). Barlow et al. (2017) conducted one of the largest RCTs to date, observing that the UP results in statistically equivalent improvements in diagnostic severity and symptoms to "gold-standard" single-diagnosis CBT protocols for treating GAD, panic disorder, social anxiety disorder, and OCD ($N = 223$; Barlow et al., 2017). Moreover, a recently completed systematic review of 77 studies summarized that the UP has been used to treat a wide range of disorders and behavioral problems in adults and has been successfully adapted (in both format [e.g., individual vs. group] and content [e.g., additions of problem-specific material]) for delivery across treatment settings (e.g., inpatient, community clinics; Cassiello-Robbins et al., 2020). The UP has also amassed growing empirical support for treating emotional disorders in children and adolescents (e.g., Ehrenreich-May et al., 2017; Kennedy et al., 2019).

As noted above, the UP has demonstrated efficacy for the treatment of disorders and complex clinical presentations commonly associated with NSSI, such as depression (Sauer-Zavala et al., 2020), BPD (Sauer-Zavala et al., 2016), and features of BPD in the context of several other comorbid internalizing and externalizing disorders (Tonarely et al., 2021). There are also preliminary data suggesting that modified versions of the UP are acceptable and feasible for delivery to suicidal adults hospitalized on psychiatric inpatient (Bentley et al., 2020) and crisis stabilization (Bentley et al., 2017b) units, as well as associated with reductions in anxiety and depressive symptoms and suicidal ideation. To date, there is only limited empirical support to treat NSSI specifically. A multiple baseline, combined series single-case experimental design study of 10 outpatients meeting criteria for NSSI disorder (American Psychiatric Association, 2013) evaluated the effects of UP Modules 3 (mindful emotion awareness) and 4 (cognitive flexibility) on NSSI urges and acts (Bentley et al., 2017a). Eight of 10 participants experienced clinically meaningful reductions in NSSI with one or both UP modules, and group-based analyses showed significant reductions in anxiety, depression, and emotion regulation skills.

Key Clinical Considerations

There are a few key clinical considerations when using (and determining whether to use) the UP to treat NSSI. First and foremost, if delivering the UP in an outpatient treatment context, it is critical to determine appropriateness for outpatient level of care. Treating any self-injuring individual in an outpatient context requires continuous monitoring and attending closely to changes in risk of both nonsuicidal and suicidal self-injurious thoughts and behaviors, which may warrant more frequent consultations (or supervision), referrals to additional supports, transitions to higher levels of care, or other modifications to the treatment plan. For example, UP therapists may decide to incorporate non-UP skills—such as DBT distress tolerance (Linehan, 1993)—or, in the case of suicidal thoughts or behaviors that often co-occur with NSSI (e.g., Nock et al., 2006), suicide risk reduction interventions such as safety planning (Stanley & Brown, 2012)—as needed for patients with NSSI. The flexible and modular nature of the UP lends itself well to weaving in such other evidence-based strategies.

When determining whether to use the UP or another evidence-based treatment for NSSI (DBT, emotion regulation group therapy [ERGT], etc.; Gratz & Gunderson, 2006), there are a few factors to consider. The UP is likely to be a good fit for patients with at least one emotional disorder (and especially, multiple comorbidities or subthreshold symptoms). As noted above, in our experience, self-injuring individuals are often more distressed by and motivated to work on anxiety or mood symptoms, for example, than NSSI; thus, the UP's emotion-focused, transdiagnostic framework, which permits simultaneously addressing multiple sets of symptoms or problems, may be especially well-received (and associated with higher treatment engagement) in these cases. The UP is less likely to effectively address NSSI when the patient reports engaging in NSSI primarily for interpersonal functions (Nock & Prinstein, 2004) rather than to relieve or regulate emotional experiences. In the case that NSSI urges or behaviors emerge during the course of treatment for emotional disorders, UP strategies may be extended and applied to these new (or recently exacerbated) concerns. Last, the UP may be a more appropriate treatment option than DBT when either the duration (one year) or multiple formats (group, consultation, phone coaching) of DBT—at least as it is traditionally delivered—are not feasible.

Clinical Case Example

The client ("L") was 17 years old and identified as a heterosexual White woman with Hispanic ethnicity. L presented for a routine checkup to her primary care provider, who noticed cuts on L's forearms. L broke down in tears and reported that, over the past year, she had been cutting herself when feeling "stressed and mad at herself," typically following "tense" or embarrassing social situations. L's physician made a therapy referral for NSSI and anxiety. In the first session, L provided a thorough overview of her symptoms via structured clinical interviews (i.e., MINI and SCID-II), reporting symptoms consistent with social anxiety disorder with panic attacks, subthreshold major depressive disorder symptoms (including passive suicidal ideation), and BPD symptoms, including intermittent past-year NSSI. The therapist told L that, given her symptoms, she felt confident they could help her better understand and manage her emotional experiences.

Over the second and third sessions, the therapist oriented L to the UP's conceptualization of emotional disorders and the main goal of treatment: to modify patterns of unhelpful reactions to emotions. The therapist and L then reviewed the symptoms and behaviors L wanted to focus on in treatment. L reported she wanted to stop "freaking out" and having panic attacks every time she was in uncomfortable social situations. Her therapist validated the importance and relevance of this goal. She then asked L if she was concerned about her NSSI. L said she wanted to stop cutting herself but didn't know how. She relied on NSSI when in crisis and felt helpless about stopping. Together they completed the UP goal-setting worksheet, recording the primary treatment goals (social anxiety, panic, NSSI) and breaking down each goal into specific, concrete steps that L could take toward accomplishing the goal. For example, for the goal of stopping NSSI, they wrote: (1) identify when urges to cut are most likely; (2) identify new coping methods for crises; (3) practice new coping methods when distressed but not in crisis; and (4) practice new coping when in crisis instead of NSSI. To increase L's sense of control and motivation, they completed a decisional balance worksheet, identifying the pros and cons of both (a) modifying her unhelpful emotional reactions like NSSI, and (b) staying the same.

The aim of the next several sessions was to begin increasing L's understanding of her emotional responses and target behaviors. In the fourth session, the therapist described the functions of primary emotions (e.g., sadness, happiness, and anxiety). L resonated with the idea that the function of anxiety is to prepare for and/or avoid a possible negative future outcome. The therapist underscored how each emotion, when accurate and in proportion to the situation, serves a necessary function that helps us meet our goals and values, and then framed NSSI and avoidance as attempts to gain short-term relief from intense and uncomfortable emotions but which lead to longer-term negative consequences. L said her avoidance made her feel trapped, stuck, lonely, and embarrassed, and engaging in NSSI made her feel defective and ashamed of her scars.

In the fifth session, the therapist broke down emotional responses into three core components: what you think (thoughts); how you feel (feelings/bodily sensations); and what you do (behaviors). Next, she introduced the Antecedent, Response, Consequence (ARC) model of emotional situations, with the UP's ARC worksheet, explaining that using this to record all the parts of emotional situations would help L increase her insight, sense of control, and the predictability of her emotional experiences. As a homework assignment, L was asked to use the ARC worksheet to track target behaviors (social anxiety, panic, and NSSI).

At the start of session 6, L disclosed that she cut herself two times over the last week. Her therapist inquired about the severity of the wounds, infection risk, and whether L had disclosed to anyone else (yes, her mom), as well as whether L had any wishes to die or other suicidal thoughts before or while cutting this past week. L told her, consistent with her reports of passive suicidal ideation at prior sessions, that she wished she could disappear at times but did not think about suicide specifically before or while cutting—on the contrary, she cut to feel better. The therapist and L then proceeded to complete an ARC worksheet in session together about her cutting episodes. L described the antecedent event as learning about her "friends making plans without her," and reviewed each component of her emotional response (fig. 55.1).

While L spoke, the therapist filled in a three-component model, asking for more details on what precisely L was thinking about the situation, herself and her friends during

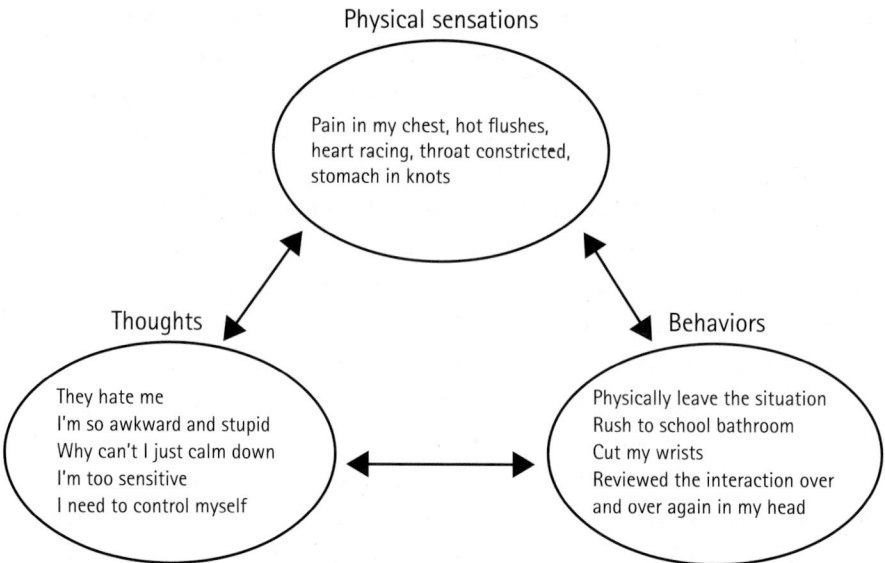

Figure 55.1 Three-Component Model of an NSSI Episode

and after the interaction, what physical sensations she experienced in her body, as well as what behaviors she engaged in during this time. The therapist asked L to try and identify the purpose or function of the behaviors she described. L reported she left her friends and rushed to the bathroom to hide how angry, rejected, and embarrassed she felt, and because she worried she might have a panic attack. However, she was not sure of the function of cutting but did notice feeling calmer and more "in control" afterward. The therapist hypothesized with L that the function of her NSSI may be to take away strong negative emotions and help her feel more in control, especially when feeling a panic attack coming on, which L agreed was possible. L then described the consequences of cutting: missing two classes as she hid in the bathroom and feeling ashamed.

Over the next two sessions, the therapist introduced the practice of mindfulness as a way for L to become more aware of her daily emotional experience in real time without judgment. L resonated with the idea that labeling emotions as bad and unwanted usually leads her to push them away, causing her emotions to magnify—especially panic symptoms. She also agreed that she felt worse (e.g., more anxious and self-critical), certainly not better, when thinking about past mistakes or what could go wrong in the future. Through a series of guided meditations in session, she found herself becoming more focused on her present experience. With practice over the next several weeks, L found that she was increasingly able to notice and "just watch" the urge to criticize herself upon noticing that her mind had wandered. Through the analogy of building her new "mindfulness" muscle, she eventually came to view her mind wandering as an opportunity to "do another rep and get stronger" by retraining her attention on her breath. L found it most difficult to just observe her emotions and bodily sensations without judgment. To practice more at home, the therapist gave L a recording of her leading a guided meditation, which included opportunities for L to validate her feelings as well as her difficulty sitting with them.

The next several sessions focused on increasing L's understanding of her negative thinking patterns and developing greater cognitive flexibility. Through her continued use of the ARC worksheets and mindfulness skills, L noticed several negative thinking patterns that tended to precede urges to engage in NSSI. For example, when feeling anxious, rejected, and "emotionally overwhelmed"/panicky, she would sometimes think, "I'm going to lose my mind if I don't cut right now." The therapist explained that many of our thoughts, especially first impressions, are automatic or reflexive; they just come to us, and when they do, it can be hard to consider other possibilities, especially when emotions are strong. Generating different possible interpretations—especially those that fit the facts of the situation—can make it easier to feel and behave consistently with the demands of the current situation. L struggled to generate alternative possibilities at first because, to her, this thought ("I'm going to lose my mind if I don't cut right now") seemed so true. In reviewing the list of challenging questions, the therapist and L wondered together, for example, whether L knew for certain that she would lose her mind if she didn't cut, what evidence she had for this thought and against it, and what the realistic chance she would actually lose her mind if she didn't cut right away. In answering these questions L was able to come up with a few more likely interpretations (e.g., "it definitely feels like I'll lose my mind if I don't cut, but I'll probably just feel really panicky; there's been times I felt like this but wasn't able to cut and it was rough for a while but I didn't actually lose my mind"). The therapist praised L for her willingness to practice thinking flexibly, and encouraged her to look for evidence that might support these new, more accurate alternatives over the next week.

Next, the therapist and L focused their efforts on countering specific maladaptive behaviors that L used to avoid experiencing unwanted emotions and "scary" situations. First, L and her therapist identified several maladaptive emotion-driven behaviors (EDBs) that reduced the intensity of unwanted emotions, like leaving social situations as soon as she felt "awkward" as well as engaging in NSSI when feeling overwhelmed, angry, and rejected. To clarify the problem with these behaviors and to increase L's motivation to work on countering them, the therapist and L identified both short- and long-term costs and benefits of continuing to engage in EDBs. They also identified a number of overt avoidance behaviors (e.g., not raising her hand in class, staying home from school to avoid a class presentation, and not letting friends know when she felt excluded), subtle avoidance behaviors (e.g., speaking softly and keeping her head down when eating around others), cognitive avoidance (e.g., pushing away embarrassing memories), and safety signals which are items that people carry with because they are comforting (e.g., the razor L hid in her backpack to potentially use to cut). The therapist reiterated that avoidance tends to maintain uncomfortable emotions, but by approaching instead of avoiding, L could begin breaking the cycle. Thus, for each emotionally avoidant behavior, the therapist and

L identified various alternative actions that L could take instead. For example, instead of engaging in NSSI when feeling overwhelmed, angry, and rejected, L might: call her cousin who was supportive and knew some of what L was going though, draw/doodle, write down her thoughts/feelings in a notebook or note on her phone, let her friends know she is upset, or play a game on her phone.

Over the next couple of sessions, the therapist began introducing the concept of emotion exposure: exercises that provide opportunities to practice choosing alternative actions when experiencing strong emotions and, in so doing, learn that they are temporary, tolerable, and not necessarily barriers to engaging in valued activities. The therapist went on to explain that by gradually choosing more challenging alternative actions and/or entering more distressing situations, L would find it easier to tolerate the uncomfortable emotions that came up, and may learn that the feared actions/situations weren't as bad as she had predicted.

First, they started with interoceptive exposures to help L learn to tolerate uncomfortable and alarming bodily sensations that commonly preceded L's panic attacks and NSSI. L's old ARC worksheets indicated that throat constriction, racing heart, and feeling suddenly hot and depersonalized were particularly distressing sensations. Her therapist explained that by gradually experiencing these unpleasant sensations, L would learn to tolerate them and not have to rely on NSSI for relief. The therapist used the UP's physical sensations test worksheet to record L's experience as she completed 60 seconds of hyperventilation, straw breathing, spinning while standing, and running in place. L found that hyperventilating and straw breathing mimicked nearly all the sensations she found aversive in real-world situations. Over the next several weeks in session and at home, L practiced eliciting uncomfortable sensations with these exercises, purposefully being curious about the sensations instead of blocking, limiting, and pushing them away and recording her experiences on the physical sensations practice worksheet. After a couple of weeks, L noticed that the exercises started to produce far less discomfort. In session, the therapist guided her through combining the exercises: L completed a round of straw breathing, then hyperventilating, then spinning in place with little to no break in between. L noticed the sensations no longer seemed so dangerous or long lasting—annoying, but temporary. She noticed she was not trying to control or push away feelings as much, which began to help her stay in uncomfortable social situations without as much fear of panicking. It also allowed her to tolerate and better resist the urge to engage in NSSI without impulsively engaging in it.

To begin the work of choosing alternative actions in real-life situations, the therapist and L began planning situational and imaginal emotion exposures. On the UP's exposure hierarchy worksheet, they ranked alternative actions and real/imagined situations in terms of the predicted distress. To help L approach and tolerate the emotions (i.e., overwhelmed, angry) that consistently preceded her NSSI urges, she completed a variety of situational exposures, including removing from her backpack the razor (safety signal) she would sometimes use for NSSI; listening to guided self-compassion meditations despite feeling she didn't deserve compassion and was "worthless"; completing previously identified alternative actions when experiencing NSSI urges (e.g., calling supportive cousin or playing game on phone); and stopping herself when thinking about NSSI (an EDB) by first shifting her attention to the uncomfortable emotions/physical sensations she was reflexively avoiding via thinking about NSSI, and then shifting her focus to what she was seeing, hearing, and smelling in the present moment. The therapist also used imaginal exposures to target emotions/situations leading to NSSI. A particularly evocative imaginal exposure involved writing in vivid, cinematic-like detail (and then repeatedly reading aloud) a story about L overhearing her friends criticize her for being too emotional and socially unskilled, making plans without her, lying about excluding her after she tearfully confronted them, then not responding to her texts, leaving L alone, rejected, and unable to make new friends. Given the potential intensity of L's emotional response to this imaginal exposure, it was important that, prior to completing it, she (a) successfully completed several other (less and equally) distressing exposures (according to her exposure hierarchy), and (b) understood and could explain the rationale and goal of this exercise (i.e., approach instead of avoid distressing emotion in order to practice responding more adaptively if/when urges arise).

The next several sessions focused on laying the groundwork for carefully concluding care with L. First, the therapist helped L take stock of her progress by reviewing her goal-setting worksheet. L was encouraged to see that she had completed many of the specific steps she had outlined. She reported "feeling like a different person" now that she was more at ease socially, no longer having panic attacks, and better able to predict when she would have strong urges to cut and not immediately give in to them. L also noted that she did not accomplish several steps relating to social anxiety, particularly purposefully volunteering for class presentations. Second, the therapist reviewed material and skills learned thus far by revisiting each core UP module. To facilitate consolidation, the therapist asked L to reflect on each component and describe how she used the material/skill, what she learned in the process, as well as the pros and cons and barriers/difficulties implementing. L reported that emotion exposures were the most difficult for her but also had the biggest impact, showing her she could change and tolerate very uncomfortable feelings. Third, the therapist and L planned for future skills practice by completing another goal-setting worksheet. L reported feeling like there was still room for improvement in feeling comfortable speaking her mind in front of others; they then brainstormed a variety of exposures L could engage in (e.g., signing up for a public speaking or improv class), thus charting a course for continued improvement and growth. Finally, together they reviewed some potential precipitants of symptom increases (e.g., transitioning from school to working in the summer), how L could use skills to navigate these stressors in order to meet her goals, and criteria indicating that L may need booster sessions with the therapist or a higher level of care. They decided that it may be wise for L to reinitiate CBT if she began having panic attacks (or avoiding situations/activities lest they bring on panic) with some regularity (twice or more per month) or if she began consistently engaging in NSSI, which they defined as at least once per week for more than two weeks. The therapist then referred L to a local psychologist in the community in order to receive supportive therapy on a weekly basis, and began seeing her less frequently (first every two weeks, then once per month for two months).

Key Considerations for Future Research

Given the relative paucity of empirical evidence for using the UP (or its core components) to treat NSSI specifically, large-scale, controlled research is clearly needed. An especially informative and clinically meaningful line of work may compare the efficacy (and potentially, cost-effectiveness) of the transdiagnostic UP to existing NSSI-specific approaches (e.g., Gratz & Gunderson, 2006) or those currently considered "gold-standard" for treating NSSI (e.g., DBT; Linehan, 1993). Other key areas for future research include personalization of UP treatment (e.g., module selection and ordering) based on preexisting and evolving patient characteristics, and technology-assisted approaches for promoting real-time skills use for those engaging in NSSI.

Conclusion

The UP was developed primarily to facilitate dissemination of and training in evidence-based psychological treatment for emotional disorders. Due to the high rates of comorbidity between NSSI and the emotional disorders, as well as striking functional overlap between NSSI and key features of emotional disorders (e.g., avoidance behaviors), the UP may also be a relevant treatment approach to consider for patients presenting with NSSI and emotional disorder diagnoses or subthreshold symptoms. The UP or its core components have demonstrated initial promise in the treatment of NSSI to date; however, more rigorous, large-scale research must be conducted. The urgent need for scalable, effective approaches to treating nonsuicidal self-injurious thoughts and behaviors underscores the importance of evaluating novel, promising approaches such as the UP for this common and perplexing behavioral phenomenon.

References

American Psychiatric Association. (2013). *Diagnostic and statistical manual of mental disorders* (5th ed.).
American Psychological Association, Division 12. (2019). Research-supported psychological treatments. Retrieved from https://www.div12.org/psychological-treatments/.
Anderson, N. L., & Crowther, J. H. (2012). Using the experiential avoidance model of non-suicidal self-injury: Understanding who stops and who continues. *Archives of Suicide Research*, *16*(2), 124–134.
Anderson, N. L., Smith, K. E., Mason, T. B., & Crowther, J. H. (2018). Testing an integrative model of affect regulation and avoidance in non-suicidal self-injury and disordered eating. *Archives of Suicide Research*, *22*(2), 295–310. https://doi.org/10.1080/13811118.2017.1340854
Andrewes, H. E., Hulbert, C., Cotton, S. M., Betts, J., & Chanen, A. M. (2017a). Ecological momentary assessment of nonsuicidal self-injury in youth with borderline personality disorder. *Personality Disorders: Theory, Research, and Treatment*, *8*(4), Article 357.

Andrewes, H. E., Hulbert, C., Cotton, S. M., & Betts, J. (2017b). An ecological momentary assessment investigation of complex and conflicting emotions in youth with borderline personality disorder. *Psychiatry Research*, *252*, 102–110. https://doi.org/10.1016/j.psychres.2017.01.100

Arkowitz, H., Miller, W. R., & Rollnick, S. (2017). *Motivational interviewing in the treatment of psychological problems*. Guilford Press.

Armey, M. F., Crowther, J. H., & Miller, I. W. (2011). Changes in ecological momentary assessment reported affect associated with episodes of nonsuicidal self-injury. *Behavior Therapy*, *42*(4), 579–588. https://doi.org/10.1016/j.beth.2011.01.002

Auerbach, R. P., Kim, J. C., Chango, J. M., Spiro, W. J., Cha, C., Gold, J., Esterman, M., & Nock, M. K. (2014). Adolescent nonsuicidal self-injury: Examining the role of child abuse, comorbidity, and disinhibition. *Psychiatry Research*, *220*(1–2), 579–584. https://doi.org/10.1016/j.psychres.2014.07.027

Barlow, D. H., Ellard, K. K., Sauer-Zavala, S., Bullis, J. R., & Carl, J. R. (2014). The origins of neuroticism. *Perspectives on Psychological Science*, *9*(5), 481–496. https://doi.org/10.1177/1745691614544528

Barlow, D. H., Farchione, T. J., Bullis, J. R., Gallagher, M. W., Murray-Latin, H., Sauer-Zavala, S., Bentley, K. H., Thompson-Hollands, J., Conklin, L. R., Boswell, J. F., Ametaj, A., Carl, J. R., Boettcher, H. T., & Cassiello-Robbins, C. (2017). The Unified Protocol for Transdiagnostic Treatment of Emotional Disorders compared with diagnosis-specific protocols for anxiety disorders: A randomized clinical trial. *JAMA Psychiatry*, *74*(9), Article 875. https://doi.org/10.1001/jamapsychiatry.2017.2164

Barlow, D. H., Ellard, K. K., Fairholme, C. P., Farchione, T. J., Boisseau, C. L., Allen, L. B., & Ehrenreich-May, J. (2011a). *Unified Protocol for Transdiagnostic Treatment of Emotional Disorders: Client workbook*. Oxford University Press.

Barlow, D. H., Farchione, T. J., Fairholme, C. P., Ellard, K. K., Boisseau, C. L., Allen, L. B., & Ehrenreich-May, J. (2011b). *The Unified Protocol for Transdiagnostic Treatment of Emotional Disorders: Therapist guide* (1st ed.). Oxford University Press.

Barlow, D. H., Farchione, T. J., Sauer-Zavala, S., Murray Latin, H., Ellard, K. K., Bullis, J. R., Bentley, K. H., Boettcher, H. T., & Cassiello-Robbins, C. (2018a). *The Unified Protocol for Transdiagnostic Treatment of Emotional Disorders: Therapist guide* (2nd ed.). Oxford University Press.

Barlow, D. H., Sauer-Zavala, S., Farchione, T. J., Murray-Latin, H., Ellard, K. K., Bullis, J. R., Bentley, K. H., Boettcher, H. T., & Cassiello-Robbins, C. (2018b). *Unified Protocol for Transdiagnostic Treatment of Emotional Disorders: Client workbook* (2nd ed.). Oxford University Press.

Bentley, K. H., Nock, M. K., Sauer-Zavala, S., Gorman, B. S., & Barlow, D. H. (2017a). A functional analysis of two transdiagnostic, emotion-focused interventions on nonsuicidal self-injury. *Journal of Consulting and Clinical Psychology*, *85*(6), 632–646. https://doi.org/10.1037/ccp0000205

Bentley, K. H., Sauer-Zavala, S., Cassiello-Robbins, C. F., Conklin, L. R., Vento, S., & Homer, D. (2017b). Treating suicidal thoughts and behaviors within an emotional disorders framework: Acceptability and feasibility of the Unified Protocol in an inpatient setting. *Behavior Modification*, *41*(4), 529–557. https://doi.org/10.1177/0145445516689661

Bentley, K. H., Sauer-Zavala, S., Stevens, K. T., & Washburn, J. J. (2020). Implementing an evidence-based psychological intervention for suicidal thoughts and behaviors on an inpatient unit: Process, challenges, and initial findings. *General Hospital Psychiatry*, *63*, 76–82. https://doi.org/10.1016/j.genhosppsych.2018.09.012

Brown, S. A., Williams, K., & Collins, A. (2007). Past and recent deliberate self-harm: Emotion and coping strategy differences. *Journal of Clinical Psychology*, *63*(9), 791–803. https://doi.org/10.1002/jclp

Bullis, J. R., Boettcher, H., Sauer-Zavala, S., Farchione, T. J., & Barlow, D. H. (2019). What is an emotional disorder? A transdiagnostic mechanistic definition with implications for assessment, treatment, and prevention. *Clinical Psychology: Science and Practice*, *26*(2), Article e12278. https://doi.org/10.1111/cpsp.12278

Carlucci, L., Aristide, S., & Michela, B. (2021). On the efficacy of the Barlow Unified Protocol for Transdiagnostic Treatment of Emotional Disorders: A systematic review and meta-analysis. *Clinical Psychology Review*, *87*, Article 101999. https://doi.org/10.1016/j.cpr.2021.101999

Cassiello-Robbins, C., Southward, M. W., Tirpak, J. W., & Sauer-Zavala, S. (2020). A systematic review of Unified Protocol applications with adult populations: Facilitating widespread dissemination via adaptability. *Clinical Psychology Review*, *78*, Article 101852. https://doi.org/10.1016/j.cpr.2020.101852

Chapman, A. L., Gratz, K. L., & Brown, M. Z. (2006). Solving the puzzle of deliberate self-harm: The experiential avoidance model. *Behaviour Research and Therapy*, *44*(3), 371–394. https://doi.org/10.1016/j.brat.2005.03.005

Claes, L., Vandereycken, W., & Vertommen, H. (2004). Personality traits in eating-disordered patients with and without self-injurious behaviors. *Journal of Personality Disorders, 18*(4), 399–404.

Ehrenreich-May, J., Rosenfield, D., Queen, A. H., Kennedy, S. M., Remmes, C. S., & Barlow, D. H. (2017). An initial waitlist-controlled trial of the unified protocol for the treatment of emotional disorders in adolescents. *Journal of Anxiety Disorders, 46*, 46–55. https://doi.org/10.1016/j.janxdis.2016.10.006

Gámez, W., Chmielewski, M., Kotov, R., Ruggero, C., & Watson, D. (2011). Development of a measure of experiential avoidance: The Multidimensional Experiential Avoidance Questionnaire. *Psychological Assessment, 23*, 692–713. https://doi.org/10.1037/a0023242

Ghinea, D., Edinger, A., Parzer, P., Koenig, J., & Resch, F. (2020). Non-suicidal self-injury disorder as a stand-alone diagnosis in a consecutive help-seeking sample of adolescents. *Journal of Affective Disorders, 274*(February), 1122–1125. https://doi.org/10.1016/j.jad.2020.06.009

Glenn, C. R., & Klonsky, E. D. (2013). Nonsuicidal self-injury disorder: an empirical investigation in adolescent psychiatric patients. *Journal of Clinical Child & Adolescent Psychology, 42*(4), 496–507. https://doi.org/10.1080/15374416.2013.794699

Gratz, K. L., & Gunderson, J. G. (2006). Preliminary data on an acceptance-based emotion regulation group intervention for deliberate self-harm among women with borderline personality disorder. *Behavior Therapy, 37*(1), 25–35. https://doi.org/10.1016/j.beth.2005.03.002

Hamza, C. A., Goldstein, A., Heath, N., & Ewing, L. (2021). Stressful experiences in university predict non-suicidal self-injury through emotional reactivity. *Frontiers in Psychology, 12*, Article 1209.

Hayes, S. C., Strosahl, K., Wilson, K. G., Bissett, R. T., Pistorello, J., Toarmino, D., Polusny, M. A., Dykstra, T. A., Batten, S. V., Bergan, J., Stewart, S. H., Zvolensky, M. J., Eifert, G. H., Bond, F. W., Forsyth, J. P., Karekla, M., & McCurry, S. M. (2004). Measuring experiential avoidance: A preliminary test of a working model. *The Psychological Record, 54*, 553–578. https://doi.org/10.1007/BF03395492

Hielscher, E., Whitford, T. J., Scott, J. G., & Zopf, R. (2019). When the body is the target—Representations of one's own body and bodily sensations in self-harm: A systematic review. *Neuroscience & Biobehavioral Reviews, 101*, 85–112. https://doi.org/10.1016/j.neubiorev.2019.03.007

Howe-Martin, L. S., Murrell, A. R., & Guarnaccia, C. A. (2012). Repetitive nonsuicidal self-injury as experiential avoidance among a community sample of adolescents. *Journal of Clinical Psychology, 68*(7), 809–829. https://doi.org/10.1002/jclp.21868

Kennedy, S. M., Bilek, E. L., & Ehrenreich-May, J. (2019). A randomized controlled pilot trial of the Unified Protocol for Transdiagnostic Treatment of Emotional Disorders in children. *Behavior Modification, 43*(3), 330–360. https://doi.org/10.1177/0145445517753940

Klonsky, E. D. (2007). The functions of deliberate self-injury: A review of the evidence. *Clinical Psychology Review, 27*(2), 226–239. https://doi.org/10.1016/j.cpr.2006.08.002

Linehan, M. (1993). *Cognitive-behavioral treatment of borderline personality disorder*. Guilford Press.

Liu, S., You, J., Ying, J., Li, X., & Shi, Q. (2020). Emotion reactivity, nonsuicidal self-injury, and regulatory emotional self-efficacy: A moderated mediation model of suicide ideation. *Journal of Affective Disorders, 266*(July 2019), 82–89. https://doi.org/10.1016/j.jad.2020.01.083

Lloyd-Richardson, E. E., Perrine, N., Dierker, L., & Kelley, M. L. (2007). Characteristics and functions of non-suicidal self-injury in a community sample of adolescents. *Psychological Medicine, 37*(8), 1183–1192. https://doi.org/10.1017/S003329170700027X

Maclaren, V. V, & Best, L. A. (2010). Nonsuicidal self-injury, potentially addictive behaviors, and the five factor model in undergraduates. *Personality and Individual Differences, 49*(5), 521–525. https://doi.org/10.1016/j.paid.2010.05.019

McHugh, R. K., & Barlow, D. H. (2010). The dissemination and implementation of evidence-based psychological treatments: A review of current efforts. *American Psychologist, 65*(2), 73–84. https://doi.org/10.1037/a0018121

Mettler, J., Stern, M., Lewis, S. P., & Heath, N. L. (2021). Perceived vs. actual emotion reactivity and regulation in individuals with and without a history of NSSI. *Frontiers in Psychology, 12*, Article 479.

Muehlenkamp, J. J., Engel, S. G., Wadeson, A., Crosby, R. D., Wonderlich, S. A., Simonich, H., & Mitchell, J. E. (2009). Emotional states preceding and following acts of non-suicidal self-injury in bulimia nervosa patients. *Behaviour Research and Therapy, 47*(1), 83–87.

Nock, M. K., Joiner Jr, T. E., Gordon, K. H., Lloyd-Richardson, E., & Prinstein, M. J. (2006). Non-suicidal self-injury among adolescents: Diagnostic correlates and relation to suicide attempts. *Psychiatry Research, 144*(1), 65–72. https://doi.org/10.1016/j.psychres.2006.05.010

Nock, M. K., & Mendes, W. B. (2008). Physiological arousal, distress tolerance, and social problem-solving deficits among adolescent self-injurers. *Journal of Consulting and Clinical Psychology, 76*(1), 28. https://doi.org/10.1037/0022-006X.76.1.28

Nock, M. K., & Prinstein, M. J. (2004). A functional approach to the assessment of self-mutilative behavior. *Journal of Consulting and Clinical Psychology, 72*(5), 885–890. https://doi.org/10.1037/0022-006X.72.5.885

Nock, M. K., Prinstein, M. J., & Sterba, S. K. (2009). Revealing the form and function of self-injurious thoughts and behaviors: A real-time ecological assessment study among adolescents and young adults. *Journal of Abnormal Psychology, 118*(4), Article 816. https://doi.org/10.1037/a0016948

Nock, M. K., Wedig, M. M., Holmberg, E. B., & Hooley, J. M. (2008). The emotion reactivity scale: development, evaluation, and relation to self-injurious thoughts and behaviors. *Behavior Therapy, 39*(2), 107–116.

Sakiris, N., & Berle, D. (2019). A systematic review and meta-analysis of the Unified Protocol as a transdiagnostic emotion regulation based intervention. *Clinical Psychology Review, 72*, 101751. https://doi.org/10.1016/j.cpr.2019.101751

Sauer-Zavala, S., Bentley, K. H., Steele, S. J., Tirpak, J. W., Ametaj, A. A., Nauphal, M., Cardona, N., Wang, M., Farchione, T. J., & Barlow, D. H. (2020). Treating depressive disorders with the Unified Protocol: A preliminary randomized evaluation. *Journal of Affective Disorders, 264*, 438–445. https://doi.org/10.1016/j.jad.2019.11.072

Sauer-Zavala, S., Bentley, K. H., & Wilner, J. G. (2016). Transdiagnostic treatment of borderline personality disorder and comorbid disorders: A clinical replication series. *Journal of Personality Disorders, 30*(1), 35–51. https://doi.org/10.1521/pedi_2015_29_179

Schoenleber, M., Berenbaum, H., & Motl, R. (2014). Shame-related functions of and motivations for self-injurious behavior. *Personality Disorders: Theory, Research, and Treatment, 5*(2), Article 204. https://doi.org/10.1037/per0000035

Selby, E. A., Bender, T. W., Gordon, K. H., Nock, M. K., & Joiner Jr, T. E. (2012). Non-suicidal self-injury (NSSI) disorder: A preliminary study. *Personality Disorders: Theory, Research, and Treatment, 3*(2), Article 167. https://doi.org/10.1037/a0024405

Shingleton, R. M., Eddy, K. T., Keshaviah, A., Franko, D. L., Swanson, S. A., Yu, J. S., Krishna, M., Nock, M. K., & Herzog, D. B. (2013). Binge/purge thoughts in nonsuicidal self-injurious adolescents: An ecological momentary analysis. *International Journal of Eating Disorders, 46*(7), 684–689. https://doi.org/10.1002/eat.22142

Smith, N. B., Steele, A. M., Weitzman, M. L., Trueba, A. F., & Meuret, A. E. (2015). Investigating the role of self-disgust in nonsuicidal self-injury. *Archives of Suicide Research, 19*(1), 60–74. https://doi.org/10.1080/13811118.2013.850135

Stanley, B., & Brown, G. K. (2012). Safety planning intervention: A brief intervention to mitigate suicide risk. *Cognitive and Behavioral Practice, 19*(2), 256–264. https://doi.org/10.1016/j.cbpra.2011.01.001

Taylor, P. J., Jomar, K., Dhingra, K., Forrester, R., Shahmalak, U., & Dickson, J. M. (2018). A meta-analysis of the prevalence of different functions of non-suicidal self-injury. *Journal of Affective Disorders, 227*(November 2017), 759–769. https://doi.org/10.1016/j.jad.2017.11.073

Tonarely, N. A., Sherman, J. A., Grossman, R. A., & Ehrenreich-May, J. (2021). Targeting elevated borderline features in adolescents using the Unified Protocol for Transdiagnostic Treatment of Emotional Disorders in Adolescents (UP-A). *Evidence-Based Practice in Child and Adolescent Mental Health, 6*(1), 47–64. https://doi.org/10.1080/23794925.2020.1805821

Turner, B. J., Dixon-Gordon, K. L., Austin, S. B., Rodriguez, M. A., Rosenthal, M. Z., & Chapman, A. L. (2015). Non-suicidal self-injury with and without borderline personality disorder: Differences in self-injury and diagnostic comorbidity. *Psychiatry Research, 230*(1), 28–35. https://doi.org/10.1016/j.psychres.2015.07.058

Williams, J., & Hassanyeh, F. (1983). Deliberate self-harm, clinical history and extreme scoring on the EPQ. *Personality and Individual Differences, 4*(3), 347–350.

You, J., Lin, M., Xu, S., & Hu, W. (2016). Big Five personality traits in the occurrence and repetition of nonsuicidal self-injury among adolescents: The mediating effects of depressive symptoms. *Personality and Individual Differences, 101*, 227–231.

You, J., Ren, Y., Zhang, X., Wu, Z., Xu, S., & Lin, M. (2018). Emotional dysregulation and nonsuicidal self-injury: A meta-analytic review. *Neuropsychiatry, 8*(2), 733–748.

CHAPTER 56

Cognitive-Behavioral and Dialectical Behavior Therapy for Nonsuicidal Self-Injury

Alexander L. Chapman, Philippa Hood, *and* Cassandra J. Turner

> **Abstract**
>
> The primary aim of this chapter is to discuss and illustrate core cognitive-behavioral (CBT) principles and practices in the treatment of nonsuicidal self-injury (NSSI). CBT principles emphasize the context in which NSSI occurs, along with the transaction of cognitive, emotional, and behavioral factors in the maintenance of NSSI. Dialectical behavior therapy (DBT) is an example of an effective treatment for NSSI with unique elements, including a comprehensive treatment structure, a biosocial developmental and dialectical theoretical perspective, and a focus on skills deficits, emotions, and emotion regulation. Broadly, DBT includes many core CBT strategies that can help clients overcome NSSI, build more effective coping strategies, and build lives they experience as worth living. Throughout this chapter, the authors discuss key, overarching CBT and DBT principles and strategies applied to the treatment of NSSI.
>
> **Key Words:** nonsuicidal self-injury, self-harm, emotion regulation, cognitive-behavioral therapy, dialectical behavior therapy

Conceptualized as the intentional self-infliction of acute bodily harm without the intent or expectation of death, nonsuicidal self-injury (NSSI; International Society for the Study of Self-Injury, 2007) often presents significant clinical challenges. Although once considered unique to psychiatric populations, NSSI occurs in community populations as well, with rates of NSSI being particularly high among adolescents and emerging adults ranging from (15%–38%; Claes et al., 2010; Gratz, 2001; Whitlock et al., 2011; see Kiekens et al., this volume). NSSI places a substantial burden on the healthcare system (Burke et al., 2015; Lieb et al., 2004; Skodol et al., 2002), and it is one of the strongest and most robust predictors of suicide attempts and death by suicide (Franklin et al., 2017; Guan et al., 2012; Hamza et al., 2012; Kiekens et al., 2018). Therefore, clinicians treating NSSI also must be adept in the assessment and management of suicide risk (see Victor et al., this volume).

NSSI also presents other clinical challenges. Despite increasing awareness of the risk factors, developmental progression, and functions of NSSI (see Taylor et al., this volume), it can be difficult to understand why somebody would go so far against the natural instinct of self-preservation as to intentionally harm themselves. Another clinical challenge is that many clients have internalized stigma and shame about this behavior. As a result, they may either not disclose NSSI to a clinician or mental health professional or underreport or minimize the occurrence of NSSI. Indeed, some research suggests that at least a minority of people who engage in NSSI might prefer to disclose and seek support from loved ones than from mental health providers (Simone & Hamza, 2020).

Notwithstanding these challenges, from a cognitive-behavioral therapy (CBT) perspective, NSSI is simply another behavior that warrants clinical attention. Clinicians with a firm grounding in CBT principles are already in a good position to help clients engaging in NSSI. From a CBT perspective, many of the factors that influence and maintain NSSI are transdiagnostic mechanisms that influence and maintain other behaviors, such as depressive behaviors (e.g., staying in bed and avoiding people), anxiety-related avoidance, aggression, substance use, disordered eating, and so forth. Although clinicians should have specific knowledge of the phenomenology and developmental psychopathology of NSSI, the literature on effective treatments, and NSSI's specific functions and risk factors, in many ways, treating NSSI is not substantially different from treating many other clinically relevant behaviors.

The primary aim of this chapter is to discuss key CBT principles and practices in the treatment of NSSI. As dialectical behavior therapy (DBT; Linehan, 1993a, 2015) is a comprehensive form of CBT originally designed to treat chronically suicidal individuals, we also illustrate unique theoretical and practical elements that DBT brings to the effective treatment of NSSI. Additionally, we briefly summarize the research on CBT and DBT for NSSI.

A CBT and DBT View of the Development and Maintenance of NSSI

Clinicians using a CBT approach with NSSI can benefit from understanding how this behavior might develop. At the same time, both CBT and DBT are present-oriented therapies; thus, clinicians should also understand factors that maintain NSSI currently. Below, we discuss the development of NSSI as well as factors that might maintain this behavior over time.

The Development of NSSI

From a standard CBT viewpoint, NSSI develops through a combination of early social learning (e.g., modeling of NSSI by peers), a deficient repertoire of alternative coping strategies, and reinforcement of NSSI in the form of emotion regulation or social consequences (Nock & Prinstein, 2004), among other factors. DBT theory helps to place NSSI within a developmental psychopathology (Cicchetti, 2014) context emphasizing social (rearing and social environments, cultural contexts) and individual (temperament, biology, genetics) factors contributing to the development of NSSI, suicidal behavior, borderline personality disorder (BPD), and transdiagnostic, emotion regulation difficulties.

According to DBT's biosocial developmental theory, BPD and NSSI develop through the interaction and transaction of core temperament characteristics with aspects of the child's rearing environment (Crowell et al., 2009; Crowell et al., 2014; Linehan, 1993a, 1993b, 2015). Temperament-based characteristics include high trait impulsivity and the tendency to have an emotional temperament (often referred to as emotion vulnerability). Trait impulsivity, in particular, is a highly heritable, neurobiologically based characteristic including poor delay of gratification (i.e., difficulty resisting impulses to seek an immediate reward despite knowing that waiting will lead to something of greater value) and difficulty with behavioral inhibition and learning from negative consequences (e.g., someone with high trait impulsivity may repeatedly overspend, struggling to learn to inhibit the behavior despite the stress of incurring increasing debt), among other features. Children with high trait impulsivity may be especially prone to the negative effects of adverse childhood environments, including those that involve invalidation of the child's emotional experience, abuse, neglect, and/or trauma (Beauchaine et al., 2019).

Within this framework, in invalidating environments, highly impulsive children have difficulty learning how to understand and regulate emotions. Instead, they learn to escalate emotional expression or behavior (e.g., yelling, threats, and physical aggression) to get their needs met or navigate conflict. Over time, the environment shapes emotion dysregulation, consisting of labile, intense emotional responses, combined with difficulty regulating emotions in the service of goal-directed behavior (Beauchaine, 2015; Chapman, 2019). As emotion dysregulation worsens throughout later childhood and early adolescence, maladaptive coping strategies that help the individual to escape or avoid emotions emerge and become entrenched. These coping strategies often include NSSI, drug use, or reckless behaviors. Along with interpersonal difficulties, emotion dysregulation and maladaptive coping can escalate into suicidal behavior and coalesce into BPD in later adolescence. This type of developmental model of NSSI suggests that effective prevention and treatment should focus primarily on interventions to change risky rearing environments (e.g., parenting interventions) and improve emotion regulation capabilities (Beauchaine et al., 2019). Please see box 56.1 for a case example illustrating a biosocial developmental model of NSSI.

The Maintenance of NSSI

Within a CBT framework, a transaction of cognition (see Browning & Muehlenkamp, this volume), emotion, behavior, and context influence and maintain NSSI. DBT similarly focuses on these factors and enriches the formulation of NSSI by emphasizing an emotion regulation framework. Starting from the foundation provided by a broad theoretical model of how NSSI develops, CBT/DBT therapists determine how this model applies (or doesn't) ideographically to maintaining factors for specific clients.

> **Box 56.1** Case Example of the Biosocial Developmental Model
>
> "Morey" is a single, unemployed, partnered transgendered man who self-injures via cutting two to three times per week. He grew up in a deeply religious, high-achieving, and strict family environment. He often felt different from his family members, who did not seem to understand his often-changing moods and were frustrated by his erratic, impulsive behaviors. His family relied largely on punishment to try to control Morey's reckless behavior at home (e.g., breaking things, making messes, playing aggressively with siblings, and absconding) and at school. As Morey increasingly recognized that his gender identity did not match his assigned sex, he increasingly isolated himself from his family, suppressing his emotions and concealing his gender identity out of concern that he would be rejected or punished. He learned to invalidate his own experiences, including his need to explore his identity, as it was painful to contemplate the consequences of coming out as a trans boy. He began to experience periods of depression but was often emotionally labile even between depressive episodes. As he spent more time with kids who drank, cut, and used drugs, he learned that cutting, in particular, helped to distract him from and soothe his overwhelming emotions, and became a way to express his anger toward himself. He began to cut more often, hiding this behavior and his injuries from his family, until he accidentally harmed himself severely enough to require medical attention. At that point, he came out, in terms of both self-injury and his gender identity. His family members were alarmed and concerned, and although they had great difficulty understanding and accepting Morey's behavior and identity, they did help him seek treatment for his mental health concerns. It was a rocky road for the family, and the relationship remains tenuous, but they are working on acceptance and reconciliation. Meanwhile, Morey continues to struggle with NSSI and depression and a conflictual relationship with his current partner.

COGNITION

Although relatively understudied, clinically, we have observed that several cognitive patterns are often related to NSSI. Such patterns often include the client's negative self-referential core beliefs (that the client is deficient, unlovable, etc.), the client's self-efficacy beliefs about their ability to cope with stress or regulate emotions, along with expectations about how difficult these situations or stressors will be or about their negative consequences (e.g., that a fight with a partner will result in rejection, and that the client will end up alone). Clients may also have positive beliefs or expectations about the likely effectiveness of NSSI in terms of coping with a variety of emotional and interpersonal stressors. Additionally, some clients have stigma-promoting beliefs about NSSI, believing that NSSI is a shameful behavior. Please see table 56.1 for examples of questions a therapist might ask to better understand cognitions related to NSSI.

EMOTIONS

Emotional factors are particularly relevant to a DBT conceptualization of NSSI. Indeed, NSSI most commonly appears to be an emotion regulation behavior (Chapman et al., 2006; Linehan, 1993a), functioning to avoid or escape aversive or unwanted emotional states (thoughts or sensations). Although a significant minority of self-injuring individuals report engaging in this behavior for interpersonal reasons (e.g., to communicate or

Table 56.1 Questions about Cognitions Related to NSSI

What types of thoughts go through your mind before you self-injure?
How do you think of your ability to cope with or tolerate stress or painful emotions?
Can you describe what you think will happen when you self-injure?
How do you think self-injury changes how you feel or think, or effects on others who know about it?
What do you think about others who self-injure?
What do you think about your own self-injury?

influence others; Brown et al., 2002), the most commonly reported function or purpose of NSSI is to downregulate or reduce negative emotional states (Brown et al., 2002; Chapman et al., 2006; Klonsky, 2007). As a result, it is useful to assess negative emotional states occurring prior to NSSI, such as shame, guilt, tension, anxiety, anger, and so forth (Kleindienst et al., 2008). NSSI can also upregulate emotions, through stimulating feelings of excitement or a "rush"; thus, states of boredom and numbness or even curiosity can also be relevant to explore.

An emotion regulation framework helps to clarify how emotions relate to NSSI and suggests important areas to assess. DBT therapists conceptualize emotions as multicomponent, full-system responses (Chapman & Dixon-Gordon, 2020; Linehan, 1993a, 2015). Components of emotion include biological changes, such as changes in brain activity, neurochemistry, hormones, sympathetic and parasympathetic nervous system activity, and physiological changes that we can experience, such as changes in heart rate, perspiration, body temperature, or muscle tension. Other changes that we can experience can include what we feel like doing when emotions arise, such as the desire to escape or avoid in the presence of fear or anxiety, the desire to yell or act aggressively when anger arises, and so forth (in DBT, these desires are often referred to as "action urges"; Linehan, 2015). Emotions also often include expressive components, such as the types of facial expressions or body language that accompany emotional states, as well as emotion-related changes in cognition, attention, and perception and action tendencies. Therefore, to understand a particular client's NSSI, it can be useful to explore the different components of emotions related to this behavior.

Consistent with a functional view of emotions and emotion regulation, it can also be helpful to understand what function or purpose the client's emotion might serve. Shame about not having a job or struggling with mental health problems, for example, might prevent these factors from coming to light in situations where the client might be criticized, ostracized, or rejected. Strong feelings of anger toward himself, for example, might not seem to serve much of a purpose for Morey, but it could suggest that there are things about his life that he's dissatisfied with or that he's not achieving goals that are important to him (e.g., not having established a career and having difficulty functioning in daily living). NSSI, in this case, might help to temporarily alleviate self-directed anger, or might

Table 56.2 Questions about Emotions Related to NSSI

Which emotions do you think you were feeling before you self-injured?
Is it common that you feel these things before self-injuring?
Which emotion or emotions did you (or do you usually) have the hardest time coping with or tolerating?
What types of body/physical sensations do you have before you self-injure?
What do you feel like doing (in addition to or aside from self-injuring)?
How about how your face or body might be expressing how you feel?
How do you think your facial expression looks?
What changes happen in your posture or body language?
If you're interacting with someone, what kinds of words do you find yourself using?
How about actions? What do you see yourself doing (before or after you self-injure)?
What do you think your emotion might be doing for you? Is there anything your emotions were/are telling you?

be self-validating, confirming that Morey is "bad" and needs to be punished. It can be helpful to ask clients what purpose emotion related to self-injury might be serving. Please see table 56.2 for examples of questions a therapist might ask to better understand emotions related to NSSI.

BEHAVIORAL FACTORS

We include both the *topography* (the specific nature of the self-injury) and *function* of NSSI under this category of "behavioral factors." In terms of topography, it is useful to assess type (cutting, burning, hitting, or banging oneself, etc.), frequency (i.e., is it a daily, couple of times a week, or less often), duration (how long does a particular episode of self-injury last?), and intensity (how serious or injurious the NSSI is, and whether medical attention is needed) of NSSI. Additionally, it is useful to assess behaviors that are related to or facilitate NSSI, such as researching NSSI methods, acquiring means (e.g., razors and lighters), threatening to engage in NSSI, and imagining or fantasizing about the behavior, among others.

When it comes to the function or purpose of NSSI, it can be helpful to understand what consequences tend to follow this behavior, as well as (noted previously) the client's expectations about what might happen if they were to engage in NSSI. As discussed above, intrapersonal functions or consequences in the form of downregulation of emotion are most common; however, it can be helpful to consider a broader array of functions. The four-function model (Nock & Prinstein, 2004; see Hird et al., this volume), for example, proposes that the reinforcers for NSSI can be social or automatic, and positive or negative. Social reinforcers involve changes in others' behavior, such as when Morey's partner backs down and stops confronting him about why he hasn't applied for a job yet after Morey self-injures. Automatic reinforcers involve changes in the client's internal states, such as when Morey feels less angry with himself after cutting. This model results in four categories of reinforcers: social/positive, social/negative, automatic/positive, and automatic/negative. A detailed CBT/DBT formulation of NSSI should ideally incorporate these four categories, as applicable.

Early Therapy Strategies: Assessment, Orientation, and Commitment

Early in CBT or DBT, therapy often involves assessing the client's patterns of NSSI and securing a commitment to work on this behavior in therapy. During this phase of treatment, often called the "pretreatment phase" in DBT, the therapist might use motivational interviewing (Miller & Rollick, 2013) or DBT commitment strategies (Linehan, 1993a) to help the client commit to this work. Given the association of NSSI with suicide risk, safety planning is also useful at this stage. The therapist also orients the client to treatment, including the use of phone coaching, which is a key component of DBT aiming to help clients generalize skills learned in therapy to everyday life (Chapman, 2018; Linehan, 1993a). In addition, typically in DBT, the client begins to use a self-monitoring form (e.g., the DBT diary card) to keep track of relevant emotions, thoughts, and actions (such as NSSI) that might become a focus of therapy. Please see box 56.2 for a case example illustrating some of these early therapy strategies.

> **Box 56.2 Early CBT/DBT Therapy Strategies with Morey**
>
> Early in therapy, Morey was ambivalent about reducing or eliminating cutting, stating, "You're asking me to stop something I've been doing for ten years, and I don't know what else I'd do when I start to get that buzzing or humming feeling." Modeling dialectical thinking, the therapist replied, "I know, it would be incredibly hard to imagine just giving up a helpful coping strategy and I'd like us to work together to find other skills that could replace it. Therapy is not being stuck on an arctic expedition without a warm jacket; it's trying to find a better one that will last." Morey's therapist also used motivational and DBT commitment strategies to help Morey consider (a) how cutting fits with the life he wants to have, (b) the pros and cons of continuing versus stopping cutting, and (c) what his life would look like and how he'd like to be coping if he were to develop alternative skills and reduce or move away from cutting. Morey concluded that, whereas cutting does make him feel better (and serves other purposes as described earlier), he would ultimately feel better about himself if he could learn to cope with life without cutting. Morey agreed to monitor his cutting weekly using a DBT diary card and to at least work on learning new coping skills and reducing cutting. He and the therapist came up with a plan to make Morey's preferred cutting implements less easily accessible and constructed a safety plan. The safety plan was meant to address both suicide risk and risk of NSSI and included people he could contact for support or in the event of an emergency, places he could go if he believes he is at risk, and at least five DBT skills he agreed to use before doing anything to harm himself. Additionally, Morey agreed to call his therapist for coaching in skills he could use to manage overwhelming emotions, before he got to the point of cutting.

Ongoing Functional/Chain Analyses to Illuminate Patterns of NSSI

As therapy progresses, the client and therapist come to a clearer understanding of factors maintaining NSSI and start to use interventions to address these factors. One way that CBT/DBT therapists often seek to understand the maintaining factors for NSSI is through a *functional analysis* (Farmer & Chapman, 2016; Goldfried & Davison, 1976), often referred to as a *chain analysis* in DBT (Linehan, 1993a; Rizvi, 2019). A functional analysis is a detailed assessment of a particular instance of a clinically relevant behavior, such as Morey's cutting last Thursday evening after a fight with his partner. The therapist and client collaboratively discuss the specific events preceding NSSI, including events in the environment, emotional states, thoughts, sensations, and actions, as well as the consequences following the behavior. Repeated functional analyses can illuminate the client's typical patterns of NSSI and the function or purpose this behavior seems to serve (i.e., what reinforces and maintains NSSI). Functional analyses, therefore, form the building blocks of a CBT/DBT formulation of NSSI and highlight possibly effective intervention strategies. Please see box 56.3 for a case example illustrating how therapy can use chain or functional analyses to build a case formulation of NSSI.

Core CBT and DBT Interventions for NSSI

DBT addresses NSSI and other clinically relevant behaviors using core, evidence-based CBT intervention strategies, within the overall structure of a comprehensive treatment. In terms of therapy structure, DBT consists of four components: Weekly individual

---

Box 56.3 Case Formulation of Morey's NSSI

Each week, if Morey had reported cutting on his DBT diary card, he and the therapist would make this behavior top priority. They conducted chain analyses to understand how he ended up cutting, and considered alternative skills and solutions he could implement next time he is in a similar situation. It became clear that the highest-risk situations for cutting included (a) conflict with Morey's partner, particularly when his partner criticized him; (b) anticipation of a family gathering; and (c) the aftermath of a family gathering. The most salient emotions related to cutting included shame, anxiety, and self-directed anger. He also struggled with shame about gender identity when he had to interact with his family, and anxiety before family events. At times, before self-injuring, he felt angry with himself for "not just being normal" like most people. Thoughts typically included self-denigration ("I'm a freak. I can't do anything. What's wrong with me? All our problems are my fault. I'm odd, awkward. I'm a mistake."). Cutting typically temporarily alleviated Morey's negative emotions but often resulted in increases in shame. At times, Morey reported cutting to punish himself. Morey has said he believes cutting releases tension and anger toward himself, and is a way to express or atone for (through self-punishment) his "flaws." Typically, Morey cuts about two to three times per week with a razor in his bathroom, usually involving two to three moderately shallow cuts at a time on his arms or thighs. Following cutting, Morey reported feeling tired, detached, and ashamed. He sometimes cuts during fights with his partner, and when this happens, his partner becomes solicitous and backs down from the fight.

therapy, weekly group skills training, as-needed telephone consultation (often referred to as phone coaching), and weekly therapist consultation team meetings. Many authors have described these components in other volumes and articles (Chapman & Dixon-Gordon, 2020; Linehan, 1993a, 1993b, 2015), so rather than delving into each one here, we will illustrate them as needed throughout this section.

As illustrated in box 56.2, in individual DBT, the therapist and client typically monitor NSSI, use chain analyses to clarify treatment targets, and then solve problems collaboratively. The problem-solving component of DBT could entail coaching or training in particular DBT or CBT coping skills, or any of a plethora of core, evidence-based CBT intervention strategies. These core CBT strategies are often used across other clinical problem areas and include a combination of psychoeducation, motivational interventions, cognitive restructuring, behavioral activation, skills training (i.e., in coping or interpersonal skills), exposure therapy, and behavioral contingency management (Farmer & Chapman, 2016; Tolin, 2016). Typically, many forms of CBT also include mindfulness and acceptance-based interventions and skills or strategies to improve emotion regulation.

DBT includes all these core CBT interventions, within a dialectical framework balancing acceptance and change. The therapist seeks to balance validation and understanding of the client's experiences, thoughts, and emotions, with problem-solving efforts to help the client learn to change behavior and build a life worth living. Based in part on a skill-deficit model, one of the primary ways to help clients change behavior is to teach them new skills. As a result, DBT includes both formal skills training and active efforts to ensure that therapy is a learning-oriented process (e.g., having clients learn and practice new behaviors in individual therapy sessions, on the phone, and during group skills training) (Chapman, 2018). DBT also balances the way in which the therapist communicates with the client, with warmth and responsiveness (often called "reciprocity" in DBT; Linehan, 1993a) balanced with irreverence, involving an unexpected, matter-of-fact, deadpan, or humorous therapeutic style. Irreverence can be used to shift the mood in a therapy session, to capture the client's attention, or to reframe something the client has said (e.g., Patient: "I am going to kill myself," Therapist: "I thought we agreed you weren't going to quit therapy"; Linehan, 1993a). In addition, DBT balances acceptance and change in terms of the skills that clients learn in therapy, with some skills emphasizing ways to change interpersonal situations, emotions, or actions and others focusing on acceptance of reality as it is (e.g., the distress tolerance skill of "radical acceptance"; Linehan, 2015). Please see box 56.4 for an illustration of some core treatment strategies within a DBT framework with Morey.

Evidence for CBT and DBT in the Treatment of NSSI

With regard to the use of CBT and DBT, prior reviews and meta-analyses have examined both therapies and their use in the treatment of NSSI. Broadly, DBT or DBT for adolescents (DBT-A) has been found to be most effective for treatment of NSSI. Meta-analyses

Box 56.4 Core Treatment Strategies with Morey

Morey and his therapist began to use treatment strategies to address key patterns related to cutting. Of note, therapy did not focus only on cutting. Indeed, many of the problems (emotions, thinking patterns, etc.) related to cutting also hampered Morey's quality of life and made it difficult for him to reach his goals. As a result, therapy focused on both improving Morey's quality of life and reducing cutting. Using **mindfulness and acceptance** interventions and skills, Morey learned to mindfully observe difficult emotions, such as shame, anxiety, and anger toward himself. He began to pick up on cues for these emotions and high-risk situations for cutting, and as a result, was more able to come up with effective coping plans. Mindfully accepting his emotions also helped Morey counter his normal tendency to avoid or escape emotions; he learned that these emotions, while incredibly uncomfortable, were tolerable and often come and go. As DBT is an **emotion-focused** therapy, the therapist would often coach Morey in DBT skills in the moment during therapy sessions if he was, for example, showing signs of shame (eyes averted, head down, avoiding particular topics). **Cognitive restructuring** addressed Morey's negative thoughts about himself and helped him think more flexibly about criticism from others, for example, "When Andy [Morey's partner] asks if I looked for jobs, this probably means he's worried about our finances and wants me to feel productive and happy. He's not necessarily saying I'm a deadbeat." Using **contingency management**, Morey and his therapist spoke to Andy about what to do if Morey does cut himself. They came up with a plan to reduce reinforcement of cutting by (a) Morey using interpersonal skills to express how he feels and what he needs from Andy (sometimes, to take a time out, or for Andy to validate how difficult it is for Morey to function), (b) Andy not becoming more attentive and solicitous when Morey has cut himself. Through **exposure interventions** and the DBT skill of **opposite action**, Morey worked on his fear, anxiety, and shame before family gatherings. Morey started by imagining going to family gatherings repeatedly (imaginal exposure), and progressed to imagining his ultimate fear, that his family would criticize and reject him. Then, working on the skill of opposite action for shame (and fear), he showed up at get-togethers, mindfully made eye contact with others, presented himself in a way that was congruent with his gender identity, and resisted his urge to avoid people. In addition, through his **DBT skills training group**, Morey learned a variety of mindfulness, interpersonal effectiveness, emotion regulation, and distress tolerance skills that helped equip him with tools he needed to move away from cutting and build a life worth living. Although the road to becoming more free of NSSI and building a better life was not always smooth, Morey did stop cutting around Week 9 of therapy, and by the time he'd finished a year of DBT, he had started meaningful volunteer work with a group supporting allyship for gender-diverse people, felt much better about how things were going with Andy, and had begun to heal some of the problems in his family relationships.

and systematic reviews with a focus on adolescents are common in research on treatment of NSSI and indicate that DBT reduces both self-injury and depressive symptoms (Cook & Gorraiz, 2016; Freeman et al., 2016) and may be a promising route for the treatment of NSSI (Flaherty, 2018). DBT has been found to reduce hospitalizations and CBT interventions have been found to reduce factors that maintain self-injury (Brausch & Girresch, 2012). Some studies indicate mixed results for CBT (Muehlenkamp, 2006); however, more recent systematic reviews show that CBT is effective in reducing self-harm or self-injurious behavior more broadly, but many studies fail to differentiate between suicide attempts and NSSI (Labelle et al., 2015). In a systematic review, Turner et al. (2014) found mixed results for DBT in the reduction of self-harm. In a more recent systematic review that combined DBT-A and CBT into one CBT category, Iyengar et al. (2018) found that CBT was the only therapy that demonstrated reduction of NSSI in replicated results. Many of these systematic reviews showed the efficacy of both CBT and DBT in the treatment of NSSI while also indicating there is a dearth of RCTs on CBT for NSSI.

A variety of subgroups or adaptations of CBT have been utilized to treat nonsuicidal self-injury in the past including family-based CBT (Kothgassner et al., 2020), problem-solving therapy (Brausch & Girresch, 2012; Muehlenkamp, 2006), and standard CBT with a problem-solving component (Brausch & Girresch, 2012). Randomized control trials (RCTs) examining these adaptations, however, are limited (Brausch & Girresch, 2012). RCTs have been conducted on the Cutting Down Program (CDP) which is an adaptation of manual assisted cognitive-behavioral therapy adapted for adolescents (Fischer et al., 2013; Kaess et al., 2020). Historically, MACT has been shown to significantly decrease NSSI when compared to treatment as usual, as has CDP (Fischer et al., 2013). One trial for the CDP conducted in Germany randomized participants to two conditions; a CDP intervention and a treatment as usual condition (75% of whom received CBT). The researchers reported that both the treatment-as-usual group and the CDP group showed approximately a 70% reduction in NSSI with large effect sizes for both groups (Kaess et al., 2020). Given that both CDP and the treatment as usual (75% CBT), showed no difference and reduced symptoms, both versions of treatment show promising efficacy.

With regard to DBT, several RCTs investigated the use of DBT for individuals who self-injure and do or do not have borderline personality disorder or co-occurring suicidal behaviors. Trials broadly show support for the use of DBT to reduce NSSI. McCauley et al. (2018) and Adrian et al. (2019) used the same data and compared a DBT intervention for self-harm to an individual/group supportive therapy (IGST) intervention in a randomized clinical trial (Adrian et al., 2019; McCauley et al., 2018). Individuals in the DBT condition reported lower numbers of NSSI episodes than those in the IGST condition during treatment and at the 12-month follow-up. DBT was found to be associated with a greater percentage of individuals (51.2%) being NSSI free after the 12-month follow-up than the IGST was (32.2%) (McCauley et al., 2018). The results of both studies demonstrate the effectiveness of DBT for NSSI even when it is accompanied by more complex or severe mental health problems such as suicidality. Berk et al. (2020) also found a significant decrease in participants' number of self-injury episodes during treatment in their trial of DBT-A. Another trial of DBT for NSSI utilized a wait-list control design RCT to examine a 20-week DBT intervention and its reduction of borderline symptoms (Krantz et al., 2018; McMain et al., 2017). The DBT group showed significant reductions in self-injuring behavior on one measure of NSSI. Secondary analyses also indicated a significant effect of DBT on the reduction of NSSI (Krantz et al., 2018).

Both CBT, DBT, and their various adaptations show promise and efficacy in the treatment of NSSI; however, more RCTs are needed to replicate previous findings, particularly for CBT. DBT-A seems to show efficacy for adolescents who exhibit nonsuicidal self-injury (Glenn et al., 2019).

Conclusions

As an overarching framework for the treatment of NSSI, CBT emphasizes a transaction of cognitive, emotional, behavioral, and contextual factors in the development and maintenance of this behavior. DBT adds a unique focus on developmental pathways toward emotion dysregulation and NSSI, a skill-deficit model emphasizing ways to replace NSSI with skillful behaviors and develop tools to build a life worth living, and a dialectical framework directing the balance and synthesis of treatment strategies and therapeutic styles.

Core treatment strategies stemming from CBT can help address factors maintaining NSSI. Cognitive strategies help to address beliefs and thoughts that facilitate NSSI, exposure and other core behavioral strategies can help to improve emotion tolerance and reduce avoidance, and contingency management can help modify reinforcement contingencies for NSSI and reinforce effective alternative behaviors. We should note that working on NSSI does not mean that the client must cease the behavior immediately, as this is often unrealistic and may not be consistent with the client's goals. Recovery from NSSI also might involve the client improving their quality of life, working toward valued goals, and still having urges and thoughts related to self-injury, and possibly periodic lapses (but without the behavior becoming uncontrollable or causing significant distress or dysfunction) (Lewis & Hasking, 2020; also see Whitlock et al., this volume).

A DBT framework helps to maintain a treatment focus on learning and incorporating new behaviors into daily life. DBT skills training helps clients learn to effectively regulate and tolerate emotions, navigate interpersonal situations or stressors related to NSSI, and mindfully accept rather than avoid overwhelming emotions associated with NSSI. DBT phone coaching aims to generalize these skills to relevant situations in the client's daily life, including high-risk situations for NSSI. DBT individual therapy also helps to maintain a focus on NSSI as a high priority, as well as maintain the client's commitment to change and build a life worth living.

References

Adrian, M., McCauley, E., Berk, M. S., Asarnow, J. R., Korslund, K., Avina, C., Gallop, R., & Linehan, M. M. (2019). Predictors and moderators of recurring self-harm in adolescents participating in a comparative treatment trial of psychological interventions. *Journal of Child Psychology and Psychiatry and Allied Disciplines*, *60*(10), 1123–1132. https://doi.org/10.1111/jcpp.13099

Beauchaine, T. P. (2015). Future directions in emotion dysregulation and youth psychopathology. *Journal of Clinical Child and Adolescent Psychology*, *44*(5), 875–896. https://doi.org/10.1080/15374416.2015.1038827

Beauchaine, T. P., Hinshaw, S. P., & Bridge, J. A. (2019). Nonsuicidal self-injury and suicidal behaviors in girls: The case for targeted prevention in preadolescence. *Clinical Psychological Science*, *7*(4), 643–667. https://doi.org/10.1177/2167702618818474

Berk, M. S., Starace, N. K., Black, V. P., & Avina, C. (2020). Implementation of dialectical behavior therapy with suicidal and self-harming adolescents in a community clinic. *Archives of Suicide Research, 24*(1), 64–81. https://doi.org/10.1080/13811118.2018.1509750

Brausch, A. M., & Girresch, S. K. (2012). A review of empirical treatment studies for adolescent nonsuicidal self-injury. *Journal of Cognitive Psychotherapy, 26*(1), 3–18. https://doi.org/10.1891/0889-8391.26.1.3

Brown, M. Z., Comtois, K. A., & Linehan, M. M. (2002). Reasons for suicide attempts and nonsuicidal self-injury in women with borderline personality disorder. *Journal of Abnormal Psychology, 111*(1), 198–202. https://doi.org/10.1037/0021-843X.111.1.198

Burke, T. A., Hamilton, J. L., Abramson, L. Y., & Alloy, L. B. (2015). Non-suicidal self-injury prospectively predicts interpersonal stressful life events and depressive symptoms among adolescent girls. *Psychiatry Research, 228*, 416–424.

Chapman, A. L. (2018). *Phone coaching in dialectical behavior therapy*. Guilford Press.

Chapman, A. L. (2019). Borderline personality disorder and emotion dysregulation. *Development and Psychopathology, 31*(3), 1143–1156. https://doi.org/10.1017/s0954579419000658

Chapman, A. L., & Dixon-Gordon, K. L. (2020). *Dialectical behavior therapy*. American Psychological Association Books. https://doi.org/10.1037/0000188-000

Chapman, A. L., Gratz, K. L., & Brown, M. Z. (2006). Solving the puzzle of deliberate self-harm: The experiential avoidance model. *Behaviour Research and Therapy, 44*(3), 371–394. https://doi.org/10.1016/j.brat.2005.03.005

Cicchetti, D. (2014). Illustrative developmental psychopathology perspectives on precursors and pathways to personality disorder: Commentary on the special issue. *Journal of Personality Disorders, 28*(1), 172–179. https://doi.org/10.1521/pedi.2014.28.1.172

Claes, L., Houben, A., Vandereycken, W., Bijttebier, P., & Muehlenkamp, J. (2010). Brief report: The association between non-suicidal self-injury, self-concept and acquaintance with self-injurious peers in a sample of adolescents. *Journal of Adolescence, 33*(5), 775–778. https://doi.org/10.1016/j.adolescence.2009.10.012

Cook, N. E., & Gorraiz, M. (2016). Dialectical behavior therapy for nonsuicidal self-injury and depression among adolescents: Preliminary meta-analytic evidence. *Child and Adolescent Mental Health, 21*(2), 81–89. https://doi.org/10.1111/camh.12112

Crowell, S. E., Beauchaine, T. P., & Linehan, M. M. (2009). A biosocial developmental model of borderline personality: Elaborating and extending Linehan's theory. *Psychological Bulletin, 135*(3), 495–510. https://doi.org/10.1037/a0015616

Crowell, S. E., Kaufman, E. A., & Beauchaine, T. P. (2014). A biosocial model of BPD: Theory and empirical evidence. In C. Sharp & J. Tackett (Eds.), *Handbook of borderline personality disorder in children and adolescents* (pp. 143–157). New York: Springer. https://doi.org/10.1007/978-1-4939-0591-1_11

Farmer, R. F., & Chapman, A. L. (2016). *Behavioral interventions in cognitive behavior therapy: Practical guidance for putting theory into action* (2nd ed.). American Psychological Association Books. https://doi.org/10.1037/14691-000

Fischer, G., Brunner, R., Parzer, P., Resch, F., & Kaess, M. (2013). Short-term psychotherapeutic treatment in adolescents engaging in non-suicidal self-injury: A randomized controlled trial. *Trials, 14*, 294. https://doi.org/10.1186/1745-6215-14-294

Flaherty, H. B. (2018). Treating adolescent nonsuicidal self-injury: A review of psychosocial interventions to guide clinical practice. *Child and Adolescent Social Work Journal, 35*(1), 85–95. https://doi.org/10.1007/s10560-017-0505-5

Franklin, J. C., Ribeiro, J. D., Fox, K. R., Bentley, K. H., Kleiman, E. M., Huang, X., Musacchio, K. M., Jaroszewski, A. C., Chang, B. P., & Nock, M. K. (2017). Risk factors for suicidal thoughts and behaviors: A meta-analysis of 50 years of research. *Psychological Bulletin, 143*(2), 187–232. https://doi.org/10.1037/bul0000084

Freeman, K. R., James, S., Klein, K. P., Mayo, D., & Montgomery, S. (2016). Outpatient dialectical behavior therapy for adolescents engaged in deliberate self-harm: Conceptual and methodological considerations. *Child and Adolescent Social Work Journal, 33*(2), 123–135. https://doi.org/10.1007/s10560-015-0412-6

Glenn, C. R., Esposito, E. C., Porter, A. C., & Robinson, D. J. (2019). Evidence base update of psychosocial treatments for self-injurious thoughts and behaviors in youth. *Journal of Clinical Child and Adolescent Psychology, 48*(3), 357–392. https://doi.org/10.1080/15374416.2019.1591281

Goldfried, M. R., & Davison, G. R. (1976). *Clinical behavior therapy*. Holt, Rinehart, & Winston.

Gratz, K. L. (2001). Measurement of deliberate self-harm: Preliminary data on the deliberate self-harm inventory. *Journal of Psychopathology and Behavioral Assessment, 23*(4), 253–263. https://doi.org/10.1023/A:1012779403943

Guan, K., Fox, K., & Prinstein, M. (2012). Nonsuicidal self-injury as a time-invariant predictor of adolescent suicide ideation and attempts in a diverse community sample. *Journal of Consulting and Clinical Psychology, 80*(5), 842–849. https://doi.org/10.1037/a0029429

Hamza, C. A., Stewart, S. L., & Willoughby, T. (2012). Examining the link between nonsuicidal self-injury and suicidal behavior: A review of the literature and an integrated model. *Clinical Psychology Review, 32*(6), 482–495. https://doi.org/10.1016/j.cpr.2012.05.003

International Society for the Study of Self-Injury. (2007). *What is self-injury?* https://itriples.org/about-self-injury/what-is-self-injury.

Iyengar, U., Snowden, N., Asarnow, J. R., Moran, P., Tranah, T., & Ougrin, D. (2018). A further look at therapeutic interventions for suicide attempts and self-harm in adolescents: An updated systematic review of randomized controlled trials. *Frontiers in Psychiatry, 9*, 1–16. https://doi.org/10.3389/fpsyt.2018.00583

Kaess, M., Edinger, A., Fischer-Waldschmidt, G., Parzer, P., Brunner, R., & Resch, F. (2020). Effectiveness of a brief psychotherapeutic intervention compared with treatment as usual for adolescent nonsuicidal self-injury: A single-centre, randomised controlled trial. *European Child and Adolescent Psychiatry, 29*(6), 881–891. https://doi.org/10.1007/s00787-019-01399-1

Kiekens, G., Hasking, P., Boyes, M., Claes, L., Mortier, P., Auerbach, R. P., Cuijpers, P., Demyttenaere, K., Green, J. G., Kessler, R. C., Myin-Germeys, I., Nock, M. K., & Bruffaerts, R. (2018). The associations between non-suicidal self-injury and first onset suicidal thoughts and behaviors. *Journal of Affective Disorders, 239*, 171–179. https://doi.org/10.1016/j.jad.2018.06.033

Kleindienst, N., Bohus, M., Ludaescher, P., Limberger, M. F., Kuenkele, K., Ebner-Priemer, U., Chapman, A. L., Reicherzer, M., Stieglitz, R. D., & Schmahl, C. (2008). Motives for non-suicidal self-injury among women with borderline personality disorder. *Journal of Nervous and Mental Disease, 196*, 230–236.

Klonsky, E. D. (2007). The functions of deliberate self-injury: A review of the evidence. *Clinical Psychology Review, 27*(2), 226–239. https://doi.org/10.1016/j.cpr.2006.08.002

Kothgassner, O. D., Robinson, K., Goreis, A., Ougrin, D., & Plener, P. L. (2020). Does treatment method matter? A meta-analysis of the past 20 years of research on therapeutic interventions for self-harm and suicidal ideation in adolescents. *Borderline Personality Disorder and Emotion Dysregulation, 7*(1), Article 9, 1–16. https://doi.org/10.1186/s40479-020-00123-9

Krantz, L. H., McMain, S., & Kuo, J. R. (2018). The unique contribution of acceptance without judgment in predicting nonsuicidal self-injury after 20-weeks of dialectical behaviour therapy group skills training. *Behaviour Research and Therapy, 104*, 44–50. https://doi.org/10.1016/j.brat.2018.02.006

Labelle, R., Pouliot, L., & Janelle, A. (2015). A systematic review and meta-analysis of cognitive behavioural treatments for suicidal and self-harm behaviours in adolescents. *Canadian Psychology, 56*(4), 368–378. https://doi.org/10.1037/a0039159

Lewis & Hasking, P. A. (2020). Rethinking self-injury recovery: A commentary and conceptual reframing. *BJPsych Bulletin, 44*(2), 44–46. https://doi.org/10.1192/bjb.2019.51

Lieb, K., Zanarini, M. C., Schmahl, C., Linehan, M. M., & Bohus, M. (2004). Borderline personality disorder. *The Lancet, 364*, 453–461.

Linehan, M. (1993a). *Cognitive-behavioral treatment of borderline personality disorder*. Guilford Press.

Linehan, M. (1993b). *Skills training manual for treating borderline personality disorder*. Guilford Press.

Linehan, M. (2015). *DBT skills training manual*. Guilford Press.

McCauley, E., Berk, M. S., Asarnow, J. R., Adrian, M., Cohen, J., Korslund, K., Avina, C., Hughes, J., Harned, M., Gallop, R., & Linehan, M. M. (2018). Efficacy of dialectical behavior therapy for adolescents at high risk for suicide a randomized clinical trial. *JAMA Psychiatry, 75*(8), 777–785. https://doi.org/10.1001/jamapsychiatry.2018.1109

McMain, S. F., Guimond, T., Barnhart, R., Habinski, L., & Streiner, D. L. (2017). A randomized trial of brief dialectical behaviour therapy skills training in suicidal patients suffering from borderline disorder. *Acta Psychiatrica Scandinavica, 135*(2), 138–148. https://doi.org/10.1111/acps.12664

Miller, W. R., & Rollnick, S. (2013). *Motivational interviewing: Helping people change* (3rd ed.). Guilford Press.

Muehlenkamp, J. J. (2006). Empirically supported treatments and general therapy guidelines for non-suicidal self-injury. *Journal of Mental Health Counseling, 28*(2), 166–185. https://doi.org/10.17744/mehc.28.2.6w61cut2lxjdg3m7

Nock, M. K., & Prinstein, M. J. (2004). A functional approach to the assessment of self-mutilative behavior. *Journal of Consulting and Clinical Psychology, 72*(5), 885–890. https://doi.org/10.1037/0022-006x.72.5.885

Rizvi, S. L. (2019). *Chain analysis in dialectical behavior therapy*. Guilford Press.

Simone, A. C., & Hamza, C. A. (2020). Examining the disclosure of nonsuicidal self-injury to informal and formal sources: A review of the literature. *Clinical Psychology Review, 82*, Article 101907. https://doi.org/10.1016/j.cpr.2020.101907

Skodol, A. E., Siever, L. J., Livesley, W. J., Gunderson, J. G., Pfohl, B., & Widiger, T. A. (2002). The borderline diagnosis II: Biology, genetics, and clinical course. *Biological Psychiatry, 51*, 951–963.

Tolin, D. F. (2016). *Doing CBT: A comprehensive guide to working with behaviors, thoughts, and emotions*. Guilford Press.

Turner, B. J., Austin, S. B., & Chapman, A. L. (2014). Treating nonsuicidal self-injury: A systematic review of psychological and pharmacological interventions. *Canadian Journal of Psychiatry, 59*(11), 576–585. https://doi.org/10.1177/070674371405901103

Whitlock, J., Muehlenkamp, J., Purington, A., Eckenrode, J., Barreira, P., Baral Abrams, G., Marchell, T., Kress, V., Girard, K., Chin, C., & Knox, K. (2011). Nonsuicidal self-injury in a college population: General trends and sex differences. *Journal of American College Health, 59*(8), 691–698. https://doi.org/10.1080/07448481.2010.529626

CHAPTER 57

Family Therapy for NSSI

Imke Baetens, Lisa Van Hove, *and* Tinne Buelens

Abstract

Over the past few decades, an increasing number of researchers have studied the treatment of nonsuicidal self-injury (NSSI) in adolescent and adult samples in both clinical and nonclinical settings. Various scholars have emphasized the importance of a motivated family, satisfactory attachment relationships, and family support in obtaining a desirable NSSI treatment outcome. Also, several forms of family-based/systemic therapies, hereinafter identified as family therapy (FT), have shown relative efficacy for the treatment of NSSI (and broader self-injurious thoughts and behaviors). Therefore, the current chapter presents an overview of the available methods and evidence for using family-based approaches (e.g., attachment-based family therapy, emotionally focused family therapy) to treat NSSI. The chapter includes guidelines for FT based on both common elements for psychotherapy (e.g., countertransference) and FT elements (e.g., addressing attachment ruptures and supporting parents or caregivers suffering from secondary stress). Challenges and future directions for clinical practice and research on FT and NSSI are discussed in the concluding paragraph, stressing the need for more tailored interventions and critical view on outcome measurements.

Key Words: nonsuicidal self-injury, treatment, family therapy, psychotherapy, interventions, family

Introduction

Nonsuicidal self-injury (NSSI) is defined "*as the deliberate, self-inflicted damage of body tissue without suicidal intent and for purposes not socially or culturally sanctioned*" (International Society for the Study of Self-Injury, n.d.), and includes methods such as cutting, burning and hitting (Baetens et al., 2011). NSSI is prevalent among all populations and age groups, with lifetime prevalence rates of approximately 9% of children ages 9–10 (Deville et al., 2020), 17% of adolescents ages 10–17, 13.7% of young adults ages 18–24 years old, and 5% of adults (Swannell et al., 2014). Using the criteria according to the fifth edition of *Diagnostic and Statistical Manual of Mental Disorders* (DSM-5; American Psychiatric Association, 2013) (e.g., presence of repetitive NSSI behaviors on at least five days in the past year), prevalence rates of 1.5%–7.6% were found in child and adolescent community samples (Buelens et al., 2020; Zetterqvist, 2015; Zetterqvist et al., 2013).

NSSI is commonly identified as a way to regulate intense emotions. In a meta-analysis of NSSI functions (see Taylor et al., this volume), researchers found intrapersonal functions, in which NSSI is a way to manage or change one's own internal state (feelings, thoughts, or physical sensations), were prevalent among 66%–81% of the individuals engaging in NSSI. Interpersonal functions, in which NSSI is used as a way to regulate their social environment (e.g., increase social support) or to communicate distress (e.g., "to show others how I'm feeling"), were endorsed by 32%–52% of the individuals engaging in NSSI (Taylor et al., 2018). Beyond the relational-related functions NSSI serves for individuals, there are a several notable interpersonal risk factors, such as childhood trauma (see Serafini et al., this volume), family factors and dynamics (see James & Gibb, this volume) and peer relationship factors (see Pollak et al., this volume, and Jarvi Steele et al., this volume).

As described in James and Gibb (this volume), NSSI is also bidirectionally related to interpersonal factors, meaning that NSSI-linked social dynamics are reinforced through engagement in NSSI. This is especially the case for family environments where families often report heightened stress and intense emotions and conflicts within the family after the disclosure of NSSI (Whitlock et al., 2018), which can, in turn, heighten risk for NSSI. For example, Baetens et al. (2014) demonstrated changes in parenting after the disclosure of NSSI, where parents tend to withdraw support (i.e., showing less warmth) and increase controlling behaviors (i.e., more harsh punishment) after the disclosure of the engagement in NSSI by their child. Furthermore, Guo et al. (2022) showed that the association between parental controlling behaviors and NSSI is mediated by parental depressive symptoms and parent-related loneliness, suggesting that NSSI-linked family dynamics may be reinforced by the presence of NSSI.

The NSSI Family Cascade Theory (Waals et al., 2018) describes the reciprocal and reinforcing cycle of families in distress after NSSI disclosure. First, parents may experience overwhelmingly intense emotions, such as fear, anger and grief. Growing escalation can cause parents to attempt to gain control over the adolescent's NSSI behavior (Baetens et al., 2015). Often, these attempts are experienced as intrusive by the adolescent, and may elevate the frequency and severity of NSSI. This, in turn, increases the pressure on the already tense family dynamic and hinders connection between family members (Waals et al., 2018). Also, this theory posits that the emotional intensity that parents may experience when trying to cope with their child's NSSI engagement may lead to what "empathy burnout," where the parent is increasingly unable to respond in an attuned manner to the adolescent's needs (Thomas, 2013; Waals et al., 2018). Empathy burnout, which may be combined with confusion, misunderstanding, or fear (Kelada et al., 2016), can lead to a sense of hopelessness, which in turn can be experienced as unsupportive, harsh, or cold for the adolescent. These negative feelings, which can result in feeling "left alone or abandoned," reinforce the likelihood of more severe and extreme forms of NSSI (and may elicit suicidal thoughts and behaviors). This reinforcing cycle prevents connection between family members and often contributes to already tense family dynamics.

Notwithstanding these negative reciprocal effects between adolescents and parents, several studies have also highlighted positive reciprocal effects and underscore the importance of supportive social networks as protective factors for NSSI continuation (e.g., Nixon & Heath, 2008; Tabaac et al. 2016). For example, Tatnell et al. (2014) described the importance of family support and connection for NSSI recovery. Also, Taliaferro et al. (2019) found that parent connectedness may buffer against adolescent NSSI engagement and youth moving from NSSI to suicide (Whitlock et al., 2013).

Treatment of NSSI

The past few decades, an increasing number of researchers have studied the treatment of NSSI in adolescent and adult samples, both in clinical and nonclinical settings. In a recent meta-analysis, based on 591 published articles with 1,125 unique RCTs over the past 50 years, Fox et al. (2020) concluded that the overall effects of intervention is significant yet small with a RR of 0.91 across all SITB (i.e., self-injurious thoughts and behaviors) outcomes. When focusing only on NSSI as a discrete outcome (based on 46 studies), Fox et al. (2020) reported no overall decrease in frequency and/or intensity of NSSI, and no moderator effect of specific intervention types. Despite the increase in interventions studies and RCTS examining treatments for NSSI, intervention efficacy has not been improved and no treatment for NSSI currently meets criteria for well "established" (Fox et al., 2020; Nock et al., 2019).

Notwithstanding the small effect sizes, several meta-reviews (Flaherty, 2021; Ougrin et al., 2015; Turner et al., 2014) point toward the following interventions as most promising for treatment of NSSI in adolescent samples: cognitive behavioral therapy (CBT-A; see Chapman et al., this volume), dialectic behavioral therapy (DBT-A; see Chapman et al., this volume), and mentalization-based treatment for adolescents (MBT-A; see Motz et al., this volume). Treatment protocols with a strong family component appear to be particularly effective in addressing NSSI, especially in an adolescent population (e.g., Brent et al., 2013; Ougrin et al., 2015). For example, Glenn et al. (2019) performed a systematic review on psychosocial treatments for NSSI in youth and concluded that NSSI was most reduced in studies that applied treatment models with family involvement. Indeed, various scholars have emphasized the importance of a motivated family, satisfactory attachment relationships, and family support to obtain a desirable NSSI treatment outcome (e.g., Muehlenkamp et al., 2013; Turner et al., 2014). Several types of family-based/systemic therapies, hereinafter identified as family therapy (FT), have shown relative efficacy for the treatment of NSSI (and broader self-injurious thoughts and behaviors, or SITBs) (Nock et al., 2019) and are therefore the main focus of this chapter.

This chapter presents a current state of the evidence for FT and an overview of the available types for a family-based approach to treat NSSI (e.g., attachment-based family therapy and emotionally focused family therapy). Opposed to other psychotherapies (such as CBT, which is more protocolized), there is less agreement among family therapists on key elements for FT. Therefore, we present some common elements for treatments of NSSI and provide an oversight of important FT techniques and approaches (e.g., addressing attachment ruptures and supporting parents or caregivers suffering from secondary stress). Next, a case example is discussed. Finally, the challenges and future directions for clinical practice and research on FT and NSSI are discussed.

Current State of Evidence for Family Therapy

Taken together, Nock et al. (2019) described family-based interventions as probably efficacious treatments for SIBTs. Although only a few studies have systematically researched the effectivity of FT approaches for SIBTs, and only a paucity focus on NSSI specifically, preliminary results are promising.

The largest randomized control trial (RCT) study to date is the SHIFT (Self-Harm Intervention: Family Therapy) study by Cottrell et al. (2018), who examined the effectiveness of FT (N = 415) on self-harm (i.e., both suicidal and nonsuicidal self-injury) compared to one-on-one treatment as usual (TAU; N = 417) in one of the 40 participating CAMHS (Child and Adolescent Mental Health Services) locations. FT was not significantly different from TAU with regard to reducing the number of emergency department visits due to self-harm (primary outcome). With regard to the secondary outcomes, FT was demonstrated to be superior to TAU with regard to improvements in prosocial behaviors and decreases in emotional problems, problems with peers, and internalizing problems at 12 and 18-months follow-up. Taking into account quality-adjusted life-years (QALY) of both adolescents and caregivers, FT was overall superior to TAU. Effects of FT are most beneficial for adolescents who reported less difficulties communicating about their emotions and/or those who reported family problems. Vice versa, the FT group was at a higher risk of engaging in self-harm in comparison to the TAU group if they reported more communicative difficulties about emotions or less family problems. These findings indicate both that FT is likely to be an efficacious dimension of NSSI treatment and that assessing and working with adolescent capacity for talking about emotions and family dynamics may augment treatment efficacy, regardless of approach.

Overall, these findings are in line with other literature in this area finding little effects of FT on SITB frequency but positive effects on an array of secondary outcomes. For example, Witt et al. (2021) recently performed a systematic review of RCTs and concluded that there is no significant effect of family interventions over (E-)TAU (i.e., enhanced treatment as usual) with regard to frequency of SITB, neither immediately after the intervention (Asarnow et al., 2017) nor at an 18-month follow-up (Cottrell et al., 2018; Witt et al., 2021). Witt et al. (2021) concluded that, overall, the currently available RCTs show little to no effect of home-based (Harrington et al., 1998) or clinic-based (Asarnow et al., 2017; Cottrell et al., 2018) family interventions for SITB. This conclusion, although tentative given the heterogeneity[1] in the operationalization of (E-)TAU, is in line with the meta-analysis of Fox et al. (2020), that no medical or psychotherapeutic treatments to date can satisfactorily decrease NSSI/SITB. However, when it comes to secondary outcomes, FT did outperform TAU and enhanced usual care (EUC). These secondary outcomes included treatment adherence, depression, hopelessness, general functioning of all family members, social functioning, suicidal ideation, and suicide (Witt et al., 2021). Given these secondary benefits, FT is likely to be an efficacious dimension of NSSI treatment and assessing and working with the family may augment treatment efficacy. For example, one key obstacle in most NSSI treatment is low adherence rates to treatment protocols. Notably, several studies show that more adolescents completed the full course of treatment when their family was involved (Cottrell et al., 2018; Harrington et al., 1998). Also, FT outperforms TAU when taken into account outcomes of all family members. Several studies have shown the detrimental effect of NSSI on the surrounding, especially family members. For example, Whitlock et al. (2018) showed that NSSI often puts a great objective and subjective strain on parents. Therefore, taking into account the outcomes of all family members, FT may be recommended for treatment of NSSI, especially when the psychological distress of family members is heightened and they find themselves trapped in negative reinforcing cycles.

In sum, we conclude that FT is a promising treatment for some adolescents engaging in NSSI, especially taking into account secondary favorable outcomes (e.g., treatment adherence) and benefits (low cost, fewer than 10 sessions, outcome for all family members). FT may be especially helpful for those adolescents who do not show any signs of alexithymia (and/or more general difficulties talking about emotions) and those families who seem to be caught in a negative distress cascade after disclosure of NSSI.

Overview of Family Therapy for the Treatment of NSSI

Family therapy is an umbrella term for several different types of systemic or FT interventions. In the following paragraph, we present a brief overview of the different FT types that might be feasible for NSSI treatment in adolescence.

In 2011, Kissil was the first to suggest attachment-based family therapy (ABFT) as a family-based approach to treat NSSI. ABFT was developed by Diamond et al. (2007) and is an empirically supported therapy treatment for adolescents who struggle with suicidality and depression. It assumes that ruptured attachment can withhold adolescents from developing adequate coping skills. In ABFT, the ruptured attachment is restored by rebuilding trust, rectifying impasses in the attachment relationship, and fostering parents' or caregivers' positive involvement in the parent-child relationship. Kissil (2011) used a case study to illustrate how ABFT improved an adolescent girl's emotion regulation by restoring a sense of security and supportive interactions with her parents. Diamond et al. (2010) conducted an RCT with two conditions, either ABFT ($n = 35$) or the EUC condition ($n = 31$) (i.e., monitored referrals to external aid providers). During the 12 weeks of treatment, the ABFT group showed a significantly greater rate of improvement in self-reported suicidal ideation and clinician-rated suicidality compared to EUC, with a strong overall effect size (ES = 0.97). However, these differences were not significant at the 24-week posttreatment follow-up visit. In 2019, Diamond et al. performed a new RCT in which suicidal and depressed adolescents (12–18 years) were either assigned to ABFT or to the Family Enhanced Non-Directive Supportive Therapy (FE-NST) condition. In FE-NST, the relationship between an adolescent and therapist is centralized as a way to enhance the adolescent's access to supportive relationships with other adults. Findings showed that the ABFT group reported a significant decrease of suicide ideation and depressive symptoms. Yet, this was also the case for FE-NST, which implies that these decreases cannot be solely attributed to ABFT. It is more likely that these decreases can be explained by elements that were used in both systems-based approaches. No studies thus far, except for the case study of Kissil (2011), has specifically examined the feasibility of ABFT to reduce NSSI, but ABFT has shown relative efficacy for the treatments of SITB and may be a promising FT approach for treatment of NSSI behaviors in adolescence.

Aside from ABFT, researchers have also examined emotionally focused family therapy (EFFT; Schade, 2013) and structural family therapy (SFT; Miner et al., 2016) to treat NSSI. Like ABFT, EFFT and SFT are also aimed at restoring a secure relationship with the parents or caregivers, as this may lead to an expansion of emotion regulation alternatives (Johnson et al., 1998; Miner et al., 2016; Schade, 2013). In EFFT, the therapist acts as a process consultant to help the family unclog emotional blockage and alter negative behavioral patterns that interrupt a family's ability to respond effectively to the needs of one another (Furrow & Palmer, 2019). In SFT, on the other hand, the therapist initially creates space between the adolescents and caregivers as this allows the therapist to assess the possible presence of disruptive family structures (e.g., coalition) and to outline clear boundaries for both the child and parents or caregivers (Minuchin, 1974). Unfortunately, the empirical evidence on both treatments is scarce. Regarding EFFT, Schade (2013) described a single case study in his article, in which the application of EFFT led to NSSI cessation. In the article in which SFT was first proposed (Miner et al., 2016), prior research was used to strengthen the suggestion to apply SFT for NSSI treatment. However, no studies to date have systematically researched the efficacy of these treatments.

Regarding psychiatric populations specifically, multifamily therapy (MFT; Asen, 2002) has been mentioned as a possible efficacious family-based treatment for SIBT (Ougrin et al., 2015) but to date has not been examined for NSSI specifically. For the treatment of anorexia nervosa, MFT has been widely studied and shows benefits over systemic single-family therapy with decreases in eating disorder (ED) symptomatology, increases in family functioning, lower dropout rates, and higher satisfaction of all family members (Terache et al., 2023). Especially, the sharing of experience with other group members, role playing in empathic responses, and diminished feelings of social isolations are key outcomes for parents (e.g., Salaminiou et al., 2017). For adolescents, several studies showed decreases in ED symptoms and elevated levels of family functioning (less conflict, more support, e.g., Depestele et al., 2017).

Another family-based intervention which yielded positive results is the Resourceful Adolescent Parent Program (RAP-P; Shochet et al., 2001), a brief interactive psychoeducation program for parents of adolescents implemented over four two-hour sessions in four weeks. Pineda and Dadds (2013) examined the feasibility for RAP-P in an outpatient adolescent population and found greater improvement in family functioning and greater reductions in adolescents' suicidal behavior and psychiatric symptoms, with a strong overall effect size. Benefits were maintained at follow-up. Interestingly, results showed that decreases in adolescent's suicidal thoughts and behaviors were largely mediated by changes in family functioning. Pineda and Dadds (2013) also point out that they managed an excellent overall participant retention rate and high satisfaction ratings from parents, despite the challenges inherent in the socioeconomically disadvantaged clientele pool.

Finally, a two-therapist model, with one therapist focusing on the youth and the other therapist on the family, showed evidence in reducing the risk for a broad range of self-harming behaviors and might therefore be a promising approach for the treatment of NSSI. For example, Esposito-Smythers et al. (2011) examined an integrated CBT (I-CBT) protocol for suicidality and co-occurring addictions. The I-CBT protocol is founded on the social cognitive learning theory, which states that adolescents must relearn adaptive ways to acquire and apply skills such as coping strategies (Bandura, 1986). To accomplish this, I-CBT is aimed at identifying the underlying behaviors and beliefs which foster substance abuse and suicidality in adolescents, and simultaneously invest in parenting skills such as monitoring and communication. The I-CBT protocol includes individual sessions with the adolescent (e.g., affect regulation), individual sessions with the parents (e.g., monitoring) and family sessions (e.g., communication) (Esposito-Smythers et al., 2011). They found a significant effect for I-CBT, with fewer suicide attempts after 18 months compared to those in the control condition. Also, Asarnow et al. (2015, 2017) developed a cognitive-behavioral family treatment (SAFETY), which aims to strengthen cognitive, behavioral, and regulatory processes in both youth and parents and to increase support and protection within the family and social environment via joint family sessions, next to individual sessions with the adolescent. Results showed a significant advantage for SAFETY in decreasing suicide attempts over the three-month treatment period and reducing the risk of a first incident suicide attempt in the follow-up period. Weaker (nonsignificant) group differences were also found for NSSI. While results of these studies are promising, caution in interpretation is needed due to relatively small trials.

In sum, these findings show that several types of FT may be efficacious for the treatment of NSSI in adolescence and that they all have similar goals which are addressed with different approaches. Next to diminishing NSSI symptomatology, several findings, as described above, highlight the extra beneficial outcomes of FT such as family satisfaction, minimizing dropout rates, and long-term effects of treatment.

FT Guidelines for Treatment of NSSI in Adolescence

As a guideline for clinicians, there is a NSSI-specific FT guideline—that can be applied in addition to individual therapy—which integrates both common factors for psychotherapy (and how to handle these as a FT) and more specific FT components.

COMMON FACTORS FOR PSYCHOTHERAPY

Three major common factors (i.e., therapeutic alliance, dealing with countertransference, and the client factors (e.g., motivation for change) are the basis for any effective psychotherapeutic treatments of NSSI.

First, the most significant common element in treatment of NSSI is the quality of the *therapeutic alliance* and an open and unprejudiced stance of the therapist toward NSSI (Miller et al., 2009). Building a strong therapeutic alliance is a necessity for any intervention for NSSI. For example, fewer NSSI episodes were reported during a DBT treatment if the client experienced the therapist as warm and protective (Bedics et al., 2012). In a FT approach, the family therapist will build and monitor the working alliance with both the adolescent and the parents. Simultaneously, the family therapist will work on establishing overarching goals within the family (Friedlander et al., 2011). The framework of multi-directed partiality as described by Boszormenyi-Nagy (2013) may guide family therapists to attune with all family members. Often this is particularly difficult in the case of NSSI behaviors as they evoke intense emotions in parents, whereas adolescents are often not motivated to cease the behavior, let alone talk about their emotions and/or NSSI in front of their parents. A family therapist should balance this line and attune with the emotions, expectations, and perspectives of the parents as well as with those of the adolescent. Furthermore, NSSI can evoke tension within FT as the adolescent often feels distrust regarding the parents and/or the parents who initially tend to focus on NSSI cessation as their primary goal. In such cases, the family therapist should avoid split alliance at all costs (i.e., the strength of the therapist's alliance differs substantially between family members) and foster both a safe environment for and a warm, empathic relationship with all family members (Friedlander et al., 2006).

A typical challenge for the family therapist in the face of working with NSSI patients is dealing with their own emotions during the session. In some cases, for example, adolescents will keep wounds "on display" in therapy and this may shock/alarm the therapist and other family members (Thompson et al., 2008). Metacommunication (i.e., communication on the mechanisms, what is happening in the room) could be helpful to handle the countertransference. The therapist may reflect on this pattern and explore which reactions this evokes from parents and themselves. This reaction in turn might challenge the therapeutic alliance or test the unconditional love of family members. On the other hand, and more often the case, adolescents refuse to talk about their NSSI behaviors, especially when parents are present. This might evoke a shift toward individual therapy (unconsciously taking over the position of safe haven of the parent) or feelings of frustration from the therapist (in line with the frustration of the parents). In sum, in case of either hiding or showing NSSI, recognizing and handling the evoked countertransference by self-reflection and metacommunication can be helpful in keeping the therapeutic alliance safe.

Next, client factors, such as, for example, *client's and system's willingness to change* (Kruzan & Whitlock, 2019) and a *tailored treatment* (Turner et al., 2014), have been identified as common factors in successful NSSI treatment. First, the focus is on a core mechanism, namely, willingness to change. This can take several forms, including understanding of what specific behaviors, attitudes, or dynamics individuals are willing and able to actually modify and how these align within families. For example, a young person may want to focus on reducing severity and urges, without full cessation as an immediate goal (see also Whitlock et al., this volume). Parents, however, may want to focus solely on NSSI cessation. Because of this, it will be important for parents and therapists to explore and establish shared goals. In most cases, dealing with NSSI urges and learning how to react/talk about NSSI are treatment goals most family members can agree upon. Furthermore, most effective therapies take into account the complexity of the client system as a whole and are therefore in nature tailored, flexible, multifaceted, and adapted (Mustafa, 2018). This might also be why protocolized treatments are not more effective than TAU, as TAU is usually multicomponent, more adapted to the person's needs, and more flexible. One should always consider that a one-fits-all protocol rarely works and the FT should invest in maximizing tailored treatments to the client system to benefit the effectivity of the treatment.

The elements described in this section (i.e., therapeutic alliance, countertransference, and client factors) are common elements relevant for all NSSI treatments. When treating NSSI from a FT approach, these will be colored by the different voices and perspectives of all family members and may sometimes feel challenging for therapists, but on the other side may bring multiple layers and dialogues when the FT embraces the complexity.

CORE COMPONENTS OF A FT APPROACH

This section present cores FT elements for NSSI treatment, including the overarching FT goal, addressing family stressors, addressing the family distress cascade, talking about the "not yet said," supporting emotion regulation of all family members, and building connection among family members (including (re)discovering positivity within the family dynamic).

First, the key goal of each family therapy is to restore connection in the family while fostering the adolescent's autonomy and individuality. In line with Erikson's developmental theory, the main developmental task in adolescence is to build autonomy and identity and shift from a strong familial focus to a strong connection with peers. This developmental task poses new challenges for all families in this life stage. Often connection and autonomy might feel as irreconcilable opposites, especially for adolescents. Nonetheless, FT will handle this conflict from a dialogical viewpoint (Rober, 2002) and considers connection and autonomy are intertwined: Where autonomy is only possible within a context of a safe family connection with the family (a safe haven to return to in times of distress), and vice versa, feeling a strong connection with family members is only possible when all family members have the feeling they can/may be autonomous individuals. Therefore, the family therapist will help parents to foster and support their child's identity formation and slowly become more independent while keeping a strong, safe connection. Parents will be supported to trust the strengths and growth of their child while being present as a safe haven.

Second, the family therapist will address family stressors, if present. Several metareviews (e.g., Arbuthnott & Lewis, 2015) have been devoted to describing some *family-related factors to increase the risk* for onset and maintenance of NSSI (for more information, James & Gibb, this volume). Therefore, addressing adverse family circumstances and patterns (e.g., high levels of conflict and criticism or familial stressors (e.g., abuse) are core elements of nearly all family therapy approaches. As discussed by Cottrell et al. (2018), FT might be particularly effective in those families with more family problems. For example, in the case of a high-conflict divorce in which negative family dynamics have a negative impact on the well-being of the child and in turn heighten the risk for NSSI (Arbuthnott & Lewis, 2015), FT often focuses on helping adolescents to handle loyalty conflicts. Overall, one key feature of FT is to explore patterns and roles of each family member and install new relational skills and dynamics. For example, emotion-focused child-rearing practices can be provided (e.g., Havighurst et al., 2020), as increasing connectedness with a caring adult is one of the mechanisms for recovery of NSSI.

That said, the FT therapist should always take into account the complexity of the relationship between symptoms and the family dynamics (Eisler et al., 2005). For some individuals, family-related risk factors may be a part of a multifaceted interaction between intra- and interpersonal risk factors (for more information, see Fox, this volume, and James & Gibb, this volume). For others, a different cause/mechanism (also see Bastiaens & Claes, this volume) may explain the onset and maintenance of the NSSI behavior. But for all, NSSI has an impact on the environment, both positive (e.g., positive changes; Whitlock et al., 2018) and negative, and this in turn is bidirectionally related to NSSI. When treating NSSI, mental health professionals should always be mindful to not (un)consciously blame the family or get trapped in a linear way of reasoning or thinking.

Indeed, in line with the *distress cascade* theory (Waals et al., 2018), a FT therapist always considers the reinforcing cycles in the family dynamics and may consider that disclosure of NSSI can lead to the parents experiencing overwhelmingly intense emotions, such as fear, anger, and grief. Parent escalation of emotion and/or empathy burnout may cause parents to increase efforts to gain control over the adolescent's NSSI behavior (Baetens et al., 2015). Often, the adolescent experiences these attempts as intrusive, which may elevate the severity of NSSI, increase the pressure on the already tense family dynamic, and hinder connection between family members (Waals et al., 2018). First, it is imperative to provide parent psychoeducation and to broaden both indirect and direct help as support networks for the family in crisis. This is in line with a review by Arbuthnott and Lewis (2015), which showed that indirect and direct help for parents is protective. Second, therapists should assist parents in learning to support their own self-care as a means to avoid feelings of "empathy burnout" and parental secondary stress.

One of the most important things a family therapist can do is to create a safe environment to talk about the "*not yet said*," such as, for example, parents' fear that their child's NSSI will lead to suicide. From a narrative perspective, the family therapist can accomplish this by examining the story behind the wounds, "If your wounds could speak, what would they say?" For example, families can be asked to reflect on emotional stresses (e.g., conflict, anger, and sadness), in such a way that family stress may manifest itself in the behavior of one of the family members. Then, the adolescent may signal to the outside world through NSSI that certain tensions in the family (e.g., absent father) are too difficult to bear. Being able to speak and listen to each other, where the different narratives are allowed to stand side by side, is thus an important cornerstone in FT.

Next enhancing emotion regulation strategies and coping capacity among all family members is another FT key element. In crisis phases, it can be helpful to introduce an emotion thermometer. The adolescent is asked to communicate about how they are feeling each day via an emotion thermometer (e.g., on a scale from 1 to 10, ranging from red 1—I cannot bear this feeling and I'm afraid of myself—vs. green 10—life is perfect). Via this technique, parents get some insight on what is going on with their child, without forcing the adolescent to talk to the parents if they do not want to. A crisis plan is made based on this thermometer, where, for example, in case of a score 1 and 2, it is a signal that the adolescent is suffering from suicidal thoughts, and they will immediately be sent to the emergency room. Gradually, parents and adolescents learn how to talk about feelings, how to cope with stressful events, and sooth oneself and others. Investing in emotional awareness and emotion labeling during sessions and at home is an important mechanism for change (for more information, see Swerdlow et al., this volume). Finally, it is worth noting that FT might work best for those adolescents who can talk about their feelings, at least with a little support and coaxing. Adolescents with alexithymia or severe deficits in emotion recognition and communication are better referred to individual treatments before engaging in FT approaches.

Furthermore, all systemic approaches have another main goal, which is restoring trust and connection between family members. As such, adolescents will regain trust and experience a corrective attachment experience. The family therapist should emphasize the importance of being together in the same space, being able to speak and listen to each other, and allowing the different narratives to stand side by side. The family therapist may also emphasize the importance of engaging in joint activities to strengthen the sense of connection. Preferably these joint activities do not entail any communication in the beginning of the therapy (such as movie night or going for a run together without talking). While the therapy process evolves, the family therapist might explore activities that are focused on connection (e.g., family rituals such as pizza night or game evenings). These joint activities aim to focus on the family's strengths and help to (re)discover positivity within the family dynamic. Whitlock and Lloyd-Richardson (2019) also developed an exercise "List of family strengths" where parents and their adolescents could be invited to indicate which items apply most to their family. This varied list, containing among others "*We have enjoyable memories with each other*" and "*We trust each other*," ensures that most families will be able to find one or more shared strengths (i.e., Whitlock & Lloyd-Richardson, 2019). The parents and their child can then be invited to come up with a written/visual/metaphorical/... reminder of this shared strength, which can be helpful for each family member to foster resilience during current or later times of crisis.

Case Example

This case example illustrates the FT approach and its common effective components in youth who engage in NSSI.

Mr. and Mrs. Doe have been married for 23 years and are parents to John, age 17, and Jane, age 14. The teenage years of both their children have been tumultuous. With John, they constantly clashed over his nonchalant attitude when it came to his grades and fulfilling his academic potential. At age 16, John nearly dropped out of high school after an incident where he was caught using and selling drugs on the school grounds. The incident left Mr. and Mrs. Doe feeling confounded and ashamed as they could not grasp how this could have happened. Around the same time, Jane, who had been an exemplary and high-achieving pupil in primary school, had started her adolescence with a vengeance. Mr. and Mrs. Doe felt like they did not recognize their once soft-tempered daughter, as she suddenly rebelled against every boundary they tried to set. After two years of high school, Jane had become a stranger to her parents, both in the way she looked with her now brightly dyed hair and multiple ear piercings, as in their relationship, which had become strained and distant.

At a doctor's visit for her daughter, Mrs. Doe panicked as she noticed recent cuts and burn wounds on her daughter's forearms. Feeling overwhelmed by worry and anxiousness about Jane being suicidal, Mrs. Doe broke down crying in the car on the way home. What follows is a fierce conflict between her and her daughter, where a terribly upset Mrs. Doe fires endless questions about when, where, and how Jane has self-injured and Jane reacting first hostile and then careless and distant about the self-injury. Mrs. Doe is left with no answers to her questions and Jane feels attacked, misunderstood, and annoyed by the whole situation. For the next month, Mrs. Doe brings up the self-injury constantly and persists for so long that Jane agrees to go to therapy in an attempt to stop her mother's nagging.

Despite her initial suspicion, Jane quickly opens up to her individual therapist about the confusion she experiences about who she is (identity crisis): She feels caught between wanting to belong to a group of popular but sometimes vicious girls at school and wanting to stand out as an individual. She often ends up feeling lonely, confused, and tearful. After discovering self-injury through a friend at school, she shares with her therapist how self-injury "tones down my mind when I feel like I'm in overdrive." Jane comes across as a confused and emotionally volatile adolescent but also intelligent and able to reflect upon her inner world with some support from her therapist in identifying and labeling her emotions. With Jane's permission, Mr. and Mrs. Doe are invited to a separate FT intake session with the goal of later seeing all three of them together for a series of family therapy sessions.

During Mr. and Mrs. Doe's FT intake, it quickly becomes clear how their marriage is starting to show some cracks under the pressure of their teens' difficulties. Mrs. Doe has started to work part time in an attempt to keep an eye on Jane as she states feeling like "Jane is slipping through my fingers." Mr. Doe disagrees very strongly and openly with his wife's decision. He feels like Jane is manipulating Mrs. Doe and "her cutting has our whole family in a stranglehold." He additionally outs his frustration on Jane defying all the restrictions that were previously put in place, specifically her curfew, as he sees her group of friends as part of the problem. Wanting to avoid conflict with his wife on this subject, Mr. Doe feels powerless and excluded from his own family. Mrs. Doe interprets her husband stepping aside as carelessness and feels isolated and helpless with her daughter. Their different approaches and loss of connection were adding fuel to the fire, but in therapy some ruptures are repaired by pointing out their shared anger, sadness, disappointment, and fear about Jane's self-injury. Additionally, efforts are made to put additional support systems in place, with monthly couple consultations and encouragement to reach out to their mutual friends and some trusted family members.

FT sessions allow the Doe family neutral ground to speak about the self-injury for the first time without the conversation escalating into a conflict. The therapist supports each family member to share their perspective and listen carefully to others, accepting that someone else's experience can be somewhat different from their own. With the therapist modeling respectful and empathic curiosity about each perspective, all three family members start to slowly open up to each other, leading to some early signs of reconnection and reestablished communication. For instance, when Mrs. Doe disclosed that she interpreted Jane's initial secrecy about the self-injury as a lack of trust in their mother-daughter bond, Jane was able to verbalize how she hid her self-injury because she was ashamed and scared to upset or disappoint her mother. As another example, when Jane spoke about how she perceived her father's lack of interest in her as a confirmation of her self-image as "worthless" and "a hopeless case," she shared a vulnerable and tearful moment with her father, who expressed how his feeling of powerlessness and frustration had resulted in him taking a step back. Although by no means every session leads to these breakthrough moments, the foundation is laid for a more communicative and less overheated family dynamic.

Besides fostering this new communication, Mr. and Mrs. Doe are supported in setting age-appropriate boundaries for Jane. Psychoeducation on the nonsuicidal aspect of self-injury, normalizing some of the developmental issues Jane is facing, and reassuring the importance of providing limits even in the face of crisis provides sufficient groundwork for Mr. and Mrs. Doe to pick up some of the rules they had let go and stick with them, but also fostering the wish for autonomy of Jane and giving her more "freedom." Additionally, John is invited to a family therapy session and some mutual shame and sadness about letting go of the image of a "picture-perfect family" even gets addressed. The presence of John makes Jane feel less singled out as the "problem child" and is the therapist's cue to start moving from a focus on self-injury to a broader perspective on family functioning. The aim is to bring the moments of (re)connection as they happen in therapy to the family home, and the therapist introduces some tools such as a "weekly check-in" and a crisis plan. Although a long road might lie ahead of the Doe family, family therapy provided some gear for along the way and reintroduced tranquility in their family dynamic.

Discussion

Although most of NSSI treatments are mainly individual-focused and behaviorally based (Bean et al., 2021), systems-based approaches are gradually gaining more attention as a useful addition to individual behaviorally based NSSI treatment (Freeman et al., 2016). Researchers have confirmed the importance of including the family system in NSSI treatment. For example, studies found a larger decrease in the number of NSSI episodes if the family system was involved in the treatment (Brent et al., 2013; Ougrin et al., 2015).

In family systems therapy, the focus lies on providing each person in the system the opportunity to understand their own role in the family process and to try newly learned relational skills to recover trust between family members (Diamond et al., 2016). For parents or caregivers, this entails being resilient and having enough mental space in the midst of an emotional and stressful context (Arbuthnott & Lewis, 2015), elicited by NSSI disclosure (Whitlock et al., 2018). FT may counter the negative distress cascade of families after discovery of NSSI by supporting families in connecting again through facilitating communication. Indeed, studies show that striving for connection may lead to successful NSSI treatment outcomes (Baetens et al., 2021).

Future Directions in Research

Preliminary research shows that FT (or at least a dual-therapist model) might be a promising approach for treatment of NSSI in adolescence, especially given the unique benefits of FT superior to other forms of treatments such as treatment adherence, QALY for all family members, less intensive treatments (opposed to, for example, IPT/DBT). Future research is urgently needed on different fronts: first, more robust RCT research is needed to examine the potential effects and outcome relevant for FT, such as treatment adherence, satisfaction (of all family members), long-term sustainability of effects, and general family functions. Also, longer follow-up measurements should be taken into account to examine the potential long-term effects of psychotherapy. Furthermore, treatment studies should also broaden our scope when examining effectivity of treatment, based on recovery research (e.g., see Whitlock et al., this volume), where cessation of NSSI is often not a target but feelings of personal growth, connectedness with others (especially family members), beliefs in one's own strength, and resilience are important outcomes to take into account. Also, next to empirically robust RCT research, future research needs to use more naturalistic and ecologically valid intervention studies and noninferiority designs (Leichsenring et al., 2018). Finally, several metareviews (i.e., Ougrin et al., 2015) have shown TAU (especially enhanced TAU) is often as effective as the targeted psychological treatment protocol, which might be explained by the flexibility of the (enhanced) TAU to individually tailor the treatment. In line with several other scholars in this book (i.e., Westlund Schreiner et al., this volume, and Rockstroh & Kaess, this volume), our NSSI research field should first and foremost invest research on individually tailored interventions. Systematic process monitoring (Stinckens et al., 2012) is a promising approach to support tailored treatments. With regard to the potential negative effects of continuous tracking of NSSI behaviors (and therefore prompting the attention to NSSI acts and urges), the main focus should be on process monitoring (and not as much on behavioral outcome monitoring), as this will benefit the work alliance between therapists and clients, the attunement of the therapist, and work with potential (counter)transference, which are common elements for psychotherapies, especially when working with clients who engage in NSSI.

Conclusion

NSSI is relatively common in adolescence and has a demonstrated and pronounced impact on both the adolescent and those around them. Systematic research on the effectiveness of family therapy has been limited to date but shows some promising results. In this chapter we have described some key elements for FT treatment of NSSI such as strengthening family cohesion and communication and repairing attachment issues, among others. Future research is urgently needed to examine the effectivity of FT robustly, taking into account these key elements.

Note

1. Specifically, E-TAU as implemented by Asarnow et al. (2017) did include an in-clinic parent session, psychoeducation for parents, and follow-up parent telephone calls aimed at improving treatment attendance. Cottrell et al. (2018), on the other hand, deemed it impossible to specify TAU in their study, given the large number of practitioners involved. They did anticipate the TAU to be diverse and possibly to include both individual and family-orientated work.

References

American Psychiatric Association. (2013). *Diagnostic and statistical manual of mental disorders* (5th ed., text rev.). https://doi.org/10.1176/appi.books.9780890425787

Arbuthnott, A. E., & Lewis, S. P. (2015). Parents of youth who self-injure: A review of the literature and implications for mental health professionals. *Child and Adolescent Psychiatry and Mental Health*, *9*(1), 1–20. https://doi.org/10.1186/s13034-015-0066-3

Asarnow, J. R., Berk, M., Hughes, J. L., & Anderson, N. L. (2015). The SAFETY program: A treatment-development trial of a cognitive-behavioral family treatment for adolescent suicide attempters. *Journal of Clinical Child & Adolescent Psychology*, *44*(1), 194–203. https://doi.org/10.1080/15374416.2014.940624

Asarnow, J. R., Hughes, J. L., Babeva, K. N., & Sugar, C. A. (2017). Cognitive-behavioral family treatment for suicide attempt prevention: A randomized controlled trial. *Journal of the American Academy of Child & Adolescent Psychiatry*, *56*(6), 506–514. https://doi.org/10.1016/j.jaac.2017.03.015

Asen, E. (2002). Multiple family therapy: An overview. *Journal of Family Therapy*, *24*, 3–16. https://doi.org/10.1111/1467-6427.00197

Baetens, I., Claes, L., Martin, G., Onghena, P., Grietens, H., Van Leeuwen, K., Pieters, C., Wiersema, J. R., & Griffith, J. W. (2014). Is nonsuicidal self-injury associated with parenting and family factors? *Journal of Early Adolescence*, *34*(3), 387–405. https://doi.org/10.1177/0272431613494006

Baetens, I., Claes, L., Muehlenkamp, J., Grietens, H., & Onghena, P. (2011). Non-suicidal and suicidal self-injurious behavior among Flemish adolescents: A web-survey. *Archives of Suicide Research*, *15*(1), 56–67. https://doi.org/10.1080/13811118.2011.540467

Baetens, I., Claes, L., Onghena, P., Grietens, H., Van Leeuwen, K., Pieters, C., Wiersema, J. R., & Griffith, J. W. (2015). The effects of nonsuicidal self-injury on parenting behaviors: A longitudinal analyses of the perspective of the parent. *Child and Adolescent Psychiatry and Mental Health*, *9*(1), 1–6. https://doi.org/10.1186/s13034-015-0059-2

Baetens, I., De ridder, L., & Buelens, T. (2021). Systeemtherapeutische behandeling bij opzettelijk zelfverwondend gedrag. *Tijdschrift Systeemtherapie*, *34*(1).

Bandura, A. (1986). *Social foundations of thought and action: A social cognitive theory*. Prentice Hall.

Bean, R. A., Keenan, B. H., & Fox, C. (2021). Treatment of adolescent non-suicidal self-injury: A review of family factors and family therapy. *The American Journal of Family Therapy*, *50*(3), 264–279. https://doi.org/10.1080/01926187.2021.1909513

Bedics, J. D., Atkins, D. C., Comtois, K. A., & Linehan, M. M. (2012). Treatment differences in the therapeutic relationship and introject during a 2-year randomized controlled trial of dialectical behavior therapy versus nonbehavioral psychotherapy experts for borderline personality disorder. *Journal of Consulting and Clinical Psychology*, *80*(1), 66–77. https://doi.org/10.1037/a0026113

Boszormenyi-Nagy, I. K. (2013). *Between give and take: A clinical guide to contextual therapy*. Routledge.

Brent, D. A., McMakin, D. L., Kennard, B. D., Goldstein, T. R., Mayes, T. L., & Douaihy, A. B. (2013). Protecting adolescents from self-harm: A critical review of intervention studies. *Journal of the American Academy of Child & Adolescent Psychiatry*, *52*(12), 1260–1271. https://doi.org/10.1016/j.jaac.2013.09.009

Buelens, T., Luyckx, K., Kiekens, G., Gandhi, A., Muehlenkamp, J. J., & Claes, L. (2020). Investigating the DSM-5 criteria for non-suicidal self-injury disorder in a community sample of adolescents. *Journal of Affective Disorders*, *260*, 314–322. https://doi.org/10.1016/j.jad.2019.09.009

Cottrell, D. J., Wright-Hughes, A., Collinson, M., Boston, P., Eisler, I., Fortune, S., Graham, E. H., Green, J., House, A. O., Kerfoot, M., Owens, D. W., Saloniki, E., Smic, M., Lambert, F., Rothwell, J., Tubeuf, S., & Farrin, A. J. (2018). Effectiveness of systemic family therapy versus treatment as usual for young people after self-harm: A pragmatic, phase 3, multicentre, randomised controlled trial. *Lancet Psychiatry*, *5*(3), 203–216. https://doi.org/10.1016/S2215-0366(18)30058-0

Depestele, L., Claes, L., Dierckx, E., Colman, R., Schoevaerts, K., & Lemmens, G. M. D. (2017). An adjunctive multi-family group intervention with or without patient participation during an inpatient treatment for adolescents with an eating disorder: A pilot study. *European Eating Disorders Review*, *35*(6), 570–578. https://doi.org/10.1002/erv.2556

Deville, D. C., Whalen, D., Breslin, F. J., Morris A. S., Khalsa, S. S., Paulus, M. P., & Barch, D. M. (2020). Prevalence and family-related factors associated with suicidal ideation, suicide attempts, and self-injury in children aged 9 to 10 years. *JAMA Network Open*, *3*(2), e1920956. https://doi.org/10.1001/jamanetworkopen.2019.20956

Diamond, G. M., Diamond, G. S., & Hogue, A. (2007). Attachment-based family therapy: Adherence and differentiation. *Journal of Marital and Family Therapy*, *33*(2), 177–191. https://doi.org/10.1111/j.1752-0606.2007.00015.x

Diamond, G. S., Kobak, R. R., Ewing, E. S. K., Levy, S. A., Herres, J. L., Russon, J. M., & Gallop, R. J. (2019). A randomized-controlled trial: Attachment-based family and non-directive supportive treatments for suicidal youth. *Journal of the American Academy of Child & Adolescent Psychiatry*, *58*(7), 721–731. https://doi.org/10.1016/j.jaac.2018.10.006

Diamond, G. S., Russon, J., & Levy, S. (2016). Attachment-based family therapy: A review of the empirical support. *Family Process*, *55*(3), 595–610. https://doi.org/10.1111/famp.12241

Diamond, G. S., Wintersteen, M. B., Brown, G. K., Diamond, G. M., Gallop, R., Shelef, K., & Levy, S. (2010). Attachment-based family therapy for adolescents with suicidal ideation: A randomized controlled trial. *Journal of the American Academy of Child & Adolescent Psychiatry*, *49*(2), 122–131. https://doi.org/10.1016/j.jaac.2009.11.002

Eisler, I. (2005). The empirical and theoretical base of family therapy and multiple family day therapy for adolescent anorexia nervosa. *Journal of Family Therapy*, *27*(2), 104–131. https://doi.org/10.1111/j.1467-6427.2005.00303.x

Esposito-Smythers, C., Spirito, A., Kahler, C. W., Hunt, J., & Monti, P. (2011). Treatment of co-occurring substance abuse and suicidality among adolescents: A randomized trial. *Journal of Consulting & Clinical Psychology*, *79*(6), 728–739. https://doi.org/10.1037/a0026074

Flaherty, H. B. (2021). Treating adolescent non-suicidal self-injury: Guidelines for clinical practice. *Child & Youth Services*, *42*(4), 393–410. https://doi.org/10.1080/0145935X.2021.1938525

Fox, K. R., Huang, X., Guzmán, E. M., Funsch, K. M., Cha, C. B., Ribeiro, J. D., & Franklin, J. C. (2020). Interventions for suicide and self-injury: A meta-analysis of randomized controlled trials across nearly 50 years of research. *Psychological Bulletin*, *146*(12), 1117. https://doi.org/10.1037/bul0000305

Freeman, K. R., James, S., Klein, K. P., Mayo, D., & Montgomery, S. (2016). Outpatient dialectical behavior therapy for adolescents engaged in deliberate self-harm: Conceptual and methodological considerations. *Child and Adolescent Social Work Journal*, *33*(2), 123–135. https://doi.org/10.1007/s10560-015-0412-6

Friedlander, M. L., Escudero, V., & Heatherington, L. (2006). *Therapeutic alliances in couple and family therapy: An empirically informed guide to practice*. American Psychological Association.

Friedlander, M. L., Escudero, V., Heatherington, L., & Diamond, G. M. (2011). Alliance in couple and family therapy. *Psychotherapy*, *48*(1), 25–33. https://doi.org/10.1037/a0022060

Furrow, J. L., & Palmer, G. (2019). Emotionally focused family therapy. In J. L. Lebow, A. L. Chambers, & D. C. Breunlin (Eds.), *Encyclopedia of couple and family therapy* (pp. 879–884). Springer, Cham. https://doi.org/10.1007/978-3-319-49425-8_900

Glenn, C. R., Esposito, E. C., Porter, A. C., & Robinson, D. J. (2019). Evidence based update of psychosocial treatments for self-injurious thoughts and behaviors in youth. *Journal of Clinical Child & Adolescent Psychology*, *48*(3), 357–392. https://doi.org/10.1080/15374416.2019.1591281

Guo, J., Gao, Q., Wu, R., Ying, J., & You, J. (2022). Parental psychological control, parent-related loneliness, depressive symptoms, and regulatory emotional self-efficacy: A moderated serial mediation model of nonsuicidal self-injury. *Archives of Suicide Research*, *26*(3), 1462–1477.

Harrington, R., Whittaker, J., & Shoebridge, P. (1998). Psychological treatment of depression in children and adolescents: A review of treatment research. *British Journal of Psychiatry*, *173*(4), 291–298. https://doi.org/10.1192/bjp.173.4.291

Havighurst, S. S., Radovini, A., Hao, B., & Kehoe, C. E. (2020). Emotion-focused parenting interventions for prevention and treatment of child and adolescent mental health problems: A review of recent literature. *Current Opinion in Psychiatry*, *33*(6), 586–601. https://doi.org/10.1097/YCO.0000000000000647

International Society for the Study of Self-Injury. (n.d.). What is non-suicidal self-injury? https://www.itriples.org/what-is-nssi

Johnson, S. M., Maddeaux, C., & Blouin, J. (1998). Emotionally focused family therapy for bulimia: Changing attachment patterns. *Psychotherapy*, *35*(2), 238–247. https://doi.org/10.1037/h0087728.

Kelada, L., Whitlock, J., Hasking, P., & Melvin, G. (2016). Parents' experiences of nonsuicidal self-injury among adolescents and young adults. *Journal of Child and Family Studies*, *25*(11), 3403–3416. https://doi.org/10.1007/s10826-016-0496-4

Kissil, K. (2011). Attachment-based family therapy for adolescent self-injury. *Journal of Family Psychotherapy*, *22*(4), 313–327. https://doi.org/10.1080/08975353.2011.627801

Kruzan, K. P., & Whitlock, J. (2019). Processes of change and nonsuicidal self-injury: A qualitative interview study with individuals at various stages of change. *Global Qualitative Nursing Research*, *6*, 1–15. https://doi.org/10.1177/2333393619852935

Leichsenring, F., Abbass, A., Driessen, E., Hilsenroth, M., Luyten, P., Rabung, S., & Steinert, C. (2018). Equivalence and non-inferiority testing in psychotherapy research. *Psychological Medicine*, *48*(11), 1917–1919. https://doi.org/10.1017/S0033291718001289

Miller, A. L., Muehlenkamp, J. J., & Jacobson, C. M. (2009). Special issues in treating adolescent nonsuicidal self-injury. In M. K. Nock (Ed.), *Understanding nonsuicidal self-injury: Origins, assessment, and treatment* (pp. 251–270). American Psychological Association. https://doi.org/10.1037/11875-013

Miner, C. L., Love, H. A., & Paik, S. E. (2016). Non-suicidal self-injury in adolescents: Addressing the function and the family from the perspective of systemic family therapies. *The American Journal of Family Therapy*, *44*(4), 211–220. https://doi.org/10.1080/01926187.2016.1150798

Minuchin, S. (1974). *Families and family therapy*. Harvard University Press.

Muehlenkamp, J., Brausch, A., Quigley, K., & Whitlock, J. (2013). Interpersonal features and functions of nonsuicidal self-injury. *Suicide and Life-Threatening Behavior*, *43*(1), 67–80. https://doi.org/10.1111/j.1943-278X.2012.00128.x

Mustafa, F. A. (2018). Randomised controlled trials for multisystemic therapy: When is enough, enough? *The Lancet Psychiatry*, *5*(5), 390. https://doi.org/10.1016/S2215-0366(18)30098-1

Nixon, M. K., & Heath, N. L. (Eds.). (2008). *Self-injury in youth: The essential guide to assessment and intervention*. Taylor & Francis.

Nock, M. K., Boccagno, C. E., Kleiman, E. M., Ramirez, F., & Wang, S. B. (2019). Suicidal and nonsuicidal self-injury. In M. J. Prinstein, E. A. Youngstrom, E. J. Mash, & R. A. Barkley (Eds.), *Treatment of disorders in childhood and adolescence* (pp. 258–277). Guilford Press.

Ougrin, D., Tranah, T., Stahl, D., Moran, P., & Asarnow, J. R. (2015). Therapeutic interventions for suicide attempts and self-harm in adolescents: Systematic review and meta-analysis. *Journal of the American Academy of Child & Adolescent Psychiatry*, *54*(2), 97–107. https://doi.org/10.1016/j.jaac.2014.10.009

Pineda, J., & Dadds, M. R. (2013). Family intervention for adolescents with suicidal behavior: A randomized controlled trial and mediation analysis. *Journal of the American Academy of Child & Adolescent Psychiatry*, *52*(8), 851–862. https://doi.org/10.1016/j.jaac.2013.05.015

Rober, P. (2002). *Samen in therapie: Gezinstherapie als dialoog*. Acco.

Salaminiou, E., Campbell, M., Simic, M., Kuipers, E., & Eisler, I. (2017). Intensive multi-family therapy for adolescent anorexia nervosa: An open study of 30 families. *Journal of Family Therapy*, *39*(4), 498–513. https://doi.org/10.1111/1467-6427.12075

Schade, L. C. (2013). Non-suicidal self-injury (NSSI): A case for using Emotionally Focused Family Therapy. *Contemporary Family Therapy*, *35*(3), 568–582. https://doi.org/10.1007%2Fs10591-013-9236-8

Shochet, I. M., Dadds, M. R., Holland, D., Whitefield, K., Harnett, P. H., & Osgarby, S. M. (2001). The efficacy of a universal school-based program to prevent adolescent depression. *Journal of Clinical Child & Adolescent Psychology*, *30*(3), 303–315. https://doi.org/10.1207/S15374424JCCP3003_3

Stinckens, N., Smits, D., Claes, L., & Soenen, S. (2012). Meaningful romming (routine outcome monitoring): Seeking a balance between user friendliness and clinical relevance. *Tijdschrift Voor Psychiatrie*, *54*(2), 161–165.

Swannell, S. V., Martin, G. E., Page, A., Hasking, P., & St. John, N. J. (2014). Prevalence of nonsuicidal self-injury in nonclinical samples: Systematic review, meta-analysis and meta-regression. *Suicide and Life-Threatening Behavior*, *44*(3), 273–303. https://doi.org/10.1111/sltb.12070

Tabaac, A. R., Perrin, P. B., & Rabinovitch, A. E. (2016). The relationship between social support and suicide risk in a national sample of ethnically diverse sexual minority women. *Journal of Gay & Lesbian Mental Health*, *20*(2), 116–126. https://doi.org/10.1080/19359705.2015.1135842

Taliaferro, L. A., McMorris, B. J., Rider, G. N., & Eisenberg, M. E. (2019). Risk and protective factors for self-harm in a population-based sample of transgender youth. *Archives of Suicide Research*, *23*(2), 203–221. https://doi.org/10.1080/13811118.2018.1430639

Tatnell, R., Kelada, L., Hasking, P., & Martin, G. (2014). Longitudinal analysis of adolescent NSSI: The role of intrapersonal and interpersonal factors. *Journal of Abnormal Child Psychology*, *42*(6), 885–896. https://doi.org/10.1007/s10802-013-9837-6

Taylor, P. J., Jomar, K., Dhingra, K., Forrester, R., Shahmalak, U., & Dickson, J. M. (2018). A meta-analysis of the prevalence of different functions of non-suicidal self-injury. *Journal of Affective Disorders*, *227*, 759–769. https://doi.org/10.1016/j.jad.2017.11.073

Terache, J., Wollast, R., Simon, Y., Marot, M., Van der Linden, N., Franzen, A., & Klein, O. (2023). Promising effect of multi-family therapy on BMI, eating disorders and perceived family functioning in adolescent anorexia nervosa: An uncontrolled longitudinal study. *Eating Disorders, 31*(1), 64–84. https://doi.org/10.1080/10640266.2022.2069315

Thomas, J. (2013). Association of personal distress with burnout, compassion fatigue, and compassion satisfaction among clinical social workers. *Journal of Social Service Research, 39*(3), 365–379. https://doi.org/10.1080/01488376.2013.771596

Thompson, A. R., Powis, J., & Carradice, A. (2008). Community psychiatric nurses' experience of working with people who engage in deliberate self-harm. *International Journal of Mental Health Nursing, 17*(3), 153–161. https://doi.org/10.1111/j.1447-0349.2008.00533.x

Turner, B. J., Austin, S. B., & Chapman, A. L. (2014). Treating nonsuicidal self-injury: A systematic review of psychological and pharmacological interventions. *La Revue Canadienne de Psychiatrie, 59*(11), 576–585. https://doi.org/10.1177/070674371405901103

Waals, L., Baetens, I., Rober, P., Lewis, S., Van Parys, H., Goethals, E. R., & Whitlock, J. (2018). The NSSI family distress cascade theory. *Child and Adolescent Psychiatry and Mental Health, 12*(1), 1–6. https://doi.org/10.1186/s13034-018-0259-7

Whitlock, J., & Lloyd-Richardson, E. E. (2019). *Healing self-injury: A compassionate guide for parents and other loved ones*. Oxford University Press.

Whitlock, J., Lloyd-Richardson, E. E., Fisseha, F., & Bates, T. (2018). Parental secondary stress: The often hidden consequences of nonsuicidal self-injury in youth. *Journal of Clinical Psychology, 74*(1), 178–197. https://doi.org/10.1002/jclp.22488

Whitlock, J., Muehlenkamp, J., Eckenrode, J., Purington, A., Barrera, P., Baral-Abrams, G., Kress, V., Grace Martin, K, Smith, E., (2013). Non-suicidal self-injury as a gateway to suicide in adolescents and young adults. *Journal of Adolescent Health, 52*(4), 486–492. https://doi.org/10.1016/j.jadohealth.2012.09.010

Witt, K. G., Hetrick, S. E., Rajaram, G., Hazell, P., Salisbury, T. L. T., Townsend, E., & Hawton, K. (2021). Psychosocial interventions for self-harm in adults. *Cochrane Database of Systematic Reviews, 4*(5), Article CD013668. https://doi.org/10.1002/14651858.CD013668.pub2

Zetterqvist, M. (2015). The DSM-5 diagnosis of nonsuicidal self-injury disorder: A review of the empirical literature. *Child and Adolescent Psychiatry and Mental Health, 9*(1), 1–13. https://doi.org/10.1186/s13034-015-0062-7

Zetterqvist, M., Lundh, L., Dahlström, Ö., & Svedin, C. G. (2013). Prevalence and function of non-suicidal self-injury (NSSI) in a community sample of adolescents, using suggested DSM-5 criteria for a potential NSSI disorder. *Journal of Abnormal Child Psychology, 41*(5), 759–773. https://doi.org/10.1007/s10802-013-9712-5

CHAPTER 58
Mentalizing and Psychodynamic Approaches to Nonsuicidal Self-Injury

Anna Motz, Anthony Bateman, Peter Fonagy, *and* Patrick Luyten

Abstract

This chapter covers the mentalizing and psychodynamic approaches to nonsuicidal self-injury (NSSI). It explains that the communicative and meaningful aspects of NSSI can be found in mentalization-based treatment approaches, which are part of the family of psychodynamic treatments. The mentalization-based therapy (MBT) model conceptualizes NSSI and provides further elaboration on the more traditional psychodynamic approaches to self-harm. MBT operates using an approach that addresses the underlying difficulties in integrating thoughts and feelings while also resisting the urge to find action-based interventions for painful thoughts and emotions. The chapter also mentions the efficacy of the treatment in reducing the major public health issue of NSSI.

Key Words: mentalizing, psychodynamic approaches, nonsuicidal self-injury, self-harm, mentalization-based therapy, thoughts, emotions, public health issue

Introduction

Nonsuicidal self-injury (NSSI) is a major public health concern (García-Nieto et al., 2015), with lifetime prevalence rates in adulthood reported as ranging between 5.9% (Klonsky, 2011) and 23.2% (Muehlenkamp & Gutierrez, 2007). The lifetime prevalence of NSSI in international adolescent community-based populations has been found to be between 18% and 25% (Muehlenkamp et al., 2012; Swannell et al., 2014). There are also indications that NSSI is becoming more prevalent. A recent report in the United Kingdom, for instance, reported that the prevalence of NSSI in young women and girls nearly tripled since the year 2000, but this was not matched by a rise in the use of health or other support services by patients who self-harm (Agenda and the National Centre for Social Research, 2020). While we consider self-injury without suicidal intent (NSSI) to be a distinct phenomenon from those acts committed with an intention to die, it is evident that NSSI increases the risk of actual suicide and is in itself an urgent area for assessment and treatment (Gillies et al., 2018). An emphasis on the communicative and meaningful aspects of NSSI can be found in mentalization-based treatment approaches, which are part of the family of psychodynamic treatments.

In addition to suicidal ideation and behavior, NSSI has increasingly been a subject generating significant interest. While NSSI is an important clinical issue in its own right (American Psychiatric Association, 2013) it is now recognized as being a more robust prospective predictor of suicide attempts than a past history of suicide attempts (Ribeiro et al., 2016; see Victor et al., this volume). NSSI in women and girls occurs at a greater frequency than for men and boys; women ages 18–33 were significantly more likely to report past-year NSSI than men and their greater psychological distress contributed to their higher NSSI prevalence (Lutz et al., 2022). Various factors can be cited as contributory to the higher rates of NSSI in recent years including the prevalence of self-harm sites on social media (see Westers, this volume), the increasing pressures on young people created by social media, and the restrictions and anxiety created by the COVID-19 pandemic. Differences in rates of NSSI according to gender are also found in particular populations, including the female prison population (Ministry of Justice, 2021).

This chapter offers an overview of the development of NSSI using a mentalization-based framework. First, we outline a psychodynamic understanding of NSSI and describe how a mentalization-based therapy (MBT) model conceptualizes it. This is followed by a synopsis of how MBT conceptualizes NSSI, as a psychodynamic treatment approach that also incorporates aspects of DBT, CBT, and systemic therapy. We offer two clinical case examples to illustrate basic treatment principles of MBT, and to describe how such treatment addresses the important issues of NSSI. The first focuses on the principles of treatment using MBT for NSSI, and the second for treatment of someone presenting with both violence against herself and against others. We then conclude, with recommendations for treatment using the MBT approach.

Development of NSSI

A Psychodynamic Understanding of the Development and Maintenance of NSSI

A psychodynamic perspective on self-harm and suicidal behavior focuses on emotional experience, unconscious meaning, and interpretation within a relational framework (Yakeley & Burbridge-James, 2018). An understanding of the possible unconscious meanings and functions of apparently self-destructive acts informs the assessment, treatment, and management of people who engage in these. This model further holds that early experience, particularly in relation to primary caregivers, shapes an infant's sense of self and creates a template for development that can influence their relationship with others and with themselves across the lifespan, often without their conscious awareness. Attacks on their own bodies by adolescents can be viewed as attempts to create a separation from their primary carer, and may also express unconscious acts of hostility toward them. The force of sexual and aggressive impulses that strengthen in adolescence can now find their expression in action, rather than simply fantasy, and the guilt over these unacceptable feelings may also contribute to the young person wanting to punish themselves, and their bodies, through NSSI, sometimes taking risks that result in their death, though this was not their intention (Anderson, 2008).

This view is consistent with high rates of early adversity and attachment trauma in particular young people who self-harm, and the emergence of these problems typically increases in adolescence coinciding with emergence of sexuality and physical aggression (Wright et al., 2005).

As Freud (1923) described, the body ego is the first ego, and so infants gain a sense of themselves, their boundaries, and their feelings through this body and how it is treated by another. Freud proposed that the mind and its experiences originally develop from the body and its experiences (Freud, 1923). The centrality of and deep connection between body and mind have further been explored and described by psychoanalytic authors including the child psychoanalyst Esther Bick (1968), in her discussion of how maternal care directly impacts on the infant's sense of its skin, and Didier Anzieu (2016), whose discussion of the containing envelope of the skin helps us to see how attacks on this essential organ can serve as means of both locating and displacing aggression onto the body. This kind of self-directed violence can also serve as unconscious punishment toward the self and significant others, notably the parents, who have given birth to this individual. In suicidal states of mind, the person is enacting unconscious fantasies whose meaning can be understood in various ways, as contemporary analyst (Stephen Briggs et al., 2008; Briggs, 2022) has outlined:

- *Revenge:* The solution to a grievance; "the child wishes to rob the parent of her most precious possession" (Stekel, 1910/1967).
- *(Self)-punishment:* Punishment of self will remove the problem (for others) or bring atonement—masochistic solutions.
- *"Dicing with Death":* On the model of "Russian roulette" in which an individual does not intentionally seek to die but engages in activities that could easily result in death (Campbell & Hale, 2017; Hale, 2008; Maltsberger & Buie, 1980, 1996).
- *Elimination fantasy:* A further unconscious fantasy fueling nonsuicidal and suicidal acts is what Campbell and Hale (2017) refer to as the "elimination fantasy" in which sources of pain and humiliation are split off and evacuated. The elimination fantasy involves the identification of one part of the body as toxic and is therefore attacked in order to purify another part, to preserve a good object. When the sources of pain and humiliation are, for example, the sexual organs that have been abused by another, these may directly be attacked, and injured, as a symbolic as well as actual form of protest.

- *Self-harm as a sign of hope:* Motz (2009b) has described this in terms of NSSI serving as a form of purification and release for those who engage in it, as well as a sign of hope, in that it is testing the environment to see that it can survive assault. This is a development of Donald Winnicott's notion of the "antisocial tendency as a sign of hope" (Winnicott, 1956/2012), in that the person who behaves aggressively is searching to re-discover a good object that can withstand their aggression and remain intact. In a similar way, the woman attacking her own body is searching for containment and survival, using this as an act of relating both to herself and to another in order to obtain a response. There is the hope of positive relating (Briggs et al., 2008; Briggs, 2022).

Underpinning these psychodynamic approaches is the notion of non-suicidal self-harm developing and being maintained in the context of interpersonal relationships, as comprehensively explicated by Briggs et al. (2008), who incorporate suicidal ideation in their understanding of NSSI. This model is supported by Stänicke et al. (2018) in their study of adolescent NSSI, who describe how the action of self-harm may contain and reveal important emotional and relational content and an intention or wish to connect and communicate with others. Stänicke et al. (2018) emphasize the importance of relating self-harm to developmental psychological needs and challenges in adolescence, such as separation, autonomy, and identity formation. They suggest that NSSI in adolescence may reveal both a need to express affective experiences and a relational need for care. NSSI does not take place in a void, but often occurs in an interpersonal context. Motz (2009a) emphasizes the communicative function of NSSI, "self-harm is a communication to oneself and others that serves several functions for the individual by offering them a variety of ways of relating to themselves and enacting certain essential roles. In this sense, self-harm reflects a split and divided self, and its enactment offers a sequential series of rewards and compensations" (p. 18).

Hence, from a psychodynamic perspective, the treatment priorities include the therapist working carefully with the patient to understand and identify underlying emotional states and experiences that lead to the self-injurious action, offering containment to them, helping the patient to tolerate feelings that are contradictory or ambivalent, and ensuring that the therapist themselves is able to manage disturbing countertransference feelings that may include anger, hopelessness, despair, or confusion.

A recent meta-analysis involving 12 clinical trials showed that psychodynamic therapies were effective in reducing suicide (pooled odds ratio = 0.469; 95% CI [0.274, 0.804]) and self-harm at 6-month, but not 12-month, follow-up. There was also evidence for improvements in psychosocial functioning and reduction in number of hospital admissions (Briggs et al., 2019).

A Mentalization-Based Understanding of the Development of NSSI

Mentalizing and Self-Harm

The MBT model can be seen as a further elaboration and extension of more traditional psychodynamic approaches to self-harm as its starting point is that many patients presenting with self-harm lack—either temporarily or more permanently—the capacities to mentalize (i.e., to reflect on their self-states and those of others). As a consequence, more insight-oriented approaches may not only be ineffective but even harmful as they assume high-level abilities of mental function. While traditional psychoanalytic therapies rely on a less active approach by the analyst, and sometimes adopt a more silent and neutral presence, this can activate the patient's already disturbed attachment systems and create levels of arousal that interfere with their capacity to self-monitor and self-reflect. Their high-level self-appraisal capacities are reduced. MBT is based on an attachment model that pays close attention to the activation or deactivation of the individual's level of emotional arousal and dysregulation. The therapeutic relationship serves as the secure environment within which the patient can learn to reflect on their mental and emotional experiences, their thoughts and assumptions that trigger behavior designed to change these experiences, such as NSSI. In essence, MBT focuses on preconscious processing, that is at the level of working memory, rather than unconscious process.

What is mentalizing? Mentalizing is the process by which we understand our own and others' behaviors from a reading of underlying mental states. Mentalizing can be understood as attentiveness to thinking and feeling in oneself and others, with central emphasis on the mental states of others. It can be thought of as "holding mind in mind." This approach was initially developed in the treatment of individuals with borderline personality disorder (BPD; Bateman & Fonagy, 2004). People with BPD have considerable problems with mentalizing and are well known to self-harm and make suicide attempts frequently. Improving the stability and effective deployment of mentalizing within the interpersonal and social world of the individual is the target of MBT on the basis that stability of mental function and ability to engage in constructive social relationships allows the individual to give up their reliance on harmful self-destructive action as a method of self-control. In sum, MBT is an effective integration of a mentalizing/attachment model, informed by psychodynamic principles. Relatively easy to train in, and continuously subject to rigorous evaluations, MBT has been demonstrated to be effective across a range of psychological difficulties, throughout the age range (Storebø et al., 2020). This model has been developed for individuals presenting with high levels of self-harm such as BPD and therefore it is possible to extend the model to self-harm more generally.

THE DEVELOPMENT OF MENTALIZING AND ITS ROLE IN NSSI

Mentalizing theory is rooted in Bowlby's attachment theory (1969) and its elaboration by contemporary developmental psychologists, while paying attention to constitutional vulnerabilities. We are all philosophers of minds as we negotiate the social world and devote substantial amounts of "headspace" to wondering what is going on in other people's heads, and tracking our own thoughts of feelings. We see things beyond, behind, or simply different from physical objects, moving bodies, and expressive faces. Such mind-wondering, which is termed "mentalizing," is central to social interaction, culture, and morality. It is also central to psychotherapy in which minds are the target of scrutiny.

It is a developmentally determined mental capacity starting in infancy and childhood within the context of attachment and probably only becomes stable by the mid-20s. Attachment problems lead to mentalizing problems and mentalizing problems fuel further attachment difficulties. Failures in early maternal/carer mirroring and reflective processes result in later developmental difficulties in mentalizing, so that the individual becomes overwhelmed by unstable self-experience, dysregulated negative feelings, distressing thoughts, and misinterpretations of others' behavior and intentions, all of which lead to the perceived need to take action to maintain mental stability. Problems with mentalizing lead to failure to regulate self-experience and internal emotional states and to understand others' motives accurately. The argument here is that mentalizing is the very process that is required to maintain a subjective experience of a self over time and in social interaction which is stable and coherent.

Prior to a self-harming act, whether or not suicidal in nature, there is a collapse in mental functioning, a disorganized and painful mental state, and a disruption to an experiential self. Mentalizing failures may lead to self-harm because the individual may revert to states of mind that antedate the full capacity for mentalizing. Examples of these include "psychic equivalence" functioning in which the person believes that what they think another person is thinking about them must actually be true—so "I think he thinks I'm ugly" becomes a certain and rigid truth, rather than a speculation about another mind. Another nonmentalizing form of functioning is "teleological mode" in which the behavior of another person is taken to be clear evidence of their mental state, so that "she did not smile at me" becomes the basis for the assumption that "she does not like me, she does not want to speak to me, she hates me." Finally, in the pretend or as-if mode, the individual loses the capacity to distinguish between thoughts and feelings that are rooted in real lived experience and thoughts and feelings that are no longer related to such experiences. Mental states are decoupled from reality and the person lives in their own world, isolated and separated from others. At an extreme, their inner life becomes fantasy with no grounding in external reality and they lose an ability to calibrate their inner experience with others. They are alone and unreachable.

The pain and distress that results from these mentalizing failures is such that the individual becomes emotionally dysregulated and these unmentalized or "alien-self" experiences are then discharged through physical means, such as drug or alcohol use, or violence against others or themselves. For instance, in psychic equivalence mode, the feeling that

"I am ugly and useless" may lead to such painful feelings of helplessness and despair that the individual increasingly has the feeling that she needs to self-harm to "prove"—in teleological mode—that she is indeed ugly and useless. Hence, according to the MBT model, self-harm actions can be conceptualized as teleological attempts to get rid of feelings that are felt to be intolerable and have the potential to reinstate stability to a sense of self even if this is negative. But that does not actually address the underlying confusion surrounding mental states.

The MBT approach to understanding the generation of non-suicidal self-harm has been well described by Anthony Bateman (2019). Even verbalizing "I am suicidal" or "I have suicidal thoughts", indicates that a mental escape procedure has been activated; a subsequent action itself means the escape procedure has been ineffective and the state of mind has become increasingly painful and threatening to self- coherence and self-existence. Suicide attempts and self-harm are a result of a disorganized and painful mind state. They are an end product rather than the problem creating pain. It is far too easy for clinicians to become focused on the thoughts or actions themselves because they are anxious and frightened about the level of risk. This results in a failure to explore the mental circumstances and interpersonal contexts that are leading to thoughts and actions about self-harm and suicide.

THE EVIDENCE BASE FOR MBT

In treatment of individuals who self-harm, there is emerging evidence base for taking into account the vulnerabilities in their mentalizing in the context of disturbed attachments. Randomized control trials have demonstrated the efficacy of MBT for adolescents presenting with NSSI (Rossouw & Fonagy, 2012) in reducing self-harm and depression, which was mediated by improvements in mentalizing and reduced attachment avoidance. This finding was replicated in other studies, (Hawton et al., 2016), highlighting that MBT in combination with emotion regulation-based group therapy was associated with a significant reduction in repeated self-injury. These authors found significant treatment effects of MBT after an 18-month treatment period with fewer engaging in self-harming behaviors. In the recent Cochrane review, evidence was found that MBT was more effective in reducing self-harm in BPD when compared with well-conducted control treatments and showed high effect sizes (Storebø et al., 2020).

Evidence that MBT may be superior to other psychodynamic therapy in addressing the specific issue of NSSI has also been found, by Calati and Courtet (2016) in their meta-analysis, concluding that there was no significant evidence to suggest any other psychodynamic approach apart from MBT is effective for treatment of nonsuicidal self-harm.

MBT treatment principles for self-harm can be seen in action in the following clinical case examples, anonymized and created for the purposes of this chapter, but based on actual presenting problems of a typical referrals. We present two cases, the first to illustrate the principles of MBT in NSSI and the second to illustrate MBT where harm to others as well as the self coexist.

MBT is a structured treatment with an initial psychoeducation phase followed by focused individual and/or group therapy using a collaborative formulation agreed with the patient at the beginning of treatment. The psychoeducation includes information about good mentalizing, poor mentalizing, emotions and how to manage them, and attachment relationships. The patient uses the information provided to map their own mentalizing pattern and attachment style and how they relate to others. In general terms, as we have mentioned, the greater the activation of attachment process, the more vulnerable an individual is to a collapse in mentalizing, which potentially results in self-harm as a way of reinstating mental stability. Most serious risk-taking behaviors involve interpersonal sensitivity and attachment activation; hence, a focus on relationships and attachment and mentalizing in treatment is likely to be helpful. The therapist will be exploring the patient's past mental states from the perspective of current mentalizing and keeping a close eye on the patient's capacity to mentalize in the session, and bringing them back to the optimal state of arousal that enables this.

Case Illustration: Freya

The application of an MBT approach to a typical presentation of a young woman with borderline traits is described below. Here, we focus on its use as a treatment of violent actions that are primarily self-directed.

Freya is a 19-year-old woman, in her first year of university. Always prone to perfectionism, she has struggled with the transition from being top of her class at school to being one of many excellent students, where she is not the best, and in fact, considers herself to be performing in the bottom range of her class. She is constantly worried that she will not meet others' expectations of her. She is not being treated for clinical depression currently, but her self-esteem is lower than usual, and she has been feeling isolated, alone and ashamed and had on occasions picked at her skin enough to make it bleed. When she learned that she had obtained a lower second in the exams at the end of her first term she felt hopeless and despairing, convinced that this meant she would either fail the course altogether, or, at best, get a third-class degree. She was convinced that her parents would be devastated, and that her friends would reevaluate her, having discovered that she was not the clever, accomplished girl she had always appeared. Disgusted with herself she reached for her razor and for, the first time ever, cut into her skin, making several delicate marks on the insides of her thighs, where the marks would not be visible. She has a history of depression and, when she developed a serious eating disorder at 16 was seen in an adolescent psychiatric unit where it was suggested that she had emergent personality disorder of a borderline type. Her depression and eating disorder stabilized after a brief period of inpatient treatment but seems to have resurfaced recently. Since that first occasion she has cut herself at least four times, generally following her submission of coursework, and the anticipation of it being marked low, but on one occasion it was after she found out about a party that she had not been invited to, though several of her close friends had been. Disturbed by her growing preoccupation with self-harm, Freya has decided, at last, that she needs to discuss this in therapy and presents at the clinic, explaining that she is "addicted" to self-harm and is worried that it will leave permanent scars, and become a lifelong habit.

How Would We Work with Freya Using an MBT Perspective?

The therapist will follow the principles outlined in this section to ensure that they remain adherent to the MBT model, retaining authenticity and an exploratory "not-knowing" stance throughout, and validating and empathizing with the patient's experiences.

PRINCIPLES OF MBT MODEL IN TREATMENT OF SELF-HARM

The "not-knowing" stance is one in which the therapist expresses curiosity and interest in the patient's mind, rather than presenting themselves as an expert or making interpretations. This models the notion, central to MBT, that minds are not transparent. The validation of the patient's experience and empathy for their pain or distress is essential for engagement and also to reduce high levels of emotional arousal that can interfere with mentalizing. It is vital for therapeutic engagement and establishing trust. This is the first step to engaging patients in a thoughtful process, where they feel that it is possible to understand the feelings that underlie their self-harm or other acts of violence. The basic stance of the MBT therapist can be summarized as follows:

- Maintain a not-knowing stance when exploring a theme; for example, if a patient says "All women hate me, including you, and I know it," the therapist could inquire about what feelings are evoked by that, where they get that thought from in that very moment, and most importantly what that means to the person, rather than assuming anything about what being hated means, challenging the cognition directly, or making an interpretation about why and how that belief and its attendant pain developed.
- See things from the patient's perspective.
- Validate their emotional pain—contingent and marked responsiveness.
- Join with mentalizing and provide judicious praise for successful mentalizing.
- Do not join nonmentalizing.

The clinical guidance is for interventions that apply in the following circumstances:

1. At the beginning of treatment, when assessing a patient who has history of suicide and self-harm behaviors.
2. Suicide or self-harm attempt has occurred.
3. Patient threatens imminent suicide attempt or self-harm.
4. Suicidal ideation is persistent.
5. Other recurrent self-destructive action occurs (e.g., violence).

One of the most significant aspects to address is the risk of harm increasing. There are certain well-known warning signs of change in risk that could turn an act of self-harm into one with suicidal intention. The clinician needs to be aware of these and keep them in mind throughout treatment. They include the following:

- Increase in statements and thoughts of suicide, anxiety and depressive symptoms;
- Uncontrolled emotion;
- Change in illicit drug use;
- Recent loss events including failure of treatment and discharge from support due to breaking of a contract;
- Social withdrawal;
- Interpersonal strife in close relationships; and
- Describing and planning a method of dying and arranging personal matters with the aim of closure.

Initial Phase

The formulation in MBT is developed between clinician and patient, identifying the patient's mentalizing vulnerabilities in detail, their mentalizing profile, which outlines their pattern of use of the main dimensions of mentalizing, and their propensity to use nonmentalizing modes and the circumstances in which they are deployed. Mentalizing is loosely coupled with attachment and so the interaction between attachment and mentalizing in their lives is also identified. In treatment of self-harm, the clinician uses a formulation coupled with psychoeducation, and in conjunction with goal-setting (Grove & Smith, 2022).

In the case of Freya, for example, the initial case formulation outlines Freya's vulnerabilities and also defines a crisis plan, in case her self-harm increases in frequency or intensity. The aim of psychoeducation is not solely transfer of knowledge. It is to support development of a joint framework for treatment and to increase collaboration and engagement in the MBT process in which Freya will identify her mentalizing and nonmentalizing modes of functioning and the attachment styles activated in her relationships. In addition, the clinician sets out part of the agreement about the responsibilities for destructive behavior being shared, rather than either party carrying the weight of it alone. An example of how this could be expressed is as follows:

> *You and I have to work on understanding what goes on in your mind before you self-harm, when mentalizing goes "offline." This may mean we also go back to the point just before it went "offline" and trace what was going on for you just then. This can help us to identify how best to manage and mentalize those thoughts and feelings rather than to self-harm, which we know can be dangerous for you. We need to agree that whenever you have dark thoughts and certainly if you do try to harm yourself, that we look at it in detail however painful it might be. We cannot ignore it, even if only*

for the benefit of my understanding, as it will be difficult to work on all your problems with the danger of serious injuries hanging over us both. Can we talk about this for a moment so we both have some understanding of our views on this?

The agreement of joint goals early in treatment specifies self-harm and suicide attempts and other destructive behaviors as a clear focus for the initial sessions. Reducing risk is the most important step. As part of this process the clinician takes a thorough history of Freya's attachment relationships and details of her actions of self-harm including the context of events that led to the self-harm and what happened before she self-harmed, in terms of her thoughts and feelings. Exploring attachment histories can be done effectively by mapping the patient's description of former important relationships not only with parents but also with partners and friends. Using basic attachment strategies as a template, the clinician considers the characteristics of two aspects of insecure attachment—overinvolved and anxious or anxious and avoidant. This is done in MBT, initially in a MBT introductory psychoeducation phase in which patients can be given prototypes of attachment strategies and asked to rate themselves in relation to these, in discussion with the clinician. Importantly, the clinician probes for triggers of attachment processes which are likely to have led to destabilization of mentalizing, asking the patient to think backward to a point at which they felt calm and stable prior to the event. This intervention is one often used in the beginning of an MBT intervention and is known as "Stop and Rewind." This initial phase of developing a framework and using it to explore Freya's mental processes leading to events of self-harm might help her begin to restore mental stability and reduce the risk of further self-harm episodes. This formulation (see fig. 58.1) is revisited throughout treatment as more information and better understanding of her self-harm is developed.

The introduction to MBT will help Freya understand the collaborative approach, and its aims of emotional regulation, cognitive and affective balance, and the goal of restoring mentalizing, with less reliance on evacuating painful feelings into self-directed acts of violence, or, alternatively, overdosing on drugs, withdrawing altogether from social situations and becoming isolated, afraid of the negative judgement she perceives that others will definitely have of her now, based on her exam performance.

Treatment Phase

The intervention steps followed by an MBT clinician with a patient who has reported a suicidal or self-harming event are as follows:

(a) Fact-find about the incident followed by using a not-knowing stance. The therapist needs to gather a full picture of the events around the self-harming incident, particularly focusing on the interpersonal situation that led to it, or any thoughts and beliefs that the patient had. This is the essential "fact finding" component that might give some indication of the current level of risk.

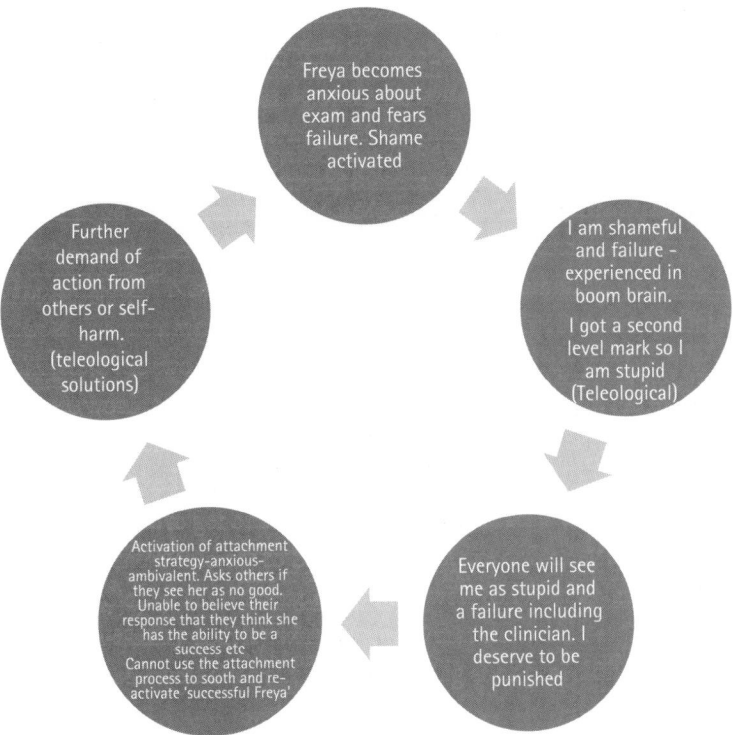

Figure 58.1 Initial Formulation Agreed with Freya of her Cycle of Self-Harm

The clinician is instructed in MBT to empathically validate the painful experiences that the patient was struggling with. Empathic validation in MBT required the clinician to show that they can see how the patient was experiencing things and also what effects this is having or has had on them. In other words, it relates to both the past in terms of when the event occurred and also in the present in the sense of the effects this experience is **now** having on the patient.

> As you talk to me I am getting a sense of you keeping a picture in your mind of you as someone who can do well and be respected and well thought of by others like your parents but that seems to get lost when you are anxious. The effect on you **now** is that you doubt yourself terribly and feel a failure and this was confirmed by your exam results. You fear that now everyone sees you as a failure and you have lost that sense of yourself as someone who can succeed not just for others but for yourself.

The move to the current experience is a step toward generating "we-mode", indicating that the patient and therapist are working together to learn more about events leading to NSSI. Strong attempts are made, once this picture is painted, to identify the point where mentalizing went offline, the rewind, and the patient either decided to or felt compelled to take action. This requires the therapist to slowly, tenaciously and without judgment or ascribing meaning to the action, help the patient identify their feelings at each point in the story. Asking the patient to rewind to the point before mentalization went 'offline' is key to this, and the empathic validation of their feelings at each point enables the work to take place in 'we' mode, as together, clinician and patient piece together what was going on at each stage in their narrative.

MBT is seeking the point of vulnerability for the patient in terms of when anxiety undermines mentalizing and Freya no longer can access a self that can do well, meeting her own standard and be seen as a success by others. This can only be identified by going back to find a point when mentalizing is stable and tracing this forward toward the point at which it is apparent to the patient that their mentalizing became less stable but prior to the uncontrollable cascade into the low mentalizing which results in action.

(b) Managing mind states. Most patients in treatment will have some understanding of mind states from the MBT Introductory phase. Like Freya, the patient needs to become sensitive to their changing mind states and, in particular, to be increasingly aware of the development of low mentalizing functioning such as psychic equivalence and teleological function, both of which become common during the onset of self-harming thoughts and behaviors. These prototypical low mentalizing states are fixed formations of mental function. In psychic equivalence, the person considers that whatever they are thinking is a reality. Thoughts and feelings become facts. They have no doubt and fail to question the accuracy of their thoughts—a thought of being a bad person is experienced as a reality and unquestioned and not balanced by uncertainty or additional self-experience making the whole thought or feeling exquisitely painful. In teleological mode, mental states are based not on impressionistic internal scrutiny and attunement with others' states of mind but on what happens in reality. So, I can only be understood through my actions, and others' actions inform me of their motives—you are what you do and not what you say; self-harm expresses an otherwise inexpressible mental state. Inevitably, dominance of this mode of understanding of the world leads to considerable confusion and serious misunderstandings between people.

The MBT clinician locates the beginnings of psychic equivalence and the context in which Freya begins to realize that her thoughts became rigid and certain. For many patients, it is possible to label these mind states and help them to rewind themselves once they realize they are in them. Once psychic equivalence is recognized by the patient, you may find a short-hand term with the patient describing the specific state of mind that proceeds self-harm. For instance, Freya found a description of her mental state at the point in terms of the "Boom Brain Time"; when in teleological mode she learned to recognize this as her "Action Brain" being active. This may help the patient become more sensitive to the onset of these states and begin to stop them before they dominate.

(c) Identify the core domain of problem—interpersonal and affective. The evidence shows that many suicide and self-harm attempts in BPD occur in interpersonal contexts and

in a state of high emotion. In Freya's case, she is convinced that her parents, tutors, and others will judge her negatively on the basis of her exam results, and that the fact her friends have not sought her out is evidence of this. Negative interpersonal events predict self-harm. It is not an easy task to differentiate interpersonal/social interaction disturbance from problems with intrapersonal emotional regulation as both mutually influence each other. Identifying a hierarchy between interpersonal process and emotional regulation as the primary pathology in BPD and related conditions is impossible as there is circularity. High emotions distort how a person reads social meaning and how they understand others' mind states, resulting in interpersonal discord and confusion; interpersonal discord stimulates problematic intrapersonal emotions and misperceptions of others' motives. Nevertheless, the clinician uses a "not-knowing" stance to explore the interaction between interpersonal process and emotional dysregulation, trying but never succeeding to identify the "chicken from the egg."

The most common error is to assume that the problem is primarily related solely to managing emotion and then trying to implement emotional management strategies without generating the detail of the interpersonal context to identify the patient's personal sensitivities. Only if their interpersonal sensitivities are recognized will it be possible to start exploring the relational and attachment processes that are central to the problems of people with BPD and many others who self-harm. Their often insecure early attachments are evident in the ways that they respond to these interpersonal slights, and the impact of these experiences on their fragile sense of self.

Within the therapeutic relationship, a secure attachment would enable a patient like Freya to begin to make sense of her nonmentalizing activities and generate a sense of control and capacity in relation to these, essentially becoming able to integrate aspects of the "alien self" as she is increasingly able to reflect on her own states of mind and to identify and regulate them. This relates clearly to the use of nonmentalizing modes of functioning, as Fonagy and Luyten (2018) explain in their work in attachment, mentalizing and the self:

> Understanding and recognizing the pre-mentalizing modes is important because they often appear alongside a pressure to externalize unmentalized and self-hating aspects of the self (so-called "alien-self" parts). Torturing feelings of badness, possibly linked to experiences of abuse that are felt to be part of the self but are not integrated with it (the "alien-self" parts), can come to dominate self-experience. We assume that these discontinuities in internal experience (when the person feels aspects of their self-experience to be of themselves or their own, and yet also to be alien) generate a sense of incongruence, which is dealt with through externalizing. (p. 129)

Through MBT, Freya can focus on the painful feelings that she finds overwhelming by discovering an empathic other who validates these feelings, and helps her to identify them.

This is essentially the therapist offering a form of contingent marked mirroring that she may not have received from a carer earlier in life. In terms of identifying and working with Freya's attachment strategies which are activated as soon as she thinks about her close relationships and undermine her mentalizing, the MBT clinician follows a number of steps. First, the attachment strategies deployed by Freya are identified in the first phase of psychoeducation and placed in the formulation (see earlier); second, the way in which they play out in current life with friends and others are noted; third, the effects they have within her relationships are mapped; and fourth, Freya and the clinician agree to sensitize themselves to when they may be active within the interaction between them and use this to explore in detail what it tells them about Freya and her relationships in the "real" world.

(d) Therapist stance. In MBT, the therapist must be mindful of the main aim of the work, which is to enable the patient to gain a sense of curiosity and reflection over their mind, and will approach this task with compassion and without judgment or an interpretative stance. Empathy and seeing things from Freya's perspective serve to offer a form of reflective functioning of which she, like so many other patients, was often deprived early in life, and can help them stand back from the feelings and behavior with which they are preoccupied, in order to reflect on what triggered them, and restore a mentalizing capacity. Therapists must avoid the stance, offered by clinicians in other modalities, by resisting the temptation to take over the patient's mentalizing, even if it is poor, to tell them what is in their mind or what they feel. Because therapists are generally good mentalizers it is tempting to use this capacity to manage the patient's low mentalizing but this will not help the patient to name their feelings, explore their impact, and shift the focus away from their certain, rigid and unhelpful thoughts about events, and reliance on behavior to alleviate the pain of their mental states.

The therapist stance in this treatment model is one of humility, authenticity, transparency, empathy, and "not knowing." There is plenty in Freya's history and current experiences to be empathic with. Freya does not have a formal psychiatric diagnosis of BPD, but her early experiences include being sent to boarding school at an early age, feeling rejected by her parents and misunderstood by those around her. She is the only child of older parents, from a Northern European country, who were themselves rather alienated in the United Kingdom. Her mother suffered from depression, and her father worked long hours. Her reliance on self-harm and sense of abject failure due to lower-than-expected exam results, her difficulty tolerating painful feelings, and her wish to simply have people around her care for her, or if not, to drop out of life altogether, indicates that she does not have the inner resources to manage her subjective experience of self. This implies she may not have had an early experience of reflective parenting, when her feelings were named, reflected back to her in contingent (accurate) marked (related to her mental experience) mirroring, whereby a parent or carer shows the child that they understand what she is feeling, enabling that child to internalize this sense of their own mind—we learn about ourselves through the mind of others. This lack of interpersonal reciprocity leaves her with an impoverished capacity to mentalize—that is to identify, regulate, and differentiate her own mental states and feelings from those of others. In interpersonal situations where her attachment system is triggered, she quickly feels overwhelmed and wholly inadequate, unsure how to self-soothe, or even how to understand what she feels. Empathic validation of her experiences of being seen negatively by others is essential to the therapeutic process.

(e) Managing nonmentalizing modes. When a series of events, like the work-related failure perceived by Freya, destabilizes her and awakens fear of punishment, loss, and abandonment by those on whom she relies, she collapses into a nonmentalizing mode and seeks comfort and care. But as she desperately tries to manage her instability the fears of punishment begin to be increasingly experienced in psychic equivalence and so gain a reality that is increasingly painful. Her fear of punishment becomes "I deserve punishment" and "I am a failure." She will enter a kind of "fight-or-flight" mode where she attempts to exert influence over her sense of vulnerability and change something external in order to manage such painful internal feelings. She will engage in nonmentalizing, including teleological thinking, whereby only behavioral outcomes are important, and where any expression of emotional response from others does not "count" and is not perceived as valid, or meaningful. Only external outcomes, like being given a good mark, or having a friend come over to take her out, matter. Being told by a teacher she perceives her as good and valuable, or by a friend that they care about her, does not have credibility. She believes she is only as good as the mark she achieved on the test, and does not give weight to her internal worth; her sense of self is fragile and she is destabilized.

Freya is also likely to make assumptions about the mental states of others, and this is an important aspect of nonmentalizing modes. When distressed and feeling low she will equate what she believes another person to be thinking to be the truth, thereby equating what she believes with the actual truth, expressing certainty about another's mental states. This mode of psychic equivalence can clearly be seen in people with depression, BPD, and antisocial personality disorder, conditions associated with self-harm, who typically act with certainty about other people's mental states, assuming that what they believe about them, based on their own fears and rigid interpretation of someone's behavior, is the truth. Their beliefs become facts.

In violent individuals, this misinterpretation of mind states can lead to retaliatory violence as an attempt to restore the sense of self that has been lost through what they believe is the other person's disrespect of them. The violent action is an attempt to reset their sense of self. When someone is depressed and interprets the behavior or mental state of someone else as a rejection of them, self-harm is an attempt to get rid of the painful state of mind, through action. Again, this is a means to try to stabilize the self, and may also serve as an attempt to generate a response from others, to glean attention and care from others. This will meet teleological needs, that is, will give the person a sense that the other person is attending to them, something they do not experience from the emotional expression of care or concern.

Using an MBT approach can help the self-harming person to understand the various distortions in their thinking, and their own lack of faith that others can respond to their distress, and care for them, without needing to take particular actions to elicit these responses, or in the absence of certain behaviors being demonstrated by others that "prove" their care.

Case Illustration: Rita

Our second case illustration demonstrates how MBT can be used to help a woman who uses both self-harm and violence against others, with a complex personality and long history of disturbance. Although we are not explicitly describing the application of MBT to people with antisocial personality disorder (ASPD) here, the use of MBT with antisocial personalities specifically is increasingly considered an effective intervention. MBT is used to target symptomatology in individuals with antisocial traits or personality disorders who struggle to mentalize other people's minds and their own, with destructive consequences (Fonagy et al., 2020). The following case shows how both antisocial and borderline traits can coexist in a vulnerable and risky woman and how both are amenable to modification through MBT, as well as suggesting that an MBT-informed approach can also be of use to the staff who are working with her.

Rita is a 42-year-old prisoner, who has a long history of violence against others, substance misuse and self-harm through overdose of illegal and prescribed medication and ligatures. Although she was known to mental health services since adolescence, she has not had a sustained period of psychiatric and psychological care as an outpatient, as she would disengage frequently, and was eventually arrested for criminal damage and grievous bodily harm in her early 20s. Her crimes took place in the context of substance misuse. She is diagnosed with "emotionally unstable personality disorder" and also shows clear traits of antisocial personality disorder. Her understanding of her difficulties is that she has been badly treated and/or neglected for most of her life, and that others consider her to "have a PD," which she sees as an unhelpful label, and does not understand how she can be considered both antisocial and borderline, as she thought only men were given the former diagnosis. She largely considers herself a victim of other people's attempts to control her.

In prison, she has frequent self-harm episodes and occasional verbal outbursts at staff, particularly when instructed to go back to her room, or when asking about appointments, and not being given the answers clearly or quickly enough. When she erupts most aggressively, she displays physical violence, generally throwing objects at others, and has been "adjudicated" for these offenses, leading to time in the segregation unit. She has little hope of leaving prison in the near future, as she becomes violent and "disruptive" as the prospect of release comes nearer, a behavioral pattern she recognizes as destructive and familiar, and, at some level, wants to break free from. She has been moved from prison to prison as staff describe her as a "heartsink prisoner" because she is so "demanding" of their time and attention. A closer look at her history reveals that she came to the UK as an unaccompanied minor, and spent considerable time in the care system, with infrequent contact with relatives who had immigrated her, and no contact with her parents or sister, who remained in Ethiopia. She will not talk about her past and often presents a confusing and chaotic picture of her life in England prior to prison, which appears to have elements of fantasy, in that she describes a highly glamorous lifestyle where she associated with celebrities and went to nightclubs.

Her self-harm at points of transition increases dramatically and she is more or less constantly placed on an Accessing Safer Care in Custody and Teamwork (ACCT) book, a record of those prisoners deemed at significant risk of suicide or self-harm. She is clear that she does not want to die, but that self-harm is an effective coping method for distress, alleviating her depression and turning psychic pain into physical pain. It distracts her from her traumatic memories of previous abuse, and of her offense, which was a near-fatal assault on her partner. Additionally, when she self-harms she is tended to by the nurse on the spur, and prison officers are required to have at least four conversations with her per day, something that would otherwise not happen. She describes a sense of pure release when she has tied ligatures, and although she is aware that it could be fatal if she tied one too tightly, and was not checked on at regular intervals by an officer, she is adamant that this is a way of trying to stay alive, rather than an attempt to die.

Rita has a long history of being abandoned, rejected, and abused, and clearly does not trust those in positions of authority. She has no experience of benevolent authority, but only of being betrayed and punished by those in charge. She has little sense of her own mind, let alone that of others, and only feels safe when she is able to evacuate her feelings through actions, that is to use teleological modes to get away from painful mental states. Furthermore, these actions lead to direct consequences, behavioral manifestations of other people's care, that are the only kind of expressions of care she can understand. This reinforces her perceived need to remain a person who self-harms, who is checked on at regular and frequent times (known in the criminal justice and psychiatric services as being "under observation" or "observed") with records being made of the number of times she is observed, and the numbers of conversations that are held with her. The ACCT book itself becomes a concrete example of care, and even if she leaves the unit where she is resident, the book will go with her, outlining her self-harming risks and acts, and ensuring that staff document events in the requisite pages. The book has great significance for her, as demonstrated when Rita gave a favored prison officer a "Thank you" card, depicting him, herself, and the orange ACCT book, placed carefully between them.

Rita, while fearful and distrustful, also has a strong need for others to take care of her, as she was so deprived of this in her earlier life, and so she is constantly monitoring the behavior of the prison staff, nursing staff, and clinicians who attend the unit, and who see her because of her status as a "prolific self-harmer." She derives a sense of identity from this, and closely watches the workers to see if other women receive more care than she does, as measured in terms of their number of daily "observations." She was outraged when she saw that another woman in the houseblock was being observed more frequently than she was, and demanded to know why this was, escalating her self-harm in the form of ligatures, as if deliberately creating a risky situation *to ensure the attendance of prison officers at her cell door more often. The irony of this situation is that this attendance, or "observation" was hardly a meaningful interaction, but simply involved the officer looking through the hatch to see if Rita appeared to be alive or moving. If she could not be seen, as she was lying under the bedclothes, and not fully visible, the officer would enter the room, talk to her, ask her if she was okay, and if Rita didn't respond, would remove the covers to see her neck, where often she would have tied a ligature. The officer would simply reach for their ligature cutter and remove the tie, sometimes without saying a word.*

When the clinician began to meet Rita for a brief series of sessions with an MBT focus, to help her mentalize and reduce the focus on self-harm, she explored with her in what sense this ligature-cutting could be seen as an example of care, or could help her to understand what particular mental state or feeling had led her to tie it. It took six or seven weeks before Rita was able to distinguish between the rote act of cutting a ligature and the act of an officer asking to talk to her about her feelings. She saw the former in teleological terms as far more indicative of care than talking as she found it impossible to mentalize other people's minds. In this case, Rita was so far from having an awareness of her own mental states when the clinician first met with her, that the goal of her being able to mentalize the other, (i.e., to see that an officer who sat with her, cared about her, and wanted to help her, at least as much as one who simply, silently, cut her tie), was not one she could achieve easily. The roots of her difficulty in understanding her own mind, and then being able to see herself from the outside, as others saw her, and interpreted her challenging behavior, could be found in her early parenting. She had not had another mind to hold her in mind, to name her different feelings and thoughts, that underlay her behavior in infancy, and so the only means she had of expressing herself was in action, unarticulated. This parental function, which enables mentalizing in those lucky enough to have good enough care in early life, is known as "reflective functioning" and it is the mechanism through which the infant learns, from their carer, how to name and understand their feelings. Without reflective functioning, the growing child is simply caught up in a feeling, acting it out, devoid of a sense of what is going on inside of them and how to manage it. Furthermore, Rita had almost no way of understanding that what she imagined, if she did, what the officers were thinking, could be altogether different from what they actually were thinking or feeling, as she judged this solely on the basis of their behavior. If they checked on someone else more than Rita, or spoke to her but didn't ask specifically about tying ligatures, this proved to her that they did not care about her. She often repeated to staff her certain belief that staff did not care whether she lived or died.

In order to work with this challenging behavior and help the staff to manage their countertransference feelings of frustration, boredom, and anger, or, alternatively, the wish to rescue Rita, or placate her and meet her needs for care by keeping her on the ACCT book constantly, and observing her several times a day, the clinician organized regular meetings with the prison officers, including those from the Safer Custody Team, and nurses, as well as a care coordinator on the Mental Health In-reach Team, to share the formulation of Rita's self-harming, following a collaborative introductory session with her. There was also reflective space provided for the staff to try to mentalize their own countertransference feelings and to reflect on ways that they sometimes responded unhelpfully or teleologically. For example, Rita would often buzz through to the office on her cell bell repeatedly and the officers would assume that they knew what was in her mind, and sometimes neglect to answer this persistent calling. This, they realized, was an example of their nonmentalizing, assuming that they knew what was in her mind, a state that could lead to a dangerous situation where a sudden decline in her mental state could lead to a fatal act of self-injury while they assumed it was "just another cry for more attention." High frequency of an action by an individual with repeated consequential interpersonal reaction easily induces assumptions about mental states in the reactor who may be desensitized against the severity of the action and begin to see it as of low importance. As well as using a mentalization-based approach to understanding Rita and supporting the staff, a short-term series of focused individual MBT sessions were offered, in which Rita could begin to identify and explore her nonmentalizing modes, and reflect on what triggered them. She could also identify times when she could mentalize well. Through this combined approach, Rita was able to reduce her self-harm in frequency to fewer than three times a week, while before treatment she was self-harming at least twice a day on average.

A self-harm strategy has been implemented throughout the prison, using a mentalization-based approach to help the prison and probation officers, teachers, chaplaincy, nurses, GPs, psychologists, and senior managers to focus on the feelings and thoughts that underlie behavior, rather than making rigid assumptions and responding in equally non-mentalizing ways. The evaluation of this project is in process.

Summary and Conclusion

As we have emphasized, violence and self-harm are often the expression of dysregulation in people with highly disturbed early attachments commonly based on developmental trauma. Earlier vulnerabilities, whether genetic or environmental, and usually both, sensitize an individual to current stressors. These are then experienced as unbearable challenges to which the patient has limited resilience. Stress reactions, anxieties, and painful mental states automatically trigger attachment processes which further dysregulate the person and activate proximity seeking. The patient will try to get support from a partner, friends, or services, only to find that the response they receive lacks appropriate contingency to their desperation. Further panic ensues as this frantic attempt challenges their self-existence further and mentalizing is disrupted, leading to experiences being processed in nonmentalizing modes. This makes any affective and cognitive experience increasingly acute and painful because the mind loses the capacity to differentiate reality from inner experience. Doubt is lost and certainty of belief dominates. Only action can then change mental processing, and teleological solutions are required. The use of action to relieve anxiety is part of the function of NSSI, as it is intended to focus the mind away from painful thoughts, memories, and experiences, locating a place for these on the body itself. It therefore offers a temporary solution to overwhelming and unwanted feelings. By engaging in self-injury, the person feels that they are taking charge, and changing their inner experience through this externally directed action.

MBT treatment operates using an approach that addresses the underlying difficulties in integrating thoughts and feelings, and in being able to resist the urge to find teleological or action-based interventions for painful thoughts and emotions. MBT is founded on attachment-based models, and has an emerging empirical basis. The underlying premise is that individuals with an insecure attachment system will find this is activated at times of transition, separation, reunion, and loss, with the result that they will be destabilized in terms of their mental functioning; that is, the arousal of this system will tip them over into a "nonmentalizing" mode in which certain attempts will be made to stabilize the system. These attempts will be frantic, and not ones in which thought and reason are predominant, but ones in which action is sought to bring about a reduction in the painful affect. Examples of actions include use of alcohol or substances, risk-taking of various kinds, violent actions including violence against the self—self-harm and, for those with antisocial personality traits, violence against others.

Other methods of coping with painful feelings, induced by a destabilized attachment system, include dissociation, which can also be found in traumatized individuals and can take the form of emotional shutdown and psychological defensiveness, as expressed through "pretend mode" functioning. Here the individual engages in a kind of pseudo self-exploration in which the language of emotional expressiveness is used but there is a paucity of emotional content.

When working with individuals in nonmentalizing modes, it is essential to bring them back into a mentalizing state, and what must first occur is that their arousal levels need to be reduced, to enable them to regulate their thoughts and feelings—overwhelming feelings will blow rationality out of the water and make any kind of therapeutic contact involving thought impossible. MBT attempts to balance out the affective and cognitive, and to restore a sense of connection between the two poles, which for individuals with personality disorder, or highly disrupted attachments, has often oscillated to extremes, leading to a failure of integration and reliance on violent, nonmentalizing action to evacuate feelings. As the authors have shown, this model of treatment has efficacy in reducing the major public health issue of NSSI, and is applicable to individuals who demonstrate not just borderline personality traits but also those with coexisting antisocial traits.

References

Agenda and the National Centre for Social Research. (2020). *Often overlooked: Young women, poverty and self-harm. A briefing by agenda, the alliance for women and girls at risk, and the National Centre for Social Research.* https://weareagenda.org/wp-content/uploads/2017/03/Often-Overlooked-Young-women-poverty-and-self-harm-2.pdf

American Psychiatric Association. (2013). *Diagnostic and statistical manual of mental disorders* (5th ed.).

Anderson, R. (2008). A psychoanalytic approach to suicide in adolescents. In S. Briggs, A. Lemma & W. Crouch (Eds.), *Relating to self-harm and suicide: Psychoanalytic perspectives on practice, theory and prevention* (pp. 61–71). Routledge.

Anzieu, D. (2016). The notion of the skin ego. In *The Skin Ego: A new translation by Naomi Segal* (pp 39–48). Routledge.

Bateman, A. W. (2019). *MBT for suicide and self-harm: Clinical guidance for intervention*. Anna Freud Centre.

Bateman, A., & Fonagy, P. (2004). Mentalisation based treatment of borderline personality disorder. *Journal of Personality Disorder, 18*, 35–50. https://doi.org/10.1521/pedi.18.1.36.32772

Bick, E. (1968). The experience of the skin in early object relations. *International Journal of Psychoanalysis, 49*, 558–566.

Bowlby, J. (1969). *Attachment and loss: Vol. 1. Attachment*. Basic Books.

Briggs, S. (2022). *Suicidality* [Powerpoint-*slides*]. Confer Diploma Course on Psychopathology.

Briggs, S., Lemma, A., & Crouch, W. (2008). *Relating to self-harm and suicide: Psychoanalytic perspectives on practice, theory and prevention*. Routledge.

Briggs, S., Netuveli, G., Gould, N., Gkaravella, A., Gluckman, N., Kangogyere, P., Farr, R., Goldblatt, M. J., & Lindner, R. (2019). The effectiveness of psychoanalytic/psychodynamic psychotherapy for reducing suicide attempts and self-harm: Systematic review and meta-analysis. *British Journal of Psychiatry, 214*(6), 320–328. https://doi.org/10.1192/bjp.2019.33

Calati, R., & Courtet, P. (2016). Is psychotherapy effective for reducing suicide attempt and non-suicidal self-injury rates? Meta-analysis and meta-regression of literature data. *Journal of Psychiatric Research, 79*, 8–20. https://doi.org/10.1016/j.jpsychires.2016.04.003

Campbell, D., & Hale, R. (2017). *Working in the dark: Understanding the pre-suicide state of mind*. Oxon.

Fonagy, P., & Luyten, P. (2018). Attachment, mentalizing, and the self. In W. J. Livesley & R. Larstone (Eds.), *Handbook of personality disorders: Theory, research, and treatment* (pp. 123–140). Guilford Press.

Fonagy, P., Yakeley, J., Gardner, T., Simes, E., McMurran, M., Moran, P., Crawford, M., Frater, A., Barrett, B., Cameron, A., Wason, K., Pilling, S., Butler, S., & Bateman, A. (2020). Mentalization for offending adult males (MOAM): Study protocol for a randomized controlled trial to evaluate mentalization-based treatment for antisocial personality disorder in male offenders on community probation. *Trials, 21*(1), 1–17. https://doi.org/10.1186/s13063-020-04896-w

Freud, S. (1923). The ego and the id. In J. Strachey (Ed.), *The standard edition of the complete psychological works of Sigmund Freud* (Vol. 19, pp. 13–27). Hogarth Press.

García-Nieto, R., Carballo, J. J., Díaz de Neira Hernando, M., de León-Martinez, V., & Baca-García, E. (2015). Clinical correlates of non-suicidal self-injury (NSSI) in an outpatient sample of adolescents. *Archives of Suicide Research, 19*(2), 218–230. https://doi.org/10.1080/13811118.2014.957447

Gillies, D., Christou, M. A., Dixon, A. C., Featherston, O. J., Rapti, I., Garcia-Anguita, A., Villasis-Keever, M., Reebye, P., Christou, E., Al Kabir, N., & Christou, P. A. (2018). Prevalence and characteristics of self-harm in adolescents: Meta-analyses of community-based studies 1990-2015. *Journal of the American Academy of Child and Adolescent Psychiatry, 57*(10), 733–741. https://doi.org/10.1016/j.jaac.2018.06.018

Grove, P., & Smith, E. (2022). A framework for MBT formulations: The narrative formulation and MBT passport. *Journal of Contemporary Psychotherapy, 52*(3), 1–8. https://doi.org/10.1007/s10879-022-09531-0

Hale, R. (2008). Psychoanalysis and suicide: Process and typology. In S. Briggs, A. Lemma, & W. Crouch (Eds.), *Relating to self-harm and suicide: Psychoanalytic perspectives on practice, theory and prevention* (pp. 13–24). Routledge.

Hawton, K., Witt, K. G., Taylor Salisbury, T. L., Arensman, E., Gunnell, D., Hazell, P., Townsend, E., & van Heeringen, K. (2016). Psychosocial interventions for self-harming adults. *Lancet Psychiatry, 3*(8), 740–750. https://doi.org/10.1016/S2215-0366(16)30070-0

Klonsky, E. D. (2011). Non-suicidal self-injury in United States adults: Prevalence, sociodemographics, topography and functions. *Psychological Medicine, 41*(9), 1981–1986. https://doi.org/10.1017/S0033291710002497

Lutz, N. M., Neufeld, S. A., Hook, R. W., Jones, P. B., Bullmore, E. T., Goodyer, I. M., Ford, T. J., Chamberlain, S. R., & Wilkinson, P. O. (2022). Why is non-suicidal self-injury more common in women? Mediation and moderation analyses of psychological distress, emotion dysregulation, and impulsivity. *Archives of Suicide Research*. Advance online publication. https://doi.org/10.1080/13811118.2022.2084004

Maltsberger, J. T., & Buie, D. H. (1980). The devices of suicide revenge, riddance, and rebirth. *International Review of Psycho-Analysis, 7*, 61–72.

Maltsberger, J. T., & Buie Jr, D. H. (1996). Countertransference hate in the treatment of suicidal patients. *Essential Papers on Suicide, 20,* Article 269.

Ministry of Justice (2021, October 28). *Safety in custody statistics, England and Wales: Deaths in prison custody to September 2021, assaults and self-harm to June 2021.* Retrieved from https://www.gov.uk/government/statistics/safety-in-custody-quarterly-update-to-june-2021/safety-in-custody-statistics-england-and-wales-deaths-in-prison-custody-to-september-2021-assaults-and-self-harm-to-june-2021

Motz, A. (2009a). *Managing self-harm: Psychological perspectives.* Routledge.

Motz, A. (2009b). Self-harm as a sign of hope. In A. Motz (Ed.), *Managing self-harm: Psychological perspectives* (pp. 15–41). Routledge.

Muehlenkamp, J. J., Claes, L., Havertape, L., & Plener, P. L. (2012). International prevalence of adolescent non-suicidal self-injury and deliberate self-harm. *Child and Adolescent Psychiatry and Mental Health, 6*(1), 1–9. https://doi.org/10.1186/1753-2000-6-10

Muehlenkamp, J. J., & Gutierrez, P. M. (2007). Risk for suicide attempts among adolescents who engage in non-suicidal self-injury. *Archives of Suicide Research, 11*(1), 69–82. https://doi.org/10.1080/13811110600992902

Ribeiro, J. D., Franklin, J. C., Fox, K. R., Bentley, K. H., Kleiman, E. M., Chang, B. P., & Nock, M. K. (2016). Self-injurious thoughts and behaviors as risk factors for future suicide ideation, attempts, and death: A meta-analysis of longitudinal studies. *Psychological Medicine, 46*(2), 225–236. https://doi.org/10.1017/S0033291715001804

Rossouw, T. I., & Fonagy, P. (2012). Mentalization-based treatment for self-harm in adolescents: A randomized controlled trial. *Journal of the American Academy of Child Adolescent Psychiatry, 51*(12), 1304–1313. https://doi.org/10.1016/j.jaac.2012.09.018.

Stänicke, L. I., Haavind, H., & Gullestad, S. E. (2018). How do young people understand their own self-harm? A meta-synthesis of adolescents' subjective experience of self-harm. *Adolescent Research Review, 3,* 173–191. https://doi.org/10.1007/s40894-018-0080-9

Stekel, W. (1967). On suicide. In P. Friedman (Ed) *On suicide with particular reference to suicide among young students, discussions of the Vienna psychoanalytic society* (pp. 89). International Universities Press. (Original work published 1910)

Storebø, O. J., Stoffers-Winterling, J. M., Völlm, B. A., Kongerslev, M. T., Mattivi, J. T., Jørgensen, M. S., Faltinsen, E., Todorovac, A., Sales, C. P., Callesen, H. E., Lieb, K., & Simonsen, E. (2020). Psychological therapies for people with borderline personality disorder. *Cochrane Database of Systematic Reviews, 5*(5), Article CD012955. https://doi.org/10.1002/14651858.CD012955.pub2

Swannell, S. V., Martin, G. E., Page, A., Hasking, P., & St John, N. J. (2014). Prevalence of nonsuicidal self-injury in nonclinical samples: Systematic review, meta-analysis and meta-regression. *Suicide and Life-Threatening Behavior, 44*(3), 273–303. https://doi.org/10.1111/sltb.12070

Winnicott, D.W. (2012). The antisocial tendency. In C. Winnicott, R. Shepherd, & M. Davis (Eds.), *Deprivation and delinquency* (pp. 103–112). Routledge. (Original work published 1956)

Wright, J., Briggs, S., & Behringer, J. (2005). Attachment and the body in suicidal adolescents. *Clinical Child Psychology and Psychiatry, 10*(4), 477–491. https://doi.org/10.1177/1359104505056310

Yakeley, J., & & Burbridge-James, W. (2018). Psychodynamic approaches to suicide and self-harm. *BJPsych Advances, 24*(1), 37–45. https://doi.org/10.1192/bja.2017.6

CHAPTER 59

Experiential Therapies and Nonsuicidal Self-Injury

Victoria E. Kress, Julia Whisenhunt, Nicole A. Stargell, *and* Christine A. McAllister

Abstract

Nonsuicidal self-injury (NSSI) is widely considered to be a form of emotion regulation. Experiential approaches generally address the here and now rather than the past or the future, and they focus on clients processing emotions and behaviors in the current moment. There are a number of experiential techniques that may be helpful when counseling those who self-injure. Expressive arts activities (e.g., visual arts, music, dance, writing, and drama) may be helpful techniques to use in facilitating experiential awareness when counseling those who self-injure. Additionally, guided imagery is a system of visualization that may be used to promote relaxation and allow clients to imagine a future that does not include NSSI. Experiential therapies that focus on relationships are well suited for NSSI. Emotion-focused therapy addresses insecure attachment patterns and increasing emotional regulation. Accelerated experiential dynamic psychotherapy (AEDP) is helpful in addressing trauma and dissociation; clients mindfully reflect on the present moment and make healthier choices in real time. Enhancing self-compassion in those who use NSSI may also be helpful. Additionally, mindfulness techniques may facilitate emotion regulation and promote acceptance and change. The emotional freedom technique (EFT) blends cognitive therapy, behavioral exposure, and acupressure to help clients reprocess their thoughts and feelings. Eye movement desensitization and reprocessing (EMDR) is a therapeutic approach to help clients work toward changing maladaptive thoughts. Resource development and installation (RDI) is a method for clients to recognize adaptive coping mechanisms and put them into practice.

Key Words: nonsuicidal self-injury, experiential therapies, expressive arts, guided imagery, emotion-focused therapy, accelerated experiential dynamic psychotherapy, self-compassion, emotional freedom technique, eye movement desensitization and reprocessing, resource development and installation

This chapter explores experiential therapies and their use with those who engage in nonsuicidal self-injury (NSSI). Although there is limited research on the use of experiential approaches with those whose self-injure, many practitioners report these methods as being helpful when counseling this population (Bentley et al., 2017; Bjureberg et al., 2018; Kress et al., 2013). The chapter addresses examples of experiential approaches that may be helpful when counseling those who self-injure, including expressive arts therapies/techniques, guided imagery, experiential approaches that focus on relationships, and experiential approaches that focus on thought and behavior change. This chapter also discusses implications for clinical practice, the limitations of these approaches, and future research directions.

Experiential Counseling Approaches

NSSI is widely considered to be a form of emotion regulation and is believed to occur secondary to clients struggling with their ability to regulate their emotions and get their needs met in alternative ways (Hamza & Willoughby, 2015). Experiential therapies involve the use of interventions that focus on experiencing emotions and behaviors in the current moment (Baer et al., 2019; Heath, Joly, and Carsley, 2016). Experiential approaches generally address the here and now rather than the past or the future, although the boundaries around this time concept can be blurry. Experiential awareness (i.e., What am I currently experiencing and consciously aware of?; Sebastián, 2012) is crucial to understanding oneself. An increased awareness of one's self (e.g., thoughts, feelings, impulses, and urges) can help clients become more proficient at accessing, identifying, understanding, and regulating their emotions and experiences so they can live more fully (Heath, Carsley, et al., 2016).

Those who self-injure often struggle with alexithymia, an inability to express and identify their emotions (Bedi et al., 2014). Alexithymia is a deficit in emotion processing which manifests itself in difficulties identifying and communicating emotions and in an externally orient ed thinking style. Alexithymia rates are significantly higher among people with a history of NSSI (Greene et al., 2020). Experiential therapies, with their focus on the present and affective states, may encourage awareness of thoughts and feelings; help clients access and process subconscious thoughts, feelings, and behaviors; and give them an opportunity to practice behavior changes that can be replicated independently.

Experiential Therapies and Associated Interventions

When working with clients who self-injure, awareness is facilitated in the safe environment of the counseling session. In-session experiencing helps clients to become better aware of their emotional experiences. Through this awareness, clients are able to create new self-narratives and meanings that incorporate a more resilient, self-actualized, and authentic sense of self (Kress et al., 2021).

Expressive Arts Therapy

Expressive therapies involve the use of the creative arts as a vehicle for achieving therapy goals. It is through the process and experience of creation that clients connect with a richer awareness of their inner lives. Creative and expressive arts interventions that integrate visual arts, music, dance, writing, and drama may be helpful when working with those who self-injure (Whisenhunt & Kress, 2013). Expressive art techniques are experiential, by definition, in that clients—through expressive techniques—create, and thus experience.

Creative and expressive arts interventions that pull from media such as drawing, painting, making symbolic objects out of materials, and collaging can be helpful when working with those who self-injure (Martin et al., 2012; Whisenhunt & Kress, 2013). Because those who self-injure struggle with verbal expression and feeling identification, counseling approaches that focus on creative expression and not solely on verbal communication may be helpful (Martin et al., 2012; Whisenhunt & Kress, 2013). The act of creating is, by definition, experiential. The artistic, experiential process can help clients connect with their feelings and emotions. Creating and experiencing can, at times and for some clients, be more effective than communicating through language when navigating painful emotions (Kress et al., 2021). Although there is a limited body of research to support the use of expressive arts when counseling those who self-injure, expressive arts have demonstrated effectiveness with a wide array of populations, including those who experience depression, anxiety, and trauma, struggles that those who self-injure often co-navigate (MacIntosh, 2017; Martin et al., 2012).

There are many advantages to the use of art and creativity in counseling those who self-injure. One benefit of using visual arts is that it may enhance a client's sense of control over themselves and their counseling experience (Edgar-Bailey & Kress, 2010). Because many clients who self-injure have ambivalence regarding the change process (Kress & Hoffman, 2008), it may be especially important to the therapeutic relationship and the counseling process that clients feel in control of their counseling experience. When using expressive arts, the client has the freedom to choose the words, colors, artistic media, and therapeutic topics. Expressive arts can also facilitate a catharsis or emotional release. Clients typically look to NSSI for an emotional release or regulation, but expression and creativity may provide an alternative to this behavior. Self-disclosure can be intimidating for clients, and those who self-injure may feel shame when discussing their experiences. Particularly for those with a trauma history, expressive arts may provide a safe, controlled form of communication and sharing (MacIntosh, 2017; Martin et al., 2012).

Collage is one example of an expressive arts activity that may be helpful with those who self-injure (Whisenhunt & Kress, 2013). Collage involves assembling parts to create a whole. A collage can be constructed using images or quotes obtained from the internet, newspaper or magazine clippings, photographs, recycled gift cards, or any other small objects. The counselor provides the client with a directive and these objects are then placed on a piece of paper or a canvas, or arranged in any other creative way. Collage requires no artistic skill and the creative possibilities are endless.

An application of collage to work with those who self-injure is the *Before and After Collage* (Whisenhunt & Kress, 2013). In this activity, the client develops a collage that demonstrates the negative ways NSSI impacts their life. Using symbols, images, or words, the client then develops a future collage in which they depict what life will be like when they have control of the behavior. Prompts that may be helpful in processing the collage include (Whisenhunt & Kress, 2013): (a) explain your collages—what stood out for you? How did it feel to develop each of these? What did you learn about yourself?; (b) compare the first and second collage, examine which elements are consistent and which differ; (c) consider what resources and supports you will need to help you move toward the future collage; and (d) consider what barriers might get in the way of you reaching your future collage vision and how you can work toward overcoming those barriers.

Guided Imagery

Guided imagery is an experiential counseling technique that is grounded in a behavioral therapy framework and may be helpful when counseling those who self-injure (Kress et al., 2013; Kress et al., 2021). Guided imagery is a focused meditation technique that involves the use of descriptive language to pull in several or all senses to invoke strong mental imagery with the aim of helping a client experience an improved reality. Guided imagery is a system of visualization that may also be used to promote relaxation (Kress et al., 2021). In terms of application, it may be used to help clients develop an ability to connect with a safe or relaxing mental place during times of distress. Guided imagery may also be used as a form of distraction from unpleasant emotions. Clients may find guided imagery increases their ability to relax, while also distracting from urges to self-injure. Using guided imagery, clients may condition themselves such that urges to self-injure are replaced with an ability to self-soothe (Kress et al., 2013). Guided imagery may also assist clients in visualizing an improved life circumstance. Additionally, guided imagery may help clients connect with a better way of managing a problematic situation. Finally, guided imagery may facilitate an increase in self-awareness of psychological and physiological experiences and sensations, and it may help clients visualize desired circumstances and connect with possibilities. Instilling hope and supporting clients in using imagery to connect with an image of a positive future has been supported as an effective treatment for various mental health concerns (Kress & Paylo, 2019).

Guided imagery can help clients to imagine a future that does not include NSSI (Kress et al., 2013). Also, as previously stated, those who self-injure struggle with emotion regulation, and guided imagery may enhance relaxation and promote different ways of responding to urges to self-injure. Guided imagery techniques may also be used to help clients deepen their awareness and insight related to their emotions, thoughts, and behaviors. No empirical research to date has assessed the effectiveness of these techniques; however, a plethora of research suggests that guided imagery is helpful in minimizing the distress caused by a wide variety of physical and mental health disorders including trauma, anxiety, and depression (Kress et al., 2021). Guided imagery has earned the right to be considered a research-based approach for use in helping clients engage in behavioral change (Kress et al., 2021).

Prior to using guided imagery techniques with clients, counselors should assess the client's ability to maintain sustained concentration and stay present. After these issues have been determined, the counselor may then discuss with the client the risks and benefits associated with using guided imagery techniques. The following is a brief script that can be used in describing guided imagery to a client (Kress et al., 2013):

> *Guided imagery may help you connect with your thoughts, feelings, strengths, and internal resources. This may or may not be a helpful activity for you, but others in similar situations to yours have found this process to improve their ability to relax and ultimately cope with their thoughts and feelings about self-injury. I am extremely interested in how this intervention will work for you. How would you feel about trying out this technique? At any time, you can tell me you would like to stop and we will halt the process. I am hopeful that you will be able to discover some new insights, as well as feel empowered to manage the impulses to self-injure.*

Once the counselor and client have set the intention of the guided imagery activity, the following steps may be helpful in focusing the guided imagery activity (Kress et al., 2021): (a) assess, educate, and promote relaxation skills as a foundation to the intervention; (b) help the client develop an imagery scene that promotes security, safety, and health; (c) during the guided imagery process, present the client with a task or question related to the intent of the activity (e.g., the purpose of this activity is to help you gain a sense of control over your behavior); (d) aid clients in visualizing themselves as empowered and successful throughout the process; and (e) request the client say goodbye to the activity facilitator and gradually leave the imagery scene and enter back into the present.

To encourage client engagement and empowerment, the counselor should provide the client with as much control over the guided imagery process as possible. Additionally, questions such as the following might be used to help the client process during the postguided imagery time. These questions attempt to increase clients' learning and awareness related to the guided imagery, and the answers to these questions will impact how the counselor manages future sessions. The following questions can be used (Kress et al., 2013):

- Describe the guided imagery process. How did the session feel or go for you?
- What were your thoughts and feelings about the relaxation aspect of the guided imagery, the part before your actual imagery began?
- Is there anything that seemed to make guided imagery better or more effective for you?
- Is there anything that seemed to inhibit it or make it less effective?
- Have you experienced any personal changes, for example, in your health or healing, that you associate with your participation in guided imagery?

- Is there anything else you would like to add about your experience using guided imagery that I have not asked you?

The provider must consider that the skill of visualization is a learned practice. Visualization needs to be practiced repeatedly and used over time for it to be effective. After the client has demonstrated mastery of this process, the counselor may consider assigning imagery activities weekly, daily, or even in reaction to certain situations. The counselor can record short, guided imagery activities (e.g., 3 to 5 min) for the client or have the client co-construct a script or tape to aid in this process.

An example of a guided imagery technique is the *Protective Shields* activity (Kress et al., 2013), in which clients are guided through an imagery exercise in which they imagine a protective shield that can be used to prevent NSSI. This activity is intended to promote bodily and affective awareness, and it is a skill that can be used by clients to prevent NSSI. The materials that are needed include paper and drawing materials such as paint, markers, oils, pastels, or crayons. The client is first educated on the purpose and intention of the activity. The client is invited to relax with their eyes closed or open, depending upon which feels most comfortable to them. The client is then invited to focus on the area of their body where they most commonly injure. The following script is read to the client:

> *Focus on the area of your body where you most often want to self-injure. Focus your attention on that part of the body and notice: the color, its weight, texture, movements, shape, and form. Take a few minutes to connect with this area of your body: feel its weight, texture, shape . . . consider the function this part of your body serves, and take a moment to honor it . . . be aware of its function, its mobility, its ability to support and work together with the rest of your body. How does this part of your body connect you to the world? Take a few minutes to continue to relax and connect with your body. Now, imagine you have some type of a protective shield over this area of your body: What texture is it? What is the shield's color? Is it just one color? How intense is the color? What is the shape of the shield? When do you need to connect with this shield? Take a few minutes to connect with your image of this shield. When you have a clear image, open your eyes and draw what came to you.*

Questions that can be used in processing this activity include the following: "What was this activity like for you?" "How did you see the area of your body where you self-injured?" "What was it like for you to resurrect this shield?" "When do you think you need to use this shield?"

A study conducted by Toussaint et al. (2021) utilized guided imagery as an intervention to promote physiological and psychological relaxation. Again, guided imagery has shown positive effects in coping with trauma, depression, anxiety and other various mental health conditions (Kress et al., 2021). In the context of this study, guided imagery is a potential way to decrease the frequency of NSSI related to mental health disorders.

Researchers gathered 60 undergraduate students and implemented techniques such as progressive muscle relaxation and deep breathing in addition to guided imagery (Toussaint et al., 2021). When compared to the baseline before intervention as well as the outcome of the control group, results displayed that the participants using guided imagery had the greatest change from their baseline of psychological relaxation and the results were statistically significant (Toussaint et al., 2021). Participants were the most relaxed after completing guided imagery. In terms of physiological relaxation, both guided imagery and progressive muscle relaxation interventions displayed significant changes from baseline to completion (Toussaint et al., 2021). Because these techniques are relatively feasible to teach clients, they can yield promising results in decreasing maladaptive coping mechanisms (including NSSI). Though this particular study does not focus on NSSI, the displayed results of increasing physical and mental relaxation are effective replacements for partaking in NSSI.

Not all clients have the capacity to visualize, and some clients respond better than others to this activity. Future research might empirically evaluate the usefulness of guided imagery as an intervention in working with those who self-injure.

Experiential Therapies that Focus on Relationships

Because NSSI is often a result of insecure attachments and an attempt to regulate emotions, experiential therapies that focus on relationships are well suited for integration into counseling with this population (Gleiser, 2021; Kimball, 2009; see Pollak et al., this volume, for review of social processes in NSSI). The two experiential therapies that focus on relationships that will be discussed in this chapter are emotion-focused therapy (EFT) and accelerated experiential dynamic psychotherapy (AEDP). Both of these therapies are founded on attachment theory, which suggests that individuals who have insecure attachments have a higher likelihood of self-injuring and experiencing mental health issues. EFT and AEDP both aim to create a strong therapeutic relationship to facilitate a corrective emotional experience, thus reducing NSSI (Bridges, 2006; Fosha, 2021).

EMOTION-FOCUSED THERAPY

EFT (also known as process-experiential therapy or focusing-oriented therapy) foundational themes focus on attachments and emotion regulation. As such, it may be useful with those who self-injure since insecure attachment patterns and an aim to regulate emotions are common predictors of NSSI (Kimball, 2009). EFT addresses the etiology of NSSI by encouraging the use of emotion expression, teaching emotion regulation skills, and enhancing healthy relationships which in turn may decrease the likelihood of NSSI. EFT, which has been around for more than 40 years, focuses on meaning-making through self-awareness and language, which create emotion schemes (Greenberg, 2006). Emotion schemes are made up of emotions, cognitions, and motivation, which evolve from people's experiences with their environment and interactions with other individuals. Emotion schemes often predict behavior and act as lenses through which individuals perceive their world, relationships, and themselves.

A core component of EFT is attachment theory (Kimball, 2009). When individuals have secure attachments, they are more likely to develop healthy emotion schemes, whereas when they have insecure attachments, they are more likely to experience unhealthy emotion schemes. Differing attachments are based on differing experiences during childhood. For example, when children experience trauma, such as neglect or abuse from their caregivers, an insecure attachment is likely to form. Within mental health counseling, therapists aim to provide a corrective emotional experience through the therapeutic relationship to combat previous harmful interpersonal relationships by creating a safe and empathetic environment (Bridges, 2006; Kimball, 2009). When clients are provided a safe space to process their emotions through interpersonal interactions, they are more likely to form positive emotions (Greenberg, 2006). Additionally, therapists aim to show empathy and unconditional positive regard, enhancing the likelihood of transforming insecure attachments into secure attachments, thus reducing NSSI.

EFT also focuses on tolerating and experiencing negative emotions through the use of experiential activities, and this may also enhance emotion regulation (Kimball, 2009). For example, mindful emotion awareness is an intervention that can be used to help clients notice their emotions through acceptance and a nonjudgmental attitude. This directly goes against the experiential avoidance model, which often maintains NSSI (Anderson & Crowther, 2012; see Hird et al., this volume, for comparison of theoretical models). Research suggests that individuals who self-injure often have deficits in self-awareness, and this approach's focus on awareness may be helpful (Dixon-Gordon et al., 2014). Additionally, mindfulness often alleviates the effects of depression, which can mitigate the relationship between depression and NSSI (Heath, Carsley, et al., 2016). When clients have self-awareness of their negative emotions, as well as awareness of the triggers of their emotions, they are better equipped to transform their negative emotions into positive emotions. Emotion schemes can be identified, explored, and transformed by creating new meaning from experiences. When emotion schemes are explored, new emotion schemes with more pleasant emotions, cognitions, and behaviors are within reach. EFT also aims to teach clients new emotion regulation skills to manage unpleasant emotions in more effective ways.

Another EFT intervention that is highly effective and can be used to reduce NSSI is cognitive reappraisal (Voon et al., 2014). Cognitive reappraisal involves identifying thoughts related to a situation that produces emotions and then changing the thoughts so that they are more helpful and accurate, ideally reducing the intensity of the emotions. This gives individuals the opportunity to create new meaning and new perspectives that improve well-being and reduce NSSI (Bentley et al., 2017).

ACCELERATED EXPERIENTIAL DYNAMIC PSYCHOTHERAPY

AEDP (Fosha, 2000) has been around for about two decades, and it is helpful in addressing trauma and dissociation, two issues commonly associated with NSSI (Gleiser, 2021; Polk & Liss, 2009; Saxe et al., 2002; Zlotnik et al., 2001). AEDP is commonly delivered across 16 sessions, and it has been shown to effect desirable mental health outcomes in a clinical and subclinical sample of individuals across the United States, Canada, Israel, Japan, and Sweden (Iwakabe et al., 2020). AEDP has been found to increase psychological functioning and decrease distress, both of which can contribute to a reduction in NSSI (Iwakabe et al., 2020; Kress et al., 2021).

Through a combination of neurobiology, attachment theory, body-focused approaches, and transformational studies, AEDP is used to support the process of neuroplasticity. Neuroplasticity is the brain's ability to change and adapt, which can occur at any point in the lifespan, not just during childhood (Fuchs & Flügge, 2014). The combination of attachment theory and transformational studies allows an individual to identify sources of trauma and dissociation in their life and process the emotions surrounding such stressors. Healthy attachment within the therapeutic relationship is leveraged and processed as the physical state of being secure (Lipton & Fosha, 2011). This physical state promotes healthy body-focused shifts in the present moment, and this experience can be generalized outside the session.

Unhealthy attachment experiences can lead to physical changes in the structure of the brain. When an individual is stressed, the brain responds by retreating and protecting from pain as much as possible. However, these protective changes in the brain are not desirable long term and can lead to unhealthy relational behaviors and unhelpful coping skills (e.g., avoidance, dissociation, and NSSI). According to AEDP, however, the brain defenses that are developed over time in the context of stressful life experiences can be altered using the transformational power of secure attachment between client and therapist (Lipton & Fosha, 2011). Clients are able to heal from past insecure attachments by experiencing a secure attachment within the therapeutic relationship. Furthermore, the healthy attachment experienced in therapy allows clients to experience healthier relationships outside therapy. AEDP aims to heal past stress and promote posttraumatic growth as clients develop an ability to feel safer and more secure in their relationships.

AEDP assumes a healing orientation in which it is believed that all individuals are inherently able to rebuild and thrive despite past challenges (Fosha, 2021). The therapeutic process involves intentionally building relational safety between client and counselor in order to process emotions in healthy ways rather than through NSSI or the use of other unhealthy coping skills. When clients feel safe with their therapist, they are able to come into contact with painful emotions and process them in healthy ways. They learn that they have the inherent power to heal from past relationships and to foster new, healthier ways of relating to others and themselves.

Therapeutic techniques associated with AEDP are used with two ultimate goals: to promote secure attachment within the therapeutic relationship and to harness the transformational power of secure attachment in order to create meaningful and lasting psychological changes in the client's brain (Lipton & Fosha, 2011). Tracking is an essential technique used in AEDP in order to foster secure attachment within the therapeutic relationship (Hanakawa, 2021). Therapists should track each moment with a client and explore past and present sources of stress. Therapists should focus on accurately identifying client feelings, uncovering sources of client defensiveness, exploring client anxieties, tracking relationship shifts within the dyad, and tracking therapist emotions as therapeutically relevant. This relational attunement creates the secure attachment needed to process past relational difficulties and grow through somatic changes that can be observed in the moment (Hanakawa, 2021). Overall, AEDP therapists should foster a genuine relationship with clients through emotional attunement and tracking of the therapeutic process.

In AEDP, the experience of secure attachment within the therapeutic relationship creates insight and lasting change (Fosha, 2021). As clients encounter their core selves and experience healthy attachment, physical transformation happens in the brain and the body (Fosha, 2021). The therapist helps clients process past experiences in the context of the safe and secure therapeutic relationship, and these physical experiences help clients connect with baseline feelings of safety and security. In addition to healthier neurobiology, the therapeutic relationship empowers clients and provides them with a greater sense of resiliency against future stressors.

When clients focus on the thoughts and feelings associated with healthy attachment, they are able to mindfully reflect on the present moment and make healthier choices (Hanakawa, 2021). These choices can lead to stronger mental health. For example, an individual who feels secure and believes that they are loved and worthwhile might choose going on a walk with a friend instead of self-injuring. The experience of healthy attachment is a transformational process.

Experiential Therapies That Focus on Thought and Behavior Change

Helping those who self-injure to connect with greater self-compassion may be helpful. The research base indicates that people who self-injure tend to experience elevated levels of negative affect, such as anger, guilt, and self-loathing (Armey et al., 2011); self-criticism (Hooley & St. Germain, 2014); shame ; inferiority (Gilbert et al., 2010); and lower levels of self-compassion (Gregory et al., 2017). Moreover, Per et al. (2022) found that "self-coldness" was a strong predictor of NSSI (Per et al., 2022, p. 9). These findings are probably not surprising to most mental health professionals, who typically observe high levels of self-deprecation among their clients who self-injure.

SELF-COMPASSION

Neff (2021) explains self-compassion as a way of being in which, "instead of mercilessly judging and criticizing yourself for various inadequacies or shortcomings . . . you are kind and understanding when confronted with personal failings" (para. 3). Neff (2021) further explains that self-compassion consists of three characteristics. The first characteristic is self-kindness, which Neff describes as "being warm and understanding toward ourselves when we suffer, fail, or feel inadequate, rather than ignoring our pain or flagellating ourselves with self-criticism" (para. 5). The second characteristic is recognizing that suffering is common to humanity. Neff explains that self-compassion involves "recognizing that suffering and personal inadequacy is part of the shared human experience—something that we all go through rather than being something that happens to 'me' alone" (para. 6). Finally, Neff states that self-compassion involves the ability to mindfully experience negative emotions so that they are "neither suppressed nor exaggerated" (para. 7). In sum, self-compassion is the ability to extend to oneself the compassion one would extend to others (Neff, 2015).

Bluth and Blanton (2014) extended Neff's work on self-compassion, finding that self-compassion and mindfulness are important mediators for emotional well-being in adolescents. This is particularly important due to the characteristic tendency of adolescence to involve ample self-criticism and negative self-evaluation (Bluth & Blanton, 2014). Bluth (2017) further proposed a model of mindful self-compassion for teens that may prove helpful in mediating the risk of NSSI.

COMPASSION-FOCUSED THERAPY

Compassion-focused therapy (CFT) is a relatively new therapeutic approach, which Vliet and Kalnins (2011) describe as a "form of cognitive behavioral therapy aimed at helping people with mental health problems that are related to shame and self-directed hostility" (p. 296). Gilbert (2010), who proposed the CFT model, stated that it was developed as an offspring of cognitive behavioral therapy (CBT) for clients who experience shame and self-criticism, particularly those whose family-of-origin dynamics were challenging. Gilbert (2010) described CFT as an approach that integrates Buddhist teachings, evolution, neuroscience, and social psychology. Although it is beyond the scope of this chapter to present a full review of CFT, we will offer a summary of some key aspects of the approach.

First, according to Gilbert (2010), CFT is based on the premise that clients must develop self-compassion, compassion for others, and the ability to understand and be receptive to compassion from others. This does not mean that clients should avoid painful memories and experiences. Rather, they can learn to tolerate their strong feelings and approach those experiences and feelings with acceptance and compassion. Second, interactions with others that involve compassion or self-criticism tend to trigger a mirror response in the client (Gilbert, 2010). Accordingly, critical relationships tend to foster engrained self-criticism, whereas compassionate relationships tend to foster self-compassion.

Although CFT utilizes several strategies founded in a traditional CBT approach, focus is given to compassionate imagery and affect regulation (Gilbert, 2010). In so doing, the therapist works with clients to help them experience compassion rather than simply understand it from a cognitive perspective. For this reason, it is imperative that the therapist works to establish a sense of safety and trust in the therapeutic relationship, wherein the client can be sufficiently vulnerable to receive the therapist's compassion—an experience that may be acutely unfamiliar to the client (see Gilbert, 2010). Gilbert described this process as experiencing togetherness, and it is this interpersonal-experiential component that forms the basis for therapeutic efficacy.

Vliet and Kalnins (2011) proposed a model for applying CFT to the treatment of NSSI. They stated that through practice of CFT techniques, clients who self-injure can become better aware and more tolerant of their moment-to-moment experiences and learn how to soothe themselves in the face of emotional distress. A compassion-focused approach may also help clients minimize self-directed hostility as they better learn to direct patience, understanding, and kindness toward themselves (Vliet & Kalnins, 2011). CFT aligns well with mindfulness-based practice, which is described next.

MINDFULNESS

Mindfulness is defined as "the awareness that emerges through paying attention on purpose, in the present moment, and nonjudgmentally to the unfolding of experiences moment by moment" (Kabat-Zinn, 2003, p. 145). Mindfulness is a form of meditation in which one suspends interpretation or judgment and focuses attention on both internal and external stimuli (Hooker & Fodor, 2008). Mindfulness helps in shifting one's mood and enhancing affect modulation to promote acceptance and change. This includes the development of "enhanced self-regulation," which includes attention regulation, emotional regulation, and body awareness (Treleaven, 2018, p. 31). Mindfulness includes a number of components, which Treleaven (2018) describes as (a) paying purposeful attention, (b) maintaining a present-moment focus, and (c) practicing nonjudgmental attention.

The use of mindfulness-based practice (MBP) in mental health has gained momentum in recent years. Hofmann et al. (2010) found that mindfulness can be advantageous in addressing processes that occur across a range of disorders, including anxiety and depression. Further, mindfulness can help facilitate self-soothing and awareness of negative emotions, thereby reducing emotional reactivity (Vliet & Kalnins, 2011). Combined with stress reduction strategies, mindfulness can increase well-being, restfulness, and the regulation of the body's physiological responses (Ernhout & Whitlock, 2014). And, perhaps most relevant to working with clients who self-injure, mindfulness can increase present-moment focus, self-compassion, and self-regulation (Treleaven, 2018).

The relationship between mindfulness and self-injury is becoming clearer through emergent literature, which suggests that lower levels of mindfulness may be related to higher rates of NSSI (Caltabiano & Martin, 2017; Garisch & Stewart Wilson, 2015). Relatedly, Heath, Joly, and Carsley (2016) found that participants who reported recent NSSI also reported lower levels of mindfulness and coping self-efficacy. This research provides a foundation for understanding the role mindfulness may play in understanding NSSI, although further research is needed to clarify the nature of the relationship between mindfulness and NSSI.

Conversely, when exploring the aspects of mindfulness that may be implicated in protecting against NSSI, Per et al. (2022) found that the "nonjudging and acting with awareness" aspects of mindfulness had a negative correlation with NSSI (p. 9). In a related study, Heath, Joly, and Carsley (2016) examined the roles of mindfulness and coping self-efficacy, or "solve problems and cope with difficult emotions" in the experience of NSSI. They found that participants who reported higher levels of mindfulness also had a higher perceived level of coping self-efficacy. These findings provide compelling evidence for the utilization of mindfulness in a therapeutic intervention with NSSI, which is further supported by some preliminary evidence that mindfulness practice may help to reduce the risk of repeated self-injury among clients who experience marked anxiety (Bock et al., 2021) and that mindfulness practice may help to mediate (or reduce) the risk of suicide among clients who self-injure (Warner, 2017). To this end, Heath, Joly, and Carsley (2016) suggested that teaching mindfulness may decrease rumination, increase acceptance and tolerance of difficult emotions, and, thereby, lead to a reduction in the need to self-injure. As the literature base continues to evolve, we are likely to see mindfulness play a more prominent role in the treatment of NSSI.

EMOTIONAL FREEDOM TECHNIQUE

EFT (Craig & Fowlie, 1995) is an experiential approach that blends cognitive therapy, behavioral exposure, and acupressure. Acupressure follows the ancient Chinese theory in which energy flows through pathways in our bodies called meridians, and the starting and ending points to these meridians are especially powerful for healing (Callahan & Trubo, 2001). For example, under the eye lies the end point for the meridian that runs through the stomach. Imaginal exposure is achieved in session by having clients reflect upon bothersome problems, and cognitive therapy is used to reframe irrational thoughts. A therapist using EFT would guide the client to develop a setup statement that is repeated while the client engages in a specific sequence of tapping points in order to help reprocess their thoughts and feelings.

More than 100 randomized control trials, outcome studies, and meta-analyses have provided evidence for the effectiveness of EFT (Church & Nelms, 2016). EFT meets the American Psychological Association's Division 12 Task Force criteria to be considered an empirically validated treatment for anxiety, depression, and posttraumatic stress disorder (PTSD; Church et al., 2014). EFT has also been found to contribute to significant improvement in physical conditions such as tension headaches, and pain (Bougea et al., 2013; Church, 2014). In general, EFT has been found to effectively improve mental and physical health in university students (Boath et al., 2013) and in a clinical population (Stewart et al., 2013). EFT is a promising technique for individuals who use NSSI due to the frequency with which NSSI is associated with mood disorders and trauma. Visit EFTuniverse for more information.

There is growing support for the use of EFT as a safe and effective method for addressing psychological and physical challenges (Church, 2013). A sequence of tapping on various acupressure points can address a wide variety of concerns, rather than having to find the specific acupressure point associated with the specific thought and feeling (Callahan & Trubo, 2001). EFT works to desensitize the power of uncomfortable feelings by shifting the underlying thought while simultaneously applying acupressure.

When starting EFT, clients should be encouraged to think about something that bothers them. The problem statement in EFT identifies specifically what is bothering a client with an emphasis on reframing the idea. This process of reframing is facilitated by starting the problem statement with "Even though . . ." and stating after it, "I deeply and completely accept myself." (Church, 2013, p. 649). For example, a client who self-injures might say, "Even though I self-injure, I deeply and completely accept myself." This problem statement is therapeutic in itself as it allows clients to reframe shame and judgment about the behavior so that they can deeply and completely accept themselves. The cognitive reframe is enhanced by sequential tapping while repeating the statement setup (Craig & Fowlie, 1995). This helps to process the thoughts in healthier ways and releases the body from the burden of the feeling associated with the problematic thought.

EFT is an innovative and integrative mental health intervention that is picking up traction in helping fields. Through the process of EFT, individuals who typically self-injure can be encouraged to use tapping in the moment to make cognitive, emotional, and physical shifts. EFT is an evidence-based practice (Church et al., 2014), and therapists should introduce this intervention to clients intentionally when it is therapeutically indicated.

EYE MOVEMENT DESENSITIZATION AND REPROCESSING

EMDR is a therapeutic approach primarily utilized to help clients cope with trauma and work toward changing maladaptive thoughts (Shapiro & Laliotis, 2011; Slotema et al., 2019). The adaptive information processing (AIP) model accompanies EMDR, stating that symptoms of mental illness are considered to be a result of repressed, negative memories in the brain (Proudlock & Peris, 2020). The process itself is relatively groundbreaking, with little research in regard to NSSI. However, because it is a treatment that focuses on cognition and behavior, it is a plausible therapy for NSSI. In addition, EMDR has previously shown to be an effective treatment for PTSD and other trauma-related disorders (Slotema et al., 2019).

EMDR therapy contains eight stages, each working to aid clients in emotion regulation and preventing behaviors of self-harm. The first stage involves investigating the client's history of NSSI. Without knowing the client's background and patterns of behavior, clinicians struggle with treating NSSI (Mosquera & Ross, 2016). Once clinicians understand why a client self-injures, creating a proper, individualized treatment plan becomes feasible (Mosquera & Ross, 2016). The second phase encompasses stabilization of behavior. Aspects of dialectical behavior therapy (DBT), a treatment typically used for borderline personality disorder (BPD), can be utilized during the early stages of EMDR (Linehan, 1993; Mosquera & Ross, 2016). The remaining phases of EMDR encompass aiding clients in reconstructing their maladaptive thoughts. However, because trauma can be so complex, confronting adversity during these phases may trigger thoughts and actions of self-harm (Mosquera & Ross, 2016).

NSSI is a maladaptive coping mechanism for trauma. Considering self-injury is a mere thought, but once it is acted upon, the behavior cannot be taken back (Kress et al., 2021). Not only can these behaviors become visible to others, but they can also have lasting negative impacts. People may become comfortable with NSSI, therefore deeming it unproblematic. Circumventing decision-making, or inaction (Kress et al., 2021), about reducing NSSI behaviors is harmful as well. Cognitions are involved alongside behavior. EMDR can be effective for both aiding clients in making changes in their self-injurious behavior and ensuring that inaction is ceased.

RESOURCE DEVELOPMENT AND INSTALLATION

RDI is a method for clients to recognize adaptive coping mechanisms and put them into practice (Ibadi et al., 2018). This practice is the second stage of the EMDR therapeutic intervention. EMDR is primarily used to treat trauma or mental illness directly related to intense, stressful events (Shapiro & Laliotis, 2011).NSSI is often used by distressed individuals as a maladaptive coping mechanism. The ultimate goal of this intervention is to decrease negative feelings and maladaptive coping mechanisms, therefore decreasing and ultimately preventing NSSI.

Ibadi et al. (2018) conducted a study utilizing RDI to discover its relation to self-injury. The research was a case study, covering only one participant: a 16- year-old female. The teenager turned to NSSI when feeling anxiety regarding her performance in school, potential rumors being spread about her, and other various situations that caused her distress (Ibadi et al., 2018). Ibadi et al. (2018) also reported that the participant's thoughts were self-deprecating as she stated that she was "a disappointment" and "not good enough" (p. 119). Implementing RDI, however, displayed success for the teenager. Though thoughts of NSSI did not completely vanish, the behavior ceased as she began changing her thinking: her thoughts became positive and she began taking part in hobbies she enjoyed when she felt like she might perform NSSI (Ibadi et al., 2018).

This study displays promising information in terms of treatment for NSSI. RDI and EMDR were successful in the case of this research and though the literature is limited, this study opens multiple doors for future replication.

Limitations and Implications

Although experiential therapies have the potential to be particularly effective and powerful when working with clients who self-injure, caution is necessary. We present recommendations here to assist therapists in utilizing experiential therapies from a trauma-informed perspective, but this list is not exhaustive. As such, and in consideration of the changing landscape of this topic, it is imperative that therapists remain abreast of the current research and literature related to the treatment of NSSI and techniques for utilizing experiential therapies. Many of the recommendations herein are extended from literature regarding the clinical application of mindfulness.

Perhaps most important, therapists should remember that trauma resolution therapy should be a primary treatment focus when trauma is present. Experiential therapies may assist with achieving treatment goals, helping clients learn to manage trauma symptoms, and supporting clients' overall adaptive functioning, but these therapies are part of a larger clinical approach that must address the underlying factors that contributed to the development of NSSI. Equally important, therapists should work to create a safe and comfortable physical environment that is conducive to therapy and minimizes trauma triggers and NSSI triggers. This is part of utilizing a trauma-informed lens, which is described as "recogniz[ing] and respond[ing] to the impact of traumatic stress" on those who have contact with the system of care (National Child Traumatic Stress Network, n.d.). Trauma-informed care involves remaining aware of the effects of trauma, viewing behavior and symptoms through a trauma-informed lens, being sensitive to factors that may exacerbate trauma symptoms, and empowering clients to take control of their own treatment. Although not all clients who self-injure have experienced trauma, therapists should remain attuned to the possible influence of trauma and monitor clients' responses accordingly. This is a particularly important clinical task because the experiential nature of the interventions described herein may trigger interoceptive experiences, which could lead to trauma re experiencing. Accordingly, therapists should be prepared to manage transcrisis symptoms, which may require crisis stabilization.

When using interventions that have the potential to be particularly emotionally evocative, therapists should monitor clients' reaction and adapt interventions as needed to match client needs. It is important to utilize a compassionate, empathetic, caring therapeutic approach that supports client empowerment (Baer et al., 2019), intentionally practicing non judg ment of trauma and NSSI to facilitate a sense of safety and acceptance in the therapeutic relationship. Likewise, therapists can work with clients to emphasize nonjudgmental present-moment awareness and make efforts to avoid rumination or judgmental present-moment awareness, as these can be harmful (Baer et al., 2019). Therapists may utilize psychoeducation to prepare clients for experiential therapies (Baer et al., 2019) and allow them to make treatment decisions.

When utilizing experiential therapies, therapists may incorporate multiple strategies to manage emotional reactivity. First, it is important to monitor the duration and intensity of interventions to avoid over stimulation (Baer et al., 2019). It may be helpful to start with brief, concrete exercises to build competency and efficacy while avoiding retraumatization (Treleaven, 2018) or triggering NSSI. Treleaven proposed a "window of tolerance" (p. 87), which is the "zone that lies between the two extremes of hyper- and hypoarousal" (Treleaven, 2018, p. 93). Therapists may utilize an "arousal scale" to help clients monitor their arousal and stay within the window of tolerance (Treleaven, 2018, p. 109). Treleaven (2018) further described a "mindful gauge," which can help clients measure their response to various stimuli (e.g., physical sensations, moods, feelings, and thoughts) in the moment when practicing mindfulness, but this gauge may be useful across experiential therapies to avoid retraumatization and to identify the interventions or strategies that are effective for the client.

Although some level of emotional discomfort is expected, when clients begin to feel overwhelmed with trauma memories or sensations, they may use anchors to help them refocus their attention on a safe stimulus (Treleaven, 2018). Therapists can help to taper their clients' emotional reactivity by utilizing strategies that slow the experiential without entirely interrupting it. Examples may include opening the eyes, taking additional breaths, taking a short pause/break, or doing a grounding exercise (see Treleaven, 2018).

To allow for the development of self-efficacy and self-regulation, it might be advantageous to begin with guided exercises during therapeutic sessions that provide safety, guidance, and support before inviting clients to use experiential techniques outside of session. As clients' skills begin to improve related to self-regulation when using experiential therapies, therapists may encourage clients to use psychoeducational materials or short guided exercises outside of session (Baer et al., 2019). As clients build confidence and skill in the use of experiential therapies, clients may practice using these skills to support positive social interaction within the window of tolerance (Treleaven, 2018).

Case Study

Cassandra is a 21-year-old transgender female presenting to individual counseling primarily due to PTSD, a history of self-injurious behaviors, difficulty regulating emotions, and instability in interpersonal relationships. When asked what her primary goal for seeking counseling is, she reported that she wants to "stop self-injuring and learn about healthy relationships." In a recent counseling session, Cassandra reported that she had a difficult childhood due to her parents divorcing when she was young, and she reports a history of emotional and physical abuse. Throughout Cassandra's counseling sessions, Cassandra and her counselor collaboratively explored how Cassandra's insecure attachments as a young child have impacted her experiences with emotion regulation and unhealthy interpersonal relationships. Cassandra developed an insight that she was never taught how to notice or name her emotions and she was often punished for expressing emotions. As an adult, she self-injures secondary to frustration, and she reports that it is how she expresses her emotions. Additionally, Cassandra disclosed to her counselor that her parents do not accept her for who she is and that they often misgender her and tell her that her shift toward identifying as a female is "a phase." Because of this, the counselor utilized the therapeutic relationship as a tool for growth by creating a safe, empathetic, and accepting environment in which Cassandra was taught how to notice and identify emotions as they arise, as well as begin the journey of self-acceptance. With Cassandra's consent, the counselor integrated various experiential activities into the therapeutic process. Because of Cassandra's difficulty regulating emotions, the counselor integrated an experiential activity called the Self-Injury Before and After collage (described earlier in this chapter). As Cassandra engaged in the creation of her collage, she was able to identify feelings that developed during the "before" collage. The "before" collage included pictures of isolation, hiding, darkness, and crying, and she identified feelings of shame, guilt, and sadness. During the development of the "after" collage, Cassandra identified feelings of "freedom, self-acceptance, and hope" and chose pictures that included belongingness, positive affirmations, and sunshine. Cassandra identified social supports that she can utilize as she moves forward with the experiences of the "after" collage to reduce self-injurious behavior and find healthy relationships. Cassandra disclosed that she is hopeful for the future and feels more empowered to regulate her emotions in more effective ways.

Future Research Directions

Although previous research has highlighted the significance of the therapeutic alliance to overall treatment outcomes (Horvath et al., 2011; Wampold, 2015), future research may examine the impact, if any, of the use of experiential techniques on the therapeutic relationship. Similarly, although research is emerging to address the impact of the therapist's attachment on the therapeutic alliance (Rizou & Giannouli, 2020) and the impact of the client's attachment style on the therapeutic alliance (Smith et al., 2010), additional research might examine the interactions between attachment, experiential therapies, and therapeutic alliance. These two lines of inquiry could help to expand our understanding of therapist qualities and therapeutic practices that can most effectively support treatment when using an experiential approach.

A compelling line of inquiry is related to the potential for retraumatization when using experiential therapies, particularly those that involve mindfulness, projection, and/or interoceptive experiencing. Such research could yield evidence-based practices for trauma-informed application of experiential therapies.

Conclusion

This chapter provided an overview of experiential therapies that can be utilized while working with individuals who self-injure. Experiential therapies are particularly helpful because they address many of the common reasons people self-injure, including alexithymia, emotion regulation, and emotion expression. Experiential therapies focus on the here and now rather than the past and the future. By gaining awareness of one's emotions and experiences, individuals are more likely to engage in more effective emotion regulation skills. Experiential therapies also focus greatly on the therapeutic alliance and hold that through corrective emotional experiences, healing can occur (Bridges, 2006; Fosha, 2021). Additionally, experiential therapies give individuals the opportunity to learn various behavioral and cognitive strategies to cope with emotions, thus reducing NSSI (Church, 2013; Treleaven, 2018; Vliet & Kalnins, 2011).

References

Anderson, N. L., & Crowther, J. H. (2012). Using the experiential avoidance model of non-suicidal self injury: Understanding who stops and who continues. *Archives of Suicide Research*, *16*, 124–134. https://doi.org/10.1080/13811118.2012.667329

Armey, M. F., Crowther, J. H., & Miller, I. W. (2011). Changes in ecological momentary assessment reported affect associated with episodes of nonsuicidal self-injury. *Behavior Therapy*, *42*(4), 579–588.

Baer, R., Crane, C., Miller, E., & Kuyken, W. (2019). Doing no harm in mindfulness-based programs: Conceptual issues and empirical findings. *Clinical Psychology Review*, *71*, 101–114. https://doi.org/10.1016/j.cpr.2019.01.001

Bedi, R., Muller, R. T., & Classen, C. C. (2014). Cumulative risk for deliberate self-harm among treatment-seeking women with histories of childhood abuse. *Psychological Trauma: Theory, Research, Practice, and Policy*, *6*(6), 600–609.

Bentley, K. H., Nock, M. K., Sauer-Zavala, S., Gorman, B. S., & Harlow, D. H. (2017). A functional analysis of two transdiagnostic, emotion-focused interventions on nonsuicidal self-injury. *Journal of Consulting and Clinical Psychology*, *85*(6), 632–646. https://dx.doi.org/10.1037/ccp0000205

Bjureberg, J., Sahlin, H., Hedman-Lagerlof, E., Gratz, K. L., Tull, M. T., Jokinen, J., Hellner, C., & Ljotsson, B. (2018). Extending research on emotion regulation individual therapy for adolescents (ERITA) with nonsuicidal self-injury disorder: Open pilot trial and mediation analysis of a novel online version. *BMC Pyschiatry*, *18*, 1–13, https://doi.org/10.1186/s12888-018-1885-6

Bluth, K. (2017). *The self-compassion workbook for teens: Mindfulness and compassion skills to overcome self-criticism and embrace who you are*. Instant Help.

Bluth, K., & Blanton, P. (2014). Mindfulness and self-compassion: Exploring pathways to adolescent emotional well-being. *Journal of Child & Family Studies*, *23*(7), 1298–1309. https://doi.org/10.1007/s10826-013-9830-2

Boath, E., Stewart, A., & Carryer, A. (2013). Tapping for success: A pilot study to explore if emotional freedom techniques (EFT) can reduce anxiety and enhance academic performance in university students. *Innovative Practice in Higher Education*, *1*, 1–13.

Bock, R. C., Berghoff, C. R., Baker, L. D., Tull, M. T., & Gratz, K. L. (2021). The relation of anxiety to nonsuicidal self injury is indirect through mindfulness. *Mindfulness*, *12*(8), 2022–2033. https://doi.org/10.1007/s12671-021-01660-2

Bougea, A. M., Spandideas, N., Alexopoulos, E. C., Thomaides, T., Chrousos, G. P., & Darviri, C. (2013). Effect of the emotional freedom technique on perceived stress, quality of life, and cortisol salivary levels in tension-type headache sufferers: A randomized controlled trial. *Explore: The Journal of Science and Healing*, *9*, 91–99. http://dx.doi.org/10.1016/j.explore.2012.12.005

Bridges, M. R. (2006). Activating the corrective emotional experience. *Journal of Clinical Psychology: In Session*, *62*(5), 551–568.

Callahan, R. J., & Trubo, R. (2001). *Tapping the healer within: Using thought field therapy to instantly conquer your fears, anxieties, and emotional distress.* McGraw-Hill.

Caltabiano, G., & Martin, G. (2017). Mindless suffering: The relationship between mindfulness and non-suicidal self-injury. *Mindfulness, 8*(3), 788–796. https://doi.org/10.1007/s12671-016-0657-y

Church, D. (2013). Clinical EFT as an evidence-based practice for the treatment of psychological and physiological conditions. *Psychology, 4,* 645–654. https://doi.org/10.4236/psych.2013.48092

Church, D. (2014). Reductions in pain, depression, and anxiety symptoms after PTSD remediation in veterans. *Explore: The Journal of Science and Healing, 10,* 162–169. https://doi.org/10.1016/j.explore.2014.02.005

Church, D., Feinstein, D., Palmer-Hoffman, J., Stein, P. K., & Tranguch, A. (2014). Empirically supported psychological treatments: The challenge of evaluating clinical innovations. *Journal of Nervous and Mental Disease, 202,* 699–709. http://doi.org/10.1097/NMD.0000000000000188

Church, D., & Nelms, J. (2016). Pain, range of motion, and psychological symptoms in a population with frozen shoulder: A randomized controlled dismantling study of clinical EFT (emotional freedom techniques). *Archives of Scientific Psychology, 4,* 38–48. https://doi.org/proxy181.nclive.org/10.1037/arc0000028.supp

Craig, G., & Fowlie, A. (1995). *Emotional freedom techniques: The manual.* Gary Craig.

Dixon-Gordon, K. L., Tull, M. T., & Gratz, K. L. (2014). Self-injurious behaviors in posttraumatic stress disorder: An examination of potential moderators. *Journal of Affective Disorders, 166,* 359–367. http://doi.org/10.1016/j.jad.2014.05.033

Edgar-Bailey, M., & Kress, V. E. (2010). Resolving child and adolescent traumatic grief: Creative techniques and interventions. *Journal of Creativity in Mental Health, 5*(2), 158–176. doi: 10.1080/15401383.2010.485090.

Fosha, D. (2000). *The transforming power of affect: A model for accelerated change.* Basic Books.

Fosha, D. (2021). Introduction. In D. Fosha (Ed.), *Undoing aloneness & the transformation of suffering into flourishing: AEDP 2.0* (pp. 3–24). American Psychological Association. https://doi.org./10.1037/0000232-002

Fuchs, E., & Flügge, G. (2014). Adult neuroplasticity: More than 40 years of research. *Neural Plasticity, 2014,* Article 541870. https://doi.org/10.1155/2014/541870

Garisch, J. A., & Stewart Wilson, M. (2015). Prevalence, correlates, and prospective predictors of non-suicidal self-injury among New Zealand adolescents: Cross-sectional and longitudinal survey data. *Child & Adolescent Psychiatry & Mental Health, 9*(1), 1–11. https://doi.org/10.1186/s13034-015-0055-6

Gilbert, P. (2010). *Compassion focused therapy: Distinctive features.* Routledge.

Gilbert, P., McEwan, K., Irons, C., Bhundia, R., Christie, R., Broomhead, C., & Rockliff, H. (2010). Self-harm in a mixed clinical population: The roles of self-criticism, shame, and social rank. *British Journal of Clinical Psychology, 49*(4), 563–576.

Gleiser, K. A. (2021). Relational prisms: Navigating experiential attachment work with dissociation and multiplicity in AEDP. In D. Fosha (Ed.), *Undoing aloneness & the transformation of suffering into flourishing: AEDP 2.0* (pp. 321–345). American Psychological Association. https://doi.org/proxy181.nclive.org/10.1037/0000232-013

Greenberg, L. (2006). Emotion-focused therapy: A synopsis. *Journal of Contemporary Psychotherapy, 36,* 87–93. https://doi.org/10.1007/s10879-006-9011-3.

Greene, D., Boyes, M., & Hasking, P. (2020). The associations between alexithymia and both non-suicidal self-injury and risky drinking: A systematic review and meta-analysis. *Journal of Affective Disorders, 1*(260), 140–166. https://doi.org/10.1016/j.jad.2019.08.088

Gregory, W., Glazer, J., & Berenson, K. (2017). Self-compassion, self-injury, and pain. *Cognitive Therapy & Research, 41*(5), 777–786. https://doi.org/10.1007/s10608-017-9846-9

Hamza, C. A., & Willoughby, T. (2015). Nonsuicidal self-injury and affect regulation: Recent findings from experimental and ecological momentary assessment studies and future directions. *Journal of Clinical Psychology, 71,* 561–574. https://doi.org/10.1002/jclp.22174

Hanakawa, Y. (2021). What just happened? And what is happening now? The art and science of moment-to-moment tracking in AEDP. In D. Fosha (Ed.), *Undoing aloneness & the transformation of suffering into flourishing: AEDP 2.0* (pp. 107–131). American Psychological Association. https://doi.org/proxy181.nclive.org/10.1037/0000232-005

Heath, N. L., Carsley, D., De Riggi, M. E., Mills, D., & Mettler, J. (2016). The relationship between mindfulness, depressive symptoms and non-suicidal self-injury amongst adolescents. *Archives of Suicide Research, 20,* 635–649. http://doi.org/10.1080/13811118.2016.1162243

Heath, N. L., Joly, M., & Carsley, D. (2016). Coping self-efficacy and mindfulness in non-suicidal self-injury. *Mindfulness, 7*(5), 1132–1141. https://doi.org/10.1007/s12671-016-0555-3

Hofmann, S. G., Sawyer, A. T., Witt, A. A., & Oh, D. (2010). The effect of mindfulness-based therapy on anxiety and depression: A meta-analytic review. *Journal of Consulting and Clinical Psychology, 78*(2), 169–183.

Hooker, K. E., & Fodor, I. E. (2008). Teaching mindfulness to children. *Gestalt Review, 12*(1), 75–91.

Hooley, J. M., & St. Germain, S. A. (2014). Nonsuicidal self-injury, pain, and self-criticism: Does changing self-worth change pain endurance in people who engage in self-injury? *Clinical Psychological Science, 2*(3), 297–305. https://doi.org/10.1177/2167702613509372

Horvath, A. O., Del Re, A. C., Flückiger, C., & Symonds, D. (2011). Alliance in individual psychotherapy. *Psychotherapy, 48*(1), 9–16. https://doi.org/10.1037/a0022186

Ibadi, A., Kuntoro, I. A., & Iswardani, T. (2018). The implementation of resource development and installation (RDI) for an adolescent with non-suicidal self-injury (NSSI). *Advances in Social Science, Education, and Humanities Research, 135*, 107–122.

Iwakabe, S., Edlin, J., Fosha, D., Gretton, H., Joseph, A. J., Nunnink, S. E., Nakamura, K., & Thoma, N. C. (2020). The effectiveness of accelerated experiential dynamic psychotherapy (AEDP) in private practice settings: A transdiagnostic study conducted within the context of a practice-research network. *Psychotherapy, 57*(4), 548–561. https://doi.org/10.1037/pst0000344

Kabat-Zinn, J. (2003). Mindfulness-based interventions in context: Past, present, and future. *Clinical Psychology: Science and Practice, 10*(2), 144–156. https://doi.org/10.1093/clipsy.bpg016

Kimball, J. S. (2009). Treatment for deliberate self-harm: Integrating emotion-focused therapy. *Journal of Contemporary Psychotherapy, 39*, 197–202. https://doi.org/10.1007/s10879-008-9093-1

Kress, V. E., Adamson, N., DeMarco, C., Paylo, M., & Zoldan, C. A. (2013). The use of guided imagery as an intervention in treating non-suicidal self-injury. *Journal of Creativity in Mental Health, 8*, 35–47. https://doi.org/10.1080/15401383.2013.763683

Kress, V. E., & Hoffman, R. M. (2008). Non-suicidal self-injury and motivational interviewing: Enhancing readiness for change. *Journal of Mental Health Counseling, 30*(4), 311–329. https://doi.org/10.17744/mehc.30.4.n2136170r5732u6h

Kress, V. E., & Paylo, M. (2019). *Treating those with mental disorders: A comprehensive approach to case conceptualization and treatment* (2nd ed.). Pearson.

Kress, V. E., Seligman, L. W., & Reichenberg, L. W. (2021). *Theories of counseling and psychotherapy: Systems, strategies, and skills.* Pearson.

Linehan, M. M. (1993). *Cognitive-behavioral treatment of borderline personality disorder.* Guilford Press.

Lipton, B., & Fosha, D. (2011). Attachment as a transformative process in AEDP: Operationalizing the intersection of attachment theory and affective neuroscience. *Journal of Psychotherapy Integration, 21*(3), 253–279. https://doi.org/10.1037/a0025421

MacIntosh, H. B. (2017). A bridge across silent trauma: Enactment, art, and emergence in the treatment of a traumatized adolescence. *Psychoanalytic Dialogues, 27*, 433–453. https://doi.org/10.1080/10481885.2017.1328188

Martin, S., Martin, G., Lequertier, B., Swannell, S., Follent, A., & Choe, F. (2012). Voice movement therapy: Evaluation of a group-based expressive arts therapy for nonsuicidal self-injury in young adults. *Music and Medicine, 5*, 31–38. https://doi.org/10.1177/1943862112467649

Mosquera, D., & Ross, C.A. (2016). Application of EMDR therapy to self-harming behaviors. *Journal of EMDR Practice and Research, 10*(2), 119–128. http://doi.org/10.1891/1933-3196.10.2.119

National Child Traumatic Stress Network. (n.d.). *Creating trauma informed systems.* https://www.nctsn.org/trauma-informed-care/creating-trauma-informed-systems

Neff, K. (2015). *Self-compassion: The proven power of being kind to yourself.* William Morrow.

Neff, K. (2021, October 25). *Definition of self-compassion.* Self-Compassion. https://self-compassion.org/the-three-elements-of-self-compassion-2/#definition

Per, M., Simundic, A., Argento, A., Khoury, B., & Heath, N. (2022). Examining the relationship between mindfulness, self-compassion, and emotion regulation in self-injury. *Archives of Suicide Research, 26*(3), 1286–1301. https://doi.org/10.1080/13811118.2021.1885534

Polk, E., & Liss, M. (2009). Exploring the motivations behind self-injury. *Counselling Psychology Quarterly, 22*(2), 233–241. https://doi.org/proxy181.nclive.org/10.1080/09515070903216911

Proudlock, S., & Peris, J. (2020). Using EMDR therapy with patients in an acute mental health crisis. *BMC Psychiatry, 20*, Article 14. https://doi.org/10.1186/s12888-019-2426-7

Rizou, E., & Giannouli, V. (2020). An exploration of the experience of trainee integrative psychotherapists on therapeutic alliance in the light of their attachment style. *Health Psychology Research*, *8*(3), Article 9177. https://doi.org/10.4081/hpr.2020.9177

Saxe, G. N., Chawla, N., & Van Der Kolk, B. (2002). Self-destructive behavior in patients with dissociative disorders. *Suicide and Life-Threatening Behavior*, *32*, 313–320.

Sebastián, M.A. (2012). Experiential awareness: Do you prefer "it" to "me"? *Philosophical Topics*, *40*(2), 155–177.

Shapiro, F., & Laliotis, D. (2011). EMDR and the adaptive information processing model: Integrative treatment and case conceptualization. *Clinical Social Work Journal*, *39*(2), 191–200. https://doi.org/10.1007/s10615-010-0300-7

Slotema, C. W., van der Berg, D. P.G., Driessen, A., Wilhelmus, B., & Franken I. H. A. (2019). Feasibility of EMDR for posttraumatic stress disorder in patients with personality disorders: A pilot study. *European Journal of Psychotraumatology*, *10*(1), 1–10. https://doi.org/10.1080/20008198.2019.1614822

Smith, A. E. M., Msetfi, R. M., & Golding, L. (2010). Client self-rated adult attachment patterns and the therapeutic alliance: A systematic review. *Clinical Psychology Review*, *30*(3), 326–337. https://doi.org/10.1016/j.cpr.2009.12.007

Stewart, A., Boath, E., Carryer, A., Walton, I., & Hill, L. (2013). Can emotional freedom techniques (EFT) be effective in the treatment of emotional conditions? Results of a service evaluation in Sandwell. *Journal of Psychological Therapies in Primary Care*, *2*, 71–84.

Toussaint, L., Nguyen, Q. A., Roettger, C., Dixon, K., Offenbächer, M., Kohls, N., Hirsch, J., & Sirois, F. (2021). Effectiveness of progressive muscle relaxation, deep breathing, and guided imagery in promoting psychological and physiological states of relaxation. *Evidence Based Complementary and Alternative Medicine*, *2021*, Article 5924040. https://doi.org/10.1155/2021/5924040

Treleaven, D. A. (2018). *Trauma-sensitive mindfulness: Practices for safe and transformative healing*. W. W. Norton.

Van Vliet, K. J., & Kalnins, G. R. C. (2011). A compassion-focused approach to nonsuicidal self-injury. *Journal of Mental Health Counseling*, *33*(4), 295–311. https://doi.org/10.17744/mehc.33.4.j7540338q223t417

Voon, D., Hasking, P., & Martin, G. (2014). The roles of emotion regulation and ruminative thoughts in nonsuicidal self-injury. *British Journal of Clinical Psychology*, *53*, 95–113.

Wampold, B. E. (2015). How important are the common factors in psychotherapy? An update. *World Psychiatry: Official Journal of the World Psychiatric Association (WPA)*, *14*(3), 270–277. https://doi.org/10.1002/wps.20238

Warner, A. (2017). Mindfulness as a protective factor for the relationship between self-injury and suicide [ProQuest Information & Learning]. *Dissertation Abstracts International: Section B: The Sciences and Engineering*, *78* (4–B(E)).

Whisenhunt, J., & Kress, V. E. (2013). The use of visual arts in counseling clients who engage in nonsuicidal self-injury. *Journal of Creativity in Mental Health*, *8*, 120–135.

Zlotnick, C., Mattia, J. I., & Zimmerman, M. (2001). The relationship between posttraumatic stress disorder, childhood trauma and alexithymia in an outpatient sample. *Journal of Traumatic Stress*, *14*, 177–188.

CHAPTER 60

Collaborative Strengths-Based Family Therapy with Nonsuicidal Self-Injuring Adolescents and Their Families

Matthew D. Selekman

Abstract

This chapter presents an innovative ecosystemic strengths-based family therapy approach for nonsuicidal self-injuring adolescents and their families. Unlike most individual and family therapy approaches typically used with nonsuicidal self-injuring adolescents that tend to view these youths' difficulties from problem and deficit-based lens, collaborative strengths-based family therapy focuses its attention on and utilizes what is *right* with the adolescents and their families to empower them to resolve whatever difficulties they wish to change. Celebrating and accentuating nonsuicidal self-injuring adolescents and their families' strengths triggers positive emotions, helps foster cooperative partnerships with them, and co-creates a therapeutic climate ripe for change. Collaborative strengths-based family therapy capitalizes on the strengths, resources, and past successes of the adolescents, their families, involved key resource people from their social networks, and involved helping professionals from larger systems to rapidly co-construct solutions. After presenting the key theoretical influences and core assumptions of the model, major therapeutic tools and change strategies are presented. Although only qualitative research studies have been conducted with the collaborative strengths-based family therapy model, client outcome feedback regarding the benefits they experienced in receiving this approach have been highly positive. The chapter closes with a case example of a nonsuicidal self-injuring adolescent female presenting with multiple difficulties and treatment experiences, which nicely illustrates the collaborative strengths-based family therapy approach in action.

Key Words: Clients as experts, exceptions, family therapy, tailor-fit treatment

This chapter presents a collaborative strengths-based family therapy (CSBFT) approach to working with nonsuicidal self-injuring adolescents and their families. Many nonsuicidal self-injuring adolescents have grave difficulty coping with negative emotions and higher levels of stress, and they may not think they have a problem. They may have already had multiple treatment experiences, and are being forced to see us by their parents or the referring person who can enforce response and action. For them, the CSBFT approach is a pleasant surprise. CSBFT is a highly positive and upbeat treatment approach that places a strong emphasis on what is *right* with nonsuicidal self-injuring adolescents and their families, rather than what is supposed to be wrong with them. This approach is all about utilizing to the maximum degree clients' pretreatment changes, strengths, resourcefulness, resiliencies, life passions, and past successes to empower them to achieve their goals.

After providing a comprehensive overview of the CSBFT model, a case example demonstrates the use of the major therapeutic tools and strategies of this approach in action. In conclusion, this chapter presents implications for future research on CSBFT.

Theoretical Overview of the CSBFT Approach

The CSBFT model is a competency-based, integrative, and ecosystemic family therapy approach that capitalizes on the strengths and resources of adolescents, their families, key resource people from their social networks, and involved helping professionals from larger systems to rapidly co-construct solutions. The model integrates the best elements of solution-focused brief therapy (De Shazer, 1991; De Shazer et al., 2007; Gingerich et al., 1988; Ratner et al., 2012; McKeel, 2012; Ratner & Yusuf, 2015; Weiner-Davis et al., 1987); MRI brief strategic therapy (Fisch et al., 1982; Fisch & Schlanger, 1999); narrative therapy (Durrant & Coles, 1991; White, 2007; White & Epston, 1990), postmodern systemic therapy approaches (Andersen, 1991; Anderson, 1997; Anderson & Gehart, 2007; Anderson & Goolishian, 1988; Boscolo et al., 1987; Goolishian & Anderson, 1988; Hoffman, 2002); client-directed, outcome-informed therapy (Duncan, 2010, 2019; Duncan & Miller, 2000; Duncan et al., 2010; Prescott et al., 2017); harm-reduction psychotherapy (Denning & Little, 2017; Tatarsky, 2007); positive psychology (Fredrickson, 1999; Lopez & Snyder, 2009; Seligman, 2011); mindfulness meditation practices (Bowen et al., 2011; Gemer & Neff, 2019; Hanh, 1999, 2001; Kabat-Zinn, 1994; Kissel-Wegela, 2014; Pollak et al., 2014); art therapy (Malchiodi, 2003, 2006); and expressive writing (Pennebaker, 2004). As I have continued to allow the CSBFT model to evolve, I have incorporated empirically supported ideas from both individual and family therapy approaches (Alexander et al., 2013; Clark & Beck, 2011; Diamond et al., 2014; Henggeler & Sheidow, 2011; Miller et al., 2007; Miller & Rollnick, 2013; Prochaska, Norcross, & DiClemente, 1994; Rathus & Miller, 2015; Robin & Le Grange, 2010; Selekman, 2017, 2021; Selekman & Beyebach, 2013; Szapocznik & Hervis, 2020; Szapocznik et al., 2012) to offer additional therapeutic tools and strategies to choose from and as a way to best tailor fit what we do with the unique needs, goals, preferences, theories of change, family characteristics, and families' presenting difficulties.

CSBFT therapists are sensitive to gender, cultural, and social justice issues with their clients. CSBFT therapists give themselves permission to be free to make maximum creative use of themselves to serve as catalysts for change in the therapeutic process. In any given family session, CSBFT therapists work both sides of the generational fence striving to help both the parents and the adolescents to get their needs and goals met and to strengthen their alliances with them. They also actively collaborate with involved helping professionals and key resource people from families' social networks throughout the course of therapy. Seven of the nine major components of the CSBFT model are:

1. Guiding assumptions about nonsuicidal self-injuring adolescents and therapy;
2. Effective engagement, alliance-building, and retention strategies;
3. Purposeful systemic interviewing: questions as intervention tools for creating possibilities;
4. Solution-oriented parent management skills training;
5. Use of mindfulness practices, visualizations, and resilience-enhancing thinking tools and strategies;
6. Finding fit: guidelines for intervention design and selection; and
7. Covering the back door: family-social network relapse prevention tools and strategies.

Guiding Assumptions about Nonsuicidal Self-Injuring Adolescents and Therapy

CSBFT is both a philosophy and a highly practical method of doing therapy with nonsuicidal self-injuring (NSSI) adolescents and their families. Therapeutic thinking and intervention choice-making are guided by seven core assumptions.

ASSUMPTION 1: NSSI ADOLESCENTS AND THEIR FAMILIES HAVE THE STRENGTHS AND RESOURCES TO CHANGE

Having worked with NSSI adolescents and their families for close to 30 years, I have been in awe and struck by their multitude of strengths—how creative, resourceful, and resilient they have been. In fact, often prior to entering treatment, they have already taken some important steps with beginning to resolve and better cope with the original concerns they had reported in their intake calls for service (Selekman, 2017; Selekman & Beyebach, 2013). Without any therapeutic input, family members on their own have co-generated novel and effective coping and problem-solving strategies and/or made use of successful problem-solving strategies they had used with their past difficulties to begin to resolve their current difficulties (McKeel, 2012; Weiner-Davis et al., 1987). This is why as therapists, at both the beginning of and throughout the treatment process, we should be eliciting our clients' expertise, which includes not only inquiring about their self-generated pretreatment and between-sessions changes but utilizing to the maximum degree family members' top strengths to empower them to achieve their goals. Research indicates that 40% of what counts for treatment success has to do with clients' *extra-therapeutic factors*, that is therapists' making skillful use of all that their clients bring to the therapeutic relationship (Duncan, 2010; Duncan et al., 2010; Norcross & Wampold, 2011).

ASSUMPTION 2: COOPERATION IS INEVITABLE

All NSSI clients and their families will cooperate with us when we listen generously to them from a position of respectful curiosity and utilize their key words, metaphors, and belief system material and take a deep interest in their life passions and top strengths. We need to look for clues for how best to foster cooperative partnerships with them. Thus, as therapists, we also need to pay close attention to our clients' nonverbal responses and listen carefully to how they respond to our questions, our positive relabeling of negative behaviors, and our reflections on their situation and how they manage both in- and out-of-session therapeutic tools and strategies offered to them to experiment with. When we observe *yes-set* hypnotic responses like head nods and smiles from family members in response to our questions and new ideas, this indicates that what we shared either comes close to fitting how they view their situation or is acceptable to their belief system, which helps deepen our therapeutic alliances with them. Finally, we also can help foster cooperative partnerships with our clients when we punctuate or celebrate the sparkling moments they report in sessions, for example, by complimenting them on going a few days without self-injuring and inquiring in great detail about how they pulled it off. Such action invites them to compliment themselves on their resourcefulness and to be proud of their accomplishments.

ASSUMPTION 3: NSSI BEHAVIOR AND OTHER SELF-DESTRUCTIVE HABITS ARE ATTEMPTED SOLUTIONS TO COPE

Research and clinical practice evidence-based experience has indicated that the majority of NSSI adolescents use self-injuring to get quick relief from emotional distress in response to a variety of stressors in their lives (Adler & Adler, 2011; Gratz & Chapman, 2009; Hawton & Rodham, 2006; Selekman, 2009, 2017; Selekman & Beyebach, 2013; Selekman & Shulem, 2007; Whitlock & Lloyd-Richardson, 2019). Additionally, the longer career adolescents have had with self-injuring, the more functions for its use they will find for coping with family, peer, and intimate relationship difficulties and school stressors (Andover et al., 2007; Gratz & Chapman, 2009; Klonsky, 2007; Selekman & Beyebach, 2013). For many NSSI adolescents, the calming, numbing, and pleasurable effects they receive from self-injuring make it a highly inviting habit to protect at all costs. This is why self-injurers often cut or burn themselves on places on their bodies that are hard to see and that they can cover up. Some adolescent clients have reported that they use self-injury to ward off suicidal thoughts, to release or purge painful thoughts and feelings, to disrupt negative thoughts, and for anger management purposes. Other adolescents report symptom switching, moving back and forth from self-injuring to bulimia or binge-eating, to substance-abusing, and engaging in sexually risky behaviors, which all serve unique functions for them as attempted solutions to cope with specific stressors in their lives.

ASSUMPTION 4: THERE ARE ALWAYS EXCEPTIONS TO THE RULE

No self-injurer harms themselves continuously throughout a given day; there are always exceptions or lulls in between. Our job as therapists is to play skillful super-sleuth detectives and inquire what is happening instead during the periods of time that NSSI adolescents are refraining from self-injuring: specifically, what are they, family members, and/or concerned resource people from their social networks doing that promotes their abstinence from this behavior. For NSSI adolescents, they may be using self-talk, immersing themselves in healthier and meaningful hobbies and activities during their free time, steering clear from toxic peers, spending high-quality time with a parent or close relative, and so forth. We may discover that when the NSSI adolescents are not self-injuring, their parents are not yelling at or criticizing them, or putting pressure on them to bring in "A" grades in school. Exceptions are new ways of thinking, feeling, and doing that contribute to the reduction or absence of self-injuring behavior. Once we identify these key exception patterns, it is important to have NSSI adolescents and their families increase doing more of what works until the self-injuring behavior and other presenting difficulties are stabilized.

ASSUMPTION 5: THE THERAPIST PARTICIPATES IN CO-CREATING THE NEW THERAPY SYSTEM'S REALITY

As members of the new therapist-client system, our constructions of or formulations about the clients' self-injuring behavior and other presenting difficulties will be primarily based on our own theoretical maps, professional experiences working with clients with similar presentations, and our personal experiences in the world (Efran & Lukens, 1985; Maturana & Varela, 1988; von Foerster, 1981). For example, a psychodynamic therapist's major focus will be on assessing for unresolved conflicts and psychic deficits in the client. Strengths-based therapists will inquire about clients' strengths, resiliency protective factors, life passions, pretreatment changes, and past successes and coauthor compelling future realities with clients. Strengths-based therapists also engage in *solution talk* with their clients; that is, they converse with them using the language of change, such as embedding presuppositional words like *when*, *will*, and *going to do* in their questions and reflections, which engenders hope and optimism and can help co-create positive self-fulfilling prophecies (De Shazer et al., 2007; Gingerich et al., 1988; Selekman, 2017).

Many therapists make the assumptions that self-injuring adolescents are on the road to suicide or that their intimidating and provocative cutting behavior confirms a BPD diagnosis or sexual or physical abuse, and they don't take the time to gather any further information about how clients are functioning in all areas of their lives. However, what they see is what they will get. There is no such thing as a "God's eye" view to look at clients from a truly objective perspective; we and any other involved helping professionals are part of the same therapist-client treatment system. Therefore, in our conversations with clients we must make careful use of language, maintain an open and curious mind, honor their theories of change and preferences, and solicit from them session-by-session feedback about the quality of our therapeutic relationships with them and their perceptions of the change process. We must tailor-fit what our clients need us to be in our relationships with them and deliver by providing a therapeutic climate ripe for them to achieve their ideal treatment outcomes.

ASSUMPTION 6: CLIENTS DETERMINE THEIR GOALS AND ARE CO-AUTHORS OF THEIR TREATMENT PLANS

Our clients should have the lead voice in determining their treatment goals, choosing which therapeutic tools and strategies they would like to try, deciding who participates in sessions and the frequency of visits, and determining when they are done with therapy. Research indicates that when clients think they have personal control over their destinies, they will persist at mastering tasks, do better at managing them, and become more committed to the change process. In fact, when clients choose a course of action among alternatives, they are more likely to adhere to it and succeed (Miller & Rollnick, 2013). Honoring clients' preferences, in terms of their choosing which combination of treatment modalities and therapeutic tools and strategies they wish to pursue and identifying what their goals are, will help increase their motivation levels, strengthen our alliances with them, and optimize their chances for treatment success (Selekman, 2017).

ASSUMPTION 7: ADOLESCENT NSSI IS BEST TREATED IN A FAMILY THERAPY CONTEXT

Although many NSSI adolescents struggle individually with mood management and coping with high levels of stress, there are certain family dynamics that play a major role in the development and maintenance of their self-injuring behaviors, such as emotional invalidating patterns of interaction, family difficulties with open affective expression and conflict avoidance, and parental emotional disconnection and excessive criticism (Miller et al., 2007; Rathus & Miller, 2015; Selekman, 2009, 2017; Selekman & Beyebach, 2013; Selekman & Shulem, 2007). Unless these problem-maintaining patterns of interaction are disrupted and replaced with more positive and adaptive family interactions, they will continue to be a powerful force in the perpetuation of the adolescent's self-injuring and other behavioral difficulties. Family therapy provides therapists with a great opportunity for observing the family problem-maintaining interactions in action, listening for narrow and unhelpful family beliefs about the NSSI adolescent's behavior, and learning about the family's unproductive attempts at solutions. Once they have gained access to this important information, therapists can directly begin to dismantle the NSSI problem life support system by disrupting the family problem-maintaining patterns, offering the family more positive ways of interacting, alter their outmoded family beliefs, and coauthor with them a solution-determined story.

Research on the CSBFT Approach

The only research studies that have been conducted on the CSBFT approach have combined family ethnographic and qualitative methodology (Cohn-Siver, 2009; Kuehl, 1987; Newfield et al., 1991; Selekman & Shulem, 2007). With the family ethnographic research approach, research interviewers have had no previous contact with and do know anything about the families they will be interviewing in a given study. Ideally, they want to have family members share their perceptions about their therapists, what they are doing with them in sessions, and what they found both helpful and not useful to them. Both the families and the therapists are interviewed separately on a random basis, every few sessions, about what their experiences have been like in the therapeutic process. In fact, to better find a fit with strengthening therapeutic alliances and making necessary adjustments, as well as to gain access to family members' treatment satisfaction levels with the change process, the research interviewers give direct feedback to their therapists about what families have liked and disliked about their work together and what specifically therapists need to do more of or differently to optimize positive treatment outcomes with them. In an effort to analyze the wealth of data provided by families, we need to come up with domain or subject areas that are derived from what the families thought were important about their therapists and their treatment experiences, both positive and negative, such as, for example, the use of *scaling questions* for goal-setting and as a measurement of progress across the course of treatment (see Annex D). Another important finding in our qualitative study with 20 NSSI adolescents with concurrent eating-distressed and substance abuse behaviors and their families was that all the adolescents reported their strong desire to "grow into" their relationships with their parents, no matter how much conflict, emotional distance, and invalidation was present. They wanted to know that their parents loved and appreciated them (Selekman & Shulem, 2007).

In reviewing the empirically supported short-term and family-based treatment outcome research on NSSI adolescents, most of the studies had small sample sizes, which greatly impacts the generalizability of the treatment results. Cognitive behavioral therapy (CBT) integrating problem-solving strategies and dialectical behavior therapy (DBT) have been the most widely tested treatment methods for NSSI adolescents (Brausch & Girresch, 2012). Eskin et al. (2007) found that their short-term and structural cognitive behavioral problem-solving treatment (PST) approach achieved 96.3% treatment outcome success with stabilizing the depressive symptoms and suicide ideation of adolescents and young adults as compared to the waiting-list control group achieving 21.1% full to partial stabilization of their symptoms. In a multisite study from 2014 to 2019, Mehlum et al. (2019) found up to three years follow-up that individual DBT combined with a multifamily group treatment (DBT-A) remained superior to treatment as usual (TAU) at reducing self-injuring behavior. DBT-A also was found to be the treatment of choice for adolescents who have longer careers of self-injury and engage in this behavior on a more regular basis. However, as compared to TAU NSSI adolescents, there was no marked difference in the reduction of suicidal ideation, hopelessness, and depressive and BPD symptoms.

As far as family-based treatment studies with NSSI adolescents go, Sitton et al. (2020) found in their study examining the relationship between family factors (family communications, role behaviors, problem-solving, affective involvement, affective responsiveness, behavioral control, and conflict) and the development and maintenance of adolescent self-injuring behavior that when families have positive communications, they can resolve conflicts and problem-solve well together. The family environment is most conducive for NSSI adolescents to successfully implement the use of their coping tools and strategies and reduce the likelihood of self-injuring episodes. Cottrell et al. (2018) found that their Leeds Systemic Family Therapy (LSFT) approach did no better at treatment outcome than the TAU control group, which had been randomly assigned to one of the following three treatments: DBT, mentalization-based therapy, or CBT. However, those NSSI adolescents who received LSFT reported at outcome that family members became more caring toward them and that affective expression in family relationships had improved, particularly for the adolescents in expressing their emotions, which led to a reduction in self-injuring episodes. Their caregivers also reported marked improvements in the adolescents' emotional and behavioral functioning. Finally, when adolescents had grave difficulty expressing their emotions and concerns to family members, they experienced better treatment outcome results from one of the TAU therapies.

Effective Adolescent and Family Alliance Building and Retention Strategies

Many NSSI adolescents enter therapy under duress because their parents are making them do it out of love and concern and/or the referring person has the power to enforce action and response. Thus, they are not happy about being forced to go for treatment; in fact, they may not think they have a problem to begin with. Additionally, their self-injuring practices may have been serving them well as a coping strategy for internal and external stressors and they will not be receptive in the beginning of treatment to trying alternative and more healthy coping strategies. Finally, they may be in the *precontemplative* stage of readiness for change and therefore they do not see the benefit of changing a coping strategy that has worked for them or have already had negative past experiences in therapy and don't want to do it again (Prochaska et al., 1994). In Annex A, I present five effective engagement strategies for NSSI adolescents.

Family therapy and psychotherapy treatment outcome studies have identified five major engagement and retention strategies to employ with families to prevent premature therapy dropouts from occurring, to co-create a therapeutic climate ripe for change, and to optimize for clients' treatment success (Alexander et al., 2013; Diamond et al., 2014; Duncan, 2019; Duncan et al., 2010; Escudero et al., 2010; Friedlander et al., 2011; Henggeler & Schaeffer, 2010; Liddle, 2010; Prescott et al, 2017; Robbins et al., 2010, 2006; Robin & Le Grange, 2010; Lambert, 2010; Norcross & Wampold, 2013;

Swift & Greenberg, 2015). The five therapeutic operations are *providing emotional safety and establishing a strong connection with each family member*; *multipartiality: validating all family members' perspectives*; *therapist structuring skills*; *establishing systemic treatment goals and mutual sense of purpose*; and *soliciting session-by-session feedback from family members on both their perceptions of the quality of therapeutic relationship and the change process*. In Annex B, I describe each one of these important therapeutic operations.

Purposeful Systemic Interviewing: Questions as Interventive Tools for Creating Possibilities
Therapeutic questions are interventive tools for eliciting clients' expertise, establishing realistic and solvable goals, and co-creating compelling future realities with them. Each family member's unique cooperative response pattern will determine which category of questions to select and use. For example, if clients are hard-pressed to identify any past successes or self-generated pretreatment changes or entertain the notion of hypothetical future successes, we need to shift gears and better cooperate with their pessimism. We can ask a pessimistic mother who is burned out with her NSSI daughter's intractable difficulties, "It sounds like Kim's (the NSSI daughter) struggles have been stressing you out for a long time. Tell me, what steps have you taken to prevent her situation from getting much worse?" After a brief pause while reflecting on their situation, she responded with, "Well, I have been trying to refrain from yelling at her." The therapist can respond with, "How has she responded to your cutting back on your yelling?" The mother shared, "Well, I don't think she is cutting herself as much and she has stayed away from her friends I don't like her to associate with." Just by shifting gears and better cooperating with the mother's pessimism, the therapist learned about a new solution-building exception pattern to have the mother increase doing: "refraining from yelling at Kim." By doing so, we are getting a reduction in Kim's self-injuring behavior and an increase in her making better choices by staying away from toxic peers.

In Annex C, D, and E, I present three major categories of questions: *key assessment questions to learn about NSSI adolescents' self-injuring practices and stories, goal-setting questions*, and *questions for highly pessimistic and demoralized NSSI adolescents and their families*. Under each major category of questions, I provide examples of a variety of practical questions to choose from. Once we find questions that produce valuable information and meaningful dialogue and open up space for possibilities, we want to continue to ask similar questions and do more of what is working.

KEY SELF-HARMING ASSESSMENT QUESTIONS

The key self-harming assessment questions to ask NSSI adolescents are designed to learn more about why they gravitated to self-injury, the positive benefits or effects they receive from engaging in this habit or practice, and how it is intimately connected to their family and life stories. These questions are asked from a position of respectful curiosity. Gradually, I move from nonthreatening open-ended questions to more heavy questions about any past trauma experiences or suicide attempts. It also is important to learn about other self-destructive habits NSSI adolescents may switch to, such as bulimic or binge-eating, substance abuse, or engaging in sexually risky behaviors and the various functions each of these habits serve for them (see Annex C).

GOAL-SETTING QUESTIONS

Once we know what NSSI adolescents and their families view as the *right* problems to work on changing first, we can use *goal-setting* questions to secure from them crystal-clear descriptions of the *what, who, where,* and *how* both short- and long-term goal achievement will look like to them. We can invite our clients to share with us specific details about how they will know they are making progress toward achieving these goals. The bottom line is, if we don't know where we are going with our clients' we will end up somewhere else, lost and confused. Vague treatment goals lead to vague, unfocused therapy. As therapists, our jobs are to negotiate realistic and solvable goals with our clients.

It also is critical to engage in *mental contrasting* with our clients, that is, exploring with them any obstacles they may anticipate running into as they pursue their goals (Oettingen, 2014). Together, we can problem-solve how to best remove or work around these possible obstacles so that all family members know what concrete steps to take to manage them or, in case they get temporarily tripped up by them, know what to quickly do to bounce back and get back on track. Annex D presents some examples of useful goal-setting questions to ask in initial family therapy sessions to help secure from families their initial short-term and preferred future treatment outcome goals. The questions have been developed and inspired by the late and brilliant hypnotist and solution-focused brief therapy theorist Milton H. Erickson (De Shazer et al., 2007; Havens, 2003; O'Hanlon & Weiner-Davis, 1989; Ratner et al., 2012; Ratner & Yusuf, 2015; Selekman, 2017).

QUESTIONS FOR HIGHLY PESSIMISTIC AND DEMORALIZED NSSI ADOLESCENTS AND THEIR FAMILIES

It may be quite difficult for highly pessimistic, and demoralized NSSI adolescents and their families to either identify short- or long-term treatment goals in initial family meetings. They often have long stories to tell about the chronicity of their presenting difficulties and their multiple treatment failures where they felt misunderstood and mishandled by their treatment professionals. In addition, they may have certain constraints related to past traumatic events, painful losses, and family secrets. Like cultural anthropologists, as their treatment providers we have to be good listeners and ask open-ended questions from a position of respectful curiosity to better come to know their stories and avoid at all costs being narrative editors. The questions described in Annex E have been developed and inspired by solution-focused brief therapy (De Shazer et al., 2007), narrative therapy (White, 2007), and postmodern systemic theorists (Andersen, 1991; Anderson, 1997; Anderson & Gehart, 2007; Boscolo et al., 1987; Hoffman, 2002). The coping, pessimistic, and sub-zero scaling questions are effective with highly pessimistic and demoralized clients who have had lots of treatment. The coping and pessimistic questions are particularly useful with parents who are negative and skeptical about any new treatment experience working and may have grave difficulty responding to the aforementioned treatment outcome questions or may respond to them in a "yes, but" manner. Sub-zero scaling questions can engender hope with even the most pessimistic and veteran long-term therapy clients.

Externalizing questions work really well with NSSI adolescents and their families who report having been oppressed by their present difficulties for a long time. It is as if their NSSI or other major presenting problem has had a life of its own. Through these questions we learn about the NSSI problem life support system—that is, the key family interactions, unproductive attempted solutions, and rigid and limiting beliefs that maintain and further perpetuate the NSSI behavior in the family. Externalizing the problem, which was developed by narrative therapy pioneer Michael White, is a non-blame therapy strategy where the problem is viewed as a problem, and they are all being victimized by the problem (White, 2007).

Finally, conversational questions are helpful to use when therapists are picking up on innuendos, secrets, and constraints that are keeping the treatment process at a standstill, or keeping the clients feeling confused or stuck. Conversational questions tend to be open-ended and are asked from a position of respectful curiosity.

Solution-Oriented Parent Management Skills Training

A very important dimension of the CSBFT approach is *solution-oriented parenting management skills training*. Many parents of NSSI adolescents struggle with being too emotionally reactive when self-injuring episodes occur, are not empathically-attuned with their kids, are being too critical and controlling, and emotionally invalidate and/or may disconnect from them. In some families with NSSI adolescents, the parents may be struggling with their own mental health and substance abuse difficulties and/or marital discord or postdivorce conflicts, which may be fueling high stress and can contribute to the maintenance of their NSSI and other self-destructive behaviors. In Annex F, I present nine parenting skills and change strategies that have shown good clinical results with adolescents presenting with self-injury and other self-destructive behaviors.

Mindfulness Meditation, Visualization, and Resilience-Enhancing Thinking Tools and Strategies

Annex G presents a wide range of therapeutic tools and strategies designed to quiet the inner emotional storms occurring in NSSI adolescents' minds, which are triggered by certain thoughts, feelings, memories, images, negative interactions with their parents and peers, and a high level of stress. Since self-injury has been like a fast-acting analgesic and has served them well in quickly numbing bad thoughts and feelings, they will not be quick to give up their beloved self-harming habits. After we build trusting partnerships with them, NSSI adolescents will be more open to experimenting with mindfulness meditation, visualization, and resilience-enhancing thinking tools and strategies. Once NSSI adolescents have mastered the use of the therapeutic tools and strategies, it is helpful to put them in charge of teaching their parents and siblings how to use these highly practical coping methods.

MINDFULNESS MEDITATION

Mindfulness meditation has been shown to have many physical health and psychological benefits. Physically, it strengthens our immune systems; calms our neurological systems; improves the quality of our sleeping; and lowers our breathing, heart, and pulse rates (Kabat-Zinn, 1994; Kisella Wegela, 2014). Psychologically, mindfulness enhances our concentration and creative problem-solving abilities; increases positive emotions, hope, and optimism levels; balances our moods; and helps us to be much more present and compassionate with others (Fredrickson, 1999). Individuals with self-injuring and other self-destructive difficulties have responded well to mindfulness meditation because it teaches them distress tolerance by learning how to observe their negative emotions and thoughts without caving into the impulse to self-injure, binge eat, binge and purge, or abuse substances to get quick relief (Bowen et al., 2011; Miller et al., 2007; Rathus & Miller, 2015; Selekman, 2017; Selekman & Beyebach, 2013). For the sake of brevity, I present below three of the most popular mindfulness practices my NSSI adolescent clients have found helpful: *the sound meditation, take six deep breathes slowly*, and *mindful walking*.

VISUALIZATION

There are two visualization strategies I use with NSSI adolescents which are easy to do and trigger positive emotions: *visualizing a movie of success* and *visualizing a movie of joy* (see Annex H). Kids who are strong in visual-spatial intelligence and are into art and photography make excellent visualizers. Some NSSI adolescents are quite ambitious and create three or four movies of success and joy so they have multiple options to visualize when experiencing negative emotions, unpleasant thoughts, and higher levels of stress. They also have used certain movies for coping with particular stressors in their lives or to naturally elevate their moods and self-confidence levels prior to taking on a challenging tasks or performances.

RESILIENCE-ENHANCING THINKING TOOLS AND STRATEGIES

Wise Mind thinking tools and strategies integrates ideas from DBT, CBT, Buddhist mindfulness practices, and self-control management skills (Brier, 2014; Clark & Beck, 2011; Pollak et al, 2014; Kross et al., 2014; Rathus & Miller, 2015). These tools and strategies are to be practiced both in sessions and at home daily by the NSSI adolescents. It is important that their parents also learn them, particularly those tools and strategies that their adolescents have found most effective so that they can say to their kids, "You look like you just got triggered, what do you think could help you the most at this time, *counting all of the objects in the room* or *5-4-3-2-1*." For the sake of brevity, I present nine of the resilience-enhancing thinking tools and strategies (see Annex I).

Finding Fit: Guidelines for Intervention Design, Selection, and Matching
When it comes to offering NSSI adolescents and their families therapeutic experiments to try both in and out session, it is critical that these experiments are in line with family members' goals, their unique stages of readiness for change, theories of change, their strengths, and their life passions. The rationales designed for pursuing particular therapeutic experiments have to incorporate family members' language, metaphors, and beliefs. This helps foster client cooperation with implementing proposed change strategies offered to them. Annex J presents four classes of therapeutic experiments that we can select from that best match family members' strengths, goals, and ways of expressing themselves and are designed to strengthen family relationship bonds: *using the imaginary time machine*, *family connection-building rituals and therapeutic experiments*, *art therapy experiments*, and *expressive writing experiments*.

FAMILY CONNECTION BUILDING RITUALS AND THERAPEUTIC EXPERIMENTS
Family connection-building rituals and therapeutic experiments are designed to help strengthen relationship bonds. They tap the strengths and creativity of family members to transform their relationships. For the sake of brevity, two family connection-building rituals and one therapeutic experiment are presented in Annex J.

ART THERAPY EXPERIMENTS
Over the years, I have been impressed with how artistically talented NSSI adolescents are. Since many of these kids express their creative selves best through art and/or may have grave difficulty putting words to the emotional turmoil and conflicts they are experiencing, art and photography can be a nonthreatening and fun way to express what is going on in their minds and families. When using art and photography methods with NSSI adolescents it is important to refrain from making any interpretations of the meaning of their final products. Instead, ask open-ended questions from a position of curiosity and invite them to tell you the meanings of the objects in their art products and photographs. With all of the art experiments I use with NSSI adolescents, it is up to them to decide whether or not they share with their families their final products. Annex J describes five of the most popular art activities among NSSI adolescents I have worked.

EXPRESSIVE WRITING EXPERIMENTS
Some NSSI adolescents are strong in linguistic intelligence, that is they express themselves best through writing creative stories, raps, and poetry, and they may like to journal about their thoughts, feelings, and life experiences. They are often avid readers as well. Therefore,

the use of expressive writing experiments would be a good fit for them. Annex J describes five popular expressive writing experiments I frequently use with NSSI adolescents.

Covering the Back Door: Family Social Network Relapse Prevention Tools and Strategies
NSSI relapse prevention needs to be a family-social network affair. In addition to having family members helping the NSSI adolescents to stay on track and stave off powerful triggers from derailing them, having key resource people from their social networks as integral members of the relapse prevention team can be a solid support structure for outside family therapy sessions—working like co-therapists. The key resource people from their social networks can be close relatives, adult inspirational others, close friends, clergy, and so forth. Additionally, it is important at the beginning of family therapy and when collaborative work begins with the relapse prevention team that therapists normalize the inevitably of slips or relapses happening; they are part of the change process, and they offer us valuable wisdom for where we need to tighten up with the structure. Thus, when minor slips or relapses do occur the clients and their relapse prevention team will not view them as disastrous events but great opportunities for comeback practice. Annex K presents four major family-social network relapse prevention tools and strategies.

Case Example

Artemis, a 16-year-old, who came out recently as lesbian to her parents, was referred to me for follow-up family therapy by a colleague working in an adolescent partial hospitalization program.

Artemis had been admitted into the program for daily self-injuring, fleeting suicidal thoughts, anxiety and depressed moods, angry outbursts, attention/deficit hyperactivity disorder (ADHD), and intense conflict with her father, which often resulted in heated arguments. Artemis also was grappling with posttraumatic stress syndrome (PTSD) symptoms for the past three years after being sexually assaulted by an older boy at a party. As far as her strengths go, Artemis was an accomplished oboe player, a talented artist and poet, and quite knowledgeable about crystals and their healing powers for a wide range of psychological and physical maladies. Artemis had a very close relationship with her mother Barbara who often would take her side when her husband Sidney would fly off the handle with his anger toward her or be unreasonable and inflexible with her. Sidney had a hot temper, a very stressful job, sleeping difficulties, and apparently was quite controlling and inflexible with family members. Artemis had participated in both individual and family therapy four times in the past and was psychiatrically hospitalized twice before for self-injuring and suicidal ideation.

Key Family Therapy Highlights: A Session-By-Session Summary

I saw the family five times before we terminated. For the sake of brevity, I will summarize the key highlights and therapeutic operations employed in each session to help the family eventually achieve their ideal outcome goals.

First Family Therapy Session

After establishing rapport with each family member and determining with them what they wished to change, I asked the *beyond your wildest dreams questions* in an attempt to establish both short- and long-term goals. Barbara responded that she would have "a happy family" where all members would enjoy being together and there was "no arguing." Sidney shared that he and Artemis would be "closer and doing more things together" like in the past. For Artemis, her father would be "less controlling and not taking out his anger on us and more chilled." Next, I asked them the following *scaling question* to help secure their best hopes and treatment goals: "On a scale from 1 to 10, with 1 being when you first were referred to me two weeks ago and 10 being the day after your wildest dreams just happened, where would you rate today?" Barbara shared that they are at a 6. Both Artemis and her father rated their situation at a 5. In an effort to establish small behavioral goals over the next week, I asked the family the following question, "What are each of you going to do over the next week to get one step higher up on the scale to a 7 and 6, respectively." Barbara shared that she would try to be more supportive of Sidney and be a "better team player with him." Sidney shared that he would work on "better managing" his anger and do some "high-quality activity with Artemis" that she would enjoy doing with him. Artemis shared that she would refrain from "swearing at or provoking" her father and try to get along with him.

During my individual session time with Artemis, I took a deep interest in learning more about her top strengths and life passions. Artemis read me one of her favorite poems and showed me two of her best pottery pieces on her iPhone. I was curious to learn more about her interest in crystals and how she had used them to help heal herself. Apparently, they had helped her to combat negative emotions and sleeping difficulties and to reduce her self-injuring and flashback activity. Before she started crystals to help herself, she relied on self-injuring a few times a day to "numb out bad thoughts and feelings," to release anger toward her father, and to disrupt flashback activity. An imaginary light bulb had lit up above my head while discussing Artemis's use of crystals to heal herself. I offered her to try as an experiment over the next week the *adolescent mentoring her parent ritual*. I proposed to Artemis the idea of putting her in charge of teaching her father about the healing powers of crystals. Artemis thought this would be "cool." She shared with me that there was a specific crystal that has been found to be effective for better managing one's anger. Since her father wanted to do something high-quality with her, I suggested she have him take them to her favorite rock store and she could use the time to educate him about different crystals, particularly the ones that seem to work best for anger management and sleeping difficulties. Artemis became quite animated and fired up to do this with him. Prior to briefly meeting with her parents, I offered her the *sound meditation, taking six deep breathes slowly*, and *counting all of the objects in her bedroom* as alternatives to self-injuring whenever she was triggered by her negative emotions or flashbacks.

After complimenting all family members on their strengths and desire to improve their family relationships, I encouraged them to keep track of all that they will do to achieve their goals. I shared with Sidney the adolescent mentoring her parent ritual that Artemis would be doing with him over the next week. Sidney shared that it sounded interesting and he was looking forward to it.

SECOND FAMILY THERAPY SESSION

The family came to the second session with smiles and were in great spirits. They had achieved their initial goals and there had been positive gains on both the parental and father-Artemis relationship fronts. Barbara and Sidney worked better as a co-parenting team and she had been quite supportive of her husband after some highly stressful work days. Sidney eagerly shared that not only had he had learned a lot about crystals from Artemis but they had a delicious lunch together at their favorite vegetarian restaurant. He further added that he was highly impressed with how knowledgeable Artemis was about the healing powers of crystals. In fact, not only did Artemis point out specific crystals that were known to help people with both anger management and sleeping difficulties but Sidney experimented with placing one of the crystals in his pants pocket daily and placing the other one under his pillow at night to sleep better. Sidney reported that he had better control over his anger and had some better nights of sleep over the past week. Artemis chimed in that she had a great day with her father and was pleased that he wanted to learn about crystals and use them to help himself. Also, Artemis reported not cutting herself once over the week and that there was a marked reduction in her posttraumatic stress symptoms. She found the combination of her crystals and the mindfulness practices she was using daily had helped. After amplifying and consolidating family members' gains, I encouraged them to keep track of what they would do over the next week to get one step higher on their scales to 8 and 7s. Sidney contracted another week with Artemis to do the adolescent mentoring her parent ritual to learn from her how to write poetry, which was something he always wanted to learn how to do. Artemis was happy to do this.

THIRD FAMILY THERAPY SESSION

When asked what further progress they had made, Sidney was eager to read me the poem that he had written that both Artemis and Barbara really loved. I was most impressed by Sidney's poem and his great use of metaphor. He praised Artemis for being a great teacher. Artemis was smiling and happy that she could do this with her father. Over the past week, there was not one argument between Artemis and Sidney. Artemis had not cut herself once and her posttraumatic stress symptoms were minimal. Sidney was finding that the crystals were both helping him better manage his anger and sleep better. There had been one minor clash between Sidney and Barbara but they quickly resolved it. To test the waters, I asked the family, "What would you have to do to go backward at this point?" Sidney shared that he would "blow his stack" and take out his anger on family members.

Barbara shared that she would "fuel Sidney's anger by siding with the kids against him." Artemis shared that she would start "swearing at" her dad and "provoking him." I invited family members to share what else they had been doing that was 8- and 7-like and making a difference for them in getting along. They all had been making a conscious effort to speak to one another in a respectful way and be more playful with one another. I amplified and consolidated their gains and offered them a mini vacation from therapy as a vote of confidence and due to all of their progress. To help keep the family on their toes, I pointed out to them that slips go with the territory of change, that they might encounter a minor setback over the next week or two but that I was confident they would rapidly bounce back and get on track again. The family chose to come back in two weeks.

FOURTH FAMILY THERAPY SESSION

Although that family had made further progress during their vacation from counseling, Sidney had "two blowups," one with Barbara and one with Artemis. Prior to exploring with them about the blowup situations, I wanted to learn what was working despite these incidents. The family reported that they had a few nice dinners together and had seen a movie together that they all enjoyed. Overall, the family interactions had been quite positive for most of the week. I inquired if Sidney had forgotten to put the special crystal in his pants pocket on the days that he had blown up. He did admit that on one of the days he had forgotten to put the crystal in his pocket. Apparently, the days that he had blown up were related to having very stressful and bad days at work and rather than going to the gym, he got lead-footed with his anger and wrongly unleashed it at his wife and daughter. I decided to meet alone with Sidney to teach him some mindfulness practices for backup coping strategies. I taught him the *sound meditation, taking six deep breaths slowly,* and *mindful walking*. I strongly encouraged him to practice each of these mindfulness practices daily to help combat anger and work stress. He agreed to try them out over the next week. After I amplified and consolidated the family's gains, I asked them when they wished to come back in three or four weeks due to their progress. They chose to come back in three weeks.

FIFTH AND FINAL FAMILY THERAPY SESSION

When asked, "What further progress have you made?" Barbara responded with, "We broke the scale and we are at an 11!" Artemis and her father agreed with Barbara's rating of their situation. Everyone laughed. Sidney proudly pointed out that he had gone three weeks without one blowup. He had found the mindfulness practices to be most beneficial to him. Both Barbara and Artemis were pleased with Sidney's progress. For the first time, Artemis and her father had had a deep conversation about the latter's trauma history. Artemis shared that she had learned that Sidney's father used to blow up at and criticize him growing up and how he is now making a concerted effort to be different as a father with her and the family. Also, they made the connection between their past traumas and how they had been mutually triggering one another's fight response, leading to heated destructive verbal exchanges with one another. Artemis was pleased to share that she was now symptom free and had not had one cutting episode for several weeks. To help consolidate her gains, I asked Artemis, "If I were to work with another 16-year-old just like you, what advice would you have for me that I should share with her?" Artemis recommended to use crystals, meditate, and have lots of interests and passions to pursue when triggered and to own your part in the family dynamics and try and be less reactive. The family and I mutually agreed to terminate due to their tremendous progress.

TREATMENT OUTCOME FOLLOW-UPS

The family and I met at 6 and 12 months to assess the staying power of their changes and further progress they made. In both follow-up sessions, the family reported that not only had the changes they had made in our earlier work together persisted over time, but they all had grown closer together as a family. There were no reports of self-injury or anger management difficulties.

Conclusion: Implications for Future Research on CSBFT

In this chapter, I have presented a highly practical strengths-based family therapy approach that has shown positive clinical outcome results with NSSI adolescents and their families as reported by families who participated in small-scale qualitative research studies conducted by my colleagues and I. However, the small sample sizes, the lack of comparison control groups, and quantitative measures make it difficult to generalize our results. In the future, what is needed is a well-controlled, manualized, experimental-designed research format with a large sample size, combining qualitative and quantitative analysis methods. Additionally, to truly determine the efficacy of the CSBFT approach with NSSI adolescents and their families, we would have to compare the CSBFT treatment outcome results to both empirically supported individual and family therapy approaches such as DBT, CBT, functional family therapy, or attachment-based family therapy at treatment outcome (Alexander et al., 2013; Clark & Beck, 2011; Diamond et al., 2014; Miller, Rathus, & Linehan, 2007).

References

Adler, P. A., & Adler, P. (2011). *The tender cut: Inside the hidden world of self-injury*. New York University Press.
Alexander, J. F., Waldron, H. B., Robbins, M. S., & Neeb, A. A. (2013). *Functional family therapy for adolescent behavioral problems*. American Psychological Association.
Andersen, T. (1991). *The reflecting team: Dialogues about the dialogues about the dialogues*. Norton.
Anderson, H. (1997). *Conversation, language, and possibilities: A postmodern approach to therapy*. Basic Books.
Anderson, H., & Gehart, D. (Eds.). (2007). *Collaborative therapy: Relationships and conversations that make a difference*. Routledge.
Anderson, H., & Goolishian, H. (1988). Human systems as linguistic systems: Evolving ideas about the implications for theory and practice. *Family Process, 27*, 371–393.
Andover, M. S., Pepper, C. M., & Gibb, B. E. (2007). Self-mutilation and coping strategies in a College sample. *Suicide and Life-Threatening Behavior, 37*, 238–243.

Boscolo, L., Cecchin, G., Hoffman, L., & Penn, P. (1987). *Milan systemic therapy: Conversations in theory and practice.* Basic Books.

Bowen, S., Chawla, N., & Marlatt, G. A. (2011). *Mindfulness-based relapse prevention for addictive behaviors.* Guilford Press.

Brausch, A. M., & Girresch, S. K. (2012). A review of empirical treatment studies of adolescent non-suicidal self-injury. *Journal of Cognitive Psychotherapy, 26*(1), 3–18.

Brier, N. B. (2014). *Enhancing self-control in adolescents: Treatment strategies derived from psychological science.* Routledge.

Clark, D. A., & Beck, A. T. (2011). *The anxiety & worry workbook: The cognitive behavioral solution.* Guilford Press.

Cohn-Siver, S. (2009). *Using clients' perceptions in family therapy with at-risk adolescents and their families.* University of Michigan Dissertation Information Service.

Cottrell, D. J., Wright-Hughes, A., Collinson, M., Boston, P., Eisler, I., Fortune, S., Graham, E. H., Green, J., House, A. O., Kerfoot, M., Owens, D. W., Saloniki, E.-C., Simic, M., Lambert, F., Rothwell, J., Tubeuf, S., & Farrin, A. J. (2018, March). Effectiveness of systemic family therapy versus treatment-as-usual for young people after self-harm: A pragmatic, phase 3, multi-center, randomized control group. *The Lancet Psychiatry, 5*(3), 203–216

Denning, P., & Little, J. (2017). *Overcoming the influence: The harm-reduction guide to controlling your drug and alcohol use* (2nd ed.). Guilford Press.

De Shazer, S. (1991). *Putting difference to work.* Norton.

De Shazer, S., Dolan, Y., Korman, H., Trepper, T., McCollum, E., & Berg, I. K. (2007). *More than miracles: The state of the art of solution-focused brief therapy.* Haworth.

Diamond, G. S., Diamond, G. M., & Levy, S. A. (2014). *Attachment-based family therapy for depressed adolescents.* American Psychological Association.

Duncan, B. L. (2010). *On becoming a better therapist.* American Psychological Association.

Duncan, B. L. (2019). *Strategies for getting better with couples.* Workshop presented at the Harvard Medical School's Treating Couples Conference, Boston, MA.

Duncan, B. L., & Miller, S. D. (2000). *The heroic client: Doing client-directed, outcome-informed therapy.* Jossey-Bass.

Duncan, B. L., Miller, S. D., Wampold, B. E., & Hubble, M. A. (Eds.). (2010). *The heart and soul of change: Delivering what works in therapy* (2nd ed.). American Psychological Association.

Durrant, M., & Coles, D. (1991). The Michael White approach. In T. C. Todd & M. D. Selekman (Eds.), *Family therapy approaches with adolescent substance abusers* (pp. 135–175). Allyn & Bacon.

Efran, J., & Lukens, M. (1985, May-June). The world according to Humberto Maturana. *Family Therapy Networker,* 23–28, 72–75.

Eskin, M., Ertekin, K., & Demir, H. (2007, April). Efficacy of a problem-solving therapy for depression and suicidal potential in adolescents and young adults. *Cognitive Therapy and Research,* 32 (2), 227–245.

Escudero, V., Heatherington, L., & Friedlander, M. L. (2010). Therapeutic alliances and alliance- building in family therapy. In J. C. Muran & J. P. Barber (Eds.). *Therapeutic alliance: An evidence-based guide to practice* (pp. 240–263). Guilford Press.

Fisch, R., & Schlanger, K. (1999). *Brief therapy with intimidating cases: Changing the unchangeable.* Jossey-Bass.

Fisch, R., Weakland, J., & Segal, L. (1982). *The tactics of change: Doing therapy briefly.* Jossey-Bass.

Fredrickson, B.L. (1999). *Positivity: Groundbreaking research reveals how to embrace the hidden strength of positive emotions, overcome negativity, and thrive.* Crown.

Friedlander, M. L., Escudero, V., Heatherington, L., & Diamond, G. (2011). Alliance in couple and family therapy. In J. C. Norcross (Ed.), *Psychotherapy relationships that work: Evidence-based responsiveness* (2nd ed.), (pp. 92–110). Oxford University Press.

Gemer, C., & Neff, K. (2019). *Teaching the mindful self-compassion program: A guide for professionals.* Guilford Press.

Gingerich, W., De Shazer, S., & Weiner-Davis, M. (1988). Constructing change: A research view of interviewing. In E. Lipchik (Ed.), *Interviewing* (pp. 21–31). Aspen Systems.

Goolishian, H., & Anderson, H. (1988). *The therapeutic conversation.* Three-Day intensive training sponsored by the Institute of Systemic Therapy, Chicago, IL.

Gratz, K. L., & Chapman, A. L. (2009). *Freedom from self-harm: Overcoming self-injury with skills from DBT and other treatments.* New Harbinger.

Hanh, T. N. (1999). *The heart of the Buddha's teachings: Transforming suffering into peace, joy, and liberation*. Broadway Books.

Hanh, T. N. (2001). *Thich Nhat Hanh essential writings*. Orbis Books.

Havens, R. A. (2003). *The wisdom of Milton H. Erickson: The complete volume*. Crown House.

Hawton, K., & Rodham, K. (2006). *By their own young hand: Deliberate self-harm and suicidal ideas in adolescents*. Jessica Kingsley.

Henggeler, S. W., & Schaeffer, C. (2010). Treating serious antisocial behavior using multisystemic therapy. In J. R. Weisz & A. E. Kazdin (Eds.), *Evidence-based psychotherapies for children and adolescents* (pp. 259–277). Guilford Press.

Henggeler, S. W., & Sheidow, A. J. (2011). Empirically-supported family-based treatment for conduct disorders and delinquent adolescents. *Journal of Marital and Family Therapy, 39*(1), 30–58.

Hoffman, L. (2002). *Family therapy: An intimate journey*. Norton.

Kabat-Zinn, J. (1994). *Wherever you go, there you are: Mindfulness meditation in everyday life*. Hyperion.

Kissel-Wegela, K. (2014). *Contemplative psychotherapy essentials: Enriching your practice with Buddhist psychology*. Norton.

Klonsky, E. D. (2007). The function of deliberate self-injury: A review of the empirical evidence. *Clinical Psychology Review, 27*, 226–239.

Kross, E., Bruehlman-Senecal, E., Park, J., Burson, A., Dougherty, A., Shablack, H., Bremner, R., Moser, J., & Ayduk, O. (2014). Self-talk as a regulatory mechanism: How you do it matters. *Journal of Personality and Social Psychology, 106*(2), 304–324.

Kuehl, B. P. (1987). *The family therapy of adolescent drug abuse: Family members describe their experience*. University of Michigan Dissertation Information Service.

Lambert, M. J. (2010). *Prevention of treatment failure: The use of measuring, monitoring, and feedback in clinical practice*. American Psychological Association.

Liddle, H. A. (2010). Treating adolescent substance abuse using multidimensional family therapy. In J. R. Weisz & A. E. Kazdin (Eds.), *Evidence-based psychotherapies for children and adolescents* (pp.416–435). Guilford Press.

Lopez, S. J., & Snyder, C. R. (Eds.). (2009). *The Oxford handbook of positive psychology* (2nd ed.). Oxford University Press.

Malchiodi, C. A. (2003). *Handbook of art therapy*. Guilford Press.

Malchiodi, C. A. (2006). *Expressive therapies*. Guilford Press.

Maturana, H., & Varela, F. (1988). *The tree of knowledge: The biological roots to human understanding*. New Science Library.

McKeel, J. (2012). What works in solution-focused brief therapy: A review of change process research. In C. Franklin, T. S Trepper, W. J. Gingerich, & E. E. McCollum (Eds.), *Solution-focused brief therapy: A handbook of evidence-based practice* (pp. 130–144). Oxford University Press.

Mehlum, L., Ramleth, R. K., Tormoen, A. J., Haga, E., Diep, L. M., Stanley, B. H. Miller, A. L., Larsson, B., Sund, A. M., & Grøholt, B. (2019, May 25). Long-term effectiveness of dialectical behavior therapy versus enhanced usual care for adolescents with self-harming and suicidal behavior. *The Journal of Child Psychology and Psychiatry, 60*(10), 1112–1122.

Miller, A. L., Rathus, J. H., & Linehan, M. M. (2007). *Dialectical behavior therapy with suicidal adolescents*. Guilford Press.

Miller, W. R., & Rollnick, S. (2013). *Motivational interviewing: Helping people change* (2nd ed.). Guilford Press.

Newfield, N. A., Kuehl, B. P., Joanning, H. P., & Quinn, W. H. (1991). We can tell you about "Psychos" and "Shrinks": An ethnography of the family therapy of adolescent drug abuse. In T. C. Todd & M. D. Selekman (Eds.), *Family approaches with adolescent substance Abusers* (pp. 275–307). Allyn & Bacon.

Norcross, J. C., & Wampold, B. E. (2011). Evidence-based therapy relationships research Conclusions and clinical practices. In J. C. Norcross (Ed.). *Psychotherapy relationships that work: Evidence-based responsiveness* (2nd ed.) (pp. 423–431). Oxford University Press.

Norcross, J. C., & Wampold, B. E. (2013). Compendium of treatment applications. *Psychotherapy in Australia, 19*(3), 34–37.

Oettingen, G. (2014). *Re-thinking positive thinking: Inside the new science of motivation*. Current.

O'Hanlon, W. H., & Weiner-Davis, M. (1989). *In search of solutions: A new direction in psychotherapy*. New York: Norton.

Pennebaker, J. W. (2004). *Writing to heal: A guided journal for recovering from trauma and emotional upheaval.* New Harbinger.

Pollak, S. M., Pedulla, T., & Siegel, R. D. (2014). *Sitting together: Essential skills for mindfulness-based psychotherapy.* Guilford Press.

Prescott, D. S., Maeschalck, C. L., & Miller, S. D. (Eds.). (2017). *Feedback-informed treatment in clinical practice: Reaching for excellence.* American Psychological Association.

Prochaska, J. O., Norcross, J. C., & DiClemente, C. C. (1994). *Changing for good: A revolutionary six-stage program for overcoming bad habits and moving your life positively forward.* HarperCollins.

Rathus, J. H. & Miller, A. L. (2015). *DBT skills manual for adolescents.* Guilford Press.

Ratner, H., George, E., & Iveson, C. (2012). *Solution-focused brief therapy: 100 key points and techniques.* Routledge.

Ratner, H., & Yusuf, D. (2015). *Brief coaching with children and young people: A solution-focused approach.* Routledge.

Robin, A. L., & Le Grange, D. (2010). Family therapy for adolescents with anorexia nervosa. In J. R. Weisz & A. E. Kazdin (Eds.), *Evidence-based psychotherapies for children and Adolescents* (pp. 345–359). Guilford Press.

Robbins, M. S., Horigian, V., Szapocznik, J., & Ucha, J. (2010). Treating Hispanic youths using brief strategic family therapy. In J. R. Weisz & A. E. Kazdin (Eds.), *Evidence-based psychotherapies for children and adolescents* (pp. 375–391). Guilford Press.

Robbins, M. S., Turner, C. W., Dakof, G. A. & Alexander, J. F. (2006). Adolescent and parent therapeutic alliances as predictors of dropout in multidimensional family therapy. *Journal of Family Psychology, 20,* 108–116.

Selekman, M. D. (2009). *The adolescent and young adult self-harming treatment manual: A collaborative strengths-based therapy approach.* Norton.

Selekman, M. D. (2017). *Working with high-risk adolescents: A collaborative strengths-based approach.* Guilford Press.

Selekman, M. D. (2021). COVID-19 as a transformative opportunity for families and therapists: Harnessing the possibilities that constraints offer us. *Australian & New Zealand Journal of Family Therapy, 42*(1), 70–84.

Selekman, M. D., & Beyebach, M. (2013). *Changing self-destructive habits: Pathways to solutions with couples and families.* Routledge.

Selekman, M. D., & Shulem, H. (2007). The self-harming adolescents and their families' expert consultants project: A qualitative study [Unpublished manuscript].

Seligman, M. E. P. (2011). *Flourish: A visionary new understanding of happiness and well-being.* Free Press.

Sitton, M., Schudlich, T., Du Rocher, B., Byrne, C., Ochrach, C.M., & Erwin, E. A. (2020). Family functioning and self-injury in treatment-seeking adolescents: Implications for counselors. *Professional Counselor, 10*(3), 351–364.

Swift, J. K. & Greenberg, R. P. (2015). *Premature termination in psychotherapy: Strategies for engaging clients and improving outcomes.* American Psychological Association.

Szapocznik, J., & Hervis, O. E. (2020). *Brief strategic family therapy.* American Psychological Association.

Szapocznik, J., Schwartz, S. J., Muir, J. A., & Brown, C. H. (2012). Brief strategic family therapy: An intervention to reduce adolescent risk behavior. *Couple and Family Psychology, 1*(2), 134–145.

Tatarsky, A. (2007). *Harm-reduction psychotherapy: A new treatment for drug and alcohol problems.* Rowman & Littlefield.

von Foerster, H. (1981). *Observing systems.* Intersystems.

Weiner-Davis, M., De Shazer, S., & Gingerich, W. (1987). Building pretreatment change to construct the therapeutic solution: An exploratory study. *Journal of Marital and Family Therapy, 13*(4), 359–363.

White, M. (2007). *Maps of narrative practice.* Norton.

White, M., & Epston, D. (1990). *Narrative means to therapeutic ends.* Norton.

Whitlock, J., & Lloyd-Richardson, E. (2019). *Healing self-injury: A compassionate guide for parents and other loved ones.* Oxford University Press.

Annex A. Five Effective Engagement Strategies for NSSI Adolescents

Annex A presents five effective engagement strategies for NSSI adolescents: *utilize to the maximum degree adolescents' strengths and resources; make it safe for adolescents to share their self-injury stories; go with whatever goals and preferences the adolescents wish to pursue; honor and respect adolescents' silence;* and *use the two-step tango strategy when adolescents are in the precontemplative stage of readiness for change.*

Utilize to the Maximum Degree Adolescents' Strengths and Resources

When NSSI adolescents' come to us under duress, we need to strive to make the therapeutic context as inviting, nonthreatening, and positive as possible. A great starting place is to invite NSSI adolescents to share their major interests, hobbies, talents, skills, and life passions. Have them share with you examples of successfully mastering life challenges in the past using their strengths and skills. While hearing them share their past success stories, listen intently for the steps they were taking to be successful and how they were thinking and feeling about their performances at the time. Not only does this trigger positive emotions for them but it provides therapists with a treasure chest of potential building blocks for solution construction with the NSSI adolescents. As far as life passions go, our conversations need to incorporate the keywords and metaphors the adolescents use to describe their most meaningful and pleasurable activities to excite them for solution-finding and therapeutic intervention design. Adolescents are more likely to try out therapeutic experiments that are couched in what is meaningful to them. For example, if the adolescent really loves the *Marvel Comics* superhero the *Black Widow*, the therapist could ask, "If the Black Widow knew your situation, what advice would she have for you to try out that might have a great shot at working?" Adolescents like talking about what is important to them, not about problems or being lectured at about the dangers of self-injuring.

Make It Safe for Adolescents to Share Their Self-Injuring Stories

Once we have come to know NSSI adolescents by their strengths, talents, and life passions, we need to inquire about what positive effects they receive from their self-injuring practices a nd whether they are concurrently engaging in any other self-destructive habits, and we need to explore with them how the self-injuring behavior is connected to their family stories. By learning what positive psychological and physiological effects they receive from their self-injuring behavior and building an alliance, we can introduce them to alternative coping strategies like mindfulness meditation and visualization, which can produce similar comforting effects. For risk management purposes, it is critical to separate adolescents' cutting behavior from their substance abuse behavior. It is important to have them schedule these coping strategies at different times of the day since they are a dangerous combination together. Finally, we want to learn about how their self-injuring behavior fits with their family stories, that is, what family dynamics seem to maintain and exacerbate their behavior. Adolescents make excellent family systems' consultants and will not hesitate to tell us about the negative interactions and unresolved conflicts with their parents and siblings that stress them out the most and are integral parts of the NSSI family problem life support system.

Go With Whatever Goals and Preferences the Adolescents Wish to Pursue

Often, NSSI adolescents do not enter treatment wanting to change their self-injuring behaviors. Even if the parents and referring person think this should be the main focus of therapy, as therapists we need to go with whatever the adolescents wish to change and work on first. What may be most pressing for them are difficulties with their peers, challenges they are experiencing in their intimate romantic relationships, or behaviors they would like to see changed with their parents, such as being yelled at, not listened to, or having too much pressure put on them for high academic achievement. Helping them meet with success in their target goals areas usually has a positive impact on reducing their self-injuring and other self-destructive behaviors. It is not necessary to have goal consensus with adolescents and their parents. We can establish separate treatment goals and work projects with adolescents and their parents and still have a positive treatment outcome. Some NSSI adolescents have already had negative family therapy experiences in the past and would like to be seen individually in the early stages of treatment. It is still possible to maintain a relational systemic treatment focus seeing adolescents and parents separately. While working separately with each subsystem, we can give the adolescents and the parents therapeutic experiments to try that are geared to disrupt their negative interactions, increase more positive interactions, and strengthen their relationship bonds. At some point in the treatment process as changes are occurring, they may be more receptive to working together in improving the quality of their relationships.

Honor and Respect Adolescents' Silence

Some NSSI adolescents initially say very little in the first few sessions. This could be due to a lack of trust for therapists—often as a result of having their confidentiality violated by past therapists, who also had an interrogative style of questioning them or talked too much because of their own anxiety and pushed the adolescents to sign off on no-self-harming contracts before getting to know them and before they were ready to pursue total abstinence goals. What is important to remember is that these adolescents are not being resistant, but in silence they are sizing us up and asking themselves the following questions: "Do I like this therapist? How is the therapist different than the other therapists I've seen? Has the therapist made it comfortable enough to open up?" Silent adolescents are active participants in the alliance-building process, not passive recipients. Whether or not the adolescents are talking, it is important to stay connected and not give up on them. When it feels safe and comfortable, they will lower their drawbridges and let us in. One strategy that works well with silent adolescents is to ask them to bring in an MP4 or to burn a CD of their favorite music which they can turn you on to so that you can better get to know them.

Use the Two-Step Tango Strategy

The *two-step tango* is engagement strategy that works really well with reluctant adolescents in the precontemplative stage of readiness for change (Prochaska et al., 1994) (Selekman,

2009). The first step of the tango is to empathize with their dilemma about being forced to see us and refrain from demanding immediate change by using "go slow" messages: "We have plenty of time and I respect your desire not to change anything at this time. Unlike your past therapists, change is your choice and if down the road you choose to do so, I will be right by your side to help make it happen with you." Often, an NSSI adolescent's guard comes down after hearing the therapists giving them permission not to change. The second step of the tango is to gently and in a nonchalant manner begin to plant seeds in the minds of the NSSI adolescents about the benefits of change. The therapists can do so by sharing stories of other NSSI adolescents whose self-injuring behavior cost them in some way, such as a long-career female adolescent's scars from cutting herself which turned off a boy she was seriously interested in, or sharing a few examples of NSSI adolescents who ended up in psychiatric hospitals after wrongly being deemed suicidal. The seeds we are planting in the NSSI adolescents' minds are designed to raise their consciousness that their self-injuring behavior may have become problematic for them and to have them arrive at the conclusion that they want to consider trying to change it. By going back and forth with restraining them from changing and planting seeds, NSSI adolescents will move from not even being window-shoppers for therapy and precontemplators to advancing to the *contemplative stage* of readiness for change where they begin to view their self-injuring behavior in a new light and something they might possibly want to change.

Annex B. Therapeutic Operations

Provide Emotional Safety and Establish a Strong Connection With Each Family Member
One of the most important therapist-facilitated operations that must occur for alliance-building with families is providing a therapeutic climate that is emotionally safe for family members to allow themselves to be vulnerable and share with one another their thoughts, feelings, needs, concerns, and even secrets without any fear of being invalidated, yelled at, shamed, blamed, rejected, or physically threatened or harmed (Friedlander et al., 2011; Robbins et al., 2006). At the beginning of their initial family sessions, therapists can share with their clients that their house rule is that everyone's voice will be heard and celebrated throughout the therapeutic process and this will be actively enforced. Therapists should strive to build strong emotional connections with each family member through the use of such relationship skills as empathy, warmth, genuineness, validating, and conveying understanding.

Multipartiality: Validate All Family Members' Perspectives
Therapists need to simultaneously honor and embrace all family members' unique perspectives, theories of change, expectations, preferences, and best hopes they would like to achieve in family therapy. When using multipartiality, the therapist needs to be careful not to privilege any one family member's perspective or their own therapeutic perspectives

or ideas. Therapists need to operate from a position of *not knowing* and employ curiosity to keep therapeutic conversations going and to learn more about families' stories. It is the telling and retelling of the various chapters of the family's story that can lead to the co-generation of new meanings and opening up space for possibilities (Anderson & Goolishian, 1988; Friedlander et al., 2011).

Structuring Skills

Alexander et al. (2013) have found in their functional family therapy outcome research that clients in their studies reported that therapists' use of *structuring skills* greatly contributed to their treatment satisfaction and positive outcomes. Structuring skills consist of the therapist providing a safe therapeutic climate, actively taking charge in sessions to disrupt and stop negative and destructive family interactions, timing with breaking up the family and meeting alone with parents and adolescents, and the timing with offering families' specific therapeutic tools, strategies, and rituals when they were ready to try them out. Additionally, families in their studies reported being more hopeful and confident that change would occur with their situations when their therapists appeared confident and competent.

Establish Systemic Treatment Goals and Mutual Sense of Purpose

Whenever it is possible, therapists should strive to establish treatment goals that all family members agree upon. There needs to be clarity on what family members want to work on changing and how they will know that they have achieved their ideal treatment outcome. We need to listen carefully for any consensus around what family members would like to change first, and this can become their initial target goal area for change. The therapist's job is to negotiate with family members a solvable behavioral goal. By agreeing as a group what they would like to change first, they are conveying to one another, "We are in this together and it will be a team effort." Having systemic goals and a sense of purpose have been identified as critical alliance-building factors that contribute to positive treatment outcomes (Escudero et al., 2010; Friedlander, Escudero, & Heatherington, 2006; Friedlander, Escudero, Heatherington, & Diamond, 2011).

Solicit Session-by-Session Feedback From Family Members on Both Their Perceptions of the Quality of the Therapeutic Relationship and the Change Process

The therapeutic enterprise is an ambiguous process. As therapists, the only way we can ever truly know where we stand in the therapeutic process with our clients is after the initial family therapy meeting and in subsequent sessions by soliciting feedback from them on how they perceive both the quality of our relationships with them and the change process. At the end of every family session, we can ask family members the questions in Annex A.

By securing this valuable feedback from our clients at each family session, we can make the necessary therapeutic adjustments to deepen our alliances with them and deliver better, thereby optimizing their chances for treatment success. Therapeutic feedback research indicates that not only does this therapeutic operation help prevent premature client dropouts, but therapists who routinely do this with their clients tend to have better treatment outcomes (Duncan, 2010, 2019; Duncan et al., 2010; Lambert, 2010; Prescott et al., 2017).

- "What ideas from today's session did you find most useful that you plan to try out over the next week?"
- "Was there anything we did not talk about or address today that you wish for us to discuss in our next session?"
- "Was there anything I said or did in our meeting that you did not like or you would like me to stop doing in future sessions?"
- "Are you feeling satisfied with how things are going in our work together or is there anything you would like me to do differently with you in terms of what we are working on or what you would like more help with?"

Annex C. Key Questions for Self-Harming Assessment

- "Now that I know you are cutting/burning yourself, how has the habit benefited you?"
- "What effects do you like the most from doing it?"
- "What does it mean to you as a practice and how does it fit into your life story?"
- "In what situations and relationships do you find cutting/burning yourself helps you the most?"
- "What results do you get that you are hoping for?"
- "Can you think of any times lately or in the past where cutting/burning yourself really backfired or cost you in a big-time way?"
- "How long have you been cutting/burning yourself?"
- "In a given day and week, how often do you cut/burn yourself?"
- "What would be the disadvantages of giving your cutting/burning habit up?"
- "If 'cutting' were to pack its bags and leave your life for good, what would you miss the most about it?"
- "If there were any aspects of 'cutting' you would wish to keep, what would those be?"
- "If you could put a voice to 'cutting' or your most meaningful scar, what would it say about you as a person and your life situation?"
- "What is different during the times you avoid caving into cutting/burning; what do you tell yourself and do instead?"

- "In the past, what was the longest stretch of time you went without cutting/burning yourself and what worked to pull that off?"
- "When stressed out or feeling out of control, do you ever binge eat, starve yourself, overexercise, or take diet pills/laxatives for weight control?"
- "Do you ever abuse drugs or alcohol to get rid of bad thoughts or feelings or to escape from your problems?"
- "Do you ever engage in risky unprotected sex when seeking comfort or as a way to hurt yourself?"
- "This is a routine question I often ask, 'Has anyone ever seriously hurt you emotionally or physically in the past?'"
- "Another routine question I often ask, 'Have you ever thought about or tried to take your life in the past?'"

Annex D. Examples of Useful Goal-Setting Questions

Best Hopes Questions
- "What are your best hopes that will come out of our conversation today?"
- "Let's say our meeting today met all of your best hopes and expectations and you left here completely satisfied. What is now better with your situation?"
- "I'm curious, have there been any times lately or in the past where your best hopes happened, even a little bit?"
- "Are you aware of what you did to get that to happen?"
- "How will you really know that you achieved your best hopes?"

The Tomorrow Question
- "Suppose you achieved your best hopes overnight, what would you be doing differently tomorrow?"
- "Who will be the first to notice you at your best tomorrow?"
- "What will they notice you doing that will surprise them the most?"
- "What else will be better tomorrow?"

Beyond Your Wildest Dreams Questions:
- "Let's say our session today proves to be helpful beyond your wildest dreams. What will have changed with your situation?"
- "How will that change make a big difference in your life?"
- "While driving home from my office today, how else will you be able to tell that your wildest dreams are really happening?"
- "On a scale from 1 to 10, with 1 being when you were first referred to me two weeks ago and 10 being the day after your wildest dreams just happened, with your best estimate, where would you rate your situation today?"

- "Sometimes out of the blue parts of people's wildest dreams had already started to happen a little bit well before seeing me for the first time. Have any of you noticed this happening, even a little bit in your relationships or individually?"

Scaling Questions

- "So, if there is a conflict between the three of you, rather than sweeping it under the rug you quickly will resolve it in a calm way. On a scale from 1 to 10, with 10 being you can more consistently resolve conflicts together and 1 not at all, where would you have rated your situation a month ago?"
- "All of you say at a 1. How about two weeks ago?"
- "At a 3 (the parents) and a 4 (the NSSI daughter). Are you aware of what you told yourselves and the steps you took to get two and three steps higher on the scale, respectively?"
- "It sounds like mom and dad, by approaching Alice (daughter) in a calm way, you have been able to better manage disagreements with her. Alice, it sounds like when your parents don't fly off the handle with you and are calmer, it is easier for you to work out your disagreements with them. Where would you rate your situation today on that scale?"
- "Wow! At a 6 and 7, respectively. Are you aware of how the three of you pulled that off?"
- "'Staying calm,' 'trying to listen to each other's point of view,' and 'three times quickly resolving your disagreements.' Great work! So, over the next week what are each of you going to do to get one step higher on that scale to a 7 and 8, respectively?"

Annex E. Other Questions Developed and Inspired by Solution-Focused Brief Therapy, Narrative Therapy, and Postmodern Systemic Theorists

Coping Questions

- "It sounds like there are times where you feel really stressed out and frustrated. Tell me, what steps have you taken to prevent your situation from getting much worse?"
- "Are you aware of how you pulled that off?"
- "Is that different for you to not lose your cool with your daughter?"
- "What else are you doing to prevent this situation from getting much worse?"

Pessimistic Sequence Questions
- "(For parents who are burned out and too laissez-faire with limit-setting) Let's say this Saturday morning at 2 AM a police officer rings your front doorbell to say your son is no longer with us. What effect would his loss have on you individually as parents?"
- "What impact would his loss have on your marital relationship?"
- "What would both of you miss the most not having him around?"
- "Who will attend his funeral?"
- "What will the eulogies be?"
- "Some parents in your situation would have thrown in the towel with counseling a long time ago. What keeps you hanging in there and willing to give it another try?"
- In fact, some parents in your situation would have considered putting their daughter in residential treatment or a boarding school, making their kid a state ward, or, better yet, putting her up for adoption! Have you ever considered those options?"

Sub-Zero Scaling Questions
- "On a scale from -10 to -1, with -10 being your situation is totally hopeless and irresolvable and -1 being you have a glimmer of hope that your situation may improve just a little bit, where would you have rated your situation a month ago?"
- "At a -8. How come not lower on the rating scale?"
- "Oh, she had been 'cooperating better' with the two of you. Anything else your daughter started to do differently that prevented all of you at being at rock bottom -10?"
- "Okay nothing else. What about two weeks ago, where would you have rated your situation?"
- "At a -6. What steps was she taking and what adjustments were you making to move you up to that -6?"
- "Wow, she was 'doing her homework without reminders' and 'being more respectful' with how she spoke to you?"
- "Were the two of you doing anything different with her?"
- "So, you 'refrained from criticizing her' and cut back on your 'yelling at' her?"
- "Where would you rate your situation today on the scale?"
- "At a -5. What steps have you (the parents) and Karen taken to get up one step higher on the scale?"
- "So, you have 'not had any arguments.' What else has been a little bit better?"

- "So, Karen has been coming to you for support when she has been triggered. As parents, are you aware of what you are doing differently that has made it more inviting for Karen to come to you instead of self-harming?"
- "Staying calm and 'being better listeners.' Karen, have you noticed that and other things your parents have been doing differently that has made it more comfortable to go to them?"
- "So, 'being calm, being better listeners, not criticizing' you, and 'not threatening to put you back into the psychiatric hospital' has helped. Since all of you are on a roll, what steps are you going to take over the next week to get up to a -4?"

Externalizing Questions

- "How long has 'cutting' gotten the best of you and your parents?"
- "Can you think of any times lately where you stood up to 'cutting' and did not cave into its wishes?"
- "What did you tell yourself and do instead to frustrate it and loosen 'cutting's' grip on you?"
- "Have there been any times recently Carolyn where 'cutting' deceived you as a comforting friend and instead betrayed you in a really negative way?"
- "In what ways does 'cutting' divide the two of you (the parents) in how best to help Carolyn out?"
- "Can the two of you (the parents) think of any times lately or in the past where you were a dynamic duo in thwarting 'cutting's' attempts to compel Carolyn to brutalize her arms?"
- "What percentage of the time would you say 'cutting' is now in charge of your lives?"
- "About 60% of the time. As a family team, what steps will you need to take over the next week to take back control from 'cutting' 50% of the time?"

Conversational Questions

- "Before we started working together was there anything that you told yourselves that you weren't going to bring up in our meetings together?"
- "It feels like we have all of sudden run into a brick wall in our work together. What's not being talked about that we may need to talk about here?"
- "What's missing in your relationship with your father that if it were present would make a big difference to you (the NSSI daughter)?"
- "Are there any questions that you are hoping I would ask you while we are working together?"
- "Are there any questions you hope I don't ask you?"

- "Is there a courageous conversation you have not yet had with your father that once it happens, could potentially take your relationship with him to a better place?"
- "If I were to work with another family just like your family, what advice would you have for me to help them out in the best way possible?"

Annex F. Nine Solution-Oriented Parenting Skills and Change Strategies

Parenting Like Buddhist Monks and Parental Presence

As part of the parent management skills training process, it is important to teach parents the core Buddhist principles of loving-kindness and compassion and the benefits of adopting a daily mindfulness practice. Once parents come to the realization that their NSSI adolescents are not acting-out teenagers trying to make their lives stressful but are suffering and experiencing emotional distress, they will see the need to respond with loving support and compassionate understanding. By responding in this manner, NSSI adolescents will come to know that they can count on their parents to be truly present and to validate and support them both prior to and after self-harming episodes. Once this occurs, they will no longer have to take matters into their own hands to comfort themselves (Selekman, 2017; Selekman & Beyebach, 2013).

Parental presence can be strengthened by the parents adopting a daily mindfulness meditation practice and making themselves available for high-quality activities that their kids would like to do with them. The more skillful parents get at meditating and being able to observe their thoughts and feelings without allowing them to own and control them, the more they can be truly empathically attuned to and present with their kids (Selekman, 2017).

Be Calm, Listen, Validate, and Soothe

Be calm, listen, validate, and soothe is an exercise we can have NSSI adolescents and their families practice both in sessions and at home. For the parents, they learn a positive and constructive way to respond to their kids when they are triggered or following a self-harming episode. In the family session, we can have the NSSI adolescents think of both powerful triggers for them and recent self-harming episodes they had experienced. First, we can have the NSSI adolescent pretend that she had just experienced a powerful trigger and her parents can practice responding to her in a calm way, listening intently to their daughter's triggering story, validating her thoughts and feelings, and then comforting her in a soothing way. Next, we can have the adolescent and her family reenact a recent self-harming episode, and the parents can practice this new constructive and positive way of responding. The NSSI adolescent can then offer feedback to her parents on what worked and any proposed adjustments she would like her parents to make to help her in the best way possible following a self-harming episode. To further solidify this more positive way of parental responding, it is helpful to have families practice this exercise at home daily.

Become Solution Detectives and Capture Your Kids' Sparkling Moments

As mentioned earlier, self-injuring and other behavioral difficulties with adolescents do not happen every hour of the day, there are always exceptions to the rule. However, when a particular problem becomes habitual there is a tendency for parents to anticipate or look for problems to happen with their kids, particularly the identified client. To help counter this unproductive mindset, it is helpful to coach parents to pull out their imaginary magnifying glasses and on a daily basis carefully observe for sparkling moments with their kids. The sparkling moments can be responsible and respectful behaviors, not showing any signs of self-harming behaviors, or steering clear of toxic peers who the parents have had concerns about. The parents can celebrate these sparkling moments with praise and reward their kids with privileges the kids desire (Selekman, 2010, 2017).

The Compliment/Gratitude Box

The compliment/gratitude box is a great family ritual to help generate more positive family communications, create more warmth, and strengthen their bonds in their family relationships. In order to do this ritual, the family needs to find an old shoebox and cut a slit in the lid top. On a daily or every-other-day basis, family members are to write down on slips of paper things they appreciate about one another and are grateful about that they have experienced together, sign them, and then drop their slips into the shoebox. A few times a week after dinner or in the evenings they are to take turns blindly reaching in and reading the slips. Often, family members discover certain qualities that they never knew family members appreciated about them or certain vacations or life experiences that meant a lot to them (Selekman, 2009, 2017).

Reserve and Protect Weekly High-Quality Bonding Time

Spending time together has been found to be an important characteristic of strong families (DeFrain, 2007). I would argue that 90% of the family problems we see in our offices involving kids has to do with the fact that they spend very little time together engaging in high-quality offline activities together. A lot of parents today are failing to put in place firm boundaries between their work and family lives and have not laid down any consistently enforced guidelines around their kids' screen usage. When they do spend time together, it is often about what the parents would like to do with them or what they think would be good for their kids. Kids need to pick what they would like to do with one or both parents that would be meaningful and enjoyable to them. During this high-quality bonding time all parties involved have to agree to disconnect from their digital devices so they can truly be present with one another.

Use Positive Consequences Instead of Punishment
The use of positive consequences with kids can elevate their self-esteem and help build character. Rather than the old parental consequences of grounding and taking away meaningful possessions, privileges, and activities, positive consequences can be a great alternative to punishment. So, when the NSSI adolescent breaks a parental rule or gets into trouble outside the home, they will have to do a good deed for a family member or some form of service work in the community. The parents can determine the length of the positive consequence based on the nature of the adolescent's infraction. The NSSI adolescent may balk at wanting to do the positive consequence initially, but often once they do it, they feel great about the experience. In some cases, the kids' service work experiences have led to more volunteer work, summer employment, or potential future career paths for them (Selekman, 2009, 2017).

If It Is Not Working, Do Something Dramatically Different
When parents become stuck, find themselves being too super-responsible with, disengaging from out of frustration, or yelling at their NSSI adolescents all of the time, the "do something dramatically different" strategy can be a useful option (De Shazer, 1991; Selekman, 2009). To help break parental unproductive and redundant attempted solution patterns, we can share with them the following:

> *"Your kid has gotten your number and you have become too predictable with your responses to her. So, over the next week, whenever your daughter pushes your buttons, breaks your rules, or gets into trouble at school, I want the two of you to respond to her in a dramatically different way. It can be really off-the-wall and really out of character for you two; the important thing is that whatever you come up with, your daughter has never encountered this before from you. I want the two of you to go for Academy Award performances and have fun with this. Keep track of what you do that seems to have a positive effect in promoting more cooperation, a reduction in self-harming, and more responsible behaviors from her."*

Often, parents come back in the next session eager to share with their therapists what worked and how they had fun with their homework. Once the parents have found strategies that work, we want to have them continue to do more of what works until their NSSI adolescent's presenting difficulties have stabilized.

Externalize Oppressive Intergenerational Parenting Practices
More often than not, the same redundant negative patterns of parental emotional reactivity—yelling, criticizing, being too overprotective and controlling—parents fall prey to often are intergenerational parenting styles and practices that have taken on a life all of their own and are now wreaking havoc in the families they helped co-create. In family sessions, we observe how these patterns play a central role in the maintenance of the NSSI

problem life support system by noticing how anxious, shut down, or defensive the NSSI adolescent becomes in response to their parents. One effective way to disrupt these negative intergenerational parenting patterns is to externalize them (Selekman, 2017; White, 2007). For example, if the lead parent is constantly falling prey to criticizing her NSSI daughter about everything, we can ask the parent, "Tell me, when you were growing up did 'criticizing' get the best of your relationship with you and your parents?" If the parent responds with, "Yes and I didn't like it." We can inquire with the parent, "How did that make you feel toward them and about yourself?" After the parent describes the unpleasant thoughts and feelings she had experienced from being treated this way, we can offer the parent an invitation to rewrite family history and work with their family team to conquer the 'criticizing' intergenerational pattern. A great ritual to offer the parent and her family to help conquer the pattern is the habit control ritual (Durrant & Coles, 1991; Selekman, 2009, 2017). First, we have the family get a large sheet of flipchart paper or tag board and create two columns. The family is to come up with a team name and write it at the top of the left column. In the right column, they can write at the top The Criticizing Pattern. Second, they are to daily keep track of their victories over The Criticizing Pattern, that is, what they tell themselves or do to not allow it to get the best of them individually or in their relationships. Finally, they also have to keep track of The Criticizing Pattern's victories over them and as a family strategize for reducing these sneak attacks. Once they find problem-solving and coping strategies that work, they are to keep doing more of what works until the pattern has been conquered.

Regularly Solicit Feedback From Your Kids on Your Parenting Performance
As parents, we don't always know where we stand with our kids in terms of what we do that they like and dislike. A highly practical parenting strategy parents can use with their kids to find out what they should increase doing and what they need to discontinue doing is to solicit weekly feedback on their parenting performance (Selekman, 2017). Parents can ask and share with their kids, "What are we doing as parents that you find helpful and appreciate, and where do we need to make adjustments so that we can improve the quality of our relationships with you? It is important to us that you are happy and satisfied with how we are as parents and you are getting your needs met." Adolescents in particular appreciate hearing that their parents really care about making their relationships better and are willing to change their negative behaviors to strengthen their relationships with them.

Annex G. Three Mindfulness Practices

The Sound Meditation
The NSSI adolescent is to first get comfortable in a chair or couch and sit back with an open ribcage to enhance their breathing. Next, the adolescent is to pay close attention to

everything they hear around them, silently labeling each sound they hear. The adolescent is not to try to figure out why they are hearing certain sounds but just to label them. They are to do this for 12 to 15 minutes. Often, adolescents become so relaxed doing this meditation that they fall asleep both in my sessions when we practice together and at home.

Take Six Deep Breaths Slowly
The NSSI adolescent is to first get comfortable in a chair or couch and sit back with an open ribcage to enhance their breathing. Next, they are to slowly take an inhalation breath to the count of five then slowly exhale to the count of five. They are to repeat the same breathing method five more times slowly. Often, adolescents report feeling mentally and physically cleansed and relaxed after doing this mindfulness practice.

Mindful Walking
This powerful and relaxing mindfulness practice really grounds adolescents in the miraculous moment. While walking on a forest preserve park path ideally, they are to carefully pay close attention to everything they see, hear, and smell. Adolescents often report multi-sensory experiences in the woods that they never encountered before. Being out in nature is healing in its own right, but this mindfulness practice really enhances the experience for them. Some adolescents have branched out to mindful biking or running.

Annex H. Visualization Strategies

Visualizing a Movie of Success
To begin with, have the NSSI adolescent get comfortable on a chair or couch, sitting back with an open ribcage. The adolescent is to share with the therapist what movie theater they typically go to with family or friends. Next, they are to picture in their mind the blank movie screen at this theater prior to the advertisements for future TV shows or movies. The adolescent is asked to think of a time in the past where they achieved something that they were really proud of. Using all their senses, including color and motion, the adolescent is to create a movie of their top accomplishment and project it on to the blank movie screen in their mind. While they are creating the movie, they should access more details regarding the setting of the achievement, who else is present, and what they are thinking and feeling as they are succeeding with the accomplishment. Reliving their past successes triggers a wide range of positive emotions for adolescents and reminds them of all of their strengths and resources and how resilient they are (Selekman, 2009).

Visualizing a Movie of Joy
Some NSSI adolescents have grave difficulty accessing any past achievements where they were proud of themselves. A great visualization option is to have them create movies of joy. The adolescents are to access in their minds past experiences on vacations or at camps that brought them great joy, had sparked exuberant feelings in them, and/or put them in

awe of what they saw and did. Using the same format as described above with visualizing movies of success, they are to create in great detail movies of joy that they can project on to the blank movie screens in their minds (Selekman, 2009).

Annex I. Nine Resilience-Enhancing Thinking Tools and Strategies

The Impossibility of Certainty

When stressed out by or worried about an upcoming event going badly or by the aftermath of a situation that did not go well, the adolescent can ask themselves, "How can I be absolutely certain X will happen?" The truth of the matter is that we cannot be absolutely certain about anything.

Implications

After a negative situation occurs involving the adolescent's peers, family members, or a poor performance, it makes matters worse to ruminate about it. This is a great way to put oneself in emotional quicksand and make oneself even more depressed and anxious. It is helpful for the adolescent to ask themselves, "By dwelling on what happened over and over again, does it make me happier or more miserable?"

Decatastrophize

Many NSSI adolescents are prone to catastrophizing when they are worried about something or when negative life events occur. A great question to ask oneself is, "Really, come on, what is the ultimate worst thing that could happen?" (Antony & Norton, 2020).

Use Your Mind Like a Kaleidoscope

One way we can help NSSI adolescents not latch on to the first explanation for why bad things happen to them is to have them pretend that their minds are like kaleidoscopes. By doing so, and using curiosity, they can open their minds up to the second, third, fourth, and fifth possible explanations for why bad things happened to them, such as being let down by friends.

Count All the Objects in the Room

This thinking strategy helps NSSI adolescents get their heads away from rumination and has them focus their attention on counting all the objects in their bedrooms. It helps them to successfully disrupt negative thought processes that are driving the emotional storms in their heads (Antony & Norton, 2020).

5-4-3-2-1

This multisensory strategy helps NSSI adolescents move away from ruminating and being owned by their negative thoughts and feelings by having them focus on five things they can see, four things they can touch, three things they can hear, two things they can smell, and one thing they can touch. Most adolescents in general have reported that they found this coping strategy to be very helpful (Antony & Norton, 2020).

Detachment

Once NSSI adolescents adopt a daily mindfulness practice, over time they will get better at observing their visiting negative thoughts and feelings whenever they enter their minds, rather than allowing them to own and control them. These negative thoughts and feelings are not solid and permanent residents, so it is important to remind adolescents that there is no need to flinch or cave into impulse because if they are patient and remain calm, they will do them no harm and will exit on their own. I like to have NSSI adolescents imagine in their minds a flashing neon sign with the following mantra: "Don't let your negative thoughts and feelings own you, detach from them!

Self-Talk in the Third Person

Research indicates that when we use self-talk in the third-person we gain a big-picture view of the situations that triggered us, have more self-control, and are better able to regulate our emotions (Kross et al., 2014). We can instruct an adolescent to do third-person self-talk in the following way: "Jane is a kind and caring person. She is popular and has many friends. She knows there is always drama going on with her friends and not to worry about it because the conflicts that occur are often resolved quickly. Jane also is a good pianist and now can play more complicated classical music pieces."

If X, Then Y Intentions

"When I am triggered by X, I will do Y" (Listen to my favorite tune, text my best friend for support, count all of the objects in the room, take six deep breaths slowly, visualize a movie of success or joy). The more Y options NSSI adolescents have, the less likely they will cave into self-injuring and engaging in other self-destructive behaviors. Implementation intentions have been found to be quite effective as a self-control management intervention for adolescents with behavioral difficulties (Brier, 2014).

Annex J. Four Classes of Therapeutic Experiments

Using the Imaginary Time Machine

The imaginary time machine is one of the most versatile in-session therapeutic experiments to use in family therapy sessions for solution-finding and strengthening relationship bonds. It can be used at any stage of the treatment process. This annex illustrates two major ways to use it (Selekman, 2009, 2017).

Bring Back the Best From the Past

The NSSI adolescents and their parents will have separate opportunities to hop into the imaginary time machine in my office and take it back to a place where they felt closer and were getting along well (Selekman, 2009, 2017). Using all of their senses, including color and motion, they are to describe where in time they traveled back to, what they are doing and talking about together, and what is most special about their time traveling experiences. Often, we discover a goldmine of past successful ways of being with one another that sparks positive emotions, warmth, and closeness in their relationships. We can then explore with the NSSI adolescents and their parents what pieces of their past positive experiences they could put in place in the here and now to improve their current relationships.

Experience Future Selves to Establish New Parent-Adolescent Relationships in the Here and Now

Using the same instructions as above, the NSSI adolescents are to hop into the imaginary machine into the future and when they exit from it, they are now 22 years old and are having Sunday night dinner at their parents' house (Selekman, 2009, 2017). They are now college graduates, completing college, working, and have their own apartments or sharing them with friends. As successful and productive adults, they can be asked to share with their parents all the great accomplishments they have made in their lives that they think their parents would be proud of. We can ask the parents in the family meeting not only how they will be responding to their transformed adult children but what questions they would be asking them and changes they would be most delighted to hear about. Using the future in this way can engender hope with demoralized parents who are feeling burned out with their NSSI adolescents' behaviors. This can lead to more positive interactions between them and the establishment of treatment goals growing out of some of the changes the NSSI adolescents had made in the future. We can have the NSSI adolescents pick two of the major changes they made in the future and walk their way back to the here and now speculating the steps they took to get on their pathways to success. The steps can be negotiated into treatment goals.

Family Connection Building Rituals and Therapeutic Experiments

In this section, I describe family connection-building rituals and therapeutic experiments that are designed to help strengthen relationship bonds. They tap the strengths and creativity of family members to transform their relationships. For the sake of brevity, two family connection-building rituals and one therapeutic experiment are presented below (Selekman, 2009, 2017).

NSSI Adolescents Mentoring One or Both Parents

The NSSI adolescents are to pick one of their top strengths or specific skills that they possess and teach one or both parents over the next week their selected strengths or skills. They can be playing an instrument, some form of artwork, dancing, a sports skill, sewing, wood-working, writing poetry, and so forth. They are to come up with a class schedule of a minimum of two times over the next week for 45 minutes to an hour of lesson times. No digital devices are allowed or disruptions from uninvolved family members. One or both parents have to be respectful students and can ask questions but cannot challenge their teachers' authority. The beauty in this ritual is that it is a great opportunity for the NSSI adolescents to shine with their competencies and for the parents to see sides of their kids that they lost sight of due their NSSI and other behavioral difficulties (Selekman, 2009, 2017). Parents often enjoy their special time with their kids and it can infuse more warmth and closeness in their relationships. Some parents have had such great times with their kids that they have contracted with them for more classes.

The Secret Surprise

This therapeutic experiment can be quite effective at creating more warmth and closeness and sparking positive interactions in NSSI adolescents' relationships with their parents. While meeting alone with the NSSI adolescents in a family session, we have them think about one secret surprise they could pull off for each of their parents over the next week that their parents will really notice and appreciate and will shock them in a positive way. They are not to tell the parents what the surprises were. When we reconvene the family, we instruct the parents to play detectives over the next week and try to figure out what the NSSI adolescents' surprises were. This will be discussed in the next family session (Selekman, 2009, 2010).

Invisible Family Inventions

The NSSI adolescents are asked, "If you were to invent a machine or gadget that would benefit other kids and families like yours, what would it look like, how would it work, and how could it really make a difference with transforming your family situation?" While meeting alone with them, they are to draw a prototype sketch with crayons or colored pencils. Next, they are to think about all of its cool and practical features and how it would work. They also have to come up with a name for their new product. We then reconvene their families and have them present their inventions to them. The added fun bonus to this therapeutic experiment is that the kids want to go home and build their new inventions with their families (Selekman, 2009, 2010, 2017).

Art Therapy Experiments

Over the years, I have been impressed with how artistically talented NSSI adolescents are. Since many of these kids express their creative selves best through art and/or may have grave difficulty putting words to the emotional turmoil and conflicts they are experiencing, art and photography can be a nonthreatening and fun way to express what is going on in their heads and families. When using art and photography methods with NSSI adolescents, it is important to refrain from making any interpretations of the meaning of their final products. Instead, ask open-ended questions from a position of curiosity and invite them to tell you the meanings of the objects in their art products and photographs. With all of the art experiments I use with NSSI adolescents, it is up to them to decide whether or not they share with their families their final products. Below, I describe five of the most popular art activities among NSSI adolescents I have worked with (Selekman, 2009, 2017).

My Soul Collage

My Soul Collage is great to use at the beginning of treatment as a way to gain access to the inner emotional worlds of the NSSI adolescents, certain habits or behaviors and beliefs they wish to change about themselves, and what is most pressing for them to first try to stabilize or change. This can become their initial treatment goals. When introducing this art experiment, we first have a discussion about what they think a soul is and where it is housed. Most kids think it is inside their brains. They are given the following directive, "If we were to take the top of your head off and peer into your soul, what images, words, and phrases would emanate out?" It is critical when doing this exercise that we have on hand a tall stack of varied topic magazines, old newspapers, scissors, glue, and colored markers and pencils to write or draw things they could not find in the magazines or newspapers (Selekman, 2017).

Surrealist Art Solutions

Surrealist artists like Salvador Dali and Rene Magritte used their imagination powers to depict their unique ways of interpreting historic events, time distortion, dreams and nightmares, the random, injecting an element of surprise in their works, and made it impossible to give a definitive grand interpretation of the meaning of their final art products. After sharing with NSSI adolescents' examples of these two leading Surrealist artists to get their creative juices activated, it is up to them to depict certain difficulties they are experiencing, including reoccurring dreams and nightmares, in a Surrealist way. Some NSSI adolescents like to include in their Surrealist work both their current difficulty in their life and what an ideal outcome would look like. In fact, one of my NSSI adolescents thought it was best for therapists to use this art therapy experiment after three to four sessions into the treatment process with adolescents after their more immediate issues had been addressed to then show how their ideal outcomes will look like when their difficulties are resolved. It is helpful to do this activity alone with the NSSI adolescents and offer them the options of using crayons, color pencils, or different color paints (Selekman, 2017).

Imaginary Feelings X-Ray Machine

This art experiment is a great way to gain access to NSSI adolescents' emotional worlds and where in their bodies these feelings live. It is also helpful to have them draw important scenes from their life that specific feelings are connected to. For this art experiment, we need to use a thicker meat-wrapping quality paper that does not tear easily for the NSSI adolescent to lay down on. The paper has to be long enough for the adolescent to get their entire body on it. The first step is to have a family draw the outline of the adolescent's body on the paper. The directive given is as follows, "Suppose we had a special machine that could show us pictures of what your feelings look like and where they live in your body. While drawing how your feelings look like and where they live in your body, please draw important scenes from your life that those feelings are connected to." They can use crayons, colored markers, and pencils. It is amazing how powerful NSSI adolescents' X-Ray drawings have been in revealing strong negative emotions they had been keeping locked up inside and unresolved conflicts with certain family members and peers (Selekman, 2010, 2009).

My Superhero Comic Strip

Today, a lot of NSSI adolescents are into Marvel Comics superheroes. A fun art experiment is to have the NSSI adolescents really stretch their imagination powers and come up with a new superhero they would like to become. I ask them, "What kind of superpowers do you have? How would you look? What strategies would you use to defeat a clever and powerful villain?" Next, we can externalize and objectify their number one presenting problem, which may be "cutting," "anxiety," "depression," into a super villain. Again, the NSSI adolescents are to use their imaginative powers to come up with a super villain who is smart, clever, and strong. Similar to a comic strip format, on a long sheet of paper they are to depict how they will conquer their super villains in boxes. It is important that they depict their super villains as challenging opponents who also will use their powers to counterstrike and try to defeat them. Often, what grows out of NSSI adolescents' superhero comic strips are potential creative solutions they can use to try to resolve their difficulties (Selekman, 2017).

My Strengths Collage

NSSI adolescents really love doing this fun collage art exercise. On a long sheet of paper, they can either draw themselves or have someone draw the outline of their bodies on it. They are to think about all of their strengths, talents, skills, and personal qualities they and others like about them. We need to have a tall stack of varied topic magazines, old newspapers, colored markers and pencils, scissors, and glue. The therapeutic power of this art exercise is that it triggers positive emotions for the NSSI adolescents and it increases their self-awareness of all of the positive inner jewels that they possess. Additionally, we can utilize the NSSI adolescents' strengths in their target goal areas to empower them to resolve their difficulties (Selekman, 2017).

Expressive Writing Experiments

Some NSSI adolescents are strong in linguistic intelligence, that is, they express themselves best through writing creative stories, raps, poetry, and may like to journal about their thoughts, feelings, and life experiences. They are often avid readers as well. Therefore, the use of expressive writing experiments with them would be a good fit. Below, I describe five popular expressive writing experiments I frequently use with NSSI adolescents.

My Favorite Author Rewrites My Story

This expressive writing experiment begins with finding out who the NSSI adolescent's favorite authors are and which central characters really resonate with them and why. The following directive is given, "If _____ were to rewrite your story, what kind of character would you become? Would you have any magical powers and/or truly unique qualities? Would any of your family members or close friends be characters in this new story about you? What would be the central themes your favorite author would try to convey in this new story about you?" Next, I have the NSSI adolescents write the first page of the first chapter that they imagine their favorite author would write to set the tone for this new story about them. Some NSSI adolescents became so enthusiastic about this writing exercise that they went home and generated a whole first chapter of this new story about them! For co-generating solutions, we can ask them what advice the new characters they have become would have for them off the page to help resolve their current difficulties. You can also ask them what advice their favorite authors would have for them as well (Selekman, 2017).

You-At-Your-Best Story

The NSSI adolescents are to write a few paragraphs of something that they had accomplished that they were really proud of. They are to include their agency thinking, that is, what they told themselves to get fired up for the achievement and/or who were the key people that got behind them and cheered them on. They are also to include their pathway thinking, that is, the steps that they took to make their achievements happen. I like to have them underline in different color ink their agency and pathway thinking. These past successful problem-solving strategies can be used to help them to achieve their present goals. This expressive writing exercise not only triggers positive emotions for the writer but when read before going to bed each night, helps them to sleep better (Peterson, 2006).

My Epiphany Log

Over the years, I have had a number of NSSI adolescents come to my sessions reporting experiencing epiphanies about their difficulties and life situations. They were randomly sparked by something they read, heard, or saw in a movie, TV show, news interviews, or conversations with family and friends. Now, I routinely ask NSSI adolescents about whether or not they have experienced any recent epiphanies about their difficulties or life situations and have them fill out the My Epiphany Log (Selekman, 2009). There are five headings on the form: Date, My Epiphany, Sparked By, Wisdom Gained, and Applied To. Epiphanies can be transformative in changing people's beliefs about themselves and their life situations and lead to new ways of being with others.

My Gratitude Log

Gratitude is one of the key characteristics of individuals who are reporting high levels of life satisfaction and flourishing in their lives (Seligman, 2011). In fact, keeping a gratitude log by adding new entries two to three days per week has been found to benefit us in the following ways: increases our hope, optimism, and happiness levels; neutralizes negative emotions; calms our nervous systems; improves the quality of our sleep; and both helps us to strengthen our relationship bonds and be more empathic with family members and friends (Emmons, 2007; Niemiec, 2018; Selekman, 2009, 2021). When we feel grateful, our brains release dopamine, which makes us want to feel good again, which can become a new virtuous habit for us. Once we start regularly looking for new things to be grateful for, our brains start looking for more things to be grateful for.

Habit Diary

The habit diary has been found to be quite effective with women trying to lose weight and keep it off at treatment outcome (Hollis et al., 2008). The women who had received the habit diary intervention were to daily document the highs and lows of how they lost weight through changing their diets, exercising, changing who they socialized with, steering clear of risky places that involved food, having slips, and how they bounced back from them across their change journeys. My colleagues and I have found the habit diary to be equally effective with clients with other types of eating difficulties and with self-injuring and substance-abusing clients (Selekman & Beyebach, 2013; Selekman, 2017). It is empowering for clients to keep track of their progress, discover what works, be proud of bouncing back more quickly from slips, and having longer stretches of abstinence.

Annex K. Four Major Family-Social Network Relapse Prevention Tools and Strategies

Consolidating Questions

Consolidating questions are great to ask once NSSI adolescents start to make progress toward achieving their goals, report stretches of abstinence from self-injury and other self-destructive habits, and relate improvements in school (Selekman, 2009, 2017; Selekman & Beyebach, 2013). Some examples of consolidating questions are as follows:

- "Let me test the waters with you, what would you have to do to go backward at this point?"

- "Let's say, you get triggered and have a slip over the next week. What steps will you take to get quickly back on track?"
- "What could your parents say or do that you would find most empowering after a slip?"
- "What steps could your friends Sally and Jill take to help you to quickly bounce back from a slip?"
- "If you were to join me in a session as a guest consultant, what advice would you share with my teen client to help her to conquer her self-injuring habit?"
- "What else would you share with her that really worked for you?"
- "Let's say we had an anniversary party in my office one year from today so I can learn about what further changes the four of you had made. What will each of you be the most eager to share with me?"
- "What else will be better?"

These questions are great for solidifying clients' gains and offer them an opportunity to share what works and new insights they have gained about themselves. Inviting NSSI adolescents and their parents to speculate about their future successes can co-create positive self-fulfilling prophecies for them.

Honor Storylines of Courage and Resilience

As part of the relapse prevention process, we want to underscore NSSI adolescents' storylines of courage and resilience, that is where they staved off slips after experiencing very stressful or painful life situations. It is helpful to explore with them what the useful self-talk was and the problem-solving steps they took to stand strong and not cave into impulse. By doing so, it triggers positive emotions for them, makes them feel proud of themselves, and boosts their self-confidence.

Use of My Positive Trigger Log

In the addiction field and Twelve Step-oriented programs for other types of self-destructive behaviors like self-injury, the staff spend a lot of time having their clients identify their negative triggers and very little time if any on their positive triggers, which lead to successful coping and problem-solving and positive emotional states. To help fill this gap in the treatment process and in the literature, I have developed the My Positive Trigger Log (Selekman, 2009). On this form, NSSI adolescents are to keep track of and write in what they do individually and what their parents and/or siblings, close friends, adult inspirational others, and involved helping professionals say or do that helps them to stave off slips and triggers positive emotions for them. I have them circle what specifically they and the other involved key resource people do that seems to help the best and can become their main go-to coping and problem-solving strategies to not cave into a slip.

Worst-Case Scenario Planning

Another great way to consolidate NSSI adolescents' gains and help prevent slips from happening is to use worst-case scenario planning (Selekman, 2009, 2017). The worst-case scenario planning form should be filled out and discussed with NSSI adolescents' relapse prevention teams early in family treatment. The NSSI adolescents are first to identify in column one at least four worst-case scenario situations that might occur in the future. In Column two, they are to write in their most effective coping and problem-solving go-to tools and strategies. In the last column, the NSSI adolescents are to share with the parents and key resource people from their social networks the steps they need to take to help them to stave off slips and bounce back quickly if they should occur. When all parties involved are very clear about what they need to do that works, the NSSI adolescents will eventually be able to achieve abstinence and maintain it with high levels of confidence.

References

Alexander, J. F., Waldron, H. B., Robbins, M. S., & Neeb, A. A. (2013). *Functional family therapy foradolescent behavior problems*. American Psychological Association.

Anderson, H. (1997). *Conversation, language, and possibilities: A post-modern approach to therapy*.Basic Books.

Anderson, H., & Goolishian, H. (1988). Human systems as linguistic systems: Evolving ideas about the implications of theory and practice. *Family Process, 27*, 371–393.

Antony, M. M., & Norton, P.J. (2020). *The anti-anxiety program*. 2nd ed. Guilford Press.

Brier, N. M. (2015). *Enhancing self-control in adolescents: Treatment strategies derived from psychological science*. Routledge.

DeFrain, J. (2007). *Family treasures: Creating strong families*. iUniverse.

De Shazer, S., Dolan, Y., Korman, H., Trepper, T., McCollum, E., & Berg, I. K. (2007). *More than miracles: The state-of-the-art of solution focused brief therapy*. Haworth Press.

Duncan, B. L. (2010). *On becoming a better therapist*. American Psychological Association.

Duncan, B. L. (2019). *8 lessons learned from the Norway couple project*. Workshop presented at the Harvard University Couple Therapy Conference, Cambridge, MA.

Duncan, B.L., Miller, S. D ., Wampold, B. E., Hubble, M. A. (Eds.). (2010). *The heart and soul of change: Delivering what works*. 2nd ed. American Psychological Association.

Durrant, M., & Coles, D. (1991). The Michael White's cybernetic approach. In T. C. Todd & M. D. Selekman (Eds.), *Family therapy approaches with adolescent substance abusers* (pp. 135–174). Pearson.

Emmons, R.A. (2007). *Thanks! How the new science of gratitude can make you happier*. Houghton Mifflin.

Escudero, V., Heatherington, L., & Friedlander, M. L. (2010). Therapeutic alliances and alliance building in family therapy. In J. C. Muran & J. P. Barber (Eds.), *The therapeutic alliance: An evidence-based guide to practice* (pp. 240–263). Guilford Press.

Friedlander, M. L., Escudero, V., & Heatherington, L. (2006). *Therapeutic alliances in couple and family therapy: An empirically-informed guide to practice*. American Psychological Association.

Friedlander, M. L., Escudero, V., Heatherington, L., & Diamond, G.M. (2011). Alliance in couple and family therapy. In J. C. Norcross (Ed.), *Psychotherapy relationships that work: Evidence-based responsiveness* (2nd ed., pp. 92–110). Oxford University Press.

Hollis, J.F.,Gullion, C.M., Stevens, V.J., Brantley, P.J., Appel, I.J., Ard, J.D., & Svetkey, L.P. (2008). Weight loss during the intensive intervention phase of the weight-loss maintenance trial. *Journal of Preventaive Medicine, 35* (2), 118–126.

Lambert, M. J. (2010). *Prevention of treatment failure: The use of measuring, monitoring, and feedback in clinical practice*. American Psychological Association.

Prescott, D. S., Maeschalck, C. L., & Miller, S. D. (Eds.). (2017). *Feedback-informed treatment in clinical practice: Reaching for excellence*. American Psychological Association.

Ratner, H., George, E., & Iveson, C. (2012). *Solution-focused brief therapy: 100 key points and techniques*. Routledge.

Selekman, M. D. (2009). *The adolescent and young adult self-harming manual: A collaborative strengths-based brief therapy approach*. W. W. Norton.
Selekman, M. D. (2010). *Collaborative brief therapy with children*. Guilford Press.
Selekman, M. D. (2017). *Working with high-risk adolescents: A collaborative strengths-based approach*. Guilford Press.
Selekman, M. D., & Beyebach, M. (2013). *Changing self-destructive habits: Pathways to solutions with couples and families*. Routledge.
White, M. (2007). *Maps of narrative practice*. W. W. Norton.

CHAPTER 61

Conclusion and Future Directions

Elizabeth E. Lloyd-Richardson, Imke Baetens, *and* Janis L. Whitlock

> **Abstract**
>
> This chapter considers the possible directions of the field of NSSI research in the future. It details the development of the NSSI field that started from a diverse array of unaligned terms and measures of self-injury. The epidemiological outlines of NSSI presented several notions over the past 20 years, which include the recognition of NSSI as a clinical disorder and the relationship between NSSI and suicidal thoughts and behaviors. Moreover, future research could also look into themes of populations, lived experiences, operationalization, assessment of NSSI, novel research methods, and bio-neuro processes. The chapter also explores themes correlated with prevention, intervention, and treatment.
>
> **Key Words:** NSSI research, self-injury, suicidal thoughts and behaviors, prevention, intervention, treatment, populations, operationalization

It is our hope that readers of this volume come away with appreciation for the many advances that have been made over the past two decades in the field of nonsuicidal self-injury (NSSI) research. It is hard to overstate what we have accomplished as a field in a relatively short time. We have made progress in moving from using a diverse array of unaligned terms and measures of self-injury to using a (largely) consensus definition that allows for international comparison and clearly differentiates NSSI from suicidal thoughts and behavior (STB) while simultaneously acknowledging the place NSSI occupies on a self-harm continuum. We have also moved from knowing very little about NSSI epidemiology across the globe to having a well-established set of internationally relevant baseline prevalence and incidence markers. Our conjoined efforts have also resulted in a fairly robust understanding of secondary epidemiological characteristics across a number of diverse populations and have deepened insight into the phenomenology of NSSI, particularly related to the role of pain, blood, and wound site in self-injury practice and ritual. And, as part of the growing movement to more fully understand and include lived experience perspectives in understanding and treating mental health, our field has begun to fully embrace the vital importance of assuring that the lived experience perspective is fully represented in all phases of NSSI-related knowledge development and application. These are but a few of the many advancements we have made as a field over the past two decades, as this nearly 60-chapter volume so clearly demonstrates.

On the shoulders of these accomplishments, current and emerging research address some of the most important and challenging questions of the field. It is our hope that this volume will firmly establish what is known about NSSI while simultaneously laying the groundwork for articulating and exploring the raft of emerging questions and possibilities with implications for both research and clinical application. Although by no means exhaustive, what follows are some of our high-level takeaways about the most pressing questions and promising directions for future NSSI-linked research.

Themes Related to NSSI Epidemiology

The epidemiological contours of NSSI have been well explored in the past two decades and have yielded important understanding of primary and secondary features across community and clinical populations. As a field, we have collectively amassed information that warrants consideration of NSSI as a free-standing disorder and have learned much about the landscape of NSSI in and outside clinical and community populations. However, a number of important unanswered questions, ripe for future research, remain.

First, irrespective of whether NSSI is officially recognized as a clinical disorder in the next DSM, greater uniformity is needed in (a) developing standards for defining and measuring NSSI, (b) identifying features and thresholds salient to assessing and measuring NSSI severity, (c) understanding the progression of NSSI within and between individuals across the life course, and (d) exploring cross-cultural differences in epidemiological presentation and evolution. As many authors point out, in order to do this, cross-sectional studies must yield to longitudinal approaches that will allow for greater understanding of the sequencing and features of NSSI across time, developmental stage, and as a phenomenon embedded within larger cultural contexts. For example, representation of non-Western, minority, and indigenous groups in NSSI research is limited, as is empirical research dedicated to exploring cross-cultural similarities and differences. Because of this, little is understood about cultural variation in the subjective meaning of NSSI (e.g., wound location, presence/absence of pain, and role of blood) and the ways these influence pathways into and away from self-injury. Culturally responsive intervention and treatment are equally limited. Large, high-quality, cross-cultural studies that use both within- and between-person methods are needed, as are the development of culturally nuanced and sensitive assessment methods. Nor do we understand much about NSSI in children, adults, and older adults in and outside clinical contexts. Understanding the unique developmental trajectories of NSSI is an area ripe for research.

Second, while significant progress has been made in understanding the relationship between NSSI and STB, research intended to explicate how specific components of NSSI (urges, behaviors, recency, functions) dynamically amplify or protect against risk of STB over time is needed. Coupling this with deeper understanding of intrapersonal risk factors, the interplay of antecedents and consequences, and the perceived and behavioral function of NSSI and STB, will assist in identifying and supporting individuals at greatest risk of both NSSI and STB.

Parts II and IV include reviews of research related to protective and risk factors for onset and maintenance of NSSI behaviors. Future researchers should consider potential complex interactions across risk factors, with a focus on untangling the complexities and mechanisms not yet explicated, such as how pain and biological mechanisms work, how we can understand differential pathways in NSSI, whether or not NSSI should be interpreted as an addiction, and which special populations are most affected. Another area in need of attention is understanding the way in which risk and protective factors interact within individuals and across life events, characteristics, and identities. Finally, there is little clear understanding of what specific and dynamic combinations of factors elevate risk for onset and continuation of NSSI over time. Contributors to this volume consistently point to the need for longitudinal and real-time investigation of current theoretical models in this area as a way to explore the interplay of early risk factors, inter- and intrapersonal risk and protective factors, and NSSI-specific outcome expectancies in predicting onset and/or NSSI progression over time.

In line with this thought, research on resilience and promotive factors are warranted, particularly since most extant research focuses on understanding risk factors. Deeper insight into protective and resilience factors will improve understanding of how to assist individuals, families, and institutions to leverage these in service of healing, recovery, and growth. Research on, for example, supportive social networks, peer and family support, feelings of self-compassion and competency, and positive coping strategies in protecting against NSSI engagement are urgently needed.

Finally, while Nock and Favazza (2009) established a foundational topography for understanding distinctions in NSSI type and severity, the bulk of NSSI-linked research to date relates to community and, to a lesser degree, clinical populations. There is a dearth of understanding of NSSI that presents outside these domains, such as atypical, severe NSSI. Since this group evidences a higher number of risk indicators than those with more common forms, more research is needed to understand unique epidemiological features and pathways.

Themes Related to Special Populations and Contexts

There are also a number of other, population-specific research questions that merit additional attention. For example, although research on NSSI in adolescents and young adulthood is quite advanced, there remain important basic epidemiological questions about NSSI in elementary age children, adults, and older adults. Methodological adaptations for accommodating the vulnerability associated with specific groups, such as children or adults of advanced age, also require attention. Understanding the way NSSI is affected by developmental stage and across time are natural extensions of this line of inquiry. As such, future research is needed on homotypical and heterotypical continuity of NSSI and related behaviors and symptoms across the lifespan.

In addition to deepening understanding of NSSI in individuals of various ages and developmental stages, there remain many open questions about NSSI presentation and trajectory of various groups already shown to be disproportionately affected. These include but are not limited to prison populations, where rates of NSSI have been shown to be more than 30%, and military populations, where rates of both NSSI and STB are higher than civilian populations. In both of these instances, the study of NSSI requires thoughtful consideration of the way that it interacts with institutional contexts and cultures. Individuals with intellectual and developmental disabilities are another population with unique NSSI features, setting-specific considerations and, potentially, sequelae. In each of these cases, robust empirical and theoretical work is needed to expand the small but important body of empirical work on epidemiology as well as in areas related to detection, treatment, intervention, and prevention in ways that take into consideration the nuanced and complex external settings within which NSSI occurs which often limit personal autonomy and which may pose challenges to compassionate, person-centered treatment and intervention.

Finally, the current literature regarding the social contagion of NSSI is limited by broad definitions of the concept, particularly the term "exposure," which refers to various contexts and levels of exposure to NSSI. Additionally, there is a lack of standardized measures designed to assess social contagion of NSSI, and therefore an array of methods, surveys, and measures used to capture these experiences in the published literature. Particularly salient methodologies for future work in this area include ecological momentary assessment (EMA) to collect real-time, temporally dense data, and single-case experimental design to test possible interventions targeted at reducing the effects of social contagion on both NSSI onset and maintenance.

Themes Related to Lived Experience Perspective

One of the themes that clearly emerges across many of this volume's chapters is the importance of including the lived experience in study formation, execution, and interpretation of results. As several authors point out, exploring NSSI primarily from the external object-oriented perspective omits vital understanding available only through deep understanding of internal, subjective experience. To fully understand the lived experience perspective, however, it is important to include it not as an object but as a fundamental part of study question formulation, investigation, and interpretation. For example, whereas important work has been accomplished in understanding the meaning of NSSI from the emic perspective, there remain important and useful questions about how individuals with lived experience subjectively experience healing and recovery pathways and processes, what constitutes "recovery," and ways in which lived experience of NSSI and related challenges can foster deeper awareness and growth. Similarly, the role of ritual, the importance of wound formation, site of injury, and the role of blood would benefit from emic-focused investigation.

To more robustly understand and integrate the lived experience perspective, it is imperative to involve individuals with lived experience at all stages of clinical care and advocacy settings to increase the potential long-term impact on the society and individually tailoring the support that is offered to people. In general, authors have urged adopting a person-centered approach in NSSI research and treatment, in which idiographic within-person knowledge is gathered. Through better use of methods designed to capture short-term changes in NSSI-linked thoughts, emotions, and behaviors in daily life, researchers and clinicians will be better equipped to understand patterns of NSSI and risk and protective features from a lived experience perspective. Finally, by working with people with lived experience in research, outreach, and clinical work, we can create and consolidate nonstigmatizing language and understanding of NSSI.

Themes Related to Operationalization and Assessment of NSSI

While it is clear that NSSI and STB share many commonalities, they are discrete phenomena from both an intervention and clinical care perspective because they imply a differential level of distress and approach to intervention and care. Although there are multiple prominent conceptualizations of how they are interrelated, longitudinal studies that directly evaluate mediators of this association are needed. Thus, robust and nuanced assessment methods for clearly differentiating NSSI and STB are another area where work is needed. With the advent of new assessment approaches, including EMA, implicit association tests, and therapeutic assessment, there are new opportunities to differentially assess, address, and intervene on behaviors that increase the likelihood of future NSSI engagement. Authors in this volume provide useful information on how to capture these therapeutic opportunities as part of assessment processes and protocols.

Clear strategies for best employing the multiple assessment approaches currently available for assessing NSSI and the NSSI-STB relationship is another area ripe for attention. Currently, assessment of self-injury is conducted through direct assessment (i.e., via self-reported nonsuicidal and suicidal self-injury) and indirectly through assessment of implicit processes thought to be closely linked to NSSI and STB (i.e., laboratory tasks or implicit association assessments). Self-report measures and interview assessments play critical roles in both research and clinical practice, with regular assessment needed to accommodate natural fluctuations. Diagnostic tools such as interviews or self-report symptom scales with established clinical thresholds are useful for aiding evaluation of NSSI among those meeting criteria for different disorders. Structured assessment tools can serve a valuable role in supplementing psychosocial assessment as part of clinical and community assessment approaches. Although these direct assessments are most commonly used to assess for and differentiate between NSSI and STB, they are limited by respondent willingness to disclose behavior, variation in interpretation of the NSSI and suicidal behavior, and awareness of and/or ability to accurately communicate behavioral intent. With regard to prediction of future NSSI or suicide attempts, no tool has provided both sensitivity and positive predictive value. Finally, differential assessment of NSSI and suicide is complicated by the fact that clinical guidelines in some nations (e.g., UK, New Zealand, Australia) recommend against using tools to replace face-to-face clinical assessment, while other nations (e.g., United States) are more lenient in their use of valid, reliable non-face-to-face tools for aiding in evaluating risk.

Themes Related to Novel Research Methods

There are other fruitful and methodological novel ways to broaden operationalization and assessment of NSSI, such as examining NSSI among clinical samples or conducting chart reviews to understand prevalence, demographic, and other health-related factors associated with NSSI. These approaches would also be helpful in deepening understanding of NSSI from the vantage point of transdiagnostic frameworks and would allow for examination of similarities and differences across the severity continuum and between different subgroups. Unique opportunities to capture events, emotions, and behaviors in daily life and real time are also available through real-time digital monitoring (e.g., digital phenotyping and wearable technology). These methods are all ripe for research into the nuanced way that emotion, thoughts, and behavior interact directly before and after NSSI or other self-harm continuum experiences in ways that minimize recall biases and other state-dependent memory effects. Ultimately, combining participant data from wearable technology (e.g., heart rate and sleep) and other psychophysiological markers (e.g., neurocircuitry and cortisol) and self-report surveys (e.g., feelings and activities) would allow researchers to link NSSI-related biological and daily events in ways that may better isolate precursors and consequences of NSSI behavior.

Other areas of methodological promise include neuroimaging, implicit tests, EMA, digital phenotyping, artificial intelligence risk algorithms, network analysis, and wearable monitoring of autonomic processes. While promising, the infrequent nature of NSSI and STB makes it challenging to assess these in real time and/or in ecologically valid settings so theoretical and empirical work in how to best apply these techniques to NSSI and STB are warranted. Also needed is research on strategies for understanding the detailed landscape of risk and protective factors in on- and offline contexts. For example, online material can be text, image, or video based and platforms often rely on all these in tandem. Text-based analysis and the use of meta- and big data offer opportunities to employ qualitative and mixed-method approaches for creatively and systematically making use of large multifaceted data rich sources (e.g., in-depth text descriptions or detailed video).

Themes Related to Transdiagnostic and Bioneural Processes

Transdiagnostic frameworks are useful in helping elucidate the complexity of NSSI and in highlighting some important pathways for future research. Many of the findings detailed in this volume underscore the bidirectional relationship between NSSI and negative affect and counter the assumption that NSSI might effectively mitigate negative mood states for more than short period; it is clear that use of NSSI for short-term relief contributes to negative affect over time. More nuanced understanding of the temporal and long-term bidirectional relationship between NSSI and negative affect will also enhance intervention efforts aimed at interrupting this negative cycle. In line with this, additional research on the biological underpinnings of the negative bidirectional affect cycle is a clear research need. For example, better understanding of NSSI is needed in cases where trauma history results in hypothalamic-pituitary-adrenal (HPA) axis dysfunction which, in turn, increases vulnerability and decreases resilience in the face of (inter)personal stressors (such as bullying, an argument with loved ones, or academic pressure) and results in use of NSSI to manage the resulting overwhelming feelings and thoughts. Similarly, research on the link between NSSI and psychophysiological markers is essential for identifying novel intervention pathways that focus on alleviating distress associated with NSSI urges in the moment and for countering urges and the related short-term increase in positive affect that serves as a positive reinforcer for some individuals in the aftermath of NSSI.

To date, the most extensive body of work in this area focuses on domains related to negative affectivity, positive affectivity, cognition, and social processes. While laying critical groundwork, there is a lacuna in studies on NSSI focused on the arousal and regulatory systems and the sensorimotor domains. Furthermore, there is a need for a more nuanced understanding of interpersonal and contextual mechanisms of risk and protective factors (such as the role of online environments, peers, family dynamics, and broader societal influences) in relation to dynamic processes of the brain and physiological systems. Also needed are studies dedicated to surfacing congruences and incongruences of different levels of analyses (e.g., self-report and physiological markers) and on understanding interactions between the Research Domain Criteria (RDoC) domains, such as the link between negative affectivity and cognitive processes, or the relationship between the threat system and social processes. We expect that more robust understanding of these core interactions and bidirectional relationships will inform treatment innovation and prevention strategies. It will be important for all research in transdiagnostic processes to take into account the fact that NSSI is heavily interlinked with other forms of (in)direct self-harming behaviors (e.g., substance abuse, disordered eating, and obsessive-compulsive behaviors) and psychological symptoms. A dynamic perspective, one that accounts for symptom shifting over time, is warranted both in research and in clinical work.

Themes Related to Prevention

Research on effective approaches to prevention in diverse settings and with diverse populations is sorely needed. Although there have been important gains in this area, this is an area ripe for research that sheds light on identification of core components as well as how these are affected by setting, population, and cultural context. It is clear that provision of evidence-informed, NSSI-focused psychoeducation serves as a first step in addressing NSSI and that it is needed to support all stakeholders (e.g., parents, peers, and professional healthcare workers) in effectively identifying and productively addressing NSSI, but much more remains to be done. Research into how NSSI prevention efforts can best incorporate an array of messages, delivery modalities, and interactive and/or multifaceted techniques using tiered intervention approaches is strongly needed. Universal prevention approaches that couple psychoeducation, mental health literacy, and enhanced well-being and resilience skills are critically needed along with evaluations that help to identify the most effective individual and interlinked components. Moreover, in addition to strong tertiary prevention efforts, there is need for secondary prevention strategies aimed at identifying and intervening with at-risk populations and for protocols for assisting mental health professionals in a variety of settings using stepped approaches to address NSSI in their professional contexts. Future research should also rigorously evaluate short-term and long-term effectiveness of tiered approaches.

Beyond the physical clinical and community settings within which prevention typically occurs, many scholars in this book argue for multilevel approaches that move beyond place-focused approaches to encompass societal, digital, and media contexts. For example, more research is needed on how portrayals of NSSI in all forms of print, audio, visual, and digital media, as well as in psychoeducational materials, (a) produce or reduce stigma (e.g., such as references to "self-injurer" or "cutter"), (b) enhance or minimize "Werther effects" that lead to social contagion, and (c) inhibit or promote the Papageno effect ("portraying positive coping") and help-seeking. Related to this, understanding of the scope, nature and effects of online NSSI activity have emerged in recent years, but several important avenues remain understudied. These include but are not limited to (a) who is most impacted by their online activities, (b) what kinds of online posts and exchanges have the most impact on NSSI activity and why, and (c) what kinds of online interventions are likely to be most effective and with whom and under what circumstances. Future investigation of online NSSI activity should explicate the interactive and dynamic effects of both risk (e.g., triggering and reinforcing) and benefits (e.g., reductions of NSSI and increasing motivation for cessation) associated with online NSSI-related activity.

Themes Related to Intervention and Treatment

While recent and multiple meta-analytic studies have concluded that psychotherapeutic interventions remain the gold standard for treatment of NSSI (in some cases this are augmented by psychopharmacological interventions to treat comorbid conditions such as depression), most studies conclude that the efficacy for treatment of NSSI and STB is weak despite the growing number of randomized controlled trial (RCT) research that has taken place in recent decades. Most authors conclude that more research is needed to identify and untangle key ingredients of NSSI treatment, and are cautious about over-interpretation of often modest results. Future research in this area is needed to identify

(a) novel, promising, and efficacious NSSI-specific treatments approaches; (b) identification of core underlying NSSI-specific and transdiagnostic processes, and (c) efficacious approaches to creating individually tailored treatments from a person-centered perspective. Furthermore, future research is urgently needed to understand and address barriers and facilitators to healthcare and ascertain the optimal dose of intervention, and develop treatments that foster healing in a broad sense.

Another area in need of urgent attention is research on ecological validity in intervention and prevention studies, ascertaining factors that affect treatment outcomes outside controlled research protocols, and development of methods of monitoring and understanding how treatment in daily life/routine care is working. A growing number of treatment specialists and scholars argue for investment in personalized or precision medicine, where individual biological characteristics and transdiagnostic features inform treatment. We argue for a bottom-up approach for creating interventions, specifically targeting unique features of NSSI. For example, NSSI urges and gradual increases in NSSI severity (part of an addictive process, as described by some scholars) may be targeted by behavioral extinction procedures and sensorial attention shift techniques (e.g., the role of touch or scent). Also, findings from psychophysiological markers (such as neurocircuitry and heart rate variability) suggest the importance of alleviating distress associated with NSSI.

As the digital landscape expands, it also offers possibilities to examine the role of e-treatments (e.g., app-based, VR, or other digital interventions) as stand-alone or blended interventions. The very limited findings to date are promising, especially with regard to otherwise hard-to-access populations who experience significant barriers to seeking professional help (e.g., individuals in rural areas or who are economically disadvantaged or hesitant to disclose NSSI experience). Also, e-treatments may be particularly suitable for intervening in the moment of need: many individuals who engage in NSSI experience overwhelming in-the-moment distress by NSSI urges and thoughts and may benefit from short, easily accessible e-interventions. For instance, individuals could be prompted by wearable technology when increases in distress levels are noted, directing them just-in-time and with the right doses to e-treatment modules.

Finally, future research may explore biologically oriented treatment methods such as different models of stimulation. To date, there are some preliminary results of open label trials on transcranial repetitive magnetic stimulation, transcranial direct current stimulation, and transauricular vagal nerve stimulation. Future research can explore the effectiveness of these models of stimulation, adjacent to psychological interventions.

In conclusion, we hope you will agree that the chapters that comprise this substantial handbook are full of knowledge, novel considerations, and avenues for future research possibilities. Indeed, the areas we touch on briefly above represent just a fraction of the conversations we, the editors, had as we compiled the extraordinary set of chapters contained in this volume. For each future direction identified above, there are several more we are certain dedicated readers will detect and, we hope, pursue (or encourage graduate students to pursue). It has been such a privilege to serve as editors of this volume. It is our hope that readers come away as in awe of and inspired by the wisdom and insight amassed in an area of study that barely existed two decades ago as we have.

Reference

Nock, M. K., & Favazza, A. R. (2009). Nonsuicidal self-injury: Definition and classification. In M. K. Nock (Ed.), *Understanding nonsuicidal self-injury: Origins, assessment, and treatment* (pp. 9–18). American Psychological Association.

INDEX

For the benefit of digital users, indexed terms that span two pages (e.g., 52–53) may, on occasion, appear on only one of those pages.

Tables, figures, and boxes are indicated by *t*, *f*, and *b* following the page number

A

abusive relationships, 57–58
accelerated experiential dynamic psychotherapy (AEDP), 1175, 1177–78
acceptance, online self-injury activity, 789
acceptance and commitment therapy (ACT)
  major depressive disorder (MDD) and, 379
  NSSI and, 136
  NSSI and co-occurring conditions, 319–20
  obsessive-compulsive disorder (OCD), 321–22
  university intervention, 988–89
"ACCEPTS" skill, dialectical behavior therapy (DBT), 461
Accessibility, digital intervention, 1016
acquired capability, NSSI and suicidality, 974
adaptive information processing (AIP), 1182–83
addiction
  behavioral, 188
  cognitive control, 316–17
  emotional dysregulation, 191–95
  evidence for NSSI as addictive behavior, 195–96
  framing of self-injury as, 188–90
  implications of NSSI addiction, 196–97
  NSSI as, 188, 459
addictive model of self-harm, 190–91
administrators, NSSI policy, 934, 942–43

adolescence and emerging adulthood, 514, 530
  age of onset and incidence, 516–17
  cognitive vulnerabilities, 520–21
  developmental risk and protective factors in, 518–23
  developmental variation, 528
  early life trauma, 518
  emotion regulation, 519–20
  evidence-based assessment and intervention, 526–27
  interventions for schools and postsecondary institutions, 525–26
  normative course of NSSI in, 516–18
  parenting and family influences, 521–22
  peer influences, 522–23
  personality and identity development, 519
  potential consequences of engaging in NSSI, 523–25
  prevalence and features of NSSI, 516
  psychopathology and mental disorders, 521
  as sensitive periods for NSSI, 515
  stress-response systems, 815
  See also adults with NSSI
adolescents
  age of NSSI onset and incidence, 516–17, 753–54
  algorithm on treatment of NSSI, 1048–52
  COVID-19 pandemic and, 157–58

Dialectical Behavior Therapy Skills in Schools: Skills Training for Emotional Problem Solving for Adolescents (DBT STEPS-A), 957, 959–60, 962–63
  emotion regulation individual therapy for adolescents (ERITA), 1079–80
  family alliance building and retention, 1198–99
  family therapy guidelines for NSSI treatment, 1134–38
  friendship stress, 812–13
  goal-setting questions, 1200
  NSSI of minority groups, 170–71
  peer relationship quality, 812–13
  peer victimization, 813–15
  Project SAVE (Stop Adolescent Violence Everywhere), 1083–84
  proposed treatment algorithm for NSSI in, 1050*f*
  risk factors for NSSI, 725–27
  social contagion in, 832–35
  socialization with friends and peers, 817–18
  stepped-care approach to treat NSSI, 1043*f*
  See also adolescence and emerging adulthood; sexual and gender diverse (SGD) youth; youth in custody
adulthood. *See* adolescence and emerging adulthood
adults with NSSI, 540
  age of onset, 540–41
  assessments of NSSI, 548–49

adults with NSSI (*cont.*)
  clinical implications, 549–50
  community advocates, 549–50
  comorbidity of, 545–46
  functions of NSSI, 546–47
  NSSI prevalence and
    course, 541–43
  NSSI scarring, 547–48
  NSSI severity, 543–45
  treatment for, 549
  See also older adults with NSSI
Adult Temperament
  Questionnaire (ATQ), 284
Adverse Childhood Experiences
  (ACE) study, 740
adverse psychosocial outcomes,
  NSSI as risk factor
  for, 524–25
advocacy and outreach
  applications, lived experience
  of self-injury, 406–7, 406t
affective disorders, NSSI
  and, 351
affect regulation, NSSI
  outcome, 30
affect-related conditions, military
  service and veterans, 643–44
affiliation and attachment, NSSI
  within construct of, 330–31
African Americans, NSSI
  prevalence in, 170–71
age, military service members and
  veterans, 642–43
agency and engagement, NSSI
  recovery, 423
alcohol use disorder (AUD)
  military service and veterans,
    646, 650
  NSSI and, 55–56
alexithymia, 175–76
  emotional processing, 704–5
  emotional processing
    deficit, 1170
  intervention for, 712
algorithmic modeling culture,
  1029–30
algorithms, digital
  interventions, 1017
alien self, 1159
allostatic overload,
  definition, 254–55
American Foundation for Suicide
  Prevention (AFSP), 980
American Psychiatric
  Association, 12

American Psychological
  Association (APA), 924–25,
  1181–82
American Society of Addiction
  Medicine (ASAM), 413–14
Anamnestic Comparative Self-
  Assessment (ACSA), 436
anorexia nervosa (AN), 50, 60
  binge-purge subtype, 50–51
  multifamily therapy
    (MFT), 1132
  NSSI and, 50–51
ANS. *See* autonomic nervous
  system (ANS) function
antagonistic function, 353
Antecedent, Response,
  Consequence (ARC) model,
  emotional situations, 1103,
  1105, 1106
antecedents, NSSI, 855
anthropology, self-injury
  and, 472–74
anti-depressants, 1066–67
antipsychotics, 1065–67
antisocial personality disorder
  (ASPD), mentalization-based
  therapy (MBT), 1162
anxiety disorders
  adults with NSSI and, 545–46
  COVID-19 pandemic, 152, 158
  emotional freedom technique
    (EFT), 1181–82
  NSSI and, 687
  selective serotonin reuptake
    inhibitors (SSRIs), 1065–66
apathy, 211–12
Apathy Evaluation Scale, 211–12
aripiprazole, 384
Arousal and Regulatory Systems,
  Research Domain Criteria
  (RDoC), 214
arrested flight model, suicidal
  thinking, 76
artificial intelligence (AI)
  digital interventions, 1017
art therapy, experiments, 1203
Asian societies, suicide reporting
  in media, 780
Asperger's syndrome, self-injurious
  behavior (SIB), 602
assessment(s), 5, 847–48
  adults with NSSI, 548–49
  alternative approaches
    to, 860–62
  challenges, 904–5

confidentiality, 849–50
co-production, 864
differentiating suicidal and
  NSSI, 897–902, 905–6
digital monitoring
  technologies, 865–66
digital phenotyping, 903
ecological momentary
  assessment (EMA), 861
engagement, 849
health services research, 865
implementation science, 865
Implicit Association Test
  (IAT), 861–62
laboratory-based methods,
  899–901
linguistic, acoustic, and visual
  data analysis, 903–4
machine learning, 865
neurobiological correlates and
  pain perception, 866
neuroimaging, 901–2
non healthcare
  professionals, 864
NSSI in community, 848–49
NSSI in military personnel, 649
online self-injury
  activity, 797–98
primary care/family
  medicine, 863
psychosocial, 852–57
risk assessment tools, 858–
  60, 859t
schools and educational
  settings, 864
self-report, 898–99
sexual and gender diverse
  (SGD) youth, 667–68
structural assessment tools, 857–58
suicidal intent and suicide
  risk, 850–51
summary of questions, 851t
themes related to NSSI,
  1241–42
therapeutic assessment, 862
therapeutic modalities, 862
virtual reality (VR), 902–3
wearable technology, 904
See also fine-grained assessment
  of NSSI; psychosocial
  assessment
at-risk college students, 985
attachment avoidance, major
  depressive disorder
  (MDD), 379

attachment-based family therapy (ABFT), 1131–32
Attachment-Based Family Therapy (ABFT) for Lesbian, Gay, and Bisexual (LGB) Youth, 665
attachment theory
  Bowlby's, 1150–51
  emotion-focused therapy (EFT), 1176
  See also mentalization-based therapy (MBT)
attentional bias, cognitive process, 312–13
attention deficit/hyperactivity disorder (ADHD), 189
  co-occurring with NSSI, 130
  military service and veterans, 647
  NSSI and, 132–33, 687
  parental self-injury and, 756
  selective serotonin reuptake inhibitors (SSRIs), 1065–66
attention-seeking, NSSI, 94
atypical, severe nonsuicidal self-injury (NSSI), 555
  client examples re treatment, 565–66
  foreign body ingestion (FBI) as form of, 559, 563*t*
  functions of, 561–62, 561*t*, 562*t*, 563*t*
  hierarchy of risk, 563
  public health problem, 556
  requiring medical intervention, 557–59, 561*t*
  research implications, 566–67
  risk indicators, 560
  sequential, multimodal treatments, 564–65
  study of findings for, 560–61
  subgroups of, 555, 556–57, 567–68
  treating individuals with, 562–65
  unusual body locations for, 557–59, 562*t*
Australia
  indigenous people, 173
  NSSI research, 169
  studies of NSSI in older adults, 577*t*
  suicide surveillance system, 155–56
Australian Twin Registry, 189, 194–95

autism or autism spectrum disorder (ASD), 190, 848
  adults living with, 542–43
  NSSI and, 11, 267–69
  self-injurious behaviors (SIB) and, 594, 599*t*, 602
autobiographical self-enhancement training (ASET)
  digital interventions, 1002–03
  online treatment, 1081–83
  university intervention, 989–90
autonomic nervous system (ANS)
  activation of, 253–54
  stress-response, 815
autonomic nervous system (ANS) function
  blood pressure, 354*t*, 356, 364
  breathing, 354*t*, 355, 364
  cardiovascular activity, 354–56, 354*t*
  common measures and metrics in psychopathology research, 354*t*
  diurnal variation findings of, in NSSI, 367–68
  diurnal variation of ANS activity, 357–58
  EDA (electrodermal activity), 353–54, 354*t*, 358–64
  heart rate, 354*t*, 355, 365–67
  heart rate variability, 354*t*, 355, 365–67
  measures of, 353–56
  in NSSI, 358–67, 370
  pupillometry, 354*t*, 356
  pupil size, 354*t*, 356, 367
  rationale for ANS involvement in NSSI, 351
  Research Domain Criteria (RDoC) framework, 349–51
  respiration, 354*t*, 355
  resting state, responsivity, and recovery, 357

B

Barratt Impulsivity Scale (BIS), 859–60
Barriers and Benefits
  model, 35
  NSSI, 32–34, 35–36
behavior(s), 2–3
  criterion A for NSSI-D, 12–14
  NSSI policy for help-seeking, 940

  NSSI recovery, 425–28
  three-component model of NSSI episode, 1104*f*
  See also self-injurious behavior (SIB)
behavior activation system (BAS), motivation system, 286–87, 295
Behavioral Activation for Depression Scale, 211–12
behavioral and self-report data, NSSI and, 335–36
Behavioral Approach System (BAS), Research Domain Criteria (RDoC), 214–15
behavioral factors, topography and function of NSSI, 1117–18
behavioral management plans, prison populations, 627
behavioral markers, NSSI recovery and, 420
behavior inhibition system (BIS), motivation system, 286–87, 295
Benefits and Barriers Model, 724–25
benzodiazepines, 1065–66
Big Five personality model, extraversion, 286, 294–95
binge-eating disorder (BED)
  cognitive control, 316–17
  NSSI and, 50–51
  pain and anxiety, 42
biological interventions, nonpharmaceutical, for NSSI, 1067
biologically driven self-injury, 617, 624
biological treatments, 1062
biology
  indices of treatment response in NSSI-adjacent disorders, 380–82
  NSSI case example, 386
  preliminary findings of factors for NSSI intervention, 382–84
  psychopharmacological approaches to NSSI, 384
  psychotherapeutic approaches in NSSI, 383–84
  strategies and interventions targeting NSSI, 385*t*
  tools for studying NSSI factors, 379–80

bioneural processes, NSSI and, 1242–43
biosocial developmental model, 1115b
biosocial developmental theory, dialectical behavior therapy (DBT), 1114
bipolar disorder (BP), NSSI and, 253
Black, Asian minority ethnic groups (BAME), COVID-19 pandemic and, 159
Black, Indigenous, and People of Color, lived experience of self-injury, 405–6
blood
  imitation of Christ, 470
  role of, and Indigenous motives and explanations, 475–76
  role of seeing, 469
  See also self-injury
blood pressure, 360t, 364
  autonomic nervous system (ANS) function study, 354t, 356
body. See endocrine and neural threat system
body disregard, self-injurious behavior (SIB) and, 683f, 686
body ego, 1148
body locations
  atypical, severe NSSI and unusual, 557–59, 562t
  NSSI, 854
  See also self-injury location
borderline personality disorder (BPD), 9, 189, 284–85
  adults with NSSI and, 331, 335–36, 545
  college students, 979
  ecological momentary assessment (EMA) and, 283–84
  emotional cascade model, 27–28
  eye movement desensitization and reprocessing (EMDR), 1183
  features overlapping with NSSI, 336–37
  mentalizing approach, 1150
  military service and veterans, 644
  NSSI and, 10, 132–33, 138, 253, 351, 378–79, 380–82

NSSI functions, 96
neurocircuitry, 334–35
pain analgesia findings for, 454–55
prison populations, 623–24
psychopharmacological interventions, 1065–66
self-injury by proxy and, 46–47
as symptom of NSSI, 519
brain. See endocrine and neural threat system
brain activation, NSSI and, 382
brain structures
  neurotransmitters, 290
  positive valence systems, 288–90
  reward circuitry (fMRI studies), 288–90
breathing
  autonomic nervous system (ANS) function study, 354t, 355
  findings on, 360t, 364
Brief Risk-Resilience Index for Screening (BRISC), 211–12
bulimia nervosa (BN)
  blood important group and, 474
  ecological momentary assessment (EMA) and, 283–84
  NSSI and, 50–51
  selective serotonin reuptake inhibitors (SSRIs), 1065–66
buprenorphine, 384

C

Cambridge Dictionary, recovery definition, 423–24
CAMHS (Child and Adolescent Mental Health Services), 1130
Campus Connect, gatekeeper, 981
Canada
  elementary school staff and children with NSSI, 503, 504–6, 505t, 506t
  studies of NSSI in older adults, 577t
  suicide reporting in media, 780
cannabis use, NSSI and, 54–55
cardiovascular activity, autonomic nervous system (ANS) function study, 354–56, 354t
caregivers, secondary schools informing, 965
caretaker relationships, 763–64

CASHAS, culturally accepted self-harming acts/activities, 41
Centers for Disease Control and Prevention (CDC), Youth Risk Behavior Surveillance System, 172–73
central neurophysiology, NSSI and, 231–32
cessation, as unrealistic measure of recovery, 419
chatbots, digital technology, 1005t, 1013
Child and Adolescent Self-Harm in Europe Study (CASE), 117
childhood adversity, 231
Childhood Disorder and Mood Disorder Work Groups, 9
childhood maltreatment, 739–40
  abuse and neglect, 739
  Adverse Childhood Experiences (ACE) study, 740
  child neglect, 742
  definition, 739
  depression, 744–45
  dissociation, 743–44
  emotional abuse, 742
  emotional reactivity and regulation, 742–43
  genetic vulnerability, 747
  magnetic resonance imaging (MRI), 746–47
  neurobiological factors, 745–47
  neuroendocrine regulation, 746
  NSSI and, 740–42
  physical abuse, 741–42
  posttraumatic stress disorder (PTSD), 744
  psychache, 744–45
  self-criticism, 745
  sexual abuse, 741
childhood peer victimization, 231
childhood trauma
  different types of, 737–38
  NSSI in adolescence and emerging adulthood, 518
  prevention, 747–48
  stress response systems, 738–39
  trauma focused therapeutic approach, 747–48
child neglect, emotional abuse and, 742
children
  peer victimization, 813–15
  proposed treatment algorithm for NSSI in, 1050f

understanding NSSI in, 1239–40
See also elementary school children
China
  NSSI in prisons, 616
  studies of NSSI in older adults, 577*t*
choice and control, self-injurious behavior (SIB) and, 604*t*, 607
choking game, 59
Christianity, 471–72, 473–74
clients, questions for use about online self-injury activity, 799*b*
clinical applications, lived experience of self-injury, 404–6, 406*t*
clinical assessment
  NSSI functions, 97–98
  prevention and initial detection of, 490–91
  self-injury location, 491
clinical environment, sexual and gender diverse (SGD) youth, 667
clinical epidemiology, 127–28
  attention deficit/hyperactivity disorder (ADHD), 130
  borderline personality disorder (BPD), 130–31
  co-occurring clinical diagnoses, 129–31
  eating disorders, 130
  family connections, 136
  impulsivity, 132–34
  negative urgency, 133
  neuroticism, 132
  NSSI and suicidal thoughts and behaviors, 131
  peer engagement in NSSI, 134–35
  posttraumatic stress disorder (PTSD), 129
  prevalence of NSSI, 128–29, 140
  protective factors, 135–36
  psychiatric disorders, 131
  research and treatment implications, 138–40
  risk factors, 132–35
  self-perceptions, 135–36
  social norms, 136
  treatment considerations, 137–38
  See also epidemiology of NSSI

clinical implications
  adults with NSSI, 549–50
  military service and veterans, 651–52
  online self-injury activity, 797
  recovery, 435–36
clinical practice(s)
  assessment of NSSI, 867, 905
  elementary school children with NSSI, 508–9
  fine-grained assessment, 924–25
  interpersonal stress, 820–22
  intervention in medical settings, 884–87
  media representations of NSSI, 782–83
  NSSI as risk for suicide, 82–83
  NSSI policy, 937
  research implications for, 35–36
  self-injurious behaviors (SIBs), 691–92
  social contagion, 843–44
clinicians, digital intervention, 1017–18
Cloninger's temperament and character model, novelty seeking and reward responsiveness, 284–85
cognition
  NSSI treatment, 1115
  questions related to NSSI, 1116*t*
cognitive affordances, digital intervention, 1009–13
cognitive-behavioral suicide prevention (CBSP) therapy, 626
cognitive behavioral therapy (CBT), 5–6, 380, 1042–43
  behavioral factors, 1117–18
  clinical practice, 35–36
  cognition, 1115, 1116*t*
  "Cutting Down" approach, 1070
  early therapy strategies, 1118*b*, 1118
  emotions, 1115–17, 1117*t*
  evidence in NSSI treatment, 1120–23
  family-based treatment, 1197–98
  functional analysis in, 1119
  interventions for NSSI, 1119–20
  maintenance of NSSI, 1114–18
  major depressive disorder (MDD) and, 379
  NSSI and co-occurring conditions, 319–20

  NSSI intervention, 339–40
  NSSI treatment, 862, 1064–65, 1123
  obsessive-compulsive disorder (OCD), 321–22
  parent and parent-child factors, 760
  perfectionism, 711
  prison populations, 625–26
cognitive behavioral therapy for adolescents (CBT-A), 1129
cognitive biases
  positive valence systems, 295
  suicidal ideation, 73–74
cognitive control, 317
cognitive distortions, self-injurious behavior (SIB) and, 683*f*, 685–86
cognitive-emotional model of NSSI, 30–31, 520–21
cognitive-emotional perspective
  alexithymia, 704–5
  clinical implications, 710–13
  emotional processing, 703–5
  emotion reactivity, 703–4
  experiential avoidance, 705
  NSSI behaviors, 702–3, 714
  theoretical implications, 709–10
  transdiagnostic cognitive processes, 705–7
cognitive perspectives, self-injury location, 486
cognitive processes, 309–10, 322–23
  attentional bias, 312–13
  cognitive control, 315–17
  expectancies and rule-governed behavior, 313–15
  integrated conceptualization and model, 317–18
  psychopathology, 310
  rumination, 310–12
  treatment implications, 319–20
cognitive restructuring
  DBT treatment for Morey, 1121*b*
  PTSD, 564
Cognitive Systems, Research Domain Criteria (RDoC), 212, 213, 215
cognitive vulnerabilities, emotion and, 520–21
collaborative assessment and management of suicidality (CAMS), NSSI in military personnel, 650–51

collaborative strengths-based
    family therapy (CSBFT),
    1191–92
art therapy experiments, 1203
effective adolescent and family
    alliance building and
    retention strategies, 1198–99
expressive writing
    experiments, 1203–4
family connection building
    rituals, 1203
family social network
    relapse prevention tools/
    strategies, 1204
goal-setting questions, 1200
guidelines for intervention
    design, selection, and
    matching, 1203–4
guiding assumptions about
    NSSI adolescents and
    therapy, 1193–96
mindfulness meditation, 1202
purposeful systemic
    interviewing, 1199–201
questions for pessimistic
    and demoralized
    NSSI adolescents and
    families, 1200–1
resilience-enhancing thinking
    tools/strategies, 1202–3
self-harming assessment
    questions, 1199–200
session summary, 1204–8
solution-oriented parent
    management skills
    training, 1201
theoretical overview of
    approach, 1192–96
visualization, 1202
collectivism, individualism
    vs., 177
college. *See* higher education
college samples, social contagion
    of NSSI, 835–37
college settings
    identifying NSSI among
        students, 939
    interventions for NSSI, 525–26
    NSSI among students, 938–39
    NSSI literacy, 941
    NSSI responses by staff, 942–43
communication
    NSSI outcome, 30
    self-injurious behavior (SIB)
        and, 599*t*, 602–3

community advocates, adults with
    NSSI, 549–50
community-based prevention,
    interpersonal stress, 820–22
community inclusion, self-
    injurious behavior (SIB) and,
    604*t*, 607
community settings, NSSI
    in, 848–49
comorbidity
    adults with NSSI, 545–46
    military service and
        veterans, 643–47
compassion-focused therapy
    (CFT), experiential therapy,
    1179–80
complementary function, 353
compliance and retention, fine-
    grained assessment, 918–19
compromised self-care, 46
compulsive exercise, NSSI
    and, 52–53
compulsivity, neurocognitive
    model of, 318
conduct disorder (CD), NSSI
    and, 687
confidentiality, assessment of
    NSSI, 849–50
consent, obtaining, for online
    treatment for NSSI, 1086
contagion effects, peer groups, 817
contingency management, DBT
    treatment for Morey, 1121*b*
cooperative function, 353
coping capacity and efficacy, NSSI
    recovery, 430
coping mechanisms, NSSI, 856
coping strategies, protective factor
    for NSSI, 728
coping styles and temperaments,
    prison populations, 623
Cornell Research Program on Self-
    injury and Recovery, 801*b*
Cornell Self-Injury and Recovery
    Resources, 983
correctional facilities
    barriers to conducting clinical
        research in, 632
    See also prison(s)
cortisol awakening response,
    HPA, 256–57
cortisol reactivity, 232
COVID-19 pandemic, 3
    adolescents and, 157–58
    at-risk groups, 160

Black, Asian minority ethnic
    groups (BAME), 159
changing health and safety
    protocols, 150
decreasing deliberate self-harm
    during, 154–57
deliberate self-harm and, 149–50
eating disorders and, 159–60
family relationships and, 158
family support and NSSI
    during, 522
identity-related factors
    for deliberate self-harm
    and, 157–60
impact on NSSI behavior, 265
increasing deliberate self-harm
    during, 150–54
increasing pressure on young
    people, 1147
LGBTQ community and
    deliberate self-harm, 158–59
NSSI and, 108, 114–15
online self-injury activity, 790, 802
self-injurious behavior and, 611
crisis-intervention cell, 624
crisis plan, 856–57
cross-cultural representations
    of NSSI
    across nations, 169–70
    among minority groups within
        nations, 170–71
    culture, 167–69, 175–79
    forms and functions of
        NSSI, 174–75
    gender, 178
    in Indigenous peoples, 172–74
    in non-Western nations, 171–72
    religion, 178–79
    sexuality, 178
    youth subcultures, 179
cultural concepts of distress, 168–69
culturally sanctioned body
    modifications, NSSI-D, 15
cultural pressures, self-injurious
    behavior (SIB) and,
    683*f*, 684–85
culture
    appreciation of, 169
    definition, 167
    importance of, 168–69
    notion of cultural scripts, 177
    relationship between NSSI
        and, 175–77
    See also cross-cultural
        representations of NSSI

curiosity and understanding, online self-injury activity, 789–90
cut the cut (CTC), 1045–46
cutting down program (CDP), 196, 527, 1042–43, 1122
digital interventions, 1003

D

data modeling culture, 1029–30
Defective Self Model, NSSI theory, 724–25
deliberate self-harm, 8, 43
deliberate self-harm behavior, 832–33
social contagion, 832–33
Deliberate Self-Harm Inventory, 173
deliberate self-harm syndrome, 9
demographics, risk factor, 725–27
depression
adults with NSSI and, 545
bargaining model of, 190–91
cannabis and, 54–55
childhood maltreatment, 744–45
COVID-19 pandemic and, 150, 152
emotional freedom technique (EFT), 1181–82
NSSI and, 351, 687
selective serotonin reuptake inhibitors (SSRIs), 1065–66
Derges, Jane, 470–71
developmental assessment, study of pain, 446
developmental course
age of onset, 109
incidence rates, 109–10
increases over time, 110
NSSI and, 109–10
persistence rates, 110
developmental disabilities, NSSI and, 11
developmental factors
cognitive vulnerabilities, 520–21
early life trauma, 518
emotion regulation, 519–20
NSSI in adolescence and emerging adulthood, 518–23
parenting and family influences, 521–22
peer influences, 522–23
personality and identity development, 519

psychopathology and mental disorders, 521
See also adolescence and emerging adulthood
developmental group psychotherapy (DGP), 196
Diagnostic and Statistical Manual of Mental Disorders (DSM), 848
Diagnostic and Statistical Manual of Mental Disorders (DSM-5), 1–2, 3, 9, 107–8, 168–69, 204–5, 329, 516, 681, 877, 972, 1031, 1039–40, 1127–28
algorithms for syndrome diagnosis/heterogeneity, 205–6
Cultural Formulation Interview, 169
inclusion of NSSI in, 398
lack of dimensionality, 206
NSSI definition, 13
NSSI inclusion in, 417
NSSI prevalence and course, 541–42
overlap in diagnostic criteria/multimorbidity, 205
problems with DSM-ICD assumptions, 205–7
RDoC project, 206–7
See also Research Domain Criteria (RDoC)
Diagnostic and Statistical Manual of Mental Disorders (DSM-IV), 195, 474
Diagnostic and Statistical Manual of Mental Disorders-Text Revised (DSM-5TR), 130–31
diagnostic categories, NSSI and, 140
dialectical behavior therapy (DBT), 5–6, 196, 238–39, 1042–43, 1077–78
"ACCEPTS" skill, 461
adolescents (DBT-A), 1042
behavioral factors, 1117–18
case formulation of Morey's NSSI, 1119*b*
chain analysis in, 1119
childhood trauma, 748
cognition, 1115, 1116*t*
college students, 979
core treatment strategies with Morey, 1121*b*
DBT Coach, 1078

digital interventions, 1000, 1001–02
early therapy strategies, 1118*b*, 1118
emotions, 1115–17, 1117*t*
evidence in NSSI treatment, 1120–23
eye movement desensitization and reprocessing (EMDR), 1183
family-based treatment, 1197–98
frequency of NSSI among adolescents, 527
inpatient program, 381
intervention, 711–12
interventions for NSSI, 1119–20
maintenance of NSSI, 1114–18
neurocircuitry with NSSI behaviors, 383
NSSI and, 138, 241–42, 268–69
NSSI and co-occurring conditions, 319–20
NSSI in military personnel, 650–51
NSSI intervention, 339–40
NSSI treatment, 862, 1064–65, 1123
prison populations, 626–27
obsessive-compulsive disorder (OCD), 321–22
parent and parent-child factors, 760
pharmacology and, 383
"TIPP" skill, 461
dialectical behavior therapy for adolescents (DBT-A), 340, 1129
Dialectical Behavior Therapy Skills in Schools: Skills Training for Emotional Problem Solving for Adolescents (DBT STEPS-A), 957, 959–60, 962–63
"Dicing with Death," 1148
Difficulties and Coping Profile, 631
Difficulties and Coping Profiles Questionnaire (DCP), 630
diffusion imaging, white matter connections, 260
diffusion weighted imaging (DWI), biology in NSSI, 379
digital interventions, 998–99
Autobiographical Self-Enhancement Training (ASET), 1002–03

digital interventions (cont.)
  challenges with, 1004
  current state of empirical evidence on NSSI, 999–1008
  dialectical behavior therapy (DBT), 1000, 1001–02
  efficacy trials of, for NSSI, 1001
  emotion regulation individual therapy for adolescents (ERITA), 1000, 1002
  ethics and accessibility, 1016
  NSSI and, 999, 1001–03
  possible benefits and constraints of, 1011t
  safety, privacy, and risk management, 1015
  Self-injury: Treatment, Assessment and Recovery (STAR), 1003
  summary of desired content or platform features, 1005t
  Therapeutic Evaluative Conditioning (TEC), 1002
  understanding needs and preferences of, 1004–08
  user engagement, 1014–15
  See also digital technologies
digital monitoring technologies, assessment of NSSI, 865–66
digital natives, 60
digital phenotyping, 895
  assessment, 903
digital technologies
  affective affordances, 1013
  affordances of, 1008–14
  virtual reality, 1008–09, 1011t
Direct and Indirect Self-Harm Inventory (DISH), 649
direct self-injurious behavior (SIB)
  definition, 42–43
  overview of indirect and, 43f
  relationship between indirect and, 47–49
disclosures
  lived experience of self-injury, 400
  NSSI policy promoting, 940
disease-based language, NSSI recovery, 424
dissociation
  childhood trauma, 743–44
  definition, 743
  NSSI and, 487–88
  self-injurious behavior (SIB) and, 687–88

distal risk factors of self-injurious behavior (SIB), 682–85
  cultural pressures, 684–85
  family environment, 684
  model of interactive risk factors for direct and indirect SIB, 683f
  personality, 683
  temperament, 682–83
  traumatic experiences, 684
distress cascade theory, 1136–37
distress intolerance, NSSI and, 230–31
distress or impairment, NSSI-D, 15–16
distress response, NSSI in prisons, 619
distress tolerance
  case for, 714
  intervention for, 712
  transdiagnostic process, 705–6
diurnal variation
  autonomic nervous system (ANS) activity, 357–58
  findings on, 367–68
dopamine, NSSI addiction, 194
dorms/student houses, NSSI policy, 943–44
Down syndrome, 608–9
drive for thinness, eating, 42
duration, assessment, 916–17
dysregulated neuropeptides, NSSI risk and, 333

E
Early Adolescents Temperament Questionnaire (EATQ), 284
early childhood. See childhood maltreatment; childhood trauma
eating disorders (EDs), 190, 284–85, 309–10
  adults with NSSI and, 545
  attentional bias, 313
  characteristics of persons with SIB and, 51–52
  cognitive control, 315–17
  comorbidity between NSSI and, 292
  compulsive exercise and NSSI, 52–53
  co-occurring with NSSI, 130
  COVID-19 pandemic and, 159–60
  cross-sectional studies, 292–93

  direct and indirect SIB, 61
  family environment and, 684
  indirect SIB, 680–81
  longitudinal studies, 293–94
  multifamily therapy (MFT), 1132
  NSSI and, 49–52, 138, 267–68
  outcome expectancy theory, 313–14
  positive valence systems, 299
  psychophysiology of positive affective processing, 296
  reactivity of positive valence systems, 291
  reactivity of reward system in brain, 295–96
  rumination, 310–11
  temperamental/personality traits as mechanism for NSSI and, 294–95
  temporal relationship between SIB and, 52
EBSCOHost database, 574
ecological momentary assessment (EMA)
  adolescents with NSSI, 336
  automatic/social positive reinforcement, 283–84, 293–94
  designs, 914
  digital intervention, 1009–13
  dynamic processes of change, 434
  emotion-regulatory properties of NSSI, 519–20
  episodes of NSSI, 707, 710
  future work in NSSI, 1240
  importance of anger, 643–44
  method, 915
  negative affect and NSSI, 230, 233–34, 236–38, 242
  NSSI assessment, 861
  self-injury research, 35, 369–70
  self-report assessment, 898–99
  service members and veterans, 649–50
  social attachment of people with NSSI, 330–31
  social contagion, 841
  digital intervention, 1009–13
ecological sampling studies, negative affect and NSSI, 233–34, 236–38
ecological systems theory, Bronfenbrenner, 2–3

education, parental, about
  NSSI, 759
educational settings
  NSSI assessment, 864
  research-informed NSSI policy
    in, 932–33
  See also higher education; NSSI
    policy
elders. See older adults with NSSI
electrocardiogram (ECG), 355
electroconvulsive therapy
    (ECT), 1061
  major depressive disorder
    (MDD), 379
electrodermal activity (EDA)
  autonomic nervous system
    (ANS) function study, 353–
    54, 354t
  findings on, 358–64, 360t
electromyography (EMG),
    communication assessment
    with facial, 331
elementary school children
  Belgian school staff, 503, 504–6,
    505t, 506t
  Canadian school staff, 503,
    504–6, 505t, 506t
  experiences of school staff with
    NSSI of, 504–7
  method for engaging with, 504–5
  methods of engagement in
    NSSI, 506t
  NSSI in school settings, 503
  perspectives of staff regarding
    NSSI, 505–6, 505t
  prevalence and etiology of NSSI
    in, 500, 511
  research on NSSI in, 501–3
  school response
    principles, 509–10
  suicide ideation, 501–2
  supportive needs of school
    staff, 506–7
elimination fantasy, 1148
emerging adulthood. See
    adolescence and emerging
    adulthood
emotional abuse, child neglect
    and, 742
emotional cascade, 27–28
emotional cascade model
  negative emotions, 228
  risky health behaviors, 27–28
Emotional Cascade Model
    (ECM), 450–51, 520

emotional dysregulation
  addictive mechanisms, 191
  neurobiological
    mechanisms, 193–95
  NSSI with addictive
    characteristics, 191–95
  psychological
    mechanisms, 191–93
emotional freedom technique
    (EFT), experiential
    approach, 1181–82
emotionally focused family
    therapy (EFFT), 1132
emotional processing
  alexithymia, 704–5
  clinical implications, 668–69
  emotion reactivity, 703–4
  experiential avoidance, 705
  See also cognitive-emotional
    perspective; transdiagnostic
    cognitive processes
emotional reactivity, childhood
    maltreatment, 742–43
emotional regulation
  childhood
    maltreatment, 742–43
  NSSI in prisons, 619
emotional regulation individual
    therapy for adolescents
    (ERITA), 196
emotion dysregulation
  pain experience, 450–51
  self-injurious behavior (SIB)
    and, 683f, 685
emotion-focused therapy (EFT)
  experiential, 1175–76
  intervention for, 712
emotion reactivity, emotional
    processing, 703–4
emotion regulation
  adults with NSSI and, 545, 546
  NSSI and, 132
  NSSI as form of, 1170
  NSSI in adolescence and
    emerging adulthood, 519–20
emotion regulation group therapy
    (ERGT), 383–84
  adults with NSSI, 549
  NSSI and, 138, 241–42
emotion regulation group
    treatment, NSSI
    intervention, 339–40
emotion regulation individual
    therapy for adolescents
    (ERITA), 60, 383–84

digital interventions, 596–
    97, 1000
  NSSI and, 138
  online treatment, 1079–80
emotions
  NSSI treatment, 1115–17
  questions related to
    NSSI, 1117t
empathy burnout, 1128, 1136–37
employment, self-injurious
    behavior (SIB) and,
    604t, 608
endocannabinoid system, NSSI
    addiction, 194–95
endocrine and neural threat
    systems
  clinical implications of
    alterations in, 268–69
  concordance and discordance
    across levels of, 262–63
  developmental changes
    to, 255–56
  hypothalamic-pituitary-adrenal
    (HPA) axis in NSSI, 253–
    54, 256–59
  overview of, 253–55
  potential avenues of future
    exploration, 263–68
  See also neural threat systems
    in NSSI
endogenous opioid, 290
endogenous opioid release
    hypothesis, pain
    analgesia, 455–56
endogenous opioid system, NSSI
    addiction, 193–94
engagement, assessment of
    NSSI, 849
engagement NSSI recovery,
    423, 429
England, studies of NSSI in older
    adults, 577t
English Adult Psychiatric
    Morbidity survey, 848
enhanced self-awareness skills,
    NSSI recovery, 429
environment, NSSI in
    prison, 620
environmental contexts, NSSI
    recovery, 430
environmental factors,
    research on threat-system
    function, 263–65
environmental stress, NSSI
    and, 231

epidemiology of NSSI
  age of onset, 109
  developmental course, 109–10
  ethnicity and race, 112
  incidence rates, 109–10
  increases over time, 110
  lifetime prevalence, 108
  low- and middle-income countries (LMICs), 113
  in older adults, 573–74
  persistence rates, 110
  prevalence, 108–9
  sex, 112
  sexuality and gender identity, 112
  sociodemographic correlates and risk factors, 111–13
  socioeconomic status, 113
  themes related to, 1238–39
  thoughts-behavior transitions, 110–11
  twelve-month prevalence, 108–9
  See also clinical epidemiology
Erickson, Milton H., 1200
ethical considerations, media representation of NSSI, 780–81
ethics
  digital intervention, 1016
  machine learning, 1033
ethnicity
  military service members and veterans, 643
  NSSI and, 112
  NSSI prevalence by, 129
  risk factors for NSSI, 726–27
etiology
  distal risk factors, 682–85
  model of interactive risk factors for direct and indirect SIB, 683f
  proximal risk factors, 685–88
  self-injurious behaviors (SIBs), 682–88
evidence-based assessment, interventions for NSSI, 526–27
excoriation, NSSI and, 11
experience sampling methodology (ESM), 118
  investigation of NSSI, 449, 459
  pain analgesia findings, 455
  study of pain, 444–45
Experiences in Close Relationships Inventory-Revised (ECR), 339

experiential avoidance model deliberate self-harm, 26–27
emotional processing, 705
experiential counseling, approaches, 1170
experiential therapies and interventions, 1170–84
  accelerated experiential dynamic psychotherapy (AEDP), 1177–78
  compassion-focused therapy (CFT), 1179–80
  emotional freedom technique (EFT), 1181–82
  emotion-focused therapy, 1175–76
  expressive arts therapy, 1170–72
  eye movement desensitization and reprocessing (EMDR), 1182–83
  focusing on relationships, 1175–78
  focus on thought and behavior change, 1178–84
  guided imagery, 1172–75
  limitations and implications, 1184–85
  mindfulness, 1180–81
  resource development and installation (RDI), 1183–84
  self-compassion, 1179
exposure, 839–40
exposure interventions, DBT treatment for Morey, 1121b
exposure to pain, suicide, 79–80
expressive arts therapy, 1170–72
expressive writing (EW), 1081–82, 1203–4
extended evolutionary metamodel (EEMM), 421, 414, 433–34
eye movement desensitization and reprocessing (EMDR), experiential therapy, 1182–83

F

Facebook, 686–87, 795–96
facial electromyography, 291
facilitation processes, NSSI recovery and, 421
families
  connection of, and NSSI, 136
  COVID-19 pandemic and relationships, 158
  impact of self-injurious behaviors (SIB), 595

NSSI in adolescents and emerging adulthood, 521–22
  protective factor, 819–20
  self-injurious behavior (SIB) and environment of, 683f, 684
Family Cascade Theory, NSSI, 1128
Family Enhanced Non-Directive Supportive Therapy (FE-NST), 1131–32
family medicine, NSSI assessment, 863
family-social network affair, 1204
family therapy (FT), 1129–30
  attachment-based family therapy (ABFT), 1131–32
  common factors for psychotherapy, 1134–35
  core components of FT approach, 1135–38
  current state of evidence for, 1130–31
  emotionally focused family therapy (EFFT), 1132
  guidelines for treatment of NSSI in adolescence, 1134–38
  NSSI treatment, 1131–33, 1140, 1198–99
  session-by-session summary, 1204–8
  structural family therapy (SFT), 1132
  See also collaborative strengths-based family therapy (CSBFT)
father-child relationship, fathers and, 763–64
feature engineering, machine learning, 1030–31
Federal Correctional Institution, Pennsylvania, 624–25
Fight Club (novel/movie), 782
Fight/Flight/Freeze System (FFFS), 214–15
Fight/Flight System (FFS), 214–15, 1161
fine-grained assessment of NSSI, 912–13
  clinical practice implications, 924–25
  compliance and retention, 918–19
  frequency of, 914–16
  key decision points in designing, 913–18

recruitment and selection
bias, 920–21
research advances, 925
research implications, 922–24
resolving ethical and technical
issues, 918–22
risk assessment and
response, 921–22
technological
challenges, 919–20
timing and duration of, 916–17
variables of, 917–18
first responders, 873
aftercare, 881
as conduits of health, 874–76
continuing the
conversation, 879–84
cultivating safety, 874–76
ethical considerations, 888–89
lived experience of self-
injury, 877–78
onset, frequency and
methods, 880–81
perspective of lived experience
of self-injury, 883–84
reasons for self-injuring, 882
risk assessment, intervention
and guidance for, 874
Screen for Nonsuicidal Self-
Injury (SNSI), 877, 887
SOARS model, 879–80, 884,
886, 887, 888, 889–90
stage of change, 880
STOPS FIRE mnemonic
strategy, 879, 887
suicidal ideation, 882
flu (1918) epidemic, 150
food addiction (FA), 190
foreign body ingestion (FBI)
atypical, severe NSSI, 559, 563t
Forms of Self-Criticizing/
Attacking and Self-Reassuring
Scale (FSCRS), 338–39
Four-Function Model (FFM) of
NSSI, 25–26, 114, 282–84
automatic negative
reinforcement, 689
automatic positive
reinforcement, 282–84, 689
categories, 853
cross-sectional and prospective
survey studies, 282–83
direct and indirect SIB, 682
ecological momentary assessment
(EMA) studies, 283–84

processes of, 689
relationship between
processes, 690
social negative
reinforcement, 689
social positive reinforcement,
282–84, 689
frequency, 894–95
fine-grained assessment, 914–16
Freud, Sigmund, 1148
friendships
socialization of NSSI
within, 816–19
stress in, 812–13
function, 90
See also nonsuicidal self-injury
(NSSI) functions
functional affordances, digital
intervention, 1013–14
Functional Assessment of Self-
Mutilation (FASM), 91–92,
93, 97–98, 337–38, 548
functional equivalence, direct
and indirect self-injurious
behavior (SIB), 682, 688–91
functional magnetic resonance
imaging (fMRI), 232
adolescents with NSSI, 335–36
biology in NSSI, 379
communication assessment
with, 331
reward circuitry in
brain, 288–90
task-based, 261

G

gatekeeper interventions
impact and effectiveness of, 982
NSSI applicability and, 983
university level, 980
gatekeeper trainings
assessment and evaluation
challenges, 984–87
Campus Connect, 981
Kognito, 981–82, 985, 987
peer vignettes, 985–87, 986t
question, persuade, refer
(QPR), 981
recommendations for, 983–84, 983t
university settings, 980–82
gateway theory, NSSI and
suicidality, 974
Gay, Lesbian & Straight
Education Network
(GLSEN), 664, 669

gender
difference in NSSI by, 178
military service members and
veterans, 641–42
NSSI and identity, 112
risk factors for NSSI, 726
gender minority status, military
service members and
veterans, 642
Gender Minority Stress and
Resilience Model, 660
general anxiety disorder (GAD),
NSSI and, 1092–93
genetic vulnerability, childhood
maltreatment, 747
Global Severity Index
(GSI), 859–60
Goal Attraction System (GAS),
proximity, 215, 216f
Goal Inhibition System (GIS),
proximity, 215, 216f
Goal Repulsion System (GRS),
proximity, 215, 216f
goal-setting questions, 1200
Google app store, 924–25
Gray's reinforcement sensitivity
theory (RST), 286–87
Greece, studies of NSSI in older
adults, 577t
growth, NSSI recovery, 430–31
guided imagery, experiential
counseling, 1172–75
guidelines. See NSSI policy

H

habituation model, pain of self-
injury, 456–57, 459
hair pulliing (trichotillomania), 11
HappylesPLUS program, 956
Happyles program, 99–100, 932–33
healing
definition, 431
intervention planning with
goals of, 432–34
NSSI recovery, 430–31
health services, NSSI
responses, 944
health services research,
assessment of NSSI, 865
healthy prison, 628, 633
heart rate
autonomic nervous system
(ANS) function study,
354t, 355
findings on, 360t, 365–67

heart rate variability (HRV)
  autonomic nervous system (ANS) function study, 354t, 355
  findings on, 360t, 365–67
  physiological component of NSSI, 380
  vagal activity, 1068–69
HEEADSSS psychosocial interview, 876
hegemonic masculinity, 648–49
help-seeking and help-giving, online self-injury activity, 790–91
help-seeking behavior, NSSI policy, 940
Her Majesty's Inspectorate of Prisons, 628
"H-EX-A-GO-N" model, rumination, 311
Hierarchical Taxonomy of Psychopathology (HiTOP), 219–20, 681
hierarchy of risk, atypical, severe NSSI, 563
higher education
  assessment and evaluation of gatekeeper trainings/interventions, 984–87
  building multifaceted intervention efforts on NSSI, 978–79
  Campus Connect, 981
  classroom- and campus-based interventions, 987–90
  contribution of college environment to NSSI, 976–77
  counseling center-based interventions, 979–80
  factors preventing seeking support, 977
  future research directions, 991–92
  gatekeeper interventions, 980
  gatekeeper interventions and applicability to NSSI, 983
  gatekeeper trainings, 980–82
  impact and effectiveness of gatekeeper, 982
  implications for university mental health services, 990–91
  intervention strategies, 979–87
  Kognito intervention program, 981–82

  peer vignette activity, 985–87, 986t
  question, persuade, refer (QPR) model, 981
  rates of NSSI on college campuses, 971–73
  reasons for engaging in NSSI, 976
  relationship between NSSI and suicide, 974
  risk factors for NSSI among university students, 973
  understanding typologies and latent classes of NSSI, 975–76
Hinduism, self-injuring acts of rituals, 471–72
Hispanic adolescents, NSSI prevalence in, 170–71
homophily, friends and peers, 818
hopelessness, suicidal ideation, 73–74
human development, Bronfenbrenner's model of, 416–17
Human Services Research Institute, 596–97
hypothalamic-pituitary-adrenal (HPA) axis, 232
  activation of, 253–54
  assessing cortisol output, 258
  cortisol levels, 256–57, 258–59
  cortisol reactivity of, 255–56
  heightened activation of, 263–64
  intervention as risk of NSSI, 269
  neuroendocrine regulation, 746
  in NSSI, 256–59
  stress-response, 815
  stress responses and NSSI, 333–34

I
Iceberg Model, self-harm, 848
ideation-to-action, suicide, 73, 110–11
identity, risk factor, 725–27
identity affordances, digital intervention, 1013
identity development, NSSI in adolescence and emerging adulthood, 519
illness, management, and recovery (IMR), atypical, severe NSSI, 564–65

imitation, phrase, 831
Impact NSSI Scale (INS), 339
implementation science, assessment of NSSI, 865
Implicit Association Test (IAT), 95–96
  differentiating suicidal and NSSI, 899–900
  NSSI assessment, 861–62
impulsivity
  cognitive control, 315–17
  NSSI and, 78–79, 132–34
independent risk factor, suicidal behavior, 83
Indigenous people, NSSI in, 172–74
indirect self-injurious behavior (SIB), 45
  active, 45–46, 48t
  behaviors by categories, 48t
  categorization of, 44–47
  correlations between NSSI and, 49–53
  definition, 44
  overview of direct and, 43f
  passive, 46, 48t
  relationship between direct and, 47–49
  risk-taking behavior, 47f, 47, 48t
  self-injury by proxy, 46f, 46, 48t
  See also nonsuicidal self-injury (NSSI)
individual and group supportive therapy (IGST), NSSI and, 268, 1122
individual differences, suicide capability, 78–79
individualism, collectivism vs., 177
individuals, impact of self-injurious behaviors (SIB), 595
Indonesia
  role of blood, 476
  self-injuring acts in rituals, 471–72
informal relationships and support, NSSI recovery, 429
injury location. See self-injury location
Inmate Observer Program, 627
inpatient treatment, NSSI, 1051b
Instagram, 686–87, 838
integrated cognitive-behavioral therapy (I-CBT), 1133
integrated model, self-injury, 29–30

Integrated Motivational-Volitional model, 117
  suicide, 76–77, 78, 79, 80
intellectual disability, 848
International Affective Picture System (IAPS), 288, 289–90
International Classification of Diseases (ICD-11), 204–5, 848
  problems with DSM-ICD assumptions, 205–7
International Consortium on Self-injury in Educational Settings (ICSES), 936, 978–79
International Society for the Study of Self-Injury (ISSS), 12
  media guide for NSSI reporting, 777–78
international Study to Predict Optimized Treatment for Depression (iSPOT-D), 379
internet. *See* digital interventions; online self-injury activity
internet addiction (IA), 190
interpersonal and social factors NSSI, 807–9, 808f
  See also social context of NSSI
interpersonal processes, suicide ideation, 74–76
Interpersonal Psychological Theory, 117
interpersonal stress, NSSI and, 231
Interpersonal Theory of Suicide, 585–86
interpersonal theory of suicide (IPTS), 523–24, 880–81, 974
intervention, 5–6
  NSSI functions, 98–99
  NSSI themes, 1244–46
  prison populations, 624–28
  self-injury, 491–92
  sexual and gender diverse (SGD) youth, 667–68
  See also digital interventions
interviewing
  goal-setting questions, 1200
  purposeful systemic, 1199–201
  questions for highly pessimistic/demoralized NSSI adolescents and families, 1200–1
  self-harming assessment questions, 1199–200

interview methods, study of pain, 443–44
intimate partner violence (IPV), NSSI and, 57
Inventory of Statements about Self-Injury (ISAS), 91–92, 93, 97–98, 337–38, 548, 858
Islam, 471–72, 473–74
Italy, studies of NSSI in older adults, 577t

J
just-in-time adaptive interventions (JITAIs)
  digital interventions, 1000–01
  technology, 1028–29

K
Kognito, 985, 987
  gatekeeper, 981–82
Korea, studies of NSSI in older adults, 577t

L
laboratory-based methods
  differentiating suicidal and NSSI, 899–901
  study of pain, 445–46
laboratory studies, negative affect and NSSI, 234–36
language, lived experience of self-injury, 401
Latent Dirichlet Allocation (LDA), 1026
Leeds Systemic Family Therapy (LSFT), 1198
LEGO® lion, properties and functionalities of, 218, 219f
LGBTQ+ individuals/community
  COVID-19 pandemic and, 158–59
  inclusion in online NSSI treatment, 1087
  lived experience of self-injury, 405–6
  NSSI and, 112
  self-injury risks, 24
  sexual and gender diverse (SGD) youth, 663, 664–65, 669, 672–73
  victimization, 814
Life Attitudes Schedule (LAS), 629–30
Life Problem Inventory (LPI), 338

lifetime history of NSSI, risk factor, 725
linguistic, acoustic, and visual data analysis, assessment, 903–4
literature on NSSI research
  lived experience, 397–402
  See also lived experience
lived experience, 393, 407–8
  adopting a person-centered approach, 401–2
  advocacy and research applications, 406–7, 406t
  barriers to, initiatives, 394–95
  clinical applications, 404–6, 406t
  conceptualization of NSSI, 398
  literature including perspectives of, 397–402
  navigating disclosures, 400
  NSSI recovery, 398–99
  NSSI stigma, 400–1
  online self-injury activity, 787, 790
  practical applications, 402–7, 406t
  rationale for, 394–97
  reasons to include voices of, 395–97
  research applications, 402–4, 406t
  themes related to, 1240–41
location. *See* self-injury location
loneliness, suicide ideation, 75
longitudinal designs, 35, 913, 914
low- and middle-income countries (LMICs), NSSI and, 113
low-lethality deliberate physical self-harm, 9
Lynam and Miller's UPPS-P model, Sensation Seeking and Positive Urgency, 285–86

M
McGilvray, Dennis, 470
machine learning (ML), 1024–26
  applications in MSSI research, 1026–29
  detection of NSSI, 1026–27
  developing good models and testing theory, 1029–30
  digital interventions, 1017
  ethics, 1033
  feature engineering, 1030–31
  implications, 1033–34

machine learning (ML) (*cont.*)
  just-in-time adaptive
    interventions (JITAIs),
    1028–29
  missing data, 1032
  occurrence of NSSI, 865
  outcome measurement, 1031–32
  prediction of NSSI, 1027–28
  research directions, 1017
  study design and data
    collection, 1030
  treatment of NSSI, 1028–29
magnetic resonance
  imaging (MRI)
  biology in NSSI, 379
  childhood
    maltreatment, 746–47
  major depressive disorder (MDD)
    chemical imbalance theory
    for, 378
  military service and veterans,
    644, 646
  NSSI and, 138, 190, 253, 378–
    79, 380–81, 1092–93
  NSSI functions, 96
  symptom-guided
    intervention, 379
maltreatment. *See* childhood
  maltreatment
Manchester Self-Harm Rule
  (MSHR), 859–60
manual assisted cognitive-
  behavioral therapy, 1122
manual-assisted cognitive
  therapy, 549
media
  ethical considerations, 780–81
  influence on human life, 998
  reporting of suicide, 772
  See also digital interventions
media representations of NSSI
  clinical practice
    implications, 782–83
  guidelines for appropriate, of
    NSSI, 777–78
  Papageno effect, 772, 776–77
  protective factors of NSSI, 772–
    73, 776–77
  risk factors of NSSI, 772–76
  Werther effect, 771–72, 773–76
medical attention
  requirements, 555
  atypical, severe NSSI, 557–59,
    561*t*
medical lethality, 894–95

medical professionals, 873
medical settings
  continuing the
    conversation, 879–84
  intervention in, 884–87
  risk assessment, intervention
    and guidance for, 874
  starting the conversation, 876–
    78, 878*t*
  See also first responders
medications
  prison populations, 625
  psychopharmacological
    interventions, 384
mental disorders
  NSSI engagement and, 521
  Research Domain Criteria for
    understanding, 329–30
  self-injurious behavior (SIB)
    and, 683*f*, 687
mental health, 1–2
  COVID-19 pandemic and
    preexisting, 152
  prison populations, 623–24
Mental Health Media Guide, 778
mental health professionals
  (MHPs), 873
  cultural considerations, 936
  NSSI policy, 935–36
  NSSI responses of
    college, 944–45
  risk assessment by MHPs, 935
  social antecedents and
    consequences, 935–36
mental health promotion,
  university policy, 939–40
mental health services,
  university, 990–91
mental illness, self-injurious
  behavior (SIB) and, 601
mental imagery, self-injury
  location, 486
mentalization-based therapy
  (MBT), 1147
  approach, 1152
  evidence base for, 1152–53
  fact-find and not-knowing
    stance about incident,
    1156–58
  identifying core domain of
    problem, 1158–60
  initial phase, 1155–56, 1157*f*
  managing mind states, 1158
  managing nonmentalizing
    modes, 1161–62

mentalizing and self-harm,
    1150–53
  NSSI development, 1150–65
  NSSI intervention, 339–40
  NSSI treatment, 862, 1064–65
  principles of, in treatment of
    self-harm, 1154–62
  role of mentalizing in NSSI,
    1150–52
  therapist stance, 1160–61
  treatment phase, 1156–62
mentalization-based treatment for
  adolescents (MBT-A), 340–
  41, 1042, 1129
Merriam-Webster Dictionary
  healing, 431
  proxy, 46
Meta-Analyses and Systematic
  Reviews of Observational
  Studies in Epidemiology
  (MOOSE)
  selection process, 574–76,
    575*f*, 586
  See also older adults with NSSI
Mighty's Guide to Understanding
  Self-harm, 801*b*
military service members and
  veterans
  affect-related
    conditions, 643–44
  age and military service
    era, 642–43
  assessment of NSSI in, 649
  attention-deficit/hyperactivity
    disorder (ADHD), 647
  clinical practice
    implications, 651–52
  comorbidities, 643–47
  demographic
    differences, 641–43
  forms and functions of
    NSSI, 647–49
  future research priorities, 652–53
  gender, 641–42
  innovative methodological
    approaches to study
    NSSI, 649–50
  NSSI and suicide risk, 644–45
  NSSI vulnerability of, 638–39
  obsessive-compulsive disorder
    (OCD), 646–47
  posttraumatic stress disorder
    (PTSD) in, 640
  prevalence of NSSI in, 639–41
  race and ethnicity, 643

sexual and gender minority
status, 642
substance use, 646
trauma exposure, 645–46
treatment of NSSI in, 650–51
understanding NSSI in, 1240
military sexual trauma (MST),
military service and veterans,
641–42, 645–46
mindfulness
definition, 1180
experiential therapy, 1180–81
mindfulness-based practice
(MBP), 1180
self-injury and, 1181
mindfulness and acceptance, DBT
treatment for Morey, 1121b
mindfulness meditation, family
therapy, 1202
mind states, mentalization-
based therapy (MBT) for
managing, 1158
minoritized populations/groups
inclusion in online NSSI
treatment, 1087
NSSI among, within
nations, 170–71
Minority Stress Model, sexual and
gender diverse (SGD) youth,
660–61, 662–63
missing data, machine
learning, 1032
Mobile Health, 1043–44
mobile health (mHealth), 924–25
modeling, phrase, 831
model of cognitive control of
emotion (MCCE), 1069
models. See theoretical models;
theoretical models of suicidal
ideation; theoretical models
of suicide capability
mood stabilizers, 1065–67
moral climate, prison, 618–19
motivational interviewing (MI),
NSSI treatment, 862
MTURK (Amazon Mechanical
Turk), 55–56
Multidimensional Scale of
Perceived Social Support
(MSPS), 339
multifamily therapy (MFT), 1132

N

N-acetylcysteine, 1065–67
naloxone, 290, 385–86

naltrexone, 290, 384, 385–86,
1065–66
National Alliance on Mental
Illness (NAMI), 623
National Association of State
Directors of Developmental
Disabilities Services, 596–
97, 613–14
National Core Indicators (NCI)
collaboration of disability
agencies, 596–97
dataset, 609–10
In-Person Survey (IPS), 593–94,
597, 610
public policy
considerations, 611–12
See also self-injurious
behavior (SIB)
National Health Service (NHS)
public health care through, 544
UK's, 851–52
National Institute for Health and
Care Excellence (NICE), 851,
857, 1048–49
National Institute of Mental
Health (NIMH), 204–5, 279
National Scientific Council on the
Developing Child, 738
National Self-harm Registry,
Ireland, 116–17
nations
NSSI among minority groups
within, 170–71
NSSI functions, 170
NSSI in non-Western, 171–72
NSSI prevalence, 169–70
See also cross-cultural
representations of NSSI
Native Americans, NSSI
in, 172–74
negative affect
findings from ecological
sampling studies, 233–34
findings from laboratory
studies, 234–35
function of NSSI in context
of, 227–29
long-term consequences of
NSSI engagement for, 238
NSSI acts typically preceded by
heightened, 232–35
NSSI and, 229
NSSI regulating and
reducing, 235–38
as risk factor for NSSI, 229–32

theories of, as trigger, 227
negative life event, NSSI and, 134
negative reinforcement, NSSI
addiction, 192
negative self beliefs, NSSI
outcome, 30
negative social outcomes,
NSSI, 30
negative urgency, NSSI
and, 230–31
Negative Valence Systems
reinforcement sensitivity theory
(RST), 214–15
Research Domain Criteria
(RDoC), 207, 209, 211–
13, 218
negative views of the self, suicide
ideation, 76–77
NEO-Personality Inventory-
Revised (NEO-PI-R), 286
Netflix series, 13 Reasons
Why, 771–72
neural threat systems in NSSI
brain structure and
NSSI, 259–60
multimodal imaging, 261
overview of endocrine
and, 253–55
potential future
research, 263–68
resting-state functional
connectivity and NSSI, 260
task-based functional
imaging, 261
white matter connectivity and
NSSI, 260
See also endocrine and neural
threat systems
neurobiological factors
childhood
maltreatment, 745–47
endocrine regulation, 746
genetic vulnerability, 747
magnetic resonance imaging
(MRI), 746–47
neurobiological mechanisms,
NSSI addiction, 193–95
neurobiological research, pain
perception and, 866
neurobiology
NSSI, 1062–64
of social exclusion, 334–35
neurocircuitry, NSSI and, 334–35
neurocognitive model of
compulsivity, 318

neuroendocrine regulation, childhood maltreatment, 746
neuroimaging
  biology in NSSI, 379
  differentiating suicidal and NSSI, 901–2
neuropeptides, NSSI risk and, 333
neurophysiology, NSSI and, 231–32
neuropsychology, NSSI functions, 91
neurostimulation approaches, 1061
neuroticism, NSSI and, 132, 230
Neurotransmitters, positive valence systems and, 290
New Zealand
  indigenous people, 173
  NSSI research, 169
  studies of NSSI in older adults, 577t
nonpharmaceutical "biological" interventions, NSSI, 1067
nonsuicidal self-injury (NSSI), 1–3
  age of onset, 109
  assessment in military personnel, 649
  background on, 556
  behavior, 2–3, 4
  biological correlates of, 382
  borderline personality disorder (BPD) and, 10
  childhood maltreatment and, 740–42
  compulsive exercise and, 52–53
  conceptualization of, 398
  continuing the conversation, 879–84
  correlations with active and passive indirect SIB, 49–53
  COVID-19 pandemic, 114–15
  definition, 42, 43, 72, 329, 938, 1127–28
  developmental course, 109–10
  development of, 1113–14
  diagnosis of, 107–8
  differentiating from other diagnoses and behaviors, 10–11
  early conceptualizations and discussions of, as syndrome, 8–9
  early conceptualizing as clinical form or threshold, 9
  eating disorders and, 49–52
  epidemiology, 3, 4–5, 6
  epidemiology themes, 1238–39
  evidence as addictive behavior, 195–96
  excoriation, trichotillomania, and self-harm in developmental disabilities, 11
  frequency, 894–95
  history of early identification of, as behavior and "condition," 8
  hypothalamic-pituitary-adrenal (HPA) axis in, 253–54, 256–59
  incidence rates, 109–10
  increases over time, 110
  intervention and treatment themes, 1244–46
  lifetime prevalence, 108
  lifetime rates of NSSI behavior, 7
  lived experience perspective, 1240–41
  maintenance of, 1114–18
  medical lethality, 894–95
  mentalization-based understanding of development of, 1150–65
  methods, 113–14
  negative affectivity as risk factor for, 229–32
  neurobiological background of, 1062–64
  novel research methods, 1242
  operationalization and assessment, 1241–42
  outcome expectancies and self-efficacy beliefs, 702–3, 707–9
  overlapping features with borderline personality disorder (BPD), 336–37
  parental awareness and disclosure of, 758–59
  persistence rates, 110
  prevalence, 108–9, 490–91
  prevalence and comorbidity of, 1040
  prevention themes, 1243–44
  psychodynamic understanding of development and maintenance of, 1147–49
  psychopharmacological approaches to, 384
  psychotherapeutic approaches to, 383–84
  recovery from, 398–99
  Research Domain Criteria (RDoC) and, 212–14
  research in elementary school, 501–3
  screening for, 876–78
  self-harm risk, 5
  self-injurious behavior, 4–5
  severity in adults, 543–45
  sociodemographic correlates and risk factors, 111–13
  special populations and, 1239–40
  substance use and, 53–56
  suicide and, 10–11
  theoretical frameworks for, 754–55
  thoughts-behavior transitions, 110–11
  transdiagnostic and bioneural processes, 1242–43
  transdiagnostic phenomenon, 253
  twelve-month prevalence, 108–9
  See also atypical, severe nonsuicidal self-injury (NSSI); elementary school children; epidemiology of NSSI; negative affect; NSSI policy; recovery
nonsuicidal self-injury (NSSI) functions, 89–90, 114
  adults, 546–47
  characteristics of, 96–97
  clinical assessment of, 97–98
  contextualizing, 94–95
  forms and, 174–75
  implications for intervention, 98–99
  implications for prevention, 99–100
  implications for research, 100–1
  inferred and implicit functions, 95–96
  neuropsychology of, 91
  prevalence of, 92–94
  in prisons, 619–20
  self-injury and therapeutic relationship, 99
  service members and veterans, 647–49
  structure of, 91–92
  variety of, 90–91
  See also prison(s)
Nonsuicidal Self-Injury Assessment Tool (NSSI-AT), 93, 96–97, 459, 548

nonsuicidal self-injury disorder
	(NSSI-D), 42
	anti-NSSI-D arguments, 18–19
	articulating and differentiating
		criteria B and C, 14–15
	categorizing and specifying, 16
	challenges with current
		NSSI-D criteria and
		categorization, 12–16
	criteria D, E, and F, 15–16
	current status of, 12
	determining the threshold for
		criterion A, 12–14
	diagnosis of, 7–8, 9
	first attempt of inclusion in
		DSM-5, 11–12
	NSSI functions, 96
	prevalence and features of, 516
	pro-NSSI-D arguments, 16–18
Non-Suicidal Self-Injury
	Expectancy Questionnaire
	(NEQ), 337–38
Norway, studies of NSSI in older
	adults, 577t
novel sensory interventions, 463
NSSI. *See* nonsuicidal self-injury
	(NSSI)
NSSI episode, three-component
	model of, 1104f
NSSI Family Cascade Theory, 1128
NSSI policy
	administrators, 934
	clinical practice, 937
	cultural considerations, 936
	mental health professionals
		(MHPs), 935–36
	risk assessment by MPHs, 935
	school and university staff, 934
	social antecedents and
		consequences, 935–36
	students and caregivers, 934–35
NSSI reinforcement, online self-
	injury activity and, 794

O

obsessive-compulsive disorder
	(OCD), 309–10
	cognitive control, 315–17
	military service and
		veterans, 646–47
	NSSI and, 267–68, 853
	outcome expectancy
		theory, 313–14
	rumination, 310–11
older adults with NSSI, 1239–40

clinician implications, 587
	epidemiology and etiology
		of, 573–74
	future research
		implications, 586–87
	included studies, 576–86, 577t
	Meta-Analyses and Systematic
		Reviews of Observational
		Studies in Epidemiology
		(MOOSE) as selection
		process, 574–76, 575f
	method, 574–76, 575f
	systemic review of risk and
		protective factors, 574
online self-injury activity, 787–
	88, 802–3
	acceptance and validation, 789
	assessment, 797–98
	clinical implications, 797
	curiosity and
		understanding, 789–90
	help-seeking and help-
		giving, 790–91
	motives for engaging in, 788–91
	NSSI resources, 801b
	outreach and training, 801–2
	potential benefits of, 791–93
	potential risks of, 793–96
	questions for use with
		clients, 799b
	research implications, 796–97
	school responses to, 963–64
	self-expression, 791
	social contagion of
		NSSI, 838–39
	treatment approaches, 798–801
	types of, 788
online self-injury activity
	benefits, 791–93
	improving NSSI
		outcomes, 792–93
	recovery encouragement, 793
	reduced social isolation, 792
	resource provision, 793
online self-injury activity
	risks, 793–96
	NSSI reinforcement, 794
	stigma, 795–96
	triggering effects, 794–95
online survey platforms, 919–20
online treatments for NSSI,
	1077–84
	autobiographic self-
		enhancement training
		(ASET), 1081–83

blueprint for the future of,
	1087–88
challenges and opportunities,
	1084–87
DBT (dialectical behavioral
	therapy), 1077–78
emotion regulation individual
	therapy for adolescents
	(ERITA), 1079–80
inclusion of minoritized
	populations, 1087
managing risk, 1084–85
obtaining consent, 1086
Project SAVE (Stop Adolescent
	Violence Everywhere),
	1083–84
therapeutic evaluative
	conditioning, 1080–81
operationalization themes related
	to NSSI, 1241–42
Operation Enduring Freedom
	(OEF) veterans, 643
Operation Iraqi Freedom (OIF)
	veterans, 643
opioids, 290, 333
opposite action, DBT treatment
	for Morey, 1121b
oppositional defiant disorder
	(ODD), NSSI and, 687
Ostracism Experience Scale for
	Adolescents (OES-A), 338
Ostracism Short Scale (OSS), 338
others, perception and
	understanding of, 332
Ottawa Self-Injury Inventory
	(OSI), 188
outcome expectancy, 317
	cognitive processes, 313–15
	NSSI, 702–3, 707–9
outcomes of NSSI, online self-
	injury activity and, 792–93
outreach and training, online self-
	injury activity, 801–2
oxytocin, NSSI risk and, 333

P

pain, 4, 443
	definition of, 443
	NSSI outcome, 30
	perception of, as self-injury
		continues, 458–59
pain analgesia, 447
	during NSSI, 454
	endogenous opioid release
		hypothesis, 455–56

INDEX | 1263

pain analgesia (cont.)
  habituation model, 456–57
  hypothesis, 33
  pain tolerance and, 462–63
  self-injury and, 448
pain experience, 463
  after self-injury ceases, 449–50
  clinical implications for understanding, 460–61
  dose-effect functions of severity and method, 462
  emotion dysregulation theories of NSSI, 450–51
  etiological relevance, 441
  mood alteration after, 450–52
  pain substitution intervention strategies, 461
  psychotherapy, 460
  public health policy and, 442
  research relevance, 441–42
  self-punishment model of NSSI, 451–52
  treatment relevance, 442
  understanding, 441–42
pain in NSSI
  cross-sectional self-report and interview methods, 443–44
  defining pain, 443
  developmental assessment considerations, 446
  experience sample methods, 444–45
  laboratory-based methods, 445–46
  measuring and assessing, 443
  methodological approaches to study, 443–46
pain offset, 447
  additive nature of NSSI in relief mechanism, 192
  evidence supporting theories, 453–54
  self-injury and, 447
  theory, 452–53
pain of self-injury, 448–50
  alternative hypotheses, 456–57
  continuation of, after ceasing, 449–50
  developmental dynamics of, 457
  dose-effect functions of NSSI pain severity and method, 462
  endogenous opioid release hypothesis, 455–56

evidence supporting pain-offset theories, 453–54
experience and perception of, 441–42
habituation model, 456–57, 459
novel sensory interventions, 463
onset of initial, 457–58
pain analgesia, 448, 462–63
pain analgesia during NSSI, 454
pain analgesia findings, 454–55
pain offset, 447, 452–53
pain onset, 447, 448–49
perception of, with continuing NSSI, 458–59
qualitative research, 461–62
questioning, 440–41
"reward" of, 452–59
understanding intentionality of causing, 446–48
pain onset, 447
  during NSSI, 448–49
  self-injury and, 447
  self-injury onset, 457–58
pain perception, 4, 866
  NSSI addiction, 193
pain substitution intervention strategies, 461
pain threshold, 443
pain tolerance, 443
  pain analgesia and, 462–63
Palestinian youth, NSSI of minority groups, 171
panic disorder
  co-occurring with NSSI, 129
  NSSI and, 1092–93
Papageno effect, 777–78, 780–81, 783
  protective factors of NSSI media representation, 772, 776–77
parasuicide, 8
parasympathetic nervous system (PNS), 352
parental awareness
  education about NSSI, 759
  influence of, on NSSI in adolescents and emerging adulthood, 521–22
  NSSI disclosure and, 758–59
  well-being, 758–59
parental self-injury, psychopathology and, 756
parental substance use disorder, 189
parent-child relationship

interventions, 760–61
protective factors, 759–60
risk factors, 756–58
passive and active audio recordings, fine-grained assessment, 922–23
pathological bondage, recovery, 414
pathological self-injury
  NSSI, 398
  NSSI-D, 15
peer groups
  affiliation and NSSI, 32
  contagion effects, 817
  engagement in NSSI, 134–35
  protective factor, 819–20
  relationship quality, 812–13
  socialization of NSSI within, 816–19
  victimization, 813–15
peer influences
  NSSI in adolescents and emerging adulthood, 522–23
  self-injurious behavior (SIB) and, 683f, 686–87
peer prevention programs, prison populations, 627
peer support networks, NSSI responses by, 943
peer victimization, definition, 813–14
perceived burdensomeness
  concept of, 74–75
  suicide, 76–77
Perceived Criticism Measure (PCM), 338–39
perception of self and others, NSSI within construct of, 332
Perceval, John, 412, 413
perfectionism
  avenue for intervention, 711
  NSSI and, 133–34
  transdiagnostic process, 707
peripheral neurophysiology, NSSI and, 231–32
personality
  NSSI and disorders of, 687
  NSSI in adolescence and emerging adulthood, 519
  self-injurious behavior (SIB) and, 683f, 683
  suicide capability, 78–79
personal safety, self-injurious behavior (SIB) and, 604t, 606

person-centered approach
  lived experience of self-
    injury, 401–2
  NSSI research, 529–30
pharmacological interventions
  childhood trauma, 748
  NSSI and, 384
photoplethysmography (PPG), 355
physical abuse, childhood, 741–42
physical activity, sleep and,
    1067–68
physical health and longevity,
    atypical, severe NSSI, 560
physical sensations, three-
    component model of NSSI
    episode, 1104f
physiology
  stress responses and
    NSSI, 333–34
Positive and Negative Affect
    Schedule (PANAS), 284
positive behavior supports,
    self-injurious behavior
    (SIB), 612–14
positive emotions
  psychopathology, 279
  temporal course of, 279
positive psychology,
    growth, 430–31
positive reinforcement
  NSSI addiction, 192
  See also four-function model
    of NSSI
Positive Valence Systems
  behavioral activation system
    (BAS), 286–87
  behavioral inhibition system
    (BIS), 286–87
  Big Five personality model, 286
  brain circuitry in brain (fMRI
    studies), 288–90
  brain structures
    comprising, 288–90
  Cloninger's temperament and
    character model, 284–85
  cognitive biases related
    to, 287–88
  constructs and subconstructs
    in, 280t
  future research
    suggestions, 298–99
  Gray's reinforcement sensitivity
    theory (RST), 286–87
  Lynam and Miller's UPPS-P
    model, 285–86

neurotransmitters and, 290
NSSI and, 278–79, 299
reinforcement sensitivity theory
    (RST), 214–15
Research Domain Criteria
    (RDoC), 207–8, 211–12, 213,
    218, 279–81
reward learning, 280t
reward responsiveness, 280t
reward valuation, 280t
Rothbart's temperament
    model, 284
sensation seeking and positive
    urgency, 285–86
temperament and personality
    traits related to, 284–87
transdiagnostic treatment focus
    on, 296–97
postsecondary institutions,
    interventions for
    NSSI, 525–26
posttraumatic stress
    disorder (PTSD)
  abusive relationships, 57–58
  adults with NSSI and, 545, 546
  atypical, severe NSSI and, 558
  cannabis and, 54–55
  childhood trauma, 744, 748
  cognitive restructuring (CR)
    for, 564
  co-occurring with NSSI, 129
  COVID-19 pandemic and, 150
  emotional freedom technique
    (EFT), 1181–82
  military service and veterans,
    644, 647, 650, 651–52
  military service members and
    veterans, 640
  NSSI and, 687, 1092–93
  NSSI functions, 96
prediction, real-time assessment of
    NSSI, 729–30
prevalence
  clinical samples, 128–29
  lifetime, 108
  NSSI and, 108–9
  twelve-month, 108–9
primary and secondary
    prevention, 956–57
primary care settings
  NSSI assessment, 863
  screening for NSSI, 876–78
prison(s)
  barriers to conducting clinical
    research in, 632

behavioral outcome
    measures, 631
  definitional variances, 630–31
  distress response and emotional
    regulation, 619
  facility characteristics, 621
  function of NSSI in, 619–20
  methods for NSSI in, 617
  nature of self-harm
    in, 631
  NSSI influencing the
    environment, 620
  research limitations
    in, 630–32
  self-punishment in, 620
  study design, 631
prison populations
  behavioral management
    plans, 627
  cognitive behavioral therapy
    (CBT), 625–26
  demographic factors, 621–22
  dialectical behavioral therapy
    (DBT), 626–27
  individual coping styles and
    temperaments, 623
  institution-level
    interventions, 628
  interventions for NSSI, 624–28
  interventions for youth in
    custody, 629–30
  medication, 625
  mental health disorders, 623–24
  peer prevention programs, 627
  psychological distress, 622
  risk factors for NSSI, 620–24
  risk factors for youth in
    custody, 629
  risk screening, 627–28
  self-injury among, 616–18
  solitary confinement, 624–25
  suicide rates in, 616–17
  theoretical model for NSSI
    in, 618–19
  youth in custody, 628–30
privacy, digital intervention, 1015
problem-solving treatment (PST),
    family-based treatment,
    1197–98
professional guidance,
    assessment, 851–52
professionals, non healthcare,
    NSSI assessment, 864
professional support, NSSI
    recovery, 428–29

progress markers for NSSI
  recovery, 425–30
  articles and factors associated
    with, 426t
  engagement and sense of
    mastery, 429
  enhanced coping capacity and
    efficacy, 430
  enhanced self-awareness skills, 429
  informal relationships and
    support, 429
  NSSI behavior, 425–28
  professional support, 428–29
  shifts in environmental
    contexts, 430
Project SAVE (Stop Adolescent
  Violence Everywhere), online
  treatment, 1083–84
Project Youth Affirm, 666
propinquity theory, 818
protective factors
  clinical epidemiology, 135–36
  defining, 720–21
  family, peer, and romantic
    partner support, 819–20
  future research for, 728
  intrapersonal, 727–28, 732
  NSSI and, 135–36
  parent-child relationship, 759–60
  youth NSSI, 762–63
  See also risk factors
Protective Shields Activity, guided
  imagery, 1174
proximal biological traits,
  autonomic nervous system
  (ANS) as, 368
proximal risk factors of self-
  injurious behavior
  (SIB), 685–88
  body disregard, 686
  dissociation and SIB, 687–88
  emotion dysregulation, 685
  mental disorders, 687
  model of interactive risk factors
    for direct and indirect
    SIB, 683f
  peer influence, 686–87
  vulnerable cognitions, 685–86
proxy
  Merriam-Webster Dictionary
    on, 46
  self-injury by, 46f, 46, 48t
psychache
  childhood maltreatment, 744–45
  definition, 73, 745

psychiatric comorbidity,
  NSSI, 855–56
psychiatric disorders, co-
  occurrence of NSSI and, 131
psychiatric institutions, using
  staff of, for self-injury for
  proxy, 58
psychic equivalence, 1151–52
psychodynamic approaches, NSSI
  development, 1147–49
psychological architecture, NSSI
  recovery, 424–25, 429
psychological distress, prison
  populations, 622
psychological function, NSSI, 853
psychological mechanisms, NSSI
  addiction, 191–93
psychopathology
  cognitive control, 315–17
  cognitive processes for
    understanding, 310
  cognitive systems, 215
  experimental, and seeing
    blood, 474–75
  Goal Attraction System (GAS),
    215, 216f
  Goal Inhibition System (GIS),
    215, 216f
  Goal Repulsion System (GRS),
    215, 216f
  introducing a proximity
    dimension, 215
  McNaughton's hierarchy, 216f
  NSSI and, 137–38, 189, 190
  NSSI as symptom of, 18
  NSSI engagement, 521
  NSSI in context of
    broader, 267–68
  NSSI risk factor, 723–24
  parental self-injury and, 756
  positive emotions in, 279
  reinforcement sensitivity theory
    (RST), 214–15
  Research Domain Criteria
    (RDoC), 214–17
  Sensorimotor Systems, 217
  Social Systems of
    RDoC, 216–17
psychopharmacological
  interventions, 1061
  NSSI, 384, 1065–67
  selective serotonin reuptake
    inhibitors (SSRIs), 1065–67
psychophysiology of positive
  affective processing

automatic/social positive
  reinforcement and
  transdiagnostic
  mechanism, 292–94
cognitive biases related to
  positive valence systems, 295
comorbidity of NSSI and
  eating disorder/substance use
  disorder (ED/SUD), 292
reactivity of positive valence
  systems, 291
reactivity of reward system in
  brain, 295–96
reflexive and facial
  electromyography, 291–96
related to NSSI, ED, and
  SUD, 296
temperament/personality
  traits as common
  mechanism, 294–95
psychosis, recovery from, 413
psychosocial assessment,
  849, 852–57
  clinician approach, 852
  consequences, 855
  coping mechanisms, 856
  detailed assessment of NSSI
    episode, 852–54
  history of NSSI, 854–55
  location of NSSI, 854
  method of NSSI, 853–54
  psychiatric comorbidity, 855–56
  psychological function of
    NSSI, 853
  risk management planning, 856–57
  safeguarding and social
    circumstances, 856
  social networks in place, 856
  suicide risk, 856
  timing, 854
  triggers and antecedents, 855
  See also assessment(s)
psychosocial treatments,
  childhood trauma, 748
psychotherapeutic interventions
  aims and general elements in,
    1046–48
  core elements across, 1046b
  efficacy of, 1070
  as first treatment of choice,
    1064–65
  NSSI, 383–84
psychotherapy
  common factors for, 1134–35
  pain experience, 460

psychotic episodes and substance intoxication, NSSI-D, 15
public health policy
  impact of self-injurious behaviors (SIB), 595–96
  National Health Service, 544
  pain experience, 442
  self-injurious behavior (SIB) and, 611–12
public safety, atypical, severe NSSI, 560
PubMed, 574
pupillometry
  autonomic nervous system (ANS) function study, 354t, 356
  findings on, 360t, 367

Q
question, persuade, refer (QPR) model, gatekeeper, 981

R
race
  military service members and veterans, 643
  NSSI and, 112
  NSSI prevalence by, 129
  risk factors for NSSI, 726–27
ReACT Self-Harm Rule (ReACT), 859–60
Reading the Mind in the Eyes paradigm, 209
recovery
  community-supported and aligned dimension, 416
  conceptualization of NSSI recovery, 417
  conceptualizing milestones, 424–25
  defining and measuring process of, 419–23
  definition of, 414, 423–24
  Diagnostic and Statistical Manual of Mental Disorders (DSM-5) in 2013, 417
  dynamic dimension, 415
  engagement and sense of mastery, 429
  enhanced coping capacity and efficacy, 430
  enhanced self-awareness skills, 429
  growth and healing stemming from adversity, 430–31
  idea and importance of, 412–13
  individually situated, 416
  informal relationships and support in, 429
  intentional dimension, 415
  intervention planning with healing goals for case studies, 432–34
  as journey or process, 434
  markers for progress toward, 425–30
  models of, 413–17
  NSSI, 398–99
  NSSI behavior as progress marker, 425–28
  NSSI recovery-focused articles and factors associated, 426t
  online self-injury activity and encouragement for, 793
  policy and program affected, 416
  professional support, 428–29
  relational dimension, 415
  research implications for, 434–35
  self-injury, 491–92
  shifts in environmental contexts, 430
  spiritually-supporting dimension, 416
  wellness and growth focused dimension, 415
Recovery Science Research Collaborative (RSRC), 413–14
recruitment and selection bias, fine-grained assessment, 920–21
reinforcement sensitivity theory (RST), Gray's, 286–87
rejection sensitivity, NSSI and, 230–31
relationships with friends/family
  NSSI recovery support, 429
  self-injurious behavior (SIB) and, 604t, 606–7
religion, difference in NSSI by, 178–79
religious rituals
  self-injuring acts of, 471–72
  South Asia, 470–71
repetitive self-mutilation, 9
repetitive transcranial magnetic stimulation (rTMS), 1061
  NSSI and, 1069–70
transcranial direct current stimulation, 1070
Research Domain Criteria (RDoC), 2–3, 4, 204–5, 681, 1243
  assumed unidirectionality, 218–19
  autonomic nervous system (ANS) function under, 349–51
  case examples, 211–12
  cognitive systems, 310
  developmental course, 209–10
  emergent properties at higher level: functionalities of LEGO® lion, 218, 219f
  emergent properties at higher levels of hierarchical systems, 218–20
  environmental influences, 210
  high-order research domains and comprising constructs, 207–9
  integrated research framework, 329–30
  levels of analysis, 209
  limitations and alternative approaches, 217–20
  matrix, 207–10, 208f
  National Institute of Mental Health (NIMH), 279
  negative affect, 227
  NSSI and, 212–14, 253
  properties emerging from interaction between domains/constructs/subconstructs, 218
  as (re)conceptualization of psychopathology, 214–17
  reinforcement sensitivity theory (RST), 214–15
  transdiagnostic approaches, 219–20
  See also psychopathology
researchers, digital intervention, 1016–17
resilience-enhancing thinking tools and strategies, family therapy, 1202–3
resource development and installation (RDI), experiential therapy, 1183–84
Resourceful Adolescent Parent Program (RAP-P), 1133

resources
  NSSI, 801b
  online NSSI policy, 946–47
  online self-injury activity and, 793
respiration
  autonomic nervous system (ANS) function study, 354t, 355
  findings on, 360t, 364
respiratory sinus arrhythmia (RSA), NSSI and, 334
resting state, responsivity and recovery, autonomic nervous system (ANS) function study, 357
resting-state functional connectivity (RSFC), 260, 261
retention and compliance, fine-grained assessment, 918–19
revenge, 1148
reward, pain during self-injury, 452–59
reward circuitry, brain based on fMRI studies, 288–90
rights and respect, self-injurious behavior (SIB) and, 604t, 607–8
risk assessment, 5
  fine-grained assessment, 921–22
  first responders and medical settings, 874
  sample statements/responses, 878t
risk assessment tools, 858–60, 859t
risk factors
  adolescent, 725–27
  barriers to research, 721–22
  causes and explanations, 730
  defining, 720–21
  demographic and identity characteristics, 725–27
  friendship stress, 812–13
  future NSSI, 822
  intrapersonal, 721–27, 732
  intrapersonal NSSI, 723–27
  lifetime history of NSSI and, 725
  NSSI among university students, 973
  NSSI and, 132–35
  parental and parent-child relational, 755–58
  peer relationship quality, 812–13
  peer victimization, 813–15
  prediction, 729–30
  psychopathology, 723–24
  research and clinical approaches to understand NSSI, 731–32
  romantic relationship stress, 810–11
  self-criticism, 724–25
  self-punishment desire, 724–25
  Werther effect in NSSI media representation, 771–72, 773–76
  youth NSSI, 762–63
  See also protective factors
risk management
  digital intervention, 1015
  online treatment for NSSI, 1084–85
  planning of NSSI assessment, 856–57
risk screening, prison populations, 627–28
risk-taking behavior
  correlations between NSSI and, 58–60
  definition, 58–59
  direct self-injury and, 59
  indirect self-injury, 47f, 47, 48t
  youth and, 59
romantic relationships
  protective factor, 819–20
  risk factors for NSSI, 810–11
Rosenberg Self-Esteem Scale (RSES), 338–39
Rothbart's temperament model, positive affectivity/positive reactivity, 284
rule-governed behavior (RGB)
  cognitive processes, 314
  expectancies and, 313–15
rumination, 317
  cognitive process, 310–12
  evidence-based interventions, 711
  intervention for, 713
  transdiagnostic process, 706–7
rumination-focused cognitive behavioral therapy (RF-CBT), 385
"Russian roulette," 1148

S

SAFE Alternatives, 801b
Safe Alternatives for Teens and Youth (SAFETY), 760–61, 1133
safeguarding, NSSI, 856
safety
  digital intervention, 1015
  first responders as conduits of health, 874–76
safety plan, 856–57
Samaritans, mental health charity, 99
SARS (2003) outbreak, 152
Saving and Empowering Young Lives in Europe (SEYLE), 956–57
SAVRY assessment, 631
scaling questions, goal-setting, 1197
scarring
  adults with NSSI, 547–48
  school responses to, 963
school children. See elementary school children
School Climate Survey, 664
school closure, adolescents during pandemic, 157–58
school settings
  address NSSI in, 931–32
  interventions for NSSI, 525–26
  NSSI assessment, 864
  NSSI policy, 934
  See also NSSI policy; secondary school settings
Screen for Nonsuicidal Self-Injury (SNSI), 877
screening, NSSI, 876–78, 878t
Screening for Mental Health, Inc., 956
secondary school settings
  background of NSSI in, 953–55
  current state of empirical evidence, 955–57
  Dialectical Behavior Therapy Skills in Schools: Skills Training for Emotional Problem Solving for Adolescents (DBT STEPS-A), 957, 959–60, 962–63
  HappylesPLUS, 956
  informing caregivers, 965
  NSSI in, 962–63, 966, 967
  NSSI online activities, 963–64
  prevention and intervention in, 958–63
  primary and secondary prevention, 956–57
  primary prevention and intervention, 958–60

response to wounds or
  scarring, 963
Saving and Empowering
  Young Lives in Europe
  (SEYLE), 956–57
secondary prevention and
  intervention, 960–61
Signs of Self-Injury (SOSI)
  program, 956
social contagion, 964–65
tertiary prevention and
  intervention, 961–62
tertiary prevention
  program, 956
selection bias and
  recruitment, fine-grained
  assessment, 920–21
selection effects, friends and
  peers, 818
selective serotonin reuptake
  inhibitors (SSRIs), 384,
  1065–67
self, perception and understanding
  of, 332
self-assault, 8
self-compassion
  experiential therapy, 1179
  protective factor for
    NSSI, 727–28
self-criticism, 189, 724–25
  childhood maltreatment, 745
  NSSI and, 33, 77, 133–34
  risk factors for NSSI, 724–
    25, 727–28
  transdiagnostic process, 707
self-defeating behavior, 8
self-destructive behaviors, 8
  atypical, severe NSSI, 560
self-directed aggression, 8
self-efficacy, 30
self-efficacy beliefs, NSSI, 702–
  3, 707–9
self-esteem
  NSSI and, 77, 133–34
  protective factor for NSSI, 728
self-expression, online self-injury
  activity, 791
self-harm, 43
  addictive model of, 190–91
  assessment questions, 1199–200
  COVID-19 pandemic, 114–15
  decreasing deliberate, during
    COVID-19, 154–57
  developmental disabilities and
    NSSI, 11

digital interventions, 1003–04
direct and indirect forms of, 5
increasing deliberate, during
  COVID-19, 150–54
mentalization-based therapy
  (MBT) model principles in
  treatment of, 1154–62
nature of, 631
NSSI and, 118
as sign of hope, 1149
stress and, 150
Self-Harm Behavior
  Questionnaire, 858
self-harm in older adults
  epidemiology and etiology
    of, 573–74
  See also older adults with NSSI
Self-Harm Inventory (SHI), 42–43
self-identity, self-injury
  location, 488–89
self-injurious behavior (SIB),
  41, 593–94
  age, 599t, 601
  behavior support and
    medication needs, 599t, 603
  categorization of indirect
    SIB, 44–47
  challenges of, 60, 691
  choice and control, 604t, 607
  clinical and treatment
    reforms, 612–13
  community inclusion,
    participation and leisure,
    604t, 607
  correlations between NSSI
    and active/passive indirect
    SIB, 49–53
  correlations between NSSI and
    self-injury by proxy, 56–60
  definition and characteristics of,
    42–49, 594
  demographics, 608–9
  diagnoses/conditions, 599t, 602
  direct SIB, 42–43, 680–82, 692
  distal risk factors, 682–85
  employment, 604t, 608
  examples of behaviors included
    and excluded from indirect
    categories, 48t
  experience with service
    coordination, 604t, 608
  forms and levels of severity, 42
  functional equivalence, 688–91
  future research
    directions, 610–11

guardianship, 599t, 602
impact on individuals and
  families, 595
incidence by state, 598
indirect SIB, 44–47, 680–82, 692
intellectual and developmental
  disabilities (IDD) and, 593, 594
key points of, 62
level of ID, 599t, 601
mental illness as co-occurring
  condition, 599t, 601
methods for studying, 596–98
model of interactive risk factors
  for direct and indirect self-
  injury, 683f
mode of communication, 599t,
  602–3
NSSI and substance use, 53–56
outcomes, 609
outcomes of respondents and
  support needs for, 603–8, 604t
overview of, 43f
perception of personal safety,
  604t, 606
personal characteristics, 598–
  603, 599t, 608–9
prevalence and etiology, 594–95
proximal risk factors, 685–88
public policy
  considerations, 611–12
relationship between direct and
  indirect, 47–49
relationships with friends and
  family, 604t, 606–7
respondent race/ethnicity, 598–
  603, 599t
results from studies, 598–608
rights and respect, 604t, 607–8
risk-taking behavior, 47f, 47
satisfaction with supports,
  604t, 606
self-injury by proxy, 46f, 46
shared etiology, 682–88
supports for people with IDD,
  593, 613–14
temporality of damage and
  desired effect of direct and
  indirect, 45f
therapeutic interventions and
  public policies, 595–96
where people life, 599t, 603
See also lived experience
Self-Injurious Thoughts and
  Behaviors Interview (SITBI),
  548–49, 858

Self-Injurious Thoughts and
    Behaviors Interview - revised
    (SITBI-R), 863, 1031
Self-injury: Treatment, Assessment
    and Recovery (STAR), digital
    interventions, 1003
self-injury by proxy
    correlations between NSSI
        and, 56–60
    indirect self-injurious behavior,
        46f, 46, 48t
    risk-taking behavior and
        NSSI, 58–60
    sex as self-injury (SASI), 56–57
    staying in abusive
        relationships, 57–58
    using staff in psychiatric
        institutions for, 58
Self-Injury Implicit Association
    Task (SI-IAT), 287–88
self-injury location, 481, 494
    beyond western-based
        studies, 483
    clinical assessment, 491
    cognitive perspectives, 486
    factors determining, and
        meaning, 489–90
    functional perspectives, 484–86
    intervention and
        recovery, 491–92
    intrapersonal processes and
        reenactment, 487–88
    mental imagery, 486
    practical implications, 490–92
    prevalence and cultural
        perspectives of, 482–83
    prevention and initial detection
        of NSSI, 490–91
    psychodynamic
        perspectives, 487–89
    relationship between NSSI
        function and, 485–86
    research implications, 492–94
    self-identity and
        communicative and scarred
        body, 488–89
Self-Injury Outreach and Support
    (SiOS), 801b
self-injury scars (SIS), adults with
    NSSI, 547–48
Self-Injury Trauma Scale, 493–94
self-mutilation, 8
self-perceptions, NSSI and, 135–36
self-punishment, 32, 1148
    in prison, 620

self-punishment desire, risk factors
    for NSSI, 724–25
Self-Punishment Hypothesis,
    NSSI theory, 724–25
self-punishment model of
    NSSI, 451–52
self-punishment
    motivation, 446–47
self-report, study of pain, 443–44
self-report assessments,
    differentiating suicidal and
    NSSI, 898–99
self-report data, NSSI and, 335–36
semantic obfuscation, 8
    NSSI helping mitigate, 17
Sensitivity to Punishment
    and Sensitivity to
    Reward Questionnaire
    (SPSRQ), 286–87
sensitizing hypothesis, NSSI
    addiction, 193
Sensorimotor Systems,
    Research Domain Criteria
    (RDoC), 217
Sequenced Treatment Alternatives
    to Relieve Depression
    (STAR*D) trial, 378
serotonin and norepinephrine
    reuptake inhibitors
    (SNRIs), 380
serotonin reuptake inhibitors
    (SSRIs), 380, 384, 625
Serotonin Transporter-Linked
    Polymorphic Region (5-
    HTTLPR), NSSI risk
    and, 333
service coordination, self-
    injurious behavior (SIB) and,
    604t, 608
service members. *See* military
    service members and veterans
sex, NSSI and, 112
sex as self-injury (SASI)
    definition, 56
    NSSI and, 56–57
sexual abuse, childhood, 741
sexual and gender diverse
    (SGD) youth
    assessment, 667–68
    case vignette (Ash), 665, 669–71
    clinical considerations, 665
    clinic environment, 667
    community-level
        factors, 663–64
    considerations for, 668–69

definition, 659–60
empirically supported risk and
    protective factors, 660–65
future research
    directions, 671–73
individual factors, 661–62
interpersonal factors, 662–63
intervention, 667–68
linking care to, 666–67
Minority Stress Model, 660–61,
    662–63, 665
NSSI among, 660
societal factors, 664–65
treatments for NSSI
    among, 665–66
sexual and gender
    minorities (SGM)
    military service members and
        veterans, 642
    threat-system
        development, 264–65
sexuality
    difference in NSSI by, 178
    NSSI and, 112
    risk factors for NSSI, 726
shame proneness, NSSI
    and, 230–31
Shedding Light on Self-
    injury, 801b
SHIFT (Self-Harm Intervention:
    Family Therapy), 1130
shifts in environmental contexts,
    NSSI recovery, 430
SIB. *See* self-injurious
    behavior (SIB)
Signs of Self-Injury (SOSI)
    program, 956
single-case experimental
    design (SCED), social
    contagion, 841
skin conductance levels (SCL),
    NSSI and, 334
skin conductance response (SCR)
    autonomic nervous system
        (ANS) activity, 353–54, 354t
    autonomous nervous system
        (ANS), 380
    findings on, 358–64, 360t
    physiological component of
        NSSI, 380
skin picking (excoriation), 11
sleep and physical activity, NSSI
    and, 1067–68
Snapchat, 686–87
SOARS model, 526–27

aftercare, 879, 881
assessment domains of, 879
first responders using, 879–80
onset, frequency and methods, 879, 880–81
reasons, 879, 882
stage of change, 879, 880
suicidal ideation, 879, 882
social affordances, digital intervention, 1009
social cognitive theory, Bandura's, 837
social communication, NSSI within construct of, 331
social contagion, 5, 830–31
in adolescent samples, 832–35
definition, 831
description of, 831–32
ecological momentary assessment (EMA), 841
future research directions, 839–41
NSSI, 1240
NSSI in online samples, 838–39
secondary school settings, 964–65
single-case experimental design (SCED), 841
social context of NSSI, 806–9
acute interpersonal stress responses, 815–16
clinical practice implications, 820–22
community-based prevention and intervention, 820–22
developmental psychopathology and systems theory, 807
friendship stress, 812–13
interpersonal and social factors, 807–8, 808f
interpersonal stress and socially themes correlates, 809–15
peer relationship quality, 812–13
peer victimization, 813–15
protective factors of family, peer and romantic partner, 819–20
romantic relationship stress and breakups, 810–11
socialization within friendships and peer networks, 816–19
social distancing, COVID-19 lockdowns and, 153, 154–55
social interactions, health and well-being, 328–29

social isolation, online self-injury activity and, 792
socialization effects, peer groups, 818
social learning, phrase, 831
social learning hypothesis, self-injury behavior, 32–33
social learning theory, Bandura's, 831
social media, 5, 686–87
COVID-19 lockdowns and, 153
digital technology, 1005t
identity affordances, 1013
peer victimization, 814–15
social contagion, 838–39
See also online self-injury activity
social networks
protective factor for NSSI, 727
support of NSSI, 856
social norms
barrier to NSSI, 33–34
NSSI and, 136
social platforms, digital interventions, 1017
Social Problem-Solving Inventory-Revised (SPSI-R), 339
Social Processes
assessment, 337–39
interventions, 339–41
NSSI within construct affiliation and attachment, 330–31
NSSI within construct perception and understanding of self and others, 332
NSSI within construct social communication, 331
overlapping features between NSSI and BPD, 336–37
Research Domain Criteria (RDoC), 212, 213–14
social stressors, 333–36
See also social stressors and NSSI
social stressors and NSSI, 329
behavior and self-report as units of analysis, 335–36
genes and molecules as units of analyses, 333
neurocircuitry as unit of analysis, 334–35
physiology as unit of analysis, 333–34
See also social processes in NSSI

Social Systems, Research Domain Criteria (RDoC), 216–17, 218
sociodemographic factors
ethnicity and race, 112
low- and middle-income countries, 113
sexuality and gender identity, 112
socioeconomic status, 113
socioeconomic status (SES), NSSI and, 113
solitary confinement, prison populations, 624–25
solution-oriented parenting management skills training, 1201
South America, NSSI research, 169
South Asia
comparing ritual and nonritual self-injury, 476–78
ritual self-injury in, 470–71
role of blood, 476
Southeast Asia, self-injuring acts in rituals, 471–72
South Korea, studies of NSSI in older adults, 577t
Spanish flu epidemic, 150
speculations, 561
Sri Lanka, comparing ritual and nonritual self-injury, 477–78
STAR Consortium, 1043–44
state of the science, 2
stepped-care approach, treatment of NSSI, 1042, 1043f, 1054
stigma
NSSI, 400–1
online self-injury activity and, 795–96
seeking support for NSSI, 977
stress
acute interpersonal, responses, 815–16
childhood trauma, 738–39
friendships, 812–13
NSSI recovery, 430
peer relationship quality, 812–13
peer victimization, 813–15
romantic relationships, 810–11
structural assessment tools, 857–58
structural family therapy (SFT), 1132
students and caregivers, NSSI policy, 934–35
subcultures, NSSI of youth, 179

Substance Abuse and Mental Health Services Administration (SAMHSA), 413–14
substance use
  alcohol, 55–56
  cannabis, 54–55
  direct and indirect SIB, 61
  military service and veterans, 646
  NSSI and, 53–56
  tobacco, 54
substance use disorders (SUDs), 309–10
  attentional bias, 313
  cognitive control, 315–17
  comorbidity between NSSI and, 292
  cross-sectional studies, 292–93
  longitudinal studies, 293–94
  NSSI addiction, 194
  outcome expectancy theory, 313–14
  parental, 756
  positive valence systems, 299
  psychophysiology of positive affective processing, 296
  reactivity of positive valence systems, 291
  reactivity of reward system in brain, 295–96
  rumination, 310–11
  temperamental/personality traits as mechanism for NSSI and, 294–95
suicidal behavior (SB)
  addiction to, 188–89
  concept of, 188
  See also addiction
suicidal ideation (SI), 380–81
  See also theoretical models of suicidal ideation
suicidal intent, suicide risk and, 850–51
suicidality, NSSI and, 938
suicidal self-injury
  assessment of NSSI and, 897–902
  differentiating nonsuicidal from, 895–97
  false dichotomy between NSSI and, 18
  laboratory-based methods, 899–901
  neuroimaging, 901–2
  self-report assessments, 898–99

suicidal thoughts and behavior (STB)
  NSSI and, 1237–38
  NSSI as risk factor for, 523–24
suicide
  assessing risk of, 856
  commonalities, 73
  co-occurrence of NSSI and, 131
  interpersonal theory of, 266
  NSSI and, 10–11
suicide attempts (SA), 380–81
Suicide Attempt Self-Injury Interview (SASII), 97–98, 548–49
suicide capability. *See* theoretical models of suicide capability
suicide contagion, 80
suicide deaths, 80–81
Suicide Prevention Resource Center (SPRC), 985
suicide risk, 1–2
  military service and veterans, 644–45
  suicidal intent and, 850–51
suicide surveillance system, Australia, 155–56
support needs, self-injurious behavior (SIB) and, 604t, 606
sustained movement toward wellness, recovery, 414
Sweden, studies of NSSI in older adults, 577t
sympathetic nervous system (SNS), 352
Symptom Checklist-90 Revised (SCL-90-R), 338
syndrome of delicate self-cutting, 8
syndrome of the wrist cutter, 8
Systems for Social Processes, Research Domain Criteria (RDoC), 329

T

tailored treatment, family therapy (FT), 1135
Taiwan, studies of NSSI in older adults, 577t
task-shifting, cognitive control, 315–17
tattooing, form of NSSI, 15
technology challenges, fine-grained assessment, 919–20
temperament, self-injurious behavior (SIB) and, 682–83, 683f

Temperament and Character Inventory-(Revised) (TCI/TCI-R), 284–85, 294
temporal course, positive emotions, 279
tertiary prevention program, 956
text-messaging (SMS), digital technology, 1005t, 1009
theoretical models of NSSI
  barriers and benefits model, 32–34
  cognitive-emotional model, 30–31
  emotional cascade model, 27–28
  experiential avoidance model, 26–27
  four-function model, 25–26
  implications for clinical practice, 35–36
  integrated model, 29–30
  understanding of NSSI, 34–35
theoretical models of suicidal ideation
  arrested flight model, 76
  cognitive biases and hopelessness, 73–74
  integrated motivational-volitional model, 76–77
  interpersonal processes and challenges, 74–76
  interpersonal theory of suicide, 74–75
  negative view of the self, 76–77
  self-esteem, 77
  three-step theory, 74, 75
theoretical models of suicide capability
  clinical practice, 82–83
  exposure and habituation to injury and pain, 79–80
  impulsivity, 78–79
  integrated motivational-volitional model, 78, 79, 80
  personality and individual differences, 78–79
  practical capability and access to lethal means, 80–81
  three-step theory, 78, 80
therapeutic alliance, family therapy (FT), 1134
therapeutic assessment, NSSI, 862
Therapeutic Evaluative Conditioning (TEC)
  digital interventions, 1002
  online treatment, 1080–81

therapeutic interventions, impact of self-injurious behaviors (SIB), 595–96
therapeutic relationship, self-injury and, 99
therapist stance, mentalization-based therapy (MBT), 1160–61
13 Reasons Why (Netflix series), 771–72
thoughts, three-component model of NSSI episode, 1104f
threat system
  clinical implications of alterations in, 268–69
  considering a broader systems approach, 266–67
  environmental factors as mechanisms of risk and protection, 263–65
  NSSI in context of broader psychopathology, 267–68
  sustained engagement in NSSI, 265–66
  See also endocrine and neural threat system; neural threat system in NSSI
three-component model, NSSI episode, 1104f
three-step theory, 117
  practical capability, 80
  suicidal ideation, 74, 75, 78
thwarted belongingness
  concept of, 74–75
  suicide, 76–77
timing
  assessment, 916–17
  NSSI, 854
TIPP skill, dialectical behavior therapy (DBT), 461
tobacco use, NSSI and, 54
Toronto Alexithymia Scale (TAS-20), 175–76
trait rumination NSSI and, 230–31
transcranial direct current stimulation (tDCS), 1061, 1070
transcutaneous auricular vagus nerve stimulation (taVNS), 1061, 1068–69
transdiagnostic behavior, NSSI and, 140
transdiagnostic cognitive processes
  distress tolerance, 705–6
  perfectionism, 707
  rumination, 706–7
  self-criticism, 707

transdiagnostic frameworks, NSSI and, 1242–43
transgender/gender diverse (TGD)
  military service members and veterans, 642
  risk factors for NSSI, 726
transtheoretical model (TTM), NSSI recovery, 398–99, 418–19, 431
trauma
  atypical, severe NSSI, 560
  See also childhood trauma
trauma-informed care (TIC), childhood trauma, 748
traumatic brain injury (TBI), service members and veterans, 650
traumatic experiences
  military service and veterans, 645–46
  self-injurious behavior (SIB) and, 683f, 684
treatment of NSSI, 5–6, 137–38
  adults with NSSI, 549
  aims and general elements in psychotherapeutic, 1046–48
  algorithm on, in adolescents, 1048–52
  atypical, severe NSSI, 564–65
  core elements across psychotherapeutic, 1046b
  efficacy of different settings, 1044–46
  indicators for inpatient, 1051b
  mentalization-based therapy (MBT), 1156–62
  military personnel, 650–51
  online self-injury activity, 798–801
  pain experience, 442
  proposed stepped-care approach, 1043f
  proposed treatment algorithm in childhood and adolescence, 1050f
  self-injurious behavior, 138, 527
  sexual and gender diverse youth, 665–66
  stepped-care approach to treat NSSI, 1043f
trichotillomania, NSSI and, 11
Trier Social Stress Test (TSST), 257–58, 262–63, 333–34, 358–64

triggers
  NSSI, 855
  online self-injury activity and, 794–95

U

understanding of self and others, NSSI within construct of, 332
Unified Protocol for Transdiagnostic Treatment of Emotional Disorders (UP), 241–42
  adaptive nature of emotion (Module 2), 1095–96
  applicability to NSSI, 1092–100
  brief introduction to, 1091–92
  clinical considerations, 1101–2
  cognitive flexibility (Module 4), 1097
  comorbidity, 1092–93
  countering emotional behaviors (Module 5), 1098
  emotion exposure (Module 7), 1099–100
  empirical evidence and clinical theory, 1092–94
  empirical evidence to date, 1100–1
  functional framework, 1093–94
  future research considerations, 1108
  initial session, 1094–95
  interoceptive exposure (Module 6), 1098–99
  mindful emotion awareness (Module 3), 1096–97
  motivational enhancement (Module 1), 1095
  relapse prevention (Module 8), 1100
  treatment modules and relevance to NSSI, 1094–100
United Kingdom (UK)
  National Health Service (NHS), 851–52
  NSSI research, 169
  self-harm during COVID-19 pandemic, 155–56
  studies of NSSI in older adults, 577t
  teen suicide, 158
United States
  NSSI research, 169
  studies of NSSI in older adults, 577t

university
  NSSI policy for staff, 934
  self-injury risks of students, 24
  See also higher education; NSSI policy
unusual body locations, 555
  atypical, severe NSSI, 557–59, 562t
UPPS-P Model, sensation seeking and positive urgency, 285–86, 294
user engagement, digital intervention, 1014–15

V

vagal stimulation, NSSI and, 1068–69
validation, online self-injury activity, 789
vasopressin, NSSI risk and, 333
Vera Institute of Justice, 621, 624–25, 628
veterans. *See* military service members and veterans
veterinary professionals, medications for euthanasia, 80
virtual reality (VR), 895
  assessment, 902–3
  digital technology, 1005t, 1008–09
  research directions, 1017
visualization, family therapy, 1202
Vrije Universiteit Brussel (VUB) NSSI policy, 938–46
  college administration/faculty, 942–43
  college mental health professionals, 944–45
  definition of NSSI, 938
  dorms/student houses, 943–44
  general mental health promotion, 939–40
  health services, 944
  identifying NSSI among college students, 939
  improving NSSI literacy at all levels, 941
  NSSI among college students, 938–39
  online resources, 946–47
  peer support networks and VUB buddies, 943
  promoting disclosures and help-seeking behavior, 940
  protocol for VUB, 945–46
  reasons people engage in NSSI, 938
  referral process, 947f
  responding effectively, 941–45
  roles in referral process, 946f
VUB. *See* Vrije Universiteit Brussel (VUB) NSSI policy
vulnerability, NSSI in prison, 618–19

W

wearables, 895
wearable technologies
  assessment, 904
  fine-grained assessment, 922–23, 924
web-based interventions/resources, digital technology, 1005t, 1009–13
web-based programs, affective affordances, 1013
Web of Science, 574
WEIRD (Western, Educated, Industrialized, Rich, and Democratic) samples, NSSI and self-harm, 116
Werther effect, 777–78, 780–81
  risk factors of NSSI media representation, 771–72, 773–76
White Mountain Apache Surveillance System, 172
Wise Mind thinking tools and strategies, 1202–3
working memory, cognitive control, 315–17
World Health Organization (WHO), 394, 739
  International Classification of Diseases, 848
  media guide for reporting on suicide, 777
World Mental Health International College Student Initiative, 117, 972
wounds, school responses to, 963
wrist cutting syndrome, 8

Y

youth
  impact of parent factors on NSSI in, 757–58
  interventions for NSSI, 760–61
  NSSI and, 753–54
  parental and parent-child relational risk factors, 755–58
  parental criticism and, 757
  risk-taking behavior, 59
  See also adolescents; adolescence and emerging adulthood; sexual and gender diverse (SGD) youth
Youth Aware of Mental Health Program (YAM), 932–33
youth in custody
  Coping Course, 629–30
  incarceration considerations, 628–30
  interventions for, 629–30
  risk factors for NSSI among, 629
Youth Self-Report, 631
youth subcultures, difference in NSSI by, 179

Z

ziprasidone, 384, 1066–67